Contents

II	European driving: cut through the confusion	
IV	Driving regulations	
VII	Ski resorts	

1 Route planning maps

1 Key to route planning map pages

24 Road maps

24 Key to road map pages · Distance table

201 City plans and approach maps

Alicante C	201	Luxembourg C	215
Amsterdam CU	202	Lyon CU	215
Antwerpen C	201	Madrid UC	215
Athina UC	202	Málaga C	216
Barcelona CU	203	Marseille C	216
Basel C	203	Milano CU	217
Beograd C	205	Moskva CU	218
Berlin CU	204	München CU	218
Bordeaux CU	205	Nápoli CU	219
Bruxelles UC	205	Oslo UC	219
Budapest CU	206	Paris CU	220
Dublin CU	207	Praha CU	222
Düsseldorf CU	207	Roma CU	223
Edinburgh C	207	Rotterdam C	222
Firenze Florence C	209	Sankt Peterburg U	222
Frankfurt C	209	Sevilla C	224
Genève Geneva C	209	Stockholm CU	225
Génova Genoa C	209	Strasbourg CU	224
Göteborg C	210	Stuttgart C	224
Granada C	210	Torino UC	226
Hamburg CU	210	Venézia C	226
Helsinki CU	211	Warszawa CU	227
İstanbul U	211	Wien UC	227
København CU	212	Zagreb C	228
Köln Cologne C	212	Zürich C	228
Lisboa CU	213	C City street plan	
London CU	213	U Urban area map	

229 Index to road maps

www.philips-maps.co.uk

First published in 1998 by Philip's,
a division of Octopus Publishing Group Ltd
www.octopusbooks.co.uk
Carmelite House, 50 Victoria Embankment
London EC4Y 0DZ
An Hachette UK Company
www.hachette.co.uk

Twenty-seventh edition 2019
First impression 2019
ISBN 978-1-84907-499-5

 This product includes mapping data licensed from Ordnance Survey®, with the permission of the Controller of Her Majesty's Stationery Office © Crown copyright 2019.
All rights reserved. Licence number 100011710

® is a registered Trade Mark of the Northern Ireland Department of Finance and Personnel. This product includes mapping data licensed from Ordnance Survey of Northern Ireland®, reproduced with the permission of Land and Property Services under delegated authority from the Controller of Her Majesty's Stationery Office, © Crown Copyright 2019.

While every reasonable effort has been made to ensure that the information compiled in this atlas is accurate, complete and up-to-date at the time of publication, some of this information is subject to change and the Publisher cannot guarantee its correctness or completeness.

The information in this atlas is provided without any representation or warranty, express or implied and the Publisher cannot be held liable for any loss or damage due to any use or reliance on the information in this atlas, nor for any errors, omissions or subsequent changes in such information.

The representation in this atlas of any road, drive or track is not evidence of the existence of a right of way.

The maps of Ireland on pages 26 to 30 and the urban area map and town plan of Dublin are based upon the Crown Copyright and are reproduced with the permission of Land & Property Services under delegated authority from the Controller of Her Majesty's Stationery Office, © Crown Copyright and database right 2019, PMLPA No 100503, and on Ordnance Survey Ireland by permission of the Government © Ordnance Survey Ireland / Government of Ireland Permit number 9181.

Cartography by Philip's
Copyright © Philip's 2019

Printed in Malaysia

*Independent research survey, from research carried out by Outlook Research Limited, 2005/06

Photographic acknowledgements:
Page II: top Agencja Fotograficzna Caro / Alamy · right James Hughes · bottom Mode Images / Alamy.
Page III: centre Pete Titmuss / Alamy ·
bottom right Mim Friday / Alamy.

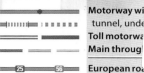

Legend to route planning maps

	Motorway with junctions tunnel, under construction
	Toll motorway
	Main through route
25 56	European road number
55	National road number
56	Distances – in kilometres
	International boundary, national boundary
LE HAVRE	Car ferry and destination
1089 ▲	Mountain pass, international airport, height (metres)

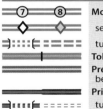

Town – population

MOSKVA ◨ ◼	5 million +		Gävle ⊙	50000–100000
BERLIN ◨ ◻	2–5 million		Nybro ◔	20000–50000
MINSK ◨ ◻	1–2 million		Ikast ◦	10000–20000
Oslo ◉ ◼	500000–1million		Skjern ◦	5000–10000
Århus ◉ ◻	200000–500000		Lillesand ◦	0–5000
Turku ◎ ◻	100000–200000			

The green version of the symbol indicates towns with Low Emission Zones

Scale · pages 2–23
1:3 200 000
1 in = 50.51 miles
1 cm = 32km

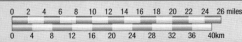

Legend to road maps pages 26–200

7 8	Motorway with junctions – full, restricted access
◇ ◇	services, rest area
	tunnel, under construction
	Toll Motorway – with toll barrier
	Pre-pay motorway – A CH CZ H SK 'Vignette' must be purchased before travel
	Principal trunk highway – single / dual carriageway
	tunnel, under construction
	Other main highway – single / dual carriageway
	Other important road, other road
E25 A49	European road number, motorway number
135	National road number
Col Bayard 1248	Mountain pass
▲	Scenic route, gradient – arrow points uphill
143	Distances – in kilometres major
28	minor
	Principal railway with tunnel
	Ferry route
	Short ferry route
	International boundary, national boundary
	National park, natural park

✈ Airport		⛷ Ski resort	
🏛 Ancient monument		☷ Theme park	
⌇ Beach		◉ World Heritage site	
⌂ Castle or house		1754▲ Spot height	
⌂ Cave		Sevilla World Heritage town	
✦ Other place of interest		Verona Town of tourist interest	
❀ Park or garden		◼ ● City or town with Low Emission Zone	
✝ Religious building			

Scale · pages 26–181
1:753 800
1 inch = 12 miles
1 cm = 7.5km

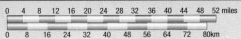

Scale · pages 182–200
1:1 507 600
1 inch = 24 miles
1 cm = 15km

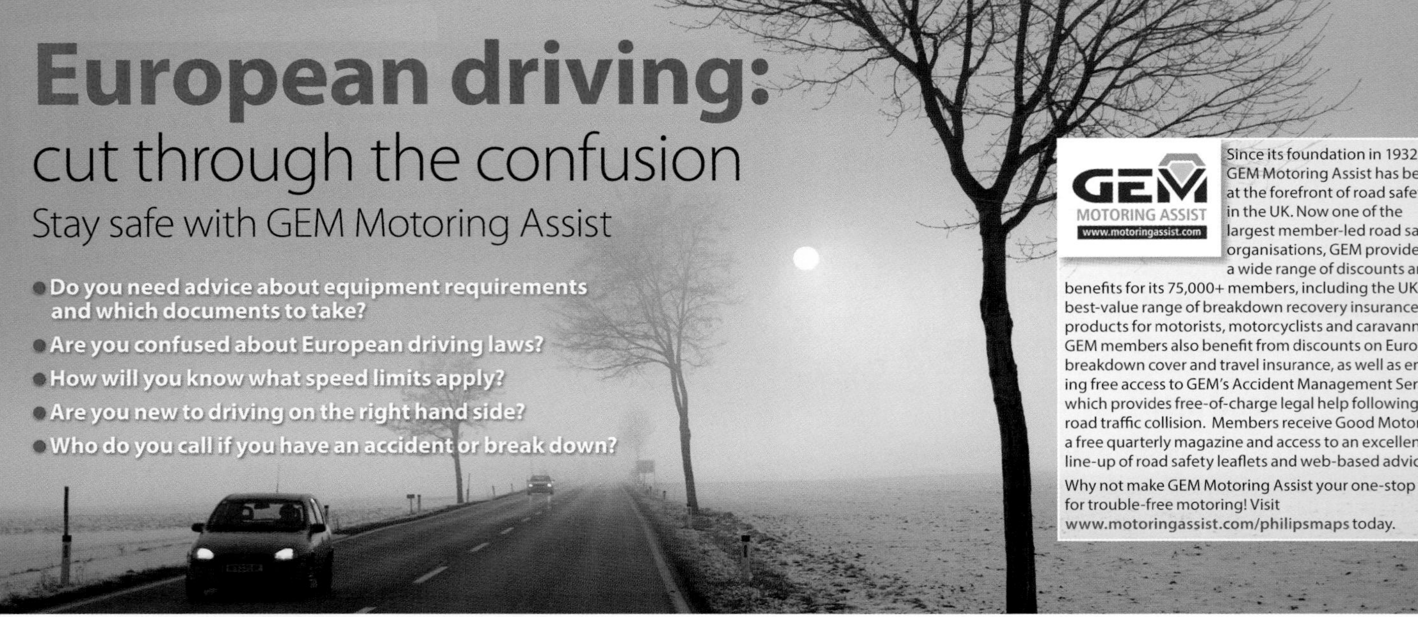

European driving:
cut through the confusion
Stay safe with GEM Motoring Assist

- Do you need advice about equipment requirements and which documents to take?
- Are you confused about European driving laws?
- How will you know what speed limits apply?
- Are you new to driving on the right hand side?
- Who do you call if you have an accident or break down?

M illions of us drive abroad on holiday each year. Perhaps it's a long motorway trip to the Mediterranean, a selection of historic cities and sites or a gentle tour along quiet country lanes. Whatever the purpose, it makes sense to ensure that both we and our vehicles are properly prepared for the journey.

It's not easy getting to grips with the finer points of driving in other countries, however experienced you may be as a motorist. Whether you have notched up thousands of miles of European driving or are preparing to make your first journey, the chances are you will always manage to find some road sign or legal requirement that will cause confusion.

What's more, 'driving in Europe' covers such a huge area. There are currently 28 countries in the European Union alone, each with its own set of road traffic laws and motoring customs. Driving in Europe can mean a spectacular and sunny coastal road that's within sight of Africa, or a snowy track amid the biting cold of the Arctic Circle, where the only others on the road are reindeer. Add to this some of the world's most congested cities, dense clusters of motorways (many with confusing numbers) and a big variation in safety standards and attitudes to risk. No wonder we often risk getting lost, taking wrong turnings or perhaps stopping where we shouldn't.

Depending on the country we're in, our errors at the wheel or our lack of familiarity with the rules of the road can sometimes bring unwelcome consequences. In any country, foreign drivers are subject to the same traffic rules as residents, enforceable in many situations by hefty on-the-spot fines and other sanctions. The situation across Europe is complex, simply because of the number of different sets of rules. For example, failure to carry a specific piece of breakdown equipment may be an offence in one country, but not in another. It's easy to see why the fun and excitement of a road trip in Europe could be spoilt by a minefield of regulations.

But we want to ensure that doesn't happen. Preparation and planning are key to a great holiday. It certainly pays to do a bit of research before you go, just to ensure you and your vehicle are up to the journey, your documents are in order and you're carrying the correct levels of equipment to keep the law enforcers happy.

Before you go

Some sensible planning will help make sure your European journey is enjoyable and – we hope – stress-free. So take some time before departure to ensure everything is in good shape: and that includes you, your travelling companions and your vehicle.

For you:

Try to become familiar with the driving laws of your holiday destination, including the local speed limits and which side of the road to drive on. You will be subject to these laws when driving abroad and if you are stopped by the police, it is not an excuse to say that you were unaware of them. Police officers in many countries have the power to impose (and collect) substantial on-the-spot fines for motoring offences, whether you are a resident or a visitor.

The European Commission's 'Driving Abroad' website http://ec.europa.eu/transport/road_safety/going_abroad gives detailed information on different road traffic rules in different European countries.

The Foreign and Commonwealth Office also gives country-specific travel advice www.gov.uk/driving-abroad with information on driving.

Passports

Check everyone's passport to make sure they are all valid.

Don't wait for your passport to expire. Unused time, rounded up to whole months (minimum one month, maximum nine months), will usually be added to your new passport.

New passports usually take two weeks to arrive. The Passport Office (0300 222 0000, www.gov.uk/renew-adult-passport) offers a faster service if you need a replacement passport urgently, but you'll have to pay a lot more.

Driving Licence

The new style photocard driving licence is currently valid in all European Union countries. Some non-EU countries may also require an International Driving Permit (£5.50, available from Post Offices). The previously used pink EU format UK paper licence is no longer a valid document. If you're planning to hire a car, the company may ask for a check code (www.gov.uk/view-driving-licence) so they can view your driving record, entitlement and any penalty points you may have. So if you haven't already done so, now is the time to update your old licence. For more information, contact the DVLA (0300 790 6802, www.gov.uk/government/organisations/driver-and-vehicle-licensing-agency)

Travel Insurance

Travel insurance is vital as it covers you against medical emergencies, accidents, thefts and cancellations, and repatriation. Ask for details before buying any travel insurance policy. Find out what it covers you for, and to what value. More important, check what's not covered. One of the key benefits of GEM membership is the excellent discount you can get on travel insurance. For more details, please visit: www.motoringassist.com/philipsmaps

European Breakdown Cover

Don't risk letting a breakdown ruin your European trip. Ensure you purchase a policy that will cover you for roadside assistance, emergency repair and recovery of your vehicle to the UK, wherever in Europe you may be heading. Once again, GEM members enjoy a specially discounted rate. You'll find the details at www.motoringassist.com/philipsmaps

EHIC

You wil need an EHIC card for everyone travelling. These are free and cover you for any medical treatment you may need during a trip to another EU or EEA country or Switzerland. However, do check at the time of requiring assistance that your EHIC will be accepted. Apply online (www.gov.uk/european-health-insurance-card), by telephone (0300 3301350) or complete an application form, available from a Post office. Allow up to 14 days for the cards to arrive.

For your vehicle:

Service

It makes sense to get your car serviced before you travel. At the very least, ensure the tyres have plenty of tread left and that coolant and oil levels are checked and topped up if required. Check them regularly during your time away.

Vehicle Registration Document

Police in many countries can demand that you prove you have the right to be driving your car. That means you need to show the registration document, or a suitable letter of authorisation if the registration document is not in your name. Remember you should never leave the registration document in the car.

Nationality plate

Your vehicle must display a nationality plate of an approved pattern, design and size.

MOT

If your car is more than three years old, make sure you take its current MOT test certificate with you.

Insurance

If you are planning a trip to Europe, you should find that your car insurance policy provides you with the minimum amount of cover you need. But it's important to contact your insurer before you go, to confirm exactly what level of cover you have and for how many days it will be valid.

Mechanical adjustments

Check the adjustments required for your headlights before you go. Beam deflectors are a legal requirement if you drive in Europe. They are generally sold at the ports, on ferries and in the Folkestone Eurotunnel terminal, but be warned – the instructions can be a little confusing! The alternative is to ask a local garage to do the job for you before you go. If you choose this, then make sure you shop around as prices for undertaking this very simple task vary enormously.

Equipment check-list

This checklist represents GEM's suggestions for what you should take with you in the car. Different countries have different rules about what's compulsory and these rules change from time to time. So it's important to check carefully before you set out. For country-by-country guidance, visit www.motoringassist.com/europe or see page IV of this atlas.

- Fire extinguisher
- First aid kit
- High-visibility jacket – one for each occupant
- Two warning triangles
- Replacement bulbs and fuses
- Spare spectacles (if worn) for each driver
- Snow chains for winter journeys into the mountains
- Camera and notebook. Keep in your glove compartment and record any collisions or damage for insurance purposes (if it is safe).

Contact details

Make sure you have all relevant emergency helpline numbers with you, including emergency services, breakdown assistance, the local British consulate and your insurance company. There are links to embassies and consulates around the world from the Foreign Office website. (www.fco.gov.uk) For information, the European emergency telephone number (our equivalent of 999) is 112.

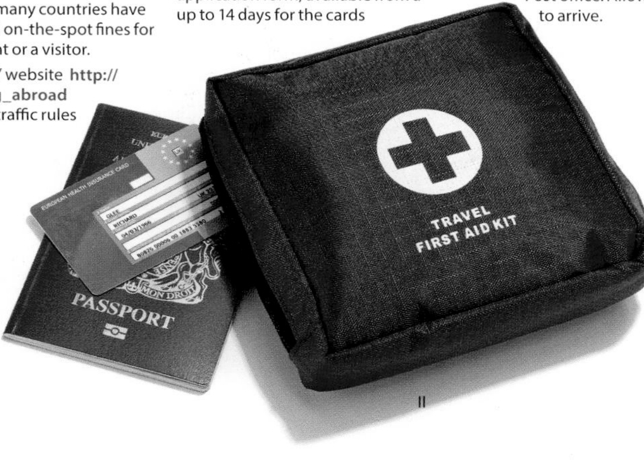

TOP AND GIVE WAY

ho has priority?
ake sure you keep a watchful eye on signs telling you who has priority on the ad. Look for a yellow diamond sign, which tells you that traffic already on the ad has priority. If you see the yellow diamond sign crossed out, then you ıst give way to traffic joining the road.

iorité a droite
espite the use of the yellow diamond signs, be aware that on some French roads specially roundabouts in Paris), the traditional 'priorité a droite' practice is followed, en though it may no longer be legal. In theory these days, the rule no longer plies unless it is clearly signed. In practice, though, it makes sense to anticipate driver pulling out in front of you, even though the priority may be yours.

eadlight flash
ar in mind that the practice of flashing headlights at a junction in France es not mean the same thing as it might in the UK. If another motorists flashes headlights at you, he's telling you that he has priority and will be coming rough in front of you.

op means stop!
ou come to a solid white line with an octagonal 'STOP' sign, then u must come to a complete stop. In other words your wheels ıst stop turning. Adherence to the 'STOP' sign is generally uch more rigorously enforced in European countries than you ay be used to here.

HELP ME, PLEASE!

If you're in a difficult situation and need local help, then the following words and phrases might prove useful if language is a problem:

(UK flag)	(French flag)	(Spanish flag)	(Italian flag)	(German flag)
Do you speak English?	Parlez-vous anglais?	¿Habla usted inglés?	Parla inglese?	Sprechen Sie Englisch?
Thank you (very much)	Merci (beaucoup)	(Muchas) Gracias	Grazie (mille)	Danke (sehr)
Is there a police station near here?	Est-ce qu'il y a un commissariat de police près d'ici?	¿Hay una comisaría cerca?	C'e' un commissariato qui vicino?	Gibt es ein Polizeirevier hier in der Nähe?
I have lost my passport.	J'ai perdu mon passeport.	He perdido mi pasaporte	Ho perso il mio passaporto.	Ich have meinen Reisepass verloren.
I have broken down.	Je suis tombé en panne	Mi coche se ha averiado.	Ho un guasto.	Ich habe eine Panne.
I have run out of fuel.	Je suis tombé en panne d'essence.	Me he quedado sin gasolina.	Ho terminato la benzina.	Ich habe kein Benzin mehr.

ORTH KNOWING

u will need a separate GB sticker in EU countries if your car esn't have a registration plate containing the GB euro-symbol.

el is generally most expensive at motorway service areas and eapest at supermarkets. However, these are usually shut on ndays and Bank Holidays. So-called '24 hour' regional fuel tions in France generally accept payment by UK credit card ese days, but some drivers still occasionally report difficulties. ould be better not to rely on them if your tank is running low ing a night-time journey.

ou see several fuel stations in short succession before a ional border, it's likely that fuel on the other side will be more pensive, so take the opportunity to fill up.

dar speed camera detectors are illegal in most European untries.

e insurance 'green card' is no longer required for journeys in ope, but it is important to make sure you have contact details your insurer in case of an accident or claim.

eed limits in France are enforced rigorously. Radar controls frequent, and any driver (including non-residents) detected nore than 25km/h above the speed limit can have their licence nfiscated on the spot. If you are caught exceeding the limit by km/h, even on a first offence, your car may be confiscated.

Spain you must carry two warning triangles, plus a spare pair glasses for every driver who needs to use them.

Luxembourg, there are specific rules relating to how you fix a nav device to your windscreen. Get it wrong and you could be ed on the spot.

Germany it is against the law to run out of fuel on the otorway. If you do run out, then you face an on-the-spot fine.

rway and Sweden have particularly low limits for ink-driving: just 20mg per 100ml of blood (compared to in the UK). In Slovakia, the limit is zero.

Hungary, the limit is also zero. If you are found to be drink-ving, your driving licence will be withdrawn by police officers the spot.

most countries, maps and signs will have the European road mber (shown in white on a green background) alongside the propriate national road number. However, in Sweden and lgium only the E-road number will be shown.

ther laws and motoring advice to be vare of across Europe:

stria Recent rules require the mandatory use of winter tyres tween 1 November and 15 April. You should not use your horn en driving near hospitals. There are also restrictions on use of hicle horns in Vienna.

lgium You will have to pay to use most public toilets – cluding those at motorway service stations • You are not rmitted to use cruise control on motorways when traffic is avy • There are also specific penalties for close-following on otorways • Roadside drug-testing of drivers (using oral fluid sting devices) forms a regular part of any police controls rivers must carry a reflective vest in case of breakdown

prus There have been important changes in how speeding and nk-driving are sanctioned. Cyprus now has a graduated system speeding fines, ranging from one euro per km/h over the limit marginal cases through to fines of up to €5,000 and a term of prisonment for the most severe infringements. There are also aduated fines for drink-driving, ranging from fixed penalties for ing slightly over the limit to terms of imprisonment and fines of to €5,000 for the most severe. Eating and drinking at the wheel e both prohibited.

enmark Cars towing caravans and trailers are prohibited from ertaking on motorways at certain times of day.

nland Speeding fines are worked out according to your income. cess to a national database allows police at the roadside to tablish a Finnish resident's income and number of dependants. ficers then impose a fine based on a specific number of days' come. The minimum speeding fine is 115 euros • If you hit an or deer, you must report the collision to the police.

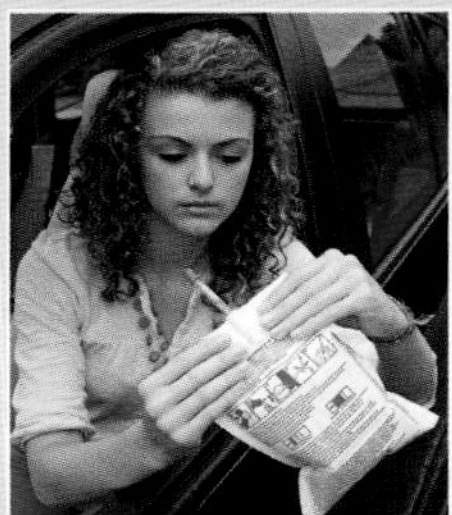

France Legislation introduced in France in 2012 requires every driver and motorcyclist to be in possession of a valid breath-alyser (displaying an 'NF' number), either electronic or chemical, to be shown to a police officer in case of control. However, the imposition of an €11 fine for failing to produce a breathalyser when required has been postponed indefinitely. So, in theory, you are required to carry a breathalyser kit, but no fine can be imposed if you don't • Motorcyclists' helmets must have four reflective stickers fitted, and there is an on-the-spot fine of €135 for non-compliance (by foreign riders as well as French). In common with other vehicle users, motorcyclists must also carry high-visibility vests to be worn on the roadside in case of emer-gency • Radar detectors, are banned with fines of €1500 for anyone using them • There are stiff penalties for driving while using a mobile phone. • The drink-drive limit for those who have held a licence for less than three years has been reduced to 20mg per 100ml of blood. For other drivers, the limit is 50mg. This compares with 80mg in England and Wales.

Germany Check your fuel contents regularly as it's an offence to run out of fuel on a German motorway • It's also an offence to make rude signs to other road users.

Greece Greece has one of Europe's highest accident rates in terms of the number of crashes per vehicle. Pay particular attention at traffic light junctions, as red lights are frequently ignored • Drivers detected with more than 110mg per 100ml of blood will face revocation of their licence, and possibly up to two years imprisonment • Carrying a petrol can in a vehicle is forbidden.

Ireland The drink-drive limit was reduced in 2011 from 80mg per 100ml of blood to 50mg • Beware of rural three-lane roads, where the middle overtaking lane is used by traffic travelling in both directions. On wider rural roads it's the accepted practice for slower vehicles to pull over to let faster traffic through.

Italy Police can impound your vehicle if you cannot present the relevant ownership documents when requested • You will need a red and white warning sign if you plan to use any rear-mounted luggage rack such as a bike rack • Zero alcohol tolerance is now applied for drivers who have held a driving licence for less than three years, as well as to drivers aged 18 to 21, professional drivers, taxi drivers and truckers.

Norway Under new legislation, police officers can perform roadside drug impairment saliva tests. There are specific limits set for the presence of 20 common non-alcohol drugs • You'll find what amounts to zero tolerance where drinking and driving is concerned. Only 10mg of alcohol per 100ml of blood is permitted (compared to 80mg in the UK) • Speeding fines are high. For example, a driver caught at 25 km/h over the 80 km/h speed limit on a national road could expect a fine of around £600. • No overtaking' signs apply to cars overtaking other cars and motorbikes overtaking cars, but curiously not to cars overtaking motorbikes.

Portugal If you are towing a caravan, you must have a current inventory of the caravan's contents to show a police officer if requested.

Slovakia It is mandatory to use dipped headlights on every road journey, regardless of the time of day, season or weather conditions.

Spain Motorway speed limits in Spain are 120km/h • If you need glasses for driving, then the law requires you to carry a spare pair with you in the car • It's compulsory to carry two spare warning triangles, spare bulbs for your car and reflective jackets.

Turkey Take great caution if you're driving at dusk. Many local drivers put off using their lights until it's properly dark, so you may find oncoming traffic very hard to spot • During the time of Ramadan, many people will not eat or drink between the hours of sunrise and sunset. This can seriously reduce levels of alertness, especially among people driving buses, trucks and taxis.

TOP TIPS FOR STAYING SAFE

Collisions abroad occur not just because of poor driving conditions locally, but also because we do not always take the same safety precautions as we might expect to take at home, for example by not wearing a seatbelt or by drinking and driving.

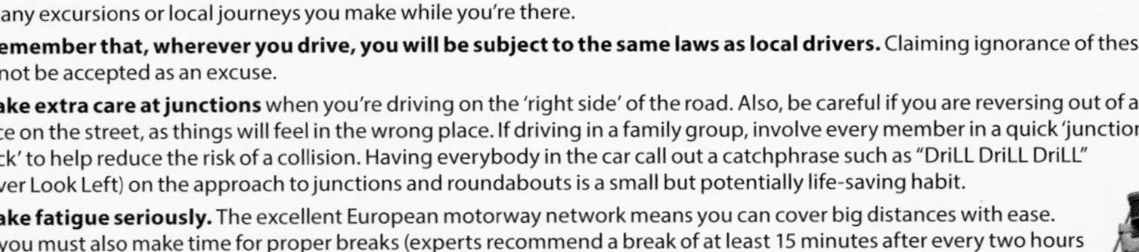

1. Plan your route before you go. That includes the journey you make to reach your destination (with sufficient breaks built in) and any excursions or local journeys you make while you're there.

2. Remember that, wherever you drive, you will be subject to the same laws as local drivers. Claiming ignorance of these laws will not be accepted as an excuse.

3. Take extra care at junctions when you're driving on the 'right side' of the road. Also, be careful if you are reversing out of a parking space on the street, as things will feel in the wrong place. If driving in a family group, involve every member in a quick 'junction safety check' to help reduce the risk of a collision. Having everybody in the car call out a catchphrase such as "DriLL DriLL DriLL" (Driver Look Left) on the approach to junctions and roundabouts is a small but potentially life-saving habit.

4. Take fatigue seriously. The excellent European motorway network means you can cover big distances with ease. But you must also make time for proper breaks (experts recommend a break of at least 15 minutes after every two hours of driving). If possible, share the driving and set strict daily limits to the number of driving hours. Watch a short video that explains the risks of driver fatigue: **www.motoringassist.com/fatigue**

5. Drink-driving limits across Europe are lower than those in the UK. The only exception is Malta, where the limit is the same. Bear this in mind if you're flying to a holiday or business destination and plan to have a drink on the plane, as the combination of unfamiliar roads and alcohol in your bloodstream is not a safe one. It's also worth remembering that drivers who cause collisions because they were drinking are likely to find their insurance policy will not cover them.

6. Expect the unexpected. Styles of driving in your destination country are likely to be very different from those you know in the UK. Drive defensively and certainly don't get involved in any altercations on the road.

7. Don't overload your car, however tempting the local bargains may appear. Make sure you have good all-round visibility by ensuring you don't pile up items on the parcel shelf or boot, and keep your windscreen clean.

8. Always wear a seatbelt and ensure everyone else on board wears one. Check specific regulations regarding the carriage of children: in some countries children under the age of 12 may not travel in the front of the car.

9. Don't use your mobile phone while driving. Even though laws on phone use while driving differ from country to country, the practice is just as dangerous wherever you are.

10. When you're exploring on foot, be wise to road safety as a pedestrian. You may get into trouble for 'jay-walking' so don't just wander across a road. Use a proper crossing, but remember that drivers may not stop for you! Don't forget that traffic closest to you approaches from the LEFT.

Driving regulations

Vehicle A national vehicle identification plate is always required when taking a vehicle abroad.

Fitting headlamp converters or beam deflectors when taking a right-hand drive car to a country where driving is on the right (every country in Europe except the UK and Ireland) is compulsory.

Within the EU, if not driving a locally hired car, it is compulsory to have either Europlates or a country of origin (e.g. GB) sticker. Outside the EU (and in Andorra) a sticker is compulsory, even with Europlates.

Documentation All countries require that you carry a valid passport, vehicle registration document, hire certificate or letter of authority for the use of someone else's vehicle, full driving licence/International Driving Permit and insurance documentation (and/or green card outside the EU). Some non-EU countries also require a visa. Minimum driving ages are often higher for people holding foreign licences. Exit checks at the Eurotunnel and ferry terminals mean that drivers taking vehicles from the UK should allow extra time. Drivers of vehicles over three years old should ensure that the MOT is up to date, and take the certificate with them..

EHIC cards are free and give you entitlement to healthcare in other EU countries and Switzerland. www.gov/european-health-insurance-card

Licence A photo licence is preferred; with an old-style paper licence, an International Driving Permit (IDP) should also be carried. In some countries, an IDP is compulsory, whatever form of licence is held. Non-EU drivers should always have both a licence and and IDP. UK (except NI) drivers should check in advance whether a hire company will wish to check for endorsements and vehicle categories. If so, visit www.gov.uk/view-driving-*licence* to create a digital code (valid for 72 hours) that allows their details to be shared. For more information, contact the DVLA (0300790 6802, www.dft.gov.uk/dvla).

Insurance Third-party cover is compulsory across Europe. Most insurance policies give only basic cover when driving abroad, so you should check that your policy provides at least third-party cover for the countries in which you will be driving and upgrade it to the level that you require. You may have to take out extra cover at the frontier if you cannot produce acceptable proof of adequate insurance. Even in countries in which a green card is not required, carrying one is recommended for extra proof of insurance.

Motorcycles It is compulsory for all motorcyclists and passengers to wear crash helmets.

Other In countries in which visibility vests are compulsory, one for each person should be carried in the passenger compartment, or panniers on a motorbike, where they can be reached easily.

Warning triangles should also be carried in the passenger compartment.

The penalties for infringements of regulations vary considerably from one country to another. In many countries the police may impose on-the-spot fines (ask for a receipt). Penalties can be severe for serious infringements, particularly for exceeding the blood-alcohol limit; in some countries this can result in immediate imprisonment.

In some countries, vignettes for toll roads are being replaced by electronic tags.

Please note that driving regulations may change, and that it has not been possible to cover all the information for every type of vehicle. The figures given for capitals' populations are for the whole metropolitan area.

The symbols used are:

- Motorway
- Dual carriageway
- Single carriageway
- Surfaced road
- Unsurfaced or gravel road
- Urban area
- Speed limit in kilometres per hour (kph). These are the maximum speeds for the types of roads listed. In some places and under certain conditions they may be considerably lower. Always obey local signs.
- Seat belts
- Children
- Blood alcohol level
- Warning triangle
- First aid kit
- Spare bulb kit
- Fire extinguisher
- Minimum driving age
- Additional documents required
- Mobile phones
- Dipped headlights
- Winter driving
- LEZ Low Emission Zone
- ★ Other information

Andorra Principat d'Andorra (AND)

Area 468 sq km (181 sq miles)
Population 85,500 **Capital** Andorra la Vella (44,000)
Languages Catalan (official), French, Castilian and Portuguese **Currency** Euro = 100 cents
Website http://visitandorra.com

	Motorway	Dual carriageway	Single carriageway	Urban area
Speed	n/a	90	60/90	50

- Compulsory
- Under 10 and below 150 cm must travel in an EU-approved restraint system adapted to their size in the rear. Airbag must be deactivated if a child is in the front passenger seat.
- 0.05% · Compulsory · Recommended
- Compulsory · Recommended · 18
- Not permitted whilst driving
- Compulsory for motorcycles during day and for other vehicles during poor daytime visibility.
- Winter tyres recommended. Snow chains compulsory in poor conditions or when indicated.
- ★ On-the-spot fines imposed
- ★ Visibility vests compulsory

Austria Österreich (A)

Area 83,859 sq km (32,377 sq miles)
Population 8,823,000 **Capital** Vienna / Wien (1,890,000) **Languages** German (official)
Currency Euro = 100 cents
Website www.austria.org

	Motorway	Dual carriageway	Single carriageway	Urban area
Speed	130	100	100	50
If towing trailer under 750kg / over 750 kg				
Speed	100	100	100/80	50

- Compulsory
- Under 14 and under 150cm cannot travel as a front or rear passenger unless they use a suitable child restraint; under 14 over 150cm must wear adult seat belt
- 0.049% • 0.01% if licence held less than 2 years
- Compulsory · Compulsory
- Recommended · Recommended
- 17 (20 for motorbikes over 50cc)
- Paper driving licences must be accompanied by photographic proof of identity.
- Only allowed with hands-free kit
- LEZ Several cities and regions have LEZs affecting HGVs that ban non-compliant vehicles, impose speed restrictions and night-time bans.
- Must be used during the day by all road users. Headlamp converters compulsory
- Winter tyres compulsory 1 Nov–15 Apr
- ★ On-the-spot fines imposed
- ★ Radar detectors and dashcams prohibited
- ★ To drive on motorways or expressways, a motorway sticker must be purchased at the border or main petrol station. These are available for 10 days, 2 months or 1 year. Vehicles 3.5 tonnes or over must display an electronic tag.
- ★ Visibility vests compulsory

Belarus (BY)

Area 207,600 sq km (80,154 sq miles)
Population 9,492,000 **Capital** Minsk (1,982,000)
Languages Belarusian, Russian (both official)
Currency Belarusian ruble = 100 kopek
Website www.belarus.by/en/government

	Motorway	Dual carriageway	Single carriageway	Urban area
Speed	110	90	90	40*
If towing trailer under 750kg				
Speed	90	70	70	

*In residential areas limit is 20 km/h • Vehicle towing another vehicle 50 kph limit • If full driving licence held for less than two years, must not exceed 70 kph

- Compulsory in front seats, and rear seats if fitted
- Under 12 not allowed in front seat and must use appropriate child restraint
- 0.00% · Compulsory · Compulsory
- Recommended · Compulsory · 18
- Visa, vehicle technical check stamp, international driving permit, green card, local health insurance. Even with a green card, local third-party insurance may be imposed at the border
- Use prohibited
- Compulsory during the day Nov–Mar and at all other times in conditions of poor visibility or when towing or being towed.
- Winter tyres compulsory; snow chains recommended
- ★ A temporary vehicle import certificate must be purchased on entry and driver must be registered
- ★ It is illegal for vehicles to be dirty
- ★ On-the-spot fines imposed
- ★ Radar-detectors prohibited
- ★ Road tax imposed at the border
- ★ To drive on main motorways an on-board unit must be acquired at the border or a petrol station in order to pay tolls. See www.beltoll.by/index.php/en

Belgium Belgique (B)

Area 30,528 sq km (11,786 sq miles)
Population 11,358,000 **Capital** Brussels/Bruxelles (1,175,000) **Languages** Dutch, French, German (all official) **Currency** Euro = 100 cents
Website www.belgium.be/en

	Motorway	Dual carriageway	Single carriageway	Urban area
Speed	120[1]	120[1]	90[2]	50[3]
If towing trailer				
Speed	90	90	60	50[3]
Over 3.5 tonnes				
Speed	90	90	60	50

[1]Minimum speed of 70 kph may be applied in certain conditions on motorways and some dual carriageways. [2]70 kph in Flanders. [3]20 kph in residential areas, 30 kph near some schools, hospitals and churches.

- Compulsory
- All under 18s under 135 cm must wear an appropriate child restraint. Airbags must be deactivated if rear-facing child seat is used in the front
- 0.049% · Compulsory · Recommended
- Recommended · Compulsory
- Motorcyclists must wear fully protective clothing
- 18 · Only allowed with a hands-free kit
- LEZ LEZs in operation in Antwerp, Brussels and areas of Flanders. Preregistration necessary and fees payable for most vehicles.
- Mandatory at all times for motorcycles and during the day in poor conditions for other vehicles
- ★ Cruise control must be deactivated on motorways where indicated ★ On-the-spot fines imposed ★ Radar detectors prohibited ★ Sticker indicating maximum recommended speed for winter tyres must be displayed on dashboard if using them ★ Visibility vest compulsory

Bosnia & Herzegovina Bosna i Hercegovina (BIH)

Area 51,197 km² (19,767 mi²) **Population** 3,872,000 **Capital** Sarajevo (643,000) **Languages** Bosnian/Croatian/Serbian **Currency** Convertible Marka = 100 convertible pfenniga
Website www.fbihvlada.gov.ba/english/index.php

	Motorway	Dual carriageway	Single carriageway	Urban area
Speed	130	100	80	50

- Compulsory if fitted
- Under 12s must sit in rear using an appropriate child restraint. Under-2s may travel in a rear-facing child seat in the front only if the airbags have been deactivated.
- 0.03% · Compulsory
- Compulsory · Compulsory
- Compulsory for LPG vehicles · 18
- Visa, International Driving Permit, green card
- Prohibited
- Compulsory for all vehicles at all times
- Winter tyres compulsory 15 Nov–15 Apr; snow chains recommended
- ★ GPS must have fixed speed camera function deactivated; radar detectors prohibited. ★ On-the-spot fines imposed ★ Visibility vest, tow rope or tow bar compulsory ★ Spare wheel compulsory, except for two-wheeled vehicles

Bulgaria Bulgariya (BG)

Area 110,912 sq km (42,822 sq miles)
Population 7,050,000 **Capital** Sofia (1,682,000)
Languages Bulgarian (official), Turkish **Currency** Lev = 100 stotinki **Website** www.government.bg

	Motorway	Dual carriageway	Single carriageway	Urban area
Speed	130	90	90	50
If towing trailer				
Speed	100	70	70	50

- Compulsory in front and rear seats
- Under 3s not permitted in vehicles with no child restraints; 3–10 year olds must sit in rear in an appropriate restraint. Rear-facing child seats may be used in the front only if the airbag has been deactivated
- 0.049% · Compulsory · Compulsory
- Recommended · Compulsory · 18
- Photo driving licence preferred; a paper licence must be accompanied by an International Driving Permit. Green card or insurance specific to Bulgaria.
- Only allowed with a hands-free kit
- Compulsory
- Winter tyres compulsory. Snow chains should be carried from 1 Nov–1 Mar. Max speed with chains 50 kph
- ★ Fee at border ★ GPS must have fixed speed camera function deactivated; radar detectors prohibited ★ On-the-spot fines imposed ★ Road tax stickers (annual, monthly or weekly) must be purchased at the border and displayed prominently with the vehicle registration number written on them. ★ Visibility vest compulsory

Croatia Hrvatska (HR)

Area 56,538 km² (21,829 mi²)
Population 4,154,000 **Capital** Zagreb (1,113,000)
Languages Croatian **Currency** Kuna = 100 lipa
Website https://vlada.gov.hr/en

	Motorway	Dual carriageway	Single carriageway	Urban area
Speed	130	110	90	50
Under 24				
Speed	120	100	80	50
If towing				
Speed	90	90	80	50

- Compulsory if fitted
- Children under 12 not permitted in front seat and must use appropriate child seat or restrai in rear. Children under 2 may use a rear-facing seat in the front only if the airbag is deactivate
- 0.05% • 0.00 % for drivers under 24
- Compulsory (two if towing) · Compulsory
- Compulsory · Recommended · 18
- Green card recommended
- Only allowed with hands-free kit
- Compulsory
- Winter tyres, snow chains and shovel compulsory in winter
- ★ On-the-spot fines imposed ★ Radar detector prohibited ★ Tow bar and rope compulsory ★ Visibility vest compulsory

Czechia Česko (CZ)

Area 78,864 sq km (30,449 sq miles)
Population 10,611,000 **Capital** Prague/Praha (2,619,000) **Languages** Czech (official), Moravian
Currency Czech Koruna = 100 haler
Website https://vlada.cz/en/

	Motorway	Dual carriageway	Single carriageway	Urban area
Speed	130	90	90	50
If towing				
Speed	80	80	80	50

- Compulsory in front seats and, if fitted, in rear
- Children under 36 kg and 150 cm must use appropriate child restraint. Only front-facing child retraints are permitted in the front in vehicles with airbags fitted. Airbags must be deactivated if a rear-facing child seat is used i the front.
- 0.00% · Compulsory · Compulsory
- Compulsory · Compulsory
- 18 (17 for motorcycles under 125 cc)
- Licences with a photo preferred. Paper licenc should be accompanied by an International Driving Permit.
- Only allowed with a hands-free kit
- LEZ Two-stage LEZ in Prague for vehicles over 3.5 and 6 tonnes. Permit system.
- Compulsory at all times
- Winter tyres compulsory November-March, roads are icy/snow-covered or snow is expected. Max speed 50 kph.
- ★ GPS must have fixed speed camera function deactivated; radar detectors prohibited ★ On-the-spot fines imposed ★ Replaceme fuses must be carried ★ Spectacles or conta lens wearers must carry a spare pair in their vehicle at all times ★ Vignette needed for motorway driving, available for 1 year, 60 day 15 days. Toll specific to lorries introduced 200 those over 12 tonnes must buy an electronic ★ Visibility vest compulsory

Denmark Danmark (DK)

Area 43,094 sq km (16,638 sq miles)
Population 5,786,000 **Capital** Copenhagen / København (1,922,000) **Languages** Danish (officia
Currency Krone = 100 øre
Website www.denmark.dk/en

	Motorway	Dual carriageway	Single carriageway	Urban area
Speed	110-130	80-90	80	50*
If towing				
Speed	80	70	70	50*

*Central Copenhagen 40 kph

- Compulsory front and rear
- Under 135cm must use appropriate child restraint; in front permitted only in an appropriate rear-facing seat with any airbags disabled
- 0.05% · Compulsory · Recommended
- Recommended · Recommended · 17
- Only allowed with a hands-free kit
- LEZ Aalborg, Arhus, Copenhagen, Frederiksberg and Odense. Proofs of emissions compliance compliant filter needed to obtain sticker. Non compliant vehicles banned.
- Must be used at all times
- Spiked tyres may be fitted 1 Nov–15 April, if used on all wheels
- ★ On-the-spot fines imposed ★ Radar detectors prohibited ★ Tolls apply on the Storebaeltsbroen and Oresundsbron bridges. ★ Visibility vest recommended

stonia Eesti (EST)

ea 45,100 sq km (17,413 sq miles)
pulation 1,319,000 **Capital** Tallinn (610,000)
nguages Estonian (official), Russian **Currency**
o = 100 cents **Website** www.valitsus.ee/en

	n/a	90*	90	50
ull driving licence held for less than two years				
	90	90	90	50

summer, the speed limit on some dual riageways may be raised to 100/110 kph

Compulsory if fitted
Children too small for adult seatbelts must wear a seat restraint appropriate to their size. Rear-facing safety seats must not be used in the front if an air bag is fitted, unless this has been deactivated.
0.00% 2 compulsory Compulsory
Recommended Compulsory 18
Only allowed with a hands-free kit
Compulsory at all times
Winter tyres are compulsory from Dec–Mar. Studded winter tyres are allowed from 15 Oct–31 Mar, but this can be extended to start 1 October and/or end 30 April
A toll system is in operation in Tallinn ★ On-the-spot fines imposed ★ Two wheel chocks compulsory ★ Visibility vest compulsory

nland Suomi (FIN)

ea 338,145 sq km (130,557 sq miles)
pulation 5,517,000 **Capital** Helsinki (1,471,000)
nguages Finnish, Swedish (both official)
rrency Euro = 100 cents
bsite https://valtioneuvosto.fi/en/frontpage

	120	100	80/100*	20/50
ns, lorries and if towing				
	80	80	60	20/50

) in summer • If towing a vehicle by rope, cable od, max speed limit 60 kph • Maximum of 80 kph vans and lorries • Speed limits are often lowered vinter

Compulsory in front and rear
Below 135 cm must use a child restraint or seat
0.05% Compulsory Recommended
Recommended Recommended
18 (motorbikes below 125cc 16)
Only allowed with hands-free kit
Must be used at all times
Winter tyres compulsory Dec–Feb
On-the-spot fines imposed ★ Radar-detectors are prohibited ★ Visibility vest compulsory

ance (F)

ea 551,500 sq km (212,934 sq miles)
pulation 65,058,000 **Capital** Paris (12,405,000)
nguages French (official), Breton, Occitan
rrency Euro = 100 cents
bsite www.diplomatie.gouv.fr/en/

	130	110	80	50
wet roads or if full driving licence held for ss than 3 years				
	110	100	70	50
owing below / above 3.5 tonnes gross				
	110/90	100/90	90/80	50

kph on all roads if fog reduces visibility to less n 50m

Compulsory in front seats and, if fitted, in rear
In rear, 4 or under must have a child safety seat (rear facing if up to 9 months); if 5–10 must use an appropriate restraint system. Under 10 permitted in the front only if rear seats are fully occupied by other under 10s or there are no rear safety belts. In front, if child is in rear-facing child seat, any airbag must be deactivated.
0.049% • If towing or with less than 2 years with full driving licence, 0.00% • All drivers/motorcyclists must carry an unused breathalyser to French certification standards, showing an NF number.
Compulsory Recommended
Recommended
18 (16 for motorbikes up to 80cc)
Use not permitted whilst driving
LEZs operate in the Mont Blanc Tunnel, Paris, Marseille and many other major cities. Crit'air vignettes must be displayed by compliant vehicles in such areas. Non-compliant vehicles are banned. See https://www.certificat-air.gouv.fr/en
Compulsory in poor daytime visibility and at all times for motorcycles
Winter tyres recommended. Carrying snow chains recommended in winter as these may have to be fitted if driving on snow-covered roads, in accordance with signage. Max speed 50kph.

★ GPS must have fixed speed camera function deactivated; radar-detection equipment is prohibited ★ Motorcyclists and passengers must have four reflective stickers on their helmets (front, back and both sides) and wear CE-certified gloves. ★ On-the-spot fines imposed ★ Tolls on motorways. Electronic tag needed if using automatic tolls. ★ Visibility vests, to be worn on the roadside in case of emergency or breakdown, must be carried for all vehicle occupants and riders. ★ Wearers of contact lenses or spectacles or lenses should carry a spare pair

Germany Deutschland (D)

Area 357,022 sq km (137,846 sq miles)
Population 82,806,000 **Capital** Berlin (6,005,000)
Languages German (official) **Currency** Euro = 100 cents **Website** www.bundesregierung.de

	*	*	100	50
If towing				
	80	80	80	50

*no limit, 130 kph recommended

Compulsory
Aged 3-12 and under 150cm must use an appropriate child seat or restraint and sit in the rear. In the front, if child under 3 is in a rear-facing seat, airbags must be deactivated
0.049% • 0.0% for drivers 21 or under or with less than two years full licence
Compulsory Compulsory
Compulsory Recommended 18
Use permitted only with hands-free kit – also applies to drivers of motorbikes and bicycles
LEZ More than 60 cities have or are planning LEZs. Proof of compliance needed to acquire sticker. Non-compliant vehicles banned.
Compulsory during poor daytime visibility and tunnels; recommended at other times. Compulsory at all times for motorcyclists.
Winter tyres compulsory in all winter weather conditions; snow chains recommended
★ GPS must have fixed speed camera function deactivated; radar detectors prohibited
★ On-the-spot fines imposed
★ Tolls on autobahns for lorries
★ Visibility vest compulsory

Greece Ellas (GR)

Area 131,957 sq km (50,948 sq miles)
Population 10,768,000 **Capital** Athens / Athina (3,781,000) **Languages** Greek (official)
Currency Euro = 100 cents
Website https://primeminister.gr/en/home

	130	110	90	50
Motorbikes, and if towing				
	90	70	70	40

Compulsory in front seats and, if fitted, in rear
Under 12 or below 135cm must use appropriate child restraint. In front if child is in rear-facing child seat, any airbags must be deactivated.
0.05% • 0.00% for drivers with less than 2 years' full licence and motorcyclists
Compulsory Compulsory Recommended
Compulsory 17 Not permitted.
Compulsory during poor daytime visibility and at all times for motorcycles
Snow chains permitted on ice- or snow-covered roads. Max speed 50 kph.
★ On-the-spot fines imposed
★ Radar-detection equipment is prohibited
★ Tolls on several newer motorways.

Hungary Magyarország (H)

Area 93,032 sq km (35,919 sq miles)
Population 9,798,000 **Capital** Budapest (3,304,000)
Languages Hungarian (official)
Currency Forint = 100 filler
Website www.kormany.hu/en

	130	110	90	50*
If towing				
	80	70	70	50*

*30 kph zones have been introduced in many cities

Compulsory
Under 135cm and over 3 must be seated in rear and use appropriate child restraint. Under 3 allowed in front only in rear-facing child seat with any airbags deactivated.
0.00% Compulsory Compulsory
Compulsory Recommended 17
Only allowed with a hands-free kit
LEZ Budapest has vehicle restrictions on days with heavy dust and is planning an LEZ.
Compulsory during the day outside built-up areas; compulsory at all times for motorcycles
Snow chains compulsory where conditions dictate. Max speed 50 kph.

★ Many motorways are toll and operate electronic vignette system with automatic number plate recognition, tickets available for 10 days, 1 month, 13 months ★ On-the-spot fines issued ★ Radar detectors prohibited ★ Tow rope recommended ★ Visibility vest compulsory

Iceland Ísland (IS)

Area 103,000 sq km (39,768 sq miles)
Population 351,000 **Capital** Reykjavík (217,000)
Languages Icelandic **Currency** Krona = 100 aurar
Website www.government.is/

	n/a	90	80	50

Compulsory in front and rear seats
Under 12 or below 150cm not allowed in front seat and must use appropriate child restraint.
0.05% Compulsory Compulsory
Compulsory Compulsory
17; 21 to drive a hire car; 25 to hire a jeep
Only allowed with a hands-free kit
Compulsory at all times
Winter tyres compulsory c.1 Nov–14 Apr (variable). Snow chains may be used when necessary.
★ Driving off marked roads forbidden
★ Highland roads unsuitable for ordinary cars
★ On-the-spot fines imposed

Ireland Eire (IRL)

Area 70,273 sq km (27,132 sq miles)
Population 4,857,200 **Capital** Dublin (1,905,000)
Languages Irish, English (both official) **Currency** Euro = 100 cents **Website** www.gov.ie/en/

	120	60–100	60–100	50*
If towing				
	80	60	60	50*

*Dublin and some other areas have introduced 30 kph zones

Compulsory where fitted. Driver responsible for ensuring passengers under 17 comply
Children 3 and under must be in a suitable child restraint system. Airbags must be deactivated if a rear-facing child seat is used in the front. Those under 150 cm and 36 kg must use appropriate child restraint.
0.05% • 0.02% for novice and professional drivers
Compulsory Recommended
Recommended Recommended
17 (16 for motorbikes up to 125cc; 18 over 125cc)
Only allowed with a hands-free kit
Compulsory for motorbikes at all times and in poor visibility for other vehicles
★ Driving is on the left ★ GPS must have fixed speed camera function deactivated; radar detectors prohibited ★ On-the-spot fines imposed ★ Tolls are being introduced on some motorways; the M50 Dublin has barrier-free tolling with number-plate recognition.

Italy Italia (I)

Area 301,318 sq km (116,338 sq miles)
Population 60,500,000 **Capital** Rome / Roma (4,356,000) **Languages** Italian (official)
Currency Euro = 100 cents **Website** www.italia.it

	130	110	90	50
If towing				
	80	70	70	50
Less than three years with full licence				
	100	90	90	50
When wet				
	110	90	80	50

Some motorways with emergency lanes have speed limit of 150 kph

Compulsory in front seats and, if fitted, in rear
Under 12 not allowed in front seats except in child safety seat; children under 3 must have special seat in the back. For foreign-registered cars, the country of origin's legislation applies.
0.05% • 0.00% for professional drivers or with less than 3 years full licence
Compulsory Recommended
Compulsory Recommended
18 (14 for mopeds, 16 up to 125cc, 20 up to 350cc)
Only allowed with hands-free kit
LEZ Most northern and several southern regions operate seasonal LEZs and many towns and cities have various schemes that restrict access. There is an LEZ in the Mont Blanc tunnel
Compulsory outside built-up areas, in tunnels, on motorways and dual carriageways and in poor visibility; compulsory at all times for motorcycles
Snow chains compulsory where signs indicate 15 Oct–15 Apr. Max speed 50 kph
★ On-the-spot fines imposed ★ Radar-detection equipment is prohibited ★ Tolls on motorways. Blue lanes accept credit cards; yellow lanes restricted to holders of Telepass pay-toll device. ★ Visibility vest compulsory

Kosovo Republika e Kosoves / Republika Kosovo (RKS)

Area 10,887 sq km (4203 sq miles) **Population** 1,921,000 **Capital** Pristina (504,000) **Languages** Albanian, Serbian (both official), Bosnian, Turkish, Roma **Currency** Euro (Serbian dinar in Serb enclaves) **Website** http://kryeministri-ks.net/en/

	130	80	80	50

Under 12 must sit in rear in appropriate restraint.
Compulsory 0.00% Compulsory
Compulsory Compulsory Compulsory
18 (16 motorbikes under 125 cc, 14 for mopeds)
International driving permit, locally purchased third-party insurance (green card is not recognised), documents with proof of ability to cover costs and valid reason for visiting. Visitors from many non-EU countries require a visa.
Only allowed with a hands-free kit
Compulsory at all times
Winter tyres or snow chains compulsory in poor winter weather conditions

Latvia Latvija (LV)

Area 64,589 sq km (24,942 sq miles)
Population 1,953,000 **Capital** Riga (1,070,000)
Languages Latvian (official), Russian **Currency** Euro = 100 cents **Website** https://www.mk.gov.lv/en

	n/a	100	90	50
If towing				
	n/a	80	80	50

In residential areas limit is 20kph • If full driving licence held for less than two years, must not exceed 80 kph

Compulsory in front seats and if fitted in rear
If under 12 years and 150cm must use child restraint in front and rear seats
0.05% • 0.02% with less than 2 years experience
Compulsory Compulsory
Recommended Compulsory 18
Only allowed with hands-free kit
Must be used at all times all year round
Winter tyres compulsory for vehicles up to 3.5 tonnes Dec–Feb, but illegal May–Sept
★ On-the-spot fines imposed ★ Pedestrians have priority ★ Radar-detection equipment prohibited ★ Visibility vests compulsory

Lithuania Lietuva (LT)

Area 65,200 sq km (25,173 sq miles)
Population 2,801,000 **Capital** Vilnius (805,000)
Languages Lithuanian (official), Russian, Polish
Currency Euro = 100 cents
Website http://lrvk.lrv.lt/en

	130	110	70–90	50
If towing				
	n/a	70	70	50
If licence held for less than two years				
	90	90	70	50

In winter speed limits are reduced by 10–20 km/h

Under 12 or below 135 cm not allowed in front seats unless in suitable restraint; under 3 must use appropriate child seat. A rear-facing child seat may be used in front only if airbags are deactivated.
0.04% • 0.00% if full licence held less than 2 years
Compulsory Compulsory Compulsory
Recommended Compulsory 18
Licences without a photograph must be accompanied by photographic proof of identity, e.g. a passport
Only allowed with a hands-free kit
Must be used at all times
Winter tyres compulsory 10 Nov–1 Apr
★ On-the-spot fines imposed
★ Visibility vest compulsory

Luxembourg (L)

Area 2,586 sq km (998 sq miles)
Population 602,000 **Capital** Luxembourg (107,000)
Languages Luxembourgian / Letzeburgish (official), French, German **Currency** Euro = 100 cents
Website http://luxembourg.public.lu/en

	130/110	90	90	50*
If towing				
	90	75	75	50*

If full driving licence held for less than two years, must not exceed 75 kph • *30 kph zones are progressively being introduced.

Compulsory
Children under 3 must use an appropriate restraint system. Airbags must be disabled if a rear-facing child seat is used in the front. Children 3–18 and/or under 150 cm must use a restraint system appropriate to their size. If over 36kg a seatbelt may be used in the back only
0.049%, 0.019 for young drivers, drivers with less than 2 years experience and drivers of taxis and commercial vehicles
Compulsory Compulsory (buses)
Compulsory 18
Compulsory (buses, transport of dangerous goods)
Use permitted only with hands-free kit
Compulsory for motorcyclists and in poor visibility and in tunnels for other vehicles
Winter tyres compulsory in winter weather
★ On-the-spot fines ★ Visibility vest compulsory

Macedonia Makedonija (MK)

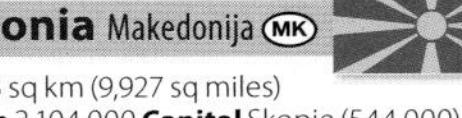

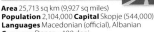

Area 25,713 sq km (9,927 sq miles)
Population 2,104,000 **Capital** Skopje (544,000)
Languages Macedonian (official), Albanian
Currency Denar = 100 deni

120	100	80	50
Newly qualified drivers or if towing			
100	80	60	50

Compulsory
Under 12 not allowed in front seats
0.05% • 0.00% for business, commercial and professional drivers and with less than 2 years experience
Compulsory Compulsory Compulsory
Recommended; compulsory for LPG vehicles
18 (mopeds 16) Compulsory at all times
International driving permit; visa
Use not permitted whilst driving
Winter tyres or snow chains compulsory 15 Nov–15 Mar. Max speed 70 kph
GPS must have fixed speed camera function deactivated; radar detectors prohibited ★ Novice drivers may only drive between 11pm and 5am if there is someone over 25 with a valid licence in the vehicle. ★ On-the-spot fines ★ Tolls apply on many roads ★ Tow rope compulsory ★ Visibility vest must be kept in the passenger compartment and worn to leave the vehicle in the dark outside built-up areas

Moldova (MD)

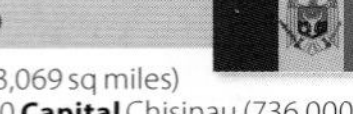

Area 33,851 sq km (13,069 sq miles)
Population 2,551,000 **Capital** Chisinau (736,000)
Languages Moldovan / Romanian (official)
Currency Leu = 100 bani **Website** www.moldova.md

90	90	90	60
If towing or if licence held under 1 year			
70	70	70	60

Compulsory in front seats and, if fitted, in rear
Under 12 not allowed in front seats
0.00% Compulsory Compulsory
Recommended Compulsory
18 (mopeds and motorbikes, 16; vehicles with more than eight passenger places, taxis or towing heavy vehicles, 21)
International Driving Permit (preferred), visa
Only allowed with hands-free kit
Must use dipped headlights at all times
Winter tyres recommended Nov–Feb

Montenegro Crna Gora (MNE)

Area 14,026 sq km, (5,415 sq miles)
Population 643,000 **Capital** Podgorica (187,000)
Languages Serbian (of the Ijekavian dialect)
Currency Euro = 100 cents
Website www.gov.me/en/homepage

n/a	100	80	50

80kph speed limit if towing a caravan

Compulsory in front and rear seats
Under 12 not allowed in front seats. Under-5s must use an appropriate child seat.
0.03 % Compulsory Compulsory
Compulsory Compulsory
18 (16 for motorbikes under 125cc; 14 for mopeds)
International Driving Permit recommended
Prohibited
Must be used at all times
From mid-Nov to March, driving wheels must be fitted with winter tyres ★ An 'eco' tax vignette must be obtained when crossing the border and displayed in the upper right-hand corner of the windscreen ★ On-the-spot fines imposed ★ Tolls on some primary roads and in the Sozina tunnel between Lake Skadar and the sea ★ Visibility vest compulsory

Netherlands Nederland (NL)

Area 41,526 sq km (16,033 sq miles)
Population 17,250,000 **Capital** Amsterdam 2,431,000 • administrative capital 's-Gravenhage (The Hague) 1,055,000 **Languages** Dutch (official), Frisian **Currency** Euro = 100 cents
Website www.government.nl

130	80/100	80/100	50

Compulsory
Under 3 must travel in the back, using an appropriate child restraint; 3–18 and under 135cm must use an appropriate child restraint. A rear-facing child seat may be used in front only if airbags are deactivated.
0.05% • 0.02% with less than 5 years experience or moped riders under 24
Compulsory Recommended
Recommended Recommended 18
Only allowed with a hands-free kit
LEZ About 20 cities operate or are planning LEZs.
Recommended in poor visibility and on open roads. Compulsory for motorcycles.
★ On-the-spot fines imposed ★ Radar-detection equipment is prohibited

Norway Norge (N)

Area 323,877 sq km (125,049 sq miles)
Population 5,303,000 **Capital** Oslo (1,588,000)
Languages Norwegian (official), Lappish, Finnish
Currency Krone = 100 øre
Website www.norway.no/en/uk

90–110	80	80	30/50
If towing trailer with brakes			
80	80	80	50
If towing trailer without brakes			
60	60	60	50

Compulsory in front seats and, if fitted, in rear
Children less than 150cm tall must use appropriate child restraint. Children under 4 must use child safety seat or safety restraint (cot). A rear-facing child seat may be used in front only if airbags are deactivated.
0.01% Compulsory Recommended
Recommended Recommended
18 (heavy vehicles 18/21)
Only allowed with a hands-free kit
Must be used at all times
Winter tyres or summer tyres with snow chains compulsory for snow- or ice-covered roads
★ On-the-spot fines imposed ★ Radar-detectors are prohibited ★ Tolls apply on some bridges, tunnels and access roads into Bergen, Haugesund, Kristiensand, Oslo, Stavangar, Tonsberg and Trondheim. Several use electronic fee collection only. ★ Visibility vest compulsory

Poland Polska (PL)

Area 323,250 sq km (124,807 sq miles)
Population 38,434,000 **Capital** Warsaw / Warszawa (3,106,000) **Languages** Polish (official)
Currency Zloty = 100 groszy
Website www.premier.gov.pl/en.html

Motor-vehicle only roads[1], under/over 3.5 tonnes			
130[2]/80[2]	110/80	100/80	n/a
Motor-vehicle only roads[1] if towing			
n/a	80	80	n/a
Other roads, under 3.5 tonnes			
n/a	100	90	50/60[3]
Other roads, 3.5 tonnes or over			
n/a	80	70	50/60[3]
Other roads, if towing			
n/a	60	60	30

[1]Indicated by signs with white car on blue background • [2]Minimum speed 40 kph • [3]50 kph 05.00–23.00; 60 kph 23.00–05.00; 20 kph in marked residential areas

Compulsory in front seats and, if fitted, in rear
Under 12 and below 150 cm must use an appropriate child restraint. Rear-facing child seats not permitted in vehicles with airbags.
0.02% Compulsory Recommended
Recommended Compulsory
18 (mopeds and motorbikes under 125cc – 16)
Only allowed with a hands-free kit
Compulsory for all vehicles
Snow chains permitted only on roads completely covered in snow
★ On-the-spot fines imposed
★ Radar-detection equipment is prohibited
★ Vehicles over 3.5 tonnes (including cars towing caravans) must have a VIAbox for the electronic toll system
★ Visibility vests compulsory

Portugal (P)

Area 88,797 sq km (34,284 sq miles)
Population 10,291,000 **Capital** Lisbon / Lisboa (2,828,000) **Languages** Portuguese (official)
Currency Euro = 100 cents
Website www.portugal.gov.pt/en/gc21

120*	90/100	90	50/20
If towing			
100*	90	80	50

*50kph minimum; 90kph maximum if licence held under 1 year

Compulsory in front seats and, if fitted, in rear
Under 12 and below 135cm must travel in the rear in an appropriate child restraint; rear-facing child seats permitted in front for under 3s only if airbags deactivated
0.049% • 0.019% if full licence held less than 3 years
Compulsory Recommended
Recommended Recommended 17
MOT certificate for vehicles over 3 years old, photographic proof of identity must be carried at all times.
Only allowed with hands-free kit
LEZ An LEZ prohibits vehicles without catalytic converters from certain parts of Lisbon. There are plans to extend the scheme city-wide
Compulsory for motorcycles, compulsory for other vehicles in poor visibility and tunnels
★ On-the-spot fines imposed ★ Radar detectors and dash-cams prohibited ★ Tolls on motorways; do not use green lanes, these are reserved for auto-payment users. Some motorways require an automatic toll device. ★ Visibility vest compulsory ★ Wearers of spectacles or contact lenses should carry a spare pair

Romania (RO)

Area 238,391 sq km (92,042 sq miles) **Population** 19,638,000 **Capital** Bucharest / Bucuresti (2,413,000) **Languages** Romanian (official), Hungarian **Currency** Romanian leu = 100 bani
Website www.gov.ro

Cars and motorcycles			
120/130	100	90	50
Vans			
110	90	80	40
Motorcycles			
100	80	80	50

For motor vehicles with trailers or if full driving licence has been held for less than one year, speed limits are 20kph lower than those listed above • Jeep-like vehicles: 70kph outside built-up areas but 60kph in all areas if diesel. For mopeds, the speed limit is 45 kph.

Compulsory
Under 12s not allowed in front and must use an appropriate restraint in the rear
0.00% Compulsory Compulsory
Compulsory Compulsory 18
Only allowed with hands-free kit
Compulsory outside built-up areas, compulsory everywhere for motorcycles
Winter tyres compulsory Nov–Mar if roads are snow- or ice-covered, especially in mountainous areas
★ Compulsory road tax can be paid for at the border, post offices and some petrol stations. Price depends on emissions category and length of stay ★ It is illegal for vehicles to be dirty ★ On-the-spot fines imposed ★ Visibility vest compulsory

Russia Rossiya (RUS)

Area 17,075,000 sq km (6,592,800 sq miles)
Population 144,427,000 **Capital** Moscow / Moskva (17,100,000) **Languages** Russian (official), and many others **Currency** Russian ruble = 100 kopeks
Website government.ru/en/

110	90	90	60/20
If licence held for under 2 years			
70	70	70	60/20

Compulsory if fitted
Under 12s permitted only in an appropriate child restraint
0.03 % Compulsory Compulsory
Compulsory Compulsory 17
International Driving Permit with Russian translation, visa, green card endorsed for Russia, International Certificate for Motor Vehicles
Only allowed with a hands-free kit
Compulsory during the day
Winter tyres compulsory 1 Dec–1 Mar
★ On-the-spot fines imposed ★ Picking up hitch-hikers is prohibited ★ Radar detectors/blockers prohibited ★ Road tax payable at the border

Serbia Srbija (SRB)

Area 77,474 sq km, 29,913 sq miles
Population 7,040,000 **Capital** Belgrade / Beogra (1,167,000) **Languages** Serbian **Currency** Dinar = 100 paras **Website** www.srbija.gov.rs

120	100	80	50
If towing			
80	80	80	50

Novice drivers limited to 90% of speed limit and n permitted to drive 11pm–5am.

Compulsory in front and rear seats
Age 3–12 must be in rear seats and wear seat belt or appropriate child restraint; under 3 in rear-facing child seat permitted in front only airbag deactivated
0.029% • 0.0% for commercial drivers, motor-cyclists, or if full licence held less than 1 year
Compulsory Compulsory
Compulsory Compulsory
18 (16 motorbikes under 125cc; 14 for moped
International Driving Permit, green card, insurance that is valid for Serbia or locally bought third-party insurance
Compulsory
Winter tyres compulsory Nov–Apr for vehicle up to 3.5 tonnes. Carrying snow chains recom mended in winter as these may have to be fit if driving on snow-covered roads, in accorda with signage.
★ 3-metre tow bar or rope ★ Spare wheel com pulsory ★ On-the-spot fines ★ Radar detect prohibited ★ Tolls on motorways and some primary roads ★ Visibility vest compulsory

Slovakia Slovenska Republika (SK)

Area 49,012 sq km (18,923 sq miles)
Population 5,435,000 **Capital** Bratislava (656,000 **Languages** Slovak (official), Hungarian **Currency** Euro = 100 cents **Website** www.government.gov

130/90	90	90	50

Compulsory
Under 12 or below 150cm must be in rear in appropriate child restraint
0.0% Compulsory Compulsory
Compulsory Recommended
18, 17 for motorbikes over 50cc, 15 for mopeds
International driving permit, proof of health insurance
Only allowed with a hands-free kit
Compulsory at all times
Winter tyres compulsory
★ On-the-spot fines imposed ★ Radar-detecti equipment is prohibited ★ Tow rope recom-mended ★ Vignette required for motorways car valid for 1 year, 30 days, 7 days; lorry vignettes carry a higher charge. ★ Visibility vests compulsory

Slovenia Slovenija (SLO)

Area 20,256 sq km (7,820 sq miles)
Population 2,067,000 **Capital** Ljubljana (538,000 **Languages** Slovene **Currency** Euro = 100 cents
Website www.vlada.si/en

130	110[1]	90[1]	50[2]
If towing			
80	80[1]	80[1]	50[2]

[1]70 kph in urban areas, [2]30 kph zones are increasingly common in cities. 50 kph in poor visibility or with snow chains

Compulsory
Below 150cm must use appropriate child restraint. A rear-facing baby seat may be usec front only if airbags are deactivated.
0.05% • 0.0% for commercial drivers, under 21 with less than one year with a full licence
Compulsory Compulsory
Compulsory Recommended
18 (motorbikes up to 125cc – 16, up to 350cc – 18)
Licences without photographs must be acco panied by an International Driving Permit
Only allowed with hands-free kit
Must be used at all times
Snow chains or winter tyres compulsory mid-Nov to mid-March, and in wintery conditions other times. Max speed 50 kph. This limit also applies if visibility is below 50m.
★ On-the-spot fines imposed ★ Radar detecto prohibited ★ Vignettes valid for variety of periods compulsory for vehicles below 3.5 tonnes for toll roads. Write your vehicle registration number on the vignette before c playing it. For heavier vehicles electronic tolli system applies; several routes are cargo-traff free during high tourist season. ★ Visibility vest compulsory

pain España (E)

ea 497,548 sq km (192,103 sq miles)
pulation 46,700,000 **Capital** Madrid (6,675,000)
nguages Castilian Spanish (official), Catalan, lician, Basque **Currency** Euro = 100 cents
ebsite www.lamoncloa.gob.es/lang/en/Paginas/ dex.aspx

)	120*	100*	90	50*
towing				
)	80	80	70	50*

ban motorways and dual carriageways 80 kph. kph zones are being introduced in many cities

- Compulsory
- Under 135cm and below 12 must use appropriate child restraint and sit in rear.
- 0.049% • 0.029% if less than 2 years full licence or if vehicle is over 3.5 tonnes or carries more than 9 passengers
- Two compulsory (one for front, one for behind)
- Recommended
- Compulsory · Recommended
- 18 (21 for heavy vehicles; 16 for motorbikes up to 125cc)
- Hands-free only
- Compulsory for motorcycles and in poor day-time visibility and in tunnels for other vehicles.
- Snow chains recommended for mountainous areas in winter
- Drivers who wear spectacles or contact lenses must carry a spare pair. ★ On-the-spot fines imposed ★ Radar-detection equipment is prohibited ★ Spare wheel compulsory ★ Tolls on motorways ★ Visibility vest compulsory

weden Sverige (S)

ea 449,964 sq km (173,731 sq les) **Population** 10,162,000 **Capital** Stockholm 227,000) **Languages** Swedish (official), Finnish urrency Swedish krona = 100 ore
ebsite www.sweden.gov.se

)	90–120	80	70–100	30–60
towing trailer with brakes				
)	80	80	70	50

- Compulsory in front and rear seats
- Under 15 or below 135cm must use an appropriate child restraint and may sit in the front only if airbag is deactivated; rear-facing baby seat permitted in front only if airbag deactivated.
- 0.019% · Compulsory · Recommended
- Recommended · Recommended · 18
- Licences without a photograph must be accompanied by photographic proof of identity, e.g. a passport
- Gothenberg, Helsingborg, Lund, Malmo, Mölndal and Stockholm have LEZs, progressively prohibiting older vehicles.
- Must be used at all times
- 1 Dec–31 Mar winter tyres, anti-freeze, screen-wash additive and shovel compulsory
- On-the-spot fines imposed ★ Radar-detection equipment is prohibited ★ Tow rope recommended ★ Visibility vest recommended

witzerland Schweiz (CH)

rea 41,284 sq km (15,939 sq miles)
opulation 8,401,000 **Capital** Bern (407,000)
anguages French, German, Italian, Romansch ll official) **Currency** Swiss Franc = 100 centimes / ppen **Website** www.admin.ch

)	120	80	80	50/30
towing up to 1 tonne / over 1 tonne				
)	80	80	80/60	50/30

- Compulsory
- Up to 12 years or below 150 cm must use an appropriate child restraint. Children 6 and under must sit in the rear.
- 0.05%, but 0.0% for commercial drivers or with less than three years with a full licence
- Compulsory · Recommended
- Recommended · Recommended
- 18 (mopeds up to 50cc – 16)
- Only allowed with a hands-free kit
- Compulsory
- Winter tyres recommended Nov–Mar; snow chains compulsory in designated areas in poor winter weather
- ★ GPS must have fixed speed camera function deactivated; radar detectors prohibited ★ Motorways are all toll and for vehicles below 3.5 tonnes a vignette must be purchased at the border. The vignette is valid for one calendar year. Vehicles over 3.5 tonnes must have an electronic tag for travel on any road. ★ On-the-spot fines imposed ★ Pedestrians have right of way ★ Picking up hitchhikers is prohibited on motorways and main roads ★ Spectacles or contact lens wearers must carry a spare pair in their vehicle at all times

Turkey Türkiye (TR)

Area 774,815 sq km (299,156 sq miles)
Population 80,811,000 **Capital** Ankara (5,445,000)
Languages Turkish (official), Kurdish
Currency New Turkish lira = 100 kurus
Website www.mfa.gov.tr/default.en.mfa

⊙	120	90	90	50
If towing				
⊙	80	80	80	40
Motorbikes				
⊙	80	70	70	50

- Compulsory if fitted
- Under 150 cm and below 36kg must use suitable child restraint. Under 3s can only travel in the front in a rear facing seat if the airbag is deactivated. Children 3–12 may not travel in the front seat.
- 0.00%
- Two compulsory (one in front, one behind)
- Compulsory
- Compulsory · Compulsory · 18
- International driving permit advised, and required for use with licences without photographs; note that Turkey is in both Europe and Asia, green card/UK insurance that covers whole of Turkey or locally bought insurance, e-visa obtained in advance.
- Prohibited
- Compulsory in daylight hours
- ★ Spare wheel compulsory ★ On-the-spot fines imposed ★ Several motorways, and the Bosphorus bridges are toll roads ★ Tow rope and tool kit must be carried

Ukraine Ukraina (UA)

Area 603,700 sq km (233,088 sq miles) **Population** 42,418,000 **Capital** Kiev / Kyviv (3,375,000) **Languages** Ukrainian (official), Russian
Currency Hryvnia = 100 kopiykas
Website www.kmu.gov.ua/control/en

⊙	130	110	90	20/60
If towing				
⊙	80	80	80	20/60

If driving licence held less than 2 years, must not exceed 70 kph

- Compulsory in front and rear seats
- Under 12 and below 145cm must use an appropriate child restraint and sit in rear
- 0.02% – if use of medication can be proved. Otherwise 0.00%
- Compulsory · Compulsory
- Optional · Compulsory · 18
- International Driving Permit, visa, International Certificate for Motor Vehicles, green card
- No legislation
- Compulsory in poor daytime and from Oct–Apr
- Winter tyres compulsory Nov–Apr in snowy conditions
- ★ A road tax is payable on entry to the country. ★ On-the-spot fines imposed ★ Tow rope and tool kit recommended

United Kingdom (GB)

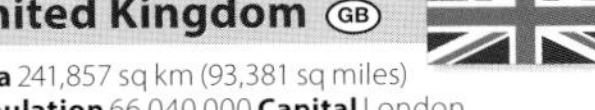

Area 241,857 sq km (93,381 sq miles)
Population 66,040,000 **Capital** London (14,040,000) **Languages** English (official), Welsh (also official in Wales), Gaelic **Currency** Sterling (pound) = 100 pence **Website** www.direct.gov.uk

⊙	112	112	96	48
If towing				
⊙	96	96	80	48

Several cities have introduced 32 kph (20 mph) zones away from main roads

- Compulsory in front seats and if fitted in rear
- Under 3 not allowed in front seats except with appropriate restraint, and in rear must use child restraint if available; in front 3–12 or under 135cm must use appropriate child restraint, in rear must use appropriate child restraint (or seat belt if no child restraint is available, e.g. because two occupied restraints prevent fitting of a third).
- 0.08% (England, Northern Ireland, Wales) • 0.05% (Scotland)
- Recommended · Recommended
- Recommended · Recommended
- 17 (16 for mopeds)
- Only allowed with hands-free kit
- LEZ London's LEZ operates by number-plate recognition; non-compliant vehicles face hefty daily charges. Foreign-registered vehicles must register.
- ★ Driving is on the left ★ On-the-spot fines imposed ★ Smoking is banned in all commercial vehicles ★ Some toll motorways, bridges and tunnels

Ski resorts

The resorts listed are popular ski centres, therefore road access to most is normally good and supported by road clearing during snow falls. However, mountain driving is never predictable and drivers should make sure they take suitable snow chains as well as emergency provisions and clothing. Listed for each resort are: the atlas page and grid square; the resort/minimum piste altitude (where only one figure is shown, they are at the same height) and maximum altitude of its own lifts; the number of lifts and gondolas (the total for lift-linked resorts); the season start and end dates (snow cover allowing); whether snow is augmented by cannon; the nearest town (with its distance in km) and, where available, the website and/or telephone number of the local tourist information centre or ski centre ('00' prefix required for calls from the UK).

The ❄ symbol indicates resorts with snow cannon

Andorra

Pyrenees

Pas de la Casa / Grau Roig 146 B2 ❄ 2050–2640m • 31 lifts • Dec–Apr • Andorra La Vella (30km) www.pasdelacasa.com • *Access via Envalira Pass (2407m), highest in Pyrenees, snow chains essential.*

Austria

Alps

Bad Gastein 109 B4 ❄ 1050/1100–2700m • 50 lifts • Dec–Mar • St Johann im Pongau (45km) +43 6432 3393 0 www.gastein.com/en

Bad Hofgastein 109 B4 ❄ 860–2295m • 50 lifts • Dec–Mar • St Johann im Pongau (40km) +43 6432 3393 0 url: www.gastein.com/en

Bad Kleinkirchheim 109 C4 ❄ 1070–2310m • 27 lifts • Dec–Mar • Villach (35km) +43 4240 8212 www.badkleinkirchheim.at

Ehrwald 108 B1 ❄ 1000–2965m • 24 lifts • Dec–Apr • Imst (30km) +43 5673 2501 www.wetterstein-bahnen.at/en

Innsbruck 108 B2 ❄ 574/850–3200m • 59 lifts • Dec–Apr • Innsbruck +43 512 5356 0 www.innsbruck.info/en/ • *Motorway normally clear. The motorway through to Italy and through the Arlberg Tunnel are both toll roads.*

Ischgl 107 B5 ❄ 1880/1400–2900m • 82 lifts • Dec–May • Landeck (25km) +43 50990 100 www.ischgl.com • *Car entry to resort prohibited between 2200hrs and 0600hrs. Lift linked to Samnaun (Switzerland).*

Kaprun 109 B3 ❄ 800/770–3030m, • 25 lifts • Nov–Apr • Zell am See (10km) +43 6542 770 www.zellamsee-kaprun.com

Kirchberg in Tirol 109 B3 ❄ 860–2000m • 197 lifts • Nov–Apr • Kitzbühel (6km) +43 57507 2100 www.kitzbueheler-alpen.com/en • *Easily reached from Munich International Airport (120 km)*

Kitzbühel (Brixen im Thale) 109 B3 ❄ 800/790–2000m • 197 lifts • Dec–Apr • Wörgl (40km) +43 57057 2000 www.kitzbueheler-alpen.com/en

Lech/Oberlech 107 B5 ❄ 1450–2810m • 97 lifts • Dec–Apr • Bludenz (50km) +43 5583 2161 0 www.lechzuers.com • *Roads normally cleared but keep chains accessible because of altitude. Linked to the other Arlberg resorts.*

Mayrhofen 108 B2 ❄ 630–2500m • 57 lifts • Dec–Apr • Jenbach (35km) +43 5285 6760 www.mayrhofen.at • *Chains rarely required.*

Obertauern 109 B4 ❄ 1740/1640–2350m • 26 lifts • Dec–Apr • Radstadt (20km) +43 6456 7252 www.obertauern.com • *Roads normally cleared but chain accessibility recommended. Camper vans and caravans not allowed; park these in Radstadt*

Saalbach Hinterglemm 109 B3 ❄ 1000/1030–2100m • 52 lifts • Nov–Apr • Zell am See (19km) +43 6541 6800-68 www.saalbach.com • *Both village centres are pedestrianised and there is a good ski bus service during the daytime*

St Anton am Arlberg 107 B5 ❄ 1300–2810m • 97 lifts • Dec–Apr • Innsbruck (104km) +43 5446 22690 www.stantonamarlberg.com • *Linked to the other Arlberg resorts.*

Schladming 109 B4 ❄ 745–1900m • 45 lifts • Dec–Mar • Schladming +43 36 87 233 10 www.schladming-dachstein.at

Serfaus 108 B1 ❄ 1427/1200–2820m • 68 lifts • Dec–Apr • Landeck (30km) +43 5476 6239 www.serfaus-fiss-ladis.at • *Private vehicles banned from village. Use Dorfbahn Serfaus, an underground funicular that runs on an air cushion.*

Sölden 108 C2 ❄ 1380–3250m, • 33 lifts • Oct–Apr • Imst (50km) +43 57200 200 www.soelden.com • *Roads normally cleared but snow chains recommended because of altitude. The route from Italy and the south over the Timmelsjoch via Obergurgl is closed Oct–May and anyone arriving from the south should use the Brenner Pass motorway.*

Zell am See 109 B3 ❄ 750–1950m • 28 lifts • Dec–Mar • Zell am See +43 6542 770 www.zellamsee-kaprun.com • *Low altitude, so good access and no mountain passes to cross.*

Zell im Zillertal (Zell am Ziller) 109 B3 ❄ 580/930–2410m • 22 lifts • Dec–Apr • Jenbach (25km) +43 5282 7165-226 www.zillertalarena.com

Zürs 107 B5 ❄ 1720/1700–2450m • 87 lifts • Dec–Apr • Bludenz (30km) +43 5583 2161 251 www.lechzuers.com • *Roads normally cleared but keep chains accessible because of altitude. Village has garage with 24-hour self-service gas/petrol, breakdown service and wheel chains supply. Linked to the other Arlberg resorts.*

France

Alps

Alpe d'Huez 118 B3 ❄ 1860–3330m • 85 lifts • Dec–Apr • Grenoble (63km) www.alpedhuez.com • *Snow chains may be required on access road to resort.*

Avoriaz 118 A3 ❄ 1800/1100–2280m • 35 lifts • Dec–May • Morzine (14km) +33 4 50 74 02 11 www.avoriaz.com/en • *Chains may be required for access road from Morzine. Car-free resort, park on edge of village.*

Chamonix-Mont-Blanc 119 B3 ❄ 1035–3840m • 49 lifts • Dec–Apr • Martigny (38km) www.chamonix.com

Chamrousse 118 B2 ❄ 1700/1420–2250m • 26 lifts • Dec–Apr • Grenoble (30km) www.chamrousse.com • *Roads normally cleared, keep chains accessible because of altitude.*

Châtel 119 A3 ❄ 1200/1110–2200m • 41 lifts • Dec–Apr • Thonon-Les-Bains (35km) +33 4 50 73 22 44 www.chatel.com

Courchevel 118 B3 ❄ 1300–2470m • 67 lifts • Dec–Apr • Moûtiers (23km) www.courchevel.com • *Roads normally cleared but keep chains accessible. Traffic 'discouraged' within the four resort bases.*

Flaine 118 A3 ❄ 1600–2500m • 26 lifts • Dec–Apr • Cluses (25km) +33 4 50 90 80 01 www.flaine.com • *Keep chains accessible for D6 from Cluses to Flaine. Car access for depositing luggage and passengers only. 1500-space car park outside resort. Near Sixt-Fer-á-Cheval.*

La Clusaz 118 B3 ❄ 1100–2600m • 55 lifts • Dec–Apr • Annecy (32km) www.laclusaz.com • *Roads normally clear but keep chains accessible for final road from Annecy.*

La Plagne 118 B3 ❄ 2500/1250–3250m • 109 lifts • Dec–Apr Moûtiers (32km) www.la-plagne.com • *Ten different centres up to 2100m altitude. Road access via Bozel, Landry or Aime normally cleared. Linked to Les Arcs by cablecar*

Les Arcs 119 B3 ❄ 1600/1200–3230m • 77 lifts • Dec–May • Bourg-St-Maurice (15km) +33 4 79 07 12 57 www.lesarcs.com • *Four base areas up to 2000 metres; keep chains accessible. Pay parking at edge of each base resort. Linked to La Plagne by cablecar*

Les Carroz d'Araches 118 A3 ❄ 1140–2500m • 80 lifts • Dec–Apr • Cluses (13km) http://winter.lescarroz.com

Les Deux-Alpes 118 C3 ❄ 1650/1300–3600m • 55 lifts • Dec–Apr • Grenoble (75km) +33 4 76 79 22 00 www.les2alpes.com/en • *Roads normally cleared, however snow chains recommended for D213 up from valley road (D1091).*

Les Gets 118 A3 ❄ 1170/1000–2000m • 52 lifts • Dec–Apr • Cluses (18km) +33 4 50 74 74 74 www.lesgets.com

Les Ménuires 118 B3 ❄ 1815/1850–3200m • 40 lifts • Dec–Apr • Moûtiers (27km) www.lesmenuires.com • *Keep chains accessible for D117 from Moûtiers.*

Les Sept Laux Prapoutel 118 B3 ❄ 1350–2400m • 24 lifts • Dec–Apr • Grenoble (38km) www.les7laux.com (in French only) • *Roads normally cleared, however keep chains accessible for mountain road up from the A41 motorway. Near St Sorlin d'Arves.*

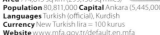

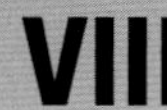

Megève 118 B3 1100/1050–2350m • 79 lifts • Dec–Apr • Sallanches (12km) www.megeve.com

Méribel 118 B3 1400/1100–2950m • 61 lifts • Dec–May • Moûtiers (18km) +33 4 79 08 60 01 www.meribel.net • *Keep chains accessible for 18km to resort on D90 from Moûtiers.*

Morzine 118 A3 1000–2460m • 67 lifts, • Dec–Apr • Thonon-Les-Bains (30km) +33 4 50 74 72 72 http://en.morzine-avoriaz.com

Pra Loup 132 A2 1500–2600m • 53 lifts • Dec–Apr • Barcelonnette (10km) www.praloup.com • *Roads normally cleared but chains accessibility recommended.*

Risoul 118 C3 1850/1650–2750m • 59 lifts • Dec–Apr • Briançon (40km) +33 4 92 46 02 60 www.risoul.com • *Keep chains accessible. Near Guillestre. Linked with Vars Les Claux*

St-Gervais Mont-Blanc 118 B3 850/1150–2350m • 27 lifts • Dec–Apr • Sallanches (10km) +33 4 50 47 76 08 www.saintgervais.com/en

Serre Chevalier 118 C3 1350/1200–2800m • 77 lifts • Dec–Apr • Briançon (10km) + 33 4 92 24 98 98 www.serre-chevalier.com • *Made up of 13 small villages along the valley road, which is normally cleared.*

Tignes 119 B3 2100/1550–3450m • 87 lifts • Jan–Dec • Bourg St Maurice (26km) +33 4 79 40 04 40 www.tignes.net • *Keep chains accessible because of altitude. Linked to Val d'Isère.*

Val d'Isère 119 B3 1850/1550–3450m • 87 lifts • Dec–Apr • Bourg-St-Maurice (30km) www.valdisere.com • *Roads normally cleared but keep chains accessible.*

Val Thorens 118 B3 2300/1850–3200m • 29 lifts • Dec–Apr • Moûtiers (37km) +33 4 79 00 08 08 www.les3vallees.com/en/ski-resort/val-thorens • *Chains essential – highest ski resort in Europe. Obligatory paid parking on edge of resort.*

Valloire 118 B3 1430–2600m • 34 lifts • Dec–Apr • Modane (20km) +33 4 79 59 03 96 www.valloire.net • *Road normally clear up to the Col du Galbier, to the south of the resort, which is closed from 1st November to 1st June. Linked to Valmeinier.*

Valmeinier 118 B3 1500–2600m • 34 lifts • Dec–Apr • St Michel de Maurienne (47km) www.valmeinier.com • *Access from north on D1006 / D902. Col du Galbier, to the south of the resort closed from 1st November to 1st June. Linked to Valloire.*

Valmorel 118 B3 1400–2550m • 90 lifts • Dec–Apr • Moûtiers (15km) www.valmorel.com • *Near St Jean-de-Belleville. Linked with ski areas of Doucy-Combelouvière and St François-Longchamp.*

Vars Les Claux 118 C3 1850/1650–2750m • 59 lifts • Dec–Apr • Briançon (40km) +33 4 92 46 51 31 www.vars.com/en/winter • *Four base resorts up to 1850 metres. Keep chains accessible. Linked with Risoul.*

Villard de Lans 118 B2 1050/1160–2170m • 28 lifts • Dec–Apr • Grenoble (32km) +33 4 76 95 10 38 www.villarddelans.com

Pyrenees

Font-Romeu 146 B3 1800/1600–2200m • 25 lifts • Nov–Apr • Perpignan (87km) www.font-romeu.fr • *Roads normally cleared but keep chains accessible.*

Saint-Lary Soulan 145 B4 830/1650/1700–2515m • 31 lifts • Dec–Mar • Tarbes (75km) +33 5 62 39 50 81 www.saintlary.com • *Access roads constantly cleared of snow.*

Vosges

La Bresse-Hohneck 106 A1 600–1370m • 33 lifts • Dec–Mar • Cornimont (6km) +33 3 29 25 41 29 www.labresse.net

Germany

Alps

Garmisch-Partenkirchen 108 B2 700–2830m • 38 lifts • Dec–Apr • Munich (95km) +49 8821 180 700 www.gapa.de • *Roads usually clear, chains rarely needed.*

Oberaudorf 108 B3 480–1850m • 30 lifts • Dec–Apr • Kufstein (15km) www.oberaudorf.de • *Motorway normally kept clear. Near Bayrischzell.*

Oberstdorf 107 B5 820/830–2200m • 26 lifts • Dec–Apr • Sonthofen (15km) +49 8322 7000 www.oberstdorf.de

Rothaargebirge

Winterberg 81 A4 700/620–830m • 19 lifts • Dec–Mar • Brilon (30km) +49 2981 925 00 www.winterberg.de (German only) • *Roads usually cleared, chains rarely required.*

Greece

Central Greece

Mount Parnassos: Kelaria-Fterolakka 182 E4 1640–2260m • 14 lifts • Dec–Apr • Amfiklia www.parnassos-ski.gr (Greek only)

Mount Parnassos: Gerondovrahos 182 E4 1800–1900m • 3 lifts • Dec–Apr • Amfiklia +30 29444 70371

Peloponnisos

Mount Helmos: Kalavrita Ski Centre 184 A3 1650–2100m • 7 lifts • Dec–Mar • Kalavrita +30 276920 24451-2 www.kalavrita-ski.gr (in Greek only)

Mount Menalo: Ostrakina 184 B3 1500–1600m • 4 lifts • Dec–Mar • Tripoli +30 27960 22227

Macedonia

Mount Falakro: Agio Pnevma 183 B6 1720/1620–2230m • 7 lifts • Dec–Apr • Drama + 30 25210 23691

Mount Vermio: Seli 182 C4 1500–1900m • 8 lifts • Dec–Mar • Kozani +30 23310 26237 www.seli-ski.gr (in Greek)

Mount Vermio: Tria-Pente Pigadia 182 C3 1420–2005m • 5 lifts • Dec–Mar • Ptolemaida +30 23320 44464

Mount Verno: Vigla 182 C3 1650–1900m • 5 lifts • Dec–Mar • Florina +30 23850 22354 www.vigla-ski.gr (in Greek)

Mount Vrondous: Lailias 183 B5 1600–1850m • 4 lifts • Dec–Mar • Serres +30 23210 53790

Thessalia

Mount Pilio: Agriolefkes 183 D5 1300–1500m • 5 lifts • Dec–Mar • Volos +30 24280 73719

Italy

Alps

Bardonecchia 118 B3 1312–2750m • 21 lifts • Dec–Apr • Bardonecchia www.bardonecchiaski.com • *Resort reached through the 11km Frejus tunnel from France, roads normally cleared.*

Bórmio 107 C5 1200/1230–3020m • 24 lifts • Dec–Apr • Tirano (40km) www.bormio.com • *Tolls payable in Ponte del Gallo Tunnel, open 0800hrs–2000hrs.*

Breuil-Cervinia 119 B4 2050–3500m • 21 lifts • Jan–Dec • Aosta (54km) +39 166 944311 www.cervinia.it • *Snow chains strongly recommended. Bus from Milan airport.*

Courmayeur 119 B3 1200–2760m • 21 lifts • Dec–Apr • Aosta (40km) www.courmayeurmontblanc.it • *Access through the Mont Blanc tunnel from France. Roads constantly cleared.*

Limone Piemonte 133 A3 1000/1050–2050m • 29 lifts • Dec–Apr • Cuneo (27km) www.limoneturismo.it • *Roads normally cleared, chains rarely required.*

Livigno 107 C5 1800–3000m • 31 lifts • Nov–May • Zernez (CH) (27km) www.livigno.com • *Keep chains accessible. The traffic direction through Munt la Schera Tunnel to/from Zernez is regulated on Saturdays. Check in advance.*

Sestrière 119 C3 2035/1840–2840m • 92 lifts • Dec–Apr • Oulx (22km) www.sestriere-online.com • *One of Europe's highest resorts; although roads are normally cleared keep chains accessible.*

Appennines

Roccaraso – Aremogna 169 B4 1285/1240–2140m • 24 lifts • Dec–Apr • Castel di Sangro (7km) https://roccaraso.net (Italian only)

Dolomites

Andalo – Fai della Paganella 121 A3 1042/1050/2125m • 17 lifts • Dec–Apr • Trento (40km) www.visitdolomitipaganella.it +39 461 585836

Arabba 108 C2 1600/1450–2950m • 29 lifts • Dec–Mar • Brunico (45km) +39 436 79130 www.arabba.it • *Roads normally cleared but keep chains accessible.*

Cortina d'Ampezzo 108 C3 1224/1050–2930m • 37 lifts • Dec–Apr • Belluno (72km) +39 436 869086 www.dolomiti.org/it/cortina • *Access from north on route 51 over the Cimabanche Pass may require chains.*

Corvara (Alta Badia) 108 C2 1568–2500m • 56 lifts • Dec–Apr • Brunico (38km) www.altabadia.it • *Roads normally clear but keep chains accessible.*

Madonna di Campiglio 121 A3 1550/1500–2600m • 72 lifts • Dec–Apr • Trento (60km) +39 465 447501 www.campigliodolomiti.it/homepage • *Roads normally cleared but keep chains accessible. Linked to Folgarida and Marilleva.*

Moena di Fassa (Sorte/Ronchi) 108 C2 1184/1450–2520m • 8 lifts • Dec–Apr • Bolzano (40km) www.fassa.com

Selva di Val Gardena/Wolkenstein Groden 108 C2 1563/1570–2450m • 81 lifts • Dec–Apr • Bolzano (40km) +39 471 777777 www.valgardena.it • *Roads normally cleared but keep chains accessible.*

Norway

Hemsedal 47 B5 700/640–1450m • 24 lifts • Nov–May • Honefoss (150km) +47 32 055030 www.hemsedal.com • *Be prepared for extreme weather conditions.*

Slovakia

Chopok (Jasna-Chopok) 99 C3 900/950–1840m • 17 lifts • Dec–Apr • Jasna +421 907 886644 www.jasna.sk

Donovaly 99 C3 913–1360m • 17 lifts • Nov–Apr • Ruzomberok +421 48 4199900 www.parksnow.sk/zima/en

Martinské Hole 98 B2 1250/1150–1456m • 8 lifts • Nov–May • Zilina +421 43 430 6000 http://leto.martinky.com/sk (Slovak only)

Plejsy 99 C4 470–912m • 9 lifts • Dec–Mar • Krompachy +421 53 429 8015 www.plejsy.sk

Strbske Pleso 99 B4 1380–1825m • 7 lifts • Dec–Mar • Poprad +421 917 682 260 www.vt.sk

Slovenia

Julijske Alpe

Kanin (Bovec) 122 A2 460/1690–2293m • 5 lifts • Dec–Apr • Bovec www.boveckanin.si

Kranjska Gora 122 A2 800–1210m • 19 lifts • Dec–Mar • Kranjska Gora +386 4 5809 440 www.kranjska-gora.si

Vogel 122 A2 570–1800m • 8 lifts • Dec–Apr • Bohinjska Bistrica +386 4 5729 712 www.vogel.si

Kawiniške Savinjske Alpe

Krvavec 122 A3 1450–1970m • 10 lifts • Dec–Apr • Kranj 386 4 25 25 911 http://www.rtc-krvavec.si/en

Pohorje

Rogla 123 A4 1517/1050–1500m • 13 lifts • Dec–Apr • Slovenska Bistrica +386 3 75 77 100 www.rogla.eu/en

Spain

Pyrenees

Baqueira-Beret/Bonaigua 145 B4 1500–2500m • 33 lifts • Dec–Apr • Vielha (15km) +34 902 415 415 www.baqueira.es • *Roads normally clear but keep chains accessible. Near Salardú.*

Sistema Penibetico

Sierra Nevada 163 A4 2100–3300m • 24 lifts • Dec–May • Granada (32km) +34 902 70 80 90 http://sierranevada.es • *Access road designed to be avalanche safe and is snow cleared.*

Sweden

Idre Fjäll 199 D9 590–890m • 33 lifts • Nov–Apr • Mora (140km) +46 253 41000 www.idrefjall.se • *Be prepared for extreme weather conditions.*

Sälen 49 A5 360m • 100 lifts • Nov–Apr • Malung (70km) +46 771 84 00 00 www.skistar.com/salen • *Be prepared for extreme weather conditions.*

Switzerland

Alps

Adelboden 106 C2 1353m • 55 lifts • Dec–Apr • Frutigen (15km) +41 33 673 80 80 www.adelboden.ch • *Linked with Lenk.*

Arosa 107 C4 1800/1740–2650m • 16 lifts • Dec–Apr • Chur (30km) +41 81 378 70 20 www.arosa.ch • *Roads cleared but keep chains accessible due to high altitude.*

Crans Montana 119 A4 1500–3000m • 34 lifts • Dec–Apr, Jul–Oct • Sierre (15km) +41 848 22 10 12 www.crans-montana.ch • *Roads normally cleared but keep chains accessible for ascent from Sierre.*

Davos 107 C4 1560/1100–2840m • 38 lifts • Nov–Apr • Davos. +41 81 415 21 21 www.davos.ch

Engelberg 106 C3 1000/1050–3020m • 26 lifts • Nov–May • Luzern (39km) +41 41 639 77 77 www.engelberg.ch • *Straight access road normally cleared.*

Flums (Flumserberg) 107 B4 1400/1000–2220m • 17 lifts • Dec–Apr • Buchs (25km) +41 81 720 18 18 www.flumserberg.ch • *Roads normally cleared, but 1000-metre vertical ascent; keep chains accessible.*

Grindelwald 106 C3 1050–2950m • 39 lifts • Dec–Apr • Interlaken (20km) +41 33 854 12 12 www.jungfrauregion.ch • *Linked with Wengen.*

Gstaad – Saanenland 106 C2 1050/950–3000 • 74 lifts • Dec–Apr • Gstaad +41 33 748 81 81 www.gstaad.ch • *Linked to Anzère.*

Klosters 107 C4 1191/1110–2840m • 52 lifts • Dec–Apr • Davos (10km). +41 81 410 20 20 www.davos.ch/klosters • *Roads normally clear but keep chains accessible.*

Leysin 119 A4 2260–2330m • 16 lifts • Dec–Apr • Aigle (6km) +41 24 493 33 00 www.aigle-leysin-lesmosses.ch

Mürren 106 C2 1650–2970m • 12 lifts • Dec–Apr • Interlaken (18km) +41 33 856 86 86 www.muerren.ch • *No road access. Park in Streche berg (1500 free places) and take the two-stage cable c*

Nendaz 119 A4 1365/1400–3300m • 20 lifts • Nov–Apr • Sion (16km) +41 27 289 55 89 www.nendaz.ch • *Roads normally cleared, howeve keep chains accessible for ascent from Sion. Near Vex.*

Saas-Fee 119 A4 1800–3500m • 23 lifts • Jan–Dec • Brig (35km) +41 27 958 18 58 www.saas-fee.ch/en/ • *Roads normally cleared bu keep chains accessible because of altitude.*

St Moritz 107 C4 1856/1730–3300m • 24 lifts • Nov–May • Chur (89km) +41 81 837 33 33 www.stmoritz.ch • *Roads normally cleared but keep chains accessible.*

Samnaun 107 C5 1846/1400–2900m • 82 lifts • Dec–May • Scuol (30km) +41 81 861 88 30 www.engadin.com/en • *Roads normally cleared b keep chains accessible. Lift linked to Ischgl (Austria).*

Verbier 119 A4 1500–3330m • 17 lifts • Nov–Apr • Martigny (27km) +41 27 775 38 88 www.verbier.ch • *Roads normally cleared.*

Villars-Gryon 119 A4 1253/1200–2100m • 16 lifts • Dec–Apr, Jun–Jul • Montreux (35km) +41 24 495 32 32 www.villars.ch • *Roads normally cleared but keep chains accessible for ascent from N9. Near Bex.*

Wengen 106 C2 1270–2320m • 39 lifts • Dec–Ap • Interlaken (12km) +41 33 856 85 85 http://wengen.ch • *No road access. Park at Lauterbrunnen and take mountain railway. Linked with Grindelwald.*

Zermatt 119 A4 1620–3900m • 40 lifts • all year • Brig (42km) +41 27 966 81 00 www.zermatt.ch • *Cars not permitted in resort, par in Täsch (3km) and take shuttle train.*

Turkey

North Anatolian Mountains

Uludag 186 B4 1770–2320m • 15 lifts • Dec–Mar • Bursa (36km) http://skiingturkey.com/resorts/uludag.html

To the best of the Publisher's knowledge the information in this table was correct at the time of going to press. No responsibility can be accepted for any errors or their consequences.

Skiing near Valmorel, France
Jacques Pierre / hemis.fr / Alamy

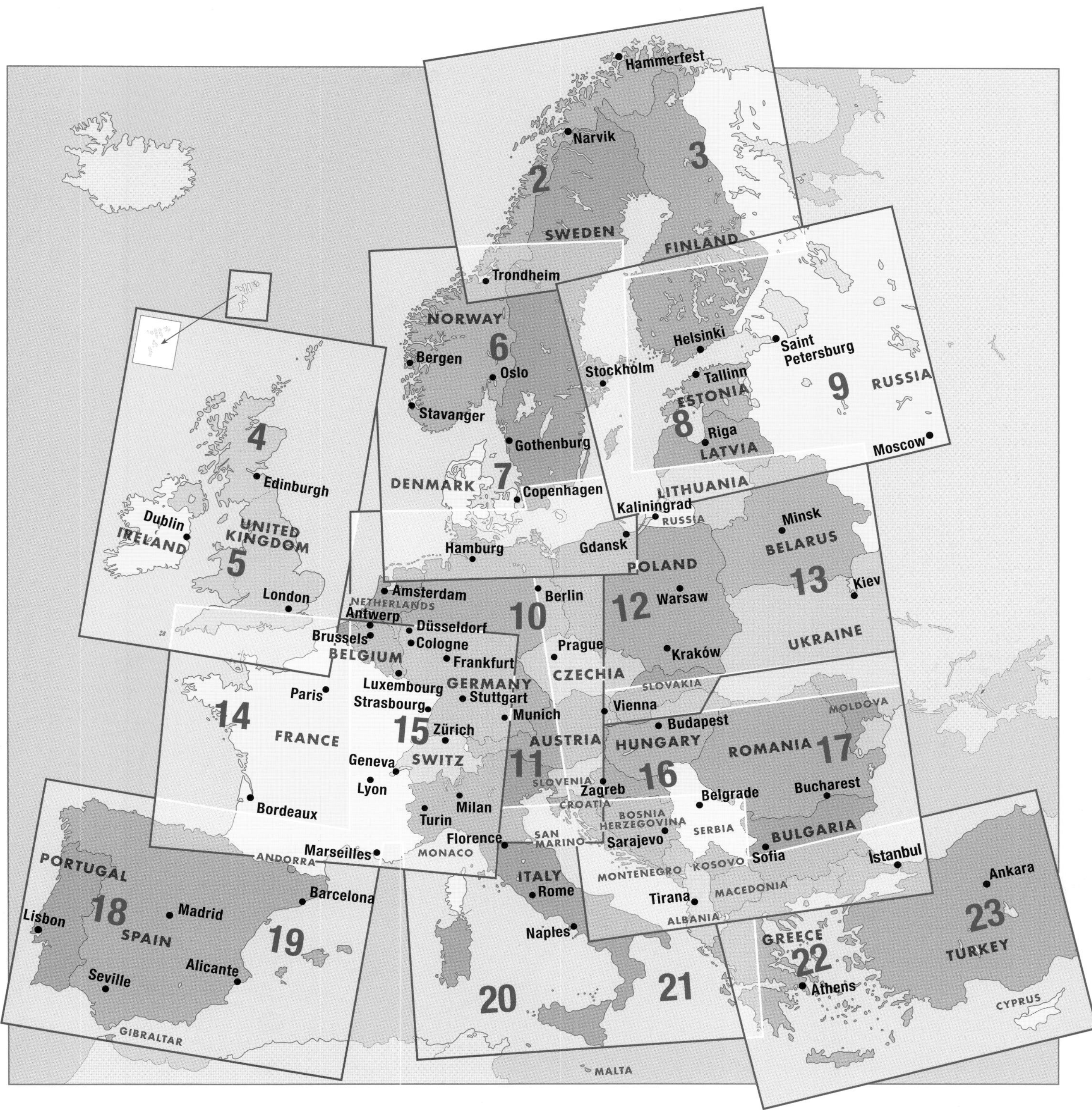

Motorway vignettes

Some countries require you to purchase (and in some cases display) a vignette before using motorways.

In Austria you will need to purchase and display a vignette on the inside of your windscreen. Vignettes are available for purchase at border crossings and petrol stations. More details from www.asfinag.at/toll/toll-sticker

In Belarus all vehicles over 3.5 tonnes and cars and vans under 3.5 tonnes registered outside the Eurasion Economic Union are required to have a *BelToll* unit installed. This device exchanges data with roadside gantries, enabling motorway tolls to be automatically deducted from the driver's account. http://beltoll.by/index.php/en/

In Czechia, you can buy a vignette at the border and also at petrol stations. Make sure you write your vehicle registration number on the vignette before displaying it. The roads without toll are indicated by a traffic sign saying "Bez poplatku". More details from www.motorway.cz

In Hungary a new e-vignette system was introduced in 2008. It is therefore no longer necessary to display the vignette, though you should make doubly sure the information you give on your vehicle is accurate. Vignettes are sold at petrol stations throughout the country. Buy online at http://toll-charge.hu/

In Slovakia, an electronic vignette must purchased before using the motorways. Vignettes may be purchased online, via a mobile app or at Slovak border crossings and petrol stations displaying the 'eznamka' logo. More details from https://eznamka.sk/selfcare/home/

In Switzerland, you will need to purchase and display a vignette before you drive on the motorway. Bear in mind you will need a separate vignette if you are towing a caravan. www.ezv.admin.ch/ezv/en/home/information-individuals/documents-for-travellers-and-road-taxes/motorway-charge-sticker--vignette-.html

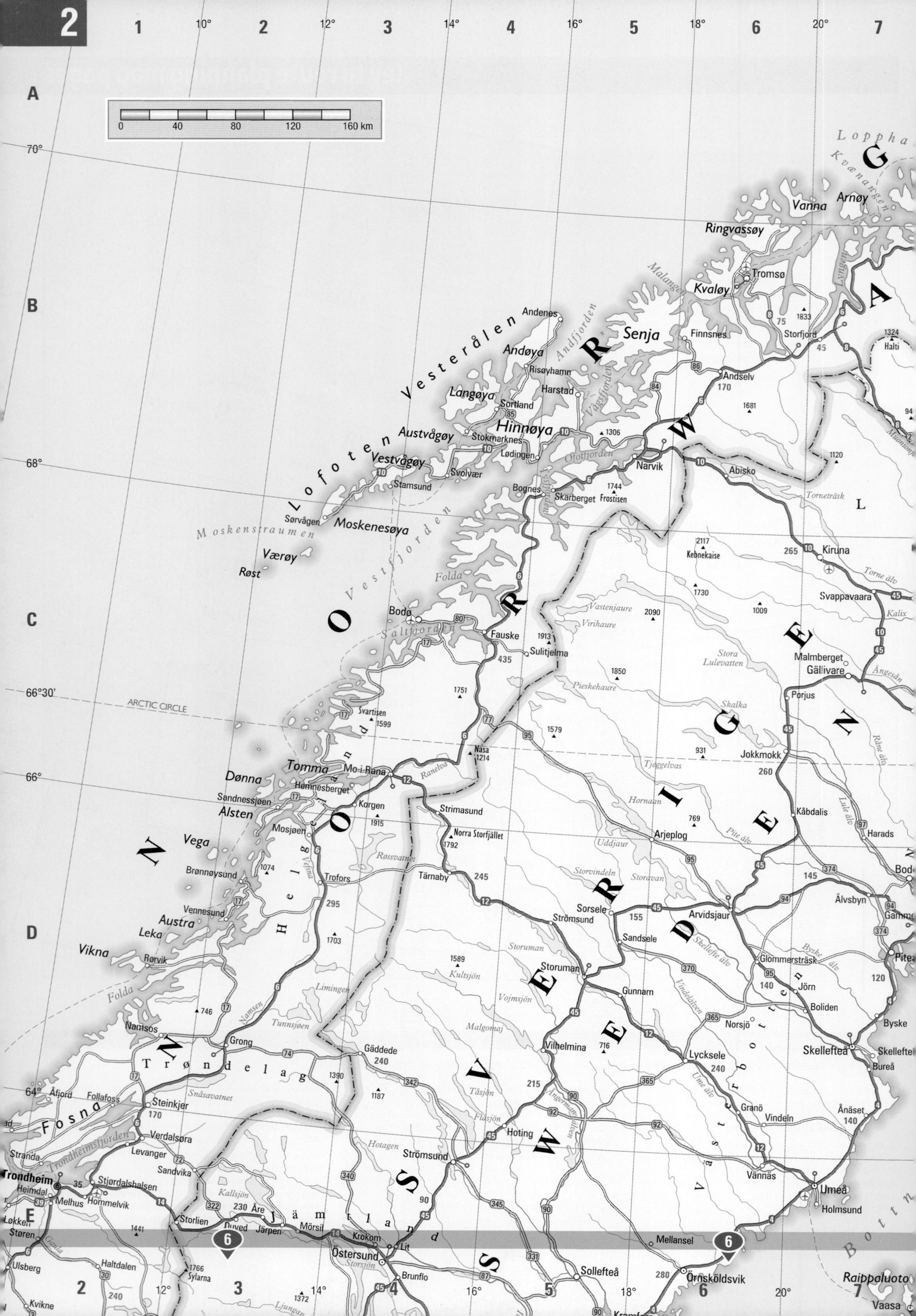
0 40 80 120 160 km
ARCTIC CIRCLE
NORWAY
SWEDEN
Lofoten
Vesterålen
Andenes
Andøya
Risøyhamn
Langøya
Sortland
Harstad
Hinnøya
Stokmarknes
Austvågøy
Vestvågøy
Lødingen
Svolvær
Stamsund
Sørvågen
Moskenesøya
Moskenstraumen
Værøy
Røst
Vestfjorden
Andfjorden
Vågsfjorden
Ofotfjorden
Senja
Finnsnes
Malangen
Kvaløy
Tromsø
Ringvassøy
Vanna
Arnøy
Loppha
Kvænangen
Lyngen
Storfjord
Halti
Andselv
Narvik
Bognes
Skarberget
Frostisen
Abisko
Torneträsk
Kebnekaise
Kiruna
Torne älv
Svappavaara
Kalix
Folda
Bodø
Saltfjorden
Fauske
Sulitjelma
Vastenjaure
Virihaure
Stora Lulevatten
Malmberget
Gällivare
Ångesån
Pieskehaure
Porjus
Skalka
Svartisen
Nasa
Jokkmokk
Råne älv
Tjeggelvas
Tomma
Mo i Rana
Ranelva
Dønna
Hemnesberget
Sandnessjøen
Alsten
Korgen
Strimasund
Hornavan
Kåbdalis
Lule älv
Harads
Mosjøen
Vega
Norra Storfjället
Arjeplog
Pite älv
Uddjaur
Røssvatnet
Vefsna
Brønnøysund
Trofors
Tärnaby
Storvindeln
Storavan
Helgeland
Sorsele
Strömsund
Arvidsjaur
Älvsbyn
Gammelstad
Vennesund
Austra
Leka
Vikna
Rørvik
Sandsele
Storuman
Skellefte älv
Glommersträsk
Piteå
Kultsjön
Limingen
Folda
Gunnarn
Vindelälven
Jörn
Boliden
Vojmsjön
Malgomaj
Namsos
Namsen
Tunnsjøen
Grong
Norsjö
Byske
Vilhelmina
Skellefteå
Bureå
Gäddede
Lycksele
Trøndelag
Ume älv
Västerbotten
Åfjord
Follafoss
Snåsavatnet
Steinkjer
Fosna
Tåsjön
Ångermanälven
Flåsjön
Hoting
Granö
Vindeln
Ånäset
Trondheimsfjorden
Verdalsøra
Stranda
Levanger
Sandvika
Hotagen
Strömsund
Trondheim
Heimdal
Stjørdalshalsen
Melhus
Hommelvik
Kallsjön
Vännäs
Umeå
Holmsund
Løkken
Støren
Storlien
Duved
Åre
Järpen
Mörsil
Krokom
Lit
Jämtland
Gaula
Mellansel
Östersund
Storsjön
Ulsberg
Haltdalen
Sylarna
Brunflo
Sollefteå
Örnsköldsvik
Raippaluoto
Botten
Kvikne
Ljungan
Kramfors
Vaasa

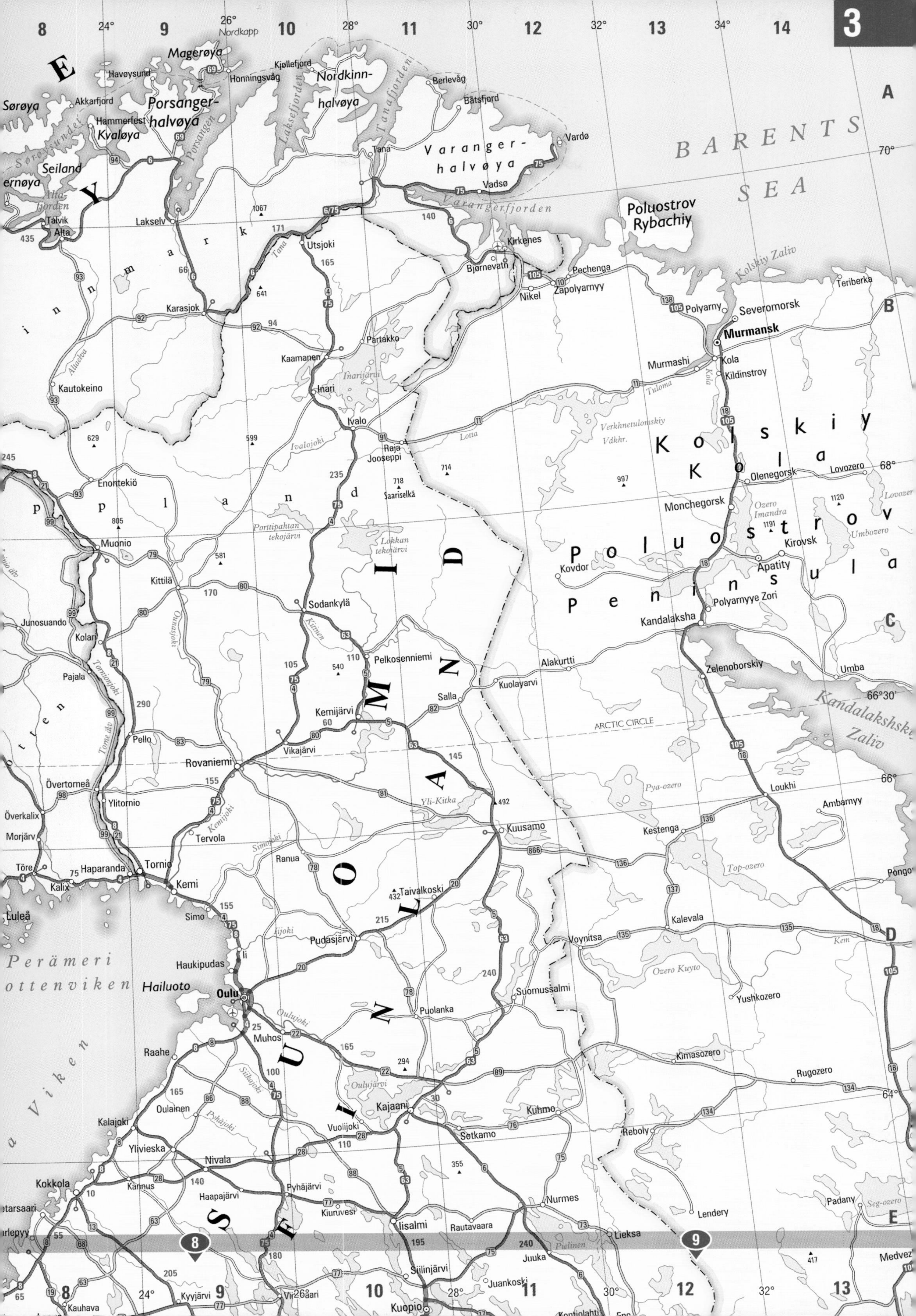
Nordkapp
Magerøya
Havøysund
Honningsvåg
Kjøllefjord
Nordkinn-
halvøya
Lakesfjorden
Tanafjorden
Berlevåg
Båtsfjord
Sørøya
Akkarfjord
Porsanger-
halvøya
Hammerfest
Kvaløya
Porsangen
Sørøysundet
Seiland
Altafjorden
Talvik
Alta
Tana
Varanger-
halvøya
Vardø
Vadsø
Varangerfjorden
BARENTS
SEA
Poluostrov
Rybachiy
Lakselv
Utsjoki
Kirkenes
Bjørnevatn
Pechenga
Nikel
Zapolyarnyy
Kolskiy Zaliv
Teriberka
Polyarny
Severomorsk
Murmansk
Kola
Kildinstroy
Murmashi
Tuloma
Karasjok
Partakko
Kaamanen
Inarijärvi
Inari
Kautokeino
Altaelva
Ivalo
Raja
Jooseppi
Ivalojoki
Lotta
Verkhnetulomskiy
Vdkhr.
Kolskiy
Kola
Poluostrov
Peninsula
Olenegorsk
Lovozero
Monchegorsk
Ozero
Imandra
Kirovsk
Umbozero
Apatity
Kovdor
Polyarnyye Zori
Kandalaksha
Enontekiö
Saariselkä
Porttipahtan
tekojärvi
Lokkan
tekojärvi
Muonio
Kittilä
Sodankylä
Kitinen
Ounasjoki
Junosuando
Kolari
Pajala
Tornionjoki
Pelkosenniemi
Alakurtti
Zelenoborskiy
Umba
Kuolayarvi
Salla
Kandalakshskiy
Zaliv
Kemijärvi
ARCTIC CIRCLE
Pello
Vikajärvi
Rovaniemi
Torne älv
Övertorneå
Ylitornio
Överkalix
Morjärv
Kemijoki
Tervola
Yli-Kitka
Pya-ozero
Loukhi
Ambarnyy
Kestenga
Kuusamo
Simojoki
Ranua
Top-ozero
Töre
Haparanda
Tornio
Kemi
Kalix
Pongoma
Luleå
Simo
Taivalkoski
Kalevala
Iijoki
Pudasjärvi
Voynitsa
Kem
Perämeri
Bottenviken
Haukipudas
Ii
Ozero Kuyto
Hailuoto
Oulu
Suomussalmi
Yushkozero
Puolanka
Oulujoki
Muhos
Raahe
Kimasozero
Siikajoki
Oulujärvi
Rugozero
Oulainen
Pyhäjoki
Kajaani
Kuhmo
Kalajoki
Vuolijoki
Sotkamo
Reboly
Ylivieska
Nivala
Kokkola
Kannus
Haapajärvi
Pyhäjärvi
Kiuruvesi
Nurmes
Padany
Seg-ozero
Lendery
Iisalmi
Rautavaara
Lieksa
Pielinen
Juuka
Siilinjärvi
Juankoski
Medvezh
Kyyjärvi
Kauhava
Kuopio
Kontiolahti
Finnmark
Lappland
SUOMI FINLAND
Barentsovo More
Kandalaksha

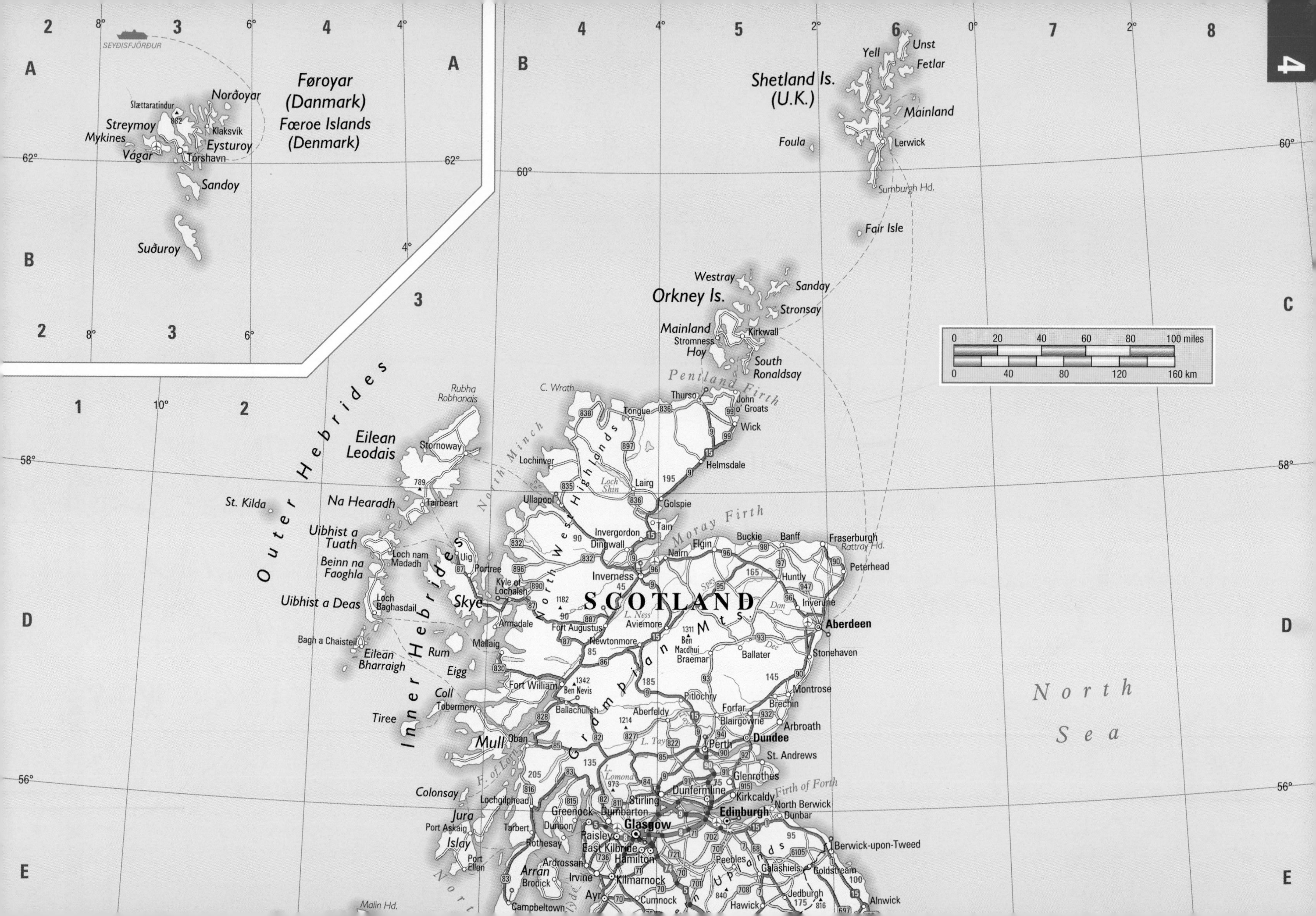

4

Føroyar
(Danmark)
Færoe Islands
(Denmark)

Norðoyar
Klaksvik
Eysturoy
Streymoy
Slættaratindur 882
Mykines
Tórshavn
Vágar
Sandoy

Suðuroy

SEYÐISFJÖRÐUR

Shetland Is.
(U.K.)

Unst
Fetlar
Mainland
Yell
Lerwick
Foula
Sumburgh Hd.

Fair Isle

Westray
Sanday
Stronsay
Orkney Is.
Mainland
Stromness
Hoy
Kirkwall
South Ronaldsay

Rubha
Robhanais

Stornoway
Tarbeart
Eilean
Leodais
789
Na Hearadh
Loch nam
Madadh
Uibhist a
Tuath
Beinn na
Faoghla
Loch
Baghasdail
Uibhist a Deas
Bagh a Chaistel
Eilean
Bharragh

St. Kilda

Outer Hebrides

North Minch

C. Wrath
Tongue
Lochinver
Ullapool
Loch
Assynt
Lairg
Loch
Shin

Durness

Thurso
John o' Groats
Wick
Helmsdale
Golspie
Dornoch

Pentland Firth

Invergordon
Dingwall
Inverness
Nairn
Elgin
Buckie

Moray Firth

Kyle of
Lochalsh
Armadale
Portree
Uig
Skye
Malaig
Fort Augustus
Aviemore
Newtonmore
Ballachulish
Fort William
828
Ben Nevis 1342

SCOTLAND

Grampian Mts.

1182
90

1311
Ben
Macdhui
Braemar
Ballater

Banff
Fraserburgh
Rattray Hd.
Peterhead
Huntly
Inverurie
Aberdeen
Stonehaven

Montrose
Brechin
Forfar
Blairgowrie
Pitlochry
Aberfeldy
L. Tay
Perth
Dundee
Arbroath
St. Andrews

Firth of Forth

Stirling
Dunfermline
Kirkcaldy
North Berwick
Dunbar

Edinburgh
Glasgow
Dumbarton
Greenock
Paisley
Hamilton
East Kilbride
Kilmarnock
Ayr
Irvine
Dunoon
Rothesay
Ardrossan
Brodick
Arran
Cumnock

Peebles
Galashiels
Hawick
Jedburgh
Berwick-upon-Tweed
Alnwick
Goldstream

Oban
Tobermory
Mull
Coll
Eigg
Rum
Tiree
Colonsay
Jura
Islay
Port Askaig
Port
Ellen
Loch Lomond
L. Lomond
Loch Fyne
Lochgilphead
Tarbert
Campbeltown

Malin Hd.

North

Inner Hebrides

N o r t h   S e a

160 km
100 miles

Dee
Don
Spey
Tay

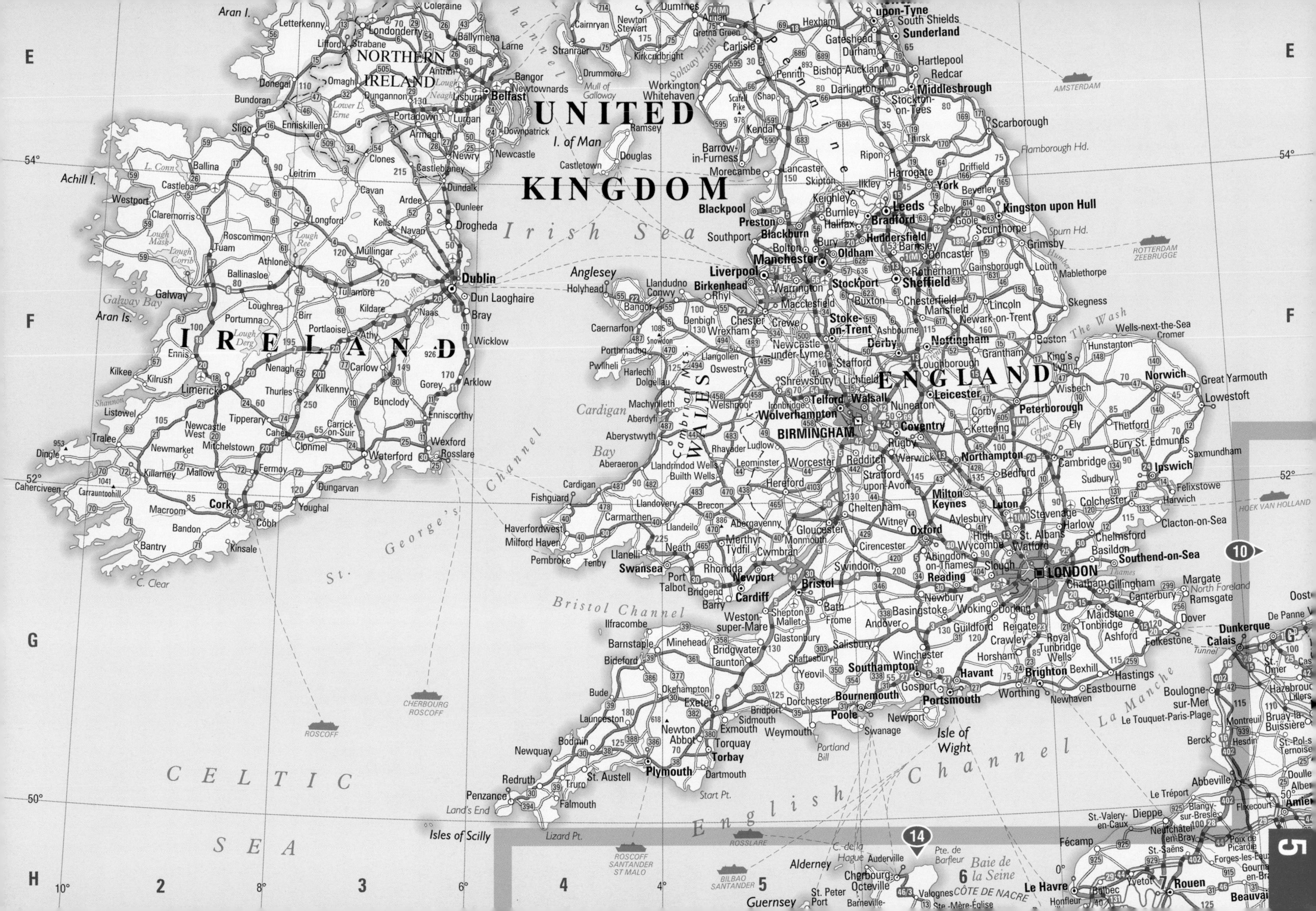
5
UNITED KINGDOM
IRELAND
NORTHERN IRELAND
ENGLAND
WALES
Irish Sea
CELTIC SEA
English Channel
La Manche
Bristol Channel
St. George's Channel
Cardigan Bay
Galway Bay
The Wash
Baie de la Seine
CÔTE DE NACRE
Isle of Wight
I. of Man
Anglesey
Isles of Scilly
Guernsey
Alderney
Aran I.
Aran Is.
Achill I.
Lough Conn
Lough Mask
Lough Corrib
Lough Ree
Lough Derg
Lough Neagh
Lower L. Erne
Solway Firth
Mull of Galloway
Pennine
Cambrian Mts.
Flamborough Hd.
Spurn Hd.
North Foreland
Land's End
Lizard Pt.
Start Pt.
Portland Bill
C. Clear
C. de la Hague
Pte. de Barfleur
AMSTERDAM
ROTTERDAM ZEEBRUGGE
HOEK VAN HOLLAND
CHERBOURG ROSCOFF
ROSCOFF
ROSSLARE
ROSCOFF SANTANDER ST MALO
BILBAO SANTANDER
10
14
54°
52°
50°
10°
8°
6°
4°
0°
E
F
G
H
2
3
4
5
6
7
LONDON
BIRMINGHAM
Dublin
Belfast
Manchester
Liverpool
Leeds
Sheffield
Bradford
Newcastle upon-Tyne
Sunderland
Middlesbrough
Kingston upon Hull
Nottingham
Leicester
Coventry
Wolverhampton
Bristol
Cardiff
Swansea
Newport
Plymouth
Southampton
Portsmouth
Bournemouth
Brighton
Norwich
Ipswich
Cambridge
Oxford
Reading
Luton
Northampton
Peterborough
Derby
Stoke-on-Trent
York
Cork
Limerick
Galway
Waterford
Calais
Dunkerque
Le Havre
Rouen
Cherbourg-Octeville
Beauvais

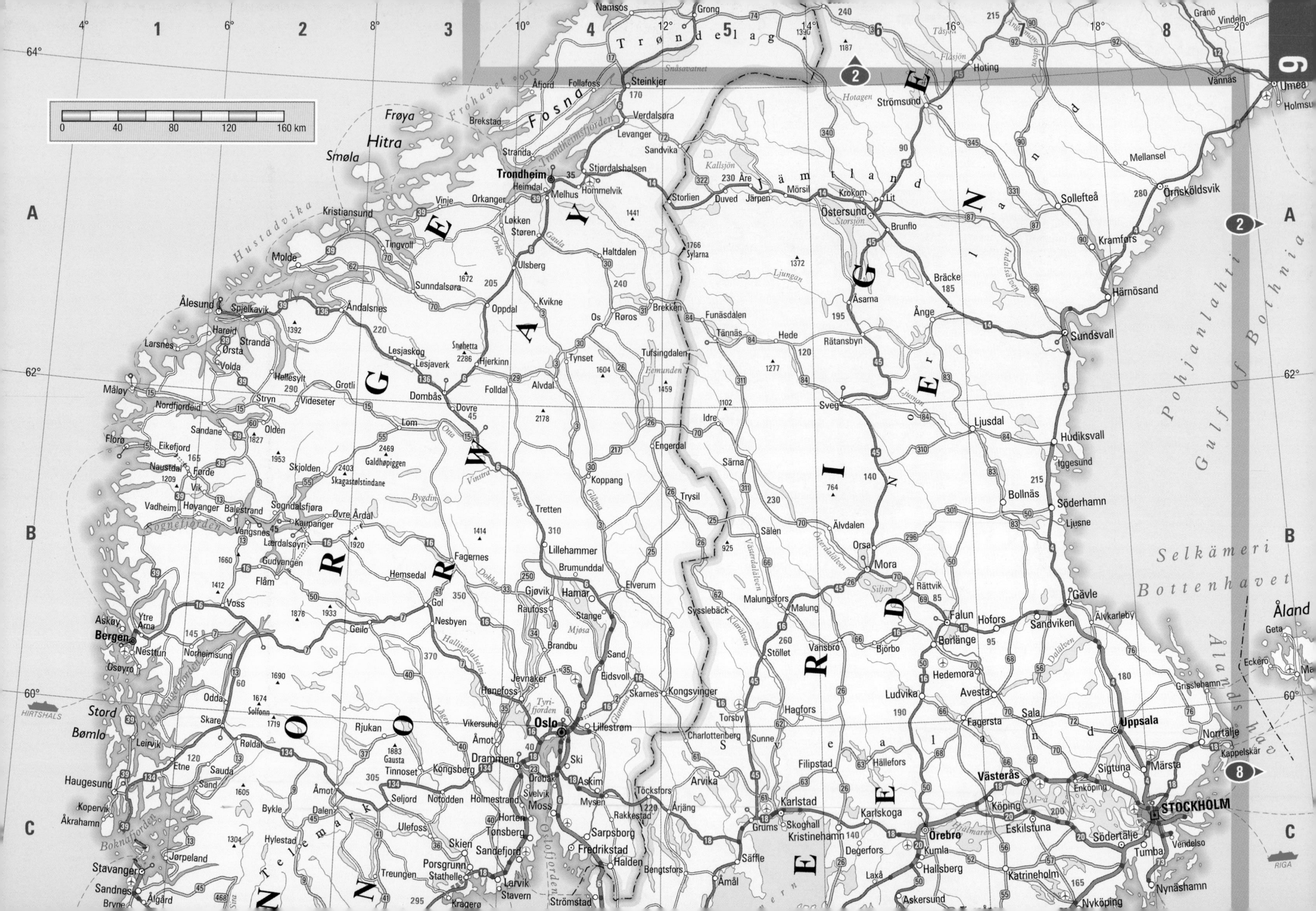

6
NORWAY
SWEDEN
Trøndelag
Jämtland
Telemark
Gulf of Bothnia
Pohjanlahti
Selkämeri
Bottenhavet
Ålands hav
Åland
Frohavet
Fosna
Hustadvika
Trondheimsfjorden
Sognefjorden
Hardangerfjorden
Boknafjorden
Oslofjorden
Mjøsa
Femunden
Siljan
Hjälmaren
Frøya
Hitra
Smøla
Stord
Bømlo
Namsos
Grong
Steinkjer
Verdalsøra
Levanger
Trondheim
Melhus
Kristiansund
Molde
Ålesund
Åndalsnes
Sunndalsøra
Oppdal
Røros
Tynset
Dombås
Lom
Måløy
Florø
Førde
Sogndalsfjøra
Flåm
Voss
Bergen
Odda
Haugesund
Stavanger
Sandnes
Gol
Fagernes
Lillehammer
Hamar
Gjøvik
Elverum
Kongsvinger
Hønefoss
Oslo
Lillestrøm
Drammen
Kongsberg
Rjukan
Skien
Porsgrunn
Larvik
Tønsberg
Moss
Sarpsborg
Fredrikstad
Halden
Storlien
Åre
Östersund
Strömsund
Sveg
Mora
Falun
Borlänge
Ludvika
Karlstad
Arvika
Örebro
Västerås
Eskilstuna
Uppsala
STOCKHOLM
Södertälje
Nyköping
Norrtälje
Gävle
Sandviken
Söderhamn
Hudiksvall
Sundsvall
Härnösand
Sollefteå
Örnsköldsvik
Umeå
Vännäs
HIRTSHALS
RIGA
0
40
80
120
160 km

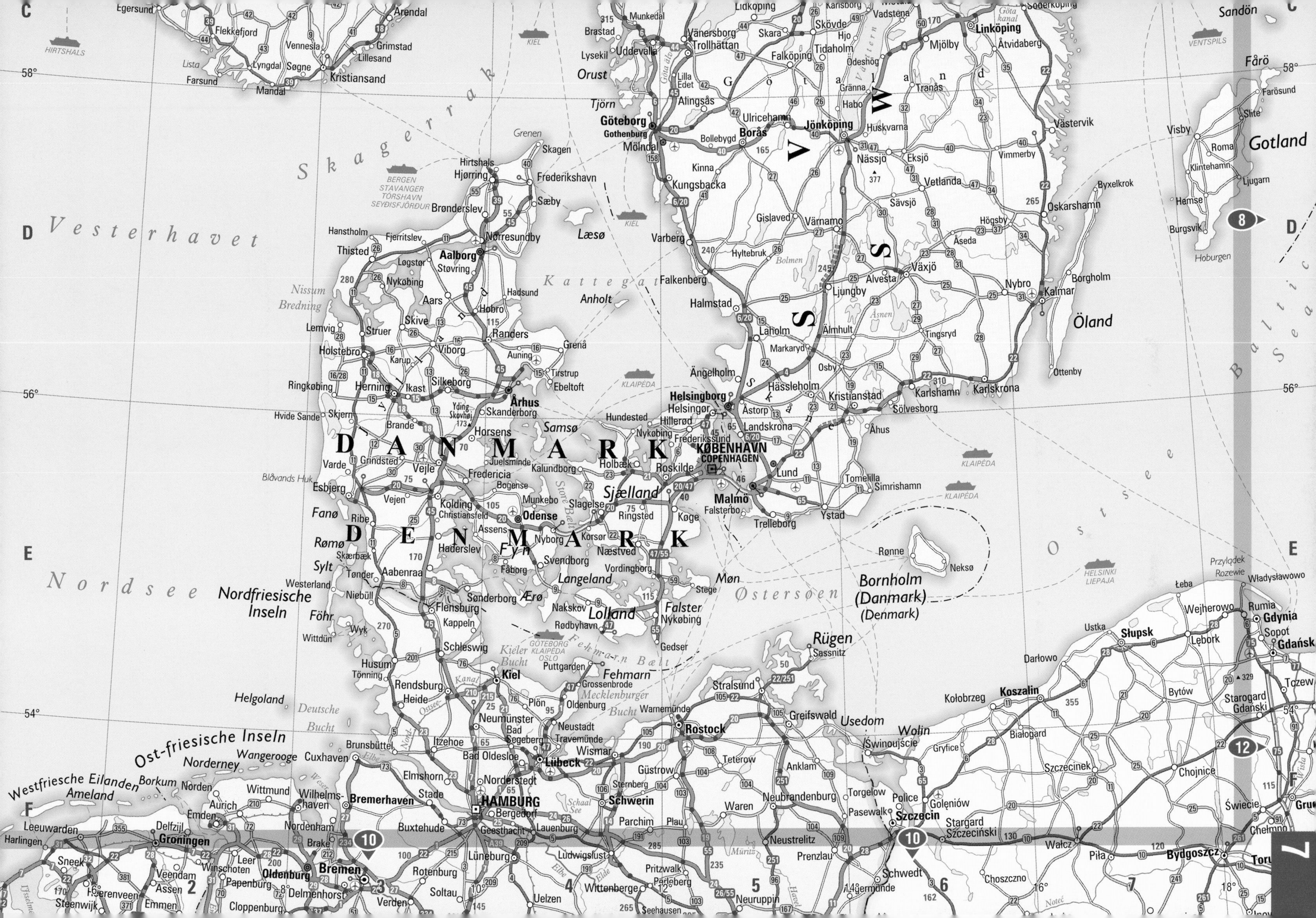
Skagerrak
Vesterhavet
Kattegat
Nordsee
Østersøen
Ostsee
Baltic Sea
DANMARK
DENMARK
SVERIGE
Götaland
Skåne
Gotland
Öland
Bornholm
(Danmark)
(Denmark)
Rügen
Usedom
Wolin
Fehmarn
Fehmarn Bælt
Sjælland
Fyn
Lolland
Falster
Møn
Langeland
Ærø
Samsø
Anholt
Læsø
Fanø
Rømø
Sylt
Föhr
Nordfriesische
Inseln
Ost-friesische Inseln
Westfriesche Eilanden
Helgoland
Deutsche
Bucht
Kieler
Bucht
Mecklenburger
Bucht
Nissum
Bredning
Store Bælt
Orust
Tjörn
Kristiansand
Mandal
Farsund
Flekkefjord
Egersund
Arendal
Grimstad
Lillesand
Göteborg
Gothenburg
Mölndal
Uddevalla
Trollhättan
Vänersborg
Borås
Jönköping
Linköping
Växjö
Kalmar
Karlskrona
Karlshamn
Kristianstad
Helsingborg
Malmö
Lund
Ystad
Trelleborg
Halmstad
Varberg
Falkenberg
Visby
KØBENHAVN
COPENHAGEN
Helsingør
Roskilde
Køge
Odense
Aalborg
Århus
Randers
Viborg
Herning
Vejle
Fredericia
Kolding
Esbjerg
Skagen
Frederikshavn
Hjørring
Hirtshals
Rønne
Nexø
Kiel
Lübeck
HAMBURG
Bremen
Bremerhaven
Oldenburg
Groningen
Rostock
Stralsund
Schwerin
Wismar
Flensburg
Schleswig
Szczecin
Koszalin
Słupsk
Gdynia
Gdańsk
Bydgoszcz
Świnoujście
HIRTSHALS
KIEL
KLAIPĖDA
VENTSPILS
HELSINKI
LIEPAJA
BERGEN
STAVANGER
TÓRSHAVN
SEYÐISFJÖRÐUR
GÖTEBORG
OSLO
8
10
12
56°
58°
54°

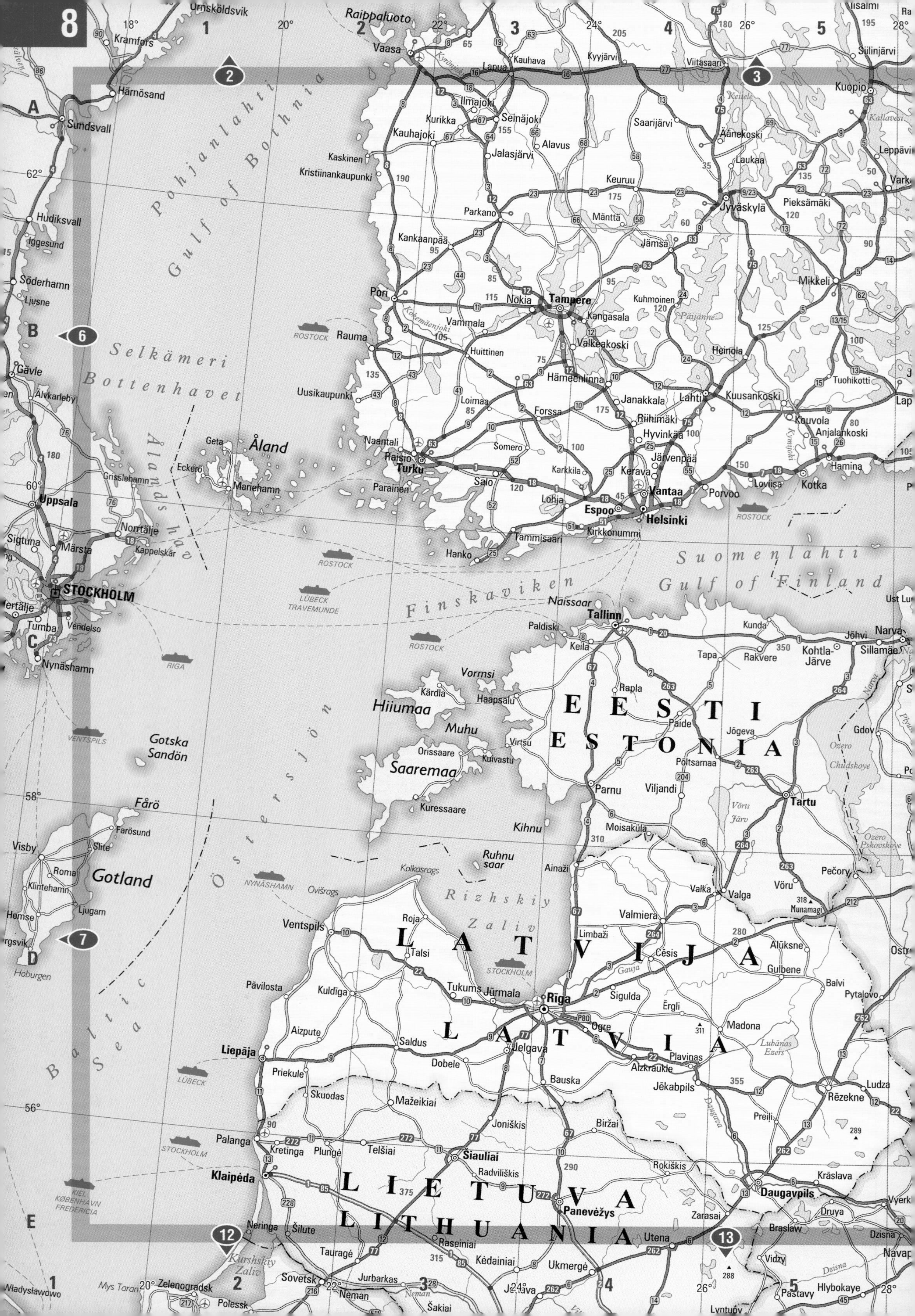
Örnsköldsvik
Kramfors
Härnösand
Sundsvall
Hudiksvall
Iggesund
Söderhamn
Ljusne
Gävle
Älvkarleby
Grisslehamn
Uppsala
Norrtälje
Sigtuna
Märsta
Kappelskär
STOCKHOLM
Tumba
Vendelsö
Nynäshamn
Visby
Fårö
Fårösund
Slite
Roma
Klintehamn
Ljugarn
Hemse
Hoburgen
Gotland
Gotska Sandön
Pohjanlahti
Gulf of Bothnia
Selkämeri
Bottenhavet
Ålands hav
Åland
Geta
Eckerö
Mariehamn
Östersjön
Baltic Sea
Finskaviken
Suomenlahti
Gulf of Finland
Raippaluoto
Vaasa
Kauhava
Lapua
Kyyjärvi
Viitasaari
Iisalmi
Siilinjärvi
Kuopio
Kallavesi
Ilmajoki
Seinäjoki
Kurikka
Kauhajoki
Alavus
Jalasjärvi
Kaskinen
Kristiinankaupunki
Saarijärvi
Äänekoski
Laukaa
Keuruu
Mänttä
Jyväskylä
Pieksämäki
Parkano
Kankaanpää
Jämsä
Mikkeli
Pori
Nokia
Tampere
Kuhmoinen
Päijänne
Kangasala
Vammala
Rauma
Huittinen
Valkeakoski
Heinola
Tuohikotti
Hämeenlinna
Uusikaupunki
Loimaa
Forssa
Janakkala
Lahti
Kuusankoski
Kouvola
Anjalankoski
Riihimäki
Hyvinkää
Naantali
Raisio
Turku
Somero
Järvenpää
Karkkila
Kerava
Salo
Parainen
Vantaa
Porvoo
Loviisa
Kotka
Hamina
Lohja
Espoo
Helsinki
Kirkkonummi
Tammisaari
Hanko
ROSTOCK
LÜBECK TRAVEMÜNDE
RIGA
VENTSPILS
NYNÄSHAMN
STOCKHOLM
LÜBECK
KIEL KØBENHAVN FREDERICIA
Naissaar
Tallinn
Paldiski
Keila
Kunda
Rakvere
Tapa
Jõhvi
Kohtla-Järve
Narva
Sillamäe
Rapla
Vormsi
Kärdla
Haapsalu
Hiiumaa
Muhu
Orissaare
Kuivastu
Virtsu
Saaremaa
Kuressaare
EESTI
ESTONIA
Paide
Jõgeva
Põltsamaa
Gdov
Ozero Chudskoye
Tartu
Viljandi
Parnu
Võrts Järv
Moisaküla
Kihnu
Ruhnu saar
Kolkasrags
Ainaži
Valka
Valga
Võru
Pečory
Munamagi
Ozero Pskovskoye
Rizhskiy Zaliv
Ovišrogs
Ventspils
Roja
Talsi
Limbaži
Valmiera
Cēsis
Alūksne
Gauja
Gulbene
Balvi
Pytalovo
Pāvilosta
Kuldīga
Tukums
Jūrmala
Rīga
Sigulda
Ērgli
Madona
Ogre
Aizpute
Saldus
LATVIJA
LATVIA
Liepāja
Jelgava
Dobele
Aizkraukle
Plavinas
Lubānas Ezers
Priekule
Bauska
Jēkabpils
Daugava
Rēzekne
Ludza
Skuodas
Mažeikiai
Preiļi
Joniškis
Biržai
Palanga
Kretinga
Plungė
Telšiai
Siauliai
Radviliškis
Rokiškis
Krāslava
Klaipėda
Daugavpils
LIETUVA
LITHUANIA
Panevėžys
Zarasai
Druya
Neringa
Šilute
Raseiniai
Utena
Braslaw
Dzisna
Tauragė
Kėdainiai
Ukmergė
Vidzy
Kurshskiy Zaliv
Sovetsk
Jurbarkas
Neman
Jonava
Pastavy
Hlybokaye
Zelenogradsk
Polessk
Šakiai
Mys Taran
Władysławowo
Lyntupy
Navap
Vyerk
Ust Lu
Leppävi
Vark
Lap
Ostr
Pc

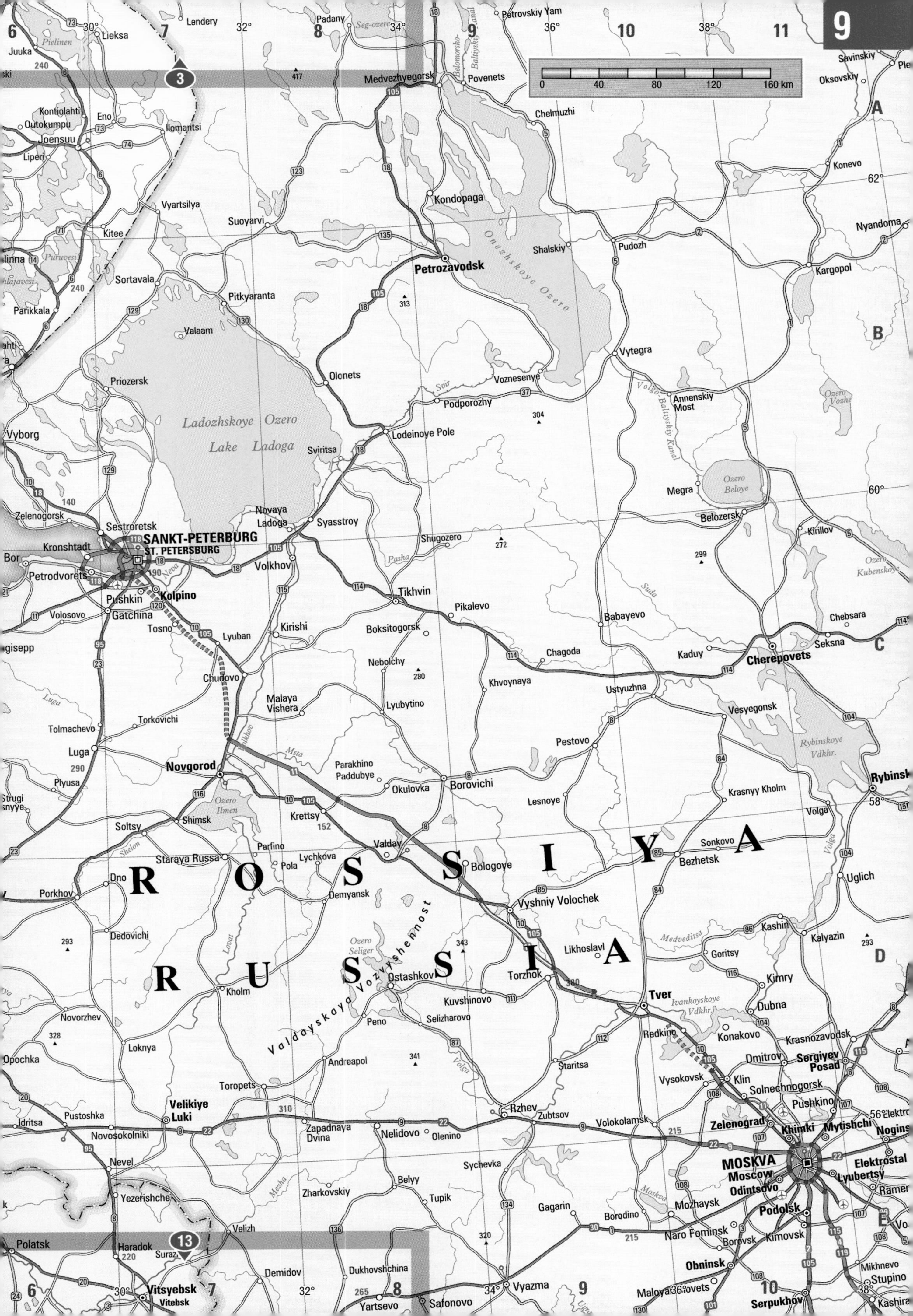

9
ROSSIYA
RUSSIA
SANKT-PETERBURG
ST. PETERSBURG
MOSKVA
Moscow
Ladozhskoye Ozero
Lake Ladoga
Onezhskoye Ozero
Rybinskoye Vdkhr.
Ozero Beloye
Ozero Ilmen
Ozero Seliger
Ozero Vozhe
Ozero Kubenskoye
Ivankovskoye Vdkhr.
Valdayskaya Vozvyshennost
Volgo-Baltiyskiy Kanal
Belomorsko-Baltiyskiy Kanal
Pielinen
Puruvesi
Seg-ozero
Svir
Pasha
Suda
Msta
Volkhov
Luga
Shelon
Lovat
Medveditsa
Volga
Mezha
Moskva
0
40
80
120
160 km
30°
32°
34°
36°
38°
56°
58°
60°
62°
A
B
C
D
E
Lieksa
Lendery
Padany
Petrovskiy Yam
Savinskiy
Oksovskiy
Juuka
Medvezhyegorsk
Povenets
Kontiolahti
Outokumpu
Eno
Joensuu
Ilomantsi
Liperi
Chelmuzhi
Konevo
Kondopaga
Vyartsilya
Suoyarvi
Kitee
Nyandoma
Shalskiy
Pudozh
Kargopol
Petrozavodsk
Sortavala
Pitkyaranta
Parikkala
Valaam
Vytegra
Olonets
Priozersk
Voznesenye
Podporozhy
Annenskiy Most
Lodeinoye Pole
Vyborg
Sviritsa
Megra
Zelenogorsk
Novaya Ladoga
Syasstroy
Belozersk
Sestroretsk
Kirillov
Kronshtadt
Shugozero
Bor
Petrodvorets
Volkhov
Pushkin
Kolpino
Tikhvin
Pikalevo
Volosovo
Gatchina
Babayevo
Chebsara
Tosno
Lyuban
Kirishi
Boksitogorsk
Seksna
Kaduy
Cherepovets
Chagoda
Nebolchy
Chudovo
Khvoynaya
Ustyuzhna
Malaya Vishera
Lyubytino
Vesyegonsk
Torkovichi
Tolmachevo
Pestovo
Luga
Novgorod
Parakhino Paddubye
Okulovka
Borovichi
Rybinsk
Plyusa
Krasnyy Kholm
Strugi Krasnyye
Lesnoye
Krettsy
Volga
Soltsy
Shimsk
Sonkovo
Parfino
Valday
Staraya Russa
Lychkova
Pola
Bologoye
Bezhetsk
Dno
Uglich
Porkhov
Demyansk
Vyshniy Volochek
Kashin
Dedovichi
Likhoslavl
Kalyazin
Goritsy
Torzhok
Kimry
Kholm
Ostashkov
Tver
Kuvshinovo
Dubna
Novorzhev
Peno
Selizharovo
Redkino
Konakovo
Loknya
Krasnozavodsk
Opochka
Andreapol
Staritsa
Dmitrov
Sergiyev Posad
Toropets
Vysokovsk
Klin
Solnechnogorsk
Velikiye Luki
Rzhev
Pushkino
Pustoshka
Zubtsov
Idritsa
Zapadnaya Dvina
Volokolamsk
Zelenograd
Khimki
Mytishchi
Nogins
Elektrostal
Novosokolniki
Nelidovo
Olenino
Nevel
Sychevka
Lyubertsy
Belyy
Odintsovo
Yezerishche
Zharkovskiy
Tupik
Gagarin
Mozhaysk
Ramen
Borodino
Podolsk
Velizh
Naro Fominsk
Borovsk
Kimovsk
Polatsk
Haradok
Suraz
Obninsk
Demidov
Dukhovshchina
Mikhnevo
Stupino
Vitsyebsk
Vitebsk
Vyazma
Maloyaroslavets
Yartsevo
Safonovo
Serpukhov
Kashira
417
313
304
272
299
280
152
343
293
341
328
320
265
240
140
290
190
215
220
310
380

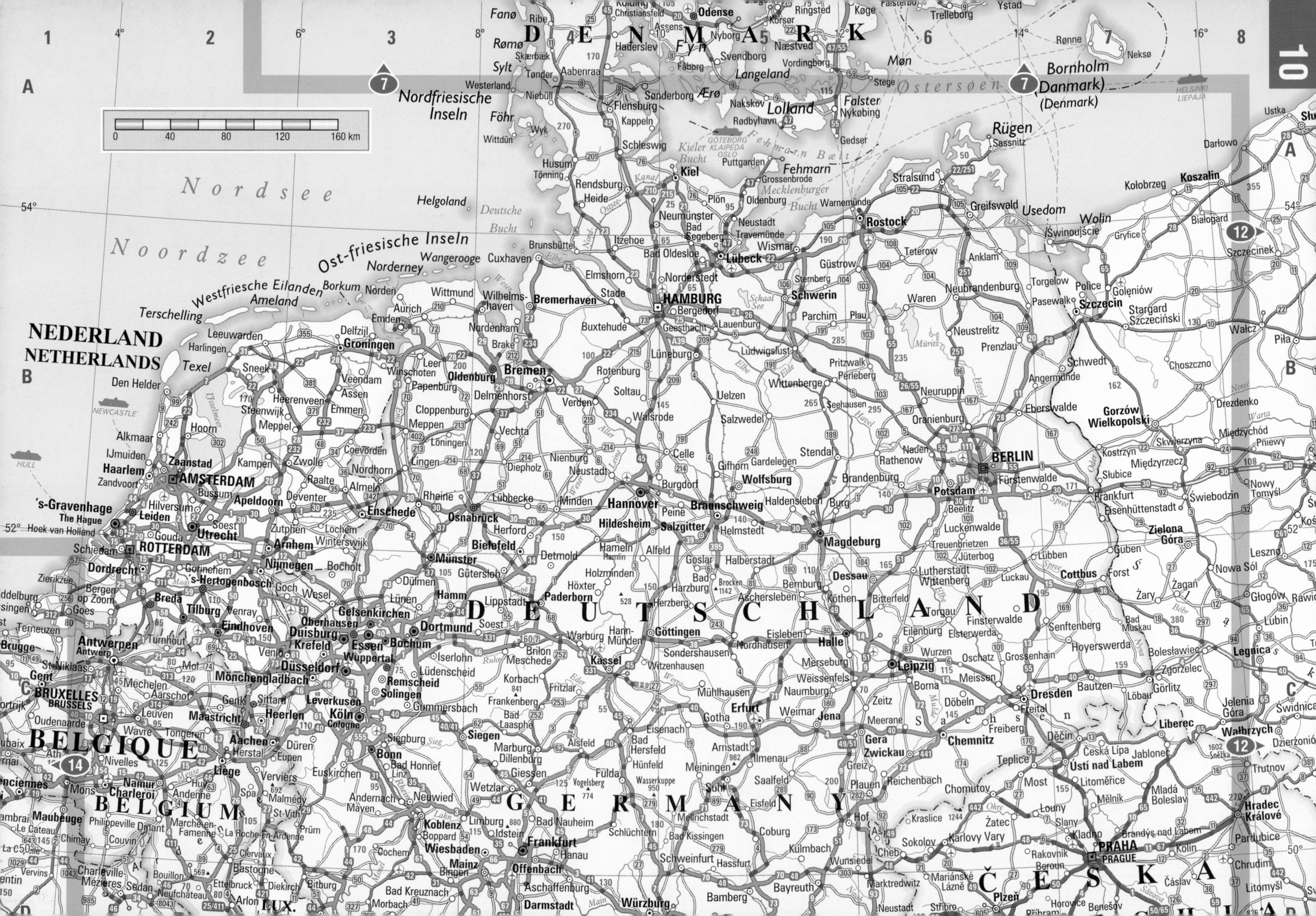

DANMARK
NEDERLAND
NETHERLANDS
BELGIQUE
BELGIUM
DEUTSCHLAND
GERMANY
ČESKÁ
Nordsee
Noordzee
Østersøen
Nordfriesische Inseln
Ost-friesische Inseln
Westfriesische Eilanden
Bornholm (Danmark)
(Denmark)
Rügen
Usedom
Wolin
Fehmarn
Lolland
Falster
Møn
Langeland
Fyn
Ærø
Sylt
Föhr
Rømø
Fanø
Helgoland
Texel
Terschelling
Ameland
Borkum
Norderney
Wangerooge
Odense
Kiel
Lübeck
HAMBURG
Bremen
Bremerhaven
Rostock
Schwerin
Szczecin
Koszalin
BERLIN
Potsdam
Magdeburg
Hannover
Braunschweig
Wolfsburg
Leipzig
Dresden
Halle
Erfurt
Chemnitz
Cottbus
Dessau
Jena
Gera
Zwickau
Göttingen
Kassel
Hildesheim
Salzgitter
Osnabrück
Münster
Bielefeld
Paderborn
Dortmund
Essen
Bochum
Duisburg
Düsseldorf
Köln
Bonn
Koblenz
Wiesbaden
Mainz
Frankfurt
Offenbach
Darmstadt
Würzburg
Bamberg
Bayreuth
Groningen
Enschede
Arnhem
Nijmegen
Utrecht
AMSTERDAM
Haarlem
Leiden
's-Gravenhage
The Hague
ROTTERDAM
Dordrecht
Breda
Tilburg
Eindhoven
Maastricht
Aachen
Liège
Antwerpen
BRUXELLES
BRUSSELS
Gent
Brugge
Namur
Charleroi
Mons
PRAHA
PRAGUE
Plzeň
Liberec
Hradec Králové
Zielona Góra
Gorzów Wielkopolski
Legnica
160 km

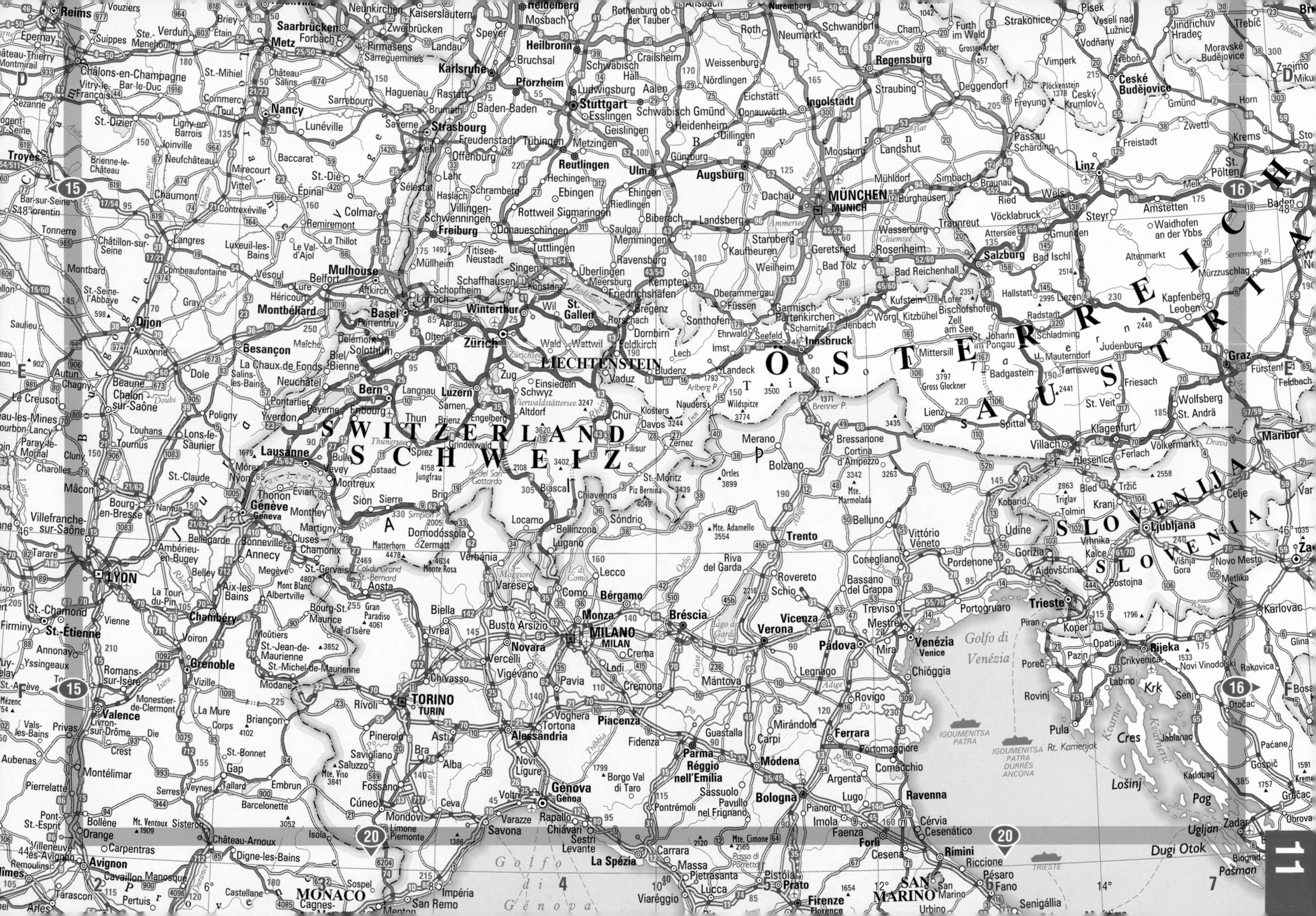
ÖSTERREICH
AUSTRIA
SWITZERLAND
SCHWEIZ
LIECHTENSTEIN
SLOVENIJA
SLOVENIA
SAN MARINO
MONACO
MÜNCHEN
MUNICH
MILANO
MILAN
TORINO
TURIN
LYON
Zürich
Bern
Basel
Genève
Lausanne
Innsbruck
Salzburg
Linz
Graz
Ljubljana
Trieste
Venézia
Verona
Bologna
Génova
Stuttgart
Strasbourg
Dijon
Grenoble
Golfo di Venézia
Golfo di Génova

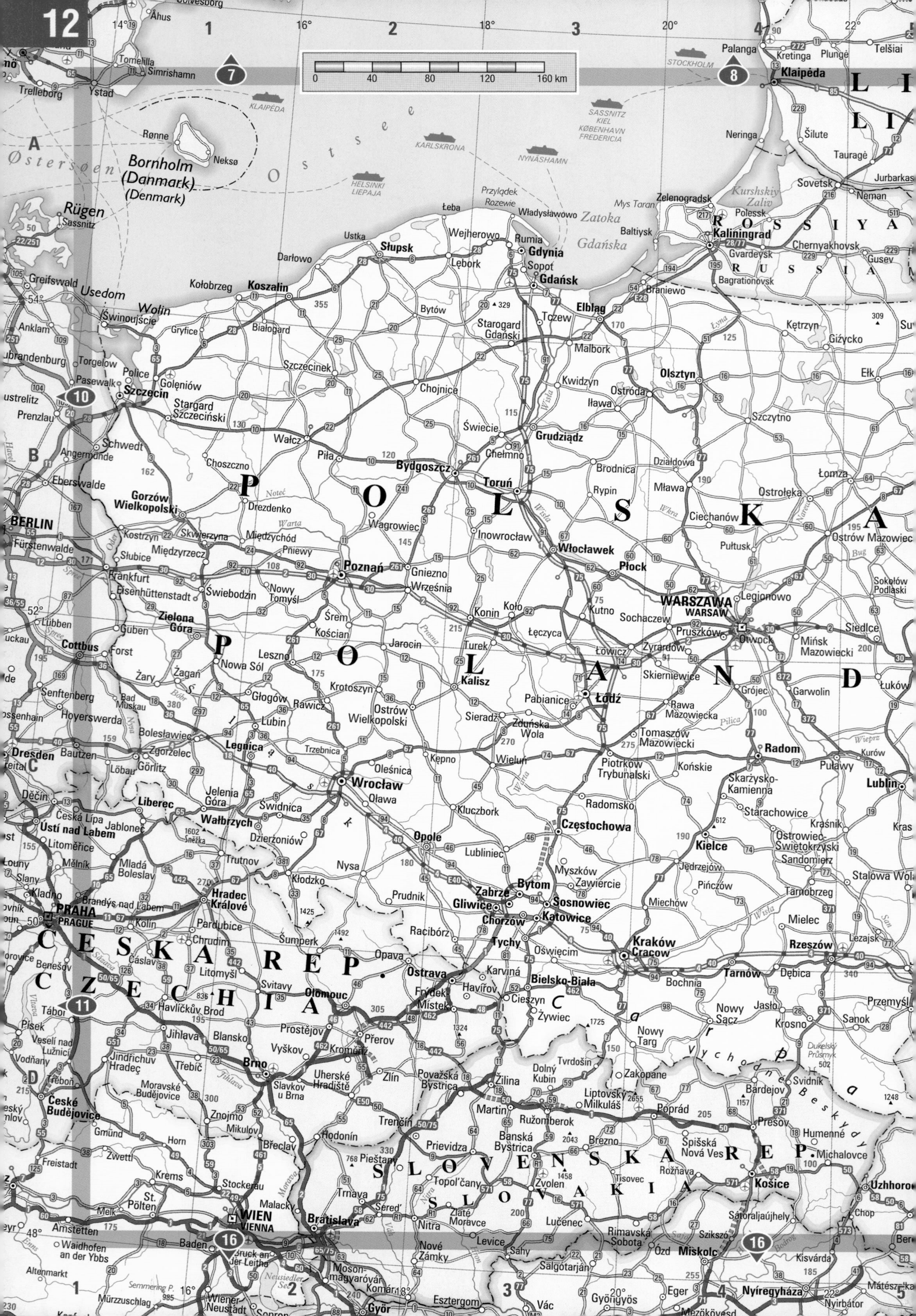
0
40
80
120
160 km
Trelleborg
Ystad
Tomelilla
Simrishamn
Rønne
Nexø
Bornholm
(Danmark)
(Denmark)
Østersøen
Ostsee
Rügen
Sassnitz
KLAIPĖDA
KARLSKRONA
NYNÄSHAMN
HELSINKI
LIEPAJA
SASSNITZ
KIEL
KØBENHAVN
FREDERICIA
STOCKHOLM
Palanga
Kretinga
Plungė
Telšiai
Klaipėda
Neringa
Šilutė
Tauragė
Jurbarkas
Sovetsk
Neman
Kurshskiy Zaliv
Zelenogradsk
Polessk
Kaliningrad
ROSSIYA
RUSSIA
Chernyakhovsk
Gusev
Gvardeysk
Bagrationovsk
Baltiysk
Mys Taran
Zatoka Gdańska
Przylądek Rozewie
Władysławowo
Łeba
Ustka
Słupsk
Wejherowo
Rumia
Gdynia
Sopot
Gdańsk
Lębork
Darłowo
Kołobrzeg
Koszalin
Greifswald
Usedom
Wolin
Świnoujście
Anklam
Gryfice
Białogard
Bytów
Starogard Gdański
Tczew
Elbląg
Braniewo
Malbork
Kętrzyn
Giżycko
Torgelow
Pasewalk
Police
Goleniów
Szczecin
Stargard Szczeciński
Szczecinek
Chojnice
Kwidzyn
Iława
Ostróda
Olsztyn
Ełk
Szczytno
Prenzlau
Schwedt
Angermünde
Wałcz
Piła
Świecie
Grudziądz
Chełmno
Bydgoszcz
Toruń
Brodnica
Działdowo
Mława
Łomża
Ostrołęka
Eberswalde
Choszczno
Gorzów Wielkopolski
Drezdenko
Noteć
Warta
Wągrowiec
Rypin
Ciechanów
Pułtusk
Ostrów Mazowiecka
BERLIN
Fürstenwalde
Kostrzyn
Skwierzyna
Międzychód
Międzyrzecz
Pniewy
Inowrocław
Włocławek
Płock
Słubice
Frankfurt
Poznań
Gniezno
Września
Eisenhüttenstadt
Świebodzin
Nowy Tomyśl
Konin
Koło
Kutno
Sochaczew
WARSZAWA
WARSAW
Legionowo
Siedlce
Sokołów Podlaski
Mińsk Mazowiecki
Lübben
Zielona Góra
Śrem
Kościan
Jarocin
Łęczyca
Łowicz
Żyrardów
Pruszków
Otwock
Guben
Cottbus
Forst
Leszno
Turek
Nowa Sól
Żagań
Żary
Krotoszyn
Kalisz
Pabianice
Łódź
Skierniewice
Grójec
Garwolin
Łuków
Senftenberg
Hoyerswerda
Głogów
Rawicz
Ostrów Wielkopolski
Sieradz
Zduńska Wola
Rawa Mazowiecka
Tomaszów Mazowiecki
Pilica
Lubin
Bolesławiec
Legnica
Trzebnica
Dresden
Bautzen
Zgorzelec
Görlitz
Löbau
Kępno
Wieluń
Piotrków Trybunalski
Końskie
Radom
Puławy
Kurów
Lublin
Oleśnica
Wrocław
Oława
Děčín
Liberec
Jelenia Góra
Świdnica
Wałbrzych
Kluczbork
Radomsko
Skarżysko-Kamienna
Starachowice
Kraśnik
Česká Lípa
Jablonec
Ústí nad Labem
Sněžka
Dzierżoniów
Opole
Częstochowa
Litoměřice
Mělník
Mladá Boleslav
Trutnov
Nysa
Lubliniec
Kielce
Ostrowiec-Świętokrzyski
Sandomierz
Stalowa Wola
Louny
Slany
Kladno
Hradec Králové
Kłodzko
Myszków
Zawiercie
Jędrzejów
Pińczów
PRAHA
PRAGUE
Brandýs nad Labem
Kolín
Pardubice
Prudnik
Zabrze
Bytom
Gliwice
Sosnowiec
Chorzów
Katowice
Miechów
Tarnobrzeg
Mielec
Chrudim
Šumperk
Racibórz
Tychy
Oświęcim
Kraków
Cracow
Rzeszów
Łańcut
Lezajsk
ČESKÁ REP.
CZECHIA
Benešov
Čáslav
Litomyšl
Svitavy
Opava
Ostrava
Karviná
Havířov
Bielsko-Biała
Tarnów
Dębica
Bochnia
Frýdek-Místek
Cieszyn
Żywiec
Olomouc
Havlíčkův Brod
Tábor
Písek
Jihlava
Blansko
Prostějov
Přerov
Nowy Sącz
Jasło
Krosno
Sanok
Przemyśl
Veselí nad Lužnicí
Vodňany
Jindřichův Hradec
Třebíč
Vyškov
Kroměříž
Nowy Targ
Brno
Uherské Hradiště
Zlín
Považská Bystrica
Žilina
Dolný Kubín
Tvrdošín
Zakopane
Bardejov
Svidník
Dukelský Průsmyk
Třeboň
Moravské Budějovice
Slavkov u Brna
Vychodné Beskydy
České Budějovice
Znojmo
Mikulov
Trenčín
Martin
Ružomberok
Liptovský Mikuláš
Poprad
Prešov
Humenné
Gmünd
Horn
Břeclav
Hodonín
Prievidza
Banská Bystrica
Brezno
Spišská Nová Ves
Michalovce
Zwettl
Freistadt
Krems
Stockerau
Piešťany
SLOVENSKÁ REP.
SLOVAKIA
Rožňava
Košice
Uzhhorod
St. Pölten
Melk
Trnava
Topoľčany
Zvolen
Tisovec
WIEN
VIENNA
Malacky
Bratislava
Sereď
Zlaté Moravce
Lučenec
Sátoraljaújhely
Chop
Amstetten
Nitra
Levice
Rimavská Sobota
Szikszó
Baden
Bruck an der Leitha
Waidhofen an der Ybbs
Nové Zámky
Šahy
Ózd
Miskolc
Kisvárda
Mosonmagyaróvár
Salgótarján
Altenmarkt
Neusiedler See
Komárno
Semmering P.
Mürzzuschlag
Wiener Neustadt
Győr
Esztergom
Vác
Gyöngyös
Eger
Mezőkövesd
Nyíregyháza
Nyírbátor
Mátészalka

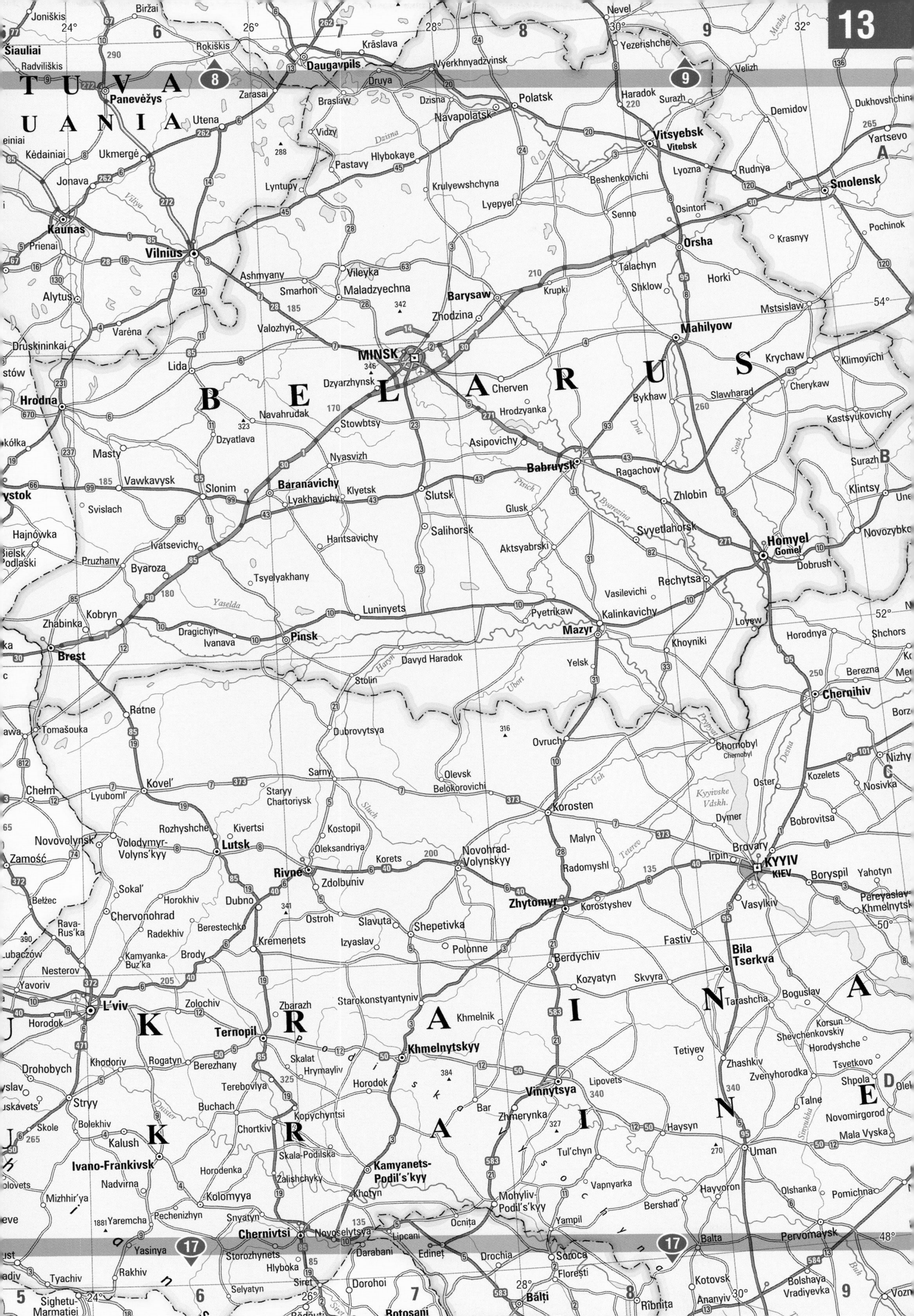
LITHUANIA
BELARUS
UKRAINE
Podilskaya vysochyna
Vilnius
Kaunas
Šiauliai
Panevėžys
Utena
Kėdainiai
Ukmergė
Jonava
Alytus
Druskininkai
Varėna
Joniškis
Biržai
Rokiškis
Radviliškis
Zarasai
Daugavpils
Krāslava
Minsk
Hrodna
Brest
Vitsyebsk
Vitebsk
Homyel
Gomel
Mahilyow
Babruysk
Polatsk
Navapolatsk
Orsha
Barysaw
Maladzyechna
Vileyka
Smarhon
Ashmyany
Lida
Navahrudak
Baranavichy
Slonim
Vawkavysk
Pinsk
Mazyr
Kalinkavichy
Rechytsa
Svyetlahorsk
Zhlobin
Slutsk
Salihorsk
Luninyets
Kobryn
Pruzhany
Smolensk
Velizh
Rudnya
Krychaw
Chernihiv
KYYIV
KIEV
Zhytomyr
Rivne
Lutsk
Kovel'
L'viv
Ternopil
Khmelnytskyy
Vinnytsya
Chernivtsi
Ivano-Frankivsk
Kamyanets-Podil's'kyy
Bila Tserkva
Uman
Korosten
Chornobyl
Novohrad-Volynskyy
Berdychiv
Bălți
Soroca
Nevel
Slawharad
Dubno
Kremenets
Stryy
Drohobych
Kolomyya
Mohyliv-Podil's'kyy
Pervomaysk
Balta
Kotovsk
Ananyiv
Haysyn
Fastiv
Brovary
Boryspil
Nizhyn
Novozybkov
Klintsy
Dobrush
Pinsk
Stowbtsy
Dzyarzhynsk
Asipovichy
Rahachow
Bykhaw
Horki
Krasnyy
Dzisna
Vilyia
Prypyat
Desna
Dnister
Sluch
Yaselda
Ubort
Teterev
Sozh
Drut
Byarezina
Uzh
Kyyivske Vdskh.

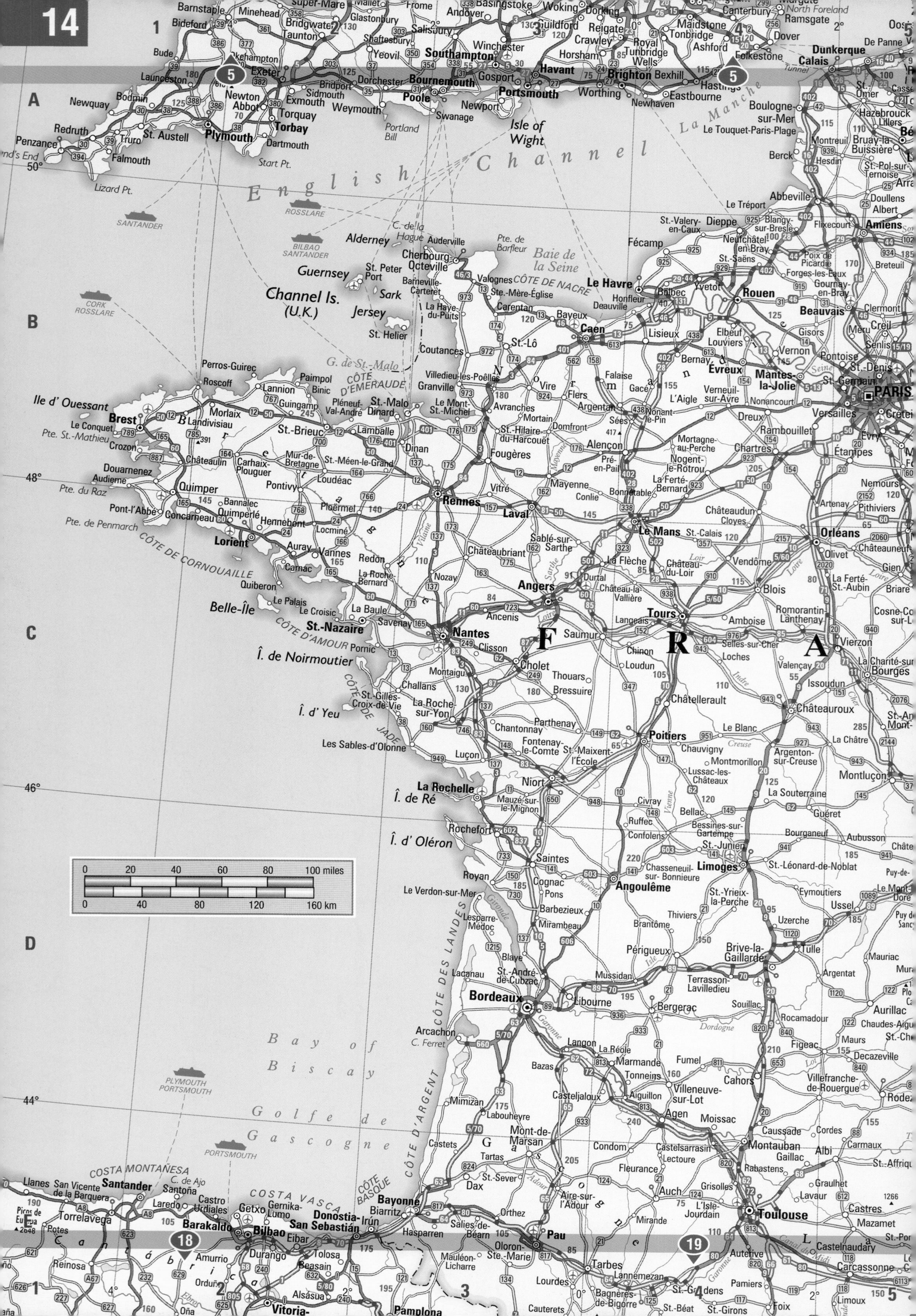
English Channel
La Manche
Channel Is. (U.K.)
Guernsey
Jersey
Alderney
Sark
St. Peter Port
St. Helier
Isle of Wight
Baie de la Seine
G. de St.-Malo
CÔTE D'EMERAUDE
CÔTE DE NACRE
CÔTE DE CORNOUAILLE
CÔTE D'AMOUR
CÔTE DE JADE
CÔTE DES LANDES
CÔTE D'ARGENT
CÔTE BASQUE
COSTA VASCA
COSTA MONTAÑESA
Bay of Biscay
Golfe de Gascogne
F R A N C E
Bretagne
Normandie
Gascogne
SANTANDER
ROSSLARE
BILBAO SANTANDER
CORK ROSSLARE
PLYMOUTH PORTSMOUTH
PORTSMOUTH
Tunnel
Barnstaple
Bideford
Minehead
Bridgwater
Taunton
Glastonbury
Frome
Andover
Basingstoke
Woking
Dorking
Guildford
Reigate
Canterbury
Ramsgate
North Foreland
Maidstone
Tonbridge
Ashford
Dover
Folkestone
Crawley
Royal Tunbridge Wells
Horsham
Brighton
Bexhill
Hastings
Eastbourne
Newhaven
Worthing
Havant
Portsmouth
Gosport
Southampton
Winchester
Salisbury
Shaftesbury
Yeovil
Bournemouth
Poole
Swanage
Newport
Portland Bill
Weymouth
Dorchester
Bridport
Sidmouth
Exmouth
Exeter
Okehampton
Bude
Launceston
Newton Abbot
Torquay
Torbay
Dartmouth
Plymouth
St. Austell
Bodmin
Newquay
Redruth
Truro
Falmouth
Penzance
Land's End
Lizard Pt.
Start Pt.
Dunkerque
Calais
Boulogne-sur-Mer
Le Touquet-Paris-Plage
St.-Omer
Hazebrouck
Montreuil
Hesdin
Berck
Abbeville
Le Tréport
Dieppe
St.-Valery-en-Caux
Fécamp
Le Havre
Honfleur
Deauville
Rouen
Yvetot
Amiens
Beauvais
Lisieux
Caen
Bayeux
Cherbourg-Octeville
Valognes
Ste.-Mère-Église
Carentan
St.-Lô
Coutances
Granville
Avranches
Le Mont-St.-Michel
Vire
Flers
Falaise
Argentan
Évreux
Vernon
Mantes-la-Jolie
PARIS
Versailles
St.-Denis
Pontoise
Rambouillet
Dreux
Chartres
Étampes
Alençon
Mayenne
Laval
Fougères
Rennes
St.-Malo
Dinard
Dinan
St.-Brieuc
Lamballe
Paimpol
Lannion
Perros-Guirec
Roscoff
Morlaix
Brest
Ile d' Ouessant
Le Conquet
Pte. St.-Mathieu
Crozon
Douarnenez
Audierne
Pte. du Raz
Quimper
Pont-l'Abbé
Pte. de Penmarch
Concarneau
Quimperlé
Lorient
Hennebont
Auray
Vannes
Carnac
Quiberon
Belle-Île
Le Palais
Le Croisic
La Baule
St.-Nazaire
Savenay
Redon
Ploërmel
Pontivy
Loudéac
Châteaulin
Carhaix-Plouguer
Le Mans
Nogent-le-Rotrou
Châteaudun
Orléans
Blois
Vendôme
Tours
Amboise
Chinon
Saumur
Angers
La Flèche
Sablé-sur-Sarthe
Châteaubriant
Nantes
Ancenis
Clisson
Cholet
Pornic
Î. de Noirmoutier
Challans
St.-Gilles-Croix-de-Vie
Î. d' Yeu
La Roche-sur-Yon
Les Sables-d'Olonne
Luçon
Fontenay-le-Comte
Parthenay
Bressuire
Thouars
Loudun
Châtellerault
Poitiers
Niort
La Rochelle
Î. de Ré
Rochefort
Î. d' Oléron
Saintes
Royan
Le Verdon-sur-Mer
Cognac
Angoulême
Limoges
St.-Junien
Confolens
Civray
Montmorillon
Le Blanc
Châteauroux
Issoudun
Vierzon
Bourges
Romorantin-Lanthenay
Montluçon
Guéret
Aubusson
Ussel
Tulle
Brive-la-Gaillarde
Uzerche
Périgueux
Brantôme
Bergerac
Libourne
Bordeaux
Arcachon
C. Ferret
Lacanau
Blaye
Langon
Bazas
Marmande
Agen
Villeneuve-sur-Lot
Cahors
Figeac
Aurillac
Rodez
Montauban
Moissac
Albi
Castres
Toulouse
Carcassonne
Castelnaudary
Mazamet
Auch
Condom
Mont-de-Marsan
Dax
Tartas
Bayonne
Biarritz
Orthez
Pau
Oloron-Ste.-Marie
Tarbes
Lourdes
Lannemezan
Bagnères-de-Bigorre
St.-Gaudens
St.-Girons
Foix
Pamiers
Limoux
Mimizan
Castets
Aire-sur-l'Adour
Mirande
Santander
Santoña
Laredo
Castro Urdiales
Torrelavega
Llanes
San Vicente de la Barquera
Barakaldo
Getxo
Bilbao
Gernika-Lumo
Durango
Eibar
Donostia-San Sebastián
Irún
Tolosa
Beasain
Alsásua
Vitoria-Gasteiz
Pamplona
Reinosa
Amurrio
Orduña
Hasparren
Mauléon-Licharre
Cauterets
Picos de Europa
Cantábrica
Loire
Seine
Garonne
Dordogne
Gironde
Charente
Vienne
Indre
Cher
Adour
Canal du Midi
0 20 40 60 80 100 miles
0 40 80 120 160 km
50°
48°
46°
44°
A
B
C
D
E
1
2
3
4
5
18
19

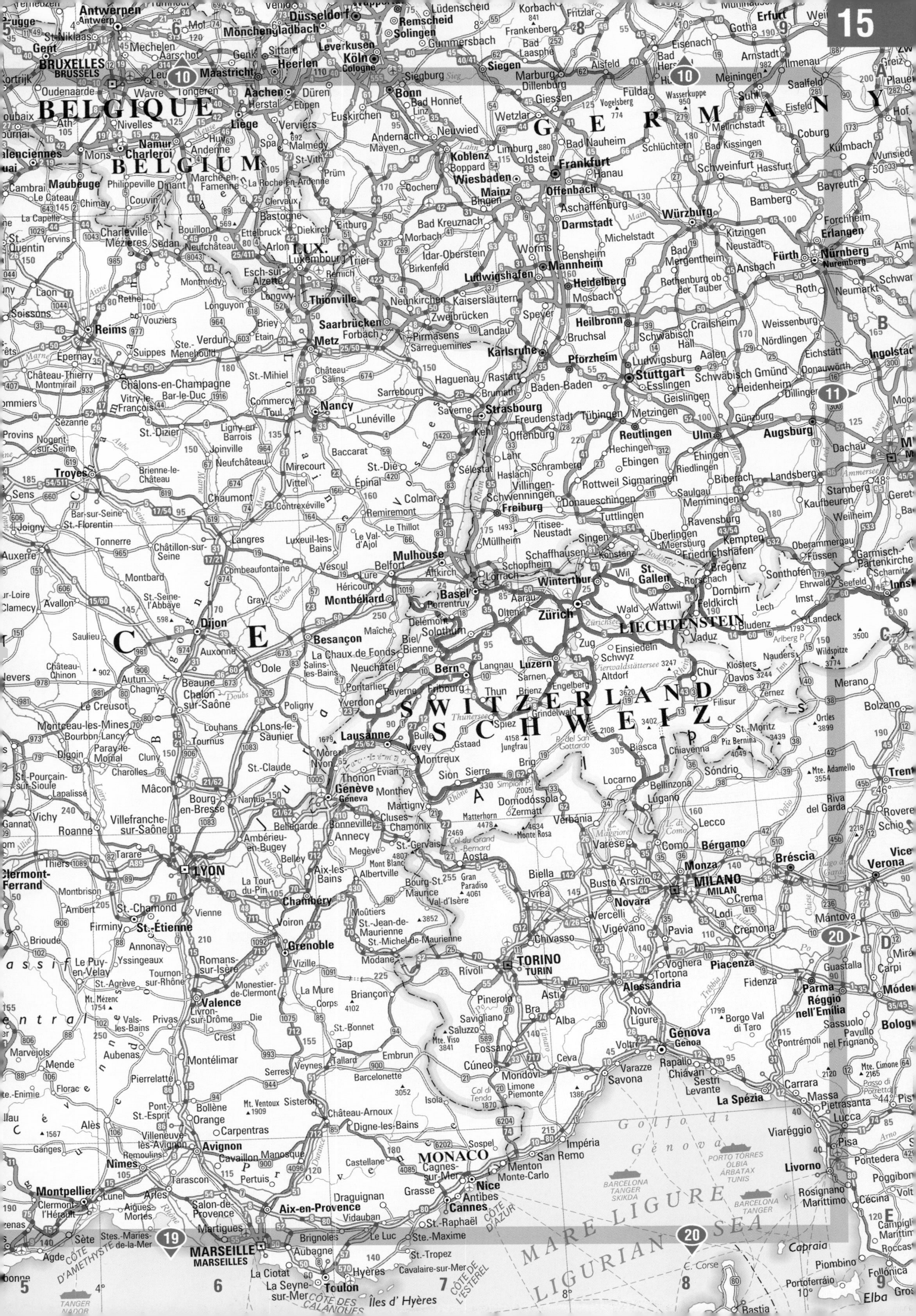

15
BELGIQUE
BELGIUM
LUX.
GERMANY
SWITZERLAND
SCHWEIZ
LIECHTENSTEIN
MONACO
MARE LIGURE
LIGURIAN SEA
Golfo di Genova
CÔTE D'AMÉTHYSTE
CÔTE D'AZUR
CÔTE DE L'ESTÉREL
CÔTE DES CALANQUES
Antwerpen
Antwerp
Düsseldorf
Mönchengladbach
Remscheid
Solingen
Leverkusen
Köln
Cologne
Lüdenscheid
Gummersbach
Korbach
Frankenberg
Erfurt
Gotha
Eisenach
Arnstadt
Ilmenau
Gent
St.-Niklaas
Mechelen
Aarschot
BRUXELLES
BRUSSELS
Leuven
Maastricht
Heerlen
Sittard
Genk
Siegburg
Siegen
Marburg
Alsfeld
Meiningen
Kortrijk
Oudenaarde
Wavre
Tongeren
Aachen
Düren
Bonn
Dillenburg
Giessen
Fulda
Wasserkuppe
Saalfeld
Plauen
Roubaix
Ath
Nivelles
Herstal
Liège
Eupen
Verviers
Bad Honnef
Euskirchen
Linz
Wetzlar
Vogelsberg
Suhl
Eisfeld
Hof
Tournai
Namur
Charleroi
Huy
Andenne
Spa
Malmédy
St-Vith
Andernach
Mayen
Neuwied
Koblenz
Boppard
Limburg
Idstein
Bad Nauheim
Frankfurt
Hanau
Schlüchtern
Bad Kissingen
Mellrichstadt
Coburg
Kulmbach
Valenciennes
Mons
Maubeuge
Philippeville
Dinant
Marche-en-Famenne
La Roche-en-Ardenne
Prüm
Wiesbaden
Mainz
Offenbach
Schweinfurt
Hassfurt
Bayreuth
Cambrai
Le Cateau
Chimay
Couvin
Clervaux
Bastogne
Cochem
Bingen
Aschaffenburg
Würzburg
Bamberg
La Capelle
Vervins
Charleville-Mézières
Sedan
Bouillon
Neufchâteau
Ettelbruck
Diekirch
Bitburg
Bad Kreuznach
Morbach
Darmstadt
Michelstadt
Kitzingen
Forchheim
Erlangen
St.-Quentin
Arlon
Luxembourg
Trier
Idar-Oberstein
Birkenfeld
Worms
Bensheim
Mannheim
Bad Mergentheim
Neustadt
Fürth
Nürnberg
Nuremberg
Laon
Rethel
Montmédy
Esch-sur-Alzette
Longwy
Remich
Thionville
Neunkirchen
Kaiserslautern
Ludwigshafen
Heidelberg
Mosbach
Rothenburg ob der Tauber
Ansbach
Roth
Neumarkt
Schwandorf
Soissons
Reims
Vouziers
Longuyon
Briey
Verdun
Étain
Metz
Saarbrücken
Forbach
Zweibrücken
Pirmasens
Landau
Speyer
Heilbronn
Schwäbisch Hall
Crailsheim
Weissenburg
Nördlingen
Épernay
Suippes
Ste.-Menehould
Sarreguemines
Karlsruhe
Bruchsal
Pforzheim
Ludwigsburg
Aalen
Schwäbisch Gmünd
Eichstätt
Ingolstadt
Château-Thierry
Montmirail
Châlons-en-Champagne
St.-Mihiel
Château-Salins
Haguenau
Rastatt
Baden-Baden
Stuttgart
Esslingen
Heidenheim
Donauwörth
Vitry-le-François
Bar-le-Duc
Commercy
Toul
Nancy
Sarrebourg
Brumath
Saverne
Strasbourg
Geislingen
Dillingen
Sézanne
St.-Dizier
Ligny-en-Barrois
Lunéville
Kehl
Freudenstadt
Tübingen
Metzingen
Reutlingen
Ulm
Günzburg
Augsburg
Provins
Nogent-sur-Seine
Joinville
Baccarat
Offenburg
Hechingen
Ebingen
Ehingen
Dachau
München
Troyes
Brienne-le-Château
Neufchâteau
Mirecourt
St.-Dié
Lahr
Sélestat
Haslach
Schramberg
Rottweil
Sigmaringen
Riedlingen
Biberach
Landsberg
Ammersee
Sens
Chaumont
Vittel
Épinal
Colmar
Villingen-Schwenningen
Saulgau
Memmingen
Starnberg
Bar-sur-Seine
St.-Florentin
Contrexéville
Remiremont
Freiburg
Donaueschingen
Tuttlingen
Ravensburg
Kaufbeuren
Weilheim
Joigny
Tonnerre
Châtillon-sur-Seine
Langres
Luxeuil-les-Bains
Le Thillot
Le Val-d'Ajol
Müllheim
Titisee-Neustadt
Singen
Überlingen
Meersburg
Kempten
Oberammergau
Auxerre
Mulhouse
Schaffhausen
Konstanz
Bodensee
Friedrichshafen
Füssen
Garmisch-Partenkirchen
Montbard
Combeaufontaine
Vesoul
Lure
Belfort
Altkirch
Lörrach
Schopfheim
Winterthur
Wil
St. Gallen
Bregenz
Sonthofen
Scharnitz
Clamecy
Avallon
St.-Seine-l'Abbaye
Gray
Héricourt
Montbéliard
Porrentruy
Basel
Aarau
Rorschach
Dornbirn
Ehrwald
Seefeld
Innsbruck
Dijon
Delémont
Olten
Zürich
Wald
Wattwil
Feldkirch
Lech
Imst
Saulieu
Besançon
Maîche
Solothurn
Biel/Bienne
Zürichsee
Bludenz
Vaduz
Landeck
Arlberg P.
Auxonne
La Chaux-de-Fonds
Zug
Einsiedeln
Schwyz
Nauders
Wildspitze
Château-Chinon
Nevers
Autun
Dole
Salins-les-Bains
Neuchâtel
Bern
Langnau
Luzern
Vierwaldstättersee
Chur
Klosters
Davos
Beaune
Chagny
Chalon-sur-Saône
Doubs
Pontarlier
Payerne
Fribourg
Thun
Sarnen
Brienz
Altdorf
Engelberg
Merano
Le Creusot
Poligny
Yverdon
Thunersee
Grindelwald
Filisur
Zernez
Bolzano
Montceau-les-Mines
Bourbon-Lancy
Louhans
Lons-le-Saunier
Bulle
Spiez
Jungfrau
P. del San Gottardo
Biasca
Chiavenna
St.-Moritz
Piz Bernina
Ortles
Digoin
Paray-le-Monial
Tournus
Cluny
Lausanne
Morez
Vevey
Gstaad
Sondrio
Mte. Adamello
Trento
St.-Pourçain-sur-Sioule
Lapalisse
Charolles
St.-Claude
Nyon
Montreux
Thonon
Évian
Sion
Sierre
Brig
Locarno
Bellinzona
Mâcon
Bourg-en-Bresse
Nantua
Genève
Geneva
Monthey
Simplon P.
Domodóssola
Lugano
Riva del Garda
Vichy
Roanne
Villefranche-sur-Saône
Martigny
Cluses
Chamonix
Zermatt
Matterhorn
Monte Rosa
Verbánia
Lecco
Rovereto
Gannat
Bellegarde
Annecy
Ambérieu-en-Bugey
Bonneville
Col du Grand St.-Bernard
Lago Maggiore
Lago di Como
Schio
Thiers
Tarare
Belley
St.-Gervais
Megève
Mont Blanc
Aosta
Varese
Como
Bérgamo
Brescia
Vicenza
Clermont-Ferrand
LYON
La Tour-du-Pin
Aix-les-Bains
Albertville
Bourg-St.-Maurice
Gran Paradiso
Biella
Busto Arsizio
Monza
MILANO
MILAN
Verona
Montbrison
St.-Chamond
Vienne
Chambéry
Val-d'Isère
Ivrea
Novara
Crema
Ambert
Firminy
St.-Étienne
Voiron
Moûtiers
St.-Jean-de-Maurienne
Vercelli
Vigévano
Lodi
Mántova
Brioude
Annonay
Grenoble
St.-Michel-de-Maurienne
Chivasso
Pavia
Cremona
Le Puy-en-Velay
Yssingeaux
Romans-sur-Isère
Tournon-sur-Rhône
Vizille
Modane
Rívoli
TORINO
TURIN
Voghera
Tortona
Piacenza
Guastalla
Carpi
St.-Agrève
Monestier-de-Clermont
La Mure
Briançon
Alessándria
Fidenza
Parma
Módena
Mt. Mézenc
Valence
Livron-sur-Drôme
Die
Corps
Pinerolo
Asti
Réggio nell'Emília
Privas
Vals-les-Bains
Crest
St.-Bonnet
Saluzzo
Savigliano
Bra
Alba
Novi Lígure
Borgo Val di Taro
Sassuolo
Bologna
Marvejols
Aubenas
Montélimar
Gap
Mte. Viso
Fossano
Génova
Genoa
Pontrémoli
Pavullo nel Frignano
Mende
Pierrelatte
Serres
Veynes
Tallard
Embrun
Cúneo
Mondovì
Ceva
Voltri
Rapallo
Chiávari
Mte. Cimone
Florac
Barcelonette
Col di Tenda
Limone Piemonte
Varazze
Savona
Sestri Levante
La Spézia
Carrara
Massa
Passo di Porretta
Pont-St.-Esprit
Bollène
Orange
Mt. Ventoux
Sisteron
Isola
Château-Arnoux
Digne-les-Bains
Pietrasanta
Pistoia
Alès
Carpentras
Villeneuve-lès-Avignon
Avignon
Remoulins
Cavaillon
Manosque
Sospel
Impéria
Lucca
Viaréggio
Ganges
Nîmes
Tarascon
Pertuis
Castellane
Menton
Monte-Carlo
San Remo
Pisa
Pontedera
Montpellier
Lunel
Arles
Aigues-Mortes
Salon-de-Provence
Cagnes-sur-Mer
Nice
Grasse
Antibes
Cannes
Draguignan
Aix-en-Provence
Vidauban
St.-Raphaël
Livorno
Poggibonsi
Clermont-l'Hérault
Martigues
Brignoles
Le Luc
Ste.-Maxime
Rosignano Marittimo
Cécina
Volterra
Campiglia Marittima
Sète
Stes.-Maries-de-la-Mer
MARSEILLE
MARSEILLES
Aubagne
St.-Tropez
Cavalaire-sur-Mer
Capraia
Rocca
Agde
La Ciotat
La Seyne-sur-Mer
Toulon
Hyères
Îles d'Hyères
C. Corse
Piombino
Portoferráio
Follonica
Elba
Bastia
Barcelona Tanger Skikda
Porto Torres Olbia Arbatax Tunis
Barcelona Tanger
Tanger Nador

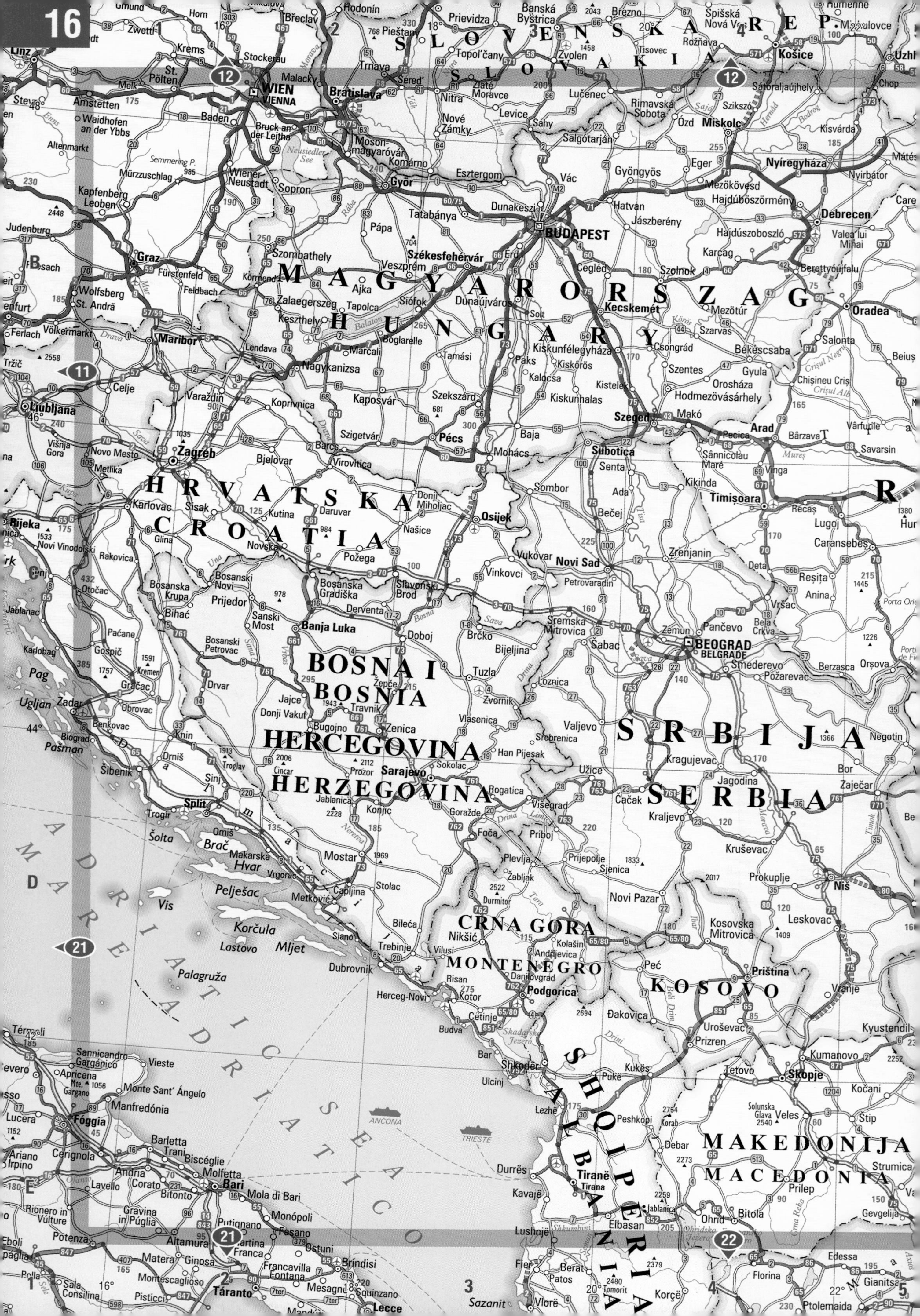
SLOVENSKÁ REP.
SLOVAKIA
MAGYARORSZÁG
HUNGARY
HRVATSKA
CROATIA
BOSNA I HERCEGOVINA
BOSNIA HERZEGOVINA
SRBIJA
SERBIA
CRNA GORA
MONTENEGRO
KOSOVO
SHQIPËRIA
ALBANIA
MAKEDONIJA
MACEDONIA
MARE ADRIATICO
ADRIATIC SEA
WIEN
VIENNA
BUDAPEST
BEOGRAD
BELGRADE
Bratislava
Zagreb
Ljubljana
Sarajevo
Podgorica
Tiranë
Tirana
Skopje
Priština
Linz
St. Pölten
Graz
Maribor
Győr
Debrecen
Miskolc
Košice
Szeged
Pécs
Kecskemét
Nyíregyháza
Oradea
Arad
Timişoara
Subotica
Novi Sad
Osijek
Banja Luka
Split
Zadar
Rijeka
Mostar
Dubrovnik
Niš
Kragujevac
Bari
Fóggia
Táranto
Lecce
Brindisi
Durrës
Elbasan
Ohrid
Bitola
Prizren
Balaton
ANCONA
TRIESTE
12
11
21
22
1
2
3
4
5
B
C
D
E
16°
18°
20°
22°
42°
44°
46°
48°

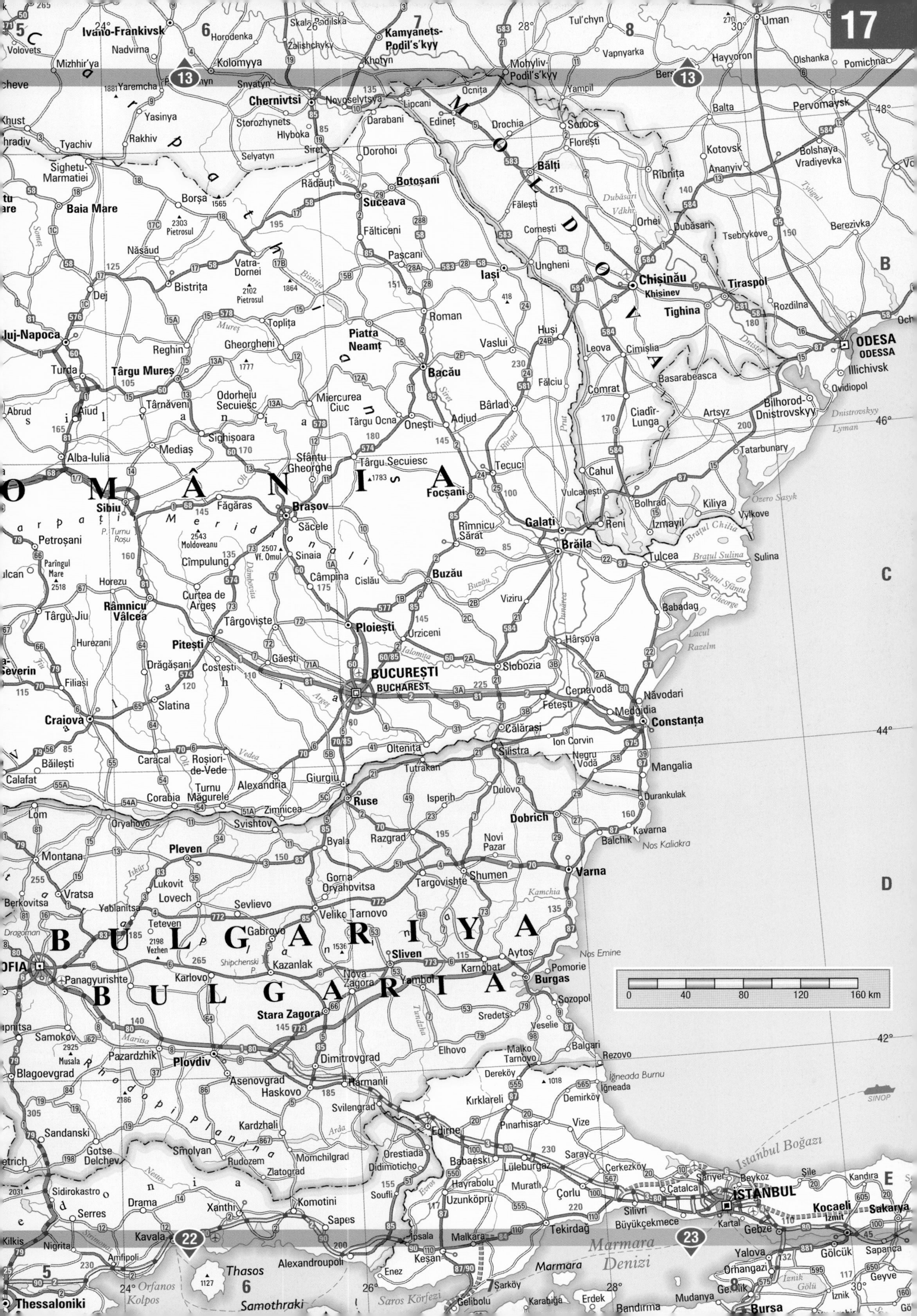
Ivano-Frankivsk
Kolomyya
Kamyanets-Podil's'kyy
Khotyn
Mohyliv-Podil's'kyy
Uman
Chernivtsi
Novoselytsya
Yaremcha
Snyatyn
Storozhynets
Hlyboka
Siret
Rakhiv
Yasinya
Tyachiv
Sighetu-Marmatiei
Baia Mare
Borșa
Dorohoi
Botoșani
Rădăuți
Suceava
Fălticeni
Pașcani
Iași
Ungheni
Bălți
Soroca
Florești
Edineț
Drochia
Ocnița
Yampil
Tul'chyn
Vapnyarka
Hayvoron
Olshanka
Pomichna
Balta
Pervomaysk
Kotovsk
Ananyiv
Bolshaya Vradiyevka
Rîbnița
Dubăsari
Fălești
Cornești
Orhei
Chișinău
Khisinev
Tiraspol
Tighina
Rozdilna
Odesa
ODESSA
Illichivsk
Ovidiopol
Berezivka
Tsebrykove
Bistrița
Năsăud
Vatra-Dornei
Dej
Cluj-Napoca
Turda
Reghin
Târgu Mureș
Toplița
Gheorgheni
Piatra Neamț
Roman
Vaslui
Bacău
Hușl
Leova
Cimișlia
Comrat
Basarabeasca
Fălciu
Bârlad
Adjud
Onești
Târgu Ocna
Miercurea Ciuc
Odorheiu Secuiesc
Târnăveni
Aiud
Abrud
Alba-Iulia
Mediaș
Sighișoara
Sfântu Gheorghe
Târgu Secuiesc
Ciadîr-Lunga
Bilhorod-Dnistrovskyy
Artsyz
Tatarbunary
Cahul
Vulcanești
Bolhrad
Reni
Izmayil
Kiliya
Vylkove
Tecuci
Focșani
Galați
Brăila
Tulcea
Sulina
ROMÂNIA
Sibiu
Făgăraș
Brașov
Săcele
Petroșani
Moldoveanu
Vf. Omul
Sinaia
Câmpina
Cislău
Rîmnicu Sărat
Buzău
Câmpulung
Horezu
Râmnicu Vâlcea
Curtea de Argeș
Târgu-Jiu
Hurezani
Târgoviște
Ploiești
Urziceni
Viziru
Babadag
Hârșova
Pitești
Drăgășani
Costești
Găești
BUCUREȘTI
BUCHAREST
Slobozia
Cernavodă
Fetești
Năvodari
Medgidia
Constanța
Severin
Filiași
Craiova
Slatina
Călărași
Ion Corvin
Oltenița
Silistra
Negru Vodă
Mangalia
Băilești
Caracal
Roșiori-de-Vede
Calafat
Corabia
Turnu Măgurele
Alexandria
Giurgiu
Tutrakan
Dulovo
Durankulak
Ruse
Isperih
Dobrich
Kavarna
Balchik
Nos Kaliakra
Lom
Oryahovo
Svishtov
Zimnicea
Byala
Razgrad
Novi Pazar
Montana
Pleven
Lukovit
Lovech
Vratsa
Berkovitsa
Gorna Oryahovitsa
Targovishte
Shumen
Varna
Yablanitsa
Sevlievo
Veliko Tarnovo
Teteven
Gabrovo
Vezhen
BULGARIYA
BULGARIA
SOFIA
Panagyurishte
Karlovo
Kazanlak
Sliven
Aytos
Nos Emine
Pomorie
Burgas
Sozopol
Karnobat
Yambol
Nova Zagora
Stara Zagora
Sredets
Veselie
Balgari
Rezovo
Samokov
Musala
Pazardzhik
Plovdiv
Dimitrovgrad
Elhovo
Malko Tarnovo
Blagoevgrad
Asenovgrad
Haskovo
Harmanli
Svilengrad
Dereköy
Iğneada
Iğneada Burnu
Kırklareli
Demirköy
Pınarhisar
Vize
Kardzhali
Sandanski
Gotse Delchev
Smolyan
Rudozem
Momchilgrad
Zlatograd
Edirne
Orestiada
Didimoticho
Babaeski
Lüleburgaz
Saray
Çerkezköy
İstanbul Boğazı
Sarıyer
Beykoz
Şile
Kandıra
ISTANBUL
Kocaeli
Izmit
Sakarya
Kartal
Gebze
Çatalca
Silivri
Büyükçekmece
Çorlu
Muratlı
Hayrabolu
Uzunköprü
Tekirdağ
Malkara
Soufli
Komotini
Xanthi
Sapes
Drama
Serres
Sidirokastro
Kavala
Nigrita
Amfipoli
Thessaloniki
Orfanos Kolpos
Thasos
Samothraki
Alexandroupoli
Enez
İpsala
Keşan
Gelibolu
Saros Körfezi
Şarköy
Marmara
Marmara Denizi
Erdek
Karabiğa
Bandırma
Mudanya
Gemlik
Orhangazi
Iznik Gölü
İznik
Yalova
Gölcük
Sapanca
Geyve
Bursa
SINOP
MOLDOVA
Carpathians
Carpații Meridionali
Rhodopi Planina
Somes
Mureș
Olt
Bistrița
Siret
Prut
Dunărea
Ialomița
Argeș
Vedea
Jiu
Buzău
Dâmbovița
Bîrlad
Dniester
Dubăsari Vdkhr.
Tyligul
Buh
Dnistrovskyy Lyman
Ozero Sasyk
Bratul Chilia
Bratul Sulina
Bratul Sfântu Gheorghe
Lacul Razelm
Kamchia
Iskar
Maritsa
Tundzha
Arda
Nestos
Strimonas
Evros
Shipchenski P.
P. Turnu Roșu
Parîngul Mare
Pietrosul
Dragoman
Stara Planina
0
40
80
120
160 km
A
B
C
D
E
48°
46°
44°
42°
24°
26°
28°
30°

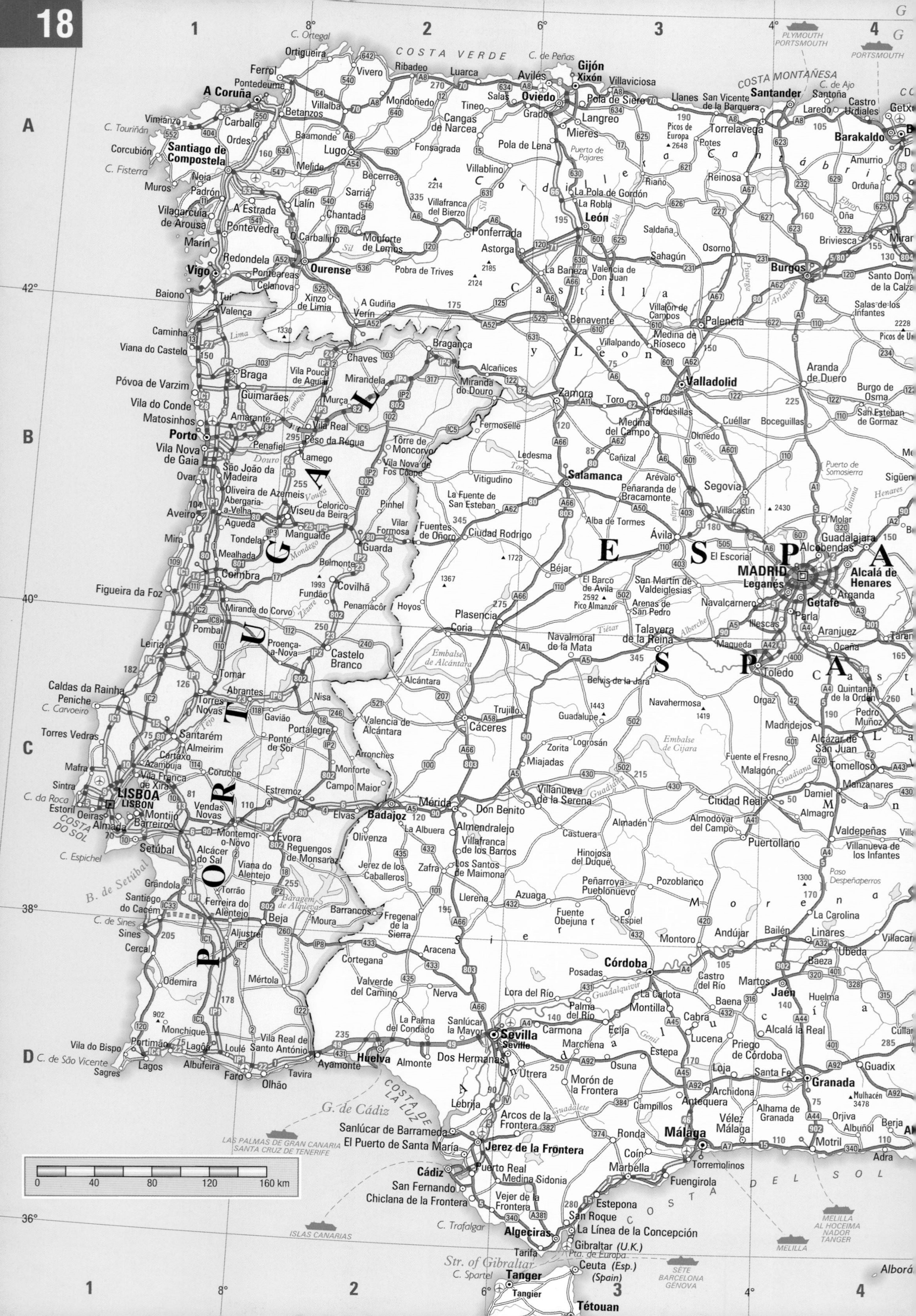

COSTA VERDE
C. Ortegal
C. de Peñas
Gijón
Xixón
Ortigueira
Ferrol
Vivero
Ribadeo
Luarca
Avilés
Villaviciosa
A Coruña
Pontedeume
Villalba
Mondoñedo
Tineo
Salas
Oviedo
Pola de Siero
Grado
Langreo
Mieres
Carballo
Betanzos
Vimianzo
C. Touriñán
Ordes
Baamonde
Cangas de Narcea
Pola de Lena
Corcubión
C. Fisterra
Santiago de Compostela
Lugo
Fonsagrada
Puerto de Pajares
Picos de Europa
COSTA MONTAÑESA
Santander
Llanes
San Vicente de la Barquera
Torrelavega
Potes
C. de Ajo
Santoña
Laredo
Castro Urdiales
Getxo
Barakaldo
Amurrio
Orduña
Reinosa
Melide
Becerrea
Villablino
Cordillera Cantábrica
Muros
Noia
Padrón
Sarria
Vilagarcía de Arousa
A Estrada
Lalín
Chantada
Villafranca del Bierzo
La Pola de Gordón
La Robla
León
Riaño
Oña
Briviesca
Pontevedra
Marín
O Carballino
Monforte de Lemos
Ponferrada
Astorga
Saldaña
Osorno
Burgos
Redondela
Vigo
Ourense
Pobra de Trives
Ponteareas
Celanova
La Bañeza
Valencia de Don Juan
Sahagún
Santo Domingo de la Calzada
Baiono
Tui
Valença
Xinzo de Limia
A Gudiña
Verín
Castilla y León
Benavente
Villalón de Campos
Palencia
Salas de los Infantes
Picos de Urbión
Caminha
Viana do Castelo
Chaves
Bragança
Villalpando
Medina de Rioseco
Aranda de Duero
Póvoa de Varzim
Braga
Vila Pouca de Aguiar
Mirandela
Alcañices
Miranda do Douro
Valladolid
Burgo de Osma
Vila do Conde
Guimarães
Murça
Zamora
Toro
Tordesillas
San Esteban de Gormaz
Matosinhos
Amarante
Vila Real
Porto
Vila Nova de Gaia
Penafiel
Peso da Régua
Fermoselle
Medina del Campo
Cuéllar
Boceguillas
Lamego
Torre de Moncorvo
Olmedo
São João da Madeira
Ovar
Vila Nova de Foz Côa
Ledesma
Cañizal
Puerto de Somosierra
Sigüenza
Oliveira de Azeméis
Vitigudino
Salamanca
Arévalo
Peñaranda de Bracamonte
Segovia
Aveiro
Albergaria-a-Velha
Viseu
Celorico da Beira
Pinhel
La Fuente de San Esteban
Villacastín
Águeda
Mangualde
Vilar Formoso
Fuentes de Oñoro
Ciudad Rodrigo
Alba de Tormes
Ávila
El Molar
Guadalajara
Mira
Tondela
Guarda
Alcobendas
Mealhada
Belmonte
El Escorial
Coimbra
ESPAÑA
PORTUGAL
Béjar
El Barco de Ávila
San Martín de Valdeiglesias
MADRID
Leganés
Alcalá de Henares
Figueira da Foz
Fundão
Covilhã
Pico Almanzor
Arenas de San Pedro
Navalcarnero
Getafe
Arganda
Miranda do Corvo
Penamacôr
Hoyos
Plasencia
Parla
Pombal
Coria
Illescas
Aranjuez
Leiria
Proença-a-Nova
Castelo Branco
Navalmoral de la Mata
Talavera de la Reina
Maqueda
Ocaña
Embalse de Alcántara
Toledo
Tomar
Alcántara
Belvís de la Jara
Quintanar de la Orden
Caldas da Rainha
Abrantes
Peniche
C. Carvoeiro
Torres Novas
Nisa
Trujillo
Navahermosa
Orgaz
Gavião
Valencia de Alcántara
Guadalupe
Madridejos
Pedro Muñoz
Torres Vedras
Santarém
Portalegre
Cáceres
Ponte de Sor
Almeirim
Cartaxo
Arronches
Zorita
Logrosán
Embalse de Cijara
Alcázar de San Juan
Mafra
Azambuja
Coruche
Monforte
Miajadas
Fuente el Fresno
Tomelloso
Sintra
Vila Franca de Xira
Malagón
C. da Roca
LISBOA
LISBON
Estremoz
Campo Maior
Manzanares
Estoril
Oeiras
Vendas Novas
Mérida
Villanueva de la Serena
Ciudad Real
Daniel
COSTA DO SOL
Montijo
Almada
Barreiro
Elvas
Badajoz
Don Benito
La Albuera
Almendralejo
Almadén
Almodóvar del Campo
Almagro
Montemor-o-Novo
Évora
Castuera
Valdepeñas
Setúbal
Olivenza
Villafranca de los Barros
Puertollano
Villanueva de los Infantes
C. Espichel
Alcácer do Sal
Reguengos de Monsaraz
Hinojosa del Duque
B. de Setúbal
Viana do Alentejo
Jerez de los Caballeros
Zafra
Los Santos de Maimona
Paso Despeñaperros
Grândola
Torrão
Peñarroya-Pueblonuevo
Pozoblanco
Santiago do Cacém
Ferreira do Alentejo
Baragem de Alqueva
Barrancos
Llerena
Azuaga
Sierra Morena
C. de Sines
Sines
Beja
Moura
Fregenal de la Sierra
Fuente Obejuna
Espiel
La Carolina
Cercal
Aljustrel
Montoro
Andújar
Bailén
Linares
Aracena
Cortegana
Córdoba
Úbeda
Baeza
Odemira
Mértola
Posadas
Valverde del Camino
Castro del Río
Martos
Nerva
Lora del Río
La Carlota
Jaén
Huelma
Palma del Río
Montilla
Baena
Monchique
La Palma del Condado
Sanlúcar la Mayor
Carmona
Écija
Cabra
Alcalá la Real
Vila do Bispo
Portimão
Lagoa
Vila Real de Santo António
Sevilla
Seville
Marchena
Lucena
Priego de Córdoba
C. de São Vicente
Sagres
Lagos
Albufeira
Loulé
Faro
Olhão
Tavira
Ayamonte
Huelva
Almonte
Dos Hermanas
Estepa
Osuna
Utrera
Loja
Santa Fe
Granada
Guadix
Morón de la Frontera
Archidona
Mulhacén
COSTA DE LA LUZ
G. de Cádiz
Lebrija
Antequera
Campillos
Alhama de Granada
LAS PALMAS DE GRAN CANARIA
SANTA CRUZ DE TENERIFE
Sanlúcar de Barrameda
El Puerto de Santa María
Arcos de la Frontera
Vélez Málaga
Orjiva
Berja
Albuñol
Ronda
Málaga
Jerez de la Frontera
Motril
Adra
Coín
Torremolinos
Cádiz
Puerto Real
Marbella
San Fernando
Medina Sidonia
Fuengirola
Chiclana de la Frontera
COSTA DEL SOL
Vejer de la Frontera
Estepona
C. Trafalgar
San Roque
ISLAS CANARIAS
Algeciras
La Línea de la Concepción
MELILLA
AL HOCEIMA
NADOR
TANGER
Tarifa
Gibraltar (U.K.)
Pta. de Europa
Str. of Gibraltar
Ceuta (Esp.)
(Spain)
SÈTE
BARCELONA
GÉNOVA
C. Spartel
Tanger
Tangier
Tétouan
Alborán
PLYMOUTH
PORTSMOUTH
0
40
80
120
160 km

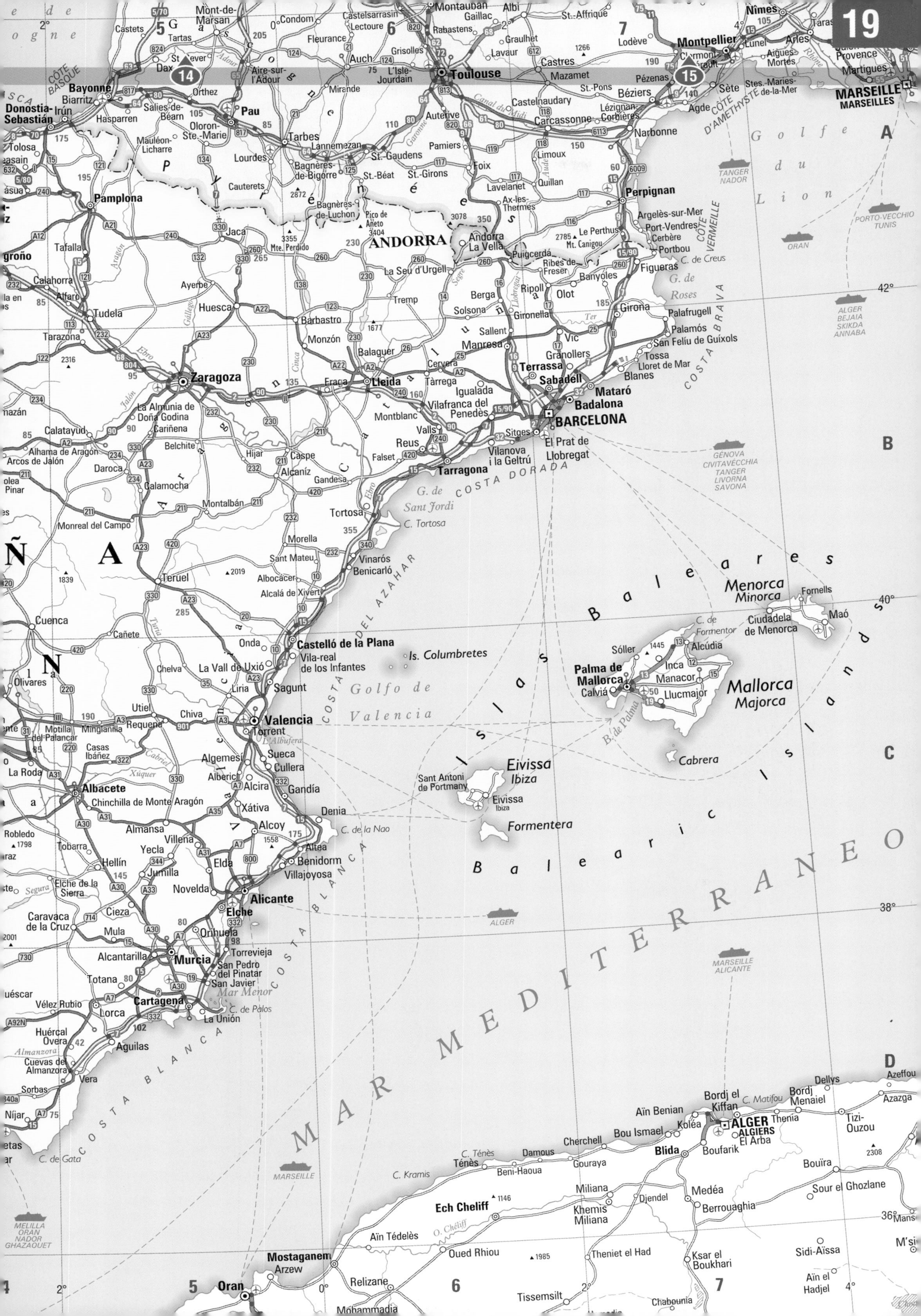

Mont-de-Marsan
Condom
Castelsarrasin
Lectoure
Montauban
Gaillac
Albi
St.-Affrique
Nîmes
Castets
Tartas
Fleurance
Rabastens
Graulhet
Lodève
Montpellier
Lunel
Arles
Provence
Dax
Aire-sur-l'Adour
Auch
Grisolles
L'Isle-Jourdain
Lavaur
Castres
Mazamet
Aigues-Mortes
Martigues
CÔTE BASQUE
Bayonne
Biarritz
Orthez
Mirande
Toulouse
Pézenas
Béziers
St.-Pons
Sète
Stes.-Maries-de-la-Mer
MARSEILLE
MARSEILLES
Donostia-Sebastián
Irún
Salies-de-Béarn
Pau
Hasparren
Oloron-Ste.-Marie
Castelnaudary
Lézignan-Corbières
Carcassonne
Agde
CÔTE D'AMETHYSTE
Narbonne
Mauléon-Licharre
Tarbes
Lannemezan
Lourdes
St.-Gaudens
Pamiers
Bagnères-de-Bigorre
St.-Béat
St.-Girons
Foix
Limoux
Quillan
Golfe du Lion
Cauterets
Lavelanet
Perpignan
TANGER
NADOR
Pamplona
Bagnères-de-Luchon
Pico de Aneto
Ax-les-Thermes
Argelès-sur-Mer
Port-Vendres
Cerbère
Portbou
CÔTE VERMEILLE
PORTO-VECCHIO
TUNIS
ORAN
Jaca
Mte. Perdido
ANDORRA
Andorra La Vella
Le Perthus
Mt. Canigou
Puigcerdà
Ribes de Freser
Tafalla
Logroño
Calahorra
Alfaro
Ayerbe
La Seu d'Urgell
Figueras
C. de Creus
Banyoles
G. de Roses
Berga
Ripoll
Olot
Tremp
Solsona
Gironella
Girona
Palafrugell
Palamós
San Feliú de Guíxols
ALGER
BEJAIA
SKIKDA
ANNABA
Tudela
Huesca
Barbastro
Sallent
Manresa
Vic
Granollers
Tossa
Lloret de Mar
Blanes
COSTA BRAVA
Tarazona
Monzón
Balaguer
Cervera
Terrassa
Sabadell
Mataró
Badalona
Zaragoza
Fraga
Lleida
Tàrrega
Igualada
Vilafranca del Penedès
BARCELONA
La Almunia de Doña Godina
Cariñena
Montblanc
Valls
Calatayud
Alhama de Aragón
Arcos de Jalón
Belchite
Hijar
Caspe
Reus
Falset
Sitges
Vilanova i la Geltrú
El Prat de Llobregat
Tarragona
GÉNOVA
CIVITAVÉCCHIA
TANGER
LIVORNA
SAVONA
Daroca
Calamocha
Alcañiz
Gandesa
G. de Sant Jordi
COSTA DORADA
Montalbán
Tortosa
C. Tortosa
Monreal del Campo
Morella
Sant Mateu
Vinarós
Benicarló
Teruel
Albocàcer
Alcalà de Xivert
COSTA DEL AZAHAR
Menorca
Minorca
Fornells
Ciudadela de Menorca
Maó
C. de Formentor
Cuenca
Cañete
Onda
Castelló de la Plana
Vila-real de los Infantes
Is. Columbretes
Sóller
Alcúdia
Chelva
La Vall de Uxió
Palma de Mallorca
Inca
Manacor
Calviá
Llucmajor
Mallorca
Majorca
Olivares
Liria
Sagunt
Golfo de Valencia
Utiel
Chiva
Valencia
Torrent
Motilla del Palancar
Minglanilla
Requena
Casas Ibáñez
L'Albufera
B. de Palma
Cabrera
La Roda
Algemesí
Sueca
Cullera
Alberic
Alcira
Eivissa
Ibiza
Sant Antoni de Portmany
Albacete
Chinchilla de Monte Aragón
Gandía
Xátiva
Dénia
C. de la Nao
Almansa
Alcoy
Formentera
Robledo
Tobarra
Villena
Yecla
Altea
Hellín
Elda
Benidorm
Jumilla
Villajoyosa
Elche de la Sierra
Novelda
Alicante
Elche
Caravaca de la Cruz
Cieza
Mula
Orihuela
ALGER
Alcantarilla
Murcia
Torrevieja
San Pedro del Pinatar
San Javier
Mar Menor
Totana
Cartagena
C. de Palos
La Unión
MARSEILLE
ALICANTE
Vélez Rubio
Lorca
Huércal Overa
Aguilas
Cuevas del Almanzora
Vera
Sorbas
Níjar
C. de Gata
COSTA BLANCA
MAR MEDITERRANEO
Islas Baleares
Balearic Islands
Dellys
Azeffoun
Azazga
Bordj el Kiffan
C. Matifou
Bordj Menaiel
Aïn Benian
ALGER
ALGIERS
Thenia
Tizi-Ouzou
Koléa
Bou Ismael
Cherchell
Blida
Boufarik
El Arba
C. Ténès
Ténès
Damous
Gouraya
Beni-Haoua
C. Kramis
Bouïra
Sour el Ghozlane
Miliana
Khemis Miliana
Djendel
Médéa
Berrouaghia
Ech Cheliff
O. Chéliff
Aïn Tédelès
MELILLA
ORAN
NADOR
GHAZAOUET
Mostaganem
Arzew
Oued Rhiou
Theniet el Had
Ksar el Boukhari
Sidi-Aïssa
M'sila
Relizane
Oran
Tissemsilt
Chabounia
Aïn el Hadjel
Mohammadia

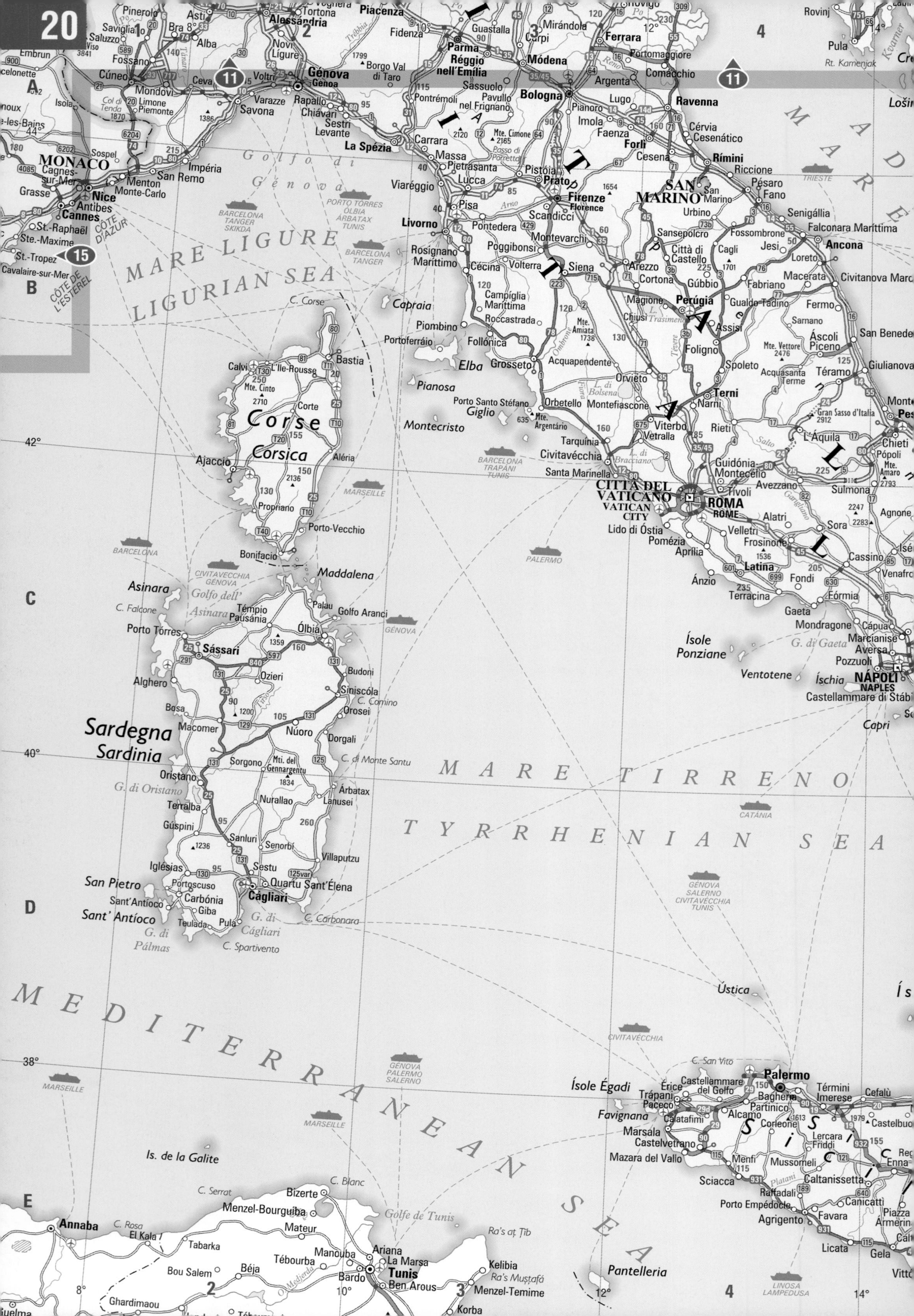

Pinerolo
Asti
Tortona
Piacenza
Guastalla
Mirándola
Ferrara
Rovinj
Saluzzo
Saviglia
Bra
Alessándria
Fidenza
Carpi
Portomaggiore
Pula
Viso
3841
Fossano
Alba
Novi Lígure
1799
Borgo Val di Taro
Parma
Réggio nell'Emília
Módena
Comacchio
Rt. Kamenjak
Kvarner
Embrun
Cúneo
Mondovi
Ceva
Voltri
Génova
Genoa
Sassuolo
Bologna
Argenta
Lugo
Ravenna
Lošinj
Isola
Col di Tenda
1870
Limone Piemonte
Varazze
Savona
Rapallo
Chiávari
Sestri Levante
Pontrémoli
Pavullo nel Frignano
Pianoro
Imola
Faenza
Forlì
Cérvia
Cesenático
Cesena
1386
2120
Mte. Cimone
2165
Passo di Porretta
La Spézia
Carrara
Massa
Pietrasanta
Rímini
Riccione
MONACO
Sospel
Cagnes-sur-Mer
Grasse
Nice
Antibes
Cannes
St.-Raphaël
Ste.-Maxime
St.-Tropez
Cavalaire-sur-Mer
Menton
Monte-Carlo
Impéria
San Remo
Golfo di Génova
Viaréggio
Lucca
Pistóia
Prato
Firenze
Florence
1654
SAN MARINO
San Marino
Pésaro
Fano
Urbino
Senigállia
Falconara Marittima
Ancona
CÔTE D'AZUR
CÔTE DE L'ESTEREL
BARCELONA
TANGER
SKIKDA
PORTO TORRES
ÓLBIA
ARBATAX
TUNIS
TRIESTE
Pisa
Livorno
Pontedera
Scandicci
Montevarchi
Sansepolcro
Fossombrone
Jesi
Rosignano Marittimo
Poggibonsi
Cécina
Volterra
Siena
Arezzo
Città di Castello
Cagli
1701
Loreto
Cortona
Gúbbio
Fabriano
Macerata
Civitanova Marche
MARE LIGURE
LIGURIAN SEA
C. Corse
Capraia
Campíglia Marittima
Roccastrada
Magione
Perúgia
Gualdo Tadino
Fermo
Chiusi
L. Trasimeno
Assisi
Sarnano
Piombino
Portoferráio
Follónica
Mte. Amiata
1738
Foligno
Mte. Vettore
2476
Áscoli Piceno
San Benedetto
Bastia
Calvi
L'Île-Rousse
Mte. Cinto
2710
Elba
Grosseto
Acquapendente
Spoleto
Acquasanta Terme
Téramo
Giulianova
Pianosa
Corte
Orvieto
L. di Bolsena
Terni
Narni
Corse
Corsica
Porto Santo Stéfano
Giglio
Mte. Argentário
Orbetello
Montefiascone
Gran Sasso d'Italia
2912
Montecristo
Viterbo
Vetralla
Rieti
L'Áquila
Chieti
Pópoli
42°
Ajaccio
Aléria
2136
Tarquínia
Civitavécchia
L. di Bracciano
Guidónia-Montecélio
Mte. Amaro
2793
BARCELONA
TRAPANI
TUNIS
Santa Marinella
Avezzano
Sulmona
CITTÀ DEL VATICANO
VATICAN CITY
ROMA
ROME
Tívoli
MARSEILLE
Propriano
Porto-Vecchio
Lido di Óstia
Pomézia
Velletri
Alatri
Sora
Agnone
Frosinone
Aprília
1536
Cassino
Bonifacio
Maddalena
PALERMO
Latina
Fondi
Venafro
BARCELONA
CIVITAVECCHIA
GÉNOVA
Ánzio
Terracina
Fórmia
Asinara
Golfo dell' Asinara
Palau
C. Falcone
Témpio Pausánia
Golfo Aranci
Gaeta
Mondragone
Cápua
Porto Torres
Ólbia
GÉNOVA
Ísole Ponziane
Marcianise
G. di Gaeta
Aversa
Pozzuoli
Sássari
1359
Budoni
Ventotene
Íschia
NÁPOLI
NAPLES
Alghero
Ozieri
Siniscóla
C. Comino
Castellammare di Stábia
Bosa
1200
Orosei
Capri
Sardegna
Sardinia
Macomer
Núoro
Dorgali
40°
Oristano
Sorgono
Mti. del Gennargentu
1834
C. di Monte Santu
MARE TIRRENO
G. di Oristano
Árbatax
Lanusei
Terralba
Nurallao
CATÁNIA
Gúspini
TYRRHENIAN SEA
Sanluri
Senorbì
1236
Villaputzu
Iglésias
Sestu
San Pietro
Portoscuso
Quartu Sant'Élena
GÉNOVA
SALERNO
CIVITAVECCHIA
TUNIS
Sant'Antíoco
Carbónia
Cágliari
Sant' Antíoco
Giba
G. di Cágliari
C. Carbonara
Teulada
Pula
G. di Pálmas
C. Spartivento
MEDITERRANEAN SEA
Ústica
CIVITAVÉCCHIA
38°
GÉNOVA
PALERMO
SALERNO
C. San Vito
Palermo
MARSEILLE
Ísole Égadi
Érice
Castellammare del Golfo
Términi Imerese
Cefalù
Trápani
Paceco
Bagheria
Partinico
Favignana
Calatafimi
Alcamo
Corleone
1613
1979
Castelbuono
MARSEILLE
Marsala
Castelvetrano
Lercara Friddi
Sicilia
Is. de la Galite
Mazara del Vallo
Menfi
Mussomeli
Enna
Sciacca
Caltanissetta
C. Serrat
Bizerte
C. Blanc
Raffadali
Porto Empédocle
Canicattì
Menzel-Bourguiba
Agrigento
Favara
Piazza Armerina
Annaba
C. Rosa
El Kala
Golfe de Tunis
Mateur
Ra's at Tib
Tabarka
Manouba
Ariana
La Marsa
Licata
Gela
Béja
Tébourba
Bou Salem
Tunis
Kelibia
Ra's Mustafá
Pantelleria
Bardo
Ben Arous
Menzel-Temime
LINOSA
LAMPEDUSA
Ghardimaou
Korba
8°
10°
12°
14°
A
B
C
D
E
1
2
3
4
11
15

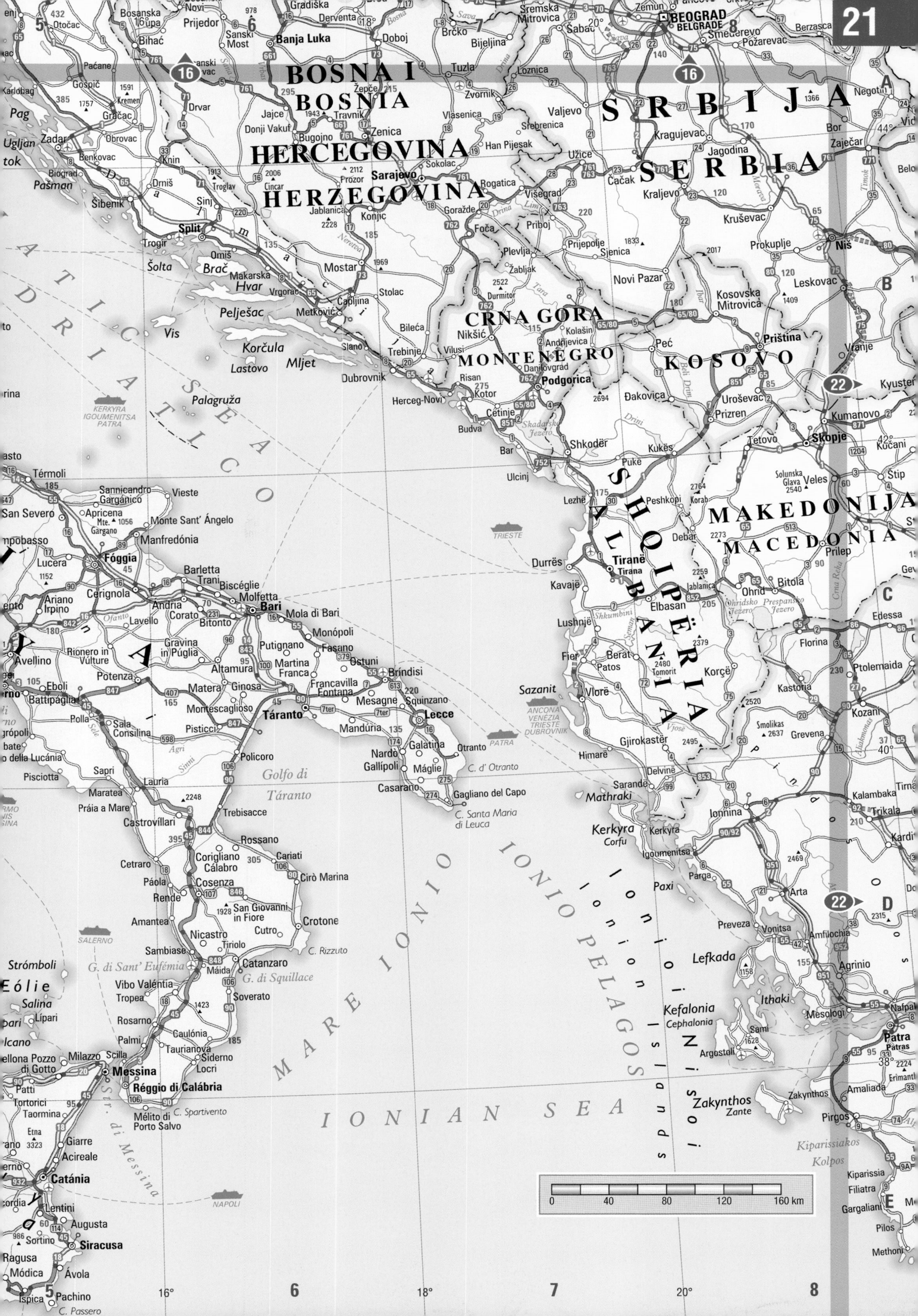
BOSNA I HERCEGOVINA
BOSNIA HERZEGOVINA
SRBIJA
SERBIA
CRNA GORA
MONTENEGRO
KOSOVO
SHQIPËRIA
ALBANIA
MAKEDONIJA
MACEDONIA
BEOGRAD
BELGRADE
Sarajevo
Podgorica
Priština
Skopje
Tiranë
Tirana
Banja Luka
Split
Dubrovnik
Mostar
Niš
Zadar
Šibenik
Bari
Bríndisi
Lecce
Táranto
Fóggia
Cosenza
Catanzaro
Messina
Réggio di Calábria
Catánia
Siracusa
Durrës
Shkodër
Vlorë
Kerkyra
Corfu
Ioannina
Patra
Patras
Kefalonia
Cephalonia
Zakynthos
Zante
Lefkada
Ithaki
Paxi
Mare Adriatico
Adriatic Sea
Golfo di Táranto
MARE IONIO
IONIO PELAGOS
IONIAN SEA
Ionioi Nisoi
Ionian Islands
Kiparissiakos Kolpos
Str. di Messina
Eólie
Strómboli
Salina
Lípari
G. di Sant' Eufémia
G. di Squillace
C. Spartivento
C. Rizzuto
C. d' Otranto
C. Santa Maria di Leuca
C. Passero
Pag
Ugljan
Pašman
Šolta
Brač
Hvar
Vis
Korčula
Lastovo
Mljet
Pelješac
Palagruža
Sazanit
Mathraki
0
40
80
120
160 km
16°
18°
20°
5
6
7
8
A
B
C
D
E
16
22

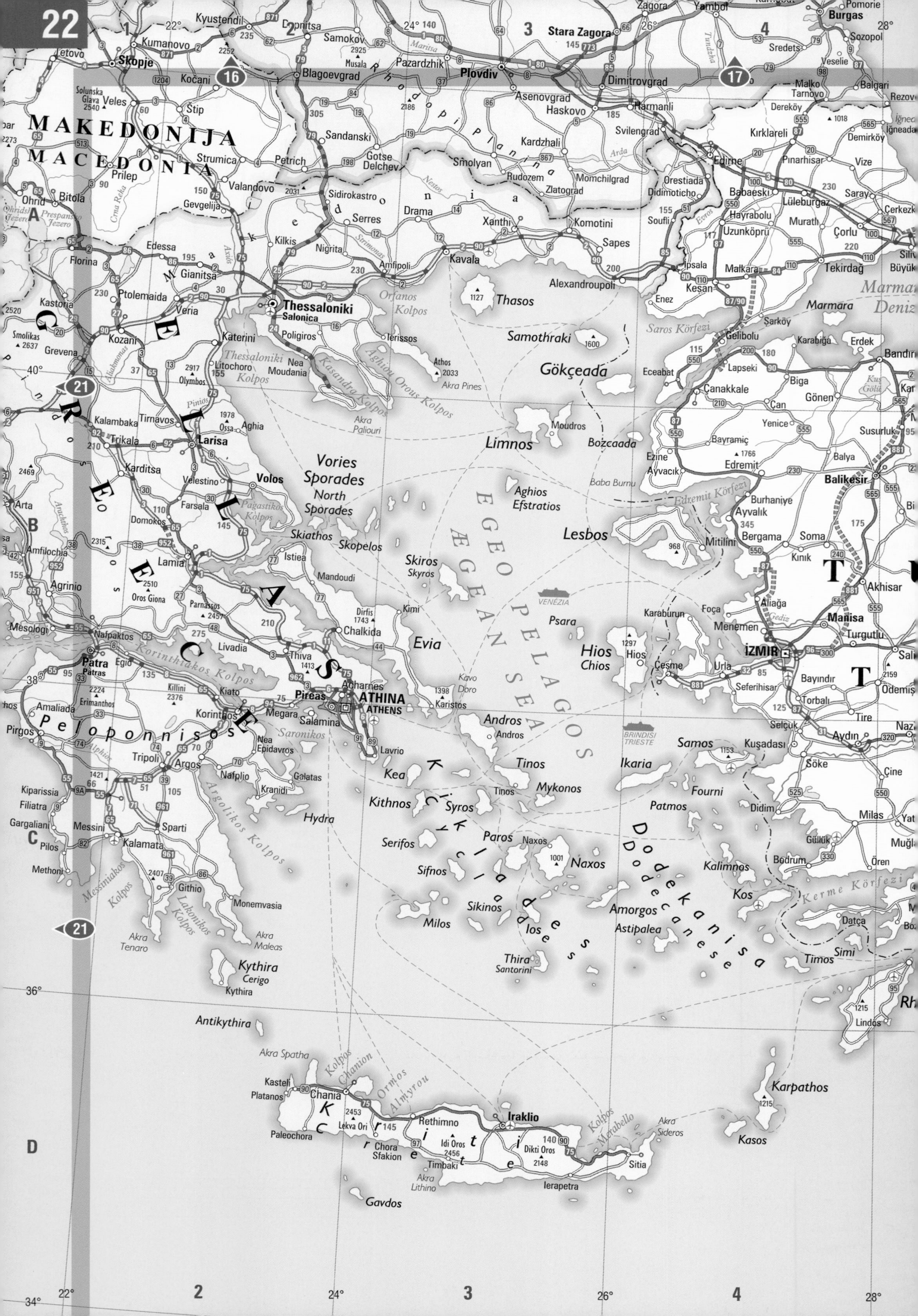
MAKEDONIJA
MACEDONIA
GREECE
ELLAS
Peloponnisos
EGEO PELAGOS
AEGEAN SEA
Kikladhes
Dodekanisa
Dodecanese
Kriti
Skopje
Kumanovo
Tetovo
Kyustendil
Dupnitsa
Samokov
Musala 2925
Pazardzhik
Plovdiv
Stara Zagora
Zagora
Yambol
Burgas
Pomorie
Sozopol
Sredets
Veselie
Malko Tarnovo
Bulgari
Rezovo
Dimitrovgrad
Asenovgrad
Haskovo
Harmanli
Svilengrad
Kardzhali
Momchilgrad
Zlatograd
Rudozem
Smolyan
Rhodopi Planina
Maritsa
Tundzha
Arda
Nestos
Blagoevgrad
Sandanski
Gotse Delchev
Petrich
Kočani
Štip
Veles
Solunska Glava 2540
Strumica
Prilep
Bitola
Ohrid
Ohridsko Jezero
Prespansko Jezero
Crna Reka
Valandovo
Gevgelija
Sidirokastro
Serres
Drama
Xanthi
Komotini
Sapes
Kavala
Alexandroupoli
Orestiada
Didimoticho
Soufli
Evros
Edirne
Kırklareli
Dereköy
Demirköy
İğneada
Pınarhisar
Vize
Babaeski
Lüleburgaz
Saray
Çerkezköy
Hayrabolu
Muratlı
Çorlu
Uzunköprü
Ipsala
Malkara
Tekirdağ
Keşan
Enez
Saros Körfezi
Şarköy
Marmara
Marmara Denizi
Gelibolu
Eceabat
Lapseki
Çanakkale
Biga
Çan
Karabiğa
Erdek
Bandırma
Gönen
Yenice
Bayramiç
Ezine
Ayvacık
Edremit
Edremit Körfezi
Baba Burnu
Balya
Susurluk
Balıkesir
Burhaniye
Ayvalık
Bergama
Soma
Kınık
Akhisar
Manisa
Turgutlu
Aliağa
Foça
Menemen
Karaburun
IZMIR
Urla
Çeşme
Seferihisar
Bayındır
Torbalı
Ödemiş
Tire
Selçuk
Kuşadası
Aydın
Söke
Çine
Didim
Milas
Güllük
Bodrum
Ören
Muğla
Kerme Körfezi
Datça
Simi
Timos
Rhodos
Lindos
Kilkis
Axios
Nigrita
Strimonas
Amfipoli
Edessa
Florina
Gianitsa
Ptolemaida
Kastoria
Kozani
Veria
Grevena
Smolikas 2637
Thessaloniki
Salonica
Poligiros
Ierissos
Orfanos Kolpos
Thessaloniki Kolpos
Nea Moudania
Kasandra Kolpos
Aghiou Orous Kolpos
Athos 2033
Akra Pines
Akra Paliouri
Thasos
Samothraki
Gökçeada
Limnos
Moudros
Bozcaada
Aghios Efstratios
Lesbos
Mitilini
Katerini
Litochoro
Olymbos 2917
Aliakmonas
Pinios
Ossa 1978
Aghia
Tirnavos
Larisa
Kalambaka
Trikala
Karditsa
Velestino
Volos
Pagastikos Kolpos
Farsala
Domokos
Arta
Amfilochia
Arachthos
Lamia
Agrinio
Oros Giona 2510
Parnassos 2457
Mesologi
Nafpaktos
Patra
Patras
Korinthiakos Kolpos
Egio
Livadia
Thiva
Chalkida
Dirfis 1743
Kimi
Evia
Istiea
Mandoudi
Vories Sporades
North Sporades
Skiathos
Skopelos
Skiros
Skyros
Psara
Hios
Chios
Karistos
Kavo Doro
Acharnes
Pireas
ATHINA
ATHENS
Salamina
Megara
Kiato
Killini 2376
Erimanthos 2224
Amaliada
Pirgos
Korinthos
Nea Epidavros
Saronikos
Lavrio
Tripoli
Argos
Nafplio
Galatas
Kranidi
Alphios
Kiparissia
Filiatra
Gargaliani
Messini
Kalamata
Sparti
Pilos
Methoni
Gythio
Monemvasia
Messiniakos Kolpos
Lakonikos Kolpos
Argolikos Kolpos
Akra Tenaro
Akra Maleas
Hydra
Kythira
Cerigo
Antikythira
Kea
Kithnos
Syros
Serifos
Sifnos
Milos
Paros
Naxos
Andros
Tinos
Mykonos
Ikaria
Samos
Fourni
Patmos
Kalimnos
Kos
Amorgos
Astipalea
Sikinos
Ios
Thira
Santorini
Karpathos
Kasos
Akra Sideros
Akra Spatha
Kasteli
Platanos
Chania
Kolpos Chanion
Ormos Almyrou
Rethimno
Iraklio
Paleochora
Lekva Ori 2453
Chora Sfakion
Idi Oros 2456
Timbaki
Akra Lithino
Dikti Oros 2148
Ierapetra
Kolpos Merabello
Sitia
Gavdos
VENEZIA
BRINDISI TRIESTE
16
17
21
22°
24°
26°
28°
40°
36°
34°
A
B
C
D
1
2
3
4

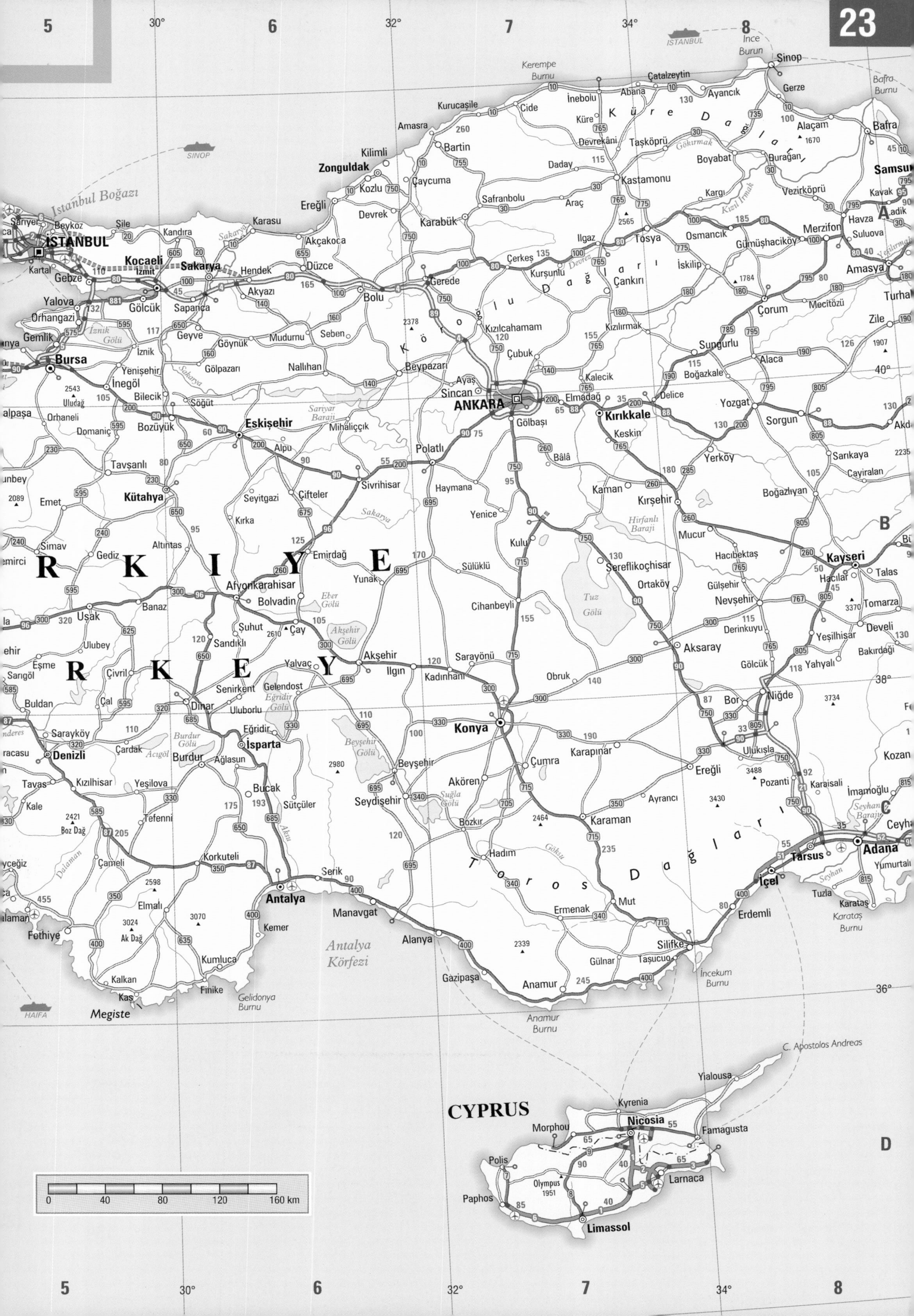
5
30°
6
32°
7
34°
8
ISTANBUL
İnce Burun
Sinop
Kerempe Burnu
Çatalzeytin
Bafra Burnu
Abana
İnebolu
Ayancık
Gerze
Kurucaşile
Cide
Küre
Küre Dağları
Alaçam
Bafra
Amasra
Bartın
Devrekâni
Taşköprü
Gökırmak
Boyabat
Durağan
Kilimli
Zonguldak
Daday
Samsun
Kozlu
Çaycuma
Kastamonu
Vezirköprü
Ereğli
Safranbolu
Araç
Kargı
Kızıl Irmak
Kavak
Devrek
Karabük
Havza
Ladik
İstanbul Boğazı
SINOP
Sarıyer
Beykoz
Şile
Karasu
Kandıra
Akçakoca
Osmancık
Merzifon
Suluova
Ilgaz
Tosya
Gümüşhacıköy
ISTANBUL
Kocaeli
Sakarya
Düzce
Çerkeş
Kurşunlu
İskilip
Amasya
Yeşilırmak
Kartal
Gebze
İzmit
Hendek
Gerede
Çankırı
Akyazı
Bolu
Yalova
Gölcük
Sapanca
Çorum
Mecitözü
Turhal
Orhangazi
İznik Gölü
Geyve
Köroğlu Dağları
Kızılcahamam
Kızılırmak
Zile
Gemlik
İznik
Göynük
Mudurnu
Seben
Bursa
Yenişehir
Gölpazarı
Nallıhan
Beypazarı
Çubuk
Sungurlu
Alaca
İnegöl
Ayaş
Sincan
Kalecik
Boğazkale
40°
Uludağ
Bilecik
Söğüt
ANKARA
Elmadağ
Delice
Yozgat
Orhaneli
Sarıyar Barajı
Kırıkkale
Sorgun
Domaniç
Bozüyük
Eskişehir
Mihalıççık
Gölbaşı
Keskin
Alpu
Polatlı
Bâlâ
Yerköy
Sarıkaya
Tavşanlı
Sivrihisar
Çayıralan
Haymana
Kaman
Kütahya
Seyitgazi
Çifteler
Kırşehir
Boğazlıyan
Emet
Kırka
Sakarya
Yenice
Hirfanlı Barajı
Mucur
Simav
Altıntaş
Emirdağ
Kulu
Hacıbektaş
Kayseri
Gediz
Yunak
Sülüklü
Şereflikoçhisar
Talas
Hacılar
Ortaköy
Gülşehir
Afyonkarahisar
Bolvadin
Eber Gölü
Tuz Gölü
Nevşehir
Tomarza
Banaz
Cihanbeyli
Uşak
Şuhut
Çay
Akşehir Gölü
Derinkuyu
Develi
Ulubey
Sandıklı
Yeşilhisar
Aksaray
Bakırdağı
Eşme
Çivril
Yalvaç
Akşehir
Ilgın
Sarayönü
Gölcük
Yahyalı
Sarıgöl
Kadınhanı
Obruk
38°
Senirkent
Gelendost
Eğridir Gölü
Bor
Niğde
Buldan
Çal
Dinar
Uluborlu
Sarayköy
Eğridir
Konya
Denizli
Çardak
Acıgöl
Burdur Gölü
Burdur
Isparta
Beyşehir Gölü
Beyşehir
Çumra
Karapınar
Ulukışla
Kozan
Ağlasun
Ereğli
Pozantı
Karaisali
Tavas
Kızılhisar
Yeşilova
Akören
İmamoğlu
Kale
Bucak
Seydişehir
Suğla Gölü
Ayrancı
Seyhan Barajı
Sütçüler
Boz Dağ
Tefenni
Bozkır
Karaman
Ceyhan
Toros Dağları
Adana
Hadım
Göksu
Tarsus
Yumurtalık
Dalaman
Korkuteli
Çameli
Serik
İçel
Seyhan
Elmalı
Antalya
Tuzla
Manavgat
Mut
Karataş
Ermenak
Erdemli
Karataş Burnu
Fethiye
Kemer
Ak Dağ
Antalya Körfezi
Alanya
Silifke
Gülnar
Taşucu
Kumluca
Kalkan
Gazipaşa
Anamur
İncekum Burnu
Kaş
Finike
36°
HAIFA
Megiste
Gelidonya Burnu
Anamur Burnu
C. Apostolos Andreas
Yialousa
CYPRUS
Kyrenia
Nicosia
Morphou
Famagusta
Polis
Olympus
Larnaca
Paphos
Limassol
A
B
C
D
0
40
80
120
160 km

Key to road map pages

- ● **Florence** *Firenze* **City plan**
- ☐ **İstanbul** **City approach map**
- ■ **Milan** *Milano* **City plan and approach map** See pages 201–228 for city plans and approach maps

97 Map pages at 1:750 000
182 Map pages at 1:1 500 000

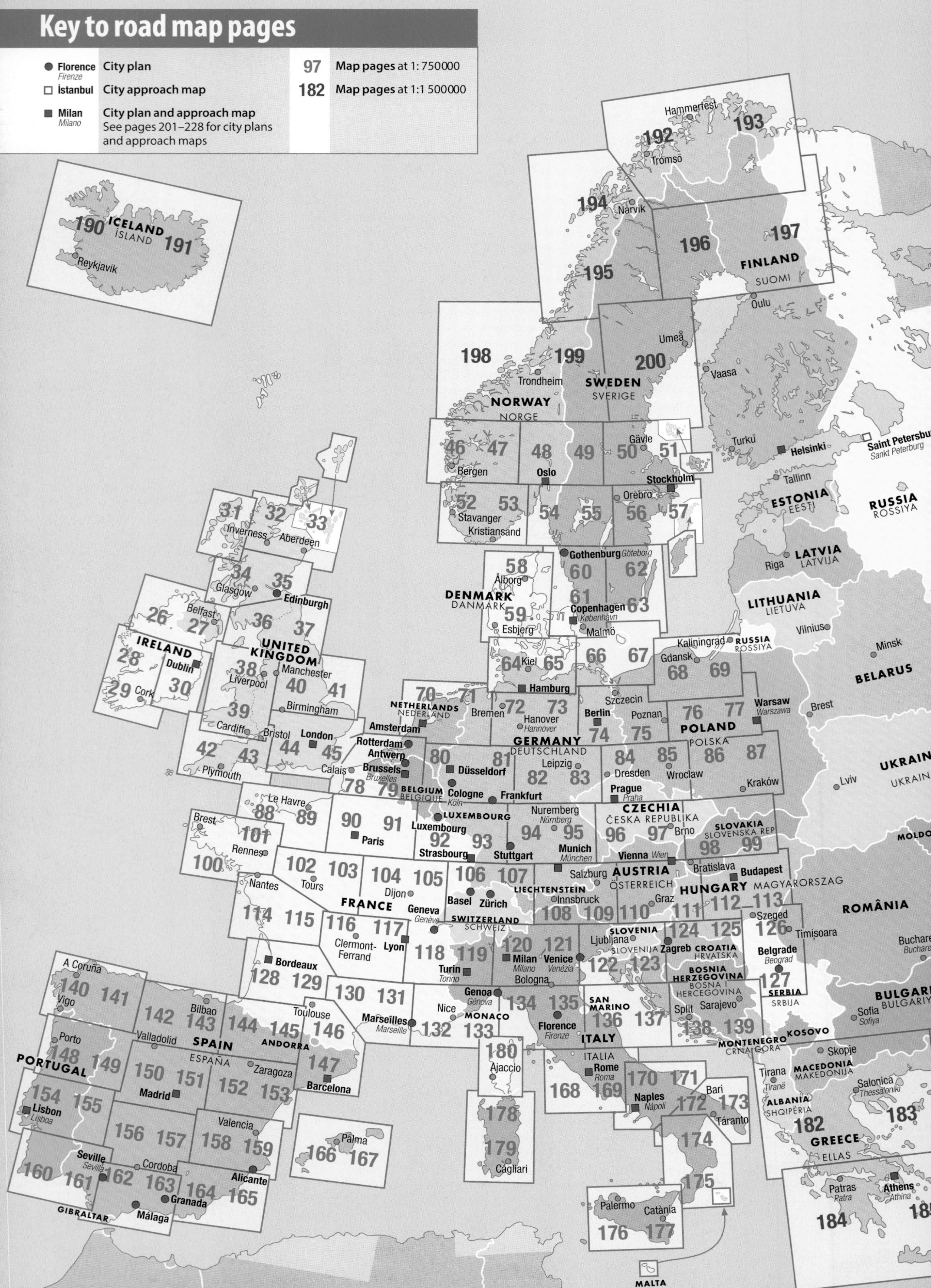

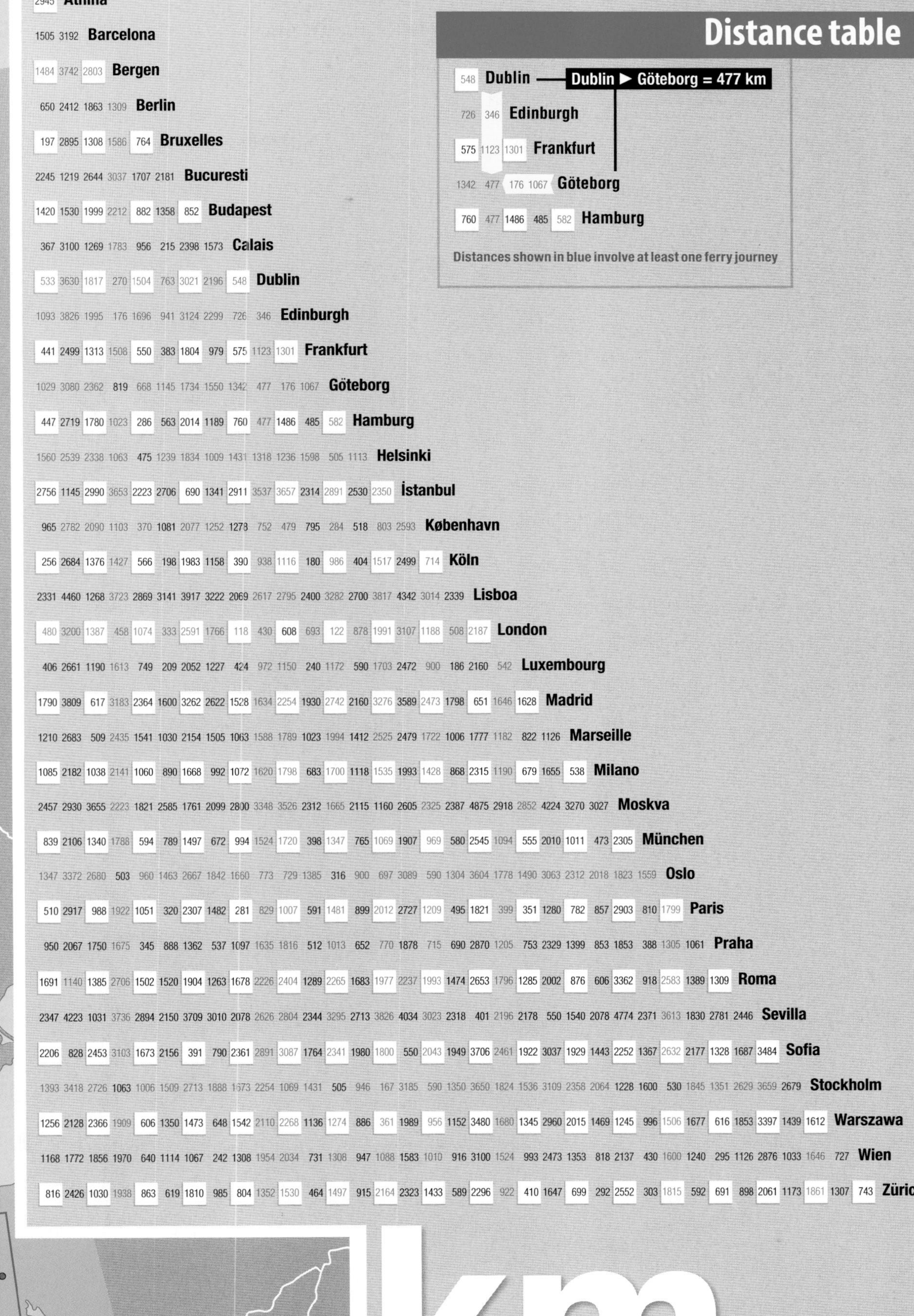

Legend:

548	Dublin	
726	346	Edinburgh
575	1123	1301 Frankfurt
1342	477 176 1067	Göteborg
760	477 1486 485 582	Hamburg

Dublin ▶ Göteborg = 477 km

Distances shown in blue involve at least one ferry journey

Distance table (km):

Amsterdam

2945 **Athina**

1505 3192 **Barcelona**

1484 3742 2803 **Bergen**

650 2412 1863 1309 **Berlin**

197 2895 1308 1586 764 **Bruxelles**

2245 1219 2644 3037 1707 2181 **Bucuresti**

1420 1530 1999 2212 882 1358 852 **Budapest**

367 3100 1269 1783 956 215 2398 1573 **Calais**

533 3630 1817 270 1504 763 3021 2196 548 **Dublin**

1093 3826 1995 176 1696 941 3124 2299 726 346 **Edinburgh**

441 2499 1313 1508 550 383 1804 979 575 1123 1301 **Frankfurt**

1029 3080 2362 819 668 1145 1734 1550 1342 477 176 1067 **Göteborg**

447 2719 1780 1023 286 563 2014 1189 760 477 1486 485 582 **Hamburg**

1560 2539 2338 1063 475 1239 1834 1009 1431 1318 1236 1598 505 1113 **Helsinki**

2756 1145 2990 3653 2223 2706 690 1341 2911 3537 3657 2314 2891 2530 2350 **İstanbul**

965 2782 2090 1103 370 1081 2077 1252 1273 752 479 795 284 518 803 2593 **København**

256 2684 1376 1427 566 198 1983 1158 390 938 1116 180 986 404 1517 2499 714 **Köln**

2331 4460 1268 3723 2869 3141 3917 3222 2069 2617 2795 2400 3282 2700 3817 4342 3014 2339 **Lisboa**

480 3200 1387 458 1074 333 2591 1766 118 430 608 693 122 878 1991 3107 1188 508 2187 **London**

406 2661 1190 1613 749 209 2052 1227 424 972 1150 240 1172 590 1703 2472 900 186 2160 542 **Luxembourg**

1790 3809 617 3183 2364 1600 3262 2622 1528 1634 2254 1930 2742 2160 3276 3589 2473 1798 651 1646 1628 **Madrid**

1210 2683 509 2435 1541 1030 2154 1505 1063 1588 1789 1023 1994 1412 2525 2479 1722 1006 1777 1182 822 1126 **Marseille**

1085 2182 1038 2141 1060 890 1668 992 1072 1620 1798 683 1700 1118 1535 1993 1428 868 2315 1190 679 1655 538 **Milano**

2457 2930 3655 2223 1821 2585 1761 2099 2800 3348 3526 2312 1665 2115 1160 2605 2325 2387 4875 2918 2852 4224 3270 3027 **Moskva**

839 2106 1340 1788 594 789 1497 672 994 1524 1720 398 1347 765 1069 1907 969 580 2545 1094 555 2010 1011 473 2305 **München**

1347 3372 2680 503 960 1463 2667 1842 1660 773 729 1385 316 900 697 3089 590 1304 3604 1778 1490 3063 2312 2018 1823 1559 **Oslo**

510 2917 988 1922 1051 320 2307 1482 281 829 1007 591 1481 899 2012 2727 1209 495 1821 399 351 1280 782 857 2903 810 1799 **Paris**

950 2067 1750 1675 345 888 1362 537 1097 1635 1816 512 1013 652 770 1878 715 690 2870 1205 753 2329 1399 853 1853 388 1305 1061 **Praha**

1691 1140 1385 2706 1502 1520 1904 1263 1678 2226 2404 1289 2265 1683 1977 2237 1993 1474 2653 1796 1285 2002 876 606 3362 918 2583 1389 1309 **Roma**

2347 4223 1031 3736 2894 2150 3709 3010 2078 2626 2804 2344 3295 2713 3826 4034 3023 2318 401 2196 2178 550 1540 2078 4774 2371 3613 1830 2781 2446 **Sevilla**

2206 828 2453 3103 1673 2156 391 790 2361 2891 3087 1764 2341 1980 1800 550 2043 1949 3706 2461 1922 3037 1929 1443 2252 1367 2632 2177 1328 1687 3484 **Sofia**

1393 3418 2726 1063 1006 1509 2713 1888 1673 2254 1069 1431 505 946 167 3185 590 1350 3650 1824 1536 3109 2358 2064 1228 1600 530 1845 1351 2629 3659 2679 **Stockholm**

1256 2128 2366 1909 606 1350 1473 648 1542 2110 2268 1136 1274 886 361 1989 956 1152 3480 1680 1345 2960 2015 1469 1245 996 1506 1677 616 1853 3397 1439 1612 **Warszawa**

1168 1772 1856 1970 640 1114 1067 242 1308 1954 2034 731 1308 947 1088 1583 1010 916 3100 1524 993 2473 1353 818 2137 430 1600 1240 295 1126 2876 1033 1646 727 **Wien**

816 2426 1030 1938 863 619 1810 985 804 1352 1530 464 1497 915 2164 2323 1433 589 2296 922 410 1647 699 292 2552 303 1815 592 691 898 2061 1173 1861 1307 743 **Zürich**

km

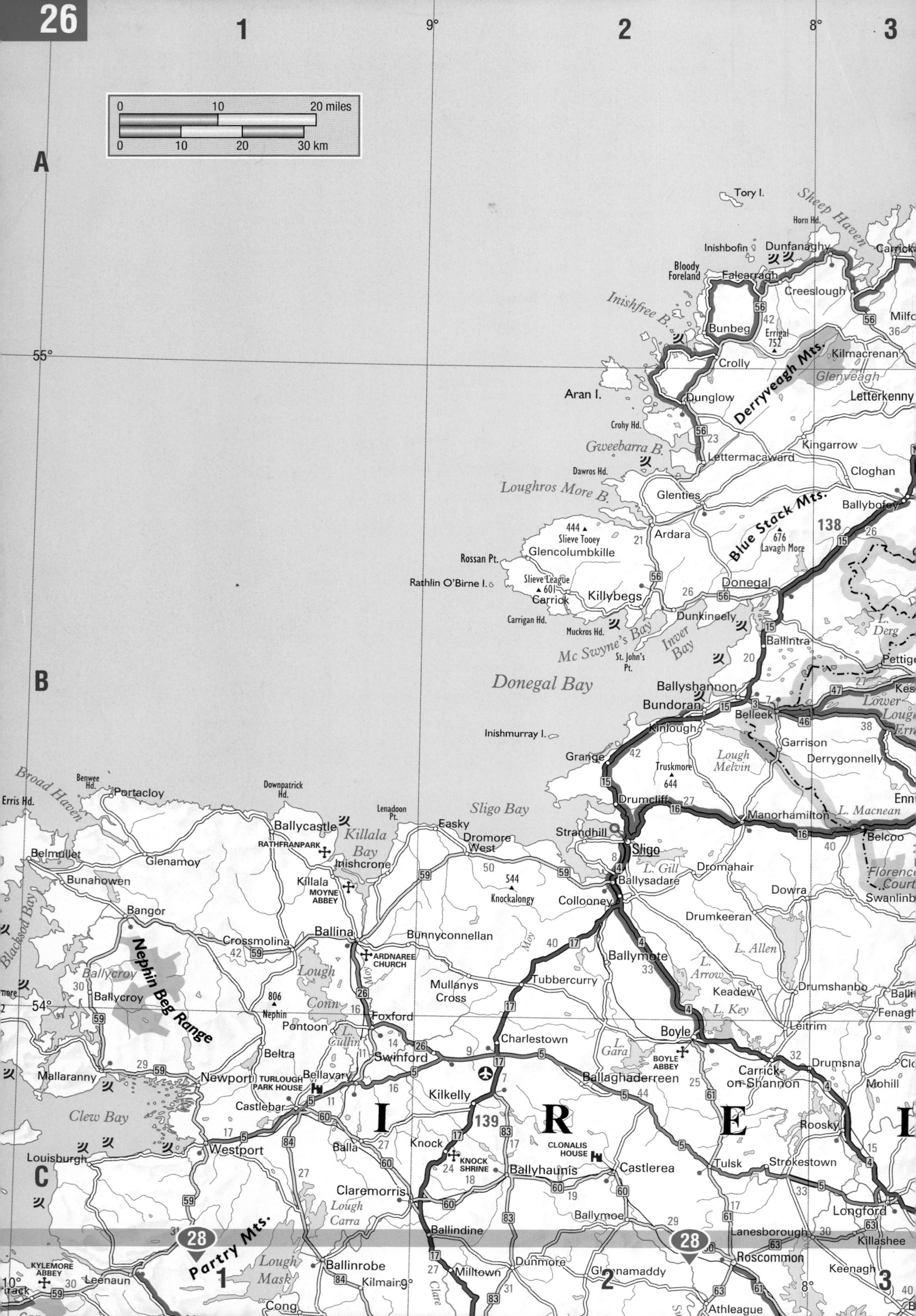
1
2
3
9°
8°
A
B
C
0 10 20 miles
0 10 20 30 km
55°
54°
10°
Tory I.
Sheep Haven
Horn Hd.
Inishbofin
Dunfanaghy
Carrick
Bloody Foreland
Falcarragh
Creeslough
Inishfree B.
Bunbeg
Errigal 752
Milford
Kilmacrenan
Derryveagh Mts.
Crolly
Glenveagh
Aran I.
Dunglow
Letterkenny
Crohy Hd.
Gweebarra B.
Lettermacaward
Kingarrow
Dawros Hd.
Cloghan
Loughros More B.
Glenties
Blue Stack Mts.
Ballybofey
444 Slieve Tooey
Ardara
676 Lavagh More
138
Rossan Pt.
Glencolumbkille
Rathlin O'Birne I.
Slieve League 601
Carrick
Killybegs
Donegal
Carrigan Hd.
Dunkineely
Muckros Hd.
Mc Swyne's Bay
Inver Bay
St. John's Pt.
L. Derg
Ballintra
Pettigo
Donegal Bay
Ballyshannon
Bundoran
Belleek
Lower Lough Erne
Kesh
Inishmurray I.
Kinlough
Garrison
Grange
Truskmore 644
Lough Melvin
Derrygonnelly
Broad Haven
Benwee Hd.
Portacloy
Downpatrick Hd.
Drumcliff
Erris Hd.
Lenadoon Pt.
Sligo Bay
Manorhamilton
L. Macnean
Enniskillen
Ballycastle
Killala Bay
Easky
Dromore West
Strandhill
Belcoo
RATHFRANPARK
Sligo
Belmullet
Glenamoy
Inishcrone
L. Gill
Dromahair
Florence Court
Bunahowen
Killala
MOYNE ABBEY
544 Knockalongy
Ballysadare
Collooney
Dowra
Swanlinbar
Blacksod Bay
Bangor
Drumkeeran
Crossmolina
Ballina
Bunnyconnellan
Moy
L. Allen
ARDNAREE CHURCH
Nephin Beg Range
Ballycroy
Lough Conn
Ballymote
L. Arrow
806 Nephin
Tubbercurry
Mullanys Cross
Keadew
Drumshanbo
L. Key
Fenagh
Pontoon
Foxford
Boyle
Leitrim
L. Cullin
Charlestown
L. Gara
Beltra
BOYLE ABBEY
Drumsna
Swinford
Mallaranny
Newport
TURLOUGH PARK HOUSE
Bellavary
Ballaghaderreen
Carrick-on-Shannon
Mohill
Kilkelly
Castlebar
Clew Bay
IRELAND
139
Rooskey
Louisburgh
Westport
Balla
Knock
KNOCK SHRINE
CLONALIS HOUSE
Ballyhaunis
Castlerea
Tulsk
Strokestown
Claremorris
Lough Carra
Ballymoe
Longford
Partry Mts.
Ballindine
Lanesborough
Killashee
28
Lough Mask
Ballinrobe
Dunmore
Glennamaddy
Roscommon
KYLEMORE ABBEY
Leenaun
Kilmaine
Milltown
Keenagh
Cong
Clare
Athleague

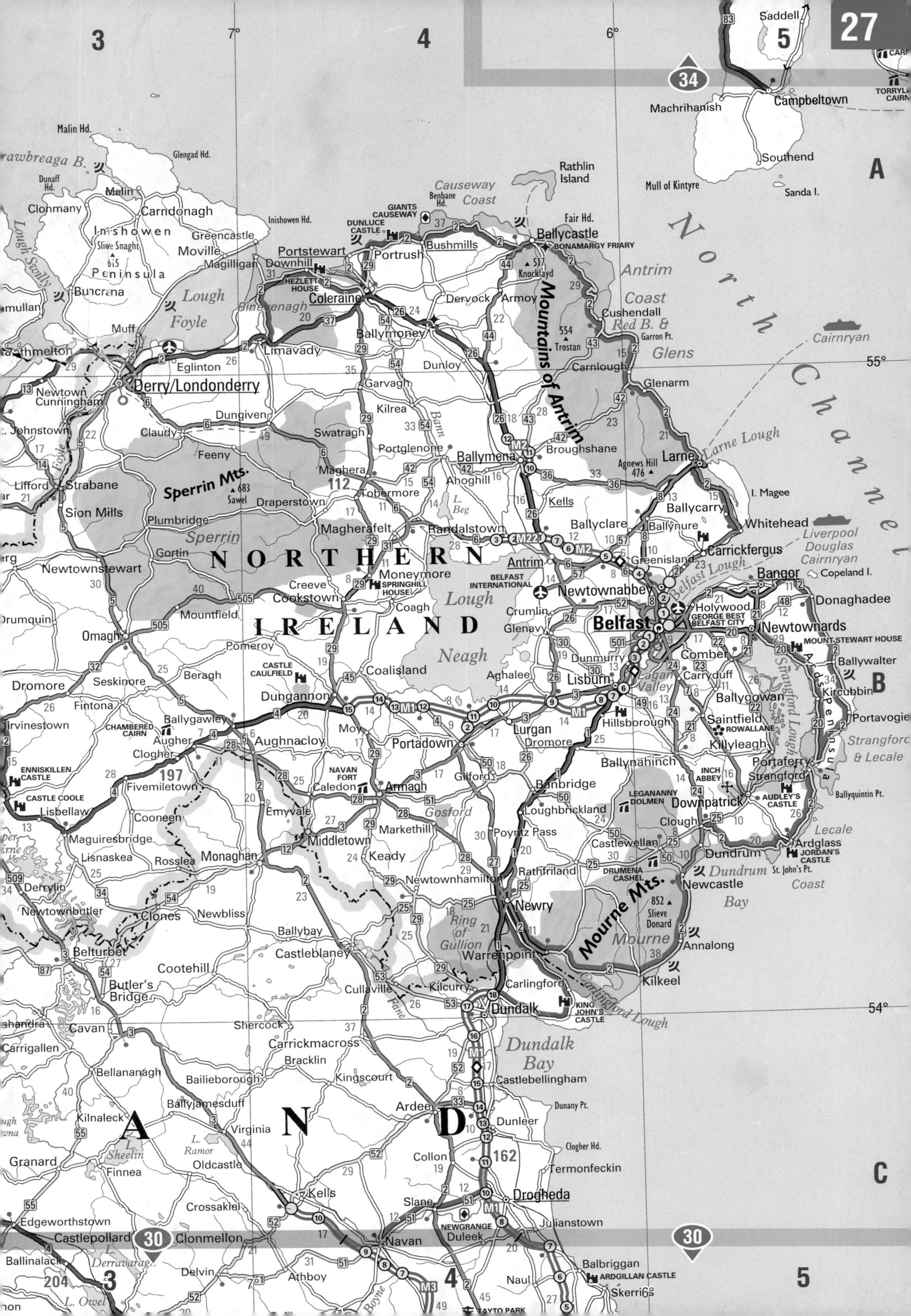

NORTHERN IRELAND
IRELAND
North Channel
Derry/Londonderry
Belfast
Lough Neagh
Lough Foyle
Sperrin Mts.
Mountains of Antrim
Mourne Mts.
Antrim Coast
Causeway Coast
Red B. & Glens
Strangford Lough
Belfast Lough
Larne Lough
Carlingford Lough
Dundalk Bay
Dundrum Bay
Rathlin Island
Campbeltown
Machrihanish
Southend
Mull of Kintyre
Saddell
Coleraine
Portrush
Portstewart
Bushmills
Ballycastle
Ballymoney
Limavady
Ballymena
Larne
Carrickfergus
Bangor
Newtownabbey
Newtownards
Lisburn
Antrim
Portadown
Lurgan
Armagh
Dungannon
Omagh
Strabane
Cookstown
Magherafelt
Banbridge
Newry
Downpatrick
Newcastle
Kilkeel
Warrenpoint
Dundalk
Drogheda
Navan
Kells
Cavan
Monaghan
Castleblaney
Carrickmacross
Ardee
Slane
Balbriggan
Sion Mills
Dungiven
Ballyclare
Whitehead
Holywood
Comber
Saintfield
Killyleagh
Portaferry
Strangford
Ardglass
Dundrum
Castlewellan
Ballynahinch
Hillsborough
Dromore
Crumlin
Randalstown
Maghera
Garvagh
Kilrea
Coalisland
Moy
Aughnacloy
Ballygawley
Clogher
Fivemiletown
Lisnaskea
Clones
Cootehill
Ballybay
Newtownbutler
Belturbet
Virginia
Oldcastle
Bailieborough
Kingscourt
Dunleer
Castlebellingham
Carlingford
Greencastle
Moville
Carndonagh
Buncrana
Malin
Clonmany
Inishowen Peninsula
Malin Hd.
Fair Hd.
Cairnryan
Liverpool Douglas Cairnryan
Giants Causeway
Belfast International
George Best Belfast City

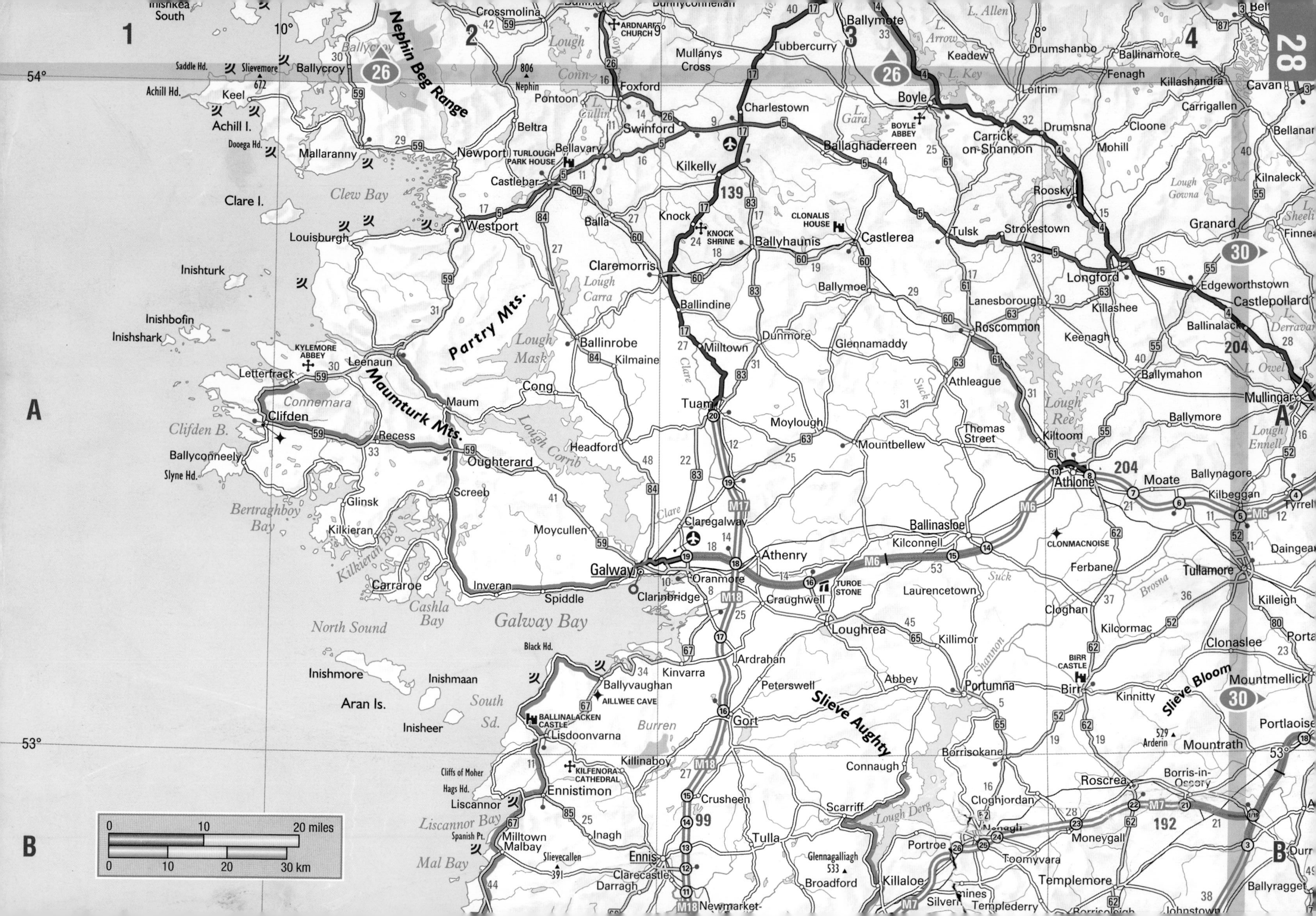

28
1
2
3
4
A
B
54°
53°
10°
8°
26
30
204
139
192
99
Nephin Beg Range
Partry Mts.
Maumturk Mts.
Slieve Aughty
Slieve Bloom
Inishkea South
Crossmolina
Ardnaree Church
Ballymote
Tubbercurry
Mullanys Cross
L. Allen
L. Arrow
Drumshanbo
Keadew
L. Key
Ballinamore
Fenagh
Killashandra
Cavan
Saddle Hd.
Slievemore
Ballycroy
Nephin
Lough Conn
Foxford
Pontoon
L. Cullin
Swinford
Charlestown
Boyle
Boyle Abbey
L. Gara
Ballaghaderreen
Leitrim
Carrick-on-Shannon
Drumsna
Cloone
Carrigallen
Bellanan
Achill Hd.
Keel
Achill I.
Dooega Hd.
Mallaranny
Newport
Turlough Park House
Bellavary
Castlebar
Beltra
Kilkelly
Mohill
Roosky
Lough Gowna
Kilnaleck
Clew Bay
Clare I.
Westport
Louisburgh
Balla
Knock
Knock Shrine
Clonalis House
Ballyhaunis
Castlerea
Tulsk
Strokestown
Granard
Lough Sheelin
Finnea
Inishturk
Claremorris
Lough Carra
Ballymoe
Lanesborough
Longford
Killashee
Edgeworthstown
Castlepollard
L. Derravaragh
Inishbofin
Inishshark
Kylemore Abbey
Leenaun
Letterfrack
Lough Mask
Ballinrobe
Kilmaine
Ballindine
Milltown
Dunmore
Glennamaddy
Roscommon
Keenagh
Ballinalack
Ballymahon
L. Owel
Connemara
Clifden
Clifden B.
Maum
Cong
Clare
Tuam
Athleague
Suck
Lough Ree
Mullingar
Ballymore
Lough Ennell
Recess
Ballyconneely
Slyne Hd.
Oughterard
Lough Corrib
Headford
Moylough
Mountbellew
Thomas Street
Kiltoom
Athlone
Moate
Ballynagore
Kilbeggan
Tyrrellspass
Screeb
Glinsk
Bertraghboy Bay
Kilkieran
Kilkieran Bay
Moycullen
Claregalway
Ballinasloe
Kilconnell
Clonmacnoise
Daingean
Galway
Athenry
Carraroe
Inveran
Clarinbridge
Oranmore
Spiddle
Turoe Stone
Craughwell
Laurencetown
Ferbane
Brosna
Tullamore
Cashla Bay
North Sound
Galway Bay
Loughrea
Cloghan
Kilcormac
Killeigh
Killimor
Shannon
Clonaslee
Black Hd.
Inishmore
Inishmaan
Kinvarra
Ardrahan
Birr Castle
Birr
Abbey
Portumna
Mountmellick
Ballyvaughan
Aillwee Cave
Peterswell
Kinnitty
Aran Is.
South Sd.
Ballinalacken Castle
Lisdoonvarna
Burren
Gort
Inisheer
Arderin
Mountrath
Portlaoise
Killinaboy
Borrisokane
Cliffs of Moher
Hags Hd.
Kilfenora Cathedral
Ennistimon
Connaugh
Roscrea
Borris-in-Ossory
Liscannor
Crusheen
Scarriff
Lough Derg
Cloghjordan
Liscannor Bay
Spanish Pt.
Milltown Malbay
Inagh
Tulla
Portroe
Moneygall
Mal Bay
Slievecallen
Ennis
Clarecastle
Darragh
Glennagalliagh
Broadford
Killaloe
Toomyvarra
Templemore
Ballyragget
Newmarket-
Silvermines
Templederry
0 10 20 miles
0 10 20 30 km

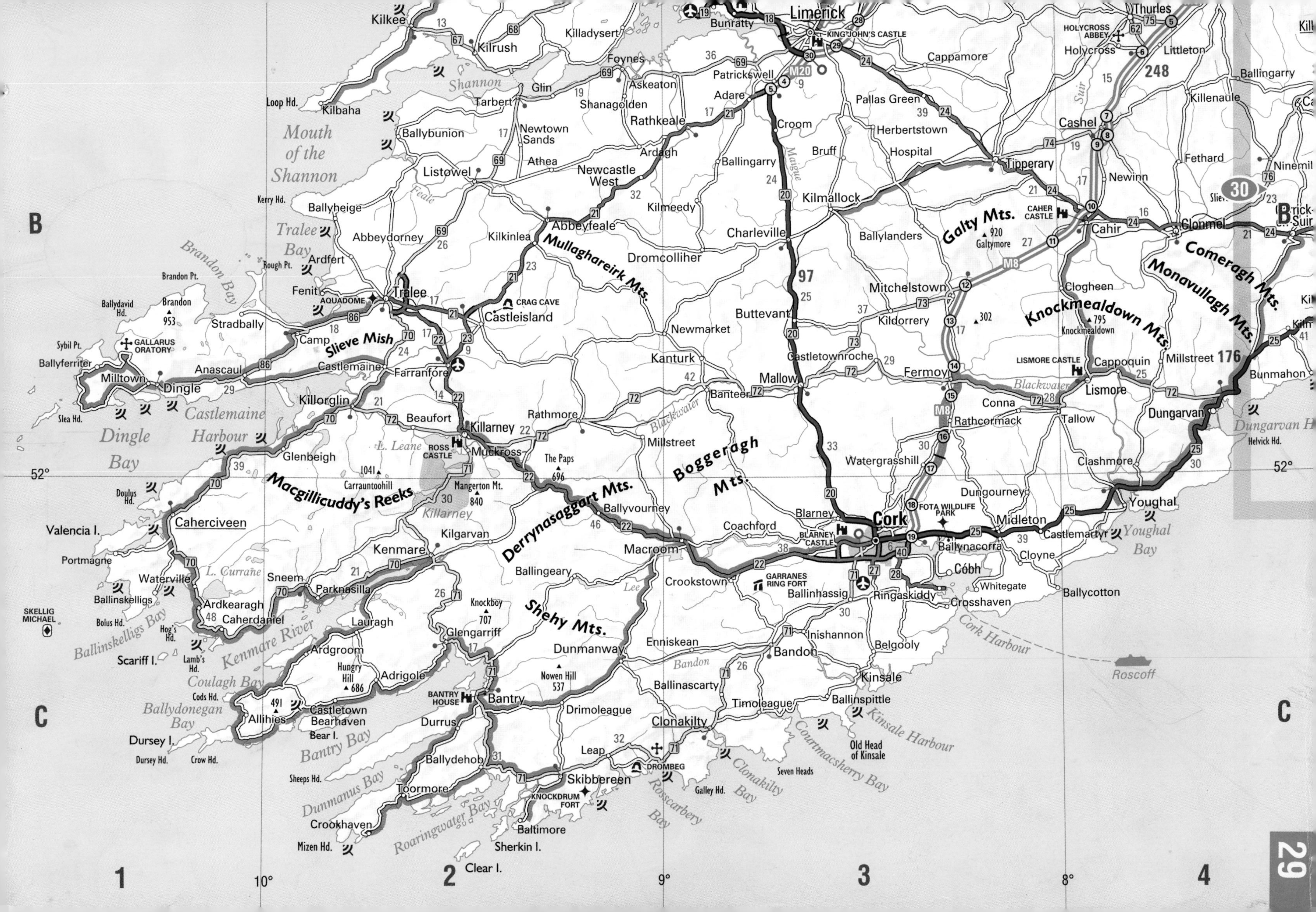
29
Limerick
King John's Castle
Bunratty
Thurles
Holycross Abbey
Holycross
Littleton
Cappamore
Ballingarry
Killenaule
Cashel
Fethard
Ninemile
Newinn
Tipperary
Caher Castle
Cahir
Clonmel
Carrick-on-Suir
Kilkee
Kilrush
Killadysert
Foynes
Askeaton
Patrickswell
Adare
Pallas Green
Herbertstown
Hospital
Croom
Bruff
Glin
Tarbert
Shanagolden
Rathkeale
Loop Hd.
Kilbaha
Mouth of the Shannon
Shannon
Ballybunion
Newtown Sands
Athea
Ardagh
Listowel
Newcastle West
Ballingarry
Kilmallock
Kilmeedy
Kerry Hd.
Ballyheige
Tralee Bay
Abbeydorney
Abbeyfeale
Kilkinlea
Mullaghareirk Mts.
Charleville
Ballylanders
Galty Mts.
Galtymore
Comeragh Mts.
Monavullagh Mts.
Brandon Bay
Brandon Pt.
Brandon
Ballydavid Hd.
Rough Pt.
Ardfert
Fenit
Aquadome
Tralee
Crag Cave
Castleisland
Dromcolliher
Mitchelstown
Clogheen
Knockmealdown Mts.
Knockmealdown
Stradbally
Camp
Slieve Mish
Buttevant
Newmarket
Kildorrery
Sybil Pt.
Gallarus Oratory
Ballyferriter
Milltown
Dingle
Anascaul
Castlemaine
Farranfore
Kanturk
Castletownroche
Mallow
Fermoy
Lismore Castle
Cappoquin
Millstreet
Bunmahon
Lismore
Slea Hd.
Dingle Bay
Castlemaine Harbour
Killorglin
Beaufort
Killarney
Rathmore
Banteer
Blackwater
Conna
Tallow
Dungarvan
Dungarvan Harbour
Helvick Hd.
L. Leane
Ross Castle
Muckross
The Paps
Millstreet
Boggeragh Mts.
Rathcormack
Watergrasshill
Clashmore
Glenbeigh
Carrauntoohill
Mangerton Mt.
Macgillicuddy's Reeks
Derrynasaggart Mts.
Ballyvourney
Dungourney
Youghal
Youghal Bay
Doulus Hd.
Valencia I.
Caherciveen
Killarney
Kilgarvan
Coachford
Blarney
Blarney Castle
Fota Wildlife Park
Cork
Midleton
Castlemartyr
Portmagne
Kenmare
Macroom
Ballynacorra
Cloyne
Cóbh
L. Currane
Waterville
Sneem
Parknasilla
Ballingeary
Crookstown
Garranes Ring Fort
Ballinhassig
Ringaskiddy
Whitegate
Crosshaven
Ballycotton
Skellig Michael
Ballinskelligs
Bolus Hd.
Ardkearagh
Caherdaniel
Knockboy
Shehy Mts.
Lee
Cork Harbour
Ballinskelligs Bay
Hog's Hd.
Kenmare River
Lauragh
Glengarriff
Dunmanway
Enniskean
Bandon
Inishannon
Belgooly
Roscoff
Scariff I.
Lamb's Hd.
Coulagh Bay
Ardgroom
Hungry Hill
Adrigole
Nowen Hill
Ballinascarty
Kinsale
Cods Hd.
Ballydonegan Bay
Allihies
Castletown Bearhaven
Bear I.
Bantry House
Bantry
Drimoleague
Clonakilty
Timoleague
Ballinspittle
Kinsale Harbour
Dursey I.
Dursey Hd.
Crow Hd.
Bantry Bay
Durrus
Leap
Drombeg
Old Head of Kinsale
Courtmacsherry Bay
Seven Heads
Sheeps Hd.
Ballydehob
Skibbereen
Clonakilty Bay
Galley Hd.
Dunmanus Bay
Toormore
Knockdrum Fort
Rosscarbery Bay
Crookhaven
Roaringwater Bay
Baltimore
Sherkin I.
Mizen Hd.
Clear I.
B
C
1
2
3
4
10°
9°
8°
52°

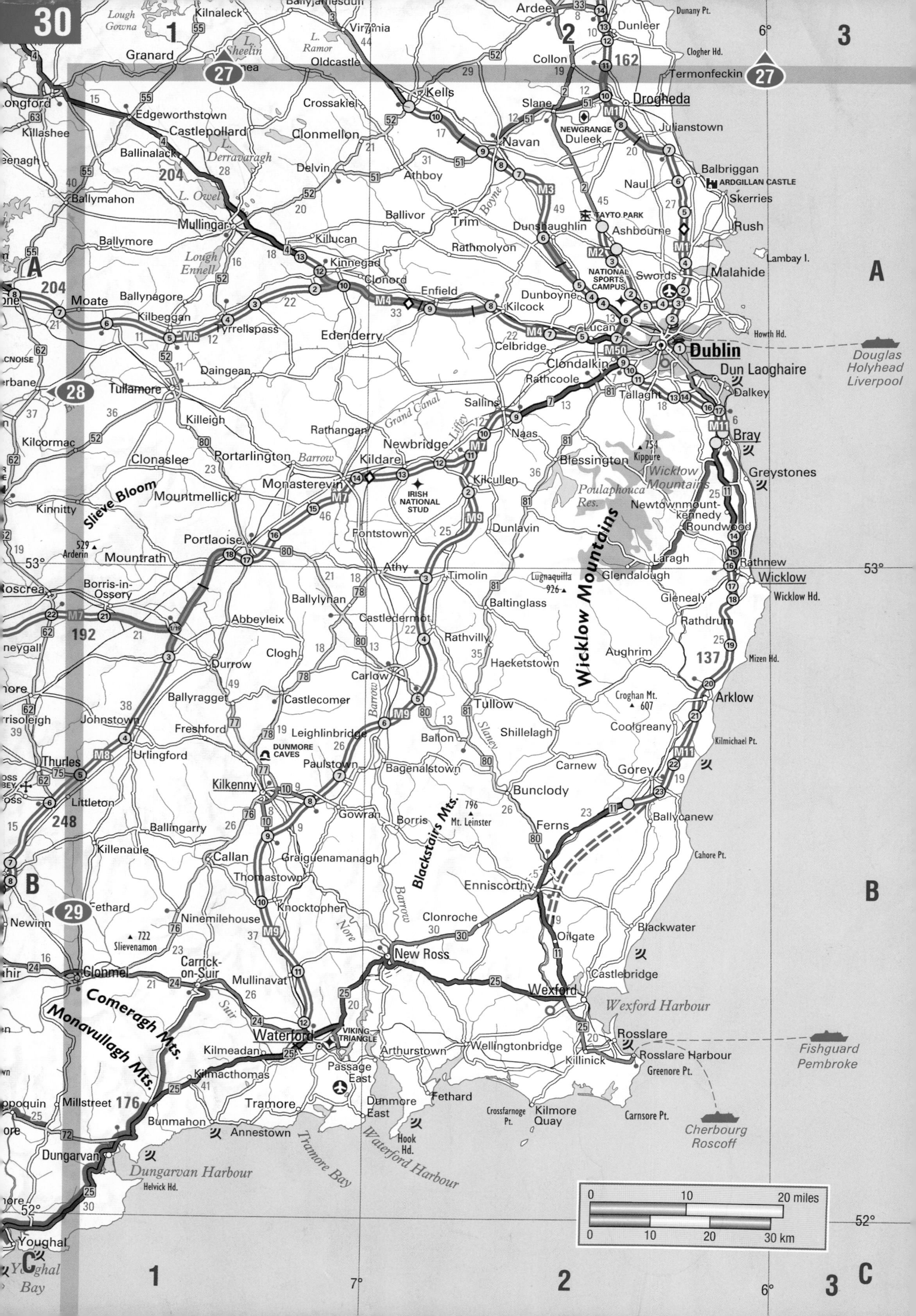

Lough Gowna
Kilnaleck
L. Sheelin
L. Ramor
Virginia
Ardee
Dunleer
Dunany Pt.
Granard
Oldcastle
Collon
Clogher Hd.
Termonfeckin
Longford
Edgeworthstown
Crossakiel
Kells
Slane
Drogheda
Killashee
Castlepollard
Clonmellon
NEWGRANGE
Duleek
Julianstown
Ballinalack
L. Derravaragh
Delvin
Navan
Athboy
Balbriggan
ARDGILLAN CASTLE
Naul
Skerries
L. Owel
Ballymahon
Boyne
TAYTO PARK
Ballivor
Trim
Dunshaughlin
Ashbourne
Rush
Mullingar
Lambay I.
Ballymore
Killucan
Rathmolyon
Lough Ennell
Kinnegad
NATIONAL SPORTS CAMPUS
Swords
Malahide
Clonard
Enfield
Dunboyne
Moate
Ballynagore
Kilcock
Kilbeggan
Tyrrellspass
Edenderry
Lucan
Howth Hd.
Celbridge
Dublin
Douglas
Holyhead
Liverpool
Clondalkin
Dun Laoghaire
Daingean
Rathcoole
Tallaght
Dalkey
Tullamore
Grand Canal
Sallins
Killeigh
Rathangan
Liffey
Naas
Bray
Kilcormac
Newbridge
Kippure
Clonaslee
Portarlington
Barrow
Kildare
Blessington
Wicklow Mountains
Greystones
Monasterevin
Kilcullen
Slieve Bloom
Mountmellick
IRISH NATIONAL STUD
Poulaphouca Res.
Newtownmount-kennedy
Kinnitty
Roundwood
Fontstown
Dunlavin
Portlaoise
Arderin
Mountrath
Athy
Laragh
Rathnew
Timolin
Lugnaquilla
Glendalough
Wicklow
Roscrea
Borris-in-Ossory
Ballylynan
Baltinglass
Glenealy
Wicklow Hd.
Abbeyleix
Castledermot
Rathdrum
Rathvilly
Clogh
Aughrim
Mizen Hd.
Durrow
Carlow
Hacketstown
Wicklow Mountains
Croghan Mt.
Arklow
Ballyragget
Castlecomer
Tullow
Johnstown
Freshford
Leighlinbridge
Shillelagh
Coolgreany
Kilmichael Pt.
DUNMORE CAVES
Ballon
Thurles
Urlingford
Paulstown
Slaney
Carnew
Bagenalstown
Gorey
Kilkenny
Bunclody
Littleton
Gowran
Borris
Blackstairs Mts.
Mt. Leinster
Ballycanew
Ballingarry
Ferns
Killenaule
Callan
Graiguenamanagh
Cahore Pt.
Thomastown
Enniscorthy
Knocktopher
Fethard
Newinn
Ninemilehouse
Clonroche
Blackwater
Nore
Slievenamon
Oilgate
Carrick-on-Suir
New Ross
Clonmel
Castlebridge
Comeragh Mts.
Mullinavat
Wexford
Monavullagh Mts.
Suir
Wexford Harbour
Waterford
VIKING TRIANGLE
Rosslare
Fishguard
Pembroke
Kilmeadan
Arthurstown
Wellingtonbridge
Rosslare Harbour
Kilmacthomas
Passage East
Killinick
Greenore Pt.
Millstreet
Tramore
Dunmore East
Fethard
Crossfarnoge Pt.
Kilmore Quay
Carnsore Pt.
Bunmahon
Annestown
Cherbourg
Roscoff
Dungarvan
Hook Hd.
Tramore Bay
Waterford Harbour
Dungarvan Harbour
Helvick Hd.
Youghal
Youghal Bay
0 10 20 miles
0 10 20 30 km
53°
52°
7°
6°

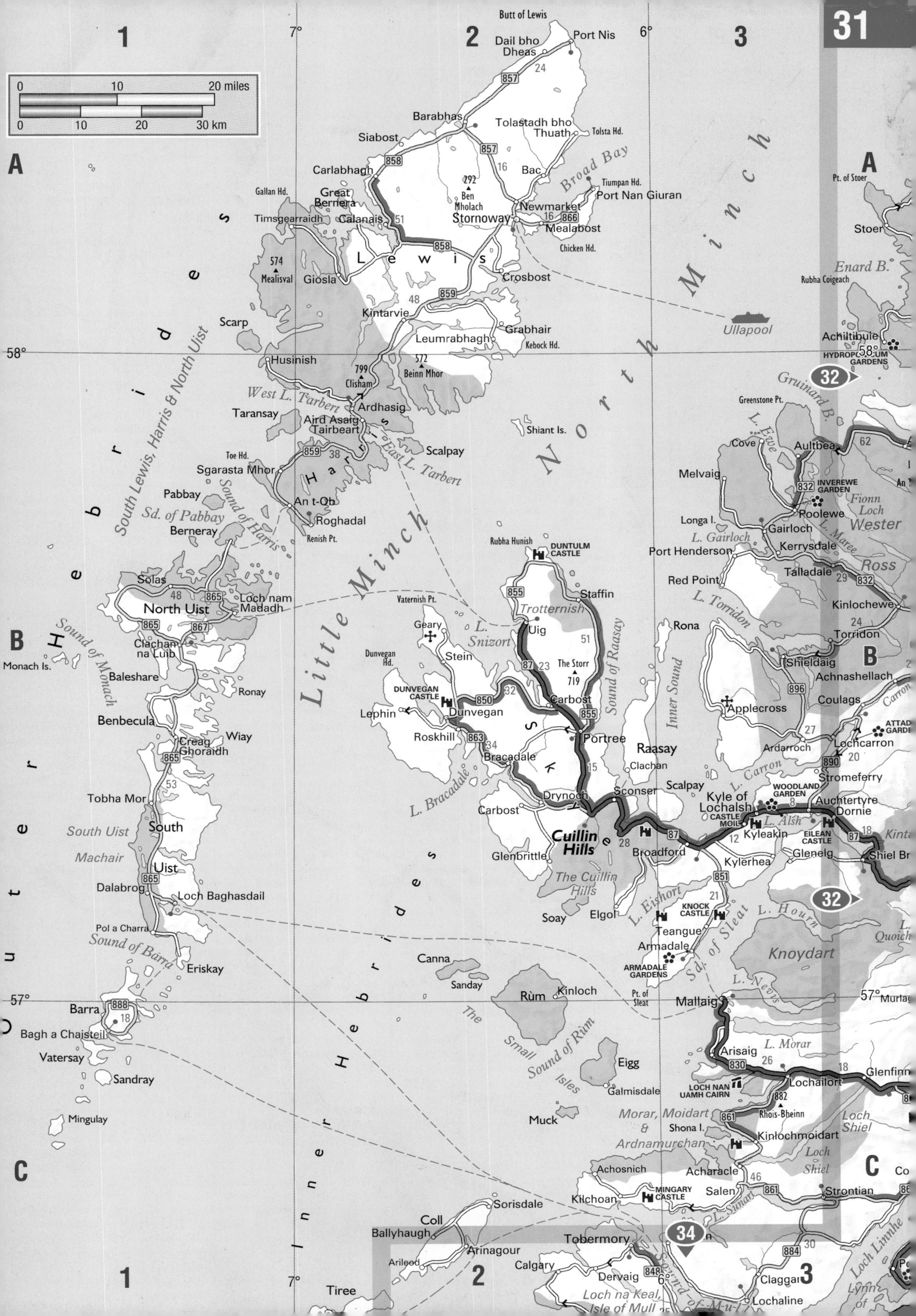
1
2
3
A
B
C
7°
6°
58°
57°
0
10
20 miles
0
10
20
30 km
Butt of Lewis
Port Nis
Dail bho Dheas
Barabhas
Tolastadh bho Thuath
Tolsta Hd.
Siabost
Carlabhagh
Bac
Broad Bay
Tiumpan Hd.
Port Nan Giuran
Gallan Hd.
Great Bernera
292 Ben Mholach
Newmarket
Timsgearraidh
Calanais
Stornoway
Mealabost
Chicken Hd.
574 Mealisval
Giosla
Lewis
Crosbost
Scarp
Kintarvie
Grabhair
Leumrabhagh
Kebock Hd.
Husinish
799 Clisham
572 Beinn Mhor
West L. Tarbert
Ardhasig
Taransay
Aird Asaig
Tairbeart
Scalpay
East L. Tarbert
Toe Hd.
Sgarasta Mhor
Harris
Pabbay
Sd. of Pabbay
Sound of Harris
An t-Ob
Roghadal
Renish Pt.
Berneray
South Lewis, Harris & North Uist
Outer Hebrides
North Minch
Ullapool
Shiant Is.
Little Minch
Rubha Hunish
DUNTULM CASTLE
Solas
North Uist
Loch nam Madadh
Clachan na Luib
Sound of Monach
Monach Is.
Baleshare
Ronay
Benbecula
Wiay
Creag Ghoraidh
Tobha Mor
South Uist
South Uist
Machair
Dalabrog
Loch Baghasdail
Pol a Charra
Sound of Barra
Eriskay
Barra
Bagh a Chaisteil
Vatersay
Sandray
Mingulay
Vaternish Pt.
Trotternish
Staffin
Geary
L. Snizort
Uig
Dunvegan Hd.
Stein
The Storr 719
Sound of Raasay
DUNVEGAN CASTLE
Lephin
Dunvegan
Carbost
Roskhill
Portree
Bracadale
Skye
Raasay
Clachan
Inner Sound
Rona
L. Bracadale
Drynoch
Sconser
Scalpay
Carbost
Cuillin Hills
The Cuillin Hills
Glenbrittle
Broadford
Soay
Elgol
L. Eishort
Inner Hebrides
Canna
Sanday
Rùm
Kinloch
The Small Isles
Sound of Rùm
Eigg
Galmisdale
Muck
Coll
Ballyhaugh
Arinagour
Arileod
Tiree
Calgary
Tobermory
Dervaig
Loch na Keal, Isle of Mull
Sound of Mull
Sorisdale
Kilchoan
MINGARY CASTLE
Achosnich
Salen
Acharacle
L. Sunart
Morar, Moidart & Ardnamurchan
Shona I.
Kinlochmoidart
Loch Shiel
Strontian
Loch Linnhe
Lochaline
Claggan
Pt. of Stoer
Stoer
Enard B.
Rubha Coigeach
Achiltibuie
HYDROPONICUM GARDENS
Gruinard B.
Greenstone Pt.
L. Ewe
Cove
Aultbea
Melvaig
INVEREWE GARDEN
Poolewe
Fionn Loch
Longa I.
Gairloch
L. Gairloch
L. Maree
Wester Ross
Kerrysdale
Port Henderson
Talladale
Red Point
L. Torridon
Kinlochewe
Torridon
Shieldaig
Achnashellach
Applecross
Coulags
Lochcarron
ATTADALE GARDENS
Ardarroch
L. Carron
Stromeferry
WOODLAND GARDEN
Kyle of Lochalsh
CASTLE MOIL
Auchtertyre
Dornie
L. Alsh
Kyleakin
EILEAN DONAN CASTLE
Glenelg
Shiel Br
Kylerhea
KNOCK CASTLE
Teangue
Sd. of Sleat
L. Hourn
Armadale
ARMADALE GARDENS
Knoydart
Quoich
Pt. of Sleat
Mallaig
L. Nevis
Murlag
Arisaig
L. Morar
Glenfinnan
Lochailort
LOCH NAN UAMH CAIRN
882 Rhois-Bheinn
32
34
857
858
859
865
866
867
855
87
850
863
851
888
830
861
884
848
832
896
890
62
29
24
27
20
18
46
30
28
21
12
8
15
23
51
32
34
53
48
38
16
24
18

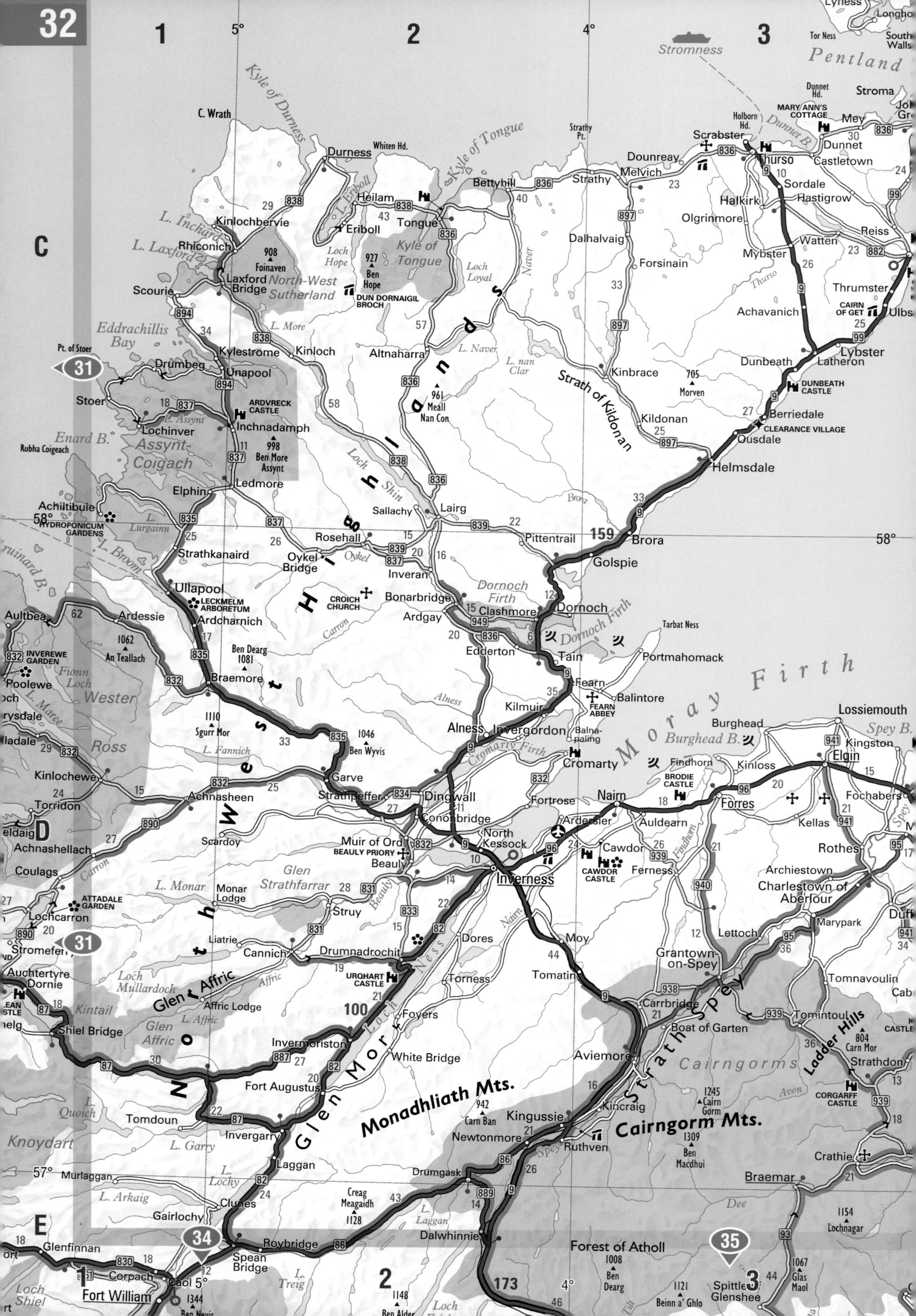
1
2
3
5°
4°
C
D
E
Stromness
Lyness
Longhope
Tor Ness
South Walls
Pentland
Stroma
Dunnet Hd.
MARY ANN'S COTTAGE
Mey
Dunnet
Dunnet B.
Holborn Hd.
Scrabster
Thurso
Castletown
Dounreay
Melvich
Strathy Pt.
Strathy
Bettyhill
Sordale
Halkirk
Hastigrow
Olgrinmore
Reiss
Watten
Mybster
Dalhalvaig
Forsinain
Thrumster
CAIRN OF GET
Ulbster
Achavanich
Lybster
Latheron
Dunbeath
DUNBEATH CASTLE
Kinbrace
705 Morven
Strath of Kildonan
Kildonan
Berriedale
CLEARANCE VILLAGE
Ousdale
Helmsdale
Brora
Pittentrail
Golspie
58°
C. Wrath
Kyle of Durness
Durness
Whiten Hd.
Kyle of Tongue
L. Eriboll
Heilam
Tongue
Eriboll
Loch Hope
927 Ben Hope
DUN DORNAIGIL BROCH
Loch Loyal
Naver
L. Naver
L. nan Clar
Altnaharra
961 Meall Nan Con
Kinlochbervie
L. Inchard
Rhiconich
L. Laxford
908 Foinaven
Laxford Bridge
North-West Sutherland
Scourie
Eddrachillis Bay
Pt. of Stoer
L. More
Kinloch
Kylestrome
Drumbeg
Unapool
Stoer
ARDVRECK CASTLE
L. Assynt
Lochinver
Inchnadamph
998 Ben More Assynt
Enard B.
Assynt-Coigach
Rubha Coigeach
Loch Shin
Ledmore
Elphin
Achiltibuie
HYDROPONICUM GARDENS
L. Lurgainn
Sallachy
Lairg
Brora
Rosehall
Oykel Bridge
Oykel
Strathkanaird
L. Broom
Gruinard B.
Inveran
Ullapool
LECKMELM ARBORETUM
Ardcharnich
CROICH CHURCH
Bonarbridge
Dornoch Firth
Dornoch
Clashmore
Ardgay
Carron
Edderton
Tain
Tarbat Ness
Portmahomack
Aultbea
Ardessie
1062 An Teallach
INVEREWE GARDEN
Fionn Loch
Poolewe
L. Maree
Wester Ross
Ben Dearg 1081
Braemore
1110 Sgurr Mor
L. Fannich
1046 Ben Wyvis
Alness
Fearn
FEARN ABBEY
Balintore
Kilmuir
Invergordon
Balnapaling
Cromarty Firth
Cromarty
Moray Firth
Burghead
Burghead B.
Lossiemouth
Spey B.
Kingston
Findhorn
BRODIE CASTLE
Kinloss
Elgin
Fochabers
Forres
Kellas
Rothes
Kinlochewe
Torridon
Achnasheen
Garve
Strathpeffer
Dingwall
Conon Bridge
Fortrose
Nairn
Ardersier
Auldearn
North Kessock
Cawdor
CAWDOR CASTLE
Ferness
Findhorn
Scardoy
Muir of Ord
BEAULY PRIORY
Beauly
Inverness
Achnashellach
Coulags
Glen Strathfarrar
L. Monar
Monar Lodge
ATTADALE GARDEN
Lochcarron
Struy
Archiestown
Charlestown of Aberlour
Marypark
Dores
Moy
Liatrie
Cannich
Drumnadrochit
Stromeferry
Auchtertyre
Dornie
Loch Mullardoch
Glen Affric
Affric Lodge
URQUHART CASTLE
Torness
Tomatin
Grantown-on-Spey
Lettoch
Tomnavoulin
Kintail
Shiel Bridge
Glen Affric
L. Affric
Foyers
Loch Ness
Carrbridge
Boat of Garten
Tomintoul
Ladder Hills
804 Carn Mor
Strathdon
Invermoriston
White Bridge
Glen Mor
Aviemore
Strath Spey
Cairngorms
Avon
CORGARFF CASTLE
Fort Augustus
Monadhliath Mts.
942 Carn Ban
Kincraig
1245 Cairn Gorm
L. Quoich
Tomdoun
Kingussie
Newtonmore
Ruthven
Cairngorm Mts.
1309 Ben Macdhui
Knoydart
Invergarry
L. Garry
Spey
Crathie
Laggan
Drumgask
Braemar
57°
Murlaggan
L. Lochy
Creag Meagaidh 1128
L. Laggan
Dee
L. Arkaig
Clunes
Gairlochy
Dalwhinnie
1154 Lochnagar
Glenfinnan
Roybridge
Spean Bridge
Forest of Atholl
1008 Ben Dearg
Corpach
Caol
Loch Shiel
Fort William
1344 Ben Nevis
L. Treig
1148 Ben Alder
1121 Beinn a' Ghlo
Spittle of Glenshee
1067 Glas Maol
Till
North West Highlands
31
34
35
159
100
173

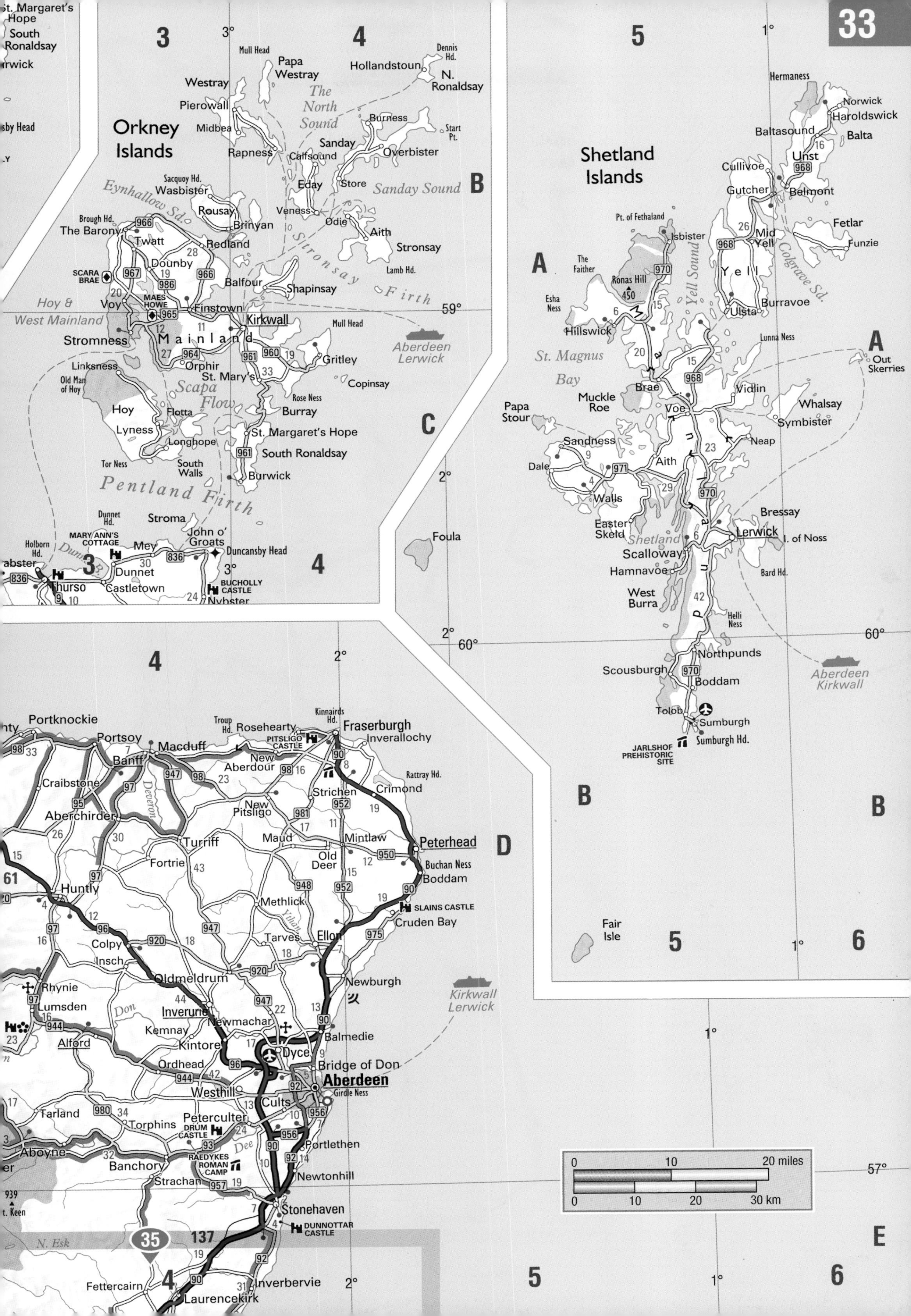
Orkney Islands
Westray
Papa Westray
Mull Head
Hollandstoun
Dennis Hd.
N. Ronaldsay
Pierowall
Midbea
The North Sound
Burness
Start Pt.
Sanday
Rapness
Calfsound
Overbister
Eday
Store
Sanday Sound
Sacquoy Hd.
Wasbister
Eynhallow Sd.
Rousay
Veness
Odie
Brinyan
Brough Hd.
The Barony
Twatt
Redland
Aith
Stronsay
Stronsay Firth
Dounby
Lamb Hd.
SCARA BRAE
Balfour
Shapinsay
MAES HOWE
Hoy & West Mainland
Voy
Finstown
Kirkwall
Stromness
Mainland
Mull Head
Aberdeen Lerwick
Orphir
Gritley
Linksness
St. Mary's
Copinsay
Old Man of Hoy
Scapa Flow
Rose Ness
Hoy
Flotta
Burray
Lyness
St. Margaret's Hope
Longhope
South Ronaldsay
Tor Ness
South Walls
Burwick
Pentland Firth
Dunnet Hd.
Stroma
John o' Groats
MARY ANN'S COTTAGE
Mey
Duncansby Head
Holborn Hd.
Dunnet B.
Dunnet
Scrabster
Thurso
Castletown
BUCHOLLY CASTLE
Nybster
St. Margaret's Hope
South Ronaldsay
Burwick
Duncansby Head
Shetland Islands
Hermaness
Norwick
Haroldswick
Baltasound
Balta
Unst
Cullivoe
Gutcher
Belmont
Pt. of Fethaland
Isbister
Mid Yell
Fetlar
Funzie
The Faither
Ronas Hill 450
Yell Sound
Yell
Colgrave Sd.
Esha Ness
Burravoe
Ulsta
Hillswick
Lunna Ness
Out Skerries
St. Magnus Bay
Brae
Vidlin
Muckle Roe
Whalsay
Papa Stour
Voe
Symbister
Sandness
Neap
Aith
Dale
Walls
Mainland
Bressay
Easter Skeld
Shetland
Lerwick
I. of Noss
Foula
Scalloway
Hamnavoe
Bard Hd.
West Burra
Helli Ness
Northpunds
Scousburgh
Boddam
Aberdeen Kirkwall
Tolob
Sumburgh
JARLSHOF PREHISTORIC SITE
Sumburgh Hd.
Fair Isle
Portknockie
Troup Hd.
Rosehearty
Kinnairds Hd.
Fraserburgh
Portsoy
PITSLIGO CASTLE
Inverallochy
Macduff
Banff
New Aberdour
Rattray Hd.
Craibstone
Strichen
Crimond
Deveron
New Pitsligo
Aberchirder
Maud
Mintlaw
Turriff
Peterhead
Old Deer
Fortrie
Buchan Ness
Boddam
Huntly
Methlick
SLAINS CASTLE
Cruden Bay
Ythan
Colpy
Tarves
Ellon
Insch
Rhynie
Oldmeldrum
Newburgh
Lumsden
Don
Inverurie
Kirkwall Lerwick
Kemnay
Newmachar
Alford
Kintore
Balmedie
Dyce
Ordhead
Bridge of Don
Westhill
Aberdeen
Girdle Ness
Cults
Tarland
Torphins
Peterculter
DRUM CASTLE
Aboyne
Dee
Portlethen
Banchory
RAEDYKES ROMAN CAMP
Strachan
Newtonhill
Mt. Keen
Stonehaven
DUNNOTTAR CASTLE
N. Esk
Fettercairn
Inverbervie
Laurencekirk
0 10 20 miles
0 10 20 30 km

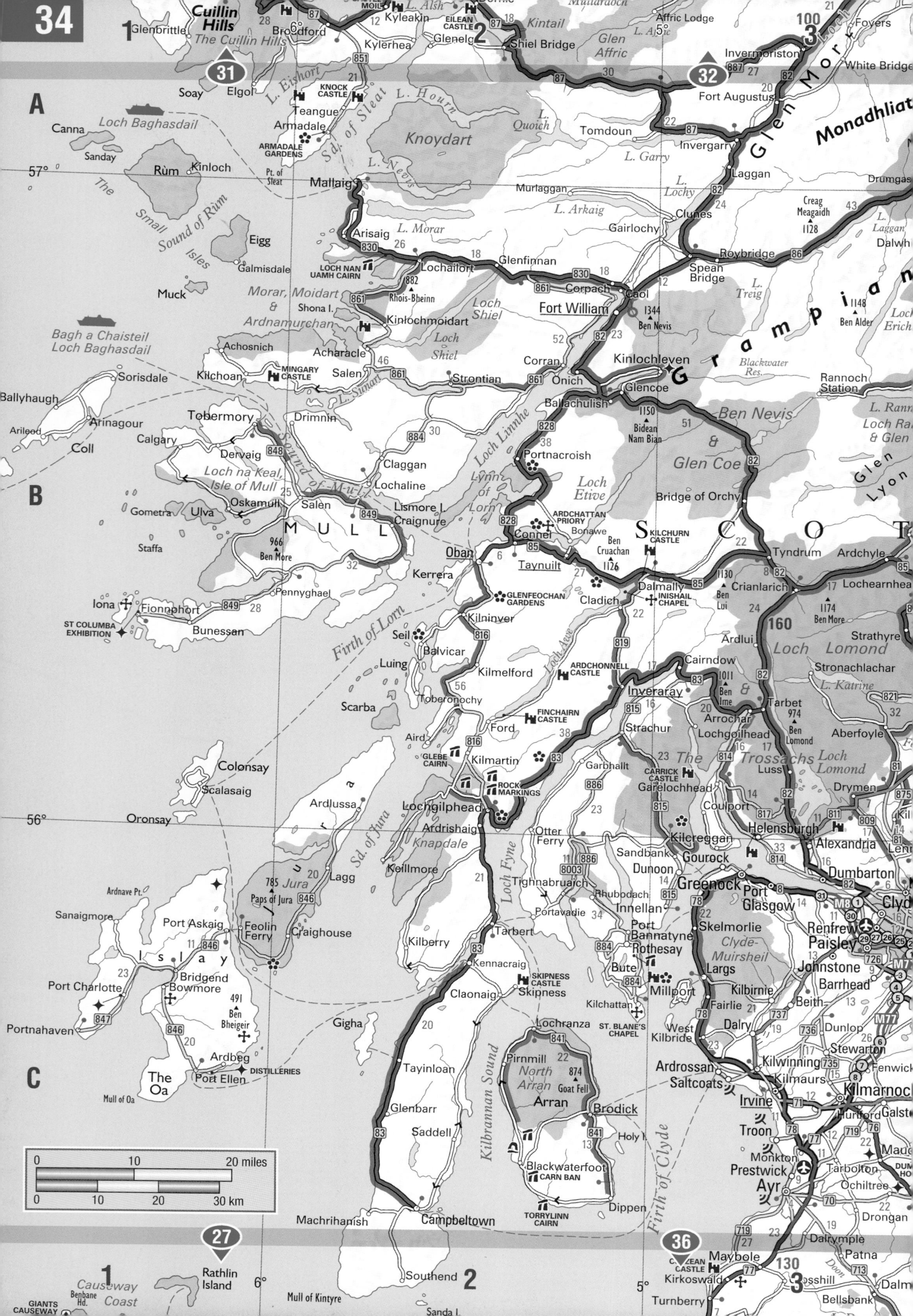

Cuillin Hills
The Cuillin Hills
Glenbrittle
Broadford
Kyleakin
Kylerhea
Eilean Castle
Glenelg
Shiel Bridge
Kintail
Glen Affric
Affric Lodge
Foyers
Invermoriston
White Bridge
Fort Augustus
Glen Mor
Monadhliath
Soay
Elgol
L. Eishort
Knock Castle
L. Hourn
Teangue
Armadale
Armadale Gardens
Sd. of Sleat
Knoydart
L. Quoich
Tomdoun
Invergarry
L. Garry
Canna
Loch Baghasdail
Sanday
Rùm
Kinloch
Pt. of Sleat
Mallaig
L. Nevis
Laggan
Murlaggan
L. Lochy
L. Arkaig
Clunes
Creag Meagaidh
1128
Drumgask
The Small Isles
Sound of Rùm
Eigg
Arisaig
L. Morar
Gairlochy
Roybridge
Spean Bridge
L. Laggan
Dalwhinnie
Galmisdale
Loch nan Uamh Cairn
Lochailort
Glenfinnan
Corpach
Caol
L. Treig
Muck
Morar, Moidart & Ardnamurchan
882
Rhois-Bheinn
Shona I.
Kinlochmoidart
Loch Shiel
Fort William
1344
Ben Nevis
Grampian
1148
Ben Alder
Loch Ericht
Bagh a Chaisteil
Loch Baghasdail
Achosnich
Acharacle
Corran
Kinlochleven
Blackwater Res.
Rannoch Station
Sorisdale
Kilchoan
Mingary Castle
Salen
L. Sunart
Strontian
Onich
Glencoe
Ballyhaugh
Ballachulish
1150
Bidean Nam Bian
Ben Nevis & Glen Coe
L. Rannoch
Loch Rannoch & Glen Lyon
Arileod
Arinagour
Coll
Tobermory
Drimnin
Calgary
Dervaig
Sound of Mull
Loch Linnhe
Portnacroish
Claggan
Lochaline
Loch na Keal, Isle of Mull
Lynn of Lorn
Loch Etive
Glen Lyon
Oskamull
Salen
Lismore I.
Craignure
Bridge of Orchy
Gometra
Ulva
Ardchattan Priory
Bonawe
Mull
Connel
Kilchurn Castle
Scotland
Staffa
966
Ben More
Oban
Ben Cruachan
1126
Taynuilt
Tyndrum
Ardchyle
Kerrera
Dalmally
1130
Ben Lui
Crianlarich
Lochearnhead
Iona
Fionnphort
Pennyghael
Glenfeochan Gardens
Cladich
Inishail Chapel
1174
Ben More
St Columba Exhibition
Bunessan
Kilninver
Seil
Firth of Lorn
Balvicar
Ardlui
Strathyre
Loch Lomond
Luing
Kilmelford
Loch Awe
Ardchonnell Castle
Cairndow
Stronachlachar
1011
Ben Ime
L. Katrine
Scarba
Toberonochy
Inveraray
Tarbet
974
Ben Lomond
Aberfoyle
Finchairn Castle
Arrochar
Ford
Strachur
Lochgoilhead
Aird
Glebe Cairn
Kilmartin
The Trossachs
Loch Lomond
Luss
Colonsay
Garbhallt
Carrick Castle
Drymen
Scalasaig
Rock Markings
Garelochhead
Jura
Ardlussa
Lochgilphead
Coulport
Oronsay
56°
Helensburgh
Ardrishaig
Sd. of Jura
Knapdale
Otter Ferry
Kilcreggan
Alexandria
Sandbank
Gourock
Dumbarton
Keillmore
Dunoon
Greenock
Port Glasgow
Clydebank
Ardnave Pt.
785
Paps of Jura
Lagg
Loch Fyne
Tighnabruaich
Rhubodach
Innellan
Sanaigmore
Port Askaig
Feolin Ferry
Craighouse
Portavadie
Port Bannatyne
Skelmorlie
Renfrew
Paisley
Islay
Kilberry
Tarbert
Rothesay
Clyde-Muirsheil
Johnstone
Bridgend
Bowmore
Kennacraig
Bute
Largs
Kilbirnie
Barrhead
Port Charlotte
491
Ben Bheigeir
Skipness Castle
Skipness
Millport
Beith
Claonaig
Kilchattan
Fairlie
Portnahaven
St. Blane's Chapel
Dalry
Dunlop
Gigha
Lochranza
West Kilbride
Stewarton
Ardbeg
Distilleries
Port Ellen
Pirnmill
North Arran
874
Goat Fell
Ardrossan
Kilwinning
Fenwick
The Oa
Tayinloan
Kilbrannan Sound
Saltcoats
Kilmaurs
Mull of Oa
Arran
Kilmarnock
Irvine
Glenbarr
Brodick
Hurlford
Galston
Troon
Saddell
Holy I.
Firth of Clyde
Monkton
Mauchline
Prestwick
Tarbolton
Blackwaterfoot
Carn Ban
Ayr
Ochiltree
Dippen
Drongan
Machrihanish
Campbeltown
Torrylinn Cairn
Dalrymple
Patna
Culzean Castle
Maybole
Kirkoswald
Dalmellington
Bellsbank
Turnberry
Southend
Mull of Kintyre
Sanda I.
Rathlin Island
Causeway Coast
Benbane Hd.
Giants Causeway
57°
6°
5°
0 10 20 miles
0 10 20 30 km

31
32
27
36
100
130
160

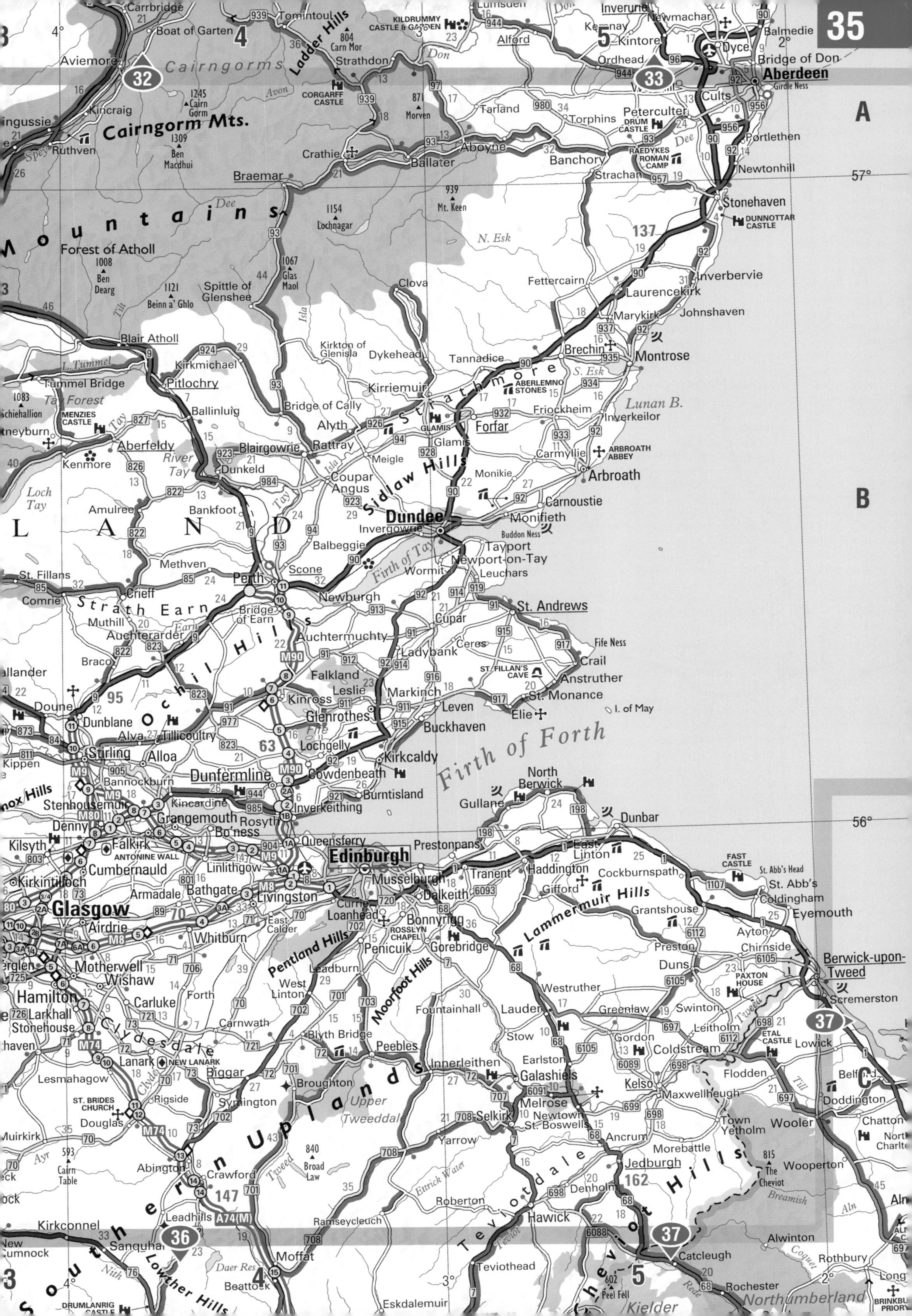
Carrbridge
Boat of Garten
Tomintoul
Ladder Hills
KILDRUMMY CASTLE & GARDEN
Lumsden
Inverurie
Newmachar
Balmedie
Aviemore
Cairngorms
804 Carn Mor
Strathdon
Don
Alford
Kemnay
Kintore
Dyce
Bridge of Don
Ordhead
Aberdeen
Girdle Ness
Kincraig
1245 Cairn Gorm
CORGARFF CASTLE
Avon
871 Morven
Tarland
Cults
Peterculter
DRUM CASTLE
Torphins
Kingussie
Cairngorm Mts.
1309 Ben Macdhui
Ruthven
Spey
Crathie
Ballater
Aboyne
Banchory
Dee
Portlethen
RAEDYKES ROMAN CAMP
Newtonhill
Braemar
Strachan
57°
939 Mt. Keen
1154 Lochnagar
Stonehaven
DUNNOTTAR CASTLE
Mountains
Forest of Atholl
1008 Ben Dearg
N. Esk
1067 Glas Maol
1121 Beinn a' Ghlo
Spittle of Glenshee
Clova
Fettercairn
Inverbervie
Laurencekirk
Johnshaven
Marykirk
Blair Atholl
L. Tummel
Tummel Bridge
Kirkmichael
Pitlochry
Kirkton of Glenisla
Dykehead
Tannadice
Brechin
Montrose
S. Esk
1083 Schiehallion
Tay Forest
MENZIES CASTLE
Ballinluig
Kirriemuir
Strathmore
ABERLEMNO STONES
Lunan B.
Bridge of Cally
Friockheim
Inverkeilor
Alyth
GLAMIS
Glamis
Forfar
Aberfeldy
Blairgowrie
Rattray
River Tay
Kenmore
Dunkeld
Meigle
Carmyllie
ARBROATH ABBEY
Arbroath
Sidlaw Hills
Coupar Angus
Monikie
Loch Tay
Amulree
Bankfoot
Carnoustie
Dundee
Monifieth
Invergowrie
Buddon Ness
Balbeggie
Tayport
Newport-on-Tay
Methven
Firth of Tay
Wormit
Leuchars
St. Fillans
Scone
Perth
Crieff
Comrie
Strath Earn
Newburgh
St. Andrews
Bridge of Earn
Muthill
Auchterarder
Auchtermuchty
Cupar
Ochil Hills
Ceres
Fife Ness
Ladybank
Braco
Crail
Falkland
ST. FILLAN'S CAVE
Anstruther
Leslie
Markinch
St. Monance
Doune
Kinross
Glenrothes
Leven
Elie
I. of May
Dunblane
Buckhaven
Alva
Tillicoultry
Stirling
Alloa
Lochgelly
Kirkcaldy
Firth of Forth
Kippen
Dunfermline
Cowdenbeath
North Berwick
Bannockburn
Burntisland
Gullane
Stenhousemuir
Kincardine
Inverkeithing
Dunbar
Denny
Grangemouth
Rosyth
Bo'ness
56°
Kilsyth
Falkirk
Queensferry
Prestonpans
East Linton
ANTONINE WALL
Edinburgh
FAST CASTLE
Cumbernauld
Linlithgow
Musselburgh
Tranent
Haddington
Cockburnspath
St. Abb's Head
Kirkintilloch
Gifford
St. Abb's
Dalkeith
Coldingham
Bathgate
Livingston
Lammermuir Hills
Eyemouth
Glasgow
Armadale
Currie
Loanhead
Grantshouse
Airdrie
East Calder
Bonnyrigg
ROSSLYN CHAPEL
Ayton
Whitburn
Penicuik
Gorebridge
Preston
Chirnside
Pentland Hills
Duns
Berwick-upon-Tweed
Motherwell
Leadburn
PAXTON HOUSE
Wishaw
Moorfoot Hills
West Linton
Westruther
Hamilton
Forth
Scremerston
Carluke
Fountainhall
Lauder
Greenlaw
Swinton
Larkhall
Stonehouse
Carnwath
Clydesdale
Blyth Bridge
Stow
Gordon
Leitholm
ETAL CASTLE
Lowick
Peebles
Coldstream
Tweed
Lanark
NEW LANARK
Innerleithen
Earlston
Galashiels
Kelso
Flodden
Lesmahagow
Biggar
Broughton
Melrose
Maxwellheugh
Doddington
ST. BRIDES CHURCH
Rigside
Symington
Upper Tweeddale
Newtown St. Boswells
Town Yetholm
Wooler
Chatton
Douglas
Selkirk
Ancrum
Muirkirk
Southern Uplands
Yarrow
Morebattle
840 Broad Law
Jedburgh
Cheviot Hills
815 The Cheviot
Wooperton
593 Cairn Table
Abington
Crawford
Ettrick Water
Teviotdale
Denholm
Breamish
Roberton
Aln
Leadhills
Kirkconnel
Ramseycleuch
Hawick
Alnwick
Alwinton
Sanquhar
New Cumnock
Moffat
Teviothead
Catcleugh
Rothbury
Coquet
Nith
Daer Res.
Lowther Hills
Beattock
602 Peel Fell
Rochester
Northumberland
Rede
Kielder
Eskdalemuir
DRUMLANRIG CASTLE
BRINKBURN PRIORY
3°
4°
2°

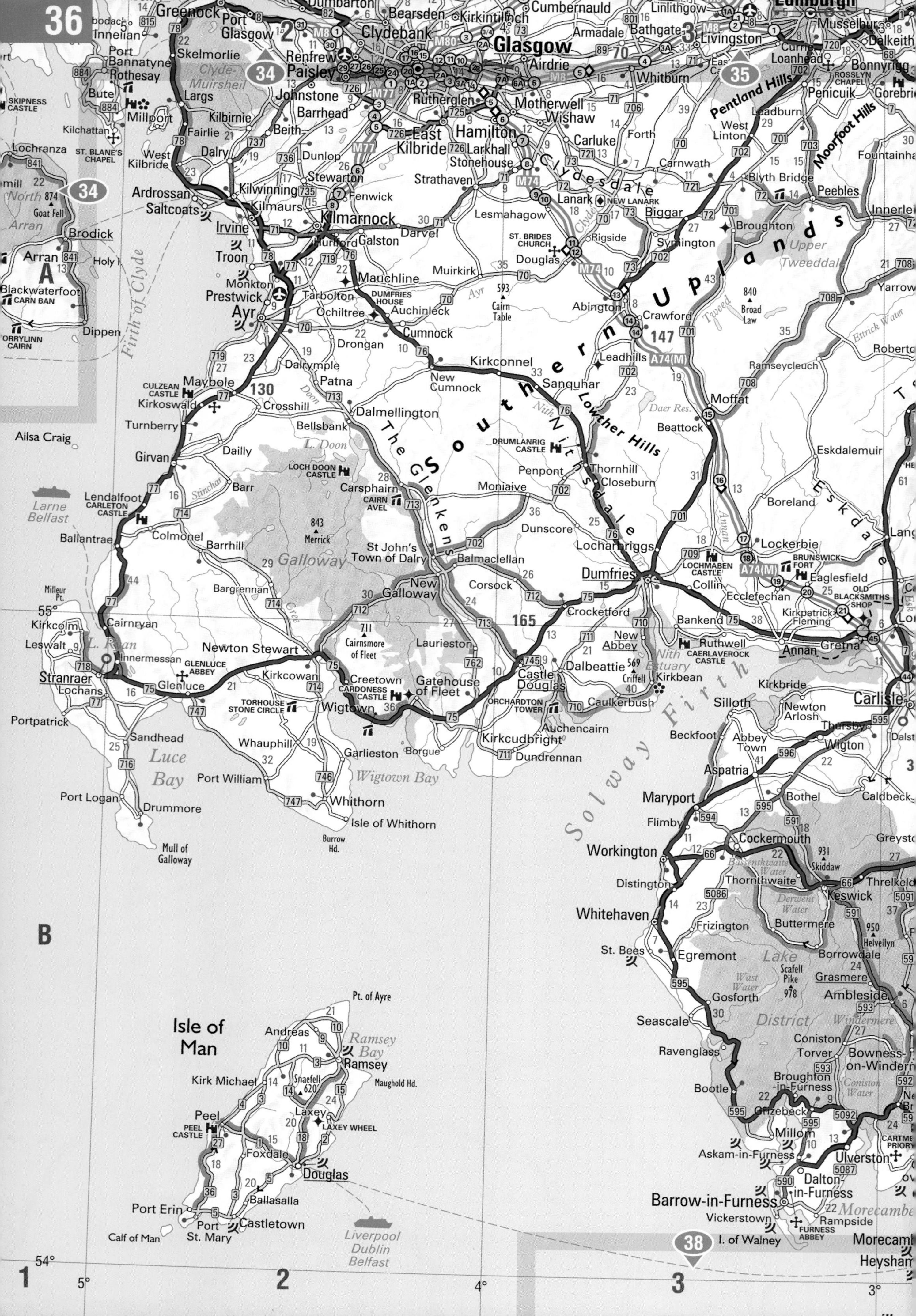
36
Greenock
Port Glasgow
Dumbarton
Bearsden
Clydebank
Kirkintilloch
Cumbernauld
Linlithgow
Edinburgh
Musselburgh
Dalkeith
Glasgow
Airdrie
Armadale
Bathgate
Livingston
Whitburn
Loanhead
Bonnyrigg
Penicuik
Gorebridge
Renfrew
Paisley
Johnstone
Barrhead
Rutherglen
Motherwell
Wishaw
East Kilbride
Hamilton
Larkhall
Stonehouse
Carluke
Forth
Carnwath
Strathaven
Lanark
NEW LANARK
Biggar
Skelmorlie
Largs
Bute
Rothesay
Port Bannatyne
Millport
Kilbirnie
Fairlie
Beith
Dalry
Dunlop
West Kilbride
Kilwinning
Stewarton
Fenwick
Ardrossan
Saltcoats
Kilmaurs
Kilmarnock
Irvine
Hurlford
Galston
Darvel
Troon
Monkton
Prestwick
Ayr
Tarbolton
Mauchline
Ochiltree
Auchinleck
Cumnock
Drongan
Dalrymple
Patna
Muirkirk
Lesmahagow
Douglas
Abington
Crawford
Leadhills
Sanquhar
Kirkconnel
New Cumnock
Lochranza
Arran
Goat Fell
Brodick
Holy I.
Blackwaterfoot
Dippen
Firth of Clyde
Maybole
Kirkoswald
CULZEAN CASTLE
Turnberry
Crosshill
Dalmellington
Bellsbank
Ailsa Craig
Girvan
Dailly
Barr
Lendalfoot
Ballantrae
Colmonel
Barrhill
Galloway
Merrick
Carsphairn
St John's Town of Dalry
Balmaclellan
New Galloway
Corsock
Moniaive
Dunscore
Penpont
Thornhill
Closeburn
Lochanbriggs
Dumfries
Southern Uplands
Lowther Hills
Nithsdale
The Glenkens
Clydesdale
Pentland Hills
Moorfoot Hills
Peebles
Broughton
Symington
Upper Tweeddale
Moffat
Beattock
Eskdalemuir
Eskdale
Boreland
Lockerbie
Lochmaben
Eaglesfield
Ecclefechan
Collin
Kirkpatrick Fleming
Annan
Gretna
Bankend
Ruthwell
CAERLAVEROCK CASTLE
New Abbey
Crocketford
Dalbeattie
Criffell
Kirkbean
Caulkerbush
Castle Douglas
Laurieston
Gatehouse of Fleet
Creetown
Newton Stewart
Kirkcowan
Wigtown
Glenluce
Cairnryan
Kirkcolm
Leswalt
Stranraer
Lochans
Portpatrick
Sandhead
Luce Bay
Port Logan
Drummore
Mull of Galloway
Port William
Whauphill
Garlieston
Whithorn
Isle of Whithorn
Wigtown Bay
Kirkcudbright
Dundrennan
Auchencairn
Solway Firth
Silloth
Kirkbride
Newton Arlosh
Carlisle
Wigton
Abbey Town
Beckfoot
Aspatria
Maryport
Bothel
Caldbeck
Flimby
Workington
Cockermouth
Skiddaw
Keswick
Thornthwaite
Threlkeld
Distington
Whitehaven
Frizington
Buttermere
Helvellyn
St. Bees
Egremont
Lake District
Borrowdale
Grasmere
Ambleside
Scafell Pike
Gosforth
Seascale
Ravenglass
Coniston
Torver
Bowness-on-Windermere
Broughton-in-Furness
Bootle
Grizebeck
Millom
Askam-in-Furness
Ulverston
Dalton-in-Furness
Barrow-in-Furness
Vickerstown
Rampside
FURNESS ABBEY
I. of Walney
Morecambe
Heysham
Isle of Man
Pt. of Ayre
Andreas
Ramsey
Ramsey Bay
Maughold Hd.
Kirk Michael
Snaefell
Laxey
LAXEY WHEEL
Peel
PEEL CASTLE
Foxdale
Douglas
Ballasalla
Port Erin
Castletown
Port St. Mary
Calf of Man
Liverpool
Dublin
Belfast
Larne
B
1
2
3
54°
55°
5°
4°
3°

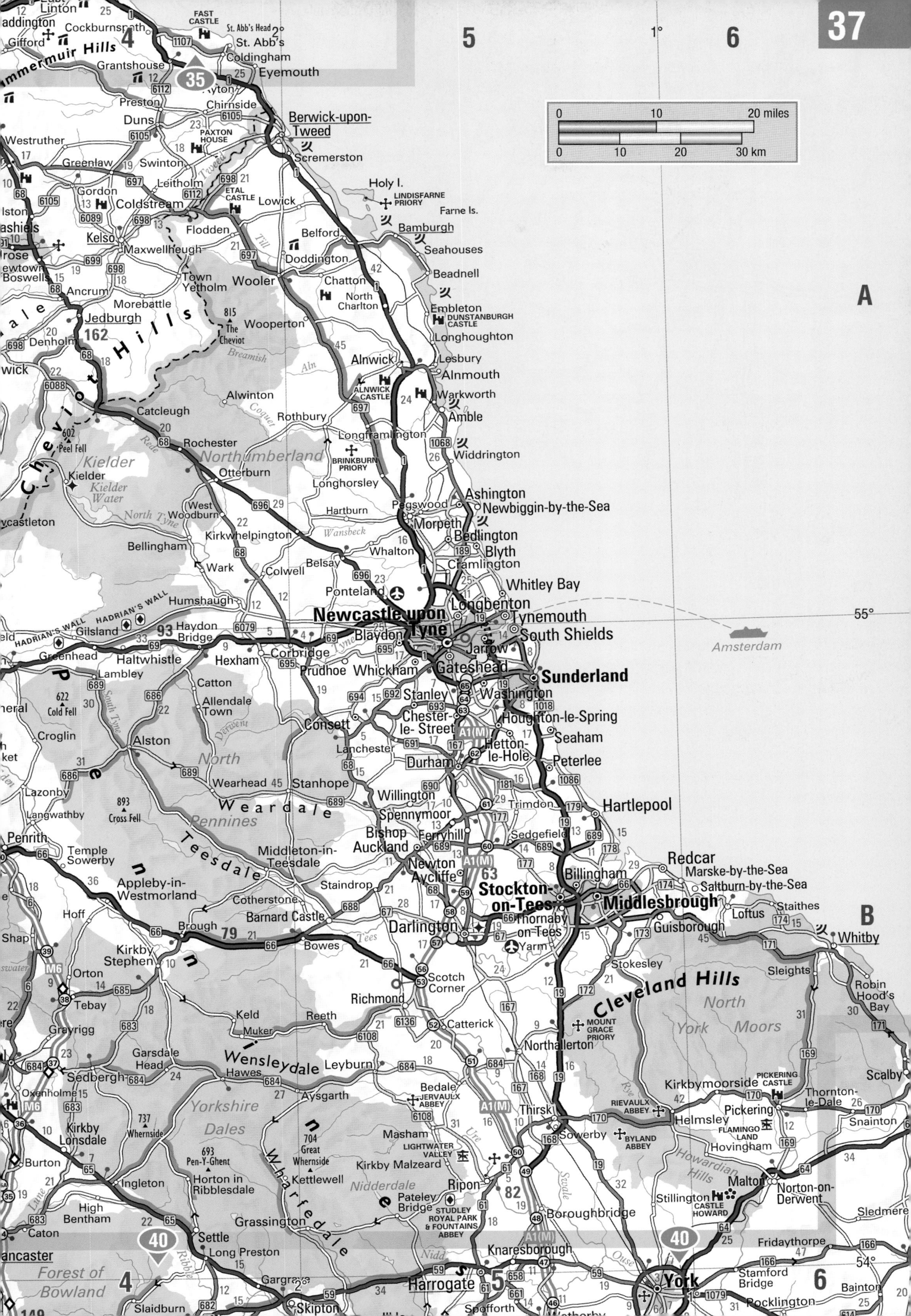

0 10 20 miles
0 10 20 30 km
Linton
Haddington
Cockburnspath
Gifford
Lammermuir Hills
FAST CASTLE
St. Abb's Head
St. Abb's
Coldingham
Grantshouse
Eyemouth
35
Ayton
Preston
Chirnside
Duns
Berwick-upon-Tweed
PAXTON HOUSE
Westruther
Scremerston
Greenlaw
Swinton
Tweed
Leitholm
Gordon
ETAL CASTLE
Lowick
Coldstream
Holy I.
LINDISFARNE PRIORY
Farne Is.
Bamburgh
Kelso
Flodden
Belford
Maxwellheugh
Seahouses
Doddington
Till
Beadnell
Boswells
Ancrum
Town Yetholm
Wooler
Chatton
North Charlton
Morebattle
Jedburgh
162
Cheviot Hills
815 The Cheviot
Wooperton
Embleton
DUNSTANBURGH CASTLE
Longhoughton
Denholm
Breamish
Aln
Alnwick
Lesbury
Alnmouth
ALNWICK CASTLE
Warkworth
Alwinton
Catcleugh
Coquet
Rothbury
Amble
Longframlington
602 Peel Fell
Rochester
Rede
Widdrington
Kielder
Northumberland
BRINKBURN PRIORY
Kielder Water
Otterburn
Longhorsley
Ashington
Newbiggin-by-the-Sea
Pegswood
Morpeth
Newcastleton
West Woodburn
North Tyne
Hartburn
Kirkwhelpington
Wansbeck
Bedlington
Bellingham
Whalton
Blyth
Wark
Colwell
Belsay
Cramlington
Ponteland
Whitley Bay
HADRIAN'S WALL
Humshaugh
Longbenton
Newcastle upon Tyne
Tynemouth
55°
Gilsland
93
Haydon Bridge
Blaydon
South Shields
Amsterdam
Greenhead
Haltwhistle
Hexham
Corbridge
Jarrow
Gateshead
Sunderland
Lambley
Prudhoe
Whickham
Catton
Stanley
Washington
622 Cold Fell
Allendale Town
South Tyne
Chester-le-Street
Houghton-le-Spring
Consett
Seaham
Croglin
Alston
Derwent
Lanchester
Hetton-le-Hole
North Pennines
Durham
Peterlee
Wearhead
Stanhope
Lazonby
Willington
Hartlepool
893 Cross Fell
Langwathby
Weardale
Trimdon
Spennymoor
Bishop Auckland
Ferryhill
Sedgefield
Penrith
Temple Sowerby
Middleton-in-Teesdale
Teesdale
Newton Aycliffe
Redcar
Marske-by-the-Sea
Appleby-in-Westmorland
Staindrop
Billingham
63
Stockton-on-Tees
Saltburn-by-the-Sea
Middlesbrough
Cotherstone
Staithes
Loftus
Hoff
Barnard Castle
Darlington
Thornaby-on-Tees
Guisborough
Whitby
Shap
Brough
79
Tees
Bowes
Yarm
Kirkby Stephen
Stokesley
Sleights
Orton
Scotch Corner
Cleveland Hills
Robin Hood's Bay
Tebay
Richmond
North York Moors
Keld
Reeth
Muker
Catterick
MOUNT GRACE PRIORY
Grayrigg
Garsdale Head
Northallerton
Wensleydale
Leyburn
Sedbergh
Hawes
Scalby
Oxenholme
Aysgarth
Bedale
Kirkbymoorside
PICKERING CASTLE
Thornton-le-Dale
Yorkshire Dales
JERVAULX ABBEY
Thirsk
RIEVAULX ABBEY
Pickering
737 Whernside
Helmsley
Kirkby Lonsdale
Sowerby
FLAMINGO LAND
Snainton
704 Great Whernside
Masham
BYLAND ABBEY
693 Pen-Y-Ghent
LIGHTWATER VALLEY
Hovingham
Howardian Hills
Burton
Kirkby Malzeard
Malton
Ingleton
Horton in Ribblesdale
Kettlewell
Nidderdale
Ripon
Norton-on-Derwent
Wharfedale
Stillington
CASTLE HOWARD
High Bentham
Pateley Bridge
STUDLEY ROYAL PARK & FOUNTAINS ABBEY
82
Boroughbridge
Caton
Grassington
Sledmere
Settle
40
Fridaythorpe
Lancaster
Long Preston
Knaresborough
54°
Forest of Bowland
Gargrave
Harrogate
York
Stamford Bridge
Bainton
Slaidburn
Skipton
Spofforth
Pocklington
A
B

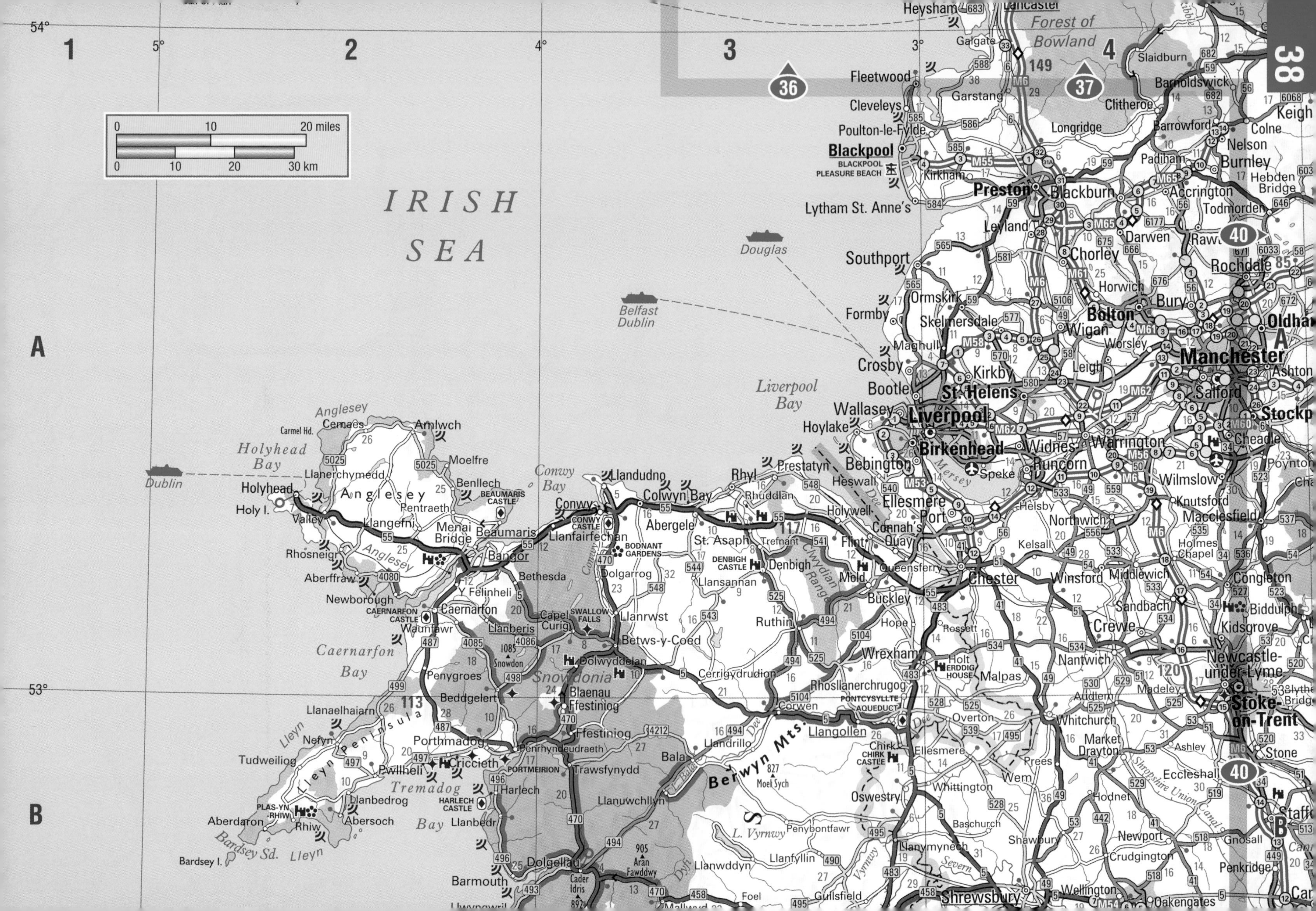

IRISH SEA
Liverpool Bay
Conwy Bay
Holyhead Bay
Caernarfon Bay
Tremadog Bay
Bardsey Sd.
Forest of Bowland
Anglesey
Lleyn Peninsula
Snowdonia
Berwyn Mts.
Clwydian Range
Mersey
Dee
Douglas
Belfast Dublin
Dublin
0 10 20 miles
0 10 20 30 km
Heysham
Lancaster
Fleetwood
Cleveleys
Poulton-le-Fylde
Blackpool
BLACKPOOL PLEASURE BEACH
Kirkham
Lytham St. Anne's
Garstang
Longridge
Clitheroe
Slaidburn
Barnoldswick
Barrowford
Colne
Nelson
Burnley
Padiham
Hebden Bridge
Todmorden
Accrington
Preston
Blackburn
Darwen
Leyland
Chorley
Horwich
Bury
Rochdale
Southport
Ormskirk
Formby
Skelmersdale
Wigan
Bolton
Worsley
Maghull
Crosby
Bootle
Kirkby
St. Helens
Leigh
Manchester
Salford
Ashton
Stockport
Cheadle
Wallasey
Liverpool
Birkenhead
Hoylake
Widnes
Warrington
Bebington
Speke
Runcorn
Wilmslow
Knutsford
Macclesfield
Heswall
Ellesmere Port
Helsby
Northwich
Holmes Chapel
Congleton
Prestatyn
Rhyl
Rhuddlan
Holywell
Connah's Quay
Flint
Queensferry
Chester
Kelsall
Winsford
Middlewich
Sandbach
Biddulph
Kidsgrove
Crewe
Mold
Buckley
Hope
Rossett
Wrexham
Holt
ERDDIG HOUSE
Malpas
Nantwich
Audlem
Madeley
Newcastle-under-Lyme
Stoke-on-Trent
Stone
Llandudno
Colwyn Bay
Abergele
St. Asaph
Trefnant
Denbigh
DENBIGH CASTLE
Llansannan
Ruthin
Conwy
CONWY CASTLE
Llanfairfechan
BODNANT GARDENS
Dolgarrog
Llanrwst
Betws-y-Coed
SWALLOW FALLS
Capel Curig
Dolwyddelan
Blaenau Ffestiniog
Ffestiniog
Cerrigydrudion
Corwen
Rhosllanerchrugog
PONTCYSYLLTE AQUEDUCT
Llangollen
Chirk
CHIRK CASTLE
Overton
Ellesmere
Whitchurch
Market Drayton
Ashley
Eccleshall
Oswestry
Whittington
Wem
Prees
Hodnet
Baschurch
Shawbury
Newport
Crudgington
Gnosall
Penkridge
Llanymynech
Wellington
Oakengates
Shrewsbury
Severn
Vyrnwy
L. Vyrnwy
Penybontfawr
Llanfyllin
Llanwddyn
Gullsfield
Foel
Dyfi
Llandrillo
Bala
Moel Sych
Llanuwchllyn
Aran Fawddwy
Cader Idris
Dolgellau
Barmouth
Trawsfynydd
Harlech
HARLECH CASTLE
Llanbedr
PORTMEIRION
Penrhyndeudraeth
Porthmadog
Criccieth
Pwllheli
Llanbedrog
Abersoch
Rhiw
PLAS-YN-RHIW
Aberdaron
Bardsey I.
Tudweiliog
Nefyn
Llanaelhaearn
Beddgelert
Penygroes
Snowdon
Llanberis
Bethesda
Y Felinheli
Caernarfon
CAERNARFON CASTLE
Waunfawr
Newborough
Aberffraw
Rhosneigr
Bangor
Menai Bridge
Beaumaris
BEAUMARIS CASTLE
Benllech
Moelfre
Pentraeth
Llangefni
Amlwch
Cemaes
Carmel Hd.
Llanerchymedd
Holyhead
Holy I.
Valley
54°
53°
5°
4°
3°
1
2
3
4
A
B
36
37
40

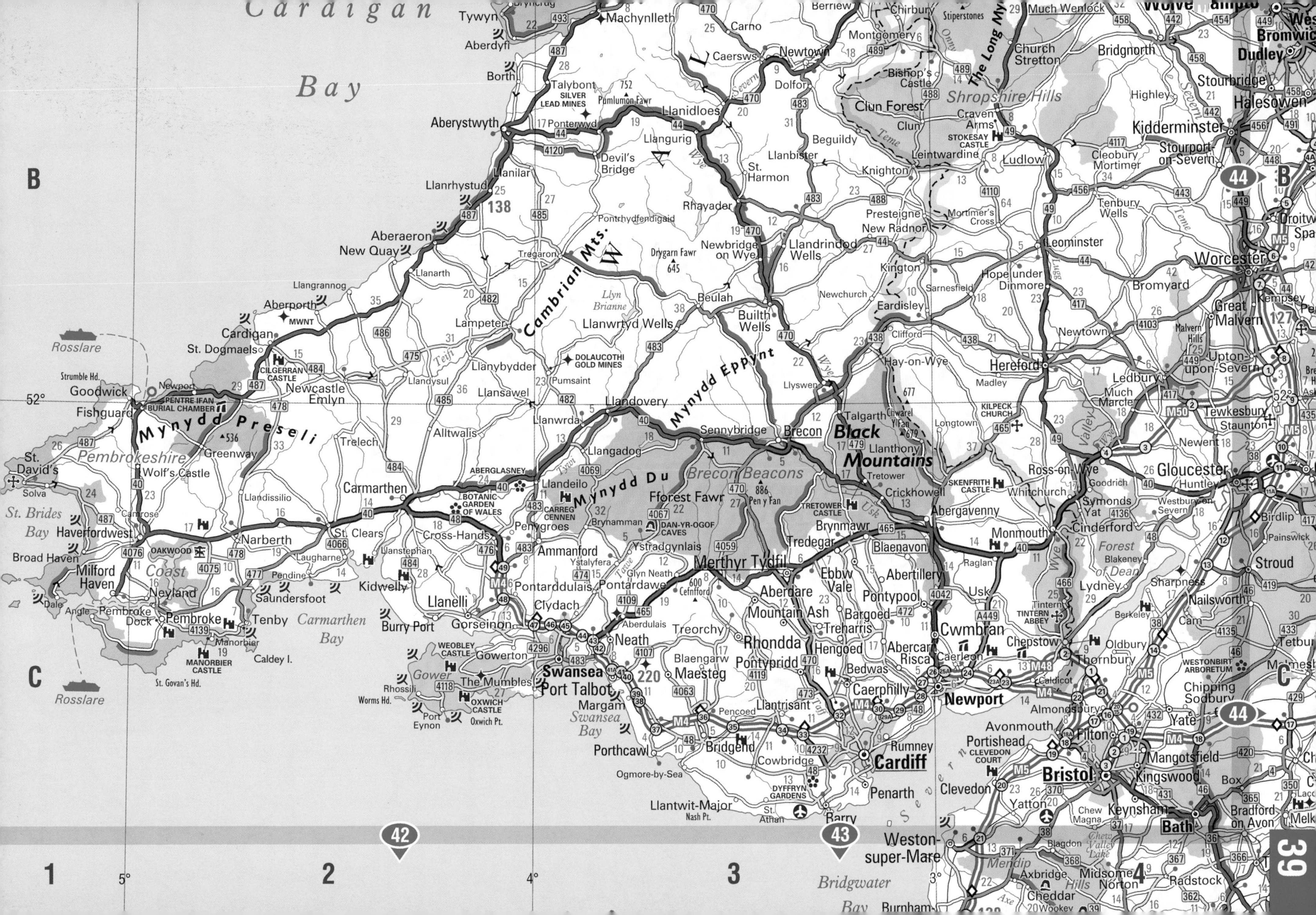
Cardigan Bay
Tywyn
Aberdyfi
Machynlleth
Borth
Talybont
SILVER LEAD MINES
Pumlumon Fawr
Aberystwyth
Ponterwyd
Devil's Bridge
Llanidloes
Llangurig
Caersws
Carno
Newtown
Dolfor
Montgomery
Chirbury
Stiperstones
The Long Mynd
Church Stretton
Much Wenlock
Bridgnorth
Bishop's Castle
Clun Forest
Clun
Shropshire Hills
Craven Arms
STOKESAY CASTLE
Leintwardine
Ludlow
Beguildy
Llanbister
Knighton
St. Harmon
Rhayader
Llanilar
Llanrhystud
Aberaeron
New Quay
Llanarth
Llangrannog
Aberporth
MWNT
Cardigan
St. Dogmaels
CILGERRAN CASTLE
Newcastle Emlyn
Rosslare
Strumble Hd.
Goodwick
Fishguard
Newport
PENTRE IFAN BURIAL CHAMBER
Mynydd Preseli
Pembrokeshire
St. David's
Solva
St. Brides Bay
Haverfordwest
Broad Haven
Milford Haven
Dale
Angle
Pembroke Dock
Pembroke
Neyland
MANORBIER CASTLE
Manorbier
St. Govan's Hd.
Tenby
Caldey I.
Saundersfoot
Narberth
OAKWOOD
Coast
Wolf's Castle
Greenway
Trelech
St. Clears
Laugharne
Pendine
Carmarthen Bay
Carmarthen
Kidwelly
Llanstephan
Cross-Hands
Llanelli
Burry Port
Gorseinon
Gower
Rhossili
Worms Hd.
Port Eynon
OXWICH CASTLE
Oxwich Pt.
WEOBLEY CASTLE
Gowerton
The Mumbles
Swansea
Swansea Bay
Port Talbot
Margam
Porthcawl
Neath
Pontardawe
Pontarddulais
Clydach
Ammanford
Penygroes
Llandeilo
CARREG CENNEN CASTLE
BOTANIC GARDEN OF WALES
ABERGLASNEY
Llangadog
Llandovery
Llanwrda
Llansawel
Pumsaint
DOLAUCOTHI GOLD MINES
Llanybydder
Lampeter
Llandysul
Alltwalis
Tregaron
Pontrhydfendigaid
Cambrian Mts.
Drygarn Fawr
Llyn Brianne
Llanwrtyd Wells
Beulah
Builth Wells
Newbridge on Wye
Llandrindod Wells
Mynydd Eppynt
Sennybridge
Brecon
Brecon Beacons
Pen y Fan
Fforest Fawr
Mynydd Du
Brynamman
DAN-YR-OGOF CAVES
Ystradgynlais
Ystalyfera
Glyn Neath
Merthyr Tydfil
Aberdare
Mountain Ash
Treorchy
Rhondda
Maesteg
Pontypridd
Bridgend
Cowbridge
Llantrisant
Pencoed
Ogmore-by-Sea
Llantwit-Major
Nash Pt.
St. Athan
DYFFRYN GARDENS
Barry
Penarth
Cardiff
Rumney
Caerphilly
Bedwas
Hengoed
Treharris
Bargoed
Abercarn
Risca
Tredegar
Ebbw Vale
Brynmawr
Blaenavon
Abertillery
Pontypool
Cwmbran
Caerleon
Newport
Usk
Raglan
Monmouth
Abergavenny
Crickhowell
TRETOWER CASTLE
Tretower
Talgarth
Black Mountains
Llanthony
Hay-on-Wye
Clifford
Llyswen
Eardisley
Kington
New Radnor
Presteigne
Newchurch
Sarnesfield
Mortimer's Cross
Leominster
Hope under Dinmore
Hereford
Madley
KILPECK CHURCH
Longtown
SKENFRITH CASTLE
Ross-on-Wye
Whitchurch
Goodrich
Symonds Yat
Cinderford
Forest of Dean
Blakeney
Lydney
Chepstow
TINTERN ABBEY
Tintern
Caldicot
Thornbury
Oldbury
Berkeley
Sharpness
Westbury-on-Severn
Gloucester
Huntley
Newent
Ledbury
Much Marcle
Newtown
Bromyard
Tenbury Wells
Cleobury Mortimer
Kidderminster
Stourport-on-Severn
Highley
Stourbridge
Halesowen
Dudley
Worcester
Droitwich Spa
Great Malvern
Malvern Hills
Kempsey
Upton-upon-Severn
Tewkesbury
Staunton
Birdlip
Painswick
Stroud
Nailsworth
Cam
Tetbury
WESTONBIRT ARBORETUM
Malmesbury
Chipping Sodbury
Yate
Almondsbury
Avonmouth
Filton
Mangotsfield
Kingswood
Bristol
Portishead
CLEVEDON COURT
Clevedon
Yatton
Keynsham
Bath
Bradford on Avon
Box
Chew Magna
Chew Valley Lake
Blagdon
Radstock
Midsomer Norton
Mendip Hills
Axbridge
Cheddar
Wookey
Weston-super-Mare
Bridgwater Bay
Burnham
Severn
Teme
Wye
Lugg
Usk
Tawe
Teifi
Tywi
B
C
1
2
3
4
42
43
44
52°
5°
4°
3°

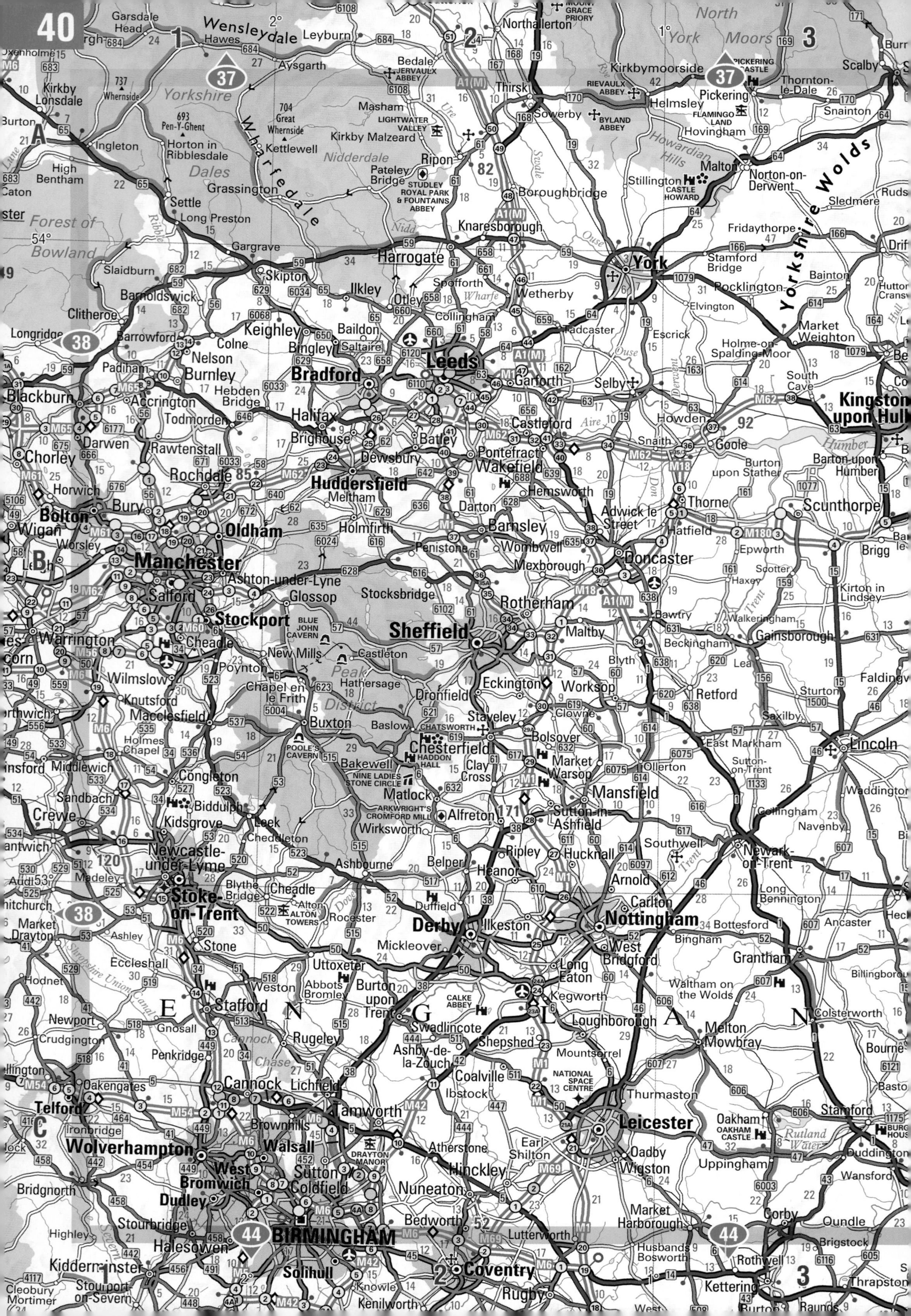
Wensleydale
Yorkshire Dales
Forest of Bowland
Wharfedale
Nidderdale
North York Moors
Howardian Hills
Yorkshire Wolds
Peak District
York
Leeds
Bradford
Harrogate
Manchester
Sheffield
Kingston upon Hull
Nottingham
Derby
Leicester
Stoke-on-Trent
Wolverhampton
BIRMINGHAM
Coventry
Lincoln
Doncaster
Huddersfield
Oldham
Stockport
Rotherham
Barnsley
Wakefield
Mansfield
Chesterfield
ENGLAND

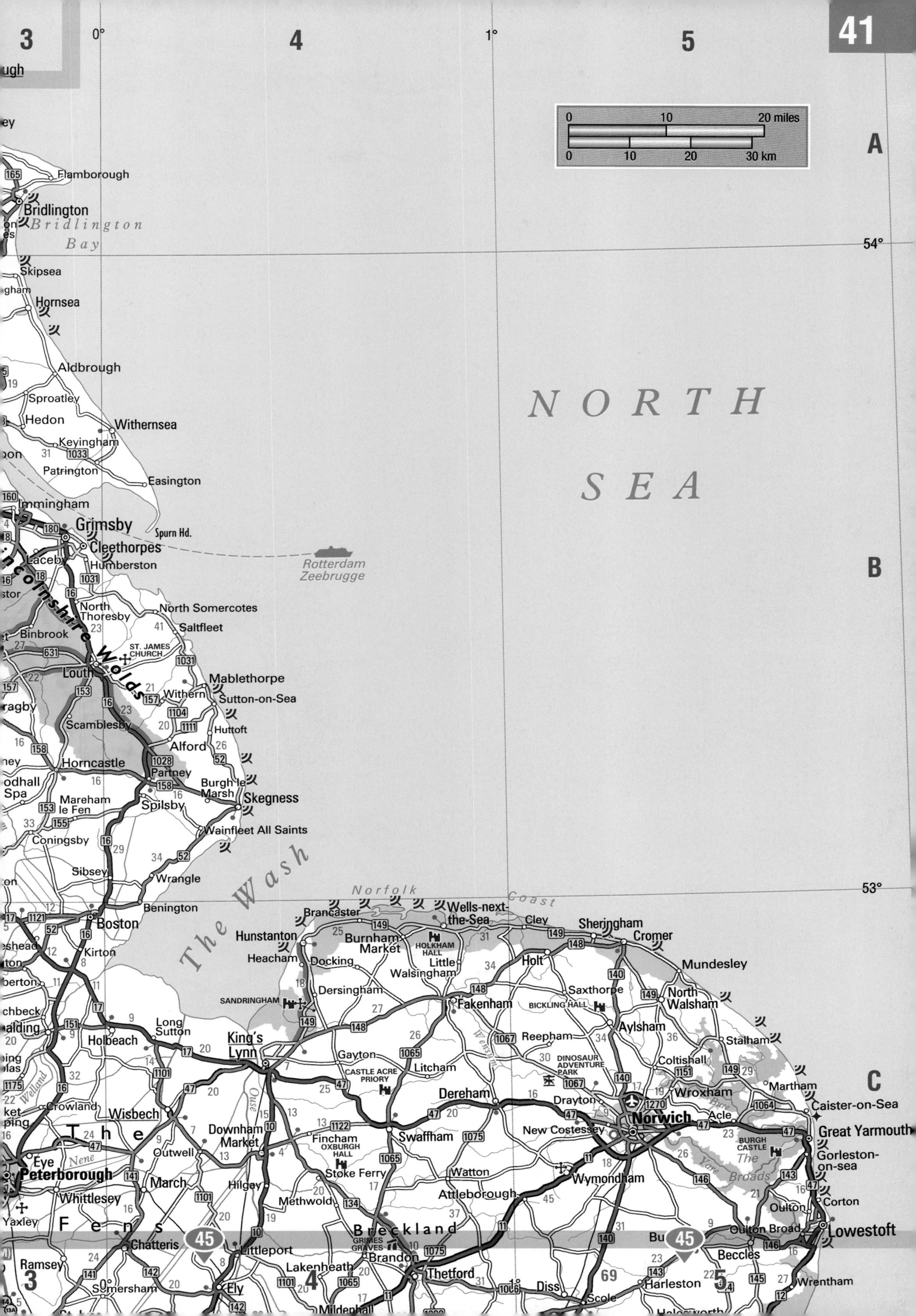

3 0° 4 1° 5

A

54°

NORTH

SEA

0 10 20 miles
0 10 20 30 km

B

Flamborough
Bridlington
Bridlington Bay

Skipsea
Hornsea
Aldbrough
Sproatley
Hedon
Withernsea
Keyingham
31 1033
Patrington
Easington
Immingham
160
Grimsby
180
Spurn Hd.
Cleethorpes
Humberston
Laceby
Rotterdam
Zeebrugge
Lincolnshire Wolds
18
1031
16
North Thoresby
North Somercotes
Binbrook
23
41
Saltfleet
631
27
ST. JAMES CHURCH
1031
22
Louth
153
21
Mablethorpe
16
157
157
Withern
Sutton-on-Sea
23
1104
157
Scamblesby
20
111
Huttoft
16
158
Alford
26
52
Horncastle
1028
Partney
Burgh le Marsh
16
158
Skegness
153
155
Mareham le Fen
Spilsby
16
Coningsby
16
29
34
52
Wainfleet All Saints
Sibsey
Wrangle
Norfolk Coast
53°

The Wash

12
Benington
1121
Boston
Brancaster
Wells-next-the-Sea
Cley
Sheringham
52
16
Hunstanton
25
Burnham Market
149
31
148
Cromer
Kirton
12
Heacham
HOLKHAM HALL
Mundesley
11
Docking
Little Walsingham
34
Holt
140
17
Dersingham
148
Saxthorpe
North Walsham
151
9
Long Sutton
18
SANDRINGHAM
27
Fakenham
BICKLING HALL
149
29
Holbeach
17
149
148
1067
Reepham
34
Coltishall
151
Stalham
1101
King's Lynn
7
Gayton
26
30
Aylsham
36
Martham
1175
20
CASTLE ACRE PRIORY
1065
Litcham
DINOSAUR ADVENTURE PARK
140
19
Wroxham
1064
Caister-on-Sea
16
Crowland
Wisbech
25
47
1067
17
Martham
Ouse
47
Dereham
16
Drayton
23
Great Yarmouth
24
15
13
Swaffham
1075
New Costessey
Norwich
BURGH CASTLE
Gorleston-on-sea
Downham Market
13
1122
47
1270
9
47
143
Eye
Nene
Outwell
4
Fincham
OXBURGH HALL
1065
Watton
Wymondham
26
The Broads
16
Peterborough
141
March
Hilgey
Stoke Ferry
17
1065
11
18
146
21
Oulton
Corton
Whittlesey
1101
Methwold
134
Attleborough
45
31
47
Yaxley
F e n s
20
10
B r e c k l a n d
11
140
Oulton Broad
146
Lowestoft
Chatteris
45
Littleport
GRIMES GRAVES
Brandon
1075
10
45
9
Beccles
Ramsey
24
141
142
20
8
Lakenheath
1101
1065
20
Thetford
31
69
23
143
145
27
Wrentham
Somersham
Ely
142
Mildenhall
17
Diss
Scole
Harleston
22
12

3 4 69 5

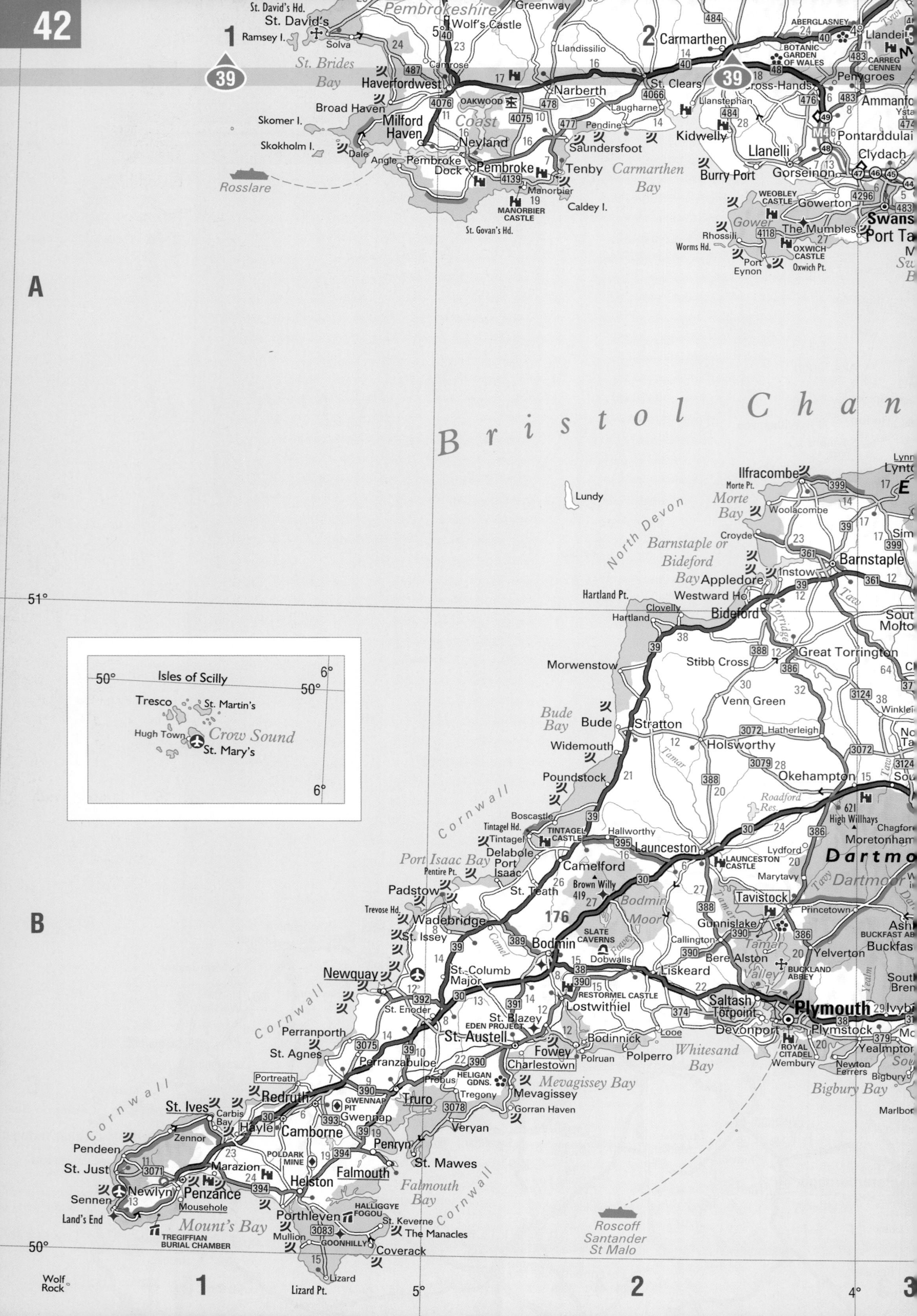

St. David's Hd.
St. David's
Ramsey I.
Solva
St. Brides Bay
Broad Haven
Skomer I.
Skokholm I.
Dale
Angle
Milford Haven
Neyland
Pembroke Dock
Pembroke
Rosslare

Pembrokeshire
Greenway
Wolf's Castle
Llandissilio
Camrose
Haverfordwest
OAKWOOD
4076
4075
477
Narberth
Laugharne
Pendine
Saundersfoot
Tenby
Manorbier
MANORBIER CASTLE
Caldey I.
St. Govan's Hd.

Carmarthen
St. Clears
4066
Kidwelly
Carmarthen Bay
Llanelli
Burry Port
Gorseinon

ABERGLASNEY
BOTANIC GARDEN OF WALES
Llanstephan
Cross Hands
Pontarddulai
Clydach
Gowerton
WEOBLEY CASTLE
Rhossili
Worms Hd.
Gower
The Mumbles
OXWICH CASTLE
Port Eynon
Oxwich Pt.
Swans
Port Ta

Llandei
CARREG CENNEN
Penygroes
Ammanfo
Ysta

A

B r i s t o l   C h a n

Lundy
North Devon

Ilfracombe
Morte Pt.
Woolacombe
Croyde
Morte Bay
Barnstaple
Instow
Appledore
Westward Ho!
Bideford
Clovelly
Hartland
Hartland Pt.
Morwenstow

Lynn
Lynto
E

Stibb Cross
Great Torrington
Venn Green
Winkle
No
Ta
Sout
Molto

51°

Isles of Scilly
Tresco
St. Martin's
Hugh Town
Crow Sound
St. Mary's
50°
6°
50°
6°
6°

Bude Bay
Bude
Stratton
Widemouth
Poundstock
Holsworthy
Hatherleigh
3072
3079
Okehampton
Roadford Res.
High Willhays
621

Dartmo
Dartmoor

Cornwall
Boscastle
Tintagel Hd.
Tintagel
TINTAGEL CASTLE
Delabole
Port Isaac
Port Isaac Bay
Pentire Pt.
Padstow
Trevose Hd.
Wadebridge
St. Issey
Hallworthy
Camelford
Brown Willy 419
Bodmin Moor
176
LAUNCESTON CASTLE
Launceston
Lydford
Marytavy
Tavistock
Princetown
Gunnislake
Callington
Bere Alston
BUCKLAND ABBEY
Chagfore
Moretonham
Buckfas
BUCKFAST ABBEY
Yelverton
Ash

B

Newquay
St. Columb Major
St. Enoder
392
Perranporth
St. Agnes
Perranzabuloe
3075
Portreath
Redruth
GWENNAP PIT
St. Ives
Carbis Bay
Zennor
Hayle
Camborne
POLDARK MINE
Pendeen
St. Just
3071
Sennen
Newlyn
Penzance
Mousehole
Land's End
Marazion
Helston
394
HALLIGGYE FOGOU
Porthleven
TREGIFFIAN BURIAL CHAMBER
Mount's Bay
Mullion
GOONHILLY
3083
Coverack
Lizard
Lizard Pt.
St. Keverne
The Manacles

St. Teath
389
Bodmin
SLATE CAVERNS
Dobwalls
RESTORMEL CASTLE
Lostwithiel
EDEN PROJECT
St. Blazey
St. Austell
Charlestown
Fowey
Polruan
Bodinnick
Looe
Polperro
Whitesand Bay
Liskeard
Saltash
Torpoint
Devonport
Plymouth
Plymstock
ROYAL CITADEL
Wembury
Newton Ferrers
Yealmpto
Sou
Bren
South
Bigbury
Ivybri
Marlbor

HELIGAN GDNS.
Tregony
Mevagissey
Gorran Haven
Mevagissey Bay
Truro
Penryn
Falmouth
St. Mawes
Veryan
Falmouth Bay
Probus
3078

Roscoff
Santander
St Malo

Bigbury Bay

Wolf Rock

50°

1
2
5°
4°

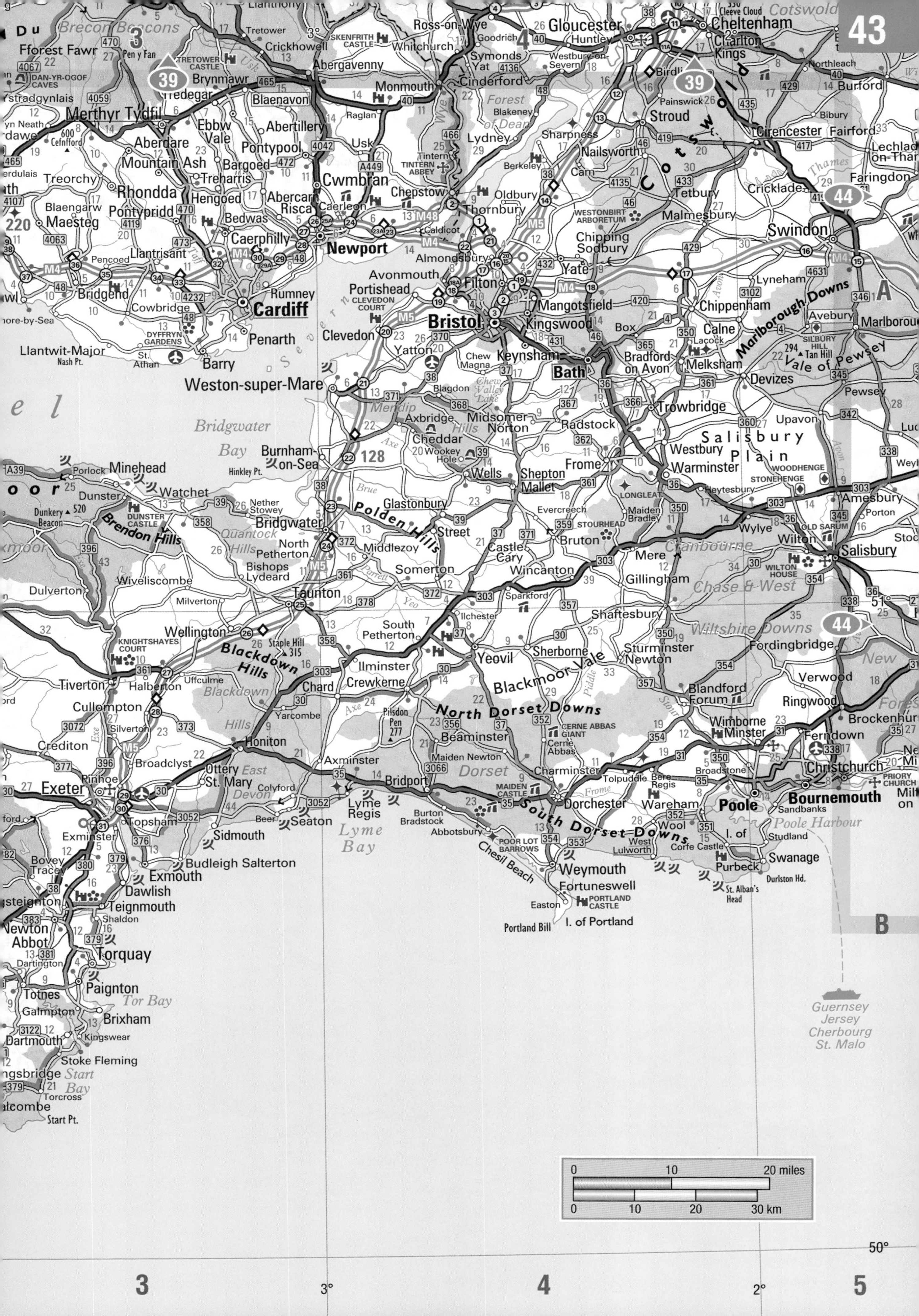
Brecon Beacons
Fforest Fawr
Pen y Fan
Tretower
Crickhowell
Tretower Castle
Skenfrith Castle
Ross-on-Wye
Goodrich
Gloucester
Huntley
Cheltenham
Charlton Kings
Cleeve Cloud
Cotswold
Northleach
Burford
Dan-yr-Ogof Caves
Ystradgynlais
Brynmawr
Abergavenny
Whitchurch
Symonds Yat
Cinderford
Westbury-on-Severn
Birdlip
Painswick
Merthyr Tydfil
Tredegar
Blaenavon
Monmouth
Raglan
Forest of Dean
Blakeney
Stroud
Bibury
Cirencester
Fairford
Lechlade on-Thames
Cefnfford
Aberdare
Ebbw Vale
Abertillery
Usk
Lydney
Sharpness
Nailsworth
Mountain Ash
Pontypool
Tintern
Tintern Abbey
Berkeley
Cam
Faringdon
Cricklade
Thames
Treorchy
Rhondda
Treharris
Bargoed
Cwmbran
Chepstow
Oldbury
Tetbury
Blaengarw
Maesteg
Pontypridd
Hengoed
Abercarn
Risca
Caerleon
Thornbury
Westonbirt Arboretum
Malmesbury
Swindon
Bedwas
Caerphilly
Newport
Caldicot
Chipping Sodbury
Llantrisant
Pencoed
Almondsbury
Yate
Avonmouth
Portishead
Clevedon Court
Filton
Lyneham
Bridgend
Cowbridge
Rumney
Cardiff
Mangotsfield
Chippenham
Marlborough Downs
Bristol
Kingswood
Avebury
Marlborough
Dyffryn Gardens
Penarth
Clevedon
Yatton
Box
Calne
Lacock
Silbury Hill
Tan Hill
Llantwit-Major
Nash Pt.
St. Athan
Barry
Chew Magna
Keynsham
Bath
Bradford on Avon
Melksham
Vale of Pewsey
Devizes
Pewsey
Weston-super-Mare
Blagdon
Chew Valley Lake
Mendip
Axbridge
Midsomer Norton
Radstock
Trowbridge
Upavon
Bridgwater Bay
Cheddar
Wookey Hole
Salisbury Plain
Westbury
Burnham-on-Sea
Frome
Warminster
Woodhenge
Stonehenge
Hinkley Pt.
Wells
Shepton Mallet
Heytesbury
Amesbury
Minehead
Porlock
Dunster
Watchet
Longleat
Dunkery Beacon
Dunster Castle
Nether Stowey
Glastonbury
Evercreech
Maiden Bradley
Porton
Brendon Hills
Bridgwater
Quantock Hills
Polden Hills
Street
Stourhead
Wylye
Old Sarum
North Petherton
Middlezoy
Castle Cary
Bruton
Mere
Cranbourne
Wilton
Salisbury
Bishops Lydeard
Wiveliscombe
Somerton
Wincanton
Gillingham
Wilton House
Chase & West
Dulverton
Taunton
Sparkford
Milverton
Shaftesbury
Ilchester
South Petherton
Wiltshire Downs
Wellington
Staple Hill
Knightshayes Court
Blackdown Hills
Ilminster
Yeovil
Sherborne
Sturminster Newton
Fordingbridge
Tiverton
Halberton
Uffculme
Chard
Crewkerne
Blackmoor Vale
Blandford Forum
Verwood
Cullompton
Yarcombe
North Dorset Downs
Ringwood
Pilsdon Pen
Silverton
Beaminster
Cerne Abbas Giant
Cerne Abbas
Wimborne Minster
Brockenhurst
Crediton
Honiton
Maiden Newton
Ferndown
Broadclyst
Ottery St. Mary
East Devon
Axminster
Dorset
Charminster
Christchurch
Priory Church
Pinhoe
Exeter
Colyford
Bridport
Maiden Castle
Tolpuddle
Bere Regis
Broadstone
Poole
Bournemouth
Frome
Dorchester
Wareham
Sandbanks
Exminster
Topsham
Beer
Seaton
Lyme Regis
Burton Bradstock
South Dorset Downs
Wool
Poole Harbour
Studland
Sidmouth
Lyme Bay
Abbotsbury
Poor Lot Barrows
West Lulworth
Corfe Castle
I. of Purbeck
Swanage
Bovey Tracey
Budleigh Salterton
Exmouth
Chesil Beach
Weymouth
Durlston Hd.
Dawlish
Fortuneswell
St. Alban's Head
Teignmouth
Shaldon
Easton
Portland Castle
Newton Abbot
Portland Bill
I. of Portland
Torquay
Dartington
Totnes
Paignton
Tor Bay
Galmpton
Brixham
Dartmouth
Kingswear
Stoke Fleming
Kingsbridge
Start Bay
Torcross
Salcombe
Start Pt.
Guernsey
Jersey
Cherbourg
St. Malo
0
10
20 miles
0
10
20
30 km
50°
3°
2°
3
4
5
A
B

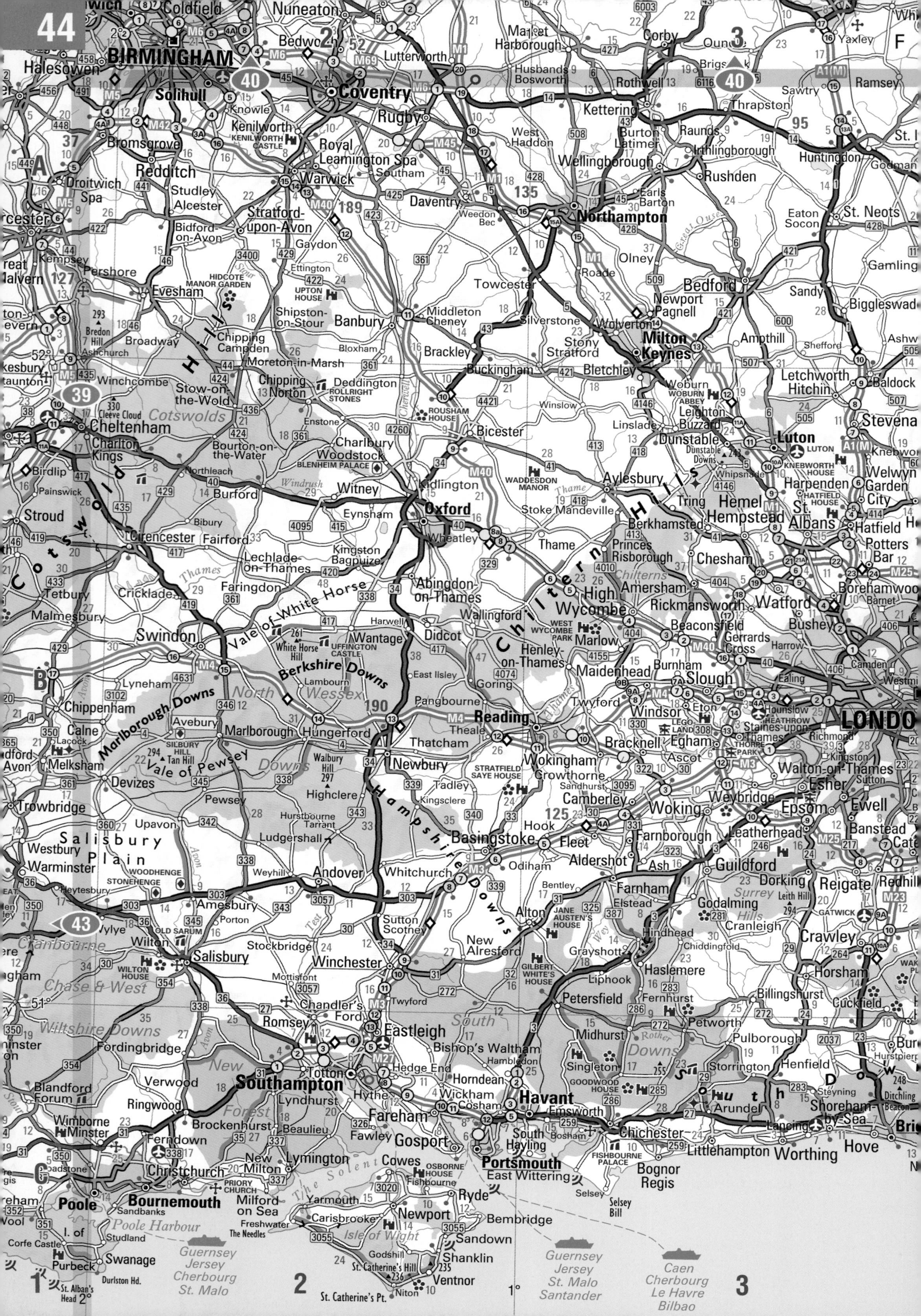

BIRMINGHAM
Coldfield
Nuneaton
Bedworth
Market Harborough
Corby
Oundle
Yaxley
Halesowen
Solihull
Coventry
Lutterworth
Husbands Bosworth
Rothwell
Sawtry
Ramsey
Knowle
Kenilworth
Kenilworth Castle
Rugby
Kettering
Thrapston
Bromsgrove
Royal Leamington Spa
Southam
West Haddon
Burton Latimer
Raunds
Irthlingborough
Huntingdon
Godmanchester
Redditch
Warwick
Wellingborough
Rushden
Droitwich Spa
Studley
Alcester
Daventry
Northampton
Earls Barton
Eaton Socon
St. Neots
Stratford-upon-Avon
Bidford-on-Avon
Weedon Bec
Gaydon
Olney
Great Ouse
Gamlingay
Kempsey
Pershore
Malvern
Ettington
Towcester
Roade
Bedford
Sandy
Biggleswade
Hidcote Manor Garden
Upton House
Evesham
Shipston-on-Stour
Banbury
Middleton Cheney
Silverstone
Newport Pagnell
Wolverton
Milton Keynes
Bredon Hill
Broadway
Chipping Campden
Ashchurch
Bloxham
Brackley
Stony Stratford
Ampthill
Shefford
Tewkesbury
Moreton-in-Marsh
Buckingham
Bletchley
Winchcombe
Stow-on-the-Wold
Chipping Norton
Deddington
Rollright Stones
Woburn
Woburn Abbey
Letchworth
Hitchin
Baldock
Cleeve Cloud
Cotswolds
Cheltenham
Enstone
Rousham House
Winslow
Leighton Buzzard
Linslade
Stevenage
Charlton Kings
Bourton-on-the-Water
Charlbury
Woodstock
Bicester
Dunstable
Dunstable Downs
Luton
Knebworth House
Birdlip
Northleach
Blenheim Palace
Waddesdon Manor
Aylesbury
Whipsnade
Welwyn Garden City
Painswick
Burford
Windrush
Witney
Kidlington
Tring
Harpenden
Hatfield House
Stroud
Bibury
Eynsham
Oxford
Stoke Mandeville
Hemel Hempstead
St. Albans
Hatfield
Berkhamsted
Cirencester
Fairford
Wheatley
Thame
Chiltern Hills
Potters Bar
Lechlade-on-Thames
Kingston Bagpuize
Princes Risborough
Chesham
Cotswold
Tetbury
Cricklade
Thames
Faringdon
Abingdon-on-Thames
High Wycombe
Amersham
Chilterns
Watford
Borehamwood
Malmesbury
Vale of White Horse
Harwell
Wallingford
Rickmansworth
Barnet
Swindon
White Horse Hill
Uffington Castle
Wantage
Didcot
West Wycombe Park
Marlow
Beaconsfield
Gerrards Cross
Bushey
Lyneham
Berkshire Downs
Lambourn
East Ilsley
Henley-on-Thames
Maidenhead
Burnham
Slough
Harrow
Camden
Chippenham
Marlborough Downs
North Wessex
Goring
Pangbourne
Twyford
Windsor
Eton
Ealing
LONDON
Calne
Avebury
Marlborough
Hungerford
Reading
Theale
Legoland
Hounslow
Heathrow
Staines-upon-Thames
Richmond
Lacock
Silbury Hill
Tan Hill
Melksham
Thatcham
Newbury
Bracknell
Wokingham
Egham
Ascot
Thorpe Park
Kingston
Devizes
Vale of Pewsey
Walbury Hill
Stratfield Saye House
Crowthorne
Walton-on-Thames
Esher
Sutton
Trowbridge
Pewsey
Highclere
Tadley
Kingsclere
Sandhurst
Camberley
Weybridge
Ewell
Epsom
Salisbury Plain
Upavon
Hurstbourne Tarrant
Hampshire Downs
Basingstoke
Hook
Woking
Leatherhead
Banstead
Westbury
Warminster
Ludgershall
Fleet
Farnborough
Aldershot
Ash
Guildford
Dorking
Reigate
Redhill
Woodhenge
Stonehenge
Weyhill
Andover
Whitchurch
Odiham
Bentley
Farnham
Surrey Hills
Leith Hill
Heytesbury
Amesbury
Old Sarum
Porton
Sutton Scotney
Alton
Jane Austen's House
Elstead
Godalming
Cranleigh
Gatwick
Crawley
Wylye
Wilton
Stockbridge
Test
New Alresford
Grayshott
Hindhead
Chiddingfold
Cranborne
Salisbury
Wilton House
Winchester
Gilbert White's House
Haslemere
Horsham
Chase & West
Mottisfont
Wey
Liphook
Petersfield
Fernhurst
Billingshurst
Cuckfield
Wiltshire Downs
Chandler's Ford
Romsey
Eastleigh
Twyford
South Downs
Midhurst
Rother
Petworth
Pulborough
Fordingbridge
Bishop's Waltham
Hambledon
Singleton
Storrington
Henfield
Hurstpierpoint
New Forest
Totton
Hedge End
Horndean
Goodwood House
Verwood
Southampton
Wickham
Havant
Arundel
Steyning
Ditchling Beacon
Blandford Forum
Ringwood
Lyndhurst
Hythe
Cosham
Emsworth
Shoreham-by-Sea
Wimborne Minster
Brockenhurst
Beaulieu
Fareham
Lancing
Fawley
Gosport
South Hayling
Bosham
Chichester
Ferndown
New Milton
Lymington
Cowes
Osborne House
Portsmouth
Fishbourne Palace
Littlehampton
Worthing
Hove
Christchurch
The Solent
Fishbourne
East Wittering
Bognor Regis
Priory Church
Milford on Sea
Yarmouth
Ryde
Selsey
Selsey Bill
Poole
Bournemouth
Sandbanks
Newport
Bembridge
Poole Harbour
Studland
I. of Purbeck
Corfe Castle
Freshwater
The Needles
Carisbrooke
Isle of Wight
Sandown
Shanklin
Godshill
St. Catherine's Hill
Swanage
Ventnor
Durlston Hd.
St. Alban's Head
St. Catherine's Pt.
Niton
Guernsey
Jersey
Cherbourg
St. Malo
Santander
Caen
Le Havre
Bilbao

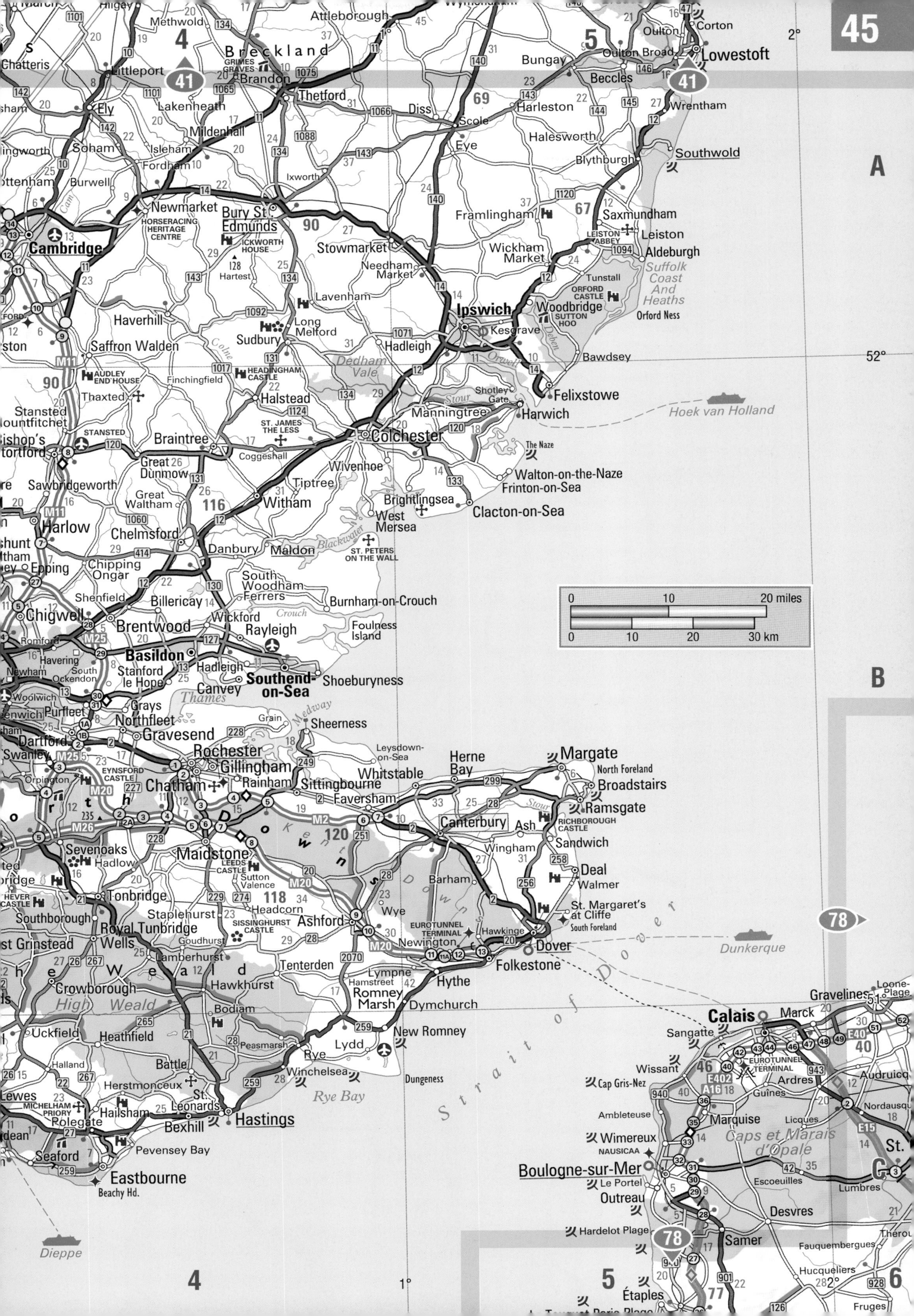
Attleborough
Corton
Oulton
Lowestoft
Oulton Broad
Bungay
Beccles
Breckland
Methwold
Chatteris
Littleport
Grimes Graves
Brandon
Thetford
Lakenheath
Ely
Mildenhall
Diss
Scole
Harleston
Wrentham
Halesworth
Eye
Soham
Isleham
Fordham
Blythburgh
Southwold
Burwell
Ixworth
Newmarket
Horseracing Heritage Centre
Bury St Edmunds
Ickworth House
Framlingham
Saxmundham
Leiston Abbey
Leiston
Aldeburgh
Cambridge
Stowmarket
Hartest
Needham Market
Wickham Market
Suffolk Coast And Heaths
Tunstall
Orford Castle
Orford Ness
Lavenham
Ipswich
Woodbridge
Sutton Hoo
Kesgrave
Haverhill
Long Melford
Sudbury
Hadleigh
Saffron Walden
Dedham Vale
Bawdsey
Audley End House
Headingham Castle
Finchingfield
Thaxted
Halstead
Shotley Gate
Felixstowe
Manningtree
Harwich
Hoek van Holland
Stansted Mountfitchet
Stansted
St. James the Less
Bishop's Stortford
Braintree
Coggeshall
Colchester
The Naze
Great Dunmow
Wivenhoe
Walton-on-the-Naze
Frinton-on-Sea
Sawbridgeworth
Tiptree
Great Waltham
Witham
Brightlingsea
West Mersea
Clacton-on-Sea
Harlow
Chelmsford
Danbury
Maldon
Blackwater
St. Peters on the Wall
Epping
Chipping Ongar
South Woodham Ferrers
Shenfield
Billericay
Burnham-on-Crouch
Crouch
Chigwell
Brentwood
Wickford
Rayleigh
Foulness Island
Romford
Havering
Basildon
Newham
South Ockendon
Stanford le Hope
Hadleigh
Canvey
Southend-on-Sea
Shoeburyness
Woolwich
Thames
Grays
Purfleet
Northfleet
Grain
Medway
Sheerness
Dartford
Gravesend
Swanley
Rochester
Gillingham
Leysdown-on-Sea
Herne Bay
Margate
North Foreland
Orpington
Eynsford Castle
Chatham
Rainham
Sittingbourne
Whitstable
Broadstairs
Faversham
Stour
Ramsgate
Canterbury
Ash
Richborough Castle
Sevenoaks
Hadlow
Maidstone
Kent Downs
Wingham
Sandwich
Leeds Castle
Sutton Valence
Barham
Deal
Walmer
Hever Castle
Tonbridge
Staplehurst
Headcorn
St. Margaret's at Cliffe
South Foreland
Southborough
Royal Tunbridge Wells
Sissinghurst Castle
Ashford
Wye
Eurotunnel Terminal
Hawkinge
Newington
Dover
Dunkerque
East Grinstead
Goudhurst
Lamberhurst
Tenterden
Folkestone
Weald
Hawkhurst
Lympne
Hamstreet
Hythe
Crowborough
Romney Marsh
Dymchurch
High Weald
Bodiam
Gravelines
Loone-Plage
Calais
Marck
Sangatte
Uckfield
Heathfield
New Romney
Lydd
Peasmarsh
Rye
Battle
Winchelsea
Dungeness
Wissant
Eurotunnel Terminal
Cap Gris-Nez
Ardres
Audruicq
Lewes
Herstmonceux
St. Leonards
Rye Bay
Guînes
Nordausques
Michelham Priory
Polegate
Hailsham
Hastings
Ambleteuse
Marquise
Licques
Bexhill
Wimereux
Caps et Marais d'Opale
St.
Seaford
Pevensey Bay
Nausicaa
Eastbourne
Beachy Hd.
Boulogne-sur-Mer
Le Portel
Escoeuilles
Lumbres
Outreau
Desvres
Hardelot Plage
Samer
Fauquembergues
Dieppe
Hucqueliers
Étaples
Fruges
Strait of Dover
0
10
20 miles
0
10
20
30 km
52°
2°
1°
A
B
C
4
5
6

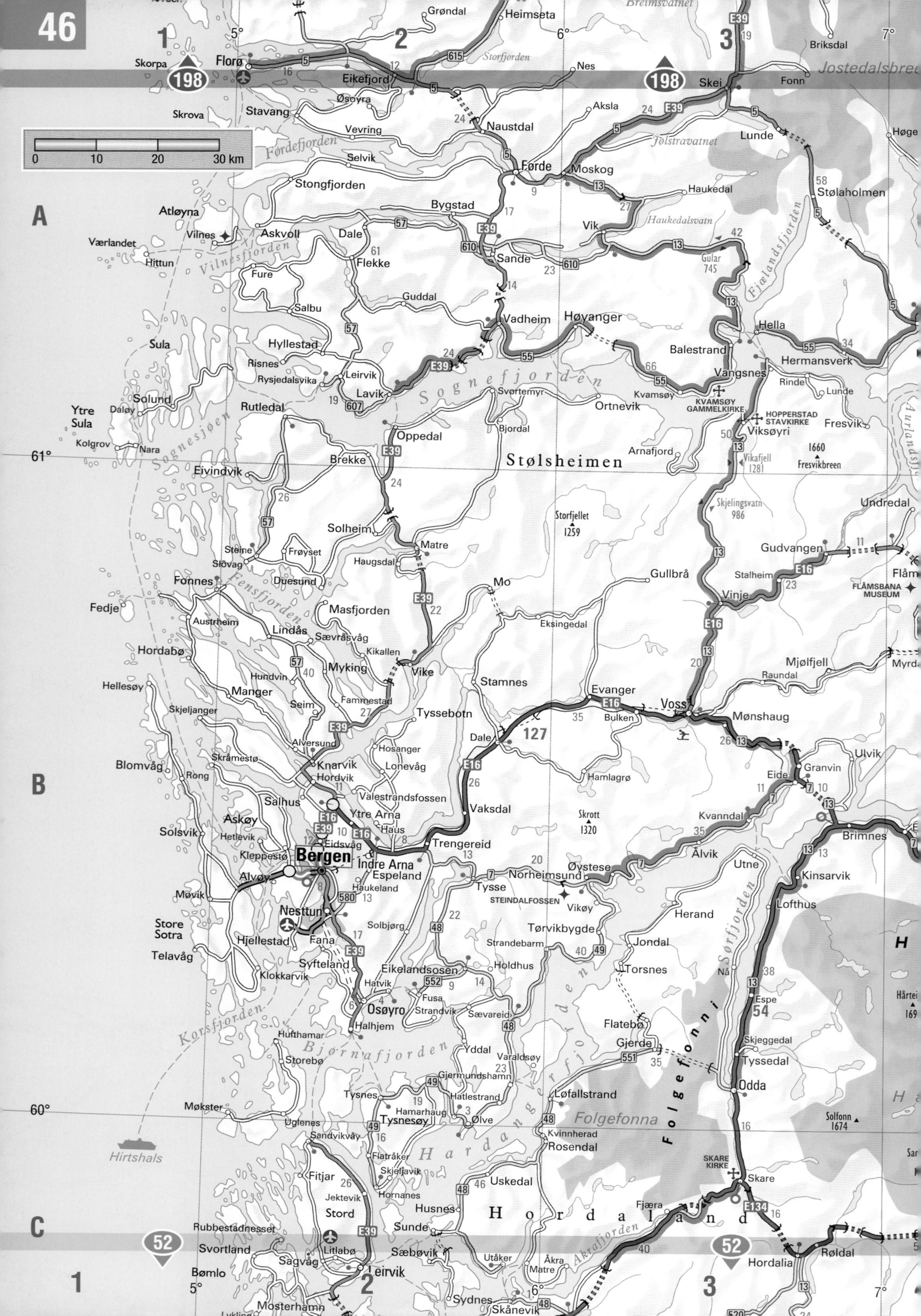
Florø
Skorpa
198
Grøndal
Heimseta
Briksdal
Eikefjord
Storfjorden
Nes
Skei
Fonn
Jostedalsbreen
Øsoyra
Stavang
Skrova
Naustdal
Aksla
Vevring
Førdefjorden
Jølstravatnet
Lunde
Høge
0
10
20
30 km
Selvik
Førde
Moskog
Stongfjorden
Haukedal
Stølaholmen
Bygstad
Atløyna
Askvoll
Dale
Vilnes
Haukedalsvatn
Vik
Værlandet
Hittun
Vilnesfjorden
Sande
Flekke
Gular
745
Fjælandsfjorden
Fure
Guddal
Salbu
Vadheim
Høyanger
Hella
Sula
Hyllestad
Balestrand
Hermansverk
Risnes
Rysjedalsvika
Leirvik
Sognefjorden
Vangsnes
Rinde
Solund
Lavik
Svørtemyr
Kvamsøy
Ortnevik
Kvamsøy Gammelkirke
Hopperstad Stavkirke
Fresvik
Ytre Sula
Daløy
Rutledal
Sognesjøen
Bjordal
Viksøyri
Kolgrov
Nara
Oppedal
Arnafjord
1660
Fresvikbreen
Vikafjell
1281
61°
Brekke
Stølsheimen
Eivindvik
Skjelingsvatn
986
Undredal
Storfjellet
1259
Solheim
Gudvangen
Steine
Frøyset
Matre
Slovag
Haugsdal
Gullbrå
Stalheim
Flåm
Flåmsbana Museum
Fonnes
Fensfjorden
Duesund
Mo
Fedje
Masfjorden
Austrheim
Eksingedal
Vinje
Lindås
Sævråsvåg
Hordabø
Kikallen
Mjølfjell
Myrdal
Myking
Vike
Raundal
Hundvin
Stamnes
Hellesøy
Manger
Evanger
Seim
Voss
Fammestad
Bulken
Mønshaug
Skjeljanger
Tyssebotn
127
Dale
Alversund
Hosanger
Ulvik
Skråmestø
Granvin
Blomvåg
Rong
Knarvik
Lonevåg
Eide
Hordvik
Hamlagrø
Valestrandsfossen
Salhus
Vaksdal
Askøy
Ytre Arna
Skrott
1320
Kvanndal
Solsvik
Hetlevik
Haus
Brimnes
Eidsvåg
Trengereid
Kleppestø
Bergen
Indre Arna
Ålvik
Alvøy
Espeland
Norheimsund
Øystese
Utne
Møvik
Haukeland
Tysse
Kinsarvik
Steindalfossen
Vikøy
Lofthus
Nesttun
Herand
Store Sotra
Solbjørg
Tørvikbygde
Sørfjorden
Hjellestad
Fana
Strandebarm
Jondal
Telavåg
Holdhus
Torsnes
Syfteland
Klokkarvik
Eikelandsosen
Nå
Hatvik
Fusa
Hårteig
Espe
Osøyro
Strandvik
Sævareid
169
Flatebø
Halhjem
Korsfjorden
Hufthamar
Gjerde
Skjeggedal
Bjørnafjorden
Yddal
Varaldsøy
Folgefonni
Tyssedal
Storebø
Gjermundshamn
Odda
Tysnes
Hatlestrand
Løfallstrand
Hamarhaug
60°
Møkster
Tysnesøy
Ølve
Folgefonna
Solfonn
1674
Uglenes
Kvinnherad
Sandvikvåg
Rosendal
Hirtshals
Flatråker
Hardangerfjorden
Skare Kirke
Skjelavik
Fitjar
Uskedal
Skare
Jektevik
Hornanes
Husnes
Hordaland
Stord
Fjæra
Rubbestadnesset
Sunde
52
Svortland
Litlabø
Akrafjorden
Sæbøvik
Røldal
Sagvåg
Utåker
Åkra
Hordalia
Bømlo
Leirvik
Matre
5°
7°
6°
Mosterhamn
Sydnes
Skånevik
A
B
C
1
2
3
E39
E16
E134

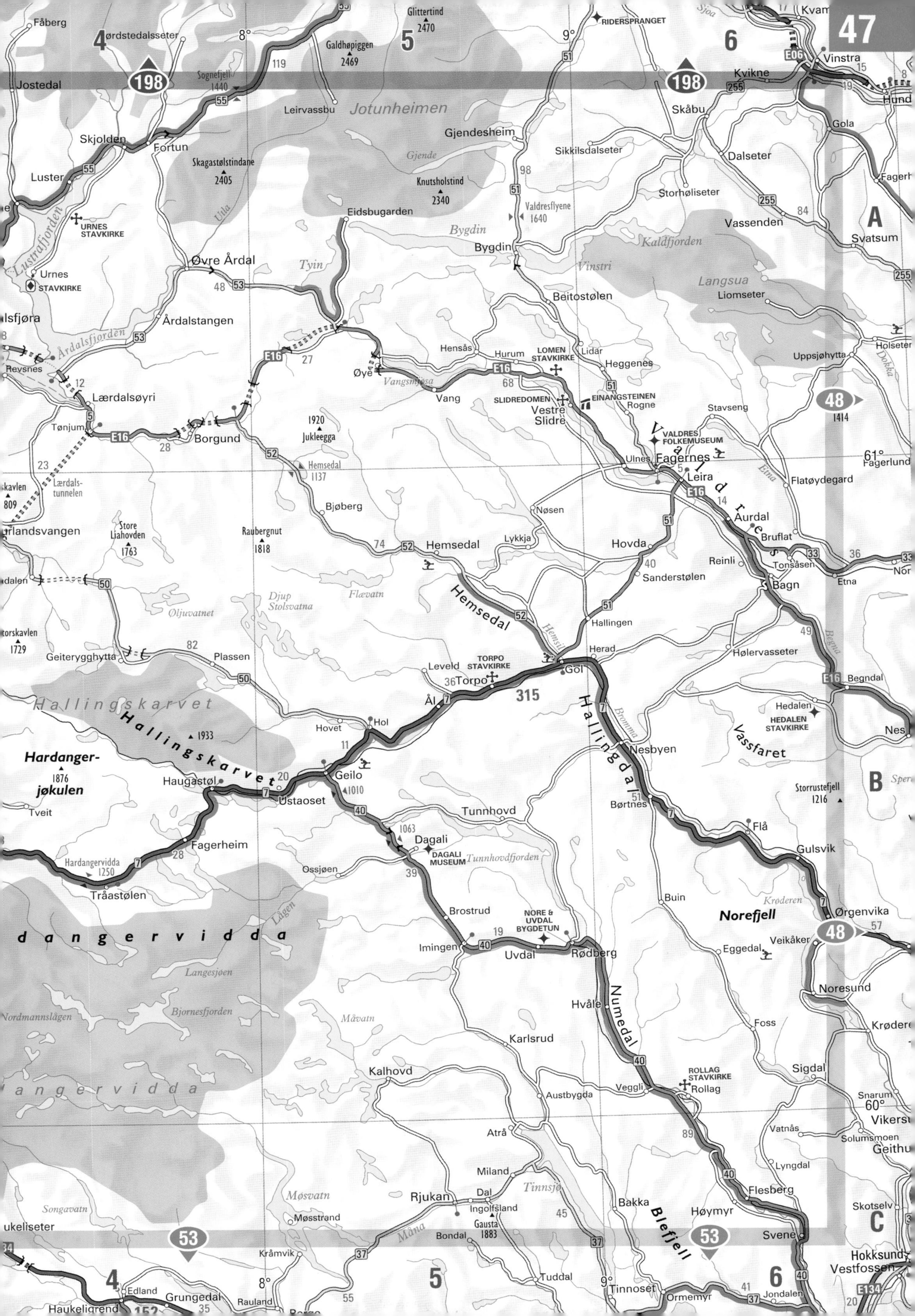
Fåberg
Jostedal
4
5
6
198
Sognefjell
1440
Glittertind
2470
Galdhøpiggen
2469
Leirvassbu
Jotunheimen
RIDERSPRANGET
Sjoa
Kvam
Vinstra
Kvikne
Hund
Skåbu
Gola
Skjolden
Fortun
Gjendesheim
Gjende
Sikkilsdalseter
Dalseter
Luster
Skagastølstindane
2405
Knutsholstind
2340
Storhøliseter
Fagerh
Valdresflyene
1640
Vassenden
A
Svatsum
Lustrafjorden
URNES STAVKIRKE
Utla
Eidsbugarden
Bygdin
Kaldfjorden
Urnes
STAVKIRKE
Øvre Årdal
Tyin
Vinstri
Langsua
Liomseter
Beitostølen
Årdalstangen
Årdalsfjorden
Revsnes
Lærdalsøyri
Hensås
Hurum
LOMEN STAVKIRKE
Lidar
Heggenes
Uppsjøhytta
Holsetei
Dokka
Øye
Vangsmjøsa
Vang
SLIDREDOMEN
EINANGSTEINEN
Rogne
Vestre Slidre
Stavseng
48
1414
Tønjum
Borgund
1920
Jukleegga
VALDRES FOLKEMUSEUM
Valdres
Ulnes
Fagernes
Leira
61°
Fagerlund
Hemsedal
1137
Lærdals-tunnelen
Flatøydegard
Bjøberg
Nøsen
Etna
Aurdal
Bruflat
Store Liahovden
1763
Raubergnut
1818
Hemsedal
Lykkja
Hovda
Reinli
Tonsåsen
Hydalen
Sanderstølen
Bagn
Djup Stolsvatna
Flævatn
Øljuvatnet
Hallingen
1729
Geiterygghytta
Plassen
Herad
Hølervasseter
Begna
Leveld
TORPO STAVKIRKE
Torpo
Gol
Begndal
Hallingskarvet
Ål
Hallingdal
Bromma
Hedalen
HEDALEN STAVKIRKE
1933
Hovet
Hol
Vassfaret
Nes
Hardanger-
1876
jøkulen
Haugastøl
Geilo
Nesbyen
B
Storrustefjell
1216
Ustaoset
1010
Tveit
Tunnhovd
Børtnes
1063
Dagali
DAGALI MUSEUM
Tunnhovdfjorden
Flå
Fagerheim
Gulsvik
Hardangervidda
1250
Ossjøen
Tråastølen
Lågen
Buin
Krøderen
Brostrud
NORE & UVDAL BYGDETUN
Norefjell
Ørgenvika
Hardangervidda
Imingen
Uvdal
Rødberg
Veikåker
Eggedal
Langesjøen
Numedal
Noresund
Hvåle
Bjornesfjorden
Nordmannslågen
Måvatn
Foss
Krøderen
Karlsrud
Kalhovd
ROLLAG STAVKIRKE
Rollag
Sigdal
Austbygda
Veggli
Snarum
60°
Vikersund
Atrå
Vatnås
Solumsmoen
Geithus
Lyngdal
Miland
Tinnsjø
Flesberg
Møsvatn
Rjukan
Dal
Ingolfsland
Bakka
Blefjell
Høymyr
Skotselv
Songavatn
Møsstrand
45
C
ukeliseter
Gausta
1883
Svene
53
Bondal
Måna
Hokksund
Vestfossen
Kråmvik
Edland
Grungedal
Tuddal
Rauland
Tinnoset
Ormemyr
Jondalen
Haukeligrend
8°
9°

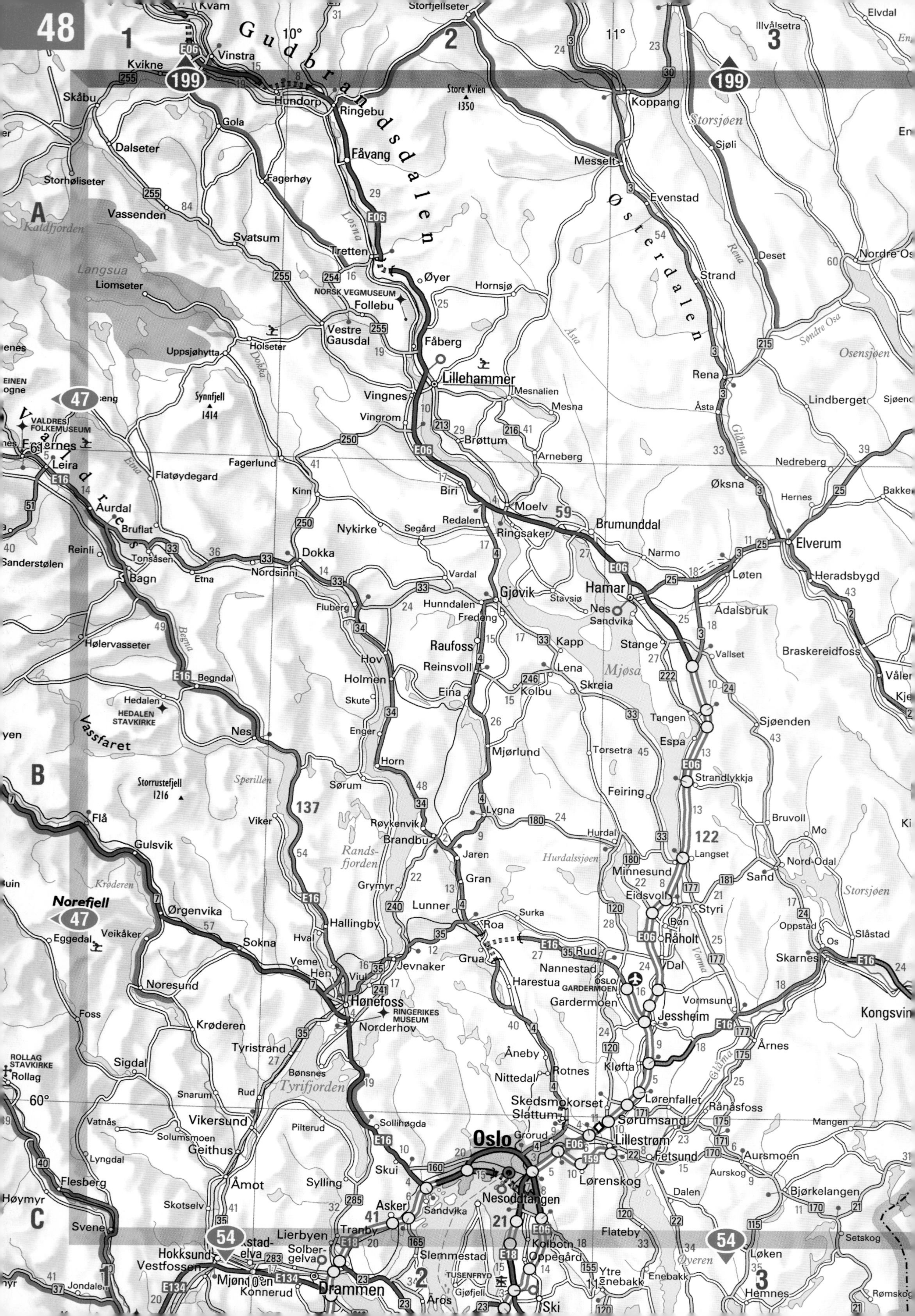
Gudbrandsdalen
Østerdalen
Valdres
Lillehammer
Gjøvik
Hamar
Elverum
Oslo
Hønefoss
Drammen
Lillestrøm
Mjøsa
Tyrifjorden
Randsfjorden
Storsjøen
Langsua
Vassfaret
Kvam
Vinstra
Kvikne
Ringebu
Hundorp
Fåvang
Tretten
Øyer
Follebu
NORSK VEGMUSEUM
Fåberg
Vestre Gausdal
Koppang
Rena
Brumunddal
Moelv
Biri
Løten
Raufoss
Dokka
Aurdal
Fagernes
Leira
Bagn
Nes
Gran
Jevnaker
Eidsvoll
Råholt
Jessheim
Gardermoen
Kløfta
Skedsmokorset
Nittedal
Sandvika
Asker
Lierbyen
Kolbotn
Oppegård
Ski
Nesoddtangen
Fetsund
Sørumsand
Årnes
Kongsvinger
Skarnes
Sigdal
Rollag
Vikersund
Geithus
Åmot
Hokksund
Vestfossen
Mjøndalen
Konnerud
Flesberg
Flå
Gulsvik
Norefjell
Eggedal
Noresund
Krøderen
Sokna
Tyristrand
Norderhov
RINGERIKES MUSEUM
HEDALEN STAVKIRKE
VALDRES FOLKEMUSEUM
ROLLAG STAVKIRKE
Synnfjell 1414
Storrustefjell 1216
Store Kvien 1350

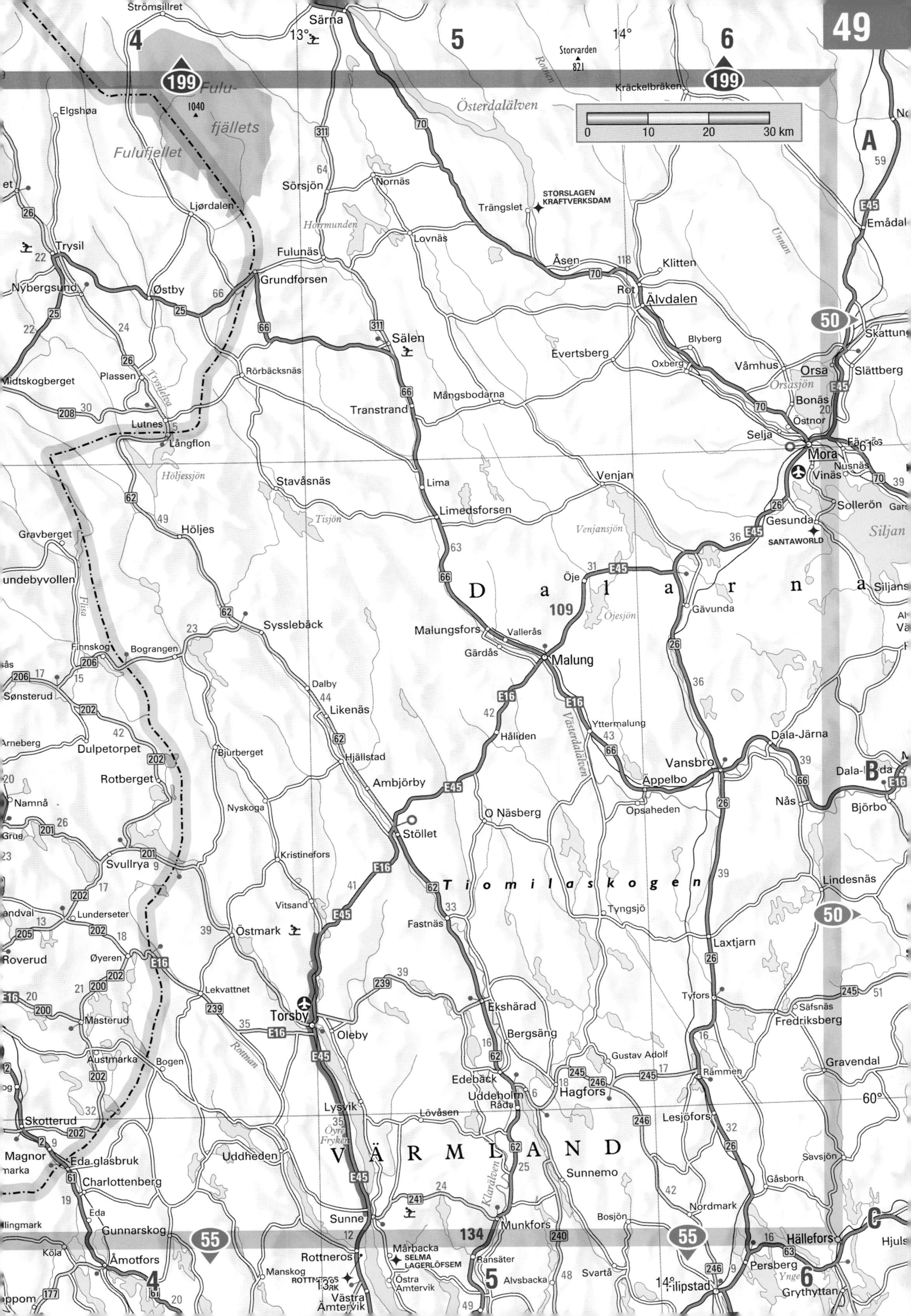

Särna
Sälen
Mora
Orsa
Älvdalen
Malung
Vansbro
Torsby
Hagfors
Sunne
Munkfors
Filipstad
Hällefors
Trysil
Dalarna
VÄRMLAND
Tiomilaskogen
Fulufjellet
Fulufjällets
Österdalälven
Västerdalälven
Siljan
STORSLAGEN KRAFTVERKSDAM
SANTAWORLD
SELMA LAGERLÖFSEM
0 10 20 30 km

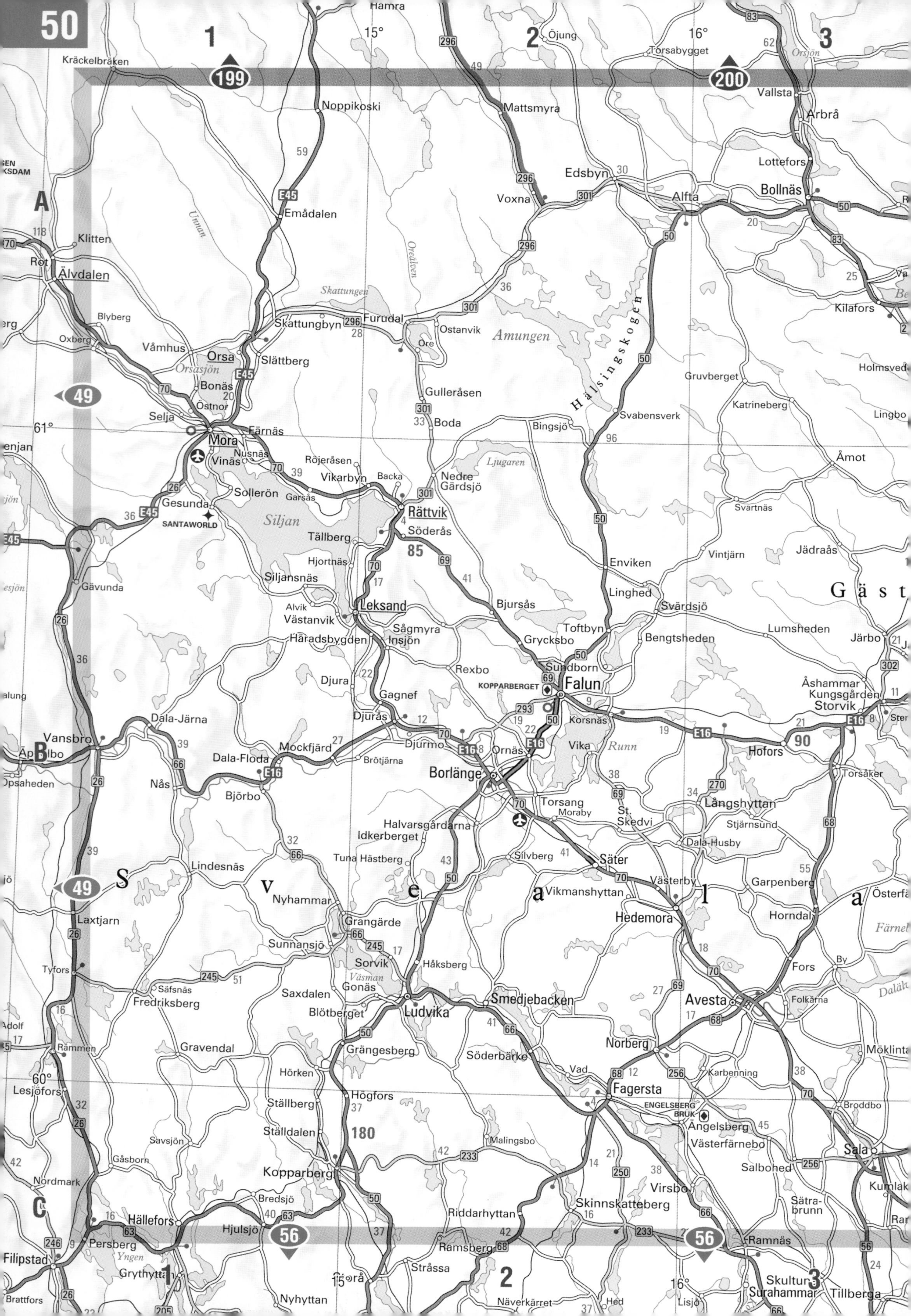

199
200
49
56
Kräckelbråken
Noppikoski
Mattsmyra
Hamra
Öjung
Torsabygget
Vallsta
Arbrå
Lottefors
Bollnäs
Edsbyn
Voxna
Alfta
Emådalen
Klitten
Rot
Älvdalen
Skattungen
Skattungbyn
Furudal
Ostanvik
Ore
Amungen
Hälsingskogen
Kilafors
Blyberg
Oxberg
Våmhus
Orsa
Orsasjön
Slättberg
Bonäs
Östnor
Selja
Mora
Färnäs
Gulleråsen
Boda
Gruvberget
Katrineberg
Holmsved
Lingbo
Svabensverk
Bingsjö
Ljugaren
Nusnäs
Vinäs
Röjeråsen
Vikarbyn
Backa
Nedre Gärdsjö
Sollerön
Garsås
Gesunda
SANTAWORLD
Siljan
Rättvik
Söderås
Tällberg
Hjortnäs
Siljansnäs
Alvik
Västanvik
Leksand
Sågmyra
Insjön
Häradsbygden
Gävunda
Åmot
Svartnäs
Vintjärn
Jädraås
Enviken
Linghed
Svärdsjö
Bjursås
Toftbyn
Grycksbo
Bengtsheden
Lumsheden
Järbo
Gäst
Rexbo
Djura
Gagnef
Djurås
Sundborn
KOPPARBERGET
Falun
Korsnäs
Åshammar
Kungsgården
Storvik
Vansbro
Äppelbo
Dala-Järna
Dala-Floda
Mockfjärd
Djurmo
Brötjärna
Ornäs
Vika
Runn
Hofors
Torsåker
Opsaheden
Nås
Björbo
Borlänge
Torsang
Moraby
St. Skedvi
Långshyttan
Stjärnsund
Halvarsgårdarna
Idkerberget
Dala-Husby
Tuna Hästberg
Silvberg
Säter
Lindesnäs
Svealand
Nyhammar
Vikmanshyttan
Västerby
Hedemora
Garpenberg
Österfärnebo
Laxtjarn
Grangärde
Horndal
Färnebofjärden
Sunnansjö
Sorvik
Håksberg
Fors
By
Dalälven
Tyfors
Väsman
Säfsnäs
Fredriksberg
Saxdalen
Gonäs
Blötberget
Ludvika
Smedjebacken
Avesta
Folkärna
Rämmen
Gravendal
Grängesberg
Söderbärke
Norberg
Möklinta
Adolf
Hörken
Vad
Karbenning
60°
Lesjöfors
Högfors
Fagersta
Broddbo
Ställberg
ENGELSBERG BRUK
Ängelsberg
Ställdalen
Västerfärnebo
Savsjön
Malingsbo
Sala
Gåsborn
Salbohed
Nordmark
Kopparberg
Kumla
Bredsjö
Virsbo
Sätrabrunn
Hällefors
Hjulsjö
Riddarhyttan
Skinnskatteberg
Persberg
Yngen
Ramsberg
Ramnäs
Filipstad
Grythyttan
Stråssa
Skultuna
Surahammar
Tillberga
Brattfors
Nyhyttan
Näverkärret
Hed
Lisjö
Unnan
Oreälven
61°
15°
16°

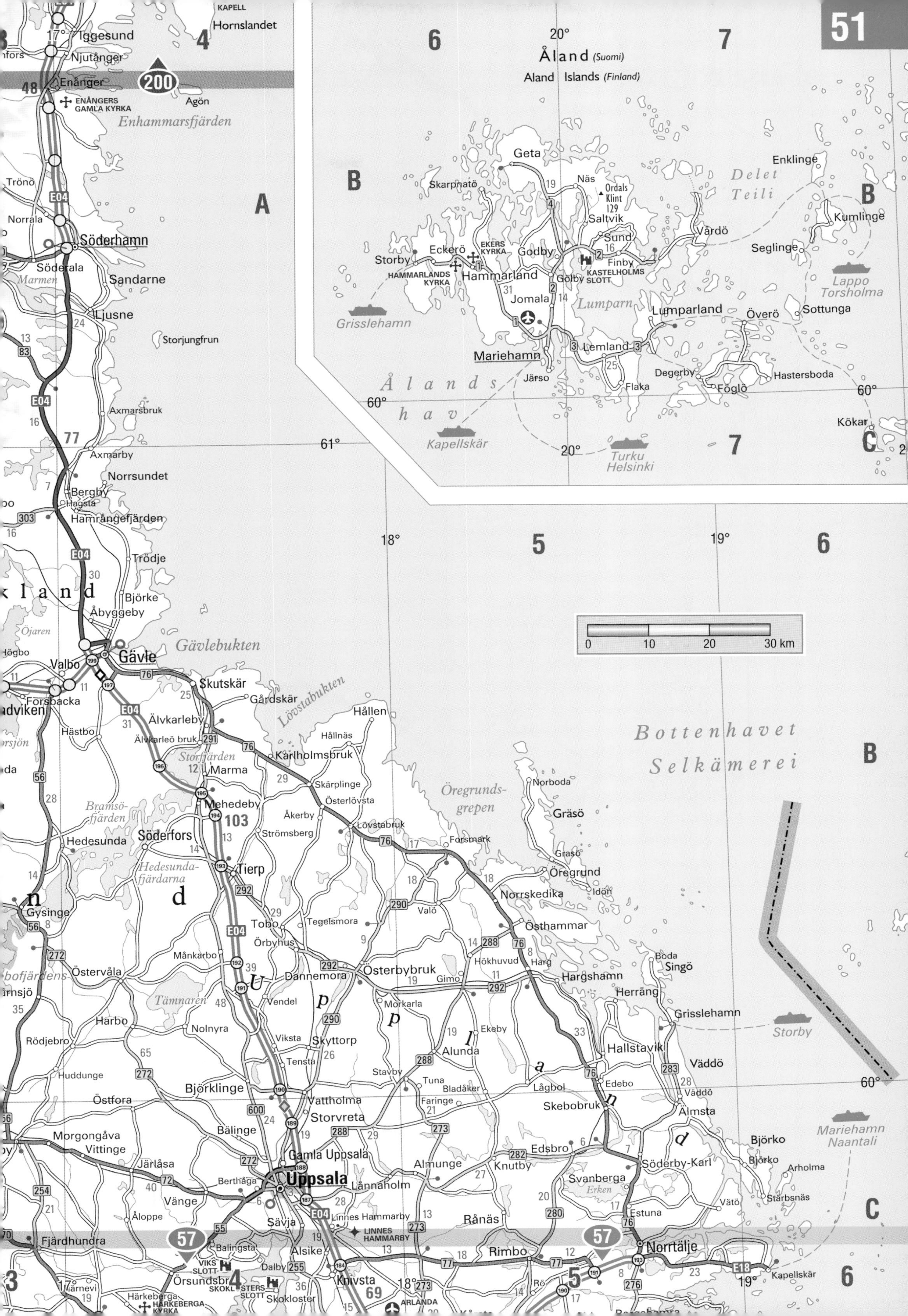
Åland (Suomi)
Aland Islands (Finland)
Geta
Skarpnatö
Näs
Ordals Klint 129
Saltvik
Delet
Teili
Enklinge
Kumlinge
Vårdö
Sund
Seglinge
Storby
Eckerö
EKERS KYRKA
Godby
Finby
KASTELHOLMS SLOTT
HAMMARLANDS KYRKA
Hammarland
Golby
Jomala
Lumparn
Lumparland
Överö
Sottunga
Lappo
Torsholma
Grisslehamn
Mariehamn
Lemland
Järso
Degerby
Föglö
Hastersboda
Flaka
Ålands hav
Kapellskär
Turku
Helsinki
Kökar
KAPELL
Hornslandet
Iggesund
Njutånger
Enånger
ENÅNGERS GAMLA KYRKA
Agön
Enhammarsfjärden
Trönö
Norrala
Söderhamn
Söderala
Marmen
Sandarne
Ljusne
Storjungfrun
Axmarsbruk
Axmarby
Norrsundet
Bergby
Hagsta
Hamrångefjärden
Trödje
Björke
Åbyggeby
Öjaren
Högbo
Valbo
Gävle
Gävlebukten
Skutskär
Gårdskär
Forsbacka
Lövstabukten
Hållen
Hållnäs
Älvkarleby
Hästbo
Älvkarleö bruk
Storfjärden
Karlholmsbruk
Marma
Skärplinge
Österlövsta
Mehedeby
Bramsöfjärden
Åkerby
Strömsberg
Lövstabruk
Hedesunda
Söderfors
Hedesundafjärdarna
Tierp
Öregrundsgrepen
Norboda
Gräsö
Forsmark
Öregrund
Idön
Norrskedika
Gysinge
Tobo
Tegelsmora
Valö
Östhammar
Örbyhus
Månkarbo
Dannemora
Österbybruk
Hökhuvud
Harg
Hargshamn
Singö
Boda
Gimo
Östervåla
Tämnaren
Vendel
Morkarla
Herräng
Grisslehamn
Nolnyra
Harbo
Rödjebro
Viksta
Skyttorp
Ekeby
Alunda
Hallstavik
Väddö
Huddunge
Tensta
Stavby
Tuna
Bladåker
Lågbol
Edebo
Björklinge
Östfora
Vattholma
Faringe
Skebobruk
Storvreta
Bälinge
Morgongåva
Vittinge
Järlåsa
Gamla Uppsala
Almunge
Knutby
Edsbro
Söderby-Karl
Björko
Arholma
Svanberga
Erken
Uppsala
Berthåga
Lännaholm
Vänge
Åloppe
Sävja
Linnes Hammarby
LINNES HAMMARBY
Rånäs
Estuna
Vätö
Stärbsnäs
Norrtälje
Fjärdhundra
Balingsta
VIKS SLOTT
Örsundsbro
SKOKLOSTERS SLOTT
Alsike
Dalby
Knivsta
Skokloster
Rimbo
Rö
Kapellskär
Härkeberga
HÄRKEBERGA KYRKA
Järnevi
ARLANDA
Bottenhavet
Selkämerei
Storby
Mariehamn
Naantali
Uppland
0 10 20 30 km

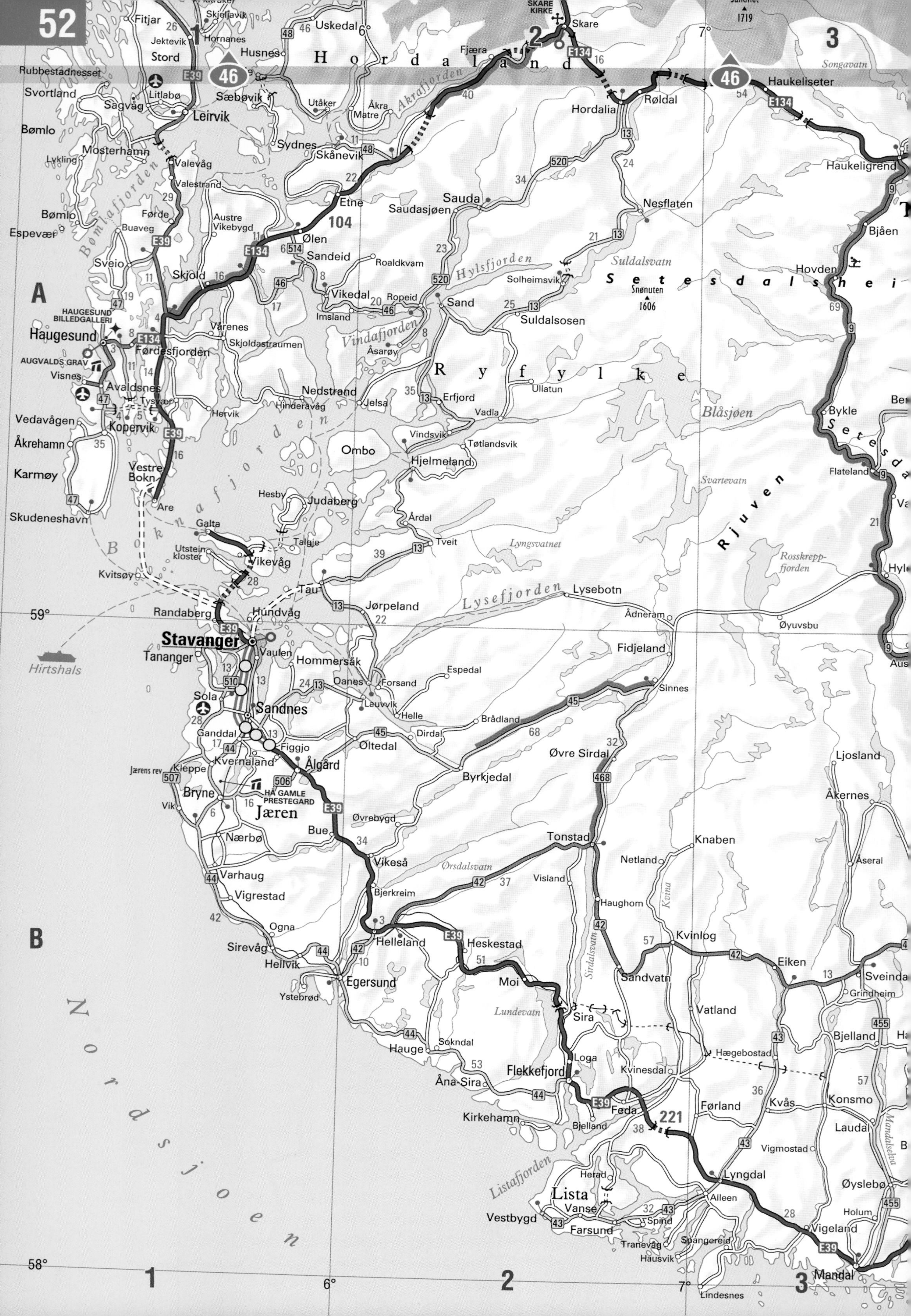
Hordaland
Fitjar
Skjelavik
Jektevik
Hornanes
Stord
Uskedal
Husnes
Rubbestadnesset
Svortland
Litlabø
Sagvåg
Sæbøvik
Leirvik
Bømlo
Utåker
Åkra
Matre
Akrafjorden
Fjæra
Skare Kirke
Skare
Sandnes
1719
Songavatn
Haukeliseter
Røldal
Hordalia
Sydnes
Skånevik
Lykling
Mosterhamn
Valevåg
Valestrand
Bømlafjorden
Førde
Austre Vikebygd
Bømlo
Espevær
Buaveg
Etne
Ølen
Sandeid
Saudasjøen
Sauda
Nesflaten
Haukeligrend
Bjåen
Hovden
Roaldkvam
Hylsfjorden
Suldalsvatn
Solheimsvik
Setesdalsheiene
Snønuten
1606
Sveio
Skjold
Vikedal
Ropeid
Sand
Imsland
Suldalsosen
A
Haugesund Billedgalleri
Haugesund
Vårenes
Skjoldastraumen
Fördesfjorden
Vindafjorden
Åsarøy
Augvalds Grav
Visnes
Avaldsnes
Tysvær
Ryfylke
Nedstrand
Hinderavåg
Jelsa
Erfjord
Ullatun
Vadla
Blåsjøen
Bykle
Vedavågen
Kopervik
Hervik
Åkrehamn
Karmøy
Vestre Bokn
Are
Boknafjorden
Ombo
Vindsvik
Tøtlandsvik
Hjelmeland
Setesdal
Flateland
Svartevatn
Rjuven
Skudeneshavn
Hesby
Judaberg
Årdal
Galta
Utstein kloster
Vikevåg
Talgje
Tveit
Lyngsvatnet
Rosskrepp-fjorden
Kvitsøy
Tau
Lysefjorden
Lysebotn
Ådneram
Øyuvsbu
59°
Randaberg
Hundvåg
Jørpeland
Stavanger
Tananger
Vaulen
Fidjeland
Hirtshals
Hommersåk
Espedal
Oanes
Forsand
Sinnes
Sola
Lauvvik
Helle
Sandnes
Brådland
Ganddal
Dirdal
Ølteda
Figgjo
Øvre Sirdal
Ljosland
Jærens rev
Kleppe
Kvernaland
Ålgård
Byrkjedal
Bryne
Hå Gamle Prestegard
Åkernes
Vik
Jæren
Øvrebygd
Bue
Tonstad
Knaben
Nærbø
Netland
Vikeså
Åseral
Varhaug
Ørsdalsvatn
Visland
Vigrestad
Bjerkreim
Haughom
Kvina
Ogna
Helleland
Heskestad
B
Sirevåg
Kvinlog
Eiken
Hellvik
Sandvatn
Sveinda
Egersund
Moi
Grindheim
Ystebrød
Lundevatn
Sira
Vatland
Sirdalsvatn
Nordsjøen
Bjelland
Hauge
Sokndal
Hægebostad
Loga
Flekkefjord
Kvinesdal
Åna-Sira
Konsmo
Kvås
Førland
Feda
Kirkehamn
Bjelland
Laudal
Vigmostad
Mandalselva
Listafjorden
Herad
Lyngdal
Lista
Alleen
Øyslebø
Vestbygd
Vanse
Spind
Holum
Farsund
Vigeland
Tranevåg
Spangereid
Hausvik
Mandal
Lindesnes
58°
1
6°
2
7°
3
E39
E134
46
104
221

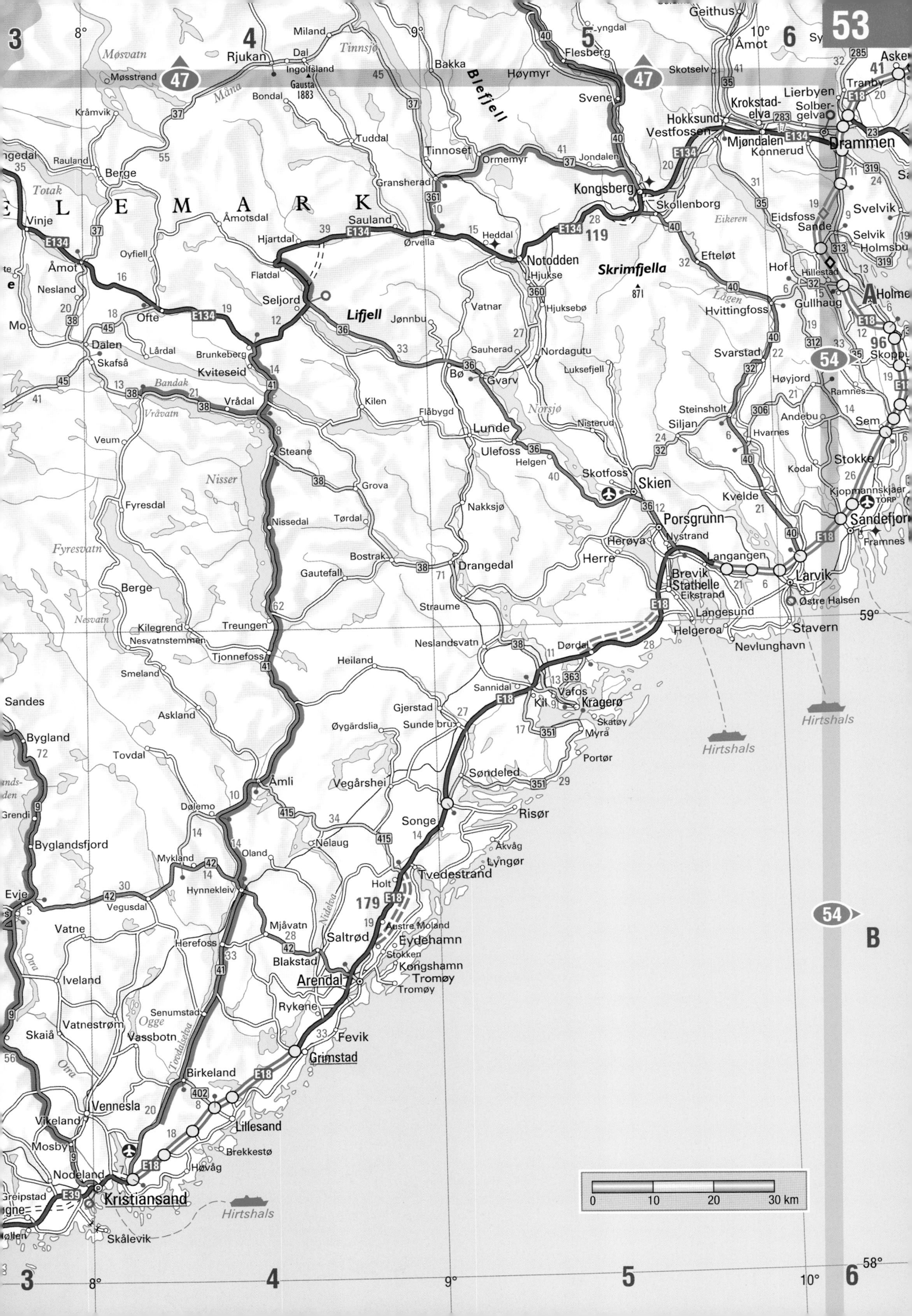
Møsvatn
Møsstrand
Rjukan
Miland
Dal
Ingolfsland
Gausta 1883
Tinnsjø
Måna
Bondal
Kråmvik
Tuddal
Bakka
Blefjell
Høymyr
Geithus
Lyngdal
Flesberg
Svene
Åmot
Skotselv
Asker
Tranby
Lierbyen
Krokstad-elva
Solbergelva
Hokksund
Vestfossen
Mjøndalen
Konnerud
Drammen
Rauland
Berge
Totak
Tinnoset
Ormemyr
Jondalen
Gransherad
Kongsberg
Skollenborg
TELEMARK
Vinje
Åmotsdal
Sauland
Hjartdal
Ørvella
Heddal
Notodden
Hjukse
Skrimfjella
871
Eikeren
Eidsfoss
Sande
Svelvik
Selvik
Holmsbu
Hillestad
Efteløt
Hof
Gullhaug
Holmestrand
Oyfiell
Åmot
Nesland
Flatdal
Seljord
Lifjell
Jønnbu
Vatnar
Hjuksebø
Lågen
Hvittingfoss
Mo
Ofte
Dalen
Lårdal
Skafså
Brunkeberg
Kviteseid
Sauherad
Nordagutu
Luksefjell
Svarstad
Skoppum
Bandak
Vrådal
Vråvatn
Kilen
Flåbygd
Bø
Gvarv
Norsjø
Høyjord
Ramnes
Andebu
Sem
Steinsholt
Siljan
Hvarnes
Lunde
Nisterud
Veum
Steane
Ulefoss
Helgen
Skotfoss
Skien
Kodal
Stokke
Nisser
Grova
Nakksjø
Kvelde
Kjopmannskjaer
TORP
Sandefjord
Fyresdal
Nissedal
Tørdal
Porsgrunn
Nystrand
Herøya
Herre
Langangen
Larvik
Framnes
Fyresvatn
Bostrak
Gautefall
Drangedal
Brevik
Stathelle
Eikstrand
Østre Halsen
Berge
Straume
Langesund
Nesvatn
Kilegrend
Nesvatnstemmen
Treungen
Helgeroa
Stavern
Nevlunghavn
59°
Neslandsvatn
Dørdal
Tjonnefoss
Heiland
Smeland
Sannidal
Vafos
Kil
Kragerø
Skatøy
Sandes
Askland
Gjerstad
Sunde bru
Øygårdslia
Myra
Hirtshals
Bygland
Tovdal
Portør
Vegårshei
Søndeled
Åmli
Dølemo
Risør
Songe
Grendi
Byglandsfjord
Nelaug
Åkvåg
Mykland
Oland
Lyngør
Hynnekleiv
Tvedestrand
Holt
Evje
Vegusdal
Mjåvatn
Austre Moland
Vatne
Herefoss
Saltrød
Eydehamn
Stokken
Blakstad
Kongshamn
Iveland
Arendal
Tromøy
Otra
Senumstad
Rykene
Vatnestrøm
Ogge
Skaiå
Vassbotn
Fevik
Grimstad
Tovdalselva
Birkeland
Vennesla
Lillesand
Vikeland
Mosby
Brekkestø
Høvåg
Nodeland
Greipstad
Kristiansand
Skålevik
0 10 20 30 km
8°
9°
10°
58°
3
4
5
6
A
B
47
54

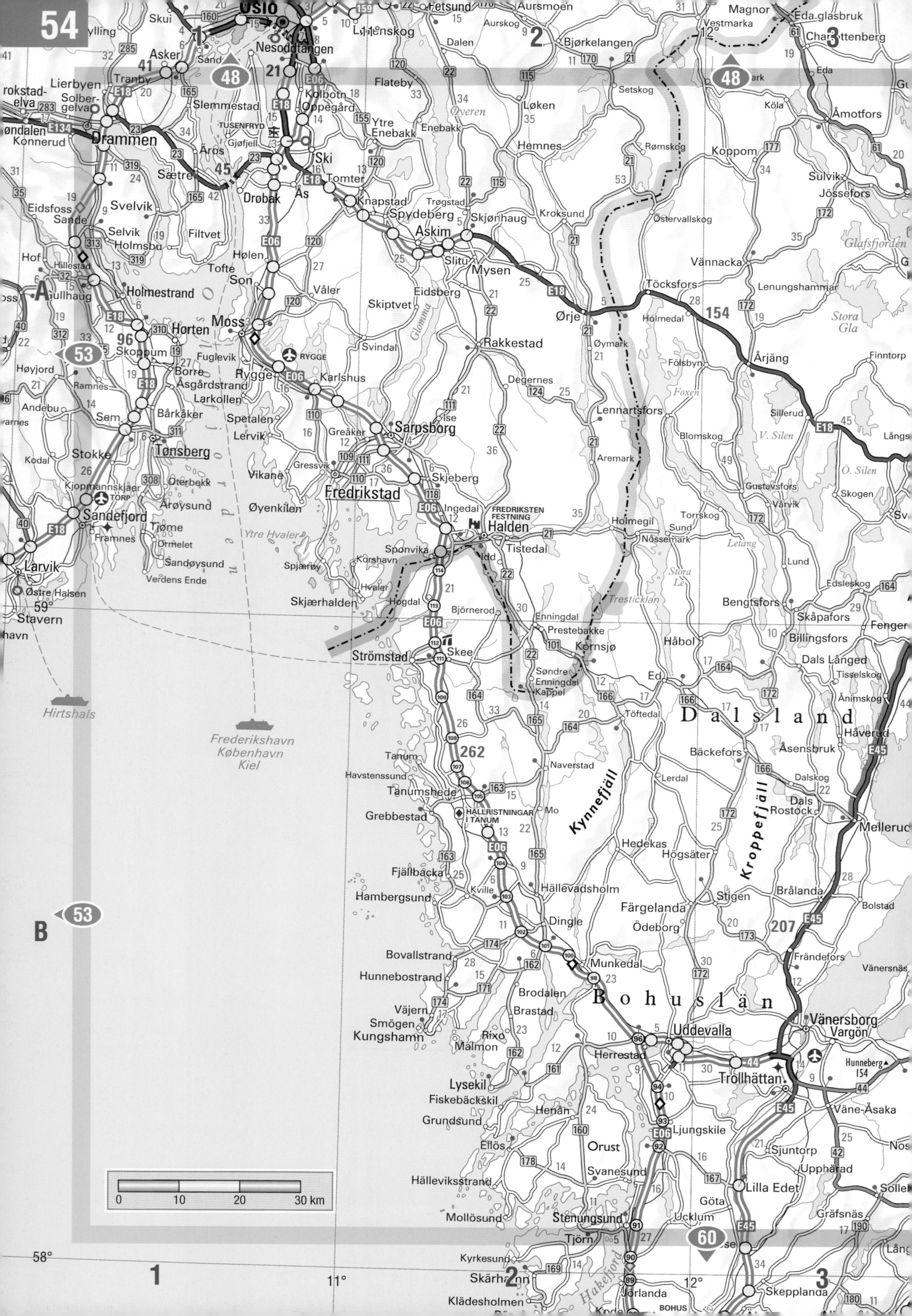

Oslo
Fetsund
Aursmoen
Magnor
Eda glasbruk
Charlottenberg
Vestmarka
Lillestrøm
Aurskog
Bjørkelangen
Skui
Asker
Nesoddtangen
Sand
Lierbyen
Tranby
Solbergelva
Drammen
Konnerud
Slemmestad
Kolbotn
Oppegård
Flateby
Dalen
Øyeren
Setskog
Løken
Eda
Köla
Åmotfors
Tusenfryd
Gjøfjell
Åros
Ytre Enebakk
Enebakk
Hemnes
Rømskog
Koppom
Sulvik
Jössefors
Sætre
Ski
Tomter
Drøbak
Ås
Eidsfoss
Sande
Svelvik
Knapstad
Trøgstad
Spydeberg
Skjønhaug
Kroksund
Østervallskog
Selvik
Holmsbu
Filtvet
Askim
Slitu
Mysen
Glafsfjorden
Hof
Hillestad
Hølen
Tofte
Son
Vännacka
Töcksfors
Lenungshammar
Gullhaug
Holmestrand
Våler
Eidsberg
Skiptvet
Ørje
Holmedal
Stora Gla
Moss
Horten
Skoppum
Glomma
Svindal
Rakkestad
Øymark
Fuglevik
Borre
Åsgårdstrand
Høyjord
Ramnes
Rygge
Karlshus
Fölsbyn
Årjäng
Finntorp
Foxen
Andebu
Sem
Larkollen
Degernes
Bårkåker
Spetalen
Lervik
Greåker
Sarpsborg
Ise
Lennartsfors
Sillerud
Blomskog
V. Silen
Långs
Tønsberg
Stokke
Kodal
Gressvik
Vikane
Fredrikstad
Skjeberg
Aremark
Ö. Silen
Gustavsfors
Skogen
Vårvik
Oterbekk
Kjopmannskjær
Torp
Årøysund
Øyenkilen
Ingedal
Fredriksten Festning
Halden
Holmegil
Torrskog
Sund
Nössemark
Letång
Sandefjord
Framnes
Tjøme
Ormelet
Ytre Hvaler
Sponvika
Tistedal
Larvik
Sandøysund
Verdens Ende
Korshavn
Spjærøy
Stora Le
Lund
Østre Halsen
Stavern
Hvaler
Skjærhalden
Hogdal
Idd
Tresticklan
Edsleskog
Bjørnerod
Enningdal
Prestebakke
Kornsjø
Bengtsfors
Skåpafors
Fenger
Billingsfors
Strömstad
Skee
Håbol
Dals Långed
Tisselskog
Hirtshals
Søndre Enningdal
Kappel
Ed
Åmål
Töftedal
Dalsland
Håverud
Åmskog
Frederikshavn
København
Kiel
Tanum
Bäckefors
Åsensbruk
Havstenssund
Tanumshede
Naverstad
Lerdal
Dalskog
Kynnefjäll
Kroppefjäll
Dals Rostock
Grebbestad
Hällristningar i Tanum
Mo
Mellerud
Hedekas
Högsäter
Fjällbacka
Kville
Hällevadsholm
Brålanda
Hambergsund
Färgelanda
Stigen
Bolstad
Dingle
Ödeborg
Bovallstrand
Frändefors
Vänersnäs
Munkedal
Hunnebostrand
Brodalen
Bohuslän
Väjern
Brastad
Smögen
Kungshamn
Vänersborg
Vargön
Uddevalla
Rixo
Malmon
Herrestad
Hunneberg
Trollhättan
Lysekil
Fiskebäckskil
Väne-Åsaka
Grundsund
Henån
Ljungskile
Ellös
Orust
Sjuntorp
Upphärad
Svanesund
Hälleviksstrand
Lilla Edet
Göta
Mollösund
Stenungsund
Ucklum
Gräfsnäs
Tjörn
Kyrkesund
Skärhamn
Hakefjord
Jörlanda
Skepplanda
Klädesholmen
Bohus
0 10 20 30 km
58°
59°
11°
12°
A
B
1
2
3
48
53
60

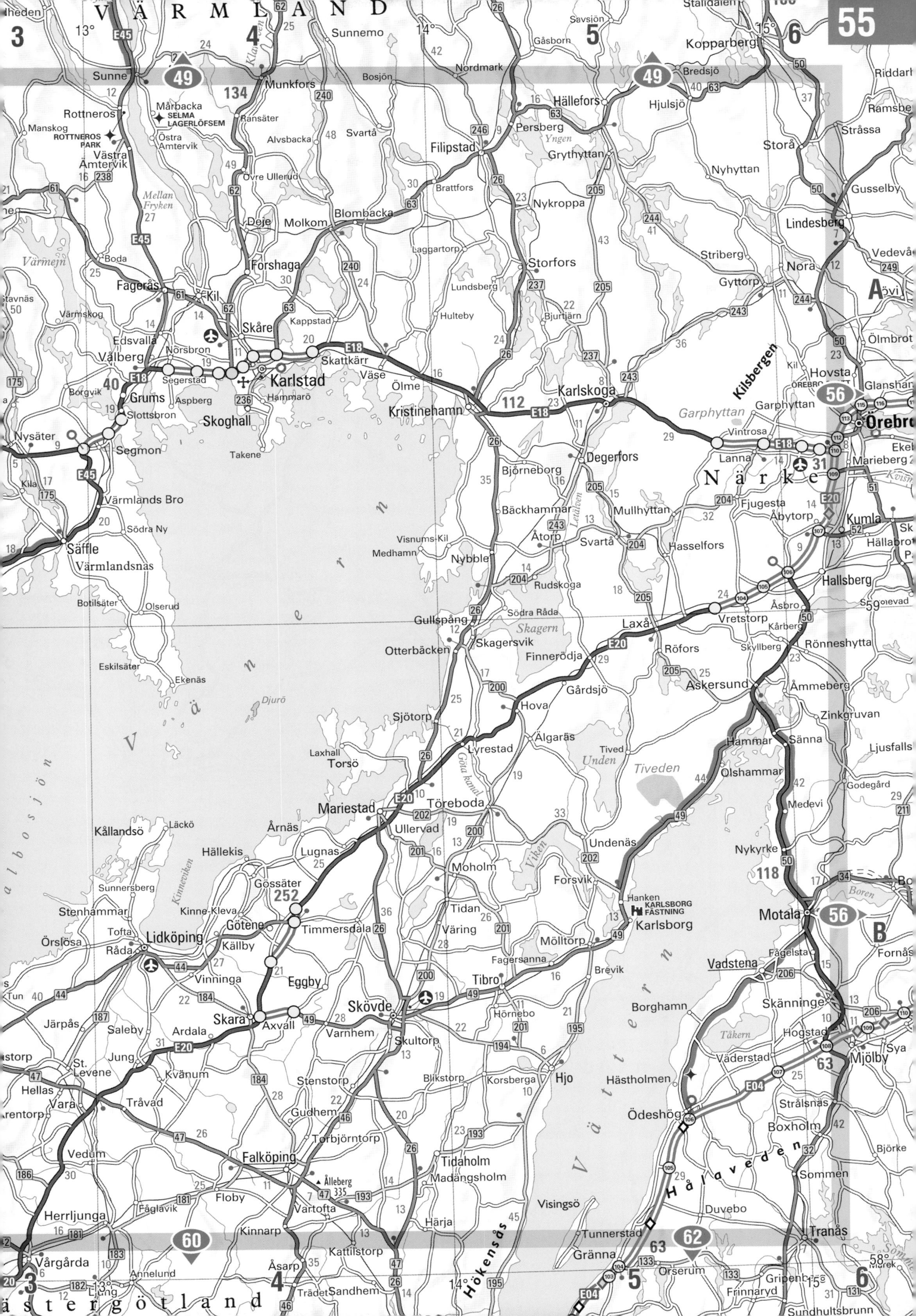
VÄRMLAND
Närke
Västergötland
Vänern
Vättern
Sunne
Munkfors
Rottneros
Mårbacka
SELMA LAGERLÖFSEM
ROTTNEROS PARK
Ransäter
Östra Ämtervik
Västra Ämtervik
Manskog
Övre Ullerud
Mellan Fryken
Deje
Molkom
Blombacka
Filipstad
Persberg
Hällefors
Grythyttan
Nykroppa
Storfors
Forshaga
Fagerås
Kil
Skåre
Edsvalla
Vålberg
Nörsbron
Segerstad
Karlstad
Hammarö
Skoghall
Skattkärr
Väse
Ölme
Kristinehamn
Karlskoga
Degerfors
Grums
Aspberg
Slottsbron
Borgvik
Nysäter
Segmon
Takene
Värmlands Bro
Södra Ny
Säffle
Värmlandsnäs
Botilsäter
Olserud
Eskilsäter
Ekenäs
Djurö
Kila
Värmskog
Boda
Värmeln
Kopparberg
Bredsjö
Hjulsjö
Gåsborn
Savsjön
Sunnemo
Nordmark
Bosjön
Svartå
Alvsbacka
Yngen
Brattfors
Laggartorp
Lundsberg
Hulteby
Bjurtjärn
Kappstad
Nyhyttan
Storå
Lindesberg
Striberg
Nora
Gyttorp
Kilsbergen
Garphyttan
Vintrosa
Lanna
Örebro
Hovsta
Glanshammar
Ekeby
Marieberg
Kumla
Fjugesta
Åbytorp
Hallsberg
Åsbro
Vretstorp
Laxå
Röfors
Mullhyttan
Hasselfors
Svartå
Åtorp
Bäckhammar
Björneborg
Letälven
Visnums-Kil
Medhamn
Nybble
Rudskoga
Södra Råda
Skagern
Gullspång
Skagersvik
Otterbäcken
Finnerödja
Gårdsjö
Askersund
Åmmeberg
Zinkgruvan
Hova
Älgarås
Tived
Unden
Tiveden
Hammar
Sänna
Olshammar
Medevi
Godegård
Ljusfalls
Rönneshytta
Kårberg
Skyllberg
Sjötorp
Lyrestad
Göta kanal
Laxhall
Torsö
Mariestad
Töreboda
Ullervad
Årnäs
Lugnås
Läckö
Kållandsö
Hällekis
Kinneviken
Sunnersberg
Gössäter
Kinne-Kleva
Götene
Timmersdala
Stenhammar
Tofta
Lidköping
Örslösa
Råda
Källby
Vinninga
Eggby
Moholm
Tidan
Väring
Viken
Undenäs
Forsvik
Hanken
KARLSBORG FÄSTNING
Karlsborg
Mölltorp
Fagersanna
Brevik
Tibro
Skövde
Hörnebo
Borghamn
Motala
Boren
Vadstena
Fågelsta
Skänninge
Tåkern
Hogstad
Väderstad
Mjölby
Sya
Fornås
Hästholmen
Ödeshög
Strålsnäs
Boxholm
Sommen
Björke
Hålaveden
Tranås
Duvebo
Visingsö
Tunnerstad
Gränna
Orserum
Gripenberg
Frinnaryd
Sundhultsbrunn
Hökensås
Tun
Järpås
Saleby
Ardala
Skara
Axvall
Varnhem
Skultorp
Blikstorp
Korsberga
Hjo
Jung
St. Levene
Kvänum
Hellas
Vara
Tråvad
Stenstorp
Gudhem
Torbjörntorp
Vedum
Falköping
Ålleberg
Tidaholm
Madängsholm
Floby
Fåglavik
Vartofta
Härja
Herrljunga
Kinnarp
Kattilstorp
Vårgårda
Annelund
Åsarp
Ljung
Trädet
Sandhem

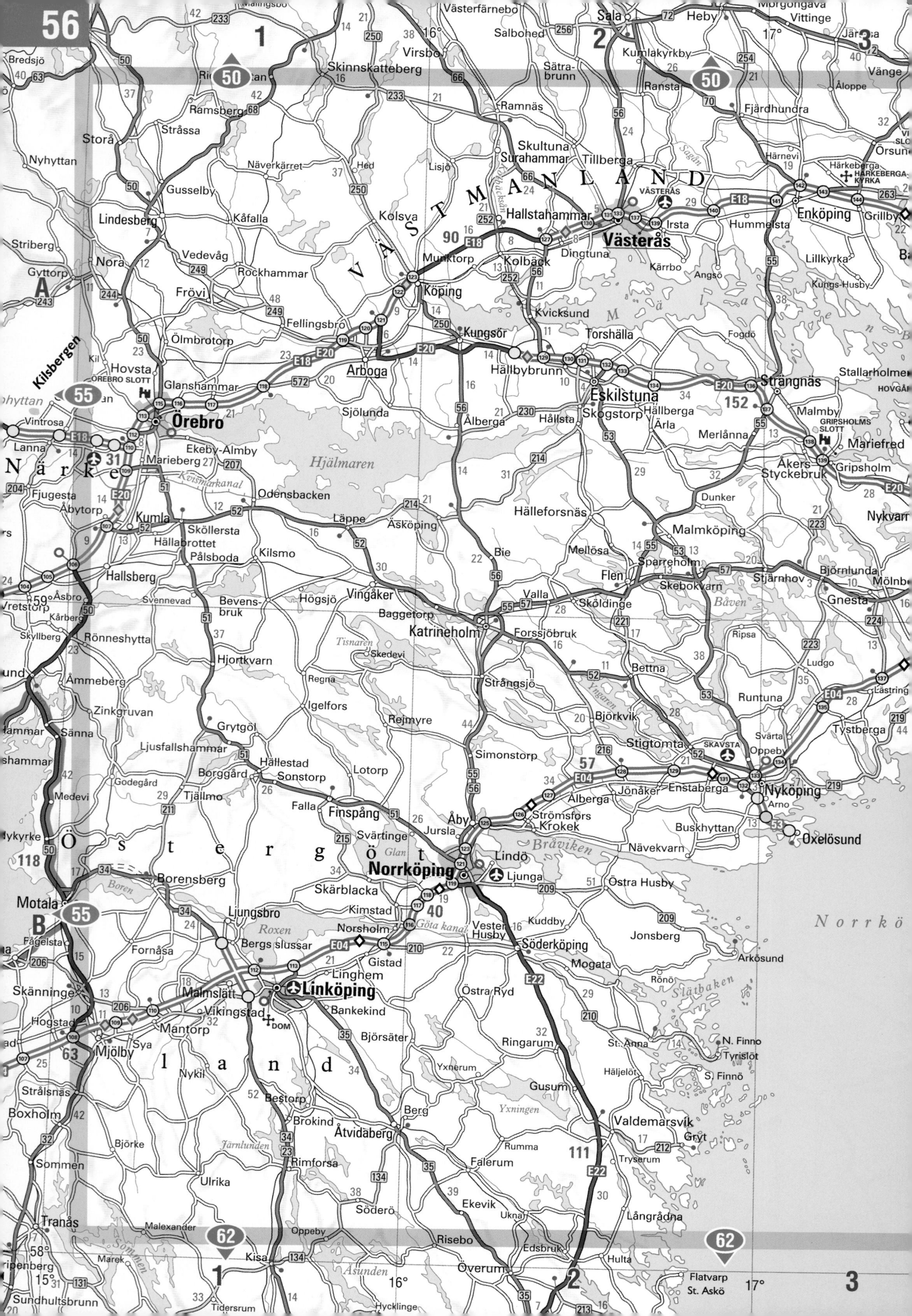
Västmanland
Närke
Östergötland
Hjälmaren
Örebro
Västerås
Eskilstuna
Norrköping
Linköping
Nyköping
Katrineholm
Köping
Arboga
Kungsör
Strängnäs
Enköping
Sala
Lindesberg
Kumla
Hallsberg
Motala
Mjölby
Finspång
Flen
Oxelösund
Söderköping
Åtvidaberg
Valdemarsvik
Mariefred
Torshälla
Hallstahammar
Surahammar
Fellingsbro
Vingåker
Skänninge
Tranås
Kisa
Norrkö

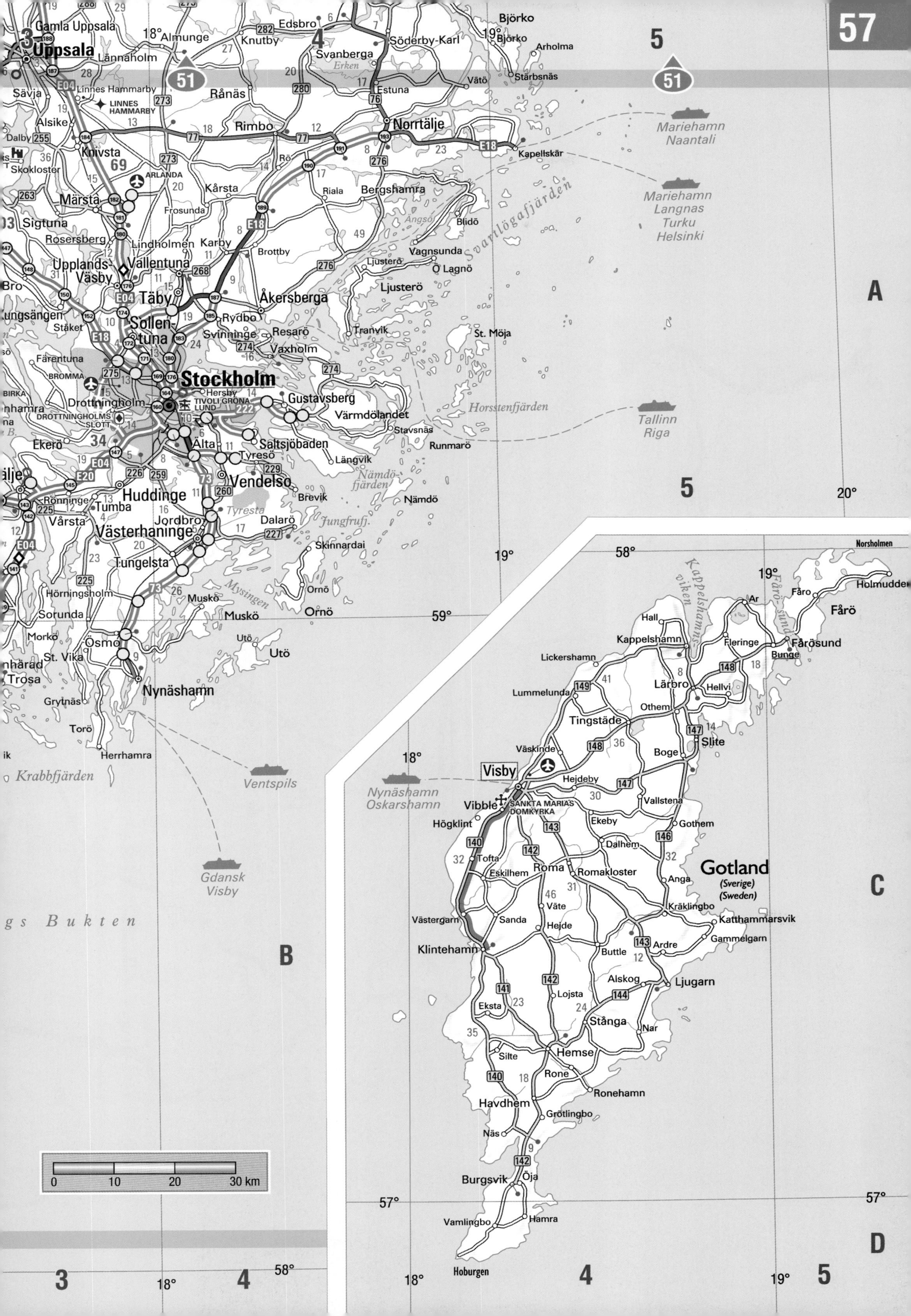

Gamla Uppsala
Uppsala
Almunge
Edsbro
Björko
Björko
Arholma
5

Lännaholm
Knutby
Svanberga
Söderby-Karl
Vätö
Stärbsnäs

Linnés Hammarby
Rånäs
Estuna
Kapellskär

Mariehamn
Naantali

Alsike
Rimbo
Norrtälje

Knivsta
Rö
Riala

Dalby
Kårsta
Bergshamra

Mariehamn
Langnas
Turku
Helsinki

Skokloster
Arlanda
Frosunda
Blidö

Märsta
Ängsö
Vagnsunda
Ljusterö
Lagnö

Sigtuna
Rosersberg
Lindholmen
Karby
Brottby

Ljusterö

Upplands
Väsby
Vallentuna
St. Möja

Täby
Åkersberga

Bro
Sollentuna
Rydbo
Svinninge
Resarö
Tranvik

Stäket
Vaxholm

Färentuna
BROMMA

Birka
Stockholm
Hersby
TIVOLI GRÖNA
LUND
Gustavsberg
Värmdölandet

Horstenfjärden

Drottningholm
DROTTNINGHOLMS
SLOTT
Stavsnäs
Runmarö

Tallinn
Riga

Ekerö
Alta
Saltsjöbaden
Längvik

Tyresö
Nämdö-
fjärden

Huddinge
Vendelso
Brevik
Nämdö

Ronninge
Tumba
Jordbro
Tyresta
Dalarö

Vårsta
Västerhaninge
Skinnardal

Tungelsta
Ornö

Mysingen
Ornö
Ornö

Hörningsholm
Muskö
Utö

Sorunda
Muskö

Mörkö
Utö

St. Vika
Trosa
Östmo

Grytnäs
Nynäshamn

Torö

Herrhamra

Krabbfjärden
Ventspils

Gdansk
Visby

g s   B u k t e n

Norsholmen

Kappelshamns-
viken
Fårö
Holmudden

Ar
Fårö
Fårö

Hall
Kappelshamn
Fleringe
Fårösund
Bunge

Lickershamn
Lärbro
Hellvi

Lummelunda
Othem

Tingstäde
Slite

Väskinde
Boge

Visby
Hejdeby

Vibble
SANKTA MARIAS
DOMKYRKA
Ekeby
Gothem

Nynäshamn
Oskarshamn

Högklint
Dalhem

Tofta
Roma
Romakloster
Anga

Eskilhem
Kräklingbo

Gotland
(Sverige)
(Sweden)

Västergarn
Väte
Katthammarsvik

Sanda
Hejde
Gammelgarn

Klintehamn
Buttle
Ardre

Alskog
Ljugarn

Eksta
Lojsta
Stånga
Nar

Silte
Hemse

Rone
Ronehamn

Havdhem
Grötlingbo

Näs

Burgsvik
Öja

Vamlingbo
Hamra

Hoburgen

0   10   20   30 km

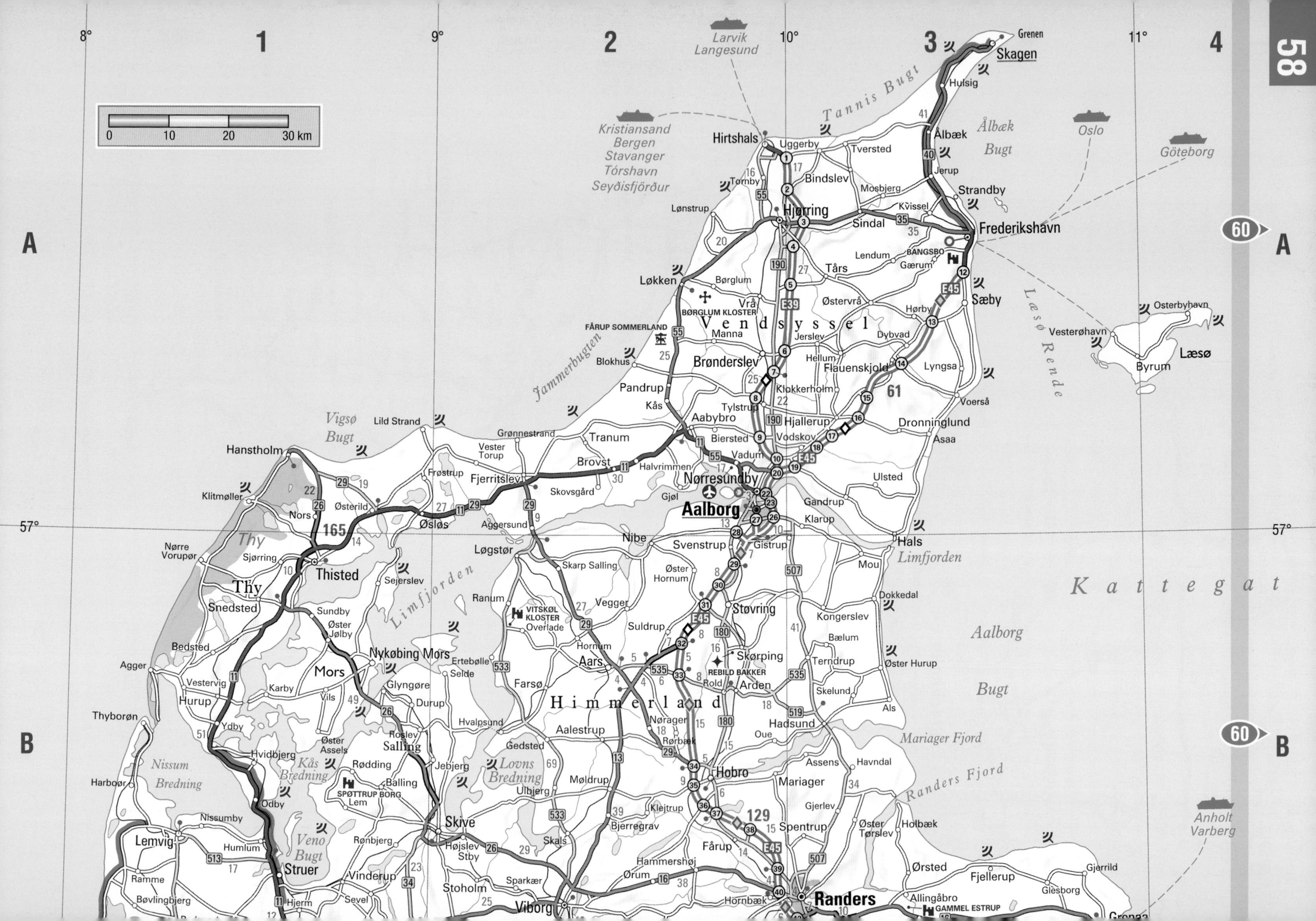
0 10 20 30 km
Skagen
Grenen
Hulsig
Tannis Bugt
Ålbæk
Ålbæk Bugt
Jerup
Strandby
Frederikshavn
Oslo
Göteborg
Larvik
Langesund
Kristiansand
Bergen
Stavanger
Tórshavn
Seyðisfjörður
Hirtshals
Uggerby
Tversted
Bindslev
Tornby
Mosbjerg
Kvissel
Hjørring
Sindal
Lønstrup
Lendum
Bangsbo
Gærum
Tårs
Løkken
Børglum
Vrå
Børglum Kloster
Vendsyssel
Manna
Østervrå
Hørby
Sæby
Læsø Rende
Vesterøhavn
Østerbyhavn
Læsø
Byrum
Dybvad
Jerslev
Fårup Sommerland
Blokhus
Brønderslev
Hellum
Flauenskjold
Lyngsa
Jammerbugten
Pandrup
Klokkerholm
Kås
Tylstrup
Voerså
Aabybro
Hjallerup
Vigsø Bugt
Lild Strand
Dronninglund
Asaa
Grønnestrand
Tranum
Biersted
Vodskov
Vadum
Hanstholm
Vester Torup
Brovst
Halvrimmen
Nørresundby
Ulsted
Frøstrup
Fjerritslev
Klitmøller
Skovsgård
Gjøl
Gandrup
Aalborg
Klarup
Nors
Østerild
Øsløs
Aggersund
Thy
Nørre Vorupør
Sjørring
Thisted
Løgstør
Nibe
Svenstrup
Gistrup
Hals
Mou
Limfjorden
Kattegat
Sejerslev
Skarp Salling
Øster Hornum
Thy
Snedsted
Ranum
Vitskøl Kloster
Overlade
Vegger
Støvring
Dokkedal
Sundby
Øster Jølby
Suldrup
Kongerslev
Aalborg Bugt
Bedsted
Nykøbing Mors
Hornum
Bælum
Agger
Ertebølle
Selde
Aars
Skørping
Rebild Bakker
Terndrup
Øster Hurup
Mors
Farsø
Vestervig
Karby
Rold
Arden
Skelund
Hurup
Vils
Glyngøre
Durup
Himmerland
Als
Thyborøn
Ydby
Hvalpsund
Aalestrup
Nørager
Hadsund
Øster Assels
Roslev
Salling
Gedsted
Rørbæk
Oue
Mariager Fjord
Nissum Bredning
Hvidbjerg
Kås Bredning
Rødding
Lovns Bredning
Møldrup
Hobro
Assens
Havndal
Harboør
Balling
Spøttrup Borg
Lem
Jebjerg
Ulbjerg
Mariager
Randers Fjord
Odby
Gjerlev
Nissumby
Skive
Bjerregrav
Klejtrup
Spentrup
Øster Tørslev
Holbæk
Anholt
Varberg
Lemvig
Humlum
Veno Bugt
Rønbjerg
Højslev
Stby
Skals
Fårup
Struer
Hammershøj
Ørsted
Gjerrild
Ramme
Vinderup
Stoholm
Sparkær
Ørum
Fjellerup
Bøvlingbjerg
Sevel
Hjerm
Viborg
Hornbæk
Randers
Allingåbro
Gammel Estrup
Glesborg
Grenaa
57°
8°
9°
10°
11°
1
2
3
4
A
B
60

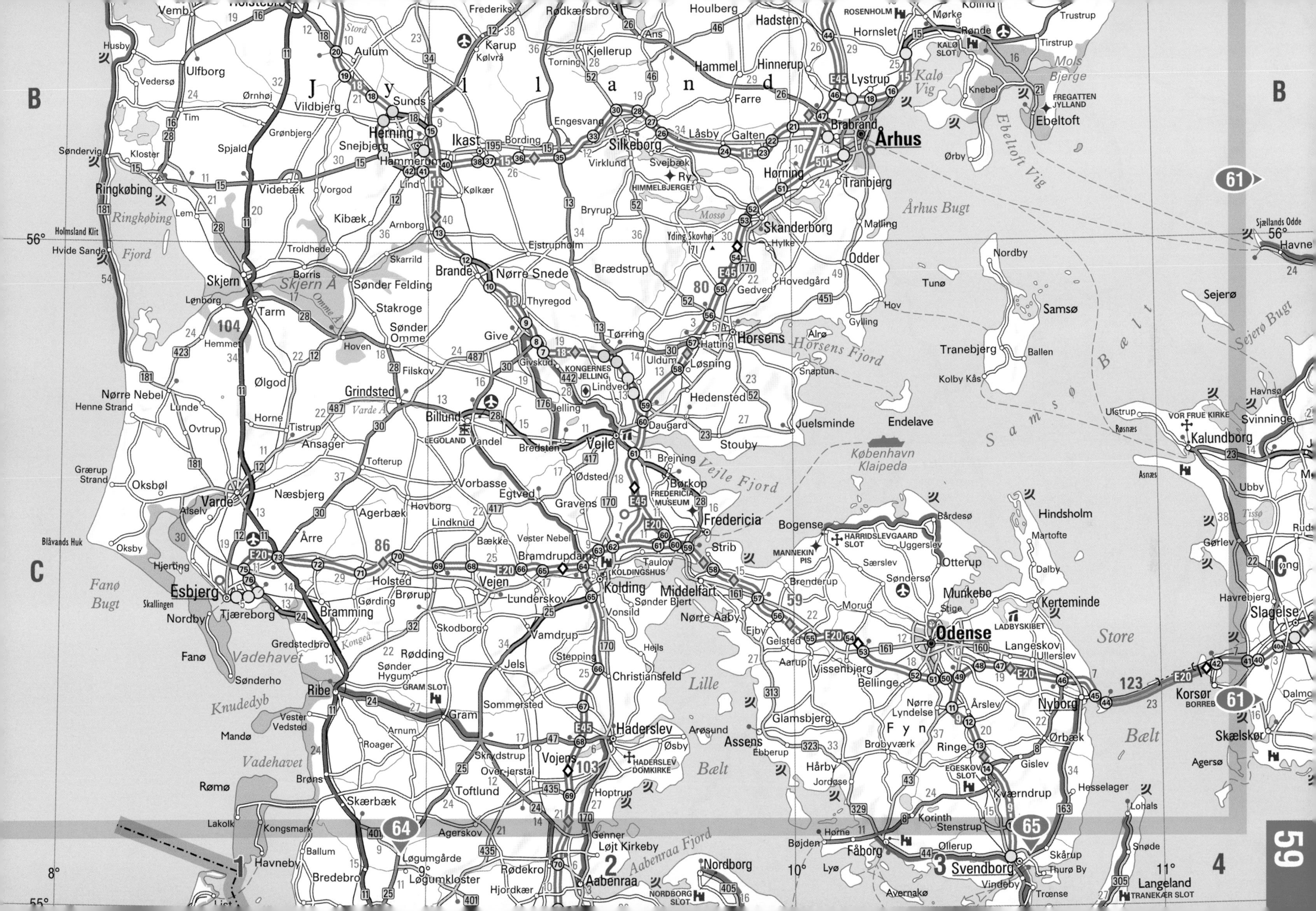
Jylland
Vemb
Husby
Vedersø
Ulfborg
Ørnhøj
Aulum
Vildbjerg
Sunds
Herning
Tim
Søndervig
Kloster
Spjald
Grønbjerg
Snejbjerg
Hammerum
Ikast
Bording
Karup
Kølvrå
Frederiks
Rødkærsbro
Kjellerup
Torning
Houlberg
Ans
Hammel
Hadsten
Hinnerup
Farre
Hornslet
Lystrup
Brabrand
Århus
ROSENHOLM
Mørke
Rønde
KALØ SLOT
Kalø Vig
Knebel
Mols Bjerge
Trustrup
Tirstrup
FREGATTEN JYLLAND
Ebeltoft
Ebeltoft Vig
Ørby
Ringkøbing
Lem
Videbæk
Vorgod
Lind
Kølkær
Engesvang
Silkeborg
Virklund
Svejbæk
Ry
HIMMELBJERGET
Låsby
Galten
Hørning
Tranbjerg
Århus Bugt
Holmsland Klit
Hvide Sande
Ringkøbing Fjord
Kibæk
Arnborg
Troldhede
Skarrild
Brande
Nørre Snede
Ejstrupholm
Bryrup
Mossø
Yding Skovhøj
Skanderborg
Hylke
Malling
Odder
Nordby
Tunø
Samsø
Sejerø
Sejerø Bugt
Sjællands Odde
Havne
Skjern
Skjern Å
Borris
Sønder Felding
Lønborg
Tarm
Omme Å
Stakroge
Sønder Omme
Hoven
Thyregod
Brædstrup
Hovedgård
Gedved
Horsens
Hatting
Horsens Fjord
Alrø
Hov
Gylling
Tranebjerg
Ballen
Kolby Kås
Snaptun
Samsø Bælt
Hemmet
Ølgod
Give
Givskud
Tørring
Uldum
Løsning
Filskov
Grindsted
KONGERNES JELLING
Lindved
Jelling
Hedensted
Juelsminde
Endelave
Nørre Nebel
Henne Strand
Lunde
Ovtrup
Horne
Tistrup
Varde Å
Billund
LEGOLAND
Vandel
Bredsten
Vejle
Daugard
Stouby
København Klaipeda
Ansager
Tofterup
Brejning
Vejle Fjord
Ulstrup
Røsnæs
VOR FRUE KIRKE
Kalundborg
Svinninge
Havnsø
Asnæs
Ubby
Tissø
Grærup Strand
Oksbøl
Varde
Alslev
Næsbjerg
Vorbasse
Egtved
Ødsted
Børkop
FREDERICIA MUSEUM
Fredericia
Gravens
Hovborg
Agerbæk
Lindknud
Blåvands Huk
Oksby
Hjerting
Årre
Bække
Vester Nebel
Bramdrupdam
Kolding
KOLDINGSHUS
Taulov
Strib
Bogense
Bårdesø
HARRIDSLEVGAARD SLOT
MANNEKIN PIS
Uggerslev
Særslev
Otterup
Hindsholm
Martofte
Dalby
Gørlev
Havrebjerg
Slagelse
Fanø Bugt
Esbjerg
Skallingen
Nordby
Tjæreborg
Holsted
Gørding
Brørup
Bramming
Vejen
Lunderskov
Sønder Bjert
Middelfart
Brenderup
Søndersø
Munkebo
Stige
Kerteminde
LADBYSKIBET
Store Bælt
Fanø
Vadehavet
Gredstedbro
Kongeå
Rødding
Sønder Hygum
Skodborg
Vamdrup
Vonsild
Stepping
Christiansfeld
Hejls
Nørre Aaby
Ejby
Gelsted
Morud
Odense
Langeskov
Ullerslev
Sønderho
Ribe
Jels
Lille Bælt
Aarup
Vissenbjerg
Bellinge
Knudedyb
Vester Vedsted
Mandø
GRAM SLOT
Gram
Arnum
Sommersted
Haderslev
Årøsund
Assens
Ebberup
Glamsbjerg
Nørre Lyndelse
Årslev
Fyn
Nyborg
Korsør
BORREB
Dalmo
Skælskør
Roager
Skrydstrup
Over-Jerstal
Vojens
Øsby
HADERSLEV DOMKIRKE
Hårby
Jordløse
Brobyværk
Ringe
EGESKOV SLOT
Ørbæk
Gislev
Agersø
Rømø
Brøns
Skærbæk
Toftlund
Hoptrup
Kværndrup
Hesselager
Lohals
Lakolk
Kongsmark
Agerskov
Genner
Løjt Kirkeby
Aabenraa Fjord
Korinth
Stenstrup
Horne
Bøjden
Fåborg
Øllerup
Svendborg
Skårup
Snøde
Ballum
Havneby
Bredebro
Løgumgårde
Løgumkloster
Rødekro
Hjordkær
Aabenraa
Nordborg
NORDBORG SLOT
Lyø
Avernakø
Thurø By
Vindeby
Trønse
Langeland
TRANEKÆR SLOT
B
C
1
2
3
4
8°
9°
10°
11°
55°
56°
61
64
65

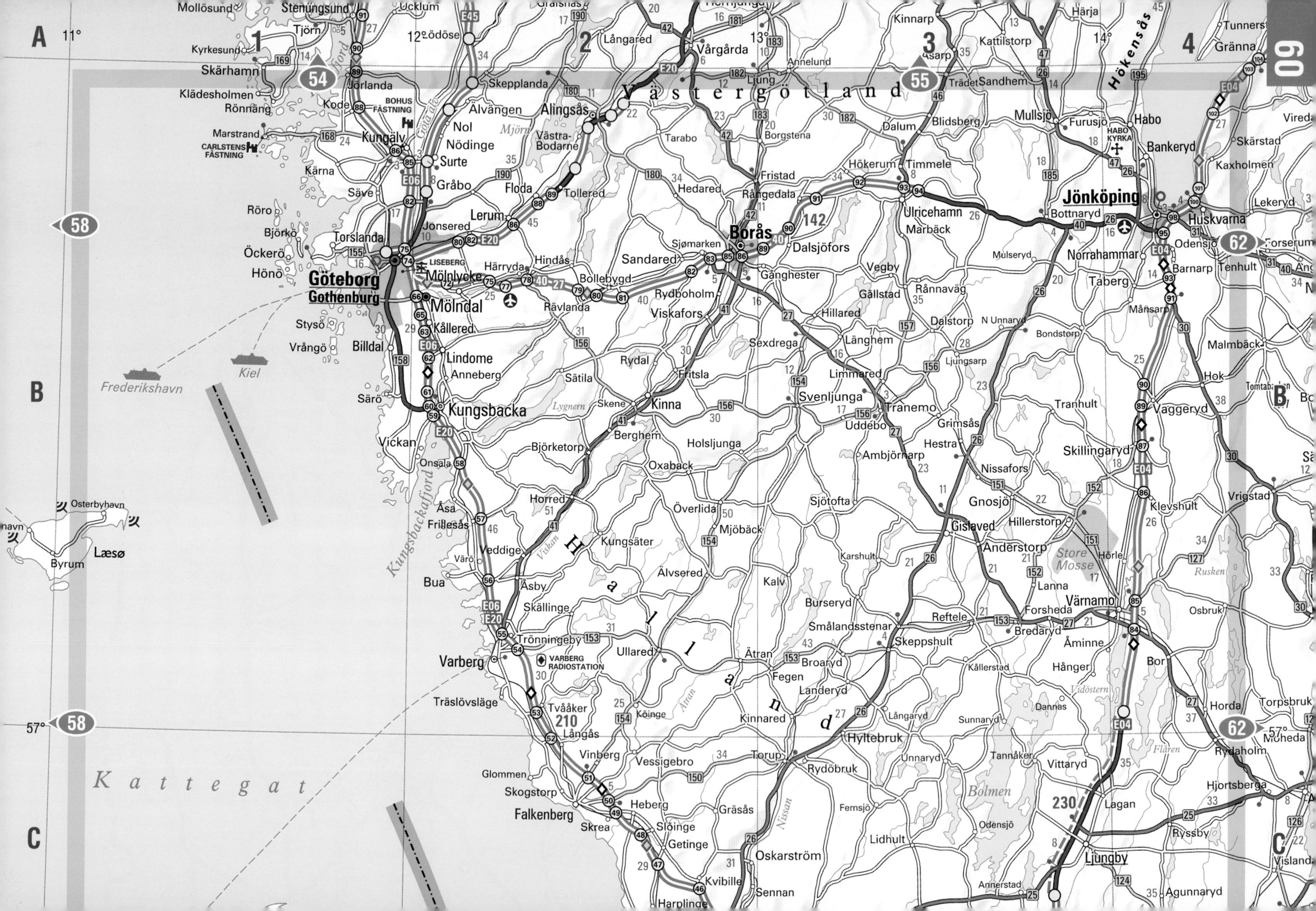
Västergötland
Halland
Kattegat
Göteborg
Gothenburg
Jönköping
Borås
Kungsbacka
Varberg
Falkenberg
Värnamo
Ljungby
Alingsås
Mölndal
Mölnlycke
Kungälv
Lerum
Ulricehamn
Huskvarna
Gislaved
Anderstorp
Gnosjö
Hyltebruk
Skillingaryd
Vaggeryd
Habo
Mullsjö
Vårgårda
Tranemo
Svenljunga
Kinna
Skene
Stenungsund
Tjörn
Skärhamn
Kyrkesund
Klädesholmen
Rönnäng
Marstrand
Mollösund
Öckerö
Hönö
Björkö
Rörö
Torslanda
Säve
Kärna
Kode
Jörlanda
Surte
Nödinge
Nol
Älvängen
Skepplanda
Lödöse
Floda
Gråbo
Jonsered
Tollered
Västra-Bodarne
Härryda
Hindås
Bollebygd
Rävlanda
Sandared
Sjömarken
Dalsjöfors
Fristad
Rångedala
Gånghester
Hedared
Tarabo
Borgstena
Längared
Annelund
Ljung
Viskafors
Rydboholm
Fritsla
Rydal
Sätila
Lindome
Anneberg
Kållered
Billdal
Särö
Vrångö
Styrsö
Vickan
Onsala
Åsa
Frillesås
Värö
Veddige
Bua
Åsby
Skällinge
Trönningeby
Tvååker
Långås
Träslövsläge
Vinberg
Glommen
Skogstorp
Skrea
Heberg
Slöinge
Getinge
Kvibille
Harplinge
Sennan
Oskarström
Gräsås
Vessigebro
Torup
Rydöbruk
Lidhult
Femsjö
Kinnared
Köinge
Ullared
Ätran
Fegen
Broaryd
Landeryd
Älvsered
Kungsäter
Horred
Björketorp
Berghem
Oxaback
Holsljunga
Överlida
Mjöback
Kalv
Karshult
Burseryd
Smålandsstenar
Skeppshult
Reftele
Forsheda
Bredaryd
Åminne
Hånger
Bor
Källerstad
Dannäs
Sunnaryd
Långaryd
Unnaryd
Tannåker
Vittaryd
Lagan
Annerstad
Agunnaryd
Ryssby
Hjortsberga
Rydaholm
Moheda
Horda
Torpsbruk
Vislanda
Osbruk
Vrigstad
Klevshult
Hörle
Lanna
Hillerstorp
Nissafors
Hestra
Sjötofta
Ambjörnarp
Uddebo
Grimsås
Limmared
Länghem
Sexdrega
Hillared
Gällstad
Rånnaväg
Dalstorp
N Unnaryd
Bondstorp
Ljungsarp
Vegby
Marbäck
Hökerum
Timmele
Dalum
Blidsberg
Kinnarp
Åsarp
Trädet
Sandhem
Kattilstorp
Härja
Furusjö
HABO KYRKA
Bankeryd
Bottnaryd
Mulseryd
Norrahammar
Taberg
Månsarp
Barnarp
Odensjö
Tenhult
Forserum
Lekeryd
Kaxholmen
Skärstad
Vireda
Gränna
Tunnerstad
Tranhult
Malmbäck
Hok
Tomtabacken
Hökensås
Store Mosse
Bolmen
Flåren
Vidöstern
Rusken
Nissan
Viskan
Ätran
Lygnern
Mjörn
Göta älv
Kungsbackafjord
Frederikshavn
Kiel
Læsø
Byrum
Österbyhavn
VARBERG RADIOSTATION
LISEBERG
BOHUS FÄSTNING
CARLSTENS FÄSTNING
Odensjö
11°
12°
13°
14°
57°
A
B
C
1
2
3
4
54
55
58
62

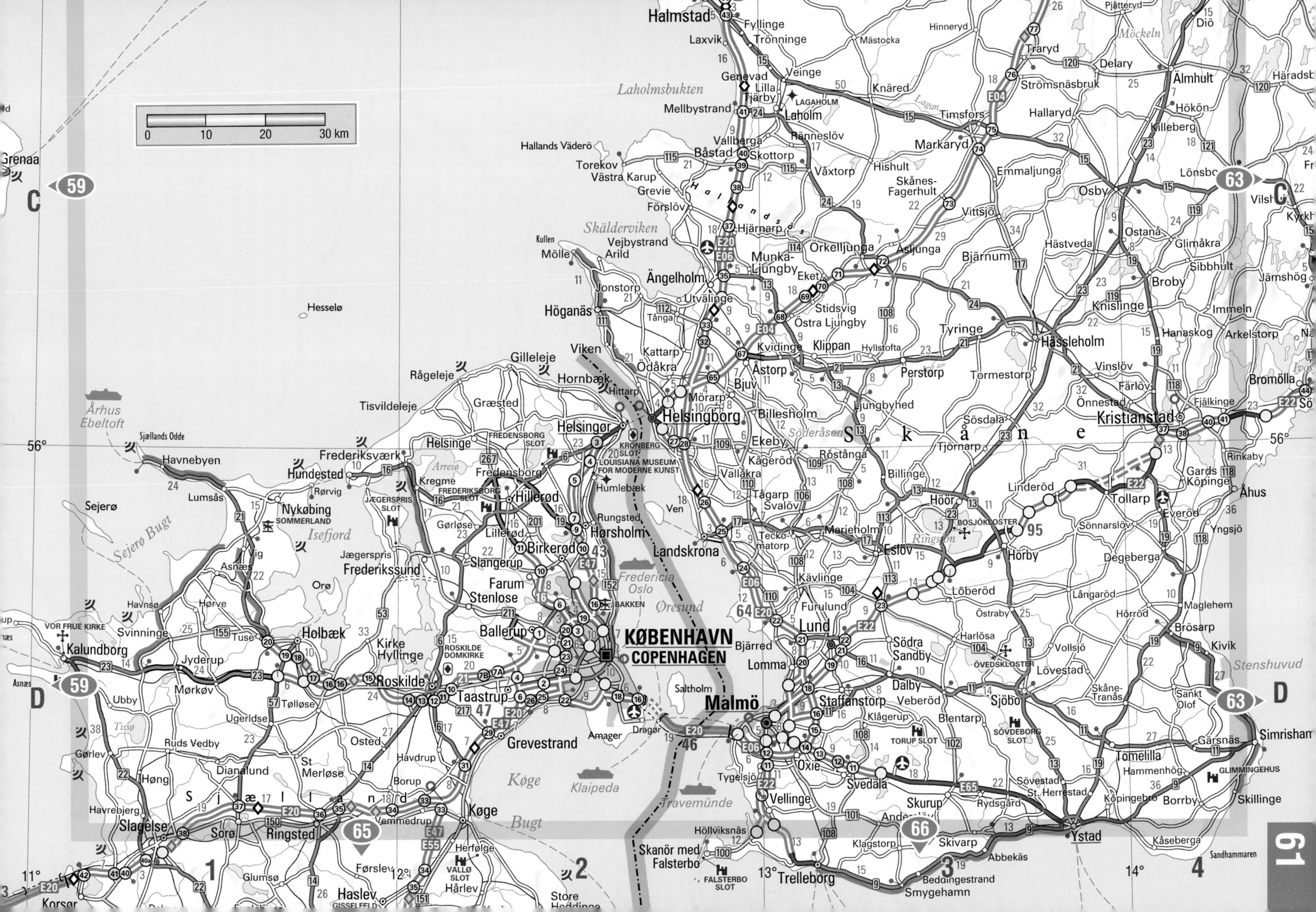
Halmstad
Laholm
Båstad
Ängelholm
Höganäs
Helsingborg
Landskrona
Lund
Malmö
Trelleborg
Ystad
Simrishamn
Kristianstad
Hässleholm
Höör
Hörby
Eslöv
Sjöbo
Skanör med Falsterbo
Älmhult
Markaryd
Osby
Klippan
Åstorp
Perstorp
Helsingør
Hillerød
Frederikssund
Roskilde
Køge
Holbæk
Kalundborg
Slagelse
Sorø
Ringsted
Hundested
Nykøbing
KØBENHAVN
COPENHAGEN
Øresund
Køge Bugt
Sejerø Bugt
Isefjord
Skälderviken
Laholmsbukten
Hallands Väderö
Hesselø
Sejerø
Grenaa
Saltholm
Amager
Skåne
Sjælland
Söderåsen
Stenshuvud
Kullen
Århus
Ebeltoft
Fredericia
Oslo
Travemünde
Klaipeda
56°
14°
13°
11°
0 10 20 30 km

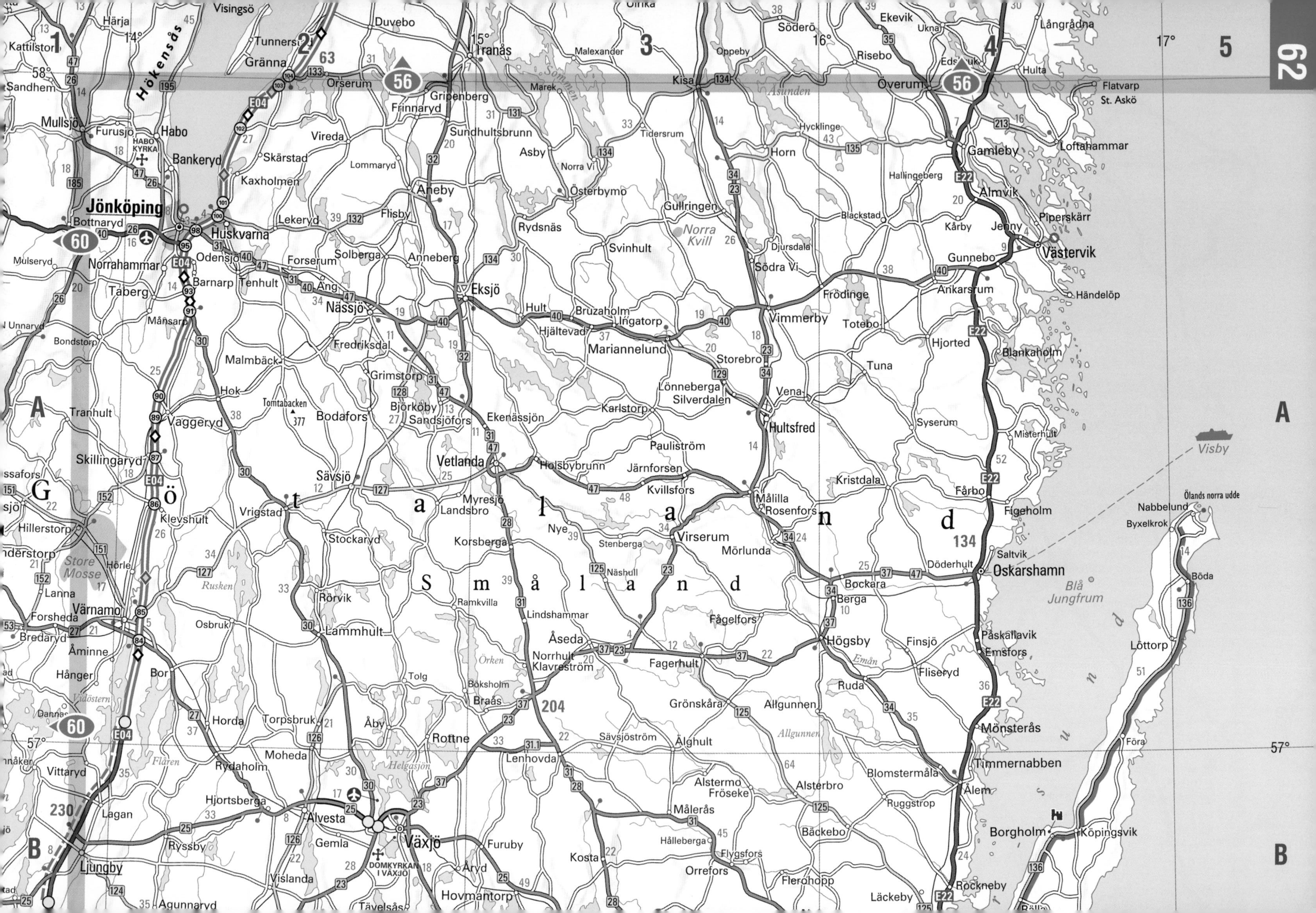
1
2
3
4
5
A
B
14°
15°
16°
17°
57°
58°
Jönköping
Huskvarna
Gränna
Tranås
Eksjö
Nässjö
Vetlanda
Västervik
Oskarshamn
Vimmerby
Hultsfred
Växjö
Alvesta
Ljungby
Värnamo
Kisa
Gamleby
Överum
Mönsterås
Borgholm
Högsby
Mörlunda
Virserum
Åseda
Lenhovda
Kosta
Orrefors
Lammhult
Braås
Rottne
Vaggeryd
Skillingaryd
Sävsjö
Aneby
Kaxholmen
Tenhult
Bankeryd
Habo
Mullsjö
Taberg
Norrahammar
Bottnaryd
Visingsö
Hökensås
Småland
Blå Jungfrum
Visby
Ölands norra udde
Nabbelund
Böda
Löttorp
Byxelkrok
Köpingsvik
Föra
Fagerhult
Kristdala
Berga
Bockara
Påskallavik
Emsfors
Figeholm
Saltvik
Döderhult
Ankarsrum
Loftahammar
Gunnebo
Almvik
Jenny
Piperskärr
Händelöp
Flatvarp
St. Askö
Långrådna
Ekevik
Totebo
Frödinge
Mariannelund
Ingatorp
Bruzaholm
Holsbybrunn
Landsbro
Myresjö
Stockaryd
Bodafors
Forserum
Lekeryd
Grimstorp
Malmbäck
Vrigstad
Rörvik
Moheda
Rydaholm
Lagan
Vislanda
Gemla
Furuby
Tolg
Åby
Hovmantorp
Älghult
Alsterbro
Läckeby
Rockneby
Ålem
Timmernabben
Fårbo
Hjorted
Tuna
Storebro
Lönneberga
Silverdalen
Pauliström
Kvillsfors
Järnforsen
Karlstorp
Hult
Hjältevad
Sommen
Norra Kvill
Asunden
Store Mosse
Helgasjön
Emån
E04
E22
56
60
63
204
230

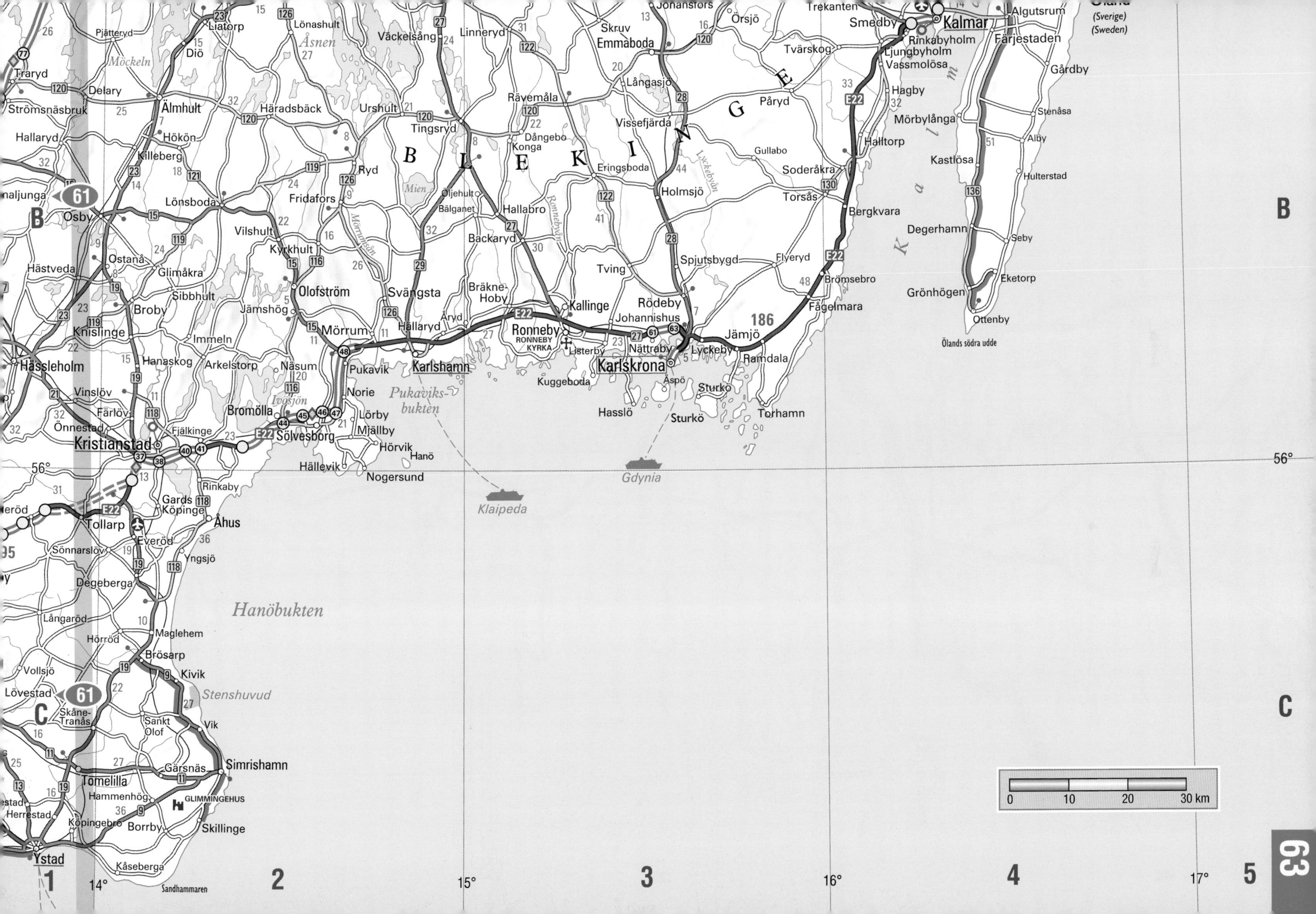
(Sverige)
(Sweden)
Kalmar
Färjestaden
Algutsrum
Gårdby
Stenåsa
Alby
Hulterstad
Seby
Eketorp
Ottenby
Ölands södra udde
Grönhögen
Degerhamn
Kastlösa
Mörbylånga
Rinkabyholm
Ljungbyholm
Vassmolösa
Hagby
Smedby
Halltorp
Bergkvara
Trekanten
Tvärskog
Påryd
Soderåkra
Torsås
Gullabo
Brömsebro
Fågelmara
Flyeryd
Torhamn
Ramdala
Jämjö
Örsjö
Johansfors
Spjutsbygd
Lyckeby
Sturkö
Äspö
Karlskrona
Nättraby
Rödeby
Johannishus
Holmsjö
Lyckebyån
Vissefjärda
Långasjö
Emmaboda
Skruv
Eringsboda
Tving
Hasslö
Gdynia
Klaipeda
Kallinge
Listerby
Kuggeboda
Ronneby
RONNEBY KYRKA
Ronnebyån
Rävemåla
Dångebo
Konga
Hallabro
Backaryd
Bräkne-Hoby
Linneryd
Tingsryd
Öljehult
Bälganet
Väckelsång
Urshult
Ryd
Mien
Svängsta
Hällaryd
Åryd
Karlshamn
Pukaviks-bukten
Pukavik
Norie
Lörby
Mjällby
Hörvik
Hanö
Nogersund
Hällevik
Sölvesborg
Mörrum
Mörrumsån
Olofström
Fridafors
Lönashult
Åsnen
Häradsbäck
Kyrkhult
Jämshög
Näsum
Ivösjön
Bromölla
Vilshult
Arkelstorp
Immeln
Liatorp
Diö
Älmhult
Hökön
Killeberg
Lönsboda
Glimåkra
Sibbhult
Hanaskog
Broby
Östanå
Knislinge
Möckeln
Pjätteryd
Delary
Strömsnäsbruk
Hallaryd
Traryd
Osby
Hästveda
Hässleholm
Vinslöv
Färlöv
Önnestad
Kristianstad
Fjälkinge
Rinkaby
Gärds Köpinge
Åhus
Yngsjö
Everöd
Tollarp
Sönnarslöv
Degeberga
Hanöbukten
Långaröd
Hörröd
Maglehem
Brösarp
Kivik
Stenshuvud
Vik
Sankt Olof
Gärsnäs
Simrishamn
GLIMMINGEHUS
Skillinge
Tomelilla
Hammenhög
Borrby
Köpingebro
Skåne-Tranås
Kåseberga
Sandhammaren
Lövestad
Vollsjö
Herrestad
Ystad
B
C
1
2
3
4
5
14°
15°
16°
17°
56°
0
10
20
30 km
E22
186

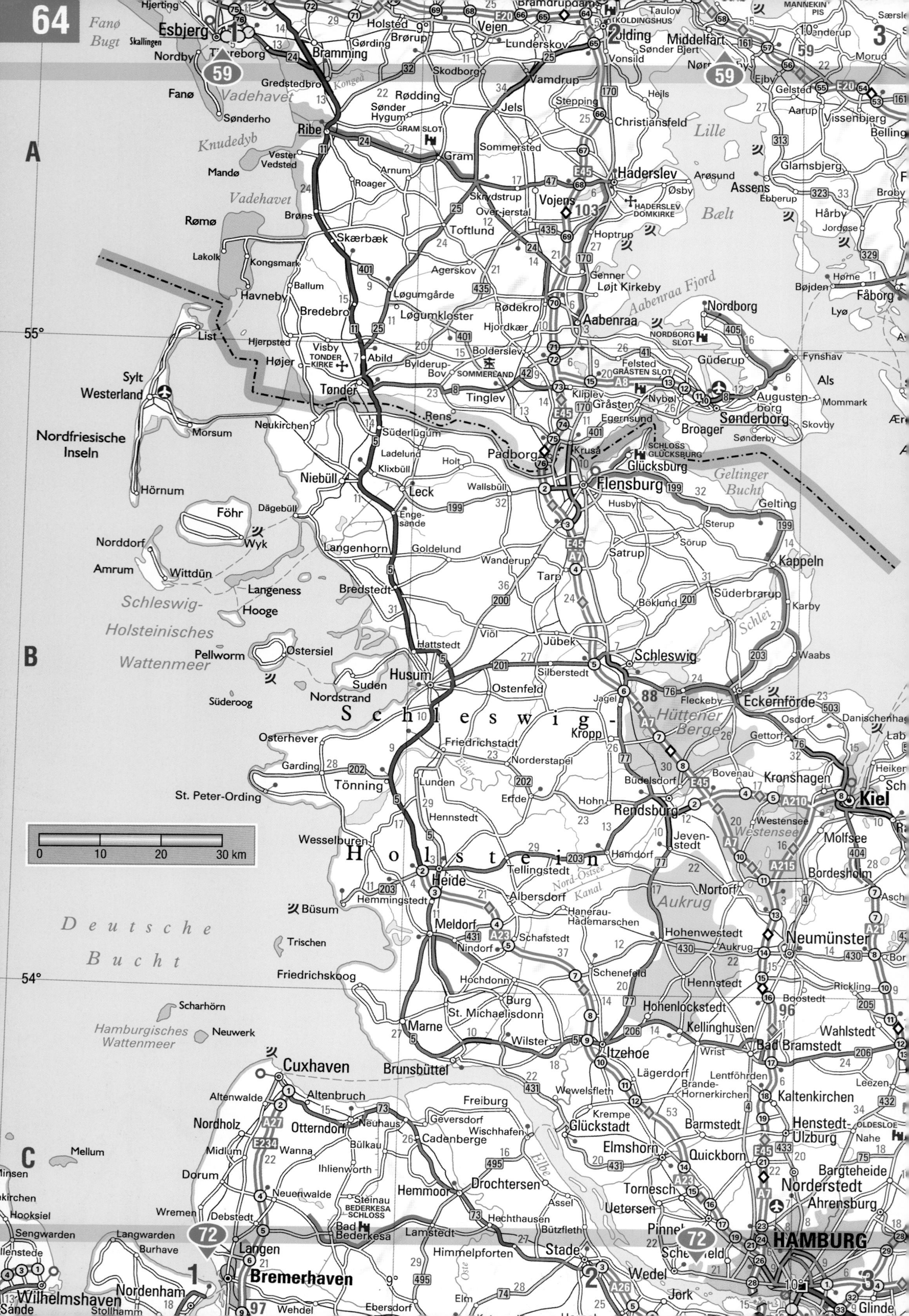
A
B
C
55°
54°
1
2
3
59
72
Fanø Bugt
Skallingen
Esbjerg
Hjerting
Nordby
Tjæreborg
Fanø
Sønderho
Vadehavet
Knudedyb
Mandø
Vester Vedsted
Rømø
Lakolk
Kongsmark
Havneby
List
Sylt
Westerland
Morsum
Hörnum
Nordfriesische Inseln
Föhr
Wyk
Dägebüll
Norddorf
Amrum
Wittdün
Langeness
Hooge
Schleswig-
Holsteinisches
Wattenmeer
Pellworm
Ostersiel
Süderoog
Nordstrand
Suden
Husum
Osterhever
Garding
Tönning
St. Peter-Ording
Wesselburen
Büsum
Deutsche
Bucht
Trischen
Friedrichskoog
Scharhörn
Neuwerk
Hamburgisches Wattenmeer
Cuxhaven
Altenwalde
Altenbruch
Nordholz
Otterndorf
Midlum
Wanna
Dorum
Mellum
Wremen
Neuenwalde
Debstedt
Langen
Bremerhaven
Sengwarden
Hooksiel
Langwarden
Burhave
Nordenham
Wilhelmshaven
Sande
Stollhamm
Wehdel
Bad Bederkesa
Bederkesa Schloss
Lamstedt
Hemmoor
Drochtersen
Himmelpforten
Stade
Ebersdorf
Elm
Wedel
Jork
Hamburg
Glinde
Schenefeld
Pinneberg
Uetersen
Tornesch
Elmshorn
Glückstadt
Krempe
Barmstedt
Quickborn
Norderstedt
Ahrensburg
Bargteheide
Henstedt-Ulzburg
Kaltenkirchen
Bad Bramstedt
Kellinghusen
Itzehoe
Wilster
Brunsbüttel
Marne
St. Michaelisdonn
Burg
Hochdonn
Meldorf
Nindorf
Schafstedt
Heide
Hemmingstedt
Albersdorf
Hanerau-Hademarschen
Hohenwestedt
Aukrug
Neumünster
Hohenlockstedt
Wahlstedt
Rendsburg
Büdelsdorf
Jevenstedt
Nortorf
Bordesholm
Kiel
Kronshagen
Molfsee
Westensee
Eckernförde
Gettorf
Hüttener Berge
Kropp
Jagel
Schleswig
Schlei
Kappeln
Süderbrarup
Böklund
Satrup
Tarp
Jübek
Silberstedt
Ostenfeld
Friedrichstadt
Norderstapel
Erfde
Lunden
Hennstedt
Tellingstedt
Hohn
Hamdorf
Nord-Ostsee Kanal
Schleswig-Holstein
Flensburg
Glücksburg
Schloss Glücksburg
Harrislee
Padborg
Kruså
Gråsten
Sønderborg
Augustenborg
Als
Nordborg
Fynshav
Broager
Aabenraa
Aabenraa Fjord
Rødekro
Haderslev
Haderslev Domkirke
Vojens
Christiansfeld
Kolding
Koldinghus
Middelfart
Lille Bælt
Assens
Fåborg
Tønder
Møgeltønder
Højer
Visby
Tønder Kirke
Abild
Bylderup-Bov
Sommerland
Tinglev
Løgumkloster
Bredebro
Skærbæk
Toftlund
Ribe
Gram
Gram Slot
Rødding
Bramming
Vejen
Holsted
Lunderskov
Vamdrup
Jels
Niebüll
Leck
Süderlügum
Bredstedt
Langenhorn
Hattstedt
Viöl
Hemmingstedt
Scale: 0 10 20 30 km

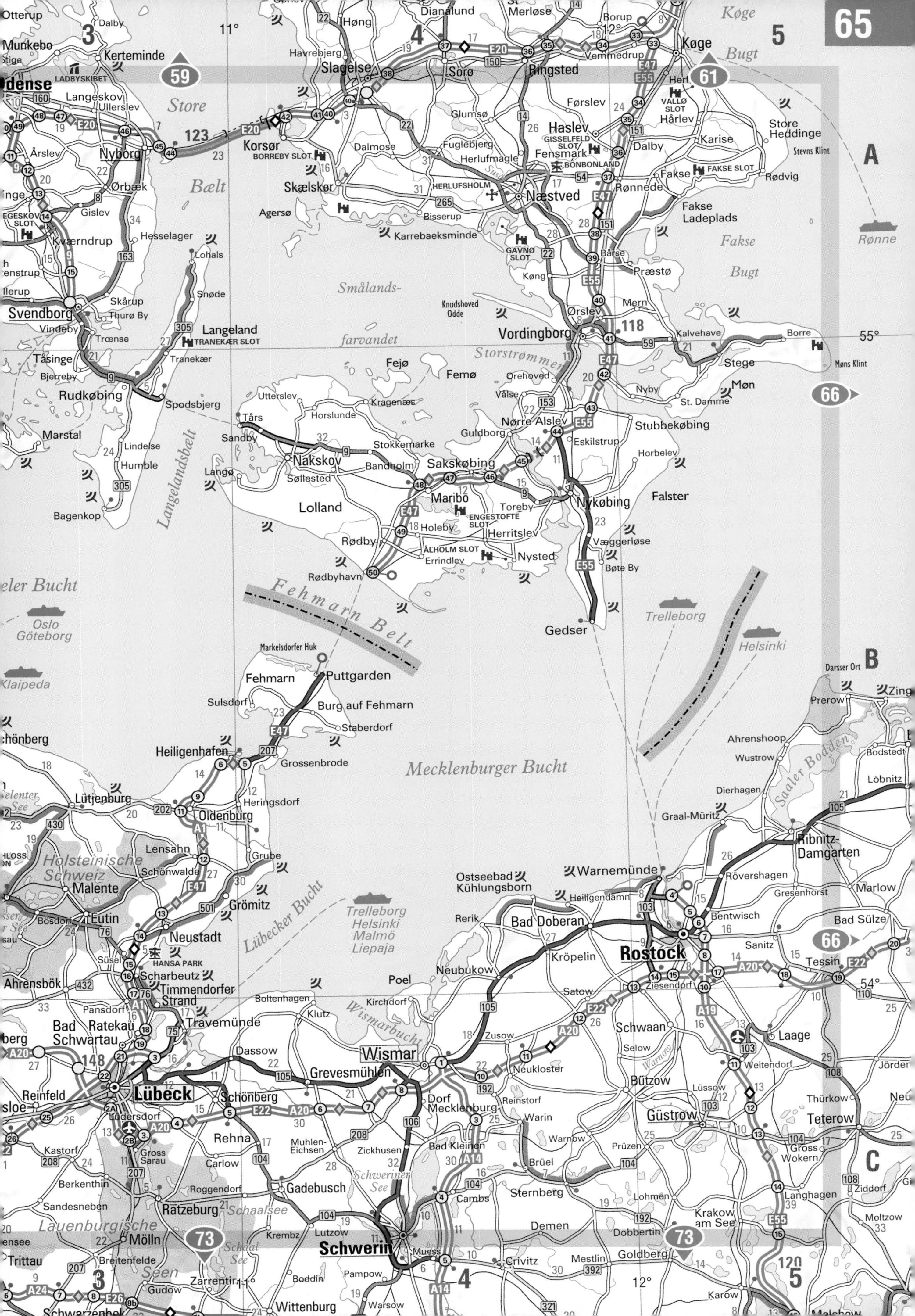

65
Otterup
Munkebo
Kerteminde
Dalby
Odense
LADBYSKIBET
Langeskov
Ullerslev
Store
Bælt
Nyborg
Korsør
BORREBY SLOT
Skælskør
Agersø
Slagelse
Havrebjerg
Høng
Dianalund
Sorø
Ringsted
Merløse
Borup
Vemmedrup
Køge
Køge Bugt
Herfølge
VALLØ SLOT
Hårlev
Førslev
Haslev
GISSELFELD SLOT
Fensmark
BONBONLAND
Glumsø
Fuglebjerg
Herlufmagle
Dalmose
HERLUFSHOLM
Næstved
Bisserup
Karrebaeksminde
GAVNØ SLOT
Store Heddinge
Stevns Klint
Karise
Dalby
Fakse
FAKSE SLOT
Rønnede
Rødvig
Fakse Ladeplads
Fakse Bugt
Rønne
Bårse
Præstø
Køng
Mern
Ørslev
Vordingborg
Kalvehave
Borre
Stege
Møns Klint
Møn
St. Damme
Nyby
Smålands-
farvandet
Knudshoved Odde
Storstrømmen
Fejø
Femø
Orehoved
Vålse
Nørre Alslev
Stubbekøbing
Eskilstrup
Horbelev
Falster
Guldborg
Utterslev
Kragenæs
Horslunde
Tårs
Sandby
Stokkemarke
Nakskov
Bandholm
Sakskøbing
Søllested
Langø
Maribo
Toreby
Nykøbing
Lolland
ENGESTOFTE SLOT
Holeby
Herritslev
Rødby
ÅLHOLM SLOT
Errindlev
Nysted
Væggerløse
Bøte By
Rødbyhavn
Gedser
Kværndrup
Gislev
Ørbæk
Hesselager
Lohals
Snøde
Egeskov Slot
Skårup
Thurø By
Svendborg
Vindeby
Trœnse
Tåsinge
Bjerreby
Rudkøbing
Langeland
TRANEKÆR SLOT
Tranekær
Spodsbjerg
Marstal
Lindelse
Humble
Bagenkop
Langelandsbælt
Kieler Bucht
Oslo
Göteborg
Klaipeda
Fehmarn Belt
Trelleborg
Helsinki
Markelsdorfer Huk
Fehmarn
Puttgarden
Sulsdorf
Burg auf Fehmarn
Staberdorf
Heiligenhafen
Grossenbrode
Mecklenburger Bucht
Darsser Ort
Prerow
Zingst
Ahrenshoop
Wustrow
Saaler Bodden
Bodstedt
Löbnitz
Dierhagen
Graal-Müritz
Schönberg
Lütjenburg
Oldenburg
Heringsdorf
Lensahn
Grube
Holsteinische Schweiz
Schönwalde
Malente
Eutin
Bosdorf
Grömitz
Neustadt
HANSA PARK
Süsel
Scharbeutz
Timmendorfer Strand
Ahrensbök
Pansdorf
Ratekau
Bad Schwartau
Travemünde
Lübecker Bucht
Trelleborg
Helsinki
Malmö
Liepaja
Ostseebad Kühlungsborn
Warnemünde
Heiligendamm
Rerik
Bad Doberan
Kröpelin
Rostock
Ribnitz-Damgarten
Rövershagen
Gresenhorst
Marlow
Bentwisch
Bad Sülze
Sanitz
Tessin
Neubukow
Poel
Boltenhagen
Klutz
Kirchdorf
Wismarbucht
Wismar
Zusow
Neukloster
Satow
Ziesendorf
Schwaan
Selow
Laage
Weitendorf
Jördenstorf
Dassow
Grevesmühlen
Lübeck
Reinfeld
Schönberg
Dorf Mecklenburg
Reinstorf
Warin
Bützow
Lüssow
Güstrow
Thürkow
Teterow
Lüdersdorf
Gross Sarau
Rehna
Carlow
Muhlen-Eichsen
Zickhusen
Bad Kleinen
Brüel
Warnow
Prüzen
Gross Wokern
Kastorf
Berkenthin
Sandesneben
Roggendorf
Ratzeburg
Schaalsee
Gadebusch
Schweriner See
Cambs
Sternberg
Lohmen
Krakow am See
Langhagen
Zidderf
Moltzow
Lauenburgische Seen
Mölln
Krembz
Lutzow
Schwerin
Demen
Dobbertin
Trittau
Breitenfelde
Zarrentin
Mueß
Crivitz
Mestlin
Goldberg
Boddin
Pampow
Warsow
Wittenburg
Gudow
Schwarzenbek
Karow
Malchow

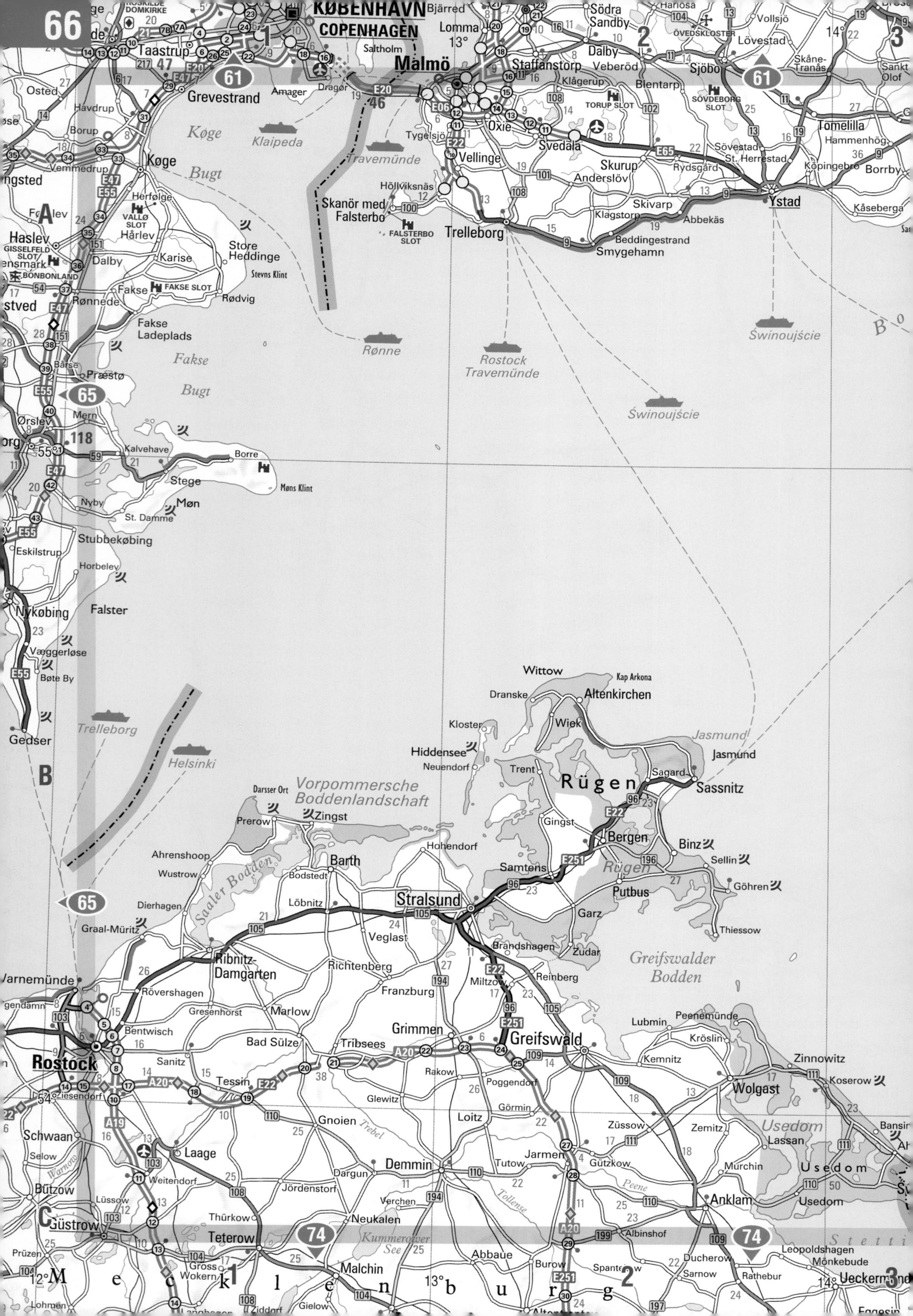
KØBENHAVN
COPENHAGEN
Roskilde Domkirke
Taastrup
Grevestrand
Amager
Dragør
Saltholm
Bjärred
Lomma
Malmö
Södra Sandby
Dalby
Staffanstorp
Veberöd
Klågerup
Blentarp
Sjöbo
Övedskloster
Vollsjö
Lövestad
Skåne-Tranås
Sankt Olof
Torup slot
Sövdeborg slot
Tomelilla
Hammenhög
Oxie
Svedala
Tygelsjö
Vellinge
Höllviksnäs
Skanör med Falsterbo
Falsterbo slot
Trelleborg
Anderslöv
Skurup
Rydsgård
Sövestad
St. Herrestad
Köpingebro
Borrby
Ystad
Kåseberga
Skivarp
Klagstorp
Abbekås
Beddingestrand
Smygehamn
Osted
Havdrup
Borup
Vemmedrup
Køge
Køge Bugt
Klaipeda
Travemünde
Herfølge
Vallø slot
Hårlev
Haslev
Gisselfeld slot
Karise
Store Heddinge
Stevns Klint
Dalby
Bonbonland
Fakse
Fakse slot
Rødvig
Rønnede
Fakse Ladeplads
Fakse Bugt
Rønne
Rostock Travemünde
Świnoujście
Præstø
Mern
Ørslev
Kalvehave
Borre
Stege
Møns Klint
Møn
Nyby
St. Damme
Stubbekøbing
Eskilstrup
Horbelev
Falster
Nykøbing
Væggerløse
Bøte By
Gedser
Trelleborg
Helsinki
Wittow
Kap Arkona
Dranske
Altenkirchen
Kloster
Wiek
Hiddensee
Neuendorf
Jasmund
Trent
Sagard
Sassnitz
Rügen
Gingst
Bergen
Binz
Sellin
Samtens
Putbus
Göhren
Garz
Thiessow
Zudar
Brandshagen
Greifswalder Bodden
Darsser Ort
Vorpommersche Boddenlandschaft
Prerow
Zingst
Hohendorf
Ahrenshoop
Wustrow
Barth
Bodstedt
Saaler Bodden
Stralsund
Löbnitz
Dierhagen
Graal-Müritz
Veglast
Ribnitz-Damgarten
Richtenberg
Franzburg
Miltzow
Reinberg
Warnemünde
Rövershagen
Gresenhorst
Marlow
Grimmen
Greifswald
Lubmin
Peenemünde
Kröslin
Bentwisch
Bad Sülze
Tribsees
Rostock
Sanitz
Tessin
Rakow
Poggendorf
Kemnitz
Zinnowitz
Wolgast
Koserow
Ziesendorf
Glewitz
Görmin
Loitz
Gnoien
Trebel
Züssow
Zemitz
Usedom
Lassan
Bansin
Schwaan
Laage
Selow
Warnow
Jarmen
Gützkow
Murchin
Demmin
Tutow
Dargun
Weitendorf
Bützow
Jördenstorf
Peene
Tollense
Verchen
Anklam
Lüssow
Thürkow
Neukalen
Güstrow
Teterow
Kummerower See
Albinshof
Leopoldshagen
Mönkebude
Prüzen
Gross Wokern
Malchin
Abbaue
Burow
Spantekow
Ducherow
Sarnow
Rathebur
Ueckermünde
Lohmen
Gielow
Mecklenburg
A
B
C
1
2
3
61
65
74
118
12°
13°
14°

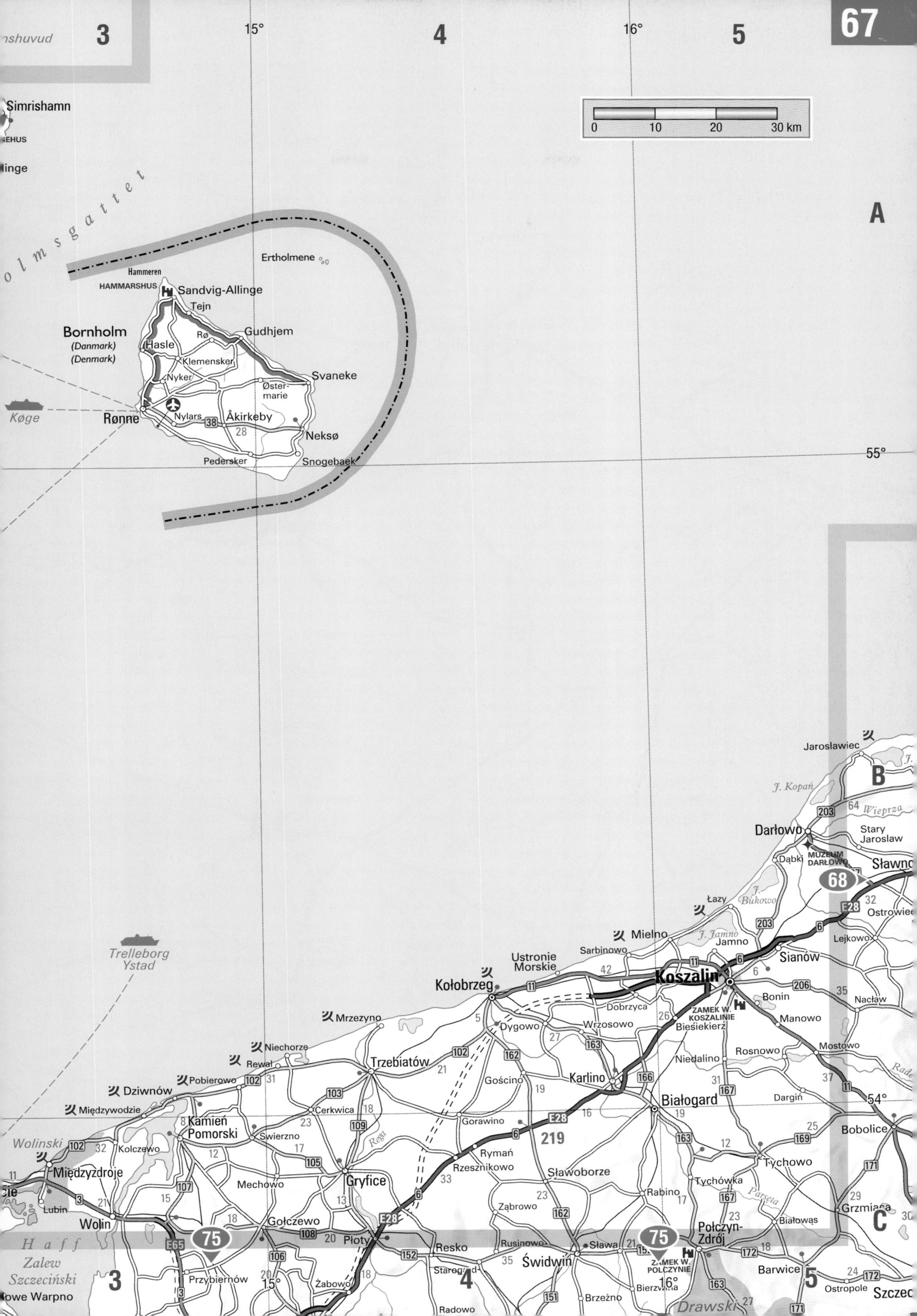

nshuvud

Simrishamn

GEHUS

linge

A

olmsgattet

Ertholmene °₀

Hammeren

HAMMARSHUS   Sandvig-Allinge

Tejn

Bornholm
(Danmark)
(Denmark)

Rø

Gudhjem

Hasle

Klemensker

Svaneke

Nyker

Øster-
marie

Køge

Rønne   Nylars 38   Åkirkeby   Neksø

28

Pedersker   Snogebaek

55°

Jaroslawiec

B

J. Kopań

203   64 *Wieprza*

Darłowo   Stary
Jaroslaw

Dąbki   MUZEUM
DARŁOWO   Sławno

Łazy   *J.*
Bukowo   **68**

203   E28   32

Mielno   *J. Jamno*   Ostrowiec

Jamno   6   Lejkowo

Sarbinowo   Sianów

Ustronie   42   **Koszalin**   6   206

Trelleborg
Ystad   Morskie   11   Bonin   35   Nacław

Kołobrzeg   Dobrzyca   26   ZAMEK W.
KOSZALINIE   Manowo

Mrzeżyno   5   Wrzosowo   Bieśiekierz   Rosnowo   Mostowo

Dygowo   27   163   Niedalino   37

Niechorze   102   162   166   31   167   Dargiń   11   54°

Rewal   Trzebiatów   Karlino   **Białogard**   169   Bobolice

Pobierowo   102   31   21   Gościno   19   E28   16   19   25

Dziwnów   103   Gorawino   6   **219**   163   12   167   Tychowo   171

Międzywodzie   Cerkwica   18   Rymań   Sławoborze   Rabino   17   Tychówka

Wolinski   8   Kamień
Pomorski   23   109   Rzesznikowo   23   162   29   Grzmiąca

102   32   Kolczewo   Swierzno   17   105   33   Ząbrowo   *Parsęta*

Międzyzdroje   12   Mechowo   13   Gryfice   162   Białowąs   Szczec

11   107   18   E28   Rusinowo   Sława   21   **75**   Połczyn-
Zdrój   18   172

Lubin   3   21   Gołczewo   108   20   Płoty   152   Resko   **C**

Wolin   **75**   E65   106   20   Staregrad   35   **Świdwin**   ZAMEK W.
POLCZYNIE   163   Barwice

Haff
Zalew
Szczeciński   **3**   Przybiernów   Żabowo   18   **4**   Bierzwina   16°   **5**   24   172

owe Warpno   15°   Radowo   Brzeżno   151   Ostropole   Szczec

Drawski   27   171

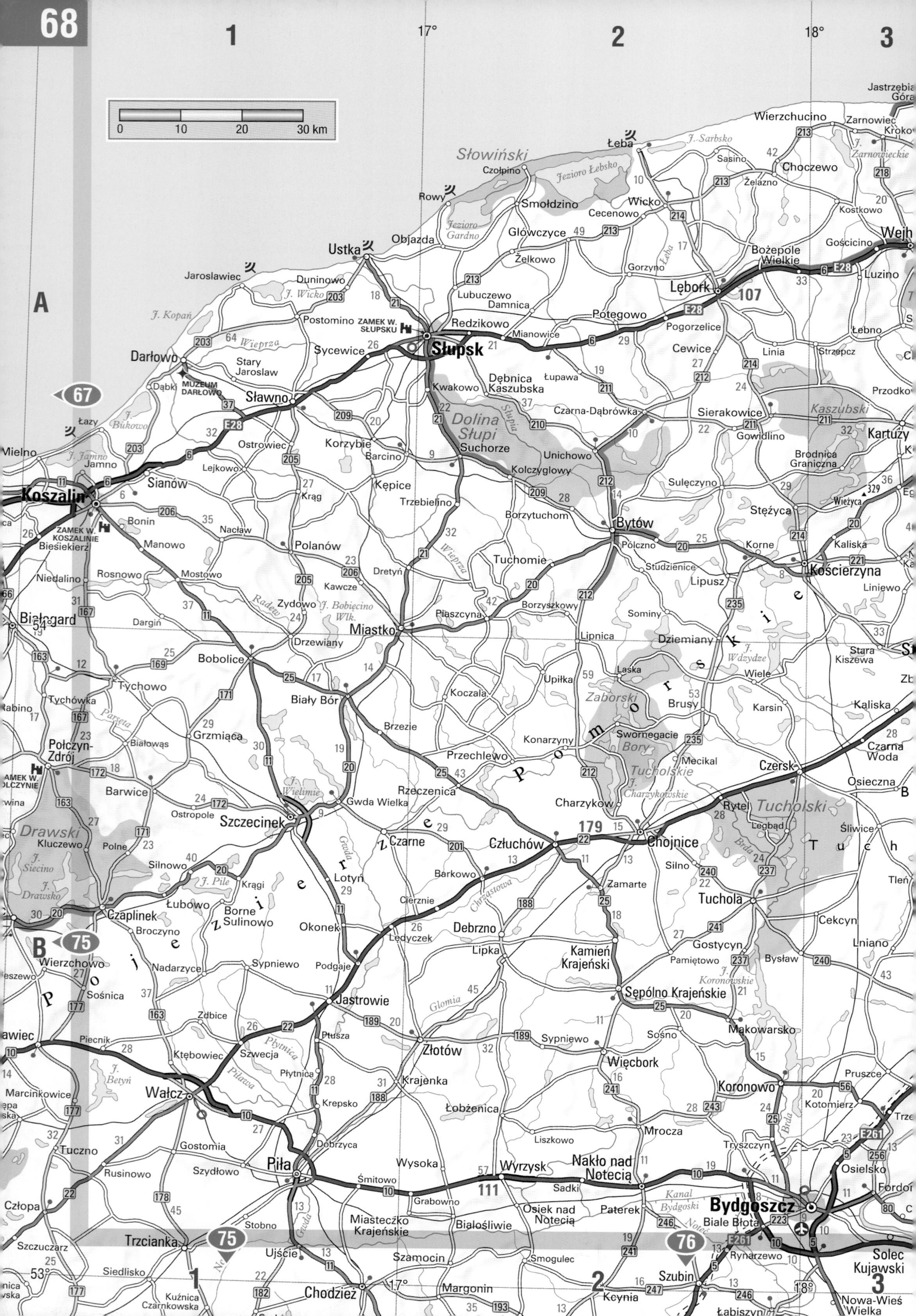
1
17°
2
18°
3
0
10
20
30 km
A
B
67
75
76
Jastrzębia Góra
Wierzchucino
Zarnowiec
Krokowa
J. Żarnowieckie
Łeba
J. Sarbsko
Słowiński
Czołpino
Jezioro Łebsko
Sasino
Choczewo
Żelazno
Rowy
Smołdzino
Wicko
Cecenowo
Kostkowo
Jezioro Gardno
Główczyce
Żelkowo
Ustka
Objazda
Bożepole Wielkie
Gościcino
Wejh
Luzino
Jarosławiec
Duninowo
J. Wicko
Gorzyno
Łeba
Lębork
107
E28
Lubuczewo
Damnica
J. Kopań
Postomino
ZAMEK W. SŁUPSKU
Redzikowo
Potęgowo
Pogorzelice
Łebno
Wieprza
Mianowice
Darłowo
Stary Jarosław
Sycewice
Słupsk
Cewice
Linia
Strzepcz
MUZEUM DARŁOWO
Dąbki
Kwakowo
Dębnica Kaszubska
Łupawa
Przodkowo
Sławno
Słupia
Czarna-Dąbrówka
Sierakowice
Kaszubski
Łazy
J. Bukowo
Dolina Słupi
Gowidlino
Kartuzy
Mielno
J. Jamno
Jamno
Ostrowiec
Korzybie
Barcino
Suchorze
Unichowo
Brodnica Graniczna
Koszalin
Lejkowo
Sianów
Kępice
Kolczyglowy
Sulęczyno
Trzebielino
Borzytuchom
Stężyca
Wieżyca
ZAMEK W. KOSZALINIE
Bonin
Nacław
Krąg
Bytów
Biesiekierz
Manowo
Polanów
Półczno
Korne
Kaliska
Wieprza
Tuchomie
Kościerzyna
Niedalino
Rosnowo
Mostowo
Dretyń
Kawcze
Studzienice
Lipusz
Liniewo
Radew
Zydowo
J. Bobięcino Wlk.
Borzyszkowy
Sominy
Białogard
Dargiń
Płaszczyna
Miastko
Lipnica
Dziemiany
Stara Kiszewa
Drzewiany
Bobolice
J. Wdzydze
Wiele
Laska
Tychowo
Upiłka
Tychówka
Koczała
Zaborski
Brusy
Karsin
Kaliska
Parsęta
Biały Bór
Pomorskie
Grzmiąca
Brzezie
Konarzyny
Swornegacie
Połczyn-Zdrój
Białowąs
Bory Tucholskie
Czersk
Czarna Woda
Mecikal
Przechlewo
J. Charzykowskie
ZAMEK W. POŁCZYNIE
J. Wielimie
Barwice
Rzeczenica
Osieczna
Gwda Wielka
Charzyków
Rytel
Tucholski
Drawski
Ostropole
Szczecinek
Legbąd
Śliwice
Kluczewo
179
Chojnice
Tuch
Polne
Czarne
Człuchów
J. Siecino
Silnowo
Gwda
Barkowo
Silno
Brda
Tleń
J. Pile
Krągi
Lotyń
Zamarte
J. Drawsko
Chrząstowa
Tuchola
Łubowo
Cierznie
Czaplinek
Borne Sulinowo
Cekcyn
Broczyno
Okonek
Debrzno
Lędyczek
Gostycyn
Lniano
Kamień Krajeński
Lipka
Wierzchowo
Pamiętowo
Bysław
Pojezierze
Nadarzyce
Sypniewo
Podgaje
J. Koronowskie
Sośnica
Glomia
Sępólno Krajeńskie
Jastrowie
Zdbice
Wałcz
Piecnik
Makowarsko
Sypniewo
Sośno
Płytnica
Ptusza
Złotów
Kłębowiec
Szwecja
Więcbork
J. Betyń
Płytnica
Piława
Pruszcz
Marcinkowice
Krajenka
Koronowo
Kotomierz
Krepsko
Łobżenica
Brda
Mrocza
Tuczno
Gostomia
Dobrzyca
Liszkowo
Tryszczyn
E261
Osielsko
Szydłowo
Rusinowo
Wysoka
Piła
Wyrzysk
Nakło nad Notecią
Fordon
Śmitowo
111
Sadki
Kanał Bydgoski
Bydgoszcz
Człopa
Grabowno
Osiek nad Notecią
Paterek
Noteć
Białe Błota
Miasteczko Krajeńskie
Białośliwie
Stobno
Trzcianka
Ujście
Szamocin
Smogulec
Szubin
Rynarzewo
Solec Kujawski
Szczuczarz
Siedlisko
Kuźnica Czarnkowska
Chodzież
Margonin
Kcynia
Łabiszyn
Nowa-Wieś Wielka

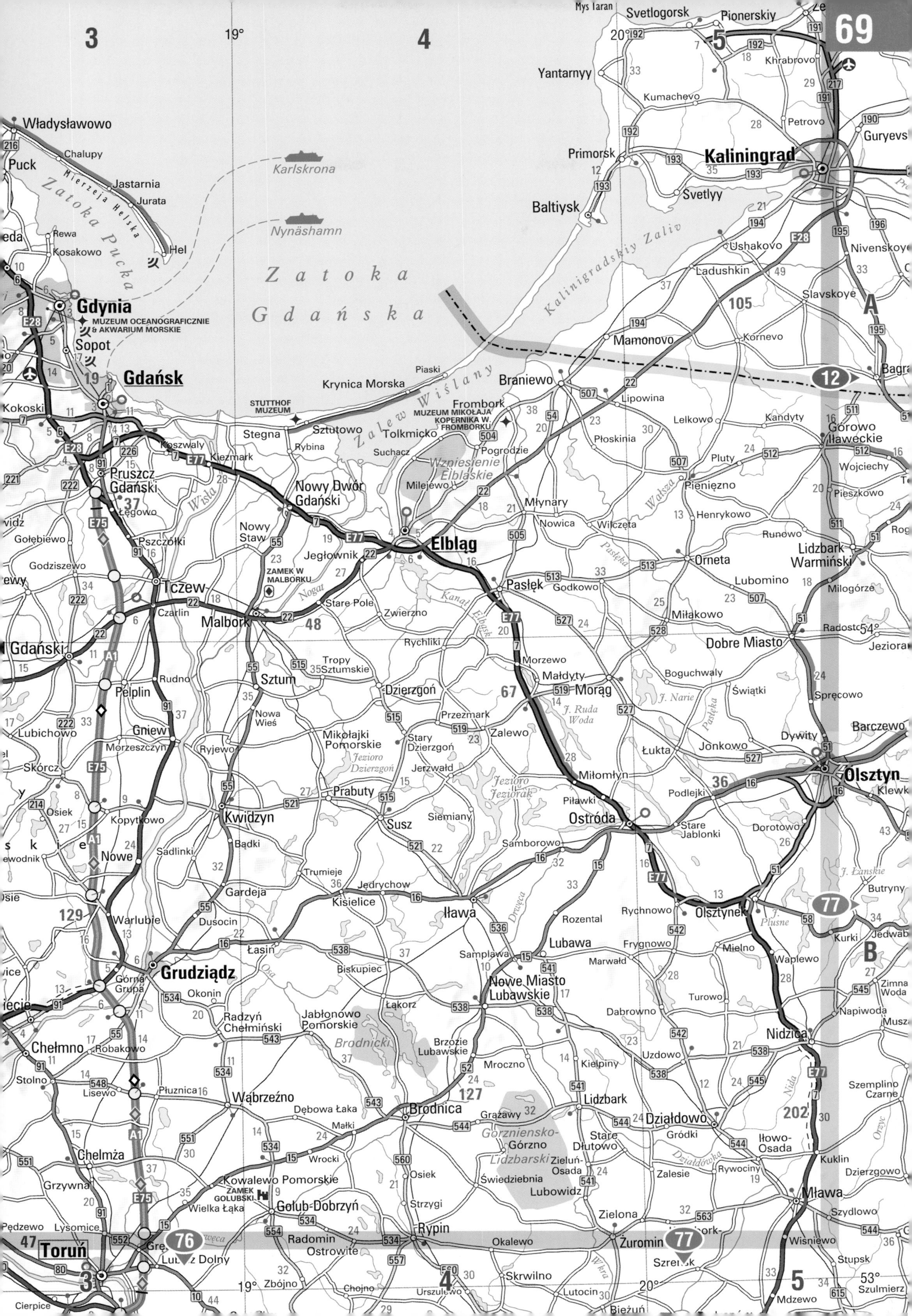
3
19°
4
Mys Taran
Svetlogorsk
Pionerskiy
20°
5
Khrabrovo
Yantarnyy
Kumachevo
Petrovo
Guryevsk
Władysławowo
Chalupy
Puck
Mierzeja Helska
Jastarnia
Jurata
Zatoka Pucka
Karlskrona
Primorsk
Kaliningrad
Svetlyy
Baltiysk
Nynäshamn
Rewa
Kosakowo
Hel
Zatoka Gdańska
Kalinigradskiy Zaliv
Ushakovo
Nivenskoye
Ladushkin
Slavskoye
Gdynia
MUZEUM OCEANOGRAFICZNIE & AKWARIUM MORSKIE
Sopot
Mamonovo
Kornevo
A
Bagra
Gdańsk
Piaski
Krynica Morska
Zalew Wiślany
Braniewo
Lipowina
Kokoski
STUTTHOF MUZEUM
Frombork
MUZEUM MIKOŁAJA KOPERNIKA W. FROMBORKU
Lelkowo
Kandyty
Górowo Iławeckie
Stegna
Sztutowo
Tolkmicko
Płoskinia
Koszwały
Kiezmark
Rybina
Suchacz
Pogrodzie
Pluty
Wojciechy
Pruszcz Gdański
Wzniesienie Elbląskie
Pieniężno
Pieszkowo
Nowy Dwór Gdański
Milejewo
Młynary
Henrykowo
Łęgowo
Wisła
Nowica
Wilczęta
Wałsza
Runowo
Lidzbark Warmiński
Gołębiewo
Nowy Staw
Pszczółki
Elbląg
Jegłownik
Orneta
Godziszewo
ZAMEK W MALBORKU
Pasłęka
Tczew
Pasłęk
Godkowo
Lubomino
Milogórze
Nogat
Stare Pole
Czarlin
Malbork
Zwierzno
Kanał Elbląski
Miłakowo
Radostowo
Gdański
Rychliki
Dobre Miasto
Jeziorany
Tropy Sztumskie
Morzewo
Rudno
Sztum
Dzierzgoń
Małdyty
Morąg
Boguchwały
Świątki
Sprecowo
Pelplin
J. Narie
Nowa Wieś
Przezmark
J. Ruda Woda
Lubichowo
Gniew
Mikołajki Pomorskie
Stary Dzierzgoń
Zalewo
Dywity
Barczewo
Morzeszczyn
Ryjewo
Jezioro Dzierzgoń
Łukta
Jonkowo
Skórcz
Jerzwałd
Miłomłyn
Olsztyn
Jezioro Jeziorak
Prabuty
Podlejki
Klewki
Osiek
Kopytkowo
Kwidzyn
Siemiany
Piławki
Susz
Ostróda
Stare Jabłonki
Dorotowo
Nowe
Sadlinki
Bądki
Samborowo
Trumieje
J. Łańskie
Gardeja
Jędrychow
Butryny
Kisielice
Iława
Drwęca
Rozental
Rychnowo
Olsztynek
J. Plusne
Kurki
Jedwabno
Warlubie
Dusocin
Lubawa
Frygnowo
B
Łasin
Samplawa
Marwałd
Mielno
Waplewo
Grudziądz
Osa
Biskupiec
Nowe Miasto Lubawskie
Górna Grupa
Okonin
Turowo
Zimna Woda
Łąkorz
Jabłonowo Pomorskie
Dąbrowno
Napiwoda
Radzyń Chełmiński
Mrocze
Chełmno
Robakowo
Brodnicki
Brzozie Lubawskie
Uzdowo
Nidzica
Mroczno
Kiełpiny
Stolno
Lisewo
Płużnica
Wąbrzeźno
Lidzbark
Szemplino Czarne
Dębowa Łąka
Brodnica
Grążawy
Działdowo
Małki
Gorznieńsko-Lidzbarski
Górzno
Stare Dłutowo
Gródki
Iłowo-Osada
Chełmża
Wrocki
Zieluń-Osada
Kuklin
Osiek
Świedziebnia
Zalesie
Rywociny
Dzierzgowo
Grzywna
Kowalewo Pomorskie
Lubowidz
Mława
ZAMEK GOLUBSKI
Strzygi
Wielka Łąka
Golub-Dobrzyń
Zielona
Szydłowo
Pędzewo
Łysomice
Toruń
Rypin
Radomin
Ostrowite
Okalewo
Żuromin
Wiśniewo
Lubicz Dolny
Szreńsk
Stupsk
Skrwilno
53°
Zbójno
Chojno
Urszulewo
Lutocin
Bieżuń
Szulmierz
Cierpice
Mdzewo
54°
E28
E77
E75
A1
12
76
77
36
37
48
67
105
127
129
202

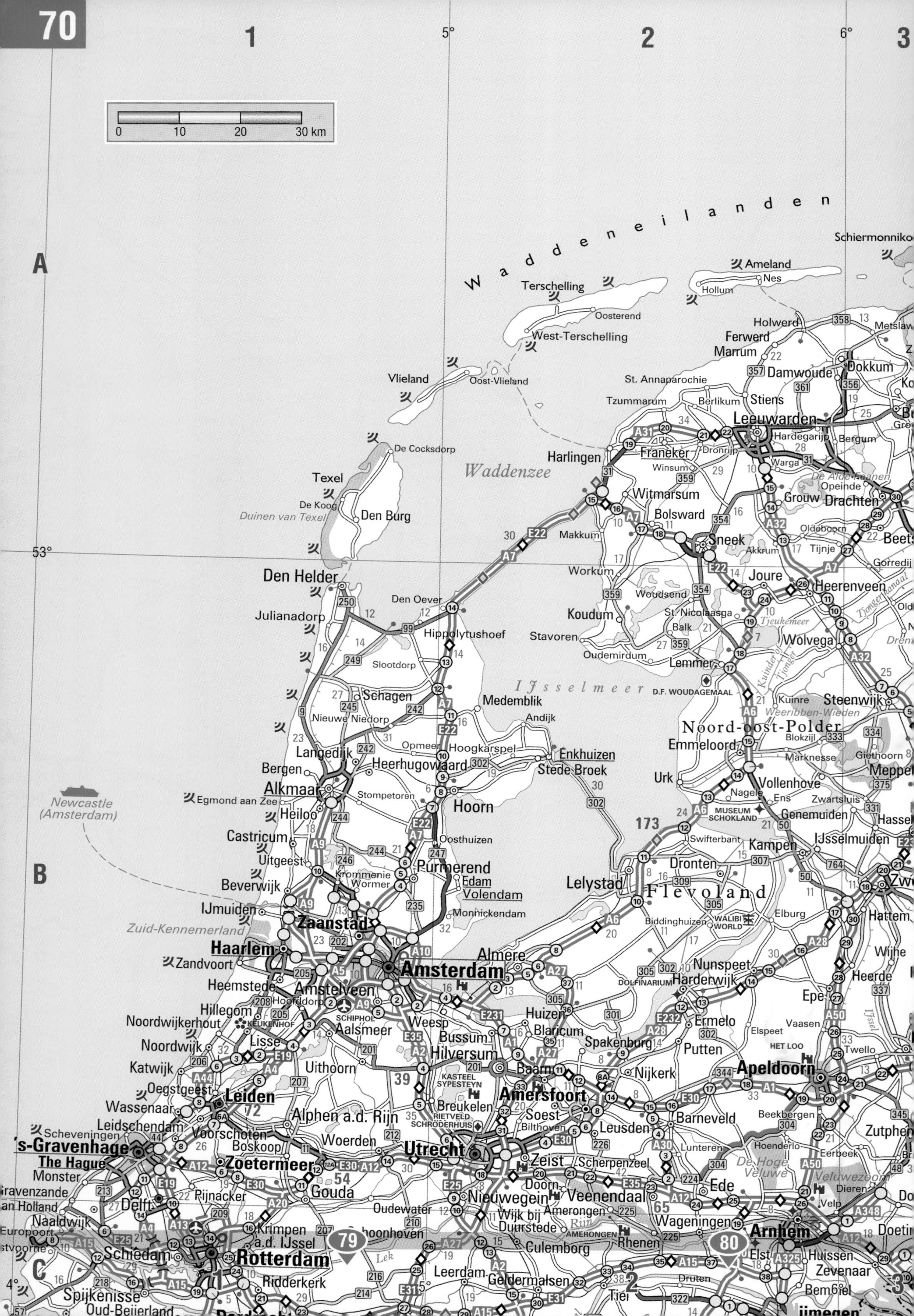
1
2
3
5°
6°
A
B
C
53°
4°
0
10
20
30 km
Waddeneilanden
Schiermonnikoog
Ameland
Nes
Hollum
Terschelling
Oosterend
West-Terschelling
Vlieland
Oost-Vlieland
Holwerd
Ferwerd
Marrum
Metslawier
Dokkum
Damwoude
St. Annaparochie
Tzummarum
Berlikum
Stiens
Leeuwarden
Hardegarijp
Bergum
Franeker
Dronrijp
Harlingen
Winsum
Warga
De Cocksdorp
Texel
De Koog
Den Burg
Duinen van Texel
Waddenzee
Witmarsum
Bolsward
Sneek
Grouw
Opeinde
Drachten
Oldeboorn
Makkum
Akkrum
Tijnje
Beetsterzwaag
Gorredijk
Workum
Joure
Heerenveen
Tjongerkanaal
Den Helder
Den Oever
Woudsend
Koudum
St. Nicolaasga
Tjeukemeer
Balk
Julianadorp
Hippolytushoef
Stavoren
Oudemirdum
Wolvega
Lemmer
Slootdorp
IJsselmeer
D.F. WOUDAGEMAAL
Kuinder of Tjonger
Schagen
Medemblik
Kuinre
Steenwijk
Nieuwe Niedorp
Andijk
Weeribben-Wieden
Noord-oost-Polder
Blokzijl
Emmeloord
Langedijk
Opmeer
Hoogkarspel
Enkhuizen
Stede Broek
Marknesse
Giethoorn
Bergen
Heerhugowaard
Meppel
Alkmaar
Urk
Vollenhove
Egmond aan Zee
Stompetoren
Hoorn
Nagele
Ens
Zwartsluis
Newcastle (Amsterdam)
Heiloo
MUSEUM SCHOKLAND
Genemuiden
Hasselt
Castricum
Oosthuizen
Uitgeest
Purmerend
Swifterbant
Kampen
IJsselmuiden
Beverwijk
Krommenie
Wormer
Edam
Volendam
Dronten
Lelystad
Flevoland
Zwolle
IJmuiden
Monnickendam
Zaanstad
Zuid-Kennemerland
Biddinghuizen
WALIBI WORLD
Elburg
Hattem
Haarlem
Almere
Wijhe
Zandvoort
Amsterdam
Nunspeet
Heerde
Heemstede
Amstelveen
DOLFINARIUM
Harderwijk
Hoofddorp
Epe
Hillegom
SCHIPHOL
Huizen
Noordwijkerhout
KEUKENHOF
Weesp
Blaricum
Ermelo
Vaassen
Lisse
Aalsmeer
Bussum
Spakenburg
Elspeet
Noordwijk
Hilversum
Putten
HET LOO
Twello
Katwijk
Uithoorn
Baarn
Nijkerk
Apeldoorn
Oegstgeest
KASTEEL SYPESTEYN
Amersfoort
Wassenaar
Leiden
Breukelen
Leidschendam
Alphen a.d. Rijn
RIETVELD SCHRÖDERHUIS
Soest
Bilthoven
Barneveld
Beekbergen
Zutphen
Scheveningen
Voorschoten
Woerden
Leusden
's-Gravenhage
The Hague
Boskoop
Utrecht
Zeist
Lunteren
Hoenderlo
Eerbeek
Monster
Zoetermeer
Scherpenzeel
De Hoge Veluwe
Veluwezoom
's-Gravenzande
Gouda
Doorn
Ede
Dieren
Naaldwijk
Delft
Pijnacker
Nieuwegein
Veenendaal
Velp
Oudewater
Wijk bij Duurstede
Amerongen
Wageningen
Europoort
Krimpen a.d. IJssel
Schoonhoven
AMERONGEN
Rhenen
Arnhem
Doetinchem
Schiedam
Culemborg
Elst
Rotterdam
Lek
Huissen
Zevenaar
Leerdam
Geldermalsen
Ridderkerk
Druten
Spijkenisse
Tiel
Bemmel
Oud-Beijerland
Nijmegen
79
80

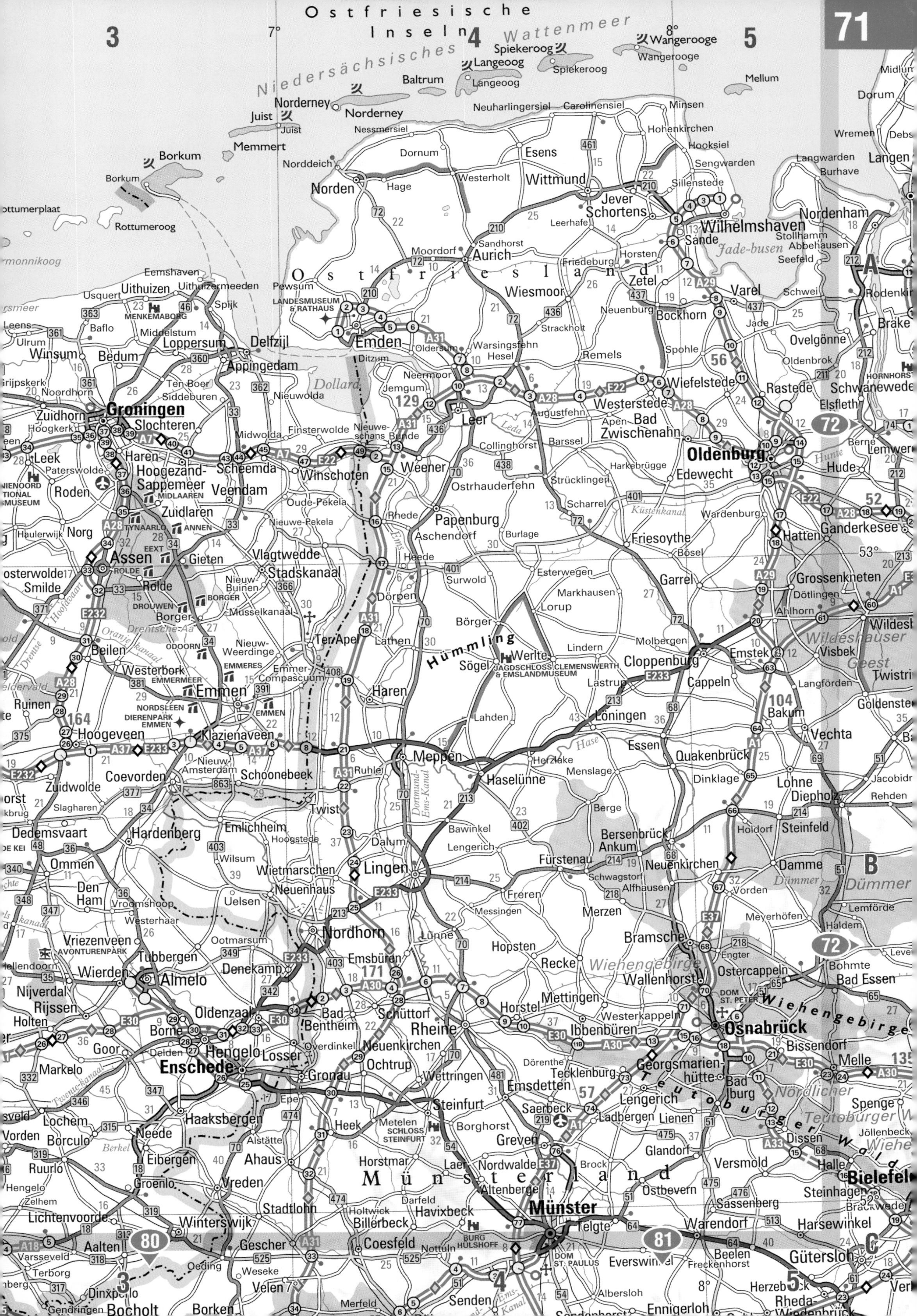

3
4
5
Ostfriesische Inseln
Niedersächsisches Wattenmeer
Wangerooge
Spiekeroog
Langeoog
Baltrum
Norderney
Juist
Memmert
Borkum
Rottumerplaat
Rottumeroog
Mellum
Minsen
Carolinensiel
Neuharlingersiel
Nessmersiel
Norddeich
Norden
Hage
Dornum
Esens
Wittmund
Westerholt
Jever
Schortens
Hohenkirchen
Hooksiel
Sengwarden
Sillenstede
Wilhelmshaven
Sande
Jade-busen
Aurich
Moordorf
Sandhorst
Leerhafe
Horsten
Friedeburg
Ostfriesland
Wiesmoor
Zetel
Neuenburg
Bockhorn
Varel
Strackholt
Remels
Pewsum
Landesmuseum & Rathaus
Emden
Oldersum
Warsingsfehn
Hesel
Ditzum
Dollard
Jemgum
Neermoor
Leer
Bunde
Weener
Augustfehn
Westerstede
Apen
Bad Zwischenahn
Wiefelstede
Rastede
Oldenburg
Edewecht
Hude
Collinghorst
Barssel
Ostrhauderfehn
Strücklingen
Harkebrügge
Scharrel
Küstenkanal
Wardenburg
Papenburg
Rhede
Aschendorf
Burlage
Friesoythe
Bösel
Heede
Surwold
Esterwegen
Garrel
Markhausen
Lorup
Dörpen
Börger
Hümmling
Werlte
Lathen
Sögel
Jagdschloss Clemenswerth & Emslandmuseum
Molbergen
Lindern
Cloppenburg
Emstek
Cappeln
Lastrup
Löningen
Lahden
Haren
Meppen
Essen
Herzlake
Menslage
Haselünne
Quakenbrück
Dinklage
Twist
Dalum
Bawinkel
Lengerich
Berge
Bersenbrück
Ankum
Fürstenau
Lingen
Wietmarschen
Neuenhaus
Freren
Schwagstorf
Alfhausen
Neuenkirchen
Nordhorn
Lünne
Messingen
Hopsten
Merzen
Bramsche
Recke
Wiehengebirge
Wallenhorst
Emsbüren
Bad Bentheim
Schüttorf
Rheine
Horstel
Mettingen
Westerkappeln
Ibbenbüren
Osnabrück
Dom St. Peter
Neuenkirchen
Ochtrup
Wettringen
Emsdetten
Dörenthe
Tecklenburg
Georgsmarienhütte
Bad Iburg
Lengerich
Teutoburger Wald
Steinfurt
Saerbeck
Ladbergen
Lienen
Borghorst
Greven
Glandorf
Metelen
Schloss Steinfurt
Heek
Horstmar
Laer
Nordwalde
Brock
Münsterland
Versmold
Altenberge
Ostbevern
Münster
Telgte
Darfeld
Havixbeck
Billerbeck
Holtwick
Burg Hülshoff
Coesfeld
Nottuln
Everswinkel
Warendorf
Sassenberg
Beelen
Freckenhorst
Dom St. Paulus
Senden
Albersloh
Enniger loh
Groningen
Delfzijl
Appingedam
Uithuizen
Uithuizermeeden
Eemshaven
Usquert
Spijk
Menkemaborg
Baflo
Winsum
Middelstum
Loppersum
Bedum
Ten Boer
Siddeburen
Nieuwolda
Noordhorn
Zuidhorn
Slochteren
Leek
Haren
Hoogezand-Sappemeer
Midwolda
Finsterwolde
Nieuweschans
Scheemda
Winschoten
Veendam
Roden
Zuidlaren
Oude-Pekela
Nieuwe-Pekela
Assen
Gieten
Vlagtwedde
Stadskanaal
Norg
Rolde
Borger
Musselkanaal
Ter Apel
Smilde
Beilen
Westerbork
Emmen
Emmer-Compascuum
Hoogeveen
Klazienaveen
Nieuw-Amsterdam
Schoonebeek
Coevorden
Zuidwolde
Dedemsvaart
Hardenberg
Emlichheim
Ommen
Den Ham
Wilsum
Uelsen
Vriezenveen
Tubbergen
Denekamp
Almelo
Wierden
Nijverdal
Rijssen
Oldenzaal
Borne
Hengelo
Losser
Enschede
Gronau
Goor
Markelo
Haaksbergen
Lochem
Borculo
Neede
Eibergen
Ahaus
Vreden
Groenlo
Ruurlo
Stadtlohn
Winterswijk
Lichtenvoorde
Aalten
Gescher
Velen
Dinxperlo
Bocholt
Borken
Nordenham
Brake
Elsfleth
Ganderkesee
Hatten
Grossenkneten
Dötlingen
Ahlhorn
Wildeshausen
Visbek
Wildeshauser Geest
Goldenstedt
Bakum
Vechta
Lohne
Diepholz
Steinfeld
Holdorf
Damme
Dümmer
Vörden
Lemförde
Bohmte
Bad Essen
Ostercappeln
Bissendorf
Melle
Dissen
Halle
Bielefeld
Steinhagen
Harsewinkel
Gütersloh
Rheda-Wiedenbrück
Herzebrock
Langen
Dorum
Wremen
72
80
81

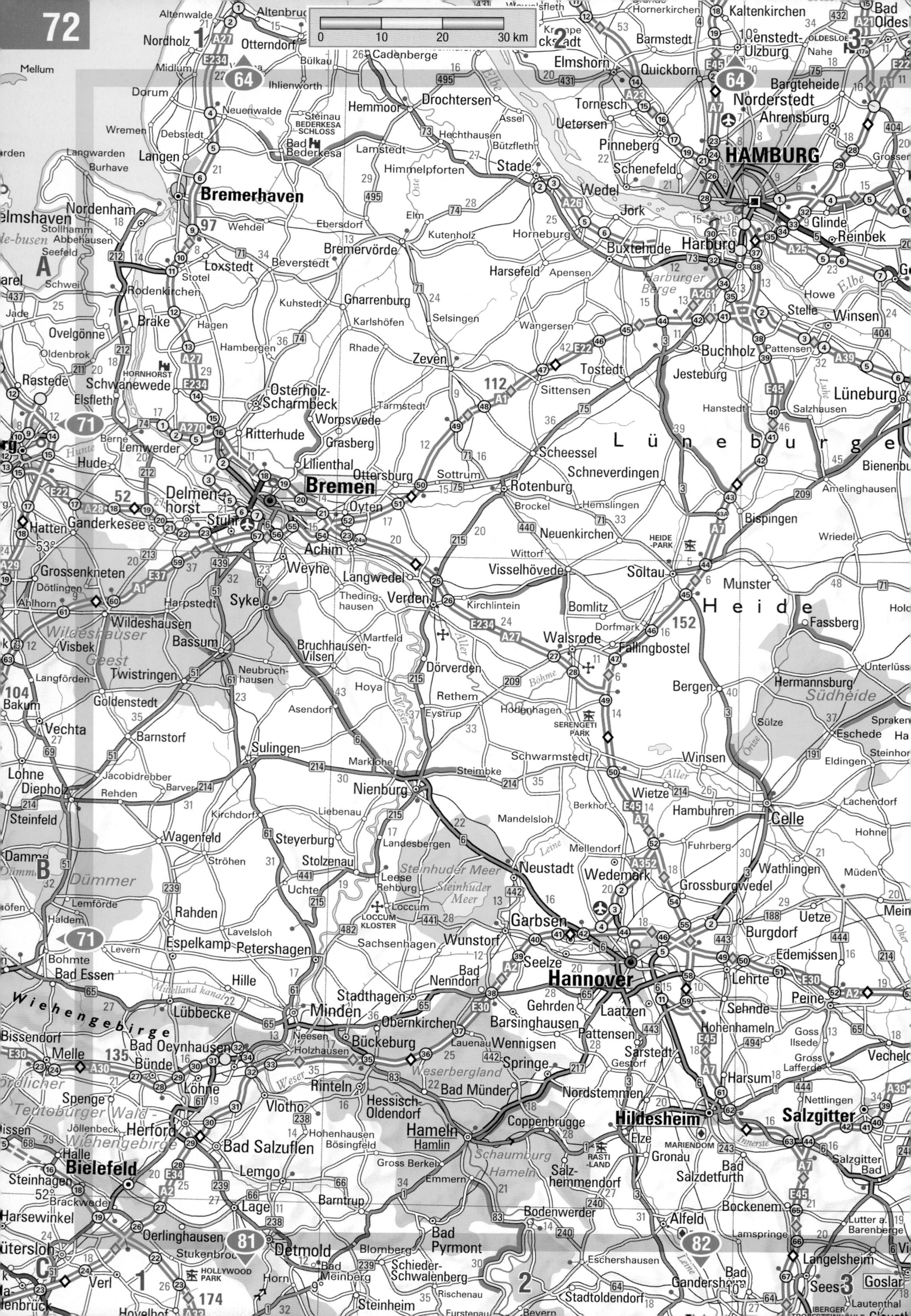
0 10 20 30 km
Altenwalde
Altenbruch
Nordholz
Otterndorf
Cadenberge
Mellum
Midlum
Bülkau
Ihlienworth
Dorum
Neuenwalde
Steinau
BEDERKESA SCHLOSS
Wremen
Debstedt
Bad Bederkesa
Hemmoor
Drochtersen
Assel
Hechthausen
Lamstedt
Bützfleth
Langwarden
Burhave
Langen
Himmelpforten
Stade
Bremerhaven
Nordenham
Stollhamm
Abbehausen
Seefeld
Wehdel
Ebersdorf
Elm
Kutenholz
Bremervörde
Loxstedt
Stotel
Beverstedt
Rodenkirchen
Schwei
Jade
Kuhstedt
Gnarrenburg
Karlshöfen
Selsingen
Brake
Hagen
Ovelgönne
Oldenbrok
Hambergen
Rhade
Zeven
HORNHORST
Rastede
Schwanewede
Elsfleth
Osterholz-Scharmbeck
Tarmstedt
Worpswede
Ritterhude
Berne
Lemwerder
Hunte
Hude
Grasberg
Lilienthal
Ottersburg
Delmenhorst
Bremen
Oyten
Stuhr
Hatten
Ganderkesee
Achim
Weyhe
Langwedel
Grossenkneten
Dötlingen
Ahlhorn
Harpstedt
Syke
Thedinghausen
Verden
Kirchlintein
Wildeshausen
Wildeshauser Geest
Visbek
Bassum
Bruchhausen-Vilsen
Martfeld
Twistringen
Neubruchhausen
Langförden
Bakum
Goldenstedt
Hoya
Dörverden
Asendorf
Vechta
Barnstorf
Eystrup
Rethem
Sulingen
Lohne
Diepholz
Jacobidrebber
Rehden
Barver
Marklohe
Nienburg
Steimbke
Steinfeld
Kirchdorf
Liebenau
Landesbergen
Wagenfeld
Steyerburg
Ströhen
Stolzenau
Leese
Rehburg
Dümmer
Uchte
Lemförde
Haldem
Rahden
Loccum
LOCCUM KLOSTER
Lavelsloh
Espelkamp
Petershagen
Sachsenhagen
Levern
Bohmte
Bad Essen
Hille
Wiehengebirge
Mittelland kanal
Lübbecke
Minden
Stadthagen
Obernkirchen
Bissendorf
Melle
Bad Oeynhausen
Neesen
Holzhausen
Bückeburg
Bünde
Löhne
Spenge
Rinteln
Teutoburger Wald
Vlotho
Hessisch-Oldendorf
Herford
Jöllenbeck
Hohenhausen
Bösingfeld
Hameln
Hamlin
Bielefeld
Halle
Bad Salzuflen
Steinhagen
Brackwede
Lemgo
Gross Berkel
Emmern
Harsewinkel
Lage
Barntrup
Oerlinghausen
Stukenbrock
Detmold
Blomberg
Bad Pyrmont
Gütersloh
Verl
HOLLYWOOD PARK
Horn
Bad Meinberg
Schieder-Schwalenberg
Rischenau
Steinheim
Hövelhof
Bevern
Fleth
Krempe
Glückstadt
Hornerkirchen
Kaltenkirchen
Barmstedt
Henstedt-Ulzburg
Elmshorn
Quickborn
Bargteheide
Tornesch
Norderstedt
Ahrensburg
Uetersen
Pinneberg
HAMBURG
Schenefeld
Wedel
Jork
Glinde
Reinbek
Horneburg
Buxtehude
Harburg
Harsefeld
Apensen
Harburger Berge
Howe
Elbe
Stelle
Winsen
Wangersen
Buchholz
Pattensen
Tostedt
Jesteburg
Sittensen
Hanstedt
Salzhausen
Lüneburg
Lüneburger Heide
Scheessel
Bienenbüttel
Schneverdingen
Sottrum
Rotenburg
Amelinghausen
Brockel
Hemslingen
Bispingen
Neuenkirchen
HEIDE-PARK
Wriedel
Wittorf
Visselhövede
Soltau
Munster
Bomlitz
Dorfmark
Fassberg
Walsrode
Fallingbostel
Unterlüss
Hermannsburg
Südheide
Bergen
Hodenhagen
SERENGETI PARK
Sülze
Eschede
Schwarmstedt
Winsen
Eldingen
Aller
Wietze
Berkhof
Hambühren
Celle
Lachendorf
Mandelsloh
Hohne
Fuhrberg
Mellendorf
Wathlingen
Neustadt
Steinhuder Meer
Wedemark
Müden
Grossburgwedel
Garbsen
Uetze
Burgdorf
Wunstorf
Seelze
Edemissen
Bad Nenndorf
Hannover
Lehrte
Gehrden
Laatzen
Sehnde
Peine
Barsinghausen
Pattensen
Hohenhameln
Wennigsen
Sarstedt
Gestorf
Springe
Weserbergland
Harsum
Bad Münder
Nordstemmen
Nettlingen
Coppenbrügge
Hildesheim
Salzgitter
Elze
MARIENDOM
Gronau
RASTI-LAND
Salzgitter Bad
Salzhemmendorf
Bad Salzdetfurth
Bodenwerder
Bockenem
Alfeld
Lutter a. Barenberge
Lamspringe
Eschershausen
Langelsheim
Bad Gandersheim
Stadtoldendorf
Goslar
Seesen
Lautenthal

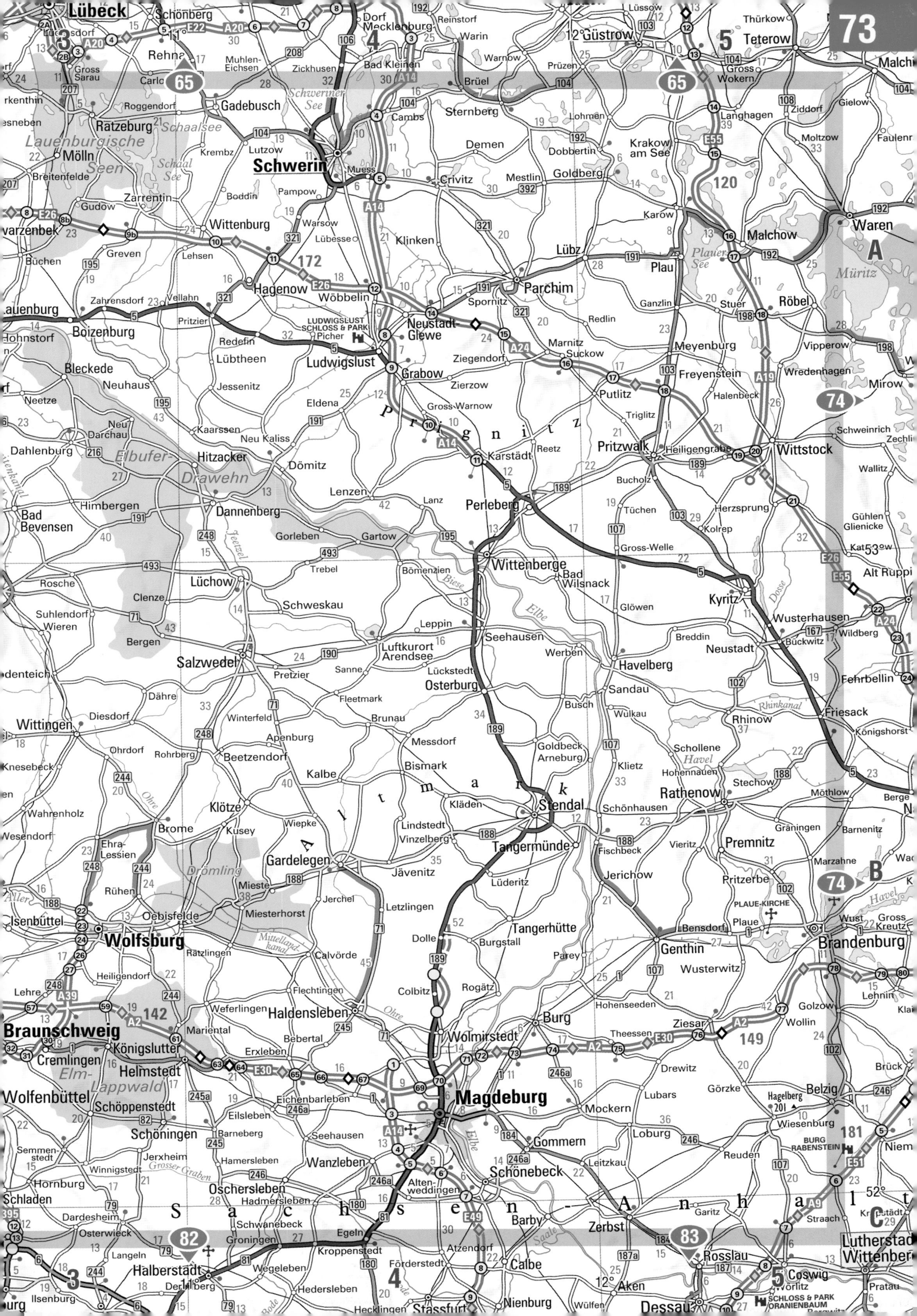
Lübeck
Schönberg
Dorf Mecklenburg
Reinstorf
Warin
Güstrow
Teterow
Malchin
Rehna
Carlow
Gadebusch
Ratzeburg
Schaalsee
Lauenburgische Seen
Mölln
Breitenfelde
Gudow
Zarrentin
Schwerin
Schweriner See
Bad Kleinen
Brüel
Sternberg
Cambs
Crivitz
Demen
Dobbertin
Goldberg
Krakow am See
Mestlin
Pampow
Boddin
Wittenburg
Hagenow
Wöbbelin
Klinken
Lübz
Parchim
Plau
Plauer See
Malchow
Waren
Müritz
Röbel
Boizenburg
Lauenburg
Zahrensdorf
Vellahn
Pritzier
Lübtheen
Redefin
Ludwigslust
Ludwigslust Schloss & Park
Neustadt-Glewe
Grabow
Spornitz
Marnitz
Suckow
Meyenburg
Freyenstein
Putlitz
Pritzwalk
Heiligengrabe
Wittstock
Bleckede
Neuhaus
Jessenitz
Eldena
Prignitz
Karstädt
Perleberg
Wittenberge
Bad Wilsnack
Kyritz
Dahlenburg
Hitzacker
Elbufer-Drawehn
Dömitz
Lenzen
Dannenberg
Bad Bevensen
Gorleben
Gartow
Lüchow
Clenze
Schweskau
Seehausen
Werben
Havelberg
Sandau
Neustadt
Wusterhausen
Salzwedel
Luftkurort Arendsee
Osterburg
Fehrbellin
Friesack
Rhinow
Wittingen
Diesdorf
Beetzendorf
Kalbe
Bismark
Stendal
Tangermünde
Rathenow
Premnitz
Klötze
Brome
Gardelegen
Altmark
Letzlingen
Tangerhütte
Genthin
Brandenburg
Wolfsburg
Oebisfelde
Drömling
Mittellandkanal
Calvörde
Burg
Ziesar
Braunschweig
Königslutter
Helmstedt
Haldensleben
Wolmirstedt
Magdeburg
Wolfenbüttel
Schöppenstedt
Elm-Lappwald
Schöningen
Wanzleben
Schönebeck
Gommern
Loburg
Belzig
Oschersleben
Barby
Zerbst
Rosslau
Dessau
Coswig
Lutherstadt Wittenberg
Halberstadt
Calbe
Aken
Stassfurt
Nienburg
Sachsen-Anhalt
Burg Rabenstein
Plaue-Kirche
Schloss & Park Oranienbaum
65
74
82
83

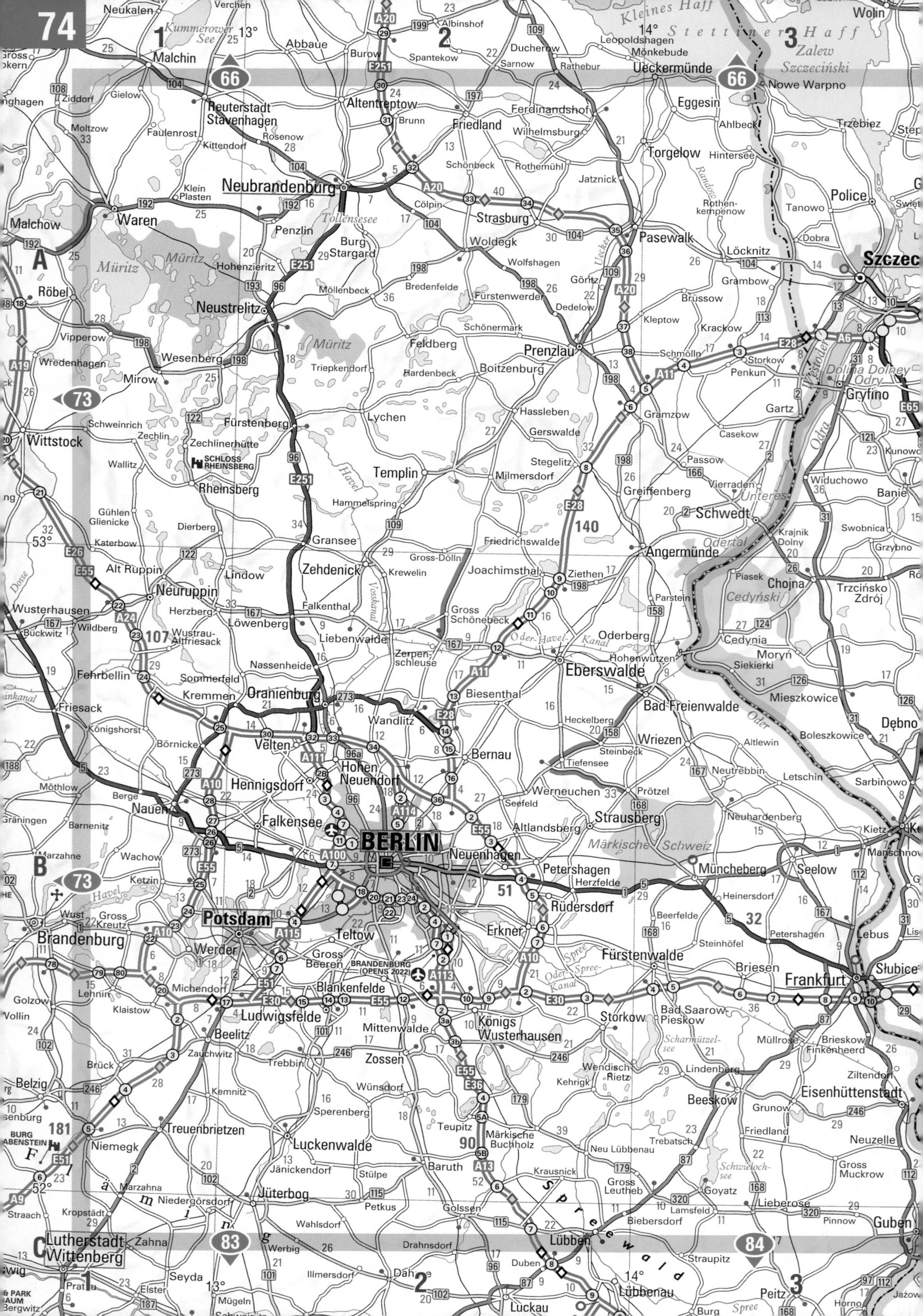

Neukalen
Verchen
Kummerower See
Malchin
Abbaue
Burow
Albinshof
Spantekow
Ducherow
Kleines Haff
Leopoldshagen
Mönkebude
Stettiner Haff
Zalew Szczeciński
Wolin
Sarnow
Rathebur
Ueckermünde
Nowe Warpno
Gielow
Reuterstadt Stavenhagen
Altentreptow
Brunn
Friedland
Ferdinandshof
Eggesin
Ahlbeck
Trzebież
Moltzow
Faulenrost
Kittendorf
Rosenow
Wilhelmsburg
Torgelow
Hintersee
Schönbeck
Rothemühl
Jatznick
Klein Plasten
Neubrandenburg
Cölpin
Strasburg
Pasewalk
Rothenkempenow
Tanowo
Police
Malchow
Waren
Tollensesee
Penzlin
Burg Stargard
Woldegk
Dobra
Löcknitz
Szczecin
Müritz
Hohenzieritz
Wolfshagen
Göritz
Grambow
Röbel
Möllenbeck
Bredenfelde
Fürstenwerder
Dedelow
Brüssow
Neustrelitz
Kleptow
Krackow
Vipperow
Schönermark
Wredenhagen
Wesenberg
Feldberg
Prenzlau
Schmölln
Storkow
Penkun
Triepkendorf
Hardenbeck
Boitzenburg
Mirow
Dolina Dolnej Odry
Gryfino
Gartz
Lychen
Hassleben
Gramzow
Schweinrich
Zechlin
Zechlinerhütte
Fürstenberg
Gerswalde
Casekow
Wittstock
Schloss Rheinsberg
Wallitz
Templin
Stegelitz
Milmersdorf
Passow
Kunowo
Rheinsberg
Widuchowo
Vierraden
Greiffenberg
Banie
Hammelspring
Gühlen Glienicke
Dierberg
Schwedt
Swobnica
Krajnik Dolny
Katerbow
Gransee
Friedrichswalde
Odertal
Grzybno
Gross-Dölln
Angermünde
Alt Ruppin
Zehdenick
Krewelin
Joachimsthal
Ziethen
Piasek
Chojna
Trzcińsko Zdrój
Lindow
Neuruppin
Wusterhausen
Herzberg
Falkenthal
Gross Schönebeck
Parstein
Cedyński
Bückwitz
Wildberg
Löwenberg
Wustrau-Altfriesack
Liebenwalde
Vosskanal
Oder-Havel-Kanal
Oderberg
Cedynia
Zerpenschleuse
Hohenwutzen
Moryń
Fehrbellin
Nassenheide
Eberswalde
Siekierki
Sommerfeld
Kremmen
Oranienburg
Biesenthal
Bad Freienwalde
Mieszkowice
Friesack
Wandlitz
Heckelberg
Dębno
Königshorst
Velten
Wriezen
Boleszkowice
Börnicke
Steinbeck
Altlewin
Hohen Neuendorf
Bernau
Tiefensee
Hennigsdorf
Neutrebbin
Letschin
Möthlow
Werneuchen
Prötzel
Sarbinowo
Berge
Nauen
Seefeld
Strausberg
Neuhardenberg
Gräningen
Barnenitz
Falkensee
Altlandsberg
Kietz
BERLIN
Märkische Schweiz
Marzahne
Wachow
Neuenhagen
Müncheberg
Seelow
Manschnow
Petershagen
Herzfelde
Ketzin
Havel
Rüdersdorf
Heinersdorf
Wust
Gross Kreutz
Potsdam
Beerfelde
Brandenburg
Teltow
Erkner
Steinhöfel
Lebus
Werder
Gross Beeren
Brandenburg (opens 2022)
Fürstenwalde
Briesen
Frankfurt
Słubice
Lehnin
Oder-Spree-Kanal
Golzow
Michendorf
Blankenfelde
Klaistow
Wollin
Ludwigsfelde
Mittenwalde
Königs Wusterhausen
Storkow
Bad Saarow-Pieskow
Beelitz
Scharmützelsee
Müllrose
Brieskow Finkenheerd
Zauchwitz
Zossen
Trebbin
Brück
Wendisch Rietz
Lindenberg
Ziltendorf
Belzig
Kemnitz
Kehrigk
Wünsdorf
Beeskow
Eisenhüttenstadt
Grunow
Sperenberg
Teupitz
Märkische Buchholz
Burg Rabenstein
Niemegk
Treuenbrietzen
Luckenwalde
Trebatsch
Neu Lübbenau
Friedland
Neuzelle
Fläming
Jänickendorf
Baruth
Krausnick
Schwielochsee
Gross Muckrow
Stülpe
Gross Leuthen
Marzahna
Niedergörsdorf
Jüterbog
Petkus
Spreewald
Goyatz
Lieberose
Strauch
Kropstädt
Golssen
Lamsfeld
Biebersdorf
Pinnow
Guben
Wahlsdorf
Lutherstadt Wittenberg
Zahna
Werbig
Drahnsdorf
Lübben
Straupitz
Duben
Seyda
Illmersdorf
Dahme
Lübbenau
Peitz
Pratau
Elster
Mügeln
Luckau
Burg
Spree
Horno
Jazów

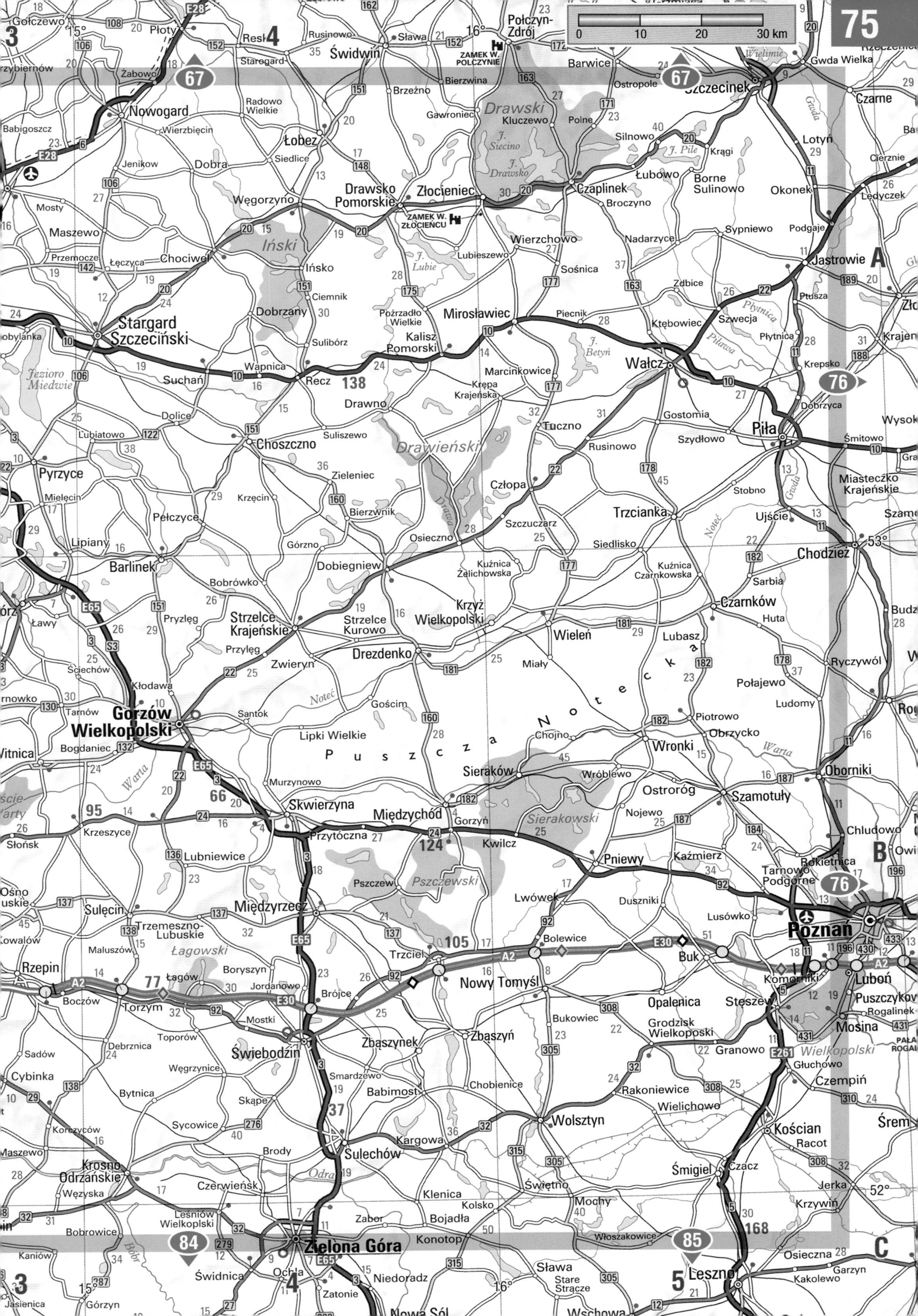

Nowogard
Świdwin
Połczyn-Zdrój
Szczecinek
Łobez
Drawsko Pomorskie
Złocieniec
Czaplinek
Stargard Szczeciński
Mirosławiec
Kalisz Pomorski
Wałcz
Piła
Recz
Choszczno
Pyrzyce
Trzcianka
Chodzież
Barlinek
Dobiegniew
Strzelce Krajeńskie
Krzyż Wielkopolski
Wieleń
Czarnków
Drezdenko
Gorzów Wielkopolski
Wronki
Oborniki
Sieraków
Szamotuły
Skwierzyna
Międzychód
Pniewy
Międzyrzecz
Poznań
Sulęcin
Rzepin
Nowy Tomyśl
Buk
Opalenica
Stęszew
Luboń
Mosina
Świebodzin
Zbąszyń
Zbąszynek
Grodzisk Wielkopolski
Wolsztyn
Kościan
Sulechów
Krosno Odrzańskie
Śmigiel
Zielona Góra
Leszno
Puszcza Notecka
Drawski
Drawieński
Iński
Pszczewski
Sierakowski
Wielkopolski

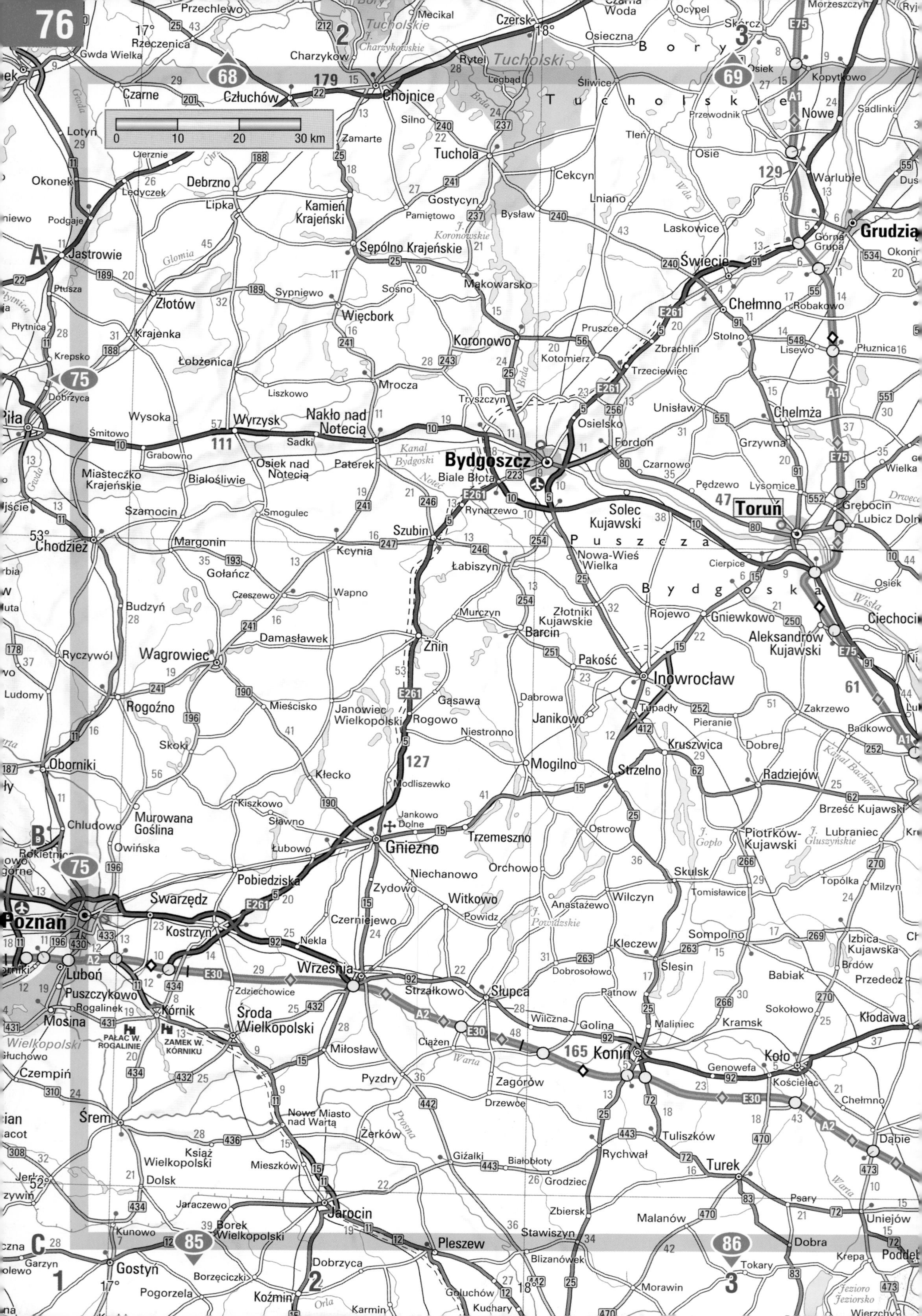
Przechlewo
Rzeczenica
Gwda Wielka
Mecikal
Charzykowy
Tucholskie
Charzykowskie
Czersk
Rytel
Tucholski
Czarna Woda
Osieczna
Ocypel
Skórcz
Bory
Morzeszczyn
Osiek
Kopytkowo
Legbąd
Śliwice
Tucholskie
Przewodnik
Nowe
Sadlinki
Czarne
Człuchów
Chojnice
Silno
Zamarte
Tuchola
Tleń
Osie
Warlubie
Lotyń
Okonek
Debrzno
Ledyczek
Lipka
Kamień Krajeński
Gostycyn
Pamiętowo
Bysław
Cekcyn
Lniano
Laskowice
Grudziądz
Górna Grupa
Podgaje
Jastrowie
Sępólno Krajeńskie
Świecie
Okonin
J. Koronowskie
Glomia
Ptusza
Złotów
Sypniewo
Sośno
Mąkowarsko
Chełmno
Robakowo
Więcbork
Płytnica
Krajenka
Koronowo
Pruszce
Stolno
Zbrachlin
Lisewo
Płużnica
Krepsko
Łobżenica
Kotomierz
Trzeciewiec
Dobrzyca
Liszkowo
Mrocza
Tryszczyn
Unisław
Chełmża
Wysoka
Wyrzysk
Nakło nad Notecią
Osielsko
Piła
Śmitowo
Sadki
Fordon
Grzywna
Grabowno
Kanał Bydgoski
Bydgoszcz
Czarnowo
Wielka
Miasteczko Krajeńskie
Białośliwie
Osiek nad Notecią
Paterek
Biale Błota
Lysomice
Pędzewo
Szamocin
Rynarzewo
Solec Kujawski
Toruń
Grębocin
Lubicz Dolny
Smogulec
Szubin
Chodzież
Margonin
Kcynia
Łabiszyn
Puszcza Bydgoska
Nowa-Wieś Wielka
Cierpice
Gołańcz
Osiek
Czeszewo
Wapno
Złotniki Kujawskie
Rojewo
Gniewkowo
Ciechocinek
Budzyń
Murczyn
Barcin
Aleksandrów Kujawski
Damasławek
Żnin
Ryczywół
Wągrowiec
Pakość
Inowrocław
Ludomy
Rogoźno
Mieścisko
Gąsawa
Dąbrowa
Janowiec Wielkopolski
Rogowo
Janikowo
Tupadły
Pieranie
Zakrzewo
Skoki
Niestronno
Kruszwica
Badkowo
Dobre
Oborniki
Mogilno
Strzelno
Radziejów
Kłecko
Modliszewko
Kanał Bachorze
Kiszkowo
Brześć Kujawski
Murowana Goślina
Sławno
Jankowo Dolne
Trzemeszno
Ostrowo
Chludowo
Gniezno
J. Gopło
Piotrków-Kujawski
Lubraniec
J. Głuszyńskie
Owińska
Łubowo
Rokietnica
Pobiedziska
Orchowo
Niechanowo
Skulsk
Topólka
Milzyn
Zydowo
Wilczyn
Tomisławice
Swarzędz
Witkowo
Poznań
Kostrzyn
Powidz
J. Powidzkie
Anastazewo
Czerniejewo
Sompolno
Nekla
Kleczew
Izbica Kujawska
Luboń
Września
Dobrosołowo
Ślesin
Brdów
Zdziechowice
Strzałkowo
Słupca
Babiak
Przedecz
Puszczykowo
Pątnów
Rogalinek
Kórnik
Środa Wielkopolski
Sokołowo
Mosina
Wilczna
Golina
Maliniec
Kramsk
Kłodawa
Pałac w Rogalinie
Zamek w Kórniku
Wielkopolski
Ciążeń
Konin
Koło
Miłosław
Warta
Genowefa
Łuchowo
Czempiń
Pyzdry
Zagórów
Kościelec
Chełmno
Drzewce
Śrem
Nowe Miasto nad Wartą
Prosna
Dąbie
Żerków
Tuliszków
Rychwał
Książ Wielkopolski
Giżałki
Białobłoty
Turek
Mieszków
Dolsk
Grodziec
Psary
Jaraczewo
Jarocin
Zbiersk
Malanów
Uniejów
Kunowo
Borek Wielkopolski
Stawiszyn
Pleszew
Dobra
Garzyn
Gostyń
Dobrzyca
Blizanówek
Tokary
Krępa
Poddębice
Borzęciczki
Pogorzela
Koźmin
Gołuchów
Kuchary
Morawin
Jezioro Jeziorsko
Orla
Karmin
Wierzchy
0 10 20 30 km
53°
52°
17°
18°
A
B
C
1
2
3
68
69
75
85
86
A1
A2
E30
E75
E261

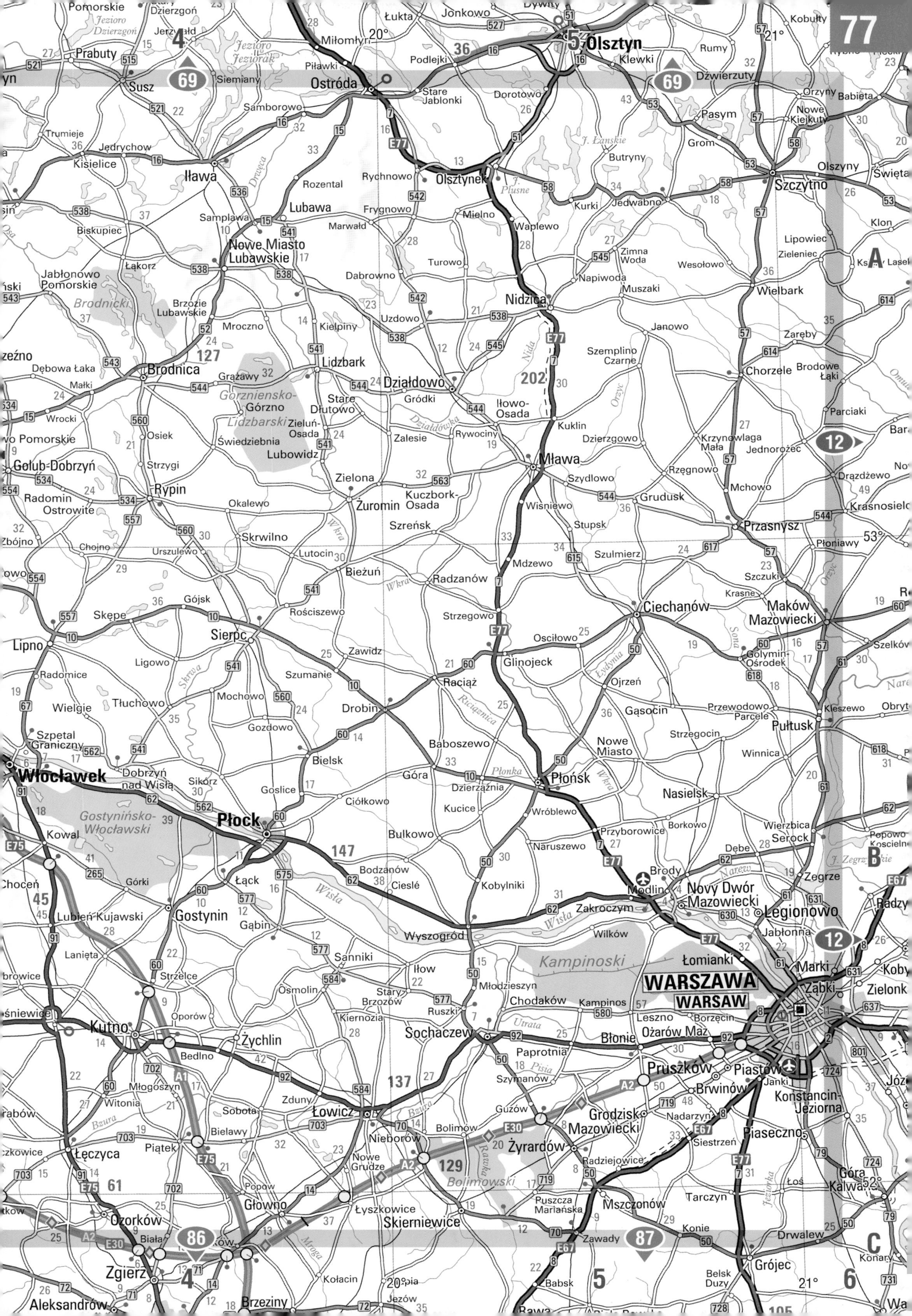
Pomorskie
Jezioro Dzierzgoń
Dzierzgoń
Jerzwałd
Prabuty
Susz
Jezioro Jeziorak
Siemiany
69
Łukta
Jonkowo
Miłomłyn
20°
Piławki
Ostróda
Podlejki
Stare Jabłonki
Dorotowo
Olsztyn
Klewki
Rumy
Dźwierzuty
Kobułty
21°
Samborowo
Trumieje
Jędrychowo
Kisielice
Iława
Drwęca
Rozental
Rychnowo
Olsztynek
J. Pluśne
J. Łańskie
Butryny
Pasym
Grom
Orzyny
Babięta
Nowe Kiejkuty
Olszyny
Szczytno
Świętaj
Lubawa
Frygnowo
Marwałd
Mielno
Waplewo
Kurki
Jedwabno
Samplawa
Biskupiec
Nowe Miasto Lubawskie
Łąkorz
Jabłonowo Pomorskie
Brodnicki
Brzozie Lubawskie
Turowo
Dąbrowno
Zimna Woda
Napiwoda
Muszaki
Wesołowo
Wielbark
Lipowiec
Zieleniec
Klon
A
Nidzica
Mroczno
Kiełpiny
Uzdowo
Janowo
Zaręby
Dębowa Łąka
Małki
Brodnica
Grążawy
127
Lidzbark
Działdowo
202
Nida
Szemplino Czarne
Chorzele
Brodowe Łąki
Wrocki
Gorznieńsko-Lidzbarski
Górzno
Stare Dłutowo
Gródki
Iłowo-Osada
Parciaki
Osiek
Świedziebnia
Zieluń-Osada
Działdówka
Rywociny
Zalesie
Kuklin
Dzierzgowo
Krzynowłoga Mała
Jednorożec
12
Golub-Dobrzyń
Lubowidz
Mława
Rzęgnowo
Drążdżewo
Radomin
Ostrowite
Strzygi
Rypin
Zielona
Kuczbork-Osada
Żuromin
Szydłowo
Grudusk
Mchowo
Krasnosielc
Okalewo
Wiśniewo
Stupsk
Przasnysz
Płoniawy
53°
Zbójno
Chojno
Skrwilno
Szreńsk
Wkra
Szulmierz
Urszulewo
Lutocin
Bieżuń
Radzanów
Mdzewo
Szczuki
Skępe
Gójsk
Rościszewo
Krasne
Ciechanów
Maków Mazowiecki
Lipno
Sierpc
Strzegowo
Osciłowo
Zawidz
Glinojeck
Gołymin-Ośrodek
Szelków
Radomice
Ligowo
Szumanie
Raciąż
Ojrzeń
Łydynia
Wielgie
Tłuchowo
Mochowo
Drobin
Rościąznica
Gąsocin
Przewodowo Parcele
Kleszewo
Obryte
Szpetal Graniczny
Gozdowo
Pułtusk
Strzegocin
Bielsk
Baboszewo
Nowe Miasto
Winnica
Włocławek
Dobrzyń nad Wisłą
Sikórz
Góra
Płonka
Płońsk
Dzierzążnia
Nasielsk
Goślice
Ciółkowo
Kucice
Wróblewo
Gostynińsko-Włocławski
Płock
Bulkowo
Przyborowice
Borkowo
Wierzbica
Serock
Popowo Kościelne
Kowal
147
Naruszewo
Dębe
Zegrzyński
B
Górki
Łąck
Bodzanów
Cieślé
Kobylniki
Brody
Modlin
Nowy Dwór Mazowiecki
Zegrze
Choceń
Gostynin
Zakroczym
Legionowo
Radzym
Lubień Kujawski
Gąbin
Wisła
Wyszogród
Wilków
Jabłonna
Łaniete
Sanniki
Kampinoski
Łomianki
Marki
Kobyłka
Strzelce
Iłów
Młodzieszyn
WARSZAWA
WARSAW
Ząbki
Zielonka
Osmolin
Stary Brzozów
Chodaków
Kampinos
Oporów
Kiernozia
Ruszki
Leszno
Borzęcin
Kutno
Żychlin
Sochaczew
Utrata
Błonie
Ożarów Maz.
Bedlno
Paprotnia
Pruszków
Piastów
Pisia
Szymanów
137
Brwinów
Janki
Józef
Młogoszyn
Witonia
Zduny
Konstancin-Jeziorna
Sobota
Łowicz
Guzów
Grodzisk Mazowiecki
Nadarzyn
Bzura
Bielawy
Nieborów
Bolimów
Żyrardów
Piaseczno
Łęczyca
Piątek
Nowe Grudze
129
Bolimowski
Rawka
Radziejowice
Siestrzeń
Góra Kalwaria
Popów
Puszcza Mariańska
Mszczonów
Tarczyn
Łoś
Ozorków
Głowno
Łyszkowice
Skierniewice
86
Biała
Zawady
87
Konie
Drwalew
C
Zgierz
Kołacin
Mroga
Grójec
Konary
Aleksandrów
Brzeziny
Jeżów
Babsk
Belsk Duży
Rawa
Kiełpiny
WARSZAWA

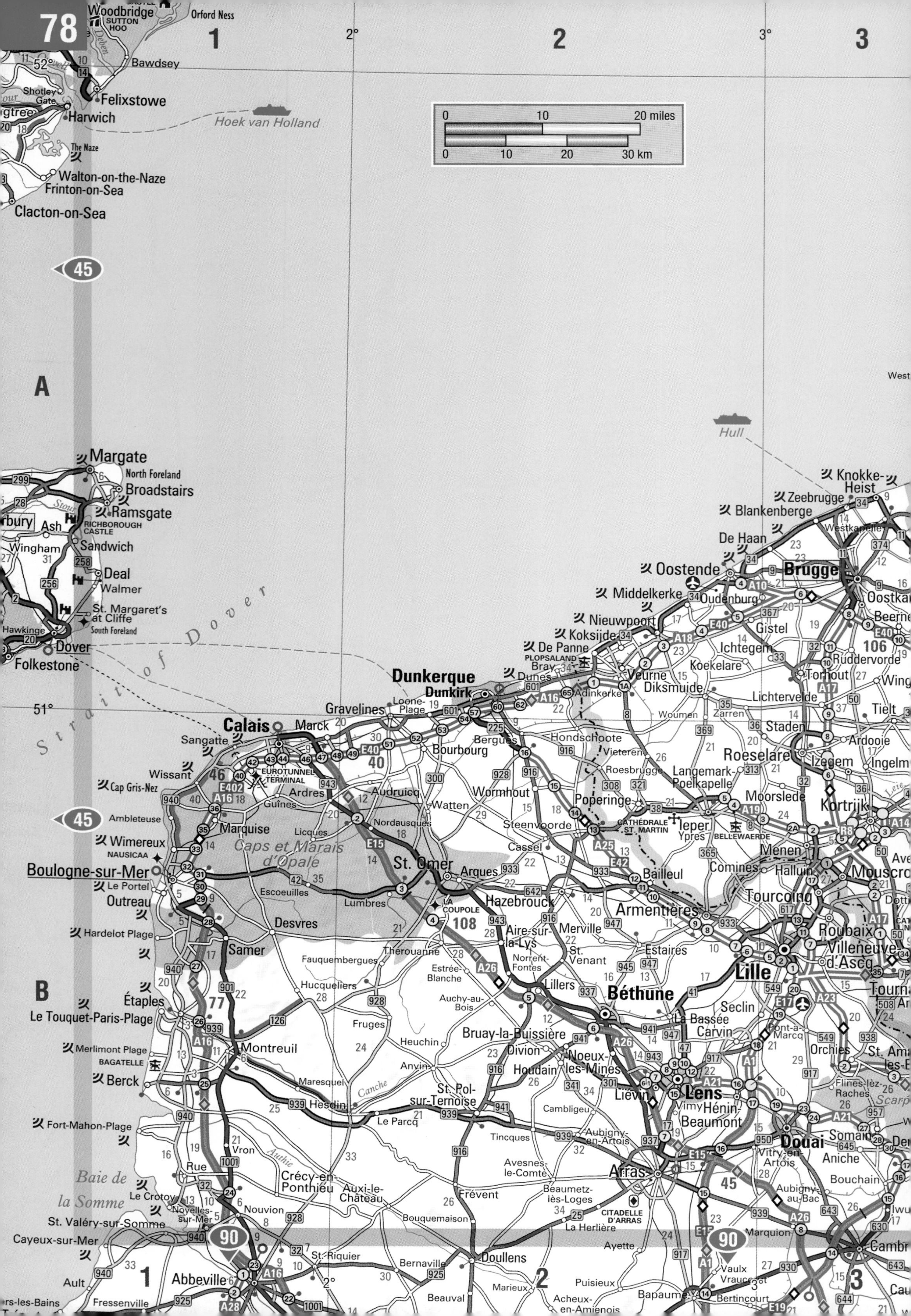

1
2
3
2°
3°
A
B
52°
51°
Woodbridge
SUTTON HOO
Orford Ness
Bawdsey
Felixstowe
Shotley Gate
Harwich
Hoek van Holland
The Naze
Walton-on-the-Naze
Frinton-on-Sea
Clacton-on-Sea
0
10
20 miles
0
10
20
30 km
45
Margate
North Foreland
Broadstairs
Ramsgate
RICHBOROUGH CASTLE
Ash
Sandwich
Wingham
Deal
Walmer
St. Margaret's at Cliffe
South Foreland
Hawkinge
Dover
Folkestone
Strait of Dover
Hull
Knokke-Heist
Zeebrugge
Blankenberge
De Haan
Oostende
Middelkerke
Oudenburg
Nieuwpoort
Koksijde
De Panne
PLOPSALAND
Bray-Dunes
Brugge
Gistel
Ichtegem
Koekelare
Torhout
Ruddervoorde
Lichtervelde
Veurne
Diksmuide
Adinkerke
Woumen
Zarren
Staden
Tielt
Ardooie
Roeselare
Izegem
Ingelm
Langemark-Poelkapelle
Moorslede
Kortrijk
Hondschoote
Vleteren
Roesbrugge
Poperinge
CATHÉDRALE ST. MARTIN
Ieper
Ypres
BELLEWAERDE
Menen
Halluin
Mouscron
Comines
Tourcoing
Roubaix
Villeneuve-d'Ascq
Lille
Tournai
Seclin
Orchies
Dunkerque
Dunkirk
Gravelines
Loone-Plage
Calais
Marck
Sangatte
Wissant
EUROTUNNEL TERMINAL
Cap Gris-Nez
Ardres
Guînes
Audruicq
Bourbourg
Bergues
Wormhout
Watten
Steenvoorde
Cassel
Bailleul
Armentières
Ambleteuse
Marquise
Licques
Nordausques
Caps et Marais d'Opale
Wimereux
NAUSICAA
Boulogne-sur-Mer
Le Portel
Outreau
Escoeuilles
Lumbres
St. Omer
Arques
LA COUPOLE
Hazebrouck
Desvres
Hardelot Plage
Samer
Fauquembergues
Thérouanne
Estrée-Blanche
Aire-sur-la-Lys
Merville
Norrent-Fontes
St. Venant
Estaires
Étaples
Le Touquet-Paris-Plage
Hucqueliers
Auchy-au-Bois
Lillers
Béthune
La Bassée
Carvin
Merlimont Plage
BAGATELLE
Montreuil
Fruges
Heuchin
Bruay-la-Buissière
Divion
Houdain
Noeux-les-Mines
Anvin
Berck
Maresquel
Canche
Hesdin
St. Pol-sur-Ternoise
Cambligeul
Liévin
Lens
Hénin-Beaumont
Fort-Mahon-Plage
Le Parcq
Tincques
Aubigny-en-Artois
Douai
Vitry-en-Artois
Aniche
Bouchain
Vron
Authie
Rue
Baie de la Somme
Le Crotoy
Crécy-en-Ponthieu
Auxi-le-Château
Avesnes-le-Comte
Arras
Beaumetz-lès-Loges
CITADELLE D'ARRAS
Frévent
Noyelles-sur-Mer
Nouvion
St. Valéry-sur-Somme
Cayeux-sur-Mer
Bouquemaison
La Herlière
Ayette
Marquion
Aubigny-au-Bac
Cambrai
St. Riquier
Doullens
Ault
Abbeville
Bernaville
Beauval
Marieux
Puisieux
Acheux-en-Amiénois
Bapaume
Bertincourt
Vaulx Vraucourt
Fressenville
77
90
106
108
40
46
E15
E40
E402
A16
A26
A25
A1
A21
E17
A23
E42
A17
A10
A18
A19
A14
A28
E19
Westkapelle
Oostkamp
Beernem
Wingene
Flines-lez-Raches
Scarpe
Pont-à-Marcq
St. Amand-les-Eaux
Somain
Denain
West

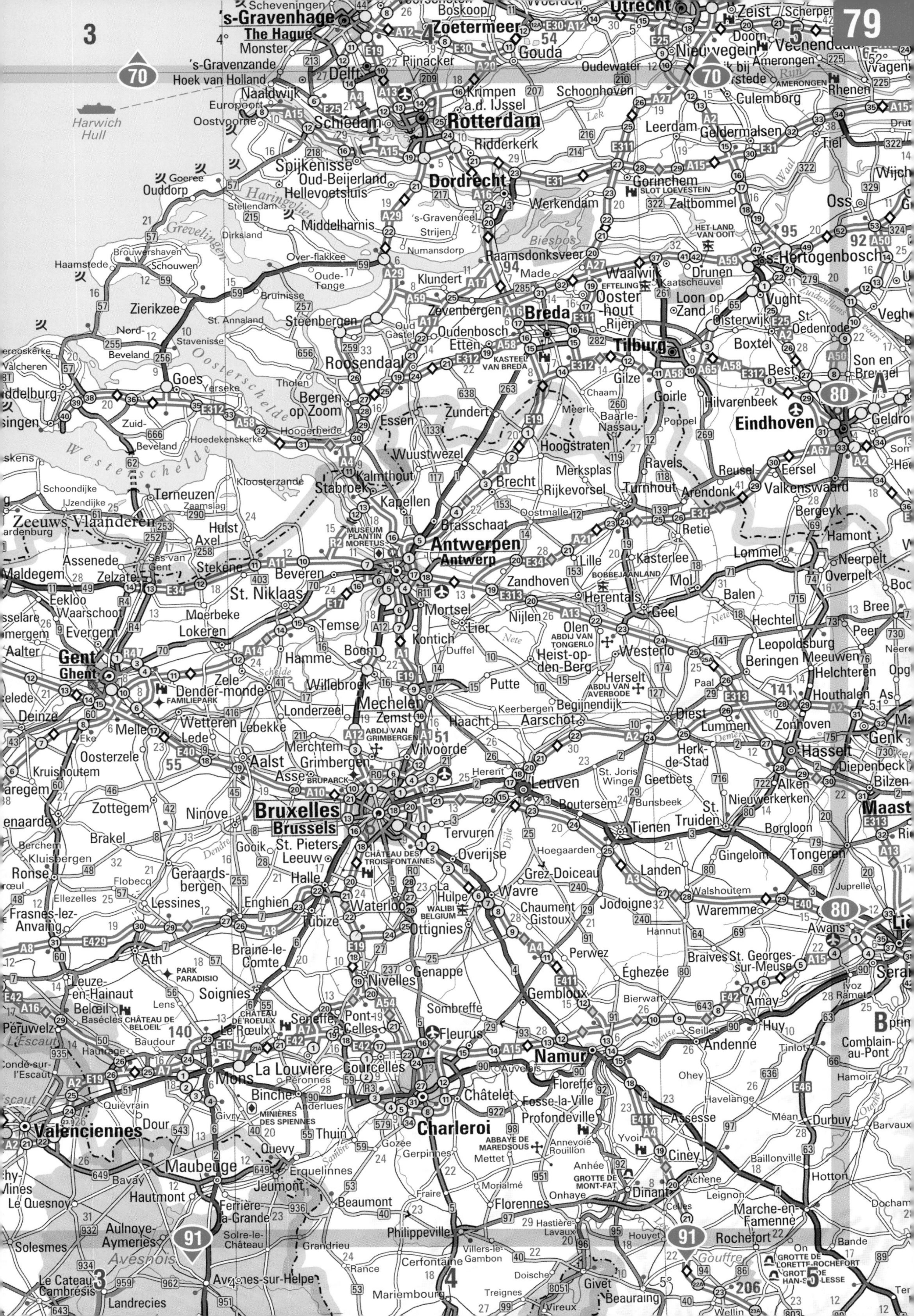

's-Gravenhage
The Hague
Scheveningen
Monster
's-Gravenzande
Hoek van Holland
Naaldwijk
Europoort
Oostvoorne
Harwich
Hull
Delft
Zoetermeer
Boskoop
Pijnacker
Gouda
Utrecht
Zeist
Nieuwegein
Doorn
Veenendaal
Amerongen
Rhenen
Culemborg
Schoonhoven
Oudewater
Krimpen a.d. IJssel
Rotterdam
Schiedam
Ridderkerk
Spijkenisse
Oud-Beijerland
Hellevoetsluis
Dordrecht
Leerdam
Geldermalsen
Tiel
Gorinchem
Zaltbommel
Werkendam
Oss
Goeree
Ouddorp
Stellendam
Haringvliet
Middelharnis
Dirksland
's-Gravendeel
Strijen
Numansdorp
Biesbos
Raamsdonksveer
Waalwijk
's-Hertogenbosch
Drunen
Grevelingen
Brouwershaven
Haamstede
Schouwen
Over-flakkee
Oude-Tonge
Klundert
Made
Bruinisse
Zierikzee
Steenbergen
Zevenbergen
Breda
Oosterhout
Loon op Zand
Vught
Nord-Beveland
Oosterschelde
Oudenbosch
Etten
Rijen
Tilburg
Oisterwijk
Boxtel
St. Oedenrode
Roosendaal
Gilze
Goirle
Best
Son en Breugel
Goes
Yerseke
Tholen
Bergen op Zoom
Zundert
Hilvarenbeek
Eindhoven
Middelburg
Vlissingen
Zuid-Beveland
Hoogerheide
Essen
Baarle-Nassau
Hoogstraten
Westerschelde
Wuustwezel
Kalmthout
Merksplas
Turnhout
Reusel
Eersel
Valkenswaard
Schoondijke
Terneuzen
Kloosterzande
Stabroek
Brecht
Rijkevorsel
Arendonk
Zeeuws Vlaanderen
Hulst
Axel
Kapellen
Brasschaat
Oostmalle
Retie
Bergeyk
Hamont
Assenede
Sas-van-Gent
Antwerpen
Antwerp
Lille
Kasterlee
Lommel
Neerpelt
Overpelt
Maldegem
Zelzate
Stekene
Beveren
Zandhoven
Mol
Eeklo
St. Niklaas
Herentals
Balen
Bree
Waarschoot
Moerbeke
Mortsel
Nijlen
Geel
Hechtel
Evergem
Lokeren
Temse
Lier
Olen
Leopoldsburg
Aalter
Gent
Ghent
Hamme
Boom
Kontich
Duffel
Heist-op-den-Berg
Westerlo
Beringen
Helchteren
Zele
Dendermonde
Willebroek
Putte
Herselt
Houthalen
Deinze
Melle
Wetteren
Lebbeke
Londerzeel
Mechelen
Zemst
Haacht
Begijnendijk
Aarschot
Diest
Lummen
Zonhoven
Genk
Lede
Merchtem
Vilvoorde
Herk-de-Stad
Hasselt
Oosterzele
Aalst
Grimbergen
Leuven
Geetbets
Alken
Diepenbeek
Bilzen
Kruishoutem
Asse
Herent
Boutersem
St. Truiden
Maastricht
Zottegem
Ninove
Bruxelles
Brussels
Tervuren
Tienen
Borgloon
Brakel
Gooik
St. Pieters-Leeuw
Overijse
Hoegaarden
Gingelom
Tongeren
Kluisbergen
Geraardsbergen
Halle
Grez-Doiceau
Landen
Ronse
Flobecq
La Hulpe
Wavre
Ellezelles
Lessines
Enghien
Waterloo
Chaumont Gistoux
Jodoigne
Waremme
Frasnes-lez-Anvaing
Tubize
Ottignies
Hannut
Awans
Liège
Ath
Braine-le-Comte
Perwez
Braives
St. Georges-sur-Meuse
Genappe
Éghezée
Seraing
Leuze-en-Hainaut
Nivelles
Gembloux
Soignies
Beloeil
Sombreffe
Bierwart
Amay
Péruwelz
Seneffe
Pont-à-Celles
Fleurus
Huy
Baudour
Le Rœulx
Namur
Andenne
Condé-sur-l'Escaut
Mons
La Louvière
Courcelles
Auvelais
Floreffe
Ohey
Binche
Châtelet
Fosse-la-Ville
Havelange
Valenciennes
Quiévrain
Dour
Anderlues
Charleroi
Profondeville
Assesse
Durbuy
Thuin
Gerpinnes
Mettet
Yvoir
Ciney
Maubeuge
Quevy
Gozée
Erquelinnes
Bavay
Jeumont
Anhée
Dinant
Achene
Hotton
Hautmont
Morialmé
Florennes
Onhaye
Leignon
Le Quesnoy
Beaumont
Ferrière-la-Grande
Celles
Marche-en-Famenne
Aulnoye-Aymeries
Solre-le-Château
Philippeville
Hastière-Lavaux
Houyet
Rochefort
Solesmes
Avesnois
Cerfontaine
Villers-le-Gambon
Doische
Le Cateau Cambrésis
Avesnes-sur-Helpe
Rance
Mariembourg
Treignes
Givet
Beauraing
Landrecies
Vireux
Wellin

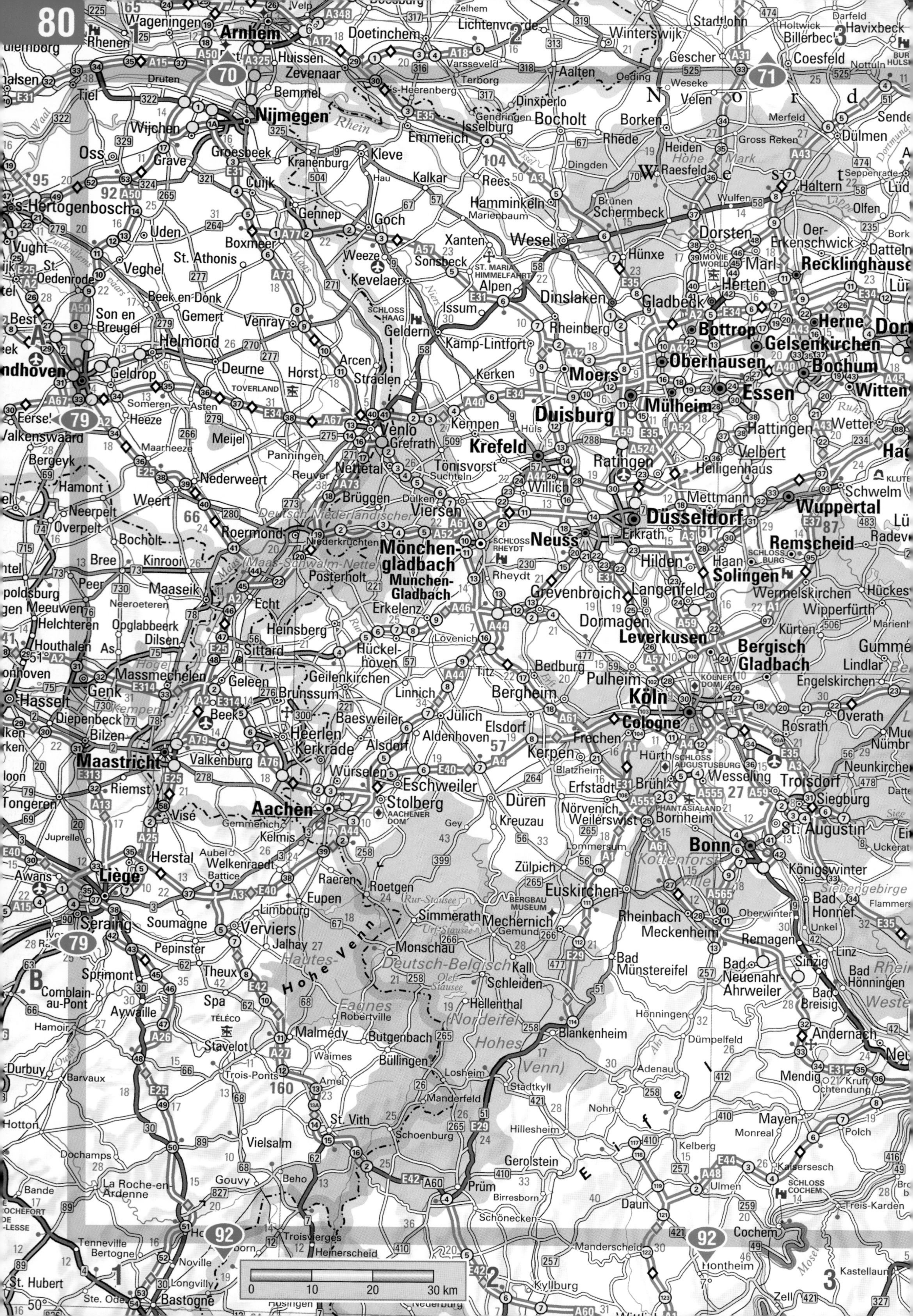

Wageningen
Arnhem
Rhenen
Doetinchem
Lichtenvoorde
Winterswijk
Stadtlohn
Billerbeck
Havixbeck
Coesfeld
Huissen
Zevenaar
Aalten
Gescher
Tiel
Bemmel
Nijmegen
Dinxperlo
Bocholt
Borken
Velen
Nord
Dülmen
Wijchen
Emmerich
Isselburg
Rhede
Heiden
Gross Reken
Oss
Groesbeek
Kleve
Kranenburg
Kalkar
Rees
Raesfeld
West
Haltern
Grave
Cuijk
Hohe Mark
's-Hertogenbosch
Gennep
Goch
Hamminkeln
Schermbeck
Olfen
Uden
Boxmeer
Xanten
Wesel
Dorsten
Marl
Recklinghausen
Vught
St. Athonis
Veghel
Weeze
Sonsbeck
Hünxe
Herten
St. Oedenrode
Kevelaer
Alpen
Dinslaken
Gladbeck
Beek en Donk
Gemert
Issum
Best
Son en Breugel
Venray
Geldern
Kamp-Lintfort
Rheinberg
Bottrop
Herne
Gelsenkirchen
Helmond
Arcen
Straelen
Oberhausen
Bochum
Eindhoven
Geldrop
Deurne
Horst
Kerken
Moers
Essen
Witten
Toverland
Someren
Asten
Duisburg
Mülheim
Eersel
Heeze
Venlo
Kempen
Hattingen
Wetter
Valkenswaard
Maarheeze
Meijel
Panningen
Grefrath
Krefeld
Ratingen
Velbert
Bergeyk
Nettetal
Tönisvorst
Heiligenhaus
Hamont
Weert
Nederweert
Reuver
Brüggen
Viersen
Willich
Mettmann
Schwelm
Wuppertal
Neerpelt
Overpelt
Roermond
Düsseldorf
Erkrath
Remscheid
Bocholt
Niederkrüchten
Mönchengladbach
München-Gladbach
Neuss
Hilden
Haan
Solingen
Bree
Kinrooi
Maaseik
Posterholt
Rheydt
Grevenbroich
Langenfeld
Wermelskirchen
Hückeswagen
Wipperfürth
Meeuwen
Neeroeteren
Echt
Erkelenz
Dormagen
Leverkusen
Helchteren
Opglabbeek
Heinsberg
Kürten
Houthalen
Dilsen
Sittard
Hückelhoven
Bedburg
Pulheim
Bergisch Gladbach
Lindlar
Gummersbach
Hasselt
Genk
Massmechelen
Geleen
Geilenkirchen
Linnich
Bergheim
Köln
Cologne
Engelskirchen
Overath
Diepenbeck
Bilzen
Beek
Brunssum
Baesweiler
Jülich
Elsdorf
Frechen
Rösrath
Maastricht
Valkenburg
Heerlen
Kerkrade
Alsdorf
Aldenhoven
Kerpen
Hürth
Wesseling
Troisdorf
Neunkirchen
Tongeren
Riemst
Würselen
Eschweiler
Erftstadt
Brühl
Siegburg
Visé
Aachen
Stolberg
Düren
Nörvenich
Weilerswist
Bornheim
St. Augustin
Gemmenich
Kelmis
Kreuzau
Bonn
Herstal
Welkenraedt
Zülpich
Kottenforst
Königswinter
Liège
Raeren
Roetgen
Euskirchen
Siebengebirge
Bad Honnef
Seraing
Limbourg
Eupen
Simmerath
Mechernich
Rheinbach
Meckenheim
Remagen
Soumagne
Verviers
Monschau
Sinzig
Linz
Pepinster
Jalhay
Hautes-Fagnes
Hohe Venn
Deutsch-Belgisch
Kall
Bad Münstereifel
Bad Neuenahr-Ahrweiler
Bad Hönningen
Sprimont
Theux
Schleiden
Bad Breisig
Comblain-au-Pont
Spa
Aywaille
Hellenthal
Nordeifel
Malmedy
Robertville
Butgenbach
Blankenheim
Hönningen
Andernach
Stavelot
Waimes
Bullingen
Hohes Venn
Dümpelfeld
Durbuy
Barvaux
Trois-Ponts
Losheim
Stadtkyll
Adenau
Mendig
Kruft
Ochtendung
Manderfeld
Eifel
Hotton
St. Vith
Schoenburg
Hillesheim
Nohn
Mayen
Monreal
Polch
Vielsalm
Dochamps
Gerolstein
Kelberg
Kaisersesch
Schloss Cochem
Beho
Gouvy
La Roche-en-Ardenne
Prüm
Birresborn
Daun
Ulmen
Treis-Karden
Schönecken
Troisvierges
Heinerscheid
Manderscheid
Cochem
Tenneville
Bertogne
Noville
Longvilly
Hontheim
Kastellaun
St. Hubert
Bastogne
Kyllburg
Zell
Mosel
0 10 20 30 km

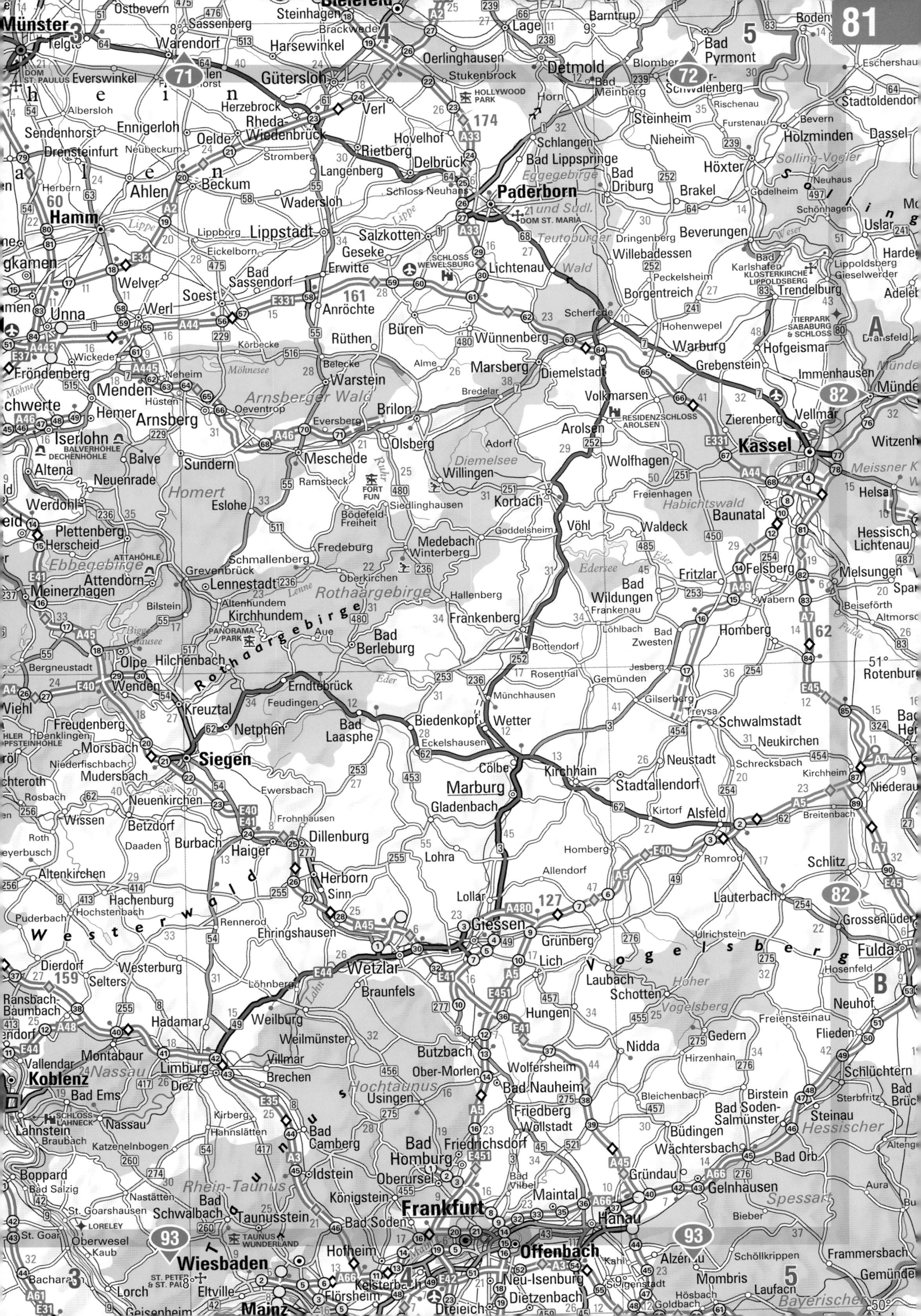
Münster
Ostbevern
Sassenberg
Steinhagen
Bielefeld
Lage
Barntrup
Bad Pyrmont
Telgte
Warendorf
Harsewinkel
Brackwede
Oerlinghausen
Detmold
Blomberg
Schwalenberg
Everswinkel
Gütersloh
Stukenbrock
Hollywood Park
Horn
Bad Meinberg
Eschershausen
Stadtoldendorf
Albersloh
Herzebrock
Verl
Steinheim
Rischenau
Sendenhorst
Ennigerloh
Rheda-Wiedenbrück
Hovelhof
Schlangen
Nieheim
Holzminden
Dassel
Drensteinfurt
Neubeckum
Oelde
Stromberg
Rietberg
Bad Lippspringe
Höxter
Solling-Vogler
Langenberg
Delbrück
Eggegebirge
Bad Driburg
Herbern
Ahlen
Beckum
Schloss Neuhaus
Paderborn
Brakel
Neuhaus
Hamm
Wadersloh
Dom St. Maria
Schönhagen
Uslar
Lippe
Lippstadt
Salzkotten
Teutoburger Wald
Dringenberg
Beverungen
Lippborg
Eickelborn
Geseke
Schloss Wewelsburg
Lichtenau
Willebadessen
Bad Karlshafen
Klosterkirche Lippoldsberg
Lippoldsberg
Gieselwerder
Bergkamen
Welver
Bad Sassendorf
Erwitte
Peckelsheim
Borgentreich
Trendelburg
Soest
Anröchte
Unna
Werl
Scherfede
Hohenwepel
Tierpark Sababurg & Schloss
Rüthen
Büren
Wünnenberg
Warburg
Hofgeismar
Körbecke
Wickede
Möhnesee
Belecke
Alme
Marsberg
Diemelstadt
Grebenstein
Immenhausen
Fröndenberg
Neheim
Warstein
Bredelar
Menden
Hüsten
Arnsberger Wald
Volkmarsen
Schwerte
Hemer
Oeventrop
Brilon
Zierenberg
Vellmar
Arnsberg
Eversberg
Residenzschloss Arolsen
Arolsen
Iserlohn
Balverhöhle
Dechenhöhle
Olsberg
Adorf
Kassel
Witzenhausen
Balve
Sundern
Meschede
Diemelsee
Wolfhagen
Altena
Neuenrade
Ramsbeck
Fort Fun
Willingen
Meissner
Homert
Eslohe
Siedlinghausen
Korbach
Freienhagen
Habichtswald
Helsa
Werdohl
Baunatal
Plettenberg
Bödefeld-Freiheit
Vöhl
Waldeck
Hessisch Lichtenau
Herscheid
Goddelsheim
Medebach
Winterberg
Fredeburg
Schmallenberg
Attahöhle
Ebbegebirge
Attendorn
Edersee
Fritzlar
Felsberg
Melsungen
Grevenbrück
Lennestadt
Oberkirchen
Rothaargebirge
Bad Wildungen
Meinerzhagen
Altenhundem
Hallenberg
Frankenau
Wabern
Beiseförth
Bilstein
Kirchhundem
Frankenberg
Löhlbach
Bad Zwesten
Homberg
Altmorschen
Panorama Park
Aue
Bad Berleburg
Bottendorf
Fulda
Biggesee
Bergneustadt
Olpe
Hilchenbach
Rosenthal
Jesberg
Gemünden
Rotenburg
Wenden
Erndtebrück
Eder
Wiehl
Kreuztal
Feudingen
Münchhausen
Gilserberg
Freudenberg
Denklingen
Netphen
Bad Laasphe
Biedenkopf
Wetter
Treysa
Schwalmstadt
Morsbach
Eckelshausen
Neukirchen
Niederfischbach
Siegen
Cölbe
Kirchhain
Neustadt
Schrecksbach
Kirchheim
Mudersbach
Marburg
Stadtallendorf
Rosbach
Neuenkirchen
Ewersbach
Gladenbach
Niederaula
Wissen
Frohnhausen
Kirtorf
Alsfeld
Breitenbach
Betzdorf
Roth
Daaden
Burbach
Haiger
Dillenburg
Homberg
Romrod
Schlitz
Altenkirchen
Lohra
Allendorf
Herborn
Sinn
Hachenburg
Lollar
Lauterbach
Hochstenbach
Puderbach
Rennerod
Ehringshausen
Giessen
Grossenlüder
Westerwald
Grünberg
Ulrichstein
Dierdorf
Selters
Westerburg
Wetzlar
Lich
Vogelsberg
Hosenfeld
Ransbach-Baumbach
Löhnberg
Braunfels
Laubach
Schotten
Höher Vogelsberg
Neuhof
Hadamar
Weilburg
Hungen
Freiensteinau
Vallendar
Weilmünster
Nidda
Gedern
Flieden
Montabaur
Villmar
Butzbach
Hirzenhain
Koblenz
Nassau
Limburg
Diez
Brechen
Ober-Morlen
Wolfersheim
Schlüchtern
Bad Ems
Hochtaunus
Bad Nauheim
Birstein
Schloss Lahneck
Usingen
Friedberg
Bleichenbach
Bad Soden-Salmünster
Sterbfritz
Steinau
Lahnstein
Kirberg
Wöllstadt
Braubach
Hahnstätten
Bad Camberg
Büdingen
Hessischer
Katzenelnbogen
Bad Homburg
Friedrichsdorf
Wächtersbach
Bad Orb
Boppard
Idstein
Oberursel
Bad Vilbel
Gründau
Bad Salzig
Rhein-Taunus
Nastätten
Königstein
Maintal
Gelnhausen
Aura
Bad Schwalbach
Frankfurt
Spessart
St. Goarshausen
Taunusstein
Hanau
Bieber
Loreley
St. Goar
Oberwesel
Kaub
Taunus Wunderland
Bad Soden
Hofheim
Offenbach
Alzenau
Schöllkrippen
Frammersbach
Wiesbaden
St. Peter & St. Paul
Kahl
Bacharach
Lorch
Eltville
Kelsterbach
Neu-Isenburg
Seligenstadt
Mombris
Gemünden
Geisenheim
Mainz
Flörsheim
Dreieich
Dietzenbach
Hösbach
Laufach
Goldbach
Bayerischer

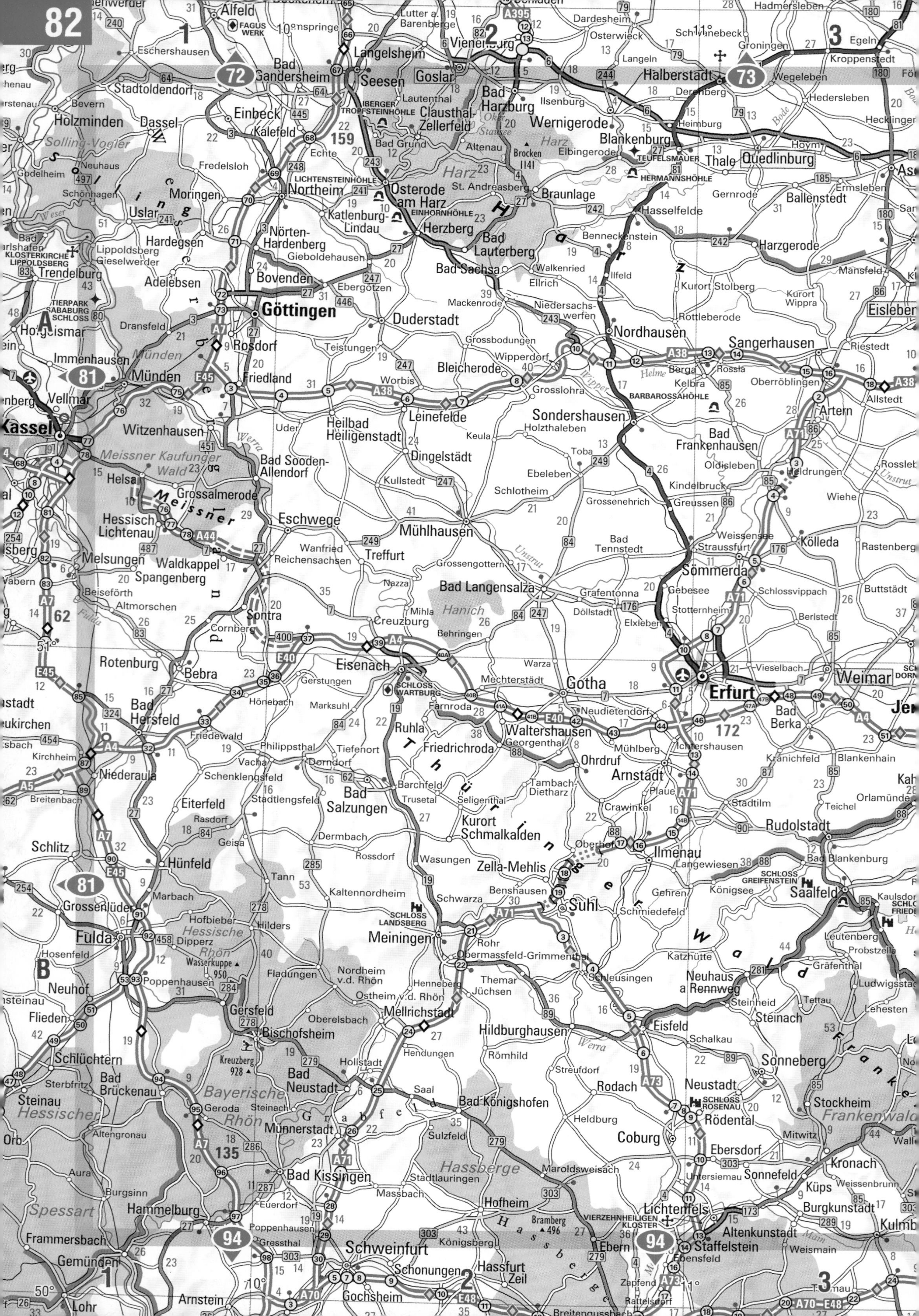

Alfeld
Langelsheim
Vienenburg
Osterwieck
Halberstadt
Bad Gandersheim
Seesen
Goslar
Bad Harzburg
Wernigerode
Stadtoldendorf
Holzminden
Einbeck
Dassel
Clausthal-Zellerfeld
Blankenburg
Thale
Quedlinburg
Northeim
Osterode am Harz
Braunlage
Ballenstedt
Uslar
Herzberg
Bad Lauterberg
Hasselfelde
Harzgerode
Hardegsen
Bovenden
Bad Sachsa
Göttingen
Duderstadt
Nordhausen
Sangerhausen
Hofgeismar
Münden
Vellmar
Kassel
Leinefelde
Heilbad Heiligenstadt
Sondershausen
Bad Frankenhausen
Artern
Witzenhausen
Bad Sooden-Allendorf
Dingelstädt
Helsa
Hessisch Lichtenau
Eschwege
Mühlhausen
Melsungen
Spangenberg
Sömmerda
Bad Langensalza
Sontra
Creuzburg
Rotenburg
Bebra
Eisenach
Gotha
Erfurt
Weimar
Bad Hersfeld
Waltershausen
Arnstadt
Bad Berka
Bad Salzungen
Rudolstadt
Schmalkalden
Zella-Mehlis
Ilmenau
Hünfeld
Suhl
Saalfeld
Fulda
Meiningen
Neuhaus a Rennweg
Schleusingen
Eisfeld
Hildburghausen
Sonneberg
Schlüchtern
Bad Brückenau
Bad Neustadt
Neustadt
Rödental
Coburg
Bad Königshofen
Bad Kissingen
Kronach
Hammelburg
Lichtenfels
Staffelstein
Schweinfurt
Gemünden
Lohr
Thüringer Wald
Harz
Solling-Vogler
Meissner
Hessische Rhön
Bayerische Rhön
Spessart
Hassberge
Frankenwald
Grabfeld

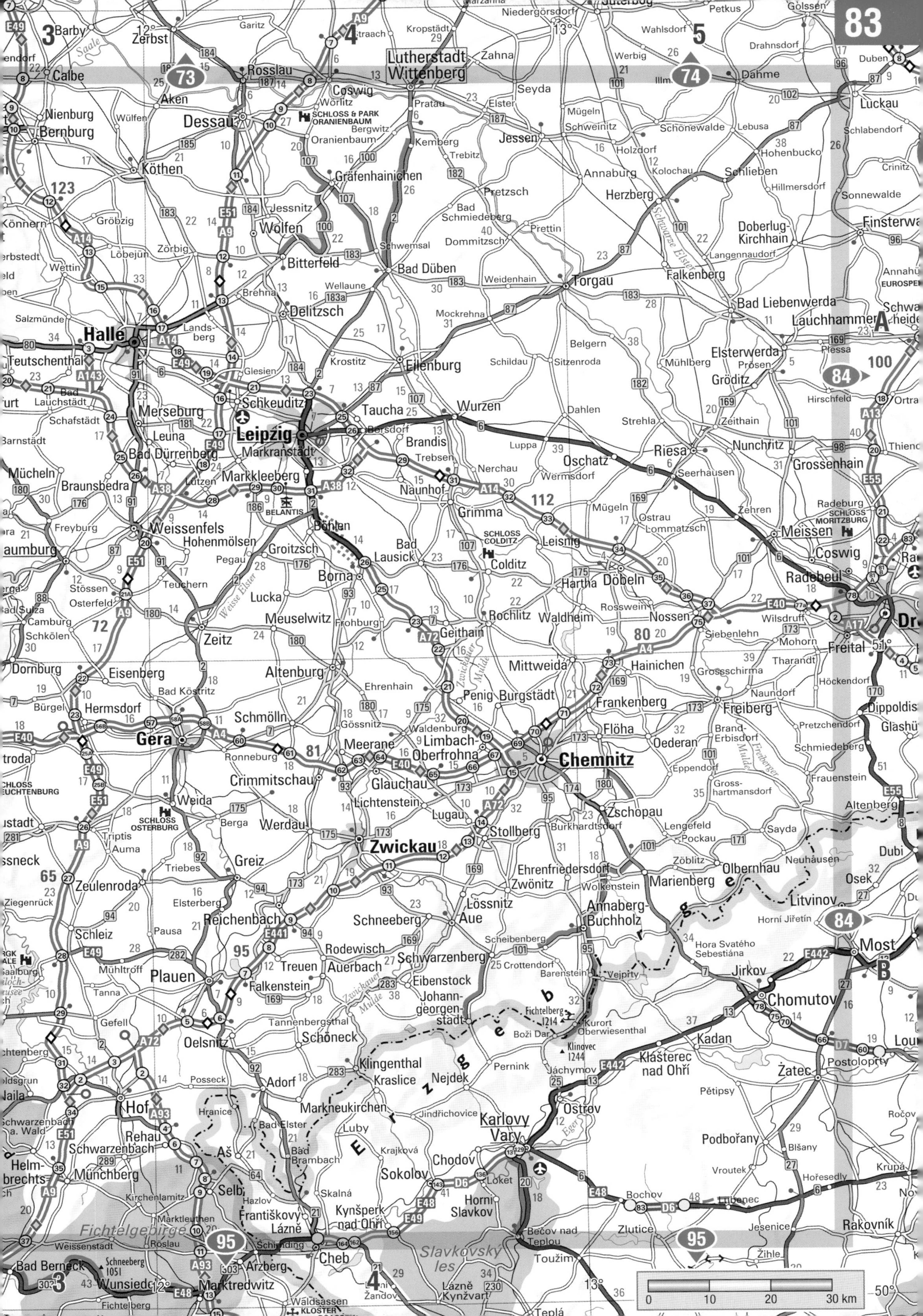
Lutherstadt Wittenberg
Dessau
Halle
Leipzig
Torgau
Riesa
Meissen
Dresden
Chemnitz
Zwickau
Gera
Plauen
Hof
Karlovy Vary
Chomutov
Most
Cheb
Erzgebirge
Fichtelgebirge
Slavkovský les
0 10 20 30 km

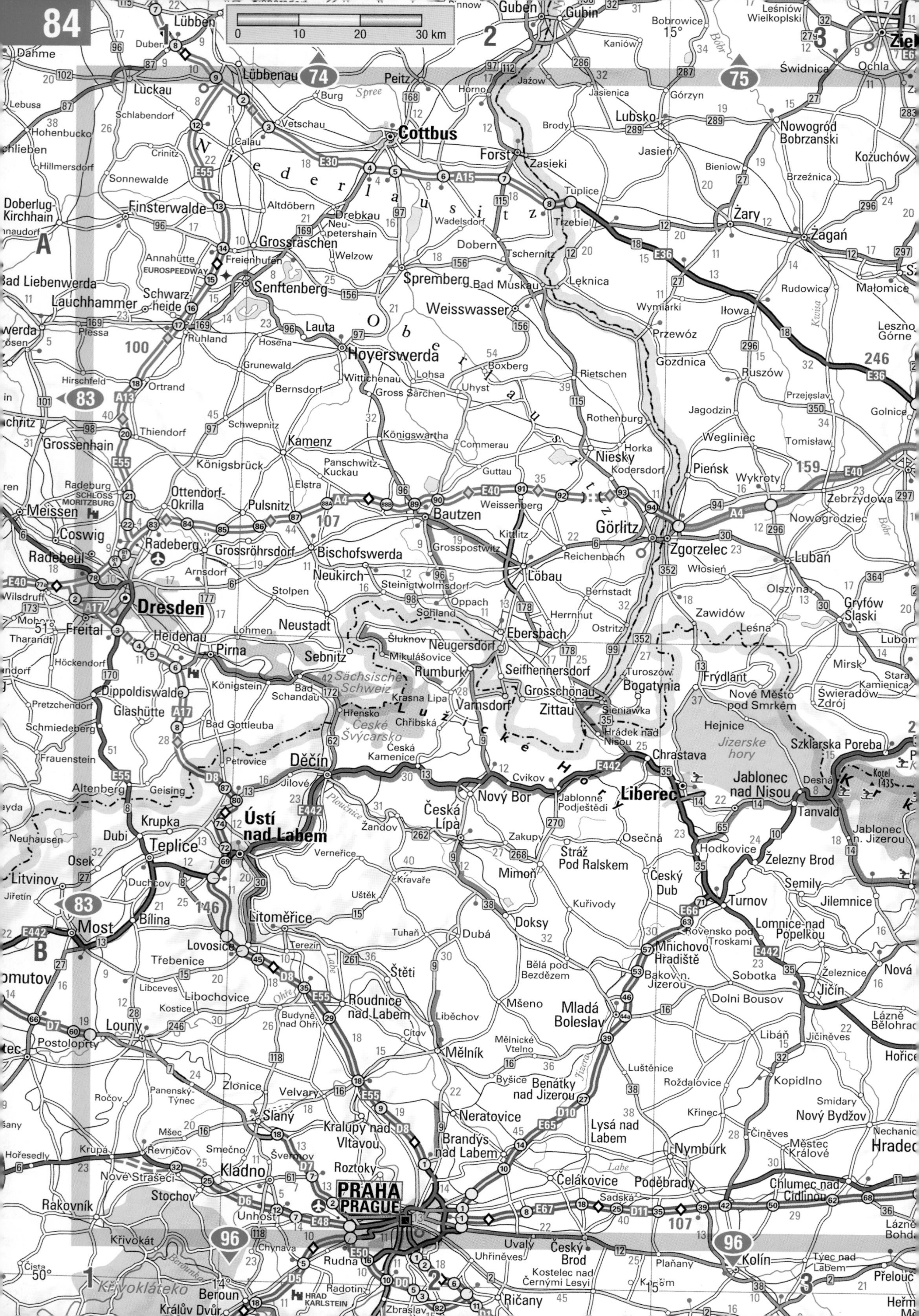
0 10 20 30 km
Lübben
Lübbenau
Luckau
Cottbus
Guben
Gubin
Peitz
Forst
Vetschau
Calau
Niederlausitz
Finsterwalde
Grossräschen
Senftenberg
Spremberg
Bad Muskau
Weisswasser
Hoyerswerda
Lauchhammer
Schwarzheide
Ruhland
Ortrand
Kamenz
Königsbrück
Grossenhain
Meissen
Coswig
Radebeul
Radeberg
Dresden
Freital
Heidenau
Pirna
Neustadt
Sebnitz
Bischofswerda
Bautzen
Löbau
Görlitz
Zgorzelec
Niesky
Rothenburg
Oberlausitz
Ebersbach
Neugersdorf
Rumburk
Varnsdorf
Zittau
Grosschönau
Bogatynia
Sächsische Schweiz
České Švýcarsko
Lužické Hory
Königstein
Bad Schandau
Dippoldiswalde
Glashütte
Altenberg
Děčín
Ústí nad Labem
Teplice
Most
Bílina
Lovosice
Litoměřice
Česká Lípa
Nový Bor
Liberec
Jablonec nad Nisou
Tanvald
Jizerske hory
Szklarska Poreba
Frýdlant
Nové Město pod Smrkem
Hejnice
Chrastava
Hrádek nad Nisou
Turnov
Železny Brod
Semily
Jilemnice
Mnichovo Hradiště
Mladá Boleslav
Jičín
Mělník
Roudnice nad Labem
Louny
Slaný
Kladno
Kralupy nad Vltavou
Neratovice
Brandýs nad Labem
PRAHA PRAGUE
Beroun
Rakovník
Nymburk
Poděbrady
Kolín
Český Brod
Říčany
Lubsko
Żary
Żagań
Nowogród Bobrzanski
Kożuchów
Bolesławiec
Lubań
Gryfów Śląski
Świeradów Zdrój
Nowogrodziec
Węgliniec
Pieńsk
Ruszów
Iłowa
Przewóz
Gozdnica
Leknica
Trzebiel
Tuplice
Jasień
Brody
Świdnica
Ochla
Zielona Góra
74
75
83
96
A
B
1
2
3
15°
50°

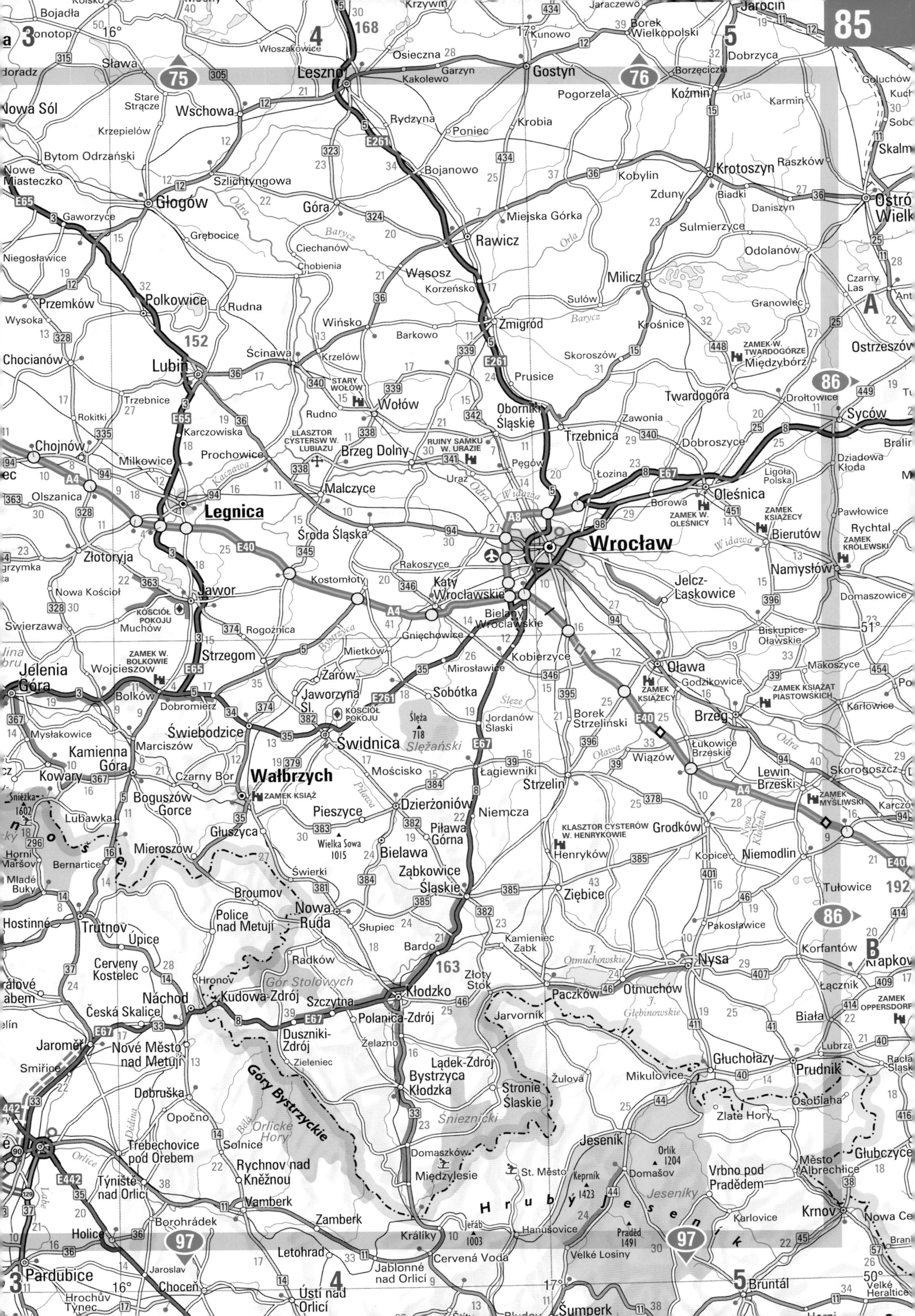

Leszno
Gostyń
Jarocin
Dobrzyca
Borek Wielkopolski
Kunowo
Krzywiń
Osieczna
Kąkolewo
Garzyn
Borzęciczki
Włoszakowice
Sława
Bojadła
Wschowa
Stare Strącze
Nowa Sól
Krzepielów
Bytom Odrzański
Nowe Miasteczko
Głogów
Gaworzyce
Grębocice
Szlichtyngowa
Góra
Rydzyna
Poniec
Krobia
Pogorzela
Koźmin
Karmin
Bojanowo
Krotoszyn
Raszków
Kobylin
Zduny
Biadki
Daniszyn
Miejska Górka
Rawicz
Sulmierzyce
Odolanów
Ciechanów
Chobienia
Wąsosz
Korzeńsko
Milicz
Czarny Las
Sułów
Granowiec
Krośnice
Żmigród
Niegosławice
Przemków
Wysoka
Polkowice
Rudna
Chocianów
Lubin
Ścinawa
Wińsko
Barkowo
Krzelów
Stary Wołów
Wołów
Prusice
Skoroszów
Zamek w. Twardogórze
Międzybórz
Ostrzeszów
Twardogóra
Drołtowice
Syców
Trzebnice
Rokitki
Rudno
Oborniki Śląskie
Trzebnica
Zawonia
Dobroszyce
Bralin
Chojnów
Karczowiska
Klasztor Cystersów w. Lubiążu
Ruiny Samku w. Urazie
Brzeg Dolny
Miłkowice
Prochowice
Pęgów
Uraz
Łozina
Oleśnica
Ligota Polska
Dziadowa Kłoda
Olszanica
Legnica
Malczyce
Borowa
Zamek w. Oleśnicy
Zamek Książęcy
Pawłowice
Rychtal
Zamek Królewski
Bierutów
Wrocław
Złotoryja
Środa Śląska
Namysłów
Nowa Kościół
Jawor
Rakoszyce
Kostomłoty
Kąty Wrocławskie
Jelcz-Laskowice
Domaszowice
Kościół Pokoju
Muchów
Świerzawa
Rogoźnica
Bielany Wrocławskie
Gniechowice
Biskupice-Oławskie
Jelenia Góra
Zamek w. Bolkowie
Wojcieszów
Strzegom
Mietków
Mirosławice
Kobierzyce
Oława
Makoszyce
Żarów
Sobótka
Godzikowice
Zamek Książąt Piastowskich
Bolków
Dobromierz
Jaworzyna Śl.
Jordanów Śląski
Borek Strzeliński
Brzeg
Karłowice
Mysłakowice
Świebodzice
Świdnica
Ślęża
718
Ślężański
Łukowice Brzeskie
Kamienna Góra
Marciszów
Wiązów
Kowary
Czarny Bór
Mościsko
Łagiewniki
Lewin Brzeski
Skorogoszcz
Zamek Myśliwski
Wałbrzych
Zamek Książ
Strzelin
Śnieżka
1602
Boguszów-Gorce
Lubawka
Pieszyce
Dzierżoniów
Niemcza
Grodków
Piława Górna
Klasztor Cysterów w. Henrykowie
Henryków
Niemodlin
Horní Maršov
Głuszyca
Wielka Sowa
1015
Bielawa
Kopice
Mieroszów
Bernartice
Mladé Buky
Świerki
Ząbkowice Śląskie
Ziębice
Tułowice
Broumov
Hostinné
Trutnov
Police nad Metují
Nowa Ruda
Słupiec
Pakosławice
Úpice
Bardo
Kamieniec Ząbk.
J. Otmuchowskie
Nysa
Korfantów
Krapkowice
Radków
Červený Kostelec
Hronov
Gór Stołowych
Złoty Stok
Łącznik
Náchod
Kudowa-Zdrój
Szczytna
Kłodzko
Paczków
Otmuchów
Zamek Oppersdorf
Česká Skalice
Polanica-Zdrój
Javorník
J. Głębinowskie
Biała
Jaroměř
Nové Město nad Metují
Duszniki-Zdrój
Żelazno
Głuchołazy
Prudnik
Lubrza
Smiřice
Zieleniec
Lądek-Zdrój
Bystrzyca Kłodzka
Żulová
Mikulovice
Dobruška
Góry Bystrzyckie
Stronie Śląskie
Osoblaha
Zlaté Hory
Opočno
Orlické Hory
Śnieżnicki
Třebechovice pod Orebem
Solnice
Domaszków
Jeseník
Orlík
1204
Město Albrechtice
Głubczyce
Rychnov nad Kněžnou
Międzylesie
St. Město
Keprník
1423
Domašov
Vrbno pod Pradědem
Týniště nad Orlicí
Vamberk
Hrubý Jeseník
Jeseníky
Krnov
Nowa Cerekwia
Borohrádek
Žamberk
Králíky
Jeřáb
1003
Hanušovice
Praděd
1491
Karlovice
Holice
Letohrad
Červená Voda
Velké Losiny
Jaroslav
Jablonné nad Orlicí
Bruntál
Pardubice
Choceň
Ústí nad Orlicí
Šumperk
Velké Heraltice
Hrochův Týnec
Odra
Barycz
Orla
Widawa
Kaczawa
Bystrzyca
Piława
Oława
Nysa Kłodzka
Ślęza
Bělá
Dědina
Orlice
Labe
A4
A8
E40
E65
E67
E261
E442
3
4
5
A
B
75
76
86
97
152
163
168
192
16°
17°
51°

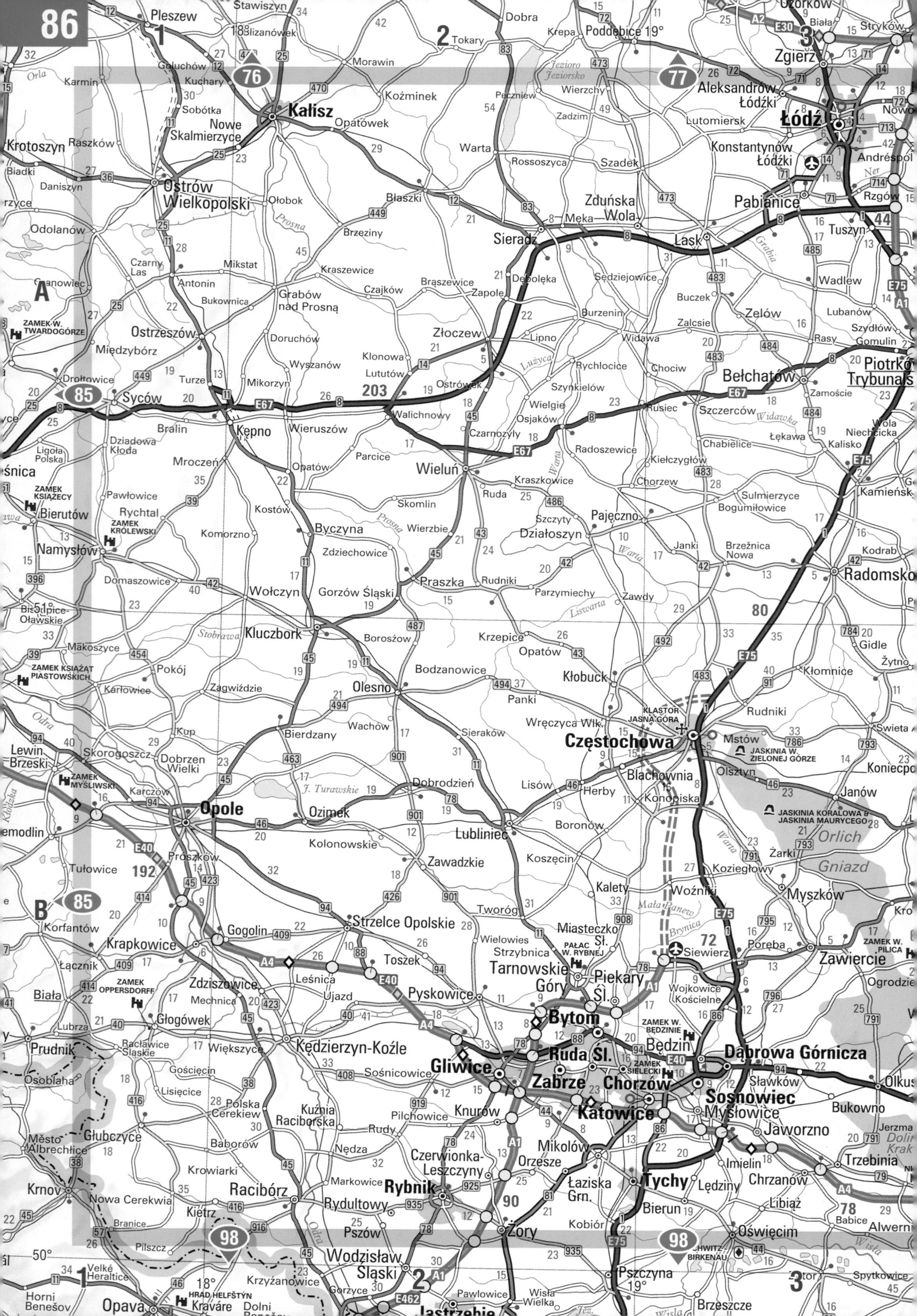

Pleszew
Stawiszyn
Blizanówek
Dobra
Krępa
Poddębice 19°
Ozorków
Biała
Stryków
Tokary
Zgierz
Morawin
Jezioro Jeziorsko
Aleksandrów Łódzki
Gołuchów
Kuchary
Karmin
Orla
Koźminek
Pęczniew
Wierzchy
Łódź
Sobótka
Kalisz
Opatówek
Zadzim
Lutomiersk
Nowe Skalmierzyce
Krotoszyn
Raszków
Warta
Konstantynów Łódzki
Andrespol
Rossoszyca
Szadek
Biadki
Daniszyn
Ostrów Wielkopolski
Ołobok
Błaszki
Zduńska Wola
Pabianice
Rzgów
Ner
Odolanów
Prosna
Brzeziny
Sieradz
Męka
Łask
Tuszyn
Grabia
Czarny Las
Mikstat
Kraszewice
Antonin
Dębołęka
Sędziejowice
Wadlew
Granowiec
Bukownica
Grabów nad Prosną
Czajków
Brąszewice
Zapole
Buczek
Zelów
Lubanów
ZAMEK W. TWARDOGÓRZE
Ostrzeszów
Burzenin
Zalcsie
Szydłów
Doruchów
Złoczew
Lipno
Widawa
Rasy
Gomulin
Międzybórz
Klonowa
Rychlocice
Chociw
Piotrków Trybunalski
Wyszanów
Lututów
Łużyca
Bełchatów
Drołtowice
Turze
Mikorzyn
Ostrówek
Szynkielów
Zamoście
Syców
Wielgie
Rusiec
Szczerców
Walichnowy
Osjaków
Widawka
Wola Niechcicka
Bralin
Kępno
Wieruszów
Czarnożyły
Radoszewice
Chabielice
Łękawa
Kalisko
Dziadowa Kłoda
Ligota Polska
Mroczeń
Opatów
Parcice
Wieluń
Kiełczygłów
Kamieńsk
Kraszkowice
Chorzew
Oleśnica
Pawłowice
Ruda
Sulmierzyce
ZAMEK KSIĄŻECY
Bierutów
Rychtal
Skomlin
Bogumiłowice
ZAMEK KRÓLEWSKI
Kostów
Szczyty
Pajęczno
Byczyna
Wierzbie
Działoszyn
Komorzno
Janki
Brzeźnica Nowa
Kodrab
Namysłów
Zdziechowice
Radomsko
Domaszowice
Wołczyn
Gorzów Śląski
Praszka
Rudniki
Parzymiechy
Zawady
Bystrzyca
Oławskie
Liswarta
Stobrawa
Kluczbork
Borószów
Krzepice
Gidle
Makoszyce
Żytno
Pokój
ZAMEK KSIĄŻĄT PIASTOWSKICH
Bodzanowice
Kłobuck
Kłomnice
Zagwiździe
Karłowice
Olesno
Panki
Odra
Wachów
Rudniki
KLASZTOR JASNA GÓRA
Wręczyca Wlk.
Kup
Sieraków
Częstochowa
Mstów
Świeta
Bierdzany
JASKINIA W. ZIELONEJ GÓRZE
Lewin Brzeski
Skorogoszcz
Dobrzeń Wielki
Koniecpol
Olsztyn
ZAMEK MYŚLIWSKI
Blachownia
J. Turawskie
Dobrodzień
Lisów
Herby
Konopiska
Janów
Karczów
Opole
Ozimek
Lubliniec
JASKINIA KORALOWA & JASKINIA MAURYCEGO
Niemodlin
Boronów
Orlich
Kolonowskie
Żarki
Gniazd
Prószków
Tułowice
Zawadzkie
Koszęcin
Koziegłowy
Kaletv
Woźniki
Myszków
Mała Panew
Brynica
Korfantów
Tworóg
Miasteczko Śl.
Gogolin
Strzelce Opolskie
Krapkowice
Wielowies
PAŁAC W. RYBNEJ
Siewierz
Poręba
ZAMEK W. PILICA
Łącznik
Toszek
Strzybnica
Zawiercie
Zdzieszowice
Leśnica
Tarnowskie Góry
Piekary Śl.
Ogrodzieniec
ZAMEK OPPERSDORFF
Ujazd
Wojkowice Kościelne
Biała
Mechnica
Pyskowice
Bytom
Głogówek
ZAMEK W. BĘDZINIE
Lubrza
Rudy
Racławice Śląskie
Większyce
Kędzierzyn-Koźle
Będzin
Prudnik
Gliwice
Ruda Śl.
Dąbrowa Górnicza
Gościęcin
ZAMEK SIELECKI
Osoblaha
Sośnicowice
Zabrze
Chorzów
Sławków
Olkusz
Lisięcice
Sosnowiec
Polska Cerekiew
Katowice
Bukowno
Kuźnia Raciborska
Pilchowice
Knurów
Mysłowice
Głubczyce
Jaworzno
Město Albrechtice
Baborów
Mikołów
Dolina Krak
Nędza
Czerwionka-Leszczyny
Orzesze
Imielin
Trzebinia
Krowiarki
Łaziska Grn.
Tychy
Lędziny
Chrzanów
Krnov
Markowice
Rybnik
Nowa Cerekwia
Racibórz
Libiąż
Kietrz
Rydultowy
Bieruń
Babice
Alwernia
Branice
Pszów
Żory
Kobiór
Oświęcim
Pilszcz
Wodzisław Śląski
AUSCHWITZ BIRKENAU
Velké Heraltice
Krzyżanowice
Pszczyna 19°
Spytkowice
Horní Benešov
HRAD HELFŠTÝN
Gorzyce
Pawłowice
Wisła Wielka
Opava
Kravaře
Dolní
Jastrzębie
Brzeszcze
Wisła
Odra
Warta
Jez.
50°
51°
18°

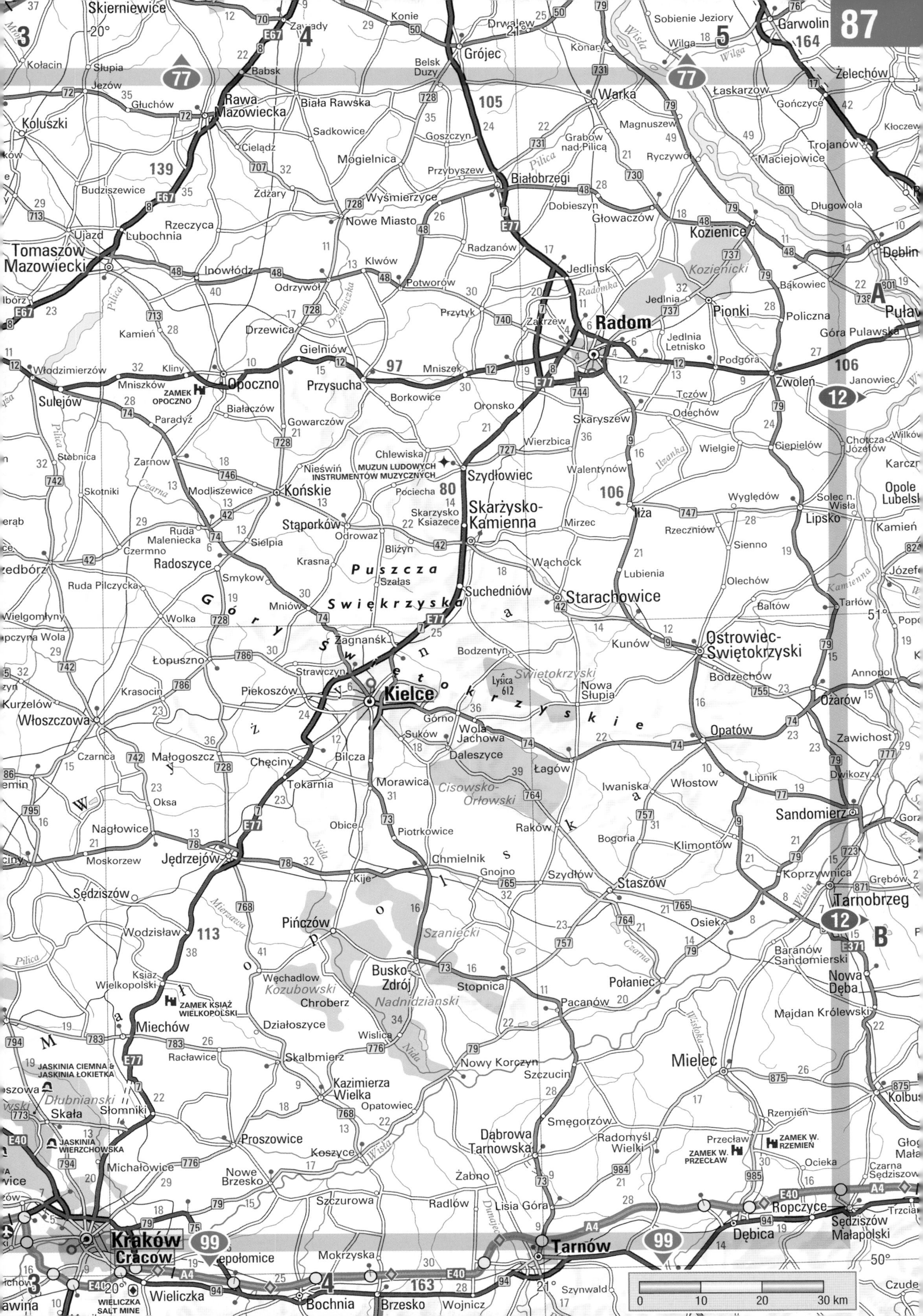
Skierniewice
Grójec
Warka
Garwolin
Żelechów
Rawa Mazowiecka
Biała Rawska
Koluszki
Białobrzegi
Tomaszów Mazowiecki
Kozienice
Dęblin
Radom
Pionki
Puławy
Opoczno
ZAMEK OPOCZNO
Przysucha
Zwoleń
Sulejów
Końskie
MUZUN LUDOWYCH INSTRUMENTÓW MUZYCZNYCH
Szydłowiec
Skarżysko-Kamienna
Iłża
Lipsko
Opole Lubelskie
Starachowice
Ostrowiec-Świętokrzyski
Puszcza Świękrzyska
Góry Świętokrzyskie
Kielce
Łysica 612
Opatów
Włoszczowa
Sandomierz
Jędrzejów
Staszów
Tarnobrzeg
Pińczów
Busko Zdrój
Miechów
ZAMEK KSIĄŻ WIELKOPOLSKI
JASKINIA CIEMNA & JASKINIA ŁOKIETKA
JASKINIA WIERZCHOWSKA
Mielec
ZAMEK W. RZEMIEŃ
ZAMEK W. PRZECŁAW
Dąbrowa Tarnowska
Kraków
Cracow
Wieliczka
WIELICZKA SALT MINE
Bochnia
Brzesko
Tarnów
Dębica
Ropczyce
Sędziszów Małopolski
0 10 20 30 km

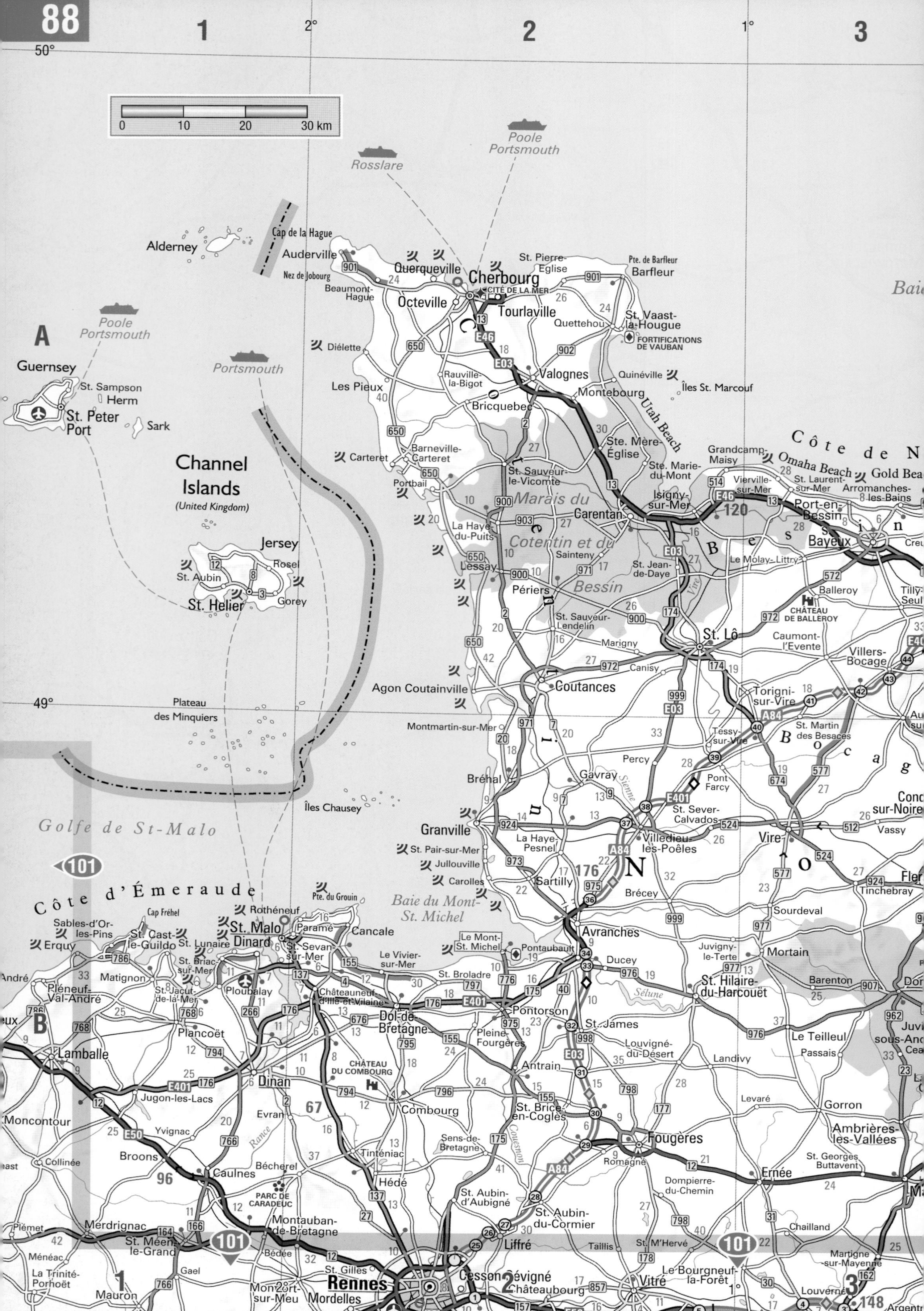

1
2
3
50°
2°
1°
49°
0 10 20 30 km
A
B
Rosslare
Poole Portsmouth
Portsmouth
Alderney
Cap de la Hague
Auderville
Nez de Jobourg
Beaumont-Hague
Querqueville
Cherbourg
Cité de la Mer
Octeville
Tourlaville
St. Pierre-Eglise
Pte. de Barfleur
Barfleur
Quettehou
St. Vaast-la-Hougue
Fortifications de Vauban
Dielette
Rauville-la-Bigot
Valognes
Quinéville
Îles St. Marcouf
Les Pieux
Montebourg
Utah Beach
Bricquebec
Guernsey
St. Sampson
Herm
St. Peter Port
Sark
Channel Islands
(United Kingdom)
Carteret
Barneville-Carteret
Portbail
Ste. Mère-Église
Ste. Marie-du-Mont
Grandcamp-Maisy
Omaha Beach
Gold Beach
Vierville-sur-Mer
St. Laurent-sur-Mer
Arromanches-les-Bains
Côte de N
St. Sauveur-le-Vicomte
Marais du Cotentin et du Bessin
Carentan
Isigny-sur-Mer
Port-en-Bessin
Bayeux
La Haye-du-Puits
Sainteny
Le Molay-Littry
Jersey
Rosel
St. Aubin
St. Helier
Gorey
Lessay
St. Jean-de-Daye
Balleroy
Château de Balleroy
Périers
St. Sauveur-Lendelin
St. Lô
Caumont-l'Evente
Villers-Bocage
Marigny
Canisy
Agon Coutainville
Coutances
Torigni-sur-Vire
Plateau des Minquiers
Montmartin-sur-Mer
Tessy-sur-Vire
St. Martin des Besaces
Bocage
Percy
Pont Farcy
Bréhal
Gavray
Sienne
St. Sever-Calvados
Conde-sur-Noireau
Îles Chausey
Golfe de St-Malo
Granville
Villedieu-les-Poêles
Vire
Vassy
La Haye-Pesnel
St. Pair-sur-Mer
Jullouville
Carolles
Sartilly
Brécey
Tinchebray
Côte d'Émeraude
Baie du Mont-St. Michel
Sourdeval
Cap Fréhel
Pte. du Grouin
Rothéneuf
Sables-d'Or-les-Pins
Erquy
St. Cast-le-Guildo
St. Malo
Paramé
Cancale
St. Lunaire
Dinard
St. Servan-sur-Mer
Avranches
Le Mont-St. Michel
Pontaubault
Juvigny-le-Terte
Mortain
St. Briac-sur-Mer
Le Vivier-sur-Mer
Ducey
Matignon
St. Broladre
Barenton
Pléneuf-Val-André
St. Jacut-de-la-Mer
Ploubalay
Châteauneuf-d'Ille-et-Vilaine
Sélune
St. Hilaire-du-Harcouët
Pontorson
Dol-de-Bretagne
St. James
Lamballe
Plancoët
Pleine-Fougères
Louvigné-du-Désert
Le Teilleul
Passais
Château du Combourg
Antrain
Landivy
Dinan
Jugon-les-Lacs
Combourg
Evran
Levaré
Gorron
Moncontour
Yvignac
Rance
St. Brice-en-Coglès
Fougères
Ambrières-les-Vallées
Broons
Sens-de-Bretagne
Couesnon
Collinée
Tinténiac
Bécherel
Romagné
St. Georges-Buttavent
Caulnes
Hédé
Ernée
Parc de Caradeuc
Dompierre-du-Chemin
St. Aubin-d'Aubigné
Merdrignac
Montauban-de-Bretagne
St. Aubin-du-Cormier
Chailland
Plémet
St. Méen-le-Grand
Liffré
Taillis
St. M'Hervé
Ménéac
Bédée
Martigné-sur-Mayenne
La Trinité-Porhoët
Gael
St. Gilles
Cesson-Sévigné
Le Bourgneuf-la-Forêt
Rennes
Châteaubourg
Vitré
Louverné
Mauron
Montfort-sur-Meu
Mordelles
Argentré
Baie

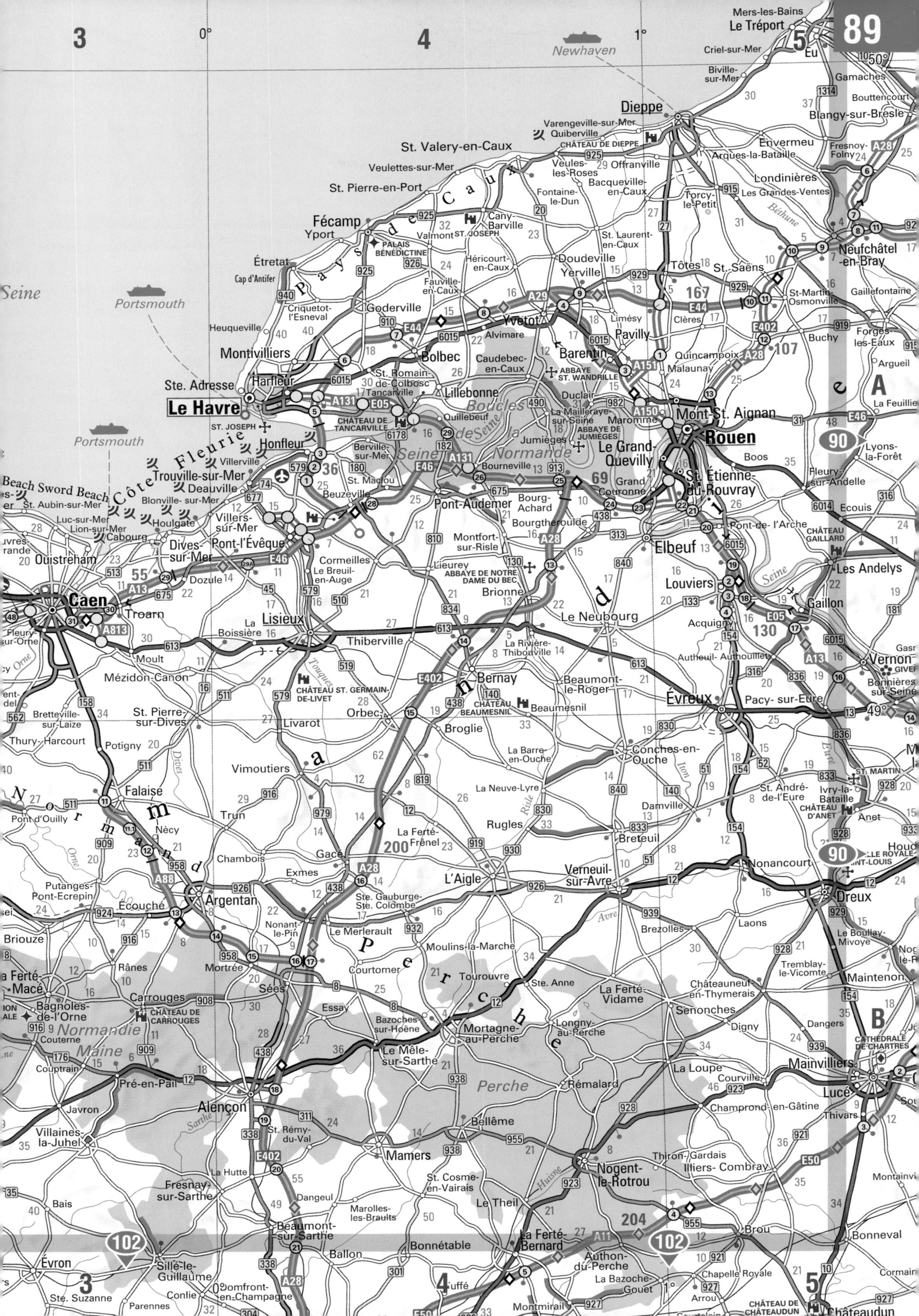

89
3
4
5
0°
1°
Newhaven
Mers-les-Bains
Le Tréport
Criel-sur-Mer
Eu
Biville-sur-Mer
Gamaches
Bouttencourt
Blangy-sur-Bresle
Dieppe
Varengeville-sur-Mer
Quiberville
CHÂTEAU DE DIEPPE
Envermeu
Arques-la-Bataille
Fresnoy-Folny
St. Valery-en-Caux
Veules-les-Roses
Offranville
Veulettes-sur-Mer
Bacqueville-en-Caux
Londinières
Les Grandes-Ventes
St. Pierre-en-Port
Fontaine-le-Dun
Torcy-le-Petit
Béthune
Fécamp
Cany-Barville
Yport
Valmont
ST. JOSEPH
St. Laurent-en-Caux
PALAIS BÉNÉDICTINE
Neufchâtel-en-Bray
Étretat
Héricourt-en-Caux
Doudeville
Tôtes
St. Saëns
Cap d'Antifer
Yerville
Fauville-en-Caux
Gaillefontaine
Seine
Portsmouth
Pays de Caux
Criquetot-l'Esneval
Goderville
Yvetot
Limésy
Clères
St-Martin-Osmonville
Heuqueville
Alvimare
Pavilly
Forges-les-Eaux
Montivilliers
Bolbec
Caudebec-en-Caux
Barentin
Quincampoix
Malaunay
Buchy
Argueil
St. Romain-de-Colbosc
ABBAYE ST. WANDRILLE
Ste. Adresse
Harfleur
Tancarville
Lillebonne
Duclair
Le Havre
CHÂTEAU DE TANCARVILLE
Quillebeuf
Boucles de Seine Normande
La Mailleraye-sur-Seine
ABBAYE DE JUMIÈGES
Maromme
Mont-St. Aignan
Rouen
La Feuillie
ST. JOSEPH
Jumièges
Le Grand-Quevilly
Lyons-la-Forêt
Portsmouth
Honfleur
Berville-sur-Mer
Bourneville
Boos
Côte Fleurie
Villerville
St. Maclou
Grand Couronne
St. Étienne-du-Rouvray
Fleury-sur-Andelle
Trouville-sur-Mer
Deauville
Beuzeville
Pont-Audemer
Bourg-Achard
Beach Sword Beach
St. Aubin-sur-Mer
Blonville-sur-Mer
Bourgtheroulde
Ecouis
Luc-sur-Mer
Lion-sur-Mer
Houlgate
Villers-sur-Mer
Cabourg
Dives-sur-Mer
Pont-l'Évêque
Montfort-sur-Risle
Elbeuf
Pont-de-l'Arche
CHÂTEAU GAILLARD
Ouistreham
Cormeilles
Le Breuil-en-Auge
Lieurey
ABBAYE DE NOTRE DAME DU BEC
Les Andelys
Dozule
Louviers
Caen
Troarn
Brionne
Le Neubourg
Gaillon
La Boissière
Lisieux
Thiberville
Acquigny
Fleury-sur-Orne
Moult
La Rivière-Thibouville
Autheuil-Authouillet
Mézidon-Canon
Bernay
Beaumont-le-Roger
Vernon
Bonnières-sur-Seine
CHÂTEAU ST. GERMAIN-DE-LIVET
Évreux
Pacy-sur-Eure
Bretteville-sur-Laize
St. Pierre-sur-Dives
Orbec
CHÂTEAU BEAUMESNIL
Beaumesnil
Livarot
Broglie
Thury-Harcourt
Potigny
Conches-en-Ouche
La Barre-en-Ouche
Vimoutiers
ST. MARTIN
Normandie
Falaise
La Neuve-Lyre
St. André-de-l'Eure
Ivry-la-Bataille
Pont d'Ouilly
Damville
CHÂTEAU D'ANET
Anet
Trun
Nècy
Rugles
Breteuil
La Ferté-Frênel
Chambois
Gacé
Exmes
L'Aigle
Verneuil-sur-Avre
Nonancourt
Putanges-Pont-Ecrepin
Argentan
Ste. Gauburge-Ste. Colombe
Dreux
Écouché
Nonant-le-Pin
Le Merlerault
Brezolles
Laons
Briouze
Moulins-la-Marche
Le Boullay-Mivoye
Rânes
Mortrée
Courtomer
Tourouvre
Tremblay-le-Vicomte
La Ferté-Macé
Sées
Ste. Anne
La Ferté-Vidame
Châteauneuf-en-Thymerais
Maintenon
Carrouges
CHÂTEAU DE CARROUGES
Essay
Senonches
Bagnoles-de-l'Orne
Bazoches-sur-Hoëne
Mortagne-au-Perche
Longny-au-Perche
Digny
Dangers
Normandie Maine
Couterne
Perche
CATHÉDRALE DE CHARTRES
Le Mêle-sur-Sarthe
Couptrain
Mainvilliers
La Loupe
Courville
Pré-en-Pail
Rémalard
Lucé
Javron
Alençon
Champrond-en-Gâtine
Thivars
Bellême
Villaines-la-Juhel
St. Rémy-du-Val
Mamers
Thiron-Gardais
Illiers-Combray
Nogent-le-Rotrou
La Hutte
St. Cosme-en-Vairais
Fresnay-sur-Sarthe
Bais
Dangeul
Le Theil
Marolles-les-Braults
Beaumont-sur-Sarthe
La Ferté-Bernard
Bonneval
Brou
Evron
Sillé-le-Guillaume
Ballon
Bonnétable
Authon-du-Perche
Chapelle Royale
La Bazoche-Gouet
Tuffé
Ste. Suzanne
Domfront-en-Champagne
Conlie
Parennes
Montmirail
Arrou
CHÂTEAU DE CHÂTEAUDUN
Châteaudun
90
102
A
B

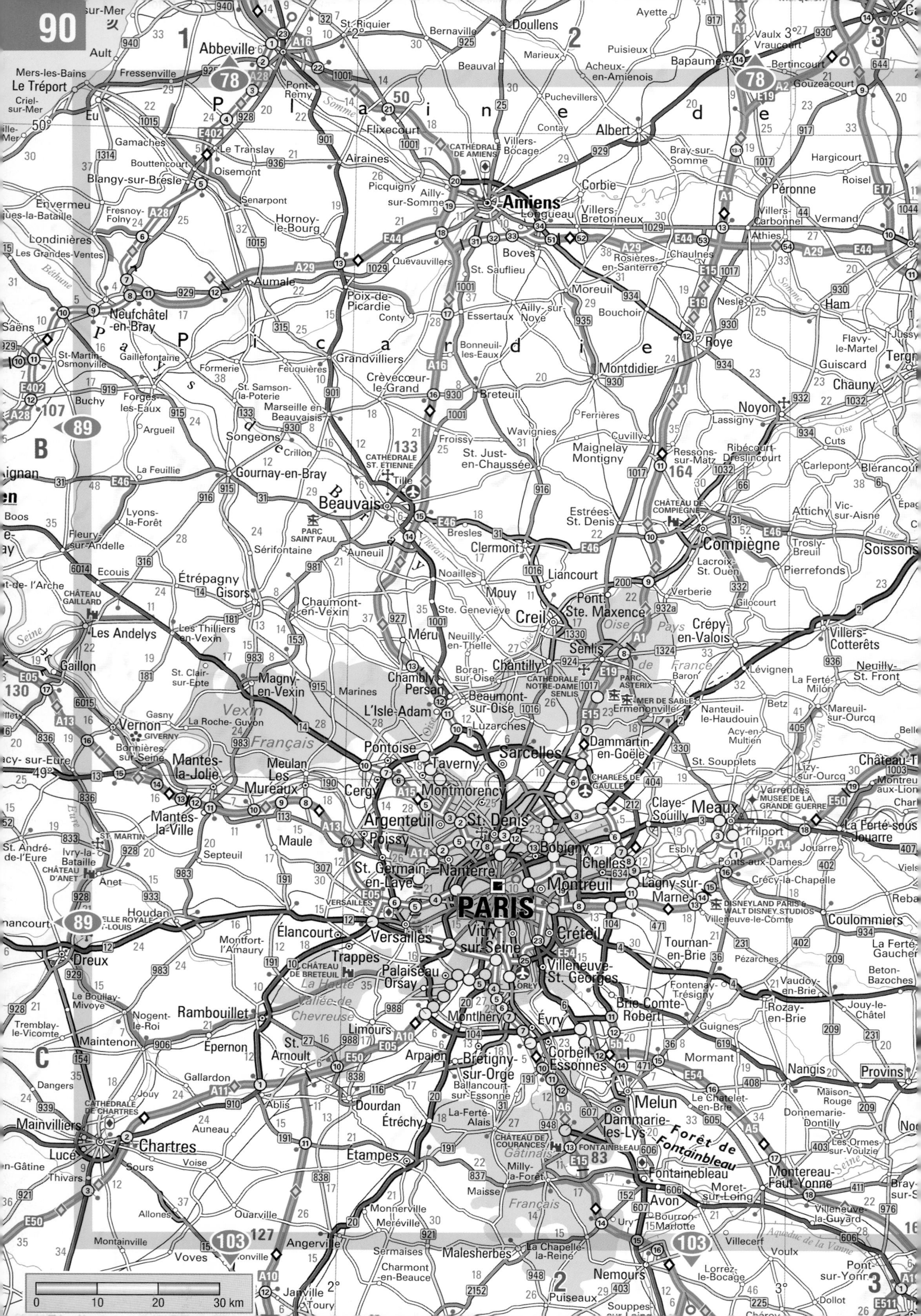

Abbeville
Doullens
Ayette
Bapaume
Vaulx Vraucourt
Bertincourt
Ault
Mers-les-Bains
Le Tréport
Criel-sur-Mer
Eu
Fressenville
Pont-Remy
Bernaville
Beauval
Marieux
Puisieux
Acheux-en-Amienois
Gouzeaucourt
Plaine de
Flixecourt
Puchevillers
Contay
Albert
Gamaches
Le Translay
Oisemont
Airaines
Cathédrale de Amiens
Villers-Bocage
Bray-sur-Somme
Hargicourt
Bouttencourt
Blangy-sur-Bresle
Picquigny
Ailly-sur-Somme
Amiens
Corbie
Péronne
Roisel
Envermeu
Senarpont
Hornoy-le-Bourg
Longueau
Villers-Bretonneux
Villers-Carbonnel
Vermand
Fresnoy-Folny
Londinières
Les Grandes-Ventes
Boves
Rosières-en-Santerre
Chaulnes
Athies
Quevauvillers
St. Sauflieu
Aumale
Moreuil
Ham
Nesle
Neufchâtel-en-Bray
Poix-de-Picardie
Conty
Essertaux
Ailly-sur-Noye
Bouchoir
St-Martin-Osmonville
Gaillefontaine
Grandvilliers
Bonneuil-les-Eaux
Roye
Flavy-le-Martel
Pays de Bray
Picardie
Montdidier
Guiscard
Chauny
Formerie
Feuquières
Crèvecœur-le-Grand
Buchy
Forges-les-Eaux
St. Samson-la-Poterie
Breteuil
Noyon
Lassigny
Marseille en Beauvaisis
Argueil
Songeons
Crillon
Froissy
Wavignies
Ferrières
Cuvilly
Ressons-sur-Matz
Ribécourt-Dreslincourt
Cuts
St. Just-en-Chaussée
Maignelay Montigny
La Feuillie
Gournay-en-Bray
Cathédrale St. Etienne
Tillé
Carlepont
Blérancourt
Lyons-la-Forêt
Beauvais
Estrées-St. Denis
Château de Compiègne
Attichy
Vic-sur-Aisne
Boos
Parc Saint Paul
Bresles
Compiègne
Trosly-Breuil
Soissons
Fleury-sur-Andelle
Sérifontaine
Auneuil
Clermont
Lacroix-St. Ouen
Pierrefonds
Ecouis
Noailles
Liancourt
Château Gaillard
Étrépagny
Gisors
Chaumont-en-Vexin
Mouy
Verberie
Gilocourt
Ste. Geneviève
Creil
Pont-Ste. Maxence
Crépy-en-Valois
Villers-Cotterêts
Les Andelys
Les Thilliers-en-Vexin
Méru
Neuilly-en-Thelle
Senlis
Gaillon
St. Clair-sur-Epte
Magny-en-Vexin
Chambly
Persan
Boran-sur-Oise
Chantilly
Cathédrale Notre-Dame Senlis
Parc Asterix
Lévignen
La Ferté-Milon
Neuilly-St. Front
Marines
Beaumont-sur-Oise
Mer de Sable
Ermenonville
Nanteuil-le-Haudouin
Betz
Mareuil-sur-Ourcq
Vexin Français
L'Isle-Adam
Luzarches
Dammartin-en-Goële
Acy-en-Multien
Gasny
Vernon
Giverny
La Roche-Guyon
Bonnières-sur-Seine
Pontoise
Sarcelles
Mantes-la-Jolie
Meulan
Les Mureaux
Cergy
Taverny
Montmorency
St. Soupplets
Lizy-sur-Ourcq
Château-Thierry
Charles de Gaulle
Claye-Souilly
Meaux
Musée de la Grande Guerre
Mantes-la-Ville
Argenteuil
St. Denis
Trilport
La Ferté-sous-Jouarre
St. Martin
Maule
Poissy
Bobigny
Esbly
Jouarre
St. André-de-l'Eure
Ivry-la-Bataille
Septeuil
Chelles
Ponts-aux-Dames
Château d'Anet
Anet
St. Germain-en-Laye
Nanterre
Montreuil
Lagny-sur-Marne
Crécy-la-Chapelle
Versailles
Paris
Disneyland Paris & Walt Disney Studios
Villeneuve-le-Comte
Houdan
Coulommiers
Élancourt
Vitry-sur-Seine
Créteil
Dreux
Montfort-l'Amaury
Tournan-en-Brie
La Ferté-Gaucher
Trappes
Pézarches
Château de Breteuil
Palaiseau
Orsay
Villeneuve-St. Georges
Orly
La Haute Vallée de Chevreuse
Fontenay-Trésigny
Vaudoy-en-Brie
Beton-Bazoches
Le Boullay-Mivoye
Nogent-le-Roi
Rambouillet
Brie-Comte-Robert
Rozay-en-Brie
Jouy-le-Châtel
Tremblay-le-Vicomte
Limours
Montlhéry
Évry
Guignes
Maintenon
Épernon
St. Arnoult
Arpajon
Brétigny-sur-Orge
Corbeil-Essonnes
Mormant
Nangis
Provins
Gallardon
Ballancourt-sur-Essonne
Dangers
Jouy
Ablis
Dourdan
Étréchy
La Ferté-Alais
Melun
Maison-Rouge
Cathédrale de Chartres
Mainvilliers
Chartres
Auneau
Château de Courances
Dammarie-les-Lys
Forêt de Fontainebleau
Donnemarie-Dontilly
Lucé
Étampes
Gâtinais Français
Fontainebleau
Les Ormes-sur-Voulzie
Sours
Voise
Milly-la-Forêt
Montereau-Fault-Yonne
Thivars
Moret-sur-Loing
Bray-sur-Seine
Avon
Maisse
Allones
Ouarville
Monnerville
Méréville
Ury
Bourron-Marlotte
Villeneuve-la-Guyard
Montainville
Voves
Angerville
Sermaises
Malesherbes
La Chapelle-la-Reine
Villecerf
Voulx
Aqueduc de la Vanne
Charmont-en-Beauce
Nemours
Lorrez-le-Bocage
Pont-sur-Yonne
Janville
Toury
Puiseaux
Souppes
Dollot
0 10 20 30 km

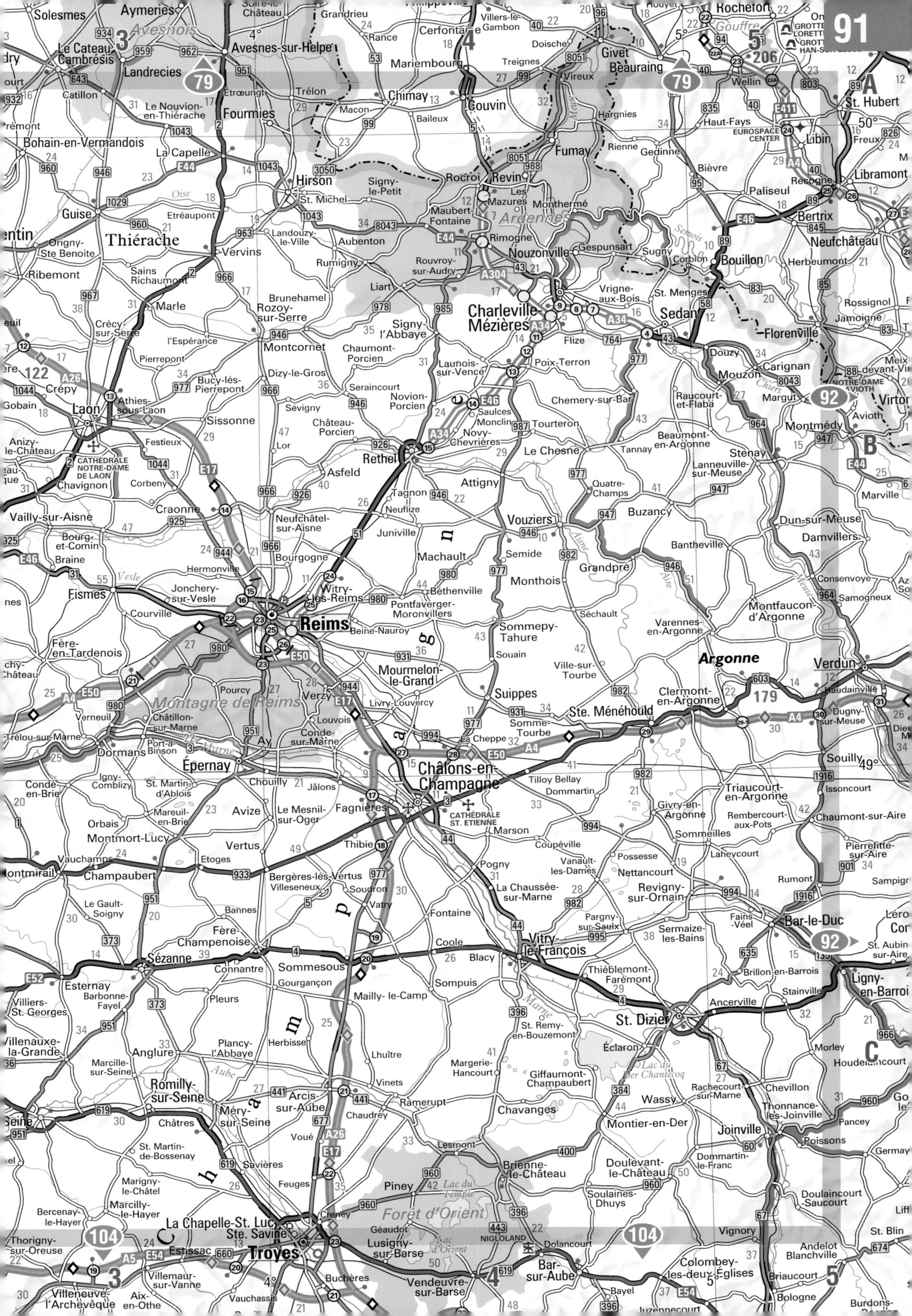
Solesmes
Aymeries
Avesnois
Le Cateau-Cambrésis
Landrecies
Avesnes-sur-Helpe
Grandrieu
Rance
Cerfontaine
Villers-le-Gambon
Doische
Philippeville
Mariembourg
Treignes
Givet
Beauraing
Rochefort
Gouffre
Grottes
Han-sur-Lesse
Wellin
St. Hubert
Catillon
Le Nouvion-en-Thiérache
Étrœungt
Fourmies
Trélon
Chimay
Macon
Baileux
Couvin
Vireux
Hargnies
Haut-Fays
Eurospace Center
Libin
Freux
Bohain-en-Vermandois
La Capelle
Hirson
St. Michel
Signy-le-Petit
Rocroi
Revin
Fumay
Rienne
Gedinne
Bièvre
Paliseul
Recogne
Libramont
Guise
Oise
Étréaupont
Maubert-Fontaine
Les Mazures
Monthermé
Ardennes
Bertrix
Neufchâteau
Origny-Ste Benoite
Thiérache
Vervins
Landouzy-le-Ville
Aubenton
Rimogne
Nouzonville
Gespunsart
Sugny
Semois
Corbion
Bouillon
Herbeumont
Ribemont
Sains Richaumont
Rumigny
Rouvroy-sur-Audry
Liart
Vrigne-aux-Bois
St. Menges
Rossignol
Marle
Brunehamel
Rozoy-sur-Serre
Signy-l'Abbaye
Charleville-Mézières
Sedan
Jamoigne
Florenville
Crécy-sur-Serre
L'Espérance
Montcornet
Chaumont-Porcien
Flize
Douzy
Carignan
Pierrepont
Bucy-lés-Pierrepont
Dizy-le-Gros
Launois-sur-Vence
Poix-Terron
Mouzon
Chiers
Margut
Notre-Dame Avioth
Avioth
Virton
Crépy
Laon
Athies-sous-Laon
Serainc ourt
Novion-Porcien
Sévigny
Saulces Monclin
Chemery-sur-Bar
Raucourt-et-Flaba
Montmédy
Anizy-le-Château
Sissonne
Château-Porcien
Novy-Chevrières
Tourteron
Beaumont-en-Argonne
Stenay
Festieux
Cathédrale Notre-Dame de Laon
Chavignon
Corbeny
Lor
Rethel
Le Chesne
Tannay
Lanneuville-sur-Meuse
Asfeld
Tagnon
Neuflize
Attigny
Quatre-Champs
Marville
Craonne
Vailly-sur-Aisne
Neufchâtel-sur-Aisne
Juniville
Vouziers
Buzancy
Dun-sur-Meuse
Damvillers
Bourg-et-Comin
Braine
Bourgogne
Machault
Semide
Aisne
Grandpré
Bantheville
Hermonville
Fismes
Vesle
Jonchery-sur-Vesle
Witry-lès-Reims
Béthenville
Monthois
Aire
Meuse
Consenvoye
Samogneux
Courville
Reims
Pontfaverger-Moronvillers
Séchault
Montfaucon-d'Argonne
Fère-en-Tardenois
Beine-Nauroy
Sommepy-Tahure
Varennes-en-Argonne
Souain
Ville-sur-Tourbe
Argonne
Verdun
Haudainville
Mourmelon-le-Grand
Montagne de Reims
Pourcy
Verzy
Suippes
Clermont-en-Argonne
Dugny-sur-Meuse
Verneuil
Châtillon-sur-Marne
Livry-Louvercy
Louvois
Conde-sur-Marne
Ste. Ménéhould
Somme-Tourbe
La Cheppe
Trélou-sur-Marne
Port-à-Binson
Dormans
Ay
Marne
Épernay
Châlons-en-Champagne
Souilly
Condé-en-Brie
Igny-Comblizy
St. Martin-d'Ablois
Chouilly
Jâlons
Tilloy Bellay
Dommartin
Triaucourt-en-Argonne
Issoncourt
Orbais
Mareuil-en-Brie
Avize
Le Mesnil-sur-Oger
Fagnières
Cathédrale St. Etienne
Marson
Givry-en-Argonne
Rembercourt-aux-Pots
Chaumont-sur-Aire
Montmort-Lucy
Vertus
Thibie
Coupéville
Sommeilles
Vauchamps
Etoges
Possesse
Laheycourt
Pierrefitte-sur-Aire
Montmirail
Champaubert
Bergères-lès-Vertus
Villeseneux
Soudron
Pogny
Vanault-les-Dames
Nettancourt
Rumont
Sampigny
Le Gault-Soigny
Vatry
La Chaussée-sur-Marne
Revigny-sur-Ornain
Bannes
Fontaine
Pargny-sur-Saulx
Fains-Véel
Bar-le-Duc
Fère-Champenoise
Coole
Sermaize-les-Bains
St. Aubin-sur-Aire
Sézanne
Connantre
Sommesous
Blacy
Vitry-le-François
Thiéblemont-Farémont
Brillon-en-Barrois
Ligny-en-Barrois
Esternay
Barbonne-Fayel
Gourgançon
Mailly-le-Camp
Sompuis
Villiers-St. Georges
Pleurs
St. Remy-en-Bouzemont
St. Dizier
Ancerville
Stainville
Villenauxe-la-Grande
Anglure
Plancy-l'Abbaye
Herbisse
Lhuître
Margerie-Hancourt
Éclaron
Lac du Der Chantecoq
Morley
Houdelaincourt
Marcilly-sur-Seine
Giffaumont-Champaubert
Romilly-sur-Seine
Aube
Arcis-sur-Aube
Vinets
Ramerupt
Rachecourt-sur-Marne
Chevillon
Wassy
Thonnance-lès-Joinville
Pancey
Méry-sur-Seine
Chaudrey
Chavanges
Montier-en-Der
Joinville
Poissons
Châtres
Voué
St. Martin-de-Bossenay
Lesmont
Brienne-le-Château
Dommartin-le-Franc
Germay
Savières
Doulevant-le-Château
Marigny-le-Châtel
Feuges
Piney
Lac du Temple
Soulaines-Dhuys
Doulaincourt-Saucourt
Marcilly-le-Hayer
Bercenay-le-Hayer
Creney
Forêt d'Orient
La Chapelle-St. Luc
Ste. Savine
Géraudot
Lusigny-sur-Barse
Lac d'Orient
Nigloland
Dolancourt
Vignory
St. Blin
Thorigny-sur-Oreuse
Estissac
Troyes
Bar-sur-Aube
Colombey-les-deux-Églises
Andelot Blanchville
Villemaur-sur-Vanne
Bréviandes
Vendeuvre-sur-Barse
Bayel
Briaucourt
Villeneuve-l'Archevêque
Aix-en-Othe
Vauchassis
Buchères
Juzennecourt
Bologne
Burdons
Champagne

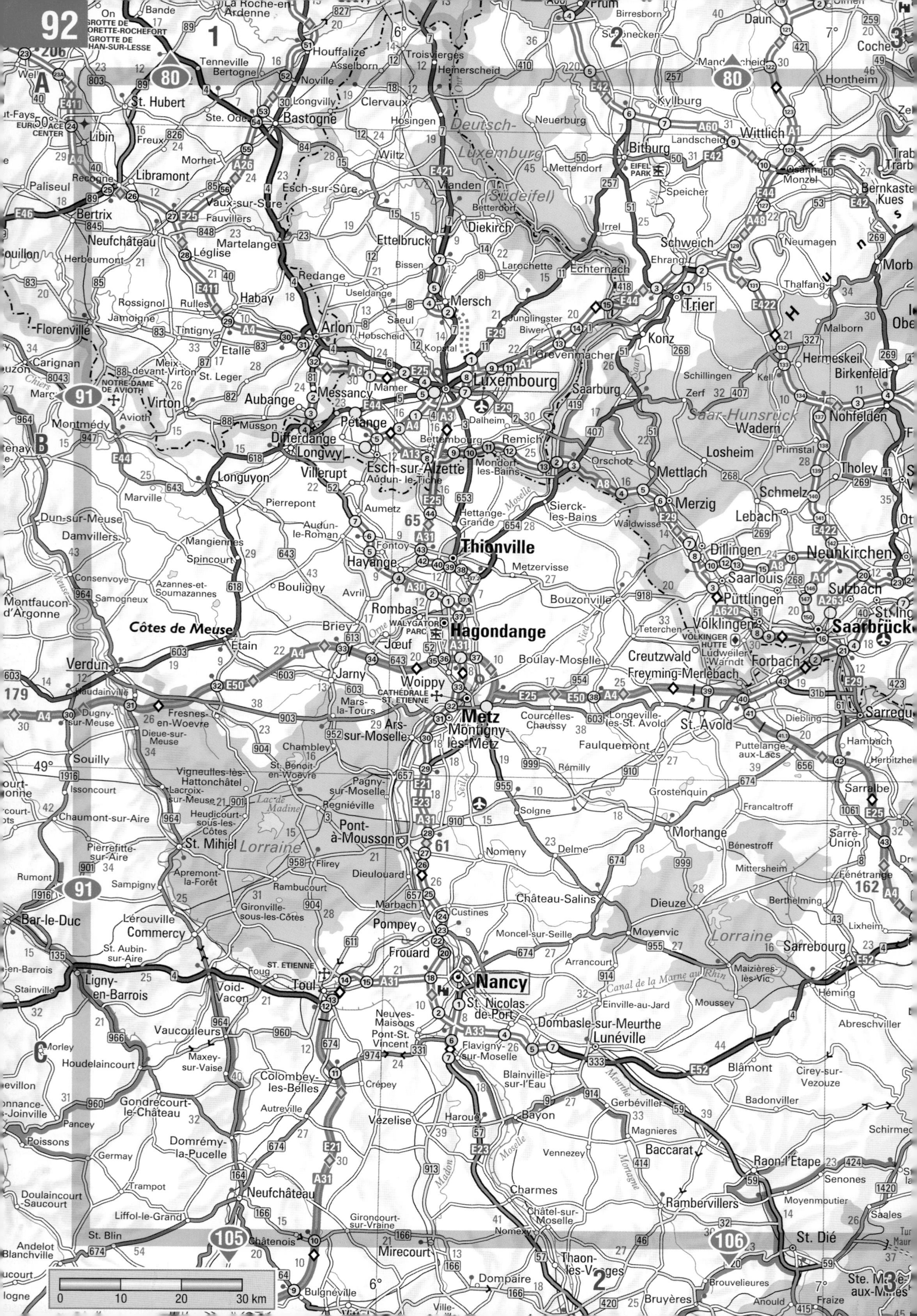

Luxembourg
Metz
Nancy
Thionville
Hagondange
Saarbrücken
Trier
Arlon
Bastogne
Verdun
Bar-le-Duc
Toul
Lunéville
St. Dié
Neufchâteau
Pont-à-Mousson
Sarrebourg
Côtes de Meuse
Lorraine
Saar-Hunsrück
Deutsch-Luxemburg (Südeifel)
0 10 20 30 km

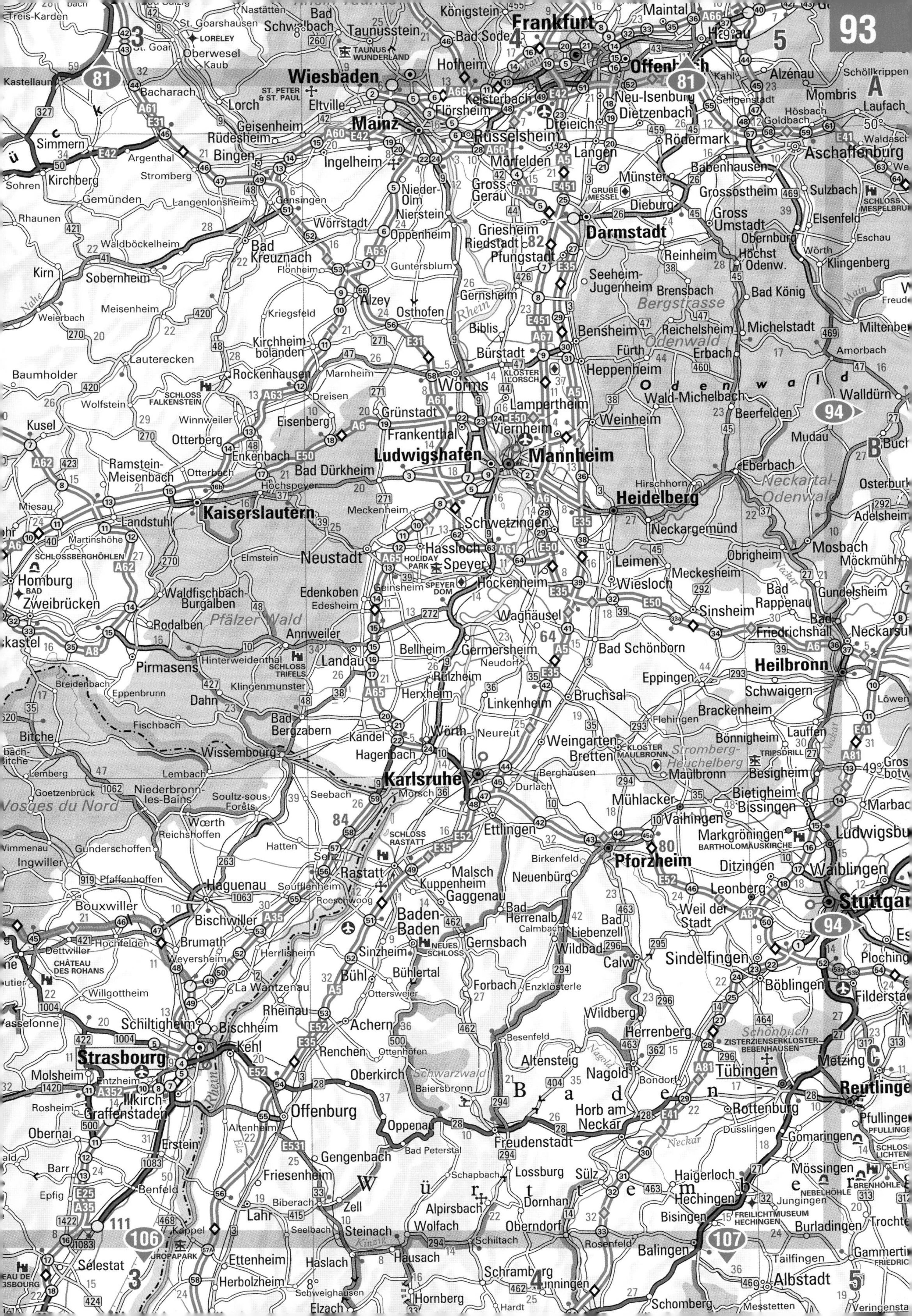

Frankfurt
Offenbach
Wiesbaden
Mainz
Königstein
Maintal
Hanau
Bad Soden
Hofheim
Kelsterbach
Flörsheim
Rüsselsheim
Neu-Isenburg
Dreieich
Dietzenbach
Rödermark
Langen
Mörfelden
Gross Gerau
Darmstadt
Dieburg
Babenhausen
Grossostheim
Aschaffenburg
Alzenau
Schöllkrippen
Mombris
Laufach
Sulzbach
Elsenfeld
Obernburg
Klingenberg
Wörth
Gross Umstadt
Höchst i. Odenw.
Reinheim
Bad König
Michelstadt
Erbach
Miltenberg
Amorbach
Walldürn
Mudau
Buchen
Beerfelden
Eberbach
Neckargemünd
Heidelberg
Mosbach
Möckmühl
Adelsheim
Osterburken
Obrigheim
Gundelsheim
Bad Rappenau
Sinsheim
Neckarsulm
Heilbronn
Bad Friedrichshall
Eppingen
Schwaigern
Brackenheim
Bönnigheim
Lauffen
Besigheim
Bietigheim-Bissingen
Markgröningen
Ludwigsburg
Waiblingen
Stuttgart
Leonberg
Ditzingen
Vaihingen
Mühlacker
Pforzheim
Maulbronn
Bretten
Bruchsal
Weingarten
Karlsruhe
Ettlingen
Durlach
Rastatt
Gaggenau
Baden-Baden
Bühl
Achern
Renchen
Oberkirch
Offenburg
Kehl
Strasbourg
Lahr
Ettenheim
Herbolzheim
Sélestat
Elzach
Haslach
Hausach
Wolfach
Schiltach
Schramberg
Hornberg
Freudenstadt
Baiersbronn
Oppenau
Nagold
Altensteig
Calw
Wildbad
Neuenbürg
Sindelfingen
Böblingen
Herrenberg
Tübingen
Reutlingen
Metzingen
Rottenburg
Horb am Neckar
Hechingen
Mössingen
Balingen
Albstadt
Oberndorf
Rosenfeld
Haigerloch
Sulz
Bisingen
Burladingen
Schwarzwald
Baden-Württemberg
Mannheim
Ludwigshafen
Worms
Frankenthal
Viernheim
Weinheim
Lampertheim
Bürstadt
Bensheim
Heppenheim
Schwetzingen
Hockenheim
Speyer
Wiesloch
Leimen
Walldorf
Waghäusel
Germersheim
Bad Schönborn
Neustadt
Landau
Bad Dürkheim
Grünstadt
Kaiserslautern
Landstuhl
Homburg
Zweibrücken
Pirmasens
Annweiler
Bad Bergzabern
Kandel
Wörth
Wissembourg
Haguenau
Bischwiller
Brumath
Schiltigheim
Illkirch-Graffenstaden
Obernai
Molsheim
Erstein
Bitche
Pfälzer Wald
Vosges du Nord
Alzey
Bad Kreuznach
Bingen
Rüdesheim
Ingelheim
Oppenheim
Nierstein
Kirchheimbolanden
Rockenhausen
Kusel
Simmern
Kirchberg
Kirn
Sobernheim
Odenwald
Bergstrasse
Rhein
Neckar
Main

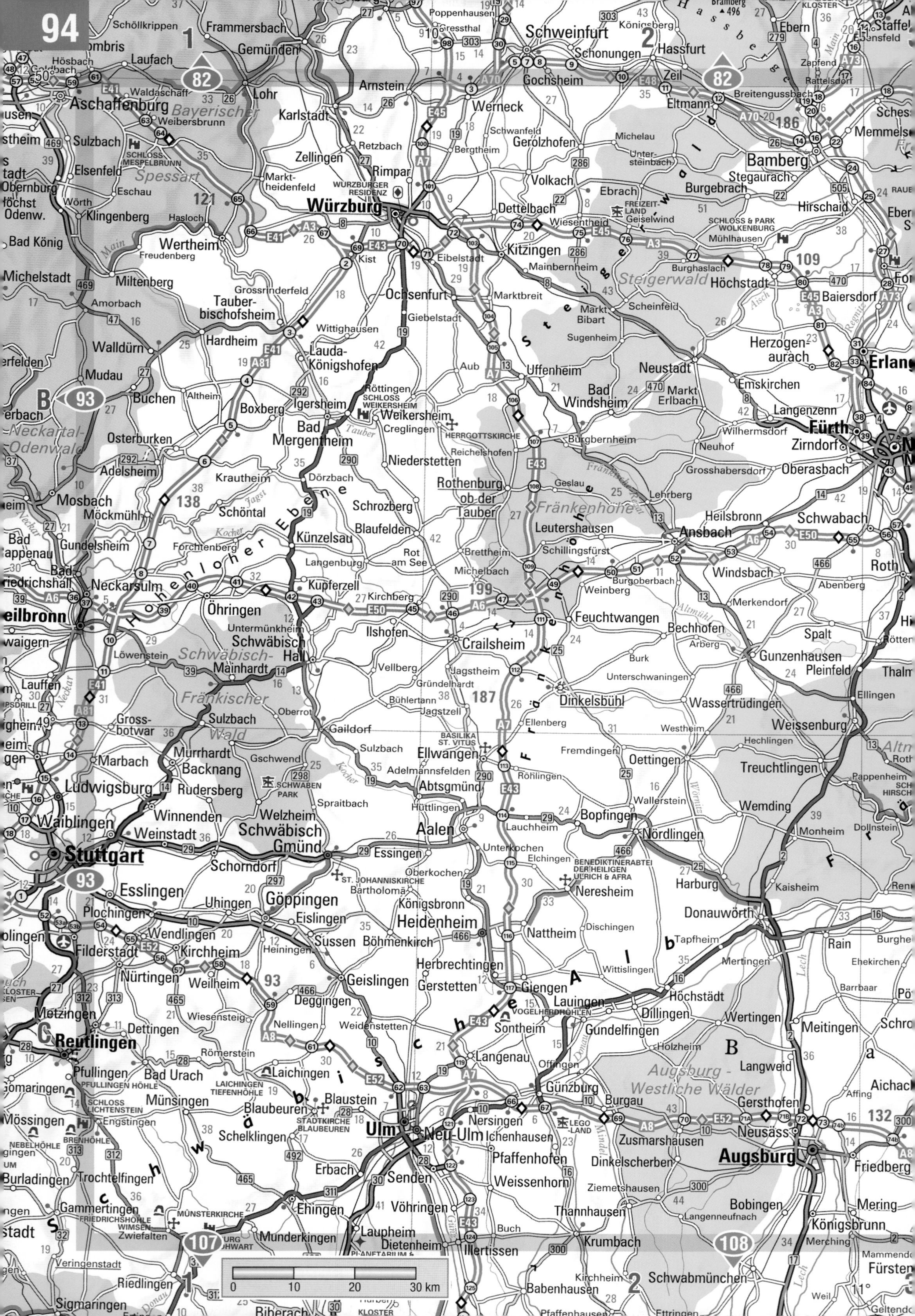
Schöllkrippen
Frammersbach
Gemünden
Poppenhausen
Gressthal
Schweinfurt
Königsberg
Schonungen
Hassfurt
Hassberge
Ebern
Staffel
Bamberg
Laufach
Hösbach
Goldbach
Aschaffenburg
Waldaschaff
Weibersbrunn
Bayerischer
Lohr
Karlstadt
Arnstein
Werneck
Gochsheim
Zeil
Eltmann
Breitengussbach
Rattelsdorf
Zapfend
Memmelsdorf
Sulzbach
Schloss Mespelbrunn
Spessart
Elsenfeld
Obernburg
Höchst Odenw.
Eschau
Wörth
Klingenberg
Hasloch
Zellingen
Retzbach
Rimpar
Markt-heidenfeld
Würzburger Residenz
Würzburg
Schwanfeld
Bergtheim
Gerolzhofen
Volkach
Dettelbach
Michelau
Unter-steinbach
Ebrach
Freizeit-Land Geiselwind
Wiesentheid
Burgebrach
Stegaurach
Hirschaid
Schloss & Park Wolkenburg
Mühlhausen
Bad König
Wertheim
Freudenberg
Kist
Eibelstadt
Kitzingen
Mainbernheim
Burghaslach
Steigerwald
Höchstadt
Baiersdorf
Michelstadt
Miltenberg
Amorbach
Grossrinderfeld
Tauber-bischofsheim
Ochsenfurt
Giebelstadt
Marktbreit
Markt Bibart
Scheinfeld
Sugenheim
Wittighausen
Walldürn
Hardheim
Lauda-Königshofen
Aub
Uffenheim
Neustadt
Herzogen-aurach
Erlangen
Mudau
Buchen
Altheim
Boxberg
Igersheim
Röttingen
Schloss Weikersheim
Weikersheim
Creglingen
Herrgottskirche
Bad Windsheim
Markt Erlbach
Emskirchen
Langenzenn
Wilhermsdorf
Fürth
Zirndorf
Neckartal-Odenwald
Osterburken
Bad Mergentheim
Tauber
Reichelshofen
Burgbernheim
Neuhof
Adelsheim
Krautheim
Dörzbach
Niederstetten
Rothenburg ob der Tauber
Geslau
Frankenhöhe
Grosshabersdorf
Oberasbach
Mosbach
Möckmühl
Schöntal
Jagst
Schrozberg
Lehrberg
Bad Rappenau
Gundelsheim
Hohenloher Ebene
Künzelsau
Blaufelden
Leutershausen
Ansbach
Heilsbronn
Schwabach
Bad Friedrichshall
Neckarsulm
Forchtenberg
Kocher
Langenburg
Rot am See
Brettheim
Schillingsfürst
Michelbach
Windsbach
Roth
Heilbronn
Öhringen
Kupferzell
Kirchberg
Weinberg
Burgoberbach
Abenberg
Merkendorf
Untermünkheim
Ilshofen
Crailsheim
Feuchtwangen
Bechhofen
Altmühl
Spalt
Weinsberg
Löwenstein
Schwäbisch Hall
Arberg
Gunzenhausen
Pleinfeld
Lauffen
Schwäbisch-Fränkischer Wald
Mainhardt
Vellberg
Jagstheim
Gründelhardt
Burk
Unterschwaningen
Bühlertann
Dinkelsbühl
Wassertrüdingen
Ellingen
Oberrot
Jagstzell
Ellenberg
Gross-bottwar
Sulzbach
Gaildorf
Basilika St. Vitus
Ellwangen
Westheim
Weissenburg
Marbach
Murrhardt
Backnang
Gschwend
Fremdingen
Oettingen
Treuchtlingen
Hechlingen
Ludwigsburg
Rudersberg
Schwaben Park
Adelmannsfelden
Abtsgmünd
Röhlingen
Pappenheim
Spraitbach
Hüttlingen
Wallerstein
Wemding
Winnenden
Waiblingen
Weinstadt
Welzheim
Schwäbisch Gmünd
Aalen
Lauchheim
Bopfingen
Nördlingen
Monheim
Dollnstein
Stuttgart
Schorndorf
Essingen
Unterkochen
Elchingen
Benediktinerabtei der Heiligen Ulrich & Afra
Neresheim
Harburg
Kaisheim
Esslingen
Göppingen
St. Johanniskirche
Bartholomä
Oberkochen
Königsbronn
Uhingen
Plochingen
Eislingen
Heidenheim
Nattheim
Dischingen
Donauwörth
Wendlingen
Filderstadt
Kirchheim
Süssen
Böhmenkirch
Heiningen
Tapfheim
Rain
Herbrechtingen
Mertingen
Nürtingen
Weilheim
Geislingen
Gerstetten
Giengen
Wittislingen
Höchstädt
Metzingen
Deggingen
Lauingen
Dillingen
Wertingen
Meitingen
Wiesensteig
Nellingen
Weidenstetten
Vogelherdhöhlen
Sontheim
Gundelfingen
Reutlingen
Dettingen
Römerstein
Schwäbische Alb
Langenau
Offingen
Holzheim
Langweid
Pfullingen
Bad Urach
Laichingen
Pfullingen Höhle
Laichingen Tiefenhöhle
Günzburg
Augsburg - Westliche Wälder
Aichach
Affing
Gomaringen
Schloss Lichtenstein
Münsingen
Blaubeuren
Blaustein
Burgau
Gersthofen
Mössingen
Engstingen
Nebelhöhle
Bärenhöhle
Stadtkirche Blaubeuren
Ulm
Neu-Ulm
Nersingen
Legoland
Neusäss
Schelklingen
Ichenhausen
Zusmarshausen
Augsburg
Friedberg
Burladingen
Trochtelfingen
Erbach
Pfaffenhofen
Dinkelscherben
Senden
Weissenhorn
Ziemetshausen
Gammertingen
Friedrichshöhle Wimsen
Münsterkirche
Ehingen
Vöhringen
Bobingen
Mering
Zwiefalten
Munderkingen
Laupheim
Thannhausen
Langenneufnach
Königsbrunn
Dietenheim
Illertissen
Buch
Krumbach
Merching
Veringenstadt
Riedlingen
Babenhausen
Kirchheim
Schwabmünchen
Sigmaringen
Biberach
Pfaffenhausen
Ettringen
Weil
Fürstenfeldbruck
Geltendorf
Lech
Donau
Neckar
Main
Wörnitz
0 10 20 30 km

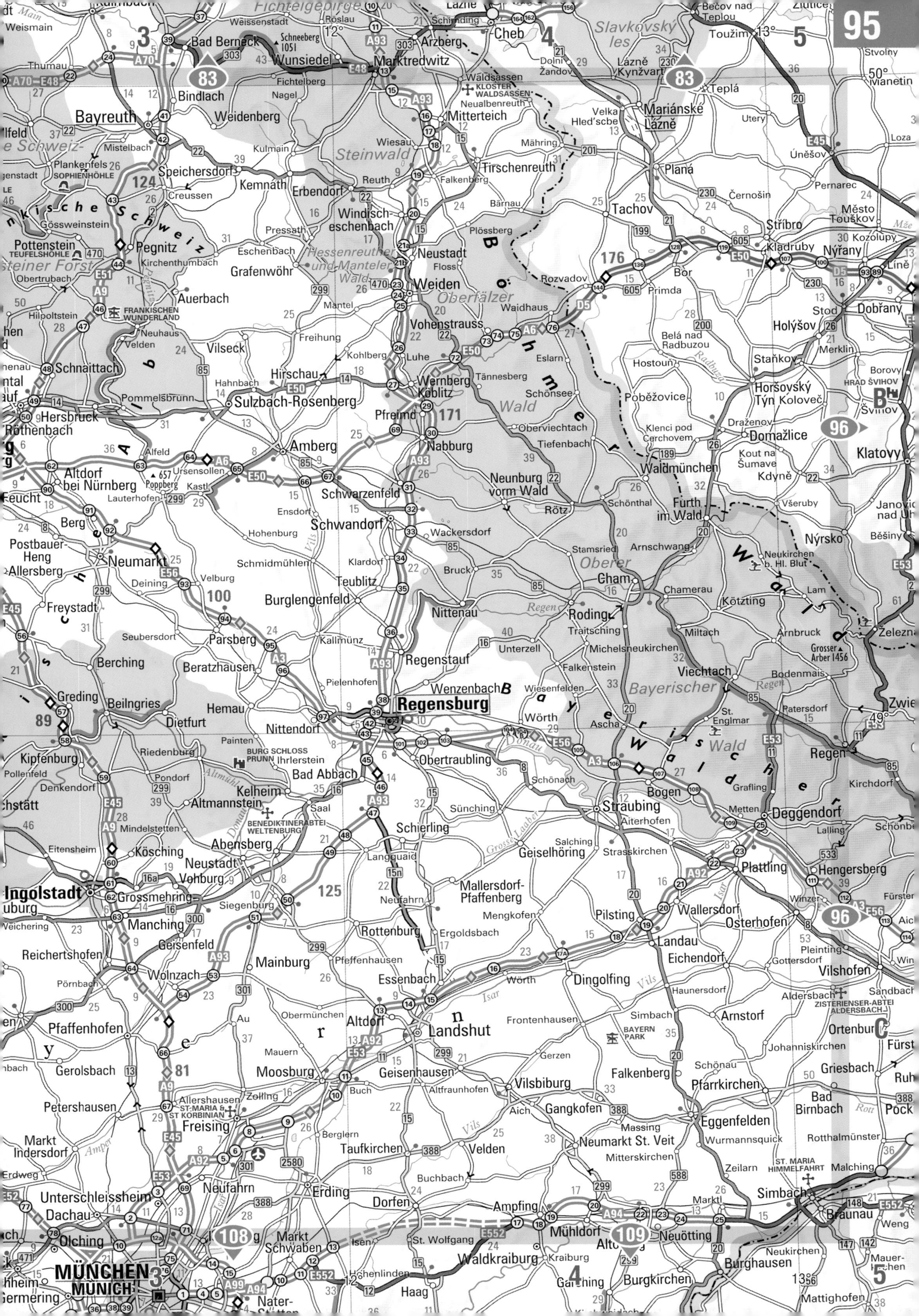
Fichtelgebirge
Weissenstadt
Röslau
Bad Berneck
Schneeberg 1051
Wunsiedel
Marktredwitz
Arzberg
Schirnding
Cheb
Slavkovský les
Bečov nad Teplou
Toužim
Weismain
Thurnau
Bindlach
Bayreuth
Weidenberg
Fichtelberg
Nagel
Waldsassen
KLOSTER WALDSASSEN
Neualbenreuth
Mitterteich
Dolní Žandov
Lázně Kynžvart
Tepla
Mariánské Lázně
Velká Hleďsebe
Mistelbach
Plankenfels
SOPHIENHÖHLE
Speichersdorf
Kulmain
Steinwald
Wiesau
Mähring
Tirschenreuth
Planá
Úněšov
Kemnath
Creussen
Erbendorf
Reuth
Falkenberg
Bärnau
Tachov
Černošín
Pernarec
Město Touškov
Gössweinstein
Pottenstein
TEUFELSHÖHLE
Pegnitz
Pressath
Windischeschenbach
Plössberg
Stříbro
Kladruby
Nýřany
Kozolupy
Eschenbach
Hessenreuther und Manteler Wald
Neustadt
Floss
Rozvadov
Bor
Primda
Obertrubach
Kirchenthumbach
Grafenwöhr
Weiden
Oberpfälzer Wald
Waidhaus
Holýšov
Stod
Dobřany
Auerbach
Hilpoltstein
FRÄNKISCHEN WUNDERLAND
Mantel
Vohenstrauss
Neuhaus
Velden
Freihung
Bělá nad Radbuzou
Merklín
Vilseck
Kohlberg
Luhe
Eslarn
Hostouň
Staňkov
Schnaittach
Hirschau
Hahnbach
Wernberg Köblitz
Tännesberg
Schönsee
Poběžovice
Horšovský Týn
Koloveč
HRAD ŠVIHOV
Švihov
Pommelsbrunn
Sulzbach-Rosenberg
Hersbruck
Röthenbach
Pfreimd
Oberviechtach
Dražeňov
Klenčí pod Čerchovem
Domažlice
Klatovy
Amberg
Alfeld
Nabburg
Tiefenbach
Altdorf bei Nürnberg
Ursensollen
Poppberg 657
Kastl
Lauterhofen
Schwarzenfeld
Neunburg vorm Wald
Waldmünchen
Kout na Šumavě
Kdyně
Feucht
Ensdorf
Rötz
Schönthal
Furth im Wald
Všeruby
Janovice nad Úhlavou
Berg
Schwandorf
Hohenburg
Wackersdorf
Nýrsko
Běšiny
Postbauer-Heng
Neumarkt
Allersberg
Schmidmühlen
Klardorf
Bruck
Stamsried
Arnschwang
Neukirchen b. Hl. Blut
Oberer
Deining
Velburg
Teublitz
Cham
Freystadt
Burglengenfeld
Nittenau
Roding
Chamerau
Kötzting
Lam
Regen
Seubersdorf
Parsberg
Kallmünz
Traitsching
Miltach
Arnbruck
Železná Ruda
Berching
Beratzhausen
Regenstauf
Unterzell
Michelsneukirchen
Grosser Arber 1456
Falkenstein
Viechtach
Bodenmais
Pielenhofen
Wenzenbach
Wiesenfelden
Bayerischer Wald
Greding
Beilngries
Hemau
Regensburg
Patersdorf
Zwiesel
Dietfurt
Nittendorf
Wörth
Ascha
St. Englmar
Painten
Riedenburg
BURG SCHLOSS PRUNN
Ihrlerstein
Obertraubling
Donau
Kipfenberg
Pollenfeld
Altmühl
Bad Abbach
Schönach
Grafling
Kirchdorf
Denkendorf
Pondorf
Kelheim
Altmannstein
Saal
Straubing
Bogen
Deggendorf
Eichstätt
BENEDIKTINERABTEI WELTENBURG
Mindelstetten
Schierling
Sünching
Aiterhofen
Metten
Lalling
Schönberg
Eitensheim
Abensberg
Salching
Geiselhöring
Strasskirchen
Kösching
Neustadt
Langquaid
Plattling
Hengersberg
Ingolstadt
Vohburg
Grossmehring
Mallersdorf-Pfaffenberg
Neufahrn
Fürstenzell
Siegenburg
Pilsting
Wallersdorf
Osterhofen
Manching
Mengkofen
Winzer
Reichertshofen
Geisenfeld
Rottenburg
Ergoldsbach
Landau
Eichendorf
Pleinting
Mainburg
Pfeffenhausen
Gottersdorf
Vilshofen
Pörnbach
Wolnzach
Essenbach
Wörth
Dingolfing
Haunersdorf
Aldersbach
Sandbach
Pfaffenhofen
Obermünchen
Altdorf
Landshut
Frontenhausen
Simbach
Arnstorf
ZISTERIENSER-ABTEI ALDERSBACH
Ortenburg
Au
BAYERN PARK
Mauern
Gerzen
Johanniskirchen
Gerolsbach
Moosburg
Geisenhausen
Falkenberg
Schönau
Griesbach
Petershausen
Allershausen
ST. MARIA & ST. KORBINIAN
Zolling
Buch
Altfraunhofen
Vilsbiburg
Pfarrkirchen
Bad Birnbach
Pocking
Rott
Freising
Gangkofen
Aich
Massing
Eggenfelden
Markt Indersdorf
Amper
Berglern
Velden
Neumarkt St. Veit
Wurmannsquick
Rotthalmünster
Taufkirchen
Mitterskirchen
Erdweg
Zeilarn
ST. MARIA HIMMELFAHRT
Malching
Neufahrn
Buchbach
Unterschleissheim
Erding
Dorfen
Ampfing
Marktl
Simbach
Braunau
Dachau
Mühldorf
Altötting
Neuötting
Olching
Markt Schwaben
Isen
St. Wolfgang
Weng
Waldkraiburg
Kraiburg
Neukirchen
Mauerkirchen
MÜNCHEN MUNICH
Germering
Hohenlinden
Haag
Gars
Burgkirchen
Burghausen
Mattighofen
Nater-Stetten
Isar
Vils
Regen
Radbuza
Grosse Laaber

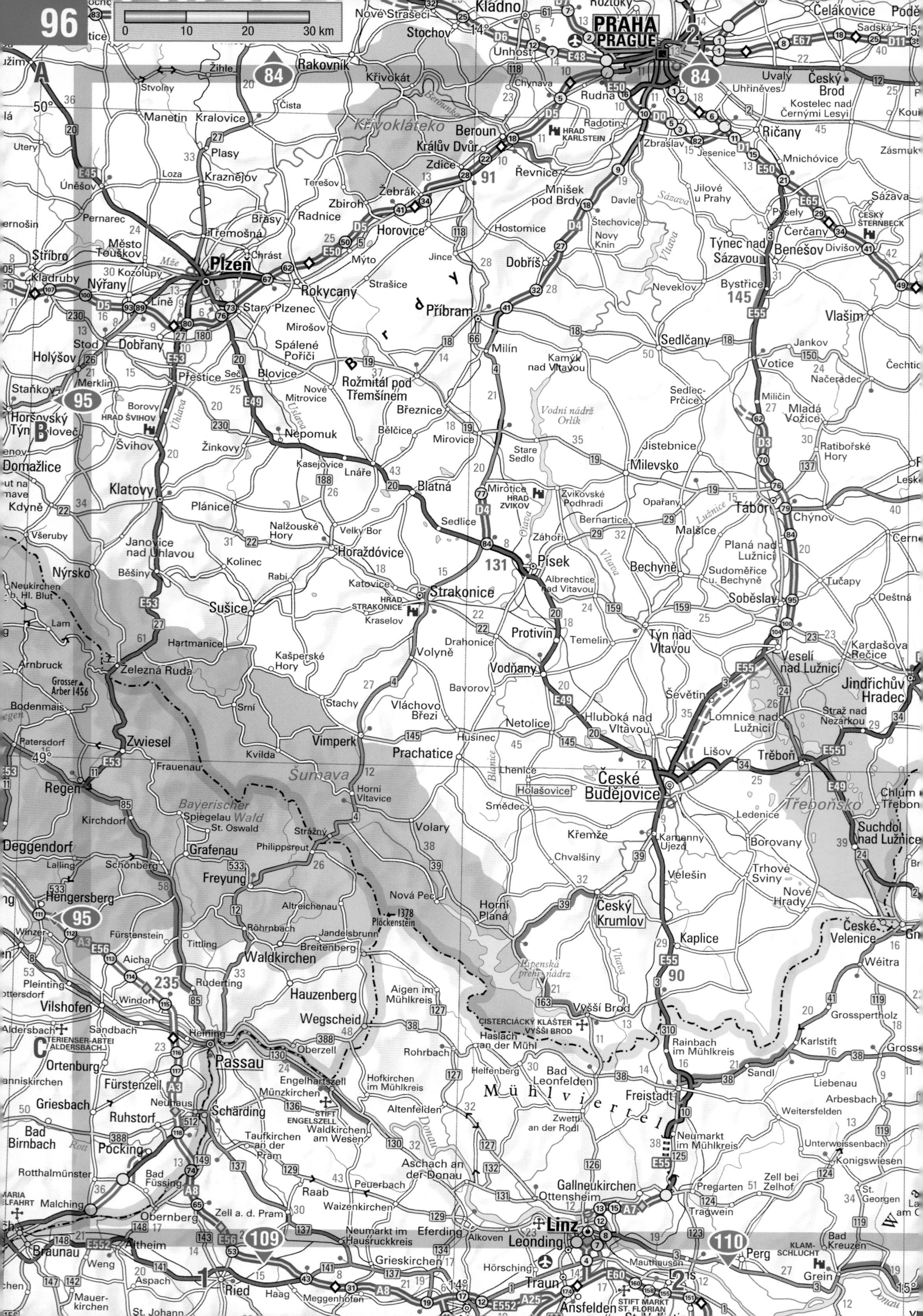
0 10 20 30 km
84
Kladno
Nové Strašecí
Stochov
Unhošť
Roztoky
PRAHA
PRAGUE
Čelákovice
Sadská
Rakovník
Křivoklát
Žihle
Stvolny
Čistá
Manetín
Kralovice
Křivoklátsko
Berounka
Beroun
Králův Dvůr
Zdice
Chýnava
Rudná
Radotín
HRAD KARLŠTEJN
Zbraslav
Jesenice
Úvaly
Uhříněves
Český Brod
Kostelec nad Černými Lesy
Říčany
Mnichovice
Plasy
Loza
Kraznějov
Úněšov
Utery
Terešov
Žebrák
Zbiroh
Hořovice
Řevnice
Mníšek pod Brdy
Davle
Jílové u Prahy
Sázava
Pyšely
ČESKÝ ŠTERNBECK
Čerčany
Benešov
Divišov
Pernarec
Třemošná
Břasy
Radnice
Hostomice
Štěchovice
Nový Knín
Týnec nad Sázavou
Město Touškov
Stříbro
Chrást
Plzeň
Mže
Mýto
Jince
Dobříš
Vltava
Kozolupy
Kladruby
Nýřany
Líně
Rokycany
Strašice
Brdy
Příbram
Neveklov
Bystřice
Vlašim
Starý Plzenec
Mirošov
Stod
Dobřany
Holýšov
Spálené Poříčí
Milín
Kamýk nad Vltavou
Sedlčany
Jankov
Votice
Načeradec
Čechtice
Staňkov
Merklín
Přeštice
Seč
Blovice
Nové Mitrovice
Rožmitál pod Třemšínem
Březnice
Sedlec-Prčice
Miličín
Mladá Vožice
Horšovský Týn
Borovy
HRAD ŠVIHOV
Úhlava
Úslava
Nepomuk
Bělčice
Mirovice
Vodní nádrž Orlík
Švihov
Žinkovy
Stare Sedlo
Jistebnice
Ratibořské Hory
Domažlice
Kasejovice
Lnáře
Milevsko
Klatovy
Blatná
Mirotice
HRAD ZVÍKOV
Zvíkovské Podhradí
Opařany
Tábor
Kdyně
Plánice
Sedlice
Bernartice
Chýnov
Všeruby
Nalžouské Hory
Velký Bor
Záhoří
Malšice
Lužnice
Janovice nad Úhlavou
Horažďovice
Otava
Písek
Bechyně
Planá nad Lužnicí
Nýrsko
Kolinec
Rabí
Albrechtice nad Vltavou
Sudoměřice u. Bechyně
Tučapy
Neukirchen b. Hl. Blut
Běšiny
Katovice
Strakonice
HRAD STRAKONICE
Kraselov
Soběslav
Deštná
Sušice
Protivín
Temelín
Týn nad Vltavou
Lam
Hartmanice
Drahonice
Volyně
Kašperské Hory
Veselí nad Lužnicí
Kardašova Řečice
Arnbruck
Železná Ruda
Vodňany
Grosser Arber 1456
Bavorov
Ševětín
Jindřichův Hradec
Stachy
Vláchovo Březí
Netolice
Hluboká nad Vltavou
Lomnice nad Lužnicí
Stráž nad Nežárkou
Bodenmais
Srní
Patersdorf
Zwiesel
Kvilda
Vimperk
Husinec
Prachatice
Lišov
Třeboň
Frauenau
Šumava
Lhenice
Blanice
České Budějovice
Holašovice
Regen
Horní Vltavice
Bayerischer Wald
Spiegelau
St. Oswald
Smědec
Ledenice
Třeboňsko
Chlum u Třeboně
Kirchdorf
Volary
Křemže
Kamenný Újezd
Borovany
Suchdol nad Lužnicí
Deggendorf
Grafenau
Philippsreut
Strážný
Chvalšiny
Lalling
Schönberg
Freyung
Velešín
Trhové Sviny
Nové Hrady
Hengersberg
Nová Pec
Horní Planá
Český Krumlov
Altreichenau
1378 Plöckenstein
Winzer
Fürstenstein
Röhrnbach
Jandelsbrunn
Breitenberg
Kaplice
České Velenice
Tittling
Aicha
Waldkirchen
Lipenská přehr. nádrž
Weitra
Pleinting
Hauzenberg
Ruderting
Aigen im Mühlkreis
Vyšší Brod
Grosspertholz
Vilshofen
Windorf
Wegscheid
CISTERCIÁCKÝ KLÁŠTER VYŠŠÍ BROD
Aldersbach
Sandbach
TERIENSER-ABTEI ALDERSBACH
Haslach an der Mühl
Rainbach im Mühlkreis
Karlstift
Heining
Passau
Oberzell
Rohrbach
Ortenburg
Helfenberg
Bad Leonfelden
Sandl
Fürstenzell
Engelhartszell
Hofkirchen im Mühlkreis
Freistadt
Liebenau
Mühlviertel
Griesbach
Neuhaus
Münzkirchen
Arbesbach
Ruhstorf
Schärding
STIFT ENGELSZELL
Altenfelden
Zwettl an der Rodl
Weitersfelden
Bad Birnbach
Rott
Taufkirchen an der Pram
Waldkirchen am Wesen
Donau
Neumarkt im Mühlkreis
Unterweissenbach
Pocking
Königswiesen
Rotthalmünster
Bad Füssing
Aschach an der Donau
Gallneukirchen
Pregarten
Zell bei Zelhof
Raab
Peuerbach
Ottensheim
St. Georgen am Gusen
Malching
Waizenkirchen
Tragwein
Obernberg
Zell a. d. Pram
Linz
Braunau
Altheim
Neumarkt im Hausruckkreis
Eferding
Alkoven
Leonding
Bad Kreuzen
Perg
KLAM-SCHLUCHT
Weng
Grieskirchen
Hörsching
Mauthausen
Aspach
Grein
Ried
Haag
Traun
Mauer-kirchen
Meggenhofen
St. Johann
Ansfelden
STIFT MARKT ST. FLORIAN
50°
49°
14°
15°
A
B
C
84
91
95
109
110
131
145
235
90

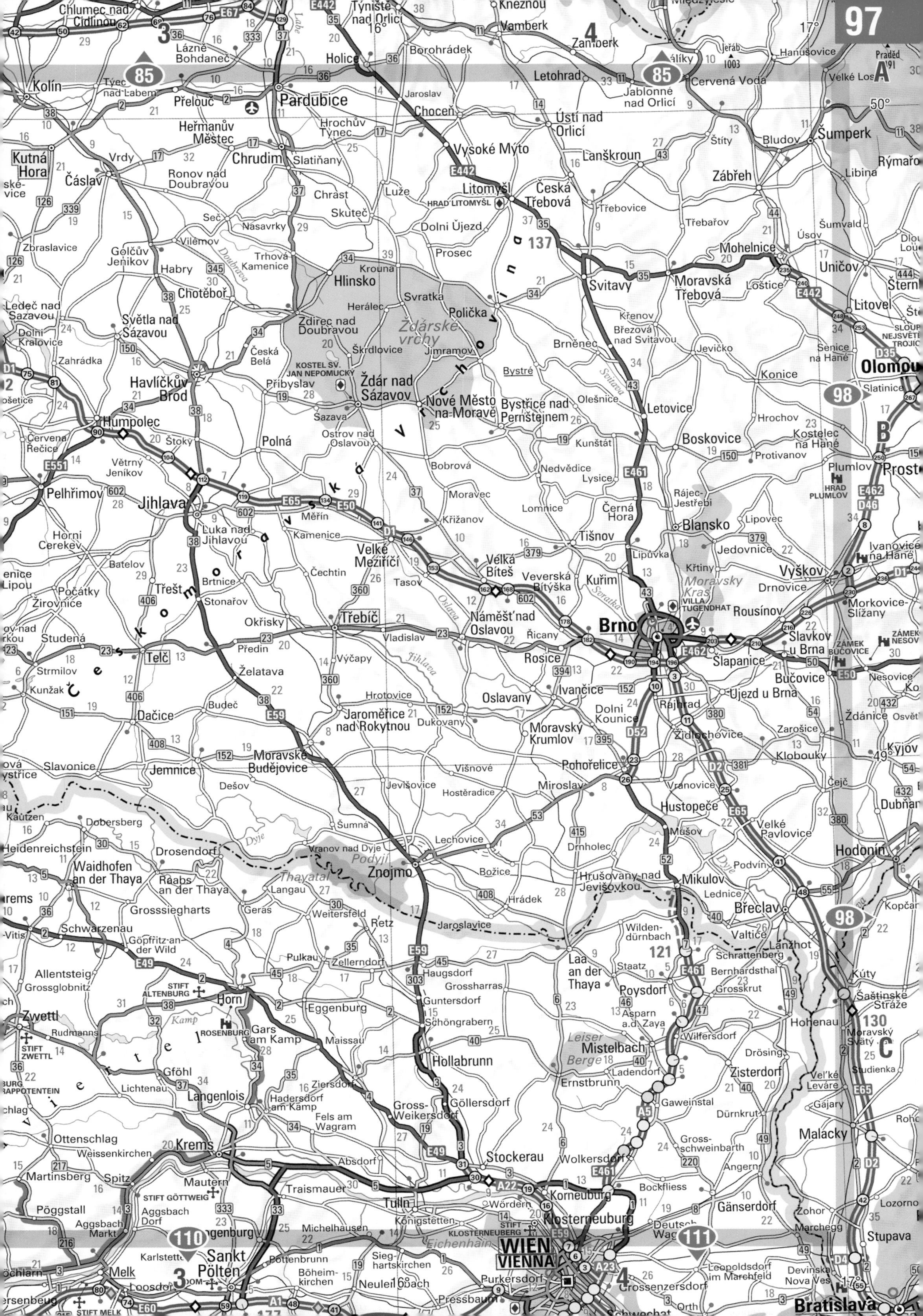

97
Chlumec nad Cidlinou
Týniště nad Orlicí
Kněžnou
Vamberk
Žamberk
Lázně Bohdaneč
Holice
Borohrádek
Kolín
Týnec nad Labem
Přelouč
Pardubice
Letohrad
Jablonné nad Orlicí
Červená Voda
Hanušovice
Praděd
Velké Losiny
Jaroslav
Choceň
Ústí nad Orlicí
Heřmanův Městec
Hrochův Týnec
Vysoké Mýto
Lanškroun
Štíty
Bludov
Šumperk
Kutná Hora
Vrdy
Chrudim
Slatiňany
Zábřeh
Rýmařov
Čáslav
Ronov nad Doubravou
Litomyšl
Česká Třebová
Libina
Chrast
Luže
HRAD LITOMYŠL
Třebovice
Skuteč
Třebařov
Šumvald
Seč
Nasavrky
Dolní Újezd
Úsov
Zbraslavice
Vilémov
Golčův Jeníkov
Trhová Kamenice
Prosec
Mohelnice
Uničov
Habry
Krouna
Hlinsko
Svitavy
Moravská Třebová
Loštice
Šternberk
Chotěboř
Heralec
Svratka
Polička
Litovel
Ledeč nad Sázavou
Světlá nad Sázavou
Zdírec nad Doubravou
Žďárské vrchy
Křenov
Březová nad Svitavou
Dolní Kralovice
Škrdlovice
Jimramov
Brněnec
Jevíčko
Senice na Hané
Zahrádka
Česká Belá
KOSTEL SV. JAN NEPOMUCKÝ
Bystré
Konice
Olomouc
Havlíčkův Brod
Přibyslav
Žďár nad Sázavou
Nové Město na Moravě
Bystřice nad Pernštejnem
Olešnice
Slatinice
Sázava
Letovice
Humpolec
Červená Řečice
Štoky
Ostrov nad Oslavou
Polná
Kunštát
Boskovice
Hrochov
Kostelec na Hané
Větrný Jeníkov
Bobrová
Nedvědice
Lysice
Protivanov
Plumlov
Prostějov
HRAD PLUMLOV
Pelhřimov
Jihlava
Moravec
Rájec-Jestřebí
Lomnice
Černá Hora
Měřín
Křižanov
Blansko
Lipovec
Horní Cerekev
Luka nad Jihlavou
Kamenice
Velké Meziříčí
Tišnov
Jedovnice
Ivanovice na Hané
Batelov
Čechtín
Velká Bíteš
Lipůvka
Křtiny
Vyškov
Počátky
Třešť
Brtnice
Tasov
Veverská Bítýška
Kuřim
Moravský Kras
Drnovice
Žirovnice
Stonařov
VILLA TUGENDHAT
Rousínov
Morkovice-Slížany
Studená
Okříšky
Třebíč
Náměšť nad Oslavou
Brno
Slavkov u Brna
ZÁMEK NESOVICE
Telč
Předín
Vladislav
Řícany
ZÁMEK BUČOVICE
Strmilov
Výčapy
Rosice
Šlapanice
Bučovice
Nesovice
Kunžak
Želatava
Ivančice
Újezd u Brna
Hrotovice
Oslavany
Dolní Kounice
Rajhrad
Ždánice
Dačice
Budeč
Jaroměřice nad Rokytnou
Dukovany
Moravský Krumlov
Židlochovice
Zarošice
Moravské Budějovice
Klobouky
Kyjov
Slavonice
Jemnice
Višňové
Pohořelice
Čejč
Dešov
Jevišovice
Hostěradice
Miroslav
Vranovice
Dubňany
Kautzen
Hustopeče
Dobersberg
Šumná
Mušov
Velké Pavlovice
Heidenreichstein
Drosendorf
Vranov nad Dyjí
Lechovice
Drnholec
Hodonín
Podyjí
Waidhofen an der Thaya
Raabs an der Thaya
Thayatal
Znojmo
Božice
Podivín
Hrušovany nad Jevišovkou
Mikulov
Lednice
Břeclav
Kopčany
Langau
Hrádek
Gmünd
Grosssiegharts
Geras
Weitersfeld
Jaroslavice
Valtice
Retz
Wildendürnbach
Lanžhot
Schwarzenau
Göpfritz an der Wild
Pulkau
Zellerndorf
Laa an der Thaya
Staatz
Schrattenberg
Kúty
Allentsteig
Grossglobnitz
Haugsdorf
Bernhardsthal
STIFT ALTENBURG
Grossharras
Poysdorf
Grosskrut
Šaštínske Stráže
Horn
Eggenburg
Guntersdorf
Asparn a.d. Zaya
Hohenau
Zwettl
Rudmanns
Kamp
ROSENBURG
Gars am Kamp
Schöngrabern
Wilfersdorf
Moravský Svätý Ján
STIFT ZWETTL
Maissau
Hollabrunn
Leiser Berge
Mistelbach
Drösing
Studienka
Gföhl
Ziersdorf
Ladendorf
Zisterdorf
Veľké Leváre
BURG RAPPOTENTEIN
Lichtenau
Langenlois
Hadersdorf am Kamp
Ernstbrunn
Göllersdorf
Gaweinstal
Gajary
Fels am Wagram
Grossweikersdorf
Dürnkrut
Ottenschlag
Malacky
Weissenkirchen
Krems
Grossschweinbarth
Stockerau
Wolkersdorf
Angern
Martinsberg
Spitz
Absdorf
Mautern
Traismauer
Tulln
Bockfliess
Pöggstall
STIFT GÖTTWEIG
Aggsbach Dorf
Aggsbach Markt
Würdern
Korneuburg
Gänserdorf
Lozorno
Königstetten
Klosterneuburg
Zohor
Michelhausen
STIFT KLOSTERNEUBURG
Deutsch Wagram
Marchegg
Stupava
Karlstetten
Sankt Pölten
Pottenbrunn
Sieghartskirchen
Eichenhain
WIEN VIENNA
Leopoldsdorf im Marchfeld
Devínska Nová Ves
Melk
Loosdorf
Böheimkirchen
Neulengbach
Purkersdorf
Grossenzersdorf
Pressbaum
Orth
STIFT MELK
Bratislava
Schwechat
Českomoravská vrchovina
Waldviertel
85
98
110
111
A
B
C
3
4

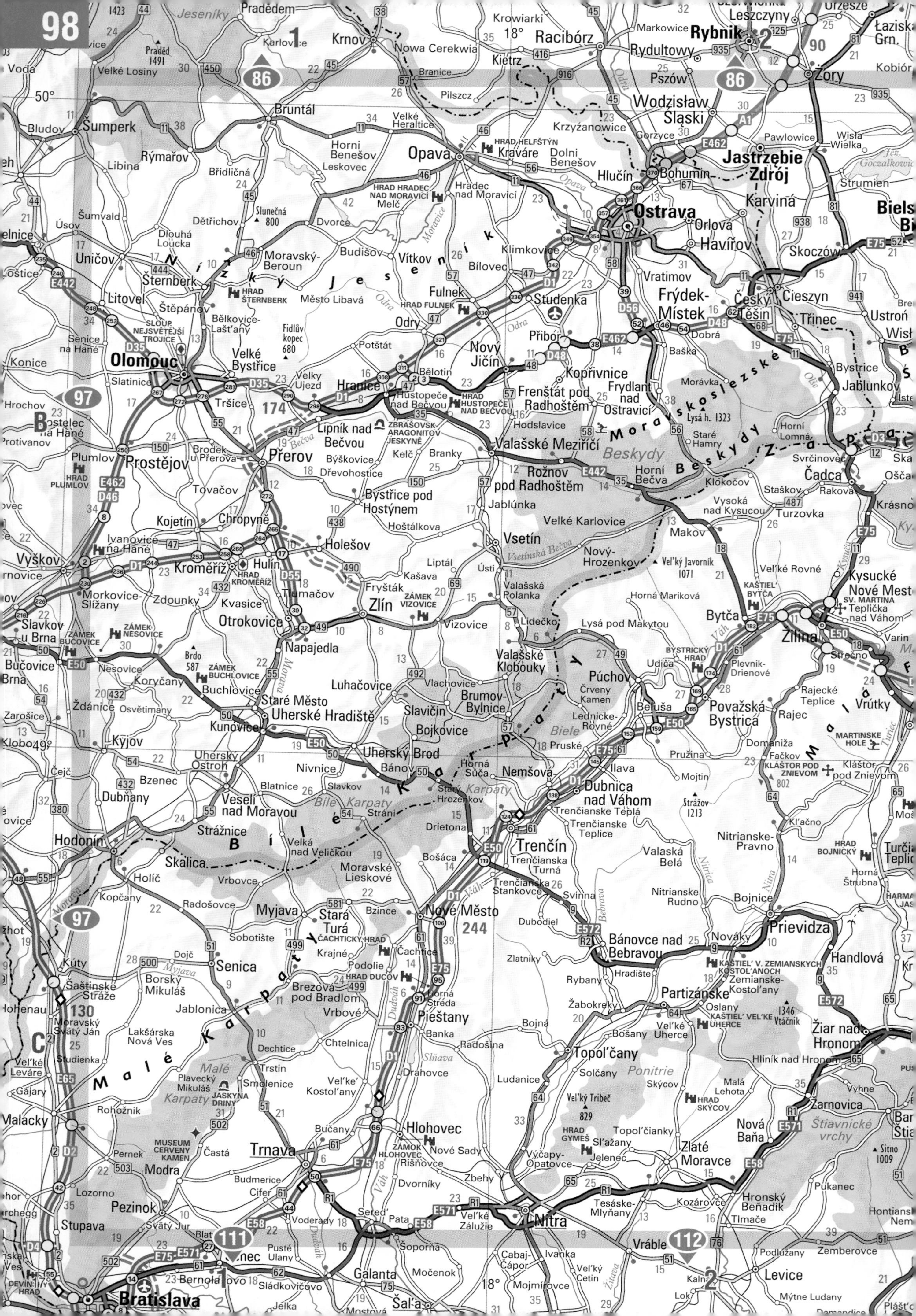
Jeseníky
Praděd 1491
Karlov
Krnov
Krowiarki
Racibórz
Markowice
Rybnik
Leszczyny
Żory
Nowa Cerekwia
Kietrz
Rydultowy
Pszów
Wodzisław Śląski
Velké Losiny
Branice
Pilszcz
Šumperk
Bruntál
Bludov
Velké Heraltice
Krzyżanowice
Gorzyce
Pawłowice
Jastrzębie Zdrój
Rýmařov
Libina
Horni Benešov
Leskovec
Opava
Kravárе
Dolni Benešov
Hlučín
Bohumín
Karviná
Břidličná
Hradec nad Moravicí
Melč
Ostrava
Orlová
Havířov
Šumvald
Úsov
Slunečná 800
Dětřichov
Dvorce
Dlouhá Loučka
Uničov
Moravský Beroun
Budišov
Vítkov
Klimkovice
Bílovec
Skoczów
Nízký Jeseník
Šternberk
Litovel
Štěpánov
Fulnek
Studenka
Vratimov
Frýdek-Místek
Český Těšín
Cieszyn
Třinec
Ustroń
Město Libavá
Odry
Příbor
Dobrá
Baška
Senice na Hané
Bělkovice-Lašťany
Fidlův kopec 680
Potštát
Nový Jičín
Kopřivnice
Frydlant nad Ostravicí
Bystrice
Jablunkov
Olomouc
Velké Bystřice
Bělotín
Hranice
Velky Ujezd
Slatinice
Konice
Hrochov
Kostelec na Hané
Tršice
Hustopeče nad Bečvou
Frenštát pod Radhoštěm
Morávka
Lysá h. 1323
Moravskoslezské Beskydy
Lipník nad Bečvou
Zbrašovské aragonitové jeskyně
Hodslavice
Horní Lomná
Protivanov
Plumlov
Prostějov
Brodek u Přerova
Přerov
Býškovice
Kelč
Branky
Valašské Meziříčí
Rožnov pod Radhoštěm
Horní Bečva
Staré Hamry
Svrčinovec
Čadca
Drevohostice
Bystřice pod Hostýnem
Jablůnka
Klokočov
Staškov
Raková
Tovačov
Vysoká nad Kysucou
Turzovka
Kojetín
Chropyně
Hoštálkova
Velké Karlovice
Makov
Ivanovice na Hané
Holešov
Vsetín
Vyškov
Kroměříž
Hulín
Liptál
Nový Hrozenkov
Veľký Javorník 1071
Veľké Rovné
Kysucké Nové Mesto
Morkovice-Slížany
Zdounky
Kvasice
Tlumačov
Fryšták
Kašava
Zámek Vizovice
Zlín
Ústí
Valašská Polanka
Horná Mariková
Slavkov u Brna
Otrokovice
Vizovice
Lidečko
Lysá pod Makytou
Bytča
Teplička nad Váhom
Žilina
Zámek Bučovice
Zámek Nesovice
Napajedla
Brdo 587
Valašské Klobouky
Púchov
Bučovice
Nesovice
Koryčany
Buchlovice
Luhačovice
Vlachovice
Brumov-Bylnice
Udiča
Plevnik-Drienové
Strečno
Vrútky
Ždánice
Osvětimany
Staré Město
Uherské Hradiště
Slavičin
Bojkovice
Červený Kamen
Lednické-Rovné
Beluša
Považská Bystrica
Rajecké Teplice
Rajec
Kunovice
Kyjov
Zarošice
Uherský Ostroh
Uherský Brod
Nivnice
Bánov
Horná Súča
Nemšová
Ilava
Pružina
Domaniža
Fačkov
Martinske hole
Klaštor pod Znievom
Čejč
Bzenec
Dubňany
Blatnice
Slavkov
Veselí nad Moravou
Strání
Starý Hrozenkov
Bílé Karpaty
Dubnica nad Váhom
Mojtín
Strážov 1213
Trenčianske Teplá
Trenčianske Teplice
Drietoma
Strážnice
Hodonín
Velká nad Veličkou
Trenčín
Trenčianska Turná
Valaská Belá
Nitrianske Pravno
Kl'ačno
Skalica
Holíč
Vrbovce
Moravské Lieskové
Bošáca
Trenčianske Stankovce
Svinná
Nitrianske Rudno
Bojnice
Kopčany
Radošovce
Myjava
Stará Turá
Bzince
Nové Mesto
Dubodiel
Prievidza
Kúty
Sobotište
Čachtický hrad
Čachtice
Bánovce nad Bebravou
Nováky
Handlová
Šaštinské Stráže
Dojč
Senica
Borský Mikuláš
Krajné
Podolie
Hrad Dučov
Zlatniky
Hradište
Rybany
Kaštiel' v. Zemianskych Kostol'anoch
Zemianske-Kostol'any
Partizánske
Oslany
Vtáčnik 1346
Žiar nad Hronom
Moravský Svätý Ján
Jablonica
Brezová pod Bradlom
Vrbové
Horná Streda
Piešťany
Žabokreky
Kaštiel' Veľké Uherce
Veľké Uherce
Bošany
Lakšárska Nová Ves
Dechtice
Chtelnica
Banka
Radošina
Bojná
Topoľčany
Hliník nad Hronom
Malé Karpaty
Studienka
Veľké Leváre
Trstin
Smolenice
Plavecký Mikuláš
Jaskyna Driny
Veľké Kostoľany
Drahovce
Ludanice
Solčany
Ponitrie
Skýcov
Malá Lehota
Vyhne
Žarnovica
Gajary
Malacky
Rohožník
Veľký Tribeč 829
Hrad Skýcov
Nová Baňa
Štiavnické vrchy
Museum Cervený Kamen
Častá
Pernek
Modra
Trnava
Bučany
Hlohovec
Zámok Hlohovec
Nové Sady
Hrad Gymeš
Sľažany
Topoľčianky
Zlaté Moravce
Sitno 1009
Budmerice
Cifer
Rišňovce
Dvorníky
Zbehy
Výčapy-Opatovce
Jelenec
Pukanec
Lozorno
Pezinok
Stupava
Svätý Jur
Voderady
Sereď
Pata
Veľké Zálužie
Nitra
Tesárske-Mlyňany
Kozárovce
Hronský Beňadik
Tlmače
Hontianske Nemce
Blatné
Pusté Ulany
Šoporňa
Vráble
Podlužany
Zemberovce
Cabaj-Čápor
Ivanka
Veľký Cetín
Bernolákovo
Sládkovičovo
Galanta
Močenok
Mojmírovce
Kalná
Levice
Bratislava
Devín Hrad
Jelka
Šaľa
Lok
Mýtne Ludany
Hohenau
E462
E442
E75
E50
E65
E571
E58
E572
D1
D2
D35
D46
D48
D55
D56
R1
R2
A1
86
97
111
112
130
174
244

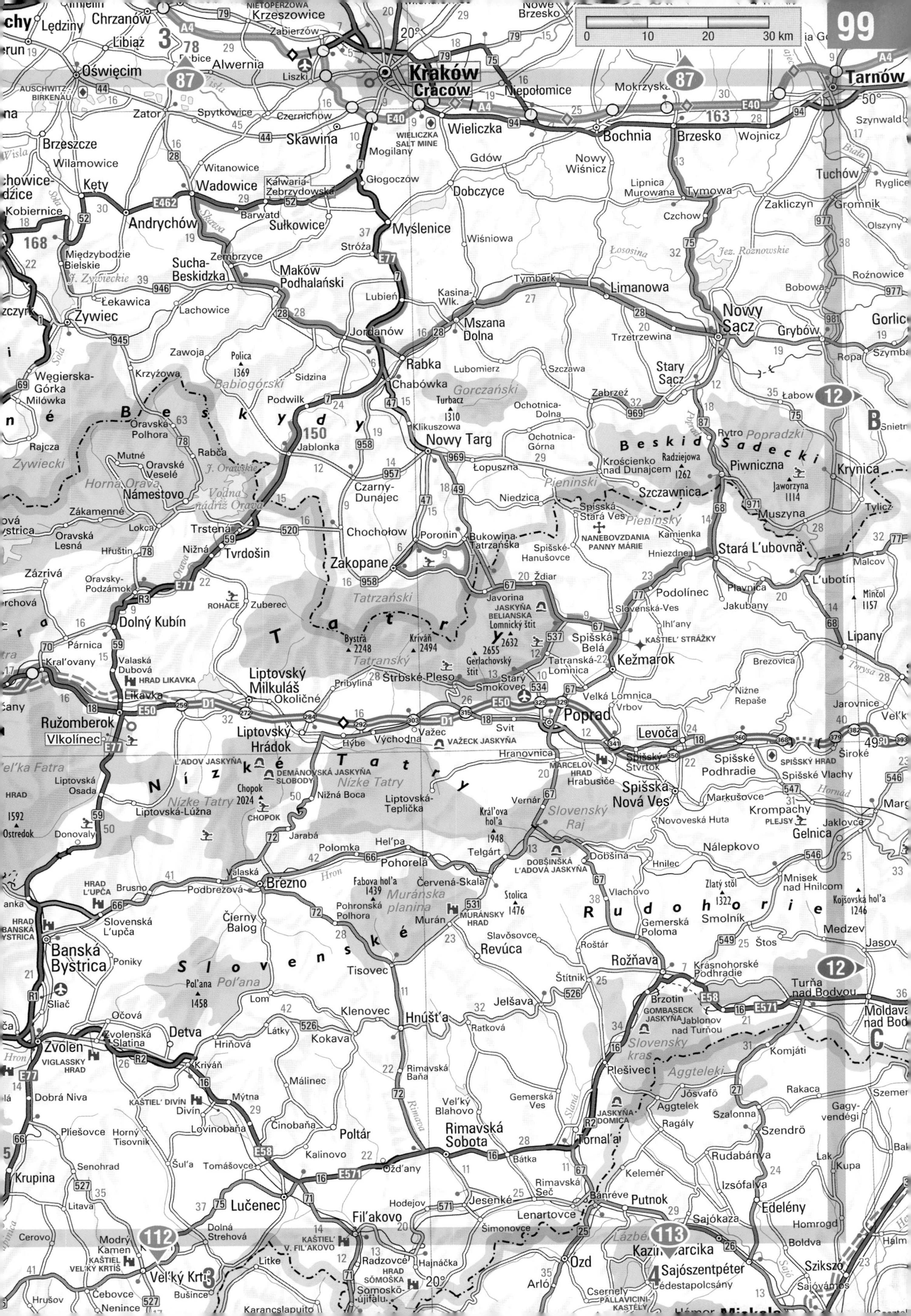
0 10 20 30 km
Chrzanów
Lędziny
Libiąż
Krzeszowice
Zabierzów
Alwernia
Liszki
Kraków
Cracow
Niepołomice
Mokrzyska
Tarnów
Oświęcim
AUSCHWITZ-BIRKENAU
Zator
Spytkowice
Czernichów
Skawina
WIELICZKA SALT MINE
Wieliczka
Bochnia
Brzesko
Wojnicz
Szynwald
Brzeszcze
Wilamowice
Mogilany
Gdów
Nowy Wiśnicz
Witanowice
Wadowice
Kalwaria-Zebrzydowska
Głogoczów
Dobczyce
Lipnica Murowana
Tymowa
Tuchów
Ryglice
Kęty
Kobiernice
Andrychów
Barwałd
Sułkowice
Myślenice
Czchow
Zakliczyn
Gromnik
Olszyny
Międzybodzie Bielskie
Zembrzyce
Stróża
Wiśniowa
Łososina
Jez. Rożnowskie
Sucha-Beskidzka
Maków Podhalański
J. Żywieckie
Łekawica
Lubień
Kasina-Wlk.
Tymbark
Limanowa
Bobowa
Rożnowice
Żywiec
Lachowice
Mszana Dolna
Nowy Sącz
Grybów
Gorlice
Jordanów
Trzetrzewina
Zawoja
Polica 1369
Rabka
Lubomierz
Szczawa
Stary Sącz
Ropa
Szymbark
Węgierska-Górka
Milówka
Krzyżowa
Babiogórski
Sidzina
Chabówka
Gorczański
Turbacz 1310
Zabrzeż
Łabow
Beskydy
Podwilk
Ochotnica-Dolna
Oravská Polhora
Jablonka
Klikuszowa
Nowy Targ
Ochotnica-Górna
Beskid Sądecki
Rytro
Popradzki
Rajcza
Żywiecki
Mutné
Oravské Veselé
Rabča
J. Oravské
Łopuszna
Krościenko nad Dunajcem
Radziejowa 1262
Piwniczna
Krynica
Horná Orava
Námestovo
Vodná nádrž Orava
Czarny-Dunajec
Niedzica
Pieniński
Szczawnica
Jaworzyna 1114
Muszyna
Tylicz
Zákamenné
Trstená
Chochołów
Spišská Stará Ves
Pieninský
NANEBOVZDANIA PANNY MÁRIE
Kamienka
Oravská Lesná
Lokca
Hruštín
Nižná
Tvrdošín
Poronin
Bukowina Tatrzańska
Spišské-Hanušovce
Hniezdne
Stará Ľubovňa
Zázrivá
Oravsky-Podzámok
Zakopane
Ždiar
Podolínec
Malcov
Ľubotín
Mincol 1157
ROHÁČE
Zuberec
Tatrzański
Javorina
JASKYŇA BELIANSKA
Lomnický štít 2632
Slovenská-Ves
Plavnica
Jakubany
Ihľany
Dolný Kubín
Tatry
Bystrá 2248
Kriváň 2494
Gerlachovský štít 2655
Spišská Belá
KAŠTIEĽ STRÁŽKY
Kežmarok
Lipany
Párnica
Valaská Dubová
Kraľovany
Tatranský
HRAD LIKAVKA
Liptovský Mikuláš
Pribylina
Štrbské Pleso
Starý Smokovec
Tatranská Lomnica
Brezovica
Toryša
Likavka
Okoličné
Veľká Lomnica
Vrbov
Nižne Repaše
Jarovnice
Veľký
Ružomberok
Vlkolínec
Liptovský Hrádok
Hýbe
Východna
Važec
VAŽECKÁ JASKYŇA
Svit
Poprad
Levoča
Široké
Veľka Fatra
Liptovská Osada
ĽADOVÁ JASKYŇA
DEMÄNOVSKÁ JASKYŇA SLOBODY
Nízke Tatry
Hranovnica
MARCELOV HRAD
Hrabušice
Spišský Štvrtok
Spišské Podhradie
SPIŠSKÝ HRAD
Spišské Vlachy
HRAD
1592 Ostredok
Chopok 2024
Nižná Boca
Liptovská-Teplička
Vernár
Spišská Nová Ves
Markušovce
Hornád
Krompachy
Margecany
Liptovská-Lúžna
CHOPOK
Donovaly
Kráľova hoľa 1948
Slovenský Raj
Novoveská Huta
PLEJSY
Jaklovce
Gelnica
Jarabá
Helpa
Polomka
Pohorelá
Telgárt
DOBŠINSKÁ ĽADOVÁ JASKYŇA
Dobšiná
Nálepkovo
Hnilec
Valaská
Brezno
Hron
Fabova hoľa 1439
Červená-Skala
Stolica 1476
Muránska planina
Vlachovo
Mnisek nad Hnilcom
Zlatý stôl 1322
Kojšovská hoľa 1246
HRAD ĽUPČA
Brusno
Podbrezová
Pohronská Polhora
MURÁNSKY HRAD
Murán
Rudohorie
Gemerská Poloma
Smolník
Medzev
HRAD BANSKÁ BYSTRICA
Slovenská Ľupča
Čierny Balog
Slavošovce
Revúca
Roštár
Rožňava
Štos
Jasov
Banská Bystrica
Poniky
Slovenské
Tisovec
Štítnik
Krásnohorské Podhradie
Turňa nad Bodvou
Poľana 1458
Lom
Klenovec
Jelšava
Brzotín
GOMBASECK JASKYŇA
Jablonov nad Turňou
Moldava nad Bodvou
Sliač
Očová
Detva
Zvolenská Slatina
Látky
Kokava
Hnúšťa
Ratková
Slovensky kras
Komjáti
Zvolen
VIGLASSKY HRAD
Hriňová
Kriváň
Rimavská Baňa
Plešivec
Aggteleki
Dobrá Niva
KAŠTIEĽ DIVÍN
Divín
Mýtna
Málinec
Veľký Blahovo
Gemerská Ves
Jósvafő
Aggtelek
Rakaca
Szemere
Gagyvendégi
Lovinobaňa
Cinobaňa
JASKYŇA DOMICA
Szalonna
Ragály
Szendrő
Pliešovce
Horný Tisovník
Poltár
Rimavská Sobota
Tornaľa
Rimava
Slaná
Senohrad
Šuľa
Tomášovce
Kalinovo
Ožďany
Bátka
Rudabánya
Lak
Kupa
Krupina
Kelemér
Izsófalva
Litava
Lučenec
Hodejov
Jesenské
Rimavská Seč
Bánréve
Putnok
Edelény
Dolná Strehová
Fiľakovo
Lenartovce
Šimonovce
Sajókaza
Homrogd
Cerovo
Modrý Kameň
KAŠTIEĽ VEĽKÝ KRTÍŠ
KAŠTIEĽ V. FIĽAKOVO
Radzovce
Hajnáčka
Boldva
Hálm
Litke
HRAD SOMOŠKA
Somoškő-újifalu
Ozd
Kazincbarcika
Sajószentpéter
Edestapolcsány
Szikszó
Sajóvámos
Veľký Krtíš
Arló
Cserneky
PALLAVICINI-KASTÉLY
Hrušov
Čebovce
Nenince
Bušince
Karancslapujtő
Sajó
A4
E40
E77
E462
E50
E58
E571
D1
R1
R2
R3
87
112
113
12
B
C
3
4
49°
50°
20°
163
168
150

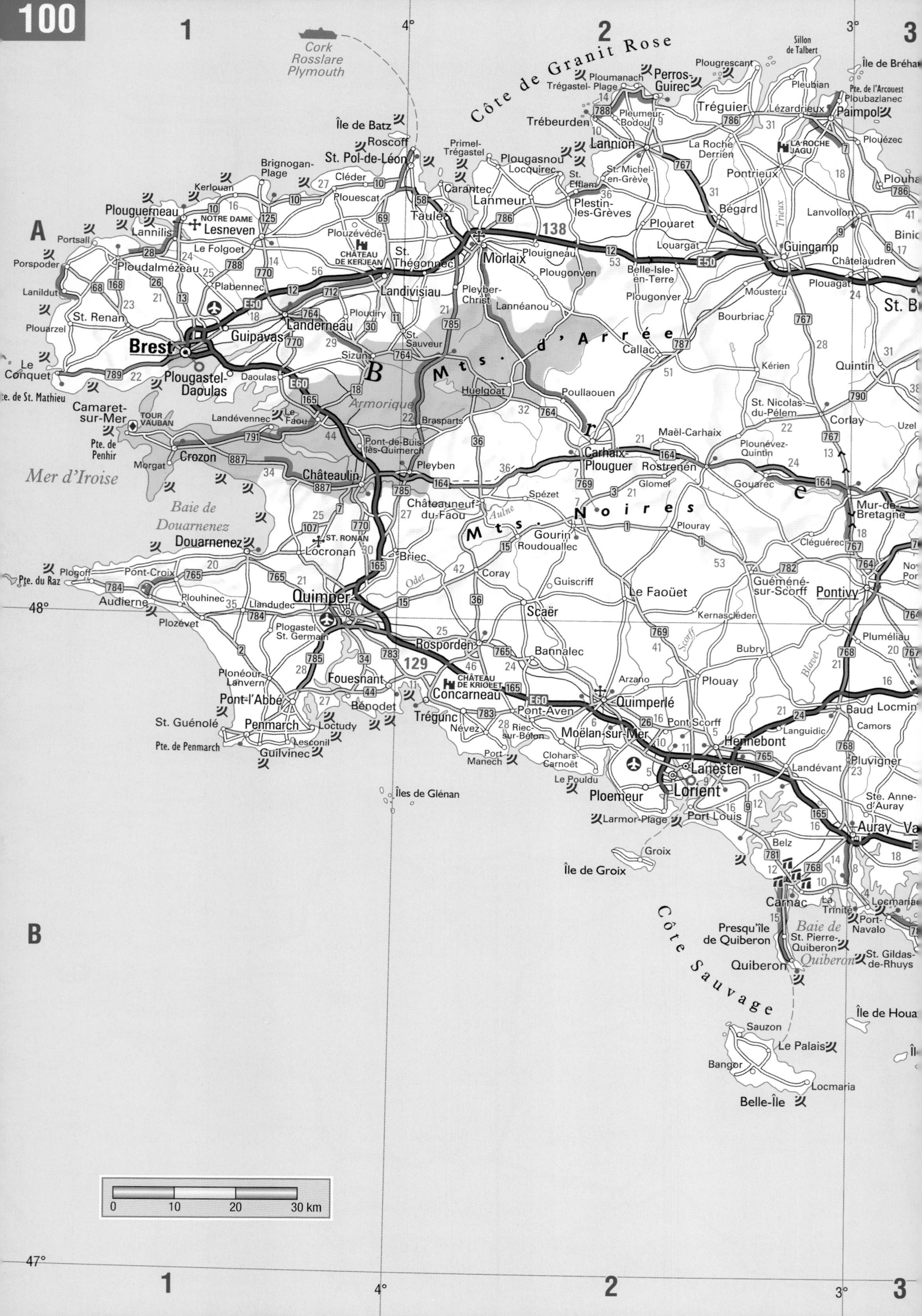

1
2
3
4°
3°
Cork
Rosslare
Plymouth
Côte de Granit Rose
Sillon de Talbert
Île de Bréhat
Plougrescant
Ploumanach
Perros-Guirec
Trégastel-Plage
Pleubian
Pte. de l'Arcouest
Ploubazlanec
Paimpol
Tréguier
Lézardrieux
Trébeurden
Pleumeur-Bodou
Lannion
La Roche Derrien
LA ROCHE JAGU
Plouézec
Île de Batz
Roscoff
St. Pol-de-Léon
Primel-Trégastel
Plougasnou
Locquirec
St. Efflam
St. Michel-en-Grève
Pontrieux
Plouha
Brignogan-Plage
Cléder
Kerlouan
Plouescat
Carantec
Lanmeur
Plestin-les-Grèves
Bégard
Lanvollon
Plouguerneau
Lannilis
NOTRE DAME
Lesneven
Plouzévédé
Taulé
Plouaret
Binic
A
Portsall
Le Folgoet
CHÂTEAU DE KERJEAN
St. Thégonnec
Morlaix
Plouigneau
Louargat
Guingamp
Châtelaudren
Porspoder
Ploudalmézeau
Plabennec
Landivisiau
Pleyber-Christ
Plougonven
Belle-Isle-en-Terre
Plouagat
Lanildut
Plougonver
Mousteru
St. B
St. Renan
Landerneau
Ploudiry
Lannéanou
Bourbriac
Plouarzel
Brest
Guipavas
St. Sauveur
Mts. d'Arrée
Callac
Le Conquet
Sizun
Kérien
Quintin
Plougastel-Daoulas
Daoulas
Huelgoat
Poullaouen
Pte. de St. Mathieu
Camaret-sur-Mer
TOUR VAUBAN
Landévennec
Le Faou
Armorique
Brasparts
St. Nicolas-du-Pélem
Corlay
Uzel
Pte. de Penhir
Crozon
Morgat
Pont-de-Buis-lès-Quimerch
Maël-Carhaix
Plounévez-Quintin
Carhaix-Plouguer
Rostrenen
Mer d'Iroise
Châteaulin
Pleyben
Glomel
Gouarec
Baie de Douarnenez
Châteauneuf-du-Faou
Spézet
Mur-de-Bretagne
Mts. Noires
Douarnenez
ST. RONAN
Locronan
Gourin
Roudouallec
Plouray
Cléguérec
Briec
Plogoff
Pont-Croix
Pte. du Raz
Coray
Audierne
Guiscriff
Guémené-sur-Scorff
Pontivy
Odet
Aulne
Plouhinec
Llandudec
Quimper
Le Faouët
48°
Plozévet
Plogastel St. Germain
Scaër
Kernascléden
Rosporden
Bannalec
Scorff
Bubry
Pluméliau
Blavet
Plonéour-Lanvern
Fouesnant
CHÂTEAU DE KRIOLET
Concarneau
Arzano
Plouay
Pont-l'Abbé
Bénodet
Trégunc
Pont-Aven
Quimperlé
Baud
Locminé
St. Guénolé
Penmarch
Loctudy
Névez
Riec-sur-Bélon
Moëlan-sur-Mer
Pont Scorff
Languidic
Camors
Pte. de Penmarch
Lesconil
Guilvinec
Port Manech
Clohars-Carnoët
Hennebont
Lanester
Landévant
Pluvigner
Le Pouldu
Îles de Glénan
Ploemeur
Lorient
Ste. Anne-d'Auray
Larmor-Plage
Port Louis
Auray
Groix
Belz
Île de Groix
B
Carnac
La Trinité
Locmariaquer
Port-Navalo
Côte Sauvage
Presqu'île de Quiberon
Baie de Quiberon
St. Pierre-Quiberon
Quiberon
St. Gildas-de-Rhuys
Île de Houat
Sauzon
Le Palais
Bangor
Locmaria
Belle-Île
E50
E60
0
10
20
30 km
47°

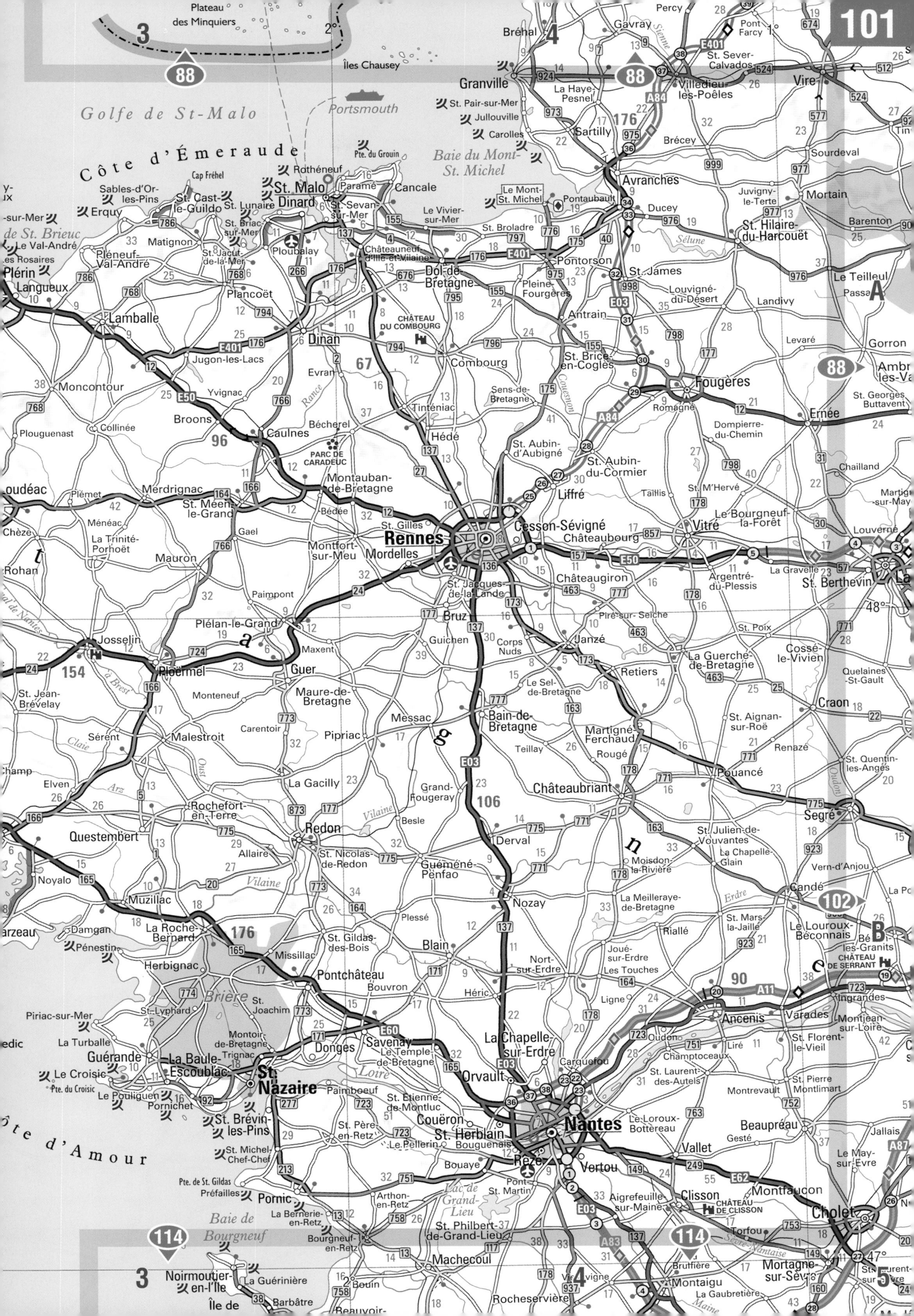
Plateau des Minquiers
Îles Chausey
Golfe de St-Malo
Portsmouth
Côte d'Émeraude
Cap Fréhel
Sables-d'Or-les-Pins
Erquy
St. Cast-le-Guildo
St. Lunaire
Dinard
St. Malo
Paramé
Cancale
Rothéneuf
Pte. du Grouin
Baie du Mont-St. Michel
Le Mont-St. Michel
Granville
St. Pair-sur-Mer
Jullouville
Carolles
Bréhal
Gavray
Percy
Pont-Farcy
Villedieu-les-Poêles
St. Sever-Calvados
Vire
La Haye-Pesnel
Sartilly
Brécey
Sourdeval
Avranches
Pontaubault
Ducey
Juvigny-le-Tertre
Mortain
St. Hilaire-du-Harcouët
Barenton
Le Teilleul
Sélune
Pontorson
St. James
Louvigné-du-Désert
Landivy
Le Vivier-sur-Mer
St. Broladre
Dol-de-Bretagne
Pleine-Fougères
Châteauneuf-d'Ille-et-Vilaine
St.-Sevan-sur-Mer
Pléneuf-Val-André
Le Val-André
Les Rosaires
Plérin
Langueux
Matignon
St. Jacut-de-la-Mer
St. Briac-sur-Mer
Ploubalay
Plancoët
Lamballe
Dinan
Jugon-les-Lacs
Moncontour
Yvignac
Broons
Caulnes
Évran
Combourg
CHÂTEAU DU COMBOURG
Antrain
St. Brice-en-Coglès
Fougères
Romagné
Levaré
Gorron
Ernée
St. Georges-Buttavent
Sens-de-Bretagne
Tinténiac
Hédé
Bécherel
PARC DE CARADEUC
Montauban-de-Bretagne
St. Aubin-d'Aubigné
St. Aubin-du-Cormier
Liffré
Dompierre-du-Chemin
Chailland
St. M'Hervé
Taillis
Le Bourgneuf-la-Forêt
Vitré
Louverné
Plouguenast
Collinée
Merdrignac
Plémet
St. Méen-le-Grand
Ménéac
La Trinité-Porhoët
Gael
Mauron
Bédée
Montfort-sur-Meu
St. Gilles
Rennes
Mordelles
Cesson-Sévigné
Châteaubourg
Châteaugiron
Argentré-du-Plessis
La Gravelle
St. Berthevin
St. Jacques-de-la-Lande
Bruz
Paimpont
Plélan-le-Grand
Josselin
Ploërmel
Maxent
Guer
Guichen
Corps Nuds
Janzé
Piré-sur-Seiche
La Guerche-de-Bretagne
Retiers
Cossé-le-Vivien
Quelaines-St-Gault
St. Poix
Craon
St. Jean-Brévelay
Monteneuf
Maure-de-Bretagne
Le Sel-de-Bretagne
Bain-de-Bretagne
Messac
Pipriac
Carentoir
Malestroit
Sérent
Teillay
Martigné-Ferchaud
Rougé
St. Aignan-sur-Roë
Renazé
St. Quentin-les-Anges
Elven
La Gacilly
Grand-Fougeray
Châteaubriant
Pouancé
Segré
Rochefort-en-Terre
Questembert
Redon
Besle
Derval
St. Julien-de-Vouvantes
La Chapelle-Glain
Vern-d'Anjou
Allaire
St. Nicolas-de-Redon
Guémené-Penfao
Moisdon-la-Rivière
Noyalo
Muzillac
Nozay
La Meilleraye-de-Bretagne
Candé
Damgan
La Roche-Bernard
Pénestin
Plessé
St. Mars-la-Jaille
Le Louroux-Béconnais
St. Gildas-des-Bois
Blain
Riallé
Joué-sur-Erdre
Les Touches
CHÂTEAU DE SERRANT
Herbignac
Missillac
Pontchâteau
Bouvron
Nort-sur-Erdre
Héric
Ligné
Ancenis
Varades
Ingrandes
Brière
St. Lyphard
St. Joachim
Piriac-sur-Mer
La Turballe
Guérande
Montoir-de-Bretagne
Trignac
Donges
Savenay
Le Temple-de-Bretagne
La Chapelle-sur-Erdre
Oudon
Liré
Champtoceaux
Montjean-sur-Loire
St. Florent-le-Vieil
Le Croisic
Pte. du Croisic
La Baule-Escoublac
Le Pouliguen
Pornichet
St. Nazaire
Paimboeuf
St. Étienne-de-Montluc
Orvault
Carquefou
St. Laurent-des-Autels
Montrevault
St. Pierre Montlimart
Côte d'Amour
St. Brévin-les-Pins
St. Michel-Chef-Chef
St. Père-en-Retz
Couëron
St. Herblain
Le Pellerin
Bouguenais
Nantes
Le Loroux-Bottereau
Beaupréau
Jallais
Vallet
Gesté
Le May-sur-Èvre
Bouaye
Rezé
Vertou
Pte. de St. Gildas
Préfailles
Pornic
Arthon-en-Retz
Lac de Grand-Lieu
Pont-St. Martin
Aigrefeuille-sur-Maine
Clisson
CHÂTEAU DE CLISSON
Montfaucon
Cholet
La Bernerie-en-Retz
Baie de Bourgneuf
Bourgneuf-en-Retz
St. Philbert-de-Grand-Lieu
Torfou
Machecoul
Bruffière
Mortagne-sur-Sèvre
Noirmoutier-en-l'Île
La Guérinière
Barbâtre
Île de
Bouin
Beauvoir-
Vieillevigne
Rocheservière
Montaigu
La Gaubretière
Sèvre Nantaise
Vilaine
Loire
Erdre
Oust
Rance
88
102
114

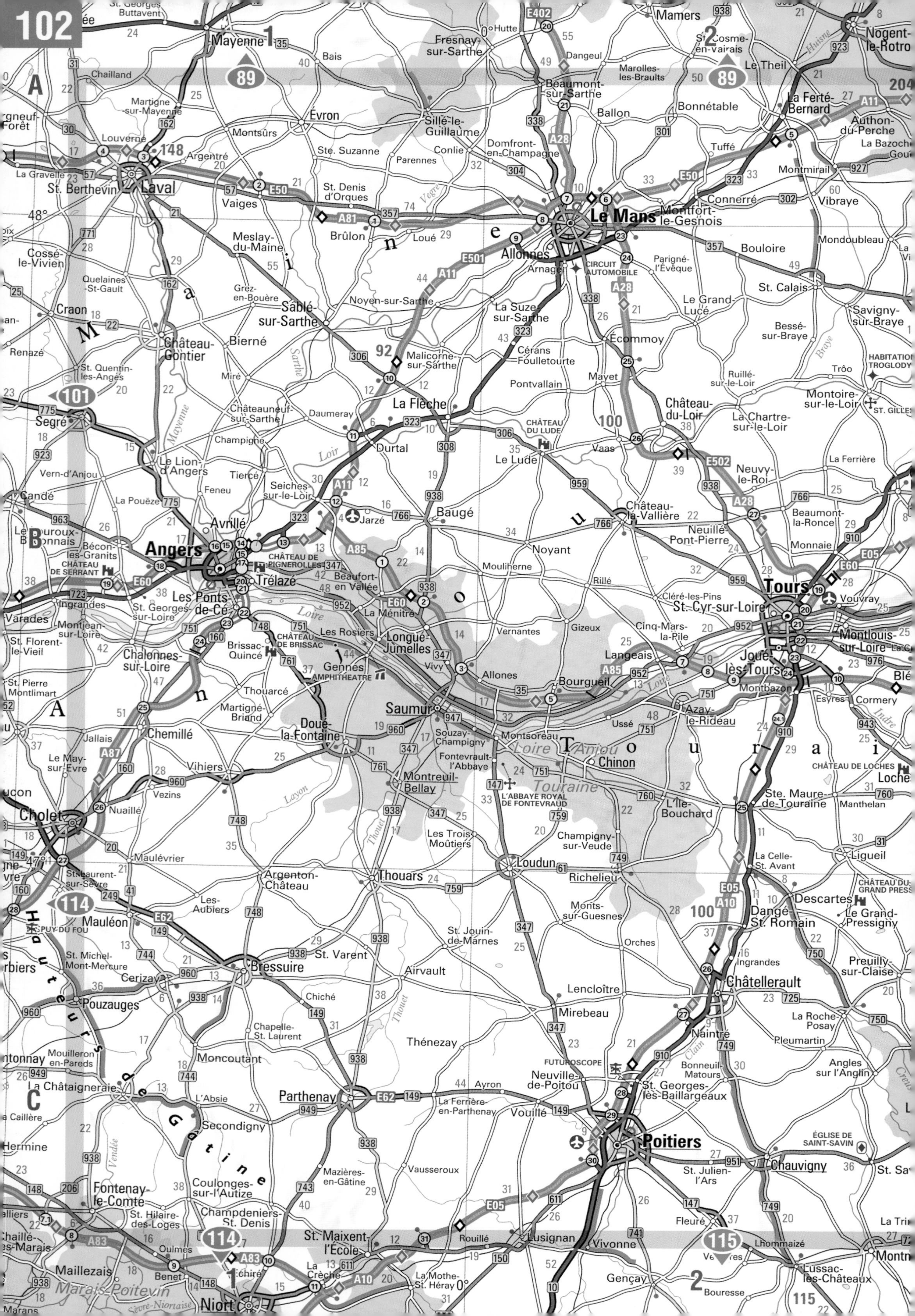
Mayenne
Bais
Fresnay-sur-Sarthe
Hutte
Mamers
St. Cosme-en-Vairais
Nogent-le-Rotrou
Le Theil
Chailland
Dangeul
Marolles-les-Braults
Beaumont-sur-Sarthe
Bonnétable
La Ferté-Bernard
Authon-du-Perche
La Bazoche-Gouet
Martigné-sur-Mayenne
Évron
Sillé-le-Guillaume
Ballon
Louverné
Montsûrs
Ste. Suzanne
Conlie
Domfront-en-Champagne
Tuffé
Argentré
Parennes
Montmirail
La Gravelle
St. Berthevin
Laval
Vaiges
St. Denis d'Orques
Le Mans
Montfort-le-Gesnois
Connerré
Vibraye
Brûlon
Loué
Meslay-du-Maine
Allonnes
Arnage
CIRCUIT AUTOMOBILE
Parigné-l'Évêque
Bouloire
Mondoubleau
Cossé-le-Vivien
Quelaines-St-Gault
Grez-en-Bouère
Sablé-sur-Sarthe
Noyen-sur-Sarthe
La Suze-sur-Sarthe
Le Grand-Lucé
St. Calais
Craon
Château-Gontier
Bierné
Écommoy
Bessé-sur-Braye
Savigny-sur-Braye
Renazé
Malicorne-sur-Sarthe
Cérans-Foulletourte
St. Quentin-les-Anges
Miré
Pontvallain
Mayet
Ruillé-sur-le-Loir
Trôo
HABITATION TROGLODYTE
Segré
Châteauneuf-sur-Sarthe
Daumeray
La Flèche
CHÂTEAU DU LUDE
Château-du-Loir
Montoire-sur-le-Loir
La Chartre-sur-le-Loir
ST. GILLES
Champigné
Durtal
Le Lude
Vaas
Le Lion-d'Angers
Vern-d'Anjou
Tiercé
Seiches-sur-le-Loir
Neuvy-le-Roi
La Ferrière
Candé
Feneu
La Pouëze
Jarzé
Baugé
Château-la-Vallière
Beaumont-la-Ronce
Le Louroux-Béconnais
Avrillé
Noyant
Neuillé-Pont-Pierre
Monnaie
Bécon-les-Granits
Angers
CHÂTEAU DE SERRANT
CHÂTEAU DE PIGNEROLLES
Beaufort-en-Vallée
Mouliherne
Trélazé
Rillé
Cléré-les-Pins
Tours
Vouvray
Ingrandes
Les Ponts-de-Cé
St. Georges-sur-Loire
La Ménitré
St. Cyr-sur-Loire
Varades
Montjean-sur-Loire
Les Rosiers
Longué-Jumelles
Vernantes
Gizeux
Cinq-Mars-la-Pile
Montlouis-sur-Loire
St. Florent-le-Vieil
CHÂTEAU DE BRISSAC
Brissac-Quincé
Chalonnes-sur-Loire
Gennes
Vivy
Langeais
Joué-lès-Tours
Allones
Bourgueil
AMPHITHÉÂTRE
St. Pierre-Montlimart
Thouarcé
Montbazon
Esvres
Cormery
Martigné-Briand
Saumur
Azay-le-Rideau
Doué-la-Fontaine
Montsoreau
Ussé
Chemillé
Jallais
Souzay-Champigny
Fontevrault-l'Abbaye
Loire Anjou Touraine
Chinon
CHÂTEAU DE LOCHES
Loches
Le May-sur-Èvre
Vihiers
Montreuil-Bellay
L'ABBAYE ROYAL DE FONTEVRAUD
L'Île-Bouchard
Ste. Maure-de-Touraine
Manthelan
Cholet
Vezins
Nuaillé
Les Trois Moûtiers
Champigny-sur-Veude
Ligueil
Maulévrier
Loudun
Richelieu
La Celle-St. Avant
St. Laurent-sur-Sèvre
Argenton-Château
Thouars
CHÂTEAU DU GRAND PRESSIGNY
Descartes
Le Grand-Pressigny
PUY-DU-FOU
Mauléon
Les Aubiers
Monts-sur-Guesnes
Dangé-St. Romain
St. Jouin-de-Marnes
Orches
Ingrandes
Preuilly-sur-Claise
St. Michel-Mont-Mercure
Bressuire
St. Varent
Airvault
Châtellerault
Cerizay
Lencloître
Pouzauges
Chiché
Mirebeau
La Roche-Posay
Chapelle-St. Laurent
Naintré
Pleumartin
Thénezay
Moncoutant
FUTUROSCOPE
Bonneuil-Matours
Angles sur l'Anglin
Fontenay
Mouilleron en-Pareds
Neuville-de-Poitou
La Châtaigneraie
Ayron
St. Georges-lès-Baillargeaux
Parthenay
La Ferrière-en-Parthenay
Vouillé
L'Absie
Secondigny
Poitiers
ÉGLISE DE SAINT-SAVIN
La Caillère
L'Hermine
Vausseroux
St. Julien-l'Ars
Chauvigny
St. Savin
Mazières-en-Gâtine
Fontenay-le-Comte
Coulonges-sur-l'Autize
Champdeniers-St. Denis
St. Hilaire-des-Loges
Fleuré
Chaillé-les-Marais
Rouillé
Lusignan
St. Maixent-l'École
Vivonne
Lhommaizé
Montmorillon
Oulmes
Maillezais
Benet
Échiré
La Crèche
La Mothe-St. Héray
Gençay
Lussac-les-Châteaux
Bouresse
Marais Poitevin
Niort
Marans
Hauteurs de Gâtine
Maine
Anjou
Touraine
Mayenne
Sarthe
Loir
Loire
Layon
Thouet
Vègre
Huisne
Braye
Indre
Vendée
Clain
Creuse
Sèvre-Niortaise
E402
E50
A81
E501
A11
A28
E502
A85
E60
E05
A87
E62
A10
A83
89
101
114
115
100
148
92
204

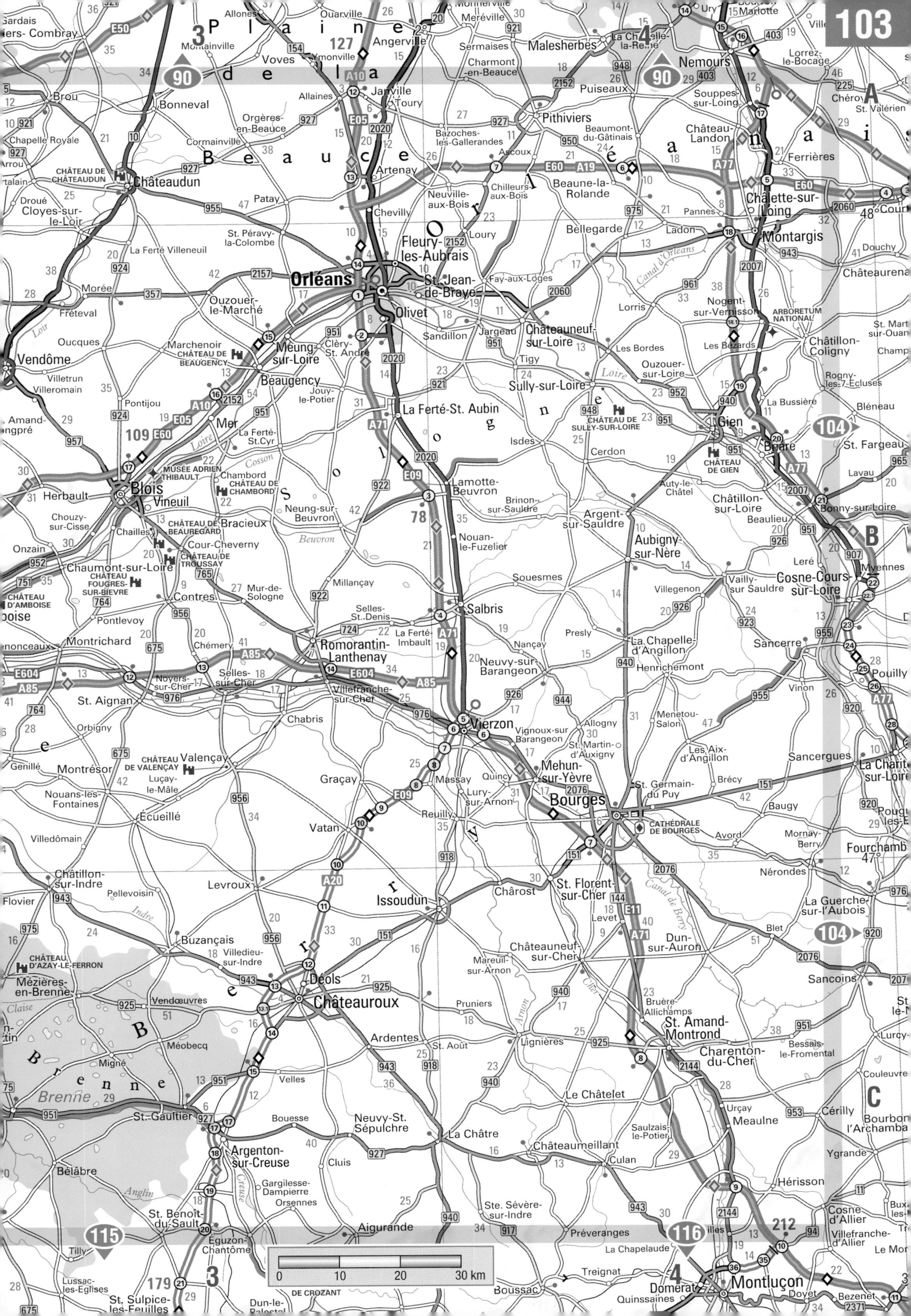

Plaine de la Beauce
Sologne
Berry
Brenne
Orléans
Fleury-les-Aubrais
St. Jean-de-Braye
Olivet
Châteaudun
Vendôme
Blois
Vineuil
Meung-sur-Loire
Beaugency
Pithiviers
Montargis
Châlette-sur-Loing
Nemours
Gien
Briare
Sully-sur-Loire
Châteauneuf-sur-Loire
Jargeau
La Ferté-St. Aubin
Lamotte-Beuvron
Salbris
Romorantin-Lanthenay
Vierzon
Mehun-sur-Yèvre
Bourges
Issoudun
Châteauroux
Déols
Argenton-sur-Creuse
La Châtre
St. Amand-Montrond
Montluçon
Cosne-Cours-sur-Loire
Sancerre
Aubigny-sur-Nère
Cour-Cheverny
Contres
Montrichard
St. Aignan
Valençay
Vatan
Levroux
Buzançais
St. Gaultier
Le Blanc
Châtillon-sur-Indre
Dun-sur-Auron
St. Florent-sur-Cher
Lignières
Châteaumeillant
Neuvy-St. Sépulchre
Aigurande
Éguzon-Chantôme
Domerat
Malesherbes
Puiseaux
Angerville
Janville
Artenay
Patay
Bonneval
Brou
Cloyes-sur-le-Loir
Château-Landon
Souppes-sur-Loing
Ferrières
Courtenay
Châtillon-Coligny
Bléneau
St. Fargeau
Bonny-sur-Loire
La Charité-sur-Loire
Sancergues
La Guerche-sur-l'Aubois
Sancoins
Cérilly
Bourbon-l'Archambault
Hérisson
Cosne-d'Allier
CHÂTEAU DE CHÂTEAUDUN
CHÂTEAU DE BEAUGENCY
CHÂTEAU DE CHAMBORD
CHÂTEAU DE BEAUREGARD
CHÂTEAU DE TROUSSAY
CHÂTEAU FOUGRES-SUR-BIEVRE
CHÂTEAU D'AMBOISE
CHÂTEAU DE VALENÇAY
CHÂTEAU D'AZAY-LE-FERRON
CHÂTEAU DE SULLY-SUR-LOIRE
CHÂTEAU DE GIEN
CATHÉDRALE DE BOURGES
MUSÉE ADRIEN THIBAULT
ARBORETUM NATIONAL
Canal d'Orléans
Canal de Berry
Loire
Cher
Indre
Creuse
A10
A19
A20
A71
A77
A85
E05
E09
E11
E60
E604
0 10 20 30 km

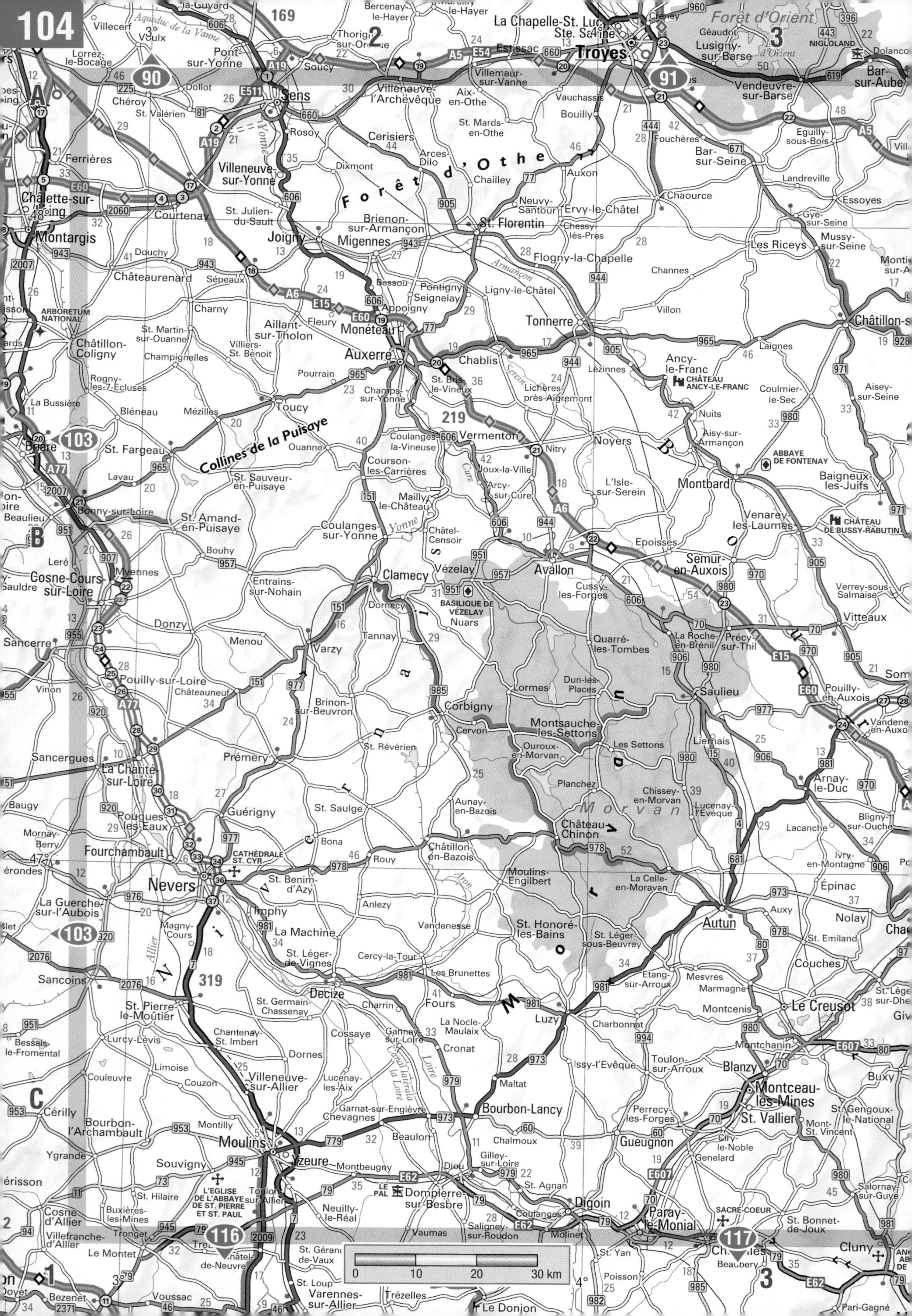

Forêt d'Orient
Troyes
La Chapelle-St. Luc
Ste. Savine
Géaudot
Lusigny-sur-Barse
Nigloland
Dolancourt
Bar-sur-Aube
Vendeuvre-sur-Barse
Estissac
Villemaur-sur-Vanne
Vauchassis
Bouilly
Bercenay-le-Hayer
Thorigny-sur-Oreuse
Soucy
Pont-sur-Yonne
Villecerf
Voulx
Aqueduc de la Vanne
Lorrez-le-Bocage
Dollot
Chéroy
St. Valérien
Sens
Villeneuve-l'Archevêque
Aix-en-Othe
St. Mards-en-Othe
Rosoy
Cerisiers
Arces-Dilo
Dixmont
Forêt d'Othe
Chailley
Auxon
Ferrières
Villeneuve-sur-Yonne
Châlette-sur-Loing
Montargis
Courtenay
St. Julien-du-Sault
Joigny
Brienon-sur-Armançon
Migennes
St. Florentin
Neuvy-Sautour
Ervy-le-Châtel
Chessy-lès-Pres
Fouchères
Bar-sur-Seine
Chaource
Landreville
Essoyes
Gyé-sur-Seine
Mussy-sur-Seine
Les Riceys
Channes
Flogny-la-Chapelle
Armançon
Ligny-le-Châtel
Tonnerre
Villon
Douchy
Châteaurenard
Sépeaux
Charny
Bassou
Pontigny
Seignelay
Appoigny
Aillant-sur-Tholon
Fleury
Monéteau
Auxerre
Chablis
Arboretum National
Châtillon-Coligny
St. Martin-sur-Ouanne
Villiers-St. Benoit
Champignelles
Rogny-les-7-Ecluses
Pourrain
Champs-sur-Yonne
St. Bris-le-Vineux
Lichères-près-Aigremont
Lézinnes
Ancy-le-Franc
Château Ancy-le-Franc
Laignes
Châtillon-sur-Seine
Coulmier-le-Sec
Aisey-sur-Seine
Nuits
Aisy-sur-Armançon
Abbaye de Fontenay
Montbard
Baigneux-les-Juifs
La Bussière
Bléneau
Mézilles
Toucy
Collines de la Puisaye
Briare
St. Fargeau
Ouanne
Coulanges-la-Vineuse
Vermenton
Nitry
Noyers
Courson-les-Carrières
Joux-la-Ville
Arcy-sur-Cure
Cure
L'Isle-sur-Serein
Lavau
St. Sauveur-en-Puisaye
Mailly-le-Château
Bonny-sur-Loire
Beaulieu
St. Amand-en-Puisaye
Coulanges-sur-Yonne
Châtel-Censoir
Venarey-les-Laumes
Château de Bussy-Rabutin
Léré
Bouhy
Epoisses
Semur-en-Auxois
Cosne-Cours-sur-Loire
Myennes
Entrains-sur-Nohain
Clamecy
Vézelay
Avallon
Basilique de Vézelay
Cussy-les-Forges
Verrey-sous-Salmaise
Donzy
Dornecy
Nuars
Quarré-les-Tombes
Vitteaux
Sancerre
Menou
Varzy
Tannay
La Roche-en-Brénil
Précy-sous-Thil
Pouilly-sur-Loire
Vinon
Châteauneuf
Brinon-sur-Beuvron
Lormes
Dun-les-Places
Saulieu
Pouilly-en-Auxois
Vandenesse-en-Auxois
Corbigny
Cervon
Montsauche-les-Settons
Les Settons
Liernais
Sancergues
La Charité-sur-Loire
Prémery
St. Révérien
Ouroux-en-Morvan
Planchez
Chissey-en-Morvan
Arnay-le-Duc
Aunay-en-Bazois
Morvan
Lucenay-l'Evêque
Baugy
Guérigny
St. Saulge
Château-Chinon
Bligny-sur-Ouche
Lacanche
Rougues-les-Eaux
Mornay-Berry
Fourchambault
Bona
Châtillon-en-Bazois
Cathédrale St. Cyr
Rouy
Ivry-en-Montagne
Nevers
St. Benin-d'Azy
Aron
Moulins-Engilbert
La Celle-en-Moravan
Epinac
La Guerche-sur-l'Aubois
Anlezy
Imphy
Magny-Cours
La Machine
Vandenesse
St. Honoré-les-Bains
St. Léger-sous-Beuvray
Autun
Auxy
Nolay
Allier
St. Léger-de-Vignes
Cercy-la-Tour
Les Brunettes
Etang-sur-Arroux
Mesvres
Marmagne
Couches
St. Emiland
Sancoins
Decize
Fours
St. Pierre-le-Moûtier
St. Germain-Chassenay
Charrin
Luzy
Montcenis
Le Creusot
Lurcy-Lévis
Chantenay-St. Imbert
Cossaye
Gannay-sur-Loire
La Nocle-Maulaix
Cronat
Charbonnat
Bessais-le-Fromental
Dornes
Loire
Canal latéral à la Loire
Issy-l'Evêque
Toulon-sur-Arroux
Montchanin
Blanzy
Limoise
Couleuvre
Couzon
Villeneuve-sur-Allier
Lucenay-les-Aix
Maltat
Montceau-les-Mines
Buxy
Cérilly
Bourbon-l'Archambault
Garnat-sur-Engièvre
Chevagnes
Bourbon-Lancy
Perrecy-les-Forges
St. Vallier
St. Gengoux-le-National
Mont-St. Vincent
Ygrande
Montilly
Moulins
Beaulon
Chalmoux
Gueugnon
Ciry-le-Noble
Genelard
Souvigny
Yzeure
Montbeugny
Dompierre-sur-Besbre
Diou
Gilley-sur-Loire
St. Agnan
L'Eglise de l'Abbaye de St. Pierre et St. Paul
St. Hilaire
Toulon-sur-Allier
Le Pal
Neuilly-le-Réal
Digoin
Coulanges
Paray-le-Monial
Sacré-Coeur
Salornay-sur-Guye
St. Bonnet-de-Joux
Buxières-les-Mines
Tronget
Cosne-d'Allier
Villefranche-d'Allier
Vaumas
Saligny-sur-Roudon
Molinet
Charolles
Cluny
Le Montet
Châtel-de-Neuvre
St. Gérand-de-Vaux
St. Yan
Poisson
Beaubery
St. Loup
Varennes-sur-Allier
Trézelles
Le Donjon
Bezenet
Voussac
0 10 20 30 km

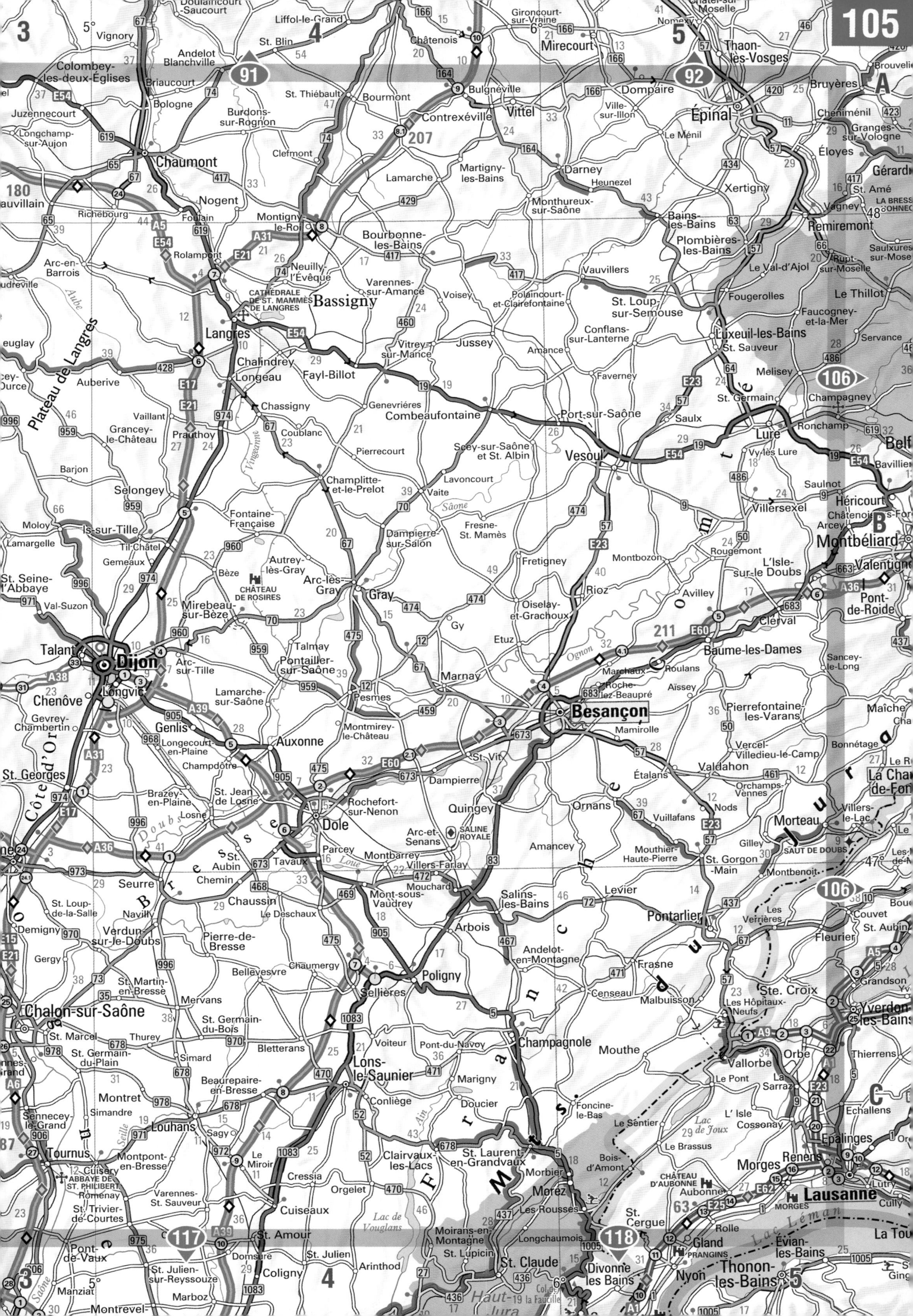

Vignory
Liffol-le-Grand
St. Blin
Andelot
Blanchville
Colombey-les-deux-Églises
Briaucourt
Bologne
Juzennecourt
Longchamp-sur-Aujon
Chaumont
Nogent
Richebourg
Foulain
Rolampont
Arc-en-Barrois
Langres
CATHÉDRALE DE ST. MAMMÈS DE LANGRES
Plateau de Langres
Auberive
Chalindrey
Longeau
Grancey-le-Château
Vaillant
Prauthoy
Barjon
Selongey
Is-sur-Tille
Lamargelle
Moloy
Til-Châtel
Gemeaux
St. Seine-l'Abbaye
Val-Suzon
Mirebeau-sur-Bèze
Bèze
CHÂTEAU DE ROSIRES
Talant
Dijon
Arc-sur-Tille
Chenôve
Longvic
Gevrey-Chambertin
Genlis
Lamarche-sur-Saône
Longecourt-en-Plaine
Champdôtre
Auxonne
St. Georges
Côte d'Or
Brazey-en-Plaine
St. Jean de Losne
Losne
Seurre
St. Aubin
Chemin
Tavaux
Dole
Rochefort-sur-Nenon
Parcey
Chaussin
Le Deschaux
St. Loup-de-la-Salle
Demigny
Navilly
Verdun-sur-le-Doubs
Gergy
Pierre-de-Bresse
Bellevesvre
St. Martin-en-Bresse
Mervans
Chalon-sur-Saône
St. Marcel
Thurey
St. Germain-du-Plain
St. Germain-du-Bois
Simard
Bletterans
Beaurepaire-en-Bresse
Montret
Simandre
Sennecey-le-Grand
Louhans
Sagy
Tournus
Cuisery
ABBAYE DE ST. PHILIBERT
Romenay
Montpont-en-Bresse
Varennes-St. Sauveur
St. Trivier-de-Courtes
Pont-de-Vaux
St. Julien-sur-Reyssouze
Manziat
Marboz
Montrevel-
Domsure
Coligny
St. Amour
St. Julien
Arinthod
Cuiseaux
Le Miroir
Cressia
Orgelet
Lac de Vouglans
Moirans-en-Montagne
St. Lupicin
St. Claude
Haut-Jura
La Faucille
Clairvaux-les-Lacs
St. Laurent-en-Grandvaux
Morbier
Morez
Les Rousses
Longchaumois
Conliège
Lons-le-Saunier
Voiteur
Pont-du-Navoy
Marigny
Doucier
Champagnole
Foncine-le-Bas
Sellières
Poligny
Chaumergy
Arbois
Mont-sous-Vaudrey
Mouchard
Villers-Farlay
Montbarrey
Arc-et-Senans
SALINE ROYALE
Quingey
Dampierre
St. Vit
Montmirey-le-Château
Pesmes
Pontailler-sur-Saône
Talmay
Gray
Arc-lès-Gray
Autrey-lès-Gray
Fontaine-Française
Dampierre-sur-Salon
Champlitte-et-le-Prelot
Coublanc
Chassigny
Fayl-Billot
Vitrey-sur-Mance
Bassigny
Neuilly-l'Évêque
Montigny-le-Roi
Bourbonne-les-Bains
Varennes-sur-Amance
Voisey
Clefmont
Burdons-sur-Rognon
Bourmont
St. Thiébault
Châtenois
Bulgnéville
Contrexéville
Vittel
Lamarche
Martigny-les-Bains
Darney
Heunezel
Monthureux-sur-Saône
Mirecourt
Gironcourt-sur-Vraine
Nomexy
Thaon-les-Vosges
Dompaire
Ville-sur-Illon
Épinal
Le Ménil
Xertigny
Bains-les-Bains
Plombières-les-Bains
Le Val-d'Ajol
Remiremont
Bruyères
Cheniménil
Granges-sur-Vologne
Éloyes
St. Amé
Vagney
Saulxures-sur-Moselle
Rupt-sur-Moselle
Le Thillot
Fougerolles
Faucogney-et-la-Mer
Servance
Luxeuil-les-Bains
St. Sauveur
Melisey
St. Germain
Champagney
Ronchamp
Lure
Vy-lès-Lure
Saulx
Vauvillers
St. Loup-sur-Semouse
Polaincourt-et-Clairefontaine
Conflans-sur-Lanterne
Amance
Jussey
Faverney
Port-sur-Saône
Genevrières
Combeaufontaine
Pierrecourt
Scey-sur-Saône et St. Albin
Vesoul
Lavoncourt
Vaite
Saône
Fresne-St. Mamès
Fretigney
Montbozon
Rougemont
Villersexel
Saulnot
Héricourt
Châtenois-les-Forges
Arcey
Montbéliard
Valentigney
L'Isle-sur-le-Doubs
Avilley
Pont-de-Roide
Clerval
Rioz
Oiselay-et-Grachoux
Gy
Etuz
Marnay
Ognon
Marchaux
Roulans
Roche-lez-Beaupré
Baume-les-Dames
Aïssey
Sancey-le-Long
Besançon
Mamirolle
Pierrefontaine-les-Varans
Maîche
Vercel-Villedieu-le-Camp
Bonnétage
Valdahon
Étalans
Orchamps-Vennes
Ornans
Vuillafans
Nods
Morteau
Villers-le-Lac
SAUT DE DOUBS
Gilley
Mouthier-Haute-Pierre
St. Gorgon-Main
Montbenoît
Amancey
Levier
Salins-les-Bains
Pontarlier
Les Verrières
Andelot-en-Montagne
Frasne
Censeau
Malbuisson
Mouthe
Les Hôpitaux-Neufs
Vallorbe
Le Pont
Le Sentier
Lac de Joux
Le Brassus
Bois-d'Amont
CHÂTEAU D'AUBONNE
Aubonne
St. Cergue
Rolle
Gland
PRANGINS
Nyon
Divonne les Bains
Thonon-les-Bains
Évian-les-Bains
Lac Léman
Lausanne
MORGES
Morges
Renens
Cully
Lutry
Épalinges
Echallens
Cossonay
L' Isle
La Sarraz
Orbe
Yverdon-les-Bains
Grandson
Ste. Croix
Fleurier
Couvet
St. Aubin
Thierrens
Jura
Doubs
Bresse
Franche-Comté
Monts du Jura
Montbéliard
Belf
Gérardmer
Bavilliers

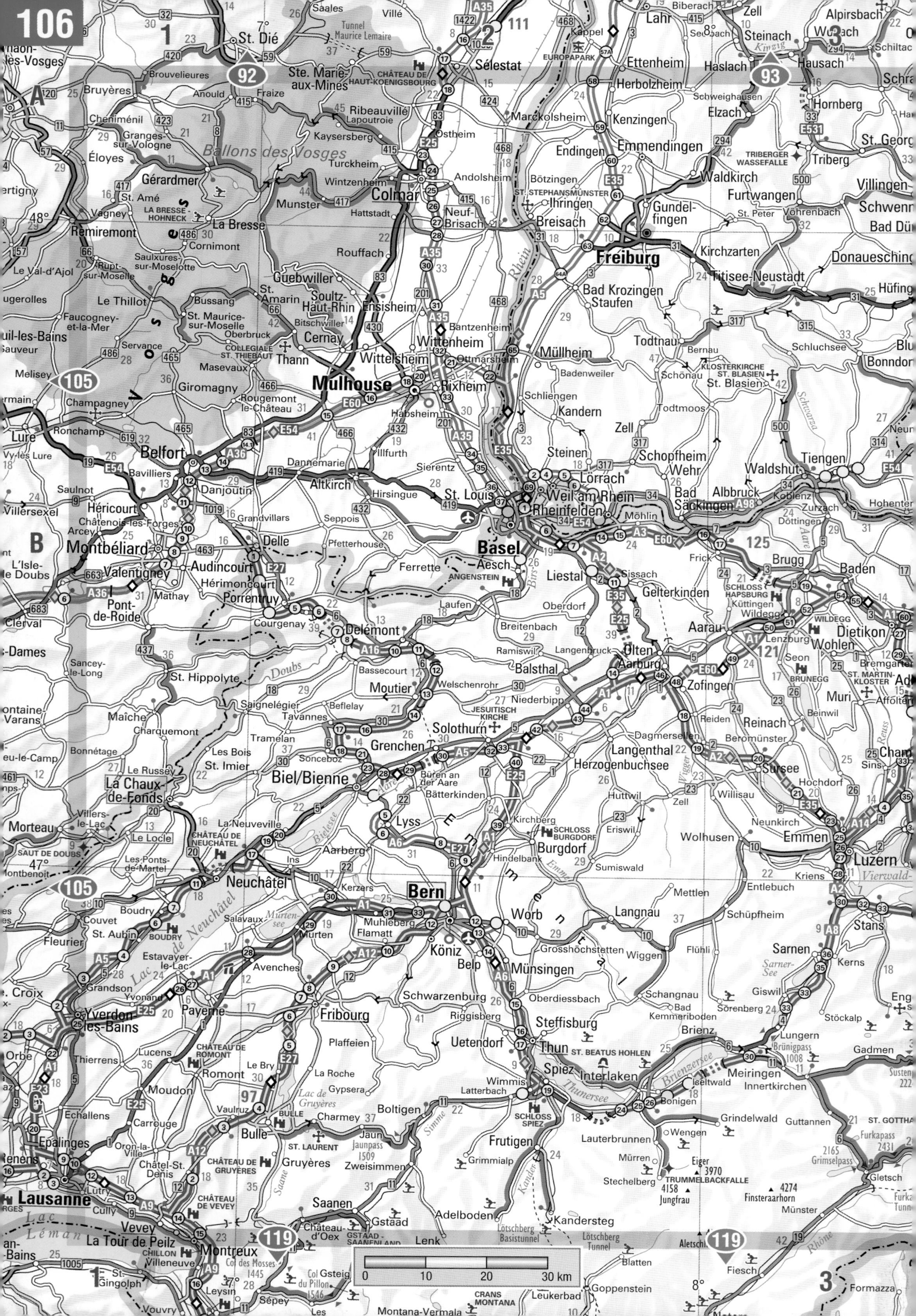
St. Dié
Saales
Villé
Tunnel Maurice Lemaire
Sélestat
Lahr
Biberach
Zell
Alpirsbach
Kappel
EUROPAPARK
Ettenheim
Steinach
Haslach
Hausach
Schiltach
Brouvelieures
Ste. Marie-aux-Mines
CHÂTEAU DE HAUT-KOENIGSBOURG
Herbolzheim
Bruyères
Anould
Fraize
Ribeauvillé
Lapoutroie
Marckolsheim
Kenzingen
Schweighausen
Elzach
Hornberg
Cheniménil
Granges-sur-Vologne
Kaysersberg
Ostheim
Endingen
Emmendingen
TRIBERGER WASSEFALLE
Triberg
St. Georg
Éloyes
Ballons des Vosges
Turckheim
Andolsheim
Bötzingen
Waldkirch
Gérardmer
Wintzenheim
Colmar
ST. STEPHANSMÜNSTER
Ihringen
Gundelfingen
Furtwangen
Villingen-Schwenningen
St. Amé
Vagney
LA BRESSE-HOHNECK
La Bresse
Munster
Hattstadt
Neuf-Brisach
Breisach
St. Peter
Vöhrenbach
Bad Dürrheim
Remiremont
Cornimont
Rouffach
Freiburg
Kirchzarten
Donaueschingen
Saulxures-sur-Moselotte
Le Val-d'Ajol
Rupt-sur-Moselle
Guebwiller
Titisee-Neustadt
Bad Krozingen
Staufen
Hüfingen
Le Thillot
Bussang
St. Amarin
Soultz-Haut-Rhin
Ensisheim
Faucogney-et-la-Mer
St. Maurice-sur-Moselle
Oberbruck
Bitschwiller
Cernay
Bantzenheim
Wittenheim
Servance
COLLEGIALE ST. THIEBAUT
Thann
Wittelsheim
Ottmarsheim
Müllheim
Todtnau
Bernau
Schluchsee
Bonndorf
Melisey
Masevaux
Mulhouse
Rixheim
Badenweiler
Schönau
KLOSTERKIRCHE ST. BLASIEN
St. Blasien
Giromagny
Rougemont le-Château
Champagney
Habsheim
Schliengen
Kandern
Todtmoos
Lure
Ronchamp
Belfort
Illfurth
Zell
Steinen
Schopfheim
Wehr
Waldshut
Tiengen
Vy-lès Lure
Bavilliers
Dannemarie
Sierentz
Lörrach
Albbruck
Saulnot
Danjoutin
Altkirch
Hirsingue
St. Louis
Weil am Rhein
Bad Säckingen
Koblenz
Hohentengen
Villersexel
Héricourt
Rheinfelden
Möhlin
Zurzach
Döttingen
Châtenois-les-Forges
Grandvillars
Seppois
Arcey
Delle
Pfetterhouse
Basel
Frick
Brugg
Baden
Montbéliard
Ferrette
Aesch
ANGENSTEIN
Liestal
Sissach
L'Isle-le Doubs
Valentigney
Audincourt
Hérimoncourt
Gelterkinden
SCHLOSS HAPSBURG
Küttingen
Wildegg
WILDEGG
Pont-de-Roide
Mathay
Porrentruy
Courgenay
Laufen
Oberdorf
Aarau
Lenzburg
Dietikon
Clerval
Delémont
Breitenbach
Wohlen
Ramiswil
Langenbruck
Olten
Seon
Bremgarten
Sancey-le-Long
Bassecourt
Balsthal
Aarburg
Zofingen
BRUNEGG
ST. MARTIN-KLOSTER
Affoltern
St. Hippolyte
Moutier
Welschenrohr
Niederbipp
Muri
Saignelégier
Beflelay
JESUITISCH KIRCHE
Maîche
Tavannes
Solothurn
Reiden
Reinach
Beinwil
Charquemont
Tramelan
Grenchen
Dagmersellen
Beromünster
Bonnétage
Les Bois
Sonceboz
Langenthal
Herzogenbuchsee
Sursee
Cham
St. Imier
Le Russey
Biel/Bienne
Büren an der Aare
Hochdorf
La Chaux-de-Fonds
Bätterkinden
Huttwil
Willisau
Zell
Lyss
Kirchberg
SCHLOSS BURGDORF
Eriswil
Villers-le-Lac
Morteau
La Neuveville
Neunkirch
Wolhusen
Emmen
Le Locle
CHÂTEAU DE NEUCHÂTEL
Aarberg
Burgdorf
Hindelbank
SAUT DE DOUBS
Les Ponts-de-Martel
Ins
Sumiswald
Luzern
Neuchâtel
Kerzers
Bern
Mettlen
Entlebuch
Kriens
Boudry
Murtensee
Langnau
Schüpfheim
Couvet
Muhleberg
Worb
Stans
St. Aubin
BOUDRY
Salavaux
Murten
Flamatt
Fleurier
Estavayer-le-Lac
Köniz
Belp
Grosshöchstetten
Wiggen
Flühli
Sarnen
Kerns
Avenches
Münsingen
Sarner-See
Grandson
Yvonand
Payerne
Schwarzenburg
Oberdiessbach
Schangnau
Giswil
Yverdon-les-Bains
Fribourg
Riggisberg
Bad Kemmeriboden
Sörenberg
Stöckalp
Orbe
Thierrens
Lucens
Plaffeien
Steffisburg
Brienz
Lungern
CHÂTEAU DE ROMONT
Uetendorf
Thun
ST. BEATUS HOHLEN
Brünigpass
Gadmen
Romont
Le Bry
La Roche
Spiez
Interlaken
Meiringen
Innertkirchen
Moudon
Gypsera
Wimmis
Brienzersee
Iseltwald
Susten
Lac de Gruyères
Latterbach
Thunersee
Bonigen
Echallens
Vaulruz
BULLE
Charmey
Boltigen
SCHLOSS SPIEZ
Grindelwald
Guttannen
ST. GOTTHARD
Carrouge
Bulle
ST. LAURENT
Jaun
Jaunpass
Frutigen
Lauterbrunnen
Wengen
Furkapass
Epalinges
Oron-la-Ville
Zweisimmen
Grimmialp
Mürren
Eiger
Grimselpass
Renens
Châtel-St. Denis
CHÂTEAU DE GRUYÈRES
Gruyères
Stechelberg
TRUMMELBACKFALLE
Jungfrau
Finsteraarhorn
Gletsch
Lausanne
Lutry
Cully
CHÂTEAU DE VEVEY
Saanen
Adelboden
Kandersteg
Münster
Lac Léman
Vevey
La Tour de Peilz
Château-d'Oex
Gstaad
GSTAAD-SAANENLAND
Lenk
Lötschberg Basistunnel
Lötschberg Tunnel
Aletsch
Montreux
CHILLON
Villeneuve
Col des Mosses
Blatten
Fiesch
St. Gingolph
Leysin
Col du Pillon
Gsteig
Sépey
Goppenstein
Leukerbad
Formazza
Vouvry
CRANS MONTANA
Montana-Vermala
Rhein
Doubs
Aare
Emmental
Rhône
0 10 20 30 km

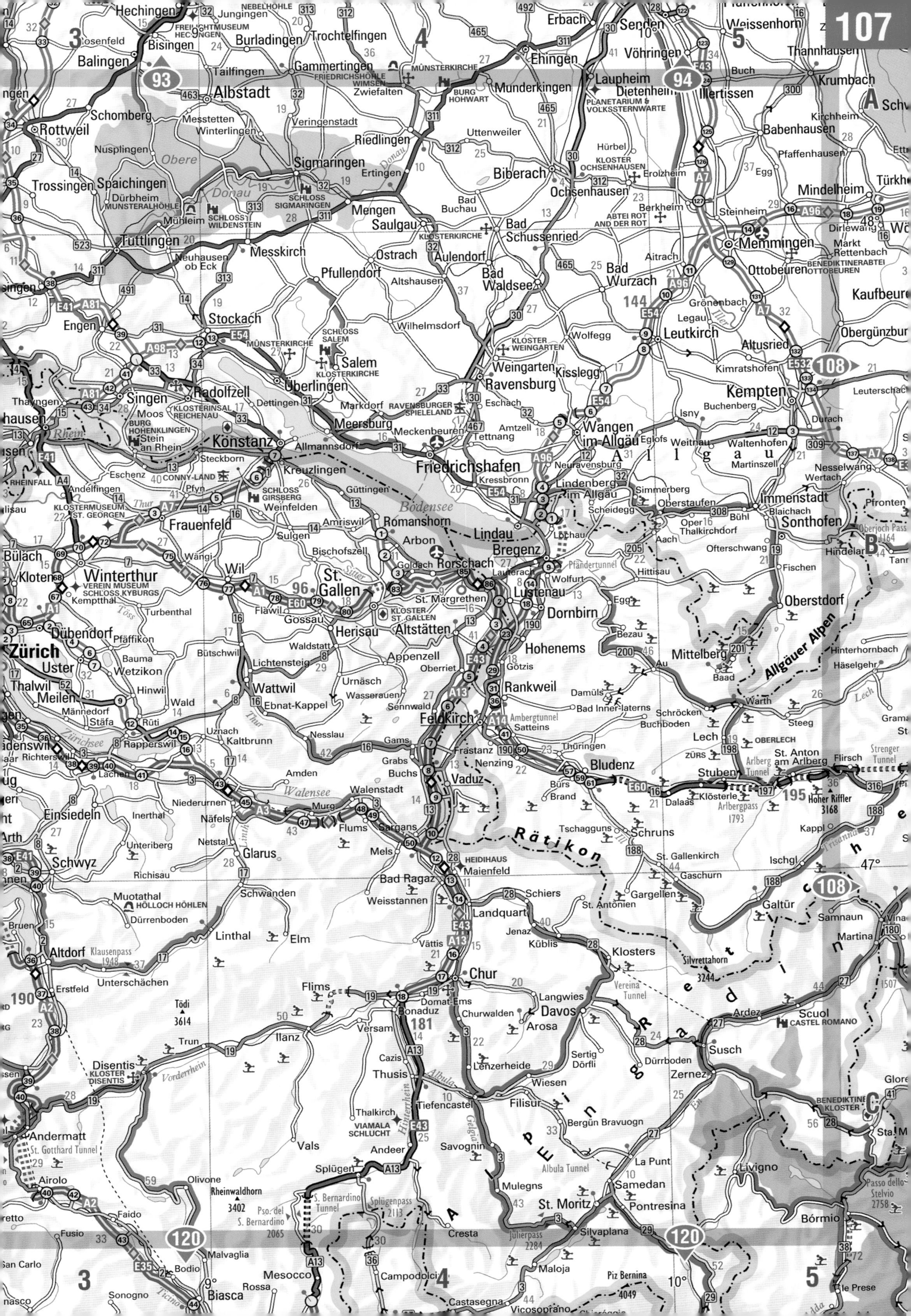
Hechingen
Bisingen
Balingen
Burladingen
Trochtelfingen
Gammertingen
Albstadt
Tailfingen
Zwiefalten
Erbach
Senden
Vöhringen
Weissenhorn
Thannhausen
Ehingen
Laupheim
Dietenheim
Illertissen
Krumbach
Munderkingen
Rottweil
Schomberg
Messtetten
Winterlingen
Veringenstadt
Riedlingen
Uttenweiler
Babenhausen
Nusplingen
Obere Donau
Sigmaringen
Ertingen
Biberach
Ochsenhausen
Erolzheim
Pfaffenhausen
Trossingen
Spaichingen
Dürbheim
Mühleim
Mengen
Saulgau
Bad Buchau
Bad Schussenried
Berkheim
Steinheim
Mindelheim
Tuttlingen
Messkirch
Ostrach
Aulendorf
Bad Waldsee
Bad Wurzach
Aitrach
Memmingen
Ottobeuren
Neuhausen ob Eck
Pfullendorf
Altshausen
Grönenbach
Kaufbeuren
Stockach
Wilhelmsdorf
Legau
Leutkirch
Engen
Salem
Wolfegg
Altusried
Obergünzburg
Weingarten
Ravensburg
Kisslegg
Kimratshofen
Kempten
Singen
Radolfzell
Überlingen
Moos
Stein an Rhein
Markdorf
Eschach
Buchenberg
Dettingen
Meersburg
Meckenbeuren
Tettnang
Amtzell
Wangen im Allgäu
Isny
Durach
Konstanz
Allmannsdorf
Weitnau
Waltenhofen
Friedrichshafen
Kreuzlingen
Steckborn
Eschenz
Neuravensburg
Lindenberg im Allgäu
Martinszell
Nesselwang
Wertach
Andelfingen
Pfyn
Güttingen
Kressbronn
Simmerberg
Oberstaufen
Immenstadt
Blaichach
Pfronten
Frauenfeld
Weinfelden
Bodensee
Amriswil
Romanshorn
Scheidegg
Oberstaufen
Bühl
Sonthofen
Sulgen
Arbon
Lindau
Bregenz
Lochau
Aach
Thalkirchdorf
Bülach
Winterthur
Wängi
Bischofszell
Rorschach
Goldach
Hittisau
Ofterschwang
Hindelang
Fischen
Kloten
Wil
St. Gallen
Lustenau
Wolfurt
Lauterach
Kemptthal
Turbenthal
Flawil
Gossau
St. Margrethen
Dornbirn
Egg
Oberstdorf
Dübendorf
Pfäffikon
Herisau
Altstätten
Zürich
Uster
Bauma
Wetzikon
Bütschwil
Waldstatt
Appenzell
Hohenems
Bezau
Mittelberg
Baad
Hinterhornbach
Häselgehr
Thalwil
Meilen
Hinwil
Lichtensteig
Wattwil
Urnäsch
Oberriet
Götzis
Rankweil
Au
Allgäuer Alpen
Männedorf
Stäfa
Rüti
Wald
Ebnat-Kappel
Wasserauen
Sennwald
Damüls
Bad Inner-laterns
Schröcken
Warth
Lech
Rapperswil
Uznach
Kaltbrunn
Nesslau
Feldkirch
Satteins
Buchboden
Steeg
Richterswil
Lachen
Gams
Grabs
Frastanz
Nenzing
Thüringen
Bludenz
Zürs
St. Anton am Arlberg
Flirsch
Einsiedeln
Amden
Buchs
Vaduz
Bürs
Brand
Stuben
Klösterle
Dalaas
Arlbergpass
Hoher Riffler 3168
Niederurnen
Näfels
Walensee
Walenstadt
Murg
Flums
Sargans
Kappl
Unteriberg
Netstal
Glarus
Mels
Rätikon
Tschagguns
Schruns
Schwyz
Richisau
Maienfeld
St. Gallenkirch
Gaschurn
Ischgl
Bad Ragaz
Weisstannen
Schiers
St. Antönien
Gargellen
Galtür
Samnaun
Muotathal
Schwanden
Dürrenboden
Landquart
Jenaz
Küblis
Klosters
Silvrettahorn 3244
Martina
Linthal
Elm
Vättis
Altdorf
Klausenpass 1948
Unterschächen
Erstfeld
Chur
Flims
Domat-Ems
Bonaduz
Langwies
Davos
Vereina Tunnel
Tödi 3614
Ilanz
Versam
Churwalden
Arosa
Ardez
Scuol
Trun
Cazis
Thusis
Lenzerheide
Sertig Dörfli
Dürrboden
Susch
Zernez
Disentis
Vorderrhein
Albula
Tiefencastel
Wiesen
Filisur
Bergün Bravuogn
Andermatt
St. Gotthard Tunnel
Thalkirch
Viamala Schlucht
Vals
Andeer
Savognin
Albula Tunnel
La Punt
Livigno
Airolo
Olivone
Splügen
Rheinwaldhorn 3402
S. Bernardino Tunnel
Splügenpass 2113
Mulegns
Samedan
Pontresina
Passo dello Stelvio 2758
Faido
Pso. del S. Bernardino 2065
St. Moritz
Julierpass 2284
Silvaplana
Bórmio
Fusio
Cresta
Malvaglia
Bodio
Maloja
Piz Bernina 4049
San Carlo
Mesocco
Campodolcino
Biasca
Rossa
Sonogno
Castasegna
Vicosoprano
Le Prese
Ticino
Alpen
Engadin
Allgäu
47°
48°
10°
93
94
96
108
120
144
181
190
195

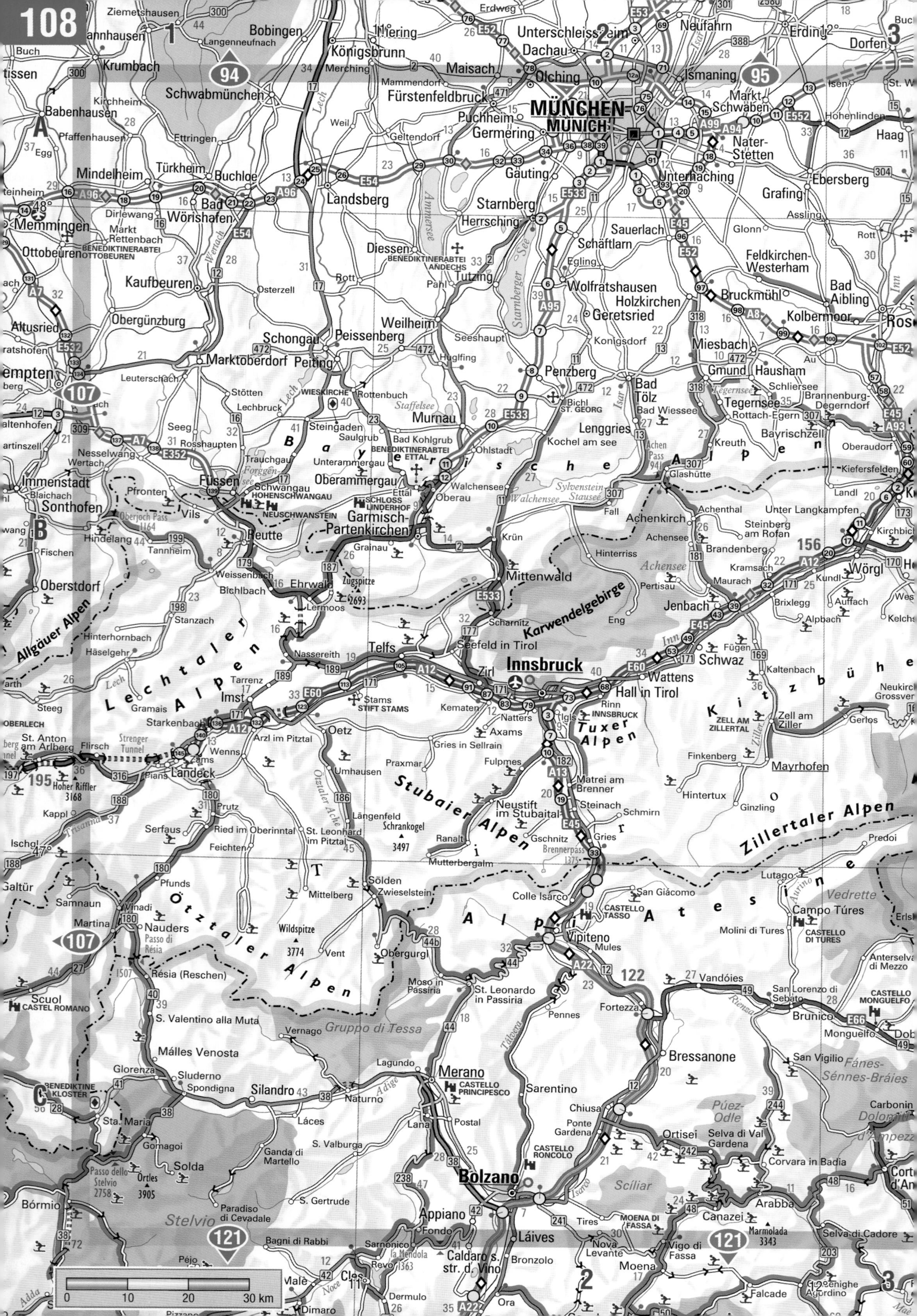

Ziemetshausen
Bobingen
Mering
Erdweg
Unterschleissheim
Neufahrn
Erding
Dorfen
Königsbrunn
Dachau
Krumbach
Maisach
Olching
Ismaning
Schwabmünchen
Fürstenfeldbruck
MÜNCHEN-MUNICH
Markt Schwaben
Babenhausen
Puchheim
Germering
Nater-Stetten
Haag
Mindelheim
Türkheim
Buchloe
Gauting
Unterhaching
Ebersberg
Grafing
Landsberg
Starnberg
Memmingen
Bad Wörishofen
Herrsching
Ottobeuren
Sauerlach
Schäftlarn
Diessen
Benediktinerabtei Andechs
Kaufbeuren
Tutzing
Wolfratshausen
Holzkirchen
Feldkirchen-Westerham
Bruckmühl
Bad Aibling
Geretsried
Kolbermoor
Obergünzburg
Weilheim
Schongau
Peissenberg
Seeshaupt
Miesbach
Altusried
Marktoberdorf
Peiting
Penzberg
Gmund
Hausham
Kempten
Wieskirche
Rottenbuch
Bad Tölz
Tegernsee
Murnau
Lenggries
Bad Wiessee
Bayrischzell
Oberammergau
Kochel am see
Immenstadt
Sonthofen
Füssen
Schwangau
Hohenschwangau
Neuschwanstein
Schloss Linderhof
Garmisch-Partenkirchen
Walchensee
Sylvenstein Stausee
Kiefersfelden
Pfronten
Vils
Reutte
Grainau
Krün
Achenkirch
Achensee
Hindelang
Oberstdorf
Ehrwald
Zugspitze
2693
Lermoos
Mittenwald
Karwendelgebirge
Jenbach
Wörgl
Allgäuer Alpen
Scharnitz
Seefeld in Tirol
Telfs
Nassereith
Innsbruck
Wattens
Schwaz
Lechtaler Alpen
Imst
Zirl
Hall in Tirol
Stams
Stift Stams
Kematen
Tuxer Alpen
St. Anton am Arlberg
Landeck
Zams
Oetz
Axams
Zell am Ziller
Strenger Tunnel
Hoher Riffler
3168
Umhausen
Stubaier Alpen
Matrei am Brenner
Mayrhofen
Fulpmes
Neustift im Stubaital
Steinach
Zillertaler Alpen
Serfaus
Längenfeld
Schrankogel
3497
Gries
Brennerpass
1375
Ischgl
Galtür
Pfunds
Sölden
Ötztaler Alpen
Zwieselstein
Colle Isarco
Campo Túres
Samnaun
Nauders
Wildspitze
3774
Vipiteno
Vent
Obergurgl
Resia (Reschen)
Scuol
Castel Romano
St. Leonardo in Passiria
Fortezza
Brunico
S. Valentino alla Muta
Gruppo di Tessa
Bressanone
Málles Venosta
Merano
Castello Principesco
San Vigilio
Glorenza
Sarentino
Silandro
Naturno
Chiusa
Ortisei
Sta. Maria
Lana
Selva di Val Gardena
Solda
Corvara in Badia
Passo dello Stelvio
2758
Ortles
3905
Bolzano
Sciliar
Arabba
Bórmio
Stelvio
Appiano
Canazei
Marmolada
3343
Láives
Moena
Caldaro s. str. d. Vino
Cles
Malè
Ora
Falcade
0
10
20
30 km

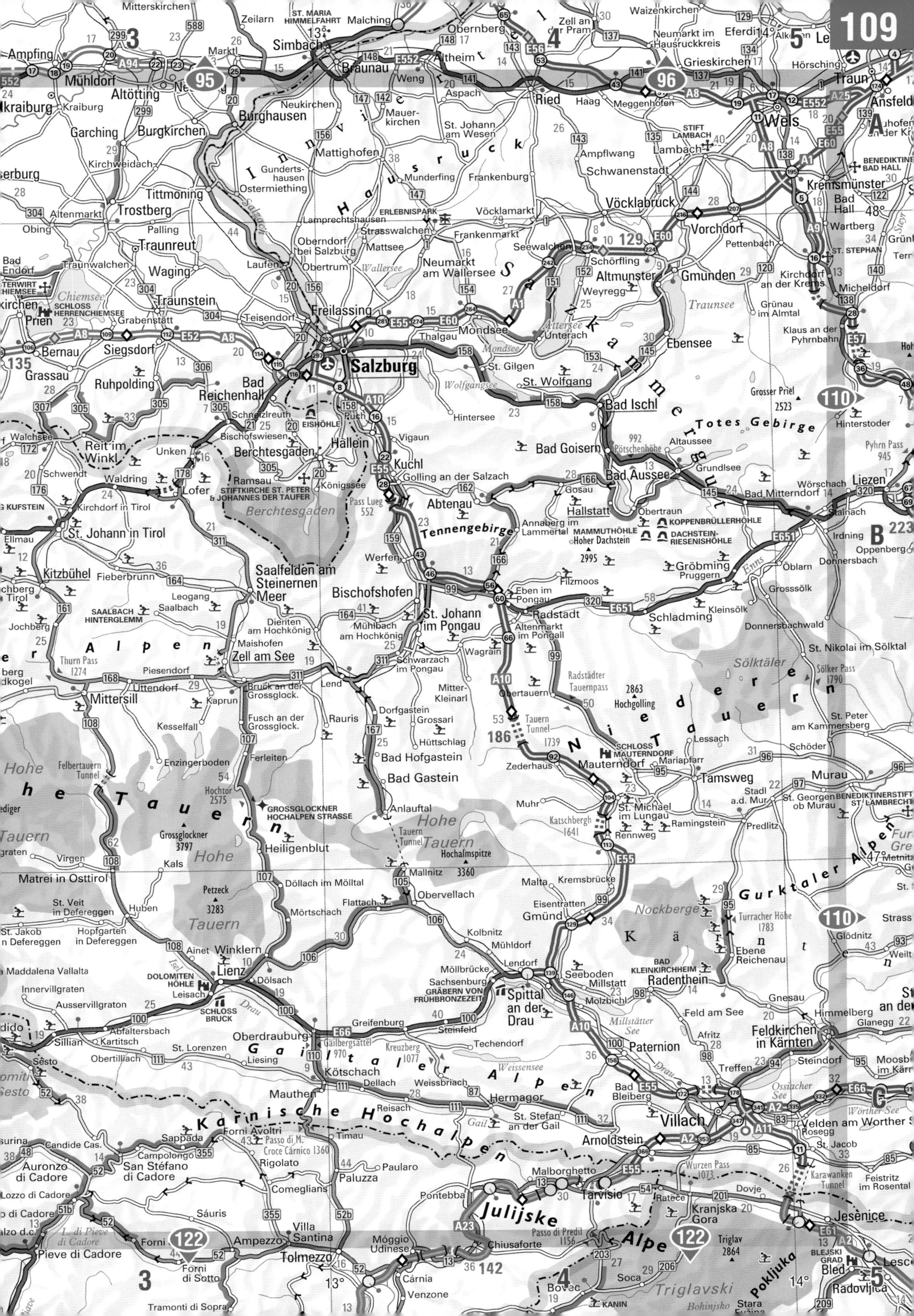

Mühldorf
Altötting
Simbach
Braunau
Burghausen
Ried
Wels
Traun
Ansfelden
Mattighofen
Vöcklabruck
Vorchdorf
Kremsmünster
Gmunden
Traunstein
Freilassing
Salzburg
Bad Reichenhall
Mondsee
St. Gilgen
St. Wolfgang
Bad Ischl
Ebensee
Traunsee
Berchtesgaden
Hallein
Kuchl
Golling an der Salzach
Abtenau
Hallstatt
Bad Goisern
Bad Aussee
Bad Mitterndorf
Liezen
Totes Gebirge
Tennengebirge
Werfen
Bischofshofen
St. Johann im Pongau
Radstadt
Schladming
Saalfelden am Steinernen Meer
Zell am See
Kitzbühel
St. Johann in Tirol
Lofer
Mittersill
Kaprun
Bad Hofgastein
Bad Gastein
Obertauern
Mauterndorf
Tamsweg
Murau
Niedere Tauern
Hohe Tauern
Grossglockner 3797
Heiligenblut
Matrei in Osttirol
Lienz
Mallnitz
Obervellach
Gmünd
Spittal an der Drau
Millstatt
Radenthein
Feldkirchen in Kärnten
Gailtaler Alpen
Villach
Arnoldstein
Hermagor
Kötschach
Karnische Hochalpen
Tarvisio
Julijske Alpe
Jesenice
Bled
Tolmezzo
Pieve di Cadore
Bovec
Triglav 2864
Gurktaler Alpen
Velden am Wörther See

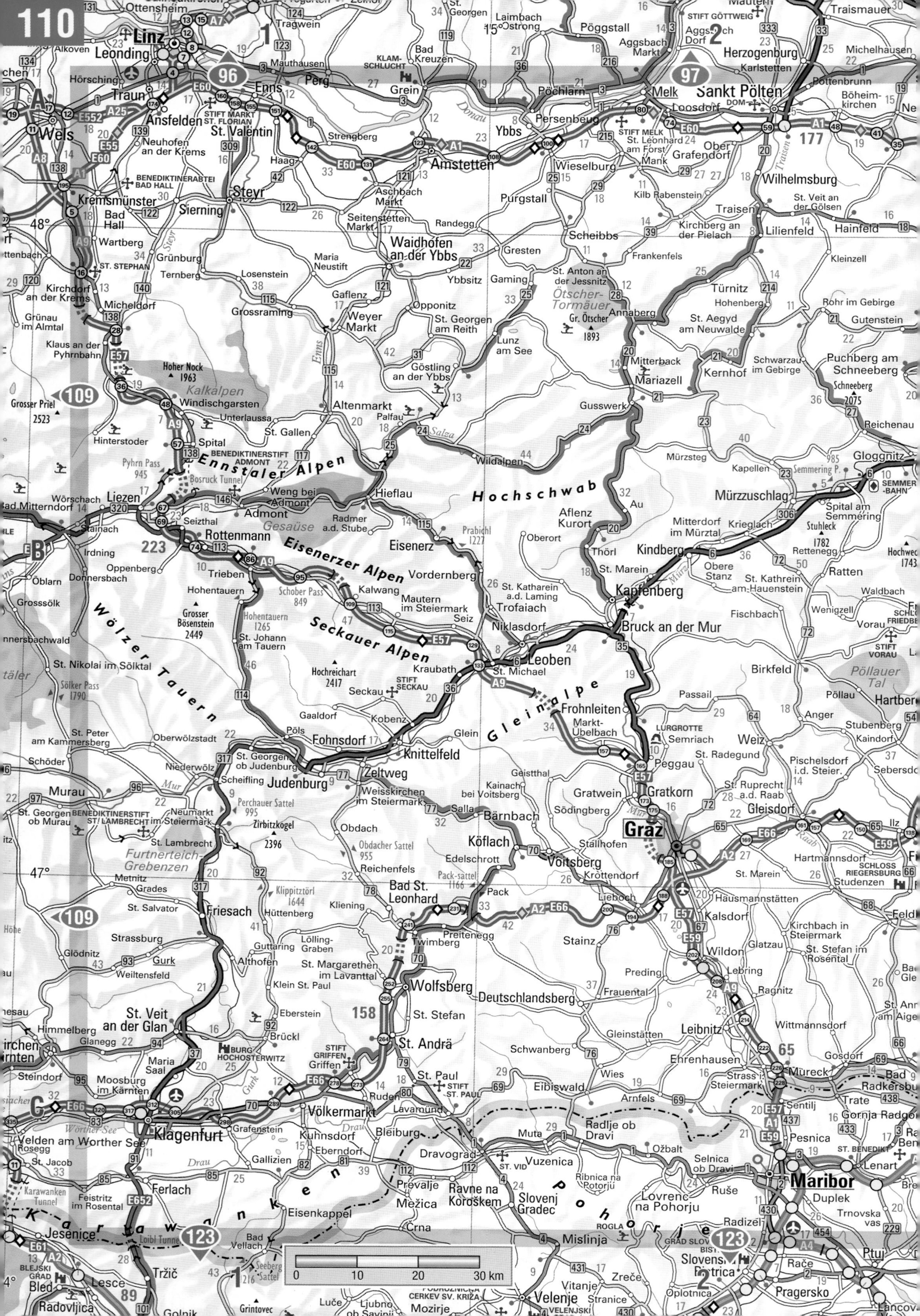
Ottensheim
Linz
Leonding
Alkoven
Tragwein
Mauthausen
Perg
Grein
Bad Kreuzen
KLAM-SCHLUCHT
St. Georgen
Laimbach
Ostrong
Pöggstall
Aggsbach Markt
Aggsbach Dorf
STIFT GÖTTWEIG
Traismauer
Herzogenburg
Michelhausen
Karlstetten
Hörsching
Traun
Enns
Pöchlarn
Melk
Sankt Pölten
Böheim-kirchen
Wels
Ansfelden
STIFT MARKT ST. FLORIAN
St. Valentin
Strengberg
Ybbs
Persenbeug
Loosdorf
DOM
STIFT MELK
St. Leonhard am Forst
Mank
Ober Grafendorf
Neuhofen an der Krems
Haag
Amstetten
Wieselburg
BENEDIKTINERABTEI BAD HALL
Steyr
Aschbach Markt
Kilb
Rabenstein
Wilhelmsburg
Kremsmünster
Bad Hall
Sierning
Seitenstetten Markt
Purgstall
Randegg
Traisen
St. Veit an der Gölsen
Hainfeld
Lilienfeld
Kirchberg an der Pielach
Scheibbs
Wartberg
Grünburg
Maria Neustift
Waidhofen an der Ybbs
Gresten
Frankenfels
Kleinzell
ST. STEPHAN
Ternberg
Losenstein
Ybbsitz
Gaming
St. Anton an der Jessnitz
Kirchdorf an der Krems
Micheldorf
Gaflenz
Opponitz
Ötscher-Tormäuer
Türnitz
Hohenberg
Rohr im Gebirge
Grünau im Almtal
Grossraming
Weyer Markt
St. Georgen am Reith
Gr. Ötscher
1893
Annaberg
St. Aegyd am Neuwalde
Gutenstein
Klaus an der Pyhrnbahn
Lunz am See
Göstling an der Ybbs
Mitterback
Mariazell
Kernhof
Schwarzau im Gebirge
Puchberg am Schneeberg
Schneeberg
2075
Hoher Nock
1963
Kalkalpen
Grosser Priel
2523
Windischgarsten
Unterlaussa
Altenmarkt
Palfau
Gusswerk
Reichenau
Hinterstoder
St. Gallen
Salza
Spital
Mürzsteg
Kapellen
Semmering P.
985
Gloggnitz
SEMMERING-BAHN
BENEDIKTINERSTIFT ADMONT
Ennstaler Alpen
Pyhrn Pass
945
Wildalpen
Bosruck Tunnel
Wörschach
Liezen
Weng bei Admont
Hieflau
Hochschwab
Mürzzuschlag
Bad Mitterndorf
Admont
Gesäuse
Radmer a.d. Stube
Au
Aflenz Kurort
Spital am Semmering
Stainach
Seizthal
Rottenmann
Eisenerz
Prabichl
1227
Oberort
Mitterdorf im Mürztal
Krieglach
Stuhleck
1782
Irdning
Eisenerzer Alpen
Thörl
Kindberg
Rettenegg
Hochwechsel
1743
Oppenberg
Trieben
Vordernberg
St. Marein
Obere Stanz
Ratten
Öblarn
Donnersbach
Kalwang
St. Kathrein am Hauenstein
Waldbach
Hohentauern
Schober Pass
849
Mautern im Steiermark
St. Katharein a.d. Laming
Trofaiach
Kapfenberg
Grosssölk
Grosser Bösenstein
2449
Seiz
Niklasdorf
Bruck an der Mur
Fischbach
Wenigzell
Vorau
Hohentauern
1265
St. Johann am Tauern
Seckauer Alpen
STIFT VORAU
Wölzer Tauern
Leoben
St. Michael
St. Nikolai im Sölktal
Kraubath
Hochreichart
2417
Birkfeld
Pöllauer Tal
Sölker Pass
1790
Seckau
STIFT SECKAU
Gleinalpe
Passail
Pöllau
Hartberg
Frohnleiten
Gaaldorf
Kobenz
Markt-Übelbach
LURGROTTE
Semriach
Anger
Stubenberg
St. Peter am Kammersberg
Oberwölzstadt
Pöls
Fohnsdorf
Glein
Weiz
Kaindorf
Schöder
St. Georgen ob Judenburg
Knittelfeld
St. Radegund
Peggau
Pischelsdorf i.d. Steier.
Sebersdorf
Niederwölz
Geistthal
Scheifling
Judenburg
Zeltweg
Kainach bei Voitsberg
Gratwein
Gratkorn
St. Ruprecht a.d. Raab
Murau
Weisskirchen im Steiermark
Perchauer Sattel
995
Salla
Söding
Gleisdorf
St. Georgen ob Murau
BENEDIKTINERSTIFT ST. LAMBRECHT
Neumarkt im Steiermark
Bärnbach
Graz
Zirbitzkogel
2396
Obdach
Köflach
Stallhofen
St. Lambrecht
Furtnerteich-Grebenzen
Obdacher Sattel
955
Edelschrott
Voitsberg
Hartmannsdorf
SCHLOSS RIEGERSBURG
Metnitz
Reichenfels
Pack-sattel
1166
Krottendorf
St. Marein
Studenzen
Grades
Bad St. Leonhard
Pack
Lieboch
Hausmannstätten
St. Salvator
Klippitztörl
1644
Friesach
Hüttenberg
Klieing
Kalsdorf
Kirchbach in Steiermark
Strassburg
Lölling-Graben
Twimberg
Preitenegg
Stainz
Glatzau
St. Stefan im Rosental
Glödnitz
Guttaring
Gurk
Weitensfeld
Althofen
St. Margarethen im Lavanttal
Wolfsberg
Preding
Wildon
Lebring
Klein St. Paul
Frauental
Deutschlandsberg
Ragnitz
St. Veit an der Glan
Himmelberg
Eberstein
St. Stefan
Wittmannsdorf
Glanegg
Brückl
St. Andrä
Leibnitz
Gleinstätten
Maria Saal
BURG HOCHOSTERWITZ
STIFT GRIFFEN
Griffen
Schwanberg
Ehrenhausen
Gosdorf
Steindorf
Moosburg im Kärnten
St. Paul
STIFT ST. PAUL
Wies
Mureck
Bad Radkersburg
Ruden
Eibiswald
Strass i. Steiermark
Arnfels
Völkermarkt
Lavamünd
Sentilj
Trate
Gornja Radgona
Wörther See
Klagenfurt
Grafenstein
Velden am Worther See
Rosegg
Kühnsdorf
Bleiburg
Muta
Radlje ob Dravi
Ožbalt
Pesnica
St. Jacob
Eberndorf
Gallizien
Dravograd
Vuzenica
Selnica ob Dravi
ST. BENEDIKT
Lenart
Ferlach
Drau
Maribor
Karawanken Tunnel
Feistritz im Rosental
Prevalje
Ravne na Koroškem
Ribnica na Pohorju
Ruše
Duplek
Mežica
Slovenj Gradec
Pohorje
Lovrenc na Pohorju
Karawanken
Eisenkappel
Radizel
Trnovska vas
Jesenice
Loibl Tunnel
Bad Vellach
Črna
ROGLA
Mislinja
Ptuj
Slovenska Bistrica
Rače
BLEJSKI GRAD
Bled
Lesce
Tržič
Seeberg Sattel
Zreče
Vitanje
Pragersko
Radovljica
Golnik
Grintovec
Luče
Ljubno ob Savinji
PODROZNICNA CERKEV SV. KRIŽA
Mozirje
Velenje
VELENJSKI
Stranice
Oplotnica
Lancova
48°
47°
0
10
20
30 km
A
B
C
1
2

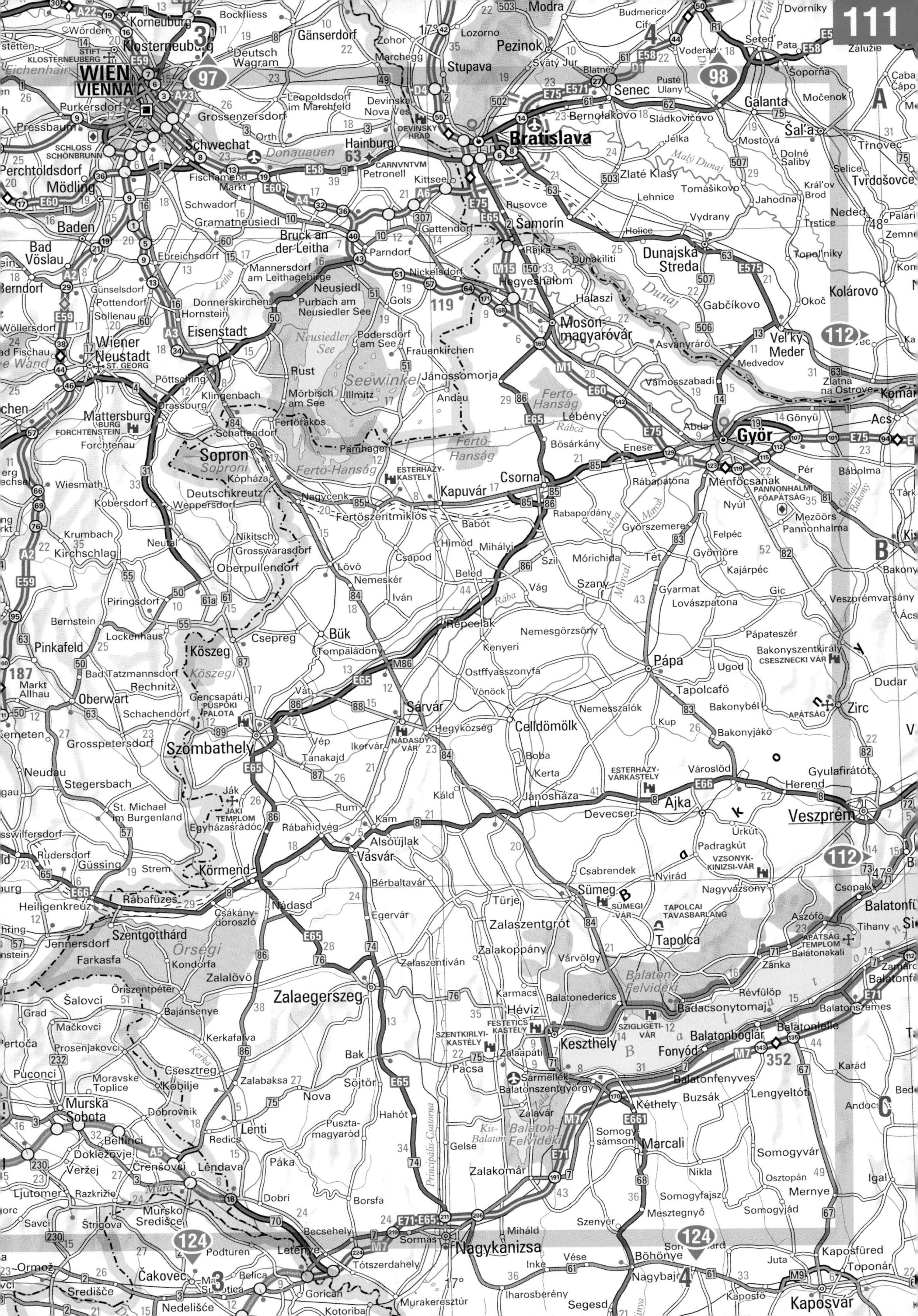
Korneuburg
Klosterneuburg
Wördern
Stetten
KLOSTERNEUBURG STIFT
WIEN
VIENNA
Purkersdorf
Pressbaum
SCHLOSS SCHÖNBRUNN
Perchtoldsdorf
Mödling
Baden
Bad Vöslau
Berndorf
Bockfliess
Deutsch Wagram
Gänserdorf
Zohor
Marchegg
Leopoldsdorf im Marchfeld
Grossenzersdorf
Orth
Schwechat
Donauauen
Fischamend Markt
Hainburg
CARNUNTUM
Petronell
Devinska Nova Ves
DEVINSKY HRAD
Kittsee
Schwadorf
Gramatneusiedl
Bruck an der Leitha
Parndorf
Gattendorf
Nickelsdorf
Ebreichsdorf
Mannersdorf am Leithagebirge
Günselsdorf
Pottendorf
Sollenau
Donnerskirchen
Hornstein
Eisenstadt
Purbach am Neusiedler See
Neusiedl
Gols
Wöllersdorf
Fischau
Wiener Neustadt
ST. GEORG
Neusiedler See
Podersdorf am See
Frauenkirchen
Rust
Seewinkel
Jánossomorja
Andau
Mörbisch am See
Illmitz
Pöttsching
Klingenbach
Drassburg
Mattersburg
BURG FORCHTENSTEIN
Forchtenau
Schattendorf
Fertörakos
Pamhagen
Sopron
Soproni
Kópháza
Fertő-Hanság
Deutschkreutz
Nagycenk
ESTERHÁZY-KASTÉLY
Kapuvár
Csorna
Wiesmath
Kobersdorf
Weppersdorf
Fertöszentmiklós
Babót
Krumbach
Kirchschlag
Neutal
Nikitsch
Grosswarasdorf
Oberpullendorf
Lövö
Csapod
Himód
Mihályi
Beled
Nemeskér
Iván
Piringsdorf
Bernstein
Lockenhaus
Csepreg
Bük
Tompaládony
Pinkafeld
Köszeg
Kőszegi
Bad Tatzmannsdorf
Rechnitz
Markt Allhau
Oberwart
Gencsapáti
PÜSPÖKI PALOTA
Schachendorf
Szombathely
Grosspetersdorf
Neudau
Stegersbach
St. Michael im Burgenland
Ják
JÁKI TEMPLOM
Egyházasrádóc
Rudersdorf
Güssing
Strem
Körmend
Heiligenkreuz
Rábafüzes
Csákány-doroszló
Szentgotthárd
Jennersdorf
Farkasfa
Őrségi
Kondorfa
Zalalövö
Öriszentpéter
Šalovci
Grad
Bajánsenye
Mačkovci
Kerkafalva
Prosenjakovci
Puconci
Moravske Toplice
Cseszteg
Kobilje
Murska Sobota
Dobrovnik
Beltinci
Dokležovje
Verzej
Črenšovci
Lendava
Ljutomer
Razkrižje
Mura
Mursko Sredisče
Savci
Štrigova
Podturen
Ormož
Čakovec
Središče
Nedelišce
Belica
Goričan
Letenye
Tótszerdahely
Kotoriba
Murakeresztúr
Nagykanizsa
Sormás
Becsehely
Borsfa
Dobri
Redics
Lenti
Páka
Puszta-magyaród
Zalabaksa
Nova
Söjtör
Hahót
Bak
Zalaegerszeg
Zalaszentiván
Egervár
Nádasd
Bérbaltavár
Vasvár
Alsóújlak
Rábahidvég
Rum
Kám
Vép
Tanakajd
Ikervár
NÁDASDY-VÁR
Sárvár
Vát
Hegyközség
Repcelak
Kenyeri
Ostffyasszonyfa
Vönöck
Celldömölk
Boba
Kerta
Káld
Jánosháza
Nemesgörzsöny
Nemesszalók
Pápa
Ugod
Tapolcafö
Bakonybél
Kup
Bakonyjákó
Városlöd
ESTERHÁZY-VÁRKASTÉLY
Ajka
Devecser
Herend
Veszprém
Gyulafirátót
Zirc
APÁTSÁG
Dudar
Bakonyszentkirály
CSESZNECKI VÁR
Pápateszér
Gic
Veszprémvarsány
Lovászpatona
Gyarmat
Szany
Vág
Szil
Mórichida
Tét
Gyömöre
Kajárpéc
Rabapordány
Györszemere
Felpéc
Rábapatona
Ménfőcsanak
PANNONHALMI FŐAPÁTSÁG
Nyúl
Mezöörs
Pannonhalma
Pér
Bábolna
Győr
Gönyü
Ács
Abda
Enese
Bösárkány
Lébény
Fertő-Hanság
Rábca
Moson-magyaróvár
Halászi
Hegyeshalom
Rajka
Dunakiliti
Ásványráró
Vámosszabadi
Medvedov
Veľký Meder
Zlatná na Ostrove
Komárno
Kolárovo
Okoč
Gabčíkovo
Dunajská Streda
Holice
Vydrany
Šamorín
Rusovce
Bratislava
Lehnice
Tomášikovo
Jahodná
Zlaté Klasy
Malý Dunaj
Mostová
Jelka
Bernolákovo
Sládkovičovo
Galanta
Šaľa
Dolné Saliby
Selice
Kráľov Brod
Trnovec
Tvrdošovce
Neded
Palárikovo
Zemné
Topoľníky
Senec
Pusté Úľany
Blatné
Svätý Jur
Pezinok
Modra
Budmerice
Cífer
Voderady
Sereď
Pata
Šoporňa
Dvorníky
Zálužie
Močenok
Caba
Lozorno
Stupava
Dunaj
Bakony
Úrkút
Padragkút
VZSONYK-KINIZSI-VÁR
Nyirád
Csabrendek
Sümeg
SÜMEGI VÁR
Nagyvázsony
TAPOLCAI TAVASBARLANG
Tapolca
Türje
Zalaszentgrót
Zalakoppány
Várvölgy
Balaton-Felvidéki
Balatonederics
Badacsonytomaj
Révfülöp
Zánka
Balatonakali
APÁTSÁG TEMPLOM
Tihany
Aszófö
Csopak
Balatonfüred
Balatonszemes
Balatonlelle
Balatonboglár
Fonyód
SZIGLIGETI VÁR
Keszthely
Hévíz
Karmacs
FESTETICS KASTÉLY
SZENTKIRLYI-KASTÉLY
Zalaapáti
Pacsa
Sármellék
Balatonszentgyörgy
Zalavár
Kis-Balaton
Balaton-Felvidéki
Gelse
Zalakomár
Principális-Csatorna
Balatonfenyves
Buzsák
Lengyeltóti
Kéthely
Somogy-sámson
Marcali
Somogyvár
Nikla
Osztopán
Mernye
Somogyfajsz
Mesztegnyö
Somogyjád
Szenyér
Miháld
Böhönye
Inke
Vése
Iharosberény
Segesd
Nagybajom
Kaposvár
Kaposfő
Juta
Kaposfüred
Toponár
Karád
Andocs
Igal
Bedegkér
97
98
112
124
352
187
119
77
63
3
4
A
B
C

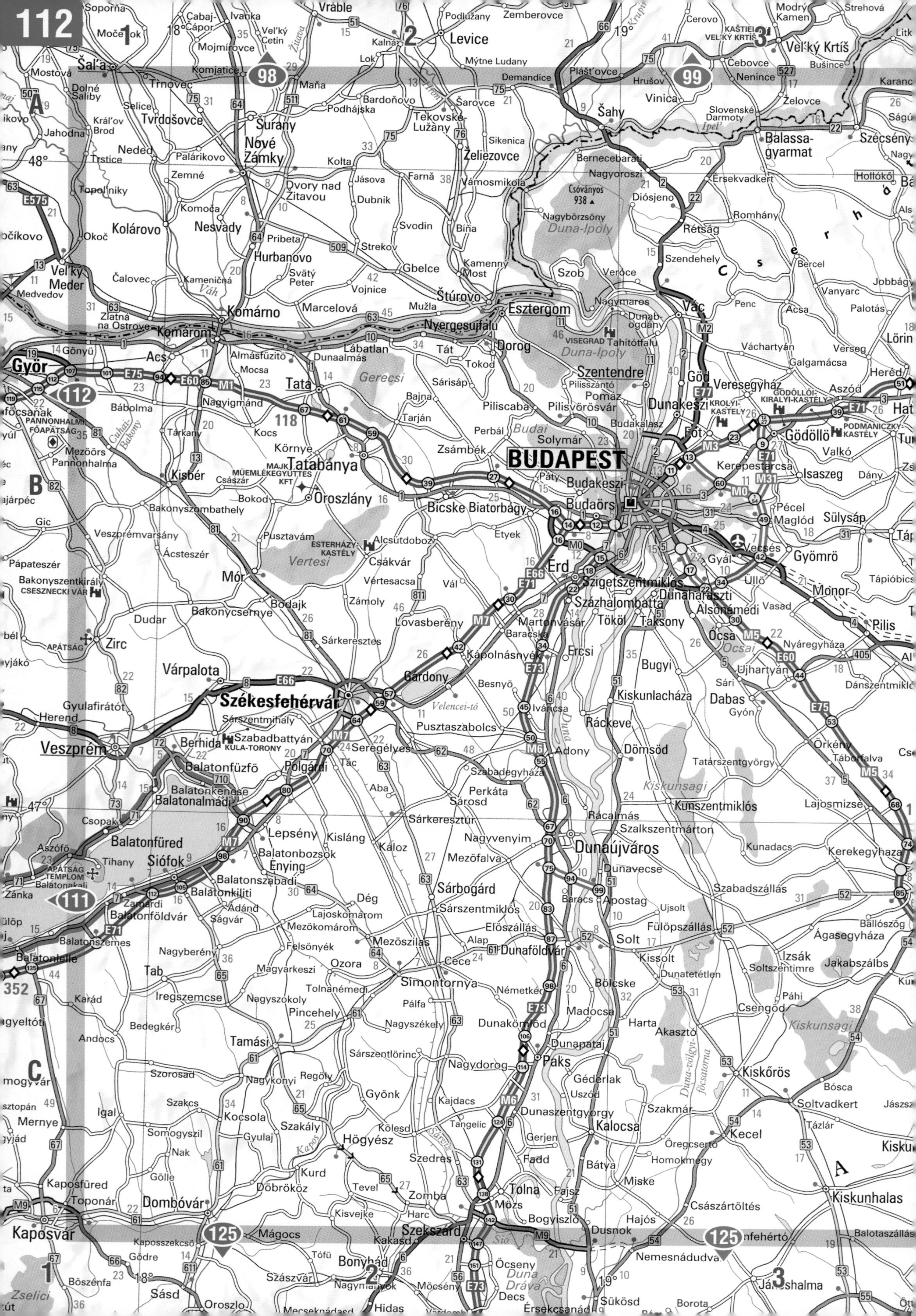

Levice
Šahy
Veľký Krtíš
Balassagyarmat
Nové Zámky
Šurany
Želiezovce
Kolárovo
Nesvady
Hurbanovo
Komárno
Komárom
Štúrovo
Esztergom
Nyergesújfalu
Vác
Győr
Tata
Tatabánya
Oroszlány
Kisbér
Pannonhalma
Szentendre
Dunakeszi
Göd
Veresegyház
Gödöllő
BUDAPEST
Budaörs
Budakeszi
Érd
Szigetszentmiklós
Százhalombatta
Dunaharaszti
Vecsés
Gyömrő
Monor
Pilis
Ócsa
Dabas
Bicske
Biatorbágy
Mór
Zirc
Várpalota
Székesfehérvár
Veszprém
Balatonfüred
Balatonalmádi
Balatonfűző
Siófok
Tihany
Gárdony
Velencei-tó
Ráckeve
Kunszentmiklós
Dunaújváros
Sárbogárd
Simontornya
Tamási
Paks
Kalocsa
Kiskőrös
Kiskunhalas
Dombóvár
Kaposvár
Szekszárd
Tolna
Bonyhád
Lajosmizse
Solt
Balaton
Duna
Duna-Ipoly
Gerecsi
Vértesi
Budai
Kiskunsági
Cserhát
Csóványos 938
Hollókő

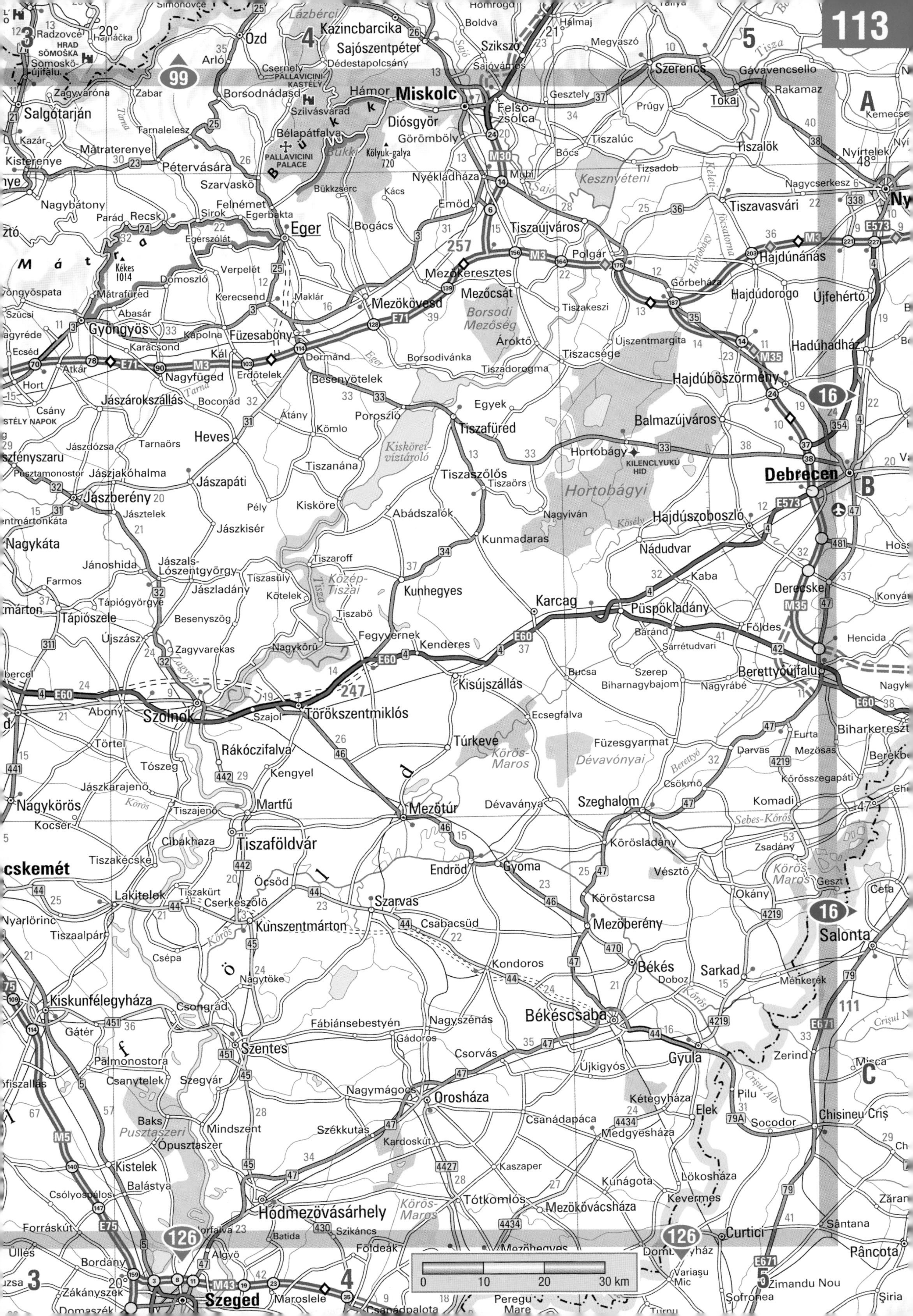
Miskolc
Eger
Ozd
Kazincbarcika
Sajószentpéter
Szerencs
Tokaj
Salgótarján
Gyöngyös
Füzesabony
Mezőkövesd
Tiszaújváros
Hajdúnánás
Hajdúböszörmény
Balmazújváros
Debrecen
Hajdúszoboszló
Hortobágy
Tiszafüred
Heves
Jászberény
Jászapáti
Kunhegyes
Karcag
Püspökladány
Berettyóújfalu
Szolnok
Törökszentmiklós
Kisújszállás
Túrkeve
Mezőtúr
Tiszaföldvár
Martfű
Szeghalom
Gyoma
Endrőd
Szarvas
Kunszentmárton
Mezőberény
Békés
Békéscsaba
Gyula
Orosháza
Szentes
Csongrád
Kiskunfélegyháza
Hódmezővásárhely
Szeged
Makó
Salonta
Curtici
Nagykőrös
Kecskemét
Hortobágyi
Bükk
Mátra
0 10 20 30 km

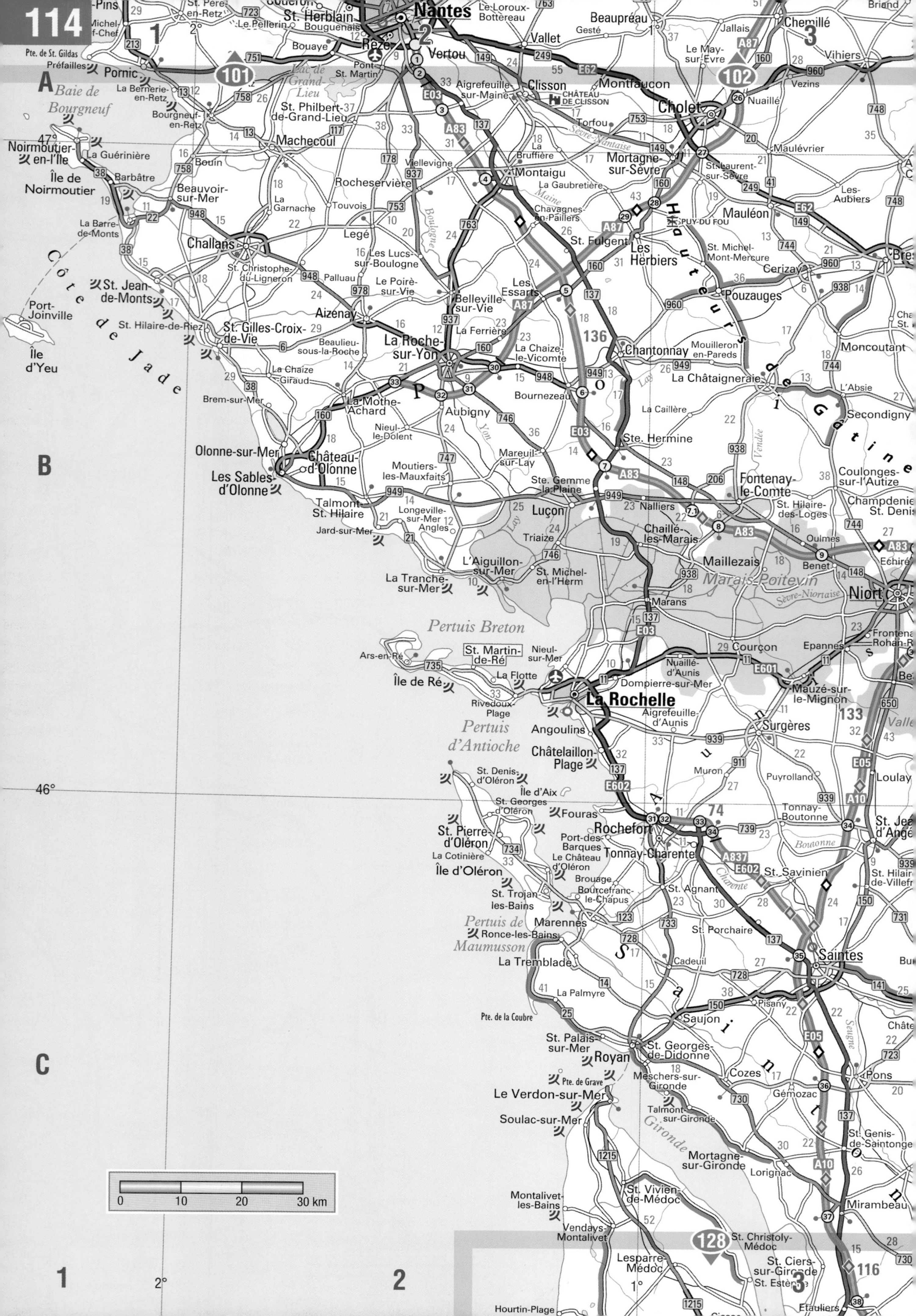
Nantes
St. Herblain
Bouguenais
Rezé
Vertou
Le Loroux-Bottereau
Beaupréau
Chemillé
Vallet
Le Pellerin
Bouaye
Pornic
Préfailles
Pte. de St. Gildas
Baie de Bourgneuf
La Bernerie-en-Retz
Bourgneuf-en-Retz
Lac de Grand-Lieu
Pont-St. Martin
St. Philbert-de-Grand-Lieu
Aigrefeuille-sur-Maine
Clisson
CHÂTEAU DE CLISSON
Montfaucon
Cholet
Nuaillé
Vihiers
Vezins
Le May-sur-Èvre
Jallais
Gesté
Torfou
Sèvre-Nantaise
Machecoul
Noirmoutier-en-l'Île
La Guérinière
Île de Noirmoutier
Barbâtre
Bouin
Beauvoir-sur-Mer
La Garnache
Rocheservière
Vieillevigne
Montaigu
La Bruffière
Mortagne-sur-Sèvre
Maulévrier
St. Laurent-sur-Sèvre
Les Aubiers
La Gaubretière
Chavagnes-en-Paillers
PUY-DU-FOU
Mauléon
La Barre-de-Monts
Challans
Touvois
Legé
Les Lucs-sur-Boulogne
St. Fulgent
Les Herbiers
St. Michel-Mont-Mercure
Cerizay
Bressuire
St. Christophe-du-Ligneron
Palluau
Le Poiré-sur-Vie
Les Essarts
Pouzauges
Côte de Jade
St. Jean-de-Monts
Port-Joinville
Île d'Yeu
St. Hilaire-de-Riez
St. Gilles-Croix-de-Vie
Aizenay
Belleville-sur-Vie
La Ferrière
La Roche-sur-Yon
Beaulieu-sous-la-Roche
La Chaize-le-Vicomte
Chantonnay
Mouilleron-en-Pareds
Moncoutant
La Chaize-Giraud
Brem-sur-Mer
La Mothe-Achard
Aubigny
Bournezeau
La Châtaigneraie
L'Absie
Secondigny
Hauteurs de la Gâtine
La Caillère
Nieul-le-Dolent
Ste. Hermine
Olonne-sur-Mer
Château-d'Olonne
Les Sables-d'Olonne
Moutiers-les-Mauxfaits
Mareuil-sur-Lay
Ste. Gemme-la-Plaine
Fontenay-le-Comte
Coulonges-sur-l'Autize
Talmont-St. Hilaire
Jard-sur-Mer
Longeville-sur-Mer
Angles
Luçon
Nalliers
St. Hilaire-des-Loges
Champdeniers-St. Denis
Triaize
Chaillé-les-Marais
Maillezais
Oulmes
Benet
Échiré
L'Aiguillon-sur-Mer
St. Michel-en-l'Herm
La Tranche-sur-Mer
Marais Poitevin
Sèvre-Niortaise
Niort
Marans
Pertuis Breton
Ars-en-Ré
St. Martin-de-Ré
Île de Ré
La Flotte
Rivedoux-Plage
Nieul-sur-Mer
Courçon
Epannes
Frontenay-Rohan-Rohan
Nuaillé-d'Aunis
Dompierre-sur-Mer
Mauzé-sur-le-Mignon
La Rochelle
Aigrefeuille-d'Aunis
Pertuis d'Antioche
Angoulins
Châtelaillon-Plage
Surgères
Muron
Puyrolland
Loulay
St. Denis-d'Oléron
Île d'Aix
St. Georges-d'Oléron
Fouras
St. Pierre-d'Oléron
La Cotinière
Île d'Oléron
Rochefort
Port-des-Barques
Le Château-d'Oléron
Tonnay-Charente
Tonnay-Boutonne
St. Jean-d'Angély
Boutonne
St. Savinien
St. Hilaire-de-Villefranche
St. Trojan-les-Bains
Brouage
Bourcefranc-le-Chapus
St. Agnant
Charente
Pertuis de Maumusson
Marennes
Ronce-les-Bains
St. Porchaire
La Tremblade
Cadeuil
Saintes
La Palmyre
Pte. de la Coubre
Saujon
Pisany
Seugne
St. Palais-sur-Mer
Royan
St. Georges-de-Didonne
Meschers-sur-Gironde
Cozes
Gémozac
Pons
Pte. de Grave
Le Verdon-sur-Mer
Talmont-sur-Gironde
Soulac-sur-Mer
Gironde
Mortagne-sur-Gironde
Lorignac
St. Genis-de-Saintonge
St. Vivien-de-Médoc
Mirambeau
Montalivet-les-Bains
Vendays-Montalivet
St. Christoly-Médoc
Lesparre-Médoc
St. Ciers-sur-Gironde
St. Estèphe
Étauliers
Hourtin-Plage
Saintonge
Aunis
Poitou
47°
46°
2°
1°
0
10
20
30 km
101
102
128
116
136
133
74
A
B
C
1
2
3

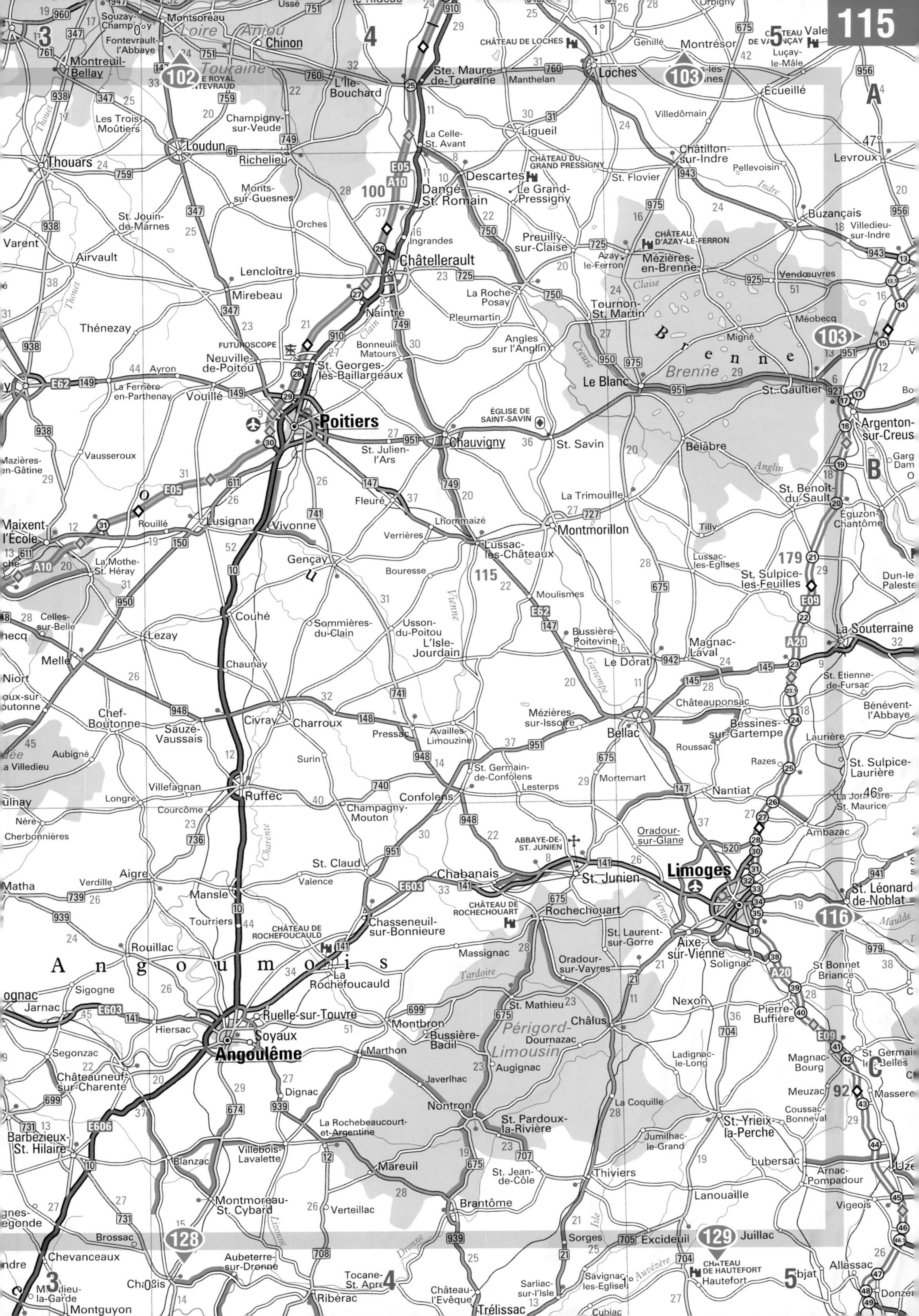
Souzay-Champigny
Montsoreau
Loire
Anjou
Chinon
Fontevrault-l'Abbaye
Montreuil-Bellay
Touraine
L'Île-Bouchard
Ste. Maure-de-Touraine
Manthelan
Loches
CHÂTEAU DE LOCHES
Genillé
Montrésor
Luçay-le-Mâle
Écueillé
Villedômain
Les Trois Moûtiers
Champigny-sur-Veude
Loudun
Richelieu
Thouars
La Celle-St. Avant
Ligueil
CHÂTEAU DU GRAND PRESSIGNY
Descartes
Le Grand-Pressigny
Châtillon-sur-Indre
Pellevoisin
Levroux
Dangé-St. Romain
Monts-sur-Guesnes
St. Flovier
Buzançais
Villedieu-sur-Indre
St. Jouin-de-Marnes
Orches
Ingrandes
Preuilly-sur-Claise
CHÂTEAU D'AZAY-LE-FERRON
Azay-le-Ferron
Mézières-en-Brenne
Vendœuvres
Varent
Airvault
Lencloître
Châtellerault
La Roche-Posay
Mirebeau
Naintré
Pleumartin
Tournon-St. Martin
Méobecq
Thénezay
Bonneuil-Matours
Angles sur l'Anglin
Brenne
Migné
FUTUROSCOPE
Neuville-de-Poitou
St. Georges-lès-Baillargeaux
Ayron
La Ferrière-en-Parthenay
Vouillé
Le Blanc
St.-Gaultier
Argenton-sur-Creuse
Poitiers
ÉGLISE DE SAINT-SAVIN
Chauvigny
St. Savin
Bélâbre
St. Julien-l'Ars
Mazières-en-Gâtine
Vausseroux
Fleuré
La Trimouille
St. Benoît-du-Sault
Éguzon-Chantôme
Lusignan
Vivonne
Lhommaizé
Montmorillon
Tilly
St.-Maixent-l'École
Rouillé
Verrières
Lussac-les-Châteaux
Lussac-les-Eglises
La Mothe-St. Héray
Gençay
Bouresse
St. Sulpice-les-Feuilles
Dun-le-Palestel
Celles-sur-Belle
Couhé
Sommières-du-Clain
Usson-du-Poitou
L'Isle-Jourdain
Moulismes
Bussière-Poitevine
La Souterraine
Lezay
Melle
Niort
Chaunay
Le Dorat
Magnac-Laval
St. Etienne-de-Fursac
Chef-Boutonne
Sauzé-Vaussais
Civray
Charroux
Pressac
Availles-Limouzine
Mézières-sur-Issoire
Bellac
Châteauponsac
Bénévent-l'Abbaye
Bessines-sur-Gartempe
Aubigné
Surin
Roussac
Laurière
Villefagnan
St. Germain-de-Confolens
Lesterps
Mortemart
Razes
St. Sulpice-Laurière
Longré
Ruffec
Confolens
Nantiat
Courcôme
Champagny-Mouton
La Jonchère-St. Maurice
Néré
Cherbonnières
Oradour-sur-Glane
Ambazac
ABBAYE-DE-ST. JUNIEN
St. Claud
Aigre
Verdille
Valence
Chabanais
St. Junien
Limoges
Matha
Mansle
CHÂTEAU DE ROCHECHOUART
Rochechouart
St. Léonard-de-Noblat
Tourriers
CHÂTEAU DE ROCHEFOUCAULD
Chasseneuil-sur-Bonnieure
St. Laurent-sur-Gorre
Aixe-sur-Vienne
Rouillac
Massignac
Oradour-sur-Vayres
Solignac
St Bonnet Briance
Angoumois
La Rochefoucauld
Sigogne
Tardoire
Jarnac
Hiersac
Ruelle-sur-Touvre
Montbron
St. Mathieu
Nexon
Pierre-Buffière
Soyaux
Angoulême
Bussière-Badil
Périgord-Limousin
Dournazac
Châlus
Segonzac
Marthon
Augignac
Ladignac-le-Long
Magnac-Bourg
St. Germain-les-Belles
Châteauneuf-sur-Charente
Javerlhac
Dignac
Meuzac
Masseret
Nontron
La Coquille
Coussac-Bonneval
La Rochebeaucourt-et-Argentine
St. Pardoux-la-Rivière
St.-Yrieix-la-Perche
Barbezieux-St. Hilaire
Villebois-Lavalette
Jumilhac-le-Grand
Blanzac
Mareuil
St. Jean-de-Côle
Thiviers
Lubersac
Arnac-Pompadour
Uzerche
Montmoreau-St. Cybard
Verteillac
Brantôme
Lanouaille
Vigeois
Brossac
Sorges
Excideuil
Juillac
Chevanceaux
Aubeterre-sur-Dronne
CHÂTEAU DE HAUTEFORT
Allassac
Tocane-St. Apre
Savignac-les-Eglises
Hautefort
Montlieu-la-Garde
Chalais
Ribérac
Château-l'Evêque
Sarliac-sur-l'Isle
Donzenac
Montguyon
Trélissac
Cubjac
Dronne
Vienne
Charente
Creuse
Indre
Claise
Anglin
Gartempe
Thouet
Clain
Auvézère
Isle
Lizonne
Maulde
Cognac

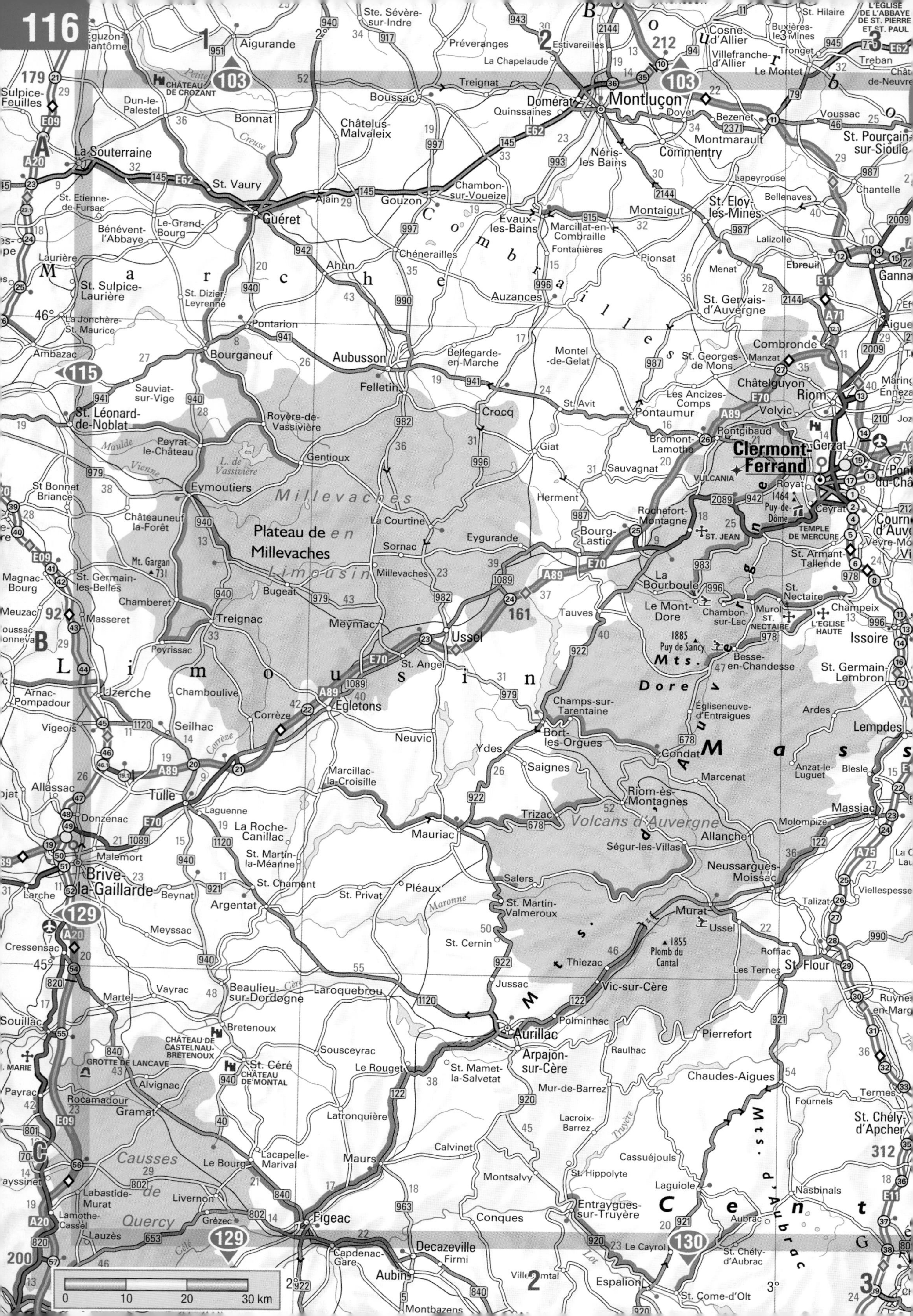
Aigurande
Ste. Sévère-sur-Indre
Préveranges
Estivareilles
La Chapelaude
Cosne-d'Allier
Villefranche-d'Allier
Buxières-les-Mines
St. Hilaire
L'EGLISE DE L'ABBAYE DE ST. PIERRE ET ST. PAUL
Tronget
Le Montet
Treban
Châteaumeillant
CHÂTEAU DE CROZANT
Treignat
Domérat
Montluçon
Quinssaines
Doyet
Bezenet
Voussac
Dun-le-Palestel
Bonnat
Boussac
Châtelus-Malvaleix
Néris-les-Bains
Commentry
Montmarault
St. Pourçain-sur-Sioule
Sulpice-Feuilles
La Souterraine
St. Vaury
Chambon-sur-Voueize
Lapeyrouse
Chantelle
St. Etienne-de-Fursac
Guéret
Ajain
Gouzon
Evaux-les-Bains
Marcillat-en-Combraille
Montaigut
St. Eloy-les-Mines
Bellenaves
Bénévent-l'Abbaye
Le-Grand-Bourg
Fontanières
Pionsat
Lalizolle
Laurière
Marche
Chénerailles
Combrailles
Menat
Ebreuil
Gannat
St. Sulpice-Laurière
St. Dizier-Leyrenne
Ahun
Auzances
St. Gervais-d'Auvergne
La Jonchère-St. Maurice
Pontarion
Aigueperse
Ambazac
Bourganeuf
Aubusson
Bellegarde-en-Marche
Montel-de-Gelat
St. Georges-de Mons
Manzat
Combronde
Sauviat-sur-Vige
Felletin
Les Ancizes-Comps
Châtelguyon
Riom
St. Léonard-de-Noblat
Royère-de-Vassivière
Crocq
St. Avit
Pontaumur
Volvic
Ennezat
Peyrat-le-Château
L. de Vassivière
Gentioux
Giat
Bromont-Lamothe
Pontgibaud
Gerzat
Clermont-Ferrand
Vienne
Maulde
St Bonnet Briance
Millevaches
Sauvagnat
VULCANIA
Eymoutiers
Herment
Royat
Puy-de-Dôme
Ceyrat
Pont-du-Château
Châteauneuf-la-Forêt
La Courtine
Rochefort-Montagne
ST. JEAN
TEMPLE DE MERCURE
Cournon-d'Auvergne
Plateau de Millevaches
Sornac
Eygurande
Bourg-Lastic
Veyre-Monton
Mt. Gargan 731
Limousin
Millevaches
St. Armant-Tallende
Magnac-Bourg
St. Germain-les-Belles
Bugeat
La Bourboule
St. Nectaire
Champeix
Chamberet
Meuzac
Masseret
Le Mont-Dore
Chambon-sur-Lac
Murol
ST. NECTAIRE
L'EGLISE HAUTE
Tauves
Treignac
Meymac
Ussel
Issoire
Peyrissac
Puy de Sancy 1885
Mts. Dore
Besse-en-Chandesse
St. Angel
St. Germain-Lembron
Arnac-Pompadour
Uzerche
Chamboulive
Egletons
Champs-sur-Tarentaine
Églisneuve-d'Entraigues
Ardes
Vigeois
Seilhac
Corrèze
Neuvic
Bort-les-Orgues
Lempdes
Ydes
Condat
Saignes
Anzat-le-Luguet
Blesle
Allassac
Tulle
Marcillac-la-Croisille
Marcenat
Riom-ès-Montagnes
Massiac
Donzenac
Laguenne
La Roche-Canillac
Mauriac
Trizac
Volcans d'Auvergne
Allanche
Molompize
Ségur-les-Villas
Malemort
St. Martin-la-Méanne
Brive-la-Gaillarde
Larche
Beynat
St. Chamant
Neussargues-Moissac
Argentat
St. Privat
Pléaux
Salers
Viellespesse
Maronne
St. Martin-Valmeroux
Talizat
Murat
Ussel
Meyssac
Cressensac
St. Cernin
1855 Plomb du Cantal
Roffiac
Thiezac
St. Flour
Les Ternes
Martel
Vayrac
Beaulieu-sur-Dordogne
Laroquebrou
Jussac
Vic-sur-Cère
Mts. du Cantal
Souillac
Bretenoux
Polminhac
Aurillac
Pierrefort
CHÂTEAU DE CASTELNAU-BRETENOUX
Sousceyrac
Arpajon-sur-Cère
Raulhac
GROTTE DE LANCAVE
St. Céré
CHÂTEAU DE MONTAL
Le Rouget
St. Mamet-la-Salvetat
Chaudes-Aigues
Alvignac
Payrac
Mur-de-Barrez
Rocamadour
Gramat
Latronquière
Fournels
St. Chély-d'Apcher
Lacroix-Barrez
Truyère
Calvinet
Cassuéjouls
Causses de Quercy
Le Bourg
Lacapelle-Marival
Maurs
Montsalvy
St. Hippolyte
Laguiole
Nasbinals
Labastide-Murat
Livernon
Mts. d'Aubrac
Lamothe-Cassel
Grèzec
Figeac
Conques
Entraygues-sur-Truyère
Aubrac
Lauzès
Célé
Capdenac-Gare
Decazeville
Firmi
Le Cayrol
St. Chély-d'Aubrac
Aubin
Villecomtal
Espalion
St. Come-d'Olt
Montbazens
0 10 20 30 km

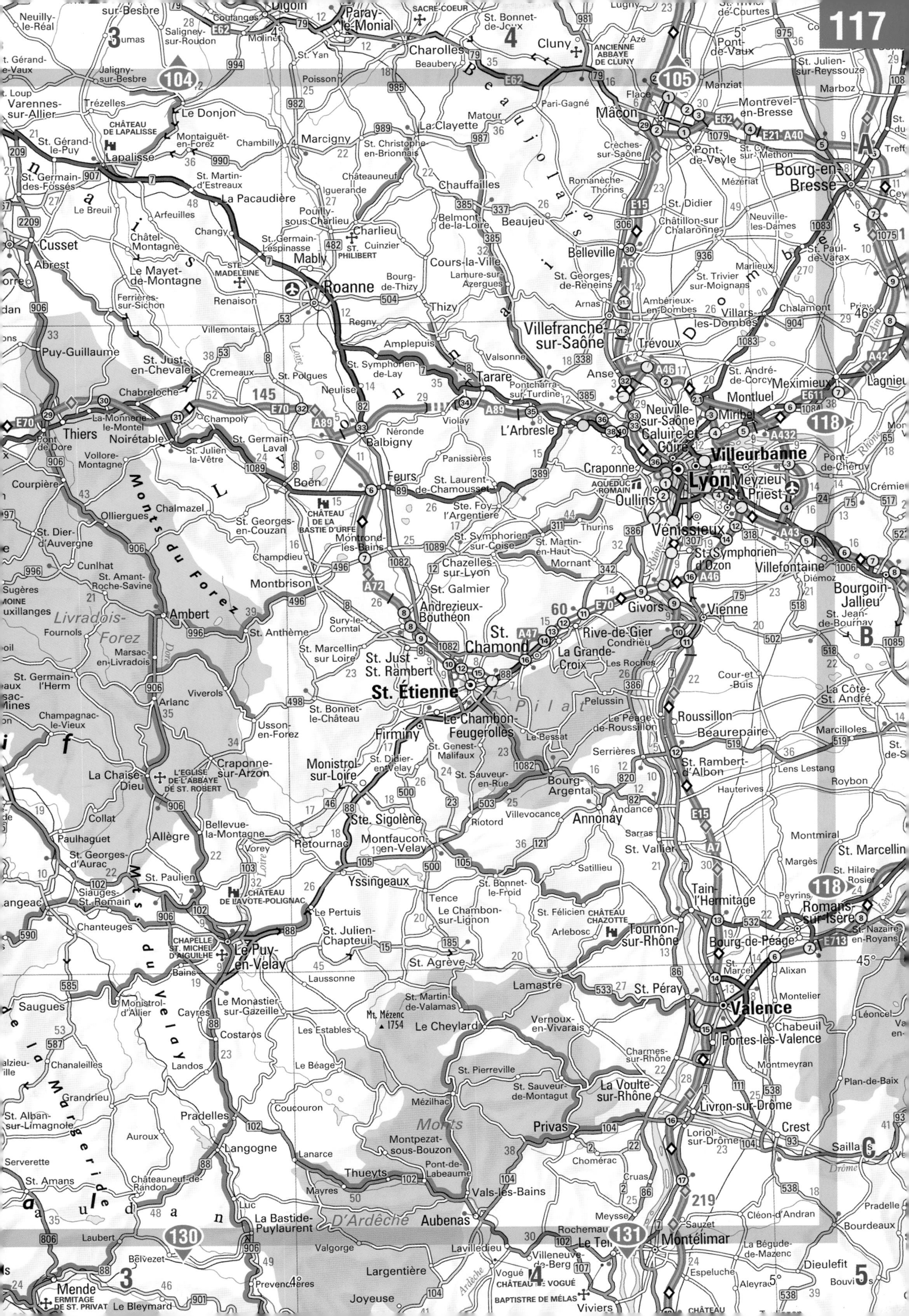
Digoin
Paray-le-Monial
Charolles
Cluny
Mâcon
Le Donjon
Lapalisse
Marcigny
La Clayette
Bourg-en-Bresse
Chauffailles
Beaujeu
Belleville
Cusset
Roanne
Mably
Thizy
Villefranche-sur-Saône
Trévoux
Tarare
Anse
Neuville-sur-Saône
Meximieux
Montluel
Thiers
Noirétable
Boën
Feurs
L'Arbresle
Villeurbanne
Lyon
Oullins
Vénissieux
Craponne
St. Priest
Montbrison
Ambert
St. Étienne
St. Chamond
Rive-de-Gier
Givors
Vienne
Andrezieux-Bouthéon
Firminy
Monistrol-sur-Loire
Annonay
Roussillon
Beaurepaire
Bourgoin-Jallieu
Villefontaine
La Chaise-Dieu
Yssingeaux
Le Puy-en-Velay
Tournon-sur-Rhône
Tain-l'Hermitage
Romans-sur-Isère
Bourg-de-Péage
Valence
St. Péray
Lamastre
Le Cheylard
La Voulte-sur-Rhône
Privas
Livron-sur-Drôme
Crest
Langogne
Aubenas
Montélimar
Mende
Monts du Forez
Monts du Lyonnais
Beaujolais
Dombes
Pilat
Mts du Velay
Livradois-Forez
Mt. Mézenc 1754
104
105
118
130
131
3
4
5
A
B
C

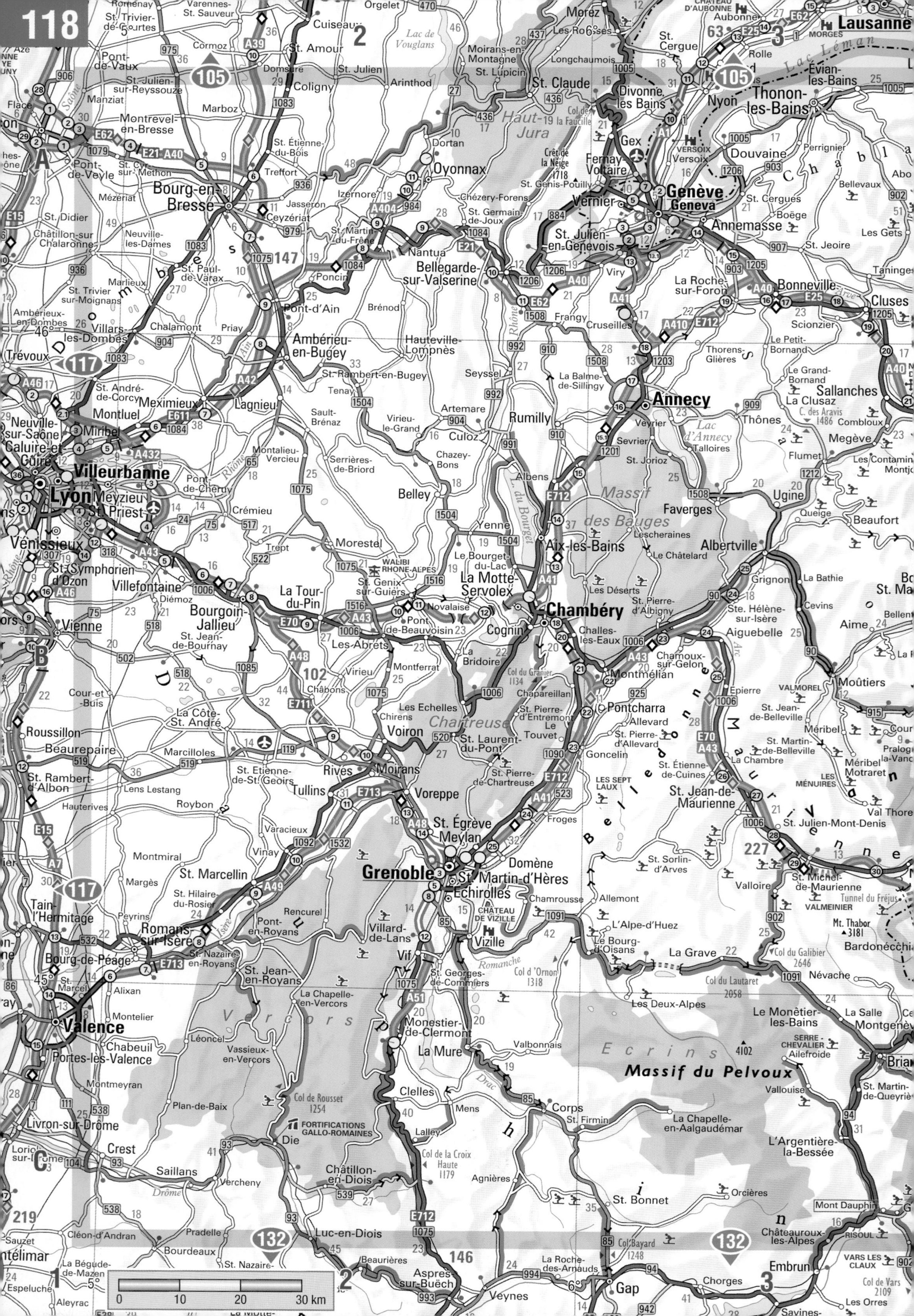

Cuiseaux
St. Amour
Lac de Vouglans
Orgelet
Moirans-en-Montagne
St. Lupicin
St. Claude
Morez
Les Rousses
Longchaumois
Haut-Jura
Col de la Faucille
Crêt de la Neige 1718
Divonne-les-Bains
Gex
Ferney-Voltaire
St. Cergue
Nyon
Versoix
Château d'Aubonne
Aubonne
Lausanne
Morges
Rolle
Lac Léman
Évian-les-Bains
Thonon-les-Bains
Douvaine
Perrignier
Chablais
Genève
Geneva
Vernier
Annemasse
St. Julien-en-Genevois
Viry
Boëge
St. Cergues
Bellevaux
Les Gets
St. Jeoire
La Roche-sur-Foron
Bonneville
Cluses
Taninges
Scionzier
Le Petit-Bornand
Thorens-Glières
Le Grand-Bornand
La Clusaz
C. des Aravis 1486
Sallanches
Combloux
Megève
Thônes
Annecy
Lac d'Annecy
Talloires
Veyrier
Sevrier
St. Jorioz
Cruseilles
Frangy
La Balme-de-Sillingy
Rumilly
Seyssel
Bellegarde-sur-Valserine
Chézery-Forens
St. Germain-de-Joux
Nantua
Oyonnax
Dortan
Izernore
Jasseron
Ceyzériat
Bourg-en-Bresse
Treffort
St. Étienne-du-Bois
Marboz
Montrevel-en-Bresse
Coligny
St. Julien
Arinthod
Domsure
Cormoz
Pont-de-Vaux
St. Trivier-de-Courtes
St. Julien-sur-Reyssouze
Manziat
Pont-de-Veyle
Mézériat
St. Didier
Châtillon-sur-Chalaronne
Neuville-les-Dames
St. Paul-de-Varax
Marlieux
St. Trivier-sur-Moignans
Ambérieux-en-Dombes
Villars-les-Dombes
Dombes
Chalamont
Priay
Pont-d'Ain
Poncin
Brénod
Ambérieu-en-Bugey
Hauteville-Lompnès
St. Rambert-en-Bugey
Tenay
Trévoux
St. André-de-Corcy
Meximieux
Montluel
Lagnieu
Miribel
Neuville-sur-Saône
Caluire-et-Cuire
Villeurbanne
Lyon
Meyzieu
St. Priest
Vénissieux
St. Symphorien-d'Ozon
Vienne
Villefontaine
Diémoz
Bourgoin-Jallieu
St. Jean-de-Bournay
Pont-de-Chéruy
Crémieu
Trept
Montalieu-Vercieu
Serrières-de-Briord
Sault-Brénaz
Virieu-le-Grand
Artemare
Culoz
Chazey-Bons
Belley
Morestel
Walibi Rhône-Alpes
St. Genix-sur-Guiers
La Tour-du-Pin
Les Abrets
Pont-de-Beauvoisin
Novalaise
Yenne
Le Bourget-du-Lac
La Motte-Servolex
Lac du Bourget
Albens
Aix-les-Bains
Massif des Bauges
Lescheraines
Le Châtelard
Les Déserts
Chambéry
Cognin
Challes-les-Eaux
St. Pierre-d'Albigny
Faverges
Ugine
Albertville
Flumet
Les Contamines-Montjoie
Queige
Beaufort
Grignon
La Bathie
Cevins
Ste. Hélène-sur-Isère
Aiguebelle
Aime
Moûtiers
Valmorel
St. Jean-de-Belleville
Méribel
Courchevel
St. Martin-de-Belleville
Méribel Motraret
Les Ménuires
Val Thorens
Montmélian
Chamoux-sur-Gelon
Épierre
Pontcharra
Allevard
St. Pierre-d'Allevard
Goncelin
Les Sept Laux
La Chambre
St. Étienne-de-Cuines
St. Jean-de-Maurienne
St. Julien-Mont-Denis
Maurienne
Belledonne
Chapareillan
St. Pierre-d'Entremont
Le Touvet
Col du Granier 1134
La Bridoire
Montferrat
Virieu
Châbons
Les Echelles
Chartreuse
St. Laurent-du-Pont
St. Pierre-de-Chartreuse
Chirens
Voiron
Moirans
Rives
Tullins
Voreppe
St. Égrève
Meylan
Grenoble
Domène
St. Martin-d'Hères
Échirolles
Froges
Crolles
La Côte-St. André
Beaurepaire
Marcilloles
St. Etienne-de-St. Geoirs
Roybon
Lens Lestang
Hauterives
Roussillon
St. Rambert-d'Albon
Cour-et-Buis
Vinay
Varacieux
Montmiral
St. Marcellin
Margès
St. Hilaire-du-Rosier
Peyrins
Romans-sur-Isère
Bourg-de-Péage
Tain-l'Hermitage
St. Marcel
Alixan
Valence
Montelier
Chabeuil
Portes-lès-Valence
Montmeyran
Livron-sur-Drôme
Loriol-sur-Drôme
Crest
Saillans
Vercheny
Plan-de-Baix
Léoncel
Vassieux-en-Vercors
Vercors
Col de Rousset 1254
Fortifications Gallo-Romaines
Die
Châtillon-en-Diois
Luc-en-Diois
Cléon-d'Andran
Pradelle
Bourdeaux
St. Nazaire-le-Désert
Montélimar
La Bégude-de-Mazenc
Espeluche
Aleyrac
Rencurel
Pont-en-Royans
St. Nazaire-en-Royans
St. Jean-en-Royans
La Chapelle-en-Vercors
Villard-de-Lans
Vif
Vizille
Château de Vizille
Chamrousse
St. Georges-de-Commiers
Monestier-de-Clermont
La Mure
Clelles
Mens
Lalley
Col de la Croix Haute 1179
Agnières
Valbonnais
Col d'Ornon 1318
Allemont
L'Alpe-d'Huez
Le Bourg-d'Oisans
Les Deux-Alpes
La Grave
Col du Lautaret 2058
Col du Galibier 2646
Valloire
St. Sorlin-d'Arves
St. Michel-de-Maurienne
Valmeinier
Tunnel du Fréjus
Mt. Thabor 3181
Bardonécchia
Névache
Le Monêtier-les-Bains
La Salle
Montgenèvre
Serre-Chevalier
Ailefroide
Briançon
Ecrins
Massif du Pelvoux
4102
Vallouise
St. Martin-de-Queyrière
L'Argentière-la-Bessée
Corps
St. Firmin
La Chapelle-en-Valgaudémar
St. Bonnet
Orcières
Mont Dauphin
Châteauroux-les-Alpes
Risoul
Embrun
Chorges
Vars les Claux
Col de Vars 2109
Les Orres
Savines
Col Bayard 1248
Gap
La Roche-des-Arnauds
Veynes
Aspres-sur-Buëch
Beaurières
0 10 20 30 km

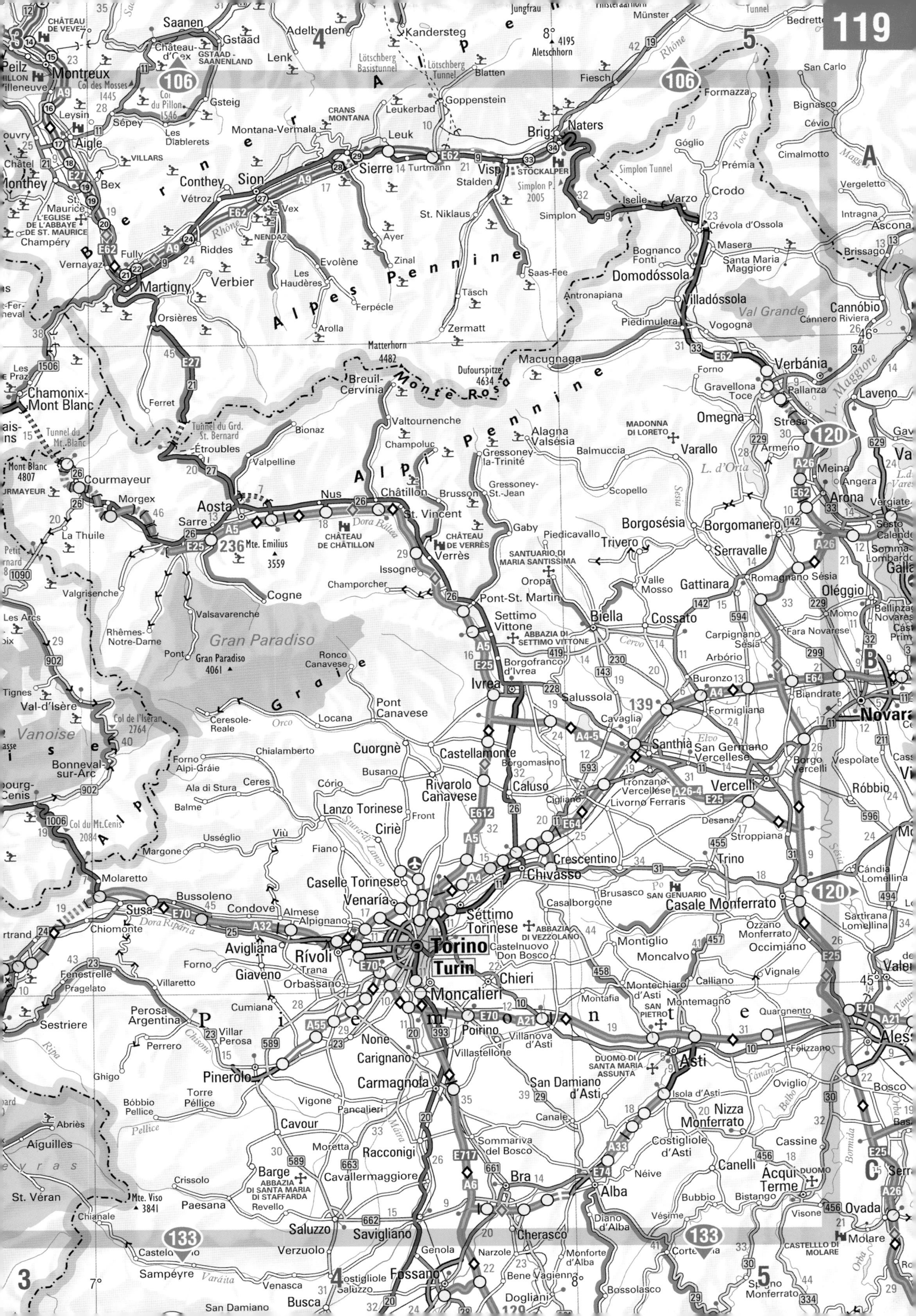
Saanen
Gstaad
Adelboden
Kandersteg
Jungfrau
Münster
Bedretto
Château-d'Oex
GSTAAD - SAANENLAND
Lenk
Lötschberg Basistunnel
Lötschberg Tunnel
Blatten
Aletschhorn
4195
Fiesch
Rhône
Montreux
Col des Mosses
1445
Col du Pillon
1546
Gsteig
Leysin
Sépey
Les Diablerets
CRANS MONTANA
Montana-Vermala
Leukerbad
Goppenstein
Leuk
Brig
Naters
Formazza
San Carlo
Bignasco
Cévio
Aigle
VILLARS
Sierre
Turtmann
Visp
STOCKALPER
Góglio
Cimalmotto
Simplon Tunnel
Prémia
Monthey
Bex
Conthey
Sion
Vétroz
Stalden
Simplon P.
2005
Crodo
Vergeletto
St. Maurice
L'EGLISE DE L'ABBAYE DE ST. MAURICE
Champéry
Vex
NENDAZ
Ayer
St. Niklaus
Simplon
Iselle
Varzo
Crévola d'Ossola
Intragna
Ascona
Riddes
Fully
Vernayaz
Zinal
Evolène
Les Haudères
Masera
Bognanco Fonti
Santa Maria Maggiore
Brissago
Martigny
Verbier
Alpes Pennine
Saas-Fee
Domodóssola
Ferpécle
Täsch
Antronapiana
Villadóssola
Cannóbio
Cánnero Riviera
Val Grande
Orsières
Arolla
Zermatt
Piedimulera
Vogogna
Matterhorn
4482
Dufourspitze
4634
Macugnaga
Verbánia
Forno
Gravellona Toce
Pallanza
L. Maggiore
Laveno
Chamonix-Mont Blanc
Ferret
Breuil-Cervínia
Monte Rosa
Alpi Pennine
Tunnel du Mt. Blanc
Tunnel du Grd. St. Bernard
Étroubles
Bionaz
Valtournenche
Alagna Valsésia
MADONNA DI LORETO
Omegna
Stresa
Mont Blanc
4807
Courmayeur
Valpelline
Champoluc
Gressoney-la-Trinité
Balmuccia
Varallo
Armeno
L. d'Orta
Meina
Angera
Morgex
Aosta
Nus
Châtillon
Brusson
Gressoney-St.-Jean
Scopello
Arona
Vergiate
La Thuile
Sarre
St. Vincent
Dora Báltea
CHÂTEAU DE CHÂTILLON
CHÂTEAU DE VERRÈS
Verrès
Gaby
Piedicavallo
Trivero
Borgosésia
Borgomanero
Sesto Calende
Mte. Emilius
3559
SANTUARIO DI MARIA SANTISSIMA
Serravalle
Issogne
Oropa
Romagnano Sésia
Valgrisenche
Cogne
Champorcher
Pont-St. Martin
Valle Mosso
Gattinara
Oléggio
Les Arcs
Valsavarenche
Settimo Vittone
Biella
Cossato
Momo
Rhêmes-Notre-Dame
Gran Paradiso
ABBAZIA DI SETTIMO VITTONE
Cervo
Carpignano Sésia
Fara Novarese
Pont
Gran Paradiso
4061
Ronco Canavese
Borgofranco d'Ivrea
Arbório
Tignes
Val-d'Isère
Alpi Graie
Ivrea
Salussola
Buronzo
Biandrate
Novara
Col de l'Iseran
2764
Pont Canavese
Locana
Orco
Cavaglia
Formigliana
Vanoise
Ceresole-Reale
Santhià
Elvo
San Germano Vercellese
Chialamberto
Cuorgnè
Castellamonte
Borgomasino
Borgo Vercelli
Vespolate
Bonneval-sur-Arc
Forno Alpi-Gráie
Busano
Caluso
Tronzano-Vercellese
Vercelli
Róbbio
Ceres
Cório
Rivarolo Canavese
Cigliano
Livorno Ferraris
Ala di Stura
Balme
Lanzo Torinese
Front
Desana
Col du Mt. Cenis
2084
Usséglio
Viù
Ciriè
Stura di Lanzo
Stroppiana
Margone
Fiano
Crescentino
Trino
Cándia Lomellina
Molaretto
Caselle Torinese
Chivasso
Po
SAN GENUARIO
Brusasco
Casale Monferrato
Bussoleno
Venaría
Casalborgone
Susa
Condove
Almese
Settimo Torinese
ABBAZIA DI VEZZOLANO
Sartirana Lomellina
Dora Riparia
Alpignano
Chiomonte
Avigliana
Torino
Turin
Castelnuovo Don Bosco
Montiglio
Ozzano Monferrato
Occimiano
Rívoli
Moncalvo
Fenestrelle
Forno
Trana
Giaveno
Chieri
Vignale
Pragelato
Villaretto
Orbassano
Moncalieri
Montechiaro d'Asti
Calliano
Cumiana
Montafia
SAN PIETRO
Montemagno
Quargnento
Perosa Argentina
Sestriere
Villar Perosa
Piemonte
Poirino
Villanova d'Asti
Chisone
None
Perrero
Villastellone
DUOMO DI SANTA MARIA ASSUNTA
Asti
Felizzano
Carignano
Ghigo
Pinerolo
Carmagnola
San Damiano d'Asti
Isola d'Asti
Oviglio
Tánaro
Bosco
Torre Péllice
Bóbbio Pellice
Vigone
Nizza Monferrato
Pancalieri
Belbo
Abriès
Pellice
Cavour
Canale
Aiguilles
Moretta
Sommariva del Bosco
Costigliole d'Asti
Cassine
Queyras
Racconigi
Bormida
Barge
ABBAZIA DI SANTA MARIA DI STAFFARDA
Cavallermaggiore
Canelli
Crissolo
Bra
Néive
Acqui Terme
DUOMO
Alba
St. Véran
Mte. Viso
3841
Paesana
Revello
Bubbio
Bistango
Chianale
Diano d'Alba
Ovada
Vésime
Visone
Saluzzo
Savigliano
Cherasco
Molare
Verzuolo
Genola
Narzole
Monforte d'Alba
Cortemilia
CASTELLO DI MOLARE
Sampéyre
Varáita
Costigliole Saluzzo
Fossano
Bene Vagienna
Venasca
Bossolasco
Spigno Monferrato
Busca
Dogliani
San Damiano
Orba

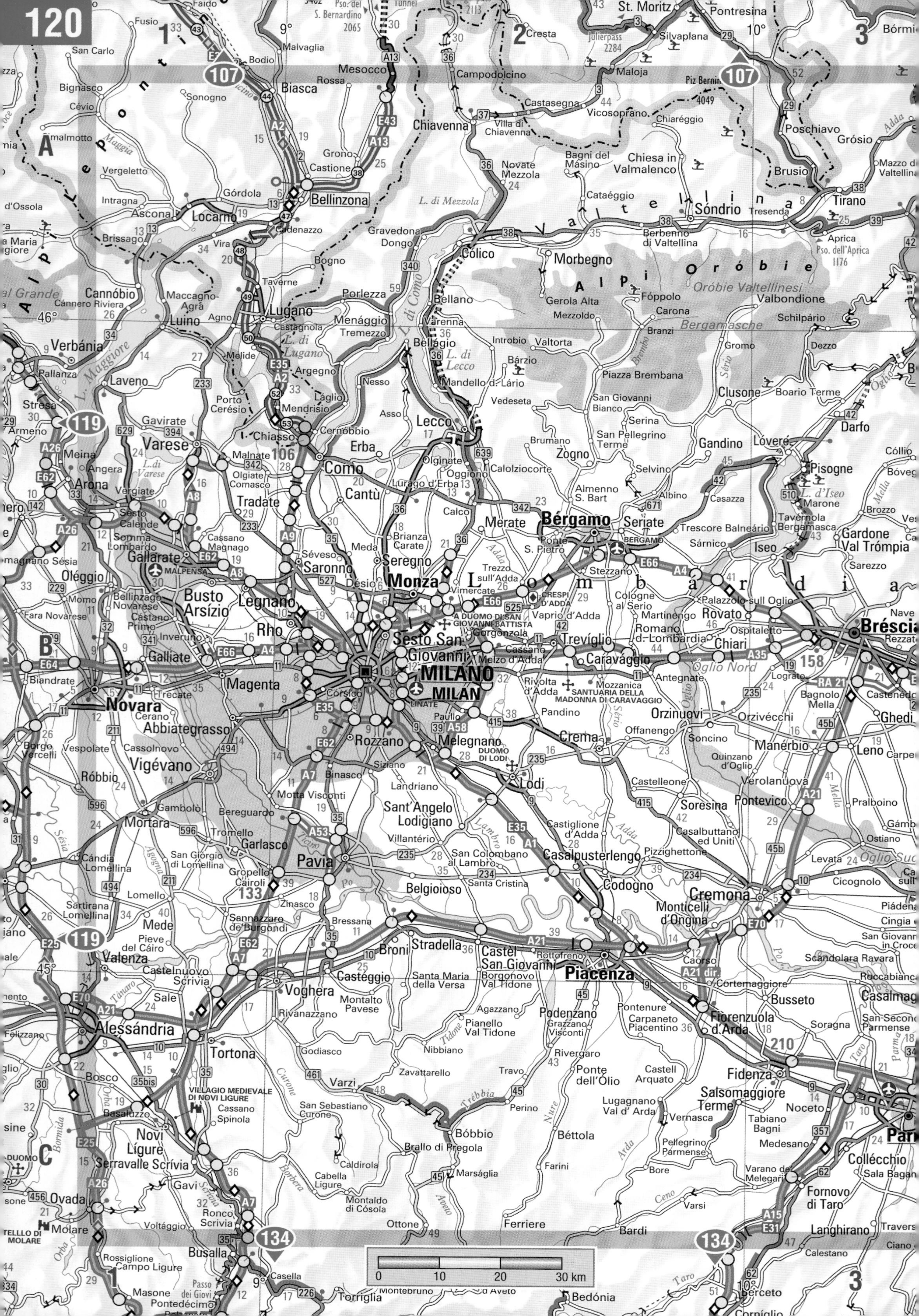
St. Moritz
Pontresina
Chiavenna
Bellinzona
Locarno
Lugano
Sóndrio
Tirano
Alpi Oróbie
Valtellina
Verbánia
Lecco
Como
Varese
Bérgamo
Monza
MILANO
MILAN
Brescia
Novara
Vigévano
Pavia
Lodi
Crema
Cremona
Piacenza
Alessándria
Tortona
Voghera
Fidenza
Novi Ligure
Ovada
Lombardia
0 10 20 30 km

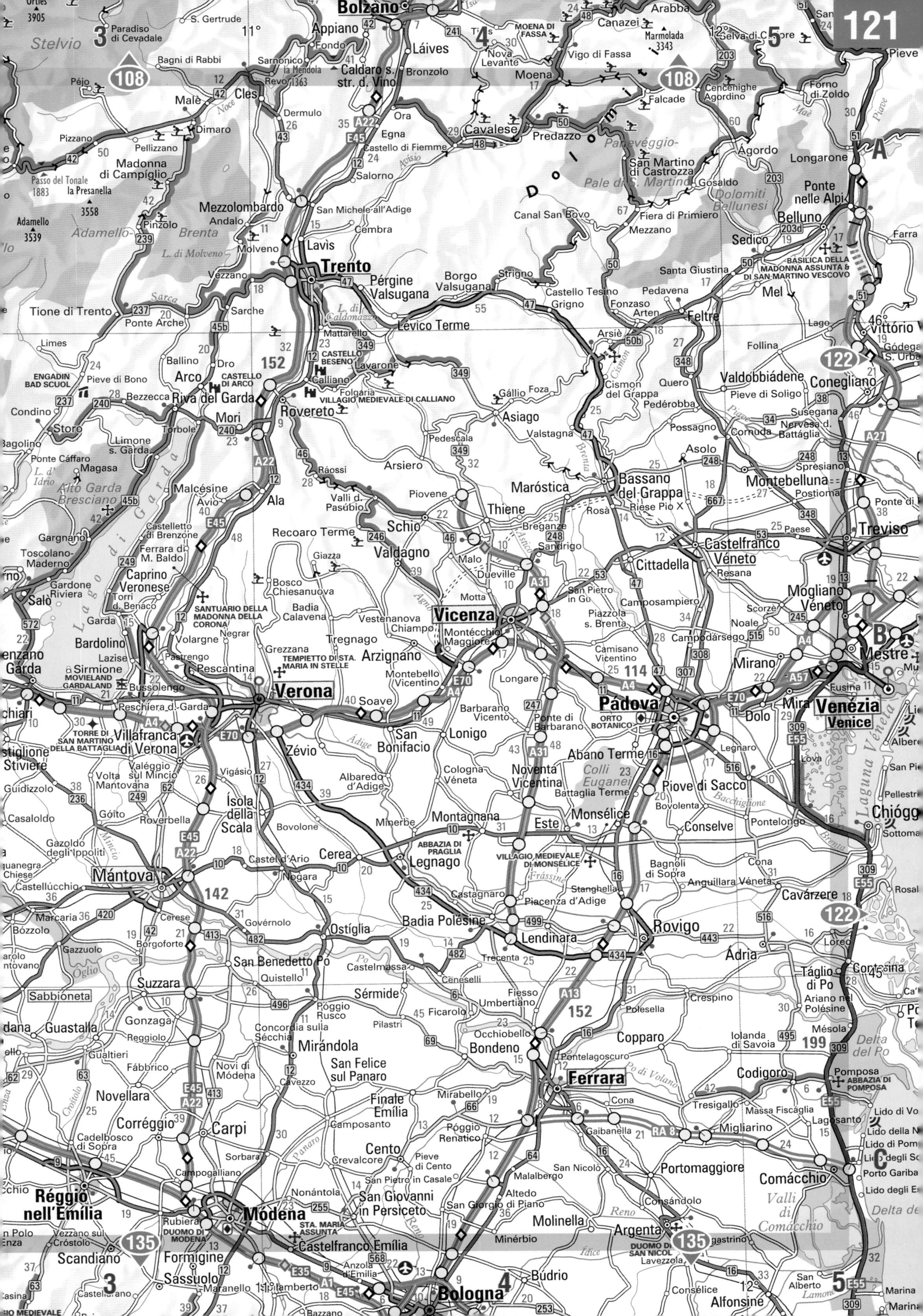
Bolzano
Appiano
Paradiso di Cevadale
S. Gertrude
Stelvio
Bagni di Rabbi
Péjo
Malè
Cles
Sarnonico
Caldaro s. str. d. Vino
Bronzolo
Láives
Moena di Fassa
Nova Levante
Moena
Canazei
Arabba
Marmolada 3343
Vigo di Fassa
Selva di Cadore
Pieve
Cencenighe Agordino
Falcade
Forno di Zoldo
Dermulo
Dimaro
Ora
Egna
Cavalese
Predazzo
Castello di Fiemme
Pizzano
Pellizzano
Madonna di Campíglio
Passo del Tonale 1883
la Presanella 3558
Adamello 3539
Dolomiti
Paneveggio
San Martino di Castrozza
Pale di S. Martino
Gosaldo
Ágordo
Longarone
Dolomiti Bellunesi
Ponte nelle Alpi
Belluno
Salorno
Mezzolombardo
Andalo
Pinzolo
Adamello-Brenta
L. di Molveno
Molveno
San Michele all'Adige
Cembra
Lavìs
Trento
Canal San Bovo
Fiera di Primiero
Mezzano
Sedico
Basilica della Madonna Assunta & di San Martino Vescovo
Vezzano
Pérgine Valsugana
Borgo Valsugana
Strigno
Castello Tesino
Grigno
Santa Giustina
Pedavena
Mel
Fonzaso
Arten
Feltre
Tione di Trento
Ponte Arche
Sarche
Lévico Terme
L. di Caldonazzo
Limes
Engadin Bad Scuol
Pieve di Bono
Ballino
Dro
Arco
Castello di Arco
Mattarello
Castello Beseno
Lavarone
Calliano
Folgaria
Villaggio Medievale di Calliano
Asiago
Gállio
Foza
Arsiè
Cismon
Cismon del Grappa
Lago
Vittório
Follina
Valdobbiádene
Quero
Conegliano
Pieve di Soligo
Pederobba
Condino
Bezzecca
Riva del Garda
Storo
Mori
Torbole
Rovereto
Limone s. Garda
Bagolino
Ponte Cáffaro
L. d'Idrio
Magasa
Alto Garda Bresciano
Pedescala
Valstagna
Arsiero
Ráossi
Possagno
Asolo
Cornuda
Nervesa d. Battáglia
Susegana
Spresiano
Montebelluna
Postioma
Bassano del Grappa
Maróstica
Riese Pio X
Rosà
Malcésine
Avio
Ala
Piovene
Valli d. Pasúbio
Thiene
Breganze
Sandrigo
Castelletto di Brenzone
Gargnano
Toscolano-Maderno
Ferrara di M. Baldo
Caprino Veronese
Recoaro Terme
Schio
Valdagno
Giazza
Bosco Chiesanuova
Castelfranco Véneto
Cittadella
Resana
Paese
Treviso
Ponte di Piave
Gardone Riviera
Salò
Torri d. Benaco
Garda
Santuario della Madonna della Corona
Lago di Garda
Badia Calavena
Vestenanova
Chiampo
Malo
Dueville
Motta
Vicenza
San Pietro in Gu
Piazzola s. Brenta
Camposampiero
Mogliano Véneto
Scorzè
Noale
Bardolino
Lazise
Volargne
Negrar
Grezzana
Tregnago
Arzignano
Montécchio Maggiore
Camisano Vicentino
Campodàrsego
Mirano
Mestre
Sirmione
Pastrengo
Pescantina
Tempietto di Sta. Maria in Stelle
Movieland Gardaland
Bussolengo
Verona
Montebello Vicentino
Longare
Pádova
Orto Botanico
Dolo
Mira
Fusina
Venézia Venice
Peschiera d. Garda
Torre di San Martino della Battáglia
Villafranca di Verona
Soave
San Bonifacio
Lonigo
Barbarano Vicento
Ponte di Barbarano
Zévio
Abano Terme
Legnaro
Lova
Laguna Véneta
Castiglione d. Stiviere
Guidizzolo
Volta Mantovana
Valéggio sul Míncio
Vigásio
Albaredo d'Adige
Cologna Véneta
Noventa Vicentina
Colli Euganei
Battaglia Terme
Piove di Sacco
Bovolenta
Casaloldo
Góito
Roverbella
Ísola della Scala
Bovolone
Minerbe
Montagnana
Este
Monsélice
Conselve
Pontelongo
Chióggia
Sottomarina
Gazoldo degli Ippoliti
Castel d'Ario
Cerea
Legnago
Abbazia di Praglia
Villaggio Medievale di Monsélice
Bagnoli di Sopra
Cona
Mántova
Nogara
Castellúcchio
Marcaria
Castagnaro
Piacenza d'Adige
Stanghella
Anguillara Véneta
Cavárzere
Bózzolo
Cerese
Govérnolo
Ostíglia
Badia Polésine
Lendinara
Rovigo
Ádria
Borgoforte
Gazzuolo
San Benedetto Po
Quistello
Castelmassa
Trecenta
Ceneselli
Loreo
Táglio di Po
Contarina
Sabbioneta
Suzzara
Sérmide
Póggio Rusco
Fiesso Umbertiano
Polesella
Crespino
Ariano nel Polésine
Guastalla
Gonzaga
Reggiolo
Concordia sulla Sécchia
Pilastri
Ficarolo
Occhiobello
Bondeno
Copparo
Iolanda di Savoia
Mésola
Delta del Po
Gualtieri
Mirándola
San Felice sul Panaro
Pontelagoscuro
Ferrara
Codigoro
Pomposa
Abbazia di Pomposa
Fábbrico
Novi di Módena
Cavezzo
Novellara
Mirabello
Finale Emília
Cona
Tresigallo
Massa Fiscáglia
Lido di Volano
Corréggio
Carpi
Camposanto
Póggio Renatico
Gaibanella
Migliarino
Lagosanto
Lido delle Nazioni
Lido di Pomposa
Lido degli Scacchi
Porto Garibaldi
Cadelbosco di Sopra
Sorbara
Cento
Crevalcore
Pieve di Cento
San Nicolò
Portomaggiore
Comácchio
Lido degli Estensi
Valli di Comácchio
Delta del Po
Campogalliano
Nonántola
San Pietro in Casale
Malalbergo
Altedo
Consándolo
Réggio nell'Emília
Módena
Rubiera
Duomo di Módena
San Giovanni in Persiceto
San Giorgio di Piano
Molinella
Argenta
Duomo di San Nicol
Vezzano sul Cróstolo
Sta. Maria Assunta
Castelfranco Emília
Minérbio
Lavezzola
Scandiano
Formigine
Sassuolo
Maranello
Anzola d'Emília
Bologna
Búdrio
Conselice
San Alberto
Alfonsine
Marina
Castellarano
Vignola
Bazzano

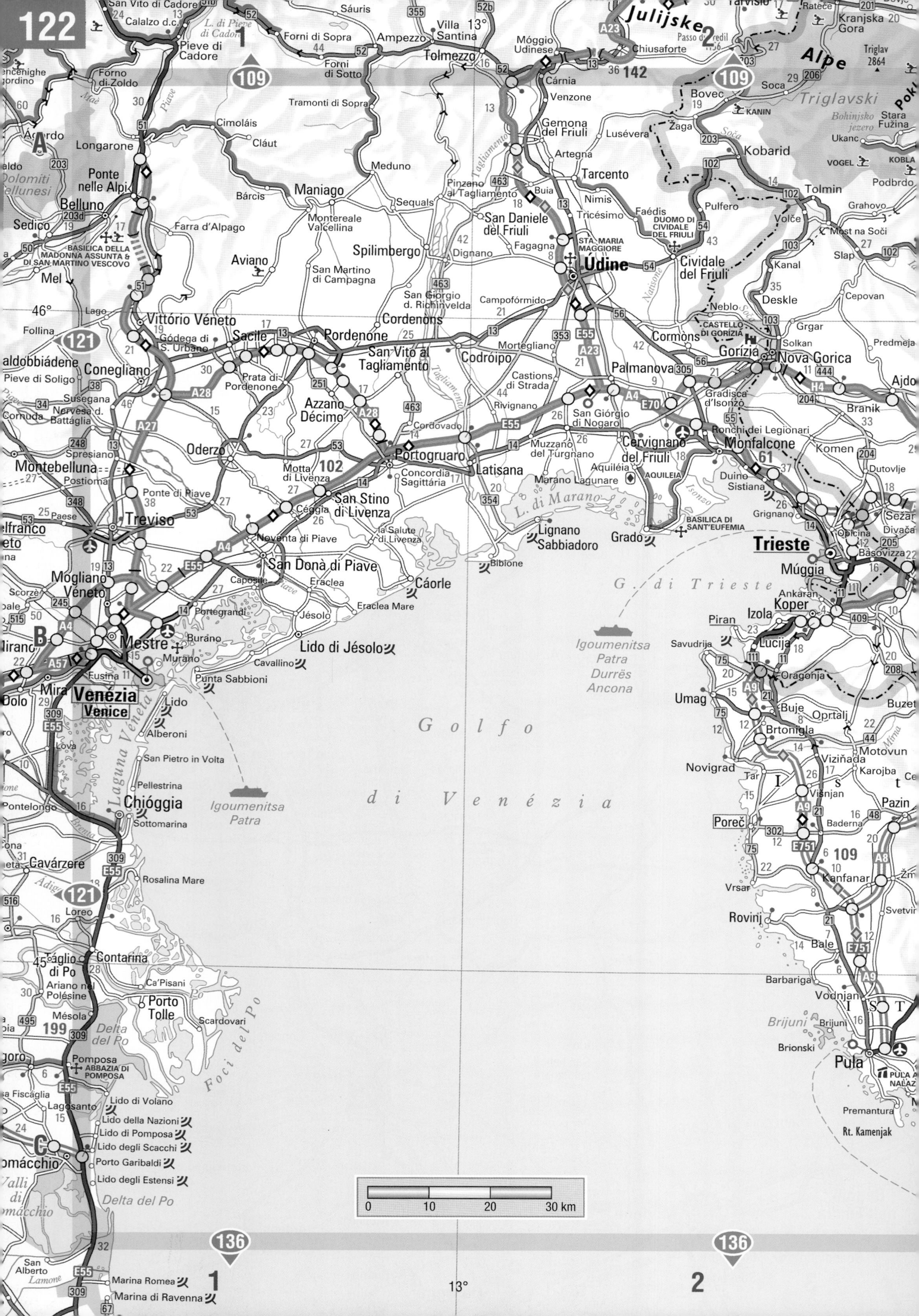

San Vito di Cadore
Calalzo d.c.
L. di Pieve di Cadore
Pieve di Cadore
Sáuris
Forni di Sopra
Ampezzo
Villa Santina
13°
Móggio Udinese
Julijske
Chiusaforte
Tarvisio
Ratece
Kranjska Gora
Alpe
Triglav 2864
Forni di Sotto
Tolmezzo
109
142
Cárnia
Venzone
Bovec
Soca
Triglavski
KANIN
Bohinjsko jezero
Stara Fužina
Ukanc
Forno di Zoldo
Tramonti di Sopra
Cimoláis
Cláut
Gemona del Friuli
Lusévera
Žaga
Kobarid
VOGEL
KOBLA
Ágordo
Longarone
Meduno
Artegna
Tarcento
Dolomiti Bellunesi
Ponte nelle Alpi
Maniago
Bárcis
Pinzano al Tagliamento
Buia
Nimis
Pulfero
Tolmin
Podbrdo
Belluno
Sequals
San Daniele del Friuli
Tricésimo
Faédis
DUOMO DI CIVIDALE DEL FRIULI
Grahovo
Volče
Sedico
Farra d'Alpago
Montereale Valcellina
Most na Soči
BASILICA DELLA MADONNA ASSUNTA & DI SAN MARTINO VESCOVO
Aviano
Spilimbergo
Dignano
Fagagna
STA. MARIA MAGGIORE
Údine
Cividale del Friuli
Slap
Kanal
Mel
San Martino di Campagna
Deskle
Cepovan
46°
Lago
San Giorgio d. Richinvelda
Campofórmido
Neblo
CASTELLO DI GORIZIA
Vittório Véneto
Cordenons
Grgar
Follina
121
Gódega di S. Urbano
Sacile
Pordenone
Cormons
Solkan
Predmeja
Valdobbiádene
Conegliano
San Vito al Tagliamento
Codróipo
Mortegliano
Gorízia
Nova Gorica
Pieve di Soligo
Prata di Pordenone
Castions di Strada
Palmanova
Gradisca d'Isonzo
Ajdo
Susegana
Azzano Décimo
Rivignano
San Giórgio di Nogaro
Branik
Nervesa d. Battáglia
Cornuda
Cordovado
Ronchi dei Legionari
Monfalcone
Komen
Montebelluna
Spresiano
Postioma
Oderzo
Motta di Livenza
102
Portogruaro
Muzzano del Túrgnano
Cervignano del Friuli
Dutovlje
Concordia Sagittária
Latisana
Aquiléia
AQUILEIA
Marano Lagunare
Duino Sistiana
Ponte di Piave
San Stino di Livenza
L. di Marano
Isonzo
Paese
Treviso
Céggia
Grignano
Sežana
Divača
Castelfranco Veneto
Noventa di Piave
La Salute di Livenza
Lignano Sabbiadoro
Grado
BASILICA DI SANT'EUFEMIA
Opicina
Trieste
Basovizza
San Donà di Piave
Bibione
Múggia
Mogliano Veneto
Scorzè
Caposile
Eraclea
Cáorle
G. di Trieste
Ankaran
Koper
Eraclea Mare
Izola
Piran
Portegrandi
Jésolo
Mestre
Burano
Murano
Lido di Jésolo
Igoumenitsa Patra Durrës Ancona
Savudrija
Lucija
Mira
Dolo
Fusina
Venézia Venice
Cavallino
Punta Sabbioni
Oragonja
Umag
Buzet
Lido
Buje
Oprtalj
Alberoni
Golfo
Brtonigla
Lova
San Pietro in Volta
Viziñada
Motovun
Novigrad
Karojba
Pellestrina
Igoumenitsa Patra
Chióggia
Sottomarina
Pontelongo
Laguna Véneta
Brenta
di Venézia
Višnjan
Pazin
Poreč
Baderna
Cavárzere
Rosalina Mare
Ádige
Kanfanar
Vrsar
Loreo
Rovinj
Svetvinčenat
Bale
Táglio di Po
Contarina
Ca'Pisani
Ariano nel Polésine
Porto Tolle
Barbariga
Vodnjan
Mésola
Scardovari
Delta del Po
Brijuni
Foci del Po
Pomposa
ABBAZIA DI POMPOSA
Brionski
Pula
Lido di Volano
Lagosanto
Lido della Nazioni
Lido di Pomposa
Lido degli Scacchi
Comácchio
Porto Garibaldi
Premantura
Rt. Kamenjak
Lido degli Estensi
Valli di Comácchio
Delta del Po
0 10 20 30 km
136
San Alberto
Lamone
Marina Romea
Marina di Ravenna
1
13°
2

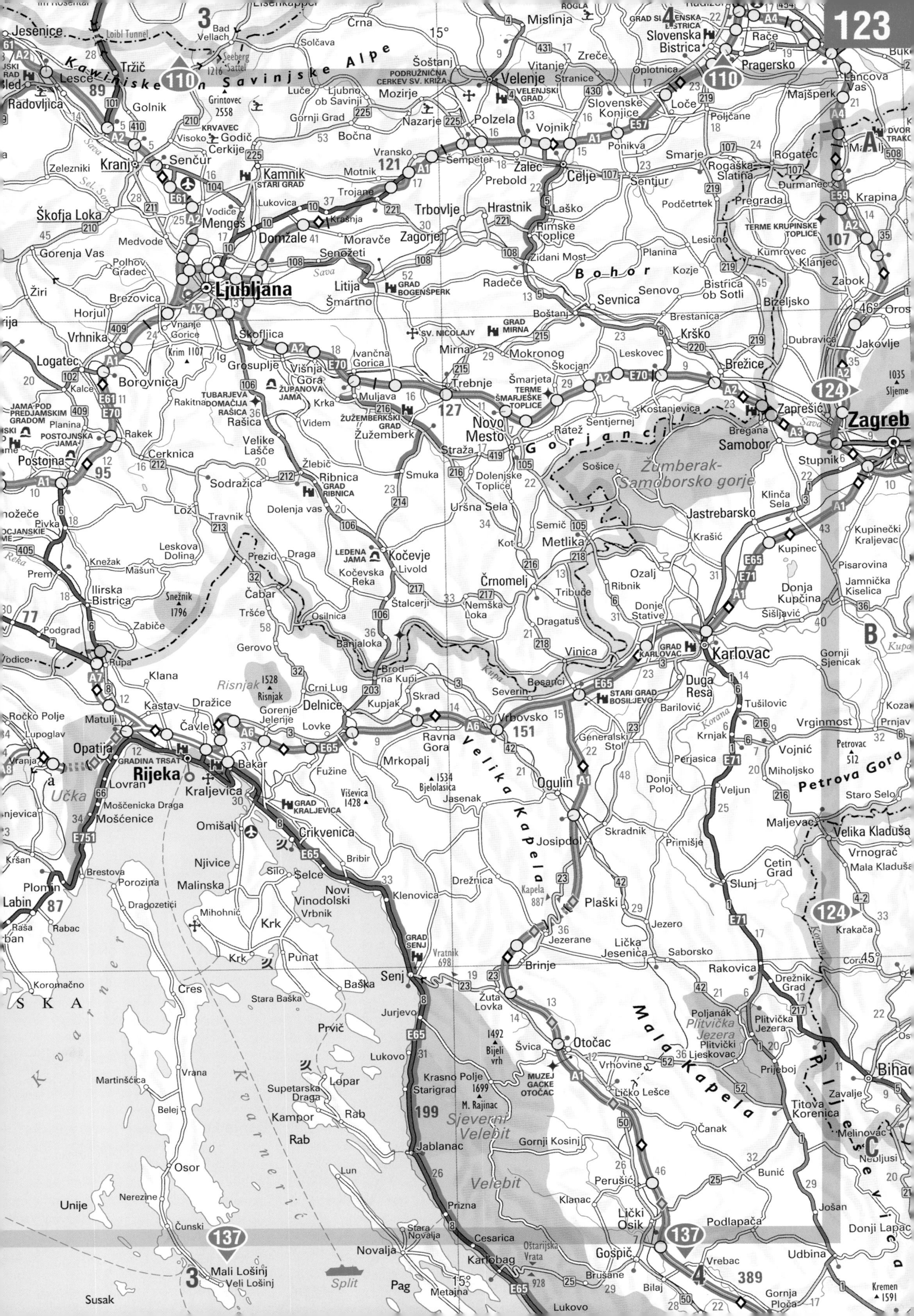

123
Jesenice
Bad Vellach
Loibl Tunnel
Seeberg Sattel
Črna
Mislinja
Slovenska Bistrica
Rače
Pragersko
Kawinjske Savinjske Alpe
Bled
Lesce
Tržič
Radovljica
Golnik
Grintovec 2558
Solčava
Luče
Ljubno ob Savinji
Mozirje
Šoštanj
Velenje
Vitanje
Zreče
Oplotnica
Ptuj
Lancova Vas
Majšperk
Slovenske Konjice
Loče
Poljčane
Gornji Grad
Bočna
Nazarje
Polzela
Vojnik
Ponikva
Kranj
Visoko
Godič
Cerkije
Šenčur
Kamnik
Vransko
Šempeter
Žalec
Celje
Šentjur
Šmarje
Rogaška Slatina
Rogatec
Zelezniki
Škofja Loka
Vodice
Menges
Lukovica
Trojane
Motnik
Prebold
Trbovlje
Hrastnik
Laško
Podčetrtek
Pregrada
Krapina
Medvode
Domžale
Moravče
Zagorje
Rimske Toplice
Lesično
Terme Krupinske Toplice
Gorenja Vas
Polhov Gradec
Senožeti
Zidani Most
Planina
Kozje
Kumrovec
Klanjec
Žiri
Ljubljana
Litija
Šmartno
Grad Bogenšperk
Radeče
Bohor
Senovo
Bistrica ob Sotli
Zabok
Brezovica
Horjul
Vrhnika
Vnanje Gorice
Škofljica
Sevnica
Boštanj
Brestanica
Bizeljsko
Krško
Dubravica
Jakovlje
Logatec
Borovnica
Krim 1107
Ig
Grosuplje
Višnja Gora
Ivančna Gorica
Mirna
Mokronog
Leskovec
Škocjan
Brežice
Šmarjeta
Terme Šmarješke Toplice
Trebnje
Muljava
Krka
Kalce
Rakitna
Tubarjeva Domačija Rašica
Žužemberk
Novo Mesto
Kostanjevica
Sentjernej
Zaprešić
Zagreb
Sljeme
Bregana
Samobor
Planina
Postojnska Jama
Postojna
Rakek
Cerknica
Velike Lašče
Ratež
Gorjanci
Stupnik
Žumberak-Samoborsko gorje
Sošice
Dolenjske Toplice
Smuka
Straža
Ribnica
Žlebič
Sodražica
Uršna Sela
Semič
Klinča Sela
Jastrebarsko
Kupinečki Kraljevac
Nožeče
Pivka
Lož
Travnik
Dolenja vas
Kot
Metlika
Krašić
Kupinec
Leskova Dolina
Prezid
Draga
Ledena Jama
Kočevje
Kočevska Reka
Livold
Ozalj
Ribnik
Pisarovina
Jamnička Kiselica
Knežak
Mašun
Prem
Čabar
Črnomelj
Tribuče
Donja Kupčina
Ilirska Bistrica
Snežnik 1796
Tršće
Štalcerji
Nemška Loka
Donje Stative
Šišljavić
Podgrad
Zabiče
Osilnica
Dragatuš
Banjaloka
Vinica
Karlovac
Gornji Sjenicak
Rupa
Gerovo
Klana
Risnjak 1528
Crni Lug
Brod na Kupi
Kupa
Severin
Bosiljevo
Duga Resa
Barilović
Tušilovic
Kastav
Dražice
Delnice
Kupjak
Skrad
Vrbovsko
Gorenje Jelenje
Lovke
Ravna Gora
Generalski Stol
Krnjak
Vrginmost
Roćko Polje
Matulji
Lupoglav
Čavle
Opatija
Vranja
Gradina Trsat
Rijeka
Bakar
Fužine
Mrkopalj
Perjasica
Vojnić
Petrovac 512
Kraljevica
Lovran
Učka
Mošćenička Draga
Mošćenice
Grad Kraljevica
Višnica 1428
1534 Bjelolasica
Jasenak
Ogulin
Donji Poloj
Miholjsko
Petrova Gora
Veljun
Staro Selo
Omišalj
Crikvenica
Velika Kapela
Skradnik
Josipdol
Primišje
Maljevac
Velika Kladuša
Vrnograč
Mala Kladuša
Kršan
Njivice
Bribir
Brestova
Porozina
Malinska
Silo
Selce
Dreznica
Cetin Grad
Plomin
Labin
Novi Vinodolski
Klenovica
Kapela 887
Plaški
Slunj
Dragozetići
Vrbnik
Mihohnić
Krk
Raša
Rabac
Jezero
Jezerane
Lička Jesenica
Saborsko
Krakača
Grad Senj
Vratnik 698
Brinje
Krk
Punat
Senj
Baška
Rakovica
Drežnik Grad
Koromačno
Cres
Stara Baška
Jurjevo
Žuta Lovka
Poljanak
Plitvička Jezera
Mala Kapela
Prvič
1492 Bijeli vrh
Švica
Otočac
Lukovo
Vrhovine
Ljeskovac
Prijeboj
Bihać
Martinšćica
Vrana
Supetarska Draga
Lopar
Krasno Polje
Starigrad
1699 M. Rajinac
Muzej Gacke Otočac
Ličko Lešce
Zavalje
Titova Korenica
Belej
Kampor
Rab
Sjeverni Velebit
Čanak
Melinovac
Jablanac
Gornji Kosinj
Nebljusi
Osor
Lun
Velebit
Perušić
Bunić
Unije
Nerezine
Klanac
Prizna
Lički Osik
Jošan
Čunski
Stara Novalja
Cesarica
Podlapača
Donji Lapac
Mali Lošinj
Veli Lošinj
Novalja
Karlobag
Ostarijska Vrata
Gospić
Vrebac
Udbina
Split
Pag
Metajna
Brušane
Bilaj
Susak
Lukovo
Gornja Ploča
Kremen 1591
Kvarner
Kvarnerić
Plješevica

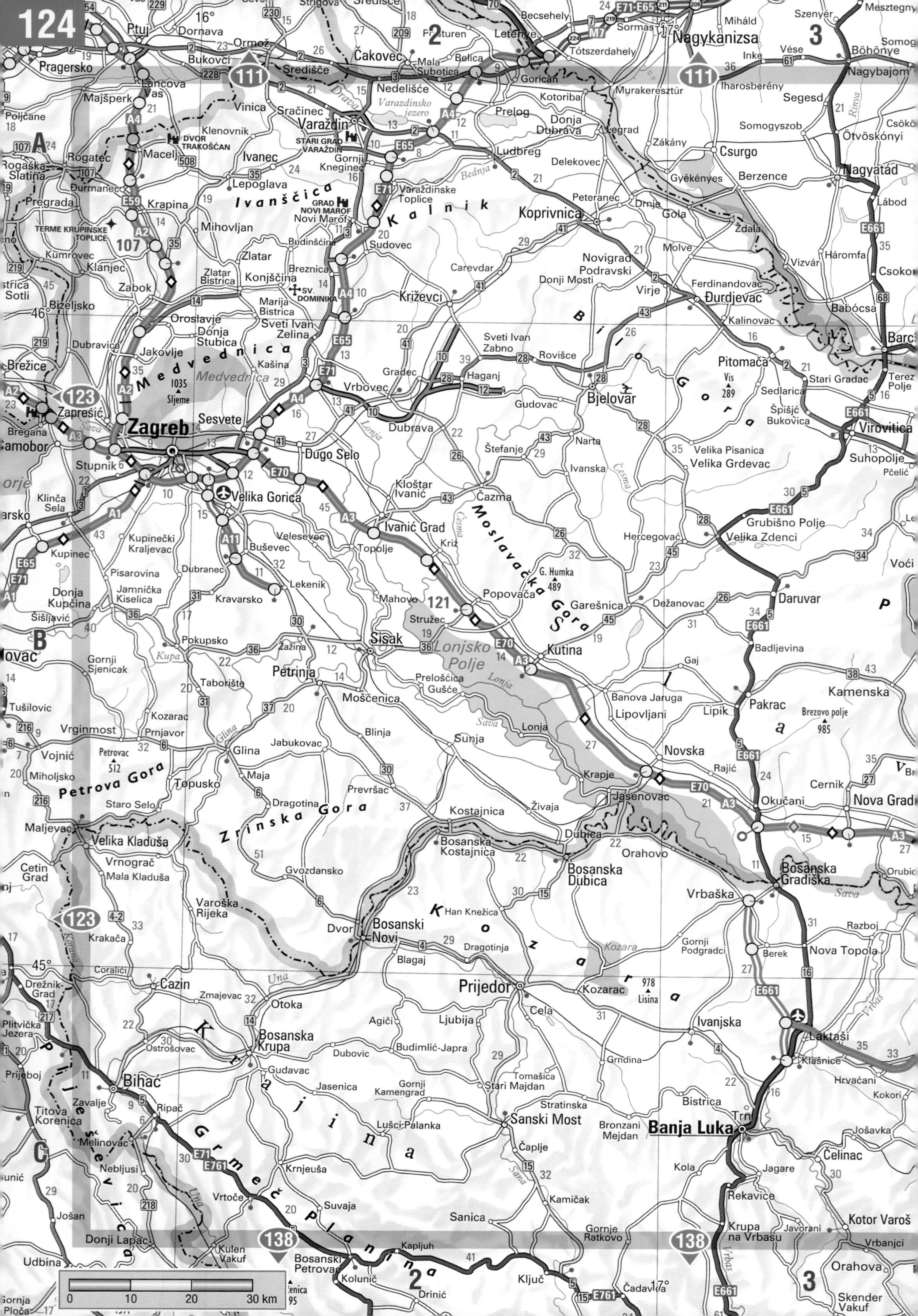
Ptuj
Dornava
Ormož
Strigova
Štrigova
Čakovec
Fertőturen
Letenye
Becsehely
Sormás
Nagykanizsa
Miháld
Szenyér
Mesztegnyő
Böhönye
Somog
Nagybajom
Pragersko
Bukovci
Središče
Mala Subotica
Belica
Goričan
Tótszerdahely
Murakeresztúr
Inke
Vése
Iharosberény
Segesd
Lancova Vas
Majšperk
Vinica
Sračinec
Nedelišće
Varaždin
Varazdinsko jezero
Prelog
Kotoriba
Donja Dubrava
Legrad
Zákány
Somogyszob
Csurgo
Ötvöskónyi
Csökö
Poljčane
Klenovnik
DVOR TRAKOŠĆAN
STARI GRAD VARAŽDIN
Gornji Kneginec
Ludbreg
Delekovec
Berzence
Nagyatád
Rogatec
Rogaška Slatina
Macelj
Ivanec
Lepoglava
Bednja
Gyékényes
Đurmanec
Pregrada
Krapina
Ivanščica
GRAD NOVI MAROF
Novi Marof
Varaždinske Toplice
Kalnik
Koprivnica
Peteranec
Drnje
Gola
Lábod
Ždala
TERME KRUPINSKE TOPLICE
Mihovljan
Budinšćina
Sudovec
Molve
Háromfa
Kumrovec
Klanjec
Zlatar
Zlatar Bistrica
Breznica
Carevdar
Novigrad Podravski
Donji Mosti
Virje
Ferdinandovac
Vizvár
Csoko
Sotli
Zabok
Konjščina
SV. DOMINIKA
Križevci
Đurđevac
Babócsa
Bizeljsko
Marija Bistrica
Oroslavje
Donja Stubica
Sveti Ivan Zelina
Kalinovac
Bilo Gora
Dubravica
Jakovlje
Medvednica
Sveti Ivan Zabno
Rovišće
Pitomača
Barc
Brežice
Kašina
Gradec
Haganj
Bjelovar
Vis 289
Stari Gradac
Terez Polje
Sljeme 1035
Sedlarica
Zaprešić
Vrbovec
Gudovac
Špišić Bukovica
Bregana
Samobor
Zagreb
Sesvete
Dubrava
Lonja
Virovitica
Stupnik
Dugo Selo
Štefanje
Narta
Velika Pisanica
Velika Grdevac
Suhopolje
Pčelić
Ivanska
Česma
Klinča Sela
Velika Gorica
Kloštar Ivanić
Čazma
Moslavačka Gora
Grubišno Polje
Velika Zdenci
Hercegovac
Kupinečki Kraljevac
Veleševec
Ivanić Grad
Križ
Kupinec
Buševec
Topolje
G. Humka 489
Voći
Pisarovina
Dubranec
Lekenik
Donja Kupčina
Jamnička Kiselica
Kravarsko
Mahovo
Popovača
Garešnica
Dežanovac
Daruvar
Šišljavić
Stružec
Pokupsko
Žažina
Sisak
Lonjsko Polje
Kutina
Badljevina
Kupa
Gornji Sjenicak
Petrinja
Prelošćica
Gušće
Gaj
Kamenska
Taborište
Mošćenica
Banova Jaruga
Lipovljani
Lipik
Pakrac
Brezovo polje 985
Tušilović
Kozarac
Vrginmost
Prnjavor
Blinja
Sava
Vojnić
Petrovac 512
Glina
Jabukovac
Sunja
Novska
Rajić
Miholjsko
Petrova Gora
Topusko
Maja
Krapje
Cernik
Nova Grad
Staro Selo
Dragotina
Prevršac
Jasenovac
Okučani
Zrinska Gora
Kostajnica
Živaja
Maljevac
Velika Kladuša
Bosanska Kostajnica
Dubica
Orahovo
Vrnograč
Mala Kladuša
Cetin Grad
Gvozdansko
Bosanska Dubica
Bosanska Gradiška
Orubic
Varoška Rijeka
Han Knežica
Vrbaška
Razboj
Kozara
Dvor
Bosanski Novi
Gornji Podgradci
Krakača
Berek
Nova Topola
Korana
Coralići
Blagaj
Dragotinja
Drežnik-Grad
Cazin
Una
Prijedor
Kozarac
978 Lisina
Zmajevac
Otoka
Cela
Plitvička Jezera
Agići
Ljubija
Ivanjska
Laktaši
Ostrošovac
Bosanska Krupa
Budimlić-Japra
Grdina
Klašnice
Prijeboj
Krajina
Dubovic
Gudavac
Tomašica
Stari Majdan
Hrvaćani
Bihać
Jasenica
Gornji Kamengrad
Kokori
Titova Korenica
Zavalje
Ripač
Stratinska
Bistrica
Melinovac
Lušci Palanka
Sanski Most
Bronzani Mejdan
Banja Luka
Trn
Jošavka
Plješevica
Nebljusi
Grmeč
Čaplje
Čelinac
Krnjeuša
Kola
Jagare
Sana
Vrtoče
Kamičak
Rekavice
Suvaja
Jošan
Sanica
Kotor Varoš
Gornje Ratkovo
Krupa na Vrbasu
Javorani
Donji Lapac
Kulen Vakuf
Grmeč Planina
Vrbanjci
Udbina
Bosanski Petrovac
Kapljuh
Ključ
Orahova
Kolunić
Drinić
Čadavica
Vrbas
Skender Vakuf
Gornja Ploča
0 10 20 30 km

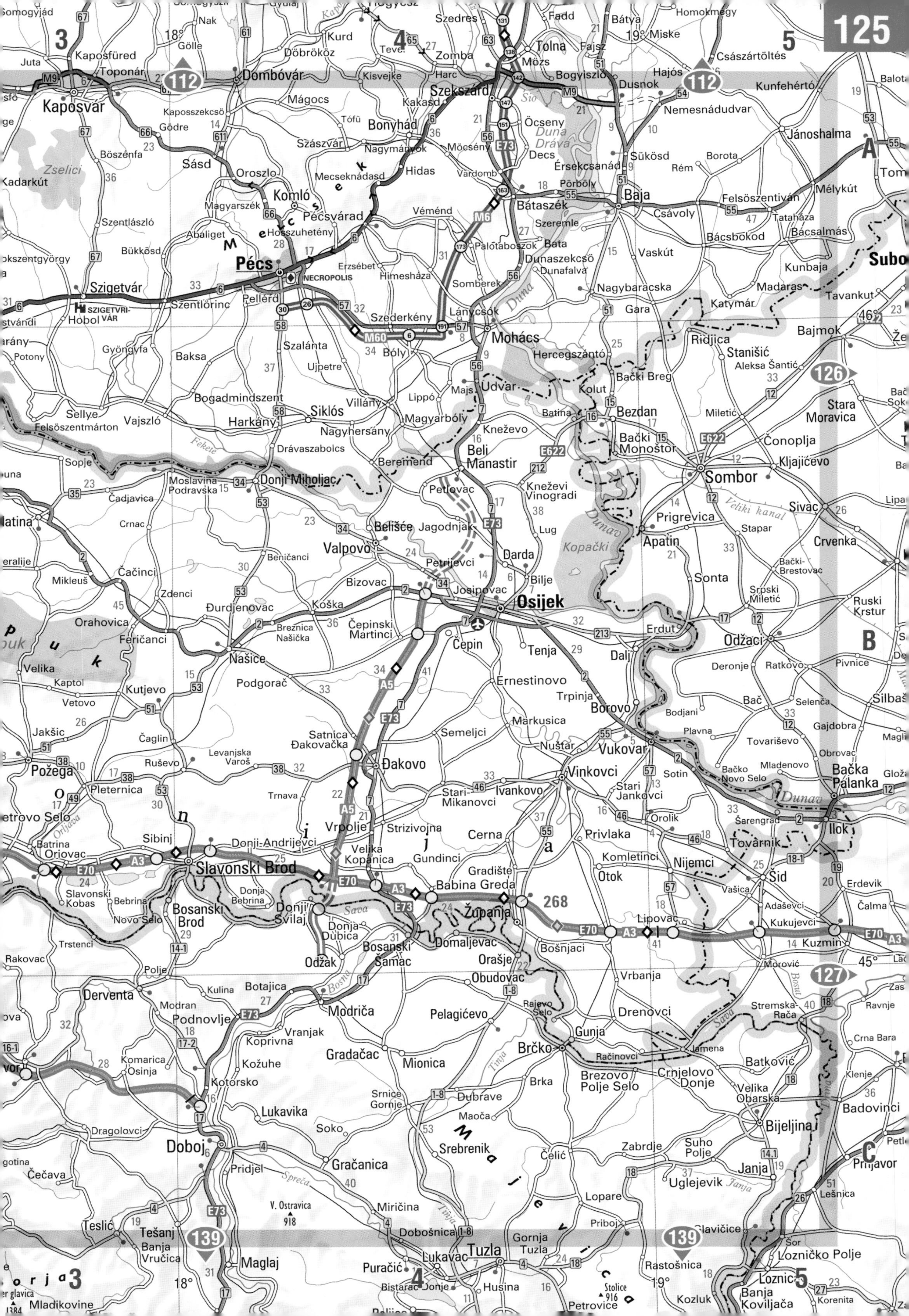
Kaposvár
Dombóvár
Szekszárd
Tolna
Bonyhád
Komló
Pécs
Szigetvár
Mohács
Baja
Bátaszék
Siklós
Harkány
Beli Manastir
Sombor
Apatin
Osijek
Valpovo
Našice
Đakovo
Vinkovci
Vukovar
Ilok
Bačka Palanka
Odžaci
Slavonski Brod
Bosanski Brod
Županja
Orašje
Brčko
Bijeljina
Gradačac
Modriča
Derventa
Doboj
Gračanica
Srebrenik
Tuzla
Lukavac
Požega
Pleternica
Šid
Subotica
126
127
112
139
268
3
4
5
A
B
C

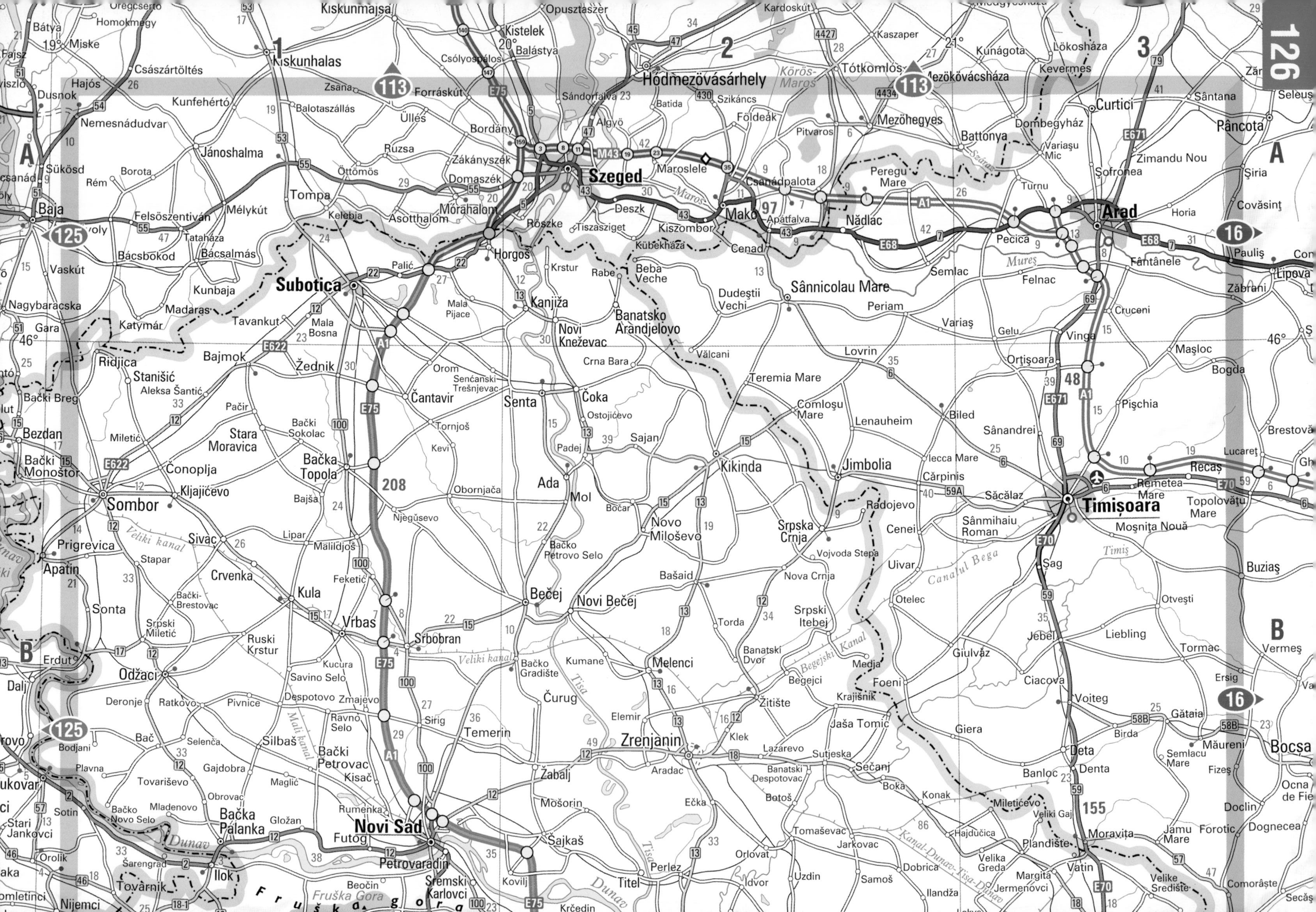

Kiskunhalas
Hódmezővásárhely
Szeged
Subotica
Sombor
Novi Sad
Zrenjanin
Kikinda
Senta
Bečej
Novi Bečej
Vrbas
Kula
Bačka Topola
Bačka Palanka
Petrovaradin
Sremski Karlovci
Titel
Baja
Apatin
Odžaci
Vukovar
Ilok
Makó
Mórahalom
Horgoš
Kanjiža
Ada
Čoka
Jimbolia
Sânnicolau Mare
Arad
Timişoara
Pecica
Nădlac
Curtici
Lipova
Recaş
Deta
Bocşa
Buziaş
Fruška Gora
Dunav
Tisa
Maros
Mureş
Timiş
Canalul Bega
Veliki kanal
Mali kanal
Begejski Kanal
Kanal-Dunav-Tisa-Dunav

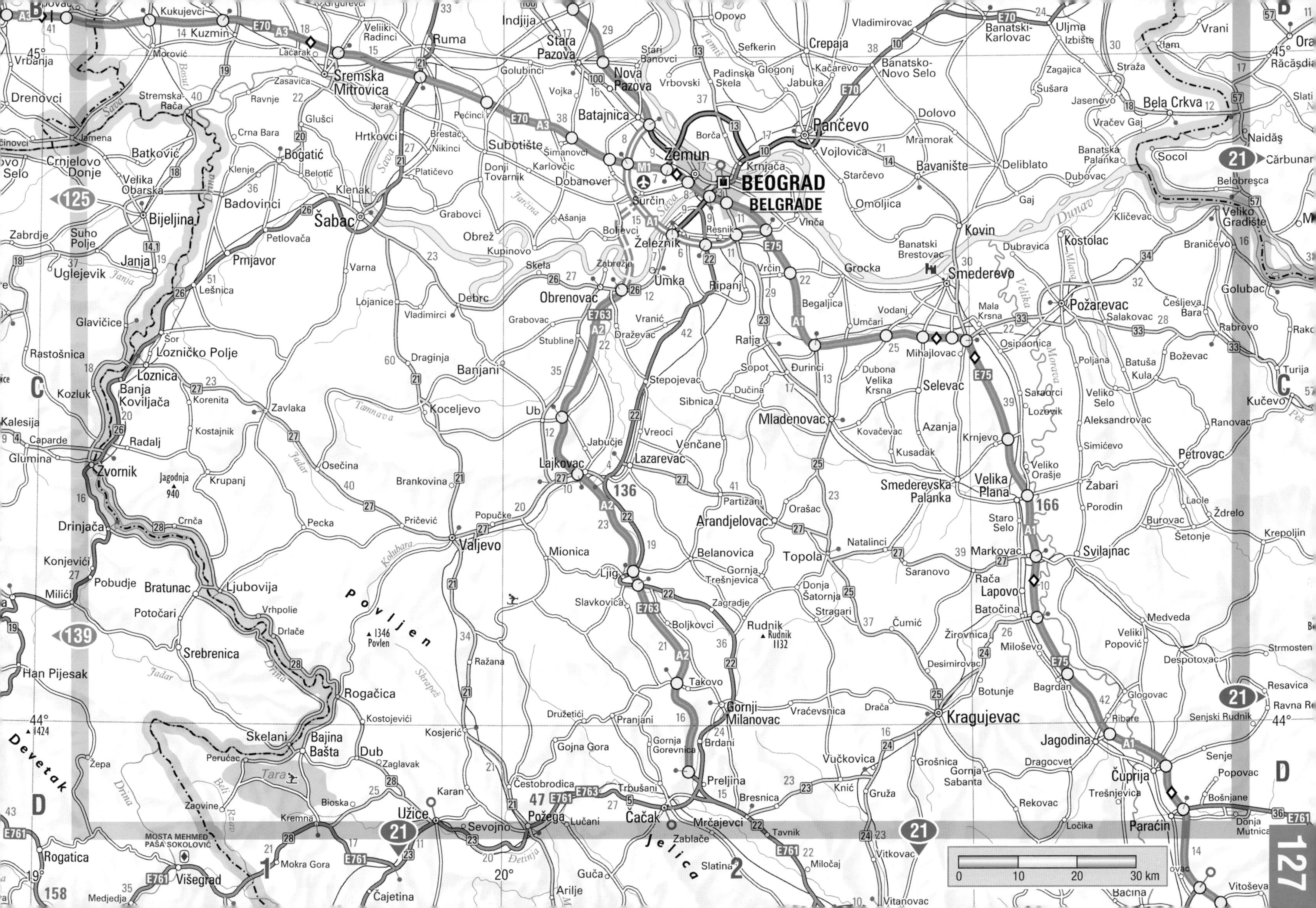
BEOGRAD
BELGRADE
Zemun
Pančevo
Smederevo
Požarevac
Kostolac
Kovin
Bela Crkva
Veliko Gradište
Golubac
Kučevo
Petrovac
Žabari
Svilajnac
Velika Plana
Smederevska Palanka
Markovac
Lapovo
Rača
Batočina
Jagodina
Ćuprija
Paraćin
Kragujevac
Topola
Arandjelovac
Mladenovac
Lazarevac
Ljig
Gornji Milanovac
Čačak
Požega
Užice
Sevojno
Kosjerić
Valjevo
Mionica
Ub
Lajkovac
Obrenovac
Šabac
Sremska Mitrovica
Ruma
Stara Pazova
Nova Pazova
Batajnica
Indjija
Bogatić
Prnjavor
Loznica
Banja Koviljača
Lozničko Polje
Zvornik
Ljubovija
Bajina Bašta
Rogačica
Srebrenica
Bratunac
Bijeljina
Janja
Višegrad
Rogatica
Han Pijesak
Milići
Povljen
Jelica
Devetak
Tara
Drina
Sava
Dunav
Velika Morava
Mlava
Jadar
Kolubara
Tamnava
MOSTA MEHMED PAŠA SOKOLOVIĆ
A1
A2
A3
E70
E75
E761
E763
21
125
139
158
136
166
0 10 20 30 km
44°
45°
20°
19°

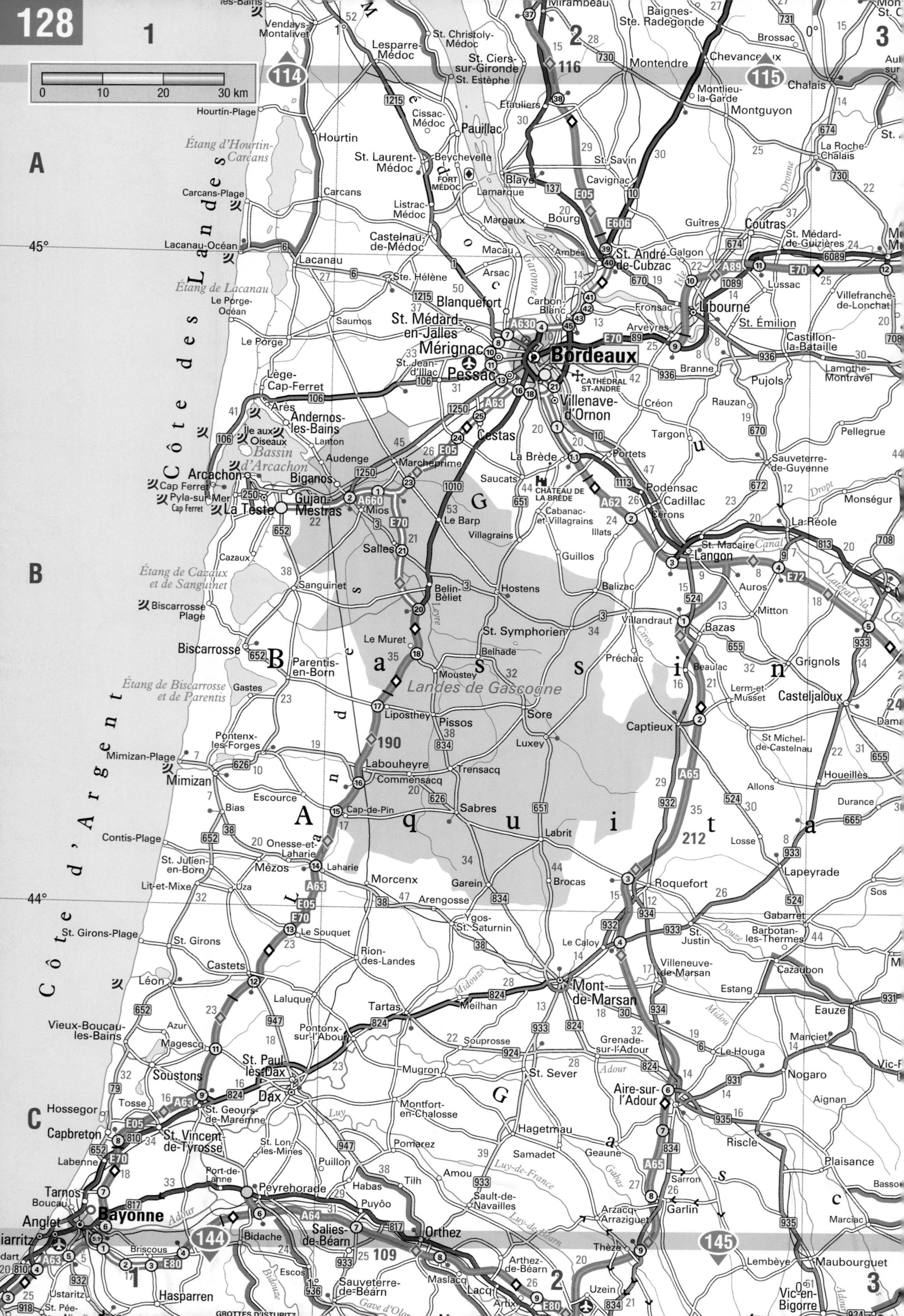
1
2
3
A
B
C
0 10 20 30 km
114
115
116
144
145
Côte des Landes
Côte d'Argent
Médoc
Aquitaine
Landes
Bassin
Gascogne
Landes de Gascogne
Vendays-Montalivet
Lesparre-Médoc
St. Christoly-Médoc
St. Ciers-sur-Gironde
St. Estèphe
Mirambeau
Baignes-Ste. Radegonde
Brossac
Montendre
Chevanceaux
Chalais
Montlieu-la-Garde
Montguyon
Hourtin-Plage
Hourtin
Étang d'Hourtin-Carcans
Cissac-Médoc
Pauillac
Etauliers
St. Laurent-Médoc
Beychevelle
Fort Médoc
Blaye
Lamarque
St. Savin
Cavignac
La Roche-Chalais
Carcans-Plage
Carcans
Listrac-Médoc
Margaux
Bourg
Guîtres
Coutras
St. Médard-de-Guizières
Lacanau-Océan
45°
Castelnau-de-Médoc
Macau
Ambès
St. André-de-Cubzac
Galgon
Lacanau
Ste. Hélène
Arsac
Garonne
Isle
Lussac
Villefranche-de-Lonchat
Étang de Lacanau
Le Porge-Océan
Blanquefort
Carbon-Blanc
Fronsac
Libourne
St. Émilion
Saumos
St. Médard-en-Jalles
Arveyres
Castillon-la-Bataille
Le Porge
Mérignac
Bordeaux
St. Jean-d'Illac
Pessac
Cathédral St-André
Branne
Pujols
Lamothe-Montravel
Lège-Cap-Ferret
Villenave-d'Ornon
Créon
Rauzan
Arès
Andernos-les-Bains
Lanton
Cestas
Targon
Pellegrue
Île aux Oiseaux
Bassin d'Arcachon
Audenge
Marcheprime
La Brède
Portets
Sauveterre-de-Guyenne
Arcachon
Biganos
Saucats
Château de la Brède
Podensac
Cap Ferret
Pyla-sur-Mer
Gujan-Mestras
La Teste
Mios
Le Barp
Cabanac-et-Villagrains
Cadillac
Cérons
Monségur
Dropt
Villagrains
Illats
La Réole
Salles
St. Macaire
Canal
Langon
Cazaux
Guillos
Étang de Cazaux et de Sanguinet
Sanguinet
Belin-Bèliet
Hostens
Balizac
Auros
Biscarrosse Plage
Leyre
Villandraut
Mitton
Bazas
Le Muret
St. Symphorien
Ciron
Biscarrosse
Belhade
Préchac
Beaulac
Grignols
Parentis-en-Born
Moustey
Étang de Biscarrosse et de Parentis
Gastes
Lerm-et-Musset
Casteljaloux
Liposthey
Pissos
Sore
Captieux
Pontenx-les-Forges
Luxey
St Michel-de-Castelnau
Mimizan-Plage
Mimizan
Labouheyre
Trensacq
Houeillès
Commensacq
Allons
Escource
Sabres
Durance
Bias
Cap-de-Pin
Labrit
Contis-Plage
Onesse-et-Laharie
Losse
Lapeyrade
St. Julien-en-Born
Mézos
Laharie
Lit-et-Mixe
Uza
Morcenx
Garein
Brocas
Roquefort
44°
Arengosse
Sos
Gabarret
Ygos-St. Saturnin
St. Girons-Plage
St. Girons
Le Caloy
St. Justin
Douze
Barbotan-les-Thermes
Rion-des-Landes
Castets
Villeneuve-de-Marsan
Cazaubon
Léon
Midouze
Mont-de-Marsan
Laluque
Estang
Tartas
Meilhan
Eauze
Midou
Vieux-Boucau-les-Bains
Azur
Magescq
Pontonx-sur-l'Adour
Souprosse
Grenade-sur-l'Adour
Manciet
Le-Houga
St. Paul-lès-Dax
Soustons
Mugron
St. Sever
Adour
Vic-F
Nogaro
Dax
Aire-sur-l'Adour
Hossegor
Tosse
St. Geours-de-Maremne
Luy
Montfort-en-Chalosse
Aignan
Capbreton
St. Vincent-de-Tyrosse
Hagetmau
Riscle
Labenne
St. Lon-les-Mines
Pomarez
Geaune
Gabas
Pouillon
Samadet
Sarron
Plaisance
Port-de-Lanne
Amou
Luy-de-France
Tarnos
Boucau
Peyrehorade
Habas
Tilh
Sault-de-Navailles
Garlin
Anglet
Bayonne
Puyôo
Arzacq-Arraziguet
Marciac
Biarritz
Bidache
Salies-de-Béarn
Orthez
Luy-de-Béarn
Briscous
Thèze
Lembeye
Maubourguet
Bidouze
Escos
Arthez-de-Béarn
Ustaritz
Sauveterre-de-Béarn
Maslacq
Lacq
Artix
Uzein
Hasparren
Vic-en-Bigorre
Gave d'Oloron
Grottes d'Isturitz

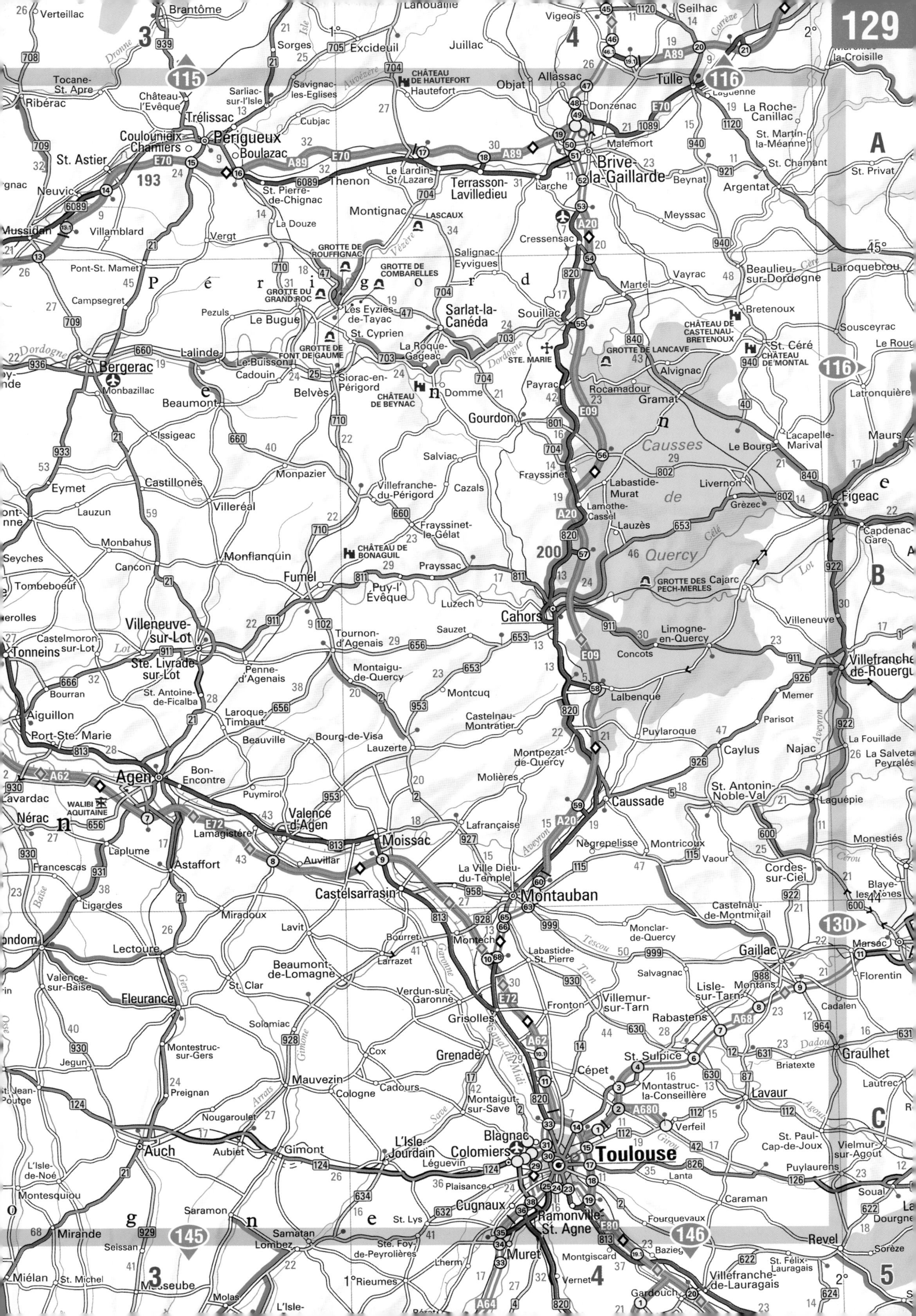
Verteillac
Brantôme
Lanouaille
Vigeois
Seilhac
Sorges
Excideuil
Juillac
Tocane-St. Apre
Ribérac
Château-l'Evêque
Sarliac-sur-l'Isle
Savignac-les-Eglises
CHÂTEAU DE HAUTEFORT
Hautefort
Objat
Allassac
Tulle
Laguenne
Donzenac
La Roche-Canillac
St. Martin-la-Méanne
Trélissac
Cubjac
Coulounieix-Chamiers
Périgueux
Boulazac
Malemort
Brive-la-Gaillarde
St. Astier
Neuvic
Le Lardin-St. Lazare
Terrasson-Lavilledieu
Larche
Beynat
Argentat
St. Chamant
St. Privat
Thenon
St. Pierre-de-Chignac
Montignac
LASCAUX
Meyssac
Mussidan
Villamblard
La Douze
Vergt
GROTTE DE ROUFFIGNAC
Cressensac
Salignac-Eyvigues
GROTTE DE COMBARELLES
Pont-St. Mamet
GROTTE DU GRAND ROC
Vayrac
Martel
Beaulieu-sur-Dordogne
Laroquebrou
Campsegret
Les Eyzies-de-Tayac
Sarlat-la-Canéda
Souillac
Bretenoux
Pezuls
Le Bugue
St. Cyprien
CHÂTEAU DE CASTELNAU-BRETENOUX
Sousceyrac
GROTTE DE FONT DE GAUME
La Roque-Gageac
STE. MARIE
GROTTE DE LANCAVE
St. Céré
CHÂTEAU DE MONTAL
Le Rouget
Dordogne
Bergerac
Lalinde
Le Buisson
Cadouin
Siorac-en-Périgord
Alvignac
Rocamadour
Gramat
Latronquière
Monbazillac
Beaumont
Belvès
CHÂTEAU DE BEYNAC
Domme
Payrac
Gourdon
Issigeac
Lacapelle-Marival
Maurs
Causses
Le Bourg
Salviac
Frayssinet
Labastide-Murat
Livernon
Monpazier
Castillonès
Eymet
Villefranche-du-Périgord
Cazals
Villeréal
Lauzun
Lamothe-Cassel
Grèzec
Figeac
Capdenac-Gare
Lauzès
Frayssinet-le-Gélat
Monbahus
Seyches
Monflanquin
CHÂTEAU DE BONAGUIL
Quercy
Cancon
Prayssac
Tombeboeuf
Fumel
Puy-l'Évêque
GROTTE DES PECH-MERLES
Cajarc
Luzech
Cahors
Villeneuve-sur-Lot
Castelmoron-sur-Lot
Tonneins
Tournon-d'Agenais
Sauzet
Limogne-en-Quercy
Villeneuve
Ste. Livrade-sur-Lot
Penne-d'Agenais
Montaigu-de-Quercy
Concots
Villefranche-de-Rouergue
Bourran
St. Antoine-de-Ficalba
Montcuq
Lalbenque
Memer
Aiguillon
Laroque-Timbaut
Castelnau-Montratier
Parisot
Port-Ste. Marie
Beauville
Bourg-de-Visa
Lauzerte
Puylaroque
Caylus
Najac
La Fouillade
La Salvetat-Peyralès
Montpezat-de-Quercy
Agen
Bon-Encontre
Molières
Lavardac
WALIBI AQUITAINE
Puymirol
Caussade
St. Antonin-Noble-Val
Laguépie
Nérac
Valence-d'Agen
Lamagistère
Lafrançaise
Monestiés
Laplume
Moissac
Nègrepelisse
Montricoux
Vaour
Francescas
Astaffort
Auvillar
La Ville Dieu-du-Temple
Cordes-sur-Ciel
Ligardes
Castelsarrasin
Montauban
Blaye-les-Mines
Castelnau-de-Montmirail
Miradoux
Lavit
Monclar-de-Quercy
Condom
Lectoure
Bourret
Montech
Labastide-St. Pierre
Gaillac
Marssac
Larrazet
Beaumont-de-Lomagne
Valence-sur-Baïse
St. Clar
Salvagnac
Florentin
Fleurance
Verdun-sur-Garonne
Fronton
Villemur-sur-Tarn
Lisle-sur-Tarn
Montans
Cadalen
Grisolles
Rabastens
Solomiac
Montestruc-sur-Gers
Cox
Grenade
St. Sulpice
Graulhet
Briatexte
Jegun
Cépet
Montastruc-la-Conseillère
Mauvezin
Cadours
Cologne
Lavaur
Lautrec
Preignan
Montaigut-sur-Save
Nougaroulet
Verfeil
Blagnac
Auch
Aubiet
Gimont
L'Isle-Jourdain
Colomiers
Toulouse
St. Paul-Cap-de-Joux
Vielmur-sur-Agout
L'Isle-de-Noé
Léguevin
Lanta
Puylaurens
Montesquiou
Plaisance
Cugnaux
Caraman
Soual
Saramon
St. Lys
Ramonville-St. Agne
Fourquevaux
Dourgne
Mirande
Samatan
Seissan
Lombez
Ste. Foy-de-Peyrolières
Muret
Bazièg
Revel
Sorèze
Lherm
Montgiscard
St. Félix-Lauragais
Miélan
St. Michel
Masseube
Rieumes
Vernet
Villefranche-de-Lauragais
Molas
L'Isle-
Gardouch
A89
A20
A62
A64
A68
A680
E70
E72
E09
E80
115
116
130
145
146
A
B
C
3
4
5
45°
44°
1°
2°

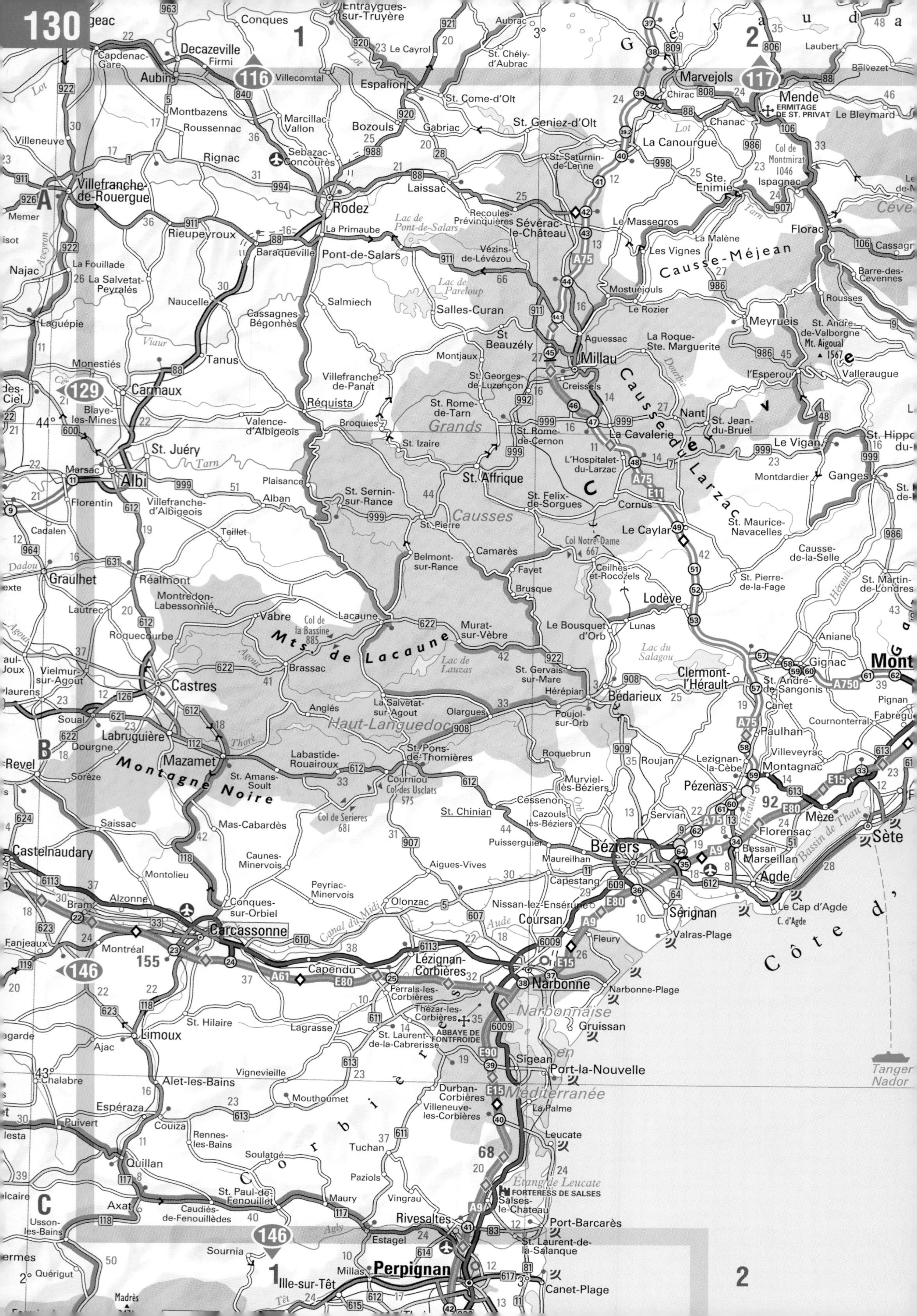

Conques
Entraygues-sur-Truyère
Aubrac
Decazeville
Firmi
Capdenac-Gare
Aubin
Villecomtal
Le Cayrol
St. Chély-d'Aubrac
Marvejols
Mende
ERMITAGE DE ST. PRIVAT
Le Bleymard
Laubert
Espalion
St. Come-d'Olt
Chirac
Montbazens
Roussennac
Marcillac-Vallon
Bozouls
Gabriac
St. Geniez-d'Olt
Chanac
Villeneuve
La Canourgue
Col de Montmirat 1046
Rignac
Sebazac-Concourès
St. Saturnin-de-Lenne
Ste. Enimie
Ispagnac
Villefranche-de-Rouergue
Rodez
Laissac
Recoules-Prévinquières
Sévérac-le-Château
Le Massegros
Florac
Rieupeyroux
La Primaube
Lac de Pont-de-Salars
La Malène
Baraqueville
Pont-de-Salars
Vézins-de-Lévézou
Les Vignes
Causse-Méjean
Cassagnes
Najac
La Fouillade
La Salvetat-Peyralés
Lac de Pareloup
Mostuéjouls
Barre-des-Cevennes
Rousses
Naucelle
Salmiech
Salles-Curan
Le Rozier
Cassagnes-Bégonhès
Meyrueis
St. André-de-Valborgne
Mt. Aigoual 1567
Laguépie
Viaur
St Beauzély
Aguessac
La Roque-Ste. Marguerite
Tanus
Montjaux
Millau
Monestiés
St. Georges-de-Luzençon
Creissels
l'Esperou
Valleraugue
Carmaux
Villefranche-de-Panat
Causse du Larzac
Blaye-les-Mines
Réquista
St. Rome-de-Tarn
Nant
St. Jean-du-Bruel
Valence-d'Albigeois
Broquiès
Grands
St. Rome-de-Cernon
La Cavalerie
St. Juéry
St. Izaire
Le Vigan
St. Hippo
Tarn
L'Hospitalet-du-Larzac
Marsac
Albi
Plaisance
St. Affrique
Montdardier
Ganges
Villefranche-d'Albigeois
Alban
St. Sernin-sur-Rance
St. Felix-de-Sorgues
Cornus
Florentin
Causses
St. Pierre
Le Caylar
St. Maurice-Navacelles
Cadalen
Teillet
Col Notre-Dame 667
Belmont-sur-Rance
Camarès
Causse-de-la-Selle
Graulhet
Réalmont
Fayet
Ceilhes-et-Rocozels
St. Pierre-de-la-Fage
St. Martin-de-Londres
Brusque
Montredon-Labessonnié
Lodève
Lautrec
Vabre
Col de la Bassine 885
Lacaune
Murat-sur-Vèbre
Le Bousquet-d'Orb
Lunas
Roquecourbe
Mts. de Lacaune
Aniane
Lac du Salagou
Vielmur-sur-Agout
Brassac
Lac de Lauzas
St. Gervais-sur-Mare
Clermont-l'Hérault
Gignac
Castres
Hérépian
Bédarieux
St. André-de-Sangonis
Pignan
Anglès
La Salvetat-sur-Agout
Olargues
Canet
Soual
Labruguière
Dourgne
Haut-Languedoc
Poujol-sur-Orb
Cournonterral
Fabrègues
Thoré
Paulhan
Revel
Montagne Noire
Mazamet
Labastide-Rouairoux
St. Pons-de-Thomières
Roquebrun
Villeveyrac
Sorèze
St. Amans-Soult
Roujan
Lezignan-la-Cèbe
Montagnac
Courniou
Col des Usclats 575
Murviel-lès-Béziers
Pézenas
Col de Serieres 681
Cessenon
Mèze
Saissac
Mas-Cabardès
St. Chinian
Cazouls-lès-Béziers
Servian
Florensac
Bassin de Thau
Sète
Castelnaudary
Puisserguier
Béziers
Bessan
Marseillan
Caunes-Minervois
Aigues-Vives
Maureilhan
Agde
Montolieu
Capestang
Peyriac-Minervois
Alzonne
Bram
Conques-sur-Orbiel
Olonzac
Nissan-lez-Ensérune
Sérignan
Le Cap d'Agde
C. d'Agde
Canal du Midi
Coursan
Carcassonne
Valras-Plage
Côte d'
Fanjeaux
Montréal
Fleury
Lézignan-Corbières
Capendu
Narbonne
Narbonne-Plage
Ferrals-les-Corbières
Narbonnaise
Thézan-les-Corbières
Gruissan
St. Hilaire
Lagrasse
ABBAYE DE FONTFROIDE
Limoux
St. Laurent-de-la-Cabrerisse
Sigean
Port-la-Nouvelle
Ajac
Tanger
Nador
Vignevieille
Chalabre
Alet-les-Bains
en Méditerranée
Durban-Corbières
Mouthoumet
Espéraza
Villeneuve-les-Corbières
La Palme
Puivert
Couiza
Rennes-les-Bains
Leucate
Quillan
Soulatgé
Tuchan
Corbières
Paziols
Étang de Leucate
St. Paul-de-Fenouillet
Maury
Vingrau
FORTERESS DE SALSES
Salses-le-Chateau
Axat
Caudiès-de-Fenouillèdes
Usson-les-Bains
Rivesaltes
Port-Barcarès
Agly
Estagel
St. Laurent-de-la-Salanque
Sournia
Millas
Perpignan
Quérigut
Ille-sur-Têt
Canet-Plage
Madrès
Têt

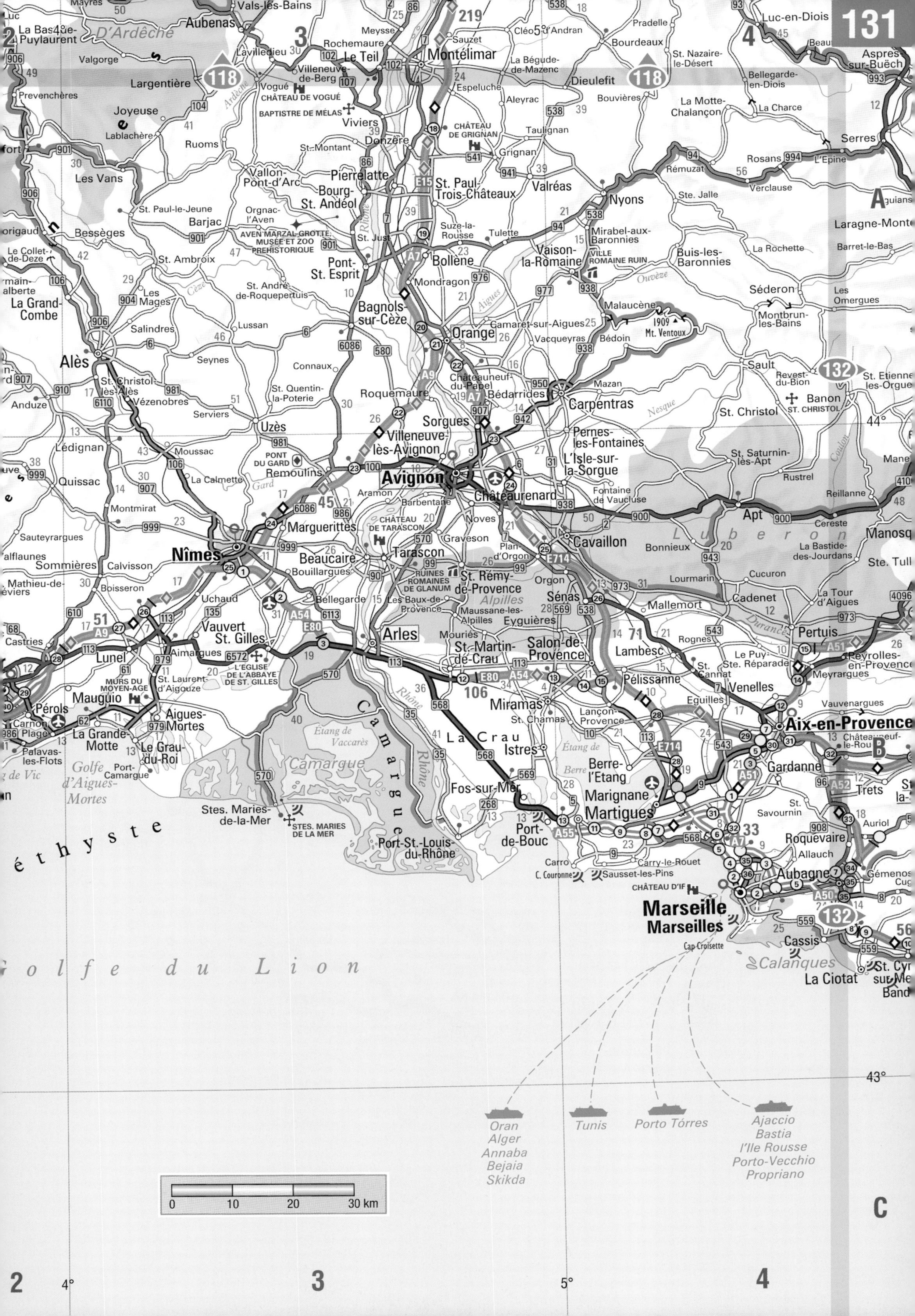
Vals-les-Bains
Aubenas
La Bastide-Puylaurent
Valgorge
Largentière
Joyeuse
Lablachère
Prevenchères
Les Vans
Ruoms
Vogüé
CHÂTEAU DE VOGÜÉ
BAPTISTRE DE MÉLAS
Villeneuve-de-Berg
Lavilledieu
Rochemaure
Le Teil
Meysse
Montélimar
Sauzet
Cléon-d'Andran
Pradelle
Bourdeaux
Luc-en-Diois
Aspres-sur-Buëch
St. Nazaire-le-Désert
La Bégude-de-Mazenc
Dieulefit
Espeluche
Aleyrac
Bouvières
Bellegarde-en-Diois
La Motte-Chalançon
La Charce
Viviers
Donzère
St.-Montant
CHÂTEAU DE GRIGNAN
Grignan
Taulignan
Serres
Rémuzat
Rosans
L'Epine
Verclause
Vallon-Pont-d'Arc
Pierrelatte
Bourg-St. Andéol
St. Paul-Trois-Châteaux
Valréas
Nyons
Ste. Jalle
St. Paul-le-Jeune
Orgnac-l'Aven
Barjac
AVEN MARZAL-GROTTE MUSÉE ET ZOO PRÉHISTORIQUE
Bessèges
St. Just
Suze-la-Rousse
Tulette
Mirabel-aux-Baronnies
Laragne-Monteglin
Le Collet-de-Deze
St. Ambroix
Pont-St. Esprit
Bollène
Vaison-la-Romaine
VILLE ROMAINE RUIN
Buis-les-Baronnies
La Rochette
Barret-le-Bas
La Grand-Combe
Les Mages
St. André-de-Roquepertuis
Mondragon
Séderon
Les Omergues
Bagnols-sur-Cèze
Malaucène
1909 Mt. Ventoux
Montbrun-les-Bains
Salindres
Lussan
Orange
Camaret-sur-Aigues
Vacqueyras
Bédoin
Alès
Seynes
Connaux
Sault
Revest-du-Bion
St. Etienne-les-Orgues
St. Christol-lès-Alès
Vézenobres
Anduze
St. Quentin-la-Poterie
Roquemaure
Châteauneuf-du-Papel
Bédarrides
Carpentras
Mazan
Banon
ST. CHRISTOL
St. Christol
Serviers
Uzès
Sorgues
Villeneuve-lès-Avignon
Pernes-les-Fontaines
Lédignan
Moussac
PONT DU GARD
Remoulins
Avignon
L'Isle-sur-la-Sorgue
St. Saturnin-lès-Apt
Quissac
La Calmette
Aramon
Barbentane
Châteaurenard
Fontaine de Vaucluse
Rustrel
Reillanne
Montmirat
Marguerittes
CHÂTEAU DE TARASCON
Noves
Apt
Céreste
Sauteyrargues
Graveson
Cavaillon
Luberon
Bonnieux
La Bastide-des-Jourdans
Manosque
Nîmes
Sommières
Calvisson
Beaucaire
Bouillargues
Tarascon
Plan-d'Orgon
RUINES ROMAINES DE GLANUM
St. Rémy-de-Provence
Orgon
Lourmarin
Cucuron
La Tour d'Aigues
Boisseron
Uchaud
Bellegarde
Les Baux-de-Provence
Alpilles
Maussane-les-Alpilles
Sénas
Eyguières
Mallemort
Cadenet
Vauvert
St. Gilles
Arles
Mouriès
St.-Martin-de-Crau
Salon-de-Provence
Lambesc
Rognes
Pertuis
Peyrolles-en-Provence
Castries
Lunel
Aimargues
L'EGLISE DE L'ABBAYE DE ST. GILLES
St. Laurent-d'Aigouze
Le Puy-Ste. Réparade
St. Cannat
Meyrargues
Mauguio
MURS DU MOYEN-AGE
Aigues-Mortes
Pélissanne
Venelles
Miramas
St. Chamas
Lançon-Provence
Eguilles
Vauvenargues
Pérols
Carnon Plage
La Grande-Motte
Le Grau-du-Roi
Palavas-les-Flots
Camargue
Étang de Vaccarès
La Crau
Istres
Étang de Berre
Aix-en-Provence
Châteauneuf-le-Rouge
Gardanne
Golfe d'Aigues-Mortes
Port-Camargue
Fos-sur-Mer
Berre-l'Etang
Marignane
Martigues
Trets
Stes. Maries-de-la-Mer
STES. MARIES DE LA MER
Port-de-Bouc
St. Savournin
Auriol
Roquevaire
Allauch
Port-St.-Louis-du-Rhône
Carro
C. Couronne
Sausset-les-Pins
Carry-le-Rouet
CHÂTEAU D'IF
Aubagne
Gémenos
Marseille
Marseilles
Cassis
Calanques
La Ciotat
St. Cyr-sur-Mer
Cap Croisette
Golfe du Lion
Oran
Alger
Annaba
Bejaia
Skikda
Tunis
Porto Tórres
Ajaccio
Bastia
l'Ile Rousse
Porto-Vecchio
Propriano
0 10 20 30 km
4°
5°
43°
44°
2
3
4
A
B
C

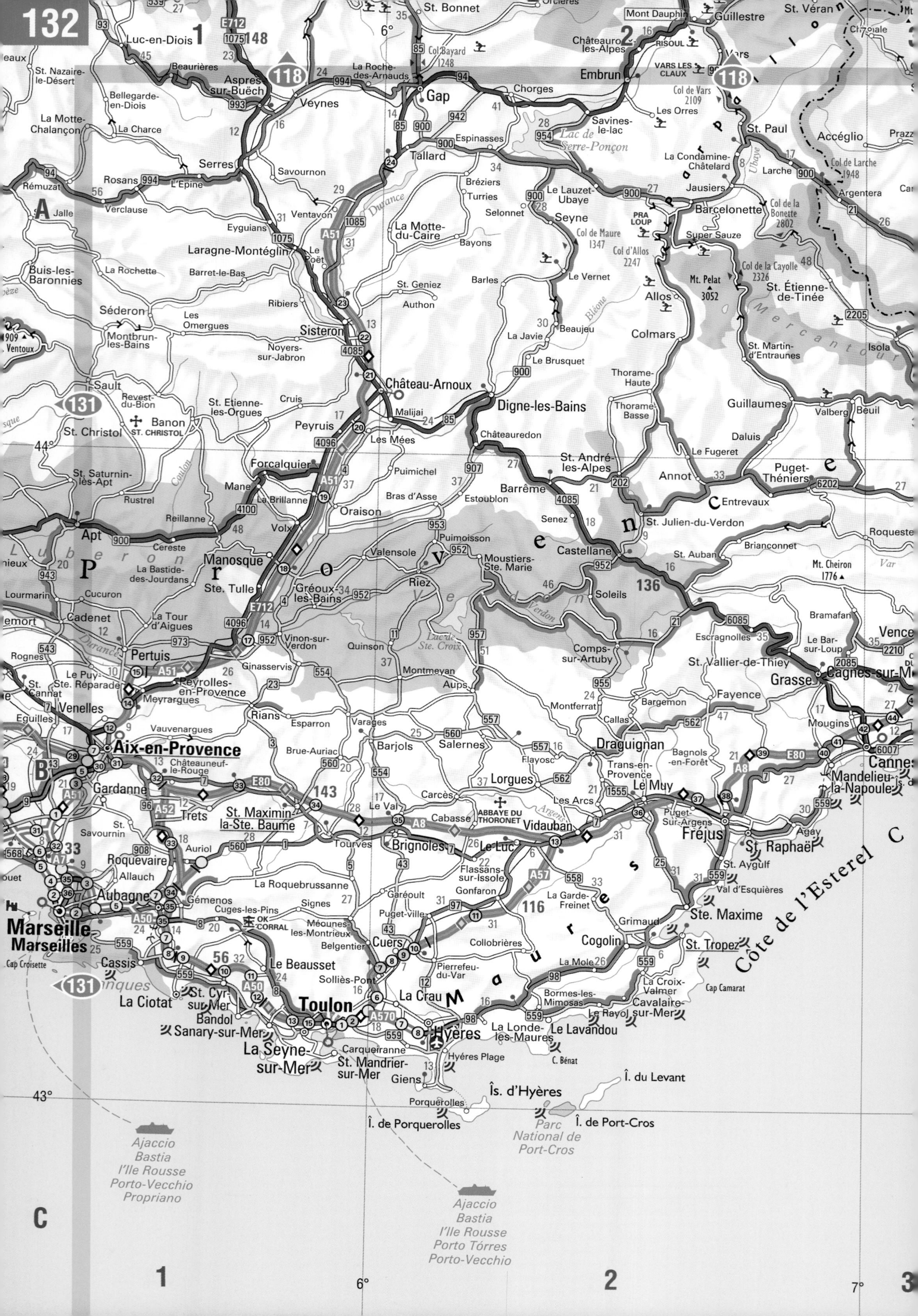
Luc-en-Diois
St. Bonnet
Mont Dauphin
Guillestre
St. Véran
Château-roux-les-Alpes
RISOUL
St. Nazaire-le-Désert
Beaurières
Aspres-sur-Buëch
La Roche-des-Arnauds
Col Bayard 1248
Embrun
VARS LES CLAUX
Vars
Bellegarde-en-Diois
Veynes
Gap
Chorges
Col de Vars 2109
Les Orres
La Motte-Chalançon
La Charce
Savines-le-lac
Lac de Serre-Ponçon
St. Paul
Acceglio
Espinasses
Tallard
La Condamine-Châtelard
Col de Larche 1948
Serres
Savournon
Larche
Rémuzat
Rosans
L'Epine
Bréziers
Turries
Le Lauzet-Ubaye
Jausiers
Argentera
Selonnet
Seyne
Barcelonette
Col de la Bonette 2802
Jalle
Verclause
Ventavon
Durance
Eyguians
La Motte-du-Caire
PRA LOUP
Super Sauze
Col de Maure 1347
Col d'Allos 2247
Laragne-Montéglin
Le Poët
Bayons
Col de la Cayolle 2326
Buis-les-Baronnies
La Rochette
Barret-le-Bas
Barles
Le Vernet
Mt. Pelat 3052
St. Étienne-de-Tinée
St. Geniez
Authon
Ribiers
Allos
Mercantour
Séderon
Les Omergues
Sisteron
Beaujeu
Colmars
Montbrun-les-Bains
Noyers-sur-Jabron
La Javie
St. Martin-d'Entraunes
Isola
Ventoux
Le Brusquet
Sault
Château-Arnoux
Thorame-Haute
Revest-du-Bion
St. Etienne-les-Orgues
Cruis
Digne-les-Bains
Thorame-Basse
Guillaumes
Valberg
Beuil
Banon
ST. CHRISTOL
St. Christol
Peyruis
Malijai
Châteauredon
Daluis
Les Mées
44°
Forcalquier
St. André-les-Alpes
Le Fugeret
Puget-Théniers
St. Saturnin-lès-Apt
Mane
Puimichel
Barrême
Annot
Entrevaux
Rustrel
La Brillanne
Bras d'Asse
Estoublon
Oraison
Reillanne
Apt
Senez
St. Julien-du-Verdon
Luberon
Cereste
Volx
Puimoisson
Roquesteron
Manosque
Valensole
Moustiers-Ste. Marie
Castellane
Brianconnet
St. Auban
La Bastide-des-Jourdans
Mt. Cheiron 1776
Var
Ste. Tulle
Gréoux-les-Bains
Riez
Soleils
Lourmarin
Cucuron
Verdon
Cadenet
La Tour d'Aigues
Bramafan
Vinon-sur-Verdon
Quinson
Lac de Ste. Croix
Escragnolles
Vence
Pertuis
Comps-sur-Artuby
Le Bar-sur-Loup
Rognes
Ginasservis
Montmeyan
St. Vallier-de-Thiey
Le Puy-Ste. Réparade
Peyrolles-en-Provence
Aups
Grasse
Cagnes-sur-Mer
St. Cannat
Venelles
Meyrargues
Montferrat
Bargemon
Fayence
Eguilles
Rians
Esparron
Varages
Callas
Mougins
Vauvenargues
Aix-en-Provence
Brue-Auriac
Barjols
Salernes
Flayosc
Draguignan
Bagnols-en-Forêt
Cannes
Châteauneuf-le-Rouge
Trans-en-Provence
Mandelieu-la-Napoule
Gardanne
Lorgues
Le Muy
Trets
St. Maximin-la-Ste. Baume
Le Val
Carcès
Cabasse
ABBAYE DU THORONET
Les Arcs
Argens
St. Savournin
Vidauban
Puget-Sur-Argens
Fréjus
St. Raphaël
Agay
Auriol
Tourves
Brignoles
Le Luc
Roquevaire
Allauch
La Roquebrussanne
Flassans-sur-Issole
St. Aygulf
Côte de l'Esterel
Aubagne
Gémenos
Gonfaron
La Garde-Freinet
Val d'Esquières
Garéoult
Signes
Maures
Marseille
Marseilles
Cuges-les-Pins
OK CORRAL
Méounes-les-Montrieux
Puget-ville
Ste. Maxime
Grimaud
Cuers
Collobrières
Cogolin
St. Tropez
Cap Croisette
Cassis
Belgentier
Le Beausset
Pierrefeu-du-Var
La Mole
Solliès-Pont
La Croix-Valmer
Cap Camarat
La Ciotat
St. Cyr-sur-Mer
Bandol
Toulon
La Crau
Bormes-les-Mimosas
Cavalaire
Le Rayol
Sanary-sur-Mer
Hyères
La Londe-les-Maures
Le Lavandou
La Seyne-sur-Mer
Carqueiranne
St. Mandrier-sur-Mer
Hyères Plage
C. Bénat
Giens
Î. du Levant
Îs. d'Hyères
43°
Porquerolles
Î. de Porquerolles
Parc National de Port-Cros
Î. de Port-Cros
Ajaccio
Bastia
I'Ile Rousse
Porto-Vecchio
Propriano
Ajaccio
Bastia
I'Ile Rousse
Porto Tórres
Porto-Vecchio
6°
7°
A
B
C
1
2
3
131
118
136
143
116
148
56
33

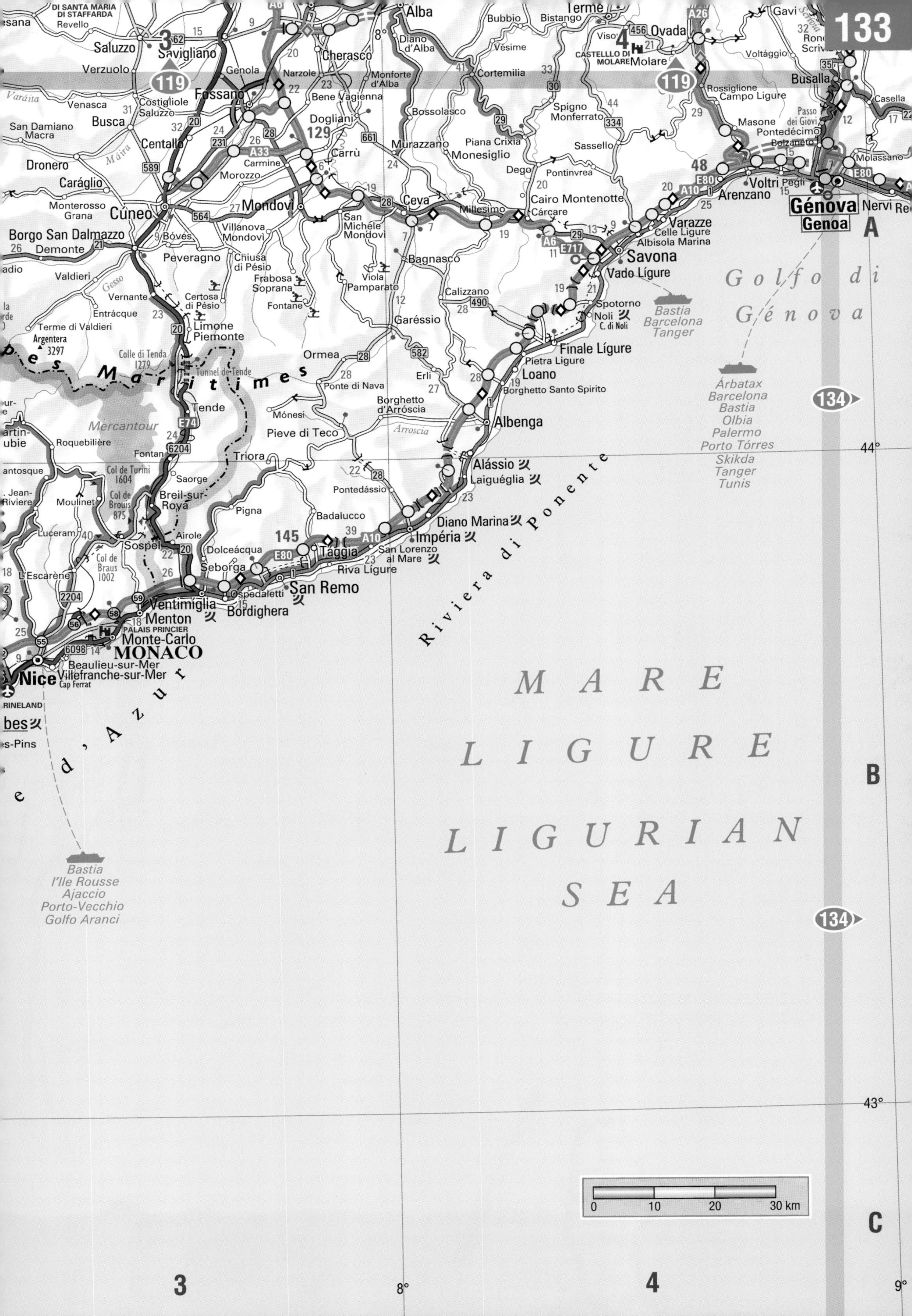
Saluzzo
Savigliano
Fossano
Cherasco
Alba
Ovada
Gavi
Busalla
Cúneo
Mondovì
Ceva
Millesimo
Cairo Montenotte
Savona
Varazze
Arenzano
Voltri
Génova
Genoa
Nervi
Vado Ligure
Spotorno
Noli
Finale Lígure
Pietra Ligure
Loano
Albenga
Alássio
Laiguéglia
Diano Marina
Impéria
San Lorenzo al Mare
Riva Ligure
Tággia
San Remo
Bordighera
Ventimiglia
Menton
Monte-Carlo
MONACO
Beaulieu-sur-Mer
Villefranche-sur-Mer
Nice
Tende
Limone Piemonte
Garéssio
Ormea
Pieve di Teco
Golfo di Génova
Riviera di Ponente
MARE LIGURE
LIGURIAN SEA
Bastia Barcelona Tanger
Árbatax Barcelona Bastia Olbia Palermo Porto Tórres Skikda Tanger Tunis
Bastia l'Ile Rousse Ajaccio Porto-Vecchio Golfo Aranci
44°
43°
8°
9°
0 10 20 30 km
A
B
C
3
4
134
119

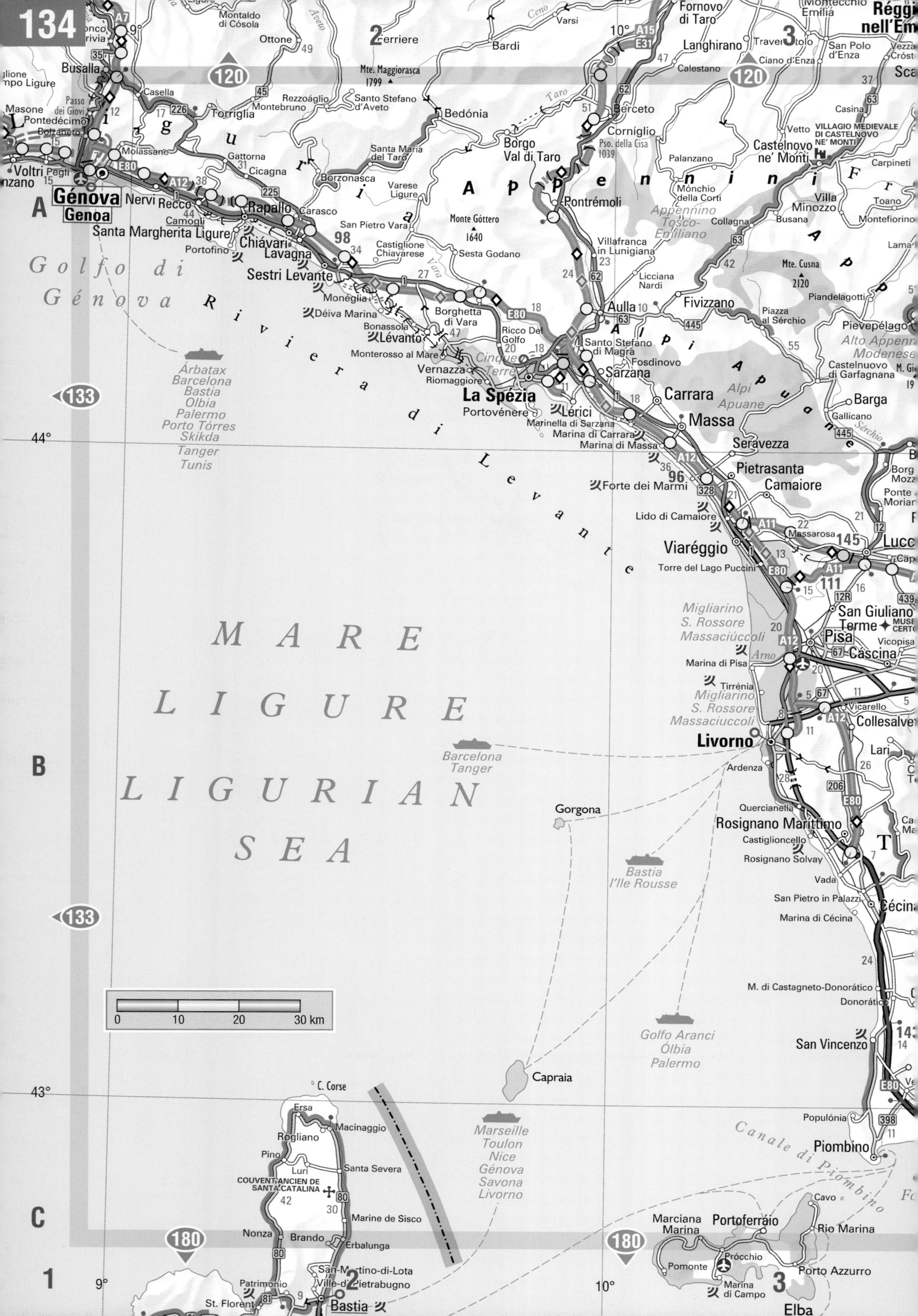
Montaldo di Cósola
Ottone
Ferriere
Bardi
Varsi
Fornovo di Taro
Langhirano
Traversetolo
San Polo d'Enza
Ciano d'Enza
Réggio nell'Emília
Busalla
Mte. Maggiorasca 1799
120
Calestano
Casella
Rezzoáglio
Santo Stefano d'Aveto
Bedónia
Berceto
Casina
Masone
Passo dei Giovi
Pontedécimo
Bolzaneto
Torriglia
Montebruno
Corníglio
Castelnuovo ne' Monti
VILLAGIO MEDIEVALE DI CASTELNUOVO NE' MONTI
Vetto
Carpineti
Molassano
Gattorna
Cicagna
Santa Maria del Taro
Borgo Val di Taro
Pso. della Cisa 1039
Palanzano
Voltri
Pegli
Génova
Genoa
Nervi
Recco
Camogli
Rapallo
Carasco
Borzonasca
Varese Ligure
Pontrémoli
Mónchio della Corti
Villa Minozzo
Toano
Montefiorino
Busana
Collagna
Appennino Tosco-Emiliano
A
Santa Margherita Ligure
Portofino
Chiávari
Lavagna
San Pietro Vara
Castiglione Chiavarese
Monte Góttero 1640
Sesta Godano
Villafranca in Lunigiana
Mte. Cusna 2120
Lama
Golfo di Génova
Sestri Levante
Mονéglia
Déiva Marina
Bonassola
Lévanto
Borghetta di Vara
Ricco Del Golfo
Licciana Nardi
Aulla
Fivizzano
Piazza al Sérchio
Piandelagotti
Pievepélago
Alto Appennino Modenese
Riviera di Levante
Monterosso al Mare
Vernazza
Riomaggiore
Cinque Terre
Santo Stefano di Magra
Fosdinovo
Sarzana
Castelnuovo di Garfagnana
Alpi Apuane
Árbatax
Barcelona
Bastia
Olbia
Palermo
Porto Tórres
Skikda
Tanger
Tunis
133
La Spézia
Portovénere
Lérici
Marinella di Sarzana
Marina di Carrara
Marina di Massa
Carrara
Massa
Barga
Gallicano
Sérchio
44°
Seravezza
Forte dei Marmi
Pietrasanta
Camaiore
Lido di Camaiore
Massarosa
Viaréggio
Torre del Lago Puccini
Lucca
Migliarino S. Rossore Massaciúccoli
San Giuliano Terme
Pisa
Vicopisa
Cáscina
Arno
Marina di Pisa
Tirrénia
Livorno
Collesalvetti
Vicarello
MARE LIGURE
LIGURIAN SEA
Barcelona
Tanger
Ardenza
Lari
B
Gorgona
Quercianella
Rosignano Maríttimo
Castiglioncello
Rosignano Solvay
Bastia
l'Ile Rousse
Vada
San Pietro in Palazzi
Cécina
Marina di Cécina
0 10 20 30 km
M. di Castagneto-Donorático
Donorático
Golfo Aranci
Ólbia
Palermo
San Vincenzo
Capraia
C. Corse
43°
Ersa
Macinaggio
Rogliano
Pino
Luri
Santa Severa
COUVENT ANCIEN DE SANTA CATALINA
Marine de Sisco
Marseille
Toulon
Nice
Génova
Savona
Livorno
Populónia
Piombino
Canale di Piombino
Cavo
Portoferráio
Marciana Marina
Rio Marina
C
Nonza
Brando
Erbalunga
180
Prócchio
Pomonte
Porto Azzurro
Marina di Campo
Elba
San-Martino-di-Lota
Ville-di-Pietrabugno
Patrimonio
St. Florent
Bastia
1
9°
2
10°
3

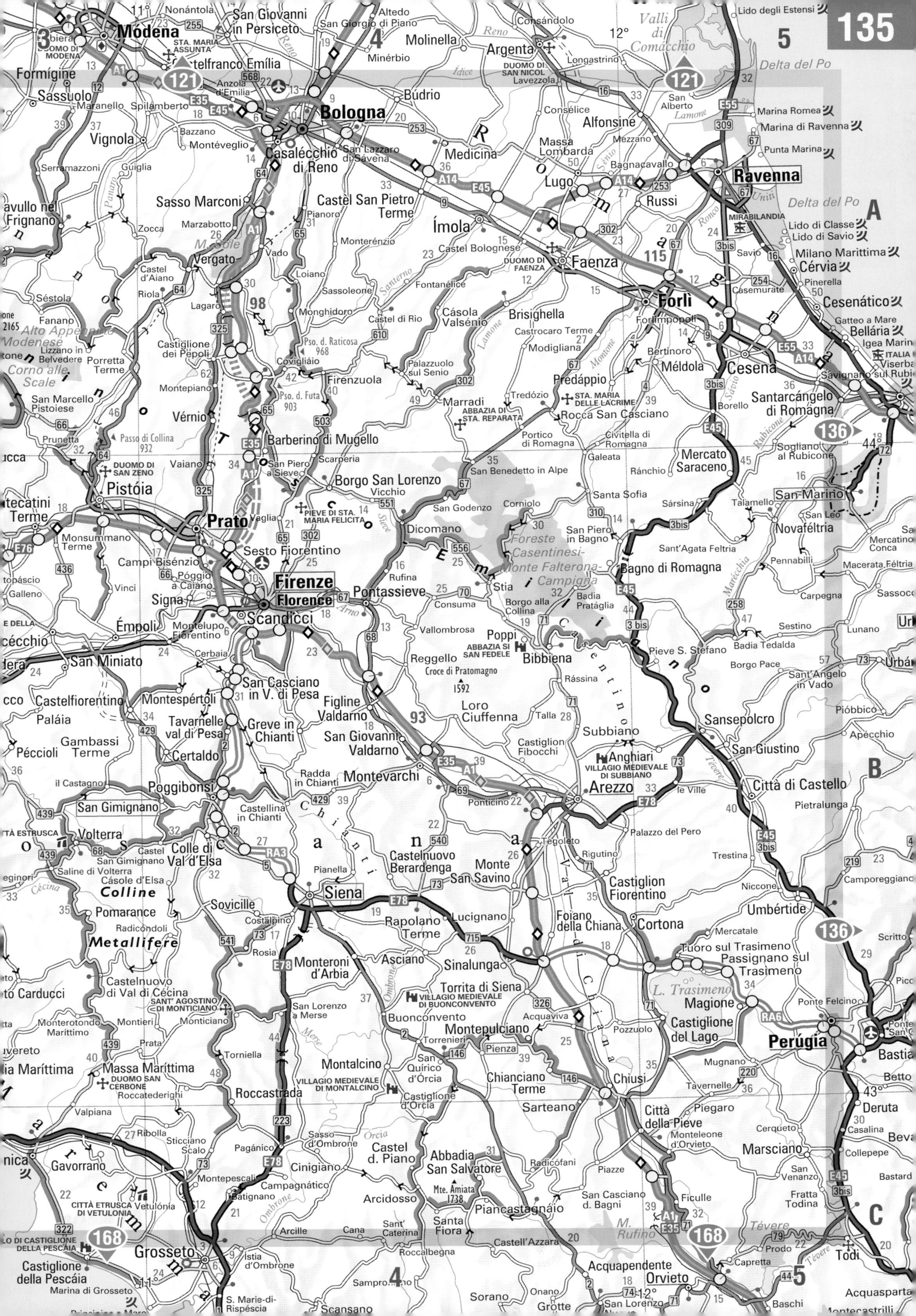

Modena
Nonántola
San Giovanni in Persiceto
Altedo
San Giorgio di Piano
Molinella
Minérbio
Consándolo
Argenta
Valli di Comácchio
Lido degli Estensi
Delta del Po
Formígine
Sassuolo
Maranello
Spilamberto
Castelfranco Emília
Anzola d'Emilia
Bologna
Búdrio
Lavezzola
Conselice
Alfonsine
San Alberto
Marina Romea
Marina di Ravenna
Punta Marina
Vignola
Bazzano
Montéveglio
Casalécchio di Reno
San Lazzaro di Sávena
Medicina
Massa Lombarda
Mezzano
Bagnacavallo
Ravenna
Serramazzoni
Guiglia
Sasso Marconi
Castel San Pietro Terme
Ímola
Lugo
Russi
Mirabilandia
Lido di Classe
Lido di Savio
Milano Marittima
Cérvia
Zocca
Marzabotto
Pianoro
Monterénzio
Castel Bolognese
Faenza
Savio
Pinerella
Cesenático
Vergato
Vado
Loiano
Sassoleone
Fontanélice
Forlì
Forlimpopoli
Casemurate
Castel d'Aiano
Riola
Lagaro
Monghidoro
Castel di Rio
Cásola Valsénio
Brisighella
Castrocaro Terme
Modigliana
Bertinoro
Méldola
Cesena
Gatteo a Mare
Bellária
Igea Marina
Viserba
Sèstola
Fanano
Alto Appennino Modenese
Lizzano in Belvedere
Corno alle Scale
Castiglione dei Pépoli
Porretta Terme
Pso. d. Raticosa
Covigliáio
Firenzuola
Palazzuolo sul Senio
Predáppio
Tredózio
Savignano sul Rubicone
Santarcángelo di Romagna
Borello
San Marcello Pistoiese
Montepiano
Vérnio
Pso. d. Futa
Marradi
Abbazia di Sta. Reparata
Sta. Maria delle Lacrime
Rocca San Casciano
Portico di Romagna
Civitella di Romagna
Galeata
Mercato Saraceno
Sogliano al Rubicone
Prunetta
Passo di Collina
Barberino di Mugello
Scarperia
San Piero a Sieve
Vaiano
Duomo di San Zeno
Pistóia
Borgo San Lorenzo
Vicchio
San Benedetto in Alpe
Ránchio
San-Marino
Montecatini Terme
Monsummano Terme
Prato
Vaglia
Pieve di Sta. Maria Felicita
San Godenzo
Corniolo
Santa Sofia
Sársina
Talamello
San Leo
Novafeltria
Sesto Fiorentino
Campi Bisénzio
Dicomano
Foreste Casentinesi-Monte Falterona-Campigna
San Piero in Bagno
Sant'Agata Feltria
Pennabilli
Mercatino Conca
Macerata Féltria
Póggio a Caiano
Vinci
Signa
Firenze
Florence
Pontassieve
Rufina
Consuma
Stia
Borgo alla Collina
Badia Prataglia
Bagno di Romagna
Carpegna
Galleno
Émpoli
Montelupo Fiorentino
Scandicci
Vallombrosa
Poppi
Abbazia si San Fedele
Bibbiena
Sestino
Lunano
San Miniato
Cerbaia
Reggello
Croce di Pratomagno
Pieve S. Stefano
Badia Tedalda
Borgo Pace
Sant'Angelo in Vado
Castelfiorentino
Montespértoli
San Casciano in V. di Pesa
Figline Valdarno
Loro Ciuffenna
Talla
Rássina
Paláia
Tavarnelle val di Pesa
Greve in Chianti
San Giovanni Valdarno
Subbiano
Sansepolcro
Piobbico
Apécchio
Gambassi Terme
Péccioli
Certaldo
Castiglion Fibocchi
Anghiari
Villaggio Medievale di Subbiano
San Giustino
il Castagno
Poggibonsi
Radda in Chianti
Montevarchi
Ponticino
Arezzo
le Ville
Città di Castello
San Gimignano
Castellina in Chianti
Pietralunga
Volterra
Colle di Val d'Elsa
Castelnuovo Berardenga
Tegoleto
Palazzo del Pero
Saline di Volterra
Cásole d'Elsa
Colline Metallifere
Pianella
Monte San Savino
Rigutino
Castiglion Fiorentino
Trestina
Camporeggiano
Siena
Sovicille
Pomarance
Radicóndoli
Costalpino
Rapolano Terme
Lucignano
Foiano della Chiana
Cortona
Niccone
Umbértide
Mercatale
Tuoro sul Trasimeno
Passignano sul Trasimeno
Rosia
Monteroni d'Arbia
Asciano
Sinalunga
Castelnuovo di Val di Cécina
Sant' Agostino di Monticiano
Torrita di Siena
Villaggio Medievale di Buonconvento
L. Trasimeno
Magione
Castiglione del Lago
Ponte Felcino
Perúgia
San Lorenzo a Merse
Monterotondo Maríttimo
Montieri
Monticiano
Buonconvento
Montepulciano
Acquaviva
Pozzuolo
Torrenieri
Pienza
Prata
Torniella
Massa Maríttima
Duomo San Cerbone
Roccatederighi
Montalcino
San Quírico d'Órcia
Chianciano Terme
Chiusi
Villaggio Medievale di Montalcino
Castiglione d'Órcia
Roccastrada
Sarteano
Città della Pieve
Piegaro
Tavernelle
Mugnano
Bastia
Betto
Deruta
Valpiana
Ribolla
Sticciano Scalo
Sasso d'Ombrone
Castel d. Piano
Abbadia San Salvatore
Monteleone d'Orvieto
Cerqueto
Casalina
Marsciano
Collepepe
Gavorrano
Pagánico
Cinigiano
Radicófani
Piazze
San Venanzo
Montepescali
Campagnático
Mte. Amiata
Fratta Todina
Bastardo
Batignano
Arcidosso
Piancastagnáio
San Casciano d. Bagni
Ficulle
Città Etrusca di Vetulonia
Vetulónia
Santa Fiora
Arcille
Cana
Sant' Caterina
Castell'Azzara
M. Rufino
Tévere
Prodo
Todi
Lo di Castiglione della Pescáia
Grosseto
Istia d'Ombrone
Roccalbegna
Acquapendente
Orvieto
Capretta
Castiglione della Pescáia
Marina di Grosseto
Samprugnano
S. Marie-di-Rispéscia
Scansano
Sorano
Onano
Grotte
San Lorenzo
Baschi
Acquasparta
Montecastrilli
Romagna
Appennino Tosco-Emiliano
Casentino
Chianti
Val di Chiana
Maremma
121
136
168

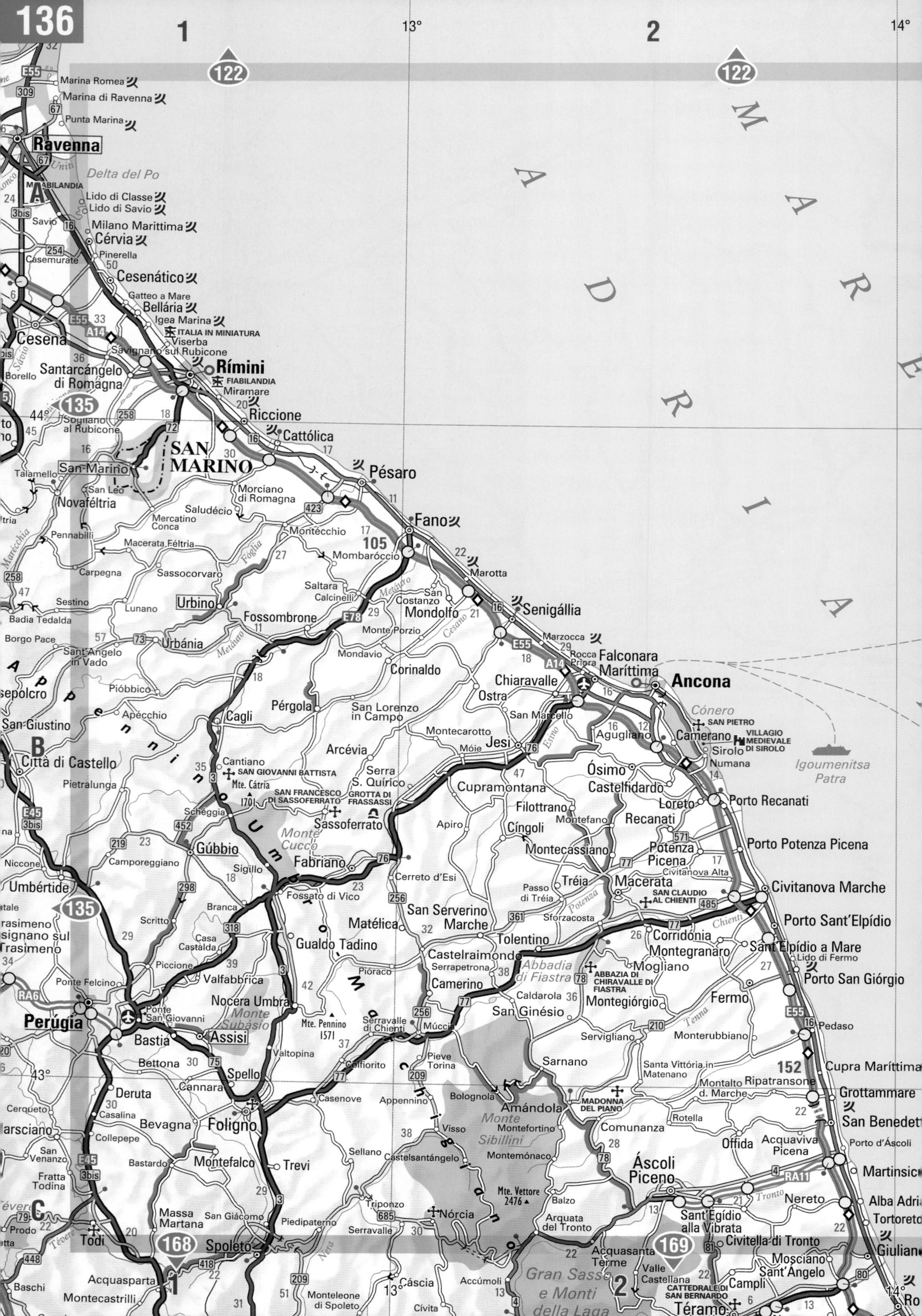
1
13°
2
14°
122
122
MARE ADRIATICO
Marina Romea
Marina di Ravenna
Punta Marina
Ravenna
Delta del Po
MIRABILANDIA
Lido di Classe
Lido di Savio
Savio
Milano Marittima
Cérvia
Pinerella
Casemurate
Cesenático
Gatteo a Mare
Bellária
Igea Marina
ITALIA IN MINIATURA
Viserba
Cesena
Savignano sul Rubicone
Santarcángelo di Romagna
Rímini
FIABILANDIA
Miramare
Riccione
135
Sogliano al Rubicone
SAN MARINO
San Marino
Cattólica
Talamello
San Leo
Novaféltria
Pésaro
Morciano di Romagna
Saludécio
Mercatino Conca
Pennabilli
Macerata Féltria
Montécchio
Fano
105
Mombaróccio
Carpegna
Sassocorvaro
Marotta
Saltara
Calcinelli
San Costanzo
Sestino
Lunano
Urbino
Mondolfo
Senigállia
Badia Tedalda
Fossombrone
Monte Porzio
Marzocca
Borgo Pace
Urbánia
Sant'Angelo in Vado
Mondavio
Corinaldo
Rocca Priora
Falconara Maríttima
Ancona
Piόbbico
Chiaravalle
Ostra
Cónero
SAN PIETRO
Camerano
VILLAGGIO MEDIEVALE DI SIROLO
Sirolo
Numana
Igoumenitsa Patra
San Marcello
Aguglìano
Pérgola
San Lorenzo in Campo
Cagli
Apécchio
San Giustino
Città di Castello
Appennino Umbro-Marchigiano
Montecarotto
Móie
Jesi
Arcévia
Ósimo
Castelfidardo
Loreto
Porto Recanati
Cantiano
SAN GIOVANNI BATTISTA
Mte. Cátria 1701
Serra S. Quírico
Cupramontana
Pietralunga
SAN FRANCESCO DI SASSOFERRATO
GROTTA DI FRASSASSI
Filottrano
Montefano
Recanati
Schéggia
Sassoferrato
Apiro
Cíngoli
Monte Cucco
Montecassiano
Potenza Picena
Porto Potenza Picena
Gúbbio
Camporeggiano
Fabriano
Civitanova Alta
Niccone
Sigillo
Cerreto d'Esi
Tréia
Macerata
Civitanova Marche
Umbértide
Fossato di Vico
Passo di Tréia
SAN CLAUDIO AL CHIENTI
Branca
San Severino Marche
Sforzacosta
Porto Sant'Elpídio
Scritto
Matélica
Corridonia
Casa Castalda
Gualdo Tadino
Tolentino
Montegranaro
Sant'Elpídio a Mare
Lido di Fermo
Piccione
Castelraimondo
Serrapetrona
Abbadia di Fiastra
ABBAZIA DI CHIARAVALLE DI FIASTRA
Mogliano
Porto San Giórgio
Ponte Felcino
Valfabbrica
Pióraco
Camerino
Caldarola
Fermo
Nocera Umbra
Monte Subásio
San Ginésio
Montegiórgio
Perúgia
Ponte San Giovanni
Mte. Pennino 1571
Serravalle di Chienti
Múccia
Pedaso
Bastia
Assisi
Servigliano
Monterubbiano
Bettona
Valtopina
Pieve Torina
Sarnano
Santa Vittória in Matenano
Cupra Maríttima
Spello
Colfiorito
Montalto d. Marche
Ripatransone
Cannara
Bolognola
Grottammare
Deruta
Casenove
Appennino
Amándola
MADONNA DEL PIANO
Cerqueto
Casalina
Bevagna
Foligno
Monte Sibillini
Montefortino
Rotella
San Benedetto
Marsciano
Collepepe
Visso
Comunanza
Porto d'Áscoli
San Venanzo
Acquaviva Picena
Offida
Bastardo
Montefalco
Sellano
Castelsantángelo
Montemónaco
Áscoli Piceno
Martinsicuro
Fratta Todina
Trevi
Mte. Vettore 2476
Nereto
Alba Adriatica
Tevere
Triponzo
Balzo
Tortoreto
Massa Martana
San Giácomo
Piediipaterno
Nórcia
Arquata del Tronto
Sant'Egídio alla Vibrata
Prodo
Todi
168
Spoleto
Serravalle
Civitella di Tronto
Giulianova
Acquasanta Terme
169
Mosciano Sant'Angelo
Valle Castellana
Acquasparta
Baschi
Cáscia
Accúmoli
Gran Sasso e Monti della Laga
CATTEDRALE DI SAN BERNARDO
Campli
Montecastrilli
Monteleone di Spoleto
Cívita
Téramo
Guardea
DUOMO DI SANTA
Notaresco
152
A
B
C
E55
E45
E78
A14
RA6
RA11

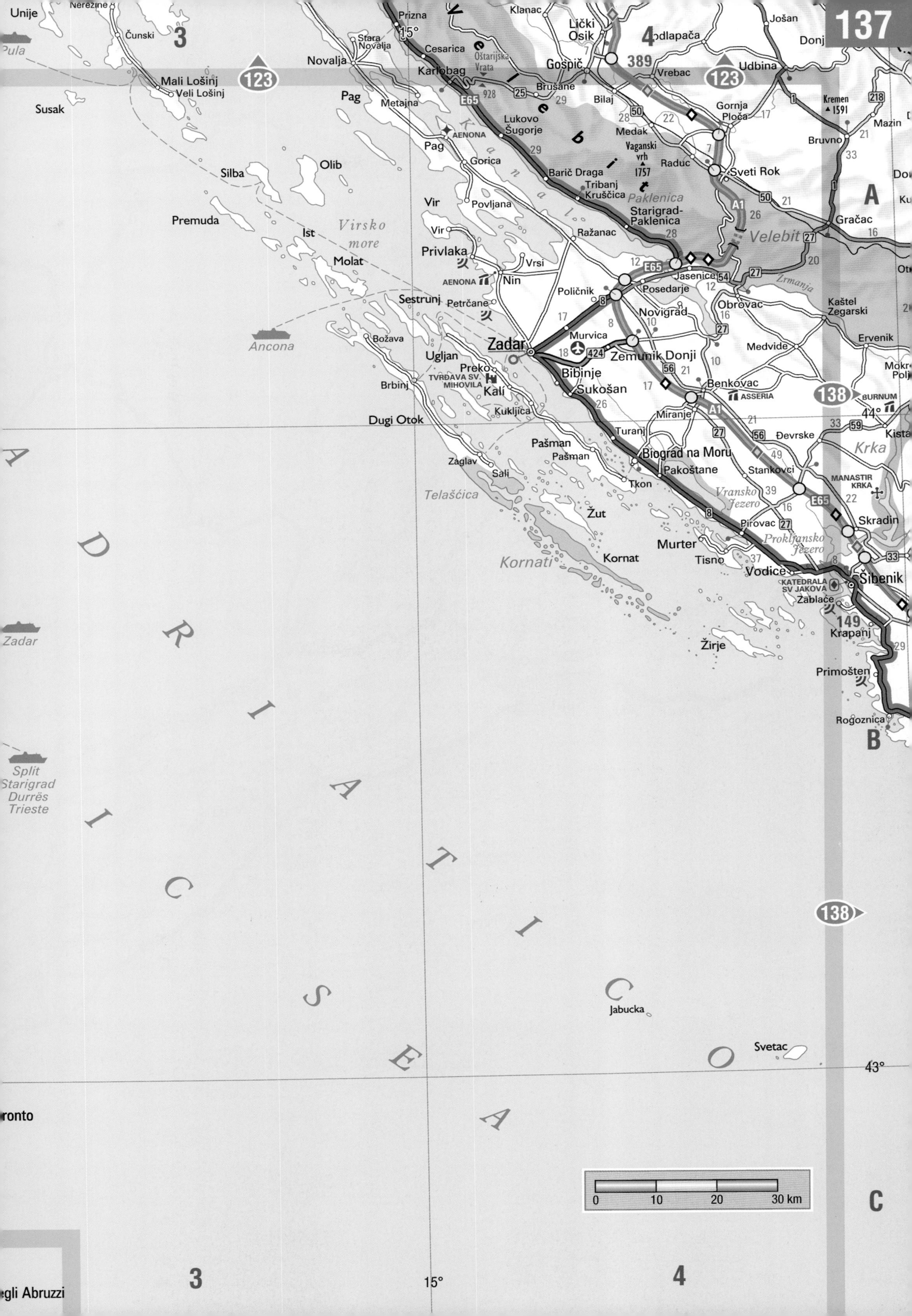
Zadar
Šibenik
Gospić
Biograd na Moru
Benkovac
Obrovac
Gračac
Velebit
Kornati
Dugi Otok
Pag
Novalja
Karlobag
Nin
Vodice
Murter
Ugljan
Pašman
Silba
Olib
Premuda
Molat
Ist
Sestrunj
Žirje
Jabucka
Svetac
Primošten
Rogoznica
Krapanj
Skradin
Mali Lošinj
Veli Lošinj
Susak
Unije
Ancona
Split
Starigrad
Durrës
Trieste
ADRIATIC SEA
123
138
0 10 20 30 km
15°
43°
44°
3
4
A
B
C

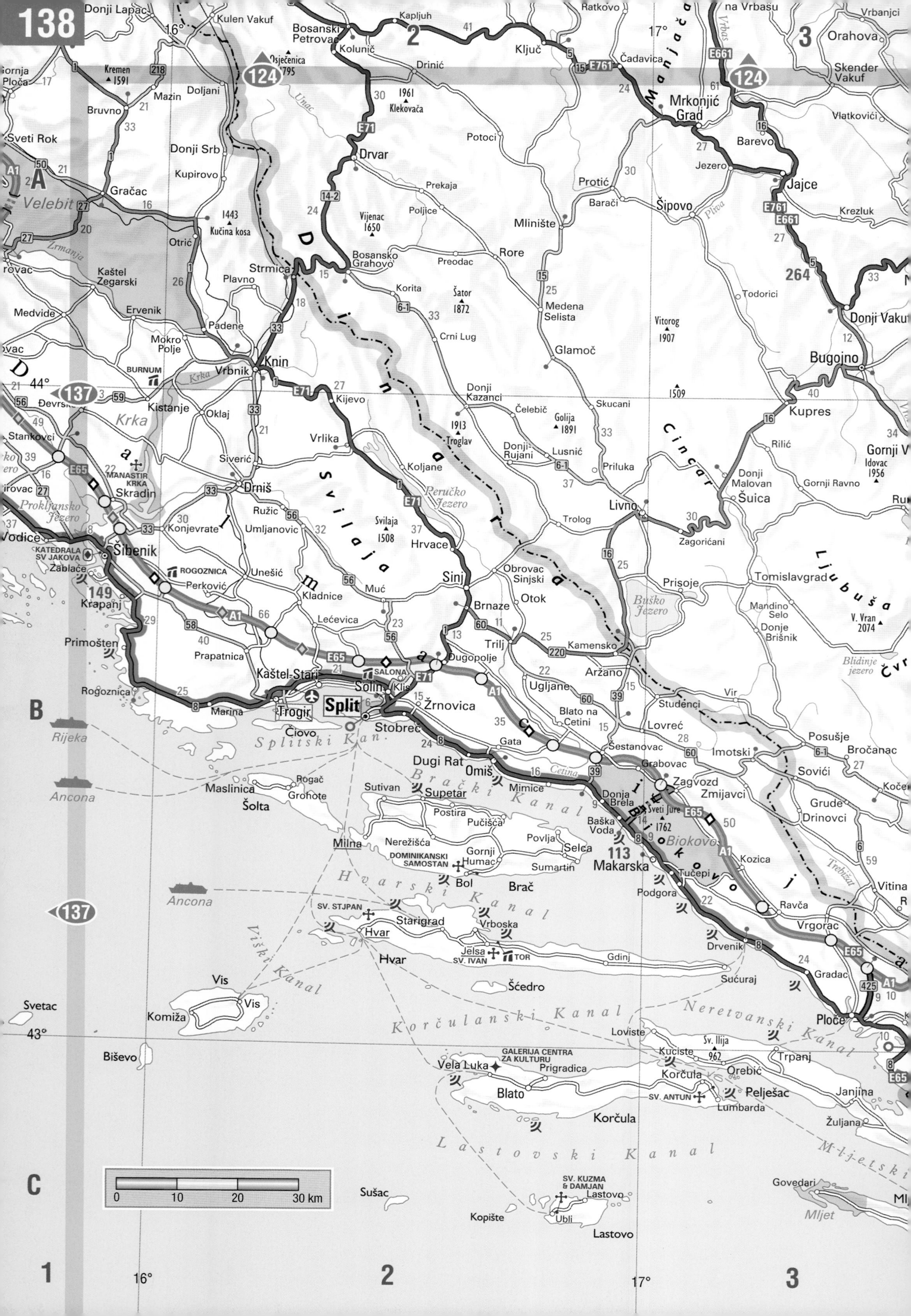
Donji Lapac
Kulen Vakuf
Bosanski Petrovac
Kapljuh
Kolunič
Ratkovo
Ključ
Čadavica
na Vrbasu
Vrbanjci
Orahova
Skender Vakuf
Osječenica 1795
Drinić
Kremen 1591
Gornja Ploča
Mazin
Doljani
Bruvno
1961 Klekovača
Mrkonjić Grad
Vlatkovići
Sveti Rok
Donji Srb
Drvar
Potoci
Barevo
Jezero
Jajce
Kupirovo
Gračac
Velebit
Prekaja
Protić
Barači
Šipovo
Krezluk
1443 Kučina kosa
Vijenac 1650
Poljice
Mliništa
Otrić
Zrmanja
Bosansko Grahovo
Preodac
Rore
Strmica
Plavno
Kaštel Zegarski
Korita
Šator 1872
Medena Selista
Todorici
Donji Vakuf
Vitorog 1907
Medvide
Ervenik
Crni Lug
Padene
Mokro Polje
Glamoč
Bugojno
BURNUM
Krka
Vrbnik
Knin
Kijevo
Donji Kazanci
1509
Kupres
Đevrske
Kistanje
Oklaj
Čelebić
Skucani
Krka
1913 Troglav
Golija 1891
Rilić
Gornji V
Idovac 1956
Stankovci
MANASTIR KRKA
Vrlika
Siverić
Donji-Rujani
Lusnić
Koljane
Priluka
Donji Malovan
Gornji Ravno
Skradin
Drniš
Peručko Jezero
Šuica
Prokljansko Jezero
Ružic
Svilaja 1508
Livno
Vodice
Konjevrate
Umljanovic
Hrvace
Trolog
Zagorićani
KATEDRALA SV JAKOVA
Šibenik
Žablaće
ROGOZNICA
Unešić
Sinj
Obrovac Sinjski
Prisoje
Tomislavgrad
Krapanj
Perković
Kladnice
Muć
Otok
Brnaze
Buško Jezero
Mandino Selo
Donje Brišnik
V. Vran 2074
Primošten
Lećevica
Trilj
Kamensko
Prapatnica
SALONA
Dugopolje
Blidinje jezero
Kaštel-Stari
Solin
Klis
Aržano
Rogoznica
Ugljane
Vir
Marina
Trogir
Split
Žrnovica
Studenci
Rijeka
Čiovo
Stobreč
Blato na Cetini
Lovreć
Posušje
Splitski Kan.
Gata
Šestanovac
Imotski
Bročanac
Dugi Rat
Omiš
Grabovac
Sovići
Rogač
Cetina
Zagvozd
Zmijavci
Ancona
Maslinica
Grohote
Sutivan
Supetar
Mimice
Donja Brela
Šolta
Bački Kanal
Sveti Jure 1762
Grude
Drinovci
Postira
Pučišća
Baška Voda
Biokovo
Milna
Nerežišća
Povlja
Selca
Gornji Humac
DOMINIKANSKI SAMOSTAN
Sumartin
Makarska
Tučepi
Kozica
Trebižat
Vitina
Hvarski Kanal
Bol
Brač
Podgora
Ancona
SV. STJPAN
Ravča
Vrboska
Starigrad
Hvar
Vrgorac
Drvenik
Jelsa
SV. IVAN
TOR
Hvar
Gdinj
Gradac
Viški Kanal
Vis
Ščedro
Sućuraj
Svetac
Komiža
Vis
Korčulanski Kanal
Neretvanski Kanal
Ploče
Loviste
Biševo
Sv. Ilija 962
Kuciste
Trpanj
GALERIJA CENTRA ZA KULTURU
Vela Luka
Prigradica
Orebić
Korčula
Blato
SV. ANTUN
Pelješac
Janjina
Lumbarda
Korčula
Žuljana
Lastovski Kanal
Mljetski
Sušac
SV. KUZMA & DAMJAN
Lastovo
Govedari
Kopište
Ubli
Lastovo
Mljet
0
10
20
30 km
Dinara
Svilaja
Cincar
Ljubuša
Manjača
A
B
C
1
2
3
16°
17°
44°
43°

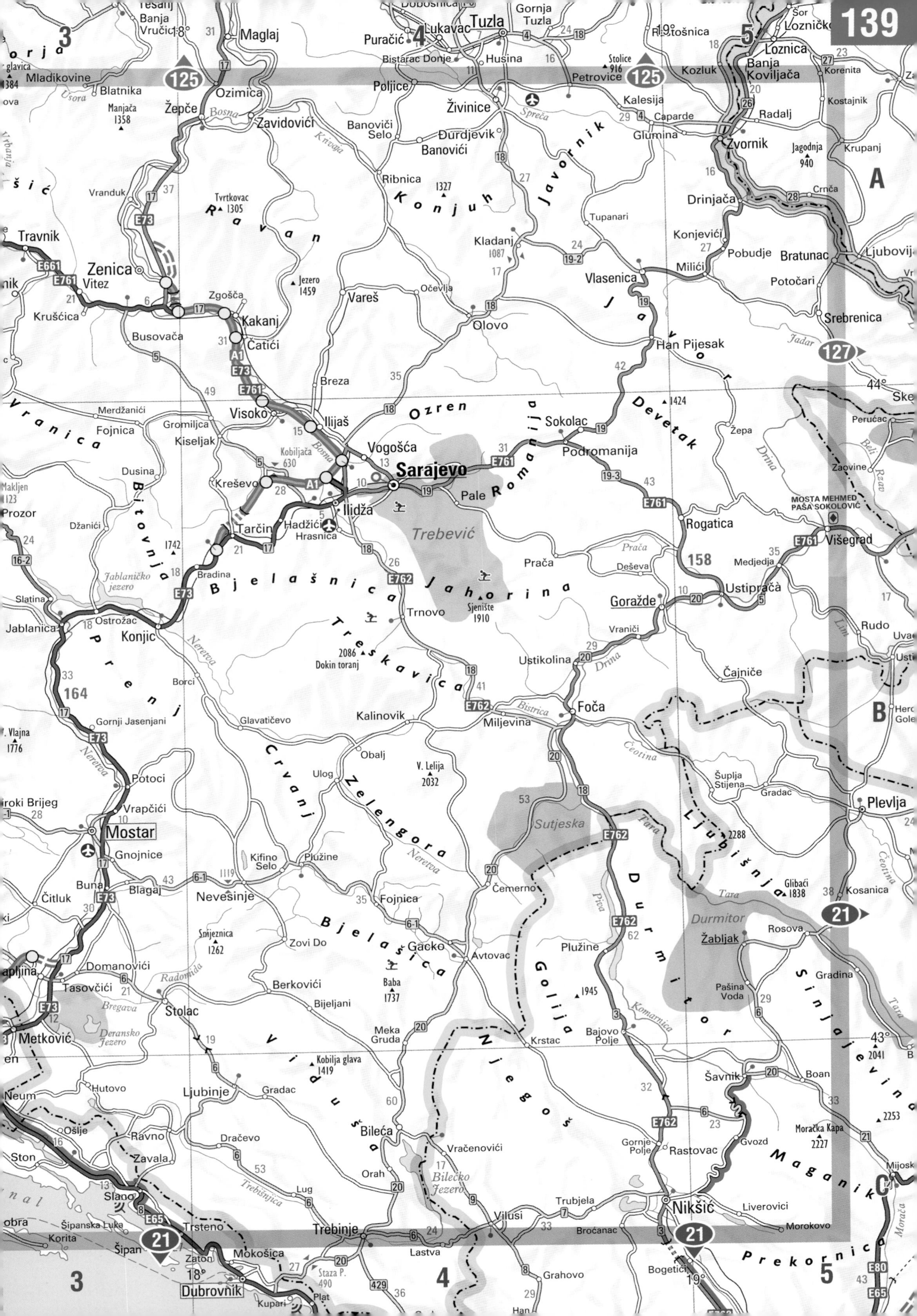
Sarajevo
Tuzla
Zenica
Mostar
Foča
Goražde
Višegrad
Zvornik
Srebrenica
Trebinje
Nikšić
Dubrovnik
Plevlja
Konjic
Visoko
Kakanj
Ilidža
Pale
Rogatica
Žabljak
Bileća
Gacko
Nevesinje
Stolac
Metković
Čapljina
Travnik
Vitez
Zavidovići
Žepče
Lukavac
Živinice
Banovići
Kladanj
Olovo
Vareš
Breza
Ilijaš
Vogošća
Kiseljak
Fojnica
Kreševo
Hadžići
Tarčin
Jablanica
Prozor
Vlasenica
Han Pijesak
Sokolac
Bratunac
Milići
Loznica
Kalinovik
Trnovo
Ustikolina
Čajniče
Šavnik
Plužine
Ljubinje
Neum
Ston
Slano
Trebević
Jahorina
Bjelašnica
Treskavica
Zelengora
Sutjeska
Durmitor
Ljubišnja
Maglić
Vranica
Prenj
Romanija
Ozren
Konjuh
Javornik
Devetak
Bjelašica
Crvanj
Golija
Njegoš
Vidušа
Sinjajevina
Maganik
Prekornica
Ravan
Bitovnja
MOSTA MEHMED PAŠA SOKOLOVIĆ
A
B
C
3
4
5
125
127
158
164
21

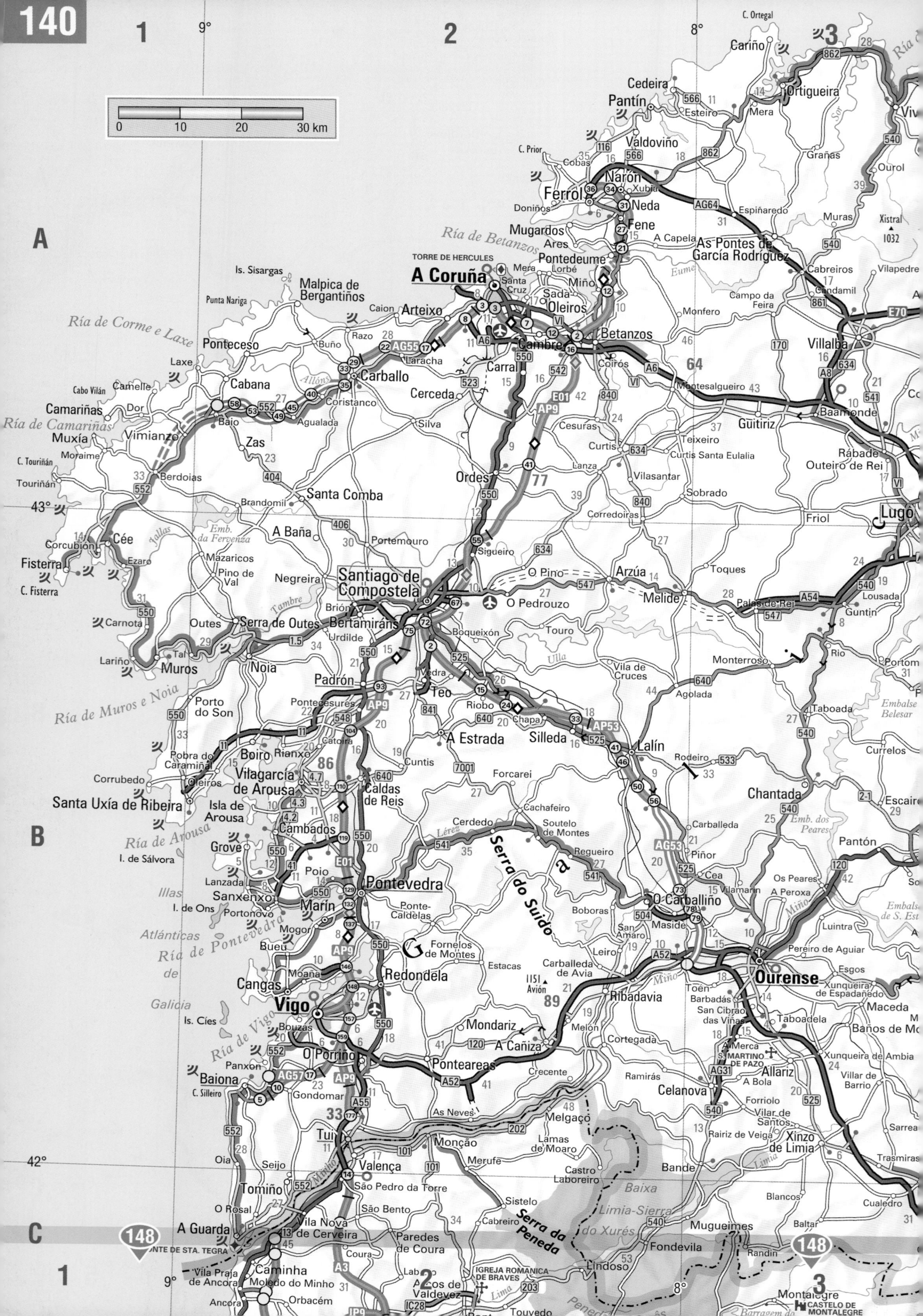

1
2
3
A
B
C
9°
8°
43°
42°
0 10 20 30 km
C. Ortegal
Cariño
Cedeira
Pantín
Esteiro
Ortigueira
Mera
Viv
Valdoviño
C. Prior
Cobas
Narón
Xubia
Ferrol
Doniños
Neda
Fene
Graňas
Ourol
Espiñaredo
Muras
Xistral
1032
AG64
Mugardos
Ares
A Capela
As Pontes de
García Rodríguez
Ría de Betanzos
Eume
TORRE DE HERCULES
Is. Sisargas
Malpica de
Bergantiños
Punta Nariga
A Coruña
Mera
Santa
Cruz
Lorbé
Pontedeume
Miño
Sada
Oleiros
Cabreiros
Vilapedre
Candamil
Campo da
Feira
Monfero
Caion
Arteixo
Ría de Corme e Laxe
Razo
Buño
AG55
Laracha
Carral
Cambre
Betanzos
Coirós
Villalba
E70
Ponteceso
Laxe
Cabana
Carballo
Allóns
Cerceda
Montesalgueiro
Cabo Vilán
Camelle
Camariñas
Dor
Coristanco
Baio
Agualada
Silva
Cesuras
Curtis
Teixeiro
Curtis Santa Eulalia
Guitiriz
Baamonde
Ría de Camariñas
Muxía
Vimianzo
Moraime
Zas
C. Touriñán
Touriñán
Berdoias
Ordes
Lanza
Vilasantar
Sobrado
Rábade
Outeiro de Rei
Santa Comba
Brandomil
Corredoiras
Friol
Lugo
Emb. da Fervenza
A Baña
Portemouro
Cée
Corcubión
Ezaro
Fisterra
C. Fisterra
Mazaricos
Pino de Val
Negreira
Santiago de Compostela
Sigueiro
O Pino
Arzúa
Toques
Melide
Palas de Rei
Lousada
Guntín
Tambre
O Pedrouzo
Brión
Bertamiráns
Carnota
Outes
Serra de Outes
Urdilde
Boqueixón
Touro
Lariño
Tal
Muros
Noia
Ulla
Vila de Cruces
Monterroso
Rio
Portom
Padrón
Vedra
Teo
Riobo
Chapa
Agolada
Porto do Son
Ría de Muros e Noia
Pontecesures
Catoira
A Estrada
Silleda
Lalín
Taboada
Embalse Belesar
Pobra do Caramiñal
Boiro
Rianxo
Cuntis
Rodeiro
Currelos
Corrubedo
Oleiros
Vilagarcía de Arousa
Forcarei
Caldas de Reis
Chantada
Escair
Santa Uxía de Ribeira
Isla de Arousa
Cachafeiro
Cambados
Cerdedo
Soutelo de Montes
Carballeda
Emb. dos Peares
Ría de Arousa
Grove
I. de Sálvora
Lérez
Serra do Suido
Regueiro
Piñor
Pantón
Poio
Lanzada
Pontevedra
Cea
Os Peares
Illas
Sanxenxo
I. de Ons
Marín
Portonovo
Ponte-Caldelas
O Carballiño
Vilamarín
A Peroxa
Miño
Embals. de S. Est
Atlánticas
Mogor
Ría de Pontevedra
Boboras
Maside
San Amaro
Luintra
Bueu
Fornelos de Montes
Leiro
Pereiro de Aguiar
Ría de Galicia
Moaña
Cangas
Estacas
Carballeda de Avia
Avión
1151
Ourense
Esgos
Xunqueira de Espadañedo
Vigo
Redondela
Ribadavia
Toén
Barbadás
San Cibrao das Viñas
Maceda
Is. Cíes
Bouzas
Mondariz
Melón
Taboadela
Baños de Mo
Ría de Vigo
Panxon
O Porriño
A Cañiza
Cortegada
A Merca
S. MARTINO DE PAZO
Xunqueira de Ambia
Baiona
C. Silleiro
Gondomar
Ponteareas
Crecente
Ramirás
Celanova
Allariz
A Bola
Villar de Barrio
Forriolo
As Neves
Melgaço
Vilar de Santos
Tui
Monção
Lamas de Moaro
Rairiz de Veiga
Xinzo de Limia
Sarrea
Oia
Seijo
Valença
Merufe
Castro Laboreiro
Bande
Trasmiras
Tomiño
Minho
São Pedro da Torre
Baixa
Limia
O Rosal
São Bento
Sistelo
Limia-Sierra do Xurés
Blancos
Cualedro
A Guarda
Vila Nova de Cerveira
Cabreiro
Serra da Peneda
Mugueimes
Baltar
Paredes de Coura
Fondevila
Randín
ONTE DE STA. TEGRA
Coura
Lindoso
Caminha
Vila Praja de Ancora
Moledo do Minho
Arcos de Valdevez
IGREJA ROMANICA DE BRAVES
Lima
Montalegre
CASTELO DE MONTALEGRE
Ancora
Orbacém
Touvedo
148

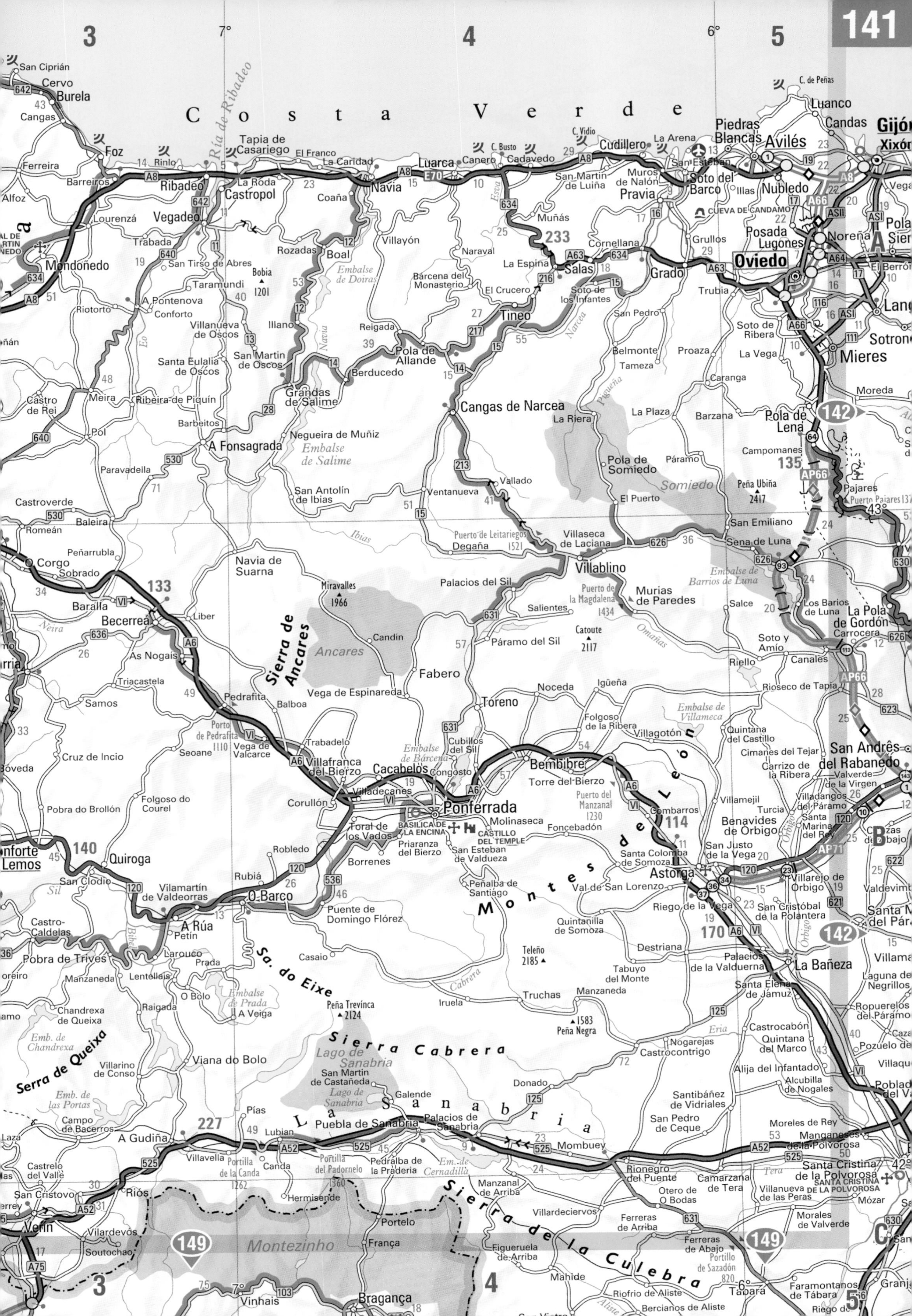
Costa Verde
Burela
Foz
Ribadeo
Castropol
Vegadeo
Mondoñedo
Navia
Luarca
Cudillero
Avilés
Gijón
Oviedo
Grado
Pravia
Salas
Tineo
Pola de Allande
Cangas de Narcea
Grandas de Salime
A Fonsagrada
Mieres
Pola de Lena
Villablino
Sierra de Ancares
Ancares
Somiedo
Becerreá
Pedrafita
Villafranca del Bierzo
Cacabelos
Ponferrada
Bembibre
Fabero
Toreno
Astorga
Montes de León
Quiroga
O Barco
A Rúa
Monforte de Lemos
Sa. do Eixe
Sierra Cabrera
Lago de Sanabria
La Sanabria
Puebla de Sanabria
A Gudiña
Verín
Sierra de la Culebra
La Bañeza
San Andrés del Rabanedo
Bragança
Montezinho
Serra de Queixa

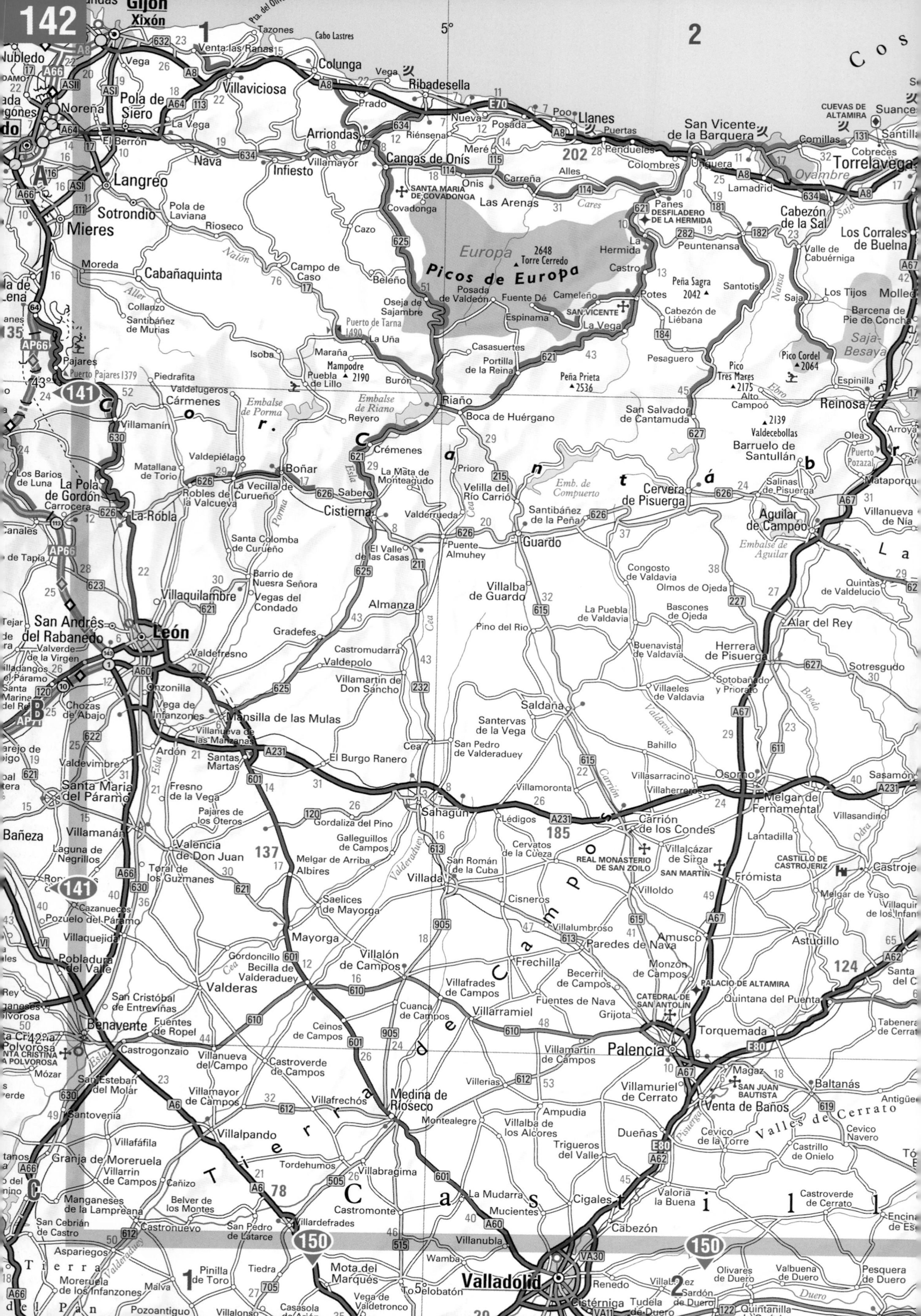
Gijón
Xixón
Pta. del Olivo
Tazones
Cabo Lastres
Venta las Ranas
Colunga
Vega
Ribadesella
Villaviciosa
Pola de Siero
Noreña
La Vega
El Berrón
Prado
Arriondas
Nueva
Posada
Poo
Llanes
Puertas
San Vicente de la Barquera
Comillas
Cuevas de Altamira
Suances
Santillana
Cobreces
Torrelavega
Nava
Infiesto
Villamayor
Riénsena
Cangas de Onís
Meré
Pendueles
Colombres
Unquera
Lamadrid
Oyambre
Langreo
Sotrondio
Mieres
Pola de Laviana
Rioseco
Onís
Carreña
Alles
Santa María de Covadonga
Covadonga
Las Arenas
Cares
Panes
Desfiladero de la Hermida
La Hermida
Cabezón de la Sal
Los Corrales de Buelna
Cazo
Europa
2648 Torre Cerredo
Picos de Europa
Hermida
Castro
Peuntenansa
Valle de Cabuérniga
Moreda
Cabañaquinta
Nalón
Campo de Caso
Beleño
Posada de Valdeón
Fuente Dé
Cameleño
Potes
Peña Sagra 2042
Santotis
Nansa
Saja
Los Tijos
Molledo
Aller
Collanzo
Santibáñez de Murias
Oseja de Sajambre
Espinama
San Vicente
La Vega
Cabezón de Liébana
Barcena de Pie de Concha
Saja-Besaya
Puerto de Tarna 1490
La Uña
Casasuertes
Portilla de la Reina
Pesaguero
Pico Cordel 2064
Isoba
Maraña
Mampodre 2190
Pajares
Puerto Pajares 1379
Piedrafita
Puebla de Lillo
Burón
Peña Prieta 2536
Pico Tres Mares 2175
Alto Campoó
Ebro
Espinilla
Reinosa
Valdelugeros
Cármenes
Embalse de Porma
Embalse de Riaño
Riaño
Reyero
Boca de Huérgano
San Salvador de Cantamuda
2139 Valdecebollas
Villamanín
Crémenes
Barruelo de Santullán
Olea
Puerto Pozazal
Arroyo
Mataporquera
Matallana de Torío
Valdepiélago
Boñar
La Mata de Monteagudo
Prioro
Los Barrios de Luna
La Pola de Gordón
Carrocera
Robles de la Valcueva
La Vecilla de Curueño
Sabero
Velilla del Río Carrión
Emb. de Compuerto
Cervera de Pisuerga
Salinas de Pisuerga
La Robla
Cistierna
Valderrueda
Santibáñez de la Peña
Aguilar de Campóo
Villanueva de Nía
Santa Colomba de Curueño
El Valle de las Casas
Puente Almuhey
Guardo
Embalse de Aguilar
Congosto de Valdavia
Olmos de Ojeda
Barrio de Nuesra Señora
Villalba de Guardo
Quintanas de Valdelucio
Villaquilambre
Vegas del Condado
Almanza
La Puebla de Valdavia
Bascones de Ojeda
San Andrés del Rabanedo
León
Gradefes
Pino del Río
Alar del Rey
Valverde de la Virgen
Valdefresno
Castromudarra
Valdepolo
Buenavista de Valdavia
Herrera de Pisuerga
Sotresgudo
Villamartín de Don Sancho
Sotobañado y Priorato
Villaeles de Valdavia
Onzonilla
Chozas de Abajo
Vega de Infanzones
Mansilla de las Mulas
Saldaña
Boedo
Villanueva de las Manzanas
Santervas de la Vega
Valdavia
Ardón
Santas Martas
El Burgo Ranero
Cea
San Pedro de Valderaduey
Bahillo
Valdevimbre
Fresno de la Vega
Villamoronta
Villasarracino
Villaherreros
Osorno
Sasamón
Santa María del Páramo
Pajares de los Oteros
Gordaliza del Pino
Sahagún
Lédigos
Carrión de los Condes
Melgar de Fernamental
Villasandino
Bañeza
Villamañán
Galleguillos de Campos
Cervatos de la Cueza
Villalcázar de Sirga
Lantadilla
Laguna de Negrillos
Valencia de Don Juan
Melgar de Arriba
San Román de la Cuba
Real Monasterio de San Zoilo
San Martín
Frómista
Castillo de Castrojeriz
Castrojeriz
Toral de los Guzmanes
Albires
Villada
Cisneros
Villoldo
Melgar de Yuso
Villaquirán de los Infantes
Cazanuecos
Pozuelo del Páramo
Saelices de Mayorga
Villaquejida
Mayorga
Villalumbroso
Amusco
Paredes de Nava
Astudillo
Pobladura del Valle
Gordoncillo
Bercilla de Valderaduey
Villalón de Campos
Frechilla
Monzón de Campos
Becerril de Campos
Palacio de Altamira
Santa ... del C...
Valderas
Villafrades de Campos
Catedral de San Antolín
Quintana del Puente
San Cristóbal de Entreviñas
Cuenca de Campos
Villarramiel
Fuentes de Nava
Grijota
Benavente
Fuentes de Ropel
Ceinos de Campos
Torquemada
Tabanera de Cerrato
Santa Cristina de la Polvorosa
Castrogonzalo
Villanueva del Campo
Castroverde de Campos
Villamartín de Campos
Palencia
Mózar
San Esteban del Molar
Villerías
Magaz
Baltanás
San Juan Bautista
Villamayor de Campos
Villafrechós
Medina de Rioseco
Villamuriel de Cerrato
Venta de Baños
Antigüedad
Santovenia
Montealegre
Ampudia
Valles de Cerrato
Villafáfila
Villalpando
Villalba de los Alcores
Dueñas
Cevico de la Torre
Cevico Navero
Granja de Moreruela
Trigueros del Valle
Castrillo de Onielo
Villarrín de Campos
Tordehumos
Villabragima
Cañizo
Tierra de Campos
Manganeses de la Lampreana
Belver de los Montes
Castromonte
La Mudarra
Mucientes
Cigales
Valoria la Buena
Castroverde de Cerrato
Encinas de Esgueva
San Cebrián de Castro
Castronuevo
San Pedro de Latarce
Villardefrades
Cabezón
Castilla
Aspariegos
Villanubla
Tierra del Pan
Pinilla de Toro
Tiedra
Mota del Marqués
Wamba
Valladolid
Renedo
Villabáñez
Olivares de Duero
Valbuena de Duero
Pesquera de Duero
Moreruela de los Infanzones
Malva
Vega de Valdetronco
Tordesillas?
Zaratán
Cistérniga
Sardón de Duero
Tudela de Duero
Quintanilla de Onésimo
Duero
Pozoantiguo
Villalonso
Casasola de Arión
Cordillera Cantábrica
Costa
135
137
141
150
185
202
124
78
5°
1
2
A
B
C

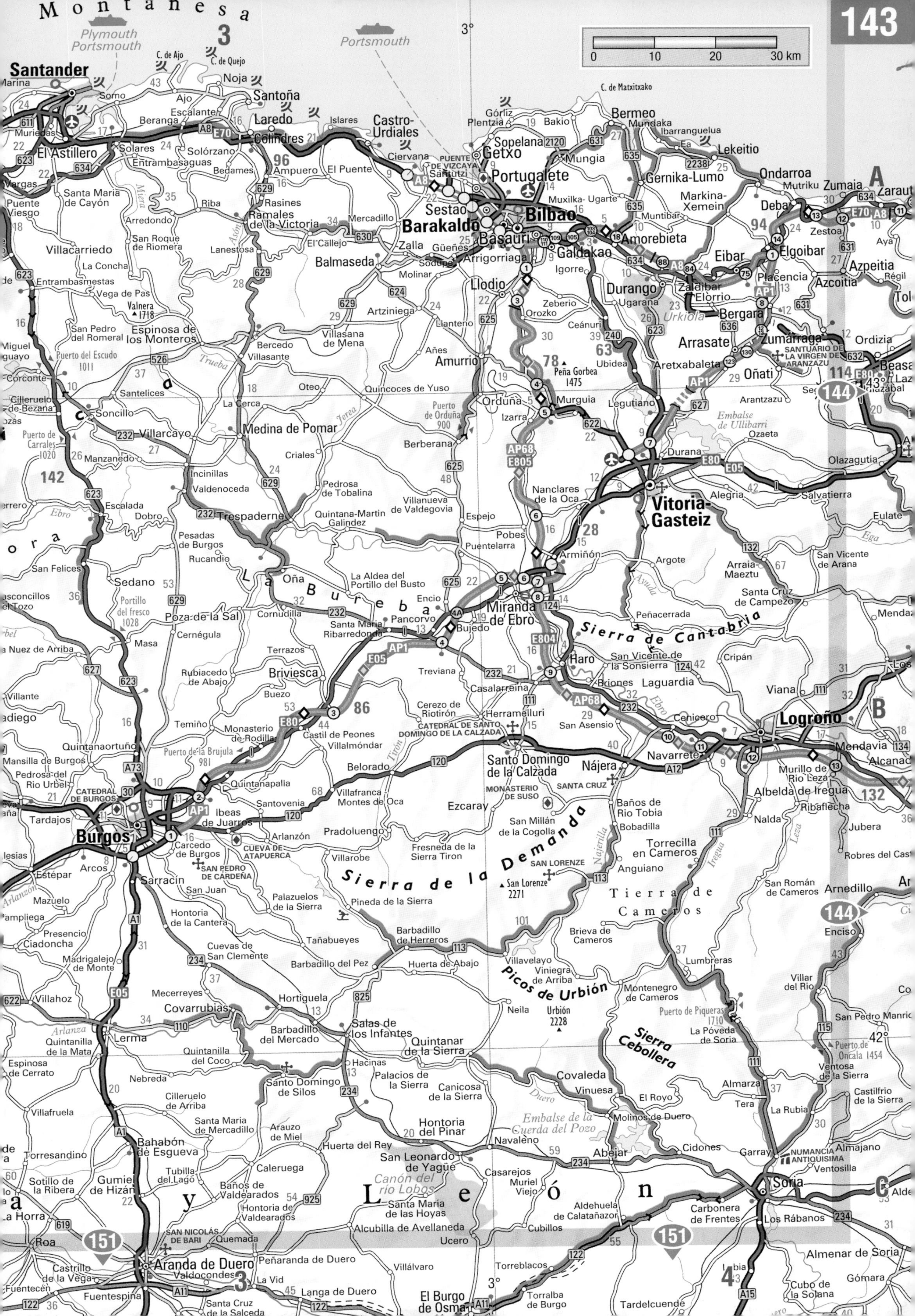

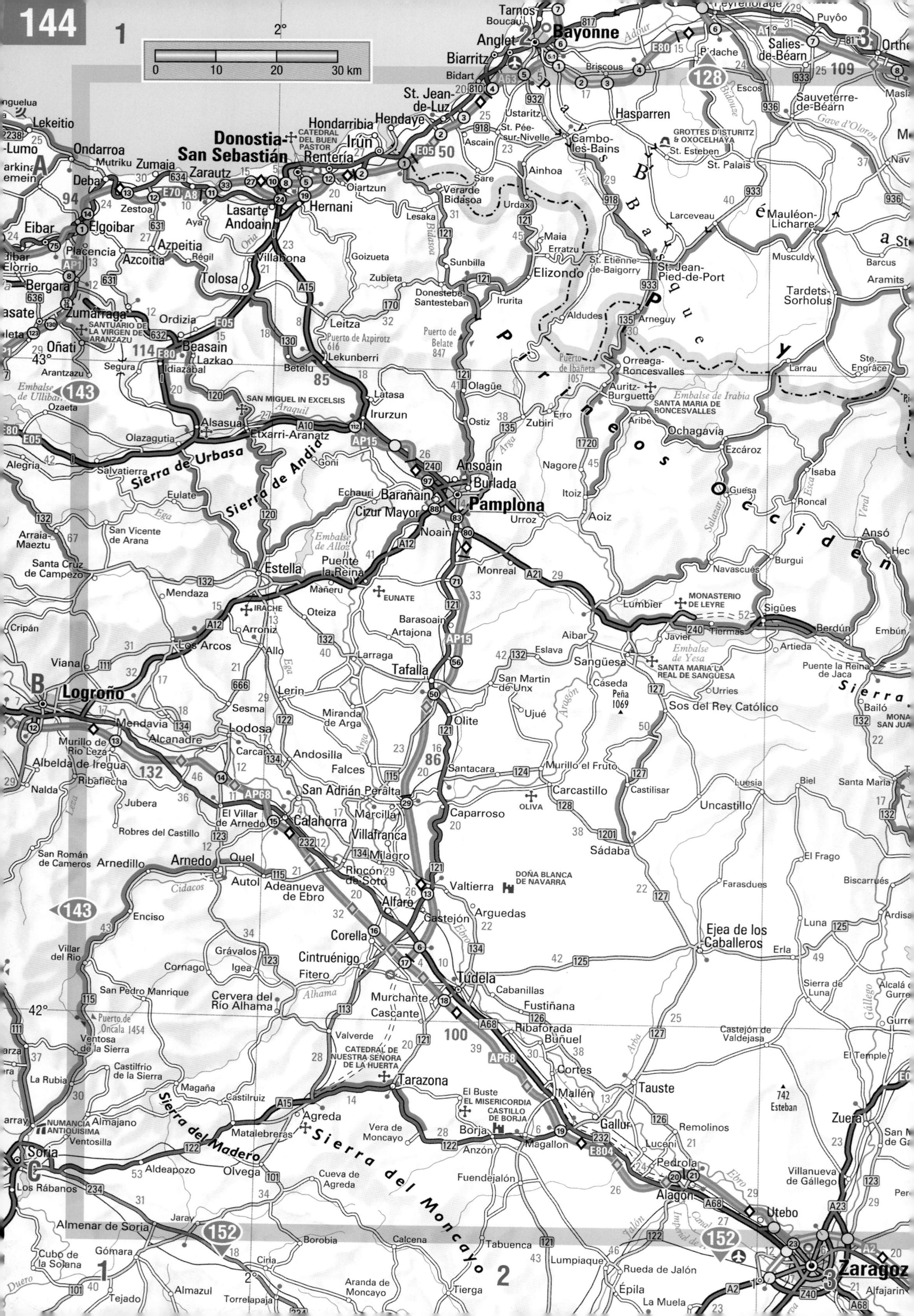
1
2°
0
10
20
30 km
Tarnos
Boucau
Bayonne
Anglet
Biarritz
Bidart
Peyrehorade
Puyôo
Salies-de-Béarn
Orthez
Bidache
Briscous
128
Escos
Sauveterre-de-Béarn
Gave d'Oloron
Masl
109
St. Jean-de-Luz
Ustaritz
St. Pée-sur-Nivelle
Ascain
Hasparren
Cambo-les-Bains
GROTTES D'ISTURITZ & OXOCELHAYA
St. Esteben
St. Palais
Hendaye
Hondarribia
CATEDRAL DEL BUEN PASTOR
Irun
Donostia-San Sebastián
Renteria
Oiartzun
Sare
Ainhoa
Verarde Bidasoa
Urdax
Lekeitio
Ondarroa
Mutriku
Zumaia
Zarautz
Lumo
Deba
Zestoa
Lasarte
Andoain
Hernani
Lesaka
Eibar
Elgoibar
Placencia
Azcoitia
Azpeitia
Régil
Aya
Villabona
Goizueta
Maia
Erratzu
Elizondo
St. Etienne-de-Baigorry
St. Jean-Pied-de-Port
Larceveau
Mauléon-Licharre
Musculdy
Barcus
Aramits
Tardets-Sorholus
Elorrio
Bergara
Tolosa
Sunbilla
Zubieta
Donestebe-Santesteban
Irurita
Aldudes
Arneguy
Zumárraga
Ordizia
SANTUARIO DE LA VIRGEN DE ARANZAZU
Oñati
Beasain
Lazkao
Leitza
Puerto de Azpirotz 616
Puerto de Belate 847
Lekunberri
Betelu
Segura
Idiazábal
Arantzazu
43°
Embalse de Ullibarri
143
Ozaeta
SAN MIGUEL IN EXCELSIS
Araquil
Alsasua
Olazagutia
Etxarri-Aranatz
Latasa
Irurzun
Puerto de Ibañeta 1057
Orreaga-Roncesvalles
Auritz-Burguette
Embalse de Irabia
SANTA MARIA DE RONCESVALLES
Larrau
Ste. Engrâce
Olagüe
Ostiz
Zubiri
Erro
Aribe
Ochagavía
Ezcároz
Isaba
Alegria
Salvatierra
Sierra de Urbasa
Sierra de Andia
Goñi
Ansoain
Burlada
Nagore
Eulate
Echauri
Barañain
Cizur Mayor
Pamplona
Itoiz
Guesa
Roncal
Urroz
Aoiz
Noain
Arraia-Maeztu
San Vicente de Arana
Embalse de Alloz
Puente la Reina
Estella
Monreal
Ansó
Santa Cruz de Campezo
Mendaza
Mañeru
EUNATE
Navascués
Burgui
Lumbier
MONASTERIO DE LEYRE
Sigües
Berdún
Embún
IRACHE
Oteiza
Barasoain
Artajona
Cripán
Arroniz
Los Arcos
Allo
Larraga
Aibar
Eslava
Javier
Tiermas
Embalse de Yesa
Artieda
Viana
Logroño
Lerin
Tafalla
Sangüesa
SANTA MARIA LA REAL DE SANGÜESA
Puente la Reina de Jaca
Sesma
San Martín de Unx
Cáseda
Peña 1069
Urries
Sos del Rey Católico
Bailó
Mendavia
Lodosa
Miranda de Arga
Olite
Ujué
Murillo de Río Leza
Alcanadre
Albelda de Iregua
Ribaflecha
Carcar
Andosilla
Falces
Santacara
Murillo el Fruto
Castilisar
Luesia
Biel
Santa María
Nalda
Jubera
El Villar de Arnedo
San Adrián
Peralta
Marcilla
Carcastillo
OLIVA
Caparroso
Uncastillo
Robres del Castillo
Calahorra
Villafranca
Sádaba
San Román de Cameros
Arnedillo
Arnedo
Quel
Autol
Milagro
Rincón de Soto
Adeanueva de Ebro
Valtierra
DOÑA BLANCA DE NAVARRA
El Frago
Cidacos
Farasdues
Biscarrués
Alfaro
Castejón
Arguedas
Enciso
Corella
Ejea de los Caballeros
Luna
Ardisa
Villar del Río
Grávalos
Cintruénigo
Fitero
Erla
Cornago
Igea
Túdela
Cabanillas
Sierra de Luna
Alcalá de Gurrea
San Pedro Manrique
Cervera del Río Alhama
Alhama
Murchante
Cascante
Fustiñana
42°
Puerto de Oncala 1454
Ribaforada
Buñuel
Castejón de Valdejasa
Gurrea
Ventosa de la Sierra
Valverde
100
CATEDRAL DE NUESTRA SEÑORA DE LA HUERTA
Cortes
El Temple
Castilfrío de la Sierra
La Rubia
Tarazona
Tauste
742 Esteban
Magaña
Castilruiz
El Buste
EL MISERICORDIA
CASTILLO DE BORJA
Mallén
Sierra del Madero
Agreda
Gallur
Remolinos
Zuera
NUMANCIA ANTIQUISIMA
Almajano
Ventosilla
Matalebreras
Sierra del Moncayo
Vera de Moncayo
Borja
Magallon
Luceni
San Mateo de Gállego
Soria
Anzón
Aldeapozo
Olvega
Cueva de Agreda
Fuendejalón
Pedrola
Villanueva de Gállego
Los Rábanos
Alagón
Ebro
Utebo
Jaray
Almenar de Soria
152
Borobia
Calcena
Tabuenca
Cubo de la Solana
Gómara
Ciria
Lumpiaque
Rueda de Jalón
Zaragoza
Duero
Tejado
Almazul
Torrelapaja
Aranda de Moncayo
Tierga
Épila
La Muela
Alfajarín
A
B
C
1
2
3
Pays Basque
Pirineos Occidentales

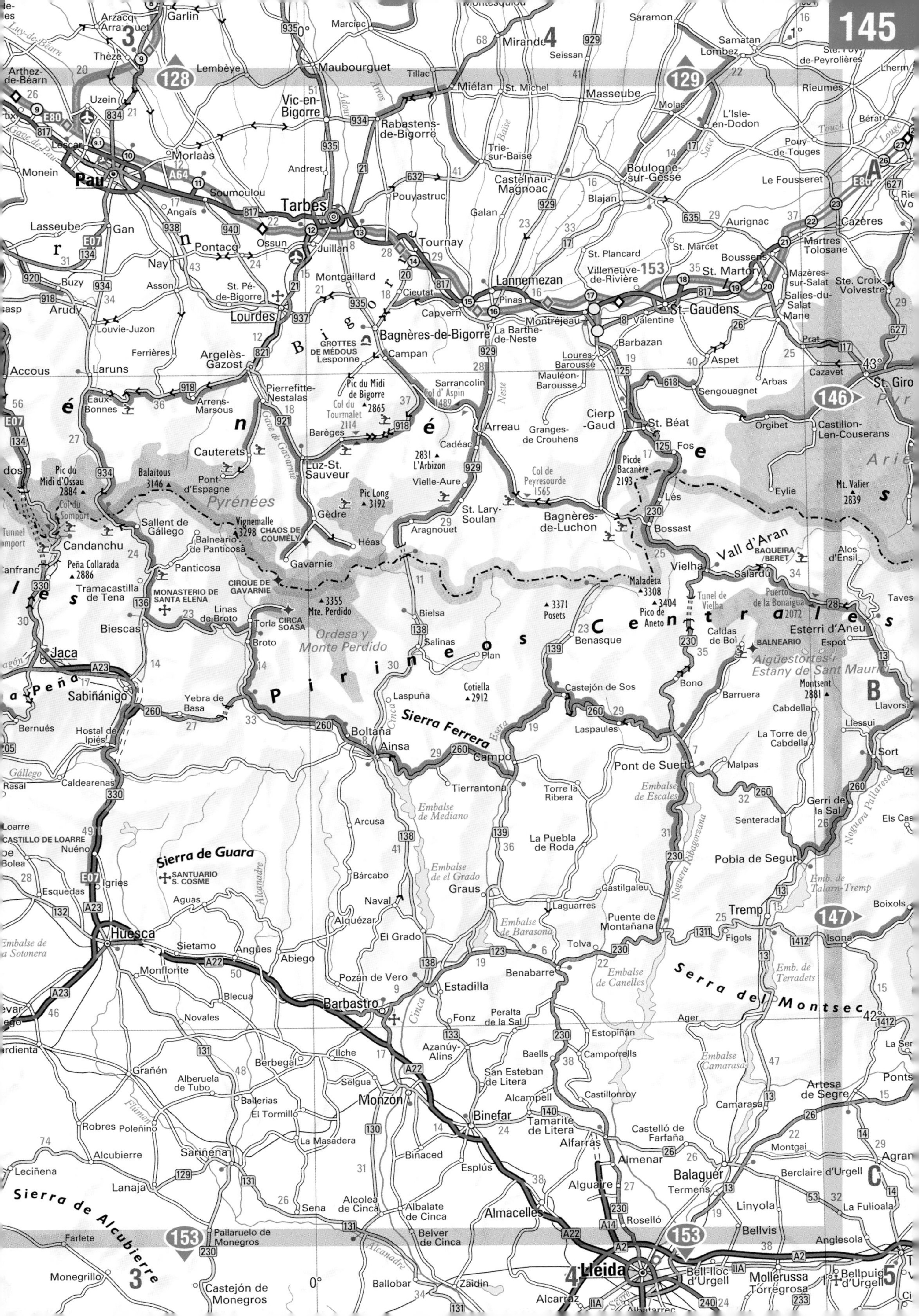

Garlin
Arzacq-Arraziguet
Thèze
Marciac
Mirande
Saramon
Samatan
Lombez
Ste. Foy-de-Peyrolières
Lembèye
Maubourguet
Tillac
Seissan
Arthez-de-Béarn
Miélan
St. Michel
Masseube
Molas
Rieumes
L'Isle-en-Dodon
Bérat
Uzein
Vic-en-Bigorre
Rabastens-de-Bigorre
Trie-sur-Baïse
Pouy-de-Touges
Lescar
Morlaàs
Boulogne-sur-Gesse
Monein
Andrest
Castelnau-Magnoac
Le Fousseret
Pau
Soumoulou
Tarbes
Pouyastruc
Blajan
Angaïs
Galan
Aurignac
Cazères
Lasseube
Gan
Ossun
Tournay
Martres Tolosane
Pontacq
Juillan
St. Plancard
St. Marcet
Boussens
Nay
Villeneuve-de-Rivière
St. Martory
Mazères-sur-Salat
Ste. Croix-Volvestre
Buzy
Asson
Montgaillard
Lannemezan
Salies-du-Salat
Arudy
St. Pé-de-Bigorre
Cieutat
Pinas
Mane
Lourdes
Capvern
Montréjeau
Valentine
St. Gaudens
Louvie-Juzon
Bagnères-de-Bigorre
La Barthe-de-Neste
Barbazan
Ferrières
Argelès-Gazost
Grottes de Médous
Lesponne
Campan
Loures-Barousse
Aspet
Prat
Cazavet
Accous
Laruns
Mauléon-Barousse
Arbas
St. Giro
Pic du Midi de Bigorre
Sarrancolin
Sengouagnet
Eaux-Bonnes
Arrens-Marsous
Pierrefitte-Nestalas
Col d'Aspin
Orgibet
Castillon-Len-Couserans
Col du Tourmalet
Arreau
Granges-de Crouhens
Cierp-Gaud
St. Béat
Barèges
Cadéac
Fos
Cauterets
L'Arbizon
Pic du Midi d'Ossau
Balaïtous
Pont-d'Espagne
Luz-St. Sauveur
Vielle-Aure
Col de Peyresourde
Picde Bacanère
Eylie
Mt. Valier
Pyrénées
Col du Somport
Pic Long
St. Lary-Soulan
Bagnères-de-Luchon
Lès
Bossost
Tunnel Somport
Candanchu
Sallent de Gállego
Vignemalle
Chaos de Coumély
Gèdre
Aragnouet
Balneario de Panticosa
Héas
Vall d'Aran
Baqueira/Beret
Alos d'Ensil
Canfranc
Peña Collarada
Panticosa
Gavarnie
Vielha
Salardú
Tramacastilla de Tena
Monasterio de Santa Elena
Cirque de Gavarnie
Maladeta
Tunel de Vielha
Puerto de la Bonaigua
Taves
Mte. Perdido
Posets
Pico de Aneto
Biescas
Linas de Broto
Torla
Circa Soasa
Bielsa
Benasque
Caldas de Boì
Esterri d'Aneu
Espot
Broto
Ordesa y Monte Perdido
Salinas
Balneario
Jaca
Plan
Aigüestortes i Estany de Sant Maurici
Pirineos Centrales
Sabiñánigo
Cotiella
Castejón de Sos
Bono
Montsent
Yebra de Basa
Laspuña
Barruera
Cabdella
Llavorsi
Sierra Ferrera
Laspaules
Llessui
Bernués
Hostal de Ipiés
Boltaña
La Torre de Cabdella
Ainsa
Campo
Sort
Pont de Suert
Malpas
Gállego
Rasal
Caldearenas
Tierrantona
Torre la Ribera
Embalse de Escales
Gerri de la Sal
Embalse de Mediano
Senterada
Els Cas
Loarre
Castillo de Loarre
Arcusa
La Puebla de Roda
Nueno
Sierra de Guara
Santuario S. Cosme
Pobla de Segur
Bolea
Embalse de el Grado
Igries
Bárcabo
Graus
Emb. de Talarn-Tremp
Esquedas
Aguas
Castilgaleu
Naval
Laguarres
Tremp
Boixols
Puente de Montañana
Alquézar
Embalse de Barasona
Huesca
El Grado
Figols
Isona
Embalse de Sotonera
Sietamo
Angües
Tolva
Abiego
Benabarre
Embalse de Canelles
Monflorite
Serra del Montsec
Emb. de Terradets
Pozán de Vero
Estadilla
Blecua
Barbastro
Novales
Fonz
Peralta de la Sal
Ager
Estopiñán
Azanúy-Alins
Baells
Camporrells
Embalse Camarasa
Grañén
Ilche
Berbegal
Alberuela de Tubo
San Esteban de Litera
Selgua
Ballerias
Monzón
Castillonroy
Artesa de Segre
Ponts
El Tormillo
Alcampell
Camarasa
Binefar
Robres
Poleñino
Tamarite de Litera
Castelló de Farfaña
La Masadera
Alfarràs
Montgai
Agran
Alcubierre
Sariñena
Binaced
Almenar
Balaguer
Berclaire d'Urgell
Leciñena
Esplús
Lanaja
Alguaire
Termens
Linyola
La Fulioala
Sierra de Alcubierre
Sena
Alcolea de Cinca
Albalate de Cinca
Almacelles
Roselló
Bellvis
Anglesola
Farlete
Pallaruelo de Monegros
Belver de Cinca
Lleida
Monegrillo
Castejón de Monegros
Ballobar
Zaidin
Bell-lloc d'Urgell
Mollerussa
Torregrosa
Bellpuig d'Urgell
Alcarraz

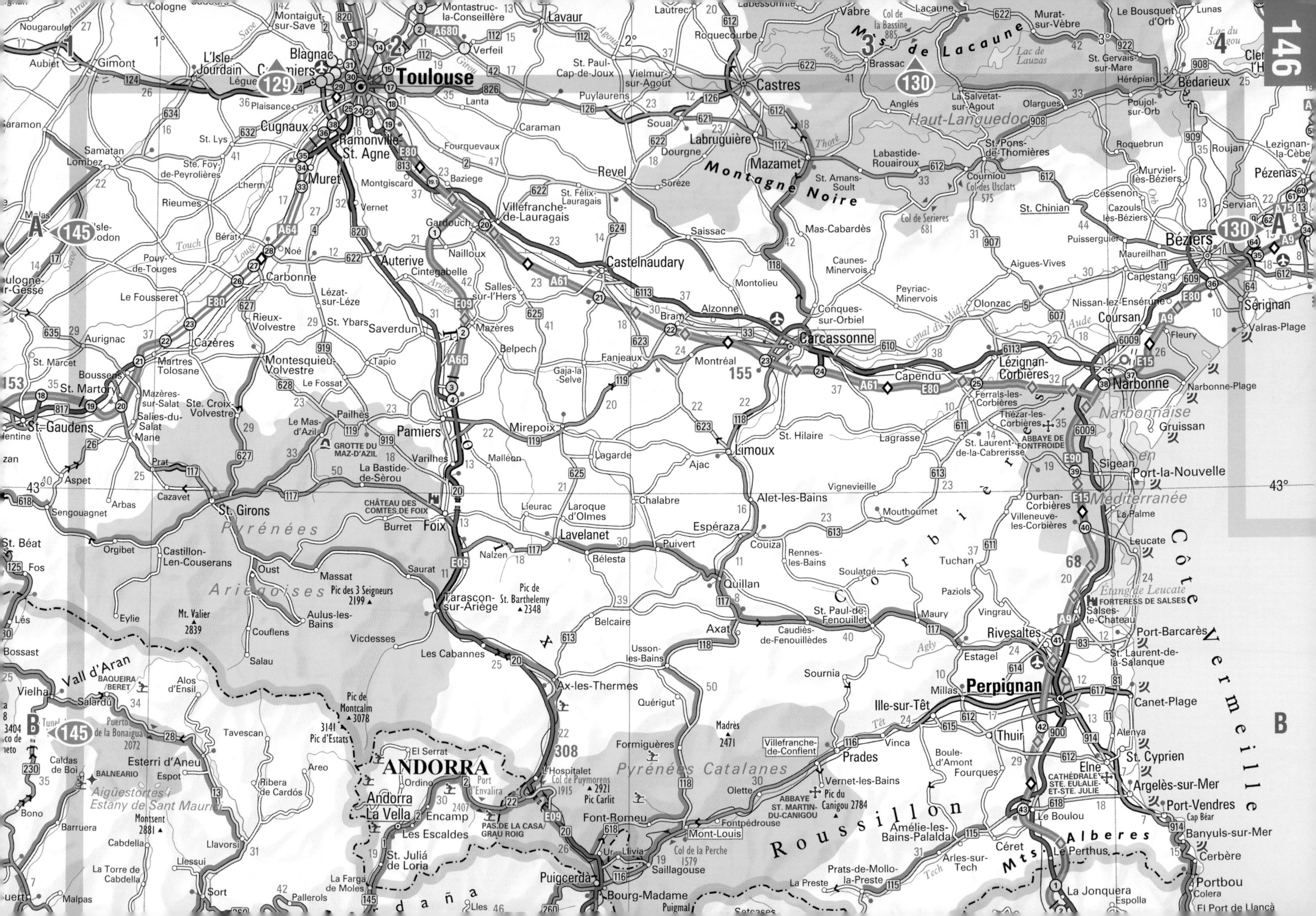
Côte Vermeille
Méditerranée
Narbonnaise
Mts. de Lacaune
Montagne Noire
Haut-Languedoc
Corbières
Roussillon
Pyrénées Catalanes
Pyrénées Ariégoises
Mts. Albères
ANDORRA
Toulouse
Carcassonne
Perpignan
Narbonne
Béziers
Castres
Mazamet
Castelnaudary
Limoux
Foix
Pamiers
Mirepoix
Muret
St. Girons
St. Gaudens
Quillan
Prades
Ille-sur-Têt
Rivesaltes
Lézignan-Corbières
Bédarieux
Pézenas
Lavaur
Revel
Villefranche-de-Lauragais
Auterive
Tarascon-sur-Ariège
Ax-les-Thermes
Puigcerdà
Mont-Louis
Font-Romeu
Bourg-Madame
Andorra La Vella
Encamp
Les Escaldes
St. Julià de Loria
Vielha
Vall d'Aran
Argelès-sur-Mer
Port-Vendres
Banyuls-sur-Mer
Cerbère
Portbou
Céret
Amélie-les-Bains-Palalda
Arles-sur-Tech
Le Perthus
La Jonquera
Thuir
Elne
Canet-Plage
St. Cyprien
Port-Barcarès
Leucate
Sigean
Port-la-Nouvelle
Gruissan
Narbonne-Plage
Valras-Plage
Sérignan
Capendu
Alzonne
Bram
Montréal
Fanjeaux
Lavelanet
Chalabre
Espéraza
Couiza
Alet-les-Bains
Axat
Blagnac
L'Isle-Jourdain
Cugnaux
Ramonville-St. Agne
Cazères
Carbonne
Rieux-Volvestre
Montesquieu-Volvestre
Saverdun
Aurignac
Castillon-en-Couserans
Massat
Aulus-les-Bains
Salau
Esterri d'Aneu
Sort
Pic de Montcalm 3078
Pic Carlit
Pic du Canigou 2784
Col de Puymorens 1915
Port d'Envalira 2407
Col de la Perche 1579
Mt. Valier 2839
Pic des 3 Seigneurs 2199
Pic de St. Barthelemy 2348
Madrès 2471
Aigüestortes i Estany de Sant Maurici
A61
A64
A66
A9
A75
E80
E15
E09
E90
129
130
145
153
155
308

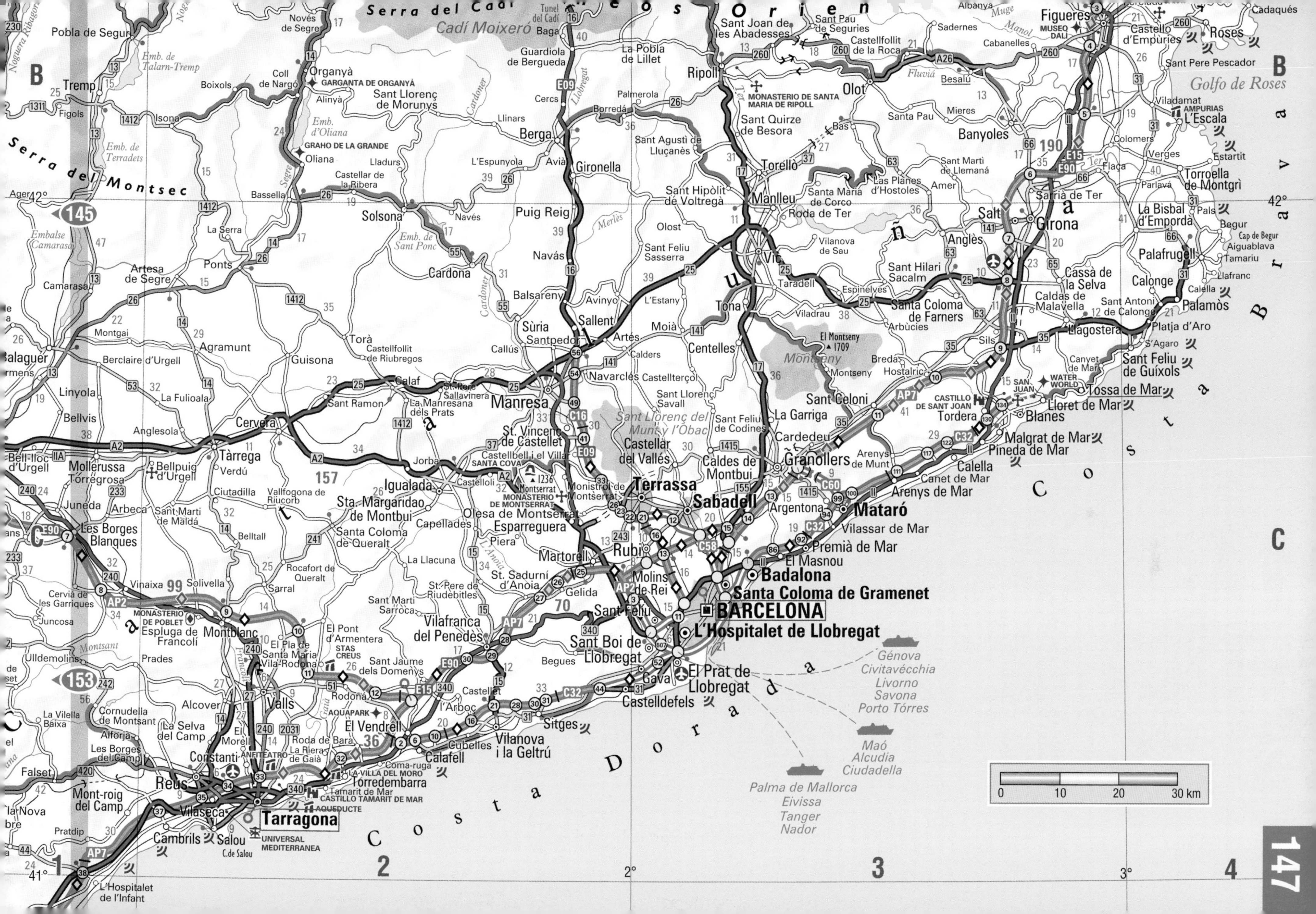
Serra del Cadí
Cadí Moixeró
Serra del Montsec
Costa Brava
Costa Daurada
Golfo de Roses
Figueres
Roses
L'Escala
Torroella de Montgrí
La Bisbal d'Empordà
Palafrugell
Palamós
Girona
Banyoles
Olot
Ripoll
Vic
Manlleu
Berga
Solsona
Cardona
Manresa
Terrassa
Sabadell
Granollers
Mataró
Badalona
Santa Coloma de Gramenet
BARCELONA
L'Hospitalet de Llobregat
El Prat de Llobregat
Castelldefels
Sitges
Vilanova i la Geltrú
Vilafranca del Penedès
Igualada
Cervera
Tàrrega
Mollerussa
Balaguer
Tremp
Pobla de Segur
Tarragona
Reus
Salou
Cambrils
Valls
El Vendrell
Lloret de Mar
Blanes
Tossa de Mar
Sant Feliu de Guíxols
Gènova
Civitavècchia
Livorno
Savona
Porto Tórres
Maó
Alcudia
Ciudadella
Palma de Mallorca
Eivissa
Tanger
Nador
0
10
20
30 km

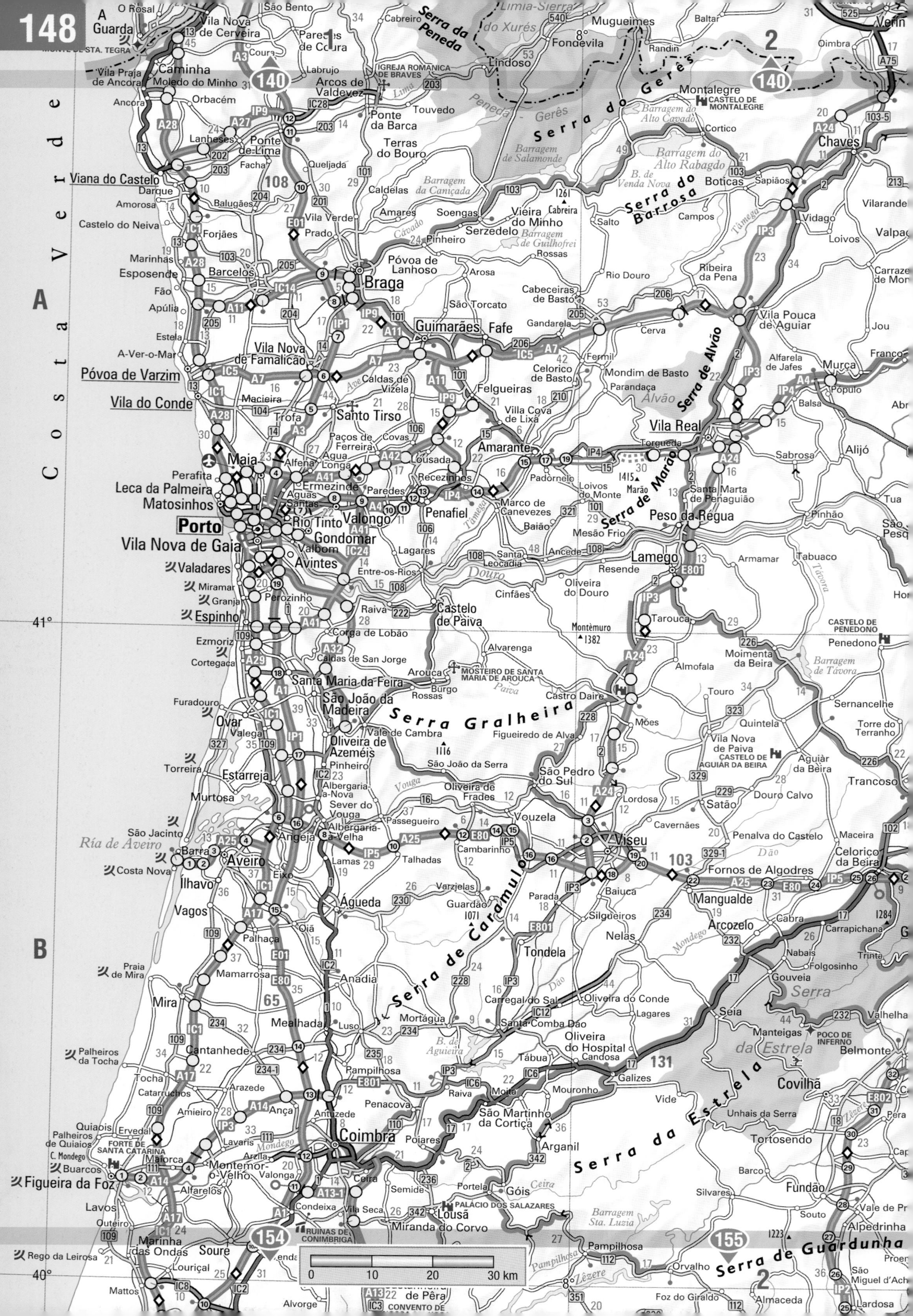

A Guarda
Vila Nova de Cerveira
Caminha
Viana do Castelo
Ponte de Lima
Arcos de Valdevez
Ponte da Barca
Terras do Bouro
Serra da Peneda
Lindoso
Mugueimes
Montalegre
Serra do Gerês
Chaves
Verín
Barragem do Alto Rabagdo
Boticas
Serra do Barrosa
Vieira do Minho
Cabreira
Salto
Vidago
Póvoa de Lanhoso
Braga
Barcelos
Esposende
Guimarães
Fafe
Cabeceiras de Basto
Vila Pouca de Aguiar
Vila Nova de Famalicão
Póvoa de Varzim
Vila do Conde
Santo Tirso
Felgueiras
Celorico de Basto
Mondim de Basto
Serra de Alvão
Murça
Amarante
Vila Real
Sabrosa
Alijó
Maia
Leca da Palmeira
Matosinhos
Porto
Vila Nova de Gaia
Valongo
Gondomar
Penafiel
Marco de Canevezes
Serra de Marão
Peso da Regua
Lamego
Espinho
Castelo de Paiva
Tarouca
Castelo de Penedono
Penedono
Moimenta da Beira
Arouca
Mosteiro de Santa Maria de Arouca
Santa Maria da Feira
São João da Madeira
Serra Gralheira
Castro Daire
Ovar
Oliveira de Azeméis
Vale de Cambra
Sernancelhe
Trancoso
Estarreja
São Pedro do Sul
Vouzela
Oliveira de Frades
Aveiro
Ílhavo
Ría de Aveiro
Viseu
Penalva do Castelo
Celorico da Beira
Fornos de Algodres
Mangualde
Águeda
Serra de Caramulo
Tondela
Nelas
Gouveia
Serra da Estrela
Mira
Mealhada
Mortágua
Santa Comba Dão
Carregal do Sal
Oliveira do Hospital
Seia
Manteigas
Poço de Inferno
Belmonte
Cantanhede
Pampilhosa
Tábua
Covilhã
Coimbra
Penacova
Figueira da Foz
Montemor-o-Velho
Forte de Santa Catarina
Arganil
Lousã
Palácio dos Salazares
Fundão
Góis
Ruinas de Conimbriga
Condeixa
Miranda do Corvo
Soure
Pampilhosa
Serra de Guardunha
Costa Verde
41°
40°
A
B
1
2
0 10 20 30 km

140
154
155

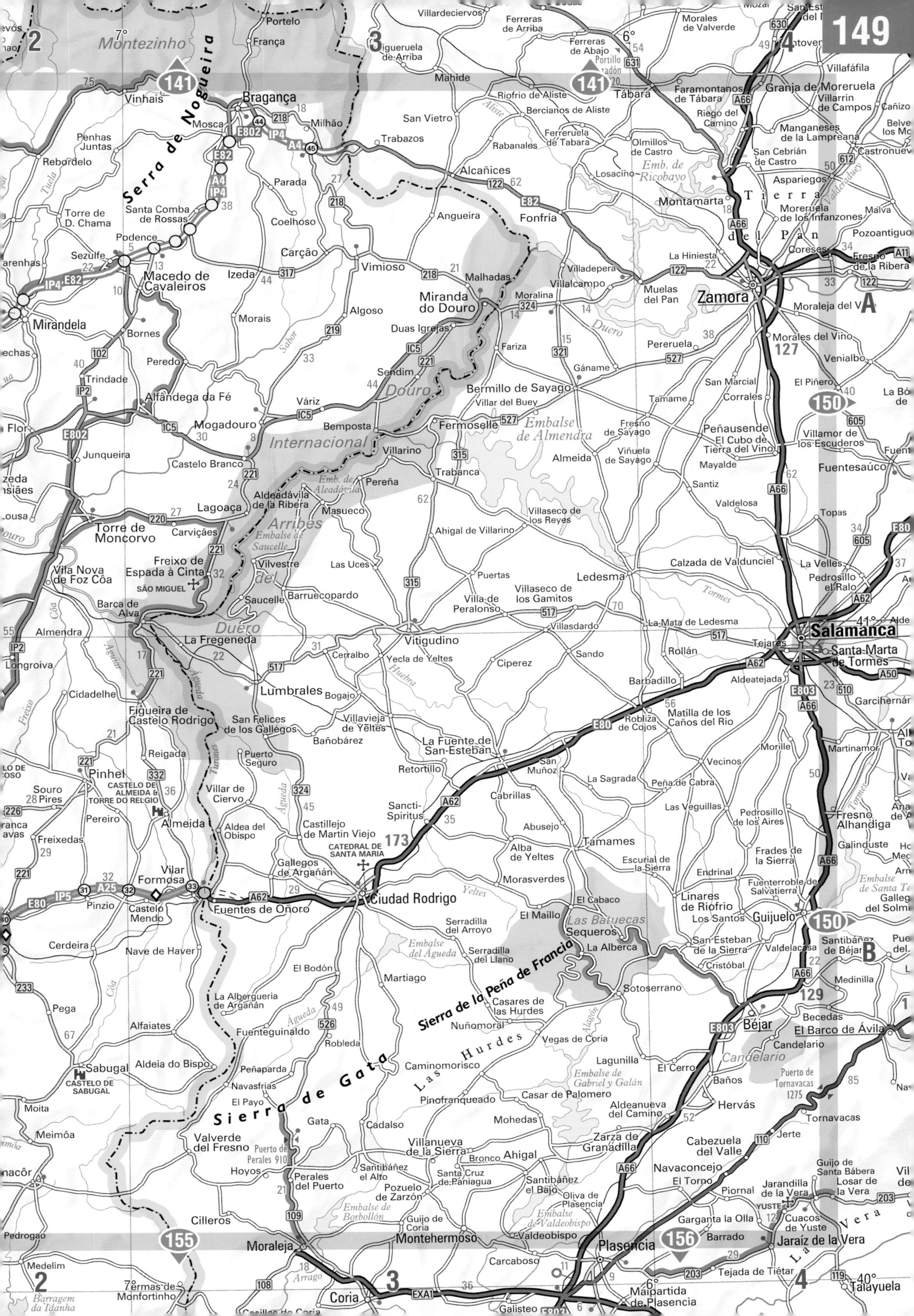
Montezinho
Serra de Nogueira
Portelo
França
Vinhais
Bragança
Mosca
Milhão
Penhas Juntas
Rebordelo
Parada
Torre de D. Chama
Santa Comba de Rossas
Coelhoso
Podence
Sezulfe
Carção
Macedo de Cavaleiros
Izeda
Mirandela
Morais
Bornes
Peredo
Trindade
Alfândega da Fé
Mogadouro
Váriz
Junqueira
Castelo Branco
Lagoaça
Torre de Moncorvo
Carviçães
Freixo de Espada à Cinta
Vila Nova de Foz Côa
SÃO MIGUEL
Barca de Alva
Almendra
La Fregeneda
Longroiva
Cidadelhe
Figueira de Castelo Rodrigo
Reigada
Pinhel
CASTELO DE ALMEIDA & TORRE DO RELGIO
Souro Pires
Pereiro
Almeida
Freixedas
Vilar Formosa
Pinzio
Castelo Mendo
Fuentes de Oñoro
Cerdeira
Nave de Haver
Pega
Alfaiates
Sabugal
CASTELO DE SABUGAL
Moita
Meimôa
Pedrogão
Medelim
Termas de Monfortinho
Barragem da Idanha
Villardeciervos
Ferreras de Arriba
Ferreras de Abajo
Morales de Valverde
Figueruela de Arriba
Mahíde
Riofrío de Aliste
Bercianos de Aliste
Tábara
Faramontanos de Tábara
Granja de Moreruela
Villafáfila
Villarrin de Campos
San Vietro
Trabazos
Rabanales
Ferreruela de Tábara
Olmillos de Castro
Riego del Camino
Manganeses de la Lampreana
San Cebrián de Castro
Castronuevo
Alcañices
Losacino
Emb. de Ricobayo
Asparigos
Montamarta
Tierra del Pan
Moreruela de los Infanzones
Angueira
Fonfría
Pozoantiguo
Vimioso
Malhadas
La Hiniesta
Coreses
Fresno de la Ribera
Villadepera
Villalcampo
Muelas del Pan
Zamora
Miranda do Douro
Moralina
Algoso
Duas Igrejas
Fariza
Moraleja del Vino
Morales del Vino
Pereruela
Sendim
Gáname
Venialbo
Bermillo de Sayago
San Marcial
Corrales
El Piñero
Villar del Buey
Tamame
Bemposta
Fermoselle
Embalse de Almendra
Fresno de Sayago
Peñausende
El Cubo de Tierra del Vino
Villamor de los Escuderos
Internacional
Villarino
Almeida
Viñuela de Sayago
Mayalde
Fuentesaúco
Pereña
Trabanca
Aldeadávila de la Ribera
Santiz
Masueco
Valdelosa
Arribes del Duero
Embalse de Saucelle
Villaseco de los Reyes
Topas
Ahigal de Villarino
Vilvestre
Las Uces
Calzada de Valdunciel
La Velles
Pedrosillo el Ralo
Ledesma
Puertas
Saucelle
Barruecopardo
Villaseco de los Gamitos
Villa de Peralonso
Villasdardo
La Mata de Ledesma
Salamanca
Vitigudino
Cerralbo
Yecla de Yeltes
Tejares
Rollán
Santa Marta de Tormes
Ciperez
Sando
Lumbrales
Bogajo
Barbadillo
Aldeatejada
Garcihernández
San Felices de los Gallegos
Villavieja de Yeltes
Robliza de Cojos
Matilla de los Caños del Río
Bañobárez
La Fuente de San Esteban
Morille
Martinamor
Puerto Seguro
Retortillo
San Muñoz
Vecinos
La Sagrada
Peña de Cabra
Villar de Ciervo
Sancti-Spiritus
Cabrillas
Las Veguillas
Pedrosillo de los Aires
Fresno Alhándiga
Aldea del Obispo
Castillejo de Martin Viejo
Abusejo
CATEDRAL DE SANTA MARIA
Tamames
Galinduste
Alba de Yeltes
Frades de la Sierra
Gallegos de Argañán
Escurial de la Sierra
Endrinal
Morasverdes
Fuenterroble de Salvatierra
Ciudad Rodrigo
El Cabaco
Linares de Riofrío
Guijuelo
El Maíllo
Las Batuecas
Los Santos
Serradilla del Arroyo
Sequeros
San Esteban de la Sierra
Santibáñez de Béjar
Embalse del Águeda
Serradilla del Llano
La Alberca
Valdelacasa
Cristóbal
El Bodón
Martiago
Sierra de la Peña de Francia
Sotoserrano
Medinilla
La Alberguería de Argañán
Casares de las Hurdes
Béjar
Becedas
Nuñomoral
El Barco de Ávila
Fuenteguinaldo
Robleda
Las Hurdes
Vegas de Coria
Candelario
Lagunilla
Peñaparda
Caminomorisco
El Cerro
Embalse de Gabriel y Galán
Puerto de Tornavacas 1275
Navasfrías
Baños
El Payo
Sierra de Gata
Pinofranqueado
Casar de Palomero
Hervás
Aldeanueva del Camino
Tornavacas
Gata
Cadalso
Mohedas
Valverde del Fresno
Puerto de Perales 910
Villanueva de la Sierra
Zarza de Granadilla
Jerte
Cabezuela del Valle
Hoyos
Santibáñez el Alto
Bronco
Ahigal
Navaconcejo
Perales del Puerto
Santa Cruz de Paniagua
El Torno
Guijo de Santa Bábara
Pozuelo de Zarzón
Santibáñez el Bajo
Piornal
Jarandilla de la Vera
Losar de la Vera
Oliva de Plasencia
Embalse de Borbollón
Guijo de Coria
Embalse de Valdeobispo
Garganta la Olla
YUSTE
Cuacos de Yuste
Cilleros
La Vera
Moraleja
Montehermoso
Valdeobispo
Plasencia
Barrado
Jaraíz de la Vera
Carcaboso
Tejada de Tiétar
Arrago
Coria
Malpartida de Plasencia
Talayuela
Galisteo
Casillas de Coria

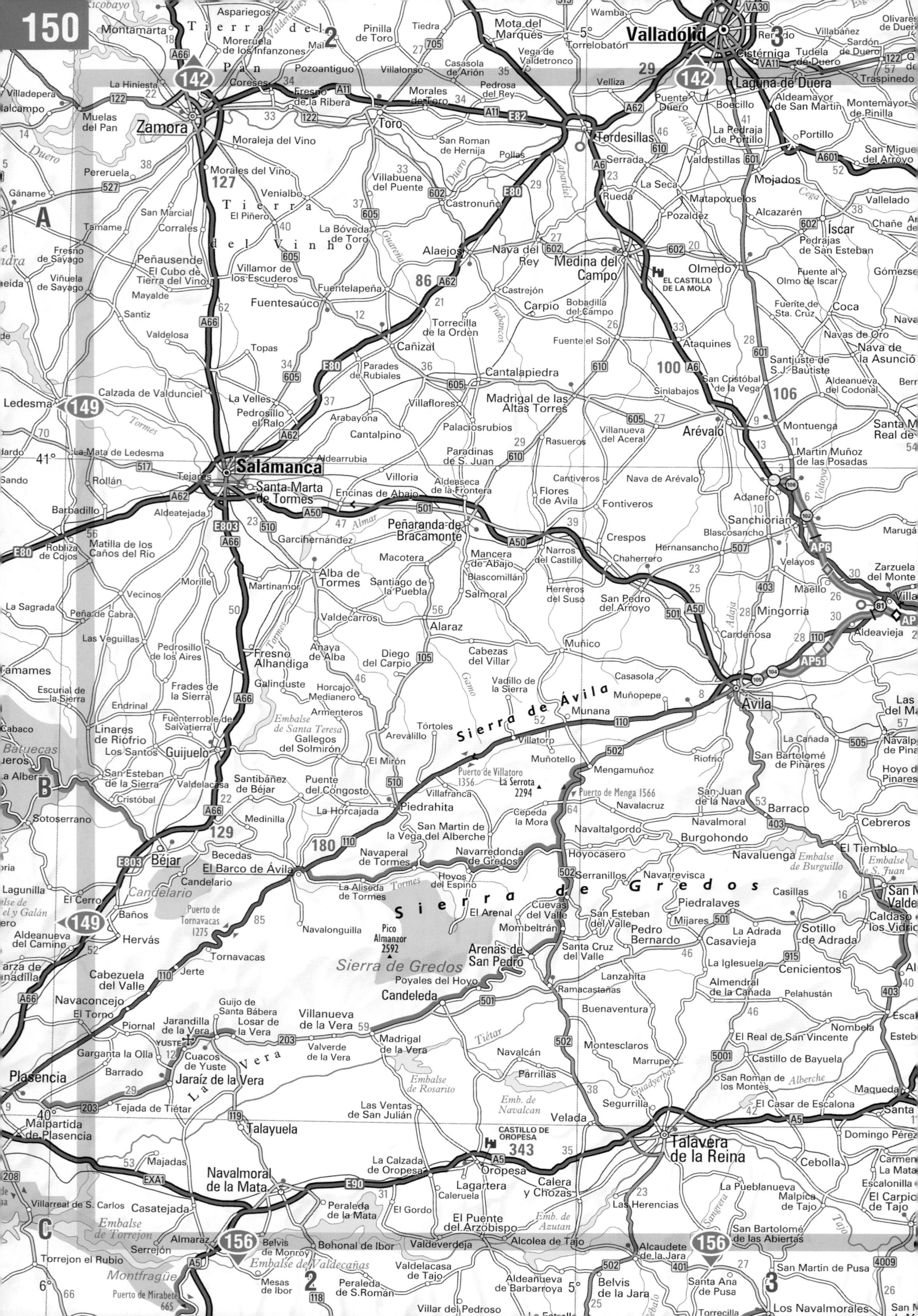
Montamarta
Aspariegos
Tierra del Pan
Moreruela de los Infanzones
Pinilla de Toro
Tiedra
Mota del Marqués
Wamba
Valladolid
Villabáñez
Sardón de Duero
Tudela de Duero
Cistérniga
Laguna de Duera
Traspinedo
Vega de Valdetronco
Torrelobatón
Villalonso
Casasola de Arión
Pozoantiguo
Coreses
La Hiniesta
Villadepera
Fresno de la Ribera
Morales de Toro
Pedrosa del Rey
Velliza
Puente Duero
Boecillo
Aldeamayor de San Martín
Montemayor de Pinilla
Zamora
Muelas del Pan
Toro
Tordesillas
La Pedraja de Portillo
Portillo
Moraleja del Vino
San Roman de Hernija
Pollos
Serrada
Valdestillas
Mojados
San Miguel del Arroyo
Duero
Pereruela
Morales del Vino
Villabuena del Puente
Gáname
Venialbo
Castronuño
La Seca
Rueda
Matapozuelos
Vallelado
Tierra del Vinho
El Piñero
San Marcial
Tamame
Corrales
Pozaldez
Alcazarén
Chañe
Íscar
Pedrajas de San Esteban
La Bóveda de Toro
Alaejos
Nava del Rey
Medina del Campo
Olmedo
Fresno de Sayago
Peñausende
El Cubo de Tierra del Vino
Villamor de los Escuderos
Viñuela de Sayago
Mayalde
Fuentelapeña
EL CASTILLO DE LA MOLA
Fuente al Olmo de Iscar
Gómezserracín
Castrejón
Carpio
Bobadilla del Campo
Fuentesaúco
Santiz
Torrecilla de la Orden
Fuente de Sta. Cruz
Coca
Valdelosa
Cañizal
Fuente el Sol
Ataquines
Navas de Oro
Nava de la Asunción
Topas
Parades de Rubiales
Cantalapiedra
San Cristóbal de la Vega
Santiuste de S.J. Bautiste
Aldeanueva del Codonal
Calzada de Valdunciel
Ledesma
La Velles
Pedrosillo el Ralo
Villaflores
Madrigal de las Altas Torres
Sinlabajos
Arabayona
Cantalpino
Palaciosrubios
Villanueva del Aceral
Arévalo
Montuenga
Santa María Real de Nieva
Tormes
La Mata de Ledesma
Paradinas de S. Juan
Rasueros
Martin Muñoz de las Posadas
Salamanca
Aldearrubia
Rollán
Tejares
Villoria
Aldeaseca de la Frontera
Cantiveros
Nava de Arévalo
Santa Marta de Tormes
Encinas de Abajo
Flores de Avila
Adanero
Fontiveros
Barbadillo
Aldeatejada
Peñaranda de Bracamonte
Sanchiorián
Almar
Crespos
Blascosancho
Garcihernández
Matilla de los Caños del Rio
Robliza de Cojos
Macotera
Mancera de Abajo
Narros del Castillo
Hernansancho
Chaherrero
Velayos
Zarzuela del Monte
Blascomillán
Alba de Tormes
Santiago de la Puebla
Morille
Martinamor
Herreros del Suso
San Pedro del Arroyo
Maello
Vecinos
Salmoral
Mingorria
La Sagrada
Peña de Cabra
Valdecarros
Alaraz
Cardeñosa
Aldeavieja
Las Veguillas
Pedrosillo de los Aires
Fresno Alhandiga
Anaya de Alba
Diego del Carpio
Cabezas del Villar
Muñico
Tamames
Escurial de la Sierra
Frades de la Sierra
Galinduste
Horcajo-Medianero
Vadillo de la Sierra
Casasola
Muñopepe
Ávila
Las Navas del Marqués
Endrinal
Fuenterroble de Salvatierra
Armenteros
Embalse de Santa Teresa
Sierra de Ávila
Munana
Linares de Riofrio
Cabaco
Batuecas
Gallegos del Solmirón
Tórtoles
Arevalillo
Villatorp
La Cañada
Los Santos
Guijuelo
Muñotello
Riofrio
San Bartolomé de Pinares
El Mirón
Mengamuñoz
Hoyo de Pinares
San Esteban de la Sierra
Valdelacasa
Santibáñez de Béjar
Puente del Congosto
Puerto de Villatoro 1356
La Serrota 2294
Puerto de Menga 1566
San Juan de la Nava
Cristóbal
Villafranca
Navalacruz
Barraco
Sotoserrano
Medinilla
La Horcajada
Piedrahita
Cepeda la Mora
Navalmoral
Navaltalgordo
Cebreros
San Martin de la Vega del Alberche
Burgohondo
El Tiemblo
Becedas
Navaperal de Tormes
Navarredonda de Gredos
Hoyocasero
Navaluenga
Embalse de Burguillo
Embalse de S. Juan
Béjar
El Barco de Ávila
Candelario
La Aliseda de Tormes
Hoyos del Espino
Serranillos
Navarrevisca
Sierra de Gredos
Lagunilla
El Cerro
Casillas
San Martín de Valdeiglesias
Puerto de Tornavacas 1275
Cuevas del Valle
Piedralaves
El Arenal
San Esteban del Valle
Mijares
Baños
Mombeltrán
Pedro Bernardo
Caldas de los Vidrios
Aldeanueva del Camino
Navalonguilla
Pico Almanzor 2592
La Adrada
Sotillo de Adrada
Hervás
Casavieja
Arenas de San Pedro
Santa Cruz del Valle
Tornavacas
La Iglesuela
Cenicientos
Cabezuela del Valle
Jerte
Lanzahita
Poyales del Hoyo
Almendral de la Cañada
Ramacastañas
Pelahustán
Navaconcejo
Candeleda
El Torno
Guijo de Santa Bábera
Buenaventura
Piornal
Jarandilla de la Vera
Losar de la Vera
Villanueva de la Vera
Nombela
Escalona
YUSTE
El Real de San Vincente
Esteban
Garganta la Olla
Cuacos de Yuste
Valverde de la Vera
Madrigal de la Vera
Tiétar
Navalcán
Montesclaros
Marrupe
Castillo de Bayuela
Barrado
Jaraíz de la Vera
Plasencia
La Vera
Parrillas
Guadyerbas
San Roman de los Montes
Alberche
Maqueda
Embalse de Rosarito
Tejada de Tiétar
Segurrilla
El Casar de Escalona
Santa Olalla
Malpartida de Plasencia
Las Ventas de San Julián
Emb. de Navalcan
Velada
Talayuela
CASTILLO DE OROPESA
Talavera de la Reina
Domingo Pérez
Majadas
Navalmoral de la Mata
La Calzada de Oropesa
Oropesa
Cebolla
Carmena
La Mata
Escalonilla
Lagartera
Caleruela
Calera y Chozas
Villarreal de S. Carlos
Casatejada
Peraleda de la Mata
El Gordo
Las Herencias
La Pueblanueva
Malpica de Tajo
El Carpio de Tajo
Embalse de Torrejon
El Puente del Arzobispo
Emb. de Azutan
Sangrera
Tajo
Almaraz
Serrejón
Belvis de Monroy
Bohonal de Ibor
Valdeverdeja
Alcolea de Tajo
Alcaudete de la Jara
San Bartolomé de las Abiertas
Torrejon el Rubio
Montfragüe
Embalse de Valdecañas
Valdelacasa de Tajo
San Martin de Pusa
Mesas de Ibor
Peraleda de S.Román
Aldeanueva de Barbarroya
Belvis de la Jara
Santa Ana de Pusa
Puerto de Mirabete 665
Villar del Pedroso
Los Navalmorales
A
B
C
2
3
41°
40°
5°
6°
142
149
156
127
129
180
86
100
106
343
A66
A11
A62
A6
A50
A5
A601
AP6
AP51
E80
E82
E803
E90
EXA1
VA30
VA11

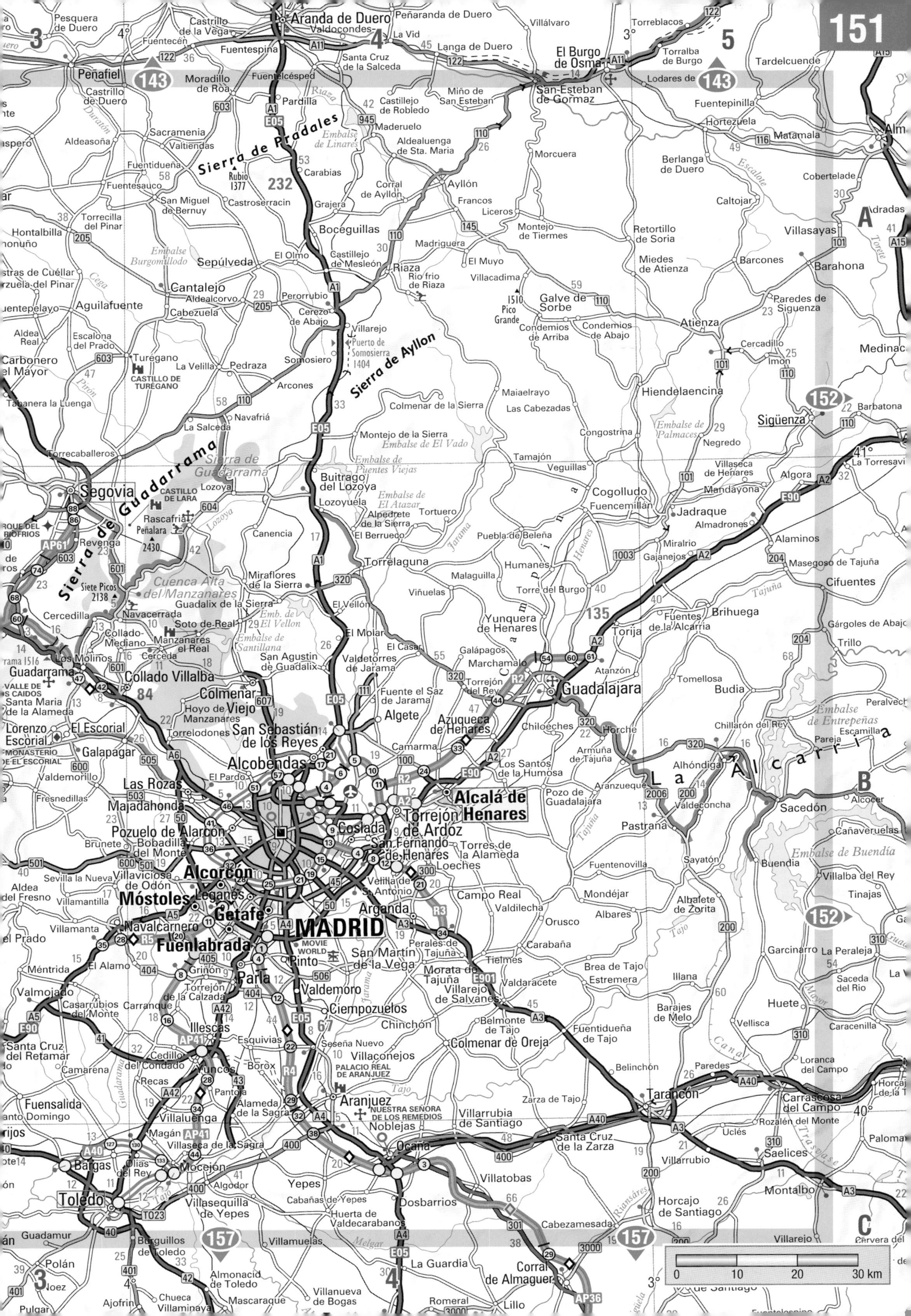
Pesquera de Duero
Castrillo de la Vega
Aranda de Duero
Peñaranda de Duero
Villálvaro
Torreblacos
Fuentecén
Valdocondes
La Vid
Langa de Duero
El Burgo de Osma
Torralba de Burgo
Tardelcuende
Fuentespina
Santa Cruz de la Salceda
Peñafiel
Moradillo de Roa
Fuentelcésped
San Esteban de Gormaz
Lodares de Osma
Castrillo de Duero
Pardilla
Castillejo de Robledo
Miño de San Esteban
Fuentepinilla
Maderuelo
Hortezuela
Sacramenia
Valtiendas
Aldeasoña
Sierra de Pradales
Embalse de Linares
Aldealuenga de Sta. Maria
Matamala
Morcuera
Fuentidueña
Rubio 1377
Carabias
Berlanga de Duero
Fuentesauco
Corral de Ayllón
Ayllón
Cobertelade
San Miguel de Bernuy
Castroserracin
Grajera
Francos
Caltojar
Torrecilla del Pinar
Liceros
Adradas
Hontalbilla
Boceguillas
Montejo de Tiermes
Retortillo de Soria
Villasayas
Madriguera
Embalse Burgomillodo
Sepúlveda
El Olmo
Castillejo de Mesleón
El Muyo
Miedes de Atienza
Barcones
Barahona
Riaza
Rio frio de Riaza
Villacadima
Cantalejo
Aldealcorvo
Perorrubio
Galve de Sorbe
Paredes de Sigüenza
Aguilafuente
Cabezuela
Cerezo de Abajo
1510 Pico Grande
Condemios de Arriba
Condemios de Abajo
Atienza
Villarejo
Puerto de Somosierra 1404
Escalona del Prado
Cercadillo
Imón
Medinaceli
Carbonero el Mayor
Turégano
La Velilla
Pedraza
Somosierra
Castillo de Turegano
Sierra de Ayllon
Arcones
Maiaelrayo
Hiendelaencina
Sigüenza
Barbatona
Tabanera la Luenga
Navafriá
Colmenar de la Sierra
Las Cabezadas
La Salceda
Montejo de la Sierra
Embalse de El Vado
Congostrina
Embalse de Palmaces
Negredo
Sierra de Guadarrama
Embalse de Puentes Viejas
Tamajón
Veguillas
Villaseca de Henares
La Torresavi
Torrecaballeros
Buitrago del Lozoya
Algora
Segovia
Castillo de Lara
Lozoya
Embalse de El Atazar
Cogolludo
Mandayona
Fuencemillán
Jadraque
Rascafría
Peñalara 2430
Lozoyuela
Alpedrete de la Sierra
Tortuero
Almadrones
Riofrío
Revenga
Canencia
El Berrueco
Puebla de Beleña
Miralrio
Alaminos
Gajanejos
Torrelaguna
Humanes
Masegoso de Tajuña
Cuenca Alta del Manzanares
Miraflores de la Sierra
Malaguilla
Torre del Burgo
Cifuentes
Siete Picos 2138
Guadalix de la Sierra
Viñuelas
El Vellón
Navacerrada
Emb. de El Vellon
Yunquera de Henares
Fuentes de la Alcarria
Brihuega
Cercedilla
Soto del Real
El Molar
Torija
Gárgoles de Abajo
Collado-Mediano
Manzanares el Real
Embalse de Santillana
Trillo
Guadarrama
Los Molinos
Cerceda
San Agustín de Guadalix
Valdetorres de Jarama
El Casar
Galápagos
Marchamalo
Atanzón
Valle de los Caídos
Collado Villalba
Tomellosa
Budia
Santa Maria de la Alameda
Colmenar Viejo
Hoyo de Manzanares
Fuente el Saz de Jarama
Torrejón del Rey
Guadalajara
Peralveche
San Lorenzo de El Escorial
El Escorial
Torrelodones
San Sebastián de los Reyes
Algete
Azuqueca de Henares
Chiloeches
Horche
Chillarón del Rey
Embalse de Entrepeñas
Monasterio de El Escorial
Galapagar
Camarma
Armuña de Tajuña
Pareja
Escamilla
Alcobendas
Los Santos de la Humosa
Alhóndiga
Valdemorillo
El Pardo
La Alcarria
Las Rozas
Alcalá de Henares
Pozo de Guadalajara
Aranzueque
Fresnedillas
Majadahonda
Torrejón de Ardoz
Valdeconcha
Sacedón
Alcocer
Pozuelo de Alarcón
Coslada
Pastrana
Cañaveruelas
Brunete
Bobadilla del Monte
San Fernando de Henares
Torres de la Alameda
Embalse de Buendía
Sevilla la Nueva
Villaviciosa de Odón
Alcorcón
Loeches
Fuentenovilla
Sayatón
Buendia
Aldea del Fresno
Villamantilla
Móstoles
Leganés
Velilla de S. Antonio
Campo Real
Mondéjar
Villalba del Rey
Tinajas
Getafe
Arganda
Valdilecha
Albalete de Zorita
Navalcarnero
Villamanta
MADRID
Orusco
Albares
El Prado
Fuenlabrada
Movie World
San Martín de la Vega
Perales de Tajuña
Carabaña
Garcinarro
La Peraleja
Méntrida
El Alamo
Griñon
Pinto
Tielmes
Brea de Tajo
Saceda del Rio
Valmojado
Torrejón de la Calzada
Parla
Morata de Tajuña
Estremera
Illana
Casarrubios del Monte
Carranque
Valdemoro
Villarejo de Salvanés
Valdaracete
Huete
Ciempozuelos
Barajes de Melo
Illescas
Chinchón
Belmonte de Tajo
Fuentidueña de Tajo
Vellisca
Caracenilla
Santa Cruz del Retamar
Esquivias
Seseña Nuevo
Villaconejos
Colmenar de Oreja
Cedillo del Condado
Palacio Real de Aranjuez
Belinchón
Loranca del Campo
Camarena
Yuncos
Borox
Paredes
Recas
Pantoja
Aranjuez
Zarza de Tajo
Tarancón
Carrascosa del Campo
Fuensalida
Santo Domingo
Alameda de la Sagra
Nuestra Señora de los Remedios
Villarrubia de Santiago
Villaluenga
Noblejas
Rozalén del Monte
Magán
Villaseca de la Sagra
Ocaña
Santa Cruz de la Zarza
Uclés
Bargas
Olías del Rey
Mocejón
Saelices
Villarrubio
Yepes
Villatobas
Toledo
Algodor
Cabañas de Yepes
Dosbarrios
Montalbo
Villasequilla de Yepes
Huerta de Valdecarabanos
Horcajo de Santiago
Cabezamesada
Guadamur
Burguillos de Toledo
Villamuelas
Melgar
Villarejo
Cervera del
Polán
Almonacid de Toledo
La Guardia
Corral de Almaguer
Chueca
Villaminaya
Villanueva de Bogas
Mascaraque
Ajofrín
Romeral
Lillo
Pulgar
143
152
157
0
10
20
30 km

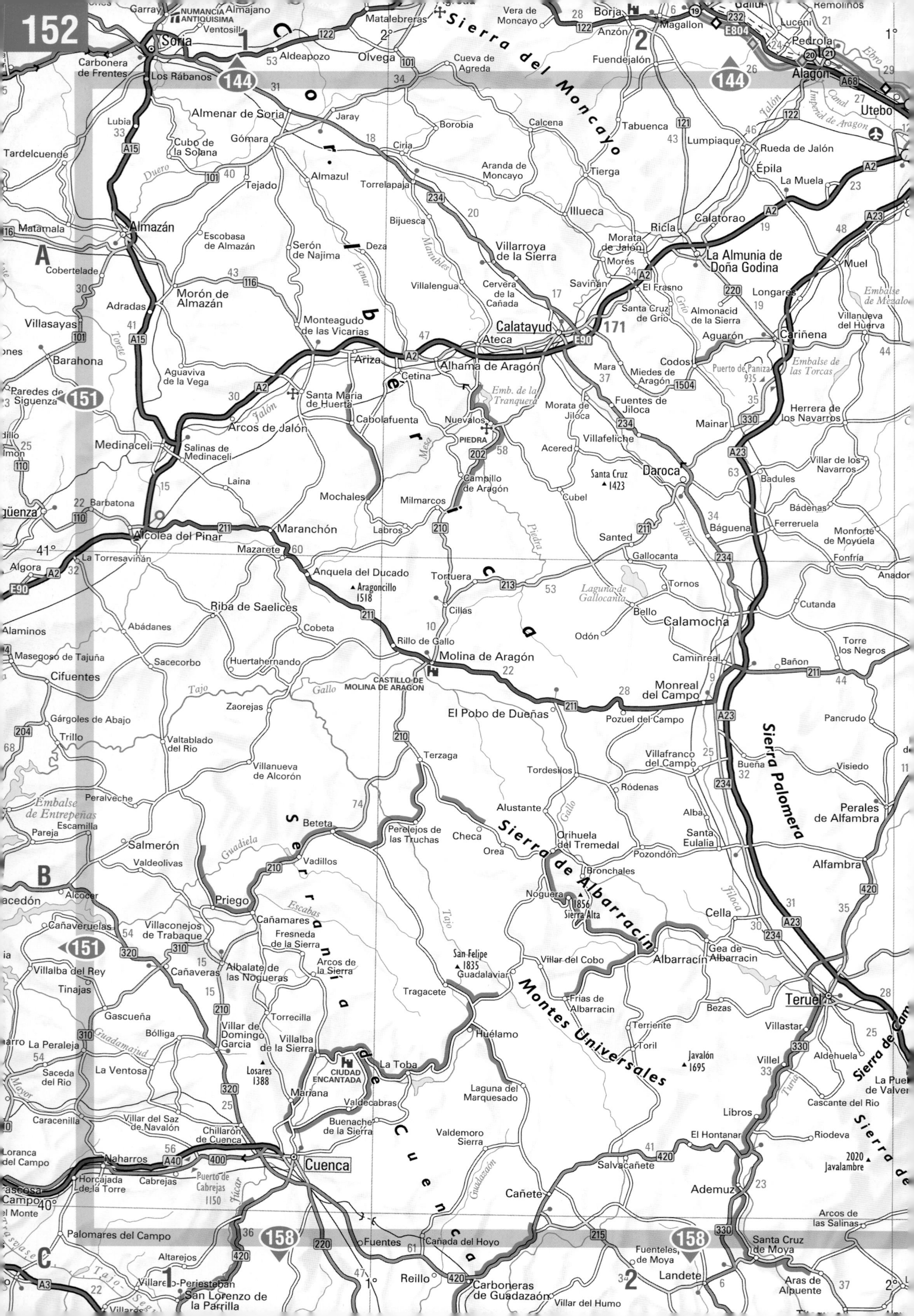
Soria
Almazán
Medinaceli
Alcolea del Pinar
Maranchón
Calatayud
Ateca
Alhama de Aragón
Daroca
Calamocha
Molina de Aragón
Monreal del Campo
Cariñena
La Almunia de Doña Godina
Borja
Alagón
Utebo
Épila
Teruel
Albarracín
Cuenca
Priego
Cifuentes
Sierra del Moncayo
Cordillera Ibérica
Sierra Palomera
Sierra de Albarracín
Montes Universales
Serranía de Cuenca
Sierra de Javalambre
Laguna de Gallocanta
Embalse de Entrepeñas
CASTILLO DE MOLINA DE ARAGON
CIUDAD ENCANTADA
PIEDRA
NUMANCIA ANTIQUISIMA
144
151
158
171

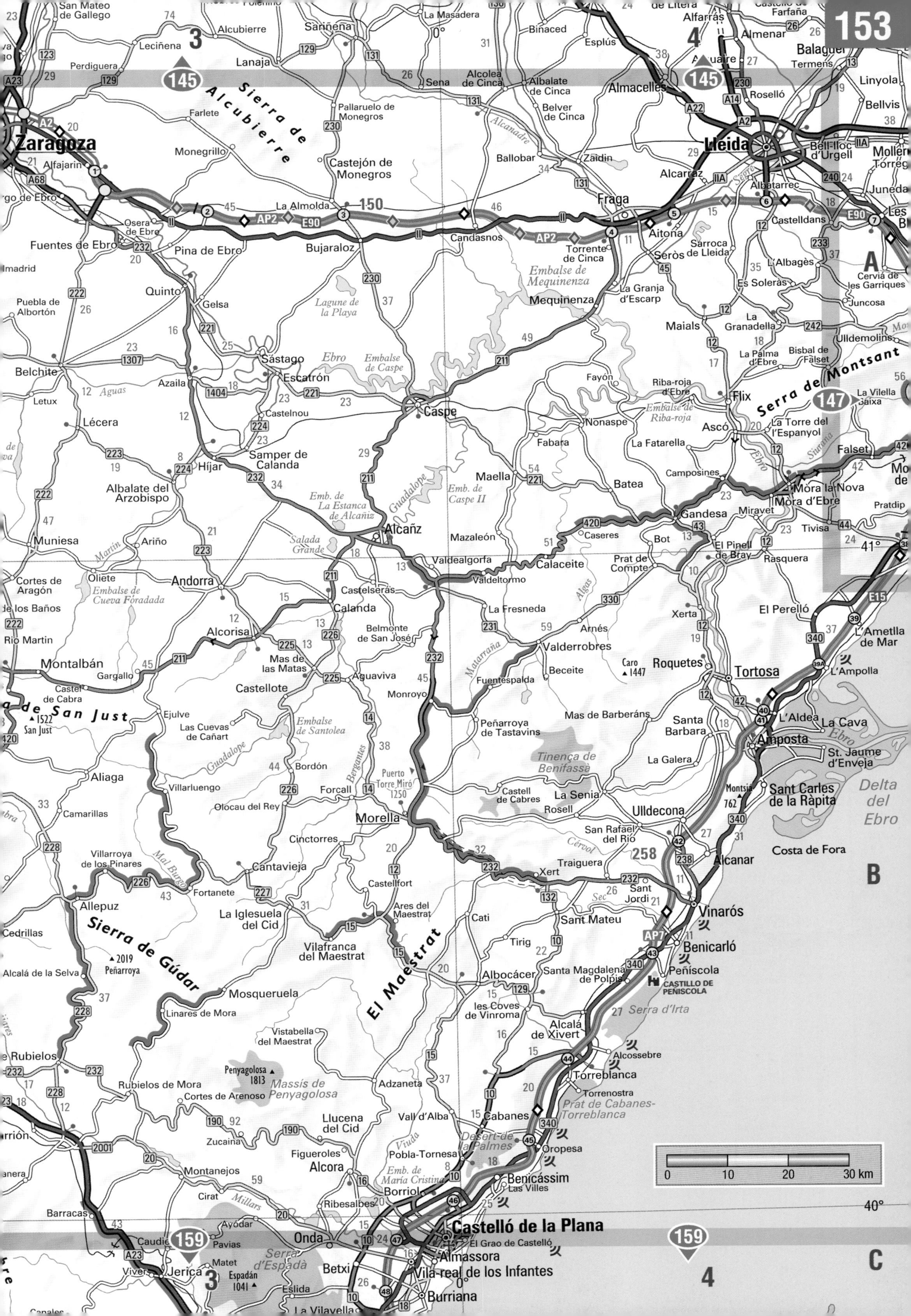
153
Zaragoza
Lleida
Alcañiz
Caspe
Fraga
Tortosa
Amposta
Vinarós
Benicarló
Peñíscola
Castelló de la Plana
Morella
Sierra de Alcubierre
Sierra de Gúdar
El Maestrat
Serra de Montsant
Delta del Ebro
Embalse de Mequinenza
Embalse de Caspe
Embalse de Riba-roja
Tinença de Benifassà
Massís de Penyagolosa
Serra d'Irta
Serra d'Espadà
Penyagolosa 1813
Peñarroya 2019
Puerto Torre Miró 1250
Costa de Fora
Sant Carles de la Ràpita
Mequinenza
Flix
Gandesa
Valderrobres
Ulldecona
Alcanar
Almacelles
Balaguer
Sariñena
Bujaraloz
Candasnos
Hijar
Andorra
Alcorisa
Calanda
Montalbán
Belchite
Quinto
Cantavieja
Vilafranca del Maestrat
Mosqueruela
Rubielos de Mora
Onda
Vila-real de los Infantes
Burriana
Almassora
Benicàssim
Oropesa
Torreblanca
Alcalà de Xivert
Sant Mateu
Albocàsser
Cabanes
Alcora
Jérica
CASTILLO DE PEÑISCOLA
0 10 20 30 km
40°
41°
A
B
C
3
4
145
147
150
159
258

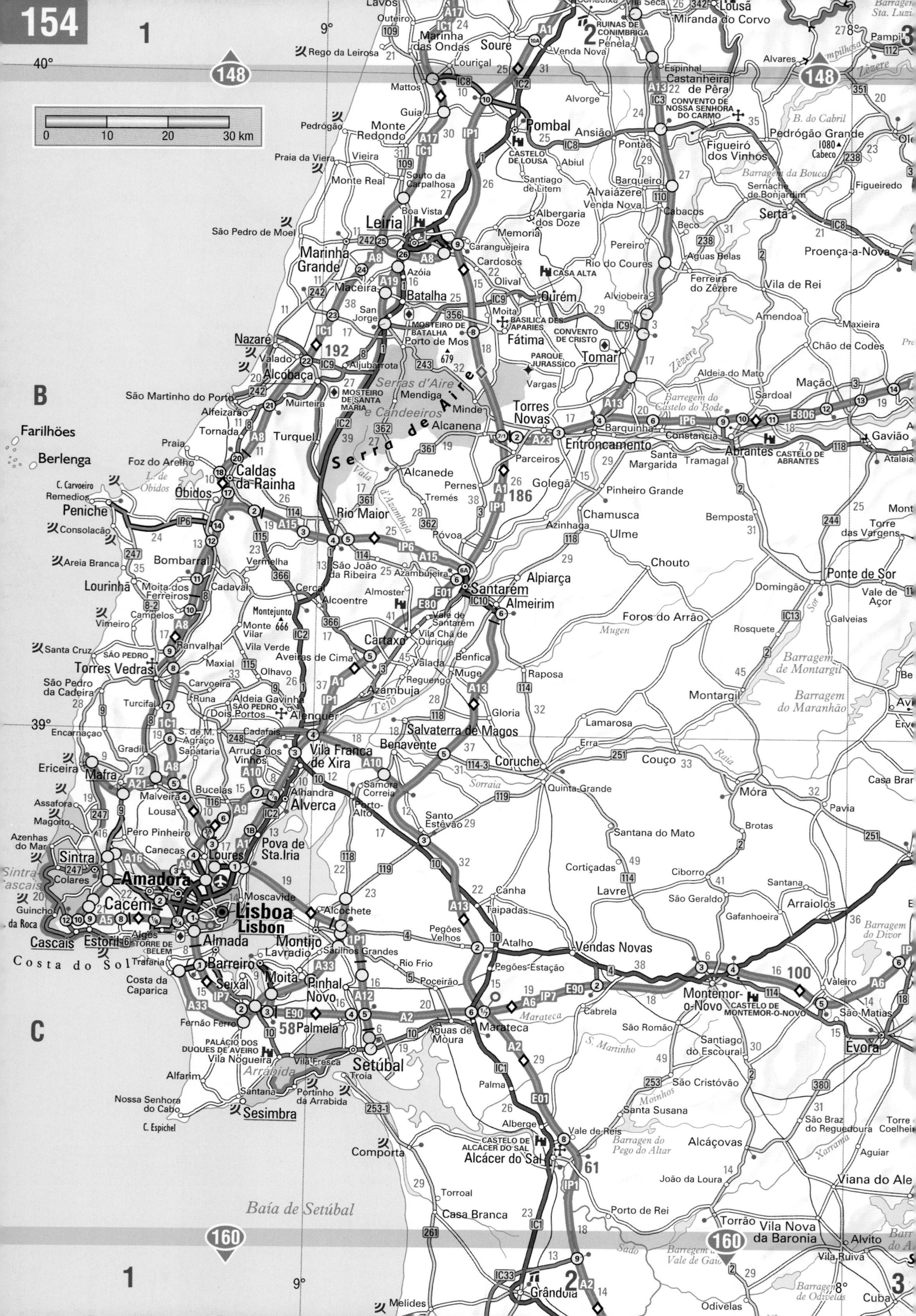
1
2
3
40°
9°
8°
39°
148
160
B
C
0
10
20
30 km
Lousã
Miranda do Corvo
Ruinas de Conimbriga
Penela
Soure
Marinha das Ondas
Outeiro
Rego da Leirosa
Louriçal
Venda Nova
Espinhal
Castanheira de Pêra
Convento de Nossa Senhora do Carmo
Mattos
Alvorge
Guia
Pombal
Ansião
Pedrógão
Monte Redondo
Castelo de Lousa
Abiul
Pontão
Figueiró dos Vinhos
Pedrógão Grande
B. do Cabril
Cabeço
Praia da Viera
Vieira
Souto da Carpalhosa
Monte Real
Santiago de Litem
Barqueiro
Barragem da Bouca
Sernache de Bonjardim
Figueiredo
Alvaiázere
Venda Nova
Cabacos
Sertã
Boa Vista
Albergaria dos Doze
São Pedro de Moel
Leiria
Memória
Beco
Marinha Grande
Caranguejeira
Pereiro
Proença-a-Nova
Cardosos
Rio do Coures
Aguas Belas
Azóia
Olival
Casa Alta
Ferreira do Zêzere
Vila de Rei
Maceira
Batalha
Ourém
Alviobeira
San Jorge
Mosteiro de Batalha
Moita
Basilica des Apariçes
Amendoa
Maxieira
Porto de Mos
Fátima
Convento de Cristo
Nazaré
Chão de Codes
Valado
Aljubarrota
Parque Jurassico
Tomar
Zêzere
Alcobaça
Serras d'Aire
Mendiga
Vargas
Aldeia do Mato
Mação
São Martinho do Porto
Mosteiro de Santa Maria
e Candeeiros
Minde
Torres Novas
Sardoal
Alfeizarão
Muirteira
Barragem do Castelo do Bode
Farilhões
Tornada
Turquel
Alcanena
Barquinha
Constancia
Abrantes
Gavião
Serra de Aire
Entroncamento
Castelo de Abrantes
Berlenga
Praia
Foz do Arelho
Parceiros
Santa Margarida
Tramagal
Atalaia
L. de Óbidos
Caldas da Rainha
Alcanede
C. Carvoeiro
Remedios
Óbidos
Pernes
Golegã
Pinheiro Grande
Peniche
Tremés
Rio Maior
Chamusca
Bemposta
Consolação
Azinhaga
Ulme
Torre das Vargens
Póvoa
Bombarral
Areia Branca
Vermelha
São João da Ribeira
Azambujeira
Alpiarça
Chouto
Ponte de Sor
Lourinhã
Moita dos Ferreiros
Cadaval
Cercal
Santarém
Domingão
Vale de Açor
Almoster
Almeirim
Alcoentre
Campelos
Montejunto
Foros do Arrão
Vimeiro
Monte Vilar
Vale de Santarém
Galveias
Mugen
Vila Chã de Ourique
Rosquete
Santa Cruz
Ranvalhal
Vila Verde
Cartaxo
Aveiras de Cima
Benfica
São Pedro
Torres Vedras
Maxial
Olhavo
Valada
Raposa
Barragem de Montargil
Reguengo
Muge
São Pedro da Cadeira
Carvoeira
Runa
Azambuja
Aldeia Gavinha
Turcifal
Tejo
Montargil
Barragem do Maranhão
Dois Portos
Alenquer
Gloria
Lamarosa
Encarnaçao
S. de M. Agraço
Cadafais
Salvaterra de Magos
Sapataria
Benavente
Gradil
Arruda dos Vinhos
Vila Franca de Xira
Erra
Raia
Ericeira
Coruche
Couço
Mafra
Samora Correia
Quinta Grande
Casa Branca
Malveira
Bucelas
Alhandra
Sorraia
Móra
Assafora
Lousa
Alverca
Pavia
Magoito
Porto Alto
Santo Estêvão
Pero Pinheiro
Brotas
Azenhas do Mar
Povo de Sta. Iria
Santana do Mato
Canecas
Loures
Sintra
Sintra-Cascais
Colares
Amadora
Corticadas
Ciborro
Santana
Moscavide
Canha
Lavre
Guincho
Cacém
Lisboa
Lisbon
Alcochete
Taipadas
São Geraldo
Arraiolos
Gafanhoeira
da Roca
Cascais
Estoril
Algés
Torre de Belem
Almada
Montijo
Pegões Velhos
Barragem do Divor
Atalho
Vendas Novas
Costa do Sol
Trafaria
Lavradio
Sarilhos Grandes
Rio Frio
Barreiro
Moita
Pegões-Estação
Valeiro
Costa da Caparica
Seixal
Pinhal Novo
Poceirão
Montemor-o-Novo
Castelo de Montemor-o-Novo
São Matias
Fernão Ferro
Palmela
Marateca
Cabrela
Evora
Palácio dos Duques de Aveiro
Vila Nogueira
Aguas de Moura
São Romão
Santiago do Escoural
Arrábida
Vila Fresca
Setúbal
S. Martinho
Alfarim
Troia
Palma
São Cristóvão
Portinho da Arrabida
Moinhos
Nossa Senhora do Cabo
Santana
Sesimbra
Santa Susana
São Braz do Regedoura
Torre Coelheiros
C. Espichel
Alberge
Vale de Reis
Barragen do Pego do Altar
Alcáçovas
Xarrama
Aguiar
Castelo de Alcácer do Sal
Comporta
Alcácer do Sal
João da Loura
Viana do Alentejo
Torroal
Baía de Setúbal
Casa Branca
Porto de Rei
Torrão
Vila Nova da Baronia
Alvito
Sado
Barragem de Vale de Gaio
Vila Ruiva
Barragem de Odivelas
Grândola
Cuba
Melides
Odivelas
Serra de Aire
192
186
100
58
61
A1
A2
A6
A8
A9
A10
A12
A13
A15
A16
A17
A19
A21
A23
A33
IC1
IC2
IC3
IC8
IC9
IC10
IC13
IC33
IP1
IP6
IP7
E01
E80
E90
E806

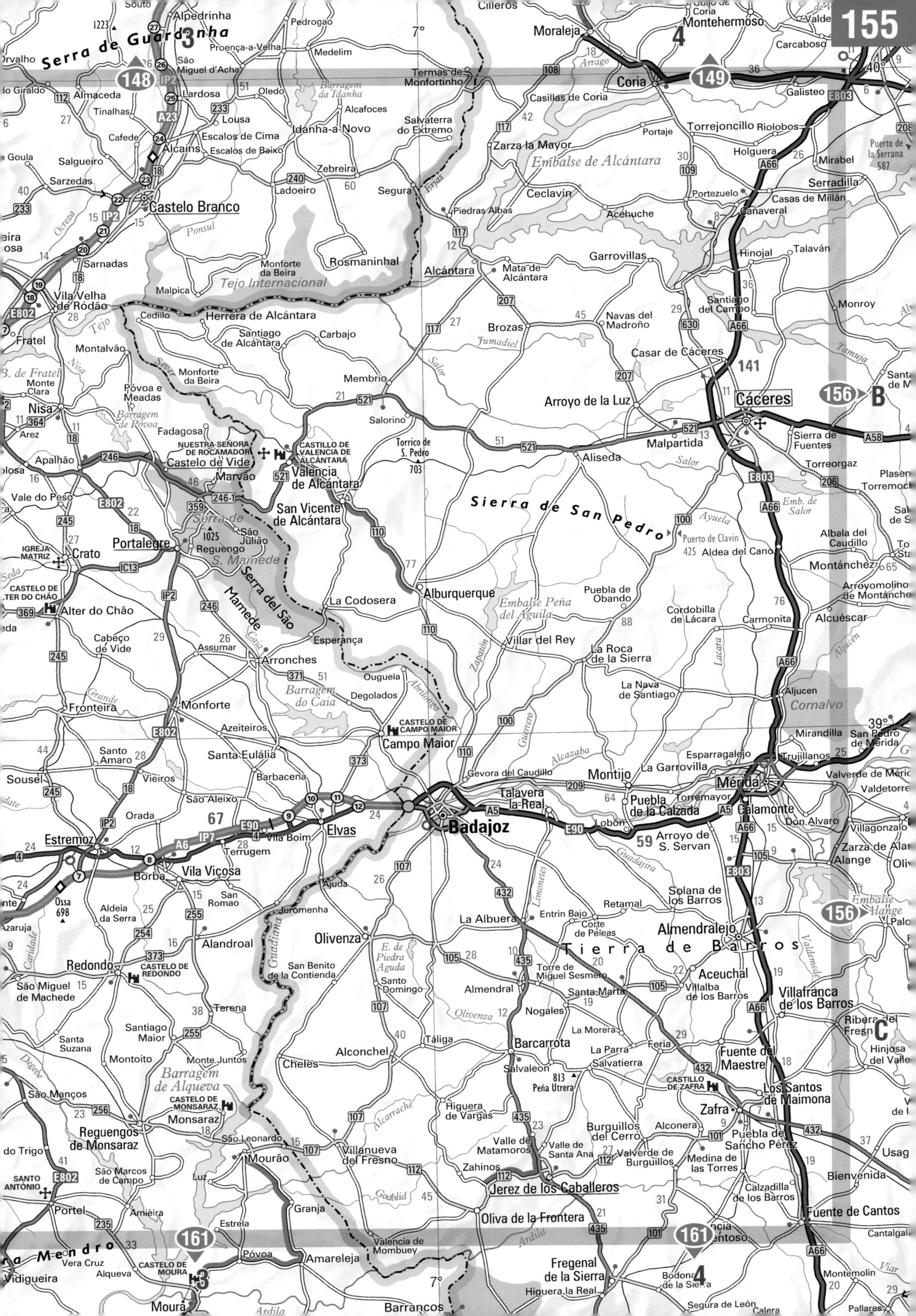
Serra de Guardunha
Alpedrinha
Pedrogão
Proença-a-Velha
Medelim
São Miguel d'Acha
Almaceda
Lardosa
Oledo
Barragem da Idanha
Alcafoces
Tinalhas
Lousa
Escalos de Cima
Escalos de Baixo
Idanha-a-Novo
Salvaterra do Extremo
Termas de Monfortinho
Cafede
Alcains
Salgueiro
Sarzedas
Zebreira
Ladoeiro
Segura
Castelo Branco
Ponsul
Rosmaninhal
Monforte da Beira
Malpica
Tejo Internacional
Sarnadas
Vila Velha de Ródão
Fratel
Cedillo
Herrera de Alcántara
Santiago de Alcántara
Carbajo
Montalvão
Monforte da Beira
Póvoa e Meadas
Barragem de Póvoa
Fadagosa
Nisa
Arez
Apalhão
Castelo de Vide
Nuestra Señora de Rocamador
Castillo de Valencia de Alcántara
Marvão
Valencia de Alcántara
San Vicente de Alcántara
Vale do Peso
Portalegre
Crato
Igreja Matriz
Serra de São Mamede
São Julião
Reguengo
Serra del São Mamede
Castelo de Alter do Chão
Alter do Chão
Cabeço de Vide
Assumar
Arronches
Esperança
La Codosera
Alburquerque
Ouguela
Degolados
Barragem do Caia
Fronteira
Monforte
Azeiteiros
Castelo de Campo Maior
Campo Maior
Santo Amaro
Santa Eulália
Barbacena
Sousel
Vieiros
São Aleixo
Orada
Estremoz
Elvas
Vila Boim
Terrugem
Borba
Vila Viçosa
Ossa 698
San Romao
Aldeia da Serra
Alandroal
Juromenha
Ajuda
Olivenza
Redondo
Castelo de Redondo
São Miguel de Machede
Terena
Santiago Maior
Santa Suzana
Montoito
Monte Juntos
Barragem de Alqueva
São Manços
Castelo de Monsaraz
Monsaraz
Reguengos de Monsaraz
São Leonardo
Mourão
São Marcos do Campo
Santo António
Portel
Amièira
Estrela
Granja
Póvoa
Amareleja
Vera Cruz
Alqueva
Castelo de Moura
Vidigueira
Moura
Ardila
Barrancos
Valencia de Mombuey
Cheles
Alconchel
Táliga
San Benito de la Contienda
Santo Domingo
E. de Piedra Aguda
Higuera de Vargas
Villanueva del Fresno
Zahinos
Oliva de la Frontera
Jerez de los Caballeros
Badajoz
Gevora del Caudillo
Talavera la Real
La Albuera
Entrín Bajo
Corte de Peleas
Torre de Miguel Sesmero
Almendral
Nogales
Barcarrota
Salvaleón
813 Peña Utrera
Valle de Matamoros
Valle de Santa Ana
Burguillos del Cerro
Valverde de Burguillos
Fregenal de la Sierra
Higuera la Real
Bodonal de la Sierra
Segura de León
Cilleros
Moraleja
Coria
Montehermoso
Carcaboso
Galisteo
Casillas de Coria
Torrejoncillo
Riolobos
Portaje
Zarza la Mayor
Embalse de Alcántara
Holguera
Mirabel
Puerto de la Serrana 587
Serradilla
Casas de Millán
Cañaveral
Portezuelo
Ceclavín
Piedras Albas
Acehuche
Alcántara
Mata de Alcántara
Garrovillas
Hinojal
Talaván
Santiago del Campo
Monroy
Brozas
Navas del Madroño
Casar de Cáceres
Membrío
Salorino
Arroyo de la Luz
Cáceres
Sierra de Fuentes
Torrico de S. Pedro 703
Malpartida
Aliseda
Torreorgaz
Sierra de San Pedro
Puerto de Clavin 425
Aldea del Cano
Emb. de Salor
Albala del Caudillo
Montánchez
Puebla de Obando
Embalse Peña del Aguila
Villar del Rey
Cordobilla de Lácara
Carmonita
Arroyomolinos de Montánchez
Alcuéscar
La Roca de la Sierra
La Nava de Santiago
Aljucen
Cornalvo
Mirandilla
San Pedro de Mérida
Trujillanos
Esparragalejo
La Garrovilla
Montijo
Mérida
Valverde de Mérida
Puebla de la Calzada
Torremayor
Calamonte
Lobón
Arroyo de S. Servan
Don Alvaro
Villagonzalo
Zarza de Alange
Alange
Embalse Alange
Solana de los Barros
Retamal
Almendralejo
Tierra de Barros
Aceuchal
Villalba de los Barros
Santa Marta
Villafranca de los Barros
La Morera
La Parra
Salvatierra
Feria
Fuente del Maestre
Ribera del Fresno
Hinojosa del Valle
Castillo de Zafra
Los Santos de Maimona
Zafra
Alconera
Puebla de Sancho Pérez
Medina de las Torres
Calzadilla de los Barros
Bienvenida
Fuente de Cantos
Montemolín
Pallares
Usagre
Cantalgallo
Mendro
Guadiana
Tejo
Salor
Ayuela
Guadajira
Olivenza
Godolid
Alcarrache
Zapatón
Guerrero
Alcazaba
Lacara
Limonetes
Caia
Sever
Nisa
Erjas
Jumadiel
Tamuja
Arrago
148
149
156
161
B
C
3
4
39°
40°
7°

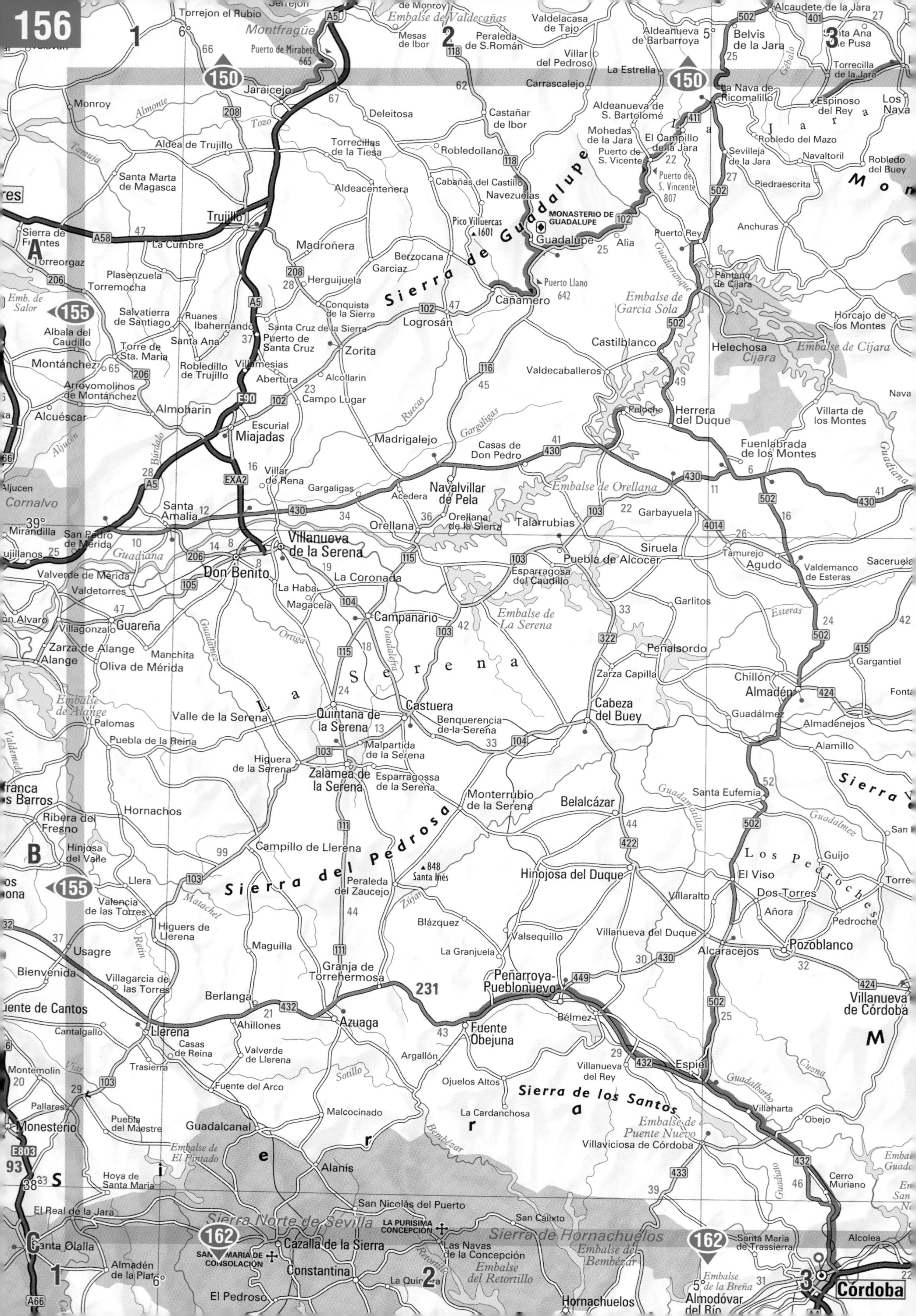

156
Torrejon el Rubio
Montfragüe
Puerto de Mirabete
665
Embalse de Valdecañas
Mesas de Ibor
Peraleda de S.Román
Valdelacasa de Tajo
Aldeanueva de Barbarroya
Villar del Pedroso
La Estrella
Belvis de la Jara
Alcaudete de la Jara
Torrecilla de la Jara
Gébalo
Jaraicejo
Puerto de Jaraicejo
Monroy
Almonte
Tozo
Deleitosa
Carrascalejo
Castañar de Ibor
Aldeanueva de S. Bartolomé
La Nava de Ricomalillo
Espinoso del Rey
Los Nava
Jara
Aldea de Trujillo
Torrecillas de la Tiesa
Robledollano
Mohedas de la Jara
El Campillo de la Jara
Puerto de S. Vicente
Robledo del Mazo
Sevilleja de la Jara
Navaltoril
Robledo del Buey
Tamuja
Santa Marta de Magasca
Aldeacentenera
Cabañas del Castillo
Navezuelas
Puerto de S. Vincente
807
Piedraescrita
Mon
Trujillo
Sierra de Fuentes
La Cumbre
Madroñera
Pico Villuercas
1601
MONASTERIO DE GUADALUPE
Guadalupe
Alia
Puerto Rey
Anchuras
Guadarranque
Torreorgaz
Plasenzuela
Torremocha
Berzocana
Garciaz
Herguijuela
Sierra de Guadalupe
Puerto Llano
642
Cañamero
Pantano de Cijara
Emb. de Salor
Salvatierra de Santiago
Ruanes
Ibahernando
Conquista de la Sierra
Santa Cruz de la Sierra
Logrosán
Embalse de García Sola
Horcajo de los Montes
Albala del Caudillo
Santa Ana
Puerto de Santa Cruz
Zorita
Castilblanco
Helechosa
Embalse de Cíjara
Cíjara
Torre de Sta. María
Montánchez
Robledillo de Trujillo
Villamesias
Abertura
Alcollarin
Valdecaballeros
Arroyomolinos de Montánchez
Campo Lugar
Nava
Alcuéscar
Almoharín
Ruecas
Gargáligas
Peloche
Herrera del Duque
Villarta de los Montes
Escurial
Miajadas
Madrigalejo
Casas de Don Pedro
Fuenlabrada de los Montes
Búrdalo
Aljucén
Villar de Rena
Gargaligas
Acedera
Navalvillar de Pela
Embalse de Orellana
Guadiana
Aljucen
Cornalvo
Santa Amalia
Orellana
Orellana de la Sierra
Talarrubias
Garbayuela
39°
Mirandilla
San Pedro de Mérida
Villanueva de la Serena
Siruela
Tamurejo
Agudo
Valdemanco de Esteras
Saceruela
Guadiana
Don Benito
La Coronada
Esparragosa del Caudillo
Puebla de Alcocer
Valverde de Mérida
Valdetorres
La Haba
Magacela
Garlitos
Esteras
Campanario
Embalse de La Serena
Guareña
Villagonzalo
Zarza de Alange
Alange
Manchita
Oliva de Mérida
Ortiga
Guadámez
Guadalefra
La Serena
Peñalsordo
Gargantiel
Zarza Capilla
Chillón
Almadén
Embalse de Alange
Valle de la Serena
Quintana de la Serena
Castuera
Benquerencia de-la-Serena
Cabeza del Buey
Guadálmez
Almadenejos
Palomas
Puebla de la Reina
Higuera de la Serena
Malpartida de la Serena
Zalamea de la Serena
Esparragossa de la Serena
Alamillo
Sierra
Franca
Barros
Ribera del Fresno
Hornachos
Monterrubio de la Serena
Belalcázar
Guadamatillas
Santa Eufemia
Guadalmez
Hinojosa del Valle
Campillo de Llerena
Sierra del Pedrosa
848
Santa Inés
Los Pedroches
Guijo
Llera
Peraleda del Zaucejo
Hinojosa del Duque
El Viso
Torre
Valencia de las Torres
Zújar
Villaralto
Dos-Torres
Añora
Pedroche
Matachel
Higuers de Llerena
Retín
Blázquez
Valsequillo
Villanueva del Duque
Alcaracejos
Pozoblanco
Usagre
Maguilla
La Granjuela
Bienvenida
Villagarcia de las Torres
Granja de Torrehermosa
Peñarroya-Pueblonuevo
Villanueva de Córdoba
Berlanga
Fuente de Cantos
Ahillones
Azuaga
Bélmez
Cantalgallo
Llerena
Casas de Reina
Fuente Obejuna
Valverde de Llerena
Argallón
Espiel
Trasierra
Villanueva del Rey
Montemolín
Viar
Sotillo
Ojuelos Altos
Sierra de los Santos
Guadalbarbo
Fuente del Arco
Villaharta
Obejo
Pallares
Malcocinado
La Cardanchosa
Cuzna
Monesterio
Puebla del Maestre
Guadalcanal
Bembézar
Embalse de Puente Nuevo
Embalse de El Pintado
Villaviciosa de Córdoba
Alanís
Guadiato
Hoya de Santa María
Cerro Muriano
San Nicolás del Puerto
El Real de la Jara
Sierra Norte de Sevilla
San Calixto
LA PURISIMA CONCEPCIÓN
Sierra de Hornachuelos
Santa María de Trassierra
Alcolea
Santa Olalla
SAN MARIA DE CONSOLACIÓN
Cazalla de la Sierra
Las Navas de la Concepción
Embalse del Bembézar
Almadén de la Plata
Constantina
Embalse del Retortillo
Retortillo
Embalse de la Breña
La Quintera
Córdoba
El Pedroso
Hornachuelos
Almodóvar del Río

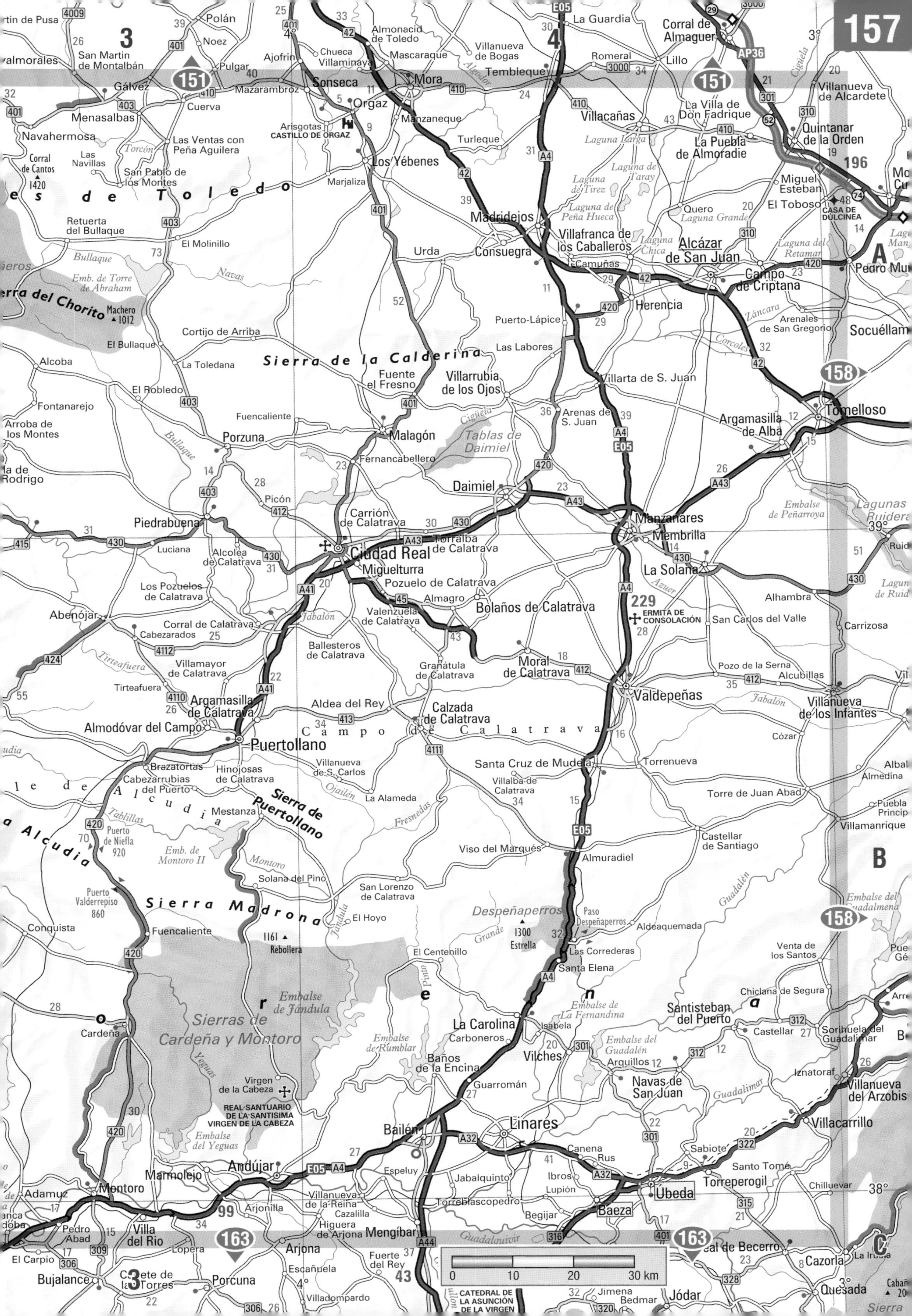

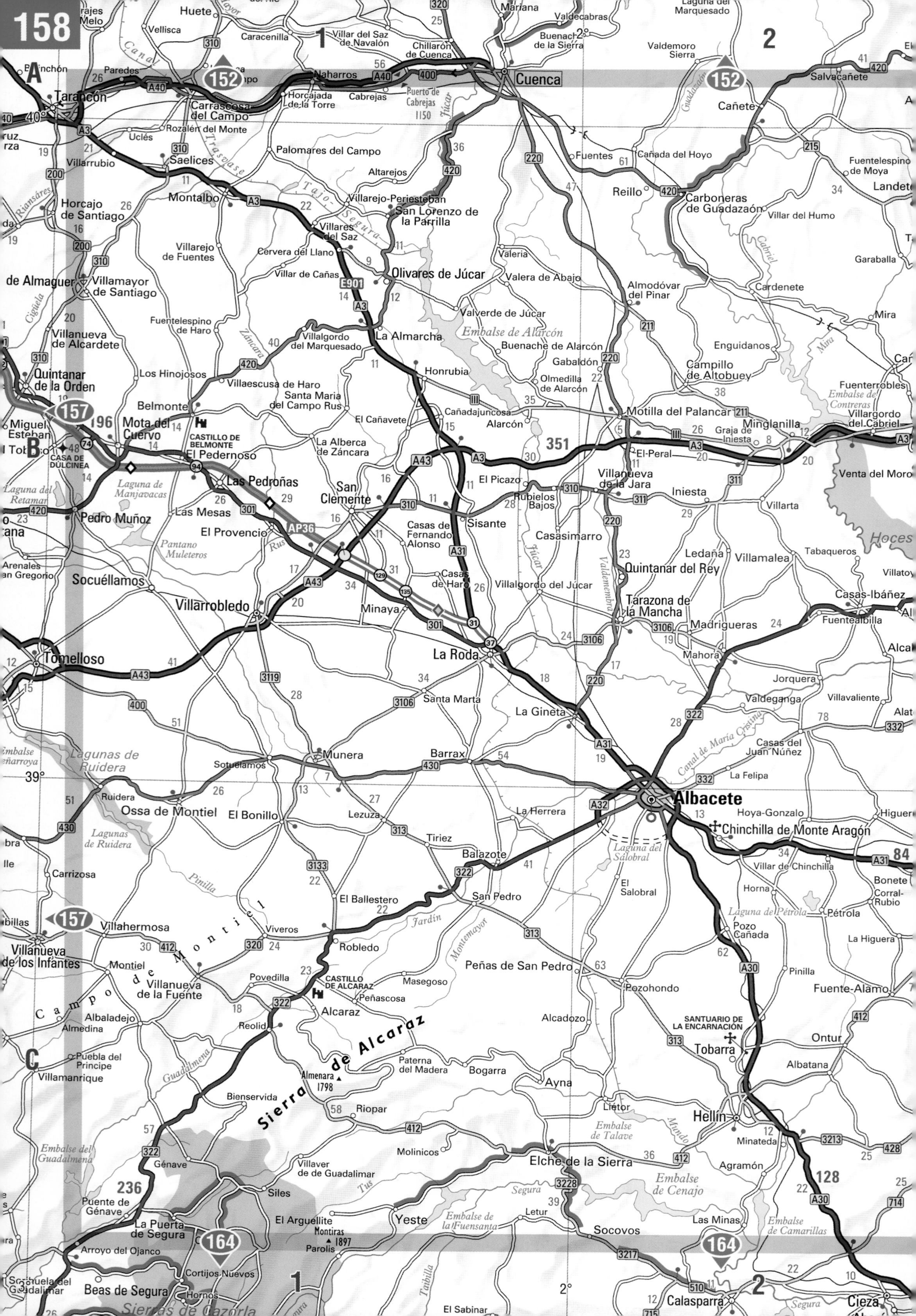
Huete
Vellisca
Caracenilla
Villar del Saz de Navalón
Chillarón de Cuenca
Mariana
Valdecabras
Buenache de la Sierra
Laguna del Marquesado
Valdemoro Sierra
Salvacañete
Cuenca
Paredes
Naharros
Tarancón
Carrascosa del Campo
Horcajada de la Torre
Cabrejas
Puerto de Cabrejas 1150
Cañete
Rozalén del Monte
Uclés
Palomares del Campo
Fuentes
Cañada del Hoyo
Villarrubio
Saelices
Altarejos
Reillo
Carboneras de Guadazaón
Fuentelespino de Moya
Landete
Horcajo de Santiago
Montalbo
Villarejo-Periesteban
San Lorenzo de la Parrilla
Villar del Humo
Villares del Saz
Villarejo de Fuentes
Cervera del Llano
Valeria
Garaballa
de Almaguer
Villamayor de Santiago
Villar de Cañas
Olivares de Júcar
Valera de Abajo
Almodóvar del Pinar
Cardenete
Fuentelespino de Haro
Valverde de Júcar
Mira
Villanueva de Alcardete
Villalgordo del Marquesado
La Almarcha
Embalse de Alarcón
Buenache de Alarcón
Enguídanos
Quintanar de la Orden
Los Hinojosos
Honrubia
Gabaldón
Campillo de Altobuey
Villaescusa de Haro
Santa María del Campo Rus
Olmedilla de Alarcón
Fuenterrobles
Embalse de Contreras
Belmonte
Cañadajuncosa
Motilla del Palancar
Villargordo del Cabriel
Mota del Cuervo
El Cañavete
Alarcón
Minglanilla
Graja de Iniesta
Castillo de Belmonte
La Alberca de Záncara
El Peral
Casa de Dulcinea
El Pedernoso
Venta del Moro
Laguna de Manjavacas
Las Pedroñas
San Clemente
El Picazo
Villanueva de la Jara
Iniesta
Laguna del Retamar
Pedro Muñoz
Las Mesas
Rubielos Bajos
Villarta
El Provencio
Casas de Fernando Alonso
Sisante
Casasimarro
Pantano Muleteros
Hoces
Arenales de San Gregorio
Quintanar del Rey
Ledaña
Villamalea
Tabaqueros
Socuéllamos
Casas de Haro
Villalgordo del Júcar
Villarrobledo
Minaya
Tarazona de la Mancha
Casas-Ibáñez
Fuentealbilla
Madrigueras
Tomelloso
La Roda
Mahora
Jorquera
Santa Marta
Valdeganga
Villavaliente
La Gineta
Casas del Juan Núñez
Lagunas de Ruidera
Munera
Barrax
Canal de María Cristina
Sotuélamos
La Felipa
Ruidera
Ossa de Montiel
El Bonillo
Lezuza
La Herrera
Albacete
Hoya-Gonzalo
Chinchilla de Monte Aragón
Tiriez
Balazote
Laguna del Salobral
Villar de Chinchilla
Carrizosa
El Salobral
Bonete
Horna
Corral-Rubio
El Ballestero
San Pedro
Laguna de Pétrola
Pétrola
Villahermosa
Viveros
Pozo Cañada
Robledo
La Higuera
Villanueva de los Infantes
Montiel
Campo de Montiel
Peñas de San Pedro
Pinilla
Povedilla
Villanueva de la Fuente
Castillo de Alcaraz
Masegoso
Pozohondo
Fuente-Álamo
Albaladejo
Almedina
Peñascosa
Alcaraz
Alcadozo
Reolid
Santuario de la Encarnación
Ontur
Puebla del Príncipe
Sierra de Alcaraz
Paterna del Madera
Bogarra
Tobarra
Villamanrique
Almenara 1798
Ayna
Albatana
Bienservida
Riopar
Liétor
Hellín
Embalse del Guadalmena
Molinicos
Embalse de Talave
Minateda
Génave
Villaverde de Guadalimar
Elche de la Sierra
Agramón
Puente de Génave
Siles
Embalse de Cenajo
La Puerta de Segura
El Arguellite
Yeste
Embalse de la Fuensanta
Letur
Socovos
Las Minas
Embalse de Camarillas
Montiras 1897
Parolis
Arroyo del Ojanco
Cortijos Nuevos
Beas de Segura
Hornos
Calasparra
Cieza
El Sabinar
Sierras de Cazorla
A40
A3
A43
A31
A32
A30
AP36
E901
39°
2°

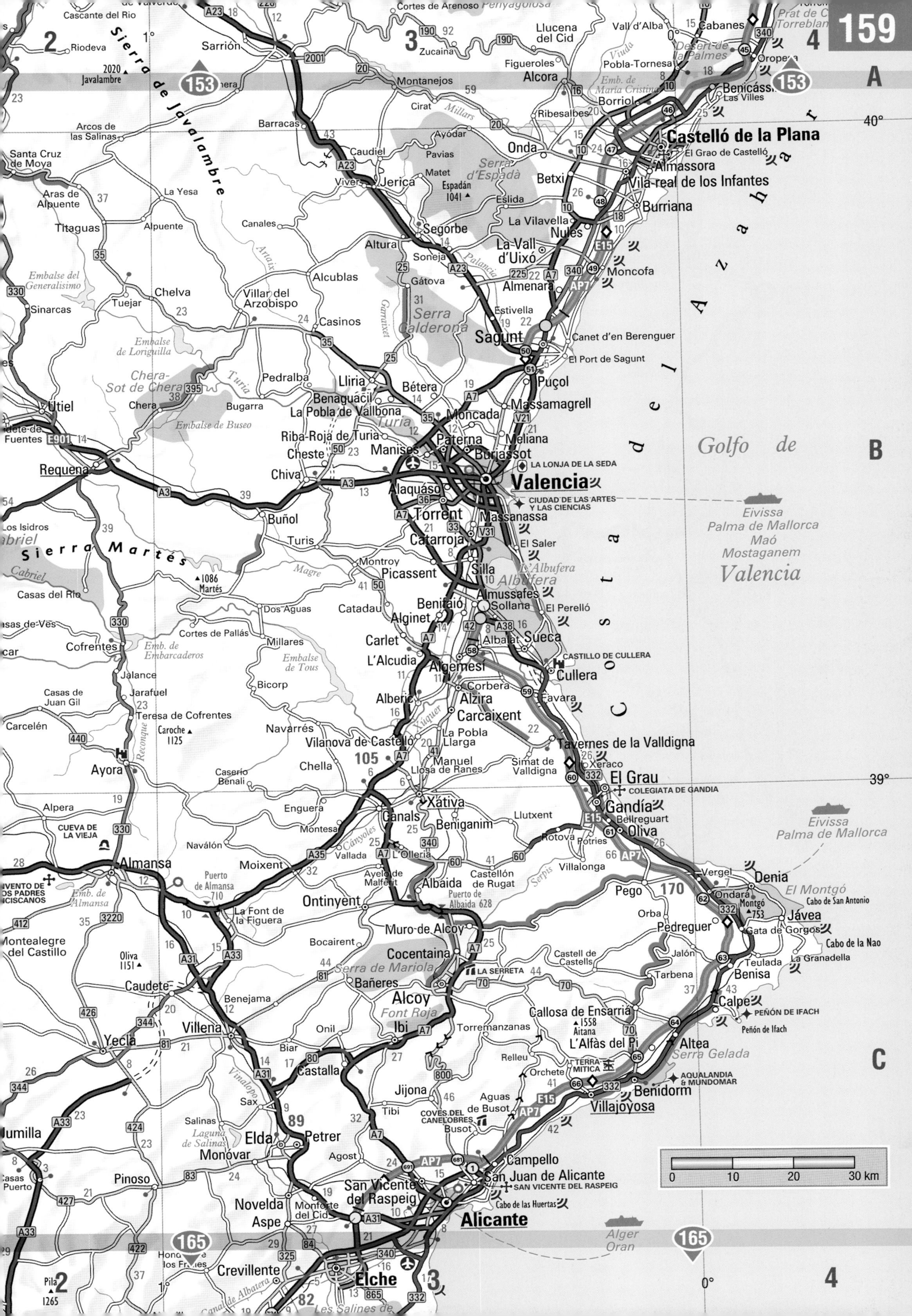
Cascante del Rio
Riodeva
Sierra de Javalambre
2020 Javalambre
Sarrión
Cortes de Arenoso
Zucaina
Llucena del Cid
Vall d'Alba
Cabanes
Desert de les Palmes
Oropesa
Figueroles
Alcora
Pobla-Tornesa
Emb. de María Cristina
Borriol
Benicàssim
Las Villes
Montanejos
Cirat
Millars
Ribesalbes
Arcos de las Salinas
Barracas
Ayódar
Castelló de la Plana
El Grao de Castelló
Almassora
Santa Cruz de Moya
Caudiel
Pavias
Onda
Serra d'Espadà
Matet
Espadán 1041
Betxi
Vila-real de los Infantes
Burriana
Aras de Alpuente
La Yesa
Viver
Jerica
Eslida
Titaguas
Alpuente
Canales
Segorbe
La Vilavella
Nules
Altura
La Vall d'Uixó
Soneja
Moncofa
Palancia
Embalse del Generalísimo
Alcublas
Gátova
Almenara
Sinarcas
Chelva
Tuejar
Villar del Arzobispo
Serra Calderona
Estivella
Casinos
Sagunt
Canet d'en Berenguer
Embalse de Loriguilla
El Port de Sagunt
Chera-Sot de Chera
Turia
Pedralba
Llíria
Bétera
Puçol
Benaguacil
Chera
Bugarra
La Pobla de Vallbona
Moncada
Massamagrell
Utiel
Embalse de Buseo
Riba-Roja de Turia
Paterna
Meliana
Fuentes
Manises
Burjassot
Golfo de
Requena
Cheste
LA LONJA DE LA SEDA
Chiva
Valencia
Alaquàs
CIUDAD DE LAS ARTES Y LAS CIENCIAS
Buñol
Torrent
Massanassa
Eivissa
Palma de Mallorca
Maó
Mostaganem
Valencia
Los Isidros
Turis
Catarroja
El Saler
Sierra Martés
Montroy
Picassent
L'Albufera
Silla
Magre
Casas del Rio
1086 Martés
Almussafes
Sollana
Dos Aguas
Catadau
Benifaió
El Perelló
Alginet
Cortes de Pallás
Sueca
Albalat
Cofrentes
Emb. de Embarcaderos
Millares
Carlet
CASTILLO DE CULLERA
Embalse de Tous
L'Alcudia
Algemesí
Cullera
Jalance
Bicorp
Corbera
Casas de Juan Gil
Jarafuel
Alberic
Alzira
Favara
Teresa de Cofrentes
Carcaixent
Costa del Azahar
Carcelén
Caroche 1125
Navarrés
La Pobla Llarga
Xúquer
Vilanova de Castelló
Tavernes de la Valldigna
Ayora
Chella
Manuel
Simat de Valldigna
Caserío Benali
Llosa de Ranes
Xeraco
El Grau
COLEGIATA DE GANDIA
Xàtiva
Gandía
Alpera
Enguera
Canals
Llutxent
Bellreguart
CUEVA DE LA VIEJA
Montesa
Beniganim
Oliva
Eivissa
Palma de Mallorca
Rotova
Potries
Navalón
Cànyoles
Vallada
L'Olleria
Almansa
Moixent
Villalonga
Vergel
Denia
Ayelo de Malferit
Castellón de Rugat
Serpis
Pego
El Montgó
Emb. de Almansa
Puerto de Almansa 710
Albaida
Puerto de Albaida 628
Ondara
Montgó 753
Cabo de San Antonio
Ontinyent
Jávea
La Font de la Figuera
Orba
Pedreguer
Muro de Alcoy
Gata de Gorgos
Montealegre del Castillo
Bocairent
Cabo de la Nao
Oliva 1151
Cocentaina
Castell de Castells
Jalón
Teulada
La Granadella
Serra de Mariola
LA SERRETA
Tarbena
Benisa
Caudete
Bañeres
Benejama
Alcoy
Callosa de Ensarriá
Calpe
PEÑÓN DE IFACH
Font Roja
1558 Aitana
Peñón de Ifach
Villena
Onil
Torremanzanas
Yecla
Ibi
L'Alfàs del Pi
Altea
Serra Gelada
Biar
Relleu
Castalla
TERRA MITICA
Orchete
AQUALANDIA & MUNDOMAR
Jijona
Benidorm
Villajoyosa
Vinalopó
Sax
Aguas de Busot
Tibi
COVES DEL CANELOBRES
Busot
Salinas
Laguna de Salinas
Elda
Petrer
Jumilla
Monóvar
Agost
Campello
San Juan de Alicante
SAN VICENTE DEL RASPEIG
Pinoso
San Vicente del Raspeig
Cabo de las Huertas
Novelda
Monforte del Cid
Aspe
Alicante
Alger
Oran
Hondón de los Frailes
Crevillente
Elche
Pila 1265
Les Salines de
0 10 20 30 km
40°
39°
0°

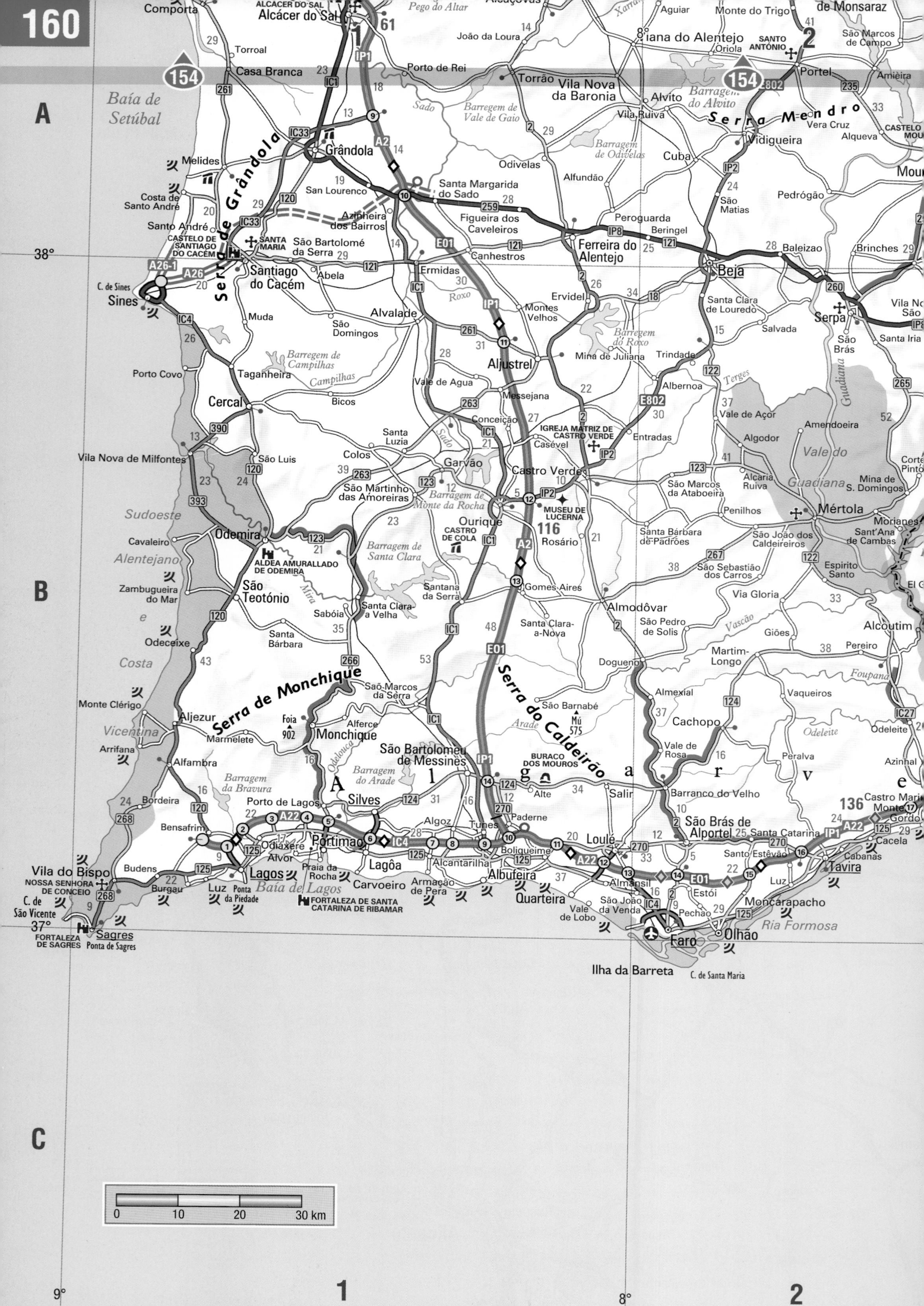
Comporta
ALCACER DO SAL
Alcácer do Sal
Pego do Altar
Aguiar
Monte do Trigo
de Monsaraz
Torroal
João da Loura
Viana do Alentejo
Oriola
SANTO ANTÓNIO
São Marcos de Campo
154
Casa Branca
Porto de Rei
Torrão
Vila Nova da Baronia
Alvito
Barragem do Alvito
Portel
Amieira
Baía de Setúbal
A
Sado
Barregem de Vale de Gaio
Vila Ruiva
Serra de Mendro
Vera Cruz
Alqueva
CASTELO
Grândola
Serra de Grândola
Barragem de Odivelas
Cuba
Vidigueira
Melides
Odivelas
Alfundão
Costa de Santo André
San Lourenço
Santa Margarida do Sado
Pedrógão
Santo André
Azinheira dos Bairros
Figueira dos Caveleiros
Peroguarda
Beringel
CASTELO DE SANTIAGO DO CACÉM
SANTA MARIA
São Bartolomé da Serra
Canhestros
Ferreira do Alentejo
Baleizao
Brinches
38°
Santiago do Cacém
Abela
Ermidas
Beja
C. de Sines
Sines
Roxo
Ervidel
Santa Clara de Louredo
Serpa
Muda
Alvalade
Montes Velhos
São Domingos
Barregem do Roxo
Salvada
São Brás
Santa Iria
Barregem de Campilhas
Aljustrel
Mina de Juliana
Trindade
Porto Covo
Taganheira
Campilhas
Vale de Agua
Albernoa
Terges
Guadiana
Cercal
Bicos
Messejana
Vale de Açor
Conceição
IGREJA MATRIZ DE CASTRO VERDE
Entradas
Amendoeira
Santa Luzia
Casével
Algodor
Vale do Guadiana
Vila Nova de Milfontes
São Luis
Colos
Garvão
Castro Verde
São Marcos da Ataboeira
Alcaria Ruiva
Corte Pinto
Mina de S. Domingos
São Martinho das Amoreiras
Barragem de Monte da Rocha
MUSEU DE LUCERNA
Sudoeste
Ourique
Penilhos
Mértola
Odemira
CASTRO DE COLA
Rosário
Santa Bárbara de Padrões
São João dos Caldeireiros
Sant'Ana de Cambas
Cavaleiro
Barragem de Santa Clara
Alentejano
ALDEA AMURALLADO DE ODEMIRA
São Sebastião dos Carros
Espirito Santo
B
Zambugueira do Mar
São Teotónio
Mira
Santana da Serra
Gomes Aires
Via Gloria
e
Sabóia
Santa Clara-a Velha
Almodôvar
São Pedro de Solis
Vascão
Alcoutim
Odeceixe
Santa Bárbara
Santa Clara-a-Nova
Gióes
Pereiro
Costa
Doguena
Martim-Longo
Foupana
Serra de Monchique
São Marcos da Serra
Serra do Caldeirão
Almexial
Vaqueiros
Monte Clérigo
Aljezur
Foia 902
São Barnabé
Mú 575
Cachopo
Vicentina
Marmelete
Alferce
Monchique
Arade
Odeleite
Arrifana
São Bartolomeu de Messines
Vale de Rosa
Peralva
Alfambra
Odelouca
BURACO DOS MOUROS
Azinhal
Barragem da Bravura
Barragem do Arade
Algarve
Bordeira
Porto de Lagos
Silves
Alte
Salir
Barranco do Velho
Castro Marim
Monte Gordo
Bensafrim
Algoz
Tunes
Paderne
São Brás de Alportel
Odiaxere
Portimão
Boliqueime
Loulé
Santa Catarina
Cacela
Alvor
Santo Estêvão
Cabanas
Vila do Bispo
Budens
Lagos
Praia da Rocha
Lagôa
Alcantarilha
Albufeira
Luz
Tavira
NOSSA SENHORA DE CONCEIO
Burgau
Baía de Lagos
Carvoeiro
Armação de Pera
Almansil
Estói
C. de São Vicente
Luz
Ponta da Piedade
FORTALEZA DE SANTA CATARINA DE RIBAMAR
Quarteira
São João da Venda
Moncarapacho
37°
Vale de Lobo
Pechão
Ria Formosa
FORTALEZA DE SAGRES
Sagres
Ponta de Sagres
Faro
Olhão
Ilha da Barreta
C. de Santa Maria
C
0
10
20
30 km
9°
1
8°
2

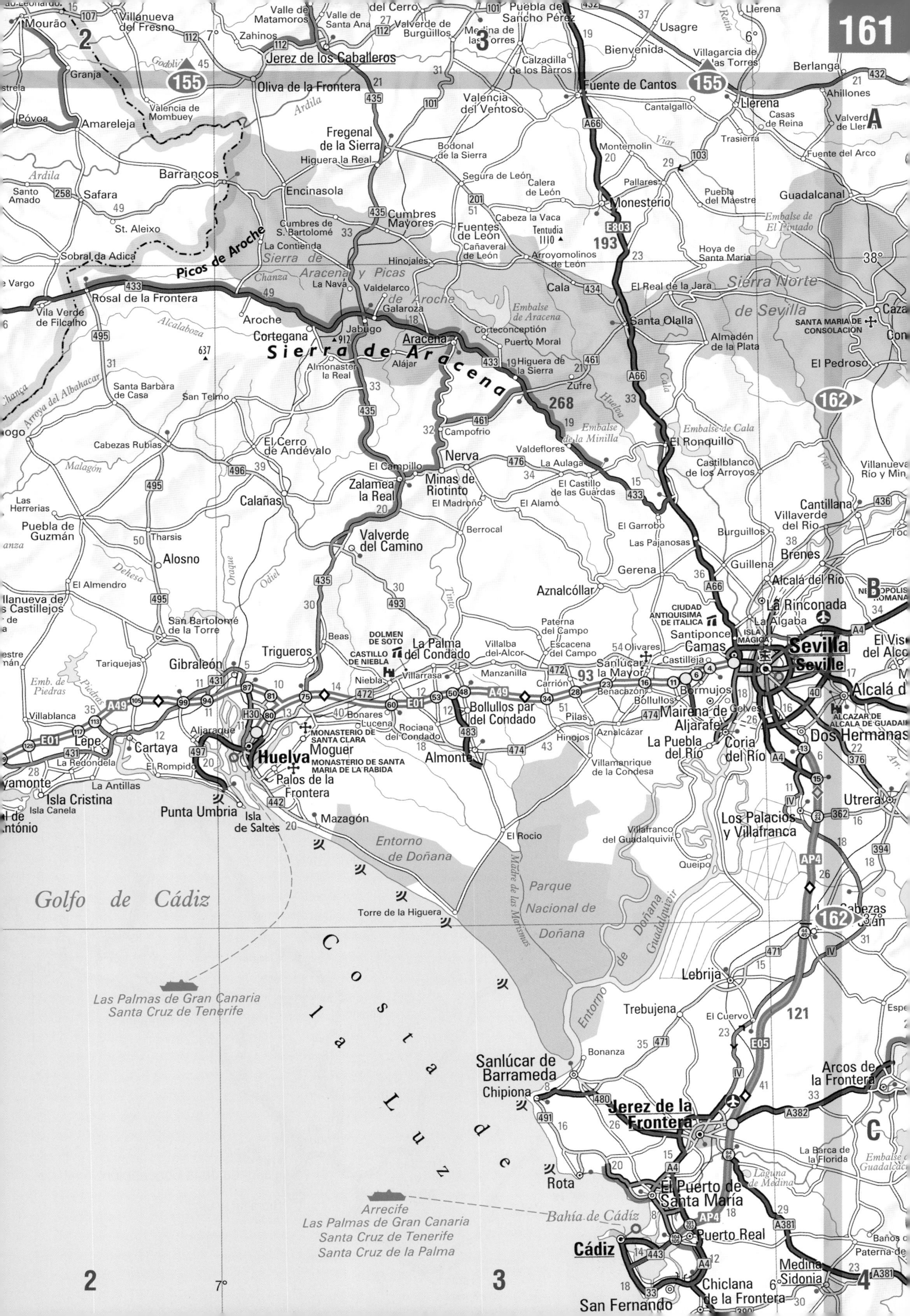

Jerez de los Caballeros
Oliva de la Frontera
Fregenal de la Sierra
Fuente de Cantos
Llerena
Monesterio
Sierra de Aracena
Picos de Aroche
Aracena
Rosal de la Frontera
Cortegana
Jabugo
Santa Olalla
Sierra Norte de Sevilla
Zalamea la Real
Minas de Riotinto
Nerva
Valverde del Camino
Calañas
Alosno
Huelva
Moguer
Palos de la Frontera
Punta Umbria
Lepe
Cartaya
Isla Cristina
La Palma del Condado
Almonte
Sevilla
Seville
Dos Hermanas
Utrera
Los Palacios y Villafranca
Lebrija
Golfo de Cádiz
Costa de la Luz
Entorno de Doñana
Parque Nacional de Doñana
Sanlúcar de Barrameda
Chipiona
Rota
Jerez de la Frontera
El Puerto de Santa María
Puerto Real
Cádiz
Bahía de Cádiz
San Fernando
Chiclana de la Frontera
Medina Sidonia
Arcos de la Frontera
Las Palmas de Gran Canaria
Santa Cruz de Tenerife
Arrecife
Santa Cruz de la Palma

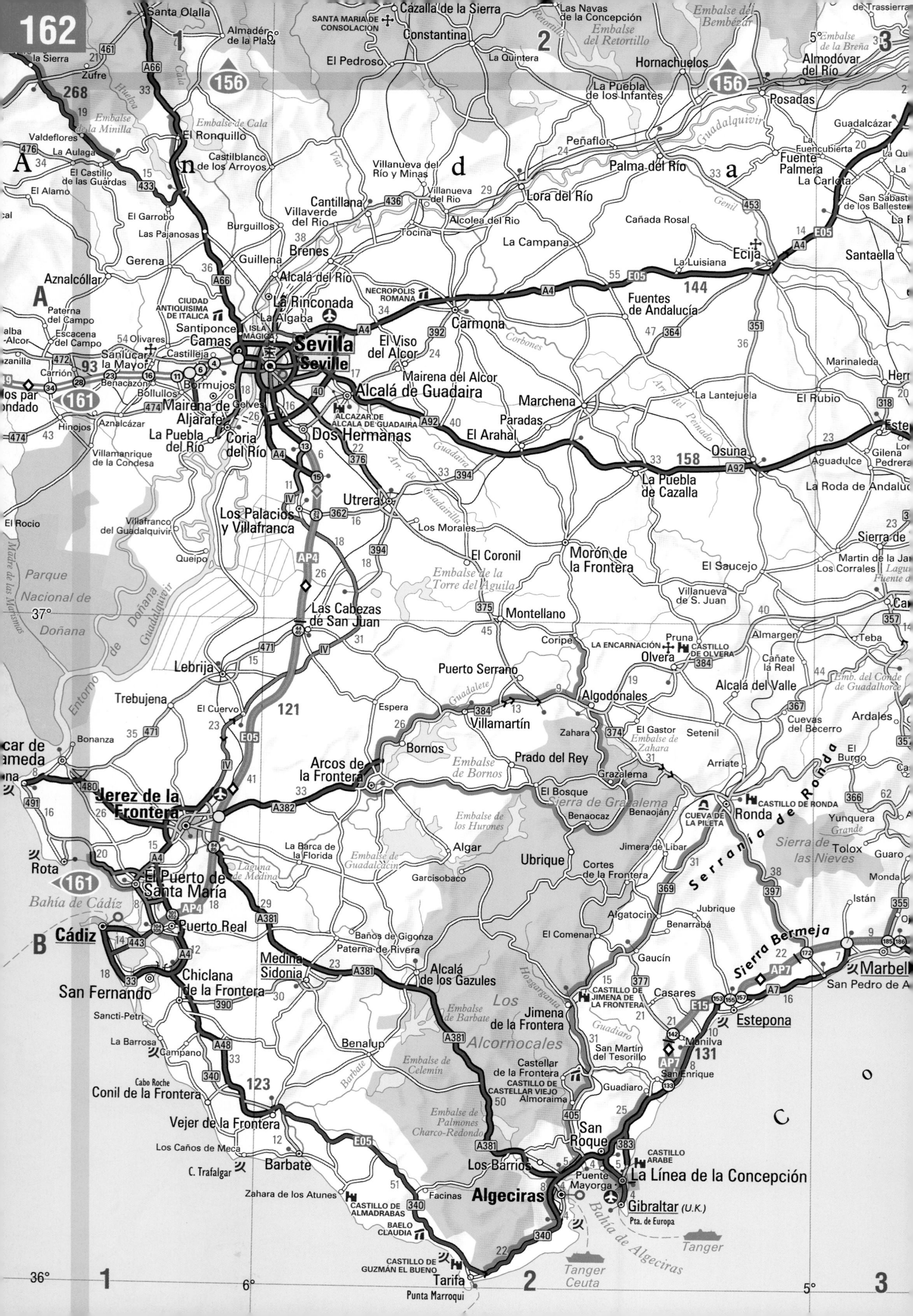
Santa Olalla
Almadén de la Plata
Cazalla de la Sierra
Las Navas de la Concepción
Embalse del Retortillo
Embalse del Bembézar
Constantina
El Pedroso
La Quintera
Hornachuelos
Almodóvar del Río
Zufre
La Puebla de los Infantes
Posadas
Embalse de la Minilla
Embalse de Cala
El Ronquillo
Peñaflor
Guadalcázar
Valdeflores
La Aulaga
Castilblanco de los Arroyos
Villanueva del Río y Minas
Palma del Río
Fuente Palmera
La Carlota
El Castillo de las Guardas
El Alamo
Villanueva del Río
Lora del Río
Cantillana
Villaverde del Río
Alcolea del Río
El Garrobo
Las Pajanosas
Burguillos
Tocina
Cañada Rosal
La Campana
Ecija
Santaella
Gerena
Guillena
Brenes
Alcalá del Río
La Luisiana
Aznalcóllar
Ciudad Antiquísima de Itálica
La Rinconada
Necropolis Romana
Carmona
Fuentes de Andalucía
Paterna del Campo
Escacena del Campo
La Algaba
Santiponce
Isla Mágica
Olivares
Camas
Sevilla
Seville
El Viso del Alcor
Sanlúcar la Mayor
Castilleja
Carrión
Benacazón
Bormujos
Bollullos
Mairena del Alcor
Alcalá de Guadaira
Marchena
Marinaleda
La Lantejuela
El Rubio
Mairena de Aljarafe
Gelves
Alcázar de Alcalá de Guadaira
Paradas
El Arahal
Hinojos
Aznalcázar
La Puebla del Río
Coria del Río
Dos Hermanas
Osuna
Aguadulce
Gilena
Villamanrique de la Condesa
La Puebla de Cazalla
La Roda de Andalucía
Utrera
El Rocío
Los Palacios y Villafranca
Villafranco del Guadalquivir
Los Morales
Queipo
El Coronil
Morón de la Frontera
El Saucejo
Los Corrales
Parque Nacional de Doñana
Entorno de Doñana
Embalse de la Torre del Aguila
Villanueva de S. Juan
Las Cabezas de San Juan
Montellano
Coripe
Pruna
La Encarnación
Castillo de Olvera
Olvera
Almargen
Teba
Cañate la Real
Lebrija
Puerto Serrano
Alcalá del Valle
Trebujena
El Cuervo
Espera
Algodonales
Villamartín
Zahara
El Gastor
Setenil
Cuevas del Becerro
Ardales
Bonanza
Bornos
Embalse de Bornos
Prado del Rey
Embalse de Zahara
Arriate
El Burgo
Arcos de la Frontera
Grazalema
Jerez de la Frontera
El Bosque
Sierra de Grazalema
Benaocaz
Benaoján
Cueva de la Pileta
Ronda
Castillo de Ronda
Serranía de Ronda
Yunquera
Embalse de los Hurones
Jimera de Líbar
Sierra de las Nieves
Tolox
Guaro
Rota
La Barca de la Florida
Algar
Ubrique
Cortes de la Frontera
Monda
El Puerto de Santa María
Laguna de Medina
Embalse de Guadalcacín
Garcisobaco
Bahía de Cádiz
Jubrique
Istán
Cádiz
Puerto Real
Algatocín
Benarrabá
El Comenar
Sierra Bermeja
Baños de Gigonza
Paterna de Rivera
Medina Sidonia
Alcalá de los Gazules
Gaucín
Marbella
San Fernando
Chiclana de la Frontera
Castillo de Jimena de la Frontera
Casares
San Pedro de Alcántara
Sancti-Petri
Los Alcornocales
Jimena de la Frontera
Estepona
La Barrosa
Campano
Embalse de Barbate
Manilva
Benalup
San Martín del Tesorillo
Cabo Roche
Embalse de Celemín
Castellar de la Frontera
San Enrique
Conil de la Frontera
Castillo de Castellar Viejo
Almoraima
Guadiaro
Vejer de la Frontera
Embalse de Palmones
Charco-Redondo
San Roque
Los Caños de Meca
Castillo Arabe
Barbate
C. Trafalgar
Los Barrios
La Línea de la Concepción
Puente Mayorga
Zahara de los Atunes
Castillo de Almadrabas
Facinas
Algeciras
Gibraltar (U.K.)
Pta. de Europa
Baelo Claudia
Bahía de Algeciras
Tanger
Castillo de Guzmán el Bueno
Tarifa
Tanger Ceuta
Punta Marroquí

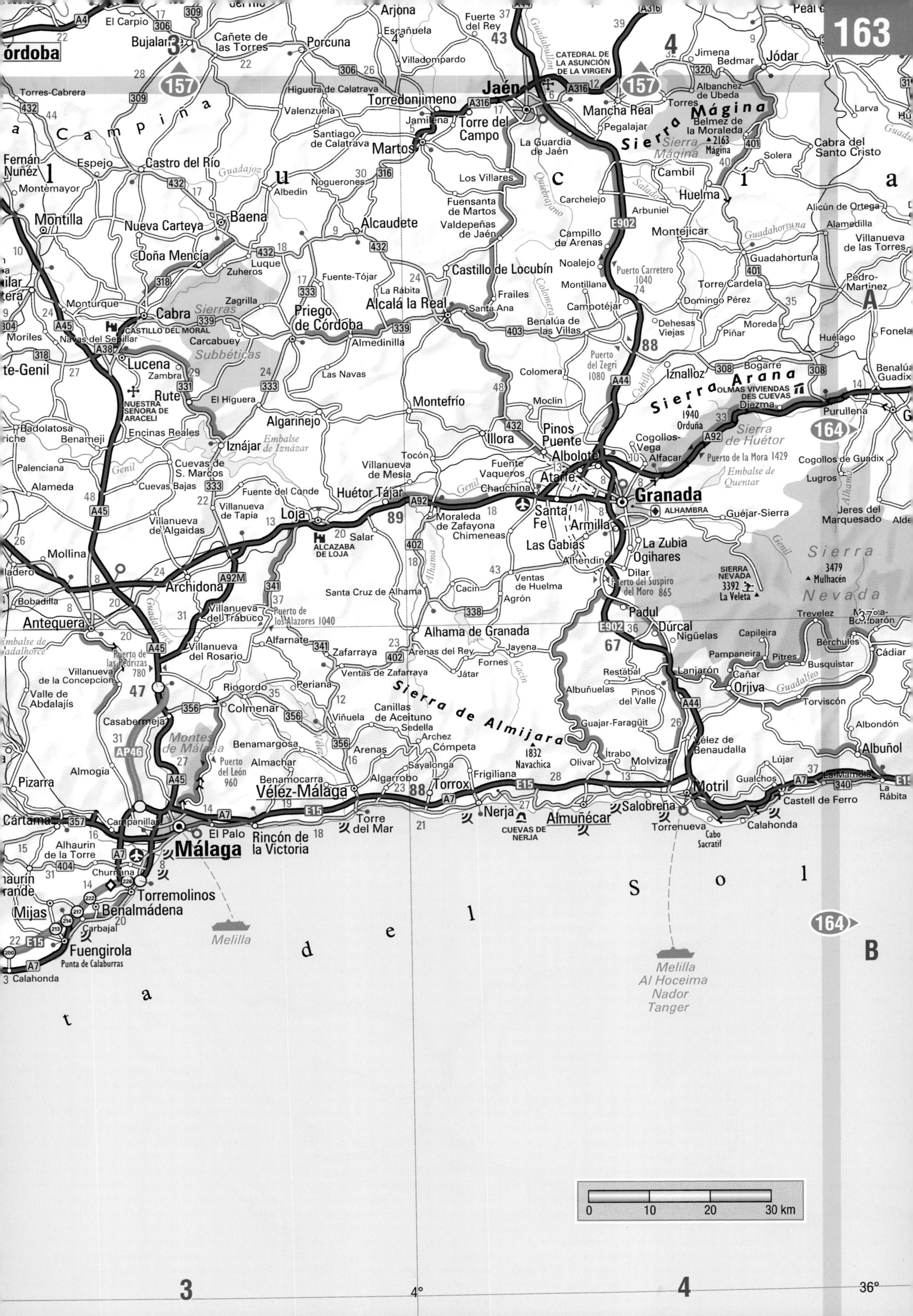
163
Córdoba
El Carpio
Bujalance
Cañete de las Torres
Porcuna
Arjona
Escañuela
Villardompardo
Fuerte del Rey
Jaén
CATEDRAL DE LA ASUNCIÓN DE LA VIRGEN
Jimena
Bedmar
Jódar
Torres-Cabrera
Campiña
Higuera de Calatrava
Torredonjimeno
Valenzuela
Jamilena
Torre del Campo
Santiago de Calatrava
Martos
Mancha Real
Pegalajar
Albanchez de Ubeda
Torres
Sierra Mágina
Belmez de la Moraleda
Mágina
2163
Larva
Cabra del Santo Cristo
Solera
La Guardia de Jaén
Fernán Nuñez
Espejo
Castro del Río
Guadajoz
Montemayor
Noguerones
Albedin
Los Villares
Cambil
Huelma
Carchelejo
Arbuniel
Alicún de Ortega
Alamedilla
Villanueva de las Torres
Montilla
Nueva Carteya
Baena
Alcaudete
Fuensanta de Martos
Valdepeñas de Jaén
Campillo de Arenas
Montejícar
Guadahortuna
Doña Mencía
Luque
Zuheros
Castillo de Locubín
Noalejo
Puerto Carretero 1040
Torre Cardela
Pedro-Martinez
Fuente-Tójar
La Rábita
Montillana
Frailes
Domingo Pérez
Monturque
Cabra
Sierras Subbéticas
Zagrilla
Priego de Córdoba
Alcalá la Real
Santa Ana
Campotéjar
Dehesas Viejas
Moreda
Fonela
CASTILLO DEL MORAL
Carcabuey
Almedinilla
Benalúa de las Villas
Piñar
Huélago
Moriles
Navas del Selpillar
Lucena
Zambra
Las Navas
Puerto del Zegri 1080
Colomera
Iznalloz
Bogarre
Benalúa
Guadix
Rute
NUESTRA SEÑORA DE ARACELI
El Higuera
Montefrío
Moclín
Sierra Arana
OLMAS VIVIENDAS DES CUEVAS
Diezma
Purullena
1940
Orduña
Badolatosa
Benameji
Encinas Reales
Algarinejo
Illora
Pinos Puente
Cogollos-Vega
Alfacar
Sierra de Huétor
Iznájar
Embalse de Iznázar
Tocón
Albolote
Puerto de la Mora 1429
Cogollos de Guadix
Palenciana
Cuevas de S. Marcos
Villanueva de Mesia
Fuente Vaqueros
Atarfe
Embalse de Quentar
Lugros
Alameda
Cuevas Bajas
Fuente del Conde
Huétor Tájar
Chauchina
Granada
ALHAMBRA
Villanueva de Tapia
Loja
Moraleda de Zafayona
Chimeneas
Santa Fe
Armilla
Güéjar-Sierra
Jeres del Marquesado
Villanueva de Algaidas
Salar
ALCAZABA DE LOJA
Las Gabias
La Zubia
Ogíhares
Alhendín
Mollina
Archidona
Cacín
Ventas de Huelma
Dilar
Puerto del Suspiro del Moro 865
SIERRA NEVADA
3392
La Veleta
3479
Mulhacén
Sierra Nevada
Bobadilla
Santa Cruz de Alhama
Agrón
Villanueva del Trabuco
Puerto de los Alazores 1040
Padul
Antequera
Embalse de Guadalhorce
Alhama de Granada
Dúrcal
Nigüelas
Capileira
Trevelez
Bérchules
Cádiar
Villanueva del Rosario
Alfarnate
Zafarraya
Arenas del Rey
Jayena
Fornes
Pampaneira
Pitres
Busquistar
Puerto de las Pedrizas 780
Villanueva de la Concepcion
Ventas de Zafarraya
Játar
Restábal
Lanjarón
Cañar
Orjiva
Sierra de Almijara
Valle de Abdalajís
Riogordo
Periana
Albuñuelas
Pinos del Valle
Torviscón
Colmenar
Canillas de Aceituno
Viñuela
Sedella
Guajar-Faragüit
Casabermeja
Archez
Cómpeta
Albondón
Montes de Málaga
Benamargosa
Arenas
1832
Navachica
Vélez de Benaudalla
Albuñol
Puerto del León 960
Almachar
Sayalonga
Ítrabo
Molvizar
Lújar
Almogia
Olivar
Pizarra
Benamocarra
Algarrobo
Torrox
Frigiliana
Motril
Gualchos
La Mamola
La Rábita
Vélez-Málaga
Castell de Ferro
Cártama
Campanillas
Nerja
Almuñécar
Salobreña
Torre del Mar
CUEVAS DE NERJA
Torrenueva
Calahonda
Alhaurin de la Torre
El Palo
Rincón de la Victoria
Cabo Sacratif
Málaga
Churriana
Torremolinos
Benalmádena
Mijas
Carbajal
Fuengirola
Punta de Calaburras
Calahonda
Melilla
Melilla
Al Hoceima
Nador
Tanger
Costa del Sol
164
0
10
20
30 km
3
4°
4
36°
A
B

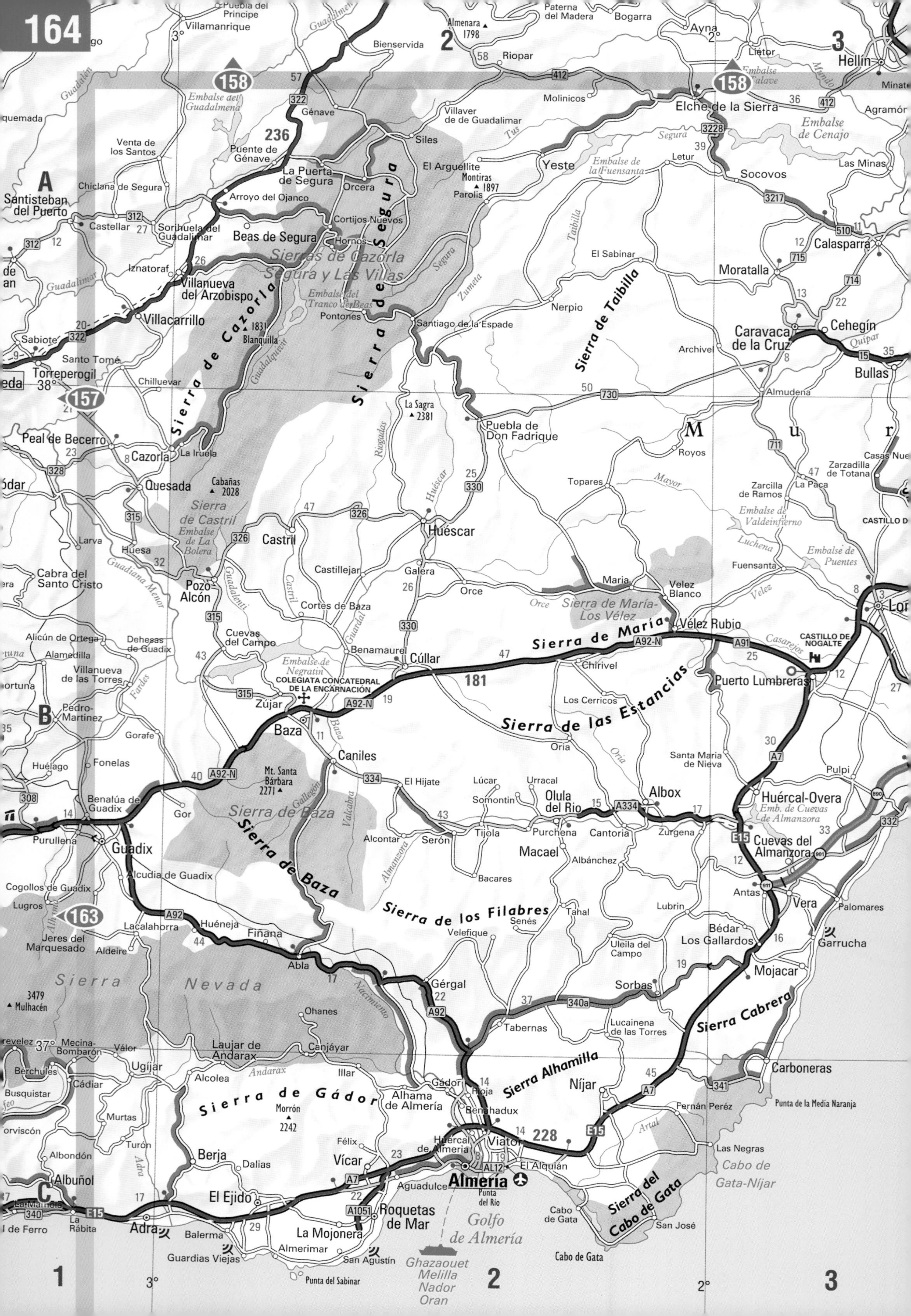
158
157
163
A
B
C
1
2
3
Villamanrique
Bienservida
Almenara 1798
Riopar
Paterna del Madera
Bogarra
Ayna
Liétor
Hellín
Génave
Villaver de de Guadalimar
Molinicos
Elche de la Sierra
Agramón
Embalse de Cenajo
Embalse del Guadalmena
Venta de los Santos
Puente de Génave
Siles
La Puerta de Segura
Orcera
El Arguellite
Montiras 1897
Parolis
Yeste
Embalse de la Fuensanta
Letur
Socovos
Las Minas
Santisteban del Puerto
Chiclana de Segura
Arroyo del Ojanco
Castellar
Sorihuela del Guadalimar
Cortijos Nuevos
Beas de Segura
Hornos
Sierras de Cazorla Segura y Las Villas
Sierra de Segura
Calasparra
Moratalla
Iznatoraf
Villanueva del Arzobispo
Embalse del Tranco de Beas
Pontones
Santiago de la Espade
El Sabinar
Nerpio
Sierra de Taibilla
Caravaca de la Cruz
Cehegín
Archivel
Bullas
Villacarrillo
Sierra de Cazorla
1831 Blanquilla
Sabiote
Santo Tomé
Torreperogil
Chilluevar
La Sagra 2381
Almudena
Puebla de Don Fadrique
Murcia
Peal de Becerro
Cazorla
La Iruela
Royos
Quesada
Cabañas 2028
Topares
Zarcilla de Ramos
La Paca
Zarzadilla de Totana
Sierra de Castril
Embalse de La Bolera
Huéscar
Castril
Embalse de Valdeinfierno
CASTILLO D
Larva
Huesa
Castillejar
Galera
Orce
Fuensanta
Embalse de Puentes
Cabra del Santo Cristo
Pozo-Alcón
Cortes de Baza
Maria
Velez Blanco
Sierra de María-Los Vélez
Lorca
Alicún de Ortega
Dehesas de Guadix
Cuevas del Campo
Vélez Rubio
Alamedilla
Villanueva de las Torres
Benamaurel
Cúllar
Sierra de María
CASTILLO DE NOGALTE
Embalse de Negratín
COLEGIATA CONCATEDRAL DE LA ENCARNACIÓN
Chirivel
Puerto Lumbreras
Zújar
Los Cerricos
Sierra de las Estancias
Pedro-Martinez
Baza
Gorafe
Oria
Caniles
Huélago
Fonelas
Mt. Santa Bárbara 2271
Santa Maria de Nieva
Pulpí
Benalúa de Guadix
El Hijate
Lúcar
Urracal
Somontín
Olula del Río
Albox
Huércal-Overa
Emb. de Cuevas de Almanzora
Gor
Sierra de Baza
Purullena
Guadix
Alcontar
Serón
Tíjola
Purchena
Cantoria
Zurgena
Cuevas del Almanzora
Macael
Albánchez
Alcudia de Guadix
Bacares
Antas
Vera
Palomares
Cogollos de Guadix
Lugros
Sierra de Baza
Sierra de los Filabres
Tahal
Lubrín
Senés
Bédar
Los Gallardos
Garrucha
Lacalahorra
Huéneja
Fiñana
Velefique
Jeres del Marquesado
Aldeire
Uleila del Campo
Abla
Mojacar
Sierra Nevada
Gérgal
Sorbas
3479 Mulhacén
Ohanes
Tabernas
Lucainena de las Torres
Sierra Cabrera
Mecina-Bombarón
Válor
Laujar de Andarax
Canjáyar
Carboneras
Bérchules
Ugíjar
Alcolea
Illar
Sierra Alhamilla
Cádiar
Gádor
Rioja
Níjar
Busquistar
Sierra de Gádor
Alhama de Almería
Punta de la Media Naranja
Morrón 2242
Benahadux
Fernán Peréz
Murtas
Turón
Félix
Huércal de Almería
Viator
Las Negras
Albondón
Berja
Dalias
Vícar
El Alquián
Cabo de Gata-Níjar
Albuñol
Almería
Punta del Río
El Ejido
Aguadulce
Roquetas de Mar
Cabo de Gata
Sierra del Cabo de Gata
San José
La Rábita
Adra
Balerma
La Mojonera
Golfo de Almería
Guardias Viejas
Almerimar
San Agustín
Cabo de Gata
Ghazaouet Melilla Nador Oran
Punta del Sabinar
A92-N
A92
A91
A7
E15
AL12
A1051
181
228
236

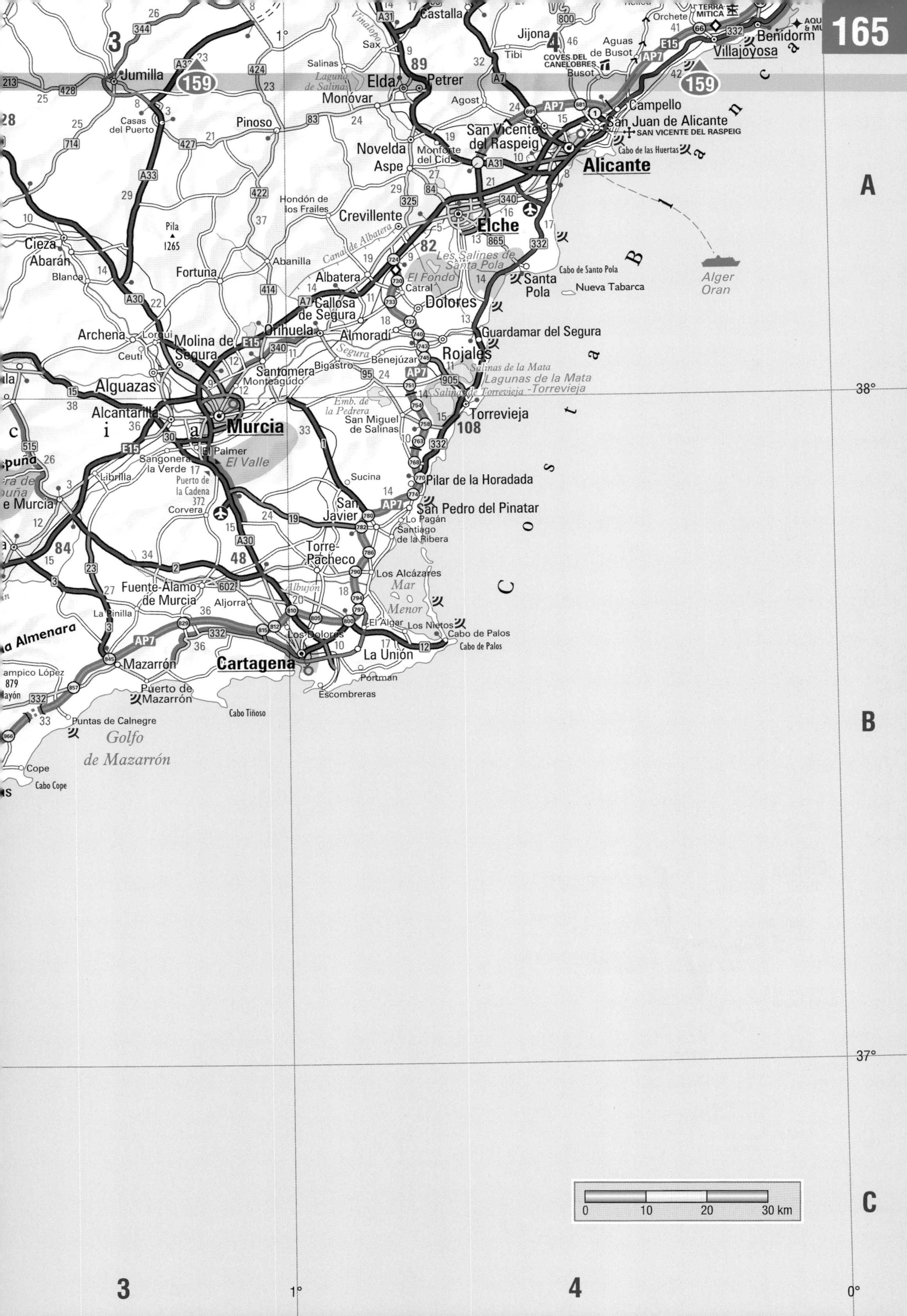
Jumilla
Castalla
Jijona
Tibi
Aguas de Busot
Busot
COVES DEL CANELOBRES
Orchete
TERRA MITICA
Benidorm
Villajoyosa
Sax
Salinas
Laguna de Salinas
Elda
Petrer
Monóvar
Agost
Campello
San Juan de Alicante
SAN VICENTE DEL RASPEIG
San Vicente del Raspeig
Cabo de las Huertas
Alicante
Casas del Puerto
Pinoso
Novelda
Monforte del Cid
Aspe
Hondón de los Frailes
Crevillente
Elche
Pila
1265
Cieza
Abarán
Blanca
Fortuna
Abanilla
Canal de Albatera
Albatera
Les Salines de Santa Pola
El Fondo
Catral
Santa Pola
Cabo de Santo Pola
Nueva Tabarca
Alger
Oran
Callosa de Segura
Dolores
Archena
Lorquí
Ceutí
Molina de Segura
Orihuela
Almoradí
Guardamar del Segura
Santomera
Bigastro
Benejúzar
Segura
Rojales
Salinas de la Mata
Lagunas de la Mata
Salinas de Torrevieja
-Torrevieja
Alguazas
Monteagudo
Alcantarilla
Murcia
Emb. de la Pedrera
San Miguel de Salinas
Torrevieja
El Palmer
Sangonera la Verde
El Valle
Librilla
Puerto de la Cadena
372
Corvera
Sucina
Pilar de la Horadada
San Javier
San Pedro del Pinatar
Lo Pagán
Santiago de la Ribera
Torre-Pacheco
Los Alcázares
Mar Menor
Fuente-Álamo de Murcia
Albujón
Aljorra
La Pinilla
El Algar
Los Nietos
Cabo de Palos
Los Dolores
La Unión
Cartagena
Mazarrón
Portman
Escombreras
Puerto de Mazarrón
Cabo Tiñoso
Puntas de Calnegre
Golfo de Mazarrón
Cope
Cabo Cope
Almenara
Costa Blanca
38°
37°
1°
0°
A
B
C
0
10
20
30 km
3
4

A

B

C

1

2°

2

40°

40°

39°

Islas
Columbretes
(España)
(Spain)

*Islas
Columbretes*

1°

ISLAS
BALEARES

BALEARIC
ISLANDS

Port de Sóller

Deia

Valldemossa

Banyalbufar   Esporles

Estellencs   39

Puigpunyent   Mar

25

11

12

Sa Dragonera   Andratx   **Palma de
Mallorca**   4

Port d'Andratx   Calvià   6

Barcelona   10   Peguera   15   13   MA1   12

1714   **Palma
Nova**   Can
Pastilla

Santa Ponça   Magaluf   S'Arer

Cap Enderrocat

Cap de Cala Figuera   *Bahía
de Palma*

Valencia   *Maó*

*Eivissa
Denia*   **Mallorca**
Majorca

Portinatx

Eivissa
Ibiza   8   Sant Joan Baptista
          Pta. Grossa

Sant Miquel   12   Sant Carlos

Santa Agnès   733   Tagomago

**Sant Antoni
de Portmany**   6   Es Caná

Sant
Rafel   16   **Santa Eulàlia des Riu**

731   11   Cala Llonga

**Sant Josep
de sa Talaia**   8   *Palma de Mallorca
Barcelona*

20   **Eivissa**
          Ibiza

Es Vedrà   Cap
Llentrisca   Sant Francesc
de ses Salines

*Denia
Valencia*   Punta Portás

S'Espardell

S'Espalmador

Formentera   Es Pujols
          Sa Savina

Sant Francesc de
Formentera   Sant Ferran

Nuestra Señora
Sa Verge des Pilar

C. de Barbària   Pta. Rotja

1

2°

2

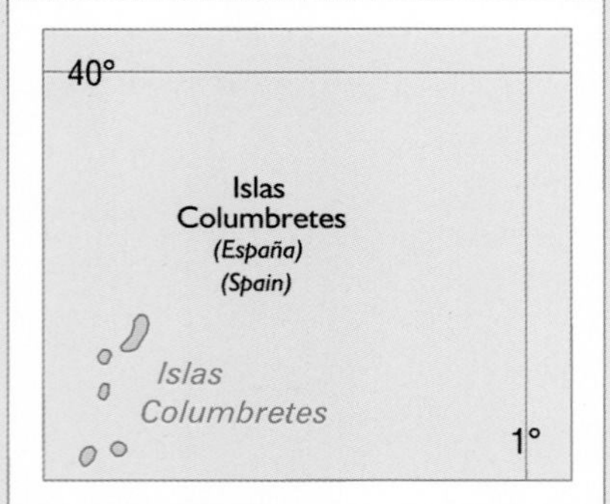

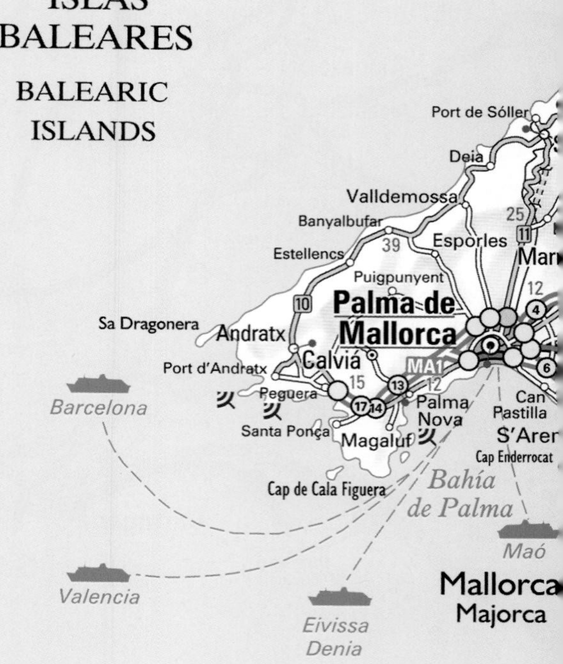

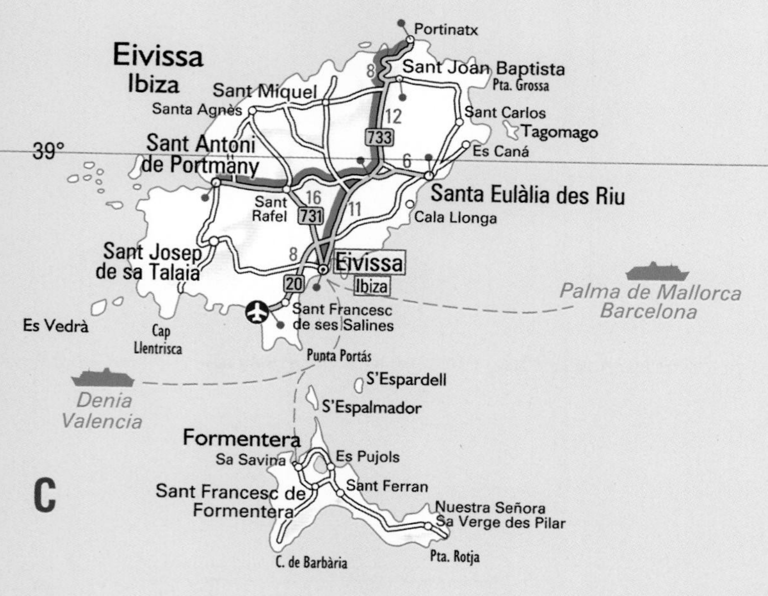

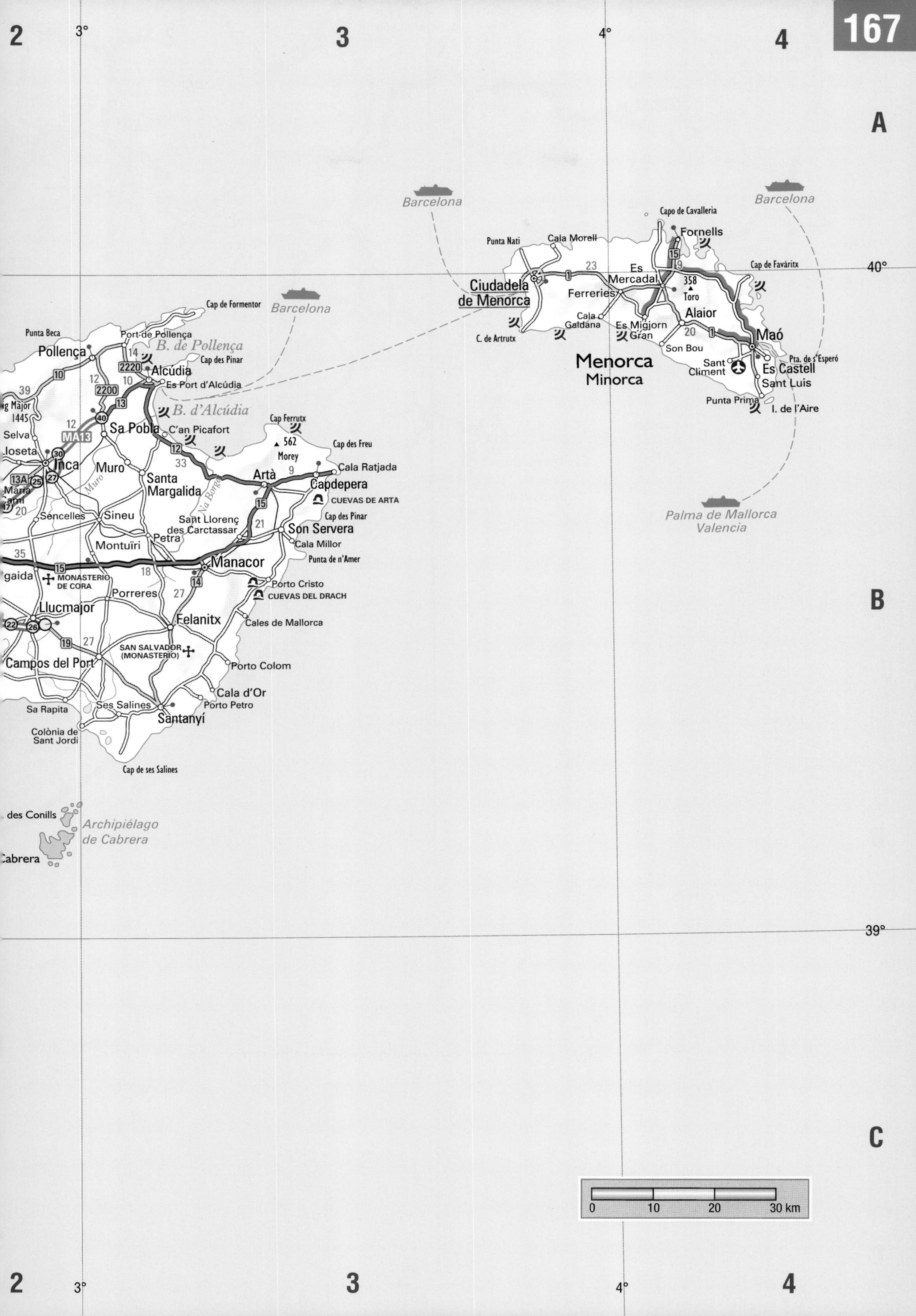

2   3°   3   4°   4

A

40°

B

39°

C

Barcelona

Barcelona

Cap de Formentor   Barcelona

Punta Nati   Cala Morell   Capo de Cavalleria   Fornells   Cap de Favàritx

Ciudadela de Menorca   Es Mercadal   358 Toro   Alaior   Maó   Cap de Favàritx

Ferreries   Es Migjorn Gran   Son Bou   Pta. de s'Esperó

C. de Artrutx   Cala Galdana   Menorca   Alaior   Maó   Es Castell

Menorca   Minorca   Sant Climent   Sant Luis

Punta Prima   I. de l'Aire

Palma de Mallorca   Valencia

Punta Beca   Port de Pollença   B. de Pollença   Cap des Pinar

Pollença   14   Alcúdia   2220

10   12   2200   10   Es Port d'Alcúdia

39   13   B. d'Alcúdia   Cap Ferrutx

g Major 1445   12   40   Sa Pobla   C'an Picafort   562 Morey   Cap des Freu

Selva   MA13   33   Cala Ratjada

Ioseta   30   Inca   Muro   Santa Margalida   Artà   9   Capdepera

13A   25   27   Sineu   Sant Llorenç des Carctassar   21   CUEVAS DE ARTA

Mària   20   Séncelles   Petra   Son Servera   Cap des Pinar

17   35   15   Montuïri   Manacor   Cala Millor

gaida   MONASTERIO DE CORA   18   14   Punta de n'Amer

Porreres   27   Porto Cristo

Llucmajor   Felanitx   CUEVAS DEL DRACH

22   26   19   27   SAN SALVADOR (MONASTERIO)   Cales de Mallorca

Campos del Port   Porto Colom

Sa Rapita   Ses Salines   Cala d'Or   Porto Petro

Colònia de Sant Jordi   Santanyí

Cap de ses Salines

des Conills   Archipiélago de Cabrera

Cabrera

0   10   20   30 km

2   3°   3   4°   4

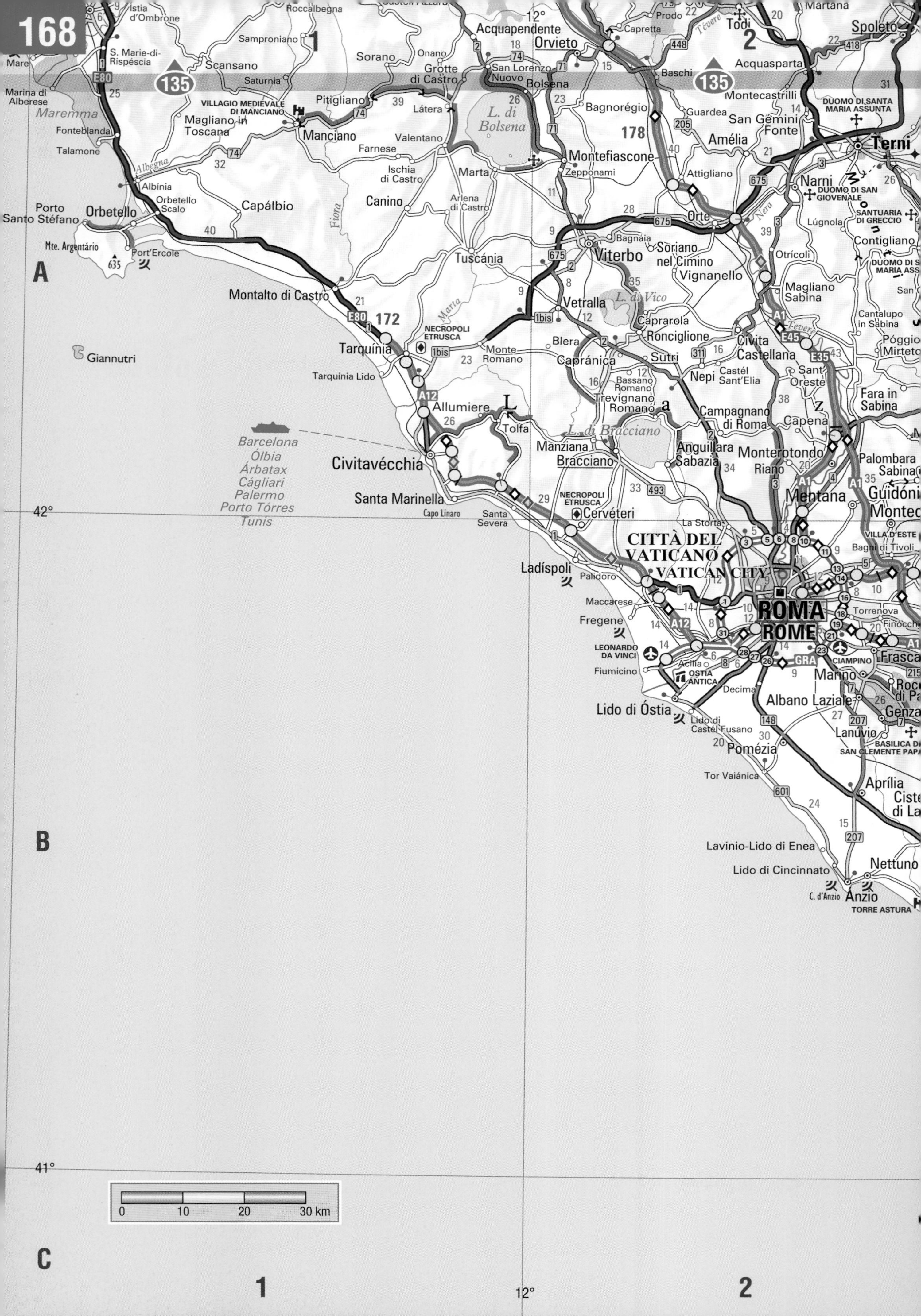

Roma
Rome
Città del Vaticano
Vatican City
Civitavécchia
Viterbo
Orvieto
Terni
Spoleto
Todi
Tarquínia
Orbetello
Porto Santo Stéfano
Montalto di Castro
Tuscánia
Bolsena
L. di Bolsena
L. di Vico
L. di Bracciano
Montefiascone
Bracciano
Cervéteri
Ladíspoli
Fiumicino
Lido di Óstia
Ostia Antica
Pomézia
Aprília
Anzio
Nettuno
Albano Laziale
Frascati
Guidónia
Mentana
Monterotondo
Civita Castellana
Narni
Orte
Amélia
Acquapendente
Pitigliano
Manciano
Sorano
Scansano
Capálbio
Canino
Santa Marinella
Allumiere
Tolfa
Barcelona
Ólbia
Árbatax
Cágliari
Palermo
Porto Tórres
Tunis
Giannutri
Mte. Argentário
Leonardo da Vinci
Ciampino
Necropoli Etrusca
Villaggio Medievale di Manciano
Duomo di Santa Maria Assunta
Duomo di San Giovenale
Santuario di Greccio
Basilica di San Clemente Papa
42°
41°
12°
A
B
C
1
2
0
10
20
30 km

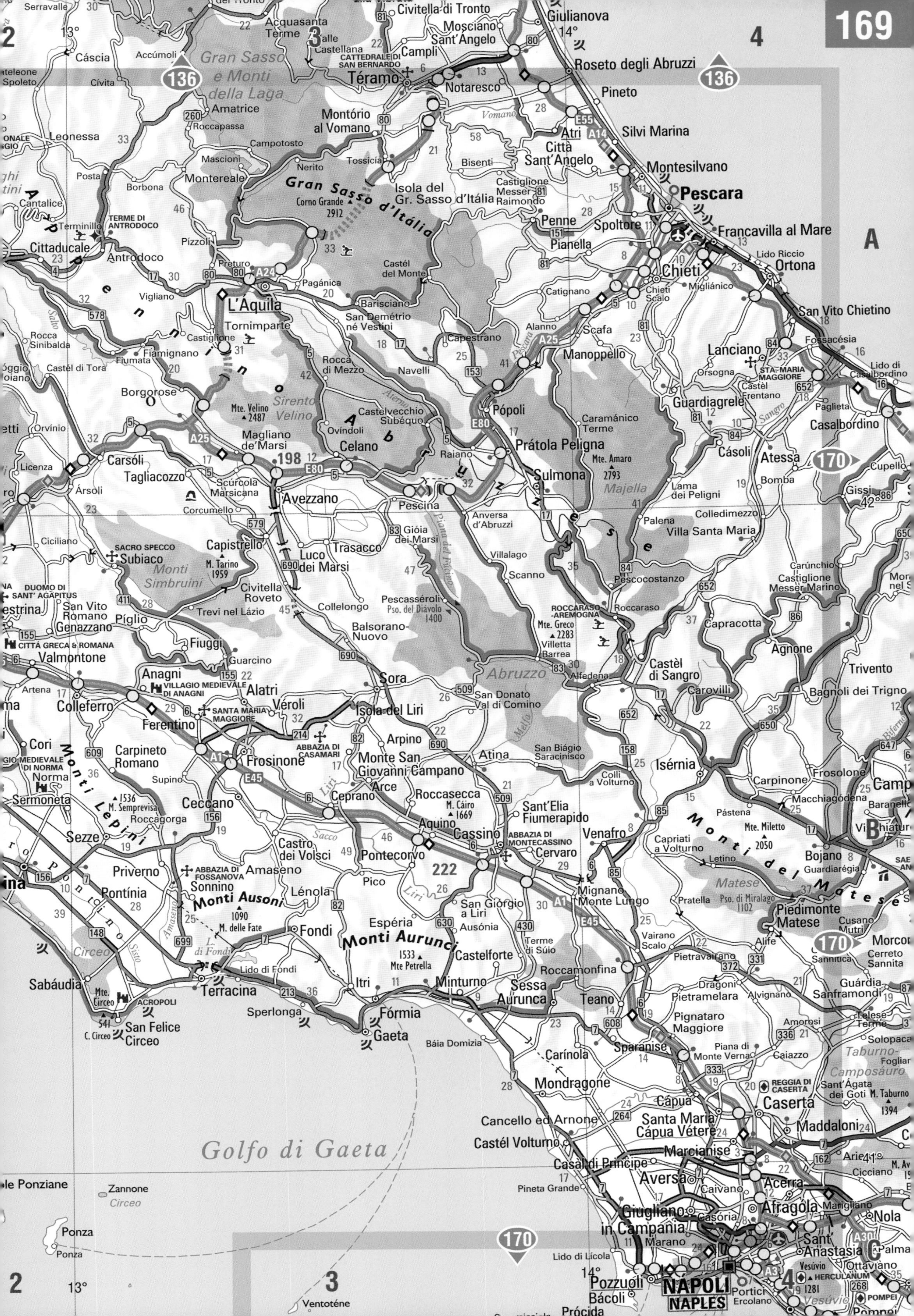
Gran Sasso e Monti della Laga
Téramo
Giulianova
Roseto degli Abruzzi
Pineto
Silvi Marina
Montesilvano
Pescara
Francavilla al Mare
Ortona
Chieti
Lanciano
San Vito Chietino
Vasto
Casalbordino
Atessa
Gran Sasso d'Itália
Corno Grande 2912
L'Aquila
Amatrice
Leonessa
Cittaducale
Antrodoco
Campotosto
Montereale
Sulmona
Pópoli
Prátola Peligna
Majella
Mte. Amaro 2793
Avezzano
Celano
Tagliacozzo
Carsóli
Mte. Velino 2487
Sirento Velino
Subiaco
Monti Simbruini
Abruzzo
Scanno
Roccaraso
Castèl di Sangro
Agnone
Isérnia
Sora
Frosinone
Anagni
Fiuggi
Valmontone
Colleferro
Ferentino
Alatri
Véroli
Isola del Liri
Cassino
Aquino
Pontecorvo
Ceprano
Ceccano
Monti Lepini
Monti Ausoni
Monti Aurunci
Sezze
Priverno
Pontínia
Sabáudia
Terracina
Fondi
Sperlonga
Gaeta
Fórmia
Minturno
Sessa Aurunca
Teano
Venafro
Monti del Matese
Piedimonte Matese
Mondragone
Cápua
Caserta
Maddaloni
Santa Maria Cápua Vétere
Marcianise
Aversa
Afragola
Giugliano in Campania
Pozzuoli
Bácoli
NAPOLI NAPLES
Nola
Vesúvio 1281
Golfo di Gaeta
Ponza
Zannone
Ventoténe
Circeo
San Felice Circeo
Próchida
136
170
A
B
C
2
3
4
13°
14°
42°
41°

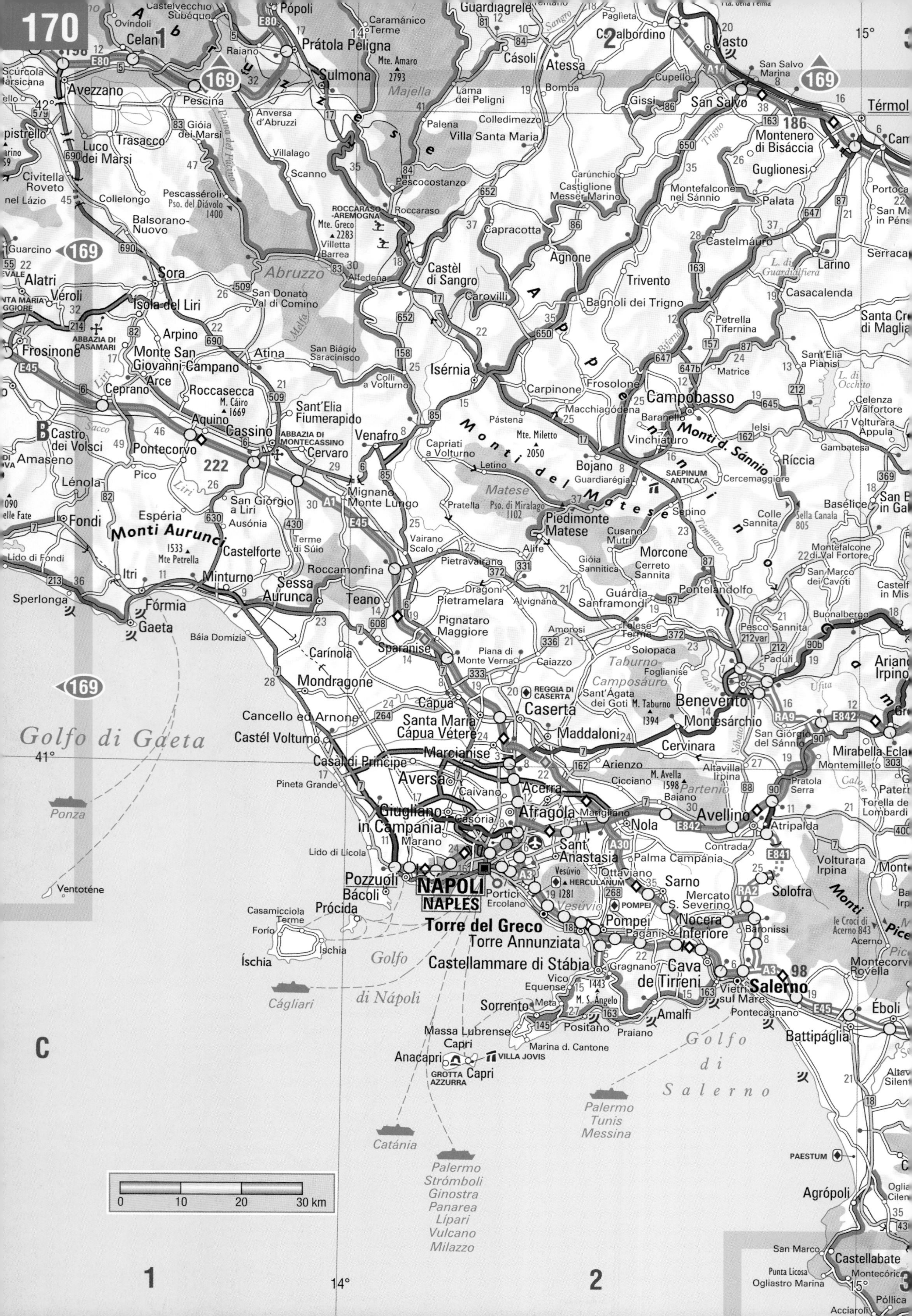
Castelvecchio Subéquo
Ovíndoli
Celano
Pópoli
Prátola Peligna
Caramánico Terme
Guardiagrele
Paglieta
Casalbordino
Vasto
Raiano
Sulmona
Mte. Amaro 2793
Majella
Cásoli
Atessa
Bomba
San Salvo Marina
Scúrcola Marsicana
Avezzano
Pescina
Gióia dei Marsi
Anversa d'Abruzzi
Lama dei Peligni
Colledimezzo
Palena
Villa Santa Maria
Cupello
Gissi
San Salvo
Térmoli
Luco dei Marsi
Trasacco
Civitella Roveto
Villalago
Scanno
Pescocostanzo
Montenero di Bisáccia
Guglionesi
Pescasséroli
Pso. del Diávolo 1400
Collelongo
Balsorano-Nuovo
ROCCARASO-AREMOGNA
Mte. Greco 2283
Villetta Barrea
Roccaraso
Capracotta
Carúnchio
Castiglione Messer Marino
Montefalcone nel Sánnio
Palata
Castelmáuro
Larino
Serracapriola
Guarcino
Alatri
Véroli
Sora
Abruzzo
Alfedena
Castèl di Sangro
Agnone
Trivento
L. di Guardialfiera
Casacalenda
Isola del Liri
San Donato Val di Comino
Carovilli
Bagnoli dei Trigno
ABBAZIA DI CASAMARI
Frosinone
Arpino
Monte San Giovanni Campano
Arce
Atina
San Biágio Saracinisco
Melfa
Isérnia
Petrella Tifernina
Santa Croce di Magliano
Sant'Elia a Pianisi
Matrice
L. di Occhito
Ceprano
Roccasecca
M. Cáiro 1669
Sant'Elia Fiumerapido
Colli a Volturno
Carpinone
Frosolone
Campobasso
Celenza Valfortore
Volturara Appula
Liri
Sacco
Castro dei Volsci
Amaseno
Aquino
Cassino
ABBAZIA DI MONTECASSINO
Cervaro
Pontecorvo
Venafro
Pástena
Mte. Miletto 2050
Macchiagódena
Baranello
Vinchiaturo
Monti d. Sánnio
Iélsi
Gambatesa
Ríccia
Lénola
Pico
Capriati a Volturno
Letino
Monti del Matese
Bojano
Guardiarégia
SAEPINUM ANTICA
Cercemaggiore
Mignano Monte Lungo
San Giórgio a Liri
Ausónia
Espéria
Fondi
Monti Aurunci
Mte Petrella 1533
Castelforte
Terme di Súio
Pratella
Matese
Pso. di Miralago 1102
Piedimonte Matese
Cusano Mutri
Sepino
Colle Sannita
Sella Canala 805
Baselice
San Bartolomeo in Galdo
Vairano Scalo
Alife
Lido di Fondi
Itri
Minturno
Sessa Aurunca
Roccamonfina
Teano
Pietravairano
Dragoni
Pietramelara
Gióia Sannitica
Morcone
Cerreto Sannita
Montefalcone di Val Fortore
San Marco dei Cávoti
Castelfranco in Miscano
Sperlonga
Fórmia
Gaeta
Báia Domizia
Alvignano
Guárdia Sanframondi
Pontelandolfo
Pignataro Maggiore
Amorosi
Telese Terme
Pesco Sannita
Buonalbergo
Carínola
Sparanise
Piano di Monte Verna
Caiazzo
Solopaca
Taburno
Foglianise
Paduli
Ariano Irpino
Mondragone
Capua
REGGIA DI CASERTA
Camposáuro
Sant'Ágata dei Goti
M. Taburno 1394
Benevento
Caserta
Santa Maria Cápua Vétere
Maddaloni
Montesárchio
San Giórgio del Sánnio
Cancello ed Arnone
Castél Volturno
Golfo di Gaeta
Cervinara
Mirabella Eclano
Marcianise
Casal di Príncipe
Arienzo
Altavilla Irpina
Montemilleto
Aversa
Caivano
Cicciano
M. Avella 1598
Partenio
Baiano
Pratola Serra
Pineta Grande
Acerra
Giugliano in Campania
Afragola
Marigliano
Nola
Avellino
Atripalda
Casória
Marano
Sant'Anastasia
Palma Campánia
Contrada
Volturara Irpina
Lido di Lícola
Pozzuoli
Bácoli
NÁPOLI
NAPLES
Vesúvio 1281
HERCULANUM
Portici
Ercolano
Ottaviano
Sarno
Mercato S. Severino
Solofra
Monti Picentini
POMPEI
Pompei
Nocera Inferiore
Baronissi
le Croci di Acerno 843
Acerno
Ponza
Ventoténe
Casamicciola Terme
Prócida
Forío
Íschia
Torre del Greco
Torre Annunziata
Pagani
Castellammare di Stábia
Gragnano
Cava de'Tirreni
Montecorvino Rovella
Golfo di Nápoli
Cágliari
Vico Equense
M. S. Ángelo 1443
Vietri sul Mare
Salerno
Éboli
Sorrento
Meta
Positano
Amalfi
Praiano
Pontecagnano
Battipáglia
Massa Lubrense
Capri
Marina d. Cantone
Anacapri
VILLA JOVIS
GROTTA AZZURRA
Golfo di Salerno
Palermo
Tunis
Messina
Catánia
PAESTUM
Strómboli
Ginostra
Panarea
Lípari
Vulcano
Milazzo
Agrópoli
0
10
20
30 km
San Marco
Castellabate
Punta Licosa
Ogliastro Marina
Montecórice
Póllica
Acciaroli
41°
42°
14°
15°
1
2
3
B
C

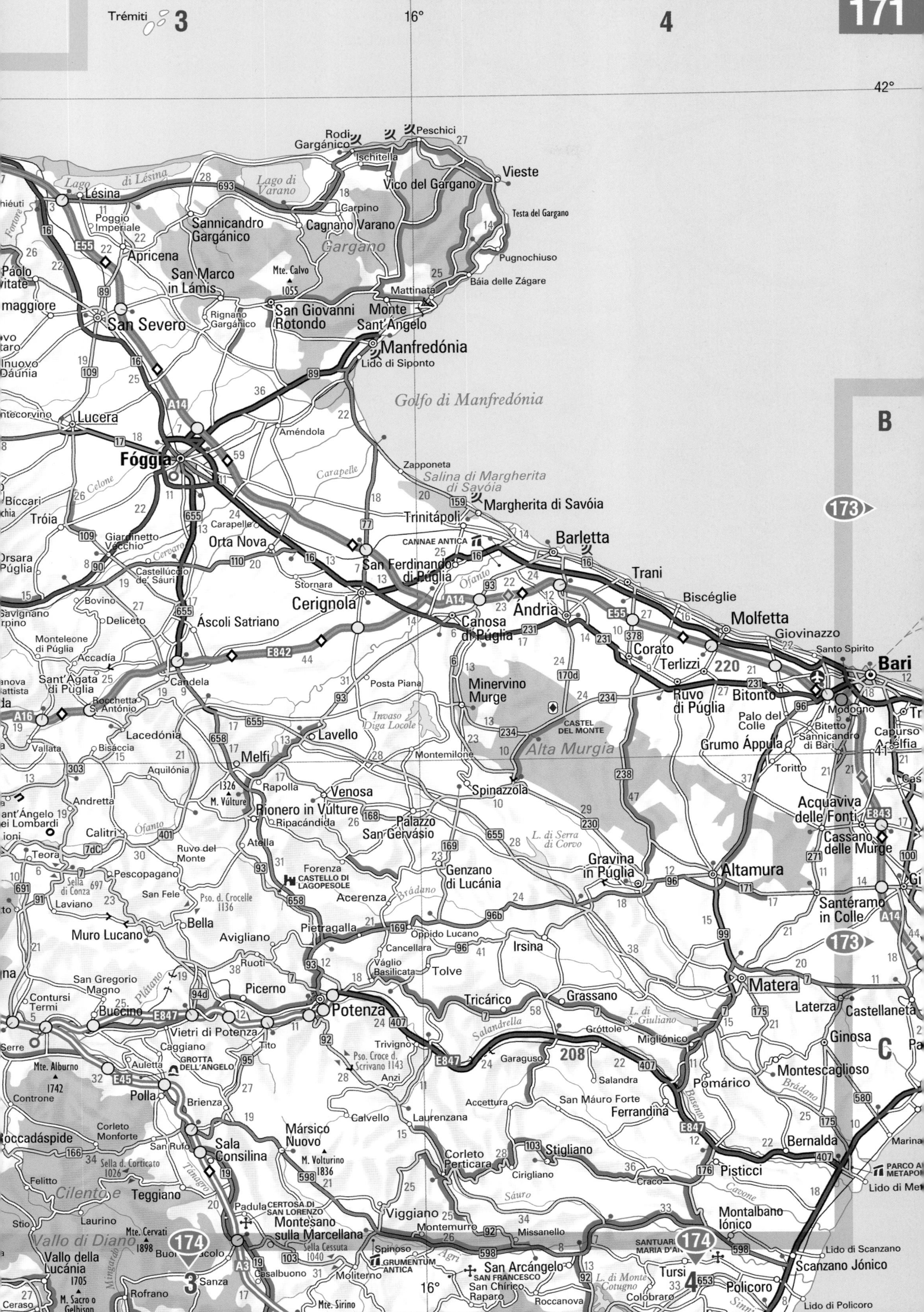

Trémiti
3
16°
4
42°
Rodi Gargánico
Peschici
Ischitella
Vieste
Lago di Lésina
Lago di Varano
Vico del Gargano
Testa del Gargano
Lésina
Carpino
Poggio Imperiale
Sannicandro Gargánico
Cagnano Varano
Gargano
Apricena
Pugnochiuso
San Marco in Lámis
Mte. Calvo 1055
Báia delle Zágare
Mattinata
San Giovanni Rotondo
Monte Sant'Angelo
Rignano Gargánico
San Severo
Manfredónia
Lido di Siponto
Lucera
Golfo di Manfredónia
B
Améndola
Fóggia
Zapponeta
Salina di Margherita di Savóia
Margherita di Savóia
Bíccari
Tróia
Carapelle
Trinitápoli
173
Orta Nova
Giardinetto Vecchio
Barletta
CANNAE ANTICA
San Ferdinando di Púglia
Castellúccio de' Sáuri
Stornara
Trani
Cerignola
Bovino
Andria
Bisceglie
Molfetta
Deliceto
Áscoli Satriano
Canosa di Púglia
Giovinazzo
Monteleone di Púglia
Corato
Santo Spirito
Accadía
Terlizzi
Bari
Sant'Agata di Púglia
Candela
Posta Piana
Minervino Murge
Ruvo di Púglia
Bitonto
Modugno
Rocchetta S. António
Invaso Diga Locone
Palo del Colle
Bitetto
Capurso
Lavello
CASTEL DEL MONTE
Lacedónia
Sannicandro di Bari
Grumo Áppula
Vallata
Bisáccia
Melfi
Montemilone
Alta Murgia
Aquilónia
Toritto
Rapolla
Spinazzola
Andretta
M. Vúlture 1326
Venosa
Acquaviva delle Fonti
Sant'Ángelo dei Lombardi
Rionero in Vúlture
Ripacándida
Palazzo San Gervásio
Cassano delle Murge
Calitri
Ófanto
L. di Serra di Corvo
Teora
Ruvo del Monte
Atella
Gravina in Púglia
Altamura
Sella di Conza 697
Pescopagano
Forenza
CASTELLO DI LAGOPESOLE
Genzano di Lucánia
Laviano
San Fele
Pso. d. Crocelle 1136
Acerenza
Bradano
Santéramo in Colle
Bella
Muro Lucano
Pietragalla
Avigliano
Oppido Lucano
Irsina
Cancellara
Ruoti
Váglio Basilicata
Tolve
San Gregorio Magno
Matera
Picerno
Contursi Terme
Tricárico
Grassano
Laterza
Castellaneta
Buccino
Potenza
L. di S. Giuliano
Vietri di Potenza
Grottole
Ginosa
Serre
Caggiano
Tito
Miglionico
Trivigno
GROTTA DELL'ANGELO
Auletta
Pso. Croce d. Scrivano 1143
Garaguso
Salandrella
Mte. Alburno 1742
Anzi
Montescaglioso
Salandra
Polla
Pomárico
Controne
Brienza
Accettura
San Máuro Forte
Ferrandina
Basento
Corleto Monforte
Calvello
Laurenzana
Occadáspide
Bernalda
Sala Consilina
Sella d. Corticato 1026
Stigliano
Marina
San Rufo
Mársico Nuovo
M. Volturino 1836
Corleto Perticara
PARCO A. METAPO
Pisticci
Cirigliano
Craco
Felitto
Cilento e
Teggiano
Sáuro
Cavone
Lido di Me
Laurino
Padula
CERTOSA DI SAN LORENZO
Viggiano
Montalbano Iónico
Stio
Mte. Cervati 1898
Montesano sulla Marcellana
Montemurro
Missanello
Vallo di Diano
174
Sella Cessuta 1040
Spinoso
Agri
SANTUARIO MARIA D'AN
Lido di Scanzano
Vallo della Lucánia
GRUMENTUM ANTICA
San Arcángelo
SAN FRANCESCO
Scanzano Jónico
M. Sacro o Gelbison 1705
Sanza
Rofrano
Casalbuono
Moliterno
San Chírico Raparo
L. di Monte Cotugno
Tursi
Policoro
Ceraso
Mte. Sirino
Roccanova
Colobraro
Sinni
Lido di Policoro
Montano Antilia
Mingardo
Tánagro
Plátano
Celone
Cervaro
Carapelle
Fortore
C
A14
A16
A3
E55
E842
E843
E847
E45

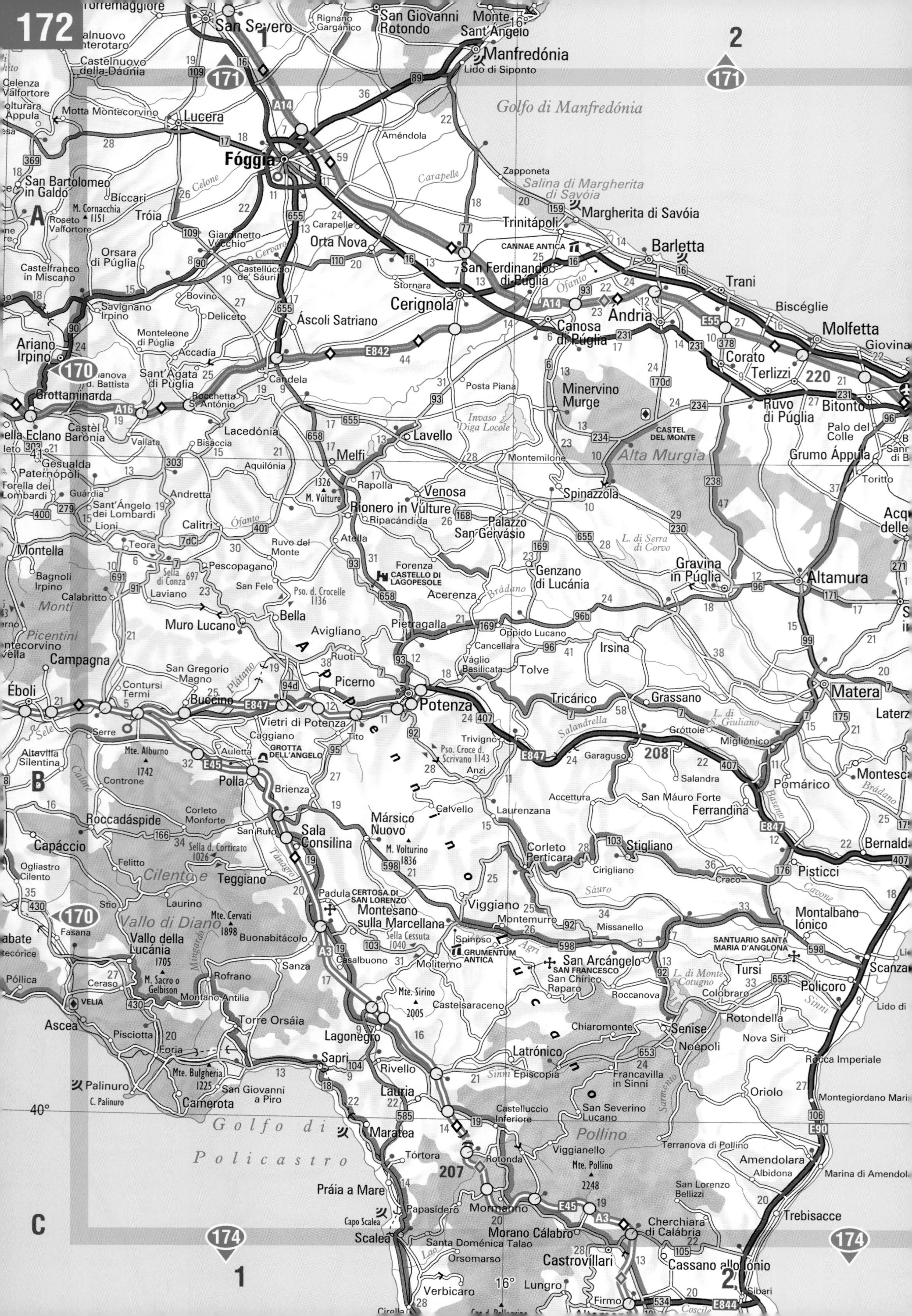

San Severo
Rignano Gargánico
San Giovanni Rotondo
Monte Sant'Angelo
Manfredónia
Lido di Siponto
Castelnuovo della Dáunia
Celenza Valfortore
Motta Montecorvino
Lucera
Fóggia
Golfo di Manfredónia
Améndola
San Bartolomeo in Galdo
Bíccari
M. Cornacchia 1151
Roseto Valfortore
Tróia
Zapponeta
Salina di Margherita di Savóia
Margherita di Savóia
Trinitápoli
Carapelle
Orta Nova
Giardinetto Vecchio
Orsara di Púglia
Castelfranco in Miscano
Castellúccio de' Sáuri
Cannae Antica
Barletta
San Ferdinando di Púglia
Stornara
Cerignola
Trani
Bisceglie
Savignano Irpino
Bovino
Deliceto
Áscoli Satriano
Canosa di Púglia
Ándria
Molfetta
Corato
Terlizzi
Ariano Irpino
Monteleone di Púglia
Accadía
Sant'Ágata di Púglia
Candela
Posta Piana
Minervino Murge
Ruvo di Púglia
Bitonto
Grottaminarda
Rocchetta S. António
Castèl Baronia
Lacedónia
Vallata
Bisáccia
Invaso Diga Locone
Lavello
Castel del Monte
Palo del Colle
Gesualdo
Paternópoli
Melfi
Montemilone
Alta Murgia
Grumo Áppula
Aquilónia
Rapolla
Venosa
Spinazzola
Toritto
Guárdia Lombardi
Sant'Ángelo dei Lombardi
Andretta
M. Vúlture 1326
Rionero in Vúlture
Ripacándida
Palazzo San Gervásio
Lioni
Calitri
Ófanto
Ruvo del Monte
Atella
Montella
Teora
Pescopagano
Forenza
Castello di Lagopesole
L. di Serra di Corvo
Genzano di Lucánia
Gravina in Púglia
Altamura
Bagnoli Irpino
Sella di Conza 697
Calabritto
Laviano
San Fele
Pso. d. Crocelle 1136
Acerenza
Brádano
Monti Picentini
Muro Lucano
Bella
Pietragalla
Óppido Lucano
Avigliano
Cancellara
Irsina
Campagna
Ruoti
Váglio Basilicata
Tolve
San Gregorio Magno
Picerno
Matera
Éboli
Contursi Terme
Buccino
Potenza
Tricárico
Grassano
Vietri di Potenza
Serre
Caggiano
Tito
Trivigno
Salandrella
Gróttole
L. di S. Giuliano
Migliónico
Laterza
Altavilla Silentina
Mte. Alburno 1742
Auletta
Grotta dell'Angelo
Pso. Croce d. Scrivano 1143
Garaguso
Anzi
Salandra
Pomárico
Montescaglioso
Calore
Controne
Polla
Brienza
Accettura
San Máuro Forte
Ferrandina
Basento
Roccadáspide
Corleto Monforte
Calvello
Laurenzana
San Rufo
Sala Consilina
Mársico Nuovo
Capáccio
Sella d. Corticato 1026
M. Volturino 1836
Corleto Perticara
Stigliano
Bernalda
Ogliastro Cilento
Felitto
Cilento e Vallo di Diano
Teggiano
Tánagro
Cirigliano
Pisticci
Craco
Sáuro
Cavone
Padula
Certosa di San Lorenzo
Montesano sulla Marcellana
Viggiano
Montemurro
Missanello
Montalbano Iónico
Stio
Laurino
Mte. Cervati 1898
Buonabitácolo
Sella Cessuta 1040
Spinoso
Grumentum Antica
Agri
San Arcángelo
San Francesco
Santuario Santa Maria d'Anglona
Scanzano
Fasana
Vallo della Lucánia
Casalbuono
Moliterno
San Chírico Raparo
L. di Monte Cotugno
Tursi
Policoro
Póllica
Ceraso
Mingardo
M. Sacro o Gelbison 1705
Rofrano
Sanza
Mte. Sirino 2005
Castelsaraceno
Roccanova
Colobraro
Sinni
Velia
Montano Antilia
Ascea
Torre Orsáia
Lagonegro
Chiaromonte
Senise
Noépoli
Rotondella
Nova Siri
Pisciotta
Foria
Latrónico
Rocca Imperiale
Sapri
Rivello
Episcopia
Francavilla in Sinni
Palinuro
C. Palinuro
Mte. Bulgheria 1225
San Giovanni a Piro
Camerota
Lauria
Oriolo
Montegiordano Marina
Sarmento
Castelluccio Inferiore
San Severino Lucano
Golfo di Policastro
Maratea
Pollino
Tórtora
Viggianello
Terranova di Pollino
Rotonda
Mte. Pollino 2248
Amendolara
Albidona
Marina di Amendolara
Práia a Mare
San Lorenzo Bellizzi
Papasídero
Mormanno
Trebisacce
Capo Scalea
Scalea
Morano Cálabro
Cherchiara di Calábria
Santa Doménica Talao
Castrovíllari
Cassano allo Iónio
Orsomarso
Lao
Verbicaro
Lungro
Sibari
Firmo
Coscile
Cirella
Appennino Lucano
40°
16°

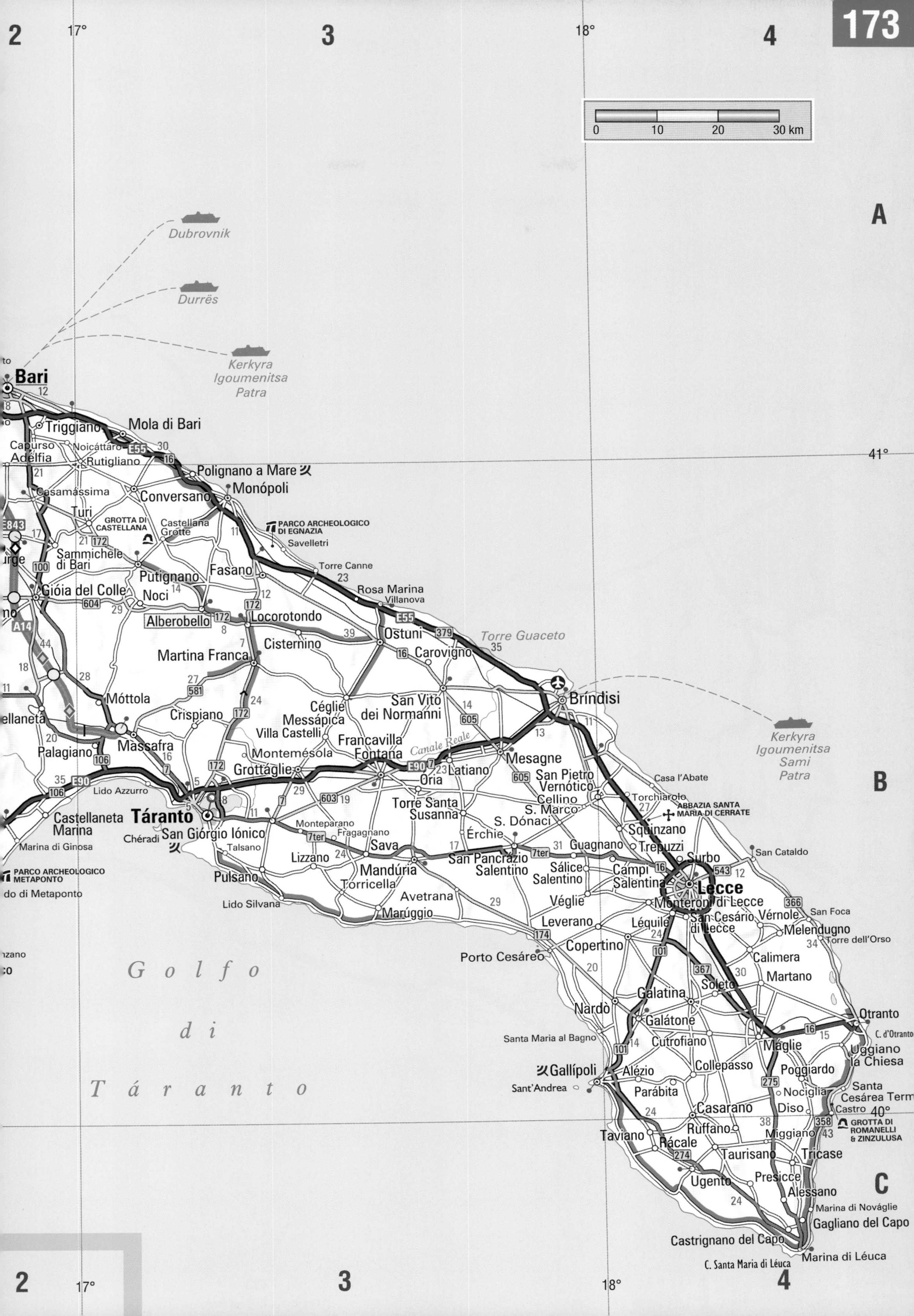

2 17°   **3**   18°   **4**

A

0 10 20 30 km

Dubrovnik

Durrës

Kerkyra
Igoumenitsa
Patra

Bari
12
Triggiano   Mola di Bari
Capurso   Noicàttaro   30   E55
Adélfia   Rutigliano   16
21   Polignano a Mare
Casamássima   Conversano   Monópoli
Turi   GROTTA DI   Castellana   PARCO ARCHEOLOGICO
CASTELLANA   Grotte   DI EGNAZIA
E843   21   172   11   Savelletri
Sammichele   Putignano   Fasano   Torre Canne
di Bari   100   Noci   14   23
604   Gióia del Colle   172   12   Rosa Marina
29   Alberobello   172   Locorotondo   Villanova
A14   8   7   Cisternino   39   E55   Ostuni   379
Martina Franca   16   Carovigno   35   Torre Guaceto
18   28   27   24   Céglie   San Vito
Móttola   581   Messápica   dei Normanni   14   Bríndisi
11   Crispiano   172   Villa Castelli   605   13   11
Massafra   Montemésola   Francavilla   Canale Reale   Mesagne   Casa l'Abate
20   172   Grottáglie   Fontana   E90   7   Latiano   605   San Pietro   Torchiarolo   ABBAZIA SANTA
106   16   7   Oria   Vernótico   27   MARIA DI CERRATE
35   E90   5   29   603   19   Torre Santa   Cellino   Squinzano   San Cataldo
106   Lido Azzurro   8   7   Susanna   S. Marco   Trepuzzi
Castellaneta   Táranto   11   Montepàrano   Érchie   S. Dónaci   31   Guagnano   Campi   Surbo
Marina   Chéradi   San Giórgio Iónico   7ter   Fragagnano   Sava   17   San Pancrazio   7ter   Sálice   Salentina   Lecce   543   12
Marina di Ginosa   Talsano   Lizzano   24   Salentino   Salentino   16   Monteroni di Lecce
PARCO ARCHEOLOGICO   Pulsano   Mandúria   Avetrana   29   Véglie   San Cesário   Vérnole   San Foca
METAPONTO   Torricella   Marúggio   Leverano   101   di Lecce   Calimera   34   Torre dell'Orso
do di Metaponto   Lido Silvana   174   Copertino   367   30   Martano
20   Porto Cesáreo   Soleto   Otranto
Galatina   16   15   C. d'Otranto
Santa Maria al Bagno   14   Nardò   Cutrofiano   Máglie   Uggiano
Gallípoli   101   Galátone   Collepasso   Poggiardo   la Chiesa
Sant'Andrea   Alézio   275   Santa
Parábita   Casarano   Nociglia   Cesárea Term
274   24   Diso   Castro   GROTTA DI
Taviano   Rácale   Ruffano   38   358   ROMANELLI
Miggiano   43   & ZINZULUSA
Ugento   Taurisano   Tricase
24   Presicce   Alessano
Marina di Nováglie
Castrignano del Capo   Gagliano del Capo
C. Santa Maria di Léuca   Marina di Léuca

Golfo

di

Táranto

B

Kerkyra
Igoumenitsa
Sami
Patra

C

41°

40°

2 17°   **3**   18°   **4**

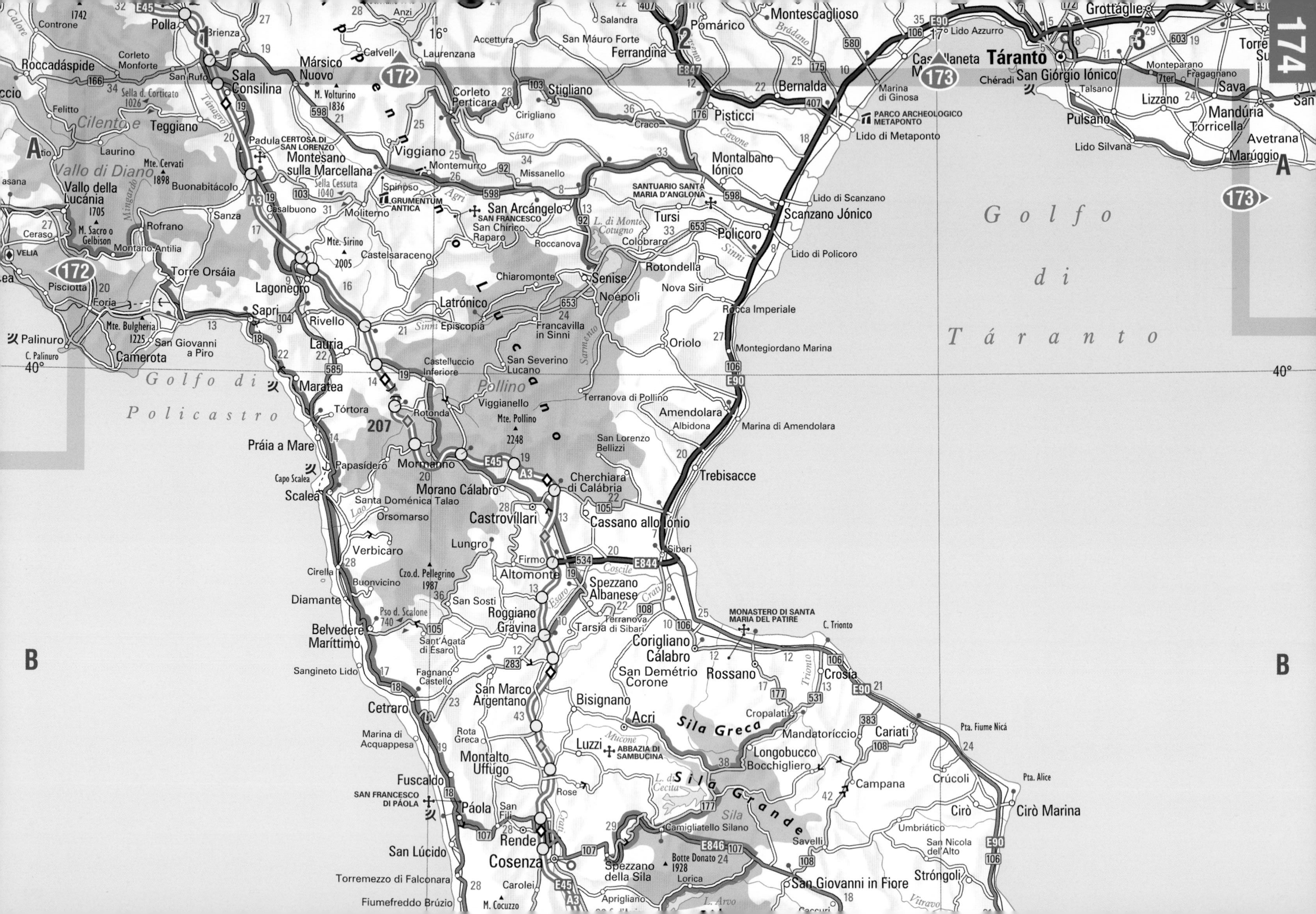
Golfo di Táranto
Golfo di Policastro
Táranto
San Giórgio Iónico
Grottáglie
Mandúria
Sava
Lizzano
Pulsano
Torricella
Avetrana
Marúggio
Lido Silvana
Talsano
Monteparano
Fragagnano
Cherádi
Castellaneta
Lido Azzurro
Marina di Ginosa
PARCO ARCHEOLOGICO METAPONTO
Lido di Metaponto
Montescaglioso
Bernalda
Pomárico
Ferrandina
Salandra
San Máuro Forte
Accettura
Pisticci
Craco
Montalbano Iónico
Scanzano Jónico
Lido di Scanzano
Policoro
Lido di Policoro
Tursi
SANTUARIO SANTA MARIA D'ANGLONA
Colobraro
Rotondella
Nova Siri
Rocca Imperiale
Montegiordano Marina
Oriolo
Amendolara
Albidona
Marina di Amendolara
Trebisacce
Senise
Noépoli
Chiaromonte
Latrónico
Episcopia
Francavilla in Sinni
San Severino Lucano
Terranova di Pollino
San Lorenzo Bellizzi
Viggianello
Mte. Pollino 2248
Pollino
Castelluccio Inferiore
Rotonda
Mormanno
Morano Cálabro
Cherchiara di Calábria
Castrovíllari
Cassano allo Iónio
Sibari
Lungro
Firmo
Altomonte
Spezzano Albanese
Terranova
Tarsia di Sibari
Roggiano Grávina
San Sosti
Corigliano Cálabro
Rossano
San Demétrio Corone
MONASTERO DI SANTA MARIA DEL PATIRE
C. Trionto
Crosia
Cropalati
Mandatoríccio
Cariati
Pta. Fiume Nicá
Longobucco
Bocchigliero
Campana
Crúcoli
Pta. Alice
Cirò
Cirò Marina
Umbriático
San Nicola dell'Alto
Stróngoli
San Giovanni in Fiore
Savelli
Sila Greca
Sila Grande
Camigliatello Silano
Botte Donato 1928
Spezzano della Sila
Lorica
Aprigliano
Acri
Bisignano
Luzzi
ABBAZIA DI SAMBUCINA
Rose
San Marco Argentano
Fagnano Castello
Sant'Ágata di Esaro
Pso d. Scalone 740
Montalto Uffugo
Rota Greca
Cosenza
Rende
San Fili
Carolei
M. Cocuzzo
Páola
SAN FRANCESCO DI PÁOLA
Fuscaldo
Marina di Acquappesa
Cetraro
Sangineto Lido
Belvedere Maríttimo
Diamante
Cirella
Buonvicino
Verbicaro
Czo.d. Pellegrino 1987
Orsomarso
Santa Doménica Talao
Scalea
Capo Scalea
Papasídero
Práia a Mare
Tórtora
Maratea
Láuria
Rivello
Lagonegro
Sapri
Mte. Sirino 2005
Castelsaraceno
San Chírico Raparo
Roccanova
San Arcángelo
SAN FRANCESCO
Moliterno
GRUMENTUM ANTICA
Spinoso
Montemurro
Missanello
Viggiano
Corleto Perticara
Stigliano
Cirigliano
Laurenzana
Calvello
Anzi
Mársico Nuovo
M. Volturino 1836
Padula
CERTOSA DI SAN LORENZO
Montesano sulla Marcellana
Sella Cessuta 1040
Casalbuono
Sanza
Buonabitácolo
Sala Consilina
Brienza
Polla
San Rufo
Teggiano
Corleto Monforte
Roccadáspide
Controne
Felitto
Sella d. Corticato 1026
Laurino
Mte. Cervati 1898
Vallo di Diano
Cilento e
Vallo della Lucánia
M. Sacro o Gelbison 1705
Rofrano
Montano Antilia
Torre Orsáia
Ceraso
VELIA
Pisciotta
Fória
Palinuro
C. Palinuro
Camerota
Mte. Bulgheria 1225
San Giovanni a Piro
Torremezzo di Falconara
Fiumefreddo Brúzio
San Lúcido
172
173
207
A
B
40°
16°
17°

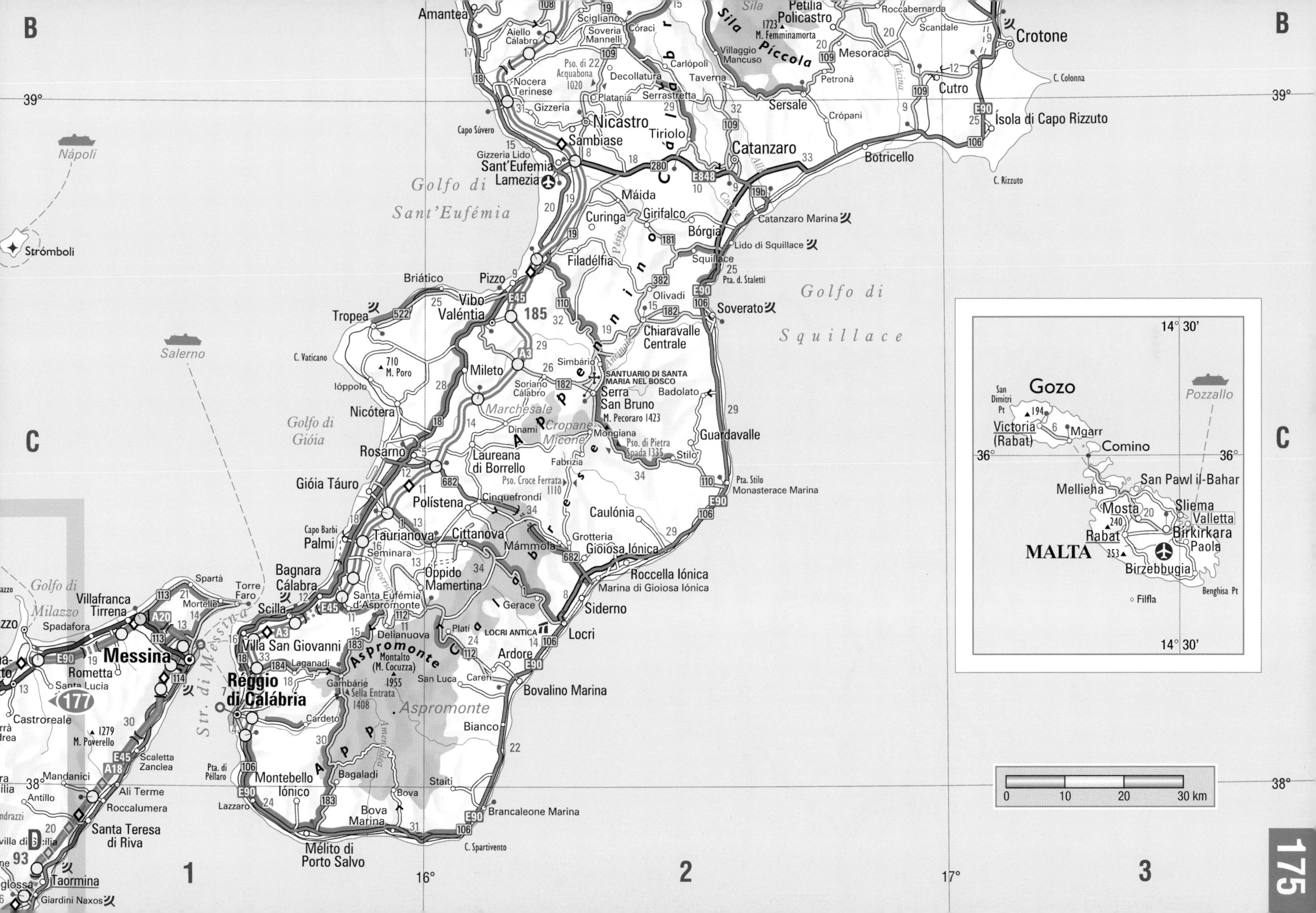

B

39°

C

C

B

B

3

2

1

C

17°

16°

38°

39°

Crotone
C. Colonna
Isola di Capo Rizzuto
C. Rizzuto
Cutro
Botricello
Roccabernarda
Scandale
Mesoraca
Petronà
Crópani
Crópani
Petilia
Policastro
M. Femminamorta
Villaggio Mancuso
Taverna
Sila Piccola
1723
Sila
Gimigliano
Catanzaro
Carlópoli
Serrastretta
Pso. di 22
Acquabona 1020
Soveria Mannelli
Decollatura
Scigliano
Nicastro
Sambiase
Platania
Gizzeria
Gizzeria Lido
Sant'Eufemia Lamezia
Nocera Terinese
Aiello Calábro
Amantea
Capo Suvero
Triolo
Tiriolo
Máida
Curinga
Girifalco
Filadélfia
Borgia
Squillace
Olivadi
Chiaravalle Centrale
SANTUARIO DI SANTA MARIA NEL BOSCO
Serra San Bruno
M. Pecoraro 1423
Pso. di Pietra Spada 1335
Badolato
Stilo
Guardavalle
Catanzaro Marina
Lido di Squillace
Pta. d. Staletti
Soverato
Golfo di Squillace
Pta. Stilo
Monasterace Marina
Roccella Iónica
Marina di Gioiosa Iónica
Siderno
Locri
LOCRI ANTICA
Gioiosa Iónica
Caulónia
Grotteria
Mámmola
Mongiana
Fabrizia
Cittanova
Polístena
Rosarno
Gióia Táuro
Palmi
Bagnara Cálabra
Scilla
Villa San Giovanni
Reggio di Calábria
Taurianova
Seminara
Oppido Mamertina
Delianuova
Santa Eufémia d'Aspromonte
Gambárie
S. Sella Entrata 1408
Montalto (M. Cocuzza) 1955
Aspromonte
Cardeto
Lazzaro
Pta. di Péllaro
Mélito di Porto Salvo
Montebello Iónico
Bagaladi
Bova
Bova Marina
C. Spartivento
Brancaleone Marina
Bovalino Marina
Ardore
Careri
Bianco
Stáiti
San Luca
Platì
Gerace
Messina
Villafranca Tirrena
Rometta
Spadafora
Santa Lucia
M. Poverello 1279
Mortelle
Torre Faro
Spartà
Scaletta Zanclea
Ali Terme
Roccalumera
Santa Teresa di Riva
Giardini Naxos
Taormina
Mandanici
Antillo
Str. di Messina
Golfo di Gióia
Nicótera
Rosarno
Tropea
C. Vaticano
Iópporo
Golfo di Gióia
Rosarno
M. Poro 710
Briático
Vibo Valéntia
Pizzo
Mileto
Soriano Cálabro
Simbário
Dinami
Laureana di Borrello
Cinquefrondi
Pso. Croce Ferrata 1110
C. Barbi
Marchesale
Méconc
Acropanc
Golfo di Sant'Eufémia
Golfo di Sant'Eufémia
Tácina
Allì
Corace
Péscara
Lámato
Amendolea
Aspromonte
Duverso
Áncinale
Golfo di Squillace
Napoli
Strómboli
Salerno
Salerno

185

93

171

17I

E90
E45
E848
106
109
108
18
280
182
382
181
280
19b
19
E45
A3
110
32
26
182
183
682
E90
106
110
112
14
E90
106
183
A20
A18
113
114
A3

14° 30'
36°
14° 30'
36°
38°
17°
Pozzallo
GOZO
San Dimitri Pt
Victoria (Rabat)
Mgarr
Comino
Mellieha
San Pawl il-Bahar
Mosta
Sliema
Valletta
Birkirkara
Paola
Rabat
Birzebbugia
MALTA
Filfla
Benghisa Pt
194
6
20
240
253

30 km
20
10
0

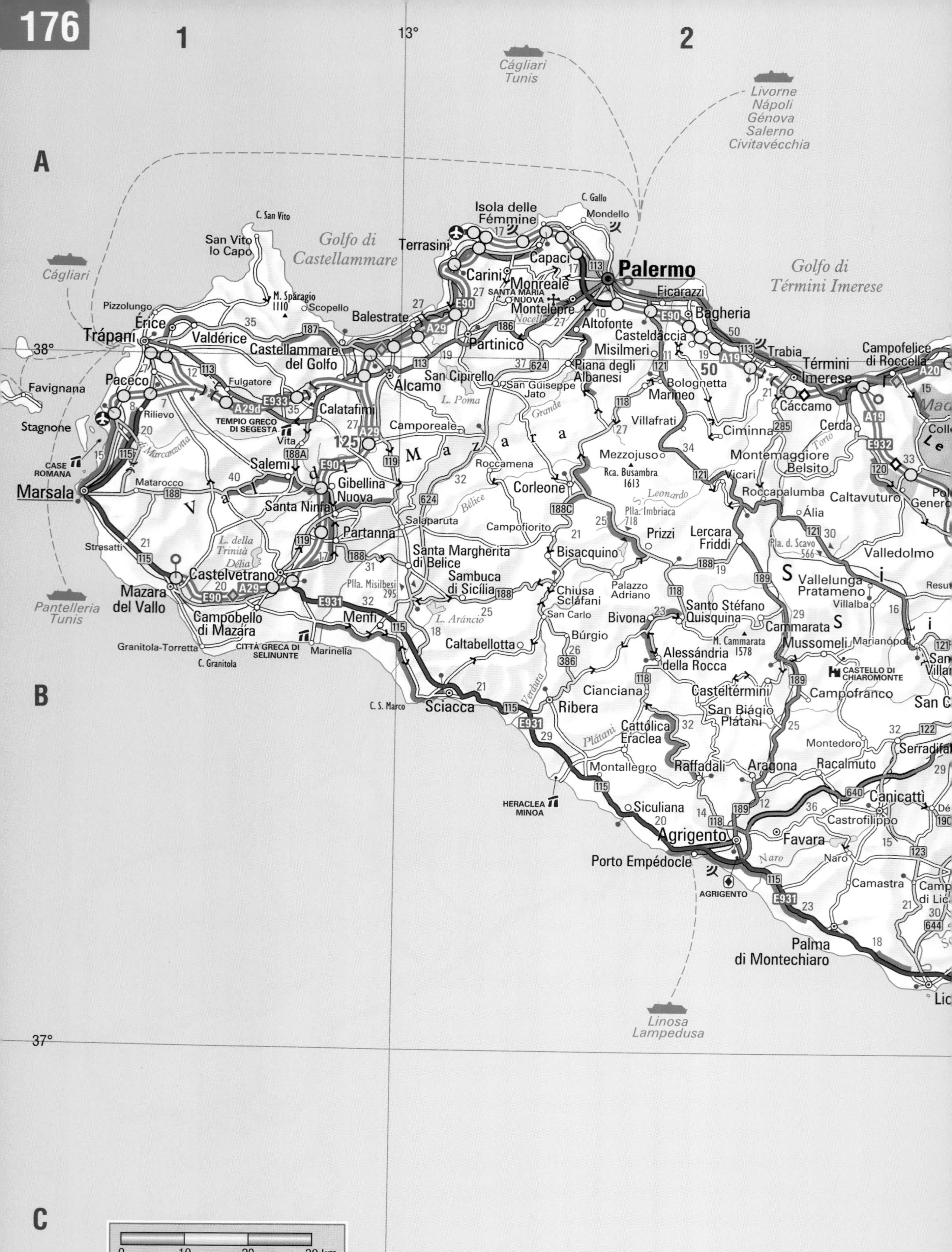
1
2
13°
A
B
C
38°
37°
Cágliari
Tunis
Livorne
Nápoli
Génova
Salerno
Civitavécchia
C. Gallo
Isola delle Fémmine
Mondello
C. San Vito
San Vito lo Capo
Golfo di Castellammare
Terrasini
Capaci
Palermo
Golfo di Términi Imerese
Carini
Monreale
Santa Maria Nuova
Montelepre
Ficarazzi
Bagheria
M. Spáragio 1110
Scopello
Pizzolungo
Érice
Trápani
Balestrate
Valdérice
Castellammare del Golfo
Partinico
Altofonte
Casteldáccia
Misilmeri
Trabia
Campofelice di Roccella
Términi Imerese
Favignana
Paceco
Fulgatore
Álcamo
San Cipirello
San Guiseppe Jato
Piana degli Albanesi
Bolognetta
Marineo
Cáccamo
Stagnone
Rilievo
Tempio Greco di Segesta
Vita
Calatafimi
L. Poma
Camporeale
Villafrati
Ciminna
Cerda
Case Romana
Salemi
Mazara
Roccamena
Mezzojuso
Rca. Busambra 1613
Montemaggiore Belsito
Marsala
Matarocco
Gibellina Nuova
Corleone
Vicari
Roccapalumba
Caltavuturo
Santa Ninfa
Salaparuta
Campofiorito
Plla. Imbriaca 718
Prizzi
Lercara Friddi
Ália
Partanna
Strasatti
L. della Trinità Délia
Santa Margherita di Belice
Bisacquino
Pla. d. Scavo 566
Valledolmo
Castelvetrano
Plla. Misilbesi 295
Sambuca di Sicília
Chiusa Sclàfani
Palazzo Adriano
Santo Stéfano Quisquina
Vallelunga Pratameno
Villalba
Pantelleria
Tunis
Mazara del Vallo
Menfi
L. Aráncio
San Carlo
Bivona
Cammarata
M. Cammarata 1578
Mussomeli
Marianópoli
Campobello di Mazara
Búrgio
Alessándria della Rocca
Castello di Chiaromonte
Granitola-Torretta
Città Greca di Selinunte
Marinella
Caltabellotta
C. Granitola
Cianciana
Casteltérmini
Campofranco
C. S. Marco
Sciacca
Ribera
San Biágio Plátani
Cattólica Eraclea
Montedoro
Montallegro
Raffadali
Aragona
Racalmuto
Heraclea Minoa
Siculiana
Canicattì
Castrofilippo
Agrigento
Favara
Porto Empédocle
Naro
Camastra
Palma di Montechiaro
Linosa
Lampedusa
0
10
20
30 km

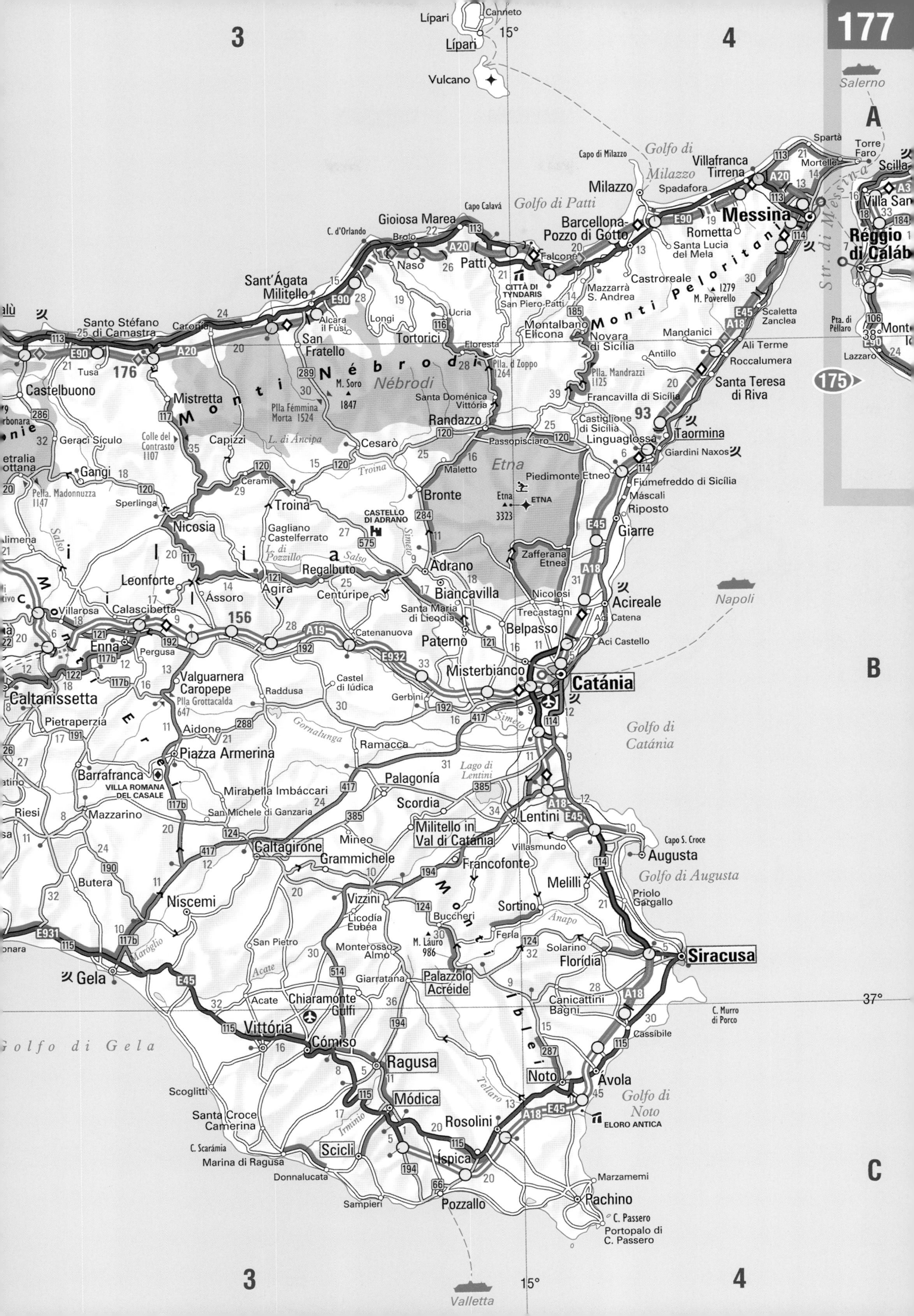

Lípari   Canneto
Lípari
Lípari   15°
Vulcano

Salerno

A

3   4

Capo di Milazzo   Golfo di   Spartà
Villafranca   Milazzo   Torre
Milazzo   Tirrena   Mortelle   Faro
Spadafora   113   21   Scilla
E90   19   Messina   114   Villa San
Barcellona-   Rometta   18   33
Pozzo di Gotto   Falconé   Santa Lucia   184   Réggio
Capo Calavá   Golfo di Patti   13   del Mela   di Caláb
Gioiosa Marea   22   113   Castroreale   106
C. d'Orlando   Brolo   Patti   Mazzarrà   1279   30   Pta. di
Naso   26   21   S. Andrea   M. Poverello   Pèllaro   Mont
Sant'Ágata   CITTÀ DI   Montalbano   Scaletta   E90   24
Militello   15   E90   28   19   TYNDARIS   185   Elicona   Mandanici   Zanclea   Lazzaro
Santo Stéfano   San Piero-Patti   Novara   Antillo   A18   Ali Terme
25 di Camastra   Caronia   Alcara   Longi   di Sicília   Roccalumera   175
113   E90   A20   il Fúsi   Ucria   Floresta   39   Francavilla di Sicília   Santa Teresa
Castelbuono   Tortorici   Plla. di Zoppo   Pla. Mandrazzi   di Riva
176   San   1264   1125   Castiglione
Tusa   24   Fratello   Santa Doménica   di Sicília   93   Taormina
286   Mistretta   20   M. Soro   Vittória   Passopisciaro   120   6   Linguaglossa   114
Geraci Sículo   117   Plla. Fémmina   1847   Randazzo   25   Giardini Naxos
Gangi   18   Colle del   Morta 1524   Cesarò   120   Maletto   16   Etna   Fiumefreddo di Sicília   114
Contrasto 1107   35   Capizzi   L. di Ancipa   25   Máscali
Pella. Madonnuzza   120   Cerami   Troina   284   Bronte   Etna   ETNA   Riposto
1147   29   575   3323   Giarre
Sperlinga   Nicosia   Gagliano   CASTELLO   Zafferana   E45
Castelferrato   DI ADRANO   11   Etnea
Leonforte   121   Regalbuto   Adrano   31   Acireale
Villarosa   9   Agira   Centúripe   17   Biancavilla   18   Nicolosi   A18
18   Calascibetta   156   28   A19   Santa Maria   Trecastagni   Aci Catena
6   Enna   192   di Licodia   Belpasso
12   117b   Pergusa   192   Catenanuova   Paterno   121   16   11   Aci Castello   Napoli
Caltanissetta   122   13   Valguarnera   E932   33   Misterbianco
Pietraperzia   Caropepe   Raddusa   Gerbini   192   Catánia
191   Pla. Grottacalda   647   30   16   417   114   Golfo di
17   Aidone   288   Ramacca   11   Catánia
26   Piazza Armerina   21   31   Lago di
27   VILLA ROMANA   Lentini   9
DEL CASALE   Palagonía   385
Barrafranca   Mirabella Imbáccari   417   A18   12
Riesi   Mazzarino   San Michele di Ganzaria   24   Scordia   34   Lentini   E45
117b   124   385   Militello in   Villasmundo   114   Capo S. Croce
Butera   190   Caltagirone   Mineo   Val di Catánia   10   Augusta
32   11   Grammichele   10   Francofonte   Golfo di Augusta
24   12   194   Melilli   Priolo
Níscemi   Vizzini   Sortino   Gargallo   21
10   124   Buccheri   Ánapo   Solarino
E931   117b   Licodía   Ferla   124   5   Siracusa
115   Eubéa   M. Láuro   Floridia
San Pietro   986   Solarino
Maróglio   Monterosso   30   Palazzolo
Almo   Acréide   28   C. Murro
Gela   San Pietro   514   Giarratana   Canicattini   A18   di Porco   37°
32   Acate   Bagni   15   30   Cassíbile
Santa Croce   Chiaramonte   194   Noto   115
Camerina   115   Gulfi   287
C. Scarámia   Vittória   Ragusa   Ávola
16   Cómiso   11   Módica   ELORO ANTICA   Golfo di
Marina di Ragusa   8   Noto   Noto
Scogliitti   115   13
Donnalucata   17   Rosolini   A18 E45
Scicli   1   115   Marzamemi
Sampieri   194   66   20   Pachino
Ispica   C. Passero
Pozzallo   Portopalo di
C. Passero

3   15°   4
Valletta

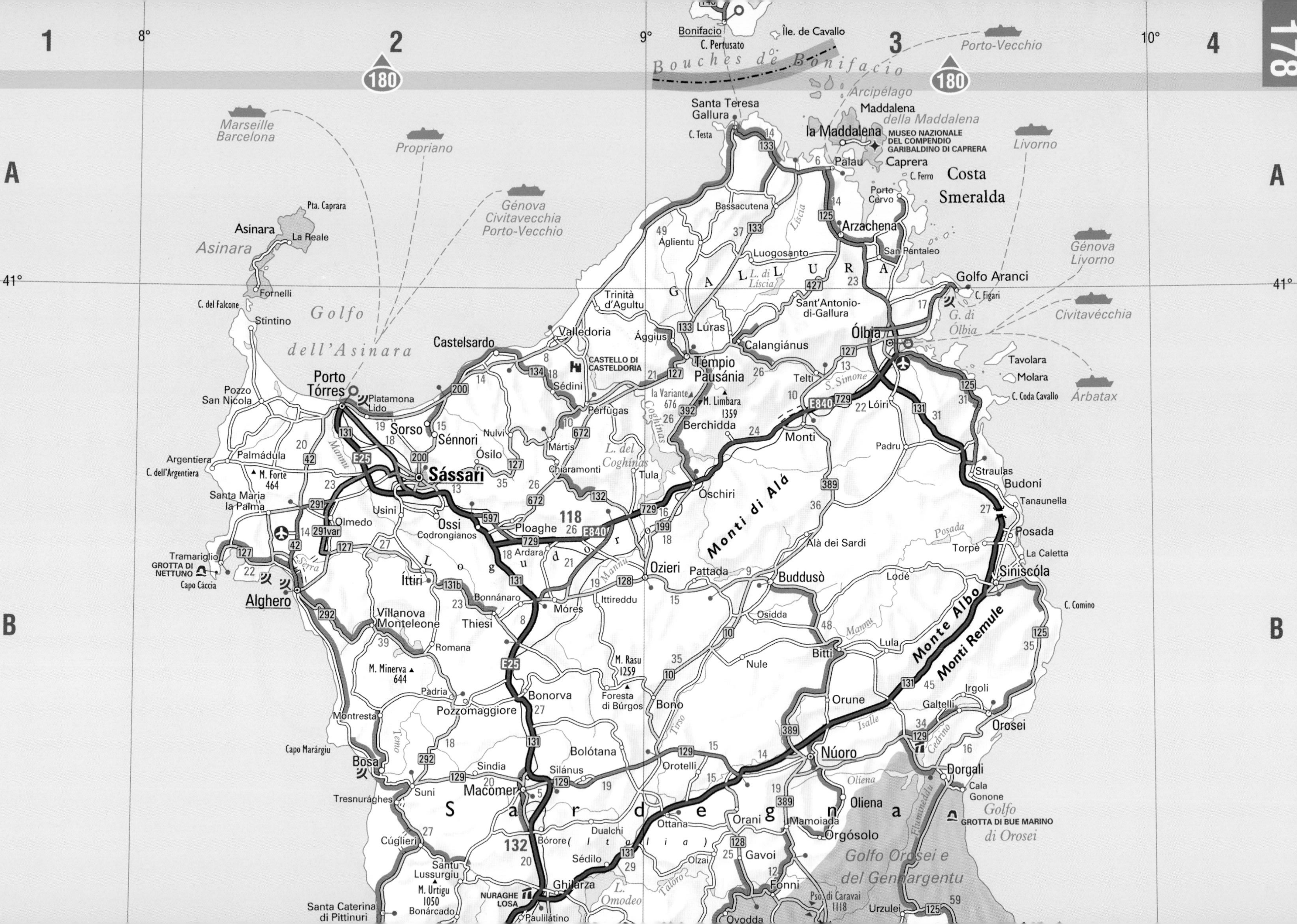

1
2
3
4
A
B
8°
9°
10°
41°
180
Bonifacio
C. Pertusato
Île. de Cavallo
Bouches de Bonifacio
Porto-Vecchio
Arcipélago della Maddalena
Maddalena
la Maddalena
MUSEO NAZIONALE DEL COMPENDIO GARIBALDINO DI CAPRERA
Caprera
C. Ferro
Costa Smeralda
Livorno
Santa Teresa Gallura
C. Testa
Palau
Porto Cervo
Arzachena
San Pantaleo
Génova Livorno
Golfo Aranci
C. Figari
G. di Ólbia
Civitavécchia
Marseille Barcelona
Propriano
Génova Civitavecchia Porto-Vecchio
Pta. Caprara
Asinara
La Reale
Fornelli
C. del Falcone
Stintino
Golfo dell'Asinara
Castelsardo
Porto Tórres
Platamona Lido
Pozzo San Nicola
Argentiera
C. dell'Argentiera
Palmádula
M. Forte 464
Santa Maria la Palma
Tramariglio
GROTTA DI NETTUNO
Capo Cáccia
Alghero
Olmedo
Usini
Sorso
Sénnori
Sássari
Nulvi
Ósilo
Ossi
Codrongianos
Ploaghe
Ardara
Íttiri
Bonnánaro
Thiesi
Villanova Monteleone
Romana
M. Minerva 644
Padria
Pozzomaggiore
Montresta
Capo Marárgiu
Bosa
Tresnurághes
Suni
Sindia
Macomer
Cúglieri
Santu Lussurgiu
M. Urtigu 1050
Bonárcado
Santa Caterina di Pittinuri
NURAGHE LOSA
Paulilátino
Ghilarza
Bórore
Sédilo
Dualchi
L. Omodeo
Valledoria
Sédini
CASTELLO DI CASTELDORIA
Pérfugas
Mártis
Chiaramonti
L. del Coghinas
Tula
Trinità d'Agultu
Ággius
Bassacutena
Aglientu
Luogosanto
L. di Liscia
Liscia
Sant'Antonio-di-Gallura
Luras
Témpio Pausánia
la Variante 676
M. Limbara 1359
Berchidda
Calangiánus
Telti
S. Simone
Ólbia
Tavolara
Molara
C. Coda Cavallo
Árbatax
Lóiri
Monti
Padru
Oschiri
Monti di Alá
Alà dei Sardi
Ozieri
Pattada
Buddusò
Ittireddu
Mores
M. Rasu 1259
Foresta di Búrgos
Bono
Bolótana
Silánus
Orotelli
Ottana
Nule
Osidda
Bitti
Lula
Lodè
Straulas
Budoni
Tanaunella
Posada
Torpè
La Caletta
Siniscóla
C. Comino
Monte Albo
Monti Remule
Irgoli
Galtellì
Orosei
Orune
Núoro
Oliena
Orgósolo
Mamoiada
Orani
Gavoi
Olzai
Fonni
Ovodda
Pso. di Caravai 1118
Urzulei
Dorgali
Cala Gonone
GROTTA DI BUE MARINO
Golfo di Orosei
Golfo Orosei e del Gennargentu
G A L L U R A
L o g u d o r o
S a r d e g n a
(I t a l i a)
Coghinas
Mannu
Tirso
Temo
Isalle
Cedrino
Flumineddu
Taloro
Serra
E25
E840

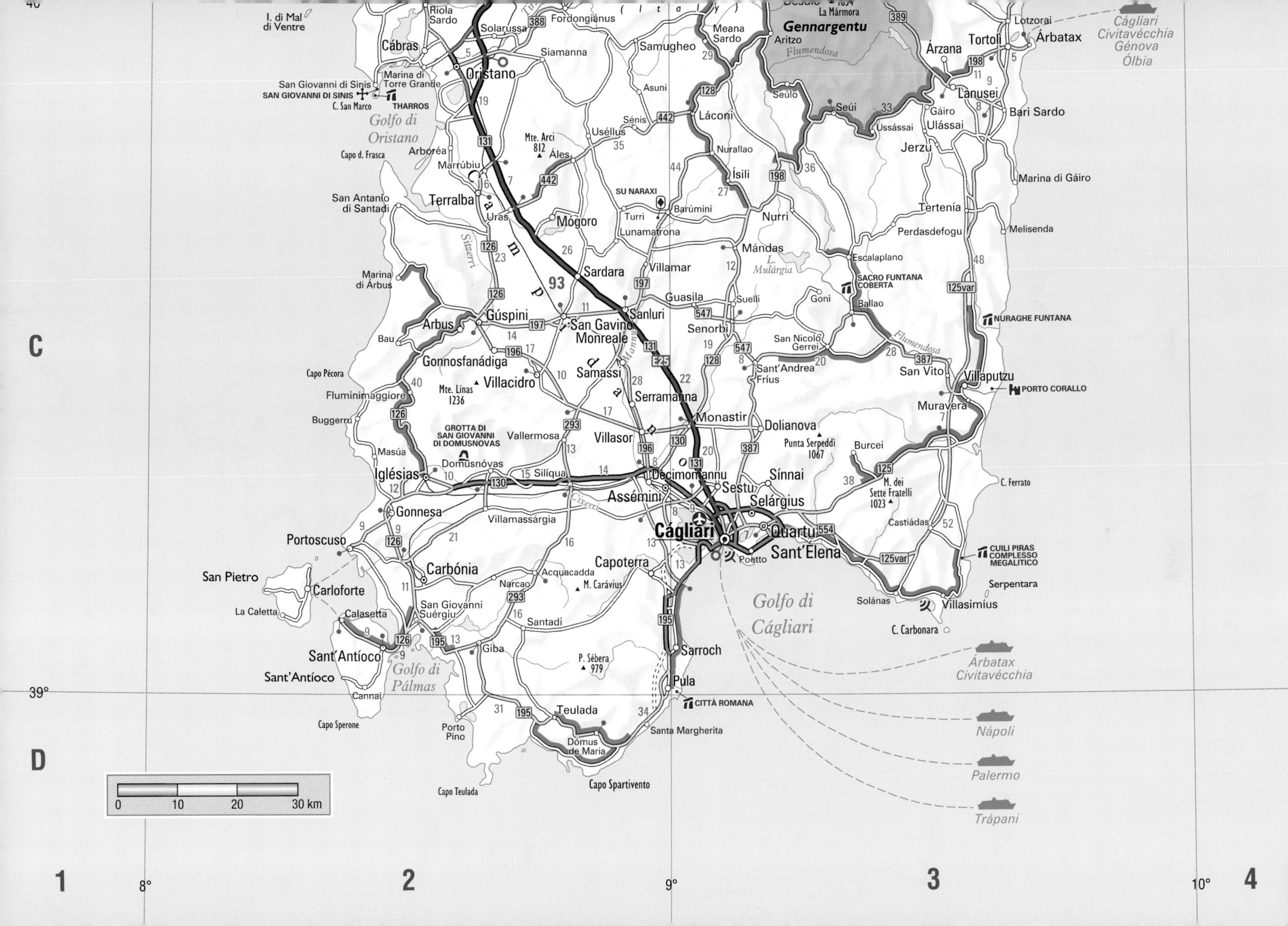

C · 4 · 3 · 2 · 1 · D
39° · 10° · 9° · 8° · 39°

Gennargentu

Cágliari

Golfo di Cágliari

Cágliari
Civitavécchia
Génova
Ólbia

Lotzorai · Arbatax · Tortolì · Árzana · Meana Sardo · Aritzo · La Mármora
Bari Sardo · Lanusei · Gáiro · Uléssai · Jerzu · Ussássai · Séui · Seúlo · Sédilo
Marina di Gáiro · Melisenda · Tertenia · Perdasdefogu · Escalaplano
NURAGHE FUNTANA · Villaputzu · PORTO CORALLO · Muravera · San Vito
Ballao · SACRO FUNTANA COBERTA · Goni · C. Ferrato · Serpentara
Villasímius · CUILI PIRAS COMPLESSO MEGALÍTICO · Castiádas · C. Carbonara
Solánas · Sant'Elena · Quartu · Selárgius · Sinnai · Dolianova
Burcei · M. dei Sette Fratelli 1023 · Punta Serpeddì 1067 · Sant'Andrea Frius
San Nicolò Gerrei · Suelli · Senorbì · Monastir · Sestu · Maracalagonis
Nurri · Mándas · L. Mulárgia · Guasila · Serramanna · Decimomannu
Ísili · Léconi · Barúmini · Villamar · Sanluri · Samassi · Serramanna · Villasor · Assémini
Nurallao · Sénis · SU NARAXI · Turri · Lunamatrona · Sardara · San Gávino Monreale
Samugheo · Asuni · Uséllus · Mógoro · Ales · Mte. Arci 812 · Guspini · Villacidro
Fordongiánus · Siamanna · Solarussa · Oristano · Marrúbiu · Terralba · Uras · Arbus · Gonnostanádiga · Mte. Linas 1236
Riola Sardo · Cábras · Marina di Torre Grande · THARROS · San Giovanni di Sinis · Arboréa · Marina di Árbus · Capo Pécora
Golfo di Oristano · Capo d. Frasca · San Antônio di Santadi · Buggerru · Fluminimaggiore
Iglésias · Gonnesa · Masúa · Narcao · GROTTA DI SAN GIOVANNI DI DOMUSNOVAS · Domusnòvas · Vallermosa · Siliqua · Villamassárgia · Carbónia
San Giovanni Suérgiu · Sant'Antíoco · Calasetta · Carloforte · Portoscuso · Cannai · Capo Sperone
San Pietro · La Caletta · Porto Pino · Capo Teulada · Giba · Teulada · Dòmus de Maria · P. Sébera 979 · M. Caráviu · Santadi · Acquacadda · Capoterra · Sarroch · Pula · CITTÀ ROMANA · Santa Margherita · Capo Spartivento
Golfo di Pálmas · Villamassárgia · Narcao
Arbatax · Civitavécchia · Nápoli · Palermo · Trápani

30 km

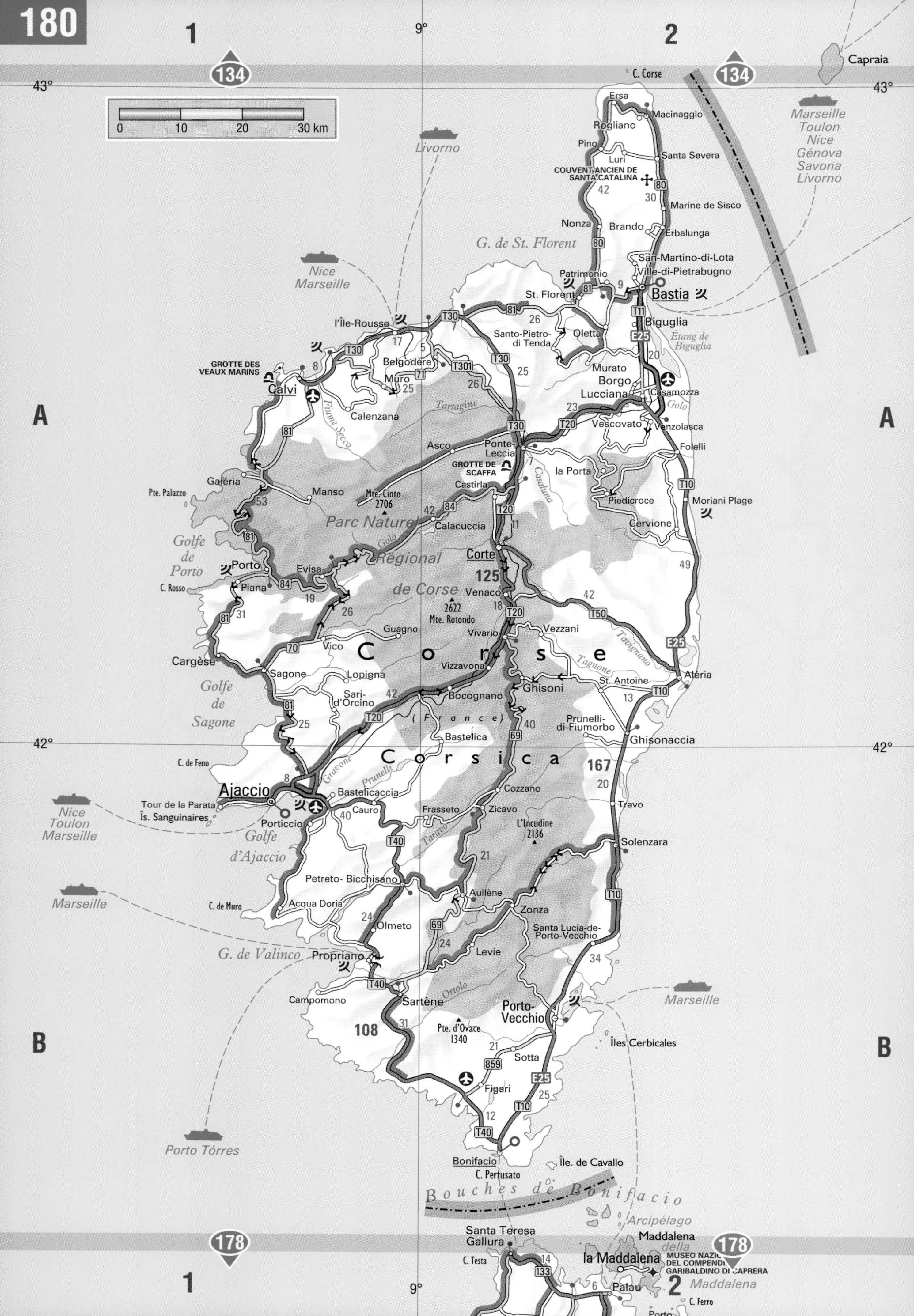

1   **2**

134   134

43°   43°

Capraia

Marseille
Toulon
Nice
Génova
Savona
Livorno

C. Corse

Ersa

Macinaggio

Rogliano

Pino   Santa Severa

Luri

COUVENT ANCIEN DE
SANTA CATALINA
42   80
30

Marine de Sisco

Nonza   Brando   Erbalunga

Livorno

80   San-Martino-di-Lota
Patrimonio   81   Ville-di-Pietrabugno
9
St. Florent   Bastia

G. de St. Florent   81   T11

Nice
Marseille   Biguglia
E25
26   20

l'Île-Rousse   T30   81   Santo-Pietro-
17   di-Tenda   Oletta   *Étang de
Biguglia*

GROTTE DES
VEAUX MARINS   T30   T301   5   Murato   20
8   Belgodère   Borgo
T30   Luciana   Casamozza
Calvi   Muro   25   25   26   *Golo*
71

A   Calenzana   Vescovato   Venzolasca   **A**
81   *Tartagine*   23   T20
T30   Folelli

Asco   Ponte-   la Porta   T10
Galéria   Leccia   7
Manso   GROTTE DE   Piedicroce   Moriani Plage
Pte. Palazzo   53   SCAFFA
Mte. Cinto   Castirla   Cervione   49
Golfe   2706   42   84
de   181   Calacuccia   11   42
Porto   *Parc Naturel*   T20
Porto   Evisa   *Régional*   Corte
C. Rosso   84   *de Corse*   **125**
Piana   19   Venaco
81   31   26   2622   18   42   T50
Mte. Rotondo   T20   Vezzani
70   Guagno   Vivario   St. Antoine   E25
Vico   Vizzavona   Ghisoni   *Tavignano*   Atéria
Cargèse   Lopigna   13   T10
Sagone   Sari-   42   *Tagnone*
Golfe   d'Orcino   Bocognano   Prunelli-
de   81   *(F r a n c e)*   40   di-Fiumorbo
Sagone   25   T20   Bastelica   69   Ghisonaccia

42°   C o r s e   42°

C o r s i c a   **167**

C. de Feno   20
Ajaccio   Cozzano
8   Bastelicaccia   Zicavo   Travo
Tour de la Parata   Cauro   Frasseto   L'Incudine
Îs. Sanguinaires   40   2136
Porticcio   21   Solenzara
Golfe   *Taravo*
d'Ajaccio   Aullène
Nice
Toulon   Petreto-Bicchisano   Zonza   T10
Marseille   Acqua Doria   Santa Lucia-de-
24   Porto-Vecchio
Olmeto   69
Marseille   24   Levie   34

G. de Valinco   Propriano

T40
Campomono   Sartène   Porto-   *Marseille*
Vecchio
B   31   Pte. d'Ovace   Îles Cerbicales   **B**
108   1340
21   Sotta
859
Figari   E25
25
T10
12

1   T40   **2**
Bonifacio
Porto Tórres   C. Pertusato   Île de Cavallo
Bouches de Bonifacio   *Arcipélago*

Santa Teresa   Maddalena
Gallura   *della*
MUSEO NAZIONALE
C. Testa   14   DEL COMPENDIO
133   GARIBALDINO DI CAPRERA
la Maddalena   *Maddalena*
6
Palau
C. Ferro
Porto

178   178

1   9°   **2**

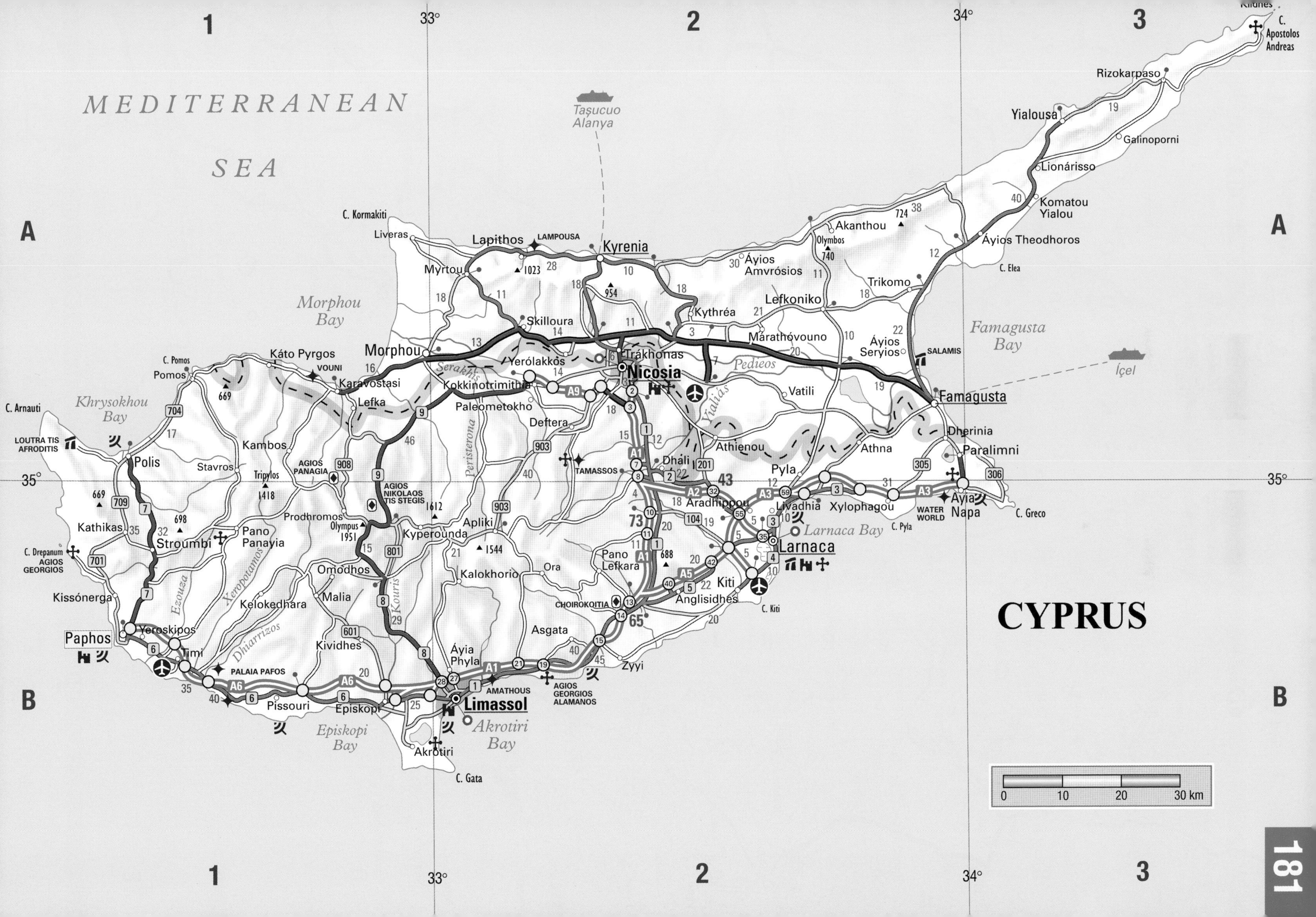
CYPRUS
MEDITERRANEAN SEA
Morphou Bay
Khrysokhou Bay
Famagusta Bay
Larnaca Bay
Episkopi Bay
Akrotiri Bay
Taşucuo Alanya
İçel
C. Apostolos Andreas
C. Kormakiti
C. Pomos
C. Arnauti
C. Drepanum
C. Elea
C. Greco
C. Pyla
C. Kiti
C. Gata
Rizokarpaso
Yialousa
Galinoporni
Lionárisso
Komatou Yialou
Áyios Theodhoros
Akanthou
Olymbos
Trikomo
Lefkoniko
Áyios Amvrósios
Kythréa
Márathóvouno
Áyios Seryios
SALAMIS
Famagusta
Dherinia
Paralimni
Ayia Napa
WATER WORLD
Athna
Xylophagou
Pyla
Athienou
Vatili
Pedieos
Yialias
Kyrenia
Lapithos
LAMPOUSA
Myrtou
Liveras
Skilloura
Morphou
Trákhonas
Nicosia
Yerólakkos
Kokkinotrimithia
Paleometokho
Deftera
Serakhis
Peristerona
Káto Pyrgos
VOUNI
Karavostasi
Lefka
Pomos
Polis
LOUTRA TIS AFRODITIS
Kambos
Stavros
Tripylos
AGIOS PANAGIA
AGIOS NIKOLAOS TIS STEGIS
Olympus
Prodhromos
Pano Panayia
Kyperounda
Apliki
TAMASSOS
Dhali
Aradhippou
Livadhia
Larnaca
Kiti
Anglisidhes
Pano Lefkara
CHOIROKOITIA
Ora
Kalokhorio
Asgata
Zyyi
AGIOS GEORGIOS ALAMANOS
AMATHOUS
Áyia Phyla
Limassol
Akrotiri
Episkopi
Pissouri
PALAIA PAFOS
Kividhes
Malia
Omodhos
Kouris
Kelokedhara
Xeropotamos
Dhiarrizos
Ezouza
Stroumbi
Kathikas
AGIOS GEORGIOS
Kissónerga
Yeroskipos
Timi
Paphos
1 2 3
A B
33° 34° 35°
0 10 20 30 km

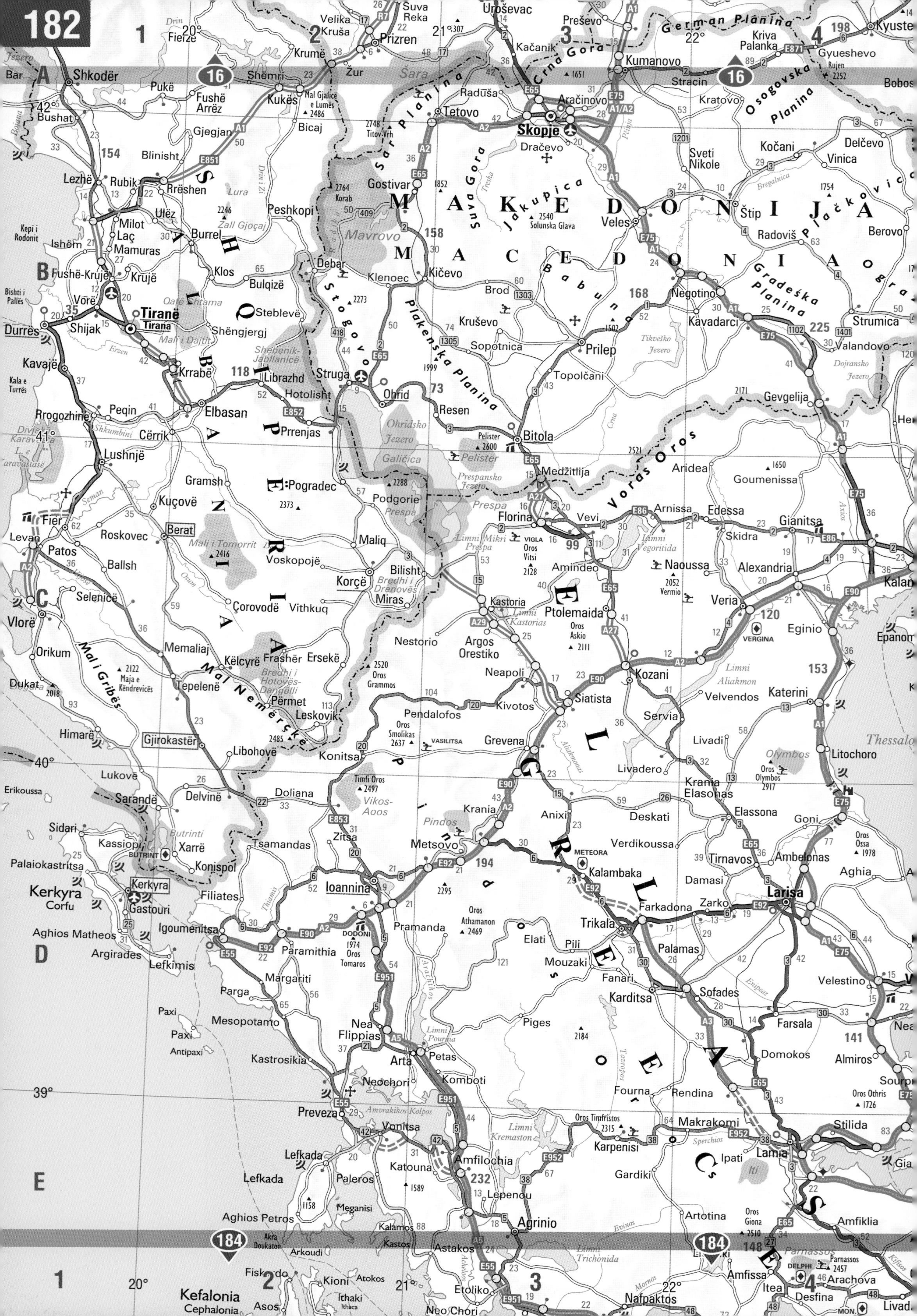
Shkodër
Lezhë
Rubik
Rrëshen
Milot
Laç
Mamuras
Burrel
Fushë-Krujë
Krujë
Vorë
Tiranë
Tirana
Durrës
Shijak
Kavajë
Krrabë
Librazhd
Elbasan
Peqin
Rrogozhinë
Cërrik
Lushnjë
Fier
Patos
Levan
Roskovec
Berat
Ballsh
Selenicë
Vlorë
Orikum
Dukat
Himarë
Tepelenë
Memaliaj
Këlcyrë
Gjirokastër
Libohovë
Përmet
Leskovik
Gramsh
Kuçovë
Pogradec
Korçë
Maliq
Bilisht
Ersekë
Frashër
Sarandë
Delvinë
Konispol
Xarrë
Kukës
Peshkopi
Bulqizë
Klos
Shëmri
Fushë Arrëz
Pukë
Bushat
Bar
Prizren
Uroševac
Kačanik
Preševo
Kumanovo
Skopje
Tetovo
Gostivar
Debar
Kičevo
Struga
Ohrid
Resen
Bitola
Prilep
Kruševo
Veles
Štip
Kočani
Delčevo
Vinica
Radoviš
Strumica
Valandovo
Gevgelija
Kavadarci
Negotino
Sveti Nikole
Kratovo
Kriva Palanka
Kyustendil
Florina
Edessa
Gianitsa
Naoussa
Veria
Alexandria
Kastoria
Ptolemaida
Kozani
Siatista
Grevena
Servia
Katerini
Litochoro
Elassona
Larisa
Trikala
Kalambaka
Karditsa
Farsala
Volos
Almiros
Lamia
Karpenisi
Amfilochia
Agrinio
Nafpaktos
Amfissa
Itea
Delphi
Arachova
Ioannina
Metsovo
Konitsa
Igoumenitsa
Parga
Preveza
Arta
Lefkada
Kerkyra
Corfu
Paxi
Kefalonia
Cephalonia
Ithaki
SHQIPËRIA
MAKEDONIJA
MACEDONIA
ELLADA
GREECE
Ohridsko Jezero
Prespansko Jezero
Limni Vegoritida
Thessaloniki
39°
40°
41°
42°
20°
21°
22°
184
16

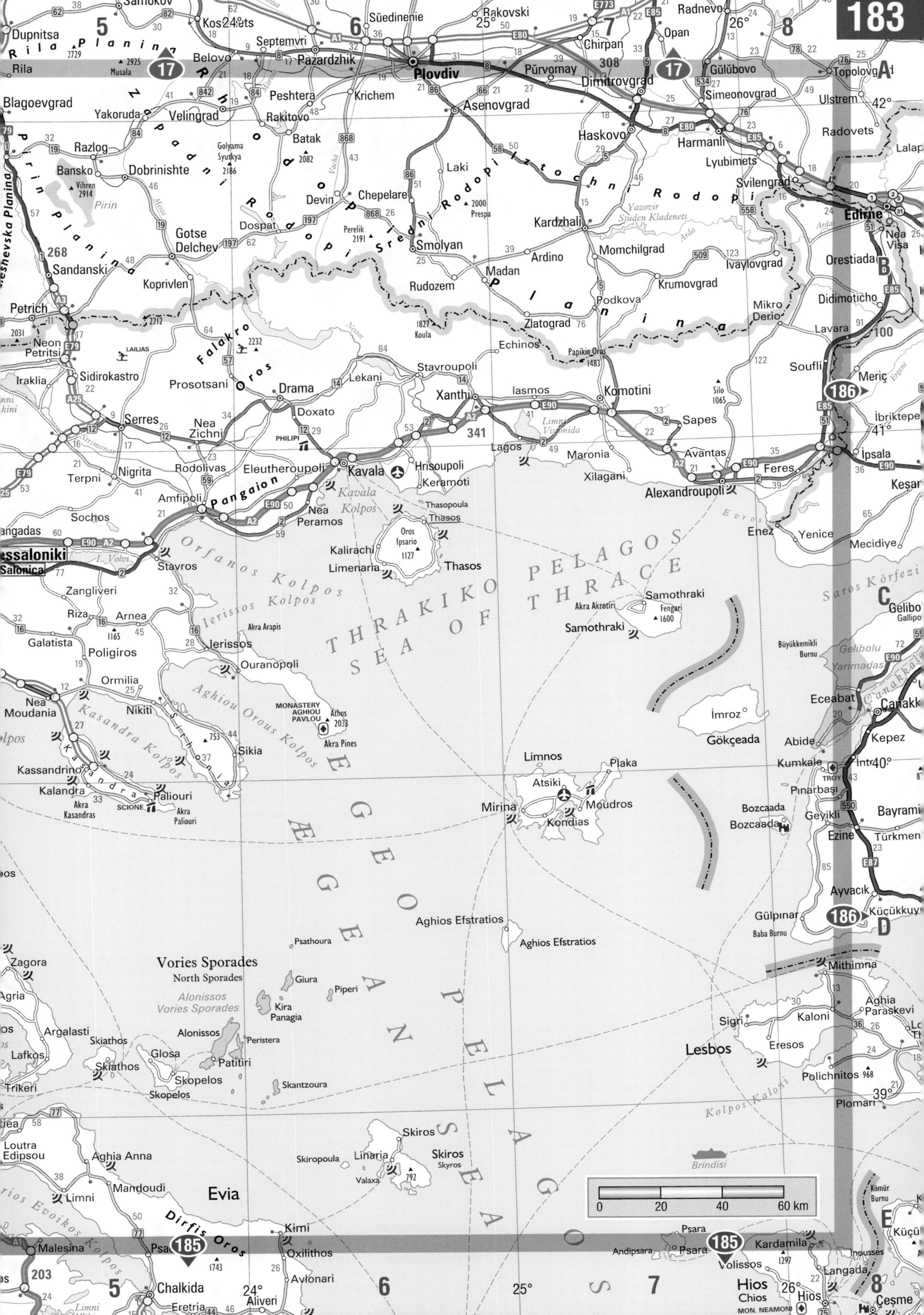

Samokov
Dupnitsa
Rila Planina
Musala
Rila
Belovo
Septemvri
Pazardzhik
Süedinenie
Plovdiv
Rakovski
Chirpan
Radnevo
Opan
Pürvomay
Dimitrovgrad
Gülübovo
Topolovgrad
Blagoevgrad
Yakoruda
Velingrad
Peshtera
Krichem
Rakitovo
Asenovgrad
Simeonovgrad
Ulstrem
Radovets
Batak
Haskovo
Harmanli
Lyubimets
Razlog
Bansko
Vihren
Dobrinishte
Pirin
Pirin Planina
Zapadni Rodopi
Golyama Syutkya
Laki
Iztochni Rodopi
Svilengrad
Edirne
Devin
Chepelare
Prespa
Sredni Rodopi
Yazovir Studen Kladenets
Gotse Delchev
Dospat
Perelik
Smolyan
Kardzhali
Momchilgrad
Nea Visa
Sandanski
Ardino
Madan
Ivaylovgrad
Orestiada
Koprivlen
Rudozem
Krumovgrad
Petrich
Podkova
Didimoticho
Mikro Derio
Zlatograd
Koula
Neon Petritsi
Falakro Oros
Echinos
Papikio Oros
Lavara
Iraklia
Sidirokastro
Prosotsani
Drama
Lekani
Stavroupoli
Soufli
Meriç
Silo
Xanthi
Iasmos
Komotini
Serres
Nea Zichni
Doxato
PHILIPPI
Limni Vistonida
Sapes
İbriktepe
Lagos
Maronia
Avantas
İpsala
Terpni
Nigrita
Rodolivas
Eleutheroupoli
Kavala
Hrisoupoli
Keramoti
Xilagani
Feres
Keşan
Amfipoli
Pangaion
Kavala Kolpos
Thasopoula
Alexandroupoli
Sochos
Nea Peramos
Thasos
Evros
Enez
Yenice
Mecidiye
Oros Ipsario
Langadas
Thessaloniki
Salonica
L. Volvi
Kalirachi
Limenaria
Thasos
Stavros
Orfanos Kolpos
THRAKIKO PELAGOS
SEA OF THRACE
Samothraki
Akra Akrotiri
Fengari
Saros Körfezi
Zangliveri
Ierissos Kolpos
Gelibolu
Riza
Arnea
Akra Arapis
Samothraki
Galatista
Poligiros
Ierissos
Büyükkemikli Burnu
Gelibolu Yarimadası
Ouranopoli
Ormilia
Nea Moudania
Nikiti
Aghiou Orous Kolpos
MONASTERY AGHIOU PAVLOU
Athos
İmroz
Eceabat
Çanakkale
Kasandra Kolpos
Sithonia
Akra Pines
Gökçeada
Abide
Kepez
Sikia
Limnos
Plaka
Kumkale
TROY
Kassandrino
Kasandra
Atsiki
Pınarbaşı
Kalandra
Paliouri
Akra Kasandras
SCIONE
Akra Paliouri
Mirina
Moudros
Kondias
Bozcaada
Geyikli
Bayramiç
Ezine
Türkmen
AEGEAN SEA
AIGAIO PELAGOS
Ayvacık
Aghios Efstratios
Gülpınar
Baba Burnu
Küçükkuyu
Psathoura
Zagora
Vories Sporades
North Sporades
Giura
Mithimna
Piperi
Alonissos
Vories Sporades
Kira Panagia
Agria
Argalasti
Skiathos
Alonissos
Peristera
Sigri
Kaloni
Aghia Paraskevi
Lafkos
Glosa
Patitiri
Eresos
Lesbos
Skiathos
Skopelos
Skopelos
Polichnitos
Trikeri
Skantzoura
Plomari
Kolpos Kaloni
Loutra Edipsou
Aghia Anna
Skiros
Skiropoula
Linaria
Skiros
Skyros
Valaxa
Bríndisi
Mandoudi
Limni
Evia
Evoikos Kolpos
Dirfis Oros
Kimi
Psara
Andipsara
Psara
Kardamila
Komür Burnu
Malesina
Oxilithos
Volissos
Inousses
Langada
Chalkida
Avlonari
Aliveri
Eretria
Hios
Chios
Hios
MON. NEAMONI
Çeşme
Limni Yliki
0 20 40 60 km

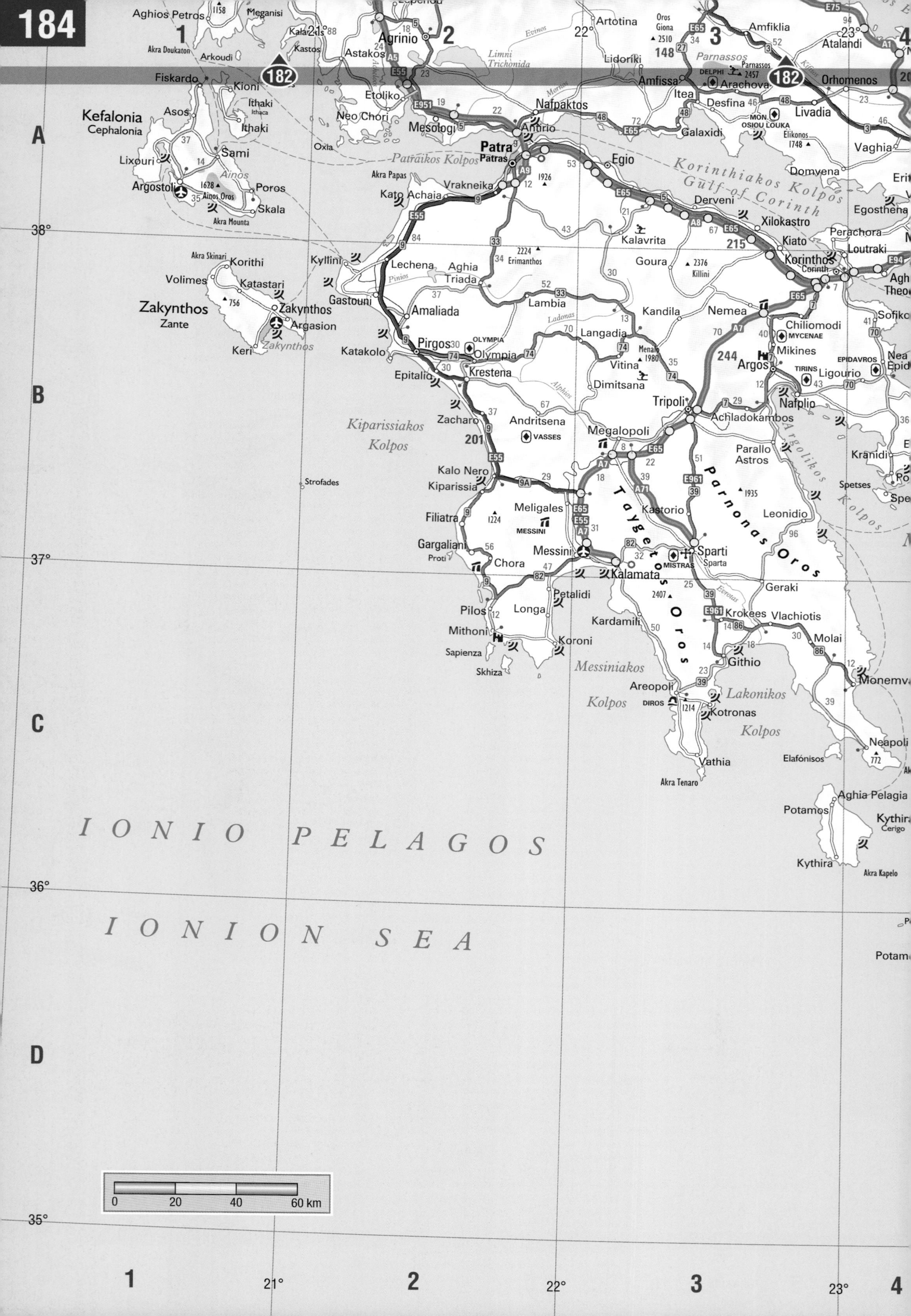

Kefalonia
Cephalonia
Argostoli
Lixouri
Sami
Poros
Skala
Fiskardo
Ithaki
Zakynthos
Zante
Patra
Patras
Patraikos Kolpos
Nafpaktos
Antirio
Mesologi
Agrinio
Egio
Korinthiakos Kolpos
Gulf of Corinth
Korinthos
Corinth
Kiato
Xilokastro
Derveni
Kalavrita
Pirgos
Olympia
Amaliada
Gastouni
Kyllini
Tripoli
Argos
Nafplio
Mikines
Megalopoli
Kalamata
Messini
Sparti
Sparta
Gythio
Monemvasia
Pilos
Methoni
Koroni
Kiparissia
Kiparissiakos Kolpos
Messiniakos Kolpos
Lakonikos Kolpos
Argolikos Kolpos
Taygetos Oros
Parnonas Oros
Kythira
Neapoli
Strofades
Amfissa
Itea
Arachova
Livadia
Loutraki
IONIO PELAGOS
IONION SEA
0
20
40
60 km
38°
37°
36°
35°
21°
22°
23°
A
B
C
D
1
2
3
4

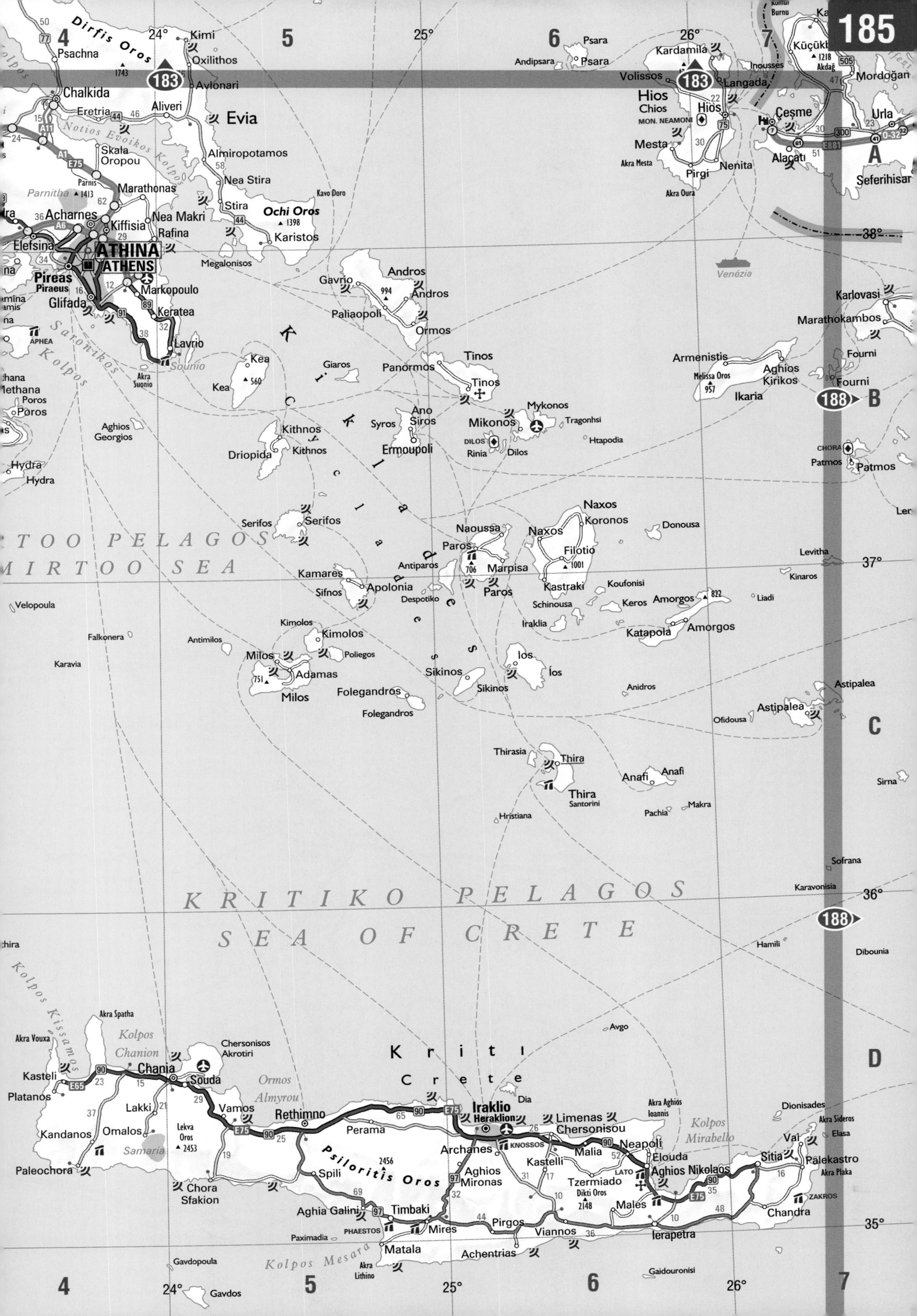

Dirfis Oros
Psachna
Kimi
Oxilithos
Avlonari
Chalkida
Eretria
Aliveri
Evia
Notios Evoikos Kolpos
Skala Oropou
Almiropotamos
Nea Stira
Stira
Kavo Doro
Ochi Oros
Karistos
Marathonas
Acharnes
Kiffisia
Nea Makri
Rafina
Elefsina
ATHINA
ATHENS
Pireas
Piraeus
Glifada
Markopoulo
Keratea
Lavrio
Sounio
Akra Sounio
Saronikos Kolpos
APHEA
Megalonisos
Andros
Gavrio
Paliaopoli
Ormos
Kea
Giaros
Tinos
Panormos
Mykonos
Mikonos
Tragonhsi
Htapodia
Ano Siros
Syros
Ermoupoli
DILOS
Rinia
Dilos
Kithnos
Driopida
Aghios Georgios
Poros
Hydra
Kiklades
Serifos
MIRTOO PELAGOS
MIRTOO SEA
Naxos
Koronos
Donousa
Naoussa
Paros
Filotio
Antiparos
Marpisa
Kastraki
Koufonisi
Kamares
Apolonia
Sifnos
Despotiko
Schinousa
Keros
Amorgos
Iraklia
Katapola
Liadi
Levitha
Kinaros
Velopoula
Kimolos
Falkonera
Antimilos
Poliegos
Karavia
Milos
Adamas
Folegandros
Sikinos
Ios
Íos
Anidros
Astipalea
Ofidousa
Thirasia
Thira
Santorini
Anafi
Pachia
Makra
Hristiana
Sirna
Sofrana
Karavonisia
KRITIKO PELAGOS
SEA OF CRETE
Hamili
Dibounia
Psara
Andipsara
Kardamila
Volissos
Hios
Chios
MON. NEAMONI
Langada
Inousses
Mesta
Akra Mesta
Pirgi
Nenita
Akra Oura
Çeşme
Alaçati
Urla
Mordoğan
Küçükbahçe
Akdağ
Seferihisar
Venézia
Karlovasi
Marathokambos
Armenistis
Melissa Oros
Aghios Kirikos
Ikaria
Fourni
CHORA
Patmos
Kolpos Kissamos
Akra Spatha
Akra Vouxa
Kolpos Chanion
Chersonisos Akrotiri
Kasteli
Chania
Souda
Platanos
Lakki
Vamos
Ormos Almyrou
Kandanos
Omalos
Lefka Oros
Samaria
Paleochora
Chora Sfakion
Kriti
Crete
Rethimno
Perama
Iraklio
Heraklion
Dia
Avgo
Limenas Chersonisou
Akra Aghios Ioannis
Dionisades
KNOSSOS
Archanes
Psiloritis Oros
Spili
Aghios Mironas
Kastelli
Malia
Neapoli
Elouda
Kolpos Mirabello
Akra Sideros
Elasa
Vai
Sitia
Palekastro
Akra Plaka
LATO
Aghios Nikolaos
Tzermiado
Dikti Oros
Males
ZAKROS
Chandra
Aghia Galini
Timbaki
PHAESTOS
Mires
Pirgos
Viannos
Ierapetra
Paximadia
Matala
Achentrias
Kolpos Mesara
Akra Lithino
Gaidouronisi
Gavdopoula
Gavdos

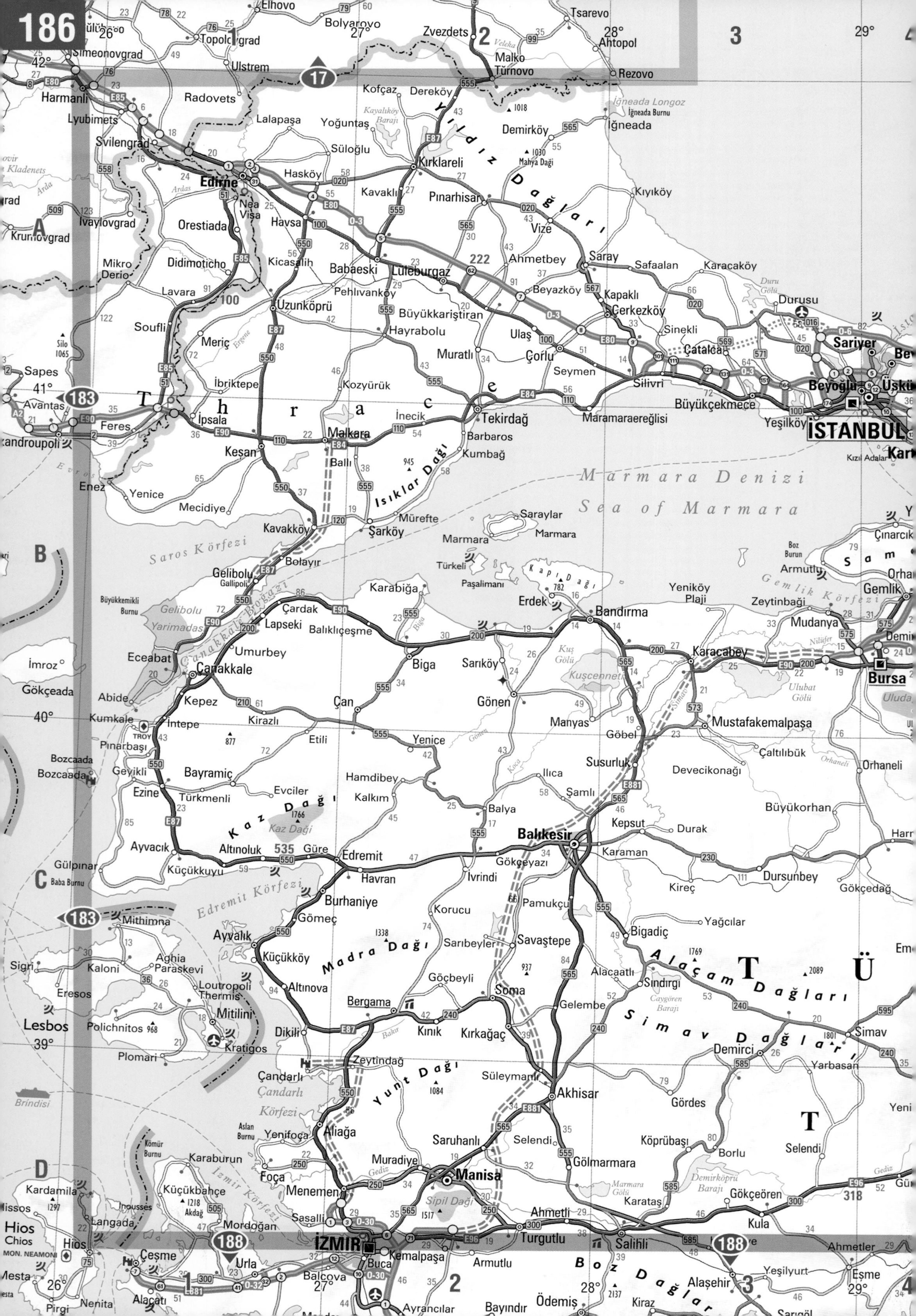
Elhovo
Bolyarovo
Zvezdets
Tsarevo
Ahtopol
Malko Türnovo
Rezovo
Topolovgrad
Simeonovgrad
Ulstrem
Harmanli
Radovets
Lyubimets
Svilengrad
Kofçaz
Dereköy
Lalapaşa
Yoğuntaş
Kayalıköy Barajı
Demirköy
İğneada Longoz
İğneada Burnu
İğneada
Süloğlu
Kırklareli
Mahya Dağı
Edirne
Hasköy
Kavaklı
Pınarhisar
Kıyıköy
Nea Visa
Orestiada
Ivaylovgrad
Krumovgrad
Havsa
Vize
Yıldız Dağları
Ahmetbey
Saray
Safaalan
Karacaköy
Mikro Derio
Didimoticho
Kicasalih
Babaeski
Lüleburgaz
Lavara
Pehlivanköy
Beyazköy
Kapaklı
Duru Gölü
Durusu
Uzunköprü
Büyükkarıştıran
Çerkezköy
Soufli
Silo
Hayrabolu
Sinekli
Meriç
Ulaş
Muratlı
Çorlu
Çatalca
Sarıyer
Seymen
Sapes
İbriktepe
Kozyürük
Silivri
Beyoğlu
Üsküdar
Avantas
Thrace
İpsala
İnecik
Tekirdağ
Büyükçekmece
Feres
Malkara
Marmaraereğlisi
Yeşilköy
İSTANBUL
Alexandroupoli
Keşan
Barbaros
Ballı
Kumbağ
Kızıl Adalar
Evros
Enez
Işıklar Dağı
Marmara Denizi
Sea of Marmara
Yenice
Mecidiye
Mürefte
Saraylar
Kavakköy
Şarköy
Marmara
Çınarcık
Saros Körfezi
Boz Burun
Bolayır
Türkeli
Armutlu
Gelibolu
Gallipoli
Paşalimanı
Kapı Dağı
Gemlik Körfezi
Orhangazi
Büyükkemikli Burnu
Karabiğa
Yeniköy Plajı
Gemlik
Erdek
Zeytinbağı
Gelibolu Yarımadası
Çardak
Bandırma
Mudanya
Lapseki
Balıklıçeşme
Biga
Çanakkale Boğazı
Umurbey
Karacabey
İmroz
Eceabat
Çanakkale
Kuş Gölü
Sarıköy
Kuşcenneti
Ulubat Gölü
Bursa
Uludağ
Gökçeada
Abide
Kepez
Çan
Gönen
Kumkale
İntepe
Kirazlı
Manyas
Mustafakemalpaşa
Troy
Pınarbaşı
Etili
Yenice
Göbel
Çaltılıbük
Bozcaada
Geyikli
Bayramiç
Hamdibey
Susurluk
Devecikonağı
Orhaneli
Ezine
Türkmenli
Evciler
Kalkım
Ilıca
Şamlı
Kaz Dağı
Balya
Büyükorhan
Ayvacık
Altınoluk
Güre
Balıkesir
Kepsut
Durak
Gülpınar
Baba Burnu
Küçükkuyu
Edremit
Gökçeyazı
Karaman
Havran
İvrindi
Dursunbey
Edremit Körfezi
Kireç
Gökçedağ
Burhaniye
Pamukçu
Mithimna
Gömeç
Korucu
Yağcılar
Ayvalık
Madra Dağı
Bigadiç
Sarıbeyler
Savaştepe
Küçükköy
Aghia Paraskevi
Sigri
Kaloni
Alaçam Dağları
Eresos
Alacaatlı
Sındırgı
Göçbeyli
Loutropoli Thermis
Altınova
Soma
Caygören Barajı
Lesbos
Mitilini
Bergama
Gelembe
Simav Dağları
Polichnitos
Dikili
Kınık
Kırkağaç
Simav
Kratigos
Demirci
Plomari
Zeytindağ
Yarbasan
Çandarlı
Yunt Dağı
Süleymanlı
Çandarlı Körfezi
Akhisar
Gördes
Brindisi
Aslan Burnu
Yenifoça
Aliağa
Saruhanlı
Selendi
Köprübaşı
Kömür Burnu
Karaburun
Borlu
Selendi
Muradiye
Gölmarmara
Foça
Manisa
İzmir Körfezi
Kardamila
Küçükbahçe
Menemen
Sipil Dağı
Marmara Gölü
Demirköprü Barajı
Karataş
Gökçeören
Akdağ
Inousses
Sasalli
Ahmetli
Hios
Chios
Langada
Mordoğan
Kula
MON. NEAMONI
İZMİR
Turgutlu
Salihli
Ahmetler
Çeşme
Urla
Buca
Kemalpaşa
Armutlu
Boz Dağlar
Yeşilyurt
Mesta
Balçova
Alaşehir
Eşme
Pirgi
Nenita
Alaçatı
Ayrancılar
Bayındır
Ödemiş
Kiraz
Sarıgöl
26°
27°
28°
29°
42°
41°
40°
39°
A
B
C
D
1
2
3
4
17
183
188
318
222
100
535

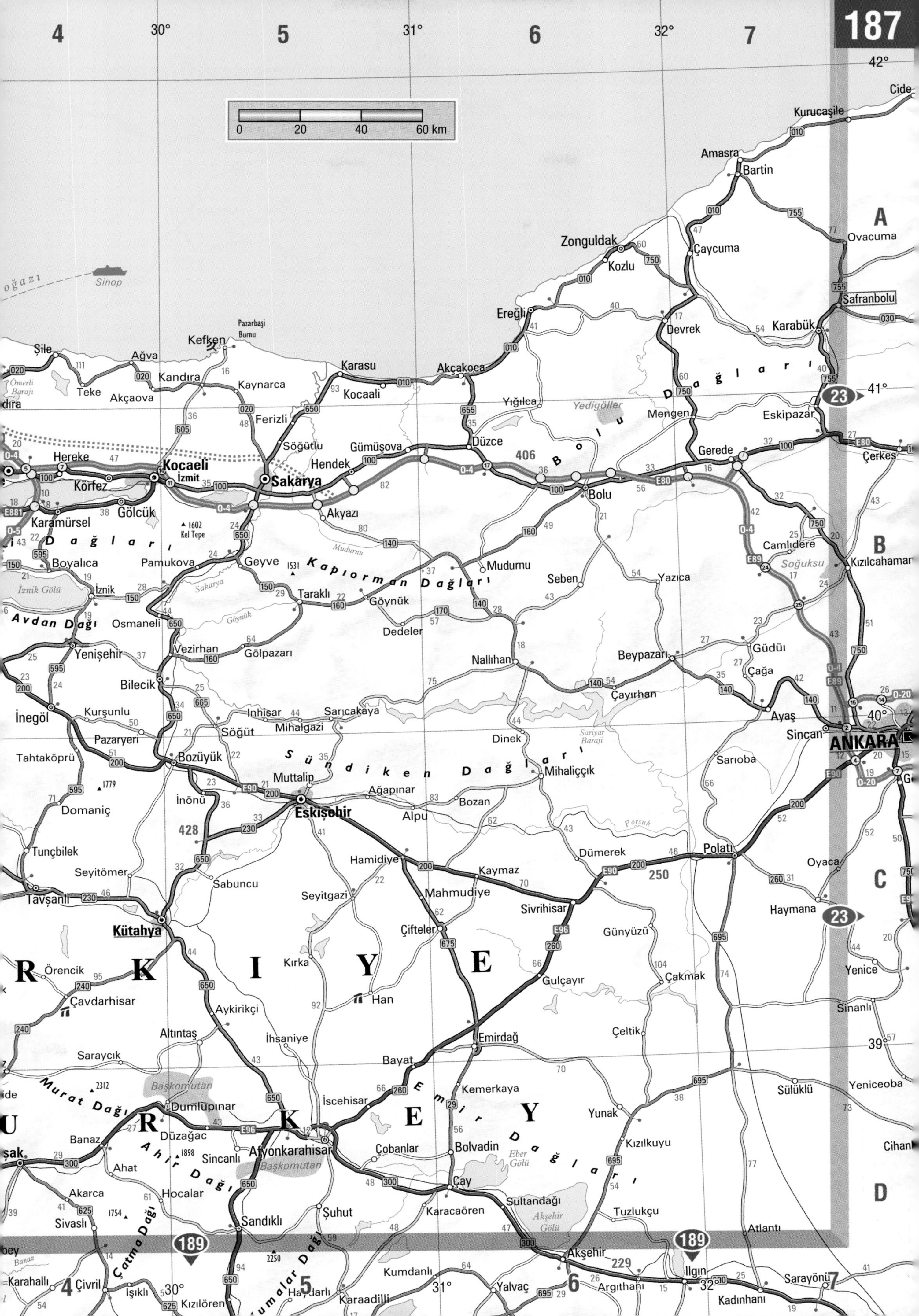

4
5
6
7
30°
31°
32°
42°
41°
40°
39°
A
B
C
D
0
20
40
60 km
Cide
Kurucaşile
Amasra
Bartin
Ovacuma
Zonguldak
Kozlu
Çaycuma
Safranbolu
Ereğli
Devrek
Karabük
Sinop
Pazarbaşi Burnu
Kefken
Şile
Ağva
Kandıra
Karasu
Akçakoca
Teke
Akçaova
Kaynarca
Kocaali
Yığılca
Yedigöller
Mengen
Eskipazar
Ferizli
Söğütlu
Gümüşova
Düzce
Bolu Dağları
Gerede
Hereke
Kocaeli
İzmit
Sakarya
Hendek
Bolu
Çerkeş
Körfez
Akyazı
Gölcük
Karamürsel
Kel Tepe
Samanlı Dağları
Camlıdere
Soğuksu
Kızılcahamam
Boyalıca
Pamukova
Geyve
Köroğlu
Kapıorman Dağları
Mudurnu
Seben
Yazıca
İznik Gölü
İznik
Taraklı
Göynük
Avdan Dağı
Osmaneli
Dedeler
Yenişehir
Vezirhan
Gölpazarı
Nallıhan
Beypazarı
Güdül
Çağa
Bilecik
Çayırhan
Ayaş
İnegöl
Kurşunlu
İnhisar
Mihalgazi
Sarıcakaya
Sincan
ANKARA
Pazaryeri
Söğüt
Dinek
Sarıyar Baraji
Tahtaköprü
Bozüyük
Sündiken Dağları
Mihalıççık
Sarıoba
Muttalip
Ağapınar
İnönü
Domaniç
Eskişehir
Bozan
Alpu
Porsuk
Tunçbilek
Hamidiye
Dümerek
Polatlı
Seyitömer
Kaymaz
Oyaca
Sabuncu
Seyitgazi
Mahmudiye
Tavşanlı
Sivrihisar
Haymana
Kütahya
Çifteler
Günyüzü
TÜRKIYE
Örencik
Kırka
Gulçayır
Çakmak
Yenice
Çavdarhisar
Han
Aykirikçi
Sinanlı
Altıntaş
İhsaniye
Emirdağ
Çeltik
Saraycık
Bayat
Murat Dağı
Başkomutan
Kemerkaya
Sülüklü
Yeniceoba
Dumlupınar
İscehisar
Emir Dağları
Yunak
Banaz
Düzağac
Kızılkuyu
Cihanbeyli
Uşak
Sincanlı
Afyonkarahisar
Çobanlar
Bolvadin
Eber Gölü
Ahat
Ahır Dağı
Akarca
Hocalar
Çay
Sultandağı
Sivaslı
Çatma Dağı
Sandıklı
Şuhut
Karacaören
Akşehir Gölü
Tuzlukçu
Atlantı
Kumalar Dağı
Akşehir
Ilgın
Banaz
Karahallı
Çivril
Işıklı
Kızılören
Haydarlı
Karaadilli
Kumdanlı
Yalvaç
Argıthanı
Sarayönü
Kadınhanı
23
189

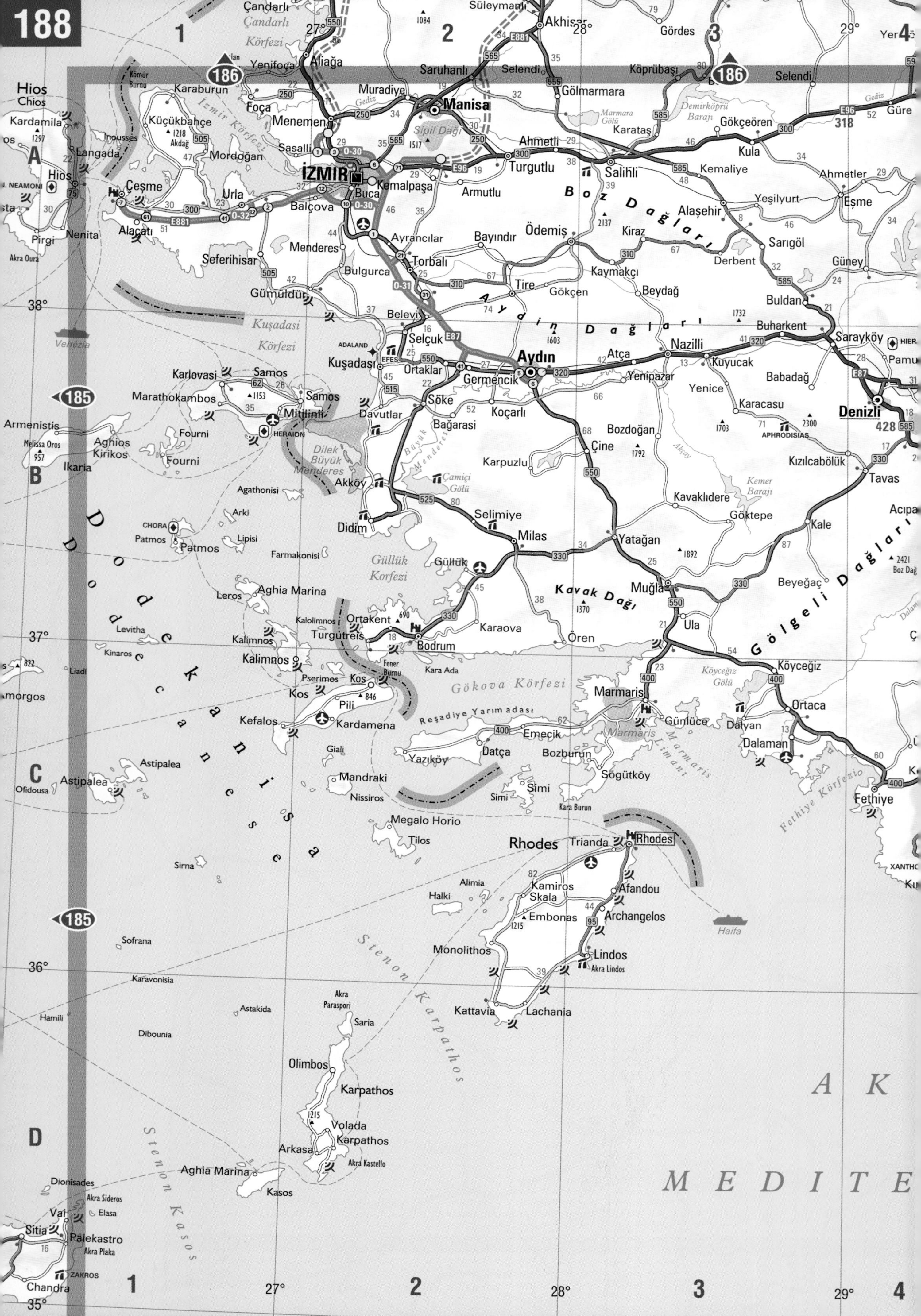
Çandarlı
Çandarlı Körfezi
Aliağa
Yenifoça
Kömür Burnu
Karaburun
Hios
Chios
Kardamila
Langada
Hios
Inousses
Küçükbahçe
Akdağ
Mordoğan
İzmir Körfezi
Foça
Menemen
Sasalli
İZMIR
Çeşme
Urla
Balçova
Buca
Kemalpaşa
Alaçatı
Nenita
Pirgi
Akra Oura
Menderes
Seferihisar
Gümüldür
Kuşadasi Körfezi
Venézia
Süleymanlı
Akhisar
Gördes
Saruhanlı
Selendi
Köprübaşı
Muradiye
Manisa
Gölmarmara
Marmara Gölü
Demirköprü Barajı
Gökçeören
Güre
Gediz
Sipil Dağı
Karataş
Ahmetli
Kula
Turgutlu
Salihli
Kemaliye
Ahmetler
Armutlu
Boz Dağları
Alaşehir
Yeşilyurt
Eşme
Ayrancılar
Bayındır
Ödemiş
Kiraz
Sarıgöl
Torbalı
Kaymakçı
Derbent
Güney
Bulgurca
Tire
Gökçen
Beydağ
Buldan
Belevi
Aydin Dağları
Buharkent
Sarayköy
Hierapolis
Selçuk
Adaland
Efes
Kuşadası
Ortaklar
Aydın
Atça
Nazilli
Kuyucak
Pamukkale
Germencik
Yenipazar
Babadağ
Yenice
Denizli
Karlovasi
Samos
Marathokambos
Mitilinii
Heraion
Söke
Davutlar
Koçarlı
Bağarasi
Karacasu
Aphrodisias
Armenistis
Melissa Oros
Ikaria
Aghios Kirikos
Fourni
Dilek Büyük Menderes
Büyük Menderes
Bozdoğan
Çine
Karpuzlu
Akçay
Kızılcabölük
Tavas
Camiçi Gölü
Akköy
Kemer Barajı
Agathonisi
Arki
Chora
Patmos
Lipisi
Didim
Selimiye
Milas
Yatağan
Kavaklıdere
Göktepe
Kale
Acıpayam
Dodecanese
Farmakonisi
Güllük Körfezi
Güllük
Muğla
Beyeğaç
Gölgeli Dağları
Boz Dağ
Leros
Aghia Marina
Kavak Dağı
Kalolimnos
Ortakent
Turgutreis
Karaova
Ören
Ula
Levitha
Kalimnos
Bodrum
Kinaros
Kalimnos
Fener Burnu
Kara Ada
Köyceğiz
Köyceğiz Gölü
Liadi
Amorgos
Pserimos
Kos
Pili
Gökova Körfezi
Marmaris
Günlüce
Dalyan
Ortaca
Kefalos
Kardamena
Reşadiye Yarımadası
Emecik
Marmaris Limanı
Dalaman
Giali
Yazıköy
Datça
Bozburun
Astipalea
Ofidousa
Mandraki
Nissiros
Sögütköy
Simi
Kara Burun
Fethiye
Fethiye Körfezio
Megalo Horio
Tilos
Rhodes
Trianda
Sirna
Alimia
Kamiros Skala
Afandou
Halki
Embonas
Archangelos
Haifa
Sofrana
Monolithos
Lindos
Akra Lindos
Stenon Karpathos
Karavonisia
Kattavia
Lachania
Akra Paraspori
Astakida
Saria
Hamili
Dibounia
Olimbos
Karpathos
Volada
Karpathos
Arkasa
Akra Kastello
Aghia Marina
Kasos
Stenon Kasos
Dionisades
Akra Sideros
Elasa
Vai
Sitia
Palekastro
Akra Plaka
Zakros
Chandra
AK
MEDITE
38°
37°
36°
35°
27°
28°
29°
A
B
C
D
1
2
3
4
185
186

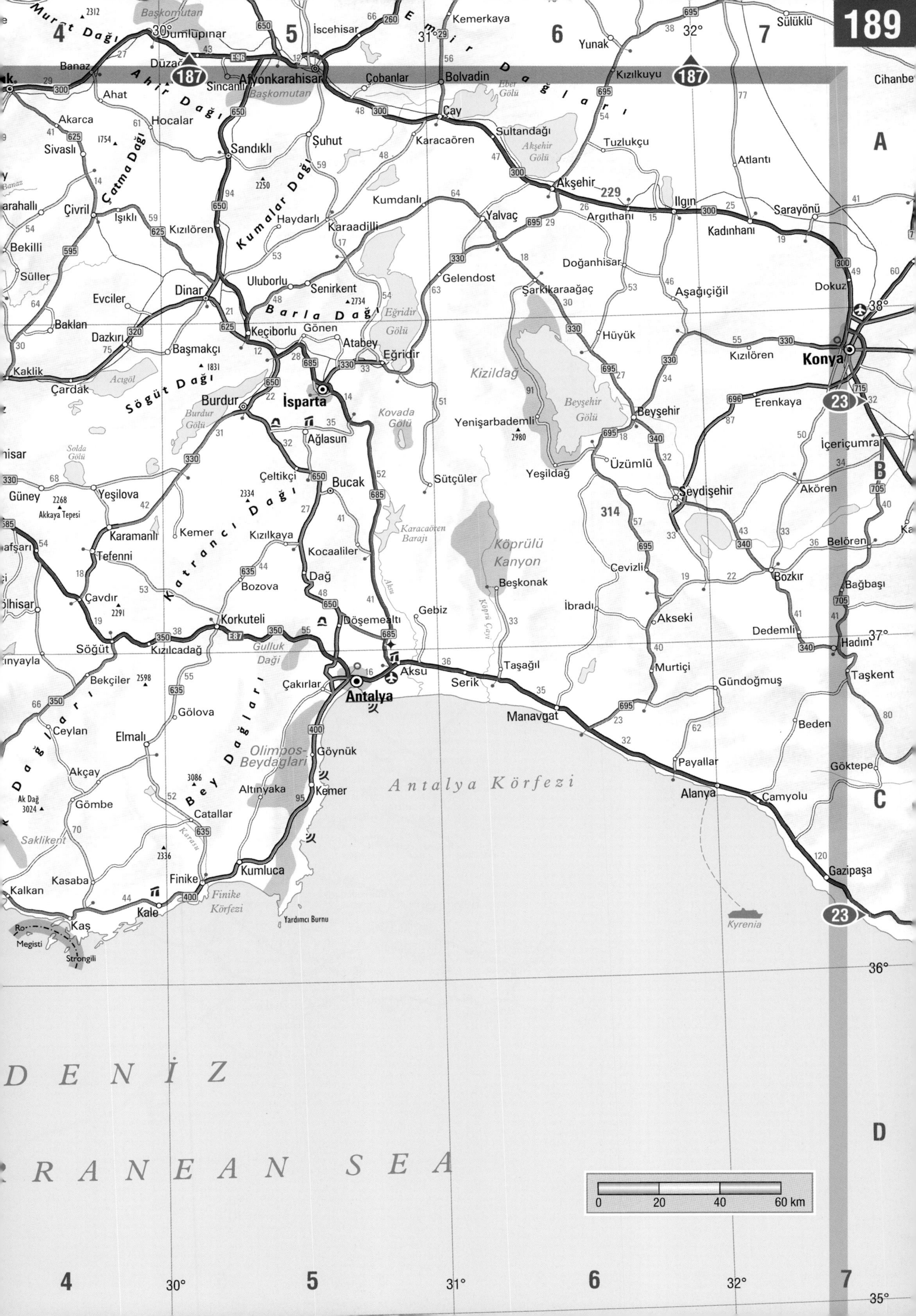
Afyonkarahisar
Isparta
Burdur
Antalya
Konya
Akşehir
Beyşehir
Seydişehir
Alanya
Manavgat
Serik
Aksu
Kemer
Kumluca
Finike
Kale
Kaş
Kalkan
Gazipaşa
Eğridir
Dinar
Sandıklı
Çay
Bolvadin
Ilgın
Sarayönü
Kadınhanı
Yalvaç
Şarkikaraağaç
Korkuteli
Elmalı
Akseki
Bozkır
Hadim
Taşkent
Antalya Körfezi
Beyşehir Gölü
Eğridir Gölü
Burdur Gölü
Akşehir Gölü
Köprülü Kanyon
Olimpos-Beydağları
Bey Dağları
Katrancı Dağı
Kumalar Dağı
Barla Dağı
Söğüt Dağı
Sultan Dağları
Emir Dağları
Kızıldağ
Finike Körfezi
Yardımcı Burnu
Megisti
Strongili
Kyrenia
DENİZ
RANEAN SEA
0
20
40
60 km
30°
31°
32°
36°
37°
38°
35°
A
B
C
D
4
5
6
7

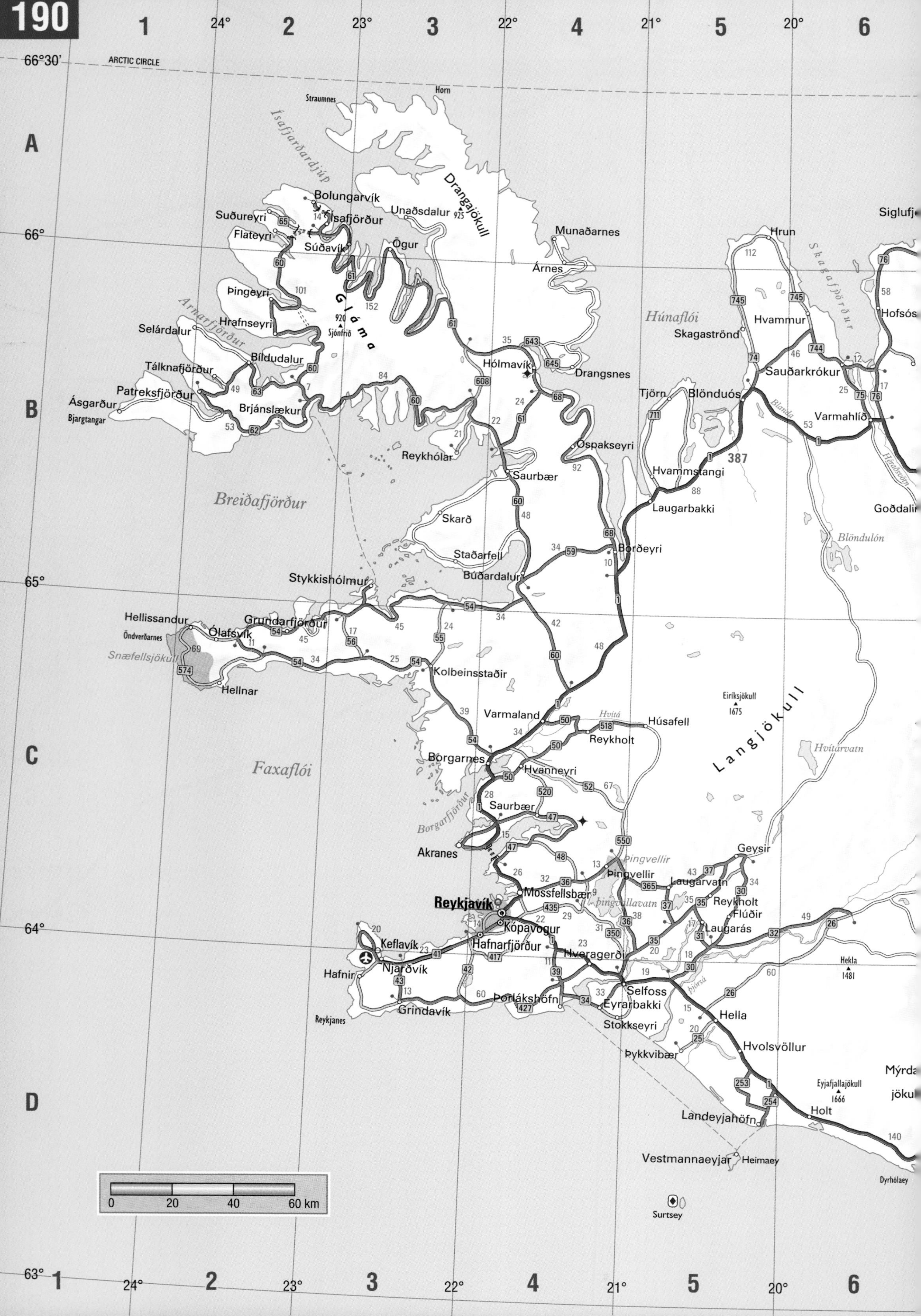

ARCTIC CIRCLE
Ísafjarðardjúp
Drangajökull
Bolungarvík
Ísafjörður
Suðureyri
Flateyri
Súðavík
Unaðsdalur
Ögur
Munaðarnes
Árnes
Þingeyri
Glámа
Hrafnseyri
Selárdalur
Arnarfjörður
Bíldudalur
Tálknafjörður
Patreksfjörður
Ásgarður
Bjargtangar
Brjánslækur
Hólmavík
Drangsnes
Reykhólar
Óspakseyri
Saurbær
Breiðafjörður
Skarð
Staðarfell
Búðardalur
Stykkishólmur
Hellissandur
Öndverðarnes
Grundarfjörður
Ólafsvík
Snæfellsjökull
Hellnar
Kolbeinsstaðir
Varmaland
Borgarnes
Faxaflói
Hvanneyri
Reykholt
Húsafell
Hvítá
Eiríksjökull
Langjökull
Hvítárvatn
Borgarfjörður
Akranes
Reykjavík
Mosfellsbær
Kópavogur
Hafnarfjörður
Keflavík
Njarðvík
Hafnir
Grindavík
Reykjanes
Þorlákshöfn
Hveragerði
Selfoss
Eyrarbakki
Stokkseyri
Þingvellir
Þingvallavatn
Laugarvatn
Geysir
Flúðir
Laugarás
Hekla
Hella
Hvolsvöllur
Þykkvibær
Landeyjahöfn
Vestmannaeyjar
Heimaey
Surtsey
Holt
Eyjafjallajökull
Mýrdalsjökull
Dyrhólaey
Húnaflói
Tjörn
Blönduós
Hvammstangi
Laugarbakki
Borðeyri
Skagaströnd
Hvammur
Hrun
Skagafjörður
Sauðárkrókur
Varmahlíð
Hofsós
Siglufjörður
Goðdalir
Blöndulón
Blanda
Héraðsvötn
Horn
Straumnes
Sjónfríð
0 20 40 60 km

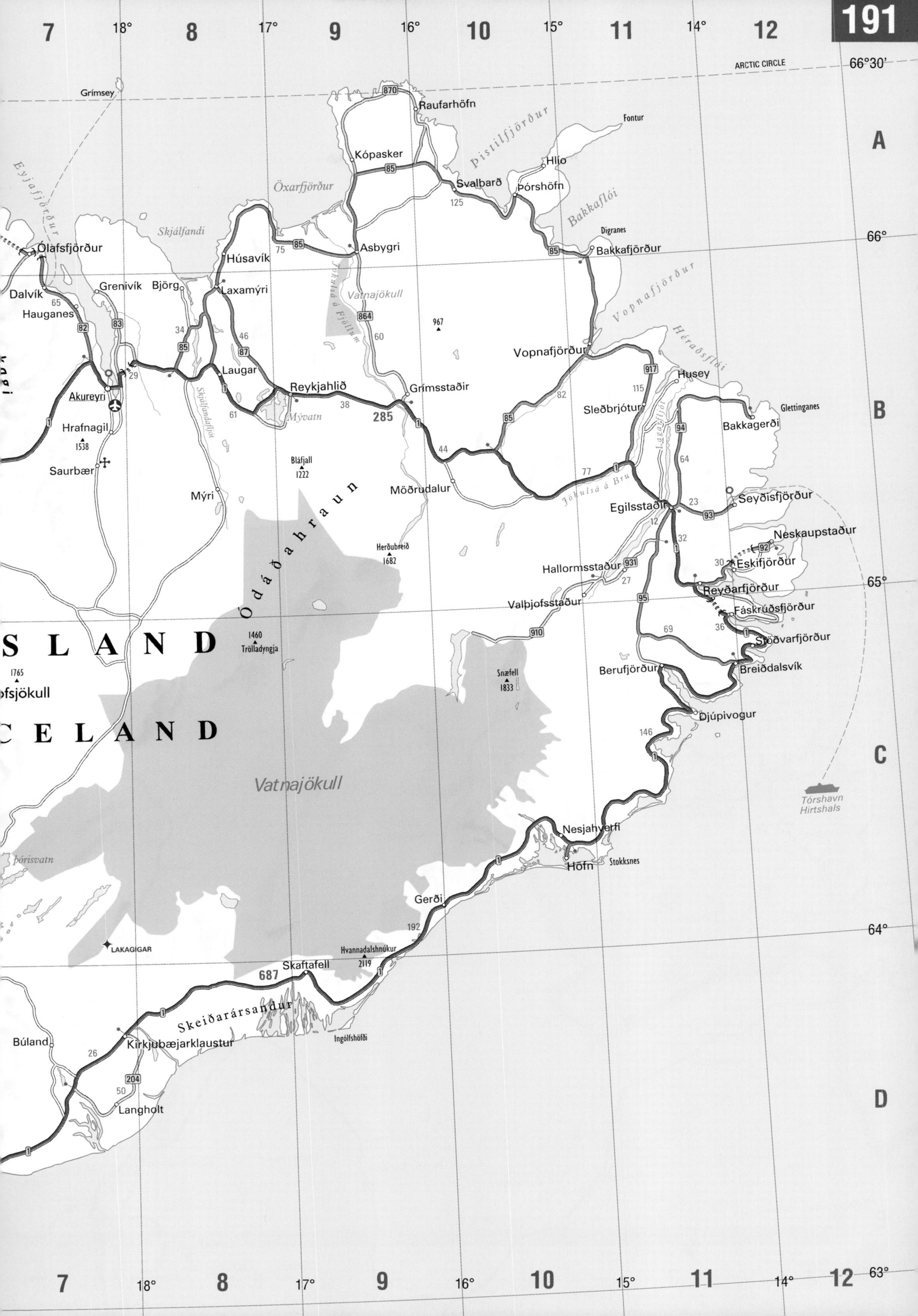
ARCTIC CIRCLE
Grímsey
Raufarhöfn
Kópasker
Svalbarð
Þórshöfn
Fontur
Öxarfjörður
Skjálfandi
Pistilfjörður
Bakkaflói
Digranes
Bakkafjörður
Eyjafjörður
Ólafsfjörður
Húsavík
Ásbygri
Dalvík
Grenivík
Björg
Laxamýri
Hauganes
Vatnajökull
Vopnafjörður
Héraðsflói
Húsey
Akureyri
Laugar
Reykjahlíð
Grímsstaðir
Mývatn
Sleðbrjótur
Bakkagerði
Glettinganes
Hrafnagil
Bláfjall
Saurbær
Möðrudalur
Egilsstaðir
Seyðisfjörður
Mýri
Ódáðahraun
Herðubreið
Neskaupstaður
Eskifjörður
Hallormsstaður
Reyðarfjörður
Valþjofsstaður
Fáskrúðsfjörður
Stöðvarfjörður
ISLAND
ICELAND
Trölladyngja
Snæfell
Berufjörður
Breiðdalsvík
Djúpivogur
Vatnajökull
Tórshavn
Hirtshals
Nesjahverfi
Höfn
Stokksnes
Þórisvatn
Gerði
LAKAGIGAR
Hvannadalshnúkur
Skaftafell
Skeiðarársandur
Búland
Kirkjubæjarklaustur
Ingólfshöfði
Langholt

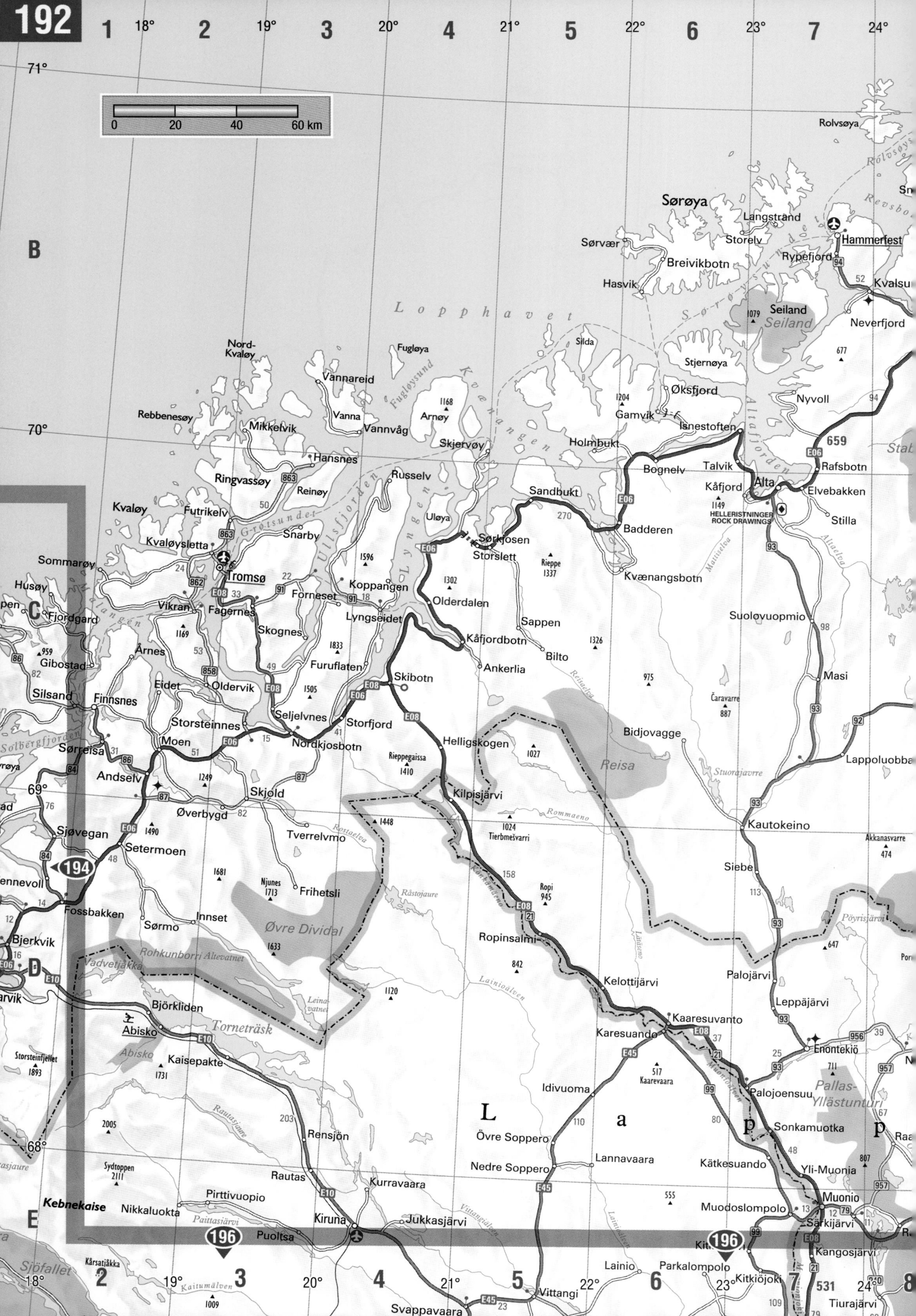

1
2
3
4
5
6
7
18°
19°
20°
21°
22°
23°
24°
71°
70°
69°
68°
B
C
D
E
0
20
40
60 km
Rolvsøya
Sørøya
Langstrand
Storelv
Hammerfest
Sørvær
Rypefjord
Breivikbotn
Hasvik
Kvalsund
Seiland
Neverfjord
Lopphavet
Silda
Stjernøya
Nord-Kvaløy
Fugløya
Vannareid
Fugløysund
Kvænangen
Øksfjord
Nyvoll
Rebbenesøy
Vanna
Vannvåg
Arnøy
Gamvik
Isnestoften
Altafjorden
Mikkelvik
Skjervøy
Holmbukt
Hansnes
Bognelv
Talvik
Rafsbotn
Ringvassøy
Russelv
Alta
Reinøy
Sandbukt
Kåfjord
Elvebakken
Kvaløy
Futrikelv
Uløya
Badderen
HELLERISTNINGER ROCK DRAWINGS
Stilla
Kvaløysletta
Snarby
Sørkjosen
Storslett
Sommarøy
Tromsø
Rieppe 1337
Kvænangsbotn
Husøy
Forneset
Koppangen
Olderdalen
Fjordgard
Vikran
Fagernes
Lyngseidet
Suolovuopmio
Sappen
Skognes
Kåfjordbotn
Årnes
Bilto
Gibostad
Furuflaten
Ankerlia
Masi
Eidet
Oldervik
Skibotn
Silsand
Finnsnes
Čaravarre 887
Seljelvnes
Storfjord
Bidjovagge
Storsteinnes
Sørreisa
Moen
Nordkjosbotn
Helligskogen
Reisa
Lappoluobbal
Andselv
Rieppegaissa 1410
Skjold
Kilpisjärvi
Øverbygd
Tverrelvmo
Rommaeno
Kautokeino
Sjøvegan
Tierbmešvarri
Akkanasvarre
Setermoen
Siebe
Fossbakken
Njunes 1713
Frihetsli
Ropi 945
Råstojaure
Innset
Sørmo
Øvre Dividal
Ropinsalmi
Bjerkvik
Rohkunborri
Altevatnet
Pöyrisjärvi
Vadvetjåkka
Kelottijärvi
Palojärvi
Björkliden
Lainioälven
Leppäjärvi
Abisko
Torneträsk
Kaaresuvanto
Karesuando
Enontekiö
Storsteinfjellet 1893
Kaisepakte
Kaarevaara
Idivuoma
Palojoensuu
Pallas-Yllästunturi
L
a
p
p
Rautasjaure
Rensjön
Sonkamuotka
Övre Soppero
Lannavaara
Nedre Soppero
Kätkesuando
Yli-Muonia
Sydtoppen 2111
Rautas
Kurravaara
Pirttivuopio
Muodoslompolo
Muonio
Kebnekaise
Nikkaluokta
Paittasjärvi
Vittangiälven
Kiruna
Jukkasjärvi
Särkijärvi
Puoltsa
196
194
Kangosjärvi
Sjöfallet
Kårsatjåkka
Lainio
Parkalompolo
Kitkiöjoki
Kaitumälven
Vittangi
Svappavaara
Tiurajärvi

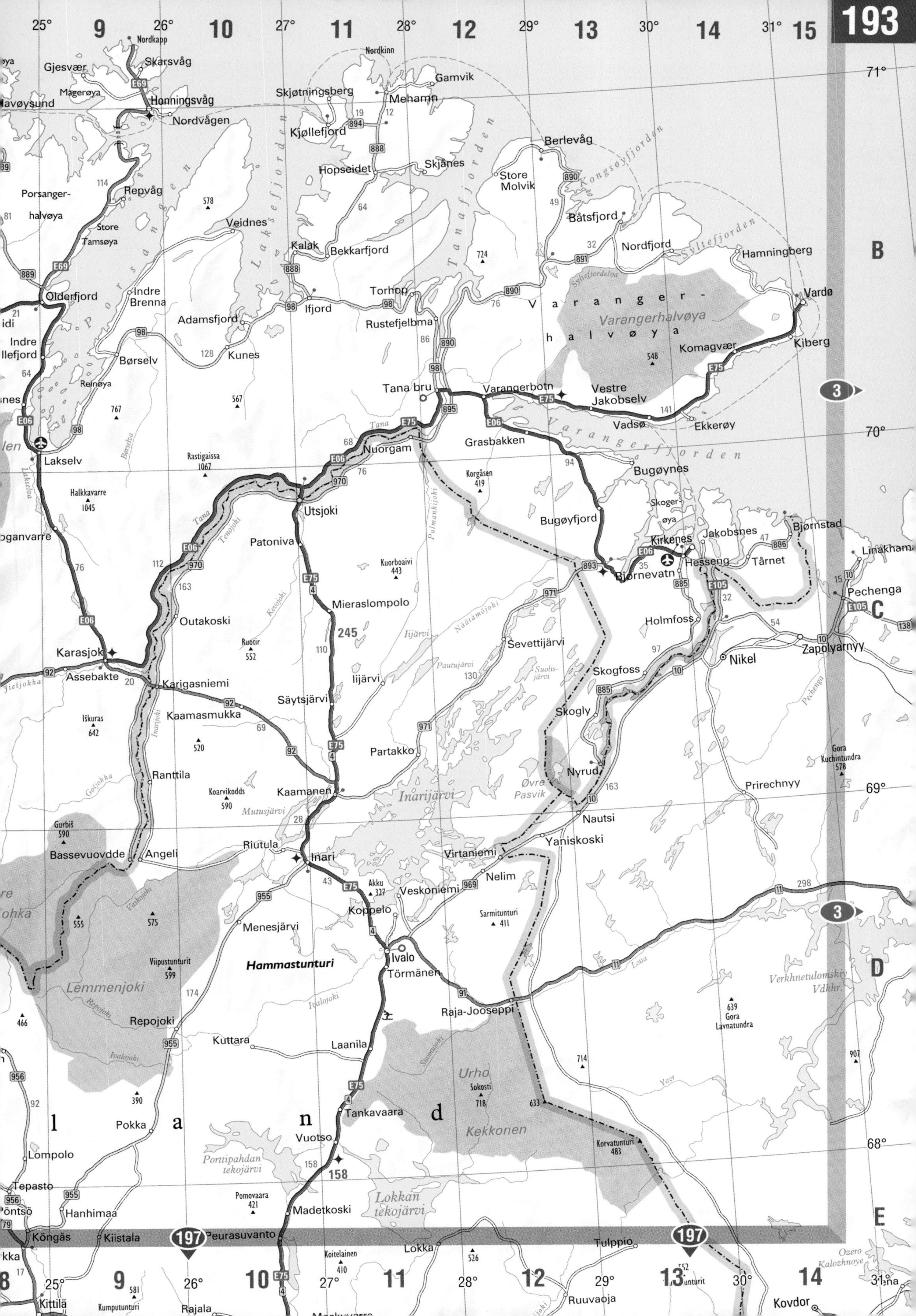
Nordkapp
Skarsvåg
Gjesvær
Magerøya
Honningsvåg
Nordvågen
Repvåg
Porsanger-
halvøya
Store
Tamsøya
Veidnes
Olderfjord
Indre
Brenna
Adamsfjord
Kunes
Børselv
Reinøya
Lakselv
Nordkinn
Gamvik
Mehamn
Skjøtningsberg
Kjøllefjord
Hopseidet
Skjånes
Kalak
Bekkarfjord
Ifjord
Torhop
Rustefjelbma
Tana bru
Berlevåg
Store
Molvik
Båtsfjord
Nordfjord
Hamningberg
Varanger-
halvøya
Varangerhalvøya
Vardø
Komagvær
Kiberg
Varangerbotn
Vestre
Jakobselv
Vadsø
Ekkerøy
Varangerfjorden
Grasbakken
Bugøynes
Nuorgam
Utsjoki
Patoniva
Mieraslompolo
Iijärvi
Säytsjärvi
Partakko
Kaamanen
Inarijärvi
Inari
Riutula
Karasjok
Assebakte
Karigasniemi
Kaamasmukka
Outakoski
Ranttila
Angeli
Bassevuovdde
Bugøyfjord
Kirkenes
Jakobsnes
Bjørnstad
Hesseng
Tårnet
Bjørnevatn
Holmfoss
Pechenga
Zapolyarnyy
Nikel
Sevettijärvi
Skogfoss
Skogly
Nyrud
Øvre
Pasvik
Nautsi
Yaniskoski
Prirechnyy
Virtaniemi
Nelim
Veskoniemi
Koppelo
Menesjärvi
Ivalo
Törmänen
Raja-Jooseppi
Hammastunturi
Lemmenjoki
Repojoki
Kuttara
Laanila
Urho
Kekkonen
Tankavaara
Vuotso
Pokka
Lompolo
Tepasto
Pöntsö
Hanhimaa
Könkäs
Kiistala
Peurasuvanto
Madetkoski
Lokkan
tekojärvi
Porttipahdan
tekojärvi
Lokka
Tulppio
Korvatunturi
Verkhnetulomskiy
Vdkhr.
Ruuvaoja
Kovdor
Kittilä
Rajala
Kumputunturi
Linakhamari

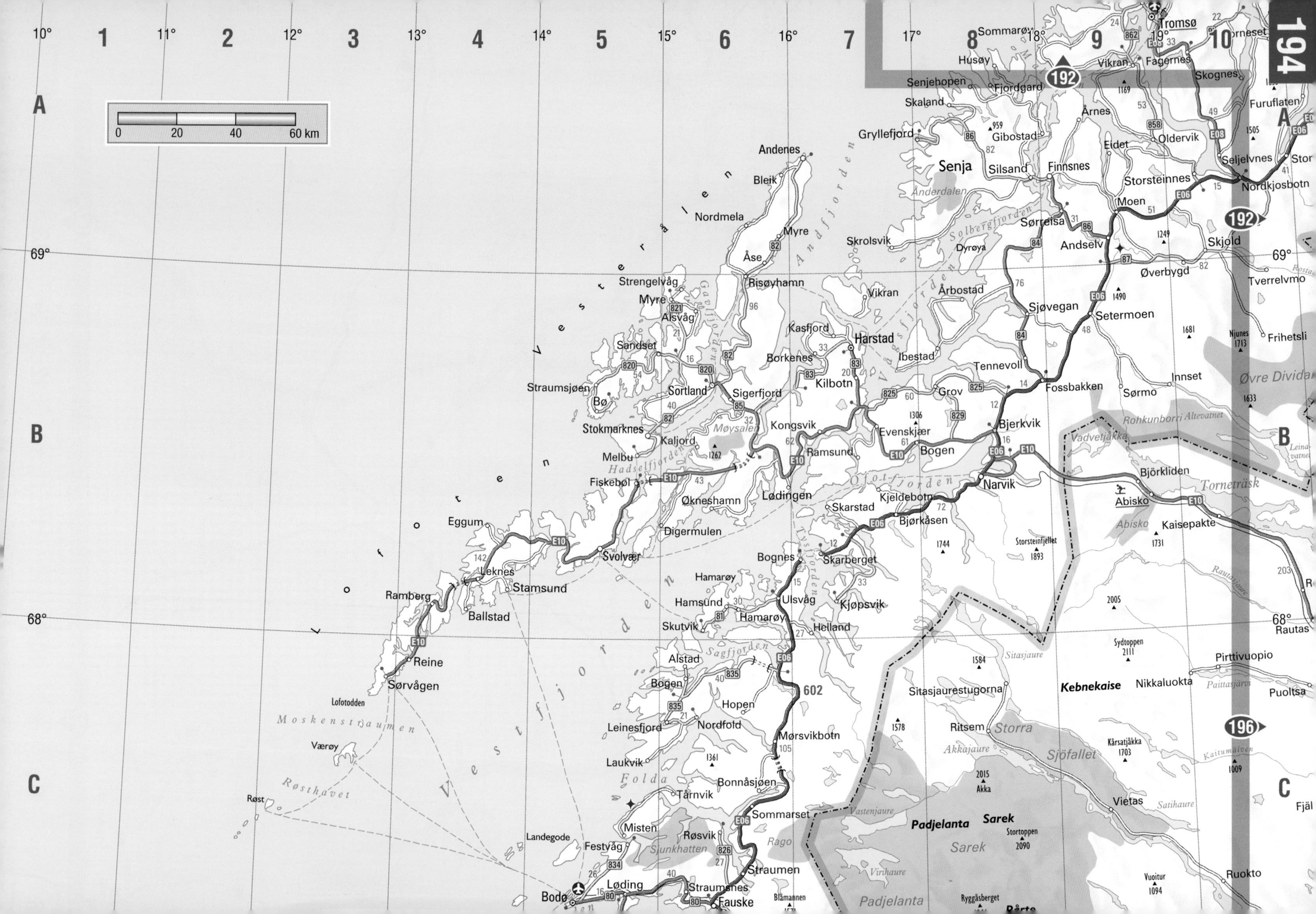

0
20
40
60 km
Vesterålen
Lofoten
Vestfjorden
Andfjorden
Senja
Tromsø
Andenes
Bleik
Nordmela
Myre
Åse
Risøyhamn
Strengelvåg
Alsvåg
Sandset
Straumsjøen
Bø
Sortland
Sigerfjord
Stokmarknes
Kaljord
Melbu
Fiskebøl
Harstad
Kasfjord
Borkenes
Kilbotn
Kongsvik
Ramsund
Lødingen
Øksneshamn
Digermulen
Svolvær
Eggum
Leknes
Stamsund
Ballstad
Ramberg
Reine
Sørvågen
Lofotodden
Moskenstraumen
Værøy
Røst
Røsthavet
Bodø
Løding
Straumsnes
Fauske
Straumen
Festvåg
Landegode
Misten
Røsvik
Tårnvik
Bonnåsjøen
Sommarset
Laukvik
Leinesfjord
Nordfold
Hopen
Bogen
Alstad
Skutvik
Hamarøy
Hamsund
Ulsvåg
Helland
Kjøpsvik
Skarberget
Bognes
Skarstad
Kjeldebotn
Bjørkåsen
Narvik
Bjerkvik
Evenskjær
Grov
Tennevoll
Fossbakken
Sjøvegan
Setermoen
Øverbygd
Andselv
Sørreisa
Moen
Finnsnes
Silsand
Gibostad
Gryllefjord
Skaland
Senjehopen
Husøy
Sommarøy
Fjordgard
Vikran
Fagernes
Skognes
Furuflaten
Seljelvnes
Nordkjosbotn
Storsteinnes
Oldervik
Eidet
Årnes
Skjold
Tverrelvmo
Frihetsli
Innset
Sørmo
Skrolsvik
Dyrøya
Årbostad
Ibestad
Vikran
Abisko
Björkliden
Torneträsk
Kaisepakte
Rautas
Pirttivuopio
Nikkaluokta
Puoltsa
Kebnekaise
Sitasjaurestugorna
Ritsem
Storra Sjöfallet
Akkajaure
Vietas
Ruokto
Padjelanta
Sarek
Storsteinfjellet
Øvre Dividal
Hadselfjorden
Møysalen
Ofotfjorden
Tysfjorden
Sagfjorden
Folda
Sjunkhatten
Rago
Vastenjaure
Virihaure
Satihaure
192
196
602

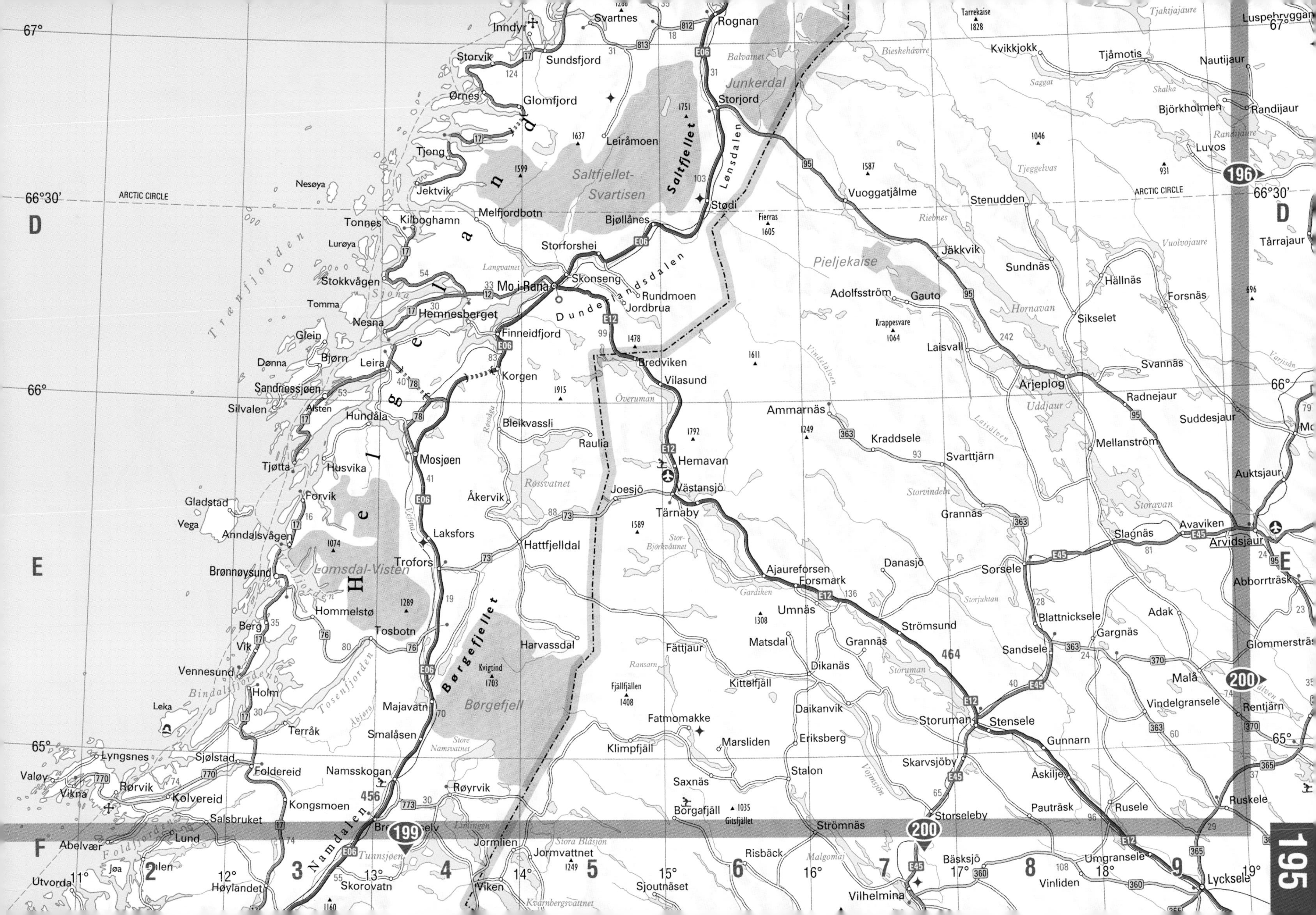
Luspebryggan
Randijaur
Nautijaur
Björkholmen
Luvos
Tårrajaur
Tjåmotis
Kvikkjokk
Tarrekaise
Sundnäs
Stenudden
Hällnäs
Sikselet
Forsnäs
Svannäs
Radnejaur
Suddesjaur
Auktsjaur
Arvidsjaur
Avaviken
Slagnäs
Mellanström
Arjeplog
Jäkkvik
Vuoggatjålme
Gauto
Adolfsström
Laisvall
Pieljekaise
Krappesvare
Kraddsele
Svarttjärn
Grannäs
Sorsele
Blattnicksele
Gargnäs
Adak
Malå
Vindelgransele
Rentjärn
Abborrträsk
Glommersträsk
Ruskele
Lycksele
Rusele
Umgransele
Vinliden
Pauträsk
Åskilje
Gunnarn
Stensele
Sandsele
Storseleby
Bäsksjö
Storuman
Skarvsjöby
Strömsund
Danasjö
Grannäs
Forsmark
Ajaureforsen
Umnäs
Dikanäs
Daikanvik
Eriksberg
Stalon
Strömnäs
Vilhelmina
Ammarnäs
Rognan
Storjord
Junkerdal
Lønsdalen
Saltfjellet
Stødi
Svartnes
Sundsfjord
Glomfjord
Inndyr
Leiråmoen
Bjøllånes
Rundmoen
Jordbrua
Saltfjellet-Svartisen
Storforshei
Skonseng
Dunderlandsdalen
Mo i Rana
Melfjordbotn
Ørnes
Storvik
Tjong
Jektvik
Kilboghamn
Tonnes
Stokkvågen
Hemnesberget
Nesna
Leira
Finneidfjord
Korgen
Bleikvassli
Raulla
Røssvatnet
Bredviken
Vilasund
Hemavan
Tärnaby
Västansjö
Joesjö
Hattfjelldal
Åkervik
Laksfors
Mosjøen
Trofors
Vefsna
Hundåla
Husvika
Forvik
Tjøtta
Sandnessjøen
Alsten
Dønna
Silvalen
Bjørn
Gleip
Tomma
Lurøya
Nesøya
Trænfjorden
Helgeland
Vega
Gladstad
Anndalsvågen
Brønnøysund
Berg
Vik
Holm
Hommelstø
Tosbotn
Lomsdal-Visten
Vennesund
Sjølstad
Salsbruket
Foldereid
Kongsmoen
Terråk
Namsskogan
Smalåsen
Majavatn
Røyrvik
Harvassdal
Børgefjellet
Børgefjell
Fättjaur
Fatmomakke
Klimpfjäll
Kittelfjäll
Matsdal
Marsliden
Saxnäs
Borgafjäll
Risbäck
Sjoutnäset
Jormvattnet
Jormlien
Viken
Skorovatn
Høylandet
Lund
Kolvereid
Rørvik
Vikna
Lyngsnes
Abelvær
Utvorda
Valøy
Leka
Namdalen
ARCTIC CIRCLE
66°30'
67°
66°
65°
D
E
F
2
3
4
5
6
7
8
9
11°
12°
13°
14°
15°
16°
17°
18°
19°
196
199
200

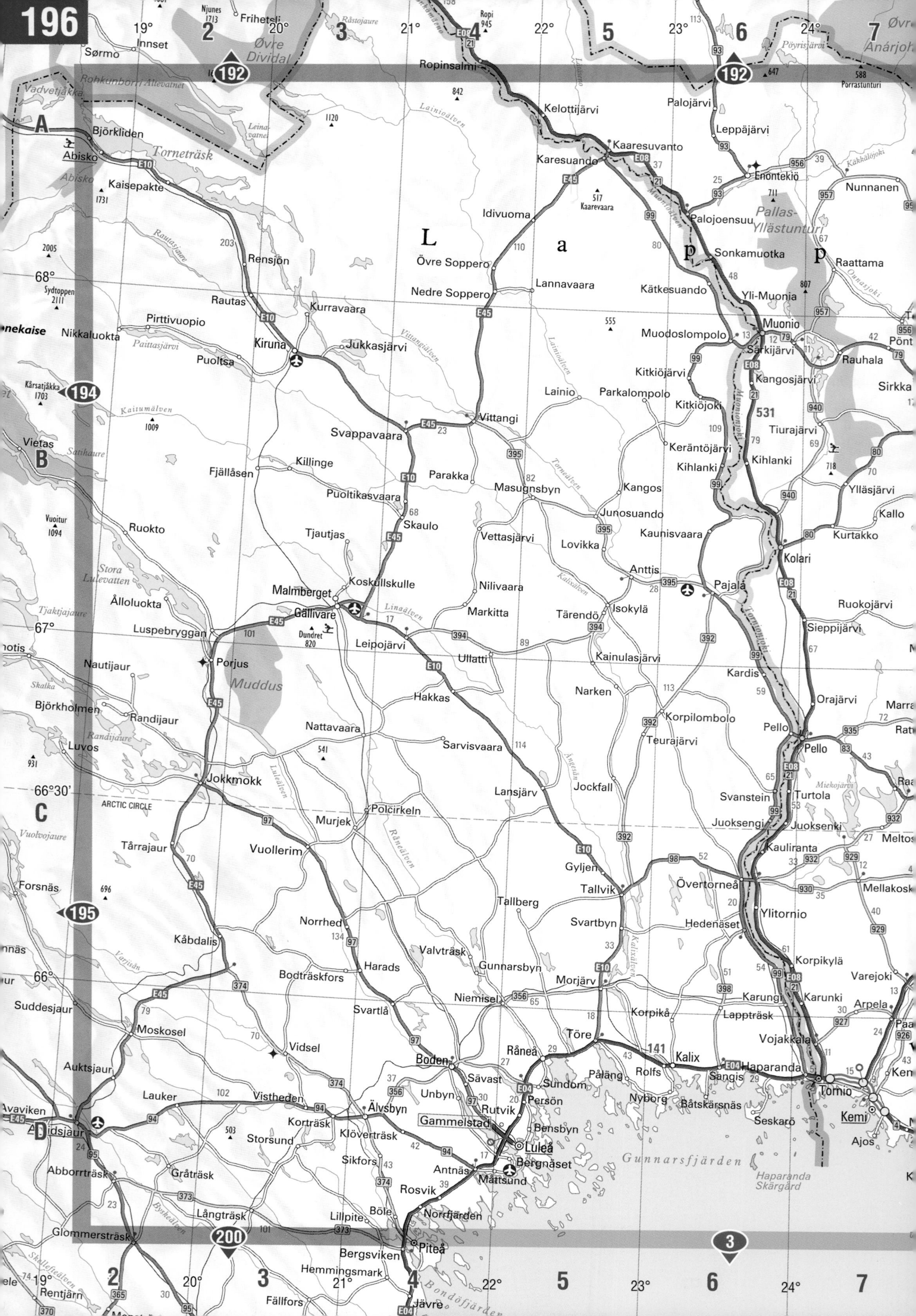

Lapp
Torneträsk
Abisko
Björkliden
Kaisepakte
Rensjön
Rautas
Kiruna
Kurravaara
Jukkasjärvi
Nikkaluokta
Pirttivuopio
Puoltsa
Svappavaara
Vittangi
Karesuando
Kaaresuvanto
Kelottijärvi
Ropinsalmi
Idivuoma
Övre Soppero
Nedre Soppero
Lannavaara
Enontekiö
Palojärvi
Leppäjärvi
Palojoensuu
Sonkamuotka
Pallas-Yllästunturi
Raattama
Kätkesuando
Yli-Muonia
Muonio
Muodoslompolo
Särkijärvi
Kangosjärvi
Kitkiöjärvi
Parkalompolo
Lainio
Kitkiöjoki
Tiurajärvi
Keräntöjärvi
Kihlanki
Kangos
Junosuando
Kaunisvaara
Masugnsbyn
Parakka
Killinge
Fjällåsen
Puoltikasvaara
Skaulo
Tjautjas
Ruokto
Vettasjärvi
Lovikka
Kolari
Kurtakko
Äkäslompolo
Ylläsjärvi
Kallo
Antti s
Pajala
Nilivaara
Markitta
Tärendö
Isokylä
Koskullskulle
Malmberget
Gällivare
Dundret 820
Leipojärvi
Ålloluokta
Luspebryggan
Porjus
Muddus
Nautijaur
Björkholmen
Randijaur
Luvos
Jokkmokk
Ullatti
Kainulasjärvi
Kardis
Narken
Hakkas
Nattavaara
Sarvisvaara
Korpilombolo
Teurajärvi
Pello
Orajärvi
Ruokojärvi
Sieppijärvi
Lansjärv
Jockfall
Svanstein
Turtola
Juoksengi
Juoksenki
Kauliranta
Polcirkeln
Murjek
ARCTIC CIRCLE
Tårrajaur
Vuollerim
Gyljen
Tallvik
Övertorneå
Ylitornio
Hedenäset
Tallberg
Svartbyn
Norrhed
Kåbdalis
Forsnäs
Valvträsk
Gunnarsbyn
Harads
Bodträskfors
Korpikylä
Morjärv
Karungi
Karunki
Niemisel
Korpikå
Lappträsk
Svartlå
Moskosel
Vidsel
Töre
Råneå
Kalix
Vojakkala
Haparanda
Tornio
Kemi
Boden
Sävast
Sundom
Pålänga
Rolfs
Sangis
Nyborg
Båtskärsnäs
Seskarö
Auktsjaur
Lauker
Vistheden
Älvsbyn
Unbyn
Rutvik
Persön
Gammelstad
Luleå
Bensbyn
Bergnäset
Mattsund
Antnäs
Arvidsjaur
Korträsk
Kloverträsk
Storsund
Sikfors
Rosvik
Abborrträsk
Gråträsk
Långträsk
Lillpite
Böle
Norrfjärden
Glommersträsk
Piteå
Bergsviken
Hemmingsmark
Fällfors
Jävre
Rentjärn
Gunnarsfjärden
Haparanda Skärgård
Bondöfjärden
Suddesjaur
Ajos
Arpela
Varejoki
Mellakoski
Meltosjärvi
Rauhala
Sirkka
Nunnanen
Pöyrisjärvi
Porrastunturi 588
Sørmo
Innset
Frihetsli
Øvre Dividal
Kårsatjäkka 1703
Vietas
Stora Lulevatten
Kebnekaise
Sydtoppen 2111
2005
192
194
195
200
3
19°
20°
21°
22°
23°
24°
68°
67°
66°30'
66°
A
B
C
D
2
3
4
5
6
7
E10
E45
E08
E04

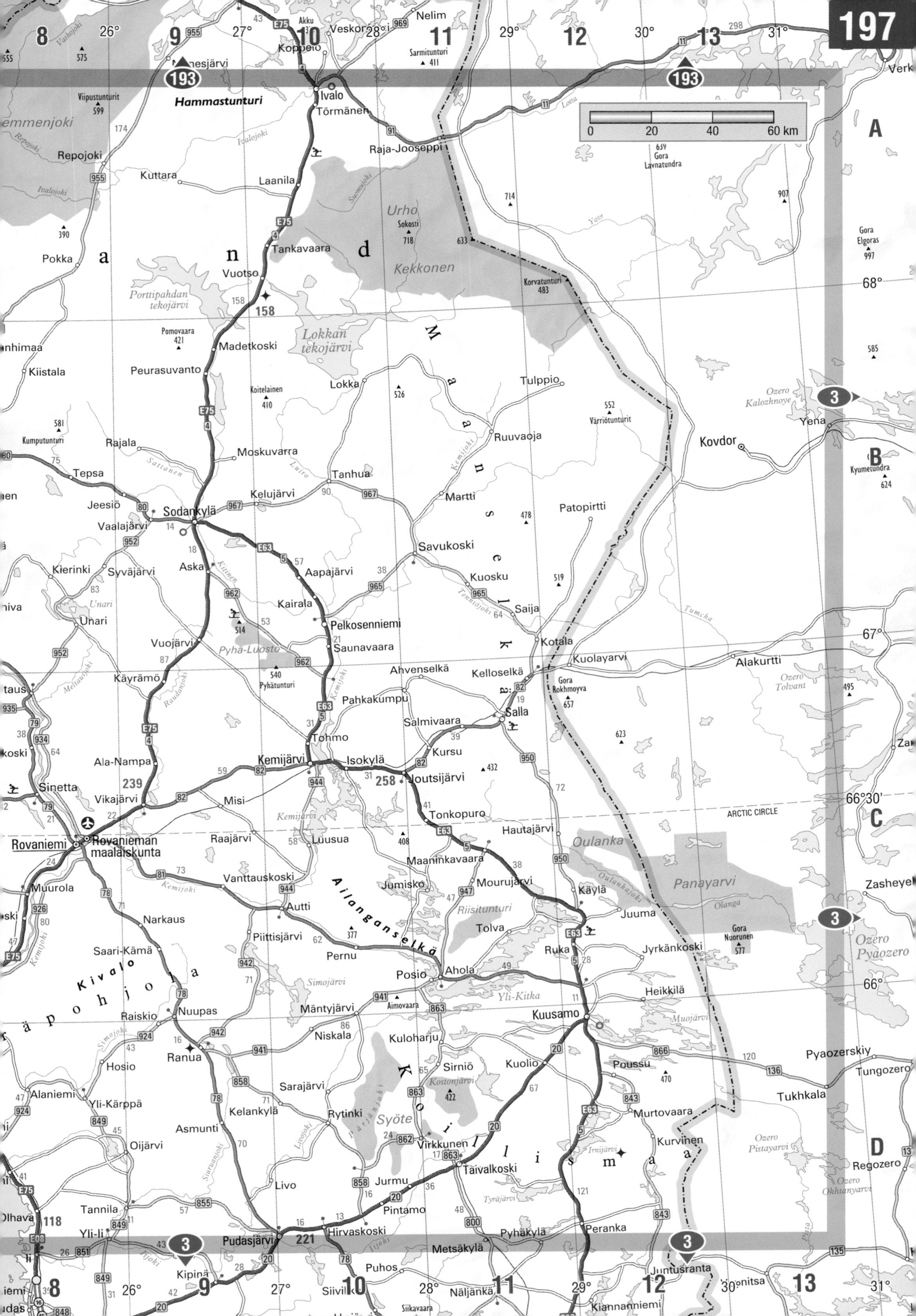
Hammastunturi
Ivalo
Törmänen
Raja-Jooseppi
Repojoki
Kuttara
Laanila
Urho
Sokosti
Kekkonen
Tankavaara
Vuotso
Pokka
Porttipahdan tekojärvi
Lokkan tekojärvi
Madetkoski
Peurasuvanto
Kiistala
Lokka
Tulppio
Korvatunturi
Ruuvaoja
Värriötunturit
Kovdor
Yena
Ozero Kalozhnoye
Rajala
Moskuvarra
Tepsa
Tanhua
Kelujärvi
Martti
Jeesiö
Sodankylä
Vaalajärvi
Patopirtti
Savukoski
Kierinki
Syväjärvi
Aska
Aapajärvi
Kuosku
Kairala
Saija
Unari
Pelkosenniemi
Vuojärvi
Saunavaara
Kotala
Kuolayarvi
Alakurtti
Ahvenselkä
Kelloselkä
Käyrämö
Pyhä-Luosto
Pyhätunturi
Pahkakumpu
Salla
Salmivaara
Tohmo
Kursu
Ala-Nampa
Kemijärvi
Isokylä
Joutsijärvi
Sinetta
Vikajärvi
Misi
Tonkopuro
ARCTIC CIRCLE
Hautajärvi
Rovaniemi
Rovaniemen maalaiskunta
Raajärvi
Luusua
Oulanka
Panayarvi
Maaninkavaara
Muurola
Vanttauskoski
Mourujärvi
Jumisko
Käylä
Zasheye
Riisitunturi
Autti
Juuma
Narkaus
Tolva
Piittisjärvi
Ailangaselkä
Ruka
Jyrkänkoski
Saari-Kämä
Pernu
Posio
Ahola
Ozero Pyaozero
Kivalo
Heikkilä
Simojärvi
Yli-Kitka
Nuupas
Mäntyjärvi
Kuusamo
Raiskio
Aimovaara
Niskala
Kuloharju
Ranua
Hosio
Kuolio
Poussu
Pyaozerskiy
Tungozero
Sirniö
Tukhkala
Alaniemi
Yli-Kärppä
Sarajärvi
Murtovaara
Kelankylä
Rytinki
Syöte
Asmunti
Oijärvi
Virkkunen
Kurvinen
Taivalkoski
Regozero
Livo
Jurmu
Pintamo
Tannila
Olhava
Yli-Ii
Pudasjärvi
Hirvaskoski
Pyhäkylä
Peranka
Metsäkylä
Puhos
Kipinä
Juntusranta
Siivikko
Näljänkä
Kiannanniemi
Siikavaara
0 20 40 60 km

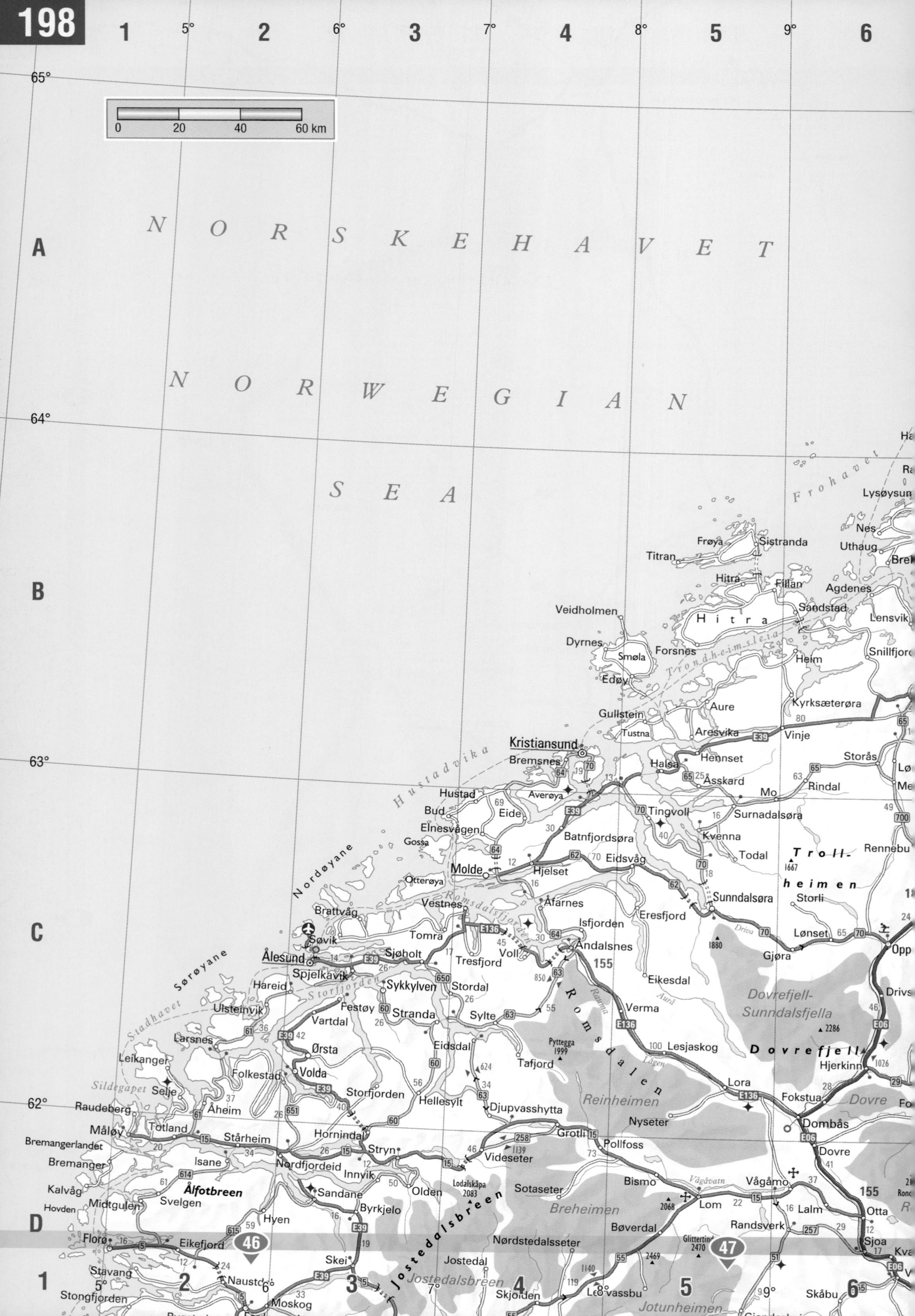
1
2
3
4
5
6
5°
6°
7°
8°
9°
65°
64°
63°
62°
A
B
C
D
0
20
40
60 km
N O R S K E H A V E T
N O R W E G I A N
S E A
Frohavet
Frøya
Sistranda
Titran
Hitra
Fillan
Sandstad
Agdenes
Lensvik
Nes
Uthaug
Lysøysund
Veidholmen
Dyrnes
Smøla
Forsnes
Edøy
Trondheimsleia
Heim
Snillfjord
Gullstein
Tustna
Aure
Aresvika
Kyrksæterøra
Vinje
Kristiansund
Bremsnes
Halsa
Hennset
Askkard
Storås
Rindal
Mo
Averøya
Hustad
Hustadvika
Bud
Eide
Elnesvågen
Gossa
Tingvoll
Surnadalsøra
Batnfjordsøra
Kvenna
Todal
Trollheimen
Rennebu
Molde
Hjelset
Eidsvåg
Otterøya
Nordøyane
Vestnes
Romsdalsfjorden
Åfarnes
Sunndalsøra
Storli
Brattvåg
Eresfjord
Isfjorden
Tomra
Søvik
Ålesund
Sjøholt
Andalsnes
Lønset
Oppdal
Voll
Tresfjord
Gjøra
Sørøyane
Spjelkavik
Storfjorden
Hareid
Sykkylven
Stordal
Eikesdal
Dovrefjell-Sunndalsfjella
Drivstua
Ulsteinvik
Festøy
Stranda
Sylte
Romsdalen
Verma
Stadhavet
Vartdal
Larsnes
Ørsta
Eidsdal
Pyttegga 1999
Lesjaskog
Dovrefjell
Leikanger
Volda
Tafjord
Hjerkinn
Folkestad
Sildegapet
Selje
Storfjorden
Hellesylt
Lora
Fokstua
Dovre
Raudeberg
Åheim
Djupvasshytta
Reinheimen
Nyseter
Dombås
Måløy
Totland
Stårheim
Hornindal
Grotli
Pollfoss
Bremangerlandet
Stryn
Videseter
Dovre
Bremanger
Isane
Nordfjordeid
Innvik
Bismo
Vågåmo
Kalvåg
Ålfotbreen
Sandane
Olden
Lodalskåpa 2083
Sotaseter
Vågåvatn
Hovden
Midtgulen
Svelgen
Byrkjelo
Breheimen
Lom
Lalm
Otta
Hyen
Jostedalsbreen
Bøverdal
Randsverk
Florø
Eikefjord
Nordstedalsseter
Sjoa
Glittertind 2470
Stavang
Skei
Jostedal
Naustdal
Jostedalsbreen
Skjolden
Leirvassbu
Skåbu
Stongfjorden
Moskog
Jotunheimen
Gjendesheim
Førde
Bygstad
46
47
155

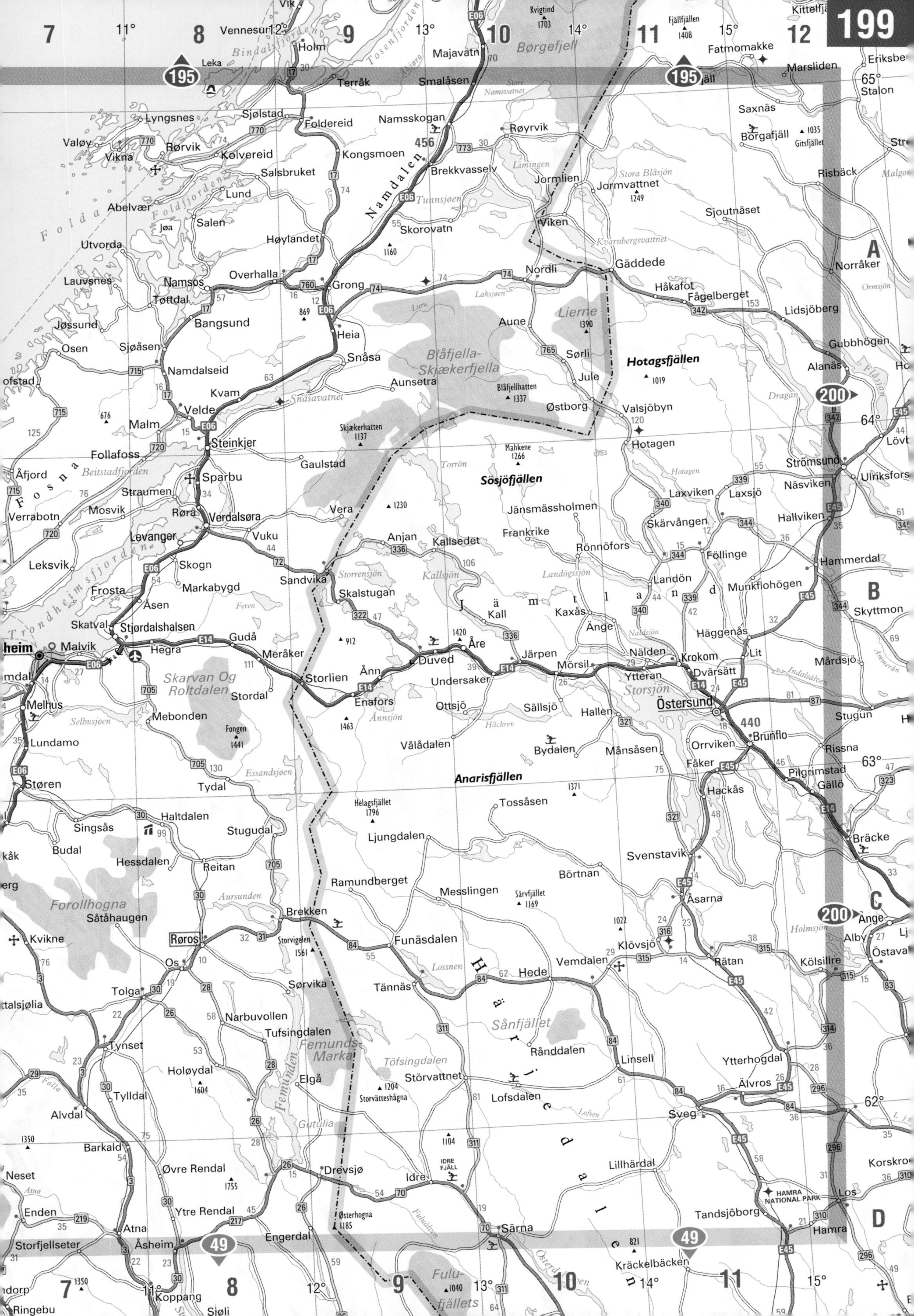

Namdalen
Bindalsfjorden
Tosenfjorden
Børgefjell
Foldfjorden
Folda
Namsos
Grong
Snåsa
Blåfjella-Skjækerfjella
Lierne
Hotagsfjällen
Steinkjer
Levanger
Verdalsøra
Trondheimsfjorden
Fosna
Stjørdalshalsen
Sösjöfjällen
Jämtland
Storsjön
Östersund
Åre
Duved
Storlien
Meråker
Skarvan Og Roltdalen
Anarisfjällen
Røros
Forollhogna
Femunden
Femundsmarka
Funäsdalen
Härjedalen
Sånfjället
Sveg
Idre
Särna
Lofsdalen
Brunflo
Bräcke
Strömsund
Gäddede
Tynset
Koppang
Fulufjällets
HAMRA NATIONAL PARK

195
195
200
200
49
49

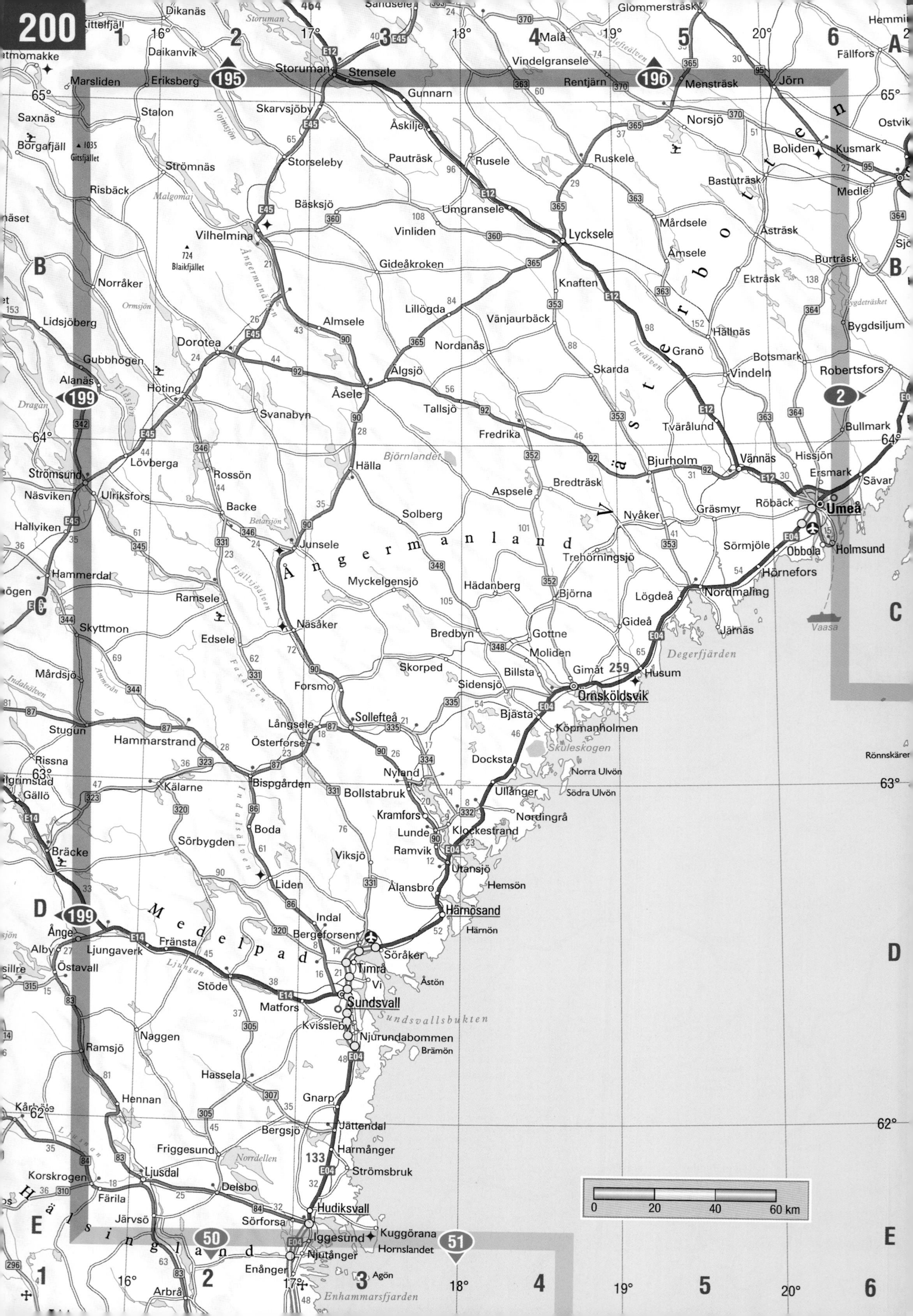

Storuman
Stensele
Vilhelmina
Dorotea
Lycksele
Åsele
Västerbotten
Ångermanland
Medelpad
Hälsingland
Umeå
Örnsköldsvik
Härnösand
Sundsvall
Hudiksvall
Sollefteå
Kramfors
Timrå
Ljusdal
Strömsund
Vännäs
Nordmaling
Bjurholm
Junsele
Ramsele
Hoting
Holmsund
Robertsfors
Vindeln
Norsjö
Malå
Boliden
Iggesund
Bollstabruk
Bräcke
Ånge
Degerfjärden
Sundsvallsbukten
Enhammarsfjärden
Vaasa
0 20 40 60 km

City plans · Plans de villes
Stadtpläne · Piante di città

Motorway	Autoroute	Autobahn	Autostrada
Major through route	Route principale majeur	Hauptstrecke	Strada di grande comunicazione
Through route	Route principale	Schnellstrasse	Strada d'importanza regionale
Secondary road	Route secondaire	Nebenstrasse	Strada d'interesse locale
Dual carriageway	Chaussées séparées	Zweispurig Schnellstrasse	Strada a carreggiate doppie
Other road	Autre route	Nebenstrecke	Altra strada
Tunnel	Tunnel	Tunnel	Galleria stradale
Limited access / pedestrian road	Rue réglementée / rue piétonne	Beschränkter Zugang/ Fussgängerzone	Strada pedonale / a accesso limitato
One-way street	Sens unique	Einbahnstrasse	Senso unico
Parking	Parc de stationnement	Parkplatz	Parcheggio
Motorway number A7	Numéro d'autoroute	Autobahnnummer A7	Numero di autostrada
National road number 447	Numéro de route nationale	Nationalstrassen- nummer 447	Numero di strada nazionale
European road number E45	Numéro de route européenne	Europäische Strassennummer E45	Numero di strada europea
Destination GENT	Destination	Ziel GENT	Destinazione
Car ferry	Bac passant les autos	Autofähre	Traghetto automobili
Railway	Chemin de fer	Eisenbahn	Ferrovia
Rail/bus station	Gare / gare routière	Bahnhof / Busstation	Stazione ferrovia / pullman
Underground, metro station	Station de métro	U-Bahnstation	Metropolitano
Cable car	Téléférique	Drahtseilbahn	Funivia
Abbey, cathedral	Abbaye, cathédrale	Abtei, Kloster, Kathedrale	Abbazia, duomo
Church of interest	Église intéressante	Interessante Kirche	Chiesa da vedere
Synagogue	Synagogue	Synagoge	Sinagoga
Hospital	Hôpital	Krankenhaus	Ospedale
Police station POL	Police	Polizeiwache POL	Polizia
Post office	Bureau de poste	Postamt	Ufficio postale
Tourist information	Office de tourisme	Informationsbüro	Ufficio informazioni turistiche
Place of interest Theatre	Autre curiosité	Sonstige Sehenswürdigkeit Theatre	Luogo da vedere

Approach maps · Agglomérations
Carte régionale · Regionalkarte

Toll motorway – with motorway number A10	Autoroute à péage – avec numéro d'autoroute	Gebührenpflichtige Autobahn – mit Autobahnnummer A10	Autostrada a pedaggio – con numero
Toll-free motorway – with European road number E51	Autoroute – avec numéro de route européenne	Gebührenfreie Autobahn – Europäische Strassennummer E51	Autostrada – con numero di strada europea
Pre-pay motorway – vignette required	Autoroute – 'vignette'	Autobahn – 'vignette'	Autostrada – 'vignette'
Motorway services	Aire de service	Autobahnservice	Area di servizio autostradale
Motorway junction full access, restricted access	Échangeur d'autoroute accès libre, accès reglémenté	Autobahnkreuz – voller/begrenzter Zugang	Raccordi autostradali – completo/parziali
Under construction	En construction	Im Bau	In construzione
Tunnel	Tunnel	Tunnel	Galleria stradale
Major route dual carriageway 14 single carriageway 14	Route principale chausées séparées chausée sans séparation	Hauptstrecke	Strada di grande communicazione carreggiata doppia carreggiata unica
Secondary route dual carriageway 96 single carriageway 96	Route secondaire chausées séparées chausée sans séparation	– zweispurige Schnellstrasse 14	Strada d'interesse locale – carreggiata doppia carreggiata unica
Other road	Autre route	Nebenstrasse – zweispurige Schnellstrasse 96	
Car ferry	Bac passant les autos	Nebenstrecke	Altra strada
Destination GIRONA	Destination	Autofähre	Traghetto automobili
Railway	Chemin de fer	Ziel GIRONA	Destinazione
Railway station Estación Central	Gare	Eisenbahn	Ferrovia
Height – in metres 234	Altitude – en mètres	Hauptbahnhof Estación Central	Stazione ferrovia
Airport	Aéroport principal	Höhe – über dem Meeresspiegel 234	Altezza in metri
Airfield	Autre aéroport	Flughafen	Aeroporto
City plan coverage area	Région de plan de ville	Flugplatz	Aerodromo/ campo d'aviazione
		Vom Stadtplan abgedecktes Gebiet	Area della pianta della città

Alicante

0 km 0.5

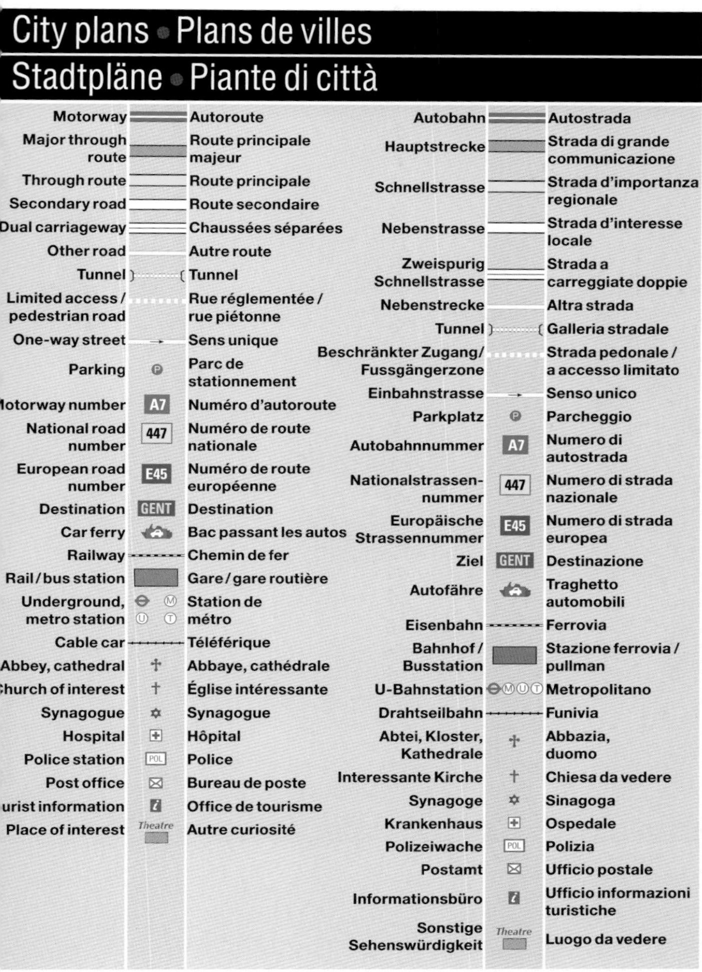
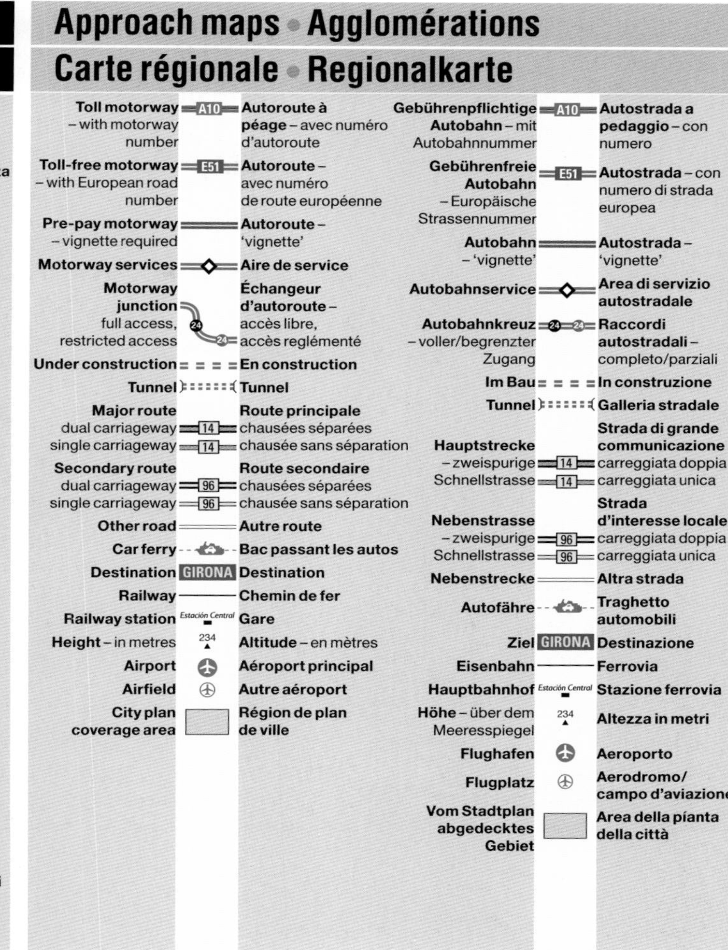

Antwerpen Antwerp

0 km 1

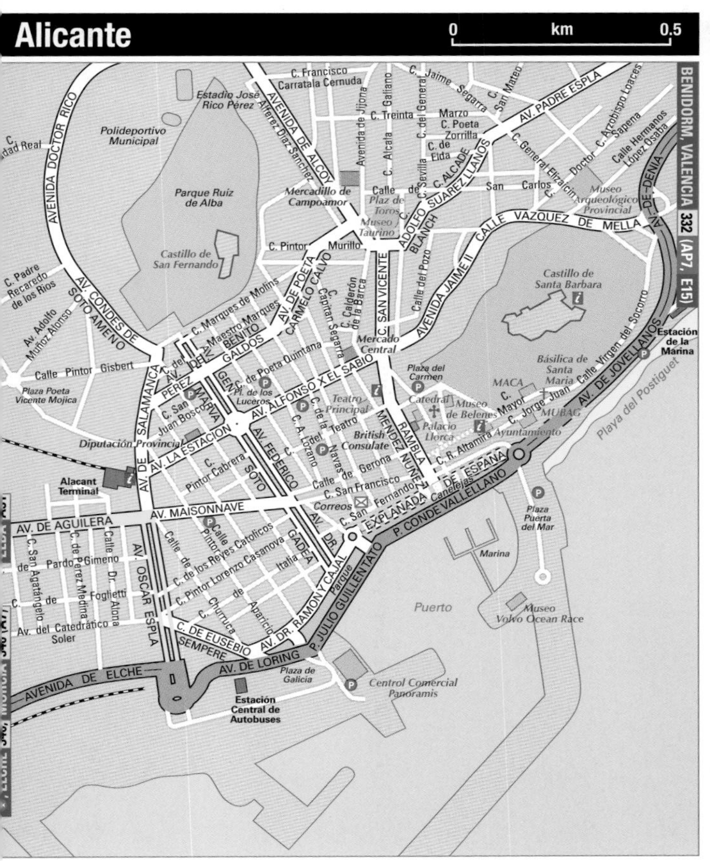
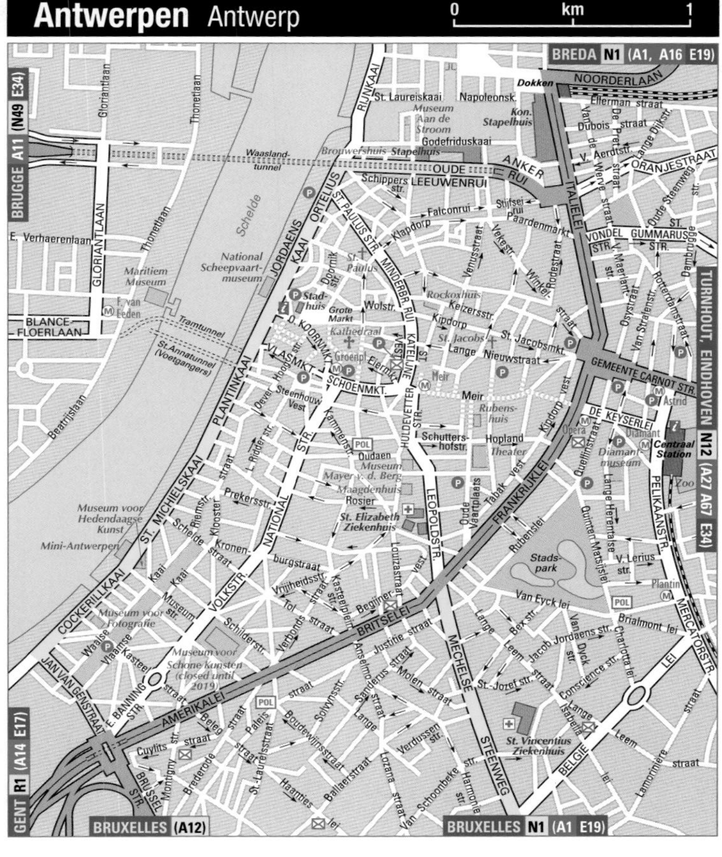

Amsterdam

0 km 2

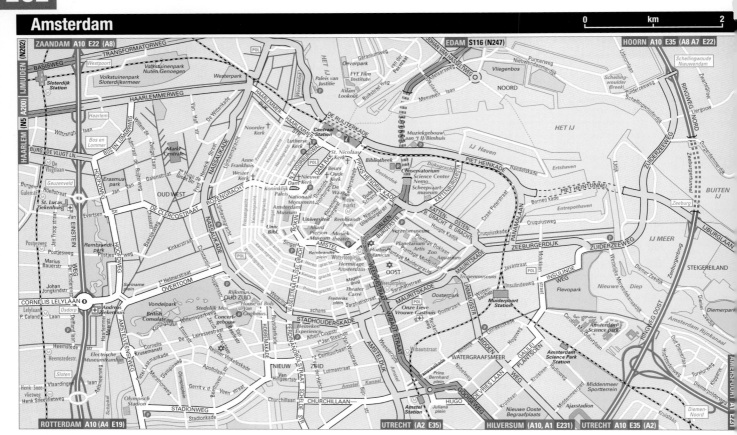

Amsterdam

0 km 5

Athina Athens

0 km 5

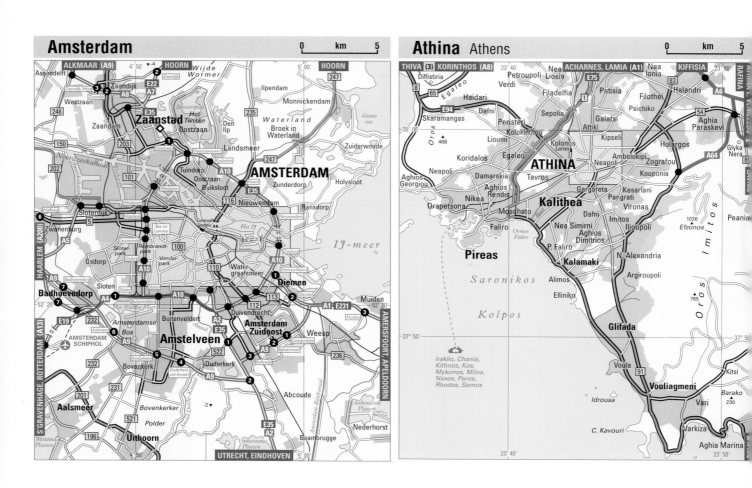

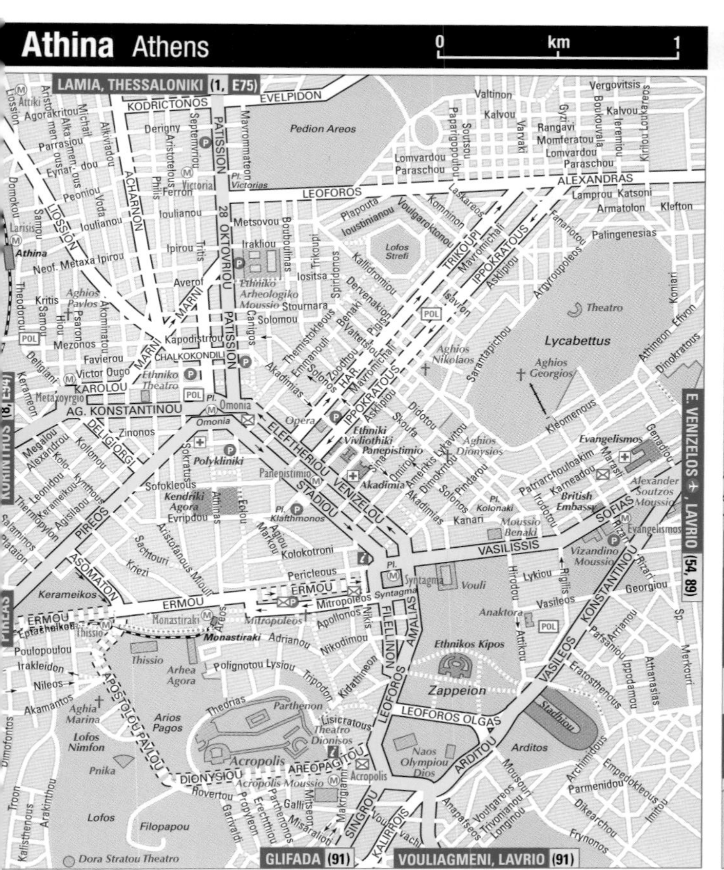

Athina Athens

0 km 1

LAMIA, THESSALONIKI (1, E75)

KODRIC-TONOS
EVELPIDON
Vergovitsis
Valtinon
Kalvou
Pedion Areos
Rangavi
Momferatou
ALEXANDRAS
Lamprou Katsoni
Palingenesias

LEOFOROS

Lycabettus

Aghios
Nikolaos
Aghios
Georgios

Evangelismos

British
Embassy

VASILISSIS

Vouli

Ethnikos Kipos

Zappeion

LEOFOROS OLGAS

Parthenon

Acropolis

Naos
Olympiou
Dios

Arditos

DIONYSIOU

Lofos
Filopapou

GLIFADA (91)   VOULIAGMENI, LAVRIO (91)

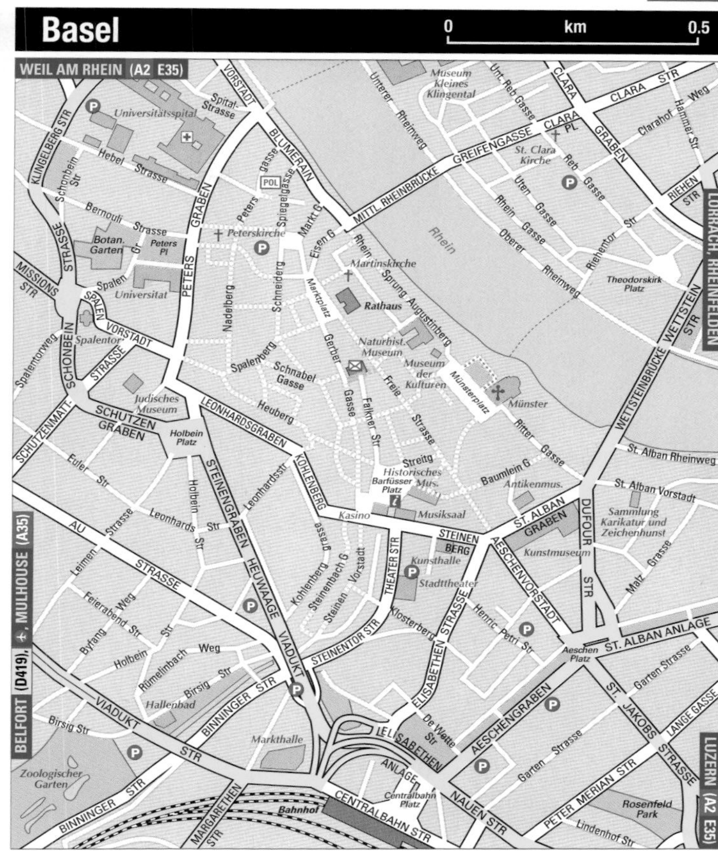

Basel

0 km 0.5

WEIL AM RHEIN (A2 E35)

Universitätsspital

Rhein

Münster

St. Alban

Bahnhof

BELFORT (D419), MULHOUSE (A35)
LÖRRACH, RHEINFELDEN
LUZERN (A2 E35)

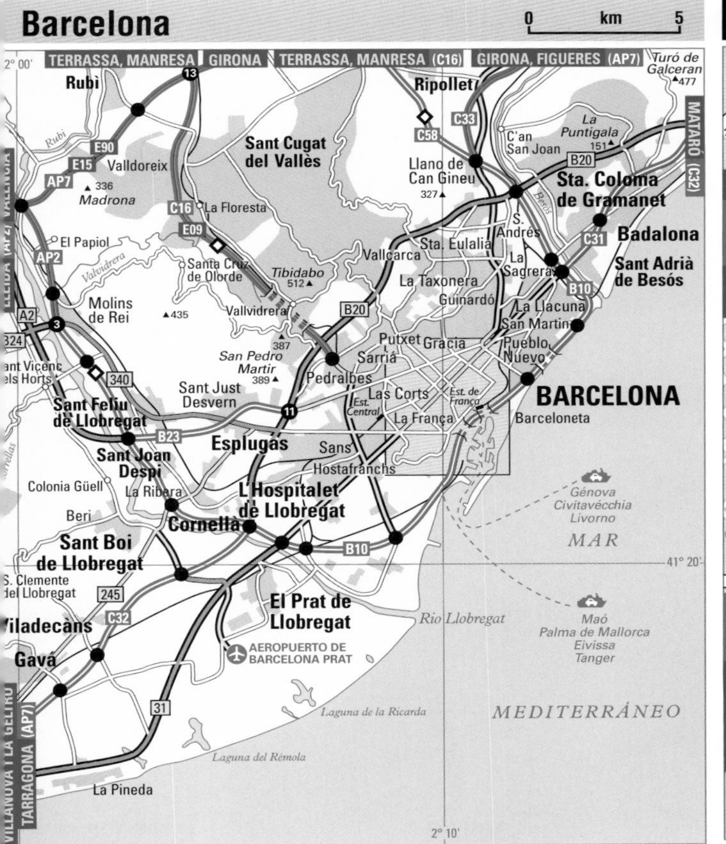

Barcelona

0 km 5

TERRASSA, MANRESA | GIRONA | TERRASSA, MANRESA (C16) | GIRONA, FIGUERES (AP7)

Turó de
Galceran
477

Rubí

Sant Cugat
del Vallès

Ripollet

Llano de
Can Gineu

Sta. Coloma
de Gramanet

Valldoreix

La Floresta

Sta. Eulalia

Badalona

El Papiol

Tibidabo

Vallcarca

La Sagrera

Sant Adrià
de Besós

Santa Cruz
de Olorde

La Taxonera

Guinardó

La Llacuna

Molins
de Rei

Vallvidrera

Putxet

San Martín

Sarrià

Gracia

Pueblo
Nuevo

San Pedro
Martir

Pedralbes

Las Corts

BARCELONA

Sant Just
Desvern

La França

Barceloneta

Sant Feliu
de Llobregat

Esplugas

Sans

Hostafranchs

Sant Joan
Despi

Colonia Güell

L'Hospitalet
de Llobregat

La Ribera

Cornellà

Beri

Sant Boi
de Llobregat

S. Clemente
del Llobregat

El Prat de
Llobregat

Rio Llobregat

Maó
Palma de Mallorca
Eivissa
Tanger

Viladecans

AEROPUERTO DE
BARCELONA PRAT

MEDITERRÁNEO

Gavà

Laguna de la Ricarda

Laguna del Rémola

La Pineda

VILLANUEVA Y LA GELTRÚ, TARRAGONA (AP7)
LLEIDA (AP2) VALLS

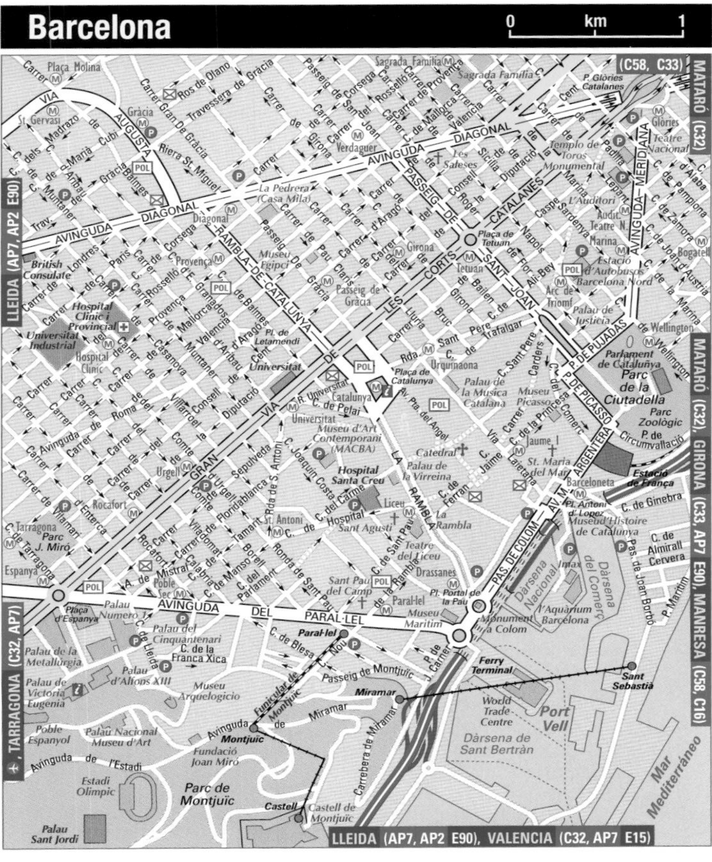

Barcelona

0 km 1

Plaça Molina

Sagrada Família

(C58, C33)
MATARÓ (C32)

La Pedrera
(Casa Milà)

DIAGONAL

British
Consulate

Universitat
Industrial

Hospital
Clinic i
Provincial

Plaça de
Catalunya

Parc
de la
Ciutadella

Universitat

Hospital
Santa Creu

RAMBLA DE CATALUNYA

Catedral

Sta. Maria
del Mar

Estació
de França

Palau
Nacional
Museu d'Art

La Rambla

PASSEIG DE COLOM

Darsena
Nacional

Plaça
d'Espanya

AVINGUDA

DEL PARAL·LEL

Ferry
Terminal

Museu
Marítim

Port
Vell

Poble
Espanyol

Fundació
Joan Miró

Passeig de Montjuïc

Monument
a Colom

Sant
Sebastià

World
Trade
Centre

Dàrsena de
Sant Bertrán

Estadi
Olímpic

Parc de
Montjuïc

Castell de
Montjuïc

Mar
Mediterráneo

Palau
Sant Jordi

TARRAGONA (AP7)
LLEIDA (AP7, AP2 E90), VALENCIA (C32, AP7 E15)
MATARÓ (C32), GIRONA (C33, AP7 E90), MANRESA (C58 C16)

Berlin

0 km 5

HAMBURG (A24), ROSTOCK (A24, A19)

ORANIENBURG, SASSNITZ (96)

HAMBURG (A24, A29)

SZCZECIN (A6)

NAUEN, KYRITZ

BRANDENBURG

MAGDEBURG (A10, A2), LEIPZIG (A10, A9)

BRANDENBURG (opening 2022)

DRESDEN (A13, E55)

Berlin

0 km 1

ORANIENBURG 96 E251

BERNAU

NAUEN 2 5

POTSDAM (A100 A115 E51 1)

POTSDAM 1 (A103)

LUCKAU 96

BERLIN-BRANDENBURG

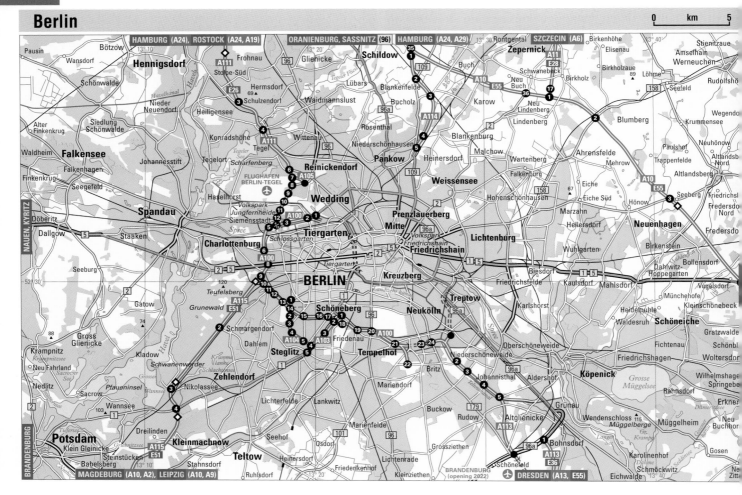

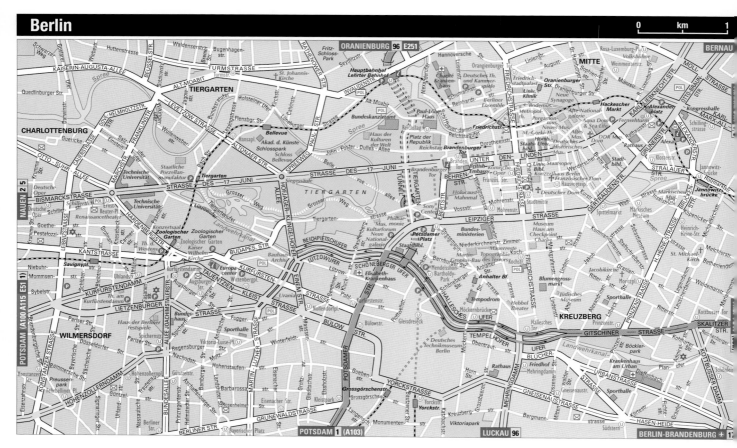

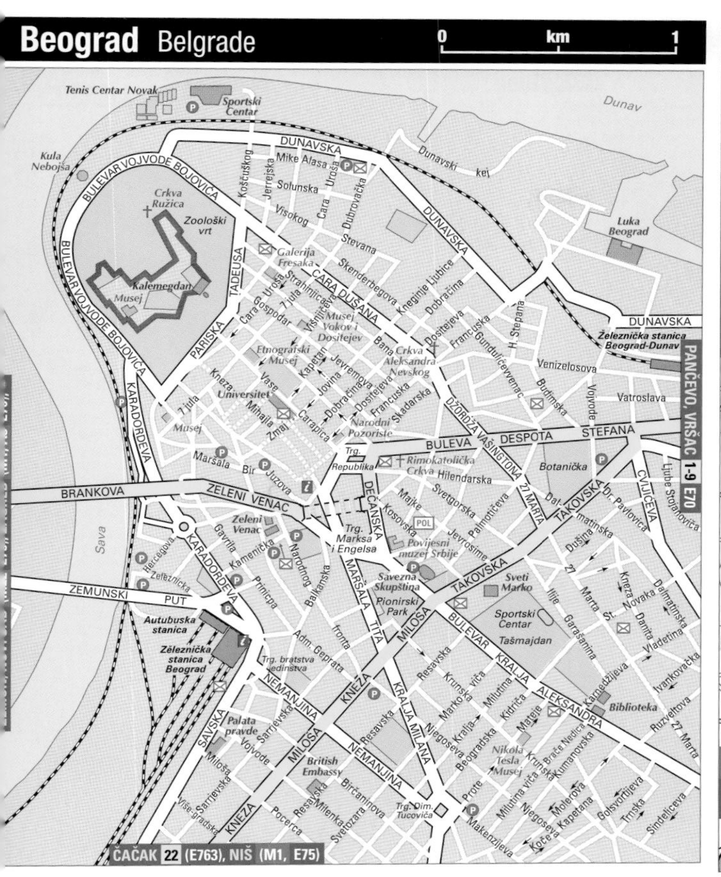

Beograd Belgrade

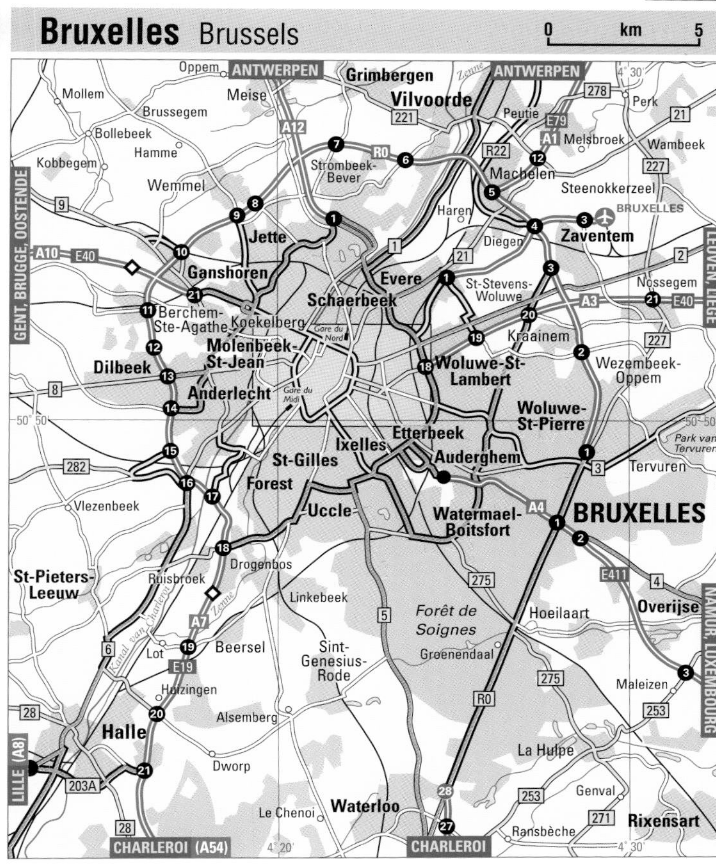

Bruxelles Brussels

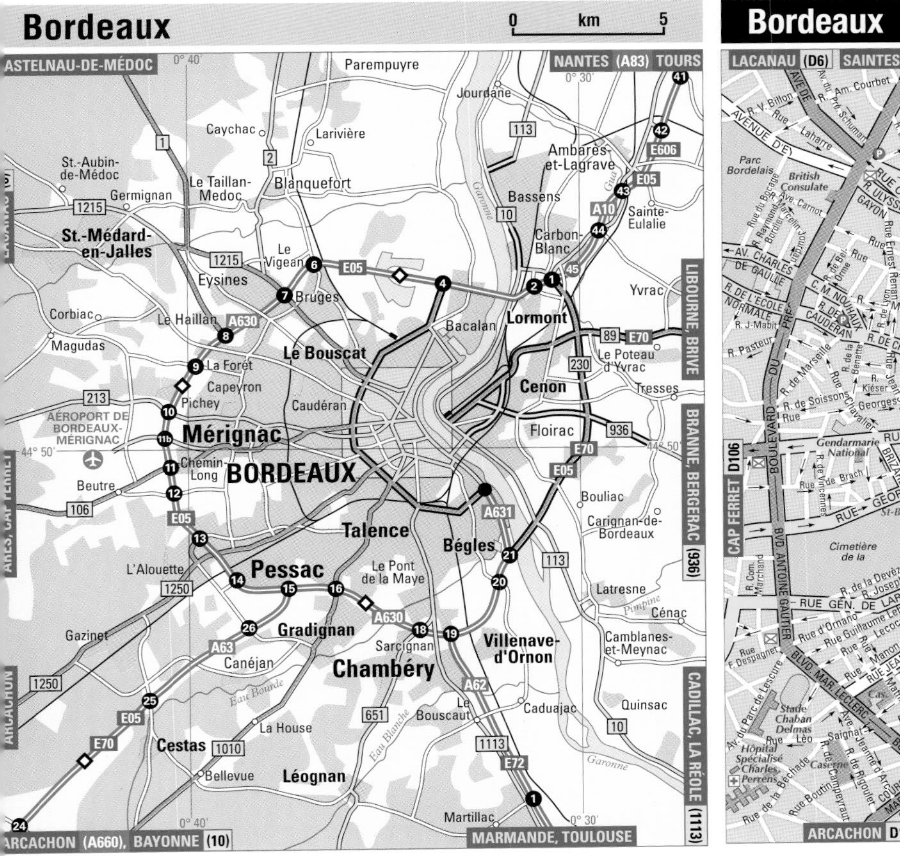

Bordeaux

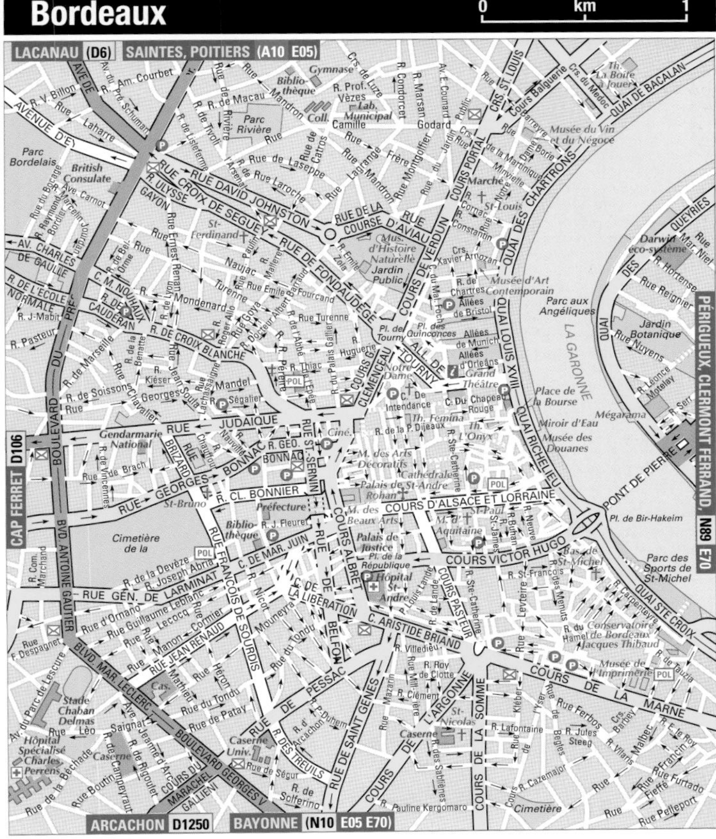

Bordeaux

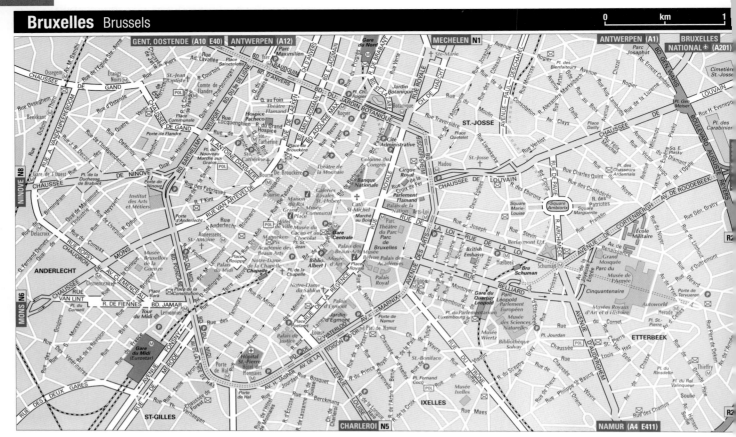

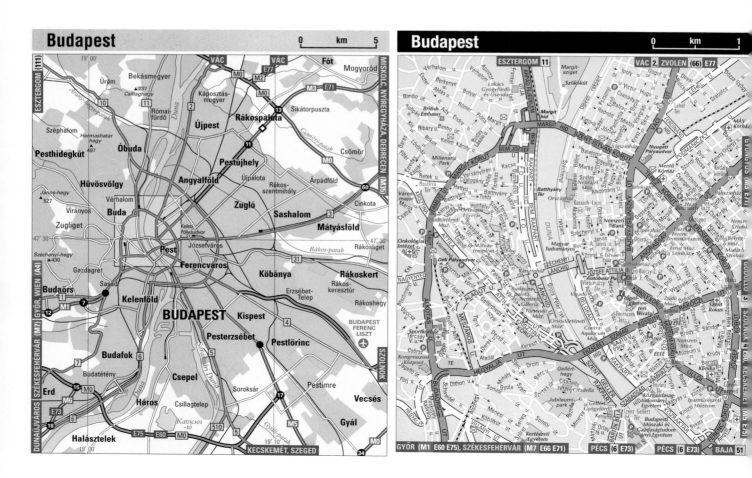

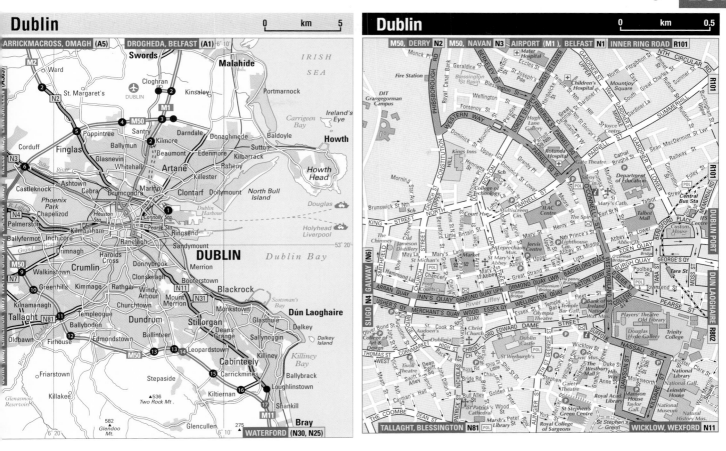

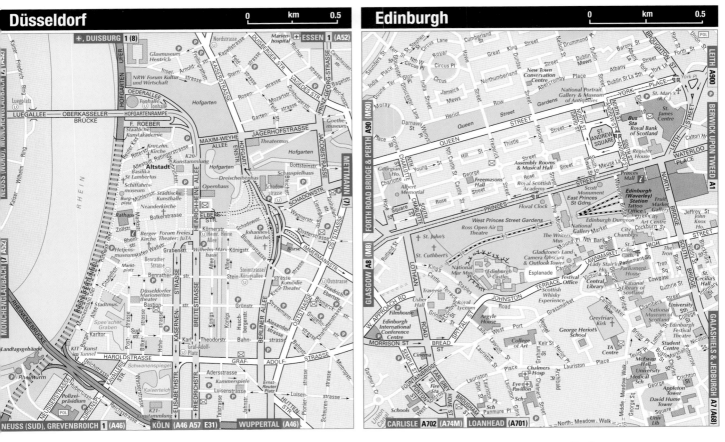

For **Cologne** see page 212
For **Copenhagen** see page 212

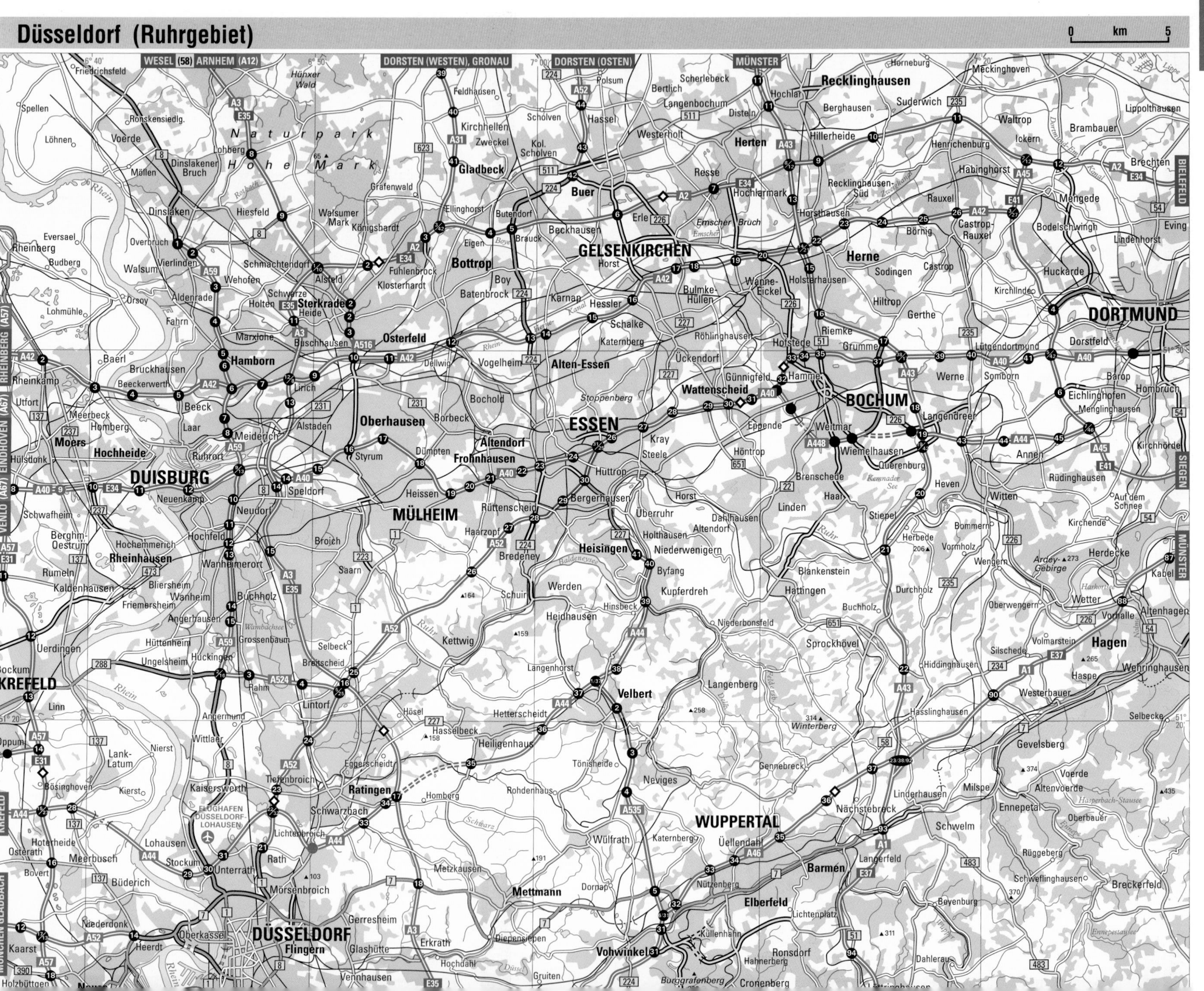
Düsseldorf (Ruhrgebiet)
0 km 5
WESEL (58) ARNHEM (A12)
DORSTEN (WESTEN), GRONAU
DORSTEN (OSTEN)
MÜNSTER
BIELEFELD
SIEGEN
RHEINBERG (A57)
VENLO (A67) EINDHOVEN (A67)
KREFELD
MÖNCHEN GLADBACH
Naturpark Hohe Mark
DORTMUND
BOCHUM
ESSEN
GELSENKIRCHEN
DUISBURG
MÜLHEIM
WUPPERTAL
DÜSSELDORF
KREFELD
Recklinghausen
Herne
Herten
Buer
Gladbeck
Bottrop
Oberhausen
Hagen
Velbert
Ratingen
Mettmann
Moers
Wattenscheid
Heisingen
Sterkrade
Osterfeld
Hamborn
Rheinhausen
Hochheide
Barmen
Elberfeld
Vohwinkel
Alten-Essen
Altendorf
Frohnhausen
FLUGHAFEN DÜSSELDORF-LOHAUSEN
Rhein
Ruhr

Firenze Florence

0 km 1

SESTO, BOLOGNA (A1 E35)

VIAREGGIO (A11 E76)

PONTASSIEVE (67), ROMA (67 A1 E35)

Frankfurt

0 km 0,5

SIEGEN, DORTMUND 3 (A5 A45 E41)

WIESBADEN (A66), KÖLN (A66 A3)

HANAU, FULDA 8 40 (A66)

OFFENBACH 43

WIESBADEN 44 (A648, A66)

MAINZ 44 (A3 A60), MANNHEIM 44 (A5)

DARMSTADT 3 (A661)

Genève Geneva

0 km 1

LAUSANNE 1 (A1, E25)

ST-GENIS-POUILLY 984

THONON-LES-BAINS (5) BONNEVILLE (205)

ANNECY 1 (201)

Génova Genoa

0 km 1

SAVONA 1, MILANO (A7 E62)

LA SPEZIA 1, FIRENZE (A12 E80, A11 E76)

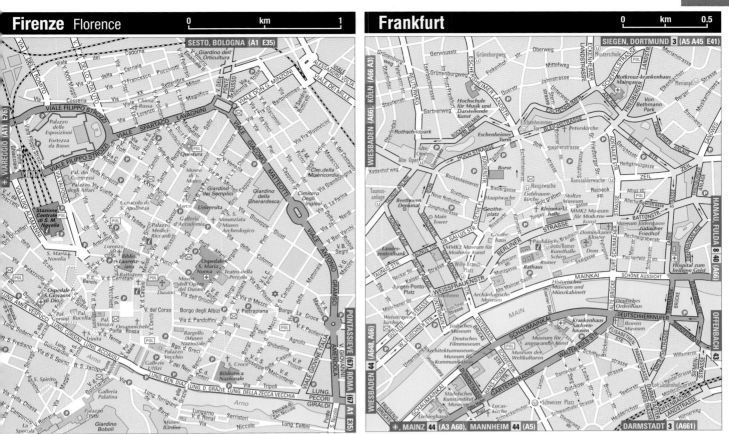

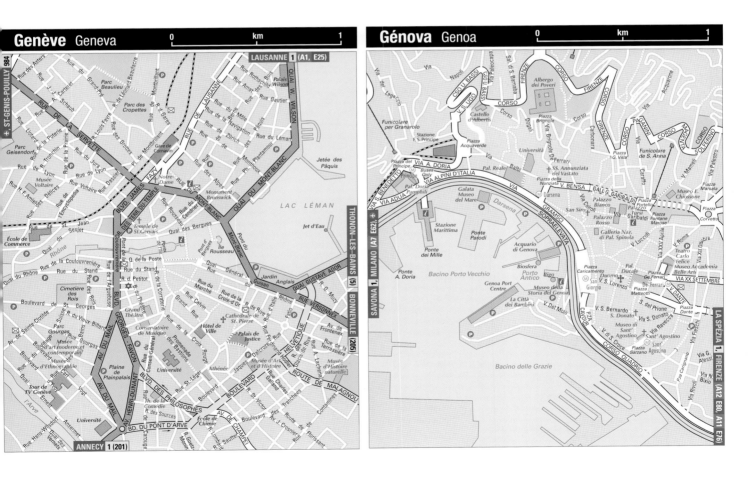

Granada

0   km   0.5

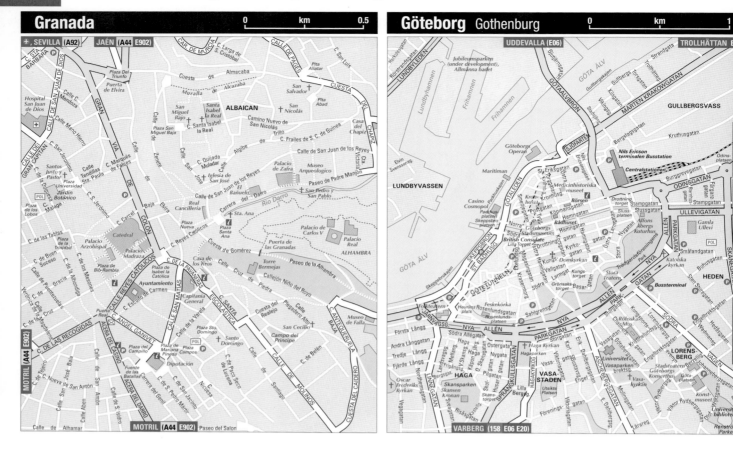

Göteborg Gothenburg

0   km   1

Hamburg

0   km   5

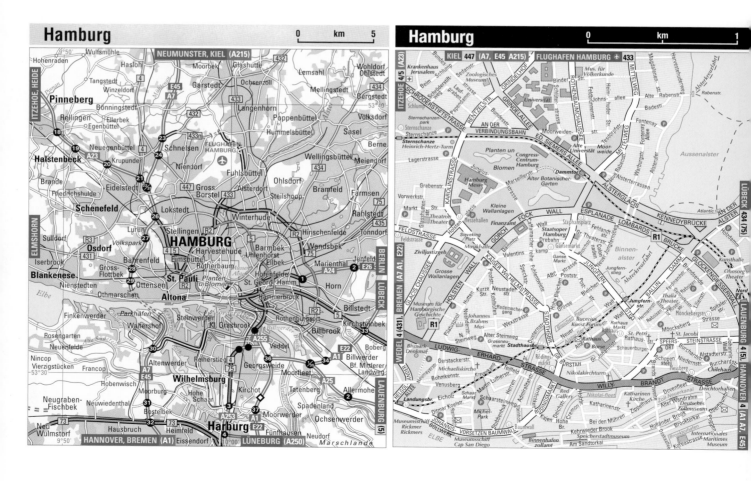

Hamburg

0   km   1

Helsinki

0 km 1

HELSINGIN LENTOASEMA (137, 45)
LAHTI 4 E75 (4)
PORVOO 170 (7, E18)
ESPOO (1 E18)
KIRKKONUMMI 51
ALPPIHARJU
ÅSHÖJDEN
Olympiastadion
BORTRE
TÖLÖ
MANNERHEIMINTIE
MECHELININKATU
HELSINGIN KATU
HÄMEENTIE
SÖRNÄISTENRANTA
SORNÄINEN
SÖRNAS
Suomen Kansallisooppera
Töölönlahti
Tölöviken
Finlandia-talo
Kansallismuseo
KLUUVI
GLOET
Eduskuntatalo
Temppeliaukion Kirkko
Sibelius Akatemia
Kiasma
KAISANIEMENKATU
ARKADIANKATU
POHJOISESPLANADI
ETELÄESPLANADI
Uspenskikatedraali
Katajanokka
Skatudden
Sörnäisten satama
Sörnäs hamn
Pohjoissatama
Norra hamnen
Eteläsatama
Södra hamnen
Olympiaterminaali
Makasiiniterminaali
Valkosaari
Blekholmen
Luoto
Klippan
Pikkuluoto
Lillklippan
Kaivopuisto
British Embassy
Hietalahti
Sandviken
LÄNSISATAMA
VÄSTRA HAMNEN
Länsiterminaali
LÖNNROTINKATU
BULEVARDI
Ruoholahti
Mikael Agricolan kirkko

İstanbul

0 km 5

Göktürk
Pirinççi
Kemerburgaz
Alibey Barajı
Cebecci
Ayazağa
Gaziosmanpaşa
Bahçeköy
Sarıyer
Anadolukavağı
Yuşa Tepesi 197
Büyükdere
Sinop
Beykoz
Tarabya
Yeniköy
İstinye
Paşabahçe
Emirgan
Boyacıköy
Çubuklu
Kanlıca
Göz Tepe 285
Rumelihisarı
Anadoluhisarı
Levent
Bebek
Kâğıthane
Alibeyköy
Mecidiyeköy
Arnavutköy
Kandilli
Küçüksu
Vaniköy
Küçükköy
Şişli
Beşiktaş
Ortaköy
Çengelköy
İnkılap
Atışalen
Bayrampaşa
Esenler
Eyüp
Hasköy
Taksim
Dolmabahçe Sarayı
Beylerbeyi
Kuzguncuk
Bağcılar
Beyoğlu
Galata
Çamlıca
Güngören
Fener
Topkapı
Bahçelıevler
Eminönü
Üsküdar
Ümraniye
Fatih
Yenikapı
Esat Paşa
Samatya
Yedikule
İSTANBUL
Kadıköy
Bakırköy
Zeytinburnu
Kızıltoprak
Fenerbahçe
Erenköy
İçerenköy
Bostancı
Marmara Denizi
İzmir
Yalova
EDIRNE
ATATÜRK
ŞİLE
SABIHA GÖKÇEN, GEBZE

Helsinki

0 km 10

HYVINKÄÄ, HÄMEENLINNA, TAMPERE (3)
TUUSULA, JÄRVENPÄÄ (145)
LAHTI
PORVOO/BORGÅ, KOTKA (7)
Järventausta
Ollila
Skogby
Kongo
Linna
Seutula
Ruotsinkylä
Myllykylä
Korso
Maantiekylä
Mäkiniitty
Hanala
Rekola
Nikinmäki
Hindsby
Gesterby
Ketunkorpi
Takkula
Lahnus
Vestra
Keimola
Kivistö
Koivupää
HELSINKI-VANTAAN LENTOASEMA
Harjusuo
Myras
Littjofs
Viirila
Heinässuo
Odilampi
Petas
Vantaanpuisto
Hiekkaharju
Kuninkaanmäki
Immersby
Massby
Veikkola
Siikajärvi
Röylä
Perusmaki
Vantaankoski
Vantaa
Simonkylä
Ita Hakkila
Ylästö
Tikkurila
Kaskela
Nybygget
Gobbacka
Askisto
Niiperi
Nuuksio
Martinkylä
Sotunki
Degermossa
Västerskog
Kolmiranta
Hämeenkylä
Friherrs
Haltiala
Tapanila
Puistola
Hakunila
Haltiavuori
Kaivoksela
HELSINKI-MALMI LENTOASEMA
Malmi
Brobacka
Paloheinä
Pukinmäki
Rajakylä
Mellunmäki
Östersundom
Kolmpera
Nupuri
Oittaa
Rastaala
Laaksolahti
Pakila
Lintuvaara
Konala
Pirkkola
Pihlajamäki
Mellunkylä
Simsalö
Västerkulla
Bemböle
Oulunkylä
Myllypuro
Vartiokylä
Grano
Espoo
Esbo
Kauniainen
Haaga
Käpylä
Viikki
Puotila
Kilo
Leppävaara
Vuosaari
Kallvik
Nuijala
Munkkiniemi
Pasila
Herttoniemi
Rastila
Roihuvuori
HELSINKI
Tuomarila
Laajalahti
Sibbo fjärden
Sipoon selkä
Kauklahti
Puolarmetsä
Henttaa
Mankkaa
Otaniemi
Tammisalo
Musta Hevonen
Boback
Olari
Tapiola
Lehtisaari
Kulosaari
Vartiosaari
Hietaniemi
Laajasalo
Vehkalahti
Vecklax
Nöykkiö
Jollas
Granlandet
Espoonlahti
Westend
Villinki
Trutlandet
Masala
Masaby
Lauttasaari
Hanskinen
Gästerby
Espoonlahti
Nokkala
Santahamina
Jorvas
Soukka
Miessaari
Pihlajasaari
Melkki
Vallisaari
Estlotan
Eestiluoto
Svinö
Björköfjärden
Stockholm, Lubeck, Travemünd, Tallinn, Rostock
Kirkkonummi
Kyrkslätt
Gunnarsby
Pentala
Lehtisaaret
Rysäkari
Harmaja
Kuivasaari
Isosaari
Medvastö
Estby

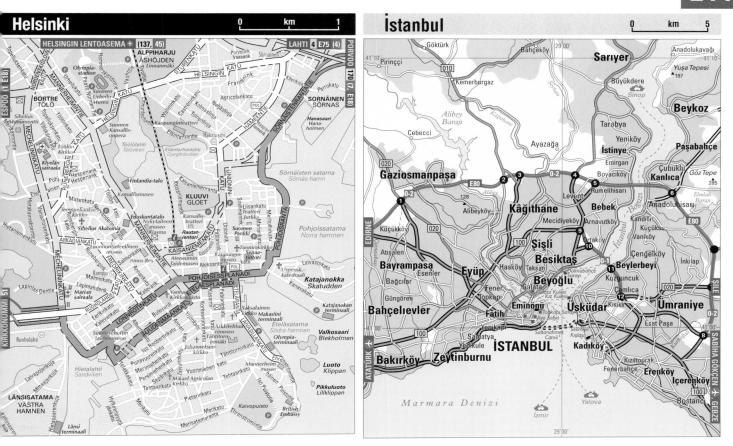

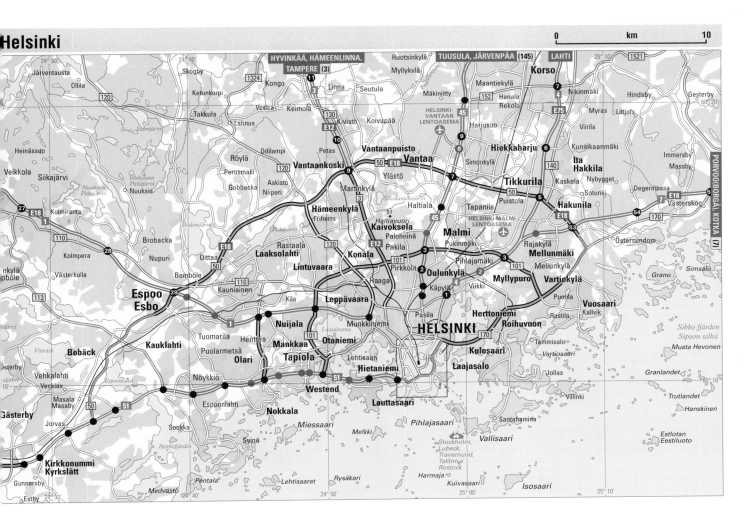

København Copenhagen

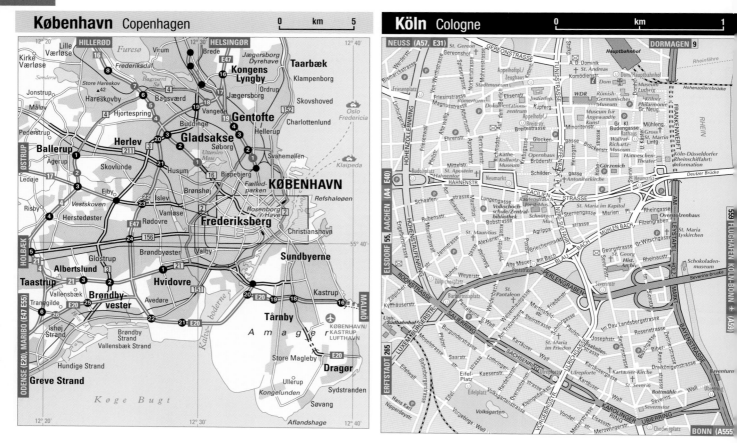

Köln Cologne

København Copenhagen

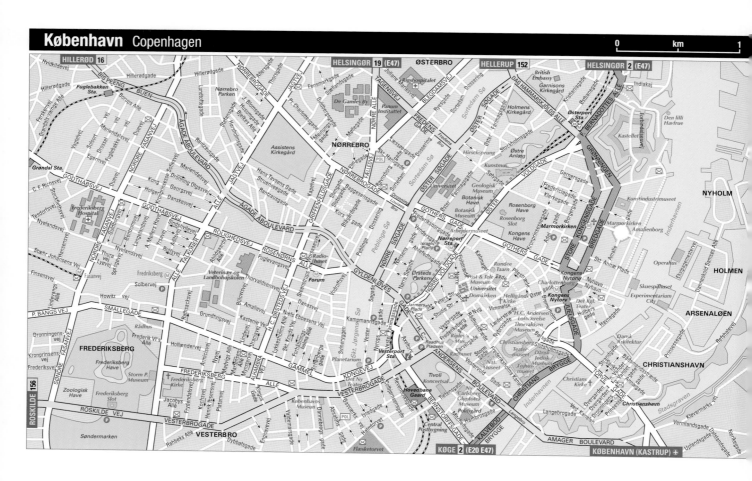

Lisboa Lisbon

Lisboa Lisbon

London

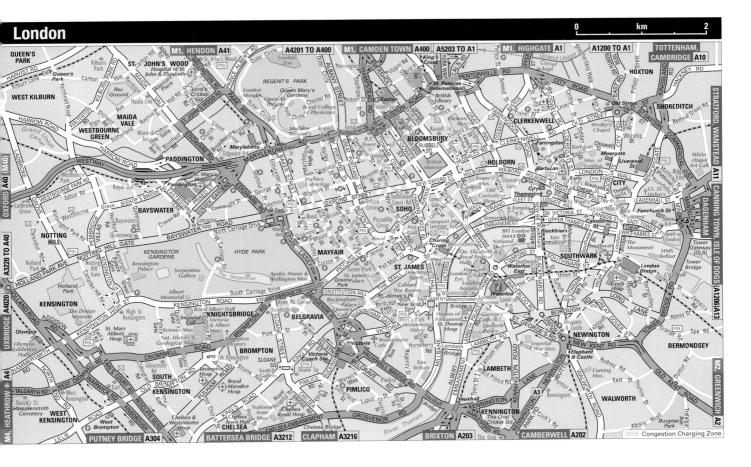

London

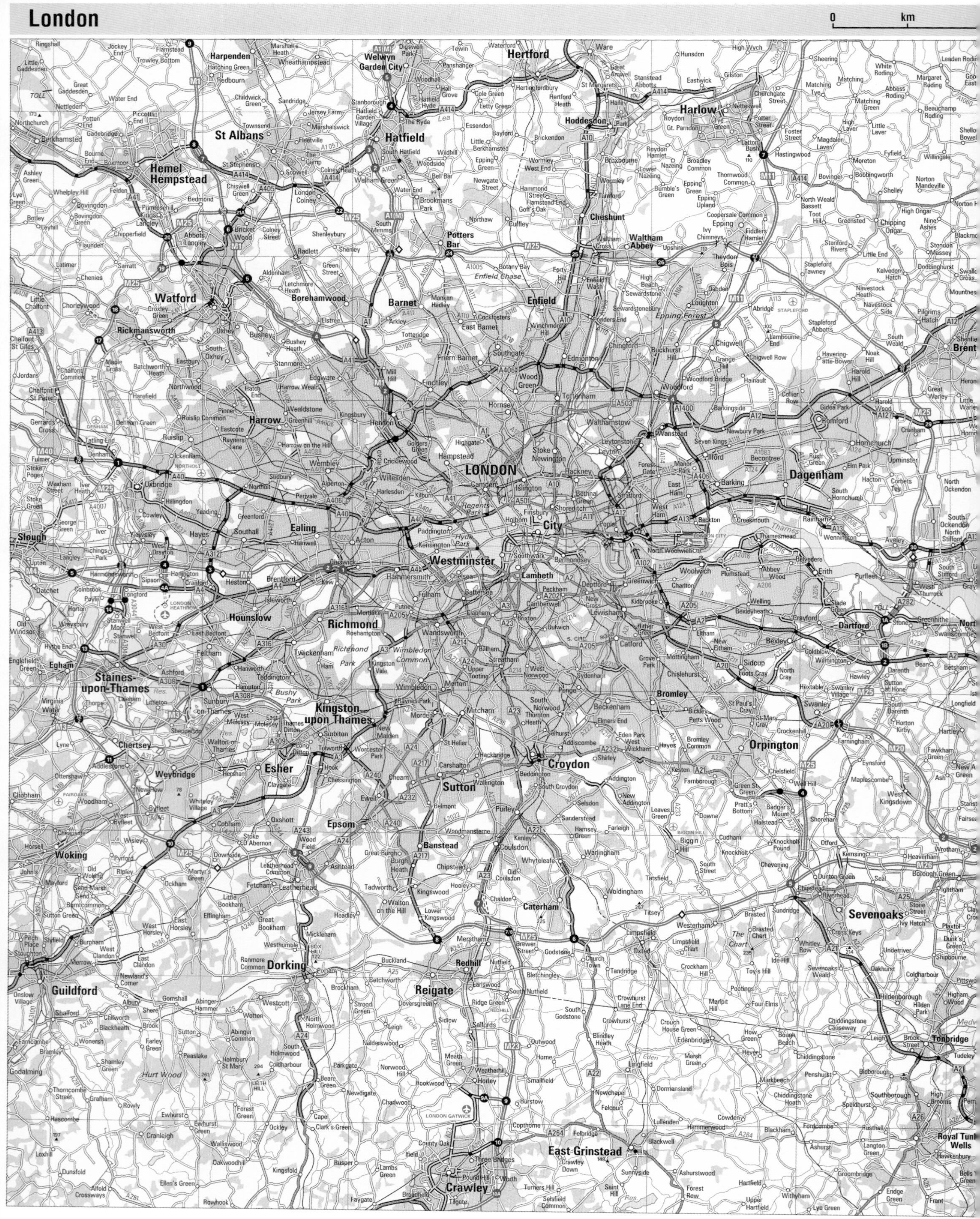
0 km
Harpenden
Welwyn Garden City
Hertford
Harlow
St Albans
Hatfield
Hemel Hempstead
Hoddesdon
Cheshunt
Potters Bar
Waltham Abbey
Watford
Borehamwood
Barnet
Enfield
Rickmansworth
Harrow
LONDON
Dagenham
Ealing
City
Slough
Westminster
Lambeth
Hounslow
Richmond
Dartford
Egham
Staines-upon-Thames
Kingston upon Thames
Bromley
Orpington
Chertsey
Weybridge
Esher
Croydon
Sutton
Epsom
Woking
Sevenoaks
Caterham
Dorking
Reigate
Guildford
Tonbridge
East Grinstead
Royal Tunbridge Wells
Crawley

Lyon

0 km 5

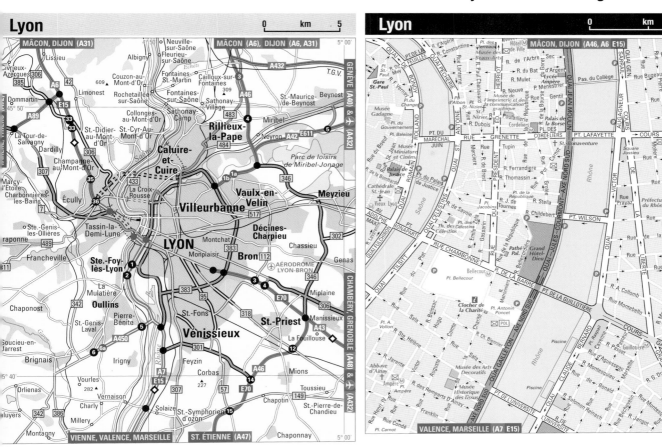
MÂCON, DIJON (A31)
MÂCON (A6), DIJON (A6, A31)
GENÈVE (A40) & ✈ (A432)
CHAMBERY, GRENOBLE (A48) & ✈ (A432)
VIENNE, VALENCE, MARSEILLE
ST. ÉTIENNE (A47)
LYON
Villeurbanne
Caluire-et-Cuire
Rillieux-la-Pape
Vaulx-en-Velin
Meyzieu
Décines-Charpieu
Bron
Vénissieux
St.-Priest
Oullins
Ste.-Foy-lès-Lyon
Tassin-la-Demi-Lune
Écully
Limonest
Chassieu
Genas
Feyzin
Corbas
Mions
AÉRODROME LYON-BRON
Parc de loisirs de Miribel-Jonage

Lyon

0 km 1

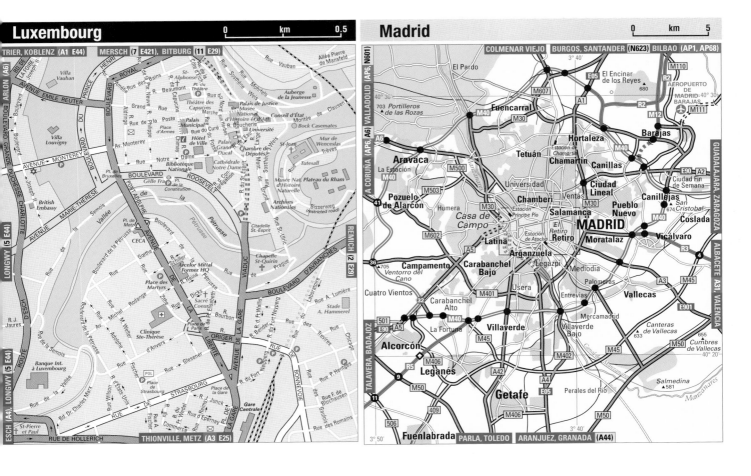
MÂCON, DIJON (A46, A6 E15)
CHAMBÉRY (A43 E70) & ✈ (A432)
VALENCE, MARSEILLE (A7 E15)
QUAI JEAN MOULIN
Saône
Rhône
Pl. Bellecour
Gare St.-Paul
Cathédrale St.-Jean
Musée Gadagne
Hôtel de Ville
Musée des Beaux-Arts
Grand Hôtel-Dieu
PT. LAFAYETTE
COURS LAFAYETTE
PT. WILSON
PT. DE LA GUILLOTIÈRE
PT. DE L'UNIVERSITÉ
Préfecture du Rhône
COURS GAMBETTA

Luxembourg

0 km 0.5

TRIER, KOBLENZ (A1 E44) · MERSCH (7 E421), BITBURG (11 E29) · ARLON (A6) · LONGWY (5 E44) · REMICH (2 E29) · ESCH (A4), LONGWY (5 E44) · THIONVILLE, METZ (A3 E25)

Avenue Emile Reuter · Boulevard Royal · Boulevard Grande Duchesse Charlotte · Avenue Monterey · Avenue Marie-Thérèse · Boulevard Roosevelt · Pont Adolphe · Avenue de la Liberté · Avenue de la Gare · Boulevard d'Avranches · Rue de Strasbourg · Rue de Hollerich · Pétrusse · Villa Vauban · Villa Louvigny · Palais Grand Ducal · Cathédrale Notre Dame · Hôtel de Ville · Place d'Armes · Palais de Justice · Musée National d'Histoire et d'Art · Bock Casemates · Musée Nat. d'Histoire Naturelle · Plateau du Rham · Citadelle St.-Esprit · Arcelor Mittal Former HQ · Clinique Ste-Thérèse · Banque Int. à Luxembourg · Gare Centrale · Viaduc

Madrid

0 km 5

COLMENAR VIEJO · BURGOS, SANTANDER (N623) · BILBAO (AP1, AP68) · VALLADOLID (AP6, N601) · LA CORUÑA (AP6, A6) · GUADALAJARA, ZARAGOZA · ALBACETE A31, VALENCIA · TALAVERA, BADAJOZ · PARLA, TOLEDO · ARANJUEZ, GRANADA (A44)

MADRID · El Pardo · Fuencarral · Hortaleza · Barajas · AEROPUERTO DE MADRID-BARAJAS · Aravaca · Tetuán · Chamartín · Canillas · Ciudad Lineal · Canillejas · Universidad · Chamberí · Salamanca · Pueblo Nuevo · Coslada · Vicálvaro · Moratalaz · Retiro · Pozuelo de Alarcón · Casa de Campo · Latina · Arganzuela · Campamento · Carabanchel Bajo · Carabanchel Alto · Mediodía · Usera · Vallecas · Villaverde · Villaverde Bajo · Alcorcón · Leganés · Getafe · Fuenlabrada · Cuatro Vientos · Mercamadrid · Perales del Río · Manzanares

Madrid

0   km   1

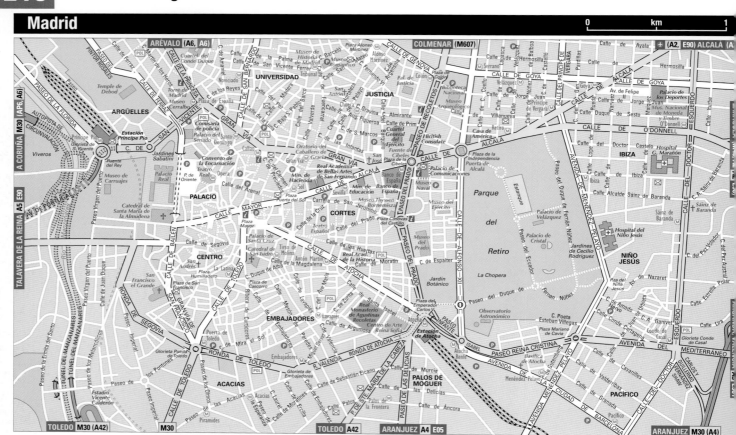

ARÉVALO (A6, A6)   COLMENAR (M607)   (A2, E90) ALCALÁ

UNIVERSIDAD · JUSTICIA · ARGÜELLES · PALACIO · CENTRO · CORTES · EMBAJADORES · ACACIAS · PALOS DE MOGUER · PACÍFICO · NIÑO JESÚS · IBIZA

Parque del Retiro

TOLEDO M30 (A42)   M30   TOLEDO A42   ARANJUEZ A4 E05   ARANJUEZ M30 (A4)

Málaga

0   km   0.5

Marseille / Marseilles

0   km   0.5

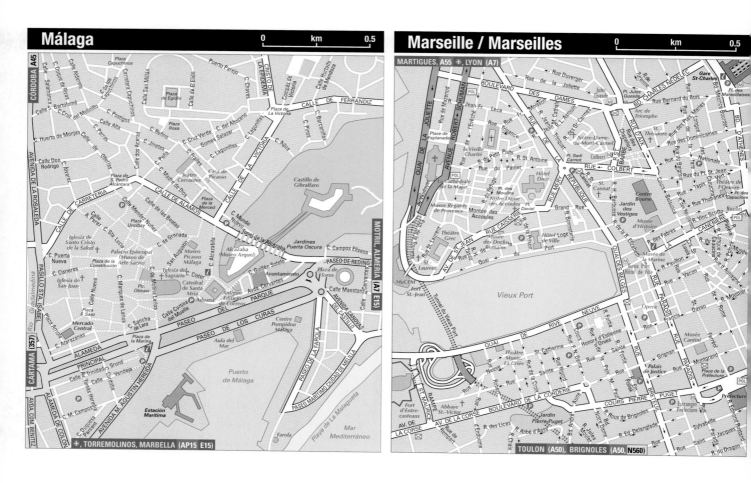

CÓRDOBA A45   CÁRTAMA (357)   MOTRIL, ALMERÍA (A7) E15

TORREMOLINOS, MARBELLA (AP15 E15)

MARTIGUES, A55, LYON (A7)

TOULON (A50), BRIGNOLES (A50, N560)

Milano Milan

0 km 5

MALPENSA ✈, VARESE
COMO, ZÜRICH (A2)
LECCO
LECCO (342d)
BÉRGAMO, BRÉSCIA
BRÉSCIA
GÉNOVA, NICE (A10)
PARMA, BOLOGNA

Limbiate
Muggiò
Monza
Concorezzo
Lainate
Garbagnate Milanese
Bollate
Paderno Dugnano
Nova Milanese
Cusano Milanino
Cinisello Balsamo
Bresso
Sesto San Giovanni
Brughério
Cologno Monzese
Cernusco sul Naviglio
Rho
Pero
Novate Milanese
Nerviano
Pogliano Milanese
Pregnana Milanese
Cornaredo
Séttimo Milanese
Magenta
MILANO
Cesano Boscone
Córsico
Trezzano sul Naviglio
Rozzano
Assago
Segrate
Pioltello
Melzo
Gorgonzola
AEROPORTO INTERNAZ. DI LINATE
San Donato Milanese
San Giuliano Milanese
Peschiera Borromeo
Melegnano
Abbiategrasso
Vigévano
Binasco
Locate di Trulzi
Lodi

Milano Milan

0 km 1

MALPENSA ✈, VARESE (A8)
VARESE 233
COMO 35 MONZA (36)
BÉRGAMO 11 (525)
LINATE ✈ BRESCIA (11)
ABBIATEGRASSO 494
GÉNOVA (A7 E62)
PAVIA 35
LODI 9 PARMA (A51, A1)

Parco Sempione
Arena
Castello Sforzesco
Staz. Ferrovie Nord
Cadorna
Stazione Centrale
Giardini Pubblici Indro Montanelli
Galleria d'Arte Moderna
Museo di Storia Naturale
Duomo
Galleria Vittorio Emanuele II
Palazzo Reale
Università Cattolica
Museo di Scienza e Tecnica
S. Maria d. Grazie
S. Ambrogio
Policlinico
Università
Staz. Genova
Porta Romana
Porta Ticinese
Porta Venezia
Piazzale Lotto
Velodromo Vigorelli
CORSO SEMPIONE
CORSO VERCELLI
CORSO MAGENTA
FORO BUONAPARTE
CORSO VENEZIA
CORSO BUENOS AIRES
VIALE PICENO
VIALE DEI MILLE
CORSO DI PORTA ROMANA
VIALE BEATRICE D'ESTE

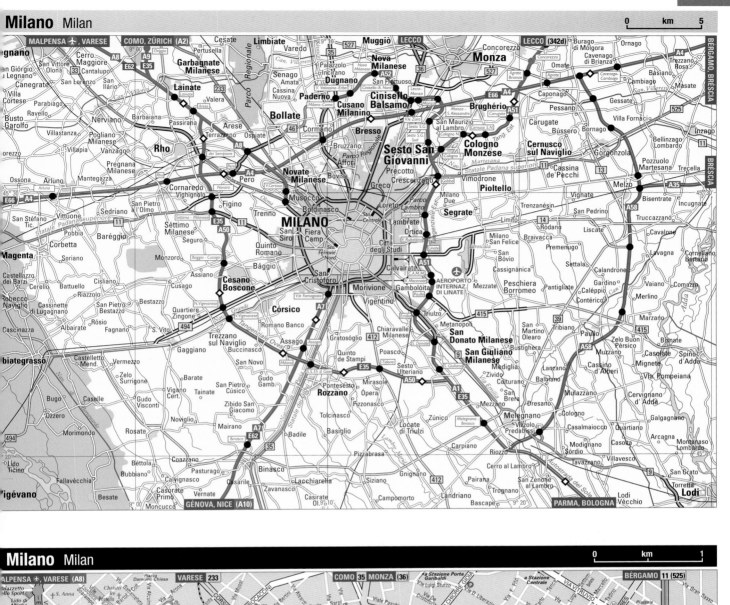

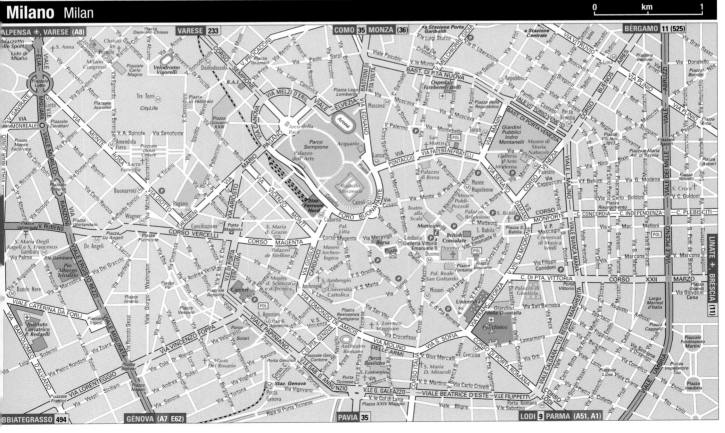

Moskva Moscow

0 km 5

Moskva Moscow

0 km 1

München Munich

0 km 5

München Munich

0 km 1

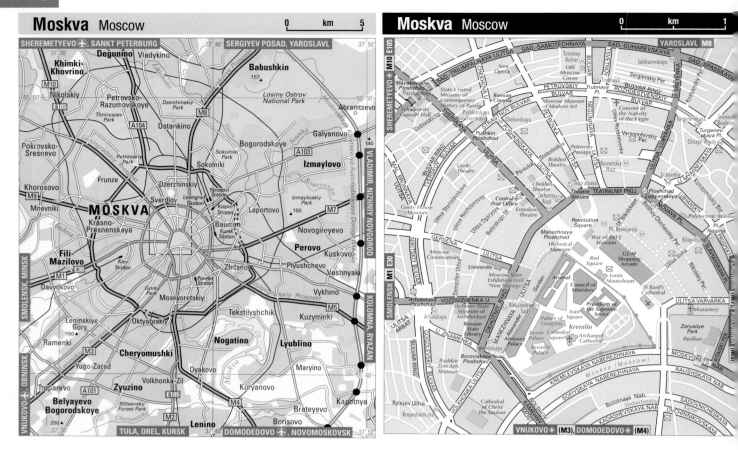

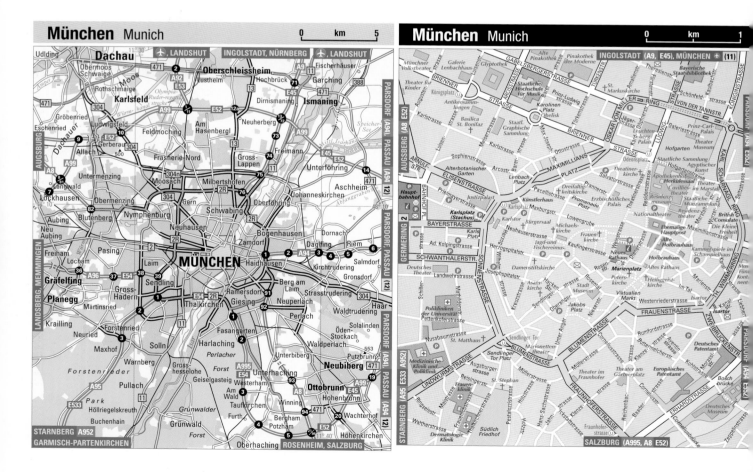

Nápoli Naples

0 km 5

CASERTA, ROMA
AVELLINO, ÁNDRIA (A14)
SALERNO, POTENZA (E847)
POZZUOLI

Aversa
Caivano
Acerra
Sant' Antimo
Giugliano in Campania
Cardito
Frattamaggiore
Villaricca
Afragola
Arzano
Casalnuovo di Nápoli
Pomigliano d'Arco
Casória
Marano di Nápoli
Secondigliano
AEROPORTO CAPODICHINO
Volla
Somma Vesuviana
Ponticelli
Sant' Anastasia
Barra
San Giórgio a Cremano
NÁPOLI
Pórtici
Ercolano
Vesúvio Vesuvius
Torre del Greco
Torre Annunziata
Golfo di Nápoli
Posillipo
Mergellina
Marechiaro
Cágliari, Catánia, Palermo, Strómboli, Ginostra, Panarea, Lipari, Vulcano, Milazzo
Prócida Ischia
Capri Sorrento

Nápoli Naples

0 km 1

MARANO DI NÁPOLI
CAPODICHINO
ROMA (A1, E45)
POMPEI, SALERNO (A3), PÓRTICI (18)
POZZUOLI

Museo Archeologico Nazionale
Accademia di Belle Arti
Policlinico
Stazione Centrale
Piazza Garibaldi
Stazione Napoli Porta Nolana
Castel Capuano
Duomo
Università
Stazione Cumana
Ospedale dei Pellegrini
Palazzo Gravina
Municipio
Castel Nuovo
Teatro San Carlo
Palazzo Reale
Piazza del Plebiscito
Stazione Funicolare
Certosa di San Martino
Stazione Marittima
Bacino del Piliero
Porto Beverello
Capri, Sorrento, Ischia, Prócida
Cágliari, Catánia, Palermo, Strómboli, Ginostra, Panarea, Lipari, Vulcano, Milazzo
Calata Villa del Popolo
Capitaneria di Porto
Molo Martello
Molo Angioino
Molo di San Vincenzo
VIA TOLEDO
CORSO UMBERTO I
VIA NUOVA MARINA
VIA CRISTOFORO COLOMBO
CORSO VITTORIO EMANUELE
Partenope

Oslo

0 km 5

BERGEN
GJØVIK, LILLEHAMMER
JESSHEIM, OSLO GARDERMOEN, HAMAR
AMMEN, TORP, KRISTIANSAND
ASKIM, KARLSTAD
MOSS, RYGGE, FREDRIKSTAD

Nordmarka
Sørkedalen
Tryvannshøgda
Holmenkollen
Maridalen
Kjelsås
Gorud
Lillestrøm
Hvam
Skjetten
Strømmen
Rud
Lørenskog
OSLO
Ullevål
Ullern
Skøyen
Bærums Verk
Kolsås
Bærum
Sandvika
Fornebu
Lysaker
Bygdøy
Hovedøya
Nesoddtangen
Oslofjorden
Bunnefjorden
Asker
Nesbru
Holsfjorden
Kolbotn
Oppegård
Ljabru
Bekkelaget
Nordstrand
Ryen
Tøyen
Alna
Sinsen
Frederikshavn København Kiel

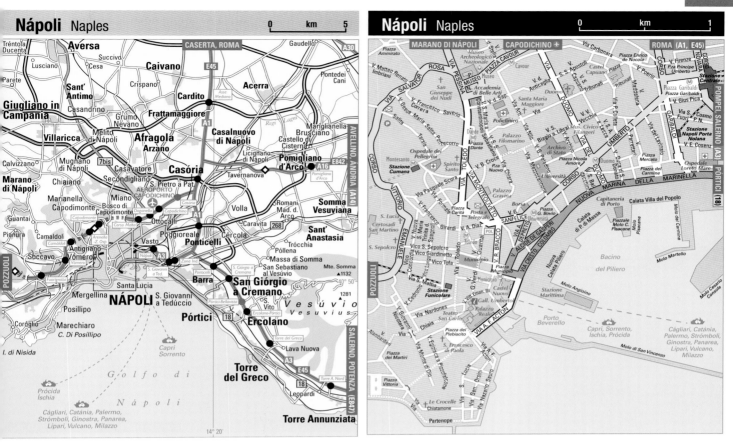

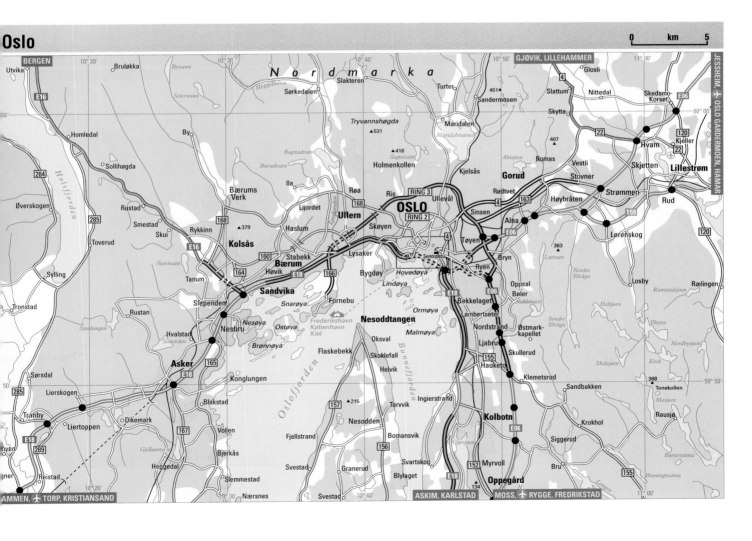

Oslo

0 km 0.5

RING 2 · RING 2/3, RØA 168 · LILLESTRØM 4 (22) · OSLO ✈ 4 (22, E06) · DRAMMEN, TORP ✈ E18 · RING 1 · KARLSTAD E18, RYGGE ✈ E18, FREDRIKSTAD E18 (E06)

Paris

0 km 1

BOULEVARD PÉRIPHÉRIQUE · ARGENTEUIL (909) · ROUEN D14 A15 · ✈ CHARLES DE GAULLE, LILLE (A1, E15 E19) · MEAUX (N3) · ST-GERMAIN-EN-LAYE N13 (A14) · ROUEN (A13 E05) · NOISY-LE-SEC (A3) · VERSAILLES 910 · ✈ ORLY (A6), LE MANS (A10 A11 E50) · REIMS (A4 E50)

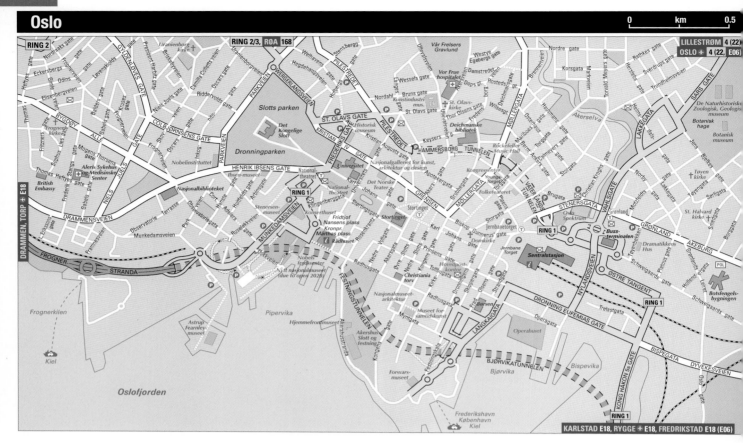

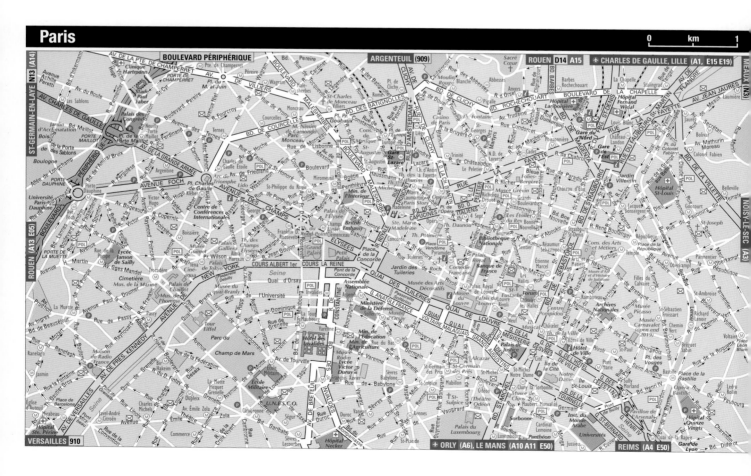

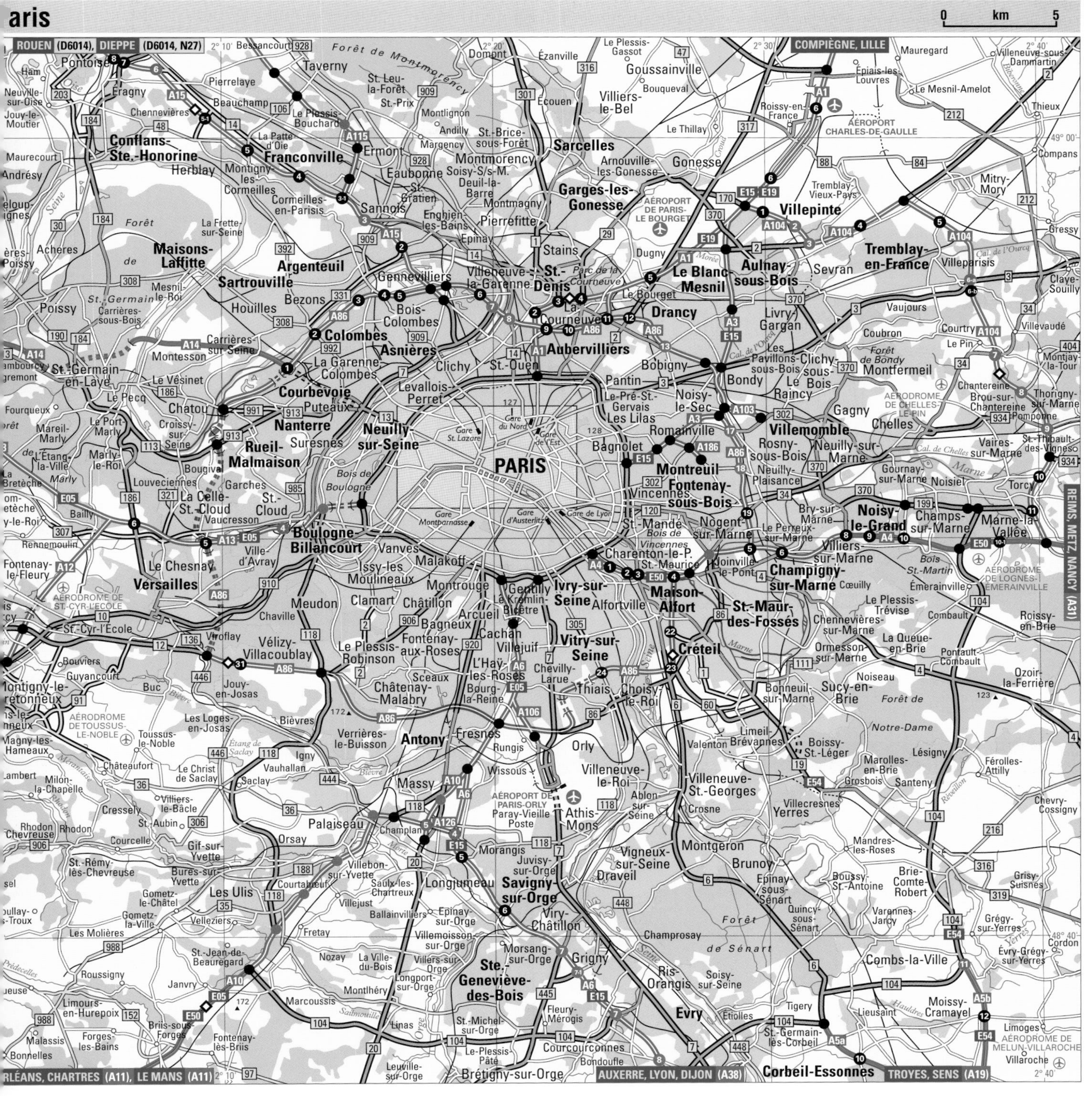
aris
0 km 5
ROUEN (D6014), DIEPPE (D6014, N27)
COMPIÈGNE, LILLE
REIMS, METZ, NANCY (A31)
ORLÉANS, CHARTRES (A11), LE MANS (A11)
AUXERRE, LYON, DIJON (A38)
TROYES, SENS (A19)
PARIS
Pontoise
Taverny
Forêt de Montmorency
Goussainville
Villiers-le-Bel
AÉROPORT CHARLES-DE-GAULLE
Roissy-en-France
Conflans-Ste.-Honorine
Franconville
Ermont
Montmorency
Sarcelles
Garges-lès-Gonesse
Gonesse
AÉROPORT DE PARIS-LE BOURGET
Villepinte
Tremblay-en-France
Aulnay-sous-Bois
Sevran
Maisons-Laffitte
Argenteuil
Sartrouville
Houilles
Bezons
Gennevilliers
Villeneuve-la-Garenne
St.-Denis
Le Blanc-Mesnil
Drancy
Aubervilliers
Colombes
Bois-Colombes
Asnières
Clichy
St.-Ouen
Bobigny
Bondy
St.-Germain-en-Laye
Le Vésinet
La Garenne-Colombes
Courbevoie
Levallois-Perret
Pantin
Noisy-le-Sec
Les Pavillons-sous-Bois
Clichy-sous-Bois
Montfermeil
Chatou
Puteaux
Nanterre
Neuilly-sur-Seine
Le Pré-St.-Gervais
Les Lilas
Romainville
Villemomble
Gagny
Chelles
Rueil-Malmaison
Suresnes
Bagnolet
Montreuil
Fontenay-sous-Bois
Rosny-sous-Bois
Neuilly-sur-Marne
Vincennes
St.-Mandé
Nogent-sur-Marne
Noisy-le-Grand
Champs-sur-Marne
Marne-la-Vallée
Versailles
Le Chesnay
La Celle-St.-Cloud
St.-Cloud
Boulogne-Billancourt
Vanves
Issy-les-Moulineaux
Malakoff
Montrouge
Gentilly
Ivry-sur-Seine
Charenton-le-P.
Maison-Alfort
Joinville-le-Pont
Champigny-sur-Marne
Villiers-sur-Marne
Meudon
Clamart
Châtillon
Arcueil
Le Kremlin-Bicêtre
Alfortville
St.-Maur-des-Fossés
Créteil
Vélizy-Villacoublay
Le Plessis-Robinson
Fontenay-aux-Roses
Bagneux
Cachan
Villejuif
Vitry-sur-Seine
Sceaux
Châtenay-Malabry
L'Haÿ-les-Roses
Bourg-la-Reine
Thiais
Choisy-le-Roi
Sucy-en-Brie
Antony
Fresnes
Rungis
Orly
Villeneuve-le-Roi
AÉROPORT DE PARIS-ORLY
Athis-Mons
Villeneuve-St.-Georges
Massy
Palaiseau
Orsay
Les Ulis
Longjumeau
Savigny-sur-Orge
Viry-Châtillon
Draveil
Montgeron
Brunoy
Ste.-Geneviève-des-Bois
Grigny
Ris-Orangis
Evry
Corbeil-Essonnes
Combs-la-Ville
Moissy-Cramayel
Brétigny-sur-Orge
Forêt de Sénart

Praha Prague

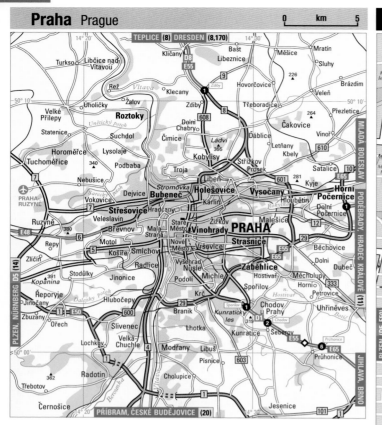

Praha Prague

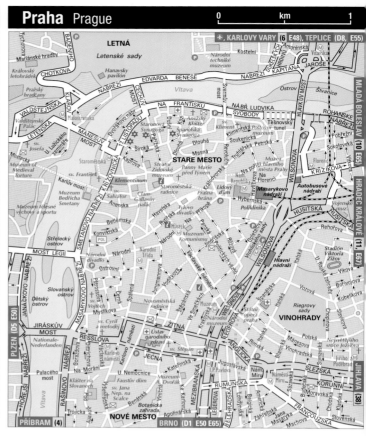

Rotterdam

Sankt-Peterburg St. Petersburg

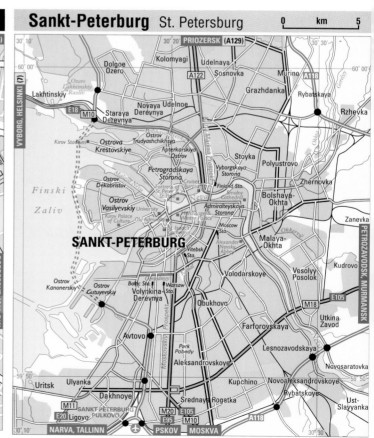

Roma Rome

0 km 5

VITERBO
CIVITA CASTELLANA
FIRENZE (A1)
RIETI
Mentana
ORTE, FIRENZE
L'AQUILA, PESCARA (A25)
FROSINONE, NAPOLI (A3)
LIDO DI ÓSTIA
LATINA, TERRACINA
APRILIA
VELLETRI

ROMA
Città Del Vaticano
Vatican City
Agro Romano
Colli Albani
AEROPORTO INTERCONTINENTALE LEONARDO DA VINCI
AEROPORTO DI CIAMPINO
AEROPORTO D. URBE
Ciampino
Frascati
Marino
Torrenova
La Ríccia
Tragliatella
Ogliata
Ost. Nuova
Isola Farnese
Santa Maria di Galéria
La Storta
Prima Porta
Settebagni
Bufalotta
Romitório
Torre Lupara
S. Ángelo Romano
Montecélio
Le Casette
Guidónia
Inviolata
Le Sprete
Cle. Centrone
La Giustiniana
San Nicola
Tragliata
Boccea
Ottávia
Tomba di Nerone
San Onófrio
Tor di Quinto
Tufello
San Basilio
Settecamini
Bagni di Tivoli
Ponte Lucano
Albuccione
Lunghezza
Salone
Torrimpietra
Torrevécchia
Primavalle
Flaminio
Parioli
Trieste
Monte Sacro
Pietralata
Torre Cervara
Nomentano
Corcolle
Casalotti
La Bottáccia
Cast. di Guido
La Monachina
La Selce
Monte-spaccato
Trionfale
Aurelio
Trastevere
Tiburtino
Tor Pignattara
Prenestino Labicano
Centocelle
Tor Sapienza
Ost. d. Osa
Cast. di Passerano
Pantano Borghese
Malagrotta
Valcannuta
Gianicolense
Monteverde Nuovo
Garbatella
Quadraro
Cinecittà
Torre Gáia
Finócchio
Laghetto
Bonifica di Maccarese
La Pisana
Corviale
Ostiense
Cast. Malnome
Magliana
L'Annunziatella
E.U.R.
Colonna
Monte Pórzio Catone
Montecómpatri
Bonifica di Porto
Ponte Galéria
Casál Morena
Cecchignola
St. Torricola
Camáldoli
Rocca Priora
Grottaferrata
Acília
Vitínia
Spinaceto
Valleranello
Castél di Leva
Santa Maria della Mole
Porto
Ostia Malpasso
Ostia Antica
Ísola Sacra
Casál Palocco
Cast. Porziano
Cast. di Décima
Mandriola
Falcognana
Frattócchie
Rocca di Papa
Mte. Iano
Mte. Cavo
Faro

Roma Rome

0 km 1

TERNI (3)
VITERBO (2)
FIRENZE 4 (A1 dir, A1 E35)
FROSINONE 6 (A1 E45)
'LEONARDO DA VINCI' (A12)
LATINA 148

CITTÀ DEL VATICANO
S. Pietro in Vaticano
Stazione Vaticana
Musei Vaticani
Piazza San Pietro
Castel S. Angelo
Villa Borghese
Galleria Nazionale d'Arte Moderna e Contemporanea
Museo Naz. di Villa Giulia
Bioparco
Piazza d. Popolo
Giardino del Pincio
Galoppatoio
Villa Medici
Mausoleo di Augusto
Piazza di Spagna
Fontana di Trevi
Pantheon
Piazza Navona
Campo d. Fiori
Palazzo Farnese
Camera dei Deputati
Giardino del Quirinale
Palazzo Venezia
Mon. a Vittorio Emanuele II
Musei Capitolini
Foro Romano
Monte Palatino
Colosseo
Arco di Costantino
Parco del Celio
Col. Traiano
Teatro di Marcello
Circo Massimo
Stazione Centrale Roma-Termini
S.M. Maggiore
Villa Albani
Villa Torlonia
Policlinico Umberto I
Sapienza Università di Roma
Biblioteca Nazionale
Castro Pretorio
Villa Abamelek
Villa Doria Pamphili
Gianicolo
Mon. a G. Garibaldi
Orto Botanico
Palazzo Corsini
S. Pietro in Montorio
S. Maria in Trastevere
Ospedale Pediatrico Bambino Gesù
Stazione di S. Pietro
S. Pancrazio
Piazza di S. Giov. in Laterano
Ospedale S. Giovanni
S. Croce in Gerus.
Porta Maggiore

Restricted Zones (ZTL)

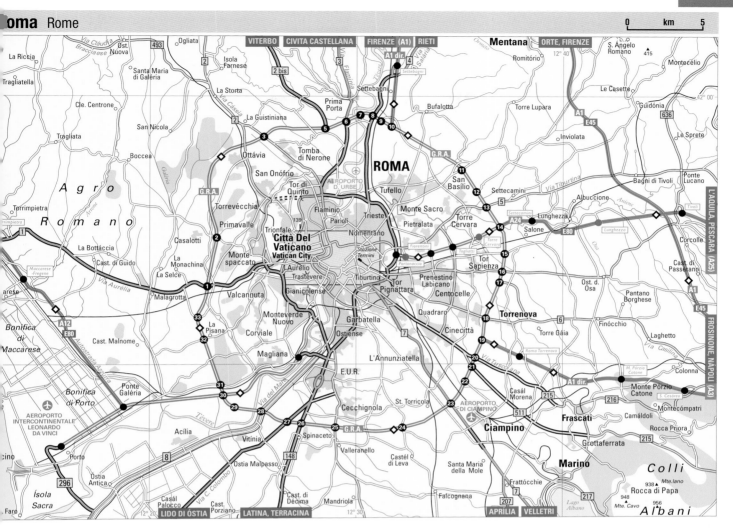

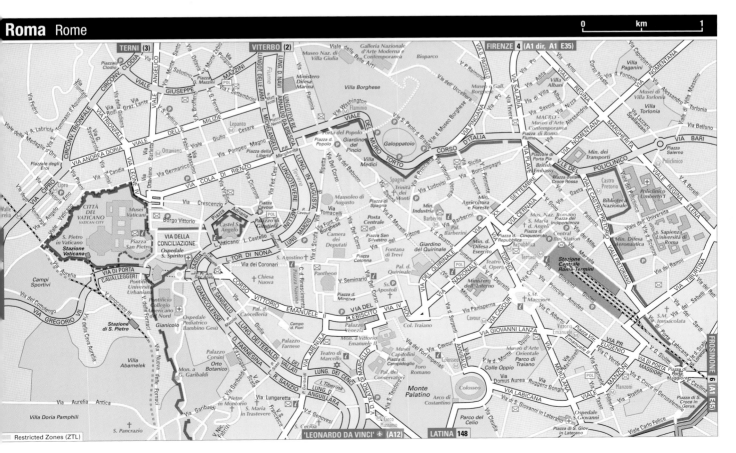

Sevilla Seville

0 km 0.5

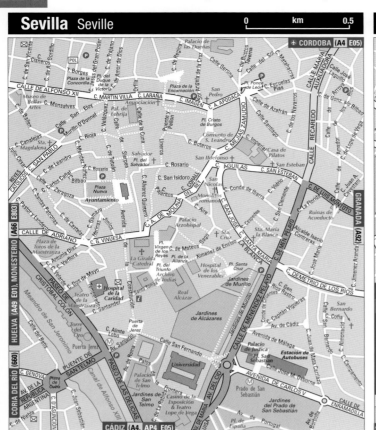

Stuttgart

0 km 0.5

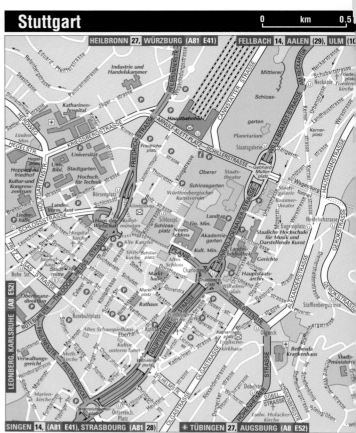

Strasbourg

0 km 5

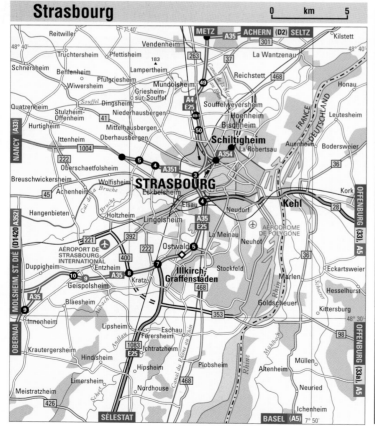

Strasbourg

0 km 0.5

Stockholm

0 km 5

VÄSTERÅS, ÖREBRO
ARLANDA, UPPSALA
NORRTÄLJE, KAPPELSKÄR
NYKÖPING, NORRKÖPING
NYNÄSHAMN
STAVSNÄS

Kallhäll
Häggvik
Edsberg
Skarpäng
Täby
Viggbyholm
Svinningeudd
Kungsängen
Görväln
Jakobsberg
Tureberg
Enebyberg
Sollentuna
Helenelund
Roslags-Näsby
Näsbypark
Näsby
Stora Värtan
Rydboholm
Österskär
Resarö
Trälhavet
Munsö
Kungsberga
Vantholmen
Barkarby
Järfälla
Akalla
Husby
Kista
Danderyd
Djursholm
Stora holmen
Frösvik
Söderby
Uteke
Vaxholm
Skarpö
Ellboda
Färentuna
Hilleshög
Ricksattra
Spånga
Rinkeby
Ursvik
Ulriksdal
Mörby
Stocksund
Sticklinge udde
Bosön
Askrikefjärden
Mariehamn
Langnas
Turku
Helsinki
Tallinn
Riga
Höggarnsfj.
Ekeby
Degerby
Sånga
Hässelby
Nälsta
Flysta
Sundbyberg
Solna
Haga
Lidingö
Ålvvik
Gåshaga
Koviksudde
Vällingby
Bromma Flygplats
Bromma
Lambarfjärden
Käppala
Kummelnäs
Svartsjölandet
Ängby
Östermalm
Norrmalm
STOCKHOLM
Lilla Värtan
Brevik
Ormingelandet
Björkö
Stenhamra
Skå
Lovö
Drottningholm
Nockeby
Alvik
Ålsten
Kungsholmen
Essingen
Djurgården
Orminge
Kil
Gustavsberg
Rasta
Kärsön
Nacka
Björknäs
Skuru
Saltsjö-Duvnäs
Eknäs
Boo
Rastaborg
Ekerön
Lovön
Fågelön
Hägersten
Mälarhöjden
Södermalm
Årsta
Hammarby
Hästhagen
Fisksätra
Igelboda
Baggensfjärden
Färstalandet
Södra Björkfj
Kungshatt
Närsta
Kaggeholm
Gällstao
Sätra
Skärholmen
Bredäng
Västertorp
Brännkyrka
Älvsjö
Enskede
Stureby
Tallkrogen
Skarpnäck
Kolarängen
Saltsjöbaden
Ingarölandet
Ekerö
Segeltorp
Örby
Älgö
Vällinge
Kyrkfjärden
Rodstensfjärden
Värby
Kungens kurva
Snättringe
Erstaviken
Slagsta
Masmo
Stuvsta
Sköndal
Flaten
Älta
Tyresö Strand
Fagersjö
Farsta
Fittja
Alby
Albysjön
Glömsta
Bollmora
Gimmersta
Tyresö
Bergaholm
Bornsjön
Botkyrka
Huddinge
Holmgård
St. Magelungen
Trångsund
Trollbäcken
Krusboda
Katrineberg
Balingsnäs
Ågesta
Kumla
Ritorp
Salem
Tullingesjön
Balingsta
Länna
Drevviken
Gudö
Brevik
Salemstaden
Tullinge
Gladökvarn
Orlången
Vidja
Vendalsö
Södertälje
Östertälje
Rönninge
Tumba
Eklundshov
Kvarnsjön
Orlångsvik
Vega
Lyckeby
Uttran

Stockholm

0 km 1

VÄSTERÅS (E04, E18)
NYNÄSHAMN 73 (73)
GUSTAVSBERG 222 (222)

Karlbergs Slott
Karlberg
Karlbergssjön
Stadshagen
STADSHAGEN
Barnklinik
Sankt Görans sjukhus
Thorildsplan
Drottningholmsvägen
Västerbron
Rålambsvägen
Västerbroplan
Rålambshovsparken
Friluftsteater
MARIEBERG
Mälaren
LÅNGHOLMEN
Långholmskanalen
Kungsholmen
KUNGSHOLMEN
Kronobergsparken
Polishuset
Rådhuset
Sankt Eriks sjukhus
Sankt Eriksplan
Vasaparken
Sabbatsbergs sjukhus
Observatoriemuseet
Strindbergsmuseum
Klarastrandsleden
Barnhusviken
NORRMALM
Norra Bantorget
Arlanda Express
City Terminalen
Stockholm Central
Stadshuset
Riddarfjärden
RIDDARHOLMEN
Riddarholmskyrkan
Johanneskyrkan
Humlegården
Kungliga Biblioteket
Kungsgatan
Hötorget
Konserthuset
Kulturhuset
Sergels torg
Hallwylska museet
Dramatiska teatern
Berzelii Park
Kungsträdgården
Karl XII Torg
Operan
Norrström
Helgeandsholmen
Riksdagshuset
Medeltidsmuseum
Kungliga Slottet
Livrustkammaren
Kungliga Myntkabinettet
Storkyrkan
Tyska kyrkan
GAMLA STAN
Nationalmuseum
Östasiatiska museet
SKEPPSHOLMEN
Moderna museet / Arkitektur- och design centrum
Kastellholmen
Strömmen
Saltsjön
Nybroviken
Ladugårdslandsviken
Nordiska museet
Junibacken
Vasamuseet
ÖSTERMALM
Karlaplan
Historiska museet
Armémuseum
Hedvig Eleonora kyrka
Valhallavägen
Stadion
Slussen
Centralbron
Stadsmuseum
SÖDERMALM
Söder Mälarstrand
Katarinavägen
Stadsgårdsleden
Hornsgatan
Götgatan

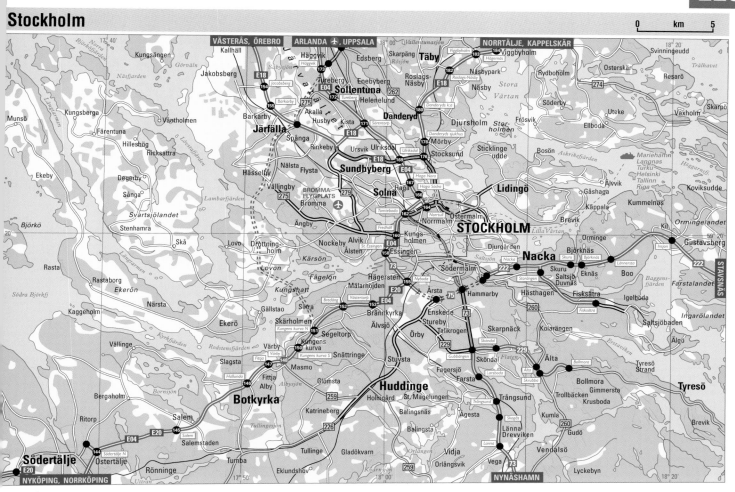

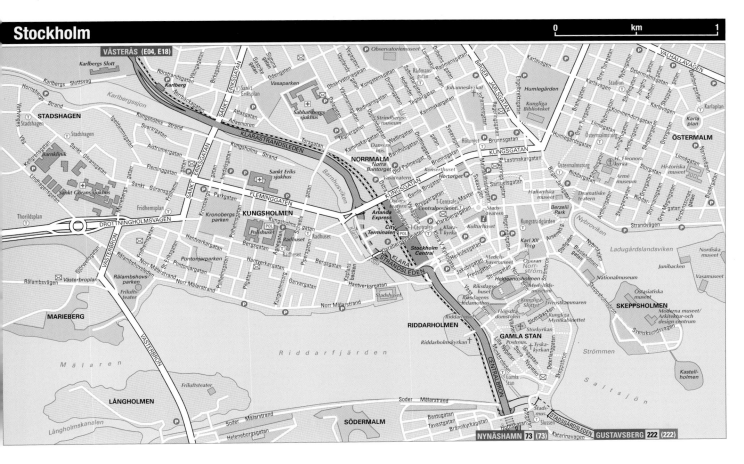

Torino Turin

0 km

AOSTA
NOVARA, MILANO
SUSA GRENOBLE (A43, A41)
PINEROLO
SAVONA
CÚNEO (20)

Bertesseno
Niquidetto
Mte. Colombano 658
Moncolombone
7° 30'
Grange
Rossignoli
Robassomero
Malanghero
AEROPORTO DI CASELLE
Caselle Tor.
S. Giacomo
Volpiano
Torassi
Rivera
Chivasso
Mte. Arpone 1600
Mte. Lera 1371
Truc di Miola
la Cassa
Parco Regionale La Mándria
Léini
Brandizzo
Mompellato
Castello
Val della Torre
Rivasacco
Givoletto
Montelera
45° 10'
Rubbianetta
Mándria
Venaria
Bórgaro Torinese
Fornacino
Cimena
S. Genésio
Castagneto Po
S. Raffaele
S. Sebastiano da Po
Piana di S. Raffaele
Rubiana
1325 Mte. Curt
Verna
S. Gillio
Druento
Cast. S. Cristina
Villaretto
Settimo Torinese
Bussolini Gassinese
Casalborgone
Brione
Grange
Laghi di Caselette
1150 Mte. Musinè
Abbadia di Stura
Gássino Torinese
Rivalba
Villár Dora
Almese
Rivera
Savonera
Tangenziale Nord
Castiglione Torinese
Caselette
S. Pancrazio
Grángia
Drubáglio
Cast. di Camerletto
Alpignano
Pianezza
Barca
S. Martino
S. Ambrógio di Torino
Dora Ripária
Lucento
Bertolla
S. Mauro Tor.
Bardassano
Sciolze
Cinzano
Avigliana
Collegno
Parco M. Carrara
Rivodora
Cordova
Regina Margherita
670 Superga
Vernone
Roccati
Molino
Buttigliere Alta
Rosta
Rívoli
TORINO
Mongreno
Pavarolo
Baldissero Tor.
Moncucco Torinese
L. Grande
Meana
Réaglie
Montaldo Tor.
Avuglione
Sala
Rivata
Reano
Corbiglia
Grugliasco
Parco del Valentino
S. Margherita
Pino Torinese
Marentino
Mombello d'Torino
L. Piccolo
Tetti Neirotti
Giaveno
Paiere
Trana
Villarbasse
Roncáglia
Gérbido
l'Éremo
Villa
S. Bernardino
Rivalta di Torino
Doirone
Tangenziale Sud
S. Vito
715 Colle d. Maddalena
Cipresso
Andezeno
Arignano
Sangano
Moranda
Bruino
Lingotto
Cavoretto
Castelvécchio
Bausone
Dalmassi
S. Giovanni
Pratovigero
Beinasco
Sangone
Mirafiori
Pecetto Tor.
S. Felice
Chieri
Buttigliera d'Asti
Mte. S. Giórgio 837
Orbassano
Borgaretto
Stupinigi
S. Pietro
S. Giovanni
Nichelino
Moncalieri
Mad. d. Scala
45° 00'
Burdini
Allivellatori
Montegrosso
Piossasco
Piazza
Parco Naturale di Stupingi
Testone
Trofarello
Oviglia
Cumiana
Cascina Parpáglia
Valle Saúglio
Riva presso Chieri
Mago
Tagliaferro
Pallera
Costa
Chisola
Tetti Rolle
Cambiano
Paschero
Valdichiesa
Tavernette
Volvera
Candiolo
la Loggia
Pessione
Sántena
Tetti Sapini
Cast. di S. Salva
Vinovo
Tetti Giro
Villanova d'Asti
Frossasco
None
Brassi
7° 40'
Marocchi
7° 50'
Banna
Corvéglia

Venézia Venice

0 km 0.5

MESTRE, PÁDOVA (A4 E70)

Stazione FF. SS. S. Lucia
Degli Scalzi
Ponte d. Scalzi
Canal Grande
Fondamenta S. Lucia
Marittima
Stazione Marittima (Main cruise and Ferry Port)
Canale di S. Chiara
Fond. S. Chiara
Sant' Andrea
Campo S. Andrea
Autorimessa
Piazzale Roma
Fond. S. Andrea
Palazzo Papadopoli
Giardino Papadopoli
Rio di S. Maria Maggiore
Fond. delle Burchielle
Rio Terra dei Pensieri
Ex Chiesa di S. Maria Maggiore
Fond. Rizzi
Fond. dei Ceren
Fond. S. Marta
Rio Terrà dei Secchi
San Nicolo dei Mendicoli
Angelo Raffaele
Campo A. Raffaele
Campo S. Sebastiano
S. Sebastiano
Sal. S. Basegio
Fond. del Bari
Stazione Marittima (San Basilio)
Canale della Giudecca
Fondamenta Beata Giuliana di Collalto
Fond. Zattere Ponte Lungo
Rio Ognissanti
Ospedale G. B. Giustinian
Calle Lunga S. Barnaba
Campo S. Barnaba
Carmini
Scuola dei Carmini
Rio Terrà della Scoazzera
Campo S. Margherita
Ca' Foscari
Ca' Rezzonico
Cllo. Squellini
Campo S. Pantalon
San Pantalon
Sal. S. Pantalon
Calle Chiovere
S. Maria dei Frari
Campo dei Frari
Casa Goldoni
Palazzo Barbarigo
Palazzo Mocenigo
Palazzo Grassi
C. Carozze
Sal. S. Samuele
San Stefano
Campo Francesco Morosini
Campo S. Vidal
Palazzo Cavalli
Galleria Accademia
Pte. Accademia
Campo Carita
Palazzo Contarini Dal Zaffo
Collezione P. Guggenheim
San Trovaso
Campo S. Trovaso
Gesuati
Campo S. Agnese
Fond. Zattere dei Gesuiti
Fond. Zattere Spirito Santo
F. Zorzi
R. Terrà S. Vio
Palazzo Dario
Terrà Catecumeni
S. Maria della Salute
Palazzo Dogana di Mare
Punta della Dogana
Canal Grande
Prefettura
Campo Maurizio
Campo S. M. Zobenigo
Campo Traghetto
Teatro La Fenice
C. Larga 22. Marzo
Campo S. Moisè
Palazzo Giustinian
Bacino di San Marco
Canale di San Marco
Isola di San Giorgio Maggiore
Campo San Giorgio
San Giorgio Maggiore
Giardini ex Reali
Molo
Palazzo Ducale
Piazza San Marco
Museo Civico Correr
San Marco (Basilica)
Ponte dei Sospiri
Riva degli Schiavoni
S. Zaccaria
S. Maria della Visitazione
Campo Bandiera e Moro
San Giovanni in Bragora
Campo S. Angelo
Calle Mandola
Campo Manin
Palazzo Corner Spinelli
Pal. Papadopoli
Palazzo Bernardo
Campo S. Polo
S. Polo
Campo S. Luca
Teatro Goldoni
Municipio
Campo S. Salvador
San Salvador
Campo S. Bartolomeo
Riva del Ferro
Ponte di Rialto
Fabbriche Nuove di Rialto
Ruga degli Orefici
Ruga Vecchia S. Giovanni
Ruga Ravano
Campo Pescaria
Ca' da Mosto
Ca' d'Oro
Strada Nuova
Ca' Pesaro
Palazzo Corner d. Regina
Campo S. Cassiano
Campo S. Giacomo
Teatro Malibran
Poste Telegafi
Sal. S. Giov. Crisostomo
Sal. S. Canciano
Santa Maria dei Miracoli
Campo S. Apostoli
R. Terrà Barba Fruttarol
Fondamenta Nuove
Fond. dei Mendicanti
Ospedale Civile
S. S. Giovani e Paolo
S. Maria della Pianta
Fond. S. Giustina
Campo S. Lorenzo
San Lorenzo
Scuola di S. Giorgio degli Schiavoni
C. Lion
C. Furlani
Campo S. Maria Formosa
S. Maria Formosa
C. Lunga
Ruga Giuffa
Calle Bande
Campo S. Zulian
S. Zulian
Merceria
Campo S. Stae
S. Stae
Campo C. S. Degola
Campo N. Sauro
Campo S. Giac. dell'Orio
Cllo. Stroppe
Campo S. Stin
Calle della Lacca
Rio Marin
Fond. Minotto
Rio Novo
Fond. Rossa
Fond. Foscarini
Rio Terra dei Pensieri
C. Amai
Cte. Case Nuove
Cpo. d. Lana
Lista dei Bari
Riva di Biasio

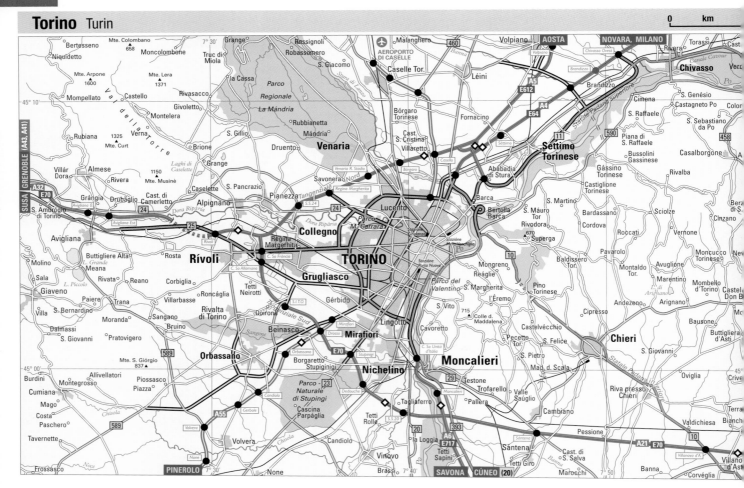

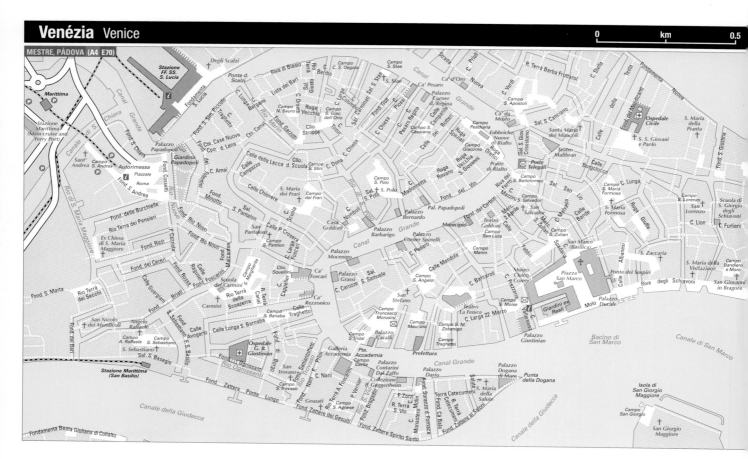

Torino Turin

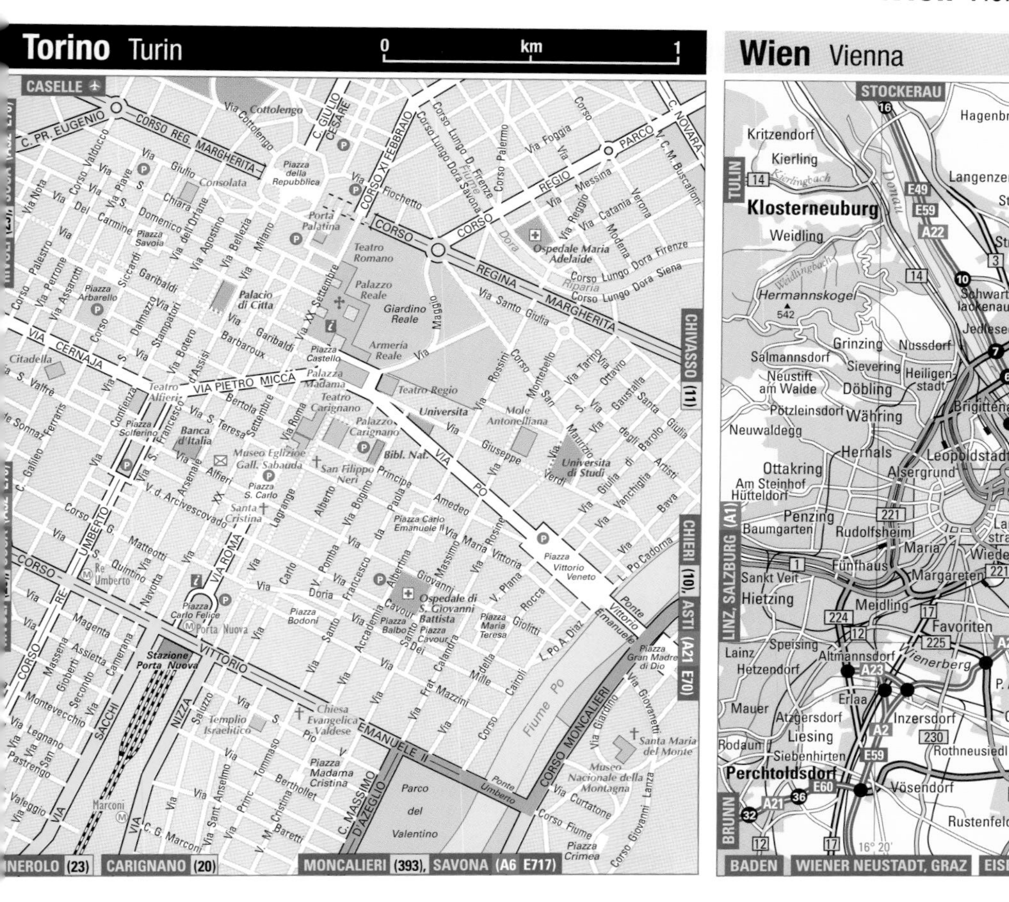

Wien Vienna

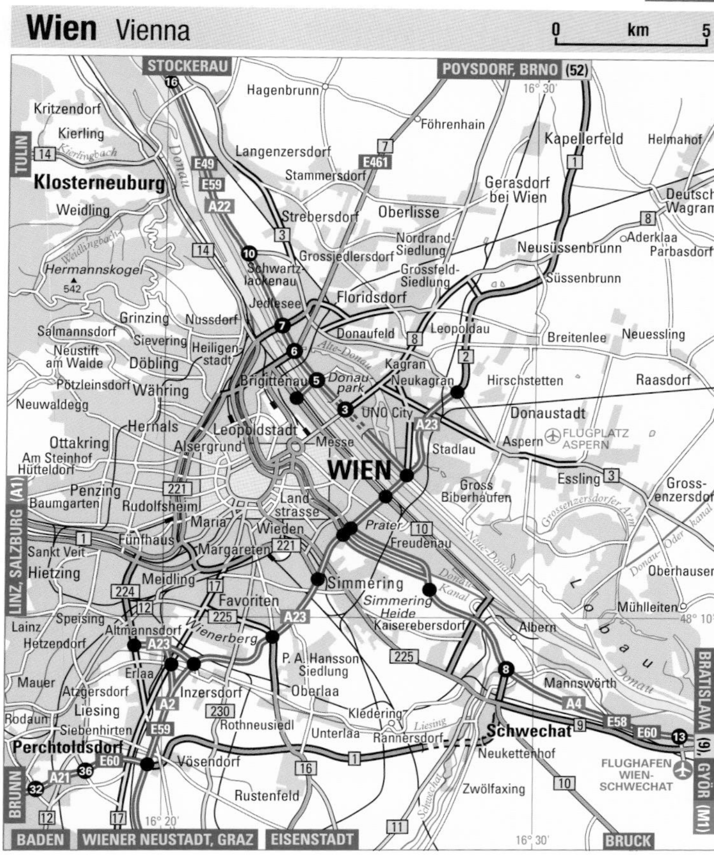

Warszawa Warsaw

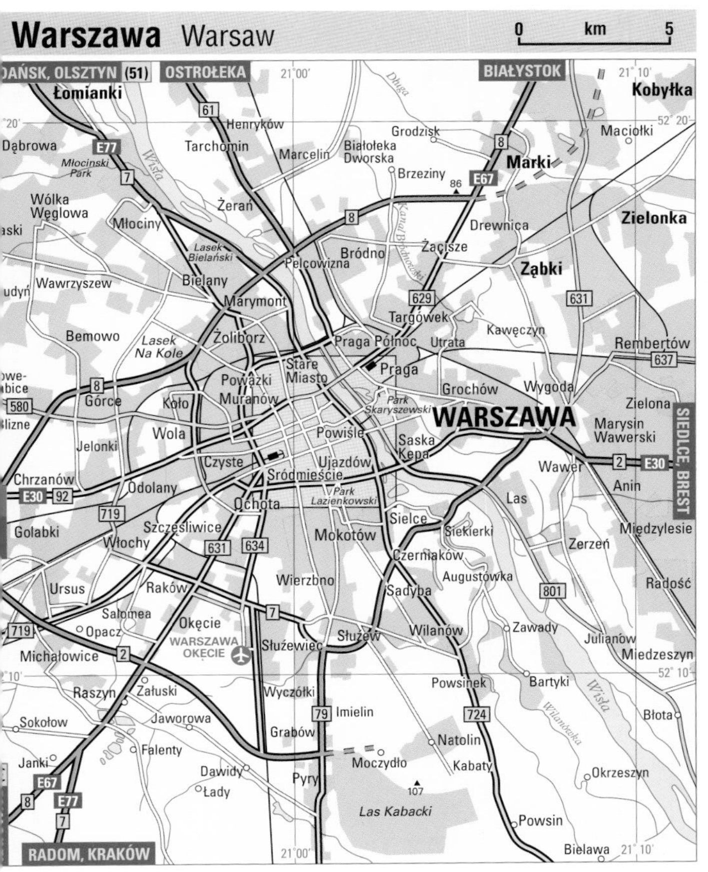

Warszawa Warsaw

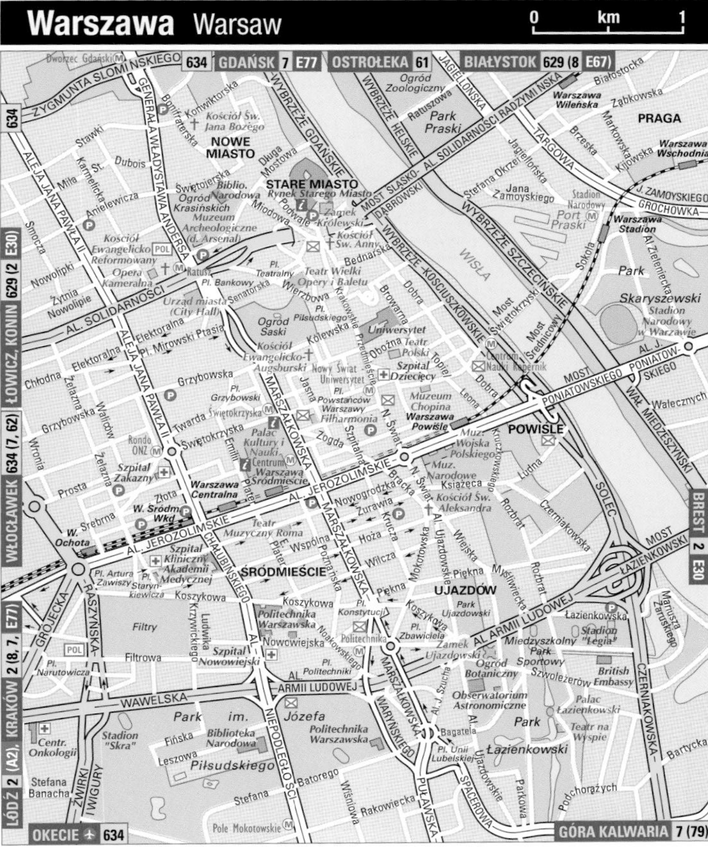

Wien Vienna

0 km 1

STOCKERAU 227 (A22 E49 E59)

DEUTSCH-WAGRAM 8

ST. PÖLTEN, LINZ 1 (A1 E60)

WIENER NEUSTADT, GRAZ 17 (A2 E59)

SCHWECHAT 225

Zagreb

0 km 0.5

LJUBLJANA (A3 E70)

KARLOVAC (A1 E65, E71)

SLAVONSKI BROD (A3 E70)

Zürich

0 km 0.5

BASEL (A1, A3 E60)

BÜLACH (A1b)

WINTERTHUR (A1, E6

UITIKON

BADEN (3)

CHUR (A3 A13)

CHUR (A3 A13)

RAPPERSWIL 17

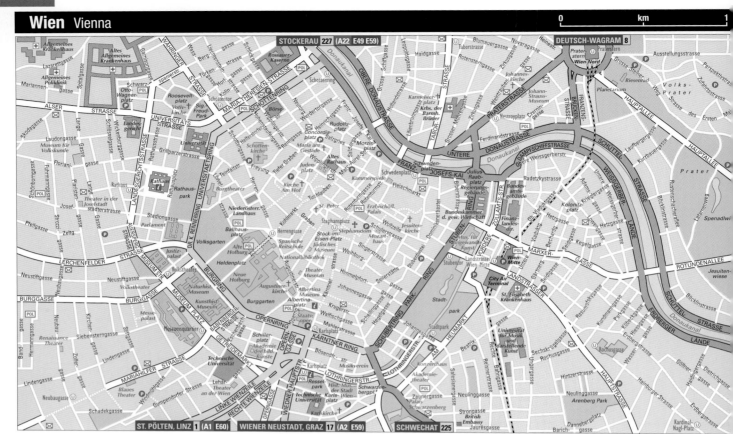

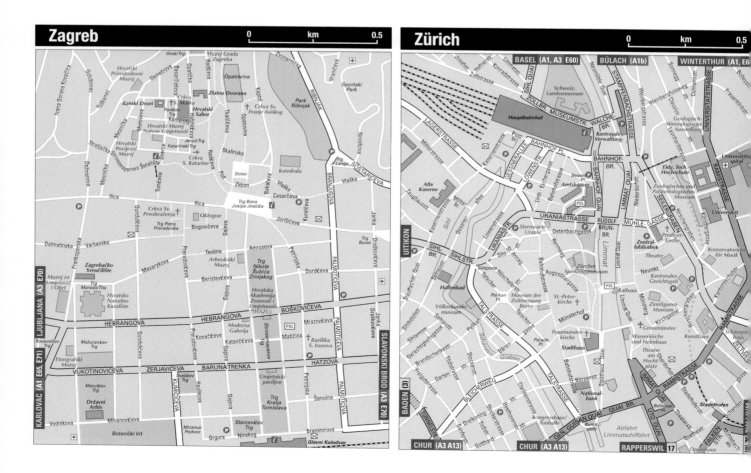

Code	English	French	German	Italian
A	Austria	Autriche	Österreich	Austria
AL	Albania	Albanie	Albanien	Albania
AND	Andorra	Andorre	Andorra	Andorra
B	Belgium	Belgique	Belgien	Belgio
BG	Bulgaria	Bulgarie	Bulgarien	Bulgaria
BIH	Bosnia-Herzegovin	Bosnia-Herzegovine	Bosnien-Herzegowina	Bosnia-Herzogovina
BY	Belarus	Belarus	Weissrussland	Bielorussia
CH	Switzerland	Suisse	Schweiz	Svizzera
CY	Cyprus	Chypre	Zypern	Cipro
CZ	Czechia	République Tchèque	Tschechische Republik	Repubblica Ceca
D	Germany	Allemagne	Deutschland	Germania
DK	Denmark	Danemark	Dänemark	Danimarca
E	Spain	Espagne	Spanien	Spagna
EST	Estonia	Estonie	Estland	Estonia
F	France	France	Frankreich	Francia
FIN	Finland	Finlande	Finnland	Finlandia
FL	Liechtenstein	Liechtenstein	Liechtenstein	Liechtenstein
FO	Faeroe Islands	Îles Féroé	Färoër-Inseln	Isole Faroe
GB	United Kingdom	Royaume Uni	Grossbritannien und Nordirland	Regno Unito
GBZ	Gibraltar	Gibraltar	Gibraltar	Gibilterra
GR	Greece	Grèce	Greichenland	Grecia
H	Hungary	Hongrie	Ungarn	Ungheria
HR	Croatia	Croatie	Kroatien	Croazia
I	Italy	Italie	Italien	Italia
IRL	Ireland	Irlande	Irland	Irlanda
IS	Iceland	Islande	Island	Islanda
KOS	Kosovo	Kosovo	Kosovo	Kosovo
L	Luxembourg	Luxembourg	Luxemburg	Lussemburgo
LT	Lithuania	Lituanie	Litauen	Lituania
LV	Latvia	Lettonie	Lettland	Lettonia
M	Malta	Malte	Malta	Malta
MC	Monaco	Monaco	Monaco	Monaco
MD	Moldova	Moldavie	Moldawien	Moldavia
MK	Macedonia	Macédoine	Makedonien	Macedonia
MNE	Montenegro	Monténégro	Montenegro	Montenegro
N	Norway	Norvège	Norwegen	Norvegia
NL	Netherlands	Pays-Bas	Niederlande	Paesi Bassi
P	Portugal	Portugal	Portugal	Portogallo
PL	Poland	Pologne	Polen	Polonia
RO	Romania	Roumanie	Rumanien	Romania
RSM	San Marino	Saint-Marin	San Marino	San Marino
RUS	Russia	Russie	Russland	Russia
S	Sweden	Suède	Schweden	Svezia
SK	Slovakia	République Slovaque	Slowak Republik	Repubblica Slovacca
SLO	Slovenia	Slovénie	Slowenien	Slovenia
SRB	Serbia	Serbie	Serbien	Serbia
TR	Turkey	Turquie	Türkei	Turchia
UA	Ukraine	Ukraine	Ukraine	Ucraina

A

Aabenraa DK 64 A2
Aabybro DK 58 A2
Aach D 107 B4
Aachen D 80 B2
Aalborg DK 58 A2
Aalen D 94 C2
Aalestrup DK 58 B2
Aalsmeer NL 70 B1
Aalst B 79 B4
Aalten NL 71 C3
Aalter B 79 A3
Äänekoski FIN 8 A4
Aapajärvi FIN 197 B10
Ağapınar TR 187 C5
Aarau CH 106 B3
Aarberg CH 106 B2
Aarburg CH 106 B2
Aardenburg NL 79 A3
Aars DK 58 B2
Aarschot B 79 B4
Aarup DK 59 C3
Aba H 112 B2
Abádanes E 152 B1
Abades E 151 B3
Abadin E 141 A3
Abádszalók H 113 B4
Abaliget H 125 A4
Abana TR 23 A8
A Baña E 140 B2
Abanilla E 165 A3
Abano Terme I 121 B4
Abarán E 165 A3
Abasár H 113 B4
Abbadia San Salvatore I 135 C4
Abbaue D 74 A2
Abbehausen D 72 A1
Abbekäs S 66 A2
Abbeville F 90 A1
Abbey IRL 28 A3
Abbeydorney IRL 29 B2
Abbeyfeale IRL 29 B2
Abbeyleix IRL 30 B1
Abbey Town GB 36 B3
Abbiategrasso I 120 B1
Abborrträsk S 196 D2
Abbots Bromley GB 40 C2
Abbotsbury GB 43 B4
Abda H 111 B4
Abejar E 143 C4
Abela P 160 B1
Abelvær N 199 A8
Abenberg D 94 B2
Abenójar E 157 B3
Abensberg D 95 C3
Aberaeron GB 39 B2
Abercarn GB 39 C3
Aberchirder GB 33 D4
Aberdare GB 39 C3
Aberdaron GB 38 B2
Aberdeen GB 33 D4
Aberdulais GB 39 C3
Aberdyfi GB 39 B2
Aberfeldy GB 35 B4
Aberffraw GB 38 A2
Aberfoyle GB 34 B3
Abergavenny GB 39 C3
Abergele GB 38 A3
Abergynolwyn GB 38 B3
Aberporth GB 39 B2
Abersoch GB 38 B2
Abertillery GB 39 C3
Abertura E 156 A2
Aberystwyth GB 39 B2
Abetone I 135 A3
Abfaltersbach A 109 C3
Abide
Çanakkale TR 186 B1
Kütahya TR 187 D4
Abiego E 145 B3
Abild DK 64 B1
Abingdon-on-Thames GB 44 B2
Abington GB 36 A3
Abisko S 194 B9
Abiul P 154 B2
Abla E 164 B2
Ablis F 90 C1
A Bola E 140 B3
Abondance F 118 A3
Abony H 113 B4
Aboyne GB 33 D4
Abrantes P 154 B2
Abreiro P 148 A2
Abreschviller F 92 C3
Abrest F 117 A3
Abriès F 119 C3
Abrud RO 17 B5
Absdorf A 97 C3
Abtenau A 109 B4
Abtsgmünd D 94 C1
Abusejo E 149 B3
Åby
Kronoberg S 62 A2
Östergötland S 56 B2
Åbyggeby S 51 B4
Åbytorp S 55 A6
A Cañiza E 140 B2
A Capela E 140 A2
Acate I 177 B3
Accadia I 171 B3
Accéglio I 132 A2
Accettura I 172 B2
Acciaroli I 170 C3
Accous F 145 A3
Accrington GB 40 B1
Accúmoli I 169 A3
Acedera E 156 A2
Acehuche E 155 B4
Acered E 152 A2
Acerenza I 172 B1
Acerno I 170 C3
Acerra I 170 C2
Aceuchal E 155 C4
Acharacle GB 34 B2
Acharnes GR 185 A4
Achavanich GB 32 C3
Achene B 79 B5
Achenkirch A 108 B2
Achensee A 108 B2
Achenthal A 108 B2
Achentrias GR 185 E6
Achern D 93 C4
Acheux-en-Amienois F 90 A2
Achiltibuie GB 32 C1
Achim D 72 A2
Achladokambos GR 184 B3
Achnasheen GB 32 D1
Achnashellach GB 32 D1
Achosnich GB 34 B1
Aci Castello I 177 B4
Aci Catena I 177 B4
Acilia I 168 B2
Acıpayam TR 189 B4
Acireale I 177 B4
Acle GB 41 C5
A Coruña E 140 A2
Acquacadda I 179 C2
Acqua Doria F 180 B1
Acquanegra sul Chiese I 121 B3
Acquapendente I 168 A1
Acquasanta Terme I 136 C2
Acquasparta I 168 A2
Acquaviva I 135 B4
Acquaviva delle Fonti I 171 C4
Acquaviva Picena I 136 C2
Acquigny F 89 A5
Acqui Terme I 119 C5
Acri I 174 B2
Acs H 112 B2
Acsa H 112 B3
Ácsteszér H 112 B1
Acy-en-Multien F 90 B2
Ada SRB 126 B2
Adak S 195 E9
Ådalsbruk N 48 B3
Adamas GR 185 C5
Adamsfjord N 193 B10
Adamuz E 157 B3
Adana TR 23 C8
Ádánd H 112 C2
Adanero E 150 B3
Adare IRL 29 B3
Adaševci SRB 125 B5
Adeanueva de Ebro E 144 B2
Adelboden CH 106 C2
Adelebsen D 82 A1
Adélfia I 173 A2
Adelmannsfelden D 94 C2
Adelsheim D 94 B1
Adelsö S 57 A3
Ademuz E 152 B2
Adenau D 80 B2
Adendorf D 72 A3
Adinkerke B 78 A2
Adjud RO 17 B7
Adliswil CH 107 B3
Admont A 110 B1
Ådneram N 52 A2
Adolfsström S 195 D7
Adony H 112 B2
Adorf
Hessen D 81 A4
Sachsen D 83 B4
Adra E 164 C1
Adradas E 152 A1
Adrall E 147 B2
Adrano I 177 B3
Ádria I 121 B5
Adrigole IRL 29 C2
Adwick le Street GB 40 B2
Adzaneta E 153 B3
Aesch CH 106 B2
A Estrada E 140 B2
Afandou GR 188 C3
Åfarnes N 198 C4
Affing D 94 C2
Affoltern CH 106 B3
Affric Lodge GB 32 D1
Åfjord N 199 B7
Aflenz Kurort A 110 B2
A Fonsagrada E 141 A3
Afragóla I 170 C2
Afritz A 109 C4
Afyonkarahisar TR 187 D5
Ágasegyháza H 112 C3
Agay F 132 B2
Agazzano I 120 C2
Agde F 130 B2
Agdenes N 198 B6
Agen F 129 B3
Ager E 145 C4
Agerbæk DK 59 C1
Agerskov DK 64 A2
Agger DK 58 B1
Aggersund DK 58 A2
Ággius I 178 B3
Aggsbach Dorf A 97 C3
Aggsbach Markt A 97 C3
Aggtelek H 99 C4
Aghalee GB 27 B4
Aghia GR 182 D4
Aghia Anna GR 183 E5
Aghia Galini GR 185 D5
Aghia Marina GR 188 D1
Aghia Paraskevi GR 186 C1
Aghia Pelagia GR 184 C3
Aghia Triada GR 184 B2
Aghiokambos GR 182 D4
Aghios Efstratios GR 183 D6
Aghios Kirikos GR 185 B7
Aghios Matheos GR 182 D1
Aghios Mironas GR 185 D6
Aghios Nikolaos GR 185 D6
Aghios Petros GR 182 E2
Aghio Theodori GR 184 B4
Agiči BIH 124 C2
Agira I 177 B3
Aglientu I 178 A3
Agnières F 118 C2
Agno CH 120 B1
Agnone I 170 B2
Agolada E 140 B2
Agon Coutainville F 88 A2
Ágordo I 121 A5
Agost E 165 A4
Agramón E 158 C2
Agramunt E 147 C2
Agreda E 144 C2
Agria GR 183 D5
Agrigento I 176 B2
Agrinio GR 182 E3
Agrón E 163 A4
Agrópoli I 170 C2
Aguadulce
Almería E 164 C2
Sevilla E 162 A3
Agualada E 140 A2
Agua Longa P 148 A1
A Guarda E 140 C2
Aguarón E 152 A2
Aguas E 145 B3
Aguas Belas P 154 B2
Aguas de Busot E 159 C3
Aguas de Moura P 154 C2
Águas Frias P 148 A2
Aguas Santas P 148 A1
Aguaviva E 153 B3
Aguaviva de la Vega E 152 A1
A Gudiña E 141 B3
Agudo E 156 B3
Águeda P 148 B1
Aguessac F 130 A2
Agugliano I 136 B2
Aguiar P 154 C3
Aguiàr da Beira P 148 B2
Aguilafuente E 151 A3
Aguilar de Campóo E 142 B2
Aguilar de la Frontera E 163 A3
Aguilas E 164 B3
Agunnaryd S 60 C4
Ahat TR 187 D4
Ahaus D 71 B3
Åheim N 198 C2
Ahigal E 149 B3
Ahigal de Villarino E 149 A3
Ahillones E 156 B2
Ahlbeck
Mecklenburg-Vorpommern D 66 C3
Mecklenburg-Vorpommern D 74 A3
Ahlen D 81 A3
Ahlhorn D 71 B5
Ahmetbey TR 186 A2
Ahmetler TR 188 A4
Ahmetli TR 188 A2
Ahoghill GB 27 B4
Ahola FIN 197 C11
Ahrensbök D 65 B3
Ahrensburg D 72 A3
Ahrenshoop D 66 B1
Ahun F 116 A2
Åhus S 63 C2
Ahvenselkä FIN 197 C11
Aibar E 144 B2
Aich D 95 C4
Aicha D 96 C1
Aichach D 94 C3
Aidone I 177 B3
Aiello Cálabro I 175 B2
Aigen im Mühlkreis A 96 C1
Aigle CH 119 A3
Aignan F 128 C3
Aignay-le-Duc F 104 B3
Aigre F 115 C4
Aigrefeuille-d'Aunis F 114 B3
Aigrefeuille-sur-Maine F 101 B4
Aiguablava E 147 C4
Aiguebelle F 118 B3
Aigueperse F 116 A3
Aigues-Mortes F 131 B3
Aigues-Vives F 130 B1
Aiguilles F 119 C3
Aiguillon F 129 B3
Aigurande F 103 C3
Ailefroide F 118 C3
Aillant-sur-Tholon F 104 B2
Ailly-sur-Noye F 90 B2
Ailly-sur-Somme F 90 B2
Aimargues F 131 B3
Aime F 118 B3
Ainaži LV 8 D4
Ainet A 109 C3
Ainhoa F 144 A2
Ainsa E 145 B4
Airaines F 90 B1
Aird GB 34 B2
Aird Asaig Tairbeart GB 31 B2
Airdrie GB 35 C4
Aire-sur-l'Adour F 128 C2
Aire-sur-la-Lys F 78 B2
Airole I 133 B3
Airolo CH 107 C3
Airvault F 102 C1
Aisey-sur-Seine F 104 B3
Aïssey F 105 B5
Aisy-sur-Armançon F 104 B3
Aiterhofen D 95 C4
Aith
Orkney GB 33 B4
Shetland GB 33 A5
Aitona E 153 A4
Aitrach D 107 B5
Aiud RO 17 B5
Aix-en-Othe F 104 A2
Aix-en-Provence F 131 B4
Aixe-sur-Vienne F 115 C5
Aix-les-Bains F 118 B2
Aizenay F 114 B2
Aizkraukle LV 8 D4
Aizpute LV 8 D2
Ajac F 146 A3
Ajaccio F 180 B1
Ajain F 116 A1
Ajaureforsen S 195 E6
Ajdovščina SLO 122 B2
Ajka H 111 B4
Ajo E 143 A3
Ajofrín E 157 A4
Ajos FIN 196 D7
Ajuda P 155 C3
Akanthou CY 181 A2
Akarca TR 189 A4
Akasztó H 112 C3
Akçakoca TR 187 A6
Akçaova TR 187 A4
Akçay TR 189 C4
Aken D 83 A4
Åkerby S 51 B4
Åkernes N 52 B3
Åkersberga S 57 A4
Åkers styckebruk S 56 A3
Åkervik N 195 E4
Akhisar TR 186 D2
Åkirkeby DK 67 A3
Akköy TR 188 B2
Akkrum NL 70 A2
Akören TR 189 B7
Åkra N 52 A2
Akranes IS 190 C3
Åkrehamn N 52 A1
Akrotiri CY 181 B1
Aksaray TR 23 B8
Akşehir TR 189 A6
Akseki TR 189 B6
Aksla N 46 A3
Aksu TR 189 C5
Aktsyabrski BY 13 B8
Akureyri IS 191 B7
Åkvåg N 53 B5
Akyazı TR 187 B5
Ål N 47 B5
Ala I 121 B4
Alaca TR 23 A8
Alacaatlı TR 186 C3
Alaçam TR 23 A8
Alaçatı TR 188 A1
Alàdei Sardi I 178 B3
Ala di Stura I 119 B4
Alaejos E 150 A2
Alagna Valsésia I 119 B4
Alagón E 144 C2
Alaior E 167 B4
Alájar E 161 B3
Alakurtti RUS 197 C13
Alakylä FIN 196 B7
Alameda E 163 A3
Alameda de la Sagra E 151 B4
Alamedilla E 163 A4
Alamillo E 156 B3
Alaminos E 151 B5
Ala-Nampa FIN 197 C9
Alanäs S 199 A12
Alandroal P 155 C3
Alange E 156 B1
Alaniemi FIN 197 D8
Alanís E 156 B2
Alanno I 169 A3
Ålansbro S 200 D3
Alanya TR 189 C7
Alap H 112 C2
Alaquáso E 159 B3
Alaraz E 150 B2
Alarcón E 158 B1
Alar del Rey E 142 B2
Alaró E 167 B2
Alaşehir TR 188 A3
Alássio I 133 A4
Ağlasun TR 189 B5
Alatoz E 158 B2
Alatri I 169 B3
Alavus FIN 8 A3
Alba
E 152 B2
I 119 C5
Alba Adriática I 136 C2
Albacete E 158 C2
Alba de Tormes E 150 B2
Alba de Yeltes E 149 B3
Albaida E 159 C3
Alba-Iulia RO 17 B5
Ålbæk DK 58 A3
Albaladejo E 158 C1
Albala del Caudillo E 156 A1
Albalat E 159 B3
Albalate de Cinca E 145 C4
Albalate del Arzobispo E 153 A3
Albalate de las Nogueras E 152 B1
Albalete de Zorita E 151 B5
Alban F 130 B1
Albánchez E 164 B2
Albanchez de Ubeda E 163 A4
Albano Laziale I 168 B2
Albanyà E 147 B3
Albaredo d'Adige I 121 B4
Albares E 151 B4
Albarracín E 152 B2
Albatana E 158 C2
Albatarrec E 153 A4
Albatera E 165 A4
Albbruck D 106 B3
Albedin E 163 A3
Albelda de Iregua E 143 B4
Albenga I 133 A4
Albens F 118 B2
Ålberga
Södermanland S 56 A2
Södermanland S 56 B2
Albergaria-a-Nova P 148 B1
Albergaria-a-Velha P 148 B1
Albergaria dos Doze P 154 B2
Alberge P 154 C2
Alberic E 159 B3
Albernoa P 160 B2
Alberobello I 173 B3
Alberoni I 122 B1
Albersdorf D 64 B2
Albersloh D 81 A3
Albert F 90 A2
Albertirsa H 112 B3
Albertville F 118 B3
Alberuela de Tubo E 145 C3
Albi F 130 B1
Albidona I 174 B2
Albinia I 168 A1
Albino I 120 B2
Albinshof D 66 C2
Albires E 142 B1
Albisola Marina I 133 A4
Albocácer E 153 B4
Albolote E 163 A4
Albondón E 164 C1
Alborea E 158 B2
Albox E 164 B2
Albrechtice nad Vltavou CZ 96 B2
Albstadt D 107 A4
Albufeira P 160 B1
Albuñol E 164 C1
Albuñuelas E 163 B4
Alburquerque E 155 B3
Alby
Öland S 63 B4
Västernorrland S 200 D1
Alcácer do Sal P 154 C2
Alcáçovas P 154 C2
Alcadozo E 158 C2
Alcafoces P 155 B3
Alcains P 155 B3
Alcaláde Guadaira E 162 A2
Alcaláde Gurrea E 144 B3
Alcaláde Henares E 151 B4
Alcaláde la Selva E 153 B3
Alcaládel Júcar E 158 B2
Alcaláde los Gazules E 162 B2
Alcaládel Rio E 162 A2
Alcaládel Valle E 162 B2
Alcaláde Xivert E 153 B4
Alcalála Real E 163 A4
Álcamo I 176 B1
Alcampell E 145 C4
Alcanadre E 144 B1
Alcanar E 153 B4
Alcanede P 154 B2
Alcanena P 154 B2
Alcañices E 149 A3
Alcántara E 155 B4
Alcantarilha P 160 B1
Alcantarilla E 165 B3
Alcañiz E 153 A3
Alcaracejos E 156 B3
Alcara il Fusi I 177 A3
Alcaraz E 158 C1
Alcaria Ruiva P 160 B2
Alcarraz E 153 A4
Alcaudete E 163 A3
Alcaudete de la Jara E 150 C3
Alcázar de San Juan E 157 A4
Alcazarén E 150 A3
Alcester GB 44 A2
Alcoba E 157 A3
Alcobaça P 154 B1
Alcobendas E 151 B4
Alcocer E 151 B5
Alcochete P 154 C2
Alcoentre P 154 B2
Alcolea
Almería E 164 C2
Córdoba E 156 C3
Alcolea de Calatrava E 157 B3

Alcolea de Cinca E 145 C4
Alcolea del Pinar E 152 A1
Alcolea del Río E 162 A2
Alcolea de Tajo E 150 C2
Alcollarín E 156 A2
Alconchel E 155 C3
Alconera E 155 C4
Alcontar E 164 B2
Alcora E 153 B3
Alcorcón E 151 B4
Alcorisa E 153 B3
Alcossebre E 153 B4
Alcoutim P 160 B2
Alcover E 147 C2
Alcoy E 159 C3
Alcsútdoboz H 112 B2
Alcubierre E 145 C3
Alcubilla de Avellaneda E 143 C3
Alcubilla de Nogales E 141 B5
Alcubillas E 157 B4
Alcublas E 159 B3
Alcúdia E 167 B3
Alcudia de Guadix E 164 B1
Alcuéscar E 155 B4
Aldbrough GB 41 B3
Aldeacentenera E 156 A2
Aldeadávila de la Ribera E 149 A3
Aldea del Cano E 155 B4
Aldea del Fresno E 151 B3
Aldea del Obispo E 149 B3
Aldea del Rey E 157 B4
Aldea de Trujillo E 156 A2
Aldealcorvo E 151 A4
Aldealuenga de Santa Maria E 151 A4
Aldeamayor de San Martin E 150 A3
Aldeanueva de Barbarroya E 150 C2
Aldeanueva del Camino E 149 B4
Aldeanueva del Codonal E 150 A3
Aldeanueva de San Bartolomé E 156 A2
Aldeapozo E 144 C1
Aldeaquemada E 157 B4
Aldea Real E 151 A3
Aldearrubia E 150 A2
Aldeaseca de la Frontera E 150 B2
Aldeasoña E 151 A3
Aldeatejada E 150 B2
Aldeavieja E 150 B3
Aldeburgh GB 45 A5
Aldehuela E 152 B2
Aldehuela de Calatañazor E 143 C4
Aldeia da Serra P 155 C3
Aldeia do Bispo P 149 B3
Aldeia do Mato P 154 B2
Aldeia Gavinha P 154 B1
Aldeire E 164 B1
Aldenhoven D 80 B2
Aldersbach D 95 C5
Aldershot GB 44 B3
Aldudes F 144 A2
Åled S 60 C2
Aledo E 165 B3
Alegria E 143 B4
Aleksandrovac SRB 127 C3
Aleksandrów Kujawski PL 76 B3
Aleksandrów Łódźki PL 86 A3
Aleksa Šantić SRB 126 B1
Ålem S 62 B4
Alençon F 89 B4
Alenquer P 154 B1
Alenya F 146 B3
Aléria F 180 A2
Alès F 131 A3
Áles I 179 C2
Alessándria I 120 C1
Alessándria della Rocca I 176 B2
Alessano I 173 C4
Ålesund N 198 C3
Alet-les-Bains F 146 B3
Alexandria
GB 34 C3
GR 182 C4
RO 17 D6
Alexandroupoli GR 183 C7
Aleyrac F 131 A3
Alézio I 173 B4
Alfacar E 163 A4
Alfaiates P 149 B3
Alfajarin E 153 A3
Alfambra
E 152 B2
P 160 B1
Alfândega da Fé P 149 A3
Alfarela de Jafes P 148 A2
Alfarelos P 148 B1
Alfarim P 154 C1
Alfarnate E 163 B3
Alfaro E 144 B2
Alfarrás E 145 C4
Alfaz del Pi E 159 C3
Alfedena I 169 B4
Alfeizarão P 154 B1
Alfeld
Bayern D 95 B3
Niedersachsen D 72 C2
Alfena P 148 A1
Alferce P 160 B1
Alfhausen D 71 B4
Alfonsine I 135 A5
Alford
Aberdeenshire GB 33 D4
Lincolnshire GB 41 B4
Alforja E 147 C1
Alfoz E 141 A3
Alfreton GB 40 B2
Alfta S 50 A3
Alfundão P 160 A1
Algaida E 167 B2
Algar E 162 B2
Älgarås S 55 B5
Ålgård N 52 B1
Algarinejo E 163 A3
Algarrobo E 163 B3
Algatocin E 162 B2
Algeciras E 162 B2
Algemesí E 159 B3
Algés P 154 C1
Algete E 151 B4
Alghero I 178 B2
Älghult S 62 A3
Alginet E 159 B3
Algodonales E 162 B2
Algodor
E 151 C4
P 160 B2
Algora E 151 B5
Algoso P 149 A3
Algoz P 160 B1
Älgsjö S 200 B3
Alguaire E 145 C4
Alguazas E 165 A3
Algutsrum S 63 B4
Algyö H 126 A2
Alhama de Almería E 164 C2
Alhama de Aragón E 152 A2
Alhama de Granada E 163 B4
Alhama de Murcia E 165 B3
Alhambra E 157 B4
Alhandra P 154 C1
Alhaurin de la Torre E 163 B3
Alhaurín el Grande E 163 B3
Alhendin E 163 A4
Alhóndiga E 151 B5
Alia E 156 A2
Ália I 176 B2
Aliağa TR 186 D1
Aliaga E 153 B3
Alibunar SRB 127 B2
Alicante E 165 A4
Alicún de Ortega E 164 B1
Alife I 170 B2
Alija del Infantado E 141 B5
Alijó P 148 A2
Alimena I 177 B3
Alingsås S 60 B2
Alinyà E 147 B2
Aliseda E 155 B4
Ali Terme I 177 A4
Aliveri GR 185 A5
Alixan F 117 C5
Aljaraque E 161 B2
Aljezur P 160 B1
Aljorra E 165 B3
Aljubarrota P 154 B2
Aljucen E 155 B4
Aljustrel P 160 B1
Alken B 79 B5
Alkmaar NL 70 B1
Alkoven A 96 C2
Allaines F 103 A3
Allaire F 101 B3
Allanche F 116 B2
Alland A 111 A3
Allariz E 140 B3
Allassac F 129 A4
Allauch F 131 B4
Alleen N 52 B3
Allègre F 117 B3
Allemont F 118 B3
Allendale Town GB 37 B4
Allendorf D 81 B4
Allentsteig A 97 C3
Allepuz E 153 B3
Allersberg D 95 B3
Allershausen D 95 C3
Alles E 142 A2
Allevard F 118 B3
Allgunnen S 62 A3
Allihies IRL 29 C1
Allingåbro DK 58 B3
Allmannsdorf D 107 B4
Allo E 144 B1
Alloa GB 35 B4
Allogny F 103 B4
Ålloluokta S 196 B2
Allones
Eure et Loire F 90 C1
Maine-et-Loire F 102 B2
Allonnes F 102 B2
Allons F 128 B2
Allos F 132 A2
Allstedt D 82 A3
Alltwalis GB 39 C2
Allumiere I 168 A1
Almaceda P 155 B3
Almacelles E 145 C4
Almachar E 163 B3
Almada P 154 C1
Almadén E 156 B3
Almadén de la Plata E 161 B3
Almadenejos E 156 B3
Almadrones E 151 B5
Almagro E 157 B4
Almajano E 144 C1
Almansa E 159 C2
Almansil P 160 B1
Almanza E 142 B1
Almaraz E 150 C2
Almargen E 162 B2
Almarza E 143 C4
Almásfüzitö H 112 B2
Almassora E 159 B3
Almazán E 152 A1
Almazul E 152 A1
Alme D 81 A4
Almedina E 158 C1
Almedinilla E 163 A3
Almeida
E 149 A3
P 149 B3
Almeirim P 154 B2
Almelo NL 71 B3
Almenar E 145 C4
Almenara E 159 B3
Almenar de Soria E 152 A1
Almendra P 149 B2
Almendral E 155 C4
Almendral de la Cañada E 150 B3
Almendralejo E 155 C4
Almenno San Bartolomeo I 120 B2
Almere NL 70 B2
Almería E 164 C2
Almerimar E 164 C2
Almese I 119 B4
Almexial P 160 B2
Älmhult S 63 B2
Almiropotamos GR 185 A5
Almiros GR 182 D4
Almodôvar P 160 B1
Almodóvar del Campo E 157 B3
Almodóvar del Pinar E 158 B2
Almodóvar del Río E 162 A2
Almofala P 148 B2
Almogia E 163 B3
Almoharin E 156 A1
Almonacid de la Sierra E 152 A2
Almonacid de Toledo E 157 A4
Almonaster la Real E 161 B3
Almondsbury GB 43 A4
Almonte E 161 B3
Almoradí E 165 A4
Almoraima E 162 B2
Almorox E 150 B3
Almoster P 154 B2
Almsele S 200 B3
Älmsta S 51 C5
Almudena E 164 A3
Almudévar E 145 B3
Almuñécar E 163 B4
Almunge S 51 C5
Almuradiel E 157 B4
Almussafes E 159 B3
Almvik S 62 A4
Alness GB 32 D2
Alnmouth GB 37 A5
Alnwick GB 37 A5
Åloppe S 51 C4
Álora E 163 B3
Alos d'Ensil E 146 B2
Alosno E 161 B2
Alozaina E 162 B3
Alpbach A 108 B2
Alpedrete de la Sierra E 151 B4
Alpedrinha P 148 B2
Alpen D 80 A2
Alpera E 159 C2
Alphen aan de Rijn NL 70 B1
Alpiarça P 154 B2
Alpignano I 119 B4
Alpirsbach D 93 C4
Alpu TR 187 C5
Alpuente E 159 B2
Alqueva P 160 A2
Alquézar E 145 B4
Als DK 58 B3
Alsasua E 144 B1
Alsdorf D 80 B2
Alselv DK 59 C1
Alsfeld D 81 B5
Alsike S 57 A3
Alskog S 57 C4
Alsleben D 83 A3
Alsónémedi H 112 B3
Alsótold H 112 B3
Alsóújlak H 111 B3
Alstad N 194 C6
Alstätte D 71 B3
Alsterbro S 62 B3
Alstermo S 62 B3
Alston GB 37 B4
Alsvåg N 194 B6
Alsvik N 194 C5
Alta N 192 C7
Älta S 57 A4
Altamura I 172 B2
Altarejos E 158 B1
Altausee A 109 B4
Altavilla Irpina I 170 B2
Altavilla Silentina I 170 C3
Altdöbern D 84 A2
Altdorf
CH 107 C3
D 95 C4
Altdorf bei Nürnberg D 95 B3
Alte P 160 B1
Altea E 159 C3
Altedo I 121 C4
Altena D 81 A3
Altenau D 82 A2
Altenberg D 84 B1
Altenberge D 71 B4
Altenbruch D 64 C1
Altenburg D 83 B4
Altenfelden A 96 C1
Altengronau D 82 B1
Altenheim D 93 C3
Altenhundem D 81 A4
Altenkirchen
Mecklenburg-Vorpommern D 66 B2
Radom D 81 B3
Altenkunstadt D 82 B3
Altenmarkt
A 110 B1
D 109 A3
Altenmarkt im Pongall A 109 B4
Altensteig D 93 C4
Altentreptow D 74 A2
Altenwalde D 64 C1
Alten-weddingen D 73 B4
Alter do Chão P 155 B3
Altfraunhofen D 95 C4
Altheim
A 109 A4
D 94 B1
Althofen A 110 C1
Altınoluk TR 186 C1
Altınova TR 186 C1
Altıntaş TR 187 C5
Altınyaka TR 189 C5
Altınyayla TR 189 B4
Altkirch F 106 B2
Altlandsberg D 74 B2
Altlewin D 74 B3
Altmannstein D 95 C3
Altmorschen D 82 A1
Altmunster A 109 B4
Altnaharra GB 32 C2
Alto Campoó E 142 A2
Altofonte I 176 A2
Altomonte I 174 B2
Alton
Hampshire GB 44 B3
Staffordshire GB 40 C2
Altopáscio I 135 B3
Altötting D 109 A3
Altreichenau D 96 C1
Alt Ruppin D 74 B1
Altshausen D 107 B4
Altstätten CH 107 B4
Altura E 159 B3
Altusried D 107 B5
Alūksne LV 8 D5
Alunda S 51 B5
Alustante E 152 B2
Alva GB 35 B4
Alvaiázere P 154 B2
Alvalade P 160 B1
Älvängen S 60 B2
Alvarenga P 148 B1
Alvares P 154 A2
Alvdal N 199 C7
Älvdalen S 49 A6
Alverca P 154 C1
Alversund N 46 B2
Alvesta S 62 B2
Alvignac F 129 B4
Alvignano I 170 B2
Ålvik N 46 B3
Alvik S 50 B1
Alvimare F 89 A4
Alviobeira P 154 B2
Alvito P 160 A2
Älvkarleby S 51 B4
Älvkarleöbruk S 51 B4
Alvor P 160 B1
Alvorge P 154 B2
Alvøy N 46 B2
Älvros S 199 C11
Alvsbacka S 55 A4
Älvsbyn S 196 D4
Älvsered S 60 B2
Alwernia PL 86 B3
Alwinton GB 37 A4
Alyth GB 35 B4
Alytus LT 13 A6
Alzénau D 93 A5
Alzey D 93 B4
Alzira E 159 B3
Alzonne F 146 A3
Amadora P 154 C1
Åmål S 55 A3
Amalfi I 170 C2
Amaliada GR 184 B2
Amance F 105 B5
Amancey F 105 B5
Amándola I 136 C2
Amantea I 175 B2
Amarante P 148 A1
Amareleja P 161 A2
Amares P 148 A1
Amaseno I 169 B3
Amasra TR 187 A7
Amatrice I 169 A3
Amay B 79 B5
Ambarnyy RUS 3 D13
Ambazac F 115 C5
Ambelonas GR 182 D4
Amberg D 95 B3
Ambérieu-en-Bugey F 118 B2
Ambérieux-en-Dombes F 117 A4
Ambert F 117 B3
Ambés F 128 A2
Ambjörby S 49 B5
Ambjörnarp S 60 B3
Amble GB 37 A5
Ambleside GB 36 B4
Ambleteuse F 78 B1
Amboise F 102 B2
Ambrières-les-Vallées F 88 B3
Amden CH 107 B4
Amel B 80 B2
Amélia I 168 A2
Amélie-les-Bains-Palalda F 146 B3
Amelinghausen D 72 A3
Amendoa P 154 B2
Amendoeira P 160 B2
Améndola I 171 B3
Amendolara I 174 B2
Amer E 147 B3
A Merca E 140 B3
Amerongen NL 70 B2
Amersfoort NL 70 B2
Amersham GB 44 B3
Amesbury GB 44 B2
Amfiklia GR 182 E4
Amfilochia GR 182 E3
Amfipoli GR 183 C5
Amfissa GR 184 A3
Amièira P 155 C3
Amieira P 154 B3
Amieiro P 148 B1
Amiens F 90 B2
Amindeo GR 182 C3
Åminne S 60 B3
Åmli N 53 B4
Amlwch GB 38 A2
Ammanford GB 39 C3
Ammarnäs S 195 E7
Åmmeberg S 55 B5
Amorbach D 94 B1
Amorebieta E 143 A4
Amorgos GR 185 C6
Amorosa P 148 A1
Amorosi I 170 B2
Åmot
Buskerud N 48 C1
Telemark N 53 A3
S 50 B3
Åmotfors S 54 A3
Åmotsdal N 53 A4
Amou F 128 C2
Ampezzo I 122 A1
Ampfing D 95 C4
Ampflwang A 109 A4
Amplepuis F 117 B4
Amposta E 153 B4
Ampthill GB 44 A3
Ampudia E 142 C2
Ampuero E 143 A3
Amriswil CH 107 B4
Åmsele S 200 B5
Amstelveen NL 70 B1
Amsterdam NL 70 B1
Amstetten A 110 A1
Amtzell D 107 B4
Amulree GB 35 B4
Amurrio E 143 A4
Amusco E 142 B2
Anacapri I 170 C2
Anadia P 148 B1
Anadon E 152 B2
Anafi GR 185 C6
Anagni I 169 B3
Anamur TR 23 C7
Ananyiv UA 17 B8
Anascaul IRL 29 B1
Ånäset S 2 D7
Åna-Sira N 52 B2
Anastażewo PL 76 B3
Anaya de Alba E 150 B2
Ança P 148 B1
Ancaster GB 40 C3
Ancede P 148 A1
Ancenis F 101 B4
Ancerville F 91 C5
Anchuras E 156 A3
Ancona I 136 B2
Ancora P 148 A1
Ancrum GB 35 C5
Ancy-le-Franc F 104 B3
Andalo I 121 A3
Åndalsnes N 198 C4
Andance F 117 B4
Andau A 111 B4
Andebu N 53 A6
Andeer CH 107 C4
Andelfingen CH 107 B3
Andelot-Blanchville F 105 A4
Andelot-en-Montagne F 105 C4
Andenes N 194 A7
Andenne B 79 B5
Anderlues B 79 B4
Andermatt CH 107 C3
Andernach D 80 B3
Andernos-les-Bains F 128 B1
Anderslöv S 66 A2
Anderstorp S 60 B3
Andijk NL 70 B2
Andoain E 144 A1
Andocs H 112 C1
Andolsheim F 106 A2
Andorra E 153 B3
Andorra La Vella AND 146 B2
Andosilla E 144 B2
Andover GB 44 B2
Andratx E 166 B2
Andreapol RUS 9 D8
Andreas GB 36 B2
Andréspol PL 86 A3
Andrest F 145 A4
Andretta I 172 B1
Andrezieux-Bouthéon F 117 B4
Ándria I 171 B4
Andrijevica MNE 16 D3
Andritsena GR 184 B2
Andros GR 185 B5
Andrychów PL 99 B3
Andselv N 194 A9
Andújar E 157 B3
Anduze F 131 A2
Åneby N 48 B2
Aneby S 62 A2
Añes E 143 A3
Anet F 90 C1
Anfo I 121 B3
Ang S 62 A2
Anga S 57 C4
Angaïs F 145 A3
Änge S 199 B11
Ånge S 200 D1
Angeja P 148 B1
Ängelholm S 61 C2
Angeli FIN 193 D9
Ängelsberg S 50 C3
Anger A 110 B2
Angera I 120 B1
Angermünde D 74 A3
Angern A 97 C4
Angers F 102 B1
Angerville F 90 C2
Anghiari I 135 B5
Angle GB 39 C1
Anglès E 147 C3
Anglés F 130 B1
Angles F 114 B2
Anglesola E 147 C2
Angles sur l'Anglin F 115 B4
Anglet F 128 C1
Anglisidhes CY 181 B2
Anglure F 91 C3
Angoulême F 115 C4
Angoulins F 114 B2
Angsö S 56 A2
Angueira P 149 A3
Angües E 145 B3
Anguiano E 143 B4
Anguillara Sabazia I 168 A2
Anguillara Véneta I 121 B4
Anhée B 79 B4
Anholt DK 60 C1
Aniane F 130 B2
Aniche F 78 B3
Ånimskog S 54 B3
Anina RO 16 C4
Anixi GR 182 D3
Anizy-le-Château F 91 B3
Anjalankoski FIN 8 B5
Anjan S 199 B9
Ankara TR 187 C7
Ankaran SLO 122 B2
Ankarsrum S 62 A4
Ankerlia N 192 C4
Anklam D 66 C2
Ankum D 71 B4
Anlauftal A 109 B4
Anlezy F 104 C2
Ånn S 199 B9
Annaberg A 110 B2
Annaberg-Buchholz D 83 B5
Annaberg im Lammertal A 109 B4
Annaburg D 83 A5
Annahütte D 84 A1
Annalong GB 27 B5
Annan GB 36 B3
Anndalsvågen N 195 E3
Anneberg
Halland S 60 B2
Jönköping S 62 A2
Annecy F 118 B3
Annelund S 60 B3
Annemasse F 118 A3
Annenskiy Most RUS 9 B10
Annerstad S 60 C3
Annestown IRL 30 B1
Annevoie-Rouillon B 79 B4
Annonay F 117 B4
Annot F 132 B2
Annweiler D 93 B3
Ano Poroia GR 183 B5
Añora E 156 B3
Ano Siros GR 185 B5
Anould F 106 A1
Anquela del Ducado E 152 B1
Anröchte D 81 A4
Ans DK 59 B2
Ansager DK 59 C1
Ansbach D 94 B2
Anse F 117 B4
Anseroeul B 79 B3
Ansfelden A 110 A1
Ansião P 154 B2
Ansó E 144 B3
Ansoain E 144 B2
Anstruther GB 35 B5
Antalya TR 189 C5
Antas E 164 B3
Antegnate I 120 B2
Antequera E 163 A3
Anterselva di Mezzo I 108 C3
Antibes F 132 B3
Antigüedad E 142 C2
Antillo I 177 B4
Antirio GR 184 A2
Antnäs S 196 D4
An t-Ob GB 31 B1
Antoing B 79 B3
Antonin PL 86 A1
Antrain F 88 B2
Antrim GB 27 B4
Antrodoco I 169 A3
Antronapiana I 119 A5
Anttis S 196 B5
Antuzede P 148 B1
Antwerp = Antwerpen B 79 A4
Antwerpen = Antwerp B 79 A4
Anversa d'Abruzzi I 169 B3
Anvin F 78 B2
Anzat-le-Luguet F 116 B3
Anzi I 172 B1
Ánzio I 168 B2
Anzola d'Emilia I 135 A4
Anzón E 144 C2
Aoiz E 144 B2
Aosta I 119 B4
Apalhão P 155 B3
Apátfalva H 126 A2
Apatin SRB 125 B5
Apatity RUS 3 C13
Apc H 112 B3
Apécchio I 136 B1
Apeldoorn NL 70 B2
Apen D 71 A4
Apenburg D 73 B4
Apensen D 72 A2
A Peroxa E 140 B3
Apiro I 136 B2
Apliki CY 181 B2
Apolda D 82 A3
Apolonia GR 185 C5
A Pontenova E 141 A3
Apostag H 112 C2
Äppelbo S 49 B6
Appennino I 136 C2
Appenzell CH 107 B4
Appiano I 108 C2
Appingedam NL 71 A3
Appleby-in-Westmorland GB 37 B4
Applecross GB 31 B3
Appledore GB 42 A2
Appoigny F 104 B2
Apremont-la-Forêt F 92 C1
Aprica I 120 A3
Apricena I 171 B3
Aprigliano I 174 B2
Aprília I 168 B2
Apt F 131 B4
Apúlia P 148 A1
Aquiléia I 122 B2
Aquilónia I 172 B1
Aquino I 169 B3
Ar S 57 C4
Arabayona E 150 A2
Arabba I 108 C2
Araç TR 23 A7
Aracena E 161 B3
Arachova GR 184 A3
Aračinovo MK 182 A3
Arad RO 126 A3
Aradac SRB 126 B2
Aradhippou CY 181 B2
Aragnouet F 145 B4
Aragona I 176 B2
Aramits F 144 A3
Aramon F 131 B3
Aranda de Duero E 143 C3
Aranda de Moncayo E 152 A2
Arandjelovac SRB 127 C2
Aranjuez E 151 B4
Arantzazu E 143 B4
Aranzueque E 151 B4
Aras de Alpuente E 159 B2
Arauzo de Miel E 143 C3
Arazede P 148 B1
Arbas F 145 B4
Árbatax I 179 C3
Arbeca E 147 C1
Arberg D 94 B2
Arbesbach A 96 C2
Arboga S 56 A1
Arbois F 105 C4
Arbon CH 107 B4
Arboréa I 179 C2
Arbório I 119 B5
Årbostad N 194 B8
Arbrå S 50 A3
Arbroath GB 35 B5
Arbùcies E 147 C3
Arbuniel E 163 A4
Arbus I 179 C2
Arcachon F 128 B1
Arce I 169 B3
Arcen NL 80 A2
Arc-en-Barrois F 105 B3
Arces-Dilo F 104 A2
Arc-et-Senans F 105 B4
Arcévia I 136 B1
Arcey F 106 B1
Archanes GR 185 D6
Archangelos GR 188 C3
Archena E 165 A3
Archez E 163 B4
Archiac F 115 C3
Archidona E 163 A3
Archiestown GB 32 D3
Archivel E 164 A3
Arcidosso I 135 C4
Arcille I 135 C4
Arcis-sur-Aube F 91 C4
Arc-lès-Gray F 105 B4
Arco I 121 B3
Arcones E 151 A4
Arcos E 143 B3
Arcos de Jalón E 152 A1
Arcos de la Frontera E 162 B2
Arcos de la Sierra E 152 B1
Arcos de las Salinas E 159 B2
Arcos de Valdevez P 148 A1
Arcozelo P 148 B2
Arc-sur-Tille F 105 B4
Arcusa E 145 B4
Arcy-sur-Cure F 104 B2
Ardagh IRL 29 B2
Årdal N 52 A2
Ardala S 55 B4
Ardales E 162 B3
Årdalstangen N 47 A4
Ardara
I 178 B2
IRL 26 B2
Ardarroch GB 31 B3
Ardbeg GB 34 C1
Ardcharnich GB 32 D1
Ardchyle GB 34 B3
Ardee IRL 27 C4
Arden DK 58 B2

Ardentes F 103 C3
Ardenza I 134 B3
Ardersier GB 32 D2
Ardes F 116 B3
Ardessie GB 32 D1
Ardez CH 107 C5
Ardfert IRL 29 B2
Ardgay GB 32 D2
Ardglass GB 27 B5
Ardgroom IRL 29 C2
Ardhasig GB 31 B2
Ardino BG 183 B7
Ardisa E 144 B3
Ardkearagh IRL 29 C1
Ardlui GB 34 B3
Ardlussa GB 34 B2
Ardón E 142 B1
Ardooie B 78 B3
Ardore I 175 C2
Ardrahan IRL 28 A3
Ardre S 57 C4
Ardres F 78 B1
Ardrishaig GB 34 B2
Ardrossan GB 34 C3
Are N 52 A1
Åre S 199 B10
Areia Branca P 154 B1
Aremark N 54 A2
Arenales de San Gregorio E 157 A4
Arenas E 163 B3
Arenas de Iguña E 142 A2
Arenas del Rey E 163 B4
Arenas de San Juan E 157 A4
Arenas de San Pedro E 150 B2
Arendal N 53 B4
Arendonk B 79 A5
Arengosse F 128 B2
Arentorp S 55 B3
Arenys de Mar E 147 C3
Arenys de Munt E 147 C3
Arenzano I 133 A4
Areo E 146 B2
Areopoli GR 184 C3
Ares E 140 A2
Arès F 128 B1
Ares del Maestrat E 153 B3
Aresvika N 198 B5
Arette F 144 A3
Aretxabaleta E 143 A4
Arevalillo E 150 B2
Arévalo E 150 A3
Arez P 155 B3
Arezzo I 135 B4
Arfeuilles F 117 A3
Argalasti GR 183 D5
Argallón E 156 B2
Argamasilla de Alba E 157 A4
Argamasilla de Calatrava E 157 B3
Arganda E 151 B4
Arganil P 148 B1
Argasion GR 184 B1
Argegno I 120 B2
Argelès-Gazost F 145 A3
Argelès-sur-Mer F 146 B4
Argenta I 121 C4
Argentan F 89 B3
Argentat F 116 B1
Argentera I 132 A2
Argenteuil F 90 C2
Argenthal D 93 B3
Argentiera I 178 B2
Argentona E 147 C3
Argenton-Château F 102 C1
Argenton-sur-Creuse F 103 C3
Argentré F 102 A1
Argentré-du-Plessis F 101 A4
Argent-sur-Sauldre F 103 B4
Argirades GR 182 D1
Argıthanı TR 189 A6
Argos GR 184 B3
Argos Orestiko GR 182 C3
Argostoli GR 184 A1
Argote E 143 B4
Arguedas E 144 B2
Argueil F 90 B1
Arholma S 51 C6
Århus DK 59 B3
Ariano Irpino I 170 B3
Ariano nel Polésine I 121 C5
Aribe E 144 B2
Aridea GR 182 C4
Arienzo I 170 B2
Arild S 61 C2
Arileod GB 34 B1
Arinagour GB 34 B1
Ariño E 153 A3
Arinthod F 118 A2
Arisaig GB 34 B2
Arisgotas E 157 A4
Aritzo I 179 C3
Ariza E 152 A1
Årjäng S 54 A3
Arjeplog S 195 D8
Arjona E 157 C3
Arjonilla E 157 C3
Arkasa GR 188 D2
Arkelstorp S 63 B2
Arklow IRL 30 B2
Arkösund S 56 B2
Ärla S 56 A2
Arlanc F 117 B3
Arlanzón E 143 B3
Arlebosc F 117 B4
Arlena di Castro I 168 A1
Arles F 131 B3
Arles-sur-Tech F 146 B3
Arló H 113 A4
Arlon B 92 B1
Armação de Pera P 160 B1
Armadale
  Highland GB 31 B3
  West Lothian GB 35 C4
Armagh GB 27 B4
Armamar P 148 A2
Armenistis GR 185 B7
Armeno I 119 B5
Armenteros E 150 B2
Armentières F 78 B2
Armilla E 163 A4
Armiñón E 143 B4
Armoy GB 27 A4
Armuña de Tajuña E 151 B4
Armutlu
  Bursa TR 186 B3
  İzmir TR 188 A2
Arnac-Pompadour F 115 C5
Arnafjord N 46 A3
Arnage F 102 B2
Arnas F 117 A4
Årnäs S 55 B4
Arnay-le-Duc F 104 B3
Arnborg DK 59 B2
Arnbruck D 95 B4
Arnea GR 183 C5
Arneberg
  Hedmark N 48 A2
  Hedmark N 49 B4
Arneburg D 73 B5
Arnedillo E 144 B1
Arnedo E 144 B1
Arneguy F 144 A2
Årnés E 153 B4
Årnes IS 190 A4
Årnes
  Akershus N 48 B3
  Troms N 194 A9
Arnfels A 110 C2
Arnhem NL 70 C2
Arnissa GR 182 C3
Arno S 56 B3
Arnold GB 40 B2
Arnoldstein A 109 C4
Arnsberg D 81 A4
Arnschwang D 95 B4
Arnsdorf D 84 A1
Årnset N 198 B6
Arnside GB 37 B4
Arnstadt D 82 B2
Arnstein D 94 B1
Arnstorf D 95 C4
Arnum DK 59 C1
Aroche E 161 B3
Ároktő H 113 B4
Arolla CH 119 A4
Arolsen D 81 A5
Arona I 119 B5
Åros N 54 A1
Arosa
  CH 107 C4
  P 148 A1
Ærøskøbing DK 65 B3
Årøsund DK 59 C2
Arouca P 148 B1
Årøysund N 54 A1
Arpajon F 90 C2
Arpajon-sur-Cère F 116 C2
Arpela FIN 196 C7
Arpino I 169 B3
Arquata del Tronto I 136 C2
Arques F 78 B2
Arques-la-Bataille F 89 A5
Arquillos E 157 B4
Arraia-Maeztu E 143 B4
Arraiolos P 154 C2
Arrancourt F 92 C2
Arras F 78 B2
Arrasate E 143 A4
Årre DK 59 C1
Arreau F 145 B4
Arredondo E 143 A3
Arrens-Marsous F 145 B3
Arriate E 162 B2
Arrifana P 160 B1
Arrigorriaga E 143 A4
Arriondas E 142 A1
Arroba de los Montes E 157 A3
Arrochar GB 34 B3
Arromanches-les-Bains F 88 A3
Arronches P 155 B3
Arroniz E 144 B1
Arrou F 103 A3
Arroya E 142 B2
Arroya de Cuéllar E 150 A3
Arroyal E 142 B2
Arroyo de la Luz E 155 B4
Arroyo del Ojanco E 164 A2
Arroyo de San Servan E 155 C4
Arroyomolinos de León E 161 A3
Arroyomolinos de Montánchez E 156 A1
Arruda dos Vinhos P 154 C1
Arsac F 128 B2
Ars-en-Ré F 114 B2
Arsiè I 121 B4
Arsiero I 121 B4
Årslev DK 59 C3
Ársoli I 169 A3
Ars-sur-Moselle F 92 B2
Årsunda S 50 B3
Artà E 167 B3
Arta GR 182 D3
Artajona E 144 B2
Artegna I 122 A2
Arteixo E 140 A2
Artemare F 118 B2
Arten I 121 A4
Artena I 169 B2
Artenay F 103 A3
Artern D 82 A3
Artés E 147 C2
Artesa de Segre E 147 C2
Arth CH 107 B3
Arthez-de-Béarn F 145 A3
Arthon-en-Retz F 101 B4
Arthurstown IRL 30 B2
Artieda E 144 B3
Artix F 145 A3
Artotina GR 182 E4
Artsyz UA 17 B8
Artziniega E 143 A3
A Rúa E 141 B3
Arudy F 145 A3
Arundel GB 44 C3
Arveyres F 128 B2
Arvidsjaur S 196 D2
Arvieux F 118 C3
Arvika S 54 A3
Åryd
  Blekinge S 63 B3
  Kronoberg S 62 B2
Arzachena I 178 A3
Arzacq-Arraziguet F 128 C2
Árzana I 179 C3
Arzano F 100 B2
Aržano HR 138 B2
Arzberg D 95 A4
Arzignano I 121 B4
Arzila P 148 B1
Arzl im Pitztal A 108 B1
Arzúa E 140 B2
As B 80 A1
Aš CZ 83 B4
Ås N 54 A1
Åsa S 60 B2
Asaa DK 58 A3
Aşağıçiğil TR 189 A6
Ašanja SRB 127 C2
Åsarna S 199 C11
Asványráró H 111 B4
Åsarøy N 52 A2
Åsarp S 55 B4
Asasp F 145 A3
Åsbro S 55 A6
Åsby S 60 B2
Asby S 62 A3
Asbygri IS 191 A9
Ascain F 144 A2
Ascea I 172 B1
Ascha D 95 B4
Aschach an der Donau A 96 C2
Aschaffenburg D 93 B5
Aschbach Markt A 110 A1
Ascheberg
  Nordrhein-Westfalen D 81 A3
  Schleswig-Holstein D 65 B3
Aschendorf D 71 A4
Aschersleben D 82 A3
Asciano I 135 B4
Ascó E 153 A4
Asco F 180 A2
Áscoli Piceno I 136 C2
Áscoli Satriano I 171 B3
Ascona CH 120 A1
Ascot GB 44 B3
Ascoux F 103 A4
Åse N 194 A6
Åseda S 62 A3
Åsele S 200 B3
Åsen
  N 199 B8
  S 49 A5
Asendorf D 72 B2
Asenovgrad BG 183 A6
Åsensbruk S 54 B3
Åseral N 52 B3
Asfeld F 91 B4
Åsgårdstrand N 54 A1
Ásgarður IS 190 B1
Asgate CY 181 B2
Ash
  Kent GB 45 B5
  Surrey GB 44 B3
Åshammar S 50 B3
Ashbourne
  GB 40 B2
  IRL 30 A2
Ashburton GB 43 B3
Ashby-de-la-Zouch GB 40 C2
Ashchurch GB 44 B1
Åsheim N 199 D8
Ashford GB 45 B4
Ashington GB 37 A5
Ashley GB 38 B4
Ashmyany BY 13 A6
Ashton Under Lyne GB 40 B1
Ashwell GB 44 A3
Asiago I 121 B4
Asipovichy BY 13 B8
Aska FIN 197 B9
Askam-in-Furness GB 36 B3
Askeaton IRL 29 B3
Asker N 48 C2
Askersund S 55 B5
Åskilje S 200 B3
Askim N 54 A2
Askland N 53 B4
Äsköping S 56 A2
Askvoll N 46 A2
Åsljunga S 61 C3
Asmunti FIN 197 D9
Asnæs DK 61 D1
As Neves E 140 B2
As Nogaís E 141 B3
Ásola I 120 B3
Asolo I 121 B4
Asos GR 184 A1
Asotthalom H 126 A1
Aspach A 109 A4
Aspang Markt A 111 B3
Aspariegos E 149 A4
Asparn an der Zaya A 97 C4
Aspatria GB 36 B3
Aspberg S 55 A4
Aspe E 165 A4
Aspet F 145 A4
Äspö S 63 B3
As Pontes de García Rodríguez E 140 A3
Aspres-sur-Buëch F 132 A1
Aspsele S 200 C4
Assafora P 154 C1
Asse B 79 B4
Assebakte N 193 C9
Assel D 72 A2
Asselborn L 92 A1
Assémini I 179 C2
Assen NL 71 B3
Assenede B 79 A3
Assens
  Aarhus Amt. DK 58 B3
  Fyns Amt. DK 59 C2
Assesse B 79 B5
Assisi I 136 B1
Åsskard N 198 B5
Assling D 108 B3
Asso I 120 B2
Asson F 145 A3
Ássoro I 177 B3
Assumar P 155 B3
Åsta N 48 A3
Astaffort F 129 B3
Astakos GR 184 A2
Asten NL 80 A1
Asti I 119 C5
Astipalea GR 188 C1
Astorga E 141 B4
Åstorp S 61 C2
Åsträsk S 200 B5
Astudillo E 142 B2
Asuni I 179 C2
Asványráró H 111 B4
Aszód H 112 B3
Aszófő H 111 C4
Atabey TR 189 B5
Atalaia P 154 B3
Atalandi GR 182 E4
Atalho P 154 C2
Átány H 113 B4
Atanzón E 151 B4
Ataquines E 150 A3
Atarfe E 163 A4
Atça TR 188 B3
Ateca E 152 A2
A Teixeira E 141 B3
Atella I 172 B1
Atessa I 169 A4
Ath B 79 B3
Athboy IRL 30 A2
Athea IRL 29 B2
Athenry IRL 28 A3
Athens = Athina GR 185 B4
Atherstone GB 40 C2
Athienou CY 181 A2
Athies F 90 B2
Athies-sous-Laon F 91 B3
Athina = Athens GR 185 B4
Athleague IRL 28 A3
Athlone IRL 28 A4
Athna CY 181 A2
Athy IRL 30 B2
Atienza E 151 A5
Atina I 169 B3
Atkár H 113 B3
Atlantı TR 189 A7
Atna N 199 D7
Åtorp S 55 A5
Åtrå N 47 C5
Ätran S 60 B2
Atri I 169 A3
Atripalda I 170 C2
Atsiki GR 183 D7
Attendorn D 81 A3
Attichy F 90 B3
Attigliano I 168 A2
Attigny F 91 B4
Attleborough GB 41 C5
Åtvidaberg S 56 B1
Atzendorf D 73 C4
Au
  Steiermark A 110 B2
  Vorarlberg A 107 B4
  Bayern D 95 C3
  Bayern D 108 B2
Aub D 94 B2
Aubagne F 132 B1
Aubange B 92 B1
Aubel B 80 B1
Aubenas F 117 C4
Aubenton F 91 B4
Auberive F 105 B4
Aubeterre-sur-Dronne F 128 A3
Aubiet F 129 C3
Aubigné F 115 B3
Aubigny F 114 B2
Aubigny-au-Bac F 78 B3
Aubigny-en-Artois F 78 B2
Aubigny-sur-Nère F 103 B4
Aubin F 130 A1
Aubonne CH 105 C5
Aubrac F 116 C2
Aubusson F 116 B2
Auch F 129 C3
Auchencairn GB 36 B3
Auchinleck GB 36 A2
Auchterarder GB 35 B4
Auchtermuchty GB 35 B4
Auchtertyre GB 31 B3
Auchy-au-Bois F 78 B2
Audenge F 128 B1
Auderville F 88 A2
Audierne F 100 A1
Audincourt F 106 B1
Audlem GB 38 B4
Audruicq F 78 B2
Audun-le-Roman F 92 B1
Audun-le-Tiche F 92 B1
Aue
  Nordrhein-Westfalen D 81 A4
  Sachsen D 83 B4
Auerbach
  Bayern D 95 B3
  Sachsen D 83 B4
Auffach A 108 B3
Augher GB 27 B3
Aughnacloy GB 27 B4
Aughrim IRL 30 B2
Augignac F 115 C4
Augsburg D 94 C2
Augusta I 177 B4
Augusten-borg DK 64 B2
Augustfehn D 71 A4
Augustów PL 12 B5
Aukrug D 64 B2
Auktsjaur S 196 D2
Auldearn GB 32 D3
Aulendorf D 107 B4
Auletta I 172 B1
Aulla I 134 A2
Aullène F 180 B2
Aulnay F 115 B3
Aulnoye-Aymeries F 79 B3
Ault F 90 A1
Aultbea GB 31 B3
Aulum DK 59 B1
Aulus-les-Bains F 146 B2
Auma D 83 B3
Aumale F 90 B1
Aumetz F 92 B1
Aumont-Aubrac F 116 C3
Aunay-en-Bazois F 104 B2
Aunay-sur-Odon F 88 A3
Aune N 199 A10
Auneau F 90 C1
Auneuil F 90 B1
Auning DK 58 B3
Aunsetra N 199 A9
Aups F 132 B2
Aura D 82 B1
Auray F 100 B3
Aurdal N 47 B6
Aure N 198 B5
Aurich D 71 A4
Aurignac F 145 A4
Aurillac F 116 C2
Auriol F 132 B1
Auritz-Burguette E 144 B2
Aurlandsvangen N 47 B4
Auronzo di Cadore I 109 C3
Auros F 128 B2
Auroux F 117 C3
Aurskog N 48 C3
Aursmoen N 48 C3
Ausónia I 169 B3
Ausservillgraton A 109 C3
Austad N 52 B3
Austbygda N 47 B5
Aústis I 178 B3
Austmarka N 49 B4
Austre Moland N 53 B4
Austre Vikebygd N 52 A1
Austrheim N 46 B1
Auterive F 146 A2
Autheuil-Authouillet F 89 A5
Authon F 132 A2
Authon-du-Perche F 102 A2
Autol E 144 B2
Autreville F 92 C1
Autrey-lès-Gray F 105 B4
Autti FIN 197 C10
Autun F 104 C3
Auty-le-Châtel F 103 B4
Auvelais B 79 B4
Auvillar F 129 B3
Auxerre F 104 B2
Auxi-le-Château F 78 B2
Auxon F 104 A2
Auxonne F 105 B4
Auxy F 104 C3
Auzances F 116 A2
Auzon F 117 B3
Ağva TR 187 A4
Availles-Limouzine F 115 B4
Avaldsnes N 52 A1
Avallon F 104 B2
Avantas GR 183 C7
Avaviken S 195 E9
Avebury GB 44 B2
A Veiga E 141 B3
Aveiras de Cima P 154 B2
Aveiro P 148 B1
Avelgem B 79 B3
Avellino I 170 C2
Avenches CH 106 C2
A-Ver-o-Mar P 148 A1
Aversa I 170 C2
Avesnes-le-Comte F 78 B2
Avesnes-sur-Helpe F 91 A3
Avesta S 50 B3
Avetrana I 173 B3
Avezzano I 169 A3
Avià E 147 B2
Aviano I 122 A1
Aviemore GB 32 D3
Avigliana I 119 B4
Avigliano I 172 B1
Avignon F 131 B3
Ávila E 150 B3
Avilés E 141 A5
Avilley F 105 B5
Avintes P 148 A1
Avinyo E 147 C2
Àvio I 121 B3
Avioth F 92 B1
Avis P 154 B3
Avize F 91 C4
Avlonari GR 185 A5
Ávola I 177 C4
Avon F 90 C2
Avonmouth GB 43 A4
Avord F 103 B4
Avranches F 88 B2
Avril F 92 B1
Avrillé F 102 B1
Avtovac BIH 139 B4
Awans B 79 B5
Axams A 108 B2
Axat F 146 B3
Axbridge GB 43 A4
Axel NL 79 A3
Ax-les-Thermes F 146 B2
Axmarby S 51 B4
Axmarsbruk S 51 A4
Axminster GB 43 B3
Axvall S 55 B4
Ay F 91 B4
Aya E 144 A1
Ayamonte E 161 B2
Ayancık TR 23 A8
Ayaş TR 187 B7
Aydın TR 188 B2
Ayelo de Malferit E 159 C3
Ayer CH 119 A4
Ayerbe E 144 B3
Ayette F 78 B2
Ayia Napa CY 181 B2
Áyia Phyla CY 181 B2
Áyios Amvrósios CY 181 A2
Áyios Seryios CY 181 A2
Áyios Theodhoros CY 181 A3
Aykirikçi TR 187 C5
Aylesbury GB 44 B3
Ayllón E 151 A4
Aylsham GB 41 C5
Ayna E 158 C1
Ayódar E 159 B3
Ayora E 159 B2
Ayr GB 36 A2
Ayrancı TR 23 C7
Ayrancılar TR 188 A2
Ayron F 115 B4
Aysgarth GB 37 B4
Ayton GB 35 C5
Aytos BG 17 D7
Ayvacık TR 186 C1
Ayvalık TR 186 C1
Aywaille B 80 B1
Azaila E 153 A3
Azambuja P 154 B2
Azambujeira P 154 B2
Azanja SRB 127 C2
Azannes-et-Soumazannes F 92 B1
Azanúy-Alins E 145 C4
Azaruja P 155 C3
Azay-le-Ferron F 115 B5
Azay-le-Rideau F 102 B2
Azcoitia E 143 A4
Azé F 117 A4
Azeiteiros P 155 B3
Azenhas do Mar P 154 C1
Azinhaga P 154 B2
Azinhal P 160 B2
Azinheira dos Barros P 160 A1
Aznalcázar E 161 B3
Aznalcóllar E 161 B3
Azóia P 154 B2
Azpeitia E 144 A1
Azuaga E 156 B2
Azuara E 153 A3
Azuqueca de Henares E 151 B4
Azur F 128 C1
Azzano Décimo I 122 B1

B

Baad A 107 B5
Baamonde E 140 A3
Baar CH 107 B3
Bağarasi TR 188 B2
Baarle-Nassau B 79 A4
Baarn NL 70 B2
Babadağ TR 188 B3
Babadag RO 17 C8
Babaeski TR 186 A2
Babayevo RUS 9 C9
Babenhausen
  Bayern D 107 A5
  Hessen D 93 B4
Babiak PL 76 B3
Babice PL 86 B3
Babigoszcz PL 75 A3
Babimost PL 75 B4
Babina Greda HR 125 B4
Babócsa H 124 A3
Bábolna H 112 B1
Baborów PL 86 B1
Baboszewo PL 77 B5
Babót H 111 B4
Babruysk BY 13 B8
Babsk PL 87 A4
Bac GB 31 A2
Bač SRB 125 B5
Bacares E 164 B2
Bacău RO 17 B7
Baccarat F 92 C2
Bacharach D 93 A3
Backa S 50 B2
Bačka Palanka SRB 126 B1
Backaryd S 63 B3
Bačka Topola SRB 126 B1
Backe S 200 C2
Bäckebo S 62 B4
Bäckefors S 54 B3
Bäckhammar S 55 A5
Bački Breg SRB 125 B4
Bački-Brestovac SRB 126 B1
Bački Monoštor SRB 125 B4
Bački Petrovac SRB 126 B1
Bački Sokolac SRB 126 B1
Backnang D 94 C1
Bačko Gradište SRB 126 B2
Bačko Novo Selo SRB 125 B5
Bačko Petrovo Selo SRB 126 B2
Bácoli I 170 C2
Bacqueville-en-Caux F 89 A5
Bácsalmás H 126 A1
Bácsbokod H 125 A5
Bad Abbach D 95 C4
Badacsonytomaj H 111 C4
Bad Aibling D 108 B3
Badajoz E 155 C4
Badalona E 147 C3
Badalucco I 133 B3
Bad Aussee A 109 B4
Bad Bederkesa D 72 A1
Bad Bentheim D 71 B4
Bad Bergzabern D 93 B3
Bad Berka D 82 B3
Bad Berleburg D 81 A4
Bad Berneck D 95 A3
Bad Bevensen D 73 A3
Bad Bibra D 82 A3
Bad Birnbach D 95 C5
Bad Blankenburg D 82 B3
Bad Bleiberg A 109 C4
Bad Brambach D 83 B4
Bad Bramstedt D 64 C2
Bad Breisig D 80 B3
Bad Brückenau D 82 B1
Bad Buchau D 107 A4
Bad Camberg D 81 B4
Badderen N 192 C6
Bad Doberan D 65 B4
Bad Driburg D 81 A5
Bad Düben D 83 A4
Bad Dürkheim D 93 B4
Bad Dürrenberg D 83 A4
Bad Dürrheim D 107 A3
Bad Elster D 83 B4
Bad Ems D 81 B3
Baden
  A 111 A3
  CH 106 B3
Bádenas E 152 A2
Baden-Baden D 93 C4
Bad Endorf D 109 B3
Badenweiler D 106 B2
Baderna HR 122 B2
Bad Essen D 71 B5
Bad Fischau A 111 B3
Bad Frankenhausen D 82 A3
Bad Freienwalde D 74 B3
Bad Friedrichshall D 93 B5
Bad Füssing D 96 C1
Bad Gandersheim D 82 A2
Bad Gastein A 109 B4
Bad Gleichenberg A 110 C2
Bad Goisern A 109 B4
Bad Gottleuba D 84 B1
Bad Grund D 82 A2
Bad Hall A 110 A1
Bad Harzburg D 82 A2
Bad Herrenalb D 93 C4
Bad Hersfeld D 82 B1
Bad Hofgastein A 109 B4
Bad Homburg D 81 B4
Bad Honnef D 80 B3
Bad Hönningen D 80 B3
Badia Calavena I 121 B4
Badia Polésine I 121 B4
Badia Pratáglia I 135 B4
Badia Tedalda I 135 B5
Bad Iburg D 71 B5
Bad Innerlaterns A 107 B4
Bad Ischl A 109 B4
Bad Karlshafen D 81 A5
Bad Kemmeriboden CH 106 C2
Bądki PL 69 B3
Bad Kissingen D 82 B2
Bad Kleinen D 65 C4
Bad Kohlgrub D 108 B2
Bad König D 93 B5
Bad Königshofen D 82 B2
Bad Köstritz D 83 B4
Badkowo PL 76 B3
Bad Kreuzen A 110 A1
Bad Kreuznach D 93 B3
Bad Krozingen D 106 B2
Bad Laasphe D 81 B4
Bad Langensalza D 82 A2
Bad Lauchstädt D 83 A3
Bad Lausick D 83 A4
Bad Lauterberg D 82 A2
Bad Leonfelden A 96 C2
Bad Liebenwerda D 83 A5
Bad Liebenzell D 93 C4
Bad Lippspringe D 81 A4

Badljevina HR 124 B3
Bad Meinberg D 81 A4
Bad Mergentheim D 94 B1
Bad Mitterndorf A 109 B4
Bad Münder D 72 B2
Bad Münstereifel D 80 B2
Bad Muskau D 84 A2
Bad Nauheim D 81 B4
Bad Nenndorf D 72 B2
Bad Neuenahr-Ahrweiler D 80 B3
Bad Neustadt D 82 B2
Bad Oeynhausen D 72 B1
Badolato I 175 C2
Badolatosa E 163 A3
Bad Oldesloe D 65 C3
Badonviller F 92 C2
Bad Orb D 81 B5
Badovinci SRB 127 C1
Bad Peterstal D 93 C4
Bad Pyrmont D 72 C2
Bad Radkersburg A 110 C2
Bad Ragaz CH 107 C4
Bad Rappenau D 93 B5
Bad Reichenhall D 109 B3
Bad Saarow-Pieskow D 74 B3
Bad Sachsa D 82 A2
Bad Säckingen D 106 B2
Bad Salzdetfurth D 72 B3
Bad Salzig D 81 B3
Bad Salzuflen D 72 B1
Bad Salzungen D 82 B2
Bad Sankt Leonhard A 110 C1
Bad Sassendorf D 81 A4
Bad Schandau D 84 B2
Bad Schmiedeberg D 83 A4
Bad Schönborn D 93 B4
Bad Schussenried D 107 A4
Bad Schwalbach D 81 B4
Bad Schwartau D 65 C3
Bad Segeberg D 64 C3
Bad Soden D 81 B4
Bad Soden-Salmünster D 81 B5
Bad Sooden-Allendorf D 82 A1
Bad Sulza D 83 A3
Bad Sülze D 66 B1
Bad Tatzmannsdorf A 111 B3
Bad Tennstedt D 82 A2
Bad Tölz D 108 B2
Badules E 152 A2
Bad Urach D 94 C1
Bad Vellach A 110 C1
Bad Vilbel D 81 B4
Bad Vöslau A 111 B3
Bad Waldsee D 107 B4
Bad Wiessee D 108 B2
Bad Wildungen D 81 A5
Bad Wilsnack D 73 B4
Bad Windsheim D 94 B2
Bad Wörishofen D 108 A1
Bad Wurzach D 107 B4
Bad Zwesten D 81 A5
Bad Zwischenahn D 71 A5
Baells E 145 C4
Baena E 163 A3
Baesweiler D 80 B2
Baeza E 157 C4
Baflo NL 71 A3
Baga E 147 B2
Bagaladi I 175 C1
Bagenkop DK 65 B3
Baggetorp S 56 A2
Bagh a Chaisteil GB 31 C1
Bagheria I 176 A2
Bagn N 47 B6
Bagnacavallo I 135 A4
Bagnáia I 168 A2
Bagnara Cálabra I 175 C1
Bagnasco I 133 A4
Bagnères-de-Bigorre F 145 A4
Bagnères-de-Luchon F 145 B4
Bagni del Másino I 120 A2
Bagni di Lucca I 134 A3
Bagni di Rabbi I 121 A3
Bagni di Tivoli I 168 B2
Bagno di Romagna I 135 B4
Bagnoles-de-l'Orne F 89 B3
Bagnoli dei Trigno I 170 B2
Bagnoli di Sopra I 121 B4
Bagnoli Irpino I 170 C3
Bagnolo Mella I 120 B3
Bagnols-en-Forêt F 132 B2
Bagnols-sur-Cèze F 131 A3
Bagnorégio I 168 A2
Bagolino I 121 B3
Bagrationovsk RUS 12 A4
Bagrdan SRB 127 C3
Báguena E 152 A2
Bahabón de Esgueva E 143 C3
Bahillo E 142 B2
Báia delle Zágare I 171 B4
Báia Domizia I 169 B3
Baia Mare RO 17 B5
Baiano I 170 C2
Baião P 148 A1
Baiersbronn D 93 C4
Baiersdorf D 94 B3
Baignes-Ste Radegonde F 115 C3
Baigneux-les-Juifs F 104 B3
Baildon GB 40 B2
Bailén E 157 B4
Băileşti RO 17 C5
Baileux B 91 A4
Bailieborough IRL 27 C4
Bailleul F 78 B2
Baillonville B 79 B5
Bailó E 144 B3
Bain-de-Bretagne F 101 B4
Bains F 117 B3
Bains-les-Bains F 105 A5
Bainton GB 40 B3
Baio E 140 A2
Baiona E 140 B2
Bais F 89 B3
Baiso I 134 A3
Baiuca P 148 B2
Baja H 125 A4
Bajánsenye H 111 C3
Bajina Bašta SRB 127 D1
Bajmok SRB 126 B1
Bajna H 112 B2
Bajovo Polje MNE 139 B4
Bajša SRB 126 B1
Bak H 111 C3
Bakar HR 123 B3
Bakewell GB 40 B2
Bakio E 143 A4
Bakka N 47 C6
Bakkafjörður IS 191 A11
Bakkagerði IS 191 B12
Bække DK 59 C2
Bakken N 48 B3
Baklan TR 189 B4
Bækmarksbro DK 58 B1
Bakonybél H 111 B4
Bakonycsernye H 112 B2
Bakonyjákó H 111 B4
Bakonyszentkirály H 111 B4
Bakonyszombathely H 112 B1
Bakov nad Jizerou CZ 84 B2
Bąkowiec PL 87 A5
Baks H 113 C4
Baksa H 125 B4
Bakum D 71 B5
Bala GB 38 B3
Bâlâ TR 23 B7
Balaguer E 145 C4
Balassagyarmat H 112 A3
Balástya H 113 C4
Balatonakali H 111 C4
Balatonalmádi H 112 B2
Balatonboglár H 111 C4
Balatonbozsok H 112 C2
Balatonederics H 111 C4
Balatonfenyves H 111 C4
Balatonföldvár H 112 C1
Balatonfüred H 112 C1
Balatonfűzfő H 112 B2
Balatonkenese H 112 B2
Balatonkiliti H 112 C2
Balatonlelle H 111 C4
Balatonszabadi H 112 C2
Balatonszemes H 111 C4
Balatonszentgyörgy H 111 C4
Balazote E 158 C1
Balbeggie GB 35 B4
Balbigny F 117 B4
Balboa E 141 B4
Balbriggan IRL 30 A2
Balchik BG 17 D8
Balçova TR 188 A2
Baldock GB 44 B3
Bale HR 122 B2
Baleira E 141 A3
Baleizao P 160 A2
Balen B 79 A5
Balerma E 164 C2
Balestrand N 46 A3
Balestrate I 176 A2
Balfour GB 33 B4
Bälganet S 63 B3
Balgari BG 17 D7
Balıkesir TR 186 C2
Balıklıçeşme TR 186 B2
Bälinge S 51 C4
Balingen D 107 A3
Balingsta S 56 A3
Balintore GB 32 D3
Balizac F 128 B2
Balk NL 70 B2
Balkbrug NL 71 B3
Balla IRL 28 A2
Ballachulish GB 34 B2
Ballaghaderreen IRL 26 C2
Ballancourt-sur-Essonne F 90 C2
Ballantrae GB 36 A2
Ballao I 179 C3
Ballasalla GB 36 B2
Ballater GB 32 D3
Ballen DK 59 C3
Ballenstedt D 82 A3
Ballerias E 145 C3
Balleroy F 88 A3
Ballerup DK 61 D2
Ballesteros de Calatrava E 157 B4
Ballı TR 186 B2
Ballina IRL 26 B1
Ballinalack IRL 30 A1
Ballinamore IRL 26 B3
Ballinascarty IRL 29 C3
Ballinasloe IRL 28 A3
Ballindine IRL 28 A3
Balling DK 58 B1
Ballingarry
Limerick IRL 29 B3
Tipperary IRL 30 B1
Ballingeary IRL 29 C2
Ballinhassig IRL 29 C3
Ballinluig GB 35 B4
Ballino I 121 B3
Ballinrobe IRL 28 A2
Ballinskelligs IRL 29 C1
Ballinspittle IRL 29 C3
Ballintra IRL 26 B2
Ballivor IRL 30 A2
Ballobar E 153 A4
Ballon
F 102 A2
IRL 30 B2
Ballószög H 112 C3
Ballsh AL 182 C1
Ballstad N 194 B4
Ballum DK 64 A1
Ballybay IRL 27 B4
Ballybofey IRL 26 B3
Ballybunion IRL 29 B2
Ballycanew IRL 30 B2
Ballycarry GB 27 B5
Ballycastle
GB 27 A4
IRL 26 B1
Ballyclare GB 27 B5
Ballyconneely IRL 28 A1
Ballycotton IRL 29 C3
Ballycroy IRL 26 B1
Ballydehob IRL 29 C2
Ballyferriter IRL 29 B1
Ballygawley GB 27 B3
Ballygowan GB 27 B5
Ballyhaunis IRL 28 A3
Ballyheige IRL 29 B2
Ballyjamesduff IRL 27 C3
Ballylanders IRL 29 B3
Ballylynan IRL 30 B1
Ballymahon IRL 28 A4
Ballymena GB 27 B4
Ballymoe IRL 28 A3
Ballymoney GB 27 A4
Ballymore IRL 28 A4
Ballymote IRL 26 B2
Ballynacorra IRL 29 C3
Ballynagore IRL 30 A1
Ballynahinch GB 27 B5
Ballynure GB 27 B5
Ballyragget IRL 30 B1
Ballysadare IRL 26 B2
Ballyshannon IRL 26 B2
Ballyvaughan IRL 28 A2
Ballyvourney IRL 29 C2
Ballywalter GB 27 B5
Balmaclellan GB 36 A2
Balmaseda E 143 A3
Balmazújváros H 113 B5
Balme I 119 B4
Balmedie GB 33 D4
Balmuccia I 119 B5
Balna-paling GB 32 D2
Balneario de Panticosa E 145 B3
Balotaszállás H 126 A1
Balsa P 148 A2
Balsareny E 147 C2
Balsorano-Nuovo I 169 B3
Bålsta S 57 A3
Balsthal CH 106 B2
Balta UA 17 A8
Baltanás E 142 C2
Baltar E 140 C3
Baltasound GB 33 A6
Bălţi MD 17 B7
Baltimore IRL 29 C2
Baltinglass IRL 30 B2
Baltiysk RUS 69 A4
Baltów PL 87 A5
Balugães P 148 A1
Bælum DK 58 B3
Balve D 81 A3
Balvi LV 8 D5
Balvicar GB 34 B2
Balya TR 186 C2
Balzo I 136 C2
Bamberg D 94 B2
Bamburgh GB 37 A5
Banatska Palanka SRB 127 C3
Banatski Brestovac SRB 127 C2
Banatski Despotovac SRB 126 B2
Banatski Dvor SRB 126 B2
Banatski-Karlovac SRB 127 B3
Banatsko Arandjelovo SRB 126 A2
Banatsko-Novo Selo SRB 127 C2
Banaz TR 187 D4
Banbridge GB 27 B4
Banbury GB 44 A2
Banchory GB 33 D4
Bande
B 79 B5
E 140 B3
Bandholm DK 65 B4
Bandırma TR 186 B2
Bandol F 132 B1
Bandon IRL 29 C3
Bañeres E 159 C3
Banff GB 33 D4
Bangor
F 100 B2
Down GB 27 B5
Gwynedd GB 38 A2
IRL 26 B1
Bangsund N 199 A8
Banie PL 74 A3
Banja Koviljača SRB 127 C1
Banjaloka SLO 123 B3
Banja Luka BIH 124 C3
Banjani SRB 127 C1
Banja Vručica BIH 125 C3
Banka SK 98 C1
Bankekind S 56 B1
Bankend GB 36 A3
Bankeryd S 62 A2
Bankfoot GB 35 B4
Bankso BG 183 B5
Banloc RO 126 B3
Bannalec F 100 B2
Bannes F 91 C3
Bannockburn GB 35 B4
Bañobárez E 149 B3
Bañon E 152 B2
Banon F 132 A1
Baños E 149 B4
Baños de Gigonza E 162 B2
Baños de la Encina E 157 B4
Baños de Molgas E 140 B3
Baños de Rio Tobia E 143 B4
Baños de Valdearados E 143 C3
Bánov CZ 98 C1
Banova Jaruga HR 124 B2
Bánovce nad Bebravou SK 98 C2
Banovići BIH 139 A4
Banoviči Selo BIH 139 A4
Bánréve H 99 C4
Bansin D 66 C3
Banská Belá SK 98 C2
Banská Bystrica SK 99 C3
Banská Štiavnica SK 98 C2
Bansko BG 183 B5
Banstead GB 44 B3
Banteer IRL 29 B3
Bantheville F 91 B5
Bantry IRL 29 C2
Bantzenheim F 106 B2
Banyalbufar E 166 B2
Banyoles E 147 B3
Banyuls-sur-Mer F 146 B4
Bapaume F 90 A2
Bar
MNE 16 D3
UA 13 D7
Barabhas GB 31 A2
Barači BIH 138 A2
Baracs H 112 C2
Baracska H 112 B2
Barahona E 151 A5
Barajes de Melo E 151 B5
Barakaldo E 143 A4
Baralla E 141 B3
Barañain E 144 B2
Baranavichy BY 13 B7
Báránd H 113 B5
Baranda SRB 127 B2
Baranello I 170 B2
Baranów Sandomierski PL 87 B5
Baraqueville F 130 A1
Barasoain E 144 B2
Barbacena P 155 C3
Barbadás E 140 B3
Barbadillo E 149 B4
Barbadillo de Herreros E 143 B3
Barbadillo del Mercado E 143 B3
Barbadillo del Pez E 143 B3
Barban HR 123 B3
Barbarano Vicento I 121 B4
Barbariga HR 122 C2
Barbaros TR 186 B2
Barbastro E 145 B4
Barbate E 162 B2
Barbatona E 152 A1
Barbâtre F 114 B1
Barbazan F 145 A4
Barbeitos E 141 A3
Barbentane F 131 B3
Barberino di Mugello I 135 A4
Barbezieux-St Hilaire F 115 C3
Barbonne-Fayel F 91 C3
Barbotan-les-Thermes F 128 C2
Barby D 73 C4
Bárcabo E 145 B4
Barca de Alva P 149 A3
Barcarrota E 155 C4
Barcellona-Pozzo di Gotto I 177 A4
Barcelona E 147 C3
Barcelonette F 132 A2
Barcelos P 148 A1
Bárcena del Monasterio E 141 A4
Barcena de Pie de Concha E 142 A2
Barchfeld D 82 B2
Barcin PL 76 B2
Barcino PL 68 A1
Bárcis I 122 A1
Barco P 148 B2
Barcones E 151 A5
Barcs H 124 B3
Barcus F 144 A3
Bardejov SK 12 D4
Bårdesø DK 59 C3
Bardi I 120 C2
Bardney GB 40 B3
Bardo PL 85 B4
Bardolino I 121 B3
Bardonécchia I 118 B3
Bardoňovo SK 112 A2
Barèges F 145 B4
Barenstein D 83 B5
Barentin F 89 A4
Barenton F 88 B3
Barevo BIH 138 A3
Barfleur F 88 A2
Barga I 134 A3
Bargas E 151 C3
Barge I 119 C4
Bargemon F 132 B2
Barghe I 120 B3
Bargoed GB 39 C3
Bargrennan GB 36 A2
Bargteheide D 64 C3
Barham GB 45 B5
Bari I 173 A2
Barič Draga HR 137 A4
Barilović HR 123 B4
Bari Sardo I 179 C3
Barisciano I 169 A3
Barjac F 131 A3
Barjols F 132 B1
Barjon F 105 B3
Bårkåker N 54 A1
Barkald N 199 D7
Barkowo
Dolnośląskie PL 85 A4
Pomorskie PL 68 B2
Bârlad RO 17 B7
Bar-le-Duc F 91 C5
Barles F 132 A2
Barletta I 171 B4
Barlinek PL 75 B4
Barmouth GB 38 B2
Barmstedt D 64 C2
Barnard Castle GB 37 B5
Barnarp S 62 A2
Bärnau D 95 B4
Bärnbach A 110 B2
Barneberg D 73 B4
Barnenitz D 74 B1
Barnet GB 44 B3
Barnetby le Wold GB 40 B3
Barneveld NL 70 B2
Barneville-Carteret F 88 A2
Barnoldswick GB 40 B1
Barnowko PL 75 B3
Barnsley GB 40 B2
Barnstädt D 83 A3
Barnstaple GB 42 A2
Barnstorf D 72 B1
Barntrup D 72 C2
Baron F 90 B2
Baronissi I 170 C2
Barqueiro P 154 B2
Barquinha P 154 B2
Barr
F 93 C3
GB 36 A2
Barra P 148 B1
Barracas E 159 A3
Barraco E 150 B3
Barrado E 150 B2
Barrafranca I 177 B3
Barranco do Velho P 160 B2
Barrancos P 161 A3
Barrax E 158 B1
Barrbaar D 94 C2
Barre-des-Cevennes F 130 A2
Barreiro P 154 C1
Barreiros E 141 A3
Barrême F 132 B2
Barret-le-Bas F 132 A1
Barrhead GB 34 C3
Barrhill GB 36 A2
Barrio de Nuesra Señora E 142 B1
Barrowford GB 40 B1
Barrow-in-Furness GB 36 B3
Barrow upon Humber GB 40 B3
Barruecopardo E 149 A3
Barruelo de Santullán E 142 B2
Barruera E 145 B4
Barry GB 39 C3
Bårse DK 65 A4
Barsinghausen D 72 B2
Barssel D 71 A4
Bar-sur-Aube F 104 A3
Bar-sur-Seine F 104 A3
Barth D 66 B1
Bartholomä D 94 C1
Bartin TR 187 A7
Barton upon Humber GB 40 B3
Barúmini I 179 C2
Baruth D 74 B2
Barvaux B 80 B1
Barver D 72 B1
Barwatd PL 99 B3
Barwice PL 68 B1
Barysaw BY 13 A8
Barzana E 141 A5
Bârzava RO 16 B4
Bárzio I 120 B2
Bas E 147 B3
Bašaid SRB 126 B2
Basaluzzo I 120 C1
Basarabeasca MD 17 B8
Basauri E 143 A4
Baschi I 168 A2
Baschurch GB 38 B4
Basconcillos del Tozo E 143 B3
Bascones de Ojeda E 142 B2
Basécles B 79 B3
Basel CH 106 B2
Basélice I 170 B2
Basildon GB 45 B4
Basingstoke GB 44 B2
Baška
CZ 98 B2
HR 123 C3
Baška Voda HR 138 B2
Bäsksjö S 200 B3
Baslow GB 40 B2
Başmakçı TR 189 B5
Basovizza I 122 B2
Bassacutena I 178 A3
Bassano del Grappa I 121 B4
Bassano Romano I 168 A2
Bassecourt CH 106 B2
Bassella E 147 B2
Bassevuovdde N 193 D9
Bassou F 104 B2
Bassoues F 128 C3
Bassum D 72 B1
Båstad S 61 C2
Bastardo I 136 C1
Bastelica F 180 A2
Bastelicaccia F 180 B1
Bastia
F 180 A2
I 136 B1
Bastogne B 92 A1
Baston GB 40 C3
Bastuträsk S 200 B6
Bata H 125 A4
Batajnica SRB 127 C2
Batak BG 183 B6
Batalha P 154 B2
Bátaszék H 125 A4
Batea E 153 A4
Batelov CZ 97 B3
Bath GB 43 A4
Bathgate GB 35 C4
Batida H 126 A2
Batignano I 135 C4
Batina HR 125 B4
Bátka SK 99 C4
Batković BIH 125 C5
Batley GB 40 B2
Batnfjordsøra N 198 C4
Batočina SRB 127 C3
Bátonyterenye H 113 B3
Batrina HR 125 B3
Båtsfjord N 193 B13
Båtskärsnäs S 196 D6
Battaglia Terme I 121 B4
Bätterkinden CH 106 B2
Battice B 80 B1
Battipáglia I 170 C2
Battle GB 45 C4
Battonya H 126 A3
Batuša SRB 127 C3
Bátya H 112 C2
Bau I 179 C2
Baud F 100 B2
Baudour B 79 B3
Baugé F 102 B1
Baugy F 103 B4
Bauma CH 107 B3
Baume-les-Dames F 105 B5
Baumholder D 93 B3
Baunatal D 81 A5
Baunei I 178 B3
Bauska LV 8 D4
Bautzen D 84 A2
Bavanište SRB 127 C2
Bavay F 79 B3
Bavilliers F 106 B1
Bavorov CZ 96 B2
Bawdsey GB 45 A5
Bawinkel D 71 B4
Bawtry GB 40 B2
Bayat TR 187 D5
Bayel F 105 A3
Bayeux F 88 A3
Bayındır TR 188 A2
Bayon F 92 C2
Bayonne F 128 C1
Bayons F 132 A2
Bayramiç TR 186 C1
Bayreuth D 95 B3
Bayrischzell D 108 B3
Baza E 164 B2
Bazas F 128 B2
Baziege F 146 A2
Bazoches-les-Gallerandes F 103 A4
Bazoches-sur-Hoëne F 89 B4
Bazzano I 135 A4
Beaconsfield GB 44 B3
Beade E 140 B2
Beadnell GB 37 A5
Beaminster GB 43 B4
Bearsden GB 34 C3
Beas E 161 B3
Beasain E 144 A1
Beas de Segura E 164 A2
Beattock GB 36 A3
Beaubery F 117 A4
Beaucaire F 131 B3
Beaufort
F 118 B3
IRL 29 B2
Beaufort-en Vallée F 102 B1
Beaugency F 103 B3
Beaujeu
Alpes-de-Haute-Provence F 132 A2
Rhône F 117 A4
Beaulac F 128 B2
Beaulieu
F 103 B4
GB 44 C2
Beaulieu-sous-la-Roche F 114 B2
Beaulieu-sur-Dordogne F 129 B4
Beaulieu-sur-Mer F 133 B3
Beaulon F 104 C2
Beauly GB 32 D2
Beaumaris GB 38 A2
Beaumesnil F 89 A4
Beaumetz-lès-Loges F 78 B2
Beaumont
B 79 B4
Beaumont *continued*
F 129 B3
Beaumont-de-Lomagne F 129 C3
Beaumont-du-Gâtinais F 103 A4
Beaumont-en-Argonne F 91 B5
Beaumont-Hague F 88 A2
Beaumont-la-Ronce F 102 B2
Beaumont-le-Roger F 89 A4
Beaumont-sur-Oise F 90 B2
Beaumont-sur-Sarthe F 102 A2
Beaune F 105 B3
Beaune-la-Rolande F 103 A4
Beaupréau F 101 B5
Beauraing B 91 A4
Beaurepaire F 117 B5
Beaurepaire-en-Bresse F 105 C4
Beaurières F 132 A1
Beauvais F 90 B2
Beauval F 90 A2
Beauville F 129 B3
Beauvoir-sur-Mer F 114 B1
Beauvoir-sur-Niort F 114 B3
Beba Veche RO 126 A2
Bebertal D 73 B4
Bebington GB 38 A3
Bebra D 82 B1
Bebrina HR 125 B3
Beccles GB 45 A5
Becedas E 150 B2
Beceite E 153 B4
Bečej SRB 126 B2
Becerreá E 141 B3
Becerril de Campos E 142 B2
Bécherel F 101 A4
Bechhofen D 94 B2
Bechyně CZ 96 B2
Becilla de Valderaduey E 142 B1
Beckfoot GB 36 B3
Beckingham GB 40 B3
Beckum D 81 A4
Beco P 154 B2
Bécon-les-Granits F 102 B1
Bečov nad Teplou CZ 83 B4
Becsehely H 111 C3
Bedale GB 37 B5
Bedames E 143 A3
Bédar E 164 B3
Bédarieux F 130 B2
Bédarrides F 131 A3
Bedburg D 80 B2
Beddgelert GB 38 A2
Beddingestrand S 66 A2
Bédée F 101 A4
Bedegkér H 112 C2
Beden TR 189 C7
Bedford GB 44 A3
Będków PL 87 A3
Bedlington GB 37 A5
Bedlno PL 77 B4
Bedmar E 163 A4
Bédoin F 131 A4
Bedónia I 134 A2
Bedretto CH 107 C3
Bedsted DK 58 B1
Bedum NL 71 A3
Bedwas GB 39 C3
Bedworth GB 40 C2
Będzin PL 86 B3
Beekbergen NL 70 B2
Beek en Donk NL 80 A1
Beelen D 71 C5
Beelitz D 74 B1
Beer GB 43 B3
Beerfelde D 74 B3
Beerfelden D 93 B4
Beernem B 78 A3
Beeskow D 74 B3
Beetsterzwaag NL 70 A3
Beetzendorf D 73 B4
Beflelay CH 106 B2
Begaljica SRB 127 C2
Bégard F 100 A2
Begejci SRB 126 B2
Begijar E 157 C4
Begijnendijk B 79 A4
Begndal N 48 B1
Begues E 147 C2
Beguildy GB 39 B3
Begur E 147 C4
Beho B 80 B1
Behringen D 82 A2
Beilen NL 71 B3
Beilngries D 95 B3
Beine-Nauroy F 91 B4
Beinwil CH 106 B3
Beiseförth D 82 A1
Beith GB 34 C3
Beitostølen N 47 A5
Beiuş RO 16 B5
Beja P 160 A2
Béjar E 149 B4
Bekçiler TR 189 C4
Békés H 113 C5
Békéscsaba H 113 C5
Bekilli TR 189 A4
Bekkarfjord N 193 B11
Bela SK 98 B2
Bélâbre F 115 B5
Bela Crkva SRB 127 C3
Belalcázar E 156 B2
Belánad Radbuzou CZ 95 B4
Belanovica SRB 127 C2
Bélapátfalva H 113 A4

Bělápod Bezdězem
CZ 84 B2
Belcaire F 146 B2
Bełchatów PL 86 A3
Belchite E 153 A3
Bělčice CZ 96 B1
Belcoo GB 26 B3
Belecke D 81 A4
Beled H 111 B4
Belej HR 123 C3
Beleño E 142 A1
Bélesta F 146 B2
Belevi TR 188 A2
Belfast GB 27 B5
Belford GB 37 A5
Belfort F 106 B1
Belgentier F 132 B1
Belgern D 83 A5
Belgioioso I 120 B2
Belgodère F 180 A2
Belgooly IRL 29 C3
Belgrade = Beograd
SRB 127 C2
Belhade F 128 B2
Belica HR 124 A2
Beli Manastir HR 125 B4
Belin-Bèliet F 128 B2
Belinchón E 151 B4
Belišće HR 125 B4
Bělkovice-Lašťany
CZ 98 B1
Bella I 172 B1
Bellac F 115 B5
Bellágio I 120 B2
Bellananagh IRL 27 C3
Bellano I 120 A2
Bellária I 136 A1
Bellavary IRL 26 C1
Belleau F 90 B3
Belleek GB 26 B2
Bellegarde
Gard F 131 B3
Loiret F 103 B4
Bellegarde-en-Diois
F 132 A1
Bellegarde-en-Marche
F 116 B2
Bellegarde-sur-
Valserine F 118 A2
Belle-Isle-en-Terre
F 100 A2
Bellême F 89 B4
Bellenaves F 116 A3
Bellentre F 118 B3
Bellevaux F 118 A3
Bellevesvre F 105 C4
Belleville F 117 A4
Belleville-sur-Vie
F 114 B2
Bellevue-la-Montagne
F 117 B3
Belley F 118 B2
Bellheim D 93 B4
Bellinge DK 59 C3
Bellingham GB 37 A4
Bellinzago Novarese
I 120 B1
Bellinzona CH 120 A2
Bell-lloc d'Urgell
E 153 A4
Bello E 152 B2
Bellpuig d'Urgell
E 147 C2
Bellreguart E 159 C3
Bellsbank GB 36 A2
Belltall E 147 C2
Belluno I 121 A5
Bellver de Cerdanya
E 146 B2
Bellvis E 147 C1
Bélmez E 156 B2
Belmez de la Moraleda
E 163 A4
Belmont GB 33 A6
Belmont-de-la-Loire
F 117 A4
Belmonte
Asturias E 141 A4
Cuenca E 158 B1
P 148 B2
Belmonte de San José
E 153 B3
Belmonte de Tajo
E 151 B4
Belmont-sur-Rance
F 130 B1
Belmullet IRL 26 B1
Belobreşca RO 127 C3
Beloeil B 79 B3
Belogradchik BG 16 D5
Belokorovichi UA 13 C8
Belorado E 143 B3
Belotić SRB 127 C1
Bělotín CZ 98 B1
Belovo BG 183 A6
Belozersk RUS 9 C10
Belp CH 106 C2
Belpasso I 177 B3
Belpech F 146 A2
Belper GB 40 B2
Belsay GB 37 A5
Belsk Duzy PL 87 A4
Beltinci SLO 111 C3
Beltra IRL 26 C1
Belturbet IRL 27 B3
Beluša SK 98 B2
Belvedere Marittimo
I 174 B1
Belver de Cinca E 153 A4
Belver de los Montes
E 142 C1
Belvès F 129 B3
Belvezet F 130 A2
Belvis de la Jara
E 150 C3
Belvis de Monroy
E 150 C2
Belyy RUS 9 E8
Belz F 100 B2
Bełżec PL 13 C5
Belzig D 73 B5
Bembibre E 141 B4
Bembridge GB 44 C2
Bemmel NL 80 A1
Bemposta
Bragança P 149 A3
Santarém P 154 B2
Benabarre E 145 B4
Benacazón E 161 B3
Benaguacil E 159 B3
Benahadux E 164 C2
Benalmádena E 163 B3
Benalúa de Guadix
E 164 B1
Benalúa de las Villas
E 163 A4
Benalup E 162 B2
Benamargosa E 163 B3
Benamaurel E 164 B2
Benameji E 163 A3
Benamocarra E 163 B3
Benaocaz E 162 B2
Benaoján E 162 B2
Benarrabá E 162 B2
Benasque E 145 B4
Benátky nad Jizerou
CZ 84 B2
Benavente
E 142 B1
P 154 C2
Benavides de Órbigo
E 141 B5
Benavila P 154 B3
Bendorf D 81 B3
Benedikt SLO 110 C2
Benejama E 159 C3
Benejúzar E 165 A4
Benešov CZ 96 B2
Bénestroff F 92 C2
Benet F 114 B3
Bene Vagienna I 133 A3
Bénévent-l'Abbaye
F 116 A1
Benevento I 170 B2
Benfeld F 93 C3
Benfica P 154 B2
Bengtsfors S 54 A3
Bengtsheden S 50 B2
Beničanci HR 125 B4
Benicarló E 153 B4
Benicássim E 153 B4
Benidorm E 159 C3
Benifaió E 159 B3
Beniganim E 159 C3
Benington GB 41 B4
Benisa E 159 C4
Benkovac HR 137 A4
Benllech GB 38 A2
Benneckenstein D 82 A2
Bénodet F 100 B1
Benquerencia de la
Serena E 156 B2
Bensafrim P 160 B1
Bensbyn S 196 D5
Bensdorf D 73 B5
Benshausen D 82 B2
Bensheim D 93 B4
Bentley GB 44 B3
Bentwisch D 65 B5
Beočin SRB 126 B1
Beograd = Belgrade
SRB 127 C2
Beragh GB 27 B3
Beranga E 143 A3
Berat AL 182 C1
Bérat F 146 A2
Beratzhausen D 95 B3
Bérbaltavár H 111 B3
Berbenno di Valtellina
I 120 A2
Berberana E 143 B3
Bercedo E 143 A3
Bercel H 112 B3
Bercenay-le-Hayer
F 91 C3
Berceto I 134 A2
Berchem B 79 B3
Berchidda I 178 B3
Berching D 95 B3
Berchtesgaden D 109 B4
Bérchules E 163 B4
Bercianos de Aliste
E 149 A3
Berck F 78 B1
Berclaire d'Urgell
E 147 C1
Berdoias E 140 A1
Berducedo E 141 A4
Berdún E 144 B3
Berdychiv UA 13 D8
Bere Alston GB 42 B2
Bereguardo I 120 B2
Berehommen N 53 A3
Berehove UA 16 A5
Berek BIH 124 B3
Beremend H 125 B4
Bere Regis GB 43 B4
Berestechko UA 13 C6
Berettyóújfalu H 113 B5
Berezhany UA 13 D6
Berezivka UA 17 B9
Berezna UA 13 C9
Berg
D 95 B3
N 195 E3
S 56 B2
Berga
Sachsen-Anhalt
D 82 A3
Thüringen D 83 B4
E 147 B2
S 62 A4
Bergama TR 186 C2
Bérgamo I 120 B2
Bergara E 143 A4
Bergby S 51 B4
Berge
Brandenburg D 74 B1
Niedersachsen D 71 B4
Berge continued
Telemark N 53 A4
Telemark N 53 A4
Bergeforsen S 200 D3
Bergen
Mecklenburg-
Vorpommern D 66 B2
Niedersachsen D 72 B2
Niedersachsen D 73 B3
N 46 B2
NL 70 B1
Bergen op Zoom
NL 79 A4
Bergerac F 129 B3
Bergères-lés-Vertus
F 91 C4
Bergeyk NL 79 A5
Berghausen D 93 C4
Bergheim D 80 B2
Berghem S 60 B2
Berg im Gau D 95 C3
Bergisch Gladbach
D 80 B3
Bergkamen D 81 A3
Bergkvara S 63 B4
Berglern D 95 C3
Bergnäset S 196 D5
Bergneustadt D 81 A3
Bergsäng S 49 B5
Bergshamra S 57 A4
Bergsjö S 200 E3
Bergs slussar S 56 B1
Bergsviken S 196 D4
Bergtheim D 94 B2
Bergues F 78 B2
Bergum NL 70 A2
Bergün Bravuogn
CH 107 C4
Bergwitz D 83 A4
Berhida H 112 B2
Beringel P 160 A2
Beringen B 79 A5
Berja E 164 C2
Berkåk N 199 C7
Berkeley GB 43 A4
Berkenthin D 65 C3
Berkhamsted GB 44 B3
Berkheim D 107 A5
Berkhof D 72 B2
Berkovići BIH 139 B4
Berkovitsa BG 17 D5
Berlanga E 156 B2
Berlanga de Duero
E 151 A5
Berlevåg N 193 B13
Berlikum NL 70 A2
Berlin D 74 B2
Berlstedt D 82 A3
Bermeo E 143 A4
Bermillo de Sayago
E 149 A3
Bern CH 106 C2
Bernalda I 174 A2
Bernardos E 150 A3
Bernartice
Jihočeský CZ 96 B2
Vychodočeský CZ 85 B3
Bernau
Baden-Württemberg
D 106 B3
Bayern D 109 B3
Brandenburg D 74 B2
Bernaville F 90 A2
Bernay F 89 A4
Bernburg D 83 A3
Berndorf A 111 B3
Berne D 72 A1
Bernecebarati H 112 A2
Bernhardsthal A 97 C4
Bernkastel-Kues D 92 B3
Bernolakovo SK 111 A4
Bernsdorf D 84 A2
Bernstadt D 84 A2
Bernstein A 111 B3
Bernués E 145 B3
Beromünster CH 106 B3
Beroun CZ 96 B2
Berovo MK 182 B4
Berre-l'Etang F 131 B4
Berriedale GB 32 C3
Berriew GB 39 B3
Berrocal E 161 B3
Bersenbrück D 71 B4
Bershad' UA 13 D8
Bertamiráns E 140 B2
Berthåga S 51 C4
Berthelming F 92 C2
Bertincourt F 90 A2
Bertinoro I 135 A5
Bertogne B 92 A1
Bertrix B 91 B5
Berufjörður IS 191 C11
Berville-sur-Mer F 89 A4
Berwick-upon-Tweed
GB 37 A4
Berzasca RO 16 C4
Berzence H 124 A3
Berzocana E 156 A2
Besalú E 147 B3
Besançon F 105 B5
Besenfeld D 93 C4
Besenyötelek H 113 B4
Besenyszög H 113 B4
Beshenkovichi BY 13 A8
Besigheim D 93 C5
Běšiny CZ 96 B1
Beška SRB 126 B2
Beşkonak TR 189 B6
Besle F 101 B4
Besnyö H 112 B2
Bessais-le-Fromental
F 103 C4
Bessan F 130 B2
Besse-en-Chandesse
F 116 B2
Bessèges F 131 A3
Bessé-sur-Braye
F 102 B2
Bessines-sur-Gartempe
F 115 B5
Best NL 79 A5
Bestorp S 56 B1
Betanzos E 140 A2
Betelu E 144 A2
Bétera E 159 B3
Beteta E 152 B1
Béthenville F 91 B4
Bethesda GB 38 A2
Béthune F 78 B2
Beton-Bazoches F 90 C3
Bettembourg L 92 B2
Betterdorf L 92 B2
Bettna S 56 B2
Béttola I 120 C2
Bettona I 136 B1
Bettyhill GB 32 C2
Betws-y-Coed GB 38 A3
Betxi E 159 B3
Betz F 90 B2
Betzdorf D 81 B3
Beuil F 132 A2
Beulah GB 39 B3
Beuzeville F 89 A4
Bevagna I 136 C1
Bevens-bruk S 56 A1
Beveren B 79 A4
Beverley GB 40 B3
Bevern D 81 A5
Beverstedt D 72 A1
Beverungen D 81 A5
Beverwijk NL 70 B1
Bex CH 119 A4
Bexhill GB 45 C4
Beyazköy TR 186 A2
Beychevelle F 128 A2
Beydağ TR 188 A3
Beyeğaç TR 188 B3
Beykoz TR 186 A4
Beynat F 129 A4
Beyoğlu TR 186 A4
Beypazarı TR 187 B6
Beyşehir TR 189 B6
Bezas E 152 B2
Bezau A 107 B4
Bezdan SRB 125 B4
Bèze F 105 B4
Bezenet F 116 A2
Bezhetsk RUS 9 D10
Béziers F 130 B2
Bezzecca I 121 B3
Biadki PL 85 A5
Biała
Łódzkie PL 77 C4
Opolskie PL 85 B5
Białaczów PL 87 A4
Biała Podlaska PL 13 B5
Biała Rawska PL 87 A4
Biale Błota PL 76 A2
Białobłoty PL 76 B2
Białobrzegi PL 87 A4
Białogard PL 67 C4
Bialośliwie PL 76 A2
Białowąs PL 68 B1
Biały Bór PL 68 B1
Białystok PL 13 B5
Biancavilla I 177 B3
Bianco I 175 C2
Biandrate I 119 B5
Biar E 159 C3
Biarritz F 144 A2
Bias F 128 B1
Biasca CH 120 A1
Biatorbágy H 112 B2
Bibbiena I 135 B4
Bibbona I 134 B3
Biberach
Baden-Württemberg
D 93 C4
Baden-Württemberg
D 107 A4
Bibinje HR 137 A4
Bibione I 122 B2
Biblis D 93 B4
Bibury GB 44 B2
Bicaj AL 182 B2
Biccari I 171 B3
Bicester GB 44 B2
Bichl D 108 B2
Bichlbach A 108 B1
Bicorp E 159 B3
Bicos P 160 B1
Bicske H 112 B2
Bidache F 128 C1
Bidart F 144 A2
Biddinghuizen NL 70 B2
Biddulph GB 40 B1
Bideford GB 42 A2
Bidford-on-Avon
GB 44 A2
Bidjovagge N 192 C6
Bie S 56 A2
Bieber D 81 B5
Biebersdorf D 74 C2
Biedenkopf D 81 B4
Biel E 144 B3
Bielany Wroclawskie
PL 85 A4
Bielawa PL 85 B4
Bielawy PL 77 B4
Biel / Bienne CH 106 B2
Bielefeld D 72 B1
Biella I 119 B5
Bielsa E 145 B4
Bielsk PL 77 B4
Bielsko-Biała PL 99 B3
Bielsk Podlaski PL 13 B5
Bienenbuttel D 72 A3
Bieniow PL 84 A3
Bienservida E 158 C1
Bienvenida E 156 B1
Bierdzany PL 86 B2
Bierné F 102 B1
Biersted DK 58 A2
Bierun PL 86 B3
Bierutów PL 85 A5
Bierwart B 79 B5
Bierzwina PL 75 A4
Bierzwnik PL 75 A4
Biescas E 145 B3
Biesenthal D 74 B2
Biesiekierz PL 67 B5
Bietigheim-Bissingen
D 93 C5
Bièvre B 91 B5
Bieżuń PL 77 B4
Biga TR 186 B2
Bigadiç TR 186 C3
Biganos F 128 B2
Bigas P 148 B2
Bigastro E 165 A4
Bigbury GB 42 B3
Biggar GB 36 A3
Biggin Hill GB 45 B4
Biggleswade GB 44 A3
Bignasco CH 119 A5
Biguglia F 180 A2
Bihać BIH 124 C1
Biharnagybajom
H 113 B5
Bijeljani BIH 139 B4
Bijeljina BIH 125 C5
Bijuesca E 152 A2
Bilaj HR 137 A4
Bila Tserkva UA 13 D9
Bilbao E 143 A4
Bilcza PL 87 B4
Bíldudalur IS 190 B2
Bileća BIH 139 C4
Bilecik TR 187 B4
Biled RO 126 B2
Biłgoraj PL 12 C5
Bilhorod-Dnistrovskyy
UA 17 B9
Bílina CZ 84 B1
Bilisht AL 182 C2
Bilje HR 125 B4
Billdal S 60 B1
Billerbeck D 71 C4
Billericay GB 45 B4
Billesholm S 61 C2
Billingborough GB 40 C3
Billinge S 61 D3
Billingham GB 37 B5
Billinghay GB 41 B3
Billingsfors S 54 B3
Billingshurst GB 44 B3
Billom F 116 B3
Billsta S 200 C4
Billund DK 59 C2
Bílovec CZ 98 B2
Bilstein D 81 A4
Bilthoven NL 70 B2
Bilto N 192 C5
Bilzen B 80 B1
Bíňa SK 112 B2
Binaced E 145 C4
Binasco I 120 B2
Binbrook GB 41 B3
Binche B 79 B4
Bindlach D 95 B3
Bindslev DK 58 A3
Binefar E 145 C4
Bingen D 93 B3
Bingham GB 40 C3
Bingley GB 40 B2
Bingsjö S 50 A2
Binic F 100 A3
Binz D 66 B2
Biograd na Moru
HR 137 B4
Bionaz I 119 B4
Bioska SRB 127 D1
Birda RO 126 B3
Birdlip GB 44 B1
Biri N 48 B2
Birkeland N 53 B4
Birkenfeld
Baden-Württemberg
D 93 C4
Rheinland-Pfalz D 92 B3
Birkenhead GB 38 A3
Birkerød DK 61 D2
Birkfeld A 110 B2
Birkirkara M 175 C3
Birmingham GB 40 C2
Birr IRL 28 A4
Birresborn D 80 B2
Birstein D 81 B5
Biržai LT 8 D4
Birzebbugia M 175 C3
Bisáccia I 172 A1
Bisacquino I 176 B2
Bisbal de Falset E 153 A4
Biscarosse F 128 B1
Biscarosse Plage
F 128 B1
Biscarrués E 144 B3
Biscéglie I 171 B4
Bischheim F 93 C3
Bischofsheim D 82 B1
Bischofshofen A 109 B4
Bischofswerda D 84 A2
Bischofswiesen D 109 B3
Bischofszell CH 107 B4
Bischwiller F 93 C3
Bisenti I 169 A3
Bishop Auckland
GB 37 B5
Bishop's Castle GB 39 B4
Bishops Lydeard
GB 43 A3
Bishop's Stortford
GB 45 B4
Bishop's Waltham
GB 44 C2
Bisignano I 174 B2
Bisingen D 93 C4
Biskupice-Oławskie
PL 85 A5
Biskupiec PL 69 B4
Bismark D 73 B4
Bismo N 198 D5
Bispgården S 200 C2
Bispingen D 72 A2
Bissen L 92 B2
Bissendorf D 71 B5
Bisserup DK 65 A4
Bistango I 119 C5
Bistarac Donje
BIH 139 A4
Bistrica BIH 124 C3
Bistrica ob Sotli
SLO 123 A4
Bistriţa RO 17 B6
Bitburg D 92 B2
Bitche F 93 B3
Bitetto I 171 B4
Bitola MK 182 B3
Bitonto I 171 B4
Bitschwiller F 106 B2
Bitterfeld D 83 A4
Bitti I 178 B3
Biville-sur-Mer F 89 A5
Bivona I 176 B2
Biwer L 92 B2
Bizeljsko SLO 123 A4
Bizovac HR 125 B4
Bjåen N 52 A3
Bjärnum S 61 C3
Bjärred S 61 D3
Bjästa S 200 C4
Bjelland
Vest-Agder N 52 B2
Vest-Agder N 52 B3
Bjelovar HR 124 B2
Bjerkreim N 52 B2
Bjerkvik N 194 B8
Bjerreby DK 65 B3
Bjerregrav DK 58 B2
Bjerringbro DK 59 B2
Bjøberg N 47 B5
Bjøllånes N 195 D5
Björbo S 50 B1
Bjordal N 46 A2
Björg IS 191 B8
Bjørkåsen N 194 B7
Björke
Gävleborg S 51 B4
Östergötland S 56 B1
Bjørkelangen N 48 C3
Björketorp S 60 B2
Björkholmen S 196 C2
Björkliden S 194 B9
Björklinge S 51 B4
Björko S 51 C6
Björkö S 60 B1
Björköby S 62 A2
Björkvik S 56 B2
Bjørn N 195 D3
Björna S 200 C4
Björneborg S 55 A5
Björnerod S 54 A2
Bjørnevatn N 193 C13
Björnlunda S 56 A3
Bjørnstad N 193 C14
Björsäter S 56 B2
Bjurberget S 49 B4
Bjurholm S 200 C5
Bjursås S 50 B2
Bjurtjärn S 55 A5
Bjuv S 61 C2
Blachownia PL 86 B2
Blackburn GB 38 A4
Blackpool GB 38 A3
Blackstad S 62 A4
Blackwater IRL 30 B2
Blackwaterfoot GB 34 C2
Blacy F 91 C4
Bladåker S 51 B5
Blaenau Ffestiniog
GB 38 B3
Blaenavon GB 39 C3
Blaengarw GB 39 C3
Blagaj
BIH 124 B2
BIH 139 B3
Blagdon GB 43 A4
Blagnac F 129 C4
Blagoevgrad BG 183 A5
Blaichach D 107 B5
Blain F 101 B4
Blainville-sur-l'Eau
F 92 C2
Blair Atholl GB 35 B4
Blairgowrie GB 35 B4
Blajan F 145 A4
Blakeney GB 39 C4
Blakstad N 53 B4
Blâmont F 92 C2
Blanca E 165 A3
Blancos E 140 C3
Blandford Forum
GB 43 B4
Blanes E 147 C3
Blangy-sur-Bresle
F 90 B1
Blankaholm S 62 A4
Blankenberge B 78 A3
Blankenburg D 82 A2
Blankenfelde D 74 B2
Blankenhain D 82 B3
Blankenheim D 80 B2
Blanquefort F 128 B2
Blansko CZ 97 B4
Blanzac F 115 C4
Blanzy F 104 C3
Blaricum NL 70 B2
Blarney IRL 29 C3
Blascomillán E 150 B2
Blascosancho E 150 B3
Błaszki PL 86 A2
Blatná CZ 96 B1
Blatné SK 111 A4
Blatnice CZ 98 C1
Blatnika BIH 139 A3
Blato HR 138 C2
Blato na Cetini
HR 138 B2
Blatten CH 119 A4
Blattnicksele S 195 E8
Blatzheim D 80 B2
Blaubeuren D 94 C1
Blaufelden D 94 B1
Blaustein D 94 C1
Blaydon GB 37 B5
Blaye F 128 A2
Blaye-les-Mines F 130 A1
Blázquez E 156 B2
Bleckede D 73 A3
Blecua E 145 B3
Bled SLO 123 A3
Bleiburg A 110 C1
Bleichenbach D 81 B5
Bleicherode D 82 A2
Bleik N 194 A6
Bleikvassli N 195 E4
Bléneau F 104 B1
Blentarp S 61 D3
Blera I 168 A2
Blérancourt F 90 B3
Bléré F 102 B2
Blesle F 116 B3
Blessington IRL 30 A2
Blet F 103 C4
Bletchley GB 44 B3
Bletterans F 105 C4
Blidö S 57 A4
Blidsberg S 60 B3
Blieskastel D 92 B3
Bligny-sur-Ouche
F 104 B3
Blikstorp S 55 B5
Blinisht AL 182 B1
Blinja HR 124 B2
Blizanówek PL 76 C3
Bliżyn PL 87 A4
Blois F 103 B3
Blokhus DK 58 A2
Blokzijl NL 70 B2
Blombacka S 55 A4
Blomberg D 72 C2
Blomskog S 54 A3
Blomstermåla S 62 B4
Blomvåg N 46 B1
Blönduós IS 190 B5
Błonie PL 77 B5
Blonville-sur-Mer F 89 A4
Blötberget S 50 B2
Blovice CZ 96 B1
Bloxham GB 44 A2
Blšany CZ 83 B5
Bludenz A 107 B4
Bludov CZ 97 B4
Blumberg D 107 B3
Blyberg S 49 A6
Blyth
Northumberland
GB 37 A5
Nottinghamshire
GB 40 B2
Blyth Bridge GB 35 C4
Blythburgh GB 45 A5
Blythe Bridge GB 40 C1
Bø
Nordland N 194 B5
Telemark N 53 A5
Boal E 141 A4
Boan MNE 139 C5
Boario Terme I 120 B3
Boat of Garten GB 32 D3
Boa Vista P 154 B2
Boğazkale TR 23 A8
Boğazlıyan TR 23 B8
Boba H 111 B4
Bobadilla
Logroño E 143 B4
Málaga E 163 A3
Bobadilla del Campo
E 150 A2
Bobadilla del Monte
E 151 B4
Bóbbio I 120 C2
Bóbbio Pellice I 119 C4
Bobigny F 90 C2
Bobingen D 94 C2
Böblingen D 93 C5
Bobolice PL 68 B1
Boboras E 140 B2
Boboshevo BG 182 A4
Bobowa PL 99 B4
Bobrová CZ 97 B4
Bobrovitsa UA 13 C9
Bobrowice PL 75 C4
Bobrówko PL 75 B4
Boca de Huérgano
E 142 B2
Bocairent E 159 C3
Bočar SRB 126 B2
Bocchigliero I 174 B2
Boceguillas E 151 A4
Bochnia PL 99 B4
Bocholt
B 80 A1
D 80 A2
Bochov CZ 83 B5
Bochum D 80 A3
Bockara S 62 A4
Bockenem D 72 B3
Bockfliess A 97 C4
Bockhorn D 71 A5
Bočna SLO 123 A3
Bocognano F 180 A2
Boconád H 113 B4
Böcs H 113 A4
Boczów PL 75 B3
Boda S 50 A2
Böda S 62 A5
Boda
Stockholm S 51 B5
Värmland S 55 A3
Västernorrland S 200 D2
Bodafors S 62 A2
Boda Glasbruk S 63 B3
Bodajk H 112 B2
Boddam
Aberdeenshire
GB 33 D5
Shetland GB 33 B5
Boddin D 73 A4
Bödefeld-Freiheit
D 81 A4
Boden S 196 D4
Bodenmais D 95 B5
Bodenteich D 73 B3
Bodenwerder D 72 C2
Bodiam GB 45 B4
Bodinnick GB 42 B2

Bodio CH 120 A1
Bodjani SRB 125 B5
Bodmin GB 42 B2
Bodø N 194 C5
Bodonal de la Sierra
E 161 A3
Bodrum TR 188 B2
Bodstedt D 66 B1
Bodträskfors S 196 C3
Bodzanów PL 77 B5
Bodzanowice PL 86 B2
Bodzechów PL 87 B5
Bodzentyn PL 87 B4
Boecillo E 150 A3
Boëge F 118 A3
Boën F 117 B3
Bogács H 113 B4
Bogadmindszent
H 125 B4
Bogajo E 149 B3
Bogarra E 158 C1
Bogarre E 163 A4
Bogatić SRB 127 C1
Bogatynia PL 84 B2
Bogda RO 126 B3
Bogdaniec PL 75 B4
Boge S 57 C4
Bogen
D 95 C4
Nordland N 194 B7
Nordland N 194 C6
S 49 B4
Bogense DK 59 C3
Bognanco Fonti I 119 A5
Bognelv N 192 B6
Bognes N 194 B7
Bogno CH 120 A2
Bognor Regis GB 44 C3
Bogoria PL 87 B5
Bograngen S 49 B4
Boguchwaly PL 69 B5
Bogumiłowice PL 86 A3
Boguslav UA 13 D9
Boguszów-Gorce
PL 85 B4
Bogyiszló H 112 C2
Bohain-en-Vermandois
F 91 B3
Böheimkirchen A 110 A2
Bohinjska Bistrica
SLO 122 A2
Böhlen D 83 A4
Böhmenkirch D 94 C1
Bohmte D 71 B5
Bohonal de Ibor E 150 C2
Böhönye H 124 A3
Bohumin CZ 98 B2
Boiro E 140 B2
Bois-d'Amont F 105 C5
Boisseron F 131 B3
Boitzenburg D 74 A2
Boixols E 147 B2
Boizenburg D 73 A3
Bojadła PL 75 C4
Bojano I 170 B2
Bojanowo PL 85 A4
Bøjden DK 64 A3
Bojkovice CZ 98 B1
Bojná SK 98 C2
Bojnice SK 98 C2
Boka SRB 126 B2
Böklund D 64 B2
Bokod H 112 B2
Böksholm S 62 A2
Boksitogorsk RUS 9 C8
Bol HR 138 B2
Bolaños de Calatrava
E 157 B4
Bolayır TR 186 B1
Bolbec F 89 A4
Bölcske H 112 C2
Bolderslev DK 64 B2
Boldog H 112 B3
Boldva H 113 A4
Böle S 196 D4
Bolea E 145 B3
Bolekhiv UA 13 D5
Bolesławiec PL 84 A3
Boleszkowice PL 74 B3
Bolewice PL 75 B5
Bólgheri I 134 B3
Bolhrad UA 17 C8
Boliden S 200 B6
Bolimów PL 77 B5
Boliqueime P 160 B1
Boljevci SRB 127 C2
Boljkovci SRB 127 C2
Bolków PL 85 B4
Bollebygd S 60 B2
Bollène F 131 A3
Bólliga E 152 B1
Bollnäs S 50 A3
Bollstabruk S 200 D3
Bollullos E 161 B3
Bollullos par del
Condado E 161 B3
Bologna I 135 A4
Bologne F 105 A4
Bolognetta I 176 B2
Bolognola I 136 C2
Bologoye RUS 9 D9
Bolótana I 178 B2
Bolsena I 168 A1
Bolshaya Vradiyevka
UA 17 B9
Bolsover GB 40 B2
Bolstad S 54 B3
Bolsward NL 70 A2
Boltaña E 145 B4
Boltenhagen D 65 C4
Boltigen CH 106 C2
Bolton GB 38 A4
Bolu TR 187 B6
Bolungarvík IS 190 A2
Bolvadin TR 187 D6
Bóly H 125 B4
Bolzaneto I 133 A4
Bolzano I 108 C2
Bomba I 169 A4
Bombarral P 154 B1
Bömenzien D 73 B4
Bomlitz D 72 B2
Bømlo N 52 A1
Bøn N 48 B3
Bona F 104 B2
Bonaduz CH 107 C4
Bonanza E 161 C3
Boñar E 142 B1
Bonarbridge GB 32 D2
Bonárcado I 178 B2
Bonares E 161 B3
Bonäs S 50 A1
Bonassola I 134 A2
Bonawe GB 34 B2
Bondal N 53 A4
Bondeno I 121 C4
Bondorf D 93 C4
Bondstorp S 60 B3
Bon-Encontre F 129 B3
Bo'ness GB 35 B4
Bonete E 158 C2
Bonifacio F 180 B2
Bonigen CH 106 C2
Bonin PL 67 B5
Bonn D 80 B3
Bonnánaro I 178 B2
Bonnåsjøen N 194 C6
Bonnat F 116 A1
Bonndorf D 106 B3
Bonnétable F 102 A2
Bonnétage F 106 B1
Bonneuil-les-Eaux
F 90 B2
Bonneuil-Matours
F 115 B4
Bonneval F 103 A3
Bonneval-sur-Arc
F 119 B4
Bonneville F 118 A3
Bonnières-sur-Seine
F 90 B1
Bonnieux F 131 B4
Bönnigheim D 93 B5
Bonnyrigg GB 35 C4
Bonny-sur-Loire F 103 B4
Bono
E 145 B4
I 178 B3
Bonorva I 178 B2
Bønsnes N 48 B2
Bonyhád H 125 A4
Boom B 79 A4
Boos F 89 A5
Boostedt D 64 B3
Bootle
Cumbria GB 36 B3
Merseyside GB 38 A3
Bopfingen D 94 C2
Boppard D 81 B3
Boqueixón E 140 B2
Bor
CZ 95 B4
S 62 A2
SRB 16 C5
TR 23 C8
Boran-sur-Oise F 90 B2
Borås S 60 B2
Borba P 155 C3
Borbona I 169 A3
Borča SRB 127 C2
Borci BIH 139 B4
Borculo NL 71 B3
Bordány H 126 A1
Bordeaux F 128 B2
Bordeira P 160 B1
Bordesholm D 64 B3
Borðeyri IS 190 B4
Bordighera I 133 B3
Bording DK 59 B2
Bordón E 153 B3
Bore I 120 C2
Borehamwood GB 44 B3
Borek Strzeliński
PL 85 B5
Borek Wielkopolski
PL 76 C2
Boreland GB 36 A3
Borello I 135 A5
Borensberg S 56 B1
Borgafjäll S 199 A12
Borgarnes IS 190 C4
Borgentreich D 81 A5
Börger D 71 B4
Borger NL 71 B3
Borggård S 56 B1
Borghamn S 55 B5
Borghetta di Vara
I 134 A2
Borghetto d'Arróscia
I 133 A3
Borghetto Santo Spirito
I 133 A4
Borgholm S 62 B4
Borghorst D 71 B4
Bórgia I 175 C2
Borgloon B 79 B5
Børglum DK 58 A2
Borgo F 180 A2
Borgo alla Collina
I 135 B4
Borgo a Mozzano
I 134 B3
Borgoforte I 121 B3
Borgofranco d'Ivrea
I 119 B4
Borgomanero I 119 B5
Borgomasino I 119 B4
Borgonovo Val Tidone
I 120 B2
Borgo Pace I 135 B5
Borgorose I 169 A3
Borgo San Dalmazzo
I 133 A3
Borgo San Lorenzo
I 135 B4
Borgosésia I 119 B5
Borgo Val di Taro
I 134 A2
Borgo Valsugana
I 121 A4
Borgo Vercelli I 119 B5
Borgstena S 60 B3
Borgue GB 36 B2
Borgund N 47 A4
Borgvik S 55 A3
Borja E 144 C2
Bork D 80 A3
Borken D 80 A2
Borkenes N 194 B7
Børkop DK 59 C2
Borkowice PL 87 A4
Borkowo PL 77 B5
Borkum D 71 A3
Borlänge S 50 B2
Borlu TR 186 D3
Bormes-les-Mimosas
F 132 B2
Bórmio I 107 C5
Bormujos E 161 B3
Borna D 83 A4
Borne NL 71 B3
Bornes P 149 A2
Borne Sulinowo PL 68 B1
Bornheim D 80 B2
Bornhöved D 64 B3
Börnicke D 74 B1
Bornos E 162 B2
Borobia E 152 A2
Borodino RUS 9 E9
Borohrádek CZ 85 B4
Boronów PL 86 B2
Bórore I 178 B2
Borosźow PL 86 B2
Borota H 126 A1
Boroughbridge GB 40 A2
Borovany CZ 96 C2
Borovichi RUS 9 C8
Borovnica SLO 123 B3
Borovo HR 125 B4
Borovsk RUS 9 E10
Borovy CZ 96 B1
Borowa PL 85 A5
Borox E 151 B4
Borrby S 66 A3
Borre
DK 65 B5
N 54 A1
Borredá E 147 B2
Borrenes E 141 B4
Borriol E 159 A3
Borris
DK 59 C1
IRL 30 B2
Borris-in-Ossory
IRL 28 B4
Borrisokane IRL 28 B3
Borrisoleigh IRL 28 B4
Borrowdale GB 36 B3
Børrud N 49 C4
Borşa RO 17 B6
Borsdorf D 83 A4
Børselv N 193 B9
Borsfa H 111 C3
Borský Mikuláš
SK 98 C1
Borsodivánka H 113 B4
Borsodnádasd H 113 A4
Börte N 53 A3
Borth GB 39 B2
Bort-les-Orgues F 116 B2
Börtnan S 199 C10
Børtnes N 47 B6
Borup DK 61 D1
Boryslav UA 13 D5
Boryspil UA 13 C9
Boryszyn PL 75 B4
Borzęciczki PL 85 A5
Borzęcin PL 77 B5
Borzonasca I 134 A2
Borzyszkowy PL 68 A2
Borzytuchom PL 68 A2
Bosa I 178 B2
Bošáca SK 98 C1
Bosanci HR 123 B4
Bosanska Dubica
BIH 124 B2
Bosanska Gradiška
BIH 124 B3
Bosanska Kostajnica
BIH 124 B2
Bosanska Krupa
BIH 124 C2
Bosanski Brod
BIH 125 B3
Bosanski Novi
BIH 124 B2
Bosanski Petrovac
BIH 124 C2
Bosanski Šamac
BIH 125 B4
Bosansko Grahovo
BIH 138 A2
Bošany SK 98 C2
Bösárkány H 111 B4
Bosau D 65 B3
Bósca H 112 C3
Boscastle GB 42 B2
Bosco I 120 C1
Bosco Chiesanuova
I 121 B4
Bösdorf D 65 B3
Bösel D 71 A4
Bosham GB 44 C3
Bösingfeld D 72 B2
Bosjön S 49 C5
Boskoop NL 70 B1
Boskovice CZ 97 B4
Bošnjaci HR 125 B4
Bošnjane SRB 127 D3
Bossast E 145 B4
Bossolasco I 133 A4
Boštanj SLO 123 A4
Boston GB 41 C3
Bostrak N 53 A4
Böszénfa H 125 A3
Bot E 153 A4
Botajica BIH 125 C4
Bøte By DK 65 B4
Bothel GB 36 B3
Boticas P 148 A2
Botilsäter S 55 A4
Botngård N 198 B6
Botoš SRB 126 B2
Botoşani RO 17 B7
Botricello I 175 C2
Botsmark S 200 B6
Bottendorf D 81 A4
Bottesford GB 40 C3
Bottnaryd S 60 B3
Bottrop D 80 A2
Botunje SRB 127 C3
Bötzingen D 106 A2
Bouaye F 101 B4
Bouça P 149 A2
Boucau F 128 C1
Bouchain F 78 B3
Bouchoir F 90 B2
Boudreville F 105 B3
Boudry CH 106 C1
Bouesse F 103 C3
Bouguenais F 101 B4
Bouhy F 104 B2
Bouillargues F 131 B3
Bouillon B 91 B5
Bouilly F 104 A2
Bouin F 114 B2
Boulay-Moselle F 92 B2
Boulazac F 129 A3
Boule-d'Amont F 146 B3
Bouligny F 92 B1
Boulogne-sur-Gesse
F 145 A4
Boulogne-sur-Mer
F 78 B1
Bouloire F 102 B2
Bouquemaison F 78 B2
Bourbon-Lancy F 104 C2
Bourbon-l'Archambault
F 104 C2
Bourbonne-les-Bains
F 105 B4
Bourbourg F 78 B2
Bourbriac F 100 A2
Bourcefranc-le-Chapus
F 114 C2
Bourdeaux F 131 A4
Bouresse F 115 B4
Bourg F 128 A2
Bourg-Achard F 89 A4
Bourganeuf F 116 B1
Bourg-Argental F 117 B4
Bourg-de-Péage
F 117 B5
Bourg-de-Thizy F 117 A4
Bourg-de-Visa F 129 B3
Bourg-en-Bresse
F 118 A2
Bourges F 103 B4
Bourg-et-Comin F 91 B3
Bourg-Lastic F 116 B2
Bourg-Madame F 146 B2
Bourgneuf-en-Retz
F 114 A2
Bourgogne F 91 B4
Bourgoin-Jallieu
F 118 B2
Bourg-St Andéol
F 131 A3
Bourg-St Maurice
F 119 B3
Bourgtheroulde F 89 A4
Bourgueil F 102 B2
Bourmont F 105 A4
Bourne GB 40 C3
Bournemouth GB 43 B5
Bourneville F 89 A4
Bournezeau F 114 B2
Bourran F 129 B3
Bourret F 129 C4
Bourron-Marlotte F 90 C2
Bourton-on-The-Water
GB 44 B2
Boussac F 116 A2
Boussens F 145 A4
Boutersem B 79 B4
Bouttencourt F 90 B1
Bouvières F 131 A4
Bouvron F 101 B4
Bouxwiller F 93 C3
Bouzas E 140 B2
Bouzonville F 92 B2
Bova I 175 D1
Bovalino Marina I 175 C2
Bovallstrand S 54 B2
Bova Marina I 175 D1
Bovec SLO 122 A2
Bóveda E 141 B3
Bóvegno I 120 B3
Bovenau D 64 B2
Bovenden D 82 A1
Bøverdal N 198 D5
Boves F 90 B2
Bóves I 133 A3
Bovey Tracey GB 43 B3
Bovino I 171 B3
Bøvlingbjerg DK 58 B1
Bovolenta I 121 B4
Bovolone I 121 B4
Bowes GB 37 B5
Bowmore GB 34 C1
Bowness-on-
Windermere GB 36 B4
Box GB 43 A4
Boxberg
Baden-Württemberg
D 94 B1
Sachsen D 84 A2
Boxholm S 55 B6
Boxmeer NL 80 A1
Boxtel NL 79 A5
Boyabat TR 23 A8
Boyalıca TR 187 B4
Boyle IRL 26 C2
Bozan TR 187 C6
Božava HR 137 A3
Bozburun TR 188 C3
Bozcaada TR 186 C1
Bozdoğan TR 188 B3
Bożepole Wielkie
PL 68 A2
Boževac SRB 127 C3
Božice CZ 97 C4
Boži Dar CZ 83 B4
Bozkır TR 189 B7
Bozouls F 130 A1
Bozova TR 189 B5
Bozüyük TR 187 C5
Bózzolo I 121 B3
Bra I 119 C4
Braås S 62 A3
Brabrand DK 59 B3
Bracadale GB 31 B2
Bracciano I 168 A2
Bracieux F 103 B3
Bräcke S 199 C12
Brackenheim D 93 B5
Brackley GB 44 A2
Bracklin IRL 27 C4
Bracknell GB 44 B3
Brackwede D 72 C1
Braco GB 35 B4
Brad RO 16 B5
Bradford GB 40 B2
Bradford on Avon
GB 43 A4
Bradina BIH 139 B4
Brådland N 52 B2
Brædstrup DK 59 C2
Brae GB 33 A5
Braemar GB 32 D3
Braemore GB 32 D1
Braga P 148 A1
Bragança P 149 A3
Brăila RO 17 C7
Braine F 91 B3
Braine-le-Comte B 79 B4
Braintree GB 45 B4
Braives B 79 B5
Brake D 72 A1
Brakel
B 79 B3
D 81 A5
Bräkne-Hoby S 63 B3
Brålanda S 54 B3
Bralin PL 86 A1
Brallo di Pregola I 120 C2
Bram F 146 A3
Bramafan F 132 B2
Bramberg am
Wildkogel A 109 B3
Bramdrupdam DK 59 C2
Bramming DK 59 C1
Brampton GB 37 B4
Bramsche D 71 B4
Branca I 136 B1
Brancaleone Marina
I 175 D2
Brancaster GB 41 C4
Brand
Nieder Östereich
A 96 C3
Vorarlberg A 107 B4
Brandbu N 48 B2
Brande DK 59 C2
Brande-Hornerkirchen
D 64 C2
Brandenberg A 108 B2
Brandenburg D 73 B5
Brand-Erbisdorf D 83 B5
Brandis D 83 A4
Brando F 180 A2
Brandomil E 140 A2
Brandon GB 45 A4
Brandshagen D 66 B2
Brandval N 49 B4
Brandýs nad Labem
CZ 84 B2
Branice PL 98 A1
Braničevo SRB 127 C3
Braniewo PL 69 A4
Branik SLO 122 B2
Brankovina SRB 127 C1
Branky CZ 98 B1
Branne F 128 B2
Brannenburg-
Degerndorf D 108 B3
Brantôme F 115 C4
Branzi I 120 A2
Bras d'Asse F 132 B2
Braskereidfoss N 48 B3
Braslaw BY 13 A7
Braşov RO 17 C6
Brasparts F 100 A2
Brassac F 130 B1
Brassac-les-Mines
F 116 B3
Brasschaat B 79 A4
Brastad S 54 B2
Břasy CZ 96 B1
Brąszewice PL 86 A2
Bratislava SK 111 A4
Brattfors S 55 A5
Brattvåg N 198 C3
Bratunac BIH 127 C1
Braubach D 81 B3
Braunau A 95 C5
Braunfels D 81 B4
Braunlage D 82 A2
Braunsbedra D 83 A3
Braunschweig D 73 B3
Bray IRL 30 A2
Bray Dunes F 78 A2
Bray-sur-Seine F 90 C3
Bray-sur-Somme F 90 B2
Brazatortas E 157 B3
Brazey-en-Plaine
F 105 B4
Brbinj HR 137 A4
Brčko BIH 125 C4
Brdani SRB 127 D2
Brdów PL 76 B3
Brea de Tajo E 151 B4
Brécey F 88 B2
Brechen D 81 B4
Brechin GB 35 B5
Brecht B 79 A4
Brecketfeld D 80 A3
Břeclav CZ 97 C4
Brecon GB 39 C3
Brécy F 103 B4
Breda
E 147 C3
NL 79 A4
Bredaryd S 60 B3
Bredbyn S 200 C4
Breddin D 73 B5
Bredebro DK 64 A1
Bredelar D 81 A4
Bredenfelde D 74 A2
Bredsjö S 50 C1
Bredstedt D 64 B1
Bredsten DK 59 C2
Bredträsk S 200 C4
Bredviken S 195 D5
Bree B 80 A1
Bregana HR 123 B4
Breganze I 121 B4
Bregenz A 107 B4
Bréhal F 88 B2
Brehna D 83 A4
Breiðdalsvík IS 191 C11
Breidenbach F 93 B3
Breil-sur-Roya F 133 B3
Breisach D 106 A2
Breitenbach
CH 106 B2
D 81 B5
Breitenberg D 96 C1
Breitenfelde D 73 A3
Breitengussbach D 94 B2
Breivikbotn N 192 B6
Brejning DK 59 C2
Brekke N 46 A2
Brekken N 199 C8
Brekkestø N 53 B4
Brekkvasselv N 199 A10
Brekstad N 198 B6
Breland N 53 B3
Bremanger N 198 D1
Bremen D 72 A1
Bremerhaven D 72 A1
Bremervörde D 72 A2
Bremgarten CH 106 B3
Bremsnes N 198 B4
Brem-sur-Mer F 114 B2
Brenderup DK 59 C2
Brenes E 162 A2
Brengova SLO 110 C2
Brenna PL 98 B2
Breno I 120 B3
Brénod F 118 A2
Brensbach D 93 B4
Brentwood GB 45 B4
Brescello I 121 C3
Bréscia I 120 B3
Breskens NL 79 A3
Bresles F 90 B2
Bresnica SRB 127 D2
Bressana I 120 B2
Bressanone I 108 C2
Bressuire F 102 C1
Brest
BY 13 B5
F 100 A1
HR 122 B2
Brestač SRB 127 C1
Brestanica SLO 123 A4
Brestova HR 123 B3
Brestovac HR 125 B3
Bretenoux F 129 B4
Breteuil
Eure F 89 B4
Oise F 90 B2
Brétigny-sur-Orge
F 90 C2
Bretten D 93 B4
Bretteville-sur-Laize
F 89 A3
Brettheim D 94 B2
Breuil-Cervínia I 119 B4
Breukelen NL 70 B2
Brevik
N 53 A5
Stockholm S 57 A4
Västra Götaland
S 55 B5
Breza BIH 139 A4
Brežice SLO 123 B4
Bréziers F 132 A2
Breznica HR 124 A2
Breznica Našička
HR 125 B4
Březnice CZ 96 B1
Brezno SK 99 C3
Brezolles F 89 B5
Březovánad Svitavou
CZ 97 B4
Brezovápod Bradlom
SK 98 C1
Brezovica
SK 99 B4
SLO 123 A3
Brezovo Polje Selo
BIH 125 C4
Briançon F 118 C3
Brianconnet F 132 B2
Briare F 103 B4
Briatexte F 129 C4
Briático I 175 C2
Briaucourt F 105 A4
Bribir HR 123 B3
Bricquebec F 88 A2
Bridgend
Argyll & Bute GB 34 C1
Bridgend GB 39 C3
Bridge of Cally GB 35 B4
Bridge of Don GB 33 D4
Bridge of Earn GB 35 B4
Bridge of Orchy
GB 34 B3
Bridgnorth GB 39 B4
Bridgwater GB 43 A4
Břidličná CZ 98 B1
Bridlington GB 41 A3
Bridport GB 43 B4
Briec F 100 A1
Brie-Comte-Robert
F 90 C2
Brienne-le-Château
F 91 C4
Brienon-sur-Armançon
F 104 B2
Brienz CH 106 C3
Brienza I 172 B1
Briesen D 74 B3
Brieskow Finkenheerd
D 74 B3
Brietlingen D 72 A3
Brieva de Cameros
E 143 B4
Briey F 92 B1
Brig CH 119 A5
Brigg GB 40 B3
Brighouse GB 40 B2
Brightlingsea GB 45 B5
Brighton GB 44 C3
Brignogan-Plage
F 100 A1
Brignoles F 132 B2
Brigstock GB 40 C3
Brihuega E 151 B5
Brijuni HR 122 C2
Brillon-en-Barrois
F 91 C5
Brilon D 81 A4
Brimnes N 46 B3
Brinches P 160 A2
Brindisi I 173 B3
Brinje HR 123 B4
Brinon-sur-Beuvron
F 104 B2
Brinon-sur-Sauldre
F 103 B4
Brinyan GB 33 B3
Brión E 140 B2
Briones E 143 B4
Brionne F 89 A4
Brioude F 117 B3
Brioux-sur-Boutonne
F 115 B3
Briouze F 89 B3
Briscous F 144 A2
Brisighella I 135 A4
Brissac-Quincé F 102 B1
Brissago CH 120 A1
Bristol GB 43 A4
Brive-la-Gaillarde
F 129 A4
Briviesca E 143 B3
Brixham GB 43 B3
Brixlegg A 108 B2
Brjánslækur IS 190 B2
Brka BIH 125 C4
Brnaze HR 138 B2
Brněnec CZ 97 B4
Brno CZ 97 B4
Bro S 57 A3
Broadclyst GB 43 B3
Broadford
GB 31 B3
IRL 28 B3
Broad Haven GB 39 C1
Broadstairs GB 45 B5
Broadstone GB 43 B4
Broadway GB 44 A2
Broager DK 64 B2
Broaryd S 60 B3
Broby S 61 C4
Brobyværk DK 59 C3
Bročanac BIH 138 B3
Brocas F 128 B2
Brock D 71 B4
Brockel D 72 A2
Brockenhurst GB 44 C2
Broczyno PL 75 A5
Brod MK 182 B3
Brodalen S 54 B2
Broddbo S 50 C3
Brodek u Přerova
CZ 98 B1
Broden-bach D 80 B3
Brodick GB 34 C2
Brod na Kupi HR 123 B3
Brodnica PL 69 B4
Brodnica Graniczna
PL 68 A3
Brodowe Łąki PL 77 A6
Brody
Lubuskie PL 75 B4
Lubuskie PL 84 A2
Mazowieckie PL 77 B5
UA 13 C6
Broglie F 89 B4
Brójce PL 75 B4
Brokind S 56 B1
Brolo I 177 A3
Brome D 73 B3
Bromley GB 45 B4
Bromölla S 63 B2
Bromont-Lamothe
F 116 B2
Brömsebro S 63 B3
Bromsgrove GB 44 A1
Bromyard GB 39 B4
Bronchales E 152 B2
Bronco E 149 B3
Brønderslev DK 58 A2
Broni I 120 B2
Brønnøysund N 195 E3
Brøns DK 59 C1
Bronte I 177 B3
Bronzani Mejdan
BIH 124 C2
Bronzolo I 121 A4
Broons F 101 A3
Broquies F 130 A1
Brora GB 32 C3
Brørup DK 59 C2
Brösarp S 63 C2
Brossac F 115 C3
Brostrud N 47 B5
Brotas P 154 C2
Brötjärna S 50 B2
Broto E 145 B3
Brottby S 57 A4
Brøttum N 48 A2

Brou F 103 A3
Brouage F 114 C2
Brough GB 37 B4
Broughshane GB 27 B4
Broughton GB 35 C4
Broughton-in-Furness GB 36 B3
Broumov CZ 85 B4
Broût-Vernet F 116 A3
Brouvelieures F 106 A1
Brouwershaven NL 79 A3
Brovary UA 13 C9
Brovst DK 58 A2
Brownhills GB 40 C2
Brozas E 155 B4
Brozzo I 120 B3
Brtnice CZ 97 B3
Brtonigla HR 122 B2
Bruay-la-Buissière F 78 B2
Bruchhausen-Vilsen D 72 B2
Bruchsal D 93 B4
Bruck D 95 B4
Brück D 74 B1
Bruck an der Grossglocknerstrasse A 109 B3
Bruck an der Leitha A 111 A3
Bruck an der Mur A 110 B2
Brückl A 110 C1
Bruckmühl D 108 B2
Brue-Auriac F 132 B1
Brüel D 65 C4
Bruen CH 107 C3
Bruère-Allichamps F 103 C4
Bruff IRL 29 B3
Bruflat N 47 B6
Brugg CH 106 B3
Brugge B 78 A3
Brüggen D 80 A2
Brühl D 80 B2
Bruinisse NL 79 A4
Brûlon F 102 B1
Brumano I 120 B2
Brumath F 93 C3
Brummen NL 70 B3
Brumov-Bylnice CZ 98 B2
Brumunddal N 48 B2
Brunau D 73 B4
Brunehamel F 91 B4
Brünen D 80 A2
Brunete E 151 B3
Brunflo S 199 B11
Brunico I 108 C2
Brunkeberg N 53 A4
Brunn D 74 A2
Brunnen CH 107 C3
Brunsbüttel D 64 C2
Brunssum NL 80 B1
Bruntál CZ 98 B1
Brušane HR 137 A4
Brusasco I 119 B5
Brusio CH 120 A3
Brusno SK 99 C3
Brusque F 130 B1
Brussels = Bruxelles B 79 B4
Brusson I 119 B4
Brüssow D 74 A3
Brusy PL 68 B2
Bruton GB 43 A4
Bruvno HR 138 A1
Bruvoll N 48 B3
Bruxelles = Brussels B 79 B4
Bruyères F 106 A1
Bruz F 101 A4
Bruzaholm S 62 A3
Brwinów PL 77 B5
Brynamman GB 39 C3
Bryncrug GB 39 B2
Bryne N 52 B1
Brynmawr GB 39 C3
Bryrup DK 59 B2
Brzeg PL 85 B5
Brzeg Dolny PL 85 A4
Brześć Kujawski PL 76 B3
Brzesko PL 99 B4
Brzeszcze PL 99 B3
Brzezie PL 68 B1
Brzeziny
Łódzkie PL 87 A3
Wielkopolskie PL 86 A2
Brzeźnica PL 84 A3
Brzeźnica Nowa PL 86 A3
Brzeźno PL 75 A4
Brzotin SK 99 C4
Brzozie Lubawskie PL 69 B4
Bua S 60 B2
Buarcos P 148 B1
Buaveg N 52 A1
Bubbio I 119 C5
Bubry F 100 B2
Buca TR 188 A2
Bucak TR 189 B5
Bučany SK 98 C1
Buccheri I 177 B3
Buccino I 172 B1
Bucelas P 154 C1
Buch
Bayern D 94 C2
Bayern D 95 C4
Buchach UA 13 D6
Bucharest = Bucureşti RO 17 C7
Buchbach D 95 C4
Buchboden A 107 B4
Buchen D 94 B1
Büchen D 73 A3
Buchenberg D 107 B5
Buchères F 104 A3
Buchholz D 72 A2
Buchloe D 108 A1
Buchlovice CZ 98 B1
Buchlyvie GB 34 B3
Bucholz D 73 A5
Buchs CH 107 B4
Buchy F 89 A5
Bückeburg D 72 B2
Buckfastleigh GB 42 B3
Buckhaven GB 35 B4
Buckie GB 33 D4
Buckingham GB 44 A3
Buckley GB 38 A3
Bückwitz D 73 B5
Bučovice CZ 97 B5
Bucsa H 113 B5
Bucureşti = Bucharest RO 17 C7
Bucy-lés-Pierreport F 91 B3
Buczek PL 86 A3
Bud N 198 C3
Budakalasz H 112 B3
Budakeszi H 112 B2
Budal N 199 C7
Budaörs H 112 B2
Budapest H 112 B3
Búðardalur IS 190 B4
Budča SK 99 C3
Buddusò I 178 B3
Bude GB 42 B2
Budeč CZ 97 B3
Büdelsdorf D 64 B2
Budens P 160 B1
Budia E 151 B5
Budimlić-Japra BIH 124 C2
Büdingen D 81 B5
Budinšćina HR 124 A2
Budišov CZ 98 B1
Budleigh Salterton GB 43 B3
Budmerice SK 98 C1
Budoni I 178 B3
Búdrio I 135 A4
Budva MNE 16 D3
Budyněnad Ohří CZ 84 B2
Budziszewice PL 87 A3
Budzyń PL 76 B1
Bue N 52 B1
Bueña E 152 B2
Buenache de Alarcón E 158 B1
Buenache de la Sierra E 152 B2
Buenaventura E 150 B3
Buenavista de Valdavia E 142 B2
Buendia E 151 B5
Bueu E 140 B2
Buezo E 143 B3
Bugac H 112 C3
Bugarra E 159 B3
Bugeat F 116 B1
Buggerru I 179 C2
Bugojno BIH 138 A3
Bugøyfjord N 193 C13
Bugøynes N 193 C13
Bugyi H 112 B3
Buharkent TR 188 B3
Bühl
Baden-Württemberg D 93 C4
Bayern D 107 B5
Bühlertal D 93 C4
Bühlertann D 94 B1
Buia I 122 A2
Builth Wells GB 39 B3
Buin N 47 B6
Buis-les-Baronnies F 131 A4
Buitenpost NL 70 A3
Buitrago del Lozoya E 151 B4
Bujalance E 157 C3
Bujaraloz E 153 A3
Buje HR 122 B2
Bujedo E 143 B3
Bük H 111 B3
Buk PL 75 B5
Bükkösd H 125 A3
Bükkzsérc H 113 B4
Bukovci SLO 124 A1
Bukowiec PL 75 B5
Bukowina Tatrzańska PL 99 B4
Bukownica PL 86 A2
Bukowno PL 86 B3
Bülach CH 107 B3
Búland IS 191 D7
Buldan TR 188 A3
Bulgnéville F 105 A4
Bulgurca TR 188 A2
Bülkau D 64 C1
Bulken N 46 B3
Bulkowo PL 77 B5
Bullas E 164 A3
Bulle CH 106 C2
Büllingen B 80 B2
Bullmark S 200 B6
Bulqizë AL 182 B2
Buna BIH 139 B3
Bunahowen IRL 26 B1
Bunbeg IRL 26 A2
Bunclody IRL 30 B2
Buncrana IRL 27 A3
Bunde D 71 A4
Bünde D 72 B1
Bundoran IRL 26 B2
Bunessan GB 34 B1
Bungay GB 45 A5
Bunge S 57 C5
Bunić HR 123 C4
Bunmahon IRL 30 B1
Bunnyconnellan IRL 26 B1
Buño E 140 A2
Buñol E 159 B3
Bunratty IRL 29 B3
Bunsbeek B 79 B4
Buñuel E 144 C2
Bunyola E 166 B2
Buonabitácolo I 172 B1
Buonalbergo I 170 B2
Buonconvento I 135 B4
Buonvicino I 174 B1
Burano I 122 B1
Burbach D 81 B4
Burcei I 179 C3
Burdons-sur-Rognon F 105 A4
Burdur TR 189 B5
Bureå S 2 D7
Burela E 141 A3
Büren D 81 A4
Büren an der Aare CH 106 B2
Burford GB 44 B2
Burg
Cottbus D 84 A2
Magdeburg D 73 B4
Schleswig-Holstein D 64 C2
Burgas BG 17 D7
Burgau
A 111 B3
D 94 C2
P 160 B1
Burg auf Fehmarn D 65 B4
Burgbernheim D 94 B2
Burgdorf
CH 106 B2
D 72 B3
Burgebrach D 94 B2
Bürgel D 83 B3
Burgess Hill GB 44 C3
Burghaslach D 94 B2
Burghausen D 109 A3
Burghead GB 32 D3
Burgheim D 94 C3
Burgh le Marsh GB 41 B4
Búrgio I 176 B2
Burgkirchen D 109 A3
Burgkunstadt D 82 B3
Burglengenfeld D 95 B4
Burgo P 148 B1
Burgoberbach D 94 B2
Burgohondo E 150 B3
Burgos E 143 B3
Burgsinn D 82 B1
Burgstädt D 83 B4
Burgstall D 73 B4
Burg Stargard D 74 A2
Burgsvik S 57 C4
Burgui E 144 B3
Burguillos E 162 A2
Burguillos del Cerro E 155 C4
Burguillos de Toledo E 151 C4
Burhaniye TR 186 C1
Burhave D 71 A5
Burie F 114 C3
Burjassot E 159 B3
Burk D 94 B2
Burkhardtsdorf D 83 B4
Burlada E 144 B2
Burladingen D 107 A4
Burlage D 71 A4
Burness GB 33 B4
Burnham GB 44 B3
Burnham Market GB 41 C4
Burnham-on-Crouch GB 45 B4
Burnham-on-Sea GB 43 A4
Burniston GB 40 A3
Burnley GB 40 B1
Burntisland GB 35 B4
Burón E 142 A1
Buronzo I 119 B5
Burovac SRB 127 C3
Burow D 74 A2
Burravoe GB 33 A5
Burrel AL 182 B2
Burret F 146 B2
Burriana E 159 B3
Burry Port GB 39 C2
Bürs A 107 B4
Bursa TR 186 B4
Burseryd S 60 B3
Bürstadt D 93 B4
Burton GB 37 B4
Burton Agnes GB 41 A3
Burton Bradstock GB 43 B4
Burton Latimer GB 44 A3
Burton upon Stather GB 40 B3
Burton upon Trent GB 40 C2
Burträsk S 200 B6
Burujón E 151 C3
Burwell GB 45 A4
Burwick GB 33 C4
Bury GB 40 B1
Bury St Edmunds GB 45 A4
Burzenin PL 86 A2
Busachi I 179 B2
Busalla I 134 A1
Busana I 134 A3
Busano I 119 B4
Busca I 133 A3
Busch D 73 B4
Buševec HR 124 B2
Bushat AL 182 B1
Bushey GB 44 B3
Bushmills GB 27 A4
Bušince SK 112 A3
Buskhyttan S 56 B2
Busko-Zdrój PL 87 B4
Busot E 159 C3
Busovača BIH 139 A3
Busquistar E 163 B4
Bussang F 106 B1
Busseto I 120 C3
Bussière-Badil F 115 C4
Bussière-Poitevine F 115 B4
Bussolengo I 121 B3
Bussoleno I 119 B4
Bussum NL 70 B2
Busto Arsízio I 120 B1
Büsum D 64 B1
Butera I 177 B3
Butgenbach B 80 B2
Butler's Bridge IRL 27 B3
Butryny PL 77 A5
Bütschwil CH 107 B4
Buttermere GB 36 B3
Buttevant IRL 29 B3
Buttle S 57 C4
Buttstädt D 82 A3
Butzbach D 81 B4
Bützfleth D 72 A2
Bützow D 65 C4
Buxières-les-Mines F 104 C1
Buxtehude D 72 A2
Buxton GB 40 B2
Buxy F 104 C3
Büyükçekmece TR 186 A3
Büyükkariştiran TR 186 A2
Büyükorhan TR 186 C3
Buzançais F 103 C3
Buzancy F 91 B4
Buzău RO 17 C7
Buzet HR 122 B2
Buziaş RO 126 B3
Buzsák H 111 C4
Buzy F 145 A3
By S 50 B3
Byala BG 17 D6
Byaroza BY 13 B6
Byczyna PL 86 A2
Bydalen S 199 B10
Bydgoszcz PL 76 A3
Bygdin N 47 A5
Bygdsiljum S 200 B6
Bygland N 53 B3
Byglandsfjord N 53 B3
Bygstad N 46 A2
Bykhaw BY 13 B9
Bykle N 52 A3
Bylderup-Bov DK 64 B2
Byrkjedal N 52 B2
Byrkjelo N 198 D3
Byrum DK 58 A3
Byšice CZ 84 B2
Byske S 2 D7
Býškovice CZ 98 B1
Bysław PL 76 A2
Bystré CZ 97 B4
Bystřice CZ 96 B2
Bystrice CZ 98 B2
Bystřice nad Pernštejnem CZ 97 B4
Bystřice pod Hostýnem CZ 98 B1
Bystrzyca Kłodzka PL 85 B4
Bytča SK 98 B2
Bytnica PL 75 B4
Bytom PL 86 B2
Bytom Odrzański PL 85 A3
Bytów PL 68 A2
Byxelkrok S 62 A5
Bzenec CZ 98 C1
Bzince SK 98 C1

C

Çağa TR 187 B7
Cabacos P 154 B2
Cabaj-Čápor SK 98 C2
Cabana E 140 A2
Cabanac-et-Villagrains F 128 B2
Cabañaquinta E 142 A1
Cabanas P 160 B2
Cabañas del Castillo E 156 A2
Cabañas de Yepes E 151 C4
Cabanelles E 147 B3
Cabanes E 153 B4
Cabanillas E 144 B2
Čabar HR 123 B3
Cabasse F 132 B2
Cabdella E 146 B2
Cabeceiras de Basto P 148 A1
Cabeço de Vide P 155 B3
Cabella Ligure I 120 C2
Cabeza del Buey E 156 B2
Cabeza la Vaca E 161 A3
Cabezamesada E 151 C4
Cabezarados E 157 B3
Cabezarrubias del Puerto E 157 B3
Cabezas del Villar E 150 B2
Cabezas Rubias E 161 B2
Cabezón E 142 C2
Cabezón de la Sal E 142 A2
Cabezón de Liébana E 142 A2
Cabezuela E 151 A4
Cabezuela del Valle E 149 B4
Cabo de Gata E 164 C2
Cabo de Palos E 165 B4
Cabolafuenta E 152 A1
Cabourg F 89 A3
Cabra
E 163 A3
P 148 B2
Cabrach GB 32 D3
Cabra del Santo Cristo E 163 A4
Cábras I 179 C2
Cabreiro P 140 C2
Cabreiros E 140 A3
Cabrejas E 152 B1
Cabrela P 154 C2
Cabrillas E 149 B3
Cabuna HR 125 B3
Cacabelos E 141 B4
Čačak SRB 127 D2
Cáccamo I 176 B2
Caccuri I 174 B2
Cacela P 160 B2
Cacém P 154 C1
Cáceres E 155 B4
Cachafeiro E 140 B2
Cachopo P 160 B2
Čachtice SK 98 C1
Cacin E 163 A4
Čačinci HR 125 B3
Cadafais P 154 C1
Cadalen F 129 C5
Cadalso E 149 B3
Cadaqués E 147 B4
Cadaval P 154 B1
Cadavedo E 141 A4
Čadavica BIH 138 A2
Čadca SK 98 B2
Cadéac F 145 B4
Cadelbosco di Sopra I 121 C3
Cadenazzo CH 120 A1
Cadenberge D 64 C2
Cadenet F 131 B4
Cadeuil F 114 C3
Cádiar E 164 C1
Cadillac F 128 B2
Cádiz E 162 B1
Čadjavica HR 125 B3
Cadouin F 129 B3
Cadours F 129 C4
Cadrete E 152 A3
Caen F 89 A3
Caerleon GB 39 C4
Caernarfon GB 38 A2
Caerphilly GB 39 C3
Caersws GB 39 B3
Cafede P 155 B3
Caggiano I 172 B1
Cagli I 136 B1
Cágliari I 179 C3
Čaglin HR 125 B3
Cagnano Varano I 171 B3
Cagnes-sur-Mer F 132 B3
Caher IRL 29 B4
Caherciveen IRL 29 C1
Caherdaniel IRL 29 C1
Cahors F 129 B4
Cahul MD 17 C8
Caiazzo I 170 B2
Caion E 140 A2
Cairndow GB 34 B3
Cairnryan GB 36 B1
Cairo Montenotte I 133 A4
Caister-on-Sea GB 41 C5
Caistor GB 41 B3
Caivano I 170 C2
Cajarc F 129 B4
Čajniče BIH 139 B5
Çakırlar TR 189 C5
Çakmak TR 187 C6
Čakovec HR 124 A2
Çal TR 189 A4
Cala E 161 B3
Calabritto I 172 B1
Calaceite E 153 B4
Calacuccia F 180 A2
Cala d'Or E 167 B3
Calaf E 147 C2
Calafat RO 17 C5
Calafell E 147 C2
Cala Galdana E 167 B3
Cala Gonone I 178 B3
Calahonda
Granada E 163 B4
Málaga E 163 B3
Calahorra E 144 B2
Calais F 78 B1
Cala Llonga E 166 C1
Calalzo di Cadore I 109 C3
Cala Millor E 167 B3
Calamocha E 152 B2
Calamonte E 155 C4
Cala Morell E 167 A3
Calanais GB 31 A2
Calañas E 161 B3
Calanda E 153 B3
Calangiánus I 178 B3
Călăraşi RO 17 C7
Cala Ratjada E 167 B3
Calascibetta I 177 B3
Calasetta I 179 C2
Calasparra E 164 A3
Calatafimi I 176 B1
Calatayud E 152 A2
Calatorao E 152 A2
Calau D 84 A1
Calbe D 73 C4
Calcena E 152 A2
Calcinelli I 136 B1
Calco I 120 B2
Caldarola I 136 B2
Caldaro sulla strada del Vino I 121 A4
Caldas da Rainha P 154 B1
Caldas de Bo i E 145 B4
Caldas de Malavella E 147 C3
Caldas de Reis E 140 B2
Caldas de San Jorge P 148 B1
Caldas de Vizela P 148 A1
Caldaso de los Vidrios E 150 B3
Caldbeck GB 36 B3
Caldearenas E 145 B3
Caldelas P 148 A1
Calders E 147 C2
Caldes de Montbui E 147 C3
Caldicot GB 39 C4
Caldirola I 120 C2
Caledon GB 27 B4
Calella
Barcelona E 147 C3
Girona E 147 C4
Calenzana F 180 A1
Calera de León E 161 A3
Calera y Chozas E 150 C3
Caleruega E 143 C3
Caleruela E 150 C2
Cales de Mallorca E 167 B3
Calestano I 134 A3
Calfsound GB 33 B4
Calgary GB 34 B1
Calimera I 173 B4
Calitri I 172 B1
Calizzano I 133 A4
Callac F 100 A2
Callan IRL 30 B1
Callander GB 35 B3
Callas F 132 B2
Calliano
Piemonte I 119 B5
Trentino Alto Adige I 121 B4
Callington GB 42 B2
Callosa de Ensarriá E 159 C3
Callosa de Segura E 165 A4
Callús E 147 C2
Čalma SRB 127 B1
Calmbach D 93 C4
Calne GB 43 A5
Calolziocorte I 120 B2
Calonge E 147 C4
Čalovec SK 112 B1
Calpe E 159 C4
Caltabellotta I 176 B2
Caltagirone I 177 B3
Caltanissetta I 177 B3
Caltavuturo I 176 B2
Çaltılıbük TR 186 C3
Caltojar E 151 A5
Caluire-et-Cuire F 117 B4
Caluso I 119 B4
Calvello I 172 B1
Calvi F 180 A1
Calviá E 166 B2
Calvinet F 116 C2
Calvisson F 131 B3
Calvörde D 73 B4
Calw D 93 C4
Calzada de Calatrava E 157 B4
Calzada de Valdunciel E 150 A2
Calzadilla de los Barros E 155 C4
Cam GB 43 A4
Camaiore I 134 B3
Camarasa E 145 C4
Camarena E 151 B3
Camarès F 130 B1
Camaret-sur-Aigues F 131 A3
Camaret-sur-Mer F 100 A1
Camarillas E 153 B3
Camariñas E 140 A1
Camarma E 151 B4
Camarzana de Tera E 141 B4
Camas E 162 A1
Camastra I 176 B2
Cambados E 140 B2
Cambarinho P 148 B1
Camberley GB 44 B3
Cambil E 163 A4
Cambligeu F 78 B2
Cambo-les-Bains F 144 A2
Camborne GB 42 B1
Cambrai F 78 B3
Cambre E 140 A2
Cambridge GB 45 A4
Cambrils E 147 C2
Cambs D 65 C4
Camburg D 83 A3
Camden GB 44 B3
Cameleño E 142 A2
Camelford GB 42 B2
Çameli TR 189 B4
Camelle E 140 A1
Camerano I 136 B2
Camerino I 136 B2
Camerota I 172 B1
Camigliatello Silano I 174 B2
Caminha P 148 A1
Caminomorisco E 149 B3
Caminreal E 152 B2
Camisano Vicentino I 121 B4
Camlıdere TR 187 B7
Cammarata I 176 B2
Camogli I 134 A2
Camors F 100 B3
Camp IRL 29 B2
Campagna I 172 B1
Campagnano di Roma I 168 A2
Campagnático I 135 C4
Campan F 145 A4
Campana I 174 B2
Campanario E 156 B2
Campanillas E 163 B3
Campano E 162 B1
Campaspero E 151 A3
Campbeltown GB 34 C2
Campello E 165 A4
Campelos P 154 B1
Campi Bisénzio I 135 B4
Campico López E 165 B3
Campíglia Marittima I 134 B3
Campillo de Altobuey E 158 B2
Campillo de Aragón E 152 A2
Campillo de Arenas E 163 A4
Campillo de Llerena E 156 B2
Campillos E 162 A3
Câmpina RO 17 C6
Campi Salentina I 173 B4
Campli I 136 C2
Campo E 145 B4
Campobasso I 170 B2
Campobello di Licata I 176 B2
Campobello di Mazara I 176 B1
Campo da Feira E 140 A3
Campodársego I 121 B4
Campo de Bacerros E 141 B3
Campo de Caso E 142 A1
Campo de Criptana E 157 A4
Campodolcino I 120 A2
Campofelice di Roccella I 176 B2
Campofiorito I 176 B2
Campofórmido I 122 A2
Campofranco I 176 B2
Campofrio E 161 B3
Campogalliano I 121 C3
Campo Ligure I 133 A4
Campolongo I 109 C3
Campo Lugar E 156 A2
Campo Maior P 155 B3
Campomanes E 141 A5
Campomarino I 170 B3
Campo Molino I 133 A3
Campomono F 180 B1
Campo Real E 151 B4
Camporeale I 176 B2
Camporeggiano I 136 B1
Camporrells E 145 C4
Camporrobles E 158 B2
Campos P 148 A2
Camposa P 148 A1
Camposampiero I 121 B4
Camposanto I 121 C4
Campos del Port E 167 B3
Camposines E 153 A4
Campotéjar E 163 A4
Campotosto I 169 A3
Campo Túres I 108 C2
Camprodón E 147 B3
Campsegret F 129 B3
Camrose GB 39 C1
Camuñas E 157 A4
Çamyolu TR 189 C7
Çan TR 186 B2
Cana I 135 C4
Cañada del Hoyo E 158 B2
Cañadajuncosa E 158 B1
Cañada Rosal E 162 A2
Čanak HR 123 C4
Çanakkale TR 186 B1
Canale I 119 C4
Canales
Asturias E 141 B5
Castellón de la Plana E 159 B3
Canals E 159 C3
Canal San Bovo I 121 A4
Cañamares E 152 B1
Cañamero E 156 A2
Cañar E 163 B4
Cañate la Real E 162 B2
Cañaveral E 155 B4
Cañaveral de León E 161 A3
Cañaveras E 152 B1
Cañaveruelas E 151 B5
Canazei I 108 C2
Cancale F 88 B2
Cancellara I 172 B1
Cancello ed Arnone I 170 B2
Cancon F 129 B3
Canda E 141 B4
Candamil E 140 A3
Candanchu E 145 B3
Çandarlı TR 186 D1
Candas E 141 A5
Candasnos E 153 A4
Candé F 101 B4
Candela I 172 A1
Candelario E 150 B2
Candeleda E 150 B2
Cándia Lomellina I 120 B1
Candide Casamazzagno I 109 C3
Candin E 141 B4
Candosa P 148 B2
Canecas P 154 C1
Canelli I 119 C5
Canena E 157 B4
Canencia E 151 B4
Canero E 141 A4
Canet F 130 B2
Canet de Mar E 147 C3
Canet d'en Berenguer E 159 B3
Cañete E 158 A2
Cañete de las Torres E 163 A3
Canet-Plage F 146 B4
Canfranc E 145 B3
Cangas
Lugo E 141 A3
Pontevedra E 140 B2

Cangas de Narcea E 141 A4
Cangas de Onís E 142 A1
Canha P 154 C2
Canhestros P 160 A1
Canicattì I 176 B2
Canicattini Bagni I 177 B4
Canicosa de la Sierra E 143 C3
Caniles E 164 B2
Canillas de Aceituno E 163 B3
Canino I 168 A1
Canisy F 88 A2
Cañizal E 150 A2
Cañizo E 142 C1
Canjáyar E 164 C2
Çankırı TR 23 A7
Cannai I 179 C2
Cannara I 136 B1
Cánnero Riviera I 120 A1
Cannes F 132 B3
Canneto
Sicilia I 177 A3
Toscana I 135 B3
Canneto sull'Oglio I 120 B3
Cannich GB 32 D2
Cannóbio I 120 A1
Cannock GB 40 C1
Canonbie GB 36 A4
Canosa di Púglia I 171 B4
Can Pastilla E 166 B2
C'an Picafort E 167 B3
Cantalapiedra E 150 A2
Cantalejo E 151 A4
Cantalgallo E 161 A3
Cantalice I 169 A2
Cantalpino E 150 A2
Cantalupo in Sabina I 168 A2
Cantanhede P 148 B1
Cantavieja E 153 B3
Čantavir SRB 126 B1
Canterbury GB 45 B5
Cantiano I 136 B1
Cantillana E 162 A2
Cantiveros E 150 B3
Cantoria E 164 B2
Cantù I 120 B2
Canvey GB 45 B4
Cany-Barville F 89 A4
Canyet de Mar E 147 C3
Caol GB 34 B2
Cáorle I 122 B1
Caorso I 120 B2
Capáccio I 172 B1
Capaci I 176 A2
Capálbio I 168 A1
Capánnori I 134 B3
Caparde BIH 139 A4
Caparroso E 144 B2
Capbreton F 128 C1
Capdenac-Gare F 116 C2
Capdepera E 167 B3
Cap-de-Pin F 128 B2
Capel Curig GB 38 A3
Capellades E 147 C2
Capena I 168 A2
Capendu F 146 A3
Capestang F 130 B2
Capestrano I 169 A3
Cap Ferret F 128 B1
Capileira E 163 B4
Capinha P 148 B2
Ca'Pisani I 122 C1
Capistrello I 169 B3
Capizzi I 177 B3
Čaplje BIH 124 C2
Čapljina BIH 139 B3
Capo di Ponte I 120 A3
Caposile I 122 B1
Capoterra I 179 C2
Cappamore IRL 29 B3
Cappeln D 71 B5
Cappoquin IRL 29 B4
Capracotta I 169 B4
Capránica I 168 A2
Caprarola I 168 A2
Capretta I 135 C5
Capri I 170 C2
Capriati a Volturno I 170 B2
Caprino Veronese I 121 B3
Captieux F 128 B2
Cápua I 170 B2
Capurso I 173 A2
Capvern F 145 A4
Carabaña E 151 B4
Carabias E 151 A4
Caracal RO 17 C6
Caracenilla E 152 B1
Caráglio I 133 A3
Caraman F 146 A2
Caramánico Terme I 169 A4
Caranga E 141 A4
Caranguejeira P 154 B2
Caransebeş RO 16 C5
Carantec F 100 A2
Carapelle I 171 B3
Carasco I 134 A2
Carate Brianza I 120 B2
Caravaca de la Cruz E 164 A3
Caravággio I 120 B2
Carbajal E 163 B3
Carbajo E 155 B3
Carballeda E 140 B3
Carballeda de Avia E 140 B2
Carballo E 140 A2
Carbis Bay GB 42 B1
Carbon-Blanc F 128 B2
Carbonera de Frentes E 143 C4
Carboneras E 164 C3
Carboneras de Guadazaón E 158 B2
Carbonero el Mayor E 151 A3
Carboneros E 157 B4
Carbónia I 179 C2
Carbonin I 108 C3
Carbonne F 146 A2
Carbost
Highland GB 31 B2
Highland GB 31 B2
Carcaboso E 149 B3
Carcabuey E 163 A3
Carcaixent E 159 B3
Carcans F 128 A1
Carcans-Plage F 128 A1
Carção P 149 A3
Carcar E 144 B2
Cárcare I 133 A4
Carcassonne F 146 A3
Carcastillo E 144 B2
Carcedo de Burgos E 143 B3
Carcelén E 159 B2
Carcès F 132 B2
Carchelejo E 163 A4
Çardak
Çanakkale TR 186 B1
Denizli TR 189 B4
Cardedeu E 147 C3
Cardeña E 157 B3
Cardenete E 158 B2
Cardeñosa E 150 B3
Cardeto I 175 C1
Cardiff GB 39 C3
Cardigan GB 39 B2
Cardona E 147 C2
Cardosos P 154 B2
Carei RO 16 B5
Carentan F 88 A2
Carentoir F 101 B3
Careri I 175 C2
Carevdar HR 124 A2
Cargèse F 180 A1
Carhaix-Plouguer F 100 A2
Caria P 148 B2
Cariati I 174 B2
Carignan F 91 B5
Carignano I 119 C4
Cariñena E 152 A2
Carini I 176 A2
Cariño E 140 A3
Carínola I 170 B1
Carisbrooke GB 44 C2
Carlabhagh GB 31 A2
Carlepont F 90 B3
Carlet E 159 B3
Carlingford IRL 27 B4
Carlisle GB 36 B4
Carloforte I 179 C2
Carlópoli I 175 B2
Carlow
D 65 C3
IRL 30 B2
Carlton GB 40 C2
Carluke GB 35 C4
Carmagnola I 119 C4
Carmarthen GB 39 C2
Carmaux F 130 A1
Carmena E 150 C3
Cármenes E 142 B1
Carmine I 133 A3
Carmona E 162 A2
Carmonita E 155 B4
Carmyllie GB 35 B5
Carnac F 100 B2
Carndonagh IRL 27 A3
Carnew IRL 30 B2
Carnforth GB 37 B4
Cárnia I 122 A2
Carnlough GB 27 B5
Carno GB 39 B3
Carnon Plage F 131 B2
Carnota E 140 B1
Carnoustie GB 35 B5
Carnwath GB 35 C4
Carolei I 174 B2
Carolinensiel D 71 A4
Carolles F 88 B2
Carona I 120 A2
Caronía I 177 A3
Carovigno I 173 B3
Carovilli I 170 B2
Carpaneto Piacentino I 120 C2
Carpegna I 135 B5
Carpenédolo I 121 B3
Carpentras F 131 A4
Carpi I 121 C3
Carpignano Sésia I 119 B5
Carpineti I 134 A3
Carpineto Romano I 169 B3
Cărpiniş RO 126 B2
Carpino I 171 B3
Carpinone I 170 B2
Carpio E 150 A2
Carquefou F 101 B4
Carqueiranne F 132 B2
Carral E 140 A2
Carranque E 151 B4
Carrapichana P 148 B2
Carrara I 134 A3
Carraroe IRL 28 A2
Carrascalejo E 156 A2
Carrascosa del Campo E 151 B5
Carratraca E 162 B3
Carrazeda de Ansiães P 148 A2
Carrazedo de Montenegro P 148 A2
Carrbridge GB 32 D3
Carregal do Sal P 148 B1
Carreña E 142 A2
Carrick IRL 26 B2
Carrickart IRL 26 A3
Carrickfergus GB 27 B5
Carrickmacross IRL 27 C4
Carrick-on-Shannon IRL 26 C2
Carrick-on-Suir IRL 30 B1
Carrigallen IRL 27 C3
Carrión E 161 B3
Carrión de Calatrava E 157 A4
Carrión de los Condes E 142 B2
Carrizo de la Ribera E 141 B5
Carrizosa E 157 B5
Carro F 131 B4
Carrocera E 142 B1
Carros F 133 B3
Carrouge CH 106 C1
Carrouges F 89 B3
Carrù I 133 A3
Carryduff GB 27 B5
Carry-le-Rouet F 131 B4
Carsóli I 169 A3
Carsphairn GB 36 A2
Cartagena E 165 B4
Cártama E 163 B3
Cartaxo P 154 B2
Cartaya E 161 B2
Carteret F 88 A2
Cartes E 142 A2
Carúnchio I 170 B2
Carviçães P 149 A3
Carvin F 78 B2
Carvoeira P 154 B1
Carvoeiro P 160 B1
Casabermeja E 163 B3
Casa Branca
Portalegre P 154 C3
Setúbal P 154 C2
Casacalenda I 170 B2
Casa Castalda I 136 B1
Casaio E 141 B4
Casa l'Abate I 173 B4
Casalarreina E 143 B4
Casalbordino I 169 A4
Casalborgone I 119 B4
Casalbuono I 174 A1
Casalbuttano ed Uniti I 120 B2
Casàl di Principe I 170 B2
Casalécchio di Reno I 135 A4
Casale Monferrato I 119 B5
Casalina I 136 C1
Casalmaggiore I 121 C3
Casalnuovo Monterotaro I 170 B3
Casaloldo I 121 B3
Casalpusterlengo I 120 B2
Casamássima I 173 B2
Casamicciola Terme I 170 C1
Casamozza F 180 A2
Casarabonela E 162 B3
Casarano I 173 B4
Casar de Cáceres E 155 B4
Casar de Palomero E 149 B3
Casarejos E 143 C3
Casares E 162 B2
Casares de las Hurdes E 149 B3
Casariche E 163 A3
Casarrubios del Monte E 151 B3
Casas de Don Pedro E 156 A2
Casas de Fernando Alonso E 158 B1
Casas de Haro E 158 B1
Casas de Juan Gil E 159 B2
Casas del Juan Núñez E 158 B2
Casas del Puerto E 159 C2
Casas del Rio E 159 B2
Casas de Millán E 155 B4
Casas de Reina E 156 B2
Casas de Ves E 159 B2
Casas-Ibáñez E 158 B2
Casasimarro E 158 B1
Casas Nuevas E 164 B3
Casasola E 150 B3
Casasola de Arión E 150 A2
Casasuertes E 142 A2
Casatejada E 150 C2
Casavieja E 150 B3
Casazza I 120 B2
Cascais P 154 C1
Cascante E 144 C2
Cascante del Rio E 152 B2
Cáscia I 169 A3
Casciana Terme I 134 B3
Cáscina I 134 B3
Cáseda E 144 B2
Casekow D 74 A3
Casella I 134 A2
Caselle Torinese I 119 B4
Casemurate I 135 A5
Casenove I 136 C1
Caseres E 153 A4
Caserio Benali E 159 B3
Caserta I 170 B2
Casével P 160 B1
Cashel IRL 29 B4
Casillas E 150 B3
Casillas de Coria E 155 B4
Casina I 134 A3
Casinos E 159 B3
Čáslav CZ 97 B3
Cásola Valsénio I 135 A4
Cásole d'Elsa I 135 B4
Cásoli I 169 A4
Casória I 170 C2
Caspe E 153 A3
Cassàde la Selva E 147 C3
Cassagnas F 130 A2
Cassagnes-Bégonhès F 130 A1
Cassano allo Iónio I 174 B2
Cassano d'Adda I 120 B2
Cassano delle Murge I 171 C4
Cassano Magnago I 120 B1
Cassano Spinola I 120 C1
Cassel F 78 B2
Cassibile I 177 C4
Cassine I 119 C5
Cassino I 169 B3
Cassis F 132 B1
Cassolnovo I 120 B1
Cassuéjouls F 116 C2
Častá SK 98 C1
Castagnaro I 121 B4
Castagneto Carducci I 134 B3
Castagnola CH 120 A1
Castalla E 159 C3
Castañar de Ibor E 156 A2
Castanheira de Pêra P 154 A2
Cástano Primo I 120 B1
Castasegna CH 120 A2
Castéggio I 120 B2
Casteição P 148 B2
Castejón E 144 B2
Castejón de Monegros E 153 A3
Castejón de Sos E 145 B4
Castejón de Valdejasa E 144 C3
Castèl Baronia I 172 A1
Castel Bolognese I 135 A4
Castelbuono I 177 B3
Casteldáccia I 176 A2
Castel d'Aiano I 135 A3
Castel d'Ario I 121 B3
Castel de Cabra E 153 B3
Casteldelfino I 132 A3
Castél del Monte I 169 A3
Castel del Piano I 135 C4
Castel di Iúdica I 177 B3
Castel di Rio I 135 A4
Castèl di Sangro I 169 B4
Castél di Tora I 169 A2
Castelfidardo I 136 B2
Castelfiorentino I 135 B3
Castelforte I 169 B3
Castelfranco Emília I 121 C4
Castelfranco in Miscano I 170 B3
Castelfranco Véneto I 121 B4
Castèl Frentano I 169 A4
Casteljaloux F 128 B3
Castellabate I 170 C2
Castellammare del Golfo I 176 A1
Castellammare di Stábia I 170 C2
Castellamonte I 119 B4
Castellana Grotte I 173 B3
Castellane F 132 B2
Castellaneta I 173 B2
Castellaneta Marina I 173 B2
Castellar E 157 B4
Castellarano I 135 A3
Castellar de la Frontera E 162 B2
Castellar de la Ribera E 147 B2
Castellar del Vallés E 147 C3
Castellar de Santiago E 157 B4
Castell Arquato I 120 C2
Castell'Azzara I 135 C4
Castellbell i Villar E 147 C2
Castelldans E 153 A4
Castell de Cabres E 153 B4
Castell de Castells E 159 C3
Castelldefels E 147 C2
Castell de Ferro E 163 B4
Castelleone I 120 B2
Castellet E 147 C2
Castelletto di Brenzone I 121 B3
Castellfollit de la Roca E 147 B3
Castellfollit de Riubregos E 147 C2
Castellfort E 153 B3
Castellina in Chianti I 135 B4
Castellina Marittima I 134 B3
Castellóde Farfaña E 145 C4
Castellóde la Plana E 159 B3
Castello d'Empùries E 147 B4
Castello di Fiemme I 121 A4
Castelloli E 147 C2
Castellón de Rugat E 159 C3
Castellote E 153 B3
Castello Tesino I 121 A4
Castellterçol E 147 C3
Castellúcchio I 121 B3
Castellúccio de'Sáuri I 171 B3
Castelluccio Inferiore I 174 B1
Castelmassa I 121 B4
Castelmáuro I 170 B2
Castelmoron-sur-Lot F 129 B3
Castelnaudary F 146 A2
Castelnau-de-Médoc F 128 A2
Castelnau-de-Montmirail F 129 C4
Castelnau-Magnoac F 145 A4
Castelnau-Montratier F 129 B4
Castelnou E 153 A3
Castelnovo ne'Monti I 134 A3
Castelnuovo Berardenga I 135 B4
Castelnuovo della Dáunia I 170 B3
Castelnuovo di Garfagnana I 134 A3
Castelnuovo di Val di Cécina I 135 B3
Castelnuovo Don Bosco I 119 B4
Castelnuovo Scrivia I 120 C1
Castelo Branco
Bragança P 149 A3
Castelo Branco P 155 B3
Castelo de Paiva P 148 A1
Castelo de Vide P 155 B3
Castelo do Neiva P 148 A1
Castelo Mendo P 149 B3
Castelraimondo I 136 B2
Castel San Gimignano I 135 B4
Castèl San Giovanni I 120 B2
Castèl San Pietro Terme I 135 A4
Castelsantángelo I 136 C2
Castél Sant'Elia I 168 A2
Castelsaraceno I 174 A1
Castelsardo I 178 B2
Castelsarrasin F 129 B4
Castelserás E 153 B3
Casteltérmini I 176 B2
Castelvecchio Subéquo I 169 A3
Castelvetrano I 176 B1
Castél Volturno I 170 B1
Castenédolo I 120 B3
Castets F 128 C1
Castiádas I 179 C3
Castiglioncello I 134 B3
Castiglione I 169 A3
Castiglione Chiavarese I 134 A2
Castiglione d'Adda I 120 B2
Castiglione dei Pepoli I 135 A4
Castiglione del Lago I 135 B5
Castiglione della Pescáia I 135 C3
Castiglione delle Stiviere I 121 B3
Castiglione di Sicília I 177 B4
Castiglione d'Órcia I 135 B4
Castiglione Messer Marino I 170 B2
Castiglione Messer Raimondo I 169 A3
Castiglion Fibocchi I 135 B4
Castiglion Fiorentino I 135 B4
Castilblanco E 156 A2
Castilblanco de los Arroyos E 161 B4
Castil de Peones E 143 B3
Castilfrío de la Sierra E 144 C1
Castilgaleu E 145 B4
Castilisar E 144 B2
Castilleja E 161 B3
Castillejar E 164 B2
Castillejo de Martin Viejo E 149 B3
Castillejo de Mesleón E 151 A4
Castillejo de Robledo E 151 A4
Castillo de Bayuela E 150 B3
Castillo de Locubín E 163 A4
Castillonès F 129 B3
Castillon-la-Bataille F 128 B2
Castillon-Len-Couserans F 146 B2
Castillonroy E 145 C4
Castilruiz E 144 C1
Castione CH 120 A2
Castions di Strada I 122 B2
Castirla F 180 A2
Castlebar IRL 28 A2
Castlebellingham IRL 27 C4
Castleblaney IRL 27 B4
Castlebridge IRL 30 B2
Castle Cary GB 43 A4
Castlecomer IRL 30 B1
Castlederg GB 27 B3
Castledermot IRL 30 B2
Castle Douglas GB 36 B3
Castleford GB 40 B2
Castleisland IRL 29 B2
Castlemaine IRL 29 B2
Castlemartyr IRL 29 C3
Castlepollard IRL 30 A1
Castlerea IRL 28 A3
Castleton GB 40 B2
Castletown
Highland GB 32 C3
Isle of Man GB 36 B2
Castletown Bearhaven IRL 29 C2
Castletownroche IRL 29 B3
Castlewellan GB 27 B5
Casto I 120 B3
Castrejón E 150 A2
Castrelo del Valle E 141 B3
Castres F 130 B1
Castricum NL 70 B1
Castries F 131 B2
Castrignano del Capo I 173 C4
Castril E 164 B2
Castrillo de Duero E 151 A4
Castrillo de la Vega E 143 C3
Castrillo de Onielo E 142 C2
Castro
E 142 A2
I 173 B4
Castrocabón E 141 B5
Castro-Caldelas E 141 B3
Castrocaro Terme I 135 A4
Castrocontrigo E 141 B4
Castro Daire P 148 B2
Castro dei Volsci I 169 B3
Castro del Río E 163 A3
Castro de Rey E 141 A3
Castrofilippo I 176 B2
Castrogonzaio E 142 B1
Castrojeriz E 142 B2
Castro Laboreiro P 140 B2
Castro Marim P 160 B2
Castromonte E 142 C1
Castromudarra E 142 B1
Castronuevo E 142 C1
Castronuño E 150 A2
Castropol E 141 A3
Castroreale I 177 A4
Castroserracin E 151 A4
Castro-Urdiales E 143 A3
Castroverde E 141 A3
Castro Verde P 160 B1
Castroverde de Campos E 142 C1
Castroverde de Cerrato E 142 C2
Castrovillari I 174 B2
Castuera E 156 B2
Catadau E 159 B3
Cataéggio I 120 A2
Çatalca TR 186 A3
Catallar TR 189 C5
Çatalzeytin TR 23 A8
Catánia I 177 B4
Catanzaro I 175 C2
Catanzaro Marina I 175 C2
Catarroja E 159 B3
Catarruchos P 148 B1
Catcleugh GB 37 A4
Catenanuova I 177 B3
Caterham GB 44 B3
Cati E 153 B4
Čatići BIH 139 A4
Catignano I 169 A3
Catillon F 91 A3
Catoira E 140 B2
Caton GB 37 B4
Catral E 165 A4
Catterick GB 37 B5
Cattólica I 136 B1
Cattólica Eraclea I 176 B2
Catton GB 37 B4
Caudebec-en-Caux F 89 A4
Caudete E 159 C3
Caudete de las Fuentes E 159 B2
Caudiel E 159 B3
Caudiès-de-Fenouillèdes F 146 B3
Caudry F 91 A3
Caulkerbush GB 36 B3
Caulnes F 101 A3
Caulónia I 175 C2
Caumont-l'Evente F 88 A3
Caunes-Minervois F 146 A3
Cauro F 180 B1
Caussade F 129 B4
Causse-de-la-Selle F 130 B2
Cauterets F 145 B3
Cava de Tirreni I 170 C2
Cavaglia I 119 B5
Cavaillon F 131 B4
Cavalaire-sur-Mer F 132 B2
Cavaleiro P 160 B1
Cavalese I 121 A4
Cavallermaggiore I 119 C4
Cavallino I 122 B1
Cavan IRL 27 C3
Cavárzere I 121 B5
Çavdarhisar TR 187 C4
Çavdır TR 189 B4
Cavernães P 148 B2
Cavezzo I 121 C4
Cavignac F 128 A2
Čavle HR 123 B3
Cavo I 134 C3
Cavour I 119 C4
Cawdor GB 32 D3
Çay TR 187 D6
Çaycuma TR 187 A7
Cayeux-sur-Mer F 78 B1
Cayiralan TR 23 B8
Çayırhan TR 187 B6
Caylus F 129 B4
Cayres F 117 C3
Cazalilla E 157 C4
Cazalla de la Sierra E 156 C2
Cazals F 129 B4
Cazanuecos E 142 B1
Cazaubon F 128 C2
Cazaux F 128 B1
Cazavet F 146 A2
Cazères F 146 A2
Cazin BIH 124 C1
Cazis CH 107 C4
Čazma HR 124 B2
Cazo E 142 A1
Cazorla E 164 B2
Cazouls-lès-Béziers F 130 B2
Cea
León E 142 B1
Orense E 140 B3
Ceánuri E 143 A4
Ceauce F 88 B3
Cebolla E 150 C3
Čebovce SK 112 A3
Cebreros E 150 B3
Čečava BIH 125 C3
Ceccano I 169 B3
Cece H 112 C2
Cecenowo PL 68 A2
Čechtice CZ 96 B3
Čechtin CZ 97 B3
Cécina I 134 B3
Ceclavín E 155 B4
Cedégolo I 120 A3
Cedeira E 140 A2
Cedillo E 155 B3
Cedillo del Condado E 151 B4
Cedrillas E 153 B3
Cedynia PL 74 B3
Cée E 140 B1
Cefalù I 177 A3
Céggia I 122 B1
Cegléd H 113 B3
Ceglédbercel H 112 B3
Céglie Messápica I 173 B3
Cehegín E 164 A3
Ceilhes-et-Rocozels F 130 B2
Ceinos de Campos E 142 B1
Ceira P 148 B1
Čejč CZ 97 C4
Cekcyn PL 76 A3
Cela BIH 124 C2
Čelákovice CZ 84 B2
Celano I 169 A3
Celanova E 140 B3
Celbridge IRL 30 A2
Čelebič BIH 138 B2
Celenza Valfortore I 170 B2
Čelić BIH 125 C4
Čelinac BIH 124 C3
Celje SLO 123 A4
Cella E 152 B2
Celldömölk H 111 B4
Celle D 72 B3
Celle Ligure I 133 A4
Celles B 79 B4
Celles-sur-Belle F 115 B3
Cellino San Marco I 173 B3
Celorico da Beira P 148 B2
Celorico de Basto P 148 A1
Çeltik TR 187 C6
Çeltikçi TR 189 B5
Cemaes GB 38 A2
Cembra I 121 A4
Čemerno BIH 139 B4
Cenad RO 126 A2
Cencenighe Agordino I 121 A4
Cenei RO 126 B2
Ceneselli I 121 B4
Cenicero E 143 B4
Cenicientos E 150 B3
Censeau F 105 C5
Čenta SRB 126 B2
Centallo I 133 A3
Centelles E 147 C3
Cento I 121 C4
Centúripe I 177 B3
Cepeda la Mora E 150 B2
Cépet F 129 C4
Čepin HR 125 B4
Čepinski Martinci HR 125 B4
Cepovan SLO 122 A2
Ceprano I 169 B3
Čeralije HR 125 B3
Cerami I 177 B3
Cerano I 120 B1
Cérans Foulletourte F 102 B2
Ceraso I 172 B1
Cerbaia I 135 B4
Cerbère F 146 B4
Cercadillo E 151 A5
Cercal
Lisboa P 154 B1
Setúbal P 160 B1
Čerčany CZ 96 B2

Cerceda E 151 B4
Cercedilla E 151 B3
Cercemaggiore I 170 B2
Cercs E 147 B2
Cercy-la-Tour F 104 C2
Cerda I 176 B2
Cerdedo E 140 B2
Cerdeira P 149 B2
Cerdon F 103 B4
Cerea I 121 B4
Ceres
GB 35 B5
I 119 B4
Cerese I 121 B3
Ceresole-Reale I 119 B4
Cereste F 132 B1
Céret F 146 B3
Cerezo de Abajo
E 151 A4
Cerezo de Riotirón
E 143 B3
Cerfontaine B 79 B4
Cergy F 90 B2
Cerignola I 171 B3
Cérilly F 103 C4
Cerisiers F 104 A2
Cerizay F 114 B3
Çerkeş TR 23 A7
Çerkezköy TR 186 A3
Cerkije SLO 123 A3
Cerknica SLO 123 B3
Cerkno SLO 122 A2
Cerkwica PL 67 B4
Cerna HR 125 B4
Černá Hora CZ 97 B4
Cernavodă RO 17 C8
Cernay F 106 B2
Cerne Abbas GB 43 B4
Cernégula E 143 B3
Cernik HR 124 B3
Cernóbbio I 120 B2
Černošin CZ 95 B4
Cernovice CZ 96 B2
Cérons F 128 B2
Cerovlje HR 123 B3
Cerovo SK 99 C3
Cerqueto I 135 C5
Cerralbo E 149 B3
Cerreto d'Esi I 136 B2
Cerreto Sannita I 170 B2
Cerrigydrudion GB 38 A3
Cërrik AL 182 B1
Cerro Muriano E 156 B3
Certaldo I 135 B4
Certosa di Pésio I 133 A3
Cerva P 148 A2
Cervaro I 169 B3
Cervatos de la Cueza
E 142 B2
Červena Řečice CZ 97 B3
Červená-Skala SK 99 C4
Cervená Voda CZ 97 A4
Cerveny Kostelec
CZ 85 B4
Cervera E 147 C2
Cervera de la Cañada
E 152 A2
Cervera del Llano
E 158 B1
Cervera del Río Alhama
E 144 B2
Cervera de Pisuerga
E 142 B2
Cervéteri I 168 B2
Cérvia I 135 A5
Cerviáde les Garriques
E 147 C1
Cervignano del Friuli
I 122 B2
Cervinara I 170 B2
Cervione F 180 A2
Cervo E 141 A3
Cervon F 104 B2
Cesana Torinese I 119 C3
Cesarica HR 137 A4
Cesarò I 177 B3
Cesena I 135 A5
Cesenático I 135 A5
Cēsis LV 8 D4
Česká Belá CZ 97 B3
Česká Kamenice
CZ 84 B2
Česká Lipa CZ 84 B2
Česká Skalice CZ 85 B4
Česká Třebová CZ 97 B4
České Budějovice
CZ 96 C2
České Velenice CZ 96 C2
Český Brod CZ 96 A2
Český Dub CZ 84 B2
Český Krumlov CZ 96 C2
Český Těšín CZ 98 B2
Češljeva Bara
SRB 127 C3
Çeşme TR 188 A1
Cessenon F 130 B2
Cesson-Sévigné
F 101 A4
Cestas F 128 B2
Čestobrodica SRB 127 D2
Cesuras E 140 A2
Cetina E 152 A2
Cetin Grad HR 123 B4
Cetinje MNE 16 D3
Cetraro I 174 B1
Ceuti E 165 A3
Ceva I 133 A4
Cevico de la Torre
E 142 C2
Cevico Navero E 142 C2
Cevins F 118 B3
Cévio CH 119 A5
Cevizli TR 189 B6
Cewice PL 68 A2
Ceylan TR 189 C4
Ceyrat F 116 B3
Ceyzériat F 118 A2
Chaam NL 79 A4
Chabanais F 115 C4
Chabeuil F 117 C5
Chabielice PL 86 A3
Chablis F 104 B2
Châbons F 118 B2
Chabówka PL 99 B3
Chabreloche F 117 B3
Chabris F 103 B3
Chagford GB 42 B3
Chagny F 105 C3
Chagoda RUS 9 C9
Chaherrero E 150 B3
Chailland F 88 B3
Chaillé-les-Marais
F 114 B2
Chailles F 103 B3
Chailley F 104 A2
Chalabre F 146 B3
Chalais F 128 A3
Chalamont F 118 B2
Châlette-sur-Loing
F 103 A4
Chalindrey F 105 B4
Chalkida GR 185 A4
Challacombe GB 42 A3
Challans F 114 B2
Challes-les-Eaux
F 118 B2
Chalmazel F 117 B3
Chalmoux F 104 C2
Chalonnes-sur-Loire
F 102 B1
Châlons-en-
Champagne F 91 C4
Chalon-sur-Saône
F 105 C3
Chalupy PL 69 A3
Châlus F 115 C4
Cham
CH 106 B3
D 95 B4
Chamberet F 116 B1
Chambéry F 118 B2
Chambilly F 117 A4
Chambley F 92 B1
Chambly F 90 B2
Chambois F 89 B4
Chambon-sur-Lac
F 116 B2
Chambon-sur-Voueize
F 116 A2
Chambord F 103 B3
Chamborigaud F 131 A2
Chamboulive F 116 B1
Chamerau D 95 B4
Chamonix-Mont Blanc
F 119 B3
Chamoux-sur-Gelon
F 118 B3
Champagnac-le-Vieux
F 117 B3
Champagney F 106 B1
Champagnole F 105 C4
Champagny-Mouton
F 115 B4
Champaubert F 91 C3
Champdeniers-St Denis
F 114 B3
Champdieu F 117 B4
Champdôtre F 105 B4
Champeix F 116 B3
Champéry CH 119 A3
Champigne F 102 B1
Champignelles F 104 B2
Champigny-sur-Veude
F 102 B2
Champlitte-et-le-Prelot
F 105 B4
Champoluc I 119 B4
Champoly F 117 B3
Champorcher I 119 B4
Champrond-en-Gâtine
F 89 B5
Champs-sur-Tarentaine
F 116 B2
Champs-sur-Yonne
F 104 B2
Champtoceaux F 101 B4
Chamrousse F 118 B2
Chamusca P 154 B2
Chanac F 130 A2
Chanaleilles F 117 C3
Chandler's Ford
GB 44 C2
Chandra GR 185 D7
Chandrexa de Queixa
E 141 B3
Chañe E 150 A3
Changy F 117 A3
Chania GR 185 D5
Channes F 104 B3
Chantada E 140 B3
Chantelle F 116 A3
Chantenay-St Imbert
F 104 C2
Chanteuges F 117 B3
Chantilly F 90 B2
Chantonnay F 114 B2
Chão de Codes P 154 B2
Chaource F 104 A3
Chapa E 140 B2
Chapareillan F 118 B2
Chapel en le Frith
GB 40 B2
Chapelle Royale F 103 A3
Chapelle-St Laurent
F 102 C1
Charbonnat F 104 C3
Chard GB 43 B4
Charenton-du-Cher
F 103 C4
Charlbury GB 44 B2
Charleroi B 79 B4
Charlestown
GB 42 B2
IRL 26 C2
Charlestown of
Aberlour GB 32 D3
Charleville IRL 29 B3
Charleville-Mézières
F 91 B4
Charlieu F 117 A4
Charlottenberg S 49 C4
Charlton Kings GB 44 B1
Charly F 90 C3
Charmes F 92 C2
Charmes-sur-Rhône
F 117 C4
Charmey CH 106 C2
Charminster GB 43 B4
Charmont-en-Beauce
F 103 A4
Charny F 104 B2
Charolles F 117 A4
Chârost F 103 C4
Charquemont F 106 B1
Charrin F 104 C2
Charroux F 115 B4
Chartres F 90 C1
Charzykow PL 68 B2
Chasseneuil-sur-
Bonnieure F 115 C4
Chassigny F 105 B4
Château-Arnoux
F 132 A2
Châteaubernard
F 115 C3
Châteaubourg F 101 A4
Châteaubriant F 101 B4
Château-Chinon
F 104 B2
Château-d'Oex
CH 106 C2
Château-d'Olonne
F 114 B2
Château-du-Loir
F 102 B2
Châteaudun F 103 A3
Châteaugiron F 101 A4
Château-Gontier
F 102 B1
Château-Landon
F 103 A4
Château-la-Vallière
F 102 B2
Château-l'Evêque
F 129 A3
Châteaulin F 100 A1
Châteaumeillant
F 103 C4
Châteauneuf
Nièvre F 104 B2
Saône-et-Loire F 117 A4
Châteauneuf-de-
Randon F 117 C3
Châteauneuf-d'Ille-et-
Vilaine F 88 B2
Châteauneuf-du-Faou
F 100 A2
Châteauneuf-du-Pape
F 131 A3
Châteauneuf-en-
Thymerais F 89 B5
Châteauneuf la-Forêt
F 116 B1
Châteauneuf-le-Rouge
F 132 B1
Châteauneuf-sur-
Charente F 115 C3
Châteauneuf-sur-Cher
F 103 C4
Châteauneuf-sur-Loire
F 103 B4
Châteauneuf-sur-
Sarthe F 102 B1
Châteauponsac F 115 B5
Château-Porcien F 91 B4
Châteauredon F 132 A2
Châteaurenard
Bouches du Rhône
F 131 B3
Loiret F 104 B1
Château-Renault
F 102 B2
Châteauroux F 103 C3
Châteauroux-les-Alpes
F 118 C3
Château-Salins F 92 C2
Château-Thierry F 91 B3
Châteauvillain F 105 A3
Châtel F 119 A3
Châtelaillon-Plage
F 114 B2
Châtelaudren F 100 A3
Châtel-Censoir F 104 B2
Châtel-de-Neuvre
F 116 A3
Châtelet B 79 B4
Châtelguyon F 116 B3
Châtellerault F 115 B4
Châtel-Montagne
F 117 A3
Châtel-St Denis
CH 106 C1
Châtel-sur-Moselle
F 92 C2
Châtelus-Malvaleix
F 116 A2
Châtenois F 105 A4
Châtenois-les-Forges
F 106 B1
Chatham GB 45 B4
Châtillon I 119 B4
Châtillon-Coligny
F 103 B4
Châtillon-en-Bazois
F 104 B2
Châtillon-en-Diois
F 118 C2
Châtillon-sur
Chalaronne F 117 A4
Châtillon-sur-Indre
F 103 C3
Châtillon-sur-Loire
F 103 B4
Châtillon-sur-Marne
F 91 B3
Châtillon-sur-Seine
F 104 B3
Châtres F 91 C3
Chatteris GB 45 A4
Chatton GB 37 A5
Chauchina E 163 A4
Chaudes-Aigues
F 116 C3
Chaudrey F 91 C4
Chauffailles F 117 A4
Chaulnes F 90 B2
Chaument Gistoux
B 79 B4
Chaumergy F 105 C4
Chaumont F 105 A4
Chaumont-en-Vexin
F 90 B1
Chaumont-Porcien
F 91 B4
Chaumont-sur-Aire
F 91 C5
Chaumont-sur-Loire
F 103 B3
Chaunay F 115 B4
Chauny F 90 B3
Chaussin F 105 C4
Chauvigny F 115 B4
Chavagnes-en-Paillers
F 114 B2
Chavanges F 91 C4
Chaves P 148 A2
Chavignon F 91 B3
Chazelles-sur-Lyon
F 117 B4
Chazey-Bons F 118 B2
Cheadle
Greater Manchester
GB 40 B1
Staffordshire GB 40 C2
Cheb CZ 83 B4
Chebsara RUS 9 C11
Checa E 152 B2
Chęciny PL 87 B4
Cheddar GB 43 A4
Cheddleton GB 40 B1
Chef-Boutonne F 115 B3
Cheles E 155 C3
Chella E 159 B3
Chelles F 90 C2
Chełm PL 13 C5
Chełmno
Kujawsko-Pomorskie
PL 76 A3
Wielkopolskie PL 76 B3
Chelmsford GB 45 B4
Chelmuzhi RUS 9 A9
Chełmża PL 76 A3
Cheltenham GB 44 B1
Chelva E 159 B2
Chémery F 103 B3
Chemery-sur-Bar F 91 B4
Chemillé F 102 B1
Chemin F 105 C4
Chemnitz D 83 B4
Chénerailles F 116 A2
Cheniménil F 105 A5
Chenonceaux F 103 B3
Chenôve F 105 B3
Chepelare BG 183 B6
Chepstow GB 39 C4
Chera E 159 B3
Cherasco I 119 C4
Cherbonnières F 115 C3
Cherbourg F 88 A2
Cherchiara di Calábria
I 174 B2
Cherepovets RUS 9 C10
Chernihiv UA 13 C9
Chernivtsi UA 17 A6
Chernobyl = Chornobyl
UA 13 C9
Chernyakhovsk
RUS 12 A4
Chéroy F 104 A1
Cherven BY 13 B8
Chervonohrad UA 13 C6
Cherykaw BY 13 B9
Chesham GB 44 B3
Cheshunt GB 44 B3
Chessy-lès-Pres
F 104 A2
Cheste E 159 B3
Chester GB 38 A4
Chesterfield GB 40 B2
Chester-le-Street
GB 37 B5
Chevagnes F 104 C2
Chevanceaux F 115 C3
Chevillon F 91 C5
Chevilly F 103 A3
Chew Magna GB 43 A4
Chézery-Forens F 118 A2
Chialamberto I 119 B4
Chiampo I 121 B4
Chianale I 119 C4
Chianciano Terme
I 135 B4
Chiaramonte Gulfi
I 177 B3
Chiaramonti I 178 B2
Chiaravalle I 136 B2
Chiaravalle Centrale
I 175 C2
Chiaréggio I 120 A2
Chiari I 120 B2
Chiaromonte I 174 A2
Chiasso CH 120 B2
Chiávari I 134 A2
Chiavenna I 120 A2
Chiché F 102 C1
Chichester GB 44 C3
Chiclana de la Frontera
E 162 B1
Chiclana de Segura
E 164 A1
Chiddingfold GB 44 B3
Chieri I 119 B4
Chiesa in Valmalenco
I 120 A2
Chieti I 169 A4
Chieti Scalo I 169 A4
Chiéuti I 171 B3
Chigwell GB 45 B4
Chiliomodi GR 184 B3
Chillarón de Cuenca
E 152 B1
Chillarón del Rey
E 151 B5
Chilleurs-aux-Bois
F 103 A4
Chillón E 156 B3
Chilluevar E 164 B1
Chiloeches E 151 B4
Chimay B 91 A4
Chimeneas E 163 A4
Chinchilla de Monte
Aragón E 158 C2
Chinchón E 151 B4
Chingford GB 45 B4
Chinon F 102 B2
Chióggia I 122 B1
Chiomonte I 119 B3
Chipiona E 161 C3
Chippenham GB 43 A4
Chipping Campden
GB 44 A2
Chipping Norton
GB 44 B2
Chipping Ongar
GB 45 B4
Chipping Sodbury
GB 43 A4
Chirac F 130 A2
Chirbury GB 39 B3
Chirens F 118 B2
Chirivel E 164 B2
Chirk GB 38 B3
Chirnside GB 35 C5
Chişinău = Khisinev
MD 17 B8
Chişineu Criş RO 113 C5
Chissey-en-Morvan
F 104 B3
Chiusa I 108 C2
Chiusa di Pésio I 133 A3
Chiusaforte I 122 A2
Chiusa Scláfani I 176 B2
Chiusi I 135 B4
Chiva E 159 B3
Chivasso I 119 B4
Chlewiska PL 87 A4
Chludowo PL 75 B5
Chlumec nad Cidlinou
CZ 84 B3
Chlum u Třeboně
CZ 96 C2
Chmielnik PL 87 B4
Chobienia PL 85 A4
Chobienice PL 75 B4
Choceň CZ 97 A4
Choceń PL 77 B4
Chochołow PL 99 B3
Chocianów PL 85 A3
Chociw PL 86 A3
Chociwel PL 75 A4
Choczewo PL 68 A2
Chodaków PL 77 B5
Chodecz PL 77 B4
Chodov CZ 83 B4
Chodzież PL 75 B5
Chojna PL 74 B3
Chojnice PL 68 B2
Chojno
Kujawsko-Pomorskie
PL 77 B4
Wielkopolskie PL 75 B5
Chojnów PL 85 A3
Cholet F 114 A3
Chomérac F 117 C4
Chomutov CZ 83 B5
Chop UA 12 D5
Chora GR 184 B2
Chora Sfakion GR 185 D5
Chorges F 132 A2
Choristanco E 140 A2
Chorley GB 38 A4
Chornobyl = Chernobyl
UA 13 C9
Chortkiv UA 13 D6
Chorzele PL 77 A5
Chorzew PL 86 A2
Chorzów PL 86 B2
Choszczno PL 75 A4
Chotěboř CZ 97 B3
Chouilly F 91 B4
Chouto P 154 B2
Chouzy-sur-Cisse
F 103 B3
Chozas de Abajo
E 142 B1
Chrast CZ 97 B3
Chrást CZ 96 B1
Chrastava CZ 84 B2
Chřibská CZ 84 B2
Christchurch GB 44 C2
Christiansfeld DK 59 C2
Chroberz PL 87 B4
Chropyně CZ 98 B1
Chrudim CZ 97 B3
Chrzanów PL 86 B3
Chtelnica SK 98 C1
Chudovo RUS 9 C7
Chueca E 157 A4
Chulmleigh GB 42 B3
Chur CH 107 C4
Church Stretton
GB 39 B4
Churriana E 163 B3
Churwalden CH 107 C4
Chvalšiny CZ 96 C2
Chwaszczyno PL 69 A3
Chynava CZ 96 A2
Chýnov CZ 96 B2
Ciacova RO 126 B3
Ciadîr-Lunga MD 17 B8
Ciadoncha E 143 B3
Cianciana I 176 B2
Ciano d'Enza I 134 A3
Ciążen PL 76 B2
Cibakhaza H 113 C4
Ciborro P 154 C2
Cicagna I 134 A2
Cicciano I 170 C2
Ciciliano I 169 B2
Cicognolo I 120 B3
Cidadelhe P 149 B2
Cide TR 23 A7
Cidones E 143 C4
Ciechanów
Dolnośląskie PL 85 A4
Mazowieckie PL 77 B5
Ciechocinek PL 76 B3
Cielądz PL 87 A4
Ciemnik PL 75 A4
Ciempozuelos E 151 B4
Ciepielów PL 87 A5
Čierny Balog SK 99 C3
Cierp-Gaud F 145 B4
Cierpice PL 76 B3
Ciervana E 143 A3
Cierznie PL 68 B2
Cieslé PL 77 B5
Cieszyn PL 98 B2
Cieutat F 145 A4
Cieza E 165 A3
Cifer SK 98 C1
Çifteler TR 187 C6
Cifuentes E 151 B5
Cigales E 142 C2
Cigliano I 119 B5
Cihanbeyli TR 23 B7
Cillas E 152 B2
Cilleros E 149 B3
Cilleruelo de Arriba
E 143 C3
Cilleruelo de Bezana
E 143 B3
Cimalmotto CH 119 A5
Cimanes del Tejar
E 141 B5
Ciminna I 176 B2
Cimişlia MD 17 B8
Cimoláis I 122 A1
Cîmpulung RO 17 C6
Çınarcık TR 186 B4
Cinctorres E 153 B3
Cinderford GB 39 C4
Çine TR 188 B3
Činěves CZ 84 B3
Ciney B 79 B5
Cinfães P 148 A1
Cingia de Botti I 120 B3
Cingoli I 136 B2
Cinigiano I 135 C4
Cinobaňa SK 99 C3
Cinq-Mars-la-Pile
F 102 B2
Cinquefrondi I 175 C2
Cintegabelle F 146 A2
Cintruénigo E 144 B2
Ciółkowo PL 77 B4
Ciperez E 149 B3
Cirat E 153 B3
Cirella I 174 B1
Cirencester GB 44 B2
Cirey-sur-Vezouze
F 92 C2
Ciria E 152 A2
Ciriè I 119 B4
Cirigliano I 174 A2
Cirò I 174 B3
Cirò Marina I 174 B3
Ciry-le-Noble F 104 C3
Cislău RO 17 C7
Cismon del Grappa
I 121 B4
Cisneros E 142 B2
Cissac-Médoc F 128 A2
Čista CZ 96 A1
Cisterna di Latina
I 169 B2
Cistérniga E 150 A3
Cisternino I 173 B3
Cistierna E 142 B1
Čitluk BIH 139 B3
Citov CZ 84 B2
Cittadella I 121 B4
Cittàdella Pieve I 135 C5
Cittádel Vaticano =
Vatican City I 168 B2
Cittàdi Castello I 135 B5
Cittaducale I 169 A2
Cittanova I 175 C2
Città Sant'Angelo
I 169 A4
Ciudadela de Menorca
E 167 B3
Ciudad Real E 157 B4
Ciudad Rodrigo E 149 B3
Ciutadilla E 147 C2
Cividale del Friuli
I 122 A2
Cívita I 169 A3
Cívita Castellana I 168 A2
Civitanova Alta I 136 B2
Civitanova Marche
I 136 B2
Civitavécchia I 168 A1
Civitella di Romagna
I 135 A4
Civitella di Tronto
I 136 C2
Civitella Roveto I 169 B3
Civray F 115 B4
Çivril TR 189 A4
Cizur Mayor E 144 B2
Clabhach GB 34 B1
Clachan GB 31 B2
Clachan na Luib
GB 31 B1
Clacton-on-Sea GB 45 B5
Cladich GB 34 B2
Claggan GB 34 B2
Clairvaux-les-Lacs
F 105 C4
Clamecy F 104 B2
Claonaig GB 34 C2
Clarecastle IRL 28 B3
Claregalway IRL 28 A3
Claremorris IRL 28 A2
Clarinbridge IRL 28 A3
Clashmore
GB 32 D2
IRL 29 B4
Claudy GB 27 B3
Clausthal-Zellerfeld
D 82 A2
Cláut I 122 A1
Clay Cross GB 40 B2
Claye-Souilly F 90 C2
Cléder F 100 A1
Cleethorpes GB 41 B3
Clefmont F 105 A4
Cléguérec F 100 A2
Clelles F 118 C2
Clenze D 73 B3
Cleobury Mortimer
GB 39 B4
Cléon-d'Andran F 117 C4
Cléré-les-Pins F 102 B2
Clères F 89 A5
Clermont F 90 B2
Clermont-en-Argonne
F 91 B5
Clermont-Ferrand
F 116 B3
Clermont-l'Hérault
F 130 B2
Clerval F 105 B5
Clervaux L 92 A2
Cléry-St André F 103 B3
Cles I 121 A4
Clevedon GB 43 A4
Cleveleys GB 38 A3
Cley GB 41 C5
Clifden IRL 28 A1
Clifford GB 39 B3
Clisson F 101 B4
Clitheroe GB 40 B1
Clogh IRL 30 B1
Cloghan
Donegal IRL 26 B3
Offaly IRL 28 A4
Clogheen IRL 29 B4
Clogher GB 27 B3
Cloghjordan IRL 28 B3
Clohars-Carnoët
F 100 B2
Clonakilty IRL 29 C3
Clonaslee IRL 30 A1
Clondalkin IRL 30 A2
Clones IRL 27 B3
Clonmany IRL 27 A3
Clonmel IRL 29 B4
Clonmellon IRL 30 A1
Clonord IRL 30 A1
Clonroche IRL 30 B2
Cloone IRL 26 C3
Cloppenburg D 71 B5
Closeburn GB 36 A3
Clough GB 27 B5
Clova GB 35 B4
Clovelly GB 42 B2
Clowne GB 40 B2
Cloyes-sur-le-Loir
F 103 B3
Cloyne IRL 29 C3
Cluis F 103 C3
Cluj-Napoca RO 17 B5
Clun GB 39 B3
Clunes GB 34 B3
Cluny F 117 A4
Cluses F 118 A3
Clusone I 120 B2
Clydach GB 39 C3
Clydebank GB 34 C3
Coachford IRL 29 C3
Coagh GB 27 B4
Coalisland GB 27 B4
Coalville GB 40 C2
Coaña E 141 A4
Çobanlar TR 187 D5
Cobas E 140 A2
Cobertelade E 151 A5
Cobeta E 152 B1
Cóbh IRL 29 C3
Cobreces E 142 A2
Coburg D 82 B2
Coca E 150 A3
Cocentaina E 159 C3
Cochem D 80 B3
Cockburnspath GB 35 C5
Cockermouth GB 36 B3
Codigoro I 121 C5
Codogno I 120 B2
Codos E 152 A2
Codróipo I 122 B1
Codrongianos I 178 B2
Coelhoso P 149 A3
Coesfeld D 71 C4
Coevorden NL 71 B3
Cofrentes E 159 B2
Cogeces del Monte
E 150 A3
Coggeshall GB 45 B4
Cognac F 115 C3
Cogne I 119 B4
Cognin F 118 B2
Cogolin F 132 B2
Cogollos de Guadix
E 164 B1
Cogollos-Vega E 163 A4
Cogolludo E 151 B4
Coimbra P 148 B1
Coín E 163 B3
Coirós E 140 A2
Čoka SRB 126 B2
Col SLO 123 B3
Colares P 154 C1
Cölbe D 81 B4
Colbitz D 73 B4
Colchester GB 45 B4
Coldingham GB 35 C5
Colditz D 83 A4
Coldstream GB 35 C5
Colebrooke GB 43 B3
Colera E 146 B4
Coleraine GB 27 A4
Colfiorito I 136 B1
Cólico I 120 A2
Coligny F 118 A2

Colindres E 143 A3
Collado-Mediano E 151 B3
Collado Villalba E 151 B4
Collagna I 134 A3
Collanzo E 142 A1
Collat F 117 B3
Coll de Nargó E 147 B2
Collécchio I 120 C3
Colledimezzo I 169 B4
Colle di Val d'Elsa I 135 B4
Colleferro I 169 B3
Colle Isarco I 108 C2
Collelongo I 169 B3
Collepasso I 173 B4
Collepepe I 136 C1
Collesalvetti I 134 B3
Colle Sannita I 170 B2
Collesano I 176 B2
Colli a Volturno I 169 B4
Collin GB 36 A3
Collinée F 101 A3
Collingham
Nottinghamshire GB 40 B2
West Yorkshire GB 40 B3
Collinghorst D 71 A4
Cóllio I 120 B3
Collobrières F 132 B2
Collon IRL 27 C4
Collooney IRL 26 B2
Colmar F 106 A2
Colmars F 132 A2
Colmenar E 163 B3
Colmenar de la Sierra E 151 A4
Colmenar de Oreja E 151 B4
Colmenar Viejo E 151 B4
Colmonel GB 36 A2
Colne GB 40 B1
Colobraro I 174 A2
Cologna Véneta I 121 B4
Cologne = Köln D 80 B2
Cologne F 129 C3
Cologne al Serio I 120 B2
Colombey-les-Belles F 92 C1
Colombey-les-deux-Églises F 105 A3
Colombres E 142 A2
Colomera E 163 A4
Colomers E 147 B3
Colomiers F 129 C4
Colònia de Sant Jordi E 167 B3
Colorno I 120 C3
Colos P 160 B1
Cölpin D 74 A2
Colpy GB 33 D4
Colsterworth GB 40 C3
Coltishall GB 41 C5
Colunga E 142 A1
Colwell GB 37 A4
Colwyn Bay GB 38 A3
Colyford GB 43 B3
Comácchio I 121 C5
Coma-ruga E 147 C2
Combarros E 141 B4
Combeaufontaine F 105 B4
Comber GB 27 B5
Comblain-au-Pont B 80 B1
Combloux F 118 B3
Combourg F 88 B2
Combronde F 116 B3
Comeglians I 109 C3
Comillas E 142 A2
Comines F 78 B3
Cómiso I 177 C3
Comloşu Mare RO 126 B2
Commensacq F 128 B2
Commentry F 116 A2
Commerau D 84 A2
Commercy F 92 C1
Como I 120 B2
Cómpeta E 163 B4
Compiègne F 90 B2
Comporta P 154 C2
Comps-sur-Artuby F 132 B2
Comrat MD 17 B8
Comrie GB 35 B4
Comunanza I 136 C2
Cona
Emilia Romagna I 121 C4
Veneto I 121 B5
Concarneau F 100 B2
Conceição P 160 B1
Conches-en-Ouche F 89 B4
Concordia Sagittária I 122 B1
Concordia sulla Sécchia I 121 C3
Concots F 129 B4
Condat F 116 B2
Condé-en-Brie F 91 C3
Condeixa P 148 B1
Condemios de Abajo E 151 A4
Condemios de Arriba E 151 A4
Condé-sur-l'Escaut F 79 B3
Conde-sur-Marne F 91 B4
Condé-sur-Noireau F 88 B3
Condino I 121 B3
Condom F 129 C3
Condove I 119 B4
Condrieu F 117 B4
Conegliano I 122 B1
Conflans-sur-Lanterne F 105 B5
Confolens F 115 B4
Conforto E 141 A3
Cong IRL 28 A2
Congleton GB 40 B1
Congosto E 141 B4
Congosto de Valdavia E 142 B2
Congostrina E 151 A4
Conil de la Frontera E 162 B1
Coningsby GB 41 B3
Coniston GB 36 B3
Conlie F 102 A1
Conliège F 105 C4
Conna IRL 29 B3
Connah's Quay GB 38 A3
Connantre F 91 C3
Connaugh IRL 28 B3
Connaux F 131 A3
Connel GB 34 B2
Connerré F 102 A2
Cononbridge GB 32 D2
Čonoplja SRB 126 B1
Conques F 116 C2
Conques-sur-Orbiel F 146 A3
Conquista E 157 B3
Conquista de la Sierra E 156 A2
Consándolo I 121 C4
Consélice I 135 A4
Conselve I 121 B4
Consenvoye F 91 B5
Consett GB 37 B5
Consolação P 154 B1
Constancia P 154 B2
Constanţa RO 17 C8
Constanti E 147 C2
Constantina E 162 A2
Consuegra E 157 A4
Consuma I 135 B4
Contarina I 122 B1
Contay F 90 B2
Conthey CH 119 A4
Contigliano I 168 A2
Contis-Plage F 128 B1
Contrada I 170 C2
Contres F 103 B3
Contrexéville F 105 A4
Controne I 172 B1
Contursi Termi I 172 B1
Conty F 90 B2
Conversano I 173 B3
Conwy GB 38 A3
Cookstown GB 27 B4
Coole F 91 C4
Coolgreany IRL 30 B2
Cooneen GB 27 B3
Cootehill IRL 27 B3
Cope E 165 B3
Copenhagen = København DK 61 D2
Copertino I 173 B4
Copparo I 121 C4
Coppenbrugge D 72 B2
Corabia RO 17 D6
Córaci I 175 B2
Coralići BIH 124 C1
Corato I 171 B4
Coray F 100 A2
Corbeil-Essonnes F 90 C2
Corbeny F 91 B3
Corbera E 159 B3
Corbie F 90 B2
Corbigny F 104 B2
Corbion B 91 B4
Corbridge GB 37 B4
Corby GB 40 C3
Corconte E 143 A3
Corcubión E 140 B1
Corcumello I 169 A3
Cordenòns I 122 B1
Cordes-sur-Ciel F 129 B4
Córdoba E 156 C3
Cordobilla de Lácara E 155 B4
Cordovado I 122 B1
Corella E 144 B2
Coreses E 150 A2
Corfe Castle GB 43 B4
Corga de Lobão P 148 B1
Cori I 169 B2
Coria E 155 B4
Coria del Río E 162 A1
Corigliano Cálabro I 174 B2
Corinaldo I 136 B1
Corinth = Korinthos GR 184 B3
Cório I 119 B4
Coripe E 162 B2
Cork IRL 29 C3
Corlay F 100 A2
Corleone I 176 B2
Corleto Monforte I 172 B1
Corleto Perticara I 174 A2
Çorlu TR 186 A2
Cormainville F 103 A3
Cormatin F 104 C3
Cormeilles F 89 A4
Cormery F 102 B2
Cormòns I 122 B2
Cormoz F 118 A2
Cornago E 144 B1
Cornberg D 82 A1
Cornellana E 141 A4
Corneşti MD 17 B8
Corníglio I 134 A3
Cornimont F 106 B1
Corniolo I 135 B4
Cornuda I 121 B5
Cornudella de Montsant E 147 C1
Cornudilla E 143 B3
Cornus F 130 B2
Çorovodë AL 182 C2
Corpach GB 34 B2
Corps F 118 C2
Corps Nuds F 101 B4
Corral de Almaguer E 157 A4
Corral de Ayllon E 151 A4
Corral de Calatrava E 157 B3
Corrales E 149 A4
Corral-Rubio E 158 C2
Corran GB 34 B2
Corredoiras E 140 A2
Corréggio I 121 C3
Corrèze F 116 B1
Corridónia I 136 B2
Corris GB 38 B3
Corrubedo E 140 B1
Córsico I 120 B2
Corsock GB 36 A3
Corte F 180 A2
Corteconceptión E 161 B3
Corte de Peleas E 155 C4
Cortegaca P 148 B1
Cortegada E 140 B2
Cortegana E 161 B3
Cortemaggiore I 120 B2
Cortemilia I 133 A4
Corte Pinto P 160 B2
Cortes E 144 C2
Cortes de Aragón E 153 B3
Cortes de Arenoso E 153 B3
Cortes de Baza E 164 B2
Cortes de la Frontera E 162 B2
Cortes de Pallás E 159 B3
Cortiçadas P 154 C2
Cortico P 148 A2
Cortijo de Arriba E 157 A3
Cortijos Nuevos E 164 A2
Cortina d'Ampezzo I 108 C3
Corton GB 41 C5
Cortona I 135 B4
Coruche P 154 C2
Corullón E 141 B4
Çorum TR 23 A8
Corvara in Badia I 108 C2
Corvera E 165 B3
Corwen GB 38 B3
Cosenza I 174 B2
Cosham GB 44 C2
Coslada E 151 B4
Cosne-Cours-sur-Loire F 104 B1
Cosne d'Allier F 103 C4
Cospeito E 140 A3
Cossato I 119 B5
Cossaye F 104 C2
Cossé-le-Vivien F 101 B5
Cossonay CH 105 C5
Costa da Caparica P 154 C1
Costa de Santo André P 160 A1
Costalpino I 135 B4
Costa Nova P 148 B1
Costaros F 117 C3
Costeşti RO 17 C6
Costigliole d'Asti I 119 C5
Costigliole Saluzzo I 133 A3
Coswig
Sachsen D 83 A5
Sachsen-Anhalt D 83 A4
Cotherstone GB 37 B5
Cotronei I 175 B2
Cottbus D 84 A2
Cottenham GB 45 A4
Cottingham GB 40 B3
Coublanc F 105 B4
Couches F 104 C3
Couço P 154 C2
Coucouron F 117 C3
Coucy-le-Château-Auffrique F 90 B3
Couëron F 101 B4
Couflens F 146 B2
Couhé F 115 B4
Couiza F 146 B3
Coulags GB 31 B3
Coulanges F 104 C2
Coulanges-la-Vineuse F 104 B2
Coulanges-sur-Yonne F 104 B2
Couleuvre F 104 C1
Coulmier-le-Sec F 104 B3
Coulommiers F 90 C3
Coulonges-sur-l'Autize F 114 B3
Coulounieix-Chamiers F 129 A3
Coulport GB 34 B3
Coupar Angus GB 35 B4
Coupéville F 91 C4
Couptrain F 89 B3
Coura P 140 C2
Courcelles B 79 B4
Courcelles-Chaussy F 92 B2
Courchevel F 118 B3
Cour-Cheverny F 103 B3
Courcôme F 115 C4
Courçon F 114 B3
Cour-et-Buis F 117 B4
Courgenay CH 106 B2
Courmayeur I 119 B3
Courniou F 130 B1
Cournon-d'Auvergne F 116 B3
Cournonterral F 130 B2
Courpière F 117 B3
Coursan F 130 B2
Courseulles-sur-Mer F 89 A3
Cours-la-Ville F 117 A4
Courson-les-Carrières F 104 B2
Courtalain F 103 A3
Courtenay F 104 A2
Courtomer F 89 B4
Courville
Eure-et-Loire F 89 B5
Marne F 91 B3
Coussac-Bonneval F 115 C5
Coutances F 88 A2
Couterne F 89 B3
Coutras F 128 A2
Couvet CH 106 C1
Couvin B 91 A4
Couzon F 104 C2
Covadonga E 142 A1
Covaleda E 143 C4
Covarrubias E 143 B3
Covas P 148 A1
Cove GB 31 B3
Coventry GB 44 A2
Coverack GB 42 B1
Covigliáio I 135 A4
Covilhã P 148 B2
Cowbridge GB 39 C3
Cowdenbeath GB 35 B4
Cowes GB 44 C2
Cox F 129 C4
Cózar E 157 B4
Cozes F 114 C3
Cozzano F 180 B2
Craco I 174 A2
Cracow = Kraków PL 99 A3
Craibstone GB 33 D4
Craighouse GB 34 C2
Craignure GB 34 B2
Crail GB 35 B5
Crailsheim D 94 B2
Craiova RO 17 C5
Cramlington GB 37 A5
Cranleigh GB 44 B3
Craon F 101 B5
Craonne F 91 B3
Craponne F 117 B4
Craponne-sur-Arzon F 117 B3
Crathie GB 32 D3
Crato P 155 B3
Craughwell IRL 28 A3
Craven Arms GB 39 B4
Crawford GB 36 A3
Crawinkel D 82 B2
Crawley GB 44 B3
Creag Ghoraidh GB 31 B1
Crecente E 140 B2
Crèches-sur-Saône F 117 A4
Crécy-en-Ponthieu F 78 B1
Crécy-la-Chapelle F 90 C2
Crécy-sur-Serre F 91 B3
Crediton GB 43 B3
Creeslough IRL 26 A3
Creetown GB 36 B2
Creeve GB 27 B4
Creglingen D 94 B2
Creil F 90 B2
Creissels F 130 A2
Crema I 120 B2
Cremeaux F 117 B3
Crémenes E 142 B1
Crémieu F 118 B2
Cremlingen D 73 B3
Cremona I 120 B3
Creney F 91 C4
Črenšovci SLO 111 C3
Créon F 128 B2
Crepaja SRB 127 B2
Crépey F 92 C1
Crépy F 91 B3
Crépy-en-Valois F 90 B2
Cres HR 123 C3
Crescentino I 119 B5
Crespino I 121 C4
Crespos E 150 B3
Cressage GB 39 B4
Cressensac F 129 A4
Cressia F 105 C4
Crest F 117 C5
Cresta CH 107 C4
Créteil F 90 C2
Creully F 88 A3
Creussen D 95 B3
Creutzwald F 92 B2
Creuzburg D 82 A2
Crevalcore I 121 C4
Crèvecoeur-le-Grand F 90 B2
Crevillente E 165 A4
Crévola d'Ossola I 119 A5
Crewe GB 38 A4
Crewkerne GB 43 B4
Criales E 143 B3
Crianlarich GB 34 B3
Criccieth GB 38 B2
Crickhowell GB 39 C3
Cricklade GB 44 B2
Crieff GB 35 B4
Criel-sur-Mer F 90 A1
Crikvenica HR 123 B3
Crillon F 90 B1
Crimmitschau D 83 B4
Crimond GB 33 D5
Crinitz D 84 A1
Cripán E 143 B4
Criquetot-l'Esneval F 89 A4
Crispiano I 173 B3
Crissolo I 119 C4
Cristóbal E 149 B4
Crivitz D 73 A4
Črna SLO 110 C1
Crna Bara
Srbija SRB 127 C1
Vojvodina SRB 126 B2
Crnac HR 125 B3
Crnča SRB 127 C1
Crni Lug
BIH 138 A2
HR 123 B3
Črni Vrh SLO 123 B3
Crnjelovo Donje BIH 125 C5
Črnomelj SLO 123 B4
Crocketford GB 36 A3
Crocq F 116 B2
Crodo I 119 A5
Croglin GB 37 B4
Crolly IRL 26 A2
Cromarty GB 32 D2
Cromer GB 41 C5
Cronat F 104 C2
Crookhaven IRL 29 C2
Crookstown IRL 29 C3
Croom IRL 29 B3
Cropalati I 174 B2
Crópani I 175 C2
Crosbost GB 31 A2
Crosby GB 38 A3
Crosía I 174 B2
Crossakiel IRL 27 C3
Cross-Hands GB 39 C2
Crosshaven IRL 29 C3
Crosshill GB 36 A2
Crossmolina IRL 26 B1
Crotone I 175 B3
Crottendorf D 83 B4
Crouy F 90 B3
Crowborough GB 45 B4
Crowland GB 41 C3
Crowthorne GB 44 B3
Croyde GB 42 A2
Croydon GB 44 B3
Crozon F 100 A1
Cruas F 117 C4
Cruceni RO 126 A3
Crúcoli I 174 B3
Cruden Bay GB 33 D5
Crudgington GB 38 B4
Cruis F 132 A1
Crumlin GB 27 B4
Cruseilles F 118 A3
Crusheen IRL 28 B3
Cruz de Incio E 141 B3
Crvenka SRB 126 B1
Črveny Kamen SK 98 B2
Csabacsüd H 113 C4
Csabrendek H 111 B4
Csákánydoroszló H 111 C3
Csákvár H 112 B2
Csanádapáca H 113 C4
Csanádpalota H 126 A2
Csány H 113 B3
Csanytelek H 113 C4
Csapod H 111 B3
Császár H 112 B2
Császártöltés H 112 C3
Csávoly H 125 A5
Csemö H 113 B3
Csengöd H 112 C3
Csépa H 113 C4
Csepreg H 111 B3
Cserkeszölö H 113 C4
Csernely H 113 A4
Csesztreg H 111 C3
Csökmö H 113 B5
Csököly H 124 A3
Csokonyavisonta H 124 A3
Csólyospálos H 113 C3
Csongrád H 113 C4
Csopak H 112 C1
Csorna H 111 B4
Csorvás H 113 C4
Csurgo H 124 A3
Cuacos de Yuste E 150 B2
Cualedro E 140 C3
Cuanca de Campos E 142 B1
Cuba P 160 A2
Cubel E 152 A2
Cubelles E 147 C2
Cubillos E 143 C4
Cubillos del Sil E 141 B4
Cubjac F 129 A3
Cubo de la Solana E 152 A1
Çubuk TR 23 A7
Cuckfield GB 44 B3
Cucuron F 131 B4
Cudillero E 141 A4
Cuéllar E 151 A3
Cuenca E 152 B1
Cuers F 132 B2
Cuerva E 157 A3
Cueva de Agreda E 144 C2
Cuevas Bajas E 163 A3
Cuevas del Almanzora E 164 B3
Cuevas del Becerro E 162 B2
Cuevas del Campo E 164 B2
Cuevas del Valle E 150 B2
Cuevas de San Clemente E 143 B3
Cuevas de San Marcos E 163 A3
Cuges-les-Pins F 132 B1
Cúglieri I 178 B2
Cugnaux F 129 C4
Cuijk NL 80 A1
Cuinzier F 117 A4
Cuiseaux F 105 C4
Cuisery F 105 C4
Culan F 103 C4
Culemborg NL 79 A5
Cúllar E 164 B2
Cullaville GB 27 B4
Cullera E 159 B3
Cullivoe GB 33 A5
Cullompton GB 43 B3
Cully CH 106 C1
Culoz F 118 B2
Cults GB 33 D4
Cumbernauld GB 35 C4
Cumbres de San Bartolomé E 161 A3
Cumbres Mayores E 161 A3
Cumiana I 119 C4
Čumić SRB 127 C2
Cumnock GB 36 A2
Çumra TR 23 C7
Cúneo I 133 A3
Cunlhat F 117 B3
Čunski HR 123 C3
Cuntis E 140 B2
Cuorgnè I 119 B4
Cupar GB 35 B4
Cupello I 170 A2
Cupra Maríttima I 136 B2
Cupramontana I 136 B2
Ćuprija SRB 127 D3
Curinga I 175 C2
Currelos E 140 B3
Currie GB 35 C4
Curtea de Argeş RO 17 C6
Curtici RO 126 A3
Curtis E 140 A2
Curtis Santa Eulalia E 140 A2
Čurug SRB 126 B2
Cusano Mutri I 170 B2
Cushendall GB 27 A4
Cusset F 117 A3
Cussy-les-Forges F 104 B3
Custines F 92 C2
Cutanda E 152 B2
Cutro I 175 B2
Cutrofiano I 173 B4
Cuts F 90 B3
Cuvilly F 90 B2
Cuxhaven D 64 C1
Cvikov CZ 84 B2
Cwmbran GB 39 C3
Cybinka PL 75 B3
Czacz PL 75 B5
Czajków PL 86 A2
Czaplinek PL 75 A5
Czarlin PL 69 A3
Czarna-Dąbrówka PL 68 A2
Czarna Woda PL 68 B3
Czarnca PL 87 B3
Czarne PL 68 B1
Czarnków PL 75 B5
Czarnowo PL 76 A3
Czarnozyly PL 86 A2
Czarny Bór PL 85 B4
Czarny-Dunajec PL 99 B3
Czarny Las PL 86 A1
Czchow PL 99 B4
Czechowice-Dziedzice PL 98 B2
Czempiń PL 75 B5
Czermno PL 87 A4
Czernichow PL 99 B3
Czerniejewo PL 76 B2
Czernikowo PL 76 B3
Czersk PL 68 B2
Czerwieńsk PL 75 B4
Czerwionka-Leszczyny PL 86 B2
Częstochowa PL 86 B3
Czeszewo PL 76 B2
Człopa PL 75 A5
Człuchów PL 68 B2
Czołpino PL 68 A2

D

Dağ TR 189 B5
Daaden D 81 B3
Dabas H 112 B3
Dąbie PL 76 B3
Dąbki PL 67 B5
Dabo F 92 C3
Dabrowa PL 76 B2
Dąbrowa Górnicza PL 86 B3
Dąbrowa Tarnowska PL 87 B4
Dąbrowice PL 77 B4
Dabrowno PL 77 A5
Dachau D 108 A2
Dačice CZ 97 B3
Daday TR 23 A7
Dagali N 47 B5
Dägebüll D 64 B1
Dagmersellen CH 106 B2
Dahlen D 83 A4
Dahlenburg D 73 A3
Dahme D 83 A5
Dahn D 93 B3
Dähre D 73 B3
Daikanvik S 195 E7
Dail bho Dheas GB 31 A2
Dailly GB 36 A2
Daimiel E 157 A4
Daingean IRL 30 A1
Đakovica KOS 16 D4
Đakovo HR 125 B4
Dal
Akershus N 48 B3
Telemark N 47 C5
Dalaas A 107 B5
Dalabrog GB 31 B1
Dala-Floda S 50 B1
Dala-Husby S 50 B2
Dala-Järna S 50 B1
Dalaman TR 188 C3
Dalarö S 57 A4
Dalbeattie GB 36 B3
Dalby
DK 59 C3
Skåne S 61 D3
Uppsala S 57 A3
Värmland S 49 B4
Dale
Pembrokeshire GB 39 C1
Shetland GB 33 A5
Hordaland N 46 B2
Sogn og Fjordane N 46 A2
Dalen
Akershus N 48 C3
Telemark N 53 A4
Daleszyce PL 87 B4
Dalhalvaig GB 32 C3
Dalheim L 92 B2
Dalhem S 57 C4
Dalías E 164 C2
Dalj HR 125 B4
Dalkeith GB 35 C4
Dalkey IRL 30 A2
Dalmally GB 34 B3
Dalmellington GB 36 A2
Dalmose DK 65 A4
Daløy N 46 A1
Dalry
Dumfries & Galloway GB 34 C3
North Ayrshire GB 36 A2
Dalrymple GB 36 A2
Dalseter N 47 A6
Dalsjöfors S 60 B3
Dalskog S 54 B3
Dals Långed S 54 B3
Dals Rostock S 54 B3
Dalston GB 36 B4
Dalstorp S 60 B3
Dalton-in-Furness GB 36 B3
Daluis F 132 A2
Dalum
D 71 B4
S 60 B3
Dalvík IS 191 B7
Dalwhinnie GB 32 E2
Dalyan TR 188 C3
Damasi GR 182 D4
Damasławek PL 76 B2
Damazan F 129 B3
Damgan F 101 B3
Dammarie-les-Lys F 90 C2
Dammartin-en-Goële F 90 B2
Damme D 71 B5
Damnica PL 68 A2
Dampierre F 105 B4
Dampierre-sur-Salon F 105 B4
Damüls A 107 B4
Damville F 89 B5
Damvillers F 92 B1
Damwoude NL 70 A2
Danasjö S 195 E7
Danbury GB 45 B4
Dångebo S 63 B3
Dangers F 89 B5
Dangé-St Romain F 102 C2
Dangeul F 89 B4
Danilovgrad MNE 16 D3
Danischenhagen D 64 B3
Daniszyn PL 85 A5
Danjoutin F 106 B1
Dannas S 60 B3
Dannemarie F 106 B2
Dannemora S 51 B4
Dannenberg D 73 A4
Dánszentmiklós H 112 B3
Dány H 112 B3
Daoulas F 100 A1
Darabani RO 17 A7
Darány H 125 B3
Darda HR 125 B4
Dardesheim D 73 C3
Darfeld D 71 B4
Darfo I 120 B3
Dargiń PL 68 A1
Dargun D 66 C1
Darlington GB 37 B5
Darłowo PL 68 A1
Darmstadt D 93 B4
Darney F 105 A5
Daroca E 152 A2
Darque P 148 A1
Darragh IRL 28 B2
Dartford GB 45 B4
Dartington GB 43 B3
Dartmouth GB 43 B3
Darton GB 40 B2
Daruvar HR 124 B3
Darvas H 113 B5
Darvel GB 36 A2
Darwen GB 38 A4
Dassel D 82 A1
Dassow D 65 C3
Datça TR 188 C2
Datteln D 80 A3
Dattenfeld D 81 B3
Daugard DK 59 C2
Daugavpils LV 8 E5
Daumeray F 102 B1
Daun D 80 B2
Daventry GB 44 A2
Davle CZ 96 B2
Davor HR 124 B3
Davos CH 107 C4
Davutlar TR 188 B2
Davyd Haradok BY 13 B7
Dawlish GB 43 B3
Dax F 128 C1
Dazkırı TR 189 B4
Deal GB 45 B5
Deauville F 89 A4
Deba E 143 A4
Debar MK 182 B2
Dębe PL 77 B5

Dębica PL 87 B5
Dębnica Kaszubska PL 68 A2
Dębno PL 74 B3
Dębołęka PL 86 A2
Dębowa Łaka PL 69 B4
Debrc SRB 127 C1
Debrecen H 113 B5
Debrznica PL 75 B4
Debrzno PL 68 B2
Debstedt D 72 A1
Decazeville F 130 A1
Dechtice SK 98 C1
Decima I 168 B2
Decimomannu I 179 C2
Děčín CZ 84 B2
Decize F 104 C2
De Cocksdorp NL 70 A1
Decollatura I 175 B2
Decs H 125 A4
Deddington GB 44 B2
Dedeler TR 187 B5
Dedelow D 74 A2
Dedemli TR 189 B7
Dedemsvaart NL 71 B3
Dédestapolcsány H 113 A4
Dedovichi RUS 9 D6
Deeping St Nicholas GB 41 C3
Deftera CY 181 A2
Dég H 112 C2
Degaña E 141 B4
Degeberga S 61 D4
Degerby FIN 51 B7
Degerfors S 55 A5
Degerhamn S 63 B4
Degernes N 54 A2
Deggendorf D 95 C4
Deggingen D 94 C1
Dego I 133 A4
Degolados P 155 B3
De Haan B 78 A3
Dehesas de Guadix E 164 B1
Dehesas Viejas E 163 A4
Deia E 166 B2
Deining D 95 B3
Deinze B 79 B3
Déiva Marina I 134 A2
Dej RO 17 B5
Deje S 55 A4
De Koog NL 70 A1
Delabole GB 42 B2
Delary S 61 C3
Delbrück D 81 A4
Delčevo MK 182 B4
Delden NL 71 B3
Deleitosa E 156 A2
Delekovec HR 124 A2
Delémont CH 106 B2
Delft NL 70 B1
Delfzijl NL 71 A3
Délia I 176 B2
Delianuova I 175 C1
Deliblato SRB 127 C3
Delice TR 23 B7
Deliceto I 171 B3
Delitzsch D 83 A4
Dellach A 109 C4
Delle F 106 B2
Delme F 92 C2
Delmen-horst D 72 A1
Delnice HR 123 B3
Delsbo S 200 E2
Delvin IRL 30 A1
Delvinë AL 182 D2
Demandice SK 112 A2
Demen D 73 A4
Demidov RUS 13 A9
Demigny F 105 C3
Demirci TR 186 C3
Demirköy TR 186 A2
Demirtaş TR 186 B4
Demmin D 66 C2
Demonte I 133 A3
Demyansk RUS 9 D8
Denain F 78 B3
Denbigh GB 38 A3
Den Burg NL 70 A1
Dender-monde B 79 A4
Denekamp NL 71 B4
Den Ham NL 71 B3
Den Helder NL 70 B1
Denholm GB 35 C5
Denia E 159 C4
Denizli TR 188 B4
Denkendorf D 95 C3
Denklingen D 81 B3
Denny GB 35 B4
Den Oever NL 70 B2
Denta RO 126 B3
Déols F 103 C3
De Panne B 78 A2
Derbent TR 188 A3
Derby GB 40 C2
Derecske H 113 B5
Dereköy TR 186 A2
Derenberg D 82 A2
Derinkuyu TR 23 B8
Dermbach D 82 B2
Dermulo I 121 A4
Deronje SRB 125 B5
Derrygonnelly GB 26 B3
Derrylin GB 27 B3
Derry/Londonderry GB 27 B3
Dersingham GB 41 C4
Deruta I 136 C1
Dervaig GB 34 B1
Derval F 101 B4
Derveni GR 184 A3
Derventa BIH 125 C3
Dervock GB 27 A4
Desana I 119 B5
Descartes F 102 C2
Desenzano del Garda I 121 B3
Deset N 48 A3
Deševa BIH 139 B4
Desfina GR 184 A3
Desimirovac SRB 127 C2
Désio I 120 B2
Deskati GR 182 D3
Deskle SLO 122 A2
Desná CZ 84 B3
Dešov CZ 97 C3
Despotovac SRB 127 C3
Despotovo SRB 126 B1
Dessau D 83 A4
Deštná CZ 96 B2
Destriana E 141 B4
Désulo I 179 B3
Desvres F 78 B1
Deszk H 126 A2
Deta RO 126 B3
Detmold D 72 C1
Dětřichov CZ 98 B1
Dettelbach D 94 B2
Dettingen
Baden-Württemberg D 94 C1
Baden-Württemberg D 107 B4
Dettwiller F 93 C3
Detva SK 99 C3
Deurne NL 80 A1
Deutschkreutz A 111 B3
Deutschlandsberg A 110 C2
Deutsch Wagram A 111 A3
Deva RO 16 C5
Dévaványa H 113 B4
Devecikonağı TR 186 C3
Devecser H 111 B4
Develi TR 23 B8
Deventer NL 70 B3
Devil's Bridge GB 39 B3
Devin BG 183 B6
Devinska Nova Ves SK 111 A3
Devizes GB 43 A5
Devonport GB 42 B2
Devrek TR 187 A6
Devrekâni TR 23 A7
Đevrske HR 137 B4
De Wijk NL 71 B3
Dewsbury GB 40 B2
Deza E 152 A1
Dežanovac HR 124 B3
Dezzo I 120 B3
Dhali CY 181 A2
Dherinia CY 181 A2
Diamante I 174 B1
Dianalund DK 61 D1
Diano d'Alba I 119 C5
Diano Marina I 133 B4
Dicomano I 135 B4
Didcot GB 44 B2
Didim TR 188 B2
Didimoticho GR 186 A1
Die F 118 C2
Diebling F 92 B2
Dieburg D 93 B4
Diego del Carpio E 150 B2
Diekirch L 92 B2
Diélette F 88 A2
Diemelstadt D 81 A5
Diémoz F 118 B2
Dienten am Hochkönig A 109 B3
Diepenbeck B 79 B5
Diepholz D 71 B5
Dieppe F 89 A5
Dierberg D 74 A1
Dierdorf D 81 B3
Dieren NL 70 B3
Dierhagen D 66 B1
Diesdorf D 73 B3
Diessen D 108 B2
Diest B 79 B5
Dietenheim D 94 C2
Dietfurt D 95 B3
Dietikon CH 106 B3
Dietzenbach D 93 A4
Dieue-sur-Meuse F 92 B1
Dieulefit F 131 A4
Dieulouard F 92 C2
Dieuze F 92 C2
Diever NL 71 B3
Diez D 81 B4
Diezma E 163 A4
Differdange L 92 B1
Digermulen N 194 B6
Dignac F 115 C4
Dignano I 122 A1
Digne-les-Bains F 132 A2
Digny F 89 B5
Digoin F 104 C2
Dijon F 105 B4
Dikanäs S 195 E7
Dikili TR 186 C1
Diksmuide B 78 A2
Dilar E 163 A4
Dillenburg D 81 B4
Dillingen
Bayern D 94 C2
Saarland D 92 B2
Dilsen B 80 A1
Dimaro I 121 A3
Dimitrovgrad BG 183 A7
Dimitsana GR 184 B3
Dinami I 175 C2
Dinan F 101 A3
Dinant B 79 B4
Dinar TR 189 A5
Dinard F 101 A3
Dinek TR 187 C6
Dingden D 80 A2
Dingelstädt D 82 A2
Dingle
IRL 29 B1
S 54 B2
Dingolfing D 95 C4
Dingtuna S 56 A2
Dingwall GB 32 D2
Dinkelsbühl D 94 B2
Dinkelscherben D 94 C2
Dinklage D 71 B5
Dinslaken D 80 A2
Dinxperlo NL 80 A2
Diö S 63 B2
Diósgyör H 113 A4
Diósjeno H 112 B3
Diou F 104 C2
Dippen GB 34 C2
Dipperz D 82 B1
Dippoldiswalde D 84 B1
Dirdal N 52 B2
Dirksland NL 79 A4
Dirlewang D 108 B1
Dischingen D 94 C2
Disentis CH 107 C3
Diso I 173 B4
Diss GB 45 A5
Dissen D 71 B5
Distington GB 36 B3
Ditzingen D 93 C5
Ditzum D 71 A4
Divača SLO 122 B2
Dives-sur-Mer F 89 A3
Divín SK 99 C3
Divion F 78 B2
Divišov CZ 96 B2
Divonne les Bains F 118 A3
Dixmont F 104 A2
Dizy-le-Gros F 91 B4
Djúpivogur IS 191 C11
Djupvasshytta N 198 C4
Djura S 50 B1
Djurås S 50 B2
Djurmo S 50 B2
Djursdala S 62 A3
Dlouhá Loucka CZ 98 B1
Długowola PL 87 A5
Dmitrov RUS 9 D10
Dno RUS 9 D6
Doade E 141 B3
Doğanhisar TR 189 A6
Dobanovci SRB 127 C2
Dobbertin D 73 A5
Dobbiaco I 108 C3
Dobczyce PL 99 B4
Dobele LV 8 D3
Döbeln D 83 A5
Doberlug-Kirchhain D 83 A5
Dobern D 84 A2
Dobersberg A 97 C3
Dobiegniew PL 75 B4
Dobieszyn PL 87 A5
Doboj BIH 125 C4
Dobošnica BIH 125 C4
Doboz H 113 C5
Dobrá CZ 98 B2
Dobra
Wielkopolskie PL 76 C3
Zachodnio-Pomorskie PL 74 A3
Zachodnio-Pomorskie PL 75 A4
Dobrá Niva SK 99 C3
Dobřany CZ 96 B1
Dobre PL 76 B3
Dobre Miasto PL 69 B5
Dobreta-Turnu-Severin RO 16 C5
Dobri H 111 C3
Dobrica SRB 126 B2
Dobrich BG 17 D7
Dobrinishte BG 183 B5
Dobříš CZ 96 B2
Dobro E 143 B3
Dobrodzień PL 86 B2
Döbrököz H 112 C2
Dobromierz PL 85 B4
Dobrosołowo PL 76 B3
Dobroszyce PL 85 A5
Dobrovnik SLO 111 C3
Dobrush BY 13 B9
Dobruška CZ 85 B4
Dobrzany PL 75 A4
Dobrzen Wielki PL 86 B1
Dobrzyca
Wielkopolskie PL 75 A5
Wielkopolskie PL 85 A5
Zachodnio-Pomorskie PL 67 B4
Dobrzyńnad Wisłą PL 77 B4
Dobšiná SK 99 C4
Dobwalls GB 42 B2
Dochamps B 80 B1
Docking GB 41 C4
Docksta S 200 C4
Doddington GB 37 A4
Döderhult S 62 A4
Doesburg NL 70 B3
Doetinchem NL 71 C3
Dogliani I 133 A3
Dogueno P 160 B2
Doische B 91 A4
Dois Portos P 154 B1
Dojč SK 98 C1
Dokka N 48 B2
Dokkedal DK 58 B3
Dokkum NL 70 A2
Dokležovje SLO 111 C3
Doksy CZ 84 B2
Dokuz TR 189 A7
Dolancourt F 104 A3
Dolceácqua I 133 B3
Dol-de-Bretagne F 88 B2
Dole F 105 B4
Dølemo N 53 B4
Dolenja vas SLO 123 B3
Dolenjske Toplice SLO 123 B4
Dolfor GB 39 B3
Dolgarrog GB 38 A3
Dolgellau GB 38 B3
Doliana GR 182 D2
Dolianova I 179 C3
Dolice PL 75 A4
Doljani HR 138 A2
Döllach im Mölltal A 109 C3
Dolle D 73 B4
Dollnstein D 94 C3
Dollot F 104 A2
Döllstadt D 82 A2
Dolná Strehová SK 99 C3
Dolné Saliby SK 111 A4
Dolni Benešov CZ 98 B2
Dolni Bousov CZ 84 B3
Dolni Kounice CZ 97 B4
Dolni Kralovice CZ 97 B3
Dolni Újezd CZ 97 B4
Dolni Žandov CZ 95 A4
Dolný Kubín SK 99 B3
Dolo I 121 B5
Dolores E 165 A4
Dolovo SRB 127 C2
Dölsach A 109 C3
Dolsk PL 76 B2
Dolwyddelan GB 38 A3
Domaljevac BIH 125 B4
Domaniç TR 187 C4
Domaniža SK 98 B2
Domanovići BIH 139 B3
Domašov CZ 85 B5
Domaszék H 126 A1
Domaszków PL 85 B4
Domaszowice PL 86 A1
Domat-Ems CH 107 C4
Domažlice CZ 95 B4
Dombås N 198 C6
Dombasle-sur-Meurthe F 92 C2
Dombegyház H 126 A3
Dombóvár H 112 C2
Domène F 118 B2
Domérat F 116 A2
Domfessel F 92 C3
Domfront F 88 B3
Domfront-en-Champagne F 102 A2
Domingão P 154 B2
Domingo Pérez
Granada E 163 A4
Toledo E 150 C3
Dömitz D 73 A4
Dommartin F 91 C4
Dommartin-le-Franc F 91 C4
Domme F 129 B4
Dommitzsch D 83 A4
Domodóssola I 119 A5
Domokos GR 182 D4
Domoszló H 113 B4
Dompaire F 105 A5
Dompierre-du-Chemin F 88 B2
Dompierre-sur-Besbre F 104 C2
Dompierre-sur-Mer F 114 B2
Domrémy-la-Pucelle F 92 C1
Dömsöd H 112 B3
Domsure F 118 A2
Dómus de Maria I 179 D2
Domusnóvas I 179 C2
Domvena GR 184 A3
Domžale SLO 123 A3
Donado E 141 B4
Donaghadee GB 27 B5
Don Alvaro E 155 C4
Doña Mencía E 163 A3
Donaueschingen D 106 B3
Donauwörth D 94 C2
Don Benito E 156 B2
Doncaster GB 40 B2
Donegal IRL 26 B2
Donestebe-Santesteban E 144 A2
Donges F 101 B3
Dongo I 120 A2
Donington GB 41 C3
Doniños E 140 A2
Donja Bebrina HR 125 B4
Donja Brela HR 138 B2
Donja Dubica BIH 125 B4
Donja Dubrava HR 124 A2
Donja Kupčina HR 123 B4
Donja Šatornja SRB 127 C2
Donja Stubica HR 124 B1
Donje Brišnik BIH 138 B3
Donje Stative HR 123 B4
Donji-Andrijevci HR 125 B4
Donji Kazanci BIH 138 B2
Donji Koričáni BIH 138 A3
Donji Lapac HR 124 C1
Donji Malovan BIH 138 B3
Donji Miholjac HR 125 B4
Donji Mosti HR 124 A2
Donji Poloj HR 123 B4
Donji-Rujani BIH 138 B2
Donji Srb HR 138 A2
Donji Svilaj BIH 125 B4
Donji Tovarnik SRB 127 C1
Donji Vakuf BIH 138 A3
Donnalucata I 177 C3
Donnemarie-Dontilly F 90 C3
Donnersbach A 110 B1
Donnersbachwald A 109 B5
Donnerskirchen A 111 B3
Donorático I 134 B3
Donostia-San Sebastián E 144 A2
Donovaly SK 99 C3
Donzenac F 129 A4
Donzère F 131 A3
Donzy F 104 B2
Doonbeg IRL 29 B2
Doorn NL 70 B2
Dor E 140 A1
Dorchester GB 43 B4
Dørdal N 53 B5
Dordrecht NL 79 A4
Dörenthe D 71 B4
Dores GB 32 D2
Dorfen D 95 C4
Dorfgastein A 109 B4
Dorfmark D 72 B2
Dorf Mecklenburg D 65 C4
Dorgali I 178 B3
Dorking GB 44 B3
Dormagen D 80 A2
Dormánd H 113 B4
Dormans F 91 B3
Dornava SLO 124 A1
Dornbirn A 107 B4
Dornburg D 83 A3
Dorndorf D 82 B2
Dornecy F 104 B2
Dornes F 104 C2
Dornhan D 93 C4
Dornie GB 31 B3
Dornoch GB 32 D2
Dornum D 71 A4
Dorog H 112 B2
Dorohoi RO 17 B7
Dorotea S 200 B2
Dorotowo PL 69 B5
Dörpen D 71 B4
Dorsten D 80 A2
Dortan F 118 A2
Dortmund D 80 A3
Doruchów PL 86 A2
Dorum D 64 C1
Dörverden D 72 B2
Dörzbach D 94 B1
Dos Aguas E 159 B3
Dosbarrios E 151 C4
Döşemealtı TR 189 B5
Dos Hermanas E 162 A2
Dospat BG 183 B6
Dos-Torres E 156 B3
Dötlingen D 72 B1
Dottignies B 78 B3
Döttingen CH 106 B3
Douai F 78 B3
Douarnenez F 100 A1
Douchy F 104 B2
Douchy-les-Mines F 78 B3
Doucier F 105 C4
Doudeville F 89 A4
Doué-la-Fontaine F 102 B1
Douglas
Isle of Man GB 36 B2
South Lanarkshire GB 36 A3
Doulaincourt-Saucourt F 91 C5
Doulevant-le-Château F 91 C4
Doullens F 90 A2
Dounby GB 33 B3
Doune GB 35 B3
Dounreay GB 32 C3
Dour B 79 B3
Dourdan F 90 C2
Dourgne F 146 A3
Dournazac F 115 C4
Douro Calvo P 148 B2
Douvaine F 118 A3
Douvres-la-Délivrande F 89 A3
Douzy F 91 B5
Dover GB 45 B5
Dovje SLO 109 C4
Dovre N 198 D6
Downham Market GB 41 C4
Downhill GB 27 A4
Downpatrick GB 27 B5
Dowra IRL 26 B2
Doxato GR 183 B6
Doyet F 116 A2
Dozule F 89 A3
Drača SRB 127 C2
Dračevo
BIH 139 C4
MK 182 B3
Drachten NL 70 A3
Draga SLO 123 B3
Drăgăşani RO 17 C6
Dragatuš SLO 123 B4
Dragichyn BY 13 B6
Draginja SRB 127 C1
Dragocvet SRB 127 D3
Dragolovci BIH 125 C3
Dragoni I 170 B2
Dragør DK 61 D2
Dragotina HR 124 B2
Dragotinja BIH 124 B2
Dragozetići HR 123 B3
Draguignan F 132 B2
Drahnsdorf D 74 C2
Drahonice CZ 96 B2
Drahovce SK 98 C1
Drama GR 183 B6
Drammen N 54 A1
Drangedal N 53 A5
Drangsnes IS 190 B4
Dransfeld D 82 A1
Dranske D 66 B2
Draperstown GB 27 B4
Drassburg A 111 B3
Drávaszabolcs H 125 B4
Dravograd SLO 110 C2
Drawno PL 75 A4
Drawsko Pomorskie PL 75 A4
Drayton GB 41 C5
Drązdżewo PL 77 A6
Draženov CZ 95 B4
Draževac SRB 127 C2
Dražice HR 123 B3
Drebkau D 84 A2
Dreieich D 93 A4
Dreisen D 93 B4
Drenovci HR 125 C4
Drensteinfurt D 81 A3
Dresden D 84 A1
Dretyń PL 68 A1
Dreux F 89 B5
Dřevohostice CZ 98 B1
Drevsjø N 199 D9
Drewitz D 73 B5
Drezdenko PL 75 B4
Drežnica HR 123 B4
Drežnik-Grad HR 123 C4
Drietona SK 98 C1
Driffield GB 40 A3
Drimnin GB 34 B2
Drimoleague IRL 29 C2
Dringenberg D 81 A5
Drinić BIH 138 A2
Drinjača BIH 139 A5
Drinovci BIH 138 B3
Driopida GR 185 B5
Drivstua N 198 C6
Drlače SRB 127 C1
Drnholec CZ 97 C4
Drniš HR 138 B2
Drnje HR 124 A2
Drnovice CZ 97 B4
Dro I 121 B3
Drøbak N 54 A1
Drobin PL 77 B5
Drochia MD 17 A7
Drochtersen D 64 C2
Drogheda IRL 30 A2
Drohobych UA 13 D5
Droitwich Spa GB 44 A1
Drołtowice PL 85 A5
Dromahair IRL 26 B2
Dromcolliher IRL 29 B3
Dromore
Down GB 27 B4
Tyrone GB 27 B3
Dromore West IRL 26 B2
Dronero I 133 A3
Dronfield GB 40 B2
Drongan GB 36 A2
Dronninglund DK 58 A3
Dronrijp NL 70 A2
Dronten NL 70 B2
Drosendorf A 97 C3
Drösing A 97 C4
Drottningholm S 57 A3
Droué F 103 A3
Drulingen F 92 C3
Drumbeg GB 32 C1
Drumcliff IRL 26 B2
Drumgask GB 32 D2
Drumkeeran IRL 26 B2
Drummore GB 36 B2
Drumnadrochit GB 32 D2
Drumquin GB 27 B3
Drumshanbo IRL 26 B2
Drumsna IRL 26 C2
Drunen NL 79 A5
Druskininkai LT 13 A5
Druten NL 80 A1
Druya BY 13 A7
Družetići SRB 127 C2
Drvar BIH 138 A2
Drvenik HR 138 B3
Drwalew PL 77 C6
Drymen GB 34 B3
Drynoch GB 31 B2
Drzewce PL 76 B2
Drzewiany PL 68 B1
Drzewica PL 87 A4
Dualchi I 178 B2
Duas Igrejas P 149 A3
Dub SRB 127 D1
Dubá CZ 84 B2
Dubăsari MD 17 B8
Duben D 74 C2
Dübendorf CH 107 B3
Dubi CZ 84 B1
Dubica HR 124 B2
Dublin IRL 30 A2
Dubna RUS 9 D10
Dubňany CZ 98 C1
Dubnica nad Váhom SK 98 C2
Dubnik SK 112 B2
Dubno UA 13 C6
Dubodiel SK 98 C2
Dubona SRB 127 C2
Dubovac SRB 127 C3
Dubovic BIH 124 C2
Dubranec HR 124 B1
Dubrava HR 124 B2
Dubrave BIH 125 C4
Dubravica
HR 123 B4
SRB 127 C3
Dubrovnik HR 139 C4
Dubrovytsya UA 13 C7
Ducey F 88 B2
Duchcov CZ 84 B1
Ducherow D 74 A2
Dučina SRB 127 C2
Duclair F 89 A4
Dudar H 112 B1
Duddington GB 40 C3
Duderstadt D 82 A2
Dudeştii Vechi RO 126 A2
Dudley GB 40 C1
Dueñas E 142 C2
Duesund N 46 B2
Dueville I 121 B4
Duffel B 79 A4
Duffield GB 40 C2
Dufftown GB 32 D3
Duga Resa HR 123 B4
Dugi Rat HR 138 B2
Dugny-sur-Meuse F 92 B1
Dugopolje HR 138 B2
Dugo Selo HR 124 B2
Duino I 122 B2
Duisburg D 80 A2
Dukat AL 182 C1
Dukovany CZ 97 B4
Duleek IRL 30 A2
Dülken D 80 A2
Dülmen D 80 A3
Dulovo BG 17 D7
Dulpetorpet N 49 B4
Dulverton GB 43 A3
Dumbarton GB 34 C3
Dümerek TR 187 C6
Dumfries GB 36 A3
Dumlupınar TR 187 D4
Dümpelfeld D 80 B2
Dunaalmás H 112 B2
Dunabogdány H 112 B3
Dunafalva H 125 A4
Dunaföldvár H 112 C2
Dunaharaszti H 112 B3
Dunajská Streda SK 111 B4
Dunakeszi H 112 B3
Dunakiliti H 111 B4
Dunakömlöd H 112 C2
Dunapataj H 112 C2
Dunaszekcsö H 125 A4
Dunaszentgyorgy H 112 C2
Dunatetétlen H 112 C3
Dunaújváros H 112 C2
Dunavecse H 112 C2
Dunbar GB 35 B5
Dunbeath GB 32 C3
Dunblane GB 35 B4
Dunboyne IRL 30 A2
Dundalk IRL 27 B4
Dundee GB 35 B5
Dundrennan GB 36 B3
Dundrum GB 27 B5
Dunfanaghy IRL 26 A3
Dunfermline GB 35 B4
Dungannon GB 27 B4
Dungarvan IRL 29 B4
Dungiven GB 27 B4
Dunglow IRL 26 B2
Dungourney IRL 29 C3
Duninowo PL 68 A1
Dunkeld GB 35 B4
Dunker S 56 A2
Dunkerque = Dunkirk F 78 A2
Dunkineely IRL 26 B2
Dunkirk = Dunkerque F 78 A2
Dun Laoghaire IRL 30 A2
Dunlavin IRL 30 A2
Dunleer IRL 27 C4
Dun-le-Palestel F 116 A1
Dun-les-Places F 104 B3
Dunlop GB 36 A2
Dunloy GB 27 A4
Dunmanway IRL 29 C2
Dunmore IRL 28 A3
Dunmore East IRL 30 B2
Dunmurry GB 27 B4
Dunnet GB 32 C3
Dunningen D 107 A3
Dunoon GB 34 C3
Duns GB 35 C5
Dunscore GB 36 A3
Dunsford GB 43 B3
Dunshaughlin IRL 30 A2
Dunstable GB 44 B3
Dunster GB 43 A3
Dun-sur-Auron F 103 C4
Dun-sur-Meuse F 91 B5
Dunvegan GB 31 B2
Duplek SLO 110 C2
Dupnitsa BG 17 D5
Durağan TR 23 A8
Durach D 107 B5
Durak TR 186 C3
Durana E 143 B4
Durance F 128 B3
Durango E 143 A4
Durankulak BG 17 D8
Duras F 128 B3
Durban-Corbières F 146 B3
Dürbheim D 107 A3
Durbuy B 79 B5
Dúrcal E 163 B4
Đurdjenovac HR 125 B4
Đurdjevac HR 124 A3
Đurdjevik BIH 139 A4
Düren D 80 B2
Durham GB 37 B5
Đurinci SRB 127 C2
Durlach D 93 C4
Đurmanec HR 124 A1
Durness GB 32 C2
Dürnkrut A 97 C4
Dürrboden CH 107 C4
Dürrenboden CH 107 C3
Durrës AL 182 B1
Durrow IRL 30 B1
Durrus IRL 29 C2
Dursunbey TR 186 C3
Durtal F 102 B1
Durup DK 58 B1
Durusu TR 186 A3
Dusina BIH 139 B3
Dusnok H 112 C2
Dusocin PL 69 B3
Düsseldorf D 80 A2
Dusslingen D 93 C5
Duszniki PL 75 B5
Duszniki-Zdrój PL 85 B4
Dutovlje SLO 122 B2
Duvebo S 55 B5
Duved S 199 B9
Düzağac TR 187 D5
Düzce TR 187 B6
Dvärsätt S 199 B11
Dvor HR 124 B2
Dvorce CZ 98 B1
Dvorníky SK 98 C1
Dvory nad Žitavou SK 112 B2
Dvůr Králové nad Labem CZ 85 B3
Dybvad DK 58 A3

Dyce GB 33 D4
Dygowo PL 67 B4
Dykehead GB 35 B4
Dymchurch GB 45 B5
Dymer UA 13 C9
Dyrnes N 198 B4
Dywity PL 69 B5
Džanići BIH 139 B3
Dziadowa Kłoda PL 86 A1
Działdowo PL 77 A5
Działoszyce PL 87 B4
Działoszyn PL 86 A2
Dziemiany PL 68 A2
Dzierzążnia PL 77 B5
Dzierzgoń PL 69 B4
Dzierzgowo PL 77 A5
Dzierżoniów PL 85 B4
Dzisna BY 13 A8
Dziwnów PL 67 B3
Dźwierzuty PL 77 A5
Dzyarzhynsk BY 13 B7
Dzyatlava BY 13 B6

E

Ea E 143 A4
Eaglesfield GB 36 A3
Ealing GB 44 B3
Eardisley GB 39 B3
Earls Barton GB 44 A3
Earl Shilton GB 40 C2
Earlston GB 35 C5
Easington GB 41 B4
Easky IRL 26 B2
Eastbourne GB 45 C4
East Calder GB 35 C4
East Dereham GB 41 C4
Easter Skeld GB 33 A5
East Grinstead GB 45 B4
East Ilsley GB 44 B2
East Kilbride GB 36 A2
Eastleigh GB 44 C2
East Linton GB 35 C5
East Markham GB 40 B3
Easton GB 43 B4
East Wittering GB 44 C3
Eaton Socon GB 44 A3
Eaux-Bonnes F 145 B3
Eauze F 128 C3
Ebberup DK 59 C2
Ebbs A 108 B3
Ebbw Vale GB 39 C3
Ebeleben D 82 A2
Ebeltoft DK 59 B3
Ebene Reichenau A 109 C4
Eben im Pongau A 109 B4
Ebensee A 109 B4
Ebensfeld D 94 A2
Eberbach D 93 B4
Ebergötzen D 82 A2
Ebermann-Stadt D 94 B3
Ebern D 82 B2
Eberndorf A 110 C1
Ebersbach D 84 A2
Ebersberg D 108 A2
Ebersdorf
Bayern D 82 B3
Niedersachsen D 72 A2
Eberstein A 110 C1
Eberswalde D 74 B2
Ebnat-Kappel CH 107 B4
Éboli I 170 C3
Ebrach D 94 B2
Ebreichsdorf A 111 B3
Ebreuil F 116 A3
Ebstorf D 72 A3
Ecclefechan GB 36 A3
Eccleshall GB 40 C1
Eceabat TR 186 B1
Echallens CH 106 C1
Echauri E 144 B2
Echinos GR 183 B7
Échiré F 114 B3
Échirolles F 118 B2
Echourgnac F 128 A3
Echt NL 80 A1
Echte D 82 A2
Echternach L 92 B2
Ecija E 162 A2
Ečka SRB 126 B2
Eckartsberga D 82 A3
Eckelshausen D 81 B4
Eckental D 94 B3
Eckernförde D 64 B2
Eckerö FIN 51 B6
Eckington GB 40 B2
Éclaron F 91 C4
Écommoy F 102 B2
Écouché F 89 B3
Ecouis F 90 B1
Ecséd H 113 B3
Ecsegfalva H 113 B4
Écueillé F 103 B3
Ed S 54 B2
Eda S 49 C4
Eda glasbruk S 49 C4
Edam NL 70 B2
Edane S 55 A3
Edderton GB 32 D2
Ede NL 70 B2
Edebäck S 49 B5
Edebo S 51 B5
Edelény H 99 C4
Edelschrott A 110 B2
Edemissen D 72 B3
Edenbridge GB 45 B4
Edenderry IRL 30 A1
Edenkoben D 93 B4
Edesheim D 93 B4
Edessa GR 182 C4
Edewecht D 71 A4
Edgeworthstown IRL 30 A1
Edinburgh GB 35 C4
Edineţ MD 17 A7
Edirne TR 186 A1
Edland N 52 A3
Edolo I 120 A3
Edøy N 198 B5
Edremit TR 186 C2
Edsbro S 51 C5
Edsbruk S 56 B2
Edsbyn S 50 A2
Edsele S 200 C2
Edsleskog S 54 A3
Edsvalla S 55 A4
Eekloo B 79 A3
Eemshaven NL 71 A3
Eerbeek NL 70 B3
Eersel NL 79 A5
Eferding A 96 C2
Effiat F 116 A3
Efteløt N 53 A5
Egeln D 73 C4
Eger H 113 B4
Egerbakta H 113 B4
Egernsund DK 64 B2
Egersund N 52 B2
Egerszólát H 113 B4
Egervár H 111 C3
Egg
A 107 B4
D 107 A5
Eggby S 55 B4
Eggedal N 47 B6
Eggenburg A 97 C3
Eggenfelden D 95 C4
Eggesin D 74 A3
Eggum N 194 B4
Egham GB 44 B3
Éghezée B 79 B4
Egiertowo PL 68 A3
Egilsstaðir IS 191 B11
Egina GR 185 B4
Eginio GR 182 C4
Egio GR 184 A3
Égletons F 116 B2
Egling D 108 B2
Eglinton GB 27 A3
Eglisau CH 107 B3
Égliseneuve-d'Entraigues F 116 B2
Eglofs D 107 B4
Egmond aan Zee NL 70 B1
Egna I 121 A4
Egosthena GR 184 A4
Egremont GB 36 B3
Egtved DK 59 C2
Eguilles F 131 B4
Eguilly-sous-Bois F 104 A3
Éguzon-Chantôme F 103 C3
Egyek H 113 B4
Egyházasrádóc H 111 B3
Ehekirchen D 94 C3
Ehingen D 94 C1
Ehra-Lessien D 73 B3
Ehrang D 92 B2
Ehrenfriedersdorf D 83 B4
Ehrenhain D 83 B4
Ehrenhausen A 110 C2
Ehringshausen D 81 B4
Ehrwald A 108 B1
Eibar E 143 A4
Eibelstadt D 94 B2
Eibenstock D 83 B4
Eibergen NL 71 B3
Eibiswald A 110 C2
Eichenbarleben D 73 B4
Eichendorf D 95 C4
Eichstätt D 95 C3
Eickelborn D 81 A4
Eide
Hordaland N 46 B3
Møre og Romsdal N 198 C4
Eidet N 194 A9
Eidfjord N 46 B4
Eidsberg N 54 A2
Eidsbugarden N 47 A5
Eidsdal N 198 C4
Eidsfoss N 53 A6
Eidskog N 49 B4
Eidsvåg
Hordaland N 46 B2
Møre og Romsdal N 198 C5
Eidsvoll N 48 B3
Eikefjord N 46 A2
Eikelandsosen N 46 B2
Eiken N 52 B3
Eikesdal N 198 C5
Eikstrand N 53 A5
Eilenburg D 83 A4
Eilsleben D 73 B4
Eina N 48 B2
Einbeck D 82 A1
Eindhoven NL 79 A5
Einsiedeln CH 107 B3
Einville-au-Jard F 92 C2
Eisenach D 82 B2
Eisenberg
Rheinland-Pfalz D 93 B4
Thüringen D 83 B3
Eisenerz A 110 B1
Eisenhüttenstadt D 74 B3
Eisenkappel A 110 C1
Eisenstadt A 111 B3
Eisentratten A 109 C4
Eisfeld D 82 B2
Eisleben D 82 A3
Eislingen D 94 C1
Eitensheim D 95 C3
Eiterfeld D 82 B1
Eitorf D 80 B3
Eivindvik N 46 A2
Eivissa = Ibiza E 166 C1
Eixo P 148 B1
Ejby DK 59 C2
Ejea de los Caballeros E 144 B2
Ejstrupholm DK 59 C2
Ejulve E 153 B3
Eke B 79 B3
Ekeby
Gotland S 57 C4
Skåne S 61 D2
Uppsala S 51 B5
Ekeby-Almby S 56 A1
Ekenäs S 55 B4
Ekenässjön S 62 A3
Ekerö S 57 A3
Eket S 61 C3
Eketorp S 63 B4
Ekevik S 56 B2
Ekkerøy N 193 B14
Ekshärad S 49 B5
Eksingedal N 46 B2
Eksjö S 62 A2
Eksta S 57 C4
Ekträsk S 200 B5
El Alamo
Madrid E 151 B4
Sevilla E 161 B3
El Algar E 165 B4
El Almendro E 161 B2
El Alquián E 164 C2
Élancourt F 90 C1
El Arahal E 162 A2
El Arenal E 150 B2
El Arguellite E 164 A2
Elassona GR 182 D4
El Astillero E 143 A3
Elati GR 182 D3
Żelazno PL 85 B4
El Ballestero E 158 C1
El Barco de Ávila E 150 B2
Elbasan AL 182 B2
El Berrón E 142 A1
El Berrueco E 151 B4
Elbeuf F 89 A4
Elbingerode D 82 A2
Elbląg PL 69 A4
El Bodón E 149 B3
El Bonillo E 158 C1
El Bosque E 162 B2
El Bullaque E 157 A3
Elburg NL 70 B2
El Burgo E 162 B3
El Burgo de Ebro E 153 A3
El Burgo de Osma E 151 A4
El Burgo Ranero E 142 B1
El Buste E 144 C2
El Cabaco E 149 B3
El Callejo E 143 A3
El Campillo E 161 B3
El Campillo de la Jara E 156 A2
El Cañavete E 158 B1
El Carpio E 157 C3
El Carpio de Tajo E 150 C3
El Casar E 151 B4
El Casar de Escalona E 150 B3
El Castillo de las Guardas E 161 B3
El Centenillo E 157 B4
El Cerro E 149 B4
El Cerro de Andévalo E 161 B3
Elche E 165 A4
Elche de la Sierra E 158 C1
Elchingen D 94 C2
El Comenar E 162 B2
El Coronil E 162 A2
El Crucero E 141 A4
El Cubo de Tierra del Vino E 149 A4
El Cuervo E 162 B1
Elda E 159 C3
Eldena D 73 A4
Eldingen D 72 B3
Elefsina GR 185 A4
El Ejido E 164 C2
Elek H 113 C5
Elemir SRB 126 B2
El Escorial E 151 B3
El Espinar E 151 B3
Eleutheroupoli GR 183 C6
El Frago E 144 B3
El Franco E 141 A4
El Frasno E 152 A2
Elgå N 199 C8
El Garrobo E 161 B3
El Gastor E 162 B2
Elgin GB 32 D3
Elgoibar E 143 A4
Elgol GB 31 B2
El Gordo E 150 C2
El Grado E 145 B4
El Granado E 161 B2
El Grao de Castelló E 159 B4
El Grau E 159 C3
Elgshøa N 49 A4
El Higuera E 163 A3
El Hijate E 164 B2
El Hontanar E 152 B2
Elhovo BG 17 D7
El Hoyo E 157 B4
Elie GB 35 B5
Elizondo E 144 A2
Ełk PL 12 B5
Ellenberg D 94 B2
Ellesmere GB 38 B4
Ellesmere Port GB 38 A4
Ellezelles B 79 B3
Ellingen D 94 B2
Ellmau A 109 B3
Ellon GB 33 D4
Ellös S 54 B2
Ellrich D 82 A2
Ellwangen D 94 C2
Elm
CH 107 C4
D 72 A2
Elmadağ TR 23 B7
El Madroño E 161 B3
El Maillo E 149 B3
Elmalı TR 189 C4
El Masnou E 147 C3
El Mirón E 150 B2
El Molar E 151 B4
El Molinillo E 157 A3
El Morell E 147 C2
Elmshorn D 64 C2
Elmstein D 93 B3
El Muyo E 151 A4
Elne F 146 B3
Elnesvågen N 198 C4
El Olmo E 151 A4
Elorrio E 143 A4
Elöszállás H 112 C2
Elouda GR 185 D6
Éloyes F 105 A5
El Palo E 163 B3
El Pardo E 151 B4
El Payo E 149 B3
El Pedernoso E 158 B1
El Pedroso E 162 A2
El Peral E 158 B2
El Perelló
Tarragona E 153 B4
Valencia E 159 B3
Elphin GB 32 C1
El Picazo E 158 B1
El Pinell de Bray E 153 A4
El Piñero E 150 A2
El Pla de Santa Maria E 147 C2
El Pobo E 153 B3
El Pobo de Dueñas E 152 B2
El Pont d'Armentera E 147 C2
El Port de la Selva E 147 B4
El Port de Llançà E 146 B4
El Port de Sagunt E 159 B3
El Prat de Llobregat E 147 C3
El Provencio E 158 B1
El Puente E 143 A3
El Puente del Arzobispo E 150 C2
El Puerto E 141 A4
El Puerto de Santa María E 162 B1
El Real de la Jara E 161 B3
El Real de San Vincente E 150 B3
El Robledo E 157 A3
El Rocio E 161 B3
El Rompido E 161 B2
El Ronquillo E 161 B3
El Royo E 143 C4
El Rubio E 162 A3
El Sabinar E 164 A2
El Saler E 159 B3
El Salobral E 158 C2
El Saucejo E 162 A2
Els Castells E 147 B2
Elsdorf D 80 B2
Elsenfeld D 93 B5
El Serrat AND 146 B2
Elsfleth D 72 A1
Elspeet NL 70 B2
Elst NL 70 C2
Elstead GB 44 B3
Elster D 83 A4
Elsterberg D 83 B4
Elsterwerda D 83 A5
Elstra D 84 A2
El Temple E 144 C3
El Tiemblo E 150 B3
Eltmann D 94 B2
El Toboso E 157 A5
El Tormillo E 145 C3
El Torno E 149 B4
Eltville D 93 A4
El Valle de las Casas E 142 B1
Elvas P 155 C3
Elvebakken N 192 C7
El Vellón E 151 B4
Elven F 101 B3
El Vendrell E 147 C2
Elverum N 48 B3
El Villar de Arnedo E 144 B1
Elvington GB 40 B3
El Viso E 156 B3
El Viso del Alcor E 162 A2
Elxleben D 82 A2
Ely GB 45 A4
Elzach D 106 A3
Elze D 72 B2
Emådalen S 50 A1
Embleton GB 37 A5
Embonas GR 188 C2
Embrun F 132 A2
Embún E 144 B3
Emden D 71 A4
Emecik TR 188 C2
Emet TR 186 C4
Emirdağ TR 187 C6
Emlichheim D 71 B3
Emmaboda S 63 B3
Emmaljunga S 61 C3
Emmeloord NL 70 B2
Emmen
CH 106 B3
NL 71 B3
Emmendingen D 106 A2
Emmer-Compascuum NL 71 B4
Emmerich D 80 A2
Emmern D 72 B2
Emöd H 113 B4
Émpoli I 135 B3
Emsbüren D 71 B4
Emsdetten D 71 B4
Emsfors S 62 A4
Emskirchen D 94 B2
Emstek D 71 B5
Emsworth GB 44 C3
Emyvale IRL 27 B4
Enafors S 199 B9
Enånger S 51 A4
Encamp AND 146 B2
Encarnação P 154 C1
Encinas de Abajo E 150 B2
Encinas de Esgueva E 142 C2
Encinasola E 161 A3
Encinas Reales E 163 A3
Encio E 143 B3
Enciso E 144 B1
Enden N 199 D7
Endingen D 106 A2
Endrinal E 149 B4
Endröd H 113 C4
Enebakk N 54 A2
Eneryda S 63 B2
Enese H 111 B4
Enez TR 183 C8
Enfield IRL 30 A2
Eng A 108 B2
Engelberg CH 106 C3
Engelhartszell A 96 C1
Engelskirchen D 80 B3
Engen D 107 B3
Enger N 48 B2
Engerdal N 199 D8
Engerneset N 49 A4
Enge-sande D 64 B1
Engesvang DK 59 B2
Enghien B 79 B4
Engstingen D 94 C1
Engter D 71 B5
Enguera E 159 C3
Enguidanos E 158 B2
Enkenbach D 93 B3
Enkhuizen NL 70 B2
Enklinge FIN 51 B7
Enköping S 56 A3
Enna I 177 B3
Ennezat F 116 B3
Ennigerloh D 81 A4
Enningdal N 54 B2
Ennis IRL 28 B3
Enniscorthy IRL 30 B2
Enniskean IRL 29 C3
Enniskillen GB 27 B3
Ennistimon IRL 28 B2
Enns A 110 A1
Eno FIN 9 A7
Enontekiö FIN 196 A6
Ens NL 70 B2
Enschede NL 71 B3
Ensdorf D 95 B3
Ensisheim F 106 B2
Enstaberga S 56 B2
Enstone GB 44 B2
Entlebuch CH 106 B3
Entrácque I 133 A3
Entradas P 160 B1
Entrains-sur-Nohain F 104 B2
Entrambasaguas E 143 A3
Entrambasmestas E 143 A3
Entraygues-sur-Truyère F 116 C2
Entre-os-Rios P 148 A1
Entrevaux F 132 B2
Entrin Bajo E 155 C4
Entroncamento P 154 B2
Entzheim F 93 C3
Envermeu F 89 A5
Enviken S 50 B2
Enying H 112 C2
Enzingerboden A 109 B3
Enzklösterle D 93 C4
Épagny F 90 B3
Epalinges CH 106 C1
Epannes F 114 B3
Epanomi GR 182 C4
Epe
D 71 B4
NL 70 B2
Épernay F 91 B3
Épernon F 90 C1
Epfig F 93 C3
Epierre F 118 B3
Épila E 152 A2
Épinac F 104 C3
Épinal F 105 A5
Episcopia I 174 A2
Episkopi CY 181 B1
Epitalio GR 184 B2
Epoisses F 104 B3
Eppenbrunn D 93 B3
Eppendorf D 83 B5
Epping GB 45 B4
Eppingen D 93 B4
Epsom GB 44 B3
Epworth GB 40 B3
Eraclea I 122 B1
Eraclea Mare I 122 B1
Erba I 120 B2
Erbach
Baden-Württemberg D 94 C1
Hessen D 93 B4
Erbalunga F 180 A2
Erbendorf D 95 B4
Érchie I 173 B3
Ercolano I 170 C2
Ercsi H 112 B2
Érd H 112 B2
Erdek TR 186 B2
Erdemli TR 23 C8
Erdevik SRB 126 B1
Erding D 95 C3
Erdötelek H 113 B4
Erdut HR 125 B5
Erdweg D 95 C3
Ereğli
Konya TR 23 C8
Zonguldak TR 187 A6
Erenkaya TR 189 B7
Eresfjord N 198 C5
Eresos GR 183 D7
Eretria GR 185 A4
Erfde D 64 B2
Erfjord N 52 A2
Erfstadt D 80 B2
Erfurt D 82 B3
Ērgli LV 8 D4
Ergoldsbach D 95 C4
Eriboll GB 32 C2
Érice I 176 A1
Ericeira P 154 C1
Eğridir TR 189 B5
Eriksberg S 195 E6
Eriksmåla S 62 B3
Eringsboda S 63 B3
Eriswil CH 106 B2
Erithres GR 185 A4
Erkelenz D 80 A2
Erkner D 74 B2
Erkrath D 80 A2
Erla E 144 B3
Erlangen D 94 B3
Erli I 133 A4
Erlsbach A 109 C3
Ermelo NL 70 B2
Ermenak TR 23 C7
Ermenonville F 90 B2
Ermezinde P 148 A1
Ermidas P 160 A1
Ermioni GR 184 B4
Ermoupoli GR 185 B5
Ermsleben D 82 A3
Erndtebrück D 81 B4
Ernée F 88 B3
Ernestinovo HR 125 B4
Ernstbrunn A 97 C4
Erolzheim D 107 A5
Erquelinnes B 79 B4
Erquy F 101 A3
Erra P 154 C2
Erratzu E 144 A2
Errindlev DK 65 B4
Erro E 144 B2
Ersa F 180 A2
Érsekcsanád H 125 A4
Ersekë AL 182 C2
Érsekvadkert H 112 B3
Ersmark S 200 C6
Erstein F 93 C3
Erstfeld CH 107 C3
Ertebølle DK 58 B2
Ertingen D 107 A4
Ervedal
Coimbra P 148 B1
Portalegre P 154 B3
Ervenik HR 138 A1
Ervidel P 160 B1
Ervy-le-Châtel F 104 A2
Erwitte D 81 A4
Erxleben D 73 B4
Erzsébet H 125 A4
Esbjerg DK 59 C1
Esbly F 90 C2
Escacena del Campo E 161 B3
Escairón E 140 B3
Escalada E 143 B3
Escalante E 143 A3
Escalaplano I 179 C3
Escalona E 150 B3
Escalona del Prado E 151 A3
Escalonilla E 150 C3
Escalos de Baixo P 155 B3
Escalos de Cima P 155 B3
Escamilla E 152 B1
Es Caná E 166 B1
Escañuela E 157 C3
Es Castell E 167 B4
Escatrón E 153 A3
Eschach D 107 B4
Eschau D 94 B1
Eschede D 72 B3
Eschenau D 95 B3
Eschenbach D 95 B3
Eschenz CH 107 B3
Eschershausen D 72 C2
Esch-sur-Alzette L 92 B1
Esch-sur-Sûre L 92 B1
Eschwege D 82 A2
Eschweiler D 80 B2
Escobasa de Almazán E 152 A1
Escoeuilles F 78 B1
Escombreras E 165 B4
Escos F 144 A2
Escource F 128 B1
Escragnolles F 132 B2
Escrick GB 40 B2
Escurial E 156 A2
Escurial de la Sierra E 149 B4
Esens D 71 A4
Esgos E 140 B3
Esher GB 44 B3
Eskdalemuir GB 36 A3
Eskifjörður IS 191 B12
Eskilhem S 57 C4
Eskilsäter S 55 B4
Eskilstrup DK 65 B4
Eskilstuna S 56 A2
Eskipazar TR 187 B7
Eskişehir TR 187 C5
Eslarn D 95 B4
Eslava E 144 B2
Eslida E 159 B3
Eslohe D 81 A4
Eslöv S 61 D3
Eşme TR 188 A3
Es Mercadal E 167 B4
Es Migjorn Gran E 167 B4
Espa N 48 B3
Espalion F 130 A1
Esparragalejo E 155 C4
Esparragosa del Caudillo E 156 B2
Esparragossa de la Serena E 156 B2
Esparreguera E 147 C2
Esparron F 132 B1
Espe N 46 B3
Espedal N 52 B2
Espejo
Alava E 143 B3
Córdoba E 163 A3
Espeland N 46 B2
Espelkamp D 72 B1
Espeluche F 131 A3
Espeluy E 157 B4
Espera E 162 B2
Esperança P 155 B3
Espéraza F 146 B3
Espéria I 169 B3
Espevær N 52 A1
Espiel E 156 B2
Espinama E 142 A2
Espiñaredo E 140 A3
Espinasses F 132 A2
Espinelves E 147 C3
Espinhal P 154 A2
Espinho P 148 A1
Espinilla E 142 A2
Espinosa de Cerrato E 143 C3
Espinosa de los Monteros E 143 A3
Espinoso del Rey E 156 A3
Espirito Santo P 160 B2
Espluga de Francolí E 147 C2
Esplús E 145 C4
Espolla E 146 B3
Espoo FIN 8 B4
Esporles E 166 B2
Es Port d'Alcúdia E 167 B3
Esposende P 148 A1
Espot E 146 B2
Es Pujols E 166 C1
Esquedas E 145 B3
Esquivias E 151 B4
Essay F 89 B4
Essen
B 79 A4
Niedersachsen D 71 B4
Nordrhein-Westfalen D 80 A3
Essenbach D 95 C4
Essertaux F 90 B2
Essingen D 94 C2
Esslingen D 94 C1
Es Soleràs E 153 A4
Essoyes F 104 A3
Estacas E 140 B2
Estadilla E 145 B4
Estagel F 146 B3
Estaires F 78 B2
Estang F 128 C2
Estarreja P 148 B1
Estartit E 147 B4
Estavayer-le-Lac CH 106 C1
Este I 121 B4
Esteiro E 140 A2
Estela P 148 A1
Estella E 144 B1
Estellencs E 166 B2
Estepa E 162 A3
Estépar E 143 B3
Estepona E 162 B2
Esternay F 91 C3
Esterri d'Aneu E 146 B2
Esterwegen D 71 B4
Estissac F 104 A2
Estivadas E 140 B3
Estivareilles F 116 A2
Estivella E 159 B3
Estói P 160 B2
Estopiñán E 145 C4
Estoril P 154 C1
Estoublon F 132 B2
Estrée-Blanche F 78 B2
Estrées-St Denis F 90 B2
Estrela P 155 C3
Estremera E 151 B4
Estremoz P 155 C3
Estuna S 51 C5
Esyres F 102 B2
Esztergom H 112 B2
Etables-sur-Mer F 100 A3
Étain F 92 B1
Étalans F 105 B5
Etalle B 92 B1
Étampes F 90 C2
Etang-sur-Arroux F 104 C3
Étaples F 78 B1
Etauliers F 128 A2
Etili TR 186 C1
Etna N 48 B1
Etne N 52 A1
Etoges F 91 C3
Etoliko GR 184 A2
Eton GB 44 B3
Etréaupont F 91 B3
Étréchy F 90 C2
Étrépagny F 90 B1
Étretat F 89 A4
Étroeungt F 91 A3
Étroubles I 119 B4
Ettal D 108 B2
Ettelbruck L 92 B2
Etten NL 79 A4
Ettenheim D 106 A2
Ettington GB 44 A2
Ettlingen D 93 C4
Ettringen D 108 A1
Etuz F 105 B4

Etxarri-Aranatz E 144 B1
Etyek H 112 B2
Eu F 90 A1
Euerdorf D 82 B2
Eulate E 144 B1
Eupen B 80 B2
Europoort NL 79 A4
Euskirchen D 80 B2
Eutin D 65 B3
Evanger N 46 B3
Évaux-les-Bains F 116 A2
Evciler
Afyon TR 189 A4
Çanakkale TR 186 C1
Evenskjær N 194 B7
Evenstad N 48 A3
Evercreech GB 43 A4
Evergem B 79 A3
Everöd S 61 D4
Eversberg D 81 A4
Everswinkel D 71 C4
Evertsberg S 49 A5
Evesham GB 44 A2
Évian-les-Bains F 118 A3
Evisa F 180 A1
Evje N 53 B3
Evolène CH 119 A4
Évora P 154 C3
Evoramonte P 155 C3
Evran F 101 A4
Evrecy F 89 A3
Évreux F 89 A5
Évron F 102 A1
Évry F 90 C2
Ewell GB 44 B3
Ewersbach D 81 B4
Excideuil F 115 C5
Exeter GB 43 B3
Exmes F 89 B4
Exminster GB 43 B3
Exmouth GB 43 B3
Eydehamn N 53 B4
Eye
Peterborough GB 41 C3
Suffolk GB 45 A5
Eyemouth GB 35 C5
Eyguians F 132 A1
Eyguières F 131 B4
Eygurande F 116 B2
Eylie F 145 B4
Eymet F 129 B3
Eymoutiers F 116 B1
Eynsham GB 44 B2
Eyrarbakki IS 190 D4
Eystrup D 72 B2
Ezaro E 140 B1
Ezcaray E 143 B4
Ezcároz E 144 B2
Ezine TR 186 C1
Ezmoriz P 148 B1

F

Fabara E 153 A4
Fábbrico I 121 C3
Fåberg N 48 A2
Fabero E 141 B4
Fábiánsebestyén H 113 C4
Fåborg DK 64 A3
Fabrègues F 130 B2
Fabriano I 136 B1
Fabrizia I 175 C2
Facha P 148 A1
Facinas E 162 B2
Fačkov SK 98 B2
Fadagosa P 155 B3
Fadd H 112 C2
Faédis I 122 A2
Faenza I 135 A4
Fafe P 148 A1
Fagagna I 122 A2
Făgăraş RO 17 C6
Fågelberget S 199 A11
Fågelfors S 62 A3
Fågelmara S 63 B3
Fågelsta S 55 B6
Fagerås S 55 A4
Fagerheim N 47 B4
Fagerhøy N 48 A1
Fagerhult S 62 A3
Fagerlund N 48 B2
Fagernes
Oppland N 47 B6
Troms N 192 C3
Fagersanna S 55 B5
Fagersta S 50 B2
Fåglavik S 55 B4
Fagnano Castello I 174 B2
Fagnières F 91 C4
Faido CH 107 C3
Fains-Véel F 91 C5
Fairford GB 44 B2
Fairlie GB 34 C3
Fajsz H 112 C2
Fakenham GB 41 C4
Fåker S 199 B11
Fakse DK 65 A5
Fakse Ladeplads DK 65 A5
Falaise F 89 B3
Falcade I 121 A4
Falcarragh IRL 26 A2
Falces E 144 B2
Fălciu RO 17 B8
Falconara I 177 B3
Falconara Maríttima I 136 B2
Falcone I 177 A4
Faldingworth GB 40 B3
Falerum S 56 B2
Făleşti MD 17 B7
Falkenberg
Bayern D 95 B4
Bayern D 95 C4
Brandenburg D 83 A5
S 60 C2
Falkensee D 74 B2
Falkenstein
Bayern D 95 B4
Sachsen D 83 B4
Falkenthal D 74 B2
Falkirk GB 35 B4
Falkland GB 35 B4
Falköping S 55 B4
Fall D 108 B2
Falla S 56 B1
Fallingbostel D 72 B2
Falmouth GB 42 B1
Falset E 147 C1
Fălticeni RO 17 B7
Falun S 50 B2
Famagusta CY 181 A2
Fammestad N 46 B2
Fana N 46 B2
Fanano I 135 A3
Fanari GR 182 D3
Fanjeaux F 146 A3
Fano I 136 B2
Fântânele RO 126 A3
Fão P 148 A1
Fara in Sabina I 168 A2
Faramontanos de Tábara E 149 A4
Fara Novarese I 119 B5
Farasdues E 144 B2
Fårbo S 62 A4
Fareham GB 44 C2
Färentuna S 57 A3
Färgelanda S 54 B2
Färila S 200 E1
Faringdon GB 44 B2
Faringe S 51 C5
Farini I 120 C2
Fariza E 149 A3
Färjestaden S 63 B4
Farkadona GR 182 D4
Farkasfa H 111 C3
Farlete E 153 A3
Färlöv S 61 C4
Farmos H 113 B3
Farnă SK 112 B2
Färnäs S 50 B1
Farnborough GB 44 B3
Farnese I 168 A1
Farnham GB 44 B3
Farnroda D 82 B2
Faro P 160 B2
Fåro S 57 C5
Fårösund S 57 C5
Farra d'Alpago I 122 A1
Farranfore IRL 29 B2
Farre DK 59 B2
Farsala GR 182 D4
Farsø DK 58 B2
Farsund N 52 B2
Farum DK 61 D2
Fårup DK 58 B2
Fasana I 172 B1
Fasano I 173 B3
Fáskrúðsfjörður IS 191 C11
Fassberg D 72 B3
Fastiv UA 13 C8
Fastnäs S 49 B5
Fátima P 154 B2
Fatmomakke S 195 E6
Fättjaur S 195 E6
Faucogney-et-la-Mer F 105 B5
Fauguerolles F 128 B3
Faulenrost D 74 A1
Faulquemont F 92 B2
Fauquembergues F 78 B2
Fauske N 194 C6
Fauville-en-Caux F 89 A4
Fauvillers B 92 B1
Fåvang N 48 A2
Favara
E 159 B3
I 176 B2
Faverges F 118 B3
Faverney F 105 B5
Faversham GB 45 B4
Favignana I 176 B1
Fawley GB 44 C2
Fay-aux-Loges F 103 B4
Fayence F 132 B2
Fayet F 130 B1
Fayl-Billot F 105 B4
Fayón E 153 A4
Fearn GB 32 D3
Fécamp F 89 A4
Feda N 52 B2
Fedje N 46 B1
Feeny GB 27 B3
Fegen S 60 B3
Fegyvernek H 113 B4
Fehrbellin D 74 B1
Fehring A 111 C3
Feichten A 108 B1
Feiring N 48 B3
Feistritz im Rosental A 110 C1
Feketić SRB 126 B1
Felanitx E 167 B3
Feld am See A 109 C4
Feldbach A 110 C2
Feldberg D 74 A2
Feldkirch A 107 B4
Feldkirchen in Kärnten A 109 C5
Feldkirchen-Westerham D 108 B2
Felgueiras P 148 A1
Felitto I 172 B1
Félix E 164 C2
Felixstowe GB 45 B5
Felizzano I 119 C5
Felletin F 116 B2
Fellingsbro S 56 A1
Felnac RO 126 A3
Felnémet H 113 B4
Felpéc H 111 B4
Fels am Wagram A 97 C3
Felsberg D 81 A5
Felsönyék H 112 C2
Felsöszentiván H 126 A1
Felsöszentmárton H 125 B3
Felsözsolca H 113 A4
Felsted DK 64 B2
Feltre I 121 A4
Femsjö S 60 C3
Fenagh IRL 26 B3
Fene E 140 A2
Fenestrelle I 119 B4
Fénétrange F 92 C3
Feneu F 102 B1
Fengersfors S 54 B3
Fenit IRL 29 B2
Fensmark DK 65 A4
Fenwick GB 36 A2
Feolin Ferry GB 34 C1
Ferbane IRL 28 A4
Ferdinandovac HR 124 A3
Ferdinandshof D 74 A2
Fère-Champenoise F 91 C3
Fère-en-Tardenois F 91 B3
Ferentillo I 168 A2
Ferentino I 169 B3
Feres GR 183 C8
Feria E 155 C4
Feričanci HR 125 B3
Ferizli TR 187 B5
Ferla I 177 B3
Ferlach A 110 C1
Ferleiten A 109 B3
Fermil P 148 A2
Fermo I 136 B2
Fermoselle E 149 A3
Fermoy IRL 29 B3
Fernancabellero E 157 A4
Fernán Nuñéz E 163 A3
Fernán Peréz E 164 C2
Fernão Ferro P 154 C1
Fernay-Voltaire F 118 A3
Ferndown GB 43 B5
Ferness GB 32 D3
Fernhurst GB 44 B3
Ferns IRL 30 B2
Ferpécle CH 119 A4
Ferrals-les-Corbières F 146 A3
Ferrandina I 172 B2
Ferrara I 121 C4
Ferrara di Monte Baldo I 121 B3
Ferreira E 141 A3
Ferreira do Alentejo P 160 A1
Ferreira do Zêzere P 154 B2
Ferreras de Abajo E 141 C4
Ferreras de Arriba E 141 C4
Ferreries E 167 B4
Ferreruela E 152 A2
Ferreruela de Tabara E 149 A3
Ferret CH 119 B4
Ferrette F 106 B2
Ferriere I 120 C2
Ferrière-la-Grande F 79 B3
Ferrières
Hautes-Pyrénées F 145 A3
Loiret F 103 A4
Oise F 90 B2
Ferrières-sur-Sichon F 117 A3
Ferrol E 140 A2
Ferryhill GB 37 B5
Fertörakos H 111 B3
Fertöszentmiklós H 111 B3
Ferwerd NL 70 A2
Festieux F 91 B3
Festøy N 198 C3
Festvåg N 194 C5
Feteşti RO 17 C7
Fethard
Tipperary IRL 29 B4
Wexford IRL 30 B2
Fethiye TR 188 C4
Fetsund N 48 C3
Fettercairn GB 35 B5
Feucht D 95 B3
Feuchtwangen D 94 B2
Feudingen D 81 B4
Feuges F 91 C4
Feuquières F 90 B1
Feurs F 117 B4
Fevik N 53 B4
Ffestiniog GB 38 B3
Fiamignano I 169 A3
Fiano I 119 B4
Ficarazzi I 176 A2
Ficarolo I 121 C4
Fichtelberg D 95 A3
Ficulle I 135 C5
Fidenza I 120 C3
Fidjeland N 52 B2
Fieberbrunn A 109 B3
Fier AL 182 C1
Fiera di Primiero I 121 A4
Fiesch CH 119 A5
Fiesso Umbertiano I 121 C4
Figari F 180 B2
Figeac F 116 C2
Figeholm S 62 A4
Figgjo N 52 B1
Figline Valdarno I 135 B4
Figols E 145 B4
Figueira da Foz P 148 B1
Figueira de Castelo Rodrigo P 149 B3
Figueira dos Caveleiros P 160 A1
Figueiredo P 154 B3
Figueiredo de Alva P 148 B2
Figueiródos Vinhos P 154 B2
Figueres E 147 B3
Figueroles E 153 B3
Figueruela de Arriba E 141 C4
Filadélfia I 175 C2
Fil'akovo SK 99 C3
Filderstadt D 94 C1
Filey GB 41 A3
Filiaşi RO 17 C5
Filiates GR 182 D2
Filiatra GR 184 B2
Filipstad S 55 A5
Filisur CH 107 C4
Fillan N 198 B5
Filotio GR 185 B6
Filottrano I 136 B2
Filskov DK 59 C2
Filton GB 43 A4
Filtvet N 54 A1
Filzmoos A 109 B4
Finale Emilia I 121 C4
Finale Lígure I 133 A4
Fiñana E 164 B2
Finby FIN 51 B7
Fincham GB 41 C4
Finchingfield GB 45 B4
Findhorn GB 32 D3
Findochty GB 33 D4
Finike TR 189 C5
Finkenberg A 108 B2
Finnea IRL 27 C3
Finneidfjord N 195 D4
Finnerödja S 55 B5
Finnskog N 49 B4
Finnsnes N 194 A9
Finntorp S 54 A3
Finócchio I 168 B2
Finsjö S 62 A4
Finsland N 52 B3
Finspång S 56 B1
Finsterwalde D 84 A1
Finsterwolde NL 71 A4
Finstown GB 33 B3
Fintona GB 27 B3
Fionnphort GB 34 B1
Fiorenzuola d'Arda I 120 C2
Firenze = Florence I 135 B4
Firenzuola I 135 A4
Firmi F 130 A1
Firminy F 117 B4
Firmo I 174 B2
Fischamend Markt A 111 A3
Fischbach
A 110 B2
D 93 B3
Fischbeck D 73 B5
Fischen D 107 B5
Fishbourne GB 44 C2
Fishguard GB 39 C2
Fiskardo GR 184 A1
Fiskebäckskil S 54 B2
Fiskebøl N 194 B5
Fismes F 91 B3
Fisterra E 140 B1
Fitero E 144 B2
Fitjar N 46 C2
Fiuggi I 169 B3
Fiumata I 169 A3
Fiumefreddo Brúzio I 174 B2
Fiumefreddo di Sicilia I 177 B4
Fiumicino I 168 B2
Fivemiletown GB 27 B3
Fivizzano I 134 A3
Fjälkinge S 63 B2
Fjällåsen S 196 B3
Fjällbacka S 54 B2
Fjæra N 46 C3
Fjärdhundra S 56 A2
Fjellerup DK 58 B3
Fjerritslev DK 58 A2
Fjordgard N 194 A8
Fjugesta S 55 A5
Flå N 47 B6
Flåbygd N 53 A4
Flaça E 147 B3
Flace F 117 A4
Fladungen D 82 B2
Flaine F 118 A3
Flaka FIN 51 B7
Flåm N 46 B4
Flamatt CH 106 C2
Flamborough GB 41 A3
Flammersfeld D 81 B3
Flassans-sur-Issole F 132 B2
Flatdal N 53 A4
Flatebø N 46 B3
Flateby N 48 C3
Flateland N 52 A3
Flateyri IS 190 A2
Flatøydegard N 47 B6
Flatråker N 46 C2
Flattach A 109 C4
Flatvarp S 62 A4
Flauenskjold DK 58 A3
Flavigny-sur-Moselle F 92 C2
Flavy-le-Martel F 90 B3
Flawil CH 107 B4
Flayosc F 132 B2
Flechtingen D 73 B4
Fleckeby D 64 B2
Fleet GB 44 B3
Fleetmark D 73 B4
Fleetwood GB 38 A3
Flehingen D 93 B4
Flekke N 46 A2
Flekkefjord N 52 B2
Flen S 56 A2
Flensburg D 64 B2
Fleringe S 57 C4
Flerohopp S 62 B3
Flers F 88 B3
Flesberg N 47 C6
Fleurance F 129 C3
Fleuré F 115 B4
Fleurier CH 105 C5
Fleurus B 79 B4
Fleury
Hérault F 130 B2
Yonne F 104 B2
Fleury-les-Aubrais F 103 B3
Fleury-sur-Andelle F 89 A5
Fleury-sur-Orne F 89 A3
Flieden D 81 B5
Flimby GB 36 B3
Flims CH 107 C4
Flines-lèz-Raches F 78 B3
Flint GB 38 A3
Flirey F 92 C1
Flirsch A 108 B1
Flisa N 49 B4
Flisby S 62 A2
Fliseryd S 62 A4
Flix E 153 A4
Flixecourt F 90 A2
Flize F 91 B4
Flobecq B 79 B3
Floby S 55 B4
Floda S 60 B2
Flodden GB 37 A4
Flogny-la-Chapelle F 104 B2
Flöha D 83 B5
Flonheim D 93 B4
Florac F 130 A2
Floreffe B 79 B4
Florence = Firenze I 135 B4
Florennes B 79 B4
Florensac F 130 B2
Florentin F 129 C5
Florenville B 91 B5
Flores de Avila E 150 B2
Floresta I 177 B3
Floreşti MD 17 B8
Florídia I 177 B4
Florina GR 182 C3
Florø N 46 A2
Flörsheim D 93 A4
Floss D 95 B4
Fluberg N 48 B2
Flúðir IS 190 C5
Flühli CH 106 C3
Flumet F 118 B3
Fluminimaggiore I 179 C2
Flums CH 107 B4
Flyeryd S 63 B3
Flygsfors S 62 B3
Foča BIH 139 B4
Foça TR 186 D1
Fochabers GB 32 D3
Focşani RO 17 C7
Foel GB 38 B3
Foeni RO 126 B2
Fogdö S 56 A2
Fóggia I 171 B3
Foglianise I 170 B2
Föglö FIN 51 B7
Fohnsdorf A 110 B1
Foiano della Chiana I 135 B4
Foix F 146 B2
Fojnica
BIH 139 B3
BIH 139 B4
Fokstua N 198 C6
Földeák H 126 A2
Foldereid N 199 A9
Földes H 113 B5
Folegandros GR 185 C5
Folelli F 180 A2
Folgaria I 121 B4
Folgosinho P 148 B2
Folgoso de la Ribera E 141 B4
Folgoso do Courel E 141 B3
Foligno I 136 C1
Folkärna S 50 B3
Folkestad N 198 C3
Folkestone GB 45 B5
Follafoss N 199 B8
Folldal N 198 C6
Follebu N 48 A2
Follina I 121 B5
Föllinge S 199 B11
Follónica I 135 C3
Fölsbyn S 54 A3
Foncebadón E 141 B4
Foncine-le-Bas F 105 C5
Fondevila E 140 C2
Fondi I 169 B3
Fondo I 121 A4
Fonelas E 164 B1
Fonfría
Teruel E 152 B2
Zamora E 149 A3
Fonn N 46 A3
Fonnes N 46 B1
Fonni I 178 B3
Fontaine F 91 C4
Fontainebleau F 90 C2
Fontaine de Vaucluse F 131 B4
Fontaine-Française F 105 B4
Fontaine-le-Dun F 89 A4
Fontan F 133 A3
Fontanarejo E 157 A3
Fontane I 133 A3
Fontanélice I 135 A4
Fontanières F 116 A2
Fontanosas E 157 B3
Fonteblanda I 168 A1
Fontenay-le-Comte F 114 B3
Fontenay-Trésigny F 90 C2
Fontevrault-l'Abbaye F 102 B2
Fontiveros E 150 B3
Fontoy F 92 B1
Fontpédrouse F 146 B3
Font-Romeu F 146 B3
Fontstown IRL 30 A2
Fonyód H 111 C4
Fonz E 145 B4
Fonzaso I 121 A4
Fóppolo I 120 A2
Föra S 62 A4
Forbach
D 93 C4
F 92 B2
Forcall E 153 B3
Forcalquier F 132 B1
Forcarei E 140 B2
Forchheim D 94 B3
Forchtenau A 111 B3
Forchtenberg D 94 B1
Ford GB 34 B2
Førde
Hordaland N 52 A1
Sogn og Fjordane N 46 A2
Förderstedt D 83 A3
Førdesfjorden N 52 A1
Fordham GB 45 A4
Fordingbridge GB 44 C2
Fordon PL 76 A3
Fordongiánus I 179 C2
Forenza I 172 B1
Foresta di Búrgos I 178 B2
Forfar GB 35 B5
Forges-les-Eaux F 90 B1
Foria I 172 B1
Forio I 170 C1
Forjães P 148 A1
Førland N 52 B3
Forlì I 135 A5
Forlimpopoli I 135 A5
Formazza I 119 A5
Formby GB 38 A3
Formerie F 90 B1
Fórmia I 169 B3
Formígine I 135 A3
Formigliana I 119 B5
Formiguères F 146 B3
Fornalutx E 166 B2
Fornåsa S 56 B1
Fornelli I 178 B2
Fornells E 167 A4
Fornelos de Montes E 140 B2
Fornes E 163 B4
Forneset N 192 C3
Forni Avoltri I 109 C3
Forni di Sopra I 122 A1
Forni di Sotto I 122 A1
Forno
Piemonte I 119 B4
Piemonte I 119 B5
Forno Alpi-Gráie I 119 B4
Forno di Zoldo I 121 A5
Fornos de Algodres P 148 B2
Fornovo di Taro I 120 C3
Foros do Arrão P 154 B2
Forráskút H 126 A1
Forres GB 32 D3
Forriolo E 140 B3
Fors S 50 B3
Forsand N 52 B2
Forsbacka S 51 B3
Forserum S 62 A2
Forshaga S 55 A4
Forsheda S 60 B3
Forsinain GB 32 C3
Førslev DK 65 A4
Förslöv S 61 C2
Forsmark
Uppsala S 51 B5
Västerbotten S 195 E6
Forsmo S 200 C3
Forsnäs S 195 D9
Forsnes N 198 B5
Forssa FIN 8 B3
Forssjöbruk S 56 B2
Forst D 84 A2
Forsvik S 55 B5
Fortanete E 153 B3
Fort Augustus GB 32 D2
Forte dei Marmi I 134 B3
Fortezza I 108 C2
Forth GB 35 C4
Fort-Mahon-Plage F 78 B1
Fortrie GB 33 D4
Fortrose GB 32 D2
Fortun N 47 A4
Fortuna E 165 A3
Fortuneswell GB 43 B4
Fort William GB 34 B2
Forvik N 195 E3
Fos F 145 B4
Fosdinovo I 134 A3
Foss N 47 B6
Fossacésia I 169 A4
Fossano I 133 A3
Fossato di Vico I 136 B1
Fossbakken N 194 B8
Fosse-la-Ville B 79 B4
Fossombrone I 136 B1
Fos-sur-Mer F 131 B3
Fót H 112 B3
Fouchères F 104 A3
Fouesnant F 100 B1
Foug F 92 C1
Fougères F 88 B2
Fougerolles F 105 B5
Foulain F 105 A4
Fountainhall GB 35 C5
Fouras F 114 C2
Fourchambault F 104 B2
Fourmies F 91 A4
Fourna GR 182 D3
Fournels F 116 C3
Fourni GR 188 B1
Fournols F 117 B3
Fourques F 146 B3
Fourquevaux F 146 A2
Fours F 104 C2
Fowey GB 42 B2
Foxdale GB 36 B2
Foxford IRL 26 C1
Foyers GB 32 D2
Foynes IRL 29 B2
Foz E 141 A3
Foza I 121 B4
Foz do Arelho P 154 B1
Foz do Giraldo P 155 B3
Frabosa Soprana I 133 A3
Frades de la Sierra E 149 B4
Fraga E 153 A4
Fragagnano I 173 B3
Frailes E 163 A4
Fraire B 79 B4
Fraize F 106 A1
Framlingham GB 45 A5
Frammersbach D 94 A1
Framnes N 54 A1
França P 141 C4
Francaltroff F 92 C2
Francavilla al Mare I 169 A4
Francavilla di Sicilia I 177 B4
Francavilla Fontana I 173 B3
Francavilla in Sinni I 174 A2
Francescas F 129 B3
Franco P 148 A2
Francofonte I 177 B3
Francos E 151 A4
Frändefors S 54 B3
Franeker NL 70 A2
Frangy F 118 A2
Frankenau D 81 A4
Frankenberg
Hessen D 81 A4
Sachsen D 83 B5
Frankenburg A 109 A4
Frankenfels A 110 B2
Frankenmarkt A 109 B4
Frankenthal D 93 B4
Frankfurt
Brandenburg D 74 B3
Hessen D 81 B4
Frankrike S 199 B10
Fränsta S 200 D2
Františkovy Lázně CZ 83 B4
Franzburg D 66 B1
Frascati I 168 B2
Frasdorf D 109 B3
Fraserburgh GB 33 D4
Frashër AL 182 C2
Frasne F 105 C5
Frasnes-lez-Anvaing B 79 B3
Frasseto F 180 B2
Frastanz A 107 B4
Fratel P 155 B3
Fratta Todina I 135 C5
Frauenau D 96 C1
Frauenfeld CH 107 B3
Frauenkirchen A 111 B3
Frauenstein D 83 B5
Frauental A 110 C2
Frayssinet F 129 B4
Frayssinet-le-Gélat F 129 B4
Frechas P 149 A2
Frechen D 80 B2
Frechilla E 142 B2
Freckenhorst D 71 C4
Fredeburg D 81 A4
Fredelsloh D 82 A1
Fredeng N 48 B2
Fredensborg DK 61 D2
Fredericia DK 59 C2
Frederiks DK 59 B2
Frederikshavn DK 58 A3
Frederikssund DK 61 D2
Frederiksværk DK 61 D2
Fredrika S 200 B4
Fredriksberg S 50 B1
Fredriksdal S 62 A2
Fredrikstad N 54 A1
Fregenal de la Sierra E 161 A3
Fregene I 168 B2
Freiberg D 83 B5
Freiburg
Baden-Württemberg D 106 B2
Niedersachsen D 64 C2
Freienhagen D 81 A5
Freienhufen D 84 A1
Freiensteinau D 81 B5
Freihung D 95 B3
Freilassing D 109 B3
Freisen D 92 B3
Freising D 95 C3
Freistadt A 96 C2
Freital D 84 A1
Freixedas P 149 B2
Freixo de Espada à Cinta P 149 A3
Fréjus F 132 B2
Fremdingen D 94 C2
Frenštát pod Radhoštěm CZ 98 B2
Freren D 71 B4
Freshford IRL 30 B1
Freshwater GB 44 C2
Fresnay-sur-Sarthe F 89 B4
Fresneda de la Sierra E 152 B1

Fresneda de la Sierra Tiron E 143 B3
Fresnedillas E 151 B3
Fresnes-en-Woevre F 92 B1
Fresne-St Mamès F 105 B4
Fresno Alhandiga E 150 B2
Fresno de la Ribera E 150 A2
Fresno de la Vega E 142 B1
Fresno de Sayago E 149 A4
Fresnoy-Folny F 90 B1
Fresnoy-le-Grand F 91 B3
Fressenville F 90 A1
Fresvik N 46 A3
Fréteval F 103 B3
Fretigney F 105 B4
Freudenberg
Baden-Württemberg D 94 B1
Nordrhein-Westfalen D 81 B3
Freudenstadt D 93 C4
Freux B 92 B1
Frévent F 78 B2
Freyburg D 83 A3
Freyenstein D 73 A5
Freyming-Merlebach F 92 B2
Freystadt D 95 B3
Freyung D 96 C1
Frias de Albarracin E 152 B2
Fribourg CH 106 C2
Frick CH 106 B3
Fridafors S 63 B2
Fridaythorpe GB 40 A3
Friedberg
A 111 B3
Bayern D 94 C2
Hessen D 81 B4
Friedeburg D 71 A4
Friedewald D 82 B1
Friedland
Brandenburg D 74 B3
Mecklenburg-Vorpommern D 74 A2
Niedersachsen D 82 A1
Friedrichroda D 82 B2
Friedrichsdorf D 81 B4
Friedrichshafen D 107 B4
Friedrichskoog D 64 B1
Friedrichstadt D 64 B2
Friedrichswalde D 74 A2
Friesach A 110 C1
Friesack D 73 B5
Friesenheim D 93 C3
Friesoythe D 71 A4
Friggesund S 200 E2
Frigiliana E 163 B4
Frihetsli N 192 D3
Frillesås S 60 B2
Frinnaryd S 62 A2
Frinton-on-Sea GB 45 B5
Friockheim GB 35 B5
Friol E 140 A3
Fristad S 60 B2
Fritsla S 60 B2
Fritzlar D 81 A5
Frizington GB 36 B3
Frödinge S 62 A4
Froges F 118 B2
Frohburg D 83 A4
Frohnhausen D 81 B4
Frohnleiten A 110 B2
Froissy F 90 B2
Frombork PL 69 A4
Frome GB 43 A4
Frómista E 142 B2
Fröndenberg D 81 A3
Fronsac F 128 B2
Front I 119 B4
Fronteira P 155 B3
Frontenay-Rohan-Rohan F 114 B3
Frontenhausen D 95 C4
Frontignan F 130 B2
Fronton F 129 C4
Fröseke S 62 B3
Frosinone I 169 B3
Frosolone I 170 B2
Frosta N 199 B7
Frøstrup DK 58 A1
Frosunda S 57 A4
Frouard F 92 C2
Frövi S 56 A1
Frøyset N 46 B2
Fruges F 78 B2
Frutigen CH 106 C2
Frýdek-Místek CZ 98 B2
Frýdlant CZ 84 B3
Frydlant nad Ostravicí CZ 98 B2
Frygnowo PL 77 A5
Fryšták CZ 98 B1
Fucécchio I 135 B3
Fuencaliente
Ciudad Real E 157 A4
Ciudad Real E 157 B3
Fuencemillán E 151 B4
Fuendejalón E 144 C2
Fuengirola E 163 B3
Fuenlabrada E 151 B4
Fuenlabrada de los Montes E 156 A3
Fuensalida E 151 B3
Fuensanta E 164 B3
Fuensanta de Martos E 163 A4
Fuente-Álamo E 158 C2
Fuente-Álamo de Murcia E 165 B3
Fuentealbilla E 158 B2
Fuente al Olmo de Iscar E 150 A3
Fuentecén E 151 A4
Fuente Dé E 142 A2
Fuente de Cantos E 155 C4
Fuente del Arco E 156 B2
Fuente del Conde E 163 A3
Fuente del Maestre E 155 C4
Fuente de Santa Cruz E 150 A3
Fuente el Fresno E 157 A4
Fuente el Saz de Jarama E 151 B4
Fuente el Sol E 150 A3
Fuenteguinaldo E 149 B3
Fuentelapeña E 150 A2
Fuentelcésped E 151 A4
Fuentelespino de Haro E 158 B1
Fuentelespino de Moya E 158 B2
Fuentenovilla E 151 B4
Fuente Obejuna E 156 B2
Fuente Palmera E 162 A2
Fuentepelayo E 151 A3
Fuentepinilla E 151 A5
Fuenterroble de Salvatierra E 150 B2
Fuenterrobles E 158 B2
Fuentes E 158 B1
Fuentesauco E 151 A3
Fuentesaúco E 150 A2
Fuentes de Andalucía E 162 A2
Fuentes de Ebro E 153 A3
Fuentes de Jiloca E 152 A2
Fuentes de la Alcarria E 151 B5
Fuentes de León E 161 A3
Fuentes de Nava E 142 B2
Fuentes de Oñoro E 149 B3
Fuentes de Ropel E 142 B1
Fuentespalda E 153 B4
Fuentespina E 151 A4
Fuente-Tójar E 163 A3
Fuente Vaqueros E 163 A4
Fuentidueña E 151 A4
Fuentidueña de Tajo E 151 B4
Fuerte del Rey E 157 C4
Fügen A 108 B2
Fuglebjerg DK 65 A4
Fuglevik N 54 A1
Fuhrberg D 72 B2
Fulda D 82 B1
Fulgatore I 176 B1
Fully CH 119 A4
Fulnek CZ 98 B1
Fülöpszállás H 112 C3
Fulpmes A 108 B2
Fulunäs S 49 A5
Fumay F 91 B4
Fumel F 129 B3
Funäsdalen S 199 C9
Fundão P 148 B2
Funzie GB 33 A6
Furadouro P 148 B1
Fure N 46 A2
Fürstenau D 71 B4
Furstenau D 81 A5
Fürstenberg D 74 A2
Fürstenfeld A 111 B3
Fürstenfeldbruck D 108 A2
Fürstenstein D 96 C1
Fürstenwalde D 74 B3
Fürstenwerder D 74 A2
Fürstenzell D 96 C1
Furta H 113 B5
Fürth
Bayern D 94 B2
Hessen D 93 B4
Furth im Wald D 95 B4
Furtwangen D 106 A3
Furuby S 62 B3
Furudal S 50 A2
Furuflaten N 192 C4
Furulund S 61 D3
Furusjö S 60 B3
Fusa N 46 B2
Fuscaldo I 174 B2
Fusch an der Grossglocknerstrasse A 109 B3
Fushë Arrëz AL 182 A2
Fushë-Krujë AL 182 B1
Fusina I 122 B1
Fusio CH 107 C3
Füssen D 108 B1
Fustiñana E 144 B2
Futog SRB 126 B1
Futrikelv N 192 C3
Füzesabony H 113 B4
Füzesgyarmat H 113 B5
Fužine HR 123 B3
Fyllinge S 61 C2
Fynshav DK 64 B2
Fyresdal N 53 A4

G

Gaaldorf A 110 B1
Gabaldón E 158 B2
Gabarret F 128 C2
Gabčíkovo SK 111 B4
Gąbin PL 77 B4
Gabriac F 130 A1
Gabrovo BG 17 D6
Gaby I 119 B4
Gacé F 89 B4
Gacko BIH 139 B4
Gäddede S 199 A11
Gadebusch D 65 C4
Gadmen CH 106 C3
Gádor E 164 C2
Gádoros H 113 C4
Gael F 101 A3
Găeşti RO 17 C6
Gaeta I 169 B3
Gafanhoeira P 154 C2
Gaflenz A 110 B1
Gagarin RUS 9 E9
Gaggenau D 93 C4
Gagliano Castelferrato I 177 B3
Gagliano del Capo I 173 C4
Gagnet S 50 B2
Gaibanella I 121 C4
Gaildorf D 94 B1
Gaillac F 129 C4
Gaillefontaine F 90 B1
Gaillon F 89 A5
Gainsborough GB 40 B3
Gairloch GB 31 B3
Gairlochy GB 34 B3
Gáiro I 179 C3
Gaj
HR 124 B3
SRB 127 C3
Gaja-la-Selve F 146 A2
Gajanejos E 151 B5
Gajary SK 97 C4
Gajdobra SRB 126 B1
Galan F 145 A4
Galanta SK 111 A4
Galapagar E 151 B3
Galápagos E 151 B4
Galaroza E 161 B3
Galashiels GB 35 C5
Galatas GR 185 B4
Galaţi RO 17 C8
Galatina I 173 B4
Galatista GR 183 C5
Galátone I 173 B4
Galaxidi GR 184 A3
Galdakao E 143 A4
Galeata I 135 B4
Galende E 141 B4
Galera E 164 B2
Galéria F 180 A1
Galgamácsa H 112 B3
Galgate GB 38 A4
Galgon F 128 B2
Galinduste E 150 B2
Galinoporni CY 181 A3
Galisteo E 155 B4
Galizes P 148 B2
Galków PL 87 A3
Gallarate I 120 B1
Gallardon F 90 C1
Gallegos de Argañán E 149 B3
Gallegos del Solmirón E 150 B2
Galleguillos de Campos E 142 B1
Galleno I 135 B3
Galliate I 120 B1
Gallicano I 134 A3
Gállio I 121 B4
Gallipoli = Gelibolu TR 186 B1
Gallípoli I 173 B3
Gällivare S 196 B3
Gallizien A 110 C1
Gallneukirchen A 96 C2
Gällö S 199 C12
Gallocanta E 152 B2
Gällstad S 60 B3
Gallur E 144 C2
Galmisdale GB 31 C2
Galmpton GB 43 B3
Galston GB 36 A2
Galta N 52 A1
Galtelli I 178 B3
Galten DK 59 B2
Galtür A 107 C5
Galve de Sorbe E 151 A4
Galveias P 154 B2
Gálvez E 157 A3
Galway IRL 28 A2
Gamaches F 90 B1
Gámbara I 120 B3
Gambárie I 175 C1
Gambassi Terme I 135 B3
Gambatesa I 170 B2
Gambolò I 120 B1
Gaming A 110 B2
Gamla Uppsala S 51 C4
Gamleby S 62 A4
Gamlingay GB 44 A3
Gammelgarn S 57 C4
Gammelstad S 196 D5
Gammertingen D 107 A4
Gams CH 107 B4
Gamvik
Finnmark N 192 B6
Finnmark N 193 A12
Gan F 145 A3
Gáname E 149 A3
Ganda di Martello I 108 C1
Gandarela P 148 A1
Ganddal N 52 B1
Ganderkesee D 72 A1
Gandesa E 153 A4
Gandía E 159 C3
Gandino I 120 B2
Gandrup DK 58 A3
Ganges F 130 B2
Gånghester S 60 B3
Gangi I 177 B3
Gangkofen D 95 C4
Gannat F 116 A3
Gannay-sur-Loire F 104 C2
Gänserdorf A 97 C4
Ganzlin D 73 A5
Gap F 132 A2
Gara H 125 A5
Garaballa E 158 B2
Garaguso I 172 B2
Garbayuela E 156 A2
Garbhallt GB 34 B2
Garbsen D 72 B2
Garching D 109 A3
Garciaz E 156 A2
Garcihernández E 150 B2
Garcillán E 151 B3
Garcinarro E 151 B5
Garcisobaco E 162 B2
Garda I 121 B3
Gardanne F 131 B4
Gärdås S 49 B5
Gårdby S 63 B4
Gardeja PL 69 B3
Gardelegen D 73 B4
Gardermoen N 48 B3
Gardiki GR 182 E3
Garding D 64 B1
Gardone Riviera I 121 B3
Gardone Val Trómpia I 120 B3
Gárdony H 112 B2
Gardouch F 146 A2
Gårdsjö S 55 B5
Gårdskär S 51 B4
Gards Köpinge S 63 C2
Garein F 128 B2
Garelochhead GB 34 B3
Garéoult F 132 B2
Garešnica HR 124 B2
Garéssio I 133 A4
Garforth GB 40 B2
Gargaliani GR 184 B2
Gargaligas E 156 A2
Gargallo E 153 B3
Garganta la Olla E 150 B2
Gargantiel E 156 B3
Gargellen A 107 C4
Gargilesse-Dampierre F 103 C3
Gargnano I 121 B3
Gargnäs S 195 E8
Gárgoles de Abajo E 152 B1
Gargrave GB 40 B1
Garitz D 73 C5
Garlasco I 120 B1
Garlieston GB 36 B2
Garlin F 128 C2
Garlitos E 156 B2
Garmisch-Partenkirchen D 108 B2
Garnat-sur-Engièvre F 104 C2
Garpenberg S 50 B3
Garphyttan S 55 A5
Garray E 143 C4
Garrel D 71 B5
Garriguella E 146 B4
Garrison GB 26 B2
Garrovillas E 155 B4
Garrucha E 164 B3
Gars-am-Kamp A 97 C3
Garsås S 50 B1
Garsdale Head GB 37 B4
Gärsnäs S 63 C2
Garstang GB 38 A4
Gartow D 73 A4
Gartz D 74 A3
Gærum DK 58 A3
Garvagh GB 27 B4
Garvão P 160 B1
Garve GB 32 D2
Garwolin PL 12 C4
Garz D 66 B2
Garzyn PL 85 A4
Gąsawa PL 76 B2
Gåsborn S 49 C6
Gaschurn A 107 C5
Gascueña E 152 B1
Gasny F 90 B1
Gąsocin PL 77 B5
Gastes F 128 B1
Gastouni GR 184 B2
Gastouri GR 182 D1
Gata
E 149 B3
HR 138 B2
Gata de Gorgos E 159 C4
Gătaia RO 126 B3
Gatchina RUS 9 C7
Gatehouse of Fleet GB 36 B2
Gátér H 113 C3
Gateshead GB 37 B5
Gátova E 159 B3
Gattendorf A 111 A3
Gatteo a Mare I 136 A1
Gattinara I 119 B5
Gattorna I 134 A2
Gaucín E 162 B2
Gaulstad N 199 B9
Gaupne N 47 A4
Gautefall N 53 A4
Gauting D 108 A2
Gauto S 195 D7
Gava E 147 C3
Gavardo I 121 B3
Gavarnie F 145 B3
Gávavencsello H 113 A5
Gavi I 120 C1
Gavião P 154 B3
Gavirate I 120 B1
Gävle S 51 B4
Gavoi I 178 B3
Gavorrano I 135 C3
Gavray F 88 B2
Gavrio GR 185 B5
Gävunda S 49 B6
Gaweinstal A 97 C4
Gaworzyce PL 85 A3
Gawroniec PL 75 A5
Gaydon GB 44 A2
Gayton GB 41 C4
Gazipaşa TR 189 C7
Gazoldo degli Ippoliti I 121 B3
Gazzuolo I 121 B3
Gbelce SK 112 B2
Gdańsk PL 69 A3
Gdinj HR 138 B2
Gdov RUS 8 C5
Gdów PL 99 B4
Gdynia PL 69 A3
Gea de Albarracin E 152 B2
Geary GB 31 B2
Géaudot F 91 C4
Geaune F 128 C2
Gebesee D 82 A2
Gebiz TR 189 B5
Gebze TR 187 B4
Géderlak H 112 C2
Gedern D 81 B5
Gedinne B 91 B4
Gediz TR 187 D4
Gèdre F 145 B4
Gedser DK 65 B4
Gedsted DK 58 B2
Geel B 79 A4
Geesthacht D 72 A3
Geetbets B 79 B5
Gefell D 83 B3
Gehrden D 72 B2
Gehren D 82 B3
Geilenkirchen D 80 B2
Geilo N 47 B5
Geinsheim D 93 B4
Geisa D 82 B1
Geiselhöring D 95 C4
Geiselwind D 94 B2
Geisenfeld D 95 C3
Geisenhausen D 95 C4
Geisenheim D 93 B4
Geising D 84 B1
Geisingen D 107 B3
Geislingen D 94 C1
Geistthal A 110 B2
Geiterygghytta N 47 B4
Geithain D 83 A4
Geithus N 48 C1
Gela I 177 B3
Geldermalsen NL 79 A5
Geldern D 80 A2
Geldrop NL 80 A1
Geleen NL 80 B1
Gelembe TR 186 C2
Gelendost TR 189 A6
Gelibolu = Gallipoli TR 186 B1
Gelida E 147 C2
Gelnhausen D 81 B5
Gelnica SK 99 C4
Gelsa E 153 A3
Gelse H 111 C3
Gelsenkirchen D 80 A3
Gelsted DK 59 C2
Geltendorf D 108 A2
Gelterkinden CH 106 B2
Gelting D 64 B2
Gelu RO 126 A3
Gelves E 162 A1
Gembloux B 79 B4
Gemeaux F 105 B4
Gémenos F 132 B1
Gemerská Poloma SK 99 C4
Gemerská Ves SK 99 C4
Gemert NL 80 A1
Gemla S 62 B2
Gemlik TR 186 B4
Gemmenich B 80 B1
Gemona del Friuli I 122 A2
Gémozac F 114 C3
Gemund D 80 B2
Gemünden
Bayern D 94 A1
Hessen D 81 B4
Rheinland-Pfalz D 93 B3
Genappe B 79 B4
Génave E 164 A2
Genazzano I 169 B2
Gençay F 115 B4
Gencsapáti H 111 B3
Gendringen NL 80 A2
Genelard F 104 C3
Genemuiden NL 70 B3
Generalski Stol HR 123 B4
Geneva = Genève CH 118 A3
Genevad S 61 C3
Genève = Geneva CH 118 A3
Genevriéres F 105 B4
Gengenbach D 93 C4
Genillé F 103 B3
Genk B 80 B1
Genlis F 105 B4
Gennep NL 80 A1
Genner DK 64 A2
Gennes F 102 B1
Genoa = Génova I 134 A1
Genola I 133 A3
Génova = Genoa I 134 A1
Genowefa PL 76 B3
Gensingen D 93 B3
Gent = Ghent B 79 A3
Genthin D 73 B5
Gentioux F 116 B1
Genzano di Lucánia I 172 B2
Genzano di Roma I 168 B2
Georgenthal D 82 B2
Georgsmarienhütte D 71 B5
Gera D 83 B4
Geraards-bergen B 79 B3
Gerace I 175 C2
Geraci Sículo I 177 B3
Geraki GR 184 C3
Gérardmer F 106 A1
Geras A 97 C3
Gerbéviller F 92 C2
Gerbini I 177 B3
Gerbstedt D 83 A3
Gerði IS 191 C9
Gerede TR 187 B7
Gerena E 161 B3
Geretsried D 108 B2
Gérgal E 164 B2
Gergy F 105 C3
Gerindote E 150 C3
Gerjen H 112 C2
Gerlos A 108 B3
Germay F 92 C1
Germencik TR 188 B2
Germering D 108 A2
Germersheim D 93 B4
Gernika-Lumo E 143 A4
Gernrode D 82 A3
Gernsbach D 93 C4
Gernsheim D 93 B4
Geroda D 82 B1
Gerola Alta I 120 A2
Geroldsgrun D 83 B3
Gerolsbach D 95 C3
Gerolstein D 80 B2
Gerolzhofen D 94 B2
Gerovo HR 123 B3
Gerpinnes B 79 B4
Gerrards Cross GB 44 B3
Gerri de la Sal E 147 B2
Gersfeld D 82 B1
Gerstetten D 94 C2
Gersthofen D 94 C2
Gerstungen D 82 B2
Gerswalde D 74 A2
Gerzat F 116 B3
Gerze TR 23 A8
Gerzen D 95 C4
Gescher D 71 C4
Geseke D 81 A4
Geslau D 94 B2
Gespunsart F 91 B4
Gesté F 101 B4
Gestorf D 72 B2
Gesualda I 170 C3
Gesunda S 50 B1
Gesztely H 113 A4
Geta FIN 51 B6
Getafe E 151 B4
Getinge S 60 C2
Getxo E 143 A4
Geversdorf D 64 C2
Gevgelija MK 182 B4
Gevora del Caudillo E 155 C4
Gevrey-Chambertin F 105 B3
Gex F 118 A3
Gey D 80 B2
Geyikli TR 186 C1
Geysir IS 190 C5
Geyve TR 187 B5
Gföhl A 97 C3
Ghedi I 120 B3
Ghent = Gent B 79 A3
Gheorgheni RO 17 B6
Ghigo I 119 C4
Ghilarza I 178 B2
Ghisonaccia F 180 A2
Ghisoni F 180 A2
Gialtra GR 182 E4
Gianitsa GR 182 C4
Giardinetto Vécchio I 171 B3
Giardini Naxos I 177 B4
Giarratana I 177 B3
Giarre I 177 B4
Giat F 116 B2
Giaveno I 119 B4
Giazza I 121 B4
Giba I 179 C2
Gibellina Nuova I 176 B1
Gibostad N 194 A9
Gibraleón E 161 B3
Gibraltar GBZ 162 B2
Gic H 111 B4
Gideå S 200 C5
Gideåkroken S 200 B3
Gidle PL 86 B3
Giebelstadt D 94 B1
Gieboldehausen D 82 A2
Gielniów PL 87 A4
Gielow D 74 A1
Gien F 103 B4
Giengen D 94 C2
Giens F 132 B2
Giera RO 126 B2
Gieselwerder D 81 A5
Giessen D 81 B4
Gieten NL 71 A3
Giethoorn NL 70 B3
Giffaumont-Champaubert F 91 C4
Gifford GB 35 C5
Gifhorn D 73 B3
Gige H 125 A3
Gignac F 130 B2
Gijón = Xixón E 142 A1
Gilena E 162 A3
Gilford GB 27 B4
Gillberga S 55 A3
Gilleleje DK 61 C2
Gilley F 105 B5
Gilley-sur-Loire F 104 C2
Gillingham
Dorset GB 43 A4
Medway GB 45 B4
Gilocourt F 90 B2
Gilserberg D 81 B5
Gilsland GB 37 B4
Gilze NL 79 A4
Gimåt S 200 C4
Gimo S 51 B5
Gimont F 129 C3
Ginasservis F 132 B1
Gingelom B 79 B5
Gingst D 66 B2
Ginosa I 171 C4
Ginzling A 108 B2
Giões P 160 B2
Gióia dei Marsi I 169 B3
Gióia del Colle I 173 B2
Gióia Sannitica I 170 B2
Gióia Táuro I 175 C1
Gioiosa Iónica I 175 C2
Gioiosa Marea I 177 A3
Giosla GB 31 A2
Giovinazzo I 171 B4
Girifalco I 175 C2
Giromagny F 106 B1
Girona E 147 C3
Gironcourt-sur-Vraine F 92 C1
Gironella E 147 B2
Gironville-sous-les-Côtes F 92 C1
Girvan GB 36 A2
Gislaved S 60 B3
Gislev DK 59 C3
Gisors F 90 B1
Gissi I 170 A2
Gistad S 56 B1
Gistel B 78 A2
Gistrup DK 58 B3
Giswil CH 106 C3
Githio GR 184 C3
Giugliano in Campania I 170 C2
Giulianova I 136 C2
Giulvăz RO 126 B2
Giurgiu RO 17 D6
Give DK 59 C2
Givet F 91 A4
Givors F 117 B4
Givry
B 79 B4
F 104 C3
Givry-en-Argonne F 91 C4
Givskud DK 59 C2
Giżałki PL 76 B2
Gizeux F 102 B2
Giżycko PL 12 A4
Gizzeria I 175 C2
Gizzeria Lido I 175 C2
Gjedved DK 59 C2
Gjegjan AL 182 B2
Gjendesheim N 47 A5
Gjerde N 46 B3
Gjerlev DK 58 B3
Gjermundshamn N 46 B2
Gjerrild DK 58 B3
Gjerstad N 53 B5
Gjesås N 49 B4
Gjesvær N 193 A9
Gjirokastër AL 182 C2
Gjøfjell N 54 A1
Gjøl DK 58 A2
Gjøra N 198 C6
Gjøvik N 48 B2
Gladbeck D 80 A2
Gladenbach D 81 B4
Gladstad N 195 E2
Glamis GB 35 B4
Glamoč BIH 138 A2
Glamsbjerg DK 59 C3
Gland CH 105 C5
Glandorf D 71 B4
Glanegg A 110 C1
Glanshammar S 56 A1
Glarus CH 107 B4
Glasgow GB 35 C3
Glashütte
Bayern D 108 B2
Sachsen D 84 B1
Glastonbury GB 43 A4
Glatzau A 110 C2
Glauchau D 83 B4
Glava S 54 A3
Glavatičevo BIH 139 B4
Glavičice BIH 127 C1
Gŭlŭbovo BG 183 A7
Glein
A 110 B1
N 195 D3
Gleinstätten A 110 C2
Gleisdorf A 110 B2
Glenamoy IRL 26 B1
Glenarm GB 27 B5
Glenavy GB 27 B4
Glenbarr GB 34 C2
Glenbeigh IRL 29 B2
Glenbrittle GB 31 B2
Glencoe GB 34 B2
Glencolumbkille IRL 26 B2
Glendalough IRL 30 A2
Glenealy IRL 30 B2
Glenelg GB 31 B3
Glenfinnan GB 34 B2
Glengarriff IRL 29 C2
Glenluce GB 36 B2
Glennamaddy IRL 28 A3
Glenrothes GB 35 B4
Glenties IRL 26 B2
Glesborg DK 58 B3
Glesien D 83 A4
Gletsch CH 106 C3
Glewitz D 66 B1
Glifada GR 185 B4
Glimåkra S 63 B2
Glin IRL 29 B2
Glina HR 124 B2
Glinde D 72 A3
Glinojeck PL 77 B5
Glinsk IRL 28 A2
Gliwice PL 86 B2
Glödnitz A 109 C5
Gloggnitz A 110 B2
Głogoczów PL 99 B3
Glogonj SRB 127 C2
Glogovac SRB 127 C3
Głogów PL 85 A4
Głogówek PL 86 B1
Glomel F 100 A2
Glomfjord N 195 D4
Glommen S 60 C2
Glommersträsk S 196 D2
Glonn D 108 B2
Glorenza I 108 C1

Gloria P 154 B2
Glosa GR 183 D5
Glossop GB 40 B2
Gloucester GB 39 C4
Głowaczów PL 87 A5
Glówczyce PL 68 A2
Glöwen D 73 B5
Głowno PL 77 C4
Gložan SRB 126 B1
Głubczyce PL 86 B1
Głuchołazy PL 85 B5
Głuchów PL 87 A4
Głuchowo PL 75 B5
Glücksburg D 64 B2
Glückstadt D 64 C2
Glumina BIH 139 A5
Glumsø DK 65 A4
Glušci SRB 127 C1
Glusk BY 13 B8
Głuszyca PL 85 B4
Glyngøre DK 58 B1
Glyn Neath GB 39 C3
Gmünd
Karnten A 109 C4
Nieder Östereich
A 96 C2
Gmund D 108 B2
Gmunden A 109 B4
Gnarp S 200 D3
Gnarrenburg D 72 A2
Gnesau A 109 C4
Gnesta S 56 A3
Gnięchowice PL 85 A4
Gniew PL 69 B3
Gniewkowo PL 76 B3
Gniezno PL 76 B2
Gnoien D 66 C1
Gnojnice BIH 139 B3
Gnojno PL 87 B4
Gnosall GB 40 C1
Gnosjö S 60 B3
Göbel TR 186 B3
Göçbeyli TR 186 C2
Goch D 80 A2
Gochsheim D 94 A2
Göd H 112 B3
Godalming GB 44 B3
Godby FIN 51 B6
Goðdalir IS 190 B6
Goddelsheim D 81 A4
Gódega di Sant'Urbano
I 122 B1
Godegård S 56 B1
Godelheim D 81 A5
Goderville F 89 A4
Godiasco I 120 C2
Godič SLO 123 A3
Godkowo PL 69 A4
Godmanchester
GB 44 A3
Gödöllö H 112 B3
Gödre H 125 A3
Godshill GB 44 C2
Godzikowice PL 85 B5
Godziszewo PL 69 A3
Goes NL 79 A3
Goetzenbrück F 93 C3
Góglio I 119 A5
Gogolin PL 86 B2
Göhren D 66 B2
Goirle NL 79 A5
Góis P 148 B1
Góito I 121 B3
Goizueta E 144 A2
Gojna Gora SRB 127 D2
Gójsk PL 77 B4
Gökçedağ TR 186 C3
Gökçen TR 188 A2
Gökçeören TR 188 A3
Gökçeyazı TR 186 C2
Göktepe TR 188 B3
Gol N 47 B5
Gola
HR 124 A3
N 48 A1
Gołańcz PL 76 B2
Gölbaşı TR 23 B7
Gölby FIN 51 B6
Gölcük
Kocaeli TR 187 B4
Niğde TR 23 B8
Golčův Jenikov CZ 97 B3
Gołczewo PL 67 C3
Goldach CH 107 B4
Goldbach D 93 A5
Goldbeck D 73 B4
Goldberg D 73 A5
Goldelund D 64 B2
Goldenstedt D 72 B1
Gołębiewo PL 69 A3
Golegã P 154 B2
Goleniów PL 75 A3
Golfo Aranci I 178 B3
Gölhisar TR 189 B4
Golina PL 76 B3
Gölle H 112 C2
Göllersdorf A 97 C4
Golling an der Salzach
A 109 B4
Gölmarmara TR 186 D2
Golnice PL 84 A3
Golnik SLO 123 A3
Gölova TR 189 C5
Gölpazarı TR 187 B5
Gols A 111 B3
Golspie GB 32 D3
Golssen D 74 C2
Golub-Dobrzyń PL 77 A4
Golubinci SRB 127 C2
Goluchów PL 86 A1
Golymin-Ośrodek
PL 77 B5
Golzow D 73 B5
Gomagoi I 108 C1
Gómara E 152 A1
Gomaringen D 93 C5
Gömbe TR 189 C4
Gömeç TR 186 C1
Gomel = Homyel
BY 13 B9
Gomes Aires P 160 B1
Gómezserracin E 150 A3
Gommern D 73 B4
Gomulin PL 86 A3
Gonäs S 50 B2
Goncelin F 118 B2
Gończyce PL 87 A5
Gondomar
E 140 B2
P 148 A1
Gondrecourt-le-
Château F 92 C1
Gondrin F 128 C3
Gönen
Balıkesir TR 186 B2
Isparta TR 189 B5
Gonfaron F 132 B2
Goñi E 144 B2
Goni
GR 182 D4
I 179 C3
Gonnesa I 179 C2
Gonnosfanádiga I 179 C2
Gönyü H 111 B4
Gonzaga I 121 C3
Goodrich GB 39 C4
Goodwick GB 39 B1
Gooik B 79 B4
Goole GB 40 B3
Goor NL 71 B3
Göpfritz an der Wild
A 97 C3
Goppenstein CH 119 A4
Göppingen D 94 C1
Gor E 164 B2
Góra
Dolnośląskie PL 85 A4
Mazowieckie PL 77 B5
Gorafe E 164 B1
Gorawino PL 67 C4
Goražde BIH 139 B4
Gőrbeháza H 113 B5
Gordaliza del Pino
E 142 B1
Gördes TR 186 D3
Gørding DK 59 C1
Górdola CH 120 A1
Gordon GB 35 C5
Gordoncillo E 142 B1
Gorebridge GB 35 C4
Gorenja Vas SLO 123 A3
Gorenje Jelenje
HR 123 B3
Gorey
GB 88 A1
IRL 30 B2
Gorgonzola I 120 B2
Gorica HR 137 A4
Gorican HR 124 A2
Gorinchem NL 79 A4
Goring GB 44 B2
Goritsy RUS 9 D10
Göritz D 74 A2
Gorizia I 122 B2
Górki PL 77 B4
Gorleben D 73 A4
Gorleston-on-sea
GB 41 C5
Gørlev DK 61 D1
Görlitz D 84 A2
Górliz E 143 A4
Görmin D 66 C2
Górna Grupa PL 69 B3
Gorna Oryahovitsa
BG 17 D6
Gornja Gorevnica
SRB 127 D2
Gornja Ploča HR 137 A4
Gornja Radgona
SLO 110 C2
Gornja Sabanta
SRB 127 D3
Gornja Trešnjevica
SRB 127 C2
Gornja Tuzla BIH 125 C4
Gornje Polje MNE 139 C4
Gornje Ratkovo
BIH 124 C2
Gornji Grad SLO 123 A3
Gornji Humac HR 138 B2
Gornji Jasenjani
BIH 139 B3
Gornji Kamengrad
BIH 124 C2
Gornji Kneginec
HR 124 A2
Gornji Kosinj HR 123 C4
Gornji Milanovac
SRB 127 C2
Gornji Podgradci
BIH 124 B3
Gornji Ravno BIH 138 B3
Gornji Sjenicak
HR 124 B1
Gornji Vakuf BIH 138 B3
Górno PL 87 B4
Görömböly H 113 A4
Górowo Iławeckie
PL 69 A5
Gorran Haven GB 42 B2
Gorredijk NL 70 A3
Gorron F 88 B3
Gorseinon GB 39 C2
Gort IRL 28 A3
Gortin GB 27 B3
Görzke D 73 B5
Gorzkowice PL 86 A3
Górzno
Kujawsko-Pomorskie
PL 77 A4
Zachodnio-Pomorskie
PL 75 A4
Gorzów Śląski PL 86 A2
Gorzów Wielkopolski
PL 75 B4
Górzyca PL 74 B3
Gorzyce PL 98 B2
Górzyn PL 84 A2
Gorzyń PL 75 B4
Gorzyno PL 68 A2
Gosaldo I 121 A4
Gosau A 109 B4
Gosberton GB 41 C3
Gościcino PL 68 A3
Gościęcin PL 86 B2
Gościm PL 75 B4
Gościno PL 67 B4
Gosdorf A 110 C2
Gosforth GB 36 B3
Goslar D 82 A2
Goslice PL 77 B4
Gospič HR 137 A4
Gosport GB 44 C2
Gössäter S 55 B4
Gossau CH 107 B4
Goss Ilsede D 72 B3
Gössnitz D 83 B4
Gössweinstein D 95 B3
Gostivar MK 182 B2
Gostkow PL 77 C4
Göstling an der Ybbs
A 110 B1
Gostomia PL 75 A5
Gostycyn PL 76 A2
Gostyń PL 85 A5
Gostynin PL 77 B4
Goszczyn PL 87 A4
Göta S 54 B3
Göteborg =
Gothenburg S 60 B1
Götene S 55 B4
Gotha D 82 B2
Gothem S 57 C4
Gothenburg =
Göteborg S 60 B1
Gotse Delchev BG 183 B5
Gottersdorf D 95 C4
Göttingen D 82 A1
Gottne S 200 C4
Götzis A 107 B4
Gouarec F 100 A2
Gouda NL 70 B1
Goudhurst GB 45 B4
Goumenissa GR 182 C4
Goura GR 184 B3
Gourdon F 129 B4
Gourgançon F 91 C4
Gourin F 100 A2
Gournay-en-Bray F 90 B1
Gourock GB 34 C3
Gouveia P 148 B2
Gouvy B 80 B1
Gouzeacourt F 90 A3
Gouzon F 116 A2
Govedari HR 138 C3
Govérnolo I 121 B3
Gowarczów PL 87 A4
Gowerton GB 39 C2
Gowidlino PL 68 A2
Gowran IRL 30 B1
Goyatz D 74 B3
Göynük
TR 187 B5
Antalya TR 189 C5
Gozdnica PL 84 A3
Gozdowo PL 77 B4
Gozee B 79 B4
Graal-Müritz D 65 B5
Grabenstätt D 109 B3
Grabhair GB 31 A2
Gråbo S 60 B2
Grabovac
HR 138 B2
SRB 127 C2
Grabovci SRB 127 C1
Grabow D 73 A4
Grabów PL 77 B4
Grabow nad Pilicą
PL 87 A5
Grabów nad Prosną
PL 86 A2
Grabowno PL 76 A2
Grabs CH 107 B4
Gračac HR 138 A1
Gračanica BIH 125 C4
Graçay F 103 B3
Grad SLO 111 C3
Gradac
BIH 139 C4
HR 138 B3
MNE 139 B5
Gradačac BIH 125 C4
Gradec HR 124 B2
Gradefes E 142 B1
Grades A 110 C1
Gradil P 154 C1
Gradina
HR 124 B3
MNE 139 B5
Gradisca d'Isonzo
I 122 B2
Gradište HR 125 B4
Grado
E 141 A4
I 122 B2
Grafenau D 96 C1
Gräfenberg D 95 B3
Gräfenhainichen D 83 A4
Grafenschlag A 97 C3
Grafenstein A 110 C1
Gräfenthal D 82 B3
Grafentonna D 82 A2
Grafenwöhr D 95 B3
Grafing D 108 A2
Grafling D 95 C4
Gräfsnäs S 54 B3
Gragnano I 170 C2
Grahovo SLO 122 A2
Graiguenamanagh
IRL 30 B2
Grain GB 45 B4
Grainau D 108 B2
Graja de Iniesta E 158 B2
Grajera E 151 A4
Gram DK 59 C2
Gramais A 108 B1
Gramat F 129 B4
Gramatneusiedl A 111 A3
Grambow D 74 A3
Grammichele I 177 B3
Gramsh AL 182 C2
Gramzow D 74 A3
Gran N 48 B2
Granada E 163 A4
Granard IRL 27 C3
Grañas E 140 A3
Granátula de Calatrava
E 157 B4
Grancey-le-Château
F 105 B4
Grandas de Salime
E 141 A4
Grandcamp-Maisy
F 88 A2
Grand-Champ F 100 B3
Grand Couronne F 89 A5
Grand-Fougeray F 101 B4
Grândola P 160 A1
Grandpré F 91 B4
Grandrieu
B 79 B4
F 117 C3
Grandson CH 106 C1
Grandvillars F 106 B1
Grandvilliers F 90 B1
Grañén E 145 C3
Grangärde S 50 B1
Grange IRL 26 B2
Grangemouth GB 35 B4
Grange-over-Sands
GB 36 B4
Grängesberg S 50 B1
Granges-de Crouhens
F 145 B4
Granges-sur-Vologne
F 106 A1
Gräningen D 73 B5
Granitola-Torretta
I 176 B1
Granja
Évora P 155 C3
Porto P 148 A1
Granja de Moreruela
E 142 C1
Granja de
Torrehermosa E 156 B2
Gränna S 55 B5
Grannäs
Västerbotten S 195 E7
Västerbotten S 195 E8
Granö S 200 B5
Granollers E 147 C3
Granowiec PL 85 A5
Granowo PL 75 B5
Gransee D 74 A2
Gransherad N 53 A5
Grantham GB 40 C3
Grantown-on-Spey
GB 32 D3
Grantshouse GB 35 C5
Granville F 88 B2
Granvin N 46 B3
Grærup Strand DK 59 C1
Gräsås S 60 C2
Grasbakken N 193 B12
Grasberg D 72 A2
Grasmere GB 36 B3
Gräsmyr S 200 C5
Grasö S 51 B5
Grassano I 172 B2
Grassau D 109 B3
Grasse F 132 B2
Grassington GB 40 A2
Græsted DK 61 C2
Gråsten DK 64 B2
Grästorp S 54 B3
Gratkorn A 110 B2
Gråträsk S 196 D2
Gratwein A 110 B2
Graulhet F 129 C4
Graus E 145 B4
Grávalos E 144 B2
Gravberget N 49 B4
Grave NL 80 A1
Gravedona I 120 A2
Gravelines F 78 A2
Gravellona Toce I 119 B5
Gravendal S 50 B1
Gravens DK 59 C2
Gravesend GB 45 B4
Graveson F 131 B3
Gravina in Púglia
I 172 B2
Gray F 105 B4
Grayrigg GB 37 B4
Grays GB 45 B4
Grayshott GB 44 B3
Graz A 110 B2
Grazalema E 162 B2
Grążawy PL 69 B4
Grazzano Visconti
I 120 C2
Greåker N 54 A2
Great Dunmow GB 45 B4
Great Malvern GB 39 B4
Great Torrington
GB 42 B2
Great Waltham GB 45 B4
Great Yarmouth
GB 41 C5
Grebbestad S 54 B2
Grebenstein D 81 A5
Grębocice PL 85 A4
Grębocin PL 76 A3
Greding D 95 B3
Gredstedbro DK 59 C1
Greencastle IRL 27 A3
Greenhead GB 37 B4
Greenisland GB 27 B5
Greenlaw GB 35 C5
Greenock GB 34 C3
Greenway GB 39 C2
Greenwich GB 45 B4
Grefrath D 80 A2
Greifenburg A 109 C4
Greiffenberg D 74 A2
Greifswald D 66 B2
Grein A 110 A1
Greipstad N 53 B3
Greiz D 83 B4
Grenaa DK 58 B3
Grenade F 129 C4
Grenade-sur-l'Adour
F 128 C2
Grenchen CH 106 B2
Grendi N 53 B3
Grenivík IS 191 B7
Grenoble F 118 B2
Gréoux-les-Bains
F 132 B1
Gresenhorst D 66 B1
Gressoney-la-Trinité
I 119 B4
Gressoney-St.-Jean
I 119 B4
Gressthal D 82 B2
Gressvik N 54 A1
Gresten A 110 B2
Gretna GB 36 B3
Greussen D 82 A2
Greve in Chianti I 135 B4
Greven
Mecklenburg-
Vorpommern D 73 A3
Nordrhein-Westfalen
D 71 B4
Grevena GR 182 C3
Grevenbroich D 80 A2
Grevenbrück D 81 A4
Grevenmacher L 92 B2
Grevesmühlen D 65 C4
Grevestrand DK 61 D2
Grevie S 61 C2
Greystoke GB 36 B4
Greystones IRL 30 A2
Grez-Doiceau B 79 B4
Grèzec F 129 B4
Grez-en-Bouère F 102 B1
Grezzana I 121 B4
Grgar SLO 122 A2
Grgurevci SRB 127 B1
Gries A 108 B2
Griesbach D 96 C1
Griesheim D 93 B4
Gries in Sellrain A 108 B2
Grieskirchen A 109 A4
Griffen A 110 C1
Grignan F 131 A3
Grignano I 122 B2
Grigno I 121 A4
Grignols F 128 B2
Grignon F 118 B3
Grijota E 142 B2
Grijpskerk NL 71 A3
Grillby S 56 A3
Grimaud F 132 B2
Grimbergen B 79 B4
Grimma D 83 A4
Grimmen D 66 B2
Grimmialp CH 106 C2
Grimsås S 60 B3
Grimsby GB 41 B3
Grimslöv S 62 B2
Grímsstaðir IS 191 B9
Grimstad N 53 B4
Grimstorp S 62 A2
Grindavík IS 190 D3
Grindelwald CH 106 C3
Grindheim N 52 B3
Grindsted DK 59 C1
Griñón E 151 B4
Gripenberg S 62 A2
Gripsholm S 56 A3
Grisolles F 129 C4
Grisslehamn S 51 B5
Gritley GB 33 C4
Grizebeck GB 36 B3
Grndina BIH 124 C2
Gröbming A 109 B4
Gröbzig D 83 A3
Grocka SRB 127 C2
Gröditz D 83 A5
Gródki PL 77 A5
Grodków PL 85 B5
Grodziec PL 76 B3
Grodzisk Mazowiecki
PL 77 B5
Grodzisk Wielkopolski
PL 75 B5
Groenlo NL 71 B3
Groesbeek NL 80 A1
Grohote HR 138 B2
Groitzsch D 83 A4
Groix F 100 B2
Grójec PL 77 C5
Grom PL 77 A5
Gromiljca BIH 139 B4
Grömitz D 65 B3
Gromnik PL 99 B4
Gromo I 120 B2
Gronau
Niedersachsen D 72 B2
Nordrhein-Westfalen
D 71 B4
Grønbjerg DK 59 B1
Grönenbach D 107 B5
Grong N 199 A9
Grönhögen S 63 B4
Groningen
D 73 C4
NL 71 A3
Grønnestrand DK 58 A2
Grono CH 120 A2
Grönskåra S 62 A3
Grootegast NL 71 A3
Gropello Cairoli I 120 B1
Grorud N 48 C2
Grósio I 120 A3
Grošnica SRB 127 D2
Grossalmerode D 82 A1
Grossarl A 109 B4
Gross Beeren D 74 B2
Gross Berkel D 72 B2
Grossbodungen D 82 A2
Gross-botwar D 94 C1
Grossburgwedel D 72 B2
Grosschönau D 84 B2
Gross-Dölln D 74 A2
Grossenbrode D 65 B4
Grossenehrich D 82 A2
Grossengottern D 82 A2
Grossenhain D 83 A5
Grossenkneten D 71 B5
Grossenlüder D 81 B5
Grossensee D 72 A3
Grossenzersdorf
A 111 A3
Grosseto I 135 C4
Gross-Gerau D 93 B4
Grossgerungs A 96 C2
Grossglobnitz A 97 C3
Grosshabersdorf D 94 B2
Grossharras A 97 C4
Grosshartmansdorf
D 83 B5
Grosshöchstetten
CH 106 C2
Gross Kreutz D 74 B1
Grosskrut A 97 C4
Gross Lafferde D 72 B3
Gross Leutheb D 74 B3
Grosslohra D 82 A2
Grossmehring D 95 C3
Gross Muckrow D 74 B3
Gross Oesingen D 72 B3
Grossostheim D 93 B5
Grosspertholz A 96 C2
Grosspetersdorf
A 111 B3
Grosspostwitz D 84 A2
Grossraming A 110 B1
Grossräschen D 84 A2
Gross Reken D 80 A3
Grossrinderfeld D 94 B1
Grossröhrsdorf D 84 A2
Gross Sarau D 65 C3
Gross Särchen D 84 A2
Grossschirma D 83 B5
Gross Schönebeck
D 74 B2
Grossschweinbarth
A 97 C4
Grosssiegharts A 97 C3
Grosssölk A 109 B4
Gross Umstadt D 93 B4
Grosswarasdorf A 111 B3
Gross Warnow D 73 A4
Gross-Weikersdorf
A 97 C3
Gross-Welle D 73 A5
Grosswilfersdorf
A 110 B2
Gross Wokern D 65 C5
Grostenquin F 92 C2
Grosuplje SLO 123 B3
Grotli N 198 C4
Grötlingbo S 57 C4
Grottáglie I 173 B3
Grottaminarda I 170 B3
Grottammare I 136 C2
Grotte di Castro I 168 A1
Grotteria I 175 C2
Gróttole I 172 B2
Grouw NL 70 A2
Grov N 194 B8
Grova N 53 A4
Grove E 140 B2
Grua N 48 B2
Grube D 65 B4
Grubišno Polje
HR 124 B3
Grude BIH 138 B3
Grudusk PL 77 A5
Grudziądz PL 69 B3
Grue N 49 B4
Gruissan F 130 B2
Grullos E 141 A4
Grumo Áppula I 171 B4
Grums S 55 A4
Grünau im Almtal
A 109 B4
Grünberg D 81 B4
Grünburg A 110 B1
Grundarfjörður IS 190 C2
Gründau D 81 B5
Gründelhardt D 94 B1
Grundforsen S 49 A4
Grundlsee A 109 B4
Grundsund S 54 B2
Grunewald D 84 A1
Grungedal N 53 A3
Grunow D 74 B3
Grünstadt D 93 B4
Gruvberget S 50 A3
Gruyères CH 106 C2
Gruža SRB 127 D2
Grybów PL 99 B4
Grycksbo S 50 B2
Gryfice PL 67 C4
Gryfino PL 74 A3
Gryfów Śląski PL 84 A3
Gryllefjord N 194 A8
Grymyr N 48 B2
Gryt S 56 B2
Grytgöl S 56 B1
Grythyttan S 55 A5
Grytnäs S 57 B3
Grzmiąca PL 68 B1
Grzybno PL 74 A3
Grzywna PL 76 A3
Gschnitz A 108 B2
Gschwend D 94 C1
Gstaad CH 106 C2
Gsteig CH 119 A4
Guadahortuna E 163 A4
Guadalajara E 151 B4
Guadalaviar E 152 B2
Guadalcanal E 156 B2
Guadalcázar E 162 A3
Guadalix de la Sierra
E 151 B4
Guadálmez E 156 B3
Guadalupe E 156 A2
Guadamur E 151 C3
Guadarrama E 151 B3
Guadiaro E 162 B2
Guadix E 164 B1
Guagnano I 173 B3
Guagno F 180 A1
Guajar-Faragüit E 163 B4
Gualchos E 163 B4
Gualdo Tadino I 136 B1
Gualtieri I 121 C3
Guarcino I 169 B3
Guarda P 149 B2
Guardamar del Segura
E 165 A4
Guardão P 148 B1
Guardavalle I 175 C2
Guardea I 168 A2
Guárdia I 172 B1
Guardiagrele I 169 A4
Guardiarégia I 170 B2
Guárdia Sanframondi
I 170 B2
Guardias Viejas E 164 C2
Guardiola de Bergueda
E 147 B2
Guardo E 142 B2
Guareña E 156 B1
Guaro E 162 B3
Guarromán E 157 B4
Guasila I 179 C3
Guastalla I 121 C3
Gubbhögen S 199 A12
Gúbbio I 136 B1
Guben D 74 C3
Gubin PL 74 C3
Gudå N 199 B8
Gudavac BIH 124 C2
Guddal N 46 A2
Güderup DK 64 B2
Gudhem S 55 B4
Gudhjem DK 67 A3
Gudovac HR 124 B2
Gudow D 73 A3
Güdül TR 187 B7
Gudvangen N 46 B3
Guebwiller F 106 B2
Guéjar-Sierra E 163 A4
Guéméné-Penfao
F 101 B4
Guéméné-sur-Scorff
F 100 A2
Güeñes E 143 A3
Guer F 101 B3
Guérande F 101 B3
Guéret F 116 A1
Guérigny F 104 B2
Guesa E 144 B2
Gueugnon F 104 C3
Guglionesi I 170 B2
Gühlen Glienicke
D 74 A1
Guia P 154 B2
Guichen F 101 B4
Guidizzolo I 121 B3
Guidónia-Montecélio
I 168 B2
Guiglia I 135 A3
Guignes F 90 C2
Guijo E 156 B3
Guijo de Coria E 149 B3
Guijo de Santa Bábera
E 150 B2
Guijuelo E 150 B2
Guildford GB 44 B3
Guillaumes F 132 A2
Guillena E 162 A1
Guillestre F 118 C3
Guillos F 128 B2
Guilsfield GB 38 B3
Guilvinec F 100 B1
Guimarães P 148 A1
Guincho P 154 C1
Guînes F 78 B1
Guingamp F 100 A2
Guipavas F 100 A1
Guisborough GB 37 B5
Guiscard F 90 B3
Guiscriff F 100 A2
Guise F 91 B3
Guisona E 147 C2
Guitiriz E 140 A3
Guîtres F 128 A2
Gujan-Mestras F 128 B1
Gulbene LV 8 D5
Gulçayır TR 187 C6
Guldborg DK 65 B4
Gullabo S 63 B3
Gullane GB 35 B5
Gullbrå N 46 B3
Gullbrandstorp S 61 C2
Gulleråsen S 50 A2
Gullhaug N 53 A6
Gullringen S 62 A3
Gullspång S 55 B5
Gullstein N 198 B5
Güllük TR 188 B2
Gülnar TR 23 C7
Gülpınar TR 186 C1
Gülşehir TR 23 B8
Gulsvik N 48 B1
Gumiel de Hizán
E 143 C3
Gummersbach D 81 A3
Gümüldür TR 188 A2
Gümüşhaciköy TR 23 A8
Gümüşova TR 187 B5
Gundelfingen D 94 C2
Gundel-fingen D 106 A2
Gundelsheim D 93 B5
Gunderschoffen F 93 C3
Gundertshausen
A 109 A3
Gundinci HR 125 B4
Gündoğmuş TR 189 C7
Güney
Burdur TR 189 B4
Denizli TR 188 A4
Gunja HR 125 C4
Günlüce TR 188 C3
Gunnarn S 195 E8
Gunnarsbyn S 196 C4
Gunnarskog S 49 C4
Gunnebo S 62 A4
Gunnislake GB 42 B2

Günselsdorf A 111 B3
Guntersblum D 93 B4
Guntersdorf A 97 C4
Guntin E 140 B3
Günyüzü TR 187 C6
Günzburg D 94 C2
Gunzenhausen D 94 B2
Güre
Balıkesir TR 186 C1
Uşak TR 186 D4
Gurk A 110 C1
Gurrea de Gállego
E 144 B3
Gürsu TR 186 B4
Gušće HR 124 B2
Gusev RUS 12 A5
Gúspini I 179 C2
Gusselby S 56 A1
Güssing A 111 B3
Gusswerk A 110 B2
Gustav Adolf S 49 B5
Gustavsberg S 57 A4
Gustavsfors S 54 A3
Güstrow D 65 C5
Gusum S 56 B2
Gutcher GB 33 A5
Gutenstein A 110 B2
Gütersloh D 81 A4
Guttannen CH 106 C3
Guttaring A 110 C1
Guttau D 84 A2
Güttingen CH 107 B4
Gützkow D 66 C2
Guzów PL 77 B5
Gvardeysk RUS 12 A4
Gvarv N 53 A5
Gvozd MNE 139 C5
Gvozdansko HR 124 B2
Gwda Wielka PL 68 B1
Gwennap GB 42 B1
Gy F 105 B4
Gyál H 112 B3
Gyarmat H 111 B4
Gyékényes H 124 A3
Gyé-sur-Seine F 104 A3
Gyljen S 196 C5
Gylling DK 59 C3
Gyoma H 113 C4
Gyömöre H 111 B4
Gyömrö H 112 B3
Gyón H 112 B3
Gyöngyfa H 125 B3
Gyöngyös H 113 B3
Gyöngyöspata H 113 B3
Gyönk H 112 C2
Györ H 111 B4
Györszemere H 111 B4
Gypsera CH 106 C2
Gysinge S 51 B3
Gyttorp S 55 A5
Gyula H 113 C5
Gyulafirátót H 112 B1
Gyulaj H 112 C2

H

Haacht B 79 B4
Haag
Nieder Östereich
A 110 A1
Ober Östereich A 109 A4
D 108 A3
Haaksbergen NL 71 B3
Haamstede NL 79 A3
Haan D 80 A3
Haapajärvi FIN 3 E9
Haapsalu EST 8 C3
Haarlem NL 70 B1
Habas F 128 C2
Habay B 92 B1
Habo S 62 A2
Håbol S 54 B3
Habry CZ 97 B3
Habsheim F 106 B2
Hachenburg D 81 B3
Hacıbektaş TR 23 B8
Hacılar TR 23 B8
Hacinas E 143 C3
Hackås S 199 C11
Hacketstown IRL 30 B2
Hackthorpe GB 37 B4
Hadamar D 81 B4
Hädanberg S 200 C4
Haddington GB 35 C5
Hadersdorf am Kamp
A 97 C3
Haderslev DK 59 C2
Haderup DK 59 B1
Hadım TR 23 C7
Hadleigh
Essex GB 45 B4
Suffolk GB 45 A4
Hadlow GB 45 B4
Hadmersleben D 73 B4
Hadsten DK 59 B3
Hadsund DK 58 B3
Hadžići BIH 139 B4
Hafnarfjörður IS 190 C4
Hafnir IS 190 D3
Hafslo N 47 A4
Haganj HR 124 B2
Hagby S 63 B4
Hage D 71 A4
Hægebostad N 52 B3
Hægeland N 53 B3
Hagen
Niedersachsen D 72 A1
Nordrhein-Westfalen
D 80 A3
Hagenbach D 93 B4
Hagenow D 73 A4
Hagetmau F 128 C2
Hagfors S 49 B5
Häggenås S 199 B11
Hagondange F 92 B2
Hagsta S 51 B4
Haguenau F 93 C3
Hahnbach D 95 B3
Hahnslätten D 81 B4
Hahót H 111 C3
Haiger D 81 B4
Haigerloch D 93 C4
Hailsham GB 45 C4
Hainburg A 111 A3
Hainfeld A 110 A2
Hainichen D 83 B5
Hajdúböszörmény
H 113 B5
Hajdučica SRB 126 B2
Hajdúdorogo H 113 B5
Hajdúnánás H 113 B5
Hajdúszoboszló
H 113 B5
Hajnáčka SK 113 A3
Hajnówka PL 13 B5
Hajós H 112 C3
Håkafot S 199 A11
Hakkas S 196 C4
Håksberg S 50 B2
Halaszi H 111 B4
Halberstadt D 82 A3
Halberton GB 43 B3
Hald Ege DK 58 B2
Haldem D 71 B5
Halden N 54 A2
Haldensleben D 73 B4
Halenbeck D 73 A5
Halesowen GB 40 C1
Halesworth GB 45 A5
Halfing D 109 B3
Halhjem N 46 B2
Håliden S 49 B5
Halifax GB 40 B2
Häljelöt S 56 B2
Halkirk GB 32 C3
Hall S 57 C4
Hälla S 200 C3
Hallabro S 63 B3
Hällabrottet S 56 A1
Halland GB 45 C4
Hällaryd S 63 B2
Hallaryd S 61 C3
Hällberga S 56 A2
Hällbybrunn S 56 A2
Halle
B 79 B4
Nordrhein-Westfalen
D 72 B1
Sachsen-Anhalt D 83 A3
Hålleberga S 62 B3
Hällefors S 55 A5
Hälleforsnäs S 56 A2
Hallein A 109 B4
Hällekis S 55 B4
Hallen S 199 B11
Hållen S 51 B4
Hallenberg D 81 A4
Hällestad S 56 B1
Hällevadsholm S 54 B2
Hällevik S 63 B2
Hälleviksstrand S 54 B2
Hallingby N 48 B2
Hallingeberg S 62 A4
Hallingen N 47 B6
Hall in Tirol A 108 B2
Hällnäs S 195 D9
Hållnäs S 51 B4
Hällnäs S 200 B5
Hallormsstaður
IS 191 B11
Hallsberg S 56 A1
Hållsta S 56 A2
Hallstahammar S 56 A2
Hallstatt A 109 B4
Hallstavik S 51 B5
Halltorp S 63 B4
Halluin F 78 B3
Hallviken S 199 B12
Hallworthy GB 42 B2
Halmstad S 61 C2
Hals DK 58 A3
Halsa N 198 B5
Halstead GB 45 B4
Haltdalen N 199 C8
Haltern D 80 A3
Haltwhistle GB 37 B4
Halvarsgårdarna S 50 B2
Halver D 80 A3
Halvrimmen DK 58 A2
Ham F 90 B3
Hamar N 48 B3
Hamarhaug N 46 B2
Hamarøy N 194 B6
Hambach F 92 B3
Hambergen D 72 A1
Hambergsund S 54 B2
Hambledon GB 44 C2
Hambuhren D 72 B2
Hamburg D 72 A3
Hamdibey TR 186 C2
Hamdorf D 64 B2
Hämeenlinna FIN 8 B4
Hameln = Hamlin D 72 B2
Hamersleben D 73 B4
Hamidiye TR 187 C5
Hamilton GB 36 A2
Hamina FIN 8 B5
Hamlagrø N 46 B3
Hamlin = Hameln D 72 B2
Hamm D 81 A3
Hammar S 55 B5
Hammarland FIN 51 B6
Hammarö S 55 A4
Hammarstrand S 200 C2
Hamme B 79 A4
Hammel DK 59 B2
Hammelburg D 82 B1
Hammelspring D 74 A2
Hammenhög S 66 A3
Hammerdal S 199 B12
Hammerfest N 192 B7
Hammershøj DK 58 B2
Hammerum DK 59 B2
Hamminkeln D 80 A2
Hamnavoe GB 33 A5
Hamneda S 60 C3
Hamningberg N 193 B14
Hamoir B 80 B1
Hamont B 80 A1
Hámor H 113 A4
Hamra
Gävleborg S 199 D12
Gotland S 57 D4
Hamrångefjärden
S 51 B4
Hamstreet GB 45 B4
Hamsund N 194 B6
Han TR 187 C5
Hanaskog S 61 C4
Hanau D 81 B4
Händelöp S 62 A4
Handlová SK 98 C2
Hanerau-Hademarschen D 64 B2
Hånger S 60 B3
Hanhimaa FIN 197 B8
Hanken S 55 B5
Hankensbüttel D 73 B3
Han Knežica BIH 124 B2
Hanko FIN 8 C3
Hannover D 72 B2
Hannut B 79 B5
Han Pijesak BIH 139 A4
Hansnes N 192 C3
Hanstedt D 72 A3
Hanstholm DK 58 A1
Hantsavichy BY 13 B7
Hanušovice CZ 85 B4
Haparanda S 196 D7
Haradok BY 13 A8
Harads S 196 C4
Häradsbäck S 63 B2
Häradsbygden S 50 B2
Harbo S 51 B4
Harboør DK 58 B1
Harburg
Bayern D 94 C2
Hamburg D 72 A2
Hårby DK 59 C3
Harc H 112 C2
Hardegarijp NL 70 A2
Hardegsen D 82 A1
Hardelot Plage F 78 B1
Hardenbeck D 74 A2
Hardenberg NL 71 B3
Harderwijk NL 70 B2
Hardheim D 94 B1
Hardt D 106 A3
Hareid N 198 C3
Haren
D 71 B4
NL 71 A3
Harestua N 48 B2
Harfleur F 89 A4
Harg S 51 B5
Hargicourt F 90 B3
Hargnies F 91 A4
Hargshamn S 51 B5
Härja S 55 B4
Harkány H 125 B4
Härkeberga S 56 A3
Harkebrügge D 71 A4
Harlech GB 38 B2
Harleston GB 45 A5
Hårlev DK 65 A5
Harlingen NL 70 A2
Harlösa S 61 D3
Harlow GB 45 B4
Harmancık TR 186 C4
Harmånger S 200 E3
Harmanli BG 183 B7
Härnevi S 56 A3
Härnösand S 200 D3
Haro E 143 B4
Haroldswick GB 33 A6
Háromfa H 124 A3
Haroué F 92 C2
Harpenden GB 44 B3
Harplinge S 60 C2
Harpstedt D 72 B1
Harrogate GB 40 A2
Harrow GB 44 B3
Härryda S 60 B2
Harsefeld D 72 A2
Harsewinkel D 71 C5
Hârşova 17 C7
Harstad N 194 B7
Harsum D 72 B2
Harsvik N 199 A7
Harta H 112 C3
Hartberg A 110 B2
Hartburn GB 37 A5
Hartennes F 90 B3
Hartest GB 45 A4
Hartha D 83 A4
Hartland GB 42 B2
Hartlepool GB 37 B5
Hartmanice CZ 96 B1
Hartmannsdorf A 110 B2
Harvassdal N 195 E5
Harwell GB 44 B2
Harwich GB 45 B5
Harzgerode D 82 A3
Häselgehr A 108 B1
Haselünne D 71 B4
Haskovo BG 183 B7
Hasköy TR 186 A1
Haslach D 106 A3
Haslach an der Mühl
A 96 C2
Hasle DK 67 A3
Haslemere GB 44 B3
Haslev DK 65 A4
Hasloch D 94 B1
Hasparren F 144 A2
Hassela S 200 D2
Hasselfelde D 82 A2
Hasselfors S 55 A5
Hasselt
B 79 B5
NL 70 B3
Hassfurt D 94 A2
Hassleben D 74 A2
Hässleholm S 61 C3
Hasslö S 63 B3
Hassloch D 93 B4
Hästbo S 51 B4
Hastersboda FIN 51 B7
Hästholmen S 55 B5
Hastière-Lavaux B 79 B4
Hastigrow GB 32 C3
Hastings GB 45 C4
Hästveda S 61 C3
Hasvik N 192 B6
Hatfield
Hertfordshire GB 44 B3
South Yorkshire
GB 40 B3
Hatherleigh GB 42 B2
Hathersage GB 40 B2
Hatlestrand N 46 B2
Hattem NL 70 B3
Hatten
D 71 A5
F 93 C3
Hattfjelldal N 195 E4
Hatting DK 59 C2
Hattingen D 80 A3
Hattstadt F 106 A2
Hattstedt D 64 B2
Hatvan H 112 B3
Hatvik N 46 B2
Hau D 80 A2
Haudainville F 92 B1
Hauganes IS 191 B7
Haugastøl N 47 B4
Hauge N 52 B2
Haugesund N 52 A1
Haughom N 52 B2
Haugsdal N 46 B2
Haugsdorf A 97 C4
Haukedal N 46 A3
Haukeland N 46 B2
Haukeligrend N 52 A3
Haukeliseter N 52 A3
Haukipudas FIN 3 D9
Haulerwijk NL 71 A3
Haunersdorf D 95 C4
Haus N 46 B2
Hausach D 106 A3
Hausham D 108 B2
Hausmannstätten
A 110 C2
Hausvik N 52 B2
Hautajärvi FIN 197 C12
Hautefort F 129 A4
Hauterives F 117 B5
Hauteville-Lompnès
F 118 B2
Haut-Fays B 91 A5
Hautmont F 79 B3
Hautrage B 79 B3
Hauzenberg D 96 C1
Havant GB 44 C3
Havdhem S 57 C4
Havdrup DK 61 D2
Havelange B 79 B5
Havelberg D 73 B5
Havelte NL 70 B3
Haverfordwest GB 39 C2
Haverhill GB 45 A4
Havering GB 45 B4
Håverud S 54 B3
Havířov CZ 98 B2
Havixbeck D 71 C4
Havlíčkův Brod CZ 97 B3
Havndal DK 58 B3
Havneby DK 64 A1
Havnebyen DK 61 D1
Havnsø DK 61 D1
Havøysund N 193 A8
Havran TR 186 C2
Havrebjerg DK 61 D1
Havsa TR 186 A1
Havstenssund S 54 B2
Havza TR 23 A8
Hawes GB 37 B4
Hawick GB 35 C5
Hawkhurst GB 45 B4
Hawkinge GB 45 B5
Haxey GB 40 B3
Hayange F 92 B2
Haydarlı TR 189 A5
Haydon Bridge GB 37 B4
Hayle GB 42 B1
Haymana TR 187 C7
Hay-on-Wye GB 39 B3
Hayrabolu TR 186 A2
Haysyn UA 13 D8
Hayvoron UA 13 D8
Haywards Heath
GB 44 C3
Hazebrouck F 78 B2
Hazlov CZ 83 B4
Heacham GB 41 C4
Headcorn GB 45 B4
Headford IRL 28 A2
Heanor GB 40 B2
Héas F 145 B4
Heathfield GB 45 C4
Hebden Bridge GB 40 B1
Heberg S 60 C2
Heby S 51 C3
Hechingen D 93 C4
Hechlingen D 94 C2
Hecho E 144 B3
Hechtel B 79 A5
Hechthausen D 72 A2
Heckelberg D 74 B2
Heckington GB 41 C3
Hecklingen D 82 A3
Hed S 56 A1
Hedalen N 48 B1
Hedared S 60 B2
Heddal N 53 A5
Hédé F 101 A4
Hede S 199 C10
Hedekas S 54 B2
Hedemora S 50 B2
Hedenäset S 196 C6
Hedensted DK 59 C2
Hedersleben D 82 A3
Hedesunda S 51 B4
Hedge End GB 44 C2
Hedon GB 41 B3
Heede D 71 B4
Heek D 71 B4
Heemstede NL 70 B1
Heerde NL 70 B3
Heerenveen NL 70 B2
Heerhugowaard NL 70 B1
Heerlen NL 80 B1
Heeze NL 80 A1
Heggenes N 47 A6
Hegra N 199 B8
Hegyeshalom H 111 B4
Hegyközség H 111 B3
Heia N 199 A9
Heide D 64 B2
Heidelberg D 93 B4
Heiden D 80 A2
Heidenau D 84 B1
Heidenheim D 94 C2
Heidenreichstein A 97 C3
Heikendorf D 64 B3
Heikkilä FIN 197 C12
Heilam GB 32 C2
Heiland N 53 B4
Heilbad Heiligenstadt
D 82 A2
Heilbronn D 93 B5
Heiligenblut A 109 B3
Heiligendamn D 65 B4
Heiligendorf D 73 B3
Heiligengrabe D 73 A5
Heiligenhafen D 65 B3
Heiligenhaus D 80 A2
Heiligenkreuz A 111 C3
Heiligenstadt D 94 B3
Heiloo NL 70 B1
Heilsbronn D 94 B2
Heim N 198 B6
Heimburg D 82 A2
Heimdal N 199 B7
Heinerscheid L 92 A2
Heinersdorf D 74 B3
Heining D 96 C1
Heiningen D 94 C1
Heinola FIN 8 B5
Heinsberg D 80 A2
Heist-op-den-Berg
B 79 A4
Hejde S 57 C4
Hejdeby S 57 C4
Hejls DK 59 C2
Hejnice CZ 84 B3
Hel PL 69 A3
Helchteren B 79 A5
Heldburg D 82 B2
Heldrungen D 82 A3
Helechosa E 156 A3
Helensburgh GB 34 B3
Helfenberg A 96 C2
Helgen N 53 A5
Helgeroa N 53 B5
Hella
IS 190 D5
N 46 A3
Helland N 194 B7
Hellas S 55 B3
Helle N 52 B2
Helleland N 52 B2
Hellendoorn NL 71 B3
Hellenthal D 80 B2
Hellesøy N 46 B1
Hellesylt N 198 C3
Hellevoetsluis NL 79 A4
Helligskogen N 192 C4
Hellín E 158 C2
Hellissandur IS 190 C2
Hellnar IS 190 C2
Hellum DK 58 A3
Hellvi S 57 C4
Hellvik N 52 B1
Helm-brechts D 83 B3
Helmond NL 80 A1
Helmsdale GB 32 C3
Helmsley GB 37 B5
Helmstedt D 73 B3
Hel'pa SK 99 C3
Helsa D 82 A1
Helsby GB 38 A4
Helsingborg S 61 C2
Helsinge DK 61 C2
Helsingør DK 61 C2
Helsinki FIN 8 B4
Helston GB 42 B1
Hemau D 95 B3
Hemavan S 195 E6
Hemel Hempstead
GB 44 B3
Hemer D 81 A3
Héming F 92 C2
Hemmet DK 59 C1
Hemmingstedt D 64 B2
Hemmoor D 64 C2
Hemnes N 54 A2
Hemnesberget N 195 D4
Hemse S 57 C4
Hemsedal N 47 B5
Hemslingen D 72 A2
Hemsworth GB 40 B2
Hen N 48 B2
Henån S 54 B2
Hendaye F 144 A2
Hendek TR 187 B5
Hendungen D 82 B2
Henfield GB 44 C3
Hengelo
Gelderland NL 71 B3
Overijssel NL 71 B3
Hengersberg D 95 C5
Hengoed GB 39 C3
Hénin-Beaumont F 78 B2
Henley-on-Thames
GB 44 B3
Hennan S 200 D1
Henneberg D 82 B2
Hennebont F 100 B2
Henne Strand DK 59 C1
Hennigsdorf D 74 B2
Hennset N 198 B5
Hennstedt
Schleswig-Holstein
D 64 B2
Hennstedt *continued*
Schleswig-Holstein
D 64 B2
Henrichemont F 103 B4
Henryków PL 85 B5
Henrykowo PL 69 A5
Hensås N 47 A5
Henstedt-Ulzburg
D 64 C2
Heppenheim D 93 B4
Herad
Buskerud N 47 B6
Vest-Agder N 52 B2
Heradsbygd N 48 B3
Heraklion = Iraklio
GR 185 D6
Herálec CZ 97 B4
Herand N 46 B3
Herbault F 103 B3
Herbern D 81 A3
Herbertstown IRL 29 B3
Herbeumont B 91 B5
Herbignac F 101 B3
Herbisse F 91 C4
Herbitzheim F 92 B3
Herbolzheim D 106 A2
Herborn D 81 B4
Herbrechtingen D 94 C2
Herby PL 86 B2
Herceg-Novi MNE 16 D3
Hercegovać HR 124 B3
Hercegszántó H 125 B4
Herchen D 80 B3
Heréd H 112 B3
Hereford GB 39 B4
Herefoss N 53 B4
Hereke TR 187 B4
Herencia E 157 A4
Herend H 111 B4
Herent B 79 B4
Herentals B 79 A4
Hérépian F 130 B2
Herfølge DK 61 D2
Herford D 72 B1
Herguijuela E 156 A2
Héric F 101 B4
Héricourt F 106 B1
Héricourt-en-Caux
F 89 A4
Hérimoncourt F 106 B1
Heringsdorf D 65 B4
Herisau CH 107 B4
Hérisson F 103 C4
Herk-de-Stad B 79 B5
Herlufmagle DK 65 A4
Hermagor A 109 C4
Hermannsburg D 72 B3
Hermansverk N 46 A3
Heřmanův Městec
CZ 97 B3
Herment F 116 B2
Hermeskeil D 92 B2
Hermisende E 141 C4
Hermonville F 91 B3
Hermsdorf D 83 B3
Hernani E 144 A2
Hernansancho E 150 B3
Herne D 80 A3
Herne Bay GB 45 B5
Hernes N 48 B3
Herning DK 59 B1
Herøya N 53 A5
Herramelluri E 143 B3
Herräng S 51 B5
Herre N 53 A5
Herrenberg D 93 C4
Herrera E 162 A3
Herrera de Alcántara
E 155 B3
Herrera del Duque
E 156 A2
Herrera de los Navarros
E 152 A2
Herrera de Pisuerga
E 142 B2
Herreros del Suso
E 150 B2
Herrestad S 54 B2
Herrhamra S 57 B3
Herritslev DK 65 B4
Herrlisheim F 93 C3
Herrljunga S 55 B4
Herrnhut D 84 A2
Herrsching D 108 A2
Hersbruck D 95 B3
Hersby S 57 A4
Herscheid D 81 A3
Herselt B 79 A4
Herso GR 182 B4
Herstal B 80 B1
Herstmonceux GB 45 C4
Herten D 80 A3
Hertford GB 44 B3
Hervás E 149 B4
Hervik N 52 A1
Herxheim D 93 B4
Herzberg
Brandenburg D 74 B1
Brandenburg D 83 A5
Niedersachsen D 82 A2
Herzebrock D 81 A4
Herzfelde D 74 B2
Herzlake D 71 B4
Herzogenaurach D 94 B2
Herzogenbuchsee
CH 106 B2
Herzogenburg A 110 A2
Herzsprung D 73 A5
Hesby N 52 A1
Hesdin F 78 B2
Hesel D 71 A4
Heskestad N 52 B2
Hessdalen N 199 C8
Hesselager DK 65 A3
Hesseng N 193 C13
Hessisch Lichtenau
D 82 A1
Hessisch-Oldendorf
D 72 B2
Hestra S 60 B3
Heswall GB 38 A3
Hetlevik N 46 B2
Hettange-Grande F 92 B2
Hetton-le-Hole GB 37 B5
Hettstedt D 82 A3
Heuchin F 78 B2
Heudicourt-sous-les-Côtes F 92 C1
Heunezel F 105 A5
Heuqueville F 89 A4
Heves H 113 B4
Héviz H 111 C4
Hexham GB 37 B4
Heysham GB 36 B4
Heytesbury GB 43 A4
Hidas H 125 A4
Hieflau A 110 B1
Hiendelaencina E 151 A5
Hiersac F 115 C4
High Bentham GB 37 B4
Highclere GB 44 B2
High Hesket GB 37 B4
Highley GB 39 B4
High Wycombe GB 44 B3
Higuera de Arjona
E 157 C4
Higuera de Calatrava
E 163 A3
Higuera de la Serena
E 156 B2
Higuera de la Sierra
E 161 B3
Higuera de Vargas
E 155 C4
Higuera la Real E 161 A3
Higuers de Llerena
E 156 B1
Higueruela E 158 C2
Híjar E 153 A3
Hilchenbach D 81 A4
Hildburghausen D 82 B2
Hilden D 80 A2
Hilders D 82 B1
Hildesheim D 72 B2
Hilgay GB 41 C4
Hillared S 60 B3
Hille D 72 B1
Hillegom NL 70 B1
Hillerød DK 61 D2
Hillerstorp S 60 B3
Hillesheim D 80 B2
Hillestad N 53 A6
Hillmersdorf D 83 A5
Hillsborough GB 27 B4
Hillswick GB 33 A5
Hilpoltstein D 95 B3
Hiltpoltstein D 94 B3
Hilvarenbeek NL 79 A5
Hilversum NL 70 B2
Himarë AL 182 C1
Himbergen D 73 A3
Himesháza H 125 A4
Himmelberg A 109 C5
Himmelpforten D 72 A2
Himód H 111 B4
Hinckley GB 40 C2
Hindås S 60 B2
Hindelang D 108 B1
Hindelbank CH 106 B2
Hinderavåg N 52 A1
Hindhead GB 44 B3
Hinjosa del Valle
E 156 B1
Hinnerup DK 59 B3
Hinneryd S 61 C3
Hinojal E 155 B4
Hinojales E 161 B3
Hinojos E 161 B3
Hinojosa del Duque
E 156 B2
Hinojosas de Calatrava
E 157 B3
Hinterhornbach A 108 B1
Hinterriss A 108 B2
Hintersee
A 109 B4
D 74 A3
Hinterstoder A 110 B1
Hintertux A 108 B2
Hinterweidenthal D 93 B3
Hinwil CH 107 B3
Hios GR 185 A7
Hippolytushoef NL 70 B1
Hirschaid D 94 B2
Hirschau D 95 B3
Hirschfeld D 83 A5
Hirschhorn D 93 B4
Hirsingue F 106 B2
Hirson F 91 B4
Hirtshals DK 58 A2
Hirvaskoski FIN 197 D10
Hirzenhain D 81 B5
Hisarcık TR 186 C4
Hishult S 61 C3
Hissjön S 200 C6
Hitchin GB 44 B3
Hitra N 198 B5
Hittarp S 61 C2
Hittisau A 107 B4
Hittun N 46 A1
Hitzacker D 73 A4
Hjallerup DK 58 A3
Hjällstad S 49 B5
Hjältevad S 62 A3
Hjärnarp S 61 C2
Hjartdal N 53 A4
Hjellestad N 46 B2
Hjelmeland N 52 A2
Hjelset N 198 C4
Hjerkinn N 198 C6
Hjerm DK 58 B1
Hjerpsted DK 64 A1
Hjerting DK 59 C1
Hjo S 55 B5
Hjordkær DK 64 A2
Hjørring DK 58 A2
Hjorted S 62 A4
Hjortkvarn S 56 B1
Hjortnäs S 50 B1
Hjortsberga S 62 B2

Hjukse N 53 A5
Hjuksebø N 53 A5
Hjulsjö S 55 A5
Hliník nad Hronom SK 98 C2
Hlinsko CZ 97 B3
Hlío IS 191 A10
Hlohovec SK 98 C1
Hlubokánad Vltavou CZ 96 B2
Hlučín CZ 98 B2
Hlyboka UA 17 A6
Hlybokaye BY 13 A7
Hniezdne SK 99 B4
Hnilec SK 99 C4
Hnúšt'a SK 99 C3
Hobol H 125 A3
Hobro DK 58 B2
Hobscheid L 92 B1
Hocalar TR 189 A4
Hochdonn D 64 B2
Hochdorf CH 106 B3
Hochfelden F 93 C3
Hochspeyer D 93 B3
Höchstadt D 94 B2
Höchstädt D 94 C2
Hochstenbach D 81 B3
Höchst im Odenwald D 93 B5
Höckendorf D 83 B5
Hockenheim D 93 B4
Hoddesdon GB 44 B3
Hodejov SK 99 C3
Hodenhagen D 72 B2
Hodkovice CZ 84 B3
Hódmezövásárhely H 113 C4
Hodnet GB 38 B4
Hodonín CZ 98 C1
Hodslavice CZ 98 B2
Hoedekenskerke NL 79 A3
Hoegaarden B 79 B4
Hoek van Holland NL 79 A4
Hoenderloo NL 70 B2
Hof
D 83 B3
N 53 A6
Hofbieber D 82 B1
Hoff GB 37 B4
Hofgeismar D 81 A5
Hofheim
Bayern D 82 B2
Hessen D 93 A4
Hofkirchen im Mühlkreis A 96 C1
Höfn IS 191 C10
Hofors S 50 B3
Hofsós IS 190 B6
Hofstad N 199 A7
Höganäs S 61 C2
Högbo S 51 B3
Hogdal S 54 A2
Høgebru N 46 A4
Högfors S 50 C2
Högklint S 57 C4
Högsäter S 54 B3
Högsby S 62 A4
Högsjö S 56 A1
Hogstad S 55 B6
Högyész H 112 C2
Hohenau A 97 C4
Hohenberg A 110 B2
Hohenbucko D 83 A5
Hohenburg D 95 B3
Hohendorf D 66 B1
Hohenems A 107 B4
Hohenhameln D 72 B3
Hohenhausen D 72 B1
Hohenkirchen D 71 A4
Hohenlinden D 108 A2
Hohenlockstedt D 64 C2
Hohenmölsen D 83 A4
Hohennauen D 73 B5
Hohen Neuendorf D 74 B2
Hohenseeden D 73 B5
Hohentauern A 110 B1
Hohentengen D 106 B3
Hohenwepel D 81 A5
Hohenwestedt D 64 B2
Hohenwutzen D 74 B3
Hohenzieritz D 74 A2
Hohn D 64 B2
Hohne D 72 B3
Hohnstorf D 73 A3
Højer DK 64 B1
Højslev Stby DK 58 B2
Hok S 62 A2
Hökerum S 60 B3
Hökhuvud S 51 B5
Hokksund N 53 A5
Hökön S 63 B2
Hol N 47 B5
Hólar IS 190 B6
Holašovice CZ 96 C2
Holbæk
Aarhus Amt. DK 58 B3
Vestsjællands Amt. DK 61 D1
Holbeach GB 41 C4
Holdenstedt D 73 B3
Holdhus N 46 B2
Holdorf D 71 B5
Holeby DK 65 B4
Hølen N 54 A1
Hølervasseter N 47 B6
Holešov CZ 98 B1
Holguera E 155 B4
Holíč SK 98 C1
Holice
CZ 97 A3
SK 111 B4
Höljes S 49 B4
Hollabrunn A 97 C4
Hollandstoun GB 33 B4
Høllen N 53 B3
Hollfeld D 95 B3
Hollókő H 112 B3
Hollstadt D 82 B2
Hollum NL 70 A2
Höllviksnäs S 66 A1
Holm N 195 E3
Hólmavík IS 190 B4
Holmbukt N 192 B5
Holmedal S 54 A2
Holmegil N 54 A2
Holmen N 48 B2
Holme-on-Spalding-Moor GB 40 B3
Holmes Chapel GB 38 A4
Holmestrand N 54 A1
Holmfirth GB 40 B2
Holmfoss N 193 C14
Holmsbu N 54 A1
Holmsjö S 63 B3
Holmsund S 200 C6
Holmsveden S 50 A3
Holmudden S 57 C5
Hölö S 57 A3
Holøydal N 199 C8
Holsbybrunn S 62 A3
Holseter N 48 A1
Holsljunga S 60 B2
Holstebro DK 59 B1
Holsted DK 59 C1
Holsworthy GB 42 B2
Holt
D 64 B2
Norfolk GB 41 C5
Wrexham GB 38 A4
IS 190 D6
N 53 B4
Holten NL 71 B3
Holtwick D 71 B4
Holum N 52 B3
Holwerd NL 70 A2
Holycross IRL 29 B4
Holyhead GB 38 A2
Holýšov CZ 95 B5
Holywell GB 38 A3
Holywood GB 27 B5
Holzdorf D 83 A5
Holzhausen D 72 B1
Holzheim D 94 C2
Holzkirchen D 108 B2
Holzminden D 81 A5
Holzthaleben D 82 A2
Homberg
Hessen D 81 A5
Hessen D 81 B5
Homburg D 93 B3
Hommelstø N 195 E3
Hommersåk N 52 B1
Homokmegy H 112 C3
Homokszentgyörgy H 124 A3
Homyel = Gomel BY 13 B9
Honaz TR 188 B4
Hondarribia E 144 A2
Hondón de los Frailes E 165 A4
Hondschoote F 78 B2
Hönebach D 82 B1
Hønefoss N 48 B2
Honfleur F 89 A4
Høng DK 61 D1
Honiton GB 43 B3
Hönningen D 80 B2
Honningsvåg N 193 B9
Hönö S 60 B1
Honrubia E 158 B1
Hontalbilla E 151 A3
Hontheim D 92 A2
Hontianske-Nemce SK 98 C2
Hontoria de la Cantera E 143 B3
Hontoria del Pinar E 143 C3
Hontoria de Valdearados E 143 C3
Hoofddorp NL 70 B1
Hoogerheide NL 79 A4
Hoogeveen NL 71 B3
Hoogezand-Sappemeer NL 71 A3
Hoogkarspel NL 70 B2
Hoogkerk NL 71 A3
Hoogstede D 71 B3
Hoogstraten B 79 A4
Hook GB 44 B3
Hooksiel D 71 A5
Höör S 61 D3
Hoorn NL 70 B2
Hope GB 38 A3
Hopen N 194 C6
Hope under Dinmore GB 39 B4
Hopfgarten A 108 B3
Hopfgarten in Defereggen A 109 C3
Hopseidet N 193 B11
Hopsten D 71 B4
Hoptrup DK 59 C2
Hora Svatého Sebestiána CZ 83 B5
Horažďovice CZ 96 B1
Horb am Neckar D 93 C4
Horbelev DK 65 B5
Hørby DK 58 A3
Hörby S 61 D3
Horcajada de la Torre E 158 A1
Horcajo de los Montes E 156 A3
Horcajo de Santiago E 151 C4
Horcajo-Medianero E 150 B2
Horche E 151 B4
Horda S 62 A2
Hordabø N 46 B1
Hordalia N 52 A2
Hordvik N 46 B2
Hořesedly CZ 83 B5
Horezu RO 17 C6
Horgen CH 107 B3
Horgoš SRB 126 A1
Horia RO 126 A3
Hořice CZ 84 B3
Horjul SLO 123 A3
Horka D 84 A2
Hörken S 50 B1
Horki BY 13 A9
Hörle S 60 B4
Horn
A 97 C3
D 81 A4
N 48 B2
S 62 A3
Horna E 158 C2
Hornachos E 156 B1
Hornachuelos E 162 A2
Horná Mariková SK 98 B2
Hornanes N 46 C2
Horná Streda SK 98 C1
Horná Štrubna SK 98 C2
Horná Súča SK 98 C1
Hornbæk
Aarhus Amt. DK 58 B2
Frederiksværk DK 61 C2
Hornberg D 106 A3
Hornburg D 73 B3
Horncastle GB 41 B3
Horndal S 50 B3
Horndean GB 44 C2
Horne
Fyns Amt. DK 64 A3
Ribe Amt. DK 59 C1
Hörnebo S 55 B5
Horneburg D 72 A2
Hörnefors S 200 C5
Horní Bečva CZ 98 B2
Horni Benešov CZ 98 B1
Horni Cerekev CZ 97 B3
Horní Jiřetín CZ 83 B5
Horní Lomná CZ 98 B2
Horni Maršov CZ 85 B3
Hornindal N 198 D3
Hørning DK 59 B3
Hörningsholm S 57 A3
Horní Planá CZ 96 C2
Horni Slavkov CZ 83 B4
Horni Vltavice CZ 96 C1
Hornnes N 53 B3
Horno D 84 A2
Hornos E 164 A2
Hornoy-le-Bourg F 90 B1
Hornsea GB 41 B3
Hornsjø N 48 A2
Hornslet DK 59 B3
Hornstein A 111 B3
Hörnum D 64 B1
Hornum DK 58 B2
Horný Tisovník SK 99 C3
Horodenka UA 13 D6
Horodnya UA 13 C9
Horodok
Khmelnytskyy UA 13 D7
Lviv UA 13 D5
Horokhiv UA 13 C6
Horovice CZ 96 B1
Horred S 60 B2
Hörröd S 61 D4
Hörsching A 110 A1
Horsens DK 59 C2
Horsham GB 44 B3
Hørsholm DK 61 D2
Horslunde DK 65 B4
Horšovský Týn CZ 95 B4
Horst NL 80 A2
Horstel D 71 B4
Horsten D 71 A4
Horstmar D 71 B4
Hort H 113 B3
Horta P 148 A2
Horten N 54 A1
Hortezuela E 151 A5
Hortiguela E 143 B3
Hortobágy H 113 B5
Horton in Ribblesdale GB 37 B4
Hørve DK 61 D1
Hörvik S 63 B2
Horwich GB 38 A4
Hosanger N 46 B2
Hösbach D 93 A5
Hosena D 84 A2
Hosenfeld D 81 B5
Hosingen L 92 A2
Hosio FIN 197 D8
Hospental CH 107 C3
Hospital IRL 29 B3
Hossegor F 128 C1
Hosszuhetény H 125 A4
Hostal de Ipiés E 145 B3
Hoštálkova CZ 98 B1
Hostalric E 147 C3
Hostens F 128 B2
Hostěradice CZ 97 C4
Hostinné CZ 85 B3
Hostomice CZ 96 B2
Hostouň CZ 95 B4
Hotagen S 199 B11
Hoting S 200 B2
Hotolisht AL 182 B2
Hotton B 79 B5
Houdain F 78 B2
Houdan F 90 C1
Houdelaincourt F 92 C1
Houeillès F 128 B3
Houffalize B 92 A1
Houghton-le-Spring GB 37 B5
Houlberg DK 59 B2
Houlgate F 89 A3
Hounslow GB 44 B3
Hourtin F 128 A1
Hourtin-Plage F 128 A1
Houthalen B 79 A5
Houyet B 79 B4
Hov
DK 59 C3
N 48 B2
Hova S 55 B5
Høvåg N 53 B4
Hovborg DK 59 C1
Hovda N 47 B6
Hovden N 52 A3
Hove GB 44 C3
Hovedgård DK 59 C2
Hovelhof D 81 A4
Hoven DK 59 C1
Hovet N 47 B5
Hovingham GB 40 A3
Hovmantorp S 62 B3
Hovsta S 56 A1
Howden GB 40 B3
Howe D 72 A3
Höxter D 81 A5
Hoya D 72 B2
Hoya de Santa Maria E 161 B3
Hoya-Gonzalo E 158 C2
Høyanger N 46 A3
Hoyerswerda D 84 A2
Høyjord N 53 A6
Hoylake GB 38 A3
Høylandet N 199 A9
Hoym D 82 A3
Høymyr N 47 C6
Hoyocasero E 150 B3
Hoyo de Manzanares E 151 B4
Hoyo de Pinares E 150 B3
Hoyos E 149 B3
Hoyos del Espino E 150 B2
Hrabusiče SK 99 C4
Hradec Králové CZ 85 B3
Hradec nad Moravicí CZ 98 B1
Hrádek CZ 97 C4
Hrádek nad Nisou CZ 84 B2
Hradište SK 98 C2
Hrafnagil IS 191 B7
Hrafnseyri IS 190 B2
Hranice
Severomoravsky CZ 98 B1
Západočeský CZ 83 B4
Hranovnica SK 99 C4
Hrasnica BIH 139 B4
Hrastnik SLO 123 A4
Hřensko CZ 84 B2
Hriňová SK 99 C3
Hrisoupoli GR 183 C6
Hrochov CZ 97 B4
Hrochův Tynec CZ 97 B3
Hrodna BY 13 B5
Hrodzyanka BY 13 B8
Hronov CZ 85 B4
Hronský Beňadik SK 98 C2
Hrotovice CZ 97 B4
Hrtkovci SRB 127 C1
Hrun IS 190 A5
Hrušov SK 112 A3
Hrušovany nad Jevišovkou CZ 97 C4
Hřuštin SK 99 B3
Hrvaćani BIH 124 C3
Hrvace HR 138 B2
Hrymayliv UA 13 D7
Huben A 109 C3
Hückel-hoven D 80 A2
Hückeswagen D 80 A3
Hucknall GB 40 B2
Hucqueliers F 78 B1
Huddersfield GB 40 B2
Huddinge S 57 A3
Huddunge S 51 B3
Hude D 72 A1
Hudiksvall S 200 E3
Huélago E 163 A4
Huélamo E 152 B2
Huelgoat F 100 A2
Huelma E 163 A4
Huelva E 161 B3
Huéneja E 164 B2
Huércal de Almeria E 164 C2
Huércal-Overa E 164 B3
Huerta de Abajo E 143 B3
Huerta del Rey E 143 C3
Huerta de Valdecarabanos E 151 C4
Huertahernando E 152 B1
Huesa E 164 B1
Huesca E 145 B3
Huéscar E 164 B2
Huete E 151 B5
Huétor Tájar E 163 A3
Hüfingen D 106 B3
Hufthamar N 46 B2
Hugh Town GB 42 B1
Huglfing D 108 B2
Huissen NL 70 C2
Huittinen FIN 8 B3
Huizen NL 70 B2
Hulin CZ 98 B1
Hüls D 80 A2
Hulsig DK 58 A3
Hulst NL 79 A4
Hult S 62 A3
Hulta S 56 B2
Hulteby S 55 A5
Hulterstad S 63 B4
Hultsfred S 62 A3
Humanes E 151 B4
Humberston GB 41 B3
Humble DK 65 B3
Humenné SK 12 D4
Humilladero E 163 A3
Humlebæk DK 61 D2
Humlum DK 58 B1
Hummelsta S 56 A2
Humpolec CZ 97 B3
Humshaugh GB 37 A4
Hundåla N 195 E3
Hundested DK 61 D1
Hundorp N 48 A1
Hundvåg N 52 A1
Hundvin N 46 B2
Hunedoara RO 17 C5
Hünfeld D 82 B1
Hungen D 81 B4
Hungerford GB 44 B2
Hunndalen N 48 B2
Hunnebostrand S 54 B2
Hunstanton GB 41 C4
Huntingdon GB 44 A3
Huntley GB 39 C4
Huntly GB 33 D4
Hünxe D 80 A2
Hurbanovo SK 112 B2
Hürbel D 107 A4
Hurdal N 48 B3
Hurezani RO 17 C5
Hurlford GB 36 A2
Hurstbourne Tarrant GB 44 B2
Hurstpierpoint GB 44 C3
Hürth D 80 B2
Hurum N 47 A5
Hurup DK 58 B1
Húsafell IS 190 C5
Húsavík IS 191 A8
Husbands Bosworth GB 44 A2
Husby
D 64 B2
DK 59 B1
Husey IS 191 B11
Huşi RO 17 B8
Husina BIH 139 A4
Husinec CZ 96 B1
Husinish GB 31 B1
Huskvarna S 62 A2
Husnes N 46 C2
Husøy N 194 A8
Hustad N 198 C4
Hüsten D 81 A3
Hustopeče CZ 97 C4
Hustopeče nad Bečvou CZ 98 B1
Husum
D 64 B2
S 200 C5
Husvika N 195 E3
Huta PL 75 B5
Hutovo BIH 139 C3
Hüttenberg A 110 C1
Hüttlingen D 94 C2
Huttoft GB 41 B4
Hutton Cranswick GB 40 B3
Hüttschlag A 109 B4
Huttwil CH 106 B2
Huy B 79 B5
Hüyük TR 189 B6
Hval N 48 B2
Hvåle N 47 B6
Hvaler N 54 A2
Hvalpsund DK 58 B2
Hvammstangi IS 190 B5
Hvammur IS 190 B6
Hvanneyri IS 190 C4
Hvar HR 138 B2
Hvarnes N 53 A5
Hveragerði IS 190 D4
Hvidbjerg DK 58 B1
Hvide Sande DK 59 C1
Hvittingfoss N 53 A6
Hvolsvöllur IS 190 D5
Hybe SK 99 B3
Hycklinge S 62 A3
Hydra GR 185 B4
Hyen N 198 D2
Hyères F 132 B2
Hyères Plage F 132 B2
Hylestad N 52 A3
Hylke DK 59 C2
Hyllestad N 46 A2
Hyllstofta S 61 C3
Hyltebruk S 60 B3
Hynnekleiv N 53 B4
Hythe
Hampshire GB 44 C2
Kent GB 45 B5
Hyvinkää FIN 8 B4

I

Iam RO 127 B3
Iaşi RO 17 B7
Iasmos GR 183 B7
Ibahernando E 156 A2
Ibarranguelua E 143 A4
Ibbenbüren D 71 B4
Ibeas de Juarros E 143 B3
Ibestad N 194 B8
Ibi E 159 C3
Ibiza = Eivissa E 166 C1
İbradı TR 189 B6
İbriktepe TR 186 A1
Ibros E 157 B4
Ibstock GB 40 C2
İçel TR 23 C8
Ichenhausen D 94 C2
Ichtegem B 78 A3
Ichtershausen D 82 B2
Idanha-a-Novo P 155 B3
Idar-Oberstein D 93 B3
Idd N 54 A2
Idiazábal E 144 B1
Idivuoma S 196 A4
Idkerberget S 50 B2
Idön S 51 B5
Idre S 199 D9
Idrija SLO 123 A3
Idritsa RUS 9 D6
Idstein D 81 B4
Idvor SRB 126 B2
Iecca Mare RO 126 B2
Ielsi I 170 B2
Ieper = Ypres B 78 B2
Ierapetra GR 185 D6
Ierissos GR 183 C5
Ifjord N 193 B11
Ig SLO 123 B3
Igal H 112 C1
Igea E 144 B1
Igea Marina I 136 A1
Igelfors S 56 B1
Igersheim D 94 B1
Iggesund S 200 E3
Iglesias E 143 B3
Iglésias I 179 C2
Igls A 108 B2
Igny-Comblizy F 91 B3
Igorre E 143 A4
Igoumenitsa GR 182 D2
Igries E 145 B3
Igualada E 147 C2
Igüeña E 141 B4
Iguerande F 117 A4
Iharosberény H 124 A3
Ihl'any SK 99 B4
Ihlienworth D 64 C1
Ihringen D 106 A2
Ihrlerstein D 95 C3
İhsaniye TR 187 C5
Ii FIN 197 D8
Iijärvi FIN 193 C11
Iisalmi FIN 3 E10
IJmuiden NL 70 B1
IJsselmuiden NL 70 B2
IJzendijke NL 79 A3
Ikast DK 59 B2
Ikervár H 111 B3
Ilandža SRB 126 B2
Ilanz CH 107 C4
Ilava SK 98 C2
Iława PL 69 B4
il Castagno I 135 B3
Ilche E 145 C4
Ilchester GB 43 B4
Ilfeld D 82 A2
Ilfracombe GB 42 A2
Ilgaz TR 23 A7
Ilgın TR 189 A6
Ílhavo P 148 B1
Ilica TR 186 C2
Ilidža BIH 139 B4
Ilijaš BIH 139 B4
Ilirska Bistrica SLO 123 B3
Ilkeston GB 40 C2
Ilkley GB 40 B2
Illana E 151 B5
Illano E 141 A4
Illar E 164 C2
Illas E 141 A5
Illats F 128 B2
Illertissen D 94 C2
Illescas E 151 B4
Ille-sur-Têt F 146 B3
Illfurth F 106 B2
Illichivsk UA 17 B9
Illiers-Combray F 89 B5
Illkirch-Graffenstaden F 93 C3
Illmersdorf D 74 C2
Illmitz A 111 B3
Íllora E 163 A4
Illueca E 152 A2
Ilmajoki FIN 8 A3
Ilmenau D 82 B2
Ilminster GB 43 B4
Ilok HR 126 B1
Ilomantsi FIN 9 A7
Iłow PL 77 B5
Iłowa PL 84 A3
Iłowo-Osada PL 77 A5
Ilsenburg D 82 A2
Ilshofen D 94 B1
Ilz A 110 B2
Iłża PL 87 A5
Imatra FIN 9 B6
Imielin PL 86 B3
Imingen N 47 B5
Immeln S 63 B2
Immenhausen D 81 A5
Immenstadt D 107 B5
Immingham GB 41 B3
Ímola I 135 A4
Imon E 151 A5
Imotski HR 138 B3
Impéria I 133 B4
Imphy F 104 C2
İmroz TR 183 C7
Imsland N 52 A1
Imst A 108 B1
Inagh IRL 28 B2
Inari FIN 193 D10
Inca E 167 B2
Inchnadamph GB 32 C2
Incinillas E 143 B3
Indal S 200 D3
Indjija SRB 127 B2
Indre Arna N 46 B2
Indre Billefjord N 193 B9
Indre Brenna N 193 B9
İğneada TR 186 A2
İnebolu TR 23 A7
İnecik TR 186 B2
İnegöl TR 187 B4
Inerthal CH 107 B3
Infiesto E 142 A1
Ingatorp S 62 A3
Ingedal N 54 A2
Ingelheim D 93 B4
Ingelmunster B 78 B3
Ingelstad S 62 B2
Ingleton GB 37 B4
Ingolfsland N 47 C5
Ingolstadt D 95 C3
Ingrandes
Maine-et-Loire F 101 B5
Vienne F 102 C2
Ingwiller F 93 C3
Inhisar TR 187 B5
Iniesta E 158 B2
Inishannon IRL 29 C3
Inishcrone IRL 26 B1
Inke H 124 A3
Inndyr N 195 C5
Innellan GB 34 C3
Innerleithen GB 35 C4
Innermessan GB 36 B2
Innertkirchen CH 106 C3
Innervillgraten A 109 C3
Innsbruck A 108 B2
Innset N 194 B9
Innvik N 198 D3
İnönü TR 187 C5
Inowłódz PL 87 A4
Inowrocław PL 76 B3
Ins CH 106 B2
Insch GB 33 D4
Insjön S 50 B2
Ińsko PL 75 A4
Instow GB 42 A2
İntepe TR 186 B1
Interlaken CH 106 C2
Intragna CH 120 A1
Introbio I 120 B2
Inverallochy GB 33 D5
Inveran
GB 32 D2
IRL 28 A2
Inveraray GB 34 B2
Inverbervie GB 35 B5
Invergarry GB 32 D2
Invergordon GB 32 D2
Invergowrie GB 35 B4
Inverkeilor GB 35 B5
Inverkeithing GB 35 B4
Invermoriston GB 32 D2
Inverness GB 32 D2
Inveruno I 120 B1
Inverurie GB 33 D4
Ioannina GR 182 D2
Iolanda di Savoia I 121 C4
Ion Corvin RO 17 C7
Ióppolo I 175 C1
Ios GR 185 C6
Ipati GR 182 E4
İpsala TR 186 B1
Ipswich GB 45 A5
Iraklia GR 183 B5
Iraklio = Heraklion GR 185 D6
Irdning A 110 B1
Iregszemcse H 112 C2
Irgoli I 178 B3
Irig SRB 127 B1
Ironbridge GB 39 B4
Irpin UA 13 C9
Irrel D 92 B2
Irsina I 172 B2
Irsta S 56 A2
Irthlingborough GB 44 A3
Iruela E 141 B4
Irún E 144 A2
Irurita E 144 A2
Irurzun E 144 B2
Irvine GB 36 A2
Irvinestown GB 27 B3
Isaba E 144 B3
Isabela E 157 B4
Ísafjörður IS 190 A2
Isane N 198 D2
Isaszeg H 112 B3
Isbister GB 33 A5
Íscar E 150 A3
İscehisar TR 187 D5
Ischgl A 107 B5
Íschia I 170 C1
Ischia di Castro I 168 A1
Ischitella I 171 B3
Isdes F 103 B4
Ise N 54 A2
Iselle I 119 A5
Iseltwald CH 106 C2
Isen D 108 A3
Isenbüttel D 73 B3
Íseo I 120 B3
Iserlohn D 81 A3
Isérnia I 170 B2
Isfjorden N 198 C4
Ishëm AL 182 B1
Isigny-sur-Mer F 88 A2
Işıklı TR 189 A4
Ísili I 179 C3
İskilip TR 23 A8
Isla Canela E 161 B2
Isla Cristina E 161 B2
Islares E 143 A3
Isleham GB 45 A4
Isle of Whithorn GB 36 B2
Ismaning D 108 A2
Isna P 154 B3
Isnestoften N 192 B6
Isny D 107 B5
Isoba E 142 A1
Isokylä
FIN 197 C10
S 196 B5
Isola F 132 A3
Isola d'Asti I 119 C5
Isola del Gran Sasso d'Itália I 169 A3
Ísola della Scala I 121 B4
Isola delle Fémmine I 176 A2
Ísola del Liri I 169 B3
Ísola di Capo Rizzuto I 175 C3
Isona E 147 B2
Ispagnac F 130 A2
Isparta TR 189 B5
Isperih BG 17 D7
Íspica I 177 C3
Isselburg D 80 A2
Issigeac F 129 B3
Issogne I 119 B4
Issoire F 116 B3
Issoncourt F 91 C5
Issoudun F 103 C4
Issum D 80 A2
Is-sur-Tille F 105 B4
Issy-l'Evêque F 104 C2

Istán E 162 B3
İstanbul TR 186 A3
Istebna PL 98 B2
Ístia d'Ombrone I 135 C4
Istiea GR 183 E5
Istres F 131 B3
Istvándi H 125 A3
Itea GR 184 A3
Ithaki GR 184 A1
Itoiz E 144 B2
Ítrabo E 163 B4
Itri I 169 B3
Ittireddu I 178 B2
Íttiri I 178 B2
Itzehoe D 64 C2
Ivalo FIN 193 D11
Iván H 111 B3
Ivanava BY 13 B6
Ivančice CZ 97 B4
Ivančna Gorica SLO 123 B3
Iváncsa H 112 B2
Ivanec HR 124 A2
Ivanić Grad HR 124 B2
Ivanjska BIH 124 C3
Ivanka SK 98 C2
Ivankovo HR 125 B4
Ivano-Frankivsk UA 13 D6
Ivanovice na Hané CZ 98 B1
Ivanska HR 124 B2
Ivatsevichy BY 13 B6
Ivaylovgrad BG 183 B8
Iveland N 53 B3
Ivoz Ramet B 79 B5
Ivrea I 119 B4
İvrindi TR 186 C2
Ivry-en-Montagne F 104 B3
Ivry-la-Bataille F 90 C1
Ivybridge GB 42 B3
Iwaniska PL 87 B5
Iwiny PL 85 A3
Iwuy F 78 B3
Ixworth GB 45 A4
Izarra E 143 B4
Izbica Kujawska PL 76 B3
Izbište SRB 127 B3
Izeda P 149 A3
Izegem B 78 B3
Izernore F 118 A2
Izmayil UA 17 C8
İzmir TR 188 A2
İzmit = Kocaeli TR 187 B4
Iznájar E 163 A3
Iznalloz E 163 A4
Iznatoraf E 164 A1
İznik TR 187 B4
Izola SLO 122 B2
Izsák H 112 C3
Izsófalva H 99 C4
Izyaslav UA 13 C7

J

Jabalquinto E 157 B4
Jablanac HR 123 C3
Jablanica BIH 139 B3
Jablonec nad Jizerou CZ 84 B3
Jablonec nad Nisou CZ 84 B3
Jablonica SK 98 C1
Jablonka PL 99 B3
Jabłonna PL 77 B5
Jablonnénad Orlicí CZ 97 A4
Jablonne Podještědi CZ 84 B2
Jablonov nad Turňou SK 99 C4
Jabłonowo Pomorskie PL 69 B4
Jablúnka CZ 98 B1
Jablunkov CZ 98 B2
Jabučje SRB 127 C2
Jabugo E 161 B3
Jabuka SRB 127 C2
Jabukovac HR 124 B2
Jaca E 145 B3
Jáchymov CZ 83 B4
Jacobidrebber D 72 B1
Jade D 71 A5
Jäderfors S 50 B3
Jädraås S 50 B3
Jadraque E 151 B5
Jaén E 163 A4
Jagare BIH 124 C3
Jagel D 64 B2
Jagenbach A 96 C3
Jægerspris DK 61 D1
Jagodina SRB 127 D3
Jagodnjak HR 125 B4
Jagodzin PL 84 A3
Jagstheim D 94 B2
Jagstzell D 94 B2
Jahodna SK 111 A4
Jajce BIH 138 A3
Ják H 111 B3
Jakabszálbs H 112 C3
Jäkkvik S 195 D8
Jakobsnes N 193 C14
Jakovlje HR 124 B1
Jakšic HR 125 B3
Jakubany SK 99 B4
Jalance E 159 B2
Jalasjärvi FIN 8 A3
Jalhay B 80 B1
Jaligny-sur-Besbre F 117 A3
Jallais F 102 B1
Jalón E 159 C3
Jâlons F 91 C4
Jamena SRB 125 C5
Jamilena E 163 A4
Jämjö S 63 B3
Jamnička Kiselica HR 124 B1
Jamno PL 67 B5
Jamoigne B 92 B1
Jämsä FIN 8 B4
Jämshög S 63 B2
Jamu Mare RO 126 B3
Janakkala FIN 8 B4
Jandelsbrunn D 96 C1
Jänickendorf D 74 B2
Janikowo PL 76 B3
Janja BIH 125 C5
Janjina HR 138 C3
Janki
Łódzkie PL 86 A3
Mazowieckie PL 77 B5
Jankov CZ 96 B2
Jankowo Dolne PL 76 B2
Jánoshalma H 126 A1
Jánosháza H 111 B4
Jánoshida H 113 B4
Jánossomorja H 111 B4
Janovice nad Uhlavou CZ 96 B1
Janów PL 86 B3
Janowiec Wielkopolski PL 76 B2
Janowo PL 77 A5
Jänsmässholmen S 199 B10
Janville F 103 A3
Janzé F 101 B4
Jarabá SK 99 C3
Jaraczewo PL 76 C2
Jarafuel E 159 B2
Jaraicejo E 156 A2
Jaraíz de la Vera E 150 B2
Jarak SRB 127 C1
Jarandilla de la Vera E 150 B2
Jaray E 152 A1
Järbo S 50 B3
Jard-sur-Mer F 114 B2
Jaren N 48 B2
Jargeau F 103 B4
Jarkovac SRB 126 B2
Järlåsa S 51 C4
Jarmen D 66 C2
Järna S 57 A3
Jarnac F 115 C3
Järnäs S 200 C5
Järnforsen S 62 A3
Jarny F 92 B1
Jarocin PL 76 C2
Jaroměř CZ 85 B3
Jaroměřice nad Rokytnou CZ 97 B3
Jaroslav CZ 97 A4
Jaroslavice CZ 97 C4
Jarosław PL 12 C5
Jaroslawiec PL 68 A1
Jarošov nad Nežarkou CZ 96 B3
Järpås S 55 B3
Järpen S 199 B10
Jarrow GB 37 B5
Järso FIN 51 B6
Järvenpää FIN 8 B4
Jarvorník CZ 85 B4
Järvsö S 200 E2
Jarzé F 102 B1
Jaša Tomic SRB 126 B2
Jasenak HR 123 B4
Jasenica BIH 124 C2
Jasenice HR 137 A4
Jasenovac HR 124 B2
Jasenovo SRB 127 C3
Jasień PL 84 A3
Jasienica PL 84 A2
Jasło PL 12 D4
Jásova SK 112 B2
Jasseron F 118 A2
Jastarnia PL 69 A3
Jastrebarsko HR 123 B4
Jastrowie PL 68 B1
Jastrzębia-Góra PL 68 A3
Jastrzębie Zdrój PL 98 B2
Jászals-Lószentgyörgy H 113 B4
Jászapáti H 113 B4
Jászárokszállás H 113 B3
Jászberény H 113 B3
Jászdózsa H 113 B4
Jászfényszaru H 113 B3
Jászjakóhalma H 113 B4
Jászkarajenö H 113 B4
Jászkisér H 113 B4
Jászladány H 113 B4
Jászszentlászló H 113 C3
Jásztelek H 113 B4
Játar E 163 B4
Jättendal S 200 E3
Jatznick D 74 A2
Jaun CH 106 C2
Jausiers F 132 A2
Jávea E 159 C4
Jävenitz D 73 B4
Javerlhac F 115 C4
Javier E 144 B2
Javorani BIH 124 C3
Javorina SK 99 B4
Javron F 89 B3
Jawor PL 85 A4
Jaworzno PL 86 B3
Jaworzyna Śl. PL 85 B4
Jayena E 163 B4
Jaźow PL 84 A2
Jebel RO 126 B3
Jebjerg DK 58 B2
Jedburgh GB 35 C5
Jedlinsk PL 87 A5
Jedlnia PL 87 A5
Jedlnia Letnisko PL 87 A5
Jednorożec PL 77 A6
Jedovnice CZ 97 B4
Jędrychow PL 69 B4
Jędrzejów PL 87 B4
Jedwabno PL 77 A5
Jeesiö FIN 197 B9
Jegłownik PL 69 A4
Jegun F 129 C3
Jēkabpils LV 8 D4
Jektevik N 46 C2
Jektvik N 195 D4
Jelcz-Laskowice PL 85 A5
Jelenec SK 98 C2
Jelenia Góra PL 85 B3
Jelgava LV 8 D3
Jelka SK 111 A4
Jelling DK 59 C2
Jels DK 59 C2
Jelsa
HR 138 B2
N 52 A2
Jelšava SK 99 C4
Jemgum D 71 A4
Jemnice CZ 97 B3
Jena D 82 B3
Jenaz CH 107 C4
Jenbach A 108 B2
Jenikow PL 75 A4
Jennersdorf A 111 C3
Jenny S 62 A4
Jerchel D 73 B4
Jeres del Marquesado E 164 B1
Jerez de la Frontera E 162 B1
Jerez de los Caballeros E 155 C4
Jerica E 159 B3
Jerichow D 73 B5
Jerka PL 75 B5
Jermenovci SRB 126 B3
Jerslev DK 58 A3
Jerte E 150 B2
Jerup DK 58 A3
Jerxheim D 73 B3
Jerzmanowice PL 87 B3
Jerzu I 179 C3
Jerzwałd PL 69 B4
Jesberg D 81 B5
Jesenice
Středočeský CZ 83 B5
Středočeský CZ 96 B2
SLO 109 C5
Jeseník CZ 85 B5
Jesenké SK 99 C4
Jesi I 136 B2
Jésolo I 122 B1
Jessen D 83 A4
Jessenitz D 73 A4
Jessheim N 48 B3
Jessnitz D 83 A4
Jesteburg D 72 A2
Jeumont F 79 B4
Jeven-stedt D 64 B2
Jever D 71 A4
Jevičko CZ 97 B4
Jevišovice CZ 97 C3
Jevnaker N 48 B2
Jezerane HR 123 B4
Jezero
BIH 138 A3
HR 123 B4
Jezów PL 87 A3
Jičín CZ 84 B3
Jičiněves CZ 84 B3
Jihlava CZ 97 B3
Jijona E 159 C3
Jilemnice CZ 84 B3
Jilové CZ 84 B2
Jilovéu Prahy CZ 96 B2
Jimbolia RO 126 B2
Jimena E 163 A4
Jimena de la Frontera E 162 B2
Jimera de Libar E 162 B2
Jimramov CZ 97 B4
Jince CZ 96 B1
Jindřichovice CZ 83 B4
Jindřichův Hradec CZ 96 B3
Jirkov CZ 83 B5
Jistebnice CZ 96 B2
Joachimsthal D 74 B2
João da Loura P 154 C2
Jobbágyi H 112 B3
Jochberg A 109 B3
Jockfall S 196 C5
Jódar E 163 A4
Jodoigne B 79 B4
Joensuu FIN 9 A6
Joesjö S 195 E5
Joeuf F 92 B1
Jõgeva EST 8 C5
Johanngeorgenstadt D 83 B4
Johannishus S 63 B3
Johanniskirchen D 95 C4
Johansfors S 63 B3
John o'Groats GB 32 C3
Johnshaven GB 35 B5
Johnstone GB 34 C3
Johnstown IRL 30 B1
Jõhvi EST 8 C5
Joigny F 104 B2
Joinville F 91 C5
Jokkmokk S 196 C2
Jöllenbeck D 72 B1
Jomala FIN 51 B6
Jönåker S 56 B2
Jonava LT 13 A6
Jonchery-sur-Vesle F 91 B3
Jondal N 46 B3
Jondalen N 53 A5
Joniškis LT 8 D3
Jönköping S 62 A2
Jonkowo PL 69 B5
Jønnbu N 53 A5
Jonsberg S 56 B2
Jonsered S 60 B2
Jonstorp S 61 C2
Jonzac F 114 C3
Jorba E 147 C2
Jordanów PL 99 B3
Jordanowo PL 75 B4
Jordanów Ślaski PL 85 B4
Jordbro S 57 A4
Jordbrua N 195 D5
Jördenstorf D 66 C1
Jordet N 49 A4
Jordøse DK 59 C3
Jork D 72 A2
Jörlanda S 60 B1
Jormlien S 199 A10
Jormvattnet S 199 A11
Jörn S 200 A6
Jørpeland N 52 A2
Jorquera E 158 B2
Jošan HR 123 C4
Jošavka BIH 124 C3
Josipdol HR 123 B4
Josipovac HR 125 B4
Jössefors S 54 A3
Josselin F 101 B3
Jøssund N 199 A7
Jostedal N 47 A4
Jósvafö H 99 C4
Jou P 148 A2
Jouarre F 90 C3
Joué-lès-Tours F 102 B2
Joué-sur-Erdre F 101 B4
Joure NL 70 B2
Joutseno FIN 9 B6
Joutsijärvi FIN 197 C10
Joux-la-Ville F 104 B2
Jouy F 90 C1
Jouy-le-Châtel F 90 C3
Jouy-le-Potier F 103 B3
Joyeuse F 131 A3
Joze F 116 B3
Juankoski FIN 8 A6
Juan-les-Pins F 132 B3
Jübek D 64 B2
Jubera E 144 B1
Jubrique E 162 B2
Jüchsen D 82 B2
Judaberg N 52 A1
Judenburg A 110 B1
Juelsminde DK 59 C3
Jugon-les-Lacs F 101 A3
Juillac F 129 A4
Juillan F 145 A4
Juist D 71 A4
Jukkasjärvi S 196 B3
Jule N 199 A10
Julianadorp NL 70 B1
Julianstown IRL 30 A2
Jülich D 80 B2
Jullouville F 88 B2
Jumeaux F 117 B3
Jumièges F 89 A4
Jumilhac-le-Grand F 115 C5
Jumilla E 159 C2
Jumisko FIN 197 C11
Juncosa E 153 A4
Juneda E 147 C1
Jung S 55 B4
Jungingen D 93 C5
Junglingster L 92 B2
Juniville F 91 B4
Junosuando S 196 B5
Junqueira P 149 A2
Junsele S 200 C2
Juoksengi S 196 C6
Juoksenki FIN 196 C6
Juprelle B 80 B1
Jurata PL 69 A3
Jurbarkas LT 12 A5
Jurjevo HR 123 C3
Jūrmala LV 8 D3
Jurmu FIN 197 D10
Juromenha P 155 C3
Jursla S 56 B2
Jussac F 116 C2
Jussey F 105 B4
Jussy F 90 B3
Juta H 125 A3
Jüterbog D 74 C2
Juuka FIN 3 E11
Juuma FIN 197 C12
Juvigny-le-Terte F 88 B2
Juvigny-sous-Andaine F 89 B3
Juzennecourt F 105 A3
Jyderup DK 61 D1
Jyrkänkoski FIN 197 C12
Jyväskylä FIN 8 A4

K

Kaamanen FIN 193 C11
Kaamasmukka FIN 193 C10
Kaaresuvanto FIN 192 D6
Kaarssen D 73 A4
Kaatscheuvel NL 79 A5
Kaba H 113 B5
Kåbdalis S 196 C3
Kačarevo SRB 127 C2
Kács H 113 B4
Kadan CZ 83 B5
Kadarkút H 125 A3
Kadınhanı TR 189 A7
Kaduy RUS 9 C10
Kåfalla S 56 A1
Kåfjord N 192 C7
Kåfjordbotn N 192 C4
Kågeröd S 61 D3
Kahl D 93 A5
Kahla D 82 B3
Kainach bei Voitsberg A 110 B2
Kaindorf A 110 B2
Kainulasjärvi S 196 C5
Kairala FIN 197 B10
Kaisepakte S 192 D3
Kaisersesch D 80 B3
Kaiserslautern D 93 B3
Kaisheim D 94 C2
Kajaani FIN 3 D10
Kajárpéc H 111 B4
Kajdacs H 112 C2
Kakanj BIH 139 A4
Kakasd H 125 A4
Kaklik TR 189 B4
Kakolewo PL 85 A4
Kál H 113 B4
Kalajoki FIN 3 D8
Kalak N 193 B11
Kalamata GR 184 B3
Kalambaka GR 182 D3
Kalamria GR 182 C4
Kalandra GR 183 D5
Kälarne S 200 D2
Kalavrita GR 184 A3
Kalbe D 73 B4
Kalce SLO 123 B3
Káld H 111 B4
Kale
Antalya TR 189 C4
Denizli TR 188 B3
Kalecik TR 23 A7
Kalefeld D 82 A2
Kalesija BIH 139 A4
Kalety PL 86 B2
Kalevala RUS 3 D12
Kalhovd N 47 B5
Kalí HR 137 A4
Kalimnos GR 188 C2
Kaliningrad RUS 69 A5
Kalinkavichy BY 13 B8
Kalinovac HR 124 A3
Kalinovik BIH 139 B4
Kalinovo SK 99 C3
Kalirachi GR 183 C6
Kaliska
Pomorskie PL 68 A3
Pomorskie PL 68 B3
Kalisko PL 86 A3
Kalisz PL 86 A2
Kalisz Pomorski PL 75 A4
Kaljord N 194 B6
Kalkan TR 189 C4
Kalkar D 80 A2
Kalkım TR 186 C2
Kall
D 80 B2
S 199 B10
Källby S 55 B4
Kållered S 60 B2
Kållerstad S 60 B3
Kallinge S 63 B3
Kallmünz D 95 B3
Kallo FIN 196 B7
Kallsedet S 199 B9
Källvik S 56 B3
Kalmar S 63 B4
Kalmthout B 79 A4
Kalná SK 112 A2
Kalocsa H 112 C2
Kalokhorio CY 181 B2
Kalo Nero GR 184 B2
Kaloni GR 186 C1
Káloz H 112 C2
Kals A 109 B3
Kalsdorf A 110 C2
Kaltbrunn CH 107 B4
Kaltenbach A 108 B2
Kaltenkirchen D 64 C2
Kaltennordheim D 82 B2
Kalundborg DK 61 D1
Kalush UA 13 D6
Kalv S 60 B3
Kalvåg N 198 D1
Kalvehave DK 65 A5
Kalwang A 110 B1
Kalwaria-Zebrzydowska PL 99 B3
Kalyazin RUS 9 D10
Kam H 111 B3
Kaman TR 23 B7
Kamares GR 185 C5
Kambos CY 181 A1
Kamen D 81 A3
Kamenice CZ 97 B3
Kamenice nad Lipou CZ 96 B3
Kameničná SK 112 B2
Kamenný Most SK 112 B2
Kamenny Ujezd CZ 96 C2
Kamenska HR 124 B3
Kamensko HR 138 B2
Kamenz D 84 A2
Kamičak BIH 124 C2
Kamień PL 87 A4
Kamieniec Zabk PL 85 B4
Kamienka SK 99 B4
Kamień Krajeński PL 76 A2
Kamienna Góra PL 85 B4
Kamień Pomorski PL 67 C3
Kamieńsk PL 86 A3
Kamiros Skala GR 188 C2
Kamnik SLO 123 A3
Kampen NL 70 B2
Kampinos PL 77 B5
Kamp-Lintfort D 80 A2
Kampor HR 123 C3
Kamyanets-Podil's'kyy UA 13 D7
Kamyanka-Buz'ka UA 13 C6
Kamýk nad Vltavou CZ 96 B2
Kanal SLO 122 A2
Kanalia GR 182 D4
Kandalaksha RUS 3 C13
Kandanos GR 185 D4
Kandel D 93 B4
Kandern D 106 B2
Kandersteg CH 106 C2
Kandila GR 184 B3
Kandıra TR 187 A5
Kandyty PL 69 A5
Kanfanar HR 122 B2
Kangasala FIN 8 B4
Kangos S 196 B5
Kangosjärvi FIN 196 B6
Kaniów PL 75 C3
Kanjiža SRB 126 A2
Kankaanpää FIN 8 B3
Kannus FIN 3 E8
Kanturk IRL 29 B3
Kapaklı TR 186 A2
Kapellen
A 110 B2
B 79 A4
Kapellskär S 57 A5
Kapfenberg A 110 B2
Kapfenstein A 110 C2
Kaplice CZ 96 C2
Kapljuh BIH 124 C2
Kápolna H 113 B4
Kápolnásnyék H 112 B2
Kaposfö H 125 A3
Kaposfüred H 125 A3
Kaposszekcsö H 125 A4
Kaposvár H 125 A3
Kapp N 48 B2
Kappel D 93 C3
Kappeln D 64 B2
Kappelshamn S 57 C4
Kappl A 107 B5
Kappstad S 55 A4
Kaprun A 109 B3
Kaptol HR 125 B3
Kapuvár H 111 B4
Karaadilli TR 189 A5
Karabiğa TR 186 B2
Karabük TR 187 A7
Karaburun TR 186 D1
Karacabey TR 186 B3
Karacaköy TR 186 A3
Karacaören TR 189 A5
Karacasu TR 188 B3
Karácsond H 113 B4
Karád H 112 C1
Karahallı TR 189 A4
Karaisali TR 23 C8
Karaman
Balıkesir TR 186 C3
Karaman TR 23 C7
Karamanlı TR 189 B4
Karamürsel TR 187 B4
Karan SRB 127 D1
Karancslapujto H 113 A3
Karaova TR 188 B2
Karapınar TR 23 C7
Karasjok N 193 C9
Karasu TR 187 A5
Karataş
Adana TR 23 C8
Manisa TR 188 A3
Karavostasi CY 181 A1
Karbenning S 50 B3
Kårberg S 55 B5
Kårböle S 199 D12
Karby
D 64 B2
DK 58 B1
Kårby S 62 A4
Karby S 57 A4
Karcag H 113 B4
Karczów PL 86 B1
Karczowiska PL 85 A4
Kardamena GR 188 C2
Kardamila GR 185 A7
Kardamili GR 184 C3
Kardašova Rečice CZ 96 B2
Kardis S 196 C6
Karditsa GR 182 D3
Kärdla EST 8 C3
Kardoskút H 113 C4
Kardzhali BG 183 B7
Karesuando S 192 D6
Kargı TR 23 A8
Kargopol RUS 9 B11
Kargowa PL 75 B4
Karigasniemi FIN 193 C9
Karise DK 65 A5
Karistos GR 185 A5
Karkkila FIN 8 B4
Karlholmsbruk S 51 B4
Karlino PL 67 B4
Karlobag HR 137 A4
Karlovac HR 123 B4
Karlovasi GR 188 B1
Karlovčic SRB 127 C2
Karlovice CZ 85 B5
Karlovo BG 17 D6
Karlovy Vary CZ 83 B4
Karłowice PL 86 B1
Karlsborg S 55 B5
Karlshamn S 63 B2
Karlshöfen D 72 A2
Karlshus N 54 A1
Karlskoga S 55 A5
Karlskrona S 63 B3
Karlsrud N 47 B5
Karlsruhe D 93 B4
Karlstad S 55 A4
Karlstadt D 94 B1
Karlstetten A 110 A2
Karlstift A 96 C2
Karlstorp S 62 A3
Karmacs H 111 C4
Karmin PL 85 A5
Kärna S 60 B1
Karnobat BG 17 D7
Karojba HR 122 B2
Karow D 73 A5
Karpacz PL 85 B3
Karpathos GR 188 D2
Karpenisi GR 182 E3
Karpuzlu TR 188 B2
Kärrbo S 56 A2
Karrebaeksminde DK 65 A4
Karshult S 60 B3
Karsin PL 68 B2
Kårsta S 57 A4
Karstädt D 73 A4
Kartal TR 186 B4
Kartitsch A 109 C3
Kartuzy PL 68 A3
Karungi S 196 C6
Karunki FIN 196 C7
Karup DK 59 B2
Karviná CZ 98 B2
Kås DK 58 A2
Kaş TR 189 C4
Kasaba TR 189 C4
Kašava CZ 98 B1
Kåseberga S 66 A3
Kasejovice CZ 96 B1
Kasfjord N 194 B7
Kashin RUS 9 D10
Kašina HR 124 B2
Kasina-Wielka PL 99 B4
Kaskinen FIN 8 A2
Kašperské Hory CZ 96 B1
Kassandrino GR 183 C5
Kassel D 81 A5
Kassiopi GR 182 D1
Kastamonu TR 23 A7
Kastav HR 123 B3
Kasteli GR 185 D4
Kastellaun D 93 A3
Kastelli GR 185 D6
Kaštel-Stari HR 138 B2
Kaštel Zegarski HR 138 A1
Kasterlee B 79 A4
Kastl D 95 B3
Kastlösa S 63 B4
Kastorf D 65 C3
Kastoria GR 182 C3
Kastorio GR 184 B3
Kastraki GR 185 C6
Kastrosikia GR 182 D2
Kastsyukovichy BY 13 B10
Kaszaper H 113 C4
Katakolo GR 184 B2
Katapola GR 185 C6
Katastari GR 184 B1
Katerbow D 74 B1
Katerini GR 182 C4
Kathikas CY 181 B1
Kätkesuando S 196 A6
Katlenburg-Lindau D 82 A2
Kato Achaia GR 184 A2
Káto Pyrgos CY 181 A1
Katouna GR 182 E3
Katovice CZ 96 B1
Katowice PL 86 B3
Katrineberg S 50 A3
Katrineholm S 56 B2
Kattarp S 61 C2
Kattavia GR 188 D2
Katthammarsvik S 57 C4
Kattilstorp S 55 B4
Katwijk NL 70 B1
Katymár H 125 A5
Kąty Wrocławskie PL 85 A4
Katzenelnbogen D 81 B3
Katzhütte D 82 B3
Kaub D 93 A3
Kaufbeuren D 108 B1
Kauhajoki FIN 8 A3
Kauhava FIN 8 A3
Kaukonen FIN 196 B7
Kauliranta FIN 196 C6
Kaulsdorf D 82 B3
Kaunas LT 13 A5
Kaunisvaara S 196 B6
Kaupanger N 47 A4
Kautokeino N 192 C7
Kautzen A 97 C3
Kavadarci MK 182 B4
Kavajë AL 182 B1
Kavakköy TR 186 B1
Kavaklı TR 186 A2
Kavaklıdere TR 188 B3
Kavala GR 183 C6
Kavarna BG 17 D8
Kävlinge S 61 D3
Kawcze PL 68 A1
Kaxås S 199 B10
Kaxholmen S 62 A2
Käylä FIN 197 C12
Kaymakçı TR 188 A3
Kaymaz TR 187 C6
Kaynarca TR 187 A5
Käyrämö FIN 197 C9
Kayseri TR 23 B8
Kaysersberg F 106 A2
Kazanlak BG 17 D6
Kazár H 113 A3
Kazimierza Wielka PL 87 B4
Kazincbarcika H 113 A4
Kaźmierz PL 75 B5
Kcynia PL 76 A2
Kdyně CZ 95 B5
Kea GR 185 B5
Keadew IRL 26 B2
Keady GB 27 B4
Kecel H 112 C3
Keçiborlu TR 189 B5
Kecskemét H 113 C3
Kėdainiai LT 13 A5
Kędzierzyn-Koźle PL 86 B2
Keel IRL 28 A1
Keenagh IRL 28 A4
Keerbergen B 79 A4
Kefalos GR 188 C1
Kefken TR 187 A5
Keflavík IS 190 C3
Kegworth GB 40 C2
Kehl D 93 C3
Kehrigk D 74 B2
Keighley GB 40 B2
Keila EST 8 C4
Keillmore GB 34 C2

Keiss GB 32 C3
Keith GB 33 D4
Kelankylä FIN 197 D10
Kelberg D 80 B2
Kelbra D 82 A3
Kelč CZ 98 B1
Kelchsau A 108 B3
Këlcyrë AL 182 C2
Keld GB 37 B4
Kelebia H 126 A1
Kelekçi TR 188 B4
Kelemér H 99 C4
Keles TR 186 C4
Kelheim D 95 C3
Kell D 92 B2
Kellas GB 32 D3
Kellinghusen D 64 C2
Kelloselkä FIN 197 C11
Kells
GB 27 B4
IRL 27 C4
Kelmis B 80 B2
Kelokedhara CY 181 B1
Kelottijärvi FIN 192 D6
Kelsall GB 38 A4
Kelso GB 35 C5
Kelsterbach D 93 A4
Keltneyburn GB 35 B3
Kelujärvi FIN 197 B10
Kemaliye TR 188 A3
Kemalpaşa TR 188 A2
Kematen A 108 B2
Kemberg D 83 A4
Kemer
Antalya TR 189 C5
Burdur TR 189 B5
Muğla TR 189 C4
Kemerkaya TR 187 D6
Kemeten A 111 B3
Kemi FIN 196 D7
Kemijärvi FIN 197 C10
Keminmaa FIN 196 D7
Kemnath D 95 B3
Kemnay GB 33 D4
Kemnitz
Brandenburg D 74 B1
Mecklenburg-Vorpommern D 66 B2
Kempen D 80 A2
Kempsey GB 39 B4
Kempten D 107 B5
Kemptthal CH 107 B3
Kendal GB 37 B4
Kenderes H 113 B4
Kengyel H 113 B4
Kenilworth GB 44 A2
Kenmare IRL 29 C2
Kenmore GB 35 B4
Kennacraig GB 34 C2
Kenyeri H 111 B4
Kenzingen D 106 A2
Kepez TR 186 B1
Kępice PL 68 A1
Kępno PL 86 A2
Kepsut TR 186 C3
Keramoti GR 183 C6
Keräntöjärvi S 196 B6
Keratea GR 185 B4
Kerava FIN 8 B4
Kerecsend H 113 B4
Kerekegyhaza H 112 C3
Kerepestarcsa H 112 B3
Keri GR 184 B1
Kérien F 100 A2
Kerkafalva H 111 C3
Kerken D 80 A2
Kerkrade NL 80 B2
Kerkyra GR 182 D1
Kerlouan F 100 A1
Kernascléden F 100 A2
Kernhof A 110 B2
Kerns CH 106 C3
Kerpen D 80 B2
Kerrysdale GB 31 B3
Kerta H 111 B4
Kerteminde DK 59 C3
Kerzers CH 106 C2
Keşan TR 186 B1
Kesgrave GB 45 A5
Kesh GB 26 B3
Keskin TR 23 B7
Kesselfall A 109 B3
Kestenga RUS 3 D12
Keswick GB 36 B3
Keszthely H 111 C4
Kétegyháza H 113 C5
Kéthely H 111 C4
Kętrzyn PL 12 A4
Kettering GB 44 A3
Kettlewell GB 40 A1
Kęty PL 99 B3
Ketzin D 74 B1
Keula D 82 A2
Keuruu FIN 8 A4
Kevelaer D 80 A2
Kevermes H 113 C5
Kevi SRB 126 B1
Keyingham GB 41 B3
Keynsham GB 43 A4
Kežmarok SK 99 B4
Khimki RUS 9 E10
Khisinev = Chişinău
MD 17 B8
Khmelnik UA 13 D7
Khmelnytskyy UA 13 D7
Khodoriv UA 13 D6
Kholm RUS 9 D7
Khotyn UA 13 D7
Khoyniki BY 13 C8
Khust UA 17 A5
Khvoynaya RUS 9 C9
Kiato GR 184 A3
Kibæk DK 59 B1
Kiberg N 193 B14
Kicasalih TR 186 A1
Kičevo MK 182 B2
Kidderminster GB 39 B4
Kidlington GB 44 B2
Kidsgrove GB 40 B1
Kidwelly GB 39 C2
Kiefersfelden D 108 B3
Kiel D 64 B3
Kielce PL 87 B4
Kiełczygłów PL 86 A3
Kielder GB 37 A4
Kiełpino PL 68 A3
Kielpiny PL 77 A4
Kierinki FIN 197 B8
Kiernozia PL 77 B4
Kierspe D 81 A3
Kietrz PL 86 B2
Kietz D 74 B3
Kiev = Kyyiv UA 13 C9
Kiezmark PL 69 A3
Kiffisia GR 185 A4
Kifino Selo BIH 139 B4
Kihlanki
FIN 196 B6
S 196 B6
Kiistala FIN 197 B8
Kije PL 87 B4
Kijevo HR 138 B2
Kikallen N 46 B2
Kikinda SRB 126 B2
Kil
N 53 B5
Örebro S 55 A6
Värmland S 55 A4
Kila S 55 A3
Kilafors S 50 A3
Kilbaha IRL 29 B2
Kilbeggan IRL 30 A1
Kilberry GB 34 C2
Kilbirnie GB 34 C3
Kilboghamn N 195 D4
Kilbotn N 194 B7
Kilb Rabenstein A 110 A2
Kilchattan GB 34 C2
Kilchoan GB 34 B1
Kilcock IRL 30 A2
Kilconnell IRL 28 A3
Kilcormac IRL 28 A4
Kilcreggan GB 34 C3
Kilcullen IRL 30 A2
Kilcurry IRL 27 B4
Kildare IRL 30 A2
Kildinstroy RUS 3 B13
Kildonan GB 32 C3
Kildorrery IRL 29 B3
Kilegrend N 53 A4
Kilen N 53 A4
Kilgarvan IRL 29 C2
Kiliya UA 17 C8
Kilkee IRL 29 B2
Kilkeel GB 27 B4
Kilkelly IRL 26 C2
Kilkenny IRL 30 B1
Kilkieran IRL 28 A2
Kilkinlea IRL 29 B2
Kilkis GR 182 B4
Killadysert IRL 29 B2
Killala IRL 26 B1
Killaloe IRL 28 B3
Killarney IRL 29 B2
Killashandra IRL 27 B3
Killashee IRL 28 A4
Killearn GB 34 B3
Killeberg S 61 C4
Killeigh IRL 30 A1
Killenaule IRL 29 B4
Killimor IRL 28 A3
Killin GB 34 B3
Killinaboy IRL 28 B2
Killinge S 196 B3
Killinick IRL 30 B2
Killorglin IRL 29 B2
Killucan IRL 30 A1
Killybegs IRL 26 B2
Killyleagh GB 27 B5
Kilmacrenan IRL 26 A3
Kilmacthomas IRL 30 B1
Kilmaine IRL 28 A2
Kilmallock IRL 29 B3
Kilmarnock GB 36 A2
Kilmartin GB 34 B2
Kilmaurs GB 36 A2
Kilmeadan IRL 30 B1
Kilmeedy IRL 29 B3
Kilmelford GB 34 B2
Kilmore Quay IRL 30 B2
Kilmuir GB 32 D2
Kilnaleck IRL 27 C3
Kilninver GB 34 B2
Kilpisjärvi FIN 192 C4
Kilrea GB 27 B4
Kilrush IRL 29 B2
Kilsmo S 56 A1
Kilsyth GB 35 C3
Kiltoom IRL 28 A3
Kilwinning GB 36 A2
Kimasozero RUS 3 D12
Kimi GR 185 A5
Kimolos GR 185 C5
Kimovsk RUS 9 E10
Kimratshofen D 107 B5
Kimry RUS 9 D10
Kimstad S 56 B1
Kinbrace GB 32 C3
Kincardine GB 35 B4
Kincraig GB 32 D3
Kindberg A 110 B2
Kindelbruck D 82 A3
Kingarrow IRL 26 B2
Kingisepp RUS 9 C6
Kingsbridge GB 43 B3
Kingsclere GB 44 B2
Kingscourt IRL 27 C4
King's Lynn GB 41 C4
Kingsteignton GB 43 B3
Kingston
Greater London
GB 44 B3
Moray GB 32 D3
Kingston Bagpuize
GB 44 B2
Kingston upon Hull
GB 40 B3
Kingswear GB 43 B3
Kingswood GB 43 A4
Kington GB 39 B3
Kingussie GB 32 D2
Kınık
Antalya TR 188 C4
İzmır TR 186 C2
Kinloch
Highland GB 31 B2
Highland GB 32 C2
Kinlochbervie GB 32 C1
Kinlochewe GB 32 D1
Kinlochleven GB 34 B3
Kinlochmoidart GB 34 B2
Kinloch Rannoch
GB 35 B3
Kinloss GB 32 D3
Kinlough IRL 26 B2
Kinn N 48 B2
Kinna S 60 B2
Kinnared S 60 B3
Kinnarp S 55 B4
Kinnegad IRL 30 A1
Kinne-Kleva S 55 B4
Kinnitty IRL 28 A4
Kinrooi B 80 A1
Kinross GB 35 B4
Kinsale IRL 29 C3
Kinsarvik N 46 B3
Kintarvie GB 31 A2
Kintore GB 33 D4
Kinvarra IRL 28 A3
Kioni GR 184 A1
Kiparissia GR 184 B2
Kipfenburg D 95 C3
Kippen GB 35 B3
Kiraz TR 188 A3
Kirazlı TR 186 B1
Kirberg D 81 B4
Kirchbach in
Steiermark A 110 C2
Kirchberg
CH 106 B2
Baden-Württemberg
D 94 B1
Rheinland-Pfalz D 93 B3
Kirchberg am Wechsel
A 110 B2
Kirchberg an der
Pielach A 110 A2
Kirchberg in Tirol
A 109 B3
Kirchbichl A 108 B3
Kirchdorf
Bayern D 96 C1
Mecklenburg-Vorpommern D 65 C4
Niedersachsen D 72 B1
Kirchdorf an der Krems
A 109 B5
Kirchdorf in Tirol
A 109 B3
Kirchenlamitz D 83 B3
Kirchenthumbach
D 95 B3
Kirchhain D 81 B4
Kirchheim
Baden-Württemberg
D 94 C1
Bayern D 108 A1
Hessen D 81 B5
Kirchheimbolanden
D 93 B4
Kirchhundem D 81 A4
Kirchlintein D 72 B2
Kirchschlag A 111 B3
Kirchweidach D 109 A3
Kirchzarten D 106 B2
Kircubbin GB 27 B5
Kireç TR 186 C3
Kırıkkale TR 23 B7
Kirillov RUS 9 C11
Kirishi RUS 9 C8
Kirka TR 187 C5
Kırkağaç TR 186 C2
Kirkbean GB 36 B3
Kirkbride GB 36 B3
Kirkby GB 38 A4
Kirkby Lonsdale
GB 37 B4
Kirkby Malzeard
GB 40 A2
Kirkbymoorside
GB 37 B6
Kirkby Stephen GB 37 B4
Kirkcaldy GB 35 B4
Kirkcolm GB 36 B1
Kirkconnel GB 36 A2
Kirkcowan GB 36 B2
Kirkcudbright GB 36 B2
Kirkehamn N 52 B2
Kirke Hyllinge DK 61 D1
Kirkenær N 49 B4
Kirkenes N 193 C14
Kirkham GB 38 A4
Kirkintilloch GB 35 C3
Kirkjubæjarklaustur
IS 191 D7
Kirkkonummi FIN 8 B4
Kırklareli TR 186 A2
Kirkmichael GB 35 B4
Kirk Michael GB 36 B2
Kirkoswald GB 36 A2
Kirkpatrick Fleming
GB 36 A3
Kirkton of Glenisla
GB 35 B4
Kirkwall GB 33 C4
Kirkwhelpington
GB 37 A5
Kirn D 93 B3
Kirovsk RUS 3 C13
Kirriemuir GB 35 B5
Kırşehir TR 23 B8
Kirton GB 41 C3
Kirton in Lindsey
GB 40 B3
Kirtorf D 81 B5
Kiruna S 196 B3
Kisa S 62 A3
Kisač SRB 126 B1
Kisbér H 112 B2
Kiseljak BIH 139 B4
Kisielice PL 69 B4
Kisköre H 113 B4
Kiskőrös H 112 C3
Kiskunfélegyháza
H 113 C3
Kiskunhalas H 112 C3
Kiskunlacháza H 112 B2
Kiskunmajsa H 113 C3
Kisláng H 112 C2
Kisslegg D 107 B4
Kissolt H 112 C3
Kissónerga CY 181 B1
Kist D 94 B1
Kistanje HR 138 B1
Kistelek H 113 C3
Kisterenye H 113 A3
Kisújszállás H 113 B4
Kisvárda H 16 A5
Kisvejke H 112 C2
Kiszkowo PL 76 B2
Kiszombor H 126 A2
Kitee FIN 9 A7
Kithnos GR 185 B5
Kiti CY 181 B2
Kitkiöjärvi S 196 B6
Kitkiöjoki S 196 B6
Kittelfjäll S 195 E6
Kittendorf D 74 A1
Kittilä FIN 196 B7
Kittlitz D 84 A2
Kittsee A 111 A4
Kitzbühel A 109 B3
Kitzingen D 94 B2
Kiuruvesi FIN 3 E10
Kivertsi UA 13 C6
Kividhes CY 181 B1
Kivik S 63 C2
Kivotos GR 182 C3
Kıyıköy TR 186 A3
Kızılcabölük TR 188 B4
Kızılcadağ TR 189 B4
Kızılcahamam TR 23 A7
Kızılırmak TR 23 A7
Kızılkaya TR 189 B5
Kızılkuyu TR 187 D6
Kızılören
Afyon TR 189 A5
Konya TR 189 B7
Kjeldebotn N 194 B7
Kjellerup DK 59 B2
Kjellmyra N 49 B4
Kjøllefjord N 193 B11
Kjopmannskjaer N 54 A1
Kjøpsvik N 194 B7
Kl'ačno SK 98 C2
Kladanj BIH 139 A4
Kläden D 73 B4
Klädesholmen S 60 B1
Kladnice HR 138 B2
Kladno CZ 84 B2
Kladruby CZ 95 B4
Klagenfurt A 110 C1
Klågerup S 61 D3
Klagstorp S 66 A2
Klaipėda LT 8 E2
Klaistow D 74 B1
Klaksvík FO 4 A3
Klana HR 123 B3
Klanac HR 123 C4
Klanjec HR 123 A4
Klardorf D 95 B4
Klarup DK 58 A3
Klašnice BIH 124 C3
Klässbol S 55 A3
Klášterec nad Ohří
CZ 83 B5
Kláštor pod Znievom
SK 98 C2
Klatovy CZ 96 B1
Klaus an der
Pyhrnbahn A 110 B1
Klazienaveen NL 71 B3
Klecko PL 76 B2
Kleczew PL 76 B3
Klein Plasten D 74 A1
Klein Sankt Paul
A 110 C1
Kleinsölk A 109 B4
Kleinzell A 110 B2
Klejtrup DK 58 B2
Klek SRB 126 B2
Klemensker DK 67 A3
Klenak SRB 127 C1
Klenci pod Cerchovem
CZ 95 B4
Klenica PL 75 C4
Klenje SRB 127 C1
Klenoec MK 182 B2
Klenovec SK 99 C3
Klenovica HR 123 B3
Klenovnik HR 124 A2
Kleppe N 52 B1
Kleppestø N 46 B2
Kleptow D 74 A2
Kleszewo PL 77 B6
Kleve D 80 A2
Klevshult S 60 B4
Klewki PL 77 A5
Kličevac SRB 127 C3
Kliening A 110 C1
Klietz D 73 B5
Klikuszowa PL 99 B3
Klimkovice CZ 98 B2
Klimontów PL 87 B5
Klimovichi BY 13 B9
Klimpfjäll S 195 E5
Klin RUS 9 D10
Klinča Sela HR 123 B4
Klingenbach A 111 B3
Klingenberg D 93 B5
Klingenmunster D 93 B4
Klingenthal D 83 B4
Klinken D 73 A4
Klintehamn S 57 C4
Kliny PL 87 A4
Kliplev DK 64 B2
Klippan S 61 C3
Klis HR 138 B2
Klitmøller DK 58 A1
Klitten S 49 A6
Klixbüll D 64 B1
Kljajićevo SRB 126 B1
Ključ BIH 138 A2
Klobouky CZ 97 C4
Kłobuck PL 86 B2
Klockestrand S 200 D3
Kłodawa
Lubuskie PL 75 B4
Wielkopolskie PL 76 B3
Kłodzko PL 85 B4
Kløfta N 48 B3
Klokkarvik N 46 B2
Klokkerholm DK 58 A3
Klokočov SK 98 B2
Kłomnice PL 86 B3
Klonowa PL 86 A2
Kloosterzande NL 79 A4
Kłopot PL 74 B3
Klos AL 182 B2
Kloštar Ivanić HR 124 B2
Kloster
D 66 B2
DK 59 B1
Klösterle A 107 B5
Klostermansfeld D 82 A3
Klosterneuburg A 97 C4
Klosters CH 107 C4
Kloten CH 107 B3
Klötze D 73 B4
Klövsjö S 199 C11
Klövsjö S 199 C11
Kluczbork PL 86 B2
Kluczewo PL 75 A5
Kluisbergen B 79 B3
Klundert NL 79 A4
Klutz D 65 C4
Klwów PL 87 A4
Klyetsk BY 13 B7
Knaben N 52 B2
Knaften S 200 B4
Knapstad N 54 A2
Knäred S 61 C3
Knaresborough GB 40 A2
Knarvik N 46 B2
Knebel DK 59 B3
Knebworth GB 44 B3
Knesebeck D 73 B3
Knesselare B 78 A3
Knežak SLO 123 B3
Kneževi Vinogradi
HR 125 B4
Kneževo HR 125 B4
Knić SRB 127 D2
Knighton GB 39 B3
Knin HR 138 A2
Knislinge S 61 C4
Knittelfeld A 110 B1
Knivsta S 57 A3
Knock IRL 28 A3
Knocktopher IRL 30 B1
Knokke-Heist B 78 A3
Knowle GB 44 A2
Knurów PL 86 B2
Knutby S 51 C5
Knutsford GB 38 A4
Kobarid SLO 122 A2
København =
Copenhagen DK 61 D2
Kobenz A 110 B1
Kobersdorf A 111 B3
Kobiernice PL 99 B3
Kobierzyce PL 85 B4
Kobilje SLO 111 C3
Kobiór PL 86 B2
Koblenz
CH 106 B3
D 81 B3
Kobryn BY 13 B6
Kobylanka PL 75 A3
Kobylin PL 85 A5
Kobylniki PL 77 B5
Kocaali TR 187 A5
Kocaaliler TR 189 B5
Kocaeli = İzmit
TR 187 B4
Kočani MK 182 B4
Koçarlı TR 188 B2
Koceljevo SRB 127 C1
Kočerin BIH 138 B3
Kočevje SLO 123 B3
Kočevska Reka
SLO 123 B3
Kochel am see D 108 B2
Kocs H 112 B2
Kocsér H 113 B3
Kocsola H 112 C2
Koczala PL 68 B2
Kodal N 53 A6
Kode S 60 B1
Kodersdorf D 84 A2
Kodrab PL 86 A3
Koekelare B 78 A2
Kofçaz TR 186 A2
Köflach A 110 B2
Køge DK 61 D2
Kohlberg D 95 B4
Kohtla-Järve EST 8 C5
Köinge S 60 B2
Kojetín CZ 98 B1
Kökar FIN 51 C7
Kokava SK 99 C3
Kokkinotrimithia 181 A2
Kokkola FIN 3 E8
Kokori BIH 124 C3
Kokoski PL 69 A3
Koksijde B 78 A2
Kola
BIH 124 C3
RUS 3 B13
Köla S 54 A3
Kołacin PL 87 A3
Kolari FIN 196 B6
Kolárovo SK 112 B1
Kolašin MNE 16 D3
Kolbäck S 56 A2
Kolbacz PL 75 A3
Kolbeinsstaðir IS 190 C3
Kolbermoor D 108 B3
Kolbnitz A 109 C4
Kolbotn N 54 A1
Kolbu N 48 B2
Kolby Kås DK 59 C3
Kolczewo PL 67 C3
Kolczyglowy PL 68 A2
Kolding DK 59 C2
Kölesd H 112 C2
Kolgrov N 46 A1
Kolín CZ 97 A3
Kolind DK 59 B3
Kolinec CZ 96 B1
Koljane HR 138 B2
Kølkær DK 59 B2
Kölleda D 82 A3
Kollum NL 70 A3
Köln = Cologne D 80 B2
Koło PL 76 B3
Kołobrzeg PL 67 B4
Kolochau D 83 A5
Kolomyya UA 13 D6
Kolonowskie PL 86 B2
Koloveč CZ 95 B5
Kolpino RUS 9 C7
Kolrep D 73 A5
Kölsillre S 199 C12
Kolsko PL 75 C4
Kolsva S 56 A1
Kolta SK 112 A2
Kolunič BIH 138 A2
Koluszki PL 87 A3
Kolut SRB 125 B4
Kolvereid N 199 A8
Kølvrå DK 59 B2
Komadi H 113 B5
Komagvær N 193 B14
Komarica BIH 125 C3
Komárno SK 112 B2
Komárom H 112 B2
Komatou Yialou
CY 181 A3
Komboti GR 182 D3
Komen SLO 122 B2
Komin HR 138 B3
Komiža HR 138 B2
Komjáti H 99 C4
Komjatice SK 112 A2
Komletinci HR 125 B4
Komló H 125 A4
Kömlo H 113 B4
Komoča SK 112 B2
Komorniki PL 75 B5
Komorzno PL 86 A2
Komotini GR 183 B7
Konak SRB 126 B2
Konakovo RUS 9 D10
Konarzyny PL 68 B2
Kondias GR 183 D7
Kondopaga RUS 9 A9
Kondorfa H 111 C3
Kondoros H 113 C4
Konevo RUS 9 A11
Køng DK 65 A4
Konga S 63 B3
Köngäs FIN 196 B7
Kongerslev DK 58 B3
Kongsberg N 53 A5
Kongshamn N 53 B4
Kongsmark DK 64 A1
Kongsmoen N 199 A9
Kongsvik N 194 B7
Kongsvinger N 48 B3
Konice CZ 97 B4
Konie PL 77 C5
Koniecpol PL 86 B3
Königsberg D 82 B2
Königsbronn D 94 C2
Königsbrück D 84 A1
Königsbrunn D 94 C2
Konigsdorf D 108 B2
Königsee D 82 B3
Königshorst D 74 B1
Königslutter D 73 B3
Königssee D 109 B3
Königstein
Hessen D 81 B4
Sachsen D 84 B2
Königstetten A 97 C4
Königswartha D 84 A2
Konigswiesen A 96 C2
Königswinter D 80 B3
Königs Wusterhausen
D 74 B2
Konin PL 76 B3
Konispol AL 182 D2
Konitsa GR 182 C2
Köniz CH 106 C2
Konjevići BIH 139 A5
Konjevrate HR 138 B2
Konjic BIH 139 B3
Konjščina HR 124 A2
Konnerud N 53 A6
Konopiska PL 86 B2
Konotop PL 75 C4
Końskie PL 87 A4
Konsmo N 52 B3
Konstancin-Jeziorna
PL 77 B6
Konstantynów Łódźki
PL 86 A3
Konstanz D 107 B4
Kontich B 79 A4
Kontiolahti FIN 9 A6
Konya TR 189 B7
Konz D 92 B2
Kópasker IS 191 A9
Kópavogur IS 190 C4
Kopčany SK 98 C1
Koper SLO 122 B2
Kopervik N 52 A1
Kópháza H 111 B3
Kopice PL 85 B5
Kopidlno CZ 84 B3
Köping S 56 A1
Köpingebro S 66 A2
Köpingsvik S 62 B4
Köpmanholmen
S 200 C4
Koppang N 48 A3
Koppangen N 192 C4
Kopparberg S 50 C1
Koppelo FIN 193 D11
Koppom S 54 A3
Koprivlen BG 183 B5
Koprivna BIH 125 C4
Koprivnica HR 124 A2
Kopřivnice CZ 98 B2
Köprübaşı TR 186 D3
Koprzywnica PL 87 B5
Kopstal L 92 B2
Kopychyntsi UA 13 D6
Kopytkowo PL 69 B3
Korbach D 81 A4
Körbecke D 81 A4
Korçë AL 182 C2
Korčula HR 138 C3
Korczyców PL 75 B3
Korenita SRB 127 C1
Korets UA 13 C7
Korfantów PL 85 B5
Körfez TR 187 B4
Korgen N 195 D4
Korinth DK 64 A3
Korinthos = Corinth
GR 184 B3
Korita
BIH 138 A2
HR 139 C3
Korithi GR 184 B1
Korkuteli TR 189 B5
Körmend H 111 B3
Korne PL 68 A2
Korneuburg A 97 C4
Kornevo RUS 69 A5
Kórnik PL 76 B2
Kornsjø N 54 B2
Környe H 112 B2
Koromačno HR 123 C3
Koroni GR 184 C2
Koronos GR 185 B6
Koronowo PL 76 A2
Körösladány H 113 C5
Köröstarcsa H 113 C5
Korosten UA 13 C8
Korostyshev UA 13 C8
Korpikå S 196 D6
Korpikylä FIN 196 C6
Korpilombolo S 196 C6
Korsberga
Jönköping S 62 A3
Skaraborg S 55 B5
Korshavn N 54 A1
Korskrogen S 200 E1
Korsnäs S 50 B2
Korsør DK 65 A4
Korsun
Shevchenkovskiy
UA 13 D9
Kortrāsk S 196 D3
Kortrijk B 78 B3
Korucu TR 186 C2
Koryčany CZ 98 B1
Korzeńsko PL 85 A4
Korzybie PL 68 A1
Kos GR 188 C2
Kosakowo PL 69 A3
Kosanica MNE 139 B5
Kösching D 95 C3
Kościan PL 75 B5
Kościelec PL 76 B3
Kościerzyna PL 68 A2
Koserow D 66 B2
Košetice CZ 97 B3
Košice SK 12 D4
Kosjerić SRB 127 D1
Koška HR 125 B4
Koskullskulle S 196 B3
Kosovska Mitrovica
KOS 16 D4
Kosta S 62 B3
Kostajnica HR 124 B2
Kostajnik SRB 127 C1
Kostanjevica SLO 123 B4
Kostelec nad Černými
Lesy CZ 96 B2
Kostelec na Hané
CZ 97 B5
Kostice CZ 84 B1
Kostkowo PL 68 A3
Kostojevići SRB 127 C1
Kostolac SRB 127 C3
Kostomłoty PL 85 A4
Kostopil UA 13 C7
Kostów PL 86 A2
Kostrzyn
Lubuskie PL 74 B3
Wielkopolskie PL 76 B2
Koszalin PL 67 B5
Koszęcin PL 86 B2
Kőszeg H 111 B3
Koszwaly PL 69 A3
Koszyce PL 87 B4
Kot SLO 123 B4
Kotala FIN 197 B11
Kötelek H 113 B4
Köthen D 83 A3
Kotka FIN 8 B5
Kotomierz PL 76 A3
Kotor MNE 16 D3
Kotoriba HR 124 A2
Kotorsko BIH 125 C4
Kotor Varoš BIH 124 C3
Kotovsk UA 17 B8
Kotronas GR 184 C3
Kötschach A 109 C3
Kötzting D 95 B4
Koudum NL 70 B2
Kouřim CZ 96 A2
Kout na Šumave
CZ 95 B5
Kouvola FIN 8 B5
Kovačevac SRB 127 C2
Kovačica SRB 126 B2
Kovdor RUS 197 B13
Kovel' UA 13 C6
Kovilj SRB 126 B2
Kovin SRB 127 C2
Kowal PL 77 B4

Kowalewo Pomorskie PL 69 B3
Kowalów PL 75 B3
Kowary PL 85 B3
Köyceğiz TR 188 C3
Kozani GR 182 C3
Kozarac
BIH 124 C2
HR 124 B1
Kozárovce SK 98 C2
Kozelets UA 13 C9
Kozica HR 138 B3
Koziegłowy PL 86 B3
Kozienice PL 87 A5
Kozina SLO 122 B2
Kozje SLO 123 A4
Kozlu TR 187 A6
Kozluk BIH 139 A5
Koźmin PL 85 A5
Koźminek PL 86 A2
Kozolupy CZ 96 B1
Kożuchów PL 84 A3
Kožuhe BIH 125 C4
Kozyatyn UA 13 D8
Kozyürük TR 186 A1
Kräckelbräken S 49 A6
Krackow D 74 A3
Kraddsele S 195 E7
Krąg PL 68 A1
Kragenæs DK 65 B4
Kragerø N 53 B5
Krągi PL 68 B1
Kragujevac SRB 127 C2
Kraiburg D 109 A3
Krajenka PL 68 B1
Krajišnik SRB 126 B2
Krajková CZ 83 B4
Krajné SK 98 C1
Krajnik Dolny PL 74 A3
Krakača BIH 124 B1
Kräklingbo S 57 C4
Kraków = Cracow PL 99 A3
Krakow am See D 73 A5
Králíky CZ 85 B4
Kraljevica HR 123 B3
Kraljevo SRB 16 D4
Kral'ovany SK 99 B3
Král'ov Brod SK 111 A4
Kralovice CZ 96 B1
Kralupy nad Vltavou CZ 84 B2
Králův Dvůr CZ 96 B2
Kramfors S 200 D3
Kramsach A 108 B2
Kramsk PL 76 B3
Krâmvik N 53 A4
Kranenburg D 80 A2
Krania GR 182 D3
Krania Elasonas GR 182 D4
Kranichfeld D 82 B3
Kranidi GR 184 B4
Kranj SLO 123 A3
Kranjska Gora SLO 109 C4
Krapanj HR 138 B1
Krapina HR 124 A1
Krapje HR 124 B2
Krapkowice PL 86 B1
Kraselov CZ 96 B1
Krašić HR 123 B4
Krāslava LV 8 E5
Kraslice CZ 83 B4
Krasna PL 87 A4
Krasna Lipa CZ 84 B2
Krasne PL 77 B5
Kraśnik PL 12 C5
Krašnja SLO 123 A3
Krásno SK 98 B2
Krásnohorské Podhradie SK 99 C4
Krasno Polje HR 123 C4
Krasnozavodsk RUS 9 D11
Krasnystaw PL 13 C5
Krasnyy RUS 13 A9
Krasnyy Kholm RUS 9 C10
Krasocin PL 87 B4
Kraszewice PL 86 A2
Kraszkowice PL 86 A2
Kratigos GR 186 C1
Kratovo MK 182 A4
Kraubath A 110 B1
Krausnick D 74 B2
Krautheim D 94 B1
Kravaře CZ 84 B2
Kraváre CZ 98 B2
Kravarsko HR 124 B2
Kraznějov CZ 96 B1
Krčedin SRB 126 B2
Kŭrdzhali BG 183 B7
Krefeld D 80 A2
Kregme DK 61 D2
Krembz D 73 A4
Kremenets UA 13 C6
Kremmen D 74 B2
Kremna SRB 127 D1
Kremnica SK 98 C2
Krempe D 64 C2
Krems A 97 C3
Kremsbrücke A 109 C4
Kremsmünster A 110 A1
Křemže CZ 96 C2
Křenov CZ 97 B4
Krepa PL 76 C3
Krępa Krajeńska PL 75 A5
Krepsko PL 68 B1
Kreševo BIH 139 B4
Kressbronn D 107 B4
Krestena GR 184 B2
Kretinga LT 8 E2
Krettsy RUS 9 C8
Kreuth D 108 B2
Kreuzau D 80 B2
Kreuzlingen CH 107 B4
Kreuztal D 81 B3
Krewelin D 74 B2
Krezluk BIH 138 A3
Krichem BG 183 A6
Krieglach A 110 B2
Kriegsfeld D 93 B3
Kriens CH 106 B3
Krimml A 108 B3
Krimpen aan de IJssel NL 79 A4
Křinec CZ 84 B3
Kristdala S 62 A4
Kristiansand N 53 B4
Kristianstad S 61 C4
Kristiansund N 198 B4
Kristiinankaupunki FIN 8 A2
Kristinefors S 49 B4
Kristinehamn S 55 A5
Kriváň SK 99 C3
Kriva Palanka MK 182 A4
Křivokát CZ 96 A1
Kriź HR 124 B2
Křižanov CZ 97 B4
Križevci HR 124 A2
Krk HR 123 B3
Krka SLO 123 B3
Krnjača SRB 127 C2
Krnjak HR 123 B4
Krnjeuša BIH 124 C2
Krnjevo SRB 127 C3
Krnov CZ 98 A1
Krobia PL 85 A4
Kroczyce PL 86 B3
Krøderen N 48 B1
Krokees GR 184 C3
Krokek S 56 B2
Krokom S 199 B11
Krokowa PL 68 A3
Krokstad-elva N 53 A5
Kroksund N 54 A2
Kroměříž CZ 98 B1
Krommenie NL 70 B1
Krompachy SK 99 C4
Kronach D 82 B3
Kronshagen D 64 B3
Kronshtadt RUS 9 C6
Kröpelin D 65 B4
Kropp D 64 B2
Kroppenstedt D 73 C4
Kropstädt D 74 C1
Krościenko nad Dunajcem PL 99 B4
Kröslin D 66 B2
Krośnice PL 85 A5
Krośniewice PL 77 B4
Krosno PL 12 D4
Krosno Odrzańskie PL 75 B4
Krostitz D 83 A4
Krotoszyn PL 85 A5
Krottendorf A 110 B2
Krouna CZ 97 B4
Krowiarki PL 86 B2
Krrabë AL 182 B1
Kršan HR 123 B3
Krško SLO 123 B4
Krstac MNE 139 B4
Krstur SRB 126 A2
Křtiny CZ 97 B4
Kruft D 80 B3
Kruishoutem B 79 B3
Krujë AL 182 B1
Krulyewshchyna BY 13 A7
Krumbach
A 111 B3
D 94 C2
Krumovgrad BG 183 B7
Krün D 108 B2
Krupá CZ 84 B1
Krupa na Vrbasu BIH 124 C3
Krupanj SRB 127 C1
Krupina SK 99 C3
Krupka CZ 84 B1
Krupki BY 13 A8
Kruså DK 64 B2
Krušćica BIH 139 A3
Kruševac SRB 16 D4
Kruševo MK 182 B3
Kruszwica PL 76 B3
Kruszyn PL 77 B4
Krychaw BY 13 B9
Krynica PL 99 B4
Krynica Morska PL 69 A4
Krzęcin PL 75 A4
Krzelów PL 85 A4
Krzepice PL 86 B2
Krzepielów PL 85 A4
Krzeszowice PL 86 B3
Krzeszyce PL 75 B4
Krzynowlaga Mała PL 77 A5
Krzywiń PL 75 C5
Krzyżanowice PL 98 B2
Krzyżowa PL 99 B3
Krzyż Wielkopolski PL 75 B5
Ksiaz Wielkopolski PL 87 B4
Książ Wielkopolski PL 76 B2
Ktębowiec PL 75 A5
Kübekháza H 126 A2
Küblis CH 107 C4
Kuchary PL 86 A1
Kuchl A 109 B4
Kucice PL 77 B5
Kuciste HR 138 C3
Kuçovë AL 182 C1
Küçükbahçe TR 188 A1
Küçükköy TR 186 C1
Küçükkuyu TR 186 C1
Kucura SRB 126 B1
Kuczbork-Osada PL 77 A5
Kuddby S 56 B2
Kudowa-Zdrój PL 85 B4
Kufstein A 108 B3
Kuggeboda S 63 B3
Kuggörana S 200 E3
Kühbach D 95 C3
Kuhmo FIN 3 D11
Kuhmoinen FIN 8 B4
Kuhnsdorf A 110 C1
Kuhstedt D 72 A1
Kuinre NL 70 B2
Kuivaniemi FIN 197 D8
Kuivastu EST 8 C3
Kukës AL 182 A2
Kuklin PL 77 A5
Kukljica HR 137 A4
Kukujevci SRB 127 B1
Kula
Srbija SRB 127 C3
Vojvodina SRB 126 B1
TR 188 A3
Kuldīga LV 8 D2
Kulen Vakuf BIH 124 C2
Kulina BIH 125 C4
Kullstedt D 82 A2
Kulmain D 95 B3
Kulmbach D 82 B3
Kuloharju FIN 197 D11
Kulu TR 23 B7
Kumachevo RUS 69 A5
Kumafşarı TR 189 B4
Kumane SRB 126 B2
Kumanovo MK 182 A3
Kumbağ TR 186 B2
Kumdanlı TR 189 A5
Kumkale TR 186 C1
Kumla S 56 A1
Kumlakyrkby S 50 C3
Kumlinge FIN 51 B7
Kumluca TR 189 C5
Kumrovec HR 123 A4
Kunadacs H 112 C3
Kunágota H 113 C5
Kunbaja H 126 A1
Kunda EST 8 C5
Kundl A 108 B2
Kunes N 193 B10
Kunfehértó H 126 A1
Kungälv S 60 B1
Kungsängen S 57 A3
Kungsäter S 60 B2
Kungsbacka S 60 B2
Kungsgården S 50 B3
Kungshamn S 54 B2
Kungs-Husby S 56 A3
Kungsör S 56 A2
Kunhegyes H 113 B4
Kunmadaras H 113 B4
Kunovice CZ 98 B1
Kunów PL 87 B5
Kunowo
Wielkopolskie PL 76 C2
Zachodnio-Pomorskie PL 74 A3
Kunštát CZ 97 B4
Kunszállás H 113 C3
Kunszentmárton H 113 C4
Kunszentmiklós H 112 B3
Kunžak CZ 97 B3
Künzelsau D 94 B1
Kuolayarvi RUS 197 C12
Kuolio FIN 197 D11
Kuopio FIN 8 A5
Kuosku FIN 197 B11
Kup
H 111 B4
PL 86 B1
Kupferzell D 94 B1
Kupinec HR 123 B4
Kupinečki Kraljevac HR 124 B1
Kupinovo SRB 127 C2
Kupirovo HR 138 A2
Kupjak HR 123 B3
Kuppenheim D 93 C4
Kupres BIH 138 B3
Küps D 82 B3
Kurd H 112 C2
Küre TR 23 A7
Kuressaare EST 8 C3
Kurikka FIN 8 A3
Kuřim CZ 97 B4
Kuřivody CZ 84 B2
Kurki PL 77 A5
Kurort Oberwiesenthal D 83 B4
Kurort Schmalkalden D 82 B2
Kurort Stolberg D 82 A2
Kurort Wippra D 82 A3
Kurów PL 12 C5
Kurowice PL 86 A3
Kurravaara S 196 B3
Kursu FIN 197 C11
Kurşunlu
Bursa TR 187 B4
Çankırı TR 23 A7
Kurtakko FIN 196 B7
Kürten D 80 A3
Kurucaşile TR 187 A7
Kurvinen FIN 197 D12
Kurzelów PL 87 B3
Kusadak SRB 127 C2
Kuşadası TR 188 B2
Kusel D 93 B3
Kusey D 73 B4
Küsnacht CH 106 B3
Kütahya TR 187 C4
Kutenholz D 72 A2
Kutina HR 124 B2
Kutjevo HR 125 B3
Kutná Hora CZ 97 B3
Kutno PL 77 B4
Kuttara FIN 193 D10
Küttingen CH 106 B3
Kúty SK 98 C1
Kuusamo FIN 197 D12
Kuusankoski FIN 8 B5
Kuvshinovo RUS 9 D9
Kuyucak TR 188 B3
Kuzmin SRB 127 B1
Kuźnia Raciborska PL 86 B2
Kuźnica Czarnkowska PL 75 B5
Kuźnica Żelichowska PL 75 B5
Kvaløysletta N 192 C2
Kvalsund N 192 B7
Kvam
Nord-Trøndelag N 199 A8
Oppland N 198 D6
Kvamsøy N 46 A3
Kvænangsbotn N 192 C6
Kvanndal N 46 B3
Kvänum S 55 B4
Kværndrup DK 59 C3
Kvås N 52 B3
Kvasice CZ 98 B1
Kvelde N 53 A5
Kvenna N 198 C5
Kvernaland N 52 B1
Kvibille S 60 C2
Kvicksund S 56 A2
Kvidinge S 61 C3
Kvikkjokk S 195 D8
Kvikne
Hedmark N 199 C7
Oppland N 47 A6
Kvilda CZ 96 B1
Kville S 54 B2
Kvillsfors S 62 A3
Kvinesdal N 52 B2
Kvinlog N 52 B2
Kvinnherad N 46 C3
Kvissel DK 58 A3
Kvissleby S 200 D3
Kviteseid N 53 A4
Kvitsøy N 52 A1
Kwakowo PL 68 A2
Kwidzyn PL 69 B3
Kwilcz PL 75 B5
Kyjov CZ 98 C1
Kyleakin GB 31 B3
Kyle of Lochalsh GB 31 B3
Kylerhea GB 31 B3
Kylestrome GB 32 C1
Kyllburg D 92 A2
Kyllini GR 184 B2
Kynšperk nad Ohří CZ 83 B4
Kyperounda CY 181 B1
Kyrenia CY 181 A2
Kyritz D 73 B5
Kyrkesund S 60 A1
Kyrkhult S 63 B2
Kyrksæterøra N 198 B6
Kysucké Nové Mesto SK 98 B2
Kythira GR 184 C3
Kythréa CY 181 A2
Kyustendil BG 16 D5
Kyyiv = Kiev UA 13 C9
Kyyjärvi FIN 8 A4

L

Laa an der Thaya A 97 C4
La Adrada E 150 B3
Laage D 65 C5
La Alameda E 157 B4
La Alberca E 149 B3
La Alberca de Záncara E 158 B1
La Albergueria de Argañán E 149 B3
La Albuera E 155 C4
La Aldea del Portillo del Busto E 143 B3
La Algaba E 162 A1
La Aliseda de Tormes E 150 B2
La Almarcha E 158 B1
La Almolda E 153 A3
La Almunia de Doña Godina E 152 A2
Laanila FIN 193 D11
La Antillas E 161 B2
La Arena E 141 A4
Laatzen D 72 B2
La Aulaga E 161 B3
La Balme-de-Sillingy F 118 B3
La Bañeza E 141 B5
La Barca de la Florida E 162 B2
La Barre-de-Monts F 114 B1
La Barre-en-Ouche F 89 B4
La Barrosa E 162 B1
La Barthe-de-Neste F 145 A4
La Bassée F 78 B2
La Bastide-de-Sèrou F 146 A2
La Bastide-des-Jourdans F 132 B1
Labastide-Murat F 129 B4
La Bastide-Puylaurent F 117 C3
Labastide-Rouairoux F 130 B1
Labastide-St Pierre F 129 C4
La Bathie F 118 B3
Lábatlan H 112 B2
La Baule-Escoublac F 101 B3
La Bazoche-Gouet F 102 A2
La Bégude-de-Mazenc F 131 A3
Labenne F 128 C1
La Bernerie-en-Retz F 114 A1
Labin HR 123 B3
La Bisbal d'Empordà E 147 C4
Łabiszyn PL 76 B2
Lablachère F 131 A3
Lábod H 124 A3
Laboe D 64 B3
La Boissière F 89 A4
Labouheyre F 128 B2
La Bourboule F 116 B2
La Bóveda de Toro E 150 A2
Łabowa PL 99 B4
La Brède F 128 B2
La Bresse F 106 A1
La Bridoire F 118 B2
La Brillanne F 132 B1
Labrit F 128 B2
Labros E 152 A2
La Bruffière F 114 A2
Labruguière F 130 B1
Labrujo P 148 A1
L'Absie F 114 B3
La Bussière F 103 B4
Laç AL 182 B1
La Caillère F 114 B3
Lacalahorra E 164 B1
La Caletta
Cágliari I 179 C2
Núoro I 178 B3
La Calmette F 131 B3
La Calzada de Oropesa E 150 C2
La Campana E 162 A2
La Cañada E 150 B3
Lacanau F 128 B1
Lacanau-Océan F 128 A1
Lacanche F 104 B3
La Canourgue F 130 A2
La Capelle F 91 B3
Lacapelle-Marival F 129 B4
Laćarak SRB 127 B1
La Cardanchosa E 156 B2
La Caridad E 141 A4
La Carlota E 162 A3
La Carolina E 157 B4
Lacaune F 130 B1
La Cava E 153 B4
La Cavalerie F 130 A2
Laceby GB 41 B3
Lacedónia I 172 A1
La Celle-en-Moravan F 104 B3
La Celle-St Avant F 102 B2
La Cerca E 143 B3
Láces I 108 C1
La Chaise-Dieu F 117 B3
La Chaize-Giraud F 114 B2
La Chaize-le-Vicomte F 114 B2
La Chambre F 118 B3
Lachania GR 188 D2
La Chapelaude F 116 A2
La Chapelle-d'Angillon F 103 B4
La Chapelle-en-Aalgaudémar F 118 C3
La Chapelle-en-Vercors F 118 C2
La Chapelle-Glain F 101 B4
La Chapelle-la-Reine F 90 C2
La Chapelle-Laurent F 116 B3
La Chapelle-St Luc F 91 C4
La Chapelle-sur-Erdre F 101 B4
La Chapelle-Vicomtesse F 103 B3
La Charce F 132 A1
La Charité-sur-Loire F 104 B2
La Chartre-sur-le-Loir F 102 B2
La Châtaigneraie F 114 B3
La Châtre F 103 C3
La Chaussée-sur-Marne F 91 C4
La Chaux-de-Fonds CH 106 B1
Lachen CH 107 B3
Lachendorf D 72 B3
La Cheppe F 91 B4
La Chèze F 101 A3
Lachowice PL 99 B3
La Ciotat F 132 B1
Łąck PL 77 B4
Läckeby S 62 B4
Läckö S 55 B4
La Clayette F 117 A4
La Clusaz F 118 B3
Lacock GB 43 A4
La Codosera E 155 B3
La Concha E 143 A3
La Condamine-Châtelard F 132 A2
Láconi I 179 C3
La Contienda E 161 A3
La Coquille F 115 C4
La Coronada E 156 B2
La Côte-St André F 118 B2
La Cotinière F 114 C2
La Courtine F 116 B2
Lacq F 145 A3
La Crau F 132 B2
La Crèche F 115 B3
La Croix F 102 B2
Lacroix-Barrez F 116 C2
Lacroix-St Ouen F 90 B2
Lacroix-sur-Meuse F 92 C1
La Croix-Valmer F 132 B2
La Cumbre E 156 A2
Łącznik PL 86 B1
Lad H 125 A3
Ladbergen D 71 B4
Lądek-Zdrój PL 85 B4
Ladelund D 64 B2
Ladendorf A 97 C4
Ladignac-le-Long F 115 C5
Ladíspoli I 168 B2
Ladoeiro P 155 B3
Ladon F 103 B4
La Douze F 129 A3
Ladushkin RUS 69 A5
Ladybank GB 35 B4
Laer D 71 B4
La Espina E 141 A4
La Estrella E 156 A2
La Farga de Moles E 146 B2
La Fatarella E 153 A4
La Felipa E 158 B2
La Fère F 90 B3
La Ferrière
Indre-et-Loire F 102 B2
Vendée F 114 B2
La Ferrière-en-Parthenay F 115 B3
La-Ferté-Alais F 90 C2
La Ferté-Bernard F 102 A2
La Ferté-Frênel F 89 B4
La Ferté-Gaucher F 90 C3
La Ferté-Imbault F 103 B3
La Ferté-Macé F 89 B3
La Ferté-Milon F 90 B3
La Ferté-sous-Jouarre F 90 C3
La Ferté-St-Aubin F 103 B3
La Ferté-St-Cyr F 103 B3
La Ferté-Vidame F 89 B4
La Ferté Villeneuil F 103 B3
La Feuillie F 90 B1
Lafkos GR 183 D5
La Flèche F 102 B1
La Flotte F 114 B2
Lafnitz A 111 B3
La Font de la Figuera E 159 C3
La Fouillade F 130 A1
Lafrançaise F 129 B4
La Fregeneda E 149 B3
La Fresneda E 153 B4
La Fuencubierta E 162 A3
La Fuente de San Esteban E 149 B3
La Fulioala E 147 C2
La Gacilly F 101 B3
La Galera E 153 B4
Lagan S 60 C3
Laganadi I 175 C1
Lagarde F 146 A2
La Garde-Freinet F 132 B2
Lagares
Coimbra P 148 B2
Porto P 148 A1
La Garnache F 114 B2
Lagaro I 135 A4
La Garriga E 147 C3
La Garrovilla E 155 C4
Lagartera E 150 C2
La Gaubretière F 114 B2
Lågbol S 51 B5
Lage D 72 C1
Lägerdorf D 64 C2
Lagg GB 34 C2
Laggan GB 32 D2
Laggartorp S 55 A5
Łagiewniki PL 85 B4
La Gineta E 158 B1
Láglio I 120 B2
Lagnieu F 118 B2
Lagny-sur-Marne F 90 C2
Lago
Calabria I 175 B2
Veneto I 121 B5
Lagôa P 160 B1
Lagoaça P 149 A3
Lagonegro I 174 A1
Lagos
GR 183 B7
P 160 B1
Lagosanto I 121 C5
Łagów
Lubuskie PL 75 B4
Świętokrzyskie PL 87 B5
La Granadella
Alicante E 159 C4
Lleida E 153 A4
La Grand-Combe F 131 A3
La Grande-Croix F 117 B4
La Grande-Motte F 131 B3
La Granja d'Escarp E 153 A4
La Granjuela E 156 B2
Lagrasse F 146 A3
La Grave F 118 B3
La Gravelle F 101 A4
Laguardia E 143 B4
La Guardia E 151 C4
La Guardia de Jaén E 163 A4
Laguarres E 145 B4
Laguenne F 116 B1
Laguépie F 129 B4
La Guerche-de-Bretagne F 101 B4
La Guerche-sur-l'Aubois F 104 C1
La Guérinière F 114 B1
Laguiole F 116 C2
Laguna de Duera E 150 A3
Laguna del Marquesado E 152 B2
Laguna de Negrillos E 142 B1
Lagundo I 108 C2
Lagunilla E 149 B3
La Haba E 156 B2
Laharie F 128 B1
La Haye-du-Puits F 88 A2
La Haye-Pesnel F 88 B2
Lahden D 71 B4
La Herlière F 78 B2
La Hermida E 142 A2
La Herrera E 158 C1
Laheycourt F 91 C5
La Higuera E 158 C2
La Hiniesta E 149 A4
Lahnstein D 81 B3
Laholm S 61 C3
La Horcajada E 150 B2
La Horra E 143 C3
Lahr D 93 C3
Lahti FIN 8 B4
La Hulpe B 79 B4
La Hutte F 89 B4
Laichingen D 94 C1
L'Aigle F 89 B4
La Iglesuela E 150 B3
La Iglesuela del Cid E 153 B3
Laignes F 104 B3
Laiguéglia I 133 B4
L'Aiguillon-sur-Mer F 114 B2
Laimbach am Ostrong A 97 C3
Laina E 152 A1
Lainio S 196 B5
Lairg GB 32 C2
La Iruela E 164 B2
Laissac F 130 A1
Laisvall S 195 D8
Láives I 121 A4
La Javie F 132 A2
Lajkovac SRB 127 C2
La Jonchère-St Maurice F 116 A1
La Jonquera E 146 B3
Lajoskomárom H 112 C2
Lajosmizse H 112 B3
Lak H 99 C4
Lakenheath GB 45 A4
Laki BG 183 B6
Lakitelek H 113 C4
Lakki GR 185 D4
Lakolk DK 64 A1
Łąkorz PL 69 B4
Lakšárska Nová Ves SK 98 C1
Lakselv N 193 B8
Laksfors N 195 E4
Laktaši BIH 124 C3
La Lantejuela E 162 A2
Lalapaşa TR 186 A1
L'Albagès E 153 A4
Lalbenque F 129 B4
L'Alcudia E 159 B3
L'Aldea E 153 B4
Lalín E 140 B2
Lalinde F 129 B3
La Línea de la Concepción E 162 B2
Lalizolle F 116 A3
La Llacuna E 147 C2
Lalley F 118 C2
Lalling D 95 C5
Lalm N 198 D6
La Londe-les-Maures F 132 B2
La Loupe F 89 B5
La Louvière B 79 B4
L'Alpe-d'Huez F 118 B3
La Luisiana E 162 A2
Laluque F 128 C1
Lam D 95 B5
La Machine F 104 C2
la Maddalena I 178 A3
Lama dei Peligni I 169 A4
Lamadrid E 142 A2
Lamagistére F 129 B3
La Mailleraye-sur-Seine F 89 A4
La Malène F 130 A2
Lama Mocogno I 135 A3
La Mamola E 163 B4
La Manresana dels Prats E 147 C2
Lamarche F 105 A4
Lamarche-sur-Saône F 105 B4
Lamargelle F 105 B3
Lamarosa P 154 B2
Lamarque F 128 A2
Lamas P 148 B1
La Masadera E 145 C3
Lamas de Moaro P 140 B2
Lamastre F 117 C4
La Mata E 150 C3
La Mata de Ledesma E 149 A4
La Mata de Monteagudo E 142 B1
Lambach A 109 A4
Lamballe F 101 A3
Lamberhurst GB 45 B4
Lambesc F 131 B4
Lambia GR 184 B2
Lambley GB 37 B4
Lambourn GB 44 B2
Lamego P 148 A2
La Meilleraye-de-Bretagne F 101 B4
La Ménitré F 102 B1
L'Ametlla de Mar E 153 B4
Lamia GR 182 E4
Lammhult S 62 A2
La Mojonera E 164 C2
La Mole F 132 B2

La Molina E 147 B2
La Monnerie-le-Montel F 117 B3
La Morera E 155 C4
La Mothe-Achard F 114 B2
Lamothe-Cassel F 129 B4
Lamothe-Montravel F 128 B3
La Mothe-St Héray F 115 B3
Lamotte-Beuvron F 103 B4
La Motte-Chalançon F 131 A4
La Motte-du-Caire F 132 A2
La Motte-Servolex F 118 B2
Lampertheim D 93 B4
Lampeter GB 39 B2
L'Ampolla E 153 B4
Lamprechtshausen A 109 B3
Lamsfeld D 74 C3
Lamspringe D 72 C3
Lamstedt D 72 A2
La Mudarra E 142 C2
La Muela E 152 A2
La Mure F 118 C2
Lamure-sur-Azergues F 117 A4
Lana I 108 C2
Lanaja E 145 C3
Lanarce F 117 C3
Lanark GB 36 A3
La Nava E 161 B3
La Nava de Ricomalillo E 156 A3
La Nava de Santiago E 155 B4
Lancaster GB 37 B4
Lanchester GB 37 B5
Lanciano I 169 A4
Lancing GB 44 C3
Lançon-Provence F 131 B4
Lancova Vas SLO 124 A1
Landau
Bayern D 95 C4
Rheinland-Pfalz D 93 B4
Landeck A 108 B1
Landen B 79 B5
Landerneau F 100 A1
Landeryd S 60 B3
Landesbergen D 72 B2
Landete E 158 B2
Landévant F 100 B2
Landévennec F 100 A1
Landeyjahöfn 190 D5
Landivisiau F 100 A1
Landivy F 88 B2
Landl A 108 B3
Landön S 199 B11
Landos F 117 C3
Landouzy-le-Ville F 91 B4
Landquart CH 107 C4
Landrecies F 91 A3
Landreville F 104 A3
Landriano I 120 B2
Landsberg D 108 A1
Lands-berg D 83 A4
Landsbro S 62 A2
Landscheid D 92 B2
Landshut D 95 C4
Landskrona S 61 D2
Landstuhl D 93 B3
Lanesborough IRL 28 A4
Lanester F 100 B2
Lanestosa E 143 A3
La Neuve-Lyre F 89 B4
La Neuveville CH 106 B2
Langå DK 59 B2
Langada GR 185 A7
Langadas GR 183 C5
Langa de Duero E 151 A4
Langadia GR 184 B3
Langangen N 53 A5
Långared S 60 A2
Långaröd S 61 D3
Långaryd S 60 B3
Långås S 60 C2
Långasjö S 63 B3
Langau A 97 C3
Langeac F 117 B3
Langeais F 102 B2
Langedijk NL 70 B1
Langeln D 73 C3
Langelsheim D 72 C3
Langemark-Poelkapelle B 78 B2
Langen
Hessen D 93 B4
Niedersachsen D 72 A1
Langenau D 94 C2
Langenberg D 81 A4
Langenbruck CH 106 B2
Langenburg D 94 B1
Längenfeld A 108 B1
Langenfeld D 80 A2
Langenhorn D 64 B1
Langenlois A 97 C3
Langenlonsheim D 93 B3
Langennaudorf D 83 A5
Langenneufnach D 94 C2
Langenthal CH 106 B2
Langenzenn D 94 B2
Langeoog D 71 A4
Langeskov DK 59 C3
Langesund N 53 A5
Langewiesen D 82 B2
Långflon S 49 A4
Langförden D 71 B5
Langhagen D 73 A5
Länghem S 60 B3
Langhirano I 120 C3
Langholm GB 36 A4
Langholt IS 191 D7
Långlöt S 62 B4
Langnau CH 106 C2
Langø DK 65 B4
Langogne F 117 C3
Langon F 128 B2
Langquaid D 95 C4
Långrådna S 56 B2
Langreo E 142 A1
Langres F 105 B4
Långsele S 200 C3
Långserud S 54 A3
Langset N 48 B3
Långshyttan S 50 B3
Langstrand N 192 B7
Långträsk S 196 D3
Langueux F 101 A3
Languidic F 100 B2
Längvik S 57 A4
Langwarden D 71 A5
Langwathby GB 37 B4
Langwedel D 72 B2
Langweid D 94 C2
Langwies CH 107 C4
Lanheses P 148 A1
Lanięta PL 77 B4
Lanildut F 100 A1
Lanjarón E 163 B4
Lanmeur F 100 A2
Lanna
Jönköping S 60 B3
Örebro S 55 A5
Lännaholm S 51 C4
Lannavaara S 196 A4
Lannéanou F 100 A2
Lannemezan F 145 A4
Lanneuville-sur-Meuse F 91 B5
Lannilis F 100 A1
Lannion F 100 A2
La Nocle-Maulaix F 104 C2
Lanouaille F 115 C5
Lansjärv S 196 C5
Lanškroun CZ 97 B4
Lanslebourg-Mont-Cenis F 119 B3
Lanta F 129 C4
Lantadilla E 142 B2
Lanton F 128 B1
Lantosque F 133 B3
La Nuez de Arriba E 143 B3
Lanusei I 179 C3
Lanúvio I 168 B2
Lanvollon F 100 A3
Lánycsók H 125 A4
Lanz D 73 A4
Lanza E 140 A2
Lanzada E 140 B2
Lanzahita E 150 B3
Lanžhot CZ 97 C4
Lanzo Torinese I 119 B4
Laole SRB 127 C3
Laon F 91 B3
Laons F 89 B5
La Paca E 164 B3
La Pacaudière F 117 A3
Lapalisse F 117 A3
La Palma d'Ebre E 153 A4
La Palma del Condado E 161 B3
La Palme F 146 B4
La Palmyre F 114 C2
La Parra E 155 C4
Łapczyna Wola PL 87 B3
La Pedraja de Portillo E 150 A3
La Peraleja E 152 B1
La Petit-Pierre F 93 C3
Lapeyrade F 128 B2
Lapeyrouse F 116 A2
Lapford GB 42 B3
La Pinilla E 165 B3
Lapithos CY 181 A2
La Plagne F 118 B3
La Plaza E 141 A4
Laplume F 129 B3
La Pobla de Lillet E 147 B2
La Pobla de Vallbona E 159 B3
La Pobla Llarga E 159 B3
La Pola de Gordón E 142 B1
la Porta F 180 A2
La Pouëze F 102 B1
Lapoutroie F 106 A2
La Póveda de Soria E 143 B4
Lapovo SRB 127 C3
Läppe S 56 A1
Lappeenranta FIN 8 B6
Lappoluobbal N 192 C7
Lappträsk S 196 C6
La Preste F 146 B3
La Primaube F 130 A1
Lapseki TR 186 B1
Lapua FIN 8 A3
La Puebla de Almoradie E 157 A4
La Puebla de Cazalla E 162 A2
La Puebla de los Infantes E 162 A2
La Puebla del Río E 162 A1
La Puebla de Montalbán E 150 C3
La Puebla de Roda E 145 B4
La Puebla de Valdavia E 142 B2
La Puebla de Valverde E 152 B3
La Pueblanueva E 150 C3
La Puerta de Segura E 164 A2
La Punt CH 107 C4
L'Áquila I 169 A3
La Quintana E 162 A3
La Quintera E 162 A2
La Rábita
Granada E 164 C1
Jaén E 163 A3
Laracha E 140 A2
Laragh IRL 30 A2
Laragne-Montéglin F 132 A1
La Rambla E 163 A3
l'Arboç E 147 C2
L'Arbresle F 117 B4
Lärbro S 57 C4
Larceveau F 144 A2
Larche
Alpes-de-Haute-Provence F 132 A2
Corrèze F 129 A4
Lårdal N 53 A4
Lærdalsøyri N 47 A4
Lardosa P 155 B3
La Reale I 178 A2
Laredo E 143 A3
La Redondela E 161 B2
La Réole F 128 B2
Largentière F 131 A3
L'Argentière-la-Bessée F 118 C3
Largs GB 34 C3
Lari I 134 B3
La Riera E 141 A4
La Riera de Gaià E 147 C2
La Rinconada E 162 A1
Lariño E 140 B1
Larino I 170 B2
Larisa GR 182 D4
La Rivière-Thibouville F 89 A4
Larkhall GB 36 A3
Larkollen N 54 A1
Larmor-Plage F 100 B2
Larnaca CY 181 B2
Larne GB 27 B5
La Robla E 142 B1
La Roca de la Sierra E 155 B4
La Roche CH 106 C2
La Rochebeaucourt-Argentine F 115 C4
La Roche-Bernard F 101 B3
La Roche-Canillac F 116 B1
La Roche-Chalais F 128 A3
La Roche Derrien F 100 A2
La Roche-des-Arnauds F 132 A1
La Roche-en-Ardenne B 80 B1
La Roche-en-Brénil F 104 B3
La Rochefoucauld F 115 C4
La Roche-Guyon F 90 B1
La Rochelle F 114 B2
La Roche-Posay F 115 B4
La Roche-sur-Foron F 118 A3
La Roche-sur-Yon F 114 B2
Larochette L 92 B2
La Rochette F 131 A4
La Roda
Albacete E 158 B1
Oviedo E 141 A4
La Roda de Andalucía E 162 A3
Laroquebrou F 116 C2
La Roquebrussanne F 132 B1
Laroque d'Olmes F 146 B2
La Roque-Gageac F 129 B4
La Roque-Ste Marguerite F 130 A2
Laroque-Timbaut F 129 B3
Larouco E 141 B3
Larraga E 144 B2
Larrau F 144 A3
Larrazet F 129 C4
Larsnes N 198 C2
La Rubia E 143 C4
Laruns F 145 A3
Larva E 164 B1
Larvik N 53 A6
La Sagrada E 149 B3
La Salceda E 151 A4
Lasalle F 131 A2
La Salle F 118 C3
la Salute di Livenza I 122 B1
La Salvetat-Peyralés F 130 A1
La Salvetat-sur-Agout F 130 B1
Las Arenas E 142 A2
La Sarraz CH 105 C5
Lasarte E 144 A1
Låsby DK 59 B2
Las Cabezadas E 151 A4
Las Cabezas de San Juan E 162 B2
Las Correderas E 157 B4
Las Cuevas de Cañart E 153 B3
La Seca E 150 A3
La Selva del Camp E 147 C2
La Senia E 153 B4
La Serra E 147 C2
La Seu d'Urgell E 146 B2
La Seyne-sur-Mer F 132 B1
Las Gabias E 163 A4
Las Herencias E 150 C3
Las Herrerias E 161 B2
Łasin PL 69 B4
Lask PL 86 A3
Laska PL 68 B2
Łaskarzow PL 87 A5
Laško SLO 123 A4
Laskowice PL 76 A3
Las Labores E 157 A4
Las Mesas E 158 B1
Las Minas E 164 A3
Las Navas E 163 A3
Las Navas de la Concepción E 156 C2
Las Navas del Marqués E 150 B3
Las Navillas E 157 A3
Las Negras E 164 C3
La Solana E 157 B4
La Souterraine F 116 A1
Las Pajanosas E 161 B3
Laspaules E 145 B4
Las Pedroñas E 158 B1
La Spézia I 134 A2
Las Planes d'Hostoles E 147 B3
Laspuña E 145 B4
Las Rozas
Cantabria E 142 B2
Madrid E 151 B4
Lassan D 66 C2
Lassay-les-Châteaux F 89 B3
Lasseube F 145 A3
Lassigny F 90 B2
La Storta I 168 B2
Lastovo HR 138 C2
Lastras de Cuéllar E 151 A3
Lästringe S 56 B3
Lastrup D 71 B4
Las Uces E 149 A3
La Suze-sur-Sarthe F 102 B2
Las Veguillas E 149 B4
Las Ventas con Peña Aguilera E 157 A3
Las Ventas de San Julián E 150 B2
Las Villes E 153 B4
Latasa E 144 B2
Látera I 168 A1
Laterza I 171 C4
La Teste F 128 B1
Lathen D 71 B4
Latheron GB 32 C3
La Thuile I 119 B3
Latiano I 173 B3
Latina I 169 B2
Latisana I 122 B2
Látky SK 99 C3
La Toba E 152 B2
La Toledana E 157 A3
La Torre de Cabdella E 146 B1
La Torre de Esteban Hambrán E 151 B3
La Torre del l'Espanyol E 153 A4
La Torresaviñán E 152 B1
La Tour d'Aigues F 132 B1
La Tour de Peilz CH 106 C1
La Tour-du-Pin F 118 B2
La Tranche-sur-Mer F 114 B2
La Tremblade F 114 C2
La Trimouille F 115 B5
La Trinité F 100 B2
La Trinité-Porhoët F 101 A3
Latrónico I 174 A2
Latronquière F 116 C2
Latterbach CH 106 C2
La Turballe F 101 B3
Laubach D 81 B4
Laubert F 117 C3
Laucha D 83 A3
Lauchhammer D 84 A1
Lauchheim D 94 C2
Lauda-Königshofen D 94 B1
Laudal N 52 B3
Lauder GB 35 C5
Lauenau D 72 B2
Lauenburg D 73 A3
Lauf D 95 B3
Laufach D 94 A1
Laufen
CH 106 B2
D 109 B3
Lauffen D 93 B5
Laugar IS 191 B8
Laugarás IS 190 C5
Laugarbakki IS 190 B5
Laugarvatn IS 190 C5
Laugharne GB 39 C2
Lauingen D 94 C2
Laujar de Andarax E 164 C2
Laukaa FIN 8 A4
Lauker S 196 D2
Laukvik N 194 C5
La Uña E 142 A1
Launceston GB 42 B2
La Unión E 165 B4
Launois-sur-Vence F 91 B4
Laupheim D 94 C1
Lauragh IRL 29 C2
Laureana di Borrello I 175 C2
Laurencekirk GB 35 B5
Laurencetown IRL 28 A3
Laurenzana I 172 B1
Lauria I 174 A1
Laurière F 116 A1
Laurieston GB 36 B2
Laurino I 172 B1
Lausanne CH 106 C1
Laussonne F 117 C4
Lauta D 84 A2
Lautenthal D 82 A2
Lauterach A 107 B4
Lauterbach D 81 B5
Lauterbrunnen CH 106 C2
Lauterecken D 93 B3
Lauterhofen D 95 B3
Lautrec F 130 B1
Lauvsnes N 199 A7
Lauvvik N 52 B2
Lauzerte F 129 B4
Lauzès F 129 B4
Lauzun F 129 B3
Lavagna I 134 A2
Laval F 102 A1
La Vall d'Uixó E 159 B3
Lavamünd A 110 C1
Lavara GR 186 A1
Lavardac F 129 B3
Lavaris P 148 B1
Lavarone I 121 B4
Lavau F 104 B1
Lavaur F 129 C4
La Vecilla de Curueño E 142 B1
La Vega
Asturias E 141 A5
Asturias E 142 A1
Cantabria E 142 A2
Lavelanet F 146 B2
La Velilla E 151 A4
La Velles E 150 A2
Lavello I 172 A1
Lavelsloh D 72 B1
Lavenham GB 45 A4
Laveno I 120 B1
La Ventosa E 152 B1
Lavezzola I 135 A4
Laviano I 172 B1
La Victoria E 162 A3
La Vid E 151 A4
Lavik N 46 A2
La Vilavella E 159 B3
La Vilella Baixa E 147 C1
La Villa de Don Fadrique E 157 A4
Lavilledieu F 131 A3
La Villedieu F 115 B3
La Ville Dieu-du-Temple F 129 B4
Lavinio-Lido di Enea I 168 B2
Lav is I 121 A4
Lavit F 129 C3
Lavoncourt F 105 B4
Lavos P 148 B1
La Voulte-sur-Rhône F 117 C4
Lavoûte-Chilhac F 117 B3
Lavradio P 154 C1
Lavre P 154 C2
Lavrio GR 185 B5
La Wantzenau F 93 C3
Lawers GB 35 B3
Ławy PL 75 B3
Laxå S 55 B5
Laxamýri IS 191 B8
Laxe E 140 A2
Laxey GB 36 B2
Laxford Bridge GB 32 C1
Laxhall S 55 B4
Laxsjö S 199 B11
Laxtjarn S 49 B6
Laxvik S 61 C2
Laxviken S 199 B11
La Yesa E 159 B3
Laza E 141 B3
Lazarevac SRB 127 C2
Lazarevo SRB 126 B2
Lazise I 121 B3
Łaziska Grn. PL 86 B2
Lazkao E 144 A1
Lázně Bělohrad CZ 84 B3
Lázně Bohdaneč CZ 97 A3
Lázně Kynžvart CZ 95 A4
Lazonby GB 37 B4
La Zubia E 163 A4
Łazy PL 67 B5
Lazzaro I 175 D1
Lea GB 40 B3
Leadburn GB 35 C4
Leadhills GB 36 A3
Leap IRL 29 C2
Leatherhead GB 44 B3
Łeba PL 68 A2
Lebach D 92 B2
Le Barp F 128 B2
Le Bar-sur-Loup F 132 B2
Le Béage F 117 C4
Le Beausset F 132 B1
Lebekke B 79 A4
Lébény H 111 B4
Le Bessat F 117 B4
Le Blanc F 115 B5
Le Bleymard F 130 A2
Łebno PL 68 A3
Leboreiro E 140 B3
Lębork PL 68 A2
Le Boullay-Mivoye F 89 B5
Le Boulou F 146 B3
Le Bourg F 129 B4
Le Bourg-d'Oisans F 118 B3
Le Bourget-du-Lac F 118 B2
Le Bourgneuf-la-Forêt F 101 A5
Le Bousquet d'Orb F 130 B2
Le Brassus CH 105 C5
Le Breuil F 117 A3
Le Breuil-en-Auge F 89 A4
Lebrija E 162 B1
Lebring A 110 C2
Le Brusquet F 132 A2
Le Bry CH 106 C2
Le Bugue F 129 B3
Le Buisson F 129 B3
Lebus D 74 B3
Lebusa D 83 A5
Leca da Palmeira P 148 A1
Le Caloy F 128 C2
Le Cap d'Agde F 130 B2
Le Cateau Cambrésis F 91 A3
Le Caylar F 130 B2
Le Cayrol F 116 C2
Lecce I 173 B4
Lecco I 120 B2
Lécera E 153 A3
Lećevica HR 138 B2
Lech A 107 B5
Le Chambon-Feugerolles F 117 B4
Le Chambon-sur-Lignon F 117 B4
Le Château d'Oléron F 114 C2
Le Châtelard F 118 B3
Le Châtelet F 103 C4
Le Chatelet-en-Brie F 90 C2
Lechbruck D 108 B1
Lechena GR 184 B2
Le Chesne F 91 B4
Le Cheylard F 117 C4
Lechlade GB 44 B2
Lechovice CZ 97 C4
Leciñena E 145 C3
Leck D 64 B1
Le Collet-de-Deze F 131 A2
Le Conquet F 100 A1
Le Creusot F 104 C3
Le Croisic F 101 B3
Le Crotoy F 78 B1
Lectoure F 129 C3
Łęczyca
Łódzkie PL 77 B4
Zachodnio-Pomorskie PL 75 A4
Ledaña E 158 B2
Ledbury GB 39 B4
Lede B 79 B3
Ledečnad Sazavou CZ 97 B3
Ledenice CZ 96 C2
Le Deschaux F 105 C4
Ledesma E 149 A3
Lédignan F 131 B3
Lédigos E 142 B2
Ledmore GB 32 C2
Lednice CZ 97 C4
Lednicke-Rovné SK 98 B2
Le Donjon F 117 A3
Le Dorat F 115 B5
Lędyczek PL 68 B1
Lędziny PL 86 B3
Leeds GB 40 B2
Leek
GB 40 B1
NL 71 A3
Leenaun IRL 28 A2
Leens NL 71 A3
Leer D 71 A4
Leerdam NL 79 A5
Leerhafe D 71 A4
Leese D 72 B2
Leeuwarden NL 70 A2
Leezen D 64 C3
Le Faou F 100 A1
Le Faoüet F 100 A2
Lefka CY 181 A1
Lefkada GR 182 E2
Lefkimis GR 182 D2
Lefkoniko CY 181 A2
Le Folgoet F 100 A1
Le Fossat F 146 A2
Le Fousseret F 146 A2
Le Fugeret F 132 A2
Leganés E 151 B4
Legau D 107 B5
Le Gault-Soigny F 91 C3
Legbąd PL 68 B2
Legé F 114 B2
Lège-Cap-Ferret F 128 B1
Legionowo PL 77 B5
Léglise B 92 B1
Legnago I 121 B4
Legnano I 120 B1
Legnaro I 121 B4
Legnica PL 85 A4
Łęgowo PL 69 A3
Legrad HR 124 A2
Le Grand-Bornand F 118 B3
Le-Grand-Bourg F 116 A1
Le Grand-Lucé F 102 B2
Le Grand-Pressigny F 102 C2
Le Grand-Quevilly F 89 A5
Le Grau-du-Roi F 131 B3
Léguevin F 129 C4
Legutiano E 143 B4
Le Havre F 89 A4
Lehesten D 82 B3
Lehnice SK 111 A4
Lehnin D 74 B1
Le Hohwald F 93 C3
Le Houga F 128 C2
Lehrberg D 94 B2
Lehre D 73 B3
Lehrte D 72 B2
Lehsen D 73 A4
Leibnitz A 110 C2
Leicester GB 40 C2
Leiden NL 70 B1
Leidschendam NL 70 B1
Leigh GB 38 A4
Leighlinbridge IRL 30 B2
Leighton Buzzard GB 44 B3
Leignon B 79 B5
Leikanger N 198 C2
Leimen D 93 B4
Leinefelde D 82 A2
Leinesfjord N 194 C6
Leintwardine GB 39 B4
Leipojärvi S 196 B4
Leipzig D 83 A4
Leira
Nordland N 195 D4
Oppland N 47 B6
Leiråmoen N 195 D5
Leiria P 154 B2
Leirvassbu N 47 A5
Leirvik
Hordaland N 52 A1
Sogn og Fjordane N 46 A2
Leisach A 109 C3
Leisnig D 83 A4
Leiston GB 45 A5
Leitholm GB 35 C5
Leitrim IRL 26 C2
Leitza E 144 A2
Leitzkau D 73 B4
Lejkowo PL 68 A1
Lekani GR 183 B6
Łękawa PL 86 A3
Łekawica PL 99 B3
Lekeitio E 143 A4
Lekenik HR 124 B2
Lekeryd S 62 A2
Leknes N 194 B4
Łęknica PL 84 A2
Leksand S 50 B1
Leksvik N 199 B7
Lekunberri E 144 A2
Lekvattnet S 49 B4
Le Lardin-St Lazare F 129 A4
Le Lauzet-Ubaye F 132 A2
Le Lavandou F 132 B2
Le Lion-d'Angers F 102 B1
Lelkowo PL 69 A5
Le Locle CH 106 B1
Le Loroux-Bottereau F 101 B4
Le Louroux-Béconnais F 101 B5
Lelów PL 86 B3
Le Luc F 132 B2
Le Lude F 102 B2
Lelystad NL 70 B2
Lem
Ringkøbing DK 59 B1
Viborg Amt. DK 58 B1
Le Malzieu-Ville F 116 C3
Le Mans F 102 A2
Le Mas-d'Azil F 146 A2
Le Massegros F 130 A2
Le Mayet-de-Montagne F 117 A3
Le May-sur-Evre F 101 B5
Lembach F 93 B3
Lemberg F 93 B3
Lembèye F 145 A3
Lemelerveld NL 71 B3
Le Mêle-sur-Sarthe F 89 B4
Le Ménil F 105 A5
Le Merlerault F 89 B4
Le Mesnil-sur-Oger F 91 C4
Lemförde D 71 B5
Lemgo D 72 B1
Le Miroir F 105 C4
Lemland FIN 51 B7
Lemmer NL 70 B2
Le Molay-Littry F 88 A3
Le Monastier-sur-Gazeille F 117 C3
Le Monêtier-les-Bains F 118 C3
Le Mont-Dore F 116 B2
Le Montet F 116 A3
Le Mont-St Michel F 88 B2
Lempdes F 116 B3
Le Muret F 128 B2
Le Muy F 132 B2
Lemvig DK 58 B1
Lemwerder D 72 A1
Lena N 48 B2
Lenart SLO 110 C2
Lenartovce SK 99 C4
Lenauheim RO 126 B2
Lencloître F 102 C2
Lend A 109 B4
Lendalfoot GB 36 A2
Lendava SLO 111 C3
Lendery RUS 3 E12
Lendinara I 121 B4
Lendorf A 109 C4
Lendum DK 58 A3
Le Neubourg F 89 A4
Lengefeld D 83 B5
Lengerich
Niedersachsen D 71 B4
Nordrhein-Westfalen D 71 B4
Lenggries D 108 B2
Lengyeltóti H 111 C4
Lenhovda S 62 B3
Lenk CH 106 C2
Lennartsfors S 54 A2
Lennestadt D 81 A4
Lennoxtown GB 35 C3
Leno I 120 B3
Lénola I 169 B3
Le Nouvion-en-Thiérache F 91 A3
Lens
B 79 B3

Lens *continued*
F 78 B2
Lensahn D 65 B3
Lens Lestang F 117 B5
Lensvik N 198 B6
Lentellais E 141 B3
Lentföhrden D 64 C2
Lenti H 111 C3
Lentini I 177 B3
Lenungshammar S 54 A3
Lenzburg CH 106 B3
Lenzen D 73 A4
Lenzerheide CH 107 C4
Leoben A 110 B2
Leogang A 109 B3
Leominster GB 39 B4
León E 142 B1
Léon F 128 C1
Leonberg D 93 C5
Léoncel F 118 C2
Leonding A 96 C2
Leonessa I 169 A2
Leonforte I 177 B3
Leonidio GR 184 B3
Leopoldsburg B 79 A5
Leopoldsdorf im Marchfeld A 111 A3
Leopoldshagen D 74 A2
Leova MD 17 B8
Le Palais F 100 B2
Le Parcq F 78 B2
Lepe E 161 B2
Le Péage-de-Roussillon F 117 B4
Le Pellerin F 101 B4
Lepenou GR 182 E3
Le Perthus F 146 B3
Le Pertuis F 117 B4
Le Petit-Bornand F 118 B3
Lephin GB 31 B2
L'Epine F 132 A1
Le Poët F 132 A1
Lepoglava HR 124 A2
Le Poirè-sur-Vie F 114 B2
Le Pont CH 105 C5
Le Pont-de-Montvert F 130 A2
Le Porge F 128 B1
Le Porge-Océan F 128 B1
Le Portel F 78 B1
Le Pouldu F 100 B2
Le Pouliguen F 101 B3
Leppäjärvi FIN 192 D7
Leppävirta FIN 8 A5
Leppin D 73 B4
le Prese I 120 A3
Lepsény H 112 C2
Le Puy-en-Velay F 117 B3
Le Puy-Ste Réparade F 131 B4
Le Quesnoy F 79 B3
Léquile I 173 B4
Le Rayol F 132 B2
Lercara Friddi I 176 B2
Lerdal S 54 B2
Leré F 103 B4
Lérici I 134 A2
Lerin E 144 B2
Lerma E 143 B3
Lerm-et-Musset F 128 B2
Lermoos A 108 B1
Le Roeulx B 79 B4
Le Rouget F 116 C2
Lérouville F 92 C1
Le Rozier F 130 A2
Lerum S 60 B2
Le Russey F 106 B1
Lervik N 54 A1
Lerwick GB 33 A5
Lés E 145 B4
Les Abrets F 118 B2
Les Aix-d'Angillon F 103 B4
Lesaka E 144 A2
Les Ancizes-Comps F 116 B2
Les Andelys F 90 B1
Les Arcs
Savoie F 119 B3
Var F 132 B2
Les-Aubiers F 102 C1
Les Baux-de-Provence F 131 B3
Les Bézards F 103 B4
Les Bois CH 106 B1
Les Bordes F 103 B4
Les Borges Blanques E 147 C1
Les Borges del Camp E 147 C2
Les Brunettes F 104 C2
Lesbury GB 37 A5
Les Cabannes F 146 B2
L'Escala E 147 B4
Lescar F 145 A3
L'Escarène F 133 B3
Lesce SLO 123 A3
Lescheraines F 118 B3
Lesconil F 100 B1
Les Contamines-Montjoie F 118 B3
les Coves de Vinroma E 153 B4
Les Déserts F 118 B2
Les Deux-Alpes F 118 C3
Les Diablerets CH 119 A4
Lesdins F 90 B3
Les Echelles F 118 B2
Le Sel-de-Bretagne F 101 B4
Le Sentier CH 105 C5
Les Escaldes AND 146 B2
Les Essarts F 114 B2
Les Estables F 117 C4
Les Eyzies-de-Tayac F 129 B4
Les Gets F 118 A3
Les Grandes-Ventes F 89 A5
Les Haudères CH 119 A4
Les Herbiers F 114 B2
Les Hôpitaux-Neufs F 105 C5
Lesično SLO 123 A4
Lésina I 171 B3
Lesjaskog N 198 C5
Lesjöfors S 49 C6
Leskovac SRB 16 D4
Leskova Dolina SLO 123 B3
Leskovec
CZ 98 B1
SLO 123 B4
Leskovice CZ 97 B3
Leskovik AL 182 C2
Leslie GB 35 B4
Les Lucs-sur-Boulogne F 114 B2
Les Mages F 131 A3
Lesmahagow GB 36 A3
Les Mazures F 91 B4
Les Mées F 132 A1
Lesmont F 91 C4
Les Mureaux F 90 C1
Leśna PL 84 A3
Lesneven F 100 A1
Leśnica PL 86 B2
Lešnica SRB 127 C1
Leśniów Wielkoplski PL 75 C4
Lesnoye RUS 9 C9
Les Omergues F 132 A1
Les Ormes-sur-Voulzie F 90 C3
Les Orres F 132 A2
Le Souquet F 128 C1
Lesparre-Médoc F 128 A2
l'Espérance F 91 B3
l'Esperou F 130 A2
Les Pieux F 88 A2
Lesponne F 145 A4
Les Ponts-de-Cé F 102 B1
Les Ponts-de-Martel CH 106 C1
Les Praz F 119 B3
L'Espunyola E 147 B2
Les Riceys F 104 B3
Les Roches F 117 B4
Les Rosaires F 101 A3
Les Rosiers F 102 B1
Les Rousses F 105 C5
Les Sables-d'Olonne F 114 B2
Lessach A 109 B4
Lessay F 88 A2
Lessebo S 62 B3
Les Settons F 104 B3
Lessines B 79 B3
L'Estany E 147 C3
Les Ternes F 116 B2
Lesterps F 115 B4
Les Thilliers en-Vexin F 90 B1
Les Touches F 101 B4
Les Trois Moûtiers F 102 B2
Les Vans F 131 A3
Les Verrières CH 105 C5
Les Vignes F 130 A2
Leswalt GB 36 B1
Leszno
Mazowieckie PL 77 B5
Wielkopolskie PL 85 A4
Leszno Górne PL 84 A3
Letchworth GB 44 B3
Le Teil F 131 A3
Le Teilleul F 88 B3
Le Temple-de-Bretagne F 101 B4
Letenye H 111 C3
Le Theil F 89 B4
Le Thillot F 106 B1
Letino I 170 B2
Letohrad CZ 97 A4
Le Touquet-Paris-Plage F 78 B1
Le Touvet F 118 B2
Letovice CZ 97 B4
Le Translay F 90 B1
Le Tréport F 90 A1
Letschin D 74 B3
Letterfrack IRL 28 A2
Letterkenny IRL 26 B3
Lettermacaward IRL 26 B2
Lettoch GB 32 D3
Letur E 164 A2
Letux E 153 A3
Letzlingen D 73 B4
Leucate F 146 B4
Leuchars GB 35 B5
Leuglay F 105 B3
Leuk CH 119 A4
Leukerbad CH 119 A4
Leumrabhagh GB 31 A2
Leuna D 83 A4
Leusden NL 70 B2
Leutenberg D 82 B3
Leuterschach D 108 B1
Leutershausen D 94 B2
Leutkirch D 107 B5
Leuven B 79 B4
Leuze-en-Hainaut B 79 B3
Le Val F 132 B2
Le Val-André F 101 A3
Le Val-d'Ajol F 105 B5
Levan AL 182 C1
Levanger N 199 B8
Levanjska Varoš HR 125 B4
Lévanto I 134 A2
Levaré F 88 B3
Levata I 120 B3
Leveld N 47 B5
Leven
East Yorkshire GB 41 B3
Fife GB 35 B5
Leverano I 173 B3
Le Verdon-sur-Mer F 114 C2
Leverkusen D 80 A2
Levern D 72 B1
Le Vernet F 132 A2
Levet F 103 C4
Levice SK 112 A2
Lévico Terme I 121 A4
Levie F 180 B2
Levier F 105 C5
Le Vigan F 130 B2
Lévignen F 90 B2
le Ville I 135 B5
Levinovac HR 124 B3
Le Vivier-sur-Mer F 88 B2
Levoča SK 99 B4
Levroux F 103 C3
Lewes GB 45 C4
Lewin Brzeski PL 85 B5
Lewisham GB 44 B3
Leyburn GB 37 B5
Leyland GB 38 A4
Leysdown-on-Sea GB 45 B4
Leysin CH 119 A4
Lezajsk PL 12 C5
Lézardrieux F 100 A2
Lézat-sur-Léze F 146 A2
Lezay F 115 B3
Lezhë AL 182 B1
Lézignan-Corbières F 130 B1
Lezignan-la-Cèbe F 130 B2
Ležimir SRB 126 B1
Lézinnes F 104 B3
Lezoux F 117 B3
Lezuza E 158 C1
Lhenice CZ 96 C2
Lherm F 146 A2
Lhommaizé F 115 B4
L'Hospitalet F 146 B2
L'Hospitalet de l'Infant E 147 D1
L'Hospitalet de Llobregat E 147 C3
L'Hospitalet-du-Larzac F 130 B2
Lhuître F 91 C4
Liancourt F 90 B2
Liart F 91 B4
Liatorp S 63 B2
Liatrie GB 32 D2
Libáň CZ 84 B3
Libceves CZ 84 B1
Liběchov CZ 84 B2
Liber E 141 B3
Liberec CZ 84 B3
Libiąż PL 86 B3
Libina CZ 98 B1
Libochovice CZ 84 B2
Libohovë AL 182 C2
Libourne F 128 B2
Libramont B 92 B1
Librazhd AL 182 B2
Librilla E 165 B3
Libros E 152 B2
Licata I 176 B2
Licciana Nardi I 134 A3
Licenza I 169 A2
Liceros E 151 A4
Lich D 81 B4
Lichères-près-Aigremont F 104 B2
Lichfield GB 40 C2
Lichtenau
A 97 C3
D 81 A4
Lichtenberg D 83 B3
Lichtenfels D 82 B3
Lichtensteig CH 107 B4
Lichtenstein D 83 B4
Lichtenvoorde NL 71 C3
Lichtervelde B 78 A3
Lička Jesenica HR 123 B4
Lickershamn S 57 C4
Lički Osik HR 123 C4
Ličko Lešce HR 123 C4
Licodía Eubéa I 177 B3
Licques F 78 B1
Lida BY 13 B6
Lidar N 47 A6
Lidečko CZ 98 B2
Liden S 200 D2
Lidhult S 60 C3
Lidköping S 55 B4
Lido I 122 B1
Lido Azzurro I 173 B3
Lido degli Estensi I 122 C1
Lido degli Scacchi I 122 C1
Lido della Nazioni I 122 C1
Lido di Camaiore I 134 B3
Lido di Casalbordino I 169 A4
Lido di Castél Fusano I 168 B2
Lido di Cincinnato I 168 B2
Lido di Classe I 135 A5
Lido di Fermo I 136 B2
Lido di Fondi I 169 B3
Lido di Jésolo I 122 B1
Lido di Licola I 170 C2
Lido di Metaponto I 174 A2
Lido di Óstia I 168 B2
Lido di Policoro I 174 A2
Lido di Pomposa I 122 C1
Lido di Savio I 135 A5
Lido di Scanzano I 174 A2
Lido di Siponto I 171 B3
Lido di Squillace I 175 C2
Lido di Volano I 122 C1
Lido Riccio I 169 A4
Lidoriki GR 184 A3
Lido Silvana I 173 B3
Lidsjöberg S 199 A12
Lidzbark PL 77 A4
Lidzbark Warmiński PL 69 A5
Liebenau
A 96 C2
D 72 B2
Liebenwalde D 74 B2
Lieberose D 74 C3
Liebling RO 126 B3
Lieboch A 110 C2
Liège B 80 B1
Lieksa FIN 3 E12
Lienen D 71 B4
Lienz A 109 C3
Liepāja LV 8 D2
Lier B 79 A4
Lierbyen N 54 A1
Liernais F 104 B3
Liesing A 109 C3
Liestal CH 106 B2
Liétor E 158 C2
Lieurac F 146 B2
Lieurey F 89 A4
Liévin F 78 B2
Liezen A 110 B1
Liffol-le-Grand F 92 C1
Lifford IRL 27 B3
Liffré F 101 A4
Ligardes F 129 B3
Lignano Sabbiadoro I 122 B2
Ligne F 101 B4
Lignières F 103 C4
Ligny-en-Barrois F 92 C1
Ligny-le-Châtel F 104 B2
Ligoła Polska PL 85 A5
Ligourio GR 184 B4
Ligowo PL 77 B4
Ligueil F 102 B2
Likavka SK 99 B3
Likenäs S 49 B5
Likhoslavl RUS 9 D9
Lild Strand DK 58 A1
L'Île-Bouchard F 102 B2
l'Île-Rousse F 180 A1
Lilienfeld A 110 A2
Lilienthal D 72 A1
Lilla Edet S 54 B3
Lilla Tjärby S 61 C3
Lille
B 79 A4
F 78 B3
Lillebonne F 89 A4
Lillehammer N 48 A2
Lillerød DK 61 D2
Lillers F 78 B2
Lillesand N 53 B4
Lillestrøm N 48 C3
Lillhärdal S 199 D11
Lillkyrka S 56 A3
Lillo E 157 A4
Lillögda S 200 B3
Lillpite S 196 D4
Lima S 49 B5
Limanowa PL 99 B4
Limassol CY 181 B2
Limavady GB 27 A4
Limbach-Oberfrohna D 83 B4
Limbaži LV 8 D4
Limbourg B 80 B1
Limburg D 81 B4
Lime DK 58 B3
Limedsforsen S 49 B5
Limenaria GR 183 C6
Limenas Chersonisou GR 185 D6
Limerick IRL 29 B3
Limes I 121 B3
Limésy F 89 A4
Limmared S 60 B3
Limni GR 183 E5
Limoges F 115 C5
Limogne-en-Quercy F 129 B4
Limoise F 104 C2
Limone Piemonte I 133 A3
Limone sul Garda I 121 B3
Limons F 117 B3
Limours F 90 C2
Limoux F 146 A3
Linares E 157 B4
Linares de Mora E 153 B3
Linares de Riofrio E 149 B4
Linaria GR 183 E6
Linas de Broto E 145 B3
Lincoln GB 40 B3
Lind DK 59 B1
Lindås N 46 B2
Lindau D 107 B4
Lindberget N 48 A3
Lindelse DK 65 B3
Lindenberg D 74 B3
Lindenberg im Allgäu D 107 B4
Lindern D 71 B4
Linderöd S 61 D3
Lindesberg S 56 A1
Lindesnäs S 50 B1
Lindesnes N 52 C3
Lindholmen S 57 A4
Lindknud DK 59 C2
Lindlar D 80 A3
Lindö S 56 B2
Lindome S 60 B2
Lindos GR 188 C3
Lindoso P 148 A1
Lindow D 74 B1
Lindsdal S 62 B4
Lindshammar S 62 A3
Lindstedt D 73 B4
Lindved DK 59 C2
Linë CZ 96 B1
Lingbo S 50 A3
Lingen D 71 B4
Linghed S 50 B2
Linghem S 56 B1
Linguaglossa I 177 B4
Linia PL 68 A2
Linie PL 74 A3
Liniewo PL 68 A3
Linkenheim D 93 B4
Linköping S 56 B1
Linksness GB 33 C3
Linlithgow GB 35 C4
Linneryd S 63 B3
Linnes Hammarby S 51 C4
Linnich D 80 B2
Linsell S 199 C10
Linslade GB 44 B3
Linthal CH 107 C4
Linyola E 147 C1
Linz
A 96 C2
D 80 B3
Liomseter N 47 A6
Lionárisso CY 181 A3
Lioni I 172 B1
Lion-sur-Mer F 89 A3
Lipany SK 99 B4
Lipar SRB 126 B1
Lipari I 177 A3
Lipcani MD 17 A7
Liperi FIN 9 A6
Liphook GB 44 B3
Lipiany PL 75 A3
Lipik HR 124 B3
Lipka PL 68 B2
Lipki Wielkie PL 75 B4
Lipnica PL 68 B2
Lipnica Murowana PL 99 B4
Lipnik PL 87 B5
Lipník nad Bečvou CZ 98 B1
Lipno
Kujawsko-Pomorskie PL 77 B4
Łódzkie PL 86 A2
Liposthey F 128 B2
Lipovac HR 125 B5
Lipovec CZ 97 B4
Lipovets UA 13 D8
Lipovljani HR 124 B2
Lipowiec PL 77 A6
Lipowina PL 69 A4
Lippborg D 81 A4
Lippó H 125 B4
Lippoldsberg D 81 A5
Lippstadt D 81 A4
Lipsko PL 87 A5
Liptál CZ 98 B1
Liptovská-Lúžna SK 99 C3
Liptovská Osada SK 99 C3
Liptovská-Teplička SK 99 C4
Liptovský Hrádok SK 99 B3
Liptovský Milkuláš SK 99 B3
Lipusz PL 68 A2
Lipůvka CZ 97 B4
Liré F 101 B4
Lisac BIH 139 A3
Lisbellaw GB 27 B3
Lisboa = Lisbon P 154 C1
Lisbon = Lisboa P 154 C1
Lisburn GB 27 B4
Liscannor IRL 28 B2
Lisdoonvarna IRL 28 A2
Lisewo PL 69 B3
Lisia Góra PL 87 B5
Lisięcice PL 86 B1
Lisieux F 89 A4
Lisjö S 56 A2
Liskeard GB 42 B2
L'Isle CH 105 C5
L'Isle-Adam F 90 B2
L'Isle-de-Noé F 129 C3
L'Isle-en-Dodon F 145 A4
L'Isle-Jourdain
Gers F 129 C4
Vienne F 115 B4
L'Isle-sur-la-Sorgue F 131 B4
L'Isle-sur-le Doubs F 105 B5
L'Isle-sur-Serein F 104 B3
Lisle-sur-Tarn F 129 C4
Lismore IRL 29 B4
Lisnaskea GB 27 B3
Lišov CZ 96 B2
Lisów
Lubuskie PL 74 B3
Śląskie PL 86 B2
Lisse NL 70 B1
Lissycasey IRL 28 B2
List D 64 A1
Listerby S 63 B3
Listowel IRL 29 B2
Listrac-Médoc F 128 A2
Liszki PL 99 A3
Liszkowo PL 76 A2
Lit S 199 B11
Litava SK 99 C3
Litcham GB 41 C4
Lit-et-Mixe F 128 B1
Litija SLO 123 A3
Litke H 112 A3
Litlabø N 52 A1
Litochoro GR 182 C4
Litoměřice CZ 84 B2
Litomyšl CZ 97 B4
Litovel CZ 98 B1
Litschau A 96 C3
Littlehampton GB 44 C3
Littleport GB 45 A4
Littleton IRL 29 B4
Little Walsingham GB 41 C4
Litvinov CZ 83 B5
Livadero GR 182 C3
Livadhia CY 181 B2
Livadi GR 182 C4
Livadia GR 184 A3
Livarot F 89 B4
Liveras CY 181 A1
Livernon F 129 B4
Liverovici MNE 139 C5
Liverpool GB 38 A4
Livigno I 107 C5
Livingston GB 35 C4
Livno BIH 138 B3
Livo FIN 197 D9
Livold SLO 123 B3
Livorno I 134 B3
Livorno Ferraris I 119 B5
Livron-sur-Drôme F 117 C4
Livry-Louvercy F 91 B4
Lixheim F 92 C3
Lixouri GR 184 A1
Lizard GB 42 C1
Lizy-sur-Ourcq F 90 B3
Lizzano I 173 B3
Lizzano in Belvedere I 135 A3
Ljig SRB 127 C2
Ljørdalen N 49 A4
Ljosland N 52 B3
Ljubija BIH 124 C2
Ljubinje BIH 139 C4
Ljubljana SLO 123 A3
Ljubno ob Savinji SLO 123 A3
Ljubovija SRB 127 C1
Ljubuški BIH 138 B3
Ljugarn S 57 C4
Ljung S 60 B3
Ljunga S 56 B2
Ljungaverk S 200 D2
Ljungby S 60 C3
Ljungbyhed S 61 C3
Ljungbyholm S 63 B4
Ljungdalen S 199 C9
Ljungsarp S 60 B3
Ljungsbro S 56 B1
Ljungskile S 54 B2
Ljusdal S 200 E2
Ljusfallshammar S 56 B1
Ljusne S 51 A4
Ljusterö S 57 A4
Ljutomer SLO 111 C3
Lŭki BG 183 B6
Lladurs E 147 B2
Llafranc E 147 C4
Llagostera E 147 C3
Llanaelhaiarn GB 38 B2
Llanarth GB 39 B2
Llanbedr GB 38 B2
Llanbedrog GB 38 B2
Llanberis GB 38 A2
Llanbister GB 39 B3
Llanbrynmair GB 39 B3
Llançà E 146 B4
Llandeilo GB 39 C3
Llandissilio GB 39 C2
Llandovery GB 39 C3
Llandrillo GB 38 B3
Llandrindod Wells GB 39 B3
Llandudec F 100 A1
Llandudno GB 38 A3
Llandysul GB 39 B2
Llanelli GB 39 C2
Llanerchymedd GB 38 A2
Llanes E 142 A2
Llanfair Caereinion GB 38 B3
Llanfairfechan GB 38 A3
Llanfyllin GB 38 B3
Llangadog GB 39 C3
Llangefni GB 38 A2
Llangollen GB 38 B3
Llangrannog GB 39 B2
Llangurig GB 39 B3
Llanidloes GB 39 B3
Llanilar GB 39 B2
Llanrhystud GB 39 B2
Llanrwst GB 38 A3
Llansannan GB 38 A3
Llansawel GB 39 B2
Llanstephan GB 39 C2
Llanteno E 143 A3
Llanthony GB 39 C3
Llantrisant GB 39 C3
Llantwit-Major GB 39 C3
Llanuwchllyn GB 38 B3
Llanwddyn GB 38 B3
Llanwrda GB 39 C3
Llanwrtyd Wells GB 39 B3
Llanybydder GB 39 B2
Llanymynech GB 38 B3
Llavorsi E 146 B2
Lleida E 153 A4
Llera E 156 B1
Llerena E 156 B1
Lles E 146 B2
Llessui E 146 B2
Llinars E 147 B2
Lliria E 159 B3
Llivia E 146 B2
Llodio E 143 A4
Lloret de Mar E 147 C3
Llosa de Ranes E 159 B3
Lloseta E 167 B2
Llucena del Cid E 153 B3
Llucmajor E 167 B2
Lluxent E 159 C3
Llwyngwril GB 38 B2
Llyswen GB 39 B3
Lnáře CZ 96 B1
Lniano PL 76 A3
Loanhead GB 35 C4
Loano I 133 A4
Loarre E 145 B3
Löbau D 84 A2
Löbejün D 83 A3
Löberöd S 61 D3
Łobez PL 75 A4
Löbnitz D 66 B1
Lobón E 155 C4
Loburg D 73 B5
Łobżenica PL 76 A2
Locana I 119 B4
Locarno CH 120 A1
Loccum D 72 B2
Loče SLO 123 A4
Lochailort GB 34 B2
Lochaline GB 34 B2
Lochans GB 36 B1
Locharbriggs GB 36 A3
Lochau A 107 B4
Loch Baghasdail GB 31 B1
Lochcarron GB 31 B3
Lochearnhead GB 34 B3
Lochem NL 71 B3
Loches F 102 B2
Lochgelly GB 35 B4
Lochgilphead GB 34 B2
Lochgoilhead GB 34 B3
Lochinver GB 32 C1
Loch nam Madadh GB 31 B1
Lochranza GB 34 C2
Ločika SRB 127 D3
Lockenhaus A 111 B3
Lockerbie GB 36 A3
Löcknitz D 74 A3
Locmaria F 100 B2
Locmariaquer F 100 B3
Locminé F 100 B3
Locorotondo I 173 B3
Locquirec F 100 A2
Locri I 175 C2
Locronan F 100 A1
Loctudy F 100 B1
Lodares de Osma E 151 A5
Lodé I 178 B3
Lodeinoye Pole RUS 9 B8
Lodève F 130 B2
Lodi I 120 B2
Løding N 194 C5
Lødingen N 194 B6
Lodosa E 144 B1
Lödöse S 54 B3
Łódź PL 86 A3
Loeches E 151 B4
Løfallstrand N 46 B3
Lofer A 109 B3
Lofsdalen S 199 C10
Loftahammar S 62 A4
Lofthus N 46 B3
Loftus GB 37 B6
Loga N 52 B2
Logatec SLO 123 B3
Lögdeå S 200 C5
Lograto I 120 B3
Logroño E 143 B4
Logrosán E 156 A2
Løgstør DK 58 B2
Løgumgårde DK 64 A1
Løgumkloster DK 64 A1
Lohals DK 65 A3
Lohiniva FIN 197 B8
Lohja FIN 8 B4
Löhlbach D 81 A4
Lohmen
Mecklenburg-Vorpommern D 65 C5
Sachsen D 84 B2
Löhnberg D 81 B4
Lohne D 71 B5
Löhne D 72 B1
Lohr D 94 B1
Lohra D 81 B4
Lohsa D 84 A2
Loiano I 135 A4
Loimaa FIN 8 B3
Lóiri I 178 B3
Loitz D 66 C2
Loivos P 148 A2
Loivos do Monte P 148 A2
Loja E 163 A3
Lojanice SRB 127 C1
Lojsta S 57 C4
Løjt Kirkeby DK 64 A2
Lok SK 112 A2
Lokca SK 99 B3
Løken N 54 A2
Lokeren B 79 A3
Loket CZ 83 B4
Lokka FIN 197 B10
Løkken
DK 58 A2
N 198 B6
Loknya RUS 9 D7
Lökösháza H 113 C5
Lokve SRB 126 B3
Lollar D 81 B4
L'Olleria E 159 C3
Lölling-Graben A 110 C1
Lom
BG 17 D5
N 198 D5
SK 99 C3
Lombez F 146 A1
Lomello I 120 B1
Łomianki PL 77 B5
Lomma S 61 D3
Lommaryd S 62 A2
Lommatzsch D 83 A5
Lommel B 79 A5
Lommersum D 80 B2
Lomnice CZ 97 B4
Lomnice nad Lužnici CZ 96 B2
Lomnice-nad Popelkou CZ 84 B3

Lompolo FIN 196 A7
Łomza PL 12 B5
Lönashult S 63 B2
Lønborg DK 59 C1
Londerzeel B 79 A4
Londinières F 89 A5
London GB 44 B3
Lonevåg N 46 B2
Longa GR 184 C2
Longare I 121 B4
Longares E 152 A2
Longarone I 122 A1
Longastrino I 135 A5
Long Bennington GB 40 C3
Longbenton GB 37 A5
Longchamp-sur-Aujon F 105 A3
Longchaumois F 118 A2
Long Eaton GB 40 C2
Longeau F 105 B4
Longecourt-en-Plaine F 105 B4
Longeville-les-St Avold F 92 B2
Longeville-sur-Mer F 114 B2
Longford IRL 28 A4
Longframlington GB 37 A5
Longhope GB 33 C3
Longhorsley GB 37 A5
Longhoughton GB 37 A5
Longi I 177 A3
Long Melford GB 45 A4
Longny-au-Perche F 89 B4
Longobucco I 174 B2
Long Preston GB 40 A1
Longré F 115 B3
Longridge GB 38 A4
Longroiva P 149 B2
Long Sutton GB 41 C4
Longtown
Cumbria GB 36 A4
Herefordshire GB 39 C4
Longueau F 90 B2
Longué-Jumelles F 102 B1
Longuyon F 92 B1
Longvic F 105 B4
Longvilly B 92 A1
Longwy F 92 B1
Lonigo I 121 B4
Löningen D 71 B4
Lonja HR 124 B2
Lönneberga S 62 A3
Lönsboda S 63 B2
Lønset N 198 C6
Lons-le-Saunier F 105 C4
Lønstrup DK 58 A2
Looe GB 42 B2
Loone-Plage F 78 A2
Loon op Zand NL 79 A5
Loosdorf A 110 A2
Lo Pagán E 165 B4
Lopar HR 123 C3
Lopare BIH 125 C4
Lopera E 157 C3
Lopigna F 180 A1
Loppersum NL 71 A3
Łopuszna PL 99 B4
Łopuszno PL 87 B4
Lor F 91 B4
Lora N 198 C5
Lora de Estepa E 162 A3
Lora del Río E 162 A2
Loranca del Campo E 151 B5
Lorbé 140 A2
Lörby S 63 B2
Lorca E 164 B3
Lorch D 93 A3
Lørenfallet N 48 B3
Lørenskog N 48 C2
Loreo I 122 B1
Loreto I 136 B2
Lorgues F 132 B2
Lorica I 174 B2
Lorient F 100 B2
Lorignac F 114 C3
Lörinci H 112 B3
Loriol-sur-Drôme F 117 C4
Lormes F 104 B2
Loro Ciuffenna I 135 B4
Lorqui E 165 A3
Lörrach D 106 B2
Lorrez-le-Bocage F 103 A4
Lorris F 103 B4
Lorup D 71 B4
Łoś PL 77 C5
Los S 199 D12
Losacino E 149 A3
Los Alcázares E 165 B4
Los Arcos E 144 B1
Losar de la Vera E 150 B2
Los Barios de Luna E 141 B5
Los Barrios E 162 B2
Los Caños de Meca E 162 B1
Los Cerricos E 164 B2
Los Corrales E 162 A3
Los Corrales de Buelna E 142 A2
Los Dolores E 165 B3
Losenstein A 110 B1
Los Gallardos E 164 B3
Losheim
Nordrhein-Westfalen D 80 B2
Saarland D 92 B2
Los Hinojosos E 158 B1
Los Isidros E 159 B2
Los Molinos E 151 B3
Los Morales E 162 A2
Los Navalmorales E 156 A3
Los Navalucillos E 156 A3
Losne F 105 B4
Los Nietos E 165 B4
Løsning DK 59 C2
Los Palacios y Villafranca E 162 A2
Los Pozuelos de Calatrava E 157 B3
Los Rábanos E 143 C4
Los Santos E 149 B4
Los Santos de la Humosa E 151 B4
Los Santos de Maimona E 155 C4
Lossburg D 93 C4
Losse F 128 B2
Losser NL 71 B4
Lossiemouth GB 32 D3
Lössnitz D 83 B4
Loštice CZ 97 B4
Los Tijos E 142 A2
Lostwithiel GB 42 B2
Los Villares E 163 A4
Los Yébenes E 157 A4
Løten N 48 B3
Lotorp S 56 B1
Lottefors S 50 A3
Löttorp S 62 A5
Lotyń PL 68 B1
Lotzorai I 179 C3
Louargat F 100 A2
Loudéac F 101 A3
Loudun F 102 B2
Loué F 102 B1
Loughborough GB 40 C2
Loughbrickland GB 27 B4
Loughrea IRL 28 A3
Louhans F 105 C4
Louisburgh IRL 28 A2
Loukhi RUS 3 C13
Loulay F 114 B3
Loulé P 160 B1
Louny CZ 84 B1
Lourdes F 145 A3
Lourenzá E 141 A3
Loures P 154 C1
Loures-Barousse F 145 A4
Louriçal P 154 A2
Lourinhã P 154 B1
Lourmarin F 131 B4
Loury F 103 B4
Lousa
Bragança P 149 A2
Castelo Branco P 155 B3
Lousã P 148 B1
Lousa P 154 C1
Lousada
E 140 B3
P 148 A1
Louth GB 41 B3
Loutra Edipsou GR 183 E5
Loutraki GR 184 B3
Loutropoli Thermis GR 186 C1
Louverné F 102 A1
Louvie-Juzon F 145 A3
Louviers F 89 A5
Louvigné-du-Désert F 88 B2
Louvois F 91 B4
Lova I 121 B5
Lovasberény H 112 B2
Lövåsen S 49 C5
Lovászpatona H 111 B4
Lövberga S 200 C1
Lovech BG 17 D6
Lövenich D 80 A2
Lóvere I 120 B3
Lövestad S 61 D3
Loviisa FIN 8 B5
Lovikka S 196 B5
Lovinobaňa SK 99 C3
Loviste HR 138 B3
Lovke HR 123 B3
Lovnäs S 49 A5
Lövö H 111 B3
Lovosice CZ 84 B2
Lovozero RUS 3 C14
Lovran HR 123 B3
Lovreć HR 138 B2
Lovrenc na Pohorju SLO 110 C2
Lovrin RO 126 B2
Lövstabruk S 51 B4
Löwenberg D 74 B2
Löwenstein D 94 B1
Lowestoft GB 41 C5
Lowick GB 37 A5
Łowicz PL 77 B4
Loxstedt D 72 A1
Loyew BY 13 C9
Lož SLO 123 B3
Loza CZ 96 B1
Łozina PL 85 A5
Loznica SRB 127 C1
Lozničko Polje SRB 127 C1
Lozorno SK 111 A4
Lozovik SRB 127 C3
Lozoya E 151 B4
Lozoyuela E 151 B4
Lozzo di Cadore I 109 C3
Luanco E 141 A5
Luarca E 141 A4
Lubaczów PL 13 C5
Lubań PL 84 A3
Lubanie PL 76 B3
Lubanów PL 86 A3
Lubars D 73 B5
Lubasz PL 75 B5
Lubawa PL 69 B4
Lubawka PL 85 B4
Lübbecke D 72 B1
Lübben D 74 C2
Lübbenau D 84 A1
Lubczyna PL 74 A3
Lübeck D 65 C3
Lubenec CZ 83 B5
Lubersac F 115 C5
Lübesse D 73 A4
Lubia E 152 A1
Lubian E 141 B4
Lubiatowo PL 75 A4
Lubichowo PL 69 B3
Lubicz Dolny PL 76 A3
Lubień PL 99 B3
Lubienia PL 87 A5
Lubień Kujawski PL 77 B4
Lubieszewo PL 75 A4
Lubin
Dolnośląskie PL 85 A4
Zachodnio-Pomorskie PL 67 C3
Lublin PL 12 C5
Lubliniec PL 86 B2
Lubmin D 66 B2
Lubniewice PL 75 B4
Lubochnia PL 87 A4
Lubomierz
Dolnośląskie PL 84 A3
Małopolskie PL 99 B4
Lubomino PL 69 A5
Luboń PL 76 B1
L'ubotín SK 99 B4
Lubowidz PL 77 A4
Łubowo
Wielkopolskie PL 76 B2
Zachodnio-Pomorskie PL 68 B1
Lubraniec PL 76 B3
Lubrin E 164 B2
Lubrza PL 85 B5
Lubsko PL 84 A2
Lübtheen D 73 A4
Lubuczewo PL 68 A2
Luby CZ 83 B4
Lübz D 73 A5
Luc F 117 C3
Lucainena de las Torres E 164 B2
Lucan IRL 30 A2
Lučani SRB 127 D2
Lúcar E 164 B2
Luçay-le-Mâle F 103 B3
Lucca I 134 B3
Lucciana F 180 A2
Lucé F 90 C1
Luče SLO 123 A3
Lucena
Córdoba E 163 A3
Huelva E 161 B3
Lucenay-les-Aix F 104 C2
Lucenay-l'Evêque F 104 B3
Luc-en-Diois F 118 C2
Lučenec SK 99 C3
Luceni E 144 C2
Lucens CH 106 C1
Lucera I 171 B3
Luceram F 133 B3
Lüchow D 73 B4
Luciana E 157 B3
Lucignano I 135 B4
Lucija SLO 122 B2
Lucka D 83 A4
Luckau D 84 A1
Luckenwalde D 74 B2
Lückstedt D 73 B4
Luco dei Marsi I 169 B3
Luçon F 114 B2
Luc-sur-Mer F 89 A3
Ludanice SK 98 C2
Ludbreg HR 124 A2
Lüdenscheid D 81 A3
Lüderitz D 73 B4
Lüdersdorf D 65 C3
Ludgershall GB 44 B2
Ludgo S 56 B3
Lüdinghausen D 80 A3
Ludlow GB 39 B4
Ludomy PL 75 B5
Ludvika S 50 B2
Ludweiler Warndt D 92 B2
Ludwigsburg D 94 C1
Ludwigsfelde D 74 B2
Ludwigshafen D 93 B4
Ludwigslust D 73 A4
Ludwigsstadt D 82 B3
Ludza LV 8 D5
Luesia E 144 B2
Luftkurort Arendsee D 73 B4
Lug
BIH 139 C4
HR 125 B4
Luga RUS 9 C6
Lugagnano Val d'Arda I 120 C2
Lugano CH 120 A1
Lugau D 83 B4
Lugnas S 55 B4
Lùgnola I 168 A2
Lugny F 105 C3
Lugo
E 140 A3
I 135 A4
Lugoj RO 16 C4
Lugones E 141 A5
Lugros E 163 A4
Luhačovice CZ 98 B1
Luhe D 95 B4
Luino I 120 B1
Luintra E 140 B3
Lújar E 163 B4
Luka nad Jihlavou CZ 97 B3
Lukavac BIH 125 C4
Lukavika BIH 125 C4
Lukovë AL 182 D1
Lukovica SLO 123 A3
Lukovit BG 17 D6
Lukovo HR 123 C3
Lukovo Šugorje HR 137 A4
Łuków PL 12 C5
Łukowice Brzeskie PL 85 B5
Luksefjell N 53 A5
Łukta PL 69 B5
Lula I 178 B3
Luleå S 196 D5
Lüleburgaz TR 186 A2
Lumbarda HR 138 C3
Lumbier E 144 B2
Lumbrales E 149 B3
Lumbreras E 143 B4
Lumbres F 78 B2
Lummelunda S 57 C4
Lummen B 79 B5
Lumparland FIN 51 B7
Lumpiaque E 152 A2
Lumsås DK 61 D1
Lumsden GB 33 D4
Lumsheden S 50 B3
Lun HR 123 C3
Luna E 144 B3
Lunamatrona I 179 C2
Lunano I 136 B1
Lunas F 130 B2
Lund
N 199 A8
Skåne S 61 D3
Västra Götaland S 54 A3
Lundamo N 199 B7
Lunde
DK 59 C1
Sogn og Fjordane N 46 A3
Sogn og Fjordane N 46 A3
Telemark N 53 A5
S 200 D3
Lundebyvollen N 49 B4
Lunden D 64 B2
Lunderseter N 49 B4
Lunderskov DK 59 C2
Lundsberg S 55 A5
Lüneburg D 72 A3
Lunel F 131 B3
Lünen D 81 A3
Lunéville F 92 C2
Lungern CH 106 C3
Lungro I 174 B2
Luninyets BY 13 B7
Lünne D 71 B4
Lunner N 48 B2
Lunteren NL 70 B2
Lunz am See A 110 B2
Luogosanto I 178 A3
Łupawa PL 68 A2
Lupión E 157 B4
Lupoglav HR 123 B3
Luppa D 83 A4
Luque E 163 A3
Lurago d'Erba I 120 B2
Lúras I 178 B3
Lurcy-Lévis F 104 C1
Lure F 105 B5
Lurgan GB 27 B4
Luri F 180 A2
Lury-sur-Arnon F 103 B4
Lušci Palanka BIH 124 C2
Lusévera I 122 A2
Lushnjë AL 182 C1
Lusignan F 115 B4
Lusigny-sur-Barse F 104 A3
Lusnić BIH 138 B2
Luso P 148 B1
Lusówko PL 75 B5
Luspebryggan S 196 B2
Luss GB 34 B3
Lussac F 128 B2
Lussac-les-Châteaux F 115 B4
Lussac-les-Eglises F 115 B5
Lussan F 131 A3
Lüssow D 65 C5
Lustenau A 107 B4
Luštěnice CZ 84 B2
Luster N 47 A4
Lutago I 108 C2
Lutherstadt Wittenberg D 83 A4
Lütjenburg D 65 B3
Lutnes N 49 A4
Lutocin PL 77 B4
Lutomiersk PL 86 A3
Luton GB 44 B3
Lutry CH 106 C1
Lutsk UA 13 C6
Lutter am Barenberge D 72 C3
Lutterworth GB 40 C2
Lututów PL 86 A2
Lützen D 83 A4
Lutzow D 73 A4
Luusua FIN 197 C10
Luvos S 196 C1
Luxembourg L 92 B2
Luxeuil-les-Bains F 105 B5
Luxey F 128 B2
Luz
Évora P 155 C3
Faro P 160 B1
Faro P 160 B2
Luzarches F 90 B2
Luže CZ 97 B4
Luzech F 129 B4
Luzern CH 106 B3
Luzino PL 68 A3
Luz-St Sauveur F 145 B3
Luzy F 104 C2
Luzzi I 174 B2
L'viv UA 13 D6
Lwówek PL 75 B5
Lwówek Śląski PL 84 A3
Lyakhavichy BY 13 B7
Lybster GB 32 C3
Lychen D 74 A2
Lychkova RUS 9 D8
Lyckeby S 63 B3
Lycksele S 200 B4
Lydd GB 45 C4
Lydford GB 42 B2
Lydney GB 39 C4
Lyepyel BY 13 A8
Lygna N 48 B2
Lykkja N 47 B5
Lykling N 52 A1
Lyme Regis GB 43 B4
Lymington GB 44 C2
Lympne GB 45 B5
Lyndhurst GB 44 C2
Lyneham GB 43 A5
Lyness GB 33 C3
Lyngdal
Buskerud N 47 C6
Vest-Agder N 52 B3
Lyngør N 53 B5
Lyngsa DK 58 A3
Lyngseidet N 192 C4
Lyngsnes N 199 A8
Lynmouth GB 42 A3
Lynton GB 42 A3
Lyntupy BY 13 A7
Lyon F 117 B4
Lyons-la-Forêt F 90 B1
Lyozna BY 13 A9
Lyrestad S 55 B5
Lysá nad Labem CZ 84 B2
Lysá pod Makytou SK 98 B2
Lysebotn N 52 A2
Lysekil S 54 B2
Lysice CZ 97 B4
Lysomice PL 76 A3
Lysøysund N 198 B6
Lyss CH 106 B2
Lystrup DK 59 B3
Lysvik S 49 B5
Łyszkowice PL 77 C4
Lytham St Anne's GB 38 A3
Lyuban RUS 9 C7
Lyubertsy RUS 9 E10
Lyubimets BG 183 B8
Lyuboml' UA 13 C6
Lyubytino RUS 9 C8

M

Maaninkavaara FIN 197 C11
Maarheeze NL 80 A1
Maaseik B 80 A1
Maastricht NL 80 B1
Mablethorpe GB 41 B4
Mably F 117 A4
Macael E 164 B2
Maçanet de Cabrenys E 146 B3
Mação P 154 B2
Macau F 128 A2
Maccagno-Agra I 120 A1
Maccarese I 168 B2
Macchiagódena I 170 B2
Macclesfield GB 40 B1
Macduff GB 33 D4
Maceda E 140 B3
Macedo de Cavaleiros P 149 A3
Maceira
Guarda P 148 B2
Leiria P 154 B2
Macelj HR 124 A1
Macerata I 136 B2
Macerata Féltria I 136 B1
Machault F 91 B4
Machecoul F 114 B2
Mchowo PL 77 A5
Machrihanish GB 34 C2
Machynlleth GB 39 B3
Macieira P 148 A1
Maciejowice PL 87 A5
Macinaggio F 180 A2
Mackenrode D 82 A2
Mačkovci SLO 111 C3
Macomer I 178 B2
Macon B 91 A4
Mâcon F 117 A4
Macotera E 150 B2
Macroom IRL 29 C3
Macugnaga I 119 B4
Madan BG 183 B6
Madängsholm S 55 B4
Madaras H 126 A1
Maddaloni I 170 B2
Made NL 79 A4
Madeley GB 38 B4
Maderuelo E 151 A4
Madetkoski FIN 197 B9
Madley GB 39 B4
Madocsa H 112 C2
Madona LV 8 D5
Madonna di Campiglio I 121 A3
Madrid E 151 B4
Madridejos E 157 A4
Madrigal de las Altas Torres E 150 A2
Madrigal de la Vera E 150 B2
Madrigalejo E 156 A2
Madrigalejo de Monte E 143 B3
Madriguera E 151 A4
Madrigueras E 158 B2
Madroñera E 156 A2
Maël-Carhaix F 100 A2
Maella E 153 A4
Maello E 150 B3
Maesteg GB 39 C3
Mafra P 154 C1
Magacela E 156 B2
Magallon E 144 C2
Magaluf E 166 B2
Magán E 151 C4
Magaña E 144 C1
Magasa I 121 B3
Magaz E 142 C2
Magdeburg D 73 B4
Magenta I 120 B1
Magescq F 128 C1
Maghera GB 27 B4
Magherafelt GB 27 B4
Maghull GB 38 A4
Magilligan GB 27 A4
Magione I 135 B5
Magioto P 154 C1
Maglaj BIH 125 C4
Maglehem S 63 C2
Magliano de'Marsi I 169 A3
Magliano in Toscana I 168 A1
Magliano Sabina I 168 A2
Maglić SRB 126 B1
Máglie I 173 B4
Maglód H 112 B3
Magnac-Bourg F 115 C5
Magnac-Laval F 115 B5
Magnieres F 92 C2
Magnor N 49 C4
Magnuszew PL 87 A5
Magny-Cours F 104 C2
Magny-en-Vexin F 90 B1
Mágocs H 125 A4
Maguilla E 156 B2
Maguiresbridge GB 27 B3
Magyarbóly H 125 B4
Magyarkeszi H 112 C2
Magyarszék H 125 A4
Mahide E 141 C4
Mahilyow BY 13 B9
Mahmudiye TR 187 C5
Mahora E 158 B2
Mahovo HR 124 B2
Mähring D 95 B4
Maia
E 144 A2
P 148 A1
Maiaelrayo E 151 A4
Maials E 153 A4
Maîche F 106 B1
Máida I 175 C2
Maiden Bradley GB 43 A4
Maidenhead GB 44 B3
Maiden Newton GB 43 B4
Maidstone GB 45 B4
Maienfeld CH 107 B4
Maignelay Montigny F 90 B2
Maijanen FIN 197 B8
Maillezais F 114 B3
Mailly-le-Camp F 91 C4
Mailly-le-Château F 104 B2
Mainar E 152 A2
Mainbernheim D 94 B2
Mainburg D 95 C3
Mainhardt D 94 B1
Maintal D 81 B4
Maintenon F 90 C1
Mainvilliers F 90 C1
Mainz D 93 A4
Maiorca P 148 B1
Mairena de Aljarafe E 162 A1
Mairena del Alcor E 162 A2
Maisach D 108 A2
Maishofen A 109 B3
Maison-Rouge F 90 C3
Maissau A 97 C3
Maisse F 90 C2
Maizières-lès-Vic F 92 C2
Maja HR 124 B2
Majadahonda E 151 B4
Majadas E 150 C2
Majavatn N 195 E4
Majs H 125 B4
Majšperk SLO 123 A4
Makarska HR 138 B3
Makkum NL 70 A2
Maklár H 113 B4
Makó H 126 A2
Makoszyce PL 85 B5
Makov SK 98 B2
Mąkowarsko PL 76 A2
Maków Mazowiecki PL 77 B6
Maków Podhalański PL 99 B3
Makrakomi GR 182 E4
Maksniemi FIN 196 D7
Malå S 195 E9
Mala Bosna SRB 126 A1
Malacky SK 97 C5
Maladzyechna BY 13 A7
Málaga E 163 B3
Malagón E 157 A4
Malaguilla E 151 B4
Malahide IRL 30 A2
Mala Kladuša BIH 124 B1
Mala Krsna SRB 127 C3
Malalbergo I 121 C4
Malá Lehota SK 98 C2
Malanów PL 76 C3
Mala Pijace SRB 126 A1
Mala Subotica HR 124 A2
Malaucène F 131 A4
Malaunay F 89 A5
Malaya Vishera RUS 9 C8
Malborghetto I 109 C4
Malbork PL 69 A4
Malborn D 92 B2
Malbuisson F 105 C5
Malcésine I 121 B3
Malchin D 74 A1
Malching D 96 C1
Malchow D 73 A5
Malcocinado E 156 B2
Malczyce PL 85 A4
Maldegem B 79 A3
Maldon GB 45 B4
Małdyty PL 69 B4
Malè I 121 A3
Malemort F 129 A4
Malente D 65 B3
Målerås S 62 B3
Males GR 185 D6
Malesherbes F 90 C2
Malesina GR 183 E5
Malestroit F 101 B3
Maletto I 177 B3
Malexander S 56 B1
Malgrat de Mar E 147 C3
Malhadas P 149 A3
Malia
CY 181 B1
GR 185 D6
Malicorne-sur-Sarthe F 102 B1
Malijai F 132 A2
Malildjoš SRB 126 B1
Målilla S 62 A3
Mali Lošinj HR 137 A3
Malin IRL 27 A3
Málinec SK 99 C3
Malingsbo S 50 C2
Maliniec PL 76 B3
Malinska HR 123 B3
Maliq AL 182 C2
Maljevac HR 123 B4
Malkara TR 186 B1
Małki PL 69 B4
Malko Tarnovo BG 17 D7
Mallaig GB 34 A2
Mallaranny IRL 28 A2
Mallemort F 131 B4
Mallén E 144 C2
Malléon F 146 A2
Mallersdorf-Pfaffenberg D 95 C4
Málles Venosta I 108 C1
Malling DK 59 B3
Mallnitz A 109 C4
Mallow IRL 29 B3
Mallwyd GB 38 B3
Malm N 199 A8
Malmbäck S 62 A2
Malmberget S 196 B3
Malmby S 56 A3
Malmédy B 80 B2
Malmesbury GB 43 A4
Malmköping S 56 A2
Malmö S 61 D3
Malmon S 54 B2
Malmslätt S 56 B1
Malnate I 120 B1
Malo I 121 B4
Małogoszcz PL 87 B4
Maloja CH 120 A2
Małomice PL 84 A3
Måløy N 198 D2
Malpartida E 155 B4
Malpartida de la Serena E 156 B2
Malpartida de Plasencia E 150 C1
Malpas
E 145 B4
GB 38 A4
Malpica P 155 B3
Malpica de Bergantiños E 140 A2
Malpica de Tajo E 150 C3
Malsch D 93 C4
Malšice CZ 96 B2
Malta A 109 C4
Maltat F 104 C2
Maltby GB 40 B2
Malung S 49 B5
Malungsfors S 49 B5
Maluszów PL 75 B4
Maluszyn PL 87 B3
Malva E 142 C1
Malvaglia CH 120 A1
Malveira P 154 C1
Malvik N 199 B7
Malyn UA 13 C8
Mamarrosa P 148 B1
Mamer L 92 B2
Mamers F 89 B4
Mamirolle F 105 B5
Mammendorf D 108 A2
Mámmola I 175 C2
Mamoiada I 178 B3
Mamonovo RUS 69 A4
Mamuras AL 182 B1
Maňa SK 112 A2
Manacor E 167 B3
Manavgat TR 189 C6
Mancera de Abajo E 150 B2
Mancha Real E 163 A4
Manchester GB 40 B1
Manching D 95 C3
Manchita E 156 B1
Manciano I 168 A1
Manciet F 128 C3
Mandal N 52 B3
Mandanici I 177 A4
Mándas I 179 C3
Mandatoriccio I 174 B2
Mandayona E 151 B5
Mandelieu-la-Napoule F 132 B2
Mandello del Lário I 120 B2
Mandelsloh D 72 B2
Manderfeld B 80 B2
Manderscheid D 80 B2
Mandino Selo BIH 138 B3
Mandoudi GR 183 E5
Mandra GR 185 A4
Mandraki GR 188 C2
Mandúria I 173 B3
Mane
Alpes-de-Haute-Provence F 132 B1
Haute-Garonne F 145 A4
Manérbio I 120 B3
Mañeru E 144 B2
Manetin CZ 96 B1
Manfredónia I 171 B3

Mangalia RO 17 D8
Manganeses de la Lampreana E 149 A4
Manganeses de la Polvorosa E 141 B5
Mangen N 48 C3
Manger N 46 B2
Mangiennes F 92 B1
Mangotsfield GB 43 A4
Mångsbodarna S 49 A5
Mangualde P 148 B2
Maniago I 122 A1
Manilva E 162 B2
Manisa TR 186 D2
Manises E 159 B3
Mank A 110 A2
Månkarbo S 51 B4
Manlleu E 147 C3
Manna DK 58 A2
Männedorf CH 107 B3
Mannersdorf am Leithagebirge A 111 B3
Mannheim D 93 B4
Manningtree GB 45 B5
Manoppello I 169 A4
Manorbier GB 39 C2
Manorhamilton IRL 26 B2
Manosque F 132 B1
Manowo PL 67 B5
Manresa E 147 C2
Månsarp S 62 A2
Månsåsen S 199 B11
Manschnow D 74 B3
Mansfeld D 82 A3
Mansfield GB 40 B2
Mansilla de Burgos E 143 B3
Mansilla de las Mulas E 142 B1
Manskog S 55 A3
Mansle F 115 C4
Manso F 180 A1
Manteigas P 148 B2
Mantel D 95 B4
Mantes-la-Jolie F 90 C1
Mantes-la-Ville F 90 C1
Manthelan F 102 B2
Mantorp S 56 B1
Mántova I 121 B3
Mänttä FIN 8 A4
Mäntyjärvi FIN 197 C10
Manuel E 159 B3
Manyas TR 186 B2
Manzanal de Arriba E 141 B4
Manzanares E 157 A4
Manzanares el Real E 151 B4
Manzaneda
León E 141 B4
Orense E 141 B3
Manzanedo E 143 B3
Manzaneque E 157 A4
Manzanera E 153 B3
Manzanilla E 161 B3
Manzat F 116 B2
Manziana I 168 A2
Manziat F 117 A4
Maó E 167 B4
Maoča BIH 125 C4
Maqueda E 150 B3
Mara E 152 A2
Maramaraereğlisi TR 186 B2
Maraña E 142 A1
Maranchón E 152 A1
Maranello I 135 A3
Marano I 170 C2
Marano Lagunare I 122 B2
Marans F 114 B2
Maratea I 174 B1
Marateca P 154 C2
Marathokambos GR 188 B1
Marathonas GR 185 A4
Marathóvouno CY 181 A2
Marazion GB 42 B1
Marbach
Baden-Württemberg D 94 C1
Hessen D 82 B1
F 92 C2
Marbäck S 60 B3
Mårbacka S 55 A4
Marbella E 162 B3
Marboz F 118 A2
Marburg D 81 B4
Marcali H 111 C4
Marčana HR 122 C2
Marcaria I 121 B3
Marcelová SK 112 B2
Marcenat F 116 B2
March GB 41 C4
Marchamalo E 151 B4
Marchaux F 105 B5
Marche-en-Famenne B 79 B5
Marchegg A 111 A3
Marchena E 162 A2
Marchenoir F 103 B3
Marcheprime F 128 B2
Marciac F 128 C3
Marciana Marina I 134 C3
Marcianise I 170 B2
Marcigny F 117 A4
Marcilla E 144 B2
Marcillac-la-Croisille F 116 B2
Marcillac-Vallon F 130 A1
Marcillat-en-Combraille F 116 A2
Marcille-sur-Seine F 91 C3
Marcilloles F 118 B2
Marcilly-le-Hayer F 91 C3
Marcinkowice PL 75 A5
Marciszów PL 85 B4
Marck F 78 B1
Marckolsheim F 106 A2
Marco de Canevezes P 148 A1
Mårdsele S 200 B5
Mårdsjö S 200 C1
Mareham le Fen GB 41 B3
Marek S 62 A3
Marennes F 114 C2
Maresquel F 78 B1
Mareuil F 115 C4
Mareuil-en-Brie F 91 C3
Mareuil-sur-Arnon F 103 C4
Mareuil-sur-Lay F 114 B2
Mareuil-sur-Ourcq F 90 B3
Margam GB 39 C3
Margariti GR 182 D2
Margate GB 45 B5
Margaux F 128 A2
Margerie-Hancourt F 91 C4
Margès F 117 B5
Margherita di Savóia I 171 B4
Margita SRB 126 B3
Margone I 119 B4
Margonin PL 76 B2
Marguerittes F 131 B3
Margut F 91 B5
Maria E 164 B2
Mariager DK 58 B2
Mariana E 152 B1
Maria Neustift A 110 B1
Mariannelund S 62 A3
Marianópoli I 176 B2
Mariánské Lázně CZ 95 B4
Mariapfarr A 109 B4
Maria Saal A 110 C1
Mariazell A 110 B2
Maribo DK 65 B4
Maribor SLO 110 C2
Marieberg S 56 A1
Mariefred S 56 A3
Mariehamn FIN 51 B6
Marieholm S 61 D3
Mariembourg B 91 A4
Marienbaum D 80 A2
Marienberg D 83 B5
Marienheide D 81 A3
Mariental D 73 B3
Mariestad S 55 B4
Marieux F 90 A2
Marigliano I 170 C2
Marignane F 131 B4
Marigny
Jura F 105 C4
Manche F 88 A2
Marigny-le-Châtel F 91 C3
Marija Bistrica HR 124 A2
Marijampolė LT 13 A5
Marín E 140 B2
Marina HR 138 B2
Marina del Cantone I 170 C2
Marina di Acquappesa I 174 B1
Marina di Alberese I 168 A1
Marina di Amendolara I 174 B2
Marina di Árbus I 179 C2
Marina di Campo I 134 C3
Marina di Carrara I 134 A3
Marina di Castagneto-Donorático I 134 B3
Marina di Cécina I 134 B3
Marina di Gáiro I 179 C3
Marina di Ginosa I 173 B2
Marina di Gioiosa Iónica I 175 C2
Marina di Grosseto I 135 C3
Marina di Léuca I 173 C4
Marina di Massa I 134 A3
Marina di Nováglie I 173 C4
Marina di Pisa I 134 B3
Marina di Ragusa I 177 C3
Marina di Ravenna I 135 A5
Marina di Torre Grande I 179 C2
Marinaleda E 162 A3
Marina Romea I 135 A5
Marine de Sisco F 180 A2
Marinella I 176 B1
Marinella di Sarzana I 134 A3
Marineo I 176 B2
Marines F 90 B1
Maringues F 116 B3
Marinha das Ondas P 154 A2
Marinha Grande P 154 B2
Marinhas P 148 A1
Marino I 168 B2
Marjaliza E 157 A4
Markabygd N 199 B8
Markaryd S 61 C3
Markdorf D 107 B4
Markelo NL 71 B3
Market Deeping GB 40 C3
Market Drayton GB 38 B4
Market Harborough GB 40 C3
Markethill GB 27 B4
Market Rasen GB 40 B3
Market Warsop GB 40 B2
Market Weighton GB 40 B3
Markgröningen D 93 C5
Markhausen D 71 B4
Marki PL 77 B6
Markina-Xemein E 143 A4
Markinch GB 35 B4
Märkische Buchholz D 74 B2
Markitta S 196 B4
Markkleeberg D 83 A4
Marklohe D 72 B2
Marknesse NL 70 B2
Markneukirchen D 83 B4
Markopoulo GR 185 B4
Markovac
Srbija SRB 127 C3
Vojvodina SRB 126 B3
Markowice PL 86 B2
Markranstädt D 83 A4
Marksuhl D 82 B2
Markt Allhau A 111 B3
Markt Bibart D 94 B2
Marktbreit D 94 B2
Markt Erlbach D 94 B2
Markt-heidenfeld D 94 B1
Markt Indersdorf D 95 C3
Marktl D 95 C4
Marktleuthen D 83 B3
Marktoberdorf D 108 B1
Marktredwitz D 95 A4
Markt Rettenbach D 108 B1
Markt Schwaben D 108 A2
Markt-Übelbach A 110 B2
Markusica HR 125 B4
Markušovce SK 99 C4
Marl D 80 A3
Marlborough
Devon GB 42 B3
Wiltshire GB 44 B2
Marle F 91 B3
Marlieux F 117 A5
Marlow
D 66 B1
GB 44 B3
Marma S 51 B4
Marmagne F 104 C3
Marmande F 128 B3
Marmara TR 186 B2
Marmaris TR 188 C3
Marmelete P 160 B1
Marmolejo E 157 B3
Marmoutier F 93 C3
Marnay F 105 B4
Marne D 64 C2
Marnheim D 93 B4
Marnitz D 73 A4
Maroldsweisach D 82 B2
Marolles-les-Braults F 89 B4
Maromme F 89 A5
Marone I 120 B3
Maronia GR 183 C7
Maroslele H 126 A2
Maróstica I 121 B4
Marotta I 136 B2
Marpisa GR 185 B6
Marquion F 78 B3
Marquise F 78 B1
Marradi I 135 A4
Marrasjärvi FIN 197 C8
Marraskoski FIN 197 C8
Marratxi E 166 B2
Marrúbiu I 179 C2
Marrum NL 70 A2
Marrupe E 150 B3
Marsac F 129 C5
Marsac-en-Livradois F 117 B3
Marságlia I 120 C2
Marsala I 176 B1
Marsberg D 81 A4
Marsciano I 135 C5
Marseillan F 130 B2
Marseille = Marseilles F 131 B4
Marseille en Beauvaisis F 90 B1
Marseilles = Marseille F 131 B4
Mársico Nuovo I 172 B1
Marske-by-the-Sea GB 37 B5
Mars-la-Tours F 92 B1
Marsliden S 195 E6
Marson F 91 C4
Märsta S 57 A3
Marstal DK 65 B3
Marstrand S 60 B1
Marta I 168 A1
Martano I 173 B4
Martel F 129 B4
Martelange B 92 B1
Martfeld D 72 B2
Martfű H 113 B4
Martham GB 41 C5
Marthon F 115 C4
Martiago E 149 B3
Martigné-Briand F 102 B1
Martigné-Ferchaud F 101 B4
Martigne-sur-Mayenne F 102 A1
Martigny CH 119 A4
Martigny-les-Bains F 105 A4
Martigues F 131 B4
Martim-Longo P 160 B2
Martin SK 98 B2
Martina CH 108 C1
Martina Franca I 173 B3
Martinamor E 150 B2
Martin de la Jara E 162 A3
Martinengo I 120 B2
Martin Muñoz de las Posadas E 150 A3
Martinsberg A 97 C3
Martinšćica HR 123 C3
Martinshöhe D 93 B3
Martinsicuro I 136 C2
Martinszell D 107 B5
Mártis I 178 B2
Martofte DK 59 C3
Martonvásár H 112 B2
Martorell E 147 C2
Martos E 163 A4
Martres Tolosane F 146 A1
Martti FIN 197 B11
Marugán E 150 B3
Marúggio I 173 B3
Marvão P 155 B3
Marvejols F 130 A2
Marville F 92 B1
Marwałd PL 77 A4
Marykirk GB 35 B5
Marypark GB 32 D3
Maryport GB 36 B3
Marytavy GB 42 B2
Marzabotto I 135 A4
Marzahna D 74 C1
Marzahne D 73 B5
Marzamemi I 177 C4
Marzocca I 136 B2
Masa E 143 B3
Mas-Cabardès F 146 A3
Máscali I 177 B4
Mascaraque E 157 A4
Mascarenhas P 149 A2
Mascioni I 169 A3
Mas de Barberáns E 153 B4
Mas de las Matas E 153 B3
Masegoso E 158 C1
Masegoso de Tajuña E 151 B5
Masera I 119 A5
Masevaux F 106 B1
Masfjorden N 46 B2
Masham GB 37 B5
Masi N 192 C7
Maside E 140 B2
Maslacq F 144 A3
Maslinica HR 138 B2
Maşloc RO 126 B3
Maslovare BIH 138 A3
Masone I 133 A4
Massa I 134 A3
Massa Fiscáglia I 121 C5
Massafra I 173 B3
Massa Lombarda I 135 A4
Massa Lubrense I 170 C2
Massamagrell E 159 B3
Massa Maríttima I 135 B3
Massa Martana I 136 C1
Massanassa E 159 B3
Massarosa I 134 B3
Massat F 146 B2
Massay F 103 B3
Massbach D 82 B2
Masseret F 116 B1
Masseube F 145 A4
Massiac F 116 B3
Massignac F 115 C4
Massing D 95 C4
Massmechelen B 80 B1
Masterud N 49 B4
Mästocka S 61 C3
Masty BY 13 B6
Masúa I 179 C2
Masueco E 149 A3
Masugnsbyn S 196 B5
Mašun SLO 123 B3
Maszewo
Lubuskie PL 75 B3
Zachodnio-Pomorskie PL 75 A4
Mata de Alcántara E 155 B4
Matala GR 185 E5
Matalebreras E 144 C1
Matallana de Torio E 142 B1
Matamala E 151 A5
Mataporquera E 142 B2
Matapozuelos E 150 A3
Mataró E 147 C3
Matarocco I 176 B1
Matélica I 136 B2
Matera I 172 B2
Mátészalka H 16 B5
Matet E 159 B3
Matfors S 200 D3
Matha F 115 C3
Mathay F 106 B1
Matignon F 101 A3
Matilla de los Caños del Rio E 149 B4
Matlock GB 40 B2
Matosinhos P 148 A1
Matour F 117 A4
Mátrafüred H 113 B3
Mátraterenye H 113 A3
Matre
Hordaland N 46 B2
Hordaland N 52 A1
Matrei am Brenner A 108 B2
Matrei in Osttirol A 109 B3
Matrice I 170 B2
Matsdal S 195 E6
Mattarello I 121 A4
Mattersburg A 111 B3
Mattighofen A 109 A4
Mattinata I 171 B4
Mattos P 154 B2
Mattsee A 109 B4
Mattsmyra S 50 A2
Måttsund S 196 D5
Matulji HR 123 B3
Maubert-Fontaine F 91 B4
Maubeuge F 79 B3
Maubourguet F 145 A4
Mauchline GB 36 A2
Maud GB 33 D4
Mauer-kirchen A 109 A4
Mauern D 95 C3
Mauguio F 131 B3
Maulbronn D 93 C4
Maule F 90 C1
Mauléon F 114 B3
Mauléon-Barousse F 145 B4
Mauléon-Licharre F 144 A3
Maulévrier F 114 A3
Maum IRL 28 A2
Maurach A 108 B2
Maure-de-Bretagne F 101 B4
Maureilhan F 130 B2
Măureni RO 126 B3
Mauriac F 116 B2
Mauron F 101 A3
Maurs F 116 C2
Maury F 146 B3
Maussane-les-Alpilles F 131 B3
Mautern A 97 C3
Mauterndorf A 109 B4
Mautern im Steiermark A 110 B1
Mauthausen A 110 A1
Mauthen A 109 C3
Mauvezin F 129 C3
Mauzé-sur-le-Mignon F 114 B3
Maxent F 101 B3
Maxey-sur-Vaise F 92 C1
Maxial P 154 B1
Maxieira P 154 B2
Maxwellheugh GB 35 C5
Mayalde E 149 A4
Maybole GB 36 A2
Mayen D 80 B3
Mayenne F 88 B3
Mayet F 102 B2
Mayorga E 142 B1
Mayres F 117 C4
Mayrhofen A 108 B2
Mazagón E 161 B3
Mazaleón E 153 A4
Mazamet F 130 B1
Mazan F 131 A4
Mazara del Vallo I 176 B1
Mazarambroz E 157 A3
Mazarete E 152 B1
Mazaricos E 140 B2
Mazarrón E 165 B3
Mažeikiai LT 8 D3
Mazères F 146 A2
Mazères-sur-Salat F 145 A4
Mazières-en-Gâtine F 115 B3
Mazin HR 138 A1
Mazuelo E 143 B3
Mazyr BY 13 B8
Mazzarino I 177 B3
Mazzarrà Sant'Andrea I 177 A4
Mazzo di Valtellina I 120 A3
Mdzewo PL 77 B5
Mealabost GB 31 A2
Mealhada P 148 B1
Méan B 79 B5
Meana Sardo I 179 C3
Meaulne F 103 C4
Meaux F 90 C2
Mebonden N 199 B8
Mecerreyes E 143 B3
Mechelen B 79 A4
Mechernich D 80 B2
Mechnica PL 86 B2
Mechowo PL 67 C4
Mechterstädt D 82 B2
Mecidiye TR 186 B1
Mecikal PL 68 B2
Mecina-Bombarón E 164 C1
Mecitözü TR 23 A8
Meckenbeuren D 107 B4
Meckenheim
Rheinland-Pfalz D 80 B3
Rheinland-Pfalz D 93 B4
Meckesheim D 93 B4
Mecseknádasd H 125 A4
Meda
I 120 B2
P 149 B2
Medak HR 137 A4
Mede I 120 B1
Medebach D 81 A4
Medelim P 155 A3
Medemblik NL 70 B2
Medena Selista BIH 138 A2
Medesano I 120 C3
Medevi S 55 B5
Medgidia RO 17 C8
Medgyesháza H 113 C5
Medhamn S 55 A4
Mediaş RO 17 B6
Medicina I 135 A4
Medinaceli E 152 A1
Medina de las Torres E 155 C4
Medina del Campo E 150 A3
Medina de Pomar E 143 B3
Medina de Rioseco E 142 C1
Medina Sidonia E 162 B2
Medinilla E 150 B2
Medja SRB 126 B2
Medjedja BIH 139 B5
Medulin HR 122 C2
Meduno I 122 A1
Medveda SRB 127 C3
Medvedov SK 111 B4
Medvezhyegorsk RUS 9 A9
Medvide HR 137 A4
Medvode SLO 123 A3
Medzev SK 99 C4
Medžitlija MK 182 C3
Meerane D 83 B4
Meerle B 79 A4
Meersburg D 107 B4
Meeuwen B 79 A5
Megalo Horio GR 188 C2
Megalopoli GR 184 B3
Megara GR 185 A4
Megève F 118 B3
Meggenhofen A 109 A4
Megra RUS 9 B10
Megyaszó H 113 A5
Mehamn N 193 A11
Mehedeby S 51 B4
Méhkerék H 113 C5
Mehun-sur-Yèvre F 103 B4
Meigle GB 35 B4
Meijel NL 80 A1
Meilen CH 107 B3
Meilhan F 128 C2
Meimôa P 149 B2
Meina I 119 B5
Meine D 73 B3
Meinersen D 72 B3
Meinerzhagen D 81 A3
Meiningen D 82 B2
Meira E 141 A3
Meiringen CH 106 C3
Meisenheim D 93 B3
Meissen D 83 A5
Meitingen D 94 C2
Meix-devant-Virton B 92 B1
Męka PL 86 A2
Meka Gruda BIH 139 B4
Mel I 121 A5
Melbu N 194 B5
Melč CZ 98 B1
Meldal N 198 B6
Méldola I 135 A5
Meldorf D 64 B2
Melegnano I 120 B2
Melenci SRB 126 B2
Melendugno I 173 B4
Melfi I 172 B1
Melfjordbotn N 195 D4
Melgaço P 140 B2
Melgar de Arriba E 142 B1
Melgar de Fernamental E 142 B2
Melgar de Yuso E 142 B2
Melhus N 199 B7
Meliana E 159 B3
Melide
CH 120 B1
E 140 B2
Melides P 160 A1
Meligales GR 184 B2
Melilli I 177 B4
Melinovac HR 124 C1
Melisenda I 179 C3
Melisey F 105 B5
Mélito di Porto Salvo I 175 D1
Melk A 110 A2
Melksham GB 43 A4
Mellakoski FIN 196 C7
Mellanström S 195 E9
Mellbystrand S 61 C2
Melle
B 79 A3
D 71 B5
F 115 B3
Mellendorf D 72 B2
Mellerud S 54 B3
Mellieha M 175 C3
Mellösa S 56 A2
Mellrichstadt D 82 B2
Mělnické Vtelno CZ 84 B2
Mělník CZ 84 B2
Melón E 140 B2
Melrose GB 35 C5
Mels CH 107 B4
Melsungen D 82 A1
Meltaus FIN 197 C8
Meltham GB 40 B2
Melton Mowbray GB 40 C3
Meltosjärvi FIN 196 C7
Melun F 90 C2
Melvaig GB 31 B3
Melvich GB 32 C3
Mélykút H 126 A1
Melzo I 120 B2
Memaliaj AL 182 C1
Membrilla E 157 B4
Membrio E 155 B3
Memer F 129 B4
Memmelsdorf D 94 B2
Memmingen D 107 B5
Memoria P 154 B2
Menággio I 120 A2
Menai Bridge GB 38 A2
Menasalbas E 157 A3
Menat F 116 A2
Mendavia E 144 B1
Mendaza E 144 B1
Mende F 130 A2
Menden D 81 A3
Menderes TR 188 A2
Mendig D 80 B3
Mendiga P 154 B2
Mendrisio CH 120 B1
Ménéac F 101 A3
Menemen TR 188 A2
Menen B 78 B3
Menesjärvi FIN 193 D10
Menetou-Salon F 103 B4
Menfi I 176 B1
Ménfőcsanak H 111 B4
Mengamuñoz E 150 B3
Mengen
D 107 A4
TR 187 B7
Mengeš SLO 123 A3
Mengíbar E 157 C4
Mengkofen D 95 C4
Menou F 104 B2
Mens F 118 C2
Menslage D 71 B4
Mensträsk S 200 A5
Mentana I 168 A2
Menton F 133 B3
Méntrida E 151 B3
Méobecq F 115 B5
Méounes-les-Montrieux F 132 B1
Meppel NL 70 B3
Meppen D 71 B4
Mequinenza E 153 A4
Mer F 103 B3
Mera
Coruña E 140 A2
Coruña E 140 A3
Meråker N 199 B8
Merano I 108 C2
Merate I 120 B2
Mercadillo E 143 A3
Mercatale I 135 B5
Mercatino Conca I 136 B1
Mercato San Severino I 170 C2
Mercato Saraceno I 135 B5
Merching D 108 A1
Merchtem B 79 B4
Merdrignac F 101 A3
Merdžanići BIH 139 B3
Meré E 142 A2
Mere GB 43 A4
Meréville F 90 C2
Merfeld D 80 A3
Méribel F 118 B3
Méribel Motraret F 118 B3
Meriç TR 186 A1
Mérida E 155 C4
Mérignac F 128 B2
Měřín CZ 97 B3
Mering D 94 C2
Merkendorf D 94 B2
Merklin CZ 96 B1
Merksplas B 79 A4
Merlånna S 56 A2
Merlimont Plage F 78 B1
Mern DK 65 A5
Mernye H 111 C4
Mersch L 92 B2
Merseburg D 83 A3
Mers-les-Bains F 90 A1
Merthyr Tydfil GB 39 C3
Mertingen D 94 C2
Mértola P 160 B2
Méru F 90 B2
Merufe P 140 B2
Mervans F 105 C4
Merville F 78 B2
Méry-sur-Seine F 91 C3
Merzen D 71 B4
Merzifon TR 23 A8
Merzig D 92 B2
Mesagne I 173 B3
Mesão Frio P 148 A2
Mesas de Ibor E 156 A2
Meschede D 81 A4
Meschers-sur-Gironde F 114 C3
Meslay-du-Maine F 102 B1
Mesna N 48 A2
Mesnalien N 48 A2
Mesocco CH 120 A2
Mésola I 122 C1
Mesologi GR 184 A2
Mesopotamo GR 182 D2
Mesoraca I 175 B2
Messac F 101 B4
Messancy B 92 B1
Messdorf D 73 B4
Messei F 88 B3
Messejana P 160 B1
Messelt N 48 A3
Messina I 177 A4
Messingen D 71 B4
Messini GR 184 B3
Messkirch D 107 B4
Messlingen S 199 C9
Messtetten D 107 A3
Mesta GR 185 A6
Mestanza E 157 B3
Městec Králové CZ 84 B3
Mestlin D 73 A4
Město Albrechtice CZ 85 B5
Město Libavá CZ 98 B1
Město Touškov CZ 96 B1
Mestre I 122 B1
Mesvres F 104 C3
Mesztegnyő H 111 C4
Meta I 170 C2
Metajna HR 137 A4
Metelen D 71 B4
Methana GR 185 B4
Methlick GB 33 D4
Methven GB 35 B4
Methwold GB 41 C4
Metković HR 139 B3
Metlika SLO 123 B4
Metnitz A 110 C1
Metsäkylä FIN 197 D11
Metslawier NL 70 A3
Metsovo GR 182 D3
Metten D 95 C4
Mettendorf D 92 B2
Mettet B 79 B4
Mettingen D 71 B4
Mettlach D 92 B2
Mettlen CH 106 C2
Mettmann D 80 A2
Metz F 92 B2
Metzervisse F 92 B2
Metzingen D 94 C1
Meulan F 90 B1
Meung-sur-Loire F 103 B3

Meuselwitz D 83 A4
Meuzac F 115 C5
Mevagissey GB 42 B2
Mexborough GB 40 B2
Meximieux F 118 B2
Mey GB 32 C3
Meyenburg D 73 A5
Meyerhöfen D 71 B5
Meylan F 118 B2
Meymac F 116 B2
Meyrargues F 132 B1
Meyrueis F 130 A2
Meyssac F 129 A4
Meysse F 117 C4
Meyzieu F 117 B4
Mèze F 130 B2
Mézériat F 117 A5
Mežica SLO 110 C1
Mézidon-Canon F 89 A3
Mézières-en-Brenne F 115 B5
Mézières-sur-Issoire F 115 B4
Mézilhac F 117 C4
Mézilles F 104 B2
Mézin F 128 B3
Mezőberény H 113 C5
Mezőcsát H 113 B4
Mezőfalva H 112 C2
Mezőhegyes H 126 A2
Mezőkeresztes H 113 B4
Mezőkomárom H 112 C2
Mezökövácsháza H 113 C4
Mezökövesd H 113 B4
Mezőörs H 111 B4
Mézos F 128 B1
Mezőszilas H 112 C2
Mezőtúr H 113 B4
Mezquita de Jarque E 153 B3
Mezzano
Emilia Romagna I 135 A5
Trentino Alto Adige I 121 A4
Mezzojuso I 176 B2
Mezzoldo I 120 A2
Mezzolombardo I 121 A4
Mgarr M 175 C3
Miajadas E 156 A2
Miały PL 75 B5
Mianowice PL 68 A2
Miasteczko Krajeńskie PL 76 A2
Miasteczko Sł. PL 86 B2
Miastko PL 68 A1
Michalovce SK 12 D4
Michałowice PL 87 B3
Michelau D 94 B2
Michelbach D 94 B2
Micheldorf A 110 B1
Michelhausen A 110 A2
Michelsneukirchen D 95 B4
Michelstadt D 93 B5
Michendorf D 74 B2
Mickleover GB 40 C2
Midbea GB 33 B4
Middelburg NL 79 A3
Middelfart DK 59 C2
Middelharnis NL 79 A4
Middelkerke B 78 A2
Middelstum NL 71 A3
Middlesbrough GB 37 B5
Middleton Cheney GB 44 A2
Middleton-in-Teesdale GB 37 B4
Middletown GB 27 B4
Middlewich GB 38 A4
Middlezoy GB 43 A4
Midhurst GB 44 C3
Midleton IRL 29 C3
Midlum D 64 C1
Midsomer Norton GB 43 A4
Midtgulen N 198 D2
Midtskogberget N 49 A4
Midwolda NL 71 A4
Mid Yell GB 33 A5
Miechów PL 87 B4
Miedes de Aragón E 152 A2
Miedes de Atienza E 151 A4
Międzybodzie Bielskie PL 99 B3
Międzybórz PL 85 A5
Międzychód PL 75 B4
Międzylesie PL 85 B4
Międzyrzec Podlaski PL 12 C5
Międzyrzecz PL 75 B4
Międzywodzie PL 67 B3
Międzyzdroje PL 67 C3
Miejska Górka PL 85 A4
Miélan F 145 A4
Mielec PL 87 B5
Mielęcin PL 75 A3
Mielno
Warmińsko-Mazurskie PL 77 A5
Zachodnio-Pomorskie PL 67 B5
Miengo E 143 A3
Mieraslompolo FIN 193 C11
Miercurea Ciuc RO 17 B6
Mieres
Asturias E 141 A5
Girona E 147 B3
Mieroszów PL 85 B4
Mierzyn PL 86 A3
Miesau D 93 B3
Miesbach D 108 B2
Mieścisko PL 76 B2
Mieste D 73 B4
Miesterhorst D 73 B4
Mieszków PL 76 B2
Mieszkowice PL 74 B3
Mietków PL 85 B4
Migennes F 104 B2
Miggiano I 173 C4
Migliánico I 169 A4
Migliarino I 121 C4
Migliónico I 172 B2
Mignano Monte Lungo I 169 B3
Migné F 115 B5
Miguel Esteban E 157 A4
Miguelturra E 157 B4
Mihajlovac SRB 127 C2
Mihàld H 111 C4
Mihalgazi TR 187 B5
Mihaliççık TR 187 C6
Mihályi H 111 B4
Mihla D 82 A2
Mihohnić HR 123 B3
Miholjsko HR 123 B4
Mihovljan HR 124 A1
Mijares E 150 B3
Mijas E 163 B3
Mike H 124 A3
Mikines GR 184 B3
Mikkeli FIN 8 B5
Mikkelvik N 192 B3
Mikleuš HR 125 B3
Mikołajki Pomorskie PL 69 B4
Mikolów PL 86 B2
Mikonos GR 185 B6
Mikorzyn PL 86 A2
Mikro Derio GR 183 B8
Mikstat PL 86 A1
Mikulášovice CZ 84 B2
Mikulov CZ 97 C4
Mikulovice CZ 85 B5
Milagro E 144 B2
Miłakowo PL 69 A5
Milan = Milano I 120 B2
Miland N 47 C5
Milano = Milan I 120 B2
Milano Marittima I 135 A5
Milas TR 188 B2
Milazzo I 177 A4
Mildenhall GB 45 A4
Milejewo PL 69 A4
Milelín CZ 85 B3
Miletić SRB 125 B5
Miletićevo SRB 126 B3
Mileto I 175 C2
Milevsko CZ 96 B2
Milford IRL 26 A3
Milford Haven GB 39 C1
Milford on Sea GB 44 C2
Milhão P 149 A3
Milići BIH 139 A5
Miličin CZ 96 B2
Milicz PL 85 A5
Milín CZ 96 B2
Militello in Val di Catánia I 177 B3
Miljevina BIH 139 B4
Milkowice PL 85 A4
Millançay F 103 B3
Millares E 159 B3
Millas F 146 B3
Millau F 130 A2
Millesimo I 133 A4
Millevaches F 116 B2
Millom GB 36 B3
Millport GB 34 C3
Millstatt A 109 C4
Millstreet
Cork IRL 29 B2
Waterford IRL 29 B4
Milltown
Galway IRL 28 A3
Kerry IRL 29 B1
Milltown Malbay IRL 28 B2
Milly-la-Forêt F 90 C2
Milmarcos E 152 A2
Milmersdorf D 74 A2
Milna HR 138 B2
Milnthorpe GB 37 B4
Milogórze PL 69 A5
Milomłyn PL 69 B4
Milos GR 185 C5
Miloševo SRB 127 C3
Milosław PL 76 B2
Milot AL 182 B1
Milówka PL 99 B3
Miltach D 95 B4
Miltenberg D 94 B1
Milton Keynes GB 44 A3
Miltzow D 66 B2
Milverton GB 43 A3
Milzyn PL 76 B3
Mimice HR 138 B2
Mimizan F 128 B1
Mimizan-Plage F 128 B1
Mimoň CZ 84 B2
Mina de Juliana P 160 B1
Mina de São Domingos P 160 B2
Minas de Riotinto E 161 B3
Minateda E 158 C2
Minaya E 158 B1
Minde P 154 B2
Mindelheim D 108 A1
Mindelstetten D 95 C3
Minden D 72 B1
Mindszent H 113 C4
Minehead GB 43 A3
Mineo I 177 B3
Minerbe I 121 B4
Minérbio I 121 C4
Minervino Murge I 171 B4
Minglanilla E 158 B2
Mingorria E 150 B3
Minnesund N 48 B3
Miño E 140 A2
Miño de San Esteban E 151 A4
Minsen D 71 A4
Minsk BY 13 B7
Mińsk Mazowiecki PL 12 B4
Minsterley GB 39 B4
Mintlaw GB 33 D4
Minturno I 169 B3
Mionica
BIH 125 C4
SRB 127 C2
Mios F 128 B2
Mira
E 158 B2
I 121 B5
P 148 B1
Mirabel E 155 B4
Mirabel-aux-Baronnies F 131 A4
Mirabella Eclano I 170 B3
Mirabella Imbáccari I 177 B3
Mirabello I 121 C4
Miradoux F 129 B3
Miraflores de la Sierra E 151 B4
Miralrio E 151 B5
Miramar P 148 A1
Miramare I 136 A1
Miramas F 131 B3
Mirambeau F 114 C3
Miramont-de-Guyenne F 129 B3
Miranda de Arga E 144 B2
Miranda de Ebro E 143 B4
Miranda do Corvo P 148 B1
Miranda do Douro P 149 A3
Mirande F 129 C3
Mirandela P 149 A2
Mirandilla E 155 C4
Mirándola I 121 C4
Miranje HR 137 A4
Mirano I 121 B5
Miras AL 182 C2
Miravet E 153 A4
Miré F 102 B1
Mirebeau F 102 C2
Mirebeau-sur-Bèze F 105 B4
Mirecourt F 105 A5
Mirepoix F 146 A2
Mires GR 185 D5
Miribel F 117 B4
Miričina BIH 125 C4
Mirina GR 183 D7
Mirna SLO 123 B4
Miroslav CZ 97 C4
Mirosławice PL 85 B4
Mirosławiec PL 75 A5
Mirošov CZ 96 B1
Mirotice CZ 96 B2
Mirovice CZ 96 B2
Mirow D 74 A1
Mirsk PL 84 B3
Mirzec PL 87 A5
Misi FIN 197 C9
Misilmeri I 176 A2
Miske H 112 C3
Miskolc H 113 A4
Mislinja SLO 110 C2
Missanello I 174 A2
Missillac F 101 B3
Mistelbach
A 97 C4
D 95 B3
Misten N 194 C5
Misterbianco I 177 B4
Misterhult S 62 A4
Mistretta I 177 B3
Misurina I 109 C3
Mitchelstown IRL 29 B3
Mithimna GR 186 C1
Mithoni GR 184 C2
Mitilini GR 186 C1
Mitilinii GR 188 B1
Mittelberg
Tirol A 108 C1
Vorarlberg A 107 B5
Mittenwald D 108 B2
Mittenwalde D 74 B2
Mitterback A 110 B2
Mitterdorf im Mürztal A 110 B2
Mitter-Kleinarl A 109 B4
Mittersheim F 92 C2
Mittersill A 109 B3
Mitterskirchen D 95 C4
Mitterteich D 95 B4
Mitton F 128 B2
Mittweida D 83 B4
Mitwitz D 82 B3
Mizhhir'ya UA 13 D5
Mjällby S 63 B2
Mjåvatn N 53 B4
Mjöbäck S 60 B2
Mjölby S 56 B1
Mjølfjell N 46 B3
Mjøndalen N 53 A6
Mjørlund N 48 B2
Mladá Boleslav CZ 84 B2
Mladá Vožice CZ 96 B2
Mladé Buky CZ 85 B3
Mladenovac SRB 127 C2
Mladenovo SRB 126 B1
Mladikovine BIH 139 A3
Mława PL 77 A5
Mlinište BIH 138 A2
Młodzieszyn PL 77 B5
Młogoszyn PL 77 B4
Młynary PL 69 A4
Mnichóvice CZ 96 B2
Mnichovo Hradiště CZ 84 B2
Mniów PL 87 A4
Mnisek nad Hnilcom SK 99 C4
Mníšek pod Brdy CZ 96 B2
Mniszek PL 87 A4
Mniszków PL 87 A4
Mo
Hedmark N 48 B3
Hordaland N 46 B2
Møre og Romsdal N 198 C5
Telemark N 53 A3
Gävleborg S 51 A3
Västra Götaland S 54 B2
Moaña E 140 B2
Moate IRL 28 A4
Mocejón E 151 C4
Močenok SK 111 A4
Mochales E 152 A1
Mochowo PL 77 B4
Mochy PL 75 B5
Mockern D 73 B4
Mockfjärd S 50 B1
Möckmühl D 94 B1
Mockrehna D 83 A4
Moclin E 163 A4
Mocsa H 112 B2
Möcsény H 125 A4
Modane F 118 B3
Modbury GB 42 B3
Módena I 121 C3
Módica I 177 C3
Modigliana I 135 A4
Modlin PL 77 B5
Mödling A 111 A3
Modliszewice PL 87 A4
Modliszewko PL 76 B2
Modogno I 171 B4
Modra SK 98 C1
Modran BIH 125 C3
Modriča BIH 125 C4
Möðrudalur IS 191 B10
Modrý Kamen SK 99 C3
Moëlan-sur-Mer F 100 B2
Moelfre GB 38 A2
Moelv N 48 B2
Moen N 194 A9
Moena I 121 A4
Moerbeke B 79 A3
Moers D 80 A2
Móes P 148 B2
Moffat GB 36 A3
Mogadouro P 149 A3
Mogata S 56 B2
Móggio Udinese I 122 A2
Mogielnica PL 87 A4
Mogilany PL 99 B3
Mogilno PL 76 B2
Mogliano I 136 B2
Mogliano Véneto I 122 B1
Mogor E 140 B2
Mógoro I 179 C2
Moguer E 161 B3
Mohács H 125 B4
Moheda S 62 A2
Mohedas E 149 B3
Mohedas de la Jara E 156 A2
Mohelnice CZ 97 B4
Mohill IRL 26 C3
Möhlin CH 106 B2
Moholm S 55 B5
Mohorn D 83 A5
Mohyliv-Podil's'kyy UA 13 D7
Moi N 52 B2
Moià E 147 C3
Móie I 136 B2
Moimenta da Beira P 148 B2
Mo i Rana N 195 D5
Moirans F 118 B2
Moirans-en-Montagne F 118 A2
Moisaküla EST 8 C4
Moisdon-la-Rivière F 101 B4
Moissac F 129 B4
Moita
Coimbra P 148 B1
Guarda P 149 B2
Santarém P 154 B2
Setúbal P 154 C1
Moita dos Ferreiros P 154 B1
Moixent E 159 C3
Mojacar E 164 B3
Mojados E 150 A3
Mojmírovce SK 112 A2
Mojtin SK 98 C2
Möklinta S 50 B3
Mokošica HR 139 C4
Mokronog SLO 123 B4
Mokro Polje HR 138 A2
Mokrzyska PL 99 A4
Møkster N 46 B2
Mol
B 79 A5
SRB 126 B2
Mola di Bari I 173 A3
Molai GR 184 C3
Molare I 133 A4
Molaretto I 119 B4
Molas F 145 A4
Molassano I 134 A1
Molbergen D 71 B4
Mold GB 38 A3
Molde N 198 C4
Møldrup DK 58 B2
Moledo do Minho P 148 A1
Molfetta I 171 B4
Molfsee D 64 B3
Moliden S 200 C4
Molières F 129 B4
Molina de Aragón E 152 B2
Molina de Segura E 165 A3
Molinar E 143 A3
Molinaseca E 141 B4
Molinella I 121 C4
Molinet F 104 C2
Molinicos E 158 C1
Molini di Tures I 108 C2
Molinos de Duero E 143 C4
Molins de Rei E 147 C3
Moliterno I 174 A1
Molkom S 55 A4
Möllbrücke A 109 C4
Mölle S 61 C2
Molledo E 142 A2
Möllenbeck D 74 A2
Mollerussa E 147 C1
Mollet de Perelada E 146 B3
Mollina E 163 A3
Mölln D 73 A3
Molló E 146 B3
Mollösund S 54 B2
Mölltorp S 55 B5
Mölnbo S 56 A3
Mölndal S 60 B2
Mölnlycke S 60 B2
Molompize F 116 B3
Moloy F 105 B3
Molsheim F 93 C3
Moltzow D 73 A5
Molve HR 124 A3
Molveno I 121 A3
Molvizar E 163 B4
Molzbichl A 109 C4
Mombaróccio I 136 B1
Mombeltrán E 150 B2
Mombris D 93 A5
Mombuey E 141 B4
Momchilgrad BG 183 B7
Mommark DK 64 B3
Momo I 119 B5
Monaghan IRL 27 B4
Monar Lodge GB 32 D2
Monasterace Marina I 175 C2
Monasterevin IRL 30 A1
Monasterio de Rodilla E 143 B3
Monastir I 179 C3
Monbahus F 129 B3
Monbazillac F 129 B3
Moncada E 159 B3
Moncalieri I 119 B4
Moncalvo I 119 B5
Monção P 140 B2
Moncarapacho P 160 B2
Moncel-sur-Seille F 92 C2
Monchegorsk RUS 3 C13
Mönchengladbach = Munchen-Gladbach D 80 A2
Mónchio della Corti I 134 A3
Monchique P 160 B1
Monclar-de-Quercy F 129 C4
Moncofa E 159 B3
Moncontour F 101 A3
Moncoutant F 114 B3
Monda E 162 B3
Mondariz E 140 B2
Mondavio I 136 B1
Mondéjar E 151 B4
Mondello I 176 A2
Mondim de Basto P 148 A2
Mondolfo I 136 B2
Mondoñedo E 141 A3
Mondorf-les-Bains L 92 B2
Mondoubleau F 102 B2
Mondovì I 133 A3
Mondragon F 131 A3
Mondragone I 170 B1
Mondsee A 109 B4
Monéglia I 134 A2
Monegrillo E 153 A3
Monein F 145 A3
Monemvasia GR 184 C4
Mónesi I 133 A3
Monesiglio I 133 A4
Monesterio E 161 A3
Monestier-de-Clermont F 118 C2
Monestiés F 130 A1
Monéteau F 104 B2
Moneygall IRL 28 B4
Moneymore GB 27 B4
Monfalcone I 122 B2
Monfero E 140 A2
Monflanquin F 129 B3
Monflorite E 145 B3
Monforte P 155 B3
Monforte da Beira
E 155 B3
P 155 B3
Monforte d'Alba I 133 A3
Monforte del Cid E 165 A4
Monforte de Lemos E 140 B3
Monforte de Moyuela E 152 A2
Monghidoro I 135 A4
Mongiana I 175 C2
Monguelfo I 108 C3
Monheim D 94 C2
Moniaive GB 36 A3
Monifieth GB 35 B5
Monikie GB 35 B5
Monistrol-d'Allier F 117 C3
Monistrol de Montserrat E 147 C2
Monistrol-sur-Loire F 117 B4
Mönkebude D 74 A2
Monkton GB 36 A2
Monmouth GB 39 C4
Monnaie F 102 B2
Monnerville F 90 C2
Monnickendam NL 70 B2
Monolithos GR 188 C2
Monópoli I 173 B3
Monor H 112 B3
Monóvar E 159 C3
Monpazier F 129 B3
Monreal
D 80 B3
E 144 B2
Monreal del Campo E 152 B2
Monreale I 176 A2
Monroy E 155 B4
Monroyo E 153 B3
Mons B 79 B3
Monsaraz P 155 C3
Monschau D 80 B2
Monségur F 128 B3
Monsélice I 121 B4
Mønshaug N 46 B3
Monster NL 70 B1
Mönsterås S 62 A4
Monsummano Terme I 135 B3
Montabaur D 81 B3
Montafia I 119 C5
Montagnac F 130 B2
Montagnana I 121 B4
Montaigu F 114 B2
Montaigu-de-Quercy F 129 B4
Montaiguët-en-Forez F 117 A3
Montaigut F 116 A2
Montaigut-sur-Save F 129 C4
Montainville F 90 C1
Montalbán E 153 B3
Montalbán de Córdoba E 163 A3
Montalbano Elicona I 177 A4
Montalbano Iónico I 174 A2
Montalbo E 158 B1
Montalcino I 135 B4
Montaldo di Cósola I 120 C2
Montalegre P 148 A2
Montalieu-Vercieu F 118 B2
Montalivet-les-Bains F 114 C2
Montallegro I 176 B2
Montalto delle Marche I 136 C2
Montalto di Castro I 168 A1
Montalto Pavese I 120 C2
Montalto Uffugo I 174 B2
Montalvão P 155 B3
Montamarta E 149 A4
Montana BG 17 D5
Montana-Vermala CH 119 A4
Montánchez E 156 A1
Montanejos E 153 B3
Montano Antilia I 172 B1
Montans F 129 C4
Montargil P 154 B2
Montargis F 103 B4
Montastruc-la-Conseillère F 129 C4
Montauban F 129 B4
Montauban-de-Bretagne F 101 A3
Montbard F 104 B3
Montbarrey F 105 B4
Montbazens F 130 A1
Montbazon F 102 B2
Montbéliard F 106 B1
Montbenoit F 105 C5
Montbeugny F 104 C2
Montblanc E 147 C2
Montbozon F 105 B5
Montbrison F 117 B4
Montbron F 115 C4
Montbrun-les-Bains F 131 A4
Montceau-les-Mines F 104 C3
Montcenis F 104 C3
Montchanin F 104 C3
Montcornet F 91 B4
Montcuq F 129 B4
Montdardier F 130 B2
Mont-de-Marsan F 128 C2
Montdidier F 90 B2
Monteagudo E 165 A3
Monteagudo de las Vicarias E 152 A1
Montealegre E 142 C2
Montealegre del Castillo E 159 C2
Montebello Iónico I 175 D1
Montebello Vicentino I 121 B4
Montebelluna I 121 B5
Montebourg F 88 A2
Montebruno I 134 A2
Monte-Carlo MC 133 B3
Montecarotto I 136 B2
Montecassiano I 136 B2
Montecastrilli I 168 A2
Montecatini Terme I 135 B3
Montécchio I 136 B1
Montécchio Emilia I 121 C3
Montécchio Maggiore I 121 B4
Montech F 129 C4
Montechiaro d'Asti I 119 B5
Monte Clara P 155 B3
Monte Clérigo P 160 B1
Montecórice I 170 C2
Montecorvino Rovella I 170 C2
Monte da Pedra P 155 B3
Monte de Goula P 155 B3
Montederramo E 141 B3
Montedoro I 176 B2
Monte do Trigo P 155 C3
Montefalco I 136 C1
Montefalcone di Val Fortore I 170 B3
Montefalcone nel Sánnio I 170 B2
Montefano I 136 B2
Montefiascone I 168 A2
Montefiorino I 134 A3
Montefortino I 136 C2
Montefranco I 168 A2
Montefrío E 163 A4
Montegiordano Marina I 174 A2
Montegiórgio I 136 B2
Monte Gordo P 160 B2
Montegranaro I 136 B2
Montehermoso E 149 B3
Montejicar E 163 A4
Montejo de la Sierra E 151 A4
Montejo de Tiermes E 151 A4
Monte Juntos P 155 C3
Montel-de-Gelat F 116 B2
Monteleone di Púglia I 171 B3
Monteleone di Spoleto I 169 A2
Monteleone d'Orvieto I 135 C5
Montelepre I 176 A2
Montelibretti I 168 A2
Montelier F 117 C5
Montélimar F 131 A3
Montella
E 146 B2
I 170 C3
Montellano E 162 A2
Montelupo Fiorentino I 135 B4
Montemaggiore Belsito I 176 B2
Montemagno I 119 C5
Montemayor E 163 A3
Montemayor de Pinilla E 150 A3
Montemésola I 173 B3
Montemilleto I 170 B2
Montemilone I 172 A1
Montemolin E 161 A3
Montemónaco I 136 C2
Montemor-o-Novo P 154 C2
Montemor-o-Velho P 148 B1
Montemurro I 174 A1
Montendre F 128 A2
Montenegro de Cameros E 143 B4
Montenero di Bisáccia I 170 B2
Monteneuf F 101 B3
Monteparano I 173 B3
Montepescali I 135 C4
Montepiano I 135 A4
Monte Porzio I 136 B2
Montepulciano I 135 B4
Monte Real P 154 B2
Montereale I 169 A3
Montereale Valcellina I 122 A1
Montereau-Faut-Yonne F 90 C2
Monte Redondo P 154 B2
Monterénzio I 135 A4
Monte Romano I 168 A1
Monteroni d'Arbia I 135 B4
Monteroni di Lecce I 173 B4
Monterosso al Mare I 134 A2
Monterosso Almo I 177 B3
Monterosso Grana I 133 A3
Monterotondo I 168 A2
Monterotondo Maríttimo I 135 B3
Monterrey E 141 C3
Monterroso E 140 B3
Monterrubio de la Serena E 156 B2
Monterubbiano I 136 B2
Montesa E 159 C3
Montesalgueiro E 140 A2
Monte San Giovanni Campano I 169 B3
Montesano sulla Marcellana I 174 A1
Monte San Savino I 135 B4
Monte Sant'Ángelo I 171 B3
Montesárchio I 170 B2
Montescaglioso I 171 C4
Montesclaros E 150 B3
Montesilvano I 169 A4
Montespértoli I 135 B4
Montesquieu-Volvestre F 146 A2
Montesquiou F 129 C3
Montestruc-sur-Gers F 129 C3
Montes Velhos P 160 B1
Montevarchi I 135 B4
Montéveglio I 135 A4
Monte Vilar P 154 B1
Montfaucon F 101 B4
Montfaucon-d'Argonne F 91 B5
Montfaucon-en-Velay F 117 B4
Montferrat
Isère F 118 B2
Var F 132 B2

Montfort-en-Chalosse F 128 C2
Montfort-l'Amaury F 90 C1
Montfort-le-Gesnois F 102 A2
Montfort-sur-Meu F 101 A4
Montfort-sur-Risle F 89 A4
Montgai E 147 C1
Montgaillard F 145 A4
Montgenèvre F 118 C3
Montgiscard F 146 A2
Montgomery GB 39 B3
Montguyon F 128 A2
Monthermé F 91 B4
Monthey CH 119 A3
Monthois F 91 B4
Monthureux-sur-Saône F 105 A4
Monti I 178 B3
Monticelli d'Ongina I 120 B2
Montichiari I 120 B3
Monticiano I 135 B4
Montiel E 158 C1
Montier-en-Der F 91 C4
Montieri I 135 B4
Montiglio I 119 B5
Montignac F 129 A4
Montigny-le-Roi F 105 B4
Montigny-lès-Metz F 92 B2
Montigny-sur-Aube F 105 B3
Montijo
E 155 C4
P 154 C2
Montilla E 163 A3
Montillana E 163 A4
Montilly F 104 C2
Montivilliers F 89 A4
Montjaux F 130 A1
Montjean-sur-Loire F 102 B1
Montlhéry F 90 C2
Montlieu-la-Garde F 128 A2
Mont-Louis F 146 B3
Montlouis-sur-Loire F 102 B2
Montluçon F 116 A2
Montluel F 117 B5
Montmarault F 116 A2
Montmartin-sur-Mer F 88 B2
Montmédy F 92 B1
Montmélian F 118 B3
Montmeyan F 132 B2
Montmeyran F 117 C4
Montmirail
Marne F 91 C3
Sarthe F 102 A2
Montmiral F 118 B2
Montmirat F 131 B3
Montmirey-le-Château F 105 B4
Montmoreau-St Cybard F 115 C4
Montmorency F 90 C2
Montmorillon F 115 B4
Montmort-Lucy F 91 C3
Montoir-de-Bretagne F 101 B3
Montoire-sur-le-Loir F 102 B2
Montoito P 155 C3
Montolieu F 146 A3
Montório al Vomano I 169 A3
Montoro E 157 B3
Montpellier F 131 B2
Montpezat-de-Quercy F 129 B4
Montpezat-sous-Bouzon F 117 C4
Montpon-Ménestérol F 128 A3
Montpont-en-Bresse F 105 C4
Montréal
Aude F 146 A3
Gers F 128 C3
Montredon-Labessonnié F 130 B1
Montréjeau F 145 A4
Montrésor F 103 B3
Montresta I 178 B2
Montret F 105 C4
Montreuil
Pas de Calais F 78 B1
Seine St Denis F 90 C2
Montreuil-aux-Lions F 90 B3
Montreuil-Bellay F 102 B1
Montreux CH 106 C1
Montrevault F 101 B4
Montrevel-en-Bresse F 118 A2
Montrichard F 103 B3
Montricoux F 129 B4
Mont-roig del Camp E 147 C1
Montrond-les-Bains F 117 B4
Montrose GB 35 B5
Montroy E 159 B3
Montsalvy F 116 C2
Montsauche-les-Settons F 104 B3
Montseny E 147 C3
Montsoreau F 102 B2
Mont-sous-Vaudrey F 105 C4
Monts-sur-Guesnes F 102 C2
Mont-St Aignan F 89 A5
Mont-St Vincent F 104 C3
Montsûrs F 102 A1
Montuenga E 150 A3
Montuïri E 167 B3
Monturque E 163 A3
Monza I 120 B2
Monzón E 145 C4
Monzón de Campos E 142 B2
Moorbad Lobenstein D 83 B3
Moordorf D 71 A4
Moorslede B 78 B3
Moos D 107 B3
Moosburg D 95 C3
Moosburg im Kärnten A 110 C1
Mór H 112 B2
Mora E 157 A4
Móra P 154 C2
Mora S 50 A1
Moraby S 50 B2
Mòra d'Ebre E 153 A4
Mora de Rubielos E 153 B3
Moradillo de Roa E 151 A4
Morąg PL 69 B4
Mórahalom H 126 A1
Moraime E 140 A1
Morais P 149 A3
Mòra la Nova E 153 A4
Moral de Calatrava E 157 B4
Moraleda de Zafayona E 163 A4
Moraleja E 149 B3
Moraleja del Vino E 150 A2
Morales del Vino E 150 A2
Morales de Toro E 150 A2
Morales de Valverde E 141 C5
Moralina E 149 A3
Morano Cálabro I 174 B2
Mörarp S 61 C2
Morasverdes E 149 B3
Morata de Jalón E 152 A2
Morata de Jiloca E 152 A2
Morata de Tajuña E 151 B4
Moratalla E 164 A3
Moravče SLO 123 A3
Moravec CZ 97 B4
Moraviţa RO 126 B3
Morávka CZ 98 B2
Moravská Třebová CZ 97 B4
Moravské Budějovice CZ 97 B3
Moravské Lieskové SK 98 C1
Moravske Toplice SLO 111 C3
Moravský-Beroun CZ 98 B1
Moravský Krumlov CZ 97 B4
Moravský Svätý Ján SK 98 C1
Morawica PL 87 B4
Morawin PL 86 A2
Morbach D 92 B3
Morbegno I 120 A2
Morbier F 105 C5
Mörbisch am See A 111 B3
Mörbylånga S 63 B4
Morcenx F 128 B2
Morciano di Romagna I 136 B1
Morcone I 170 B2
Morcuera E 151 A4
Mordelles F 101 A4
Mordoğan TR 188 A1
Moréac F 100 B3
Morebattle GB 35 C5
Morecambe GB 36 B4
Moreda
Granada E 163 A4
Oviedo E 142 A1
Morée F 103 B3
Moreles de Rey E 141 B5
Morella E 153 B3
Moreruela de los Infanzones E 149 A4
Morés E 152 A2
Móres I 178 B2
Morestel F 118 B2
Moretonhampstead GB 43 B3
Moreton-in-Marsh GB 44 B2
Moret-sur-Loing F 90 C2
Moretta I 119 C4
Moreuil F 90 B2
Morez F 105 C5
Mörfelden D 93 B4
Morgat F 100 A1
Morges CH 105 C5
Morgex I 119 B4
Morgongåva S 51 C3
Morhange F 92 C2
Morhet B 92 B1
Mori I 121 B3
Morialmé B 79 B4
Morianes P 160 B2
Moriani Plage F 180 A2
Mórichida H 111 B4
Moriles E 163 A3
Morille E 150 B2
Moringen D 82 A1
Morjärv S 196 C5
Morkarla S 51 B4
Mørke DK 59 B3
Mørkøv DK 61 D1
Morkovice-Slížany CZ 98 B1
Morlaàs F 145 A3
Morlaix F 100 A2
Morley F 91 C5
Mörlunda S 62 A3
Mormanno I 174 B1
Mormant F 90 C2
Mornant F 117 B4
Mornay-Berry F 103 B4
Morón de Almazán E 152 A1
Morón de la Frontera E 162 A2
Morović SRB 125 B5
Morozzo I 133 A3
Morpeth GB 37 A5
Morphou CY 181 A1
Mörrum S 63 B2
Morsbach D 81 B3
Mörsch D 93 C4
Mörsil S 199 B10
Morsum D 64 B1
Mørsvikbotn N 194 C6
Mortagne-au-Perche F 89 B4
Mortagne-sur-Gironde F 114 C3
Mortagne-sur-Sèvre F 114 B3
Mortágua P 148 B1
Mortain F 88 B3
Mortara I 120 B1
Morteau F 105 B5
Mortegliano I 122 B2
Mortelle I 177 A4
Mortemart F 115 B4
Mortimer's Cross GB 39 B4
Mortrée F 89 B4
Mörtschach A 109 C3
Mortsel B 79 A4
Morud DK 59 C3
Morwenstow GB 42 B2
Moryń PL 74 B3
Morzeszczyn PL 69 B3
Morzewo PL 69 B4
Morzine F 118 A3
Mosbach D 93 B5
Mosbjerg DK 58 A3
Mosby N 53 B3
Mosca P 149 A3
Moscavide P 154 C1
Moščenica HR 124 B2
Mošćenice HR 123 B3
Moščenicka Draga HR 123 B3
Mosciano Sant'Ángelo I 136 C2
Mościsko PL 85 B4
Moscow = Moskva RUS 9 E10
Mosina PL 75 B5
Mosjøen N 195 E4
Moskog N 46 A3
Moskorzew PL 87 B3
Moskosel S 196 D2
Moskuvarra FIN 197 B9
Moskva = Moscow RUS 9 E10
Moslavina Podravska HR 125 B3
Moşniţa Nouă RO 126 B3
Moso in Passíria I 108 C2
Mosonmagyaróvár H 111 B4
Mošorin SRB 126 B2
Mošovce SK 98 C2
Mosqueruela E 153 B3
Moss N 54 A1
Mossfellsbær IS 190 C4
Mössingen D 93 C5
Møsstrand N 47 C5
Most CZ 83 B5
Mosta M 175 C3
Mostar BIH 139 B3
Mosterhamn N 52 A1
Mostki PL 75 B4
Most na Soči SLO 122 A2
Móstoles E 151 B4
Mostová SK 111 A4
Mostowo PL 68 A1
Mostuéjouls F 130 A2
Mosty PL 75 A3
Mostys'ka UA 13 D5
Mosvik N 199 B7
Mota del Cuervo E 158 B1
Mota del Marqués E 150 A2
Motala S 55 B6
Motherwell GB 35 C4
Möthlow D 74 B1
Motilla del Palancar E 158 B2
Motnik SLO 123 A3
Motovun HR 122 B2
Motril E 163 B4
Motta I 121 B4
Motta di Livenza I 122 B1
Motta Montecorvino I 170 B3
Motta Visconti I 120 B1
Mottisfont GB 44 B2
Móttola I 173 B3
Mou DK 58 B3
Mouchard F 105 C4
Moudon CH 106 C1
Moudros GR 183 D7
Mougins F 132 B2
Mouilleron en-Pareds F 114 B3
Mouliherne F 102 B2
Moulinet F 133 B3
Moulins F 104 C2
Moulins-Engilbert F 104 C2
Moulins-la-Marche F 89 B4
Moulismes F 115 B4
Moult F 89 A3
Mountain Ash GB 39 C3
Mountbellew IRL 28 A3
Mountfield GB 27 B3
Mountmellick IRL 30 A1
Mountrath IRL 30 A1
Mountsorrel GB 40 C2
Moura P 160 A2
Mourão P 155 C3
Mourenx F 145 A3
Mouriés F 131 B3
Mourmelon-le-Grand F 91 B4
Mouronho P 148 B1
Mourujärvi FIN 197 C11
Mouscron B 78 B3
Mousehole GB 42 B1
Moussac F 131 B3
Moussey F 92 C2
Mousteru F 100 A2
Moustey F 128 B2
Moustiers-Ste Marie F 132 B2
Mouthe F 105 C5
Mouthier-Haute-Pierre F 105 B5
Mouthoumet F 146 B3
Moutier CH 106 B2
Moûtiers F 118 B3
Moutiers-les-Mauxfaits F 114 B2
Mouy F 90 B2
Mouzaki GR 182 D3
Mouzon F 91 B5
Møvik N 46 B2
Moville IRL 27 A3
Moy
Highland GB 32 D2
Tyrone GB 27 B4
Moycullen IRL 28 A2
Moyenmoutier F 92 C2
Moyenvic F 92 C2
Moylough IRL 28 A3
Mózar E 141 C5
Mozhaysk RUS 9 E10
Mozirje SLO 123 A3
Mözs H 112 C2
Mozzanica I 120 B2
Mramorak SRB 127 C2
Mrčajevci SRB 127 D2
Mrkonjić Grad BIH 138 A3
Mrkopalj HR 123 B3
Mrocza PL 76 A2
Mroczeń PL 86 A1
Mroczno PL 69 B4
Mrzezyno PL 67 B4
Mšec CZ 84 B1
Mšeno CZ 84 B2
Mstów PL 86 B3
Mstsislaw BY 13 A9
Mszana Dolna PL 99 B4
Mszczonów PL 77 C5
Muć HR 138 B2
Múccia I 136 B2
Much D 80 B3
Mücheln D 83 A3
Much Marcle GB 39 C4
Muchów PL 85 A4
Much Wenlock GB 39 B4
Mucientes E 142 C2
Muckross IRL 29 B2
Mucur TR 23 B8
Muda P 160 B1
Mudanya TR 186 B3
Mudau D 93 B5
Müden D 72 B3
Mudersbach D 81 B3
Mudurnu TR 187 B6
Muel E 152 A2
Muelas del Pan E 149 A4
Muess D 73 A4
Muff IRL 27 A3
Mugardos E 140 A2
Muge P 154 B2
Mügeln
Sachsen D 83 A5
Sachsen-Anhalt D 83 A5
Múggia I 122 B2
Mugnano I 135 B5
Mugron F 128 C2
Mugueimes E 140 C3
Muhi H 113 B4
Mühlacker D 93 C4
Mühlbach am Hochkönig A 109 B4
Mühlberg
Brandenburg D 83 A5
Thüringen D 82 B2
Mühldorf
A 109 C4
D 95 C4
Muhleberg CH 106 C2
Mühleim D 107 A3
Muhlen-Eichsen D 65 C4
Mühlhausen
Bayern D 94 B2
Thüringen D 82 A2
Mühltroff D 83 B3
Muhos FIN 3 D10
Muhr A 109 B4
Muine Bheag IRL 30 B2
Muirkirk GB 36 A2
Muir of Ord GB 32 D2
Muirteira P 154 B1
Mukacheve UA 12 D5
Muker GB 37 B4
Mula E 165 A3
Muğla TR 188 B3
Mulben GB 32 D3
Mulegns CH 107 C4
Mules I 108 C2
Mülheim D 80 A2
Mulhouse F 106 B2
Muljava SLO 123 B3
Mullanys Cross IRL 26 B2
Müllheim D 106 B2
Mullhyttan S 55 A5
Mullinavat IRL 30 B1
Mullingar IRL 30 A1
Mullion GB 42 B1
Müllrose D 74 B3
Mullsjö S 60 B3
Mulseryd S 60 B3
Munaðarnes IS 190 A4
Munana E 150 B2
Muñás E 141 A4
Münchberg D 83 B3
Müncheberg D 74 B3
München = Munich D 108 A2
Munchen-Gladbach = Mönchengladbach D 80 A2
Münchhausen D 81 B4
Mundaka E 143 A4
Münden D 82 A1
Munderfing A 109 A4
Munderkingen D 107 A4
Mundesley GB 41 C5
Munera E 158 B1
Mungia E 143 A4
Munich = München D 108 A2
Muñico E 150 B2
Muniesa E 153 A3
Munka-Ljungby S 61 C2
Munkebo DK 59 C3
Munkedal S 54 B2
Munkflohögen S 199 B11
Munkfors S 49 C5
Munktorp S 56 A2
Münnerstadt D 82 B2
Muñopepe E 150 B3
Muñotello E 150 B2
Münsingen
CH 106 C2
D 94 C1
Munsö S 57 A3
Münster
CH 106 C3
Hessen D 93 B4
Munster D 72 B3
Münster D 71 C4
Munster F 106 A2
Muntibar E 143 A4
Münzkirchen A 96 C1
Muodoslompolo S 196 B6
Muonio FIN 196 B6
Muotathal CH 107 C3
Muradiye TR 186 D2
Murakeresztúr H 124 A2
Murán SK 99 C4
Murano I 122 B1
Muras E 140 A3
Murat F 116 B2
Muratlı TR 186 A2
Murato F 180 A2
Murat-sur-Vèbre F 130 B1
Murau A 109 B5
Muravera I 179 C3
Murazzano I 133 A4
Murça P 148 A2
Murchante E 144 B2
Murchin D 66 C2
Murcia E 165 B3
Murczyn PL 76 B2
Mur-de-Barrez F 116 C2
Mur-de-Bretagne F 100 A2
Mur-de-Sologne F 103 B3
Mureck A 110 C2
Mürefte TR 186 B2
Muret F 146 A2
Murg CH 107 B4
Murguia E 143 B4
Muri CH 106 B3
Murias de Paredes E 141 B4
Muriedas E 143 A3
Muriel Viejo E 143 C4
Murillo de Rio Leza E 143 B4
Murillo el Fruto E 144 B2
Murjek S 196 C3
Murlaggan GB 34 B2
Murmansk RUS 3 B13
Murmashi RUS 3 B13
Murnau D 108 B2
Muro
E 167 B3
F 180 A1
Muro de Alcoy E 159 C3
Murol F 116 B2
Muro Lucano I 172 B1
Muron F 114 B3
Muros E 140 B1
Muros de Nalón E 141 A4
Murowana Goślina PL 76 B2
Mürren CH 106 C2
Murrhardt D 94 C1
Murska Sobota SLO 111 C3
Mursko Središce HR 111 C3
Murtas E 164 C1
Murten CH 106 C2
Murter HR 137 B4
Murtiçi TR 189 C6
Murtosa P 148 B1
Murtovaara FIN 197 D12
Murvica HR 137 A4
Murviel-lès-Béziers F 130 B2
Mürzsteg A 110 B2
Murzynowo PL 75 B4
Mürzzuschlag A 110 B2
Musculdy F 144 A3
Muskö S 57 A4
Mušov CZ 97 C4
Musselburgh GB 35 C4
Musselkanaal NL 71 B4
Mussidan F 129 A3
Mussomeli I 176 B2
Musson B 92 B1
Mussy-sur-Seine F 104 B3
Mustafakemalpaşa TR 186 B3
Muszaki PL 77 A5
Muszyna PL 99 B4
Mut TR 23 C7
Muta SLO 110 C2
Muthill GB 35 B4
Mutné SK 99 B3
Mutriku E 143 A4
Muttalip TR 187 C5
Mutterbergalm A 108 B2
Muurola FIN 197 C8
Muxía E 140 A1
Muxilka-Ugarte E 143 A4
Muzillac F 101 B3
Mužla SK 112 B2
Muzzano del Turgnano I 122 B2
Mybster GB 32 C3
Myckelgensjö S 200 C3
Myennes F 104 B1
Myjava SK 98 C1
Myking N 46 B2
Mykland N 53 B4
Myra N 53 B5
Myrdal N 46 B4
Myre
Nordland N 194 A6
Nordland N 194 B6
Myresjö S 62 A2
Mýri IS 191 B8
Myrtou CY 181 A2
Mysen N 54 A2
Mysłakowice PL 85 B3
Myślenice PL 99 B3
Myślibórz PL 75 B3
Mysłowice PL 86 B3
Myszków PL 86 B3
Mytishchi RUS 9 E10
Mýtna SK 99 C3
Mýtne Ludany SK 112 A2
Mýto CZ 96 B1

N

Nå N 46 B3
Naaldwijk NL 79 A4
Naantali FIN 8 B2
Naas IRL 30 A2
Nabais P 148 B2
Nabbelund S 62 A5
Nabburg D 95 B4
Načeradec CZ 96 B2
Náchod CZ 85 B4
Nacław PL 68 A1
Nadarzyce PL 75 A5
Nadarzyn PL 77 B5
Nádasd H 111 C3
Nădlac RO 126 A2
Nádudvar H 113 B5
Nadvirna UA 13 D6
Näfels CH 107 B4
Nafpaktos GR 184 A2
Nafplio GR 184 B3
Nagel D 95 B3
Nagele NL 70 B2
Naggen S 200 D2
Nagłowice PL 87 B4
Nagold D 93 C4
Nagore E 144 B2
Nagyatád H 124 A3
Nagybajom H 124 A3
Nagybaracska H 125 A4
Nagybátony H 113 B3
Nagyberény H 112 C2
Nagybörzsöny H 112 B2
Nagycenk H 111 B3
Nagycserkesz H 113 B5
Nagydorog H 112 C2
Nagyfüged H 113 B4
Nagyhersány H 125 B4
Nagyigmánd H 112 B2
Nagyiván H 113 B4
Nagykanizsa H 111 C3
Nagykáta H 113 B3
Nagykonyi H 112 C2
Nagykörös H 113 B3
Nagykörü H 113 B4
Nagylóc H 112 A3
Nagymágocs H 113 C4
Nagymányok H 125 A4
Nagymaros H 112 B2
Nagyoroszi H 112 A3
Nagyrábé H 113 B5
Nagyréde H 113 B3
Nagyszékely H 112 C2
Nagyszénás H 113 C4
Nagyszokoly H 112 C2
Nagytöke H 113 C4
Nagyvázsony H 111 C4
Nagyvenyim H 112 C2
Naharros E 152 B1
Nahe D 64 C3
Naila D 83 B3
Nailloux F 146 A2
Nailsworth GB 43 A4
Naintré F 115 B4
Nairn GB 32 D3
Najac F 129 B4
Nájera E 143 B4
Nak H 112 C2
Nakksjø N 53 A5
Nakło nad Notecią PL 76 A2
Nakskov DK 65 B4
Nalda E 143 B4
Nälden S 199 B11
Nálepkovo SK 99 C4
Nalliers F 114 B2
Nallıhan TR 187 B6
Nalzen F 146 B2
Nalžouské Hory CZ 96 B1
Namdalseid N 199 A8
Náměšť nad Oslavou CZ 97 B4
Námestovo SK 99 B3
Namnå N 49 B4
Namsos N 199 A8
Namsskogan N 199 A10
Namur B 79 B4
Namysłów PL 86 A1
Nançay F 103 B4
Nanclares de la Oca E 143 B4
Nancy F 92 C2
Nangis F 90 C3
Nannestad N 48 B3
Nant F 130 A2
Nanterre F 90 C2
Nantes F 101 B4
Nanteuil-le-Haudouin F 90 B2
Nantiat F 115 B5
Nantua F 118 A2
Nantwich GB 38 A4
Naoussa
Cyclades GR 185 B6
Imathia GR 182 C4
Napajedla CZ 98 B1
Napiwoda PL 77 A5
Naples = Nápoli I 170 C2
Nápoli = Naples I 170 C2
Nar S 57 C4
Nara N 46 A1
Naraval E 141 A4
Narberth GB 39 C2
Nærbø N 52 B1
Narbonne F 130 B1
Narbonne-Plage F 130 B2
Narbuvollen N 199 C8
Narcao I 179 C2
Nardò I 173 B4
Narkaus FIN 197 C9
Narken S 196 C5
Narmo N 48 B3
Narni I 168 A2
Naro I 176 B2
Naro Fominsk RUS 9 E10
Narón E 140 A2
Narros del Castillo E 150 B2
Narta HR 124 B2
Naruszewo PL 77 B5
Narva EST 8 C6
Narvik N 194 B8
Narzole I 133 A3
Näs FIN 51 B7
Nås S 50 B1
Näs S 57 C4
Näsåker S 200 C2
Năsăud RO 17 B6
Nasavrky CZ 97 B3
Nasbinals F 116 C3
Næsbjerg DK 59 C1
Näshull S 62 A3
Našice HR 125 B4
Nasielsk PL 77 B5
Naso I 177 A3
Nassau D 81 B3
Nassenfels D 95 C3
Nassenheide D 74 B2
Nassereith A 108 B1
Nässjö S 62 A2
Nastätten D 81 B3
Næstved DK 65 A4
Näsum S 63 B2
Näsviken S 199 B12
Natalinci SRB 127 C2
Naters CH 119 A5
Nater-Stetten D 108 A2
Nattavaara S 196 C3
Natters A 108 B2
Nattheim D 94 C2
Nättraby S 63 B3
Naturno I 108 C1
Naucelle F 130 A1
Nauders A 108 C1
Nauen D 74 B1
Naul IRL 30 A2
Naumburg D 83 A3
Naundorf D 83 B5
Naunhof D 83 A4
Naustdal N 46 A2
Nautijaur S 196 C2
Nautsi RUS 193 D13
Nava E 142 A1
Navacerrada E 151 B3
Navaconcejo E 149 B4
Nava de Arévalo E 150 B3
Nava de la Asunción E 150 A3
Nava del Rey E 150 A2
Navafriá E 151 A4
Navahermosa E 157 A3
Navahrudak BY 13 B6
Naval E 145 B4
Navalacruz E 150 B3
Navalcán E 150 B2
Navalcarnero E 151 B3
Navaleno E 143 C3
Navalmanzano E 151 A3
Navalmoral E 150 B3
Navalmoral de la Mata E 150 C2
Naválón E 159 C3
Navalonguilla E 150 B2
Navalperal de Pinares E 150 B3
Navalpino E 157 A3
Navaltalgordo E 150 B3
Navaltoril E 156 A3
Navaluenga E 150 B3
Navalvillar de Pela E 156 A2
Navan IRL 30 A2
Navaperal de Tormes E 150 B2
Navapolatsk BY 13 A8
Navarclés E 147 C2
Navarredonda de Gredos E 150 B2
Navarrenx F 144 A3
Navarrés E 159 B3
Navarrete E 143 B4
Navarrevisca E 150 B3
Navás E 147 C2
Navascués E 144 B2
Navas del Madroño E 155 B4

Navas del Rey E 151 B3
Navas del Sepillar E 163 A3
Navas de Oro E 150 A3
Navas de San Juan E 157 B4
Navasfrias E 149 B3
Nave I 120 B3
Nave de Haver P 149 B3
Nävekvarn S 56 B2
Navelli I 169 A3
Navenby GB 40 B3
Näverkärret S 56 A1
Naverstad S 54 B2
Navés E 147 C2
Navezuelas E 156 A2
Navia E 141 A4
Navia de Suarna E 141 B4
Navilly F 105 C4
Nävodari RO 17 C8
Naxos GR 185 B6
Nay F 145 A3
Nazaré P 154 B1
Nazarje SLO 123 A3
Nazilli TR 188 B3
Nazza D 82 A2
Nea Anchialos GR 182 D4
Nea Epidavros GR 184 B4
Nea Flippias GR 182 D2
Nea Kalikratia GR 183 C5
Nea Makri GR 185 A4
Nea Moudania GR 183 C5
Neap GB 33 A5
Nea Peramos GR 183 C6
Neapoli
Kozani GR 182 C3
Kriti GR 185 D6
Lakonia GR 184 C4
Nea Stira GR 185 A5
Neath GB 39 C3
Nea Visa GR 186 A1
Nea Zichni GR 183 B5
Nebljusi HR 124 C1
Neblo SLO 122 A2
Nebolchy RUS 9 C8
Nebra D 82 A3
Nebreda E 143 C3
Nechanice CZ 84 B3
Neckargemünd D 93 B4
Neckarsulm D 94 B1
Neda E 140 A2
Neded SK 112 A1
Nedelišće HR 124 A2
Nederweert NL 80 A1
Nedreberg N 48 B3
Nedre Gärdsjö S 50 B2
Nedre Soppero S 196 A4
Nedstrand N 52 A1
Nedvědice CZ 97 B4
Nędza PL 86 B2
Neede NL 71 B3
Needham Market GB 45 A5
Needingworth GB 44 A3
Neermoor D 71 A4
Neeroeteren B 80 A1
Neerpelt B 79 A5
Neesen D 72 B1
Neetze D 73 A3
Nefyn GB 38 B2
Negotin SRB 16 C5
Negotino MK 182 B4
Negrar I 121 B3
Negredo E 151 A5
Negreira E 140 B2
Nègrepelisse F 129 B4
Negru Vodă RO 17 D8
Negueira de Muñiz E 141 A4
Neheim D 81 A3
Neila E 143 B4
Néive I 119 C5
Nejdek CZ 83 B4
Nekla PL 76 B2
Neksø DK 67 A4
Nelas P 148 B2
Nelaug N 53 B4
Nelidovo RUS 9 D8
Nelim FIN 193 D12
Nellingen D 94 C1
Nelson GB 40 B1
Neman RUS 12 A5
Nemea GR 184 B3
Nemesgörzsöny H 111 B4
Nemeskér H 111 B3
Nemesnádudvar H 125 A5
Nemesszalók H 111 B4
Németkér H 112 C2
Nemours F 103 A4
Nemška Loka SLO 123 B4
Nemšová SK 98 C2
Nenagh IRL 28 B3
Nenince SK 112 A3
Nenita GR 185 A7
Nenzing A 107 B4
Neochori GR 182 D3
Neo Chori GR 184 A2
Neon Petritsi GR 183 B5
Nepi I 168 A2
Nepomuk CZ 96 B1
Nérac F 129 B3
Neratovice CZ 84 B2
Nerchau D 83 A4
Néré F 115 C3
Neresheim D 94 C2
Nereto I 136 C2
Nerezine HR 123 C3
Nerežišća HR 138 B2
Neringa LT 12 A4
Néris-les Bains F 116 A2
Nerito I 169 A3
Nerja E 163 B4
Néronde F 117 B4
Nérondes F 103 C4
Nerpio E 164 A2
Nersingen D 94 C2
Nerva E 161 B3
Nervesa della Battáglia I 121 B5
Nervi I 134 A2
Nes
Buskerud N 48 B1
Hedmark N 48 B2
NL 70 A2
Sogn og Fjordane N 46 A3
Sør-Trøndelag N 198 B6
Nesbyen N 47 B6
Neset N 199 D7
Nesflaten N 52 A2
Nesjahverfi IS 191 C10
Neskaupstaður IS 191 B12
Nesland N 53 A3
Neslandsvatn N 53 B5
Nesle F 90 B2
Nesna N 195 D4
Nesoddtangen N 48 C2
Nesovice CZ 98 B1
Nesselwang D 108 B1
Nesslau CH 107 B4
Nessmersiel D 71 A4
Nesso I 120 B2
Nesterov UA 13 C5
Nestorio GR 182 C3
Nesttun N 46 B2
Nesvady SK 112 B2
Nesvatnstemmen N 53 B4
Nether Stowey GB 43 A3
Netland N 52 B2
Netolice CZ 96 B2
Netphen D 81 B4
Netstal CH 107 B4
Nettancourt F 91 C4
Nettetal D 80 A2
Nettlingen D 72 B3
Nettuno I 168 B2
Neualbenreuth D 95 B4
Neubeckum D 81 A4
Neubrandenburg D 74 A2
Neubruchhausen D 72 B1
Neubukow D 65 B4
Neuburg D 94 C3
Neuchâtel CH 106 C1
Neu Darchau D 73 A3
Neudau A 111 B3
Neudietendorf D 82 B2
Neudorf D 93 B4
Neuenbürg D 93 C4
Neuenburg D 71 A4
Neuendorf D 66 B2
Neuenhagen D 74 B2
Neuenhaus D 71 B3
Neuenkirchen
Niedersachsen D 71 B5
Niedersachsen D 72 A2
Nordrhein-Westfalen D 71 B4
Nordrhein-Westfalen D 81 B3
Neuenrade D 81 A3
Neuenwalde D 64 C1
Neuerburg D 92 A2
Neufahrn
Bayern D 95 C3
Bayern D 95 C4
Neuf-Brisach F 106 A2
Neufchâteau
B 92 B1
F 92 C1
Neufchâtel-en-Bray F 90 B1
Neufchâtel-sur-Aisne F 91 B4
Neuflize F 91 B4
Neugersdorf D 84 B2
Neuhardenberg D 74 B3
Neuharlingersiel D 71 A4
Neuhaus
Bayern D 95 B3
Bayern D 96 C1
Niedersachsen D 64 C2
Niedersachsen D 73 A3
Niedersachsen D 81 A5
Neuhaus a Rennweg D 82 B3
Neuhausen
CH 107 B3
D 83 B5
Neuhausen ob Eck D 107 B3
Neuhof
Bayern D 94 B2
Hessen D 82 B1
Neuhofen an der Krems A 110 A1
Neuillé-Pont-Pierre F 102 B2
Neuilly-en-Thelle F 90 B2
Neuilly-le-Réal F 104 C2
Neuilly-l'Évêque F 105 B4
Neuilly-St Front F 90 B3
Neu-Isenburg D 93 A4
Neukalen D 66 C1
Neu Kaliss D 73 A4
Neukirch D 84 A2
Neukirchen
A 109 A4
Hessen D 81 B5
Schleswig-Holstein D 64 B1
Neukirchen am Grossvenediger A 109 B3
Neukirchen bei Heiligen Blut D 95 B4
Neukloster D 65 C4
Neulengbach A 110 A2
Neulise F 117 B4
Neu Lübbenau D 74 B2
Neum BIH 139 C3
Neumagen D 92 B2
Neumarkt D 95 B3
Neumarkt am Wallersee A 109 B4
Neumarkt im Hausruckkreis A 109 A4
Neumarkt im Mühlkreis A 96 C2
Neumarkt im Steiermark A 110 B1
Neumarkt Sankt Veit D 95 C4
Neumünster D 64 B2
Neunburg vorm Wald D 95 B4
Neung-sur-Beuvron F 103 B3
Neunkirch
Luzern CH 106 B3
Schaffhausen CH 107 B3
Neunkirchen
A 111 B3
Nordrhein-Westfalen D 80 B3
Saarland D 92 B3
Neunkirchen am Brand D 94 B3
Neuötting D 95 C4
Neupetershain D 84 A2
Neuravensburg D 107 B4
Neureut D 93 B4
Neuruppin D 74 B1
Neusäss D 94 C2
Neusiedl A 111 B3
Neuss D 80 A2
Neussargues-Moissac F 116 B2
Neustadt
Bayern D 94 B2
Bayern D 95 B4
Bayern D 95 C3
Brandenburg D 73 B5
Hessen D 81 B5
Niedersachsen D 72 B2
Rheinland-Pfalz D 93 B4
Sachsen D 84 A2
Schleswig-Holstein D 65 B3
Thüringen D 82 B3
Thüringen D 83 B3
Neustadt-Glewe D 73 A4
Neustift im Stubaital A 108 B2
Neustrelitz D 74 A2
Neutal A 111 B3
Neutrebbin D 74 B3
Neu-Ulm D 94 C2
Neuves-Maisons F 92 C2
Neuvic
Corrèze F 116 B2
Dordogne F 129 A3
Neuville-aux-Bois F 103 A4
Neuville-de-Poitou F 115 B4
Neuville-les-Dames F 117 A5
Neuville-sur-Saône F 117 B4
Neuvy-le-Roi F 102 B2
Neuvy-Santour F 104 A2
Neuvy-St Sépulchre F 103 C3
Neuvy-sur-Barangeon F 103 B4
Neuwied D 80 B3
Neuzelle D 74 B3
Névache F 118 B3
Neveklov CZ 96 B2
Nevel RUS 9 D6
Neverfjord N 192 B7
Nevers F 104 C2
Nevesinje BIH 139 B4
Névez F 100 B2
Nevlunghavn N 53 B5
Nevşehir TR 23 B8
New Abbey GB 36 B3
New Aberdour GB 33 D4
New Alresford GB 44 B2
Newark-on-Trent GB 40 B3
Newbiggin-by-the-Sea GB 37 A5
Newbliss IRL 27 B3
Newborough GB 38 A2
Newbridge IRL 30 A2
Newbridge on Wye GB 39 B3
Newburgh
Aberdeenshire GB 33 D4
Fife GB 35 B4
Newbury GB 44 B2
Newby Bridge GB 36 B4
Newcastle GB 27 B5
Newcastle Emlyn GB 39 B2
Newcastleton GB 37 A4
Newcastle-under-Lyme GB 40 B1
Newcastle upon Tyne GB 37 B5
Newcastle West IRL 29 B2
Newchurch GB 39 B3
New Costessey GB 41 C5
New Cumnock GB 36 A2
Newent GB 39 C4
New Galloway GB 36 A2
Newham GB 45 B4
Newhaven GB 45 C4
Newington GB 45 B5
Newinn IRL 29 B4
Newlyn GB 42 B1
Newmachar GB 33 D4
Newmarket
Suffolk GB 45 A4
Western Isles GB 31 A2
IRL 29 B3
Newmarket-on-Fergus IRL 28 B3
New Mills GB 40 B2
New Milton GB 44 C2
New Pitsligo GB 33 D4
Newport
Isle of Wight GB 44 C2
Newport GB 39 C4
Pembrokeshire GB 39 B2
Telford & Wrekin GB 38 B4
Mayo IRL 28 A2
Tipperary IRL 29 B3
Newport-on-Tay GB 35 B5
Newport Pagnell GB 44 A3
Newquay GB 42 B1
New Quay GB 39 B2
New Radnor GB 39 B3
New Romney GB 45 C4
New Ross IRL 30 B2
Newry GB 27 B4
New Scone GB 35 B4
Newton Abbot GB 43 B3
Newton Arlosh GB 36 B3
Newton Aycliffe GB 37 B5
Newton Ferrers GB 42 B2
Newtonhill GB 33 D4
Newtonmore GB 32 D2
Newton Stewart GB 36 B2
Newtown
Herefordshire GB 39 B4
Powys GB 39 B3
Newtownabbey GB 27 B5
Newtownards GB 27 B5
Newtownbutler GB 27 B3
Newtown Cunningham IRL 27 B3
Newtownhamilton GB 27 B4
Newtownmountkennedy IRL 30 A2
Newtown St Boswells GB 35 C5
Newtown Sands IRL 29 B2
Newtownstewart GB 27 B3
Nexon F 115 C5
Neyland GB 39 C2
Nibbiano I 120 C2
Nibe DK 58 B2
Nicastro I 175 C2
Niccone I 135 B5
Nice F 133 B3
Nickelsdorf A 111 B4
Nicolosi I 177 B4
Nicosia
CY 181 A2
I 177 B3
Nicótera I 175 C1
Nidda D 81 B5
Niğde TR 23 C8
Nidzica PL 77 A5
Niebla E 161 B3
Nieborów PL 77 B5
Niebüll D 64 B1
Niechanowo PL 76 B2
Niechorze PL 67 B4
Niedalino PL 67 B5
Niederaula D 82 B1
Niederbipp CH 106 B2
Niederbronn-les-Bains F 93 C3
Niederfischbach D 81 B3
Niedergörsdorf D 74 C1
Niederkrüchten D 80 A2
Niederndorf A 108 B3
Nieder-Olm D 93 B4
Niedersachswerfen D 82 A2
Niederstetten D 94 B1
Niederurnen CH 107 B4
Niederwölz A 110 B1
Niedoradz PL 85 A3
Niedzica PL 99 B4
Niegosławice PL 85 A3
Nieheim D 81 A5
Niemcza PL 85 B4
Niemegk D 74 B1
Niemisel S 196 C5
Niemodlin PL 85 B5
Nienburg
Niedersachsen D 72 B2
Sachsen-Anhalt D 83 A3
Niepołomice PL 99 A4
Nierstein D 93 B4
Niesky D 84 A2
Niestronno PL 76 B2
Nieświń PL 87 A4
Nieszawa PL 76 B3
Nieul-le-Dolent F 114 B2
Nieul-sur-Mer F 114 B2
Nieuw-Amsterdam NL 71 B3
Nieuw-Buinen NL 71 B3
Nieuwegein NL 70 B2
Nieuwe Niedorp NL 70 B1
Nieuwe-Pekela NL 71 A3
Nieuwerkerken B 79 B5
Nieuwe-schans NL 71 A4
Nieuwolda NL 71 A3
Nieuwpoort B 78 A2
Nieuw-Weerdinge NL 71 B3
Nigrita GR 183 C5
Nigüelas E 163 B4
Níjar E 164 C2
Nijemci HR 125 B5
Nijkerk NL 70 B2
Nijlen B 79 A4
Nijmegen NL 80 A1
Nijverdal NL 71 B3
Nikel RUS 193 C14
Nikinci SRB 127 C1
Nikiti GR 183 C5
Nikitsch A 111 B3
Nikkaluokta S 196 B2
Nikla H 111 C4
Niklasdorf A 110 B2
Nikšić MNE 139 C4
Nilivaara S 196 B4
Nîmes F 131 B3
Nimis I 122 A2
Nimtofte DK 58 B3
Nin HR 137 A4
Nindorf D 64 B2
Ninemilehouse IRL 30 B1
Ninove B 79 B4
Niort F 114 B3
Niš SRB 16 D4
Nisa P 155 B3
Niscemi I 177 B3
Niskala FIN 197 D10
Nissafors S 60 B3
Nissan-lez-Ensérune F 130 B2
Nissedal N 53 A4
Nissumby DK 58 B1
Nisterud N 53 A5
Niton GB 44 C2
Nitra SK 98 C2
Nitrianske-Pravno SK 98 C2
Nitrianske Rudno SK 98 C2
Nitry F 104 B2
Nittedal N 48 B2
Nittenau D 95 B4
Nittendorf D 95 B3
Nivala FIN 3 E9
Nivelles B 79 B4
Nivnice CZ 98 C1
Nižná SK 99 B3
Nižná Boca SK 99 C3
Nižne Repaše SK 99 B4
Nizza Monferrato I 119 C5
Njarðvík IS 190 D3
Njegůsevo SRB 126 B1
Njivice HR 123 B3
Njurundabommen S 200 D3
Njutånger S 200 E3
Noailles F 90 B2
Noain E 144 B2
Noale I 121 B5
Noalejo E 163 A4
Noblejas E 151 C4
Noceda E 141 B4
Nocera Inferiore I 170 C2
Nocera Terinese I 175 B2
Nocera Umbra I 136 B1
Noceto I 120 C3
Noci I 173 B3
Nociglia I 173 B4
Nodeland N 53 B3
Nödinge S 60 B2
Nods F 105 B5
Noé F 146 A2
Noépoli I 174 A2
Noeux-les-Mines F 78 B2
Noez E 157 A3
Nogales E 155 C4
Nogara I 121 B4
Nogarejas E 141 B4
Nogaro F 128 C2
Nogent F 105 A4
Nogent l'Artaud F 90 C3
Nogent-le-Roi F 90 C1
Nogent-le-Rotrou F 89 B4
Nogent-sur-Seine F 91 C3
Nogent-sur-Vernisson F 103 B4
Nogersund S 63 B2
Noguera E 152 B2
Noguerones E 163 A3
Nohfelden D 92 B3
Nohn D 80 B2
Noia E 140 B2
Noicáttaro I 173 A2
Noirétable F 117 B3
Noirmoutier-en-l'Île F 114 A1
Noja E 143 A3
Nojewo PL 75 B5
Nokia FIN 8 B3
Nol S 60 B2
Nola I 170 C2
Nolay F 104 C3
Noli I 133 A4
Nolnyra S 51 B4
Nombela E 150 B3
Nomeny F 92 C2
Nomexy F 92 C2
Nonancourt F 89 B5
Nonant-le-Pin F 89 B4
Nonántola I 121 C4
Nonaspe E 153 A4
None I 119 C4
Nontron F 115 C4
Nonza F 180 A2
Noordhorn NL 71 A3
Noordwijk NL 70 B1
Noordwijkerhout NL 70 B1
Noordwolde NL 70 B3
Noppikoski S 50 A1
Nora S 55 A6
Nørager DK 58 B2
Norberg S 50 B2
Norboda S 51 B5
Nórcia I 136 C2
Nordagutu N 53 A5
Nordanås S 200 B4
Nordausques F 78 B2
Nordborg DK 64 A2
Nordby
Aarhus Amt. DK 59 C3
Ribe Amt. DK 59 C1
Norddeich D 71 A4
Norddorf D 64 B1
Norden D 71 A4
Nordenham D 72 A1
Norderhov N 48 B2
Norderney D 71 A4
Norderstapel D 64 B2
Norderstedt D 64 C3
Nordfjord N 193 B14
Nordfjordeid N 198 D3
Nordfold N 194 C6
Nordhalben D 82 B3
Nordhausen D 82 A2
Nordheim vor der Rhön D 82 B2
Nordholz D 64 C1
Nordhorn D 71 B4
Nordingrå S 200 D4
Nordkjosbotn N 192 C3
Nordli N 199 A10
Nördlingen D 94 C2
Nordmaling S 200 C5
Nordmark S 49 C6
Nordmela N 194 A6
Nord-Odal N 48 B3
Nordre Osen N 48 A3
Nordsinni N 48 B1
Nørdstedalsseter N 198 D4
Nordstemmen D 72 B2
Nordvågen N 193 B10
Nordwalde D 71 B4
Noreña E 142 A1
Noresund N 48 B1
Norg NL 71 A3
Norheimsund N 46 B3
Norie S 63 B2
Norma I 169 B2
Nornäs S 49 A5
Norrahammar S 62 A2
Norråker S 200 B1
Norrala S 51 A3
Norra Vi S 62 A3
Nørre Aaby DK 59 C2
Nørre Alslev DK 65 B4
Nørre Lyndelse DK 59 C3
Nørre Nebel DK 59 C1
Norrent-Fontes F 78 B2
Nørre Snede DK 59 C2
Nørresundby DK 58 A2
Nørre Vorupør DK 58 B1
Norrfjärden S 196 D4
Norrhed S 196 C3
Norrhult Klavreström S 62 A3
Norrköping S 56 B2
Norrskedika S 51 B5
Norrsundet S 51 B4
Norrtälje S 57 A4
Nors DK 58 A1
Norsbron S 55 A4
Norsholm S 56 B1
Norsjö S 200 B5
Nörten-Hardenberg D 82 A1
Northallerton GB 37 B5
Northampton GB 44 A3
North Berwick GB 35 B5
North Charlton GB 37 A5
Northeim D 82 A2
Northfleet GB 45 B4
North Frodingham GB 40 B3
North Kessock GB 32 D2
Northleach GB 44 B2
North Molton GB 42 A3
North Petherton GB 43 A3
Northpunds GB 33 B5
North Somercotes GB 41 B4
North Tawton GB 42 B3
North Thoresby GB 41 B3
North Walsham GB 41 C5
Northwich GB 38 A4
Norton GB 40 A3
Nortorf D 64 B2
Nort-sur-Erdre F 101 B4
Nörvenich D 80 B2
Norwich GB 41 C5
Norwick GB 33 A6
Nøsen N 47 B5
Nossa Senhora do Cabo P 154 C1
Nossebro S 55 B3
Nössemark S 54 A2
Nossen D 83 A5
Notaresco I 169 A3
Noto I 177 C4
Notodden N 53 A5
Nottingham GB 40 C2
Nottuln D 71 C4
Nouan-le-Fuzelier F 103 B4
Nouans-les-Fontaines F 103 B3
Nougaroulet F 129 C3
Nouvion F 78 B1
Nouzonville F 91 B4
Nova H 111 C3
Nová Baňa SK 98 C2
Nová Bystrica SK 99 B3
Nová Bystřice CZ 97 B3
Nova Crnja SRB 126 B2
Novaféltria I 135 B5
Nova Gorica SLO 122 B2
Nova Gradiška HR 124 B3
Nováky SK 98 C2
Novalaise F 118 B2
Novales E 145 B3
Nova Levante I 108 C2
Novalja HR 137 A3
Nová Paka CZ 84 B3
Nova Pazova SRB 127 C2
Nová Pec CZ 96 C1
Novara I 120 B1
Novara di Sicilia I 177 A4
Nova Siri I 174 A2
Novate Mezzola I 120 A2
Nova Topola BIH 124 B3
Novaya Ladoga RUS 9 B8
Nova Zagora BG 17 D6
Nové Hrady CZ 96 C2
Novelda E 165 A4
Novellara I 121 C3
Nové Město SK 98 C1
Nové Město nad Metují CZ 85 B4
Nové Město na Moravě CZ 97 B4
Nové Město pod Smrkem CZ 84 B3
Nové Mitrovice CZ 96 B1
Noventa di Piave I 122 B1
Noventa Vicentina I 121 B4
Novés E 151 B3
Noves F 131 B3
Nové Sady SK 98 C1
Novés de Segre E 147 B2
Nové Strašeci CZ 84 B1
Nové Zámky SK 112 B2
Novgorod RUS 9 C7
Novi Bečej SRB 126 B2
Novi di Módena I 121 C3
Novigrad
Istarska HR 122 B2
Zadarsko-Kninska HR 137 A4
Novigrad Podravski HR 124 A2
Novi Kneževac SRB 126 A2
Novi Lígure I 120 C1
Noville B 92 A1
Novi Marof HR 124 A2
Novion-Porcien F 91 B4
Novi Pazar
BG 17 D7
SRB 16 D4
Novi Sad SRB 126 B1
Novi Slankamen SRB 126 B2
Novi Travnik BIH 139 A3
Novi Vinodolski HR 123 B3
Novohrad-Volynskyy UA 13 C7
Novo Mesto SLO 123 B4
Novo Miloševo SRB 126 B2
Novorzhev RUS 9 D6
Novo Selo BIH 125 B3
Novoselytsya UA 17 A7
Novosokolniki RUS 9 D6
Novoveská Huta SK 99 C4
Novovolynsk UA 13 C6
Novska HR 124 B2
Nový Bor CZ 84 B2
Nový Bydžov CZ 84 B3
Novy-Chevrières F 91 B4
Novy Dwór Mazowiecki PL 77 B5
Nový-Hrozenkov CZ 98 B2
Nový Jičín CZ 98 B2
Novy Knin CZ 96 B2
Nowa Cerekwia PL 86 B1
Nowa Dęba PL 87 B5
Nowa Karczma PL 68 A3
Nowa Kościoł PL 85 A3
Nowa Ruda PL 85 B4
Nowa Słupia PL 87 B5
Nowa Sól PL 85 A3
Nowa Wieś PL 69 B4
Nowa-Wieś Wielka PL 76 B3
Nowe PL 69 B3
Nowe Brzesko PL 87 B4
Nowe Grudze PL 77 B4
Nowe Kiejkuty PL 77 A6
Nowe Miasteczko PL 85 A3
Nowe Miasto
Mazowieckie PL 77 B5
Mazowieckie PL 87 A4
Nowe Miasto Lubawskie PL 69 B4
Nowe Miasto nad Wartą PL 76 B2
Nowe Skalmierzyce PL 86 A2
Nowe Warpno PL 74 A3
Nowica PL 69 A4
Nowogard PL 75 A4
Nowogród Bobrzanski PL 84 A3
Nowogrodziec PL 84 A3
Nowosolna PL 86 A3
Nowy Dwór Gdański PL 69 A4
Nowy Korczyn PL 87 B4
Nowy Sącz PL 99 B4
Nowy Staw PL 69 A4
Nowy Targ PL 99 B4
Nowy Tomyśl PL 75 B5
Nowy Wiśnicz PL 99 B4
Noyalo F 101 B3
Noyal-Pontivy F 100 A3
Noyant F 102 B2
Noyelles-sur-Mer F 78 B1
Noyen-sur-Sarthe F 102 B1
Noyers F 104 B2
Noyers-sur-Cher F 103 B3
Noyers-sur-Jabron F 132 A1
Noyon F 90 B2
Nozay F 101 B4
Nuaillé F 102 B1
Nuaillé-d'Aunis F 114 B3
Nuars F 104 B2
Nubledo E 141 A5
Nuéno E 145 B3
Nuestra Señora Sa Verge des Pilar E 166 C1
Nueva E 142 A2
Nueva Carteya E 163 A3
Nuevalos E 152 A2
Nuits F 104 B3
Nuits-St Georges F 105 B3

Nule I 178 B3
Nules E 159 B3
Nulvi I 178 B2
Numana I 136 B2
Numansdorp NL 79 A4
Nümbrecht D 81 B3
Nunchritz D 83 A5
Nuneaton GB 40 C2
Nunnanen FIN 196 A7
N Unnaryd S 60 B3
Nuñomoral E 149 B3
Nunspeet NL 70 B2
Nuorgam FIN 193 B11
Núoro I 178 B3
Nurallao I 179 C3
Nuremberg = Nürnberg
D 94 B3
Nurmes FIN 3 E11
Nürnberg = Nuremberg
D 94 B3
Nurri I 179 C3
Nürtingen D 94 C1
Nus I 119 B4
Nusnäs S 50 B1
Nusplingen D 107 A3
Nuštar HR 125 B4
Nuupas FIN 197 C9
Nyåker S 200 C5
Nyáregyháza H 112 B3
Nyarlörinc H 113 C3
Nyasvizh BY 13 B7
Nybble S 55 A5
Nybergsund N 49 A4
Nybøl DK 64 B2
Nyborg
DK 59 C3
S 196 D6
Nybro S 62 B3
Nybster GB 32 C3
Nyby DK 65 B5
Nye S 62 A3
Nyékládháza H 113 B4
Nyergesujfalu H 112 B2
Nyhammar S 50 B1
Nyhyttan S 55 A5
Nyírád H 111 B4
Nyirbátor H 16 B5
Nyíregyháza H 16 B4
Nyker DK 67 A3
Nykil S 56 B1
Nykirke N 48 B2
Nykøbing
Falster DK 65 B4
Vestsjællands Amt.
DK 61 D1
Nykøbing Mors DK 58 B1
Nyköping S 56 B3
Nykroppa S 55 A5
Nykvarn S 56 A3
Nykyrke S 55 B5
Nyland S 200 C3
Nylars DK 67 A3
Nymburk CZ 84 B3
Nynäshamn S 57 B3
Nyon CH 118 A3
Nyons F 131 A4
Nýřany CZ 96 B1
Nýrsko CZ 95 B5
Nyrud N 193 C13
Nysa PL 85 B5
Nysäter S 55 A3
Nyseter N 198 C5
Nyskoga S 49 B4
Nysted DK 65 B4
Nystrand N 53 A5
Nyúl H 111 B4
Nyvoll N 192 B7

O

Oadby GB 40 C2
Oakengates GB 38 B4
Oakham GB 40 C3
Oanes N 52 B2
Obalj BIH 139 B4
Oban GB 34 B2
O Barco E 141 B4
Obbola S 200 C6
Obdach A 110 B1
Obejo E 156 B3
Oberammergau D 108 B2
Oberasbach D 94 B2
Oberau D 108 B2
Oberaudorf D 108 B3
Oberbruck F 106 B1
Oberdiessbach
CH 106 C2
Oberdorf CH 106 B2
Oberdrauburg A 109 C3
Oberelsbach D 82 B2
Obere Stanz A 110 B2
Ober Grafendorf
A 110 A2
Obergünzburg D 108 B1
Obergurgl A 108 C2
Oberhausen D 80 A2
Oberhof D 82 B2
Oberkirch D 93 C4
Oberkirchen D 81 A4
Oberkochen D 94 C2
Obermassfeld-
Grimmenthal D 82 B2
Ober-Morlen D 81 B4
Obermünchen D 95 C3
Obernai F 93 C3
Obernberg A 96 C1
Obernburg D 93 B5
Oberndorf D 93 C4
Oberndorf bei Salzburg
A 109 B3
Obernkirchen D 72 B2
Oberort A 110 B2
Oberpullendorf A 111 B3
Oberriet CH 107 B4
Oberröblingen D 82 A3
Oberrot D 94 B1
Oberstaufen D 107 B5
Oberstdorf D 107 B5
Obertauern A 109 B4
Obertilliach A 109 C3
Obertraubling D 95 C4
Obertraun A 109 B4
Obertrubach D 95 B3
Obertrum A 109 B4
Oberursel D 81 B4
Obervellach A 109 C4
Oberviechtach D 95 B4
Oberwart A 111 B3
Oberwesel D 93 A3
Oberwinter D 80 B3
Oberwölzstadt A 110 B1
Oberzell D 96 C1
Obice PL 87 B4
Óbidos P 154 B1
Obing D 109 B3
Objat F 129 A4
Objazda PL 68 A2
Öblarn A 109 B5
Obninsk RUS 9 E10
O Bolo E 141 B3
Oborniki PL 75 B5
Oborniki Śląskie
PL 85 A4
Obornjača SRB 126 B1
Obrenovac SRB 127 C2
Obrež SRB 127 C1
Obrigheim D 93 B5
Obrov SLO 123 B3
Obrovac
HR 137 A4
SRB 126 B1
Obrovac Sinjski
HR 138 B2
Obruk TR 23 B7
Obrzycko PL 75 B5
Obudovac BIH 125 C4
Ocaña E 151 C4
O Carballiño E 140 B2
Occhiobello I 121 C4
Occimiano I 119 B5
Očevlja BIH 139 A4
Ochagavía E 144 B2
Ochiltree GB 36 A2
Ochla PL 84 A3
Ochotnica-Dolna
PL 99 B4
Ochotnica-Górna
PL 99 B4
Ochsenfurt D 94 B2
Ochsenhausen D 107 A4
Ochtendung D 80 B3
Ochtrup D 71 B4
Ocieka PL 87 B5
Ockelbo S 50 B3
Öckerö S 60 B1
Ocniţa MD 17 A7
O Corgo E 141 B3
Očová SK 99 C3
Ócsa H 112 B3
Öcseny H 125 A4
Öcsöd H 113 C4
Octeville F 88 A2
Ocypel PL 69 B3
Ödåkra S 61 C2
Odby DK 58 B1
Odda N 46 B3
Odder DK 59 C3
Ödeborg S 54 B2
Odeceixe P 160 B1
Odechów PL 87 A5
Odeleite P 160 B2
Odemira P 160 B1
Ödemiş TR 188 A2
Odensbacken S 56 A1
Odense DK 59 C3
Odensjö
Jönköping S 62 A2
Kronoberg S 60 C3
Oderberg D 74 B3
Oderzo I 122 B1
Odesa = Odessa
UA 17 B9
Ödeshög S 55 B5
Odessa = Odesa
UA 17 B9
Odiáxere P 160 B1
Odie GB 33 B4
Odiham GB 44 B3
Odintsovo RUS 9 E10
Odivelas P 160 A1
Odolanów PL 85 A5
Odón E 152 B2
Odorheiu Secuiesc
RO 17 B6
Odrowaz PL 87 A4
Odry CZ 98 B1
Odrzywół PL 87 A4
Ødsted DK 59 C2
Odžaci SRB 126 B1
Odžak BIH 125 B4
Oebisfelde D 73 B3
Oederan D 83 B5
Oeding D 71 C3
Oegstgeest NL 70 B1
Oelde D 81 A4
Oelsnitz D 83 B4
Oer-Erkenschwick
D 80 A3
Oerlinghausen D 72 C1
Oettingen D 94 C2
Oetz A 108 B1
Oeventrop D 81 A4
Offanengo I 120 B2
Offenbach D 81 B4
Offenburg D 93 C3
Offida I 136 C2
Offingen D 94 C2
Offranville F 89 A5
Ofte N 53 A4
Ofterschwang D 107 B5
Oggiono I 120 B2
Ogihares E 163 A4
Ogliastro Cilento I 170 C3
Ogliastro Marina I 170 C2
Ogmore-by-Sea GB 39 C3
Ogna N 52 B1
Ogre LV 8 D4
Ogrodzieniec PL 86 B3
Ogulin HR 123 B4
Ögur IS 190 A3
Ohanes E 164 B2
Ohey B 79 B5
Ohlstadt D 108 B2
Ohrdorf D 73 B3
Ohrdruf D 82 B2
Ohrid MK 182 B2
Öhringen D 94 B1
Oia E 140 B2
Oiã P 148 B1
Oiartzun E 144 A2
Oijärvi FIN 197 D8
Oilgate IRL 30 B2
Oimbra E 148 A2
Oiselay-et-Grachoux
F 105 B4
Oisemont F 90 B1
Oisterwijk NL 79 A5
Öja S 57 C4
Öje S 49 B5
Ojén E 162 B3
Ojrzeń PL 77 B5
Ojuelos Altos E 156 B2
Okalewo PL 77 A4
Okány H 113 C5
Okehampton GB 42 B2
Oklaj HR 138 B2
Økneshamn N 194 B6
Okoč SK 111 B4
Okoličné SK 99 B3
Okonek PL 68 B1
Okonin PL 69 B3
Okřisky CZ 97 B3
Oksa PL 87 B4
Oksbøl DK 59 C1
Oksby DK 59 C1
Øksfjord N 192 B6
Øksna N 48 B3
Okučani HR 124 B3
Okulovka RUS 9 C8
Ólafsfjörður IS 191 A7
Ólafsvík IS 190 C2
ÖLagnö S 57 A4
Olagüe E 144 B2
Oland N 53 B4
Olargues F 130 B1
Oława PL 85 B5
Olazagutia E 144 B1
Olbernhau D 83 B5
Ólbia I 178 B3
Olching D 108 A2
Oldbury GB 43 A4
Oldcastle IRL 27 C3
Old Deer GB 33 D4
Oldeberkoop NL 70 B3
Oldeboorn NL 70 A2
Olden N 198 D3
Oldenbrok D 71 A5
Oldenburg
Niedersachsen D 71 A5
Schleswig-Holstein
D 65 B3
Oldenzaal NL 71 B3
Olderdalen N 192 C4
Olderfjord N 193 B9
Oldersum D 71 A4
Oldervik N 192 C2
Oldham GB 40 B1
Oldisleben D 82 A3
Oldmeldrum GB 33 D4
Olea E 142 B2
Oleby S 49 B5
Olechów PL 87 A5
Oledo P 155 B3
Oléggio I 120 B1
Oleiros
Coruña E 140 A2
Coruña E 140 B1
P 154 B3
Oleksandriya UA 13 C7
Olen B 79 A4
Ølen N 52 A1
Olenegorsk RUS 3 B13
Olenino RUS 9 D8
Olesa de Montserrat
E 147 C2
Oleśnica PL 85 A5
Olešnice CZ 97 B4
Olesno PL 86 B2
Oletta F 180 A2
Olette F 146 B3
Olevsk UA 13 C7
Olfen D 80 A3
Olgiate Comasco
I 120 B1
Olginate I 120 B2
Ølgod DK 59 C1
Olgrinmore GB 32 C3
Olhão P 160 B2
Olhava FIN 197 D8
Olhavo P 154 B1
Oliana E 147 B2
Olias del Rey E 151 C4
Oliena I 178 B3
Oliete E 153 B3
Olimbos GR 188 D2
Olite E 144 B2
Oliva E 159 C3
Oliva de la Frontera
E 155 C4
Oliva de Mérida E 156 B1
Oliva de Plasencia
E 149 B3
Olivadi I 175 C2
Olival P 154 B2
Olivar E 163 B4
Olivares E 161 B3
Olivares de Duero
E 142 C2
Olivares de Júcar
E 158 B1
Oliveira de Azeméis
P 148 B1
Oliveira de Frades
P 148 B1
Oliveira do Conde
P 148 B2
Oliveira do Douro
P 148 A1
Oliveira do Hospital
P 148 B2
Olivenza E 155 C3
Olivet F 103 B3
Olivone CH 107 C3
Öljehult S 63 B3
Olkusz PL 86 B3
Ollerton GB 40 B2
Ollerup DK 65 A3
Olliergues F 117 B3
Ölmbrotorp S 56 A1
Ölme S 55 A4
Olmedilla de Alarcón
E 158 B1
Olmedillo de Roa
E 143 C3
Olmedo
E 150 A3
I 178 B2
Olmeto F 180 B1
Olmillos de Castro
E 149 A3
Olmos de Ojeda E 142 B2
Olney GB 44 A3
Ołobok PL 86 A2
Olocau del Rey E 153 B3
Olofström S 63 B2
Olomouc CZ 98 B1
Olonets RUS 9 B8
Olonne-sur-Mer F 114 B2
Olonzac F 130 B1
Oloron-Ste Marie
F 145 A3
Olost E 147 C3
Olot E 147 B3
Olovo BIH 139 A4
Olpe D 81 A3
Olsberg D 81 A4
Olsene B 79 B3
Olserud S 55 A4
Olshammar S 55 B5
Olshanka UA 13 D9
Olszanica PL 85 A3
Olsztyn
Śląskie PL 86 B3
Warmińsko-Mazurskie
PL 69 B5
Olsztynek PL 77 A5
Olszyna PL 84 A3
Olszyny PL 77 A6
Oltedal N 52 B2
Olten CH 106 B2
Olteniţa RO 17 C7
Olula del Rio E 164 B2
Ølve N 46 B2
Olvega E 144 C2
Olvera E 162 B2
Olympia GR 184 B2
Olzai I 178 B3
Omagh GB 27 B3
Omalos GR 185 D4
Omegna I 119 B5
Omiš HR 138 B2
Omišalj HR 123 B3
Ommen NL 71 B3
Omodhos CY 181 B1
Omoljica SRB 127 C2
On B 79 B5
Oña E 143 B3
Onano I 168 A1
O Näsberg S 49 B5
Oñati E 143 A4
Onda E 159 B3
Ondara E 159 C4
Ondarroa E 143 A4
Onesse-et-Laharie
F 128 B1
Oneşti RO 17 B7
Onhaye B 79 B4
Onich GB 34 B2
Onil E 159 C3
Onís E 142 A2
Önnestad S 61 C4
Onsala S 60 B2
Ontinyent E 159 C3
Ontur E 158 C2
Onzain F 103 B3
Onzonilla E 142 B1
Oostburg NL 79 A3
Oostende B 78 A2
Oosterend NL 70 A2
Oosterhout NL 79 A4
Oosterwolde NL 71 B3
Oosterzele B 79 B3
Oosthuizen NL 70 B2
Oostkamp B 78 A3
Oostmalle B 79 A4
Oost-Vlieland NL 70 A2
Oostvoorne NL 79 A4
Ootmarsum NL 71 B3
Opalenica PL 75 B5
O Páramo E 140 B3
Opařany CZ 96 B2
Opatija HR 123 B3
Opatów
Śląskie PL 86 B2
Świętokrzyskie PL 87 B5
Wielkopolskie PL 86 A2
Opatówek PL 86 A2
Opatowiec PL 87 B4
Opava CZ 98 B1
O Pedrouzo E 140 B2
Opeinde NL 70 A3
Oper Thalkirchdorf
D 107 B5
Opglabbeerk B 80 A1
Opicina I 122 B2
O Pino E 140 B2
Oplotnica SLO 123 A4
Opmeer NL 70 B1
Opochka RUS 9 D6
Opočno CZ 85 B4
Opoczno PL 87 A4
Opole PL 86 B1
Oporów PL 77 B4
O Porriño E 140 B2
Opovo SRB 127 B2
Oppach D 84 A2
Oppdal N 198 C6
Oppeby
Östergötland S 56 B1
Södermanland S 56 B2
Oppedal N 46 A2
Oppegård N 54 A1
Oppenau D 93 C4
Oppenberg A 110 B1
Oppenheim D 93 B4
Óppido Lucano I 172 B1
Óppido Mamertina
I 175 C1
Opponitz A 110 B1
Oppstad N 48 B3
Oprtalj HR 122 B2
Opsaheden S 49 B5
Ópusztaszer H 113 C4
Opuzen HR 138 B3
Ora
CY 181 B2
I 121 A4
Orada P 155 C3
Oradea RO 16 B4
Oradour-sur-Glane
F 115 C5
Oradour-sur-Vayres
F 115 C4
Oragonja SLO 122 B2
Orah BIH 139 C4
Orahova BIH 138 A3
Orahovica HR 125 B3
Orahovo BIH 124 B3
Oraison F 132 B1
Orajärvi FIN 196 C7
Orange F 131 A3
Orani I 178 B3
Oranienbaum D 83 A4
Oranienburg D 74 B2
Oranmore IRL 28 A3
Orašac SRB 127 C2
Orašje BIH 125 B4
Oravská Lesná SK 99 B3
Oravská Polhora
SK 99 B3
Oravské Veselé SK 99 B3
Oravsky-Podzámok
SK 99 B3
Orba E 159 C3
Orbacém P 148 A1
Orbais F 91 C3
Ørbæk DK 59 C3
Orbassano I 119 B4
Orbe CH 105 C5
Orbec F 89 A4
Orbetello I 168 A1
Orbetello Scalo I 168 A1
Orbigny F 103 B3
Ørby DK 59 B3
Örbyhus S 51 B4
Orce E 164 B2
Orcera E 164 A2
Orchamps-Vennes
F 105 B5
Orches F 102 C2
Orchete E 159 C3
Orchies F 78 B3
Orchowo PL 76 B3
Orcières F 118 C3
Ordes E 140 A2
Ordhead GB 33 D4
Ordino AND 146 B2
Ordizia E 144 A1
Orduña E 143 B4
Ore S 50 A2
Orea E 152 B2
Orebić HR 138 C3
Örebro S 56 A1
Öregcsertő H 112 C3
Öregrund S 51 B5
Orehoved DK 65 B4
Orellana E 156 A2
Orellana de la Sierra
E 156 A2
Ören TR 188 B2
Örencik TR 187 C4
Orestiada GR 186 A1
Organyà E 147 B2
Orgaz E 157 A4
Orgelet F 105 C4
Ørgenvika N 48 B1
Orgères-en-Beauce
F 103 A3
Orgibet F 145 B4
Orgnac-l'Aven F 131 A3
Orgon F 131 B4
Orgósolo I 178 B3
Orhaneli TR 186 C3
Orhangazi TR 187 B4
Orhei MD 17 B8
Orhomenos GR 184 A3
Oria E 164 B2
Ória I 173 B3
Origny-Ste Benoite
F 91 B3
Orihuela E 165 A4
Orihuela del Tremedal
E 152 B2
Orikum AL 182 C1
Oriola P 154 C3
Oriolo I 174 A2
Oriovac HR 125 B3
Orissaare EST 8 C3
Oristano I 179 C2
Öriszentpéter H 111 C3
Ørje N 54 A2
Orjiva E 163 B4
Orkanger N 198 B6
Örkelljunga S 61 C3
Örkény H 112 B3
Orlamünde D 82 B3
Orléans F 103 B3
Orlová CZ 98 B2
Orlovat SRB 126 B2
Ormea I 133 A3
Ormelet N 54 A1
Ormemyr N 53 A5
Ormilia GR 183 C5
Ormos GR 185 B5
Ormož SLO 124 A2
Ormskirk GB 38 A4
Ornans F 105 B5
Ornäs S 50 B2
Ørnes N 195 D4
Orneta PL 69 A5
Ørnhøj DK 59 B1
Örnö S 57 A4
Örnsköldsvik S 200 C4
Orolik HR 125 B4
Orom SRB 126 B1
Oron-la-Ville CH 106 C1
Oronsko PL 87 A4
Oropa I 119 B4
Oropesa
Castellón de la Plana
E 153 B4
Toledo E 150 C2
O Rosal E 140 C2
Orosei I 178 B3
Orosháza H 113 C4
Oroslavje HR 124 B1
Oroszlány H 112 B2
Oroszlo H 125 A4
Orotelli I 178 B3
Orozko E 143 A4
Orphir GB 33 C3
Orpington GB 45 B4
Orreaga-Roncesvalles
E 144 A2
Orrefors S 62 B3
Orrviken S 199 B11
Orsa S 50 A1
Orsara di Púglia I 171 B3
Orsay F 90 C2
Orscholz D 92 B2
Orsennes F 103 C3
Orserum S 55 B5
Orsha BY 13 A9
Orsières CH 119 A4
Örsjö S 63 B3
Ørslev DK 65 A4
Örslösa S 55 B3
Orsogna I 169 A4
Orsomarso I 174 B1
Orşova RO 16 C5
Ørsta N 198 C3
Ørsted DK 58 B3
Örsundsbro S 56 A3
Ortaca TR 188 C3
Ortakent TR 188 B2
Ortaklar TR 188 B2
Ortaköy TR 23 B8
Orta Nova I 171 B3
Orte I 168 A2
Ortenburg D 96 C1
Orth A 111 A3
Orthez F 128 C2
Ortigueira E 140 A3
Ortilla E 145 B3
Ortisei I 108 C2
Orţişoara RO 126 B3
Ortnevik N 46 A3
Orton GB 37 B4
Ortona I 169 A4
Ortrand D 84 A1
Orubica HR 124 B3
Ørum DK 58 B2
Orune I 178 B3
Orusco E 151 B4
Orvalho P 155 A3
Orvault F 101 B4
Ørvella N 53 A5
Orvieto I 168 A2
Orvínio I 169 A2
Oryahovo BG 17 D5
Orzesze PL 86 B2
Orzinuovi I 120 B2
Orzivécchi I 120 B2
Orzyny PL 77 A6
Os
Hedmark N 48 B3
Hedmark N 199 C8
Osann-Monzel D 92 B2
Osbruk S 62 A2
Øsby DK 59 C2
Osby S 61 C3
Oščadnica SK 98 B2
Oschatz D 83 A5
Oschersleben D 73 B4
Óschiri I 178 B3
Osciłowo PL 77 B5
Osdorf D 64 B3
Osečina SRB 127 C1
Osečná CZ 84 B2
Oseja de Sajambre
E 142 A1
Osek CZ 84 B1
Osen N 199 A7
Osera de Ebro E 153 A3
Osidda I 178 B3
Osie PL 69 B3
Osieczna
Pomorskie PL 68 B3
Wielkopolskie PL 75 C5
Osieczno PL 75 A4
Osiek
Kujawsko-Pomorskie
PL 76 B3
Kujawsko-Pomorskie
PL 77 A4
Pomorskie PL 69 B3
Świętokrzyskie PL 87 B5
Osiek nad Notecią
PL 76 A2
Osielsko PL 76 A3
Osijek HR 125 B4
Osilnica SLO 123 B3
Ósilo I 178 B2
Ósimo I 136 B2
Osinja BIH 125 C3
Osintorf BY 13 A9
Osipaonica SRB 127 C3
Osjaków PL 86 A2
Oskamull GB 34 B1
Oskarshamn S 62 A4
Oskarström S 60 C2
Oslany SK 98 C2
Oslavany CZ 97 B4
Ošlje HR 139 C3
Oslo N 48 C2
Øsløs DK 58 A1
Osmancık TR 23 A8
Osmaneli TR 187 B4
Ösmo S 57 B3
Osmolin PL 77 B4
Osnabrück D 71 B5
Ośno Lubuskie PL 75 B3
Osoblaha CZ 85 B5
Osor HR 123 C3
Osorno E 142 B2
Øsoyra N 46 A2
Osøyro N 46 B2
Ospakseyri IS 190 B4
Os Peares E 140 B3
Ospedaletti I 133 B3
Ospitaletto I 120 B3
Oss NL 80 A1
Ossa de Montiel E 158 C1
Ossi I 178 B2
Ossjøen N 47 B5
Ossun F 145 A3
Ostanå S 61 C4
Ostanvik S 50 A2
Ostashkov RUS 9 D8
Östavall S 200 D1
Ostbevern D 71 B4
Østborg N 199 A10
Østby N 49 A4
Osted DK 61 D1
Ostenfeld D 64 B2
Oster UA 13 C9
Øster Assels DK 58 B1
Osterburg D 73 B4
Osterburken D 94 B1
Österbybruk S 51 B4
Østerbyhavn DK 58 A4
Österbymo S 62 A3
Ostercappeln D 71 B5
Österfärnebo S 51 B3
Osterfeld D 83 A3
Österforse S 200 C3
Osterhever D 64 B1
Osterhofen D 95 C5
Osterholz-Scharmbeck
D 72 A1
Øster Hornum DK 58 B2
Øster Hurup DK 58 B3
Østerild DK 58 A1
Øster Jølby DK 58 B1
Österlövsta S 51 B4
Øster-marie DK 67 A4
Ostermiething A 109 A3
Osterode am Harz
D 82 A2
Ostersiel D 64 B1
Östersund S 199 B11
Øster Tørslev DK 58 B3
Östervåla S 51 B4
Östervallskog S 54 A2
Østervrå DK 58 A3
Osterwieck D 73 C3
Osterzell D 108 B1
Ostffyasszonyfa
H 111 B4
Östfora S 51 C4
Östhammar S 51 B5
Ostheim F 106 A2
Ostheim vor der Rhön
D 82 B2
Osthofen D 93 B4
Ostiano I 120 B3
Ostiglia I 121 B4
Ostiz E 144 B2
Östmark S 49 B4
Östnor S 50 A1
Ostojićevo SRB 126 B2
Ostra I 136 B2
Östra Amtervik S 55 A4
Östraby S 61 D3
Ostrach D 107 B4
Östra Husby S 56 B2
Östra Ljungby S 61 C3
Östra Ryd S 56 B2
Ostrau D 83 A5
Ostrava CZ 98 B2
Østre Halsen N 53 A6
Ostrhauderfehn D 71 A4
Ostritz D 84 A2
Ostróda PL 69 B4
Ostroh UA 13 C7
Ostrołęka PL 12 B4
Ostropole PL 68 B1
Ostroróg PL 75 B5
Ostrošovac BIH 124 C1
Ostrov
CZ 83 B4
RUS 8 D6
Ostrov nad Oslavou
CZ 97 B3
Ostrówek PL 86 A2
Ostrowice PL 68 A1
Ostrowiec-
Świętokrzyski PL 87 B5
Ostrowite PL 77 A4
Ostrów Mazowiecka
PL 12 B4
Ostrowo PL 76 B3
Ostrów Wielkopolski
PL 86 A1
Ostrožac BIH 139 B3
Ostrzeszów PL 86 A1
Ostseebad
Kühlungsborn D 65 B4
Ostuni I 173 B3
Osuna E 162 A2
Osvětimany CZ 98 B1
Oswestry GB 38 B3
Oświęcim PL 86 B3
Osztopán H 111 C4
Oteiza E 144 B2
Otelec RO 126 B2
Oteo E 143 A3
Oterbekk N 54 A1
Otero de Herreros
E 151 B3
Otero de O Bodas
E 141 C4
Othem S 57 C4
Otley GB 40 B2
Otmuchów PL 85 B5
Otočac HR 123 C4

Otok
Splitsko-Dalmatinska HR 138 B2
Vukovarsko-Srijemska HR 125 B4
Otoka BIH 124 C2
Otranto I 173 B4
Otrić HR 138 A2
Otricoli I 168 A2
Otrokovice CZ 98 B1
Otta N 198 D6
Ottana I 178 B3
Ottaviano I 170 C2
Ottenby S 63 B4
Ottendorf-Okrilla D 84 A1
Ottenhöfen D 93 C4
Ottenschlag A 97 C3
Ottensheim A 96 C2
Otterbach D 93 B3
Otterbäcken S 55 B5
Otterberg D 93 B3
Otterburn GB 37 A4
Otter Ferry GB 34 B2
Otterndorf D 64 C1
Ottersburg D 72 A2
Ottersweier D 93 C4
Otterup DK 59 C3
Ottery St Mary GB 43 B3
Ottignies B 79 B4
Ottmarsheim F 106 B2
Ottobeuren D 107 B5
Ottömös H 126 A1
Ottone I 120 C2
Ottsjö S 199 B10
Ottweiler D 92 B3
Otveşti RO 126 B3
Ötvöskónyi H 124 A3
Otwock PL 12 B4
Ouanne F 104 B2
Ouarville F 90 C1
Oucques F 103 B3
Oud-Beijerland NL 79 A4
Ouddorp NL 79 A3
Oudemirdum NL 70 B2
Oudenaarde B 79 B3
Oudenbosch NL 79 A4
Oudenburg B 78 A3
Oude-Pekela NL 71 A4
Oude-Tonge NL 79 A4
Oudewater NL 70 B1
Oud Gastel NL 79 A4
Oudon F 101 B4
Oue DK 58 B2
Oughterard IRL 28 A2
Ouguela P 155 B3
Ouistreham F 89 A3
Oulainen FIN 3 D9
Oulchy-le-Château F 91 B3
Oullins F 117 B4
Oulmes F 114 B3
Oulton GB 41 C5
Oulton Broad GB 41 C5
Oulu FIN 3 D9
Oulx I 119 B3
Oundle GB 40 C3
Ouranopoli GR 183 C6
Ourém P 154 B2
Ourense E 140 B3
Ourique P 160 B1
Ourol E 140 A3
Ouroux-en-Morvan F 104 B2
Ousdale GB 32 C3
Oust F 146 B2
Outakoski FIN 193 C10
Outeiro P 148 B1
Outeiro de Rei E 140 A3
Outes E 140 B2
Outokumpu FIN 9 A6
Outreau F 78 B1
Outwell GB 41 C4
Ouzouer-le-Marché F 103 B3
Ouzouer-sur-Loire F 103 B4
Ovada I 133 A4
Ovar P 148 B1
Ovelgönne D 72 A1
Overath D 80 B3
Overbister GB 33 B4
Øverbygd N 192 D3
Overdinkel NL 71 B4
Överenhörna S 56 A3
Överhalla N 199 A8
Overijse B 79 B4
Over-jerstal DK 59 C2
Overlade DK 58 B2
Överlida S 60 B2
Överö FIN 51 B7
Overpelt B 79 A5
Overton GB 38 B4
Övertorneå S 196 C6
Överum S 62 A4
Ovidiopol UA 17 B9
Oviedo E 141 A5
Oviglio I 119 C5
Ovindoli I 169 A3
Ovodda I 178 B3
Øvre Årdal N 47 A4
Øvrebygd N 52 B2
Øvre Rendal N 199 D8
Øvre Sirdal N 52 B2
Övre Soppero S 196 A4
Övre Ullerud S 55 A4
Ovruch UA 13 C8
Ovtrup DK 59 C1
Owińska PL 76 B1
Oxaback S 60 B2
Oxberg S 49 A6
Oxelösund S 56 B3
Oxenholme GB 37 B4
Oxford GB 44 B2
Oxie S 61 D3
Oxilithos GR 185 A5
Oxted GB 45 B4
Oyaca TR 187 C7
Øye N 47 A5
Øyenkilen N 54 A1
Øyer N 48 A2
Øyeren N 49 B4
Oyfiell N 53 A4
Øygärdslia N 53 B4
Oykel Bridge GB 32 D2
Øymark N 54 A2
Oyonnax F 118 A2
Øyslebø N 52 B3
Øystese N 46 B3
Oyten D 72 A2
Øyuvsbu N 52 A3
Ozaeta E 143 B4
Ozalj HR 123 B4
Ożarów PL 87 B5
Ożarów Maz PL 77 B5
Ožbalt SLO 110 C2
Ózd H 113 A4
Ožďany SK 99 C3
Ozieri I 178 B3
Ozimek PL 86 B2
Ozimica BIH 139 A4
Ozora H 112 C2
Ozorków PL 77 C4
Ozzano Monferrato I 119 B5

P

Paakkola FIN 196 D7
Paal B 79 A5
Pabianice PL 86 A3
Pacanów PL 87 B5
Paceco I 176 B1
Pachino I 177 C4
Pačir SRB 126 B1
Pack A 110 B2
Paços de Ferreira P 148 A1
Pacov CZ 96 B3
Pacsa H 111 C4
Pacy-sur-Eure F 89 A5
Paczków PL 85 B5
Padany RUS 3 E13
Padborg DK 64 B2
Padej SRB 126 B2
Padene HR 138 A2
Paderborn D 81 A4
Paderne P 160 B1
Padiham GB 40 B1
Padina SRB 126 B2
Padinska Skela SRB 127 C2
Padornelo P 148 A1
Pádova I 121 B4
Padragkút H 111 B4
Padria I 178 B2
Padrón E 140 B2
Padru I 178 B3
Padstow GB 42 B2
Padul E 163 A4
Padula I 172 B1
Paduli I 170 B2
Paesana I 119 C4
Paese I 121 B5
Pag HR 137 A4
Pagani I 170 C2
Pagánica I 169 A3
Pagánico I 135 C4
Pagl ieta I 169 A4
Pagny-sur-Moselle F 92 C2
Páhi H 112 C3
Pahkakumpu FIN 197 C11
Pahl D 108 B2
Paide EST 8 C4
Paignton GB 43 B3
Pailhès F 146 A2
Paimboeuf F 101 B3
Paimpol F 100 A2
Paimpont F 101 A3
Painswick GB 43 A4
Painten D 95 C3
Paisley GB 34 C3
Pajala S 196 B6
Pajares E 141 A5
Pajares de los Oteros E 142 B1
Pajęczno PL 86 A2
Páka H 111 C3
Pakość PL 76 B3
Pakosławice PL 85 B5
Pakoštane HR 137 B4
Pakrac HR 124 B3
Paks H 112 C2
Palacios de la Sierra E 143 C3
Palaciòs de la Valduerna E 141 B5
Palacios del Sil E 141 B4
Palacios de Sanabria E 141 B4
Palaciosrubios E 150 A2
Palafrugell E 147 C4
Palagiano I 173 B3
Palagonía I 177 B3
Paláia I 135 B3
Palaiokastritsa GR 182 D1
Palaiseau F 90 C2
Palamas GR 182 D4
Palamós E 147 C4
Påläng S 196 D5
Palanga LT 8 E2
Palanzano I 134 A3
Palárikovo SK 112 A2
Palas de Rei E 140 B3
Palata I 170 B2
Palau I 178 A3
Palavas-les-Flots F 131 B2
Palazuelos de la Sierra E 143 B3
Palazzo Adriano I 176 B2
Palazzo del Pero I 135 B4
Palazzolo Acréide I 177 B3
Palazzolo sull Oglio I 120 B2
Palazzo San Gervásio I 172 B1
Palazzuolo sul Senio I 135 A4
Paldiski EST 8 C4
Pale BIH 139 B4
Palekastro GR 185 D7
Palena I 169 B4
Palencia E 142 B2
Palenciana E 163 A3
Paleochora GR 185 D4
Paleometokho CY 181 A2
Palermo I 176 A2
Paleros GR 182 E2
Palestrina I 169 B2
Pálfa H 112 C2
Palfau A 110 B1
Palhaça P 148 B1
Palheiros da Tocha P 148 B1
Palheiros de Quiaios P 148 B1
Paliaopoli GR 185 B5
Palić SRB 126 A1
Palidoro I 168 B2
Palinuro I 172 B1
Paliouri GR 183 D5
Paliseul B 91 B5
Pallanza I 119 B5
Pallares E 161 A3
Pallaruelo de Monegros E 153 A3
Pallas Green IRL 29 B3
Pallerols E 146 B2
Palling D 109 A3
Palluau F 114 B2
Palma P 154 C2
Palma Campánia I 170 C2
Palma del Río E 162 A2
Palma de Mallorca E 166 B2
Palma di Montechiaro I 176 B2
Palmádula I 178 B2
Palmanova I 122 B2
Palma Nova E 166 B2
Palmela P 154 C2
Palmerola E 147 B3
Palmi I 175 C1
Pälmonostora H 113 C3
Palo del Colle I 171 B4
Palojärvi FIN 192 D7
Palojoensuu FIN 196 A6
Palomares E 164 B3
Palomares del Campo E 158 B1
Palomas E 156 B1
Palombara Sabina I 168 A2
Palos de la Frontera E 161 B3
Palotaboszok H 125 A4
Palotás H 112 B3
Pals E 147 C4
Pålsboda S 56 A1
Paluzza I 109 C4
Pamhagen A 111 B3
Pamiers F 146 A2
Pamiętowo PL 76 A2
Pampaneira E 163 B4
Pamparato I 133 A3
Pampilhosa
Aveiro P 148 B1
Coimbra P 148 B2
Pampliega E 143 B3
Pamplona E 144 B2
Pampow D 73 A4
Pamukçu TR 186 C2
Pamukkale TR 188 B4
Pamukova TR 187 B5
Panagyurishte BG 17 D6
Pancalieri I 119 C4
Pančevo SRB 127 C2
Pancey F 91 C5
Pancorvo E 143 B3
Pancrudo E 152 B2
Pandino I 120 B2
Pandrup DK 58 A2
Panenský-Týnec CZ 84 B1
Panes E 142 A2
Panevėžys LT 8 E4
Pangbourne GB 44 B2
Panissières F 117 B4
Panki PL 86 B2
Pannes F 103 A4
Panningen NL 80 A1
Pannonhalma H 111 B4
Pano Lefkara CY 181 B2
Pano Panayia CY 181 B1
Panormos GR 185 B6
Panschwitz-Kuckau D 84 A2
Pansdorf D 65 C3
Pantano de Cíjara E 156 A3
Panticosa E 145 B3
Pantín E 140 A2
Pantoja E 151 B4
Pantón E 140 B3
Panxon E 140 B2
Páola I 174 B2
Paola M 175 C3
Pápa H 111 B4
Papasídero I 174 B1
Pápateszér H 111 B4
Papenburg D 71 A4
Paphos CY 181 B1
Pappenheim D 94 C2
Paprotnia PL 77 B5
Parábita I 173 B4
Paraćin SRB 127 D3
Parád H 113 B4
Parada
Bragança P 149 A3
Viseu P 148 B1
Paradas E 162 A2
Paradela E 140 B3
Parades de Rubiales E 150 A2
Paradinas de San Juan E 150 B2
Paradiso di Cevadale I 108 C1
Paradyż PL 87 A4
Parainen FIN 8 B3
Parakhino Paddubye RUS 9 C8
Parakka S 196 B4
Paralimni CY 181 A2
Parallo Astros GR 184 B3
Paramé F 88 B2
Paramithia GR 182 D2
Páramo E 141 A4
Páramo del Sil E 141 B4
Parandaça P 148 A2
Paravadella E 141 A3
Paray-le-Monial F 104 C3
Parceiros P 154 B2
Parcey F 105 B4
Parchim D 73 A4
Parciaki PL 77 A6
Parcice PL 86 A2
Pardilla E 151 A4
Pardubice CZ 97 A3
Paredes
E 151 B5
P 148 A1
Paredes de Coura P 140 C2
Paredes de Nava E 142 B2
Paredes de Siguenza E 151 A5
Pareja E 151 B5
Parennes F 102 A1
Parenti I 175 B2
Parentis-en-Born F 128 B1
Parey D 73 B4
Parfino RUS 9 D7
Parga GR 182 D2
Pargny-sur-Saulx F 91 C4
Pari-Gagné F 117 A4
Parigné-l'Évêque F 102 B2
Parikkala FIN 9 B6
Paris F 90 C2
Parisot F 129 B4
Parkalompolo S 196 B5
Parkano FIN 8 A3
Parknasilla IRL 29 C2
Parla E 151 B4
Parlavá E 147 B4
Parma I 120 C3
Parndorf A 111 B3
Párnica SK 99 B3
Parnu EST 8 C4
Parolis E 164 A2
Paros GR 185 B6
Parrillas E 150 B2
Parsberg D 95 B3
Parstein D 74 B3
Partakko FIN 193 C11
Partanna I 176 B1
Parthenay F 102 C1
Partinico I 176 A2
Partizani SRB 127 C2
Partizánske SK 98 C2
Partney GB 41 B4
Påryd S 63 B3
Parzymiechy PL 86 A2
Paşcani RO 17 B7
Pasewalk D 74 A2
Pašina Voda MNE 139 B5
Påskallavik S 62 A4
Pasłęk PL 69 A4
Pašman HR 137 B4
Passage East IRL 30 B2
Passail A 110 B2
Passais F 88 B3
Passau D 96 C1
Passegueiro P 148 B1
Passignano sul Trasimeno I 135 B5
Passo di Tréia I 136 B2
Passopisciaro I 177 B4
Passow D 74 A3
Passy F 118 B3
Pastavy BY 13 A7
Pástena I 170 B2
Pastrana E 151 B5
Pastrengo I 121 B3
Pasym PL 77 A5
Pásztó H 113 B3
Pata SK 98 C1
Patay F 103 A3
Pateley Bridge GB 40 A2
Paterek PL 76 A2
Paterna E 159 B3
Paterna del Campo E 161 B3
Paterna del Madera E 158 C1
Paterna de Rivera E 162 B2
Paternion A 109 C4
Paternò I 177 B3
Paternópoli I 170 C3
Patersdorf D 95 B4
Paterswolde NL 71 A3
Patitiri GR 183 D5
Patmos GR 188 B1
Patna GB 36 A2
Patnow PL 76 B3
Patoniva FIN 193 C11
Patopirtti FIN 197 B12
Patos AL 182 C1
Patra = Patras GR 184 A2
Patras = Patra GR 184 A2
Patreksfjörður IS 190 B2
Patrickswell IRL 29 B3
Patrimonio F 180 A2
Patrington GB 41 B3
Pattada I 178 B3
Pattensen
Niedersachsen D 72 A3
Niedersachsen D 72 B2
Patterdale GB 36 B4
Patti I 177 A3
Páty H 112 B2
Pau F 145 A3
Pauillac F 128 A2
Paularo I 109 C4
Paulhaguet F 117 B3
Paulhan F 130 B2
Paulilátino I 178 B2
Pauliström S 62 A3
Paullo I 120 B2
Paulstown IRL 30 B1
Pausa D 83 B3
Pauträsk S 200 B3
Pavia
I 120 B2
P 154 C2
Pavias E 159 B3
Pavilly F 89 A4
Pāvilosta LV 8 D2
Pavullo nel Frignano I 135 A3
Pawłowice PL 86 A1
Pawlowice PL 98 B2
Paxi GR 182 D2
Payallar TR 189 C6
Payerne CH 106 C1
Paymogo E 161 B2
Payrac F 129 B4
Pazardzhik BG 183 A6
Pazaryeri TR 187 B4
Pazin HR 122 B2
Paziols F 146 B3
Pčelić HR 124 B3
Peal de Becerro E 164 B1
Peasmarsh GB 45 C4
Peć KOS 16 D4
Péccioli I 135 B3
Pécel H 112 B3
Pechao P 160 B2
Pechenga RUS 3 B12
Pechenizhyn UA 13 D6
Pecica RO 126 A3
Pećinci SRB 127 C1
Pecka SRB 127 C1
Peckelsheim D 81 A5
Pečory RUS 8 D5
Pécs H 125 A4
Pécsvárad H 125 A4
Peczniew PL 86 A2
Pedaso I 136 B2
Pedavena I 121 A4
Pedérobba I 121 B4
Pedersker DK 67 A3
Pedescala I 121 B4
Pedrafita E 141 B3
Pedrajas de San Esteban E 150 A3
Pedralba E 159 B3
Pedralba de la Praderia E 141 B4
Pedraza E 151 A4
Pedreguer E 159 C4
Pedrera E 162 A3
Pedro Abad E 157 C3
Pedro Bernardo E 150 B3
Pedroche E 156 B3
Pedrógão P 160 A2
Pedrogao P 149 B2
Pedrógão P 154 B2
Pedrógão Grande P 154 B2
Pedrola E 144 C2
Pedro-Martinez E 164 B1
Pedro Muñoz E 158 B1
Pedrosa del Rey E 150 A2
Pedrosa del Rio Urbel E 143 B3
Pedrosa de Tobalina E 143 B3
Pedrosillo de los Aires E 150 B2
Pedrosillo el Ralo E 150 A2
Pędzewo PL 76 A3
Peebles GB 35 C4
Peel GB 36 B2
Peenemünde D 66 B2
Peer B 79 A5
Pega P 149 B2
Pegalajar E 163 A4
Pegau D 83 A4
Peggau A 110 B2
Pegli I 133 A4
Pegnitz D 95 B3
Pego E 159 C3
Pegões-Estação P 154 C2
Pegões Velhos P 154 C2
Pęgów PL 85 A4
Pegswood GB 37 A5
Peguera E 166 B2
Pehlivanköy TR 186 A1
Peine D 72 B3
Peisey-Nancroix F 118 B3
Peissenberg D 108 B2
Peiting D 108 B1
Peitz D 84 A2
Péjo I 121 A3
Pelagićevo BIH 125 C4
Pelahustán E 150 B3
Pełczyce PL 75 A4
Pelhřimov CZ 97 B3
Pélissanne F 131 B4
Pelkosenniemi FIN 197 B10
Pellegrino Parmense I 120 C2
Pellegrue F 128 B3
Pellérd H 125 A4
Pellestrina I 122 B1
Pellevoisin F 103 C3
Pellizzano I 121 A3
Pello
FIN 196 C7
S 196 C6
Peloche E 156 A2
Pelplin PL 69 B3
Pelussin F 117 B4
Pély H 113 B4
Pembroke GB 39 C2
Pembroke Dock GB 39 C2
Peñacerrada E 143 B4
Penacova P 148 B1
Peña de Cabra E 149 B4
Peñafiel E 151 A3
Penafiel P 148 A1
Peñaflor E 162 A2
Peñalba de Santiago E 141 B4
Peñalsordo E 156 B2
Penalva do Castelo P 148 B2
Penamacôr P 149 B2
Peñaparda E 149 B3
Peñaranda de Bracamonte E 150 B2
Peñaranda de Duero E 143 C3
Peñarroya de Tastavins E 153 B4
Peñarroya-Pueblonuevo E 156 B2
Peñarrubla E 141 B3
Penarth GB 39 C3
Peñascosa E 158 C1
Peñas de San Pedro E 158 C2
Peñausende E 149 A4
Penc H 112 B3
Pencoed GB 39 C3
Pendalofos GR 182 C3
Pendeen GB 42 B1
Pendine GB 39 C2
Pendueles E 142 A2
Penedono P 148 B2
Penela P 154 A2
Pénestin F 101 B3
Penhas Juntas P 149 A2
Peniche P 154 B1
Penicuik GB 35 C4
Penig D 83 B4
Penilhos P 160 B2
Peñíscola E 153 B4
Penistone GB 40 B2
Penkridge GB 40 C1
Penkun D 74 A3
Penmarch F 100 B1
Pennabilli I 135 B5
Penne I 169 A3
Penne-d'Agenais F 129 B3
Pennes I 108 C2
Pennyghael GB 34 B1
Peno RUS 9 D8
Penpont GB 36 A3
Penrhyndeudraeth GB 38 B2
Penrith GB 37 B4
Penryn GB 42 B1
Pentraeth GB 38 A2
Penybontfawr GB 38 B3
Penygroes
Carmarthenshire GB 39 C2
Gwynedd GB 38 A2
Penzance GB 42 B1
Penzberg D 108 B2
Penzlin D 74 A2
Pepinster B 80 B1
Peqin AL 182 B1
Pér H 111 B4
Pera Boa P 148 B2
Perachora GR 184 A3
Perafita P 148 A1
Peraleda de la Mata E 150 C2
Peraleda del Zaucejo E 156 B2
Peraleda de San Román E 156 A2
Perales de Alfambra E 152 B2
Perales del Puerto E 149 B3
Perales de Tajuña E 151 B4
Peralta E 144 B2
Peralta de la Sal E 145 C4
Peralva P 160 B2
Peralveche E 152 B1
Perama GR 185 D5
Peranka FIN 197 D12
Perbál H 112 B2
Perchtoldsdorf A 111 A3
Percy F 88 B2
Perdasdefogu I 179 C3
Perdiguera E 145 C3
Peredo P 149 A3
Peregu Mare RO 126 A2
Pereiro
Faro P 160 B2
Guarda P 149 B2
Santarém P 154 B2
Pereiro de Aguiar E 140 B3
Perelada E 147 B4
Perelejos de las Truchas E 152 B2
Pereña E 149 A3
Pereruela E 149 A4
Pérfugas I 178 B2
Perg A 110 A1
Pérgine Valsugana I 121 A4
Pérgola I 136 B1
Pergusa I 177 B3
Periam RO 126 A2
Periana E 163 B3
Périers F 88 A2
Périgueux F 129 A3
Perino I 120 C2
Perjasica HR 123 B4
Perkáta H 112 B2
Perković HR 138 B2
Perleberg D 73 A4
Perlez SRB 126 B2
Përmet AL 182 C2
Pernarec CZ 95 B5
Pernek SK 98 C1
Pernes P 154 B2
Pernes-les-Fontaines F 131 A4
Pernik BG 17 D5
Pernink CZ 83 B4
Pernitz A 110 B2
Pernu FIN 197 C10
Peroguarda P 160 A1
Pérols F 131 B2
Péronne F 90 B2
Péronnes B 79 B4
Pero Pinheiro P 154 C1
Perorrubio E 151 A4
Perosa Argentina I 119 C4
Perozinho P 148 A1
Perpignan F 146 B3
Perranporth GB 42 B1
Perranzabuloe GB 42 B1
Perrecy-les-Forges F 104 C3
Perrero I 119 C4
Perrignier F 118 A3
Perros-Guirec F 100 A2
Persan F 90 B2
Persberg S 55 A5
Persenbeug A 110 A2
Pershore GB 44 A1
Persön S 196 D5
Perstorp S 61 C3
Perth GB 35 B4
Pertisau A 108 B2
Pertoča SLO 111 C3
Pertuis F 131 B4
Perućac SRB 127 D1
Perúgia I 136 B1
Perušić HR 123 C4
Péruwelz B 79 B3
Pervomaysk UA 13 D9
Perwez B 79 B4
Pesadas de Burgos E 143 B3
Pesaguero E 142 A2
Pésaro I 136 B1
Pescantina I 121 B3
Pescara I 169 A4
Pescasséroli I 169 B3
Peschici I 171 B4
Peschiera del Garda I 121 B3
Péscia I 135 B3
Pescina I 169 A3
Pescocostanzo I 169 B4
Pescopagano I 172 B1
Pesco Sannita I 170 B2
Peshkopi AL 182 B2
Peshtera BG 183 A6
Pesmes F 105 B4
Pesnica SLO 110 C2
Peso da Régua P 148 A2
Pesquera de Duero E 142 C2
Pessac F 128 B2
Pestovo RUS 9 C9
Petäjäskoski FIN 197 C8
Petalidi GR 184 C2
Pétange L 92 B1
Petas GR 182 D3
Peteranec HR 124 A2
Peterborough GB 41 C3
Peterculter GB 33 D4
Peterhead GB 33 D5
Peterlee GB 37 B5
Petersfield GB 44 B3
Petershagen
Brandenburg D 74 B2
Brandenburg D 74 B3
Nordrhein-Westfalen D 72 B1
Petershausen D 95 C3
Peterswell IRL 28 A3
Pétervására H 113 A4
Petília Policastro I 175 B2
Petín E 141 B3
Pětipsy CZ 83 B5
Petkus D 74 C2
Petlovac HR 125 B4
Petlovača SRB 127 C1
Petöfiszallás H 113 C3
Petra E 167 B3
Petralia Sottana I 177 B3
Petrčane HR 137 A4
Petrella Tifernina I 170 B2
Petrer E 159 C3
Petreto-Bicchisano F 180 B1
Petrich BG 183 B5
Petrijevci HR 125 B4
Petrinja HR 124 B2
Petrodvorets RUS 9 C6
Pétrola E 158 C2
Petronà I 175 B2
Petronell A 111 A3
Petroşani RO 17 C5
Petrovac SRB 127 C3
Petrovaradin SRB 126 B1
Petrovice
BIH 139 A4
CZ 84 B1
Petrovo RUS 69 A5
Petrozavodsk RUS 9 B9
Pettenbach A 109 B5
Pettigo IRL 26 B3
Petworth GB 44 C3
Peuerbach A 96 C1
Peuntenansa E 142 A2
Peurasuvanto FIN 197 B9
Pevensey Bay GB 45 C4
Peveragno I 133 A3
Pewsey GB 44 B2
Pewsum D 71 A4
Peyrat-le-Château F 116 B1
Peyrehorade F 128 C1

Portopalo di Capo Passero I 177 C4
Porto Petro E 167 B3
Porto Pino I 179 D2
Porto Potenza Picena I 136 B2
Portør N 53 B5
Porto Recanati I 136 B2
Porto San Giórgio I 136 B2
Porto Sant'Elpídio I 136 B2
Porto Santo Stéfano I 168 A1
Portoscuso I 179 C2
Porto Tolle I 122 C1
Porto Tórres I 178 B2
Porto-Vecchio F 180 B2
Portovénere I 134 A2
Portpatrick GB 36 B1
Portreath GB 42 B1
Portree GB 31 B2
Portroe IRL 28 B3
Portrush GB 27 A4
Port St Mary GB 36 B2
Portsall F 100 A1
Portsmouth GB 44 C2
Portsoy GB 33 D4
Port-Ste Marie F 129 B3
Portstewart GB 27 A4
Port-St-Louis-du-Rhône F 131 B3
Port-sur-Saône F 105 B5
Port Talbot GB 39 C3
Portugalete E 143 A4
Portumna IRL 28 A3
Port-Vendres F 146 B4
Port William GB 36 B2
Porvoo FIN 8 B4
Porzuna E 157 A3
Posada
Oviedo E 141 A5
Oviedo E 142 A2
I 178 B3
Posada de Valdeón E 142 A2
Posadas E 162 A2
Poschiavo CH 120 A3
Posedarje HR 137 A4
Posio FIN 197 C11
Positano I 170 C2
Possagno I 121 B4
Posseck D 83 B4
Possesse F 91 C4
Pössneck D 83 B3
Posta I 169 A3
Postal I 108 C2
Posta Piana I 172 A1
Postbauer-Heng D 95 B3
Posterholt NL 80 A2
Postioma I 121 B5
Postira HR 138 B2
Postojna SLO 123 B3
Postoloprty CZ 84 B1
Postomino PL 68 A1
Posušje BIH 138 B3
Potamos
Attiki GR 184 C3
Attiki GR 184 D4
Potegowo PL 68 A2
Potenza I 172 B1
Potenza Picena I 136 B2
Potes E 142 A2
Potigny F 89 B3
Potočari BIH 127 C1
Potoci
BIH 138 A2
BIH 139 B3
Potony H 125 B3
Potries E 159 C3
Potsdam D 74 B2
Potštát CZ 98 B1
Pottenbrunn A 110 A2
Pottendorf A 111 B3
Pottenstein
A 111 B3
D 95 B3
Potters Bar GB 44 B3
Pöttmes D 94 C3
Pöttsching A 111 B3
Potworów PL 87 A4
Pouancé F 101 B4
Pougues-les-Eaux F 104 B2
Pouilly-en-Auxois F 104 B3
Pouilly-sous Charlieu F 117 A4
Pouilly-sur-Loire F 104 B1
Poujol-sur-Orb F 130 B2
Poullaouen F 100 A2
Poulton-le-Fylde GB 38 A4
Poundstock GB 42 B2
Pourcy F 91 B3
Pourrain F 104 B2
Poussu FIN 197 D12
Pouyastruc F 145 A4
Pouy-de-Touges F 146 A2
Pouzauges F 114 B3
Pova de Santa Iria P 154 C1
Považská Bystrica SK 98 B2
Povedilla E 158 C1
Povenets RUS 9 A9
Povlja HR 138 B2
Povljana HR 137 A4
Póvoa
Beja P 161 A2
Santarém P 154 B2
Póvoa de Lanhoso P 148 A1
Póvoa de Varzim P 148 A1
Póvoa e Meadas P 155 B3
Powidz PL 76 B2
Poyales del Hoyo E 150 B2
Poynton GB 40 B1
Poyntz Pass GB 27 B4
Poysdorf A 97 C4
Poza de la Sal E 143 B3
Pozaldez E 150 A3
Pozán de Vero E 145 B4
Pozanti TR 23 C8
Požarevac SRB 127 C3
Požega
HR 125 B3
SRB 127 D2
Poznań PL 76 B1
Pozo Alcón E 164 B2
Pozoantiguo E 150 A2
Pozoblanco E 156 B3
Pozo Cañada E 158 C2
Pozo de Guadalajara E 151 B4
Pozo de la Serna E 157 B4
Pozohondo E 158 C2
Pozondón E 152 B2
Poźrzadło Wielkie PL 75 A4
Pozuel del Campo E 152 B2
Pozuelo de Alarcón E 151 B4
Pozuelo de Calatrava E 157 B4
Pozuelo del Páramo E 142 B1
Pozuelo de Zarzón E 149 B3
Pozzallo I 177 C3
Pozzomaggiore I 178 B2
Pozzo San Nicola I 178 B2
Pozzuoli I 170 C2
Pozzuolo I 135 B4
Prabuty PL 69 B4
Prača BIH 139 B4
Prachatice CZ 96 B1
Prada E 141 B3
Pradelle F 118 C2
Pradelles F 117 C3
Prades
E 147 C1
F 146 B3
Pradła PL 86 B3
Prado
E 142 A1
P 148 A1
Prado del Rey E 162 B2
Pradoluengo E 143 B3
Pragelato I 119 B3
Pragersko SLO 123 A4
Prägraten A 109 B3
Prague = Praha CZ 84 B2
Praha = Prague CZ 84 B2
Prahecq F 115 B3
Praia P 154 B1
Práia a Mare I 174 B1
Praia da Rocha P 160 B1
Praia da Viera P 154 B2
Praia de Mira P 148 B1
Praiano I 170 C2
Pralboino I 120 B3
Pralognan-la-Vanoise F 118 B3
Pramanda GR 182 D3
Pranjani SRB 127 C2
Prapatnica HR 138 B2
Præstø DK 65 A5
Praszka PL 86 A2
Prat F 146 A1
Prata I 135 B3
Prata di Pordenone I 122 B1
Pratau D 83 A4
Prat de Compte E 153 B4
Pratdip E 147 C1
Pratella I 170 B2
Prato I 135 B4
Prátola Peligna I 169 A3
Pratola Serra I 170 C2
Prats-de-Mollo-la-Preste F 146 B3
Prauthoy F 105 B4
Pravia E 141 A4
Praxmar A 108 B2
Prayssac F 129 B4
Prazzo I 132 A3
Prebold SLO 123 A4
Préchac F 128 B2
Précy-sur-Thil F 104 B3
Predáppio I 135 A4
Predazzo I 121 A4
Předin CZ 97 B3
Preding A 110 C2
Predjame SLO 123 B3
Predlitz A 109 B4
Predmeja SLO 122 B2
Predoi I 108 B3
Pré-en-Pail F 89 B3
Prees GB 38 B4
Preetz D 64 B3
Préfailles F 101 B3
Pregarten A 96 C2
Pregrada HR 123 A4
Preignan F 129 C3
Preiļi LV 8 D5
Preitenegg A 110 C1
Prekaja BIH 138 A2
Preko HR 137 A4
Preljina SRB 127 D2
Prelog HR 124 A2
Prelošćica HR 124 B2
Přelouč CZ 97 A3
Prem SLO 123 B3
Premantura HR 122 C2
Prémery F 104 B2
Prémia I 119 A5
Premiàde Mar E 147 C3
Premnitz D 73 B5
Prémont F 91 A3
Prenzlau D 74 A2
Preodac BIH 138 A2
Přerov CZ 98 B1
Prerow D 66 B1
Presencio E 143 B3
Presicce I 173 C4
Presly F 103 B4
Prešov SK 12 D4
Pressac F 115 B4
Pressath D 95 B3
Pressbaum A 111 A3
Prestatyn GB 38 A3
Prestebakke N 54 B2
Presteigne GB 39 B3
Přeštice CZ 96 B1
Preston
Lancashire GB 38 A4
Scottish Borders GB 35 C5
Prestonpans GB 35 C5
Prestwick GB 36 A2
Prettin D 83 A4
Preturo I 169 A3
Pretzchendorf D 83 B5
Pretzier D 73 B4
Pretzsch D 83 A4
Preuilly-sur-Claise F 115 B4
Prevalje SLO 110 C1
Prevenchères F 131 A2
Préveranges F 116 A2
Preveza GR 182 E2
Prevršac HR 124 B2
Prezid HR 123 B3
Priaranza del Bierzo E 141 B4
Priay F 118 A2
Pribeta SK 112 B2
Priboj
BIH 125 C4
SRB 16 D3
Příbor CZ 98 B2
Příbram CZ 96 B2
Pribylina SK 99 B3
Přibyslav CZ 97 B3
Pričević SRB 127 C1
Pridjel BIH 125 C4
Priego E 152 B1
Priego de Córdoba E 163 A3
Priekule LV 8 D2
Prien D 109 B3
Prienai LT 13 A5
Prievidza SK 98 C2
Prigradica HR 138 C2
Prigrevica SRB 125 B5
Prijeboj HR 123 C4
Prijedor BIH 124 C2
Prijepolje SRB 16 D3
Prilep MK 182 B3
Priluka BIH 138 B2
Primda CZ 95 B4
Primel-Trégastel F 100 A2
Primišje HR 123 B4
Primorsk
Kaliningrad RUS 69 A5
Severo-Zapadnyy RUS 9 B6
Primošten HR 138 B1
Primstal D 92 B2
Princes Risborough GB 44 B3
Princetown GB 42 B2
Principina a Mare I 135 C4
Priolo Gargallo I 177 B4
Prioro E 142 B2
Priozersk RUS 9 B7
Prirechnyy RUS 193 C14
Prisoje BIH 138 B3
Priština KOS 16 D4
Pritzerbe D 73 B5
Pritzier D 73 A4
Pritzwalk D 73 A5
Privas F 117 C4
Priverno I 169 B3
Privlaka
Vukovarsko-Srijemska HR 125 B4
Zadarska HR 137 A4
Prizna HR 123 C3
Prizren KOS 16 D4
Prizzi I 176 B2
Prnjavor
BIH 125 C3
HR 124 B1
SRB 127 C1
Proaza E 141 A4
Probstzella D 82 B3
Probus GB 42 B2
Prócchio I 134 C3
Prochowice PL 85 A4
Prócida I 170 C2
Prodhromos CY 181 B1
Prodo I 135 C5
Proença-a-Nova P 154 B3
Proença-a-Velha P 155 A3
Profondeville B 79 B4
Prokuplje SRB 16 D4
Propriano F 180 B1
Prosec CZ 97 B4
Prösen D 83 A5
Prosenjakovci SLO 111 C3
Prosotsani GR 183 B5
Prostějov CZ 98 B1
Prószków PL 86 B1
Proszowice PL 87 B4
Protić BIH 138 A2
Protivanov CZ 97 B4
Protivín CZ 96 B2
Prötzel D 74 B2
Provins F 90 C3
Prozor BIH 139 B3
Prrenjas AL 182 B2
Prudhoe GB 37 B5
Prudnik PL 85 B5
Pruggern A 109 B4
Prügy H 113 A5
Prüm D 80 B2
Pruna E 162 B2
Prunelli-di-Fiumorbo F 180 A2
Prunetta I 135 A3
Pruniers F 103 C4
Prusice PL 85 A4
Pruské SK 98 B2
Pruszce PL 76 A3
Pruszcz Gdański PL 69 A3
Pruszków PL 77 B5
Prutz A 108 B1
Prüzen D 65 C5
Pruzhany BY 13 B6
Pružina SK 98 B2
Pŭrvomay BG 183 A7
Pryzlęg PL 75 B4
Przasnysz PL 77 A5
Przechlewo PL 68 B2
Przecław PL 87 B5
Przedbórz PL 87 A3
Przedecz PL 76 B3
Przejęslav PL 84 A3
Przemków PL 85 A3
Przemocze PL 75 A3
Przemyśl PL 12 D5
Przerąb PL 87 A3
Przewodnik PL 69 B3
Przewodowo Parcele PL 77 B5
Przewóz PL 84 A2
Przezmark PL 69 B4
Przodkowo PL 68 A3
Przybiernów PL 75 A3
Przyborowice PL 77 B5
Przybyszew PL 87 A4
Przybyszów PL 86 A3
Przylęg PL 75 B4
Przysucha PL 87 A4
Przytóczna PL 75 B4
Przytyk PL 87 A4
Przywidz PL 68 A3
Psachna GR 185 A4
Psara GR 185 A6
Psary PL 76 C3
Pskov RUS 8 D6
Pszczew PL 75 B4
Pszczółki PL 69 A3
Pszczyna PL 98 B2
Pszów PL 86 B2
Pteleos GR 182 D4
Ptolemaida GR 182 C3
Ptuj SLO 124 A1
Ptusza PL 68 B1
Puch A 109 B4
Puchberg am Schneeberg A 110 B2
Puchevillers F 90 A2
Puchheim D 108 A2
Púchov SK 98 B2
Pučišća HR 138 B2
Puck PL 69 A3
Puçol E 159 B3
Puconci SLO 111 C3
Pudasjärvi FIN 197 D10
Puderbach D 81 B3
Pudozh RUS 9 B10
Puebla de Albortón E 153 A3
Puebla de Alcocer E 156 B2
Puebla de Beleña E 151 B4
Puebla de Don Fadrique E 164 B2
Puebla de Don Rodrigo E 156 A3
Puebla de Guzmán E 161 B2
Puebla de la Calzada E 155 C4
Puebla de la Reina E 156 B1
Puebla de Lillo E 142 A1
Puebla del Maestre E 161 A3
Puebla del Principe E 158 C1
Puebla de Obando E 155 B4
Puebla de Sanabria E 141 B4
Puebla de Sancho Pérez E 155 C4
Puente Almuhey E 142 B2
Puente de Domingo Flórez E 141 B4
Puente de Génave E 164 A2
Puente del Congosto E 150 B2
Puente de Montañana E 145 B4
Puente Duero E 150 A3
Puente-Genil E 162 A3
Puente la Reina E 144 B2
Puente la Reina de Jaca E 144 B3
Puentelarra E 143 B3
Puente Mayorga E 162 B2
Puente Viesgo E 143 A3
Puertas
Asturias E 142 A2
Salamanca E 149 A3
Puerto de Mazarrón E 165 B3
Puerto de Santa Cruz E 156 A2
Puerto de San Vicente E 156 A2
Puerto-Lápice E 157 A4
Puertollano E 157 B3
Puerto Lumbreras E 164 B3
Puerto Moral E 161 B3
Puerto Real E 162 B1
Puerto Rey E 156 A2
Puerto Seguro E 149 B3
Puerto Serrano E 162 B2
Puget-Sur-Argens F 132 B2
Puget-Théniers F 132 B2
Puget-ville F 132 B2
Pugnochiuso I 171 B4
Puigcerdà E 146 B2
Puigpunyent E 166 B2
Puig Reig E 147 C2
Puillon F 128 C2
Puimichel F 132 B2
Puimoisson F 132 B2
Puiseaux F 103 A4
Puisieux F 90 A2
Puisserguier F 130 B2
Puivert F 146 B3
Pujols F 128 B2
Pukanec SK 98 C2
Pukavik S 63 B2
Pukë AL 182 A1
Pula
HR 122 C2
I 179 C2
Puławy PL 12 C4
Pulborough GB 44 C3
Pulfero I 122 A2
Pulgar E 157 A3
Pulheim D 80 A2
Pulkau A 97 C3
Pulpi E 164 B3
Pulsano I 173 B3
Pulsnitz D 84 A2
Pułtusk PL 77 B6
Pumpsaint GB 39 B3
Punat HR 123 B3
Punta Marina I 135 A5
Punta Prima E 167 B4
Punta Sabbioni I 122 B1
Puntas de Calnegre E 165 B3
Punta Umbría E 161 B3
Puolanka FIN 3 D10
Puoltikasvaara S 196 B4
Puoltsa S 196 B2
Puračić BIH 125 C4
Purbach am Neusiedler See A 111 B3
Purchena E 164 B2
Purfleet GB 45 B4
Purgstall A 110 A2
Purkersdorf A 111 A3
Purmerend NL 70 B1
Purullena E 164 B1
Pushkin RUS 9 C7
Pushkino RUS 9 D10
Püspökladány H 113 B5
Pusté Ulany SK 111 A4
Pustoshka RUS 9 D6
Puszcza Mariańska PL 77 C5
Puszczykowo PL 76 B1
Pusztamagyaród H 111 C3
Pusztamonostor H 113 B3
Pusztaszabolcs H 112 B2
Pusztavám H 112 B2
Putanges-Pont-Ecrepin F 89 B3
Putbus D 66 B2
Putignano I 173 B3
Putlitz D 73 A5
Putnok H 99 C4
Putte B 79 A4
Puttelange-aux-Lacs F 92 B2
Putten NL 70 B2
Puttgarden D 65 B4
Püttlingen D 92 B2
Putzu Idu I 179 B2
Puy-Guillaume F 117 B3
Puylaroque F 129 B4
Puylaurens F 146 A3
Puy-l'Évêque F 129 B4
Puymirol F 129 B3
Puyôo F 128 C2
Puyrolland F 114 B3
Pwllheli GB 38 B2
Pyetrikaw BY 13 B8
Pyhäjärvi FIN 3 E9
Pyhäkylä FIN 197 D11
Pyla CY 181 A2
Pyla-sur-Mer F 128 B1
Pyrzyce PL 75 A3
Pysely CZ 96 B2
Pyskowice PL 86 B2
Pytalovo RUS 8 D5
Pyzdry PL 76 B2

Q

Quakenbrück D 71 B4
Quargnento I 119 C5
Quarré-les-Tombes F 104 B2
Quarteira P 160 B1
Quartu Sant'Élena I 179 C3
Quatre-Champs F 91 B4
Quedlinburg D 82 A3
Queensferry
Edinburgh GB 35 C4
Flintshire GB 38 A3
Queige F 118 B3
Queipo E 161 B3
Queixans E 146 B2
Quel E 144 B1
Quelaines-St-Gault F 102 B1
Queljada P 148 A1
Quemada E 143 C3
Queralbs E 147 B3
Quercianella I 134 B3
Querfurt D 82 A3
Quérigut F 146 B3
Quero
E 157 A4
I 121 B4
Querqueville F 88 A2
Quesada E 164 B1
Questembert F 101 B3
Quettehou F 88 A2
Quevauvillers F 90 B2
Quevy B 79 B4
Quiaois P 148 B1
Quiberon F 100 B2
Quiberville F 89 A4
Quickborn D 64 C2
Quiévrain B 79 B3
Quillan F 146 B3
Quillebeuf F 89 A4
Quimper F 100 A1
Quimperlé F 100 B2
Quincampoix F 89 A5
Quincoces de Yuso E 143 B3
Quincy F 103 B4
Quinéville F 88 A2
Quingey F 105 B4
Quinson F 132 B2
Quinssaines F 116 A2
Quinta-Grande P 154 C2
Quintana de la Serena E 156 B2
Quintana del Castillo E 141 B4
Quintana del Marco E 141 B5
Quintana del Puenta E 142 B2
Quintana-Martin Galindez E 143 B3
Quintanaortuño E 143 B3
Quintanapalla E 143 B3
Quintanar de la Orden E 157 A4
Quintanar de la Sierra E 143 C3
Quintanar del Rey E 158 B2
Quintanilla de la Mata E 143 C3
Quintanilla del Coco E 143 C3
Quintanilla de Onésimo E 150 A3
Quintanilla de Somoza E 141 B4
Quintas de Valdelucio E 142 B2
Quintela P 148 B2
Quintin F 100 A3
Quinto E 153 A3
Quinzano d'Oglio I 120 B3
Quiroga E 141 B3
Quismondo E 150 B3
Quissac F 131 B2
Quistello I 121 B3

R

Raab A 96 C1
Raabs an der Thaya A 97 C3
Raahe FIN 3 D9
Raajärvi FIN 197 C9
Raalte NL 71 B3
Raamsdonksveer NL 79 A4
Raanujarvi FIN 196 C7
Raattama FIN 196 A7
Rab HR 123 C3
Rabac HR 123 B3
Rábade E 140 A3
Rábafüzes H 111 C3
Rábahidvég H 111 B3
Rabanales E 149 A3
Rábapatona H 111 B4
Rabapordány H 111 B4
Rabastens F 129 C4
Rabastens-de-Bigorre F 145 A4
Rabat = Victoria M 175 C3
Rabat M 175 C3
Rabča SK 99 B3
Rabe SRB 126 A2
Rabi CZ 96 B1
Rabino PL 67 C4
Rabka PL 99 B3
Rabrovo SRB 127 C3
Rača SRB 127 C3
Rácale I 173 C4
Rácalmás H 112 B2
Racalmuto I 176 B2
Racconigi I 119 C4
Rače SLO 123 A4
Rachecourt-sur-Marne F 91 C5
Raciąż PL 77 B5
Racibórz PL 86 B2
Račinovci HR 125 C4
Ráckeve H 112 B2
Racławice PL 87 B4
Racławice Sląskie PL 86 B1
Racot PL 75 B5
Råda
Skaraborg S 55 B4
Värmland S 49 B5
Radalj SRB 127 C1
Rădăuţi RO 17 B6
Radda in Chianti I 135 B4
Raddusa I 177 B3
Radeberg D 84 A1
Radebeul D 84 A1
Radeburg D 84 A1
Radeče SLO 123 A4
Radekhiv UA 13 C6
Radenci SLO 111 C3
Radenthein A 109 C4
Radevormwald D 80 A3
Radicófani I 135 C4
Radicóndoli I 135 B4
Radišići BIH 138 B3
Radizel SLO 110 C2
Radków PL 85 B4
Radlje ob Dravi SLO 110 C2
Radlów PL 87 B4
Radmer an der Stube A 110 B1
Radnejaur S 195 E9
Radnice CZ 96 B1
Radohova BIH 138 A3
Radojevo SRB 126 B2
Radolfzell D 107 B3
Radom PL 87 A5
Radomice PL 77 B4
Radomin PL 77 A4
Radomsko PL 86 A3
Radomyshl UA 13 C8
Radomyśl Wielki PL 87 B5
Radošina SK 98 C1
Radošovce SK 98 C1
Radoszewice PL 86 A2
Radoszyce PL 87 A4
Radotin CZ 96 B2
Radovets BG 186 A1
Radoviš MK 182 B4
Radovljica SLO 123 A3
Radowo Wielkie PL 75 A4
Radstadt A 109 B4
Radstock GB 43 A4
Raduc HR 137 A4
Raduša MK 182 A3
Radviliškis LT 8 E3
Radzanów
Mazowieckie PL 77 B5
Mazowieckie PL 87 A4
Radziejów PL 76 B3
Radziejowice PL 77 B5
Radzovce SK 113 A3
Radzyń Chełmiński PL 69 B3
Raeren B 80 B2
Raesfeld D 80 A2
Raffadali I 176 B2
Rafina GR 185 A4
Rafsbotn N 192 B7
Ragachow BY 13 B9
Ragály H 99 C4
Rågeleje DK 61 C2
Raglan GB 39 C4
Ragnitz A 110 C2
Ragusa I 177 C3
Rahden D 72 B1
Råholt N 48 B3
Raiano I 169 A3
Raigada E 141 B3
Rain D 94 C2
Rainbach im Mühlkreis A 96 C2
Rainham GB 45 B4
Rairiz de Veiga E 140 B3
Raisdorf D 64 B3
Raisio FIN 8 B3
Raiskio FIN 197 D9
Raiva
Aveiro P 148 A1
Coimbra P 148 B1
Raja-Jooseppi FIN 193 D12
Rajala FIN 197 B9
Rajcza PL 99 B3
Rajec SK 98 B2
Rájec-Jestřebí CZ 97 B4
Rajecké Teplice SK 98 B2
Rajevo Selo HR 125 C4
Rajhrad CZ 97 B4
Rajić HR 124 B3
Rajka H 111 B4
Rakaca H 99 C4
Rakamaz H 113 A5
Rakek SLO 123 B3
Rakhiv UA 17 A6
Rakitna SLO 123 B3
Rakitovo BG 183 B6
Rakkestad N 54 A2
Rákóczifalva H 113 B4
Rakoniewice PL 75 B5
Rakoszyce PL 85 A4
Raková SK 98 B2
Rakovac BIH 125 B3
Rakovica HR 123 C4
Rakovník CZ 96 A1
Rakow D 66 B2
Raków PL 87 B5
Rakvere EST 8 C5
Ralja SRB 127 C2
Rälla S 62 B4
Ramacastañas E 150 B2
Ramacca I 177 B3
Ramales de la Victoria E 143 A3
Ramberg N 194 B4
Rambervillers F 92 C2
Rambouillet F 90 C1
Rambucourt F 92 C1
Ramdala S 63 B3
Ramerupt F 91 C4
Ramingstein A 109 B4
Ramirás E 140 B2
Ramiswil CH 106 B2
Ramkvilla S 62 A2
Ramme DK 58 B1
Rämmen S 49 B6
Ramnäs S 56 A2
Ramnes N 54 A1
Râmnicu Vâlcea RO 17 C6
Ramonville-St Agne F 129 C4
Rampside GB 36 B3
Ramsau D 109 B3
Ramsbeck D 81 A4
Ramsberg S 56 A1
Ramsele S 200 C2
Ramsey
Cambridgeshire GB 44 A3
Isle of Man GB 36 B2
Ramseycleuch GB 36 A3

Ramsgate GB 45 B5
Ramsjö S 200 D1
Ramstein-Meisenbach D 93 B3
Ramsund N 194 B7
Ramundberget S 199 C9
Ramvik S 200 D3
Ranalt A 108 B2
Rånäs S 51 C5
Rånåsfoss N 48 B3
Rance B 91 A4
Ránchio I 135 B5
Randaberg N 52 A1
Randalstown GB 27 B4
Randan F 117 A3
Randazzo I 177 B3
Rånddalen S 199 E12
Randegg A 110 A1
Randers DK 58 B3
Randijaur S 196 C2
Randin E 140 C3
Randsverk N 198 D6
Råneå S 196 D5
Rânes F 89 B3
Rångedala S 60 B3
Ranis D 82 B3
Rankweil A 107 B4
Rånnaväg S 60 B3
Ränneslöv S 61 C3
Rannoch Station GB 34 B3
Ranovac SRB 127 C3
Ransäter S 55 A4
Ransbach-Baumbach D 81 B3
Ransta S 56 A2
Ranttila FIN 193 C9
Ranua FIN 197 D9
Ranum DK 58 B2
Ranvalhal P 154 B1
Raon-l'Étape F 92 C2
Ráossi I 121 B4
Rapallo I 134 A2
Rapla EST 8 C4
Rapness GB 33 B4
Rapolano Terme I 135 B4
Rapolla I 172 B1
Raposa P 154 B2
Rapperswil CH 107 B3
Raša HR 123 B3
Rasal E 145 B3
Rascafria E 151 B4
Rasdorf D 82 B1
Raseiniai LT 13 A5
Rašica SLO 123 B3
Rasines E 143 A3
Rasquera E 153 A4
Rássina I 135 B4
Rastatt D 93 C4
Rastede D 71 A5
Rastenberg D 82 A3
Rastošnica BIH 125 C4
Rastovac MNE 139 C4
Rasueros E 150 A2
Rasy PL 86 A3
Raszków PL 86 A1
Rätan S 199 C11
Rateče SLO 109 C4
Ratekau D 65 C3
Ratež SLO 123 B4
Rathangan IRL 30 A2
Rathcoole IRL 30 A2
Rathcormack IRL 29 B3
Rathdrum IRL 30 B2
Rathebur D 74 A2
Rathenow D 73 B5
Rathfriland GB 27 B4
Rathkeale IRL 29 B3
Rathmelton IRL 27 A3
Rathmolyon IRL 30 A2
Rathmore IRL 29 B2
Rathmullan IRL 27 A3
Rathnew IRL 30 B2
Rathvilly IRL 30 B2
Ratibořské Hory CZ 96 B2
Ratingen D 80 A2
Ratková SK 99 C4
Ratkovo SRB 126 B1
Ratne UA 13 C6
Rattelsdorf D 94 A2
Ratten A 110 B2
Rattosjärvi FIN 196 C7
Rattray GB 35 B4
Rättvik S 50 B2
Ratvika N 199 B7
Ratzeburg D 65 C3
Rätzlingen D 73 B4
Raucourt-et-Flaba F 91 B4
Raudeberg N 198 D2
Raufarhöfn IS 191 A10
Raufoss N 48 B2
Rauhala FIN 196 B7
Rauland N 53 A4
Raulhac F 116 C2
Raulia N 195 E5
Rauma FIN 8 B2
Raundal N 46 B3
Raunds GB 44 A3
Rauris A 109 B4
Rautas S 196 B2
Rautavaara FIN 3 E11
Rauville-la-Bigot F 88 A2
Rauzan F 128 B2
Ravanusa I 176 B2
Rava-Rus'ka UA 13 C5
Ravča HR 138 B3
Ravels B 79 A4
Rävemåla S 63 B3
Ravenglass GB 36 B3
Ravenna I 135 A5
Ravensburg D 107 B4
Rävlanda S 60 B2
Ravna Gora HR 123 B3
Ravne na Koroškem SLO 110 C1
Ravnje SRB 127 C1
Ravno BIH 139 C3
Ravno Selo SRB 126 B1
Rawa Mazowiecka PL 87 A4
Rawicz PL 85 A4
Rawtenstall GB 40 B1
Rayleigh GB 45 B4
Ražana SRB 127 C1
Ražanac HR 137 A4
Razboj BIH 124 B3
Razes F 115 B5
Razgrad BG 17 D7
Razkrižje SLO 111 C3
Razlog BG 183 B5
Razo E 140 A2
Reading GB 44 B3
Réalmont F 130 B1
Rebais F 90 C3
Reboly RUS 3 E12
Rebordelo P 149 A2
Recanati I 136 B2
Recas E 151 B4
Recco I 134 A2
Recess IRL 28 A2
Recey-sur-Ource F 105 B3
Recezinhos P 148 A1
Rechnitz A 111 B3
Rechytsa BY 13 B9
Recke D 71 B4
Recklinghausen D 80 A3
Recoaro Terme I 121 B4
Recogne B 92 B1
Recoules-Prévinquières F 130 A1
Recsk H 113 B4
Recz PL 75 A4
Reda PL 69 A3
Redalen N 48 B2
Redange L 92 B1
Redcar GB 37 B5
Redditch GB 44 A2
Redefin D 73 A4
Redhill GB 44 B3
Redics H 111 C3
Redkino RUS 9 D10
Redland GB 33 B3
Redlin D 73 A5
Redon F 101 B3
Redondela E 140 B2
Redondo P 155 C3
Red Point GB 31 B3
Redruth GB 42 B1
Redzikowo PL 68 A2
Reepham GB 41 C5
Rees D 80 A2
Reeth GB 37 B5
Reetz D 73 A4
Reftele S 60 B3
Regalbuto I 177 B3
Regen D 95 C5
Regensburg D 95 B4
Regenstauf D 95 B4
Reggello I 135 B4
Réggio di Calábria I 175 C1
Reggiolo I 121 C3
Réggio nell'Emília I 121 C3
Reghin RO 17 B6
Régil E 144 A1
Regna S 56 B1
Regniéville F 92 C1
Regny F 117 B4
Rego da Leirosa P 154 A2
Regöly H 112 C2
Regueiro E 140 B2
Reguengo
Portalegre P 155 B3
Santarém P 154 B2
Reguengos de Monsaraz P 155 C3
Rehau D 83 B4
Rehburg D 72 B2
Rehden D 72 B1
Rehna D 65 C4
Reichelsheim D 93 B4
Reichelshofen D 94 B2
Reichenau A 110 B2
Reichenbach
Sachsen D 83 B4
Sachsen D 84 A2
Reichenfels A 110 B1
Reichensachsen D 82 A2
Reichertshofen D 95 C3
Reichshoffen F 93 C3
Reiden CH 106 B2
Reigada
E 141 A4
P 149 B3
Reigate GB 44 B3
Reillanne F 132 B1
Reillo E 158 B2
Reims F 91 B4
Reinach CH 106 B3
Reinbek D 72 A3
Reinberg D 66 B2
Reine N 194 C4
Reinfeld D 65 C3
Reinheim D 93 B4
Reinli N 47 B6
Reinosa E 142 A2
Reinstorf D 65 C4
Reinsvoll N 48 B2
Reisach A 109 C4
Reiss GB 32 C3
Reitan N 199 C8
Reit im Winkl D 109 B3
Rejmyre S 56 B1
Rekavice BIH 124 C3
Rekovac SRB 127 D3
Relleu E 159 C3
Rém H 125 A5
Remagen D 80 B3
Rémalard F 89 B4
Rembercourt-aux-Pots F 91 C5
Remedios P 154 B1
Remels D 71 A4
Remetea Mare RO 126 B3
Remich L 92 B2
Rémilly F 92 B2
Remiremont F 105 A5
Remolinos E 144 C2
Remoulins F 131 B3
Remscheid D 80 A3
Rémuzat F 131 A4
Rena N 48 A3
Renaison F 117 A3
Renazé F 101 B4
Renchen D 93 C4
Rencurel F 118 B2
Rende I 174 B2
Rendina GR 182 D3
Rendsburg D 64 B2
Renedo E 150 A3
Renens CH 105 C5
Renfrew GB 34 C3
Rengsjö S 50 A3
Reni UA 17 C8
Rennebu N 198 C6
Rennerod D 81 B4
Rennertshofen D 94 C3
Rennes F 101 A4
Rennes-les-Bains F 146 B3
Rennweg A 109 B4
Rens DK 64 B2
Rensjön S 196 A2
Rentería E 144 A2
Rentjärn S 200 A4
Répcelak H 111 B4
Repojoki FIN 193 D9
Repvåg N 193 B9
Requena E 159 B2
Réquista F 130 A1
Rerik D 65 B4
Resana I 121 B4
Resarö S 57 A4
Reschen = Résia I 108 C1
Resen MK 182 B3
Resende P 148 A2
Résia = Reschen I 108 C1
Reşiţa
RO 16 C4
RO 126 B3
Resko PL 67 C4
Resnik SRB 127 C2
Ressons-sur-Matz F 90 B2
Restábal E 163 B4
Resuttano I 177 B3
Retamal E 155 C4
Retford GB 40 B3
Rethel F 91 B4
Rethem D 72 B2
Rethimno GR 185 D5
Retie B 79 A5
Retiers F 101 B4
Retortillo E 149 B3
Retortillo de Soria E 151 A4
Retournac F 117 B4
Rétság H 112 B3
Rettenegg A 110 B2
Retuerta del Bullaque E 157 A3
Retz A 97 C3
Retzbach D 94 B1
Reuden D 73 B5
Reuilly F 103 B4
Reus E 147 C2
Reusel NL 79 A5
Reuterstadt Stavenhagen D 74 A1
Reuth D 95 B4
Reutlingen D 94 C1
Reutte A 108 B1
Reuver NL 80 A2
Revel F 146 A2
Revello I 119 C4
Revenga E 151 B3
Revest-du-Bion F 132 A1
Révfülöp H 111 C4
Revigny-sur-Ornain F 91 C4
Revin F 91 B4
Řevnice CZ 96 B2
Řevničov CZ 84 B1
Revo I 121 A4
Revsnes N 47 A4
Revúca SK 99 C4
Rewa PL 69 A3
Rewal PL 67 B4
Rexbo S 50 B2
Reyðarfjörður IS 191 B11
Reyero E 142 B1
Reykhólar IS 190 B3
Reykholt
Árnessýsla IS 190 C5
Borgarfjarðarsýsla IS 190 C4
Reykjahlið IS 191 B9
Reykjavík IS 190 C4
Rezé F 101 B4
Rēzekne LV 8 D5
Rezovo BG 17 E8
Rezzato I 120 B3
Rezzoáglio I 134 A2
Rhade D 72 A2
Rhaunen D 93 B3
Rhayader GB 39 B3
Rheda-Wiedenbrück D 81 A4
Rhede
Niedersachsen D 71 A4
Nordrhein-Westfalen D 80 A2
Rheinau D 93 C3
Rheinbach D 80 B2
Rheinberg D 80 A2
Rheine D 71 B4
Rheinfelden D 106 B2
Rheinsberg D 74 A1
Rhêmes-Notre-Dame I 119 B4
Rhenen NL 70 C2
Rhens D 81 B3
Rheydt D 80 A2
Rhiconich GB 32 C2
Rhinow D 73 B5
Rhiw GB 38 B2
Rho I 120 B2
Rhodes GR 188 C3
Rhondda GB 39 C3
Rhosllanerchrugog GB 38 A3
Rhosneigr GB 38 A2
Rhossili GB 39 C2
Rhubodach GB 34 C2
Rhuddlan GB 38 A3
Rhyl GB 38 A3
Rhynie GB 33 D4
Riala S 57 A4
Riallé F 101 B4
Riaño E 142 B1
Riano I 168 A2
Rians F 132 B1
Rianxo E 140 B2
Riaza E 151 A4
Riba E 143 A3
Ribadavia E 140 B2
Ribadeo E 141 A3
Riba de Saelices E 152 B1
Ribadesella E 142 A1
Ribaflecha E 143 B4
Ribaforada E 144 C2
Ribare SRB 127 C3
Riba-roja d'Ebre E 153 A4
Riba-Roja de Turia E 159 B3
Ribe DK 59 C1
Ribeauvillé F 106 A2
Ribécourt-Dreslincourt F 90 B2
Ribeira da Pena P 148 A2
Ribeira de Piquín E 141 A3
Ribemont F 91 B3
Ribera I 176 B2
Ribérac F 129 A3
Ribera de Cardós E 146 B2
Ribera del Fresno E 156 B1
Ribesalbes E 159 A3
Ribes de Freser E 147 B3
Ribiers F 132 A1
Ribnica
BIH 139 A4
SLO 123 B3
Ribnica na Potorju SLO 110 C2
Ribnik HR 123 B4
Rîbniţa MD 17 B8
Ribnitz-Damgarten D 66 B1
Ribolla I 135 C4
Říčany CZ 97 B4
Ričany CZ 96 B2
Ríccia I 170 B2
Riccione I 136 A1
Ricco Del Golfo I 134 A2
Richebourg F 105 A4
Richelieu F 102 B2
Richisau CH 107 B3
Richmond
Greater London GB 44 B3
North Yorkshire GB 37 B5
Richtenberg D 66 B1
Richterswil CH 107 B3
Rickling D 64 B3
Rickmansworth GB 44 B3
Ricla E 152 A2
Riddarhyttan S 50 C2
Ridderkerk NL 79 A4
Riddes CH 119 A4
Ridjica SRB 125 B5
Riec-sur-Bélon F 100 B2
Ried A 109 A4
Riedenburg D 95 C3
Ried im Oberinntal A 108 B1
Riedlingen D 107 A4
Riedstadt D 93 B4
Riegersburg A 110 C2
Riego de la Vega E 141 B5
Riego del Camino E 149 A4
Riello E 141 B5
Riemst B 80 B1
Rienne B 91 B4
Riénsena E 142 A2
Riesa D 83 A5
Riese Pio X I 121 B4
Riesi I 177 B3
Riestedt D 82 A3
Rietberg D 81 A4
Rieti I 169 A2
Rietschen D 84 A2
Rieumes F 146 A2
Rieupeyroux F 130 A1
Rieux-Volvestre F 146 A2
Riez F 132 B2
Riga LV 8 D4
Riggisberg CH 106 C2
Rignac F 130 A1
Rignano Gargánico I 171 B3
Rigolato I 109 C3
Rigside GB 36 A3
Rigutino I 135 B4
Riihimäki FIN 8 B4
Rijeka HR 123 B3
Rijen NL 79 A4
Rijkevorsel B 79 A4
Rijssen NL 71 B3
Rila BG 183 A5
Rilić BIH 138 B3
Rilievo I 176 B1
Rillé F 102 B2
Rillo de Gallo E 152 B2
Rimavská Baňa SK 99 C3
Rimavská Seč SK 99 C4
Rimavská Sobota SK 99 C4
Rimbo S 57 A4
Rimforsa S 56 B1
Rímini I 136 A1
Rîmnicu Sărat RO 17 C7
Rimogne F 91 B4
Rimpar D 94 B1
Rimske Toplice SLO 123 A4
Rincón de la Victoria E 163 B3
Rincón de Soto E 144 B2
Rindal N 198 B6
Rinde N 46 A3
Ringarum S 56 B2
Ringaskiddy IRL 29 C3
Ringe DK 59 C3
Ringebu N 48 A2
Ringkøbing DK 59 B1
Ringsaker N 48 B2
Ringsted DK 61 D1
Ringwood GB 44 C2
Rinkaby S 63 C2
Rinkabyholm S 63 B4
Rinlo E 141 A3
Rinn A 108 B2
Rinteln D 72 B2
Rio E 140 B3
Riobo E 140 B2
Riodeva E 152 B2
Rio do Coures P 154 B2
Rio Douro P 148 A2
Riofrio E 150 B3
Rio Frio P 154 C2
Riofrio de Aliste E 149 A3
Rio frio de Riaza E 151 A4
Riogordo E 163 B3
Rioja E 164 C2
Riola I 135 A4
Riola Sardo I 179 C2
Riolobos E 155 B4
Riom F 116 B3
Riomaggiore I 134 A2
Rio Maior P 154 B2
Rio Marina I 134 C3
Riom-ès-Montagnes F 116 B2
Rion-des-Landes F 128 C2
Rionegro del Puente E 141 B4
Rionero in Vúlture I 172 B1
Riopar E 158 C1
Riós E 141 C3
Rioseco E 142 A1
Rioseco de Tapia E 141 B5
Rio Tinto P 148 A1
Riotord F 117 B4
Riotorto E 141 A3
Rioz F 105 B5
Ripač BIH 124 C1
Ripacándida I 172 B1
Ripanj SRB 127 C2
Ripatransone I 136 C2
Ripley GB 40 B2
Ripoll E 147 B3
Ripon GB 40 A2
Riposto I 177 B4
Ripsa S 56 B2
Risan MNE 16 D3
Risbäck S 200 B1
Risca GB 39 C3
Rischenau D 81 A5
Riscle F 128 C2
Risebo S 56 B2
Risnes N 46 A2
Rišňovce SK 98 C1
Risør N 53 B5
Risøyhamn N 194 B6
Rissna S 199 B12
Ritsem S 194 C8
Ritterhude D 72 A1
Riutula FIN 193 D10
Riva del Garda I 121 B3
Riva Lígure I 133 B3
Rivanazzano I 120 C2
Rivarolo Canavese I 119 B4
Rivarolo Mantovano I 121 B3
Rive-de-Gier F 117 B4
Rivedoux-Plage F 114 B2
Rivello I 174 A1
Rivergaro I 120 C2
Rives F 118 B2
Rivesaltes F 146 B3
Rivignano I 122 B2
Rivne UA 13 C7
Rívoli I 119 B4
Rivolta d'Adda I 120 B2
Rixheim F 106 B2
Rixo S 54 B2
Riza GR 183 C5
Rizokarpaso CY 181 A3
Rjukan N 47 C5
Rø DK 67 A3
Rö S 57 A4
Roa
E 143 C3
N 48 B2
Roade GB 44 A3
Roager DK 59 C1
Roaldkvam N 52 A2
Roanne F 117 A4
Röbäck S 200 C6
Robakowo PL 69 B3
Róbbio I 120 B1
Röbel D 73 A5
Roberton GB 35 C5
Robertsfors S 200 B6
Robertville B 80 B2
Robin Hood's Bay GB 37 B6
Robleda E 149 B3
Robledillo de Trujillo E 156 A2
Robledo
Albacete E 158 C1
Orense E 141 B4
Robledo de Chavela E 151 B3
Robledo del Buey E 156 A3
Robledo del Mazo E 156 A3
Robledollano E 156 A2
Robles de la Valcueva E 142 B1
Robliza de Cojos E 149 B4
Robres E 145 C3
Robres del Castillo E 144 B1
Rocafort de Queralt E 147 C2
Rocamadour F 129 B4
Roccabernarda I 175 B2
Roccabianca I 120 B3
Roccadàspide I 172 B1
Rocca di Mezzo I 169 A3
Rocca di Papa I 168 B2
Roccagorga I 169 B3
Rocca Imperiale I 174 A2
Roccalbegna I 135 C4
Roccalumera I 177 B4
Roccamena I 176 B2
Roccamonfina I 170 B1
Roccanova I 174 A2
Roccapalumba I 176 B2
Roccapassa I 169 A3
Rocca Priora I 136 B2
Roccaraso I 169 B4
Rocca San Casciano I 135 A4
Roccasecca I 169 B3
Rocca Sinibalda I 169 A2
Roccastrada I 135 B4
Roccatederighi I 135 B4
Roccella Iónica I 175 C2
Rocchetta Sant'António I 172 A1
Rocester GB 40 C2
Rochdale GB 40 B1
Rochechouart F 115 C4
Rochefort
B 79 B5
F 114 C3
Rochefort-en-Terre F 101 B3
Rochefort-Montagne F 116 B2
Rochefort-sur-Nenon F 105 B4
Roche-lez-Beaupré F 105 B5
Rochemaure F 131 A3
Rocheservière F 114 B2
Rochester
Medway GB 45 B4
Northumberland GB 37 A4
Rochlitz D 83 A4
Rociana del Condado E 161 B3
Rockenhausen D 93 B3
Rockhammar S 56 A1
Rockneby S 62 B4
Ročko Polje HR 123 B3
Ročov CZ 84 B1
Rocroi F 91 B4
Rodach D 82 B2
Roda de Bara E 147 C2
Roda de Ter E 147 C3
Rodalben D 93 B3
Rødberg N 47 B5
Rødby DK 65 B4
Rødbyhavn DK 65 B4
Rødding
Sonderjyllands Amt. DK 59 C2
Viborg Amt. DK 58 B1
Rödeby S 63 B3
Rodeiro E 140 B3
Rødekro DK 64 A2
Roden NL 71 A3
Ródenas E 152 B2
Rodenkirchen D 72 A1
Rödental D 82 B3
Rödermark D 93 B4
Rodewisch D 83 B4
Rodez F 130 A1
Rodi Gargánico I 171 B3
Roding D 95 B4
Rödjebro S 51 B4
Rødkærsbro DK 59 B2
Rodolivas GR 183 C5
Rodoñá E 147 C2
Rødvig DK 65 A5
Roermond NL 80 A1
Roesbrugge B 78 B2
Roeschwoog F 93 C4
Roeselare B 78 B3
Roetgen D 80 B2
Roffiac F 116 B3
Röfors S 55 B5
Rofrano I 172 B1
Rogač HR 138 B2
Rogačica SRB 127 C1
Rogalinek PL 76 B1
Rogaška Slatina SLO 123 A4
Rogatec SLO 123 A4
Rogatica BIH 139 B5
Rogatyn UA 13 D6
Rogätz D 73 B4
Roggendorf D 65 C4
Roggiano Gravina I 174 B2
Roghadal GB 31 B2
Rogliano
F 180 A2
I 175 B2
Rognan N 195 C6
Rogne N 47 A6
Rognes F 131 B4
Rogny-les-7-Ecluses F 103 B4
Rogowo PL 76 B2
Rogoznica HR 138 B1
Rogoźnica PL 85 A4
Rogoźno PL 76 B1
Rohan F 101 A3
Röhlingen D 94 C2
Rohožnik SK 98 C1
Rohr D 82 B2
Rohrbach A 96 C1
Rohrbach-lès-Bitche F 92 B3
Rohrberg D 73 B4
Rohr im Gebirge A 110 B2
Röhrnbach D 96 C1
Roisel F 90 B3
Roja LV 8 D3
Rojales E 165 A4
Röjeråsen S 50 B1
Rojewo PL 76 B3
Rokiciny PL 87 A3
Rokietnica PL 75 B5
Rokiškis LT 8 E4
Rokitki PL 85 A3
Rokycany CZ 96 B1
Rolampont F 105 B4
Rold DK 58 B2
Røldal N 52 A2
Rolde NL 71 B3
Rolfs S 196 D6
Rollag N 47 B6
Rollán E 149 B4
Rolle CH 105 C5
Roma = Rome I 168 B2
Roma S 57 C4
Romagnano Sésia I 119 B5
Romagné F 88 B2
Romakloster S 57 C4
Roman RO 17 B7
Romana I 178 B2
Romanèche-Thorins F 117 A4
Romano di Lombardia I 120 B2
Romanshorn CH 107 B4
Romans-sur-Isère F 118 B2
Rombas F 92 B2
Rome = Roma I 168 B2
Romeán E 141 B3
Romenay F 105 C4
Romeral E 157 A4
Römerstein D 94 C1
Rometta I 177 A4
Romford GB 45 B4
Romhány H 112 B3
Römhild D 82 B2
Romilly-sur-Seine F 91 C3
Romont CH 106 C1
Romorantin-Lanthenay F 103 B3
Romrod D 81 B5
Romsey GB 44 C2
Rømskog N 54 A2
Rønbjerg DK 58 B1
Roncal E 144 B3
Ronce-les-Bains F 114 C2
Ronchamp F 106 B1
Ronchi dei Legionari I 122 B2
Ronciglione I 168 A2
Ronco Canavese I 119 B4
Ronco Scrivia I 120 C1
Ronda E 162 B2
Rønde DK 59 B3
Rone S 57 C4
Ronehamn S 57 C4
Rong N 46 B1
Rönnäng S 60 B1
Rønne DK 67 A3
Ronneburg D 83 B4
Ronneby S 63 B3
Rönneshytta S 55 B6
Rönninge S 57 A3
Rönnöfors S 199 B10
Rönö S 56 B2
Ronov nad Doubravou CZ 97 B3
Ronse B 79 B3
Roosendaal NL 79 A4
Roosky IRL 26 C3
Ropczyce PL 87 B5
Ropeid N 52 A2
Ropinsalmi FIN 192 D5
Ropuerelos del Páramo E 141 B5
Roquebilière F 133 A3
Roquebrun F 130 B2
Roquecourbe F 130 B1
Roquefort F 128 B2
Roquemaure F 131 A3
Roquesteron F 132 B3
Roquetas de Mar E 164 C2
Roquetes E 153 B4
Roquevaire F 132 B1
Røra N 199 B8
Rörbäcksnäs S 49 A4
Rørbæk DK 58 B2
Rore BIH 138 A2
Röro S 60 B1
Røros N 199 C8
Rorschach CH 107 B4
Rørvig DK 61 D1
Rørvik N 199 A8
Rörvik S 62 A2
Rosà I 121 B4
Rosal de la Frontera E 161 B2
Rosalina Mare I 122 B1
Rosa Marina I 173 B3
Rosans F 132 A1
Rosário P 160 B1
Rosarno I 175 C1
Rosbach D 81 B3

Rosche D 73 B3
Rościszewo PL 77 B4
Roscoff F 100 A2
Roscommon IRL 28 A3
Roscrea IRL 28 B4
Rosdorf D 82 A1
Rose I 174 B2
Rosegg A 109 C5
Rosehall GB 32 D2
Rosehearty GB 33 D4
Rosel GB 88 A1
Rosell E 153 B4
Roselló E 153 A4
Rosendal N 46 C3
Rosenfeld D 93 C4
Rosenfors S 62 A3
Rosenheim D 108 B3
Rosenow D 74 A2
Rosenthal D 81 A4
Rosersberg S 57 A3
Roses E 147 B4
Roseto degli Abruzzi I 169 A4
Roseto Valfortore I 170 B3
Rosheim F 93 C3
Rosia I 135 B4
Rosice CZ 97 B4
Rosières-en-Santerre F 90 B2
Rosignano Maríttimo I 134 B3
Rosignano Solvay I 134 B3
Roşiori-de-Vede RO 17 C6
Roskhill GB 31 B2
Roskilde DK 61 D2
Roskovec AL 182 C1
Röslau D 83 B3
Roslev DK 58 B1
Rosmaninhal P 155 B3
Rosnowo PL 67 B5
Rosolini I 177 C3
Rosova MNE 139 B5
Rosoy F 104 A2
Rosporden F 100 B2
Rosquete P 154 B2
Rosrath D 80 B3
Rossa CH 120 A2
Rossano I 174 B2
Rossas
Aveiro P 148 B1
Braga P 148 A1
Rossdorf D 82 B2
Rossett GB 38 A4
Rosshaupten D 108 B1
Rossiglione I 133 A4
Rossignol B 92 B1
Rossla D 82 A3
Rosslare IRL 30 B2
Rosslare Harbour IRL 30 B2
Rosslau D 83 A4
Rosslea GB 27 B3
Rossleben D 82 A3
Rossön S 200 C2
Ross-on-Wye GB 39 C4
Rossoszyca PL 86 A2
Rosswein D 83 A5
Röstånga S 61 C3
Roštár SK 99 C4
Rostock D 65 B5
Rostrenen F 100 A2
Røsvik N 194 C6
Rosvik S 196 D4
Rosyth GB 35 B4
Röszke H 126 A2
Rot S 49 A6
Rota E 161 C3
Rota Greca I 174 B2
Rot am See D 94 B2
Rotberget N 49 B4
Rotella I 136 C2
Rotenburg
Hessen D 82 B1
Niedersachsen D 72 A2
Roth
Bayern D 94 B3
Rheinland-Pfalz D 81 B3
Rothbury GB 37 A5
Rothemühl D 74 A2
Röthenbach D 95 B3
Rothenburg D 84 A2
Rothenburg ob der Tauber D 94 B2
Rothéneuf F 88 B2
Rothenklempenow D 74 A3
Rothenstein D 94 C3
Rotherham GB 40 B2
Rothes GB 32 D3
Rothesay GB 34 C2
Rothwell GB 44 A3
Rotnes N 48 B2
Rotonda I 174 B2
Rotondella I 174 A2
Rotova E 159 C3
Rott
Bayern D 108 B1
Bayern D 108 B3
Rottach-Egern D 108 B2
Röttenbach D 94 B3
Rottenbuch D 108 B1
Rottenburg
Baden-Württemberg D 93 C4
Bayern D 95 C4
Rottenmann A 110 B1
Rotterdam NL 79 A4
Rotthalmünster D 96 C1
Rottingdean GB 44 C3
Röttingen D 94 B1
Rottleberode D 82 A2
Rottne S 62 A2
Rottneros S 55 A4
Rottofreno I 120 B2
Rottweil D 107 A3
Rötz D 95 B4
Roubaix F 78 B3
Roudnice nad Labem CZ 84 B2
Roudouallec F 100 A2
Rouen F 89 A5
Rouffach F 106 B2
Rougé F 101 B4
Rougemont F 105 B5
Rougemont le-Château F 106 B1
Rouillac F 115 C3
Rouillé F 115 B4
Roujan F 130 B2
Roulans F 105 B5
Roundwood IRL 30 A2
Rousínov CZ 97 B4
Roussac F 115 B5
Roussennac F 130 A1
Rousses F 130 A2
Roussillon F 117 B4
Rouvroy-sur-Audry F 91 B4
Rouy F 104 B2
Rovanieman maalaiskunta FIN 197 C8
Rovaniemi FIN 197 C8
Rovato I 120 B2
Rovensko pod Troskami CZ 84 B3
Roverbella I 121 B3
Rovereto I 121 B4
Rövershagen D 65 B5
Roverud N 49 B4
Rovigo I 121 B4
Rovinj HR 122 B2
Rovišce HR 124 B2
Rów PL 74 B3
Rowy PL 68 A2
Royal Leamington Spa GB 44 A2
Royal Tunbridge Wells GB 45 B4
Royan F 114 C2
Royat F 116 B3
Roybon F 118 B2
Roybridge GB 34 B3
Roye F 90 B2
Royère-de-Vassivière F 116 B1
Røykenvik N 48 B2
Royos E 164 B2
Røyrvik N 199 A10
Royston GB 44 A3
Rozadas E 141 A4
Rozalén del Monte E 151 C5
Różańsko PL 75 B3
Rozay-en-Brie F 90 C2
Roždalovice CZ 84 B3
Rozdilna UA 17 B9
Rozental PL 69 B4
Rozhyshche UA 13 C6
Rožmitál pod Třemšínem CZ 96 B1
Rožňava SK 99 C4
Rožnov pod Radhoštěm CZ 98 B2
Rozoy-sur-Serre F 91 B4
Rozprza PL 86 A3
Roztoky CZ 84 B2
Rozvadov CZ 95 B4
Rozzano I 120 B2
Rrëshen AL 182 B1
Rrogozhine AL 182 B1
Ruanes E 156 A2
Rubbestadnesset N 46 C2
Rubi E 147 C3
Rubiá E 141 B4
Rubiacedo de Abajo E 143 B3
Rubielos Bajos E 158 B1
Rubielos de Mora E 153 B3
Rubiera I 121 C3
Rubik AL 182 B1
Rucandio E 143 B3
Rud
Akershus N 48 B3
Buskerud N 48 B2
Ruda
PL 86 A2
S 62 A4
Rudabánya H 99 C4
Ruda Maleniecka PL 87 A4
Ruda Pilczycka PL 87 A4
Ruda Śl. PL 86 B2
Ruddervorde B 78 A3
Ruden A 110 C1
Rudersberg D 94 C1
Rudersdorf A 111 B3
Rüdersdorf D 74 B2
Ruderting D 96 C1
Rüdesheim D 93 B3
Rudkøbing DK 65 B3
Rudmanns A 97 C3
Rudna
CZ 96 A2
PL 85 A4
Rudnik SRB 127 C2
Rudniki
Opolskie PL 86 A2
Śląskie PL 86 B3
Rudno
Dolnośląskie PL 85 A4
Pomorskie PL 69 B3
Rudnya RUS 13 A9
Rudolstadt D 82 B3
Rudowica PL 84 A3
Rudozem BG 183 B6
Rudskoga S 55 A5
Rudston GB 40 A3
Ruds Vedby DK 61 D1
Rudy PL 86 B2
Rue F 78 B1
Rueda E 150 A3
Rueda de Jalón E 152 A2
Ruelle-sur-Touvre F 115 C4
Ruerrero E 143 B3
Ruffano I 173 C4
Ruffec F 115 B4
Rufina I 135 B4
Rugby GB 44 A2
Rugeley GB 40 C2
Ruggstrop S 62 B4
Rugles F 89 B4
Rugozero RUS 3 D13
Rühen D 73 B3
Ruhla D 82 B2
Ruhland D 84 A1
Ruhle D 71 B4
Ruhpolding D 109 B3
Ruhstorf D 96 C1
Ruidera E 158 C1
Ruillé-sur-le-Loir F 102 B2
Ruinen NL 71 B3
Ruiselede B 78 A3
Ruka FIN 197 C12
Rulles B 92 B1
Rülzheim D 93 B4
Rum H 111 B3
Ruma SRB 127 B1
Rumboci BIH 138 B3
Rumburk CZ 84 B2
Rumenka SRB 126 B1
Rumia PL 69 A3
Rumigny F 91 B4
Rumilly F 118 B2
Rumma S 56 B2
Rumney GB 39 C3
Rumont F 91 C5
Runa P 154 B1
Runcorn GB 38 A4
Rundmoen N 195 D5
Rungsted DK 61 D2
Runhällen S 51 B3
Runowo PL 69 A5
Runtuna S 56 B3
Ruokojärvi FIN 196 B7
Ruokolahti FIN 9 B6
Ruokto S 196 B2
Ruoms F 131 A3
Ruoti I 172 B1
Rupa HR 123 B3
Ruppichteroth D 80 B3
Rupt-sur-Moselle F 106 B1
Rus E 157 B4
Ruse BG 17 D7
Ruše SLO 110 C2
Rusele S 200 B4
Ruševo HR 125 B4
Rush IRL 30 A2
Rushden GB 44 A3
Rusiec PL 86 A2
Rusinowo
Zachodnio-Pomorskie PL 67 C4
Zachodnio-Pomorskie PL 75 A5
Ruskele S 200 B4
Ruski Krstur SRB 126 B1
Ruskington GB 40 B3
Rusovce SK 111 A4
Rüsselsheim D 93 B4
Russelv N 192 C4
Russi I 135 A5
Rust A 111 B3
Rustefjelbma N 193 B12
Rustrel F 131 B4
Ruszki PL 77 B5
Ruszów PL 84 A3
Rute E 163 A3
Rüthen D 81 A4
Rutherglen GB 35 C3
Ruthin GB 38 A3
Ruthven GB 32 D2
Ruthwell GB 36 B3
Rüti CH 107 B3
Rutigliano I 173 A3
Rutledal N 46 A2
Rutvik S 196 D5
Ruurlo NL 71 B3
Ruuvaoja FIN 197 B11
Ruvo del Monte I 172 B1
Ruvo di Púglia I 171 B4
Ruynes-en-Margeride F 116 C3
Ružic HR 138 B2
Ružomberok SK 99 B3
Ruzsa H 126 A1
Ry DK 59 B2
Rybany SK 98 C2
Rybina PL 69 A4
Rybnik PL 86 B2
Rychliki PL 69 B4
Rychlocice PL 86 A2
Rychnov nad Kněžnou CZ 85 B4
Rychnowo PL 77 A5
Rychtal PL 86 A1
Rychwał PL 76 B3
Ryczywół PL 87 A5
Ryczywół PL 75 B5
Ryd S 63 B2
Rydaholm S 62 B2
Rydal S 60 B2
Rydbo S 57 A4
Rydboholm S 60 B2
Ryde GB 44 C2
Rydöbruk S 60 C3
Rydsgård S 66 A2
Rydsnäs S 62 A3
Rydultowy PL 86 B2
Rydzyna PL 85 A4
Rye GB 45 C4
Rygge N 54 A1
Ryjewo PL 69 B3
Rykene N 53 B4
Rymań PL 67 C4
Rýmařov CZ 98 B1
Rynarzewo PL 76 A2
Ryomgård DK 59 B3
Rypefjord N 192 B7
Rypin PL 77 A4
Rysjedalsvika N 46 A2
Ryssby S 60 C4
Rytel PL 68 B2
Rytinki FIN 197 D10
Rytro PL 99 B4
Rywociny PL 77 A5
Rzeczenica PL 68 B2
Rzeczniów PL 87 A5
Rzeczyca PL 87 A4
Rzęgnowo PL 77 A5
Rzejowice PL 87 A3
Rzemień PL 87 B5
Rzepin PL 75 B3
Rzesznikowo PL 67 C4
Rzeszów PL 12 C4
Rzgów PL 86 A3
Rzhev RUS 9 D9

S

Saal
Bayern D 82 B2
Bayern D 95 C3
Saalbach A 109 B3
Saalburg D 83 B3
Saales F 92 C3
Saalfeld D 82 B3
Saalfelden am Steinernen Meer A 109 B3
Saanen CH 106 C2
Saarbrücken D 92 B2
Saarburg D 92 B2
Saarijärvi FIN 8 A4
Saari-Kämä FIN 197 C9
Saarlouis D 92 B2
Saas-Fee CH 119 A4
Šabac SRB 127 C1
Sabadell E 147 C3
Sabáudia I 169 B3
Sabbioneta I 121 C3
Sabero E 142 B1
Sabiñánigo E 145 B3
Sabiote E 157 B4
Sables-d'Or-les-Pins F 101 A3
Sablé-sur-Sarthe F 102 B1
Sabóia P 160 B1
Saborsko HR 123 B4
Sæbøvik N 52 A1
Sabres F 128 B2
Sabrosa P 148 A2
Sabugal P 149 B2
Sabuncu TR 187 C5
Sæby DK 58 A3
Săcălaz RO 126 B3
Sacecorbo E 152 B1
Saceda del Rio E 151 B5
Sacedón E 151 B5
Săcele RO 17 C6
Saceruela E 156 B3
Sachsenburg A 109 C4
Sachsenhagen D 72 B2
Sacile I 122 B1
Sacramenia E 151 A4
Sada E 140 A2
Sádaba E 144 B2
Saddell GB 34 C2
Sadernes E 147 B3
Sadki PL 76 A2
Sadkowice PL 87 A4
Sadlinki PL 69 B3
Sadów PL 75 B3
Sadská CZ 84 B2
Saelices E 151 C5
Saelices de Mayorga E 142 B1
Saerbeck D 71 B4
Saeul L 92 B1
Safaalan TR 186 A3
Safara P 161 A2
Säffle S 55 A3
Saffron Walden GB 45 A4
Safranbolu TR 187 A7
Säfsnäs S 50 B1
Şag RO 126 B3
Sagard D 66 B2
S'Agaro E 147 C4
Sågmyra S 50 B2
Sagone F 180 A1
Sagres P 160 C1
Ságújfalu H 113 A3
Sagunt E 159 B3
Sagvåg N 52 A1
Ságvár H 112 C2
Sagy F 105 C4
Sahagún E 142 B1
Šahy SK 112 A2
Saignelégier CH 106 B1
Saignes F 116 B2
Saija FIN 197 B11
Saillagouse F 146 B3
Saillans F 118 C2
Sains Richaumont F 91 B3
St Abb's GB 35 C5
St Affrique F 130 B1
St Agnan F 104 C2
St Agnant F 114 C3
St Agnes GB 42 B1
St Agrève F 117 B4
St Aignan F 103 B3
St Aignan-sur-Roë F 101 B4
St Albans GB 44 B3
St Alban-sur-Limagnole F 117 C3
St Amand-en-Puisaye F 104 B2
St Amand-les-Eaux F 79 B3
St Amand-Longpré F 103 B3
St Amand-Montrond F 103 C4
St Amans F 117 C3
St Amans-Soult F 130 B1
St Amant-Roche-Savine F 117 B3
St Amarin F 106 B1
St Ambroix F 131 A3
St Amé F 106 A1
St Amour F 118 A2
St André-de-Corcy F 117 B4
St André-de-Cubzac F 128 B2
St André-de-l'Eure F 89 B5
St André-de-Roquepertuis F 131 A3
St André-de-Sangonis F 130 B2
St Andre-de-Valborgne F 130 A2
St André-les-Alpes F 132 B2
St Andrews GB 35 B5
St Angel F 116 B2
St Anthème F 117 B3
St Antoine F 180 A2
St Antoine-de-Ficalba F 129 B3
St Antönien CH 107 C4
St Antonin-Noble-Val F 129 B4
St Août F 103 C3
St Armant-Tallende F 116 B3
St Arnoult F 90 C1
St Asaph GB 38 A3
St Astier F 129 A3
St Athan GB 39 C3
St Auban F 132 B2
St Aubin
CH 106 C1
F 105 B4
GB 88 A1
St Aubin-d'Aubigne F 101 A4
St Aubin-du-Cormier F 101 A4
St Aubin-sur-Aire F 92 C1
St Aubin-sur-Mer F 89 A3
St Aulaye F 128 A3
St Austell GB 42 B2
St Avit F 116 B2
St Avold F 92 B2
St Aygulf F 132 B2
St Bauzille-de-Putois F 130 B2
St Béat F 145 B4
St Beauzély F 130 A1
St Bees GB 36 B3
St Benim-d'Azy F 104 C2
St Benoît-du-Sault F 115 B5
St Benoit-en-Woëvre F 92 C1
St Berthevin F 102 A1
St Blaise-la-Roche F 92 C3
St Blazey GB 42 B2
St Blin F 105 A4
St Bonnet F 118 C3
St Bonnet Briance F 115 C5
St Bonnet-de-Joux F 104 C3
St Bonnet-le-Château F 117 B4
St Bonnet-le-Froid F 117 B4
St Brévin-les-Pins F 101 B3
St Briac-sur-Mer F 101 A3
St Brice-en-Coglès F 88 B2
St Brieuc F 101 A3
St Bris-le-Vineux F 104 B2
St Broladre F 88 B2
St Calais F 102 B2
St Cannat F 131 B4
St Cast-le-Guildo F 101 A3
St Céré F 129 B4
St Cergue CH 118 A3
St Cergues F 118 A3
St Cernin F 116 B2
St Chamant F 116 B1
St Chamas F 131 B4
St Chamond F 117 B4
St Chély-d'Apcher F 116 C3
St Chély-d'Aubrac F 116 C2
St Chinian F 130 B1
St Christol F 131 A4
St Christol-lès-Alès F 131 A3
St Christoly-Médoc F 114 C3
St Christophe-du-Ligneron F 114 B2
St Christophe-en-Brionnais F 117 A4
St Ciers-sur-Gironde F 128 A2
St Clair-sur-Epte F 90 B1
St Clar F 129 C3
St Claud F 115 C4
St Claude F 118 A2
St Clears GB 39 C2
St Columb Major GB 42 B2
St Come-d'Olt F 130 A1
St Cosme-en-Vairais F 89 B4
St Cyprien
Dordogne F 129 B4
Pyrenées-Orientales F 146 B4
St Cyr-sur-Loire F 102 B2
St Cyr-sur-Mer F 132 B1
St Cyr-sur-Methon F 117 A4
St David's GB 39 C1
St Denis F 90 C2
St Denis-d'Oléron F 114 B2
St Denis d'Orques F 102 A1
St Didier F 117 A4
St Didier-en-Velay F 117 B4
St Dié F 92 C2
St Dier-d'Auvergne F 117 B3
St Dizier F 91 C4
St Dizier-Leyrenne F 116 A1
St Dogmaels GB 39 B2
Ste Adresse F 89 A4
Ste Anne F 89 B4
Ste Anne-d'Auray F 100 B3
Ste Croix CH 105 C5
Ste Croix-Volvestre F 146 A2
Ste Engrâce F 144 A3
Ste Enimie F 130 A2
St Efflam F 100 A2
Ste Foy-de-Peyrolières F 146 A2
Ste Foy-la-Grande F 128 B3
Ste Foy l'Argentiere F 117 B4
Ste Gauburge-Ste Colombe F 89 B4
Ste Gemme la Plaine F 114 B2
Ste Geneviève F 90 B2
St Égrève F 118 B2
Ste Hélène F 128 B2
Ste Hélène-sur-Isère F 118 B3
Ste Hermine F 114 B2
Ste Jalle F 131 A4
Ste Livrade-sur-Lot F 129 B3
St Eloy-les-Mines F 116 A2
Ste Marie-aux-Mines F 106 A2
Ste Marie-du-Mont F 88 A2
Ste Maure-de-Touraine F 102 B2
Ste Maxime F 132 B2
Ste Ménéhould F 91 B4
Ste Mère-Église F 88 A2
St Emiland F 104 C3
St Émilion F 128 B2
St Enoder GB 42 B2
Sainteny F 88 A2
Ste Ode B 92 A1
Saintes F 114 C3
Ste Savine F 91 C4
Ste Sévère-sur-Indre F 103 C4
Ste Sigolène F 117 B4
St Esteben F 144 A2
St Estèphe F 128 A2
Ste Suzanne F 102 A1
St Étienne F 117 B4
St Etienne-de-Baigorry F 144 A2
St Étienne-de-Cuines F 118 B3
St Etienne-de-Fursac F 116 A1
St Etienne-de-Montluc F 101 B4
St Etienne-de-St Geoirs F 118 B2
St Étienne-de-Tinée F 132 A2
St Étienne-du-Bois F 118 A2
St Étienne-du-Rouvray F 89 A5
St Etienne-les-Orgues F 132 A1
Ste Tulle F 132 B1
St Fargeau F 104 B2
St Félicien F 117 B4
St Felix-de-Sorgues F 130 B1
St Félix-Lauragais F 146 A2
Saintfield GB 27 B5
St Fillans GB 35 B3
St Firmin F 118 C3
St Florent F 180 A2
St Florentin F 104 B2
St Florent-le-Vieil F 101 B4
St Florent-sur-Cher F 103 C4
St Flour F 116 B3
St Flovier F 103 C3
St Fort-sur-le-Né F 115 C3
St Fulgent F 114 B2
St Galmier F 117 B4
St Gaudens F 145 A4
St Gaultier F 115 B5
St Gély-du-Fesc F 130 B2
St Genest-Malifaux F 117 B4
St Gengoux-le-National F 104 C3
St Geniez F 132 A2
St Geniez-d'Olt F 130 A1
St Genis-de-Saintonge F 114 C3
St Genis-Pouilly F 118 A3
St Genix-sur-Guiers F 118 B2
St Georges Buttavent F 88 B3
St Georges-d'Aurac F 117 B3
St Georges-de-Commiers F 118 B2
St Georges-de-Didonne F 114 C3
St Georges-de-Luzençon F 130 A1
St Georges-de Mons F 116 B2
St Georges-de-Reneins F 117 A4
St Georges d'Oléron F 114 C2
St Georges-en-Couzan F 117 B3
St Georges-lès-Baillargeaux F 115 B4
St Georges-sur-Loire F 102 B1
St Georges-sur-Meuse B 79 B5
St Geours-de-Maremne F 128 C1
St Gérand-de-Vaux F 117 A3
St Gérand-le-Puy F 117 A3
St Germain F 105 B5
St Germain-Chassenay F 104 C2
St Germain-de-Calberte F 130 A2
St Germain-de-Confolens F 115 B4
St Germain-de-Joux F 118 A2
St Germain-des-Fossés F 117 A3
St Germain-du-Bois F 105 C4
St Germain-du-Plain F 105 C3
St Germain-du Puy F 103 B4
St Germain-en-Laye F 90 C2
St Germain-Laval F 117 B4
St Germain-Lembron F 116 B3
St Germain-les-Belles F 116 B1
St Germain-Lespinasse F 117 A3
St Germain-l'Herm F 117 B3
St Gervais-d'Auvergne F 116 A2
St Gervais-les-Bains F 118 B3
St Gervais-sur-Mare F 130 B2
St Gildas-de-Rhuys F 100 B3
St Gildas-des-Bois F 101 B3
St Gilles
Gard F 131 B3
Ille-et-Vilaine F 101 A4
St Gilles-Croix-de-Vie F 114 B2
St Gingolph F 119 A3
St Girons
Ariège F 146 B2
Landes F 128 C1
St Girons-Plage F 128 C1
St Gobain F 91 B3
St Gorgon-Main F 105 B5
St Guénolé F 100 B1
St Harmon GB 39 B3
St Helens GB 38 A4
St Helier GB 88 A1
St Herblain F 101 B4
St Hilaire
Allier F 104 C2
Aude F 146 A3
St Hilaire-de-Riez F 114 B2
St Hilaire-des-Loges F 114 B3
St Hilaire-de-Villefranche F 114 C3
St Hilaire-du-Harcouët F 88 B2
St Hilaire-du-Rosier F 118 B2
St Hippolyte
Aveyron F 116 C2
Doubs F 106 B1
St Hippolyte-du-Fort F 130 B2
St Honoré-les-Bains F 104 C2
St Hubert B 92 A1
St Imier CH 106 B2
St Issey GB 42 B2
St Ives
Cambridgeshire GB 44 A3
Cornwall GB 42 B1
St Izaire F 130 B1
St Jacques-de-la-Lande F 101 A4
St Jacut-de-la-Mer F 101 A3
St James F 88 B2
St Jaume d'Enveja E 153 B4
St Jean-Brévelay F 101 B3
St Jean-d'Angély F 114 C3
St Jean-de-Belleville F 118 B3
St Jean-de-Bournay F 118 B2
St Jean-de-Braye F 103 B3
St Jean-de-Côle F 115 C4
St Jean-de-Daye F 88 A2
St Jean de Losne F 105 B4

St Jean-de-Luz F 144 A2
St Jean-de-Maurienne F 118 B3
St Jean-de-Monts F 114 B1
St Jean-d'Illac F 128 B2
St Jean-du-Bruel F 130 A2
St Jean-du-Gard F 131 A2
St Jean-en-Royans F 118 B2
St Jean-la-Riviere F 133 B3
St Jean-Pied-de-Port F 144 A2
St Jean-Poutge F 129 C3
St Jeoire F 118 A3
St Joachim F 101 B3
St Johnstown IRL 27 B3
St Jorioz F 118 B3
St Joris Winge B 79 B4
St Jouin-de-Marnes F 102 C1
St Juéry F 130 B1
St Julien F 118 A2
St Julien-Chapteuil F 117 B4
St Julien-de-Vouvantes F 101 B4
St Julien-du-Sault F 104 A2
St Julien-du-Verdon F 132 B2
St Julien-en-Born F 128 B1
St Julien-en-Genevois F 118 A3
St Julien-l'Ars F 115 B4
St Julien la-Vêtre F 117 B3
St Julien-Mont-Denis F 118 B3
St Julien-sur-Reyssouze F 118 A2
St Junien F 115 C4
St Just
F 131 A3
GB 42 B1
St Just-en-Chaussée F 90 B2
St Just-en-Chevalet F 117 B3
St Justin F 128 C2
St Just-St Rambert F 117 B4
St Keverne GB 42 B1
St Lary-Soulan F 145 B4
St Laurent-d'Aigouze F 131 B3
St Laurent-de-Chamousset F 117 B4
St Laurent-de-Condel F 89 A3
St Laurent-de-la-Cabrerisse F 146 A3
St Laurent-de-la-Salanque F 146 B3
St Laurent-des-Autels F 101 B4
St Laurent-du-Pont F 118 B2
St Laurent-en-Caux F 89 A4
St Laurent-en-Grandvaux F 105 C4
St Laurent-Médoc F 128 A2
St Laurent-sur-Gorre F 115 C4
St Laurent-sur-Mer F 88 A3
St Laurent-sur-Sèvre F 114 B3
St Leger B 92 B1
St Léger-de-Vignes F 104 C2
St Léger-sous-Beuvray F 104 C3
St Léger-sur-Dheune F 104 C3
St Léonard-de-Noblat F 116 B1
St Leonards GB 45 C4
St Lô F 88 A2
St Lon-les-Mines F 128 C1
St Louis F 106 B2
St Loup F 117 A3
St Loup-de-la-Salle F 105 C3
St Loup-sur-Semouse F 105 B5
St Lunaire F 101 A3
St Lupicin F 118 A2
St Lyphard F 101 B3
St Lys F 146 A2
St Macaire F 128 B2
St Maclou F 89 A4
St Maixent-l'École F 115 B3
St Malo F 88 B1
St Mamet-la-Salvetat F 116 C2
St Mandrier-sur-Mer F 132 B1
St Marcel
Drôme F 117 C4
Saône-et-Loire F 105 C3
St Marcellin F 118 B2
St Marcellin sur Loire F 117 B4
St Marcet F 145 A4
St Mards-en-Othe F 104 A2
St Margaret's-at-Cliffe GB 45 B5
St Margaret's Hope GB 33 C4
St Mars-la-Jaille F 101 B4
St Martin-d'Ablois F 91 C3
St Martin-d'Auxigny F 103 B4
St Martin-de-Belleville F 118 B3
St Martin-de-Bossenay F 91 C3
St Martin-de-Crau F 131 B3
St Martin-de-Londres F 130 B2
St Martin-d'Entraunes F 132 A2
St Martin-de-Queyrières F 118 C3
St Martin-de-Ré F 114 B2
St Martin des Besaces F 88 A3
St Martin-d'Estreaux F 117 A3
St Martin-de-Valamas F 117 C4
St Martin-d'Hères F 118 B2
St Martin-du-Frêne F 118 A2
St Martin-en-Bresse F 105 C4
St Martin-en-Haut F 117 B4
St Martin-la-Méanne F 116 B1
St Martin-Osmonville F 90 B1
St Martin-sur-Ouanne F 104 B2
St Martin-Valmeroux F 116 B2
St Martin-Vésubie F 133 A3
St Martory F 145 A4
St Mary's GB 33 C4
St Mathieu F 115 C4
St Mathieu-de-Tréviers F 131 B2
St Maurice CH 119 A3
St Maurice-Navacelles F 130 B2
St Maurice-sur-Moselle F 106 B1
St Mawes GB 42 B1
St Maximin-la-Ste Baume F 132 B1
St Méard-de-Gurçon F 128 B3
St Médard-de-Guizières F 128 A2
St Médard-en-Jalles F 128 B2
St Méen-le-Grand F 101 A3
St Menges F 91 B4
St Merløse DK 61 D1
St Město CZ 85 B4
St M'Hervé F 101 A4
St Michel
Aisne F 91 B4
Gers F 145 A4
St Michel-Chef-Chef F 101 B3
St Michel-de-Castelnau F 128 B2
St Michel-de-Maurienne F 118 B3
St Michel-en-Grève F 100 A2
St Michel-enl'Herm F 114 B2
St Michel-Mont-Mercure F 114 B3
St Mihiel F 92 C1
St Monance GB 35 B5
St Montant F 131 A3
St Moritz CH 107 C4
St Nazaire F 101 B3
St Nazaire-en-Royans F 118 B2
St Nazaire-le-Désert F 131 A4
St Nectaire F 116 B2
St Neots GB 44 A3
St Nicolas-de-Port F 92 C2
St Nicolas-de-Redon F 101 B3
St Nicolas-du-Pélem F 100 A2
St Niklaas B 79 A4
St Omer F 78 B2
St Pair-sur-Mer F 88 B2
St Palais F 144 A2
St Palais-sur-Mer F 114 C2
St Pardoux-la-Rivière F 115 C4
St Paul-Cap-de-Joux F 129 C4
St Paul-de-Fenouillet F 146 B3
St Paul-de-Varax F 118 A2
St Paulien F 117 B3
St Paul-le-Jeune F 131 A3
St Paul-lès-Dax F 128 C1
St Paul-Trois-Châteaux F 131 A3
St Pé-de-Bigorre F 145 A3
St Pée-sur-Nivelle F 144 A2
St Péravy-la-Colombe F 103 B3
St Péray F 117 C4
St Père-en-Retz F 101 B3
St Peter Port GB 88 A1
St Petersburg = Sankt-Peterburg RUS 9 C7
St Philbert-de-Grand-Lieu F 114 A2
St Pierre F 130 B1
St Pierre-d'Albigny F 118 B3
St Pierre-d'Allevard F 118 B3
St Pierre-de-Chartreuse F 118 B2
St Pierre-de-Chignac F 129 A3
St Pierre-de-la-Fage F 130 B2
St Pierre-d'Entremont F 118 B2
St Pierre-d'Oléron F 114 C2
St Pierre-Eglise F 88 A2
St Pierre-en-Port F 89 A4
St Pierre-le-Moûtier F 104 C2
St Pierre Montlimart F 101 B4
St Pierre-Quiberon F 100 B2
St Pierre-sur-Dives F 89 A3
St Pierreville F 117 C4
St Pieters-Leeuw B 79 B4
St Plancard F 145 A4
St Poix F 101 B4
St Pol-de-Léon F 100 A2
St Polgues F 117 B3
St Pol-sur-Ternoise F 78 B2
St Pons-de-Thomières F 130 B1
St Porchaire F 114 C3
St Pourçain-sur-Sioule F 116 A3
St Priest F 117 B4
St Privat F 116 B2
St Quay-Portrieux F 100 A3
St Quentin F 90 B3
St Quentin-la-Poterie F 131 A3
St Quentin-les-Anges F 102 B1
St Rambert-d'Albon F 117 B4
St Rambert-en-Bugey F 118 B2
St Raphaël F 132 B2
St Rémy-de-Provence F 131 B3
St Rémy-du-Val F 89 B4
St Remy-en-Bouzemont F 91 C4
St Renan F 100 A1
St Révérien F 104 B2
St Riquier F 90 A1
St Romain-de-Colbosc F 89 A4
St Rome-de-Cernon F 130 A1
St Rome-de-Tarn F 130 A1
St Sadurní-d'Anoia E 147 C2
St Saëns F 89 A5
St Sampson GB 88 A1
St Samson-la-Poterie F 90 B1
St Saturnin-de-Lenne F 130 A2
St Saturnin-lès-Apt F 131 B4
St Sauflieu F 90 B2
St Saulge F 104 B2
St Sauveur
Finistère F 100 A2
Haute-Saône F 105 B5
St Sauveur-de-Montagut F 117 C4
St Sauveur-en-Puisaye F 104 B2
St Sauveur-en-Rue F 117 B4
St Sauveur-Lendelin F 88 A2
St Sauveur-le-Vicomte F 88 A2
St Sauveur-sur-Tinée F 132 A3
St Savin
Gironde F 128 A2
Vienne F 115 B4
St Savinien F 114 C3
St Savournin F 131 B4
St Seine-l'Abbaye F 105 B3
St Sernin-sur-Rance F 130 B1
St Sevan-sur-Mer F 88 B1
St Sever F 128 C2
St Sever-Calvados F 88 B2
St Sorlin-d'Arves F 118 B3
St Soupplets F 90 B2
St Sulpice F 129 C4
St Sulpice-Laurière F 116 A1
St Sulpice-les-Feuilles F 115 B5
St Symphorien F 128 B2
St Symphoriende-Lay F 117 B4
St Symphorien d'Ozon F 117 B4
St Symphoriensur-Coise F 117 B4
St Teath GB 42 B2
St Thégonnec F 100 A2
St Thiébault F 105 A4
St Trivier-de-Courtes F 118 A2
St Trivier sur-Moignans F 117 A4
St Trojan-les-Bains F 114 C2
St Tropez F 132 B2
St Truiden B 79 B5
St Vaast-la-Hougue F 88 A2
St Valérien F 104 A2
St Valery-en-Caux F 89 A4
St Valéry-sur-Somme F 78 B1
St Vallier
Drôme F 117 B4
Saône-et-Loire F 104 C3
St Vallier-de-Thiey F 132 B2
St Varent F 102 C1
St Vaury F 116 A1
St Venant F 78 B2
St Véran F 119 C3
St Vincent I 119 B4
St Vincent-de-Tyrosse F 128 C1
St Vit F 105 B4
St Vith B 80 B2
St Vivien-de-Médoc F 114 C2
St Yan F 117 A4
St Ybars F 146 A2
St Yorre F 117 A3
St Yrieix-la-Perche F 115 C5
Saissac F 146 A3
Saja E 142 A2
Sajan SRB 126 B2
Šajkaš SRB 126 B2
Sajókaza H 99 C4
Sajószentpéter H 113 A4
Sajóvámos H 113 A4
Sakarya TR 187 B5
Šakiai LT 13 A5
Sakskøbing DK 65 B4
Sakule SRB 126 B2
Sala S 50 C3
Šal'a SK 111 A4
Sala Baganza I 120 C3
Sala Consilina I 172 B1
Salakovac SRB 127 C3
Salamanca E 150 B2
Salamina GR 185 B4
Salandra I 172 B2
Salaparuta I 176 B1
Salar E 163 A3
Salardú E 145 B4
Salas E 141 A4
Salas de los Infantes E 143 B3
Salau F 146 B2
Salavaux CH 106 C2
Salbertrand I 119 B3
Salbohed S 50 C3
Salbris F 103 B4
Salbu N 46 A2
Salce E 141 B4
Salching D 95 C4
Salcombe GB 43 B3
Saldaña E 142 B2
Saldus LV 8 D3
Sale I 120 C1
Saleby S 55 B4
Salem D 107 B4
Salemi I 176 B1
Salen
Argyll & Bute GB 34 B2
Highland GB 34 B2
N 199 A8
Sälen S 49 A5
Salernes F 132 B2
Salerno I 170 C2
Salers F 116 B2
Salford GB 40 B1
Salgótarján H 113 A3
Salgueiro P 155 B3
Salhus N 46 B2
Sali HR 137 B4
Sálice Salentino I 173 B3
Salientes E 141 B4
Salies-de-Béarn F 144 A3
Salies-du-Salat F 145 A4
Salignac-Eyvigues F 129 B4
Saligney-sur-Roudon F 104 C2
Salihli TR 188 A3
Salihorsk BY 13 B7
Salinas
Alicante E 159 C3
Huesca E 145 B4
Salinas de Medinaceli E 152 A1
Salinas de Pisuerga E 142 B2
Salindres F 131 A3
Saline di Volterra I 135 B3
Salins-les-Bains F 105 C4
Salir P 160 B1
Salisbury GB 44 B2
Salla
A 110 B1
FIN 197 C11
Sallachy GB 32 C2
Sallanches F 118 B3
Sallent E 147 C2
Sallent de Gállego E 145 B3
Salles F 128 B2
Salles-Curan F 130 A1
Salles-sur-l'Hers F 146 A2
Sallins IRL 30 A2
Sällsjö S 199 B10
Salmerón E 152 B1
Salmiech F 130 A1
Salmivaara FIN 197 C11
Salmoral E 150 B2
Salo FIN 8 B3
Salò I 121 B3
Salobreña E 163 B4
Salon-de-Provence F 131 B4
Salonica = Thessaloniki GR 182 C4
Salonta RO 16 B4
Salorino E 155 B3
Salornay-sur-Guye F 104 C3
Salorno I 121 A4
Salou E 147 C2
Šalovci SLO 111 C3
Salsbruket N 199 A8
Salses-le-Chateau F 146 B3
Salsomaggiore Terme I 120 C2
Salt E 147 C3
Saltaire GB 40 B2
Saltara I 136 B1
Saltash GB 42 B2
Saltburn-by-the-Sea GB 37 B6
Saltcoats GB 34 C3
Saltfleet GB 41 B4
Salto P 148 A2
Saltrød N 53 B4
Saltsjöbaden S 57 A4
Saltvik
FIN 51 B7
S 62 A4
Saludécio I 136 B1
Salussola I 119 B5
Saluzzo I 119 C4
Salvacañete E 152 B2
Salvada P 160 B2
Salvagnac F 129 C4
Salvaleon E 155 C4
Salvaterra de Magos P 154 B2
Salvaterra do Extremo P 155 B4
Salvatierra
Avila E 143 B4
Badajoz E 155 C4
Salvatierra de Santiago E 156 A1
Salviac F 129 B4
Salzburg A 109 B4
Salzgitter D 72 B3
Salzgitter Bad D 72 B3
Salzhausen D 72 A3
Salzhemmendorf D 72 B2
Salzkotten D 81 A4
Salzmünde D 83 A3
Salzwedel D 73 B4
Samadet F 128 C2
Samandıra TR 186 B4
Samassi I 179 C2
Samatan F 146 A1
Sambiase I 175 C2
Sambir UA 13 D5
Samborowo PL 69 B4
Sambuca di Sicilia I 176 B2
Samedan CH 107 C4
Samer F 78 B1
Sami GR 184 A1
Şamlı TR 186 C2
Sammichele di Bari I 173 B2
Samnaun CH 107 C5
Samobor HR 123 B4
Samoëns F 118 A3
Samogneux F 92 B1
Samokov BG 17 D5
Samora Correia P 154 C2
Šamorín SK 111 A4
Samos
E 141 B3
GR 188 B1
Samoš SRB 126 B2
Samothraki GR 183 C7
Samper de Calanda E 153 A3
Sampéyre I 133 A3
Sampieri I 177 C3
Sampigny F 92 C1
Samplawa PL 69 B4
Samproniano I 168 A1
Samtens D 66 B2
Samugheo I 179 C2
San Adrián E 144 B2
San Agustín E 164 C2
San Agustin de Guadalix E 151 B4
Sanaigmore GB 34 C1
San Alberto I 135 A5
San Amaro E 140 B2
Sânandrei RO 126 B3
San Andrês del Rabanedo E 142 B1
San Antanio di Santadi I 179 C2
San Antolín de Ibias E 141 A4
San Arcángelo I 174 A2
Sanary-sur-Mer F 132 B1
San Asensio E 143 B4
San Bartoloméde las Abiertas E 150 C3
San Bartoloméde la Torre E 161 B2
San Bartoloméde Pinares E 150 B3
San Bartolomeo in Galdo I 170 B3
San Benedetto del Tronto I 136 C2
San Benedetto in Alpe I 135 B4
San Benedetto Po I 121 B3
San Benito E 156 B3
San Benito de la Contienda E 155 C3
San Biágio Plátani I 176 B2
San Biágio Saracinisco I 169 B3
San Bonifacio I 121 B4
San Calixto E 156 C2
San Cándido I 109 C3
San Carlo
CH 119 A5
I 176 B2
San Carlos del Valle E 157 B4
San Casciano dei Bagni I 135 C4
San Casciano in Val di Pesa I 135 B4
San Cataldo
Puglia I 173 B4
Sicilia I 176 B2
San Cebrián de Castro E 149 A4
Sancergues F 104 B1
Sancerre F 103 B4
San Cesário di Lecce I 173 B4
Sancey-le-Long F 105 B5
Sanchiorian E 150 B3
San Chírico Raparo I 174 A2
Sanchonuño E 151 A3
San Cibrao das Viñas E 140 B3
San Cipirello I 176 B2
San Ciprián E 141 A3
San Clemente E 158 B1
San Clodio E 141 B3
Sancoins F 104 C1
San Colombano al Lambro I 120 B2
San Costanzo I 136 B2
San Crisóbal de Entreviñas E 142 B1
San Cristóbal de la Polantera E 141 B5
San Cristóbal de la Vega E 150 A3
San Cristovo E 141 C3
Sancti-Petri E 162 B1
Sancti-Spiritus E 149 B3
Sand
Hedmark N 48 B3
Rogaland N 52 A2
Sanda S 57 C4
San Damiano d'Asti I 119 C5
San Damiano Macra I 133 A3
Sandane N 198 D3
San Daniele del Friuli I 122 A2
Sandanski BG 183 B5
Sandared S 60 B2
Sandarne S 51 A4
Sandau D 73 B5
Sandbach
D 96 C1
GB 38 A4
Sandbank GB 34 C3
Sandbanks GB 43 B5
Sandbukt N 192 C5
Sandby DK 65 B4
Sande
D 71 A5
Sogn og Fjordane N 46 A2
Vestfold N 54 A1
Sandefjord N 54 A1
Sandeid N 52 A1
San Demétrio Corone I 174 B2
San Demétrio né Vestini I 169 A3
Sandersleben D 82 A3
Sanderstølen N 47 B6
Sandes N 53 B3
Sandesneben D 65 C3
Sandhead GB 36 B2
Sandhem S 60 B3
Sandhorst D 71 A4
Sandhurst GB 44 B3
Sandıklı TR 189 A5
Sandillon F 103 B4
Sandl A 96 C2
Sandnes N 52 B1
Sandness GB 33 A5
Sandnessjøen N 195 D3
Sando E 149 B3
Sandomierz PL 87 B5
San Dónaci I 173 B3
San Donàdi Piave I 122 B1
San Donato Val di Comino I 169 B3
Sándorfalva H 126 A2
Sandown GB 44 C2
Sandøysund N 54 A1
Sandrigo I 121 B4
Sandsele S 195 E8
Sandset N 194 B5
Sandsjöfors S 62 A2
Sandstad N 198 B6
Sandvatn N 52 B2
Sandvig-Allinge DK 67 A3
Sandvika
Akershus N 48 C2
Hedmark N 48 B3
Nord-Trøndelag N 199 B9
Sandviken S 51 B3
Sandvikvåy N 46 C2
Sandwich GB 45 B5
Sandy GB 44 A3
San Emiliano E 141 B5
San Enrique E 162 B2
San Esteban E 141 A4
San Esteban de Gormaz E 151 A4
San Esteban de la Sierra E 149 B4
San Esteban de Litera E 145 C4
San Esteban del Molar E 142 C1
San Esteban del Valle E 150 B3
San Esteban de Valdueza E 141 B4
San Fele I 172 B1
San Felice Circeo I 169 B3
San Felices E 143 B3
San Felices de los Gallégos E 149 B3
San Felice sul Panaro I 121 C4
San Ferdinando di Púglia I 171 B4
San Fernando E 162 B1
San Fernando de Henares E 151 B4
San Fili I 174 B2
San Foca I 173 B4
San Fratello I 177 B3
Sangatte F 78 B1
San Gavino Monreale I 179 C2
San Gémini Fonte I 168 A2
Sangerhausen D 82 A3
San Germano Vercellese I 119 B5
San Giácomo
Trentino Alto Adige I 108 C2
Umbria I 136 C1
San Gimignano I 135 B4
San Ginésio I 136 B2
Sangineto Lido I 174 B1
San Giórgio a Liri I 169 B3
San Giorgio della Richinvelda I 122 A1
San Giórgio del Sánnio I 170 B2
San Giórgio di Lomellina I 120 B1
San Giórgio di Nogaro I 122 B2
San Giorgio di Piano I 121 C4
San Giórgio Iónico I 173 B3
San Giovanni a Piro I 172 B1
San Giovanni Bianco I 120 B2
San Giovanni di Sinis I 179 C2
San Giovanni in Croce I 120 B3
San Giovanni in Fiore I 174 B2
San Giovanni in Persiceto I 121 C4
San Giovanni Reatino I 169 A2
San Giovanni Rotondo I 171 B3
San Giovanni Suérgiu I 179 C2
San Giovanni Valdarno I 135 B4
Sangis S 196 D6
San Giuliano Terme I 134 B3
San Giustino I 135 B5
San Godenzo I 135 B4
Sangonera la Verde E 165 B3
San Gregorio Magno I 172 B1
Sangüesa E 144 B2
Sanguinet F 128 B1
San Guiseppe Jato I 176 B2
Sanica BIH 124 C2
Sanitz D 65 B5
San Javier E 165 B4
San Jorge P 154 B2
San José E 164 C2
San Juan E 143 B3
San Juan de Alicante E 165 A4
San Juan de la Nava E 150 B3
San Justo de la Vega E 141 B4
Sankt Aegyd am Neuwalde A 110 B2
Sankt Andrä A 110 C1
Sankt Andreasberg D 82 A2
Sankt Anna S 56 B2
Sankt Anna am Aigen A 110 C2
Sankt Anton am Arlberg A 107 B5
Sankt Anton an der Jessnitz A 110 B2
Sankt Augustin D 80 B3
Sankt Blasien D 106 B3
Sankt Englmar D 95 B4
Sankt Gallen
A 110 B1
CH 107 B4
Sankt Gallenkirch A 107 B4
Sankt Georgen
A 96 C2
D 106 A3
Sankt Georgen am Reith A 110 B1
Sankt Georgen ob Judenburg A 110 B1
Sankt Georgen ob Murau A 109 B5
Sankt Gilgen A 109 B4
Sankt Goar D 81 B3
Sankt Goarshausen D 81 B3
Sankt Ingbert D 92 B3
Sankt Jacob A 109 C5

Sankt Jakob in Defereggen A 109 C3
Sankt Johann am Tauern A 110 B1
Sankt Johann am Wesen A 109 A4
Sankt Johann im Pongau A 109 B4
Sankt Johann in Tirol A 109 B3
Sankt Katharein an der Laming A 110 B2
Sankt Kathrein am Hauenstein A 110 B2
Sankt Lambrecht A 110 B1
Sankt Leonhard am Forst A 110 A2
Sankt Leonhard im Pitztal A 108 B1
Sankt Lorenzen A 109 C3
Sankt Marein
Steiermark A 110 B2
Steiermark A 110 B2
Sankt Margarethen im Lavanttal A 110 C1
Sankt Margrethen CH 107 B4
Sankt Michael A 110 B2
Sankt Michael im Burgenland A 111 B3
Sankt Michael im Lungau A 109 B4
Sankt Michaelisdonn D 64 C2
Sankt Niklaus CH 119 A4
Sankt Nikolai im Sölktal A 109 B5
Sankt Olof S 63 C2
Sankt Oswald D 96 C1
Sankt Paul
A 110 C1
F 132 A2
Sankt Peter D 106 A3
Sankt Peter am Kammersberg A 110 B1
Sankt-Peterburg = St Petersburg RUS 9 C7
Sankt Peter-Ording D 64 B1
Sankt Pölten A 110 A2
Sankt Radegund A 110 B2
Sankt Ruprecht an der Raab A 110 B2
Sankt Salvator A 110 C1
Sankt Stefan A 110 C1
Sankt Stefan an der Gail A 109 C4
Sankt Stefan im Rosental A 110 C2
Sankt Valentin A 110 A1
Sankt Veit an der Glan A 110 C1
Sankt Veit an der Gölsen A 110 A2
Sankt Veit in Defereggen A 109 C3
Sankt Wendel D 92 B3
Sankt Wolfgang
A 109 B4
D 108 A3
San Lazzaro di Sàvena I 135 A4
San Leo I 135 B5
San Leonardo de Yagüe E 143 C3
San Leonardo in Passiria I 108 C2
San Lorenzo al Mare I 133 B3
San Lorenzo a Merse I 135 B4
San Lorenzo Bellizzi I 174 B2
San Lorenzo de Calatrava E 157 B4
San Lorenzo de El Escorial E 151 B3
San Lorenzo de la Parrilla E 158 B1
San Lorenzo di Sebato I 108 C2
San Lorenzo in Campo I 136 B1
San Lorenzo Nuovo I 168 A1
San Lourenco P 160 A1
San Luca I 175 C2
Sanlúcar de Barrameda E 161 C3
Sanlúcar de Guadiana E 160 B2
Sanlúcar la Mayor E 161 B3
San Lúcido I 174 B2
Sanluri I 179 C2
San Marcello I 136 B2
San Marcello Pistoiese I 135 A3
San Marcial E 149 A4
San Marco I 170 C2
San Marco Argentano I 174 B2
San Marco dei Cavoti I 170 B2
San Marco in Lámis I 171 B3
San Marino RSM 136 B1
San Martin de Castañeda E 141 B4
San Martin de la Vega E 151 B4
San Martin de la Vega del Alberche E 150 B2
San Martin del Tesorillo E 162 B2
San Martin de Luiña E 141 A4
San Martin de Montalbán E 157 A3
San Martin de Oscos E 141 A4
San Martin de Pusa E 150 C3
San Martin de Unx E 144 B2
San Martín de Valdeiglesias E 150 B3
San Martino di Campagna I 122 A1
San Martino di Castrozza I 121 A4
San-Martino-di-Lota F 180 A2
San Martino in Pénsilis I 170 B3
San Mateo de Gallego E 144 C3
San Màuro Forte I 172 B2
San Michele all'Adige I 121 A4
San Michele di Ganzaria I 177 B3
San Michele Mondov i I 133 A3
San Miguel de Aguayo E 142 A2
San Miguel de Bernuy E 151 A4
San Miguel del Arroyo E 150 A3
San Miguel de Salinas E 165 B4
Sânmihaiu Roman RO 126 B3
San Millán de la Cogolla E 143 B4
San Miniato I 135 B3
San Muñoz E 149 B3
Sänna S 55 B5
Sannazzaro de'Burgondi I 120 B1
Sanne D 73 B4
Sannicandro di Bari I 171 B4
Sannicandro Gargânico I 171 B3
San Nicola del'Alto I 174 B2
San Nicolás del Puerto E 156 C2
Sânnicolau Mare RO 126 A2
San Nicolò I 121 C4
San Nicolò Gerrei I 179 C3
Sannidal N 53 B5
Sanniki PL 77 B4
Sanok PL 12 D5
San Pablo de los Montes E 157 A3
San Pancrázio Salentino I 173 B3
San Pantaleo I 178 A3
San Páolo di Civitate I 171 B3
San Pawl il-Bahar M 175 C3
San Pedro
Albacete E 158 C1
Oviedo E 141 A4
San Pedro de Alcántara E 162 B3
San Pedro de Ceque E 141 B4
San Pedro del Arroyo E 150 B3
San Pedro de Latarce E 142 C1
San Pedro del Pinatar E 165 B4
San Pedro del Romeral E 143 A3
San Pedro de Merida E 156 B1
San Pedro de Valderaduey E 142 B2
San Pedro Manrique E 144 B1
San Pellegrino Terme I 120 B2
San Piero a Sieve I 135 B4
San Piero in Bagno I 135 B4
San Piero Patti I 177 A3
San Pietro I 177 B3
San Pietro in Casale I 121 C4
San Pietro in Gu I 121 B4
San Pietro in Palazzi I 134 B3
San Pietro in Volta I 122 B1
San Pietro Vara I 134 A2
San Pietro Vernótico I 173 B3
San Polo d'Enza I 121 C3
Sanquhar GB 36 A3
San Quírico d'Órcia I 135 B4
San Rafael del Rio E 153 B4
San Remo I 133 B3
San Román de Cameros E 143 B4
San Roman de Hernija E 150 A2
San Román de la Cuba E 142 B2
San Roman de los Montes E 150 B3
San Romao P 155 C3
San Roque E 162 B2
San Roque de Riomera E 143 A3
San Rufo I 172 B1
San Sebastián de los Ballesteros E 162 A3
San Salvador de Cantamuda E 142 B2
San Salvo I 170 A2
San Salvo Marina I 170 A2
San Sebastián de los Reyes E 151 B4
San Sebastiano Curone I 120 C2
San Secondo Parmense I 120 C3
Sansepolcro I 135 B5
San Serverino Marche I 136 B2
San Severino Lucano I 174 A2
San Severo I 171 B3
San Silvestre de Guzmán E 161 B2
Sanski Most BIH 124 C2
San Sosti I 174 B2
San Stéfano di Cadore I 109 C3
San Stino di Livenza I 122 B1
Santa Agnès E 166 B1
Santa Amalia E 156 A1
Santa Ana
Cáceres E 156 A2
Jaén E 163 A4
Santa Ana de Pusa E 150 C3
Santa Barbara E 153 B4
Santa Bárbara P 160 B1
Santa Barbara de Casa E 161 B2
Santa Bárbara de Padrões P 160 B2
Santacara E 144 B2
Santa Catarina P 160 B2
Santa Caterina di Pittinuri I 178 B2
Santa Caterina Villarmosa I 177 B3
Santa Cesárea Terme I 173 B4
Santa Clara-a-Nova P 160 B1
Santa Clara-a-Velha P 160 B1
Santa Clara de Louredo P 160 B2
Santa Coloma de Farners E 147 C3
Santa Coloma de Gramenet E 147 C3
Santa Coloma de Queralt E 147 C2
Santa Colomba de Curueño E 142 B1
Santa Colomba de Somoza E 141 B4
Santa Comba E 140 A2
Santa Comba Dáo P 148 B1
Santa Comba de Rossas P 149 A3
Santa Cristina I 120 B2
Santa Cristina de la Polvorosa E 141 B5
Santa Croce Camerina I 177 C3
Santa Croce di Magliano I 170 B2
Santa Cruz
E 140 A2
P 154 B1
Santa Cruz de Alhama E 163 A4
Santa Cruz de Campezo E 143 B4
Santa Cruz de Grio E 152 A2
Santa Cruz de la Salceda E 151 A4
Santa Cruz de la Sierra E 156 A2
Santa Cruz de la Zarza E 151 C4
Santa Cruz del Retamar E 151 B3
Santa Cruz del Valle E 150 B2
Santa Cruz de Moya E 159 B2
Santa Cruz de Mudela E 157 B4
Santa Cruz de Paniagua E 149 B3
Santadi I 179 C2
Santa Doménica Talao I 174 B1
Santa Doménica Vittória I 177 B3
Santa Elena E 157 B4
Santa Elena de Jamuz E 141 B5
Santaella E 162 A3
Santa Eufemia E 156 B3
Santa Eufémia d'Aspromonte I 175 C1
Santa Eulália E 152 B2
Santa Eulália P 155 C3
Santa Eulalia de Oscos E 141 A3
Santa Eulàlia des Riu E 166 C1
Santa Fe E 163 A4
Santa Fiora I 135 C4
Sant'Ágata dei Goti I 170 B2
Sant'Ágata di Ésaro I 174 B1
Sant'Ágata di Puglia I 171 B3
Sant'Agata Feltria I 135 B5
Sant'Ágata Militello I 177 A3
Santa Gertrude I 108 C1
Santa Giustina I 121 A5
Sant Agust ide Lluçanès E 147 B3
Santa Iria P 160 B2
Santa Leocadia P 148 A1
Santa Lucia del Mela I 177 A4
Santa Lucia-de-Porto-Vecchio F 180 B2
Santa Luzia P 160 B1
Santa Maddalena Vallalta I 108 C3
Santa Magdalena de Polpis E 153 B4
Santa Margalida E 167 B3
Santa Margarida P 154 B2
Santa Margarida do Sado P 160 A1
Santa Margaridao de Montbui E 147 C2
Santa Margherita I 179 D2
Santa Margherita di Belice I 176 B2
Santa Margherita Ligure I 134 A2
Santa Maria
CH 108 C1
E 144 B3
Santa Maria al Bagno I 173 B3
Santa Maria Cápua Vétere I 170 B2
Santa Maria da Feira P 148 B1
Santa Maria de Cayón E 143 A3
Santa Maria de Corco E 147 B3
Santa Maria de Huerta E 152 A1
Santa Maria de la Alameda E 151 B3
Santa Maria de las Hoyas E 143 C3
Santa Maria del Camí E 167 B2
Santa Maria del Campo E 143 B3
Santa Maria del Campo Rus E 158 B1
Santa Maria della Versa I 120 C2
Santa Maria del Páramo E 142 B1
Santa Maria del Taro I 134 A2
Santa Maria de Mercadillo E 143 C3
Santa Maria de Nieva E 164 B3
Santa Maria de Trassierra E 156 C3
Santa Maria di Licodia I 177 B3
Santa Maria-di-Rispéscia I 168 A1
Santa Maria la Palma I 178 B2
Santa Maria la Real de Nieva E 150 A3
Santa Maria Maggiore I 119 A5
Santa Maria Ribarredonda E 143 B3
Santa Marina del Rey E 141 B5
Santa Marinella I 168 A1
Santa Marta
Albacete E 158 B1
Badajoz E 155 C4
Santa Marta de Magasca E 156 A1
Santa Marta de Penaguião P 148 A2
Santa Marta de Tormes E 150 B2
Santana
Évora P 154 C2
Setúbal P 154 C1
Sântana RO 126 A3
Santana da Serra P 160 B1
Sant'Ana de Cambas P 160 B2
Santana do Mato P 154 C2
Sant'Anastasia I 170 C2
Santander E 143 A3
Sant'Andrea Frius I 179 C3
Sant'Ángelo dei Lombardi I 172 B1
Sant'Angelo in Vado I 136 B1
Sant'Angelo Lodigiano I 120 B2
Santa Ninfa I 176 B1
Sant'Antíoco I 179 C2
Sant Antoni de Calonge E 147 C4
Sant Antoni de Portmany E 166 C1
Sant'Antonio-di-Gallura I 178 B3
Santanyí E 167 B3
Santa Olalla
Huelva E 161 B3
Toledo E 150 B3
Santa Pau E 147 B3
Santa Pola E 165 A4
Santa Ponça E 166 B2
Santarcángelo di Romagna I 136 A1
Santarém P 154 B2
Santa Severa
F 180 A2
I 168 A1
Santa Severina I 175 B2
Santas Martas E 142 B1
Santa Sofia I 135 B4
Santa Susana P 154 C2
Santa Suzana P 155 C3
Santa Teresa di Riva I 177 B4
Santa Teresa Gallura I 178 A3
Santa Uxía E 140 B2
Santa Valburga I 108 C1
Santa Vittória in Matenano I 136 B2
Sant Boi de Llobregat E 147 C3
Sant Carles de la Ràpita E 153 B4
Sant Carlos E 166 B1
Sant'Caterina I 135 C4
Sant Celoni E 147 C3
Sant Climent E 167 B4
Santed E 152 A2
Sant'Egídio alla Vibrata I 136 C2
Sant'Elia a Pianisi I 170 B2
Sant'Elia Fiumerapido I 169 B3
Santelices E 143 A3
San Telmo E 161 B3
Sant'Elpídio a Mare I 136 B2
Santéramo in Colle I 171 C4
Santervas de la Vega E 142 B2
Sant' Eufemia Lamezia 175 C2
Sant Feliu E 147 C3
Sant Feliu de Codines E 147 C3
Sant Feliu de Guíxols E 147 C4
Sant Feliu Sasserra E 147 C3
Sant Ferran E 166 C1
Sant Francesc de Formentera E 166 C1
Sant Francesc de ses Salines E 166 C1
Santhià I 119 B5
Sant Hilari Sacalm E 147 C3
Sant Hipòlit de Voltregà E 147 B3
Santiago de Alcántara E 155 B3
Santiago de Calatrava E 163 A3
Santiago de Compostela E 140 B2
Santiago de la Espade E 164 A2
Santiago de la Puebla E 150 B2
Santiago de la Ribera E 165 B4
Santiago del Campo E 155 B4
Santiago de Litem P 154 B2
Santiago do Cacém P 160 B1
Santiago do Escoural P 154 C2
Santiago Maior P 155 C3
Santibáñez de Béjar E 150 B2
Santibáñez de la Peña E 142 B2
Santibáñez de Murias E 142 A1
Santibáñez de Vidriales E 141 B4
Santibáñez el Alto E 149 B3
Santibáñez el Bajo E 149 B3
Santillana E 142 A2
Santiponce E 162 A1
San Tirso de Abres E 141 A3
Santisteban del Puerto E 157 B4
Santiuste de San Juan Bautiste E 150 A3
Santiz E 149 A4
Sant Jaume dels Domenys E 147 C2
Sant Joan Baptista E 166 B1
Sant Joan de les Abadesses E 147 B3
Sant Jordi E 153 B4
Sant Josep de sa Talaia E 166 C1
Sant Juliáde Loria AND 146 B2
Sant'Ilario d'Enza I 121 C3
Sant Llorençde Morunys E 147 B2
Sant Llorençdes Carctassar E 167 B3
Sant Llorenç Savall E 147 C3
Sant Luis E 167 B4
Sant Mart ide Llemaná E 147 B3
Sant Marti de Maldá E 147 C2
Sant Marti Sarroca E 147 C2
Sant Mateu E 153 B4
Sant Miquel E 166 B1
Santo Aleixo P 161 A2
Santo Amado P 161 A2
Santo Amaro P 155 C3
Santo André P 160 A1
Santo Domingo E 155 C3
Santo Domingo de la Calzada E 143 B4
Santo Domingo de Silos E 143 C3
Santo Estêvão
Faro P 160 B2
Santarém P 154 C2
Santok PL 75 B4
Santomera E 165 A3
Santoña E 143 A3
Santo-Pietro-di Tenda F 180 A2
Sant'Oreste I 168 A2
Santo Spirito I 171 B4
Santo Stefano d'Aveto I 134 A2
Santo Stéfano di Camastra I 177 A3
Santo Stefano di Magra I 134 A2
Santo Stéfano Quisquina I 176 B2
Santo Tirso P 148 A1
Santotis E 142 A2
Santo Tomé E 164 A1
Santovenia
Burgos E 143 B3
Zamora E 142 C1
Sant Pau de Seguries E 147 B3
Santpedor E 147 C2
Sant Pere de Riudebitlles E 147 C2
Sant Pere Pescador E 147 B4
Sant Pere Sallavinera E 147 C2
Sant Quirze de Besora E 147 B3
Sant Rafel E 166 C1
Sant Ramon E 147 C2
Santu Lussurgiu I 178 B2
Santutzi E 143 A3
Sant Vincençde Castellet E 147 C2
San Valentino alla Muta I 108 C1
San Venanzo I 135 C5
San Vicente de Alcántara E 155 B3
San Vicente de Arana E 144 B1
San Vicente de la Barquera E 142 A2
San Vicente de la Sonsierra E 143 B4
San Vicente de Toranzo E 143 A3
San Vietro E 149 A3
San Vigilio I 108 C2
San Vincente del Raspeig E 165 A4
San Vincenzo I 134 B3
San Vito I 179 C3
San Vito al Tagliamento I 122 B1
San Vito Chietino I 169 A4
San Vito dei Normanni I 173 B3
San Vito di Cadore I 108 C3
San Vito lo Capo I 176 A1
San Vito Romano I 169 B2
Sanxenxo E 140 B2
Sanza I 172 B1
São Aleixo P 155 C3
São Barnabé P 160 B1
São Bartoloméda Serra P 160 A1
São Bartolomeu de Messines P 160 B1
São Bento P 140 C2
São Brás P 160 B2
São Brás de Alportel P 160 B2
São Braz do Reguedoura P 154 C2
São Cristóvão P 154 C2
São Domingos P 160 B1
São Geraldo P 154 C2
São Jacinto P 148 B1
São João da Madeira P 148 B1
São João da Pesqueira P 148 A2
São João da Ribeira P 154 B2
São João da Serra P 148 B1
São João da Venda P 160 B2
São João dos Caldeireiros P 160 B2
São Julião P 155 B3
São Leonardo P 155 C3
São Luis P 160 B1
São Manços P 155 C3
São Marcos da Ataboeira P 160 B2
Saõ Marcos da Serra P 160 B1
São Marcos de Campo P 155 C3
São Martinho da Cortiça P 148 B1
São Martinho das Amoreiras P 160 B1
São Martinho do Porto P 154 B1
São Matias
Beja P 160 A2
Évora P 154 C2
São Miguel d'Acha P 155 A3
São Miguel de Machede P 155 C3
São Pedro da Torre P 140 C2
São Pedro de Cadeira P 154 B1
São Pedro de Moel P 154 B1
São Pedro de Solis P 160 B2
São Pedro do Sul P 148 B1
Saorge F 133 B3
São Romão P 154 C2
São Sebastião dos Carros P 160 B2
São Teotónio P 160 B1
São Torcato P 148 A1
Sapataria P 154 C1
Sapes GR 183 B7
Sapiãos P 148 A2
Sa Pobla E 167 B3
Sappada I 109 C3
Sappen N 192 C5
Sapri I 174 A1
Sarajärvi FIN 197 D10
Sarajevo BIH 139 B4
Saramon F 129 C3
Sarandë AL 182 D2
Saranovo SRB 127 C2
Saraorci SRB 127 C3
Sa Rapita E 167 B3
Saray TR 186 A2
Saraycık TR 187 C4
Sarayköy TR 188 B3
Saraylar TR 186 B2
Sarayönü TR 189 A7
Sarbia PL 75 B5
Sarbinowo
Zachodnio-Pomorskie PL 67 B4
Zachodnio-Pomorskie PL 74 B3
Sárbogárd H 112 C2
Sarcelles F 90 B2
Sarche I 121 A3
Sardara I 179 C2
Sardoal P 154 B2
Sardón de Duero E 150 A3
Sare F 144 A2
S'Arenal E 166 B2
Šarengrad HR 125 B5
Sarentino I 108 C2
Sarezzo I 120 B3
Sargans CH 107 B4
Sári H 112 B3
Sarıbeyler TR 186 C2
Sarıcakaya TR 187 B5
Sari-d'Orcino F 180 A1
Sarıgöl TR 188 A3
Sarıkaya TR 23 B8
Sarıköy TR 186 B2
Sarilhos Grandes P 154 C2
Sariñena E 145 C3
Sarıoba TR 187 C7
Sárisáp H 112 B2
Sariyer TR 186 A4
Sarkad H 113 C5
Sárkeresztes H 112 B2
Sárkeresztúr H 112 B2
Särkijärvi FIN 196 B6
Şarkikaraağaç TR 189 A6
Şarköy TR 186 B2
Sarlat-la-Canéda F 129 B4
Sarliac-sur-l'Isle F 129 A3
Sármellék H 111 C4
Särna S 199 D10
Sarnadas P 155 B3
Sarnano I 136 B2
Sarnen CH 106 C3
Sarnesfield GB 39 B4
Sárnico I 120 B2
Sarno I 170 C2
Sarnonico I 121 A4
Sarnow D 74 A2
Sarny UA 13 C7
Särö S 60 B1
Saronno I 120 B2
Sárosd H 112 B2
Šarovce SK 112 A2
Sarpoil F 117 B3
Sarpsborg N 54 A2
Sarracín E 143 B3
Sarral E 147 C2
Sarralbe F 92 B3
Sarrancolin F 145 B4
Sarras F 117 B4
Sarre I 119 B4
Sarreaus E 140 B3
Sarrebourg F 92 C3
Sarreguemines F 92 B3
Sárrétudvari H 113 B5
Sarre-Union F 92 C3
Sarria E 141 B3
Sarriàde Ter E 147 B3
Sarrión E 153 B3
Sarroca de Lleida E 153 A4
Sarroch I 179 C3
Sarron F 128 C2
Sársina I 135 B5
Særslev DK 59 C3
Sarstedt D 72 B2
Sárszentlörinc H 112 C2
Sárszentmihaly H 112 B2
Sárszentmiklós H 112 C2
Sarteano I 135 C4
Sartène F 180 B1
Sartilly F 88 B2
Sartirana Lomellina I 120 B1
Saruhanlı TR 186 D2
Sárvár H 111 B3

Sarvisvaara S 196 C4
Sarzana I 134 A2
Sarzeau F 101 B3
Sarzedas P 155 B3
Sasalli TR 188 A1
Sasamón E 142 B2
Sa Savina E 166 C1
Sásd H 125 A4
Sasino PL 68 A2
Sássari I 178 B2
Sassello I 133 A4
Sassenberg D 71 C5
Sassetta I 134 B3
Sassnitz D 66 B2
Sassocorvaro I 136 B1
Sasso d'Ombrone I 135 C4
Sassoferrato I 136 B1
Sassoleone I 135 A4
Sasso Marconi I 135 A4
Sassuolo I 135 A3
Sástago E 153 A3
Šaštinske Stráže SK 98 C1
Sas van Gent NL 79 A3
Såtåhaugen N 199 C7
Satão P 148 B2
Såtenäs S 55 B3
Säter S 50 B2
Sätila S 60 B2
Satillieu F 117 B4
Satnica Đakovačka HR 125 B4
Sátoraljaújhely H 16 A4
Satow D 65 C4
Sätra-brunn S 50 C3
Sætre N 54 A1
Satrup D 64 B2
Satteins A 107 B4
Satu Mare RO 17 B5
Saturnia I 168 A1
Saucats F 128 B2
Saucelle E 149 A3
Sauda N 52 A2
Sauðarkrókur IS 190 B6
Saudasjøen N 52 A2
Sauerlach D 108 B2
Saugues F 117 C3
Sauherad N 53 A5
Saujon F 114 C3
Sauland N 53 A4
Saulces Monclin F 91 B4
Saulgau D 107 A4
Saulgrub D 108 B2
Saulieu F 104 B3
Saulnot F 106 B1
Sault F 131 A4
Sault-Brénaz F 118 B2
Sault-de-Navailles F 128 C2
Saulx F 105 B5
Saulxures-sur-Moselotte F 106 B1
Saulzais-le-Potier F 103 C4
Saumos F 128 B1
Saumur F 102 B1
Saunavaara FIN 197 B10
Saundersfoot GB 39 C2
Saurat F 146 B2
Saurbær
Borgarfjarðarsýsla IS 190 C4
Dalasýsla IS 190 B4
Eyjafjarðarsýsla IS 191 B7
Sáuris I 109 C3
Sausset-les-Pins F 131 B4
Sauteyrargues F 131 B2
Sauvagnat F 116 B2
Sauve F 131 B2
Sauveterre-de-Béarn F 144 A3
Sauveterre-de-Guyenne F 128 B2
Sauviat-sur-Vige F 116 B1
Sauxillanges F 117 B3
Sauzet
Drôme F 117 C4
Lot F 129 B4
Sauzé-Vaussais F 115 B4
Sauzon F 100 B2
Sava I 173 B3
Sävar S 200 C6
Sævareid N 46 B2
Savarsin RO 16 B5
Sävast S 196 D4
Savaştepe TR 186 C2
Savci SLO 111 C3
Säve S 60 B1
Savelletri I 173 B3
Savelli I 174 B2
Savenay F 101 B4
Saverdun F 146 A2
Saverne F 93 C3
Savières F 91 C3
Savigliano I 119 C4
Savignac-les-Eglises F 129 A3
Savignano Irpino I 171 B3
Savignano sul Rubicone I 136 A1
Savigny-sur-Braye F 102 B2
Saviñán E 152 A2
Savines-le-lac F 132 A2
Savino Selo SRB 126 B1
Savio I 135 A5
Sävja S 51 C4
Šavnik MNE 139 C5
Savognin CH 107 C4
Savona I 133 A4
Savonlinna FIN 9 B6
Savournon F 132 A1
Sævråsvåg N 46 B2
Sävsjö S 62 A2
Savsjön S 50 C1
Sävsjöström S 62 A3
Savudrija HR 122 B2
Savukoski FIN 197 B11
Sawbridgeworth GB 45 B4
Sawtry GB 44 A3
Sax E 159 C3
Saxdalen S 50 B1
Saxilby GB 40 B3
Saxmundham GB 45 A5
Saxnäs S 195 F6
Saxthorpe GB 41 C5
Sayalonga E 163 B3
Sayatón E 151 B5
Sayda D 83 B5
Säytsjärvi FIN 193 C11
Sazava CZ 97 B3
Sázava CZ 96 B2
Scaër F 100 A2
Scafa I 169 A4
Scalasaig GB 34 B1
Scalby GB 40 A3
Scalea I 174 B1
Scaletta Zanclea I 177 A4
Scalloway GB 33 A5
Scamblesby GB 41 B3
Scandale I 175 B2
Scandiano I 121 C3
Scandicci I 135 B4
Scandolara Ravara I 120 B3
Scanno I 169 B3
Scansano I 168 A1
Scanzano Jónico I 174 A2
Scarborough GB 40 A3
Scardovari I 122 C1
Scardoy GB 32 D2
Scarperia I 135 B4
Scarriff IRL 28 B3
Scey-sur-Saône et St Albin F 105 B4
Schachendorf A 111 B3
Schaffhausen CH 107 B3
Schafstädt D 83 A3
Schafstedt D 64 B2
Schäftlarn D 108 B2
Schagen NL 70 B1
Schalkau D 82 B3
Schangnau CH 106 C2
Schapbach D 93 C4
Scharbeutz D 65 B3
Schärding A 96 C1
Scharnitz A 108 B2
Scharrel D 71 A4
Schattendorf A 111 B3
Scheemda NL 71 A3
Scheessel D 72 A2
Schéggia I 136 B1
Scheibbs A 110 A2
Scheibenberg D 83 B4
Scheidegg D 107 B4
Scheifling A 110 B1
Scheinfeld D 94 B2
Schelklingen D 94 C1
Schenefeld
Schleswig-Holstein D 64 B2
Schleswig-Holstein D 72 A2
Schenklengsfeld D 82 B1
Scherfede D 81 A5
Schermbeck D 80 A2
Scherpenzeel NL 70 B2
Schesslitz D 94 B3
Scheveningen NL 70 B1
Schiedam NL 79 A4
Schieder-Schwalenberg D 72 C2
Schierling D 95 C4
Schiers CH 107 C4
Schildau D 83 A4
Schillingen D 92 B2
Schillingsfürst D 94 B2
Schilpário I 120 A3
Schiltach D 93 C4
Schiltigheim F 93 C3
Schio I 121 B4
Schirmeck F 92 C3
Schirnding D 83 B4
Schkeuditz D 83 A4
Schkölen D 83 A3
Schlabendorf D 84 A1
Schladen D 73 B3
Schladming A 109 B4
Schlangen D 81 A4
Schleiden D 80 B2
Schleiz D 83 B3
Schleswig D 64 B2
Schleusingen D 82 B2
Schlieben D 83 A5
Schliengen D 106 B2
Schliersee D 108 B2
Schlitz D 81 B5
Schloss Neuhans D 81 A4
Schlossvippach D 82 A3
Schlotheim D 82 A2
Schluchsee D 106 B3
Schlüchtern D 81 B5
Schmallenberg D 81 A4
Schmelz D 92 B2
Schmidmühlen D 95 B3
Schmiedeberg D 84 B1
Schmiedefeld D 82 B2
Schmirn A 108 B2
Schmölln
Brandenburg D 74 A3
Sachsen D 83 B4
Schnaittach D 95 B3
Schneeberg D 83 B4
Schneizlreuth D 109 B3
Schneverdingen D 72 A2
Schöder A 109 B5
Schoenburg B 80 B2
Schollene D 73 B5
Schöllkrippen D 81 B5
Schomberg D 107 A3
Schönach D 95 C4
Schönau
Baden-Württemberg D 106 B2
Bayern D 95 C4
Schönbeck D 74 A2
Schönberg
Bayern D 96 C1
Mecklenburg-Vorpommern D 65 C3
Schleswig-Holstein D 65 B3
Schönebeck D 73 B4
Schöneck D 83 B4
Schönecken- D 80 B2
Schönermark D 74 A2
Schönewalde D 83 A5
Schongau D 108 B1
Schöngrabern A 97 C4
Schönhagen D 81 A5
Schönhausen D 73 B5
Schöningen D 73 B3
Schönkirchen D 64 B3
Schönsee D 95 B4
Schöntal D 94 B1
Schönthal D 95 B4
Schonungen D 94 A2
Schönwalde D 65 B3
Schoondijke NL 79 A3
Schoonebeek NL 71 B3
Schoonhoven NL 79 A4
Schopfheim D 106 B2
Schöppenstedt D 73 B3
Schörfling A 109 B4
Schorndorf D 94 C1
Schortens D 71 A4
Schotten D 81 B5
Schramberg D 106 A3
Schraplau D 83 A3
Schrattenberg A 97 C4
Schrecksbach D 81 B5
Schrems A 96 C3
Schrobenhausen D 95 C3
Schröcken A 107 B5
Schrozberg D 94 B1
Schruns A 107 B4
Schüpfheim CH 106 C3
Schüttorf D 71 B4
Schwaan D 65 C5
Schwabach D 94 B3
Schwäbisch Gmünd D 94 C1
Schwäbisch Hall D 94 B1
Schwabmünchen D 108 A1
Schwadorf A 111 A3
Schwagstorf D 71 B4
Schwaigern D 93 B5
Schwalmstadt D 81 B5
Schwanberg A 110 C2
Schwanden CH 107 C4
Schwandorf D 95 B4
Schwanebeck D 73 C4
Schwanenstadt A 109 A4
Schwanewede D 72 A1
Schwanfeld D 94 B2
Schwangau D 108 B1
Schwarmstedt D 72 B2
Schwarza D 82 B2
Schwarzach im Pongau A 109 B4
Schwarzau im Gebirge A 110 B2
Schwarzenau A 97 C3
Schwarzenbach D 83 B3
Schwarzenbach am Wald D 83 B3
Schwarzenbek D 72 A3
Schwarzenberg D 83 B4
Schwarzenburg CH 106 C2
Schwarzenfeld D 95 B4
Schwarz-heide D 84 A1
Schwaz A 108 B2
Schwechat A 111 A3
Schwedt D 74 A3
Schwei D 71 A5
Schweich D 92 B2
Schweighausen D 106 A2
Schweinfurt D 94 A2
Schweinitz D 83 A5
Schweinrich D 74 A1
Schwelm D 80 A3
Schwemsal D 83 A4
Schwendt A 109 B3
Schwenningen D 107 A3
Schwepnitz D 84 A1
Schwerin D 73 A4
Schwerte D 81 A3
Schweskau D 73 B4
Schwetzingen D 93 B4
Schwyz CH 107 B3
Sciacca I 176 B2
Scicli I 177 C3
Ściechów PL 75 B3
Scigliano I 175 B2
Scilla I 175 C1
Ścinawa PL 85 A4
Scionzier F 118 A3
Scoglitti I 177 C3
Scole GB 45 A5
Sconser GB 31 B2
Scopello
Piemonte I 119 B5
Sicilia I 176 A1
Scordia I 177 B3
Scorzè I 121 B5
Scotch Corner GB 37 B5
Scotter GB 40 B3
Scourie GB 32 C1
Scousburgh GB 33 B5
Scrabster GB 32 C3
Screeb IRL 28 A2
Scremerston GB 37 A5
Scritto I 136 B1
Scunthorpe GB 40 B3
Scuol CH 107 C5
Scúrcola Marsicana I 169 A3
Seaford GB 45 C4
Seaham GB 37 B5
Seahouses GB 37 A5
Seascale GB 36 B3
Seaton GB 43 B3
Sebazac-Concourès F 130 A1
Seben TR 187 B6
Sebersdorf A 110 B2
Sebezh RUS 8 D6
Sebnitz D 84 B2
Seborga I 133 B3
Seby S 63 B4
Seč
Vychodočeský CZ 97 B3
Západočeský CZ 96 B1
Sečanj SRB 126 B2
Secemin PL 87 B3
Séchault F 91 B4
Seckau A 110 B1
Seclin F 78 B3
Secondigny F 114 B3
Seda P 155 B3
Sedan F 91 B4
Sedano E 143 B3
Sedbergh GB 37 B4
Sedella E 163 B3
Séderon F 131 A4
Sedgefield GB 37 B5
Sedico I 121 A5
Sédilo I 178 B2
Sédini I 178 B2
Sedlarica HR 124 B3
Sedlčany CZ 96 B2
Sedlec-Prčice CZ 96 B2
Sedlice CZ 96 B1
Sędziejowice PL 86 A3
Sędziszów PL 87 B4
Sędziszów Małapolski PL 87 B5
Seebach F 93 C3
Seeboden A 109 C4
Seefeld
Brandenburg D 74 B2
Niedersachsen D 71 A5
Seefeld in Tirol A 108 B2
Seeg D 108 B1
Seehausen
Sachsen-Anhalt D 73 B4
Sachsen-Anhalt D 73 B4
Seeheim-Jugenheim D 93 B4
Seelbach D 93 C3
Seelow D 74 B3
Seelze D 72 B2
Seerhausen D 83 A5
Sées F 89 B4
Seesen D 82 A2
Seeshaupt D 108 B2
Seewalchen A 109 B4
Seferihisar TR 188 A1
Sefkerin SRB 127 B2
Segård N 48 B2
Segerstad S 55 A4
Segesd H 124 A3
Seglinge FIN 51 B7
Segmon S 55 A4
Segonzac F 115 C3
Segorbe E 159 B3
Segovia E 151 B3
Segré F 101 B5
Segura
E 144 B1
P 155 B3
Segura de León E 161 A3
Segura de los Baños E 152 B3
Ségur-les-Villas F 116 B2
Segurrilla E 150 B3
Sehnde D 72 B2
Seia P 148 B2
Seiches-sur-le-Loir F 102 B1
Seifhennersdorf D 84 B2
Seignelay F 104 B2
Seijo E 140 C2
Seilhac F 116 B1
Seilles B 79 B5
Seim N 46 B2
Seinäjoki FIN 8 A3
Seissan F 145 A4
Seitenstetten Markt A 110 A1
Seixal P 154 C1
Seiz A 110 B1
Seizthal A 110 B1
Sejerslev DK 58 B1
Seksna RUS 9 C11
Selårdalur IS 190 B1
Selárgius I 179 C3
Selb D 83 B4
Selby GB 40 B2
Selca HR 138 B2
Selce HR 123 B3
Selçuk TR 188 B2
Selde DK 58 B2
Selenča SRB 126 B1
Selendi
Manisa TR 186 D2
Manisa TR 186 D3
Selenicë AL 182 C1
Sélestat F 106 A2
Seleuš SRB 126 B2
Selevac SRB 127 C2
Selfoss IS 190 D5
Selgua E 145 C4
Selice SK 112 A1
Seligenstadt D 93 A4
Seligenthal D 82 B2
Selimiye TR 188 B2
Selizharovo RUS 9 D8
Selja S 50 A1
Selje N 198 C2
Seljelvnes N 192 C3
Seljord N 53 A4
Selkirk GB 35 C5
Sellano I 136 C1
Selles-St Denis F 103 B3
Selles-sur-Cher F 103 B3
Sellières F 105 C4
Sellin D 66 B2
Sellye H 125 B3
Selm D 80 A3
Selnica ob Dravi SLO 110 C2
Selongey F 105 B4
Selonnet F 132 A2
Selow D 65 C4
Selsey GB 44 C3
Selsingen D 72 A2
Selters D 81 B3
Seltz F 93 C4
Selva E 167 B2
Selva di Cadore I 108 C3
Selva di Val Gardena I 108 C2
Selvik
Sogn og Fjordane N 46 A2
Vestfold N 54 A1
Selvino I 120 B2
Selyatyn UA 17 B6
Sem N 54 A1
Semeljci HR 125 B4
Semič SLO 123 B4
Semide
F 91 B4
P 148 B1
Semily CZ 84 B3
Seminara I 175 C1
Semlac RO 126 A2
Semlacu Mare RO 126 B3
Semmen-stedt D 73 B3
Šempeter SLO 123 A4
Semriach A 110 B2
Semur-en-Auxois F 104 B3
Sena E 145 C3
Sena de Luna E 141 B5
Senarpont F 90 B1
Sénas F 131 B4
Senčanski Trešnjevac SRB 126 B1
Sencelles E 167 B2
Senčur SLO 123 A3
Senden
Bayern D 94 C2
Nordrhein-Westfalen D 80 A3
Sendenhorst D 81 A3
Sendim P 149 A3
Senec SK 111 A4
Seneffe B 79 B4
Séneghe I 178 B2
Senés E 164 B2
Senez F 132 B2
Senftenberg D 84 A1
Sengouagnet F 145 B4
Sengwarden D 71 A5
Senica SK 98 C1
Senice na Hané CZ 98 B1
Senigállia I 136 B2
Senirkent TR 189 A5
Sénis I 179 C2
Senise I 174 A2
Senj HR 123 C3
Senje SRB 127 D3
Senjehopen N 194 A8
Senjski Rudnik SRB 127 D3
Senlis F 90 B2
Sennan S 60 C2
Sennecey-le-Grand F 105 C3
Sennen GB 42 B1
Senno BY 13 A8
Sénnori I 178 B2
Sennwald CH 107 B4
Sennybridge GB 39 C3
Senohrad SK 99 C3
Senonches F 89 B5
Senones F 92 C2
Senorbì I 179 C3
Senovo SLO 123 A4
Senožeče SLO 123 B3
Senožeti SLO 123 A3
Sens F 104 A2
Sens-de-Bretagne F 101 A4
Senta SRB 126 B2
Senterada E 145 B4
Sentilj SLO 110 C2
Šentjernej SLO 123 B4
Šentjur SLO 123 A4
Senumstad N 53 B4
Seoane E 141 B3
Seon CH 106 B3
Sépeaux F 104 B2
Sépey CH 119 A4
Sepino I 170 B2
Sępólno Krajeńskie PL 76 A2
Seppenrade D 80 A3
Seppois F 106 B2
Septemvri BG 183 A6
Septeuil F 90 C1
Sepúlveda E 151 A4
Sequals I 122 A1
Sequeros E 149 B3
Seraincourt F 91 B4
Seraing B 80 B1
Seravezza I 134 B3
Sered' SK 98 C1
Seredka RUS 8 C6
Şereflikoçhisar TR 23 B7
Seregélyes H 112 B2
Seregno I 120 B2
Sérent F 101 B3
Serfaus A 108 B1
Sergiyev Posad RUS 9 D11
Seriate I 120 B2
Sérifontaine F 90 B1
Serifos GR 185 B5
Sérignan F 130 B2
Serik TR 189 C6
Serina I 120 B2
Serinhisar TR 188 B4
Sermaises F 90 C2
Sermaize-les-Bains F 91 C4
Sérmide I 121 C4
Sermoneta I 169 B2
Sernache de Bonjardim P 154 B2
Sernancelhe P 148 B2
Serock PL 77 B6
Serón E 164 B2
Serón de Nájima E 152 A1
Serooskerke NL 79 A3
Serós E 153 A4
Serpa P 160 B2
Serracapriola I 171 B3
Serrada E 150 A3
Serra de Outes E 140 B2
Serradifalco I 176 B2
Serradilla E 155 B4
Serradilla del Arroyo E 149 B3
Serradilla del Llano E 149 B3
Serramanna I 179 C2
Serramazzoni I 135 A3
Serranillos E 150 B3
Serrapetrona I 136 B2
Serra San Bruno I 175 C2
Serra San Quírico I 136 B2
Serrastretta I 175 B2
Serravalle
Piemonte I 119 B5
Umbria I 136 C2
Serravalle di Chienti I 136 B1
Serravalle Scrívia I 120 C1
Serre I 172 B1
Serrejón E 150 C2
Serres
F 132 A1
GR 183 B5
Serrières F 117 B4
Serrières-de-Briord F 118 B2
Sersale I 175 B2
Sertã P 154 B2
Sertig Dörfli CH 107 C4
Servance F 106 B1
Serverette F 117 C3
Servia GR 182 C4
Servian F 130 B2
Serviers F 131 A3
Servigliano I 136 B2
Serzedelo P 148 A1
Seseña Nuevo E 151 B4
Sesimbra P 154 C1
Seskarö S 196 D6
Seskinore GB 27 B3
Sesma E 144 B1
Sessa Aurunca I 170 B1
Ses Salines E 167 B3
Sesta Godano I 134 A2
Šestanovac HR 138 B2
Sestao E 143 A4
Sestino I 135 B5
Sesto I 109 C3
Sesto Calende I 120 B1
Sesto Fiorentino I 135 B4
Séstola I 135 A3
Sesto San Giovanni I 120 B2
Sestriere I 119 C3
Sestri Levante I 134 A2
Sestroretsk RUS 9 B7
Sestu I 179 C3
Sesvete HR 124 B2
Setcases E 146 B3
Sète F 130 B2
Setenil E 162 B2
Setermoen N 194 B9
Šetonje SRB 127 C3
Setskog N 54 A2
Settalsjølia N 199 C7
Séttimo Torinese I 119 B4
Settimo Vittone I 119 B4
Settle GB 40 A1
Setúbal P 154 C2
Seubersdort D 95 B3
Seùi I 179 C3
Seùlo I 179 C3
Seurre F 105 C4
Sevel DK 58 B1
Sevenoaks GB 45 B4
Sévérac-le-Château F 130 A2
Sever do Vouga P 148 B1
Severin HR 123 B4
Severomorsk RUS 3 B13
Séveso I 120 B2
Ševětin CZ 96 B2
Sevettijärvi FIN 193 C12
Sévigny F 91 B4
Sevilla = Seville E 162 A2
Sevilla la Nueva E 151 B3
Seville = Sevilla E 162 A2
Sevilleja de la Jara E 156 A3
Sevlievo BG 17 D6
Sevnica SLO 123 A4
Sevojno SRB 127 D1
Sevrier F 118 B3
Sexdrega S 60 B3
Seyches F 129 B3
Seyda D 83 A4
Seydişehir TR 189 B6
Seyðisfjörður IS 191 B12
Seyitgazi TR 187 C5
Seyitömer TR 187 C4
Seymen TR 186 A2
Seyne F 132 A2
Seynes F 131 A3
Seyssel F 118 B2
Sežana SLO 122 B2
Sézanne F 91 C3
Sezulfe P 149 A2
Sezze I 169 B3
Sfântu Gheorghe RO 17 C6
Sforzacosta I 136 B2
Sgarasta Mhor GB 31 B1
's-Gravendeel NL 79 A4
's-Gravenhage = The Hague NL 70 B1
's-Gravenzande NL 79 A4
Shaftesbury GB 43 A4
Shaldon GB 43 B3
Shalskiy RUS 9 B9
Shanagolden IRL 29 B2
Shanklin GB 44 C2
Shap GB 37 B4
Sharpness GB 43 A4
Shawbury GB 38 B4
's-Heerenberg NL 80 A2
Sheerness GB 45 B4
Sheffield GB 40 B2
Shefford GB 44 A3
Shëmri AL 182 A2
Shenfield GB 45 B4
Shëngjergj AL 182 B2
Shepetivka UA 13 C7
Shepshed GB 40 C2
Shepton Mallet GB 43 A4
Sherborne GB 43 B4
Shercock IRL 27 C4
Sheringham GB 41 C5
's-Hertogenbosch NL 79 A5
Shiel Bridge GB 32 D1
Shieldaig GB 31 B3
Shijak AL 182 B1
Shillelagh IRL 30 B2
Shimsk RUS 9 C7
Shipston-on-Stour GB 44 A2
Shklow BY 13 A9
Shkodër AL 182 A1
Shoeburyness GB 45 B4
Shoreham-by-Sea GB 44 C3
Shotley Gate GB 45 B5
Shrewsbury GB 38 B4
Shugozero RUS 9 C9
Shumen BG 17 D7
Siabost GB 31 A2
Siamanna I 179 C2
Sianów PL 67 B5
Siatista GR 182 C3
Siauges-St Romain F 117 B3
Šiauliai LT 8 E3
Sibari I 174 B2
Sibbhult S 63 B2
Šibenik HR 138 B1
Siberstedt D 64 B2
Sibinj HR 125 B3
Sibiu RO 17 C6
Sibnica SRB 127 C2
Sibsey GB 41 B4
Siculiana I 176 B2
Šid SRB 125 B5
Sidari GR 182 D1
Siddeburen NL 71 A3
Sidensjö S 200 C4
Siderno I 175 C2
Sidirokastro GR 183 B5
Sidmouth GB 43 B3
Sidzina PL 99 B3
Siebe N 192 D7
Siebenlehn D 83 A5
Siedlce PL 12 B5
Siedlice PL 75 A4
Siedlinghausen D 81 A4
Siedlisko PL 75 B5
Siegburg D 80 B3
Siegen D 81 B4
Siegenburg D 95 C3
Sieghartskirchen A 111 A3
Siegsdorf D 109 B3
Siekierki PL 74 B3
Sielpia PL 87 A4
Siemiany PL 69 B4
Siena I 135 B4
Sieniawka PL 84 B2
Sienno PL 87 A5
Sieppijärvi FIN 196 B7
Sieradz PL 86 A2
Sieraków
Śląskie PL 86 B2
Wielkopolskie PL 75 B5
Sierakowice PL 68 A2
Sierck-les-Bains F 92 B2
Sierentz F 106 B2
Sierning A 110 A1
Sierpc PL 77 B4
Sierra de Fuentes E 155 B4
Sierra de Luna E 144 B3
Sierra de Yeguas E 162 A3
Sierre CH 119 A4
Siestrzeń PL 77 B5
Sietamo E 145 B3
Siewierz PL 86 B3
Sigdal N 48 B1
Sigean F 130 B1
Sigerfjord N 194 B6
Sighetu-Marmatiei RO 17 B5
Sighişoara RO 17 B6
Sigillo I 136 B1
Siglufjörður IS 191 A7
Sigmaringen D 107 A4
Signa I 135 B4
Signes F 132 B1
Signy-l'Abbaye F 91 B4
Signy-le-Petit F 91 B4
Sigogne F 115 C3
Sigri GR 183 D7
Sigtuna S 57 A3
Sigueiro E 140 B2
Sigüenza E 151 A5
Sigües E 144 B2
Sigulda LV 8 D4
Siilinjärvi FIN 8 A5
Sikenica SK 112 A2

Sikfors S 196 D4
Sikia GR 183 C5
Sikinos GR 185 C6
Sikkilsdalseter N 47 A6
Siklós H 125 B4
Sikórz PL 77 B4
Sikselet S 195 D8
Silandro I 108 C1
Silánus I 178 B2
Silbaš SRB 126 B1
Şile TR 187 A4
Siles E 164 A2
Silgueiros P 148 B2
Silifke TR 23 C7
Siliqua I 179 C2
Silistra BG 17 C7
Silivri TR 186 A3
Siljan N 53 A5
Siljansnäs S 50 B1
Silkeborg DK 59 B2
Silla E 159 B3
Sillamäe EST 8 C5
Silleda E 140 B2
Sillé-le-Guillaume F 102 A1
Sillenstede D 71 A4
Sillerud S 54 A3
Sillian A 109 C3
Silloth GB 36 B3
Silno PL 68 B2
Silnowo PL 68 B1
Silo HR 123 B3
Sils E 147 C3
Silsand N 194 A8
Silte S 57 C4
Šilute LT 12 A4
Silvalen N 195 E3
Silvaplana CH 107 C4
Silvares P 148 B2
Silvberg S 50 B2
Silverdalen S 62 A3
Silvermines IRL 28 B3
Silverstone GB 44 A2
Silverton GB 43 B3
Silves P 160 B1
Silvi Marina I 169 A4
Simandre F 105 C3
Šimanovci SRB 127 C2
Simard F 105 C4
Simat de Valldigna E 159 B3
Simav TR 186 C3
Simbach
Bayern D 95 C4
Bayern D 95 C5
Simbário I 175 C2
Simeonovgrad BG 183 A7
Simeria RO 17 C5
Simi GR 188 C2
Simićevo SRB 127 C3
Simitli BG 183 B5
Simlångsdalen S 60 C3
Simmerath D 80 B2
Simmerberg D 107 B4
Simmern D 93 B3
Simo FIN 197 D8
Šimonovce SK 99 C4
Simonsbath GB 43 A3
Simonstorp S 56 B2
Simontornya H 112 C2
Simplon CH 119 A5
Simrishamn S 63 C2
Sinaia RO 17 C6
Sinalunga I 135 B4
Sinarcas E 159 B2
Sincan TR 187 C7
Sincanlı TR 187 D5
Sindal DK 58 A3
Sindelfingen D 93 C5
Sindia I 178 B2
Sındırgı TR 186 C3
Sinekli TR 186 A3
Sines P 160 B1
Sinetta FIN 197 C8
Sineu E 167 B3
Singen D 107 B3
Singleton GB 44 C3
Singsås N 199 C7
Siniscóla I 178 B3
Sinj HR 138 B2
Sinlabajos E 150 A3
Sinn D 81 B4
Sinnai I 179 C3
Sinnes N 52 B2
Sinop TR 23 A8
Sins CH 106 B3
Sinsheim D 93 B4
Sint Annaland NL 79 A4
Sint Annaparochie NL 70 A2
Sint Athonis NL 80 A1
Sint Nicolaasga NL 70 B2
Sint Oedenrode NL 79 A5
Sintra P 154 C1
Sinzheim D 93 C4
Sinzig D 80 B3
Siófok H 112 C2
Sion CH 119 A4
Sion Mills GB 27 B3
Siorac-en-Périgord F 129 B3
Šipanska Luka HR 139 C3
Šipovo BIH 138 A3
Sira N 52 B2
Siracusa I 177 B4
Siret RO 17 B7
Sirevåg N 52 B1
Sirig SRB 126 B1
Sirkka FIN 196 B7
Sirmione I 121 B3
Sirniö FIN 197 D11
Sirok H 113 B4
Široké SK 99 C4
Široki Brijeg BIH 139 B3
Sirolo I 136 B2
Siruela E 156 B2
Sisak HR 124 B2
Sisante E 158 B1
Šišljavić HR 123 B4
Sissach CH 106 B2
Sissonne F 91 B3
Sistelo P 140 C2
Sisteron F 132 A1
Sistiana I 122 B2
Sistranda N 198 B5
Sitasjaurestugorna S 194 C8
Sitges E 147 C2
Sitia GR 185 D7
Sittard NL 80 A1
Sittensen D 72 A2
Sittingbourne GB 45 B4
Sitzenroda D 83 A4
Sivac SRB 126 B1
Sivaslı TR 189 A4
Siverić HR 138 B2
Sivrihisar TR 187 C6
Sixt-Fer-á-Cheval F 119 A3
Siziano I 120 B2
Sizun F 100 A1
Sjenica SRB 16 D3
Sjoa N 198 D6
Sjøåsen N 199 A8
Sjöbo S 61 D3
Sjøenden
Hedmark N 48 A3
Hedmark N 48 B3
Sjøholt N 198 C3
Sjøli N 48 A3
Sjølstad N 199 A9
Sjölunda S 56 A1
Sjømarken S 60 B2
Sjørring DK 58 B1
Sjötofta S 60 B3
Sjötorp S 55 B4
Sjoutnäset S 199 A11
Sjøvegan N 194 B8
Sjuntorp S 54 B3
Skåbu N 47 A6
Skafså N 53 A4
Skaftafell IS 191 D9
Skagaströnd IS 190 B5
Skagen DK 58 A3
Skagersvik S 55 B5
Skaiå N 53 B3
Skaidi N 193 B8
Skala GR 184 A1
Skała PL 87 B3
Skaland N 194 A8
Skala Oropou GR 185 A4
Skala-Podilska UA 13 D7
Skalat UA 13 D6
Skalbmierz PL 87 B4
Skålevik N 53 B4
Skalica SK 98 C1
Skalité SK 98 B2
Skällinge S 60 B2
Skalná CZ 83 B4
Skals DK 58 B2
Skælskør DK 65 A4
Skalstugan S 199 B9
Skanderborg DK 59 B2
Skånes-Fagerhult S 61 C3
Skåne-Tranås S 61 D3
Skånevik N 52 A1
Skänninge S 55 B6
Skanör med Falsterbo S 66 A1
Skåpafors S 54 A3
Skąpe PL 75 B4
Skara S 55 B4
Skærbæk DK 64 A1
Skarberget N 194 B7
Skärblacka S 56 B1
Skarð IS 190 B3
Skarda S 200 B4
Skare N 46 C3
Skåre S 55 A4
Skärhamn S 60 B1
Skarnes N 48 B3
Skärplinge S 51 B4
Skarpnatö FIN 51 B6
Skarp Salling DK 58 B2
Skarrild DK 59 C1
Skarstad N 194 B7
Skärstad S 62 A2
Skarsvåg N 193 A9
Skarszewy PL 69 A3
Skårup DK 65 A3
Skärvången S 199 B11
Skarvsjöby S 195 F8
Skaryszew PL 87 A5
Skarżysko-Kamienna PL 87 A4
Skarzysko Ksiazece PL 87 A4
Skatøy N 53 B5
Skattkärr S 55 A4
Skattungbyn S 50 A1
Skatval N 199 B7
Skaulo S 196 B4
Skave DK 59 B1
Skawina PL 99 B3
Skebobruk S 51 C5
Skebokvarn S 56 A2
Skedala S 61 C2
Skedevi S 56 B1
Skedsmokorset N 48 B3
Skee S 54 B2
Skegness GB 41 B4
Skei N 46 A3
Skela SRB 127 C2
Skelani BIH 127 D1
Skellefteå S 2 D7
Skelleftehamn S 2 D7
Skelmersdale GB 38 A4
Skelmorlie GB 34 C3
Skelund DK 58 B3
Skender Vakuf BIH 138 A3
Skene S 60 B2
Skępe PL 77 B4
Skepplanda S 60 B2
Skeppshult S 60 B3
Skerries IRL 30 A2
Ski N 54 A1
Skiathos GR 183 D5
Skibbereen IRL 29 C2
Skibotn N 192 C4
Skidra GR 182 C4
Skien N 53 A5
Skierniewice PL 77 C5
Skillingaryd S 60 B4
Skillinge S 63 C2
Skillingmark S 49 C4
Skilloura CY 181 A2
Skinnardai S 57 A4
Skinnskatteberg S 50 C2
Skipmannvik N 195 C6
Skipness GB 34 C2
Skipsea GB 41 B3
Skipton GB 40 B1
Skiptvet N 54 A2
Skiros GR 183 E6
Skivarp S 66 A2
Skive DK 58 B2
Skjånes N 193 B12
Skjærhalden N 54 A2
Skjeberg N 54 A2
Skjeggedal N 46 B3
Skjeljanger N 46 B1
Skjeljavik N 46 C2
Skjern DK 59 C1
Skjervøy N 192 B4
Skjold
Rogaland N 52 A1
Troms N 192 C3
Skjoldastraumen N 52 A1
Skjolden N 47 A4
Skjønhaug N 54 A2
Skjøtningsberg N 193 A11
Škocjan SLO 123 B4
Skoczów PL 98 B2
Skodborg DK 59 C2
Škofja Loka SLO 123 A3
Škofljica SLO 123 B3
Skog S 51 A3
Skoganvarre N 193 C9
Skogen S 54 A3
Skogfoss N 193 C13
Skoghall S 55 A4
Skogly N 193 C13
Skogn N 199 B8
Skognes N 192 C3
Skogstorp
Halland S 60 C2
Södermanland S 56 A2
Skoki PL 76 B2
Skokloster S 57 A3
Sköldinge S 56 A2
Skole UA 13 D5
Skollenborg N 53 A5
Sköllersta S 56 A1
Skomlin PL 86 A2
Skonseng N 195 D5
Skopelos GR 183 D5
Skopje MK 182 A3
Skoppum N 54 A1
Skórcz PL 69 B3
Skorogoszcz PL 86 B1
Skoroszów PL 85 A5
Skorovatn N 199 A10
Skorped S 200 C3
Skørping DK 58 B2
Skotfoss N 53 A5
Skotniki PL 87 A3
Skotselv N 48 C1
Skotterud N 49 C4
Skottorp S 61 C2
Skovby DK 64 B2
Skövde S 55 B4
Skovsgård DK 58 A2
Skrad HR 123 B3
Skradin HR 138 B1
Skradnik HR 123 B4
Skråmestø N 46 B1
Škrdlovice CZ 97 B3
Skrea S 60 C2
Skreia N 48 B2
Skrolsvik N 194 A7
Skruv S 63 B3
Skrwilno PL 77 A4
Skrydstrup DK 59 C2
Skucani BIH 138 B2
Skudeneshavn N 52 A1
Skui N 48 C2
Skulsk PL 76 B3
Skultorp S 55 B4
Skultuna S 56 A2
Skuodas LT 8 D2
Skurup S 66 A2
Skute N 48 B2
Skuteč CZ 97 B3
Skutskär S 51 B4
Skutvik N 194 B6
Skvyra UA 13 D8
Skwierzyna PL 75 B4
Skýcov SK 98 C2
Skyllberg S 55 B5
Skyttmon S 200 C1
Skyttorp S 51 B4
Sládkovičovo SK 111 A4
Slagelse DK 61 D1
Slagharen NL 71 B3
Slagnäs S 195 E9
Slaidburn GB 40 B1
Slane IRL 30 A2
Slangerup DK 61 D2
Slano HR 139 C3
Slantsy RUS 8 C6
Slaný CZ 84 B2
Slap SLO 122 A2
Šlapanice CZ 97 B4
Slåstad N 48 B3
Slatina
BIH 139 B3
HR 125 B3
RO 17 C6
Slatiňany CZ 97 B3
Slatinice CZ 98 B1
Slättberg S 50 A1
Slattum N 48 C2
Slavičin CZ 98 B1
Slavkov CZ 98 C1
Slavkovica SRB 127 C2
Slavkov u Brna CZ 97 B4
Slavonice CZ 97 C3
Slavonski Brod HR 125 B4
Slavonski Kobas HR 125 B3
Slavŏsovce SK 99 C4
Slavskoye RUS 69 A5
Slavuta UA 13 C7
Sława
Lubuskie PL 85 A4
Zachodnio-Pomorskie PL 67 C4
Slawharad BY 13 B9
Sławków PL 86 B3
Sławno
Wielkopolskie PL 76 B2
Zachodnio-Pomorskie PL 68 A1
Sławoborze PL 67 C4
Sl'ažany SK 98 C2
Sleaford GB 40 C3
Sleðbrjótur IS 191 B11
Sledmere GB 40 A3
Sleights GB 37 B6
Slemmestad N 54 A1
Ślesin PL 76 B3
Sliač SK 99 C3
Sliema M 175 C3
Sligo IRL 26 B2
Slite S 57 C4
Slitu N 54 A2
Sliven BG 17 D7
Śliwice PL 68 B3
Slobozia RO 17 C7
Slochteren NL 71 A3
Slöinge S 60 C2
Słomniki PL 87 B4
Slonim BY 13 B6
Słońsk PL 75 B3
Slootdorp NL 70 B1
Slottsbron S 55 A4
Slough GB 44 B3
Slövag N 46 B2
Slovenj Gradec SLO 110 C2
Slovenska Bistrica SLO 123 A4
Slovenská L'upča SK 99 C3
Slovenská-Ves SK 99 B4
Slovenské Darmoty SK 112 A3
Slovenske Konjice SLO 123 A4
Słubice PL 74 B3
Sluderno I 108 C1
Sluis NL 78 A3
Šluknov CZ 84 A2
Slunj HR 123 B4
Słupca PL 76 B2
Słupia PL 87 A3
Słupiec PL 85 B4
Słupsk PL 68 A2
Slutsk BY 13 B7
Smålandsstenar S 60 B3
Smalåsen N 195 E4
Smardzewo PL 75 B4
Smarhon BY 13 A7
Smarje SLO 123 A4
Šmarjeta SLO 123 B4
Šmartno SLO 123 A3
Smečno CZ 84 B2
Smedby S 63 B4
Smědec CZ 96 C2
Smederevo SRB 127 C2
Smederevska Palanka SRB 127 C2
Smedjebacken S 50 B2
Smęgorzów PL 87 B5
Smeland N 53 B4
Smidary CZ 84 B3
Śmigiel PL 75 B5
Smilde NL 71 B3
Smiřice CZ 85 B3
Smithfield GB 36 B4
Śmitowo PL 75 A5
Smögen S 54 B2
Smogulec PL 76 A2
Smołdzino PL 68 A2
Smolenice SK 98 C1
Smolensk RUS 13 A10
Smolník SK 99 C4
Smolyan BG 183 B6
Smuka SLO 123 B3
Smygehamn S 66 A2
Smykow PL 87 A4
Snainton GB 40 A3
Snaith GB 40 B2
Snaptun DK 59 C3
Snarby N 192 C3
Snarum N 48 B1
Snåsa N 199 A9
Snedsted DK 58 B1
Sneek NL 70 A2
Sneem IRL 29 C2
Snejbjerg DK 59 B1
Snillfjord N 198 B6
Šnjegotina BIH 125 C3
Snøde DK 65 A3
Snøfjord N 193 B8
Snogebaek DK 67 A4
Snyatyn UA 13 D6
Soave I 121 B4
Sober E 140 B3
Sobernheim D 93 B3
Soběslav CZ 96 B2
Sobota
Dolnośląskie PL 85 A3
Łódzkie PL 77 B4
Sobotište SK 98 C1
Sobotka CZ 84 B3
Sobótka
Dolnośląskie PL 85 B4
Wielkopolskie PL 86 A1
Sobra HR 139 C3
Sobrado
Coruña E 140 A2
Lugo E 141 B3
Sobral da Adica P 161 A2
Sobral de Monte Agraço P 154 C1
Sobreira Formosa P 154 B3
Søby DK 64 B3
Soca SLO 122 A2
Sochaczew PL 77 B5
Sochos GR 183 C5
Socodor RO 113 C5
Socol RO 127 C3
Socovos E 164 A3
Socuéllamos E 158 B1
Sodankylä FIN 197 B9
Soderåkra S 63 B4
Söderala S 51 A3
Söderås S 50 B2
Söderbärke S 50 B2
Söderby-Karl S 51 C5
Söderfors S 51 B4
Söderhamn S 51 A4
Söderköping S 56 B2
Söderö S 56 B1
Södertälje S 57 A3
Södingberg A 110 B2
Södra Finnö S 56 B2
Södra Ny S 55 A4
Södra Råda S 55 A5
Södra Sandby S 61 D3
Södra Vi S 62 A3
Sodražica SLO 123 B3
Sodupe E 143 A3
Soengas P 148 A1
Soest
D 81 A4
NL 70 B2
Sofades GR 182 D4
Sofia BG 17 D5
Sofikon GR 184 B4
Şofronea RO 126 A3
Sögel D 71 B4
Sogliano al Rubicone I 135 A5
Sogndalsfjøra N 46 A4
Søgne N 53 B3
Sögütköy TR 188 C3
Soham GB 45 A4
Sohland D 84 A2
Sohren D 93 B3
Soignies B 79 B4
Soissons F 90 B3
Söjtör H 111 C3
Sokal' UA 13 C6
Söke TR 188 B2
Sokna N 48 B1
Sokndal N 52 B2
Soknedal N 199 C7
Soko BIH 125 C4
Sokolac BIH 139 B4
Sokółka PL 13 B5
Sokolov CZ 83 B4
Sokołowo PL 76 B3
Sokołów Podlaski PL 12 B5
Sola N 52 B1
Solana de los Barros E 155 C4
Solana del Pino E 157 B3
Solánas I 179 C3
Solares E 143 A3
Solarino I 177 B4
Solarussa I 179 C2
Solas GB 31 B1
Solberg S 200 C3
Solberga S 62 A2
Solber-gelva N 53 A6
Solbjørg N 46 B2
Solčany SK 98 C2
Solčava SLO 123 A3
Solda I 108 C1
Sölden A 108 C2
Solec Kujawski PL 76 A3
Soleils F 132 B2
Solenzara F 180 B2
Solera E 163 A4
Solesmes F 79 B3
Soleto I 173 B4
Solgne F 92 C2
Solheim N 46 B2
Solheimsvik N 52 A2
Solignac F 115 C5
Solihull GB 44 A2
Solin HR 138 B2
Solingen D 80 A3
Solivella E 147 C2
Solkan SLO 122 B2
Söll A 108 B3
Sollana E 159 B3
Sollebrunn S 54 B3
Sollefteå S 200 C3
Sollenau A 111 B3
Sollen-tuna S 57 A3
Sóller E 166 B2
Sollerön S 50 B1
Søllested DK 65 B4
Solliès-Pont F 132 B2
Sollihøgda N 48 C2
Solnechnogorsk RUS 9 D10
Solnice CZ 85 B4
Solofra I 170 C2
Solomiac F 129 C3
Solopaca I 170 B2
Solórzano E 143 A3
Solothurn CH 106 B2
Solre-le-Château F 79 B4
Solsona E 147 C2
Solsvik N 46 B1
Solt H 112 C3
Soltau D 72 B2
Soltsy RUS 9 C7
Soltszentimre H 112 C3
Soltvadkert H 112 C3
Solumsmoen N 48 C1
Solund N 46 A1
Solva GB 39 C1
Sölvesborg S 63 B2
Solymár H 112 B2
Soma TR 186 C2
Somain F 78 B3
Somberek H 125 A4
Sombernon F 104 B3
Sombor SRB 125 B5
Sombreffe B 79 B4
Someren NL 80 A1
Somero FIN 8 B3
Somersham GB 44 A3
Somerton GB 43 A4
Sominy PL 68 A2
Somma Lombardo I 120 B1
Sommariva del Bosco I 119 C4
Sommarøy N 192 C2
Sommarset N 194 C6
Sommatino I 176 B2
Sommeilles F 91 C4
Sommen S 55 B5
Sommepy-Tahure F 91 B4
Sömmerda D 82 A3
Sommerfeld D 74 B2
Sommersted DK 59 C2
Sommesous F 91 C4
Somme-Tourbe F 91 B4
Sommières F 131 B3
Sommières-du-Clain F 115 B4
Somo E 143 A3
Somogyfajsz H 111 C4
Somogyjád H 111 C4
Somogysámson H 111 C4
Somogysárd H 125 A3
Somogyszil H 112 C2
Somogyszob H 124 A3
Somogyvár H 111 C4
Somontin E 164 B2
Somosiero E 151 A4
Somosköújfalu H 113 A3
Sompolno PL 76 B3
Sompuis F 91 C4
Son N 54 A1
Son Bou E 167 B4
Sonceboz CH 106 B2
Soncillo E 143 B3
Soncino I 120 B2
Sóndalo I 120 A3
Søndeled N 53 B5
Sønder Bjert DK 59 C2
Sønderborg DK 64 B2
Sønderby DK 64 B2
Sønder Felding DK 59 C1
Sønderho DK 59 C1
Sønder Hygum DK 59 C1
Sønder Omme DK 59 C1
Sondershausen D 82 A2
Søndersø DK 59 C3
Søndervig DK 59 B1
Søndre Enningdal Kappel N 54 B2
Sóndrio I 120 A2
Soneja E 159 B3
Son en Breugel NL 80 A1
Songe N 53 B5
Songeons F 90 B1
Sonkamuotka FIN 196 A6
Sonkovo RUS 9 D10
Sönnarslöv S 61 D4
Sonneberg D 82 B3
Sonnefeld D 82 B3
Sonnewalde D 84 A1
Sonnino I 169 B3
Sonogno CH 120 A1
Sonsbeck D 80 A2
Sonseca E 157 A4
Son Servera E 167 B3
Sønsterud N 49 B4
Sonstorp S 56 B1
Sonta SRB 125 B5
Sontheim D 94 C2
Sonthofen D 107 B5
Sontra D 82 A1
Sopelana E 143 A4
Sopje HR 125 B3
Šoporňa SK 111 A4
Sopot
PL 69 A3
SRB 127 C2
Sopotnica MK 182 B3
Sopron H 111 B3
Šor SRB 127 C1
Sora I 169 B3
Soragna I 120 C3
Söråker S 200 D3
Sorano I 168 A1
Sorbara I 121 C4
Sorbas E 164 B2
Sórbolo I 121 C3
Sörbygden S 200 D2
Sordal N 52 B3
Sordale GB 32 C3
Sore F 128 B2
Sörenberg CH 106 C3
Soresina I 120 B2
Sorèze F 146 A3
Sörforsa S 200 E3
Sorges F 115 C4
Sórgono I 179 B3
Sorgues F 131 A3
Sorgun TR 23 B8
Soria E 143 C4
Soriano Cálabro I 175 C2
Soriano nel Cimino I 168 A2
Sorihuela del Guadalimar E 164 A1
Sorisdale GB 34 B1
Sørkjosen N 192 C4
Sørli N 199 A10
Sormás H 111 C3
Sörmjöle S 200 C6
Sørmo N 194 B9
Sornac F 116 B2
Sorø DK 61 D1
Soroca MD 17 A8
Sørreisa N 194 A9
Sorrento I 170 C2
Sorsele S 195 E8
Sörsjön S 49 A5
Sorso I 178 B2
Sort E 146 B2
Sortavala RUS 9 B7
Sortino I 177 B4
Sortland N 194 B6
Sørum N 48 B2
Sørumsand N 48 C3
Sorunda S 57 A3
Sörup D 64 B2
Sørvågen N 194 C3
Sørvær N 192 B6
Sorvik S 50 B2
Sørvika N 199 C8
Sos F 128 B3
Sösdala S 61 C3
Sos del Rey Católico E 144 B2
Sošice HR 123 B4
Sośnica PL 75 A5
Sośnicowice PL 86 B2
Sośno PL 76 A2
Sosnovyy Bor RUS 9 C6
Sosnowiec PL 86 B3
Sospel F 133 B3
Šoštanj SLO 123 A4
Sotaseter N 198 D4
Sotillo de Adrada E 150 B3
Sotillo de la Ribera E 143 C3
Sotin HR 125 B5
Sotkamo FIN 3 D11
Sotobañado y Priorato E 142 B2
Soto de la Marina E 143 A3
Soto del Barco E 141 A4
Soto de los Infantes E 141 A4
Soto de Real E 151 B4
Soto de Ribera E 141 A5
Sotoserrano E 149 B3
Soto y Amío E 141 B5
Sotresgudo E 142 B2
Sotrondio E 142 A1
Sotta F 180 B2
Sottomarina I 122 B1
Sottrum D 72 A2
Sottunga FIN 51 B7
Sotuelamos E 158 B1
Souain F 91 B4
Soual F 146 A3
Soucy F 104 A2
Souda GR 185 D5
Soudron F 91 C4
Souesmes F 103 B4
Soufflenheim F 93 C3
Soufli GR 186 A1
Souillac F 129 B4
Souilly F 91 B5
Soulac-sur-Mer F 114 C2
Soulaines-Dhuys F 91 C4
Soulatgé F 146 B3
Soultz-Haut-Rhin F 106 B2
Soultz-sous-Forêts F 93 C3
Soumagne B 80 B1
Soumoulou F 145 A3
Souppes-sur-Loing F 103 A4
Souprosse F 128 C2
Sourdeval F 88 B3
Soure P 154 A2
Sournia F 146 B3
Souro Pires P 149 B2
Sourpi GR 182 D4
Sours F 90 C1
Sousceyrac F 116 C2
Sousel P 155 C3
Soustons F 128 C1
Söğüt
Bilecik TR 187 B5
Burdur TR 189 B4
Soutelo de Montes E 140 B2
Southam GB 44 A2
Southampton GB 44 C2
Southborough GB 45 B4
South Brent GB 42 B3
South Cave GB 40 B3
Southend GB 34 C2
Southend-on-Sea GB 45 B4
South Hayling GB 44 C3
South Molton GB 42 A3
South Ockendon GB 45 B4
South Petherton GB 43 B4
Southport GB 38 A3
South Shields GB 37 B5
South Tawton GB 42 B3
Southwell GB 40 B3
Southwold GB 45 A5
South Woodham Ferrers GB 45 B4
Söğütlu TR 187 B5
Souto P 148 B2
Soutochao E 141 C3
Souto da Carpalhosa P 154 B2
Souvigny F 104 C2
Souzay-Champigny F 102 B1
Soverato I 175 C2
Soveria Mannelli I 175 B2
Sövestad S 66 A2
Sovetsk RUS 12 A4
Sovići BIH 138 B3
Sovicille I 135 B4
Søvik N 198 C3
Sowerby GB 37 B5
Soyaux F 115 C4
Sozopol BG 17 D7
Spa B 80 B1
Spadafora I 177 A4
Spaichingen D 107 A3
Spakenburg NL 70 B2

Spalding GB 41 C3
Spálené Poříčí CZ 96 B1
Spalt D 94 B2
Spangenberg D 82 A1
Spangereid N 52 B3
Spantekow D 74 A2
Sparanise I 170 B2
Sparbu N 199 B8
Sparkær DK 58 B2
Sparkford GB 43 A4
Sparreholm S 56 A2
Sparta = Sparti
GR 184 B3
Spartà I 177 A4
Sparti = Sparta
GR 184 B3
Spean Bridge GB 34 B3
Speicher D 92 B2
Speichersdorf D 95 B3
Speke GB 38 A4
Spello I 136 C1
Spenge D 72 B1
Spennymoor GB 37 B5
Spentrup DK 58 B3
Sperenberg D 74 B2
Sperlinga I 177 B3
Sperlonga I 169 B3
Spetalen N 54 A1
Spetses GR 184 B4
Speyer D 93 B4
Spézet F 100 A2
Spezzano Albanese
I 174 B2
Spezzano della Sila
I 174 B2
Spiddle IRL 28 A2
Spiegelau D 96 C1
Spiekeroog D 71 A4
Spiez CH 106 C2
Spigno Monferrato
I 133 A4
Spijk NL 71 A3
Spijkenisse NL 79 A4
Spilamberto I 135 A4
Spili GR 185 D5
Spilimbergo I 122 A1
Spilsby GB 41 B4
Spinazzola I 172 B2
Spincourt F 92 B1
Spind N 52 B2
Spindleruv-Mlyn
CZ 84 B3
Spinoso I 174 A1
Špišjć Bukovica
HR 124 B3
Spišská Belá SK 99 B4
Spišská Nová Ves
SK 99 C4
Spisská Stará Ves
SK 99 B4
Spišské-Hanušovce
SK 99 B4
Spišské Podhradie
SK 99 C4
Spišské Vlachy SK 99 C4
Spišský-Štvrtok
SK 99 C4
Spital A 110 B1
Spital am Semmering
A 110 B2
Spittal an der Drau
A 109 C4
Spittle of Glenshee
GB 35 B4
Spitz A 97 C3
Spjald DK 59 B1
Spjærøy N 54 A1
Spjelkavik N 198 C3
Spjutsbygd S 63 B3
Split HR 138 B2
Splügen CH 107 C4
Spodsbjerg DK 65 B3
Spofforth GB 40 B2
Spohle D 71 A5
Spoleto I 136 C1
Spoltore I 169 A4
Spondigna I 108 C1
Sponvika N 54 A2
Spornitz D 73 A4
Spotorno I 133 A4
Spraitbach D 94 C1
Sprakensehl D 72 B3
Spręcowo PL 69 B5
Spremberg D 84 A2
Spresiano I 122 B1
Sprimont B 80 B1
Springe D 72 B2
Sproatley GB 41 B3
Spydeberg N 54 A2
Spytkowice PL 99 B3
Squillace I 175 C2
Squinzano I 173 B4
Sračinec HR 124 A2
Srbac BIH 124 B3
Srbobran SRB 126 B1
Srebrenica BIH 127 C1
Srebrenik BIH 125 C4
Sredets BG 17 D7
Središče SLO 124 A2
Śrem PL 76 B2
Sremska Mitrovica
SRB 127 C1
Sremski Karlovci
SRB 126 B1
Srní CZ 96 B1
Srnice Gornje BIH 125 C4
Srock PL 86 A3
Środa Śląska PL 85 A4
Środa Wielkopolski
PL 76 B2
Srpska Crnja SRB 126 B2
Srpski Itebej SRB 126 B2
Srpski Miletić
SRB 125 B5
Staatz A 97 C4
Stabbursnes N 193 B8
Staberdorf D 65 B4
Stabroek B 79 A4
Stachy CZ 96 B1
Staðarfell IS 190 B3
Stade D 72 A2
Staden B 78 B3
Stadl an der Mur
A 109 B4
Stadskanaal NL 71 B3
Stadtallendorf D 81 B5
Stadthagen D 72 B2
Stadtilm D 82 B3
Stadtkyll D 80 B2
Stadtlauringen D 82 B2
Stadtlengsfeld D 82 B2
Stadtlohn D 71 C3
Stadtoldendorf D 82 A1
Stadtroda D 83 B3
Stadtsteinach D 82 B3
Stäfa CH 107 B3
Staffanstorp S 61 D3
Staffelstein D 82 B2
Staffin GB 31 B2
Stafford GB 40 C1
Stainach A 110 B1
Staindrop GB 37 B5
Staines-upon-Thames
GB 44 B3
Stainville F 91 C5
Stainz A 110 C2
Staithes GB 37 B6
Staïti I 175 D2
Stäket S 57 A3
Stakroge DK 59 C1
Štalcerji SLO 123 B3
Stalden CH 119 A4
Stalham GB 41 C5
Stalheim N 46 B3
Stallarholmen S 56 A3
Ställberg S 50 C1
Ställdalen S 50 C1
Stallhofen A 110 B2
Stalon S 195 F6
Stalowa Wola PL 12 C5
Stamford GB 40 C3
Stamford Bridge
GB 40 B3
Stamnes N 46 B2
Stams A 108 B1
Stamsried D 95 B4
Stamsund N 194 B4
Stanford le Hope
GB 45 B4
Stånga S 57 C4
Stange N 48 B3
Stanghella I 121 B4
Stanhope GB 37 B4
Stanišić SRB 125 B5
Staňkov CZ 95 B5
Stankovci HR 137 B4
Stanley GB 37 B5
Stans CH 106 C3
Stansted Mountfitchet
GB 45 B4
Stanzach A 108 B1
Stapar SRB 125 B5
Staphorst NL 70 B3
Staplehurst GB 45 B4
Staporków PL 87 A4
Stara Baška HR 123 C3
Starachowice PL 87 A5
Stara Fužina SLO 122 A2
Stara Kamienica
PL 84 B3
Stara Kiszewa PL 68 B3
Stará L'ubovnă SK 99 B4
Stara Moravica
SRB 126 B1
Stara Novalja HR 137 A3
Stara Pazova SRB 127 C2
Stará Turá SK 98 C1
Staraya Russa RUS 9 D7
Stara Zagora BG 17 D6
Stärbsnäs S 51 C6
Starčevo SRB 127 C2
Stare Dłutowo PL 77 A4
Staré Hamry CZ 98 B2
Stare Jablonki PL 69 B5
Staré Město CZ 98 B1
Stare Pole PL 69 A4
Stare Sedlo CZ 96 B2
Stare Strącze PL 85 A4
Stargard Szczeciński
PL 75 A4
Stårheim N 198 D2
Stari Banovci
SRB 127 C2
Starigrad
Ličko-Senjska
HR 123 C3
Splitsko-Dalmatinska
HR 138 B2
Stari Gradac HR 124 B3
Starigrad-Paklenica
HR 137 A4
Stari Jankovci HR 125 B4
Stari Majdan BIH 124 C2
Stari-Mikanovci
HR 125 B4
Staritsa RUS 9 D9
Starkenbach A 108 B1
Starnberg D 108 B2
Starogard PL 75 A4
Starogard Gdański
PL 69 B3
Starokonstyantyniv
UA 13 D7
Staro Petrovo Selo
HR 124 B3
Staro Selo
HR 124 B1
SRB 127 C3
Stary Brzozów PL 77 B5
Stary Dzierzgoń PL 69 B4
Starý Hrozenkov
CZ 98 C1
Stary Jaroslaw PL 68 A1
Stary Plzenec CZ 96 B1
Stary Sącz PL 99 B4
Starý Smokovec
SK 99 B4
Staryy Chartoriysk
UA 13 C6
Staškov SK 98 B2
Stassfurt D 82 A3
Staszów PL 87 B5
Stathelle N 53 A5
Staufen D 106 B2
Staunton GB 39 C4
Stavang N 46 A2
Stavanger N 52 B1
Stavåsnäs S 49 B4
Stavby S 51 B5
Staveley GB 40 B2
Stavelot B 80 B1
Stavenisse NL 79 A4
Stavern N 53 B6
Stavnäs S 55 A3
Stavoren NL 70 B2
Stavros
CY 181 A1
GR 183 C5
Stavroupoli GR 183 B6
Stavseng N 47 A6
Stavsiø N 48 B2
Stavsnäs S 57 A4
Stawiszyn PL 76 C3
Steane N 53 A4
Steblevë AL 182 B2
Stechelberg CH 106 C2
Štechovice CZ 96 B2
Stechow D 73 B5
Steckborn CH 107 B3
Stede Broek NL 70 B2
Steeg A 107 B5
Steenbergen NL 79 A4
Steenvoorde F 78 B2
Steenwijk NL 70 B3
Štefanje HR 124 B2
Steffisburg CH 106 C2
Stegaurach D 94 B2
Stege DK 65 B5
Stegelitz D 74 A2
Stegersbach A 111 B3
Stegna PL 69 A4
Steimbke D 72 B2
Stein GB 31 B2
Steinach
A 108 B2
Baden-Württemberg
D 106 A3
Bayern D 82 B2
Thüringen D 82 B3
Stein an Rhein CH 107 B3
Steinau
Bayern D 81 B5
Niedersachsen D 64 C1
Steinbeck D 74 B2
Steinberg am Rofan
A 108 B2
Steindorf A 109 C5
Steine N 46 B2
Steinen D 106 B2
Steinfeld
A 109 C4
D 71 B5
Steinfurt D 71 B4
Steingaden D 108 B1
Steinhagen D 72 B1
Steinheid D 82 B3
Steinheim
Bayern D 107 A5
Nordrhein-Westfalen
D 81 A5
Steinhöfel D 74 B3
Steinhorst D 72 B3
Steinigtwolmsdorf
D 84 A2
Steinkjer N 199 A8
Steinsholt N 53 A5
Stekene B 79 A4
Stelle D 72 A3
Stellendam NL 79 A4
Stenåsa S 63 B4
Stenay F 91 B5
Stenberga S 62 A3
Stendal D 73 B4
Stenhammar S 55 B4
Stenhamra S 57 A3
Stenhousemuir GB 35 B4
Stenlose DK 61 D2
Stensätra S 50 B3
Stensele S 195 E8
Stenstorp S 55 B4
Stenstrup DK 65 A3
Stenudden S 195 D8
Stenungsund S 54 B2
Štěpánov CZ 98 B1
Stephanskirchen
D 108 B3
Stepnica PL 74 A3
Stepojevac SRB 127 C2
Stepping DK 59 C2
Sterbfritz D 82 B1
Sternberg D 65 C4
Šternberk CZ 98 B1
Sterup D 64 B2
Stes Maries-de-la-Mer
F 131 B3
Stęszew PL 75 B5
Štěti CZ 84 B2
Stevenage GB 44 B3
Stewarton GB 36 A2
Steyerburg D 72 B2
Steyning GB 44 C3
Steyr A 110 A1
Stężyca PL 68 A2
Stezzano I 120 B2
Stia I 135 B4
Stibb Cross GB 42 B2
Sticciano Scalo I 135 C4
Stidsvig S 61 C3
Stiens NL 70 A2
Stige DK 59 C3
Stigen S 54 B3
Stigliano I 174 A2
Stigtomta S 56 B2
Stilida GR 182 E4
Stilla N 192 C7
Stillington GB 40 A2
Stilo I 175 C2
Stintino I 178 B2
Stio I 172 B1
Štip MK 182 B4
Stira GR 185 A5
Stirling GB 35 B4
Štítnik SK 99 C4
Štíty CZ 97 B4
Stjärnhov S 56 A3
Stjärnsund S 50 B3
Stjørdalshalsen N 199 B7
Stobnica PL 87 A3
Stobno PL 75 A5
Stobreč HR 138 B2
Stochov CZ 84 B1
Stockach D 107 B4
Stöckalp CH 106 C3
Stockaryd S 62 A2
Stockbridge GB 44 B2
Stockerau A 97 C4
Stockheim D 82 B3
Stockholm S 57 A4
Stockport GB 40 B1
Stocksbridge GB 40 B2
Stockton-on-Tees
GB 37 B5
Stod CZ 96 B1
Stöde S 200 D2
Stødi N 195 D6
Stöðvarfjörður
IS 191 C12
Stoer GB 32 C1
Stoholm DK 58 B2
Stoke Ferry GB 41 C4
Stoke Fleming GB 43 B3
Stoke Mandeville
GB 44 B3
Stoke-on-Trent GB 40 B1
Stokesley GB 37 B5
Stokke N 54 A1
Stokkemarke DK 65 B4
Stokken N 53 B4
Stokkseyri IS 190 D4
Stokkvågen N 195 D4
Stokmarknes N 194 B5
Štoky CZ 97 B3
Stolac BIH 139 B3
Stølaholmen N 46 A3
Stolberg D 80 B2
Stolin BY 13 C7
Stollberg D 83 B4
Stöllet S 49 B5
Stollhamm D 71 A5
Stolno PL 76 A3
Stolpen D 84 A2
Stolzenau D 72 B2
Stompetoren NL 70 B1
Ston HR 139 C3
Stonařov CZ 97 B3
Stone GB 40 C1
Stonehaven GB 33 E4
Stonehouse GB 36 A3
Stongfjorden N 46 A2
Stonndalen N 47 B4
Stony Stratford GB 44 A3
Stopnica PL 87 B4
Storå S 56 A1
Storås N 198 B6
Storby FIN 51 B6
Stordal
Møre og Romsdal
N 198 C4
Nord-Trøndelag
N 199 B8
Store GB 33 B4
Storebø N 46 B2
Storebro S 62 A3
Store Damme DK 65 B5
Store Heddinge DK 65 A5
Store Herrestad S 66 A2
Store Levene S 55 B3
Storelv N 192 B6
Store Molvik N 193 B12
Støren N 199 B7
Store Skedvi S 50 B2
Store Vika S 57 B3
Storfjellseter N 199 D7
Storfjord N 192 C3
Storfjorden N 198 C3
Storfors S 55 A5
Storforshei N 195 D5
Storhøliseter N 47 A6
Storjord N 195 D6
Storkow
Brandenburg D 74 B2
Mecklenburg-
Vorpommern D 74 A3
Storli N 198 C6
Storlien S 199 B9
Stornara I 171 B3
Stornoway GB 31 A2
Storo I 121 B3
Storozhynets UA 17 A6
Storrington GB 44 C3
Storseleby S 200 B2
Storsjön S 50 A3
Storslett N 192 C5
Storsteinnes N 192 C3
Storsund S 196 D3
Storuman S 195 E8
Störvattnet S 199 C9
Storvik
N 195 D4
S 50 B3
Storvreta S 51 C4
Štos SK 99 C4
Stössen D 83 A3
Stotel D 72 A1
Stötten D 108 B1
Stotternheim D 82 A3
Stouby DK 59 C2
Stourbridge GB 40 C1
Stourport-on-Severn
GB 39 B4
Støvring DK 58 B2
Stow GB 35 C5
Stowbtsy BY 13 B7
Stowmarket GB 45 A5
Stow-on-the-Wold
GB 44 B2
Straach D 73 C5
Strabane GB 27 B3
Strachan GB 33 D4
Strachur GB 34 B2
Stracin MK 182 A4
Strackholt D 71 A4
Stradbally IRL 29 B1
Stradella I 120 B2
Straelen D 80 A2
Stragari SRB 127 C2
Strakonice CZ 96 B1
Strålsnäs S 55 B6
Stralsund D 66 B2
Strand N 48 A3
Stranda N 198 C3
Strandby DK 58 A3
Strandebarm N 46 B3
Strandhill IRL 26 B2
Strandlykkja N 48 B3
Strandvik N 46 B2
Strangford GB 27 B5
Strängnäs S 56 A3
Strångsjö S 56 B2
Stráni CZ 98 C1
Stranice SLO 123 A4
Stranorlar IRL 26 B3
Stranraer GB 36 B1
Strasatti I 176 B1
Strasbourg F 93 C3
Strasburg D 74 A2
Strašice CZ 96 B1
Stråssa S 56 A1
Strassburg A 110 C1
Strass im Steiermark
A 110 C2
Strasskirchen D 95 C4
Strasswalchen A 109 B4
Stratford-upon-Avon
GB 44 A2
Strathaven GB 36 A2
Strathdon GB 32 D3
Strathkanaird GB 32 D1
Strathpeffer GB 32 D2
Strathy GB 32 C3
Strathyre GB 34 B3
Stratinska BIH 124 C2
Stratton GB 42 B2
Straubing D 95 C4
Straulas I 178 B3
Straume N 53 A5
Straumen
Nordland N 194 C6
Nord-Trøndelag
N 199 B8
Straumsjøen N 194 B5
Straumsnes N 194 C6
Straupitz D 74 C3
Strausberg D 74 B2
Straussfurt D 82 A3
Strawczyn PL 87 B4
Straža
SLO 123 B4
SRB 127 C3
Stražnad Nezárkou
CZ 96 B2
Strážnice CZ 98 C1
Strážný CZ 96 C1
Stráž Pod Ralskem
CZ 84 B2
Štrbské Pleso SK 99 B4
Strečno SK 98 B2
Street GB 43 A4
Strehla D 83 A5
Strekov SK 112 B2
Strem A 111 B3
Stremska-Rača
SRB 127 C1
Strengberg A 110 A1
Strengelvåg N 194 B6
Stresa I 119 B5
Streufdorf D 82 B2
Strib DK 59 C2
Striberg S 55 A5
Stříbro CZ 95 B4
Strichen GB 33 D4
Strigno I 121 A4
Štrigova HR 111 C3
Strijen NL 79 A4
Strizivojna HR 125 B4
Strmica HR 138 A2
Strmilov CZ 97 B3
Ströhen D 72 B1
Strokestown IRL 28 A3
Stromberg
Nordrhein-Westfalen
D 81 A4
Rheinland-Pfalz D 93 B3
Stromeferry GB 31 B3
Strömnäs S 200 B2
Stromness GB 33 C3
Strömsberg S 51 B4
Strömsbruk S 200 E3
Strömsfors S 56 B2
Strömsnäsbruk S 61 C3
Strömstad S 54 B2
Strömsund
Jämtland S 199 B12
Västerbotten S 195 E7
Stronachlachar GB 34 B3
Stróngoli I 174 B3
Stronie Ślaskie PL 85 B4
Strontian GB 34 B2
Stroppiana I 119 B5
Stroud GB 43 A4
Stroumbi CY 181 B1
Stróża PL 99 B3
Strücklingen D 71 A4
Struer DK 58 B1
Struga MK 182 B2
Strugi Krasnyye
RUS 9 C6
Strumica MK 182 B4
Strumien PL 98 B2
Struy GB 32 D2
Stružec HR 124 B2
Stryków PL 77 C4
Stryn N 198 D3
Stryy UA 13 D5
Strzałkowo PL 76 B2
Strzegocin PL 77 B5
Strzegom PL 85 B4
Strzegowo PL 77 B5
Strzelce PL 77 B4
Strzelce Krajeńskie
PL 75 B4
Strzelce Kurowo
PL 75 B4
Strzelce Opolskie
PL 86 B2
Strzelin PL 85 B5
Strzelno PL 76 B3
Strzepcz PL 68 A3
Strzybnica PL 86 B2
Strzygi PL 77 A4
Stubbekøbing DK 65 B5
Stuben A 107 B5
Stubenberg A 110 B2
Stubline SRB 127 C2
Studená CZ 97 B3
Studenci HR 138 B3
Studenka CZ 98 B2
Studenzen A 110 B2
Studienka SK 98 C1
Studland GB 43 B5
Studley GB 44 A2
Studzienice PL 68 A2
Stuer D 73 A5
Stugudal N 199 C8
Stugun S 200 C1
Stuhr D 72 A1
Stukenbrock D 81 A4
Stülpe D 74 B2
Stupava SK 111 A4
Stupnik HR 124 B1
Stupsk PL 77 A5
Sturkö S 63 B3
Sturminster Newton
GB 43 B4
Štúrovo SK 112 B2
Sturton GB 40 B3
Stuttgart D 94 C1
Stvolny CZ 96 A1
Stykkishólmur IS 190 B3
Styri N 48 B3
Stysö S 60 B1
Suances E 142 A2
Subbiano I 135 B4
Subiaco I 169 B3
Subotica SRB 126 A1
Subotište SRB 127 C1
Sučany SK 98 B2
Suceava RO 17 B7
Sucha-Beskidzka
PL 99 B3
Suchacz PL 69 A4
Suchań PL 75 A4
Suchdol nad Lužnice
CZ 96 C2
Suchedniów PL 87 A4
Suchorze PL 68 A2
Suchteln D 80 A2
Sucina E 165 B4
Suckow D 73 A4
Sućuraj HR 138 B3
Súðavík IS 190 A3
Sudbury GB 45 A4
Suddesjaur S 195 E10
Suden D 64 B1
Süderbrarup D 64 B2
Süderlügum D 64 B1
Sudoměřice u Bechyně
CZ 96 B2
Sudovec HR 124 A2
Suðureyri IS 190 A2
Sueca E 159 B3
Suelli I 179 C3
Sugenheim D 94 B2
Sugères F 117 B3
Sugny B 91 B4
Suhl D 82 B2
Suhlendorf D 73 B3
Suhopolje HR 124 B3
Suho Polje BIH 125 C5
Şuhut TR 189 A5
Šuica BIH 138 B3
Suippes F 91 B4
Sukošan HR 137 A4
Sükösd H 125 A4
Suków PL 87 B4
Šul'a SK 99 C3
Suldalsosen N 52 A2
Suldrup DK 58 B2
Sulechów PL 75 B4
Sulęcin PL 75 B4
Sulęczyno PL 68 A2
Sulejów PL 87 A3
Süleymanlı TR 186 D2
Sulgen CH 107 B4
Sulibórz PL 75 A4
Sulina RO 17 C8
Sulingen D 72 B1
Suliszewo PL 75 A4
Sulitjelma N 195 C7
Sułkowice PL 99 B3
Süller TR 189 A4
Sully-sur-Loire F 103 B4
Sulmierzyce
Łódzkie PL 86 A3
Wielkopolskie PL 85 A5
Sulmona I 169 A3
Süloğlu TR 186 A1
Sułoszowa PL 87 B3
Sulów PL 85 A5
Sulsdorf D 65 B4
Sultandağı TR 189 A6
Sülüklü TR 187 D7
Suluova TR 23 A8
Sulvik S 54 A3
Sülysáp H 112 B3
Sülz D 93 C4
Sulzbach
Baden-Württemberg
D 94 B1
Baden-Württemberg
D 94 C1
Bayern D 93 B5
Saarland D 92 B3
Sulzbach-Rosenberg
D 95 B3
Sülze D 72 B3
Sulzfeld D 82 B2
Sumartin HR 138 B2
Sumburgh GB 33 B5
Sümeg H 111 C4
Sumiswald CH 106 B2
Šumná CZ 97 C3
Šumperk CZ 97 B4
Šumvald CZ 98 B1
Sunbilla E 144 A2
Sünching D 95 C4
Sund
FIN 51 B7
S 54 A2
Sundborn S 50 B2
Sundby DK 58 B1
Sunde N 46 C2
Sunde bru N 53 B5
Sunderland GB 37 B5
Sundern D 81 A4
Sundhultsbrunn S 62 A2
Sundnäs S 195 D8
Sundom S 196 D5
Sunds DK 59 B2
Sundsfjord N 195 D5
Sundsvall S 200 D3
Sungurlu TR 23 A8
Suni I 178 B2
Sunja HR 124 B2
Sunnansjö S 50 B1
Sunnaryd S 60 B3
Sunndalsøra N 198 C5
Sunne S 49 C5
Sunnemo S 49 C5
Sunnersberg S 55 B4
Suolovuopmio N 192 C7
Suomussalmi FIN 3 D11
Suoyarvi RUS 9 A8
Super Sauze F 132 A2
Supetar HR 138 B2
Supetarska Draga
HR 123 C3
Supino I 169 B3
Šuplja Stijena
MNE 139 B5
Surahammar S 56 A2
Šurany SK 112 A2
Surazh BY 13 A9
Surbo I 173 B4
Surčin SRB 127 C2
Surgères F 114 B3
Surhuisterveen NL 70 A3
Súria E 147 C2
Surin F 115 B4
Surka N 48 B2
Surnadalsøra N 198 C5
Sursee CH 106 B3
Surte S 60 B2
Surwold D 71 B4
Sury-le-Comtal F 117 B4
Susa I 119 B4
Šušara SRB 127 C3
Susch CH 107 C5
Susegana I 122 B1
Süsel D 65 B3
Sušice CZ 96 B1
Šušnjevica HR 123 B3
Sussen D 94 C1
Susurluk TR 186 C3
Susz PL 69 B4
Sütçüler TR 189 B5
Sutivan HR 138 B2
Sutjeska SRB 126 B2
Sutri I 168 A2
Sutton GB 44 B3
Sutton Coldfield
GB 40 C2
Sutton-in-Ashfield
GB 40 B2
Sutton-on-Sea GB 41 B4
Sutton-on-Trent
GB 40 B3
Sutton Scotney GB 44 B2
Sutton Valence GB 45 B4
Suvaja BIH 124 C2
Suvereto I 135 B3
Suwałki PL 12 A5
Suze-la-Rousse F 131 A3
Suzzara I 121 C3
Svabensverk S 50 A2
Svalbarð IS 191 A10
Svalöv S 61 D3
Svanabyn S 200 B2
Svanberga S 51 C5
Svaneke DK 67 A4
Svanesund S 54 B2
Svängsta S 63 B2
Svannäs S 195 D9
Svanskog S 54 A3
Svanstein S 196 C6
Svappavaara S 196 B4
Svärdsjö S 50 B2
Svarstad N 53 A5
Svartå S 55 A5
Svärta S 56 B3
Svartå S 55 A4
Svartbyn S 196 C5
Svärtinge S 56 B2
Svartlå S 196 D4
Svartnäs S 50 B3
Svartnes N 195 C5
Svarttjärn S 195 E7
Svatsum N 48 A1
Svätý Jur SK 111 A4
Svätý Peter SK 112 B2
Svedala S 61 D3
Sveg S 199 C11
Sveindal N 52 B3
Sveio N 52 A1
Svejbæk DK 59 B2
Svelgen N 198 D2
Svelvik N 54 A1
Svendborg DK 65 A3
Svene N 53 A5
Svenljunga S 60 B3
Svennevad S 56 A1
Svenstavik S 199 C11
Svenstrup DK 58 B2
Švermov CZ 84 B2
Sveti Ivan Zabno
HR 124 B2

eti Ivan Zelina
HR 124 B2
eti Nikole MK . . . 182 B3
eti Rok HR 137 A4
ětla nad Sázavou
CZ 97 B3
etlyy RUS 69 A5
etvinčenat HR . . 122 B2
ica HR 123 C4
idník SK 12 D4
ihov CZ 96 B1
ilajnac SRB . . . 127 C3
ilengrad BG . . . 183 B8
indal N 54 A2
inhult S 62 A3
inna SK 98 C2
inninge
DK 61 D1
S 57 A4
iritsa RUS 9 B8
ishtov BG 17 D6
islach BY 13 B6
it SK 99 B4
itavy CZ 97 B4
odin SK 112 B2
olvær N 194 B5
ortemyr N 46 A2
ortland N 52 A1
ratka CZ 97 B4
rčinovec SK 98 B2
ullrya N 49 B4
yetlahorsk BY . . . 13 B8
wadlincote GB . . . 40 C2
waffham GB 41 C4
wanage GB 43 B5
wanley GB 45 B4
wanlinbar IRL 26 B3
wansea GB 39 C3
warzędz PL 76 B2
watragh GB 27 B4
wiątki PL 69 B5
widnica
Dolnośląskie PL . . . 85 B4
Lubuskie PL 84 A3
widnik PL 12 C5
widwin PL 67 C4
wiebodzice PL 85 B4
wiebodzin PL 75 B4
wiecie PL 76 A3
wiedziebnia PL . . . 77 A4
wieradów Zdrój
PL 84 B3
wierki PL 85 B4
wierzawa PL 85 A3
wierzno PL 67 C3
więta PL 74 A3
wieta Anna PL 86 B3
więtno PL 75 B5
wifterbant NL 70 B2
windon GB 44 B2
wineshead GB . . . 41 C3
winford IRL 26 C2
winoujście PL 66 C3
winton GB 35 C5
wobnica PL 74 A3
words IRL 30 A2
wornegacie PL . . . 68 B2
ya S 56 B1
yasstroy RUS 9 B8
ycewice PL 68 A1
ychevka RUS 9 E9
ycówPL 86 A1
ycowice PL 75 B4
ydnes N 52 A1
yfteland N 46 B2
yke D 72 B1
ykkylven N 198 C3
ylling N 48 C2
ylte N 198 C4
ymbister GB 33 A5
ymington GB 36 A3
ymonds Yat GB . . . 39 C4
ypniewo
Kujawsko-Pomorskie
PL 76 A2
Wielkopolskie PL . . 68 B1
yserum S 62 A4
ysslebäck S 49 B4
yväjärvi FIN 197 B8
zabadbattyán H . . 112 B2
zabadegyháza H 112 B2
zabadszállás H . . 112 C3
zadek PL 86 A2
zajol H 113 B4
zakály H 112 C2
zakcs H 112 C2
zakmár H 112 C3
zalánta H 125 B4
załas PL 87 A4
zalkszentmárton
H 112 C3
zalonna H 99 C4
zamocin PL 76 A2
zamotuły PL 75 B5
zany H 111 B4
zarvas H 113 C4
zarvaskő H 113 B4
zászvár H 125 A4
zázhalombatta
H 112 B2
zczawa PL 99 B4
zczawnica PL 99 B4
zczecin PL 74 A3
zczecinek PL 68 B1
zczekociny PL 87 B3
zczerców PL 86 A3
zczucin PL 87 B5
zczuczarz PL 75 A5
zczuki PL 77 B5
zczurowa PL 87 B4
zczyrk PL 99 B3
zczytna PL 85 B4
zczytno PL 77 A5
zczyty PL 86 A2
zécsény H 112 A3
zederkény H 125 B4
zedres H 112 C2
zeged H 126 A2
zeghalom H 113 B5
zegvár H 113 C4

Székesfehérvár
H 112 B2
Székkutas H 113 C4
Szekszárd H 125 A4
Szemplino Czarne
PL 77 A5
Szemud PL 68 A3
Szendehely H 112 B3
Szendrö H 99 C4
Szentendre H 112 B3
Szentes H 113 C4
Szentgotthárd H . . 111 C3
Szentlászló H 125 A3
Szentlörinc H 125 A3
Szentmártonkáta
H 113 B3
Szenyér H 111 C4
Szeremle H 125 A4
Szerencs H 113 A5
Szerep H 113 B5
Szigetszentmiklós
H 112 B3
Szigetvár H 125 A3
Szikáncs H 126 A2
Szikszó H 113 A4
Szil H 111 B4
Szilvásvárad H . . . 113 A4
Szklarska Poreba
PL 84 B3
Szlichtyngowa PL . . 85 A4
Szob H 112 B2
Szolnok H 113 B4
Szombathely H . . . 111 B3
Szorosad H 112 C2
Szpetal Graniczny
PL 77 B4
Szprotawa PL 84 A3
Szreńsk PL 77 A5
Sztum PL 69 B4
Sztutowo PL 69 A4
Szubin PL 76 A2
Szücsi H 113 B3
Szulmierz PL 77 B5
Szulok H 124 A3
Szumanie PL 77 B4
Szwecja PL 75 A5
Szydłów
Łódzkie PL 86 A3
Świętokrzyskie PL . 87 B5
Szydłowiec PL 87 A4
Szydlowo PL 77 A5
Szydłowo PL 75 A5
Szymanów PL 77 B5
Szynkielów PL 86 A2

T

Taastrup DK 61 D2
Tab H 112 C2
Tabanera la Luenga
E 151 A3
Tabaqueros E 158 B2
Tábara E 149 A4
Tabenera de Cerrato
E 142 B2
Taberg S 62 A2
Tabernas E 164 B2
Tabiano Bagni I . . . 120 C3
Taboada E 140 B3
Taboadela E 140 B3
Tábor CZ 96 B2
Táborfalva H 112 B3
Taborište HR 124 B2
Tábua P 148 B1
Tabuaco P 148 A2
Tabuenca E 152 A2
Tabuyo del Monte
E 141 B4
Täby S 57 A4
Tác H 112 B2
Tachov CZ 95 B4
Tadcaster GB 40 B2
Tadley GB 44 B2
Tafalla E 144 B2
Tafjord N 198 C4
Taganheira P 160 B1
Tågarp S 61 D2
Tággia I 133 B3
Tagliacozzo I 169 A3
Táglio di Po I 121 B5
Tagnon F 91 B4
Tahal E 164 B2
Tahitótfalu H 112 B3
Tahtaköprü TR 187 C4
Tailfingen D 107 A4
Taillis F 101 A4
Tain GB 32 D2
Tain-l'Hermitage
F 117 B4
Taipadas P 154 C2
Taivalkoski FIN . . . 197 D11
Takene S 55 A4
Takovo SRB 127 C2
Taksony H 112 B3
Tal E 140 B2
Talachyn BY 13 A8
Talamello I 135 B5
Talamone I 168 A1
Talant F 105 B3
Talarrubias E 156 A2
Talaván E 155 B4
Talavera de la Reina
E 150 C3
Talavera la Real E 155 C4
Talayuela E 150 C2
Talayuelas E 159 B2
Talgarth GB 39 C3
Talgje N 52 A1
Talhadas P 148 B1
Táliga E 155 C3
Talizat F 116 B3
Tálknafjörður IS . . 190 B2
Talla I 135 B4
Talladale GB 31 B3
Tallaght IRL 30 A2
Tallard F 132 A2
Tällberg S 50 B1
Tallberg S 196 C5
Tallinn EST 8 C4

Talloires F 118 B3
Tallow IRL 29 B3
Tallsjö S 200 B4
Tallvik S 196 C5
Talmay F 105 B4
Talmont-St Hilaire
F 114 B2
Talmont-sur-Gironde
F 114 C3
Talne UA 13 D9
Talsano I 173 B3
Talsi LV 8 D3
Talvik N 192 B6
Talybont GB 39 B3
Tal-Y-Llyn GB 38 B3
Tamajón E 151 B4
Tamame E 149 A4
Tamames E 149 B3
Tamarit de Mar E . . 147 C2
Tamarite de Litera
E 145 C4
Tamariu E 147 C4
Tamási H 112 C2
Tambach-Dietharz
D 82 B2
Tameza E 141 A4
Tammisaari FIN 8 B3
Tampere FIN 8 B3
Tamsweg A 109 B4
Tamurejo E 156 B3
Tamworth GB 40 C2
Tana bru N 193 B12
Tañabueyes E 143 B3
Tanakajd H 111 B3
Tananger N 52 B1
Tanaunella I 178 B3
Tancarville F 89 A4
Tandsjöborg S . . . 199 D11
Tånga S 61 C2
Tangelic H 112 C2
Tangen N 48 B3
Tangerhütte D 73 B4
Tangermünde D . . . 73 B4
Tanhua FIN 197 B10
Taninges F 118 A3
Tankavaara FIN . . 197 A10
Tann D 82 B2
Tanna D 83 B3
Tannadice GB 35 B5
Tannåker S 60 C3
Tännäs S 199 C9
Tannay
Ardennes F 91 B4
Nièvre F 104 B2
Tannenbergsthal D 83 B4
Tännesberg D 95 B4
Tannheim A 108 B1
Tannila FIN 197 D8
Tanowo PL 74 A3
Tanum S 54 B2
Tanumshede S 54 B2
Tanus F 130 A1
Tanvald CZ 84 B3
Taormina I 177 B4
Tapa EST 8 C4
Tapfheim D 94 C2
Tapia de Casariego
E 141 A4
Tapio F 146 A2
Tápióbicske H 112 B3
Tápiógyörgye H . . 113 B3
Tápióság H 112 B3
Tápiószecsö H . . . 112 B3
Tápiószele H 113 B3
Tápiószentmárton
H 113 B3
Tapolca H 111 C4
Tapolcafö H 111 B4
Tar HR 122 B2
Tarabo S 60 B2
Taradell E 147 C3
Taraklı TR 187 B5
Taramundi E 141 A3
Tarancón E 151 B4
Táranto I 173 B3
Tarare F 117 B4
Tarascon F 131 B3
Tarascon-sur-Ariège
F 146 B2
Tarashcha UA 13 D9
Tarazona E 144 C2
Tarazona de la Mancha
E 158 B2
Tarbena E 159 C3
Tarbert
GB 34 C2
IRL 29 B2
Tarbes F 145 A4
Tarbet GB 34 B3
Tarbolton GB 36 A2
Tarcento I 122 A2
Tarčin BIH 139 B4
Tarczyn PL 77 C5
Tardajos E 143 B3
Tardelcuende E . . . 151 A5
Tardets-Sorholus
F 144 A3
Tardienta E 145 C3
Tärendö S 196 B5
Targon F 128 B2
Targovishte BG 17 D7
Târgovişte RO 17 C6
Târgu-Jiu RO 17 C5
Târgu Mureş RO . . . 17 B6
Târgu Ocna RO . . . 17 B7
Târgu Secuiesc
RO 17 C7
Tarifa E 162 B2
Tariquejas E 161 B2
Tarján H 112 B2
Tárkany H 112 B2
Tarland GB 33 D4
Tarłów PL 87 A5
Tarm DK 59 C1
Tarmstedt D 72 A2
Tärnaby S 195 E6
Tarnalelesz H 113 A4
Tarnaörs H 113 B4
Târnăveni RO 17 B6
Tårnet N 193 C14

Tarnobrzeg PL 87 B5
Tarnos F 128 C1
Tarnów
Lubuskie PL 75 B3
Małopolskie PL . . . 87 B4
Tarnowo Podgórne
PL 75 B5
Tarnowskie Góry
PL 86 B2
Tärnsjö S 51 B3
Tårnvik N 194 C6
Tarouca P 148 A2
Tarp D 64 B2
Tarquínia I 168 A1
Tarquínia Lido I . . 168 A1
Tarragona E 147 C2
Tårrajaur S 196 C2
Tàrrega E 147 C2
Tarrenz A 108 B1
Tårs
Nordjyllands DK . . . 58 A3
Storstrøms DK 65 B4
Tarsia I 174 B2
Tarsus TR 23 C8
Tartas F 128 C2
Tartu EST 8 C5
Tarves GB 33 D4
Tarvísio I 109 C4
Taşağıl TR 189 C6
Täsch CH 119 A4
Taşköprü TR 23 A8
Tasov CZ 97 B4
Tasovčići BIH 139 B3
Taşucuo TR 23 C7
Tát H 112 B2
Tata H 112 B2
Tatabánya H 112 B2
Tataháza H 126 A1
Tatarbunary UA 17 C8
Tatárszentgyörgy
H 112 B3
Tatranská-Lomnica
SK 99 B4
Tau N 52 A1
Tauberbischofsheim
D 94 B1
Taucha D 83 A4
Taufkirchen D 95 C4
Taufkirchen an der
Pram A 96 C1
Taulé F 100 A2
Taulignan F 131 A3
Taulov DK 59 C2
Taunton GB 43 A3
Taunusstein D 81 B4
Tauragė LT 12 A5
Taurianova I 175 C2
Taurisano I 173 C4
Tauste E 144 C2
Tauves F 116 B2
Tavankut SRB 126 A1
Tavannes CH 106 B2
Tavarnelle val di Pesa
I 135 B4
Tavas TR 188 B4
Tavaux F 105 B4
Tävelsås S 62 B2
Taverna I 175 B2
Taverne CH 120 A1
Tavernelle I 135 B5
Tavernes de la
Valldigna E 159 B3
Tavérnola Bergamasca
I 120 B3
Taverny F 90 B2
Tavescan E 146 B2
Taviano I 173 C4
Tavira P 160 B2
Tavistock GB 42 B2
Tavşanlı TR 187 C4
Tayinloan GB 34 C2
Taynuilt GB 34 B2
Tayport GB 35 B5
Tázlár H 112 C3
Tazones E 142 A1
Tczew PL 69 A3
Tczów PL 87 A5
Teangue GB 31 B3
Teano I 170 B2
Teba E 162 B3
Tebay GB 37 B4
Techendorf A 109 C4
Tecklenburg D 71 B4
Tecko-matorp S . . . 61 D3
Tecuci RO 17 C7
Tefenni TR 189 B4
Tegelsmora S 51 B4
Tegernsee D 108 B2
Teggiano I 172 B1
Tegoleto I 135 B4
Teichel D 82 B3
Teignmouth GB . . . 43 B3
Teillay F 101 B4
Teillet F 130 B1
Teisendorf D 109 B3
Teistungen D 82 A2
Teixeiro E 140 A2
Tejada de Tiétar E 150 B2
Tejado E 152 A1
Tejares E 150 B2
Tejn DK 67 A3
Teke TR 187 A4
Tekirdağ TR 186 B2
Tekovské-Lužany
SK 112 A2
Telavåg N 46 B1
Telč CZ 97 B3
Telese Terme I 170 B2
Telford GB 38 B4
Telfs A 108 B2
Telgárt SK 99 C4
Telgte D 71 C4
Tellingstedt D 64 B2
Telšiai LT 8 E3
Telti I 178 B3
Teltow D 74 B2
Tembleque E 157 A4
Temelin CZ 96 B2
Temerin SRB 126 B1
Temiño E 143 B3

Tempio Pausánia
I 178 B3
Templederry IRL . . . 28 B3
Templemore IRL . . . 28 B4
Temple Sowerby
GB 37 B4
Templin D 74 A2
Temse B 79 A4
Tenay F 118 B2
Ten Boer NL 71 A3
Tenbury Wells GB . . 39 B4
Tenby GB 39 C2
Tence F 117 B4
Tende F 133 A3
Tenhult S 62 A2
Tenja HR 125 B4
Tenneville B 92 A1
Tennevoll N 194 B8
Tensta S 51 B4
Tenterden GB 45 B4
Teo E 140 B2
Teora I 172 B1
Tepasto FIN 196 B7
Tepelenë AL 182 C2
Teplá CZ 95 B4
Teplice CZ 84 B1
Teplička nad Váhom
SK 98 B2
Tepsa FIN 197 B8
Tera E 143 C4
Téramo I 169 A3
Ter Apel NL 71 B4
Terborg NL 71 C3
Terchová SK 99 B3
Terebovlya UA 13 D6
Teremia Mare RO . 126 B2
Terena P 155 C3
Teresa de Cofrentes
E 159 B2
Terešov CZ 96 B1
Terezín CZ 84 B2
Terezino Polje HR 124 B3
Tergnier F 90 B3
Teriberka RUS 3 B14
Terlizzi I 171 B4
Termas de Monfortinho
P 155 A4
Terme di Súio I . . . 169 B3
Terme di Valdieri I 133 A3
Termens E 145 C4
Termes F 116 C3
Términi Imerese I . 176 B2
Terminillo I 169 A2
Térmoli I 170 B3
Termonfeckin IRL . . 27 C4
Ternberg A 110 B1
Terndrup DK 58 B3
Terneuzen NL 79 A3
Terni I 168 A2
Ternitz A 111 B3
Ternopil UA 13 D6
Terpni GR 183 C5
Terracina I 169 B3
Terråk N 195 E3
Terralba I 179 C2
Terranova di Pollino
I 174 B2
Terranova di Sibari
I 174 B2
Terras do Bouro
P 148 A1
Terrasini I 176 A2
Terrassa E 147 C3
Terrasson-Lavilledieu
F 129 A4
Terrazos E 143 B3
Terriente E 152 B2
Terrugem P 155 C3
Tertenia I 179 C3
Teruel E 152 B2
Tervola FIN 196 C7
Tervuren B 79 B4
Terzaga E 152 B2
Tešanj BIH 125 C3
Tesáske-Mlyňany
SK 98 C2
Teslić BIH 125 C3
Tessin D 66 B1
Tessy-sur-Vire F . . . 88 B2
Tét H 111 B4
Tetbury GB 43 A4
Teterchen F 92 B2
Teterow D 65 C5
Teteven BG 17 D6
Tetiyev UA 13 D8
Tetovo MK 182 A2
Tettau D 82 B3
Tettnang D 107 B4
Teublitz D 95 B4
Teuchern D 83 A4
Teulada
E 159 C4
I 179 D2
Teupitz D 74 B2
Teurajärvi S 196 C5
Teutschenthal D . . . 83 A3
Tevel H 112 C2
Teviothead GB 36 A4
Tewkesbury GB . . . 39 C4
Thale D 82 A3
Thalfang D 92 B2
Thalgau A 109 B4
Thalkirch CH 107 C4
Thalmässing D 95 B3
Thalwil CH 107 B3
Thame GB 44 B3
Thann F 106 B2
Thannhausen D 94 C2
Thaon-les-Vosges
F 105 A5
Tharandt D 83 B5
Tharsis E 161 B2
Thasos GR 183 C6
Thatcham GB 44 B2
Thaxted GB 45 B4
Thayngen CH 107 B3
Theale GB 44 B2
The Barony GB 33 B3
Thebes = Thiva
GR 185 A4

Theding-hausen D . 72 B2
Theessen D 73 B5
The Hague = 's-
Gravenhage NL . . 70 B1
Themar D 82 B2
The Mumbles GB . . 39 C3
Thénezay F 102 C1
Thenon F 129 A4
Therouanne F 78 B2
Thessaloniki = Salonica
GR 182 C4
Thetford GB 45 A4
Theux B 80 B1
Thézar-les-Corbières
F 146 A3
Thèze F 145 A3
Thiberville F 89 A4
Thibie F 91 C4
Thiéblemont-Farémont
F 91 C4
Thiendorf D 84 A1
Thiene I 121 B4
Thierrens CH 106 C1
Thiers F 117 B3
Thiesi I 178 B2
Thiessow D 66 B2
Thiezac F 116 B2
Þingeyri IS 190 B2
Þingvellir IS 190 C4
Thionville F 92 B2
Thira GR 185 C6
Thiron-Gardais F . . 89 B4
Thirsk GB 37 B5
Thisted DK 58 B1
Thiva = Thebes
GR 185 A4
Thivars F 90 C1
Thiviers F 115 C4
Thizy F 117 A4
Tholen NL 79 A4
Tholey D 92 B3
Thomas Street IRL . 28 A3
Thomastown IRL . . . 30 B1
Thônes F 118 B3
Thonnance-les-
Joinville F 91 C5
Thonon-les-Bains
F 118 A3
Thorame-Basse F 132 A2
Thorame-Haute F 132 A2
Thorens-Glières F 118 A3
Thorigny-sur-Oreuse
F 91 C3
Thörl A 110 B2
Þorlákshöfn IS . . . 190 D4
Thornaby on Tees
GB 37 B5
Thornbury GB 43 A4
Thorne GB 40 B3
Thornhill
Dumfries & Galloway
GB 36 A3
Stirling GB 35 B3
Thornthwaite GB . . 36 B3
Thornton-le-Dale
GB 40 A3
Þórshöfn IS 191 A10
Thouarcé F 102 B1
Thouars F 102 C1
Thrapston GB 44 A3
Threlkeld GB 36 B3
Thrumster GB 32 C3
Thueyts F 117 C4
Thuin B 79 B4
Thuir F 146 B3
Thumau D 95 A3
Thun CH 106 C2
Thuret F 116 B3
Thurey F 105 C4
Thüringen A 107 B4
Thurins F 117 B4
Thürkow D 65 C5
Thurles IRL 29 B4
Thurmaston GB . . . 40 C2
Thurø By DK 65 A3
Thursby GB 36 B3
Thurso GB 32 C3
Thury-Harcourt F . . 89 B3
Thusis CH 107 C4
Thyborøn DK 58 B1
Þykkvibær IS 190 D5
Thyregod DK 59 C2
Tibi E 159 C3
Tibro S 55 B5
Tidaholm S 55 B4
Tidan S 55 B5
Tidersrum S 62 A3
Tiedra E 150 A2
Tiefenbach D 95 B4
Tiefencastel CH . . . 107 C4
Tiefenort D 82 B2
Tiefensee D 74 B2
Tiel NL 79 A5
Tielmes E 151 B4
Tielt B 78 A3
Tienen B 79 B4
Tiengen D 106 B3
Tiercé F 102 B1
Tierga E 152 A2
Tiermas E 144 B2
Tierp S 51 B4
Tierrantona E 145 B4
Tighina MD 17 B8
Tighnabruaich GB . 34 C2
Tignes F 119 B3
Tigy F 103 B4
Tihany H 112 C1
Tijnje NL 70 A2
Tijola E 164 B2
Tikhvin RUS 9 C8
Tilburg NL 79 A5
Til Châtel F 105 B4
Tilh F 128 C2
Tillac F 145 A4
Tillberga S 56 A2
Tille F 90 B2
Tillicoultry GB 35 B4
Tilloy Bellay F 91 B4
Tilly F 115 B5
Tilly-sur-Seulles F . 88 A3

Tim DK 59 B1
Timau I 109 C4
Timbaki GR 185 D5
Timi CY 181 B1
Timişoara RO 126 B3
Timmele S 60 B3
Timmendorfer Strand
D 65 C3
Timmernabben S . . 62 B4
Timmersdala S 55 B4
Timoleague IRL . . . 29 C3
Timolin IRL 30 B2
Timrå S 200 D3
Timsfors S 61 C3
Timsgearraidh GB . . 31 A1
Tinajas E 152 B1
Tinalhas P 155 B3
Tinchebray F 88 B3
Tincques F 78 B2
Tineo E 141 A4
Tinglev DK 64 B2
Tingsryd S 63 B2
Tingstäde S 57 C4
Tingvoll N 198 C5
Tinlot B 79 B5
Tinnoset N 53 A5
Tinos GR 185 B6
Tintagel GB 42 B2
Tinténiac F 101 A4
Tintern GB 39 C4
Tintigny B 92 B1
Tione di Trento I . . 121 A3
Tipperary IRL 29 B3
Tiptree GB 45 B4
Tirana = Tiranë
AL 182 B1
Tiranë = Tirana AL . 182 B1
Tirano I 120 A3
Tiraspol MD 17 B8
Tire TR 188 A2
Tires I 108 C2
Tiriez E 158 C1
Tirig E 153 B4
Tiriolo I 175 C2
Tirnavos GR 182 D4
Tirrénia I 134 B3
Tirschenreuth D . . . 95 B4
Tirstrup DK 59 B3
Tirteafuera E 157 B3
Tisno HR 137 B4
Tišnov CZ 97 B4
Tisovec SK 99 C3
Tisselskog S 54 B3
Tistedal N 54 A2
Tistrup DK 59 C1
Tisvildeleje DK . . . 61 C2
Tiszaalpár H 113 C3
Tiszabö H 113 B4
Tiszacsége H 113 B5
Tiszadorogma H . . 113 B4
Tiszaföldvár H . . . 113 C4
Tiszafüred H 113 B4
Tiszajenö H 113 B4
Tiszakécske H 113 C4
Tiszakeszi H 113 B4
Tiszakürt H 113 C4
Tiszalök H 113 A5
Tiszalúc H 113 A5
Tiszanána H 113 B4
Tiszaörs H 113 B4
Tiszaroff H 113 B4
Tiszasüly H 113 B4
Tiszasziget H 126 A2
Tiszaszőlős H 113 B4
Tiszaújváros H . . . 113 B5
Tiszavasvári H 113 B5
Titaguas E 159 B2
Titel SRB 126 B2
Titisee-Neustadt
D 106 B3
Tito I 172 B1
Titova Korenica
HR 123 C4
Titran N 198 B5
Tittling D 96 C1
Tittmoning D 109 A3
Titz D 80 A2
Tiurajärvi FIN 196 B7
Tived S 55 B5
Tiverton GB 43 B3
Tivisa E 153 A4
Tívoli I 168 B2
Tizsadob H 113 A5
Tjällmo S 56 B1
Tjåmotis S 195 D9
Tjæreborg DK 59 C1
Tjautjas S 196 B3
Tjøme N 54 A1
Tjong N 195 D4
Tjonnefoss N 53 B4
Tjörn IS 190 B5
Tjörnarp S 61 D3
Tjøtta N 195 E3
Tkon HR 137 B4
Tleń PL 68 B3
Tlmače SK 98 C2
Tłuchowo PL 77 B4
Tlumačov CZ 98 B1
Tóalmas H 112 B3
Toano I 134 A3
Toba D 82 A2
Tobarra E 158 C2
Tobermore GB 27 B4
Tobermory GB 34 B1
Toberonochy GB . . 34 B2
Tobha Mor GB 31 B1
Tobo S 51 B4
Tocane-St Apre F . 129 A3
Tocha P 148 B1
Tocina E 162 A2
Töcksfors S 54 A2
Tocón E 163 A4
Todal N 198 C5
Todi I 136 C1
Todmorden GB 40 B1
Todorici BIH 138 A3
Todtmoos D 106 B3

Todtnau D 106 B2
Toén E 140 B3
Tofta
Gotland S 57 C4
Skaraborg S 55 B4
Toftbyn S 50 B2
Tofte N 54 A1
Töftedal S 54 B2
Tofterup DK 59 C1
Toftlund DK 59 C2
Tófü H 125 A4
Tohmo FIN 197 C10
Tokaj H 113 A5
Tokarnia PL 87 B4
Tokary PL 76 C3
Tokod H 112 B2
Tököl H 112 B2
Tolastadh bho Thuath
GB 31 A2
Toledo E 151 C3
Tolentino I 136 B2
Tolfa I 168 A1
Tolg S 62 A2
Tolga N 199 C8
Tolkmicko PL 69 A4
Tollarp S 61 D3
Tollered S 60 B2
Tølløse DK 61 D1
Tolmachevo RUS 9 C6
Tolmezzo I 122 A2
Tolmin SLO 122 A2
Tolna H 112 C2
Tolnanémedi H 112 C2
Tolob GB 33 B5
Tolosa
E 144 A1
P 155 B3
Tolox E 162 B3
Tolpuddle GB 43 B4
Tolva
E 145 B4
FIN 197 C11
Tolve I 172 B2
Tomar P 154 B2
Tomaševac SRB 126 B2
Tomašica BIH 124 C2
Tomášikovo SK 111 A4
Tomašouka BY 13 C5
Tomášovce SK 99 C3
Tomaszów Mazowiecki
PL 87 A4
Tomatin GB 32 D3
Tombeboeuf F 129 B3
Tomdoun GB 32 D1
Tomelilla S 66 A2
Tomellosa E 151 B5
Tomelloso E 157 A4
Tomiño E 140 C2
Tomintoul GB 32 D3
Tomislavgrad BIH 138 B3
Tomisław PL 84 A3
Tomisławice PL 76 B3
Tomnavoulin GB 32 D3
Tompa H 126 A1
Tompaládony H 111 B3
Tomra N 198 C3
Tomter N 54 A1
Tona E 147 C3
Tonara I 179 B3
Tonbridge GB 45 B4
Tondela P 148 B1
Tønder DK 64 B1
Tongeren B 79 B5
Tongue GB 32 C2
Tönisvorst D 80 A2
Tønjum N 47 A4
Tonkopuro FIN 197 C11
Tonnay-Boutonne
F 114 C3
Tonnay-Charente
F 114 C3
Tonneins F 129 B3
Tonnerre F 104 B2
Tonnes N 195 D4
Tönning D 64 B1
Tonsåsen N 47 B6
Tønsberg N 54 A1
Tonstad N 52 B2
Toomyvara IRL 28 B3
Toormore IRL 29 C2
Topares E 164 B2
Topas E 150 A2
Toplița RO 17 B6
Topola SRB 127 C2
Topolčani MK 182 B3
Topoľčany SK 98 C2
Topoľčianky SK 98 C2
Topolje HR 124 B2
Topólka PL 76 B3
Topoľníky SK 111 B4
Topolovățu Mare
RO 126 B3
Toponár H 125 A3
Toporów PL 75 B4
Topsham GB 43 B3
Topusko HR 124 B1
Toques E 140 B3
Torà E 147 C2
Toral de los Guzmanes
E 142 B1
Toral de los Vados
E 141 B4
Torbalı TR 188 A2
Torbjörntorp S 55 B4
Torbole I 121 B3
Torchiarolo I 173 B4
Torcross GB 43 B3
Torcy-le-Petit F 89 A5
Torda SRB 126 B2
Tørdal N 53 A4
Tordehumos E 142 C1
Tordera E 147 C3
Tordesillas E 150 A2
Tordesilos E 152 B2
Töre S 196 D5
Töreboda S 55 B5
Toreby DK 65 B4
Torekov S 61 C2
Torella dei Lombardi
I 170 C3
Torellò E 147 B3
Toreno E 141 B4
Torfou F 114 A2
Torgau D 83 A5
Torgelow D 74 A3
Torgueda P 148 A2
Torhamn S 63 B3
Torhop N 193 B11
Torhout B 78 A3
Torigni-sur-Vire F 88 A3
Torija E 151 B4
Toril E 152 B2
Torino = Turin I 119 B4
Toritto I 171 C4
Torkovichi RUS 9 C7
Torla E 145 B3
Tormac RO 126 B3
Törmänen FIN 193 D11
Tormestorp S 61 C3
Tórmini I 121 B3
Tornada P 154 B1
Tornal'a SK 99 C4
Tornavacas E 150 B2
Tornby DK 58 A2
Tornesch D 72 A2
Torness GB 32 D2
Torniella I 135 B4
Tornimparte I 169 A3
Torning DK 59 B2
Tornio FIN 196 D7
Tornjoš SRB 126 B1
Tornos E 152 B2
Toro E 150 A2
Törökszentmiklós
H 113 B4
Toropets RUS 9 D7
Torpa S 61 C3
Torpè I 178 B3
Torphins GB 33 D4
Torpo N 47 B5
Torpoint GB 42 B2
Torpsbruk S 62 A2
Torquay GB 43 B3
Torquemada E 142 B2
Torralba de Burgo
E 151 A5
Torralba de Calatrava
E 157 A4
Torrão P 154 C2
Torre Annunziata
I 170 C2
Torreblacos E 143 C4
Torreblanca E 153 B4
Torreblascopedro
E 157 B4
Torrecaballeros E 151 A3
Torrecampo E 156 B3
Torre Canne I 173 B3
Torre Cardela E 163 A4
Torrecilla E 152 B1
Torrecilla de la Jara
E 156 A3
Torrecilla de la Orden
E 150 A2
Torrecilla del Pinar
E 151 A3
Torrecilla en Cameros
E 143 B4
Torrecillas de la Tiesa
E 156 A2
Torre das Vargens
P 154 B3
Torre de Coelheiros
P 154 C3
Torre de Dom Chama
P 149 A2
Torre de Juan Abad
E 157 B4
Torre de la Higuera
E 161 B3
Torre del Bierzo E 141 B4
Torre del Burgo E 151 B4
Torre del Campo
E 163 A4
Torre del Greco I 170 C2
Torre del Lago Puccini
I 134 B3
Torre dell'Orso I 173 B4
Torre del Mar E 163 B3
Torredembarra E 147 C2
Torre de Miguel
Sesmero E 155 C4
Torre de Moncorvo
P 149 A2
Torre de Santa Maria
E 156 A1
Torredonjimeno E 163 A4
Torre do Terranho
P 148 B2
Torre Faro I 177 A4
Torregrosa E 147 C1
Torreira P 148 B1
Torrejoncillo E 155 B4
Torrejón de Ardoz
E 151 B4
Torrejón de la Calzada
E 151 B4
Torrejón del Rey
E 151 B4
Torrejon el Rubio
E 156 A1
Torrelaguna E 151 B4
Torrelapaja E 152 A2
Torre la Ribera E 145 B4
Torrelavega E 142 A2
Torrelobatón E 150 A2
Torrelodones E 151 B4
Torre los Negros
E 152 B2
Torremaggiore I 171 B3
Torremanzanas E 159 C3
Torremayor E 155 C4
Torremezzo di
Falconara I 174 B2
Torremocha E 156 A1
Torremolinos E 163 B3
Torrenieri I 135 B4
Torrenostra E 153 B4
Torrenova I 168 B2
Torrent E 159 B3
Torrente de Cinca
E 153 A4
Torrenueva
Ciudad Real E 157 B4
Granada E 163 B4
Torreorgaz E 155 B4
Torre Orsáia I 172 B1
Torre-Pacheco E 165 B4
Torre Péllice I 119 C4
Torreperogil E 157 B4
Torres E 163 A4
Torresandino E 143 C3
Torre Santa Susanna
I 173 B3
Torres-Cabrera E 163 A3
Torres de la Alameda
E 151 B4
Torres Novas P 154 B2
Torres Vedras P 154 B1
Torrevieja E 165 B4
Torricella I 173 B3
Torri del Benaco I 121 B3
Torridon GB 31 B3
Torriglia I 134 A2
Torrijos E 151 C3
Tørring DK 59 C2
Torrita di Siena I 135 B4
Torroal P 154 C2
Torroella de Montgr i
E 147 B4
Torrox E 163 B4
Torrskog S 54 A3
Torsåker S 50 B3
Torsang S 50 B2
Torsås S 63 B4
Torsby S 49 B4
Torsetra N 48 B2
Torshälla S 56 A2
Tórshavn FO 4 A3
Torslanda S 60 B1
Torsminde DK 59 B1
Torsnes N 46 B3
Törtel H 113 B3
Tórtoles E 150 B2
Tórtoles de Esgueva
E 142 C2
Tortol i I 179 C3
Tortona I 120 C1
Tórtora I 174 B1
Tortoreto Lido I 136 C2
Tortorici I 177 A3
Tortosa E 153 B4
Tortosendo P 148 B2
Tortuera E 152 B2
Tortuero E 151 B4
Toruń PL 76 A3
Torup S 60 C3
Tor Vaiánica I 168 B2
Torver GB 36 B3
Tørvikbygde N 46 B3
Torviscón E 163 B4
Torzhok RUS 9 D9
Torzym PL 75 B4
Tosbotn N 195 E3
Toscolano-Maderno
I 121 B3
Tosno RUS 9 C7
Tossa de Mar E 147 C3
Tossåsen S 199 C10
Tosse F 128 C1
Tösse S 54 B3
Tossicía I 169 A3
Tostedt D 72 A2
Tosya TR 23 A8
Tószeg H 113 B4
Toszek PL 86 B2
Totana E 165 B3
Totebo S 62 A4
Tôtes F 89 A5
Tótkomlós H 113 C4
Totland N 198 D2
Tøtlandsvik N 52 A2
Totnes GB 43 B3
Tótszerdahely H 124 A2
Tøttdal N 199 A8
Totton GB 44 C2
Touça P 149 A2
Toucy F 104 B2
Toul F 92 C1
Toulon F 132 B1
Toulon-sur-Allier
F 104 C2
Toulon-sur-Arroux
F 104 C3
Toulouse F 129 C4
Tourcoing F 78 B3
Tour de la Parata
F 180 B1
Tourlaville F 88 A2
Tournai B 78 B3
Tournan-en-Brie F 90 C2
Tournay F 145 A4
Tournon-d'Agenais
F 129 B3
Tournon-St Martin
F 115 B4
Tournon-sur-Rhône
F 117 B4
Tournus F 105 C3
Touro
E 140 B2
P 148 B2
Tourouvre F 89 B4
Tourriers F 115 C4
Tours F 102 B2
Tourteron F 91 B4
Tourves F 132 B1
Toury F 103 A3
Touvedo P 148 A1
Touvois F 114 B2
Toužim CZ 83 B4
Tovačov CZ 98 B1
Tovariševo SRB 126 B1
Tovarnik HR 125 B5
Tovdal N 53 B4
Towcester GB 44 A3
Town Yetholm GB 35 C5
Tråastølen N 47 B4
Trabada E 141 A3
Trabadelo E 141 B4
Trabanca E 149 A3
Trabazos E 149 A3
Traben-Trarbach D 92 B3
Trabia I 176 B2
Tradate I 120 B1
Trädet S 60 B3
Trafaria P 154 C1
Tragacete E 152 B2
Tragwein A 96 C2
Traiguera E 153 B4
Trainel F 91 C3
Traisen A 110 A2
Traismauer A 97 C3
Traitsching D 95 B4
Trákhonas CY 181 A2
Tralee IRL 29 B2
Tramacastilla de Tena
E 145 B3
Tramagal P 154 B2
Tramariglio I 178 B2
Tramatza I 179 B2
Tramelan CH 106 B2
Tramonti di Sopra
I 122 A1
Tramore IRL 30 B1
Trampot F 92 C1
Trana I 119 B4
Tranås S 55 B5
Tranbjerg DK 59 B3
Tranby N 54 A1
Trancoso P 148 B2
Tranebjerg DK 59 C3
Tranekær DK 65 B3
Tranemo S 60 B3
Tranent GB 35 C5
Tranevåg N 52 B2
Trängslet S 49 A5
Tranhult S 60 B3
Trani I 171 B4
Trans-en-Provence
F 132 B2
Transtrand S 49 A5
Tranum DK 58 A2
Tranvik S 57 A4
Trápani I 176 A1
Trappes F 90 C2
Traryd S 61 C3
Trasacco I 169 B3
Trasierra E 156 B1
Träslövsläge S 60 B2
Trasmiras E 140 B3
Traspinedo E 150 A3
Trate SLO 110 C2
Trauchgau D 108 B1
Traun A 110 A1
Traunreut D 109 B3
Traunstein D 109 B3
Traunwalchen D 109 B3
Tråvad S 55 B4
Travemünde D 65 C3
Traversétolo I 120 C3
Travnik
BIH 139 A3
SLO 123 B3
Travo
F 180 B2
I 120 C2
Trawsfynydd GB 38 B3
Trbovlje SLO 123 A4
Trbušani SRB 127 D2
Treban F 116 A3
Třebařov CZ 97 B4
Trebatsch D 74 B3
Trebbin D 74 B2
Třebechovice pod
Orebem CZ 85 B3
Trebel D 73 B4
Třebenice CZ 84 B1
Trébeurden F 100 A2
Třebíč CZ 97 B3
Trebinje BIH 139 C4
Trebisacce I 174 B2
Trebitz D 83 A4
Trebnje SLO 123 B4
Třeboň CZ 96 B2
Třebovice CZ 97 B4
Trebsen D 83 A4
Trebujena E 161 C3
Trecastagni I 177 B4
Trecate I 120 B1
Trecenta I 121 B4
Tredegar GB 39 C3
Tredózio I 135 A4
Treffen A 109 C4
Treffort F 118 A2
Treffurt D 82 A2
Trefnant GB 38 A3
Tregaron GB 39 B3
Trégastel-Plage F 100 A2
Tregnago I 121 B4
Tregony GB 42 B2
Tréguier F 100 A2
Trégunc F 100 B2
Treharris GB 39 C3
Trehörningsjö S 200 C4
Tréia I 136 B2
Treignac F 116 B1
Treignat F 116 A2
Treignes B 91 A4
Treis-Karden D 80 B3
Trekanten S 63 B4
Trélazé F 102 B1
Trelech GB 39 C2
Trélissac F 129 A3
Trelleborg S 66 A2
Trélon F 91 A4
Trélou-sur-Marne F 91 B3
Tremblay-le-Vicomte
F 89 B5
Tremés P 154 B2
Tremezzo I 120 B2
Třemošná CZ 96 B1
Tremp E 145 B4
Trenčianska Stankovce
SK 98 C1
Trenčianska Turná
SK 98 C2
Trenčianske Teplá
SK 98 C2
Trenčianske Teplice
SK 98 C2
Trenčín SK 98 C2
Trendelburg D 81 A5
Trengereid N 46 B2
Trensacq F 128 B2
Trent D 66 B2
Trento I 121 A4
Treorchy GB 39 C3
Trept F 118 B2
Trepuzzi I 173 B4
Trescore Balneário
I 120 B2
Tresenda I 120 A3
Tresfjord N 198 C4
Tresigallo I 121 C4
Trešnjevica SRB 127 D3
Tresnurághes I 178 B2
Trespaderne E 143 B3
Třešť CZ 97 B3
Trestina I 135 B5
Tretower GB 39 C3
Trets F 132 B1
Tretten N 48 A2
Treuchtlingen D 94 C2
Treuen D 83 B4
Treuenbrietzen D 74 B1
Treungen N 53 A4
Trevelez E 163 B4
Trevi I 136 C1
Treviana E 143 B3
Treviglio I 120 B2
Trevignano Romano
I 168 A2
Trevi nel Lázio I 169 B3
Treviso I 122 B1
Trévoux F 117 B4
Treysa D 81 B5
Trézelles F 117 A3
Trezzo sull'Adda I 120 B2
Trhová Kamenice
CZ 97 B3
Trhové Sviny CZ 96 C2
Triacastela E 141 B3
Triaize F 114 B2
Trianda GR 188 C3
Triaucourt-en-Argonne
F 91 C5
Tribanj Kruščica
HR 137 A4
Triberg D 106 A3
Tribsees D 66 B1
Tribuče SLO 123 B4
Tricárico I 172 B2
Tricase I 173 C4
Tricésimo I 122 A2
Trieben A 110 B1
Triebes D 83 B4
Triepkendorf D 74 A2
Trier D 92 B2
Trieste I 122 B2
Trie-sur-Baïse F 145 A4
Triggiano I 173 A2
Triglitz D 73 A5
Trignac F 101 B3
Trigueros E 161 B3
Trigueros del Valle
E 142 C2
Trikala GR 182 D3
Trikeri GR 183 D5
Trikomo CY 181 A2
Trilj HR 138 B2
Trillo E 152 B1
Trilport F 90 C2
Trim IRL 30 A2
Trimdon GB 37 B5
Trindade
Beja P 160 B2
Bragança P 149 A2
Třinec CZ 98 B2
Tring GB 44 B3
Trinità d'Agultu I 178 B2
Trinitápoli I 171 B4
Trino I 119 B5
Trinta P 148 B2
Triora I 133 B3
Tripoli GR 184 B3
Triponzo I 136 C1
Triptis D 83 B3
Triste E 144 B3
Trittau D 72 A3
Trivento I 170 B2
Trivero I 119 B5
Trivigno I 172 B1
Trn BIH 124 C3
Trnava
HR 125 B4
SK 98 C1
Trnovec SK 112 A1
Trnovo BIH 139 B4
Trnovska vas
SLO 110 C2
Troarn F 89 A3
Trochtelfingen D 94 C1
Trödje S 51 B4
Troense DK 65 A3
Trofa P 148 A1
Trofaiach A 110 B2
Trofors N 195 E4
Trogir HR 138 B2
Trøgstad N 54 A2
Tróia I 171 B3
Troia P 154 C2
Troina I 177 B3
Troisdorf D 80 B3
Trois-Ponts B 80 B1
Troisvierges L 92 A2
Trojane SLO 123 A3
Troldhede DK 59 C1
Trollhättan S 54 B3
Trolog BIH 138 B2
Tromello I 120 B1
Tromøy N 53 B4
Tromsø N 192 C3
Trondheim N 199 B7
Tronget F 116 A3
Trönninge S 61 C2
Trönningeby S 60 B2
Trönö S 51 A3
Tronzano-Vercellese
I 119 B5
Trôo F 102 B2
Troon GB 36 A2
Tropea I 175 C1
Tropy Sztumskie
PL 69 B4
Trosa S 57 B3
Trösken S 50 B3
Trosly-Breuil F 90 B3
Trossingen D 107 A3
Trostberg D 109 A3
Trouville-sur-Mer F 89 A4
Trowbridge GB 43 A4
Troyes F 104 A3
Trpanj HR 138 B3
Trpinja HR 125 B4
Tršće HR 123 B3
Tršice CZ 98 B1
Trstená SK 99 B3
Trstenci BIH 125 B3
Trsteno HR 139 C3
Trstice SK 111 A4
Trstin SK 98 C1
Trubia E 141 A5
Trubjela MNE 139 C4
Truchas E 141 B4
Trujillanos E 155 C4
Trujillo E 156 A2
Trumieje PL 69 B4
Trun
CH 107 C3
F 89 B4
Truro GB 42 B1
Trusetal D 82 B2
Truskavets' UA 13 D5
Trustrup DK 59 B3
Trutnov CZ 85 B3
Tryserum S 56 B2
Trysil N 49 A4
Tryszczyn PL 76 A2
Trzcianka PL 75 A5
Trzciel PL 75 B4
Trzcińsko Zdrój PL 74 B3
Trzebiatów PL 67 B4
Trzebiel PL 84 A2
Trzebielino PL 68 A2
Trzebień PL 84 A3
Trzebiez PL 74 A3
Trzebinia PL 86 B3
Trzebnica PL 85 A5
Trzebnice PL 85 A4
Trzeciewiec PL 76 A3
Trzemeszno PL 76 B2
Trzemeszno-Lubuskie
PL 75 B4
Trzetrzewina PL 99 B4
Tržič SLO 123 A3
Tsamandas GR 182 D2
Tschagguns A 107 B4
Tschernitz D 84 A2
Tsebrykove UA 17 B9
Tsyelyakhany BY 13 B6
Tua P 148 A2
Tuam IRL 28 A3
Tubbercurry IRL 26 B2
Tubbergen NL 71 B3
Tubilla del Lago E 143 C3
Tübingen D 93 C5
Tubize B 79 B4
Tučapy CZ 96 B2
Tučepi HR 138 B3
Tuchan F 146 B3
Tüchen D 73 A5
Tuchola PL 76 A2
Tuchomie PL 68 A2
Tuchów PL 99 B5
Tuczno PL 75 A5
Tuddal N 53 A4
Tudela E 144 B2
Tudela de Duero
E 150 A3
Tudweiliog GB 38 B2
Tuejar E 159 B2
Tuffé F 102 A2
Tufsingdalen N 199 C8
Tuhaň CZ 84 B2
Tui E 140 B2
Tukhkala RUS 197 D13
Tukums LV 8 D3
Tula I 178 B2
Tulcea RO 17 C8
Tul'chyn UA 13 D8
Tulette F 131 A3
Tuliszków PL 76 B3
Tulla IRL 28 B3
Tullamore IRL 30 A1
Tulle F 116 B1
Tullins F 118 B2
Tulln A 97 C4
Tullow IRL 30 B2
Tułowice PL 85 B5
Tulppio FIN 197 B12
Tulsk IRL 28 A3
Tumba S 57 A3
Tummel Bridge GB 35 B3
Tun S 55 B3
Tuna
Kalmar S 62 A4
Uppsala S 51 B5
Tuna Hästberg S 50 B2
Tunçbilek TR 187 C4
Tunes P 160 B1
Tungelsta S 57 A4
Tunnerstad S 55 B5
Tunnhovd N 47 B5
Tunstall GB 45 A5
Tuohikotti FIN 8 B5
Tuoro sul Trasimeno
I 135 B5
Tupadły PL 76 B3
Tupanari BIH 139 A4
Tupik RUS 9 E8
Tuplice PL 84 A2
Tura H 112 B3
Turanj HR 137 B4
Turany SK 99 B3
Turbe BIH 139 A3
Turbenthal CH 107 B3
Turcia E 141 B
Turčianske Teplice
SK 98 C
Turcifal P 154 B
Turckheim F 106 A
Turda RO 17 B
Turégano E 151 A
Turek PL 76 B
Turgutlu TR 188 A
Turgutreis TR 188 B
Turi I 173 B
Turin = Torino I 119 B
Turis E 159 B
Türje H 111 C
Turka UA 12 D
Túrkeve H 113 B
Türkheim D 108 A
Türkmenli TR 186 C
Turku FIN 8 B
Turleque E 157 A
Turňa nad Bodvou
SK 99 C
Turnberry GB 36 A
Turnhout B 79 A
Türnitz A 110 B
Turnov CZ 84 B
Turnu RO 126 A
Turnu Măgurele RO 17 D
Turón E 164 C
Turoszów PL 84 B
Turowo PL 77 A
Turquel P 154 B
Turri I 179 C
Turries F 132 A
Turriff GB 33 D
Tursi I 174 A
Turtmann CH 119 A
Turtola FIN 196 C
Turze PL 86 A
Turzovka SK 98 B
Tusa I 177 B
Tuscánia I 168 A
Tuse DK 61 D
Tušilovic HR 123 B
Tuszyn PL 86 A
Tutow D 66 C
Tutrakan BG 17 C
Tuttlingen D 107 B
Tutzing D 108 B
Tuzla
BIH 125 C
TR 23 C
Tuzlukçu TR 189 A
Tvååker S 60 B
Tvärålund S 200 B
Tvärskog S 63 B
Tvedestrand N 53 B
Tveit
Hordaland N 47 B
Rogaland N 52 A
Tver RUS 9 D
Tverrelvmo N 192 D
Tversted DK 58 A
Tving S 63 B
Tvrdošin SK 99 B
Tvrdošovce SK 112 A
Twardogóra PL 85 A
Twatt GB 33 B
Twello NL 70 B
Twimberg A 110 C
Twist D 71 B
Twistringen D 72 B
Tworóg PL 86 B
Twyford
Hampshire GB 44 B
Wokingham GB 44 B
Tyachiv UA 17 A
Tychówka PL 67 C
Tychowo PL 67 C
Tychy PL 86 B
Tydal N 199 B
Týec nad Labem
CZ 97 A
Tyfors S 49 B
Tygelsjö S 61 D
Tylldal N 199 C
Tylstrup DK 58 A
Tymbark PL 99 B
Tymowa PL 99 B
Tyndrum GB 34 B
Týnec nad Sázavou
CZ 96 B
Tynemouth GB 37 A
Tyngsjö S 49 B
Týništěnad Orlicí
CZ 85 B
Týn nad Vltavou
CZ 96 B
Tynset N 199 C
Tyresö S 57 A
Tyringe S 61 C
Tyrislöt S 56 B
Tyristrand N 48 B
Tyrrellspass IRL 30 A
Tysnes N 46 B
Tysse N 46 B
Tyssebotn N 46 B
Tyssedal N 46 B
Tystberga S 56 B
Tysvær N 52 A
Tywyn GB 39 B
Tzermiado GR 185 D
Tzummarum NL 70 A

U

Ub SRB 127 C
Ubby DK 61 D
Úbeda E 157 B
Überlingen D 107 B
Ubidea E 143 A
Ubli HR 138 C
Ubrique E 162 B
Ucero E 143 C
Uchaud F 131 B
Uchte D 72 B
Uckerath D 80 B
Uckfield GB 45 C
Ucklum S 54 B

lés E ... 151 C5
ria I ... 177 A3
dbina HR ... 137 A4
ddebo S ... 60 B3
ddeholm S ... 49 B5
ddevalla S ... 54 B2
ddheden S ... 49 C4
den NL ... 80 A1
der D ... 82 A2
diča SK ... 98 B2
dine I ... 122 A2
dvar H ... 125 B4
eckermünde D ... 74 A3
elsen D ... 71 B3
elzen D ... 73 B3
etendorf CH ... 106 C2
etersen D ... 72 A2
etze D ... 72 B3
fculme GB ... 43 B3
fenheim D ... 94 B2
garana E ... 143 A4
gento I ... 173 C4
gerløse DK ... 61 D1
gerby DK ... 58 A3
gerslev DK ... 59 C3
giano la Chiesa
... 173 B4
gijar E ... 164 C1
gine F ... 118 B3
glejevik BIH ... 125 C5
glenes N ... 46 B2
glich RUS ... 9 D11
gljane HR ... 138 B2
god H ... 111 B4
herské Hradiště
CZ ... 98 B1
herský Brod CZ ... 98 B1
herský Ostroh
CZ ... 98 C1
hingen D ... 94 C1
hlířské-Janovice
CZ ... 96 B3
hříněves CZ ... 96 A2
hyst D ... 84 A2
g GB ... 31 B2
tgeest NL ... 70 B1
thoorn NL ... 70 B1
thuizen NL ... 71 A3
thuizermeeden
NL ... 71 A3
var RO ... 126 B2
azd
Łódzkie PL ... 87 A3
Opolskie PL ... 86 B2
ezd u Brna CZ ... 97 B4
hartyán H ... 112 B3
kigyós H ... 113 C5
petre H ... 125 B4
ście PL ... 75 A5
solt H ... 112 C3
szász H ... 113 B4
szentmargita H ... 113 B5
ué E ... 144 B2
kanc SLO ... 122 A2
kmergė LT ... 13 A6
kna S ... 56 B2
la TR ... 188 B3
l'anka SK ... 99 C3
laş TR ... 186 A2
lássai I ... 179 C3
lbjerg DK ... 58 B2
lbster GB ... 32 C3
lceby GB ... 40 B3
lcinj MNE ... 16 E3
ldum DK ... 59 C2
lefoss N ... 53 A5
leila del Campo
E ... 164 B2
lëz AL ... 182 B1
lfborg DK ... 59 B1
ljma SRB ... 127 B3
llånger S ... 200 C4
llapool GB ... 32 D1
llared S ... 60 B2
llatti S ... 196 B4
llatun N ... 52 A2
lldecona E ... 153 B4
lldemolins E ... 147 C1
llerslev DK ... 59 C3
llervad S ... 55 B4
llés H ... 126 A1
llö H ... 112 B3
lm D ... 94 C1
lme P ... 154 B2
lmen D ... 80 B2
lnes N ... 47 B6
log BIH ... 139 B4
lricehamn S ... 60 B3
lrichstein D ... 81 B5
lrika S ... 56 B1
lriksfors S ... 200 C1
lrum NL ... 71 A3
lsberg N ... 198 C6
lsta GB ... 33 A5
lsted DK ... 58 A3
lsteinvik N ... 198 C2
lstrup
Vestsjællands Amt.
DK ... 59 C3
Viborg Amt. DK ... 59 B2
lsvåg N ... 194 B6
lubey TR ... 188 A4
luborlu TR ... 189 A5
lukışla TR ... 23 C8
lverston GB ... 36 B3
lvik N ... 46 B3
mag HR ... 122 B2
man UA ... 13 D9
mba RUS ... 3 C14
mbértide I ... 135 B5
mbriático I ... 174 B2
mčari SRB ... 127 C2
meå S ... 200 C6
mgransele S ... 200 B4
mhausen A ... 108 B1
mka SRB ... 127 C2
mljanovic HR ... 138 B2
mnäs S ... 195 E7
murbey TR ... 186 B1
naðsdalur IS ... 190 A3
Unapool GB ... 32 C1
Unari FIN ... 197 B8
Unbyn S ... 196 D4
Uncastillo E ... 144 B2
Undenäs S ... 55 B5
Undersaker S ... 199 B10
Undredal N ... 46 B4
Unešić HR ... 138 B2
Úněšov CZ ... 96 B1
Ungheni MD ... 17 B7
Unhais da Serra P ... 148 B2
Unhošť CZ ... 84 B2
Unichowo PL ... 68 A2
Uničov CZ ... 98 B1
Uniejów PL ... 76 C3
Unisław PL ... 76 A3
Unkel D ... 80 B3
Unken A ... 109 B3
Unna D ... 81 A3
Unnaryd S ... 60 C3
Unquera E ... 142 A2
Unterach A ... 109 B4
Unterägeri CH ... 107 B3
Unterammergau D ... 108 B2
Unterhaching D ... 108 A2
Unteriberg CH ... 107 B3
Unterkochen D ... 94 C2
Unter Langkampfen
A ... 108 B3
Unterlaussa A ... 110 B1
Unterlüss D ... 72 B3
Untermünkheim D ... 94 B1
Unterschächen
CH ... 107 C3
Unterschleissheim
D ... 95 C3
Unterschwaningen
D ... 94 B2
Untersiemau D ... 82 B2
Unter-steinbach D ... 94 B2
Unterweissenbach
A ... 96 C2
Unterzell D ... 95 B4
Upavon GB ... 44 B2
Úpice CZ ... 85 B4
Upiłka PL ... 68 B2
Upphärad S ... 54 B3
Uppingham GB ... 40 C3
Upplands-Väsby S ... 57 A3
Uppsala S ... 51 C4
Uppsjøhytta N ... 48 A1
Upton-upon-Severn
GB ... 39 B4
Ur F ... 146 B2
Uras I ... 179 C2
Uraz PL ... 85 A4
Urbánia I ... 136 B1
Urbino I ... 136 B1
Urçay F ... 103 C4
Urda E ... 157 A4
Urdax E ... 144 A2
Urdilde E ... 140 B2
Urdos F ... 145 B3
Urk NL ... 70 B2
Úrkút H ... 111 B4
Urla TR ... 188 A1
Urlingford IRL ... 30 B1
Urnäsch CH ... 107 B4
Urnes N ... 47 A4
Uroševac KOS ... 16 D4
Urracal E ... 164 B2
Urries E ... 144 B2
Urroz E ... 144 B2
Ursensollen D ... 95 B3
Urshult S ... 63 B2
Uršna Sela SLO ... 123 B4
Urszulewo PL ... 77 B4
Ury F ... 90 C2
Urziceni RO ... 17 C7
Urzulei I ... 178 B3
Usagre E ... 156 B1
Uşak TR ... 187 D4
Usedom D ... 66 C2
Useldange L ... 92 B1
Uséllus I ... 179 C2
Ushakovo RUS ... 69 A5
Usingen D ... 81 B4
Usini I ... 178 B2
Usk GB ... 39 C4
Uskedal N ... 46 C2
Üsküdar TR ... 186 A4
Uslar D ... 82 A1
Úsov CZ ... 97 B5
Usquert NL ... 71 A3
Ussássai I ... 179 C3
Ussé F ... 102 B2
Usséglio I ... 119 B4
Ussel
Cantal F ... 116 B2
Corrèze F ... 116 B2
Usson-du-Poitou
F ... 115 B4
Usson-en-Forez F ... 117 B3
Usson-les-Bains
F ... 146 B3
Ustaoset N ... 47 B5
Ustaritz F ... 144 A2
Uštěk CZ ... 84 B2
Uster CH ... 107 B3
Ústi CZ ... 98 B1
Ustikolina BIH ... 139 B4
Ústínad Labem CZ ... 84 B2
Ústínad Orlicí CZ ... 97 B4
Ustiprača BIH ... 139 B5
Ustka PL ... 68 A1
Ust Luga RUS ... 8 C6
Ustroń PL ... 98 B2
Ustronie Morskie
PL ... 67 B4
Ustyuzhna RUS ... 9 C10
Uszód H ... 112 C2
Utåker N ... 52 A1
Utansjö S ... 200 D3
Utebo E ... 152 A3
Utena LT ... 13 A6
Utery CZ ... 95 B5
Uthaug N ... 198 B6
Utiel E ... 159 B2
Utne N ... 46 B3
Utö S ... 57 B4
Utrecht NL ... 70 B2
Utrera E ... 162 A2
Utrillas E ... 153 B3
Utsjoki FIN ... 193 C11
Utstein kloster N ... 52 A1
Uttendorf A ... 109 B3
Uttenweiler D ... 107 A4
Utterslev DK ... 65 B4
Uttoxeter GB ... 40 C2
Utvälinge S ... 61 C2
Utvorda N ... 199 A7
Uusikaarlepyy FIN ... 3 E8
Uusikaupunki FIN ... 8 B2
Uvaly CZ ... 96 A2
Uvdal N ... 47 B5
Uza F ... 128 B1
Uzdin SRB ... 126 B2
Uzdowo PL ... 77 A5
Uzein F ... 145 A3
Uzel F ... 100 A3
Uzerche F ... 116 B1
Uzès F ... 131 A3
Uzhhorod UA ... 12 D5
Uzhok UA ... 12 D5
Užice SRB ... 127 D1
Uznach CH ... 107 B3
Üzümlü
Konya TR ... 189 B6
Muğla TR ... 188 C4
Uzunköprü TR ... 186 A1

V

Vaalajärvi FIN ... 197 B9
Vaas F ... 102 B2
Vaasa FIN ... 8 A2
Vaasen NL ... 70 B2
Vabre F ... 130 B1
Vác H ... 112 B3
Vacha D ... 82 B2
Váchartyán H ... 112 B3
Väckelsång S ... 63 B2
Vacqueyras F ... 131 A3
Vad S ... 50 B2
Vada I ... 134 B3
Väddö S ... 51 C5
Väderstad S ... 55 B5
Vadheim N ... 46 A2
Vadillo de la Sierra
E ... 150 B2
Vadillos E ... 152 B1
Vadla N ... 52 A2
Vado I ... 135 A4
Vado Lígure I ... 133 A4
Vadsø N ... 193 B13
Vadstena S ... 55 B5
Vadum DK ... 58 A2
Vaduz FL ... 107 B4
Vafos N ... 53 B5
Vág H ... 111 B4
Vågåmo N ... 198 D6
Væggerløse DK ... 65 B4
Vaggeryd S ... 62 A2
Vaghia GR ... 184 A4
Vaglia I ... 135 B4
Váglio Basilicata I ... 172 B1
Vagney F ... 106 A1
Vagnhärad S ... 57 B3
Vagnsunda S ... 57 A4
Vagos P ... 148 B1
Vai GR ... 185 D7
Vaiano I ... 135 B4
Vaiges F ... 102 A1
Vaihingen D ... 93 C4
Vaillant F ... 105 B4
Vailly-sur-Aisne F ... 91 B3
Vailly-sur Sauldre
F ... 103 B4
Vairano Scalo I ... 170 B2
Vaison-la-Romaine
F ... 131 A4
Vaite F ... 105 B4
Väjern S ... 54 B2
Vajszló H ... 125 B3
Vaksdal N ... 46 B2
Vál H ... 112 B2
Valaam RUS ... 9 B7
Valada P ... 154 B2
Vålådalen S ... 199 B10
Valadares P ... 148 A1
Valado P ... 154 B1
Valandovo MK ... 182 B4
Valaská SK ... 99 C3
Valaská Belá SK ... 98 C2
Valaská Dubová
SK ... 99 B3
Valašská Polanka
CZ ... 98 B1
Valašské Klobouky
CZ ... 98 B2
Valašské Meziříčí
CZ ... 98 B1
Valberg F ... 132 A2
Vålberg S ... 55 A4
Valbo S ... 51 B4
Valbom P ... 148 A1
Valbondione I ... 120 A3
Valbonnais F ... 118 C2
Valbuena de Duero
E ... 142 C2
Vălcani RO ... 126 B2
Valdagno I ... 121 B4
Valdahon F ... 105 B5
Valdaracete E ... 151 B4
Valday RUS ... 9 D8
Valdealgorfa E ... 153 B3
Valdecaballeros E ... 156 A2
Valdecabras E ... 152 B1
Valdecarros E ... 150 B2
Valdeconcha E ... 151 B5
Valdeflores E ... 161 B3
Valdefresno E ... 142 B1
Valdeganga E ... 158 B2
Valdelacasa E ... 150 B2
Valdelacasa de Tajo
E ... 156 A2
Valdelarco E ... 161 B3
Valdelosa E ... 149 A4
Valdeltormo E ... 153 B4
Valdelugeros E ... 142 B1
Valdemanco de Esteras
E ... 156 B3
Valdemarsvik S ... 56 B2
Valdemorillo E ... 151 B3
Valdemoro E ... 151 B4
Valdemoro Sierra
E ... 152 B2
Valdenoceda E ... 143 B3
Valdeobispo E ... 149 B3
Valdeolivas E ... 152 B1
Valdepeñas E ... 157 B4
Valdepeñas de Jaén
E ... 163 A4
Valdepiélago E ... 142 B1
Valdepolo E ... 142 B1
Valderas E ... 142 B1
Valdérice I ... 176 A1
Valderrobres E ... 153 B4
Valderrueda E ... 142 B2
Val de San Lorenzo
E ... 141 B4
Val de Santo Domingo
E ... 150 B3
Val d'Esquières F ... 132 B2
Valdestillas E ... 150 A3
Valdetorres E ... 156 B1
Valdetorres de Jarama
E ... 151 B4
Valdeverdeja E ... 150 C2
Valdevimbre E ... 142 B1
Valdieri I ... 133 A3
Valdilecha E ... 151 B4
Val-d'Isère F ... 119 B3
Valdobbiádene I ... 121 B4
Valdocondes E ... 143 C3
Valdoviño E ... 140 A2
Valea lui Mihai RO ... 16 B5
Vale de Açor
Beja P ... 160 B2
Portalegre P ... 154 B3
Vale de Agua P ... 160 B1
Vale de Cambra P ... 148 B1
Vale de Lobo P ... 160 B1
Vale de Prazeres
P ... 148 B2
Vale de Reis P ... 154 C2
Vale de Rosa P ... 160 B2
Vale de Santarém
P ... 154 B2
Vale de Vargo P ... 160 B2
Vale do Peso P ... 155 B3
Valega P ... 148 B1
Valéggio sul Mincio
I ... 121 B3
Valeiro P ... 154 C2
Valença P ... 140 B2
Valençay F ... 103 B3
Valence
Charente F ... 115 C4
Drôme F ... 117 C4
Valence d'Agen F ... 129 B3
Valence d'Albigeois
F ... 130 A1
Valence-sur-Baise
F ... 129 C3
Valencia E ... 159 B3
Valencia de Alcántara
E ... 155 B3
Valencia de Don Juan
E ... 142 B1
Valencia de las Torres
E ... 156 B1
Valencia del Ventoso
E ... 161 A3
Valencia de Mombuey
E ... 161 A2
Valenciennes F ... 79 B3
Valensole F ... 132 B1
Valentano I ... 168 A1
Valentigney F ... 106 B1
Valentine F ... 145 A4
Valenza I ... 120 B1
Valenzuela E ... 163 A3
Valenzuela de
Calatrava E ... 157 B4
Våler
Hedmark N ... 48 B3
Østfold N ... 54 A1
Valera de Abajo E ... 158 B1
Valeria E ... 158 B1
Valestrand N ... 52 A1
Valestrandsfossen
N ... 46 B2
Valevåg N ... 52 A1
Valfabbrica I ... 136 B1
Valflaunes F ... 131 B2
Valga EST ... 8 D5
Valgorge F ... 131 A3
Valgrisenche I ... 119 B4
Valguarnera Caropepe
I ... 177 B3
Valhelhas P ... 148 B2
Valjevo SRB ... 127 C1
Valka LV ... 8 D4
Valkeakoski FIN ... 8 B4
Valkenburg NL ... 80 B1
Valkenswaard NL ... 79 A5
Valkó H ... 112 B3
Valla S ... 56 A2
Vallada E ... 159 C3
Vallado E ... 141 A4
Valladolid E ... 150 A3
Vallåkra S ... 61 D2
Vallata I ... 172 A1
Vallberga S ... 61 C3
Vall d'Alba E ... 153 B3
Valldemossa E ... 166 B2
Valle N ... 52 A3
Valle Castellana I ... 136 C2
Valle de Abdalajís
E ... 163 B3
Valle de Cabuérniga
E ... 142 A2
Valle de la Serena
E ... 156 B2
Valle de Matamoros
E ... 155 C4
Valle de Santa Ana
E ... 155 C4
Valledolmo I ... 176 B2
Valledoria I ... 178 B2
Vallelado E ... 150 A3
Vallelunga Pratameno
I ... 176 B2
Valle Mosso I ... 119 B5
Vallendar D ... 81 B3
Vallentuna S ... 57 A4
Valleräs S ... 49 B5
Valleraugue F ... 130 A2
Vallermosa I ... 179 C2
Vallet F ... 101 B4
Valletta M ... 175 C3
Valley GB ... 38 A2
Vallfogona de Riucorb
E ... 147 C2
Valli del Pasúbio I ... 121 B4
Vallo della Lucánia
I ... 172 B1
Valloire F ... 118 B3
Vallombrosa I ... 135 B4
Vallon-Pont-d'Arc
F ... 131 A3
Vallorbe CH ... 105 C5
Vallouise F ... 118 C3
Valls E ... 147 C2
Vallset N ... 48 B3
Vallsta S ... 50 A3
Vallstena S ... 57 C4
Valmadrid E ... 153 A3
Valmiera LV ... 8 D4
Valmojado E ... 151 B3
Valmont F ... 89 A4
Valmontone I ... 169 B2
Valö S ... 51 B5
Valognes F ... 88 A2
Valonga P ... 148 B1
Valongo P ... 148 A1
Válor E ... 164 C1
Valoria la Buena
E ... 142 C2
Valøy N ... 199 A7
Valozhyn BY ... 13 A7
Valpaços P ... 148 A2
Valpelline I ... 119 B4
Valpiana I ... 135 B3
Valpovo HR ... 125 B4
Valras-Plage F ... 130 B2
Valréas F ... 131 A3
Vals CH ... 107 C4
Valsavarenche I ... 119 B4
Vålse DK ... 65 B4
Valsequillo E ... 156 B2
Valsjöbyn S ... 199 A11
Vals-les-Bains F ... 117 C4
Valsonne F ... 117 B4
Valstagna I ... 121 B4
Val-Suzon F ... 105 B3
Valtablado del Rio
E ... 152 B1
Valþjofsstaður IS ... 191 B11
Val Thorens F ... 118 B3
Valtice CZ ... 97 C4
Valtiendas E ... 151 A4
Valtierra E ... 144 B2
Valtopina I ... 136 B1
Valtorta I ... 120 B2
Valtournenche I ... 119 B4
Valverde E ... 144 C2
Valverde de Burguillos
E ... 155 C4
Valverde de Júcar
E ... 158 B1
Valverde de la Vera
E ... 150 B2
Valverde de la Virgen
E ... 142 B1
Valverde del Camino
E ... 161 B3
Valverde del Fresno
E ... 149 B3
Valverde de Llerena
E ... 156 B2
Valverde de Mérida
E ... 156 B1
Valvträsk S ... 196 C4
Vamberk CZ ... 85 B4
Vamdrup DK ... 59 C2
Våmhus S ... 50 A1
Vamlingbo S ... 57 D4
Vammala FIN ... 8 B3
Vamos GR ... 185 D5
Vámosmikola H ... 112 B2
Vámosszabadi H ... 111 B4
Vanault-les-Dames
F ... 91 C4
Vandel DK ... 59 C2
Vandenesse F ... 104 C2
Vandenesse-en-Auxois
F ... 104 B3
Vandóies I ... 108 C2
Väne-Åsaka S ... 54 B3
Vänersborg S ... 54 B3
Vänersnäs S ... 54 B3
Vang N ... 47 A5
Vänge S ... 51 C4
Vangsnes N ... 46 A3
Vänjaurbäck S ... 200 B4
Vännacka S ... 54 A3
Vannareid N ... 192 B3
Vännäs S ... 200 C5
Vannes F ... 101 B3
Vannsätter S ... 51 A3
Vannvåg N ... 192 B3
Vansbro S ... 49 B6
Vanse N ... 52 B2
Vantaa FIN ... 8 B4
Vanttauskoski
FIN ... 197 C9
Vanviken N ... 199 B7
Vanyarc H ... 112 B3
Vaour F ... 129 B4
Vapnyarka UA ... 13 D8
Vaprio d'Adda I ... 120 B2
Vaqueiros P ... 160 B2
Vara S ... 55 B3
Varacieux F ... 118 B2
Varades F ... 101 B4
Varages F ... 132 B1
Varaldsøy N ... 46 B2
Varallo I ... 119 B5
Varangerbotn N ... 193 B12
Varano de'Melegari
I ... 120 C3
Varaždin HR ... 124 A2
Varaždinske Toplice
HR ... 124 A2
Varazze I ... 133 A4
Varberg S ... 60 B2
Vardal N ... 48 B2
Varde DK ... 59 C1
Vårdö FIN ... 51 B7
Vardø N ... 193 B15
Vardomb H ... 125 A4
Varejoki FIN ... 196 C7
Varel D ... 71 A5
Varėna LT ... 13 A6
Vårenes N ... 52 A1
Varengeville-sur-Mer
F ... 89 A4
Varenna I ... 120 A2
Varennes-en-Argonne
F ... 91 B5
Varennes-le-Grand
F ... 105 C3
Varennes-St Sauveur
F ... 105 C4
Varennes-sur-Allier
F ... 117 A3
Varennes-sur-Amance
F ... 105 B4
Vareš BIH ... 139 A4
Varese I ... 120 B1
Varese Ligure I ... 134 A2
Vârfurile RO ... 16 B5
Vårgårda S ... 60 A2
Vargas
E ... 143 A3
P ... 154 B2
Vargön S ... 54 B3
Varhaug N ... 52 B1
Variaş RO ... 126 A2
Variaşu Mic RO ... 126 A3
Varilhes F ... 146 A2
Varin SK ... 98 B2
Väring S ... 55 B4
Váriz P ... 149 A3
Varkaus FIN ... 8 A5
Varmahlíð IS ... 190 B6
Varmaland IS ... 190 C4
Värmlands Bro S ... 55 A4
Värmskog S ... 55 A3
Varna
BG ... 17 D7
SRB ... 127 C1
Värnamo S ... 60 B4
Varnhem S ... 55 B4
Varnsdorf CZ ... 84 B2
Värö S ... 60 B2
Varoška Rijeka
BIH ... 124 B2
Városlöd H ... 111 B4
Várpalota H ... 112 B2
Varreddes F ... 90 C2
Vars F ... 118 C3
Varsi I ... 120 C2
Varsseveld NL ... 71 C3
Vårsta S ... 57 A3
Vartdal N ... 198 C3
Vartofta S ... 55 B4
Vårvik S ... 54 A3
Várvölgy H ... 111 C4
Varzi I ... 120 C2
Varzjelas P ... 148 B1
Varzo I ... 119 A5
Varzy F ... 104 B2
Vasad H ... 112 B3
Väse S ... 55 A4
Vašica SRB ... 125 B5
Vasilevichi BY ... 13 B8
Väskinde S ... 57 C4
Vaskút H ... 125 A4
Vaslui RO ... 17 B7
Vassbotn N ... 53 B4
Vassenden N ... 47 A6
Vassieux-en-Vercors
F ... 118 C2
Vassmolösa S ... 63 B4
Vassy F ... 88 B3
Västansjö S ... 195 E6
Västanvik S ... 50 B1
Västerås S ... 56 A2
Västerby S ... 50 B2
Västerfärnebo S ... 50 C3
Västergarn S ... 57 C4
Västerhaninge S ... 57 A4
Västervik S ... 62 A4
Vasto I ... 170 A2
Västra Ämtervik S ... 55 A4
Västra-Bodarne S ... 60 B2
Västra Karup S ... 61 C2
Vasvár H ... 111 B3
Vasylkiv UA ... 13 C9
Vát H ... 111 B3
Vatan F ... 103 B3
Väte S ... 57 C4
Vathia GR ... 184 C3
Vatican City = Cittàdel
Vaticano I ... 168 B2
Vatili CY ... 181 A2
Vatin SRB ... 126 B3
Vatland N ... 52 B3
Vatnar N ... 53 A5
Vatnås N ... 48 C1
Vatne N ... 53 B3
Vatnestrøm N ... 53 B4
Vätö S ... 51 C5
Vatra-Dornei RO ... 17 B6
Vatry F ... 91 C4
Vattholma S ... 51 B4
Vättis CH ... 107 C4
Vauchamps F ... 91 C3
Vauchassis F ... 104 A2
Vaucouleurs F ... 92 C1
Vaudoy-en-Brie F ... 90 C3
Vaulen N ... 52 B1
Vaulruz CH ... 106 C1
Vaulx Vraucourt F ... 90 A2
Vaumas F ... 104 C2
Vausseroux F ... 115 B3
Vauvenargues F ... 132 B1
Vauvert F ... 131 B3
Vauvillers F ... 105 B5
Vaux-sur-Sure B ... 92 B1
Vawkavysk BY ... 13 B6
Vaxholm S ... 57 A4
Växjö S ... 62 B2
Våxtorp S ... 61 C3
Vayrac F ... 129 B4
Važec SK ... 99 B3
Veberöd S ... 61 D3
Vechelde D ... 72 B3
Vechta D ... 71 B5
Vecinos E ... 149 B4
Vecsés H ... 112 B3
Vedavågen N ... 52 A1
Veddige S ... 60 B2
Vedersø DK ... 59 B1
Vedeseta I ... 120 B2
Vedevåg S ... 56 A1
Vedra E ... 140 B2
Vedum S ... 55 B3
Veendam NL ... 71 A3
Veenendaal NL ... 70 B2
Vega
Asturias E ... 142 A1
Asturias E ... 142 A1
Vega de Espinareda
E ... 141 B4
Vega de Infanzones
E ... 142 B1
Vegadeo E ... 141 A3
Vega de Pas E ... 143 A3
Vega de Valcarce
E ... 141 B4
Vega de Valdetronco
E ... 150 A2
Vegårshei N ... 53 B4
Vegas de Coria E ... 149 B3
Vegas del Condado
E ... 142 B1
Vegby S ... 60 B3
Vegger DK ... 58 B2
Veggli N ... 47 B6
Veghel NL ... 80 A1
Veglast D ... 66 B1
Véglie I ... 173 B3
Veguillas E ... 151 B4
Vegusdal N ... 53 B4
Veidholmen N ... 198 B4
Veidnes N ... 193 B10
Veikåker N ... 48 B1
Veinge S ... 61 C3
Vejbystrand S ... 61 C2
Vejen DK ... 59 C2
Vejer de la Frontera
E ... 162 B2
Vejle DK ... 59 C2
Vejprty CZ ... 83 B5
Velada E ... 150 B3
Vela Luka HR ... 138 C2
Velayos E ... 150 B3
Velbert D ... 80 A3
Velburg D ... 95 B3
Velde N ... 199 A8
Velden
Bayern D ... 95 B3
Bayern D ... 95 C4
Velden am Worther See
A ... 109 C5
Velefique E ... 164 B2
Velen D ... 80 A2
Velenje SLO ... 123 A4
Veles MK ... 182 B3
Velesevec HR ... 124 B2
Velešin CZ ... 96 C2
Velestino GR ... 182 D4
Velez Blanco E ... 164 B2
Vélez de Benaudalla
E ... 163 B4
Vélez-Málaga E ... 163 B3
Vélez Rubio E ... 164 B2
Veliiki Radinci
SRB ... 127 B1
Velika HR ... 125 B3
Velika Gorica HR ... 124 B2
Velika Grdevac
HR ... 124 B3
Velika Greda SRB ... 126 B3
Velika Ilova BIH ... 125 C3
Velika Kladuša
BIH ... 124 B1
Velika Kopanica
HR ... 125 B4
Velika Krsna SRB ... 127 C2
Velika Obarska
BIH ... 125 C5
Velika Pisanica
HR ... 124 B3
Velika Plana SRB ... 127 C3
Velika Zdenci HR ... 124 B3
Velike Lašče SLO ... 123 B3
Velike Središte
SRB ... 126 B3
Veliki Gaj SRB ... 126 B3
Veliki Popović
SRB ... 127 C3
Velikiye Luki RUS ... 9 D7
Veliko Gradište
SRB ... 127 C3
Veliko Orašje
SRB ... 127 C3
Veliko Selo SRB ... 127 C3
Veliko Tarnovo BG ... 17 D6
Velilla del Río Carrió
E ... 142 B2
Velilla de San Antonio
E ... 151 B4
Veli Lošinj HR ... 137 A3
Velingrad BG ... 183 A5
Velizh RUS ... 9 E7
Veljun HR ... 123 B4
Velká Bíteš CZ ... 97 B4
Velka Hled'scbe CZ ... 95 B4
Velka Lomnica SK ... 99 B4
Velkánad Veličkou
CZ ... 98 C1

Velké Bystřice CZ 98 B1
Velké Heraltice CZ 98 B1
Velké Karlovice CZ 98 B2
Vel'ke'Kostol'any SK 98 C1
Vel'ké Leváre SK 97 C5
Velké Losiny CZ 98 A1
Velké Meziříčí CZ 97 B4
Velké Pavlovice CZ 97 C4
Vel'ké Rovné SK 98 B2
Vel'ké Uherce SK 98 C2
Vel'ké Zálužie SK 98 C1
Vel'ký Blahovo SK 99 C4
Velky Bor CZ 96 B1
Vel'ký Cetin SK 112 A2
Vel'ký Krtíš SK 112 A3
Vel'ký Meder SK 111 B4
Velky Ujezd CZ 98 B1
Vellahn D 73 A3
Vellberg D 94 B1
Velles F 103 C3
Velletri I 168 B2
Vellinge S 66 A2
Vellisca E 151 B5
Velliza E 150 A3
Vellmar D 81 A5
Velp NL 70 B2
Velten D 74 B2
Velvary CZ 84 B2
Velvendos GR 182 C4
Vemb DK 59 B1
Vemdalen S 199 C10
Veme N 48 B2
Véménd H 125 A4
Vemmedrup DK 61 D2
Vena S 62 A3
Venaco F 180 A2
Venafro I 169 B4
Venarey-les-Laumes F 104 B3
Venaría I 119 B4
Venasca I 133 A3
Venčane SRB 127 C2
Vence F 132 B3
Venda Nova
Coimbra P 154 A2
Leiria P 154 B2
Vendas Novas P 154 C2
Vendays-Montalivet F 114 C2
Vendel S 51 B4
Vendelso S 57 A4
Vendeuil F 91 B3
Vendeuvre-sur-Barse F 104 A3
Vendoeuvres F 115 B5
Vendôme F 103 B3
Venelles F 131 B4
Veness GB 33 B4
Venézia = Venice I 122 B1
Venialbo E 150 A2
Venice = Venézia I 122 B1
Vénissieux F 117 B4
Venjan S 49 B5
Venlo NL 80 A2
Vennesla N 53 B3
Vennesund N 195 E3
Vennezey F 92 C2
Venn Green GB 42 B2
Venosa I 172 B1
Venray NL 80 A1
Vent A 108 C1
Venta de Baños E 142 C2
Venta del Moro E 158 B2
Venta de los Santos E 157 B4
Venta las Ranas E 142 A1
Ventanueva E 141 A4
Ventas de Huelma E 163 A4
Ventas de Zafarraya E 163 B3
Ventavon F 132 A1
Ventimíglia I 133 B3
Ventnor GB 44 C2
Ventosa de la Sierra E 143 C4
Ventosilla E 143 C4
Ventspils LV 8 D2
Venturina I 134 B3
Venzolasca F 180 A2
Venzone I 122 A2
Vép H 111 B3
Vera
E 164 B3
N 199 B9
Vera Cruz P 160 A2
Vera de Bidasoa E 144 A2
Vera de Moncayo E 144 C2
Verbánia I 119 B5
Verberie F 90 B2
Verbicaro I 174 B1
Verbier CH 119 A4
Vercelli I 119 B5
Vercel-Villedieu-le-Camp F 105 B5
Verchen D 66 C1
Vercheny F 118 C2
Verclause F 131 A4
Verdalsøra N 199 B8
Verden D 72 B2
Verdens Ende N 54 A1
Verdikoussa GR 182 D3
Verdille F 115 C3
Verdú E 147 C2
Verdun F 92 B1
Verdun-sur-Garonne F 129 C4
Verdun-sur-le-Doubs F 105 C4
Veresegyház H 112 B3
Verfeil F 129 C4
Vergato I 135 A4
Vergel E 159 C4
Vergeletto CH 120 A1
Verges E 147 B4
Vergiate I 120 B1
Vergt F 129 A3
Veria GR 182 C4
Verín E 141 C3
Veringenstadt D 107 A4
Verl D 81 A4
Verma N 198 C5
Vermand F 90 B3
Vermelha P 154 B1
Vermenton F 104 B2
Vernago I 108 C1
Vernante I 133 A3
Vernantes F 102 B2
Vernár SK 99 C4
Vernasca I 120 C2
Vernayaz CH 119 A4
Vernazza I 134 A2
Vern-d'Anjou F 102 B1
Verneřice CZ 84 B2
Vernet F 146 A2
Vernet-les-Bains F 146 B3
Verneuil F 91 B3
Verneuil-sur-Avre F 89 B4
Vernier CH 118 A3
Vérnio I 135 A4
Vérnole I 173 B4
Vernon F 90 B1
Vernoux-en-Vivarais F 117 C4
Veróce H 112 B3
Verolanuova I 120 B3
Véroli I 169 B3
Verona I 121 B4
Verpelét H 113 B4
Verrabotn N 199 B7
Verrès I 119 B4
Verrey-sous-Salmaise F 104 B3
Verrières F 115 B4
Versailles F 90 C2
Versam CH 107 C4
Verseg H 112 B3
Versmold D 71 B5
Versoix CH 118 A3
Verteillac F 115 C4
Vértesacsa H 112 B2
Vertou F 101 B4
Vertus F 91 C3
Verviers B 80 B1
Vervins F 91 B3
Verwood GB 43 B5
Veryan GB 42 B2
Veržej SLO 111 C3
Verzuolo I 133 A3
Verzy F 91 B4
Vescovato F 180 A2
Vése H 124 A3
Veselie BG 17 D7
Veselínad Lužnicí CZ 96 B2
Veselínad Moravou CZ 98 C1
Vésime I 119 C5
Veskoniemi FIN 193 D11
Vesoul F 105 B5
Vespolate I 120 B1
Vessigebro S 60 C2
Vestbygd N 52 B2
Vestenanova I 121 B4
Vester Husby S 56 B2
Vester Nebel DK 59 C2
Vesterøhavn DK 58 A3
Vester Torup DK 58 A2
Vester Vedsted DK 59 C1
Vestervig DK 58 B1
Vestfossen N 53 A5
Vestmannaeyjar IS 190 D5
Vestmarka N 48 C3
Vestnes N 198 C4
Vestone I 120 B3
Vestre Gausdal N 48 A2
Vestre Jakobselv N 193 B13
Vestre Slidre N 47 A5
Vesyegonsk RUS 9 C10
Veszprém H 112 B1
Veszprémvarsány H 112 B1
Vésztő H 113 C5
Vetlanda S 62 A3
Vetovo HR 125 B3
Vetralla I 168 A2
Větrný Jeníkov CZ 97 B3
Vétroz CH 119 A4
Vetschau D 84 A2
Vettasjärvi S 196 B4
Vetto I 134 A3
Vetulónia I 135 C3
Veules-les-Roses F 89 A4
Veulettes-sur-Mer F 89 A4
Veum N 53 A4
Veurne B 78 A2
Veverská Bítýška CZ 97 B4
Vevey CH 106 C1
Vevi GR 182 C3
Vevring N 46 A2
Vex CH 119 A4
Veynes F 132 A1
Veyre-Monton F 116 B3
Veyrier F 118 B3
Vézelay F 104 B2
Vézelise F 92 C2
Vézenobres F 131 A3
Vezins F 102 B1
Vézins-de-Lévézou F 130 A1
Vezirhan TR 187 B5
Vezirköprü TR 23 A8
Vezza di Óglio I 120 A3
Vezzani F 180 A2
Vezzano I 121 A4
Vezzano sul Cróstolo I 121 C3
Vi S 200 D3
Viadana I 121 C3
Via Gloria P 160 B2
Viana E 143 B4
Viana do Alentejo P 154 C2
Viana do Bolo E 141 B3
Viana do Castelo P 148 A1
Vianden L 92 B2
Viannos GR 185 D6
Viaréggio I 134 B3
Viator E 164 C2
Vibble S 57 C4
Viborg DK 58 B2
Vibo Valéntia I 175 C2
Vibraye F 102 A2
Vic E 147 C3
Vícar E 164 C2
Vicarello I 134 B3
Vicari I 176 B2
Vicchio I 135 B4
Vicdesses F 146 B2
Vic-en-Bigorre F 145 A4
Vicenza I 121 B4
Vic-Fézensac F 129 C3
Vichy F 117 A3
Vickan S 60 B2
Vickerstown GB 36 B3
Vic-le-Comte F 116 B3
Vico F 180 A1
Vico del Gargano I 171 B3
Vico Equense I 170 C2
Vicopisano I 134 B3
Vicosoprano CH 120 A2
Vicovaro I 169 A2
Vic-sur-Aisne F 90 B3
Vic-sur-Cère F 116 C2
Victoria = Rabat M 175 C3
Vidago P 148 A2
Vidauban F 132 B2
Vide P 148 B2
Videbæk DK 59 B1
Videm SLO 123 B3
Videseter N 198 D4
Vidigueira P 160 A2
Vidin BG 16 D5
Vidlin GB 33 A5
Vidsel S 196 D3
Vidzy BY 13 A7
Viechtach D 95 B4
Vieille-Brioude F 117 B3
Vieira P 154 B2
Vieira do Minho P 148 A1
Vieiros P 155 C3
Vielha E 145 B4
Vielle-Aure F 145 B4
Viellespesse F 116 B3
Viellevigne F 114 B2
Vielmur-sur-Agout F 130 B1
Vielsalm B 80 B1
Viels Maison F 91 C3
Vienenburg D 73 C3
Vienna = Wien A 111 A3
Vienne F 117 B4
Vieritz D 73 B5
Viernheim D 93 B4
Vierraden D 74 A3
Viersen D 80 A2
Vierville-sur-Mer F 88 A3
Vierzon F 103 B4
Vieselbach D 82 B3
Vieste I 171 B4
Vietas S 194 C9
Vieteren B 78 B2
Vietri di Potenza I 172 B1
Vietri sul Mare I 170 C2
Vieux-Boucau-les-Bains F 128 C1
Vif F 118 B2
Vig DK 61 D1
Vigásio I 121 B3
Vigaun A 109 B4
Vigeland N 52 B3
Vigeois F 116 B1
Vigévano I 120 B1
Viggianello I 174 B2
Viggiano I 174 A1
Vigliano I 169 A3
Vigmostad N 52 B3
Vignale I 119 B5
Vignanello I 168 A2
Vigneulles-lès-Hattonchâtel F 92 C1
Vignevieille F 146 B3
Vignola I 135 A4
Vignory F 105 A4
Vignoux-sur Barangeon F 103 B4
Vigo E 140 B2
Vigo di Fassa I 121 A4
Vigone I 119 C4
Vigrestad N 52 B1
Vihiers F 102 B1
Viitasaari FIN 8 A4
Vik IS 190 D6
Vik
Nordland N 195 E3
Rogaland N 52 B1
Sogn og Fjordane N 46 A3
S 63 C2
Vika S 50 B2
Vikajärvi FIN 197 C9
Vikane N 54 A1
Vikarbyn S 50 B2
Vike N 46 B2
Vikedal N 52 A1
Vikeland N 53 B3
Viken
Jämtland S 199 A10
Skåne S 61 C2
Viker N 48 B2
Vikersund N 48 C1
Vikeså N 52 B2
Vikevåg N 52 A1
Vikingstad S 56 B1
Vikmanshyttan S 50 B2
Vikna N 199 A7
Vikøy N 46 B3
Vikran
Troms N 192 C2
Troms N 194 B7
Viksjö S 200 D3
Viksøyri N 46 A3
Viksta S 51 B4
Vila Boim P 155 C3
Vila Chãde Ourique P 154 B2
Viladamat E 147 B4
Vila de Cruces E 140 B2
Vila de Rei P 154 B2
Vila do Bispo P 160 B1
Vila do Conde P 148 A1
Viladrau E 147 C3
Vila Flor P 149 A2
Vila Franca das Navas P 149 B2
Vilafranca del Maestrat E 153 B3
Vilafranca del Penedès E 147 C2
Vila Franca de Xira P 154 C1
Vila Fresca P 154 C1
Vilagarcía de Arousa E 140 B2
Vilajuiga E 147 B4
Vilamarin E 140 B3
Vilamartín de Valdeorras E 141 B3
Vila Nogueira P 154 C1
Vila Nova da Baronia P 154 C2
Vilanova de Castelló E 159 B3
Vila Nova de Cerveira P 140 C2
Vila Nova de Famalicão P 148 A1
Vila Nova de Foz Côa P 149 A2
Vila Nova de Gaia P 148 A1
Vila Nova de Milfontes P 160 B1
Vila Nova de Paiva P 148 B2
Vila Nova de São Bento P 161 B2
Vilanova de Sau E 147 C3
Vilanova i la Geltrú E 147 C2
Vilapedre E 140 A3
Vila Pouca de Aguiar P 148 A2
Vila Praja de Ancora P 148 A1
Vilarandelo P 148 A2
Vilar de Santos E 140 B3
Vilardevós E 141 C3
Vila Real P 148 A2
Vila-real de los Infantes E 159 B3
Vila Real de Santo António P 160 B2
Vilar Formosa P 149 B3
Vila-Rodona E 147 C2
Vila Ruiva P 160 A2
Vilasantar E 140 A2
Vilaseca E 147 C2
Vila Seca P 148 B1
Vilassar de Mar E 147 C3
Vilasund S 195 D5
Vila Velha de Ródão P 155 B3
Vila Verde
Braga P 148 A1
Lisboa P 154 B1
Vila Verde de Filcalho P 161 B2
Vila Viçosa P 155 C3
Vilches E 157 B4
Vildbjerg DK 59 B1
Vilémov CZ 97 B3
Vileyka BY 13 A7
Vilhelmina S 200 B2
Vilia GR 184 A4
Viljandi EST 8 C4
Villabáñez E 150 A3
Villablanca E 161 B2
Villablino E 141 B4
Villabona E 144 A1
Villabragima E 142 C1
Villabuena del Puente E 150 A2
Villacadima E 151 A4
Villacañas E 157 A4
Villacarriedo E 143 A3
Villacarrillo E 164 A1
Villa Castelli I 173 B3
Villacastín E 150 B3
Villach A 109 C4
Villacidro I 179 C2
Villaconejos E 151 B4
Villaconejos de Trabaque E 152 B1
Villa Cova de Lixa P 148 A1
Villada E 142 B2
Villadangos del Páramo E 141 B5
Villadecanes E 141 B4
Villa del Prado E 150 B3
Villa del Rio E 157 C3
Villadepera E 149 A3
Villa de Peralonso E 149 A3
Villa di Chiavenna I 120 A2
Villadiego E 142 B2
Villadompardo E 163 A3
Villadóssola I 119 A5
Villaeles de Valdavia E 142 B2
Villaescusa de Haro E 158 B1
Villafáfila E 142 C1
Villafeliche E 152 A2
Villaflores E 150 A2
Villafrades de Campos E 142 B2
Villafranca
Avila E 150 B2
Navarra E 144 B2
Villafranca de Córdoba E 157 C3
Villafranca del Bierzo E 141 B4
Villafranca de los Barros E 155 C4
Villafranca de los Caballeros E 157 A4
Villafranca di Verona I 121 B3
Villafranca in Lunigiana I 134 A2
Villafranca-Montes de Oca E 143 B3
Villafranca Tirrena I 177 A4
Villafranco del Campo E 152 B2
Villafranco del Guadalquivir E 161 B3
Villafrati I 176 B2
Villafrechós E 142 C1
Villafruela E 143 C3
Villagarcia de las Torres E 156 B1
Villaggio Mancuso I 175 B2
Villagonzalo E 156 B1
Villagotón E 141 B4
Villagrains F 128 B2
Villaharta E 156 B3
Villahermosa E 158 C1
Villaherreros E 142 B2
Villahoz E 143 B3
Villaines-la-Juhel F 89 B3
Villajoyosa E 159 C3
Villalago I 169 B3
Villalba
E 140 A3
I 176 B2
Villalba de Calatrava E 157 B4
Villalba de Guardo E 142 B2
Villalba del Alcor E 161 B3
Villalba de la Sierra E 152 B1
Villalba de los Alcores E 142 C2
Villalba de los Barros E 155 C4
Villalba del Rey E 151 B5
Villalcampo E 149 A3
Villalcázar de Sirga E 142 B2
Villalengua E 152 A2
Villalgordo del Júcar E 158 B1
Villalgordo del Marquesado E 158 B1
Villalmóndar E 143 B3
Villalón de Campos E 142 B1
Villalonga E 159 C3
Villalonso E 150 A2
Villalpando E 142 C1
Villaluenga E 151 B4
Villalumbroso E 142 B2
Villálvaro E 143 C3
Villamalea E 158 B2
Villamanán E 142 B1
Villamanín E 142 B1
Villamanrique E 157 B5
Villamanrique de la Condesa E 161 B3
Villamanta E 151 B3
Villamantilla E 151 B3
Villamar I 179 C2
Villamartín E 162 B2
Villamartin de Campos E 142 B2
Villamartin de Don Sancho E 142 B1
Villamassárgia I 179 C2
Villamayor E 142 A1
Villamayor de Calatrava E 157 B3
Villamayor de Campos E 142 C1
Villamayor de Santiago E 157 A5
Villamblard F 129 A3
Villamejil E 141 B4
Villamesias E 156 A2
Villaminaya E 157 A4
Villa Minozzo I 134 A3
Villamor de los Escuderos E 150 A2
Villamoronta E 142 B2
Villamuelas E 151 C4
Villamuriel de Cerrato E 142 C2
Villandraut F 128 B2
Villanova I 173 B3
Villanova d'Asti I 119 C4
Villanova del Battista I 171 B3
Villanova Mondov ì I 133 A3
Villanova Monteleone I 178 B2
Villante E 143 B3
Villantério I 120 B2
Villanubla E 142 C2
Villanueva de Alcardete E 157 A4
Villanueva de Alcorón E 152 B1
Villanueva de Algaidas E 163 A3
Villanueva de Argaña E 143 B3
Villanueva de Bogas E 157 A4
Villanueva de Córdoba E 156 B3
Villanueva de Gállego E 144 C3
Villanueva del Aceral E 150 A3
Villanueva de la Concepcion E 163 B3
Villanueva de la Fuente E 158 C1
Villanueva de la Jara E 158 B2
Villanueva de la Reina E 157 B4
Villanueva del Arzobispo E 164 A2
Villanueva de la Serena E 156 B2
Villanueva de la Sierra E 149 B3
Villanueva de las Manzanas E 142 B1
Villanueva de las Peras E 141 C5
Villanueva de las Torres E 164 B1
Villanueva de la Vera E 150 B2
Villanueva del Campo E 142 C1
Villanueva del Duque E 156 B3
Villanueva del Fresno E 155 C3
Villanueva del Huerva E 152 A2
Villanueva de los Castillejos E 161 B2
Villanueva de los Infantes E 157 B5
Villanueva del Rey E 156 B2
Villanueva del Rio E 162 A2
Villanueva del Río y Minas E 162 A2
Villanueva del Rosario E 163 B3
Villanueva del Trabuco E 163 A3
Villanueva de Mesia E 163 A4
Villanueva de Nía E 142 B2
Villanueva de Oscos E 141 A4
Villanueva de San Carlos E 157 B4
Villanueva de San Juan E 162 A2
Villanueva de Tapia E 163 A3
Villanueva de Valdegovia E 143 B3
Villány H 125 B4
Villaputzu I 179 C3
Villaquejida E 142 B1
Villaquilambre E 142 B1
Villaquiran de los Infantes E 142 B2
Villaralto E 156 B3
Villarcayo E 143 B3
Villard-de-Lans F 118 B2
Villar de Barrio E 140 B3
Villar de Cañas E 158 B1
Villar de Chinchilla E 158 C2
Villar de Ciervo E 149 B3
Villardeciervos E 141 C4
Villar de Domingo Garcia E 152 B1
Villardefrades E 142 C1
Villar del Arzobispo E 159 B3
Villar del Buey E 149 A3
Villar del Cobo E 152 B2
Villar del Humo E 158 B2
Villar de los Navarros E 152 A2
Villar del Pedroso E 156 A2
Villar del Rey E 155 B4
Villar del Rio E 143 B4
Villar del Saz de Navalón E 152 B1
Villar de Rena E 156 A2
Villarejo E 151 A4
Villarejo de Fuentes E 158 B1
Villarejo de Orbigo E 141 B5
Villarejo de Salvanes E 151 B4
Villarejo-Periesteban E 158 B1
Villares del Saz E 158 B1
Villaretto I 119 B4
Villargordo del Cabriel E 158 B2
Villarino E 149 A3
Villarino de Conso E 141 B3
Villarluengo E 153 B3
Villarobe E 143 B3
Villarosa I 177 B3
Villar Perosa I 119 C4
Villarramiel E 142 B2
Villarrasa E 161 B3
Villarreal de San Carlos E 150 C1
Villarrin de Campos E 142 C1
Villarrobledo E 158 B1
Villarroya de la Sierra E 152
Villarroya de los Pinares E 153
Villarrubia de los Ojos E 157
Villarrubia de Santiago E 151
Villarrubio E 151
Villars-les-Dombes F 117
Villarta E 158
Villarta de los Montes E 156
Villarta de San Juan E 157
Villasana de Mena E 143
Villasandino E 142
Villa San Giovanni I 175
Villa Santa Maria I 169
Villasante E 143
Villa Santina I 122
Villasarracino E 142
Villasayas E 151
Villasdardo E 149
Villaseca de Henares E 151
Villaseca de Laciana E 141
Villaseca de la Sagra E 151
Villaseco de los Gamitos E 149
Villaseco de los Reyes E 149
Villasequilla de Yepes E 151
Villasimíus I 179
Villasmundo I 177
Villasor I 179
Villastar E 152
Villastellone I 119
Villatobas E 151
Villatorp E 150
Villatoya E 158
Villavaliente E 158
Villavelayo E 143
Villavella E 141
Villaver de Guadalimar E 158
Villaverde del Rio E 162
Villaviciosa E 142
Villaviciosa de Córdoba E 156
Villaviciosa de Odón E 151
Villavieja de Yeltes E 149
Villayón E 141
Villé F 93
Villebois-Lavalette F 115
Villecerf F 90
Villecomtal F 130
Villedieu-les-Poêles F 88
Villedieu-sur-Indre F 103
Ville-di-Pietrabugno F 180
Villedômain F 103
Villefagnan F 115
Villefontaine F 118
Villefort F 131
Villefranche-d'Albigeois F 130
Villefranche-d'Allier F 116
Villefranche-de-Lauragais F 146
Villefranche-de-Lonchat F 128
Villefranche-de-Panat F 130
Villefranche-de-Rouergue F 130
Villefranche-du-Périgord F 129
Villefranche-sur-Cher F 103
Villefranche-sur-Mer F 133
Villefranche-sur-Saône F 117
Villegenon F 103
Villel E 152
Villemaur-sur-Vanne F 104
Villemontais F 117
Villemur-sur-Tarn F 129
Villena E 159
Villenauxe-la-Grande F 91
Villenave-d'Ornon F 128
Villeneuve
CH 119
F 129
Villeneuve-d'Ascq F 78
Villeneuve-de-Berg F 131
Villeneuve-de-Marsan F 128
Villeneuve-de-Rivière F 145
Villeneuve-la-Guyard F 90
Villeneuve-l'Archevêque F 104
Villeneuve-le-Comte F 90
Villeneuve-lès-Avignon F 131
Villeneuve-les-Corbières F 146

Villeneuve-St Georges F 90 C2
Villeneuve-sur-Allier F 104 C2
Villeneuve-sur-Lot F 129 B3
Villeneuve-sur-Yonne F 104 A2
Villeréal F 129 B3
Villerias E 142 C2
Villeromain F 103 B3
Villers-Bocage
Calvados F 88 A3
Somme F 90 B2
Villers-Bretonneux F 90 B2
Villers-Carbonnel F 90 B2
Villers-Cotterêts F 90 B3
Villersexel F 105 B5
Villers-Farlay F 105 C4
Villers-le-Gambon B 79 B4
Villers-le-Lac F 106 B1
Villers-sur-Mer F 89 A3
Villerupt F 92 B1
Villerville F 89 A4
Villeseneux F 91 C4
Ville-sous-la-Ferté F 105 A3
Ville-sur-Illon F 105 A5
Ville-sur-Tourbe F 91 B4
Villetrun F 103 B3
Villetta Barrea I 169 B3
Villeurbanne F 117 B4
Villeveyrac F 130 B2
Villevocance F 117 B4
Villiers-St Benoit F 104 B2
Villiers-St Georges F 91 C3
Villingen D 106 A3
Villmar D 81 B4
Villoldo E 142 B2
Villon F 104 B3
Villoria E 150 B2
Vilnes N 46 A1
Vilnius LT 13 A6
Vils
A 108 B1
DK 58 B1
Vilsbiburg D 95 C4
Vilseck D 95 B3
Vilshofen D 96 C1
Vilshult S 63 B2
Vilusi MNE 139 C4
Vilvestre E 149 A3
Vilvoorde B 79 B4
Vimeiro P 154 B1
Vimercate I 120 B2
Vimianzo E 140 A1
Vimieiro P 154 C3
Vimioso P 149 A3
Vimmerby S 62 A3
Vimoutiers F 89 B4
Vimperk CZ 96 B1
Vimy F 78 B2
Vinadi CH 108 C1
Vinadio I 133 A3
Vinaixa E 147 C1
Vinarós E 153 B4
Vinäs S 50 B1
Vinay F 118 B2
Vinberg S 60 C2
Vinca F 146 B3
Vinča SRB 127 C2
Vinchiaturo I 170 B2
Vinci I 135 B3
Vindeby DK 65 A3
Vindelgransele S 195 E9
Vindeln S 200 B5
Vinderup DK 58 B1
Vindsvik N 52 A2
Vinets F 91 C4
Vineuil F 103 B3
Vinga RO 126 A3
Vingåker S 56 A1
Vingnes N 48 A2
Vingrau F 146 B3
Vingrom N 48 A2
Vinhais P 149 A3
Vinica
HR 124 A2
MK 182 B4
SK 112 A3
SLO 123 B4
Viniegra de Arriba E 143 B4
Vinje
Hordaland N 46 B3
Sør-Trøndelag N 198 B6
Telemark N 53 A3
Vinkovci HR 125 B4
Vinliden S 200 B3
Vinninga S 55 B4
Vinnytsya UA 13 D8
Vinon F 103 B4
Vinon-sur-Verdon F 132 B1
Vinslöv S 61 C3
Vinstra N 48 A1
Vintjärn S 50 B3
Vintrosa S 55 A5
Viñuela E 163 B3
Viñuela de Sayago E 149 A4
Viñuelas E 151 B4
Vinuesa E 143 C4
Vinzelberg D 73 B4
Viöl D 64 B2
Viola I 133 A3
Violay F 117 B4
Vipava SLO 122 B2
Vipiteno I 108 C2
Vipperow D 74 A1
Vir
BIH 138 B3
HR 137 A4
Vira CH 120 A1
Vire F 88 B3
Vireda S 62 A2
Vireux F 91 A4
Virgen A 109 B3
Virgen de la Cabeza E 157 B3
Virginia IRL 27 C3
Virieu F 118 B2
Virieu-le-Grand F 118 B2
Virje HR 124 A2
Virkkunen FIN 197 D10
Virklund DK 59 B2
Virovitica HR 124 B3
Virsbo S 50 C3
Virserum S 62 A3
Virtaniemi FIN 193 D12
Virton B 92 B1
Virtsu EST 8 C3
Viry F 118 A3
Vis HR 138 B2
Visbek D 71 B5
Visby
DK 64 A1
S 57 C4
Visé B 80 B1
Višegrad BIH 139 B5
Viserba I 136 A1
Viseu P 148 B2
Visiedo E 152 B2
Viskafors S 60 B2
Visland N 52 B2
Vislanda S 62 B2
Visnes N 52 A1
Višnja Gora SLO 123 B3
Višnjan HR 122 B2
Višnové CZ 97 C4
Visnums-Kil S 55 A5
Viso del Marqués E 157 B4
Visoko
BIH 139 B4
SLO 123 A3
Visone I 119 C5
Visp CH 119 A4
Vissefjärda S 63 B3
Visselhövede D 72 B2
Vissenbjerg DK 59 C3
Visso I 136 C2
Vistabella del Maestrat E 153 B3
Vistheden S 196 D3
Vita I 176 B1
Vitanje SLO 123 A4
Vitebsk = Vitsyebsk BY 13 A9
Viterbo I 168 A2
Vitez BIH 139 A3
Vithkuq AL 182 C2
Vitigudino E 149 A3
Vitina
BIH 138 B3
GR 184 B3
Vitis A 97 C3
Vítkov CZ 98 B1
Vitoria-Gasteiz E 143 B4
Vitré F 101 A4
Vitrey-sur-Mance F 105 B4
Vitry-en-Artois F 78 B2
Vitry-le-François F 91 C4
Vitry-sur-Seine F 90 C2
Vitsand S 49 B4
Vitsyebsk = Vitebsk BY 13 A9
Vittangi S 196 B4
Vittaryd S 60 C3
Vitteaux F 104 B3
Vittel F 105 A4
Vittinge S 51 C4
Vittória I 177 C3
Vittório Véneto I 122 B1
Vittsjö S 61 C3
Viù I 119 B4
Viul N 48 B2
Vivario F 180 A2
Viveiro E 140 A3
Vivel del Rio Martin E 152 B3
Viver E 159 B3
Viverols F 117 B3
Viveros E 158 C1
Viviers F 131 A3
Vivonne F 115 B4
Vivy F 102 B1
Vize TR 186 A2
Vizille F 118 B2
Viziňada HR 122 B2
Viziru RO 17 C7
Vizovice CZ 98 B1
Vizvár H 124 A3
Vizzavona F 180 A2
Vizzini I 177 B3
Vlachiotis GR 184 C3
Vlachovice CZ 98 B1
Vlachovo SK 99 C4
Vláchovo Březi CZ 96 B1
Vladimirci SRB 127 C1
Vladimirovac SRB 127 B2
Vladislav CZ 97 B3
Vlagtwedde NL 71 A4
Vlajkovac SRB 127 B3
Vlasenica BIH 139 A4
Vlašim CZ 96 B2
Vlatkovići BIH 138 A3
Vledder NL 70 B3
Vlissingen NL 79 A3
Vlkolinec SK 99 B3
Vlorë AL 182 C1
Vlotho D 72 B1
Vnanje Gorice SLO 123 B3
Vobarno I 121 B3
Voćin HR 124 B3
Vöcklabruck A 109 A4
Vöcklamarkt A 109 B4
Vodanj SRB 127 C2
Voderady SK 98 C1
Vodice
Istarska HR 123 B3
Šibenska HR 137 B4
SLO 123 A3
Vodňany CZ 96 B2
Vodnjan HR 122 C2
Vodskov DK 58 A3
Voe GB 33 A5
Voerså DK 58 A3
Voghera I 120 C2
Vogogna I 119 A5
Vogošća BIH 139 B4
Vogué F 131 A3
Vohburg D 95 C3
Vohenstrauss D 95 B4
Vöhl D 81 A4
Vöhrenbach D 106 A3
Vöhringen D 94 C2
Void-Vacon F 92 C1
Voiron F 118 B2
Voise F 90 C1
Voisey F 105 B4
Voiteg RO 126 B3
Voiteur F 105 C4
Voitsberg A 110 B2
Vojakkala FIN 196 D7
Vojens DK 59 C2
Vojka SRB 127 C2
Vojlovica SRB 127 C2
Vojnić HR 123 B4
Vojnice SK 112 B2
Vojnik SLO 123 A4
Vojvoda Stepa SRB 126 B2
Volada GR 188 D2
Volargne I 121 B3
Volary CZ 96 C1
Volče SLO 122 A2
Volda N 198 C3
Volendam NL 70 B2
Volga RUS 9 C11
Volimes GR 184 B1
Volissos GR 185 A6
Volkach D 94 B2
Völkermarkt A 110 C1
Volkhov RUS 9 C8
Völklingen D 92 B2
Volkmarsen D 81 A5
Voll N 198 C4
Vollenhove NL 70 B2
Vollore-Montagne F 117 B3
Vollsjö S 61 D3
Volodymyr-Volyns'kyy UA 13 C6
Volokolamsk RUS 9 D9
Volos GR 182 D4
Volosovo RUS 9 C6
Volovets UA 13 D5
Voltággio I 120 C1
Volta Mantovana I 121 B3
Volterra I 135 B3
Voltri I 133 A4
Volturara Áppula I 170 B3
Volturara Irpina I 170 C2
Volvic F 116 B3
Volx F 132 B1
Volyně CZ 96 B1
Vonitsa GR 182 E2
Vönöck H 111 B4
Vonsild DK 59 C2
Voorschoten NL 70 B1
Vopnafjörður IS 191 B11
Vorau A 110 B2
Vorbasse DK 59 C2
Vorchdorf A 109 B4
Vorden
D 71 B5
NL 71 B3
Vordernberg A 110 B1
Vordingborg DK 65 A4
Vorë AL 182 B1
Voreppe F 118 B2
Vorey F 117 B3
Vorgod DK 59 B1
Vormsund N 48 B3
Võru EST 8 D5
Voskopojë AL 182 C2
Voss N 46 B3
Votice CZ 96 B2
Voué F 91 C4
Vouillé F 115 B4
Voulx F 90 C2
Voussac F 116 A3
Vouvray F 102 B2
Vouvry CH 119 A3
Vouzela P 148 B1
Vouziers F 91 B4
Voves F 103 A3
Voxna S 50 A2
Voy GB 33 B3
Voynitsa RUS 3 D12
Voznesenye RUS 9 B9
Vrå
DK 58 A2
S 60 C3
Vráble SK 98 C2
Vračenovići MNE 139 C4
Vračev Gaj SRB 127 C3
Vraćevsnica SRB 127 C2
Vrådal N 53 A4
Vrakneika GR 184 A2
Vrana HR 123 C3
Vranduk BIH 139 A3
Vrångö S 60 B1
Vrani RO 127 B3
Vranić SRB 127 C2
Vraniči BIH 139 B4
Vranja HR 123 B3
Vranjak BIH 125 C4
Vranje SRB 16 D4
Vranovice CZ 97 C4
Vranov nad Dyje CZ 97 C3
Vransko SLO 123 A3
Vrapčići BIH 139 B3
Vratimov CZ 98 B2
Vratsa BG 17 D5
Vrbanja HR 125 C4
Vrbanjci BIH 124 C3
Vrbas SRB 126 B1
Vrbaška BIH 124 B3
Vrbnik
Primorsko-Goranska HR 123 B3
Vrbnik *continued*
Zadarsko-Kninska HR 138 A2
Vrbno pod Pradědem CZ 85 B5
Vrboska HR 138 B2
Vrbov SK 99 B4
Vrbovce SK 98 C1
Vrbové SK 98 C1
Vrbovec HR 124 B2
Vrbovski SRB 127 C2
Vrbovsko HR 123 B4
Vrchlabí CZ 84 B3
Vrčin SRB 127 C2
Vrdy CZ 97 B3
Vrebac HR 137 A4
Vreden D 71 B3
Vreoci SRB 127 C2
Vretstorp S 55 A5
Vrginmost HR 124 B1
Vrgorac HR 138 B3
Vrhnika SLO 123 B3
Vrhovine HR 123 C4
Vrhpolie SRB 127 C1
Vriezenveen NL 71 B3
Vrigne-aux-Bois F 91 B4
Vrigstad S 62 A2
Vrlika HR 138 B2
Vrnograč BIH 124 B1
Vron F 78 B1
Vroomshoop NL 71 B3
Vroutek CZ 83 B5
Vrpolje HR 125 B4
Vršac SRB 126 B3
Vrsar HR 122 B2
Vrsi HR 137 A4
Vrtoče BIH 124 C2
Vrútky SK 98 B2
Všeruby CZ 95 B4
Všestary CZ 85 B3
Vsetín CZ 98 B1
Vučkovica SRB 127 D2
Vught NL 79 A5
Vuillafans F 105 B5
Vukovar HR 125 B5
Vuku N 199 B8
Vulcan RO 17 C5
Vulcănești MD 17 C8
Vuoggatjålme S 195 D7
Vuojärvi FIN 197 B9
Vuolijoki FIN 3 D10
Vuollerim S 196 C3
Vuotso FIN 197 A10
Vuzenica SLO 110 C2
Vyartsilya RUS 9 A7
Vyborg RUS 9 B6
Výčapy CZ 97 B3
Výčapy-Opatovce SK 98 C2
Východna SK 99 B3
Vydrany SK 111 A4
Vyerkhnyadzvinsk BY 13 A7
Vyhne SK 98 C2
Vy-lès Lure F 105 B5
Vylkove UA 17 C8
Vynohradiv UA 17 A5
Vyshniy Volochek RUS 9 D9
Vyškov CZ 97 B5
Vysokánad Kysucou SK 98 B2
Vysoké Mýto CZ 97 B4
Vysokovsk RUS 9 D10
Vyšší Brod CZ 96 C2
Vytegra RUS 9 B10

W

Waabs D 64 B2
Waalwijk NL 79 A5
Waarschoot B 79 A3
Wabern D 81 A5
Wąbrzeźno PL 69 B3
Wąchock PL 87 A5
Wachow D 74 B1
Wachów PL 86 B2
Wächtersbach D 81 B5
Wackersdorf D 95 B4
Waddington GB 40 B3
Wadebridge GB 42 B2
Wadelsdorf D 84 A2
Wädenswil CH 107 B3
Wadern D 92 B2
Wadersloh D 81 A4
Wadlew PL 86 A3
Wadowice PL 99 B3
Wagenfeld D 72 B1
Wageningen NL 70 C2
Waghäusel D 93 B4
Waging D 109 B3
Wagrain A 109 B4
Wągrowiec PL 76 B2
Wahlsdorf D 74 C2
Wahlstedt D 64 C3
Wahrenholz D 73 B3
Waiblingen D 94 C1
Waidhaus D 95 B4
Waidhofen an der Thaya A 97 C3
Waidhofen an der Ybbs A 110 B1
Waimes B 80 B2
Wainfleet All Saints GB 41 B4
Waizenkirchen A 96 C1
Wakefield GB 40 B2
Wałbrzych PL 85 B4
Walchensee D 108 B2
Walchsee A 109 B3
Wałcz PL 75 A5
Wald CH 107 B3
Waldaschaff D 94 B1
Waldbach A 110 B2
Waldböckelheim D 93 B3
Waldbröl D 81 B3
Waldeck D 81 A5
Waldenburg D 83 B4
Waldfischbach-Burgalben D 93 B3
Waldheim D 83 A5
Waldkappel D 82 A1
Waldkirch D 106 A2
Waldkirchen D 96 C1
Waldkirchen am Wesen A 96 C1
Waldkraiburg D 109 A3
Wald-Michelbach D 93 B4
Waldmohr D 93 B3
Waldmünchen D 95 B4
Waldring A 109 B3
Waldsassen D 95 A4
Waldshut D 106 B3
Waldstatt CH 107 B4
Waldwisse F 92 B2
Walenstadt CH 107 B4
Walentynów PL 87 A5
Walichnowy PL 86 A2
Walincourt F 90 A3
Walkenried D 82 A2
Walkeringham GB 40 B3
Wallasey GB 38 A3
Walldürn D 94 B1
Wallenfells D 82 B3
Wallenhorst D 71 B5
Wallers F 78 B3
Wallersdorf D 95 C4
Wallerstein D 94 C2
Wallingford GB 44 B2
Wallitz D 74 A1
Walls GB 33 A5
Wallsbüll D 64 B2
Walmer GB 45 B5
Walsall GB 40 C2
Walshoutem B 79 B5
Walsrode D 72 B2
Waltenhofen D 107 B5
Waltershausen D 82 B2
Waltham Abbey GB 45 B4
Waltham on the Wolds GB 40 C3
Walton-on-Thames GB 44 B3
Walton-on-the-Naze GB 45 B5
Wamba E 142 C2
Wanderup D 64 B2
Wandlitz D 74 B2
Wanfried D 82 A2
Wangen im Allgäu D 107 B4
Wangerooge D 71 A4
Wangersen D 72 A2
Wängi CH 107 B3
Wanna D 64 C1
Wansford GB 40 C3
Wantage GB 44 B2
Wanzleben D 73 B4
Waplewo PL 77 A5
Wapnica PL 75 A4
Wapno PL 76 B2
Warburg D 81 A5
Wardenburg D 71 A5
Ware GB 44 B3
Waregem B 79 B3
Wareham GB 43 B4
Waremme B 79 B5
Waren D 74 A1
Warendorf D 71 C4
Warga NL 70 A2
Warin D 65 C4
Wark GB 37 A4
Warka PL 87 A5
Warkworth GB 37 A5
Warlubie PL 69 B3
Warminster GB 43 A4
Warnemünde D 65 B5
Warnow D 65 C4
Warnsveld NL 70 B3
Warrenpoint GB 27 B4
Warrington GB 38 A4
Warsaw = Warszawa PL 77 B6
Warsingsfehn D 71 A4
Warsow D 73 A4
Warstein D 81 A4
Warszawa = Warsaw PL 77 B6
Warta PL 86 A2
Wartberg A 110 B1
Warth A 107 B5
Warwick GB 44 A2
Warza D 82 B2
Wasbister GB 33 B3
Washington GB 37 B5
Wąsosz PL 85 A4
Wasselonne F 93 C3
Wassen CH 107 C3
Wassenaar NL 70 B1
Wasserauen CH 107 B4
Wasserburg D 108 A3
Wassertrüdingen D 94 B2
Wassy F 91 C4
Wasungen D 82 B2
Watchet GB 43 A3
Waterford IRL 30 B1
Watergrasshill IRL 29 B3
Waterloo B 79 B4
Waterville IRL 29 C1
Watford GB 44 B3
Wathlingen D 72 B3
Watten
F 78 B2
GB 32 C3
Wattens A 108 B2
Watton GB 41 C4
Wattwil CH 107 B4
Waunfawr GB 38 A2
Wavignies F 90 B2
Wavre B 79 B4
Wearhead GB 37 B4
Węchadlow PL 87 B4
Wedel D 72 A2
Wedemark D 72 B2
Weedon Bec GB 44 A2
Weener D 71 A4
Weert NL 80 A1
Weesp NL 70 B2
Weeze D 80 A2
Weferlingen D 73 B4
Wegeleben D 82 A3
Weggis CH 106 B3
Węgierska-Górka PL 99 B3
Węgliniec PL 84 A3
Węgorzyno PL 75 A4
Węgrzynice PL 75 B4
Wegscheid D 96 C1
Wehdel D 72 A1
Wehr D 106 B2
Weibersbrunn D 94 B1
Weichering D 95 C3
Weida D 83 B4
Weiden D 95 B4
Weidenberg D 95 B3
Weidenhain D 83 A4
Weidenstetten D 94 C1
Weierbach D 93 B3
Weikersheim D 94 B1
Weil D 108 A1
Weil am Rhein D 106 B2
Weilburg D 81 B4
Weil der Stadt D 93 C4
Weilerswist D 80 B2
Weilheim
Baden-Württemberg D 94 C1
Bayern D 108 B2
Weilmünster D 81 B4
Weitensfeld A 110 C1
Weimar D 82 B3
Weinberg D 94 B2
Weinfelden CH 107 B4
Weingarten
Baden-Württemberg D 93 B4
Baden-Württemberg D 107 B4
Weinheim D 93 B4
Weinstadt D 94 C1
Weismain D 82 B3
Weissbriach A 109 C4
Weissenbach A 108 B1
Weissenberg D 84 A2
Weissenbrunn D 82 B3
Weissenburg D 94 B2
Weissenfels D 83 A3
Weissenhorn D 94 C2
Weissenkirchen A 97 C3
Weissensee D 82 A3
Weissenstadt D 83 B3
Weisskirchen im Steiermark A 110 B1
Weisstannen CH 107 C4
Weisswasser D 84 A2
Weitendorf D 65 C5
Weitersfeld A 97 C3
Weitersfelden A 96 C2
Weitnau D 107 B5
Wéitra A 96 C2
Weiz A 110 B2
Wejherowo PL 68 A3
Welkenraedt B 80 B1
Wellaune D 83 A4
Wellin B 91 A5
Wellingborough GB 44 A3
Wellington
Somerset GB 43 B3
Telford & Wrekin GB 38 B4
Wellingtonbridge IRL 30 B2
Wells GB 43 A4
Wells-next-the-Sea GB 41 C4
Wels A 109 A5
Welschenrohr CH 106 B2
Welshpool GB 38 B3
Welver D 81 A3
Welwyn Garden City GB 44 B3
Welzheim D 94 C1
Welzow D 84 A2
Wem GB 38 B4
Wembury GB 42 B2
Wemding D 94 C2
Wenden D 81 B3
Wendisch Rietz D 74 B3
Wendlingen D 94 C1
Weng A 109 A4
Weng bei Admont A 110 B1
Wengen CH 106 C2
Wenigzell A 110 B2
Wennigsen D 72 B2
Wenns A 108 B1
Wenzenbach D 95 B4
Weppersdorf A 111 B3
Werben D 73 B4
Werbig D 74 C2
Werdau D 83 B4
Werder D 74 B1
Werdohl D 81 A3
Werfen A 109 B4
Werkendam NL 79 A4
Werl D 81 A3
Werlte D 71 B4
Wermelskirchen D 80 A3
Wermsdorf D 83 A4
Wernberg Köblitz D 95 B4
Werne D 81 A3
Werneck D 94 B2
Werneuchen D 74 B2
Wernigerode D 82 A2
Wertach D 108 B1
Wertheim D 94 B1
Wertingen D 94 C2
Weseke D 80 A2
Wesel D 80 A2
Wesenberg D 74 A1
Wesendorf D 73 B3
Wesołowo PL 77 A5
Wesselburen D 64 B1
Wesseling D 80 B2
West Bridgford GB 40 C2
West Bromwich GB 40 C2
Westbury
Shropshire GB 38 B4
Wiltshire GB 43 A4
Westbury-on-Severn GB 39 C4
Westendorf A 108 B3
Westensee D 64 B2
Westerbork NL 71 B3
Westerburg D 81 B3
Westerhaar NL 71 B3
Westerholt D 71 A4
Westerkappeln D 71 B4
Westerland D 64 B1
Westerlo B 79 A4
Westerstede D 71 A4
West Haddon GB 44 A2
Westheim D 94 B2
Westhill GB 33 D4
Westkapelle
B 78 A3
NL 79 A3
West Kilbride GB 34 C3
West Linton GB 35 C4
West Lulworth GB 43 B4
West Mersea GB 45 B4
Westminster GB 44 B3
Weston GB 40 C1
Weston-super-Mare GB 43 A4
Westport IRL 28 A2
Westruther GB 35 C5
West-Terschelling NL 70 A2
Westward Ho! GB 42 A2
West Woodburn GB 37 A4
Wetheral GB 37 B4
Wetherby GB 40 B2
Wetter
Hessen D 81 B4
Nordrhein-Westfalen D 80 A3
Wetteren B 79 A3
Wettin D 83 A3
Wettringen D 71 B4
Wetzikon CH 107 B3
Wetzlar D 81 B4
Wewelsfleth D 64 C2
Wexford IRL 30 B2
Weybridge GB 44 B3
Weyerbusch D 81 B3
Weyer Markt A 110 B1
Weyersheim F 93 C3
Weyhe D 72 B1
Weyhill GB 44 B2
Weymouth GB 43 B4
Weyregg A 109 B4
Węzyska PL 75 B3
Whalton GB 37 A5
Whauphill GB 36 B2
Wheatley GB 44 B2
Whickham GB 37 B5
Whipsnade GB 44 B3
Whitburn GB 35 C4
Whitby GB 37 B6
Whitchurch
Hampshire GB 44 B2
Herefordshire GB 39 C4
Shropshire GB 38 B4
White Bridge GB 32 D2
Whitegate IRL 29 C3
Whitehaven GB 36 B3
Whitehead GB 27 B5
Whithorn GB 36 B2
Whitley Bay GB 37 A5
Whitstable GB 45 B5
Whittington GB 38 B4
Whittlesey GB 41 C3
Wiązów PL 85 B5
Wick GB 32 C3
Wickede D 81 A3
Wickford GB 45 B4
Wickham GB 44 C2
Wickham Market GB 45 A5
Wicklow IRL 30 B2
Wicko PL 68 A2
Widawa PL 86 A2
Widdrington GB 37 A5
Widecombe in the Moor GB 42 B3
Widemouth GB 42 B2
Widnes GB 38 A4
Widuchowo PL 74 A3
Więcbork PL 76 A2
Wiefelstede D 71 A5
Wiehe D 82 A3
Wiehl D 81 B3
Wiek D 66 B2
Większyce PL 86 B1
Wielbark PL 77 A5
Wiele PL 68 B2
Wieleń PL 75 B5
Wielgie
Kujawsko-Pomorskie PL 77 B4
Łódzkie PL 86 A2
Mazowieckie PL 87 A5
Wielgomłyny PL 87 A3
Wielichowo PL 75 B5
Wieliczka PL 99 B4
Wielka Łąka PL 76 A3
Wielowies PL 86 B2
Wieluń PL 86 A2
Wien = Vienna A 111 A3
Wiener Neustadt A 111 B3
Wiepke D 73 B4
Wierden NL 71 B3
Wieren D 73 B3
Wieruszów PL 86 A2
Wierzbica
Mazowieckie PL 77 B6
Mazowieckie PL 87 A5
Wierzbie PL 86 A2

Wierzbięcin PL 75 A4
Wierzchowo PL 75 A5
Wierzchucino PL . . .68 A3
Wierzchy PL 86 A2
Wies A 110 C2
Wiesau D 95 B4
Wiesbaden D 93 A4
Wieselburg A 110 A2
Wiesen CH 107 C4
Wiesenburg D 73 B5
Wiesenfelden D 95 B4
Wiesensteig D 94 C1
Wiesentheid D 94 B2
Wiesloch D 93 B4
Wiesmath A 111 B3
Wiesmoor D 71 A4
Wietmarschen D . . .71 B4
Wietze D 72 B2
Wigan GB 38 A4
Wiggen CH 106 C2
Wigston GB 40 C2
Wigton GB 36 B3
Wigtown GB 36 B2
Wijchen NL 80 A1
Wijhe NL 70 B3
Wijk bij Duurstede
NL 70 C2
Wil CH 107 B4
Wilamowice PL 99 B3
Wilczęta PL 69 A4
Wilczkowice PL 77 B4
Wilczna PL 76 B3
Wilczyn PL 76 B3
Wildalpen A 110 B1
Wildbad D 93 C4
Wildberg
Baden-Württemberg
D 93 C4
Brandenburg D . . .74 B1
Wildegg CH 106 B3
Wildendürnbach A .97 C4
Wildeshausen D . . .72 B1
Wildon A 110 C2
Wilfersdorf A 97 C4
Wilhelmsburg
A 110 A2
D 74 A2
Wilhelmsdorf D . . .107 B4
Wilhelmshaven D . .71 A5
Wilków PL 77 B5
Willebadessen D . . .81 A5
Willebroek B 79 A4
Willgottheim F 93 C3
Willhermsdorf D . . .94 B2
Willich D 80 A2
Willingen D 81 A4
Willington GB 37 B5
Willisau CH 106 B3
Wilmslow GB 40 B1
Wilsdruff D 83 A5
Wilster D 64 C2
Wilsum D 71 B3
Wilton GB 44 B2
Wiltz L 92 B1
Wimborne Minster
GB 43 B5
Wimereux F 78 B1
Wimmenau F 93 C3
Wimmis CH 106 C2
Wincanton GB 43 A4
Winchcombe GB . . .44 B2
Winchelsea GB 45 C4
Winchester GB 44 B2
Windermere GB 36 B4
Windischeschenbach
D 95 B4
Windischgarsten
A 110 B1
Windorf D 96 C1
Windsbach D 94 B2
Windsor GB 44 B3
Wingene B 78 A3
Wingham GB 45 B5
Winkleigh GB 42 B3
Winklern A 109 C3
Winnenden D 94 C1
Winnica PL 77 B5
Winnigstedt D 73 B3
Winnweiler D 93 B3
Winschoten NL 71 A4
Winsen
Niedersachsen D . .72 A3
Niedersachsen D . .72 B2
Winsford GB 38 A4
Wińsko PL 85 A4
Winslow GB 44 B3
Winsum
Friesland NL 70 A2
Groningen NL 71 A3
Winterberg D 81 A4
Winterfeld D 73 B4
Winterswijk NL 71 C3
Winterthur CH 107 B3
Wintzenheim F . . .106 A2
Winzer D 95 C5
Wipperdorf D 82 A2
Wipperfürth D 80 A3
Wirksworth GB 40 B2
Wisbech GB 41 C4
Wischhafen D 64 C2
Wishaw GB 35 C4
Wisła PL 98 B2
Wisła Wielka PL . . .98 B2
Wislica PL 87 B4
Wismar D 65 C4
Wisniewo PL 77 A5
Wiśniowa PL 99 B4
Wissant F 78 B1
Wissembourg F 93 B3
Wissen D 81 B3
Witanowice PL 99 B3
Witham GB 45 B4
Withern GB 41 B4
Withernsea GB 41 B4
Witkowo PL 76 B2
Witmarsum NL 70 A2
Witney GB 44 B2
Witnica PL 75 B3
Witonia PL 77 B4
Witry-les-Reims F . .91 B4
Wittdün D 64 B1
Wittelsheim F 106 B2
Witten D 80 A3
Wittenberge D 73 A4
Wittenburg D 73 A4
Wittenheim F 106 B2
Wittichenau D 84 A2
Wittighausen D 94 B1
Wittingen D 73 B3
Wittislingen D 94 C2
Wittlich D 92 B2
Wittmannsdorf A . .110 C2
Wittmund D 71 A4
Wittorf D 72 A2
Wittstock D 73 A5
Witzenhausen D . . .82 A1
Wiveliscombe GB . .43 A3
Wivenhoe GB 45 B4
Władysławowo PL . .69 A3
Wleń PL 84 A3
Włocławek PL 77 B4
Włodawa PL 13 C5
Włodzimierzów PL .87 A3
Włosień PL 84 A3
Włostow PL 87 B5
Włoszakowice PL . .75 C5
Włoszczowa PL 87 B3
Wöbbelin D 73 A4
Woburn GB 44 B3
Wodzisław PL 87 B4
Wodzisław Śląski
PL 98 B2
Woerden NL 70 B1
Woerth F 93 C3
Wohlen CH 106 B3
Woippy F 92 B2
Wojcieszow PL 85 B3
Wojkowice Kościelne
PL 86 B3
Wojnicz PL 99 B4
Woking GB 44 B3
Wokingham GB 44 B3
Wola Jachowa PL . .87 B4
Wola Niechcicka
PL 86 A3
Wolbórz PL 87 A3
Wolbrom PL 87 B3
Wołczyn PL 86 A2
Woldegk D 74 A2
Wolfach D 93 C4
Wolfegg D 107 B4
Wolfen D 83 A4
Wolfenbüttel D 73 B3
Wolfersheim D 81 B4
Wolfhagen D 81 A5
Wolfratshausen D 108 B2
Wolfsberg A 110 C1
Wolfsburg D 73 B3
Wolf's Castle GB . .39 C2
Wolfshagen D 74 A2
Wolfstein D 93 B3
Wolfurt A 107 B4
Wolgast D 66 B2
Wolhusen CH 106 B3
Wolin PL 67 C3
Wolka PL 87 A4
Wolkenstein D 83 B5
Wolkersdorf A 97 C4
Wöllersdorf A 111 B3
Wollin D 73 B5
Wöllstadt D 81 B4
Wolmirstedt D 73 B4
Wolnzach D 95 C3
Wołów PL 85 A4
Wolsztyn PL 75 B5
Wolvega NL 70 B2
Wolverhampton
GB 40 C1
Wolverton GB 44 A3
Wombwell GB 40 B2
Woodbridge GB 45 A5
Woodhall Spa GB . .41 B3
Woodstock GB 44 B2
Wookey Hole GB . . .43 A4
Wool GB 43 B4
Woolacombe GB . . .42 A2
Wooler GB 37 A4
Woolwich GB 45 B4
Wooperton GB 37 A5
Worb CH 106 C2
Worbis D 82 A2
Worcester GB 39 B4
Wördern A 97 C4
Wörgl A 108 B3
Workington GB 36 B3
Worksop GB 40 B2
Workum NL 70 B2
Wörlitz D 83 A4
Wormer NL 70 B1
Wormhout F 78 B2
Wormit GB 35 B5
Worms D 93 B4
Worpswede D 72 A1
Wörrstadt D 93 B4
Wörschach A 110 B1
Worsley GB 38 A4
Wörth
Bayern D 93 B5
Bayern D 95 B4
Bayern D 95 C4
Rheinland-Pfalz D .93 B4
Worthing GB 44 C3
Woudsend NL 70 B2
Woumen B 78 A2
Woźniki PL 86 B3
Wragby GB 41 B3
Wrangle GB 41 B4
Wręczyca Wlk. PL . .86 B2
Wredenhagen D . . .73 A5
Wremen D 72 A1
Wrentham GB 45 A5
Wrexham GB 38 A3
Wriedel D 72 A3
Wriezen D 74 B3
Wrist D 64 C2
Wróblewo
Mazowieckie PL . . .77 B5
Wróblewo *continued*
Wielkopolskie PL . .75 B5
Wrocki PL 69 B4
Wrocław PL 85 A5
Wronki PL 75 B5
Wroxham GB 41 C5
Września PL 76 B2
Wrzosowo PL 67 B4
Wschowa PL 85 A4
Wulfen D 80 A3
Wülfen D 83 A3
Wulkau D 73 B5
Wünnenberg D 81 A4
Wünsdorf D 74 B2
Wunsiedel D 95 A4
Wunstorf D 72 B2
Wuppertal D 80 A3
Wurmannsquick D .95 C4
Würselen D 80 B2
Wurzbach D 82 B3
Würzburg D 94 B1
Wurzen D 83 A4
Wust D 74 B1
Wusterhausen D . . .73 B5
Wusterwitz D 73 B5
Wustrau-Altfriesack
D 74 B1
Wustrow D 66 B1
Wuustwezel B 79 A4
Wye GB 45 B4
Wyględów PL 87 A5
Wyk D 64 B1
Wykroty PL 84 A3
Wylye GB 43 A5
Wymiarki PL 84 A3
Wymondham GB . . .41 C5
Wyrzysk PL 76 A2
Wyśmierzyce PL . . .87 A4
Wysoka
Dolnośląskie PL . . .85 A3
Wielkopolskie PL . .76 A2
Wyszanów PL 86 A2
Wyszogród PL 77 B5

X

Xanten D 80 A2
Xanthi GR 183 B6
Xarrë AL 182 D2
Xátiva E 159 C3
Xeraco E 159 B3
Xert E 153 B4
Xerta E 153 B4
Xertigny F 105 A5
Xilagani GR 183 C7
Xilokastro GR 184 A3
Xinzo de Limia E . .140 B3
Xixón = Gijón E . . .142 A1
Xove E 140 A3
Xubia E 140 A2
Xunqueira de Ambia
E 140 B3
Xunqueira de
Espadañedo E . .140 B3
Xylophagou CY . . .181 B2

Y

Yablanitsa BG 17 D6
Yağcılar TR 186 C3
Yahyalı TR 23 B8
Yakoruda BG 183 A5
Yalova TR 187 B4
Yalvaç TR 189 A6
Yambol BG 17 D7
Yampil UA 13 D8
Yaniskoski RUS .193 D12
Yantarnyy RUS 69 A4
Yarbasan TR 186 D3
Yarcombe GB 43 B3
Yaremcha UA 13 D6
Yarm GB 37 B5
Yarmouth GB 44 C2
Yarrow GB 35 C4
Yasinya UA 17 A6
Yatağan TR 188 B3
Yate GB 43 A4
Yatton GB 43 A4
Yavoriv UA 13 D5
Yaxley GB 41 C3
Yazıca TR 187 B6
Yazıköy TR 188 C2
Ybbs A 110 A2
Ybbsitz A 110 B1
Ydby DK 58 B1
Yddal N 46 B2
Ydes F 116 B2
Yealmpton GB 42 B3
Yebra de Basa E . .145 B3
Yecla E 159 C2
Yecla de Yeltes E .149 B3
Yelsk BY 13 C8
Yelverton GB 42 B2
Yena RUS 197 B14
Yenice
Ankara TR 23 B7
Aydın TR 188 B3
Çanakkale TR . . . 186 C2
Edirne TR 183 C8
Yenifoça TR 186 D1
Yeniköy TR 186 D4
Yeniköy Plaji TR . .186 B3
Yenipazar TR 188 B3
Yenişarbademli
TR 189 B6
Yenişehir TR 187 B4
Yenne F 118 B2
Yeovil GB 43 B4
Yepes E 151 C4
Yerköy TR 23 B8
Yerólakkos CY 181 A2
Yeroskipos CY 181 B1
Yerseke NL 79 A4
Yerville F 89 A4
Yeşildağ TR 189 B6
Yeşilhisar TR 23 B8
Yeşilköy TR 186 B3
Yeşilova TR 189 B4
Yeşilyurt TR 188 A3
Yeste E 164 A2
Yezerishche BY 9 E6
Y Felinheli GB 38 A2
Ygos-St Saturnin
F 128 C2
Ygrande F 104 C1
Yialousa CY 181 A3
Yığılca TR 187 B6
Yli-Ii FIN 197 D8
Yli-Kärppä FIN 197 D8
Yli-Muonia FIN 196 A6
Ylitornio FIN 196 C6
Ylivieska FIN 3 D9
Ylläsjärvi FIN 196 B7
Ymonville F 103 A3
Yngsjö S 63 C2
York GB 40 B2
Youghal IRL 29 C4
Yoğuntaş TR 186 A2
Yozgat TR 23 B8
Yport F 89 A4
Ypres = Ieper B 78 B2
Yssingeaux F 117 B4
Ystad S 66 A2
Ystalyfera GB 39 C3
Ystebrød N 52 B1
Ystradgynlais GB . .39 C3
Ytre Arna N 46 B2
Ytre Enebakk N 54 A2
Ytre Rendal N 199 D8
Ytteran S 199 B11
Ytterhogdal S 199 C11
Yttermalung S 49 B5
Yunak TR 187 D6
Yuncos E 151 B4
Yunquera E 162 B3
Yunquera de Henares
E 151 B4
Yushkozero RUS . . .3 D13
Yverdon-les-Bains
CH 106 C1
Yvetot F 89 A4
Yvignac F 101 A3
Yvoir B 79 B4
Yvonand CH 106 C1
Yxnerum S 56 B2
Yzeure F 104 C2

Z

Zaamslag NL 79 A3
Zaanstad NL 70 B1
Žabalj SRB 126 B2
Zabar H 113 A4
Žabari SRB 127 C3
Zabiče SLO 123 B3
Zabierzów PL 87 B3
Ząbki PL 77 B6
Ząbkowice Śląskie
PL 85 B4
Zablaće HR 138 B1
Žabljak MNE 139 B5
Žabno PL 87 B4
Zabok HR 124 A1
Žabokreky SK 98 C2
Zabor PL 75 C4
Żabowo PL 75 A4
Zabrdje BIH 125 C4
Zábřeh CZ 97 B4
Zabrežje SRB 127 C2
Ząbrowo PL 67 C4
Zabrze PL 86 B2
Zabrzeź PL 99 B4
Zacharo GR 184 B2
Zadar HR 137 A4
Zadzim PL 86 A2
Zafarraya E 163 B3
Zafferana Etnea I . .177 B4
Zafra E 155 C4
Žaga SLO 122 A2
Zagajica SRB 127 C3
Żagań PL 84 A3
Zaglav HR 137 B4
Zaglavak SRB 127 D1
Zagnanśk PL 87 B4
Zagora GR 183 D5
Zagorc SLO 110 C2
Zagorićani BIH 138 B3
Zagorje SLO 123 A4
Zagórów PL 76 B2
Zagradje SRB 127 C2
Zagreb HR 124 B1
Zagrilla E 163 A3
Zagvozd HR 138 B3
Zagwiździe PL 86 B1
Zagyvarekas H . . .113 B4
Zagyvaróna H 113 A3
Zahara E 162 B2
Zahara de los Atunes
E 162 B2
Zahinos E 155 C4
Zahna D 83 A4
Záhoří CZ 96 B2
Zahrádka CZ 97 B3
Zahrensdorf D 73 A3
Zaidin E 153 A4
Zaječar SRB 16 D5
Zákamenné SK 99 B3
Zákány H 124 A2
Zákányszék H 126 A1
Zakliczyn PL 99 B4
Zakopane PL 99 B3
Zakroczym PL 77 B5
Zakrzew PL 87 A5
Zakrzewo PL 76 B3
Zakupy CZ 84 B2
Zakynthos GR 184 B1
Zalaapáti H 111 C4
Zalabaksa H 111 C3
Zalaegerszeg H . . .111 C3
Zalakomár H 111 C4
Zalakoppány H . . .111 C4
Zalalövő H 111 C3
Zalamea de la Serena
E 156 B2
Zalamea la Real E 161 B3
Zalaszentgrót H . . .111 C4
Zalaszentiván H . . .111 C3
Zalău RO 17 B5
Zalavár H 111 C4
Zalcsie PL 86 A3
Zaldibar E 143 A4
Žalec SLO 123 A4
Zalesie PL 77 A5
Zalewo PL 69 B4
Zalishchyky UA 13 D6
Zalla E 143 A3
Zaltbommel NL 79 A5
Zamárdi H 112 C1
Zamarte PL 68 B2
Zamberk CZ 85 B4
Zambra E 163 A3
Zambugueira do Mar
P 160 B1
Zámoly H 112 B2
Zamora E 149 A4
Zamość PL 13 C5
Zamoście PL 86 A3
Zams A 108 B1
Zandhoven B 79 A4
Žandov CZ 84 B2
Zandvoort NL 70 B1
Zangliveri GR 183 C5
Zánka H 111 C4
Zaorejas E 152 B1
Zaovine SRB 127 D1
Zapadnaya Dvina
RUS 9 D8
Zapfend D 94 A2
Zapole PL 86 A2
Zapolyarnyy
RUS 193 C14
Zapponeta I 171 B3
Zaprešić HR 124 B1
Zaragoza E 153 A3
Zarasai LT 13 A7
Zarautz E 144 A1
Zarcilla de Ramos
E 164 B3
Zaręby PL 77 A6
Żarki PL 86 B3
Zarko GR 182 D4
Žarnovica SK 98 C2
Zarnow PL 87 A4
Zarnowiec PL 68 A3
Zarošice CZ 97 B4
Żarów PL 85 B4
Zarren B 78 A2
Zarrentin D 73 A3
Żary PL 84 A3
Zarza Capilla E . . .156 B2
Zarza de Alange E 156 B1
Zarza de Granadilla
E 149 B3
Zarza de Tajo E . . .151 B4
Zarzadilla de Totana
E 164 B3
Zarza la Mayor E . .155 B4
Zarzuela del Monte
E 150 B3
Zarzuela del Pinar
E 151 A3
Zas E 140 A2
Zasavica SRB 127 C1
Zasieki PL 84 A2
Zásmuky CZ 96 B3
Żatec CZ 83 B5
Zaton HR 139 C4
Zatonie PL 84 A3
Zator PL 99 A3
Zauchwitz D 74 B2
Zavala BIH 139 C3
Zavalje BIH 124 C1
Zavattarello I 120 C2
Zavidovići BIH 139 A4
Zavlaka SRB 127 C1
Zawady PL 77 C5
Zawadzkie PL 86 B2
Zawdy PL 86 A2
Zawidów PL 84 A3
Zawidz PL 77 B4
Zawiercie PL 86 B3
Zawoja PL 99 B3
Zawonia PL 85 A5
Žažina HR 124 B2
Zázrivá SK 99 B3
Zbarazh UA 13 D6
Zbąszyń PL 75 B4
Zbąszynek PL 75 B4
Zbehy SK 98 C2
Zbiersk PL 76 C3
Zbiroh CZ 96 B1
Zblewo PL 69 B3
Zbójno PL 77 A4
Zbrachlin PL 76 A3
Zbraslav CZ 96 B2
Zbraslavice CZ 97 B3
Ždala HR 124 A3
Ždánice CZ 98 B1
Žďár nad Sázavov
CZ 97 B3
Zdbice PL 75 A5
Zdenci HR 125 B3
Ždiar SK 99 B4
Zdice CZ 96 B1
Zdirec nad Doubravou
CZ 97 B3
Zdolbuniv UA 13 C7
Zdounky CZ 98 B1
Zdrelo SRB 127 C3
Zduńska Wola PL . .86 A2
Zduny
Łódzkie PL 77 B4
Wielkopolskie PL . .85 A5
Żdżary PL 87 A4
Zdziechowice
Opolskie PL 86 A2
Wielkopolskie PL . .76 B2
Zdziszowice PL 86 B2
Zeberio E 143 A4
Žebrák CZ 96 B1
Zebreira P 155 B3
Zebrzydowa PL 84 A3
Zechlin D 74 A1
Zechlinerhütte D . . .74 A1
Zederhaus A 109 B4
Žednik SRB 126 B1
Zeebrugge B 78 A3
Zegrze PL 77 B6
Zehdenick D 74 B2
Zehren D 83 A5
Zeil D 94 A2
Zeilarn D 95 C4
Zeist NL 70 B2
Zeithain D 83 A5
Zeitz D 83 A4
Želatava CZ 97 B3
Želazno PL 68 A2
Zele B 79 A4
Zelenoborskiy RUS 3 C13
Zelenogorsk RUS . . .9 B6
Zelenograd RUS . . .9 D10
Zelenogradsk RUS .12 A4
Železná Ruda CZ . . .96 B1
Železnice CZ 84 B3
Železnik SRB 127 C2
Zelezniki SLO 123 A3
Železny Brod CZ . . .84 B3
Zelhem NL 71 B3
Želiezovce SK 112 A2
Želkowo PL 68 A2
Zell
CH 106 B2
Baden-Württemberg
D 93 C4
Baden-Württemberg
D 106 B2
Rheinland-Pfalz D .92 A3
Zella-Mehlis D 82 B2
Zell am See A 109 B3
Zell am Ziller A . . .108 B2
Zell an der Pram A . .96 C1
Zell bei Zellhof A . . .96 C2
Zellerndorf A 97 C3
Zellingen D 94 B1
Želovce SK 112 A3
Zelów PL 86 A3
Zeltweg A 110 B1
Zelzate B 79 A3
Zemberovce SK 98 C2
Zembrzyce PL 99 B3
Zemianske-Kostol'any
SK 98 C2
Zemitz D 66 C2
Zemné SK 112 B1
Zemst B 79 B4
Zemun SRB 127 C2
Zemunik Donji HR 137 A4
Zenica BIH 139 A3
Zennor GB 42 B1
Žepa BIH 139 B5
Žepče BIH 139 A4
Zepponami I 168 A2
Zerbst D 73 C5
Zerf D 92 B2
Zerind RO 113 C5
Żerków PL 76 B2
Zermatt CH 119 A4
Zernez CH 107 C5
Zerpen-schleuse D 74 B2
Zestoa E 144 A1
Zetel D 71 A4
Zeulenroda D 83 B3
Zeven D 72 A2
Zevenaar NL 70 C3
Zevenbergen NL . . .79 A4
Zévio I 121 B4
Zeytinbaği TR 186 B3
Zeytindağ TR 186 D2
Zgierz PL 86 A3
Zgorzelec PL 84 A3
Zgošća BIH 139 A4
Zhabinka BY 13 B6
Zharkovskiy RUS . . .9 E8
Zhashkiv UA 13 D9
Zhlobin BY 13 B9
Zhmerynka UA 13 D8
Zhodzina BY 13 A8
Zhytomyr UA 13 C8
Žiar nad Hronom
SK 98 C2
Zicavo F 180 B2
Zickhusen D 65 C4
Zidani Most SLO . .123 A4
Ziddorf D 73 A5
Židlochovice CZ . . .97 B4
Ziębice PL 85 B5
Ziegendorf D 73 A4
Ziegenrück D 83 B3
Zieleniec
Dolnośląskie PL . . .85 B4
Warmińsko-Mazurskie
PL 77 A6
Zachodnio-Pomorskie
PL 75 A4
Zielona PL 77 A4
Zielona Góra PL . . .75 C4
Zieluń-Osada PL . . .77 A4
Ziemetshausen D . .94 C2
Zierenberg D 81 A5
Zierikzee NL 79 A3
Ziersdorf A 97 C3
Zierzow D 73 A4
Ziesar D 73 B5
Ziesendorf D 65 C5
Ziethen D 74 B2
Žihle CZ 96 A1
Žilina SK 98 B2
Ziltendorf D 74 B3
Zimandu Nou RO .126 A3
Zimna Woda PL 77 A5
Zimnicea RO 17 D6
Zinal CH 119 A4
Zinasco I 120 B2
Zingst D 66 B1
Zinkgruvan S 55 B6
Žinkovy CZ 96 B1
Zinnowitz D 66 B2
Zirc H 112 B1
Žiri SLO 123 A3
Zirl A 108 B2
Zirndorf D 94 B2
Žirovnica SRB 127 C3
Žirovnice CZ 97 B3
Zisterdorf A 97 C4
Žitište SRB 126 B2
Zitsa GR 182 D2
Zittau D 84 B2
Živaja HR 124 B2
Živinice BIH 139 A4
Zlatar HR 124 A2
Zlatar Bistrica HR 124 A2
Zlate Hory CZ 85 B5
Zlaté Klasy SK 111 A4
Zlaté Moravce SK . .98 C2
Zlatnána Ostrove
SK 112 B1
Zlatniky SK 98 C2
Zlatograd BG 183 B7
Žlebič SLO 123 B3
Zlín CZ 98 B1
Złocieniec PL 75 A5
Złoczew PL 86 A2
Zlonice CZ 84 B2
Złotniki Kujawskie
PL 76 B3
Złotoryja PL 85 A3
Złotów PL 68 B2
Złoty Stok PL 85 B4
Zlutice CZ 83 B5
Zmajevac BIH 124 C2
Zmajevo SRB 126 B1
Żmigród PL 85 A4
Zmijavci HR 138 B3
Žminj HR 122 B2
Żnin PL 76 B2
Znojmo CZ 97 C4
Zöblitz D 83 B5
Zocca I 135 A3
Zoetermeer NL 70 B1
Zofingen CH 106 B2
Zogno I 120 B2
Zohor SK 111 A3
Zolling D 95 C3
Zolochiv UA 13 D6
Zomba H 112 C2
Zomergem B 79 A3
Zoñán E 141 A3
Zonguldak TR 187 A6
Zonhoven B 79 B5
Zonza F 180 B2
Zörbig D 83 A4
Zorita E 156 A2
Żory PL 98 A2
Zossen D 74 B2
Zottegem B 79 B3
Zoutkamp NL 71 A3
Zovi Do BIH 139 B4
Zreče SLO 123 A4
Zrenjanin SRB 126 B2
Žrnovica HR 138 B2
Zručnad Sazavou
CZ 97 B3
Zsadány H 113 C5
Zsámbék H 112 B2
Zsámbok H 112 B3
Zsana H 126 A1
Zschopau D 83 B5
Zuberec SK 99 B3
Zubieta E 144 A2
Zubiri E 144 B2
Zubtsov RUS 9 D9
Zucaina E 153 B3
Zudar D 66 B2
Zuera E 144 C3
Zufre E 161 B3
Zug CH 107 B3
Zuheros E 163 A3
Zuidhorn NL 71 A3
Zuidlaren NL 71 A3
Zuidwolde NL 71 B3
Zújar E 164 B2
Żukowo PL 69 A3
Žuljana HR 138 C3
Žulová CZ 85 B5
Zülpich D 80 B2
Zumaia E 144 A1
Zumárraga E 144 A4
Zundert NL 79 A4
Županja HR 125 B4
Zurgena E 164 B2
Zürich CH 107 B3
Żuromin PL 77 A4
Zurzach CH 106 B3
Zusmarshausen D . .94 C2
Zusow D 65 C4
Züssow D 66 C2
Žuta Lovka HR 123 C4
Zutphen NL 70 B3
Žužemberk SLO . .123 B3
Zvenyhorodka UA . .13 D9
Zvikovské Podhradi
CZ 96 B2
Zvolen SK 99 C3
Zvolenská Slatina
SK 99 C3
Zvornik BIH 139 A5
Zwartsluis NL 70 B3
Zweibrücken D 93 B3
Zweisimmen CH . . .106 C2
Zwettl A 97 C3
Zwettl an der Rodl
A 96 C2
Zwickau D 83 B4
Zwiefalten D 107 A4
Zwieryn PL 75 B4
Zwierzno PL 69 A4
Zwiesel D 96 B1
Zwieselstein A 108 C2
Zwoleń PL 87 A5
Zwolle NL 70 B3
Zwönitz D 83 B4
Żychlin PL 77 B4
Zydowo
Wielkopolskie PL . .76 B2
Zachodnio-Pomorskie
PL 68 A1
Żyrardów PL 77 B5
Żytno PL 86 B3
Żywiec PL 99 B3
Zyyi CY 181 B2

CONTENTS · INHALT · SOMMARIO · CONTENIDO · CONTEÚDO ·
INDHOLD · INHOUD · OBSAH ·

1

France/Belgium, Luxembourg, Netherlands · Frankre
Francia/Belgio, Lussemburgo, Paesi bassi · Franc
França/Bélgica, Luxemburgo, Holanda · Frankrig
Frankrijk/België, Luxemburg, Nederland · Franci
Francúzsko/Belgieko, Luxembursko, Holandsko · Francja/Belgia, Luksemburg, Ni

1:1 000 000

freytag & berndt
www.freytagberndt.com
© FREYTAG-BERNDT u. ARTARIA KG, 1230 VIENNA, AUSTRIA, EUROPE

2nd edition April 2012
© AA Media Limited 2012 (Original edition printed 2010)

ISBN: 978-0-7495-7367-6

The contents of this book are believed to be correct at the time of printing. Nevertheless the Publisher can accept no responsibility
for errors or omissions, or for changes in the details given. This does not affect your statutory rights.

A04924

KEY PLAN · BLATTÜBERSICHT · TAVOLA RIASSUNTIVA DELLE PAGINE · VISTA DE LA PÁGINA · VISÃO GERAL DOS MAPAS · INDDELING I KORTSIDER · BLADOVERZICHT · KLAD LISTŮ · PREHĽAD KLADU LISTOV · SKOROWIDZ ARKUSZY

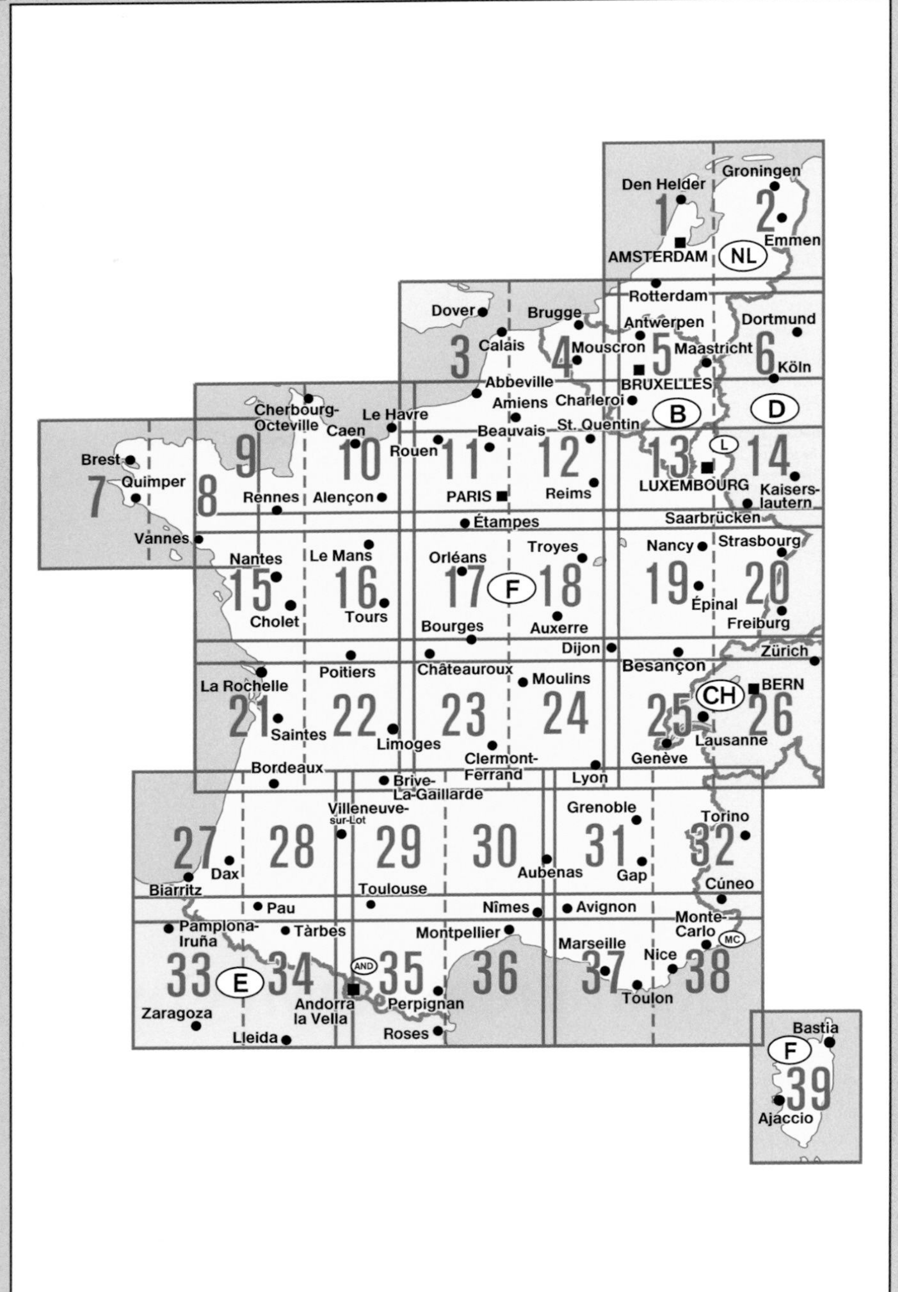

Motorway, dual carriageway
Autobahn, Fernverkehrsstraße, 4-spurig
Autostrada, strada di grande comunicazione a quattro corsie
Autovía y autopista libre, autovía
Auto-estrada, Itinerário principal com 4 faixas

Motorvej, Motortrafikvej, 4-sporet
Autosnelweg, autoweg, 4 rijstroken
Dálnice, dálková silnice, čtyřproudová
Diaľnica, diaľková cesta štvorpruhová
Autostrada, droga komunikacji dalekobieżnej, dwujezdniowe

Primary route, main road, secondary road
Fernverkehrsstraße, Hauptstraße, Nebenstraße
Strada di grande comunicazione, strada principale, strada secondaria
Carretera nacional, calle principal con número, carretera secundaria
Itinerário principal, estrada principal, estrada secundária

Vigtig hovedvej, hovedvej, bivej
Autoweg, belangrijke verkeersader, zijstraat
Dálková silnice, hlavní silnice, vedlejší silnice
Rozostavaná diaková cesta, hlavná cesta, vedľajšia cesta
Droga komunikacji dalekobieżnej, droga drugorzędna, droga drugorzędna

Motorway with interchange
Autobahn mit Anschlussstelle
Autostrada con raccordo
Intersección de autovía
Auto-estrada com ligaçao

Autosnelweg: Aansluitingen volledig
Motorvej med komplet tilkørsel
Dálnice s nájezdem
Diaľnica s nájazdom
Autostrady z węzłami

Motorway subject to toll
Autobahn mautpflichtig
Autostrada apedaggio
Autopista de peaje
Auto-estrada com portagem

Motorvej, afgiftspligtig
Autosnelweg met tol
Zpoplatněná dálnice
Spoplatnenó diaľnica
Autostrada płatna

Distances in kilometres
Entfernungen in km
Distanze in km
Distancias en km
Distância em quilómetros

5

5

Afstande i km
Afstanden in km
Vzdálenosti v km
Vzdialenosti v km
Odległości w km

Main - railway line, branch line
Hauptbahn, Nebenbahn
Linea ferrovia principale, linea ferrovia secondaria
Ferrocarril principal, ferrcarril secundario
Linha principal de caminho-de-ferro, ramal

Hovedbane, sidebane
Hoofdspoorweg, secundaire spoorweg
Hlavní trať, vedlejší trať
Hlavná železnica, vedľajšia železnica
Kolej glówna, kolej lokalna

Car ferry, International airport
Autofähre, Internationaler Flughafen
Traghetto per il trasporto, Aeroporto internazionale
Ferry, Aeropuerto internacional
Ferry-boat, Aeroporto internacional

Bilfcrge, International lufthavn
Veerdienst, Internationale vliegveld
Trajekt pro automobily, Mezinárodní letiště
Autokompa, Medzinárodné letisko
Prom samochodowy, Miedzynarodowy port lotniczy

Road numbers
Straßennummer
Numerazione delle strade
Numeración de las carreteras
Número de estrada

E25
A8
D603
D36

Vejnummer
Straatnummer
Čisla silnič
Číslo cesty
Numer drogi

Manor house, castle - ruin, antique sites, monastery
Schloss, Burg - Ruine, Antike Ruinenstätte, Kloster
Castello, fortezza - rovine, luoghi con rovine, convento
Castillo, fortaleza - ruinas, yacimineto archeológico, monasterio
Palácio, castelo - ruina, sitio arqueológico, convento/mosteiro

Slot, borg - ruin, ruin oldtidsminde, kloster
Paleis, burcht - ruïne, antieke ruïne, klooster
Zámek, hrad - zřícenina, antické zřícenimy, klášter
Zámok, ruiny hradu, antické zrúcaniny, kláštor
Zamek, Ruina zamku warownego, ruina antyczna, klasztor

Spa, marina
Heilbad, Marina
Località termale, marina
Estación termal, marina
Estância termal, marina

Kurbad, lystbådehavn
Kuurbad, jachthaven
Lázne, přistav
Kúpele, prístav
Uzdrowisko, port jachtowy

Place of particular interest, World Heritage Site
Besonders sehenswertes Objekt, Weltkulturerbe
Località di grande interesse, patrimoni dell'umanilà
Lugar de especial interés, patrimonio de la Humanidad
Sitio de interesse especial, património mundial

Scrlig sevcrdighed, verdensarv
Bijzondere bezienswaardigheden, werelderfgoed
Obzvlášť zajimavý objekt, seznam světového dědictiví
Mimoriadne pozoruhodný objekt, lokalita svetového dedičstva
Szczególnie ciekawy objekt, obiekty z listy dziedzictwa UNESCO

National boundary, international border crossing
Staatsgrenze, Internationaler Grenzübergang
Confine di Stato, posto di frontiera internazionale
Territorio nacional, internacional passo de frontera
Fronteira nacional, posto fronteiriço international

Rigsgrcnse, international grcnseovergang
Staatsgrens, internationale grensovergang
Státní hranice, mezinárodní hraniční přechod
Štátna hranica, medzinárodný hraničný priechod
Granica państwa, międzynarodowe przejście graniczne

Provincial boundary, national park
Landesgrenze, Naturschutzgebiet
Confine regionale, parco naturale
Limite regional, parque nacional
Fronteira estadual, reserva natural

N

Deltstatsgrcnse, fredet område
Provinciegrens, natuurbeschermingsgebied
Hranice země, čřírodní rezervace
Hranica krajov, chránená krajinná oblasť
Granice podziału administracyjnego, rezerwat przyrody

1 : 1 000 000

0   10   20   40   60   80km

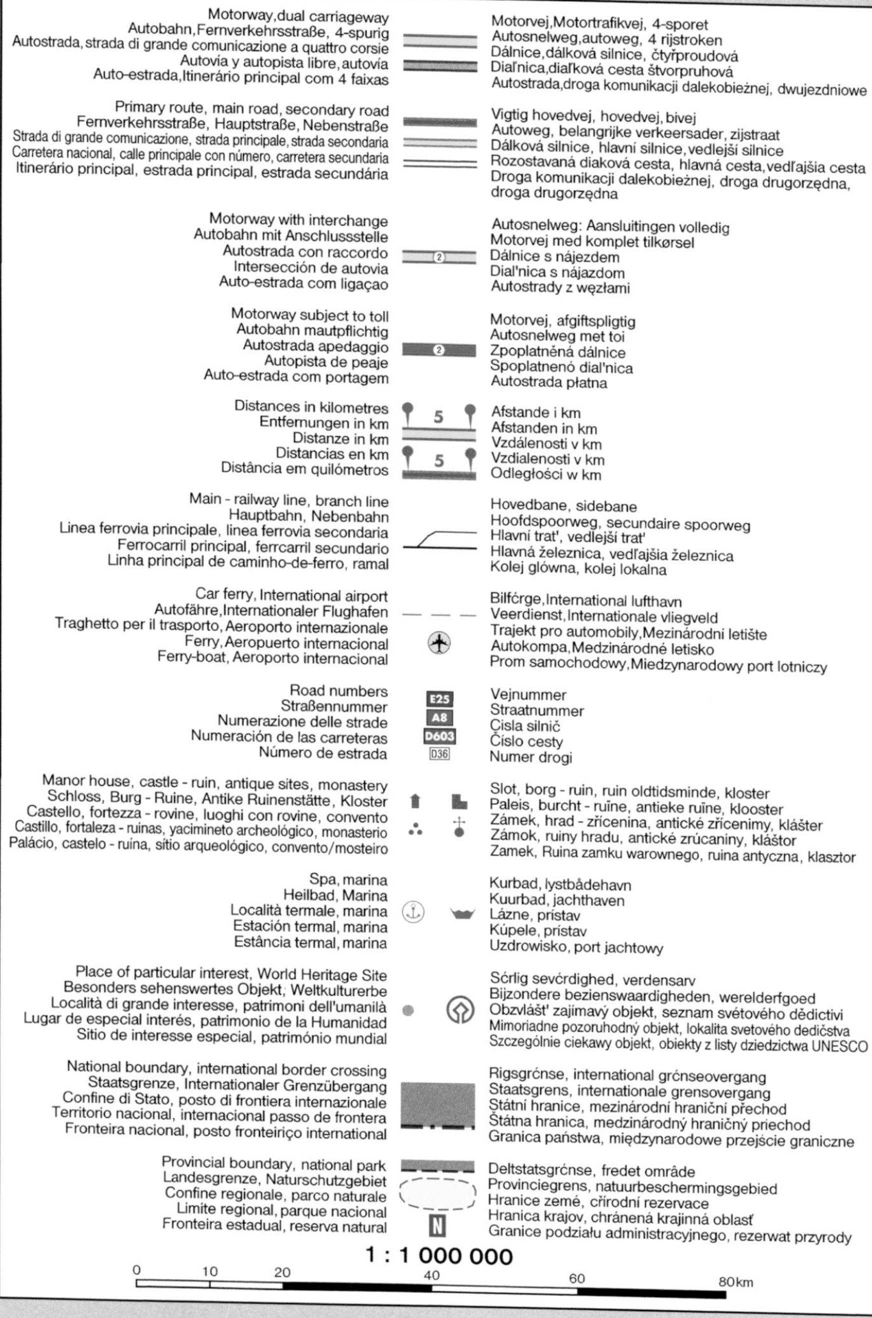

4

GENERAL MAP · VERKEHRSÜBERSICHT · CARTA SINOTTICA · VISTA
GENERAL · MAPA GERAL DE TRÁFEGO · PRIMÆRE REJSERUTER · OVER-
ZICHTSKAART · PŘEHLEDNÁ MAPA · PREHĽADNÁ MAPA · PRZEGLĄDOWA

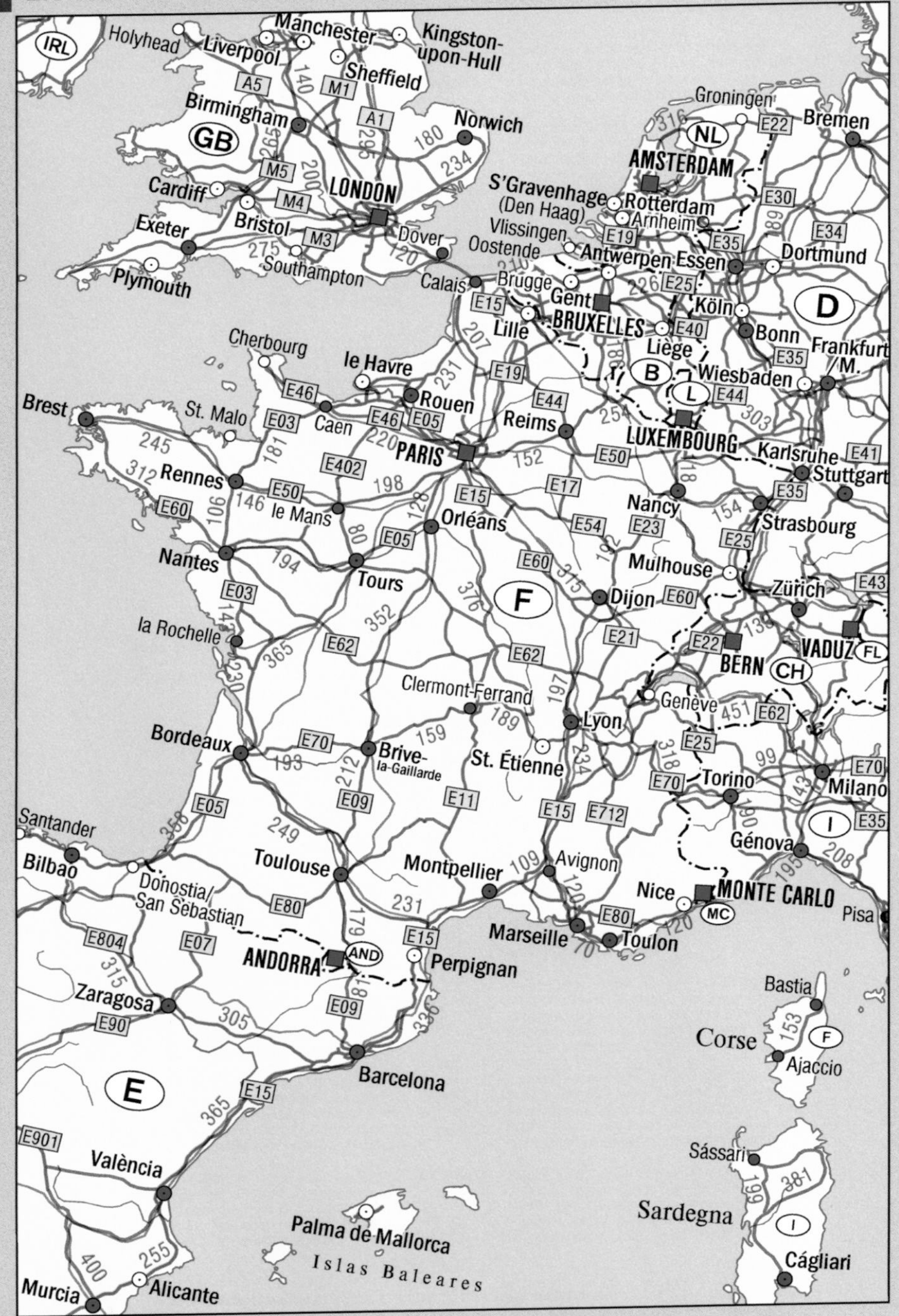

DISTANCE TABLE · ENTFERNUNGSTABELLE · TABELLA DELLE DISTANZE · TABLA DE DISTANCIAS · TABELA DE DISTÂNCIAS · AFSTANDSTABEL · AFSTANDSTABEL · TABULKA VZDÁLENOSTÍ · TABUĽKA VZDIALENOSTÍ · TABELA ODLEGŁOŚCI

Column order (left to right): Amsterdam · Andorra la Vella · Antwerpen · Arnhem · Barcelona · Bern · Bonn · Bordeaux · Brest · Brugge · Brussel/Bruxelles · Calais · Cherbourg · Clermont-Ferrand · Den Haag · Dijon · Donostia-S. Sebastián · Genève · Groningen · Le Havre · Le Mans · Liège · London · Luxembourg · Lyon · Marseille · Milano · Nantes · Nice · Oostende · Orléans · Paris · Perpignan · Reims · Rotterdam · St-Malo · Strasbourg · Toulouse · Tours · Vlissingen

Distance matrix (each row lists distances from the city named to the cities listed above, in column order):

Destination (row)	Distances (km)
Amsterdam	—
Andorra la Vella	1360
Antwerpen	159 · 1198
Arnhem	101 · 1386 · 167
Barcelona	1536 · 197 · 1374 · 1509
Bern	827 · 968 · 705 · 737 · 941
Bonn	290 · 1361 · 233 · 167 · 1356 · 565
Bordeaux	1082 · 428 · 920 · 1088 · 635 · 907 · 1085
Brest	1042 · 1273 · 858 · 924 · 1273 · 1045 · 1045 · 643
Brugge	211 · 1162 · 53 · 233 · 1338 · 771 · 395 · 830 · 830
Brussel/Bruxelles	211 · 1151 · 100 · 275 · 1327 · 713 · 352 · 846 · 947 · 99
Calais	366 · 1078 · 205 · 373 · 1273 · 884 · 432 · 794 · 643 · 115 · 210
Cherbourg	729 · 1111 · 373 · 371 · 1321 · 947 · 690 · 423 · 210 · 595 · 532 · 466
Clermont-Ferrand	1111 · 456 · 828 · 930 · 656 · 605 · 717 · 352 · 718 · 747 · 718 · 595 · 718
Den Haag	53 · 1386 · 100 · 121 · 1502 · 789 · 275 · 1088 · 1045 · 115 · 210 · 344 · 711 · 1070
Dijon	856 · 762 · 570 · 581 · 876 · 159 · 507 · 690 · 903 · 537 · 435 · 532 · 568 · 326 · 852
Donostia-San Sebastián	1321 · 350 · 1159 · 1327 · 373 · 923 · 1227 · 235 · 574 · 1227 · 1124 · 924 · 759 · 605 · 1501 · 903 · 1048
Genève	924 · 579 · 684 · 713 · 662 · 159 · 718 · 690 · 903 · 717 · 595 · 630 · 679 · 249 · 951 · 198 · 732 · 1056
Groningen	179 · 1505 · 255 · 195 · 1676 · 903 · 355 · 1190 · 1096 · 210 · 249 · 370 · 703 · 1011 · 235 · 903 · 1011 · 951
Le Havre	600 · 1046 · 325 · 445 · 1222 · 785 · 525 · 532 · 384 · 385 · 344 · 391 · 235 · 580 · 574 · 507 · 607 · 810 · 249
Le Mans	707 · 823 · 510 · 618 · 935 · 710 · 717 · 338 · 403 · 510 · 385 · 450 · 210 · 338 · 684 · 403 · 710 · 856 · 903 · 212
Liège	243 · 1227 · 144 · 229 · 1317 · 684 · 99 · 947 · 1076 · 147 · 99 · 223 · 574 · 823 · 244 · 493 · 1124 · 576 · 249 · 435 · 572
London	533 · 1313 · 371 · 487 · 1509 · 903 · 510 · 1011 · 903 · 299 · 365 · 135 · 212 · 1109 · 481 · 666 · 1285 · 742 · 403 · 216 · 301 · 491
Luxembourg	362 · 1223 · 314 · 328 · 1318 · 487 · 198 · 908 · 903 · 299 · 210 · 440 · 759 · 703 · 403 · 197 · 937 · 375 · 485 · 513 · 498 · 166 · 757
Lyon	927 · 685 · 723 · 679 · 588 · 310 · 786 · 535 · 1012 · 788 · 666 · 729 · 782 · 148 · 951 · 198 · 823 · 148 · 1038 · 601 · 604 · 572 · 791 · 507
Marseille	532 · 1080 · 270 · 314 · 816 · 614 · 821 · 588 · 442 · 821 · 732 · 766 · 633 · 326 · 892 · 326 · 732 · 460 · 1143 · 657 · 625 · 648 · 924 · 450 · 329
Milano	1237 · 875 · 1185 · 1204 · 1070 · 317 · 959 · 1100 · 1228 · 904 · 904 · 938 · 1070 · 703 · 1014 · 551 · 1185 · 317 · 1143 · 859 · 895 · 859 · 1031 · 460 · 354 · 528
Nantes	886 · 801 · 728 · 847 · 905 · 745 · 731 · 347 · 297 · 723 · 731 · 796 · 538 · 377 · 863 · 614 · 745 · 876 · 993 · 385 · 252 · 681 · 924 · 614 · 614 · 731 · 1117
Nice	1080 · 1014 · 903 · 977 · 732 · 745 · 1012 · 789 · 1070 · 1012 · 1096 · 977 · 852 · 485 · 1031 · 585 · 923 · 485 · 1143 · 901 · 899 · 931 · 1228 · 585 · 317 · 203 · 317 · 901 · —
Oostende	255 · 1176 · 116 · 312 · 1352 · 823 · 460 · 805 · 675 · 25 · 115 · 90 · 625 · 747 · 248 · 637 · 1204 · 743 · 312 · 420 · 510 · 221 · 339 · 320 · 788 · 766 · 1096 · 749 · 1096
Orléans	643 · 850 · 488 · 573 · 907 · 568 · 604 · 573 · 385 · 385 · 344 · 409 · 340 · 248 · 643 · 362 · 727 · 601 · 835 · 216 · 127 · 435 · 649 · 377 · 462 · 698 · 1052 · 300 · 749 · 436
Paris	507 · 824 · 342 · 493 · 1048 · 571 · 499 · 584 · 594 · 299 · 302 · 300 · 359 · 421 · 507 · 311 · 710 · 541 · 712 · 198 · 210 · 328 · 462 · 377 · 462 · 776 · 831 · 385 · 929 · 299 · 128
Perpignan	1082 · 199 · 920 · 1088 · 210 · 819 · 1084 · 363 · 947 · 884 · 884 · 789 · 708 · 440 · 1048 · 654 · 603 · 540 · 1315 · 895 · 739 · 862 · 1084 · 619 · 493 · 258 · 547 · 725 · 493 · 884 · 572 · 852
Reims	364 · 1000 · 229 · 316 · 1150 · 597 · 338 · 737 · 757 · 221 · 148 · 280 · 557 · 469 · 314 · 244 · 1016 · 437 · 393 · 369 · 320 · 110 · 536 · 187 · 649 · 807 · 946 · 462 · 789 · 232 · 152 · 148 · 849
Rotterdam	79 · 1313 · 119 · 147 · 1464 · 842 · 318 · 1012 · 1011 · 99 · 148 · 272 · 675 · 1000 · 25 · 789 · 1138 · 854 · 216 · 557 · 557 · 197 · 366 · 377 · 892 · 601 · 1185 · 538 · 1143 · 117 · 471 · 450 · 1001 · 314
St-Malo	914 · 915 · 730 · 810 · 1011 · 852 · 884 · 310 · 219 · 601 · 688 · 601 · 189 · 493 · 990 · 666 · 638 · 854 · 1000 · 300 · 188 · 675 · 891 · 648 · 751 · 924 · 1258 · 156 · 924 · 557 · 244 · 403 · 954 · 536 · 808
Strasbourg	632 · 964 · 498 · 464 · 1084 · 377 · 228 · 789 · 1012 · 648 · 421 · 557 · 675 · 498 · 638 · 326 · 954 · 421 · 789 · 714 · 545 · 299 · 894 · 223 · 498 · 798 · 749 · 731 · 931 · 623 · 425 · 492 · 954 · 272 · 509 · 911
Toulouse	1176 · 179 · 1014 · 1182 · 249 · 829 · 1179 · 249 · 835 · 963 · 964 · 879 · 755 · 374 · 1074 · 684 · 354 · 570 · 1323 · 849 · 705 · 735 · 1102 · 725 · 547 · 378 · 737 · 679 · 471 · 980 · 498 · 679 · 258 · 841 · 1179 · 705 · 962
Tours	738 · 768 · 472 · 548 · 845 · 705 · 741 · 340 · 340 · 541 · 528 · 474 · 194 · 340 · 705 · 362 · 627 · 577 · 934 · 249 · 65 · 365 · 579 · 307 · 462 · 798 · 1152 · 131 · 914 · 492 · 116 · 232 · 845 · 340 · 677 · 156 · 593 · 593
Vlissingen	210 · 1223 · 86 · 216 · 1473 · 730 · 310 · 946 · 908 · 91 · 135 · 212 · 655 · 767 · 129 · 648 · 1184 · 897 · 354 · 463 · 570 · 209 · 386 · 330 · 827 · 798 · 1030 · 749 · 1295 · 109 · 496 · 367 · 1212 · 403 · 109 · 705 · 557 · 1041 · 601

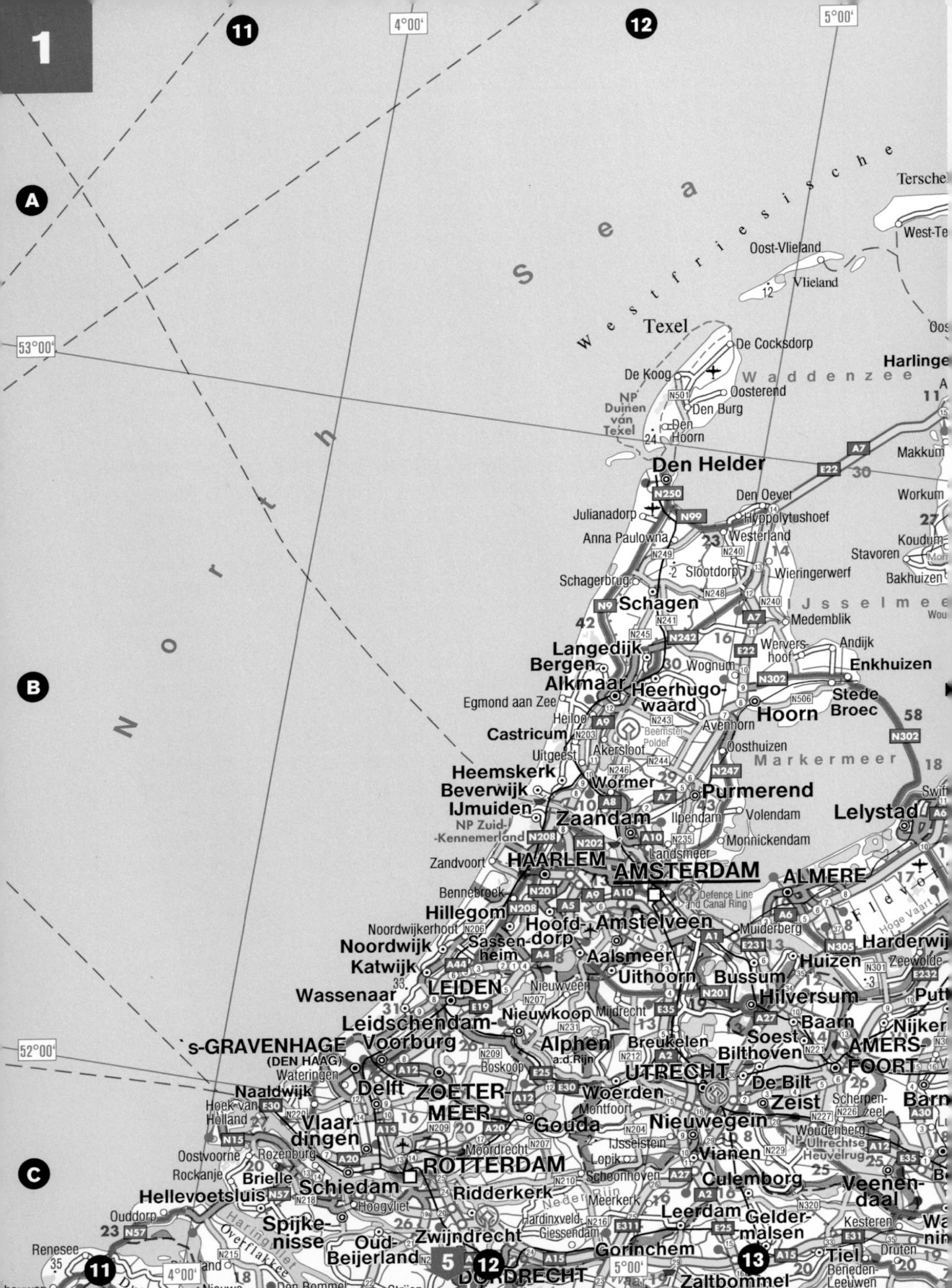

11
12
4°00'
5°00'
A
B
C
53°00'
52°00'
North Sea
Westfriesische
Terschelling
West-Terschelling
Oost-Vlieland
Vlieland
Texel
De Cocksdorp
De Koog
Oosterend
Waddenzee
NP Duinen van Texel
Den Burg
Den Hoorn
Harlingen
Makkum
Den Helder
Den Oever
Hippolytushoef
Workum
Julianadorp
Anna Paulowna
Westerland
Koudum
Stavoren
Slootdorp
Wieringerwerf
Bakhuizen
Schagerbrug
Schagen
IJsselmeer
Medemblik
Langedijk
Bergen
Wervershoof
Andijk
Enkhuizen
Wognum
Alkmaar
Heerhugowaard
Egmond aan Zee
Hoorn
Stede Broec
Heiloo
Castricum
Avenhorn
Beemster Polder
Uitgeest
Akersloot
Oosthuizen
Markermeer
Heemskerk
Wormer
Beverwijk
Purmerend
IJmuiden
Zaandam
Ilpendam
Volendam
Lelystad
NP Zuid-Kennemerland
Monnickendam
Landsmeer
Zandvoort
HAARLEM
AMSTERDAM
ALMERE
Bennebroek
Defence Line and Canal Ring
Flevoland
Hillegom
Hoofddorp
Amstelveen
Hoge Vaart
Noordwijkerhout
Muiderberg
Sassenheim
Harderwijk
Noordwijk
Aalsmeer
Huizen
Zeewolde
Katwijk
Nieuwveen
Uithoorn
Bussum
Wassenaar
LEIDEN
Hilversum
Putten
Nieuwkoop
Mijdrecht
Leidschendam-Voorburg
Baarn
Nijkerk
Soest
's-GRAVENHAGE (DEN HAAG)
Alphen a.d.Rijn
Breukelen
Bilthoven
AMERSFOORT
Boskoop
Wateringen
UTRECHT
De Bilt
Naaldwijk
Delft
ZOETERMEER
Woerden
Zeist
Barneveld
Scherpenzeel
Hoek van Holland
Montfoort
Vlaardingen
Gouda
Nieuwegein
Woudenberg
Moordrecht
IJsselstein
NP Utrechtse Heuvelrug
Oostvoorne
Rozenburg
ROTTERDAM
Lopik
Vianen
Rockanje
Brielle
Schiedam
Schoonhoven
Culemborg
Veenendaal
Hellevoetsluis
Ridderkerk
Nederrijn
Meerkerk
Ouddorp
Hoogvliet
Leerdam
Geldermalsen
Wageningen
Spijkenisse
Hardinxveld-Giessendam
Kesteren
Renesse
Oud-Beijerland
Zwijndrecht
Gorinchem
Tiel
Druten
Beneden-Leeuwen
Haringvliet
Overflakkee
DORDRECHT
Zaltbommel
Den Bommel
5
13

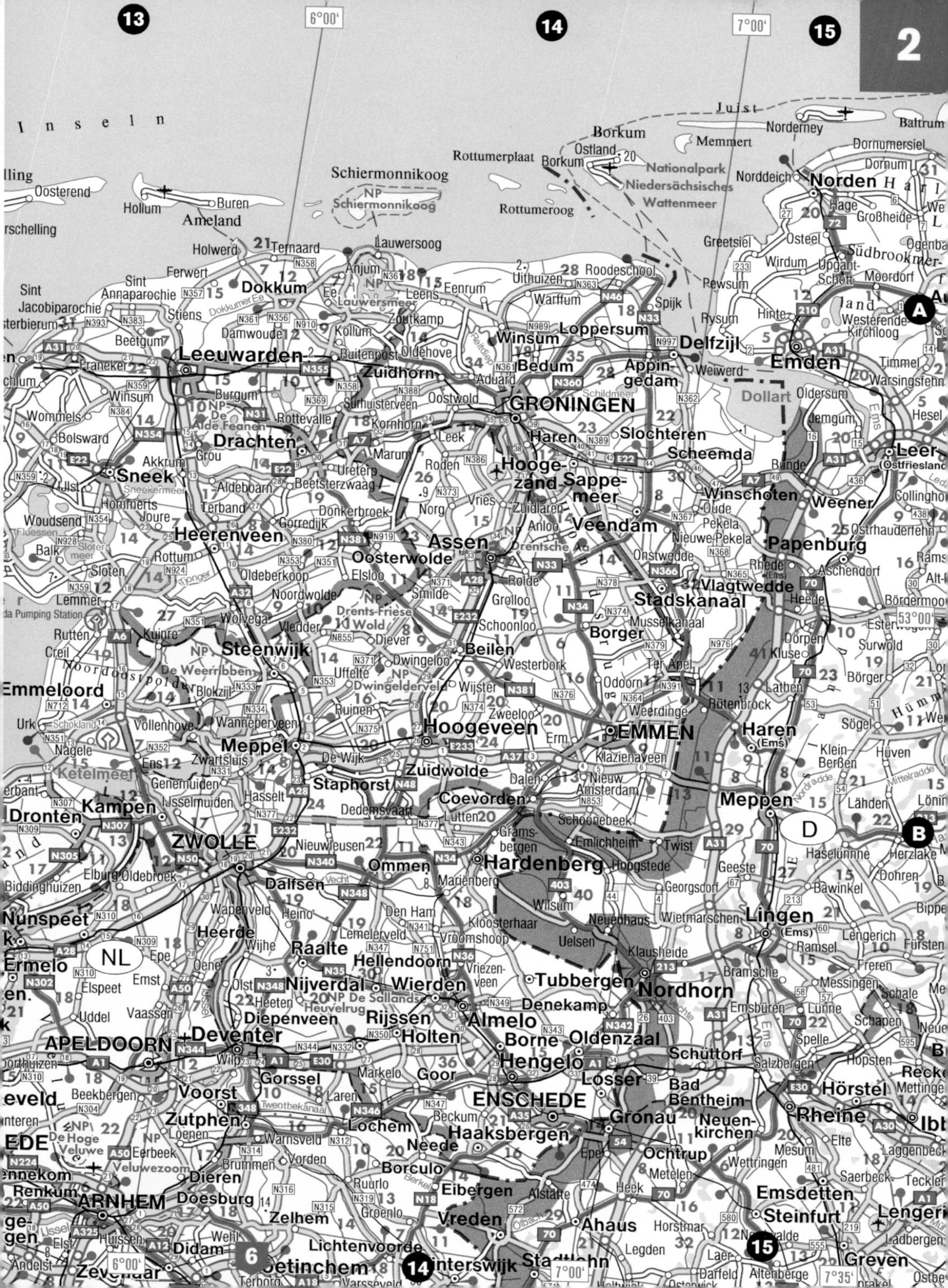

2
13
14
15
6°00'
7°00'
Inseln
Juist
Norderney
Baltrum
Borkum
Memmert
Rottumerplaat
Ostland
Nationalpark Niedersächsisches Wattenmeer
Schiermonnikoog
NP Schiermonnikoog
Rottumeroog
Oosterend
Hollum
Buren
Ameland
Terschelling
Norddeich
Norden
Dornumersiel
Dornum
Hage
Großheide
Greetsiel
Osteel
Südbrookmerland
Holwerd
Ternaard
Lauwersoog
Anjum
Roodeschool
Uithuizen
Pewsum
Wirdum
Upgant-Schott
Moordorf
Ferwert
Sint Annaparochie
Sint Jacobiparochie
Dokkum
Ee
Lauwersmeer
Leens
Eenrum
Warffum
Spijk
Rysum
Hinte
Westerende-Kirchloog
Stiens
Damwoude
Zoutkamp
Kollum
Winsum
Loppersum
Delfzijl
Emden
Beetgum
Leeuwarden
Franeker
Buitenpost
Oldehove
Bedum
Appingedam
Weiwerd
Timmel
Warsingsfehn
Zuidhorn
Aduard
Dollart
Oldersum
Winsum
Burgum
Surhuisterveen
Oostwold
GRONINGEN
Schildmeer
Jemgum
Hesel
Wommels
Bolsward
NP De Alde Feanen
Rottevalle
Kornhorn
Leek
Haren
Slochteren
Drachten
Grou
Akkrum
Marum
Roden
Hoogezand
Sappemeer
Scheemda
Bunde
Leer (Ostfriesland)
Sneek
IJlst
Sneekermeer
Aldeboarn
Ureterp
Beetsterzwaag
Vries
Winschoten
Weener
Hommerts
Joure
Terband
Donkerbroek
Norg
Zuidlaren
Oude Pekela
Collinghorst
Woudsend
Heerenveen
Gorredijk
Anloo
Veendam
Ostrhauderfehn
Balk
Rottum
Oosterwolde
Assen
Nieuwe Pekela
Papenburg
Sloten
Elsloo
Drentsche Aa
Onstwedde
Rhede (Ems)
Aschendorf
Lemmer
Oldeberkoop
Noordwolde
Smilde
Rolde
Vlagtwedde
Stadskanaal
Heede
Börgermoor
Wolvega
NP Drents-Friese Wold
Grolloo
Schoonloo
Musselkanaal
Borger
53°00'
Rutten
Kuinre
Vledder
Diever
Dörpen
Surwold
Creil
Steenwijk
Beilen
Westerbork
Kluse
Noordoostpolder
NP De Weerribben
Uffelte
Dwingeloo
NP Dwingelderveld
Ter Apel
Börger
Emmeloord
Blokzijl
Wijster
Odoorn
Lathen
Ruinen
Zweeloo
Weerdinge
Rütenbrock
Hümmling
Urk
Schokland
Vollenhove
Wanneperveen
Hoogeveen
Erm
EMMEN
Haren (Ems)
Sögel
Nagele
Meppel
Zwartsluis
De Wijk
Klazienaveen
Klein Berßen
Hüven
Ketelmeer
Ens
Genemuiden
Zuidwolde
Staphorst
Dalen
Nieuw Amsterdam
Dronten
Kampen
IJsselmuiden
Hasselt
Coevorden
Meppen
Lähden
Dedemsvaart
Lutten
Schoonebeek
D
ZWOLLE
Nieuwleusen
Gramsbergen
Emlichheim
Twist
Haselünne
Herzlake
Biddinghuizen
Elburg
Oldebroek
Ommen
Hardenberg
Hoogstede
Geeste
Dohren
Dalfsen
Vecht
Marienberg
Georgsdorf
Bawinkel
Nunspeet
Wapenveld
Heino
Den Ham
Wilsum
Neuenhaus
Wietmarschen
Lingen (Ems)
Heerde
Lemelerveld
Kloosterhaar
Uelsen
Lengerich
Ermelo
NL
Epe
Wijhe
Raalte
Vroomshoop
Klausheide
Ramsel
Fürstenau
Hellendoorn
Vriezenveen
Tubbergen
Bramsche
Freren
Elspeet
Emst
Olst
Nijverdal
Wierden
Nordhorn
Messingen
Uddel
Vaassen
Heeten
NP De Sallandse Heuvelrug
Denekamp
Emsbüren
Lünne
Schapen
Diepenveen
Rijssen
Almelo
Spelle
APELDOORN
Deventer
Wilp
Holten
Borne
Oldenzaal
Schüttorf
Salzbergen
Hopsten
Hengelo
Losser
Recke
Beekbergen
Voorst
Gorssel
Markelo
Goor
Laren
Bad Bentheim
Hörstel
Mettingen
ENSCHEDE
Rheine
Ibbenbüren
Zutphen
Lochem
Beckum
Gronau
Neuenkirchen
NP De Hoge Veluwe
Loenen
Warnsveld
Haaksbergen
Elte
EDE
Eerbeek
Neede
Epe
Ochtrup
Mesum
Laggenbeck
Veluwezoom
Brummen
Vorden
Borculo
Wettringen
Dieren
Ruurlo
Metelen
Saerbeck
Renkum
Eibergen
Alstätte
Heek
Emsdetten
ARNHEM
Doesburg
Groenlo
Vreden
Steinfurt
Lengerich
Zelhem
Ahaus
Horstmar
Nordwalde
Huissen
Wehl
Didam
Lichtenvoorde
Legden
Ladbergen
Elst
Zevenaar
Doetinchem
Winterswijk
Stadtlohn
Laer
Altenberge
Greven
Terborg
Varsseveld
Darfeld
7°35'
A
B

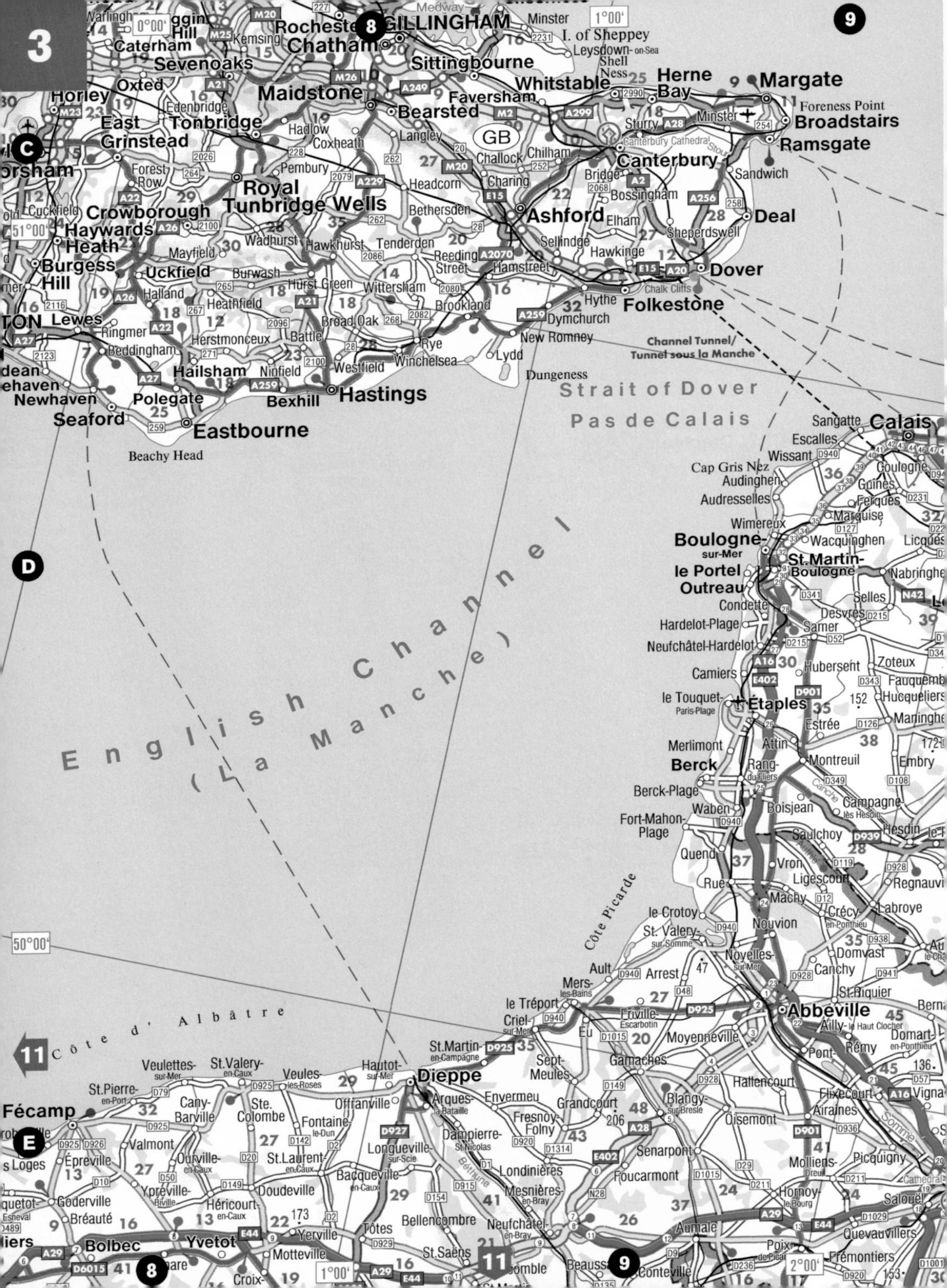

Rochester
GILLINGHAM
Chatham
Minster
I. of Sheppey
Leysdown-on-Sea
Sevenoaks
Caterham
Sittingbourne
Whitstable
Herne Bay
Margate
Foreness Point
Broadstairs
Ramsgate
Maidstone
Faversham
Bearsted
Oxted
Horley
Edenbridge
East Grinstead
Tonbridge
Canterbury
Sandwich
GB
Royal Tunbridge Wells
Ashford
Deal
Crowborough
Haywards Heath
Burgess Hill
Uckfield
Dover
Folkestone
Hythe
Dymchurch
New Romney
Lydd
Dungeness
Rye
Winchelsea
Hastings
Bexhill
Hailsham
Lewes
Newhaven
Seaford
Polegate
Eastbourne
Beachy Head
Channel Tunnel/
Tunnel sous la Manche
Strait of Dover
Pas de Calais
English Channel
(La Manche)
Calais
Sangatte
Wissant
Cap Gris Nez
Boulogne-sur-Mer
le Portel
Outreau
St.Martin-Boulogne
Hardelot-Plage
Neufchâtel-Hardelot
Camiers
le Touquet-Paris-Plage
Étaples
Merlimont
Berck
Berck-Plage
Montreuil
Fort-Mahon-Plage
Quend
Rue
Côte Picarde
le Crotoy
St. Valery-sur-Somme
Abbeville
Ault
Mers-les-Bains
le Tréport
Criel-sur-Mer
Côte d' Albâtre
Dieppe
Fécamp
St.Valery-en-Caux
Veulettes-sur-Mer
Veules-les-Roses
Yvetot
Bolbec
Neufchâtel-en-Bray
Aumale
Poix-de-Picardie
Blangy-sur-Bresle
Gamaches
Oisemont
Airaines
Picquigny
Hesdin
Crécy-en-Ponthieu
St.Riquier
51°00'
50°00'
0°00'
1°00'
2°00'

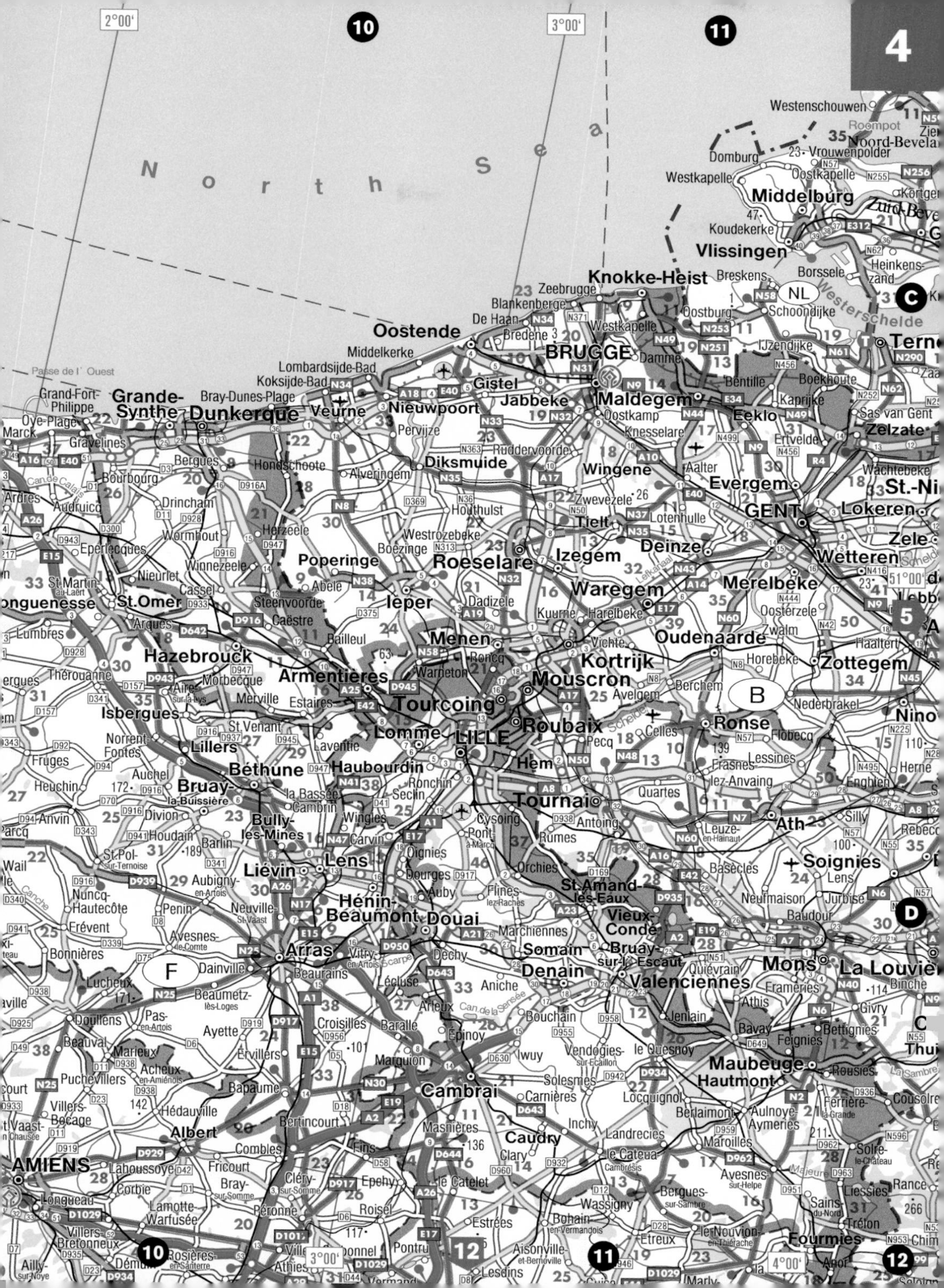
2°00'
3°00'
10
11
North Sea
Westenschouwen
Roompot
Noord-Beveland
Domburg
Vrouwenpolder
Westkapelle
Oostkapelle
Middelburg
Zuid-Beveland
Koudekerke
Vlissingen
Borssele
Heinkenszand
Knokke-Heist
Breskens
Zeebrugge
Blankenberge
NL
Westerschelde
De Haan
Oostburg
Schoondijke
Oostende
Bredene
Westkapelle
BRUGGE
Damme
IJzendijke
Terneuzen
Middelkerke
Lombardsijde-Bad
Koksijde-Bad
Gistel
Bentille
Boekhoute
Passe de l' Ouest
Grand-Fort-Philippe
Grande-Synthe
Bray-Dunes-Plage
Dunkerque
Veurne
Nieuwpoort
Jabbeke
Maldegem
Kaprijke
Oye-Plage
Marck
Gravelines
Pervijze
Oostkamp
Eeklo
Sas van Gent
Zelzate
Knesselare
Ertvelde
Ruddervoorde
Bergues
Hondschoote
Diksmuide
Wingene
Aalter
Evergem
Wachtebeke
Bourbourg
Alveringem
St.-Niklaas
Ardres
Audruicq
Drincham
Houthulst
Zwevezele
GENT
Lokeren
Tielt
Lotenhulle
Herzeele
Wormhout
Westrozebeke
Eperlecques
Boezinge
Deinze
Zele
Winnezeele
Poperinge
Roeselare
Izegem
Wetteren
St.Martin-au-Laert
Nieurlet
Cassel
Abele
Merelbeke
Longuenesse
St.Omer
Steenvoorde
Ieper
Dadizele
Waregem
Kuurne
Harelbeke
Oosterzele
Arques
Caëstre
Lumbres
Bailleul
Menen
Zwalm
Haaltert
Oudenaarde
Hazebrouck
Vichte
Roncq
Kortrijk
Horebeke
Zottegem
Thérouanne
Morbecque
Armentières
Warneton
Mouscron
Aire-sur-la-Lys
Merville
Estaires
Tourcoing
Avelgem
Berchem
B
Nederbrakel
Isbergues
Roubaix
Ninove
St.Venant
Lomme
LILLE
Pecq
Celles
Ronse
Flobecq
Norrent-Fontes
Lillers
Laventie
Hem
Lessines
Fruges
Béthune
Hauboudin
Frasnes-lez-Anvaing
Herne
Auchel
Bruay-la-Buissière
Ronchin
Enghien
Heuchin
Seclin
Quartes
la Bassée
Cambrin
Tournai
Anvin
Divion
Bully-les-Mines
Wingles
Cysoing
Antoing
Silly
Houdain
Carvin
Pont-à-Marcq
Ath
Leuze-en-Hainaut
Barlin
Rumes
St.Pol-sur-Ternoise
Oignies
Soignies
Wail
Liévin
Lens
Basècles
Dourges
Orchies
Lens
Aubigny-en-Artois
St.Amand-les-Eaux
Nuncq-Hautecôte
Auby
Flines-lez-Raches
Neufmaison
Jurbise
Penin
Hénin-Beaumont
Neuville-St.Vaast
Vieux-Condé
Baudour
Frévent
Douai
Avesnes-le-Comte
Marchiennes
Somain
Bruay-sur-l'Escaut
Bonnières
Arras
Vitry-en-Artois
Dechy
Mons
La Louvière
F
Dainville
Quiévrain
Denain
Valenciennes
Beaurains
Lucheux
Lécluse
Aniche
Frameries
Binche
Beaumetz-lès-Loges
Doullens
Pas-en-Artois
Croisilles
Arleux
Bouchain
Jenlain
Athis
Givry
Ayette
Baralle
Bavay
Beauval
Bettignies
Marieux
Ervillers
Epinoy
Vendegies-sur-Ecaillon
le Quesnoy
Feignies
Thuin
Acheux-en-Amiénois
Marquion
Iwuy
Maubeuge
Rousies
Puchevillers
Bapaume
Cambrai
Solesmes
Hautmont
Villers-Bocage
Carnières
Locquignol
Cousolre
Hédauville
Ferrière-la-Grande
Bertincourt
Masnières
Inchy
Berlaimont
Aulnoye-Aymeries
Albert
Caudry
Landrecies
Maroilles
Combles
Fins
Clary
le Cateau-Cambrésis
Solre-le-Château
AMIENS
Laboussoye
Fricourt
Cléry-sur-Somme
Epehy
le Catelet
Avesnes-sur-Helpe
Rance
Corbie
Bray-sur-Somme
Wassigny
Bergues-sur-Sambre
Liessies
Longueau
Lamotte-Warfusée
Péronne
Roisel
Estrées
Bohain-en-Vermandois
Sains-du-Nord
Trélon
Villers-Bretonneux
le Nouvion-en-Thiérache
Fourmies
Chimay
Etreux
Démuin
Rosières-en-Santerre
Aisonville-et-Bernoville
Anor
Ailly-sur-Noye
Athies
Lesdins
4°00'
12
5
C
D

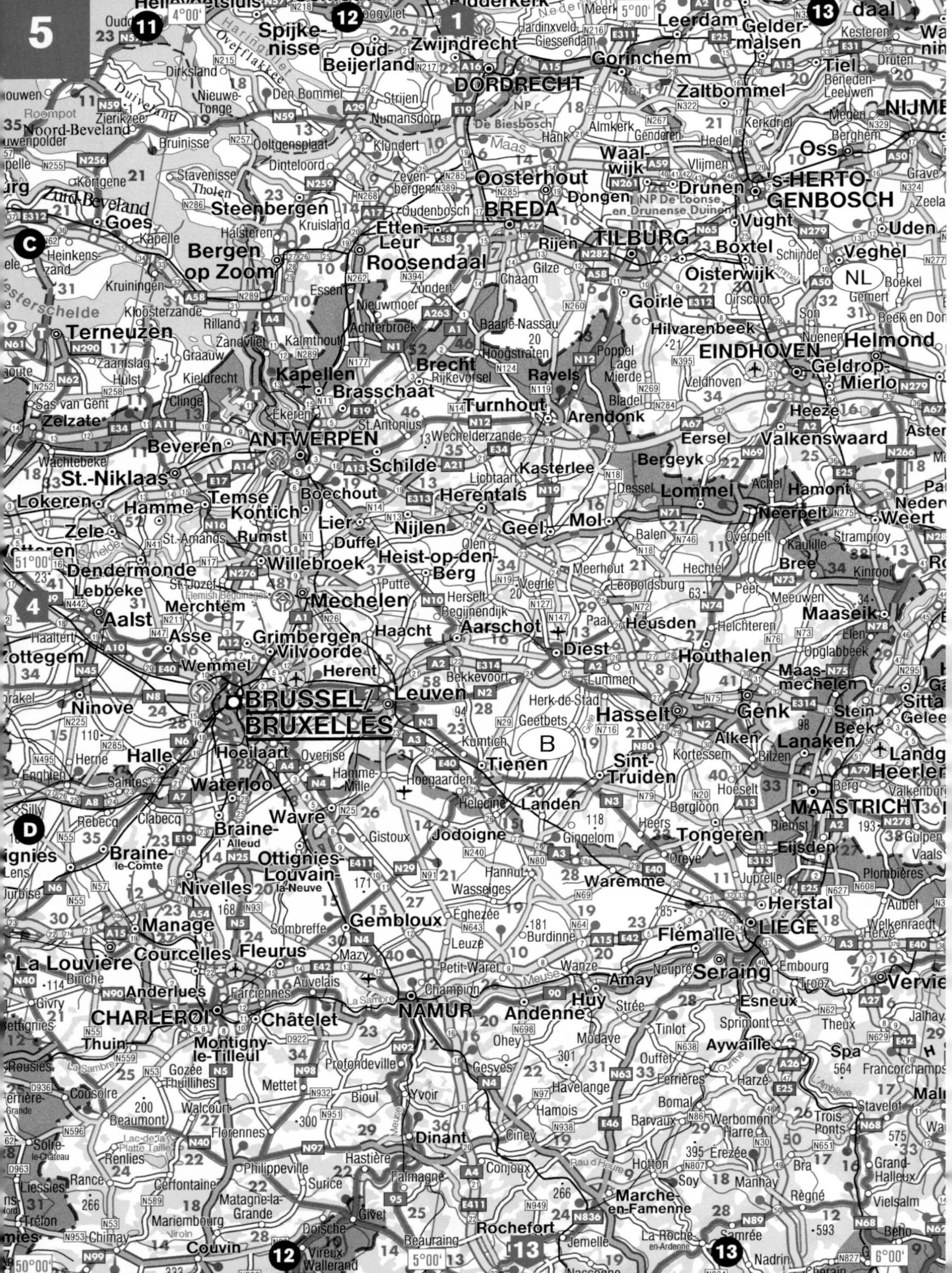
5
Hellevoetsluis
Schiedam
Ridderkerk
Spijkenisse
Oud-Beijerland
Zwijndrecht
DORDRECHT
Gorinchem
Leerdam
Geldermalsen
Tiel
Zaltbommel
Dirksland
Nieuwe-Tonge
Den Bommel
Strijen
Numansdorp
Zierikzee
Noord-Beveland
Bruinisse
Ooltgensplaat
Klundert
De Biesbosch
Maas
Almkerk
Waalwijk
Oss
Oosterhout
Dongen
Drunen
's-HERTOGENBOSCH
Dinteloord
Stavenisse
Tholen
Zevenbergen
Steenbergen
Oudenbosch
BREDA
Tilburg
Vught
Uden
Zuid-Beveland
Goes
Kapelle
Bergen op Zoom
Etten-Leur
Roosendaal
Rijen
Boxtel
Veghel
Heinkenszand
Gilze
Chaam
Oisterwijk
NL
Kruiningen
Essen
Zundert
Goirle
Oirschot
Westerschelde
Kloosterzande
Nieuwmoer
Rilland
Achterbroek
Baarle-Nassau
Hilvarenbeek
Terneuzen
Zandvliet
Kalmthout
Hoogstraten
Poppel
EINDHOVEN
Helmond
Zaamslag
Graauw
Kapellen
Brecht
Ravels
Geldrop-Mierlo
Hulst
Kieldrecht
Brasschaat
Rijkevorsel
Veldhoven
Sas van Gent
Zelzate
Ekeren
Turnhout
Arendonk
Heeze
Beveren
ANTWERPEN
Eersel
Valkenswaard
Schilde
Kasterlee
Bergeyk
St.-Niklaas
Lokeren
Hamme
Temse
Kontich
Boechout
Herentals
Lommel
Hamont
Weert
Neerpelt
Zele
Rumst
Lier
Nijlen
Geel
Mol
Dendermonde
Willebroek
Duffel
Heist-op-den-Berg
Bree
Lebbeke
Mechelen
Aalst
Merchtem
Maaseik
Asse
Grimbergen
Vilvoorde
Haacht
Aarschot
Diest
Heusden
Houthalen
Zottegem
Wemmel
Herent
Lummen
Maasmechelen
Ninove
BRUSSEL/BRUXELLES
Leuven
Hasselt
Genk
Sittard
Herk-de-Stad
Geetbets
Alken
Lanaken
Halle
Hoeilaart
Overijse
Tienen
B
Sint-Truiden
Bilzen
Waterloo
Hoegaarden
Landen
MAASTRICHT
Wavre
Braine-l'Alleud
Jodoigne
Tongeren
Braine-le-Comte
Ottignies-Louvain-la-Neuve
Hannut
Waremme
Nivelles
Wasseiges
Herstal
LIÈGE
Manage
Gembloux
Éghezée
Flémalle
Courcelles
Fleurus
Seraing
La Louvière
Binche
Anderlues
Huy
Amay
Verviers
CHARLEROI
Châtelet
NAMUR
Andenne
Esneux
Thuin
Montigny-le-Tilleul
Profondeville
Aywaille
Spa
Gesves
Havelange
Francorchamps
Mettet
Yvoir
Ferrières
Stavelot
Beaumont
Walcourt
Florennes
Dinant
Ciney
Trois-Ponts
Philippeville
Hastière
Conjoux
Hotton
Érezée
Vielsalm
Chimay
Couvin
Givet
Rochefort
Marche-en-Famenne
La Roche-en-Ardenne
Beauraing
Vireux-Wallerand
50°00'
5°00'
6°00'
4°00'
51°00'

Renkum ARNHEM Doesburg Zelhem Groenlo Eibergen Vreden Alstätte Ahaus Emsdetten Steinfurt
Ubbergen Huissen Elst Didam Wehl Lichtenvoorde Winterswijk Stadtlohn Legden Horstmar Nordwalde
Andelst Zevenaar Doetinchem Terborg Varsseveld Holtwick Osterwick Darfeld Laer Altenberge
NIJMEGEN Millingen aan de Rijn 's-Heerenberg Silvolde Ulft Dinxperlo Aalten Gescher Coesfeld Billerbeck Havixbeck Sprakel MÜNSTER
Wijchen Emmerich a. R. Elten Gendringen Bocholt Oeding Velen Borken Nottuln Roxel
Kranenburg Kleve Grieth Rees Rhede Merfeld Buldern Hiltrup Everswinkel
Cuijk Bedburg-Hau Kalkar Hamminkeln Dingden Heiden Gr. Reken Dülmen Senden Albersloh
Mill Gennep Goch Uedem Raesfeld Erle Lembeck Sythen Lüdinghausen Sendenhorst
Boxmeer Bergen Weeze Xanten Wesel Schermbeck Wulfen Haltern a. See Olfen Ascheberg Drensteinfurt Ahlen
Venray Kevelaer Sonsbeck Alpen Hünxe Voerde Dorsten Marl Recklinghausen Selm Bockum-Hövel Werne HAMM
Deurne Twisteden Issum Kamp-Lintfort Dinslaken Gladbeck Herten Waltrop Datteln Lünen
Horst Geldern Rheinberg BOTTROP Gelsenkirchen Castrop-Rauxel Bergkamen
Liessel Straelen Kerken Neukirchen-Vluyn MOERS OBERHAUSEN HERNE Kamen Bönen Unna
Wachtendonk DUISBURG MÜLHEIM AN DER RUHR ESSEN BOCHUM DORTMUND Wickede (Ruhr)
Maasbree Venlo Kempen Witten Fröndenberg
Helden Tegelen Grefrath KREFELD Heiligenhaus Hattingen Sprockhövel Schwerte Menden
Weert Nettetal Tönisvorst Meerbusch Velbert Gevelsberg Hagen Iserlohn Hemer
Swalmen Brüggen Dülken Viersen Ratingen Wülfrath Ennepetal Balve
Roermond Niederkrüchten Kaarst NEUSS DÜSSELDORF Schwelm Altena Neuenrade
Echt Wegberg MÖNCHENGLADBACH Korschenbroich Hilden Haan WUPPERTAL Radevormwald Lüdenscheid Werdohl
Wassenberg Erkelenz Langenfeld SOLINGEN REMSCHEID Halver Plettenberg
Heinsberg Hückelhoven Grevenbroich Dormagen Wermelskirchen Hückeswagen Wipperfürth Herscheid
Geilenkirchen Rommerskirchen LEVERKUSEN Marienheide Meinerzhagen Attendorn
Brunssum Linnich Titz Bedburg Pulheim Kürten Lindlar Gummersbach Bergneustadt Olpe
Übach-Palenberg Jülich Bergheim KÖLN BERGISCH-GLADBACH Engelskirchen Drolshagen
Kerkrade Alsdorf Aldenhoven Niederzier Elsdorf Frechen Overath Wiehl
Würselen Langerwehe Kerpen Hürth Rösrath Much Nümbrecht Wenden
AACHEN Eschweiler Stolberg Nörvenich Düren Brühl Wesseling Lohmar Seelscheid Freudenberg
Kelmis Kreuzau Erftstadt Bornheim Siegburg Neunkirchen Waldbröl Morsbach SIEGEN
Zweifall Vettweiß Weilerswist St. Augustin Hennef Windeck Mudersbach
Eupen Roetgen Nideggen Zülpich BONN Eitorf Uckerath Hamm (Sieg) Herdorf
Heimbach Euskirchen Bad Godesberg Königswinter Burbach
Simmerath Nationalpark Eifel Vlatten Mechernich Meckenheim Buchholz Asbach Altenkirchen (Westerwald) Daaden
Monschau Rheinbach Bad Honnef Neustadt (Wied) Hachenburg Marienberg
Schleiden Kall Bad Münstereifel Bad Neuenahr-Ahrweiler Remagen Linz am Rhein Puderbach Höchstenbach
Hellenthal Elsenborn Hollerath Tondorf Sinzig Herschbach Rennerod
Bütgenbach Bad Breisig Bad Hönningen Rengsdorf Dierdorf Selters Westerburg
Büllingen Blankenheim Dümpelfeld Niederzissen Neuwied Bansbach-Baumbach Dornburg
Amel Hallschlag Dahlem Müsch Hohe Acht 747 Kempenich Andernach Wallmerod
St. Vith Stadtkyll Wiesbaum Adenau Bendorf Wirges Hadamar
Auw bei Prüm Steffeln Kelberg Mendig Kottenheim Mülheim-Kärlich Montabaur
Bleialf Olzheim Hillesheim Hirten Mayen Neuhäusel Diez
Prüm Büdesheim Pelm Dockweiler Monreal Kaisersesch Polch Lahnstein KOBLENZ Bad Ems Limburg an der Lahn

Westerwald Ebbegebirge Lenneberglande Münsterland Hohe Eifel

52°00' 51°00' 6°00' 7°00' 8°00'

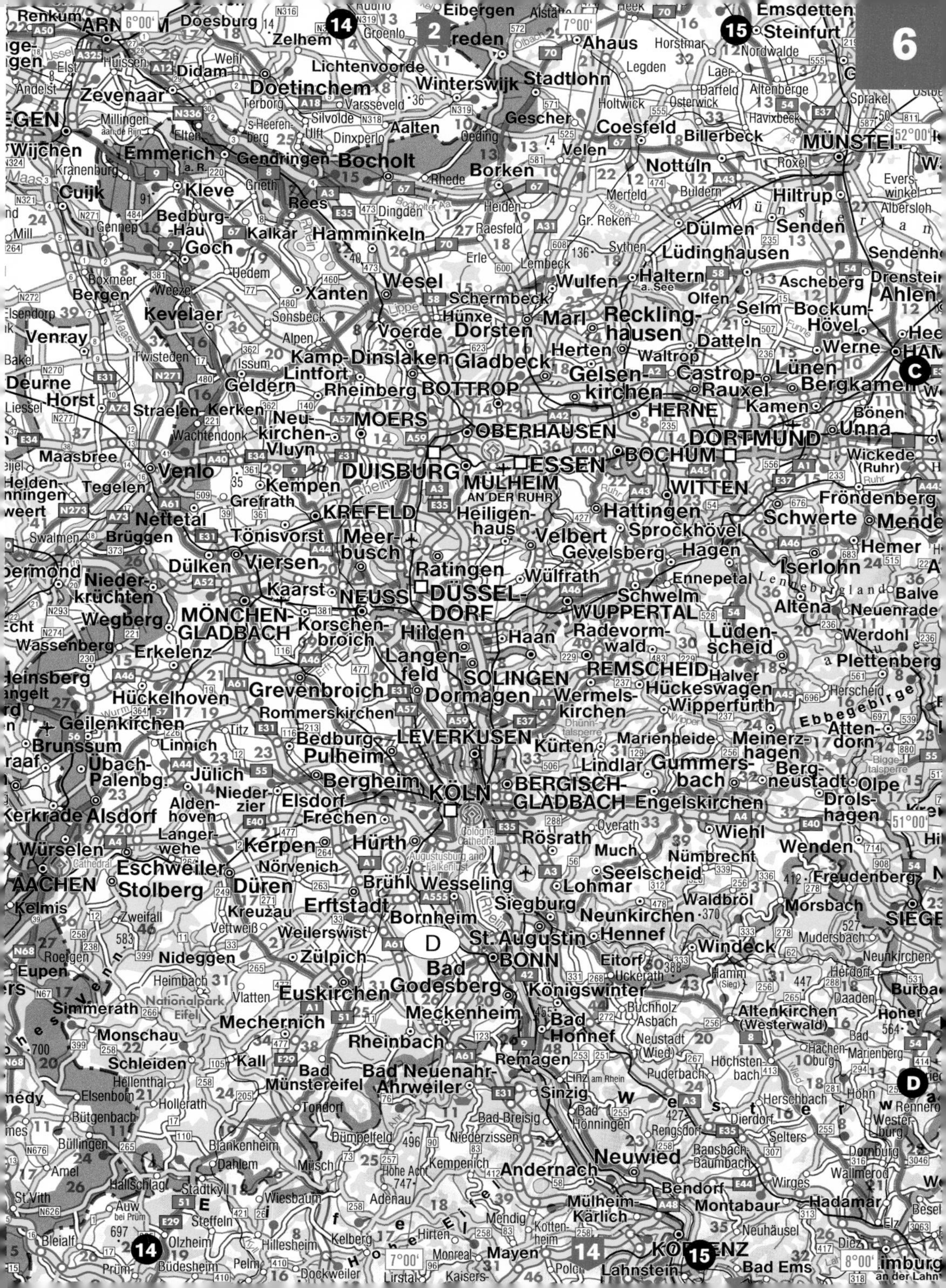

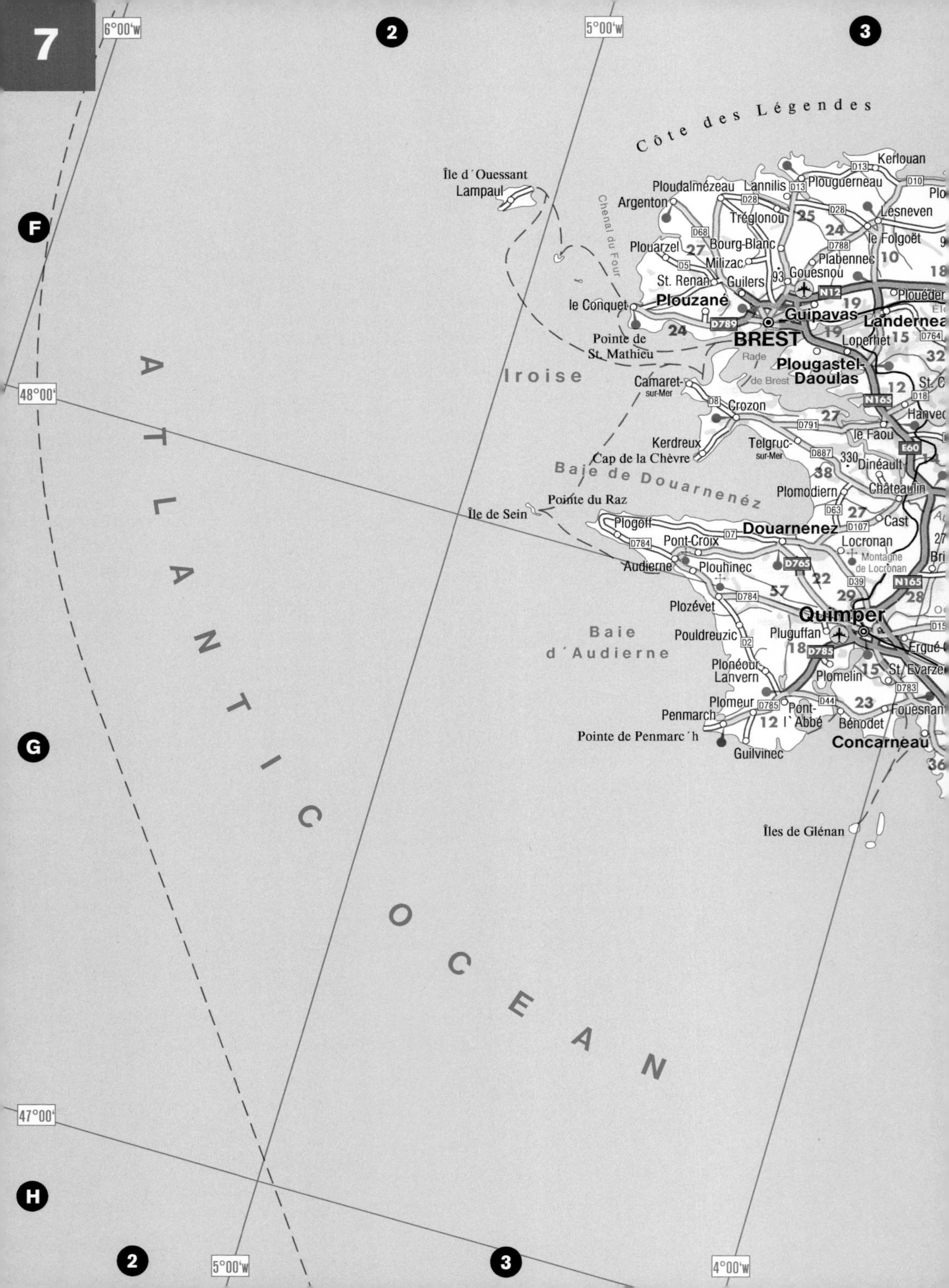

6°00'w   **2**   5°00'w   **3**

F

Côte des Légendes

Kerlouan
Ploudalmézeau   Lannilis   Plouguerneau
D13
D10
Île d´Ouessant   Chenal du Four
Lampaul
D28   Lesneven
Argenton   Tréglonou   **25**   **24**   le Folgoët
D68
Plouarzel   **27**   Bourg-Blanc   D788   Plabennec   **10**   **18**
Milizac
D5
St. Renan   Guilers   93   Gouesnou
le Conquet   **Plouzané**   N12   **19**   Plouéder
Guipavas
24   D789   **19**   Lopernet   **15**   D764
Pointe de   **BREST**   **Landernea**
St. Mathieu
Rade   **Plougastel-**   **32**
Iroise   de Brest   **Daoulas**
Camaret-   **12**   St. C
sur-Mer   D8   N165   D18
Crozon   D791   **27**   Hanved
le Faou
Kerdreux   Telgruc-   D887   330   Dinéault   E60
Cap de la Chèvre   sur-Mer   **38**   Châteaulin
Plomodiern   D63
Baie de Douarnenéz   **27**   Cast
Pointe du Raz   D107
Île de Sein   Plogoff   **Douarnenez**   Locronan   27
D7   Montagne   Bri
Pont-Croix   de Locronan
D784   **29**   **28**
Audierne   Plouhinec   **22**   D39   N165
57   D765
Plozévet   **Quimper**   D15
D784
Baie   Pouldreuzic   Pluguffan
d´Audierne   **18**   D785   Ergué-   St. Évarze
Plonéour-   D783   **15**
Lanvern   Plomelin
D44   **23**   Fouesnan
Penmarch   Plomeur   Pont-   D785   **12**   l´Abbé   Bénodet
Pointe de Penmarc´h   Guilvinec   **Concarneau**
36

G   A T L A N T I C

Îles de Glénan

O C E A N

48°00'

47°00'

H

2   5°00'w   **3**   4°00'w

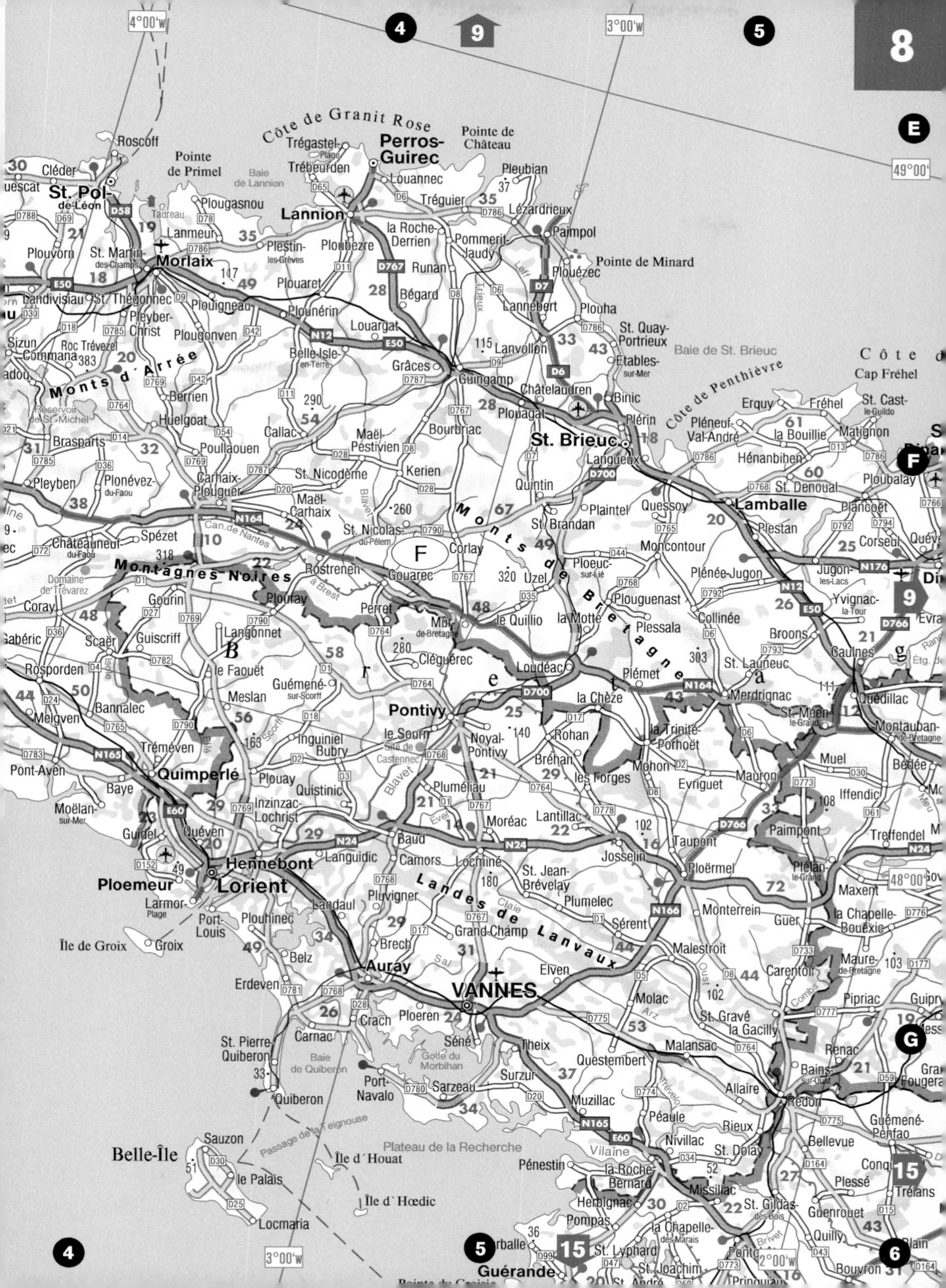
8
4
9
5
4°00'W
3°00'W
49°00'
48°00'
2°00'W
E
F
G
Côte de Granit Rose
Roscoff
Pointe de Primel
Baie de Lannion
Trégastel-Plage
Trébeurden
Perros-Guirec
Pointe de Château
Pleubian
Louannec
Tréguier
Lézardrieux
Paimpol
Pointe de Minard
Cléder
St. Pol-de-Léon
Plougasnou
Lannion
Taureau
Lanmeur
Plestin-les-Grèves
Ploubezre
la Roche-Derrien
Pommerit-Jaudy
Plouézec
Plouvorn
St. Martin-des-Champs
Morlaix
Runan
Plouaret
Bégard
Lannebert
Plouha
Landivisiau
St. Thégonnec
Plouigneau
Plounérin
Pleyber-Christ
Plougonven
Louargat
St. Quay-Portrieux
Sizun
Roc Trévezel
Commana
Belle-Isle-en-Terre
Lanvollon
Étables-sur-Mer
Baie de St. Brieuc
Côte de Penthièvre
Côte d
Cap Fréhel
Monts d'Arrée
Grâces
Guingamp
Châtelaudren
Binic
Berrien
Erquy
Fréhel
St. Cast-le-Guildo
Réservoir de St.-Michel
Huelgoat
Callac
Bourbriac
Plouagat
Plérin
Pléneuf-Val-André
la Bouillie
Matignon
Brasparts
Poullaouen
Maël-Pestivien
St. Brieuc
Langueux
Hénanbihen
Carhaix-Plouguer
St. Nicodème
Kerien
Quintin
Ploubalay
Pleyben
Plonévez-du-Faou
St. Denoual
Maël-Carhaix
Plaintel
Quessoy
Lamballe
Plancoët
Can. de Nantes
St. Nicolas-du-Pélem
Monts de Bretagne
St. Brandan
Plestan
Corseul
Châteauneuf-du-Faou
Spézet
Corlay
Moncontour
Montagnes Noires
Rostrenen
Gouarec
Ploeuc-sur-Lié
Uzel
Plénée-Jugon
Jugon-les-Lacs
Domaine de Trévarez
Gourin
Plouray
Perret
Mûr-de-Bretagne
le Quillio
la Motte
Plouguenast
Collinée
Yvignac-la-Tour
Coray
Langonnet
Plessala
Broons
Gabéric
Scaër
Guiscriff
Caulnes
Cléguérec
Loudéac
St. Launeuc
Rosporden
le Faouët
Guémené-sur-Scorff
Plémet
Meslan
Pontivy
la Chèze
Merdrignac
Quédillac
Bannalec
Melgven
St.-Méen-le-Grand
Le Sourn
Noyal-Pontivy
Rohan
la Trinité-Porhoët
Montauban-de-Bretagne
Tréméven
Inguiniel
Bubry
Site de Castennec
Pont-Aven
Quimperlé
Plouay
Quistinic
Pluméliau
Bréhan
les Forges
Mohon
Evriguet
Mauron
Muel
Bédée
Baye
Moëlan-sur-Mer
Inzinzac-Lochrist
Moréac
Lantillac
Iffendic
Guidel
Quéven
Baud
Paimpont
Treffendel
Josselin
Taupont
Hennebont
Languidic
Camors
Locminé
Ploërmel
Plélan-le-Grand
Ploemeur
Lorient
Larmor-Plage
St. Jean-Brévelay
Maxent
Landes de Lanvaux
Pluvigner
Plumelec
Monterrein
la Chapelle-Bouëxic
Port-Louis
Plouhinec
Landaul
Sérent
Guer
Île de Groix
Groix
Grand-Champ
Brech
Malestroit
Belz
Maure-de-Bretagne
Auray
Elven
Carentoir
Erdeven
VANNES
Molac
Pipriac
Carnac
Crach
Ploeren
St. Gravé
la Gacilly
St. Pierre-Quiberon
Baie de Quiberon
Séné
Golfe du Morbihan
Theix
Malansac
Renac
Questembert
Bains-sur-Oust
Port-Navalo
Sarzeau
Surzur
Allaire
Quiberon
Muzillac
Redon
Péaule
Passage de la Teignouse
Rieux
Guémené-Penfao
Sauzon
Plateau de la Recherche
Vilaine
Nivillac
St. Dolay
Bellevue
Belle-Île
Île d'Houat
Pénestin
la Roche-Bernard
le Palais
Herbignac
Missillac
Plessé
St. Gildas-des-Bois
Guenrouet
Île d'Hœdic
Pompas
la Chapelle-des-Marais
Locmaria
St. Lyphard
St. Joachim
Bouvron
Guérande
E50
N12
N164
N165
E60
N24
N166
N176
D700
D766
D767
D7
D6
D58

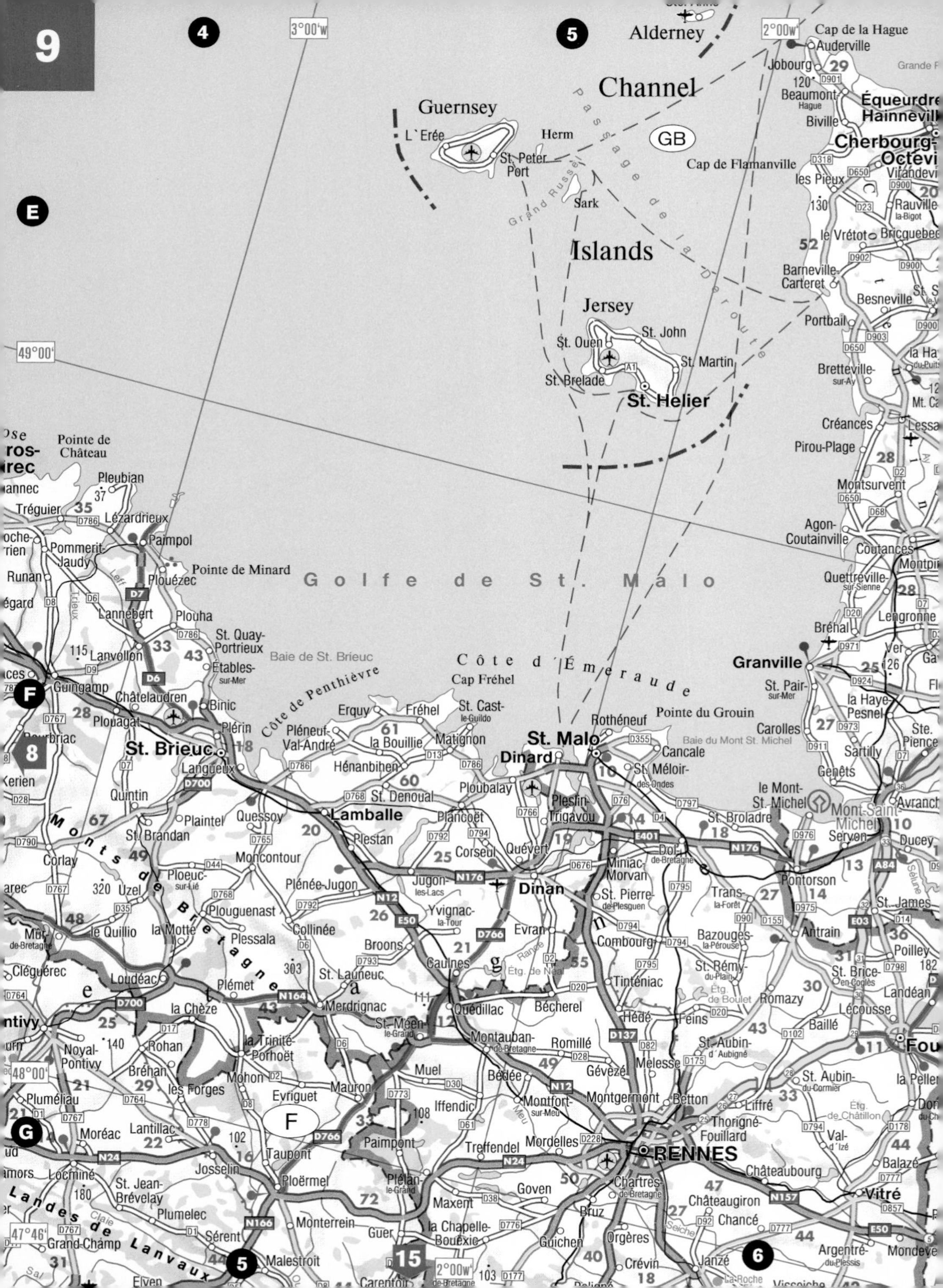

9
4
5
3°00'W
2°00'W
Alderney
Cap de la Hague
Auderville
Jobourg
Beaumont-Hague
Biville
Équeurdre
Hainneville
Cherbourg-Octeville
Grande
Channel
Islands
Guernsey
L'Erée
Herm
St. Peter Port
Sark
Grand Russel
Passage de la Déroute
GB
Cap de Flamanville
les Pieux
Virandeville
Rauville-la-Bigot
le Vrétot
Bricquebec
Barneville-Carteret
Besneville
Portbail
Jersey
St. John
St. Ouen
St. Martin
St. Brelade
St. Helier
Bretteville-sur-Ay
la Haye-du-Puits
Mt. Ca
Créances
Lessay
Pirou-Plage
Montsurvent
Agon-Coutainville
Coutances
Montpinchon
Quettreville-sur-Sienne
Lengronne
Bréhal
Granville
Ver
Gavray
St. Pair-sur-Mer
la Haye-Pesnel
Carolles
Sartilly
Genêts
Ste. Pience
E
49°00'
Pointe de Château
Pleubian
Tréguier
Lézardrieux
Paimpol
Pommerit-Jaudy
Pointe de Minard
Plouézec
Runan
Lannebert
Plouha
St. Quay-Portrieux
Lanvollon
Étables-sur-Mer
Baie de St. Brieuc
Golfe de St. Malo
Côte d'Émeraude
Cap Fréhel
Côte de Penthièvre
Guingamp
Châtelaudren
Binic
Plouagat
Plérin
St. Brieuc
Langueux
Erquy
Fréhel
St. Cast-le-Guildo
Pléneuf-Val-André
la Bouillie
Matignon
Hénanbihen
St. Malo
Rothéneuf
Pointe du Grouin
Cancale
Baie du Mont St. Michel
Dinard
St. Méloir-des-Ondes
le Mont-St.-Michel
Mont-Saint-Michel
Avranches
F
8
Quintin
St. Denoual
Ploubalay
Pleslin-Trigavou
Lamballe
Plancoët
Plaintel
Quessoy
Monts de Bretagne
St. Brandan
Plestan
Corseul
Quévert
Dol-de-Bretagne
Miniac-Morvan
St. Broladre
Servon
Ducey
Pontorson
Corlay
Moncontour
Ploeuc-sur-Lié
Plénée-Jugon
Jugon-les-Lacs
Dinan
St. Pierre-de-Plesguen
Trans-la-Forêt
St. James
Uzel
Plouguenast
Yvignac-la-Tour
Combourg
Bazouges-la-Pérouse
Antrain
Mûr-de-Bretagne
le Quillio
la Motte
Plessala
Collinée
Broons
Evran
Poilley
Cléguérec
Loudéac
Plémet
St. Launeuc
Caulnes
Étg. de Néal
Tinténiac
St. Rémy-du-Plain
St. Brice-en-Coglès
Landéan
Étg. de Boulet
Romazy
la Chèze
Merdrignac
Quédillac
Bécherel
Lécousse
Pontivy
St. Méen-le-Grand
Hédé
Feins
Baillé
Noyal-Pontivy
Rohan
la Trinité-Porhoët
Montauban-de-Bretagne
Romillé
St. Aubin-d'Aubigné
Fougères
48°00'
Bréhan
Mohon
Muel
Bédée
Gévezé
Melesse
St. Aubin-du-Cormier
la Pellerine
Pluméliau
les Forges
Evriguet
Mauron
Iffendic
Montfort-sur-Meu
Montgermont
Betton
Liffré
Étg. de Châtillon
Moréac
Lantillac
Paimpont
Treffendel
Mordelles
Thorigné-Fouillard
Val-d'Izé
G
Taupont
RENNES
Balazé
Locminé
Josselin
Ploërmel
Plélan-le-Grand
Châteaubourg
Vitré
St. Jean-Brévelay
Goven
Chartres-de-Bretagne
Châteaugiron
Landes de Lanvaux
Plumelec
Maxent
Bruz
Chancé
Monterrein
la Chapelle-Bouëxic
Seiche
Grand-Champ
Sérent
Guer
Guichen
Orgères
Argentré-du-Plessis
Mondevert
47°46'
Malestroit
15
Crévin
Janzé
6
Elven
Carentoir
la Roche

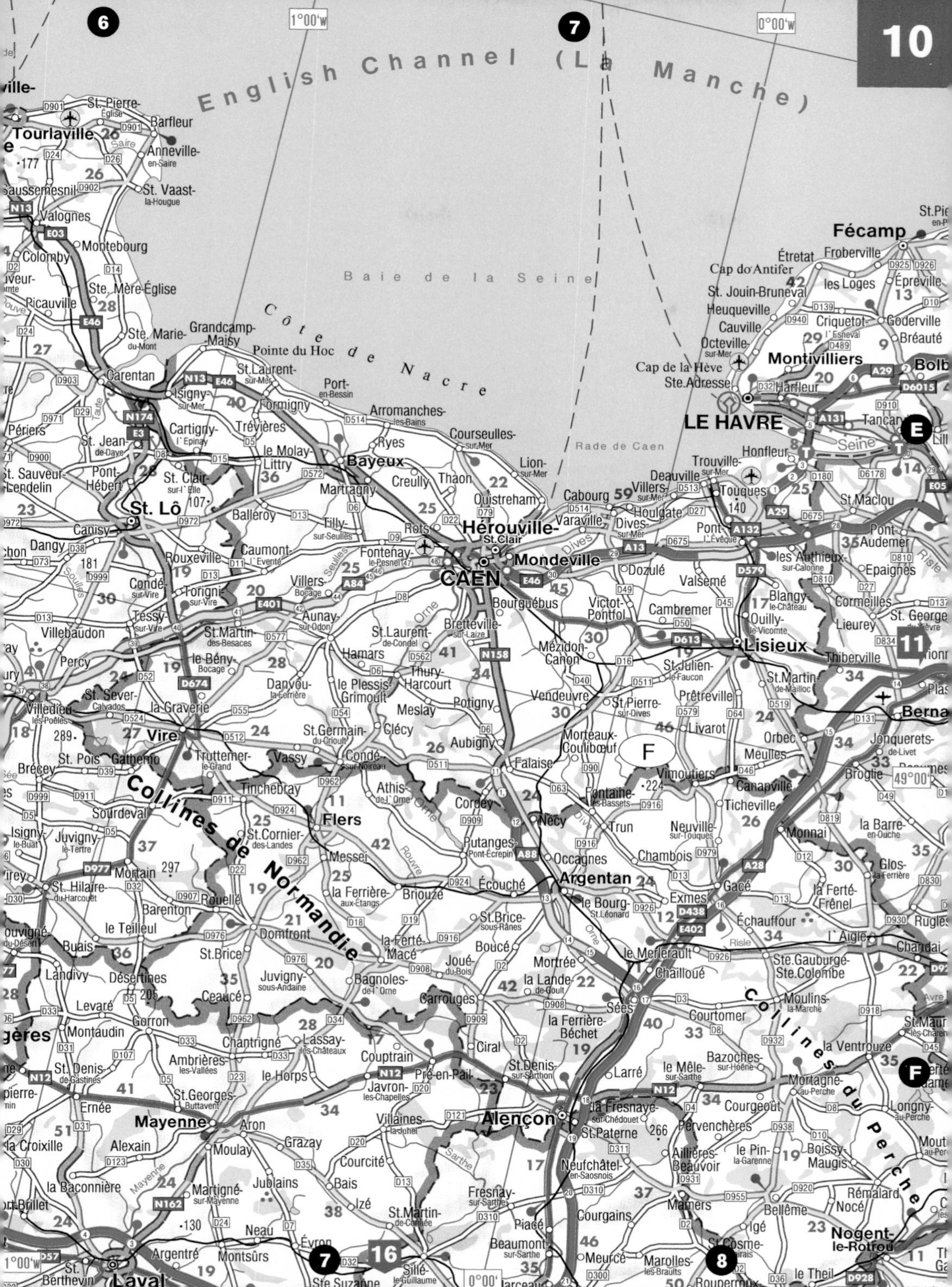

10
6
7
1°00'w
0°00'w
English Channel (La Manche)
Tourlaville
St. Pierre-Église
Barfleur
Anneville-en-Saire
Saussemesnil
St. Vaast-la-Hougue
Valognes
Montebourg
Colomby
Picauville
Ste. Mère-Église
Ste. Marie-du-Mont
Carentan
Grandcamp-Maisy
Pointe du Hoc
St. Laurent-sur-Mer
Baie de la Seine
Côte de Nacre
Port-en-Bessin
Arromanches-les-Bains
Isigny-sur-Mer
Formigny
Trévières
Cartigny-l'Epinay
Périers
St. Jean-de-Daye
Courseulles-sur-Mer
Ryes
Bayeux
Le Molay-Littry
Lion-sur-Mer
Rade de Caen
Creully
Thaon
Ouistreham
St. Sauveur-Lendelin
Pont-Hébert
St. Clair-sur-l'Elle
St. Lô
Martragny
Balleroy
Tilly-sur-Seulles
Hérouville-St.Clair
Canisy
Dangy
Rots
Caumont-l'Eventé
Rouxeville
Fontenay-le-Pesnel
CAEN
Mondeville
Condé-sur-Vire
Torigni-sur-Vire
Villers-Bocage
Aunay-sur-Odon
Bourguébus
Tessy-sur-Vire
Villebaudon
St. Martin-des-Besaces
St. Laurent-de-Condel
Bretteville-sur-Laize
Percy
Le Bény-Bocage
Hamars
Thury-Harcourt
Danvou-la-Ferrière
Le Plessis-Grimoult
Potigny
Meslay
Villedieu-les-Poêles
St. Sever-Calvados
la Graverie
Vire
St. Germain-du-Crioult
Clécy
Aubigny
St. Pois
Gathemo
Truttemer-le-Grand
Vassy
Condé-sur-Noireau
Falaise
Brécey
Tinchebray
Athis-de-l'Orne
Sourdeval
Collines de Normandie
Flers
Cordey
Nécy
Isigny-le-Buat
Juvigny-le-Tertre
St. Cornier-des-Landes
Putanges-Pont-Écrepin
Mortain
Messei
Occagnes
Argentan
St. Hilaire-du-Harcouët
la Ferrière-aux-Étangs
Briouze
Écouché
Barenton
Rouellé
St. Brice-sous-Rânes
le Teilleul
Domfront
la Ferté-Macé
Buais
St. Brice
Bouce
Joué-du-Bois
Landivy
Désertines
Juvigny-sous-Andaine
Bagnoles-de-l'Orne
Carrouges
Ceaucé
Levaré
Gorron
Montaudin
Chantrigné
Lassay-les-Châteaux
Ciral
Ambrières-les-Vallées
Couptrain
St. Denis-de-Gastines
le Horps
Pré-en-Pail
Javron-les-Chapelles
Ernée
St. Georges-Buttavent
Mayenne
Aron
Villaines-la-Juhel
Alençon
Alexain
Moulay
Grazay
Courcité
la Croixille
la Baconnière
Martigné-sur-Mayenne
Jublains
Bais
Izé
St. Martin-de-Connée
Fresnay-sur-Sarthe
Neau
Évron
Argentré
Montsûrs
St. Berthevin
Laval
Ste Suzanne
Sillé-le-Guillaume
Beaumont-sur-Sarthe
Piacé
16
Fécamp
Étretat
Froberville
Cap d'Antifer
les Loges
Épreville
St. Jouin-Bruneval
Heuqueville
Criquetot-l'Esneval
Goderville
Bréauté
Cauville
Octeville-sur-Mer
Montivilliers
Cap de la Hève
Ste.Adresse
Harfleur
LE HAVRE
Tancarville
Honfleur
Seine
Trouville-sur-Mer
Deauville
Villers-sur-Mer
Cabourg
Houlgate
Touques
Varaville
Dives-sur-Mer
Pont-l'Évêque
St. Maclou
Pont-Audemer
les Authieux-sur-Calonne
Epaignes
Dozulé
Valsemé
Blangy-le-Château
Cormeilles
Victot-Pontfol
Cambremer
Quilly-le-Vicomte
Lieurey
St. Georges-du-Vièvre
Mézidon-Canon
Lisieux
Thiberville
St. Julien-le-Faucon
St. Martin-de-Mailloc
Vendeuvre
St. Pierre-sur-Dives
Prêtreville
Livarot
Orbec
Jonquerets-de-Livet
Morteaux-Coulibœuf
Meulles
Vimoutiers
Canapville
Broglie
49°00'
Fontaine-les-Bassets
Ticheville
Trun
Neuville-sur-Touques
Monnai
la Barre-en-Ouche
Chambois
Glos-la-Ferrière
le Bourg-St.Léonard
Exmes
Gacé
la Ferté-Frênel
Échauffour
Rugles
l'Aigle
Chandai
le Merlerault
Chailloué
Ste. Gauburge-Ste. Colombe
Mortrée
la Lande-de-Goult
Sées
Moulins-la-Marche
Collines du Perche
la Ferrière-Béchet
Courtomer
Bazoches-sur-Hoëne
la Ventrouze
St. Denis-sur-Sarthon
Larré
le Mêle-sur-Sarthe
Mortagne-au-Perche
la Fresnaye-sur-Chédouet
Courgeout
Pervenchères
Longny-au-Perche
St.Paterne
Aillières-Beauvoir
le Pin-la-Garenne
Boissy-Maugis
Neufchâtel-en-Saosnois
Mamers
Rémalard
Noce
Courgains
Bellême
Igé
Nogent-le-Rotrou
St. Cosme-en-Vairais
Meurcé
Marolles-les-Braults
le Theil
Bernay
E
F
8
11

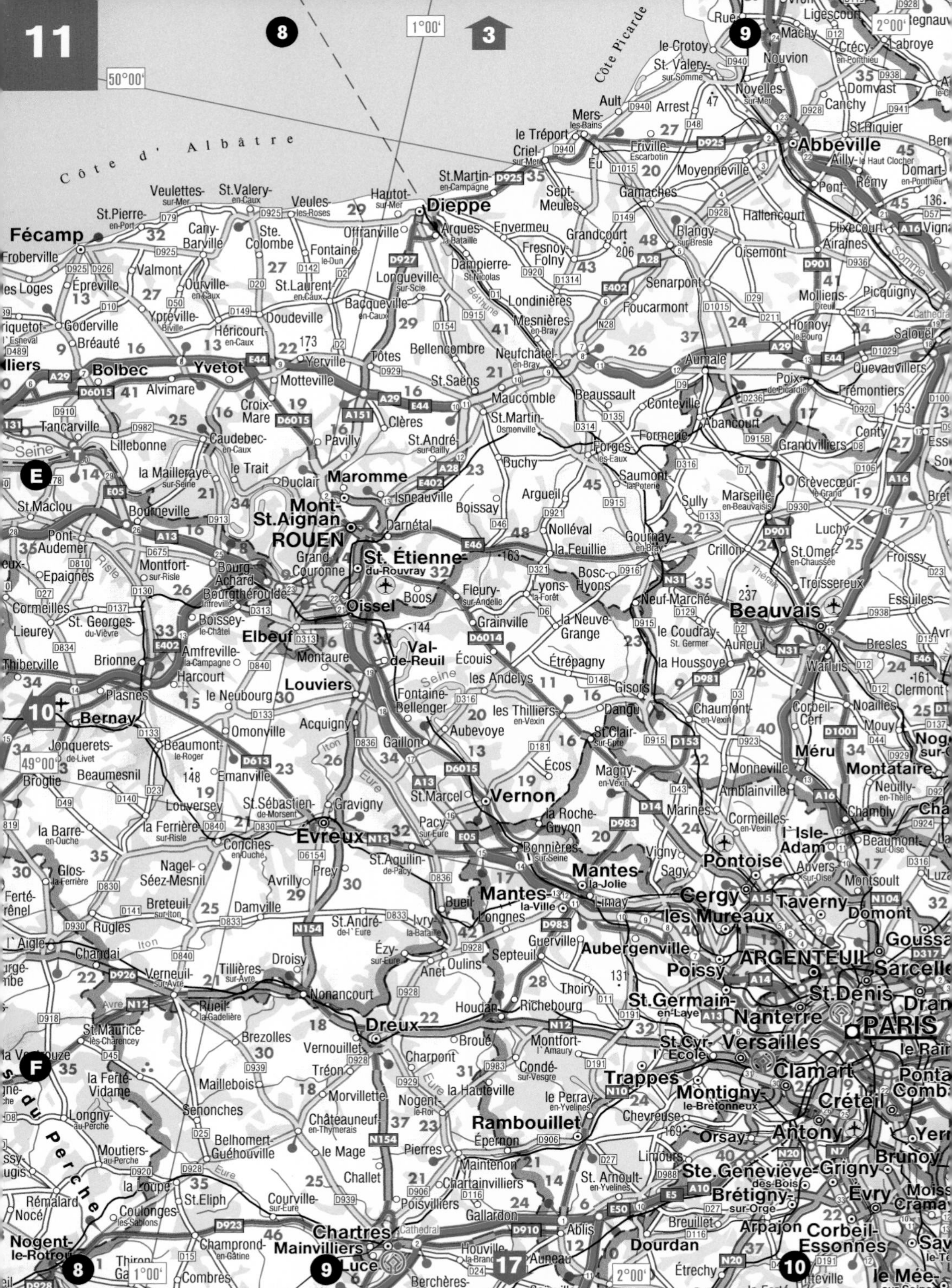

11
8
1°00'
3
50°00'
Côte Picarde
Côte d' Albâtre
9
2°00'
Rue
Ligescourt
Machy
Crécy-en-Ponthieu
Labroye
le Crotoy
Nouvion
St. Valery-sur-Somme
Noyelles-sur-Mer
Domvast
Canchy
Ault
Arrest
Mers-les-Bains
St. Riquier
le Tréport
Criel-sur-Mer
Friville-Escarbotin
Abbeville
Eu
Ailly-le Haut Clocher
Domart-en-Ponthieu
Moyenneville
Rémy
St. Martin-en-Campagne
Sept-Meules
Gamaches
Pont-
Veulettes-sur-Mer
St. Valery-en-Caux
Veules-les-Roses
Hautot-sur-Mer
Dieppe
Hallencourt
Flixecourt
St. Pierre-en-Port
Cany-Barville
Ste. Colombe
Offranville
Arques-la-Bataille
Envermeu
Grandcourt
Blangy-sur-Bresle
Airaines
Fécamp
Froberville
Fontaine-le-Dun
Fresnoy-Folny
Oisemont
Valmont
Dampierre-St. Nicolas
Épreville
Longueville-sur-Scie
Senarpont
Les Loges
Ourville-en-Caux
St. Laurent-en-Caux
Molliens-Dreuil
Picquigny
Londinières
Foucarmont
Ypréville-Biville
Bacqueville-en-Caux
Doudeville
Mesnières-en-Bray
Goderville
Héricourt-en-Caux
Hornoy-le-Bourg
Bréauté
Saloue
Yerville
Tôtes
Bellencombre
Neufchâtel-en-Bray
Aumale
Bolbec
Yvetot
Quevauvillers
Motteville
St. Saëns
Poix-de-Picardie
Alvimare
Maucomble
Beaussault
Conteville
Frémontiers
Croix-Mare
Tancarville
Clères
St. Martin-Osmonville
Abancourt
Lillebonne
Caudebec-en-Caux
Pavilly
St. André-sur-Cailly
Formerie
Conty
Seine
Forges-les-Eaux
Grandvilliers
Buchy
E
la Mailleraye-sur-Seine
le Trait
Duclair
Maromme
Saumont-la-Poterie
Crèvecœur-le-Grand
Isneauville
Argueil
Sully
Marseille-en-Beauvaisis
St. Maclou
Bourneville
Mont-St. Aignan
Boissay
Darnétal
Nolléval
Luchy
Pont-Audemer
ROUEN
Gournay-en-Bray
Crillon
St. Omer-en-Chaussée
Froissy
Epaignes
Montfort-sur-Risle
Grand-Couronne
St. Étienne-du-Rouvray
la Feuillie
Bourg-Achard
Bosc-Hyons
Cormeilles
Bourgthéroulde-Infreville
Fleury-sur-Andelle
Lyons-la-Forêt
Oissel
Boos
Neuf-Marché
Troissereux
Essuiles
St. Georges-du-Vièvre
Boissey-le-Châtel
Beauvais
Lieurey
Elbeuf
Grainville
la Neuve-Grange
le Coudray-St. Germer
Bresles
Amfreville-la-Campagne
Montaure
Val-de-Reuil
Écouis
Auneuil
Brionne
Harcourt
Étrépagny
la Houssoye
Warluis
Thiberville
Louviers
les Andelys
Gisors
Clermont
le Neubourg
Fontaine-Bellenger
Noailles
Plasnes
Chaumont-en-Vexin
Corbeil-Cerf
10
Bernay
Acquigny
les Thilliers-en-Vexin
Dangu
Mouy
Omonville
Aubevoye
Jonquerets-de-Livet
Beaumont-le-Roger
Gaillon
St. Clair-sur-Epte
Méru
Montataire
49°00'
Broglie
Beaumesnil
Emanville
Écos
Magny-en-Vexin
Monneville
Neuilly-en-Thelle
St. Marcel
Vernon
Amblainville
Louversey
St. Sébastien-de-Morsent
Gravigny
la Roche-Guyon
Marines
Chambly
la Barre-en-Ouche
la Ferrière-sur-Risle
Évreux
Pacy-sur-Eure
Cormeilles-en-Vexin
l'Isle-Adam
Beaumont-sur-Oise
Conches-en-Ouche
Bonnières-sur-Seine
Vigny
Glos-la-Ferrière
St. Aquilin-de-Pacy
Prey
Mantes-la-Jolie
Sagy
Pontoise
Auvers-sur-Oise
Nagel-Séez-Mesnil
Avrilly
Montsoult
Ferté-Frênel
Breteuil-sur-Iton
Damville
Bueil
Mantes-la-Ville
Limay
Cergy
Taverny
Domont
St. André-de-l'Eure
Ivry-la-Bataille
Longnes
les Mureaux
Rugles
l'Aigle
Chandai
Ézy-sur-Eure
Guerville
Aubergenville
ARGENTEUIL
Sarcelles
Droisy
Oulins
Septeuil
Poissy
Tillières-sur-Avre
Anet
Thoiry
Verneuil-sur-Avre
St. Denis
Nonancourt
Richebourg
St. Germain-en-Laye
Nanterre
Rueil-la-Gadelière
Houdan
PARIS
Dreux
St. Maurice-lès-Charencey
Brezolles
Vernouillet
Broué
Montfort-l'Amaury
St. Cyr-l'École
Versailles
la Ventrouze
F
Charpont
Condé-sur-Vesgre
Clamart
Tréon
la Ferté-Vidame
Maillebois
Morvillette
la Hauteville
Trappes
Montigny-le-Bretonneux
Créteil
Nogent-le-Roi
le Perray-en-Yvelines
Senonches
Longny-au-Perche
Châteauneuf-en-Thymerais
Rambouillet
Chevreuse
Orsay
Antony
Épernon
Belhomert-Guéhouville
Moutiers-au-Perche
le Mage
Pierres
Limours
Ste. Geneviève-des-Bois
Grigny
Brunoy
Maintenon
Challet
St. Arnoult-en-Yvelines
Évry
la Loupe
Chartainvilliers
Brétigny-sur-Orge
Rémalard
Coulonges-les-Sablons
St. Eliph
Courville-sur-Eure
Poisvilliers
Noce
Gallardon
Breuillet
Arpajon
Corbeil-Essonnes
Perche
Chartres
Ablis
Nogent-le-Rotrou
Champrond-en-Gâtine
Mainvilliers
Cathedral
Houville-la-Branche
Dourdan
8
Thiron-Gardais
Combres
9
Lucé
17
Auneau
Étrechy
10
le Mée-sur-Seine
Berchères-les-Pierres
Sainville
la Ferté-

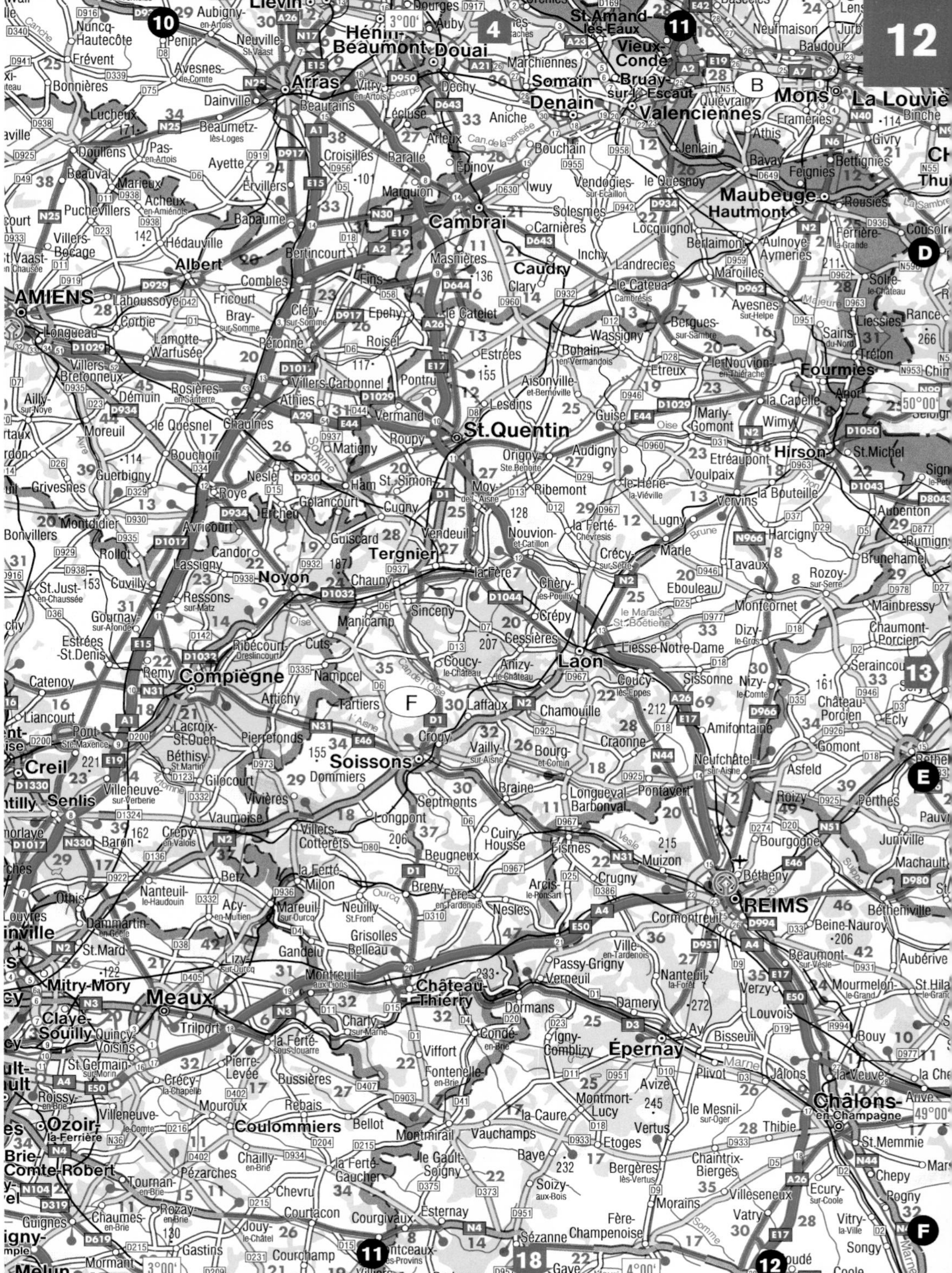

12
Lievin
Hénin-Beaumont
Douai
Arras
St.Amand-les-Eaux
Vieux-Condé
Somain
Denain
Valenciennes
Mons
La Louvière
Maubeuge
Hautmont
Cambrai
Caudry
Le Cateau-Cambrésis
Avesnes-sur-Helpe
Fourmies
Hirson
Doullens
Albert
AMIENS
Péronne
Bapaume
St.Quentin
Guise
Vervins
Montdidier
Roye
Ham
Tergnier
Chauny
Noyon
Compiègne
Laon
Soissons
Creil
Senlis
Villers-Cotterêts
Crépy-en-Valois
Meaux
Château-Thierry
Reims
Épernay
Châlons-en-Champagne
Coulommiers
Melun
Sézanne
Montmirail
Fismes
Rethel
Marle
Montcornet
Craonne
Sissonne
Frévent
Nuncq-Hautecôte
Avesnes-le-Comte
Beaumetz-lès-Loges
Bohain-en-Vermandois
Le Quesnoy
Landrecies
Pierrefonds
La Ferté-Milon
La Ferté-sous-Jouarre
Dammartin-en-Goële
Mitry-Mory
Claye-Souilly
Ozoir-la-Ferrière
Brie-Comte-Robert
Nangis
Vertus
Avize
Ay
3°00'
4°00'
49°00'
50°00'

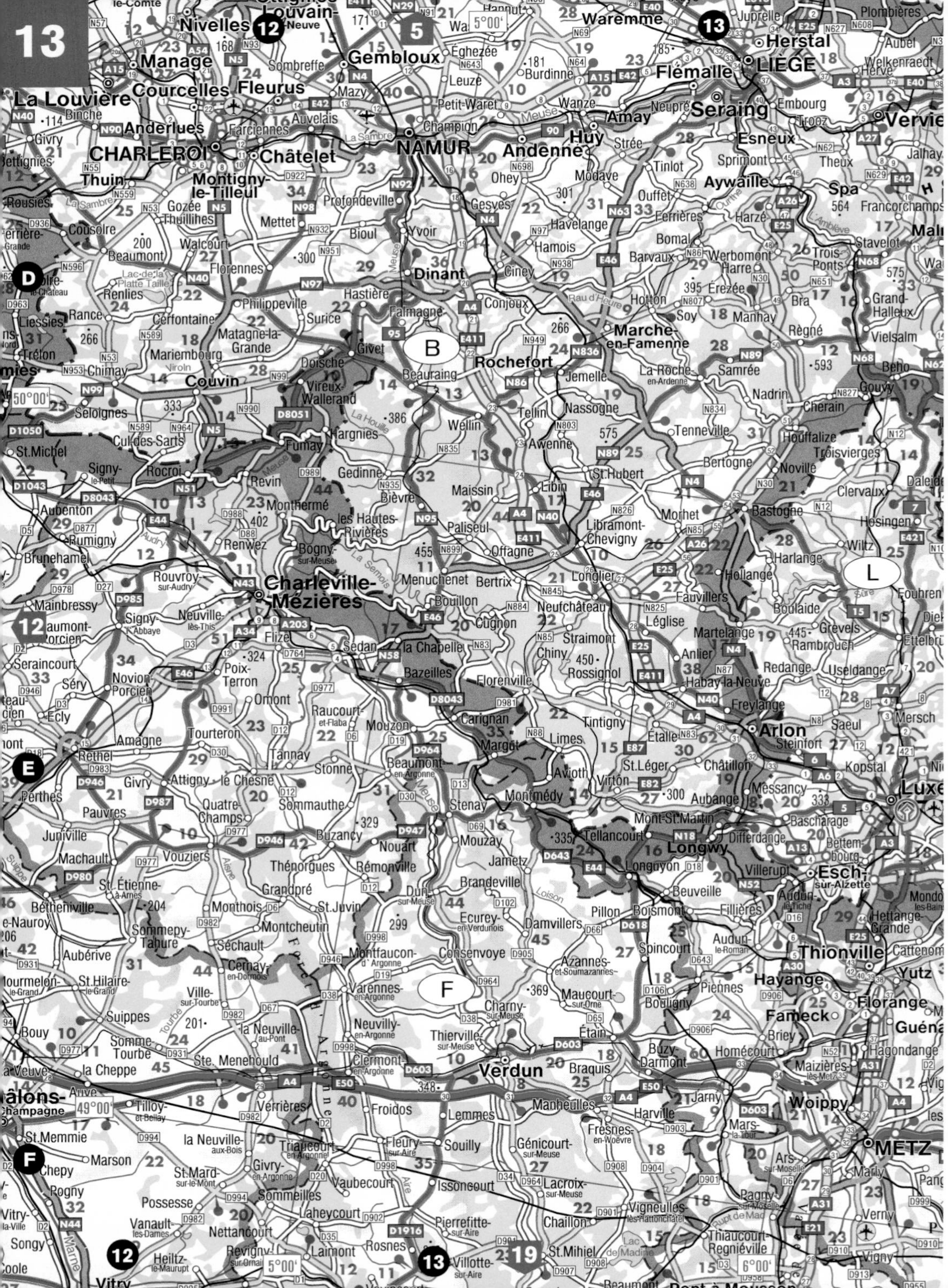

Nivelles
Louvain-la-Neuve
Waremme
Herstal
Manage
Gembloux
Eghezée
Burdinne
Flémalle
LIÈGE
Courcelles
Fleurus
Sombreffe
Leuze
Mazy
Petit-Waret
Wanze
Seraing
Embourg
La Louvière
Binche
Anderlues
Auvelais
Farciennes
Champion
Amay
Trooz
Verviers
Givry
CHARLEROI
Châtelet
NAMUR
Andenne
Huy
Strée
Esneux
Jalhay
Thuin
Montigny-le-Tilleul
Ohey
Modave
Tinlot
Sprimont
Theux
Rousies
Gozée
Thuillies
Profondeville
Gesves
Ouffet
Aywaille
Spa
Francorchamps
Cousolre
Mettet
Yvoir
Havelange
Ferrières
Harzé
Beaumont
Walcourt
Bioul
Hamois
Bomal
Stavelot
Florennes
Dinant
Ciney
Barvaux
Werbomont
Trois-Ponts
Liessies
Renlies
Philippeville
Hastière
Conjoux
Hotton
Érezée
Grand-Halleux
Rance
Cerfontaine
Surice
Falmagne
Soy
Manhay
Trélon
Chimay
Matagne-la-Grande
Mariembourg
Givet
Marche-en-Famenne
Regné
Vielsalm
Couvin
Doische
Beauraing
Rochefort
Jemelle
La Roche-en-Ardenne
Samrée
Beho
Vireux-Wallerand
Nadrin
Gouvy
Seloignes
Cherain
Wellin
Tellin
Nassogne
Tenneville
Houffalize
Cul-des-Sarts
Hargnies
Awenne
St.Michel
Fumay
Troisvierges
Signy-le-Petit
Rocroi
Revin
Gedinne
Maissin
St.Hubert
Bertogne
Noville
Libin
Clervaux
Aubenton
Monthermé
Bièvre
Paliseul
Libramont-Chevigny
Morhet
Bastogne
Hosingen
Rumigny
Renwez
les Hautes-Rivières
Offagne
Wiltz
Brunehamel
Bogny-sur-Meuse
Harlange
Rouvroy-sur-Audry
Charleville-Mézières
Menuchenet
Bertrix
Longlier
Fauvillers
Hollange
Mainbressy
Bouillon
Neufchâteau
Léglise
Boulaide
Signy-l'Abbaye
Neuville-lès-This
Cugnon
Martelange
Grevels
Flize
Sedan
la Chapelle
Straimont
Anlier
Rambrouch
Ettelbruck
Seraincourt
Poix-Terron
Bazeilles
Chiny
Rossignol
Redange
Useldange
Séry
Novion-Porcien
Florenville
Habay-la-Neuve
Omont
Raucourt-et-Flaba
Carignan
Tintigny
Freylange
Mersch
Ecly
Tourteron
Mouzon
Étalle
Arlon
Saeul
Amagne
Margut
Limes
Steinfort
Rethel
Tannay
St.Léger
Châtillon
Kopstal
Givry
Attigny
le Chesne
Stonne
Beaumont-en-Argonne
Avioth
Virton
Messancy
Luxembourg
Perthes
Stenay
Montmédy
Aubange
Pauvres
Quatre-Champs
Sommauthe
Mont-St.Martin
Bascharage
Juniville
Buzancy
Tellancourt
Longwy
Differdange
Nouart
Mouzay
Machault
Vouziers
Thénorgues
Rémonville
Jametz
Longuyon
Villerupt
Esch-sur-Alzette
St.Étienne-à-Arnes
Grandpré
Brandeville
Audun-le-Tiche
Bétheniville
Monthois
St.Juvin
Dun-sur-Meuse
Beuveille
Ecurey-en-Verdunois
Pillon
Boismont
Fillières
Hettange-Grande
Sommepy-Tahure
Montcheutin
Damvillers
Séchault
Spincourt
Audun-le-Roman
Thionville
Cattenom
Aubérive
Montfaucon-d'Argonne
Consenvoye
Cernay-en-Dormois
Azannes-et-Soumazannes
Hayange
Yutz
St.Hilaire-le-Grand
Varennes-en-Argonne
Ville-sur-Tourbe
Maucourt-sur-Orne
Piennes
Charny-sur-Meuse
Bouligny
Florange
Suippes
la Neuville-au-Pont
Neuvilly-en-Argonne
Fameck
Bouy
Somme-Tourbe
Thierville-sur-Meuse
Étain
Briey
Ste. Menehould
Clermont-en-Argonne
Buzy-Darmont
Homécourt
Hagondange
la Cheppe
Verdun
Braquis
Maizières-lès-Metz
Auve
Verrières
Manheulles
Jarny
Woippy
Châlons-en-Champagne
Tilloy-et-Bellay
Froidos
Lemmes
Harville
St.Memmie
la Neuville-aux-Bois
Triaucourt-en-Argonne
Fleury-sur-Aire
Souilly
Génicourt-sur-Meuse
Fresnes-en-Woëvre
Mars-la-Tour
METZ
Marson
St.Mard-sur-le-Mont
Givry-en-Argonne
Ars-sur-Moselle
Chepy
Vaubecourt
Issoncourt
Lacroix-sur-Meuse
Marly
Pogny
Sommeilles
Pagny-sur-Moselle
Possesse
Vigneulles-lès-Hattonchâtel
Vitry-la-Ville
Vanault-les-Dames
Laheycourt
Pierrefitte-sur-Aire
Chaillon
Verny
Nettancourt
Thiaucourt-Regniéville
Songy
Revigny-sur-Ornain
Laimont
Rosnes
St.Mihiel
Lac de Madine
Heiltz-le-Maurupt
Villotte-sur-Aire
Vigny
Coole
Vitry
Beaumont
Pont-à-Mousson
La Sambre
Meuse
Moselle
La Semois
Aisne
Marne
Ourthe
L'Amblève
50°00'
49°00'
5°00'
6°00'
B
L
F
D
E
12
13
5
19

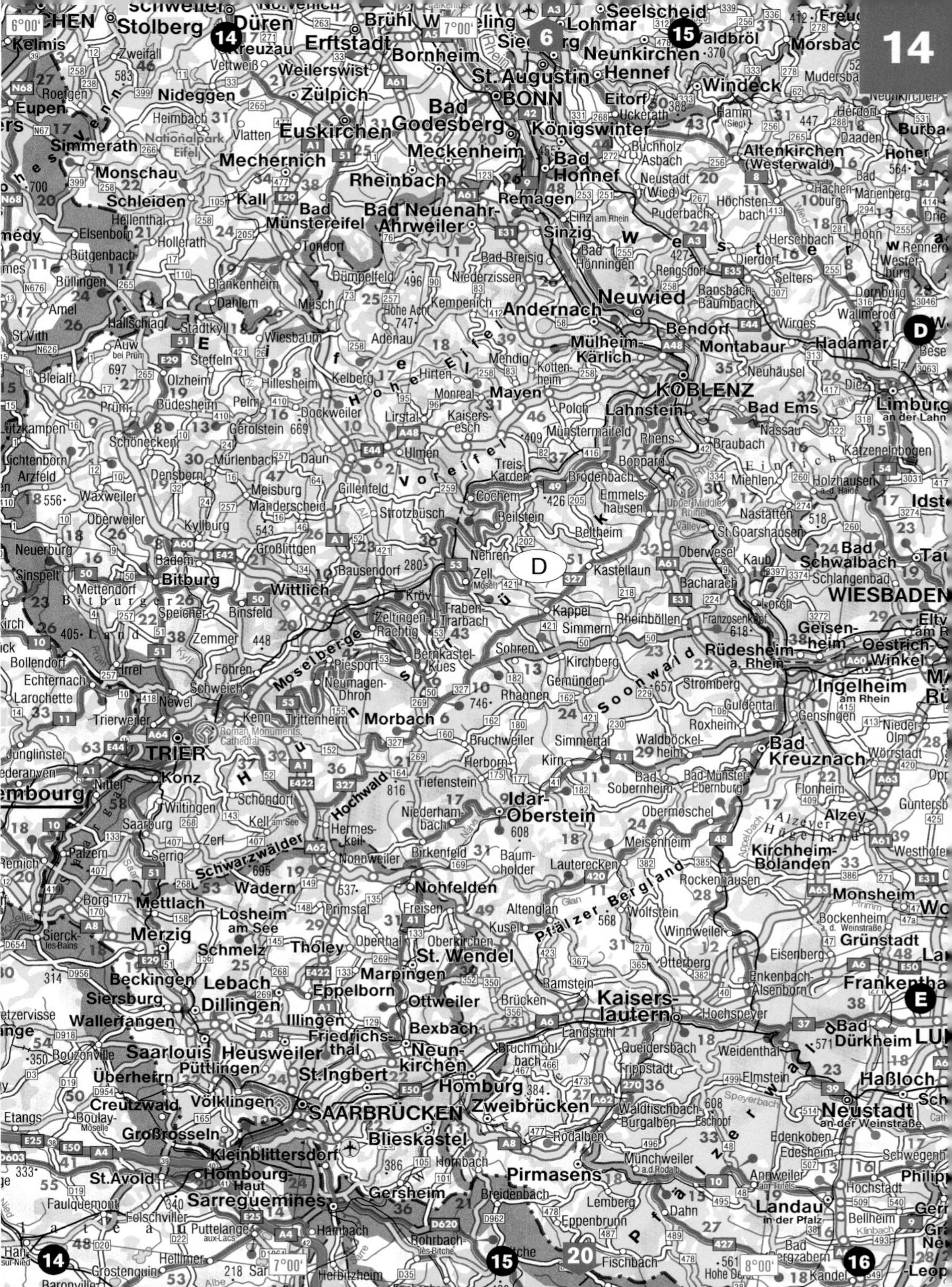

14
6°00'
7°00'
8°00'
Stolberg
Düren
Erftstadt
Brühl
Siegburg
Lohmar
Seelscheid
Waldbröl
Kelmis
Kreuzau
Bornheim
Neunkirchen
Morsbach
Weilerswist
St. Augustin
Hennef
Nideggen
Zülpich
BONN
Windeck
Eupen
Bad Godesberg
Eitorf
Euskirchen
Königswinter
Simmerath
Nationalpark Eifel
Mechernich
Meckenheim
Altenkirchen (Westerwald)
Monschau
Rheinbach
Bad Honnef
Schleiden
Kall
Bad Münstereifel
Bad Neuenahr-Ahrweiler
Remagen
Elsenborn
Hellenthal
Hollerath
Sinzig
Bütgenbach
Tondorf
Bad Breisig
Bad Hönningen
Büllingen
Blankenheim
Dümpelfeld
Niederzissen
Rengsdorf
Selters
Dahlem
Kempenich
Andernach
Neuwied
Amel
Hallschlag
Hohe Acht
Stadtkyll
Adenau
Bendorf
St.Vith
Wiesbaum
Mülheim-Kärlich
Montabaur
Hadamar
Steffeln
Mendig
Bleialf
Olzheim
Hillesheim
Kelberg
Mayen
KOBLENZ
Prüm
Büdesheim
Gerolstein
Dockweiler
Lahnstein
Bad Ems
Limburg an der Lahn
Daun
Ulmen
Kaisersesch
Münstermaifeld
Nassau
Mürlenbach
Treis-Karden
Boppard
Arzfeld
Densborn
Meisburg
Gillenfeld
Cochem
Brodenbach
Holzhausen
Idstein
Waxweiler
Manderscheid
Strotzbüsch
Emmelshausen
Upper Middle Rhine Valley
Nastätten
Kyllburg
Beilstein
Beltheim
St.Goarshausen
Neuerburg
Bitburg
Großlittgen
Bausendorf
Nehren
Oberwesel
Bad Schwalbach
Zell (Mosel)
Kastellaun
Kaub
Wittlich
Kröv
Bacharach
Schlangenbad
WIESBADEN
Speicher
Binsfeld
Traben-Trarbach
Kappel
Simmern
Rheinböllen
Lorch
Zemmer
Sohren
Geisenheim
Oestrich-Winkel
Rüdesheim a. Rhein
Bollendorf
Irrel
Moselberge
Bernkastel-Kues
Kirchberg
Echternach
Föhren
Piesport
Gemünden
Stromberg
Ingelheim am Rhein
Schweich
Neumagen-Dhron
Rhaunen
Soonwald
Guldental
Trierweiler
Trittenheim
Morbach
Roxheim
Gensingen
Bruchweiler
Simmertal
Waldböckelheim
Bad Kreuznach
Wörrstadt
TRIER
Konz
Herborn
Kirn
Tiefenstein
Bad Sobernheim
Bad Münster-Ebernburg
Hochwald
Schöndorf
Wiltingen
Idar-Oberstein
Flonheim
Saarburg
Kell am See
Niederhambach
Obermoschel
Alzey
Hermeskeil
Zerf
Meisenheim
Kirchheim-Bolanden
Palzem
Serrig
Schwarzwälder
Nonnweiler
Birkenfeld
Baumholder
Lauterecken
Rockenhausen
Remich
Wadern
Nohfelden
Pfälzer Bergland
Monsheim
Mettlach
Losheim am See
Primstal
Freisen
Altenglan
Wolfstein
Bockenheim
Merzig
Schmelz
Tholey
Oberkirchen
Kusel
Winnweiler
Grünstadt
Sierck-les-Bains
St. Wendel
Otterberg
Eisenberg
Beckingen
Lebach
Marpingen
Ramstein
Enkenbach-Alsenborn
Frankenthal
Siersburg
Dillingen
Eppelborn
Ottweiler
Brücken
Kaiserslautern
Wallerfangen
Illingen
Bexbach
Landstuhl
Hochspeyer
Bad Dürkheim
Friedrichsthal
Neunkirchen
Saarlouis
Heusweiler
Bouzonville
Püttlingen
St.Ingbert
Homburg
Bruchmühlbach
Queidersbach
Weidenthal
Überherrn
Trippstadt
Elmstein
Haßloch
Creutzwald
Völklingen
Zweibrücken
Waldfischbach-Burgalben
Neustadt an der Weinstraße
SAARBRÜCKEN
Boulay-Moselle
Großrosseln
Eschopf
Edenkoben
Blieskastel
Rodalben
Edesheim
Kleinblittersdorf
Münchweiler a.d.Rodalb
Hornbach
St.Avold
Hombourg-Haut
Pirmasens
Annweiler am Trifels
Hochstadt
Sarreguemines
Gersheim
Breidenbach
Lemberg
Dahn
Landau in der Pfalz
Faulquemont
Folschviller
Puttelange-aux-Lacs
Hambach
Eppenbrunn
Bellheim
Rohrbach-lès-Bitche
Bad Bergzabern
Hellimer
Fischbach
Kandel
Grostenquin
Herbitzheim
Hohe Derst
A
B
C
D
E
15
16
20

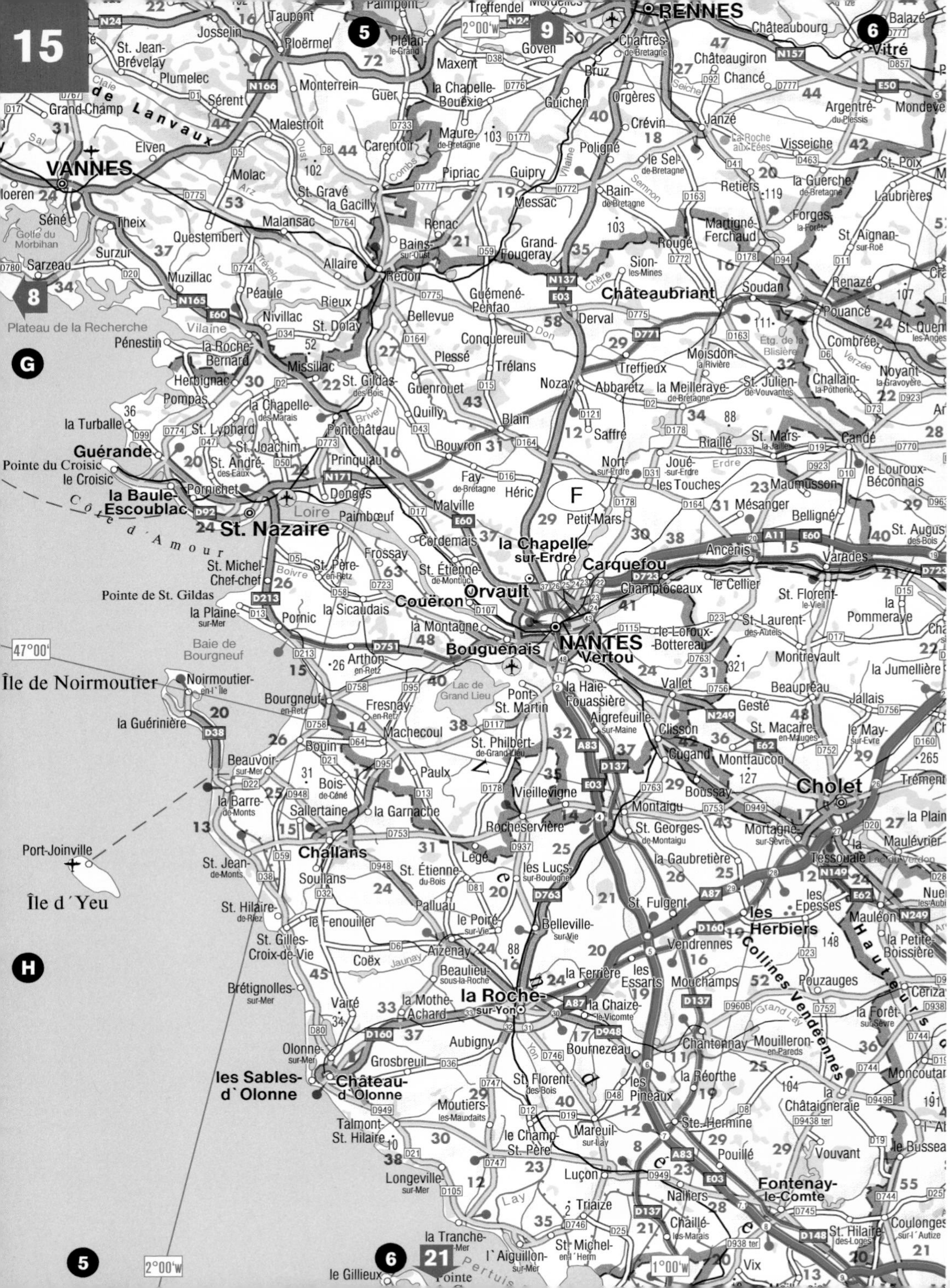

15
RENNES
Vitré
Châteaubourg
Châteaugiron
Chancé
Janzé
Argentré-du-Plessis
Mondevert
Balazé
Treffendel
Paimpont
Taupont
Josselin
Ploërmel
Plélan-le-Grand
Maxent
Goven
Bruz
Chartres-de-Bretagne
Orgères
Guichen
Crévin
Poligné
Le Sel-de-Bretagne
Visseiche
Retiers
la Guerche-de-Bretagne
St. Poix
Laubrières
Forges-la-Forêt
Martigné-Ferchaud
St. Aignan-sur-Roë
Renazé
Pouancé
Combrée
St. Quentin-les-Anges
St. Jean-Brévelay
Plumelec
Monterrein
Guer
la Chapelle-Bouëxic
Maure-de-Bretagne
Sérent
Grand-Champ
Lanvaux
Malestroit
Carentoir
Elven
VANNES
Molac
Pipriac
Guipry
Messac
Bain-de-Bretagne
St. Gravé
la Gacilly
Séné
Theix
Golfe du Morbihan
Questembert
Malansac
Renac
Bains-sur-Oust
Grand-Fougeray
Rougé
Sion-les-Mines
Surzur
Sarzeau
Muzillac
Allaire
Redon
Péaule
Rieux
Guémené-Penfao
Châteaubriant
Soudan
Derval
Conquereuil
Plateau de la Recherche
Nivillac
St. Dolay
Pénestin
la Roche-Bernard
Missillac
Herbignac
Pompas
St. Gildas-des-Bois
Plessé
Trélans
Nozay
Abbaretz
la Meilleraye-de-Bretagne
Moisdon-la-Rivière
St. Julien-de-Vouvantes
Challain-la-Potherie
Noyant-la-Gravoyère
Treffieux
Guenrouet
Quilly
Blain
Saffré
Riaillé
St. Mars-la-Jaille
Candé
la Turballe
la Chapelle-des-Marais
St. Lyphard
Pontchâteau
Bouvron
Guérande
St. Joachim
St. André-des-Eaux
Prinquiau
Pointe du Croisic
le Croisic
Pornichet
la Baule-Escoublac
St. Nazaire
Donges
Fay-de-Bretagne
Héric
Nort-sur-Erdre
Joué-sur-Erdre
les Touches
Maumusson
le Louroux-Béconnais
Malville
Paimbœuf
Petit-Mars
Mésanger
Belligné
Côte d'Amour
Cordemais
la Chapelle-sur-Erdre
Carquefou
Ancenis
Varades
St. Augustin-des-Bois
St. Michel-Chef-chef
Frossay
St. Père-en-Retz
St. Étienne-de-Montluc
Orvault
Champtoceaux
le Cellier
St. Florent-le-Vieil
la Pommeraye
Pointe de St. Gildas
la Plaine-sur-Mer
Pornic
la Sicaudais
Couëron
la Montagne
NANTES
Bouguenais
Vertou
le Loroux-Bottereau
St. Laurent-des-Autels
Montrevault
la Jumellière
47°00'
Baie de Bourgneuf
Arthon-en-Retz
Lac de Grand Lieu
Pont-St. Martin
la Haie-Fouassière
Vallet
Beaupréau
Jallais
Île de Noirmoutier
Noirmoutier-en-l'Île
Bourgneuf-en-Retz
Fresnay-en-Retz
Aigrefeuille-sur-Maine
Clisson
Gesté
St. Macaire-en-Mauges
le May-sur-Evre
la Guérinière
Machecoul
St. Philbert-de-Grand-Lieu
Bouin
Cugand
Montfaucon
Beauvoir-sur-Mer
Paulx
Vieillevigne
Boussay
Cholet
Trémentines
Bois-de-Céné
la Barre-de-Monts
Sallertaine
la Garnache
Montaigu
Rocheservière
St. Georges-de-Montaigu
Mortagne-sur-Sèvre
la Plaine
Maulévrier
Port-Joinville
Challans
Legé
la Gaubretière
Tessoualle
St. Jean-de-Monts
Soullans
St. Étienne-du-Bois
les Lucs-sur-Boulogne
Île d'Yeu
St. Hilaire-de-Riez
le Fenouiller
Palluau
le Poiré-sur-Vie
Belleville-sur-Vie
St. Fulgent
les Herbiers
les Epesses
Mauléon
la Petite-Boissière
St. Gilles-Croix-de-Vie
Coëx
Aizenay
Vendrennes
Collines Vendéennes
Hauteurs de la Gâtine
Brétignolles-sur-Mer
Beaulieu-sous-la-Roche
la Ferrière
les Essarts
Mouchamps
Pouzauges
Vairé
la Mothe-Achard
la Roche-sur-Yon
la Chaize-le-Vicomte
la Forêt-sur-Sèvre
Aubigny
Bournezeau
Chantonnay
Mouilleron-en-Pareds
Olonne-sur-Mer
Grosbreuil
les Sables-d'Olonne
Château-d'Olonne
St. Florent-des-Bois
les Pineaux
la Réorthe
Moncoutant
Moutiers-les-Mauxfaits
la Châtaigneraie
Talmont-St. Hilaire
le Champ-St. Père
Mareuil-sur-Lay
Ste. Hermine
Pouillé
Vouvant
l'Absie
Longeville-sur-Mer
Luçon
Nalliers
Fontenay-le-Comte
Triaize
Chaillé-les-Marais
St. Hilaire-des-Loges
Coulonges-sur-l'Autize
la Tranche-sur-Mer
St. Michel-en-l'Herm
l'Aiguillon-sur-Mer
Vix
le Gillieux
Pointe
Pertuis
2°00'W
1°00'W

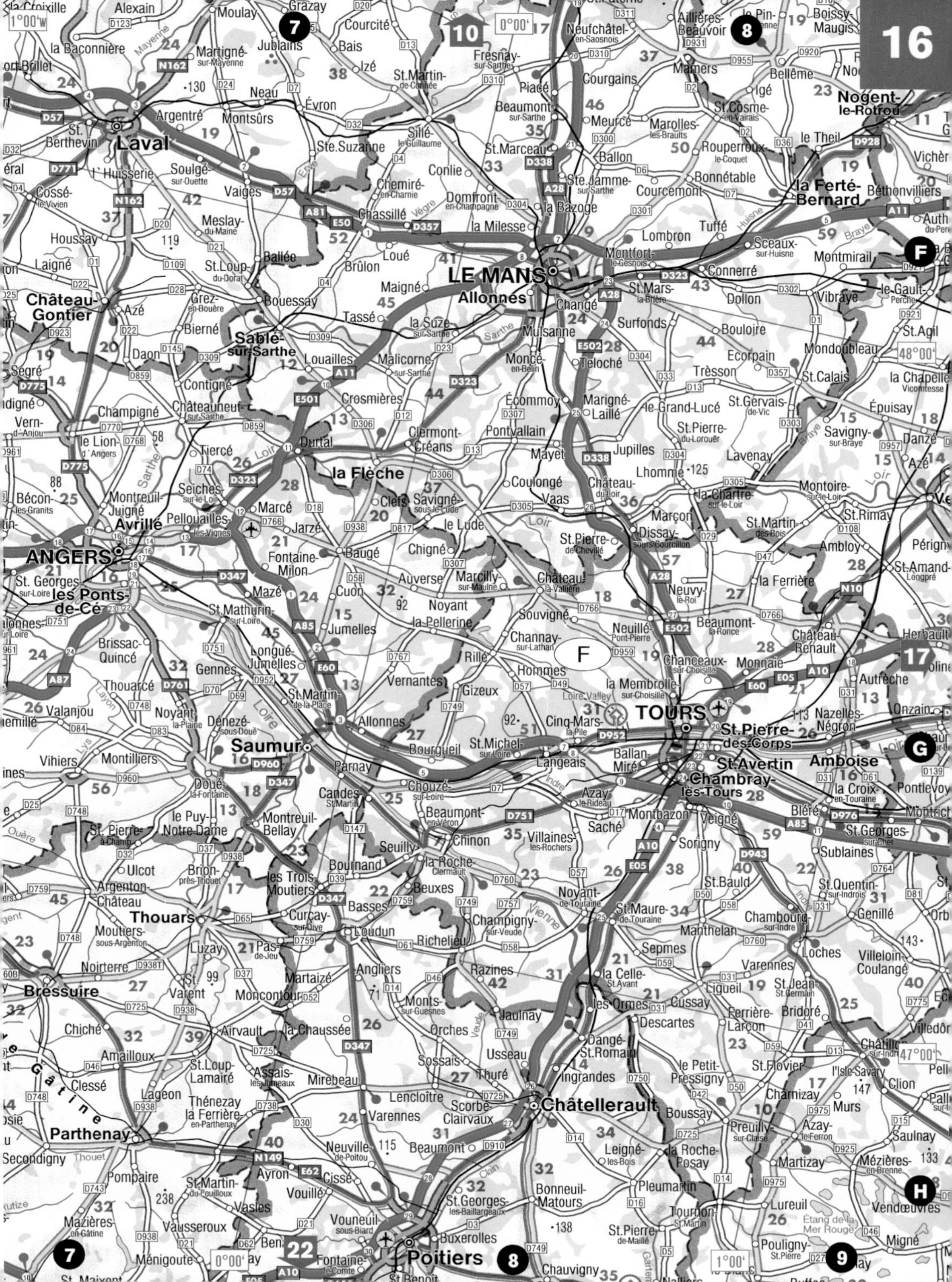
Laval
LE MANS
Allonnes
Château-Gontier
Sablé-sur-Sarthe
la Flèche
ANGERS
Avrillé
les Ponts-de-Cé
Saumur
TOURS
St.Pierre-des-Corps
St.Avertin
Chambray-lès-Tours
Amboise
Thouars
Bressuire
Parthenay
Châtellerault
Poitiers
Nogent-le-Rotrou
la Ferté-Bernard
Chinon
Loudun
Loches
Mamers
Montfort-le-Gesnois
Château-Renault
Montoire-sur-le-Loir
Château-du-Loir
Durtal
Baugé
Doué-la-Fontaine
Montreuil-Bellay
Langeais
Azay-le-Rideau
Richelieu
Mirebeau
la Roche-Posay
Chauvigny
Montbazon
Ste.Maure-de-Touraine
Bourgueil
Écommoy
Sillé-le-Guillaume
Évron
Beaumont-sur-Sarthe
Bonnétable
Vibraye
Mondoubleau
St.Calais
Bléré
Preuilly-sur-Claise
Neuville-de-Poitou
Vouillé
Airvault
Argenton-Château
Vihiers
Brissac-Quincé
Gennes
Candes-St.Martin
Château-la-Vallière
Neuillé-Pont-Pierre
Descartes
le Grand-Lucé
Loire Valley
A11
A28
A81
A85
A87
A10
E50
E60
E05
E502
E501
E62
N162
N10
N149
D323
D338
D347
D751
D952
D960
D976
D943
1°00'W
0°00'
48°00'
47°00'
1°00'
F
7
8
9
10
17
22
G
H

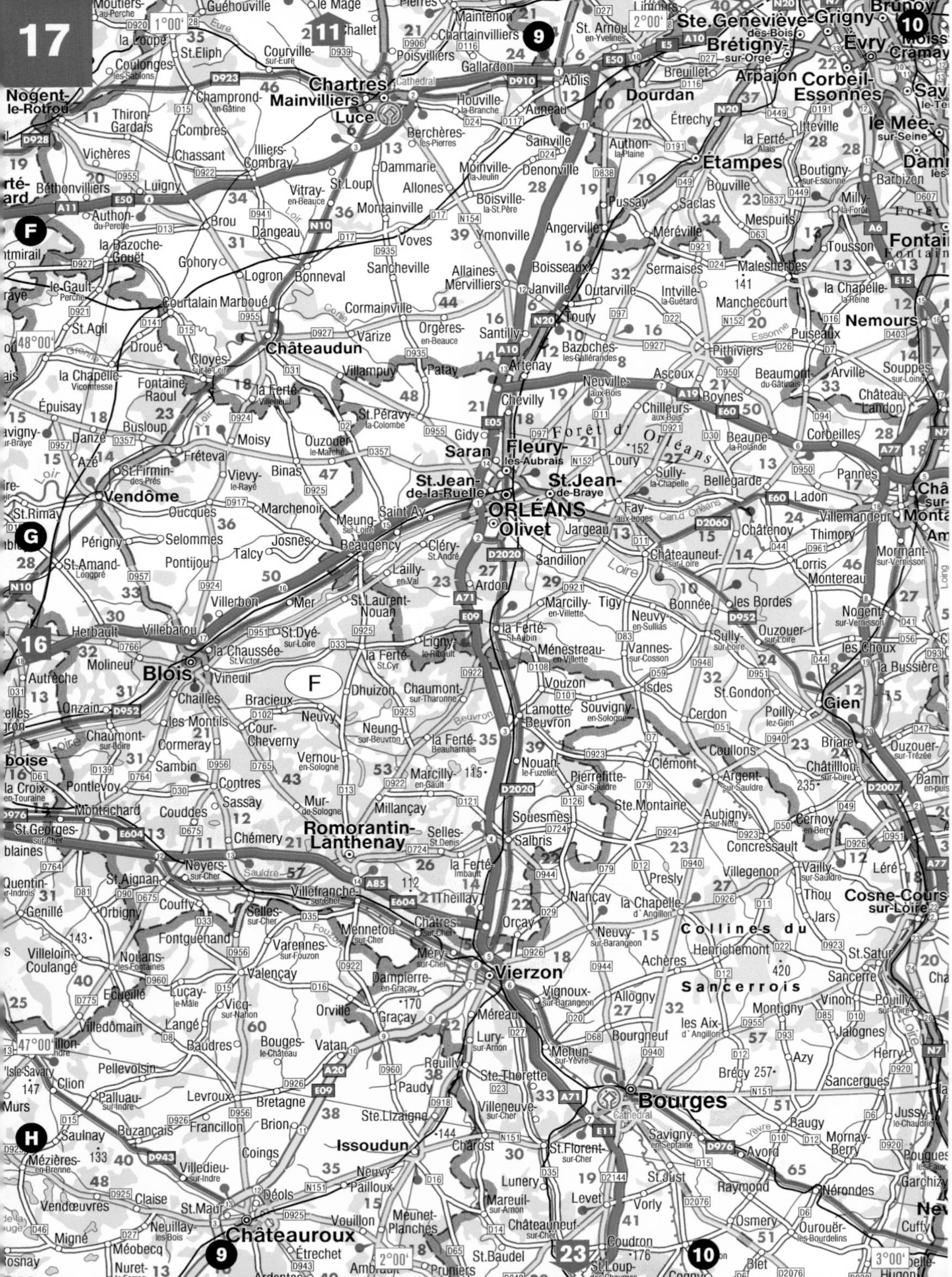

Moutiers-au-Perche
Guéhouville
le Mage
Pierres
Maintenon
Limours
Ste.Geneviève-des-Bois
Grigny
Brunoy
la Loupe
St.Eliph
Courville-sur-Eure
Challet
Chartainvilliers
St. Arnoult-en-Yvelines
Brétigny-sur-Orge
Evry
Coulonges-les-Sablons
Poisvilliers
Gallardon
Breuillet
Arpajon
Corbeil-Essonnes
Nogent-le-Rotrou
Champrond-en-Gâtine
Chartres
Mainvilliers
Luce
Houville-la-Branche
Ablis
Dourdan
Thiron-Gardais
Combres
Berchères-les-Pierres
Auneau
Étrechy
Itteville
le Mée-sur-Seine
Vichères
Chassant
Illiers-Combray
Dammarie
Sainville
Authon-la-Plaine
la Ferté-Alais
Étampes
Béthonvilliers
Luigny
Vitray-en-Beauce
St.Loup
Allones
Moinville-la-Jeulin
Denonville
Boutigny-sur-Essonne
Barbizon
Authon-du-Perche
Brou
Dangeau
Montainville
Boisville-la-St.Père
Pussay
Saclas
Bouville
Milly-la-Forêt
la Bazoche-Gouët
Gohory
Voves
Ymonville
Angerville
Méréville
Mespuits
Tousson
Fontainebleau
le Gault-Perche
Logron
Bonneval
Sancheville
Allaines-Mervilliers
Boisseaux
Sermaises
Malesherbes
Courtalain
Marboué
Cormainville
Janville
Outarville
Intville-la-Guétard
Manchecourt
la Chapelle-la-Reine
Nemours
St.Agil
Droué
Châteaudun
Varize
Orgères-en-Beauce
Santilly
Toury
Bazoches-les-Gallerandes
Pithiviers
Puiseaux
la Chapelle-Vicomtesse
Cloyes-sur-le-Loir
Fontaine-Raoul
Villampuy
Patay
Artenay
Ascoux
Beaumont-du-Gâtinais
Arville
Souppes-sur-Loing
Épuisay
la Ferté-Villeneuil
St.Péravy-la-Colombe
Chevilly
Neuville-aux-Bois
Chilleurs-aux-Bois
Boynes
Château-Landon
Busloup
Danzé
Moisy
Ouzouer-le-Marché
Gidy
Saran
Fleury-les-Aubrais
Forêt d' Orléans
Loury
Beaune-la-Rolande
Corbeilles
Fréteval
Azé
St.Firmin-des-Prés
Vievy-le-Rayé
Binas
St.Jean-de-la-Ruelle
St.Jean-de-Braye
Sully-la-Chapelle
Bellegarde
Pannes
Vendôme
St.Rimay
Oucques
Marchenoir
Meung-sur-Loire
Saint Ay
ORLÉANS
Olivet
Fay-aux-Loges
Ladon
Châtenoy
Villemandeur
Montargis
Périgny
Selommes
Josnes
Beaugency
Cléry-St.André
Jargeau
Thimory
St.Amand-Longpré
Talcy
Pontijou
Lailly-en-Val
Sandillon
Châteauneuf-sur-Loire
Lorris
Mormant-sur-Vernisson
Ardon
Montereau
Villerbon
Mer
St.Laurent-Nouan
Marcilly-en-Villette
Tigy
Bonnée
les Bordes
Nogent-sur-Vernisson
Herbault
Villebarou
St.Dyé-sur-Loire
Ligny-le-Ribault
la Ferté-St.Aubin
Neuvy-en-Sullias
Sully-sur-Loire
Ouzouer-sur-Loire
les Choux
la Chaussée-St.Victor
Molineuf
Blois
la Ferté-St.Cyr
Ménestreau-en-Villette
Vannes-sur-Cosson
la Bussière
Autrèche
Vineuil
Chailles
Bracieux
Dhuizon
Chaumont-sur-Tharonne
Vouzon
Isdes
St.Gondon
Gien
Onzain
les Montils
Neuvy
Lamotte-Beuvron
Souvigny-en-Sologne
Cerdon
Poilly-lez-Gien
Chaumont-sur-Loire
Cour-Cheverny
Neung-sur-Beuvron
la Ferté-Beauharnais
Coullons
Briare
Ouzouer-sur-Trézée
Amboise
Cormeray
Sambin
Vernou-en-Sologne
Nouan-le-Fuzelier
Clémont
Argent-sur-Sauldre
Châtillon-sur-Loire
la Croix-en-Touraine
Pontlevoy
Contres
Marcilly-en-Gault
Pierrefitte-sur-Sauldre
Sassay
Mur-de-Sologne
Millançay
Ste.Montaine
Aubigny-sur-Nère
Cernoy-en-Berry
Montrichard
Couddes
Souesmes
St.Georges-sur-Cher
Chémery
Romorantin-Lanthenay
Selles-St.Denis
Salbris
Concressault
Noyers-sur-Cher
St.Aignan
la Ferté-Imbault
Presly
Villegenon
Vailly-sur-Sauldre
Léré
Genillé
Orbigny
Couffy
Villefranche-sur-Cher
Theillay
Nançay
la Chapelle-d'Angillon
Thou
Cosne-Cours-sur-Loire
Selles-sur-Cher
Mennetou-sur-Cher
Châtres-sur-Cher
Orçay
Jars
Fontguenand
Varennes-sur-Fouzon
Neuvy-sur-Barangeon
Collines du Sancerrois
Henrichemont
St.Satur
Villeloin-Coulangé
Nouans-les-Fontaines
Méry-sur-Cher
Vierzon
Achères
Sancerre
Valençay
Dampierre-en-Graçay
Vignoux-sur-Barangeon
Allogny
Ecueillé
Luçay-le-Mâle
Vicq-sur-Nahon
Orville
Graçay
Montigny
Vinon
Pouilly-sur-Loire
Villedômain
Langé
Méreau
Les Aix-d'Angillon
Jalognes
Baudres
Bouges-le-Château
Vatan
Lury-sur-Arnon
Mehun-sur-Yèvre
Bourgneuf
Azy
Herry
Pellevoisin
Reuilly
Ste.Thorette
Brécy
Sancergues
Clion
Palluau-sur-Indre
Levroux
Bretagne
Paudy
Villeneuve-sur-Cher
Bourges
Jussy-le-Chaudrier
Buzançais
Francillon
Brion
Ste.Lizaigne
Baugy
Saulnay
Mézières-en-Brenne
Coings
Issoudun
Charost
St.Florent-sur-Cher
Savigny-en-Septaine
Avord
Mornay-Berry
Pougues-les-Eaux
Villedieu-sur-Indre
Neuvy-Pailloux
Lunery
St.Just
Raymond
Garchizy
Vendœuvres
Claise
St.Maur
Déols
Mareuil-sur-Arnon
Levet
Vorly
Nérondes
Neuilly-les-Bois
Vouillon
Meunet-Planches
Châteauneuf-sur-Cher
Osmery
Ourouër-les-Bourdelins
Cuffy
Migné
Méobecq
Châteauroux
Étrechet
St.Baudel
Coudron
Rosnay
Nuret-le-Ferron
Ardentes
Ambrault
Pruniers
St.Loup-des-Chaumes
Cogny
Blet

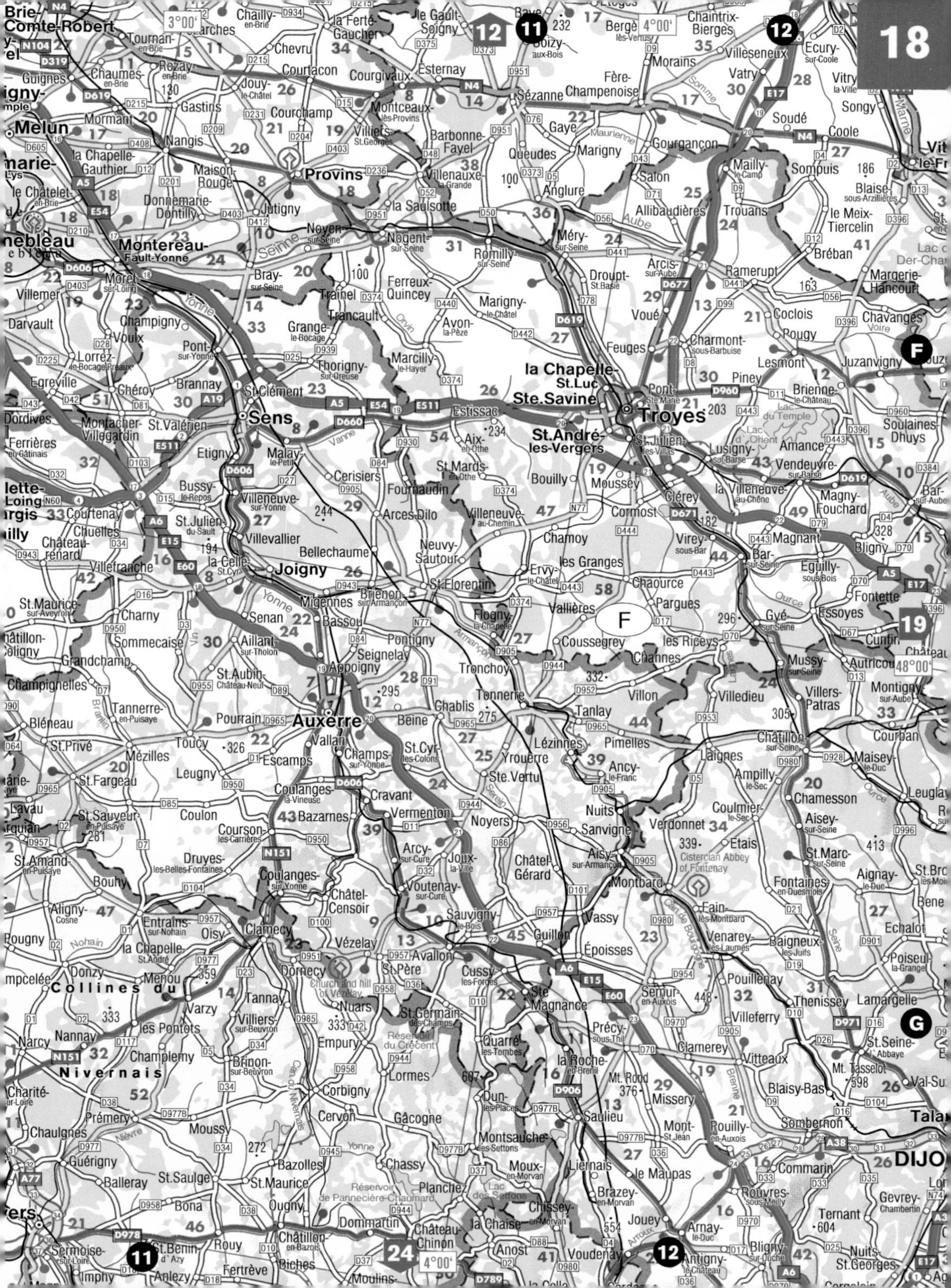

Brie-Comte-Robert
Tournan-en-Brie
Chailly-en-Brie
la Ferté-Gaucher
le Gault-Soigny
Baye
Étoges
Bergères-lès-Vertus
Chaintrix-Bierges
Ecury-sur-Coole
Guignes
Chaumes-en-Brie
Rozay-en-Brie
Jouy-le-Châtel
Chevru
Courtacon
Courgivaux
Esternay
Sézanne
Fère-Champenoise
Morains
Villeseneux
Vatry
Vitry-la-Ville
Melun
Mormant
Gastins
Courchamp
Montceaux-lès-Provins
Villiers-St.Georges
Barbonne-Fayel
Queudes
Gaye
Marigny
Gourgançon
Soudé
Coole
Songy
Nangis
la Chapelle-Gauthier
Maison-Rouge
Provins
Villenauxe-la-Grande
Anglure
Salon
Mailly-le-Camp
Sompuis
Blaise-sous-Arzillières
le Châtelet-en-Brie
Donnemarie-Dontilly
Jutigny
la Saulsotte
Allibaudières
Trouans
le Meix-Tiercelin
Fontainebleau
Montereau-Fault-Yonne
Noyen-sur-Seine
Nogent-sur-Seine
Romilly-sur-Seine
Méry-sur-Seine
Arcis-sur-Aube
Ramerupt
Bréban
Margerie-Hancourt
Moret-sur-Loing
Villemer
Bray-sur-Seine
Traînel
Ferreux-Quincey
Marigny-le-Châtel
Droupt-St.Basle
Voué
Chavanges
Darvault
Champigny
Voulx
Trancault
Grange-le-Bocage
Avon-la-Pèze
Charmont-sous-Barbuise
Coclois
Pougy
Lorrez-le-Bocage-Préaux
Pont-sur-Yonne
Thorigny-sur-Oreuse
Marcilly-le-Hayer
Feuges
Lesmont
Juzanvigny
Egreville
Chéroy
Brannay
St.Clément
la Chapelle-St.Luc
Ste.Savine
Pont-Ste.Marie
Piney
Brienne-le-Château
Dordives
Montacher-Villegardin
St.Valérien
Sens
Estissac
Troyes
Lac du Temple
Lac d'Orient
Soulaines-Dhuys
Ferrières-en-Gâtinais
Etigny
Malay-le-Petit
Aix-en-Othe
St.André-les-Vergers
St.Julien-les-Villas
Lusigny-sur-Barse
Amance
Cerisiers
St.Mards-en-Othe
Bouilly
Mousseyy
Vendeuvre-sur-Barse
Nargis
Courtenay
Bussy-le-Repos
Villeneuve-sur-Yonne
Fournaudin
Villeneuve-au-Chemin
Cormost
Clérey
la Villeneuve-au-Chêne
Magny-Fouchard
Bar-sur-Aube
Chuelles
St.Julien-du-Sault
Arces-Dilo
Château-Renard
Villevallier
Neuvy-Sautour
Chamoy
Virey-sous-Bar
Magnant
Bligny
Villefranche
la Celle-St.Cyr
Joigny
Bellechaume
Ervy-le-Châtel
les Granges
Chaource
Bar-sur-Seine
Eguilly-sous-Bois
Fontette
St.Maurice-sur-Aveyron
Charny
Migennes
Brienon-sur-Armançon
St.Florentin
Flogny-la-Chapelle
Vallières
Pargues
Gyé-sur-Seine
Essoyes
Châtillon-Coligny
Sommecaise
Senan
Aillant-sur-Tholon
Bassou
Pontigny
Coussegrey
les Riceys
Cunfin
Grandchamp
Seignelay
Appoigny
Tronchoy
Channes
Mussy-sur-Seine
Autricourt
Champignelles
St.Aubin-Château-Neuf
Villon
Villedieu
Villers-Patras
Montigny-sur-Aube
Tannerre-en-Puisaye
Auxerre
Chablis
Tonnerre
Tanlay
Bléneau
Pourrain
Beine
Châtillon-sur-Seine
Courban
St.Privé
Mézilles
Toucy
Vallan
St.Cyr-les-Colons
Lézinnes
Pimelles
Laignes
Maisey-le-Duc
Leugny
Escamps
Champs-sur-Yonne
Yrouerre
Ancy-le-Franc
Ampilly-le-Sec
St.Fargeau
Coulanges-la-Vineuse
Ste.Vertu
Chamesson
Leuglay
Lavau
St.Sauveur-en-Puisaye
Coulon
Cravant
Vermenton
Noyers
Nuits
Coulmier-le-Sec
Aisey-sur-Seine
Bazarnes
Sanvigne
Verdonnet
Courson-les-Carrières
Arcy-sur-Cure
Joux-la-Ville
Châtel-Gérard
Aisy-sur-Armançon
Etais
Cistercian Abbey of Fontenay
St.Marc-sur-Seine
St.Amand-en-Puisaye
Druyes-les-Belles-Fontaines
Montbard
Fontaines-en-Duesmois
Aignay-le-Duc
Bouhy
Coulanges-sur-Yonne
Voutenay-sur-Cure
Châtel-Censoir
Fain-lès-Montbard
Aligny-Cosne
Entrains-sur-Nohain
Oisy
Clamecy
Sauvigny-le-Bois
Vassy
Echalot
Rougny
la Chapelle-St.André
Vézelay
Avallon
Guillon
Époisses
Venarey-les-Laumes
Baigneux-les-Juifs
Poiseul-la-Grange
Donzy
Menou
Dornecy
Church and hill of Vézelay
St.Père
Cussy-les-Forges
Collines du Nivernais
Tannay
Nuars
Ste.Magnance
Semur-en-Auxois
Pouillenay
Thenissey
Lamargelle
Varzy
Villiers-sur-Beuvron
St.Germain-des-Champs
Précy-sous-Thil
Villeferry
St.Seine-l'Abbaye
Narcy
Nannay
les Pontots
Empury
Réservoir du Crescent
Quarré-les-Tombes
Clamerey
Vitteaux
Mt. Tasselot
Champlemy
Brinon-sur-Beuvron
la Roche-en-Brenil
Mt. Rond
Missery
Blaisy-Bas
Val-Suzon
Charité-sur-Loire
Lormes
Corbigny
Dun-les-Places
Saulieu
Mont-St.Jean
Sombernon
Prémery
Cervon
Gâcogne
Pouilly-en-Auxois
Chaulgnes
Moussy
Montsauche-les-Settons
Commarin
Dijon
Guérigny
Bazolles
Chassy
Moux-en-Morvan
Liernais
le Maupas
Balleray
St.Saulge
St.Maurice
Planchez
Lac des Settons
Réservoir de Pannecière-Chaumard
Rouvres-sous-Meilly
Gevrey-Chambertin
Bona
Ougny
la Chaise
Chissey-en-Morvan
Brazey-en-Morvan
Jouey
Ternant
Nevers
Dommartin
Château-Chinon
Arnay-le-Duc
Sermoise-sur-Loire
St.Benin-d'Azy
Rouy
Châtillon-en-Bazois
Anost
Voudenay
Bligny-sur-Ouche
Nuits-St.Georges
Imphy
Anlezy
Fertrève
Biches
Moulins
Antigny-le-Château
3°00'
4°00'
48°00'

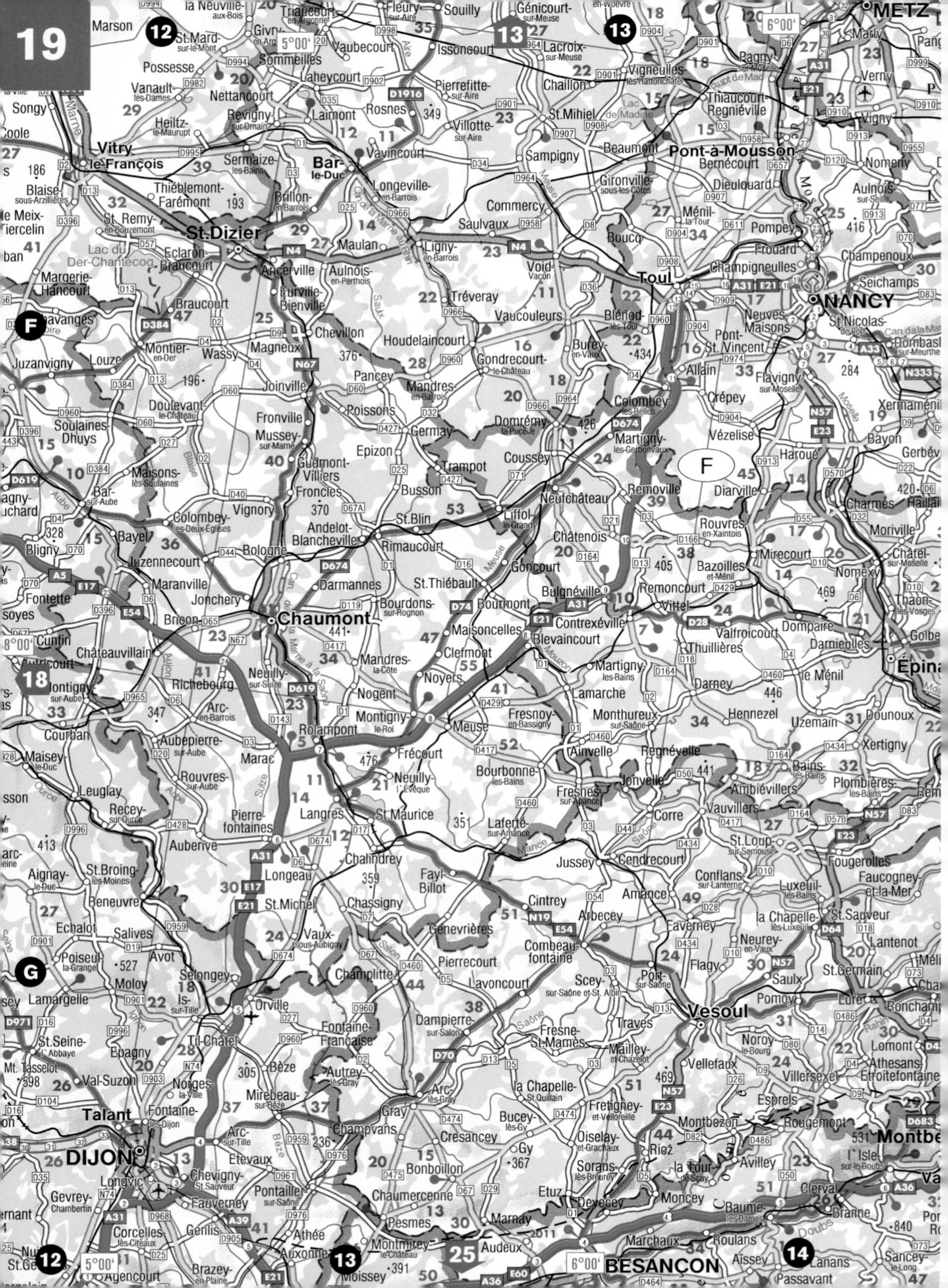
METZ
NANCY
Pont-à-Mousson
Toul
St.Dizier
Vitry le-François
Bar-le-Duc
Commercy
St.Mihiel
Chaumont
Langres
Neufchâteau
Vittel
Contrexéville
Épinal
Vesoul
DIJON
BESANÇON
Montbéliard
Gray
Talant
Longvic
Chevigny-St.Sauveur
Auxonne
Genlis
Pontailler-sur-Saône
Pesmes
Marnay
Is-sur-Tille
Til-Châtel
Selongey
Champlitte
Fontaine-Française
Mirebeau-sur-Bèze
Chalindrey
Fayl-Billot
Jussey
Port-sur-Saône
Scey-sur-Saône et St. Albin
Combeaufontaine
Luxeuil-les-Bains
Lure
Villersexel
Rougemont
Baume-les-Dames
Clerval
Rioz
Plombières-les-Bains
Bains-les-Bains
Darney
Lamarche
Bourbonne-les-Bains
Mirecourt
Charmes
Vézelise
Colombey-les-Belles
Vaucouleurs
Joinville
Wassy
Montier-en-Der
Bar-sur-Aube
Colombey-les-Deux-Églises
Châteauvillain
Nogent
Montigny-le-Roi
Auberive
Recey-sur-Ource
Aignay-le-Duc
St.Seine-l'Abbaye
Gevrey-Chambertin
Ligny-en-Barrois
Void-Vacon
Thiaucourt-Regniéville
Vigneulles-lès-Hattonchâtel
Lac de Madine
Lac du Der-Chantecoq
Dombasle-sur-Meurthe
St.Nicolas-de-Port
Neuves-Maisons
Pompey
Frouard
Champigneulles
Sermaize-les-Bains
Revigny-sur-Ornain
Ancerville
Eurville-Bienville
Chevillon
Gondrecourt-le-Château
Domrémy-la-Pucelle
Liffol-le-Grand
Bulgnéville
Andelot-Blancheville
Rolampont
Vaux-sous-Aubigny
Dampierre-sur-Salon
Champvans
Cresancey
Chaumercenne
Fresne-St.Mamès
Amance
Faverney
Vauvillers
Corre
Jonvelle
Monthureux-sur-Saône
Dompaire
Rambervillers
Bayon
Haroué
Xertigny
Fougerolles
Faucogney-et-la-Mer
St.Sauveur
Pomoy
Noroy-le-Bourg
Athesans-Etroitefontaine
l'Isle-sur-le-Doubs
Roulans
Marchaux
Audeux
Montmirey-le-Château
5°00'
6°00'
8°00'
12
13
14
18
25
F
G
A31
A5
A36
A39
E17
E21
E23
E54
E60
N4
N19
N57
N67
D674
D619
Marne
Meuse
Moselle
Saône
Aube
Doubs

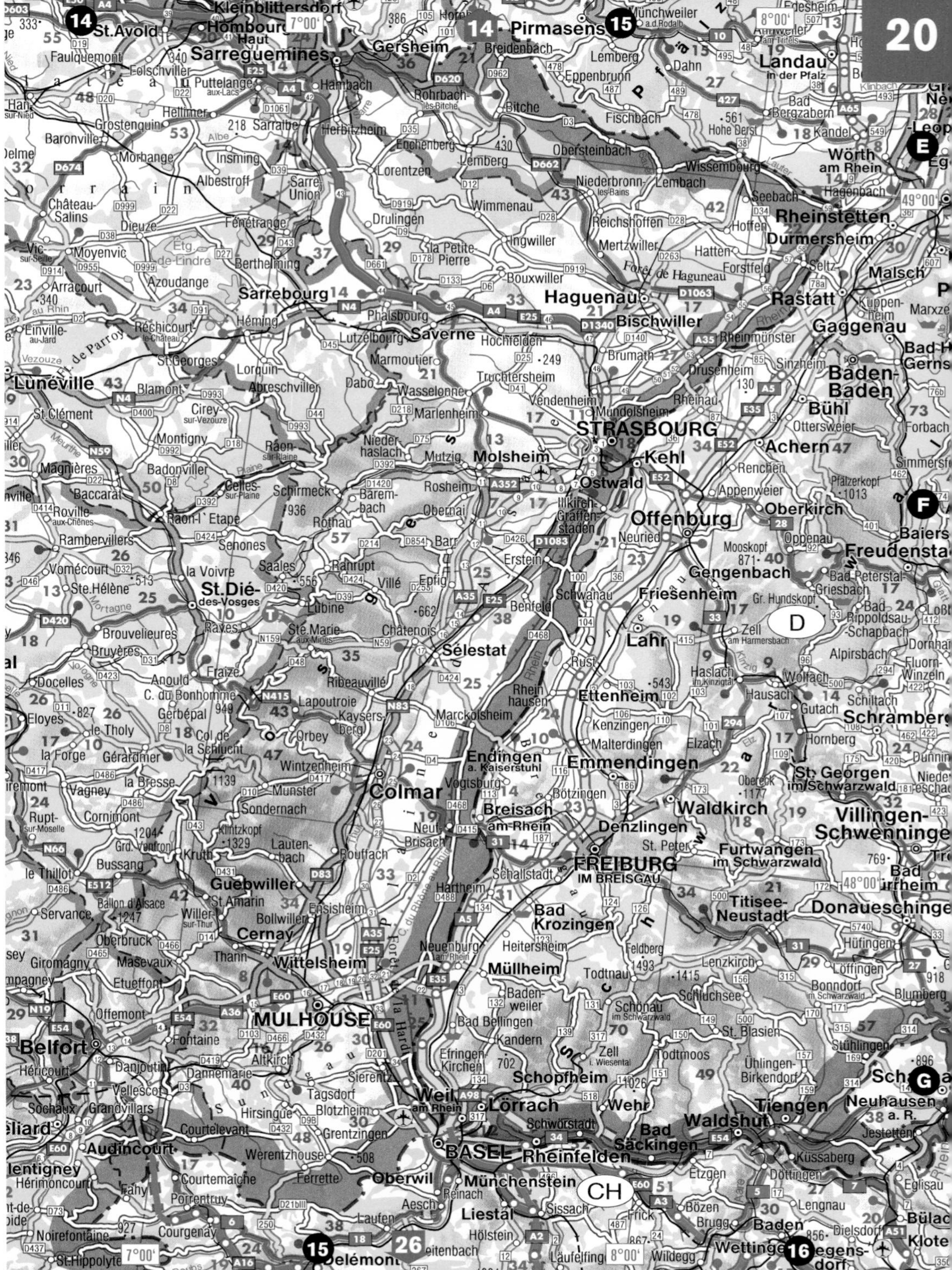
14
St.Avold
Kleinblittersdorf
Homburg
Sarreguemines
Gersheim
Pirmasens
15
Münchweiler a.d.Rodalb
Landau in der Pfalz
Faulquemont
Folschviller
Puttelange-aux-Lacs
Hambach
Rohrbach-lès-Bitche
Breidenbach
Lemberg
Dahn
Eppenbrunn
Hellimer
Sarralbe
Herbitzheim
Bitche
Fischbach
Bad Bergzabern
Hohe Derst
Kandel
Grostenquin
Baronville
Morhange
Insming
Enchenberg
Obersteinbach
Wissembourg
Wörth am Rhein
E
Sarre-Union
Lorentzen
Niederbronn-les-Bains
Lembach
Seebach
Hagenbach
Rheinstetten
Albestroff
Château-Salins
Dieuze
Fénétrange
Drulingen
Wimmenau
Reichshoffen
Hoffen
Durmersheim
Vic-sur-Seille
Moyenvic
Étg. de Lindre
Berthelming
la Petite-Pierre
Ingwiller
Mertzwiller
Hatten
Forstfeld
Seltz
Malsch
Azoudange
Arracourt
Bouxwiller
Forêt de Haguenau
Sarrebourg
Haguenau
Rastatt
Kuppenheim
Gaggenau
Héming
Réchicourt-le-Château
Phalsbourg
Lutzelbourg
Saverne
Hochfelden
Bischwiller
Rheinmünster
Einville-au-Jard
St.Georges
Lorquin
Marmoutier
Brumath
Sinzheim
Baden-Baden
Lunéville
Blâmont
Abreschviller
Dabo
Wasselonne
Truchtersheim
Drusenheim
Rheinau
Bühl
Forbach
St.Clément
Cirey-sur-Vezouze
Marlenheim
Vendenheim
Mundolsheim
Ottersweier
Montigny
Nieder-haslach
Mutzig
Molsheim
STRASBOURG
Kehl
Achern
Raon-sur-Plaine
Magnières
Badonviller
Celles-sur-Plaine
Schirmeck
Rosheim
Ostwald
Renchen
Baccarat
Barembach
Obernai
Illkirch-Graffenstaden
Appenweier
Oberkirch
F
Roville-aux-Chênes
Raon-l'Etape
Rothau
Offenburg
Pfälzerkopf
Rambervillers
Senones
Barr
Erstein
Neuried
Oppenau
Baiersbronn
Freudenstadt
Mooskopf
Gengenbach
Vomécourt
Ste.Hélène
la Voivre
Saales
Rahrupt
Epfig
Bad Peterstal-Griesbach
St.Dié-des-Vosges
Villé
Schwanau
Friesenheim
Gr. Hundskopf
Bad Rippoldsau-Schapbach
Lubine
Benfeld
D
Zell am Harmersbach
Brouvelieures
Raves
Ste.Marie-aux-Mines
Châtenois
Lahr
Bruyères
Sélestat
Alpirsbach
Rust
Haslach im Kinzigtal
Wolfach
Docelles
Anould
Fraize
Ribeauvillé
Fluorn-Winzeln
C. du Bonhomme
Lapoutroie
Rheinhausen
Ettenheim
Hausach
Schiltach
Eloyes
le Tholy
Gerbépal
Kaysersberg
Marckolsheim
Gutach
Schramberg
Col de la Schlucht
Orbey
Kenzingen
Elzach
Hornberg
la Forge
Gérardmer
Wintzenheim
Endingen a. Kaiserstuhl
Emmendingen
Malterdingen
St. Georgen im Schwarzwald
la Bresse
Munster
Colmar
Vogtsburg
Oberreck
Vagney
Sondernach
Breisach am Rhein
Bötzingen
Waldkirch
Villingen-Schwenningen
Rupt-sur-Moselle
Cornimont
Klintzkopf
Neuf-Brisach
Denzlingen
Grd. Ventron
Lautenbach
St. Peter
Furtwangen im Schwarzwald
Kruth
Rouffach
FREIBURG IM BREISGAU
Bussang
le Thillot
Guebwiller
Schallstadt
Hartheim
Ballon d'Alsace
St.Amarin
Ensisheim
Titisee-Neustadt
Donaueschingen
Servance
Willer-sur-Thur
Bollwiller
Bad Krozingen
Oberbruck
Cernay
Heitersheim
Feldberg
Hüfingen
Giromagny
Masevaux
Thann
Wittelsheim
Neuenburg am Rhein
Müllheim
Todtnau
Lenzkirch
Löffingen
Etueffont
Badenweiler
Schluchsee
Bonndorf im Schwarzwald
Blumberg
Offemont
MULHOUSE
Bad Bellingen
Schönau im Schwarzwald
Fontaine
Kandern
St. Blasien
Stühlingen
Belfort
Danjoutin
Dannemarie
Altkirch
Efringen-Kirchen
Zell i. Wiesental
Todtmoos
Héricourt
Sierentz
Schopfheim
Ühlingen-Birkendorf
G
Vellescot
Tagsdorf
Wehr
Sochaux
Grandvillars
Hirsingue
Blotzheim
Weil am Rhein
Lörrach
Schwörstadt
Tiengen
Neuhausen a. R.
Courtelevant
Grentzingen
Bad Säckingen
Waldshut
Jestetten
Audincourt
Werentzhouse
BASEL
Rheinfelden
Küssaberg
Courtemaîche
Ferrette
Oberwil
Münchenstein
CH
Etzgen
Döttingen
Eglisau
Porrentruy
Fahy
Reinach
Aesch
Liestal
Sissach
Frick
Bözen
Lengnau
Noirefontaine
Courgenay
Laufen
Hölstein
Brugg
Baden
Dielsdorf
15
Delémont
26
Läufelfingen
Wildegg
Wettingen
16
St.Hippolyte
7°00'
8°00'
48°00'
49°00'

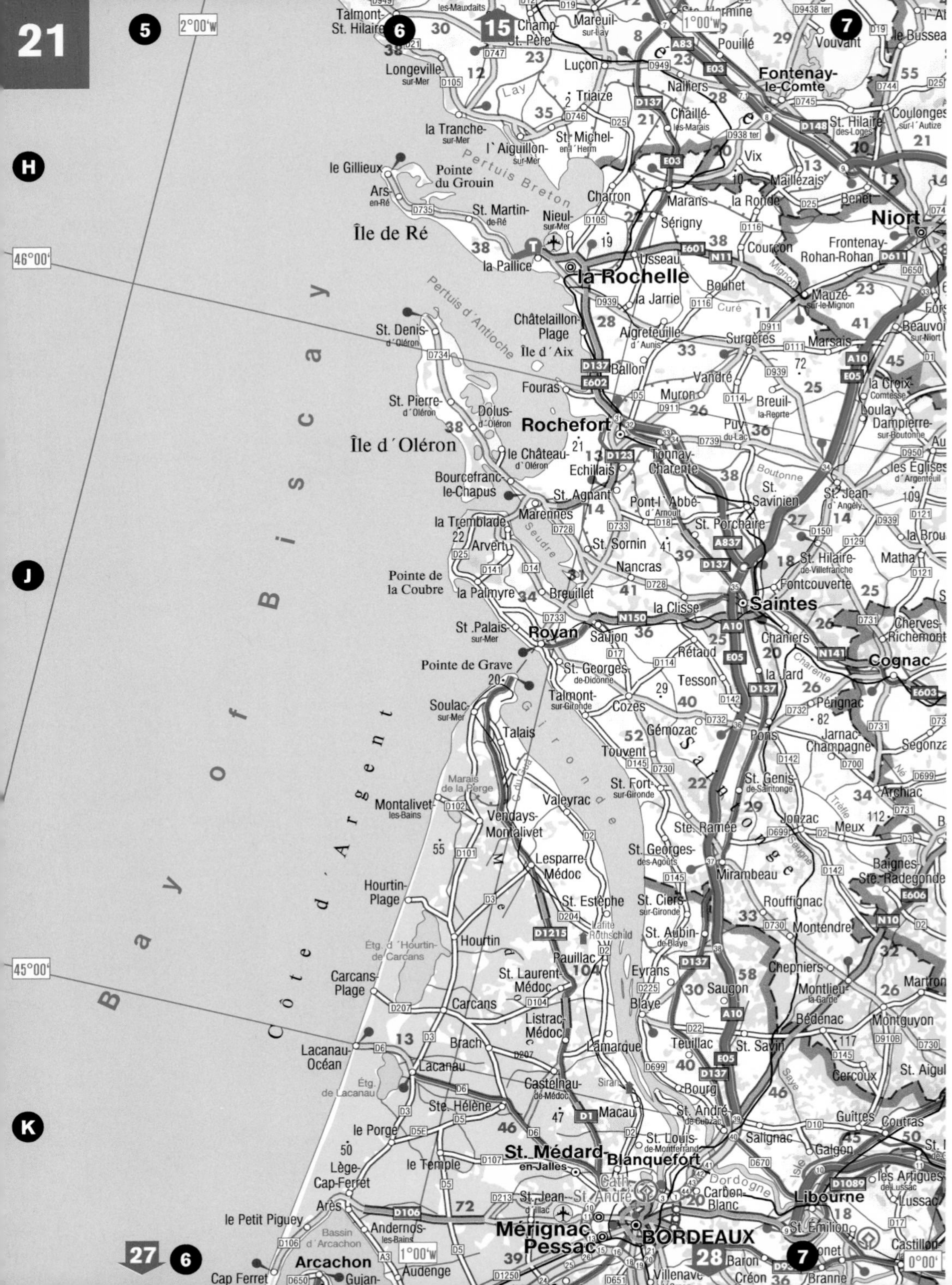

5
2°00'W
6
15
1°00'W
7
H
J
K
46°00'
45°00'
Bay of Biscay
Côte d'Argent
Pertuis Breton
Pertuis d'Antioche
Gironde
Saintonge
Talmont-St. Hilaire
Champ-St. Père
Mareuil-sur-Lay
Ste. Hermine
Vouvant
Longeville-sur-Mer
Luçon
Pouillé
Fontenay-le-Comte
Triaize
Nalliers
la Tranche-sur-Mer
l'Aiguillon-sur-Mer
St. Michel-en-l'Herm
Chaillé-les-Marais
St. Hilaire-des-Loges
Coulonges-sur-l'Autize
le Gillieux
Pointe du Grouin
Ars-en-Ré
Vix
Maillezais
St. Martin-de-Ré
Charron
Marans
la Ronde
Benet
Niort
Île de Ré
Nieul-sur-Mer
Sérigny
Courçon
Frontenay-Rohan-Rohan
la Pallice
Usseau
la Rochelle
Bouhet
Mauzé-sur-le-Mignon
la Jarrie
Châtelaillon-Plage
Aigrefeuille-d'Aunis
Surgères
Marsais
Beauvoir-sur-Niort
St. Denis-d'Oléron
Île d'Aix
Ballon
Vandré
Fouras
Muron
Breuil-la-Réorte
la Croix-Comtesse
St. Pierre-d'Oléron
Dolus-d'Oléron
Loulay
Dampierre-sur-Boutonne
Rochefort
Puy-du-Lac
Île d'Oléron
le Château-d'Oléron
Tonnay-Charente
les Églises-d'Argenteuil
Bourcefranc-le-Chapus
Echillais
St. Agnant
Pont-l'Abbé-d'Arnoult
St. Savinien
St. Jean-d'Angély
Marennes
la Tremblade
St. Porchaire
Arvert
St. Sornin
St. Hilaire-de-Villefranche
Matha
Pointe de la Coubre
Nancras
la Palmyre
Breuillet
Fontcouverte
la Clisse
Saintes
St. Palais-sur-Mer
Royan
Saujon
Chaniers
Cherves-Richemont
Cognac
Pointe de Grave
Rétaud
St. Georges-de-Didonne
Tesson
la Jard
Soulac-sur-Mer
Talmont-sur-Gironde
Cozes
Pérignac
Talais
Gémozac
Jarnac-Champagne
Segonzac
Touvent
Pons
Marais de la Perge
St. Fort-sur-Gironde
St. Genis-de-Saintonge
Archiac
Montalivet-les-Bains
Valeyrac
Vendays-Montalivet
Jonzac
Meux
Ste. Ramée
St. Georges-des-Agoûts
Lesparre-Médoc
Mirambeau
Baignes-Ste. Radegonde
Hourtin-Plage
St. Estèphe
St. Ciers-sur-Gironde
Rouffignac
Lafite Rothschild
St. Aubin-de-Blaye
Montendre
Étg. d'Hourtin-de Carcans
Hourtin
Pauillac
Eyrans
Chepniers
St. Laurent-Médoc
Carcans-Plage
Saugon
Montlieu-la-Garde
Martron
Carcans
Blaye
Listrac-Médoc
Bédenac
Montguyon
Brach
Lacanau-Océan
Lamarque
Teuillac
St. Savin
Lacanau
Cercoux
St. Aiguli
Étg. de Lacanau
Castelnau-de-Médoc
Bourg
Ste. Hélène
Macau
St. André-de-Cubzac
Guîtres
Coutras
le Porge
St. Louis-de-Montferrand
Salignac
Galgon
St. Médard-en-Jalles
Blanquefort
le Temple
Lège-Cap-Ferret
Dordogne
les Artigues-de-Lussac
St. Jean-d'Illac
St. André
Carbon-Blanc
Libourne
Lussac
Arès
le Petit Piquey
Andernos-les-Bains
Mérignac
Pessac
BORDEAUX
St. Émilion
Castillon
Bassin d'Arcachon
27
28
Arcachon
Audenge
Cap Ferret
Gujan-
Baron
Créon
Branne
0°00'
A83
A10
A837
E03
E05
E601
E602
E603
E606
N11
N10
N141
N150
D137
D148
D123
D1215
D106
D1089

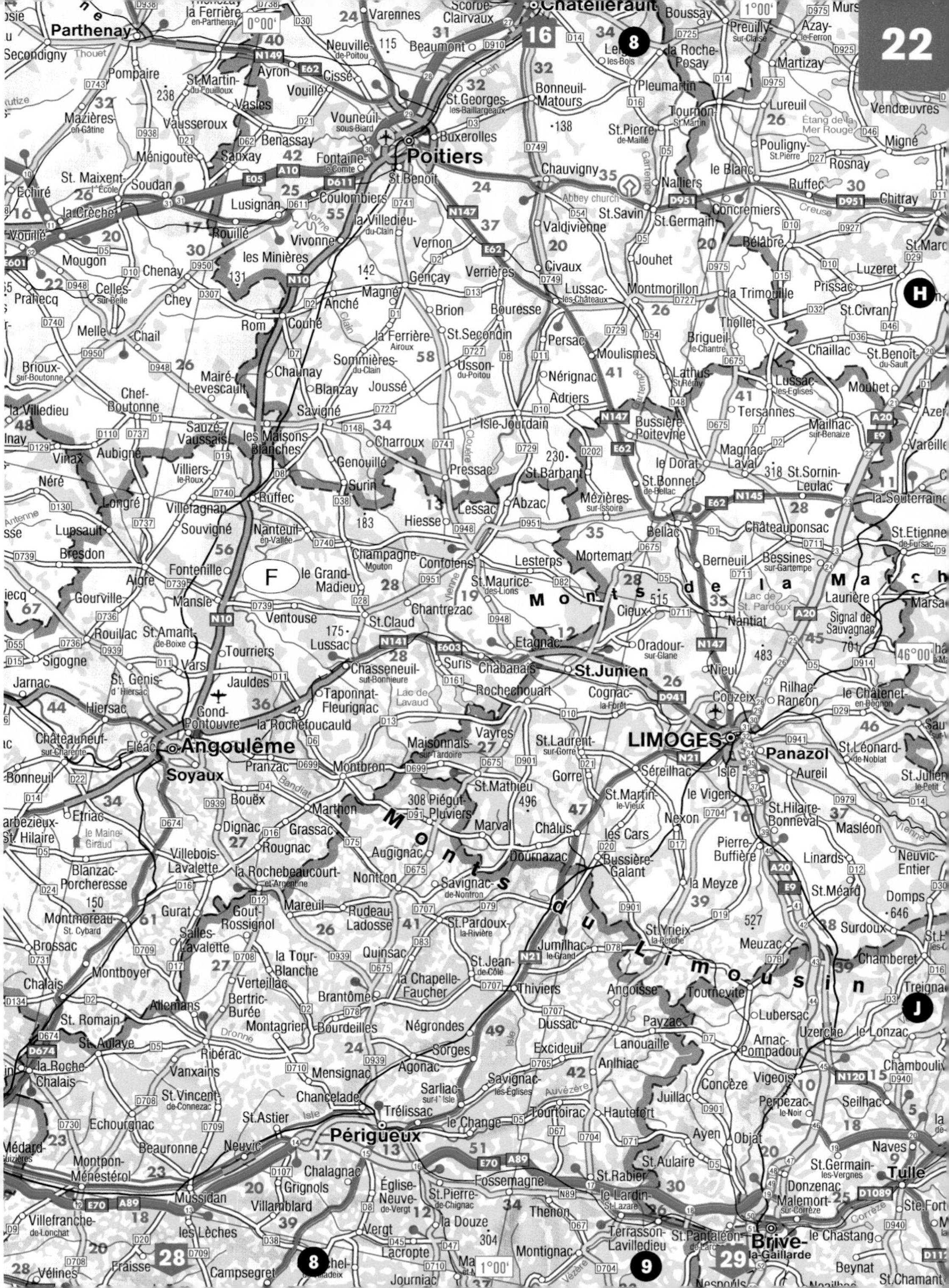
Parthenay
Châtellerault
Poitiers
Chauvigny
St. Savin
Montmorillon
le Blanc
Lusignan
Vivonne
Gençay
Civaux
Lussac-les-Châteaux
Melle
Chef-Boutonne
Ruffec
Mansle
l'Isle-Jourdain
le Dorat
Bellac
Confolens
Chabanais
St. Junien
Rochechouart
la Rochefoucauld
Angoulême
Soyaux
LIMOGES
Panazol
St. Léonard-de-Noblat
Châlus
Nontron
Brantôme
St.Yrieix-la-Perche
Uzerche
Tulle
Brive-la-Gaillarde
Périgueux
Ribérac
Mussidan
Montignac
Terrasson-Lavilledieu
Monts de la Marche
Monts du Limousin
Abbey church
0°00'
1°00'
46°00'

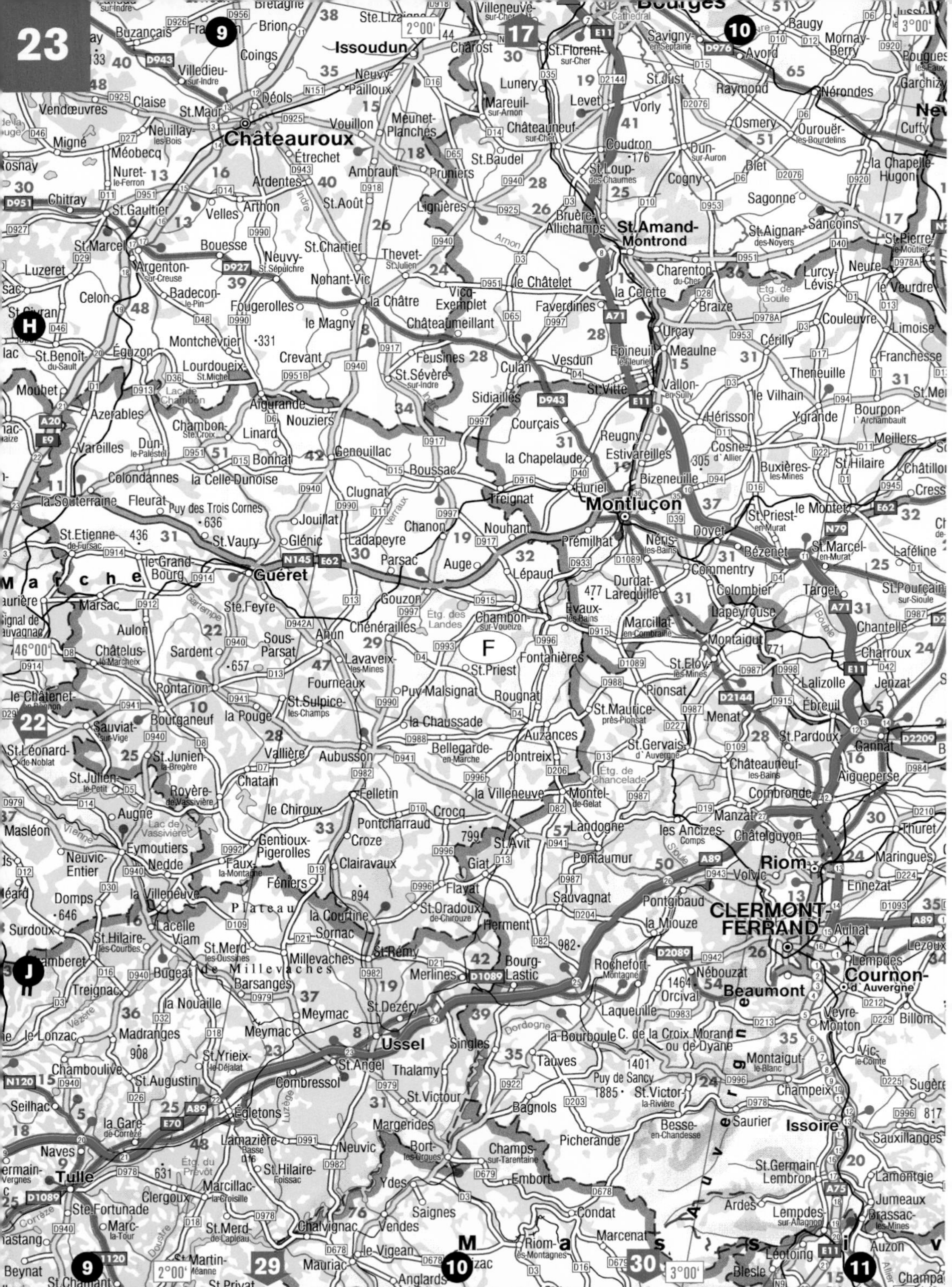
23
Bourges
Issoudun
Châteauroux
Buzançais
Villedieu-sur-Indre
Déols
Vendœuvres
Neuillay-les-Bois
Migné
Méobecq
Nuret-le-Ferron
Chitray
St.Gaultier
Velles
Arthon
Ardentes
Étrechet
St.Août
Ambrault
Neuvy-Pailloux
Vouillon
Meunet-Planches
Charost
St.Florent-sur-Cher
Lunery
Mareuil-sur-Arnon
Châteauneuf-sur-Cher
St.Baudel
Pruniers
Lignières
Levet
Vorly
St.Just
Savigny-en-Septaine
Avord
Baugy
Mornay-Berry
Raymond
Nérondes
Osmery
Ourouër-les-Bourdelins
Dun-sur-Auron
Coudron
St.Loup-des-Chaumes
Cogny
Blet
Sagonne
Bruère-Allichamps
St.Amand-Montrond
St.Aignan-des-Noyers
Sancoins
Charenton-du-Cher
La Celette
Le Châtelet
Vicq-Exemplet
Châteaumeillant
Thevet-St.Julien
Nohant-Vic
la Châtre
St.Chartier
Neuvy-St.Sépulchre
Bouesse
St.Marcel
Argenton-sur-Creuse
Luzeret
Celon
Badecon-le-Pin
Fougerolles
le Magny
Montchevrier
Éguzon
St.Benoît-du-Sault
Crevant
Lourdoueix-St.Michel
Aigurande
Nouziers
Linard
Chambon-Ste.Croix
Dun-le-Palestel
Azerables
Vareilles
Colondannes
la Celle-Dunoise
Bonnat
Genouillac
la Souterraine
Fleurat
Puy des Trois Cornes
St.Etienne-de-Fursac
St.Vaury
Glénic
Jouillat
le Grand-Bourg
Guéret
Marsac
Ste.Feyre
Aulon
Châtelus-le-Marcheix
Sardent
Sous-Parsat
Ahun
Pontarion
Bourganeuf
la Pouge
Sauviat-sur-Vige
St.Léonard-de-Noblat
St.Junien-la-Bregère
St.Julien-le-Petit
Royère-de-Vassivière
Augne
Lac de Vassivière
Masléon
Eymoutiers
Neuvic-Entier
Nedde
Faux-la-Montagne
Gentioux-Pigerolles
le Chiroux
Chatain
Vallière
Aubusson
Felletin
Domps
Surdoux
St.Hilaire-les-Courbes
Lacelle
Viam
la Villeneuve
Plateau de Millevaches
St.Merd-les-Oussines
Bugeat
Barsanges
Millevaches
Treignac
Madranges
le Lonzac
Chamboulive
St.Augustin
St.Yrieix-le-Déjalat
Meymac
Seilhac
la Gare-de-Corrèze
Égletons
Naves
Tulle
Lamazière-Basse
Marcillac-la-Croisille
Clergoux
Ste.Fortunade
Marc-la-Tour
St.Merd-de-Lapleau
St.Martin-la-Méanne
Beynat
St.Chamant
St.Privat
Neuvic
St.Hilaire-Foissac
Combressol
Ussel
St.Angel
St.Dezéry
Sornac
St.Rémy
la Courtine
Clairavaux
Féniers
Croze
Pontcharraud
Crocq
Flayat
St.Oradoux-de-Chirouze
Merlines
Bourg-Lastic
Giat
St.Avit
Herment
Thalamy
St.Victour
Margerides
Bort-les-Orgues
Ydes
Saignes
Vendes
Chalvignac
le Vigean
Mauriac
Anglards
Champs-sur-Tarentaine
Embort
Condat
Riom-ès-Montagnes
Marcenat
Singles
Tauves
la Bourboule
Bagnols
Picherande
Puy de Sancy
St.Victor-la-Rivière
Besse-en-Chandesse
Saurier
Laqueuille
Orcival
Rochefort-Montagne
Nébouzat
C. de la Croix Morand ou de Dyane
Montaigut-le-Blanc
Champeix
Issoire
Sauxillanges
St.Germain-Lembron
Lamontgie
Ardes
Lempdes-sur-Allagnon
Jumeaux
Brassac-les-Mines
Auzon
Léotoing
Blesle
Beaumont
Clermont-Ferrand
Aulnat
Lempdes
Cournon-d'Auvergne
Veyre-Monton
Vic-le-Comte
Billom
Pontgibaud
la Miouze
Sauvagnat
Pontaumur
Volvic
Riom
Ennezat
Maringues
Thuret
Châtelguyon
les Ancizes-Comps
Manzat
Combronde
Aigueperse
Gannat
St.Pardoux
Ébreuil
Lalizolle
Jenzat
Charroux
Chantelle
Menat
Châteauneuf-les-Bains
St.Gervais-d'Auvergne
St.Maurice-près-Pionsat
Rionsat
St.Eloy-les-Mines
Montaigut
Lapeyrouse
Marcillat-en-Combraille
Evaux-les-Bains
Durdat-Larequille
Commentry
Colombier
Néris-les-Bains
Montluçon
Prémilhat
Lépaud
Chambon-sur-Voueize
Fontanières
St.Priest
Rougnat
Auzances
Dontreix
Bellegarde-en-Marche
la Chaussade
Puy-Malsignat
St.Sulpice-les-Champs
Fourneaux
Lavaveix-les-Mines
Chénérailles
Étg. des Landes
Gouzon
Parsac
Auge
Nouhant
Chanon
Ladapeyre
Clugnat
Boussac
Treignat
Huriel
la Chapelaude
Courçais
Sidiailles
St.Sévère-sur-Indre
Feusines
Culan
Vesdun
St.Vitte
Faverdines
Epineuil-le-Fleuriel
Meaulne
Urçay
Braize
Vallon-en-Sully
Reugny
Estivareilles
Bizeneuille
Cosne-d'Allier
Hérisson
le Vilhain
Cérilly
Theneuille
Ygrande
Bourbon-l'Archambault
Buxières-les-Mines
St.Hilaire
Meillers
Le Montet
St.Priest-en-Murat
Doyet
Bézenet
St.Marcel-en-Murat
Target
St.Pourçain-sur-Sioule
Laféline
Lurcy-Lévis
Neure
le Veurdre
Couleuvre
Limoise
Franchesse
St.Pierre-le-Moûtier
la Chapelle-Hugon
Pougues-les-Eaux
Garchizy
Cuffy
Marche
Auvergne
Millevaches
46°00'
2°00'
3°00'

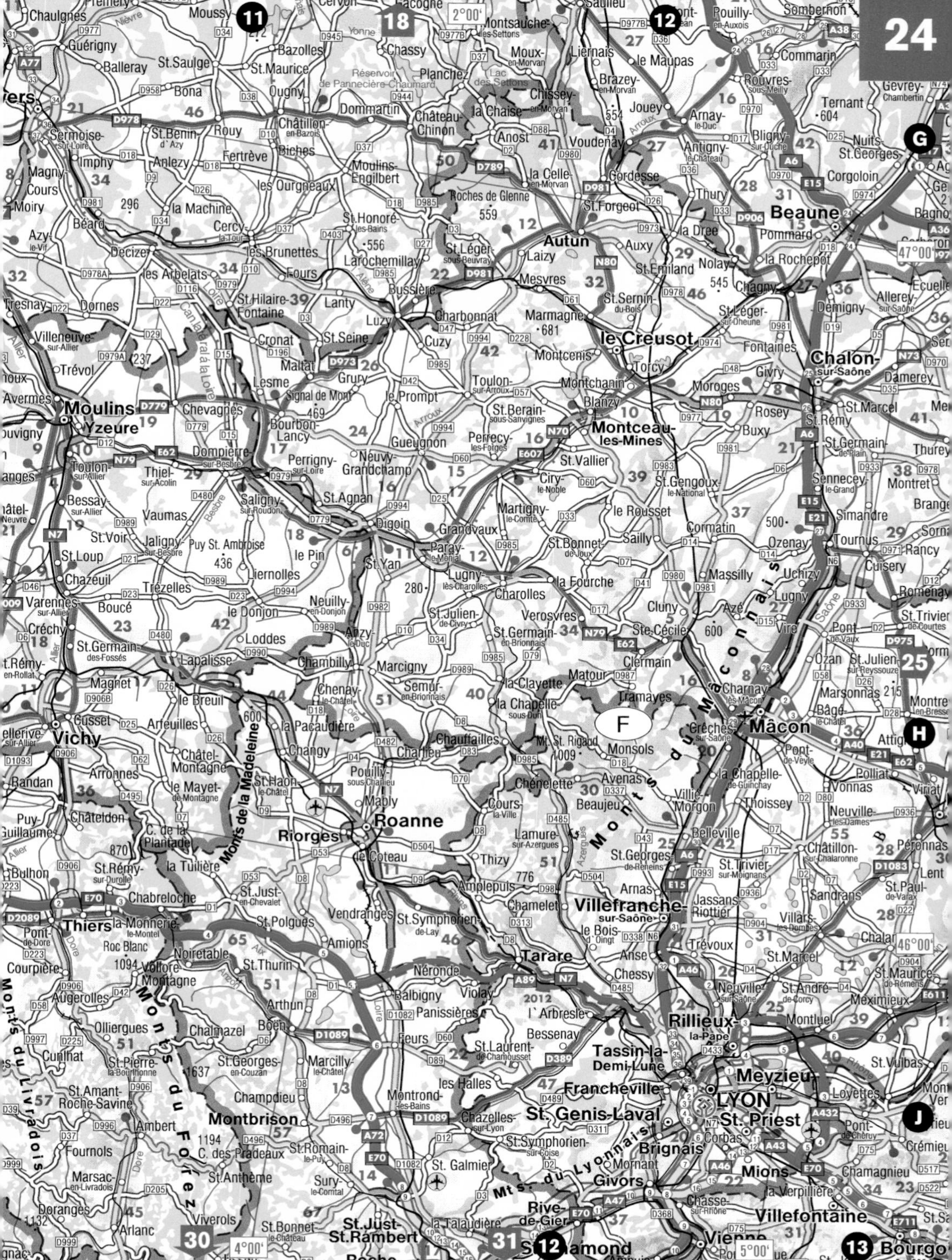

24
Chaulgnes
Prémery
Moussy
Cervon
Gâcogne
Montsauche-les-Settons
Saulieu
Pouilly-en-Auxois
Sombernon
Guérigny
Balleray
St.Saulge
Bazolles
St.Maurice
Chassy
Réservoir de Pannecière-Chaumard
Lac des Settons
Planchez
Moux-en-Morvan
Liernais
le Maupas
Commarin
Bona
Ougny
Dommartin
Château-Chinon
la Chaise
Chissey-en-Morvan
Brazey-en-Morvan
Jouey
Arnay-le-Duc
Rouvres-sous-Meilly
Ternant
Gevrey-Chambertin
Sermoise-sur-Loire
St.Benin-d'Azy
Rouy
Châtillon-en-Bazois
Anost
Voudenay
Antigny-le-Château
Bligny-sur-Ouche
Nuits-St.Georges
Imphy
Anlezy
Fertrève
Biches
Moulins-Engilbert
la Celle-en-Morvan
Cordesse
Corgoloin
Magny-Cours
les Ourgneaux
Roches de Glenne
Thury
Moiry
la Machine
Beaune
Azy-le-Vif
Béard
Cercy-la-Tour
St.Honoré-les-Bains
St.Forgeot
Pommard
Decize
les Brunettes
Larochemillay
St.Léger-sous-Beuvray
Autun
Laizy
Auxy
la Dree
Nolay
la Rochepot
47°00'
les Arbelats
Fours
Bussière
Mesvres
St.Emiland
St.Sernin-du-Bois
Chagny
Allerey-sur-Saône
Ecuelle
Tresnay
Dornes
St.Hilaire-Fontaine
Lanty
Luzy
Charbonnat
Marmagne
St.Léger-sur-Dheune
Demigny
Villeneuve-sur-Allier
Cronat
St.Seine
Cuzy
le Creusot
Fontaines
Chalon-sur-Saône
Trévol
Maltat
Grury
Montcenis
Torcy
Givry
Damerey
Avermes
Moulins
Yzeure
Chevagnes
Lesme
Signal de Mont
le Prompt
Toulon-sur-Arroux
Montchanin
Moroges
St.Marcel
Bourbon-Lancy
St.Berain-sous-Sanvignes
Blanzy
Rosey
St.Rémy
Gueugnon
Perrecy-les-Forges
Montceau-les-Mines
Buxy
St.Germain-de-Plain
Thurey
Toulon-sur-Allier
Thiel-sur-Acolin
Dompierre-sur-Besbre
Perrigny-sur-Loire
Neuvy-Grandchamp
St.Vallier
Ciry-le-Noble
St.Gengoux-le-National
Sennecey-le-Grand
Montret
Bessay-sur-Allier
Vaumas
Saligny-sur-Roudon
St.Agnan
Digoin
Martigny-le-Comte
le Rousset
Brange
St.Voir
Jaligny-sur-Besbre
Puy St. Ambroise
Grandvaux
Paray-le-Monial
St.Bonnet-de-Joux
Sailly
Cormatin
Simandre
Tournus
St.Loup
le Pin
St.Yan
Ozenay
Rancy
Chazeuil
Trézelles
Liernolles
Lugny-lès-Charolles
Charolles
la Fourche
Massilly
Uchizy
Cuisery
Varennes-sur-Allier
Boucé
Neuilly-en-Donjon
le Donjon
Verosvres
Cluny
Lugny
Romenay
Créchy
St.Germain-des-Fossés
Loddes
Anzy-le-Duc
St.Julien-de-Civry
St.Germain-en-Brionnais
Ste.Cécile
Azé
Viré
Pont-de-Vaux
St.Trivier-de-Courtes
St.Rémy-en-Rollat
Lapalisse
Chambilly
Marcigny
Clermain
Ozan
St.Julien-sur-Reyssouze
Magnet
le Breuil
Chenay-le-Châtel
Semur-en-Brionnais
la Clayette
Matour
Tramayes
Charnay-lès-Mâcon
Marsonnas
Montrevel-en-Bresse
Cusset
Arfeuilles
la Pacaudière
la Chapelle-sous-Dun
Bâgé-le-Châtel
Vichy
Châtel-Montagne
Changy
Charlieu
Chauffailles
Mt. St. Rigaud
Monsols
Crêches-sur-Saône
Mâcon
Pont-de-Veyle
Attig
Randan
Arronnes
le Mayet-de-Montagne
St.Haon-le-Châtel
Pouilly-sous-Charlieu
Chénelette
Avenas
la Chapelle-de-Guinchay
Polliat
Vonnas
Viriat
Puy-Guillaume
Châteldon
C. de la Plantade
Mably
Roanne
Cours-la-Ville
Beaujeu
Villié-Morgon
Thoissey
Neuville-les-Dames
Riorges
le Coteau
Lamure-sur-Azergues
Belleville
Châtillon-sur-Chalaronne
Péronnas
Bulhon
St.Rémy-sur-Durolle
la Tuilière
Thizy
St.Georges-de-Reneins
St.Trivier-sur-Moignans
Lent
Chabreloche
St.Just-en-Chevalet
Amplepuis
Arnas
Jassans-Riottier
Sandrans
St.Paul-de-Varax
Thiers
la Monnerie-le-Montel
St.Polgues
Vendranges
St.Symphorien-de-Lay
Chamelet
Villefranche-sur-Saône
Villars-les-Dombes
Pont-de-Dore
Roc Blanc
Amions
le Bois-d'Oingt
Trévoux
Chalar
46°00'
Courpière
Noiretable
St.Thurin
Tarare
Anse
St.Marcel
St.Maurice-de-Rémens
Vollore-Montagne
Néronde
Violay
Chessy
Augerolles
Arthun
Balbigny
Neuville-sur-Saône
St.André-de-Corcy
Meximieux
Olliergues
Chalmazel
Boën
Panissières
l'Arbresle
Rillieux-la-Pape
Montluel
Cunlhat
St.Pierre-la-Bourlhonne
St.Georges-en-Couzan
Marcilly-le-Châtel
Feurs
St.Laurent-de-Chamousset
Bessenay
Tassin-la-Demi-Lune
St.Vulbas
St.Amant-Roche-Savine
Champdieu
les Halles
Francheville
Meyzieu
Loyettes
Montbrison
Montrond-les-Bains
Chazelles-sur-Lyon
St. Genis-Laval
LYON
St.Priest
Ambert
C. des Pradeaux
St.Romain-le-Puy
St.Symphorien-sur-Coise
Corbas
Pont-de-Chéruy
Crémieu
Fournols
St.Anthème
Sury-le-Comtal
St. Galmier
Mornant
Brignais
Mions
Chamagnieu
Marsac-en-Livradois
Givors
la Verpillière
Dorangès
Viverols
Rive-de-Gier
Chasse-sur-Rhône
Villefontaine
Arlanc
St.Bonnet-le-Château
St.Just-St.Rambert
la Talaudière
St.Chamond
Vienne
Bourgoin-Jallieu
Monts de la Madeleine
Monts du Forez
Monts du Livradois
Monts du Mâconnais
Mts. du Lyonnais
2°00'
4°00'
5°00'

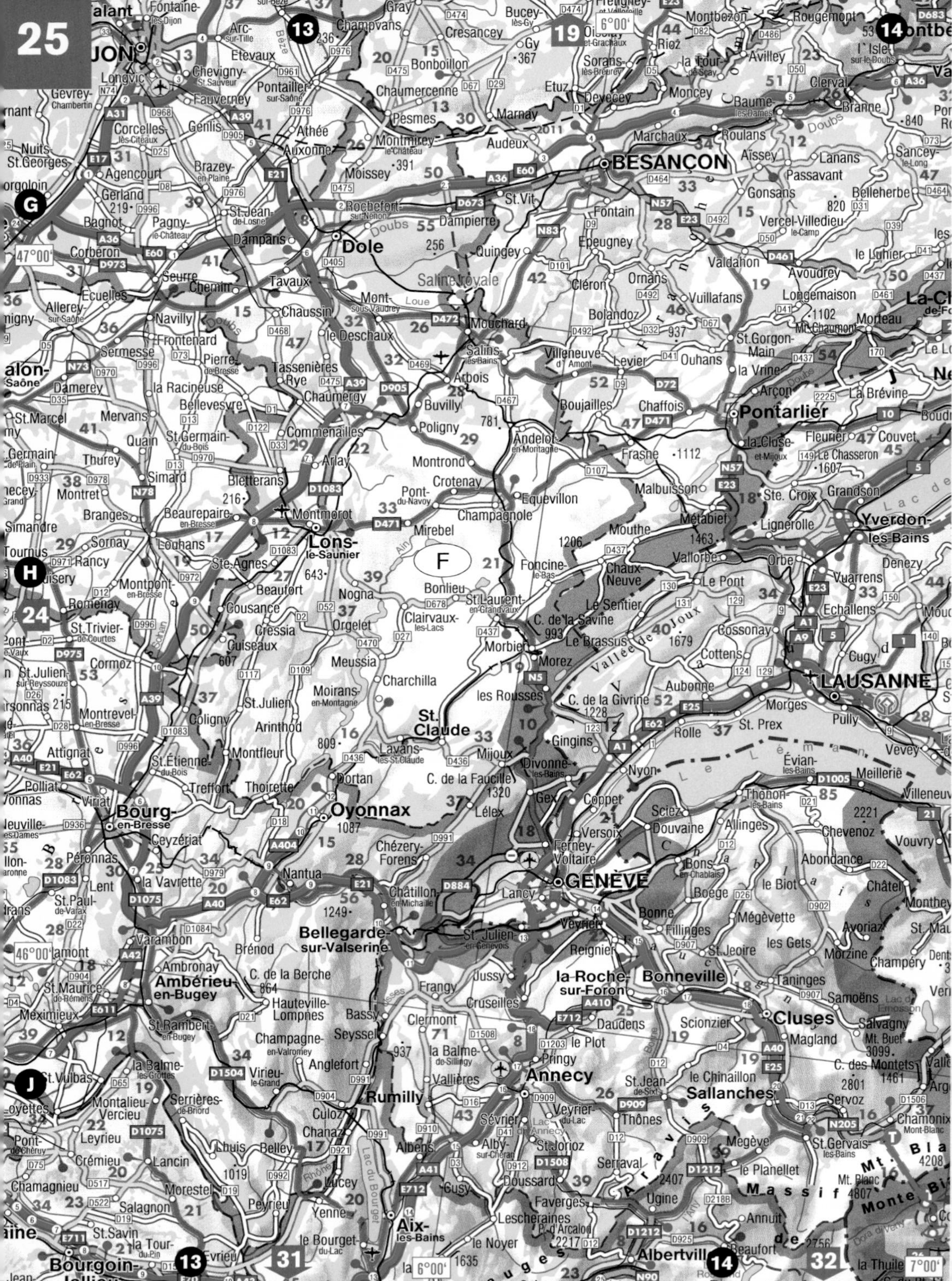

Dijon
Besançon
Dole
Lons-le-Saunier
Pontarlier
Yverdon-les-Bains
Lausanne
Genève
Annecy
Bourg-en-Bresse
Oyonnax
Bellegarde-sur-Valserine
Ambérieu-en-Bugey
Aix-les-Bains
Albertville
Chamonix Mont-Blanc
Cluses
Bonneville
la Roche-sur-Foron
St. Claude
Champagnole
Poligny
Arbois
Salins-les-Bains
Mouchard
Ornans
Baume-les-Dames
Auxonne
Seurre
Louhans
Nantua
Rumilly
Sallanches
Thonon-les-Bains
Évian-les-Bains
Morges
Nyon
Vevey
Morez
les Rousses
Massif des Aravis
Mt. Blanc 4807
Lac du Bourget
Le Léman
Vallée de Joux
6°00'
7°00'
47°00'
46°00'

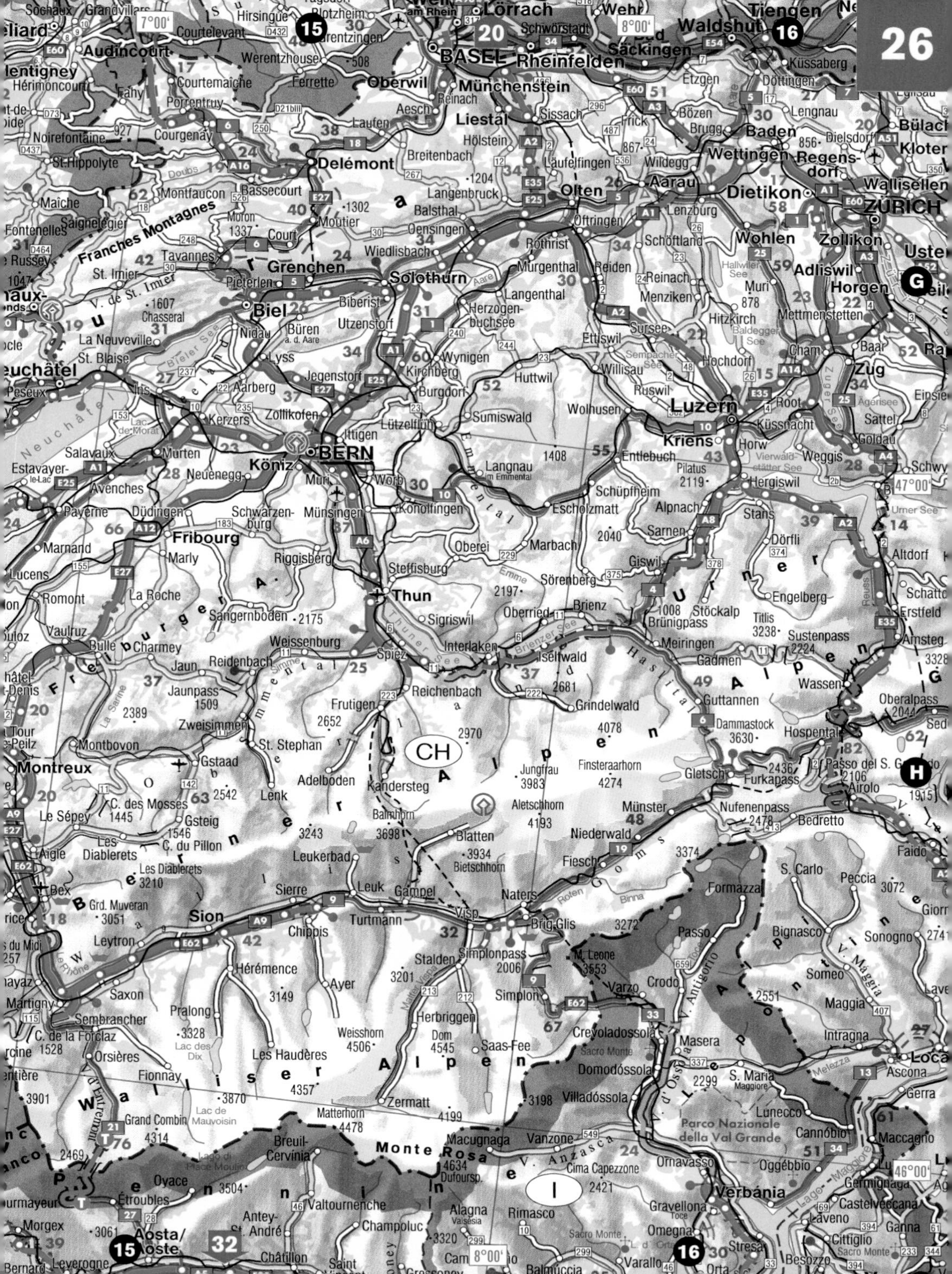
26
Lörrach
BASEL
Rheinfelden
Bad Säckingen
Waldshut
Tiengen
Audincourt
Hérimoncourt
Courtemaîche
Porrentruy
Oberwil
Münchenstein
Reinach
Aesch
Liestal
Sissach
Frick
Bözen
Brugg
Baden
Lengnau
Bülach
Kloten
Dielsdorf
Regensdorf
Wettingen
Dietikon
Wallisellen
ZÜRICH
Delémont
Laufen
Breitenbach
Hölstein
Läufelfingen
Wildegg
Aarau
Olten
Langenbruck
Balsthal
Oensingen
Moutier
Court
Bassecourt
Montfaucon
Saignelégier
Franches Montagnes
St. Hippolyte
Noirefontaine
Courgenay
Tavannes
Grenchen
Pieterlen
St. Imier
Solothurn
Wiedlisbach
Rothrist
Oftringen
Murgenthal
Reiden
Lenzburg
Schöftland
Wohlen
Zollikon
Adliswil
Horgen
Uster
Biel
Nidau
Chasseral
Büren a. d. Aare
Biberist
Utzenstorf
Herzogenbuchsee
Langenthal
Sursee
Reinach
Menziken
Hitzkirch
Muri
Mettmenstetten
Cham
Baar
Zug
La Neuveville
St. Blaise
Neuchâtel
Lyss
Jegenstorf
Kirchberg
Burgdorf
Wynigen
Huttwil
Willisau
Ettiswil
Ruswil
Hochdorf
Luzern
Kriens
Horw
Küssnacht
Root
Peseux
Aarberg
Kerzers
Zollikofen
Ittigen
Lützelflüh
Sumiswald
Wolhusen
Entlebuch
Murten
BERN
Köniz
Muri
Worb
Langnau im Emmental
Schüpfheim
Pilatus 2119
Hergiswil
Weggis
Goldau
Schwyz
Salavaux
Estavayer-le-Lac
Avenches
Neuenegg
Payerne
Düdingen
Schwarzenburg
Münsingen
Konolfingen
Escholzmatt
Alpnach
Stans
Sarnen
Dörfli
Altdorf
Fribourg
Marly
Marnand
Riggisberg
Oberei
Marbach
Giswil
Steffisburg
Sörenberg
Lucens
Romont
La Roche
Sangernboden
Thun
Sigriswil
Oberried
Brienz
Brünigpass
Stöckalp
Engelberg
Titlis 3238
Erstfeld
Vaulruz
Bulle
Charmey
Weissenburg
Spiez
Interlaken
Iseltwald
Meiringen
Sustenpass
Amsteg
Jaun
Reidenbach
Gadmen
Wassen
Jaunpass
Reichenbach
Frutigen
Grindelwald
Guttannen
Oberalppass
Zweisimmen
Montbovon
St. Stephan
Dammastock 3630
Hospental
Montreux
Gstaad
Adelboden
Kandersteg
CH
Jungfrau 3983
Finsteraarhorn 4274
Gletsch
Furkapass
Passo del S. Gottardo
Airolo
C. des Mosses
Le Sépey
Gsteig
Lenk
Balmhorn 3698
Aletschhorn 4193
Münster
Nufenenpass
Bedretto
C. du Pillon
Les Diablerets
Aigle
Leukerbad
Blatten
Bietschhorn 3934
Niederwald
Fiesch
Faido
Bex
Grd. Muveran 3051
Sion
Sierre
Leuk
Gampel
Visp
Naters
Brig-Glis
Formazza
S. Carlo
Peccia
Leytron
Chippis
Turtmann
Stalden
Simplonpass 2006
Bignasco
Sonogno
Hérémence
Ayer
M. Leone 3553
Varzo
Crodo
Someo
Saxon
Martigny
Pralong
Simplon
Maggia
Sembrancher
C. de la Forclaz
Herbriggen
Crevoladossola
Intragna
Orsières
Les Haudères
Weisshorn 4506
Dom 4545
Saas-Fee
Masera
Locarno
Ascona
Fionnay
Domodóssola
S. Maria Maggiore
Walliser Alpen
Zermatt
Villadóssola
Gerra
Grand Combin 4314
Lac de Mauvoisin
Matterhorn 4478
Parco Nazionale della Val Grande
Lunecco
Cannóbio
Maccagno
Breuil-Cervinia
Macugnaga
Vanzone
Monte Rosa 4634 Dufoursp.
Ornavasso
Oggébbio
Cima Capezzone 2421
Oyace
Étroubles
Valtournenche
Alagna Valsesia
Verbánia
Germignaga
Courmayeur
Gravellona Toce
Castelveccana
Laveno
Morgex
Antey-St. André
Champoluc
Rimasco
Omegna
Cittiglio
Aosta/Aoste
Châtillon
Varallo
Stresa
Besozzo
Lago Maggiore
Berner Alpen
Urner Alpen
Freiburger Alpen
Jura
Emmental
Simmental
Goms
Haslital
Vierwaldstätter See
Thuner See
Brienzer See
Bieler See
Lac de Neuchâtel
Zuger See
Urner See
7°00'
8°00'
47°00'
46°00'
I

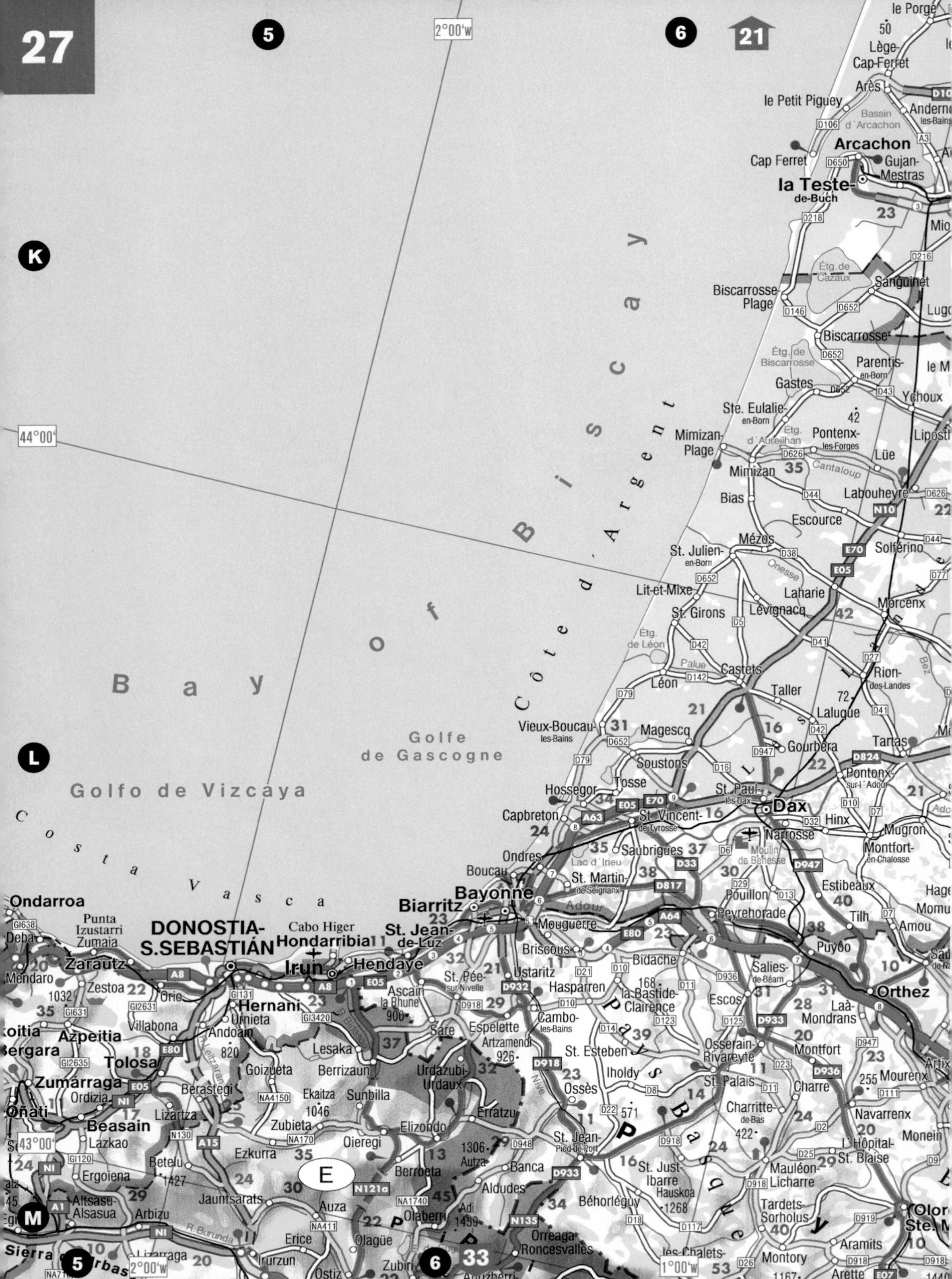
27
5
6
21
2°00'W
44°00'
43°00'
1°00'W
K
L
M
Bay of Biscay
Golfe de Gascogne
Golfo de Vizcaya
Costa Vasca
Côte d'Argent
le Porge
Lège-Cap-Ferret
Arès
le Petit Piquey
Bassin d'Arcachon
Andernos-les-Bains
Arcachon
Cap Ferret
Gujan-Mestras
la Teste-de-Buch
Étg. de Cazaux
Sanguinet
Biscarrosse-Plage
Biscarrosse
Étg. de Biscarrosse
Parentis-en-Born
Gastes
Ychoux
Ste. Eulalie-en-Born
Mimizan-Plage
Étg. d'Aureilhan
Pontenx-les-Forges
Mimizan
Lüe
Bias
Labouheyre
Escource
Mézos
St. Julien-en-Born
Solférino
Onesse
Lit-et-Mixe
Laharie
St. Girons
Lévignacq
Morcenx
Étg. de Léon
Palue
Castets
Léon
Rion-des-Landes
Taller
Vieux-Boucau-les-Bains
Magescq
Laluque
Gourbera
Tartas
Soustons
Pontonx-sur-l'Adour
Hossegor
Tosse
St. Paul-lès-Dax
Dax
Capbreton
St. Vincent-de-Tyrosse
Hinx
Narrosse
Mugron
Ondres
Saubrigues
Moulin de Benesse
Montfort-en-Chalosse
Lac d'Irieu
Boucau
St. Martin-de-Seignanx
Pouillon
Estibeaux
Bayonne
Biarritz
Adour
Peyrehorade
Tilh
Amou
Mouguerre
Puyoo
St. Jean-de-Luz
Briscous
Bidache
Salies-de-Béarn
Orthez
Hendaye
Ustaritz
St. Pée-sur-Nivelle
Hasparren
la Bastide-Clairence
Escos
Laà-Mondrans
Ascain
la Rhune 900
Cambo-les-Bains
Sare
Espelette
Artzamendi 926
Osserain-Rivareyte
Montfort
St. Esteben
Pays Basque
Iholdy
St. Palais
Mourenx
Ossès
Charre
Charritte-de-Bas
Navarrenx
L'Hôpital-St. Blaise
Monein
St. Jean-Pied-de-Port
Banca
Mauléon-Licharre
St. Just-Ibarre
Hauskoa 1268
Aldudes
Béhorléguy
Tardets-Sorholus
Aramits
Montory
Arette
les Chalets
Orreaga-Roncesvalles
Ondarroa
Punta Izustarri
Deba
Zumaia
DONOSTIA-S.SEBASTIÁN
Cabo Higer
Hondarribia
Irun
Zarautz
Mendaro
Zestoa
Orio
Hernani
Urnieta
Andoain
Villabona
Azpeitia
Bergara
Tolosa
Zumárraga
Ordizia
Oñati
Beasain
Lazkao
Lizartza
Berastegi
Goizueta
Lesaka
Berrizaun
Urdazubi-Urdaux
Ekaitza 1046
Sunbilla
Zubieta
Elizondo
Erratzu
Oieregi
Ezkurra
Betelu
Ergoiena
Altsasu-Alsasua
Arbizu
Jauntsarats
Auza
Berroeta
Autza
Olaberri
Olagüe
Erice
Irurzun
Lizarraga
Zubiri
Ostiz
R. Burunda
Sierra
E
A8
A63
A64
E05
E70
E80
A15
N121a
N135
D932
D933
D918
D936
D947
D817
D824
D33
N10
N1
33

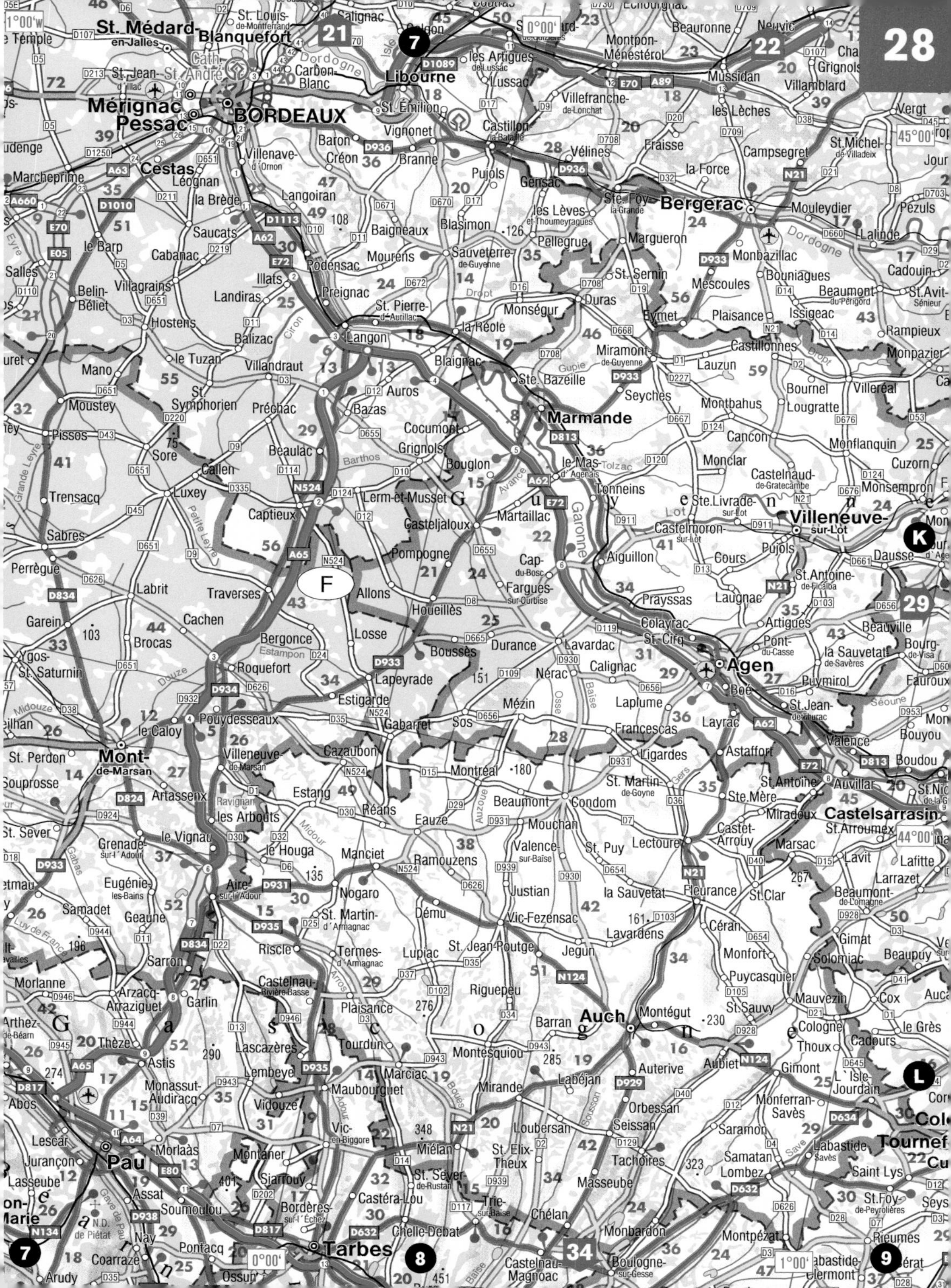
St. Médard-en-Jalles
Blanquefort
St. Louis-de-Montferrand
Salignac
Galgon
Coutras
Echourgnac
Beauronne
Neuvic
Montpon-Ménestérol
Mussidan
Grignols
Villamblard
Le Temple
St. Jean-d'Illac
St. André
Carbon-Blanc
Libourne
les Artigues-de-Lussac
Lussac
Mérignac
Pessac
BORDEAUX
St. Émilion
Castillon-la-Bataille
Villefranche-de-Lonchat
les Lèches
Vergt
Baron
Vignonet
Fraisse
Campsegret
St. Michel-de-Villadeix
Cestas
Villenave-d'Ornon
Créon
Branne
Vélines
la Force
Marcheprime
Léognan
Pujols
Gensac
Ste. Foy-la-Grande
Bergerac
Mouleydier
Pezuls
la Brède
Langoiran
les Lèves-et-Thoumeyragues
Lalinde
Saucats
Baigneaux
Blasimon
Margueron
Monbazillac
le Barp
Cabanac
Podensac
Mourens
Sauveterre-de-Guyenne
Pellegrue
Cadouin
Salles
Villagrains
Illats
St. Sernin
Bouniagues
Belin-Béliet
Landiras
Preignac
Mescoules
Beaumont-du-Périgord
St. Avit-Sénieur
Hostens
St. Pierre-d'Aurillac
Monségur
Duras
Eymet
Plaisance
Issigeac
Balizac
Langon
la Réole
Rampieux
le Tuzan
Villandraut
Blaignac
Miramont-de-Guyenne
Lauzun
Castillonnès
Monpazier
Mano
St. Symphorien
Préchac
Auros
Ste. Bazeille
Seyches
Bournel
Villeréal
Moustey
Bazas
Marmande
Montbahus
Lougratte
Pissos
Sore
Beaulac
Cocumont
Grignols
Cancon
Monflanquin
Callen
Bouglon
le Mas-d'Agenais
Monclar
Cuzorn
Trensacq
Luxey
Lerm-et-Musset
Tonneins
Castelnaud-de-Gratecambe
Monsempron
Captieux
Casteljaloux
Martaillac
Ste. Livrade-sur-Lot
Villeneuve-sur-Lot
Sabres
Pompogne
Castelmoron-sur-Lot
Aiguillon
Cours
Pujols
Dausse
Perrègue
Labrit
Traverses
Allons
Cap-du-Bosc
Fargues-sur-Ourbise
St. Antoine-de-Ficalba
Prayssas
Laugnac
Garein
Cachen
Houeillès
Colayrac-St. Cirq
Artigues
Beauville
Brocas
Bergonce
Losse
Boussès
Durance
Lavardac
Pont-du-Casse
Bourg-de-Visa
Ygos-St. Saturnin
Roquefort
Lapeyrade
Nérac
Calignac
Agen
la Sauvetat-de-Savères
Puymirol
Fauroux
Estigarde
Mézin
Laplume
Boé
St. Jean-de-Thurac
Pouydesseaux
Gabarret
Sos
Francescas
Layrac
le Caloy
Mont-de-Marsan
Villeneuve-de-Marsan
Cazaubon
Ligardes
Astaffort
Valence
Bouyou
Boudou
St. Perdon
Montréal
St. Martin-de-Goyne
St. Antoine
Auvillar
Soprosse
Artassenx
Estang
Beaumont
Condom
Ste. Mère
Miradoux
Castelsarrasin
St. Arroumex
les Arbouts
Réans
Eauze
Mouchan
Lectoure
Castet-Arrouy
Marsac
Lavit
Lafitte
St. Sever
le Vignau
le Houga
Manciet
Valence-sur-Baïse
St. Puy
Larrazet
Grenade-sur-l'Adour
Ramouzens
Aire-sur-l'Adour
Nogaro
Justian
la Sauvetat
Fleurance
St. Clar
Beaumont-de-Lomagne
Eugénie-les-Bains
Samadet
Geaune
St. Martin-d'Armagnac
Dému
Vic-Fezensac
Lavardens
Céran
Gimat
Sarron
Riscle
Termes-d'Armagnac
Lupiac
St. Jean-Poutge
Jegun
Monfort
Solomiac
Beaupuy
Morlanne
Castelnau-Rivière-Basse
Puycasquier
Arzacq-Arraziguet
Garlin
Plaisance
Riguepeu
Mauvezin
Cox
Arthez-de-Béarn
Thèze
Barran
Auch
Montégut
St. Sauvy
Cologne
le Grès
Lascazères
Tourdun
Montesquiou
Thoux
Cadours
Astis
Lembeye
Marciac
Labéjan
Auterive
Aubiet
Gimont
L'Isle-Jourdain
Monassut-Audiracq
Maubourguet
Mirande
Orbessan
Monferran-Savès
Abos
Vidouze
Vic-en-Bigorre
Loubersan
Seissan
Saramon
Lescar
Pau
Morlaàs
Montaner
Miélan
St. Elix-Theux
Tachoires
Samatan
Lombez
Labastide-Savès
Tournefeuille
Jurançon
Siarrouy
St. Sever-de-Rustan
Masseube
Saint Lys
Lasseube
Assat
Bordères-sur-l'Échez
Castéra-Lou
Trie-sur-Baïse
Chélan
Montpézat
St. Foy-de-Peyrolières
Soumoulou
N.D. de Piétat
Nay
Chelle-Debat
Monbardon
Rieumes
Pontacq
Tarbes
Castelnau-Magnoac
Boulogne-sur-Gesse
Labastide-Clermont
Coarraze
Arudy
Ossun
Dordogne
Garonne
Lot
Adour
Gers
Baïse
Midouze
Douze
Estampon
Ciron
Dropt
Barthos
Avance
Tolzac
Gupie
Séoune
Save
Arros
Bouès
Osse
Auzoue
Gabas
Luy de France
Gave de Pau
Grande Leyre
Petite Leyre
Eyre
Sousson
G a s c o g n e
G u y e n n e
0°00'
1°00'W
1°00'
45°00'
44°00'

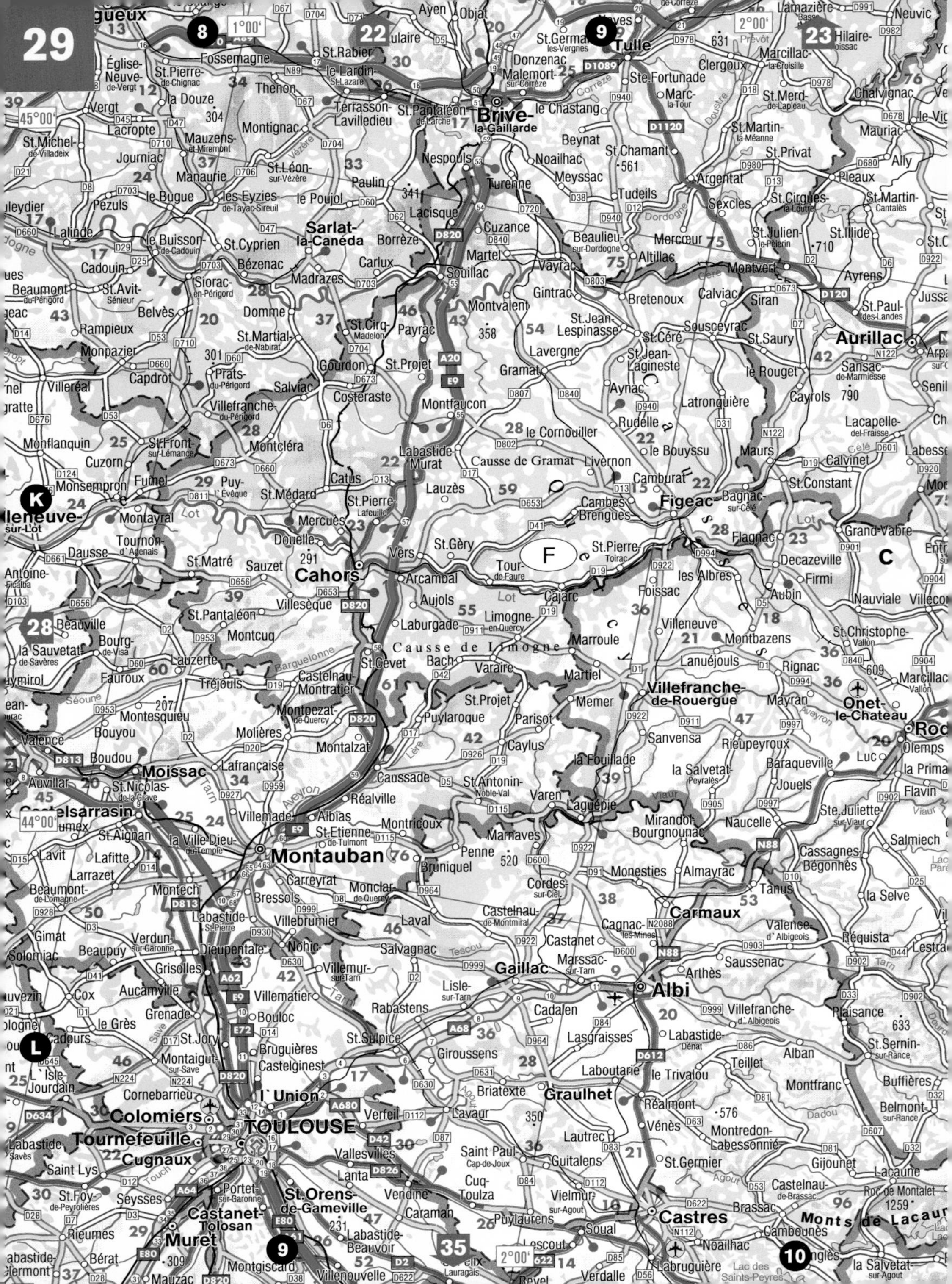
Périgueux
Fossemagne
St.Rabier
le Lardin-St.Lazare
Terrasson-Lavilledieu
Ayen
Objat
St.Germain-les-Vergnes
Tulle
Donzenac
Malemort-sur-Corrèze
Brive-la-Gaillarde
St.Pantaléon-de-Larche
le Chastang
Ste.Fortunade
Marc-la-Tour
Clergoux
Marcillac-la-Croisille
Lamazière-Basse
Neuvic
St.Merd-de-Lapleau
Chalvignac
Mauriac
Église-Neuve-de-Vergt
St.Pierre-de-Chignac
Thenon
la Douze
Vergt
Lacropte
Mauzens-et-Miremont
Montignac
St.Michel-de-Villadeix
Journiac
Manaurie
St.Léon-sur-Vézère
Paulin
Nespouls
Noailhac
Beynat
St.Chamant
Argentat
St.Martin-la-Méanne
St.Privat
Pleaux
Ally
le Bugue
les Eyzies-de-Tayac-Sireuil
le Poujol
Lacisque
Turenne
Meyssac
Tudeils
Sexcles
St.Cirgues-la-Loutre
St.Martin-Cantalès
Pezuls
Lalinde
le Buisson-de-Cadouin
St.Cyprien
Sarlat-la-Canéda
Borrèze
Cuzance
Beaulieu-sur-Dordogne
Mercœur
St.Julien-le-Pèlerin
St.Illide
Cadouin
Bézenac
Carlux
Martel
Vayrac
Altillac
Montvert
Ayrens
Beaumont-du-Périgord
St.Avit-Sénieur
Siorac-en-Périgord
Madrazès
Souillac
Gintrac
Bretenoux
Calviac
Siran
St.Paul-des-Landes
Belvès
Domme
Montvalent
St.Jean-Lespinasse
Sousceyrac
St.Saury
Aurillac
Rampieux
St.Martial-de-Nabirat
St.Cirq-Madelon
Payrac
St.Céré
St.Jean-Lagineste
Lavergne
Sansac-de-Marmiesse
Monpazier
Capdrot
Prats-du-Périgord
Gourdon
St.Projet
Gramat
le Rouget
Villeréal
Salviac
Costeraste
Aynac
Latronquière
Cayrols
Villefranche-du-Périgord
Montfaucon
Rudelle
Lacapelle-del-Fraisse
Monflanquin
St.Front-sur-Lémance
Montcléra
le Cornouiller
le Bouyssu
Cuzorn
Labastide-Murat
Causse de Gramat
Livernon
Maurs
Calvinet
Monsempron
Fumel
Puy-l'Évêque
St.Médard
Catus
Lauzès
Camburat
St.Constant
Villeneuve-sur-Lot
Montayral
Mercuès
St.Pierre-Lafeuille
Cambes
Brengues
Figeac
Bagnac-sur-Célé
Tournon-d'Agenais
Douelle
St.Géry
St.Pierre-Toirac
Flagnac
Grand-Vabre
Dausse
St.Matré
Sauzet
Cahors
Vers
Arcambal
Tour-de-Faure
Cajarc
les Albres
Decazeville
Firmi
Villesèque
Aujols
Foissac
Aubin
Nauviale
Beauville
St.Pantaléon
Laburgade
Limogne-en-Quercy
Villeneuve
Montbazens
St.Christophe-Vallon
Bourg-de-Visa
Montcuq
Causse de Limogne
Marroule
la Sauvetat-de-Savères
Lauzerte
St.Cevet
Bach
Varaire
Lanuéjouls
Rignac
Marcillac-Vallon
Fauroux
Tréjouls
Castelnau-Montratier
Martiel
Villefranche-de-Rouergue
Montesquieu
Montpezat-de-Quercy
St.Projet
Memer
Mayran
Onet-le-Château
Rodez
Bouyou
Molières
Puylaroque
Parisot
Sanvensa
Valence
Montalzat
Caylus
Rieupeyroux
Olemps
Boudou
Moissac
Lafrançaise
la Fouillade
la Salvetat-Peyralès
Baraqueville
Luc
Auvillar
St.Nicolas-de-la-Grave
Caussade
St.Antonin-Noble-Val
Jouels
Flavin
Castelsarrasin
Réalville
Varen
Laguépie
Mirandol-Bourgnounac
Villemade
Albias
Ste.Juliette-sur-Viaur
St.Aignan
la Ville-Dieu-du-Temple
St.Etienne-de-Tulmont
Montricoux
Marnaves
Naucelle
Salmiech
Lavit
Lafitte
Montauban
Penne
Cassagnes-Bégonhès
Larrazet
Carreyrat
Bruniquel
Monestiès
Almayrac
Beaumont-de-Lomagne
Montech
Bressols
Monclar-de-Quercy
Cordes-sur-Ciel
Tanus
la Selve
Labastide-St.Pierre
Villebrumier
Castelnau-de-Montmiral
Carmaux
Gimat
Verdun-sur-Garonne
Nohic
Laval
Cagnac-les-Mines
Valence-d'Albigeois
Réquista
Solomiac
Beaupuy
Dieupentale
Salvagnac
Castanet
Saussenac
Grisolles
Villemur-sur-Tarn
Gaillac
Marssac-sur-Tarn
Arthès
Cox
Aucamville
Villematier
Lisle-sur-Tarn
Albi
le Grès
Grenade
Bouloc
Rabastens
Cadalen
Villefranche-d'Albigeois
Plaisance
Cadours
St.Jory
St.Sulpice
Lasgraisses
Labastide-Dénat
Montaigut-sur-Save
Bruguières
Giroussens
Alban
St.Sernin-sur-Rance
L'Isle-Jourdain
Castelginest
Teillet
Cornebarrieu
l'Union
Briatexte
Graulhet
Laboutarie
le Trivalou
Montfranc
Buffières
Colomiers
Toulouse
Verfeil
Lavaur
Réalmont
Belmont-sur-Rance
Tournefeuille
Vénès
Montredon-Labessonnié
Labastide-Savès
Cugnaux
Vallesvilles
Saint Paul-Cap-de-Joux
Lautrec
Guitalens
St.Germier
Gijounet
Lacaune
Saint Lys
Portet-sur-Garonne
Lanta
Cuq-Toulza
Castelnau-de-Brassac
St.Foy-de-Peyrolières
Seysses
St.Orens-de-Gameville
Vendine
Vielmur-sur-Agout
Brassac
Roc de Montalet
Monts de Lacaune
Castanet-Tolosan
Caraman
Puylaurens
Castres
Rieumes
Muret
Labastide-Beauvoir
Soual
Noailhac
Cambounès
Bérat
Lescout
Anglès
la Salvetat-sur-Agout
Labastide-Clermont
Montgiscard
Villenouvelle
Revel
Verdalle
Labruguière
Lac des Saints-Peyres
Mauzac
Lot
Tarn
Aveyron
Dordogne
Garonne
Agout
Viaur
Vézère
Corrèze
Cère
Célé
Barguelonne
Séoune
Save
Touch
Tescou
Lère
Causses du Quercy
A20
E9
A62
A64
A68
A680
E72
E80
D820
D1089
D1120
D120
N88
N122
N2088
D813
D612
1°00'
2°00'
45°00'
44°00'

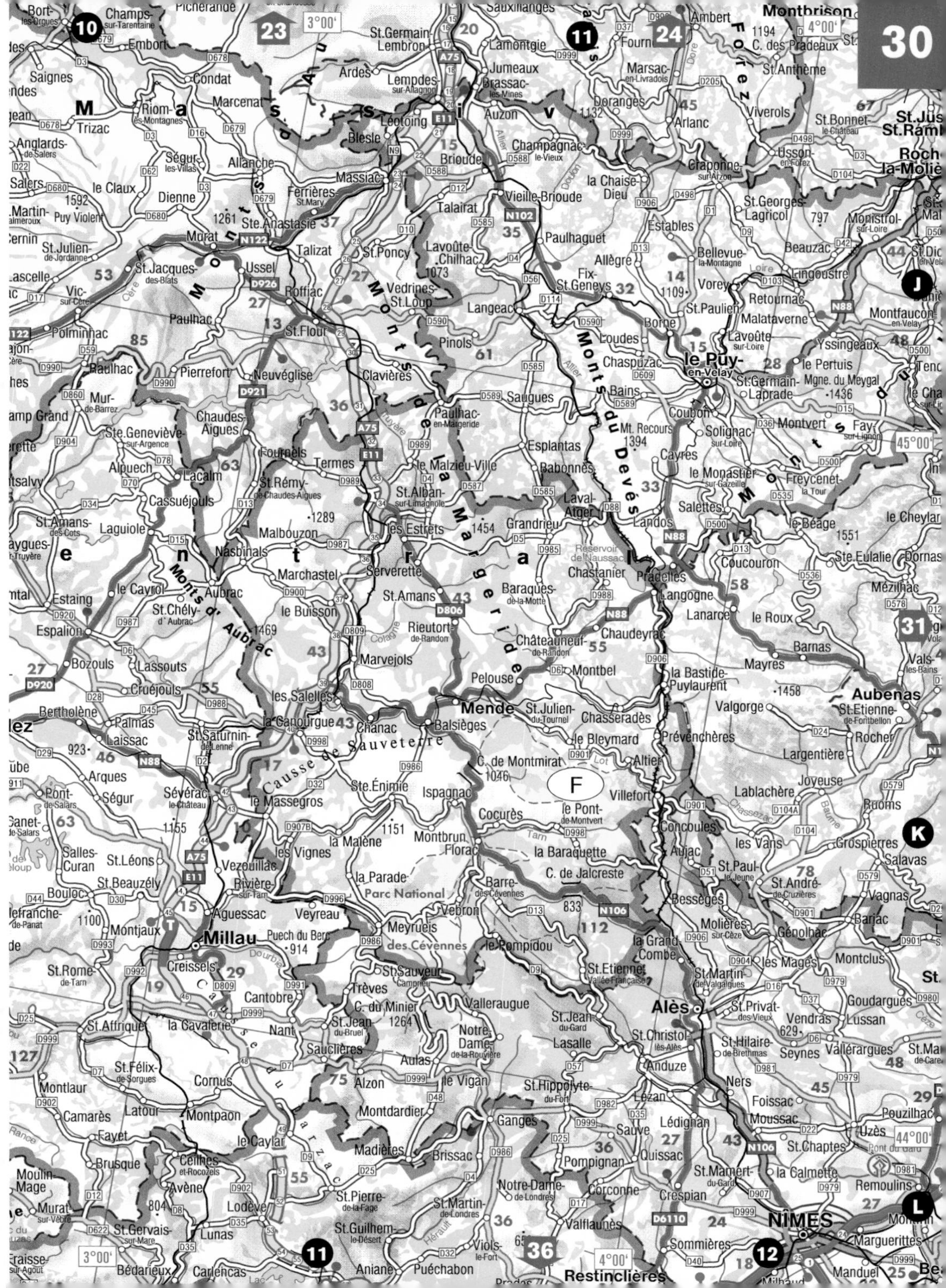

Bort-les-Orgues
Champs-sur-Tarentaine
Embort
Saignes
Condat
Marcenat
Riom-ès-Montagnes
Trizac
Anglards-de-Salers
Ségur-les-Villas
Allanche
Salers
le Claux
Dienne
Puy Violent
1592
Murat
1261
Ste.Anastasie
Ferrières-St.Mary
Massiac
St.Julien-de-Jordanne
St.Jacques-des-Blats
Ussel
Talizat
Vic-sur-Cère
Polminhac
Paulhac
St.Flour
Roffiac
Raulhac
Pierrefort
Neuvéglise
Mur-de-Barrez
Chaudes-Aigues
Ste.Geneviève-sur-Argence
Alpuech
Lacalm
Cassuéjouls
St.Amans-des-Cots
Laguiole
Nasbinals
Aubrac
St.Chély-d'Aubrac
le Cayrol
Estaing
Espalion
Bozouls
Lassouts
Cruéjouls
Bertholène
Palmas
Laissac
St.Saturnin-de-Lenne
Arques
Ségur
Sévérac-le-Château
Pont-de-Salars
Salles-Curan
St.Léons
St.Beauzély
Bouloc
Montjaux
Millau
Creissels
St.Rome-de-Tarn
St.Affrique
St.Félix-de-Sorgues
Montlaur
Camarès
Fayet
Brusque
Latour
Montpaon
Cornus
le Caylar
Ceilhes-et-Rocozels
Avène
Lodève
Lunas
Murat-sur-Vèbre
St.Gervais-sur-Mare
Bédarieux
Carlencas
Sauxillanges
St.Germain-Lembron
Ardes
Lempdes-sur-Allagnon
Lamontgie
Jumeaux
Brassac-les-Mines
Léotoing
Blesle
Auzon
Brioude
Champagnac-le-Vieux
Talairat
Vieille-Brioude
Lavoûte-Chilhac
St.Poncy
Paulhaguet
Vedrines-St.Loup
Langeac
Pinols
Clavières
Saugues
Paulhac-en-Margeride
Termes
le Malzieu-Ville
St.Alban-sur-Limagnole
St.Rémy-de-Chaudes-Aigues
Malbouzon
les Estrets
Serverette
Marchastel
St.Amans
le Buisson
Rieutort-de-Randon
Marvejols
les Salelles
la Canourgue
Chanac
Mende
Balsièges
le Massegros
Ste.Énimie
Ispagnac
les Vignes
la Malène
Montbrun
Florac
Vezouillac
Rivière-sur-Tarn
Aguessac
la Parade
Parc National des Cévennes
Veyreau
Meyrueis
Puech du Berc
Cantobre
Nant
la Cavalerie
St.Sauveur-Camprieu
Trèves
C. du Minier
St.Jean-du-Bruel
Sauclières
Alzon
Aulas
le Vigan
Montdardier
Madières
Brissac
Ganges
St.Pierre-de-la-Fage
St.Guilhem-le-Désert
St.Martin-de-Londres
Aniane
Puéchabon
Viols-le-Fort
Ambert
Montbrison
Fournols
Marsac-en-Livradois
Doranges
Arlanc
Viverols
St.Anthème
C. des Pradeaux
Craponne-sur-Arzon
la Chaise-Dieu
Usson-en-Forez
St.Bonnet-le-Château
St.Georges-Lagricol
Estables
Allègre
Bellevue-la-Montagne
Beauzac
Monistrol-sur-Loire
Fix-St.Geneys
Vorey
Retournac
St.Paulien
Lavoûte-sur-Loire
Malataverne
Yssingeaux
Montfaucon-en-Velay
Loudes
Borne
Chaspuzac
le Puy-en-Velay
le Pertuis
St.Germain-Laprade
Mgne. du Meygal
Bains
Coubon
Solignac-sur-Loire
Montvert
Fay-sur-Lignon
Mt. Recours
Esplantas
Cayres
le Monastier-sur-Gazeille
Freycenet-la-Tour
Babonnès
Laval-Atger
Salettes
Landos
Grandrieu
le Béage
le Cheylard
Réservoir de Naussac
Chastanier
Pradelles
Coucouron
Ste.Eulalie
Langogne
Lanarce
le Roux
Mézilhac
Baraques-de-la-Motte
Châteauneuf-de-Randon
Chaudeyrac
Barnas
Mayres
Vals-les-Bains
Montbel
la Bastide-Puylaurent
Pelouse
Aubenas
St.Julien-du-Tournel
Chasseradès
Valgorge
St.Etienne-de-Fontbellon
le Bleymard
Prévenchères
Rocher
C. de Montmirat
Altier
Largentière
Villefort
Joyeuse
Lablachère
Cocurès
le Pont-de-Montvert
Concoules
Ruoms
la Baraquette
Aujac
les Vans
Grospierres
C. de Jalcreste
St.Paul-le-Jeune
St.André-de-Cruzières
Salavas
Barre-des-Cévennes
Bessèges
Vagnas
Vebron
Molières-sur-Cèze
Génolhac
Barjac
le Pompidou
la Grand-Combe
St.Etienne-Vallée-Française
les Mages
Montclus
St.Martin-de-Valgalgues
Valleraugue
St.Jean-du-Gard
Alès
St.Privat-des-Vieux
Vendras
Goudargues
Notre-Dame-de-la-Rouvière
Lasalle
St.Christol-lès-Alès
St.Hilaire-de-Brethmas
Lussan
Seynes
Vallérargues
Anduze
St.Hippolyte-du-Fort
Lézan
Ners
Foissac
Lédignan
Moussac
Pouzilhac
Sauve
Quissac
St.Chaptes
Uzès
Pompignan
St.Mamert-du-Gard
la Calmette
Notre-Dame-de-Londres
Corconne
Crespian
Remoulins
Valflaunès
NÎMES
Marguerittes
Sommières
Restinclières
Manduel
Monts du Cantal
Monts de la Margeride
Monts d'Aubrac
Monts du Devès
Causse de Sauveterre
Causse du Larzac
Monts du Forez
Monts du Vivarais
Massif Central
3°00'
4°00'
45°00'
44°00'

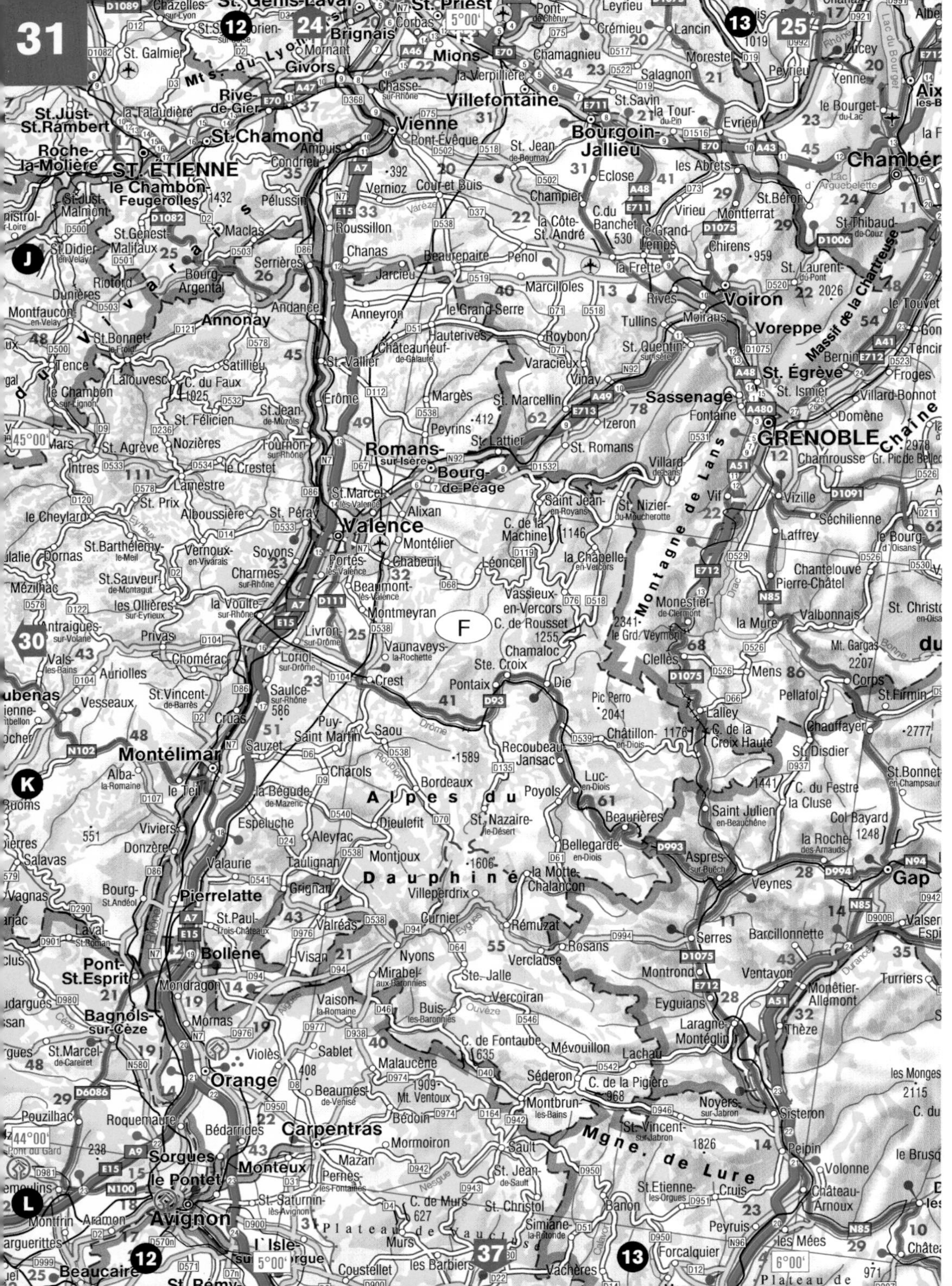

Chazelles-sur-Lyon
St. Genis-Laval
St. Priest
5°00'
Pont-de-Chéruy
Leyrieu
Crémieu
Lancin
Lac du Bourget
St. Galmier
St. Symphorien-sur-Coise
Brignais
Corbas
Mornant
Mions
Chamagnieu
Morestel
Lucey
Yenne
Aix-les-Bains
Mts. du Lyonnais
Givors
la Verpillière
Salagnon
Peyrieu
Rive-de-Gier
Chasse-sur-Rhône
Villefontaine
St. Savin
la Tour-du-Pin
Evrieu
le Bourget-du-Lac
St. Just-St. Rambert
la Talaudière
Vienne
Bourgoin-Jallieu
St. Chamond
Pont-Évêque
St. Jean-de-Bournay
Chambéry
Roche-la-Molière
St. ÉTIENNE
Ampuis
Condrieu
les Abrets
le Chambon-Feugerolles
Vernioz
Cour-et-Buis
Eclose
Lac d'Aiguebelette
St. Just-Malmont
Pélussin
Champier
St. Béron
Montferrat
Virieu
St. Thibaud-de-Couz
St. Genest-Malifaux
Maclas
Roussillon
la Côte-St. André
C. du Banchet
le Grand-Lemps
St. Didier-en-Velay
Chanas
Beaurepaire
Penol
Chirens
St. Laurent-du-Pont
Serrières
Bourg-Argental
Riotord
Jarcieu
Marcilloles
la Frette
Rives
Voiron
Massif de la Chartreuse
le Touvet
Dunières
Andance
Anneyron
le Grand-Serre
Tullins
Moirans
Voreppe
Montfaucon-en-Velay
Annonay
Hauterives
Roybon
St. Quentin-sur-Isère
St. Bonnet-le-Froid
Châteauneuf-de-Galaure
Bernin
Tencin
Tence
St. Vallier
Varacieux
Vinay
St. Égrève
Froges
Lalouvesc
Satillieu
C. du Faux
St. Ismier
Villard-Bonnot
le Chambon-sur-Lignon
Érôme
Margès
St. Marcellin
Sassenage
Fontaine
Domène
St. Félicien
St. Jean-de-Muzols
Peyrins
Izeron
GRENOBLE
Chaîne
45°00'
Mars
St. Agrève
Nozières
Tournon-sur-Rhône
Romans-sur-Isère
St. Lattier
St. Romans
Villard-de-Lans
Chamrousse
Gr. Pic de Belledonne
Intres
le Crestet
Bourg-de-Péage
Lamastre
St. Marcel-lès-Valence
Saint Jean-en-Royans
St. Nizier-du-Moucherotte
Vif
Vizille
St. Prix
Alixan
le Cheylard
Alboussière
St. Péray
Valence
C. de la Machine
Montagne de Lans
Séchilienne
St. Barthélemy-le-Meil
Vernoux-en-Vivarais
Montélier
Laffrey
le Bourg-d'Oisans
Dornas
Soyons
Portes-lès-Valence
Chabeuil
Léoncel
la Chapelle-en-Vercors
St. Sauveur-de-Montagut
Charmes-sur-Rhône
Beaumont-lès-Valence
Chantelouve
Pierre-Châtel
Mézilhac
Vassieux-en-Vercors
Monestier-de-Clermont
Drac
les Ollières-sur-Eyrieux
la Voulte-sur-Rhône
Montmeyran
St. Christophe-en-Oisans
Valbonnais
Antraigues-sur-Volane
F
C. de Rousset
la Mure
Livron-sur-Drôme
Vaunaveys-la-Rochette
le Grd. Veymont
Mt. Gargas
Privas
Chomérac
Loriol-sur-Drôme
Chamaloc
Clelles
Vals-les-Bains
Auriolles
Ste. Croix
Mens
Corps
Crest
Pontaix
Die
Pellafol
St. Firmin
Aubenas
St. Vincent-de-Barrès
Pic Perro
Vesseaux
Saulce-sur-Rhône
Cruas
Lalley
Chauffayer
C. de la Croix Haute
Puy-Saint Martin
Saou
Châtillon-en-Diois
Drôme
Montélimar
Sauzet
Recoubeau-Jansac
St. Disdier
Charols
Roubion
Alba-la-Romaine
le Teil
Bordeaux
Luc-en-Diois
St. Bonnet-en-Champsaur
C. du Festre
la Cluse
Ruoms
la Bégude-de-Mazenc
Poyols
Alpes du Dauphiné
Espeluche
Dieulefit
St. Nazaire-le-Désert
Beaurières
Saint Julien-en-Beauchêne
Col Bayard
Viviers
Aleyrac
la Roche-des-Arnauds
Donzère
Montjoux
Bellegarde-en-Diois
Aspres-sur-Buëch
Salavas
Valaurie
Taulignan
la Motte-Chalancon
Veynes
Gap
Bourg-St. Andéol
Grignan
Villeperdrix
Pierrelatte
St. Paul-Trois-Châteaux
Valréas
Curnier
Rémuzat
Serres
Barcillonnette
Valserres
Laval-St. Roman
Eygues
Rhône
Bollène
Visan
Nyons
Rosans
Verclause
Pont-St. Esprit
Mondragon
Mirabel-aux-Baronnies
Ste. Jalle
Montrond
Ventavon
Turriers
Vaison-la-Romaine
Vercoiran
Monêtier-Allemont
Bagnols-sur-Cèze
Mornas
Buis-les-Baronnies
Ouvèze
Eyguians
Laragne-Montéglin
Cèze
Thèze
St. Marcel-de-Careiret
Violès
Sablet
C. de Fontaube
Mévouillon
Lachau
Orange
Malaucène
Séderon
C. de la Pigière
les Monges
Mt. Ventoux
Beaumes-de-Venise
Montbrun-les-Bains
Noyers-sur-Jabron
Sisteron
Pouzilhac
Roquemaure
Bédarrides
Carpentras
Bédoin
St. Vincent-sur-Jabron
Mgne. de Lure
44°00'
Pont du Gard
Mormoiron
Sault
Peipin
le Brusquet
Sorgues
Monteux
Mazan
Volonne
Remoulins
le Pontet
Pernes-les-Fontaines
Nesque
St. Jean-de-Sault
St. Etienne-les-Orgues
Cruis
Château-Arnoux
Montfrin
Aramon
Avignon
St. Saturnin-lès-Avignon
C. de Murs
St. Christol
Banon
Plateau de Vaucluse
Simiane-la-Rotonde
Peyruis
Marguerittes
L'Isle-sur-la-Sorgue
Murs
les Mées
Beaucaire
5°00'
Coustellet
les Barbiers
Vachères
Forcalquier
6°00'
Plateau de
Château
St. Rémy
12
24
13
25
30
37
J
K
L

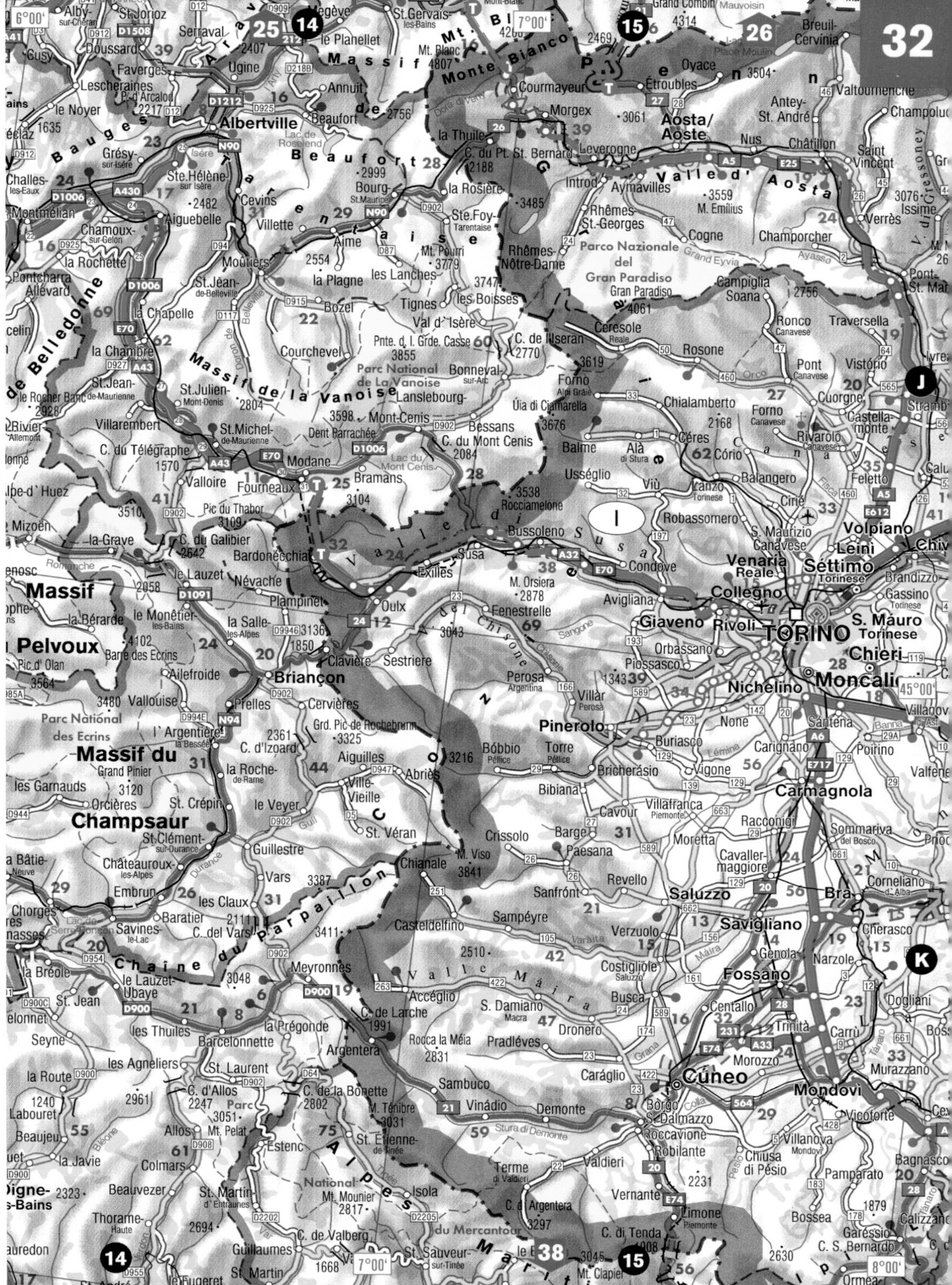
6°00'
7°00'
8°00'
45°00'
25
14
15
26
38
J
K
I
Alby-sur-Chéran
St.Jorioz
Megève
St.Gervais-les-Bains
Mont-Blanc
Grand Combin
4314
Mauvoisin
Breuil-Cervinia
Serraval
Doussard
Gusy
Faverges
Ugine
le Planellet
Mt. Blanc 4807
Massif du Mt. Blanc
Monte Bianco
Lescheraines
P.d'Arcalod 2217
Annuit
Courmayeur
Oyace
Étroubles
Valtournenche
le Noyer
1635
Albertville
Beaufort
2756
Morgex
3061
Aosta/Aoste
Antey-St. André
Champoluc
Bauges
Lac de Roselend
la Thuile
C. du Pt. St. Bernard 2188
Leverogne
Nus
Châtillon
Saint Vincent
Grésy-sur-Isère
Beaufortain
2999
Bourg-St.Maurice
la Rosière
Introd
Aymavilles
Valle d'Aosta
3559
M. Emilius
Verrès
Issime
3076
Challes-les-Eaux
Ste.Hélène-sur Isère
Cevins
2482
3485
Rhêmes-St.-Georges
Cogne
Champorcher
Montmélian
Aiguebelle
Villette
Aime
Ste.Foy-Tarentaise
Chamoux-sur-Gelon
Tarentaise
Mt. Pourri 3779
Rhêmes-Nôtre-Dame
Parco Nazionale del Gran Paradiso
Gran Paradiso 4061
la Rochette
Moûtiers
2554
la Plagne
les Lanches
3747
Pontcharra
Allevard
St.Jean-de-Belleville
Bozel
Tignes
les Boisses
Campiglia Soana
2756
Pont-St. Martin
Belledonne
la Chapelle
Val d'Isère
Ceresole Reale
Ronco Canavese
Traversella
Courchevel
Pnte. d. l. Grde. Casse 3855
C. de l'Iseran 2770
Rosone
Pont Canavese
Vistrorio
Ivrea
la Chambre
Massif de la Vanoise
Parc National de La Vanoise
Bonneval-sur-Arc
3619
St.Jean-de-Maurienne
le Rocher Blanc 2928
St.Julien-Mont-Denis
2804
Lanslebourg-Mont-Cenis
Forno Alpi Graie
Chialamberto
Forno Canavese
Cuorgnè
Castellamonte
Strambino
Villarembert
St.Michel-de-Maurienne
3598
Dent Parrachée
Bessans
Úia di Ciamarella 3676
2168
Rivarolo Canavese
C. du Télégraphe 1570
Modane
C. du Mont Cenis 2084
Lac du Mont Cenis
Balme
Alà di Stura
Céres
Cório
Balangero
Feletto
Valloire
Fourneaux
Bramans
Usséglio
Lanzo Torinese
Alpe-d'Huez
Pic du Thabor 3109
3104
3538 Rocciamelone
Viù
Ciriè
Robassomero
3510
Mizoën
Bussoleno
Valle di Susa
S. Maurizio Canavese
Volpiano
Leinì
la Grave
C. du Galibier 2642
Bardonécchia
Susa
Exilles
Venaria Reale
Settimo Torinese
Brandizzo
Condove
le Lauzet
Névache
M. Orsiera 2878
Collegno
Gassino Torinese
Massif
2058
Plampinet
Oulx
Fenestrelle
Avigliana
le Monêtier-les-Bains
la Berarde
Giaveno
Rivoli
TORINO
S. Mauro Torinese
Pelvoux
4102
Barre des Ecrins
la Salle-les-Alpes
3136
1850
3043
Val Chisone
Orbassano
Chieri
Pic d'Olan 3564
Clavière
Sestriere
Piossasco
Ailefroide
Briançon
Perosa Argentina
1343
Nichelino
Moncalieri
3480
Vallouise
Prelles
Cervières
Villar Perosa
Parc National des Ecrins
Grd. Pic de Rochebrune 3325
Pinerolo
Santena
Villanova d'Asti
l'Argentière-la-Bessée
2361
C. d'Izoard
Bóbbio Pellice
Torre Pellice
Buriasco
Carignano
Poirino
Massif du Champsaur
Grand Pinier 3120
la Roche-de-Rame
Aiguilles
Abriès
3216
Bricherásio
Vigone
les Garnauds
Orcières
St. Crépin
Ville-Vieille
Bibiana
Carmagnola
le Veyer
Villafranca Piemonte
Cavour
Racconigi
St. Véran
Barge
Sommariva del Bosco
St.Clément-sur-Durance
Guillestre
Crissolo
Paesana
Moretta
Cavallermaggiore
la Bâtie-Neuve
Châteauroux-les-Alpes
Chianale
M. Viso 3841
Revello
Vars
3387
Embrun
les Claux
Sanfront
Saluzzo
Bra
Corneliano d'Alba
Chorges
Baratier
2111
Sampéyre
Savigliano
Cherasco
Savines-le-Lac
C. del Vars
3411
Casteldelfino
Verzuolo
Lac de Serre-Ponçon
2510
Genola
Narzole
la Bréole
le Lauzet-Ubaye
Meyronnes
Valle Máira
Costigliole Saluzzo
Fossano
St. Jean
3048
Acceglio
S. Damiano Macra
Busca
Centallo
Dogliani
Chaîne du Parpaillon
C. de Larche 1991
Dronero
Trinità
Carrù
Seyne
les Thuiles
Barcelonnette
la Prégonde
Argentera
Rocca la Méia 2831
Pradléves
Morozzo
les Agneliers
St. Laurent
Caráglio
Cúneo
Mondovì
Murazzano
la Route
C. d'Allos 2247
C. de la Bonette 2802
Sambuco
1240
Labouret
2961
3051
Mt. Pelat
Parc
M. Ténibre 3031
Vinádio
Demonte
Borgo S.Dalmazzo
Vicoforte
Beaujeu
Allos
Estenc
St. Etienne-de-Tinée
Stura di Demonte
Roccavione
Villanova Mondovì
la Javie
Colmars
Alpes
Robilante
Chiusa di Pésio
Bagnasco
Terme di Valdieri
Valdieri
2231
Pamparato
Digne-les-Bains
2323
Beauvezer
St. Martin-d'Entraunes
National
Mt. Mounier 2817
Isola
Vernante
1879
C. d'Argentera 3297
Limone Piemonte
Bossea
Calizzano
Thorame-Haute
2694
du Mercantour
C. di Tenda 1908
Garéssio
C. S. Bernardo
Guillaumes
C. de Valberg
St. Sauveur-sur-Tinée
Alpes Maritimes
3045
Mt. Clapier
2630
1668
St. Martin
le Fugeret
St. André
Ormea

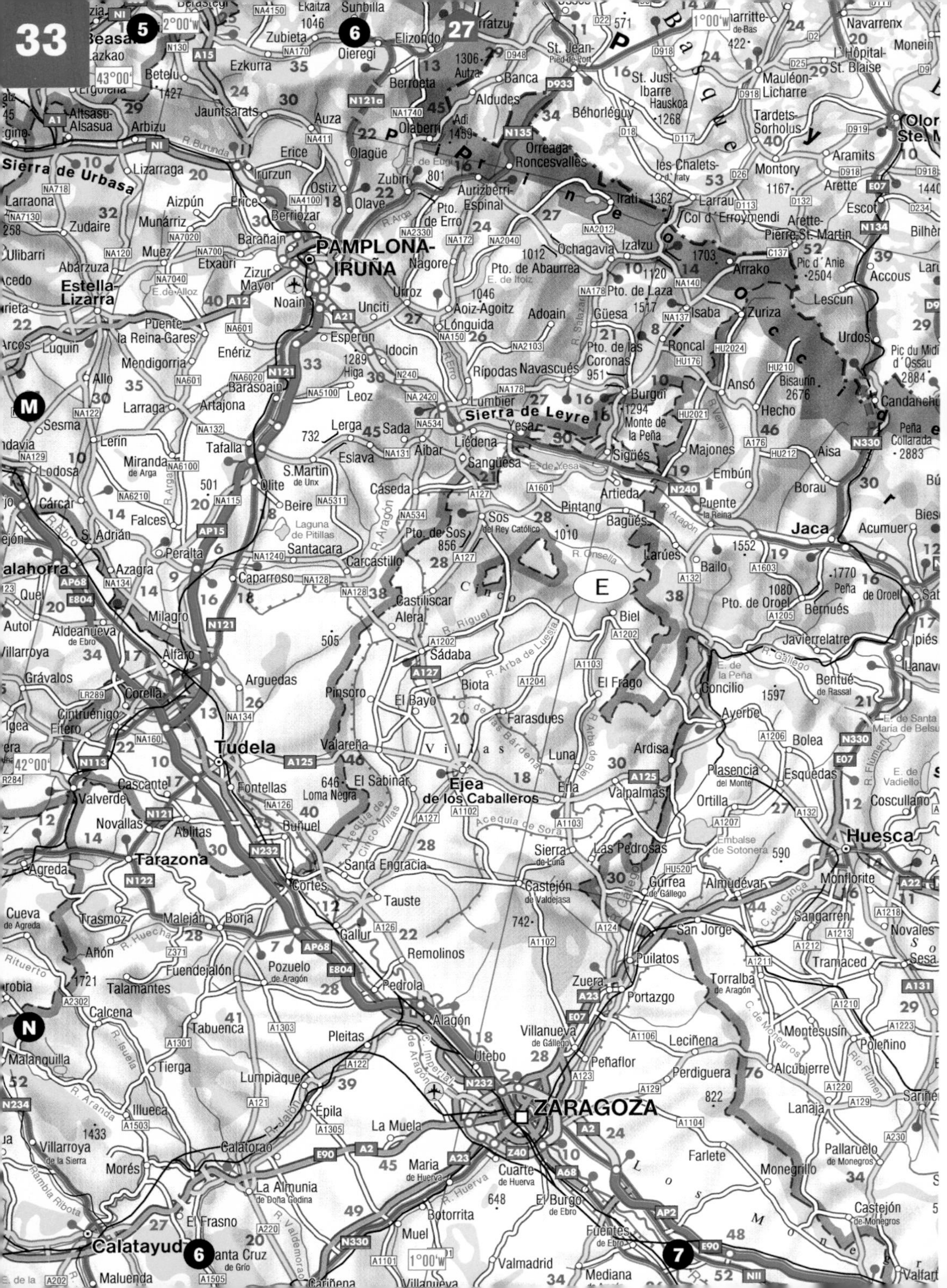

Beasain
Lazkao
Betelu
Ezkurra
Zubieta
Oieregi
Elizondo
Sunbilla
Ekaitza
Autza
Berroeta
Banca
Aldudes
St. Jean-Pied-de-Port
St. Just-Ibarre
Hauskoa
Béhorléguy
Mauléon-Licharre
Navarrenx
Monein
L'Hôpital-St. Blaise
Tardets-Sorholus
Altsasu-Alsasua
Arbizu
Jauntsarats
Auza
Olaberri
Adi
Sierra de Urbasa
Lizarraga
Irurzun
Erice
Olagüe
Zubiri
Orreaga-Roncesvalles
les Chalets-d'Iraty
Montory
Aramits
Arette
Larrau
Col d'Erroymendi
Arette-Pierre-St. Martin
Escot
Larraona
Zudaire
Aizpún
Munárriz
Ericé
Berriozar
Ostiz
Olave
Pto. de Erro
Aurizberri-Espinal
Irati
Ochagavia
Izalzu
Pic d'Anie
Arrako
Lescun
Accous
Barañain
PAMPLONA-IRUÑA
Nagore
Pto. de Abaurrea
Ulibarri
Abárzuza
Muez
Etxauri
Zizur Mayor
Noain
Estella-Lizarra
E. de Alloz
E. de Itoiz
Urroz
Aoiz-Agoitz
Unciti
Pto. de Laza
Güesa
Isaba
Zuriza
Urdos
Pic du Midi d'Ossau
Puente la Reina-Gares
Esperun
Lónguida
Adoain
Pto. de las Coronas
Roncal
Luquin
Mendigorria
Enériz
Idocin
Higa
Rípodas
Navascués
Ansó
Bisaurín
Candanchú
Allo
Barasoain
Leoz
Lumbier
Burgui
Hecho
Larraga
Artajona
Sierra de Leyre
Yesa
Monte de la Peña
Sesma
Lerín
Tafalla
Lerga
Sada
Aibar
Liédena
Majones
Aisa
Peña Collarada
Lodosa
Miranda de Arga
Olite
S. Martin de Unx
Eslava
Sangüesa
E. de Yesa
Sigüés
Embún
Cárcar
Beire
Cáseda
Artieda
Borau
Falces
Laguna de Pitillas
Pto. de Sos
Sos del Rey Católico
Pintano
Bagüés
Puente la Reina
Jaca
Acumuer
S. Adrián
Peralta
Santacara
Carcastillo
R. Onsella
Larúes
Bailo
Calahorra
Azagra
Caparroso
Cinco
Peña de Oroel
Pto. de Oroel
Bernués
Autol
Milagro
Castiliscar
Alera
Biel
Aldeanueva de Ebro
Villarroya
Alfaro
Sádaba
Javierrelatre
Grávalos
Arguedas
R. Riguel
R. Arba de Luesia
El Frago
Bentué de Rassal
Corella
Cintruénigo
Fitero
Pinsoro
El Bayo
Biota
Farasdues
Concilio
Ayerbe
Tudela
Valareña
Villas
Luna
Ardisa
Bolea
Cascante
Fontellas
El Sabinar
Loma Negra
Ejea de los Caballeros
Erla
Valpalmas
Plasencia del Monte
Esquedas
Valverde
Novallas
Ablitas
Buñuel
Acequia de Cinco Villas
Acequia de Sora
Ortilla
Coscullano
Agreda
Tarazona
Santa Engracia
Sierra de Luna
Las Pedrosas
Embalse de Sotonera
Huesca
Cortes
Castejón de Valdejasa
Gurrea de Gállego
Almudévar
Monflorite
Cueva de Agreda
Trasmoz
Maleján
Borja
Tauste
Sangarrén
Añón
Gallur
Remolinos
San Jorge
Novales
Rituerto
Talamantes
Fuendejalón
Pozuelo de Aragón
Pedrola
Pulilatos
Zuera
Portazgo
Torralba de Aragón
Tramaced
Calcena
Tabuenca
Alagón
Villanueva de Gállego
Montesusín
Poleñino
Malanquilla
Tierga
Pleitas
Utebo
Leciñena
Peñaflor
Perdiguera
Alcubierre
Lumpiaque
Illueca
Épila
La Muela
ZARAGOZA
Lanaja
Sariñena
Villarroya de la Sierra
Calatorao
Farlete
Pallaruelo de Monegros
Morés
La Almunia de Doña Godina
Maria de Huerva
Cuarte de Huerva
Monegrillo
El Burgo de Ebro
Los Monegros
Castejón de Monegros
Calatayud
El Frasno
Santa Cruz de Grío
Botorrita
Muel
Fuentes de Ebro
Maluenda
Valmadrid
Mediana
Villanueva
Cariñena
Valfarta
Pyrénées
Pirineo
Basque
E
M
N

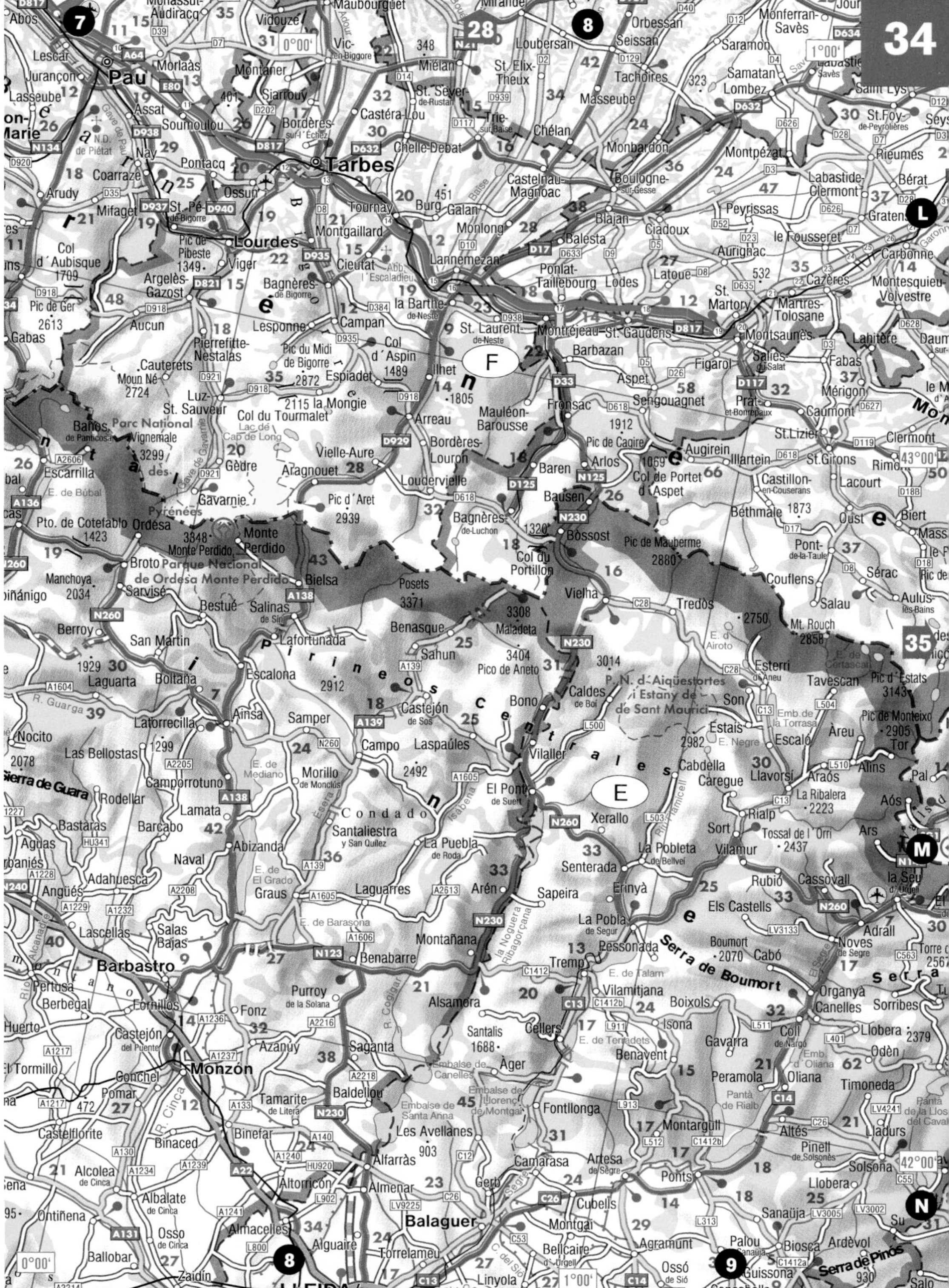

Pau
Lescar
Jurançon
Lasseube
Abos
Morlaàs
Montaner
Vidouze
Maubourguet
Vic-en-Bigorre
Sarrouy
Soumoulou
Assat
Bordères-sur-l'Échez
Castéra-Lou
Tarbes
Chelle-Debat
Nay
Pontacq
Coarraze
Ossun
Arudy
Mifaget
St. Pé-de-Bigorre
Lourdes
Pic de Pibeste
1349
Viger
Col d'Aubisque
1709
Argelès-Gazost
Pic de Ger
2613
Gabas
Aucun
Bagnères-de-Bigorre
Cauterets
Moun Né
2724
Pierrefitte-Nestalas
Luz-St. Sauveur
Pic du Midi de Bigorre
2872
Col du Tourmalet
Lac de Cap de Long
Vignemale
3299
Gèdre
Gavarnie
Baños de Panticosa
Escarrilla
E. de Búbal
Pto. de Cotefablo
1423
Ordesa
Parc National des Pyrénées
Monte Perdido
3348
Broto
Parque Nacional de Ordesa Monte Perdido
Manchoya
2034
Sarvisé
Bielsa
Bestué
Salinas de Sin
Berroy
San Martin
Lafortunada
Escalona
Boltaña
Laguarta
1929
R. Guarga
Ainsa
Latorrecilla
Nocito
Las Bellostas
Sierra de Guara
Rodellar
Camporrotuno
E. de Mediano
Lamata
Bastaràs
Barcabo
Abizanda
Naval
Adahuesca
Angüés
E. de El Grado
Graus
Lascellas
Salas Bajas
Barbastro
Pertusa
Berbegal
Fornillos
Fonz
Castejón del Puente
Azanúy
El Tormillo
Monzón
Conchel
Pomar
Castelflorite
Binaced
Binéfar
Alcolea de Cinca
Albalate de Cinca
Ontiñena
Osso de Cinca
Ballobar
Zaidín
Almacelles
Alguaire
Tamarite de Litera
Baldellou
Altorricón
Almenar
Alfarràs
Les Avellanes
903
Balaguer
Torrelameu
Linyola
Benabarre
Purroy de la Solana
Saganta
Montañana
Alsamora
Santalis
1688
Àger
Embalse de Canelles
Embalse de Santa Anna
Embalse de Llorenç de Montgai
Fontllonga
Camarasa
Gerb
Artesa de Segre
Cubells
Montgai
Bellcaire d'Urgell
Agramunt
Ossó de Sió
Ponts
Guissona
Palou
Biosca
Sanaüja
Ardèvol
Serra de Pinós
Tremp
Vilamitjana
Cellers
Isona
E. de Terradets
Benavent
Boixols
Gavarra
Peramola
Oliana
Montargull
La Pobla de Segur
Pessonada
E. de Talam
Serra de Boumort
Boumort
2070
Cabó
Organyà
Canelles
Coll de Nargó
Emb. d'Oliana
Sorribes
Llobera
2379
Odèn
Timoneda
Altés
Pinell de Solsonès
Lladurs
Solsona
Noves de Segre
Adrall
la Seu d'Urgell
Els Castells
Cassovall
Rubió
Vilamur
Sort
Tossal de l'Orri
2437
Rialp
La Ribalera
2223
Llavorsí
Caregue
Araós
Alins
Àreu
Pic de Monteixo
2905
Tor
Aós
Ars
Escaló
Estaís
E. Negre
Cabdella
2982
Emb. de la Torrasa
Son
Esterri d'Àneu
Tavescan
Pic d'Estats
3143
E. de Cortascar
P. N. d'Aigüestortes i Estany de Sant Maurici
Caldes de Boí
Bono
3014
Vilaller
El Pont de Suert
Xerallo
La Pobleta de Bellveí
Senterada
Erinyà
Sapeira
Arén
La Puebla de Roda
Laguarres
Santaliestra y San Quílez
Condado
Morillo de Monclús
Campo
Laspaúles
2492
Samper
Castejón de Sos
Sahun
2912
Benasque
Maladeta
3308
3404
Pico de Aneto
Posets
3371
Pirineos centrales
Vielha
Col du Portillon
Bossòst
Bausen
Pic de Mauberme
2880
Tredòs
2750
Mt. Rouch
2858
E. d'Airoto
Couflens
Salau
Aulus-les-Bains
Sérac
Pont-de-la-Taule
Oust
Biert
Béthmale
1873
Castillon-en-Couserans
Lacourt
St. Girons
St. Lizier
Clermont
Caumont
Mérigon
Illartein
Augirein
Col de Portet d'Aspet
1069
Arlos
Baren
Pic de Cagire
1912
Fronsac
Mauléon-Barousse
Bagnères-de-Luchon
1320
Loudervielle
Bordères-Louron
Pic d'Aret
2939
Aragnouet
Vielle-Aure
Arreau
Ilhet
1805
Col d'Aspin
1489
Espiadet
La Mongie
2115
Lesponne
Campan
la Barthe-de-Neste
St. Laurent-de-Neste
Montréjeau
St. Gaudens
Barbazan
Aspet
Sengouagnet
Figarol
Salies-du-Salat
Fabas
Prat-et-Bonrepaux
Lahitère
Montsaunès
Martres-Tolosane
Cazères
Montesquieu-Volvestre
Carbonne
St. Martory
Latoue
Aurignac
532
le Fousseret
Peyrissas
Gratens
Montpézat
Labastide-Clermont
Bérat
Rieumes
St.Foy-de-Peyrolières
Saint Lys
Labastide-Savès
Samatan
Lombez
Saramon
Monferran-Savès
Orbessan
Seissan
Tachoires
Masseube
Monbardon
Boulogne-sur-Gesse
Ciadoux
Blajan
Balesta
Pontat-Taillebourg
Lodes
Lannemezan
Montlong
Castelnau-Magnoac
Galan
Burg
451
Tournay
Montgaillard
Cieutat
Abb. l'Escaladieu
Chélan
Trie-sur-Baïse
St. Sever-de-Rustan
Miélan
348
Mirande
Loubersan
St. Elix-Theux
Monassut-Audiracq
Mauléon
Montréjeau

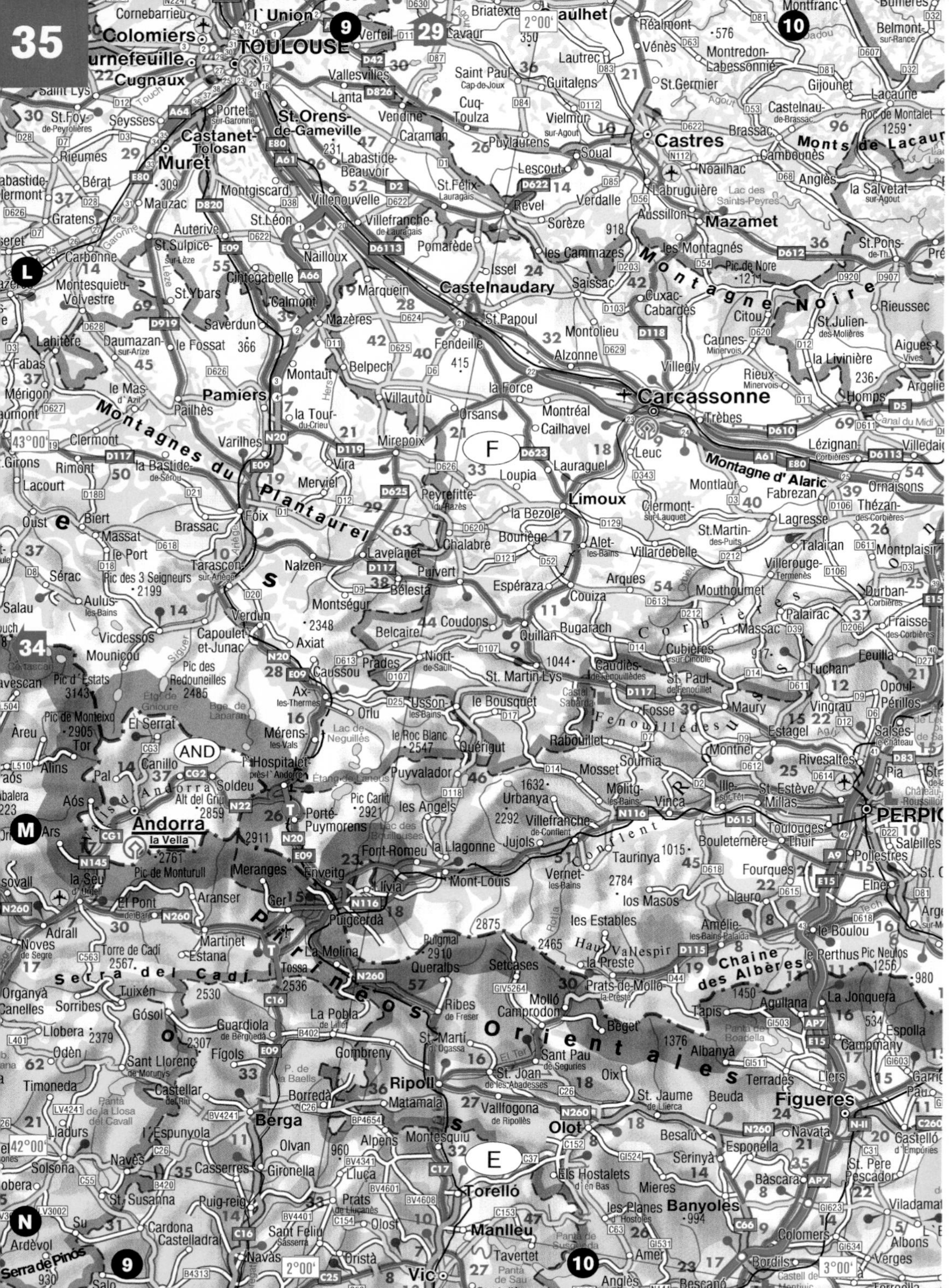

Cornebarrieu
Colomiers
Tournefeuille
Cugnaux
L'Union
TOULOUSE
Verfeil
29
Briatexte
Graulhet
Réalmont
Vénès
Montfranc
Belmont-sur-Rance
Montredon-Labessonnié
Lautrec
Saint Paul-Cap-de-Joux
Guitalens
St.Germier
Gijounet
Lacaune
Vallesvilles
Lanta
Vendine
Cuq-Toulza
Vielmur-sur-Agout
Castelnau-de-Brassac
Roc de Montalet 1259
St.Foy-de-Peyrolières
Seysses
Portet-sur-Garonne
St.Orens-de-Gameville
Caraman
Puylaurens
Castres
Brassac
Monts de Lacaune
Rieumes
Castanet-Tolosan
Muret
Labastide-Beauvoir
Soual
Cambounès
Bérat
Montgiscard
Lescout
Noailhac
Anglès
Mauzac
Villenouvelle
St.Félix-Lauragais
Revel
Verdalle
Labruguière
Lac des Saints-Peyres
la Salvetat-sur-Agout
Gratens
St.Léon
Villefranche-de-Lauragais
Sorèze
Aussillon
Mazamet
Carbonne
Auterive
St.Sulpice-sur-Lèze
Nailloux
Pomarède
les Cammazes
les Montagnés
Pic de Nore 1211
St.Pons-de-Th.
Montesquieu-Volvestre
Cintegabelle
Issel
Castelnaudary
Saissac
Cuxac-Cabardès
Montagne Noire
Rieussec
St.Ybars
Calmont
Marquein
Citou
St.Julien-des-Molières
Saverdun
Mazères
St.Papoul
Montolieu
Lahitère
Daumazan-sur-Arize
le Fossat
Fendeille
Alzonne
Caunes-Minervois
Aigues-Vives
Fabas
Belpech
Villegly
la Livinière
Mérigon
le Mas-d'Azil
Montaut
Rieux-Minervois
Pamiers
Villautou
la Force
Carcassonne
Homps
Argeliers
Pailhès
la Tour-du-Crieu
Orsans
Montréal
Trèbes
Montagnes du Plantaurel
Clermont
Varilhes
Mirepoix
Cailhavel
Canal du Midi
Lézignan-Corbières
Villedaigne
St.Girons
Rimont
la Bastide-de-Sérou
Vira
F
Leuc
Montagne d'Alaric
Lacourt
Merviel
Loupia
Lauraguel
Montlaur
Fabrezan
Ornaisons
Peyrefitte-du-Razès
Limoux
Clermont-sur-Lauquet
Thézan-des-Corbières
Oust
Biert
Brassac
Foix
la Bezole
Lagresse
Massat
le Port
Tarascon-sur-Ariège
Lavelanet
Chalabre
Bouriège
Alet-les-Bains
St.Martin-des-Puits
Talairan
Montplaisir
Villardebelle
Sérac
Pic des 3 Seigneurs 2199
Nalzen
Puivert
Espéraza
Arques
Villerouge-Termenès
Salau
Aulus-les-Bains
Bélesta
Couiza
Mouthoumet
Durban-Corbières
Montségur
Verdun
Coudons
Bugarach
Palairac
Fraisse-des-Corbières
34
Vicdessos
Capoulet-et-Junac
Axiat
Belcaire
Quillan
Corbières
Massac
Mounicou
Pic des Redouneilles 2485
Prades
Niort-de-Sault
Cubières-sur-Cinoble
Tuchan
Eeuilla
Caussou
St.Martin-Lys
Caudiès-de-Fenouillèdes
St.Paul-de-Fenouillet
Pic d'Estats 3143
Ax-les-Thermes
Usson-les-Bains
le Bousquet
Castel Sabarda
Fosse
Maury
Vingrau
Opoul-Périllos
Pic de Montcalm
El Serrat
Orlu
Fenouillèdes
Estagel
Salses-le-Château
Àreu
Pic de Medecourbe 2905
Tor
Mérens-les-Vals
Lac de Naguilles
le Roc Blanc 2547
Quérigut
Rabouillet
Montner
Rivesaltes
AND
Alins
Pal
Canillo
l'Hospitalet-près-l'Andorre
Puyvalador
Mosset
Sournia
Pia
Soldeu
Étang de Lanoux
Pic Carlit 2921
les Angels
Urbanya
Molitg-les-Bains
Ille-sur-Têt
St. Estève
Aós
Alt del Griu 2859
Porté-Puymorens
2292
Villefranche-de-Conflent
Vinça
Millas
Ars
Andorra la Vella
2911
Lac des Bouillouses
Jujols
Conflent
Toulouges
Thuir
PERPIGNAN
Saleilles
Pic de Monturull
Font-Romeu
la Llagonne
Taurinya
Bouleternère
Pollestres
Meranges
Enveitg
Llívia
Mont-Louis
Vernet-les-Bains
Fourques
Elne
la Seu d'Urgell
El Pont de Bar
Aranser
Ger
Puigcerdà
2784
los Masos
Llauro
Adrall
Noves de Segre
Martinet
Torre de Cadí 2567
Estana
La Molina
Puigmal 2910
2875
les Estables
Amélie-les-Bains-Palalda
le Boulou
Queralbs
Setcases
Haut Vallespir
la Preste
le Perthus
Pic Neulos 1256
Serra del Cadí
Tossa 2536
Prats-de-Mollo-la-Preste
Chaîne des Albères
Organyà
Canelles
Tuixén
2530
Molló
Camprodon
La Jonquera
Sorribes
Gósol
La Pobla de Lillet
Ribes de Freser
Pirineos Orientales
Agullana
Espolla
Llobera
Guardiola de Berguedà
St. Martí d'Ogassa
Beget
Albanyà
Campmany
Odèn
Sant Llorenç de Morunys
Fígols
Gombreny
Sant Pau de Seguries
Timoneda
Castellar del Riu
Borredà
Ripoll
St. Joan de les Abadesses
Oix
St. Jaume de Llierca
Beuda
Terrades
Llers
Figueres
Lladurs
Berga
Matamala
Vallfogona de Ripollès
Olot
Navata
Espunyola
Olvan
Alpens
Montesquiu
Besalú
Esponella
Castelló d'Empúries
Solsona
Navès
Casserres
Gironella
Lluçà
E
Els Hostalets d'en Bas
Serinyà
Bàscara
St. Pere Pescador
St. Susanna
Puig-reig
Prats de Lluçanès
Torelló
Mieres
Banyoles
Viladamat
Ardèvol
Cardona
Castelladral
Sant Feliu Sasserra
Olost
Manlleu
les Planes d'Hostoles
Colomers
Albons
Serra de Pinós
Navàs
Orís
Tavertet
Amer
Bordils
Verges
Salo
Vic
Anglès
Bescanó

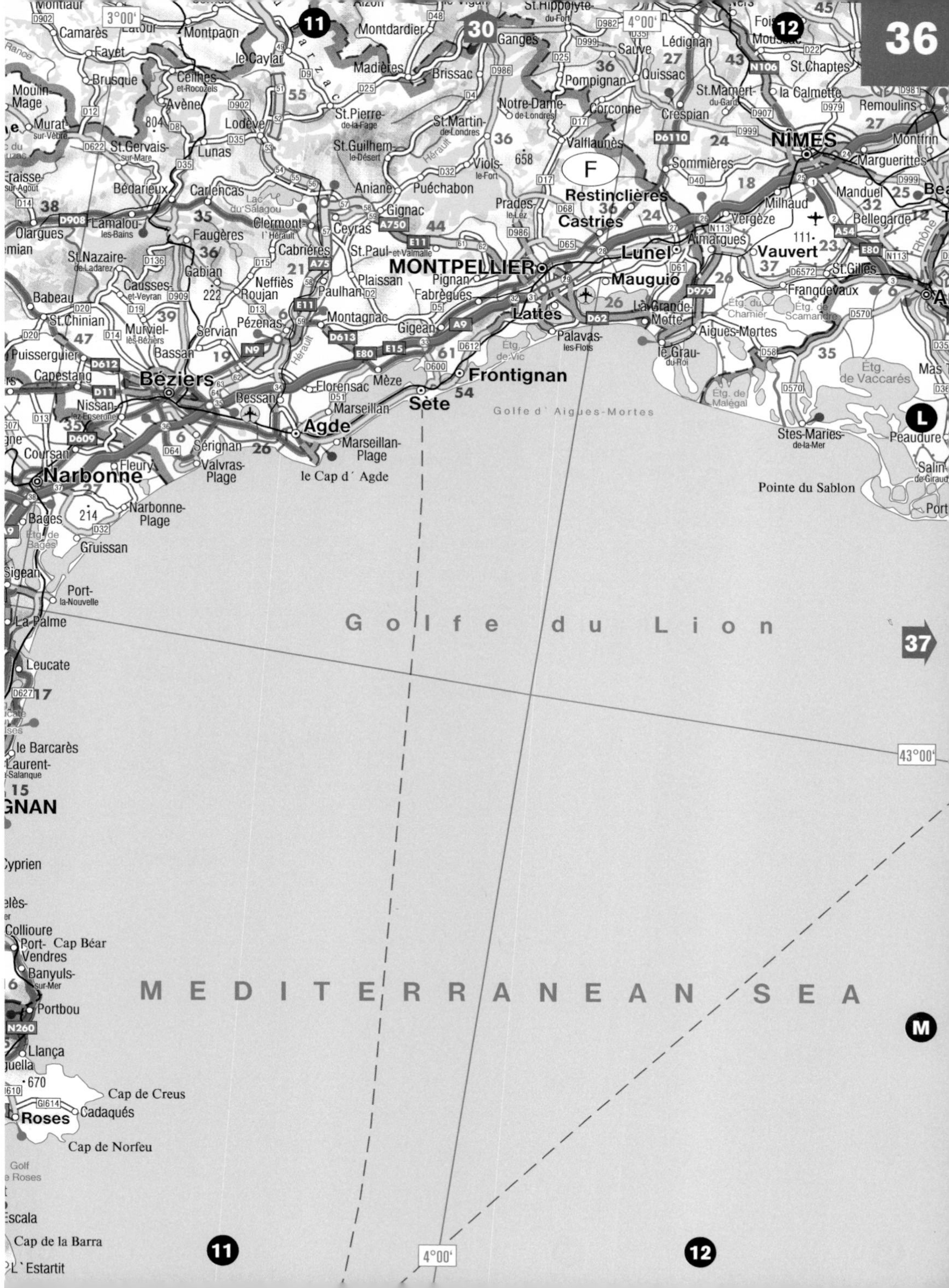
Camarès
Montpaon
le Caylar
Montdardier
Ganges
St.Hippolyte-du-Fort
Lédignan
Sauve
Fayet
Brusque
Ceilhes-et-Rocozels
Madières
Brissac
Pompignan
Quissac
St.Chaptes
Moulin-Mage
Avène
Lodève
St.Pierre-de-la-Fage
Notre-Dame-de-Londres
Corconne
Crespian
St.Mamert-du-Gard
la Calmette
Remoulins
Murat-sur-Vèbre
St.Gervais-sur-Mare
Lunas
St.Guilhem-le-Désert
St.Martin-de-Londres
Valflaunès
NÎMES
Montfrin
Marguerittes
Sommières
Fraisse-sur-Agout
Bédarieux
Carlencas
Lac du Salagou
Aniane
Puéchabon
Viols-le-Fort
F
Restinclières
Manduel
Milhaud
Prades-le-Lez
Castries
Olargues
Lamalou-les-Bains
Clermont-l'Hérault
Gignac
Ceyras
Vergèze
Bellegarde
Faugères
Aimargues
St.Nazaire-de-Ladarez
Cabrières
St.Paul-et-Valmalle
MONTPELLIER
Lunel
Vauvert
Gabian
Causses-et-Veyran
Neffiès
Roujan
Plaissan
Pignan
Mauguio
St.Gilles
Franquevaux
Babeau
St.Chinian
Paulhan
Fabrègues
Lattes
La Grande-Motte
Étg. du Charnier
Étg. de Scamandre
Murviel-lès-Béziers
Servian
Pézenas
Montagnac
Gigean
Palavas-les-Flots
Aigues-Mortes
Bassan
Étg. de Vic
le Grau-du-Roi
Puisserguier
Capestang
Béziers
Florensac
Mèze
Frontignan
Étg. de Vaccarès
Nissan-lez-Enserune
Bessan
Marseillan
Sète
Golfe d' Aigues-Mortes
Étg. de Malégal
Agde
Coursan
Sérignan
Marseillan-Plage
Stes-Maries-de-la-Mer
Peaudure
Narbonne
Fleury
Valvras-Plage
le Cap d' Agde
Pointe du Sablon
Bages
Narbonne-Plage
Étg. de Bages
Gruissan
Sigean
Port-la-Nouvelle
La Palme
Golfe du Lion
37
Leucate
le Barcarès
43°00'
3°00'
4°00'
GNAN
Collioure
Port-Vendres
Cap Béar
Banyuls-sur-Mer
MEDITERRANEAN SEA
Portbou
Llança
Cap de Creus
Cadaqués
Roses
Cap de Norfeu
Golf de Roses
Escala
Cap de la Barra
L' Estartit
11
12
L
M

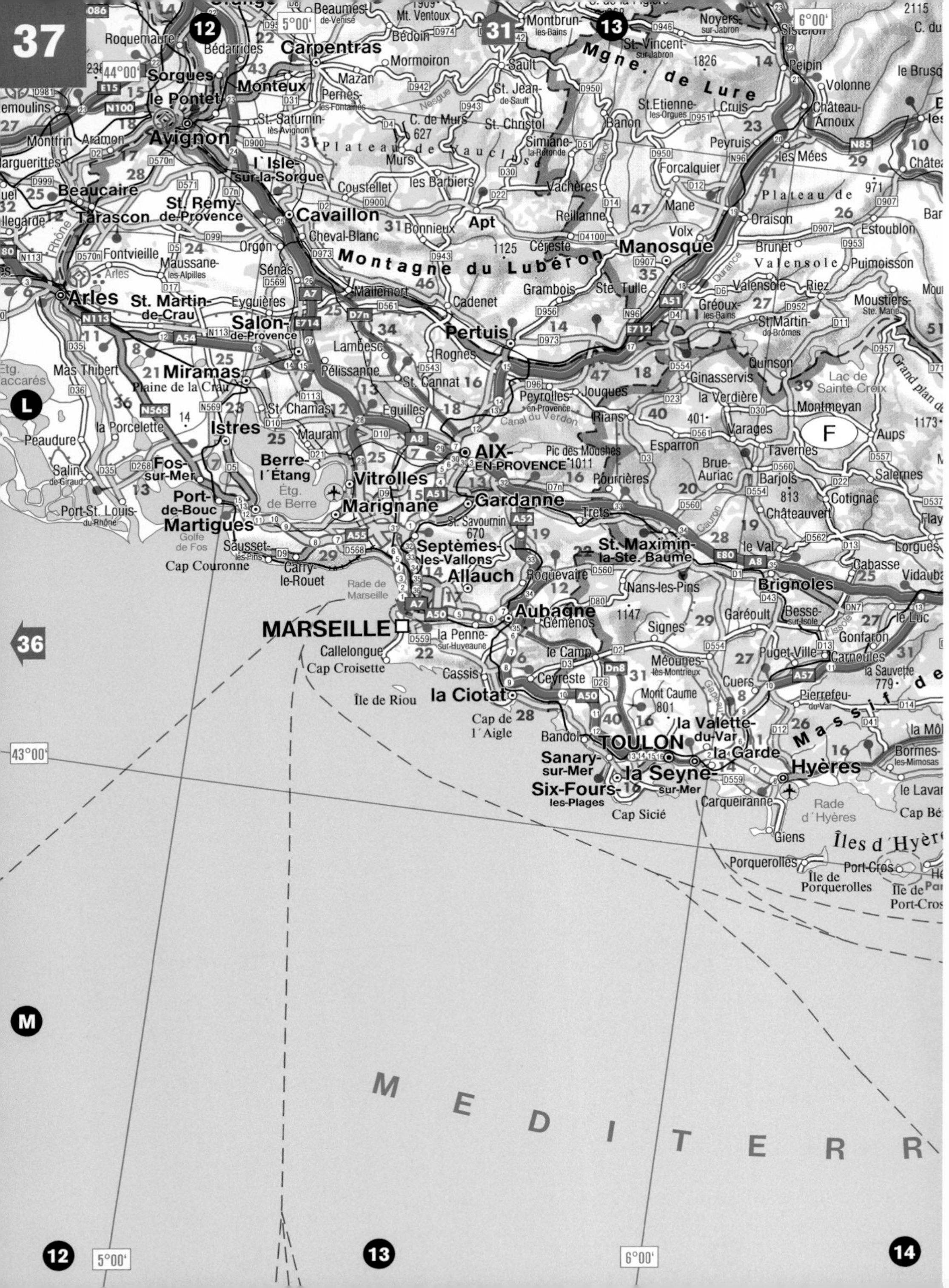

12
13
31
5°00'
6°00'
44°00'
43°00'
Beaumes-de-Venise
Mt. Ventoux
Montbrun-les-Bains
Noyers-sur-Jabron
Sisteron
Roquemaure
Bédarrides
Carpentras
Bédoin
St. Vincent-sur-Jabron
Mgne. de Lure
1826
Peipin
le Brusq
Sorgues
Monteux
Mazan
Mormoiron
Sault
Volonne
le Pontet
Pernes-les-Fontaines
St. Jean-de-Sault
St. Etienne-les-Orgues
Cruis
Château-Arnoux
Avignon
St. Saturnin-lès-Avignon
C. de Murs
627
St. Christol
Banon
Montfrin
Aramon
Plateau de Vaucluse
Murs
Simiane-la-Rotonde
Peyruis
les Mées
Château
l`Isle-sur-la-Sorgue
Forcalquier
Beaucaire
Coustellet
les Barbiers
Vachères
Plateau de
971
St. Rémy-de-Provence
Cavaillon
Apt
Reillanne
Mane
Oraison
Tarascon
Bonnieux
Volx
Estoublon
Fontvieille
Cheval-Blanc
Orgon
Montagne du Lubéron
1125
Céreste
Manosque
Brunet
Valensole
Puimoisson
Maussane-les-Alpilles
Sénas
Grambois
Ste. Tulle
Riez
Moustiers-Ste. Marie
Arles
St. Martin-de-Crau
Eyguières
Mallemort
Cadenet
Gréoux-les-Bains
St. Martin-de-Brômes
Salon-de-Provence
Pertuis
Lambesc
Rognes
Quinson
Grand plan de
Mas Thibert
Miramas
Plaine de la Crau
Pélissanne
St. Cannat
Peyrolles-en-Provence
Jouques
Ginasservis
Lac de Sainte Croix
la Verdière
Montmeyan
St. Chamas
Eguilles
Canal du Verdon
Rians
401
Varages
Aups
1173
la Porcelette
Istres
Mauran
Esparron
Tavernes
Peaudure
Berre-l'Étang
AIX-EN-PROVENCE
Pic des Mouches 1011
Brue-Auriac
Barjols
Salernes
Fos-sur-Mer
Vitrolles
Pourrières
813
Cotignac
Port-de-Bouc
Étg. de Berre
Marignane
Gardanne
Trets
Châteauvert
Port-St. Louis-du-Rhône
Martigues
Golfe de Fos
St. Savournin
670
Septèmes-les-Vallons
St. Maximin-la-Ste. Baume
le Val
Sausset-les-Pins
Carry-le-Rouet
Cap Couronne
Allauch
Roquevaire
Cabasse
Vidauban
Brignoles
Rade de Marseille
Nans-les-Pins
Aubagne
Gémenos
1147
Garéoult
Besse-sur-Issole
le Luc
MARSEILLE
la Penne-sur-Huveaune
Signes
Gonfaron
Callelongue
le Camp
Méounes-lès-Montrieux
Puget-Ville
Carnoules
Cap Croisette
Cassis
Ceyreste
Cuers
la Sauvette 779
Île de Riou
la Ciotat
Mont Caume 801
Pierrefeu-du-Var
Cap de l´Aigle
Bandol
TOULON
la Valette-du-Var
Massif de
Sanary-sur-Mer
la Garde
Bormes-les-Mimosas
Six-Fours-les-Plages
la Seyne-sur-Mer
Hyères
le Lavan
Cap Sicié
Carqueiranne
Rade d´Hyères
Cap Bé
Giens
Îles d'Hyè
Porquerolles
Port-Cros
Île de Porquerolles
Île de Port-Cros
M E D I T E R R
L
F
M
36
14

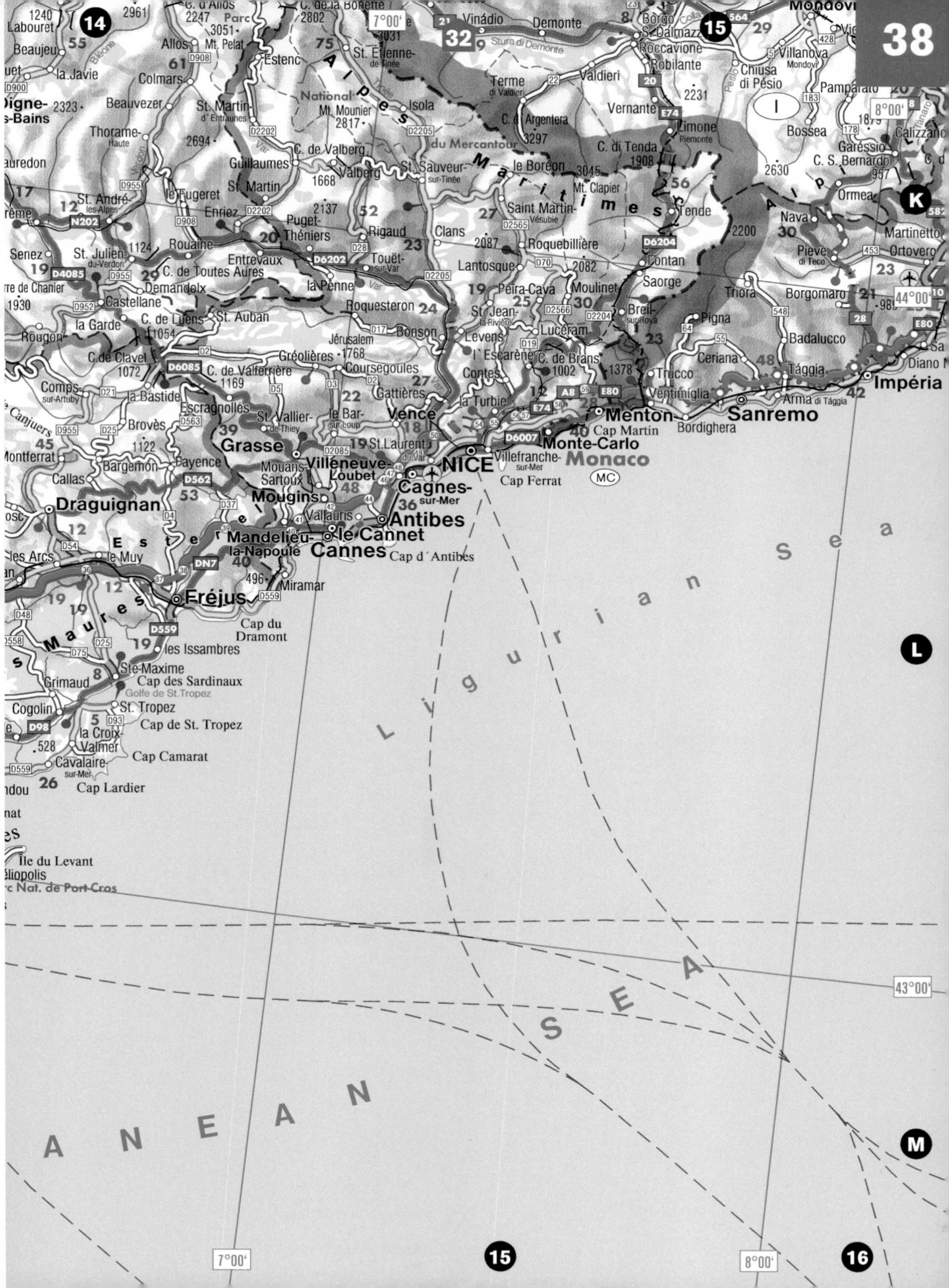
Digne-les-Bains
Castellane
Draguignan
Fréjus
Grasse
Cannes
Antibes
Mandelieu-la-Napoule
le Cannet
Vallauris
Mougins
Villeneuve-Loubet
Cagnes-sur-Mer
NICE
Vence
Villefranche-sur-Mer
Monte-Carlo
Monaco
Menton
Ventimiglia
Bordighera
Sanremo
Impéria
Tággia
Cap Ferrat
Cap d´Antibes
Cap Martin
Cap du Dramont
Miramar
les Issambres
Ste-Maxime
Cap des Sardinaux
Golfe de St.Tropez
St. Tropez
Cap de St. Tropez
Cap Camarat
Cap Lardier
Cavalaire-sur-Mer
la Croix-Valmer
Grimaud
Cogolin
Île du Levant
Alpes Maritimes
Parc National du Mercantour
Esterel
Maures
Ligurian Sea
SEA
Tende
Limone Piemonte
Borgo S. Dalmazzo
Roccavione
Robilante
Valdieri
Vernante
Vinádio
Demonte
Mondovì
Villanova Mondovì
Chiusa di Pésio
Ormea
Garéssio
Calizzano
Triora
Pigna
Saorge
Breil-sur-Roya
Sospel
Roquebillière
Saint Martin-Vésubie
Lantosque
Levens
Contes
l`Escarène
Lucéram
la Turbie
Puget-Théniers
Entrevaux
Guillaumes
Valberg
Isola
St. Étienne-de-Tinée
St. Sauveur-sur-Tinée
Colmars
Allos
Beauvezer
Thorame-Haute
Senez
St. Julien-du-Verdon
St. André-les-Alpes
Annot
Demandolx
Comps-sur-Artuby
Bargemon
Callas
Fayence
Montferrat
le Muy
les Arcs
St.Vallier-de-Thiey
Gréolières
Coursegoules
Roquesteron
Bonson
Gattières
St.Laurent-du-Var
Mouans-Sartoux
7°00'
8°00'
44°00'
43°00'
14
15
16
K
L
M

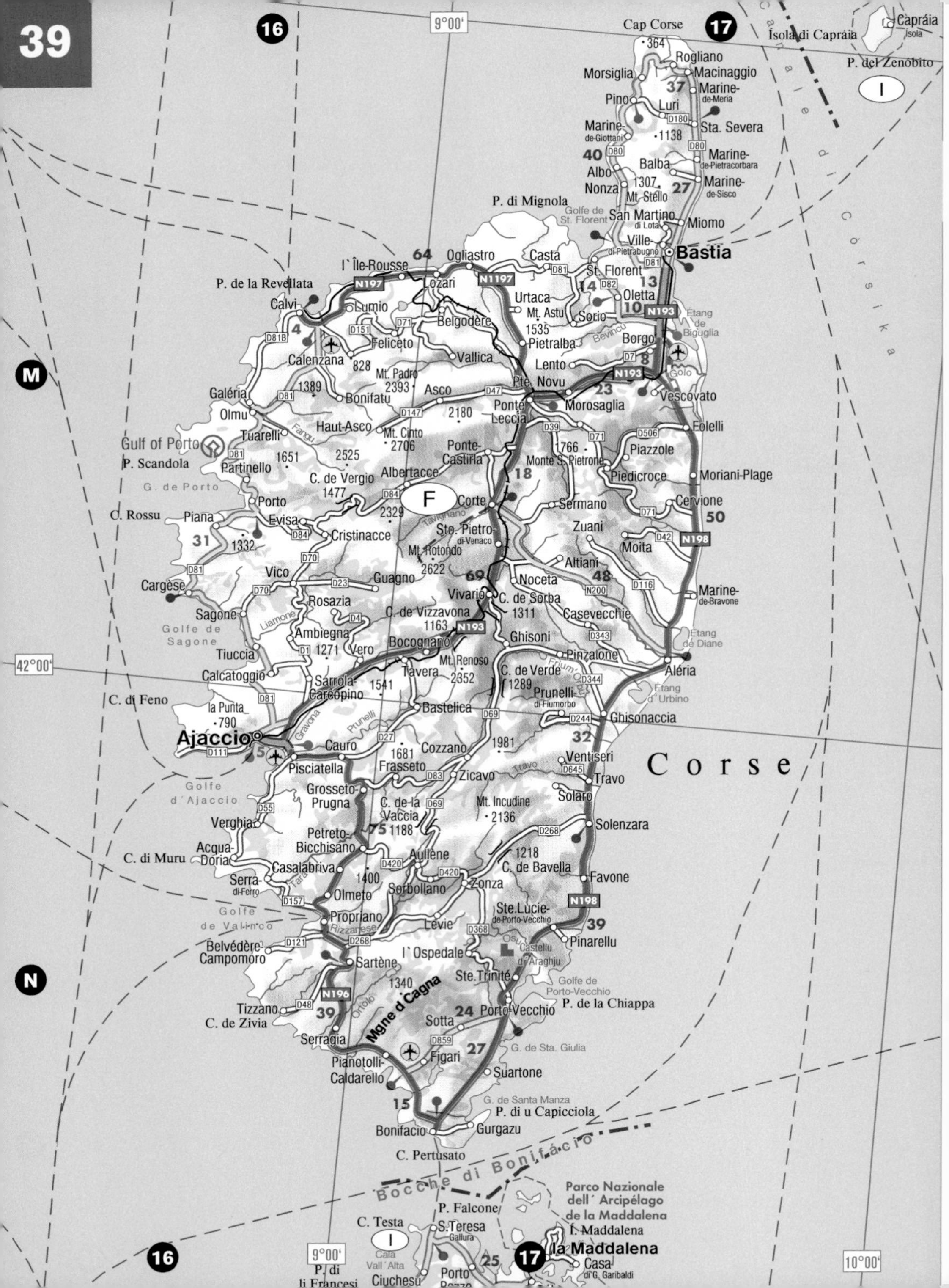

16
9°00'
Cap Corse
17
Capráia
Ísola di Capráia
P. del Zenóbito
I
Rogliano
Macinaggio
Morsiglia
Marine-de-Meria
Pino
Luri
Sta. Severa
Marine-de-Giottani
1138
Marine-de-Pietracorbara
Albo
Balba
Nonza
1307
Mt. Stello
Marine-de-Sisco
P. di Mignola
Golfe de St. Florent
San Martino di Lota
Miomo
Ville-di-Pietrabugno
Bastia
Ogliastro
Casta
St. Florent
l'Île-Rousse
P. de la Revellata
Calvi
Lozari
Urtaca
Oletta
Lumio
Belgodère
Mt. Astu
Sorio
Étang de Biguglia
Feliceto
1535
Pietralba
Borgo
Calenzana
Vallica
Lento
828
Mt. Padro
2393
Pte. Novu
Golo
1389
Galéria
Bonifatu
Asco
Morosaglia
Vescovato
Olmu
2180
Ponte Leccia
Folelli
Gulf of Porto
Tuarelli
Haut-Asco
Mt. Cinto
2706
1766
Piazzole
P. Scandola
Ponte-Castirla
Monte S. Pietrone
1651
2525
Partinello
Piedicroce
Moriani-Plage
G. de Porto
C. de Vergio
Albertacce
1477
F
Corte
Sermano
Cervione
C. Rossu
Porto
Piana
Evisa
2329
Sto. Pietro-di-Venaco
Zuani
1332
Cristinacce
Moita
Mt. Rotondo
2622
Altiani
Cargèse
Vico
Guagno
Noceta
Vivario
C. de Sorba
1311
Marine-de-Bravone
Sagone
Rosazia
Casevecchie
Golfe de Sagone
C. de Vizzavona
1163
Étang de Diane
Ambiegna
Bocognano
Ghisoni
Tiuccia
1271
Vero
Mt. Renoso
Pinzalone
42°00'
Calcatoggio
Tavera
2352
C. de Verde
1289
Aléria
C. di Feno
Sarrola-Carcopino
1541
Prunelli-di-Fiumorbo
Étang d'Urbino
la Punta
790
Bastelica
Ghisonaccia
Ajaccio
Gravona
Prunelli
Cauro
1681
Cozzano
1981
Pisciatella
Frasseto
Ventiseri
Corse
Golfe d'Ajaccio
Zicavo
Travo
Grosseto-Prugna
C. de la Vaccia
1188
Solaro
Verghia
Mt. Incudine
2136
Solenzara
Petreto-Bicchisano
Acqua-Doria
C. di Muru
Aullène
1218
C. de Bavella
Casalabriva
1400
Serra-di-Ferro
Sorbollano
Zonza
Favone
Olmeto
Golfe de Valinco
Propriano
Ste.Lucie-de-Porto-Vecchio
Rizzanese
Levie
Pinarellu
Belvédère-Campomoro
l'Ospedale
Castellu di Araghju
Sartène
1340
Ste.Trinité
Golfe de Porto-Vecchio
N
M
Mgne d'Cagna
Tizzano
Porto-Vecchio
P. de la Chiappa
C. de Zivia
Sotta
Serragia
G. de Sta. Giulia
Figari
Pianotolli-Caldarello
Suartone
G. de Santa Manza
P. di u Capicciola
Bonifacio
Gurgazu
C. Pertusato
Bocche di Bonifácio
Parco Nazionale dell' Arcipélago de la Maddalena
P. Falcone
C. Testa
S.Teresa Gallura
I. Maddalena
I
la Maddalena
Casa di G. Garibaldi
Cala Vall'Alta
P. di li Francesi
Ciuchesu
10°00'

INDEX WITH POST CODES · ORTSREGISTER MIT POSTLEITZAHLEN · INDICE CON CODICI POSTALI · ÍNDICE CON CÓDIGOS POSTALES · INDICE DE LUGARES COM CÓDIGOS POSTAIS · STEDREGISTER MED POSTNUMRE · PLAATSNAMENREGISTER MET POSTCODE · REJSTŘÍK MÍST S PSČ · ZOZNAM OBCÍ S PSČ · INDEKS MIEJSCOWOŚCI Z KOD POCZTOWY

40

Andorra la Vella · ·   Erstfeld

 AND

AD500 Andorra la Vella 35 M 9
AD100 Canillo 35 M 9
AD300 El Serrat 35 M 9
AD400 Pal 35 M 9
AD100 Soldeu 35 M 9

B

9300 Aalst 5 D 12
9880 Aalter 4 C 11
3200 Aarschot 5 C 12
8700 Aarsele 4 D 11
8970 Abele 4 D 10
3930 Achel 5 C 13
2920 Achterbroek 5 C 12
3570 Alken 5 D 12
8690 Alveringem 4 D 10
4540 Amay 5 D 13
4770 Amel 14 D 14
5300 Andenne 5 D 12
6150 Anderlues 5 D 12
6721 Anlier 13 E 13
7640 Antoing 4 D 11
2000 Antwerpen 5 C 12
2370 Arendonk 5 C 13
6700 Arlon 13 E 13
1730 Asse 5 D 12
7800 Ath 4 D 11
7387 Athis 4 D 11
6790 Aubange 13 E 13
4460 Aubel 5 D 13
5060 Auvelais 5 D 12
8580 Avelgem 4 C 11
6870 Awenne 13 D 13
4920 Aywaille 5 D 13
2490 Balen 5 C 12
6940 Barvaux 13 D 13
7971 Basècles 4 D 11
6600 Bastogne 13 E 13
7331 Baudour 4 D 11
6500 Beaumont 13 D 12
5570 Beauraing 13 D 13
3130 Begijnendijk 5 C 12
6672 Beho 13 D 14
3460 Bekkevoort 5 D 12
9982 Bentille 4 C 11
9690 Berchem 4 D 11
6687 Bertogne 13 D 13
6880 Bertrix 13 E 13
9120 Beveren 5 C 12
5555 Bièvre 13 E 13
3740 Bilzen 5 D 13

7130 Binche 5 D 12
5537 Bioul 13 D 12
8370 Blankenberge 4 C 11
2530 Boechout 5 C 12
9961 Boekhoute 4 C 11
8904 Boezinge 4 D 10
6941 Bomal 13 D 13
3840 Borgloon 5 D 13
6830 Bouillon 13 E 13
4990 Bra 13 D 13
1420 Braine-l'Alleud 5 D 12
7090 Braine-le-Comte 5 D 12
2930 Brasschaat 5 C 12
2960 Brecht 5 C 12
8450 Bredene 4 C 10
3960 Bree 5 C 13
8000 Brugge 4 C 11
1000 Brussel/Bruxelles 5 D 12
4760 Büllingen 14 D 14
4210 Burdinne 5 D 13
4750 Bütgenbach 14 D 14
7760 Celles 4 D 11
5630 Cerfontaine 13 D 12
5020 Champion 5 D 12
6000 Charleroi 5 D 12
6200 Châtelet 5 D 12
6747 Châtillon 13 E 13
6673 Cherain 13 D 13
6460 Chimay 13 D 12
6810 Chiny 13 E 13
5590 Ciney 13 D 13
1480 Clabecq 5 D 12
5590 Conjoux 13 D 13
6180 Courcelles 5 D 12
5660 Couvin 13 D 12
6880 Cugnon 13 E 13
5660 Cul-des-Sarts 13 E 12
8890 Dadizele 4 D 11
8340 Damme 4 C 11
9200 De Haan 4 C 11
9200 Dendermonde 5 C 12
2480 Dessel 5 C 13
3290 Diest 5 D 13
8600 Diksmuide 4 C 10
5500 Dinant 13 D 12
5680 Doische 13 D 12
2570 Duffel 5 D 12
9900 Eeklo 4 C 11
5310 Éghezée 5 D 12
3350 Ekeren 5 C 12
3650 Elen 5 C 13
4750 Elsenborn 14 D 14
4053 Embourg 5 D 13
7850 Enghien 5 D 12
6997 Erezée 13 D 13
9940 Ertvelde 4 C 11
4130 Esneux 5 D 13
2910 Essen 5 C 12

6740 Étalle 13 E 13
4700 Eupen 6 D 14
9940 Evergem 4 C 11
5500 Falaën 13 D 12
6240 Farcienne 5 D 12
6637 Fauvillers 13 E 13
4190 Ferrières 5 D 13
4400 Flémalle 5 D 13
6220 Fleurus 5 D 12
7880 Flobecq 4 D 11
5620 Florennes 13 D 12
6820 Florenville 13 E 13
7080 Frameries 4 D 11
4970 Francorchamps 5 D 13
7910 Frasnes-iez-Anvaing 4 D 11
6700 Freylange 13 E 13
5575 Gedinne 13 E 13
2440 Geel 5 C 12
3450 Geetbets 5 D 13
5030 Gembloux 5 D 12
3600 Genk 5 D 13
9000 Gent 4 C 11
5340 Gesves 5 D 12
3890 Gingelom 5 D 13
8470 Gistel 4 C 10
1325 Gistoux 5 D 12
7041 Givry 4 D 12
6670 Gouvy 13 D 13
6534 Gozée 5 D 12
6698 Grand-Halleux 13 D 13
1850 Grimbergen 5 D 12
3150 Haacht 5 D 12
9450 Haaltert 5 D 12
6720 Habay-la-Neuve 13 E 13
1500 Halle 5 D 12
9220 Hamme 5 D 12
1320 Hamme-Mille 5 D 12
5360 Hamois 13 D 13
3930 Hamont 5 C 13
4280 Hannut 5 D 13
8530 Harelbeke 4 D 11
6960 Harre 13 D 13
4920 Harzé 5 D 13
3500 Hasselt 5 D 13
5540 Hastière 13 D 12
5370 Havelange 13 D 13
3940 Hechtel 5 C 13
3870 Heers 5 D 13
2220 Heist-op-den-Berg 5 C 12
3530 Heichteren 5 C 13
1357 Helecine 5 D 12
3600 Herent 5 D 12
2200 Herentals 5 C 12
1540 Herne 5 D 12
2230 Herselt 5 C 12
4040 Herstal 5 D 13
4650 Herve 5 D 13
3550 Heusden 5 C 13

3320 Hoegaarden 5 D 12
1560 Hoeilaart 5 D 12
3730 Hoeselt 5 D 13
6637 Hollange 13 E 13
2320 Hoogstraten 5 C 12
9667 Horebeke 4 D 11
6990 Hotton 13 D 13
5660 Houffalize 13 D 13
3530 Houthalen 5 C 13
8650 Houthulst 4 D 10
4500 Huy 5 D 13
8900 Ieper 4 D 10
8870 Izegem 4 D 11
8490 Jabbeke 4 C 11
4845 Jalhay 5 D 13
5580 Jemelle 13 D 13
1370 Jodoigne 5 D 12
4450 Juprelle 5 D 13
7050 Jurbise 4 D 11
2920 Kalmthout 5 C 12
2950 Kapellen 5 C 12
9970 Kaprijke 4 C 11
2460 Kasterlee 5 C 12
3950 Kaulille 5 C 13
4720 Kemis 6 D 14
9130 Kieldrecht 5 C 12
3640 Kinrooi 5 C 13
9100 Knesselare 4 C 11
1880 Knokke-Heist 4 C 11
8670 Koksijde-Bad 4 C 10
2550 Kontich 5 C 12
3720 Kortessem 5 D 13
8500 Kortrijk 4 D 11
3300 Kumtich 5 D 12
8520 Kuurne 4 D 11
7100 La Louvière 5 D 12
6980 La Roche-en-Ardenne 13 D 13
3620 Lanaken 5 D 13
3400 Landen 5 D 13
9280 Lebbeke 5 D 12
6860 Léglise 13 E 13
7870 Lens 4 D 11
3970 Leopoldsburg 5 C 13
7860 Lessines 4 D 11
3000 Leuven 5 D 12
5310 Leuze 5 D 12
7900 Leuze-en-Hainaut 4 D 11
6890 Libin 13 E 13
1630 Libramont-Chevigny 13 E 13
2460 Lichtaart 5 C 12
4000 Liège 5 D 13
2500 Lier 5 D 12
6769 Limes 13 E 13
9160 Lokeren 5 C 12
8434 Lombardsijde-Bad 4 C 10
3920 Lommel 5 C 13
6840 Longlier 13 E 13
9880 Lotenhulle 4 C 11

3560 Lummen 5 D 13
3680 Maaseik 5 C 13
3630 Maasmechelen 5 D 13
6852 Maissin 13 E 13
9990 Maldegem 4 C 11
4960 Malmedy 14 D 14
7170 Manage 5 D 12
6960 Manhay 13 D 13
6900 Marche-en-Famenne 13 D 13
5660 Mariembourg 13 D 12
6680 Matagne-la-Grande 13 D 12
5032 Mazy 5 D 12
2800 Mechelen 5 C 12
2450 Meerhout 5 C 13
3670 Meeuwen 5 C 13
8930 Menen 4 D 11
6851 Menuchenet 13 E 13
1785 Merchtem 5 D 12
9820 Merelbeke 4 D 11
6780 Messancy 13 E 13
5640 Mettet 13 D 12
8430 Middelkerke 4 C 10
4577 Modave 5 D 13
2400 Mol 5 C 13
7000 Mons 4 D 11
6110 Montigny-le-Tilleul 5 D 12
6643 Mont 13 E 13
7700 Mouscron 4 D 11
6600 Nadrin 13 D 13
5000 Namur 5 D 12
6950 Nassogne 13 D 13
9660 Nederbrakel 4 D 11
3910 Neerpelt 5 C 13
6840 Neufchâteau 13 E 13
7332 Neufmaison 4 D 11
4120 Neupré 5 D 13
8620 Nieuwpoort 4 C 10
2560 Nijlen 5 C 12
9400 Ninove 5 D 12
1400 Nivelles 5 D 12
6600 Noville 13 D 13
6850 Offagne 13 E 13
5350 Ohey 5 D 13
2250 Olen 5 C 12
8400 Oostende 4 C 10
9860 Oosterzele 4 D 11
8020 Oostkamp 4 C 11
3660 Opglabbeek 5 C 13
4360 Oreye 5 D 13
1340 Ottignies-Louvain-la-Neuve 5 D 12
9700 Oudenaarde 4 D 11
4590 Ouffet 5 D 13
3090 Overijse 5 D 12
3900 Overpelt 5 C 13
8580 Paal 5 C 13
6850 Paliseul 13 E 13
7740 Pecq 4 D 11
3990 Peer 5 C 13
8600 Pervijze 4 C 10
5300 Petit-Waret 5 D 13
5600 Philippeville 13 D 12
4850 Plombières 5 D 13
8970 Poperinge 4 D 10
2382 Poppel 5 C 13
5170 Profondeville 5 D 12
2580 Putte 5 C 12
7540 Quartes 4 D 11
7380 Quiévrain 4 D 11
4730 Rance 13 D 12
2380 Ravels 5 C 13
1430 Rebecq 5 D 12
4990 Régné 13 D 13
6500 Renlies 13 D 12
3770 Riemst 5 D 13
2310 Rijkevorsel 5 C 12
5580 Rochefort 13 D 13
8680 Roeselare 4 D 11
9600 Ronse 4 D 11
6730 Rossignol 13 E 13
8020 Ruddervoorde 4 C 11
7610 Rumes 4 D 11
2840 Rumst 5 C 12
6870 Saint Hubert 13 D 13
6747 Saint Léger 13 E 13
1480 Saintes 5 D 12
6860 Samrée 13 D 13
4780 Saint Vith 14 D 14
2970 Schilde 5 C 12
6596 Seloignes 13 D 12
4100 Seraing 5 D 13
7830 Silly 4 D 11
2980 Sint Antonius 5 C 12
9100 Sint Niklaas 5 C 12
3800 Sint Truiden 5 D 13
2890 Sint-Amands 5 C 12
1840 Sint-Jozef 5 C 12
7060 Soignies 5 D 12
5140 Sombreffe 5 D 12
6997 Soy 13 D 13
4900 Spa 5 D 13
4140 Sprimont 5 D 13
4970 Stavelot 13 D 13
6887 Straimont 13 E 13
4577 Strée 5 D 13
5600 Surice 13 D 12
6927 Tellin 13 D 13
9140 Temse 5 C 12
4910 Theux 5 D 13
6536 Thuillies 13 D 12
6530 Thuin 5 D 12
3390 Tielt 4 D 11

3300 Tienen 5 D 12
4557 Tinlot 5 D 13
6730 Tintigny 13 E 13
3700 Tongeren 5 D 13
7500 Tournai 4 D 11
4980 Trois-Ponts 13 D 13
4870 Trooz 5 D 13
2300 Turnhout 5 C 12
2431 Veerle 5 C 12
4800 Verviers 5 D 13
8630 Veurne 4 C 10
8570 Vichte 4 D 11
6690 Vielsalm 13 D 13
1800 Vilvoorde 5 D 12
6760 Virton 13 E 13
9185 Wachtebeke 5 C 11
4950 Waimes 14 D 14
5650 Walcourt 13 D 12
4520 Wanze 5 D 13
4300 Waremme 5 D 13
7784 Warneton 4 D 10
4219 Wasseiges 5 D 13
1410 Waterloo 5 D 12
1300 Wavre 5 D 12
2275 Wechelderzande 5 C 12
4650 Welkenraedt 5 D 13
6920 Wellin 13 D 13
1780 Wemmel 5 D 12
4190 Werbomont 13 D 13
8300 Westkapelle 4 C 11
8840 Westrozebeke 4 D 11
9230 Wetteren 4 D 11
2830 Willebroek 5 C 12
8750 Wingene 4 C 11
5530 Yvoir 13 D 12
2040 Zandvliet 5 C 12
8380 Zeebrugge 4 C 11
9240 Zele 5 C 12
9060 Zelzate 4 C 11
9620 Zottegem 4 D 11
9630 Zwalm 4 D 11
8750 Zwevezele 4 C 11

 CH

5000 Aarau 26 G 16
3270 Aarberg 26 G 16
3715 Adelboden 26 H 15
8134 Adliswil 26 G 16
4147 Aesch 26 G 15
6982 Agno 26 H 16
1860 Aigle 26 H 14
6780 Airolo 26 H 16
6055 Alpnach 26 H 16
6463 Altdorf 26 H 16
6474 Amsteg 26 H 16
6612 Ascona 26 H 16
1170 Aubonne 25 H 14
1580 Avenches 26 H 15
3961 Ayer 26 H 15
6340 Baar 26 G 16
5400 Baden 26 G 16
4710 Balsthal 26 G 15
4000 Basel 20 G 15
2854 Bassecourt 26 G 15
6781 Bedretto 26 H 16
3000 Bern 26 H 15
1880 Bex 26 H 15
4562 Biberist 26 G 15
2500 Biel 26 G 15
6676 Bignasco 26 H 16
3914 Blatten 26 H 15
2017 Boudry 26 H 14
1698 Boudoz 26 H 14
5076 Bözen 26 G 16
4226 Breitenbach 26 G 15
3853 Brienz 26 H 16
3900 Brig-Glis 26 H 15
5200 Brugg 26 G 16
6440 Brunnen 26 H 16
8180 Bülach 26 G 16
1630 Bulle 26 H 15
3294 Büren an der Aare 26 G 15
3400 Burgdorf 26 G 15
6330 Cham 26 G 16
1874 Champery 25 H 14
1637 Charmey 26 H 15
3965 Chippis 26 H 15
1618 Châtel-St-Denis 26 H 14
1296 Coppet 25 H 14
1304 Cossonay 25 H 14
1116 Cottens 25 H 14
2950 Courgenay 26 G 15
2738 Court 26 G 15
2923 Courtemaîche 20 G 15
2108 Couvet 25 H 14
1053 Cugy 25 H 14
2800 Delémont 26 G 15
5116 Denezy 25 H 14
8157 Dielsdorf 26 G 16
8953 Dietikon 26 G 16
6386 Dörfli 26 H 16
5312 Döttingen 20 G 16
3186 Düdingen 26 H 15
1040 Echallens 25 H 14
8307 Effretikon-Illnau 26 G 16
8193 Eglisau 20 G 16
8840 Einsiedeln 26 G 16
6390 Engelberg 26 H 16
6162 Entlebuch 26 H 16
6472 Erstfeld 26 H 16

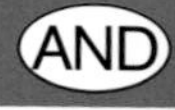

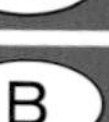

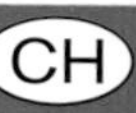

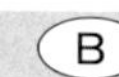

41 INDEX WITH POST CODES · ORTSREGISTER MIT POSTLEITZAHLEN · INDICE CON CODICI POSTAIS · STEDREGISTER MED POSTNUMRE · PLAATSNAMENREGISTER MET POSTCODE ·

CH
D

Escholzmatt (CH) · (D) Monsheim

6182 Escholzmatt 26 H 15
1470 Estavayer-le-Lac 26 H 14
6218 Ettiswil 26 G 16
5275 Etzgen 20 G 16
2916 Fahy 26 G 14
6760 Faido 26 H 16
3984 Fiesch 26 H 16
1948 Fionnay 26 H 15
2114 Fleurier 25 H 14
1700 Fribourg 26 H 15
5070 Frick 26 G 16
3714 Frutigen 26 H 15
3863 Gadmen 26 H 16
3945 Gampel 26 H 15
1200 Genève 25 H 14
6576 Gerra 26 H 16
1276 Gingins 25 H 14
6074 Giswil 26 H 16
3999 Gletsch 26 H 16
6410 Goldau 26 G 16
6596 Gordola 26 H 16
1422 Grandson 25 H 14
2540 Grenchen 26 G 15
3918 Grindelwald 26 H 16
3780 Gstaad 26 H 15
3785 Gsteig 26 H 15
3864 Guttannen 26 H 16
3927 Herbriggen 26 H 15
1987 Hérémence 26 H 15
6133 Hergiswil 26 H 16
3360 Herzogenbuchsee 26 G 15
6285 Hitzkirch 26 G 16
6280 Hochdorf 26 G 16
4434 Hölstein 26 G 15
8810 Horgen 26 G 16
6048 Horw 26 G 16
6493 Hospental 26 H 16
4950 Huttwil 26 G 15
3232 Ins 26 G 15
3800 Interlaken 26 H 15
6655 Intragna 26 H 16
3807 Iseltwald 26 H 15
3063 Ittigen 26 H 15
1656 Jaun 26 H 15
3303 Jegenstorf 26 G 15
3718 Kandersteg 26 H 15
3210 Kerzers 26 H 15
3422 Kirchberg 26 G 15
8302 Kloten 26 G 16
3098 Köniz 26 H 15
3510 Konolfingen 26 H 15
6010 Kriens 26 G 16
8700 Küssnacht 26 G 16
2406 La Brévine 25 H 14
2520 La Neuveville 26 G 15
1634 La Roche 26 H 15
1814 La Tour-de-Peilz 25 H 14
2300 La-Chaux-de-Fonds 26 G 14
1212 Lancy 25 H 14
4438 Langenbruck 26 G 15
4900 Langenthal 26 G 15
3550 Langnau im Emmental 26 H 15
4448 Läufelfingen 26 G 15
4242 Laufen 26 G 15
1000 Lausanne 25 H 14
6633 Lavertezzo 26 H 16
1348 Le Brassus 25 H 14
2400 Le Locle 25 G 14
1342 Le Pont 25 H 14
1347 Le Sentier 25 H 14
1863 Le Sépey 26 H 15
5426 Lengnau 26 G 16
3775 Lenk 26 H 15
5600 Lenzburg 26 G 16
1865 Les Diablerets 26 H 15
1984 Les Haudères 26 H 15
3953 Leuk 26 H 15
3954 Leukerbad 26 H 15
1912 Leytron 26 H 15
4410 Liestal 26 G 15
1357 Lignerolle 25 H 14
6600 Locarno 26 H 16
1522 Lucens 26 H 14
3432 Lützelflüh 26 G 15
6000 Luzern 26 G 16
3250 Lyss 26 G 15
6673 Maggia 26 H 16
9437 Marbach 26 H 15
1723 Marly 26 H 15
1524 Marnand 26 H 14
1920 Martigny 26 H 15
8706 Meilen 26 G 16
3860 Meiringen 26 H 16
5737 Menziken 26 G 16
8932 Mettmenstetten 26 G 16
1835 Montbovon 26 H 15
2875 Montfaucon 26 G 15
1870 Monthey 26 H 14
1820 Montreux 26 H 14
1110 Morges 25 H 14
1510 Moudon 25 H 14
2740 Moutier 26 G 15
4142 Münchenstein 20 G 15
3110 Münsingen 26 H 15
3985 Münster 26 H 16
4853 Murgenthal 26 G 15
5630 Muri/Adliswil 26 G 16
3074 Muri/Bern 26 H 15
3280 Murten 26 H 15
3904 Naters 26 H 15
2000 Neuchâtel 26 H 14
3176 Neuenegg 26 H 15
8212 Neuhausen am Rhein 20 G 16
2560 Nidau 26 G 15
3981 Niederwald 26 H 16
1260 Nyon 25 H 14
3618 Oberei 26 H 15
3854 Oberried 26 H 15
4104 Oberwil 20 G 15
4702 Oensingen 26 G 15
4665 Oftringen 26 G 15
4600 Olten 26 G 15
1350 Orbe 25 H 14
1937 Orsières 26 H 15
1530 Payerne 26 H 14
6695 Peccia 26 H 16
2034 Peseux 26 H 14
2542 Pieterlen 26 G 15
2900 Porrentruy 26 G 15
1987 Pralong 26 H 15
1009 Pully 25 H 14
8105 Regensdorf 26 G 16
3713 Reichenbach 26 H 15
6260 Reiden 26 G 15
3766 Reidenbach 26 H 15
4153 Reinach/Basel 20 G 15
4153 Reinach/Menziken 26 G 16
3132 Riggisberg 26 H 15
1180 Rolle 25 H 14
1680 Romont 26 H 14
6037 Root 26 G 16
4852 Rothrist 26 G 15
6017 Ruswil 26 G 16
3906 Saas-Fee 26 H 15
2350 Saignelégier 26 G 15
2072 Saint Blaise 26 G 14
2610 Saint Imier 26 G 15
1162 Saint Prex 25 H 14
1450 Sainte Croix 25 H 14
1585 Salavaux 26 H 15
6690 San Carlo 26 H 16
1738 Sangernboden 26 H 15
1890 Sankt Maurice 26 H 14
3772 Sankt Stephan 26 H 15
6060 Sarnen 26 H 16
6417 Sattel 26 G 16
1907 Saxon 26 H 15
8200 Schaffhausen 20 G 16
6467 Schattdorf 26 H 16
5040 Schöftland 26 G 16
6170 Schüpfheim 26 H 16
3150 Schwarzenburg 26 H 15
6430 Schwyz 26 G 16
7188 Sedrun 26 H 16
1933 Sembrancher 26 H 15
3960 Sierre 26 H 15
3655 Sigriswil 26 H 15
3907 Simplon 26 H 16
1950 Sion 26 H 15
4450 Sissach 26 G 15
4500 Solothurn 26 G 15
6674 Someo 26 H 16
6637 Sonogno 26 H 16
6174 Sörenberg 26 H 16
3700 Spiez 26 H 15
8712 Stäfa 26 G 16
3922 Stalden 26 H 15
6370 Stans 26 H 16
3612 Steffisburg 26 H 15
6067 Stöckalp 26 H 16
3454 Sumiswald 26 G 15
6210 Sursee 26 G 16
2710 Tavannes 26 G 15
3600 Thun 26 H 15
3946 Turtmann 26 H 15
8610 Uster 26 G 16
3427 Utzenstorf 26 G 15
1337 Vallorbe 25 H 14
1627 Vaulruz 26 H 14
1904 Vernayaz 26 H 15
1290 Versoix 25 H 14
1800 Vevey 25 H 14
1844 Villeneuve 26 H 14
3930 Visp 26 H 15
1896 Vouvry 25 H 14
1418 Vuarrens 25 H 14
8304 Wallisellen 26 G 16
6484 Wassen 26 H 16
6353 Weggis 26 G 16
3764 Weissenburg 26 H 15
5430 Wettingen 26 G 16
4537 Wiedlisbach 26 G 15
5103 Wildegg 26 G 16
6130 Willisau 26 G 16
5610 Wohlen 26 G 16
6110 Wolhusen 26 G 16
3076 Worb 26 H 15
3472 Wynigen 26 G 15
1400 Yverdon-les-Bains 25 H 14
3920 Zermatt 26 H 15
3052 Zollikofen 26 G 15
8702 Zollikon 26 G 16
6300 Zug 26 G 16
8000 Zürich 26 G 16
3770 Zweisimmen 26 H 15

D

52062 Aachen 6 D 14
77855 Achern 20 F 16
53518 Adenau 14 D 14
48683 Ahaus 2 B 14
59227 Ahlen 6 C 15
48324 Albersloh 6 C 15
52457 Aldenhoven 6 D 14
46519 Alpen 6 C 14
72275 Alpirsbach 20 F 16
52477 Alsdorf 6 D 14
48683 Alstätte 2 B 14
26817 Alt-Burlage 2 A 15
58762 Altena 6 C 15
48341 Altenberge 6 B 15
66885 Altenglan 14 E 15
57610 Altenkirchen(Westerwald) 6 D 15
55232 Alzey 14 E 16
56626 Andernach 14 D 15
76855 Annweiler am Trifels 14 E 15
77767 Appenweier 20 F 15
54687 Arzfeld 14 D 14
53567 Asbach 6 D 15
59387 Ascheberg 6 C 15
26871 Aschendorf 2 A 15
57439 Attendorn 6 C 15
26603 Aurich 2 A 15
54597 Auw bei Prüm 14 D 14
55422 Bacharach 14 D 15
79415 Bad Bellingen 20 G 15
48455 Bad Bentheim 2 B 15
76887 Bad Bergzabern 20 E 16
53498 Bad Breisig 14 D 15
67098 Bad Dürkheim 14 E 16
78073 Bad Dürrheim 20 F 16
56130 Bad Ems 14 D 15
53177 Bad Godesberg 6 D 15
76332 Bad Herrenalb 20 F 16
53604 Bad Honnef 6 D 15
53557 Bad Hönningen 14 D 15
55545 Bad Kreuznach 14 E 15
79189 Bad Krozingen 20 G 15
56470 Bad Marienberg 6 D 15
55583 Bad Münster-Ebernburg 14 E 15
53902 Bad Münstereifel 6 D 14
53474 Bad Neuenahr-Ahrweiler 14 D 15
77740 Bad Peterstal-Griesbach 20 F 16
77776 Bad Rippoldsau-Schapbach 20 F 16
79713 Bad Säckingen 20 G 16
65307 Bad Schwalbach 14 D 16
55566 Bad Sobernheim 14 E 15
54657 Badem 14 D 14
76530 Baden-Baden 20 F 16
79410 Badenweiler 20 G 15
26629 Bagband 2 A 15
72270 Baiersbronn 20 F 16
58802 Balve 6 C 15
55774 Baumholder 14 E 15
54538 Bausendorf 14 D 14
49844 Bawinkel 2 B 15
66701 Beckingen 14 E 14
50181 Bedburg 6 D 14
47551 Bedburg-Hau 6 C 14
56814 Beilstein 14 D 15
76756 Bellheim 14 E 16
56290 Beltheim 14 D 15
56170 Bendorf 14 D 15
49626 Berge/Bippen 2 B 15
50126 Bergheim 6 D 14
51465 Bergisch-Gladbach 6 D 15
59192 Bergkamen 6 C 15
51702 Bergneustadt 6 C 15
54470 Bernkastel-Kues 14 E 15
65614 Beselich 14 D 16
66450 Bexbach 14 E 15
48727 Billerbeck 6 C 15
54518 Binsfeld 14 E 14
49626 Bippen 2 B 15
55765 Birkenfeld 14 E 15
54634 Bitburg 14 E 14
53945 Blankenheim 14 D 14
54608 Bleialf 14 D 14
66440 Blieskastel 14 E 15
78176 Blumberg 20 G 16
46395 Bocholt 6 C 14
44787 Bochum 6 C 15
67278 Bockenheim an der Weinstraße 14 E 16
59073 Bockum-Hövel 6 C 15
54669 Bollendorf 14 E 14
59199 Bönen 6 C 15
53103 Bonn 6 D 15
79848 Bonndorf im Schwarzwald 20 G 16
56154 Boppard 14 D 15
46706 Borg 14 E 14
26903 Börgermoor 2 A 15
46325 Borken 6 C 14
26757 Borkum 2 A 14
53322 Bornheim 6 D 14
46236 Bottrop 6 C 14
79268 Bötzingen 20 F 15
49565 Bramsche 2 B 15
56338 Braubach 14 D 15
65611 Brechen 14 D 16
79206 Breisach am Rhein 20 F 15
28195 Bremen 6 C 15
56332 Brodenbach 14 D 15
66849 Bruchmühlbach-Miesau 14 E 15
55758 Bruchweiler 14 E 15
66904 Brücken 14 E 15
41379 Brüggen 6 C 14
50321 Brühl 6 D 14
56379 Buchholz 6 D 15
54610 Büdesheim 14 D 14
77815 Bühl 20 F 16
48249 Buldern 6 C 15
26831 Bunde 2 A 15
57299 Burbach 6 D 16
44575 Castrop-Rauxel 6 C 15
56812 Cochem 14 D 15
48653 Coesfeld 6 C 15
26817 Collinghorst 2 A 15
57567 Daaden 6 D 15
53949 Dahlem 14 D 14
66994 Dahn 14 E 15
54689 Daleiden 14 D 14
48720 Darfeld 6 B 15
45711 Datteln 6 C 15
54550 Daun 14 D 14
54570 Densborn 14 D 14
79211 Denzlingen 20 F 15
56269 Dierdorf 14 D 15
65582 Diez 14 D 16
66763 Dillingen 14 E 14
46499 Dingden 6 C 14
46535 Dinslaken 6 C 14
54552 Dockweiler 14 D 14
49770 Dohren/Haselünne 2 B 15
78166 Donaueschingen 20 G 16
41539 Dormagen 6 C 14
65599 Dornburg 14 D 16
72175 Dornhan 20 F 16
72280 Dornstetten 20 F 16
26553 Dornum 2 A 15
26553 Dornumersiel 2 A 15
26892 Dörpen 2 B 15
46282 Dorsten 6 C 14
44135 Dortmund 6 C 15
48317 Drensteinfurt 6 C 15
57489 Drolshagen 6 C 15
47051 Duisburg 6 C 14
41747 Dülken 6 C 14
48249 Dülmen 6 C 15
53520 Dümpelfeld 14 D 14
78655 Dunningen 20 F 16
52349 Düren 6 D 14
76448 Durmersheim 20 F 16
40213 Düsseldorf 6 C 14
67480 Edenkoben 14 E 16
67483 Edesheim 14 E 16
79588 Efringen-Kirchen 20 G 15
76344 Eggenstein-Leopoldshafen 20 E 16
67304 Eisenberg/Grünstadt 14 E 16
53783 Eitorf 6 D 15
67471 Elmstein 14 E 15
51089 Elsdorf 6 D 14
48432 Elte 2 B 15
46446 Elten 6 C 14
65343 Eltville am Rhein 14 D 16
65604 Elz 14 D 16
79215 Elzach 20 F 16
26721 Emden 2 A 15
49824 Emlichheim 2 B 14
56281 Emmelshausen 14 D 15
79312 Emmendingen 20 F 15
46446 Emmerich am Rhein 6 C 14
48488 Emsbüren 2 B 15
48282 Emsdetten 2 B 15
79346 Endingen am Kaiserstuhl 20 F 15
51766 Engelskirchen 6 D 15
67677 Enkenbach-Alsenborn 14 E 15
58256 Ennepetal 6 C 15
48594 Epe 2 B 15
66571 Eppelborn 14 E 14
66957 Eppenbrunn 20 E 15
50374 Erftstadt 6 D 14
41812 Erkelenz 6 C 14
46348 Erle 6 C 14
52249 Eschweiler 6 D 14
45127 Essen 6 C 15
77955 Ettenheim 20 F 15
76275 Ettlingen 20 F 16
53879 Euskirchen 6 D 14
48351 Everswinkel 6 C 15
57413 Finnentrop 6 C 15
67693 Fischbach 20 E 15
55237 Flonheim 14 E 16
78737 Fluorn-Winzeln 20 F 16
54343 Föhren 14 E 14
76596 Forbach 20 F 16
50226 Frechen 6 D 14
79098 Freiburg im Breisgau 20 F 15
66629 Freisen 14 E 15
49832 Freren 2 B 15
57610 Freudenberg/Siegen 6 D 15
72250 Freudenstadt 20 F 16
66299 Friedrichsthal 14 E 15
77948 Friesenheim 20 F 15
58730 Fröndenberg 6 C 15
49584 Fürstenau 2 B 15
78120 Furtwangen im Schwarzwald 20 F 16
76571 Gaggenau 20 F 16
52538 Gangelt 6 D 13
49744 Geeste 2 B 15
52511 Geilenkirchen 6 D 14
65366 Geisenheim 14 E 15
78187 Geisingen 20 G 16
47608 Geldern 6 C 14
45879 Gelsenkirchen 6 C 15
55490 Gemünden/Rhaunen 14 E 15
77723 Gengenbach 20 F 16
55457 Gensingen 14 E 15
49828 Georgsdorf 2 B 15
76726 Germersheim 14 E 16
76593 Gernsbach 20 F 16
54568 Gerolstein 14 D 14
66453 Gersheim 14 E 15
48712 Gescher 6 C 15
58285 Gevelsberg 6 C 15
54558 Gillenfeld 14 D 14
45964 Gladbeck 6 C 15
47574 Goch 6 C 14
26736 Greetsiel 2 A 15
47929 Grefrath 6 C 14
48268 Greven 2 B 15
41515 Grevenbroich 6 C 14
77740 Griesbach-Bad Peterstal 20 F 16
47546 Grieth 6 C 14
48599 Gronau 2 B 15
48734 Groß-Reken 6 C 15
26532 Großheide 2 A 15
54534 Großlittgen 14 D 14
66352 Großrosseln 14 E 14
67269 Grünstadt 14 E 16
55452 Guldental 14 E 15
51643 Gummersbach 6 C 15
77793 Gutach 20 F 16
42781 Haan 6 C 15
57627 Hachenburg 6 D 15
65589 Hadamar 14 D 16
26524 Hage 2 A 15
59846 Hagen/Iserlohn 6 C 15
76767 Hagenbach 20 E 16
54611 Hallschlag 14 D 14
45721 Haltern am See 6 C 15
58553 Halver 6 C 15
59065 Hamm 6 C 15
57577 Hamm (Sieg) 6 D 15
46499 Hamminkeln 6 C 14
49733 Haren (Ems) 2 B 15
79258 Hartheim 20 G 15
49740 Haselünne 2 B 15
77716 Haslach im Kinzigtal 20 F 16
67454 Haßloch 14 E 16
45525 Hattingen 6 C 15
77756 Hausach 20 F 16
48329 Havixbeck 6 C 15
26892 Heede 2 B 15
48619 Heek 2 B 15
59073 Heessen 6 C 15
46359 Heiden 6 C 14
42579 Heiligenhaus 6 C 14
52396 Heimbach 6 D 14
52525 Heinsberg 6 C 14
79423 Heitersheim 20 G 15
53940 Hellenthal 14 D 14
58675 Hemer 6 C 15
53773 Hennef 6 D 15
35745 Herborn 14 E 15
57562 Herdorf 6 D 15
54411 Hermeskeil 14 E 14
44623 Herne 6 C 15
56249 Herschbach 14 D 15
58849 Herscheid 6 C 15
45699 Herten 6 C 15
49770 Herzlake 2 B 15
26835 Hesel 2 A 15
66265 Heusweiler 14 E 14
40721 Hilden 6 C 14
54576 Hillesheim 14 D 14
48163 Hiltrup 6 C 15
26759 Hinte 2 A 15
56729 Hirten 14 D 15
67691 Hochspeyer 14 E 15
76879 Hochstadt 14 E 16
57629 Höchstenbach 6 D 15
56462 Höhn 14 D 15
53940 Hollerath 14 D 14
26835 Holtland 2 A 15
48720 Holtwick 6 B 15
56357 Holzhausen an der Haide 14 D 15
66424 Homburg 14 E 15
49846 Hoogstede 2 B 14
48496 Hopsten 2 B 15
66500 Hornbach 14 E 15
78132 Hornberg 20 F 16
48477 Hörstel 2 B 15
48612 Horstmar 2 B 15
41836 Hückelhoven 6 C 14
42499 Hückeswagen 6 C 15
78183 Hüfingen 20 G 16
46569 Hünxe 6 C 14
50354 Hürth 6 D 14
59755 Hüsten 6 C 15
49751 Hüven 2 B 15
49477 Ibbenbüren 2 B 15
55743 Idar-Oberstein 14 E 15
66557 Illingen 14 E 15
55218 Ingelheim am Rhein 14 E 16
54666 Irrel 14 E 14
58636 Iserlohn 6 C 15
47661 Issum 6 C 14
26844 Jemgum 2 A 15
79798 Jestetten 20 G 16
52428 Jülich 6 D 14
41564 Kaarst 6 C 14
56759 Kaisersesch 14 D 15
67657 Kaiserslautern 14 E 15
47546 Kalkar 6 C 14
53925 Kall 6 D 14
59174 Kamen 6 C 15
47475 Kamp-Lintfort 6 C 14
76870 Kandel 20 E 16
79400 Kandern 20 G 15
55483 Kappel 14 E 15
76133 Karlsruhe 20 E 16
56288 Kastellaun 14 D 15
56368 Katzenelnbogen 14 D 15
56349 Kaub 14 D 15
77694 Kehl 20 F 15
53539 Kelberg 14 D 14
54427 Kell am See 14 E 14
47906 Kempen 6 C 14
56746 Kempenich 14 D 15
54344 Kenn 14 E 14
79341 Kenzingen 20 F 15
47647 Kerken 6 C 14
50171 Kerpen 6 D 14
47623 Kevelaer 6 C 14
55481 Kirchberg/Simmern 14 E 15
67292 Kirchheim-Bolanden 14 E 16
55606 Kirn 14 E 15
48531 Klausheide 2 B 15
49777 Klein Berßen 2 B 15
66271 Kleinblittersdorf 14 E 15
47533 Kleve 6 C 14
26892 Kluse 2 B 15
56068 Koblenz 14 D 15
50667 Köln 6 D 14
53639 Königswinter 6 D 15
54329 Konz 14 E 14
41352 Korschenbroich 6 C 14
56736 Kottenheim 14 D 15
47559 Kranenburg 6 C 14
47796 Krefeld 6 C 14
52372 Kreuzau 6 D 14
57223 Kreuztal 6 C 15
54536 Kröv 14 E 15
76456 Kuppenheim 20 F 16
51515 Kürten 6 C 15
66869 Kusel 14 E 15
79790 Küssaberg 20 G 16
54655 Kyllburg 14 D 14
49549 Ladbergen 2 B 15
48366 Laer 6 B 15
49479 Laggenbeck 2 B 15
49774 Lähden 2 B 15
56112 Lahnstein 14 D 15
77933 Lahr 20 F 15
76829 Landau in der Pfalz 14 E 16
66849 Landstuhl 14 E 15
40764 Langenfeld 6 C 14
52379 Langerwehe 6 D 14
49762 Lathen 2 B 15
67742 Lauterecken 14 E 15
66822 Lebach 14 E 14
26789 Leer(Ostfriesland) 2 A 15
48739 Legden 6 B 15
46286 Lembeck 6 C 14
66969 Lemberg 14 E 15
49838 Lengerich 2 B 15
57368 Lennestadt 6 C 16
79853 Lenzkirch 20 G 16
76344 Leopoldshafen-Eggenstein 20 E 16
51373 Leverkusen 6 C 14
54619 Lichtenborn 14 D 14
65594 Limburg an der Lahn 14 D 16
51789 Lindlar 6 C 15
49808 Lingen (Ems) 2 B 15
52441 Linnich 6 D 14
53545 Linz am Rhein 14 D 15
56767 Lirstal 14 D 15
79843 Löffingen 20 G 16
53797 Lohmar 6 D 15
56391 Lorch/Bacharach 14 D 15
79539 Lörrach 20 G 15
26901 Lorup 2 B 15
66679 Losheim am See 14 E 14
72290 Loßburg 20 F 16
58507 Lüdenscheid 6 C 15
59348 Lüdinghausen 6 C 15
44532 Lünen 6 C 15
48480 Lünne 2 B 15
54617 Lützkampen 14 D 14
55116 Mainz 14 E 16
76316 Malsch 20 F 16
79364 Malterdingen 20 F 15
54531 Manderscheid 14 D 14
51709 Marienheide 6 C 15
45768 Marl 6 C 15
66646 Marpingen 14 E 15
76359 Marxzell 20 F 16
56727 Mayen 14 D 15
53894 Mechernich 6 D 14
53340 Meckenheim 6 D 15
40667 Meerbusch 6 C 14
58540 Meinerzhagen 6 C 15
54570 Meisburg 14 D 14
55590 Meisenheim 14 E 15
58706 Menden 6 C 15
56743 Mendig 14 D 15
35794 Mengerskirchen 14 D 16
48249 Merfeld 6 C 15
66663 Merzig 14 E 14
49832 Messingen 2 B 15
48432 Mesum 2 B 15
48629 Metelen 2 B 15
54675 Mettendorf 14 E 14
49497 Mettingen 2 B 15
66693 Mettlach 14 E 14
56357 Miehlen 14 D 15
47441 Moers 6 C 14
41061 Mönchen Gladbach 6 C 14
56729 Monreal 14 D 15
52156 Monschau 6 D 14
67590 Monsheim 14 E 16

56410 Montabaur 14 D 15
26624 Moordorf 2 A 15
54497 Morbach 14 E 15
51597 Morsbach 6 D 15
53804 Much 6 D 15
57555 Mudersbach 6 D 15
45438 Mülheim an der Ruhr 6 C 14
56218 Mülheim-Kärlich 14 D 15
79379 Müllheim 20 G 15
66981 Münchweiler an der Rodalb 14 E 15
48143 Münster 6 C 15
56294 Münstermaifeld 14 D 15
54570 Mürlenbach 14 D 14
53533 Müsch 14 D 14
56377 Nassau 14 D 15
56355 Nastätten 14 D 15
59755 Neheim 6 C 15
56820 Nehren 14 D 15
57250 Netphen 6 D 16
41334 Nettetal 6 C 14
79395 Neuenburg am Rhein 20 G 15
41517 Neuenhaus 2 B 14
48485 Neuenkirchen/Rheine 2 B 15
58809 Neuenrade 6 C 15
54673 Neuerburg 14 D 14
56335 Neuhäusel 14 D 15
47506 Neukirchen-Vluyn 6 C 14
54347 Neumagen-Dhron 14 E 14
66538 Neunkirchen/Saarbrücken 14 E 15
53819 Neunkirchen/Siegburg 6 D 15
97290 Neunkirchen/Siegen 6 D 16
77743 Neuried 20 F 15
41460 Neuss 6 C 14
67433 Neustadt an der Weinstraße 14 E 16
53577 Neustadt (Wied) 6 D 15
56564 Neuwied 14 D 15
54309 Newel 14 E 14
52385 Nideggen 6 D 14
55268 Nieder-Olm 14 E 16
78078 Niedereschach 20 F 16
55767 Niederhambach 14 E 15
41372 Niederkrüchten 6 C 14
52382 Niederzier 6 D 14
56651 Niederzissen 14 D 15
54453 Nittel 14 E 14
66625 Nohfelden 14 E 15
66620 Nonnweiler 14 E 14
26506 Norddeich 2 A 15
26506 Norden 2 A 15
26548 Norderney 2 A 15
48527 Nordhorn 2 B 15
48356 Nordwalde 2 B 15
52388 Nörvenich 6 D 14
48301 Nottuln 6 C 15
51588 Nümbrecht 6 D 15
46045 Oberhausen 6 C 14
77704 Oberkirch 20 F 16
66629 Oberkirchen 14 E 15
67823 Obermoschel 14 E 15
66649 Oberthal 14 E 15
54636 Oberweiler 14 D 14
55430 Oberwesel 14 D 15
48607 Ochtrup 2 B 15
46354 Oeding 6 C 14
65375 Oestrich-Winkel 14 D 16
77652 Offenburg 20 F 15
26802 Oldersum 2 A 15
59399 Olfen 6 C 15
57462 Olpe 6 C 15
54597 Olzheim 14 D 14
77728 Oppenau 20 F 16
48346 Ostbevern 6 B 15
26529 Osteel 2 A 15
48720 Osterwick 6 B 15
67574 Osthofen 14 E 16
26757 Ostland 2 A 14
26842 Ostrhauderfehn 2 A 15
67697 Otterberg 14 E 15
77833 Ottersweier 20 F 16
66564 Ottweiler 14 E 15
51491 Overath 6 D 15
54439 Palzem 14 E 14
26871 Papenburg 2 A 15
54570 Pelm 14 D 14
26736 Pewsum 2 A 15
54498 Piesport 14 E 14
66953 Pirmasens 14 E 15
58840 Plettenberg 6 C 15
56751 Polch 14 D 15
66620 Primstal 14 E 14
54595 Prüm 14 D 14
56305 Puderbach 6 D 15
50259 Pulheim 6 C 14
66346 Püttlingen 14 E 14
66851 Queidersbach 14 E 15
42477 Radevormwald 6 C 15
46348 Raesfeld 6 C 14
49811 Ramsel 2 B 15
66892 Ramstein 14 E 15
56235 Ransbach-Baumbach 14 D 15
76437 Rastatt 20 F 16
40878 Ratingen 6 C 14
49509 Recke 2 B 15
45657 Recklinghausen 6 C 15
46459 Rees 6 C 14
66780 Rehlingen-Siersburg 14 E 14
53424 Remagen 6 D 15
42853 Remscheid 6 C 15
77871 Renchen 20 F 16
56579 Rengsdorf 14 D 15
56477 Rennerod 14 D 16
55624 Rhaunen 14 E 15
46414 Rhede 6 C 14
26899 Rhede(Ems) 2 A 15
77866 Rheinau 20 F 15
53359 Rheinbach 6 D 14
47495 Rheinberg 6 C 14
55494 Rheinböllen 14 D 15
48431 Rheine 2 B 15
79618 Rheinfelden 20 G 15
79365 Rheinhausen 20 F 15
77836 Rheinmünster 20 F 16
76287 Rheinstetten 20 F 16
58566 Rhens 14 D 15
67806 Rockenhausen 14 E 15
66976 Rodalben 14 E 15
52159 Roetgen 6 D 14
41569 Rommerskirchen 6 C 14
51503 Rösrath 6 D 15
48161 Roxel 6 C 15
55595 Roxheim 14 E 15
65385 Rüdesheim am Rhein 14 E 15
65594 Runkel 14 D 16
77977 Rust 20 F 15
49733 Rütenbrock 2 B 15
26736 Rysum 2 A 15
66111 Saarbrücken 14 E 14
54439 Saarburg 14 E 14
66740 Saarlouis 14 E 14
48369 Saerbeck 2 B 15
48499 Salzbergen 2 B 15
53757 Sankt Augustin 6 D 15
79837 Sankt Blasien 20 G 16
78112 Sankt Georgen im Schwarzwald 20 F 16
56346 Sankt Goarshausen 14 D 15
66386 Sankt Ingbert 14 E 15
79271 Sankt Peter 20 F 16
66606 Sankt Wendel 14 E 15
48496 Schale 2 B 15
79227 Schallstadt 20 G 15
48480 Schapen 2 B 15
46514 Schermbeck 6 C 14
67105 Schifferstadt 14 E 16
77761 Schiltach 20 F 16
26605 Schirum 2 A 15
65388 Schlangenbad 14 D 16
53937 Schleiden 6 D 14
79859 Schluchsee 20 G 16
66839 Schmelz 14 E 14
79677 Schönau im Schwarzwald 20 G 15
54316 Schöndorf 14 E 14
54614 Schönecken 14 D 14
76650 Schopfheim 20 G 15
78713 Schramberg 20 F 16
48465 Schüttorf 2 B 15
77963 Schwanau 20 F 15
67365 Schwegenheim 14 E 16
54338 Schweich 14 E 14
58332 Schwelm 6 C 15
58239 Schwerte 6 C 15
79739 Schwörstadt 20 G 15
53819 Seelscheid 6 D 15
59379 Selm 6 C 15
56242 Selters 14 D 15
48308 Senden 6 C 15
48324 Sendenhorst 6 C 15
54455 Serrig 14 E 14
53721 Siegburg 6 D 15
57072 Siegen 6 D 16
52152 Simmerath 6 D 14
55469 Simmern 14 E 15
72226 Simmersfeld 20 F 16
55618 Simmertal 14 E 15
54675 Sinspelt 14 E 14
76547 Sinzheim 20 F 16
53489 Sinzig 14 D 15
49751 Sögel 2 B 15
55487 Sohren 14 E 15
42659 Solingen 6 C 15
47665 Sonsbeck 6 C 14
54662 Speicher 14 E 14
48480 Spelle 2 B 15
48157 Sprakel 6 B 15
45549 Sprockhövel 6 C 15
54589 Stadtkyll 14 D 14
48703 Stadtlohn 6 C 14
54597 Steffeln 14 D 14
48565 Steinfurt 2 B 15
52222 Stolberg 6 D 14
47638 Straelen 6 C 14
55442 Stromberg 14 E 15
54552 Strotzbüsch 14 D 14
79780 Stühlingen 20 G 16
59846 Sundern 6 C 16
26903 Surwold 2 B 15
45721 Sythen 6 C 15
65232 Taunusstein 14 D 16
49545 Tecklenburg 2 B 15
5931 Tegelen 6 C 14
48291 Telgte 6 C 15
66636 Tholey 14 E 15
55743 Tiefenstein 14 E 15
26629 Timmel 2 A 15
79822 Titisee-Neustadt 20 G 16
79822 Titisee-Neustadt 20 G 16
52445 Titz 6 C 14
79682 Todtmoos 20 G 16
79674 Todtnau 20 G 15
53947 Tondorf 14 D 14
47918 Tönisvorst 6 C 14
56841 Traben-Trarbach 14 E 15
56253 Treis-Karden 14 D 15
54290 Trier 14 E 14
54311 Trierweiler 14 E 14
67705 Trippstadt 14 E 15
54349 Trittenheim 14 E 14
49767 Twist 2 B 15
47624 Twisteden 6 C 14
52531 Übach-Palenberg 6 D 14
66802 Überherrn 14 E 14
53773 Uckerath 6 D 15
47589 Uedem 6 C 14
49843 Uelsen 2 B 14
79777 Ühlingen-Birkendorf 20 G 16
56766 Ulmen 14 D 15
59423 Unna 6 C 15
26529 Upgant-Schott 2 A 15
42549 Velbert 6 C 15
46342 Velen 6 C 14
52391 Vettweiß 6 D 14
41747 Viersen 6 C 14
78048 Villingen-Schwenningen 20 F 16
52396 Vlatten 6 D 14
46562 Voerde 6 C 14
79235 Vogtsburg 20 F 15
66333 Völklingen 14 E 14
48691 Vreden 2 B 14
47669 Wachtendonk 6 C 14
66687 Wadern 14 E 14
55596 Waldböckelheim 14 E 15
51545 Waldbröl 6 D 15
67714 Waldfischbach-Burgalben 14 E 15
79183 Waldkirch 20 F 15
90993 Waldshut-Tiengen 20 G 16
90993 Waldshut-Tiengen 20 G 16
66798 Wallerfangen 14 E 14
56414 Wallmerod 14 D 15
45731 Waltrop 6 C 15
26802 Warsingsfehn 2 A 15
41849 Wassenberg 6 C 14
54649 Waxweiler 14 D 14
26826 Weener 2 A 15
47652 Weeze 6 C 14
41844 Wegberg 6 C 14
79664 Wehr 20 G 15
67475 Weidenthal 14 E 15
79576 Weil am Rhein 20 G 15
53919 Weilerswist 6 D 14
59514 Welver 6 C 15
57482 Wenden 6 D 15
58791 Werdohl 6 C 15
59457 Werl 6 C 15
42929 Wermelskirchen 6 C 15
59368 Werne 6 C 15
49757 Werlte 2 B 15
46483 Wesel 6 C 14
50389 Wesseling 6 D 14
56457 Westerburg 14 D 15
26632 Westerende-Kirchloog 2 A 15
26556 Westerholt 2 A 15
67593 Westhofen 14 E 16
48493 Wettringen 2 B 15
58739 Wickede(Ruhr) 6 C 15
51674 Wiehl 6 D 15
65183 Wiesbaden 14 D 16
54578 Wiesbaum 14 D 14
49835 Wietmarschen 2 B 15
57234 Wilnsdorf 6 D 16
49849 Wilsum 2 B 14
54459 Wiltingen 14 E 14
51570 Windeck 6 D 15
67722 Winnweiler 14 E 15
51688 Wipperfürth 6 C 15
26529 Wirdum 2 A 15
56422 Wirges 14 D 15
58452 Witten 6 C 15
54516 Wittlich 14 E 14
77709 Wolfach 20 F 16
67752 Wolfstein 14 E 15
55286 Wörrstadt 14 E 16
76744 Wörth am Rhein 20 E 16
46286 Wulfen 6 C 15
42489 Wülfrath 6 C 15
42275 Wuppertal 6 C 15
52146 Würselen 6 D 14
46509 Xanten 6 C 14
77736 Zell am Harmersbach 20 F 16
79669 Zell im Wiesental 20 G 15
56856 Zell (Mosel) 14 D 15
54492 Zeltingen-Rachtig 14 E 14
54313 Zemmer 14 E 14
54314 Zerf 14 E 14
53909 Zülpich 6 D 14
66482 Zweibrücken 14 E 15
52224 Zweifall 6 D 14

(E)

31178 Abárzuza 33 M 5
22392 Abizanda 34 M 8
31523 Ablitas 33 N 6
31282 Acedo 33 M 5
22612 Acumuer 33 M 7
22147 Adahuesca 34 M 8
31448 Adoain 33 M 6
25797 Adrall 34 M 9
25691 Àger 34 M 8
25310 Agramunt 34 N 9
42100 Ágreda 33 N 6
22141 Aguas 34 M 7
17707 Agullana 35 M 10
31460 Aibar 33 M 6
22330 Ainsa 34 M 8
22860 Aisa 33 M 7
31172 Aizpún 33 M 6
50630 Alagón 33 N 6
22534 Albalate de Cinca 34 N 8
17733 Albanyà 35 M 10
17136 Albons 35 M 11
22410 Alcolea de Cinca 34 N 8
25660 Alcoletge 34 N 8
22251 Alcubierre 33 N 7
01117 Alda 33 M 5
26559 Aldeanueva de Ebro 33 M 6
50679 Alera 33 M 6
26540 Alfaro 33 M 6
25120 Alfarràs 34 N 8
25125 Alguaire 34 N 8
25574 Alins 34 M 9
25100 Almacelles 34 N 8
25126 Almenar 34 N 8
22270 Almudévar 33 M 7
08587 Alpens 35 M 10
25632 Alsamora 34 M 8
25289 Altés 34 M 9
22540 Altorricón 34 N 8
31800 Altsasu-Alsasua 33 M 5
31262 Allo 33 M 5
17170 Amer 35 M 10
20140 Andoain 27 L 5
17160 Anglès 35 N 10
22123 Angüés 34 M 7
22728 Ansó 33 M 7
50590 Añón 33 N 6
31430 Aoiz-Agoitz 33 M 6
25799 Aós 35 M 9
25762 Aranser 35 M 9
20567 Arantzazu 27 M 5
25573 Araós 34 M 9
22121 Arbaniés 34 M 7
31839 Arbizu 33 M 5
25287 Ardèvol 34 N 9
50614 Ardisa 33 M 7
22583 Arén 34 M 8
25575 Àreu 34 M 9
31513 Arguedas 33 M 6
26580 Arnedo 33 M 5
31417 Arrako 33 M 7
25799 Ars 35 M 9
31140 Artajona 33 M 6
25730 Artesa de Segre 34 N 9
31480 Artrieda 33 M 7
31694 Aurizberri-Espinal 33 M 6
26513 Ausejo 33 M 5
26560 Autol 33 M 5
31797 Auza 33 M 6
22800 Ayerbe 33 M 7
31560 Azagra 33 M 6
22421 Azanúy 34 N 8
20720 Azkoitia 27 L 5
20730 Azpeitia 27 L 5
50685 Bagüés 33 M 7
22760 Baílo 33 M 7
25600 Balaguer 34 N 8
22571 Baldellou 34 N 8
22234 Ballobar 34 N 8
17820 Banyoles 35 M 10
22650 Baños de Panticosa 34 M 7
31396 Barañain 33 M 6
31395 Barásoain 33 M 6
22300 Barbastro 34 M 8
22148 Barcabo 34 M 8
17483 Bàscara 35 M 10
22141 Bastaras 34 M 7
25549 Bausen 34 M 8
20200 Beasain 27 L 5
17867 Beget 35 M 10
31393 Beire 33 M 6
25337 Bellcaire d'Urgell 34 N 8
22580 Benabarre 34 M 8
22440 Benasque 34 M 8
25658 Benavent 34 M 9
22150 Bentué de Rasal 33 M 7
20492 Berastegi 27 L 6
22131 Berbegal 34 N 7
08600 Berga 35 M 9
20570 Bergara 27 L 5
22711 Bernués 33 M 7
31013 Berriozar 33 M 6
31790 Berrizaun 27 L 6
31796 Berroeta 27 L 6
22373 Berroy 34 M 7
17850 Besalú 35 M 10
17162 Bescanó 35 N 10
22362 Bestué 34 M 8
31890 Betelu 27 L 6
17850 Beuda 35 M 10
50619 Biel 33 M 7
22350 Bielsa 34 M 8
22630 Biescas 34 M 7
50316 Bijuesca 33 N 6
22510 Binaced 34 N 8
22500 Binéfar 34 N 8
25752 Biosca 34 N 9
50695 Biota 33 M 6
25652 Boixols 34 M 9
22160 Bolea 33 M 7
22340 Boltaña 34 M 8
22487 Bono 34 M 8
22860 Borau 33 M 7
17462 Bordils 35 M 10
50540 Borja 33 N 6
42138 Borobia 33 N 6
08619 Borredà 35 M 9
25550 Bòssost 34 M 8
50441 Botorrita 33 N 6
22370 Broto 34 M 7
22665 Búbal 34 M 7
31540 Buñuel 33 N 6
31412 Burgui 33 M 6
25515 Cabdella 34 M 8
25794 Cabó 34 M 9
17488 Cadaqués 36 M 11
26500 Calahorra 33 M 6
50300 Calatayud 33 N 6
50280 Calatorao 33 N 6
50268 Calcena 33 N 6
25528 Caldes de Boí 34 M 8
25613 Camarasa 34 N 8
17723 Campmany 35 M 10
22450 Campo 34 M 8
22395 Camporrotuno 34 M 8
17867 Camprodon 35 M 10
22889 Candanchú 33 M 7
25794 Canelles 34 M 9
31380 Caparroso 33 M 6
31579 Cárcar 33 M 6
31310 Carcastillo 33 M 6
08261 Cardona 35 N 9
25594 Caregue 34 M 9
50400 Cariñena 33 N 6
31520 Cascante 33 M 6
31490 Cáseda 33 M 6
08693 Casserres 35 M 9
25714 Cassovall 34 M 9
22222 Castejón de Monegros 33 N 7
22466 Castejón de Sos 34 M 8
50612 Castejón de Valdejasa 33 N 7
22310 Castejón del Puente 34 N 8
22215 Castelflorite 34 N 7
08671 Castelladral 35 N 9
08619 Castellar del Riu 35 M 9
17486 Castelló d'Empúries 35 M 11
50696 Castiliscar 33 M 6
25631 Cellers 34 M 8
26520 Cervera del Río Alhama 33 M 6
31592 Cintruénigo 33 M 6
17144 Colomers 35 M 10
25793 Coll de Nargó 34 M 9
25212 Concabella 34 N 9
22808 Concilio 33 M 7
22414 Conchel 34 N 8
31591 Corella 33 M 6
31530 Cortes 33 N 6
22141 Coscullano 33 M 7
50410 Cuarte de Huerva 33 N 7
25737 Cubells 34 N 8
42107 Cueva de Ágreda 33 N 6
20820 Deba 27 L 5
20070 Donostia-San Sebastián 27 L 6
01260 Egino 33 M 5
20600 Eibar 27 L 5
50600 Ejea de los Caballeros 33 M 6
50694 El Bayo 33 M 6
50730 El Burgo de Ebro 33 N 7
50610 El Frago 33 M 7
50320 El Frasno 33 N 6
25723 El Pont de Bar 35 M 9
25520 El Pont de Suert 34 M 8
50617 El Sabinar/Ejea de los Caballeros 33 M 6
22215 El Tormillo 34 N 7
20870 Elgoibar 27 L 5
31700 Elizondo 27 L 6
25795 Els Castells 34 M 9
17177 Els Hostalets d'en Bas 35 M 10
22740 Embún 33 M 7
31153 Enériz 33 M 6
50290 Épila 33 N 6
20211 Ergoiena 27 M 5
31867 Erice 33 M 6
31867 Erice 33 M 6
25516 Erinyà 34 M 8
50611 Erla 33 M 7
31714 Erratzu 27 L 6
25596 Escaló 34 M 9
22363 Escalona 34 M 8
22760 Escarrilla 34 M 7
31494 Eslava 33 M 6
31119 Esperun 33 M 6
17753 Espolla 35 M 11
17832 Esponellà 35 M 10
22810 Esquedas 33 M 7
25597 Estaís 34 M 9
25725 Estana 35 M 9
31200 Estella-Lizarra 33 M 5
25580 Esterri d'Àneu 34 M 9
31174 Etxauri 33 M 6
31749 Ezkurra 27 L 6
31370 Falces 33 M 6
50619 Farasdues 33 M 6
50163 Farlete 33 N 7
25794 Fígols 35 M 9
17600 Figueres 35 M 10
31593 Fitero 33 M 6
31512 Fontellas 33 M 6
25615 Fontllonga 34 N 8
22422 Fonz 34 M 8
22415 Fornillos 34 N 8
50529 Fuendejalón 33 N 6
50740 Fuentes de Ebro 33 N 7
50650 Gallur 33 N 6
17780 Garriguella 35 M 11
25793 Gavarra 34 M 9
17539 Ger 35 M 9
25614 Gerb 34 N 8
17070 Girona/Gerona 35 N 10
08680 Gironella 35 M 9
31754 Goizueta 27 L 6
17531 Gombreny 35 M 10
08697 Gósol 35 M 9
22430 Graus 34 M 8
26587 Grávalos 33 M 6
08694 Guardiola de Berguedà 35 M 9
31452 Güesa 33 M 6
25210 Guissona 34 N 9
22280 Gurrea de Gállego 33 M 7
22720 Hecho 33 M 7
20120 Hernani 27 L 6
20280 Hondarribia 27 L 6
22210 Huerto 34 N 7
22070 Huesca 33 M 7
31473 Idocin 33 M 6
26525 Igea 33 M 5
50250 Illueca 33 N 6
22621 Ipiés 33 M 7
31680 Irati 33 M 6
20300 Irun 27 L 6
31860 Irurzun 33 M 6
31417 Isaba 33 M 7
25650 Isona 34 M 9
31689 Izalzu 33 M 6
22700 Jaca 33 M 7
31866 Jauntsarats 33 M 6
22624 Javierrelatre 33 M 7
08614 l'Espunyola 35 M 9
08148 l' Estany 35 N 10
17130 L'Escala 35 M 11
17258 L'Estartit 36 M 11
50100 La Almunia de Doña Godina 33 N 6
17700 La Jonquera 35 M 10
17537 La Molina 35 M 9
50196 La Muela 33 N 6
08696 La Pobla de Lillet 35 M 9
25500 La Pobla de Segur 34 M 8
25513 La Pobleta de Bellveí 34 M 8
22482 La Puebla de Roda 34 M 8
25798 la Seu d'Urgell 35 M 9
22364 Lafortunada 34 M 8
22587 Laguarres 34 M 8
22623 Laguarta 34 M 7
22393 Lamata 34 M 8
22250 Lanaja 33 N 7
22621 Lanave 33 M 7
31251 Larraga 33 M 6
31270 Larraona 33 M 5
22761 Larúes 33 M 7
22149 Las Bellostas 34 M 7
50612 Las Pedrosas 33 M 7
22124 Lascellas 34 M 7
22471 Laspaúles 34 M 8
22349 Latorrecilla 34 M 8
31588 Lazagurría 33 M 5
20210 Lazkao 27 L 5
50160 Leciñena 33 N 7
20230 Legazpi 27 L 5
20250 Legorreta 27 L 5
48280 Lekeitio 27 L 5
31395 Leoz 33 M 6
31494 Lerga 33 M 6
31260 Lerín 33 M 6
25612 Les Avellanes 34 N 8
17172 les Planes d'Hostoles 35 M 10
31770 Lesaka 27 L 6
31487 Liédena 33 M 6
25240 Linyola 34 N 8
31829 Lizarraga 33 M 5
20490 Lizartza 27 L 5
31580 Lodosa 33 M 5
31481 Lónguida 33 M 6
31210 Los Arcos 33 M 5
31440 Lumbier 33 M 6
50295 Lumpiaque 33 N 6
50610 Luna 33 M 7
31243 Luquin 33 M 5
25283 Lladurs 35 M 9
17490 Llançà 36 M 11
25595 Llavorsí 34 M 9
17730 Llers 35 M 10
17527 Llívia 35 M 9
25281 Llobera 34 N 9
25794 Llobera 34 M 9
08514 Lluça 35 M 10
22771 Majones 33 M 7
50315 Malanquilla 33 N 6
50549 Maleján 33 N 6
50340 Maluenda 33 N 6
08560 Manlleu 35 M 10
50430 María de Huerva 33 N 7
48270 Markina-Xemein 27 L 5
25724 Martinet 35 M 9
17515 Matamala 35 M 10
50135 Mediana de Aragón 33 N 7
20850 Mendaro 27 L 5
31587 Mendavia 33 M 5
31150 Mendigorría 33 M 6
17539 Meranges 35 M 9
17830 Mieres 35 M 10
31320 Milagro 33 M 6
31253 Miranda de Arga 33 M 6
17868 Molló 35 M 10
50164 Monegrillo 33 N 7
22111 Monflorite 33 M 7
22584 Montañana 34 M 8
25738 Montargull 34 N 9

22351 Monte Perdido 34 M 8
08585 Montesquiu 35 M 10
22269 Montesusín 33 N 7
25616 Montgai 34 N 8
22400 Monzón 34 N 8
50240 Morés 33 N 6
22336 Morillo de Monclús 34 M 8
50450 Muel 33 N 6
31176 Muez 33 M 6
31172 Munárriz 33 M 6
31280 Murieta 33 M 5
31438 Nagore 33 M 6
22320 Naval 34 M 8
08670 Navàs 35 N 9
31450 Navascués 33 M 6
17744 Navata 35 M 10
25286 Navès 35 N 9
31110 Noain 33 M 6
22622 Nocito 34 M 7
22113 Novales 33 M 7
50510 Novallas 33 N 6
25795 Noves de Segre 34 M 9
31680 Ochagavía 33 M 6
25283 Odèn 34 M 9
31720 Oieregi 27 L 6
17856 Oix 35 M 10
31638 Olaberri 33 L 6
31798 Olagüe 33 M 6
31799 Olave 33 M 6
25790 Oliana 34 M 9
31390 Olite 33 M 6
08516 Olost 35 N 10
17800 Olot 35 M 10
08611 Olvan 35 M 9
42110 Ólvega 33 N 6
48700 Ondarroa 27 L 5
22232 Ontiñena 34 N 8
20560 Oñati 27 L 5
22376 Ordesa 34 M 7
20240 Ordizia 27 L 5
25794 Organyà 34 M 9
20810 Orio 27 L 5
08518 Oristà 35 N 10
31650 Orreaga-Roncesvalles 33 L 6
22811 Ortilla 33 M 7
22532 Osso de Cinca 34 N 8
25318 Ossó de Sió 34 N 9
31799 Ostiz 33 M 6
25211 Palou de Sanaüja 34 N 9
22221 Pallaruelo de Monegros 33 N 7
31070 Pamplona-Iruña 33 M 6
17133 Parlavà 35 M 11
17494 Pau 36 M 11
50690 Pedrola 33 N 6
50193 Peñaflor 33 N 7
31350 Peralta 33 M 6
25790 Peramola 34 M 9
50161 Perdiguera 33 N 7
22132 Pertusa 34 M 7
25518 Pessonada 34 M 9
25286 Pinell de Solsonès 34 N 9
50694 Pinsoro 33 M 6
50685 Pintano 33 M 6
88210 Plasencia del Monte 33 M 7
50297 Pleitas 33 N 6
22216 Poleñino 33 N 7
22413 Pomar 34 N 8
25740 Ponts 34 N 9
50800 Portazgo 33 N 7
17497 Portbou 36 M 11
50529 Pozuelo de Aragón 33 N 6
26510 Pradejón 33 M 5
08513 Prats de Lluçanès 35 M 10
22753 Puente la Reina 33 M 7
31100 Puente la Reina-Gares 33 M 6
08692 Puig-reig 35 N 9
17520 Puigcerdà 35 M 9
50810 Puilatos 33 N 7
22589 Purroy de la Solana 34 M 8
26570 Quel 33 M 5
17534 Queralbs 35 M 10
50637 Remolinos 33 N 6
25594 Rialp 34 M 9
17534 Ribes de Freser 35 M 10
31448 Rípodas 33 M 6
17500 Ripoll 35 M 10
22144 Rodellar 34 M 7
31415 Roncal 33 M 7
17480 Roses 36 M 11
25737 Rubió 34 M 9
22600 Sabiñánigo 33 M 7
31491 Sada 33 M 6
50670 Sádaba 33 M 6
22572 Saganta 34 N 8
22468 Sahun 34 M 8
22314 Salas Bajas 34 M 8
22366 Salinas de Sin 34 M 8
08269 Salo 35 N 9
08650 Sallent 35 N 9
22452 Samper 34 M 8
31570 San Adrián 33 M 6
22283 San Jorge 33 N 7
22372 San Martín 34 M 7
31495 San Martín de Unx 33 M 6
25753 Sanaüja 34 N 9
22100 Sangarrén 33 M 7
31400 Sangüesa 33 M 6
31220 Sansol 33 M 5
08274 Sant Feliu Sasserra 35 N 10
17854 Sant Jaume de Llierca 35 M 10
17860 Sant Joan de les Abadesses 35 M 10
08504 Sant Julià de Vilatorta 35 N 10
25282 Sant Llorenç de Morunys 35 M 9
17861 Sant Martí d'Ogassa 35 M 10
17864 Sant Pau de Segúries 35 M 10
17470 Sant Pere Pescador 35 M 11
50324 Santa Cruz de Grío 33 N 6
50669 Santa Engracia 33 N 6
02529 Santa Susanna 35 N 9
31314 Santacara 33 M 6
22461 Santaliestra y San Quílez 34 M 8
22583 Sapeira 34 M 8
22200 Sariñena 33 N 7
22374 Sarvisé 34 M 7
20214 Segura 27 L 5
22230 Sena 34 N 7
25514 Senterada 34 M 8
17852 Serinyà 35 M 10
22110 Sesa 33 N 7
31293 Sesma 33 M 5
17869 Setcases 35 M 10
50612 Sierra de Luna 33 M 7
50682 Sigüés 33 M 6
25280 Solsona 35 N 9
25589 Son 34 M 9
08697 Sorribes 35 M 9
25560 Sort 34 M 9
50680 Sos del Rey Católico 33 M 6
25287 Su 35 N 9
31791 Sunbilla 27 L 6
08260 Súria 35 N 9
50547 Tabuenca 33 N 6
31300 Tafalla 33 M 6
50546 Talamantes 33 N 6
22550 Tamarite de Litera 34 N 8
17721 Tapis 35 M 10
50500 Tarazona 33 N 6
50660 Tauste 33 N 6
08511 Tavertet 35 N 10
25577 Tavescan 34 M 9
17731 Terrades 35 M 10
50269 Tierga 33 N 6
25288 Timoneda 34 M 9
20400 Tolosa 27 L 5
25574 Tor 35 M 9
08570 Torelló 35 M 10
22254 Torralba de Aragón 33 N 7
25138 Torrelameu 34 N 8
17257 Torroella de Montgrí 35 M 11
22268 Tramaced 33 N 7
50583 Trasmoz 33 N 6
25598 Tredòs 34 M 8
25620 Tremp 34 M 8
31500 Tudela 33 M 6
25717 Tuixén 35 M 9
31283 Ulibarri 33 M 5
31422 Unciti 33 M 6
31711 Urdazubi-Urdaux 27 L 6
20130 Urnieta 27 L 6
31420 Urroz 33 M 6
50180 Utebo 33 N 7
50617 Valareña 33 M 6
22223 Valfarta 33 N 7
50138 Valmadrid 33 N 7
50615 Valpalmas 33 M 7
26528 Valverde/Agreda 33 N 6
17862 Vallfogona de Ripollès 35 M 10
22528 Velilla de Cinca 34 N 8
17142 Verges 35 M 11
08500 Vic 35 N 10
25530 Vielha 34 M 8
17137 Viladamat 35 M 11
25552 Vilaller 34 M 8
25654 Vilamitjana 34 M 8
25566 Vilamur 34 M 9
20150 Villabona 27 L 5
50216 Villalengua 33 N 6
50830 Villanueva de Gállego 33 N 7
26187 Villarroya 33 M 5
50310 Villarroya de la Sierra 33 N 6
25555 Xerallo 34 M 8
31410 Yesa 33 M 6
22530 Zaidín 34 N 8
50070 Zaragoza 33 N 7
20800 Zarautz 27 L 5
20740 Zestoa 27 L 5
31180 Zizur Mayor 33 M 6
31746 Zubieta 27 L 6
31630 Zubiri 33 M 6
31272 Zudaire 33 M 5
50800 Zuera 33 N 7
20750 Zumaia 27 L 5
22728 Zuriza 33 M 7

F

60220 Abancourt 11 E 9
44170 Abbaretz 15 G 6
80100 Abbeville 3 D 9
78660 Ablis 17 F 9
74360 Abondance 25 H 14
64360 Abos 28 L 7
57560 Abreschviller 20 F 15
05460 Abriès 32 K 14
16500 Abzac 22 H 8
64490 Accous 33 M 7
18250 Achères 17 G 10
80560 Acheux-en-Amiénois 12 D 10
20138 Acqua-Doria 39 N 16
27400 Acquigny 11 E 9
60620 Acy-en-Multien 12 E 10
86430 Adriers 22 H 8
34300 Agde 36 L 11
47000 Agen 28 K 8
21700 Agencourt 25 G 13
50230 Agon-Coutainville 9 E 6
12520 Aguessac 30 K 11
23150 Ahun 23 H 10
21510 Aignay-le-Duc 18 G 12
17290 Aigrefeuille-d'Aunis 21 H 7
44140 Aigrefeuille-sur-Maine 15 G 6
73220 Aiguebelle 32 J 14
63260 Aigueperse 23 H 11
30220 Aigues-Mortes 36 L 12
11800 Aigues-Vives 35 L 10
05470 Aiguilles 32 K 14
47190 Aiguillon 28 K 8
36140 Aigurande 23 H 9
05340 Ailefroide 32 K 14
89110 Aillant-sur-Tholon 18 G 11
72600 Aillières-Beauvoir 10 F 8
80690 Ailly-le Haut Clocher 3 D 9
80250 Ailly-sur-Noye 12 E 10
30470 Aimargues 36 L 12
73210 Aime 32 J 14
88320 Ainvelle 19 G 13
80270 Airaines 11 E 9
40800 Aire-sur-l'Adour 28 L 7
62120 Aire-sur-la-Lys 4 D 10
79600 Airvault 16 H 7
21400 Aisey-sur-Seine 18 G 12
02110 Aisonville-et-Bernoville 12 E 11
25360 Aissey 25 G 14
89390 Aisy-sur-Armançon 18 G 12
10160 Aix-en-Othe 18 F 11
13100 Aix-en-Provence 37 L 13
73100 Aix-les-Bains 31 J 13
85190 Aizenay 15 H 6
20000 Ajaccio 39 N 16
07400 Alba-la-Romaine 31 K 12
81250 Alban 29 L 10
73410 Albens 25 J 13
80300 Albert 12 D 10
20224 Albertacce 39 M 17
73200 Albertville 32 J 14
57670 Albestroff 20 F 14
81000 Albi 29 L 10
82350 Albias 29 K 9
20217 Albo 39 M 17
07440 Alboussière 31 K 12
74540 Alby-sur-Cheran 25 J 14
64430 Aldudes 27 L 6
61000 Alençon 10 F 8
20270 Aléria 39 M 17
30100 Alès 30 K 12
11580 Alet-les-Bains 35 L 10
53240 Alexain 10 F 7
26770 Aleyrac 31 K 12
58200 Aligny-Cosne 18 G 11
26300 Alixan 31 K 13
54170 Allain 19 F 13
28310 Allaines-Mervilliers 17 F 9
56350 Allaire 15 G 5
15160 Allanche 30 J 10
13190 Allauch 37 L 13
43270 Allègre 30 J 11
71350 Allerey-sur-Saône 25 H 12
38580 Allevard 32 J 14
10700 Allibaudières 18 F 12
74200 Allinges 25 H 14
18110 Allogny 17 G 10
28150 Allones 17 F 9
72700 Allonnes/le Mans 16 G 8
49650 Allonnes/Saumur 16 G 8
47420 Allons 28 K 7
04260 Allos 32 K 14
15700 Ally 29 J 10
81190 Almayrac 29 K 10
38750 Alpe-d'Huez 32 J 14
12210 Alpuech 30 K 10
20251 Altiani 39 M 17
48800 Altier 30 K 11
19120 Altillac 29 K 9
68130 Altkirch 20 G 15
76640 Alvimare 11 E 8
30770 Alzon 30 L 11
11170 Alzonne 35 L 10
08300 Amagne 13 E 12
79350 Amailloux 16 H 7
10140 Amance/Troyes 18 F 12
70160 Amance/Vesoul 19 G 14
01500 Ambérieu-en-Bugey 25 J 13
63600 Ambert 24 J 11
20151 Ambiegna 39 M 16
70210 Ambiévillers 19 G 14
60110 Amblainville 11 E 10
41310 Ambloy 16 G 8
37400 Amboise 16 G 8
36120 Ambrault 23 H 9
53300 Ambrières-les-Vallées 10 F 7
01500 Ambronay 25 H 13
66110 Amélie-les-Bains-Palalda 35 M 10
27370 Amfreville-la-Campagne 11 E 8
80000 Amiens 12 E 10
02190 Amifontaine 12 E 11
45200 Amilly 17 G 10
42260 Amions 24 J 12
40330 Amou 27 L 7
21400 Ampilly-le-Sec 18 G 12
69550 Amplepuis 24 J 12
69420 Ampuis 31 J 12
44150 Ancenis 15 G 6
55170 Ancerville 19 F 13
86700 Anché 22 H 8
89160 Ancy-le-Franc 18 G 12
07340 Andance 31 J 12
52700 Andelot-Blancheville 19 F 13
39110 Andelot-en-Montagne 25 H 13
33510 Andernos-les-Bains 27 K 6
49220 Andigné 16 G 7
30140 Anduze 30 K 11
28260 Anet 11 F 9
49000 Angers 16 G 7
91670 Angerville 17 F 9
15380 Anglards-de-Salers 30 J 10
01350 Anglefort 25 J 13
81260 Anglès 35 L 10
86330 Angliers 16 H 8
51260 Anglure 18 F 11
24270 Angoisse 22 J 9
34150 Aniane 36 L 11
59580 Aniche 4 D 11
02320 Anizy-le-Château 12 E 11
58270 Anlezy 24 H 11
24160 Anlhiac 22 J 9
74000 Annecy 25 J 14
50760 Anneville-en-Saire 10 E 6
26140 Anneyron 31 J 12
07100 Annonay 31 J 12
73590 Annuit 32 J 14
59186 Anor 12 E 12
71550 Anost 24 G 12
88650 Anould 20 F 14
69480 Anse 24 J 12
06600 Antibes 38 L 15
21230 Antigny-le-Château 24 G 12
92160 Antony 11 F 10
07530 Antraigues-sur-Volane 31 K 12
35560 Antrain 9 F 6
62134 Anvin 4 D 10
71110 Anzy-le-Duc 24 H 12
89380 Appoigny 18 G 11
84400 Apt 37 L 13
65710 Aragnouet 34 M 8
64570 Aramits 33 L 7
30390 Aramon 37 L 12
70120 Arbecey 19 G 13
39600 Arbois 25 H 13
52210 Arc-en-Barrois 19 G 13
70100 Arc-lès-Gray 19 G 13
21560 Arc-sur-Tille 19 G 13
33120 Arcachon 27 K 6
46090 Arcambal 29 K 9
89320 Arces-Dilo 18 F 11
17520 Archiac 21 J 7
51170 Arcis-le-Ponsart 12 E 11
10700 Arcis-sur-Aube 18 F 12
25300 Arçon 25 H 14
89270 Arcy-sur-Cure 18 G 11
36120 Ardentes 23 H 9
63420 Ardes 23 J 11
45160 Ardon 17 G 9
62610 Ardres 4 D 9
33740 Arès 21 K 6
64570 Arette 33 L 7
64570 Arette-Pierre-Saint Martin 33 M 7
03120 Arfeuilles 24 H 11
65400 Argelès-Gazost 34 L 7
66700 Argelès-sur-Mer 35 M 11
11120 Argeliers 36 L 10
18410 Argent-sur-Sauldre 17 G 10
61200 Argentan 10 F 7
19400 Argentat 29 J 9
95100 Argenteuil 11 F 10
74400 Argentière 25 J 14
29840 Argenton 7 F 3
79150 Argenton-Château 16 H 7
36200 Argenton-sur-Creuse 23 H 9
53210 Argentré 16 F 7
35370 Argentré-du-Plessis 15 F 6
76780 Argueil 11 E 9
39240 Arinthod 25 H 13
63220 Arlanc 30 J 11
39140 Arlay 25 H 13
13200 Arles 37 L 12
59151 Arleux 4 D 11
31440 Arlos 34 M 8
59280 Armentières 4 D 10
19230 Arnac-Pompadour 22 J 9
69400 Arnas 24 H 12
21230 Arnay-le-Duc 24 G 12
53440 Aron 10 F 7
91290 Arpajon 11 F 10
15130 Arpajon-sur-Cère 29 K 10
11190 Arques/Limoux 35 M 10
12290 Arques/Rodez 30 K 10
62510 Arques/Saint Omer 4 D 10
76880 Arques-la-Bataille 11 E 9
58310 Arquian 18 G 10
54370 Arracourt 20 F 14
62000 Arras 4 D 10
65240 Arreau 34 M 8
80820 Arrest 3 D 9
14117 Arromanches-les-Bains 10 E 7
03250 Arronnes 24 H 11
17590 Ars-en-Ré 21 H 6
57130 Ars-sur-Moselle 13 E 14
40090 Artassenx 28 L 7
45410 Artenay 17 F 9
81160 Arthès 29 L 10
64370 Arthez-de-Béarn 28 L 7
36330 Arthon 23 H 9
44320 Arthon-en-Retz 15 G 6
42130 Arthun 24 J 12
47480 Artigues 28 K 8
64170 Artix 28 L 7
64260 Arudy 34 L 7
17530 Arvert 21 J 6
77890 Arville 17 F 10
64410 Arzacq-Arraziguet 28 L 7
64310 Ascain 27 L 6
20276 Asco 39 M 17
45300 Ascoux 17 F 10
08190 Asfeld 12 E 12
31160 Aspet 34 L 8
05140 Aspres-sur-Buëch 31 K 13
79600 Assais-les-Jumeaux 16 H 7
64510 Assat 34 L 7
47720 Astaffort 28 K 8
64450 Astis 28 L 7
21130 Athée 25 G 13
70110 Athesans-Etroitefontaine 19 G 14
80200 Athies 12 E 10
61430 Athis-de-l'Orne 10 F 7
60350 Attichy 12 E 11
01340 Attignat 25 H 13
08130 Attigny 13 E 12
62170 Attin 3 D 9
13400 Aubagne 37 L 13
07200 Aubenas 31 K 12
02500 Aubenton 12 E 12
52210 Aubepierre-sur-Aube 19 G 12
78410 Aubergenville 11 F 9
52160 Auberive 19 G 13
51600 Aubérive 13 E 12
27940 Aubevoye 11 E 9
32270 Aubiet 28 L 8
79110 Aubigné 22 H 7
14700 Aubigny/Falaise 10 F 7
79390 Aubigny/la Roche-sur-Yon 15 H 6
62690 Aubigny-en-Artois 4 D 10
18700 Aubigny-sur-Nere 17 G 10
12110 Aubin 29 K 10
12470 Aubrac 30 K 10
23200 Aubusson 23 J 10
59950 Auby 4 D 11
82600 Aucamville 29 L 9
32000 Auch 28 L 8
62260 Auchel 4 D 10
65400 Aucun 34 M 7
33980 Audenge 28 K 6
45300 Auderville 9 E 6
25170 Audeux 25 G 13
29770 Audierne 7 F 3
02120 Audigny 12 E 11
25400 Audincourt 20 G 14
62179 Audinghen 3 D 9
62164 Audresselles 3 D 9
62370 Audruicq 4 D 10
54560 Audun-le-Roman 13 E 13
57390 Audun-le-Tiche 13 E 13
23170 Auge 23 H 10
63930 Augerolles 24 J 11
09800 Augirein 34 M 8
87120 Augne 23 J 9
30450 Aujac 30 K 12
46090 Aujols 29 K 9
30120 Aulas 30 K 11
20116 Aullène 39 N 17
63510 Aulnat 23 J 11
17470 Aulnay 22 H 7
55170 Aulnois-en-Perthois 19 F 13
57590 Aulnois-sur-Seille 19 F 14
59620 Aulnoye-Aymeries 12 D 11
23210 Aulon 23 H 9
80460 Ault 3 D 9
09140 Aulus-les-Bains 35 M 9
76390 Aumale 11 E 9
14260 Aunay-sur-Odon 10 E 7
28700 Auneau 17 F 9
60390 Auneuil 11 E 9
83630 Aups 37 L 14
56400 Auray 8 G 5
87220 Aureil 22 J 9
31420 Aurignac 34 L 8
15000 Aurillac 29 K 10
07200 Auriolles 31 K 12
33124 Auros 28 K 7
81200 Aussillon 35 L 10
32550 Auterive/Auch 28 L 8
31190 Auterive/Muret 35 L 9
28330 Authon-du-Perche 17 F 8
91410 Authon-la-Plaine 17 F 9
37110 Autrèche 16 G 8
70100 Autrey-lès-Gray 19 G 13
21570 Autricourt 18 G 12
71400 Autun 24 H 12
51800 Auve 13 E 12
95430 Auvers-sur-Oise 11 E 10
49490 Auverse 16 G 8
82340 Auvillar 28 K 8
89000 Auxerre 18 G 11
62390 Auxi-le-Château 3 D 10
21130 Auxonne 25 G 13
71400 Auxy 24 H 12
23700 Auzances 23 H 10
43390 Auzon 30 J 11
89200 Avallon 18 G 11
69430 Avenas 24 H 12
34260 Avène 30 L 11
03000 Avermes 24 H 11
62810 Avesnes-le-Comte 4 D 10
59440 Avesnes-sur-Helpe 12 D 11
84000 Avignon 37 L 12
25680 Avilley 19 G 14
55600 Avioth 13 E 13
51190 Avize 12 F 12
10290 Avon-la-Pèze 18 F 11
18520 Avord 17 G 10
74110 Avoriaz 25 H 14
21580 Avot 19 G 13
25690 Avoudrey 25 G 14
50300 Avranches 9 F 6
60130 Avrechy 12 E 10
60310 Avricourt 12 E 10
49240 Avrillé 16 G 7
27240 Avrilly 11 F 9
09110 Ax-les-Thermes 35 M 9
09250 Axiat 35 M 9
51160 Ay 12 E 11
19310 Ayen 22 J 9
62116 Ayette 4 D 10
46120 Aynac 29 K 9
15250 Ayrens 29 K 10
86190 Ayron 16 H 8
55150 Azannes-et-Soumazannes 13 E 13
36290 Azay-le-Ferron 16 H 9
37190 Azay-le-Rideau 16 G 8
53200 Azé/Château Gontier 16 G 7
71260 Azé/Mâcon 24 H 12
41100 Azé/Vendôme 17 G 9
23160 Azerables 23 H 9
57810 Azoudange 20 F 14
18220 Azy 17 G 10
58240 Azy-le-Vif 24 H 11
34360 Babeau 36 L 10
43170 Babonnès 30 K 11
54120 Baccarat 20 F 14
46230 Bach 29 K 9
76730 Bacqueville-en-Caux 11 E 8
36200 Badecon-le-Pin 23 H 9
54540 Badonviller 20 F 14
01380 Bâgé-le-Châtel 24 H 12
11100 Bages/Narbonne 36 L 10
66670 Bages/Perpignan 35 M 10
46270 Bagnac-sur-Célé 29 K 10
65200 Bagnères-de-Bigorre 34 L 8
31110 Bagnères-de-Luchon 34 M 8
61140 Bagnoles-de-l'Orne 10 F 7
63810 Bagnols 23 J 10
30200 Bagnols-sur-Cèze 31 K 12
21700 Bagnot 25 G 13
33760 Baigneaux 28 K 7
16360 Baignes-Sainte Radegonde 21 J 7
21450 Baigneux-les-Juifs 18 G 12
35460 Baillé 9 F 6
59270 Bailleul 4 D 10
35600 Bain-de-Bretagne 15 G 6
43370 Bains 30 J 11
88240 Bains-les-Bains 19 G 14
35600 Bains-sur-Oust 15 G 5
53160 Bais 10 F 7
35500 Balazé 9 F 6
20233 Balba 39 M 17
42510 Balbigny 24 J 12
31580 Balesta 34 L 8
33730 Balizac 28 K 7
37510 Ballan-Miré 16 G 8
53340 Ballée 16 G 7
58130 Balleray 18 G 11
14490 Balleroy 10 E 7
17290 Ballon/la Rochelle 21 H 7
72290 Ballon/le Mans 16 F 8
48000 Balsièges 30 K 11
64430 Banca 27 L 6
83150 Bandol 37 L 13
29380 Bannalec 8 G 4
04150 Banon 37 K 13
66650 Banyuls-sur-Mer 36 M 11
62450 Bapaume 12 D 10
55000 Bar-le-Duc 19 F 13
10200 Bar-sur-Aube 19 F 12
10110 Bar-sur-Seine 18 F 12
62860 Baralle 4 D 11
48170 Baraques-de-la-Motte 30 K 11
12160 Baraqueville 29 K 10
05200 Baratier 32 K 14
31510 Barbazan 34 L 8
16300 Barbezieux-Saint Hilaire 22 J 7
77630 Barbizon 17 F 10
51120 Barbonne-Fayel 18 F 11
04400 Barcelonnette 32 K 14
05110 Barcillonnette 31 K 13
67130 Barembach 20 F 15
31440 Baren 34 M 8
50720 Barenton 10 F 7
50760 Barfleur 10 E 6
83830 Bargemon 38 L 14
30430 Barjac 30 K 12
83670 Barjols 37 L 14
62620 Barlin 4 D 10
07330 Barnas 30 K 12
50270 Barneville-Carteret 9 E 6
33750 Baron/Bordeaux 28 K 7
60300 Baron/Senlis 12 E 10
57340 Baronville 20 F 14
67140 Barr 20 F 15

POSTALI · ÍNDICE CON CÓDIGOS POSTALES · INDICE DE LUGARES COM CÓDIGOS
REJSTŘÍK MÍST S PSČ · ZOZNAM OBCÍ S PSČ · INDEKS MIEJSCOWOŚCI Z KOD POCZTOWY

44

F

Barran · F · Bidache

32350 Barran 28 L 8
48400 Barre-des-Cévennes 30 K 11
04330 Barrème 38 L 14
19170 Barsanges 23 J 10
34290 Bassan 36 L 11
86200 Basses 16 G 8
89400 Bassou 18 G 11
74910 Bassy 25 J 13
20119 Bastelica 39 N 17
20200 Bastia 39 M 17
56150 Baud 9 G 4
36110 Baudres 17 G 9
49150 Baugé 16 G 7
18800 Baugy 17 G 10
25110 Baume-les-Dames 25 G 14
59570 Bavay 4 D 11
51270 Baye/Montmirail 12 F 11
29300 Baye/Quimperlé 8 G 4
10310 Bayel 19 F 12
14400 Bayeux 10 E 7
54290 Bayon 19 F 14
64100 Bayonne 27 L 6
89460 Bazarnes 18 G 11
33430 Bazas 28 K 7
08140 Bazeilles 13 E 13
45480 Bazoches-les-Gallérandes 17 F 10
61560 Bazoches-sur-Hoëne 10 F 8
88500 Bazoilles-et-Ménil 19 F 14
58110 Bazolles 18 G 11
35560 Bazouges-la-Pérouse 9 F 6
58160 Béard 24 H 11

30300 Beaucaire 37 L 12
73270 Beaufort/Albertville 32 J 14
39190 Beaufort/Lons-le-Saunier 25 H 13
45190 Beaugency 17 G 9
04420 Beaujeu/Digne-les-Bains 32 K 14
69430 Beaujeu/Villefranche-sur-Saône 24 H 12
33430 Beaulac 28 K 7
85190 Beaulieu-sous-la-Roche 15 H 6
19120 Beaulieu-sur-Dordogne 29 K 9
84190 Beaumes-de-Venise 31 K 13
27410 Beaumesnil 11 E 8
62123 Beaumetz-lès-Loges 4 D 10
24440 Beaumont/Bergerac 29 K 8
86490 Beaumont/Châtellerault 16 H 8
63110 Beaumont/Clermont-Ferrand 23 J 11
32100 Beaumont/Condom 28 L 8
54470 Beaumont-Fort-à-Mousson 19 F 13
82500 Beaumont-de-Lomagne 28 L 8
77890 Beaumont-du-Gâtinais 17 F 10
08210 Beaumont-en-Argonne 13 E 13
37420 Beaumont-en-Véron 16 G 8
50440 Beaumont-Hague 9 E 6

37360 Beaumont-la-Ronce 16 G 8
27170 Beaumont-le-Roger 11 E 8
26760 Beaumont-lès-Valence 31 K 12
95260 Beaumont-sur-Oise 11 E 10
72170 Beaumont-sur-Sarthe 16 F 8
51360 Beaumont-sur-Vesle 12 E 12
21200 Beaune 24 G 12
45340 Beaune-la-Rolande 17 F 10
49600 Beaupréau 15 G 7
82600 Beaupuy 29 L 9
62217 Beaurains 4 D 10
38270 Beaurepaire 31 J 13
71580 Beaurepaire-en-Bresse 25 H 13
26310 Beaurières 31 K 13
76870 Beaussault 11 E 9
60000 Beauvais 11 E 10
80630 Beauval 4 D 10
04370 Beauvezer 38 K 14
47470 Beauville 29 K 8
85230 Beauvoir-sur-Mer 15 H 5
79360 Beauvoir-sur-Niort 21 H 7
43590 Beauzac 30 J 12
35190 Bécherel 9 F 6
49370 Bécon-les-Granits 16 G 7
71270 Bédarieux 35 L 9
84370 Bédarrides 31 K 12
35137 Bédée 9 F 6
36210 Bédenac 21 J 7
22140 Bégard 9 F 4

64220 Béhoriéguy 27 L 6
89800 Beine 18 G 11
51490 Beine-Nauroy 12 E 12
36370 Bélâbre 22 H 9
11340 Bélcaire 35 M 9
09300 Bélesta 35 M 9
90000 Belfort 20 G 14
20226 Belgodère 39 M 17
28240 Belhomert-Guéhouville 11 F 9
33830 Belin-Béliet 28 K 7
87300 Bellac 22 H 9
22810 Belle-Isle-en-Terre 8 F 4
12400 Belleau 12 E 11
89210 Bellechaume 18 F 11
30127 Bellegarde/Arles 36 L 12
45270 Bellegarde/Châtenoy 17 G 10
26470 Bellegarde-en-Diois 31 K 13
23190 Bellegarde-en-Marche 23 J 10
01200 Bellegarde-sur-Valserine 25 H 13
25380 Belleherbe 25 G 14
61130 Bellême 10 F 8
76680 Bellencombre 11 E 9
03700 Bellerive-sur-Allier 24 H 11
69220 Belleville 24 H 12
85170 Belleville-sur-Vie 15 H 6
44460 Bellevue 15 G 5
43350 Bellevue-la-Montagne 30 J 11
01300 Bellley 25 J 13

44370 Belligné 15 G 6
77510 Bellot 12 F 11
12370 Belmont-sur-Rance 29 L 10
11420 Belpech 35 L 9
20110 Belvédère-Campomoro 39 N 16
24170 Belvès 29 K 8
56550 Belz 8 G 4
86470 Benassay 22 H 8
85490 Benet 21 H 7
21290 Beneuvre 19 G 12
67230 Benfeld 20 F 15
29950 Bénodet 7 G 3
31370 Bérat 35 L 9
28630 Berchères-les-Pierres 17 F 9
62600 Berck 3 D 9
62600 Berck-Plage 3 D 9
22600 Bergerac 28 K 8
51130 Bergères-les-Vertus 12 F 12
40120 Bergonce 28 K 7
59380 Bergues 4 D 10
02450 Bergues-sur-Sambre 12 D 11
86170 Berfaimont 12 D 11
80370 Bernaville 3 D 10
27300 Bernay 11 E 8
54470 Bernécourt 19 F 13
87300 Berneuil 22 H 8
38190 Bernin 31 J 13
13130 Berre-l'Étang 37 L 13
29690 Berrien 8 F 4
57930 Berthelming 20 F 15
12310 Bertholène 30 K 10

62124 Bertincourt 12 D 10
25000 Besançon 25 G 14
50390 Besneville 9 E 6
34550 Bessan 36 L 11
73480 Bessans 32 J 14
03340 Bessay-sur-Allier 24 H 11
63610 Besse-en-Chandesse 23 J 10
83890 Besse-sur-Issole 37 L 14
30190 Bessèges 30 K 12
69690 Bessenay 24 J 12
87250 Bessines-sur-Gartempe 22 H 9
51490 Béthenivílle 12 E 12
51450 Bétheny 12 E 12
60320 Béthisy-Saint Martin 12 E 10
09800 Bethmale 34 M 9
28330 Béthonvilliers 17 F 8
62490 Béthune 4 D 10
59600 Bettignies 4 D 11
35830 Betton 9 F 6
60620 Betz 12 E 10
02210 Beugneux 12 E 11
54260 Beuveille 13 E 13
86120 Beuxes 16 G 8
19190 Beynat 29 J 9
21310 Bèze 19 G 13
24220 Bézenac 29 K 9
03170 Bézenet 23 H 10
34500 Béziers 36 L 11
64200 Biarritz 27 L 6
40170 Bias 27 K 6
58110 Biches 24 G 11
64520 Bidache 27 L 6

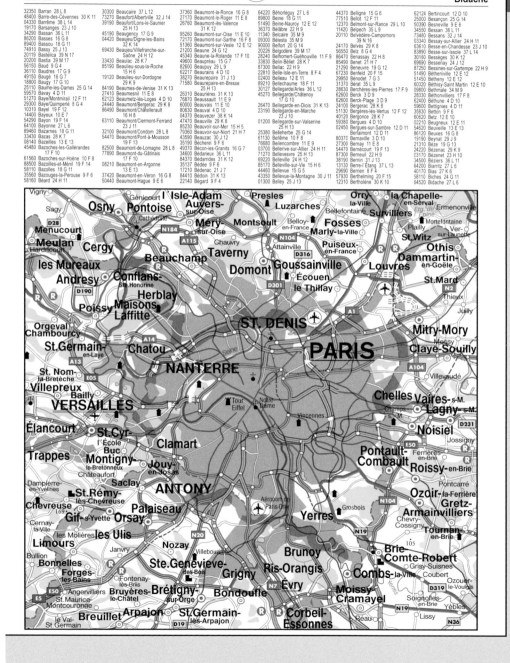

53290 Bierné 16 G 7
09320 Biert 35 M 9
64260 Bilhères 34 L 7
63160 Billom 23 J 11
41240 Binas 17 G 9
22520 Binic 9 F 5
40600 Biscarrosse 27 K 6
40600 Biscarrosse-Plage 27 K 6
67240 Bischwiller 20 F 15
51150 Bisseuil 12 E 12
57230 Bitche 20 E 15
50440 Biville 9 E 6
03170 Bizeneuille 23 H 10
33190 Blaignac 28 K 7
44130 Blain 15 G 6
51300 Blaise-sous-Arzillières 19 F 12
21540 Blaisy-Bas 18 G 12
31350 Blajan 34 L 8
54450 Blamont 20 F 14
14130 Blangy-le-Château 10 E 8
76340 Blangy-sur-Bresle 11 E 9
32290 Blanquefort 21 K 7
86400 Blanzay 22 H 8
71450 Blanzy 24 H 12
33540 Blasimon 28 K 7
33390 Blaye 21 J 7
89220 Bléneau 18 G 10
54113 Blénod-lès-Toul 19 F 13
37150 Bléré 16 G 8
43450 Blesle 30 J 11
18350 Blet 23 H 10
39140 Bletterans 25 H 13
88320 Blevaincourt 19 F 13
10200 Bligny 18 F 12
21360 Bligny-sur-Ouche 24 G 12
41000 Blois 17 G 9
68730 Blotzheim 20 G 15
20136 Bocognano 39 M 17
47550 Boé 28 K 8
74420 Boege 25 H 14
42130 Boën 24 J 12
08120 Bogny-sur-Meuse 13 E 12
02110 Bohain-en-Vermandois 12 E 11
85710 Bois-de-Céné 15 H 6
62170 Boisjean 3 D 9
54620 Boismont 13 E 13
76750 Boissay 11 E 9
45480 Boisseaux 17 F 9
27520 Boissey-le-Châtel 11 E 8
61110 Boissy-Maugis 10 F 8
28150 Boisville-la-Saint Père 17 F 9
25330 Bolandoz 25 G 14
76210 Bolbec 11 E 8
84500 Bollène 31 K 12
68540 Bollwiller 20 G 15
52310 Bologne 19 F 13
58330 Bona 18 G 11
70150 Bonboillon 19 G 13
20169 Bonifacio 39 N 17
20214 Bonifatu 39 M 16
39130 Bonlieu 25 H 13
23200 Bonnat 23 H 9
74380 Bonne 25 H 14
45460 Bonnée 17 G 10
72110 Bonnétable 16 F 8
16120 Bonneuil 22 J 7
86210 Bonneuil-Matours 16 H 8
28800 Bonneval 17 F 9
74130 Bonneville 25 H 14
62270 Bonnières 4 D 10
78270 Bonnières-sur-Seine 11 E 9
84480 Bonnieux 37 L 13
74890 Bons-en-Chablais 25 H 14
06830 Bonson 38 L 15
60120 Bonvillers 12 E 10
76520 Boos 11 E 9
26460 Bordeaux/Montélimar 31 K 13
33000 Bordeaux/Pessac 28 K 7
65590 Bordères-Louron 34 M 8
65320 Bordères-sur-l'Échez 34 L 8
20290 Borgo 39 M 17
83230 Bormes-les-Mimosas 37 L 14
43350 Borne 30 J 11
24590 Borrèze 29 K 9
19110 Bort-les-Orgues 23 J 10
76220 Bosc-Hyons 11 E 9
64340 Boucau 27 L 6
61570 Boucé/Argentan 10 F 7
03150 Boucé/Varennes-sur-Allier 24 H 11
59111 Bouchain 4 D 11
80910 Bouchoir 12 E 10
54200 Boucq 19 F 13
82200 Boudou 29 K 9
53290 Bouessay 16 G 7
36200 Bouesse 23 H 9
36110 Bouges-le-Château 17 G 9
47250 Bouglon 28 K 8
44340 Bouguenais 15 G 6
17540 Bouhet 21 H 7
58310 Bouhy 18 G 11
10320 Bouilly 18 F 11
85230 Bouin 15 H 6
25560 Boujailles 25 H 14
57220 Boulay-Moselle 14 E 14
66130 Bouleternère 35 M 10
55240 Bouligny 13 E 13
12410 Bouloc/Millau 30 K 10
82110 Bouloc/Toulouse 29 L 9
31350 Boulogne-sur-Gesse 34 L 8
62200 Boulogne-sur-Mer 3 D 9
72440 Bouloire 16 G 8
24560 Bouniagues 28 K 8
71140 Bourbon-Lancy 24 H 11
52400 Bourbonne-les-Bains 19 G 13
59630 Bourbourg 4 D 10
22390 Bourbriac 9 F 4
17560 Bourcefranc-le-Chapus 21 J 6
52700 Bourdons-sur-Rognon 19 F 13
86410 Bouresse 22 H 8
33710 Bourg 21 J 7
27310 Bourg-Achard 11 E 8
42220 Bourg-Argental 31 J 12
29860 Bourg-Blanc 7 F 3
26300 Bourg-de-Péage 31 J 13
82190 Bourg-de-Visa 29 K 8
01000 Bourg-en-Bresse 25 H 13
02160 Bourg-et-Comin 12 E 11
63760 Bourg-Lastic 23 J 10
07700 Bourg-Saint Andéol 31 K 12
73700 Bourg-Saint Maurice 32 J 14
23400 Bourganeuf 23 J 9
18000 Bourges 17 G 10
18110 Bourgneuf 17 G 10
44580 Bourgneuf-en-Retz 15 G 6
51110 Bourgogne 12 E 12
38300 Bourgoin-Jallieu 31 J 13
27520 Bourgthéroulde-Infreville 11 E 8
14540 Bourguébus 10 E 7
37140 Bourgueil 16 G 8
11300 Bouriège 35 M 10
52150 Bourmont 19 F 13
86120 Bournand 16 G 8
47210 Bournel 28 K 8
27500 Bourneville 11 E 8
85480 Bournezeau 15 H 6
03160 Bourpon-l'Archambault 23 H 11
23600 Boussac 23 H 10
37290 Boussay/Châtellerault 16 H 8
44190 Boussay/Cholet 15 G 6
47420 Boussès 28 K 8
91820 Boutigny-sur-Essonne 17 F 10
91880 Bouville 17 F 10
44130 Bouvron 15 G 6
67330 Bouxwiller 20 F 15
51400 Bouy 12 E 12
82400 Bouyou 29 K 9
57320 Bouzonville 14 E 14
45300 Boynes 17 F 10
73350 Bozel 32 J 14
12340 Bozouls 30 K 10
33480 Brach 21 J 7
41250 Bracieux 17 G 9
02220 Braine 12 E 11
03360 Braize 23 H 10
73500 Bramans 32 J 14
55150 Brandeville 13 E 13
71500 Branges 25 H 13
89150 Brannay 18 F 11
25340 Branne/Baume-les-Dames 25 G 14
33420 Branne/Bordeaux 28 K 7
55400 Braquis 13 E 13
29190 Brasparts 8 F 4
81260 Brassac/Castres 35 L 10
09000 Brassac/Foix 35 M 9
63570 Brassac-les-Mines 30 J 11
52290 Braucourt 19 F 12
59123 Bray-Dunes-Plage 4 C 10
77480 Bray-sur-Seine 18 F 11
80340 Bray-sur-Somme 12 E 10
21430 Brazey-en-Morvan 18 G 12
21470 Brazey-en-Plaine 25 G 13
76110 Bréauté 11 E 8
51320 Bréban 18 F 12
50370 Brécey 10 F 6
56400 Brech 8 G 5
18220 Brécy 17 G 10
50290 Bréhal 9 F 6
56580 Bréhan 9 F 5
57570 Breidenbach 14 E 15
06540 Breil-sur-Roya 38 L 15
46320 Brengues 29 K 9
01110 Brénod 25 H 13
02210 Breny 12 E 11
17490 Bresdon 22 J 7
60510 Bresles 11 E 10
82710 Bressols 29 L 9
79300 Bressuire 16 H 7
29200 Brest 7 F 3
36110 Bretagne 17 H 9
46130 Bretenoux 29 K 9
60120 Breteuil 11 E 10
27160 Breteuil-sur-Iton 11 F 8
85470 Brétignolles-sur-Mer 15 H 6
91220 Brétigny-sur-Orge 11 F 10
50430 Bretteville-sur-Ay 9 E 6
14680 Bretteville-sur-Laize 10 E 7
17700 Breuil-la-Reorte 21 H 7
91650 Breuillet/Dourdan 11 F 10
17920 Breuillet/Royan 21 J 6
28270 Brezolles 11 F 8
05100 Briançon 32 K 14
45250 Briare 17 G 10
81390 Briatexte 29 L 9
52120 Bricon 19 F 12
50260 Bricquebec 9 E 6
37600 Bridoré 16 G 9
77170 Brie-Comte-Robert 12 F 10
29510 Briec 8 F 4
10500 Brienne-le-Château 18 F 12
89210 Brienon-sur-Armançon 18 G 11
54150 Briey 13 E 13
69530 Brignais 24 J 12
83170 Brignoles 37 L 14
86290 Brigueil-le-Chantre 22 H 9
55000 Brillon-en-Barrois 19 F 13
58420 Brinon-sur-Beuvron 18 G 11
86160 Brion/Gençay 22 H 8
36110 Brion/Issoudun 17 H 9
79290 Brion-près-Thouet 16 G 7
27800 Brionne 11 E 8
43100 Brioude 30 J 11
79170 Brioux-sur-Boutonne 22 H 7
61220 Briouze 10 F 7
64240 Briscous 27 L 6
34190 Brissac 30 L 11
49320 Brissac-Quincé 16 G 7
19100 Brive-la-Gaillarde 29 J 9
40420 Brocas 28 K 7
27270 Broglie 10 E 8
22250 Broons 9 F 5
16480 Brossac 22 J 7
28160 Brou 17 F 9
28410 Broué 11 F 9
88600 Brouvelieures 20 F 14
83440 Brovès 38 L 14
62700 Bruay-la-Buissière 4 D 10
59860 Bruay-sur-l'Escaut 4 D 11
83119 Brue-Auriac 37 L 13
18200 Bruère-Allichamps 23 H 10
31150 Bruguières 29 L 9
72350 Brûlon 16 G 7
67170 Brumath 20 F 15
02360 Brunehamel 12 E 12
04210 Brunet 37 L 14
82800 Bruniquel 29 K 9
91800 Brunoy 11 F 10
12360 Brusque 30 L 10
88600 Bruyères 20 F 14
35170 Bruz 9 F 6
50640 Buais 10 F 7
56310 Bubry 8 G 4
70700 Bucey-lès-Gy 19 G 13
76750 Buchy 11 E 9
27730 Bueil 11 F 9
12370 Buffières 30 L 10
11190 Bugarach 35 M 10
19170 Bugeat 23 J 9
26170 Buis-les-Baronnies 31 K 13
88140 Bulgnéville 19 F 13
63350 Bulhon 24 J 11
62160 Bully-les-Mines 4 D 10
55140 Burey-en-Vaux 19 F 13
65190 Burg 34 L 8
41160 Busloup 17 G 9
88540 Bussang 20 G 14
58170 Bussière 24 H 12
87230 Bussière-Galant 22 J 9
87320 Bussière-Poitevine 22 H 8
77760 Bussières 12 F 11
52700 Busson 19 F 13
89500 Bussy-le-Repos 18 F 11
39800 Buvilly 25 H 13
86180 Buxerolles 22 H 8
03440 Buxières-les-Mines 23 H 10
71390 Buxy 24 H 12
36500 Buzançais 17 H 9
08240 Buzancy 13 E 12
55400 Buzy-Darmont 13 E 13
33650 Cabanac 28 K 7
83340 Cabasse 37 L 14
14390 Cabourg 10 E 7
34800 Cabrières 36 L 11
40120 Cachen 28 K 7
81600 Cadalen 29 L 9
84160 Cadenet 37 L 13
24480 Cadouin 29 K 8
31480 Cadours 29 L 9
14000 Caen 10 E 7
59190 Caëstre 4 D 10
81130 Cagnac-les-Mines 29 L 10
06800 Cagnes-sur-Mer 38 L 15
46000 Cahors 29 K 9
11240 Cailhavel 35 L 10
46160 Cajarc 29 K 9
62100 Calais 3 D 9
20111 Calcatoggio 39 M 16
20214 Calenzana 39 M 16
47600 Calignac 28 K 8
22160 Callac 8 F 4
83830 Callas 38 L 14
13008 Callelongue 37 L 13
40430 Callen 28 K 7
31560 Calmont 35 L 9
20260 Calvi 39 M 16
46190 Calviac 29 K 10
15340 Calvinet 29 K 10
12360 Camarès 30 L 10
29570 Camaret-sur-Mer 7 F 3
46100 Cambes 29 K 9
64250 Cambo-les-Bains 27 L 6
81260 Cambounès 35 L 10
59400 Cambrai 4 D 11
14340 Cambremer 10 E 8
62149 Cambrin 4 D 10
46100 Camburat 29 K 9
62176 Camiers 3 D 9
56330 Camors 9 G 4
62870 Campagne-lès-Hesdin 3 D 9
65710 Campan 34 L 8
24140 Campsegret 28 K 8
61120 Canapville 10 F 8
35260 Cancale 9 F 6
80115 Canchy 3 D 9
47290 Cancon 28 K 8
49440 Candé 15 G 6
37500 Candes-Saint Martin 16 G 8
60310 Candor 12 E 10
12290 Canet-de-Salars 30 K 10
50750 Canisy 10 E 6
06400 Cannes 38 L 15
12230 Cantobre 30 K 11
76450 Cany-Barville 11 E 8
33970 Cap Ferret 27 K 6
47430 Cap-du-Bosc 28 K 8
40130 Capbreton 27 L 6
24540 Capdrot 29 K 8
34310 Capestang 36 L 11
09400 Capoulet-et-Junac 35 M 9
33840 Captieux 28 K 7
31460 Caraman 35 L 9
33560 Carbon-Blanc 21 K 7
31390 Carbonne 35 L 9
33121 Carcans 21 J 6
33121 Carcans-Plage 21 J 6
11000 Carcassonne 35 L 10
50500 Carentan 10 E 6
56910 Carentoir 15 G 5
20130 Cargèse 39 M 16
29270 Carhaix-Plouguer 8 F 4
08110 Carignan 13 E 13
34600 Carlencas 36 L 11
24370 Carlux 29 K 9
81400 Carmaux 29 K 10
56340 Carnac 8 G 4
59217 Carnières 12 D 11
83660 Carnoules 37 L 14
50740 Carolles 9 F 6
84200 Carpentras 31 K 13
44470 Carquefou 15 G 6
83320 Carqueiranne 37 L 14
82000 Carreyrat 29 L 9
61320 Carrouges 10 F 7
13620 Carry-le-Rouet 37 L 13
14330 Cartigny-l'Epinay 10 E 6
62220 Carvin 4 D 10
20140 Casalabriva 39 N 16
20270 Casevecchie 39 M 17
12120 Cassagnes-Bégonhès 29 K 10
59670 Cassel 4 D 10
13260 Cassis 37 L 13
12210 Cassuéjouls 30 K 10
29150 Cast 7 F 3
20246 Casta 39 M 17
81150 Castanet 29 L 10
31320 Castanet-Tolosan 35 L 9
31780 Castelginest 29 L 9
47700 Casteljaloux 28 K 8
04120 Castellane 38 L 14
47260 Castelmoron-sur-Lot 28 K 8
81260 Castelnau-de-Brassac 35 L 10
33480 Castelnau-de-Médoc 21 J 7
81140 Castelnau-de-Montmiral 29 L 9
65230 Castelnau-Magnoac 34 L 8
46170 Castelnau-Montratier 29 K 9
65700 Castelnau-Rivière-Basse 28 L 7
47290 Castelnaud-de-Gratecambe 28 K 8
11400 Castelnaudary 35 L 9
82100 Castelsarrasin 29 K 9
65350 Castéra-Lou 34 L 8
32340 Castet-Arrouy 28 L 8
40260 Castets 27 L 6
09800 Castillon-en-Couserans 34 M 9
33350 Castillon-la-Bataille 28 K 7
47330 Castillonnes 28 K 8
81100 Castres 35 L 10
34160 Castries 36 L 11
60840 Catenoy 12 E 10
57570 Cattenom 13 E 14
46150 Catus 29 K 9
76490 Caudebec-en-Caux 11 E 8
66220 Caudiès-de-Fenouillèdes 35 M 10
59540 Caudry 12 D 11
22350 Caulnes 9 F 5
09160 Caumont 34 L 9
14240 Caumont-l'Eventé 10 E 7
11160 Caunes-Minervois 35 L 10
20117 Cauro 39 N 16
82300 Caussade 29 K 9
34490 Causses-et-Veyran 36 L 11
09250 Caussou 35 M 9
65110 Cauterets 34 M 7
76930 Cauville 10 E 8
84300 Cavaillon 37 L 13
83240 Cavalaire-sur-Mer 38 L 14
82160 Caylus 29 K 9
43510 Cayres 30 K 11
15290 Cayrols 29 K 10
32150 Cazaubon 28 L 7
31220 Cazères 34 L 9
61330 Ceaucé 10 F 7
34260 Ceilhes-et-Rocozels 30 L 11
79370 Celles-sur-Belle 22 H 7
88110 Celles-sur-Plaine 20 F 14
36200 Celon 23 H 9
70500 Cendrecourt 19 G 13
32500 Céran 28 L 8
17270 Cercoux 21 J 7
58340 Cercy-la-Tour 24 H 11
45620 Cerdon 17 G 10
04280 Céreste 37 L 13
95000 Cergy 11 E 10
03350 Cérilly 23 H 10
89320 Cerisiers 18 F 11
79140 Cerizay 15 H 7
68700 Cernay 20 G 15
51800 Cernay-en-Dormois 13 E 12
45360 Cernoy-en-Berry 17 G 10
05100 Cervières 32 K 14
20221 Cervione 39 M 17
58800 Cervon 18 G 11
02320 Cessières 12 E 11
33610 Cestas 28 K 7
73730 Cevins 32 J 14
34800 Ceyras 36 L 11
13600 Ceyreste 37 L 13
01250 Ceyzériat 25 H 13
26120 Chabeuil 31 K 13
89800 Chablis 18 G 11
63250 Chabreloche 24 J 11
25300 Chaffois 25 H 14
71150 Chagny 24 H 12
79500 Chail 22 H 7
36310 Chaillac 22 H 9
85450 Chaillé-les-Marais 21 H 6
41120 Chailles 17 G 9
55210 Chaillon 19 F 13
61500 Chailloué 10 F 8
77120 Chailly-en-Brie 12 F 11
51130 Chaintrix-Bierges 12 F 12
11230 Chalabre 35 M 10
01320 Chalamont 25 J 13
45120 Châlette-sur-Loing 17 F 10
52600 Chalindrey 19 G 13
49440 Challain-la-Potherie 15 G 6
85300 Challans 15 H 6
73190 Challes-les-Eaux 32 J 13
28300 Challet 11 F 9
42920 Chalmazel 24 J 11
71100 Chalon-sur-Saône 24 H 12
49290 Chalonnes-sur-Loire 16 G 7
51000 Châlons-en-Champagne 12 F 12
15200 Chalvignac 29 J 10
38460 Chamagnieu 24 J 13
26150 Chamaloc 31 K 13
19370 Chamberet 23 J 9
73000 Chambéry 31 J 13
71110 Chambilly 24 H 12
60230 Chambly 11 E 10
61160 Chambois 10 F 8
23220 Chambon-Sainte Croix 23 H 9
23170 Chambon-sur-Voueize 23 H 10
19450 Chamboulive 23 J 9
37310 Chambourg-sur-Indre 16 G 8
37170 Chambray-lès-Tours 16 G 8
69620 Chamelet 24 J 12
21400 Chamesson 18 G 12
74400 Chamonix-Mont-Blanc 25 J 14
02860 Chamouille 12 E 11
73390 Chamoux-sur-Gelon 32 J 14
10130 Chamoy 18 F 11
15130 Champ Grand 29 K 10
43440 Champagnac-le-Vieux 30 J 11
01260 Champagne-en-Valromey 25 J 13
70290 Champagney 20 G 14
39300 Champagnole 25 H 13
58150 Champcelée 18 G 11
42600 Champdieu 24 J 12
63320 Champeix 23 J 11
54280 Champenoux 19 F 14
38260 Champier 31 J 13
49330 Champigné 16 G 7
89350 Champignelles 18 G 11
54240 Champigneulles 19 F 14
89340 Champigny 18 F 11
37120 Champigny-sur-Veude 16 G 8
58210 Champlemy 18 G 11
70600 Champlitte 19 G 13
28240 Champrond-en-Gâtine 17 F 9
15270 Champs-sur-Tarentaine 23 J 10
89290 Champs-sur-Yonne 18 G 11
49270 Champtoceaux 15 G 6
70100 Champvans 19 G 13
38410 Chamrousse 31 J 13
48230 Chanac 30 K 11
38150 Chanas 31 J 12
73310 Chanaz 25 J 13
35680 Chancé 15 F 6
37390 Chanceaux-sur-Choisille 16 G 8
61300 Chandai 11 F 8
72560 Changé 16 G 8
42310 Changy 24 H 11
17610 Chaniers 21 J 7
37330 Channay-sur-Lathan 16 G 8
10340 Channes 18 G 12
23600 Chanon 23 H 10
03140 Chantelle 23 H 11
38740 Chantelouve 31 K 13
60500 Chantilly 12 E 10
85110 Chantonnay 15 H 6
53300 Chantrigné 10 F 7
10210 Chaource 18 F 12
71320 Charbonnat 24 H 12
39260 Charchilla 25 H 13
18210 Charenton-du-Cher 23 H 10
08000 Charleville-Mézières 13 E 12
42190 Charlieu 24 H 12
02310 Charly-sur-Marne 12 F 11
88130 Charmes 19 F 14
07800 Charmes-sur-Rhône 31 K 12
10150 Charmont-sous-Barbuise 18 F 12
71850 Charnay-lès-Mâcon 24 H 12
37290 Charnizay 16 H 8
89120 Charny 18 G 11
55100 Charny-sur-Meuse 13 E 13
71120 Charolles 24 H 12
26450 Charols 31 K 12
18290 Chârost 17 H 10
28500 Charpont 11 F 9
64190 Charre 27 L 7
64130 Charritte-de-Bas 27 L 7
17230 Charron 21 H 6
86250 Charroux 22 H 8
03140 Charroux 23 H 11
28130 Chartainvilliers 11 F 9
28000 Chartres 17 F 9
35131 Chartres-de-Bretagne 9 F 6
43320 Chaspuzac 30 J 11
28480 Chassant 17 F 9
38670 Chasse-sur-Rhône 31 J 12
48250 Chasseradès 30 K 11
52190 Chassigny 19 G 13
72540 Chassillé 16 F 7
89110 Chassy 18 G 11
48300 Chastanier 30 K 11
23340 Chatain 23 J 9
04160 Château-Arnoux 37 K 14
58120 Château-Chinon 24 G 11
85180 Château-d'Olonne 15 H 6
72500 Château-du-Loir 16 G 8
53200 Château-Gontier 16 G 7
37330 Château-la-Vallière 16 G 8
77570 Château-Landon 17 F 10
08360 Château-Porcien 12 E 12
37110 Château-Renault 16 G 8
57170 Château-Salins 20 F 14
02400 Château-Thierry 12 E 11
35220 Châteaubourg 9 F 6
44110 Châteaubriant 15 G 6
28200 Châteaudun 17 F 9
35410 Châteaugiron 9 F 6
29150 Châteaulin 7 F 3
18370 Châteaumeillant 23 H 10
26330 Châteauneuf-de-Galaure 31 J 12
48170 Châteauneuf-de-Randon 30 K 11
29520 Châteauneuf-du-Faou 8 F 4
28170 Châteauneuf-en-Thymerais 11 F 9
63390 Châteauneuf-les-Bains 23 H 10
16120 Châteauneuf-sur-Charente 22 J 7
18190 Châteauneuf-sur-Cher 23 H 10
45110 Châteauneuf-sur-Loire 17 G 10
49330 Châteauneuf-sur-Sarthe 16 G 7
87290 Châteauponsac 22 H 9
04270 Châteauredon 37 K 14
45220 Châteaurenard 18 G 10
36000 Châteauroux 23 H 9
05380 Châteauroux-les-Alpes 32 K 14
83670 Châteauvert 37 L 14
52120 Châteauvillain 19 F 12
74390 Châtel 25 H 14
89660 Châtel-Censoir 18 G 11
03500 Châtel-de-Neuvre 24 H 11
89310 Châtel-Gérard 18 G 12
03250 Châtel-Montagne 24 H 11
88330 Châtel-sur-Moselle 19 F 14
17340 Châtelaillon-Plage 21 H 6
22170 Châtelaudren 9 F 5
63290 Châteldon 24 J 11
63140 Châtelguyon 23 J 11
86100 Châtellerault 16 H 8
23430 Châtelus-le-Marcheix 23 J 9
88170 Châtenois/Neufchâteau 19 F 13
67730 Châtenois/Sélestat 20 F 15
45260 Châtenoy 17 G 10
03210 Châtillon 23 H 11
45230 Châtillon-Coligny 17 G 10
58110 Châtillon-en-Bazois 24 G 11
26410 Châtillon-en-Diois 31 K 13
01200 Châtillon-en-Michaille 25 H 13
01400 Châtillon-sur-Chalaronne 24 H 12
36700 Châtillon-sur-Indre 16 H 9
45360 Châtillon-sur-Loire 17 G 10
21400 Châtillon-sur-Seine 18 G 12
41310 Châtres-sur-Cher 17 G 9
15110 Chaudes-Aigues 30 K 10
48170 Chaudeyrac 30 K 11
71170 Chauffailles 24 H 12
05800 Chauffayer 31 K 14
58400 Chaulgnes 18 G 11
80320 Chaulnes 12 E 10
70140 Chaumercenne 25 G 13
39230 Chaumergy 25 H 13
77390 Chaumes-en-Brie 12 F 10
52000 Chaumont 19 F 13
60240 Chaumont-en-Vexin 11 E 9
08220 Chaumont-Porcien 12 E 12
41150 Chaumont-sur-Loire 17 G 9

41600 Chaumont-sur-Tharonne 17 G 9
86510 Chaunay 22 H 8
02300 Chauny 12 E 11
39120 Chaussin 25 H 13
86300 Chauvigny 22 H 8
25240 Chaux-Neuve 25 H 14
10330 Chavanges 19 F 12
42140 Chazelles-sur-Lyon 24 J 12
03150 Chazeuil 24 H 11
79110 Chef-Boutonne 22 H 7
32140 Chélan 34 L 8
65350 Chelle-Debat 34 L 8
41700 Chémery 17 G 9
49120 Chemillé 16 G 7
39120 Chemin 25 H 13
72540 Chemiré-en-Charnie 16 F 7
79120 Chenay 22 H 7
71340 Chenay-le-Châtel 24 H 11
69430 Chénelette 24 H 12
23270 Chénérailles 23 H 10
17210 Chepniers 21 J 7
51240 Chepy 12 F 12
50100 Cherbourg-Octeville 10 E 6
89690 Chéroy 18 F 10
16370 Cherves-Richemont 21 J 7
02000 Chéry-les-Pouilly 12 E 11
69380 Chessy 24 J 12
03230 Chevagnes 24 H 11
84460 Cheval-Blanc 37 L 13
74500 Chevenoz 25 H 14
21800 Chevigny-Saint Sauveur 19 G 13
52170 Chevillon 19 F 13
45520 Chevilly 17 F 9
78460 Chevreuse 11 F 10
77320 Chevru 12 F 11
79120 Chey 22 H 7
01410 Chézery-Forens 25 H 13
79350 Chiché 16 H 7
49490 Chigné 16 G 8
45170 Chilleurs-aux-Bois 17 F 10
37500 Chinon 16 G 8
38850 Chirens 31 J 13
71540 Chissey-en-Morvan 24 G 12
36800 Chitray 23 H 9
49300 Cholet 15 G 7
07210 Chomérac 31 K 12
05230 Chorges 32 K 14
37140 Chouzé-sur-Loire 16 G 8
45220 Chuelles 18 F 10
31350 Ciadoux 34 L 8
65200 Cieutat 34 L 8
87520 Cieux 22 J 9
37130 Cinq-Mars-la-Pile 16 G 8
31550 Cintegabelle 35 L 9
70120 Cintrey 19 G 13
61320 Ciral 10 F 7
54480 Cirey-sur-Vezouze 20 F 14
71420 Ciry-le-Noble 24 H 12
86170 Cissé 16 H 8
11160 Citou 35 L 10
86320 Civaux 22 H 8
23500 Clairavaux 23 J 10
39130 Clairavaux-les-Lacs 25 H 13
36500 Claise 23 H 9
92140 Clamart 11 F 10
58500 Clamecy 18 G 11
21390 Clamerey 18 G 12
06420 Clans 38 L 15
59225 Clary 12 D 11
15320 Clavières 30 K 11
77410 Claye-Souilly 12 F 10
14570 Clécy 10 F 7
29233 Cléder 8 F 3
52240 Clefmont 19 F 13
49150 Clefs 16 G 7
56480 Cléguérec 9 F 4
38930 Clelles 31 K 13
18410 Clémont 17 G 10
76690 Clères 11 E 9
10390 Clérey 18 F 12
19320 Clergoux 23 J 9
71520 Clermain 24 H 12
09420 Clermont/Daumazan-sur-Arize 35 L 9
60600 Clermont/Nogent-sur-Oise 12 E 10
74270 Clermont/Rumilly 25 J 13
72200 Clermont-Créans 16 G 7
55120 Clermont-en-Argonne 13 E 13
63000 Clermont-Ferrand 23 J 11
34800 Clermont-l'Hérault 36 L 11
11250 Clermont-sur-Lauquet 35 L 10
25330 Cléron 25 G 14
25340 Clerval 19 G 14
45370 Cléry-Saint André 17 G 9
80200 Cléry-sur-Somme 12 E 10
71260 Clessé 16 H 7
36700 Clion 17 H 9
44190 Clisson 15 G 6
28220 Cloyes-sur-le-Loir 17 G 9
23270 Clugnat 23 H 10
71250 Cluny 24 H 12
74300 Cluses 25 H 14
64800 Coarraze 34 L 7
10240 Coclois 18 F 12
47250 Cocumont 28 K 8
48400 Cocurès 30 K 11
85220 Coëx 15 H 6
16100 Cognac 21 J 7
87310 Cognac-la-Forêt 22 J 9
18130 Cogny 23 H 10
83310 Cogolin 38 L 14
36130 Coings 17 H 9
47450 Colayrac-Saint Cirq 28 K 8
01270 Coligny 25 H 13
22330 Collinée 9 F 5
66190 Collioure 36 M 11
68000 Colmar 20 F 15
04370 Colmars 32 K 14
32430 Cologne 28 L 8
54170 Colombey-les-Belles 19 F 13
52330 Colombey-les-Deux-Églises 19 F 12
03600 Colombier 23 H 10
50700 Colomby 10 E 6
31770 Colomiers 29 L 9
23800 Colondannes 23 H 9
70120 Combeaufontaine 19 G 13
80360 Combles 12 D 10
35270 Combourg 9 F 6
49520 Combrée 15 G 6
28480 Combres 17 F 9
19250 Combressol 23 J 10
63460 Combronde 23 J 11
29450 Commana 8 F 4
21320 Commarin 18 G 12
39140 Commenailles 25 H 13
03600 Commentry 23 H 10
55200 Commercy 19 F 13
60200 Compiègne 12 E 10
83840 Comps-sur-Artuby 38 L 14
29900 Concarneau 7 G 4
19350 Concèze 22 J 9
27190 Conches-en-Ouche 11 F 8
30450 Concoules 30 K 11
36300 Concremiers 22 H 9
18260 Concressault 17 G 10
15190 Condat 23 J 10
02330 Condé-en-Brie 12 E 11
14110 Condé-sur-Noireau 10 F 7
78113 Condé-sur-Vesgre 11 F 9
50890 Condé-sur-Vire 10 E 6
62360 Condette 3 D 9
32100 Condom 28 L 8
69420 Condrieu 31 J 12
70800 Conflans-sur-Lanterne 19 G 14
16500 Confolens 22 H 8
72240 Conlie 16 F 7
72160 Connerré 16 F 8
44290 Conquereuil 15 G 6
55110 Consenvoye 13 E 13
06390 Contes 38 L 15
76390 Conteville 11 E 9
49330 Contigné 16 G 7
41700 Contres 17 G 9
88140 Contrexéville 19 F 13
80160 Conty 11 E 10
51320 Coole 18 F 12
29370 Coray 8 F 4
69960 Corbas 24 J 12
60110 Corbeil-Cerf 11 E 10
91100 Corbeil-Essonnes 11 F 10
45490 Corbeilles 17 F 10
21250 Corberon 25 G 13
80800 Corbie 12 E 10
58800 Corbigny 18 G 11
21910 Corcelles-lès-Cîteaux 25 G 13
30260 Corconne 30 L 11
44360 Cordemais 15 G 6
81170 Cordes-sur-Ciel 29 K 9
71540 Cordesse 24 G 12
14700 Cordey 10 F 7
21700 Corgoloin 24 G 12
22320 Corlay 9 F 4
28140 Cormainville 17 F 9
71460 Cormatin 24 H 12
27260 Cormeilles 10 E 8
60120 Cormeilles-en-Vexin 11 E 10
41120 Cormeray 17 G 9
51350 Cormontreuil 12 E 12
10800 Cormost 18 F 12
01560 Cormoz 25 H 13
31700 Cornebarrieu 29 L 9
88310 Cornimont 20 G 14
12580 Cornus 30 L 11
38970 Corps 31 K 13
70500 Corre 19 G 13
22130 Corseul 9 F 5
20250 Corte 39 M 17
58200 Cosne-Cours-sur-Loire 17 G 10
03430 Cosne-d'Allier 23 H 10
53230 Cossé-le-Vivien 16 G 7
46300 Costeraste 29 K 9
83570 Cotignac 37 L 14
43700 Coubon 30 K 11
07470 Coucouron 30 K 11
02380 Coucy-le-Château 12 E 11
02840 Coucy-lès-Eppes 12 E 11
41700 Couddes 17 G 9
11500 Coudons 35 M 10
18190 Coudron 23 H 10
44220 Couëron 15 G 6
41110 Couffy 17 G 9
09140 Couflens 34 M 9
86700 Couhé 22 H 8
11190 Couiza 35 M 10
89580 Coulanges-la-Vineuse 18 G 11
89480 Coulanges-sur-Yonne 18 G 11
03320 Couleuvre 23 H 10
45720 Coullons 17 G 10
21400 Coulmier-le-Sec 18 G 12
62137 Coulogne 3 D 9
86600 Coulombiers 22 H 8
77120 Coulommiers 12 F 11
89560 Coulon 18 G 11
72800 Coulongé 16 G 8
61110 Coulonges-les-Sablons 11 F 8
79160 Coulonges-sur-l'Autize 21 H 7
53250 Couptrain 10 F 7
41700 Cour-Cheverny 17 G 9
38121 Cour-et Buis 31 J 13
21520 Courban 19 G 12
03370 Courçais 23 H 10
72110 Courcemont 16 F 8
77560 Courchamp 18 F 11
73120 Courchevel 32 J 14
53700 Courcité 10 F 7
17170 Courçon 21 H 7
72260 Courgains 16 F 8
61560 Courgeoût 10 F 8
51310 Courgivaux 18 F 11
63800 Cournon-d'Auvergne 23 J 11
63120 Courpière 24 J 11
47360 Cours 28 K 8
69470 Cours-la-Ville 24 H 12
11110 Coursan 36 L 11
06140 Coursegoules 38 L 14
14470 Courseulles-sur-Mer 10 E 7
89560 Courson-les-Carrières 18 G 11
77560 Courtacon 18 F 11
28290 Courtalain 17 F 9
90100 Courtelevant 20 G 15
45320 Courtenay 18 F 11
61390 Courtomer 10 F 8
28190 Courville-sur-Eure 11 F 9
39190 Cousance 25 H 13
59149 Cousolre 13 D 12
10210 Coussegrey 18 G 12
88630 Coussey 19 F 13
84220 Coustellet 37 L 13
50200 Coutances 9 E 6
33230 Coutras 21 J 7
87270 Couzeix 22 J 9
31480 Cox 29 L 9
17120 Cozes 21 J 7
20148 Cozzano 39 N 17
56950 Crach 8 G 5
53400 Craon 16 G 7
02160 Craonne 12 E 11
43500 Craponne-sur-Arzon 30 J 11
89460 Cravant 18 G 11
50710 Créances 9 E 6
71680 Crèches-sur-Saône 24 H 12
03150 Créchy 24 H 11
80150 Crécy-en-Ponthieu 3 D 9
77580 Crécy-la-Chapelle 12 F 10
02270 Crécy-sur-Serre 12 E 11
60100 Creil 12 E 10
12520 Creissels 30 K 11
38460 Crémieu 25 J 13
33670 Créon 28 K 7
54170 Crépey 19 F 13
02870 Crépy 12 E 11
60800 Crépy-en-Valois 12 E 10
70100 Cresancey 19 G 13
30260 Crespian 30 L 12
03240 Cressanges 23 H 11
39270 Cressia 25 H 13
26400 Crest 31 K 13
94000 Créteil 11 F 10
14480 Creully 10 E 7
57150 Creutzwald 14 E 14
36140 Crevant 23 H 9
60360 Crèvecœur-le-Grand 11 E 10
35320 Crévin 15 G 6
76910 Criel-sur-Mer 3 D 9
60112 Crillon 11 E 9
76280 Criquetot-l'Esneval 10 E 8
20126 Cristinacce 39 M 16
23260 Crocq 23 J 10
61230 Croisilles 4 D 10
76190 Croix-Mare 11 E 8
71140 Cronat 24 H 11
72200 Crosmières 16 G 7
39300 Crotenay 25 H 13
02880 Crouy 12 E 11
23500 Croze 23 J 10
29160 Crozon 7 F 3
07350 Cruas 31 K 12
12340 Cruéjouls 30 K 10
51170 Crugny 12 E 11
04230 Cruis 37 K 13
74350 Cruseilles 25 H 14
11190 Cubières-sur-Cinoble 35 M 10
83390 Cuers 37 L 14
18150 Cuffy 23 H 11
85610 Cugand 15 G 6
31270 Cugnaux 29 L 9
02480 Cugny 12 E 11
02220 Cuiry-Housse 12 E 11
71480 Cuiseaux 25 H 13
71290 Cuisery 24 H 12
18270 Culan 23 H 10
01350 Culoz 25 J 13
10360 Cunfin 18 F 12
63590 Cunlhat 24 J 11
49150 Cuon 16 G 7
81470 Cuq-Toulza 35 L 9
86120 Curçay-sur-Dive 16 G 7
26110 Curnier 31 K 13
37310 Cussay 16 G 8
03300 Cusset 24 H 11
89420 Cussy-les-Forges 18 G 12
74540 Cusy 25 J 14
60400 Cuts 12 E 11
60490 Cuvilly 12 E 10
11390 Cuxac-Cabardès 35 L 10
46600 Cuzance 29 K 9
47500 Cuzorn 29 K 8
71320 Cuzy 24 H 12
59830 Cysoing 4 D 11
57850 Dabo 20 F 15
62000 Dainville 4 D 10
71620 Damerey 25 H 12
51480 Damery 12 E 11
28360 Dammarie 17 F 9
45420 Dammarie-en-Puisaye 17 G 10
77190 Dammarie-les-Lys 17 F 10
77230 Dammartin-en-Goële 12 E 10
39500 Damparis 25 G 13
39700 Dampierre 25 G 13
18310 Dampierre-en-Graçay 17 G 9
76510 Dampierre-Saint Nicolas 11 E 9
17470 Dampierre-sur-Boutonne 21 H 7
70180 Dampierre-sur-Salon 19 G 13
27240 Damville 11 F 9
55150 Damvillers 13 E 13
86220 Dangé-Saint Romain 16 H 8
28160 Dangeau 17 F 9
27720 Dangu 11 E 9
50750 Dangy 10 E 6
90400 Danjoutin 20 G 14
68210 Dannemarie 20 G 15
14770 Danvou-la-Ferrière 10 F 7
41160 Danzé 17 G 9
53200 Daon 16 G 7
52700 Darmannes 19 F 13
76160 Darnétal 11 E 9
88260 Darney 19 F 14
88390 Darnieulles 19 F 14
77140 Darvault 18 F 10
74570 Daudens 25 H 14
09350 Daumazan-sur-Arize 35 L 9
47140 Dausse 29 K 8
40100 Dax 27 L 6
14800 Deauville 10 E 8
12300 Decazeville 29 K 10
59187 Dechy 4 D 11
58300 Decize 24 H 11
57590 Delme 20 F 14
04120 Demandolx 38 L 14
71150 Demigny 24 H 12
32190 Dému 28 L 8
80110 Démuin 12 E 10
59220 Denain 4 D 11
49700 Dénezé-sous-Doué 16 G 7
28700 Denonville 17 F 9
36130 Déols 23 H 9
44590 Derval 15 G 6
37160 Descartes 16 H 8
53190 Désertines 10 F 7
62240 Desvres 3 D 9
25870 Devecey 25 G 14
41220 Dhuizon 17 G 9
54930 Diarville 19 F 14
26150 Die 31 K 13
15300 Dienne 30 J 10
76200 Dieppe 3 E 9
26220 Dieulefit 31 K 13
54380 Dieulouard 19 F 14
82170 Dieupentale 29 L 9
57260 Dieuze 20 F 14
04000 Digne-les-Bains 37 K 14
71160 Digoin 24 H 11
21000 Dijon 19 G 13
22100 Dinan 9 F 5
35800 Dinard 9 F 5
29150 Dinéault 7 F 3
72500 Dissay-sous-Courcillon 16 G 8
14160 Dives-sur-Mer 10 E 7
62460 Divion 4 D 10
01220 Divonne-les-Bains 25 H 14
02340 Dizy-le-Gros 12 E 12
88460 Docelles 20 F 14
35120 Dol-de-Bretagne 9 F 6
39100 Dole 25 G 13
72390 Dollon 16 F 8
17550 Dolus-d'Oléron 21 J 6
80620 Domart-en-Ponthieu 3 D 10
54110 Dombasle-sur-Meurthe 19 F 14
38420 Domène 31 J 13
61700 Domfront 10 F 7
72240 Domfront-en-Champagne 16 F 8
58120 Dommartin 24 G 11
24250 Domme 29 K 9
02600 Dommiers 12 E 11
95330 Domont 11 E 10
88270 Dompaire 19 F 14
35210 Dompierre-du-Chemin 9 F 6
03290 Dompierre-sur-Besbre 24 H 11
87120 Domps 23 J 9
88630 Domrémy-la-Pucelle 19 F 13
80150 Domvast 3 D 9
44480 Donges 15 G 5
77520 Donnemarie-Dontilly 18 F 11
23700 Dontreix 23 J 10
19270 Donzenac 22 J 9
26290 Donzère 31 K 12
58220 Donzy 18 G 11
63220 Doranges 30 J 11
45680 Dordives 18 F 10
51700 Dormans 12 E 11
07160 Dornas 31 K 12
58530 Dornecy 18 G 11
58390 Dornes 24 H 11
01590 Dortan 25 H 13
59500 Douai 4 D 11
29100 Douarnenez 7 F 3
76560 Doudeville 11 E 8
49700 Doué-la-Fontaine 16 G 7
46140 Douelle 29 K 9
52130 Doulevant-le-Château 19 F 12
80600 Doullens 4 D 10
88220 Dounoux 19 F 14
91410 Dourdan 17 F 10
62119 Dourges 4 D 10
74210 Doussard 25 J 14
74140 Douvaine 25 H 14
03170 Doyet 23 H 10
14430 Dozulé 10 E 7
83300 Draguignan 38 L 14
92700 Drancy 11 F 10
28100 Dreux 11 F 9
59630 Drincham 4 D 10
27320 Droisy 11 F 9
41270 Droué 17 F 9
10170 Droupt-Saint Basle 18 F 11
67320 Drulingen 20 F 15
67410 Drusenheim 20 F 15
89560 Druyes-les-Belles-Fontaines 18 G 11
50220 Ducey 9 F 6
76480 Duclair 11 E 8
23800 Dun-le-Palestel 23 H 9
58230 Dun-les-Places 18 G 12
18130 Dun-sur-Auron 23 H 10
56110 Dun-sur-Meuse 13 E 13
43220 Dunières 31 J 12
59140 Dunkerque 4 C 10
47420 Durance 28 K 8
47120 Duras 28 K 8
11360 Durban-Corbières 35 M 10
03310 Durdat-Larequille 23 H 10
49430 Durtal 16 G 7
24270 Dussac 22 J 9
32800 Eauze 28 L 8
02350 Ebouleau 12 E 11
03450 Ébreuil 23 H 11
21510 Échalot 19 G 12
61370 Échauffour 10 F 8
17620 Échillais 21 J 7
79410 Échiré 22 H 7
52290 Eclaron-Braucourt 19 F 12
38300 Eclose 31 J 13
08300 Écly 12 E 12
72220 Écommoy 16 G 8
72120 Écorpain 16 G 8
27630 Écos 11 E 9
61150 Écouché 10 F 7
27440 Écouis 11 E 9
36240 Ecueillé 17 G 9
71350 Ecuelles 25 H 13
55150 Ecurey-en-Verdunois 13 E 13
51240 Écury-sur-Coole 12 F 12
19300 Égletons 23 J 10
77620 Egreville 18 F 10
13510 Éguilles 37 L 13
10110 Éguilly-sous-Bois 18 F 12
36270 Éguzon 23 H 9
54370 Einville-au-Jard 20 F 14
76500 Elbeuf 11 E 9
88510 Eloyes 20 F 14
56250 Elven 8 G 5
27190 Emanville 11 E 8
15270 Embort 23 J 10
05200 Embrun 32 K 14
62990 Embry 3 D 9
58140 Empury 18 G 11
57415 Enchenberg 20 E 15
63720 Ennezat 23 J 11
04320 Enriez 38 L 14
68190 Ensisheim 20 G 15
58410 Entrains-sur-Nohain 18 G 11
12140 Entraygues-sur-Truyère 30 K 10
04320 Entrevaux 38 L 14
66760 Enveitg 35 M 9
76630 Envermeu 11 E 9
21380 Epagny 19 G 13
27260 Epaignes 10 E 8
80740 Epehy 12 D 11
62910 Éperlecques 4 D 10
51200 Épernay 12 E 11
28230 Épernon 11 F 9
25290 Epeugney 25 G 14
67680 Epfig 20 F 15
88000 Épinal 19 F 14
18360 Épineuil-le-Fleuriel 23 H 10
62860 Épinoy 4 D 11
52230 Épizon 19 F 13
21460 Époisses 18 G 12
76400 Épreville 11 E 8
41360 Épuisay 17 G 8
50120 Équeurdreville-Hainneville 9 E 6
39300 Equevillon 25 H 13
80400 Ercheu 12 E 10
56410 Erdeven 8 G 4
29500 Ergué-Gabéric 7 F 3
53500 Ernée 10 F 7
26600 Érôme 31 J 12
22430 Erquy 9 F 5
67150 Erstein 20 F 15
62121 Ervillers 4 D 10
10130 Ervy-le-Châtel 18 F 11
62179 Escalles 3 D 9
89240 Escamps 18 G 11
64120 Escos 27 L 7
64490 Escot 33 L 7
40210 Escource 27 K 6
06460 Escragnolles 38 L 14
12500 Espalion 30 K 10
83560 Esparron 37 L 13
64250 Espelette 27 L 6
26780 Espeluche 31 K 12
11260 Espéraza 35 M 10
65710 Espiadet 34 M 8
05190 Espinasses 32 K 14
43170 Esplantas 30 K 11
70110 Esprels 19 G 14
80160 Essertaux 11 E 10
10360 Essoyes 18 F 12
60510 Essuiles 11 E 10
43350 Estables 30 J 11
66310 Estagel 35 M 10
12190 Estaing 30 K 10
59940 Estaires 4 D 10
32240 Estang 28 L 7
06470 Estenc 32 K 14
51310 Esternay 18 F 11
40290 Estibeaux 27 L 7
40240 Estigarde 28 K 7
10190 Estissac 18 F 11
03190 Estivareilles 23 H 10
04270 Estoublon 37 L 14
62170 Estrée 3 D 9
02420 Estrées 12 E 11
60190 Estrées-Saint Denis 12 E 10
22680 Étables-sur-Mer 9 F 5
55400 Étain 13 E 13
21500 Étais 18 G 12
91150 Étampes 17 F 10
62630 Étaples 3 D 9
21270 Etevaux 19 G 13
89510 Etigny 18 F 11
51270 Etoges 12 F 11
02580 Etréaupont 12 E 11
36120 Étrechet 23 H 9
91580 Étrechy 17 F 10
27150 Étrépagny 11 E 9
14420 Étretat 10 E 8
02510 Etreux 12 E 11
16250 Etriac 22 J 7
90170 Etueffont 20 G 14
70150 Etuz 19 G 13
76260 Eu 3 D 9
40320 Eugénie-les-Bains 28 L 7
52410 Eurville-Bienville 19 F 13
23110 Évaux-les-Bains 23 H 10
74500 Évian-les-Bains 25 H 14
20126 Evisa 39 M 16
22630 Évran 9 F 6
27000 Évreux 11 E 9
38110 Evrieu 31 J 13
56490 Évriguet 9 F 5
53600 Évron 16 F 7
91000 Évry 11 F 10
24160 Excideuil 22 J 9
61310 Exmes 10 F 8
05300 Eyguians 31 K 13
13430 Eyguières 37 L 13
24500 Eymet 28 K 8
87120 Eymoutiers 23 J 9
33390 Eyrans 21 J 7
27530 Ézy-sur-Eure 11 F 9
09230 Fabas 34 L 9
34690 Fabrègues 36 L 11
11200 Fabrezan 35 L 10
21500 Fain-lès-Montbard 18 G 12
14700 Falaise 10 F 7
57290 Fameck 13 E 14
47700 Fargues-sur-Ourbise 28 K 8
70310 Faucogney-et-la-Mer 19 G 14
34600 Faugères 36 L 11
57380 Faulquemont 14 E 14
62560 Fauquembergues 4 D 10
82190 Fauroux 29 K 9
21110 Fauverney 19 G 13
23340 Faux-la-Montagne 23 J 9
18360 Faverdines 23 H 10
74210 Faverges 25 J 14
70160 Faverney 19 G 14
20135 Favone 39 N 17
45450 Fay-aux-Loges 17 G 10
44130 Fay-de-Bretagne 15 G 6
43430 Fay-sur-Lignon 30 K 12
83440 Fayence 38 L 14
12360 Fayet 30 L 10
52500 Fayl-Billot 19 G 13
76400 Fécamp 11 E 8
59750 Feignies 4 D 11
35440 Feins 9 F 6
20225 Feliceto 39 M 16
23500 Felletin 23 J 10
11400 Fendeille 35 L 9
57930 Fénétrange 20 F 15
23100 Féniers 23 J 10
51230 Fère-Champenoise 18 F 11
02130 Fère-en-Tardenois 12 E 11
01210 Ferney-Voltaire 25 H 14
62250 Ferques 3 D 9
68480 Ferrette 20 G 15
10400 Ferreux-Quincey 18 F 11
59680 Ferrière-la-Grande 12 D 12
37350 Ferrière-Larçon 16 H 8
45210 Ferrières 18 F 10

47

INDEX WITH POST CODES · ORTSREGISTER MIT POSTLEITZAHLEN · INDICE CON CODICI POSTAIS · STEDREGISTER MED POSTNUMRE · PLAATSNAMENREGISTER MET POSTCODE ·

F

Ferrières-Saint Mary   F   **la Graverie**

POSTALI · ÍNDICE CON CÓDIGOS POSTALES · INDICE DE LUGARES COM CÓDIGOS
REJSTŘÍK MÍST S PSČ · ZOZNAM OBCÍ S PSČ · INDEKS MIEJSCOWOŚCI Z KOD POCZTOWY

48

la Guerche-de-Bretagne   (F)   **Loué**   **F**

47290 Lougratte 28 K 8
71500 Louhans 25 H 13
17330 Loulay 21 H 7
11300 Loupia 35 L 10
65100 Lourdes 34 L 7
36140 Lourdoueix-Saint Michel 23 H 9
45470 Loury 17 G 10
27190 Louversey 11 F 8
27400 Louviers 11 E 9
35420 Louvigné-du-Désert 10 F 6
51150 Louvois 12 E 12
95380 Louvres 12 E 10
52220 Louze 19 F 12
01360 Loyettes 25 J 13
20226 Lozari 39 M 17
19210 Lubersac 22 J 9
88490 Lubine 20 F 15
12450 Luc 29 K 10
26310 Luc-en-Diois 31 K 13
36360 Luçay-le-Mâle 17 G 9
28110 Luce 17 F 9
06440 Lucéram 38 L 15
73170 Lucey 25 J 13
80600 Lucheux 4 D 10
60260 Luchy 11 E 10
85400 Luçon 15 H 6
40210 Lüe 27 K 7
71260 Lugny/Cluny 24 H 12
02140 Lugny/Marle 12 E 11
71120 Lugny-lès-Charolles 24 H 12
33830 Lugos 28 K 7
28480 Luigny 17 F 9
62380 Lumbres 4 D 10
20260 Lumio 39 M 16
34650 Lunas 36 L 11
34400 Lunel 36 L 12
18400 Lunery 17 H 10
54300 Lunéville 20 F 14
32290 Lupiac 28 L 8
16140 Lupsault 22 J 7
03320 Lurcy-Lévis 23 H 10
70200 Lure 19 G 14
36220 Lureuil 22 H 9
20228 Luri 39 M 17
18120 Lury-sur-Arnon 17 G 10
86600 Lusignan 22 H 8
10270 Lusigny-sur-Barse 18 F 12
33570 Lussac/Libourne 21 K 7
86320 Lussac-les-Châteaux 22 H 8
87360 Lussac-les-Eglises 22 H 9
30580 Lussan 30 K 12
57820 Lutzelbourg 20 F 15
70300 Luxeuil-les-Bains 19 G 14
40430 Luxey 28 K 7
65120 Luz-Saint Sauveur 34 M 7
95270 Luzarches 11 E 10
79100 Luzay 16 H 7
36800 Luzeret 23 H 9
58170 Luzy 24 H 11
69000 Lyon 24 J 12
27480 Lyons-la-Forêt 11 E 9
42300 Mably 24 H 12
33460 Macau 21 J 7
08310 Machault 13 E 12
44270 Machecoul 15 H 6
80150 Machy 3 D 9
20248 Macinaggio 39 M 17
42520 Maclas 31 J 12
21320 Mâcon 24 H 12
34520 Madières 30 L 11
19470 Madranges 23 J 9
24200 Madrazès 29 K 9
22340 Maël-Carhaix 8 F 4
22160 Maël-Pestivien 8 F 4
40140 Magescq 27 L 6
74300 Magland 25 H 14
87190 Magnac-Laval 22 H 9
10110 Magnant 18 F 12
79460 Magné 22 H 8
03260 Magnet 24 H 11
52130 Magneux 19 F 13
54129 Magnières 20 F 14
58470 Magny-Cours 24 H 11
95420 Magny-en-Vexin 11 E 9
10140 Magny-Fouchard 18 F 12
25120 Maîche 26 G 14
72210 Maigné 16 G 7
87160 Mailhac-sur-Benaize 22 H 9
28170 Maillebois 11 F 9
70000 Mailley-et-Chazelot 19 G 14
85420 Maillezais 21 H 7
10230 Mailly-le-Camp 18 F 12
08220 Mainbressy 12 E 12
28130 Maintenon 11 F 9
28300 Mainvilliers 17 F 9
79190 Mairé-Levescault 22 H 8
21400 Maisey-le-Duc 18 G 12
77370 Maison-Rouge 18 F 11
52240 Maisoncelles 19 F 13
10200 Maisons-lès-Soulaines 19 F 12
57280 Maizières-lès-Metz 13 E 14
56220 Malansac 15 G 5
43200 Malataverne 30 J 12
84340 Malaucène 31 K 13
89100 Malay-le-Petit 18 F 11
48270 Malbouzon 30 K 11
25160 Malbuisson 25 H 14
19360 Malemort-sur-Corrèze 29 J 9
45330 Malesherbes 17 F 10
56140 Malestroit 8 G 5
72270 Malicorne-sur-Sarthe 16 G 7
13370 Mallemort 37 L 13
71140 Maltat 24 H 11
44260 Malville 15 G 6
72600 Mamers 10 F 8
24620 Manaurie 29 K 8
45300 Manchecourt 17 F 10
32370 Manciet 28 L 8
06210 Mandelieu-la-Napoule 38 L 14
55290 Mandres-en-Barrois 19 F 13
52800 Mandres-la-Côte 19 F 13
30129 Manduel 36 L 12
04300 Mane 37 L 13
55160 Manheulles 13 E 13
02300 Manicamp 12 E 11
62650 Maninghem 3 D 9
40410 Mano 28 K 7
04100 Manosque 37 L 13
78200 Mantes-la-Jolie 11 E 9
78200 Mantes-la-Ville 11 F 9
37240 Manthelan 16 G 8
63410 Manzat 23 J 10
52260 Marac 19 G 13
17230 Marans 21 H 7
52370 Maranville 19 F 12
28200 Marboué 17 F 9
19150 Marc-la-Tour 29 J 9
49140 Marcé 16 G 7
15190 Marcenat 30 J 10
48260 Marchastel 30 K 11
25640 Marchaux 25 G 14
41370 Marchenoir 17 G 9
33380 Marcheprime 28 K 7
59870 Marchiennes 4 D 11
32230 Marciac 28 L 8
71110 Marcigny 24 H 12
19320 Marcillac-la-Croisille 23 J 10
12330 Marcillac-Vallon 29 K 10
03420 Marcillat-en-Combraille 23 H 10
38260 Marcilloles 31 J 13
41210 Marcilly-en-Gault 17 G 9
45240 Marcilly-en-Villette 17 G 10
42130 Marcilly-le-Chatel 24 J 12
10290 Marcilly-le-Hayer 18 F 11
37330 Marcilly-sur-Maulne 16 G 8
62730 Marck 4 D 9
67390 Marckolsheim 20 F 15
72340 Marçon 16 G 8
17320 Marennes 21 J 6
18290 Mareuil-sur-Arnon 23 H 10
85320 Mareuil-sur-Lay 15 H 6
60890 Mareuil-sur-Ourcq 12 E 11
19200 Margerides 23 J 10
51290 Margerie-Hancourt 18 F 12
26260 Margès 31 J 13
30320 Marguerittes 36 L 12
33220 Margueron 28 K 8
08370 Margut 13 E 13
80560 Marieux 4 D 10
13700 Marignane 37 L 13
72220 Marigné-Laillé 16 G 8
51230 Marigny 18 F 11
10350 Marigny-le-Châtel 18 F 11
20230 Marine-de-Bravone 39 M 17
20228 Marine-de-Giottani 39 M 17
20287 Marine-de-Meria 39 M 17
20233 Marine-de-Pietracorbara 39 M 17
20233 Marine-de-Sisco 39 M 17
95640 Marines 11 E 9
63350 Maringues 23 J 11
02250 Marle 12 E 11
67520 Marlenheim 20 F 15
57155 Marly 13 E 14
02120 Marly-Gomont 12 E 11
71710 Marmagne 24 H 12
47200 Marmande 28 K 8
67440 Marmoutier 20 F 15
81170 Marnaves 29 K 9
70150 Marnay 25 G 13
59550 Maroilles 12 D 11
72260 Marolles-les-Braults 16 F 8
76150 Maromme 11 E 9
11410 Marquein 35 L 9
62860 Marquion 4 D 11
62250 Marquise 3 D 9
12200 Marroule 29 K 9
07320 Mars 31 J 12
54800 Mars-la-Tour 13 E 13
23210 Marsac/Guéret 23 H 9
82120 Marsac/Lectoure 28 L 8
63940 Marsac-en-Livradois 24 J 11
17700 Marsais 21 H 7
34340 Marseillan 36 L 11
34340 Marseillan-Plage 36 L 11
13001 Marseille 37 L 13
60690 Marseille-en-Beauvaisis 11 E 9
51240 Marson 13 F 12
01340 Marsonnas 24 H 13
81150 Marssac-sur-Tarn 29 L 10
47250 Martaillac 28 K 8
86330 Martaizé 16 H 8
46600 Martel 29 K 9
12200 Martiel 29 K 9
35640 Martigné-Ferchaud 15 G 6
53470 Martigné-sur-Mayenne 10 F 7
71220 Martigny-le-Comte 24 H 12
88320 Martigny-les-Bains 19 F 13
88300 Martigny-les-Gerbonvaux 19 F 13
13500 Martigues 37 L 13
36220 Martizay 16 H 9
14740 Martragny 10 E 7
31220 Martres-Tolosane 34 L 9
17270 Martron 21 J 7
48100 Marvejols 30 K 11
13200 Mas Thibert 37 L 12
68290 Masevaux 20 G 15
87130 Masléon 22 J 9
59241 Masnières 12 D 11
11330 Massac 35 M 10
09320 Massat 35 M 9
32140 Masseube 28 L 8
15500 Massiac 30 J 11
71250 Massilly 24 H 12
17160 Matha 21 J 7
22550 Matignon 9 F 5
80400 Matigny 12 E 11
71520 Matour 24 H 12
59600 Maubeuge 4 D 11
65700 Maubourguet 28 L 8
76680 Maucomble 11 E 9
55400 Maucourt-sur-Orne 13 E 13
34130 Mauguio 36 L 12
55500 Maulan 19 F 13
79700 Mauléon 15 H 7
65370 Mauléon-Barousse 34 M 8
64130 Mauléon-Licharre 27 L 7
49360 Maulévrier 15 G 7
44540 Maumusson 15 G 6
13130 Mauran 37 L 13
35330 Maure-de-Bretagne 15 G 6
15200 Mauriac 29 J 10
56430 Mauron 9 F 5
15600 Maurs 29 K 10
66460 Maury 35 M 10
13520 Maussane-les-Alpilles 37 L 12
32120 Mauvezin 28 L 8
31560 Mauzac 35 L 9
79210 Mauzé-sur-le-Mignon 21 H 7
24260 Mauzens-et-Miremont 29 K 8
35380 Maxent 9 G 5
53100 Mayenne 10 F 7
72360 Mayet 16 G 8
12390 Mayran 29 K 10
07330 Mayres 30 K 12
81200 Mazamet 35 L 10
84380 Mazan 31 K 13
49630 Mazé 16 G 7
09270 Mazères 35 L 9
79310 Mazières-en-Gâtine 22 H 7
03360 Meaulne 23 H 10
77100 Meaux 12 F 10
74120 Megève 25 J 14
74490 Mégevette 25 H 14
18500 Mehun-sur-Yèvre 17 G 10
40400 Meilhan 28 L 7
74500 Meillerie 25 H 14
03210 Meillers 23 H 11
35520 Melesse 9 F 6
29140 Melgven 8 G 4
70270 Mélisey 19 G 14
79190 Melle 22 H 7
77000 Melun 18 F 10
12200 Memer 29 K 9
63560 Menat 23 H 10
48000 Mende 30 K 11
45240 Ménestreau-en-Villette 17 G 10
79340 Ménigoute 22 H 7
54200 Ménil-la-Tour 19 F 13
41320 Mennetou-sur-Cher 17 G 9
58210 Menou 18 G 11
38710 Mens 31 K 13
06500 Menton 38 L 15
36500 Méobecq 23 H 9
83136 Méounes-lès-Montrieux 37 L 13
41500 Mer 17 G 9
53230 Méral 16 G 7
46090 Mercuès 29 K 9
19430 Mercœur 29 J 9
22230 Merdrignac 9 F 5
18120 Méreau 17 G 10
09110 Mérens-les-Vals 35 M 9
91660 Méréville 17 F 10
33700 Mérignac 28 K 7
09230 Mérigon 34 L 9
62155 Merlimont 3 D 9
19340 Merlines 23 J 10
80350 Mers-les-Bains 3 D 9
67580 Mertzwiller 20 F 15
60110 Méru 11 E 10
71310 Mervans 25 H 13
09600 Merviel 35 L 9
59660 Merville 4 D 10
18100 Méry-sur-Cher 17 G 9
10170 Méry-sur-Seine 18 F 11
44522 Mésanger 15 G 6
24240 Mescoules 28 K 8
56320 Meslan 8 G 4
14220 Meslay 10 F 7
53170 Meslay-du-Maine 16 G 7
76270 Mesnières-en-Bray 11 E 9
91150 Mespuits 17 F 10
35480 Messac 15 G 6
61440 Messei 10 F 7
71190 Mesvres 24 H 12
25370 Métabief 25 H 14
57000 Metz 13 E 14
57940 Metzervisse 13 E 14
14290 Meulles 10 F 8
36100 Meunet-Planches 23 H 9
45130 Meung-sur-Loire 17 G 9
72170 Meurcé 16 F 8
52140 Meuse 19 G 13
39260 Meussia 25 H 13
17500 Meux 21 J 7
87380 Meuzac 22 J 9
26560 Mévouillon 31 K 13
01800 Meximieux 25 J 13
19250 Meymac 23 J 10
19250 Meymac 23 J 10
04530 Meyronnes 32 K 14
48150 Meyrueis 30 K 11
19500 Meyssac 29 J 9
69330 Meyzieu 24 J 12
34140 Mèze 36 L 11
14270 Mézidon-Canon 10 E 7
36290 Mézières-en-Brenne 16 H 9
87330 Mézières-sur-Issoire 22 H 8
07530 Mézilhac 31 K 12
89130 Mézilles 18 G 11
47170 Mézin 28 K 8
40170 Mézos 27 K 6
32170 Miélan 28 L 8
64800 Mifaget 34 L 7
89400 Migennes 18 G 11
36800 Migné 23 H 9
01170 Mijoux 25 H 13
30540 Milhaud 36 L 12
29290 Milizac 7 F 3
41200 Millançay 17 G 9
66170 Millas 35 M 10
12100 Millau 30 K 11
19290 Millevaches 23 J 10
91490 Milly-la-Forêt 17 F 10
40200 Mimizan 27 K 6
40200 Mimizan-Plage 27 K 6
35540 Miniac-Morvan 9 F 6
20200 Miomo 39 M 17
69780 Mions 24 J 12
33380 Mios 28 K 7
26110 Mirabel-aux-Baronnies 31 K 13
32340 Miradoux 28 L 8
06590 Miramar 38 L 14
13140 Miramas 37 L 13
17150 Mirambeau 21 J 7
47800 Miramont-de-Guyenne 28 K 8
32300 Mirande 28 L 8
81190 Mirandol-Bourgnounac 29 K 10
86110 Mirebeau 16 H 8
21310 Mirebeau-sur-Bèze 19 G 13
39570 Mirebel 25 H 13
88500 Mirecourt 19 F 14
09500 Mirepoix 35 L 9
21210 Missery 18 G 12
44780 Missillac 15 G 5
77290 Mitry-Mory 12 F 10
38142 Mizoën 32 J 14
73500 Modane 32 J 14
29350 Moëlan-sur-Mer 8 G 4
56490 Mohon 9 F 5
28700 Moinville-la-Jeulin 17 F 9
38430 Moirans 31 J 13
39260 Moirans-en-Montagne 25 H 13
58490 Moiry 24 H 11
44520 Moisdon-la-Rivière 15 G 6
82200 Moissac 29 K 9
39290 Moissey 25 G 13
77550 Moissy-Cramayel 11 F 10
41160 Moisy 17 G 9
20270 Moita 39 M 17
56230 Molac 8 G 5
82220 Molières 29 K 9
30410 Molières-sur-Cèze 30 K 12
41190 Molineuf 17 G 9
66500 Molitg-les-Bains 35 M 10
80540 Molliens-Dreuil 11 E 10
21120 Moloy 19 G 12
67120 Molsheim 20 F 15
40700 Momuy 28 L 7
64160 Monassut- Audiracq 28 L 7
32420 Monbardon 34 L 8
24240 Monbazillac 28 K 8
72230 Moncé-en-Belin 16 G 8
25870 Moncey 19 G 14
47380 Monclar 28 K 8
82230 Monclar-de-Quercy 29 L 9
22510 Moncontour/Saint Brieuc 9 F 5
86330 Moncontour/Thouars 16 H 8
79320 Moncoutant 15 H 7
35370 Mondevert 15 F 6
14120 Mondeville 10 E 7
41170 Mondoubleau 16 G 8
84430 Mondragon 31 K 12
64360 Monein 28 L 7
38650 Monestier-de-Clermont 31 K 13
81640 Monestiés 29 K 10
05110 Monêtier-Allemont 31 K 13
32490 Monferran-Savès 28 L 8
47150 Monflanquin 28 K 8
32120 Monfort 28 L 8
43120 Monistrol-sur-Loire 30 J 12
65670 Monlong 34 L 8
61470 Monnai 10 F 8
37380 Monnaie 16 G 8
60240 Monneville 11 E 9
24540 Monpazier 29 K 8
33580 Monségur 28 K 8
47500 Monsempron 29 K 8
69860 Monsols 24 H 12
40000 Mont-de-Marsan 28 L 7
66210 Mont-Louis 35 M 10
76130 Mont-Saint Aignan 11 E 9
21320 Mont-Saint Jean 18 G 12
54350 Mont-Saint Martin 13 E 13
39380 Mont-sous-Vaudrey 25 H 13
89150 Montacher-Villegardin 18 F 11
34530 Montagnac 36 L 11
85600 Montaigu 15 H 6
63700 Montaigut 23 H 10
63320 Montaigut-le-Blanc 23 J 11
31530 Montaigut-sur-Save 29 L 9
28150 Montainville 17 F 9
38390 Montalieu-Vercieu 25 J 13
33930 Montalivet-les-Bains 21 J 6
82270 Montalzat 29 K 9
64460 Montaner 28 L 7
45200 Montargis 17 G 10
60160 Montataire 11 E 10
82000 Montauban 29 K 9
35360 Montauban-de-Bretagne 9 F 5
53220 Montaudin 10 F 7
27400 Montaure 11 E 9
09700 Montaut 35 L 9
47500 Montayral 29 K 8
47290 Montbahus 28 K 8
21500 Montbard 18 G 12
12220 Montbazens 29 K 10
37250 Montbazon 16 G 8
48170 Montbel 30 K 11
25200 Montbéliard 20 G 14
70230 Montbozon 19 G 14
42600 Montbrison 24 J 12
48210 Montbrun 30 K 11
26570 Montbrun-les-Bains 31 K 13
71300 Montceau-les-Mines 24 H 12
77151 Montceaux-lès-Provins 18 F 11
71710 Montcenis 24 H 12
71210 Montchanin 24 H 12
08250 Montcheutin 13 E 12
36140 Montchevrier 23 H 9
46250 Montcléra 29 K 9
30630 Montclus 30 K 12
02340 Montcornet 12 E 12
46800 Montcuq 29 K 9
30120 Montdardier 30 L 11
80500 Montdidier 12 E 10
50310 Montebourg 10 E 6
82700 Montech 29 L 9
32550 Montégut 28 L 8
63380 Montel-de-Gelat 23 J 10
26120 Montélier 31 K 13
26200 Montélimar 31 K 12
17130 Montendre 21 J 7
45260 Montereau 17 G 10
77130 Montereau-Fault-Yonne 18 F 10
56800 Monterrein 15 G 5
82200 Montesquieu 29 K 9
31310 Montesquieu-Volvestre 35 L 9
32320 Montesquiou 28 L 8
84170 Monteux 31 K 12
49230 Montfaucon/Cholet 15 G 6
46240 Montfaucon/Labastide-Murat 29 K 9
55270 Montfaucon-d'Argonne 13 E 13
43290 Montfaucon-en-Velay 31 J 12
38620 Montferrat/Chambéry 31 J 13
83131 Montferrat/Draguignan 38 L 14
39320 Montfleur 25 H 13
64190 Montfort 27 L 7
40380 Montfort-en-Chalosse 27 L 7
78490 Montfort-l'Amaury 11 F 9
72450 Montfort-le-Gesnois 16 F 8
35160 Montfort-sur-Meu 9 F 6
27290 Montfort-sur-Risle 11 E 8
12380 Montfranc 29 L 10
30490 Montfrin 37 L 12
65200 Montgaillard 34 L 8
35760 Montgermont 9 F 6
31450 Montgiscard 35 L 9
17270 Montguyon 21 J 7
08800 Monthermé 13 E 12
08400 Monthois 13 E 12
88410 Monthureux-sur-Saône 19 F 13
52220 Montier-en-Der 19 F 12
24290 Montignac 29 J 9
18250 Montigny/Bourges 17 G 10
54540 Montigny/Lunéville 20 F 14
78180 Montigny-le-Bretonneux 11 F 10
52140 Montigny-le-Roi 19 F 13
21520 Montigny-sur-Aube 19 G 12
49310 Montilliers 16 G 7
76290 Montivilliers 10 E 8
12490 Montjaux 30 K 10
26220 Montjoux 31 K 13
12400 Montlaur/Camarès 30 L 10
11220 Montlaur/Carcassonne 35 L 10
17210 Montlieu-la-Garde 21 J 7
03100 Montluçon 23 H 10
01120 Montluel 24 J 13
55600 Montmédy 13 E 13
73800 Montmélian 32 J 14
83670 Montmeyan 37 L 14
26120 Montmeyran 31 K 12
51210 Montmirail/Coulommiers 12 F 11
72320 Montmirail/la Ferté-Bernard 16 F 8
39290 Montmirey-le-Château 25 G 13
86500 Montmorillon 22 H 8
39570 Montmorot 25 H 13
51270 Montmort-Lucy 12 F 11
66720 Montner 35 M 10
41800 Montoire-sur-le-Loir 16 G 8
11170 Montolieu 35 L 10
64470 Montory 33 L 7
12540 Montpaon 30 L 11
34000 Montpellier 36 L 11
32220 Montpézat 34 L 8
82270 Montpezat-de-Quercy 29 K 9
50210 Montpinchon 10 E 6
11360 Montplaisir 35 L 10
71470 Montpont-en-Bresse 25 H 13
11290 Montréal/Carcassonne 35 L 10
32250 Montréal/Condom 28 L 8
81360 Montredon-Labessonnié 29 L 10
31210 Montréjeau 34 L 8
71440 Montret 25 H 13
62170 Montreuil 3 D 9
02310 Montreuil-aux-Lions 12 E 11
49260 Montreuil-Bellay 16 G 7
49460 Montreuil-Juigné 16 G 7
49110 Montrevault 15 G 6
01340 Montrevel-en-Bresse 25 H 13
41400 Montrichard 17 G 9
82800 Montricoux 29 K 9
39300 Montrond/Poligny 25 H 13
05700 Montrond/Serres 31 K 13
42210 Montrond-les-Bains 24 J 12
86420 Monts-sur-Guesnes 16 H 8
15120 Montsalvy 29 K 10
58230 Montsauche-les-Settons 18 G 12
32160 Montsaunès 34 L 8
09300 Montségur 35 M 9
95560 Montsoult 11 E 10
53150 Montsûrs 16 F 7
50200 Montsurvent 9 E 6
46600 Montvalent 29 K 9
15150 Montvert/Aurillac 29 K 10
43260 Montvert/le Puy-en-Velay 30 J 12
51130 Morains 12 F 11
59190 Morbecque 4 D 10
39400 Morbier 25 H 14
40110 Morcenx 27 K 7
35310 Mordelles 9 F 6
56500 Moréac 9 G 5
38510 Morestel 25 J 13
77250 Moret-sur-Loing 18 F 10
80110 Moreuil 12 E 10
39400 Morez 25 H 14
57340 Morhange 20 F 14
20230 Moriani-Plage 39 M 17
88330 Moriville 19 F 14
64160 Morlaàs 28 L 7
29600 Morlaix 8 F 4
64370 Morlanne 28 L 7
77720 Mormant 18 F 10
45700 Mormant-sur-Vernisson 17 G 10
84570 Mormoiron 31 K 13
69440 Mornant 24 J 12
84550 Mornas 31 K 12
18350 Mornay-Berry 17 G 10
71390 Moroges 24 H 12
20218 Morosaglia 39 M 17
20238 Morsiglia 39 M 17
61400 Mortagne-au-Perche 10 F 8
85290 Mortagne-sur-Sèvre 15 H 7
50140 Mortain 10 F 7
25500 Morteau 25 G 14
14620 Morteaux-Coulib+uf 10 F 7
87330 Mortemart 22 H 8
61570 Mortrée 10 F 8
28170 Morvillette 11 F 9
74110 Morzine 25 H 14
66500 Mosset 35 M 10
76970 Motteville 11 E 8
06370 Mouans-Sartoux 38 L 14
85640 Mouchamps 15 H 6
32330 Mouchan 28 L 8
39330 Mouchard 25 H 13
06250 Mougins 38 L 14
79370 Mougon 22 H 7
64990 Mouguerre 27 L 6
36170 Mouhet 23 H 9
85390 Mouilleron-en-Pareds 15 H 7
53100 Moulay 10 F 7
24520 Mouleydier 28 K 8
81320 Moulin-Mage 36 L 10
06380 Moulinet 38 L 15
03000 Moulins 24 H 11
58290 Moulins-Engilbert 24 H 11
61380 Moulins-la-Marche 10 F 8
86500 Moulismes 22 H 8
09220 Mounicou 35 M 9
33410 Mourens 28 K 7
64150 Mourenx 27 L 7
51400 Mourmelon-le-Grand 12 E 12
77120 Mouroux 12 F 11
30190 Moussac 30 L 12
10800 Moussey 18 F 12
58700 Moussy 18 G 11
40410 Moustey 28 K 7

04360 Moustiers-Sainte Marie 37 L 14
25240 Mouthe 25 H 14
11330 Mouthoumet 35 M 10
73600 Moûtiers 32 J 14
61110 Moutiers-au-Perche 11 F 8
85540 Moutiers-les-Mauxfaits 15 H 6
79150 Moutiers-sous-Argenton 16 H 7
58230 Moux-en-Morvan 18 G 12
60250 Mouy 11 E 10
55700 Mouzay 13 E 13
08210 Mouzon 13 E 13
02610 Moy-de-l'Aisne 12 E 11
62121 Moyenneville 3 D 9
57630 Moyenvic 20 F 14
35290 Muel 9 F 5
40250 Mugron 27 L 7
51140 Muizon 12 E 11
68100 Mulhouse 20 G 15
72230 Mulsanne 16 G 8
67450 Mundolsheim 20 F 15
68140 Munster 20 F 15
12600 Mur-de-Barrez 30 K 10
22530 Mûr-de-Bretagne 9 F 5
41230 Mur-de-Sologne 17 G 9
15300 Murat 30 J 10
81320 Murat-sur-Vèbre 36 L 10
31600 Muret 35 L 9
17430 Muron 21 H 7
84220 Murs/Cavaillon 37 L 13
36700 Murs/Châtillon-sur-Indre 16 H 9
34490 Murviel-lès-Béziers 36 L 11
52300 Mussey-sur-Marne 19 F 13
10250 Mussy-sur-Seine 18 G 12
67190 Mutzig 20 F 15
56190 Muzillac 8 G 5
62142 Nabringhen 3 D 9
27190 Nagel-Séez-Mesnil 11 F 8
31560 Nailloux 35 L 9
85370 Nalliers/Fontenay-le-Comte 15 H 6
86310 Nalliers/Poitiers 22 H 8
09300 Nalzen 35 M 9
60400 Nampcel 12 E 11
18330 Nançay 17 G 10
17600 Nancras 21 J 7
54000 Nancy 19 F 14
77370 Nangis 18 F 11
58350 Nannay 18 G 11
83860 Nans-les-Pins 37 L 13
12230 Nant 30 K 11
92000 Nanterre 11 F 10
44000 Nantes 15 G 6
16700 Nanteuil-en-Vallée 22 H 8
51480 Nanteuil-la-Forêt 12 E 11
60440 Nanteuil-le-Haudouin 12 E 10
87140 Nantiat 22 H 9
01130 Nantua 25 H 13
11100 Narbonne 36 L 10
11100 Narbonne-Plage 36 L 11
58400 Narcy 18 G 11
40180 Narrosse 27 L 6
48260 Nasbinals 30 K 11
12800 Naucelle 29 K 10
12330 Nauviale 29 K 10
64190 Navarrenx 27 L 7
19460 Naves 23 J 9
71270 Navilly 25 H 13
64800 Nay 34 L 7
37530 Nazelles-Négron 16 G 8
53150 Neau 16 F 7
63210 Nébouzat 23 J 10
61160 Nécy 10 F 7
87120 Nedde 23 J 9
34320 Neffiès 36 L 11
77140 Nemours 17 F 10
47600 Nérac 28 K 8
17510 Néré 22 J 7
86150 Nérignac 22 H 8
03310 Néris-les-Bains 23 H 10
42510 Néronde 24 J 12
18350 Nérondes 17 H 10
30360 Ners 30 K 12
80190 Nesle 12 E 10
02130 Nesles 12 E 11
19600 Nespouls 29 J 9
55800 Nettancourt 19 F 12
68600 Neuf-Brisach 20 F 15
76220 Neuf-Marché 11 E 9
88300 Neufchâteau 19 F 13
76270 Neufchâtel-en-Bray 11 E 9
72600 Neufchâtel-en-Saosnois 10 F 8
62152 Neufchâtel-Hardelot 3 D 9
02190 Neufchâtel-sur-Aisne 12 E 12
36500 Neuillay-les-Bois 23 H 9
37360 Neuillé-Pont-Pierre 16 G 8
03130 Neuilly-en-Donjon 24 H 11
60530 Neuilly-en-Thelle 11 E 10
52360 Neuilly-l'Évêque 19 G 13
02470 Neuilly-Saint Front 12 E 11
52000 Neuilly-sur-Suize 19 F 13
41210 Neung-sur-Beuvron 17 G 9
03320 Neure 23 H 10
70160 Neurey-en-Vaux 19 G 14
15260 Neuvéglise 30 K 10
54230 Neuves-Maisons 19 F 14
19160 Neuvic/Ussel 23 J 10
87130 Neuvic-Entier 23 J 9
45170 Neuville-aux-Bois 17 F 10
86170 Neuville-de-Poitou 16 H 8
01400 Neuville-les-Dames 24 H 13
08090 Neuville-lès-This 13 E 12
62580 Neuville-Saint Vaast 4 D 10
69250 Neuville-sur-Saône 24 J 12
61120 Neuville-sur-Touques 10 F 8
55120 Neuvilly-en-Argonne 13 E 13
41250 Neuvy 17 G 9
45510 Neuvy-en-Sullias 17 G 10
71130 Neuvy-Grandchamp 24 H 11
37370 Neuvy-le-Roi 16 G 8
36100 Neuvy-Pailloux 17 H 9
36230 Neuvy-Saint Sépulchre 23 H 9
89570 Neuvy-Sautour 18 F 11
18330 Neuvy-sur-Barangeon 17 G 10
05100 Névache 32 J 14
58000 Nevers 24 H 11
87800 Nexon 22 J 9
06000 Nice 38 L 15
67110 Niederbronn-les-Bains 20 F 15
67280 Niederhaslach 20 F 15
87510 Nieul 22 J 9
17137 Nieul-sur-Mer 21 H 6
59143 Nieurlet 4 D 10
30000 Nîmes 36 L 12
79000 Niort 21 H 7
11140 Niort-de-Sault 35 M 10
34440 Nissan-lez-Enserune 36 L 11
56130 Nivillac 8 G 5
02150 Nizy-le-Comte 12 E 12
19500 Noailhac/Brive-la-Gaillarde 29 J 9
81490 Noailhac/Castres 35 L 10
60430 Noailles 11 E 10
61340 Nocé 10 F 8
20242 Noceta 39 M 17
32110 Nogaro 28 L 7
52800 Nogent 19 F 13
28210 Nogent-le-Roi 11 F 9
28400 Nogent-le-Rotrou 17 F 8
60180 Nogent-sur-Oise 12 E 10
10400 Nogent-sur-Seine 18 F 11
45290 Nogent-sur-Vernisson 17 G 10
39570 Nogna 25 H 13
36400 Nohant-Vic 23 H 9
82370 Nohic 29 L 9
25190 Noirefontaine 26 G 14
42440 Noiretable 24 J 11
85330 Noirmoutier-en-l'Île 15 H 5
79300 Noirterre 16 H 7
21340 Nolay 24 H 12
76780 Nolléval 11 E 9
54610 Nomeny 19 F 14
88440 Nomexy 19 F 14
27320 Nonancourt 11 F 9
20217 Nonza 39 M 17
21490 Norges-la-Ville 19 G 13
70000 Noroy-le-Bourg 19 G 14
62120 Norrent-Fontes 4 D 10
44390 Nort-sur-Erdre 15 G 6
30570 Notre-Dame-de-la-Rouvière 30 K 11
34380 Notre-Dame-de-Londres 36 L 11
41600 Nouan-le-Fuzelier 17 G 10
37460 Nouans-les-Fontaines 17 G 9
08240 Nouart 13 E 13
23170 Nouhant 23 H 10
80860 Nouvion 3 D 9
02270 Nouvion-et-Catillon 12 E 11
23350 Nouziers 23 H 9
08270 Novion-Porcien 13 E 12
56920 Noyal-Pontivy 9 F 5
49490 Noyant 16 G 8
37800 Noyant-de-Touraine 16 G 8
49520 Noyant-la-Gravoyère 15 G 7
49700 Noyant-la-Plaine 16 G 7
80860 Noyelles-sur-Mer 3 D 9
77114 Noyen-sur-Seine 18 F 11
52240 Noyers/Chaumont 19 F 13
89310 Noyers/Vermenton 18 G 11
41140 Noyers-sur-Cher 17 G 9
04200 Noyers-sur-Jabron 31 K 13
60400 Noyon 12 E 10
44170 Nozay 15 G 6
07270 Nozières 31 J 12
58190 Nuars 18 G 11
79250 Nueil-les-Aubiers 16 H 7
89390 Nuits 18 G 12
21700 Nuits-Saint Georges 25 G 12
62270 Nuncq-Hautecôte 4 D 10
36800 Nuret-le-Ferron 23 H 9
26110 Nyons 31 K 13
68290 Oberbruck 20 G 14
67210 Obernai 20 F 15
67510 Obersteinbach 20 E 15
19130 Objat 22 J 9
61200 Occagnes 10 F 7
76930 Octeville-sur-Mer 10 E 8
90300 Offemont 20 G 14
76550 Offranville 11 E 9
20217 Ogliastro 39 M 17
62590 Oignies 4 D 10
70700 Oiselay-et-Grachaux 19 G 13
80140 Oisemont 11 E 9
76350 Oissel 11 E 9
58500 Oisy 18 G 11
34390 Olargues 36 L 10
12510 Olemps 29 K 10
20232 Oletta 39 M 17
45160 Olivet 17 G 9
63880 Olliergues 24 J 11
20113 Olmeto 39 N 16
20245 Olmu 39 M 16
85340 Olonne-sur-Mer 15 H 6
64400 Oloron-Sainte Marie 33 L 7
08430 Omont 13 E 12
76730 Omonville 11 E 8
40440 Ondres 27 L 6
12850 Onet-le-Chateau 29 K 10
41150 Onzain 17 G 9
66600 Opoul-Périllos 35 M 10
87520 Oradour-sur-Glane 22 J 9
04700 Oraison 37 L 13
84100 Orange 31 K 12
14290 Orbec 10 E 8
32260 Orbessan 28 L 8
68370 Orbey 20 F 15
37460 Orbigny 17 G 9
41300 Orçay 17 G 10
86230 Orches 16 H 8
59310 Orchies 4 D 11
05170 Orcières 32 K 14
63210 Orcival 23 J 10
39270 Orgelet 25 H 13
35230 Orgères 15 G 6
28140 Orgères-en-Beauce 17 F 9
13660 Orgon 37 L 13
02390 Origny-Sainte Benoite 12 E 11
45000 Orléans 17 G 9
09110 Orlu 35 M 9
11200 Ornaisons 35 L 10
25290 Ornans 25 G 14
11270 Orsans 35 L 9
91400 Orsay 11 F 10
64300 Orthez 27 L 7
44700 Orvault 15 G 6
36210 Orville 17 G 9
21260 Orville 19 G 13
18130 Osmery 23 H 10
64390 Osserain-Rivareyte 27 L 7
64780 Ossès 27 L 6
65380 Ossun 34 L 7
67540 Ostwald 20 F 15
77280 Othis 12 E 10
41290 Oucques 17 G 9
58110 Ougny 24 G 11
25520 Ouhans 25 H 14
14100 Ouilly-le-Vicomte 10 E 8
14150 Ouistreham 10 E 7
28260 Oulins 11 F 9
18350 Ourouër-les-Bourdelins 23 H 10
76450 Ourville-en-Caux 11 E 8
09140 Oust 34 M 9
45480 Outarville 17 F 10
62230 Outreau 3 D 9
41240 Ouzouer-le-Marché 17 G 9
45570 Ouzouer-sur-Loire 17 G 10
45250 Ouzouer-sur-Trézée 17 G 10
62215 Oye-Plage 4 D 10
01100 Oyonnax 25 H 13
01190 Ozan 24 H 12
71700 Ozenay 24 H 12
77330 Ozoir-la-Ferrière 12 F 10
27120 Pacy-sur-Eure 11 E 9
21250 Pagny-le-Château 25 G 13
54530 Pagny-sur-Moselle 19 F 14
09130 Pailhès 35 L 9
44560 Paimbœuf 15 G 5
22500 Paimpol 9 F 4
35380 Paimpont 9 F 5
11330 Palairac 35 M 10
34250 Palavas-les-Flots 36 L 11
85670 Palluau 15 H 6
36500 Palluau-sur-Indre 17 H 9
12310 Palmas 30 K 10
09100 Pamiers 35 L 9
87350 Panazol 22 J 9
52230 Pancey 19 F 13
57530 Pange 13 E 14
42360 Panissières 24 J 12
45700 Pannes 17 F 10
71600 Paray-le-Monial 24 H 12
40160 Parentis-en-Born 27 K 6
10210 Pargues 18 F 12
75001 Paris 11 F 10
82160 Parisot 29 K 9
49730 Parnay 16 G 8
23140 Parsac 23 H 10
79200 Parthenay 16 H 7
20147 Partinello 39 M 16
79100 Pas-de-Jeu 16 H 7
62760 Pas-en-Artois 4 D 10
25360 Passavant 25 G 14
51700 Passy-Grigny 12 E 11
45310 Patay 17 F 9
64000 Pau 28 L 7
36260 Paudy 17 G 9
33250 Pauillac 21 J 7
15430 Paulhac 30 J 10
48140 Paulhac-en-Margeride 30 K 11
43230 Paulhaguet 30 J 11
34230 Paulhan 36 L 11
24590 Paulin 29 J 9
44270 Paulx 15 H 6
08310 Pauvres 13 E 12
76570 Pavilly 11 E 8
46350 Payrac 29 K 9
24270 Payzac 22 J 9
13200 Peaudure 37 L 12
56130 Péaule 8 G 5
04200 Peipin 31 K 13
06440 Peïra-Cava 38 L 15
13330 Pélissanne 37 L 13
38970 Pellafol 31 K 13
33790 Pellegrue 28 K 8
36180 Pellevoisin 17 H 9
49112 Pellouailles-les-Vignes 16 G 7
48000 Pelouse 30 K 11
42410 Pélussin 31 J 12
56760 Pénestin 8 G 5
62127 Penin 4 D 10
29760 Penmarch 7 G 3
81140 Penne 29 K 9
38260 Penol 31 J 13
55410 Percy 10 F 6
50190 Périers 10 E 6
17800 Pérignac 21 J 7
41100 Périgny 17 G 9
84210 Pernes-les-Fontaines 31 L 13
01960 Péronnas 25 H 13
80200 Péronne 12 E 10
19410 Perpezac-le-Noir 22 J 9
66000 Perpignan 35 M 10
71420 Perrecy-les-Forges 24 H 12
40630 Perrègue 28 K 7
22570 Perret 9 F 4
71160 Perrigny-sur-Loire 24 H 11
22700 Perros-Guirec 9 F 4
86320 Persac 22 H 8
08300 Perthes 13 E 12
84120 Pertuis 37 L 13
61360 Pervenchères 10 F 8
70140 Pesmes 25 G 13
33600 Pessac 28 K 7
44390 Petit-Mars 15 G 6
20140 Petreto-Bicchisano 39 N 16
11230 Peyrefitte-du-Razès 35 L 10
40300 Peyrehorade 27 L 6
01300 Peyrieu 25 J 13
26380 Peyrins 31 J 13
31420 Peyrissas 34 L 8
13860 Peyrolles-en-Provence 37 L 13
04310 Peyruis 37 K 13
77131 Pézarches 12 F 10
34120 Pézenas 36 L 11
24510 Pezuls 29 K 8
57370 Phalsbourg 20 F 15
66380 Pia 35 M 10
72170 Piacé 16 F 8
20115 Piana 39 M 16
20131 Pianotolli-Caldarello 39 N 17
20229 Piazzole 39 M 17
50360 Picauville 10 E 6
63113 Picherande 23 J 10
80310 Picquigny 11 E 10
20229 Piedicroce 39 M 17
54490 Piennes 13 E 13
87260 Pierre-Buffière 22 J 9
38119 Pierre-Châtel 31 K 13
71270 Pierre-de-Bresse 25 H 13
77580 Pierre-Levée 12 F 11
70600 Pierrecourt 19 G 13
83390 Pierrefeu-du-Var 37 L 14
65260 Pierrefitte-Nestalas 34 M 7
55260 Pierrefitte-sur-Aire 19 F 13
41300 Pierrefitte-sur-Sauldre 17 G 10
60350 Pierrefonds 12 E 10
52160 Pierrefontaines 19 G 13
15230 Pierrefort 30 K 10
26700 Pierrelatte 31 K 12
28130 Pierres 11 F 9
20218 Pietralba 39 M 17
34570 Pignan 36 L 11
55230 Pillon 13 E 13
89740 Pimelles 18 G 12
20124 Pinarellu 39 N 17
10220 Piney 18 F 12
20228 Pino 39 M 17
43300 Pinols 30 J 11
20227 Pinzalone 39 M 17
63330 Pionsat 23 H 10
35550 Pipriac 15 G 6
50770 Pirou-Plage 9 E 6
20129 Pisciatella 39 N 16
40410 Pissos 28 K 7
45300 Pithiviers 17 F 10
29860 Plabennec 7 F 3
22940 Plaintel 9 F 5
12550 Plaisance/Albi 29 L 10
24560 Plaisance/Bergerac 28 K 8
32160 Plaisance/Marciac 28 L 8
34230 Plaissan 36 L 11
05100 Plampinet 32 K 14
58230 Planchez 18 G 12
22130 Plancoët 9 F 5
27300 Plasnes 11 E 8
15700 Pleaux 29 J 10
35380 Plélan-le-Grand 9 F 5
22210 Plémet 9 F 5
22640 Plénée-Jugon 9 F 5
22370 Pléneuf-Val-André 9 F 5
22190 Plérin 9 F 5
22490 Pleslin-Trigavou 9 F 5
22330 Plessala 9 F 5
44630 Plessé 15 G 5
22640 Plestan 9 F 5
22310 Plestin-les-Grèves 8 F 4
22610 Pleubian 9 F 4
86450 Pleumartin 16 H 8
29190 Pleyben 8 F 4
29410 Pleyber-Christ 8 F 4
51150 Plivot 12 E 12
56270 Ploemeur 8 G 4
56880 Ploeren 8 G 5
56800 Ploërmel 9 G 5
22150 Ploeuc-sur-Lié 9 F 5
29770 Plogoff 7 F 3
88370 Plombières-les-Bains 19 G 14
29700 Plomelin 7 G 3
29120 Plomeur 7 G 3
29550 Plomodiern 7 F 3
29720 Plonéour-Lanvern 7 G 3
29530 Plonévez-du-Faou 8 F 4
22170 Plouagat 9 F 5
22420 Plouaret 8 F 4
29810 Plouarzel 7 F 3
56270 Plouay 8 G 4
22650 Ploubalay 9 F 5
22300 Ploubezre 8 F 4
29830 Ploudalmézeau 7 F 3
29800 Plouédern 7 F 3
29430 Plouescat 8 F 3
22470 Plouézec 9 F 5
29630 Plougasnou 8 F 4
29470 Plougastel-Daoulas 7 F 3
29640 Plougonven 8 F 4
22150 Plouguenast 9 F 5
29880 Plouguerneau 7 F 3
22580 Plouha 9 F 5
56680 Plouhinec/Lorient 8 G 4
29780 Plouhinec/Quimper 7 F 3
29610 Plouigneau 8 F 4
22780 Plounérin 8 F 4
56770 Plouray 8 F 4
29420 Plouvorn 8 F 3
29280 Plouzané 7 F 3
29710 Plozévet 7 G 3
29700 Pluguffan 7 G 3
56420 Plumelec 8 G 5
56930 Pluméliau 9 G 5
56330 Pluvigner 8 G 4
33720 Podensac 28 K 7
51240 Pogny 13 F 12
35420 Poilley 9 F 6
45500 Poilly-lez-Gien 17 G 10
21440 Poiseul-la-Grange 19 G 12
52230 Poissons 19 F 13
78300 Poissy 11 F 10
28300 Poisvilliers 11 F 9
86000 Poitiers 22 H 8
80290 Poix-de-Picardie 11 E 9
08430 Poix-Terron 13 E 12
35320 Poligné 15 G 6
39800 Poligny 25 H 13
66450 Pollestres 35 M 10
01310 Polliat 25 H 13
15800 Polminhac 30 K 10
11400 Pomarède 35 L 9
21630 Pommard 24 G 12
22450 Pommerit-Jaudy 9 F 4
70240 Pomoy 19 G 14
79200 Pompaire 16 H 7
44410 Pompas 8 G 5
54340 Pompey 19 F 14
30170 Pompignan 30 L 11
47420 Pompogne 28 K 8
31210 Ponlat-Taillebourg 34 L 8
17800 Pons 21 J 7
27500 Pont-Audemer 11 E 8
29930 Pont-Aven 8 G 4
59710 Pont-à-Marcq 4 D 11
54700 Pont-à-Mousson 19 F 14
29790 Pont-Croix 7 F 3
38230 Pont-de-Chéruy 24 J 13
63920 Pont-de-Dore 24 J 11
09140 Pont-de-la-Taule 34 M 9
25150 Pont-de-Roide 26 G 14
12290 Pont-de-Salars 30 K 10
01190 Pont-de-Vaux 24 H 12
01290 Pont-de-Veyle 24 H 12
47480 Pont-du Casse 28 K 8
39300 Pont-du-Navoy 25 H 13
38780 Pont-Évêque 31 J 12
50880 Pont-Hébert 10 E 6
29120 Pont-l'Abbé 7 G 3
17250 Pont-l'Abbé-d'Arnoult 21 J 7
14130 Pont-l'Évêque 10 E 8
80580 Pont-Rémy 3 D 9
30130 Pont-Saint Esprit 31 K 12
44860 Pont-Saint Martin 15 G 6
54550 Pont-Saint Vincent 19 F 14
10150 Pont-Sainte Marie 18 F 12
60700 Pont-Sainte Maxence 12 E 10
89140 Pont-sur-Yonne 18 F 11
64530 Pontacq 34 L 7
21270 Pontailler-sur-Saône 19 G 13
26150 Pontaix 31 K 13
23250 Pontarion 23 J 9
25300 Pontarlier 25 H 14
77340 Pontault-Combault 12 F 10
63380 Pontaumur 23 J 10
02160 Pontavert 12 E 11
38530 Pontcharra 32 J 14
23260 Pontcharraud 23 J 10
44160 Pontchâteau 15 G 5
20218 Ponte Leccia 39 M 17
20235 Ponte Novu 39 M 17
20236 Ponte-Castirla 39 M 17
40200 Pontenx-les-Forges 27 K 6
63230 Pontgibaud 23 J 10
89230 Pontigny 18 G 11
41500 Pontijou 17 G 9
56300 Pontivy 9 F 5
41400 Pontlevoy 17 G 9
95300 Pontoise 11 E 10
40465 Pontonx-sur-l'Adour 27 L 7
50170 Pontorson 9 F 6
02490 Pontru 12 E 11
72510 Pontvallain 16 G 8
44210 Pornic 15 G 5
44380 Pornichet 15 G 5
83400 Porquerolles 37 M 14
12330 Port Saint Louis-du-Rhône 37 L 12
53410 Port-Brillet 16 F 7
83400 Port-Cros 37 L 14
13110 Port-de-Bouc 37 L 12
14520 Port-en-Bessin 10 E 7
85350 Port-Joinville 15 H 5
11210 Port-la-Nouvelle 36 L 11
56290 Port-Louis 8 G 4
56640 Port-Navalo 8 G 5
70170 Port-sur-Saône 19 G 14
66660 Port-Vendres 36 M 11
50580 Portbail 9 E 6
66760 Porté-Puymorens 35 M 9
26800 Portes-lès-Valence 31 K 12
31120 Portet-sur-Garonne 35 L 9
20150 Porto 39 M 16
20137 Porto-Vecchio 39 N 17
51330 Possesse 13 F 12
14420 Potigny 10 F 7
49420 Pouancé 15 G 6
58200 Pougny 18 G 11
58320 Pougues-les-Eaux 18 G 11
10240 Pougy 18 F 12
85570 Pouillé 15 H 7
21150 Pouillenay 18 G 12
40350 Pouillon 27 L 7
21320 Pouilly-en-Auxois 18 G 12
42720 Pouilly-sous-Charlieu 24 H 12
58150 Pouilly-sur-Loire 17 G 10
29710 Pouldreuzic 7 G 3
36300 Pouligny-Saint Pierre 22 H 9
29246 Poullaouen 8 F 4
89240 Pourrain 18 G 11
83910 Pourrières 37 L 13
40120 Pouydesseaux 28 L 7
85700 Pouzauges 15 H 7
30210 Pouzilhac 31 K 12
26310 Poyols 31 K 13
43420 Pradelles 30 K 11
09110 Prades 35 M 9
34730 Prades-le-Lez 36 L 11
79230 Prahecq 22 H 7
09160 Prat-et-Bonrepaux 34 L 9
66230 Prats-de-Mollo-la-Preste 35 M 10
24550 Prats-du-Périgord 29 K 9
47360 Prayssas 28 K 8
53140 Pré-en-Pail 10 F 7
33730 Préchac 28 K 7
21390 Précy-sous-Thil 18 G 12
33210 Preignac 28 K 7
05120 Prelles 32 K 14
58700 Prémery 18 G 11
34390 Prémian 36 L 10
03410 Prémilhat 23 H 10
18380 Presly 17 G 10
86460 Pressac 22 H 8
14140 Prêtreville 10 E 8
37290 Preuilly-sur-Claise 16 H 8
48800 Prévenchères 30 K 11
27220 Prey 11 F 9
74370 Pringy 25 J 14
44260 Prinquiau 15 G 5
36370 Prissac 22 H 9
07000 Privas 31 K 12
20110 Propriano 39 N 16
77160 Provins 18 F 11
20243 Prunelli-di-Fiumorbo 39 M 17
36120 Pruniers 23 H 10
80560 Puchevillers 12 D 10
34150 Puéchabon 36 L 11
06260 Puget-Théniers 38 L 14
83390 Puget-Ville 37 L 14
04410 Puimoisson 37 L 14
45390 Puiseaux 17 F 10
34620 Puisserguier 36 L 11
11230 Puivert 35 M 10
33350 Pujols/Bordeaux 28 K 7
47300 Pujols/Villeneuve-sur-Lot 28 K 8
91740 Pussay 17 F 9
61240 Putanges-Pont-Écrepin 10 F 7
57510 Puttelange-aux-Lacs 20 E 14
17380 Puy-du-Lac 21 J 7
63290 Puy-Guillaume 24 J 11
46700 Puy-l'Évêque 29 K 9
23130 Puy-Malsignat 23 H 10
26450 Puy-Saint Martin 31 K 12
32120 Puycasquier 28 L 8
82240 Puylaroque 29 K 9
81700 Puylaurens 35 L 10
47270 Puymirol 28 K 8
64270 Puyôo 27 L 7
66210 Puyvalador 35 M 10
71330 Quain 25 H 13
89630 Quarré-les-Tombes 18 G 11
08400 Quatre-Champs 13 E 12
35290 Quédillac 9 F 5
80120 Quend 3 D 9
09460 Quérigut 35 M 10
22120 Quessoy 9 F 5
56230 Questembert 8 G 5
50660 Quettreville-sur-Sienne 9 F 6
51120 Queudes 18 F 11
80710 Quevauvillers 11 E 10
56530 Quéven 8 G 4

22100 Quévert 9 F 5
56170 Quiberon 8 G 4
11500 Quillan 35 M 10
44750 Quilly 15 G 6
29000 Quimper 7 G 3
29300 Quimperlé 8 G 4
77860 Quincy-Voisins 12 F 10
25440 Quingey 25 G 13
04500 Quinson 37 L 14
22800 Quintin 9 F 5
30260 Quissac 30 L 12
56310 Quistinic 8 G 4
81800 Rabastens 29 L 9
66730 Rabouillet 35 M 10
88700 Rambervillers 20 F 14
78120 Rambouillet 11 F 9
10240 Ramerupt 18 F 12
32800 Ramouzens 28 L 8
24440 Rampieux 29 K 8
71290 Rancy 25 H 13
63310 Randan 24 H 11
62180 Rang-du-Fliers 3 D 9
67420 Ranrupt 20 F 15
88110 Raon-l'Etape 20 F 14
88110 Raon-sur-Plaine 20 F 15
08450 Raucourt-et-Flaba 13 E 12
15800 Raulhac 30 K 10
50260 Rauville-la-Bigot 9 E 6
88520 Raves 20 F 15
18130 Raymond 17 H 10
37120 Razines 16 H 8
81120 Réalmont 29 L 10
82440 Réalville 29 K 9
32800 Réans 28 L 8
77510 Rebais 12 F 11
21290 Recey-sur-Ource 19 G 12
54370 Réchicourt-le-Château 20 F 14
26310 Recoubeau-Jansac 31 K 13
35600 Redon 15 G 5
62140 Regnauville 3 D 10
88410 Regnévelle 19 G 13
67110 Reichshoffen 20 F 15
74930 Reignier 25 H 14
04110 Reillanne 37 L 13
51100 Reims 12 E 12
61110 Rémalard 11 F 8
88200 Remiremont 20 F 14
88800 Remoncourt 19 F 14
08240 Rémonville 13 E 13
30210 Remoulins 37 L 12
88170 Removille 19 F 13
26510 Rémuzat 31 K 13
60190 Remy 12 E 10
35660 Renac 15 G 6
53800 Renazé 15 G 6
35000 Rennes 9 F 6
08150 Renwez 13 E 12
12170 Réquista 29 K 10
60490 Ressons-sur-Matz 12 E 10
34160 Restinclières 36 L 12
17460 Rétaud 21 J 7
08300 Rethel 13 E 12
35240 Retiers 15 G 6
43130 Retournac 30 J 12
03190 Reugny 23 H 10
36260 Reuilly 17 G 10
31250 Revel 35 L 10
55800 Revigny-sur-Ornain 19 F 12
08500 Revin 13 E 12
44440 Riaillé 15 G 6
83560 Rians 37 L 13
68150 Ribeauvillé 20 F 15
60170 Ribécourt-Dreslincourt 12 E 10
02240 Ribemont 12 E 11
52120 Richebourg/Chaumont 19 F 13
78550 Richebourg/Trappes 11 F 9
37120 Richelieu 16 G 8
31370 Rieumes 34 L 9
12240 Rieupeyroux 29 K 10
34220 Rieussec 35 L 10
48700 Rieutort-de-Randon 30 K 11
56350 Rieux 15 G 5
11160 Rieux-Minervois 35 L 10
04500 Riez 37 L 14
06260 Rigaud 38 L 15
12390 Rignac 29 K 10
32320 Riguepeu 28 L 8
87570 Rilhac-Rancon 22 J 9
37340 Rillé 16 G 8
69140 Rillieux-la-Pape 24 J 12
52700 Rimaucourt 19 F 13
09420 Rimont 35 M 9
63200 Riom 23 J 11
15400 Riom-ès-Montagnes 30 J 10
40370 Rion-des-Landes 27 L 7
42153 Riorges 24 H 12
43220 Riotord 31 J 12
70190 Rioz 19 G 14
32400 Riscle 28 L 7
42800 Rive-de-Gier 31 J 12
38140 Rives 31 J 13
66600 Rivesaltes 35 M 10
12640 Rivière-sur-Tarn 30 K 11
42300 Roanne 24 H 12
42230 Roche-la-Molière 31 J 12
17300 Rochefort 21 J 7
63210 Rochefort-Montagne 23 J 10
39700 Rochefort-sur-Nenon 25 G 13
07110 Rocher 30 K 12
85620 Rocheservière 15 H 6
08230 Rocroi 13 E 12
12000 Rodez 29 K 10
15100 Roffiac 30 J 11
20247 Rogliano 39 M 17
13840 Rognes 37 L 13
56580 Rohan 9 F 5
57410 Rohrbach-lès-Bitche 20 E 15
80240 Roisel 12 E 11
77680 Roissy-en-Brie 12 F 10
08190 Roizy 12 E 12
52260 Rolampont 19 G 13
80500 Rollot 12 E 10
79120 Rom 22 H 8
26100 Romans-sur-Isère 31 J 13
35490 Romazy 9 F 6
71470 Romenay 25 H 13
35850 Romillé 9 F 6
10100 Romilly-sur-Seine 18 F 11
41200 Romorantin-Lanthenay 17 G 9
70250 Ronchamp 20 G 14
59790 Ronchin 4 D 11
59223 Roncq 4 D 11
06450 Roquebillière 38 K 15
40120 Roquefort 28 K 7
30150 Roquemaure 31 K 12
06910 Roquesteron 38 L 15
13360 Roquevaire 37 L 13
05150 Rosans 31 K 13
20121 Rosazia 39 M 16
29680 Roscoff 8 F 4
71390 Rosey 24 H 12
67560 Rosheim 20 F 15
80170 Rosières-en-Santerre 12 E 10
36300 Rosnay 22 H 9
55260 Rosnes 19 F 13
29140 Rosporden 8 G 4
22110 Rostrenen 8 F 4
67570 Rothau 20 F 15
35400 Rothéneuf 9 F 6
14980 Rots 10 E 7
04240 Rouaine 38 L 14
59100 Roubaix 4 D 11
61700 Rouellé 10 F 7
76000 Rouen 11 E 9
68250 Rouffach 20 G 15
17130 Rouffignac 21 J 7
44660 Rougé 15 G 6
25680 Rougemont 19 G 14
23700 Rougnat 23 H 10
04120 Rougon 38 L 14
16170 Rouillac 22 J 7
86480 Rouillé 22 H 8
34320 Roujan 36 L 11
25640 Roulans 25 G 14
72110 Rouperroux-le-Coquet 16 F 8
02590 Roupy 12 E 11
59131 Rousies 4 D 12
38150 Roussillon 31 J 12
88500 Rouvres-en-Xaintois 19 F 14
21320 Rouvres-sous-Meilly 18 G 12
52160 Rouvres-sur-Aube 19 G 12
08150 Rouvroy-sur-Audry 13 E 12
50810 Rouxeville 10 E 7
58110 Rouy 24 G 11
88700 Roville-aux-Chênes 20 F 14
17200 Royan 21 J 6
38940 Roybon 31 J 13
80700 Roye 12 E 10
23460 Royère-de-Vassivière 23 J 9
77540 Rozay-en-Brie 12 F 10
02360 Rozoy-sur-Serre 12 E 12
46120 Rudelle 29 K 9
80120 Rue 3 D 9
28270 Rueil-la Gadelière 11 F 8
36300 Ruffec 22 H 9
16700 Ruffec 22 H 8
27250 Rugles 11 F 8
08290 Rumigny 13 E 12
74150 Rumilly 25 J 13
22260 Runan 9 F 4
07120 Ruoms 30 K 12
88360 Rupt-sur-Moselle 20 G 14
39230 Rye 25 H 13
14400 Ryes 10 E 7
67420 Saales 20 F 15
72300 Sablé-sur-Sarthe 16 G 7
84110 Sablet 31 K 13
40630 Sabres 28 K 7
37190 Saché 16 G 8
91690 Saclas 17 F 10
44390 Saffré 15 G 6
20118 Sagone 39 M 16
18600 Sagonne 23 H 10
95450 Sagy 11 E 9
15240 Saignes 23 J 10
71250 Sailly 24 H 12
59177 Sains-du-Nord 12 D 12
12400 Saint Affrique 30 L 10
41170 Saint Agil 17 F 8
71160 Saint Agnan 24 H 11
17620 Saint Agnant 21 J 7
07320 Saint Agrève 31 J 12
82100 Saint Aignan/Castelsarrasin 29 K 9
41110 Saint Aignan/Romorantin-Lanthenay 17 G 9
18600 Saint Aignan-des-Noyers 23 H 10
53390 Saint Aignan-sur-Roë 15 G 6
17360 Saint Aigulin 22 J 7
48120 Saint Alban-sur-Limagnole 30 K 11
58310 Saint Amand-en-Puisaye 18 G 11
59230 Saint Amand-les-Eaux 4 D 11
41310 Saint Amand-Longpré 17 G 9
18200 Saint Amand-Montrond 23 H 10
48700 Saint Amans 30 K 11
12460 Saint Amans-des-Cots 30 K 10
63890 Saint Amant-Roche-Savine 24 J 11
68550 Saint Amarin 20 G 15
01390 Saint André-de-Corcy 24 J 12
07460 Saint André-de-Cruzières 30 K 12
33240 Saint André-de-Cubzac 21 K 7
27220 Saint André-de-l'Eure 11 F 9
44117 Saint André-des-Eaux 8 G 5
04170 Saint André-les-Alpes 38 L 14
10120 Saint André-les-Vergers 18 F 12
76690 Saint André-sur-Cailly 11 E 9
19200 Saint Angel 23 J 10
63660 Saint Anthème 24 J 11
32340 Saint Antoine 28 K 8
47340 Saint Antoine-de-Ficalba 28 K 8
82140 Saint Antonin-Noble-Val 29 K 9
36120 Saint Août 23 H 9
27120 Saint Aquilin-de-Pacy 11 E 9
78730 Saint Arnoult-en-Yvelines 11 F 9
82210 Saint Arroumex 29 L 8
04160 Saint Auban 38 L 14
89110 Saint Aubin-Château-Neuf 18 G 11
35250 Saint Aubin-d'Aubigné 9 F 6
33820 Saint Aubin-de-Blaye 21 J 7
35140 Saint Aubin-du-Cormier 9 F 6
19390 Saint Augustin 23 J 9
49170 Saint Augustin-des-Bois 16 G 7
19130 Saint Aulaire 22 J 9
37550 Saint Avertin 16 G 8
63380 Saint Avit 23 J 10
24440 Saint Avit-Sénieur 29 K 8
57500 Saint Avold 14 E 14
45130 Saint Ay 17 G 9
87330 Saint Barbant 22 H 8
07160 Saint Barthélemy-le-Meil 31 K 12
18160 Saint Baudel 23 H 10
37310 Saint Bauld 16 G 8
12620 Saint Beauzély 30 K 10
58270 Saint Benin-d'Azy 24 H 11
86280 Saint Benoît 22 H 8
36170 Saint Benoît-du-Sault 23 H 9
71300 Saint Berain-sous-Sanvignes 24 H 12
73520 Saint Béron 31 J 13
53940 Saint Berthevin 16 F 7
52700 Saint Blin 19 F 13
87300 Saint Bonnet-de-Bellac 22 H 8
71220 Saint Bonnet-de-Joux 24 H 12
05500 Saint Bonnet-en-Champsaur 31 K 14
42380 Saint Bonnet-le-Château 30 J 12
43290 Saint Bonnet-le-Froid 31 J 12
22800 Saint Brandan 9 F 5
61700 Saint Brice 10 F 7
35460 Saint Brice-en-Coglès 9 F 6
61150 Saint Brice-sous-Rânes 10 F 7
22000 Saint Brieuc 9 F 5
21290 Saint Broing-les-Moines 19 G 12
35120 Saint Broladre 9 F 6
29450 Saint Cadou 8 F 3
72120 Saint Calais 16 G 8
13760 Saint Cannat 37 L 13
22380 Saint Cast-le-Guildo 9 F 5
46400 Saint Céré 29 K 9
15310 Saint Cernin 29 J 10
46230 Saint Cevet 29 K 9
19380 Saint Chamant 29 J 9
13250 Saint Chamas 37 L 13
42400 Saint Chamond 31 J 12
30190 Saint Chaptes 30 L 12
36400 Saint Chartier 23 H 9
12470 Saint Chély-d'Aubrac 30 K 10
34360 Saint Chinian 36 L 10
84390 Saint Christol 37 K 13
30380 Saint Christol-lès-Alès 30 K 12
38520 Saint Christophe-en-Oisans 32 K 14
12330 Saint Christophe-Vallon 29 K 10
33820 Saint Ciers-sur-Gironde 21 J 7
19220 Saint Cirgues-la-Loutre 29 J 10
46300 Saint Cirq-Madelon 29 K 9
36170 Saint Civran 23 H 9
95770 Saint Clair-sur-Epte 11 E 9
50680 Saint Clair-sur-l'Elle 10 E 6
32380 Saint Clar 28 L 8
39200 Saint Claude 25 H 13
54590 Saint Clément/Lunéville 20 F 14
89100 Saint Clément/Sens 18 F 11
05600 Saint Clément-sur-Durance 32 K 14
15600 Saint Constant 29 K 10
61800 Saint Cornier-des-Landes 10 F 7
72110 Saint Cosme-en-Vairais 16 F 8
05600 Saint Crépin 32 K 14
66750 Saint Cyprien/Perpignan 35 M 11
24220 Saint Cyprien/Sarlat-le-Canédan 29 K 9
78210 Saint Cyr-l'Ecole 11 F 10
89800 Saint Cyr-les-Colons 18 G 11
93200 Saint Denis 11 F 10
17650 Saint Denis-d'Oléron 21 H 6
53500 Saint Denis-de-Gastines 10 F 7
61420 Saint Denis-sur-Sarthon 10 F 7
22400 Saint Denoual 9 F 5
19200 Saint Dezéry 23 J 10
43140 Saint Didier-en-Velay 31 J 12
88100 Saint Dié-des-Vosges 20 F 14
05250 Saint Disdier 31 K 13
52100 Saint Dizier 19 F 12
56130 Saint Dolay 15 G 5
41500 Saint Dyé-sur-Loire 17 G 9
38120 Saint Egrève 31 J 13
28240 Saint Eliph 11 F 9
32300 Saint Elix-Theux 28 L 8
63700 Saint Eloy-les-Mines 23 H 10
71490 Saint Emiland 24 H 12
33330 Saint Emilion 28 K 7
64640 Saint Esteben 27 L 6
33180 Saint Estèphe 21 J 7
66240 Saint Estève 35 M 10
42000 Saint Etienne 31 J 12
08310 Saint Etienne-à-Arnes 13 E 12
07200 Saint Etienne-de-Fontbellon 31 K 12
23290 Saint Etienne-de-Fursac 23 H 9
44360 Saint Etienne-de-Montluc 15 G 6
06660 Saint Etienne-de-Tinée 32 K 14
82410 Saint Etienne-de-Tulmont 29 K 9
01370 Saint Etienne-du-Bois/Bourg-en-Bresse 25 H 13
85670 Saint Etienne-du-Bois/Legé 15 H 6
76800 Saint Etienne-du-Rouvray 11 E 9
04230 Saint Etienne-les-Orgues 37 K 13
48330 Saint Etienne-Vallée-Française 30 K 11
29170 Saint Evarzec 7 G 3
89170 Saint Fargeau 18 G 11
07410 Saint Félicien 31 J 12
12400 Saint Félix-de-Sorgues 30 L 10
31450 Saint Félix-Lauragais 35 L 9
05800 Saint Firmin 31 K 14
41100 Saint Firmin-des-Prés 17 G 9
20217 Saint Florent 39 M 17
85310 Saint Florent-des-Bois 15 H 6
49410 Saint Florent-le-Vieil 15 G 6
18400 Saint Florent-sur-Cher 17 H 10
89600 Saint Florentin 18 G 11
15100 Saint Flour 30 J 11
37600 Saint Flovier 16 H 9
71400 Saint Forgeot 24 G 12
17240 Saint Fort-sur-Gironde 21 J 7
47500 Saint Front-sur-Lémance 29 K 8
85250 Saint Fulgent 15 H 6
42330 Saint Galmier 24 J 12
31800 Saint Gaudens 34 L 8
36800 Saint Gaultier 23 H 9
42660 Saint Genest-Malifaux 31 J 12
71460 Saint Gengoux-le-National 24 H 12
17240 Saint Genis-de-Saintonge 21 J 7
69230 Saint Genis-Laval 24 J 12
57830 Saint Georges 20 F 14
53100 Saint Georges-Buttavent 10 F 7
17110 Saint Georges-de-Didonne 21 J 7
85600 Saint Georges-de-Montaigu 15 H 6
69830 Saint Georges-de-Reneins 24 H 12
17150 Saint Georges-des-Agoûts 21 J 7
27450 Saint Georges-du-Vièvre 11 E 8
42990 Saint Georges-en-Couzan 24 J 11
43500 Saint Georges-Lagricol 30 J 11
86130 Saint Georges-les-Baillargeaux 16 H 8
41400 Saint Georges-sur-Cher 17 G 9
49170 Saint Georges-sur-Loire 16 G 7
70200 Saint Germain/Lure 19 G 14
86310 Saint Germain/Saint Savin 22 H 8
89630 Saint Germain-des-Champs 18 G 11
03260 Saint Germain-des-Fossés 24 H 11
71330 Saint Germain-du-Bois 25 H 13
14110 Saint Germain-du-Crioult 10 F 7
71370 Saint Germain-du-Plain 24 H 12
71800 Saint Germain-en-Brionnais 24 H 12
78100 Saint Germain-en-Laye 11 F 10
43700 Saint Germain-Laprade 30 J 11
63340 Saint Germain-Lembron 23 J 11
19330 Saint Germain-les-Vergnes 22 J 9
77860 Saint Germain-sur-Morin 12 F 10
81210 Saint Germier 29 L 10
63390 Saint Gervais-d'Auvergne 23 H 10
72120 Saint Gervais-de-Vic 16 G 8
74170 Saint Gervais-les-Bains 25 J 14
34610 Saint Gervais-sur-Mare 36 L 11
46330 Saint Géry 29 K 9
44530 Saint Gildas-des-Bois 15 G 5
30800 Saint Gilles 36 L 12
85800 Saint Gilles-Croix-de-Vie 15 H 6
40560 Saint Girons/Castets 27 L 6
09200 Saint Girons/Saint Lizier 34 M 9
45500 Saint Gondon 17 G 10
25520 Saint Gorgon-Main 25 G 14
56220 Saint Gravé 15 G 5
34150 Saint Guilhem-le-Désert 36 L 11
42370 Saint Haon-le-Châtel 24 H 11
03440 Saint Hilaire 23 H 11
87260 Saint Hilaire-Bonneval 22 J 9
30560 Saint Hilaire-de-Brethmas 30 K 12
85270 Saint Hilaire-de-Riez 15 H 6
17770 Saint Hilaire-de-Villefranche 21 J 7
85240 Saint Hilaire-des-Loges 21 H 7
50600 Saint Hilaire-du-Harcouët 10 F 6
19550 Saint Hilaire-Foissac 23 J 10
58300 Saint Hilaire-Fontaine 24 H 11
51600 Saint Hilaire-le-Grand 13 E 12
19170 Saint Hilaire-les-Courbes 23 J 9
25190 Saint Hippolyte 26 G 14
30170 Saint Hippolyte-du-Fort 30 L 11
58360 Saint Honoré-les-Bains 24 H 11
15310 Saint Illide 29 J 10
38330 Saint Ismier 31 J 13
15800 Saint Jacques-des-Blats 30 J 10
50240 Saint James 9 F 6
04140 Saint Jean 32 K 14
56660 Saint Jean-Brévelay 9 G 5
17400 Saint Jean-d'Angély 21 J 7
33127 Saint Jean-d'Illac 28 K 7
73440 Saint Jean-de-Belleville 32 J 14
38440 Saint Jean-de-Bournay 31 J 13
45800 Saint Jean-de-Braye 17 G 9
50620 Saint Jean-de-Daye 10 E 6
45140 Saint Jean-de-la-Ruelle 17 G 9
21170 Saint Jean-de-Losne 25 G 13
64500 Saint Jean-de-Luz 27 L 6
73300 Saint Jean-de-Maurienne 32 J 14
85160 Saint Jean-de-Monts 15 H 5
07300 Saint Jean-de-Muzols 31 J 12
84390 Saint Jean-de-Sault 31 K 13
74450 Saint Jean-de-Sixt 25 J 14
47270 Saint Jean-de-Thurac 28 K 8
12230 Saint Jean-du-Bruel 30 K 11
30270 Saint Jean-du-Gard 30 K 11
26190 Saint Jean-en-Royans 31 J 13
06450 Saint Jean-la-Rivière 38 L 15
46400 Saint Jean-Lagineste 29 K 9
46400 Saint Jean-Lespinasse 29 K 9
64220 Saint Jean-Pied-de-Port 27 L 6
32190 Saint Jean-Poutge 28 L 8
37600 Saint Jean-Saint Germain 16 G 9
74490 Saint Jeoire 25 H 14
44720 Saint Joachim 8 G 5
74410 Saint Jorioz 25 J 14
31790 Saint Jory 29 L 9
76280 Saint Jouin-Bruneval 10 E 8
39320 Saint Julien 25 H 13
71800 Saint Julien-de-Civry 24 H 12
15590 Saint Julien-de-Jordanne 30 J 10
44670 Saint Julien-de-Vouvantes 15 G 6
34210 Saint Julien-des-Molières 35 L 10
89330 Saint Julien-du-Sault 18 F 11
48190 Saint Julien-du-Tournel 30 K 11
04170 Saint Julien-du-Verdon 38 L 14
05140 Saint Julien-en-Beauchêne 31 K 13
40170 Saint Julien-en-Born 27 K 6
74890 Saint Julien-en-Genevois 25 H 14
14140 Saint Julien-le-Faucon 10 E 8
19430 Saint Julien-le-Pèlerin 29 J 10
87460 Saint Julien-le-Petit 23 J 9
10800 Saint Julien-les-Villas 18 F 12
73870 Saint Julien-Mont-Denis 32 J 14
01560 Saint Julien-sur-Reyssouze 25 H 13
23400 Saint Junien-la-Bregère 23 J 9
18340 Saint Just 17 H 10
60130 Saint Just-en-Chaussée 12 E 10
42430 Saint Just-en-Chevalet 24 J 11
64120 Saint Just-Ibarre 27 L 6
43240 Saint Just-Malmont 31 J 12
42170 Saint Just-Saint Rambert 31 J 12
08250 Saint Juvin 13 E 12
38840 Saint Lattier 31 J 13
22230 Saint Launeuc 9 F 5
04400 Saint Laurent 32 K 14
69930 Saint Laurent-de-Chamousset 24 J 12
14220 Saint Laurent-de-Condel 10 E 7
66250 Saint Laurent-de-la-Salanque 35 M 10
65150 Saint Laurent-de-Neste 34 L 8
49270 Saint Laurent-des-Autels 15 G 6
38380 Saint Laurent-du-Pont 31 J 13
06700 Saint Laurent-du-Var 38 L 15
76560 Saint Laurent-en-Caux 11 E 8
39150 Saint Laurent-en-Grandvaux 25 H 13
33112 Saint Laurent-Médoc 21 J 7
41220 Saint Laurent-Nouan 17 G 9
14710 Saint Laurent-sur-Mer 10 E 7
71990 Saint Léger-sous-Beuvray 24 H 12
71510 Saint Léger-sur-Dheune 24 H 12
31560 Saint Léon 35 L 9
24290 Saint Léon-sur-Vézère 29 J 9
87400 Saint Léonard-de-Noblat 22 J 9
12780 Saint Léons 30 K 10
09190 Saint Lizier 34 L 9
50000 Saint Lô 10 E 6
33440 Saint Louis-de-Montferrand 21 K 7
28360 Saint Loup 17 F 9
03150 Saint Loup/Varennes-sur-Allier 24 H 11
18190 Saint Loup-des-Chaumes 23 H 10
53290 Saint Loup-du-Dorat 16 G 7
79600 Saint Loup-Lamairé 16 H 7
70800 Saint Loup-sur-Semouse 19 G 14
44410 Saint Lyphard 8 G 5
31470 Saint Lys 29 L 9
49450 Saint Macaire-en-Mauges 15 G 7
27210 Saint Maclou 10 E 8
79400 Saint Maixent-l'Ecole 22 H 7
35400 Saint Malo 9 F 6
30730 Saint Mamert- du-Gard 36 L 12
21450 Saint Marc-sur-Seine 18 G 12
72170 Saint Marceau 16 F 8
71380 Saint Marcel/Chalon-sur-Saône 24 H 12
36200 Saint Marcel/Châteauroux 23 H 9
01390 Saint Marcel/Rillieux-la-Pape 24 J 12
27950 Saint Marcel/Vernon 11 E 9
30330 Saint Marcel-de-Careiret 31 K 12
03390 Saint Marcel-en-Murat 23 H 11
26320 Saint Marcel-les-Valence 31 K 12
38160 Saint Marcellin 31 J 13
77230 Saint Mard 12 E 10
51330 Saint Mard-sur-le-Mont 13 F 12

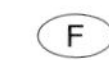

POSTALI · ÍNDICE CON CÓDIGOS POSTALES · INDICE DE LUGARES COM CÓDIGOS
REJSTŘÍK MÍST S PSČ · ZOZNAM OBCÍ S PSČ · INDEKS MIEJSCOWOŚCI Z KOD POCZTOWY

52

Saint Mards-en-Othe (F) — Surzur (F)

32260 Tachoires 28 L 8
68130 Tagsdorf 20 G 15
11220 Talairan 35 L 10
43100 Talairat 30 J 11
33590 Talais 21 J 6
21240 Talant 19 G 12
41370 Talcy 17 G 9
15170 Talizat 30 J 11
40260 Taller 27 L 6
85440 Talmont-Saint Hilaire 15 H 6
17120 Talmont-sur-Gironde 21 J 7
76430 Tancarville 11 E 8
74440 Taninges 25 H 14
89430 Tanlay 18 G 12
58190 Tannay/Clamecy 18 G 11
08390 Tannay/le Chesne 13 E 12
89350 Tannerre-en-Puisaye 18 G 11
81190 Tanus 29 K 10
69170 Tarare 24 J 12
13150 Tarascon 37 L 12
09400 Tarascon-sur-Ariège 35 M 9
65000 Tarbes 34 L 8
64470 Tardets-Sorholus 33 L 7
03140 Target 23 H 11
40400 Tartas 27 L 7
02990 Tartiers 12 E 11
72430 Tassé 16 G 7
39120 Tassenières 25 H 13
69160 Tassin-la-Demi-Lune 24 J 12
26770 Taulignan 31 K 12
56800 Taupont 9 G 5
66500 Taurinya 35 M 10
63690 Tauves 23 J 10
39500 Tavaux/Dole 25 G 13
02250 Tavaux/Laon 12 E 11
20163 Tavera 39 M 17
83670 Tavernes 37 L 14
95150 Taverny 11 E 10
81120 Teillet 29 L 10
29560 Telgruc-sur-Mer 7 F 3
54260 Tellancourt 13 E 13
72220 Teloché 16 G 8
43190 Tence 31 J 12
38570 Tencin 31 J 13
06430 Tende 38 K 15
02700 Tergnier 12 E 11
48310 Termes 30 K 11
32400 Termes-d'Armagnac 28 L 7
21220 Ternant 24 G 12
24120 Terrasson-Lavilledieu 29 J 9
87360 Tersannes 22 H 9
17460 Tesson 21 J 7
50420 Tessy-sur-Vire 10 F 6
33710 Teuillac 21 J 7
19200 Thalamy 23 J 10
68800 Thann 20 G 15
14610 Thaon 10 E 7
88150 Thaon-les-Vosges 19 F 14
41300 Theillay 17 G 10
56450 Theix 8 G 5
03350 Theneuille 23 H 10
79390 Thénezay 16 H 7
21150 Thenissey 18 G 12
24210 Thenon 22 J 9
08240 Thénorgues 13 E 12
62129 Thérouanne 4 D 10
36400 Thevet-Saint Julien 23 H 10
11200 Thézan-des-Corbières 35 L 10
64450 Thèze/Pau 28 L 7
04200 Thèze/Sisteron 31 K 13
54470 Thiaucourt-Regniéville 19 F 13
27230 Thiberville 10 E 8
51510 Thibie 12 F 12
51300 Thiéblemont-Farémont 19 F 12
03230 Thiel-sur-Acolin 24 H 11
63300 Thiers 24 J 11
55840 Thierville-sur-Meuse 13 E 13
45260 Thimory 17 G 10
57100 Thionville 13 E 14
28480 Thiron-Gardais 17 F 8
69240 Thizy 24 H 12
39240 Thoirette 25 H 13
78770 Thoiry 11 F 9
01140 Thoissey 24 H 12
86290 Thollet 22 H 9
74230 Thônes 25 J 14
74200 Thonon-les-Bains 25 H 14
04170 Thorame-Haute 38 K 14
35235 Thorigné-Fouillard 9 F 6
89260 Thorigny-sur-Oreuse 18 F 11
18260 Thou 17 G 10
49380 Thouarcé 16 G 7
79100 Thouars 16 H 7
32430 Thoux 28 L 8
88260 Thuillières 19 F 14
66300 Thuir 35 M 10
86540 Thuré 16 H 8
63260 Thuret 23 J 11
71440 Thurey 25 H 13
21340 Thury 24 G 12
14220 Thury-Harcourt 10 F 7
61120 Ticheville 10 F 8
49125 Tiercé 16 G 7
73320 Tignes 32 J 14
45510 Tigy 17 G 10
21120 Til-Châtel 19 G 13
40360 Tilh 27 L 7
27570 Tillières-sur-Avre 11 F 9
51460 Tilloy-et-Bellay 13 E 12
14250 Tilly-sur-Seulles 10 E 7
61800 Tinchebray 10 F 7
35190 Tinténiac 9 F 6
20111 Tiuccia 39 M 16
20100 Tizzano 39 N 16
17430 Tonnay-Charente 21 J 7
47400 Tonneins 28 K 8
89700 Tonnerre 18 G 11
71210 Torcy 24 H 12
50160 Torigni-sur-Vire 10 E 7
40230 Tosse 27 L 6
76890 Tôtes 11 E 9
89130 Toucy 18 G 11
06710 Touët-sur-Var 38 L 15
54200 Toul 19 F 13
83000 Toulon 37 L 13
03400 Toulon-sur-Allier 24 H 11
71320 Toulon-sur-Arroux 24 H 12
66350 Toulouges 35 M 10
31000 Toulouse 29 L 9
14800 Touques 10 E 8
46330 Tour-de-Faure 29 K 9
59200 Tourcoing 4 D 11
32230 Tourdun 28 L 8
50110 Tourlaville 10 E 6
77220 Tournan-en-Brie 12 F 10
65190 Tournay 34 L 8
31170 Tournefeuille 29 L 9
19210 Tournevite 22 J 9
47370 Tournon-d'Agenais 29 K 9
36220 Tournon-Saint Martin 16 H 8
07300 Tournon-sur-Rhône 31 J 12
71700 Tournus 24 H 12
37000 Tours 16 G 8
08130 Tourteron 13 E 12
24390 Tourtoirac 22 J 9
28310 Toury 17 F 9
77123 Tousson 17 F 10
17120 Touvent 21 J 7
10400 Trainel 18 F 11
71520 Tramayes 24 H 12
88350 Trampot 19 F 13
10290 Trancault 18 F 11
35610 Trans-la-Forêt 9 F 6
78190 Trappes 11 F 9
40120 Traverses 28 K 7
70360 Traves 19 G 13
20240 Travo 39 N 17
11800 Trèbes 35 L 10
22560 Trébeurden 8 F 4
35380 Treffendel 9 F 5
44170 Treffieux 15 G 6
01370 Treffort 25 H 13
22730 Trégastel-Plage 8 F 4
29870 Tréglonou 7 F 3
22220 Tréguier 9 F 4
19260 Treignac 23 J 9
03380 Treignat 23 H 10
82110 Tréjouls 29 K 9
48340 Trélans 15 G 6
59132 Trélon 12 D 12
49340 Trémentines 15 G 7
29300 Tréméven 8 G 4
40630 Trensacq 28 K 7
28500 Tréon 11 F 9
58240 Tresnay 24 H 11
72440 Tresson 16 G 8
13530 Trets 37 L 13
55130 Tréveray 19 F 13
30750 Trèves 30 K 11
14710 Trévières 10 E 7
03460 Trévol 24 H 11
01600 Trévoux 24 J 12
03220 Trézelles 24 H 11
85580 Triaize 21 H 6
55250 Triaucourt-en-Argonne 13 F 13
65220 Trie-sur-Baïse 34 L 8
77470 Trilport 12 F 10
15400 Trizac 30 J 10
60112 Troissereux 11 E 10
89700 Tronchoy 18 G 11
10700 Trouans 18 F 12
14360 Trouville-sur-Mer 10 E 8
10000 Troyes 18 F 12
67370 Truchtersheim 20 F 15
61160 Trun 10 F 8
14500 Truttemer-le-Grand 10 F 7
20245 Tuarelli 39 M 16
11350 Tuchan 35 M 10
19120 Tudeils 29 J 9
72160 Tuffé 16 F 8
19000 Tulle 23 J 9
38210 Tullins 31 J 13
19500 Turenne 29 J 9
04250 Turriers 31 K 14
71700 Uchizy 24 H 12
73400 Ugine 25 J 14
79150 Ulcot 16 G 7
66500 Urbanya 35 M 10
03360 Urçay 23 H 10
64490 Urdos 33 M 7
20218 Urtaca 39 M 17
86230 Usseau/Châtellerault 16 H 8
17220 Usseau/la Rochelle 21 H 6
15300 Ussel/Murat 30 J 10
19200 Ussel/Saint Angel 23 J 10
86350 Usson-du-Poitou 22 H 8
42550 Usson-en-Forez 30 J 11
11140 Usson-les-Bains 35 M 10
64480 Ustaritz 27 L 6
22460 Uzel 9 F 5
88220 Uzemain 19 F 14
19140 Uzerche 22 J 9
30700 Uzès 30 K 12
72500 Vaas 16 G 8
04110 Vachères 37 L 13
07150 Vagnas 30 K 12
88120 Vagney 20 F 14
53480 Vaiges 16 F 7
02370 Vailly-sur-Aisne 12 E 11
18260 Vailly-sur-Sauldre 17 G 10
85150 Vairé 15 H 6
84110 Vaison-la-Romaine 31 K 13
73150 Val d'Isère 32 J 14
35450 Val-d'Izé 9 F 6
27100 Val-de-Reuil 11 E 9
21121 Val-Suzon 19 G 12
49670 Valanjou 16 G 7
26230 Valaurie 31 K 12
06470 Valberg 38 K 14
38740 Valbonnais 31 K 13
25800 Valdahon 25 G 14
86300 Valdivienne 22 H 8
36600 Valençay 17 G 9
82400 Valence/Moissac 28 K 8
26000 Valence/Romans-sur-Isère 31 K 12
32310 Valence sur-Baïse 28 L 8
81340 Valence-d'Albigeois 29 K 10
59300 Valenciennes 4 D 11
04210 Valensole 37 L 13
25700 Valentigney 20 G 14
33340 Valeyrac 21 J 7
34270 Valflaunès 36 L 11
88270 Valfroicourt 19 F 14
07110 Valgorge 30 K 12
89580 Vallan 18 G 11
06220 Vallauris 38 L 15
30580 Vallérargues 30 K 12
30570 Valleraugue 30 K 11
31570 Vallesvilles 29 L 9
44330 Vallet 15 G 6
20259 Vallica 39 M 17
23120 Vallière 23 J 10
10210 Vallières/Chaource 18 G 12
74150 Vallières/Rumilly 25 J 13
73450 Valloire 32 J 14
03190 Vallon-en-Sully 23 H 10
74660 Vallorcine 25 H 14
05290 Vallouise 32 K 14
76540 Valmont 11 E 8
50700 Valognes 10 E 6
84600 Valréas 31 K 12
07600 Vals-les-Bains 31 K 12
14340 Valsemé 10 E 8
05130 Valserres 31 K 14
34350 Valvras-Plage 36 L 11
51340 Vanault-les-Dames 19 F 12
54500 Vand+uvre-les-Nancy 19 F 14
17700 Vandré 21 H 7
56000 Vannes 8 G 5
45510 Vannes-sur-Cosson 17 G 10
38470 Varacieux 31 J 13
44370 Varades 15 G 6
83670 Varages 37 L 13
46260 Varaire 29 K 9
01160 Varambon 25 H 13
14390 Varaville 10 E 7
23300 Vareilles 23 H 9
82330 Varen 29 K 9
37600 Varennes/Ligueil 16 G 8
86110 Varennes/Mirebeau 16 H 8
55270 Varennes-en-Argonne 13 E 13
03160 Varennes-sur-Allier 24 H 11
36210 Varennes-sur-Fouzon 17 G 9
09120 Varilhes 35 L 9
28140 Varize 17 F 9
05560 Vars/Guillestre 32 K 14
58210 Varzy 18 G 11
79340 Vasles 22 H 7
26420 Vassieux-en-Vercors 31 K 13
89420 Vassy/Guillon 18 G 12
14410 Vassy/Vire 10 F 7
36150 Vatan 17 G 9
51320 Vatry 12 F 12
55250 Vaubecourt 13 F 13
51210 Vauchamps 12 F 11
55140 Vaucouleurs 19 F 13
03220 Vaumas 24 H 11
60117 Vaumoise 12 E 10
26400 Vaunaveys-la-Rochette 31 K 13
79420 Vausseroux 22 H 7
30600 Vauvert 36 L 12
70210 Vauvillers 19 G 14
52190 Vaux-sous-Aubigny 19 G 13
55000 Vavincourt 19 F 13
46110 Vayrac 29 K 9
48400 Vebron 30 K 11
15100 Vedrines-Saint Loup 30 J 11
37250 Veigné 16 G 8
24230 Vélines 28 K 8
70000 Vellefaux 19 G 14
36330 Velles 23 H 9
90100 Vellescot 20 G 15
21150 Venarey-les-Laumes 18 G 12
06140 Vence 38 L 15
33930 Vendays-Montalivet 21 J 6
67550 Vendenheim 20 F 15
15240 Vendes 23 J 10
02800 Vendeuil 12 E 11
14170 Vendeuvre 10 E 7
10140 Vendeuvre-sur-Barse 18 F 12
31460 Vendine 29 L 9
36500 Vend+uvres 17 H 9
59213 Vendogies-sur-Ecaillon 4 D 11
41100 Vendôme 17 G 9
42590 Vendranges 24 J 12
30580 Vendras 30 K 12
85250 Vendrennes 15 H 6
81440 Vénès 29 L 10
38520 Venosc 32 K 14
05300 Ventavon 31 K 13
20240 Ventiseri 39 N 17
50450 Ver 9 F 6
25530 Vercel-Villedieu-le-Camp 25 G 14
26510 Verclause 31 K 13
26170 Vercoiran 31 K 13
81110 Verdalle 35 L 10
21330 Verdonnet 18 G 12
09310 Verdun/les Cabannes 35 M 9
55100 Verdun/Thierville-sur-Meuse 13 E 13
82600 Verdun-sur-Garonne 29 L 9
31590 Verfeil 29 L 9
30310 Vergèze 36 L 12
20138 Verghia 39 N 16
02490 Vermand 12 E 11
89270 Vermenton 18 G 11
49220 Vern-d'Anjou 16 G 7
49390 Vernantes 16 G 8
66820 Vernet-les-Bains 35 M 10
51700 Verneuil 12 E 11
27130 Verneuil-sur-Avre 11 F 8
38150 Vernioz 31 J 12
27200 Vernon/Mantes-la-Jolie 11 E 9
86340 Vernon/Poitiers 22 H 8
41230 Vernou-en-Sologne 17 G 9
28500 Vernouillet 11 F 9
07240 Vernoux-en-Vivarais 31 K 12
57420 Verny 19 E 14
20172 Vero 39 M 16
71220 Verosvres 24 H 12
86410 Verrières/Poitiers 22 H 8
08390 Verrières/Sainte Menehould 13 E 12
46090 Vers 29 K 9
78000 Versailles 11 F 10
44120 Vertou 15 G 6
51130 Vertus 12 F 12
02140 Vervins 12 E 11
51380 Verzy 12 E 12
20215 Vescovato 39 M 17
18360 Vesdun 23 H 10
70000 Vesoul 19 G 14
07200 Vesseaux 31 K 12
76980 Veules-les-Roses 11 E 8
76450 Veulettes-sur-Mer 3 E 8
05400 Veynes 31 K 13
63960 Veyre-Monton 23 J 11
12720 Veyreau 30 K 11
74290 Veyrier 25 H 14
74290 Veyrier-du-Lac 25 J 14
89450 Vézelay 18 G 11
54330 Vézelise 19 F 14
12520 Vezouillac 30 K 11
19170 Viam 23 J 9
72320 Vibraye 16 F 8
65500 Vic-en-Biggore 28 L 8
32190 Vic-Fezensac 28 L 8
63270 Vic-le-Comte 23 J 11
15800 Vic-sur-Cère 30 K 10
57630 Vic-sur-Seille 20 F 14
09220 Vicdessos 35 M 9
28480 Vichères 17 F 8
03200 Vichy 24 H 11
20160 Vico 39 M 16
36400 Vicq-Exemplet 23 H 10
36600 Vicq-sur-Nahon 17 G 9
14430 Victot-Pontfol 10 E 7
83550 Vidauban 38 L 14
65700 Vidouze 28 L 7
43100 Vieille-Brioude 30 J 11
44116 Vieillevigne 15 H 6
65170 Vielle-Aure 34 M 8
81570 Vielmur-sur-Agout 35 L 10
38200 Vienne 31 J 12
18100 Vierzon 17 G 10
40800 Vieux-Boucau-les-Bains 27 L 6
59690 Vieux-Condé 4 D 11
41290 Vievy-le-Rayé 17 G 9
38450 Vif 31 J 13
02540 Viffort 12 F 11
19410 Vigeois 22 J 9
65100 Viger 34 L 7
80650 Vignacourt 11 D 10
55210 Vigneulles-lès-Hattonchâtel 13 F 13
33330 Vignonet 28 K 7
52320 Vignory 19 F 13
18500 Vignoux-sur-Barangeon 17 G 10
57420 Vigny/Pont-à-Mousson 19 F 14
95450 Vigny/Pontoise 11 E 9
57640 Vigy 13 E 14
49310 Vihiers 16 G 7
33650 Villagrains 28 K 7
53700 Villaines-la-Juhel 10 F 7
37190 Villaines-les-Rochers 16 G 8
28200 Villampuy 17 F 9
33730 Villandraut 28 K 7
38190 Villard-Bonnot 31 J 13
38250 Villard-de-Lans 31 J 13
11580 Villardebelle 35 L 10
73300 Villarembert 32 J 14
01330 Villars-les-Dombes 24 J 13
11420 Villautou 35 L 9
67220 Villé 20 F 15
20200 Ville-di-Pietrabugno 39 M 17
51170 Ville-en-Tardenois 12 E 11
51800 Ville-sur-Tourbe 13 E 12
05350 Ville-Vieille 32 K 14
41000 Villebarou 17 G 9
50410 Villebaudon 10 F 6
82370 Villebrumier 29 L 9
12580 Villecomtal 29 K 10
11200 Villedaigne 35 L 10
21330 Villedieu 18 G 12
50800 Villedieu-les-Poêles 10 F 6
36320 Villedieu-sur-Indre 17 H 9
37460 Villedômain 17 G 9
16240 Villefagnan 22 H 8
21350 Villeferry 18 G 12
38090 Villefontaine 31 J 13
48800 Villefort 30 K 11
89120 Villefranche 18 G 11
81430 Villefranche-d'Albigeois 29 L 10
66500 Villefranche-de-Conflent 35 M 10
31290 Villefranche-de-Lauragais 35 L 9
24610 Villefranche-de-Lonchat 28 K 8
12430 Villefranche-de-Panat 30 K 10
12200 Villefranche-de-Rouergue 29 K 10
24550 Villefranche-du-Périgord 29 K 9
41200 Villefranche-sur-Cher 17 G 9
06230 Villefranche-sur-Mer 38 L 15
69400 Villefranche-sur-Saône 24 J 12
18260 Villegenon 17 G 10
11600 Villegly 35 L 10
37460 Villeloin-Coulangé 17 G 9
82130 Villemade 29 K 9
45700 Villemandeur 17 G 10
31340 Villematier 29 L 9
77250 Villemer 18 F 10
31340 Villemur-sur-Tarn 29 L 9
10370 Villenauxe-la-Grande 18 F 11
33140 Villenave-d'Ornon 28 K 7
12260 Villeneuve 29 K 10
10130 Villeneuve-au-Chemin 18 F 11
25270 Villeneuve-d'Amont 25 H 14
40190 Villeneuve-de-Marsan 28 L 7
77174 Villeneuve-le-Comte 12 F 10
06270 Villeneuve-Loubet 38 L 15
03460 Villeneuve-sur-Allier 24 H 11
18400 Villeneuve-sur-Cher 17 G 10
47300 Villeneuve-sur-Lot 28 K 8
60410 Villeneuve-sur-Verberie 12 E 10
89500 Villeneuve-sur-Yonne 18 F 11
31290 Villenouvelle 35 L 9
26510 Villeperdrix 31 K 13
41000 Villerbon 17 G 9
47210 Villeréal 28 K 8
11330 Villerouge-Termenès 35 L 10
80260 Villers-Bocage/Amiens 12 D 10
14310 Villers-Bocage/Caen 10 E 7
80800 Villers-Bretonneux 12 E 10
80200 Villers-Carbonnel 12 E 10
02600 Villers-Cotterêts 12 E 11
21400 Villers-Patras 18 G 12
14640 Villers-sur-Mer 10 E 8
70110 Villersexel 19 G 14
54190 Villerupt 13 E 13
51130 Villeseneux 12 F 12
46090 Villesèque 29 K 9
73210 Villette 32 J 14
89330 Villevallier 18 F 11
69910 Villié-Morgon 24 H 12
16240 Villiers-le-Roux 22 H 8
77560 Villiers-Saint Georges 18 F 11
58210 Villiers-sur-Beuvron 18 G 11
89740 Villon 18 G 12
55260 Villotte-sur-Aire 19 F 13
61120 Vimoutiers 10 F 8
17510 Vinax 22 H 7
38470 Vinay 31 J 13
66320 Vinça 35 M 10
41350 Vineuil 17 G 9
66600 Vingrau 35 M 10
18300 Vinon 17 G 10
42780 Violay 24 J 12
84150 Violès 31 K 12
34380 Viols-le-Fort 36 L 11
09120 Vira 35 L 9
50690 Virandeville 9 E 6
71260 Vire/Lugny 24 H 12
71260 Vire/Vassy 10 F 7
08320 Vireux-Wallerand 13 D 12
50600 Virey 10 F 6
10260 Virey-sous-Bar 18 F 12
01440 Viriat 25 H 13
38730 Virieu 31 J 13
01510 Virieu-le-Grand 25 J 13
84820 Visan 31 K 12
35130 Visseiche 15 G 6
28360 Vitray-en-Beauce 17 F 9
35500 Vitré 9 F 6
13127 Vitrolles 37 L 13
62490 Vitry-en-Artois 4 D 10
51240 Vitry-la-Ville 12 F 12
51300 Vitry-le-François 19 F 12
21350 Vitteaux 18 G 12
88800 Vittel 19 F 13
20219 Vivario 39 M 17
63840 Viverols 30 J 11
02600 Vivières 12 E 11
07220 Viviers 31 K 12
86370 Vivonne 22 H 8
85770 Vix 21 H 7
38220 Vizille 31 J 13
55190 Void-Vacon 19 F 13
38500 Voiron 31 J 13
63120 Vollore-Montagne 24 J 11
04290 Volonne 31 K 14
63530 Volvic 23 J 11
04130 Volx 37 L 13
88700 Vomécourt 20 F 14
01540 Vonnas 24 H 12
38340 Voreppe 31 J 13
43800 Vorey 30 J 11
18340 Vorly 17 H 10
21230 Voudenay 24 G 12
10150 Voué 18 F 12
79230 Vouillé/Niort 22 H 7
86190 Vouillé/Poitiers 16 H 8
36100 Vouillon 23 H 9
02140 Voulpaix 12 E 11
77940 Voulx 18 F 10
86580 Vouneuil-sous-Biard 22 H 8
89270 Voutenay-sur-Cure 18 G 11
85120 Vouvant 15 H 7
08400 Vouziers 13 E 12
41600 Vouzon 17 G 10
28150 Voves 17 F 9
80120 Vron 3 D 9
25840 Vuillafans 25 G 14
62180 Waben 3 D 9
62250 Wacquinghen 3 D 9
62770 Wail 4 D 10
60430 Warluis 11 E 10
67310 Wasselonne 20 F 15
02630 Wassigny 12 D 11
52130 Wassy 19 F 12
68480 Werentzhouse 20 G 15
68760 Willer-sur-Thur 20 G 15
62930 Wimereux 3 D 9
67290 Wimmenau 20 F 15
02500 Wimy 12 E 12
62410 Wingles 4 D 10
59670 Winnezeele 4 D 10
68920 Wintzenheim 20 F 15
62179 Wissant 3 D 9
67160 Wissembourg 20 E 15
68310 Wittelsheim 20 G 15
57140 Woippy 13 E 14
59470 Wormhout 4 D 10
54300 Xermaménil 19 F 14
88220 Xertigny 19 F 14
40160 Ychoux 27 K 7
15210 Ydes 23 J 10
73170 Yenne 25 J 13
91330 Yerres 11 F 10
76760 Yerville 11 E 8
40110 Ygos-Saint Saturnin 28 L 7
03160 Ygrande 23 H 10
28150 Ymonville 17 F 9
76540 Ypreville-Biville 11 E 8
89700 Yrouerre 18 G 11
43200 Yssingeaux 30 J 12
57970 Yutz 13 E 14
76190 Yvetot 11 E 8
22350 Yvignac-la-Tour 9 F 5
03400 Yzeure 24 H 11
20132 Zicavo 39 N 17
20124 Zonza 39 N 17
62650 Zoteux 3 D 9
20272 Zuani 39 M 17

Ashford 3 C 8
Battle 3 D 8
Bearsted 3 C 8
Beddingham 3 D 8
Bethersden 3 C 8
Bexhill 3 D 8
Biggin Hill 3 C 8
Bossingham 3 C 9
Bridge 3 C 9
Brighton 3 D 7
Broad Oak 3 D 8
Broadstairs 3 C 9
Brookland 3 D 8
Burgess Hill 3 D 7
Burwash 3 D 8
Canterbury 3 C 9
Caterham 3 C 7
Challock 3 C 8
Charing 3 C 8
Chatham 3 C 8
Chilham 3 C 8
Cobham 3 C 7
Cowfold 3 D 7
Coxheath 3 C 8
Crawley 3 C 7
Crowborough 3 C 8
Cuckfield 3 C 7
Deal 3 C 9
Dorking 3 C 7
Dover 3 C 9
Dymchurch 3 C 9

POSTALI · ÍNDICE CON CÓDIGOS POSTALES · INDICE DE LUGARES COM CÓDIGOS
REJSTŘÍK MÍST S PSČ · ZOZNAM OBCÍ S PSČ · INDEKS MIEJSCOWOŚCI Z KOD POCZTOWY

54

East Grinstead   GB · I · L · MC · NL   **Bergeyk**

East Grinstead 3 C 7
Eastbourne 3 D 8
Edenbridge 3 C 8
Elham 3 C 8
Faversham 3 C 8
Folkestone 3 C 8
Forest Row 3 C 8
Gillingham 3 D 8
Grain 3 C 8
Gravesend 3 C 8
Hadlow 3 C 8
Hailsham 3 D 8
Halland 3 D 8
Hamstreet 3 C 8
Hastings 3 D 8
Hawkhurst 3 C 8
Hawkinge 3 C 9
Haywards Heath 3 D 7
Headcorn 3 C 8
Heathfield 3 D 8
Henfield 3 D 7
Herne Bay 3 C 9
Herstmonceux 3 D 8
Horley/Reigate-Redhill 3 C 7
Horsham 3 C 7
Hurst Green 3 C 8
Hythe/Folkestone 3 C 9
Kemsing 3 C 8
Keymer 3 D 7
L'Eree 9 E 5
Langley 3 C 8
Leatherhead 3 C 7
Lewes 3 D 7
Leysdown-on Sea 3 C 8
Lydd 3 D 8
Maidstone 3 C 8
Margate 3 C 9
Mayfield 3 C 8
Minster 3 C 9
New Addington 3 C 7
New Romney 3 D 8
Newhaven 3 D 8
Ninfield 3 D 8

Oxted 3 C 8
Peacehaven 3 D 7
Pembury 3 C 8
Polegate 3 D 8
Ramsgate 3 C 9
Reeding Street 3 C 8
Reigate-Redhill 3 C 7
Ringmer 3 D 8
Rochester/London 3 C 8
Rottingdean 3 D 7
Royal Tunbridge Wells 3 C 8
Rye 3 D 8
Saint Brelade 9 E 5
Saint Helier 9 E 5
Saint John 9 E 5
Saint Martin 9 E 5
Saint Ouen 9 E 5
Saint Peter Port 9 E 5
Sainte Anne 9 E 5
Sandwich 3 C 9
Seaford 3 D 8
Sellindge 3 C 8
Sevenoaks 3 C 8
Sheerness 3 C 8
Shepherdswell 3 C 9
Sittingbourne 3 C 8
Sturry 3 C 9
Swanley 3 C 8
Tenderden 3 C 8
Tonbridge 3 C 8
Uckfield 3 D 8
Wadhurst 3 C 8
Warlingham 3 C 7
Westfield 3 D 8
Whitstable 3 C 9
Winchelsea 3 D 8
Wittersham 3 C 8

(I)

12021 Accéglio 32 K 14
17021 Alassio 38 K 16

12051 Alba 32 K 16
12010 Argentera 32 K 14
18018 Arma di Tàggia 38 L 15
18010 Badalucco 38 L 15
12071 Bagnasco 32 K 16
13020 Balmuccia 26 J 16
10052 Bardonécchia 32 J 14
12032 Barge 32 K 15
21023 Besozzo 26 J 16
12060 Bibiana 32 K 15
10060 Bòbbio Péllice 32 K 15
18012 Bordighera 38 L 15
12011 Borgo San Dalmazzo 32 K 15
18021 Borgomaro 38 L 15
12082 Bossea 38 K 15
12060 Bossolasco 32 K 16
12042 Bra 32 K 15
10060 Bricherásio 32 K 15
12060 Buriasco 32 K 15
12032 Busca 32 K 15
17020 Calizzano 38 K 16
13023 Campertogno 26 J 16
28822 Cannóbio 26 H 16
57032 Capràia Isola 39 L 17
12023 Caràglio 32 K 15
10041 Carignano/Nichelino 32 K 15
10022 Carmagnola 32 K 15
12061 Carrù 32 K 15
07020 Casa di Garibaldi 39 N 17
12020 Casteldelfino 32 K 15
21010 Castelveccana 26 J 16
12030 Cavallermaggiore 32 K 15
10061 Cavour 32 K 15
12044 Centallo 32 K 15
18034 Ceriana 38 L 15
12073 Ceva 32 K 16
12062 Cherasco 32 K 15
20020 Chianale 32 K 14
12013 Chiusa di Pésio 32 K 15
21033 Cittiglio 26 J 16
07028 Ciuchesu 39 N 17
10050 Claviere 32 K 14

12040 Corneliano d'Alba 32 K 15
12024 Costigliole Saluzzo 32 K 15
11013 Courmayeur 32 J 14
28865 Crevoladossola 26 H 16
12030 Crissolo 32 K 15
28862 Crodo 26 H 16
12100 Cúneo 32 K 15
12014 Demonte 32 K 15
18013 Diano Marina 38 L 16
12063 Dogliani 32 K 15
28845 Domodóssola 26 H 16
12025 Dronero 32 K 15
12050 Exilles 32 J 14
12063 Formazza 26 H 16
12045 Fossano 32 K 15
21039 Garena 26 J 16
12075 Garéssio 38 K 16
12040 Genola 32 K 15
21010 Germignaga 26 J 16
28883 Gravellona Toce 26 J 16
18100 Impéria 38 L 16
07024 la Maddalena/Arzachena 39 N 17
11016 la Thuile 32 J 14
17020 Laigueglia 38 L 16
12024 Laveno 26 J 16
21016 Lirone Piemonte 38 K 15
21016 Luino 26 J 16
28825 Lunecco 26 H 16
21010 Maccagno 26 H 16
17035 Martinetto 38 K 16
28885 Masera 26 H 16
12084 Mondovì 32 K 15
12033 Moretta 32 K 15
12040 Morozzo 32 K 15
12030 Murazzano 32 K 16
12068 Narzole 32 K 15
18020 Nava 38 K 15
10042 Nichelino 32 K 15
10060 None 32 K 15
12084 Oggèbbio 26 J 16
28887 Omegna 26 J 16
12078 Ormea 38 K 15
28877 Ornavasso 26 J 16

28016 Orta San Giulio 26 J 16
17037 Ortovero 38 K 16
10056 Oulx 32 J 14
12034 Paesana 32 K 15
07020 Palau 39 N 17
12087 Pamparato 32 K 15
28868 Passo 26 H 16
10063 Perosa Argentina 32 K 15
18026 Pieve di Teco 38 K 15
18037 Pigna 38 L 15
10064 Pineròlo 32 K 15
10045 Piossasco 32 K 15
07020 Poirino 32 K 15
07020 Porto Pozzo 39 N 17
12027 Pradlèves 32 K 15
12035 Racconigi 32 K 15
12036 Revello 32 K 15
13026 Rimasco 26 J 16
12017 Robilante 32 K 15
12018 Roccavione 32 K 15
12037 Saluzzo 32 K 15
12010 Sambuco 32 K 15
12020 Sampeyre 32 K 15
18016 San Bartolomeo al Mare 38 L 16
12029 San Damiano Macra 32 K 15
18030 Sanfront 32 K 15
18038 San Remo 38 L 15
28857 Santa Maria Maggiore 26 H 16
07028 Santa Teresa Gallura 39 N 17
10026 Santena 32 K 15
12038 Savigliano 32 K 15
10058 Sestriere 32 K 14
12048 Sommariva del Bosco 32 K 15
28838 Stresa 26 J 16
18018 Tàggia 38 L 15
12010 Terme di Valdieri 32 K 15
12010 Torre Péllice 32 K 15
12049 Trinità 32 K 15
18010 Triora 38 L 15
18039 Trucco 38 L 15

12010 Valdieri 32 K 15
14017 Valfenera 32 K 15
28879 Vanzone 26 J 16
13019 Varallo 26 J 16
21100 Varese 26 J 16
28868 Varzo 26 H 16
18039 Ventimiglia 38 L 15
28900 Verbània 26 J 16
12019 Vernante 32 K 15
12039 Vierzuolo 32 K 15
12080 Vicoforte 32 K 15
21059 Viggiù 26 J 16
10047 Vigone 32 K 15
28844 Villadóssola 26 H 16
12018 Villafranca Piemonte 32 K 15
14019 Villanova d'Asti 32 K 15
28089 Villanova Mondovì 32 K 15
10069 Villar Perosa 32 K 15
12010 Vinádio 32 K 15

(L)

4901 Baschárage 13 E 13
9237 Bettembourg 13 E 14
9633 Boulaide 13 E 13
9706 Clervaux 13 E 14
9201 Diekirch 13 E 14
4501 Differdange 13 E 13
6440 Echternach 14 E 14
4001 Esch-sur-Alzette 13 E 13
9001 Ettelbrück 13 E 14
9454 Fouhren 14 E 14
8618 Grevels 13 E 13
9655 Harlange 13 E 14
9801 Hosingen 13 D 14
6101 Junglinster 14 E 14
8179 Kopstal 13 E 14
7601 Larochette 14 E 14
1009 Luxembourg 13 E 14
8823 Martelange 13 E 13
7410 Mersch 13 E 14
5601 Mondorf-les-Bains 14 E 14
6905 Niederanven 14 E 14
8801 Rambrouch 13 E 13
8501 Redange 13 E 13
5501 Remich 14 E 14
7470 Saeul 13 E 13
8401 Steinfort 13 E 13
9901 Troisvierges 13 D 14
8701 Useldange 13 E 13
9501 Wiltz 13 E 13

(MC)

98000 Monte-Carlo 38 L 15

(NL)

1431 Aalsmeer 1 B 12
7123 Aalten 6 C 14
8806 Achlum 2 A 13
9831 Aduard 2 A 14
1921 Akersloot 1 B 12
8491 Akkrum 2 A 13
8495 Aldeboarn 2 A 13
1811 Alkmaar 1 B 12
7607 Almelo 2 B 14
1811 Almere 1 B 13
4286 Almkerk 5 C 12
2402 Alphen aan den Rijn 1 B 12
3811 Amersfoort 1 B 13
1181 Amstelveen 1 B 12
1012 Amsterdam 1 B 12
6673 Andelst 6 C 13
1619 Andijk 1 B 13
9133 Anjum 2 A 14
9467 Anloo 2 A 14
9901 Anna Paulowna 1 B 12
7311 Apeldoorn 2 B 13
9901 Appingedam 2 A 14
6811 Arnhem 2 C 13
9401 Assen 2 A 14
5721 Asten 5 C 13
1633 Avenhorn 1 B 12
4881 Baarle-Nassau 5 C 12
3741 Baarn 1 B 13
5761 Bakel 6 C 13
8574 Bakhuizen 2 B 13
8561 Balk 2 B 13
3772 Barneveld 1 B 13
7554 Beckum 2 B 14
9781 Bedum 2 A 14
6191 Beek 5 D 12
5741 Beek en Donk 5 C 13
7361 Beekbergen 2 B 13
9044 Beetgum 2 A 13
9244 Beetsterzwaag 2 A 14
9411 Beilen 2 B 14
6658 Beneden-Leeuwen 5 C 13
2121 Bennebroek 1 B 12
6721 Bennekom 2 C 13
6325 Berg 5 D 13
1861 Bergen 1 B 12
5854 Bergen 6 C 14
4611 Bergen op Zoom 5 C 12
5571 Bergeyk 5 C 13

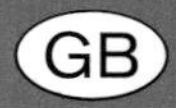

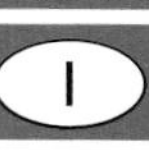

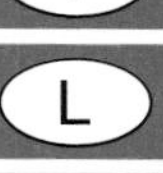

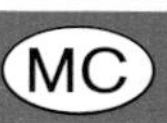

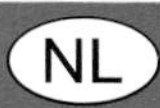

55

INDEX WITH POST CODES · ORTSREGISTER MIT POSTLEITZAHLEN · INDICE CON CODICI POSTALI · ÍNDICE CON CÓDIGOS POSTALES · INDICE DE LUGARES COM CÓDIGOS POSTAIS · STEDREGISTER MED POSTNUMRE · PLAATSNAMENREGISTER MET POSTCODE · REJSTŘÍK MÍST S PSČ · ZOZNAM OBCÍ S PSČ · INDEKS MIEJSCOWOŚCI Z KOD POCZTOWY

NL

Berghem   NL   **Zwolle**

5351 Berghem 5 C 13	3247 Dirksland 5 C 12	5361 Grave 6 C 13	8501 Joure 2 B 13
1944 Beverwijk 1 B 12	6981 Doesburg 2 B 14	7141 Groenlo 2 B 14	1788 Julianadorp 1 B 12
8256 Biddinghuizen 2 B 13	7001 Doetinchem 6 C 14	9443 Grolloo 2 B 14	8261 Kampen 2 B 13
3721 Bilthoven 1 B 13	9101 Dokkum 2 A 14	9712 Groningen 2 A 14	4421 Kapelle 5 C 11
5531 Bladel 5 C 13	4357 Domburg 4 C 11	9001 Grou 2 A 13	2225 Katwijk 1 B 12
8356 Blokzijl 2 B 13	5104 Dongen 5 C 12	6271 Gulpen 5 D 13	5331 Kerkdriel 5 C 13
5427 Boekel 5 C 13	8435 Donkerbroek 2 A 14	7481 Haaksbergen 2 B 14	6461 Kerkrade 6 D 13
8701 Bolsward 2 A 13	3311 Dordrecht 5 C 12	2012 Haarlem 1 B 12	4041 Kesteren 1 C 13
7271 Borculo 2 B 14	9203 Drachten 2 A 14	4661 Halsteren 5 C 12	7891 Klazienaveen 2 B 15
9531 Borger 2 B 14	8251 Dronten 2 B 13	4273 Hank 5 C 12	7894 Kloosterhaar 2 B 14
7622 Borne 2 B 14	5151 Drunen 5 C 13	7772 Hardenberg 2 B 14	4587 Kloosterzande 5 C 12
4454 Borssele 4 C 11	6651 Druten 5 C 13	3841 Harderwijk 2 B 13	4791 Klundert 5 C 12
2771 Boskoop 1 B 12	7991 Dwingeloo 2 B 14	3371 Hardinxveld-Giessendam	9291 Kollum 2 A 14
5831 Boxmeer 6 C 13	6101 Echt 6 C 13		9864 Kornhorn 2 A 14
5281 Boxtel 5 C 13	6711 Ede 2 B 13	9751 Haren 2 A 14	4484 Kortgene 5 C 11
4811 Breda 5 C 12	9131 Ee 2 A 14	8861 Harlingen 2 A 13	4371 Koudekerke 4 C 11
4511 Breskens 4 C 11	9967 Eenrum 2 A 14	8061 Hasselt 2 B 14	8723 Koudum 2 B 13
3621 Breukelen 1 B 13	6961 Eerbeek 2 B 14	5321 Hedel 5 C 13	4756 Kruisland 5 C 12
3232 Brielle 1 C 12	5521 Eersel 5 C 13	1964 Heemskerk 1 B 12	8374 Kuinre 2 B 13
4311 Bruinisse 5 C 12	1931 Egmond aan Zee 1 B 12	8181 Heerde 2 B 13	5094 Lage Mierde 5 C 13
6971 Brummen 2 B 14	7151 Eibergen 2 B 14	8442 Heerenveen 2 B 13	6371 Landgraaf 6 D 13
6441 Brunssum 6 D 13	6245 Eijsden 5 D 13	1702 Heerhugowaard 1 B 12	1121 Landsmeer 1 B 12
9285 Buitenpost 2 A 14	5611 Eindhoven 5 C 13	6411 Heerlen 6 D 13	1721 Langedijk 1 B 12
9164 Buren 2 A 14	8081 Elburg 2 B 13	8111 Heeten 2 B 14	7245 Laren 2 B 14
9251 Burgum 2 A 13	5424 Elsendorp 6 C 13	5591 Heeze 5 C 13	9976 Lauwersoog 2 A 14
1401 Bussum 1 B 12	8424 Elsloo 2 B 14	1851 Heiloo 1 B 12	3531 Leek 2 A 14
1402 Castricum 1 B 12	8075 Elspeet 2 B 13	4455 Heinkenszand 5 C 11	9965 Leens 2 A 14
4861 Chaam 5 C 12	6661 Elst 6 C 13	8141 Heino 2 B 14	4141 Leerdam 1 C 13
4567 Clinge 5 C 12	6301 Emmeloord 2 B 13	5988 Helden-Panningen 6 C 14	8911 Leeuwarden 2 A 13
7741 Coevorden 2 B 14	7811 Emmen 2 B 14	7447 Hellendoorn 2 B 14	2312 Leiden 1 B 12
8312 Creil 2 B 13	8166 Emst 2 B 13	3221 Hellevoetsluis 1 C 12	2261 Leidschendam-Voorburg
5431 Cuijk 6 C 13	1601 Enkhuizen 1 B 13	5707 Helmond 5 C 13	
4101 Culemborg 1 C 13	8307 Ens 2 B 13	7255 Hengelo 2 B 14	8232 Lelystad 1 B 13
7751 Dalen 2 B 14	7511 Enschede 2 B 14	2181 Hillegom 1 B 12	8152 Lemelerveld 2 B 14
7721 Dalfsen 2 B 14	8161 Epe 2 B 14	5081 Hilvarenbeek 5 C 13	8532 Lemmer 2 B 13
9104 Damwoude 2 A 14	3851 Ermelo 2 B 13	1171 Hilversum 1 B 13	7131 Lichtenvoorde 6 C 14
3731 De Bilt 1 B 13	4872 Etten-Leur 5 C 12	3151 Hoek van Holland 1 C 12	5757 Liessel 6 C 13
1795 De Cocksdorp 1 A 12	9172 Ferwert 2 A 13	9161 Hollum 2 A 13	7242 Lochem 2 B 14
1796 De Koog 1 A 12	8802 Franeker 2 A 13	7451 Holten 2 B 14	7371 Loenen 2 B 14
7957 De Wijk 2 B 14	4191 Geldermalsen 5 C 13	9151 Holwerd 2 A 13	3411 Lopik 1 C 13
7701 Dedemsvaart 2 B 14	5665 Geldrop-Mierlo 5 C 13	8622 Hommerts 2 B 13	9919 Loppersum 2 A 14
2611 Delft 1 B 12	6161 Geleen 5 D 13	2131 Hoofddorp 1 B 12	7581 Losser 2 B 15
9934 Delfzijl 2 A 14	5421 Gemert 5 C 13	7801 Hoogeveen 2 B 14	6741 Lunteren 1 B 13
3258 Den Bommel 5 C 12	4265 Genderen 5 C 13	9601 Hoogezand-Sappemeer	7775 Lutten 2 B 14
7681 Den Burg 1 A 12	7081 Gendringen 2 B 14	2 A 14	5993 Maasbree 6 C 14
7683 Den Ham 2 B 14	8281 Genemuiden 2 B 14	3191 Hoogvliet 1 C 12	6211 Maastricht 5 D 13
1782 Den Helder 1 B 12	6591 Gennep 6 C 13	8896 Hoorn 1 B 13	8754 Makkum 2 A 13
1797 Den Hoorn 1 A 12	5126 Gilze 5 C 12	5961 Horst 6 C 13	7692 Marienberg 2 B 14
1779 Den Oever 1 B 13	4461 Goes 5 C 11	6851 Huissen 6 C 13	7475 Markelo 2 B 14
7591 Denekamp 2 B 15	5051 Goirle 5 C 13	1211 Huizen 1 B 13	9363 Marum 2 A 14
5751 Deurne 6 C 13	7471 Goor 2 B 14	4561 Hulst 5 C 12	1671 Medemblik 1 B 13
7418 Deventer 2 B 14	4201 Gorinchem 5 C 12	1777 Hippolytushoef 1 B 12	4231 Meerkerk 1 C 13
6952 Didam 6 C 14	6901 Gorredijk 2 A 14	8651 IJlst 2 A 13	5366 Megen 5 C 13
7991 Diepenveen 2 B 14	7213 Gorssel 2 B 14	1972 IJmuiden 1 B 12	5768 Meijel 6 C 13
6951 Dieren 2 B 14	2801 Gouda 1 B 12	8271 IJsselmuiden 2 B 13	7944 Meppel 2 B 14
7981 Diever 2 B 14	4569 Graauw 4 C 11	3401 IJsselstein 1 B 13	4331 Middelburg 4 C 11
4671 Dinteloord 5 C 12	7783 Gramsbergen 2 B 14	4515 IJzendijke 4 C 11	3641 Mijdrecht 1 B 12
7091 Dinxperlo 6 C 14		1452 Ilpendam 1 B 12	

5451 Mill 6 C 13	6171 Stein 5 D 13
6566 Millingen aan de Rijn 6 C 14	9051 Stiens 2 A 13
1141 Monnickendam 1 B 13	6039 Stramproy 5 C 13
3417 Montfoort 1 B 12	3291 Strijen 5 C 12
2841 Moordrecht 1 C 12	9231 Surhuisterveen 2 A 14
1399 Muiderberg 1 B 13	6071 Swalmen 6 C 13
9581 Musselkanaal 2 B 15	8255 Swifterbant 2 B 13
2671 Naaldwijk 1 C 12	2511 s-Gravenhage (den Haag) 1 B 12
8308 Nagele 2 B 13	5211 s-Hertogenbosch 5 C 13
6031 Nederweert 5 C 13	9561 Ter Apel 2 B 15
7161 Neede 2 B 14	8449 Terband 2 B 13
7833 Nieuw Amsterdam 2 B 14	7061 Terborg 6 C 14
9963 Nieuwe-Pekela 2 A 14	9145 Ternaard 2 A 13
3244 Nieuwe-Tonge 5 C 12	4531 Terneuzen 5 C 11
3434 Nieuwegein 1 B 13	4001 Tiel 5 C 13
2421 Nieuwkoop 1 B 12	5011 Tilburg 5 C 13
7711 Nieuwleusen 2 B 14	7651 Tubbergen 2 B 14
2990 Nieuwpoort 5 C 12	3888 Uddel 2 B 13
2441 Nieuwveen 1 B 12	5401 Uden 5 C 13
3861 Nijkerk 1 B 13	7975 Uffelte 2 B 14
6511 Nijmegen 6 C 13	1911 Uitgeest 1 B 12
7441 Nijverdal 2 B 14	1422 Uithoorn 1 B 12
2202 Noordwijk 1 B 12	9981 Uithuizen 2 A 14
2211 Noordwijkerhout 1 B 12	7071 Ulft 6 C 14
8391 Noordwolde 2 B 14	9247 Ureterp 2 A 14
9301 Norg 2 A 14	8321 Urk 2 B 13
5671 Nuenen 5 C 13	3311 Utrecht 1 B 13
9362 Numansdorp 5 C 12	6291 Vaals 6 D 13
8071 Nunspeet 2 B 13	8171 Vaassen 2 B 13
7871 Odoorn 2 B 14	6301 Valkenburg 5 C 13
8167 Oene 2 B 14	5554 Valkenswaard 5 C 13
8168 Oirschot 5 C 13	7051 Varsseveld 6 C 14
5062 Oisterwijk 5 C 13	9641 Veendam 2 A 14
8421 Oldeberkoop 2 B 14	3901 Veenendaal 1 B 13
8096 Oldebroek 2 B 13	5461 Veghel 5 C 13
8883 Oldehove 2 A 14	5501 Veldhoven 5 C 13
7572 Oldenzaal 2 B 14	5911 Venlo 6 C 14
8121 Olst 2 B 14	5801 Venray 6 C 13
7731 Ommen 2 B 14	4132 Vianen 1 C 13
9591 Onstwedde 2 A 15	3131 Vlaardingen 1 C 12
3257 Ootgensplaat 5 C 12	9541 Vlagtwedde 2 A 15
8899 Oost-Vlieland 1 A 13	8381 Vledder 2 B 14
4501 Oostburg 4 C 11	5251 Vlijmen 5 C 13
8854 Oosterbierum 2 A 13	4381 Vlissingen 4 C 11
8897 Oosterend 2 B 14	3131 Volendam 1 B 13
8897 Oosterend 2 A 13	8325 Vollenhove 2 B 13
4901 Oosterhout 5 C 12	7383 Voorst 2 B 14
8097 Oosterwolde 2 B 14	3781 Voorthuizen 1 B 13
1477 Oosthuizen 1 B 13	7251 Vorden 2 B 14
4356 Oostkapelle 4 C 11	9481 Vries 2 A 14
3233 Oostvoorne 1 C 12	7671 Vriezenveen 2 B 14
9682 Oostwold 2 A 14	7681 Vroomshoop 2 B 14
5341 Oss 5 C 13	4354 Vrouwenpolder 4 C 11
3262 Oud-Beijerland 1 C 12	5261 Vught 5 C 13
3253 Ouddorp 1 C 11	5141 Waalwijk 5 C 13
9665 Oude Pekela 2 A 15	6701 Wageningen 2 C 13
4731 Oudenbosch 5 C 12	7946 Wanneperveen 2 B 14
1441 Purmerend 1 B 12	8191 Wapenveld 2 B 13
3882 Putten 2 B 13	9989 Warffum 2 A 14
8102 Raalte 2 B 14	7231 Warnsveld 2 B 14
4325 Renesse 5 C 11	2242 Wassenaar 1 B 12
6871 Renkum 2 C 13	2291 Wateringen 1 B 12
2982 Ridderkerk 1 C 12	7814 Weerselo 2 B 14
5121 Rijen 5 C 12	6001 Weert 5 C 13
7461 Rijssen 2 B 14	7031 Wehl 6 C 14
4411 Rilland 5 C 12	9936 Weiwerd 2 A 14
3235 Rockanje 1 C 12	1693 Wervershoof 1 B 13
9301 Roden 2 A 14	8896 West-Terschelling 1 A 13
6041 Roermond 6 C 14	4328 Westenschouwen 5 C 11
9451 Rolde 2 B 14	9431 Westerbork 2 B 14
9983 Roodeschool 2 A 14	1778 Westerland 1 B 13
4701 Roosendaal 5 C 12	4361 Westkapelle 4 C 11
3011 Rotterdam 1 C 12	7641 Wierden 2 B 14
9221 Rottevalle 2 A 14	1771 Wieringerwerf 1 B 13
8461 Rottum 2 B 13	6601 Wijchen 6 C 13
1437 Rozenburg 1 C 12	8131 Wijhe 2 B 14
7963 Ruinen 2 B 14	9418 Wijster 2 B 14
8313 Rutten 2 B 13	7384 Wijk 2 B 14
7261 Ruurlo 2 B 14	9671 Winschoten 2 A 15
7041 s-Heerenberg 6 C 14	8831 Winsum 2 A 14
4551 Sas van Gent 4 C 11	8831 Winsum 2 A 13
2171 Sassenheim 1 B 12	3441 Woerden 1 B 12
1741 Schagen 1 B 12	1687 Wognum 1 B 13
1751 Schagerbrug 1 B 12	8471 Wolvega 2 B 14
9679 Scheemda 2 A 14	8731 Wommels 2 A 13
8483 Scherpenzeel 1 B 13	8731 Workum 2 B 13
3111 Schiedam 1 C 12	1531 Wormer 1 B 12
5482 Schijndel 5 C 13	3931 Woudenberg 1 B 13
4507 Schoondijke 4 C 11	8551 Woudsend 2 B 13
7761 Schoonebeek 2 B 14	4543 Zaamslag 5 C 11
2871 Schoonhoven 1 C 12	1501 Zaandam 1 B 12
9443 Schoonloo 2 B 14	5301 Zaltbommel 5 C 13
7064 Silvolde 6 C 14	2042 Zandvoort 1 B 12
9076 Sint Annaparochie 2 A 13	5411 Zeeland 5 C 13
9079 Sint Jacobiparochie 2 A 13	3891 Zeewolde 1 B 13
6131 Sittard 5 C 13	3701 Zeist 1 B 13
9621 Slochteren 2 A 14	7021 Zelhem 2 B 14
1774 Slootdorp 1 B 12	6901 Zevenaar 6 C 14
8556 Sloten 2 B 13	4761 Zevenbergen 5 C 12
9422 Smilde 2 B 14	4301 Zierikzee 5 C 11
8603 Sneek 2 A 13	2711 Zoetermeer 1 B 12
3762 Soest 1 B 13	9974 Zoutkamp 2 A 14
5691 Son 5 C 13	9801 Zuidhorn 2 A 14
9909 Spijk 2 A 14	9471 Zuidlaren 2 A 14
3203 Spijkenisse 1 C 12	9785 Zuidwolde 2 B 14
9501 Stadskanaal 2 B 15	4881 Zundert 5 C 12
7951 Staphorst 2 B 14	7201 Zutphen 2 B 14
4696 Stavenisse 5 C 12	8064 Zwartsluis 2 B 14
8715 Stavoren 1 B 13	7554 Zweeloo 2 B 14
1614 Stede Broec 1 B 13	3331 Zwijndrecht 5 C 12
4651 Steenbergen 5 C 12	8011 Zwolle 2 B 14
8331 Steenwijk 2 B 14